Nursing Malpractice

Volume II: Roots of Nursing Malpractice
Fourth Edition

Compiled and edited by

Patricia W. Iyer, MSN, RN, LNCC
Barbara J. Levin, BSN, RN, ONC, LNCC
Kathleen C. Ashton, PhD, APRN, BC
Victoria Powell, RN, CCM, LNCC, CNLCP, CLCP, MSCC, CEAS

Contributors

Carol Ann Armenti, MA, JD
Gretchen Aumann, PhD, RN
Jenny Beerman, MN, RN, LNCC
David M. Benjamin, PhD, FCP, FCLM
Barbara Mladenetz Weber Berry, MSN, RN
Georgette M. Bieber, RNC, LNCC
Gloria Blackmon, AAS, RN, BSN, RN-BC, LNHA
Rose Clifford, RN
Beth Cohen, MSN, RNC, ARNP
Mindy Cohen, RN, MSN, LNCC
Trish Councell, BSN RN
Luke Curtis, MD, MS, CIH
Dana DeVito, RN
Elaine K. Diegmann, CNM, ND, FACNM
Sean J. Doolan, Esq.
Kelly L. Dyar, RN, CNN
Susan G. Engleman, MSN, RN, APRN-BC, PNP, CLCP
Linda Esposito, PhD, MPH, MSN, APRN-BC
Austin A. Evans, Esq.

Mary E. Fakes, RN, MSN
Hilary J. Flanders, MPH, RN-BC, RRT
Patricia Goode, RN, ANP/FNP
M. Elizabeth Greenberg, RN-BC, C-TNP, PhD
Agnes Grogan, BS, RN
Lorraine M. Harkavy, RN, MS
Martie Hawkins, RN-BC, BSN, CWOCN, CCM
Elizabeth Hill, PhD, RN, PLNC
Donna Hunter-Adkins, BSN, RN, CEN, CCM, CRRN, CLCP, LNCC
Monica Kenny, Esq.
Peter A. Kolbert, Esq.
Ginny Lee, BBM, MBA/HCM, MSN, RN
Mary K. Leverock, RN, BSN, QAUR
Susan Masoorli, RN
Dianna McCorkle, BSN, RN, CNOR
Joanne McDermott, MA, RN
Wanda K. Mohr, PhD, RN, FAAN

Nancy E. Mooney, MA, RNC, ONC
Scott A. Mullins, AAS, EMT-P
Tammy J. Murphy, ASN, RN, CAP III
Marian Nowak, RN, MSN, M.Ed., MPH
James O'Donnell, PharmD, FCP, ABCP
Valerie V. Parisi, RN, CRRN, CLCP
Ann M. Peterson, EdD, MSN, RN, CS, LNCC
JoAnn Pietro, JD, RN
Katherine Ramsland, PhD
F. David Rodden, CRNA, MSN, MS
Marlene Roman, MSN, RN, ARNP, CMSRN
Carol Rutenberg, RN-BC, C-TNP, MNSc
Kelly Shanley, MSN, RN
Nanette Sulik, MSN, RN, CSN
Jacqueline Vance RNC, CDONA/LTC
M. Terese Verklan, PhD, CCNS, RNC
John C. Webber, Esq.

 Lawyers & Judges
Publishing Company, Inc.
Tucson, Arizona

This publication is designed to provide accurate and authoritative information in regard to the subject matter covered. It is sold with the understanding that the publisher is not engaged in rendering legal, accounting, or other professional service. If legal advice or other expert assistance is required, the services of a competent professional person should be sought.

—From a Declaration of Principles jointly adopted by
a Committee of the American Bar Association
and a Committee of Publishers and Associations.

The publisher, editors and authors must disclaim any liability, in whole or in part, arising from the information in this volume. The reader is urged to verify the reference material prior to any detrimental reliance thereupon. Since this material deals with legal, medical and engineering information, the reader is urged to consult with an appropriate licensed professional prior to taking any action that might involve any interpretation or application of information within the realm of a licensed professional practice.

 **Lawyers & Judges
Publishing Company, Inc.**

P.O. Box 30040 • Tucson, AZ 85751-0040
(800) 209-7109 • FAX (800) 330-8795
e-mail: sales@lawyersandjudges.com
www.lawyersandjudges.com

Library of Congress Cataloging-in-Publication Data

Nursing malpractice / compiled and edited by Patricia W. Iyer ; contributors Tonia D. Aiken ...[et al.]. -- 4th ed.
    p. cm.
  Includes index.
  ISBN-13: 978-1-933264-96-7 (hardcover : alk. paper)
  ISBN-10: 1-933264-96-9 (hardcover : alk. paper)
  1. Nurses--Malpractice--United States. 2. Nursing--Law and legislation--United States. 3. Nursing errors. I. Iyer, Patricia W. II. Aiken, Tonia D.
  KF2915.N83N874 2011
  344.7304'14--dc22

                    2010053436

Printed in the United States of America
10 9 8 7 6 5 4 3 2 1

Dedications

Thank you to Kathleen Ashton and Victoria Powell for stepping up to assist with this revision. This revision would not have happened without their eager help. This book is dedicated to those affected by nursing malpractice—the nurses who are caught up in the legal system, sometimes without reason, and the patients and their families who are irreparably harmed. It is my great hope that application of the information provided in this work will provide a higher level of patient safety and avoid some of the tragedies that occur.

—Pat Iyer

Many thanks to my family and friends for affording me the luxury and opportunity to write and create. "The best and most beautiful things in the world cannot be seen or even touched. They must be felt with the heart." (Helen Keller) I give great appreciation to my friends Sue, Lesley, Michelle and Eileen for their continued friendship and support. Thank you, Pat Iyer, for inviting me on this journey and being an inspiration! A warm thank you to Kathleen and Victoria for their assistance with this book.

—With love, Barbara Levin

With gratitude to God, through whom all things are possible. With love and thanks to my husband, John, my best friend and the love of my life. With appreciation to Pat Iyer whose wonderful wit and wisdom have guided me since I first became a legal nurse consultant. And with warmest regards to my co-editors who lightened the load in so many ways and made the journey enjoyable.

—Kathleen Ashton

To my strongest supporter: my husband, Robert, who pushed me out of my comfort zone and thoroughly expected me to spread my wings so I could finally learn to soar. Thanks to my children, Lacy and John-Michael, for sitting patiently while I completed an e-mail or phone call before I could visit or tend to a concern. And a big hug goes to Remington Grace for helping me to find the smiles even when the pressure was on. Thank you to Pat Iyer for having faith in me and supporting us through this lengthy process. I appreciate your not laughing at my less-than-intelligent questions and not firing me for the incessant e-mails. I have learned so much, and I am grateful to have had the opportunity.

—Victoria Powell

Contents

Preface..vii

Part I:
Areas of Nursing Liability

Chapter 1: Obstetrical Nursing Malpractice Issues 3
*Joanne McDermott, MA, RN and
Gretchen Aumann, PhD, RN*

Chapter 2: Neonatal Nursing Malpractice Issues........51
M. Terese Verklan, PhD, CCNS, RNC

Chapter 3: Pediatric Nursing Malpractice Issues........93
Susan G. Engleman, MSN, RN, APRN-BC, PNP, CLCP

Chapter 4: Critical Care Malpractice Issues..............109
*Kathleen C. Ashton, PhD, APRN, BC and
Jenny Beerman, MN, RN, LNCC*

**Chapter 5: Perioperative Nursing Malpractice
Issues** 131
*JoAnn Pietro, JD, RN and
Dianna McCorkle, BSN, RN, CNOR*

Chapter 6: Psychiatric Nursing Liability 179
*Linda Esposito, PhD, MPH, MSN, APRN-BC and
Wanda K. Mohr, PhD, RN, FAAN*

Chapter 7: Medical Surgical Malpractice Issues.......197
*Marlene Roman, MSN, RN, ARNP, CMSRN and
Beth Cohen, MSN, RNC, ARNP*

Chapter 8: Respiratory Malpractice...........................227
Hilary J. Flanders, MPH, RN-BC, RRT

**Chapter 9: Orthopaedic Nursing Malpractice
Issues** 253
*Barbara J. Levin BSN, RN, ONC, LNCC and
Nancy E. Mooney, MA, RNC, ONC*

**Chapter 10: Subacute and Long-Term Care Nursing
Malpractice Issues**...................................279
*Patricia W. Iyer, MSN, RN, LNCC, Gloria Blackmon,
AAS, RN, BSN, RN-BC, LNHA, and
Georgette M. Bieber, RNC, LNCC*

Chapter 11: Assisted Living Liability 325
Sean J. Doolan, Esq. and Monica Kenny, Esq.

**Chapter 12: Legal Issues in School Nursing
Practice**..347
Marian Nowak, RN, MSN, M.Ed., MPH

Chapter 13: Managed Care Liability..........................363
Peter A. Kolbert, Esq. and John C. Webber, Esq.

Chapter 14: Dialysis Therapy Malpractice 371
Kelly L. Dyar, RN, CNN

**Chapter 15: Home Healthcare Nursing Malpractice
Issues** 401
*Nanette Sulik, MSN, RN, CSN, Valerie V. Parisi, RN,
CRRN, CLCP, Barbara Mladenetz Weber Berry, MSN,
RN, and Mindy Cohen, RN, MSN*

Chapter 16: Emergency Medical Services..................429
*Mary E. Fakes, RN, MSN and
Scott A. Mullins, AAS, EMT-P*

Chapter 17: Emergency Nursing Malpractice 469
*Christine B. Macaulay, MSN, RN, CEN, Tammy J.
Murphy, ASN, RN, CAP III, and Donna Hunter-Adkins,
BSN, RN, CEN, CCM, CRRN, CLCP, LNCC*

**Chapter 18: Telephone Triage: A Primer for
Lawyers and LNCs** 541
*Carol Rutenberg, RN-BC, C-TNP, MNSc, M. Elizabeth
Greenberg, RN-BC, C-TNP, PhD, Trish Councell, BSN
RN, and Austin A. Evans, Esq.*

Part II:
Advanced Roles

Chapter 19: Nurse Practitioner Liability Issues 561
Patricia Goode, RN, ANP/FNP

Chapter 20: Nurse Anesthesia Malpractice Issues 569
F. David Rodden, CRNA, MSN, MS

Chapter 21: Midwifery Malpractice and Litigation...637
Elaine K. Diegmann, CNM, ND, FACNM

Part III:
Causes of Action

Chapter 22: Preventing Healthcare-Acquired Conditions Means Never Having to Say You're Sorry 661
Carol Ann Armenti, MA, JD

Chapter 23: Infections in Hospitals and Nursing Homes 673
Ginny Lee, BBM, MBA/HCM, MSN, RN, Luke Curtis, MD, MS, CIH, Jacqueline Vance RNC, CDONA/LTC, and Lorraine M. Harkavy, RN, MS

Chapter 24: Intravenous Therapy Malpractice 707
Susan Masoorli, RN

Chapter 25: Wounds...725
Martie Hawkins, RN-BC, BSN, CWOCN, CCM

Chapter 26: Falls and their Consequences 769
*Barbara J. Levin, BSN, RN, ONC, LNCC,
Kelly Shanley, MSN, RN, and
Elizabeth Hill, PhD, RN, PLNC*

Chapter 27: Significance of Healthcare Fraud in Nursing..791
*Rose Clifford, RN, Agnes Grogan, BS, RN, and
Mary K. Leverock, RN, BSN, QAUR*

Chapter 28: Medication Errors 821
*Patricia W. Iyer, MSN, RN, LNCC, James O'Donnell,
PharmD, FCP, ABCP, and David M. Benjamin, PhD,
FCP, FCLM*

Chapter 29: Nurses Who Kill.......................................861
Katherine Ramsland, PhD and Dana DeVito, RN

Appendix A: Medical Terminology, Abbreviations, Acronyms, and Symbols 877
Ann M. Peterson, EdD, MSN, RN, CS, LNCC

About the Editors..927

About the Contributors 929

Index..939

Preface

Since its original publication in 1996, this book has become THE most comprehensive book on nursing malpractice. Written by experienced attorneys and nursing experts, this is the book needed to litigate nursing malpractice cases, assist in the screening and preparation of cases, and reduce risks of patient injury.

The efforts to reduce risks and improve patient safety have become more visible since the publication of the third edition of this book. The nursing shortage has worsened since the book was first published, raising concerns about patient safety. Faculty shortages and waiting lists for seats in nursing schools exacerbate the problem.

The chapters in this text have been updated to reflect the changes in nursing. A comprehensive review of the content of the third edition resulted in the identification of the need to add new material to broaden the range of the text. The publication of this edition includes nine new chapters to expand on the 45 in the third edition, 30 in the second edition, and 18 in the first edition.

The book is organized into two volumes. Volume I, *Foundations of Nursing Malpractice Claims*, contains four sections. Part One, *Patient Safety*, presents a comprehensive look at the factors that influence medical errors. All of the chapters in this section have been revised to detail the factors that contribute to patient injury and drive plaintiffs to seek attorneys.

Part Two, *Nursing Practice*, presents information on how nursing is practiced and documented. This section will enable attorneys to use the correct language when requesting documents or questioning nurses during depositions or trial.

Part Three, *Damages*, addresses the impact of injuries on a patient's future medical needs, vocational losses, economic claims, and pain and suffering. These chapters, like all of the chapters in the previous edition, were extensively updated.

Part Four, *Litigation of Nursing Malpractice Cases*, has the highest concentration of attorney authors. Experienced plaintiff and defense attorneys present their perspectives on nursing malpractice. This section includes two new chap-

ters: Chapter 17, *View of the Actuary* and Chapter 18, *E-Discovery*. Chapter 17 covers the types of malpractice policies, premiums, and rating variables. Chapter 18 covers rules, cases, and challenges associated with electronic discovery.

Volume II, *Roots of Nursing Malpractice*, begins with Part One, *Common Areas of Nursing Liability*. This consists of clinical topics written by nurses and attorneys to explain the clinical and liability issues specific to a wide range of nursing practice. New chapters have been added. Chapter 8, *Respiratory Malpractice*, discusses the role of healthcare providers in their care and treatment of a patient who has respiratory issues. Clinical issues, diagnostic tests and malpractice areas are discussed in this chapter. Chapter 14, *Dialysis Therapy Malpractice*, is another new chapter which educates the reader on types of dialysis therapy and the common complications and causes of action in this clinical area. Chapter 18, *Telephone Triage*, another new chapter, discusses the liability risks associated with telephone triage.

Part Two, *Advanced Roles*, focuses on the role of the nurse anesthetist, the nurse midwife and the newest chapter on the role of the nurse practitioner. All of these nurses work on the cusp of advanced practice nursing.

Part Three, *Causes of Action*, examines nursing liability from the perspective of sources of liability. Chapter 22, *Preventing Healthcare Acquired Complications Means You Never Have to Say You're Sorry*, a new chapter, focuses on the "never events" or hospital-acquired injury. Falls are one such type of injury. Another new chapter, Chapter 26, *Falls and Their Consequences*, addresses a widespread safety concern affecting all age groups, across both public and private locations as well as community and healthcare settings. Patient safety in hospitals has the attention of accreditation agencies, public health organizations, private insurance companies, and the government. This chapter provides the reader with important information to assist with the review of a medical record.

Key concepts are highlighted in figures throughout the book. An extensive appendix consisting of medical terms, abbreviations, and definitions, as well as websites, has been added to Volume II. This book is geared to attorneys who represent either plaintiffs or defendants and to legal nurse consultants. Insurance personnel such as claims investigators and risk management personnel who work in acute care settings will benefit from the information in this text. Legal nurse consultants and risk managers have come to rely on the comprehensive perspective of nursing malpractice presented in prior editions. Healthcare facility leaders are encouraged to use this valuable resource to educate and make a positive impact on the delivery of health care to patients. A unique blend of attorneys, nurse attorneys, nurse expert witnesses, legal nurse consultants, physicians, pharmacists, toxicologists, jury consultants, actuaries and legal photographers contributed chapters for this book. To our knowledge, this text remains the only one on the market written for attorneys on nursing malpractice using such a broad base of expert authors.

We would like to thank all of the authors for contributing their time and talents to this project. They poured enormous amounts of effort into the creation of this book. We appreciate having Kathleen Ashton and Victoria Powell join us as editors for this fourth edition of *Nursing Malpractice*. We hope you will find this book to be of great value.

Patricia W. Iyer, MSN, RN, LNCC
Barbara J. Levin, BSN, RN, ONC, LNCC

Part I:

Areas of Nursing Liability

Chapter 1

Obstetrical Nursing Malpractice Issues

Joanne McDermott, MA, RN and Gretchen Aumann, PhD, RN

Synopsis
1.1 Introduction
1.2 Standards of Care
    A. Categories of Obstetrical Services
    B. Other Sources of Standards
1.3 Deviations from the Standards of Care
1.4 Screening Cases
1.5 Managing Pregnancy
    A. Diagnosis and Initial Visit
    B. Subsequent Prenatal Visits
    C. Identifying and Assessing the High-Risk Pregnancy
        1. Ultrasound
        2. Biophysical profile
        3. Non-stress test and contraction stress test
        4. Nursing responsibilities
    D. Amniocentesis
        1. Use and complications
        2. Nursing responsibilities
1.6 Labor
    A. Labor and Delivery Units
    B. Labor/Delivery/Recovery/Postpartum (LDRP) Units
    C. Physiology of Labor
    D. Abnormal Labor
1.7 Delivery
    A. Overview
    B. Use of Forceps
    C. Vacuum Extraction Assisted Births
    D. Shoulder Dystocia
        1. Fundal versus suprapubic pressure
1.8 Cesarean Section
1.9 Vaginal Birth after a Cesarean Section (VBAC)
1.10 Cord Blood-Gas Analysis
1.11 Apgar Score
1.12 Neonatal Resuscitation
1.13 Recovery Period
1.14 Postpartum Period
1.15 Normal Newborn Care
1.16 Areas of Specific Nursing Liability
    A. Failure to Appropriately Monitor Maternal and Fetal Status; Failure to Correctly Interpret Fetal Monitor Strips
    B. Inappropriate Oxytocin Administration, Use, or Monitoring
    C. Miscommunication
    D. Initiation of Procedures Without Adequate Client Information or Consent
    E. Improper Sponge and Instrument Counts During Cesarean Surgery
    F. Failure to Use Chain of Command When Physician Does Not Respond Quickly or Appropriately
    G. Failure to Recognize Signs of Uterine Rupture
1.17 Charting and Documentation
1.18 Identification of High-Risk Patients
1.19 Staffing
1.20 Defenses
    A. Brain Damage
        1. Lymphocytes and normoblasts
        2. Meconium stained amniotic fluid (MSAF)
    B. Shoulder Dystocia
    C. Cesarean Section "30-Minute Rule"
1.21 Summary
Endnotes

1.1 Introduction

Expectant parents want the perfect baby, and pregnancy is often an exciting and happy time. When labor and delivery do not go as planned and the baby is physically or mentally compromised, parents may seek answers in the office of a plaintiff's attorney.[1]

The great changes and progress in obstetrical care in the past decades have resulted in a close-working relationship and interreliance between nursing and medical professionals. Obstetrics, perhaps more than any other field of health care, relies on a team approach to patient care. Such an approach involves cooperation, collaboration, communication, and mutual respect among the health professionals to reach the goal of quality obstetrical care for all patients. The field of obstetrics is concerned with a patient's prenatal period (encompassing her pregnancy and any complications), obstetric procedures during labor and delivery, and the postpartum period. Obstetrical nursing also includes considerations of preconception counseling and care, as well as avoidance of disease and injury to the woman and her infant. No other specialty in medicine or nursing concerns itself with two patients at any given time, one of whom is contained within the body of the other. Medically mandated treatment or care often requires the use of invasive techniques, increasing the risk of injury to one or both. Further, the vast majority of women will receive care for obstetrical reasons at least once during their lives.

More often than not, having a baby is a time of great anticipation, high hopes, and joy for the parents and their families. It also represents a period during which many women, in the course of their prenatal care, experience their first long-term contact with a physician, midwife, or nurse practitioner. Because pregnancy is a normal physiological process, most women progress through their prenatal course with expectations that everything will be absolutely normal, and that the infant will be healthy. When these expectations are not met, and the baby or mother is injured, joy turns to despair and grief. Plaintiffs seek explanations of how, when, and why it happened and who was responsible. If they cannot get reasonable answers from their healthcare providers, the plaintiffs may turn to the legal system for relief. The costs associated with caring for a damaged infant or mother can be enormous. The death or persistent coma of a previously healthy woman can profoundly affect the family. This factor alone can induce plaintiffs to consider legal action against the healthcare providers. Many prenatal and perinatal factors lead to cerebral palsy and other types of birth injuries. The obstetrical case must be carefully evaluated by both plaintiff and defense counsel.

1.2 Standards of Care

The obstetrical healthcare team is charged with the responsibility of practicing obstetrics within the standard of care. Failing to do so may establish a basis for litigation. A nursing standard of care is defined as those acts performed by a reasonably prudent nurse in a similar situation and with similar background. Standards of care in obstetrics arise from many different sources. Chief among these are the standards promulgated by the American College of Obstetricians and Gynecologists (ACOG) and the Association of Women's Health, Obstetric and Neonatal Nurses (AWHONN, formerly NAACOG, the Nurses Association of the American College of Obstetricians and Gynecologists).

TIP: Nursing standards in the obstetrical field emerge primarily from AWHONN (Association of Women's Health, Obstetric and Neonatal Nurses, formerly NAA-COG).

Obstetrical nursing standards have historically been based on standards and policies promulgated through ACOG. In 1974, NAACOG published its first set of independently developed nursing standards under the auspices of and with the approval of ACOG. At that time, a joint *Statement on Maternity Care* was also published, delineating the aims of obstetrical care and identifying the need for a multidisciplinary approach as necessary to reach those goals. In the intervening years, this collaborative approach to obstetrical care has been adopted by the majority of OB caregivers.

The nature of OB care, in its continuum from preconception through pregnancy, labor, delivery, and postpartum, makes it clear that shared responsibility between nurses and physicians is a necessity. Thus it is not hard to understand the interreliance of each profession on the other regarding the development of standards of care.

ACOG provides publications of guidelines and opinions to assist the physician in clinical practice. Technical, practice, and educational bulletins summarize current information on techniques and clinical management guidelines for the practice of OB-GYN (obstetrics-gynecology). Practice bulletins are evidence-based documents focusing on current clinical management issues with recommendations linked directly to medical research. ACOG periodically reviews, revises, or renders obsolete these bulletins to ensure they are updated frequently. See Chapter 6, *The Foundations of Nursing Practice*, in Volume 1, for more information about evidence-based practice.

The College also publishes a series of "committee opinions" prepared by standing ACOG committees. The opinions are intended to "provide timely information on controversial issues, ethical concerns, and emerging approaches to clinical management. They represent the considered views of the sponsoring committee based on interpretation of published data in peer reviewed journals."[2] These are also periodically reviewed by the College for obsolete information. For example, the Committee on Obstetric Practice first published *Scope and Services for Uncomplicated Obstetric Care* in September 1996, and this was later reaffirmed in 1998. In February 1998, the Committee published *Inappropriate Use of the Terms Fetal Distress and Birth Asphyxia*. As of December 1998, ACOG has published 213 Committee opinions, with only 93 considered to be current at that time. ACOG notifies its members as to which committee opinions have been withdrawn from circulation and instructs the physicians to remove them from their files.[3]

AWHONN has similarly published practice resources and standards for nurses. The first *Obstetric, Gynecologic and Neonatal Nursing Functions and Standards* manual was published in 1974. Likewise, practice resources for nurses first appeared in the late 1970s and continue to be published today. AWHONN's sixth edition of *Standards and Guidelines for Professional Nursing Practice in the Care of Women and Newborns* was published in 2003. This edition continues to integrate the art and science of nursing, with a new emphasis on evidence-based practice. The publication is intended to guide practice and shape institutional guidelines. Other AWHONN publications include education guides, such as *Clinical Competencies and Education Guide: Basic, High Risk and Critical Care Intrapartum Nursing*. AWHONN offers clinical practice guidelines and monographs, which provide in-depth clinical information on the care of women and newborns. Titles offered include *Nursing Care of the Woman Receiving Regional Analgesia/Anesthesia in Labor* (2001), *Cervical Ripening, Induction and Augmentation of Labor* (2002), and *Nursing Management of the Second Stage of Labor* (2000). The publications of ACOG and AWHONN contain much information regarding standards of care for obstetrical nurses, and in many cases are accepted in toto as the medical and nursing standard of care for a particular hospital. These standards are recognized as the national obstetrical nursing standards. However, there are other significant sources of information regarding guidelines for obstetrical nursing care. An important text in this regard is a joint publication by the American Academy of Pediatrics (AAP) and ACOG, entitled *Guidelines for Perinatal Care*. This book contains the recommendations and guidelines of the AAP and ACOG, which are frequently used by physicians and healthcare providers in formulating plans for the care of pregnant women and their fetuses and newborns.[4]

A. Categories of Obstetrical Services

Hospital-based obstetrical services offer varied levels of care, based on their degree of technology and staff qualifications. These services have traditionally been divided into three levels, defined in a seminal document by the March of Dimes Committee on Perinatal Health, *Toward Improving the Outcome of Pregnancy* (TIOP). This small book, first published in 1976, defines the regional concept for organizing perinatal care and issues recommendations for developing regional networks, including a delineation of the responsibilities and services appropriate to community hospitals with basic Level I nurseries, secondary care facilities with special care or Level II nurseries, and tertiary referral centers with Level III neonatal intensive care units (NICUs). The principal goal was the development of regionalized perinatal care services. This approach consisted of a hierarchical taxonomy of care provided by hospitals to prevent unnecessary duplication of services and maximize access to high-risk care.

Level I hospitals were identified as hospitals that provide care for uncomplicated maternity and newborn cases. Level II hospitals provide care for both uncomplicated and moderately complicated obstetrical and neonatal cases. Level III institutions are almost always found in university hospitals, and are responsible for providing perinatal care and services for all pregnant women and neonates.[5] The Committee has since published *TIOP II: the '90s and Beyond*, in 1993. This publication recommends changes in the designation of the various types of nurseries. The fourth edition of *Guidelines*

for Perinatal Care also follows this recommendation. The terms "basic," "specialty," and "subspecialty" are recommended to replace the previous designations of Level I, II, and III, respectively. The reason given for this change is to allow for a more functional description of each of these nurseries. However, the structure, facility, personnel, and function of the three types of nurseries are essentially unchanged. The exception appears to be that there are more specific descriptions of the level of acuity of care in the specialty nursery (previously Level II).[6] The recommendations continue to emphasize early recognition and triage of potential prenatal problems before or early in pregnancy.[7] Attempts to share responsibilities among hospitals have not been uniformly successful and have resulted in different levels of care for different services at a single hospital. This imbalance in the provision of services has resulted from a growing market of competitive health care and prepaid health plans. A further complicating issue is the uneven distribution of subspecialists in neonatal and maternal-fetal medicine throughout the United States.[8] The recommendation is now for a functional descriptive designation of basic, specialty, and subspecialty, as opposed to Levels I, II, and III. Recent studies suggest that "deregionalization" of perinatal care may adversely affect outcome, especially for low-birth-weight deliveries. The changes in the provider and payment systems led to a type of competition between Level II and Level III centers, creating real or implied disincentives to referral.[9]

Specialty care (formerly Level II) of the newborn should be reserved for stable or moderately ill newborns who have problems that are expected to resolve rapidly. Preterm labor and impending delivery at less than 32 weeks of gestation warrant maternal transfer to a subspecialty center (formerly Level III). Infants with birth weights of less than 1500 grams and born at less than 32 weeks of gestation should usually be transferred to a subspecialty center. Also, mothers with complex medical or surgical problems should be transferred to a subspecialty center.[10] These organizing principles assume legal importance when a hospital, physician, or nurse accepts a patient who requires a higher level of care than the hospital is prepared to handle.

TIP: Find out the designated (or advertised) level of the obstetrical service of the institution involved in the specific legal case. Look at the hospital's obstetrical department mission statement or philosophy of care to help identify the level of care the hospital claims to offer. Most OB units qualify as Level II facilities (specialty units). Level I (basic) units are rare and primarily found in freestanding birthing centers and geographically isolated hospitals.

Failure to appropriately transfer can result in lawsuits arising from any subsequent poor outcome. It could be argued the outcome might have been prevented if subspecialty care services had been available. The following case involves a failure to timely transfer to a higher level hospital.

The plaintiff mother was 32 weeks pregnant and undergoing weekly non-stress tests (NST) for a suspected small-for-gestational-age fetus. The mother reported the baby had not moved for two days, and the NST performed at that time was noted to be non-reassuring with poor fetal heart rate variability. The mother was discharged home and instructed to come back the next day for a biophysical profile. When she arrived for the biophysical profile she was told the technician was ill and the test could not be performed. She was placed on an external fetal monitor, where the variability was noted to be poor and the fetal heart tones were non-reassuring throughout this day. She was admitted to the hospital for a possible cesarean section. The hospital was a Level I hospital and the obstetrician was the only obstetrician on staff. The fetal heart tones continued to be non-reassuring into the following day. A cesarean section was performed and the baby was noted to be distressed at birth. The baby was transferred to another hospital after birth and diagnosed with cerebral palsy. The plaintiffs claimed the obstetrician should have transferred the mother to a higher-level hospital, which would have allowed for better supportive treatment and an improved outcome. A $3.4 million settlement was reached in this case.[11]

The unfortunate outcome of this case involved many issues, including the failure to obtain high-risk care for the mother prior to the birth. When non-reassuring fetal status was initially identified, immediate measures should have been taken for further evaluation of fetal well-being. The attorney litigating this type of case would need to review the referral and transfer policies to identify the usual procedure for obtaining appropriate medical attention.

B. Other Sources of Standards
More general information regarding professional standards can be found in the following sources:

1. Professional organization standards, such as the American Nurses Association

2. State and other licensing requirements for nurses, such as the state Nurse Practice Act, and special credentialing requirements for advanced practitioners such as clinical specialists

3. Accreditation standards, such as the American Hospital Association (AHA), The Joint Commission (TJC), and the ACOG accreditation of hospital obstetrical services

4. Learned treatises in the specialty, such as *Williams Obstetrics*[12] and *Danforth's Obstetrics and Gynecology*[13]

5. Basic professional education standards, such as the nursing process, as discussed in Chapter 6, *The Foundations of Nursing Practice*, in Volume 1

6. Manufacturers' product instructions and warnings

TIP: Professional standards in obstetrics may also be found in specific hospital materials, such as policies, procedures, and protocols developed in the respective departments. Job descriptions are frequently helpful. See Figure 1.1 for a listing of typical policies and procedures.

1.3 Deviations from the Standards of Care
In general, the causes of injury to a pregnant or newly "delivered" woman or her fetus/infant are divided into three categories. These deviations from the obstetrical nursing standards of care are described in reports of jury verdicts and settlements of OB/GYN cases, as well as the nursing professional literature regarding nursing malpractice.

1. The most frequently cited cause of obstetrical injury is related to general medical and nursing management. This category involves the overall planning and handling of patient care, including the use and management of medications, deviations from nursing standards, and deviations from medical standards.

2. Injuries caused by a specific procedure or treatment are a close second in frequency of citation. These cases involve, for instance, surgical procedures performed incorrectly. The majority of these cases involve physicians, although nurse midwives may also be included.

3. Injuries caused by problems in diagnosis are the third category of cases. This involves both misdiagnosis and failure to diagnose a condition.[14]

- Administration of Pitocin, magnesium sulfate, terbutaline, ritodrine
- Admission and standard orders
- Fetal heart-rate monitoring
- Management of preterm labor
- Use of IV pumps
- Management of premature rupture of the membranes
- Storage of tracings
- Use of cervical ripening agents
- Admission for induction of labor
- Cesarean section
- Identification of high-risk pregnancy
- Diabetes in pregnancy
- Pregnancy-induced hypertension or toxemia
- Critical care in obstetrics
- Use of Swan-Ganz lines
- Apgar scoring
- Staffing
- Chain of command
- Nonreassuring fetal heart patterns
- Nonstress test/contraction stress test
- Biophysical profile
- Amniocentesis
- Documentation
- Amnioinfusion

Figure 1.1 *Common Obstetrical Nursing Policies and Procedures*

1.4 Screening Cases

High-risk obstetrical problems and unexpected and untoward outcomes usually come to the attention of risk managers and defense counsel before plaintiff's attorneys become involved in litigation. The following outcomes are usually investigated immediately by the risk management personnel:

1. A mother's death
2. Severe, permanent, neurological impairment of a mother
3. A neonate's death
4. Stillbirth (death of a fetus)
5. Low Apgar scores (in newborn)
6. Blood transfusion(s) for a mother in response to excessive blood loss
7. Any delivery unattended by a physician
8. Transfer of a mother or infant to a critical care unit

9. Unplanned, emergency surgery on a mother after delivery, such as removal of the uterus for excessive uterine bleeding or atony
10. Undiagnosed twins at time of delivery
11. Emergency cesarean section
12. Infant abduction

Assuming the efforts of the doctors, nurses, and risk management team are unable to alleviate the patient's or family's concerns about the care received, the patient or family may decide to consult an attorney. Careful, thorough evaluation of these outcomes is warranted to determine if the healthcare professionals followed the standard of care. Obstetrical malpractice cases are complex and warrant cautious and complete investigation. The cost of pursuing the claim is high, but the potential settlement or jury award can run into the millions. Hence, both defense and plaintiff's attorneys need to recognize what is at stake.

In order to screen obstetrical cases for potential deviations from the standard of care, it is important to have an idea of where to look and what to look for. Obstetrical care involves a team of nurses, physicians, and other health professionals. Each shares in the responsibility to assess the patient on a continuing basis, and to pass on the information to other healthcare providers. The attorney should keep in mind the following points:

1. It is necessary to obtain complete medical records for both the mother and the infant. The prenatal records should be reviewed to determine if the mother
   a. received care during her pregnancy, and at what gestational age the care was initiated;
   b. had any risk factors during her pregnancy such as diabetes, high blood pressure, sickle cell disease, infectious diseases, seizure disorder, or other chronic illnesses (see Figure 1.2);
   c. was taking any medication during her pregnancy, and if so, what risks these posed to the fetus;
   d. had any history or suspicion of drug, alcohol, or tobacco abuse observed during pregnancy;
   e. had an unusually large weight gain or loss during pregnancy; or
   f. appeared to have complied with the medical care and kept her appointments for care.
2. If the placenta was sent for pathology review at the time of delivery, obtain the report. If slides were taken of the placenta, obtain these through discovery and have them reviewed.

Socioeconomic factors
- inadequate finances
- poor housing
- severe social problems
- unwed, especially adolescent
- minority status
- nutritional deprivation

Demographic factors
- maternal age under 16 or over 35 years
- overweight or underweight prior to pregnancy
- height under five feet
- maternal education less than 11 years
- family history of severe inherited disorder

Obstetric history
- history of infertility
- ectopic pregnancy or spontaneous abortion
- grandmultiparity (more than seven pregnancies)
- stillbirth(s) or deaths of neonates
- uterine or cervical abnormality
- multiple gestation
- preterm labor or delivery
- prolonged labor
- cesarean section
- low-birth-weight infant (less than 2500 gms at term)
- macrosomic infant (greater than 4000 gms at term or delivery)
- midforceps delivery
- baby with neurological deficit, birth injury, or malformation
- hydatidiform mole or choriocarcinoma

Mother's medical history and status
- cardiac disease
- disease
- maternal metabolic disease (especially diabetes mellitus, thyroid disease)

- chronic renal disease, repeated urinary tract infections, repeated bacteriuria
- gastrointestinal disease
- endocrine disorders (pituitary, adrenal)
- chronic hypertension
- hemoglobinopathies
- seizure disorder
- venereal or other infectious disease, positive GBS (group beta strep)
- weight loss greater than five pounds
- malignancy
- surgery during pregnancy
- major congenital anomalies of the reproductive tract
- mental retardation, major emotional or psychiatric disorders

Current obstetrical status
- late or no prenatal care
- Rh sensitization
- fetus inappropriately large or small for gestational age
- pre-term labor
- pregnancy-induced hypertension (PIH)
- multiple gestation
- polyhydramnios
- premature rupture of the membranes (PROM)
- antepartum bleeding—placenta previa or abruptio placentae
- abnormal presentation
- postdates (pregnancy continuing beyond due date)
- abnormality in tests of fetal well-being
- maternal anemia

Habits/habituation
- smoking during pregnancy
- regular alcohol intake
- drug use or abuse

Figure 1.2 Categories of high-risk pregnancy factors

3. Consider obtaining records from the mother's previous deliveries, if any. This may help identify previously existing problems that went undetected or untreated in the subsequent pregnancy. Examples of this include shoulder dystocia, maternal gestational diabetes, excessively large infant, or pre-eclampsia or PIH (pregnancy-induced hypertension).

4. Obtain all fetal monitoring strips, including antepartum tracings. It is usually necessary to request the monitor tracings separately.

5. The neonatal medical records must be carefully reviewed. Look for documentation of the infant's condition and any abnormalities noted. Examine any photographs of the newborn for obvious abnormalities.

6. If a product was involved in the injury to the infant, obtain information about the device used.

TIP: Women are described in terms of their gravida and parity. Gravida means the number of pregnancies, parity is the number of pregnancies carried to the point of viability. There is also a five-digit description used: GT-PAL-gravida, term births, preterm births, abortions, and living children.

To determine if the hospital has supplied complete medical records, look for the following documentation, which is commonly found in an obstetrical medical record:

1. A copy of the woman's prenatal chart, including initial visit history, physical, lab work, as well as data recorded at subsequent visits (this is described in more detail below).

2. Admission assessment form filled out by the labor and delivery (L&D) nurse; this will contain basic data about the patient including a previous obstetrical history, exposure to infectious diseases before going into labor, the time the membranes were ruptured, the onset of labor, the last food and fluid intake, the name of the pediatrician, and so on

3. Labor record/flow sheet, including vital signs, assessments of contraction and fetal heart rate, identification of abnormal fetal monitoring strip patterns, medications given, and time

4. Laboratory reports and the results of any diagnostic studies performed, such as an ultrasound

5. Narrative notes from the nurses who cared for the patient during labor

6. Physician's orders

7. Physician's or nurse midwife's progress notes, which should also include the assessment of the patient when the physician or nurse midwife first examined her at the hospital

8. Delivery record, which includes the times of various events, the Apgar scores, the names of the people in attendance

9. Anesthesia record, if the patient had a cesarean section or anesthesia such as an epidural

10. Physician summary of delivery

11. Postpartum recovery record

12. Postpartum nursing notes and medication records

13. Postpartum flow sheets which record data about the patient's dietary intake, elimination patterns, activity, status of her breasts and vaginal drainage (lochia), incision (for a cesarean section), or episiotomy (for a vaginal delivery)

14. Vital sign record including temperature, pulse, blood pressure, and respirations

15. Patient education sheet documenting the teaching given to the mother and an evaluation of her ability to comprehend the instructions

16. Nursing care plans, which are often preprinted forms applicable to the patient's needs, such as a normal vaginal delivery or a cesarean section

17. Consents for all procedures such as a cesarean section or a concurrent tubal ligation

18. The fetal heart rate tracing, including any performed during pregnancy and before delivery

19. Discharge summary by the doctor and the nurse and instructions given to the mother documenting routine postpartum care and reasons for contacting the obstetrician (i.e., fever, increased discharge, and so on)

Many lawyers believe obstetricians are competent to comment only on the obstetrical standard of care, not on causation. This necessitates having an obstetrician, a pediatric neurologist or neonatologist, and an obstetrical nursing expert review the case before the complaint is filed. The records should be organized by a legal nurse consultant and a timeline prepared before sending the material to the experts for their comments. The plaintiff's attorney should also secure statements from the follow-up treating physicians, particularly any neonatologists and pediatric neurologists, before the suit is filed.

1.5 Managing Pregnancy

The following is an overview of typical standards of care for pregnancy management, including labor and delivery. From this content the attorney can begin to identify possible deviations from the standard of care.

A. Diagnosis and Initial Visit

Depending on the setting, the obstetrical practitioner may be a physician, a nurse practitioner, or a nurse midwife. Nurse practitioners and nurse midwives handle low-risk pregnancies, with varying degrees of collaboration with a physician. As part of the discovery process, it is important the attorney identify the credentials of the individuals who provided prenatal care.

Normal pregnancy care begins with the diagnosis of pregnancy. Many women use home pregnancy tests which, when positive, prompt the patient to seek care from an obstetrical practitioner. Establishing the diagnosis of pregnancy is of fundamental importance in OB care. The diagnosis is confirmed at an early visit to the obstetrician by correlation with historical information, physical examination, and laboratory tests. The estimation of gestational age and due date, or "estimated date of confinement" (EDC), minimizes confusion as the pregnancy progresses. Initial estimation of gestational age is most accurate in the early first trimester (weeks 1 through 13 out of 40), and becomes increasingly subject to error later on because of individual variations in fetal growth in the late second and third trimesters.

Dating the pregnancy—that is, identifying the correct due date for a patient—is important not solely as a matter of convenience. When a pregnancy is appropriately diagnosed, fetal status can be monitored by correctly comparing fetal age with fetal growth. Establishing an accurate due date has implications for the end of pregnancy, in identifying if or when a delivery is overdue, and in planning if or when to intervene for delivery. In decreasing order of accuracy, the criteria for estimating the date of birth are shown in Figure 1.3.

---

1. Basal body temperature chart with coital record
2. Ultrasound between seven and ten weeks gestational age, documenting crown-rump length
3. Serum HCG (human chorionic gonadatropin, a blood test)
4. Urine pregnancy testing, depending on type of test
5. Two serial ultrasounds prior to 26 weeks gestation
6. Last menstrual period, in which the cycle is normal and regular

---

Figure 1.3 Criteria for estimating date of birth or confinement (EDC)

The first visit with the obstetrician is important in evaluating patient risk and establishing a plan of care, and should include:

1. A careful screening history, including demographic information, obstetrical, contraceptive, and menstrual history.
2. A general and specific physical exam to exclude risk factors.
3. Routine labs (see Table 1.1).
4. Indicated special labs (see Table 1.2).
5. Careful fetal assessment including fetal heart rate (when possible), fundal height, and gestational age assessment.
6. Obstetrical and medical history including other pregnancies, hospitalizations, surgeries, and so on. This should specifically investigate maternal history of medical conditions that may complicate this pregnancy, including diabetes, hypertension, thyroid disorders, cardiac disease, seizure disorders, as well as any medication currently being taken. Previous obstetrical problems should also be noted, such as preeclampsia (PIH) or difficult delivery.
7. Significant family medical history (diabetes, preeclampsia/eclampsia, bleeding problems, and so on) and hereditary illnesses should also be noted.
8. Specialized studies to ascertain fetal well-being, fetal maturity, or both, as individually indicated.

Although the studies may not be performed at the first visit, the obstetrician may discuss the reason for and timing of these studies. The following case illustrates the importance of screening for hereditary illnesses:

The plaintiff's father was of Portuguese descent and the plaintiff's mother was of Syrian, Portuguese, and Irish descent. The mother had long-standing problems with anemia, which persisted despite treatment with iron. The woman was at increased risk for the blood disorder thalassemia due to her Mediterranean descent. The plaintiff was seen by a nurse practitioner for administration of a birth control injection. At that time there were concerns the plaintiff might have thalassemia, which was recorded in the records. No further steps were taken to evaluate this, nor was the plaintiff advised of potential risks to a child should she become pregnant. The supervising physician cosigned the note from the visit, but took no steps to further evaluate the plaintiff for thalassemia or advise her of the risks

Table 1.1
General Laboratory Tests

Tests	Initial visit	26-30 weeks	36 weeks	Findings that signal further assessment
Blood Tests: 1. Complete Blood Count (CBC): a) Hemoglobin (HgB) or b) Hematocrit (Hct) c) White blood cell count (WBC) d) Differential (diff)	X X X	X	X	Hgb<10 g/dl Hct ≤ 32% 15,000mm or > Cellular abnormalities and/or decreased platelets
Blood Group	X			
Rh Factor	X			Mother: Rh-neg Partner: Rh-pos or unknown
Antibody Screen	X			Titer defined by laboratory
Serologic test for syphilis (STS)	X		Repeat if at risk for reinfection	Positive
Rubella Screen	X			Titer of 1:8 or less, or a significant rise in the titer
Hepatitis B	X		Repeat if in high-risk group or known to have been exposed	Positive
Two-hour post-prandial blood sugar	Obtain if high-risk pregnancy or if history is inadequate	X	X	145 mg/dl or >
1 hour-50 gram glucose load screen for gestational diabetes	Obtain if + family history, at risk, or gestational diabetic in prior pregnancy	Obtain on all patients at 26-28 weeks		140 mg/dl or >
Urine Tests 1. Bacteria screen 2. Urine glucose and protein	X AT EACH VISIT	X		Positive Protein 1+ or > Glucose 1+ or >
Cervical Tests: 1. Pap smear	X			Positive
2. Culture for gonorrhea	X		Repeat if at risk for reinfection	Positive

Table 1.2
Specific Laboratory Tests

Tests	Initial Visit	24-28 weeks	36 weeks	Findings that Signal Further Assessment
Blood tests: Antibody screen (Rh-neg woman)	X	X	X	
Oral glucose tolerance test (OGTT)		X		Plasma threshold 140mg/dl
Human Immuno-deficiency virus (HIV)	Offer screening to at-risk women at initial visit			Positive
Maternal Serum-Alpha Fetal Protein (MSAFP)	Initial visit counsel; offer test to be done at 15-18 weeks			≥ 2.0 MoMs
Sickle-cell Screen	X			Positive for trait or anemia
Tay-Sachs Screen	X			Carrier (if positive, test the woman's partner)
Cervical test: Herpes	When physical findings indicate at any prenatal visit		X	Positive
Skin test: Tuberculosis	X			Positive

associated with pregnancy. Two years later the plaintiff became pregnant with her first child. The health history at her first prenatal visit indicated she had a positive family history of anemia/hemoglobinopathy. The plaintiff's blood work was also worrisome relative to thalassemia. The plaintiff's daughter was diagnosed shortly after birth with thalassemia major. Both parents were found to be carriers of the thalassemia minor trait. The child began receiving transfusions when she was seven-months-old and has undergone nightly treatments. She is not expected to have a normal life expectancy. The plaintiff claimed she and her husband should have been tested for the thalassemia trait and that testing such as chorionic villi sampling or amniocentesis should have been performed to detect or rule out thalassemia in the fetus. A $900,000 settlement was reached in mediation.[15]

Based on the review of the client's history, referral for genetic screening and counseling would have been the appropriate action. It is the responsibility of the healthcare provider to inform the client of appropriate and available testing and screening that can detect potential adverse outcomes of the pregnancy.

B. Subsequent Prenatal Visits

The recommended frequency of prenatal visits is monthly from the first indication of pregnancy until 28 weeks gestation; every two weeks until 36 weeks; and weekly thereafter. Frequency of visits will be predicated on the risk status of the pregnant woman. Many obstetrical practitioners see the patient weekly starting at 11 weeks and continuing until fetal heart tones can be heard with an ultrasonic Doppler (usually between ten and 12 weeks). Some see the patient weekly at 18 weeks to document hearing fetal heart tones with a non-Doppler fetascope (usually by 20 weeks). These aid in further documenting the due date and gestational age.

At each subsequent prenatal visit the following information should be documented:

1. Interval history: patient-related changes in physical, emotional, and social status (e.g., complaints of nausea, bleeding, or contractions since the previous visit).
2. Physical assessment: maternal weight, BP, urinalysis, evaluation of edema, uterine growth, fetal gestational age, quickening and daily fetal movements, fundal height, fetal heart tones, specific assessments as necessary [ultrasound, amniocentesis,

non-stress and stress testing, biophysical profile (BPP)]. The biophysical profile is described in more detail below.
3. Laboratory tests at appropriate intervals.
4. Information provided to the patient, particularly regarding maternal serum alpha-fetal protein testing (MSAFP) for neural tube defects. Information should be offered early in the pregnancy, and the test should be offered between 16 and 18 weeks gestation.

TIP: The office nurse is often involved in documenting the interval history. It is usually written on the patient's chart and is available for the obstetrical practitioner's review.

C. Identifying and Assessing the High-Risk Pregnancy

A high-risk pregnancy is one during which the mother or fetus has a significantly increased chance of death or disability. To eliminate or decrease risk, all factors contributing to mortality and morbidity should be identified and acted upon as early as possible. Evidence that the obstetrical practitioner has assessed the patient for such risk should be documented in the prenatal chart. Such assessments should be part of each prenatal visit. The low-risk pregnancy being managed by the nurse practitioner or nurse midwife should be referred to a physician as high-risk factors become evident. Consultations, referrals to other physicians for higher level care, medical problems, and so forth, should be documented in the chart.

The following case illustrates a failure to treat abnormal fundal height measurements, which can indicate intrauterine fetal growth restriction:

The minor plaintiff's mother received prenatal care at a clinic owned and operated by the defendant health plan. Fundal height measurements were always within 1 cm of gestational age until approximately 36 weeks of gestation, where it was recorded at 31 cm, from a previous recording of 35 cm. The following week the fundal height was again measured at 31 cm. Two weeks later, when the client was 39 weeks gestation, the fundal height was recorded at 32 cm, and the next weekly visit the measurement was the same. The mother then went into spontaneous labor and presented to the labor and delivery unit, and an external monitor was attached. It showed severe variable decelerations and fetal tachycardia with a baseline of 170. Internal monitors and amnioinfusion were started. She was 3 cm dilation, 90 percent effaced, and 0 station of the fetal head. Ten minutes later, the mother was transferred to the operating room where a cesarean section delivery was performed. At delivery the plaintiff had Apgar scores of three and six (with ten as the highest possible score), with thick meconium noted, and a birth weight of 5 pounds. Two months later a pediatric neurologist diagnosed cerebral palsy, consistent with hypoxic or ischemic insult. The plaintiff claimed the defendant failed to recognize and diagnose intrauterine growth retardation. According to published accounts, the case settled for $4.1 million.[16]

The premise here is that the practitioner had the duty to refer the patient for evaluation of the discordant fundal heights at the time it was initially identified. Early recognition and treatment could have prevented the poor outcome.

Family-centered care is promoted throughout the nation, and many women opt to have nurse midwives provide their care and attend to their delivery. Nurse midwives function through private practice, clinics, and hospitals. A certified nurse midwife needs to consult with a physician in situations in which risk factors are identified. The following case illustrates allegations of a failure to provide obstetrical consultation for a patient being managed by a nurse midwife:

The plaintiff's mother delivered her first child by cesarean section because of a diagnosis of cephalopelvic disproportion. The first child weighed approximately 8 pounds, 12 ounces. The plaintiff's mother consulted physicians affiliated with the United States government for delivery of her second child, but was cared for by a midwife. The plaintiff's mother advised the midwife about her first pregnancy. Her estimated due date was May 30. On June 17, over two weeks after the mother's due date, the nurse midwife estimated the weight of the fetus to be nine and one quarter pounds with an unfavorable cervix and a fetal head that was not engaged. The plaintiff's mother was admitted to the hospital for an induction of labor. Meconium was noted in the amniotic fluid when rupture of the membranes occurred at 9:05 A.M. The labor was monitored by the nurse midwife. The plaintiff child was born at 5:40 P.M. by cesarean section. The weight was 11 pounds, two ounces. Apgars were 1 at one minute and 4 at five minutes. Evidence of fetal distress was noted on the fetal heart-tone monitor strips before delivery.

Perinatal asphyxiation was diagnosed following delivery and plaintiff's mother lost her uterus because of uterine rupture. The plaintiff's expert opined there was negligence in failing to consult with an obstetrician-gynecologist during the later part of the pregnancy because there were many indications the fetus was large, including a large baby previously delivered for cephalopelvic disproportion, significant weight gain during pregnancy, 42-week gestational age, and high presenting part. It was further the expert's opinion an ultrasound should have been done between 37 and 38 weeks to assess the size of the fetus. The child was diagnosed with cerebral palsy following delivery. According to a published account, the case settled with the establishment of a medical needs trust for the baby. The present value cost of the settlement was $1,915,101 with an expected lifetime payout of $12,923,355.[17]

Related to this patient's risk factors, there should have been physician evaluation during her prenatal course, labor, and delivery. The midwife would have the responsibility to consult with the physician for management of a woman who is past due date, who has a fetus that is large for gestational age, or who has had a cesarean birth for cephalopelvic disproportion. Please see Chapter 21, *Midwifery Malpractice and Litigation*, for another perspective on the role of this practitioner.

1. Ultrasound

Diagnostic ultrasonography (US) is used in pregnancy to assess both the pregnancy and the fetus. Many obstetricians routinely use US on all their pregnant patients; some physicians use it only on selected patients. Ultrasound is defined as high-frequency sound waves that produce an image when aimed at an echogenic object. Thus, a fetus in utero will produce an image while the amniotic fluid in which she is floating will not. Technological changes in the past 25 years have led to significant improvements in image production and resolution. Ultrasonographic scanning now allows for real-time images that readily detect fetal body motion, cardiac activity, and breathing movements. This enables the operator to evaluate both structural and functional characteristics of the fetus.

Indications for prenatal US examination are varied (see Figure 1.4). The type of exam will also vary depending on the information needed. Figure 1.5 shows some of the information that can be obtained from an ultrasound. Information about specific conditions or procedures can also be obtained through US. Examples of these include:

- Estimation of gestational age for patients with uncertain dates, or verification of dates for patients who are to undergo scheduled repeat elective cesarean section, indicated induction of labor, or other elective termination of pregnancy
- Evaluation of fetal growth
- Vaginal bleeding of undetermined etiology in pregnancy
- Determination of fetal presentation
- Suspected multiple gestation
- Guided amniocentesis
- Significant uterine size or dates discrepancy
- Estimation of fetal weight
- Serial evaluation of fetal growth in multiple gestation
- Suspected oligohydramnios or polyhydramnios
- Biophysical profile

Figure 1.4 Some Indications for Ultrasonography During Pregnancy

- Fetal presentation
- Fetal lie (position)
- Number of fetuses
- Placental location
- Assessment of amniotic fluid volume
- Estimation of gestational age
- Survey of fetal anatomy for gross malformations
- Evaluation for maternal pelvic masses

Figure 1.5 Information Available through Ultrasound

- External cephalic version—turning the fetus in utero from breech to vertex presentation
- Localization of the placenta in antepartum hemorrhage
- Confirmation of fetal life or death
- Evaluation of fetal growth and development
- US-guided amniocentesis
- Fetal biophysical profile testing (BPP)

Ultrasound performed during the first trimester is done primarily for dating or confirmation of an intrauterine pregnancy. Measuring the crown-rump length will provide the former information; presence of intrauterine fetal cardiac activity will document the latter. Second trimester ultrasounds are most frequently employed to confirm dates, and

to monitor fetal growth rate and pattern. Ultrasound studies for anomalies are done when there is a clinical indication to do so, such as elevated alpha-fetoprotein.[18] The placenta is localized and evaluated for maturity during this time. A third trimester ultrasound allows for some estimation of fetal weight, but is not nearly as accurate as in the earlier trimesters because of the great individual variation in fetal growth rate in later pregnancy. The same difficulty holds true for estimates of fetal age. Nevertheless, serial ultrasounds can help identify the growth-retarded fetus.

Registered nurses in various clinical settings are performing limited ultrasounds. The AWHONN has developed an educational guideline and practice competency recommendations for nurses and institutions that incorporate RN-performed limited ultrasounds. The publication is entitled *Clinical Competencies and Education Guide: Limited Ultrasound Examinations in Obstetrics and Gynecologic/Infertility Settings*, revised in 1998 and reviewed in 2003. This booklet emphasizes that nurses should verify that limited ultrasound examinations are within their scope of practice as defined by the appropriate licensing body in their state, and that these are consistent with regulations applicable to the institution in which they practice.[19]

TIP: Performing limited ultrasound examinations represents an expanded nursing role and, as such, is not to be undertaken by the novice or inexperienced obstetric/gynecologic RN.

Malpractice suits related to ultrasound arise from many causes, with missing an anomaly on a sonogram as the most frequent source of litigation. According to Sanders, other causes of malpractice problems have been identified as[20]

1. failure to communicate the results of an ultrasound in a timely fashion,
2. failure to inform the patient of the findings about the sonogram at the time the patient is seen,
3. failure to perform ultrasound studies for anomalies when there is clinical indication to do so; i.e., elevated MSAFP (maternal serum alpha-fetoprotein) or polyhydramnios (excessive amniotic fluid), and
4. erroneous reporting of anomalies when none exists.

As indicated in Figure 1.5, the amount of amniotic fluid is an important assessment parameter that can be determined with an ultrasound examination. In the following case, significant ultrasound findings included polyhydramnios, irregular heartbeat, and cerebral bleeding.

A pregnant woman at 30 weeks gestation went to the defendant hospital complaining of lower back pain and contractions for two days. An external monitor indicated an irregular fetal heartbeat. An ultrasound technician suspected cerebral bleeding and reported his suspicions to the radiologist, who overruled the technician and reported the findings as normal. The patient returned to the hospital six days later complaining of lower back pain and decreased fetal movement for three days. There was also increased amniotic fluid, but she was discharged and told to return the next day. The next day she returned to the defendant hospital, where another ultrasound report indicated polyhydramnios, as well as irregular brain structure in the fetus. The doctors could not rule out intracerebral or subdural bleed, and they performed a cesarean section. The infant showed markedly abnormal brain morphology, probably secondary to chronic compression from large extra-axial fluid collections, consistent with subdural hematomas and cerebral bleeding. The plaintiff claimed her child should have been delivered after the first questionable monitor strip. The parties settled for $3.4 million in mediation.[21]

There appears to have been evidence of the bleed from the very first ultrasound, and an expeditious delivery would have offered earlier intervention to prevent further morbidity to the child. This case also demonstrates where second, or even third, opinions should be obtained when there are discrepancies between examiners. Although it was the opinion of a technician versus a physician, there should be respect for a trained personnel's ability. Advocacy for the client would require the technician seek out another practitioner to also view the ultrasound findings.

2. Biophysical profile

Assessment of fetal status is the most common use of ultrasound exams in late pregnancy. The biophysical profile, a series of ultrasonic assessments evaluated in conjunction with a non-stress test, can give a clearer idea of fetal condition, particularly in high-risk pregnancies. The ultrasonic components of a BPP consist of number of fetal breathing movements, number of fetal body movements, fetal tone as measured by episodes of extension (straightening out) of an extremity with return to flexion (bending), and quantification of amniotic fluid. A score of 2 (normal) or 0 (abnormal) is assigned to each of the observations. A score of 10 (including a reactive NST) is normal; a 6 is considered equivocal and should be repeated in 12 to 24 hours; and 4 or less is

abnormal.[22] Any oligohydramnios (decreased amniotic fluid levels) warrant further investigation. Ultrasound can also be used to assess fetal anatomy for malformations, particularly in the heart, abdomen, spine, and head.

The importance of correct interpretation of a biophysical profile is illustrated in the following case, which resulted in a $111.7 million verdict in New York:

> The plaintiff's mother had an uneventful pregnancy until five weeks before her due date, at which time she detected a change in fetal movement, and did not detect any movement after performing a fetal kick test. A biophysical profile was done, with a score of eight out of ten, with the non-stress test non-reactive. She was sent home with instructions to continue to monitor changes in fetal movement. Five days later, the mother reported an absence in fetal movement and met the physician at the hospital. A cesarean section was subsequently performed, and the infant was hypoglycemic and acidotic, and later diagnosed with a periventricular leukomalacia. The infant plaintiff, six at the time of the suit, is only able to walk a few steps at a time and suffers seizure disorder, spastic quadriparesis, and cortical blindness. The suit asserted the doctor misinterpreted the biophysical profile, and an immediate cesarean section should have been performed at that time. The $111.7 million jury verdict was reduced to a $6 million settlement under a high/low agreement.[23]

3. Non-stress test and contraction stress test

Other types of antepartum fetal surveillance techniques include the non-stress test (NST) and the contraction stress test (CST). Both use a fetal heart rate monitor to document fetal heart rate and body movements, as well as uterine contractions. The principle behind the NST is that the heart rate of a fetus who is not acidotic or neurologically depressed will transiently accelerate in response to fetal movement. This response is felt to indicate good fetal autonomic function. Loss of reactivity can be associated with a fetal sleep cycle, but continued non-reactivity may be a sign of central nervous system depression. The results of a NST are classified as reactive (normal) or non-reactive (abnormal).

The CST is based on the response of the fetal heart rate to uterine contractions. It relies on the premise that when fetal oxygenation is only marginally adequate with the uterus at rest, oxygenation will transiently deteriorate in response to contractions. The resultant intermittent fetal hypoxemia will in turn cause late decelerations of the fetal heart rate.

Persistent late decelerations have been shown to be a reliable indicator of suboptimal fetal oxygenation. The results of a CST are categorized as negative (no late decelerations), positive (late decelerations with 50 percent or more of the uterine contractions), suspicious or equivocal (intermittent late or significant variable decelerations), and unsatisfactory (poor quality tracing or too few contractions).[24]

TIP: The indication for non-stress tests and contraction stress tests or biophysical profiles includes any pregnancy at increased risk for antepartum fetal demise.

Some of the indicated conditions for non-stress and contraction stress tests or biophysical profiles include decreased fetal movement, hypertensive disorders, maternal diabetes (insulin dependent), oligohydramnios (inadequate amount of amniotic fluid), intrauterine growth retardation, postdate pregnancy (overdue), and so forth. Testing is typically performed weekly (after 28 weeks gestation) unless a problem indicates further or more frequent testing is necessary. Any time there is a change or deterioration in maternal condition, the test should be repeated. A recent normal test should not preclude intrapartum fetal monitoring, as labor constitutes a major change in both maternal and fetal status.

A $2 million New Jersey settlement was reached in the following case when a non-stress test was misread. The non-stress test was being performed to rule out placental insufficiency, which was suspected from the dropping height of the fundus during the weeks leading up to the plaintiff child's birth. The child was subsequently born with meconium aspiration and transferred to another facility for intensive care. Respiratory failure triggered cardiac arrest en route, causing brain damage and seizures. He cannot walk, speak, or feed himself, and requires 24 hour care at age 14.[25]

TIP: NSTs and CSTs may be performed in the physician's office, the L&D unit of the hospital, or (at a Level III facility) in an entirely separate unit (e.g., prenatal testing unit). Occasionally, patients are admitted for such tests. The attorney should request all tracings, not just the labor and delivery tracings. It may take several attempts before they are supplied.

---

4. Nursing responsibilities

Nurses have significant responsibilities regarding many aspects of antepartum testing. Some hospitals allow nurses to perform BPPs. Nurses hold primary responsibility for performing NSTs and CSTs. However, nursing duties include not only performing the tests correctly and appropriately; nurses may be responsible in some institutions for interpreting the results and accurately communicating those results to the physician. In addition, proper documentation and storage or filing of the tracings are included in the nursing responsibilities. In institutions where a physician is not readily available for interpretation of NSTs and CSTs, specific procedures and protocols should be in place for handling antepartum test-result interpretation and reporting. It is not enough for the nurse to perform the test. The nurse must also correctly and timely communicate to the appropriate persons the results and any concerns regarding the test. The nurse should not have the responsibility for the final interpretation, since the medical management of the woman and her fetus depends on the test's interpretation. It is recommended there be documented evidence of a physician's interpretation within 24 hours of the test. ACOG guidelines require that official interpretation be placed in the patient's chart.[26]

D. Amniocentesis

1. Use and complications

Amniocentesis is a prenatal test in which amniotic fluid is withdrawn through a needle inserted transabdominally into the uterus. This test is commonly used to diagnose genetic problems, document fetal lung maturity, and diagnose fetal hemolytic disease (Rh isoimmunization). Amniocentesis is possible after the fourteenth week of pregnancy, when the uterus becomes an abdominal organ and when there is adequate amniotic fluid for the procedure. In recent years, it has become more common to perform an amniocentesis under ultrasonic guidance to avoid hitting the fetus, placenta, or umbilical cord.

The risk of complications arising from an amniocentesis is less than 1 percent for both woman and fetus. Maternal complications include feto-maternal hemorrhage with possible maternal Rh isoimmunization, infection, labor, abruptio placentae, inadvertent damage to the intestines or bladder, and amniotic fluid embolism. Fetal complications include death, hemorrhage, infection (amnionitis), direct injury from the needle, abortion or preterm labor, and leakage of amniotic fluid.

An amniocentesis may be done early in the second trimester to identify fetal genetic problems including:

1. Inborn errors of metabolism (e.g., galactosemia, maple sugar urine disease, Tay-Sachs)
2. Cystic fibrosis

3. Sickle cell disease
4. Thalassemia
5. Duchenne's muscular dystrophy
6. Hemophilia
7. Down's syndrome

Amniocentesis is also used in conjunction with maternal serum alpha-fetal protein (MSAFP) testing and diagnostic ultrasound to diagnose Down's syndrome and neural tube defects such as spina bifida, meningomyelocele, and anencephaly. The risk of having a baby with Down's syndrome is correlated with the age of the mother. Attorneys screening a case involving the birth of a Down's syndrome baby should carefully review the standard of care relating to the prenatal diagnosis of Down's syndrome. Children born with Down's syndrome often have other physical problems that increase the costs associated with their care. Plaintiff's attorneys should question the mother regarding what diagnostic tests were offered to her during the pregnancy. It is within the standard of care to educate the pregnant women regarding potential genetic problems, and to offer an MSAFP with a subsequent follow up amniocentesis for positive MSAFP results along with an ultrasound estimation of fetal size and structure. The standard of care holds regardless of the maternal or parental stance regarding abortion. The duty to offer information related to genetic testing is not contingent upon parental decisions or feelings regarding abortion. Some parents just want to know ahead of time what to expect and plan for.

In later pregnancy, amniocentesis is used to estimate lung maturity, particularly when pregnancy is threatened by preterm labor. Lung maturation is also of interest when considering induction of labor in diabetic women and in scheduled repeat cesarean sections. Amniotic fluid analysis is also occasionally performed when there is a question of intrauterine infection, as in preterm labor.

2. Nursing responsibilities

Amniocentesis done in later pregnancy is usually always preceded and followed by a period of monitoring of the fetal heart rate and uterine activity. The rationale for this is both patient-oriented and professionally protective. The prior tracing reflects fetal condition before the invasive procedure. Any problems during the amniocentesis that may cause fetal difficulties may well be reflected in the subsequent fetal heart rate tracing. If the pre-amniocentesis tracing shows a fetus in poor condition, the decision may be made to forego the amniocentesis and observe the fetus further. If a problem arises during the amniocentesis, such as obtaining blood, the attending nurse is responsible for communicating

this information to the appropriate people. Post procedure monitoring usually lasts for a minimum of 20 minutes, and evidence of fetal well-being needs to be present. These policies and procedures should all be specified in the OB unit's policy and procedure manual.

Coordination and delivery of patient care and services requires optimal communication among members of the multidisciplinary team. Nurses share responsibility in communicating relevant information to the physician, who holds the primary responsibility for patient diagnosis, treatment, evaluation of response to treatment, and follow-up.[27] In prenatal testing, it is often the nurses' responsibility to obtain results of prenatal screening tests. Systems need to be in place for procuring, reporting, and filing test results. Results need to be obtained timely, and any abnormal results need to be reported to the physician at that time. If a patient is being managed by a nurse midwife or nurse practitioner, he is responsible for the surveillance of all diagnostic and laboratory testing as well as reporting abnormalities to the appropriate physician.

The following case involved an amniocentesis with complications, and issues concerned with the subsequent fetal monitoring:

The plaintiff was at 38 weeks gestation. An amniocentesis was performed to assess fetal lung maturity prior to an elective cesarean section. The plaintiff had a history of two prior cesareans. The amniocentesis was performed with ultrasound guidance. The placenta was identified in a fundal location, meaning the placenta was attached to the top portion of the uterus. The tap was performed in the left upper quadrant—the top portion of the uterus. The first tap was bloody and the second tap also contained blood-tinged fluid. The amniotic fluid volume was described as normal. The fetal lungs were determined to be mature and the plaintiff was told to return to the hospital the next day for the cesarean. When the plaintiff came to the hospital for the cesarean the baby's heartbeat could not be found and a diagnosis of intrauterine fetal demise was made. The plaintiff then underwent a cesarean to deliver the male stillborn infant. The amniotic fluid was noted to be meconium stained. The baby was described as extremely pale and had a nuchal cord (around his neck). There was no sign of placental abruption. The autopsy report confirmed a feto-maternal bleed, meaning the baby lost blood that entered the mother's blood stream. The lab report noted that 34 fetal cells were noted in the mother's blood. The plaintiff claimed the defendant was negligent in sending the plaintiff home after two bloody taps during the amniocentesis. The plaintiff claimed a KB blood test should have been performed to check for ongoing bleeding. A settlement of $265,000 was reached.[28]

Related to the bloody taps, there should have been ongoing assessment of maternal and fetal status, and testing to identify any mixing of maternal and fetal blood. The KB test referred to in this case is the Kleihauer-Betke blood test, which is a quantitative test for fetal-maternal hemorrhage.

1.6 Labor

The majority of obstetrical nursing malpractice claims revolve around the standards of care associated with labor and delivery. To provide the attorney with a frame of reference for review in these cases, the following section defines some basic concepts included in nursing care of the laboring woman. Figure 1.6 summarizes potential sources of negligence in obstetrical nursing.

A. Labor and Delivery Units

In the typical hospital, the labor and delivery unit is a section of a floor devoted to the care of maternity patients. Traffic in and out of the area is controlled to minimize the spread of infections. In recent years there has been an effort to soften the coldness of the labor and delivery area by redecorating the rooms to make them more home-like. Although the room may contain furniture that looks non-institutional, all of the safety, resuscitation, and medical equipment are kept close at hand. In a traditional setting, once the mother has delivered the child, she is transferred to a recovery room within the obstetrical unit and then to a postpartum bed. In more progressive units, the patient labors, delivers and recovers in one room, usually referred to as a LDR (labor, delivery, recovery), and then is transferred to the postpartum unit.

Most labor and delivery units contain an operating room for cesarean sections. The obstetrical nurses are expected to possess the skills needed to assist with this operation. If the unit is dependent on the general operating room for the performance of cesarean sections, policies and procedures must be in place to insure the expedient management of any emergency situation.

Administration of oxytocin
- Failure to administer correctly or appropriately (increased too quickly, did not use infusion pump, etc.)
- Failure to assess maternal or fetal condition
- Failure to recognize, identify, respond to, or intervene for hyperstimulation

Fetal monitoring
- Failure to monitor appropriately
- Failure to recognize fetal heart-rate abnormalities
- Failure to respond to fetal heart-rate abnormalities
- Failure to assess fetal or maternal status or condition
- Failure to document adequately
- Failure to notify physician appropriately and timely

General obstetrics
- Failure to access the chain of command
- Failure to provide for patients' safety
- Medication errors
- Inadequate patient assessment
- Failure to adhere to standards of care
- Failure to adhere to hospital-derived policy
- Failure to properly supervise student nurses or other ancillary personnel
- Failure to recognize or identify a high-risk patient
- Failure to identify risk factors during labor
- Failure to document adequately or appropriately
- Failure to take vital signs at appropriate intervals
- Failure to monitor maternal and fetal condition
- Failure to provide adequate staffing
- Inadequate or inappropriate nursing qualifications to care for the patient
- Inadequate knowledge base for the type of patient care undertaken
- Improper sponge or instrument count during a cesarean section

Figure 1.6 *Potential Malpractice Issues for Obstetrical Nurses*

B. Labor/Delivery/Recovery/Postpartum (LDRP) Units

LDRP units were established in the 1980s when obstetrical practitioners recognized the disadvantages of constantly transferring a mother to several different rooms over the course of a brief admission to the hospital. In a LDRP unit, the mother labors, delivers, recovers, and is discharged from the same room. LDRP units are commonly set up so the newborn stays with her mother, rather than in a central nursery. The same standard of care should be followed whether the mother is laboring in a traditional labor and delivery unit or in a LDRP.

C. Physiology of Labor

Labor is the physiologic process that expels the fetus and is characterized by uterine contractions that progressively increase in frequency, intensity, and duration, causing the cervix to efface (thin out) and dilate (open), and the fetus to descend through the birth canal. Normal labor is divided into three stages (see Figure 1.7). The first stage is divided into three phases: latent, active, and transition.[29] During the latent phase of labor's first stage, uterine contractions are typically infrequent and irregular, resulting in very gradual effacement (thinning) and some dilation (opening) of the cervix. Although it varies greatly, a prolonged latent phase is one that exceeds 20 hours in a first pregnancy, and 14 hours in a subsequent delivery.[30]

First Stage: regular contractions cause cervical dilation, up to full dilation of the cervix (10 cms, "complete," or "fully"); consists of three phases (latent, active, and transition)

Second Stage: full dilation through delivery of the infant.

Third Stage: immediately following delivery of the infant through delivery of the placenta

---

Figure 1.7 Stages of Labor

Table 1.3
First Stage of Labor

Phase of labor	Cervical dilation
Latent	0–3 cm
Active	4–7 cm
Transition	8–10 cm

The active phase of the first stage encompasses cervical dilation from about 3 to 7 centimeters, with transition from 8 to 10 cm (completely dilated). It is signaled by an abrupt upswing in the curve of the slope of dilation plotted against time. Cervical changes are used in assessing progression through each phase. First stage ends at complete dilation and effacement. The typical length of time for active phase of labor is four to eight hours.[31] The length of the first stage can therefore normally extend up to approximately 30 hours. See Table 1.3.

The second stage encompasses full cervical dilation through delivery of the infant. The average second stage length is short, approximately 50 minutes for women having a first baby, and 20 minutes for subsequent deliveries. A prolonged second stage of labor is one that exceeds two hours.[32] The third stage of labor extends from delivery of the infant to delivery of the placenta.

D. Abnormal Labor

Abnormalities in labor patterns can arise at any of several points. Identification of an abnormal labor pattern requires assessment of several parameters:

1. The powers: force or strength of uterine contractions
2. The passenger: the fetus, including its presentation, estimated weight, position, and attitude
3. The pelvis: size and shape of maternal pelvis and soft-tissue factors relative to the fetus
4. The position: maternal position affects the strength and frequency of uterine contractions, duration of labor, descent of the fetus, perinatal outcome, maternal comfort, and maternal satisfaction
5. The psyche (maternal psychological status): psyche can alter the normal physiologic process of labor and birth[33]

Dysfunctional labor is frequently referred to as dystocia, meaning difficult labor or childbirth. Dystocia can be more readily identified when cervical dilation and fetal descent are regularly charted and plotted on a Friedman curve or labor graph (see Figure 1.8). Developed by Dr. Emmanuel A. Friedman of Harvard University, the labor curve presents a graphical representation of normal labor for both nulliparous (no previous births) and multiparous (more than one prior birth) women, as well as deviations from the norms.

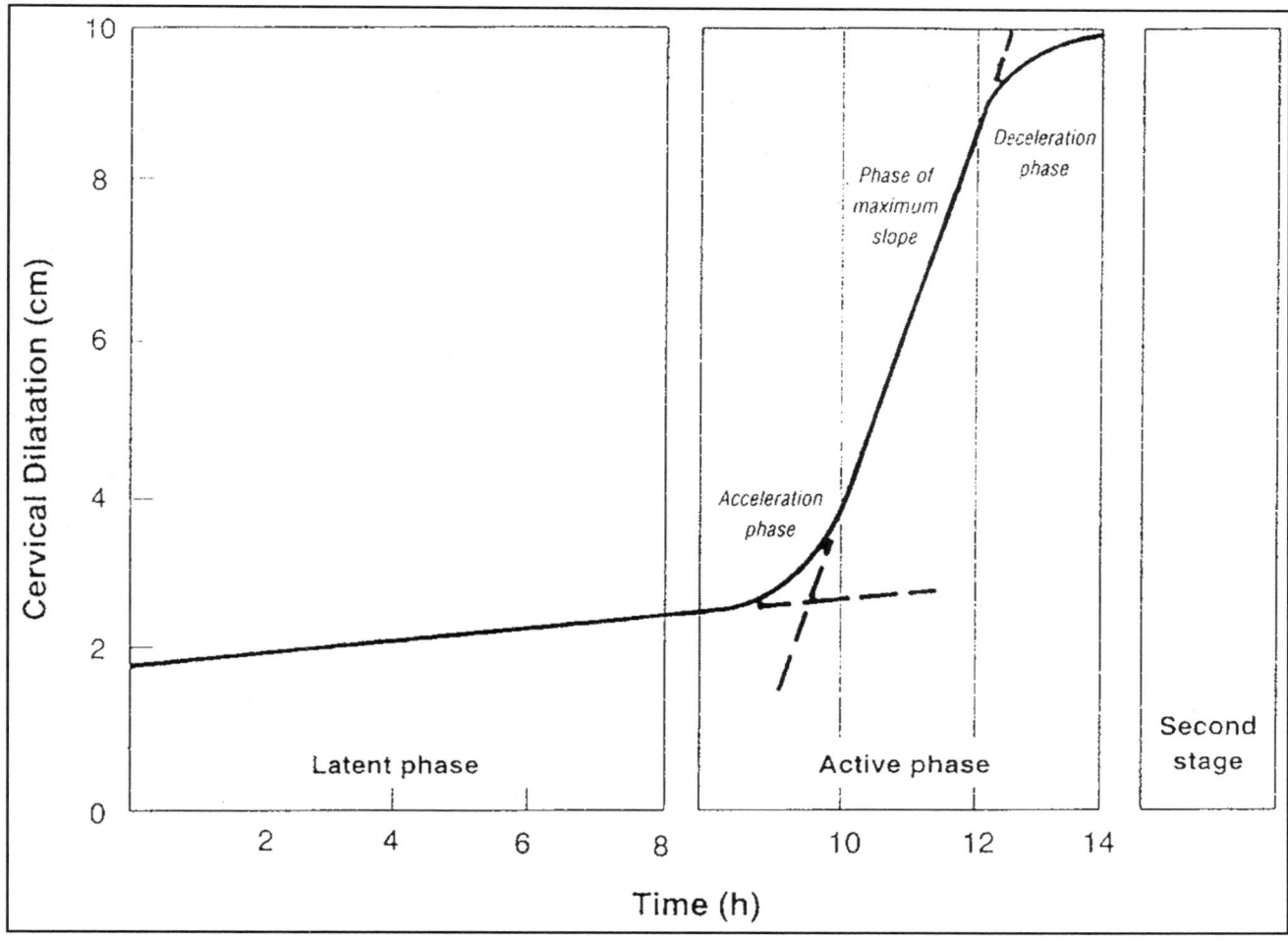

Figure 1.8 *Friedman Labor Curve. Reprinted with permission of Appleton and Lange, Stamford, Connecticut (F. Gary Cunningham, Paul C. MacDonald and Norman F. Gant), Williams Obstetrics, Seventeenth Edition, 1985.*

TIP: Use of a labor graph allows earlier diagnosis and management of labor progress difficulties, and can assist in identifying those pregnancies complicated by cephalo-pelvic disproportion. Most all commercially produced labor and delivery records include a Friedman curve along with a place to graphically document the individual patient's progress.

Occasionally, a hospital has a separate graph used in specified or other circumstances, such as upon starting Pitocin. Once a labor curve is started, it becomes part of the medical record and should be supplied to the attorney when records are requested.

Dystocia is a broad category that includes a number of more specific problems, including cephalo-pelvic disproportion (CPD) and failure to progress (FTP). Absolute CPD is a disparity between the size of the maternal pelvis and the fetal head that precludes vaginal delivery. Relative CPD results when extension of the fetal head presents bony diameters too great to allow passage through the maternal pelvis (e.g., a chin or forehead presenting part). Failure to progress includes lack of progressive cervical dilation, or lack of descent of the fetal head, or both. This term is synonymous with Friedman's arrest disorders. The diagnosis of FTP should not be made until adequate uterine contractions have been achieved and maintained for a reasonable period of time.[34] Prolonged labor and its complications have been the subjects of medical malpractice actions. Undiagnosed or poorly handled dystocia in labor can have drastic effects on the fetus, as the following case illustrates:

The plaintiff mother was hospitalized for labor and was showing signs of fetal compromise during her almost seven-hour second stage. The plaintiff claimed the midwife in charge of the delivery, as well as the nurse and the resident, failed to consult the obstetrician on duty that night. The child was born essentially dead, but was revived by the code blue team. The delivery was complicated by shoulder dystocia. The obstetrician on duty testified that if she had been notified she would have delivered the child two to three hours earlier. The child has permanent speech and coordination problems, but was showing some improvement with therapy. A $6.185 million verdict was returned.[35]

This case involved other serious issues besides the management of the labor dystocia, including a failure by the midwife to consult with the attending physician and a failure of the nurse to advocate for the patient by notifying the obstetrician of the abnormal second stage.

1.7 Delivery
A. Overview

Although the actual delivery of the infant constitutes a short time relative to pregnancy and labor, it is fraught with potential problems and potential areas of liability for staff nurses in labor and delivery as well as nurse midwives. The following is an overview of some of the major concepts involved in delivery.

Fetal presentation during labor and delivery is important. Presentation involves the part of the fetus lowermost in the birth canal when labor starts. The most common presentation is vertex, or head first. In this presentation, the top back of the fetus's head (referred to as the occipital region or occiput) presents first. The chin is tucked onto the fetus' chest. Variations of the vertex presentation include chin (mentum) or brow presentations. Each of these variations make vaginal delivery more difficult. In some cases, a fetus with a chin or brow presentation may not be able to be delivered vaginally, and will not convert to a normal vertex presentation. Use of oxytocin is inadvisable in these cases, as severe fetal neck injury may result. Nurses should question an order to start Pitocin in any case involving an unusual presentation.

Vertex presentations are the most common and best adapted for vaginal delivery. The vertex presentation is further examined for position, that is, the relation of fetal occiput (back of the head) to the maternal sacrum. Position is reported as OA or OP with further orientation to maternal left or right. For instance, LOA position refers to left occiput anterior, meaning the fetal occiput is anterior and to the left of the maternal midline (the mother's left, not the examiner's). Occiput anterior positions deliver more readily; OP positions tend to cause "back labor." The position must be identified correctly before placement of forceps so as to prevent fetal injury from misapplication.

TIP: The attorney will find that the labor flow sheet or the obstetrical practitioner's record commonly identify the presenting part.

A second mode of presentation is the transverse lie, which refers to the longitudinal axis of the infant. The fetus lies across the uterus, in a plane parallel to the floor (when the patient is standing). The fetus's back may be facing up or down. Rarely, a transverse lie may convert to a breech presentation prior to or early in labor, but generally, any fetus in a transverse lie is delivered by cesarean section. Transverse lies are more common in multiparous women (a multipara is a woman who has completed two or more pregnancies to viability),[36] and in women with uterine malformations or obstructions (e.g., a fibroid tumor low in the uterus).

In a breech presentation the fetal buttocks is the presenting part. There are three main types of breech presentation:

1. Frank breech (thighs flexed, knees extended, in a "pike" or "V" position)
2. Complete breech (thighs and knees are flexed, the fetus is "sitting tailor fashion")
3. Incomplete breech (foot or knee extends below the buttocks: a "footling breech")

Breech presentation can be identified before and during labor by palpation, vaginal exam, ultrasound, or x-ray.

Vaginal breech deliveries constitute a "hot" topic in contemporary obstetrics. Generally, first babies that present as breeches will be delivered by cesarean, as will most preterm breech infants. Vaginal breech delivery is associated with very high rates of fetal morbidity and mortality which relate to head entrapment, cord compression, and resultant hypoxia during delivery. The primary problem in a vaginal breech delivery is not knowing whether the fetus' head will fit through the maternal pelvis. If the head is the largest bony structure of the fetus, the rest of the baby will follow readily after the head delivers. This does not hold for a breech delivery: once the infant's body has been delivered, it is too late to discover that the baby's head will not fit through the pelvis or an incompletely dilated cervix. The incidence of significant fetal injury is 12 times higher in the vaginally delivered breech infant compared with vertex presentations. Therefore, vaginal delivery of breech babies is not uncommon, and should be undertaken only with very good reasons and many precautions.

Nurses participating in vaginal breech deliveries should be aware of the inherent problems in the situation and therefore anticipate difficulties. They also should communicate with the nursing supervisor as well as the pediatric staff before the delivery. Nurse midwives who encounter a breech delivery may suddenly find themselves in a high-risk situation which warrants advanced skills.

B. Use of Forceps

Forceps may be used to ease or speed delivery of an infant when maternal pushing efforts are inadequate and the fetal skull is well down in the vagina. Forceps deliveries are classified as high, mid, and low. High forceps deliveries have no place in modern obstetrics, and are not performed. Mid-forceps operations are rare and reserved for special circumstances. Low forceps delivery may be indicated by fetal or maternal distress. Elective low forceps are used at the discretion of the obstetrical practitioner when maternal expulsive efforts are inadequate or when the baby's head no longer progresses to the opening of the birth canal. This frequently results from maternal soft-tissue resistance.

Problems arising from forceps deliveries include misapplications that may cause fetal injury such as a fractured skull, cephalohematoma (collection of blood on the head), brain damage, eye injuries, and facial palsies. Most problems occur because too much traction is used or the forceps are placed and replaced multiple times. While nurses do not apply or use forceps, they do participate in caring for the patient during forceps use. Consequently, the OB nurse is responsible for communicating with her supervisor when difficulties are anticipated or present.

Improper forcep technique was the allegation in the following Florida case:

> The defendant obstetrician was concerned the baby would be too large for normal delivery, leading him to induce labor and use forceps to aid delivery. He suffered severe brain damage at birth leaving him with the physical abilities of an infant and requiring around-the-clock care. Since birth, he has undergone 14 operations on his brain and spine. The plaintiff's suit included allegations the defendant obstetrician used a technique with the forceps disavowed by the medical community because of the high incidence of brain damage resulting from its use. The jury awarded the plaintiff $63 million.[37]

This case demonstrates how an improper forcep delivery can result in devastating consequences. Because of cases like this, ACOG has provided opinions regarding the use of forceps in obstetrical practice.

C. Vacuum Extraction Assisted Births

Some physicians choose to use vacuum extraction when birth needs to be facilitated. Use of the vacuum extractor involves specific practice parameters. Vacuum applications are limited to three and the time of application to no more than 20 minutes.[38] Complications from both vacuum extraction and forceps are similar, depending primarily on the skill of the practitioner. The nurse must be aware of potential maternal complications such as vaginal and cervical tears, uterine rupture, bladder trauma, and increased vaginal bleeding with uterine atony. The nurse must be prepared for newborn resuscitation and observe the infant for lacerations, bruising, skull fracture, and intracranial hemorrhages.[39]

D. Shoulder Dystocia

Shoulder dystocia refers to an obstetrical emergency in which the infant's anterior fetal shoulder becomes lodged under the maternal pubic bone, preventing delivery of the fetal body even after the head has been delivered. Several maneuvers exist to attempt to dislodge the shoulder. These maneuvers are described in standard obstetrical tests. The attorney should read about these maneuvers and use this knowledge when questioning the obstetrical practitioner. Injuries arising from a shoulder dystocia include Erb's palsy, Klumpke's palsy, and evulsion of the brachial plexus nerves. Occasionally, a fractured clavicle or fracture of the contralateral upper arm, or both, may result from alternative maneuvers employed to deliver the infant. Shoulder dystocia may be associated with significant fetal morbidity and even mortality.[40]

1. Fundal versus suprapubic pressure

A nurse may be called upon to provide fundal or suprapubic pressure during the second stage of labor. Fundal pressure is the application of gentle, steady pressure on the fundus of the uterus. Suprapubic pressure is steady pressure on the suprapubic area of the body as it directs the anterior shoulder of the infant posteriorly behind the pubic bone and under the symphysis.[41] Suprapubic pressure is manual pressure used in cases of shoulder dystocia. The need for fundal pressure has not been well documented in literature and efficacy of the procedure has not been proved. However, it has been documented in literature that fundal pressure is contraindicated in a shoulder dystocia situation.[42]

TIP: Fundal pressure should never be applied with a shoulder dystocia, because it can further affect the fetal shoulder, resulting in an inability to deliver the fetal body.

The following case illustrates this issue:

> The infant son of a 32-year-old attorney was born with Erb's palsy, and suffers from reduced movement and strength in his right arm. The attorney mother claimed that during the vaginal delivery of her son in the defendant hospital, his shoulders became stuck (shoulder dystocia) and the defendant obstetrician used improper maneuvers to free them. Specifically, she claimed the nurse, operating under the direction of the defendant obstetrician, applied fundal pressure, which is contraindicated in shoulder dystocia, and that the excessive traction caused injury to his brachial plexus nerves. The jury returned a $3,165,000 verdict for the plaintiff.[43]

Fundal pressure used during shoulder dystocia can further impact the fetal shoulder, contributing to brachial plexus injuries and fractures of the humerus and clavicle. Suprapubic pressure can dislodge the impacted shoulder while gentle downward pressure is applied by the physician. It is usually left to the nurse to apply pressure during the emergency situation encountered in a case of shoulder dystocia. In most situations she is taking direction from the delivering physician on how and where to apply pressure in the maneuvers used to deliver the infant. The perinatal nurse has the right to refuse application of fundal pressure if she is uncomfortable with the clinical situation.[44] It is recommended hospitals adopt protocols addressing the issue of the nurse's applying fundal pressure.

Infants of diabetic mothers are especially prone to shoulder dystocia as they tend to be macrosomic and have disproportionately wide shoulders relative to the widest diameter of the head. Infants estimated to be larger than 4,500 grams at term generally should not be considered for vaginal delivery. The route of delivery for any large infant should be carefully considered, and labor should be monitored for any sign of dysfunction. The biggest risk factor for shoulder dystocia has been identified as a failure to descend in the second stage of labor.[45]

Shoulder dystocia can occur without warning, so the intrapartal nurse must always be ready for such an emergency. Practice sessions using simulations, assisting with McRoberts maneuver (flexing the woman's legs against her abdomen), and notifying staff when extra help is needed should be routine practice. A step stool which is often needed for applying suprapubic pressure should be part of the labor room equipment.[46]

1.8 Cesarean Section

When Julius Caesar was allegedly born by cesarean delivery, it changed obstetrics forever. Before, all children were born vaginally, but after this first cesarean delivery, practitioners had an alternative way to deliver infants.[47] The rates for cesarean section (C/S) delivery have risen in recent years, primarily because of major advances in antepartum and neonatal care and increased neonatal survival rates. Some observers believe increased awareness of liability risks has prompted an increase in cesarean section rates, as well as desire for planning a convenient delivery date. However, an effort is being made to decrease the national cesarean section birth rate, and this effort has become a priority for many payors and providers.[48] The largest increase in C/S rates is in the group of preterm labor infants. Maternal risks from cesarean section are very low. Most studies reported in literature cite no maternal deaths related to C/S in large numbers of deliveries. The most common problems associated with C/S are infection, injury to bowel or bladder, and retained laparotomy sponges. Fetal complications most commonly arise from failure to begin the surgery promptly when necessitated by fetal condition. Any hospital that provides labor and delivery services should be equipped to perform an emergency C/S. The nursing, anesthesia, neonatal resuscitation, and obstetric personnel required must be either in the hospital or readily available. It should be possible to commence a C/S within 30 minutes of the time the decision is made to operate. There can be several sources of delay in performing a C/S. These include:

1. Delay in recognizing signs of non-reassuring fetal heart-rate patterns
2. Lack of communication between the nurse and the obstetrician
3. Lack of institutional preparedness for an emergency C/S

The following case includes an allegation of failure to perform an indicated cesarean section in a timely manner:

> The fetal heart rate tracing showed some decelerations starting at the time of the patient's admission at 9:45 A.M., with complaints of abdominal pain. At 11:00 A.M., the resident ordered an emergency cesarean section for a non-reassuring pattern, which was overruled by the defendant attending physician. At 12:25 P.M., the tracing became non-reassuring again, and the defendant physician ordered the emergency cesarean section. The infant was not delivered until 1:11 P.M., 46 minutes after the order.

At the time of delivery, a 20 percent placental abruption was discovered. The plaintiff argued the delay was the defendant's fault. The defendant agreed the delay after his 12:15 P.M. order was inexcusable, arguing the hospital must have been responsible for the delay. The former director of obstetrics at the hospital testified that sometimes delays are caused by the unavailability of anesthesia personnel. The hospital settled pre-trial for $6 million, and there was a $90.9 million verdict against the obstetrician for failure to diagnose the placental abruption and deliver in a timely manner.[49]

The policies and procedures related to surgical team response for an emergency cesarean section could be at issue, because it is an ACOG standard that when a decision is made to perform an emergency cesarean section, no more than 30 minutes should elapse before the incision is made. This case also involved a failure in the diagnosis of the placental abruption, which compromised fetal oxygenation.

1.9 Vaginal Birth after a Cesarean Section (VBAC)

In 1916, Dr. Cragin coined the phrase, "Once a cesarean section, always a cesarean section." At that time, it was thought to be too dangerous to allow a mother to have a vaginal delivery after a cesarean delivery.[50] VBAC is now recognized as an acceptable alternative to routinely performing repeat cesarean deliveries. However, this area continues to be a controversial issue in obstetrical practice. Although a trial of labor after a previous cesarean birth (TOLAC) is considered safe, there is now almost two decades of research to consider. This research suggests there is a significantly elevated risk for both mother and child attempting a VBAC. Studies continue to conclude that the benefits of a trial of labor more than outweigh the risks. However, there is concern that these studies lack reliability because they are conducted in university or tertiary care centers with in-house staff coverage and the availability of anesthesia 24 hours a day.[51] It is important to ascertain whether patients are being adequately informed about the medical risks of VBAC before they agree to accept their physicians' recommendations for a trial of labor after a previous cesarean birth. ACOG recommends all potential complications be discussed with the patient and documented in the chart.[52] Each patient's risk factors and the benefits of VBAC should be discussed in a counseling session. ACOG has also expressed opposition to any mandating of trials of labor by any third party payor. Physicians could find themselves pressured to attempt VBACs when they feel the situation is unsuitable, or if the patient desires a repeat cesarean

section.[53] ACOG recommends obstetrical care include continuous fetal monitoring and the presence of personnel familiar with VBAC complications, including non-reassuring fetal monitoring tracings and signs of inadequate labor progress. TOLAC is specifically contraindicated in situations in which there is an inability to perform emergency cesarean section because of unavailable surgeons, anesthetist, nursing staff, or equipment.[54]

The nurse caring for a patient attempting a VBAC needs to know that the previous uterine incision increases the risk for uterine rupture. The nurse is responsible for accurate ongoing assessment, including monitoring the mother and fetus for any change in condition. A uterine rupture can present in a variety of ways. Obstetric nurses must understand the signs and symptoms of uterine rupture, including abdominal, shoulder, or back pain which is usually not masked by an epidural. Patients have reported pain even with an epidural that had previously been giving them pain relief. Vaginal bleeding may also be a symptom of uterine rupture. Occult bleeding may cause reduced blood volume and altered vital signs.[55]

The nursing management includes a thorough history of the patient's description of abdominal pain, uterine contraction activity, amount of vaginal bleeding, and presence or absence of fetal movement. The nurse should also monitor the rate of cervical dilation and fetal descent, being alert to abnormal progress. Loss of station is a possible sign of uterine rupture. Station is defined as the level of the presenting part in the birth canal in relation to the ischial spines, which are halfway between the pelvic inlet and the pelvic outlet.[56] If the fetus had been at a zero station (even with the ischial spines) and then was determined to be above this level, that would constitute a loss of station.

Other vaginal examination findings in the situation of a ruptured uterus can be that the fetus is ballotible (ballotment—upon tapping on its head, the fetus floats up from the fingertips, and then rebounds), and the fetus may be palpable outside the uterus.[57] Close attention must be paid to any complaints of severe pain in the area of the prior incision. Impending rupture may be preceded by increasing uterine hypertonus. The most significant sign of uterine rupture described in literature is a change in the fetal heart rate tracing. Several authors have indicated that when uterine rupture occurs, variable decelerations are frequently seen, or they have reported cases of variable decelerations followed by a slowed heart rate. Others have reported that a slow heart rate may occur without preceding decelerations, or that decelerations may come before the slow heart rate.[58]

Plans for appropriate management, rapid diagnosis, and immediate intervention by the perinatal staff should be in place before undertaking a trial of labor.[59] Also, in consideration of unit staffing, care of patients during a trial of labor should not be left to a novice nurse.

TIP: Highly skilled, knowledgeable, and experienced labor and delivery nurses should be used to provide care to patients during a trial of labor after cesarean (TOLAC).

The following Texas case involves a failure to recognize signs of uterine rupture during a trial of labor for vaginal birth after cesarean section; the infant suffered cerebral palsy and mental retardation, as well as neurologic impairment. A jury found in favor of the plaintiff, against the hospital for $9.675 million.

> The plaintiff's mother, age 29, was admitted to the defendant hospital for a trial of labor by vaginal birth after cesarean section. This was her third child. Her first was delivered by cesarean section and the second by vaginal delivery. Pitocin was administered. During labor the plaintiff suffered a uterine rupture. The baby was delivered by emergency cesarean section. At birth the infant showed no signs of life, with an Apgar score of 0 and a pH of 6.7. Plaintiffs maintained the hospital had deficient policies and procedures governing the monitoring of a VBAC patient on Pitocin, the Pitocin was improperly used, and the nurses failed to recognize the signs of uterine rupture. Allegations also included that the nurses failed to notify the obstetrician of fetal monitor strip changes and failed to timely prepare for an emergency cesarean section, and that the hospital failed to have equipment and personnel immediately available to respond to an emergency. Plaintiffs claimed the obstetrician failed to timely recognize and respond to the signs of uterine rupture.[60]

This case illustrates the importance of early evaluation of potential signs of uterine rupture, and the need for available personnel in case of an emergency. Policies and procedures should be requested to verify plans are in place to handle the adverse outcome of a ruptured uterus when attempting a VBAC delivery.

1.10 Cord Blood-Gas Analysis

Umbilical cord blood-gas analysis can provide evidence either confirming or refuting the presence of intrapartum acidemia, and the results are carefully reviewed in cases with medicolegal risks. It is important to ascertain the different values between the arterial and venous blood gases, as it is

the arterial gas that depicts the status of the baby. Although the arterial results can diagnose hypoxemia and metabolic acidosis, the results will give no indication of the duration of the asphyxia.[61] It has been believed the presence of acidosis in the umbilical arterial cord blood is a good measure of the severity or duration of intrauterine asphyxia. However, the actual relationship of acidosis at birth to adverse neurologic outcome is poor. Although ACOG considers an umbilical arterial pH less than 7.00 to reflect pathologic or severe fetal acidemia, it remains unclear what best defines the umbilical arterial pH associated with asphyxia. Studies have shown that even when infants with severe fetal acidemia are admitted to the neonatal intensive care unit (NICU), 80 to 90 percent exhibit a benign neurologic course. The fetus has a remarkable adaptive ability to maintain cerebral perfusion. It would be better to evaluate the coupling of bradycardia with severe fetal acidosis, which necessitates intensive resuscitation in the delivery room for correction. This data may provide initial objective evidence of a severe intrapartum insult that is of sufficient duration to compromise cerebral perfusion and oxygen delivery.[62]

In studying infants that developed hypoxic-ischemic encephalopathy, the presence of certain peripartum markers was found to increase the risk for neonatal seizures.[63] These were identified as:

1. Five-minute Apgar scored less than 5 (see discussion below)
2. Need for delivery room intubation, or CPR, or both
3. Umbilical cord arterial pH less than 7.00

The correlation between the blood-gas analysis and the Apgar score can be significant in recognizing any disparity between the two. A blood-gas analysis of the cord blood, if performed properly, may help in determining the accuracy of the Apgars and the condition of the fetus at delivery. Table 1.4 shows cord blood-gas results with the implications of the values obtained.

1.11 Apgar Score

The Apgar score at one and five minutes has been used for years as a primary tool to evaluate the degree of resuscitative effort required for an infant (see Figure 1.9). A score of 0 to 3 indicates severe distress and the need for immediate vigorous resuscitative measures. Infants with Apgars of 4 to 7 are in moderate distress and may require vigorous resuscitation. Infants with Apgars of 8 to 10 usually only require observation.[64] Close monitoring is necessary for all infants, as delayed respiratory depression may occur because of drugs, anesthesia, or a variety of anatomic defects.

Table 1.4
Umbilical Cord Blood Gas Test Results

<u>Cord Blood Gases*:</u>		
Cord Arterial Norms	**Cord Venous Norms**	
pH ≥ 7.20 pO_2 16 – 20 mmHg pCO_2 40 – 50 mmHg BE 0 – (-10) mEq/l	pH ≥ 7.25 pO_2 28 – 32 mmHg pCO_2 ≤ 40 mmHg BE 0 – (-5) mEq/l	

<u>Using the arterial norms:</u>	
Hypoxia	pO_2 < 16 mmHg : cells lack oxygen
Respiratory acidosis	pH < 7.20, pCO_2 > 60: pre-acidotic 51-59, CO_2 retention
Metabolic acidosis	pH < 7.20, BE < - 10 mEq/l: lactic acid retention
Asphyxia	pH < 7.20, pO2 < 16 mmHg, pCO_2 > 60, BE < - 10mEq/l

*adapted from information from Fetal Monitoring Certification Seminar, Michelle Murray, Houston, Texas, December 11 – 13, 1995

Criteria for Apgar Scoring

Sign	0	1	2
Heart rate	Absent	Below 100	Over 100
Respiratory effort	Absent	Slow, irregular	Good, crying
Muscle tone	Flaccid	Some flexion of extremities	Active motion
Reflex irritability	No response	Grimace	Vigorous cry
Color	Blue, pale	Body pink, extremities blue	Completely pink

Figure 1.9 Criteria for Apgar Scoring

The mere presence of a low Apgar score is not necessarily indicative of intrapartum asphyxia. Several studies have demonstrated both false-positive and false-negative results. False positives (low Apgar score, normal cord pH) can be seen with analgesia and prematurity. False negatives (normal Apgar, low pH) can be seen with acute asphyxia and maternal metabolic acidosis. Infants that demonstrate a persistent low Apgar score at five, ten, or twenty minutes despite resuscitation are associated with increasing mortality and morbidity.[65]

Apgar scores are most commonly assigned by the nurse attending the delivery, who then records them on the delivery summary and record. The nurse's initials may appear next to the Apgar score to identify the person who evaluated the infant. The standard of care requires nurses to be honest in their assessments, and communicate their findings to the obstetrician and, when indicated, the pediatrician. Attorneys often scrutinize Apgar scores. A disparity between the Apgar score and the subsequent clinical condition of the infant can raise questions about the accuracy of the score.

1.12 Neonatal Resuscitation

Some of the most anxiety-producing moments in the obstetrical suite occur when a newborn infant requires active resuscitation. Neonatal resuscitation is the responsibility of both obstetric and neonatal and pediatric personnel. The anesthesia department may also be held responsible. At least one person attending a delivery must be capable of performing neonatal resuscitation. The resuscitation must be skillfully performed with equipment in good working order.

For example, the following case involves a failure to have the proper equipment in the delivery room, as well as not having skilled personnel immediately available to perform infant resuscitation:

The minor plaintiff was born with the umbilical cord wrapped around her neck. As a result she required resuscitation following delivery. The family practitioner and the nurses attempted resuscitation. The resuscitation equipment required to be available in the delivery room, including a positive pressure breathing bag, and a stylet for intubation, and oxygen, was not available. The positive pressure bag was not previously used in the labor and delivery area and was unassembled at the time of the baby's delivery. The nurse providing for positive pressure did not immediately know how to put together the bag and may have incorrectly supplied oxygen to the baby. In addition, intubation was not

accomplished for 12 minutes. As a result the child suffered a hypoxic/ischemic event which caused a stroke in the right side of the child's brain, resulting in left-sided partial paralysis greater in the arm than the leg. There was apparently no cognitive deficit. The defendants asserted the delay in resuscitation was of short duration, the resuscitation was effective and that the child's brain damage must have resulted from another unknown cause. A jury returned a verdict of $780,000 for the minor plaintiff.[66]

Checking the resuscitation equipment is the ultimate responsibility of the labor and delivery nursing staff. This is one of the essential responsibilities that cuts across all areas of nursing. If the nurses attending the delivery are incapable of performing neonatal resuscitation, either the charge nurse or the nurse caring for the patient is responsible for making arrangements for someone with those skills to attend the delivery. The nursing staff is also responsible for notifying the pediatrician or neonatologist when a high-risk delivery is anticipated.

Many institutions require that all nurses who attend deliveries complete the Neonatal Resuscitation Program, developed by the AAP and the American Heart Association (AHA). The content of this program is accepted as the standard of care for infant resuscitation across the nation. Competency validation is required every two years.[67]

1.13 Recovery Period

After delivery, the patient typically recovers in the OB unit's recovery area. With the trend in single-setting deliveries, though, the recovery phase now often takes place in the room where the delivery occurred. The exception would be a patient having a cesarean section, in which case a more traditional recovery setting is often used. The nurse is responsible for providing postpartum monitoring which includes frequent (every 15 minutes for the first hour after delivery) vital signs, fundus (the top of the uterus) checks to watch for postpartum hemorrhage, assessments of bleeding, and follow-up of any preexisting or incipient signs or symptoms of problems such as pre-eclampsia or diabetes. Conditions such as pre-eclampsia (toxemia or pregnancy-induced hypertension) at times do not become evident until after delivery. Other problems, such as postpartum hemorrhage, may be a logical consequence of circumstances that arose during labor, such as overuse of Pitocin or uterine atony. The postpartum recovery nurse is responsible for observing for these problems.

1.14 Postpartum Period

The postpartum period is a critical transition time for a woman, from both physiological and psychological perspectives. After birth, the woman's body undergoes significant changes as it returns to its prepregnancy state.[68] During the short hospital stay post delivery, the maternal newborn staff helps the woman and her family care for her general needs and those of her newborn. It is also the time when any potential problems or complications need to be identified. One of the most serious concerns in the immediate postpartum period is excessive maternal blood loss. "Hemorrhage remains one of the leading causes of maternal mortality."[69] Hospitals that provide obstetrical services have to be prepared to manage maternal hemorrhage.

There are many factors associated with obstetrical hemorrhage. These include uterine atony, uterine inversion, obstetrical lacerations, retained placental fragments, placental abnormalities, and maternal coagulopathies.[70] Nursing responsibilities include close maternal postpartum observations for timely identification of signs of excessive blood loss, including hypotension and tachycardia. The uterine fundus needs to be evaluated for its size and degree of contraction, and massaged as needed. Medications such as Oxytocin, Hemabate, and Methergine should be readily available for the treatment of uterine atony.

The following scenario involves a patient who experienced a devastating postpartum hemorrhage (PPH). A primigravida delivers an 11-pound, ten-ounce baby boy and is subsequently transferred to the postpartum unit. The nurse notices the patient is experiencing bright red vaginal bleeding in large amounts with few clots. The nurse documents her findings and rechecks the patient in 30 minutes. She finds the patient has heavily saturated eight pads. The nurse notifies the physician, who instructs her to continue observing the patient. A change of shift occurs, and the oncoming nurse determines on her initial assessment the patient has excessive bleeding and unstable vital signs. The nurse calls the physician to come immediately to the hospital. The patient subsequently suffers cardiac arrest and a code blue is called. Resuscitative measures are unsuccessful.[71] The nurse should have taken reasonable care in monitoring the client's condition, as the client had an increased risk of postpartum hemorrhage related to the overdistention of the uterus caused by a macrosomic infant.

Even when prompt identification and treatment are instituted, maternal hemorrhage can still cause devastating consequences, as seen in the following case:

A 37-year-old woman delivers her third child three minutes after arriving in labor and delivery, with a nurse midwife present but no attending physician. She delivered a nine-pound, two-ounce infant. The woman's postpartum course was complicated by uterine atony with intermittent bleeding. Oxytocin and methergine was administered and vigorous fundal massage was tried. The woman's uterus remained atonic, however, and she continued to bleed intermittently over the next hour. The physician, who had just finished an emergency cesarean section, also tried fundal massage and ordered hemabate. He ordered blood for crossmatch, coagulation studies, and continued to monitor her status. When her vital signs dropped significantly, he took her to surgery and performed a dilation and curettage (D&C). He found no retained products of conception, but the bleeding, though somewhat controlled, did not stop completely. Over the next hour the midwife and nurse continued to provide fundal massage and medications and the woman continued to bleed intermittently. She received 4 units of packed red blood cells and several thousand milliliters of IV fluids and plasma expander. The physician then determined the patient needed an emergency hysterectomy. As he was removing the woman's uterus, he noted continued pelvic bleeding and summoned another surgeon for help. After a number of vessels were sutured and ligated, the patient continued to bleed. The patient then went to the ICU, in critical but stable condition. She continued to receive IV fluid support and additional transfusions of blood products until she developed a fatal cardiac arrhythmia and died. A defense verdict was returned in this case.[72]

1.15 Normal Newborn Care

The first 28 days of life are considered the neonatal period. During this time numerous physiological changes occur as the newborn adapts to life after birth.[73] Healthcare providers need to be diligent in being aware of any deviations from normal; early identification and prompt intervention is crucial in optimizing healthy newborn outcomes.

All institutions that provide maternity services have to include an overall security program to protect the physical safety of newborns. There should be policies and procedures in place for visitation, newborn identification, verification of personnel, transfer, and discharge.[74]

There are numerous commercial newborn security systems on the market, which have state of the art abduction thwarting systems. Not only are these necessary for legal reasons, but they protect against unnecessary grief and anguish of parents, as well as the unfavorable publicity that can have long-lasting repercussions.[75]

An article from the *Reno Gazette Journal* relates the story of Olga Lopez, who kidnapped a ten-hour-old newborn from a maternity ward in Reno, Nevada. Lopez devised an elaborate scheme to save her failing marriage by faking pregnancy. Her scheme included showing her husband two sonograms of a baby boy and made non-existent appointments with doctors. She tried to take a baby from another hospital but was asked to leave after nurses noted suspicious behavior. In the successful abduction, she went into the hospital room posing as a social worker and told the new mother she needed to take the baby for tests. She never came back. Lopez was later apprehended after being recognized from a description. She was at another hospital, where she had called relatives to pick her up after she claimed she had delivered her infant.[76]

This is a typical profile of an infant abductor. Usually the abductor is a female of childbearing age, often overweight, may indicate she has lost a baby, and is married or cohabitating with a companion who desires to have a baby. She often has a strong desire to give birth, frequently impersonates a nurse or other allied healthcare personnel, frequently visits maternity units at more than one facility, asks questions about the routine, learns the layout of the unit, and plans the abduction.[77]

The National Council of Missing and Exploited Children (NCMEC) has a publication entitled *For Healthcare Providers: Guidelines on Prevention of and Response to Infant Abductions*.[78] In a case involving an infant abduction, the attorney should request the institution's policies and procedures regarding infant safety. Critical incident response plans should include a detailed written plan of what should occur in the event of an infant abduction.

According to a NCMEC report, the greatest number of hospital abductions occurs from the mother's room. There has been a decrease in the number of abductions, speculated to be from an increased focus on prevention and education of staff and parents of abduction-thwarting strategies, and availability of more sophisticated security equipment. In infant abduction cases, the hospital has potential liability on the basis that it has a duty to prevent foreseeable harm to its patients.[79] Individuals that have a strong determination to abduct a newborn are a real danger. Hospitals need to take reasonable measures to thwart abductions by having security measures in place that make abductions as difficult as possible.

1.16 Areas of Specific Nursing Liability

Some practices in obstetrical nursing are especially vulnerable to problems and subsequent allegations of malpractice. Some would argue that the increase in litigation of obstetrical cases is directly proportional to advances in technological capabilities during pregnancy, labor, and delivery. However, while cases involving problems with fetal monitoring do constitute a significant percentage of liability claims against nurses, the majority of nursing liability problems arises from other "low-tech" sources.[80] Seven major omissions that form the basis for many obstetrical nursing malpractice cases include:

A. Failure to appropriately monitor maternal and fetal status; failure to correctly interpret fetal monitor strips
B. Inappropriate oxytocin administration, use, or monitoring
C. Failure to notify the physician in a timely fashion
D. Initiation of procedures without adequate client information or consent
E. Improper sponge and instrument counts during cesarean surgery
F. Failure to use chain of command when physician does not respond quickly or appropriately
G. Failure to recognize signs of uterine rupture

A. Failure to Appropriately Monitor Maternal and Fetal Status; Failure to Correctly Interpret Fetal Monitor Strips

The Controlled Risk Insurance Company (CRICO) provides professional liability insurance to all Harvard-affiliated physicians, healthcare institutions, and their employees. Between 1987 and 1996, nurses were named in 70 percent of all CRICO claims that named non-physicians, and 14 percent of all CRICO claims. The most frequent allegation in CRICO's perinatal case is delay in diagnosis of fetal distress. Delay in diagnosis of fetal distress is a national phenomenon and was reported in 1998 to be a factor in 88 percent of malpractice cases related to neurologically impaired newborns, up from 41 percent ten years earlier.[81] Liability regarding fetal heart-rate monitoring most frequently attaches to the nursing staff, as the nurse is the primary healthcare provider for a woman in labor. Before the advent of electronic fetal heart-rate monitoring, nurses and physicians auscultated the fetal heart tones with a weighted, oversized stethoscope or a "fetascope" (a stethoscope with an additional metal headpiece that relies on bone conduction through the listener's skull to pick up fetal heart tones). Fetal heart rates were counted manually by the individual listener, which obviously built in great variations in accuracy.

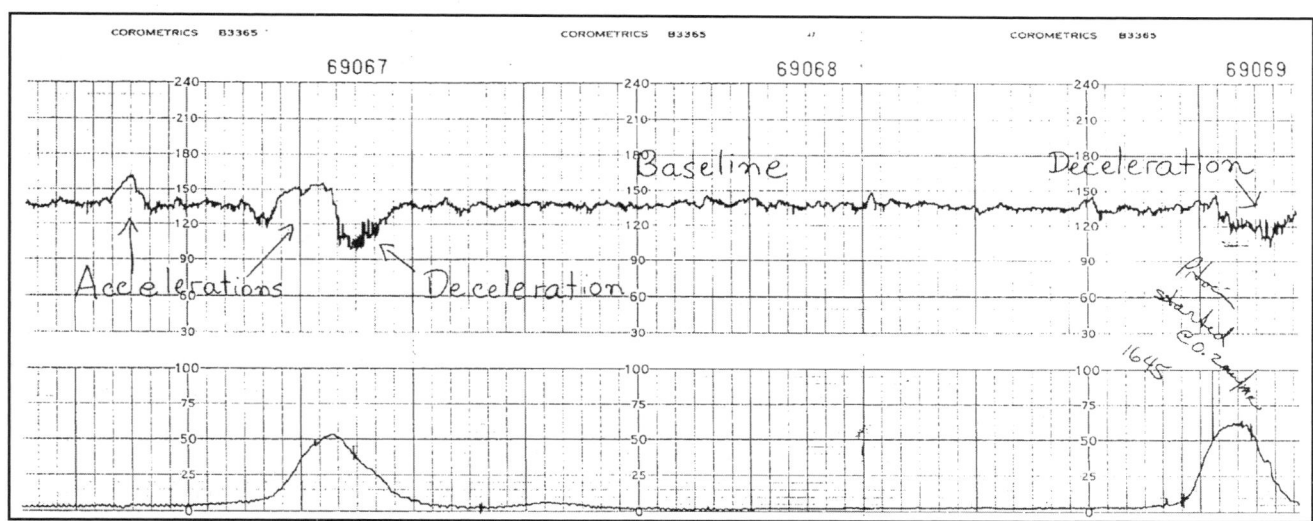

Figure 1.10 *Monitoring Strip. Reprinted with permission of Corometrics Medical Systems, Wallingford, Connecticut from Rabello and Lapidus, Fundamentals of Electronic Fetal Heart Monitoring, 1988.*

The invention of the electronic fetal heart-rate monitor permitted more accurate assessment of fetal response to contractions and labor. Electronic fetal heart-rate monitoring (EFM) is accomplished by means of an ultrasonic transducer placed externally, or an electrode placed internally on the fetal presenting part (usually the infant's scalp). The heart rate is printed on a continuous strip of graph paper as a continuous line or tracing (see Figure 1.10). Uterine contractions are most frequently measured by an externally placed device. An internal uterine pressure monitor is also available, but is used less often than the external monitor, primarily when the adequacy of contractions is questionable such as in labor arrest difficulties. This information is printed continuously on a two-channel recorder.

Obtaining and interpreting fetal monitoring strips are essential steps in the litigation of obstetrical malpractice cases. For the attorney examining the fetal monitoring strip, the following will be evident. The fetal heart rate (FHR) is printed on the upper channel, and the uterine activity is printed on the lower panel. The tracing prints in real-time, allowing for precise timing of events. When run at the standard 3 centimeters per minute paper speed, each small block on the paper represents ten seconds. Dark vertical lines mark off increments of one minute. Reference numbers in ascending order are found on the top of each sheet between paper perforations. Depending on the monitor's manufacturer, each sheet represents either three or three and one-third minutes. Any nurse, nurse midwife, or obstetrician caring for a monitored patient is obligated to be able to read and interpret the fetal monitoring strip. It is highly recommended

nurses chart all pertinent information on the FHR tracing first, and then in the patient's chart.[82] This allows for correlation between maternal condition and interventions with the resulting effect exhibited in the FHR. With the advent of central fetal surveillance stations, such as the Watch Child system, much of the documentation is done electronically and is automatically printed on the fetal monitor strip.

TIP: The labor and delivery nurse is responsible for assessing, recognizing, intervening for, and responding to any abnormalities in the tracing. The nurse is further charged with adequately documenting, and notifying the physician of, fetal and maternal status.

According to ACOG standards, EFM is not required in all patients, particularly low-risk patients. However, intensive monitoring of both fetal heart rate and contractions is mandated in high-risk laboring patients. If the nurse is not available to listen to the fetal heart rate at the required intervals, EFM is a better modality. Electronic fetal monitoring can detect at least some cases of fetal distress.[83]

The nurse applies external fetal monitors. In several states, the nurse, after specific certification, may apply internal FHR as well as uterine contraction monitors. This is dictated by the state Nurse Practice Acts. The rationale behind certification for placement of internal monitors is related to the potential complications of placement, as well as the need for the membranes to be ruptured before using internal monitors. Few state Nurse Practice Acts allow nurses to artificially rupture amniotic membranes.

In a North Carolina case, the infant was born with severe asphyxia. The plaintiff's physician experts testified it was a gross deviation from the standards of practice to fail to use an electronic fetal monitor on the mother in light of her high-risk factors. The obstetrician and the labor and delivery nurses, the defendants in the trial, testified the doctor never used the electronic fetal monitor on any of his patients. The plaintiff's nursing experts testified it was negligent for the nurses to fail to question the doctor's refusal to institute electronic fetal monitoring on the mother, given the risk factors present. Further, these experts were of the opinion it was negligent for the nurses, including the head nurse in labor and delivery, to fail to notify their superiors about the doctor's constant failure to use fetal monitoring. In the opinion of all these experts, had fetal monitoring been used on the mother during her labor, abnormal fetal heart-rate patterns would have been detected. This would have permitted and necessitated intervention by cesarean section, which would in all likelihood have prevented the permanent brain damage suffered by the infant before his birth. The plaintiffs settled with the defendants just before trial for $3 million.[84]

The obstetrician's failure to follow the prevailing standard of care placed a further duty on the nurses to intervene on the patients' behalf and provide adequate, if not good, care. These nurses failed to do so. This case also points out the independent status of the nurse in contemporary health care. The nurse's role as the patient's advocate is a standard of practice in the profession of nursing.

Nurses are responsible not only for placing monitors, they are also charged with maintaining tracing quality or "readability" as well as the assessment of the fetal heart rate and uterine patterns on the tracings. Electronic fetal heart-rate monitoring increases the accountability of nurses. In addition to the knowledge and skills required to provide care to patients, nurses must know how to use, adjust, and maintain the equipment. The interpretation of the tracing is based on an understanding of fetal and maternal physiology and their separate and combined effects on fetal heart rate. The accuracy of the tracing depends on the elimination of artifact or extraneous lines caused by patient movement. Interpretation of the strip depends upon the nurse's ability to recognize patterns of the fetal heart rate and uterine activity. It is essential the nurse be able to recognize and report any

heart-rate patterns that indicate fetal hypoxia. To provide appropriate patient care, the nurse also must know the appropriate interventions for responding to these patterns. See Figure 1.11 for an overview of FHR patterns and causes.

The following case illustrates a failure to appropriately monitor:

The mother had a long history of hypertension. Upon admission she was assessed by the hospital's nursing staff as "high risk." She labored through the night, morning, and early afternoon, and was slowly progressing without evidence of complications. At 4:00 P.M. she was started on Pitocin, and her blood pressure was periodically spiking at a high rate. She had been on and was continued on a fetal monitoring machine, pursuant to the policies and procedures of the hospital as well as the doctor's orders. While on the monitor, the nurse had the client use a birthing ball and walk in the room, and the external monitor showed no discernible tracing. At 6:43 P.M., the mother went into a seizure, and an internal fetal monitor was applied. Immediate signs of fetal compromise were observed. The nursing staff began decreasing the Pitocin and then turned it off completely by 6:53 P.M. The mother was then experiencing a massive, uncontrolled seizure and the baby's fetal heart tones dropped into a low and dangerous pattern. An on-site physician was called who rendered care immediately and a vaginal delivery was performed. The infant was born with low Apgars and had seizure activity soon after birth. The plaintiff's experts testified that due to the failure to properly monitor the mother for approximately one and one-half hours, the nursing staff was unaware whether the baby was being deprived of oxygen. A settlement was made in this case for $1.4 million.[85]

This case demonstrates the accountability of the nurses to obtain a "readable" fetal monitor tracing. If the nurses are able to observe signs of fetal well-being, measures need to be taken to evaluate the status of the fetus. In this case, with evidence of increased maternal blood pressure, nursing care should have included maintaining the mother in a lateral position. With the mother in the bed as opposed to up and about in the room, a fetal monitor tracing could have been obtained. Other assessment parameters such as maternal deep tendon reflexes should also have been evaluated.

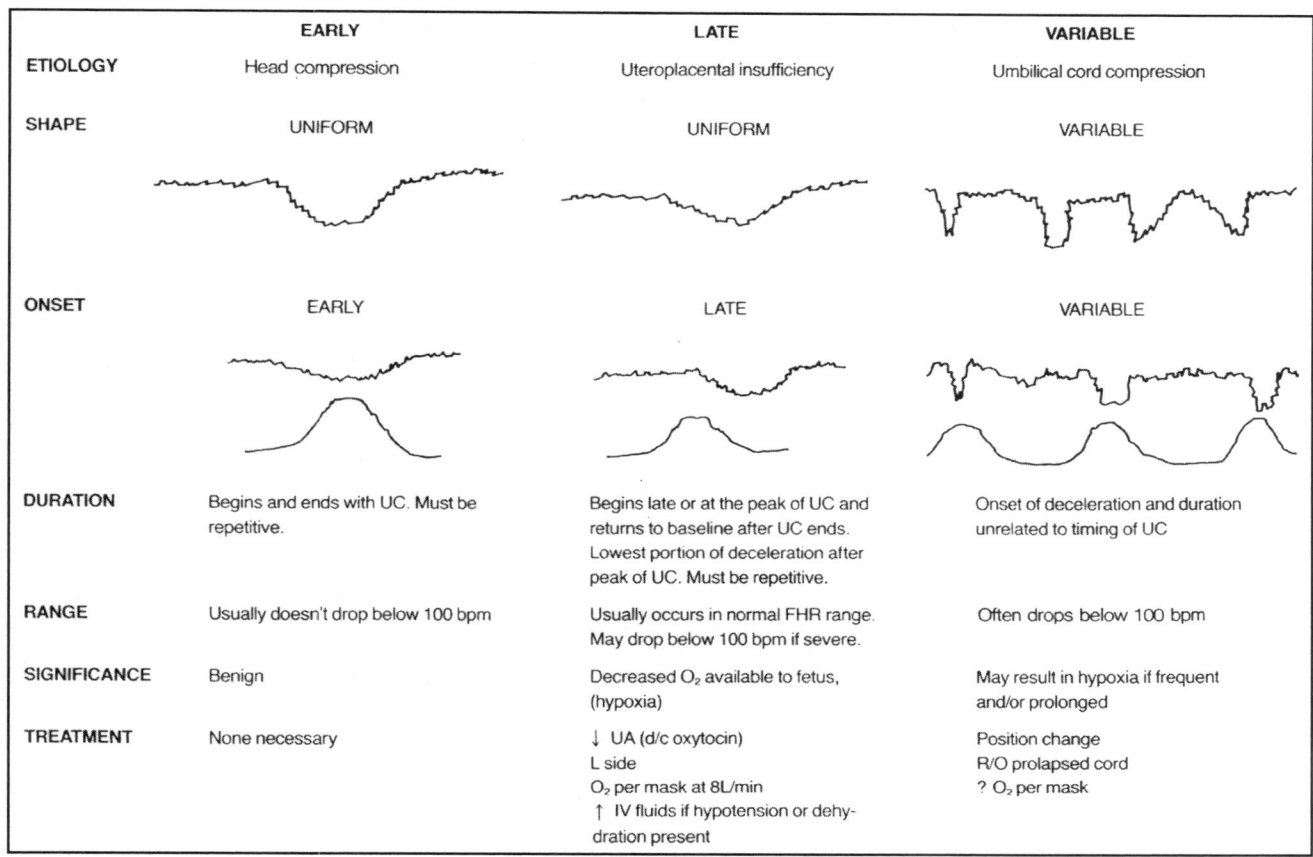

	EARLY	LATE	VARIABLE
ETIOLOGY	Head compression	Uteroplacental insufficiency	Umbilical cord compression
SHAPE	UNIFORM	UNIFORM	VARIABLE
ONSET	EARLY	LATE	VARIABLE
DURATION	Begins and ends with UC. Must be repetitive.	Begins late or at the peak of UC and returns to baseline after UC ends. Lowest portion of deceleration after peak of UC. Must be repetitive.	Onset of deceleration and duration unrelated to timing of UC
RANGE	Usually doesn't drop below 100 bpm	Usually occurs in normal FHR range. May drop below 100 bpm if severe.	Often drops below 100 bpm
SIGNIFICANCE	Benign	Decreased O_2 available to fetus, (hypoxia)	May result in hypoxia if frequent and/or prolonged
TREATMENT	None necessary	↓ UA (d/c oxytocin) L side O_2 per mask at 8L/min ↑ IV fluids if hypotension or dehydration present	Position change R/O prolapsed cord ? O_2 per mask

Figure 1.11 Characteristics of FHR Deceleration Patterns. Reprinted with permission of Corometrics Medical Systems, Wallingford, CT from Rabello and Lapidus, Fundamentals of Electronic Fetal Heart Monitoring, 1988.

Competency validation is an important factor that needs to be confirmed for all staff functioning in the perinatal clinical setting. AWHONN provides multiple publications to assist the nurse in this endeavor, including a text entitled *Competence Validation*. Another valuable tool is entitled *Fetal Assessment of Well-Being: AWHONN Competence Assessment Tool* (1999, reviewed in 2004). Nurses working in obstetrics need to be judicious in their efforts to keep current, and should have yearly educational updates and competency verification. A joint statement by ACOG and NAACOG in March 1986 regarding EFM addressed the hospital's responsibility to verify the knowledge base of its health professionals in the clinical application of electronic fetal monitoring. Hospital administrators therefore may not place inexperienced nurses in situations for which they are unprepared in terms of fetal heart-rate monitoring education.[86] All perinatal nurses are responsible for pattern recognition, interpretation, nursing intervention, documentation, and maintenance of current knowledge base.[87] The fetal heart-rate tracing is a permanent part of the patient's chart. It should also be retrievable, as is the chart itself. Hospital medical record departments vary in practices regarding where the tracing is actually filed. Some file them with the maternal chart, others with the neonatal chart. Some facilities microfilm or microfiche the tracings and keep them separately from the medical record. It is also possible, in some institutions, to record the FHR tracing on tape at the time of the event, thus reducing the need to keep multiple paper copies of the tracing. Copies of the tracing can be made by printing the tape by computer. The end result is a clear, clean, essentially original tracing printed on monitor paper that allows for better interpretation. When used with monitors that allow typed computer input of nursing and other notations and interventions, the problems with unclear or over-handled tracings become obsolete. This type of tracing is available in only some hospitals, and therefore it behooves the attorney to inquire if a particular hospital has this capability.

Some labor and delivery units have central monitoring systems that place a second view of the tracing on a monitor screen for viewing outside the patient's room. These monitors may also have a tape drive that allows similar regeneration of the tracing. Presumably, a functioning central monitoring system in a labor unit extends the responsibility for interpretation of FHR tracings to other nurses who may observe them. The attorney should find out if the unit has such a system, and arrange to talk with other nurses working at the time of the problem in question.

Failure to provide adequate or appropriate fetal monitoring is a common allegation in medical malpractice in the labor and delivery area. Negligence can be based on the deviations listed in Figure 1.12. The following case illustrates the nurse's responsibility both to interpret the FHR tracing appropriately and to notify the physician of non-reassuring FHR patterns:

> The plaintiff's mother was admitted to the defendant hospital after her bag of water broke. The fetal monitor indicated the fetus had experienced approximately two periods of brief decelerated heart rate about one-half hour after admission, with periods of moderate decelerations in the half-hour following this. There were subsequent periods of decelerated heart rate, and the nurse reported the fetus was fine. More variable decelerations occurred shortly after this. The nurse contacted the doctor and reported the mother was 8 centimeters dilated, but did not report the nature and extent of the variable decelerations. A stat cesarean section was ordered shortly after this, and the baby was delivered 38 minutes after the section was called. The plaintiff child had Apgars of 0 at one minute, but was resuscitated. The child suffered brain damage, cannot walk or talk, and has cerebral palsy. The plaintiff argued the nurses failed to timely contact the physician regarding the decelerations, and the hospital failed to have an operating room ready in a timely manner. A $23.3 million verdict was returned against the hospital.[88]

The ACOG Committee on Obstetric Practice is encouraging clinicians to cease using the term "fetal distress," and to use the phrase "non-reassuring fetal status."[89] The committee opinion states the term fetal distress has a low positive predictive value. Clinicians are counseled to be descriptive of the clinical findings in any non-reassuring fetal tracing.[90] However, there is no agreement among OB-GYN practitioners regarding this issue, and inconsistency continues in the terminology used in interpreting electronic fetal monitoring. Some observers believe the change in terminology is a direct result of the current litigation climate. The term "fetal distress" is a red flag for attorneys.

B. Inappropriate Oxytocin Administration, Use, or Monitoring

Ironically, one of the most common grounds for litigation in obstetrics arises not from use or misuse of new technology but from aspects of a medication commercially available to U.S. obstetricians since 1928. Oxytocin had been used in Germany since 1910 to induce labor by causing uterine contractions, and was marketed by Parke-Davis in the United States under the brand name Pitocin. In the 1950s, a synthetic version was developed and marketed by Parke-Davis under the same name.[91] Contraindications for the use of Pitocin (oxytocin) began to appear in the Physicians' Desk Reference (PDR) in 1962. The list of precautions and contraindications grew throughout the 1960s and 1970s. Restrictions on the amounts and routes of administration became tighter until, in the mid-1970s, the recommended route of administration of intrapartum oxytocin was solely by intravenous (IV) infusion pump. The pump strictly regulates the rate of flow. This remains the standard form of administration today. A pump controls the rate of flow in one of two ways: by counting drops or by regulating flow itself. The latter method is preferable, as it does not rely on anyone's calculations or type of IV tubing to deliver an accurate amount of medication. Oxytocin administration rates should always be ordered by the healthcare provider as milliunits per minute (mU/min). Nursing documentation indicates the amount of milliunits per minute that is being infused.[92] A potential side effect of oxytocin is that it can produce maternal water intoxication; therefore intake and output should also be measured.[93]

---

1. Inadequate training regarding the use of the fetal monitor
2. Inadequate education regarding the interpretation of fetal monitoring tracings
3. Failure to observe the monitor frequently enough
4. Discontinuing the monitor too soon
5. Failure to notify the physician, or timely notify the physician, regarding fetal monitor results (Grossman, 1993)

Figure 1.12 *Deviations from the Standards of Care Associated with Fetal Heart-Rate Monitoring*

TIP: It is conceivable a pump may malfunction and administer too much medication too fast. If this is suspected, request the incident report and biomedical logs that show when the machine was last checked.

All labor and delivery units must have a policy or procedure for Pitocin administration; this policy or procedure is obtainable during discovery. This will specify the method of administration, the concentration of the drug, and the nursing responsibilities for monitoring the patient. A one-to-one nurse-to-patient ratio is recommended during oxytocin dosage adjustment. Maternal-fetal assessment during oxytocin infusion should occur at least before each dosage increase; however, other factors such as stage of labor and maternal-fetal risk status should be considered when determining frequency.[94] ACOG recommends that when oxytocin is being administered, the fetal heart rate, resting tone of the uterus, and frequency and duration of contractions should be monitored appropriately, either by electronic fetal monitor or palpation and auscultation, every 15 minutes during the first stage of labor and every five minutes during the second stage of labor.[95] Oxytocin should not be used unless fetal status is reassuring. If exceptions are made because of unusual clinical circumstances, a physician's note documenting the circumstances and rationale must be in the record.[96] The nurse needs to ensure that the nursing supervisor is aware of the clinical situation, and that the appropriate support staff to handle an emergency is readily available.

Administration of oxytocin must be carefully controlled and monitored, as too large a dose results in excessive uterine contractions which can injure the fetus or rupture the uterus. (See Figure 1.13.) "Nursing responsibility during oxytocin infusion involves careful titration of the drug to the maternal-fetal response."[97] This process includes decreasing or discontinuing the oxytocin infusion when the contractions are too frequent or fetal status is nonreassuring. Hyperstimulation describes contractions less than two minutes apart and greater than 90 seconds in duration. A uterine resting tone of greater than 20 mmHg by an intrauterine pressure catheter is also considered hyperstimulation.[98] Murray[99] identifies hyperstimulation as the interval between contractions being less than one minute and contractions occurring closer than every two minutes. The patient's progress (e.g., cervical dilation rate, fetal descent rate) should be periodically communicated to the physician. A physician capable of performing a cesarean section must be readily available when the nurse is administering Pitocin to a labor patient.[100]

Reference	Initial Dose (mU/min)	Incremental Dose (mU/min)	Incremental Time Interval (min)
Seitchik et al. (1983)	0.5–1	1–2	40–60
Hauth et al. (1986)	1 or 2	1	15

Figure 1.13 *Protocols for Oxytocin Infusion Rates*

TIP: Required assessments during Pitocin administration during labor include the following:
- Every 15 minutes: evaluation of uterine contractions including frequency, duration, intensity, and uterine tone
- Every 15 minutes: evaluation of fetal heart rate including baseline rate, variability, and periodic changes (i.e., accelerations and decelerations)

- Monitoring of intake and output
- Maternal vital signs before dosage adjustment, and as stage of labor and patient condition indicate, in accordance with institution protocol

Issues in lawsuits in cases involving the use of oxytocin usually fall into two categories: (1) injudicious use of the drug, and (2) failure to appropriately monitor the patient during its administration. Physicians are most often charged with the former, while nurses more frequently are held responsible for the latter.

TIP: Review the nursing documentation of Pitocin administration for completeness of maternal and fetal monitoring including vital signs and assessments of fetal status at required intervals.

The majority of cases involving injudicious drug use occur in conjunction with augmentation (intensification) of labor, as opposed to induction (initiation of labor). Augmentation of labor may be needed when labor slows down, contractions space out or become less forceful, or progress of cervical dilation slows or stops. Administration of oxytocin is commonly ordered to restore contractions and labor progress. However, arrest of labor may be an indication of a complication such as cephalo-pelvic disproportion (CPD). In this situation, the fetus's head, which is its largest anatomical part, is too large to fit through the maternal pelvis. It is occasionally possible to predict this circumstance before labor, as in large infants of diabetic women. It is possible and desirable to identify the problem once it presents during labor. The combination of inappropriate oxytocin augmentation with the natural forces of labor causes some of the worst neonatal injuries observed. Oxytocin use can also result in uterine hyperstimulation, which in turn may cause uteroplacental insufficiency as seen in the following case:

> The plaintiff was admitted to the labor and delivery unit with contractions every three to five minutes. Her labor was augmented with the use of Pitocin. The plaintiff contended that the Pitocin was used to the point of uterine hyperstimulation. This jeopardized the placental gas exchange, leading to fetal acidosis, resulting in hypoxic ischemic encephalopathy. The plaintiff presented evidence that the hospital nurses and residents failed to follow a standing order for the administration of Pitocin, that the hospital staff failed to respond appropriately to non-reassuring fetal heart tracing, and that the order to restart the Pitocin after it had been discontinued by the nurse for a period of 14 minutes should have been questioned or overturned. The infant's Apgar scores were 3 at one minute, and 6 at 15 minutes, exhibiting signs of severe metabolic acidosis. The child now has static encephalopathy with spasticity in her extremities, decreased mental development and microcephaly. The jury awarded the plaintiff $6.5 million.[101]

C. Miscommunication

One of the major responsibilities of the obstetrical nurse after assessing the patient is to notify the physician of the findings. Physicians cannot act on information they have not received. Implicit in this nursing obligation is the duty to assess the patient correctly, as well as the responsibility for having the requisite level of knowledge and education. The nurse should document all conversations with the physician, including the information conveyed to the physician as well as any responses received.

The Joint Commission has identified communication as a factor most frequently involved in sentinel events.[102] The high stress environment of an obstetrical unit contributes to the opportunities for missed communication. The following strategies are recommended by the Association of Women's Health, Obstetric and Neonatal Nurses:[103]

- The provider is asked to see the patient immediately if the mother and/or fetus are at risk.

- Speech is clear; tone is congenial.
- All relevant facts, including concerns and abnormal findings, are communicated.
- Facts are presented in a methodical and chronological style.
- Clarification of orders is requested at the time the nurse has the physician or midwife's full attention.
- Reasons for disagreement with the treatment plan are conveyed at the time of the encounter.
- The provider is informed if the chain of command process is to be enforced.

TIP: During discovery, obtain the nursing department's policies and procedures regarding documentation. Look for a policy that addresses what the nurse should document when the physician is notified of adverse changes in the patient's condition.

One of the most important responsibilities of labor and delivery nurses is the notification of the physician regarding non-reassuring fetal heart-rate patterns, as is illustrated in the following case:

> The plaintiff mother, age 22, was admitted for induction of labor after passing her due date in September. Within four hours the fetal heart monitor showed repetitive variable decelerations. The Pitocin was stopped and the decelerations stopped. The attending physician ordered the Pitocin to be restarted after an epidural was started. The fetal heart monitor became non-reactive. The labor and delivery nurse did not notify anyone of this fact. Almost three and one-half hours later the fetal heart monitor showed persistent late decelerations. The labor and delivery nurse did not notify anyone of this fact. Almost two hours later the fetal heart rate crashed to 60 beats per minute. No physician saw the mother during the entire labor until the fetal heart rate crashed. The woman was taken to the operating room for an emergency cesarean section and the baby was delivered within ten minutes. The Apgars were 3 at one minute and 9 at five minutes. The baby was diagnosed with mental retardation and cerebral palsy at three months of age. A $2.3 million settlement was reached.[104]

In this case the nurse failed to properly evaluate and monitor the patient, interpret the data, and notify the physician. The labor and delivery nurse had the responsibility to have a physician review fetal status related to the non-reactive pattern and decelerations.

The nurse is charged with the responsibility of being the patient's advocate. The nurse is likely to be with the patient during the entire course of labor and is therefore required to evaluate the condition of the mother and notify the physician if a problem is identified. If the physician fails to respond or does not respond appropriately in the nurse's judgment, the nurse must notify the supervisor on call, another physician, or both.[105] In many obstetrical cases, the time for intervention may be a narrow window, so another physician may be asked to intervene. Fisher[106] recommends that unless there is an emergency, the nurse should call the doctor, wait ten minutes, and then call again. If the nurse cannot reach the doctor, the next person in the chain of command should be notified. The Joint ACOG/NAACOG Statement on Electronic Fetal Monitoring states that, in the face of non-reassuring FHR patterns, the nurse is responsible "for notifying the physician. Once the physician is notified of a non-reassuring pattern, the nurse can expect the physician to respond. There should be established hospital policy for the nurse to follow in the event the physician is unable to respond in a timely fashion."[107]

D. Initiation of Procedures Without Adequate Client Information or Consent

During the unpredictable perinatal period, the patient may be required to make planned or unplanned decisions about treatments or interventions relating to the pregnancy. In these situations, the patient can either provide or refuse authorization for those treatments or interventions.[108] However, in some emergency situations (e.g., placental abruption, ruptured uterus, cord prolapse) there is little time to provide information. For this reason, it is very important the physician or nurse midwife discuss the labor and delivery process, possible related complications, and the general management of maternal and fetal complications during the prenatal period. Failure to obtain valid consent may result in litigation if the expectant mother or the infant sustains an injury as a result of the provider's negligently failing to inform the client of known risks. The responsibility for obtaining informed consent for medical procedures rests with the physician.[109] The nurse, in the role as patient advocate, has the responsibility to ensure informed consent has been obtained. The nurse has an ethical duty to the patient to facilitate complete understanding of pertinent information, but must not assume responsibility for providing specific content.

E. Improper Sponge and Instrument Counts During Cesarean Surgery

Obstetrical units performing surgical procedures (e.g., cesarean sections, postpartum tubal ligations) need to adhere to the same standards of care as the perioperative nurses. Refer to Chapter 5, *Perioperative Nursing Malpractice Issues*, for a complete discussion on this topic. The perinatal nurse should receive didactic orientation to preoperative, intraoperative, and postoperative care.[110] Surgical counts should be the same as those used in the main hospital operating room. The institution's policies and protocols need to address procedures to be taken when there is an inconsistency in surgical counts. The following case reports a surgical sponge being retained following a cesarean section.

> The plaintiff maintained that several days following her surgery she developed severe abdominal pain and the cause of the pain was found to be a retained surgical sponge, which required a second surgery for removal. The plaintiff alleged the surgeon failed to remove the sponge after the cesarean section, the radiologist failed to detect the sponge when x-rays were taken of the abdomen, and the surgical staff of the hospital failed to properly count the sponges before and after the procedure. A $175,000 verdict was returned.[111]

F. Failure to Use Chain of Command When Physician Does Not Respond Quickly or Appropriately

When a high-risk condition is identified in a patient, it is incumbent on the nurse to intervene to provide adequate care. The duty to provide reasonable care must be carried out by the hospital's agents, and the staff members that have the most contact with the patients are the nurses. "If the attending physician is not providing appropriate care for the patient, the hospital, through its agents, has a legal duty to intervene."[112]

For the nurse, this involves knowing about and actively accessing the chain of command and following up any actions taken by his supervisors. Failure to access chain of command was an allegation in the following case:

> The plaintiff mother was pregnant with twins. At approximately 32 weeks gestation she was admitted to the hospital in preterm labor. Labor was stopped with magnesium sulfate and she was given betamethasone to mature the fetal lungs. Four days after admission the mother again went into labor. Throughout the first stage of labor both babies had reactive fetal heart-rate patterns, indicating that both were well during that time. The plaintiff began pushing at approximately 1:40 P.M. After several hours, the presenting twin had descended to

+1/+2 station, and the heart-rate pattern had deep variable decelerations, diminished fetal heart rate variability, and a rising baseline. No intrauterine resuscitative measures were made and no cesarean ordered. At 6:20 P.M. the defendant physician noted that the presenting part had descended to +3 station. The plaintiff claimed the fetal heart-rate pattern for the presenting baby mandated immediate delivery and the nurse did not summon another physician when it was apparent the defendant physician was not responding appropriately. At 6:42 P.M. the fetal heart rate of the presenting twin decreased to 50 beats per minute and thereafter did not record. At 6:50 P.M. a cesarean section was ordered for failure to descend. At 7:33 P.M. the presenting twin was delivered by cesarean section. She was limp, blue and white, and without respiratory effort or heart rate. Resuscitative efforts were halted at three minutes, as the baby had died prior to delivery. The plaintiff alleged negligence by the nurse for failing to activate the chain of command when the physician failed to properly respond to the fetal distress. A $740,000 settlement was reached.[113]

This case illustrates that the nurse has the responsibility to recognize non-reassuring fetal heart-rate patterns, take measures to provide intrauterine resuscitation, and notify the supervisor if the physician is not responding appropriately.

G. Failure to Recognize Signs of Uterine Rupture

This area is discussed under Section 1.9, Vaginal Birth After Cesarean (VBAC), and it includes the nurses' role in recognizing a potential uterine rupture. However, any uterus can rupture, and besides the increased risk inherent in having a previously scarred uterus from a cesarean section, the following factors can also contribute to an increased risk for uterine rupture:

1. high dosages of oxytocin;
2. prostaglandin preparations;
3. hyperstimulation;
4. hypertonus;
5. grand multiparity;
6. blunt or penetrating abdominal trauma;
7. midforceps rotation;
8. maneuvers with the uterus;
9. obstructed labor; and
10. abnormal fetal lie.[114]

1.17 Charting and Documentation

The chart is the best evidence of what was done for and to the patient. An incomplete chart may be construed as an indication of incomplete care. Nurses must chart their own observations and actions thoroughly. It is important to document items such as vital signs, labor progress, assessments of fetal heart-rate patterns and uterine contractions, treatments, and medications given. Other notations that should be recorded include position changes, responses to interventions, oxygen, and so forth. It is preferable pertinent notations be written directly on the labor tracing. This allows instantaneous documentation, because the nurse may write the interventions for a particular problem at the time the problem becomes evident in the tracing. Because the fetal monitor tracing is continuous, it is also possible to reconstruct the timing of events when the information is written on the tracing itself. It is acceptable for nurses to document on the tracing first and then write the narrative notes in the nursing notes at a later time.

Nurses are not faulted for caring for a patient and then completing the chart after the delivery has occurred or after the complication has been resolved. However, such entries should be noted as "late entry," and should be made as soon as feasible, preferably the same day the nurse cared for the patient.[115] See Chapter 7, *Nursing Documentation*, in Volume I, for more information regarding late entries.

Commercially available records for labor and delivery (e.g., Hollister) have made nurses' charting a great deal easier. Because of the repetitive nature of some of the necessary assessments, many hospitals have adopted these record systems to facilitate better, more comprehensive, and easier charting. As noted previously, some monitors include the capability for direct information input through a bedside computer keyboard connected to the monitor. Information entered in this manner appears as typed information on the tracing, thus alleviating problems with illegible penmanship, among other things. Documentation by nurses is important for both patient care as well as support of the nurse in adversarial situations with a physician, as the next case illustrates:

> The plaintiff went to the hospital at 32 weeks gestation complaining of headaches, chest pain, nausea, vomiting, blurred vision, and abdominal pain. When the nurse first called the physician regarding the plaintiff's status at 4:00 A.M., the physician did not come to the hospital to examine the plaintiff. The nurse called the defendant again at 6:00 A.M. The defendant testified if he had a clear understanding of everything wrong with the mother and baby,

he would have come to the hospital immediately. The defendant's medical center's nurse testified she would have reported all of the plaintiff's symptoms and test results to the defendant doctor when she called. The defendant obstetrician's partner arrived on the unit at 6:30 A.M., diagnosed pre-eclampsia, and ordered the plaintiff be transferred to a larger hospital better equipped to perform a cesarean at 32 weeks gestation. Before the transfer to another hospital, the mother's condition worsened. Her experts testified she suffered a three-minute seizure. An emergency cesarean was then performed at the defendant medical center. The experts testified the lack of timely treatment, combined with the systemic strain of the mother's seizure, deprived the fetus of needed oxygen. The plaintiffs claimed the defendants failed to timely diagnose and treat pre-eclampsia, allowing the condition to progress to a seizure stage. The plaintiffs alleged a maternal seizure caused oxygen deprivation to the fetus, resulting in permanent injuries to the newborn. The plaintiff child suffers from pulmonary problems and cognitive deficits. The plaintiff was awarded $4.1 million in damages.[116]

This case illustrates one of the classic liability dilemmas seen in many clinical areas. Lack of communication between a nurse and physician resulting in injury to a patient can become a finger-pointing nightmare. The cohesive obstetrical team managing the labor and delivery can begin fighting for self-protection when something goes wrong. The absence of documentation verifying notification of a patient's status complicates the nurse's defense and provides the plaintiff with another potential defendant. It is in the nurse's best interest to document the content of any conversations with physicians, supervisors, and others, regarding a patient. This helps eliminate questions regarding what was reported by the nurse, when the conversation took place, and the nurse's follow up or interventions.

TIP: Computer-generated or commercially available obstetrical charts (e.g., Hollister Co., ACOG) have made charting for nurses and physicians much easier and more uniform. If a hospital uses one form, most likely it uses all of them: this is important for discovery purposes, to make certain all records are obtained.

1.18 Identification of High-Risk Patients

Identifying a high-risk patient is a responsibility that falls on both physician and nurse. When an obstetrical patient arrives at the hospital, the nurse assumes the role of the primary caregiver. High-risk status in pregnancy frequently does not become evident until the patient's labor has begun. For this reason, nurses in labor and delivery (or any unit in which the patient is seen during her pregnancy) are responsible for reviewing any clinical information available regarding the patient. This includes the summary of her prenatal visits, her history and physical, and so forth. Although prenatal forms are generated and filled out in the obstetrician's office, any nurse who cares for the patient becomes responsible for reviewing extant information when seeing the patient subsequently. Consequently, each nurse should be accurate and timely in documenting and passing on pertinent information about every patient. This includes office nurses and antepartum unit nurses, as well as labor and delivery and postpartum caregivers.

Diagnosis of a high-risk condition may become manifest based on the patient's previous and present clinical information. Conditions that may become apparent as pregnancy progresses include gestational diabetes, pregnancy-induced hypertension, fetal growth restriction, multiple gestation (discovery of more than one fetus), premature rupture of membranes, bleeding, alcohol or drug abuse, fever, and so forth.

During labor, high-risk conditions can become evident as well. These conditions may include:

1. A prolapsed umbilical cord (the cord slips down between the uterine wall and the fetal presenting part, compressing it and reducing blood flow to the fetus)
2. Placenta previa (the placenta is implanted low in the uterus, partially or completely covering the cervical os (opening), and begins to "separate" as the cervix dilates away from it before the fetus is delivered)
3. The presence of meconium (fetal feces) in the amniotic fluid, which may indicate prior or current fetal stress
4. Placental abruption (premature separation of the placenta from the uterine wall resulting in covert or overt bleeding)
5. Non-reassuring fetal heart-rate pattern

Table 1.5
Recommended Staffing Patterns in the Obstetrical Unit*

Nurse to Patient Ratio	Specialty Area	Type of Care Provided
1:2	Labor and Delivery	Uncomplicated laboring patients
1:1	Labor and Delivery	Patients in second stage
1:1	Labor and Delivery	Medical or Obstetrical complications
1:2	Labor and Delivery	Oxytocin induction or augmentation
1:1	Labor and Delivery	Initiation of epidural
2:1	Labor and Delivery	Cesarean deliveries
1:6	Antepartum	Patients without complication
1:3	Antepartum	Complications but stable
1:6	Postpartum	Patients without complication
1:3	Postpartum	Complications but stable
1:3-4‡	Mother-Baby Units	Routine Care
1:4	Newborn	Transitional and close observation
1:6-8	Newborn	Routine Care
1:3-4	Newborn/NICU†	Requiring continuing care
1:2-3	Newborn/NICU	Requiring intermediate care
1:1-2	NICU	Requiring Intensive Care
1:1	NICU	Multisystem support, Ventilation support
1:1 or more	NICU	Unstable, complex care

*Adapted from AAP/ACOG Guidelines for Perinatal Care,1997; Calfee, B. Risk management guidance for short-staffed units and nurses asked to float, 1995,; and NAACOG's Considerations for Professional Nurse Staffing in Perinatal Units, OGN Nursing Practice Resource, 1988.
†Neonatal Intensive Care Unit
‡Mother-baby pairs

1.19 Staffing

Specialty guidelines need to be considered in staffing perinatal units. Guidelines for Perinatal Care staffing recommendations are provided in Table 1.5.[117] Although the principles are sound, they are based on assumed conditions, rather than real-life conditions unique to each patient. In any given situation many factors are involved in determining staffing requirements. Inherent to staffing decisions are adequate numbers of competent staff to meet the needs of the patients. Hospital administrations are responsible for providing adequate staffing and ensuring staff members are competent to perform their assigned duties. The nurse is required to communicate any individual limitations when assigned a patient whose care is beyond the nurse's competence. The institution has the responsibility to provide adequate training, orientation, competence assessment, and validation for each nurse. Staffing considerations must also look at the overall knowledge and experience of the mix of the nurses on duty during any particular shift. When scheduling staff, the plan should balance the number of inexperienced nurses with an adequate number of experienced nurses as much as possible.

The following case illustrates some of the problems that can arise when an inexperienced nurse is put in charge of caring for a laboring patient:

The plaintiff's mother was expecting her first child and had an uneventful pregnancy. At 42 weeks gestation she was admitted to the hospital in early labor. A Pitocin augmentation was undertaken. The progress of labor was slow. The nurse caring for the mother continued the administration of Pitocin despite evidence of hyperstimulation and fetal distress. Because of prolonged hyperstimulation, the fetus' condition deteriorated and electronic fetal monitor tracings showed changes in the baseline, loss of variability and late decelerations. Despite continuing evidence of fetal distress, the nurse failed to contact the treating obstetrician. The nurse testified at her deposition that she did not believe the fetal monitor tracings showed evidence of fetal distress, even after it was pointed out by her peers and physicians following the baby's birth. The treating obstetrician testified the nurse departed from accepted standards of nursing practice in failing to recognize the evidence of fetal distress and in failing to contact a physician to report the deteriorating condition of the fetus. As a result of prolonged fetal distress, the infant sustained severe hypoxic ischemic encephalopathy, resulting in brain damage. A structured settlement with a present value of $2 million was reached in May 1992.[118]

In situations such as this, both the individual nurse and the hospital can be held liable for the tragic outcome. The hospital has the responsibility of validating the nurse's competency in interpretation of fetal monitor tracings.

TIP: Many L&D units maintain a log of all deliveries, including time, date, place, physician, nurses, complications, Apgars, and so forth. Request a copy of the appropriate page to get an idea of unit activity, staffing, overcrowding, and so forth on the date or dates at issue.

There is a high risk of liability when understaffing results in an inability to meet standards of practice. Contingency staffing can be an effective way for a healthcare institution to plan for the unpredictable patient volume and complications that can occur at any time in the perinatal setting. Each organization should have a written planned approach for dealing with a staffing crisis and a contingency plan in place to deal with variable staffing needs for times of increased patient volume and/or increased acuity.

No matter how experienced the staff may be, staffing shortages may have a dramatic effect on the outcome of labor and delivery, as is illustrated in this case:

A United States District Court in Anchorage, Alaska, awarded $8.1 million to the plaintiff and his parents for negligently inflicted injuries. The judge found the United States liable for the negligent conduct of the Alaska Native Medical Center Hos-

pital which resulted in the child's cerebral palsy. Suit was brought under the Federal Tort Claims Act. The award was the largest medical malpractice award in Alaska's history and one of the largest under the Federal Tort Claims Act. The judge specially found the defendant violated the standard of care, which requires that when a prolapsed cord is present, the hospital must be staffed and equipped to be able to perform a cesarean section within 30 minutes from the time of assessment. If the hospital is unable to provide safe care for this emergency, it has an obligation to transfer the patient to another medical facility where that care could be provided. The obstetrical department was negligent because it was not appropriately staffed. The nurse on duty failed to assess the potentially life-threatening but addressable condition of a prolapsed cord as she had insufficient experience to assess, define and react to this emergency. The hospital did not have backup personnel arrangements necessary to deal adequately with this problem. The hospital's defense was complicated by the absence of a fetal monitoring strip, a labor and delivery record, nurses' progress notes, and physician's progress notes, all of which are customarily found in medical records of this type.[119]

1.20 Defenses

It is important to keep in mind there are many reasons for bad outcomes in obstetrics, not all of which are related to negligence by a healthcare provider. Common defenses include attributing the child's neurological deficits to genetic errors or in utero exposure to environmental toxins such as alcohol, medications, recreational drugs, lawn sprays, household chemicals, pesticides, oral contraceptives, x-rays, or cigarettes. The attorney should determine if the pregnant woman had a viral infection and the point in the pregnancy when it occurred. Falls, blows to the abdomen or motor vehicle accidents may also affect the developing fetus. The attorney's legal nurse consultant should determine when these incidents occurred and the nature of their severity. Before proceeding further, plaintiff's attorneys may have the parents and the infant screened for possible genetic disorders or exposure to chemicals.

According to ACOG, OB-GYN practitioners can expect an average of 2.53 medical malpractice lawsuits to be filed against them during their career. However, more than half of all claims (53.9 percent) were either dropped or settled without payment on behalf of the OB-GYN. OB-GYNs also won 65.5 percent of all claims resolved by arbitration, jury verdict, or judge's decision.[120] The expanded scope of nursing practice, in addition to the specialty technology involved, has also been associated with a greater degree of liability for professional practice. Perinatal nurses have historically experienced increased liability exposure, and have some of the highest rates for nursing malpractice insurance premiums.

A. Brain Damage

When cases involving hypoxic brain damage first began to appear a number of years ago, insurance companies, physicians, and hospitals were reluctant to defend them. The thought of a severely brain-damaged infant sitting in the courtroom was daunting. The insurance companies' willingness to settle such cases was positive reinforcement to plaintiff's attorneys to file more cases. Successful defenses of these cases increased after the cost of not defending them became evident. The defense bar's courage to begin fighting these claims and the defenses' successes in the courtroom have resulted in a decrease in the number of these lawsuits.

Plaintiff's attorneys may be confronted with the sight of an obviously neurologically damaged infant brought into the attorney's office by upset parents interested in pursuing a lawsuit against the doctor, nurse, and hospital. The attorney should see the infant before filing suit to look for obvious genetic defects and to estimate the extent of damages. Family history is very important: the attorney should attempt to identify a preexisting family disorder such as a history of genetic disorders or seizures. The attorney should determine if the infant was premature and if so, how early the child was born. Prematurity is associated with a substantial risk of injuries in direct correlation with the degree of prematurity. The earlier the delivery and the lower the birth weight, the greater the risk of intracranial hemorrhage, respiratory difficulties from immature lungs, and other problems related solely to fetal age at the time of delivery.[121]

Plaintiffs usually contend that the cause of brain damage in the infant was perinatal trauma or hypoxia due to malpractice. The defense frequently contends the act or omission did not occur and the cause of brain damage was not of intrapartum origin. Common causation defenses include:

1. The infant was unavoidably premature, and damage was due to the fragility of the preterm infant's neurological system.
2. The timing of the event, particularly in an intracranial hemorrhage, was prior to labor.
3. The fetus was growth-restricted, particularly if there is evidence of prenatal infection.

4. The problem was caused by a prenatal incident or infection.
5. Allegations that the mother used street drugs during pregnancy are often quite damaging to the plaintiff's case.
6. Placental pathology report shows a prenatal rather than a perinatal problem.

Medical literature about placental pathology has provided a proximate cause argument that attributes some of the infant's hypoxic damage to prenatal factors. For this reason, in anticipation of litigation, some obstetricians ask national experts to examine the placenta when a hypoxic infant is born.[122] Besides the advances in placental pathology, other important research findings have had important defense implications. There is increasing evidence that in most cases the brain injury associated with cerebral palsy (CP) is not related to perinatal events.[123] CP is defined as a nonprogressive motor disorder of early onset that affects approximately two to three per 1000 school-aged children. The origin of the brain injury resulting in CP may occur at anytime during the pregnancy, labor, or postnatal period. Overwhelming evidence suggests that in approximately 70 to 80 percent of CP cases, the origin has been attributed to the antepartum period. This correlates to the estimate that only 20 percent of CP is attributable to a perinatal event such as birth asphyxia.[124] The U.S. Preventive Services Task Force[125] reports that most cases of CP occur in persons without evidence of birth asphyxia or other intrapartum events.

Mental retardation must be distinguished from cerebral palsy. The etiology of severe mental retardation unaccompanied by CP is primarily genetic, viral, or developmental in origin and not related to perinatal events. Mild mental retardation also does not appear to be related to peripartum events, but rather to social and environmental conditions.[126]

Impaired cerebral blood flow is the principal mechanism attributed to intrapartum hypoxia ischemia. This occurrence is most likely a consequence of interruption in placental blood flow and gas exchange, which is more commonly referred to as asphyxia. Most infants that have impaired cerebral blood flow will respond with adaptive systemic and cerebral circulatory responses to maintain cerebral perfusion. Even when asphyxia is prolonged or severe, most newborn infants recover with minimal or no neurologic sequelae.[127]

Many factors have been associated with these antenatal hypoxic-ischemic cerebral injuries. These include maternal drug use (e.g., cocaine), multiple pregnancies, and bleeding in the third trimester. However, in most cases the cause is idiopathic (not known).

Table 1.6
Gestational Ages at which Ischemia Occurs and Resultant Type of Cerebral Lesion Identified*

Gestational Age	Lesion
Before 20th week	Neuromigrational defect, e.g. schizencephaly
Between 28th and 34th week	Periventricular leukomalacia
Between 34th and 40th week	Focal/multifactorial cerebral injury
*Adapted from information from Perlman (1997, June).	

As previously discussed, the incidence of hypoxic-ischemic cerebral injury in most cases of CP is before labor and delivery. Studies have shown that the timing of the antepartum insult is critical to the evolution of a specific lesion. Table 1.6 shows the different gestational ages at which cerebral ischemia occurs, and what type of lesion results. In attempting to determine whether an intrapartum timing of asphyxia is a proximate cause of CP, a set of conditions need to be met.[128] These are:

1. No clinical evidence for potential antenatal injury (i.e., microcephaly, multiple pregnancy, hypothyroidism, chromosomal disorders, and so forth)
2. Absence of antenatal cerebral injury by neuroimaging
3. Evidence of severe perinatal asphyxia (i.e., cord arterial pH less than 7.00, depressed neonate requiring intensive resuscitation, a postnatal syndrome of hypoxia-ischemic encephalopathy including seizures, and associated systemic abnormalities)
4. Exclusion of other causes of neonatal encephalopathy

Careful monitoring of patients in labor is performed to detect changes in the fetal heart-rate pattern that might identify asphyxia in utero. The nurse has great responsibility in the ongoing assessment, instituting appropriate interventions, ongoing evaluation, and communicating in a timely manner with the physician. Measures to identify infants at risk for asphyxia continue during the delivery process and into the initial neonatal period.

1. Lymphocytes and normoblasts

Other studies can assist the defense when events during labor and delivery are being alleged as the cause of fetal injury. Dr. Richard Naeye, a renowned pathologist, has postulated that finding large numbers of lymphocytes and normoblasts in the blood of neonates should raise the possibility of severe hypoxemia within the 24 hours that preceded the finding. Dr. Naeye reports that the time of the hypoxemia can be calculated by counting back 24 hours from the time blood lymphocyte counts rapidly decreased from high to normal or subnormal levels. Studies have shown that lymphocytes can enter the blood in large numbers within 15 minutes and normoblasts within 30 minutes of the start of severe hypoxemia-ischemia. It was also discovered the interval between the start of severe hypoxia-ischemia and the first recognized neonatal seizure in most infants is between 20 to 30 hours.[129] The defense can use these types of analysis to reveal that a child's hypoxic-ischemic brain damage took place before its mother entered a healthcare facility in labor.

2. Meconium stained amniotic fluid (MSAF)

The incidence of meconium-stained amniotic fluid during labor is approximately 20 percent. It has been considered that meconium, when thick, reflects fetal stress in utero. However, some studies report no association with fetal hypoxia, acidosis, or asphyxia. It has been further suggested the vast majority of infants with MSAF do not develop CP.[130] Studies have examined the incidence of CP associated with meconium in the amniotic fluid. It was usually assumed that acute hypoxia caused both the fetus to defecate and the brain injury. This assumption is incorrect according to Dr. Naeye.[131] Dr. Naeye describes the usual cause of defecation as being (1) the fetus aspirating amniotic fluid that contains the products of acute bacterial chorioamnitis, (2) chronic low uteroplacental blood flow and (3) congenital malformations that stress the fetus during labor.

It has been demonstrated that long-standing meconium in the amniotic fluid may itself be toxic. The presence of meconium in the amniotic fluid for a period of time before birth can induce veins on the surface of the placenta and in the umbilical cord to constrict for up to 10 to 14 hours. This could result in fetal hypoxemia-ischemia which sometimes will produce widespread hypoxic-ischemic cortical brain necrosis. After 12 to 14 hours the vasoconstriction appears to end, permitting fetuses to recover at least partially from the hypoxemia and acidosis before delivery. However, the reoxygenation of the fetus will not alter any brain damage that may have already taken place.[132] CP caused by this sequence has often occurred before the intrapartum period.

Another area concerned with MSAF is the risk to the fetus of meconium aspiration. When the potential for meconium aspiration in utero is clinically identified, it is now being treated with amnioinfusions to dilute the thick meconium. Perineal suctioning is routine, and a team capable of intubation and deep tracheal suction should be in attendance for resuscitation when thick meconium is present.[133]

B. Shoulder Dystocia

The current medicolegal climate appears to presume that brachial plexus injuries are the result of delivery trauma. Of all obstetrics-related claims and suits filed against CRICO-insured healthcare providers from 1991-2000, 18 percent involved shoulder dystocia. While 62 percent of shoulder dystocia cases were closed without indemnity payments to the plaintiffs, it nonetheless costs an average of $50,000 to successfully defend those cases.[134]

It has been suggested fetal malposition in utero may be a factor in brachial plexus impairment, arguing that injury is not necessarily dependent on the birth process. Fetal movement is constrained by the absence of amniotic fluid, and this may predispose the fetus to this insult.[135] Another study concluded that in pregnancies resulting in delivery of neonates weighing more than 4000 grams, the occurrence of shoulder dystocia cannot be predicted from clinical characteristics or labor abnormalities. The defense can argue that the ability to predict shoulder dystocia is not reasonably probable to a degree of medical certainty. The following case illustrates this concept:

> The plaintiff mother was seen for prenatal care by the defendant, an obstetrician. The defendant estimated the baby's weight to be approximately nine and one-half pounds at term. Shoulder dystocia developed during delivery and the plaintiff infant suffered a permanent brachial plexus injury. The plaintiffs claimed the defendant was negligent in failing to obtain a sonogram at term to confirm the fetus's weight, in failing to recommend a cesarean

section for a macrosomic baby, and in applying excessive traction on the infant's head. The defendant contended the standard of care did not require a sonogram or cesarean section and the shoulder dystocia had been managed properly. According to Metro Verdicts Monthly, a defense verdict was returned.[136]

Current obstetrical practice requires diligence in assessing risk factors for shoulder dystocia, careful conduct of labor following well-established guidelines, and prompt and judicious intervention when the clinical problem of shoulder dystocia is manifest.[137]

C. Cesarean Section "30-Minute Rule"

The issue of timeliness in performing an emergent cesarean section is often at the forefront in claims of medical negligence. However, successful defenses can be based on other factors besides the time to delivery. These factors can adversely affect neonatal outcome, and include chronic uteroplacental insufficiency, the presence of prolonged meconium-stained fluid, and laboratory data. Some studies do not support the 30-minute guideline as having clinical significance in terms of neonatal mortality or morbidity. When pairing these other factors with the results of the studies done on the outcome of timing of the cesarean section, a solid defense can often be presented.[138]

1.21 Summary

Contrary to popular belief, the literature supports the fact that, while the absolute number of obstetrical claims may be rising, the proportion of obstetrical cases filed to estimated numbers of negligent acts remains small.[139] Several lines of evidence suggest that medical malpractice during labor is rare. Even with the judicious monitoring of labor patients, there are sudden intrapartum fetal deaths. These are often associated with acute, unpredictable obstetrical events that clearly do not represent negligence. Another important issue to address is whether different management would have altered the outcome in a positive manner, or whether the outcome was an unavoidable accident or an act of God. The fetus is a remarkable being, with many adaptive mechanisms that enable it to maintain cerebral perfusion and metabolism. The fetus's brain also has an inherent tolerance of or resistance to intrapartum asphyxia. Given these factors, it is difficult to render a legal opinion with any degree of certainty, as to whether an alternate medical strategy could have been adopted or whether the outcome was an unavoidable act.[140] In cases that go to court, jury verdicts overwhelmingly favor the defense. When the plaintiffs prevail, it is likely to be in situations that do not involve specific procedures but do involve severe injuries and older technologies. Recent research illustrates that perinatal hypoxic-ischemic cerebral injury that is secondary to intrapartum asphyxia that results in CP is a rare event in most delivery rooms and NICUs.[141] However, when a plaintiff is successful, the award tends to be high but not excessive, given the serious nature of the injuries. Life care planners play a key role in calculating costs for maintaining a brain-damaged baby.

Current trends in obstetrical care (and health care in general) make some areas of practice vulnerable to mistakes and consequent litigation. The growth of managed health care and increased use of cost-containing, short-stay programs have resulted in earlier hospital discharge for the postpartum mother and her newborn. It has become apparent this is too little time for the careful evaluation and teaching of mother and baby that should take place. In response to this trend, some states have passed laws mandating a specific length of stay after a hospital delivery. Hospital downsizing and cost-cutting measures are a reality affecting nurse-patient ratios, staffing patterns, and number of experienced personnel available to work with patients. Refer to Chapter 2, *Where Have All the Nurses Gone?*, in Volume I, for another perspective on the nursing shortage.

Nurses are therefore charged with being advocates for patients at a time when financial and other pressures are high. Members of the nursing profession will do well to review, remember, and practice their profession based on both ethical and clinical care standards. Members of the legal profession need to choose or defend their cases carefully, in light of the changes in both health care and nursing practice.

Endnotes

1. Connors, P., "High-risk Perinatal Issues: Delay in the Diagnosis of Fetal Distress and Insufficient Documentation," *Journal of Nursing Law* 9, no. 1 (2003): 19–26.

2. ACOG Committee Opinions. List of Titles. Washington, D.C., December 1998.

3. *Id.*

4. Oh, W. and G. Merenstein, "Fourth edition of the Guidelines for Perinatal Care: Summary of Changes," *Pediatrics* 100, no. 6 (December 1997).

5. Gagnon, D. and S. Allison-Cooke, "Adaptations to perinatal regionalization," In *High-Risk Pregnancy: A Team Approach*, Second edition, eds. R. A. Knuppel and J. E. Drukker. Philadelphia: W. B. Saunders Co., 1993.

6. See note 4.

7. American Academy of Pediatrics and American College of Obstetricians and Gynecologists, *Guidelines for Perinatal Care*, Fourth edition, Washington, D.C., 2002.

8. *Id.*

9. Yeast, J., M. Poskin, J. Stockauer, and S. Shaffer, "Changing patterns in regionalization of perinatal care and the impact on neonatal mortality," *American Journal of Obstetrics and Gynecology* 178, no. 1 (January 1998).

10. See note 7.

11. Laska, L. (ed.), "Woman with suspected small gestational age fetus at 32 weeks and non-reassuring fetal heart tones not transferred from Level I hospital," *Medical Malpractice Verdicts, Settlements and Experts* (June 2005): 28.

12. Cunningham et al. *Williams Obstetrics*. Stamford, Connecticut: Appleton and Lange, 2005.

13. Scott, J., R. Gibbs, B. Karlan, and A. Haney, *Danforth's Obstetrics and Gynecology*, Ninth edition, Lippincott, Williams and Wilkins, 2003.

14. Daniels, S. and L. Andrews, "The shadow of the law: jury decisions in obstetrics and gynecology cases," In *Medical Professional Liability and the Delivery of Obstetrical Care, Vol. II*: An *Interdisciplinary Review*, eds. V. Rostow and R. Bulger, 161–193. Washington, D.C.: Academy Press, 1989.

15. Laska, L. (ed.), "Failure to test mother, father, or fetus for thalassemia despite mother's abnormal blood work," *Medical Malpractice Verdicts, Settlements and Experts* (March 2005): 31.

16. Laska, L. (ed.), "Failure to treat abnormal fundal height measurements," *Medical Malpractice Verdicts, Settlements and Experts* (September 2004): 36.

17. Laska, L. (ed.), "Midwife delivers large infant," *Medical Malpractice Verdicts, Settlements and Experts* (November 1998): 32.

18. Sanders, R. C., "Legal problems related to obstetrical ultrasound," *Annals of the New York Academy of Sciences* 847 (June 18, 1998): 220–27.

19. AWHONN, *Clinical Competencies and Education Guide: Limited Ultrasound Examinations in Obstetric and Gynecologic/Infertility Settings*. Washington, D.C., 1998.

20. See note 18.

21. Laska, L. (ed.), "Failure to perform cesarean section when fetal monitoring abnormal," *Medical Malpractice Verdicts, Settlements and Experts* (July 2004): 30.

22. *ACOG Tech, Bulletin #188: Antepartum Fetal Surveillance*. Washington, D.C., January 1994.

23. Laska, L. (ed.), "Doctor mistakenly interprets biophysical test," *Medical Malpractice Verdicts, Settlements and Experts* (August 2004): 30.

24. See note 22.

25. Laska, L. (ed.), "Failure to diagnose uterine insufficiency," *Medical Malpractice Verdicts, Settlements and Experts* (September 2004): 38.

26. Rommal, C., "Documentation issues in electronic fetal monitoring," *Journal of Healthcare Risk Management* 17, no. 2 (Spring 1997).

27. Rostant, D. and R. Cady, *AWHONN: Liability Issues in Perinatal Nursing*. Philadelphia: Lippincott, 1999.

28. Laska, L. (ed.), "Fetal demise follows amniocentesis," *Medical Malpractice Verdicts, Settlements and Experts* (April 2005): 28.

29. Lowdermilk, D. and S. Perry, *Maternity and Women's Health Care*, Eighth edition. St. Louis: Mosby, Inc., 2004.

30. ACOG Tech. *Bulletin #218: Dystocia and the Augmentation of Labor*. Washington, D.C., December 1995.

31. *Id.*

32. *Id.*

33. See note 29.

34. See note 30.

35. Laska, L. (ed.), "$6.185 million verdict in Illinois where child suffers birth injuries from delayed delivery," *Medical Malpractice Verdicts, Settlements and Experts* (December 2004): 28.

36. See note 29.

37. Laska, L. (ed.), "Newborn suffers brain damage after use of improper forceps technique," *Medical Malpractice Verdicts, Settlements and Experts* (August 2004): 32.

38. Simpson, K. and P. Creehan, *AWHONN's Perinatal Nursing*. Philadelphia: Lippincott, 2001.

39. *Id.*

40. Cunningham et al. *Williams Obstetrics*. Stamford, Connecticut: Appleton and Lange, 1997.

41. See note 27.

42. *Id.*

43. Laska, L. (ed.), "Improper maneuvers in face of shoulder dystocia during delivery blamed for Erb's palsy," *Medical Malpractice Verdicts, Settlements and Experts* (September 2004): 38.

44. See note 38.

45. Knox, G., K. Simpson, and T. Garite, "High reliability perinatal units: an approach to the prevention of patient injury and medical malpractice claims," *Journal of Healthcare Risk Management* 19, no. 2 (Spring 1999).

46. See note 1.

47. Dauphinee, J., "VBAC: Safety for the Patient and the Nurse," *JOGNN* (January-February 2004): 105–115.

48. Schnitker, K., "Uterine rupture during trial of labor: risk management recommendations," *Journal of Healthcare Risk Management* 19, no. 4 (Fall 1999).

49. Laska, L. (ed.), "Failure to diagnose placental abruption," *Medical Malpractice Verdicts, Settlements and Experts* (January 2003): 39.

50. See note 47.

51. Apfel, D., "A primer on vaginal birth after cesarean," *TRIAL* (February 2000): 38–44.

52. *Id.*

53. *Id.*

54. See note 47.

55. *Id.*

56. See note 40.

57. See note 27.

58. See note 47.

59. See note 38.

60. Laska, L. (ed.), "Vaginal birth after cesarean section results in cerebral palsy, mental retardation and neurological impairment," *Medical Malpractice Verdicts, Settlements and Expert*s (September 2004): 33.

61. See note 38.

62. Perlman, J., "Intrapartum hypoxic-ischemic cerebral injury and subsequent cerebral palsy: medicolegal issues," *Pediatrics* 99, no. 6 (1997).

63. *Id.*

64. ACOG Tech. *Bulletin #163: Fetal and Neonatal Neurologic Injury.* Washington, D.C., January 1992.

65. See note 63.

66. Laska, L. (ed.), "Family practice physician delivers child in need of resuscitation," *Medical Malpractice Verdicts, Settlements and Experts* (December 1998): 23.

67. See note 27.

68. Ricci, S., *Essentials of Maternity, Newborn, and Women's Health Nursing.* Philadelphia: Lippincott, 2007.

69. See note 7 at 179.

70. *Id.*

71. Blair, P., "Solid standards guard against malpractice," *Nursing Management* 34, no. 7 (2003): 10–11.

72. Collins, D., "Legally Speaking," *Contemporary OB/GYN* (2005). Retrieved August 1, 2005 from http://www.contemporaryobgyn.net/obgyn/content/printContentPopup.jsp?id=150180.

73. See note 69.

74. See note 7.

75. Burns, A., "Protecting infants in healthcare facilities from abduction," *Journal of Perinatal and Neonatal Nursing* 17, no. 2 (2003): 139–147.

76. Thompson, M., "Woman gets life in baby kidnapping," *Reno Gazette Journal* (March 29, 2002). Retrieved April 1, 2006 from http://www.rgj.com.

77. Burgess, A. and K. Lanning, *An analysis of infant abductions,* Second edition. United States Department of Justice: National Center for Missing and Exploited Children, July 2003.

78. See note 76 at 142.

79. Id at 143.

80. McMullen, P., "Liability in obstetrical nursing," *Nursing Connections* 3 (1990).

81. See note 1.

82. Murray, M., *Antepartal and Intrapartal Fetal Monitoring: Essentials of Electronic Fetal Monitoring.* Washington, D.C.: NAACOG, 1989.

83. U.S. Preventive Services Task Force, "Guidelines for intrapartum electronic fetal monitoring," *Guide to Clinical Preventive Services*, Second edition, 1996.

84. Laska, L. (ed.), "101 Brain-damaged babies: the nation's largest collection of obstetrical disasters," Nashville, Tennessee: *Medical Malpractice Verdicts, Settlements and Experts* (1993): 31–33.

85. Laska, L. (ed.), "Failure to appropriately monitor mother and infant during final stage of labor," *Medical Malpractice Verdicts, Settlements and Experts* (November 2003): 33.

86. ACOG/NAACOG. *Joint Statement on Electronic Fetal Monitoring.* Washington, D.C., March 1986.

87. Simpson, K. and P. Creehan, *AWHONN's Competence Validation for Perinatal Care Providers.* Philadelphia: Lippincott, 1998.

88. Laska, L. (ed.), "Failure to properly monitor and timely delivery child despite decelerations," *Medical Malpractice Verdicts, Settlements and Experts* (November 2004): 29.

89. ACOG Committee Opinion #197: *Inappropriate Use of the Terms Fetal Distress and Birth Asphyxia.* Washington, D.C., February 1998.

90. Boehm, F., "Intrapartum fetal heart rate monitoring." *Obstetrics and Gynecology Clinics* 26, no. 4 (December 1999).

91. See note 14.

92. See note 38.

93. ACOG Tech. *Bulletin #217: Induction of Labor.* Washington, D.C., December 1995.

94. Simpson, K. and P. Creehan, *AWHONN's Perinatal Nursing.* Philadelphia: Lippincott, 1996.

95. ACOG. *Precis V-An Update in Obstetrics and Gynecology.* Washington, D.C., 1994.

96. See note 45.

97. See note 38 at 344.

98. See note 27.

99. Murray, M., *Antepartal and Intrapartal Fetal Monitoring*, Second edition, Learning Resources International, 1997.

100. See note 7.

101. Laska, L. (ed.), "Failure to respond appropriately to non-reassuring signs results in hypoxic ischemic encephalopathy, microcephaly, mental retardation, and spasticity," *Medical Malpractice Verdicts, Settlements and Experts* (March 2004): 47.

102. www.jchao.org.

103. Association of Women's Health, Obstetrics, and Neonatal Nurses, *Liability Issues in Prenatal Nursing,* New York, Lippincott, 1999.

104. Laska, L. (ed.), "Failure to timely deliver child," *Medical Malpractice Verdicts, Settlements and Experts* 26 (July 2005).

105. Fiesta, J., "Obstetrical liability update-part II," *Nursing Management* 26, no. 8 (August 1995): 22–25.

106. Fisher, C., "The abnormal infant: protecting yourself against blame," *RN* (April 1990): 69–72.

107. See note 87.

108. See note 27.

109. *Id.*

110. See note 95.

111. Laska, L. (ed.), "Surgical sponge retained following cesarean section," *Medical Malpractice Verdicts, Settlements and Experts* (September 2004): 35.

112. See note 106.

113. Laska, L. (ed.), "One twin dies due to failure to respond to fetal distress," *Medical Malpractice Verdicts, Settlements and Experts* (July 2004): 27.

114. See note 38 at 197.

115. Grossman, S. Z., "The nature of lawsuits related to obstetrical care," In *High-Risk Pregnancy: A Team Approach*, Second edition, eds. R. A. Knuppel and J. E. Drukker. Philadelphia: Saunders, 1993.

116. Laska, L. (ed.), "Failure to timely treat pre-eclampsia and perform indicated cesarean results in mother's seizures, precipitating infant hypoxic damage, with consequent seizures, mild brain damage and physiological impairment for infant boy," *Medical Malpractice Verdicts, Settlements and Experts* (June 2003): 37–38.

117. See note 7.

118. Laska, L. (ed.), "Child suffers brain damage due to delayed delivery caused by nurse's failure to diagnose fetal distress on fetal monitor tracings," *Medical Malpractice Verdicts, Settlements and Experts* (January 1993): 40.

119. Laska, L. (ed.), "101 Brain-damaged babies: the nation's largest collection of obstetrical disasters," *Medical Malpractice Verdicts, Settlements and Experts* (1993): 60–61.

120. ACOG news release (embargoed until January 31, 2000). *ACOG's Latest Professional Liability Survey Reveals Increase in Liability Claims.* Washington, D.C.

121. Peters, J., "Litigating the brain-damaged baby case," *TRIAL* (May 1989): 32–40.

122. Fiesta, J., "Obstetrical liability update-part I," *Nursing Management* 26, no. 7 (July 1995): 24.

123. See note 63.

124. *Id.*

125. See note 84.

126. See note 63.

127. *Id.*

128. *Id.*

129. Naeye, R., "Hypoxic-ischemic antenatal brain injury: determining how and when it took place," American Association of Legal Nurse Consultants, Eighth National Educational Conference, Syllabus book, 1997.

130. See note 63.

131. See note 130.

132. *Id.*

133. See note 45.

134. See note 1.

135. Lavery, J., "Shoulder dystocia: a risk management perspective," *Journal of Healthcare Risk Management* 16, no. 2 (Spring 1996).

136. Laska, L., (ed.), "Failure to perform sonogram or cesarean section for large baby-shoulder dystocia with Erb's palsy," *Medical Malpractice Verdicts, Settlements and Experts* (July 1999): 29.

137. See note 136.

138. Lavery, J., J. Janssen, and L. Hutchinson, "Is the obstetric guideline of 30 minutes from decision to incision for cesarean delivery clinically significant?" Journal of Healthcare Risk Management 19, no. 1 (Winter 1999).

139. See note 14.

140. See note 63.

141. *Id.*

Chapter 2

Neonatal Nursing Malpractice Issues

M. Terese Verklan, PhD, CCNS, RNC

Synopsis
2.1 Introduction
2.2 Standard of Care
2.3 Scope of Practice
    A. The Neonatal Nurse
    B. The Advanced Practice Nurse
2.4 Common Causes of Liability
    A. Resuscitation Situations
    B. Respiratory Distress
    C. Intravenous Therapy
    D. Medication Errors
    E. Sepsis
    F. Hypoglycemia
    G. Hyperbilirubinemia
    H. Retinopathy of Prematurity (ROP)
    I. Stabilization and Transport of the High-Risk Neonate
    J. Neonatal Kidnapping
    K. Videotapes
    L. Iatrogenic Injuries
2.5 Prevention of Liability
    A. Risk Management
    B. Clinical Knowledge and Skills
2.6 Issues Related to Informed Consent
2.7 Documentation
2.8 Summary
Endnotes

2.1 Introduction

Neonatal nursing is a specialty practice area contained within maternal-child nursing. Nurses working in the special care or intensive care nurseries are considered to have a subspecialty practice. Thus, whether the nurse cares for the low- or high-risk neonate, it is essential the neonatal nurse be a professional healthcare provider with specialized knowledge, skills, and training in the care of neonates and their families. The skill mix demanded by the high-technology, high-acuity environment found in the neonatal intensive care unit (NICU) often blurs the line between nursing and medical practice. Knowledge of scope of practice and professional responsibilities of the other members of the healthcare team will keep the nurse within the legal limits of practice.

For the majority of families, the birth of a baby is a happy, major life event, and the extended family eagerly anticipates the newborn's arrival. Whenever anything other than a routine labor, delivery, and birth is encountered, the already intense emotions of all involved parties become even more charged. Many families feel a loss of control in the noisy NICU or special care nursery (SCN) environment. These feelings may heighten anxieties related to the circumstances surrounding the infant's admission, treatment options, and the unfamiliarity with personnel, medical language and surroundings. Ineffective diffusion of these emotions may pave the way for a lawsuit should a mistake be made.

The neonatal nurse is accountable to the patient, the family, the employer, and the profession. Establishing a rapport with the family, always placing their interests first, keeping them informed, and anticipating the next step, are some measures neonatal nurses may take to reduce the possibility that the family bring legal action. This chapter reviews the standard of care, scope of practice, common causes of liability, prevention of liability, issues related to informed consent, as well as documentation related to neonatal nursing.

2.2 Standard of Care

Due to the advances in communication, technology, transportation, and the law, the "locality rule" is considered obsolete, replaced by a national standard.[1] Thus, it is expected the standard of care given to all neonates is the same, regardless of geographical location. The standard of care is established by defining what a reasonable and prudent nurse would have done given the same or similar circumstances. A reasonable and prudent nurse is a nurse with a comparable background, education, and level of experience who would behave in an analogous manner given an equivalent set of circumstances.

The unique vulnerability of a neonate mandates that the nurse be cognizant of both internal and external standards of care. In 1988, *Ewing v. Aubert* established that a maternal-child nurse is held to the standard of care of a nurse who practiced in the maternal-child specialty.[2] Attorneys should expect that neonatal nurses, a subspecialty within maternal-child nursing, are aware of the professional practice standards for that subspecialty:

> A nurse who practices her profession in a particular specialty owes to the patients the duty of possessing the degree of knowledge or skill ordinarily possessed by members of the profession actively practicing in such a specialty under similar circumstances. It is the nurse's duty to exercise the degree of such skill ordinarily employed, under similar circumstances, by members of the nursing profession in good standing who practice their profession in the same specialty and to use reasonable care and diligence, along with his/her best judgment, in the application of his/her skill to the case.[3]

The internal standards are delineated by the institution's policies, procedures, and protocols. The policy outlines the purposes for which the procedure is performed. The policy is the guideline that dictates how the procedure needs to be carried out. Both the policy and procedure must reflect the standard of care, be reviewed at least annually, and be revised to reflect current nursing practice.[4] The policies, procedures, and protocols must be:

- developed by a qualified committee of professionals who practice in the specialty;
- consistent with current research and practice literature;
- archived for the length of liability; and,
- accessible to staff members.[5]

In addition, both the unit and hospital's nursing and medical administrators must approve of the policy and procedure manual.

TIP: Hospitals are aware the institutional policy and procedure manual lays out the specific standards by which to evaluate the care given by the nurse. It is becoming increasingly difficult to obtain the institution's policy and procedure manual due to a reluctance to place these documents on hard copy or on computer files. Professional associations have developed standards with measurable criteria that define professional nursing practice. Specialty organizations such as Association of Women's Health, Obstetric and Neonatal Nurses (AWHONN), American Association of Critical Care Nurses (AACN), and National Association of Neonatal Nurses (NANN) have adopted these standards in the form of recommendations and general guidelines for specific practice situations.

The external standards of care are established by state and federal regulations, current professional literature, expert witnesses, and professional organizations. The resultant national standards tend to be written in broad language to permit flexibility without compromising those set out in the individual state's Nurse Practice Act as mandated by each state's legislature. As mentioned in Chapter 6, *The Foundations of Nursing Practice*, in Volume I, standards of nursing practice are also regulated by the Department of Health, TJC, Centers for Medicare and Medicaid Services, and other regulatory agencies. Professional literature, such as textbooks, clinical and research articles, and case reports, assists in determining the standard of care by virtue of its focus on management issues, the state of the science, and nursing techniques in place at the time of the malpractice suit. The nurse expert witness is also used to establish the standard of care. The expert should be a neonatal nurse who possesses special knowledge, skill, and experience in the care of neonates. An expert witness has knowledge of the standards applicable at the time of the incident and is used to articulate the deviations from or adherence to the customary standard of care.

> Terry Lynn Hanson, a registered nurse, was charged by the Mississippi Board of Nursing with abuse of neonatal patients. Her clinical practice included holding a baby around its neck with only one hand, carrying babies by holding them under their axillae, and carrying babies naked to the sink for bathing. She was also noted to endanger babies by rapidly flipping the levers on incubators to stimulate them. The Board found her guilty on all charges and revoked her license. On appeal, the Supreme Court of Mississippi held that Nurse Hanson's behavior constituted a reckless disregard for the health and safety of the neonates. The Court also ruled that she was negligent by holding babies under their axillae, permitting their bodies to dangle; that removing them naked from incubators to bathe compromised thermoregulation and exposed them to risks of infection; and that overstimulation increased the risk of intraventricular hemorrhage.[6]

Professional associations represent the interests of the nurse. The American Nurses Association has developed standards along with measurable criteria to define professional nursing practice. Specialty organizations such as NANN, AWHONN, AACN and National Association of Pediatric Nurse Associates and Practitioners (NAPNAP) have adopted these standards in the form of recommendations and general guidelines for specific practice situations. For example, NANN's publication, S*cope and Standards of Practice*, identifies practice characteristics, settings, and roles of neonatal nurses and advanced practice neonatal nurses along with education, advanced practice criteria, and certification.[7] *Guidelines for Perinatal Care* outlines recommendations for nursing ratios, staffing guidelines, nurse providers, and outreach education for inpatient perinatal care facilities providing basic, specialty, and sub-specialty care.[8]

TIP: *Guidelines for Perinatal Care*,[9] considered a gold standard for perinatal/neonatal medical and nursing care, outlines the latest policies and practice guidelines of the American Academy of Pediatrics and the American College of Obstetricians and Gynecologists for the care of pregnant women and their fetuses and neonates. Expert witnesses will refer to these guidelines as well as to the standards developed by specialty organizations when evaluating the actions of the nurse.

2.3 Scope of Practice

In many instances, the lines distinguishing medical practice from that of neonatal nursing have become blurred due to the expanded role of the neonatal nurse given major advances in technology routinely used in neonatal care. Skills once performed only by physicians have become part of everyday nursing practice, such as placement of percutaneous lines, intubation, and diagnostic testing. Most often, these "grey areas" are found in the sub-specialty units such as the Special Care Nursery and the Intensive Care Nursery. The basic concern underlying scope of practice questions is whether the procedure performed by the nurse is legally within or beyond the scope of a nursing license to practice. Two roles of nurses most commonly found in neonatal areas are those of the neonatal nurse and the advanced practice nurse.

TIP: Increasing the scope of practice, autonomy and authority may result in greater exposure to liability situations. Scope of practice and critical liability issues are most likely to arise when the nurse assumes independent patient care functions that (a) have typically been solely within the province of physicians, (b) are not the subject of standing orders, (c) have no support in nursing practice acts, and (d) are not generally recognized as legitimate nursing procedures by professional organizations.[10]

A. The Neonatal Nurse

"A neonatal nurse is a professional who provides skilled nursing care for low-risk, high-risk and critically ill neo-

nates; high-risk neonates; and their families. The neonatal nurse has specialized knowledge, and develops and maintains clinical competence through standardized practice and continuing education."[11] "In addition to providing basic neonatal care, neonatal nurses may focus on one or more areas of expertise, such as intensive or critical neonatal care, transport, lactation, grief, extracorporeal membrane oxygenation (ECMO) or developmental care."[12] National certification in low- and high-risk neonatal nursing (RNC) can be obtained through the National Certification Corporation (NCC) for obstetric, gynecologic, and neonatal nurses. Neonatal nurses in the NICU may also be certified as critical care registered nurses (CCRN) through the American Association of Critical Care Nurses Certification Corporation.

B. The Advanced Practice Nurse

The advanced practice nurse (APN) is a professional registered nurse who has obtained advanced education in the sub-specialty of neonatal nursing to provide specialized knowledge and skills to function in an expanded role. The APN may provide direct patient care, staff or patient/family education, and/or act as a neonatal case manager.[13-16] Inherent in the expanded role is the concurrent increase in both professional and legal responsibility.

TIP: Role definition of the advanced practice nurse must begin at the professional level with a review of the specific perinatal and neonatal professional organizations' policy statements as well as the nursing literature.[17] Because there are no national laws or regulations applicable to APNs, each state decides the scope of practice for the APN as well as the identity of the regulating authority.[18]

The two types of APNs functioning in the nurseries are the neonatal nurse practitioner (NNP) and the clinical nurse specialist (CNS). The NNP is a professional "registered nurse with clinical practice in neonatal nursing who has obtained a master's degree with supervised clinical experience in the management of newborn infants and their families. The NNP manages patients in collaboration with a physician, usually a pediatrician or neonatologist. Using the acquired knowledge of pathophysiology, pharmacology, and physiology, the NNP may exercise independent judgment in the assessment, diagnosis, and management of infants and in the performance of certain procedures. The NNP may also be responsible for education of staff, research, and developing standards of nursing care."[19] The NNP manages a caseload of neonates using independent judgment, the nursing process, and medical management and procedures that reflect the Nurse Practice Act and other state laws, institutional guidelines, education and experience in consultation, and collaboration under the supervision of a physician.[20,21] Certification for the NNP is obtained through the NCC. Since January 2000, a minimum of a master's degree has been required to be eligible for certification as an NNP.

The neonatal CNS is a professional "registered nurse with a master's degree in nursing who, through study and supervised practice at the graduate level, has become an expert in the theory and practice of neonatal care. The neonatal CNS is responsible for fostering continuous quality improvement in neonatal nursing care and developing and educating staff. The neonatal CNS models expert nursing practice and applies and promotes evidence-based nursing practice."[22] In addition, the CNS educates families as well as consults with staff, members of the healthcare team, and multidisciplinary team members. The CNS may be responsible for initiating research projects, participating in data collection, and implementing and evaluating evidence-based practice. Certification can be obtained through either the NCC (high-risk neonatal nursing) or the AACN Certification Corporation. Successful candidates are permitted to use the initials RNC (registered nurse certified) and CCNS (critical care clinical nurse specialist-neonatal), respectively.

Advanced practice is controlled by the licensing statute of each state, thereby protecting the use of the title of APN. Each state Board of Nursing has defined the scope of practice of the APN, and has included diagnosis and treatment, areas once exclusive to medicine. Several states have both the state Board of Nursing and the state board of medicine jointly oversee licensing and scope of practice.[23] Depending on the state, the APN may have her own independent practice, or may be required to practice with a supervising or collaborating physician. Many states are moving toward removing statutory requirements to allow full independent practice. The issue of independence remains a point of controversy between the NNP and neonatologist/pediatrician.

2.4 Common Causes of Liability

The increase in the neonatal nurse's scope of practice, autonomy, and authority may translate into greater exposure to liability situations as a consequence. The impact of liability involving a neonate is high for three reasons:[24]

- costs of health care for a damaged neonate with a normal life expectancy are high;
- a long statute of limitations for minors may permit suits to be filed years later, applicable to other medical malpractice actions; and,
- there is sympathy toward the family, who may not

be able to afford the needed expensive care for the baby.

Because neonatal nurses are in constant, close contact with the neonate, physicians and APNs depend upon them (and the neonatologist depends on the NNP) to detect and communicate any signs of distress or compromise as early as possible.

Baby R was born after a stressful labor complicated by the passage of meconium and episodes of hypoxia. Despite risk factors for hypoglycemia, only routine orders for a newborn admission were given. The baby's glucose level decreased from 104 mg/dL to 28 mg/dL by three hours of life. Although the nurse fed her, the nurse did not call the physician. Baby R experienced hypoglycemia throughout the night, and returned to a normal glucose level after a morning feeding. The physician examined her shortly afterward, noting that she was a healthy newborn at risk for hypoglycemia. The physician did not give further orders, including the need to begin intravenous glucose, nor was there consultation with a neonatologist. Later that afternoon seizures developed due to profound hypoglycemia. The nurse did not contact the physician until late that night when the seizure activity became more pronounced. The physician returned to the hospital, observed the seizures, and transferred the neonate to another facility. The hospital settled before trial for $1.75 million.[25]

Liability for negligence and the standard of care may be determined by:[26]

- Training and experience of the neonatal nurse
- Manuals and textbooks written for the specialty
- Action and inactions of the nurse
- Instructions and protocols referred to by the nurse
- Accepted professional nursing practice

The above case highlights that the inactions of the nurse and the failure to call the physician fall below expectations of accepted professional practice. The hospital is ultimately responsible for the quality of care given by employees (*respondeat superior*); thus, the defensibility of the case fundamentally depends on nursing care that has been rendered. This section discusses the more common high-risk situations that may expose neonatal nurses to litigation.

A. Resuscitation Situations

Although healthcare professionals are taught to expect the unexpected, resuscitation situations are often the central issue in malpractice cases. Ten percent of all neonates require assistance to initiate respiration at birth, while 1 percent require extensive resuscitative interventions at time of birth to survive.[27] The Neonatal Resuscitation Program was developed to encourage the presence of an individual at each delivery who would possess the requisite skills necessary to perform or assist in the resuscitation of the newly born infant. Although the intent of these "guidelines" was not to establish a standard of care, the program has evolved into just that. Textbooks in neonatal medicine and nursing, as well as the *Guidelines for Perinatal Care*,[28] convey that resuscitation is provided according to the American Academy of Pediatrics/American Heart Association Neonatal Resuscitation Program.

It is recommended at each delivery there be at least one person skilled in initiating resuscitative therapies, with the primary responsibility being the care of the newborn.[29] Another healthcare provider must be immediately available if that person is incapable of performing all steps of the resuscitative process.[30] In the circumstance the delivery is anticipated to be high-risk (fetal distress or suspected perinatal insult) with the possibility that advanced resuscitative efforts will be required, the AAP/AHA recommends there be at least two people present to manage the neonate: one capable of performing all the necessary resuscitation skills and one or more to assist with resuscitation efforts. The need for resuscitation can often be predicted, facilitating opportunities to select the optimal setting, prepare equipment, and have trained personnel in attendance at the delivery.[31] A full set of personnel and equipment should be available for each baby in the case of multiple births. Many hospitals have implemented dedicated resuscitation teams that have a specified leader, with all members aware of their roles and responsibilities.

TIP: The Neonatal Resuscitation Program was jointly developed in the 1980s by the American Academy of Pediatrics and the American Heart Association to assist neonatal and obstetrical healthcare providers in gaining the proper knowledge to enable them to provide optimal care to newborns immediately after birth. The basic principles of that program are supported by the American College of Obstetrics and Gynecology (ACOG), the American Society of Anesthesiology, the American Academy of Family Physicians, and the Canadian Pediatric Society.[32]

Initial steps of resuscitation include:

- preventing heat loss: placing the baby under a radiant warmer source and drying the neonate;
- clearing the airway: positioning and, if needed, suctioning;
- initiation of breathing-tactile stimulation, or bag/mask ventilation; and,
- evaluation of the neonate: beginning of adaptation to extrauterine life.

These steps support the newborn's respiratory, circulatory, and metabolic systems as he begins the transition to life outside the uterus.

When the delivery is complicated by known or suspected asphyxia (lack of oxygen and ventilation, and decreased circulation), the goal of resuscitation is to reverse the hypoxia (decreased oxygenation), hypercarbia (increased carbon dioxide), and acidosis (low pH). It is never known whether a non-breathing neonate is displaying primary apnea (first time the baby has stopped breathing and will breathe again on her own) or secondary apnea (baby has stopped breathing, and will not initiate respirations again without intervention). Therefore, secondary apnea is always assumed and resuscitation procedures should begin immediately. For every one-minute delay after a neonate's last breath (gasp) when in secondary apnea, the time to the first breath is increased by approximately two minutes, and the time to the onset of spontaneous breathing is delayed by greater than four minutes.[33] If resuscitation efforts are ineffective, the lack of ventilation, oxygenation, and circulation will cause progressive biochemical deterioration:[34]

- Arterial oxygen level (PaO_2) will be zero in less than five minutes
- Arterial carbon dioxide level ($PaCO_2$) will increase at a rate of 8 millimeters of mercury (mm Hg) per minute
- The baby will demonstrate progressive acidosis (pH will decrease by 0.04 units/minute and the bicarbonate will decrease by 2 milliequivalents (mEq) per minute)

As the hypoxemia and acidosis continue, myocardial function deteriorates, cardiac output decreases, and perfusion to vital organs diminishes. If not corrected, the process becomes self-perpetuating, leading to tissue hypoxia, ischemia, and ultimately irreversible organ damage.[35] The case located in Appendix 2.1 illustrates some of the standards of care involved in the resuscitation of a newborn.

The standard of care requires the neonatal nurse to anticipate the need for action, ensure all necessary equipment is assembled and at hand, and ensure the appropriate skilled people are available. Hospital policies should indicate where resuscitation equipment is located, the identity of the members of the resuscitation team, and the protocol for notifying them of emergent situations. A policy should reflect how and when the resuscitation supplies and equipment are to be checked. Equipment must be in working order and display an identifier indicating the date it was last inspected by the biomedical department. All nursing staff must know how to operate the necessary equipment. Use of the equipment in resuscitative situations may be designated as a competency in some institutions with annual dates for review of the nurse's skill level.

> Baby M developed respiratory distress in the delivery room. The nurse suctioned the infant and administered oxygen; however, the baby become apneic. The physician intubated the infant for the purpose of suctioning. The nurse could not locate the suction tubing to fit the endotracheal tube (ETT). The physician removed the ETT, gave blow-by oxygen and re-intubated the neonate. When asked for an Ambu-bag, the nurse could only provide one with a mask attached to it. Neither the nurse or physician could remove the mask from the bag. Baby M continued to deteriorate, necessitating the need for the physician to provide mouth to ETT resuscitation until the proper equipment was provided. Baby M developed hypoxic ischemic encephalopathy and later, cerebral palsy.
>
> Based on the nurse's testimony, the court returned a verdict against the hospital, but not against the physician. The nurse testified (a) it was her responsibility to have proper equipment in the delivery room and know how to use that equipment; (b) she hadn't restocked equipment in the resuscitation area because she didn't think she would need any; (c) she had never participated in an emergent situation in which an Ambu-bag was required; and (d) she didn't know why she could not remove the mask from the Ambu-bag. Expert testimony noted that the hospital breached the standard of care by failing to have its employees properly trained in the use of resuscitation and by failing to have necessary resuscitation equipment available. The physician testified the nurse's actions contributed to the extent and seriousness of Baby M's injuries. Plaintiffs were awarded a $9 million verdict.[36,37]

In addition to the nurse being responsible for her actions, the case illustrates the concept of *respondeat superior*, in which the hospital, as the nurse's employer, is also responsible for her actions. However, given the increase in accountability nursing has today, it is likely the nurse would have been named as an individual defendant.

Attorneys handling a neonatal resuscitation case may find it useful to explore the facility's practices relating to equipment and medications. Many institutions keep the resuscitation equipment and medications in a locked cart. Checking this cart may mean ensuring the lock is intact, and then signing off on an emergency cart checklist or permanent log book. In institutions that do not keep the equipment and medications locked, someone should be assigned once-a-shift to document that all medications, supplies, and equipment are present in sufficient quantity, and that no expiration dates are met, and then document the check in a permanent log book. Medical, nursing, and respiratory staff participation in mock codes will hone skills and give all an opportunity to practice a number of roles in different resuscitation scenarios. Maintaining competency-based records and up-to-date neonatal resuscitation program certification will help ensure the healthcare team is prepared for emergency situations.

TIP: Records for nurses, physicians, and respiratory therapists related to the NRP can be obtained through discovery. Determine if the healthcare provider is currently certified and when the certification expires (certification by the APA/AHA is for a two year period). It may also be helpful to determine their level of "responder" and what roles they assume during mock codes. Mock codes are especially useful for those institutions that do not have a high volume of deliveries and/or high-risk neonates because certification in neonatal resuscitation does not always mean competency.

Resuscitation of the pre-viable infant, considered to be less than 23 weeks postmenstrual age (PMA) and/or weighing less than 400 grams, is controversial due to the poor survival rate.[38,39] If time permits, the healthcare team should develop a plan of care in discussion with the family prior to delivery. In any resuscitation, interventions should rarely continue past 15 minutes when the neonate demonstrates no heart rate or response to adequate ventilation, chest compressions, and fluids/medications based on the severity of neurological damage or death in those who show a response after 15 minutes.[40]

Continuation of support after resuscitation is also key in ameliorating or preventing further damage to body systems.

However, as illustrated in the case above, many healthcare providers fail to do this. Obtaining vital signs, maintaining body temperature, evaluating cardiopulmonary status, and providing sufficient glucose are essential. There should be evidence of the nurse's critical thinking in the approach to designing a plan of care. Documentation should reflect the nurse's observations, the assessment as to the etiology, the neonate's response to interventions, and the revision of the plan of care based on the baby's response.

B. Respiratory Distress

Respiratory symptoms are typically the first signs there is something wrong with the baby. Because signs of respiratory distress are associated with numerous etiologies, not just pulmonary ones, it is the standard to rule out "common" causes quickly with diagnostic interventions such as temperature, blood glucose, blood gases, blood chemistries, complete blood count and differential, radiographs, ultrasounds, and septic workups (cultures). Prompt recognition of the onset and progression of symptomatology, as well as communication of changes in condition to the neonatologist or advanced practice nurse, is essential in the competent care of neonates.

> Shortly after birth, a newborn developed symptoms of respiratory distress, including subcostal retractions, tachypnea, grunting, gasping, and colour changes. The neonatalogist, Dr. V, was consulted and came to the hospital. Dr. V ordered that the neonate be transferred to the NICU and have a chest radiograph, complete blood count, blood gases and oxygen by oxyhood. After he left the hospital, the NICU called him to report the results of the blood gas. Dr. V maintained that the nurse reassured him that the baby was in no respiratory distress and was in excellent clinical condition, despite the abnormal blood gas results. The next day in the early morning hours, the nurse found that the baby was tachypneic, cyanotic and clinically deteriorating. Dr. V was called and after arrival, attempted to resuscitate the newborn without success. The baby died at approximately 20 hours of age. The plaintiffs claimed that the baby's persistent pulmonary hypertension did not receive the proper careful respiratory monitoring nor the proper respiratory support through intubation and other medical therapies, which contributed to her death. A $250,000 settlement was reached. [41]

Signs and symptoms of respiratory distress account for the majority of admissions to the special care and intensive care nurseries. A prompt diagnosis is essential because not all neonates who have respiratory sequelae have respiratory disease. The nurse's understanding of the pathophysiology is essential in assisting the physician and advanced practice nurse in ruling out the underlying disorder and guiding the correct comprehensive management.

TIP: Cyanosis (bluish tinge to the skin) is not a reliable indicator of the neonate's oxygenation status. Color is dependent on the oxygen-carrying capability of the blood, measured by the amount of hemoglobin present. Hematocrit is also a major factor as a high value can cause the blood flow through peripheral blood vessels to be sluggish. A complete blood count should be obtained to verify the amount of hemoglobin and hematocrit.

The standard of care requires that the nurse begin the assessment with a basic observation of the neonate in the undisturbed state if possible. This will permit evaluation of resting posture, muscle tone, and lethargy or alertness. Neonates will become less alert/arousable and lose muscle tone and appear floppy as they become increasingly compromised. Color changes may also be evident as the baby is disturbed or changes behavioral state. Generalized color of the skin peripherally and centrally, as well as evaluation of the color of the mucous membranes should be noted. Documentation should include the appearance, quality, and amount of oral and nasal secretions, as well as the presence of nasal flaring. Visual observation of the chest should include symmetry, synchrony, and depth and rate of respiration (which can also be evaluated by auscultation). Respirations are typically irregular and abdominal at a rate of approximately 40 to 60 breaths per minute after the first hour of life. Tachypnea (breathing faster than 60 breaths per minute) is usually the earliest symptom of both respiratory and non-respiratory disorders. Periodic breathing, common in both the term and preterm baby, involves cycles of breathing (for 10 to 15 seconds) and cessation of breathing (for five to ten seconds). Apnea is cessation of breathing for longer than 20 seconds, or cessation of breathing less than 20 seconds if accompanied by decreased heart rate, color changes, hypotonia or loss of muscle tone.

Retractions (pulling in of the chest with each breath) are common because of the soft cartilage of the airway and rib cage. Grunting may be heard with or without a stethoscope as the neonate attempts to maintain open alveoli. Moderate to severe retractions may add to an already compromised lung expansion as they cause a decrease in lung volume. Accessory muscles are used in times of decreased pulmonary compliance (stiff lungs) or increased airway resistance.

The greater the retractions, the worse the respiratory disease. Seesaw respirations and retractions, in which the chest is pulled in and the abdomen flares out on inspiration, are never normal, and indicate severe respiratory distress or failure.

The standard of care requires careful listening to the lungs. Auscultation should include each lung lobe, with the nurse comparing and contrasting each to evaluate the quality of the breath sounds. It is common for the nurse to hear referred (extraneous) sounds because sound is easily transmitted through the small, hyper-resonant chest of the neonate. The Silverman-Andersen scale may be used to quantify the level of respiratory distress.[42] Similar to that of the Apgar score, the neonate is given a 0, 1 or 2 on 5 parameters assessing work of breathing. Unlike the Apgar score, the higher the value, the worse the respiratory distress. A high score generally indicates the need for endotracheal intubation. The nurse is expected to note the quality of breath sounds after intubation and compare with the pre-intubation assessment, chest excursion and symmetry of movement, infant tolerance of the intubation procedure, as well as any secretions obtained from endotracheal suctioning.

Examination of non-respiratory systems is a frequently overlooked component of the chest assessment. The muscle tone and posture of the neonate communicates essential information. A healthy baby is able to hold himself in flexion, while the compromised neonate proceeds from flexion to flaccidity, sometimes termed a "position of surrender," as the degree of hypoxia and fatigue worsen. A scaphoid abdomen may indicate the distress is due to a diaphragmatic hernia. Evaluation of the cardiovascular system may reveal bounding or weak pulses, changing location of the point of maximal impulse (the place where the heartbeat sounds the loudest), unequal blood pressures, murmurs indicative of patent ductus arteriousus (fetal pathway connecting aorta and pulmonary artery) or tricuspid atresia (abnormal closure of the valve between the right atrium and right ventricle of the heart), congestive heart failure, or congenital heart defects. Muffled heart sounds may indicate a pneumopericardium, in which air is being trapped inside the pericardial sac.

C. Intravenous Therapy

Both short- and long-term intravenous access are typically required when the healthcare team is caring for the high-risk neonate. Depending upon the severity of the illness, both the pre- and full-term neonate may require invasive procedures to provide constant physiologic monitoring, fluid and electrolyte therapy, medication, and parenteral (intravenous) nutrition. In the NICU, intravenous (IV) access is often initially achieved by cannulation of the umbilical vein, umbilical artery, or peripheral vein or artery. Prior to removing these central lines, placement of a percutaneous line (also known as a peripherally inserted central catheter, or PICC) has become routine in many institutions. A percutaneous line is an intravenous catheter inserted into a peripheral vein and then advanced to a position near the heart. It is used to provide long-term intravenous access in the preterm neonate for the provision of parenteral nutrition, fluids, and/or medications.

Except in delivery room resuscitations, peripheral IV line placement is the most easily performed procedure and has untoward effects; in the delivery room, the fastest method of IV access is to sterilely cannulate the umbilical vein. The most common sites of placement are the veins located in the foot, hand, and scalp. The risk of infiltration and subsequent damage to surrounding tissue is highest when the site is the foot, and least when a scalp vein is used. A padded armboard or footboard may be used to limit the mobility of the extremity to prevent the neonate from dislodging the IV catheter. The armboard or footboard and tape securing the IV must be placed in such a way that stabilization of the IV catheter is ensured and visual inspection of the IV site and surrounding area can easily occur at least hourly.

TIP: The standard of care is to place the tape, dressing, and restraint devices to allow for easy inspection of the IV insertion site, circulation of the distal extremity, and patency of the IV catheter. Placement of tape and stabilizing devices should be done so as to not interfere with venous return. Tape circumventing a finger, toe, or even extremity, could act as a tourniquet and increase the risk of venous congestion and tissue damage in the event of an infiltration. The IV site should be assessed at least hourly, and the inspection documented in the patient's record.

Insertion of percutaneous venous lines, peripheral arterial lines, and umbilical arterial/venous lines are within the realm of advanced practice nursing or a staff nurse functioning in an advanced role. Just as there is a policy and procedure for peripheral venous access, a policy and procedure is also necessary for the insertion of percutaneous lines. In addition, there needs to be clearly identified practice protocols that distinguish who is authorized to perform the procedure, the competencies required to be skillful in the procedure and the attending physician's signature under whose authority the nurse is able to function in the advanced role. Percutaneous venous lines using Silastic catheters are increasingly replacing the need for the large-bore Broviac IV catheter. A

Broviac catheter is surgically placed into the jugular or femoral veins, leaving the distal end on the anterior chest wall or thigh, respectively. The percutaneous catheter is most often inserted into the antecubital or axillary veins, although veins in the leg, scalp, and external jugular vein may also be used. It is recommended these veins not be used for routine peripheral IV placement in those neonates likely to require a percutaneous line. Unlike the peripheral IV, which may be used immediately after the catheter is secure, fluids should never be infused until the position of the central and percutaneous line is confirmed by radiograph. Neonatal nurses are expected to be attuned to this and obtain a physician order that it is permissible to begin infusion of fluids after the x-ray has been reviewed. The tip of the central venous line should be located in the superior vena cava approximately 1 centimeter outside the cardiac silhouette in the preterm infant and 2 centimeters in the term infant.[43] If the percutaneous line is placed in an upper extremity, it is considered centrally placed once it crosses the midclavicular line with the tip located in the superior vena cava.[44] If the percutaneous line is inserted in a lower extremity, it is considered centrally placed once it crosses to the pelvic cavity and the tip is positioned in the inferior vena cava.[45]

In the newly born infant, the umbilical artery is often cannulated to continuously monitor the blood pressure when connected to a pressure transducer, as well as to obtain arterial blood gases. The umbilical arterial catheter (UAC) is inserted under sterile conditions so the tip of the UAC is either in the low position placed between the third and fourth lumbar vertebrae, or is at the "high" position placed between the sixth and tenth thoracic vertebrae. The umbilical venous catheter (UVC) is most often used for administration of medications and hypertonic fluids, exchange transfusions, blood transfusions, or central venous pressure monitoring when connected to a pressure transducer. In an emergency soon after delivery, the UVC may be placed into the vein a short distance ("just under the skin") until blood is aspirated (confirms its placement), for the purpose of infusing emergent medications, fluids, and measurement of pH and PaCO2 (the amount of carbon dioxide in the blood). The UVC should be removed once the emergency is resolved. When the neonate is admitted to the NICU another UVC should be inserted under sterile conditions such that the tip is positioned at or just above the level of the diaphragm. The UAC and UVC are considered central lines, and should not be used to infuse fluids until tip placement has been confirmed by radiograph. It is the nurse's responsibility to securely tape the central lines in place once site placement has been verified.

Irrespective of whether the IV is a peripheral, percutaneous, or central line, the standard of care is to evaluate and document the site at least once per hour. The visual inspection as well as the "hands-on" evaluation should be described in the policy and procedure manual. Visual observation of the IV site should include color changes at, above, and below the site, presence of swelling/edema, leakage of fluid and the condition of the dressing. The "hands-on" evaluation should include gently palpating the site for signs of edema, pain, or discomfort; examining the intravenous tubing connections for tightness; and checking for ease of flushing the line and presence of blood return. The nurse should also visually inspect (and document) the IV pump to ensure the correct drip rate is set and the correct amount per hour has been infused. New generation IV pumps (Smart Infusion pumps) have safety mechanisms that require the nurse to enter the dose of medications, such as vasopressors and narcotics, as well as the baby's weight to enable the pump to display additional information such as how many micrograms per kilogram per minute the baby is receiving. Smart pump technology incorporates comprehensive libraries of medications, typical concentrations, dosing units and dosing limits along with software to verify the medication is being delivered at the right dose and flow rates based on safety parameters.[46] The smart pump technology decreases the reliance on human factors such as fatigue and staffing patterns, and should ultimately decrease the amount of medication errors. The pump will need to be manually overridden in the event the prescribed dosage is outside of typical parameters of normal. Should this occur, the nurse should question the dosage to ensure there was not an error in ordering the medication. Intravenous delivery of medications presents the biggest potential for harm to the neonate.

TIP: Intravenous fluids and medications should only be delivered using a neonatal infusion pump as an adult pump is capable of delivering greater volumes at faster speeds in the event an error is made in entering either the drip rate or the volume to be infused. Latest generation IV pumps have pre-set limits for medications given as continuous drips and will alarm or give an alert that the dosage programmed is outside the allowable limits. Many models of IV pumps have pressure limits that can be set, such that the pump will alarm when the pressure limit is exceeded. This may be the first sign of an extravasation.

As part of the initial assessment of the baby when beginning a shift, the nurse should also inspect the labels on the fluids to be sure they are properly labeled with the baby's name, as well as to ensure that the syringes and bags of fluids contain the correct fluids and additives, and are delivering them at the correct rate. At this time the pump should also be checked to verify that it is a neonatal infusion pump, as adult pumps are capable of delivering larger volumes at faster hourly rates. The nurse should also check that the pressure limits on the pump are set low enough to give an alert when the pump is requiring higher pressures to infuse the fluid. An alarm noting "occlusion" may be the first sign of an extravasation, and the nurse needs to immediately inspect the IV site. The nurse also needs to verify the label on the IV tubing as to when it was last changed. Tubing containing hyperalimentation or clear fluids should be allowed to hang no more than 72 hours. Tubings containing vasopressors, narcotics, and intralipids are required to be changed at least once every 24 hours. Umbilical artery and venous catheter lines are also changed once every 24 hours and the transducers re-zeroed during the initial assessment.

As with any procedure, there are inherent risks to receiving intravenous therapy, especially that of extravasation. The immaturity of the neonate's skin often compounds the damage from the extravasation, tending to result in involvement of a larger percentage of skin surface than would occur in an adult. Calcium is notorious for causing "IV burns"; however other substances such as vasopressors, sodium bicarbonate, and parenteral nutrition will also produce similar damage. Infiltration of caustic substances necessitates immediate attention and care.

> Dr. Bloom ordered a bolus of normal saline (unconcentrated) to be given over 30 minutes to treat Baby Wright's hypotension. Both unconcentrated and concentrated normal saline were stocked in the hospital. Nurse Diltz obtained a vial of normal saline that had "CONCENTRATE" and "CAUTION: MUST BE DILUTED FOR I.V. USE" in capital red letters. A written warning also noted the fluid was a 14.6% solution. In addition to not noting the warnings on the vial, Nurse Diltz did not read the physician's order. Baby Wright suffered severe brain damage after the second bolus. The Wrights sued the suppliers of the sodium chloride solution, Abbott Laboratories, who had never sent a warning letter to the hospital. The Food and Drug Administration had warned them to change the label as well as the packet inserts for both the concentrated and unconcentrated normal saline solutions. It was argued that Abbott had a duty to warn the hospital regarding the dangers of administering the incorrect concentration, and that failure to do so was a proximate cause of Baby Wright's injury. The court granted summary judgment for Abbott Laboratories

because it found that the hospital and nurses should have been aware of the dangers of stocking in close proximity medications that appear similar. Had Nurse Diltz actually read the physician's order and the labels on the sodium chloride vial, the incorrect solution would not have been administered.[47]

There are a number of ways the nurse documents the IV site assessment. These documents become crucial exhibits in a lawsuit related to an IV injury. It is customary to note a comprehensive assessment of the IV site when charting the initial shift physical assessment of the infant. Thereafter, it is acceptable to note "no change in IV site." Flow sheets, frequently used in nurseries to decrease redundant charting, may simply have a box the nurse checks as an indication the hourly IV site evaluation was performed, and there was nothing untoward noted. All flow sheets should contain a legend that explains the symbol, letter, or abbreviation the nurse used to place in the box, as this is the same information that previously would have been found in a narrative note. An example would be an "N" written in a box, which would translate into "site non-reddened, non-edematous," or "W" meaning "warm to touch."

TIP: There are pharmacologic interventions that may reduce or prevent tissue injury from an extravasation. Hyaluronidase (Amphase) should be injected in five 0.2 cc injections subcutaneously around the periphery of the infiltration of an extravasation that involves hypertonic solutions or those containing calcium, such as total parenteral nutrition, sodium bicarbonate, potassium chloride, and aminophylline. Ideally given within the first hour for best results, Hyaluronidase may be given up to three hours after the infiltration. Phentolamine is indicated for treatment of an infiltrate of vasoactive medications such as dopamine, epinephrine, and nor-epinephrine, and should be given within 12 hours of the extravasation.

Changes from previous assessments must be documented in detail along with the interventions the nurse used to rectify the situation. Infiltrations require prompt action as the neonate's muscles and tissues are still developing and are at higher risk for permanent damage. If the nurse suspects the IV may be infiltrating, the standard of care requires the IV be removed immediately, or be inspected at least once every 15 minutes, depending on the appearance of the site, the type of fluid infusing, the flow rate, as well as the status of the neonate. Even with the utmost vigilance on the part of the nurse, the IV may infiltrate and result in permanent damage.

This was the case when a scalp IV infiltrated, and after healing, left a small area of discoloration on the forehead near the hair line of a preterm baby. The mother was extremely upset at the complication "because the twins were no longer identical." A careful review of the medical record revealed the babies were born at 26 weeks post-menstrual age and required invasive intensive care therapies for a prolonged period of time due to complications of extreme prematurity. At time of discharge the infants were 35 weeks post-menstrual age with no residual pulmonary, neurologic, gastrointestinal, or ophthalmologic sequelae. When the IV infiltration was suspected, the nurse carefully monitored the site, documented her concerns/findings, and removed the IV immediately upon confirming the infusate was not remaining within the vein. Another IV was promptly started.

The review of medical records noted that during the course of the twin's hospitalization, they received the highest standard of medical and nursing care. However, it must be remembered that there is a risk-benefit ratio for all medical and nursing therapies given. Please refer to Chapter 24, *Intravenous Therapy Malpractice,* for additional information.

D. Medication Errors

Babies admitted to the normal newborn nursery typically are given only Vitamin K, a sterile ophthalmic ointment and hepatitis B vaccine. High-risk neonates admitted to the special care and intensive care nurseries may be expected to receive countless doses of a variety of medications, some given under stressful emergent conditions. It is estimated there is a 1.6 percent error rate for all medications administered, and a reporting rate of only 25 percent of all medication errors.[48] Medication dosages and fluid volumes are calculated individually for each baby based upon the baby's weight. Because of their small size, an error in calculation can easily result in drug or fluid overdoses or underdoses, and therefore, an increased potential for harm exists when compared to the adult.

TIP: Medication doses and fluid volumes are calculated individually based on the baby's weight. The weight used initially is the birthweight, as all babies lose weight over the first days of life. Once the baby regains the birthweight the doses/volumes will be recalculated according to changes in the weight. For example, a medication dose may be written as 100 mg/kilogram every 12 hours, and a daily fluid volume as 120 cc/kilogram/day.

Nurses are taught the five "rights" of medication delivery early in their training: right patient, right medication, right dose, right time, and right route. It is the standard of care for the nurse to perform this check on every medication and volume of fluid before administering it to the baby. When taking the order from the physician's medication order sheet, it is a nursing responsibility to verify the medication dose and route of delivery are correct before sending the order to be filled in the pharmacy. The pharmacist should also verify the medication dose and route of delivery are correct before filling the order. The professional nurse is responsible for understanding the pharmaceutical actions of the medications being administered. Whenever circumstances are unclear, the nurse must question the prescribing physician/APN before administering the medication. It is the standard for the nurse to also re-verify the medication order if the writing is illegible or if the details with respect to the five rights are not explicit.

Automated drug-dispensing units or automated dispensing machines stock commonly used medications. They may lead to elimination of errors in dispensing and administration.[49] The use of bar code scanning involves a unique identifier for the patient that matches the correct patient to the medication at the right time prior to administration. The bar code system has been effective in decreasing patient identification error. However, the small extremities of high-risk neonates are not very conducive to having a large point-of-care bar code system. Commonly, the bar code is affixed to a card that is at the baby's bedside and may not be scanned until after the medication has been given. Thus, testing in the NICU environment for bar coding effectiveness is still ongoing.[50] Please refer to Chapter 28, *Medication Errors,* for more information.

TIP: The systems approach does not absolve the individual from being responsible and accountable for practice. The professional recognizes a duty to report, pursue, and develop safe methods in the delivery of care for the purpose of decreasing errors.[51]

The National Patient Safety Foundation was established in 1997 by the American Medical Association, CNA HealthPro, and 3M as an independent, nonprofit research and education organization dedicated to the measurable improvement of patient care safety. Healthcare errors have been thrust into the public's attention since the Institute of Medicine published its report, "To Err is Human: Building a Safer Health System," on the failure in health care due to a lack of safety systems, even under the best of intentions. "Crossing the Quality Chasm: A New Health System for the 21st Century" and "Keeping Patients Safe: Transforming the Work Environment of Nurses" followed, calling for redesign and sweeping changes in the healthcare delivery system with equitable patient-driven care delivered by teams of healthcare professionals.[52] The Leapfrog Group, Joint Commission, and professional nursing/medical organizations have since joined with nonprofit organizations to collaborate with healthcare clinicians, institutional providers, health product manufacturers, researchers, legal advisors, consumer advocates, regulators, and policymakers to build a knowledge base, create a forum for sharing knowledge and facilitate the implementation of "best practices" and "evidence-based practice" to improve patient safety and outcomes. Refer to Chapter 4, *Patient Safety Initiatives*, and Chapter 6, *The Foundations of Nursing Practice*, both in Volume I, for more information on these topics.

A neonatal nurse practitioner (NNP) and two neonatal nurses were accused of negligent homicide in a famous Denver case. The baby was in the Level I nursery and was scheduled to be discharged with his mother that afternoon. Care of the baby had been transferred to a neonatologist due to a question regarding management of prenatal exposure to syphilis. The neonatologist ordered the correct dose of benzathine penicillin G to be given intramuscularly (IM); the mother-baby nurse signed off the order, and sent it to pharmacy. The pharmacist made a ten-fold error, dispensing 1,500,000 units of benzathine penicillin G in 2.5 cc rather than 150,000 units in 0.25 cc. The two syringes had a label to "note dosage strength." The mother-baby nurse remarked that it looked like a lot to give IM as it would taken five injections to give the medication. The mother-baby nurse became busy with another patient, leading the Level II nurse and NNP to check pharmaceutical references (*Neofax*[53] and *Drug Administration in the NICU*[54]) to determine if the medication could be given intravenously. It was wrongly deduced from the reference books that the medication could be given IV. The two nurses volunteered to administer the medication as the Level I nurse did not have neonatal IV experience. The NNP changed the physician's order to administer the medication IV. Neither the Level II nurse nor the NNP observed that the dose was a ten-fold amount. The baby had a cardiopulmonary arrest and died.

Two of the three nurses were disciplined by the Board of Nursing; however, the prosecutor accused them of negligent homicide and a grand jury indicted them. After 45 minutes of deliberation, the jury acquitted the mother-baby nurse. The other two nurses plea-bargained days before the trial.[55-57]

The Institute of Safe Medication Practices found more than 50 failures that contributed to the error that resulted in the death of the neonate.[58-60] "System errors" have now been recognized, rather than having one person, typically the nurse as the end user, shoulder the entire responsibility for the error (Figure 2.1). Most serious errors are system errors, with the nurse being the patient's last line of defense. Thus, it is expected the nurse will question the prescribing physician if issues arise related to the ordering and administering of medications.

- The five "rights" must be employed without fail with each medication or fluid administration. Double check with another registered nurse:
    - The neonate using the hospital identification band
    - Correct medication, volume, dose, and route
- Notify the pharmacist if the medication is not labeled correctly. The medication should be sent back to the pharmacy and the pharmacy should reissue another dose.
- A medication volume over 1.5 cc should be re-verified if unfamiliar with the medication.
- Know therapeutic medication parameters and monitor medication blood levels, if appropriate.
- Use medication administration equipment only after orientation and demonstrated competency has been proven and documented.
- The medication area should be user-friendly, with proper lighting and limited distractions.
- Adhere to state and federal agency rules for storage of medications.
- Report all medication errors, including interventions undertaken once the error was discovered.

Figure 2.1 Strategies to Decrease Medication Errors

E. Sepsis

Neonatal sepsis, defined as an actual or potential infection, is a major cause of death in the first month of life. Diagnosing early-onset sepsis, infection occurring in the first 72 hours of life, is one of the most difficult diagnostic tasks of the physician, APN, and neonatal nurse.[61] Failure to identify early-onset sepsis results contributes to a high mortality rate, and increased morbidity, especially in the preterm neonate.[62] Group B streptococci (GBS), *Escherichia coli, Haemophilius influenzae*, and coagulase-negative staphylococcus are the organisms most frequently isolated. Neonates are particularly susceptible to the hazards of sepsis and meningitis (infection isolated in the cerebrospinal fluid and brain tissue) as a result of being subjected to the variety of invasive procedures common in the special care and neonatal intensive care nurseries. The incidence of sepsis in the full-term baby is one to eight per 1,000 live births and increases to approximately 24 percent of very low birthweight infants.[63] Nosocomial or late-onset sepsis occurs in approximately 250 infants per 1,000 live births.[64] Unfortunately, these neonates have a high risk of developing meningitis, with 40 percent of survivors exhibiting neurologic sequelae.[65,66]

All healthcare providers are expected to follow strict handwashing protocols and use scrupulous sterile techniques because of the immunocompromised status of the preterm and ill neonate. Nurses, as the key healthcare providers at the bedside, have a responsibility to ensure health professionals as well as the baby's family wash their hands upon entering the unit, as well as prior to touching the infant or the infant's equipment. It is also a nursing responsibility, as discussed above, to communicate any findings in the physical assessment of the neonate, including the results of inspection of an IV site that would suggest sepsis. The observational skills of the nurse are key in the early detection of infection. The earlier the nurse communicates presumptive findings to the physician or NNP, the earlier treatment can begin. The majority of malpractice cases appear to involve delayed or missed diagnosis and treatment because of delayed recognition of symptoms, or lack of communication between nursing and medical personnel. In the following case, the plaintiff alleged, in part, the failure of the nurses to notify the physician of the birth of a newborn with sepsis led to serious injury:

> Baby N displayed symptoms of Group B step sepsis and meningitis on the first day of life. The mother had not received prophylactic antibiotics during labor despite experiencing a urinary tract infection of GBS etiology during the pregnancy. Based on the mother's history as well as the results

of diagnostic testing, Baby N should have received antibiotics prior to developing symptoms. The defense argued the lack of standards in 1990 related to prophylactic intrapartum antibiotics. It was also argued antibiotics did not need to be given prior to the onset of symptoms based on the laboratory tests. The jury returned defense verdicts for the obstetrician and pediatrician. The hospital and nurse were dismissed after settling for $2,750,000.[67]

Many women are carriers of GBS as well as other organisms responsible for early-onset sepsis; however, these organisms may be extremely difficult to isolate at times. Early-onset sepsis presents subtly and/or rapidly as a fulminant multisystem disease during the first few days of life, with the most critically ill displaying symptoms within the first 12 hours of life. Many of the affected neonates are premature as the incidence is inversely related to gestational age. The neonate's perinatal history should be reviewed by the neonatal nurse at time of admission to the nursery to note significant events that may place the baby at higher risk. These risk factors may include prolonged premature rupture of membranes (greater than 18 hours), premature delivery, low birth weight baby, chorioamnionitis, peripartum maternal fever, Group B streptococcal bacteriuria during current pregnancy, previous delivery of an infant with group B streptococcal disease, and prolonged duration of intrauterine monitoring.[68] Since 2003, the overall rate of early-onset GBS disease has increased; however, the late-onset disease has remained stable.[69]

TIP: Universal screening is recommended at 35 or more weeks of gestation and intrapartum antibiotic prophylaxis for GBS-colonized women by The Centers for Disease Control and Prevention (CDC)[70] and the American College of Obstetricians and Gynecologists.[71] The woman's GBS status should be documented on the labor and delivery units admitting form. Neonatal nurses should be aware of the risk factors for GBS sepsis in the neonate and, if present, verify the mother's GBS status and use of antibiotic therapy from the obstetrical record.

The symptoms of early-onset sepsis tend to be sudden and follow a fulminant course involving many organ systems. Respiratory distress is the most common initial sign. It is challenging for nursing/medicine to make a diagnosis regarding etiology of disease in the neonate as signs typically present with many of the same nonspecific symptoms irrespective of the underlying disease process. Very frequently these presenting signs are varying degrees of respiratory distress. However, it is the responsibility of the nurse to note deviations from the expected in both the physical examination and any laboratory results, and communicate the findings and nursing diagnosis to the neonatologist or APN as soon as possible. Subtle signs of temperature instability, lethargy, poor feeding, glucose instability, irritability, and increased oxygen requirements are commonly noted. Assessments and observations, along with the symptomatology reported to the physician and APN, should be carefully documented. Reviewing both the mother's prenatal and intrapartum history, as well as the baby's may provide clues as to the causative organism. It must be kept in mind that antibiotics are only one part of the treatment strategy in managing sepsis. The nurse must pay meticulous attention to other body systems that may be affected and need supportive management, as for example, cardiac (hypotension), respiratory (distress), metabolic (hypoglycemia; temperature instability) and acid-base imbalance.[72]

TIP: Often a nurse will experience the feeling that "I just can't tell what's wrong for sure, but there is something wrong. The baby just isn't himself." The nurse is likely observing subtle changes that could be early nonspecific symptoms of sepsis. The change in appearance or behavior should be documented and communicated to the healthcare team so that surveillance of the baby is increased.

Late-onset sepsis, acquired as early as 72 hours, but more commonly after the first seven days of life, is acquired by horizontal transmission (nosocomial). Gram-positive organisms are the predominate invaders, although fungal infections, especially *Candida* species, are the second most common infection in those infants who weigh less than 1500 grams.[73] Technological advances in the NICU, along with the increase in low birth weight survivors, has increased the opportunity for organisms to cause sepsis. The invasive therapies required for physiologic support (endotracheal intubation, central or peripheral intravenous lines, indwelling urinary catheters, duration and number of courses of antibiotic therapy, and so on) are significant risk factors. Symptoms of late-onset sepsis, much like those evidenced in early-onset sepsis, are nonspecific; however, by this time other disease processes such as respiratory distress syndrome, congenital heart disease, and metabolic pathologies have been ruled out. Thus, a presumptive diagnosis of suspected sepsis must be communicated to the physician and APN for immediate management. If positive cultures indicate systemic fungal infection, the neonate must have urine analyzed and cultured, an ophthalmologic examination, an echocardiogram

for endocarditis and renal ultrasound to look for fungal balls (mycetomas).[74]

Late-onset sepsis must always be ruled out in a neonate with nonspecific symptoms who presents to the emergency room or pediatrician's or APN's office after having been discharged home as healthy.

F. Hypoglycemia

Changes in practice, since early research outlined normal parameters of glucose values in the pre- and full-term babies, have led to current recommendations for upward modifications in the definition of neonatal hypoglycemia. There is a continuum of low blood glucose values of varied duration and severity influenced by factors such as gestational age, general health status, adequacy of gluconeogenic factors, and presence or absence of symptoms.[75-77] Clinicians typically use a plasma glucose concentration of 40 mg/dL as the cutoff for intervention; an acceptable level should be 50-70 mg/dL. The literature has established a link between a decrease in both mental and motor neurodevelopmental scores with an increased incidence of hypoglycemia in the preterm neonate.[78] Despite a lack of consensus regarding the absolute definition of hypoglycemia, the incidence is thought to be approximately 1-5 per 1,000 neonates, with the incidence increasing to about 30 percent in the high-risk neonate.[79]

Clinicians do agree that the critical value for hypoglycemia should be individualized according to the baby's clinical status.[80-82] The lowest level of blood glucose and the length of time it can be tolerated without cellular or cerebral injury are unknown. It is important to remember that the serum or plasma glucose levels only provide an approximation of the cerebral glucose level—therefore, the lowest critical blood glucose level may be altered by conditions that impair cerebral blood flow or increase cerebral glucose use.[83]

TIP: Indications for testing glucose levels in the baby include growth restriction, jitteriness, lethargy, cold stress, suspected sepsis, perinatal stress, prematurity and if the baby is the infant of a woman with diabetes mellitus. In addition to treating the predisposing condition, immediate interventions must occur to return the glucose levels to normal. This may require glucose bolus and the establishment of a continuous intravenous infusion of glucose.

Babies demonstrating hypoglycemia either have inadequate production/substrate delivery, hyperinsulinism, or a combination of these two etiologies. Inadequate supply or production of glucose is the most common, and is related to decreased fat and glycogen stores accumulated during fetal life. Babies most at risk are those born preterm and those who have delayed or insufficient feedings, growth restriction, perinatal stress, hypoxia, respiratory distress, hypothermia, polycythemia/hyperviscosity, sepsis, and congenital heart failure. It should be a priority that on admission to the high-risk nursery, the neonatal nurse evaluate the baby's risk of hypoglycemia by obtaining a plasma glucose (point of care testing) and complete blood count (CBC) with differential, and assess the physical needs of the neonate. The CBC gives values for hemoglobin (oxygen-carrying capacity), hematocrit (rule out polycythemia) and white count (sepsis).

The baby's weight, length, and head circumference are obtained and plotted on standardized growth charts. The Colorado Intrauterine Growth Chart is used in almost every nursery in the United States as it is supplied free of charge by the companies who produce neonatal formulas. Aligning the baby's age with growth assists in determining if the baby is large (90th percentile), small (10th percentile), or appropriate for gestational age. The physical assessment will also detect the presence of asymmetric growth. The growth pattern, symmetrical versus asymmetrical, determines the timing of the appearance of hypoglycemia, and therefore helps the nurse anticipate when to monitor the glucose level to optimally detect hypoglycemia.

Growth is considered to be asymmetrical (brain-sparing) if there is a disproportionate reduction in weight and length as compared to the head circumference. Such an infant is likely to displays symptoms of hypoglycemia within the first hours of birth because the glucose requirements of the brain may quickly deplete the liver's glucose stores and ability to produce sufficient glucose to keep up with the body's needs (inadequate supply/production of glucose). Neonates found to be small for gestational age may demonstrate symptoms of hypoglycemia later, approximately 12 to 18 hours after birth.

Hyperinsulinemia or an increased rate of glucose use is the second etiology for hypoglycemia. The most common etiology is the mother having diabetes mellitus. During fetal life, high levels of glucose are transferred across the placenta. The fetal pancreas is stimulated to produce high levels of insulin, causing the glucose to be stored as fat. When the umbilical cord is cut at time of delivery, the glucose load is abruptly stopped; however, the neonate continues to produce high levels of insulin. The excessive insulin level inhibits both the production of new glucose and the breakdown of glycogen. Due to increased metabolic demands as the neonate transitions to extrauterine life, there is a rapid depletion of available glucose.

- Majority of neonates are symptomatic
- Tremors; jitteriness; exaggerated Moro reflex; irritability
- High-pitched or weak cry
- Respiratory distress: tachypnea, apnea, cyanosis
- Hypotonia, lethargy, stupor
- Temperature instability
- Poor intake: weak suck, takes very little at one feeding, refuses to eat
- Seizure activity
- Cardiopulmonary arrest

Figure 2.2 *Clinical Manifestations of Neonatal Hypoglycemia*

An increased rate of glucose use may also be found in the neonate who is appropriate for gestational age, and has sufficient glycogen stores and glucose availability to meet normal metabolic needs. However, the mechanisms for glucose production may be quickly overwhelmed when the metabolic drive is heightened. Thus, in addition to infants of diabetic mothers and those who are large for gestational age, the nurse should screen for hypoglycemia in any neonate with concomitant conditions that alter metabolic drive. The nursing plan of care should be revised accordingly. Examples would include the neonate with cold stress, hypoxic-ischemic encephalopathy, metabolic acidosis, sepsis, or respiratory distress. Detecting hypoglycemia is difficult as the majority of neonates are symptom free or they display non-specific symptoms that, in conjunction with other clinical conditions such as respiratory distress, mask the signs of hypoglycemia. Please refer to Figure 2.2 for symptoms of hypoglycemia.

TIP: Whipple's triad must be met in order for clinical symptoms to be attributed to hypoglycemia:[84]
- Reliable low blood glucose
- Symptoms consistent with hypoglycemia are evident
- Symptoms resolve after euglycemia is achieved

Four principles guide management of hypoglycemia:[85,86]

- high-risk neonates need to be monitored;
- confirmation that the glucose level is low;
- symptoms resolve after euglycemia is achieved; and,
- the events are carefully observed and documented.

Potential risk factors that may predispose the neonate to hypoglycemia may be found from the mother's history or intrapartum experience. The nurse should be aware of a maternal history of gestational or insulin-dependent diabetes, any medications received during labor that may predispose the neonate to a low blood sugar, or any intravenous fluids during labor and delivery that contained dextrose that may trigger an increase in insulin secretion in the neonatal period. The Apgar scores, as well as the events surrounding the birth, should also be noted because perinatal asphyxia is an etiology of hypoglycemia. The physical assessment should include careful measurement of head (frontal-occipital) circumference, length, abdominal circumference, and weight, along with the determination of the growth pattern with respect to gestational age.

TIP: Infants of mothers with diabetes have a characteristic appearance. They are plethoric (very red due to increased hematocrit levels), and have big chubby cheeks (tomato faces) and big chubby thighs. While they are typically large for gestational age, close inspection and measurement of the head circumference will reveal that the head is small in relation to the large body. This is because insulin does not cross the blood brain barrier and thus, cannot cause increased brain and head growth.

Immediately upon suspecting a neonate is hypoglycemic, the nurse should obtain a plasma glucose level (Chemstrip®) and communicate the results to the physician and APN. "Stat" laboratory confirmation using whole blood is also recommended; however, it is essential treatment not be delayed while awaiting the results from the laboratory. Some asymptomatic infants may be managed by frequent formula feedings and observing the glucose level either before or after the feeding. Enteral feedings of dextrose 5 percent or 10 percent are not recommended because they provide few calories. If the baby is able to tolerate enteral feeds, then formula or breast milk is the fluid of choice as they contain fats, proteins, and carbohydrates that provide more energy over longer periods of time.

Intravenous glucose therapy is required by the majority of symptomatic neonates. The nurse should know that the standard of care is to use a "mini-bolus" of 2 ml/kg of 10 percent dextrose in water (D10W), followed immediately by an infusion of glucose to provide 4-6 mg/kg/minute (approximately 80 ml/kg/day). The mini-bolus does not result in hyperglycemia, and there is little risk of rebound hypoglycemia. Very importantly, the mini-bolus helps raise the serum glucose much faster than simply starting an intravenous glucose infusion. It is the nurse's responsibility to obtain a plasma blood glucose concentration 15 to 30 minutes after the mini-bolus to determine the infant's response and whether re-bolusing is required. Subsequent monitoring of, and frequency of monitoring, the plasma and the serum blood glucose concentrations are based upon the neonate's underlying clinical condition, presenting symptoms and glucose values. Typically, the nurse evaluates the blood glucose every one to two hours until the glucose level is stable, decreasing to once every four hours, then eight, then 24 hours as the hypoglycemia resolves.

The pregnancy was uncomplicated and the neonate was delivered without difficulty. Within 18 hours of birth, the neonate demonstrated tachycardia, lethargy, poor feeding and a poor suck. A glucose value of 17 was obtained about 12 hours after the symptoms presented. The value decreased to 15 minutes later. The neonate suffered brain damage which progressed to cerebral palsy and partial blindness. It was claimed that the hospital was understaffed with nurses, the nurses were not properly trained, and the nurses ignored the physician's orders that he be contacted if tachycardia or poor feeding presented. It was also claimed that the nurses failed to instruct this first-time mother on how to properly breast feed. A $1.8 million settlement was reached.[87]

Hypoglycemia is considered a medical emergency, in that immediate treatment is required. Nurses must communicate their concerns rapidly to the physician/APN as the goal of medical management is to return the blood glucose level to normal, and maintain it at normal levels. Glucose is essential for cerebral metabolism because it is the brain's primary source of fuel. Hypoglycemic brain damage occurs mainly in grey matter structures; however, the severely compromised neonate may also have white matter injury. Thus, one of the most serious sequelae of hypoglycemia is neurologic impairment, including both intellectual and motor deficits. Head ultrasounds, magnetic resonance imaging, and positron emission tomography scans have shown brain abnormalities in neonates who have experienced hypoglycemia.[88] Outcome studies report that neonates with seizure-associated hypoglycemia exhibit the worst neurologic prognosis.

G. Hyperbilirubinemia

Jaundice, or hyperbilirubinemia, is found in varying degrees in almost every newborn. However, bilirubin is potentially so toxic to the central nervous system that it must be closely evaluated. When the serum total bilirubin (STB) is approximately 6-7 mg/dl, the baby begins to appear yellow. Jaundice usually appears first on the face and progresses down toward the lower extremities. While the majority of neonates experience no residual effects, some neonates are devastated by the effects of unconjugated bilirubin on the central nervous system. The precise identification of the level at which unconjugated bilirubin is harmful for an individual neonate remains unknown.[89]

Kernicterus is a term often used to characterize a range of clinical sequelae caused by high levels of unconjugated bilirubin. Kernicterus really refers to the yellow staining found in specific regions of the brain during autopsy. *Bilirubin encephalopathy* is the term appropriate for the central nervous system effects of bilirubin. The symptoms may include subtle behavioral changes such as lethargy and irritability, to more severe signs such as seizures, hearing deficits, developmental delays, and death. In recent years, there has been an increase in neonates presenting to the emergency department with symptoms of bilirubin encephalopathy. Upon investigation, it has been found that the typical infant presenting to the emergency department is a late-preterm male discharged by 48 hours of life who is exclusively breastfeeding.

The increase in the number of episodes prompted The Joint Commission to release a Sentinel Event Alert and undertake a root cause analysis.[90] Risk factors that played a role in recent severe hyperbilirubinemia cases include those normally observed for in all babies (Figure 2.3). The root cause analysis identified factors related to four patient care processes: patient assessment, continuum of care, patient and family education, and treatment.[91] (See Figure 2.4.) In response to the apparent increase in bilirubin toxicity, the American Academy of Pediatrics released an updated clinical practice guideline, *Management of Hyperbilirubinemia in the Newborn Infant 35 or More Weeks of Gestation*.[92] The

Undersecretion of Bilirubin
- Perinatal distress/asphyxia
- Sepsis
- Biliary obstruction

Overproduction of Bilirubin
- Polycythemia
- Infant of a Diabetic Mother
- Increased enterohepatic circulation
  - Delayed feeding/poor feeder
  - Intestinal obstruction
- Hemolytic disease
  - ABO/Rh incompatibilities
  - Anomalies of red blood cell membrane or enzyme defects
- Sepsis
- Extravascular blood
  - Cephalohematoma
  - Swallowed blood
  - Enclosed hemorrhage
- Intracranial
- Pulmonary

Breastfeeding

Miscellaneous
- Hypothyroidism
- Hypopituitarism
- Inborn errors of metabolism

Figure 2.3 Etiologies and Risk Factors for Severe Hyperbilirubinemia

Patient Assessment
- Visual assessment of jaundice is unreliable in neonates with dark skin
- Failure to recognize jaundice and its severity based on visual assessment
- Failure to measure bilirubin level in the infant jaundiced in the first 24 hours

Continuum of Care
- Discharge prior to 48 hours with no follow-up within 24-48 hours of discharge
- Failure to provide follow-up for those neonates discharged displaying jaundice prior to discharge
- Failure to provide lactation support to ensure that the neonate has an adequate intake

Education
- Failure to provide appropriate information to parents regarding jaundice
- Failure to respond to parental concerns about their baby: jaundiced, poor feeding, change in behaviour/activity level

Treatment
- Failure to recognize and treat the increased bilirubin level
- Failure to aggressively treat severe hyperbilirubinemia in a timely manner

Figure 2.4 Root Cause Analysis: Severe Hyperbilirubinemia. www.jointcommission.org

guideline provides healthcare providers with specific information to prevent kernicterus, and educational guidelines for parents as well as the public regarding the risk of severe hyperbilirubinemia. One of the key elements of the guideline is the recognition that the late-preterm baby (34 to 36 weeks gestation), especially those who are breast-fed, is at an increased risk, and therefore requires a higher level of surveillance.

Luca Vaia was born at full term with a normal delivery and Apgar scores. Despite facial jaundice and an above-normal bilimeter reading of 16, he was discharged on day of life two from Elmhurst Memorial Hospital. He did well for two days and then began to demonstrate poor feeding, irritability and restlessness. The mother called the pediatrician's office twice and was told to feed him with a syringe, and bring him to the office in the morning. When the parents noted Luca had turned yellow, they took him to an emergency department. His bilirubin level was 38.2. A transport was arranged to a tertiary center for a double volume exchange transfusion to be performed. The transport team picked the baby up and arrived at the receiving hospital approximately four hours after he was taken to the emergency department. At the tertiary hospital, an umbilical venous catheter (UVC) was inserted and an order given to obtain whole blood for the exchange transfusion. When the exchange transfusion was started, blood could not be withdrawn through the UVC. After multiple attempts to obtain an arterial line failed, pediatric surgery was called. Pediatric surgery finally placed an arterial line into the brachial artery on the fifth attempt. Within an hour after the exchange transfusion, the bilirubin level decreased to 18.8. Luca suffered bilirubin encephalopathy as a result of excess bilirubin crossing the blood-brain barrier. He requires 24-hour care due to severe cerebral palsy, spastic quadriplegia, profound hearing loss and upward gaze palsy. It was alleged that the delay in performing an exchange transfusion caused the brain damage. It was also claimed that the delay in leaving the first hospital and the delay caused by the blood not being available when Luca got to the receiving hospital contributed to the brain damage, as well as negligence in placing the UVC. The defendant claimed that Luca's bilirubin level had been critical for more than 24 hours prior to the receiving hospital being contacted, that the transport was within the standard of care, and that it was not the standard to pre-order blood. A defense verdict was returned. Elmhurst hospital settled for $5,750,000 and Dr. Jeanette Edwards and Elmhurst Pediatric Association settled for $2 million prior to trial.[93]

TIP: Joint Commission recommends:[94]
- All newborns be assessed prior to hospital discharge for their risk of developing severe hyperbilirubinemia
- A follow-up visit within three to five days of hospital discharge be scheduled (bilirubin level is at its peak)
- Breastfeeding women should receive adequate oral and written instructions regarding newborn jaundice

---

Bilirubin is produced mainly from the breakdown of red blood cells. It is released in the unconjugated form (indirect bilirubin) from the liver and spleen, and binds tightly to circulating albumin. The albumin circulates the bilirubin back to the hepatocyte (liver cells) where it is metabolized into the water-soluble form of conjugated bilirubin (direct bilirubin), and is ready for excretion through the small intestine. Bilirubin bound to albumin is not toxic because it cannot cross the blood-brain barrier. However, when albumin is no longer available for binding, unconjugated bilirubin can be found freely in the blood, and is able to cross the blood-brain barrier to be deposited in the brain, laying the groundwork for bilirubin encephalopathy and kernicterus.

The two types of jaundice are physiologic and pathologic. Physiologic jaundice occurs in approximately 60 percent of term neonates and 80 percent of premature neonates.[95] This is due to the increased red blood cell production and the inability of the liver to adequately process the increased bilirubin load it receives. Additionally, neonates have an increased reabsorption of bilirubin from the intestine. The bilirubin level should peak on day three in the full-term baby and day five or six in the preterm baby.

Pathologic jaundice needs to be ruled out if any of the following criteria are present:[96,97]

- Clinical jaundice appearing within the first 24 hours of life
- Total serum bilirubin concentration increasing by more than 5 mg/dl
- Total serum bilirubin concentration greater than 12.9 mg/dl in a full-term neonate
- Total serum bilirubin concentration greater than 15 mg/dl in a preterm neonate

- Direct serum bilirubin greater than 1.5-2 mg/dl
- Clinical jaundice lasting longer than one week in a full-term neonate or two weeks in the preterm neonate

The physician or APN must investigate any suspicion of pathologic jaundice, as it is never normal. The bedside nurse has the responsibility of observing for the presence and progression of jaundice, being aware of the individual neonate's risk factors, and reviewing the baby's serum indirect and direct bilirubin levels. The nurse also has a professional responsibility and accountability for being aware of the symptoms of bilirubin encephalopathy, and communicating concerns or findings to the physician or APN. Early signs include nonspecific symptoms such as lethargy, high-pitched crying, weak suck/poor feeding, and hypotonia. As the encephalopathy progresses, the baby may demonstrate hypertonia, temperature instability, and opisthotonic posturing. Survivors commonly display neurologic sequelae of hearing loss, cerebral palsy, and severe developmental delays.

The goal of medical management is to prevent hyperbilirubinemia and its effects in order to decrease the risk of bilirubin encephalopathy. There is no treatment once damage has been done to the central nervous system. The nurse has a responsibility to be aware of the expected medical management of hyperbilirubinemia, including the normal ranges of laboratory values for serum total bilirubin. Algorithms and guidelines offer assistance and guidance for the healthcare provider's management plan of the baby in the hospital, as well as for the baby readmitted for phototherapy or an exchange transfusion.[98] The low-risk nursery has incorporated a nomogram into the baby's medical record that plots the bilirubin level at the hour at which it was taken prior to the baby's discharge. The hour-specific bilirubin level is predictive of the likelihood of a subsequent bilirubin level falling into the high-risk zone (95th percentile).[99] Low-risk nursery nurses have standing orders to obtain a transcutaneous bilirubin on any neonate that looks jaundiced prior to discharge. If that level is above normal (a level set by the institution), the nurse is to obtain a serum total bilirubin and report the findings to the physician. Anticipation of medical management strategies in combination with knowledge of the physiologic basis of hyperbilirubinemia structure the framework for the nurse to tailor the nursing care plan to the neonate.

TIP: Visual estimation of jaundice has been shown to be inaccurate. The healthcare provider is responsible for assessing the neonate with a transcutaneous or serum total bilirubin any time concern for hyperbilirubinemia

exists. The bilirubin level should be interpreted based on the baby's age in hours at the time the level was obtained and plotted on Bhutani's normogram to determine if the neonate falls into the high-risk zone. The neonate who falls above the 95th percentile or is "jumping the tracks" (moving into higher risk zones quickly) should not be discharged and likely requires treatment for hyperbilirubinemia.

The most commonly used management strategy to decrease bilirubin levels is placing the baby under a bright light or a fluorescent bank of lights. Effective phototherapy decreases the serum total bilirubin at a rate of 0.5 to 1 mg percent per hour, and by 30 to 40 percent after 24 hours.[100] The effectiveness is determined by the energy output of the phototherapy unit, the spectrum of light emitted, the distance from the unit to the baby's skin, and the amount of the neonate's body surface area exposed to the light. A light irradiance of 4 to 6 W/cm^2 per nanometer at a distance of approximately 40 to 50 cms from the skin surface is required for optimal phototherapy efficacy.[101] The nurse should measure the light irradiance and document it in the medical record once per shift.

The nurse is responsible for using the phototherapy apparatus according to the manufacturer's recommendations. For maximal effectiveness, the phototherapy units should be checked by nursing or bioengineering for adequacy of light levels (hours in use).[102] Halogen lamps are more compact than fluorescent lamps; however they cannot be brought close enough to the neonate to increase the irradiance without elevating the risk of burning the skin. Fiberoptic systems are convenient for home phototherapy since eye shields do not have to be worn unless the baby is placed prone on the blanket. However, they have a major disadvantage in that the irradiance emitted is low because of the pad's small surface area. The Wallabye® and the Bili-Blanket® have been very useful when double phototherapy is required to expose more of the baby's surface area, as either system can be placed under the baby while the fluorescent lights are overhead. Plexiglass should cover the lamps when banks of fluorescent lights are used to protect the neonate from ultraviolet light. Because the lights generate energy, there is a risk of temperature instability, especially overheating inside an incubator. Monitoring the neonate's skin temperature with servocontrol while in an incubator will provide the nurse with essential information related to temperature.

TIP: After initiating phototherapy, the total serum bilirubin level must be monitored on a regular basis (every 4–12 hours) because visual assessment of the jaundice will not be reliable.[103] The bilirubin level should be monitored for a minimum of 24 hours after phototherapy is discontinued to detect significant rebound.[104]

As much of the baby's skin surface as possible should be exposed to the light to maximize phototherapy effectiveness. The eyes, however, must be covered with eye shields at all times during phototherapy to protect them from the intense light. Repositioning and turning of the baby is necessary to allow the lights access to all sides of the body. The nurse should document on the medical record the position of the baby, type of phototherapy used, and that the eyes are protected with a "bili-mask." The mask should be removed at least every four hours with the phototherapy unit off so that the baby can be exposed to visual stimuli and interact with the parents.

TIP: Bili-masks are required to protect the baby's eyes from the intense light of phototherapy. A nursing responsibility is to routinely check that the mask is covering the baby's eyes, and that it is positioned so as to not obstruct breathing.

Known side effects of phototherapy include increased insensible water loss and the risk of frequent, watery stools. Medical management of the baby may involve increasing basic fluid requirements by as much as 20 ml/kg/day. Thus, the nurse is responsible for monitoring intake and output closely. All diapers should be weighed in grams, making note of the number and consistency of stools. The nurse should document the output on the flow record, along with the enteral and intravenous intake, and note if the infant is in positive or negative fluid balance. Many low-risk nurseries check that the baby has voided/stooled rather than weighing the diapers. If the neonate is breastfeeding, it is important that the low-risk nursery nurse ensure that the baby has adequate intake and output to prevent complications. Nursing is also accountable for observing for any other adverse effects of phototherapy such as hyperthermia, dehydration, and skin rashes. Any adverse effects must be communicated to the physician or APN in a timely manner.

Effective use of phototherapy and a decrease in the numbers of babies born with Rh hemolytic disease has reduced the number of exchange transfusions performed in NICUs today. The baby with rapidly rising total serum bilirubin levels that are not amenable to treatment with phototherapy will likely be transferred to a tertiary center for management of the hyperbilirubinemia. A single-volume exchange removes approximately 75 percent of the neonate's red blood cell mass, while a double-volume exchange removes approximately 85-90 percent. An exchange removes about 45-85 percent of the total serum bilirubin.[105] It is expected that there will be a "rebound" in the bilirubin levels of as much as 60 percent of the pre-exchange level[106] as the bilirubin leaves the extravascular space and enters the vascular space, with the possibility of a subsequent exchange transfusion needed. The most common adverse effects of an exchange transfusion are pressure changes, volume fluctuations and biochemical imbalances, which can be ameliorated by withdrawing small aliquots of blood slowly and slowly replacing the volume. Adverse effects may occur more frequently if routes other than the umbilical vein are used.[107]

The decision to undertake an exchange transfusion should be made based on the bilirubin level, how quickly the level is increasing, post-menstrual age of the neonate, as well as the baby's age in days and hours.[108] The nurse will closely monitor the baby, and assist in stabilization as preparations are made for an exchange transfusion. It is the nurse's responsibility to position the baby on the radiant warmer, monitor vital signs continuously with a cardiopulmonary monitor, ensure adequate intravenous access, and have oxygen and suction at the beside. The baby should be in as stable a condition as possible prior to the initiation of the procedure. During the procedure the nurse is responsible for monitoring the baby's heart rate, blood pressure, the overall condition and observing for signs of hypocalcemia and hypoglycemia. Typically small aliquots of blood (3 to 5 ml/kg) are removed in the preterm or critically ill patient whereas larger volumes (10 ml/kg) are removed in the term baby.[109] With the removal of each aliquot of blood, the neonate must be observed for symptoms of hypocalcemia: irritability, tachycardia, and prolongation of the Q-T interval on the cardiopulmonary monitor. As a precaution, calcium gluconate 10 percent should be available at the bedside. Because of the invasiveness of the procedure, it is common to have the emergency cart close by the bedside, possibly with emergency medications prepared in advance. In addition to the vital signs, the nurse may also be responsible for recording the times the blood aliquots were removed and replaced and any medications given.

The nurse must remain at the bedside to observe the baby's response to the exchange transfusion and to assist the physician if necessary. After the blood is checked by two registered nurses to ensure it is the proper type for the neonate, the requisition must be signed by the nurses and placed in the appropriate section in the medical record. The baby typically receives type O Rh-negative blood. Before signing for the blood, the nurses must verify the blood is irradiated to minimize the risk of graft-versus-host disease and verify it is cytomegalovirus (CMV) negative. The nurse will also send the first and last aliquot to the laboratory for bilirubin, calcium, hematocrit, and cultures. A type and cross will also be done on the last aliquot in anticipation of a subsequent exchange transfusion.

TIP: Blood products used for neonates must always be checked by two registered nurses prior to being infused. CMV negative blood is always used for transfusions.

At completion of the exchange transfusion, phototherapy is re-initiated, thus the nurse needs to replace the protective eye coverings and position the baby appropriately. Blood needs to be drawn to evaluate bilirubin levels at least once every four hours, as well as to monitor blood glucose levels until they are stable or there is no longer a risk of hypoglycemia.[110] In conjunction with the neonatologist and APN, the nurse is responsible for assisting in educating the parents with respect to phototherapy, exchange transfusion, bilirubin, and the baby's changing clinical condition.

H. Retinopathy of Prematurity (ROP)

TIP: All newborn infants born at less than 28 weeks post-menstrual age, or with a birth weight of less than 1500 grams, and selected infants between 1500 and 2000 grams with an unstable clinical course, should have an initial eye examination by a trained pediatric ophthalmologist within four to six weeks after birth, or within 31 to 33 weeks post-menstrual age, whichever is later.[111]

Formerly known as retrolental fibroplasias, ROP is one of the major causes of blindness in infants. The most important clinical factors associated with the development of retinopathy of prematurity (ROP) are birth weight and post-menstrual age. The cause of ROP is multifactorial, thus oxygen by itself is not to blame for its development. Incidence of ROP increases significantly as birth weight and post-menstrual age decrease. Eighty-two percent of infants weighing less than 1 kilogram will develop ROP, with 9.5 percent progressing to vision-threatening sequelae.[112] Forty-seven percent of those who weigh between 1 and 1.5 kilograms will develop ROP, with 2 percent in danger of becoming blind.[113] Thus, of those who develop ROP, approximately 80 percent will have spontaneous regression with no visual loss.[114] The standard treatment for ROP is laser therapy.[115] The standard of care is to schedule retinal examinations at times corresponding to the sequential nature of the progression of ROP.[116] The American Academy of Pediatrics, American Association for Pediatric Ophthalmology and Strabis-

mus, and the American Academy of Ophthalmology have suggested guidelines on which a screening program may be developed to detect ROP in infants at risk:[117]

- All newborn infants born at less than 28 weeks post-menstrual age, or with a birth weight of less than 1500 grams, and selected infants between 1500 and 2000 grams with an unstable clinical course, should have at least two eye examinations by a trained pediatric ophthalmologist. Retinal changes should be documented using the *International Classification of Retinopathy of Prematurity*.[118]
- The first examination should take place within four to six weeks after birth, or within 31 to 33 weeks post-menstrual age, whichever is later.
- Infants with areas of retinal immaturity on initial examination should have serial examinations every two to three weeks until vascularization has reached the ora serrata.
- If ROP is present during the initial examination, the infant should be examined weekly or every other week, depending upon the severity of the findings.
- Treatment should take place within 72 hours of finding any stage with plus disease in Zone I ROP, stage 3, no plus disease in Zone I ROP and stage 2 or 3 with plus disease in Zone II ROP to decrease the risk of retinal detachment prior to treatment.
- NICU-specific criteria should define who is responsible for examination and follow-up of neonates at risk. Transfer to another unit or healthcare facility should be accompanied by what eye examinations are needed and their required timing, and discharge or transfer should not be made if timely follow-up cannot be accomplished.

Baby B was born 25 weeks post-menstrual age (PMA) and admitted to the NICU requiring ventilatory support. He was weaned to CPAP at 28 weeks PMA, and to nasal cannula 1 litre at 21 percent oxygen (room air). Debra, a neonatal APN and his primary healthcare provider, noted on the medical record he was now 31 weeks PMA, and given his history, was in need of an eye examination to rule out ROP. Debra noted this again on the medical record the next day, Thursday. Friday, Brenda, another APN on the same team, was responsible for Baby B's care and also noted Baby B was in need of his initial eye examination. Both Debra and Brenda had time off and Baby B's care was left to the attending physician and other APN's on the team. When they returned five days later, neither followed up on whether Baby B had the initial eye examination, nor did they question the lack of documentation regarding ROP in the daily medical progress note. Baby B was discharged home at 36 weeks PMA. His mother took him for his first follow-up visit with the pediatrician three days after discharge. The pediatrician found Stage 3 ROP with plus disease. The left eye was noted to have a complete retinal detachment and the retina of the right eye to be partially attached. The pediatrician immediately arranged to have Baby B admitted to another tertiary facility for surgery. Despite attempts at treatment, the baby is completely blind in both eyes. The parents filed a lawsuit against the hospital, APNs, and physician. All parties settled in mediation (unpublished settlement).

It was the responsibility of the APN, who was the primary healthcare provider for Baby B, to follow up with his treatment plan and ensure the proper eye examinations were done at the appropriate times. Because APNs function under protocols approved by the neonatologist, the physician is ultimately responsible for the plan of care.

Laser surgery and cryotherapy have been shown to decrease the risk of blinding complications of ROP by 50 percent.[119] The nurse's responsibility preoperatively for the infant undergoing laser photocoagulation is to instill the eye drops as ordered, in addition to the standard nursery monitoring protocol. Postoperatively, the nurse will administer the eye drops as ordered to decrease postoperative complications. The nurse should also ensure that the neonate's eyes are not directly exposed to bright light. Observation for signs of feeding intolerance and gastric distention should also be done if the neonate was given mydriatic medications during surgery.[120]

I. Stabilization and Transport of the High-Risk Neonate

The concept of regionalization of perinatal care to increase access to the appropriate level of care for each neonate led to the need for neonatal transport teams. The goal is to transport critically ill neonates in the most stable condition possible whether the transport is intrafacility or interfacility. Optimal stabilization at a referring hospital will vary based upon the baby's clinical condition, and may constitute an emergent return (providing extraordinary care under adverse conditions). Modes of transport between facilities vary according to distance, region, condition of the neonate, and weather patterns. The level of care given during the transport should

be the same as what is standard at the receiving institution: that is, intubation, UVC/UAC line placement, thoracentesis, administration and delivery of fluids and medications, and physiologic monitoring capabilities (vital signs, oxygen saturation, and so on). The American Academy of Pediatrics and the National Association of Neonatal Nurses, among others, have provided lists of suggested transport equipment and supplies.[121–126] Transports typically done for diagnostic or invasive procedures are less likely to be an emergency, and as such, the level of care must be maintained or increased.

The principles of respondeat superior set out that the hospital is the party responsible for approving and maintaining the protocols followed by the transport team. The neonatal transport team is an extension of the NICU. Although the composition of the team will vary among institutions, all involved need the combined skills to care for any anticipated clinical condition the neonate may exhibit while at the referring hospital, and more importantly, while en route to the receiving hospital. Advanced knowledge of physiology, pathophysiology, management principles of acute problems and technical skills must be demonstrated, and these competencies should be documented annually.

Many centers utilize an extensively trained NICU registered nurse as the predominant team member. The nurse must be aware of her specific state's Nurse Practice Act to determine the scope of acceptable nursing practice. Protocols must be in place to permit them to use an expanded scope of practice, based upon documented competencies, under the guidelines approved by the Boards of Nursing. Generally two basic principles guide the operation of a transport program: (1) the receiving institution has a properly trained transport team for which it has assumed responsibility; and (2) the team is operating under the direction of a medical director.[127–129] The institution is ultimately responsible for the acts and omissions of the transport nurse, and should ensure the nurse possesses the requisite skills and knowledge, is properly supervised, and is operating under established policies and procedures. It is the nurse's responsibility to work within the scope of practice and the specific protocols, policies, and procedures relating to transport.

Communication is the foundation for a successful transport program. It provides the referring facility a point of access and coordinates activities of the transport team. The main responsibilities of the referring hospital are to provide adequate stabilization and resuscitation for the neonate, and to arrange the appropriate referral and transport.[130,131] The transport nurse should obtain sufficient information during the referral call to adequately prepare for and anticipate the needs of the neonate. The information should include the baby's name and gender, referring physician and institution, maternal prenatal, labor and delivery history, date and time of birth, gestational age and weight, Apgar scores, details of delivery room stabilization, and current hospital course with laboratory data, including the reason for the transfer.[132,133] Thus, the referral record is used as the beginning of documentation, and should reflect the time the team received the call, recommendations given to the referring hospital, the time the team left the receiving hospital, and the time of arrival at the receiving hospital. The referring hospital is responsible for obtaining all necessary consents and providing a copy of the neonate's entire medical record.

The receiving hospital has the responsibility of accepting the patient, communicating with the referring physician, assuming responsibility and accountability for team composition, selecting the mode of transport, and directing clinical care providing during transport.[134–136] When answering the transport request, the transport nurse or healthcare professional should document all information received as well as all recommendations given to the referring center directly on the transport record. The transport record then becomes part of the neonate's medical record. The receiving hospital should also have a medical director of transport to oversee the entire program, develop and approve policies and procedures, supervise training of transport personnel, and review transport cases. A transport coordinator, usually a nurse, is assigned to supervise the daily activities of the transport service under the direction of the medical director.[137,138]

Upon arrival at the referring facility, the neonatal transport nurse is responsible for performing a primary assessment of the baby to prioritize immediate interventions. The nurse should obtain an update on the medical condition, review laboratory and radiographic data, and consult with the transport physician regarding the management plan. The nurse should document interventions as well as the baby's response to the intervention. Documentation of patient care during transport varies among institutions. The referring hospital's staff may stop documentation and "discharge" the neonate to the transport team if their policy states the transport team assumes responsibility for the baby upon its arrival. On the other hand, the receiving facility's staff may be uncomfortable providing care to someone else's patient, and thus, their policy may be that once the transport team arrives, the baby is considered to be "admitted" to the receiving hospital, and assumes all care functions. Other institutions may continue to document care provided by the transport team until the team leaves its hospital. The transport nurse and the referring bedside nurse need to be familiar with their respective institution's policies and procedures for documentation.

TIP: When functioning on the transport team, the nurse may be held to a different standard of care than when he performs that task in the NICU, because he performs advanced practice functions during transport.[139,140]

Once the infant is stabilized, she should be secured inside the transport incubator, and continuously monitored during the transport to the tertiary center. The nurse must be able to communicate with the receiving physician or medical transport coordinator at all times during the transport. Documentation of vital signs, color, ventilator settings and status of the neonate should be performed every five to 30 minutes, depending upon the severity of the neonate's condition. Narrative notes must record any complications or unusual situations in detail. A deterioration of the infant's condition during the transport may raise questions about the advisability of the transfer. Documentation on the transport record should reflect the time the team left the referring hospital, time of arrival at the receiving hospital, where the baby was admitted (i.e., Special Care Nursery or NICU), and the name of the nurse who received report from the transport team. The transport nurse should also document on the transport record the patient status on arrival in the unit, including vital signs and monitor readings.

J. Neonatal Kidnapping

Between 1983 and 2008, there were 124 infant abductions (birth to six months) by non-family members from healthcare facilities.[141] Abductions most often occur from the mother's room (57 percent), the nursery (14 percent), pediatric floor (14 percent) and other areas on hospital grounds (15 percent).[142] Many hospitals practice "family-centered care" or have rooming-in policies in which the baby spends most of the time in the mother's room, making it easier for "strangers" to gain access to the neonate.

The National Center for Missing and Exploited Children (NCMEC) was founded in 1984. The Center has developed close working relationships with the Association of Women's Health, Obstetric and Neonatal Nurses, the National Association of Neonatal Nurses, and the International Association for Healthcare Security and Safety. Together these associations have developed a comprehensive program that outlines hospital policy, teamwork by staff, parents and security, and the use of electronic and physical security devices.[143] A component of the guideline, the Self Assessment for Healthcare Facilities, reviews four broad categories that include general issues, proactive measures, physical-security safeguards, and critical incident-response plans. Hospitals can use the self-assessment to review current processes and develop policies and procedures.[144]

TIP: The Joint Commission requires mock abduction drills. "The plan for preventing or thwarting an abduction should be tested to the extent and with the frequency necessary to ensure that the plan is effective as would apply to any other plans for responses to potentially hazardous, unusual or emergency situations. Any testing should ensure that staff knowledge and competence is adequate as it relates to their role in responding. The need for drills should be addressed by the organization as part of their risk assessment and planning process."[145]

The Joint Commission requires emergency management plans be in place for newborn abductions. The Commission also requires the plan be tested to ensure it is effective, just like any other hospital emergency.[146] A newborn abduction is considered a sentinel event that requires immediate investigation. A thorough root cause analysis and action plan must be submitted by the healthcare facility to TJC within 45 days.[147] The root cause analysis will review areas such as staffing levels, orientation and competency assessment of staff, lines of communication to staff as well as family, the physical environment, and security processes.[148] Joint Commission will place the facility on Accreditation Watch if the plan is not acceptable.[149]

A heavyset woman was asking when the babies went out to the mothers. The nurse immediately notified the charge nurse and nursing supervisor of a possible abduction. All mother-baby unit staff began looking for the baby. Two staff members immediately went to the exits until security arrived. A Code Pink went over the hospital public announcement system. The baby's nurse asked the mother when she last had her baby. She stayed with the mother in her private room and only let her family in. Security personnel monitored the entrances to the mother-baby unit so no one could leave or enter. The incident occurred at change of shift; however, all staff were required to remain in the unit.

Staff in the emergency department heard the overhead page. They had noticed a woman in a lab coat entering the parking garage carrying an odd-shaped sport bag that appeared to be moving. The woman was looking over her shoulder and scanning the parking area as she was getting into her car. Security was given her location, a physical description, and the license number of her vehicle. Security notified the local law enforcement authorities and sent a patrol car to the garage. In the meantime, the nurse manager was informing hospital administration and the community relations department about the abduction. Within hours of the kidnapping, the police apprehended the abductor with the unharmed newborn a few miles from the hospital.[150]

Because hospital personnel are the key to preventing newborn abductions, staff education is essential. Orientation and yearly competencies should include the hospital emergency plan, abductor profile, and abductor behaviors. The typical abductor is:[151]

- Female, age 12 to 53
- Overweight
- Lives in the community where the abduction occurred
- Has had a miscarriage or is unable to conceive
- Is married or living with a significant other—kidnapping the baby may be an attempt to save or maintain the relationship
- Has visited nurseries and maternity units in more than one hospital prior to the abduction asking detailed questions about procedures and the layout of the nursery/maternity areas
- Plans the abduction, but takes advantage of whatever opportunity presents itself—no specific baby is the target
- Impersonates hospital personnel
- Is able to provide "good" care for the baby after the abduction

All babies should have an identification band that matches their mother's numbers. It is the nurse's responsible to place the baby's identification number, footprints or photograph, and a complete physical assessment of the baby in the medical record. After the birth of the baby, the nurse should remind the parents not to leave the baby unattended or give the baby to anyone without proper hospital identification. Some hospitals have a special marking on their employee identification badges that permit access to the newborn area.

Although not foolproof, electronic alarms and surveillance equipment support hospital policy and nursing practice. Installation of alarms on exit doors and security cameras positioned to see faces of all persons using the main entrance of the maternal-child area are examples of recommended physical-security safeguards.[152] It is common to have infant bracelet or identification band alarms, access control, and closed-circuit television. The monitors may document the abduction, providing valuable evidence to aid in capturing the abductor if the kidnapping is successful.

The critical incident-response plan should include a written plan that details what should occur in the event of a newborn abduction. It is the nurse's responsibility to immediately search the entire unit and notify security. One nurse is to remain with the mother to provide emotional support. A head count of all newborns needs to be immediately carried out. The crime scene should also be protected to preserve any possible forensic evidence. The director of the maternal-child area in conjunction with security personnel should hold mock abductions to evaluate competencies of nursing and security in their response to the critical incident.[153]

TIP: The Joint Commission (TJC) requires hospitals to perform at least one annual proactive risk assessment of a high-risk process as part of its Patient Safety initiative. The Infant Security Program is included in the Patient Safety initiatives.

In the event of an abduction, a comprehensive program that includes staff education and an electronic security system may help the position of the hospital.[154] Litigation is pursued whether the baby was kidnapped from the mother's room or the nursery; however, the risk of being sued increases if the abductor impersonated a hospital employee.[155] Healthcare institutions may be liable because of their general duty to take reasonable care to prevent foreseeable harm to their patients, and therefore, may be held responsible for any physical or psychological harm suffered by the newborn.[156] The hospital's liability may also be based on a contractual duty to use reasonable care to prevent foreseeable injury to third parties, and thus, may be held accountable to the parents for the cost of any searches and psychological harm.[157]

K. Videotapes

Parents want to capture the birth experience along with their baby's progression during prolonged hospital stays. Digital cameras, digital phones, and videotapes are commonly seen in the labor and delivery and nursery areas. Healthcare providers need to be aware of what their hospital's policy on videotaping. The policy needs to[158]

- Identify the person responsible for informing the mother or parents of the existence of the policy;
- Establish requirements regarding the videotaping equipment brought into the areas;
- Decide exactly where videotaping is permitted;
- Determine who decides whether videotaping continues or stops when complications or the unexpected arise;

- Specify what to do when the healthcare personnel do not wish to be videotaped or audiotaped; and
- State where in the medical record to document the existence of the videotape.

Having a videotape has advantages in the event of a lawsuit that proceeds to trial. The jury does not need to rely on events reconstructed from the interested parties' memories. Timely responses to emergency situations may be captured on the videotape or audiotape. If negligence has been documented, the videotape may encourage fact-based mediation discussions.

The author was a plaintiff's expert for a malpractice case in which it was alleged that a nurse failed to recognize the infant's distress and properly institute resuscitation measures. The father videotaped the birth, as well as the healthcare personnel providing initial delivery room care to Twin A. A few minutes later Twin B was delivered. On the audiotape, a brief, weak cry could be heard as the baby was handed to the nurse. The videotape showed Twin B being placed on the radiant warmer and dried, and wet blankets being removed. The baby became hypotonic, stopped moving, and had a poor color. The nurse examining the baby began tapping on the diaphragm of the stethoscope, saying "Something is wrong with this thing. I can't hear anything. Can someone get me another?" She continued to tap on the stethoscope instead of observing the baby as he became more cyanotic with no evidence of chest movement.

When the nurse failed to hear a heartbeat through the stethoscope, she could have palpated the umbilical cord for pulsation, rather than blame the equipment for being faulty. When it was recognized the baby was in need of resuscitation, someone in the room turned the videotape lens toward the floor as the father continued to videotape. The tape then ended.

In situations involving unexpected or complicated nursing and medical procedures, it may be helpful for the nurse or physician to view the videotape with the family to explain what is happening, answer any questions, and offer emotional support. Having a duplicate of the videotape will be helpful if a lawsuit is filed. The defense attorney and nurse should review the videotape to help the nurse remember the events and prepare for testimony. Keeping a duplicate tape will also decrease the risk the tape is tampered with by the plaintiff. If the tape is overly edited, having a full copy will enable the defense to illustrate to the jury all the events that occurred in the proper sequence, as well as the nursing and medical interventions used to resolve the situation.[159]

TIP: There are advantages to having videotapes in the event the lawsuit proceeds to trial: (a) the jury does not need to rely on events reconstructed from the interested parties' memories; (b) timely responses to emergency situations may be captured on the videotape/audiotape; and (c) the videotape may encourage fact-based mediation discussions.

L. Iatrogenic Injuries

The high-tech world of the Level II and III nurseries uses many medical and nursing interventions that are invasive and risky. It is the nurse's responsibility to follow the manufacturer's recommendations when using any piece of equipment. In light of safety initiatives by TJC, manufacturers, and professional organizations, there has been a move to decrease some of these hazards. For example, pumps to infuse enteral feedings should not accept intravenous tubing, and tubing that connects to enteral feeding tubes should not accept extension tubing made for intravenous infusions. One of the biggest dangers is infusing fluids that cannot be given intravenously directly into a vein or artery if the nurse connects the tubing in error.

> An infant was admitted because of coughing, a fever, and vomiting. He was noted to be in a poor nutritional state on admission. Intravenous fluids were started and tapered over the course of four days. He was being given enteral feeds via a nasogastric tube. The night nurse on day four was administering the enteral feed when the infant suddenly had a respiratory arrest and became cyanotic. Resuscitation was carried out for one hour but was unsuccessful. The nurse later admitted she may have done something wrong.
>
> The cause of death was noted to be cardiac arrest due to lung embolization with enteral material and air. The feeding solution had been injected accidentally into the intravenous catheter. The nurse confirmed her error when confronted with the results of the autopsy. The excess amount of air in the heart was explained by the nurse in that she had found it difficult to infuse the enteral feeding, and thus refilled the syringe with air several times to re-inject into the feeding tube. In a subsequent court trial the nurse was convicted of involuntary manslaughter.[160]

Many iatrogenic injuries occur as a result of negligence, and are thus preventable (Figure 2.5). As in the above case, an inappropriate, or lack of appropriate, intervention increases the nurse's risk of liability.

- Intravenous infiltration
- Unrecognized respiratory or cardiac arrest due to malfunctioning cardiopulmonary monitor, or alarms disengaged by staff
- Burns from devices used to warm the skin before obtaining blood
- Infections due to contamination during invasive procedures
- Reactions to blood or blood products due to incorrect blood type
- Aspiration due to an uncoordinated suck/swallow reflux or improper position of the orogastric/nasogastric tube
- Fluid overload from failure to properly set the rate on the intravenous pump
- Tissue necrosis from constrictive dressings
- Tissue or organ damage resulting from medication therapeutic levels abnormally low or high
- Tissue or organ damage from insertion of tubes or intravenous lines, such as an orogastric or urinary catheter, or from an umbilical arterial/venous catheter perforating the cardiac intra-atrial septum

Figure 2.5 *Common Iatrogenic Injuries in High-risk Nurseries*

One of the most frequent nursing interventions is to administer medications. All medications have a risk-benefit ratio that should be evaluated daily with respect to the neonate's clinical condition. Long-term antibiotics not only result in superinfections in the individual, but also increase the risk the microorganism will develop resistance to the medication, as for example, methicillin-resistant staphylococcus aureus (MRSA).

Many medications require blood level monitoring to assist in titrating the dose for maximum effectiveness and to minimize harm. Gentamycin, Vancomycin, Digoxin, Theophylline and Phenobarbital are examples of medications that require serum levels to be evaluated at specific times during initiation of treatment, with subsequent monitoring depending on the serum level and the baby's clinical condition. It is the responsibility of the nurse to obtain the therapeutic drug level at the correct time (trough, peak, random), and inform the physician/APN of the laboratory results. The nurse must be familiar with the normal ranges for the therapeutic drug level obtained, as adverse results—such as hearing loss—are not always reversible. Therapeutic drug levels should be charted on the flow sheet in the area used for laboratory data.

Overheating of the neonate is another common iatrogenic injury. The radiant warmers typically used for the sickest of infants utilize an infrared heating system to keep a neonate's temperature within a desired range. "Servo-control" is a probe placed on the baby's skin which sends information back to the bed's computer such that the bed will produce more or less heat given the degree the nurse has chosen. A full-term baby may have the set-point as low as 35.5°C (95.9°F), and a preterm baby may have it set at 37°C (98.6°F). The aim is to have an axilla temperature of 36.5 to 37.5°C (97.7 to 99.5°F) for the term baby, and 36.4 to 37.1°C (97.6 to 98.8°F) in the preterm baby. The nurse is responsible for documenting the thermoregulation and the temperature of the baby on the flow sheet. The nurse must note the set-point of the bed, the baby's skin temperature, and the axillary temperature. If the baby is in an incubator, the nurse must also document its interior temperature, and note whether the bed is on manual control or servo-control. Improper parameters can result in cold stress or heat stress in the baby. Weight loss, metabolic acidosis, hypothermia or hyperthermia, increased oxygen needs, prolongation of time on a ventilator, and apnea are possible symptoms if the baby is not in proper heat balance.

TIP: A nurse assumes liability any time equipment or supplies are faulty or used in a manner not recommended by the manufacturer. To do so is a violation of the standard of care in that the nurse must provide a safe environment for the patient and family.

It is the nurse's responsibility to be familiar with equipment and use it correctly. The institution must have a management plan that documents the nurse's competency validations for the proper use of medical equipment.[161] Nurses are responsible for any injuries or errors that result from equipment failure. The standard of care that the nurse must provide a safe environment for the patient and family is violated if the nurse continues to use equipment that he knows is faulty or damaged.

A 27-week neonate was admitted to the NICU for intrauterine growth restriction. He was later diagnosed with apnea and bradycardia, and anemia related to multiple blood draws. Head ultrasounds were reported to be normal. At two weeks of age he received a blood transfusion, during which the baby coded and was successfully resuscitated. Several days later brain imaging studies showed white spots that were identified as air emboli introduced during the transfusion. A head ultrasound at one month of age showed a loss of brain volume and cystic lesions that corresponded to the white spots seen on previous studies. The plaintiff claimed negligence during the blood transfusion allowed the air emboli to be introduced which resulted in brain damage. The baby was diagnosed with developmental delay, spastic quadriplegia, left-side hemiplegia and speech difficulties. The hospital admitted negligence with respect to the air emboli, but claimed the air emboli were not responsible for the baby's brain damage. A jury returned a verdict for $35,341,585.[162]

Equipment may sometimes be used for purposes other than those for which it was originally intended:

Elijah Dodson, a two-week-old infant, was admitted to Westchester Medical Center in Valhalla, where doctors determined his extremities were unusually cool. A nurse soaked a diaper in hot water and applied it to his feet to warm them. Four of his right foot's toes subsequently became gangrenous and fell off. The baby's mother, acting individually and on her baby's behalf, sued the hospital's operating agency, Westchester County Healthcare Corporation. It was alleged the nurse's treatment was improper because the temperature of the diaper could not be accurately monitored. The jury awarded $2.3 million to the plaintiffs. *Gray v. Westchester County Healthcare Corp.*[163]

A nurse assumes liability any time equipment or supplies are used in a manner not recommended by the manufacturer. The hospital must have policies, procedures, or protocols that outline nursing management strategies in the event of an emergency or complications that arise due to an iatrogenic injury.

2.5 Prevention of Liability

Nurses are professionals responsible and accountable for the care they give their patients.[164] Neonates are viewed as a "special" population in need of increased protection. Thus, the cost of liability is high in a neonatal malpractice case. It is costly to provide medical care to a damaged infant with a normal life expectancy. The longer statute of limitations permits claims to be made years later, and there is always sympathy for the family who may not be able to afford the care the baby requires. Two general areas can be examined to determine if a nurse is practicing preventative legal maintenance: (1) risk management, and (2) clinical skills and knowledge level.

A. Risk Management

Nurses strive to provide quality care that results in an optimal outcome for their patients and families in a safe environment. However, merely to be in a special care or intensive care nursery invites an element of risk. The risk-management department needs to work collaboratively with the nursing department to identify risks that can be controlled. Communication between the two is essential to completely investigate untoward events, promote changes to decrease adverse situations, and follow risk-management concerns.

The hospital administration also has a responsibility to ensure nurses employed in neonatal areas possess certain training and specialized knowledge. For example, all neonatal nurses need to be competent in neonatal resuscitation. Documentation that neonatal nurses are certified in the American Academy of Pediatrics and American Heart Association's Neonatal Resuscitation Program should be completed, along with ensuring the certification is current. A record should be maintained documenting all competency-based practice required for the hospital's specific unit.

TIP: The hospital is responsible for evaluating and documenting the nurse's clinical competencies every two years.[165]

Effective communication with the family is an essential risk-management strategy. The majority of parents filed a malpractice claim because they were upset their baby's permanent problems or likelihood of dying was never discussed with them.[166] The neonatal nurse is expected to care for two patients: the baby and the family.

Eight-week-old Baby Perez was taken to Randelman Medical Clinic because of nausea, diarrhea, and poor intake. Dr. Steward Kossover examined him and determined he had a viral condition. Telling Brian's parents this was "nothing serious," he prescribed Amoxycillin. Brian's condition did not improve. Because he vomited at least eight times during the night, Brian's father took Brian back to the Medical Center at 10:00 A.M. the next morning. Dr. James Little examined him and determined he was "fine." Dr. Little instructed a nurse to give Brian an injection of Rocephin. She told the parents, in Spanish, that Brian had a "minor stomach infection." When the nurse injected Brian with Ro-

cephin, he began to convulse involuntarily. Brian's father asked the nurse what was wrong. The nurse explained that this was a "natural reaction to the medication." Brian never stopped having seizures. Brian appeared to be turning grey while Brian's father was paying the bill. Brian's father found a nurse and begged her for help. The nurse said "nothing was wrong." They arrived home about 20 minutes after leaving the Medical Center. Brian's father noted Brian's lips had turned a "blackish" color. Shortly thereafter, he received a call from the nurse at the Medical Center. He told her that Brian "looked terrible, was having trouble breathing, and was dying." The nurse said he was having "a normal reaction to the medicine." He desperately held the phone close to Brian's mouth so the nurse could hear Brian having difficulty breathing. He demanded to know what injection Brian received. The nurse refused to answer and told him to return to the hospital immediately. When they arrived, the nurse and Dr. Little were waiting for them. Dr. Little noticed greenish brown fluid coming from Brian's mouth and nose. Brian was barely breathing and had no heart tones. A nurse tried to force Brian's parents out of the room. They refused to leave. Dr. Little began mouth-to-mouth resuscitation but was unsuccessful. Brian was pronounced dead on arrival at Randall Memorial Hospital at 11:45 A.M. that morning.

The Perez's brought suit against the Medical Center and Dr. Little. Dr. Peter Curtis testified for the plaintiffs. At the close of the plaintiff's evidence, the defendants' motion for directed verdict was granted because the plaintiff failed to elicit specific testimony from Dr. Curtis indicating he was "familiar with the standard of care applicable to healthcare providers in Randolph County, North Carolina." Brian's parents' motion for a new trial was denied. They appealed. The Court of Appeals of North Carolina affirmed the judgment of the lower court. It ruled that expert medical witness testimony must be elicited from one "familiar" with the standard of care in the community. *Ramirez v. Little*, 609 S.E.2d 499-NC (2005).[167]

It is harder for parents to bring a claim against a caring and helpful nurse than it is to sue an inattentive nurse. Just like the baby, the family requires attention, the use of good communication skills, reassurance, and the use of the medical and nursing hierarchies to obtain the care and information each require.

B. Clinical Knowledge and Skills

Although there appears to be a trend in which hospitals place less of their policies and procedures in writing, there must be a means by which the standards of care are incorporated into daily nursing practice. Professional associations, such as NANN, AWHONN, and AACN, develop measurable criteria that define professional nursing practice for specialty areas. For example, the *Standards and Guidelines for Professional Nursing Practice in the Care of Women and Newborns* has been published by AWHONN. Nurses can adapt these suggestions for use in their own facility to help ensure they are providing care consistent with similar healthcare facilities.[168]

Encouraging certification in the nurse's specialty is another way of promoting professional growth and competent nursing care. There is an increase in the number of nurses seeking certification, because it is one of the criteria evaluated when a hospital undergoes review for Magnet designation. Refer to Chapter 8, *Inside the Healthcare Environment*, in Volume I, for more on Magnet status. Reading relevant professional journals, attending inservice training and national conferences, and continuing formal education are additional avenues to maintain and enhance professional nursing competence. By keeping abreast of the latest issues, clinical advances, and evidence-based practice, the nurse should be successful in supporting the clinical knowledge and skills necessary to provide competent nursing care. Importantly, because of the neonate's status as a minor, the nurse must be able to rely on perceptions gleaned during the nursing assessment, and be able to make critical judgments based on that assessment. This is a refined skill lacking in those with limited neonatal clinical experience.

2.6 Issues Related to Informed Consent

Neonates do not meet criteria to legally give informed consent. The parents are usually the best surrogate decision makers for the baby, as long as they are acting in her best interest. Parents married to each other may both grant consent on behalf of their baby. In the case of divorce, custody battles, and teenage or foster parenting, issues related to informed consent and patient privacy can become very complex.[169] Occasionally, the court may appoint a guardian *ad litem* to act in the best interest of the baby instead of, or in addition to, the parent or parents. To meet the legal standard for consent, the decision maker must receive sufficient information regarding the procedure, including the risks and benefits of the treatment, any alternate treatment strategies, and the consequences of not consenting.[170] One exception to obtaining consent is an emergent situation in which harm could befall the baby if treatment is delayed. The name of the person who is able to give informed consent on behalf of the baby should be documented in the medical record.

TIP: Providing the patient and family with information regarding medical surgical risks and benefits of treatment, or to suggest alternative medical surgical therapies, is outside the scope of nursing practice. Obtaining informed consent is the responsibility of the physician or APN providing the treatment.

The physician or APN should document the content of the pertinent discussion in the medical record. The nurse certainly may be a witness to the process. It is encouraged the nurse be present when the consent is obtained to assist in evaluating the parent's level of understanding. It is also appropriate for the nurse to inform the physician or APN the family needs further clarification to comfortably make a decision.

"If the nurse is required to obtain the parent's signature on a consent form, he should limit the clarification of the family's understanding to two questions: (a) Has your physician/APN discussed your baby's central line placement (i.e., medical or surgical strategy) with you? and (b) Are you ready to sign this consent form? This means you are consenting to the procedure."[171]

Three possibilities may happen if the parents or guardian do not grant consent.[172] First, if the physician/APN respects the family's wished to not treat the baby, the he or she may be guilty of child abuse or neglect, as laws stipulate that parents must provide needed medical care. Second, if the baby is treated over the parent's or guardian's objections, the physician or APN could be liable for battery, as their touching was intentional and without consent. Third, a court order may be obtained to provide the necessary treatment, which is almost always granted. If the parents refuse to permit treatment for other reasons, the court will base its decisions on several other factors: (a) infant's overall health and development; (b) immediacy of danger to the baby if the treatment is withheld; and (c) risk and benefits of the proposed treatment strategy.[173,174]

2.7 Documentation

The nurse has a professional responsibility to document observations, assessment, interventions, and the baby's response to medical and nursing care. The medical chart promotes coordination and continuity of care, assists in the evaluation of the baby's response to the treatment plan, and provides a legal and official record of the care provided. A range of charting systems is in use in hospitals, including a combination of flow sheets, narrative charting, problem-oriented charting, and Charting By Exception, as described in Chapter 7, *Nursing Documentation*, in Volume 1.

The medical record is used during legal proceedings to provide evidence that care was carried out. The record verifies the nurse provided the standard of care and performed within the scope of nursing practice. The chart should outline the sequence of events, the time frame in which they occurred, and the healthcare providers involved in the care of the neonate. The portion of recording done by nurses in the course of a hospitalization makes up the bulk of the medical record, and thus, is the most important evidence of the care rendered and the outcomes of that care. The record, and the recorder, are immediately suspect if omissions, inaccuracies, or breaks are detected in the notes. For a detailed discussion of nursing documentation, please refer to Chapter 7, *Nursing Documentation*, in Volume 1.

2.8 Summary

In the past, obstetrics was considered the "high-risk" area. Today, litigation involving neonatal nurses is not uncommon. By holding themselves as a professional nurse, neonatal nurses are held to a high level of accountability. Accountability and responsibility increase the nurse's unique role, both as a staff nurse and APN, and better define that role. Joint liability, in which the nurse and the hospital or the nurse and the physician or APN are both held liable, is one reflection of the increased accountability of the neonatal nurse.

Endnotes

1. Verklan, M. T., "Core Curriculum for Neonatal Intensive Care Nursing," In *Legal Issues*, Fourth edition, 865–881. Philadelphia: Elsevier, 2010.

2. Brent, N. J., "Concepts of negligence, professional negligence, and liability," In *Nurses and the Law,* 2nd edition, ed. N. J. Brent, 53–74. Philadelphia: W. B. Saunders, 2001.

3. *King v. Department of Health & Hospitals*, 728 So. 2d 1027, 1030 (La. Ct. App.). writ denied, 741 So. 2d 656, La. 1999.

4. Hospital Accreditation Standards. Joint Commission for Accreditation of Healthcare Organizations. Oakbrook Terrace, Illinois, 2010.

5. Rottkamp, J., "Inside the healthcare environment," *Nursing Malpractice*, Third Edition, 4149-174. Tucson, Arizona: Lawyers and Judges Publishing Co., 2007.

6. Tammelleo, A. D., "Neonatal nurse's reprehensible conduct results in revocation," *Reagan Report on Nursing Law* 38, no. 9 (1998).

7. National Association of Neonatal Nurses, *Neonatal Nursing: Scope and Standards of Practice*. Washington, D.C.: American Nurses Association, 2004.

8. American Academy of Pediatrics and American College of Obstetricians and Gynecologists, *Guidelines for Perinatal Care*, Sixth edition. Elk Grove Village, Illinois, 2007.

9. *Id.*

10. See note 1.

11. Association of Women's Health, Obstetric and Neonatal Nurses and National Association of Neonatal Nurses, *Neonatal nursing: Orientation and development for registered and advanced practice nurses in basic and intermediate care settings*. Washington, D.C., 1997.

12. *Id.* p. 8-9.

13. See note 7.

14. See note 11.

15. American Nurses Association. *Scope and standards of advanced practice registered nursing*. Washington, D.C., 2004.

16. American Academy of Pediatrics Committee on Fetus and Newborn. Advanced practice in neonatal nursing. *Pediatrics*, 123 (2009):1606-1607.

17. Henry, P., *Nurses and the Law. The nurse in advanced practice. A Guide to Principles and Applications,* Second edition, 459–489. Philadelphia: W. B. Saunders Co., 2001.

18. See note 1.

19. See note 16.

20. See note 1.

21. See note 17.

22. See note 11.

23. See note 1.

24. *Id.*

25. Laska. L. (ed.), "Failure to treat newborn's hypoglycemia," *Medical Malpractice Verdicts, Settlements and Experts* (April 2005): 26.

26. See note 2.

27. Kattwinkel, J. (Ed). *Textbook of Neonatal Resuscitation,* Sixth edition. Elk Grove Village, Illinois: American Academy of Pediatrics and American Heart Association, 2006.

28. See note 8.

29. See note 27.

30. *Id.*

31. Kattwinkel, J., S. Niermeyer, V. Nadkarni, J. Tibballsl, B. Phillips, D. Zideman, P. Van Reempts, and M. Osmond, "An advisory statement from the pediatric working group of the international liaison committee on resuscitation," 2005. http://www.pediatrics.org/cgi/content/full/103/4/e5X. Accessed October 6, 2005.

32. Merrill, J. D. and R. A. Ballard, "Resuscitation in the delivery room," In *Avery's Diseases of the Newborn,* Eighth edition, eds. H. W. Taeusch, R. A. Ballard, and C. A. Gleason, 349–363. Philadelphia: Elsevier Saunders, 2005.

33. Niermeyer, S. and S. Clarke. "Delivery room care," In *Handbook of Neonatal Intensive Care*, Sixth edition, eds. S. L. Gardner, B. Carter, M. I. Enzman-Hines, and J. A. Hernandez, 52-77. St. Louis: Mosby, 2011.

34. *Id.*

35. *Id.*

36. See note 2.

37. *Mather v. Griffin Hospital.* 540 A.2d 666 (Conn.), 1988.

38. See note 27.

39. See note 32

40. *Id.*

41. Laska, L. (Editor), "Failure to Treat Newborn's Persistent Pulmonary Hypertension Blamed for Death—$250,000 Texas Settlement," *Medical Malpractice Verdicts, Settlements and Experts*, May 2009, page 28-29.

42. Askin, D. F. and W. Diehl-Jones, "Assisted Ventilation," In *Core Curriculum for Neonatal Intensive Care Nursing,* Fourth edition, eds. M. T. Verklan and M. Walden, 494–520. Philadelphia: Elsevier, 2010.

43. Heiss-Harris, G. M. and T. Bailey, "Common invasive procedures," In *Core Curriculum for Neonatal Intensive Care Nursing,* Fourth edition, eds. M. T. Verklan and M. Walden, 299–332. Philadelphia: Elsevier, 2010.

44. Lane, L, "Radiologic evaluation," In: *Core Curriculum for Neonatal Intensive Care Nursing,* Fourth edition, eds. M. T. Verklan and M. Walden, 270–298. Philadelphia: Elsevier, 2010.

45. *Id.*

46. Smith, J. R., "Patient Safety," In *Core Curriculum for Neonatal Intensive Care Nursing*, Fourth edition, eds. M. T. Verklan and M. Walden, 361-382. Philadelphia: Elsevier, 2010.

47. *Wright v. Abbott Lab.*, No 99-333 I, 2001.

48. Verklan, M. T., "Malpractice and the neonatal intensive-care nurse," *JOGNN's Clinical Issues* 33 (2004): 116–123.

49. See note 46.

50. *Id.*

51. *Id.*

52. *Id.*

53. Young, T. E. and O. B. Magnum, *Neofax: A Manual of Drugs Used in Neonatal Care*, Eighth edition. Raleigh, North Carolina: Acorn Publishing, 1995.

54. Pawlak, R. P. and L. A. T. Herfert, *Drug Administration in the NICU: A Handbook for Nurses*. Second edition. Petaluma, California: Neonatal Network, 1991.

55. Cady, R. F., "Criminal prosecution for nursing errors" *JONA's Healthcare Law, Ethics, and Regulation* 11 (2009): 10-16.

56. Horns, K. M. and M. B. Gills, "Neonatal nurse knowl-edge of penicillin therapy," *Neonatal Network* 17 (1998): 52–55.

57. Horns, K. M. and D. L. Loper, "Medication errors: Analysis not blame," *Journal of Obstetric, Gynecologic and Neonatal Nurses* 31 (2002): 347–354.

58. See note 55.

59. See note 56.

60. See note 57.

61. Lott, J. W., "Immunology and infectious disease," In *Core Curriculum for Neonatal Intensive Care Nurs-ing*, Fourth edition, eds. M. T. Verklan and M. Walden, 694–723. Philadelphia: Elsevier, 2010.

62. Venkatesh, M. P., K. M. Adams, and L. E. Weisman, "Infection in the neonate," In *Handbook of Neonatal Intensive Care*, Sixth edition, eds. S. L. Gardner, B. Carter, M. I. Enzman-Hines, and J. A. Hernandez, 553-580. St. Louis: Mosby, 2011.

63. See note 61.

64. *Id.*

65. *Id.*

66. See note 62.

67. Laska, L. (ed.), "Newborn Develops Meningitis," *Med-ical Malpractice Verdicts, Settlements and Experts* (Au-gust 2003): 30.

68. See note 62.

69. Center for Disease Control. Perinatal group B strepto-coccal disease after universal screening recommenda-tions—United States, 2003–2005. *MMWR*, 56 (2007): 701-705.

70. Schrag, S., R. Gorwitz, K. Fultz-Butts, and A. Schuchat, "Prevention of perinatal group B streptococcal disease. Revised guidelines from CDC." *MMWR Recommenda-tions Rep.* 51, RR-11 (2002): 1–22.

71. American College of Obstetricians and Gynecologists Committee Opinion Number 279, "Prevention of early-onset group B streptococcal disease in newborns," *Ob-stetrics and Gynecology* 100 (December 2002): 1405–1412.

72. See note 62.

73. *Id.*

74. *Id.*

75. Armentrout, D., "Glucose management," In *Core Cur-riculum for Neonatal Intensive Care Nursing*, Fourth edition, eds. M. T. Verklan and M. Walden, 172–181. Philadelphia: Elsevier, 2010.

76. Cornblath, M. and R. Ichord, "Hypoglycemia in the ne-onate," *Seminars in Perinatology* 24 (2000): 136–149.

77. McGowan, J. E., P. J. Rozance, W. Price-Douglas and W. W. Hay, "Glucose homeostasis," In *Handbook of Neonatal Intensive Care*, Sixth edition, eds. S. L. Gard-ner, B. Carter, M. I. Enzman-Hines, and J. A. Hernan-dez, 353-377. St. Louis: Mosby, 2011.

78. Volpe, J. J., *Neurology of the Newborn*, Fifth edition. Philadelphia: W. B. Saunders, 2008.

79. See note 75

80. See note 78.

81. See note 77.

82. See note 75.

83. See note 78.

84. See note 76.

85. See note 77.

86. See note 75.

87. Laska, L. (ed.), "Failure to Respond to Symptoms Indi-cating Possible Hypoglycemia in Newborn—Cerebral Palsy and Partial Blindness—$1.8 Million Utah Settle-ment," *Medical Malpractice Verdicts, Settlements and Experts* (July 2009): 29.

88. See note 78.

89. Kamath, B. D., E. H. Thilo and J. A. Hernandez, "Jaun-dice," In *Handbook of Neonatal Intensive Care*, Sixth edition, eds. S. L. Gardner, B. Carter, M. I. Enzman-Hines, and J. A. Hernandez, 531-552. St. Louis: Mosby, 2011.

90. Joint Commission for Accreditation of Healthcare Organizations, "Kernicterus threatens healthy newborns," *Sentinel Event Alert* 18 (2004): 1–3.

91. *Id.*

92. American Academy of Pediatrics Subcommittee on Hyperbilirubinemia, "Management of hyperbilirubinemia in the newborn infant 35 or more weeks of gestation," *Pediatrics* 114 (2004): 297–316.

93. Laska. L. (ed.), "Child discharged two days after birth with high bilimeter reading—returns to hospital with hyperbilirubinemia—delay in performing transfer and double volume exchange transfusion blamed for brain injury—severe cerebral palsy, spastic quadriplegia, profound hearing loss and upward gaze palsy—$7.75 million In settlements before Illinois defense verdict." *Medical Malpractice Verdicts, Settlements and Experts* (April 2009): 32-33.

94. See note 90.

95. Bradshaw, W. T. "Gastrointestinal disorders," In *Core Curriculum for Neonatal Intensive Care Nursing*, Fourth edition, eds. M. T. Verklan and M. Walden, 589–637. Philadelphia: Elsevier, 2010.

96. *Id.*

97. See note 89.

98. *Id.*

99. Bhutani, V., K., L. Johnson, and E. M. Sivieri. Predictive ability of a predischarge hour-specific serum bilirubin for subsequent significant hyperbilirubinemia in healthy and near-term newborns. *Pediatrics*, 103 (1999): 6-14.

100. See note 89.

101. Bagwell, G. A., "Hematologic system," In *Comprehensive Neonatal Nursing: A Physiologic Perspective*, Fourth edition, eds. C. Kenner and J. W. Lott, 201-253. Philadelphia: Saunders, 2007.

102. *Id.*

103. See note 89.

104. *Id.*

105. *Id.*

106. *Id.*

107. Patra, K., A. Storfer-Isser, B. Siner, J. Moore, and M. Hack, "Adverse events associated with neonatal exchange transfusion in the 1990s," *Journal of Pediatrics* 114 (2004): 626–631.

108. See note 89.

109. *Id.*

110. See note 95.

111. American Academy of Pediatrics, "Report of Committee on Infectious Diseases," Elk Grove Village, IL (2006). American Academy of Pediatrics.

112. Askin, D. F. and W. Diehl-Jones, "Ophthalmologic and auditory disorders," In *Core Curriculum for Neonatal Intensive Care Nursing*, Fourth edition, eds. M. T. Verklan and M. Walden, 832-849. Philadelphia: Elsevier, 2010.

113. Isenberg, S. J., "Eye disorders," In *Avery's Diseases of the Newborn*, Eighth edition, eds. H. W. Taeusch, R. A. Ballard, and C. A. Gleason, 1469–1484. Philadelphia: Elsevier Saunders, 2005.

114. Gardner, S. L., M. Enzman-Hines, and L. A. Dickey, "Respiratory diseases," In *Handbook of Neonatal Intensive Care*, Sixth edition, eds. S. L. Gardner, B. Carter, M. I. Enzman-Hines, and J. A. Hernandez, 581-677. St. Louis: Mosby, 2011.

115. *Id.*

116. American Academy of Pediatrics, "Screening Examination of Premature Infants for Retinopathy of Prematurity," *Pediatrics* 108 (2001): 809-811.

117. *Id.*

118. Committee for the Classification of Retinopathy of Prematurity, "An international classification of retinopathy of prematurity," *AMA Archives of Ophthalmology* 102 (1984): 1130–1134.

119. See note 112.

120. *Id.*

121. See note 7.

122. American Academy of Pediatrics, Task Force on Interhospital Transport. *Guidelines for air and ground transport of neonatal and pediatric patients.* Elk Grove Village, Illinois: American Academy of Pediatrics, 1999.

123. National Association of Neonatal Nurses. *Neonatal nursing transport guidelines.* Petaluma, California: NANN, 1998.

124. Jaimovich, D. G. and D. Vidyasagar, *Handbook of Pediatric and Neonatal Transport Medicine*, Second edition. Philadelphia: Hanley & Belfus, 2002.

125. Bowen, L. S., "Intrafacility and Interfacility Neonatal Transport," In *Core Curriculum for Neonatal Intensive Care Nursing*, Fourth edition, eds. M. T. Verklan and M. Walden, 415–433. Philadelphia: Elsevier, 2010.

126. Wood, K. S. and C. L. Bose, "Neonatal Transport," In *Avery's Neonatology. Pathophysiology and Management of the Newborn*, Sixth edition, eds. M. G. MacDonald, M. D. Mullett, and M. M. K. Seshia, 40–53. Philadelphia: Lippincott Williams & Wilkins, 2005.

127. See note 123.

128. See note 125.

129. *Id.*

130. See note 123.

131. See note 125.

132. See note 124.

133. See note 125.

134. See note 123.

135. See note 124.

136. See note 126.

137. See note 123.

138. See note 126.

139. See note 124.

140. See note 125.

141. Rabin, J. B., *For Healthcare Professionals: Guidelines on Prevention of and Response to Infant Abductions.* Ninth Edition, Alexandria, Virginia: National Center for Missing & Exploited Children, 2009.

142. *Id.*

143. Burns, A. L., "Protecting infants in healthcare facilities from abduction. A facility's search for a sound infant security system," *Journal of Perinatal and Neonatal Nursing* 17 (2003): 139–147.

144. *Id.*

145. See note 4.

146. *Id.*

147. *Id.*

148. See note 141.

149. See note 4.

150. Shogan, M. G., "Emergency management plan for newborn abduction," *JOGNN Clinical Issues* 31 (2002): 340–346.

151. See note 141.

152. See note 150.

153. See note 142.

154. See note 150.

155. See note 142.

156. See note 150.

157. *Id.*

158. Rommal, C., "Risk management issues in the perinatal setting," *Journal of Perinatal and Neonatal Nursing* 10 (1996): 1–31.

159. Eitel, D., J. Yakowitz, and J. Ely, "Legal implications of birth videos," *Journal of Family Practice* 46 (1998): 251–256.

160. Fechner, G., A. Du Chesne, C. Ortmann, and B. Brinkmann, "Death due to intravenous application of enteral feed," *International Journal of Legal Medicine* 116 (2002): 354–356.

161. See note 4.

162. Laska, L. (ed.), "Air Embolisms in Brain Introduced During Blood Transfusion for Two-Week Old Premature Baby—Brain Damage—$35.3 Million Wisconsin Verdict," *Medical Malpractice Verdicts, Settlements and Experts* (January 2009): 26.

163. See note 2.

164. See note 1.

165. See note 4.

166. Ament, L., "Risk management and continuous quality improvement," In *Legal Aspects of Maternal-Child Nursing Practice: Concepts and Strategies in Risk Management,* eds. S. L. Gardner and M. I. E. Hagedorn, 51–66. Menlo Park, California: Addison-Wesley, 1997.

167. Tammelleo, A. D., "Did nurses 'stonewall' parents of dead infant?" *Nursing Law's Regan Report* (May 2005): 4.

168. Standards and Guidelines for Professional Nursing Practice in the Care of Women and Newborns AWHONN, 2009.

169. Swaney, J. R., N. English and B. S. Carter, "Ethics, Values, and Palliative Care in Neonatal Intensive Care," In *Handbook of Neonatal Intensive Care*, Sixth edition, eds. S. L. Gardner, B. Carter, M. I. Enzman-Hines, and J. A. Hernandez, 962-989. St. Louis: Mosby, 2011.

170. *Id.*

171. See note 1.

172. *Id.*

173. See note 2.

174. See note 169.

Appendix 2.1

Baby H was born October 30, 1998 at 38 weeks gestation to a 22-year-old G3 P2 (third pregnancy with two living children) woman with prenatal care. Birth was via an emergency Cesarean section due to decreased fetal heart rate variability and profound bradycardia. At delivery it was noted that the umbilical cord was wrapped around the neck three times. Baby H was born in a depressed condition and required resuscitation measures. His Apgar scores were 0 and 3 (HR1, tone1, color1) at one and five minutes respectively. (Ten is the best possible score). After resuscitation, and admission to the Special Care Nursery, he was transferred to the neonatal intensive care unit at the tertiary hospital. The nursing care provided to Baby H fell below the minimum acceptable standards of care required by a nurse practicing in a Level II Nursery, particularly in the following areas:

1. Failure to follow the guidelines/recommendations of the Neonatal Resuscitation Program in effect October 1998;
2. Failure to appropriately assess Baby H's condition post-resuscitation;
3. Failure to appropriately assess Baby H's condition at admission to the Special Care Nursery;
4. Failure to provide post-resuscitation care and institute the appropriate nursing interventions which might be required to stabilize the neonate's condition; and,
5. Failure to appropriately document and record the clinical events/patient's condition while in the Special Care Nursery.

The Facts of the Case

07??-The obstetrical team should have anticipated that this was a high-risk delivery based on the fetal heart rate pattern and had qualified healthcare professionals skilled in all aspects of neonatal resuscitation present at delivery.

The delivery room record notes time of birth at 0749, "baby bagged with 100% oxygen, intubated at 0752, chest compressions 0750, drugs 0756-HR 100 at 0757. Baby to NICU. Dr. J here at 0805."

0752: Placed in warmer, quickly dried, no tone, respiratory effort, heart rate, pale/dusky with decreased perfusion. Immediately bagged with face mask with 100% oxygen. Suction required for moderate (3-4cc) clear mucus orally/nasally.

The Standard of Care/Violations of the Standard of Care

0749-0752: Although there is some controversy over what time the birth actually occurred, there were indications at least by 0640 that this was a high risk delivery. The standard of care is to anticipate the need for resuscitation and have adequately trained personnel that can perform all aspects of resuscitation. The standard was violated by having a nursery nurse present who was skilled in assisting in resuscitation rather than trained to initiate all steps if needed (intubation, medications, line placement). The other personnel present were the anesthesiologist, circulator nurse, and the scrub nurse, whose first duty should have been to the mother. Dr. J should have been paged early enough to permit attendance at delivery.

0752: The standard of care is to place the baby in the warmer, quickly dry while providing tactile stimulation, assess the physical appearance/vital signs and establish the airway (should take approximately 15-20 seconds). Positive pressure ventilation (PPV) should then be provided via face mask with 100% oxygen as preparation for endotracheal intubation is underway. After 15-30 seconds of PPV the baby's breathing and heart rate should be reassessed. Violation of the standard: the heart rate was found to be 0—the adequacy of the PPV via the mask the adequacy of the PPV via the mask (seal, adequate pressures, chest expansion, etc.) should have been reassessed. Chest compressions should have been started after 15-30 seconds of adequate ventilation given. Chest compressions and ventilation rate should be done as one breath for every three compressions (30 breaths and 90 compressions in one minute). The baby should then have been intubated as he was not responding to the PPV by face mask as evidenced by absent heart rate.

0753: No heart tones noted. Apgar 0. Chest compressions begun.

0753: Standard of care: Baby H should have been intubated and chest compressions underway for approximately 30 seconds. Epinephrine 1:10,000. 0.1-0.3 cc/kg (.36-1.0 cc) should have been given via the ETT as the heart rate was less than 60 beats/minute after 30 seconds of PPV and another 30 seconds of PPV with chest compressions. A check every 30 seconds should be done to evaluate heart rate and spontaneous breathing. Based upon the heart rate, epinephrine can be repeated every 3-5 minutes, with subsequent doses given via the umbilical venous catheter (UVC).

0754: Baby H intubated with #3.0 per Dr. K, the anesthesiologist. Chest has bilateral breath sounds and chest movement.

0754: The standard of care is to provide PPV at a rate of 30 breaths/minute and chest compressions at a rate of 90/minute. As the baby is still unresponsive, volume replacement needs to be considered as well as a direct route for medications. Preparations should be underway to place a low-lying UVC to deliver medications and fluids to support the cardiovascular system. The UVC should be placed within 5-15 minutes if the baby remains unresponsive to PPV and epinephrine. A violation of the standard of care occurred when the UVC or any intravenous/intraosseous route was not made available.

0755: No heart rate noted by auscultation, no spontaneous respiratory effort noted.

0755: The standard of care requires that an assessment be done of why there is no heart rate—i.e. assessment of the adequacy of PPV, ETT dislodged, secretions in airway, shock, etc. Consideration of volume expansion also should have been done as the baby remains unresponsive to resuscitative efforts.

0756: 0.1 mg (1cc) epinephrine given via the ETT. Dr. J (neonatologist) notified to come stat.

0756: The reviewer was uncertain as to what dose of epinephrine was actually given. The standard of care requires accurate documentation of the time/amount/route of medications delivered. Baby H should have received 0.1-0.3 mg/kg of epinephrine 1:10,000 (.3-.9 cc). If 0.1 mg/kg was given, then Baby H would have received 0.3 cc. If he received 1 cc of epinephrine the dose would have been ~0.3 mg/kg. Ideally a code sheet should contain times of the medications as well as recording significant events in the resuscitation. A violation of the care is the lack of proper documentation and possibly too little epinephrine being given.

0757: Heart rate 80-100, PPV continues. Chest compressions stopped. Heart rate quickly increases to 150.

0757: Apgar score of 3 (0 = dead; 10 = optimal).

0758: Spontaneous respiratory effort noted. PPV stopped. 100% oxygen delivered blow-by per ETT. ETT secured by

0758: The standard of care is to provide respiratory support by PPV at a rate of 40-60 breaths per minute with enough

tape at 10 cm. Coarse breath sounds noted, color very pale with perfusion greater than 5 seconds. Decreased tone with slight movement when stimulated.

positive pressure to have the chest gently moving. Violation of the standard occurred by providing "blow-by" via the ETT as well as not recognizing that the cardiovascular system also needed support. 10 cc/kg (35 cc slow push over 5-15 minutes) of an isotonic solution (NS, Ringer's Lactate) should have been given via the UVC to support the cardiovascular system.

0800: Heart rate and tones strong, now—180s. Infant quickly dried and placed in warm blankets.

0800: Baby H is further evidencing signs of cardiovascular insufficiency. He requires further stabilization with volume expanders. He still has an ETT in place—how is ventilation being provided as handbagging has stopped to provide free flow oxygen?

0802: "Transferred to warmed radiant warmer (how?) in the Special Care Nursery (SCN) with spontaneous respiratory effort (ETT securely in place). Remains pale, poor tone, poor perfusion (> 5 sec)."

0802: The standard of care is to assign the Apgar score until a "7" is achieved; this was not done. Baby H should have been transferred to the SCN via a warmed incubator so as to maintain heat. Violation of the standard occurred with allowing a neonate to breathe spontaneously through an ETT with no means of pressure support. Nursing continues to fail to recognize/evaluate signs of cardiovascular compromise.

0803: "Dr. J arrived as infant being transferred from OR to SCN"

0803: Dr. J arrived 7 minutes after being called "stat." As stated above, Dr. J should have been paged prior to the emergent Cesarean section to enable him to attend the delivery and initiate all aspects of the resuscitation (assessment, intubation, medications, UVC placement).

0804: Placed on ventilator 24/6, 40 and 100%.

0806: Oxygen saturation monitor "not picking up yet." "Set up for UAC/UVC placement by Dr. J."

0806: The standard of care entailed that an assessment of the cardiovascular system should have been done, including pulses, perfusion and blood pressure. Oxygen saturation monitors require adequate blood flow to function—they do not need time "to pick up." The standard of care was violated as nursing did not interpret the poor reading as evidence of vascular insufficiency. The standard of care was further violated when an axilla temperature was not taken to assess for cold stress or blood glucose/Chemstrip obtained to rule out hypoglycemia in a stressed neonate. In addition, an arterial blood gas should have been obtained via an arterial sample.

0807: ?? 15 minute Apgar score. The standard of care is to evaluate the baby until a score of 7 is obtained.

0809: No blood pressure, temperature or glucose obtained. Weaning oxygen to 40% based on oxygen saturations.

0809: Nursing is not evaluating the total picture of this stressed neonate. The standard of care is to formulate a care plan to address his cardiorespiratory condition. The standard is violated as this is not implemented, nor are nursing interventions to begin to stabilize his condition put in place. Charting is functional and does not evidence critical thinking of how to support a baby who was born in a depressed condition after fetal distress and nuchal cord x3. Rather than weaning oxygen, attention should be focused on support of the cardiovascular system, with likely metabolic acidosis and the need for adequate oxygenation. The standard of care requires that hypothermia, hypoglycemia and hypovolemia be ruled out as etiologies of continuing cardiovascular insufficiency—this was not done. The standard of care also requires that a chest x-ray be done to evaluate the lungs and confirm ETT location (was taped at 10 cm and should have been at ~9 cm given the baby's weight) as soon as possible, especially if the baby is giving a poor response to resuscitative measures.

0815: Dr. J places UVC.

0815: 12 minutes after his arrival, Dr. J places the UVC. The standard of care is to have skilled personnel available at resuscitation.

0816: The standard of care is to give 10 cc/kg (36 cc) of replacement volume slow IV push (5-15 minutes) as soon as the line is in place. The standard was violated as volume replacement should have been anticipated—the fluids should have been ready for administration immediately after the line was in place.

0817: 30 cc of 5% albumin given over 2-3 minutes.

0817: No assessment of the Baby H's response to treatment or evidence of nursing care plan. The standard is to formulate a plan of care that will allow for the observation of symptoms, intervention and evaluation of the intervention/baby's response to the plan of care.

0820: "Blood gases and CBC with differential drawn from UVC." Hgb: 9 and Hct: 27.8.

0820: The reviewer is uncertain as to when the results of the Hgb and Hct were known. The standard requires that the laboratory notify the nursery of the abnormal results and that these results, as well as the action taken, be documented.

0827: Oxygen weaned to room air (21%) as color slowly improving and oxygen saturation is 92%.

0827: Color is improving due to an increase in volume. The blood gas demonstrates that he was hypoxic on 30% oxygen but nursing weans to room air. A saturation of 92% indicates a PaO2 of approximately 60 mmHg in a baby with normal hemoglobin and hematocrit levels. The violation of the standard of care occurred when Baby H's nurses did not evaluate his blood oxygen with consideration given to his hemoglobin of 9 and hematocrit of 27.8. Nursing is focusing on one measurement, rather than a total assessment, to guide their interventions.

0836: Dr. J places the UAC.

0836: The standard of care would be to send an arterial blood gas as quickly as possible to evaluate ventilation and acid-base, as well as blood glucose/Chemstrip and CBC with differential (blood loss).

0838: Arterial blood gas drawn with oxygen saturations at 87%: 7.10/30.9/47/9.7/??

0838: The reviewer is uncertain as to when the lab called the values (or even if they did) to the nursery.

D10W 1:1 heparin at 8 cc/hr now infusing through UVC.

8 cc/hr is equivalent to 53 cc/kg/day of D10W which is not sufficient volume or glucose. The standard of care would be to receive 9.8-12 cc/hr. This is the first glucose Baby H has received. The glucose value and blood pressure remain unknown. The blood gas shows severe metabolic acidosis with decreased oxygenation. The violation of the standard: does not appear that any medical/nursing interventions were implemented to address the metabolic acidosis/hypoxemia based on this gas.

0844: Chest and abdominal x-ray done.

The standard of care is to place a low-lying UVC for the administration of emergency fluids and medications. Once the baby is stabilized the line is pulled, and a UVC is inserted to the level of the diaphragm. The violation occurred when fluids were infusing through lines that did not have placement confirmed by x-ray. It is uncertain as to the time that the UAC fluids of 1/4 NS 1:1 heparin at 5 cc/hr were started. The standard is to document time/dose and route of administration of all medications and fluids. Nursing should have questioned the rate of fluid infusing through the UAC. The total fluids (UAC + UVC) now equal 90 cc/kg/day. The rate of the UAC should be decreased to allow the UVC rate to increase to provide glucose at a total fluid volume of 65-80 cc/kg/day (standard of care).

0845—0900: Oxygen saturations decrease and oxygen continues to be increased in increments. Although the saturations are 73% in 60% oxygen, the baby is assessed as being pink with improved tone and perfusion (> 4 sec). Arterial blood gas drawn.

0845—0900: Violation of the standard: No nursing assessment as to what physiologic events are occurring nor nursing intervention to help stabilize Baby H.

The reviewer is uncertain when values were called to nursery: 7.04/36.5/28/10.1/??

0905: ETT pulled back 1 cm.

ETT placement was not a priority as ventilation was satisfactory. Once the baby was stabilized, the ETT could have been manipulated. There is the risk of extubation in an unstable baby who is ventilating well.

0908: Oxygen is decreased to 55% because the saturations are 100%.

Violation: nursing has not formulated a plan of care—the ABG is demonstrating hypoxia and metabolic acidosis.

0909-0910: 20 cc of 5% albumin given slowly via UVC. Oxygen is decreased to 50%.

0909-0910: ?? results of ABG known. The standard of care is to document significant events as well as to assess why the intervention is given and the baby's response to the intervention. Nursing continues to wean the oxygen.

The bolus of albumin is given. The volume should have been 36 cc (10 cc/kg) of an isotonic expander. Albumin promotes 3rd spacing and as such consideration should be given to using normal saline/ringer's lactate as volume expanders.

0911: Blood pressure of 31/19 with a mean pressure of 23 is obtained. Oxygen is further decreased.

0911: This is the first blood pressure noted in a critically ill baby over one hour of age. Vital signs should have been obtained immediately on admission. Additionally, the standard requires that blood pressure be continuously monitored via a transducer as an UAC was in place—this enables constant assessment of central blood pressure. Until that time, the peripheral blood pressure should have been obtained every 5-15 minutes at a minimum to evaluate adequacy of the cardiovascular system. The standard of care is to anticipate that the mean blood pressure is approximately the gestational age. Nursing should have anticipated the mean blood pressure to be approximately 35-40 mmHg. The violation of the standard was that the nurses are not assessing/recognizing that Baby H is hypotensive. They are falsely reassured by the pulse oximetry and are inappropriately decreasing the oxygen.

0912: 5 mEq of NaHCO3 is given over 15 minutes via the UAC.

0912: The standard of care was that Baby H should have received 7.2 mEq (2 mEq/kg) of NaHCO3 as effective ventilation was occurring. The results of the ABG are known for certain, thus, nursing should have increased the oxygen to help correct the hypoxemia.

0916: Oxygen is decreased to 35%. Chemstrip is 13.

0916: The standard of care is to evaluate the blood glucose in a stressed neonate on admission to the nursery. Violation of the standard—this is the first glucose determination (baby almost 90 minutes old) and the value is critically low. Nursing continues to violate the standard of care by not formulating a nursing plan of care that evaluates Baby H's symptomatolgy, decreasing the oxygen despite the proven hypotension, hypoxemia, severe metabolic acidosis and hypoglycemia.

0918: 10 cc D10W given over 1-2 minutes via the UVC.

0918: The standard of care is to give 2-2.5 cc/kg of D10W push intravenously (7.2-9 cc D10W). The maintenance D10W fluids should have also been immediately increased from 53 cc/kg/day to 80 cc/kg/day. Nursing should have rechecked the blood glucose 15-30 minutes after the bolus of D10 to evaluate the result and determine further treatment.

0923: Blood pressure 36/17 with a mean of 22.

0923: There continues to be no nursing plan of care to evaluate the cardiovascular system and the baby's response to therapies. Baby H is severely hypotensive.

0924: Erythromycin eye care and Vitamin K is given.

The Vitamin K should have been given as soon as possible on admission as this is a compromised term baby at risk for bleeding.

0937: Baby H continues to evidence hypotension.

No nursing/medical intervention to address Baby H's condition.

0940: Transport team arrives and assumes care of Baby H.

The lack of proper resuscitative techniques and nursing interventions at time of birth and during admission to the special care nursery prolonged Baby H's depressed state and further contributed to the extent and seriousness of the injury. He suffered permanent damage that will require a lifetime of support.

Chapter 3

Pediatric Nursing Malpractice Issues

Susan G. Engleman, MSN, RN, APRN-BC, PNP, CLCP

Synopsis
3.1 Introduction
3.2 Initial Review of the Pediatric Case
3.3 Five Litigation Issues in Pediatric Nursing
    A. Assessment and Monitoring of the Patient
    B. Reporting and Documenting Changes in the Patient's Condition
    C. Following the Appropriate Chain of Command
    D. Medication and Treatment Errors
    E. Appropriate Delegation of Nursing Tasks
3.4 Critical Illnesses in the Pediatric Population Causing Injury that May Lead to Litigation
    A. Septic Shock
    B. Hypovolemic Shock
    C. Increased Intracranial Pressure
    D. Respiratory Failure
    E. Hypoxia
3.5 Cardiopulmonary Resuscitation in Children
3.6 Pediatrics as a Specialty
3.7 Standards of Care for Pediatric Nursing
3.8 Scope of Practice
3.9 Psychosocial Aspects of the Pediatric Case
3.10 Summary
Endnotes

3.1 Introduction

Since the publication of "To Err is Human" in 1999, patient safety has become a focus in health care. Fortunately this spotlight has not overlooked the pediatric population. In fact it has been suggested that pediatric patients may be even more at risk than the adult population when it comes to medical errors.[1] The Harvard Medical Practice Study that reviewed 30,000 hospital admissions from 1984 in New York State identified that 3.7 percent of hospitalized patients experienced an adverse event.[2] This study included pediatric patients and found children experienced 12.91 adverse events per 1,000 discharges.[3] In addition to errors similar to those noted in the adult population, there are issues unique to the care of children. These include potential errors related to changes in weight and physiologic immaturity, the dependency that children have on others, and the healthcare provider's lack of familiarity with the care of pediatric patients.[4] Children are generally resilient, but there is little room for error, especially in treatments such as medication dosing and fluid administration. Children's small bodies make these errors more serious than the same errors affecting adults. Children often have less ability to compensate for the physiologic changes that occur during illness due to physiologic immaturity. A good example of this is the respiratory syncytial virus (RSV). In adults this virus is manifested as the common cold. Adults may whine and complain while sick with this virus but rarely do they develop complications of any severity. In children, however, RSV can have severe consequences. Children less than three years of age have very small airways, which swell when attacked by this virus. This can lead to respiratory distress and develop into a life-threatening pneumonia. A child's airway cannot always accommodate this swelling, whereas an adult's airway is nearly unaffected.

This chapter addresses those issues pertinent to litigation that differentiate the pediatric population from other populations in health care. This chapter begins with a discussion of the initial review of a pediatric case. Following that is an extended examination of five frequently encountered issues that may lead to litigation. These include:

1. Assessment or monitoring of the patient
2. Reporting or documenting changes in the patient's condition
3. Following the appropriate chain of command
4. Appropriate delegation of nursing tasks
5. Medication or treatment errors

Each issue is followed by examples of cases involving those particular issues.

This chapter also covers several critical illnesses frequently seen in the pediatric population, including sepsis, hypovolemic shock, increased intracranial pressure, and respiratory failure. These may cause injury or death, thereby leading to litigation. The definitions, early and late signs and symptoms, and general management principles of these critical illnesses are also discussed. Finally, a discussion of hypoxia, a condition that may result from the illnesses listed above, is examined. This chapter concludes with a discussion of pediatric resuscitation.

3.2 Initial Review of the Pediatric Case

Of note in pediatric malpractice cases is the statute of limitations. This differs from state to state, but may be as long as two years following the child reaching the age of majority. If the injury occurred during the child's first year of life, the review of the case could begin as long as 20 years later. This makes discovery an interesting challenge. It can also cause difficulty in finding appropriate expert witnesses for the case. It is very uncommon for a parent or guardian to wait this length of time to pursue such an action.

The pediatric case logically originates with the search for and a meeting with an attorney prompted by the parents' interpretation of some injury to their child. The initial review generally begins with an interview of the parents or caregivers by a plaintiff's attorney. This may be an emotional meeting, as dealing with the perceived effects of the breach of the standard of care may bring up intense issues for the parents. The attorney should be very cautious in giving opinions at this meeting based only on oral accounts from the parents. It is helpful to make clear to the parents that the attorney is not qualified, in most cases, to give opinions regarding the care rendered to the child. A review of the chart by a person with the appropriate medical background is necessary to form a preliminary opinion.

TIP: If a breach of the standard of care is not associated with the child's injury, it may be advantageous for the medical consultant who reviewed the chart to meet with the attorney and family to explain why the definition of negligence was not met.

As discovery proceeds, other items beneficial to the case include: policies and procedures related to that specific area of care, employee files of the nurses involved (if discoverable in the respective state), orientation and continuing education files of the nurses involved, and information about staffing for the particular unit to which the patient was admitted at the time of the incident.

The attorney defending a suit begins with a review of the chart for potential breaches of the standard of care. The defense attorney usually then investigates by speaking with the caregivers involved in the case to clarify information in the chart or gather more detail about other factors that may have influenced the care of this patient. The defense also reviews policies and procedures, employee files, and continuing education information.

TIP: Nursing policies and procedures from the institution in which the nursing care took place are key in establishing the standards that the institution finds acceptable. Many facilities maintain these electronically on an intranet and should be able to readily produce them.

Further development of the case by either defense or plaintiff from this point will be dictated by the facts of the specific case. This development can be greatly enhanced and simplified by the use of a strong legal nurse consultant to guide the attorney regarding the medical and nursing nuances of the case. This consultant may serve many purposes in assisting the attorney including:

1. recommending specific documents that may be needed to support the case,
2. assisting in identifying the specific pediatric medical specialists the attorney may need to consult to assess the case or address specific questions,
3. drafting questions the attorney may wish to ask specific parties in depositions, and
4. developing educational materials used to educate the jury at trial.

TIP: Pediatric medical and nursing specialists with expertise in medical specialties such as pediatric pulmonology and pediatric gastroenterology may be useful in evaluating the care given to the patient.

It is strongly recommended a pediatric nurse be used to review the case. The expert witness will be a pediatric nurse who may have a subspecialty in a specific pediatric area, but the attorney may also wish to have a legal nurse consultant who can work behind-the-scenes. The nursing consultant should aid the attorney in deciding which nursing liability issue forms the strongest basis for the case. This information will also influence how the case is developed.

3.3 Five Litigation Issues in Pediatric Nursing

Litigation issues in nursing cases are often similar regardless of the age of the patient. Generally these issues fall into one of five categories:

1. Assessment or monitoring of the patient
2. Reporting or documenting changes in the patient's condition
3. Following the appropriate chain of command
4. Appropriate delegation of nursing tasks
5. Medication or treatment errors

Each of these is addressed in the following sections with a focus on unique pediatric aspects.

A. Assessment and Monitoring of the Patient

Assessment is a professional skill that sets the nurse apart from other professionals. It is the ability to recognize, process, and synthesize patient information.[5] Two elements differentiate the nurse's assessment from that of other professionals: the time factor and the comprehensive nature of that assessment. Many healthcare professionals visit a hospitalized patient throughout the course of a day. Of these professionals, the nurse spends the most time at the patient's bedside. This affords the nurse a particular advantage by lending a perspective to his care that other professionals lack. Other professionals see a snapshot of the patient while the nurse has a videographer's view. Second, nurses are taught to view the patient as a whole rather than in systems. A nursing assessment generally encompasses a "head-to-toe" assessment, whereas other professionals, for example a respiratory therapist, focus on a specific aspect of the patient.

Timely assessment is a critical factor. Pediatric patients have a tendency to compensate for a limited period of time. When they lose the ability to further compensate, they decompensate quickly.[6] Compensation refers to the body's involuntary mechanisms to offset inadequacies in one system by stepping up the function in another system. For example, when a patient is dehydrated, the issue is an inadequate circulation of blood volume, which leads to an inadequate circulation of nutrients and oxygen throughout the body. To compensate for this, the heart rate increases to pump the existing blood volume throughout the body at a faster rate. According to Broughton, "the nurse's astuteness in detecting changes in the patient's condition can profoundly affect the patient's outcome."[7]

A key factor in determining assessment skill is the nurse's knowledge. The nurse must first become aware of the need to focus on assessment, which is dependent upon several factors including the nurse's knowledge and clinical experience.[8] The nurse must then recognize what is normal for the patient, be able to differentiate from that norm, and determine the importance of that information. This is the primary reason it is preferable to treat pediatric patients in pediatric facilities or at least have pediatric patients cared for by nurses well-versed in the care of children. This often becomes problematic in a community hospital having no pediatric unit or in a community hospital emergency room where children are infrequently seen as patients. Nurses who commonly care for adult patients find it difficult to recognize a departure from normal in a pediatric patient because they are unfamiliar with the pediatric norm. Cholowski and Chan[9]

contend that the key factor in making good nursing judgments from the assessment process is recognition of cues as well as appreciation of the relevance of this data in the clinical situation. Given this assumption, it would be difficult for the nonpediatric nurse to identify signs and symptoms of decompensation different from those of adults. This is specifically a problem in evaluating vital signs, which differ among age groups of children; in determining drug dosages, which in pediatric patients are based on weight; and in behavioral norms such as incontinence in a previously continent child.

A common example of failure to assess or monitor is the failure to measure vital signs. This can occur with children or adults; however, vital signs are generally monitored more frequently in the pediatric patient. In most hospital units, the pediatric patient's vital signs are measured every four hours, whereas adults' are generally measured every eight hours. In the pediatric intensive care unit, the child's vital signs may be taken as often as every 15 minutes, especially post procedurally or postoperatively, but generally at least hourly. As discussed earlier in this chapter, the pediatric patient can decompensate very quickly.

TIP: Trends in vital signs, rather than a single set of vital signs, can be an early indicator of a patient's impending distress.

A five-year-old male with a history of cerebral palsy, seizure disorder, spastic quadriplegia and mental retardation was admitted to a general pediatric unit following an osteotomy of the left femur with a lengthening of the tendons of both legs with spica cast application. His heart rate and respiratory rate were taken every 15 minutes for the first two hours of his stay; however, his blood pressure was not obtained during this time period. At the two hour mark, the nurse documented that the child had stable vital signs despite the fact that the child was markedly tachycardic with a heart rate of 177 beats per minute even though he had been given a dose of morphine. The nurse then stopped her frequent vital sign monitoring. The child became agitated shortly after with circumoral cyanosis and began to require supplemental oxygen. No vital signs were obtained. The nurse called a physician and requested a dose of Valium for the agitation. The order was given and the dose was administered. Within the hour the child arrested and following a lengthy resuscitation, died. The hospital was sued based upon the nurses' failure to monitor appropriately. The case was settled prior to trial.

Agitation in the pediatric population must be carefully assessed. It is common for the child experiencing hypoxia to become agitated and even combative as a result. The exact mechanism of the problem in the child above most likely related to a decrease in circulating blood volume leading to a shock-like state. It is common following a long period of NPO (nothing by mouth) status prior to surgery followed by conservative fluid administration in the operating room. Had the signs and symptoms of this child's problem been appropriately recognized, fluid boluses would have been the appropriate treatment. As the child experienced a decrease in circulating blood volume, the heart rate increased in order to carry the same amount of oxygen throughout the child's body. The child compensated by constricting the vessels carrying the blood, thus maintaining an acceptable blood pressure for a period of time. However, the blood pressure eventually fell as the vessels were less filled with blood. Careful monitoring of the heart rate and blood pressure would have shown a trend of instability. Should the trend be in the direction of shock as described above, it should be immediately related to the physician. Because the patient's vital signs were not properly monitored, the trend was not detected until the patient lost his ability to further compensate. The normal heart rate for this child's age range was approximately 70-110 bpm.[10] A heart rate of 177 bpm was markedly elevated and the patient was already in serious jeopardy.

Another aspect of pediatric nursing that can be problematic in assessing and monitoring the patient is the use of intravenous (IV) catheters. Placing an IV catheter in a small child can be a challenging task; the nurse generally tries once or twice and then asks someone else to try. An IV should be placed in a reasonable period of time. The American Heart Association states that during CPR of children age six years or younger, intraosseous access (a large bore needle placed directly into the tibia) should be established if reliable venous access cannot be achieved within three attempts or 90 seconds, whichever comes first.[11]

TIP: Even in a nonemergency, if the nursing staff is unsuccessful in placing an ordered venous line, the physician should be notified so another method of giving the child fluids can be provided. This is standard practice.

Keeping a patent IV in place in a child can be even more difficult than placing it. The child's movement may displace an IV from the vein, with the catheter remaining within the child's tissues. The technical term for this is an IV infiltration. The fluid infiltrates into the tissues rather than flowing into the vein. Adults, when informed, usually understand that dislodging their IV will lead to the need to place another, so they guard their IV sites carefully. If the IV becomes dislodged, creating an infiltration, it is generally reported quickly because it causes pain. Lacking mature reasoning skills, small children often do not conclude that should the IV be pulled out, the nurse will have to place another. A second problem is that small children are often unable to pinpoint the exact location of pain in the case of an IV infiltration and will not promptly report this problem. Nonverbal children may just exhibit signs of fussiness. To complicate matters further, a child's IV is generally regulated by an IV pump which pumps fluid into the vein at a specified rate of flow. Because a child's tissues can be very yielding or because the pressure gauge on the pump is set incorrectly, the pump may not sense the infiltration and continue to pump fluid for an indefinite period of time despite the catheter's being dislodged.

When an IV infiltrates, it causes pain. If the fluid is mixed with medications, an infiltration can cause a serious burn in which the tissues die, leading to the necessity of plastic surgery. Proper treatment of an infiltration includes stopping the infusion, removing the IV catheter, and elevating the extremity. Research reveals the application of compresses should not be used routinely, as either warm or cool compresses may have a detrimental effect on the skin and tissues involved.[12] Infiltrations can also be treated with hyaluronidase, a medication that breaks down the connective tissue surrounding the infiltrate, allowing the infiltrating fluid to be more quickly absorbed, which may decrease the complications of tissue sloughing and burns. Hyaluronidase can be used for most medications; however, phentolamine is the appropriate medication for use of infiltration of vasopressor agents such as dopamine or epinephrine.[13]

Another less common, but serious, complication of an infiltration can be an entrapment injury or compartment syndrome. This is most commonly seen when the IV is placed in an extremity. As the fluid continues to pump into the tissues surrounding the IV site, the extremity becomes tighter. This can cut off the oxygenation to the nerve tissue, leading to the death of the surrounding nerves. This can also occur when a limb containing the IV is wrapped circumferentially.

For all of these reasons, it is very important the IV site of a child be checked thoroughly and frequently. Most pediatric facilities have a policy and procedure addressing this aspect of care. The policy is usually to check the site hourly and document the findings.[14] Often the policy addresses how the site should be protected with dressings. The site of an IV should be visible or easily accessible. It is against the standard to circumferentially wrap an IV or totally cover the site to the degree that it cannot be properly assessed.

An example of failure to appropriately assess an IV site occurred in *Villaneuva v. Hayes Green Beach Memorial Hospital* in Michigan Superior Court (Case No. 03 268-NH). The jury awarded damages of $225,000 after a six-month-old child was admitted to the hospital for croup. An IV was started in the child's right wrist. It became dislodged some time between midnight and 6:30 A.M. Fluids ran into the interstitial tissues of the hand, wrist, and forearm. At 8:30 A.M. the notes indicated the extremity was swollen into the shoulder and anterior chest. The child suffered from compartment syndrome and required two surgical procedures to relieve the pressure. Further surgeries were endured later following skin graft for scar revision and debridements. The hospital admitted liability with only issues of damages to be submitted to the jury.

The following is an example of the consequences of failing to monitor a patient following the administration of narcotics:

A 14-week-old male child was admitted to a pediatric surgical unit following a cleft lip repair. The physician's orders included placement of the child into a car seat when not being held and this was accomplished by the child's nurse. The infant appeared to be in pain and the nurse administered a dose of morphine intravenously as ordered. Once the child was quiet the parents decided to go home to check on their other children. Upon returning to the room, the nurse noted that the child was not in the position in which she had placed him and so went to check on him. The child was noted to be cyanotic and apneic and a code was called. The child was successfully resuscitated but had sustained severe anoxic brain damage. The hospital was sued based upon the nurse's failure to either place the child on an oxygen saturation monitor or physically monitor the child following the administration of the narcotic. The case was settled prior to trial.

TIP: Failure to assess or monitor is usually easily recognized in a patient's chart. Blanks on a vital signs record or an intake and output record are fairly evident. An astute nurse consultant will easily note that the appropriate parameters of assessment were not followed for the particular disease process or injury.

Although the nurse may fail to assess a particular parameter, this failure may be completely unrelated to the injury that befell the patient. This is frequently the case during a preliminary review of the chart. There may be evidence of general sloppiness, but keep in mind those elements necessary to prove negligence. The nurse's actions may have fallen below the standard of care, but unless the failure to assess was a cause of the injury, the nurse may not be liable for the care.

B. Reporting and Documenting Changes in the Patient's Condition

Communication is critical to the safety of the patient. A patient in a hospital is seen by numerous healthcare providers in the course of a day. Because the physician is not standing at the bedside of the patient all day, the nurse must report any change in the patient's status so the physician may intervene on the patient's behalf.

The nurse's knowledge is essential. A nurse without an understanding of the assessment data will not grasp the importance of reporting the data to a physician. Experience can also influence the effectiveness of a nurse's communications. Not only must the nurse understand the importance of the data, but the data must be placed in the context of this particular patient's situation to determine the significance and seriousness of the information.

A nine-year-old female was admitted to a hospital one morning to be treated with intravenous antibiotics for mastoiditis, an infection that may be an extension of an ear infection. The child complained of a headache and vomited several times throughout the day and evening shifts. During the night shift the nurse documented that the child would awaken, cry out, and then go back to sleep. At 6:00 A.M. the patient was incontinent of urine. The nurse did not report any of these events to the physician. She later stated that she felt the headache and vomiting were normal for the child's illness and that the incontinence was just because the child did not wish to get up to go to the bathroom. A knowledgeable pediatric nurse should have recognized the headache, vomiting, and changes in level of consciousness as signs and symptoms of increased intracranial pressure. This can occur in mastoiditis if the infection spreads beyond the mastoids into the intracranial contents of the brain causing swelling. Incontinence should have been seen as an ominous sign in a child of this age with no history of bed-wetting. This child died and the case was settled before trial.

Nursing documentation is critical. The patient's chart is heavily relied upon by all caregivers because most health-care professionals work shifts. Once the professional has completed an assigned shift, other professionals assume that the professional documented her observances of the patient and the care that was rendered. Decisions regarding a patient's status and further care are based on the information as it was documented.

TIP: It is rare that a telephone call is made to question events on a previous shift. It is assumed the professional documented what occurred during that shift.

Appropriate and accurate documentation cannot be stressed heavily enough. The physician is potentially unable to make appropriate decisions without all of the information or without the correct information clearly documented in the patient's chart.

What follows is an example of what may occur when a nurse fails to report or document:

A six-week-old infant was admitted to a pediatric intensive care unit (PICU) in Texas following an extensive craniotomy. The registered nurse assessed the patient upon admission to the PICU at 1:40 P.M. and documented the assessment. At 3:25 P.M., the baby was noted to experience an apneic episode in which he momentarily ceased to breathe. There was no documentation of a physician being notified of this happening until 8:50 P.M. despite there being repeated episodes of apnea documented. At 8:50 P.M., the nurse notified an unspecified person (only the first name of the person was documented) of her concerns about the patient's breathing and bradycardia (slowing of the heart). The unspecified person spoke with the neurosurgeon about this and the nurse was instructed to watch the patient for worsening episodes of bradycardia and apnea. The surgeon called the nurse to order blood work on the patient at 11:15 P.M. at which time she told him of her concerns about the patient's increasingly labored breathing and longer periods of apnea. The surgeon came to the bedside at that time and the patient was returned to the operating room shortly thereafter, where it was found he had bleeding and swelling of the brain. It was later revealed that the registered nurse believed these apneic episodes were related to a recent respiratory infection with respiratory syncytial virus (RSV), which may be associated with apnea (periods of not breathing).[15]

Apnea, however, especially when associated with bradycardia in a patient having just undergone a craniotomy, is also a classic sign of increased intracranial pressure.[16] Because the nurse felt she understood why the patient was having apnea, she did not report these repeated episodes to the surgeon in an expeditious manner. Consequently, the patient showed signs of neurological damage beginning the day after his surgery; however, the long-term outcome of the patient will be in question for years to come. The case settled before trial.

TIP: Failure to report or document is a fairly common allegation, but once again, that failure must be linked to the patient's injury for there to be liability for that injury. Should the nurse fail to report something to the physician, he may be a less than stellar nurse, but may not have a legal responsibility unless that failure to report caused the patient's injury.

C. Following the Appropriate Chain of Command

The profession of nursing began by carrying out care as prescribed by physicians. Initially, nursing lacked a well-defined base of knowledge. As time progressed, nurses performed more independent thinking. With growing knowledge and advances in practice came greater responsibility. In today's society greater responsibility is accompanied by a greater potential for litigation.

Litigation based on chain of command issues is not nearly as common as cases involving the previously discussed issues. This aspect of litigation has emerged as the role of the nurse has evolved from handmaiden to the doctor to that of a more autonomous and complex role. As early as 1936 in the case of *Hallinan v. Prindle*, nurses were found to have liability for their own actions.[17] The nurse has an independent license and an independent duty to the patient. Nor is ignorance defensible. The nurse is charged with having sufficient knowledge to provide appropriate care.

TIP: Over time, the registered nurse has been held more responsible and independent of the physician for the care rendered to the patient. No longer can a nurse hide behind the cloak of, "I was following the doctor's orders."

TIP: Failure to follow the appropriate chain of command generally occurs as a result of a nurse not recognizing or not pointing out a breach of the standard of care being practiced by another healthcare provider.

This can be a difficult situation for a nurse because it often requires the nurse to question a physician about decision-making. Many nurses are not accustomed to such assertive actions and do not possess the necessary interpersonal skills. This may be attributed in part to the unequal relationship between physicians and nurses over the years. The "doctor-nurse game" was first described in 1967 by Dr. Stein. This relationship between physician and nurse ensured that open disagreement between the professions did not occur. Accepting advice from a nonphysician threatened the physician's omnipotence. Nurses were taught they could not act independently but were a great asset to the physician. Based on these two assumptions, the professionals played the doctor-nurse game in which the nurse subtly suggested to the physician how a specific aspect of care might be handled while making it appear it was the physician's idea. The physician accepted well-cloaked advice and proceeded with the care as suggested.

Today, the doctor-nurse game is played less often. In more recent studies, especially involving direct observation of doctor-nurse interactions, it is found the nurse has much informal overt decision-making power and is involved more openly in the decision-making process.[18] However, even as the nurse may venture to give opinions to doctors, not all doctors have given up the doctor-nurse game. In recognition of this issue, the nursing profession has tried to overcome this difficulty through policy and procedure development. This is accomplished by having nurses report doubts about the care provided by other professionals up the chain of command, especially if the bedside nurse's attempt to intervene is unsuccessful. These issues are generally not raised about trivial situations; these types of challenges are usually reserved for situations that may place the patient at harm or in danger.

The usual chain of command is as follows. The bedside nurses report to a charge nurse. The charge nurse supervises the unit for that particular shift. This position may be a permanently assigned position within the unit or may consist of a pool of nurses who rotate the responsibility. In some institutions the bedside registered nurse may communicate directly with the next level. Licensed practical and vocational nurses report to the charge nurse. The level above the charge nurse is usually the manager of the unit, but in absence of that person, for instance at night, some type of "house" or nursing supervisor is in charge of the entire facility for the given shift. If the house supervisor is unable to resolve the issue with the physician, she may contact either the director of nurses or, if at night, the administrator on call. The administrator on call may contact the medical director or chairperson of the medical department. This chain and the position titles vary among institutions, but the principles remain the same. Further information about the hierarchy of the healthcare system is found in Chapter 8, *Inside the Healthcare Environment*, in Volume I.

TIP: The nurse at the bedside is not alone if she believes other caregivers are not acting in the best interest of the patient.

An example of this type of issue follows:

> A one-year-old male was admitted through the emergency room of a community hospital following a seizure experienced the previous day. He had a history of minor head trauma two weeks previous and flu-like symptoms the day prior to admission. He was taken emergently to the operating room where an external ventricular drain was placed to relieve increased intracranial pressure as noted on the CT scan. The child was admitted to the neonatal intensive care unit as the hospital only had a general pediatric unit and the child was intubated and mechanically ventilated. It was clear from the physician's progress notes that the child was being regularly examined by several physicians; however, there was no clear differential diagnosis noted. At 36 hours postoperative, documentation of changes in neurological status began to appear in the chart. These changes were not reported to the physician in a timely fashion; however, even when reported, interventions were slow or inappropriate. Documentation revealed that the child slowly deteriorated neurologically day by day and on the fifteenth day of hospitalization the child arrested and died. On autopsy, the child was found to have tuberculosis meningitis. The physicians were sued for misdiagnosis and failure to treat the child's signs and symptoms of neurological deterioration. The hospital was sued based upon the failure of the nursing staff to inform the physician regarding the child's deteriorations in a timely fashion and for failure to activate the appropriate chain of command related to the hospital's lack of resources to treat this particular patient appropriately. This case was settled before trial.

D. Medication and Treatment Errors

Medication errors abound in pediatrics for several reasons. Pediatric medications are dosed based upon weight. This leads to calculation errors and also requires pediatric medications to be available in multiple concentrations. In addition, young pediatric patients are unable to recognize and communicate an error themselves. A recent study found 616 medication errors of 10,778 orders reviewed in two academic pediatric institutions. This represents 5.7 percent. Of these, one in five errors was a near miss so did not actually reach the patient.[19] See Chapter 1, *The Roots of Patient Injury*, in Volume I, for more information.

TIP: Near misses, in which a medication error has been averted by the attentiveness of a nurse, physician, or pharmacist, are generally not reported.

Unit dose preparation of medications, in which each dose comes individually prepared from the hospital pharmacy, has decreased the number of medication errors. However, some medications are unstable when mixed hours before administration and so the nurse must mix them in the nursing unit. In addition, there are many opportunities for errors other than dosage errors. Medications may be given at the wrong time, increasing the blood level of that specific medication with many possible harmful effects. Medications may inadvertently be given to patients other than the patient for whom the medication was prescribed. Giving the medication by the wrong route is a very serious error. For example, an oral medication administered intravenously can lead to disastrous consequences.

TIP: Another large arena for medication errors is the practice of admixture, in which medications are added to IV bags. A specific and dangerous example of this is the addition of potassium chloride to IV solutions. An overdosage of potassium chloride can lead to serious cardiac events and even death. Many potassium chloride errors have been averted by the removal of this medication from nursing units.

What follows is an example of a case that contained numerous errors of different kinds:

An 18-month-old child was brought to an emergency room by his parents because of symptoms of respiratory distress. The child had an elevated respiratory rate as well as retractions (skin of the chest is sucked in between the ribs at each breath) and labored breathing. The child had no fever or history of any other signs of illness. In the emergency room, numerous laboratory samples were drawn from the child but the results were not back at the time it was decided to take the child to the

operating room for a bronchoscopy to look for a foreign body that might have been blocking the airway. There was no history of a foreign-body ingestion nor did an x-ray confirm the presence of a foreign body, but the physician believed this was the most logical etiology of the child's distress. During the bronchoscopy the lab results returned. They revealed the child was very acidotic and the blood sugar was very elevated. The child was diagnosed with diabetic ketoacidosis, a potentially life-threatening situation characterized by a high glucose level and the development of ketones in the blood stream leading to acidosis.[20] It was now apparent the child's symptoms had nothing to do with foreign-body aspiration, but because the child had been placed under anesthesia, the physician decided this toddler should be admitted to the surgical intensive care unit rather than the medical intensive care unit, where patients with ketoacidosis are generally treated. The medication error occurred when the child's IV bag was changed from a 500-milliliter bag to a 250-milliliter bag. The nurse failed to reduce the potassium dose by half, the patient received twice the dose prescribed, and the patient's heart stopped approximately one hour after the bag containing the excessive dose of potassium was hung. The resuscitation effort continued unsuccessfully until laboratory results came back revealing a potassium level of 9.2. With that knowledge, efforts were then turned to treating this particular problem but not soon enough to prevent the child from suffering severe brain damage and anoxia to the spinal cord, which caused the child to be a paraplegic. This case was settled before trial.

More information on medication issues can be found in Chapter 28, *Medication Errors*.

E. Appropriate Delegation of Nursing Tasks

Lawsuits based on inappropriate delegation are not as common as those based on failures to assess, failures to report, or medication errors. Delegation is the act of asking another to act in one's place. The delegator gives the delegatee the authority to act on his part. In the case of the professional nurse the accountability and responsibility remain with the nurse.[21]

Issues of liability generally come into play when a nurse delegates to an unlicensed person or a licensed vocational nurse activities which that person does not have the capability or training to perform. These cases have become more common as hospitals and other healthcare facilities are replacing professional nurses with unlicensed personnel. The nurse is not responsible for an institution's decision to reorganize and, as an employee, is obligated to follow the care delivery model used in the facility. Therefore, the staff nurse may assume that an unlicensed individual is competent should the institution present this employee as such. However, if the nurse recognizes the unlicensed person is incompetent, the nurse is obligated to notify her manager and refrain from delegating tasks to the unlicensed person.[22]

> A severe example of inappropriate delegation occurred when a registered nurse requested an unlicensed nursing assistant to feed a child receiving his feedings through a nasogastric tube. The nursing assistant prepared the formula and proceeded to instill the formula through the tube. At deposition the nursing assistant stated that the formula did not flow easily so she used the syringe stopper to help push in the formula. The child coughed and became distressed immediately upon instillation of the formula. The nursing assistant stopped the feeding and went to get the registered nurse to check the patient. The patient was found in severe respiratory distress with retractions, labored breathing, cyanotic (blue) color, and extreme tachycardia (rapid heart rate). It was determined the nursing assistant had instilled a total of approximately 60 milliliters of formula into the lungs of the child. The child developed severe aspiration pneumonia, required intubation with mechanical ventilation and at one point required a chest tube during his prolonged, complicated course. This case was settled before trial.

In the state where this injury occurred, only licensed nurses were to feed a child through a nasogastric tube. The reasoning behind forbidding the delegation of this task is that nasogastric tubes may migrate or be easily displaced in children. The skill of feeding through a nasogastric tube requires assessment of the placement of the tube before beginning the feeding to prevent exactly what occurred in this case. See Chapter 1, *The Roots of Patient Injury*, and Chapter 8, *Inside the Healthcare Environment*, both in Volume I, for more information about unlicensed assistive personnel.

Breaches of the standards of care of the types just discussed may lead to injuries. Children experience a multitude of illnesses and injuries. It would be impossible to cover all of the injuries or illnesses that might be involved in a pediatric nursing malpractice case in this text; however, several critical illnesses are fairly common in children. These are the subject of the following section.

3.4 Critical Illnesses in the Pediatric Population Causing Injury that May Lead to Litigation

As previously stated, numerous disease processes and accidents may occur in childhood. Fortunately, because pediatric patients are resilient, many recover completely. For those who do not recover completely, it is often not the primary accident that causes the final injury from which the patient suffers, but the terminal pathway upon which the child was set by the breach of the standard of care. For example, the child who underwent the liver biopsy described in the scenario for failure to assess was originally admitted for liver dysfunction. The primary illness was serious, but that is not what ultimately led to his death. The child died from hemorrhaging from his liver biopsy site.

As the condition of a child worsens, several common illnesses can lead to injuries. This section discusses four such illnesses: septic shock, hypovolemic shock, increased intracranial pressure, and respiratory failure. These conditions may result in the patient's death or in severe injury, leaving the patient with numerous functional deficits. Finally, a brief discussion of cardiopulmonary resuscitation and of hypoxic and ischemic injuries is provided.

It is important for the attorney to recognize that these critical illnesses, while resulting in severe damage, may not have resulted from a breach of the standard of care. The illnesses described below may be characterized by a rapid development or a resistance to treatment. These qualities readily provide defenses for healthcare professionals. Carefully analyze the symptoms of the child, the attempts by the parents to obtain medical attention, and the chronology of events before making judgments about the liability issues. Many of these critical illnesses result in the death of the child. These malpractice cases can produce substantial damage awards because of the emotional appeal they have for jurors. Calculation of the lost earning potential of a child is discussed in Chapter 11, *Vocational Evaluations in Nursing Malpractice Cases,* in Volume I. A brain-damaged child (which may result from hypoxia) requires a significant amount of money to be cared for over his lifetime. A life care plan will be essential to calculate future costs. See Chapter 12, *Life Care Planning*, and Chapter 13, *The Role of the Forensic Economist in Nursing Malpractice Actions*, both in Volume I, for more information regarding these issues.

A. Septic Shock

Systemic inflammatory response syndrome (SIRS) results from a severe infectious process. Sepsis is when SIRS occurs in the face of an infection proven by a culture sampled from a bodily fluid of the clinically ill patient. Septic shock is present when hypotension and signs of poor perfusion continue after fluid resuscitation.[23] Septic shock is an important cause of death, especially in the infant population, responsible for 5.9 deaths per 100,000 infants. In the one- to four-year-old age range the mortality rate is 0.6 deaths per 100,000 children, and in the five- to fourteen-year-old group the mortality rate is 0.2 deaths per 100,000 children.[24]

Septic shock is a complicated process. It occurs in response to an infection, but the response of the body to the infection appears to determine whether the patient experiences sepsis. The most important element in the treatment of septic shock is early recognition. As mentioned earlier, children decompensate rapidly; therefore, the earlier the intervention, the better the outcome. According to Schexnayder,[25] the signs of sepsis vary and can be insidious or dramatic. The signs may depend upon which organism caused the initial infection. It is important to remember that septic shock may result in an increased temperature, but infants often may present with decreased temperature. See Figure 3.1 for early and late symptoms of septic shock. If the septic state continues without treatment, the patient will deteriorate and enter a hypodynamic state involving hypotension, metabolic acidosis, and a decline in the cardiac output.

Medical management goals are directed toward rapid treatment of perfusion failure and identification and control of the infection.[26] Further explanation of the management of septic shock extends beyond the scope of this text as it is extremely complicated. It is also important to recognize that severe injury or death of a child from septic shock does not necessarily support the conclusion that the standards of care were breached. There is still much research being carried out in this area to identify all the host reactions the body may have to invading pathogens.

TIP: Textbook treatment for septic shock and strict adherence to the standards of care can be accomplished and the patient may still die.

B. Hypovolemic Shock

Hypovolemic shock is a type of circulatory failure characterized by inadequate tissue perfusion that fails to meet the metabolic needs of the body.[27] It generally results from fluid loss in the form of vomiting or diarrhea, but may result from blood or plasma losses as well. This is the most common type of shock seen in the pediatric population. Shock occurs because the amount of blood in the vascular system is decreased in relation to the size of the vasculature whether from an actual loss of fluids or from a dilation of the vascular system. Because of this loss of fluids or dilation of the vessels, less blood returns to the heart, which in turn decreases the amount of blood pumped from the heart with each beat. This can lead to inadequate oxygenation of the tissues and organs, which may lead to cellular injury if untreated.

Early or compensated hypovolemic shock is characterized by persistent tachycardia with vasoconstriction. As it progresses, the patient demonstrates decreased perfusion as seen with mottling of the skin (an uneven distribution of color with patches of pale and reddened areas), decreased capillary refill, and cool extremities.[28] Blood pressure is generally unaffected in early shock. Should fluid losses continue or this state be left untreated, shock will become decompensated, characterized by extreme tachycardia, hypotension, mental lethargy, cold extremities with weakened or absent peripheral pulses, and decreased or absent urine output.[29]

Whatever the cause of the hypovolemia, the primary management is the same.[30] Because the common endpoint in hypovolemia is deprivation of the tissues of needed nutrients, attention to airway and breathing is the first treatment. Oxygen is delivered and assurance of adequate ventilation is necessary. Following this, measures to restore the volume to adequate levels are instituted. It is also necessary to control the losses based on the etiology of this critical problem. Fluid resuscitation is the primary treatment.[31]

Early Signs
- Tachycardia or increased heart rate
- Tachypnea or increased respiratory rate
- High fever
- Mental confusion
- Vital signs may not reflect the degree of illness

Late Signs
- Marked tachycardia followed by bradycardia or decreased heart rate
- Hypotension or decreased blood pressure
- Increases in respiratory rate
- Decreased level of consciousness
- Deficits in capillary refill
- Absent peripheral pulses with weakening central pulses
- Cool extremities

Figure 3.1 Signs and Symptoms Encountered in Septic Shock

TIP: It is important to remember that although the child may have had a severe injury or died, the treatment may have been appropriate. Especially in cases of major trauma, appropriate treatment may have begun too late or have been ineffective because of the extent of the child's injuries.

C. Increased Intracranial Pressure

The Monroe-Kellie doctrine is the principle by which increased intracranial pressure is defined. The basic premise of this doctrine is that the skull is a bony, rigid encasement that contains the intracranial contents: the brain, cerebrospinal fluid, and blood; therefore, the volume is nearly the same at all times. It is recognized that reciprocal change among the intracranial compartments may occur with blood or cerebrospinal fluid being expelled to accommodate an increase in another component. However, if the decrease in the amount of one constituent is not adequate to accommodate the increase of another, intracranial pressure will increase.[32] An uncompensated increase in intracranial pressure can result from numerous causes. Some of the most common etiologies in children include: head trauma, arteriovenous malformations, tumors, meningitis, encephalitis, and obstructive hydrocephalus.

TIP: One of the earliest signs of increased intracranial pressure in a child is a change in the child's level of consciousness.

Increased intracranial pressure is often exhibited in infants by periods of irritability interspersed with periods of lethargy. Infants often emit a high-pitched cry, and may have bulging fontanelles (area where the skull plates meet) and "sunset eyes" in which the eyes are deviated downward. An older child may be confused or disoriented. Decreased responsiveness or decreased ability to follow commands may also be noted. Parents are often important resources in the early recognition of these signs and symptoms because they are most familiar with the child's behavior patterns. Often they will be the first to report, "He's just not himself." Early on, the child may also exhibit tachycardia (rapid heart rate) and tachypnea (rapid breathing rate), and may complain of a headache. Vomiting may occur, especially following a position change from lying to upright. Other later signs and symptoms include pupil dilation with decreased reactivity to light, bradycardia (slowed heart rate), and alterations in the respiratory rate or pattern. Cushing's Triad, which consists of hypertension, bradycardia, and apnea, is often seen with increased intracranial pressure in adults, but in children may occur only as a late sign.[33] Papilledema, or edema of the optic nerve or disc in the eye, must be viewed by ophthalmoscope and would not normally be noted by the nurse, but is also a sign of increased intracranial pressure that develops when the intracranial pressure has been elevated 48 hours or more.

Management of a child with increased intracranial pressure is directed toward meeting three goals: maintenance of effective cerebral perfusion through excellent systemic perfusion and control of intracranial pressure; preservation of cerebral function; and prevention of secondary insults to the brain.[34] To fulfill these goals, one of the first requirements is accurate and timely identification and treatment of the cause of the increased intracranial pressure. These children may deteriorate quickly and also require intubation with mechanical ventilation.

The detailed treatment of the child with increased intracranial pressure is beyond the scope of this text. Increased intracranial pressure can be difficult to treat. Early recognition is important. Some instances of increased intracranial pressure may be difficult to reverse and do not respond to interventions. The endpoint of untreated or unsuccessfully treated intracranial pressure is brain death that occurs when the brain herniates, or moves downward through the bony opening at the base of the skull. This permanently and fatally injures the brain's ability to perform basic bodily functions such as respiration.

D. Respiratory Failure

Respiratory illnesses are by far the most common illnesses in children. In a recent study comparing school-age children living in rural versus non-rural settings, the most frequent diagnoses leading to outpatient physician visits in a non-rural setting were routine health check, asthma, and acute respiratory infections. In rural settings the most common diagnoses were attention deficit disorder, otitis media, chronic rhinitis, and influenza.[35]

TIP: Most emergencies faced in dealing with children are respiratory. This is due in part to the small size of the respiratory organs and to a child's poor respiratory reserve, which is based much on size as well.

Respiratory failure occurs when alveolar gas exchange (the gas exchange that takes place at the capillary-alveolar level in the lungs) is abnormal. The patient exhibits hypoxemia (decreased oxygen levels in the blood), hypercarbia (increased carbon dioxide levels in the blood), or both.[36] Any respiratory illness and many injuries may result in respiratory failure. Respiratory failure may develop after a head injury impairs the brain's control of the respiratory center. It may occur when a patient develops a pneumonia that remains untreated or worsens despite therapy because oxygen cannot be exchanged in alveoli that are filled with infectious material. An injury to the chest wall in a motor vehicle accident may cause respiratory failure by inducing uncoordinated respirations. A child with muscular dystrophy who has progressively weakened respiratory muscles may develop respiratory failure because the diaphragm, which is the primary respiratory muscle, does not function appropriately. Most commonly, in small children, it is a problem with the airway itself. Because of edema and mucous production during a respiratory viral illness, the infant may be unable to clear her airways so effective respiration can occur, which leads to respiratory failure.

Signs and symptoms of respiratory failure are shown in Figure 3.2. Management of respiratory failure is geared toward two goals: to maximize oxygen delivery and to decrease oxygen demand. This seems simple on paper but can be exceptionally difficult to accomplish. It involves the administration of oxygen in a modality tolerable and effective to overcome the problems of the disease process from which the patient suffers, while minimizing all possible demands for oxygen the body might make. Careful monitoring by a trained and educated professional to prevent movement away from these goals is imperative. Refer to Chapter 8, *Respiratory Malpractice*, for more information.

E. Hypoxia

This term is used interchangeably with many others and sometimes inappropriately. Hypoxia is defined as reduced oxygenation of brain tissue, whereas hypoxemia is defined as reduced oxygenation of the blood.[37] Ischemia is a decrease in regional blood flow, with hypoxic-ischemic injury referring to brain hypoxia combined with ischemia.

Hypoxia may result from each of the above-described critical illnesses. Should a child be left untreated, be treated ineffectively, or progress beyond the point of treatment's ability to be successful, hypoxia may well be the endpoint. Certainly there are causes of hypoxia beyond the above-discussed critical illnesses, but these are fairly common ones. These particular pathophysiologic issues are frequently associated with pediatric nursing malpractice cases.

Brain tissue and nerves are extremely sensitive to injury from hypoxia and ischemia. It is now recognized that brain injuries that occur with hypoxia and ischemia are related not just to the lack of oxygen to the brain. The presence of hypoxia and ischemia begins a complex chemical reaction which may injure the entire brain.

An altered level of consciousness is one presenting sign of the child who has suffered an ischemic-hypoxic injury. Other signs and symptoms may include: alterations in pupil size and response to light, acidotic state as determined by laboratory tests, and signs and symptoms of damage to other oxygen-sensitive organs such as the heart, kidney, and liver. Generally, CT scans and MRI studies will show infarcted (dead) areas of the brain or global cerebral edema (swelling). Management of ischemic-hypoxic injury is based on treatment of symptoms and the underlying event that led to the insult.

3.5 Cardiopulmonary Resuscitation in Children

Cardiopulmonary resuscitation (CPR) is performed when a child has a cardiac arrest or when a respiratory arrest deteriorates to severe bradycardia. The causes of pediatric arrests are more diverse than those seen in adults. Generally, pediatric emergencies are respiratory in nature, and cardiac arrests occur because of a respiratory problem. The decreased oxygenation of the blood and increased carbon dioxide that

Early Signs and Symptoms	Late Signs or Symptoms	Signs and Symptoms Just Prior to Respiratory Arrest
<ul><li>Increased respiratory rate</li><li>Increased heart rate</li><li>Increased work of breathing including retractions, stridor, see-saw respirations, grunting and nasal flaring</li><li>Irritability or lethargy</li><li>Pale skin</li><li>Decreased breath sounds</li><li>Delayed capillary refill</li><li>Mottled color</li></ul>	<ul><li>Severe respiratory effort including severe retractions, decreased chest movement, absent or severely decreased breath sounds upon auscultation</li><li>Depressed level of consciousness</li><li>Cyanosis or bluish skin color</li><li>Extreme increase in heart rate</li><li>Absent peripheral pulses</li><li>Cool extremities</li></ul>	<ul><li>Bradycardia or slowed heart rate</li><li>Episodes of apnea</li><li>Gasping</li><li>Agonal or uncoordinated and ineffective respirations</li><li>Hypotension</li><li>Absence of breath sounds</li><li>No response to painful stimuli</li></ul>

Figure 3.2 Signs and Symptoms of Respiratory Failure

occur in a respiratory emergency impair the function of the myocardium of the heart, and a cardiac arrest or severe bradycardia may then result.

Outcomes of cardiac arrest differ based upon the location of the arrest. For those children who suffer an arrest outside a hospital setting, the outcome is generally poor.[38] Should the arrest occur within a hospital, the outcome is slightly better. This is thought to be due to the fact that the predominant rhythm when a child arrests appears to be asystole or complete cessation of the heart that is associated with an outcome somewhat better than that of the adult who generally suffers a ventricular arrhythmia. In this particular study, 27 percent of children survived to hospital discharge, and of these 65 percent of the children had good neurological outcomes.[39]

For these reasons it is important to prevent cardiac arrest in children. This is accomplished by treating the underlying disease process and by giving prompt attention to airway and breathing management.

TIP: Basic life support and advanced life support for pediatric patients is reviewed thoroughly in the Pediatric Advanced Life Support Textbook, published by the American Heart Association. New standards went into effect in 2005.

3.6 Pediatrics as a Specialty

Although pediatric nursing has long been a subspecialty of nursing, the first professional organization dedicated to pediatric nursing, the Society of Pediatric Nurses, was not begun until the early 1990s. Before that time pediatric nurses often joined subspecialty professional organizations having a pediatric division. The emergence of the Society of Pediatric Nurses has led to a network for the professionals working in the pediatric nursing arena. This network allows nurses in the specialty area to share information and experiences in a variety of manners. The Society has its own journal. Chapters are forming across the United States, with regular meetings for local members. There is an annual national meeting. Publications through subcommittees of the Society are becoming available including the standards of practice for pediatric nurses. All these resources assist the pediatric nurse to grow in knowledge of and experience with the pediatric population and may be useful as evidence in a pediatric nursing malpractice case.

Although no professional group of nurses was devoted to the pediatric population before the 1990s, information about pediatric nursing was and continues to be available through various media sources. Numerous journals are dedicated to the care of pediatric patients, several of which are specifically nursing journals. These journals discuss appropriate care for a given disease process as it occurs in the pediatric population. See Figure 3.3 for a listing of some important pediatric journals. In addition to journals, numerous nursing texts address pediatric issues. *Wong's Nursing Care of Infants and Children*, a textbook written by noted authorities in pediatric nursing, is now in its ninth edition. This has been a standard pediatric text in many nursing schools for years.

- Advances in Neonatal Care
- Issues in Comprehensive Pediatric Nursing
- Journal for Specialist in Pediatric Nursing
- Journal of Child and Adolescent Psychiatric Nursing
- Journal of Family Nursing
- Journal of Neonatal Nursing
- Journal of Pediatric Health Care
- Journal of Pediatric Nursing
- Journal of Pediatric Oncology Nursing
- Journal of Perinatal and Neonatal Nursing
- Journal of School Nursing
- MCN: American Journal of Maternal/Child Nursing
- Neonatal Network
- Pediatric Nursing
- School Nurse News

Figure 3.3 Important Pediatric Nursing Journals

3.7 Standards of Care for Pediatric Nursing

The Society of Pediatric Nurses has developed and published the standards of practice for pediatric nursing. Other sources for pediatric nursing standards of care include the texts listed above as well as the pediatric nursing journals. Should the standard of care issue be applicable to a specific specialty, a standard may be available from the professional organization related to that specialty.

TIP: Standards of practice for pediatric nursing can be obtained by contacting the Society of Pediatric Nursing online at www.pedsnurses.org.

3.8 Scope of Practice

The scope of practice for a licensed nurse is dictated by the board of nurse examiners for that particular state, although in the near future this information may not differ significantly from state to state because of the trend toward interstate agreements among the existing boards. Until that time, however, the Nurse Practice Act for the particular state is the most logical place to begin to investigate if the nurse was practicing within his realm. The Nurse Practice Act generally addresses the line between nursing and medicine, what types of activities can be delegated to unlicensed personnel, and what basic activities the nurse is responsible for in patient care.

Several types of advanced practitioners practice in the realm of pediatric nursing. These include: the pediatric nurse practitioner, the pediatric clinical nurse specialist, the nurse anesthetist, and the family nurse practitioner, who often sees pediatric patients. The scope of practice for these nurses is different from those in general practice. Generally, because these nurses have advanced education (master's degrees), they are held to a higher standard of care. The Nurse Practice Act for the state in which the nurse is practicing also addresses scope of practice issues for advanced practice nurses.

3.9 Psychosocial Aspects of the Pediatric Case

The emotions involved in the injury or illness of a child cannot be overemphasized. Every parent believes it is the parent's job to nurture and protect children. When a child is injured, the parent feels responsible. This tends to lead to a great deal of guilt regardless of whether the parent has any degree of fault whatsoever. This often occurs even when the fault can be placed elsewhere. In some instances the parents file a lawsuit to place the blame elsewhere, in hopes of alleviating some of the guilt.

When children are injured or ill, it affects the entire family. When the injured child requires ongoing care at home, this places heavy burdens, demands, and responsibilities on the caregivers. The stressors associated with these may lead to many feelings including chronic sorrow.[40] Unlike the theories on grieving that end with acceptance of the loss, chronic sorrow considers cyclic grief when a child is disabled. Grief may cycle in when the parent is starkly reminded of the loss suffered.[41] It has also been noted that the physical and psychological health of parents caring for a child with a disability may suffer.[42] Even the seemingly stable family with substantial resources can be stressed by such a happening. Financial strains, constant stress on the family unit, potential divorce, or other disruptions may be the impetus for the family to pursue a lawsuit.

TIP: Insurance policy limits are often capped and children with such injuries or illnesses often quickly expend a policy of substantial limits, sometimes before their initial discharge from the hospital.

If such events are associated with a child's injury, imagine what the consequences may be when a child dies. All of the emotions are magnified. Parents believe children should not predecease them: children do not die; old people die.

But children do die sometimes and many times in today's healthcare setting parents' questions are unanswered. Parents want to know why their child died. Often the healthcare team does not know why, especially immediately following the death. In addition, grieving persons have a difficult time hearing information during the beginning stages of grief. Based on the work of Lindemann, grief reactions are characterized by four phases: shock and disbelief, expression of grief, disorganization and despair, and reorganization.[43] In the first stage, shock and disbelief, parents are often numb and have a feeling of being in another reality. Frequently, they remember little of this time period. This is generally the period during which the healthcare team is most available to the family; however, the family members are unable to hear the explanations of what occurred given to them at this time.

As the numbness subsides, parents experience an overwhelming sense of grief and loss. There is a tendency to review the child's life and their part as parents. At this time parents begin to question why the death occurred. By this time the involved healthcare team has moved on to care for other children and is less available to the parents of the deceased child. This may upset the parents further and they may attempt to draw their own conclusions. Often, they conclude that someone did something very wrong for this death to have occurred. Sometimes a lawsuit can be diverted once the questions of "why" are answered. If parents are treated with respect, supported in their grief, and communicated with following the death, a lawsuit may never be filed.

Then there are the cases in which no breaches of the standards of care are found. Children are injured and die even when there are no mistakes. It is extremely difficult to explain to a family that sometimes things do just happen, meaning that although the child has died or has been severely affected and will remain so for life, there was no error or mistake that caused this trauma.

TIP: Often parents are seeking an explanation and find it comforting to pursue the lawsuit in order to be told by outside sources not connected with the medical team that there was no wrongdoing.

3.10 Summary

Pediatric patients are not just small adults. They are a unique population with issues pertinent to them as a whole, such as a high incidence of accidental injuries and the propensity for respiratory illnesses because of their small anatomy. They are developing individuals, and injuries may interrupt the developmental processes as well as injure physical aspects of the body. Issues affecting children tend to be visited upon the parents or siblings of the child.

Today's society is often viewed as being very litigious. In the case of a perceived mistake involving the health or safety of a child, it is even more likely to develop into a lawsuit than a similar issue involving an adult. Many emotional factors affect the parents' decision to pursue a lawsuit. Grief, perceived inability to deal with a long-term illness, death of a child, disruption of family relationships: all of these factors may be involved. For all of these reasons it is even more important to closely examine the merit or lack of merit in the potential pediatric case. Proper evaluation involves all of the factors discussed in this chapter. It is a huge disservice to a grieving family to pursue litigation in the face of a pediatric case that lacks merit. Carefully explaining to a family exactly what occurred in the hospital in terms that they can easily understand at a time when they can listen to the explanation can be of great benefit to the family, whether or not negligence actually occurred. This can be achieved by the attorney with the assistance of an appropriate medical consultant. Once all of the events are made clear through appropriate evaluation, it is left to the attorney and the family to jointly decide whether to pursue a claim. This is done with a clear picture of what has occurred and what the possible battles may be in the future.

Endnotes

1. Napper, C., J. Battles, and C. Fargason, "Pediatrics and patient safety," *Journal of Pediatrics* (2003): 359.

2. Brennan, T., L. Leape, N. Laird, L. Hebert, A. Localio, A. Lawthers, J. Newhouse, P. Weiler, H. Heatt, and Harvard Practice Medical Study I, "Incidence of adverse events and negligence in hospitalized patients: results from the Harvard Medical Practice Study I," *New England Journal of Medicine* (1991): 370.

3. See note 2.

4. Lannon, C., J. Coven, F. France, G. Hickson, P. Miles, J. Swanson, J. Takayama, D. Wood, and Yamamoto, "Principles of patient safety in pediatrics," *Pediatrics* (2001): 1473.

5. Broughton, V., "Critical thinking: linking assessment data and knowledge," *Nursing Connections* (1998): 59.

6. Haziniski, M., "Children are different." In *Manual of Pediatric Critical Care*, ed. M. F. Hazinski, 1. St. Louis: Mosby, 1999.

7. See note 5.

8. *Id.*

9. Reischman, R. and H. Yarandi, "Critical care cardiovascular nurse expert and novice diagnostic cue utilization," *Journal of Advanced Nursing* (2002): 24.

10. See note 6.

11. American Academy of Pediatrics and American Heart Association, "Vascular access," In *Pediatric Advanced Life Support*, eds. L. Chameides and M. F. Hazinski, Emergency Cardiac Care Committee and Subcommittees, American Heart Association, 2002.

12. Fabian, B., "Intravenous complication: infiltration," *Journal of Intravenous Nursing* (2000): 229.

13. Wynsma, L., "Negative outcomes of intravascular therapy in infants and children," *American Association of Critical Care Nurses Clinical Issues* (1998): 49.

14. Pettit, J., "Assessment of the infant with a peripheral intravenous device," *Advances in Neonatal Care* (2003): 230.

15. Park, J. and D. Barnett, "Respiratory syncytial virus infection and the primary care physician," *Southern Medical Journal* (2003): 353.

16. Kline, N. and J. O'Neill, "The child with cerebral dysfunction," In *Wong's Nursing Care of Infants and Children*, eds. D. Wilson, M. L. Winkelstein, and N. E. Kline, 1641. St. Louis: Mosby, 2003.

17. Bailey-Allen, A., "Changing liability of the nurse over the past decade," *Orthopaedic Nursing* (1990): 13.

18. Manias, E. and A. Street, "The interplay of knowledge and decision making between nurses and doctors in critical care," *International Journal of Nursing Studies* (2001): 129.

19. Landrigan, C., "The safety of inpatient pediatrics: preventing medical errors and injuries among hospitalized children," *Pediatric Clinics of North America* (2005): 979.

20. "Child with endocrine dysfunction," In *Wong's Nursing Care of Infants and Children*, eds. D. Wilson, M. L. Winkelstein, and N. E. Kline, 1734. St. Louis: Mosby, 2003.

21. Standing, T., M. Anthony, and J. Hertz, "Nurses' narratives of outcomes after delegation to unlicensed assistive personnel," *Outcomes Management for Nursing Practice* (2001): 18.

22. Standing, T., M. Anthony, and J. Hertz, "Nurses' beliefs about their abilities to delegate within changing models of care," *Journal of Continuing Education in Nursing* (2001): 210.

23. Novotny, W. and R. Perkin, "Shock," In *Pediatric Hospital Medicine*, eds. R. Perkin, J. Swift, and D. Newton, 199. Philadelphia: Lippincott, Williams & Wilkins, 2003.

24. Schexnayder, S., "Pediatric septic shock," *Pediatrics in Review* (1999): 303.

25. *Id.*

26. Sparrow, A. and F. Willis, "Management of septic shock in children," *Emergency Medicine Australia* 16 (2004): 125.

27. Novotny, W. and R. Perkin, "Shock," In *Pediatric Hospital Medicine,* eds. R. Perkin, J. Swift, and D. Newton, 199–208. Philadelphia: Lippincott, Williams & Wilkins, 2003.

28. Sevier, N. and N. Kline, "Conditions that produce fluid and electrolyte imbalance," In Wong's Nursing Care of Infants and Children, eds. D. Wilson, M. L. Winkelstein, and N. E. Kline, 1207. St. Louis: Mosby, 2003.

29. *Id.*

30. *Id.*

31. *Id.*

32. Knapp, J., "Hyperosmolar therapy in the treatment of severe head injury in children: mannitol and hypertonic saline," *AACN Clinical Issues* (2005): 199.

33. Kline, N. and J. O'Neill, "The child with cerebral dysfunction," In *Wong's Nursing Care of Infants and Children*, eds. D. Wilson, M. L. Winkelstein, and N. E. Kline, 1641. St. Louis: Mosby, 2003.

34. See note 32.

35. Cayce, K., D. Krowchuk, S. Feldman, F. Camacho, R. Balkrishnan, and A. Fleischer, "Healthcare utilization for acute and chronic diseases of young, school-age children in the rural and non-rural setting," *Clinical Pediatrics* (2005): 491.

36. Katz, A. and E. Grayck, "Respiratory failure," In *Pediatric Hospital Medicine*, eds. R. Perkin, J. Swift, and D. Newton, 273. Philadelphia: Lippincott, Williams & Wilkins, 2003.

37. Biagas, K., "Hypoxic-ischemic brain injury: advancements in the understanding of mechanisms and potential avenues for therapy," *Current Opinions in Pediatrics* (1999): 223.

38. Donoghue, A., V. Nadkarni, R. Berg, M. Osmond, G. Wells, L. Nesbitt, and I. Stiell, "Out-of-hospital pediatric cardiac arrest: an epidemiologic review and assessment of current knowledge," *Annals of Emergency Medicine* (2005): 512.

39. See note 6.

40. Northington, L., "Chronic sorrow in caregivers of school age children with sickle cell disease: a grounded theory approach," *Issues in Comprehensive Pediatric Nursing* (2000): 141.

41. "Parental grief and adjustment to a child with a disability," www.office-for-children.vic.gov.au/children/ ccd-nav.nsf/childdocs. Downloaded April 11, 2006.

42. Raina, P., M. O'Donnell, P. Rosenbaum, J. Brehaut, S. Walter, D. Russell, M. Swinton, B. Zhu, and E. Wood, "The health and well-being of caregivers of children with cerebral palsy," *Pediatrics* (2005): 626.

43. Corless, I., "Bereavement," In *Textbook of Palliative Nursing,* eds. B. Ferrell and N. Coyle, 352. New York: Oxford University Press, 2001.

Chapter 4

Critical Care Malpractice Issues

Kathleen C. Ashton, PhD, APRN, BC and Jenny Beerman, MN, RN, LNCC

Synopsis
4.1 Introduction
4.2 Scope of Practice
    A. Types of Practice
    B. Unit-Based Protocols and Standing Orders
4.3 Use of the Nursing Process in Critical Care
    A. Assessment
    B. Nursing Diagnoses
    C. Expected Outcomes
    D. Planning
    E. Implementation
    F. Evaluation
4.4 Criteria for Practice
    A. Orientation
    B. Personnel in Critical Care
    C. Prerequisites for Critical Care Nursing
    D. Certification
    E. Continuing Education
4.5 Standards of Care
4.6 Sources of Liability
    A. Airway Maintenance
        1. Paralysis of the diaphragm with neuromuscular blocking agents
        2. Suctioning
        3. Ventilation without intubation
        4. Weaning from the ventilator
        5. Ventilator-associated pneumonia
    B. Consent
    C. Advance Directives and Organ Procurement
    D. Pressure Ulcers
    E. Falls and Use of Restraints
    F. Response to Alarms and Changes in Condition
    G. Nursing Research
4.7 Trends that Influence the Liability of Critical Care Nurses
    A. Aging of America
    B. Increased Reliance on Computers
    C. Nursing in the Telemedicine Setting
    D. Use of Unlicensed Assistive Personnel
    E. Managed Care
    F. ICU Occupancy
    G. Cost Containment in ICU
    H. Admission and Discharge to the Critical Care Unit
4.8 Screening Critical Care Cases
4.9 Summary
Endnotes
Additional Reading

4.1 Introduction

As the healthcare industry moves into the second decade of the twenty-first century, some of the greatest changes and challenges will be those related to critical care nursing. Critical care nursing in the United States began with the recognition that specialty nursing was necessary to more adequately care for seriously ill patients with complex needs. Ongoing technological advancements in diagnostics and treatment of the critically ill led to the emergence of specialty intensive care units, the first being a coronary care unit at Abington Memorial Hospital outside Philadelphia.[1] The modern-day Intensive Care Unit (ICU) developed because of three major forces:

1. grouping patients according to special needs encourages specialty nursing and concentrates expensive equipment;
2. complex technology and medical procedures demand more extensive and specialized observation in one location; and
3. ICUs relieve recovery rooms or postanesthesia care units (PACUs) from pressure to extend the patient stay from hours to days.[2]

Nurses working in these units sought more knowledge in meeting the growing needs of sicker patients.[3] The American Association of Critical Care Nurses (AACN), born out of this need for knowledge, continues to be a major force in providing educational support, as well as certification opportunities for the critical care nurse. Many definitions have been used to describe critical care nursing, but the AACN defines it as "the specialty of nursing that deals with human responses to life-threatening problems."[4] It is a specialty that is practiced in a setting where direct observation, monitoring, and rapid intervention are possible.

Today, we are in the middle of a revolution permanently altering how health care is delivered and how its quality is assessed. An emphasis placed on primary, preventive, and holistic care, and the rise of managed care has substantially altered the roles and philosophies of multiple healthcare providers, especially critical care nurses. Patients are often admitted to hospitals because they need intensive nursing care. Nurses have become primary care providers in some instances. These recent changes in the healthcare environment have led to greater identification and reliance on knowledge, expertise, and services of all healthcare providers, but especially the critical care nurse.[5]

4.2 Scope of Practice

Critical care nurses no longer focus only on the patient's acute illness event. In the rapidly changing healthcare environment, critical care nurses must expand their care to include education on prevention and risk factor modification to decrease future patient admissions to acute care facilities. "Critical care nursing recognizes that the boundaries of specialty practice are often fluid, responding to changing patient needs in the healthcare environment."[6] Professional accountability must be maintained through adherence to standards of nursing care of the critically ill and through a commitment to act in accordance with ethical principles.[7] Certification and special skills are needed to perform Advanced Cardiac Life Support (ACLS). Continuing education is necessary for critical care nurses to be knowledgeable and proficient about emergency cardiovascular care.

TIP: The nurse is the key person in the intensive care or critical care unit (CCU), with the potential to directly influence patient outcomes.

A. Types of Practice

Critical care nurses do not practice in isolation but rather in concert with other healthcare providers. Through exchange of ideas and demonstration of clinical expertise, each practitioner is able to evaluate professional competence. Trust can then be established, and new collaborative roles for all healthcare providers in the critical care environment become possible. Areas of nursing activities are dependent, independent, and interdependent, as outlined in the AACN standards of care. Orders and medical care plans, defined as those directed primarily by physicians, are dependent nursing interventions. Independent nursing interventions are unique to nursing, assessment, diagnosis, teaching, counseling, and manipulation of the patient's environment. Today's ICU environment reveals increasingly interdependent activities of shared interest, such as quality improvement and mutual responsibility for unit operation, organization, and administration. Professional obligations and responsibilities become clearer when dependent, independent, and interde-

pendent areas of activity are considered. Critical care nurses must accept professional, ethical, and legal responsibility for their actions and, to some extent, the actions of the entire healthcare team.[8]

TIP: Lawyers may need to investigate if problems of trust and communication affected the patient outcome with incidents involving both doctors and nurses.

Collaboration and communication form the cornerstone of effective care. Knaus concluded that involvement and interaction of critical care personnel could actually influence the outcome of critical illness. The outcome is affected by the degree of interaction and communication between nurses and physicians.[9] Communication and collaboration are responsibilities of not only the nurses, but also the physicians to mutually update each other on information from diagnostic studies, and physiological and psychosocial parameters affecting the patient or family.[10] Daily multidisciplinary rounds, end-of-shift reporting, and timely and appropriate telephone calls combine to maintain an esprit de corps essential in a setting where a patient's condition changes rapidly and often.[11]

Several studies have shown that the implementation of an integrated medical record, clinical pathways and protocols, and other products of a more collaborative arrangement may improve patient outcomes.[12]

B. Unit-Based Protocols and Standing Orders

Unit-based protocols and standing orders are frequently used in the critical care unit. These documents serve as a guide for the critical care nurse, permitting rapid intervention when life-threatening symptoms are present.

TIP: Protocols and standing orders should be dated and signed by the physician, and periodically updated as changes in medical and nursing practice mandate.

The highly sophisticated nature of critical care nursing and the expanded scope of clinical practice make nurses vulnerable to liability. There is no question the critical care nurse can be held to a higher standard of care than the staff nurse on a regular unit.[13] The critical care nurse is often required to perform highly technical procedures without the direct and immediate supervision of a physician. These activities must be based on established protocols created by medical and nursing departments of the hospital. The protocols should be reviewed frequently so healthcare professionals can determine if they reflect current medical and nursing standards of care. Unit protocols and procedures serve as evidence to assist with the establishment of the applicable standard of care.[14]

The legal responsibility of critical care nurses is the same as that of other nurses, that is, they are responsible for their own conduct, including any negligence or tort.[15] However, the complexity of patient problems, their rapidly changing condition, and ongoing technological innovations place a higher demand on the critical care nurse.[16] To complicate matters further, gray areas of legal authority surround certain situations, such as when the nurse makes the clinical diagnosis of a dysrhythmia (a heart rhythm disturbance), and implements standing orders. In essence she is making a medical diagnosis—independent of the physician—and treating it based on established protocol.

TIP: Critical care nurses must immediately assess and treat conditions such as dysrhythmias, hypotension, or bleeding.

If the patient's outcome is a good recovery, no questions are raised. If the opposite occurs and the patient dies, can the nurse be found guilty of practicing medicine? This is the vacuum in which critical care nursing is practiced and the uncertainty that attorneys face as they review critical care malpractice suits.[17]

> In *Sermchief v. Gonsales*, the court upheld the use of standing orders and protocol because these practices were in effect when the legislature amended the State of Missouri Nurse Practice Act. Though the statute did not address these practices, the fact that they existed when the legislature broadly amended the statute implied to the court that the practices were authorized. 660 S.W. 2d 683 (MO) 1983.[18]

The Joint Commission, an organization that accredits hospitals, requires the appointment of a medical director for each ICU. Attorneys must not lose sight of the fact that, more often than not, nurses are the overall protectors and primary caregivers of the patients admitted to the critical care unit. But critical care nursing is a multidisciplinary team approach and open communication should exist among the physician, the critical care nurse, and other health team members, including the medical director.

TIP: The medical director oversees the quality of care in the ICU and is often involved when it comes time to decide which patients are stable enough to be transferred out of the critical care area to make way for someone in need of the bed.

4.3 Use of the Nursing Process in Critical Care

The nursing process serves as the organizational framework for the practice of critical care nursing. The nurse takes the following steps:

1. performing patient assessment;
2. identifying actual and potential alterations in health (nursing diagnosis);
3. defining expected patient outcomes and designing a plan of care;
4. implementing nursing interventions; and
5. evaluating the patient's response to the plan of care.

A. Assessment

The first and most important step of the nursing process, patient assessment, is essential in critical care because it forms a scientific basis for the nursing process. On the patient's admission to the critical care unit, the nurse performs a comprehensive history and initial assessment. It is crucial that the critical care nurse adequately assesses the patient in a systematic fashion, and correctly identifies the patient's needs, preferences, abilities, actual problems, and potential for complications in order to implement the remaining steps of the nursing process. In the following case, critical assessment data demonstrated that the patient was experiencing a retroperitoneal hemorrhage:

> The plaintiff's decedent went to Sharp Grossmont Hospital with an occluded femoral artery graft. After the defendant radiologist performed a scheduled angiogram, the decedent was transferred to the ICU for post-procedure monitoring by a registry nurse. (A registry nurse is a temporary nurse who works for a nursing agency. He receives assignments from the nursing agency to work either short term or long term at a facility.) During the monitoring phase, her condition deteriorated and she ultimately died from a retroperitoneal hemorrhage (internal bleeding). The plaintiffs (three adult children of the decedent) alleged wrongful death and malpractice. The plaintiffs contended the radiologist pierced the graft while performing the angiogram, which caused their mother to bleed to death. They also asserted that Sharp Grossmont staff, including the nurses, misapplied pressure to the wound site, failed to recognize the internal bleeding, and otherwise failed to appropriately monitor the patient, allowing her to essentially bleed to death while

under their direct care. The defendants contended the decedent's health condition was already poor and there were no signs she was bleeding internally while in the ICU. The plaintiffs settled their claim for $160,000, which was paid by the nursing registry.[19]

In this case, the failure to adequately monitor and assess the patient led to charges of nursing negligence. Careful monitoring to determine changing conditions should be noted in a timely fashion and recognized as one of the key activities of the critical care nurse.

Continuous ongoing assessment based on hospital policy guidelines, or practice guidelines, is usually performed every one to two hours, or more frequently as needed in the critical care units. A complete assessment is repeated at least once every 8 to 12 hours in critical care, usually at the beginning of the nurse's shift. A modified assessment to detect any changes is repeated every two to four hours, depending on the changing condition and complexity of the patient. An inappropriate assessment that fails to identify early subtle changes exhibited by the critical care patient could result in irreversible and untreatable complications, for example, hemorrhage, shock, cauda equina syndrome, paralysis, side effects or misuse of medication, or increased intracranial pressure.[20]

The subjective data from the patient and objective data from nursing observations are included at each assessment. The initial admission assessment must be completed within eight hours. In most critical care settings, the assessment is performed shortly after the patient arrives on the critical care unit. The assessment includes:

1. patient interview (if the patient is able to cooperate)
2. astute observations about the patient
3. past nursing and social history from the patient and old medical records
4. vital signs
5. physical assessment
6. identification of psychosocial needs
7. review of diagnostic tests

This important baseline information forms the basis for comparison throughout the patient's hospitalization and is referred to by all members of the multidisciplinary critical care team. Parts of the assessment may have to be deferred if the patient has an altered level of consciousness, is intubated (has a breathing tube in her throat), or is so critically ill that a complete assessment cannot be performed.[21]

B. Nursing Diagnoses

Critical care nurses analyze the data to establish nursing diagnoses or priority problems typical to most patients with deviations of health in the identified body system, for example, chest trauma or respiratory failure. Critical care nurses are responsible for establishing nursing diagnoses using the most current North American Nursing Diagnosis Association (NANDA) terminology, which is endorsed by the American Nurses Association (ANA).[22] Refer to Chapter 5, *Medical Errors: Roots of Litigation*, in Volume I, for additional information on nursing diagnoses.

C. Expected Outcomes

After identification and documentation of the patient's nursing diagnoses, the critical care nurse must establish the desired or expected patient outcomes for each nursing diagnosis during the critical phase of the patient's illness. Without well-defined patient outcomes, interventions have no focus, making it difficult to measure patient progress. In addition, The Joint Commission has made it a priority that patient-specific, multidisciplinary interactions be identified and that outcomes need to be documented for all patients in the ICU.[23]

D. Planning

To achieve expected patient outcomes, the critical care nurse designs a plan of care, applying practice guidelines. He then initiates that plan of care, outlining and prioritizing nursing interventions. With today's complex critical care issues, multidisciplinary planning is becoming the norm. All members of the treating team contribute planning components to achieve the overall expected patient outcomes. For example, the cardiologist, the cardiothoracic surgeon, the traumatologist, and the critical care nurse may all contribute interventions for the patient with decreased cardiac output. Each member of the team expects the patient to regain a cardiac output within normal limits. In addition to expected outcomes, the care plan includes discharge planning, patient and family education, and nursing process standards in consultation with other members of the treatment team.[24]

E. Implementation

It is the critical care nurse's responsibility to implement the identified plan, protocol, or guideline in anticipation that the patient will achieve the expected outcome in the critical care environment. Nursing interventions can be based on established protocols or guidelines, but should be individualized to meet the needs of the patient. A lower nurse-patient ratio assignment in the critical care environment fosters a therapeutic relationship among the nurse, patient, and family. Ideally, this humanizes the sophisticated state-of-the-art technology and level of care in critical care units.[25]

F. Evaluation

The nurse evaluates the patient's response to critical care interventions and the extent to which the expected outcomes have been achieved, the patient's degree of compliance, any variances from the plan, the need for change, as well as the patient's and family's satisfaction. A review of diagnostic studies and medication, along with consultation with members of the clinical team, may be necessary to determine if the expected outcome has been met.[26]

4.4 Criteria for Practice

Critical care is the largest specialty in nursing. Nurses enter critical care nursing with different levels of experience. All entry-level critical care nurses complete a special course in critical care nursing, an extensive orientation, and on-the-job training. A precepting program is an effective tool in placing a non-experienced critical care nurse with a more experienced ICU nurse. This approach ensures that shared knowledge and experience will translate into high-quality care.[27]

TIP: Many hospitals insist that a critical care nurse have at least one year of experience in medical surgical nursing. This recommendation builds upon the nurse's foundation of knowledge.

In contrast, critical care medicine is a subspecialty made up of the following four disciplines:

1. surgery
2. anesthesiology
3. internal medicine
4. pediatrics

The Council of the Society of Critical Care Medicine (SCCM) approved guidelines in 2004 for critical care fellowships with a list of cognitive and procedural skills felt to be fundamental to the training of a specialist in critical care.[28] While critical care staff nurses lack the post-graduate formal education of critical care medicine, nurses may advance their knowledge and skills through graduate programs with a specialty in critical care as clinical nurse specialists (CNS) or nurse practitioners (NP).[29] Obtaining national certification is another means of demonstrating advanced knowledge.

A. Orientation

Orientation for all new employees begins with a general introduction to the hospital.

TIP: Entry-level critical care nurses are required to complete a critical care course and become certified in Advanced Cardiac Life Support (ACLS).

Some courses include a clinical experience with structured performance objectives, which must be satisfactorily met. Areas of competence include:

1. pathophysiology
2. patient assessment
3. hemodynamic monitoring
4. cardiac monitoring and interpretation of arrhythmias
5. emergency equipment and drugs
6. cardiopulmonary resuscitation
7. advanced computer technology
8. proficiency in the specific diseases treated in the particular critical care unit

---

TIP: ICU nurses provide care to patients received directly from the operating room following procedures such as open-heart surgery, or unstable patients from the postanesthesia care unit.

B. Personnel in Critical Care

The intensivist is a physician who specializes in the care of patients in intensive care units with severe illnesses. These illnesses may include respiratory failure, heart failure, kidney failure, liver failure, sepsis, or gastrointestinal bleeding. This role is being driven by the patient safety movement and is seen as vital since intensive care medicine is considered a specialty practice.

The traditional all-RN-staffed ICU with one registered nurse providing care to one or two patients has dramatically changed in the last few years, with cost-cutting moves due to managed care, budget cuts, nursing department reorganization, and downsizing. These changes are creating critical care staff shortages and new staff combinations in hospitals throughout the country. In January 2002, The Joint Commission noted that 35 percent of all ventilator-related deaths and injuries in ICUs were caused by insufficient staffing levels.[30] Registered nurses are often hired after graduating from nursing schools, with little or no nursing experience. Senior students may be hired to carry out nursing tasks, but are not allowed to do procedures that require a nursing license, such as irrigating tubes, starting blood, or suctioning an endotracheal tube. Unlicensed assistive personnel (UAP), formerly known as nurses' aides, who may receive only one to six weeks of training, are being hired to handle nursing tasks.[31] Medical surgical nurses are also being cross-trained to work in various units, including critical care units. Likewise, critical care and emergency department nurses are also participating in cross-training for other departments of nursing. In many institutions, staff from other departments such as radiology and respiratory therapy have been cross-trained to handle nursing duties.

TIP: The use of UAP in critical care is creating controversy as hospitals change staffing to replace highly paid RNs and investigate ways to better use the specialized skills of senior nurses with advanced expertise and knowledge.

A recent research survey of nurses concluded that short staffing has put patients in danger. Many nurses report a short-staffing situation on a weekly basis.[32] Due to seriously ill patients with complex needs, many critical care units can face unsafe staffing. Most understaffing-related malpractice actions against hospitals arise from the failure to adequately monitor or report significant patient changes. Regardless of staffing issues, nurses are expected to comply with the applicable standards of care.[33] Informing the nurse manager and the ICU medical director of unsafe staffing, and documenting the issues in an internal memo or incident report are appropriate actions for nurses. By documenting the incident, the onus of ensuring adequate staffing levels rests on the facility.[34]

C. Prerequisites for Critical Care Nursing

The ability to closely monitor, rapidly interpret, and immediately respond is the goal in critical care nursing and has led to the term "high tech, high touch" nurse. Knowledge is required to implement common medical and surgical interventions, evaluate medication efficacy and side effects, interpret laboratory studies, and perform the technical skills to operate and troubleshoot complex equipment such as an intra-aortic balloon counter-pulsation device, a ventilator, a defibrillator, or an electrocardiogram machine.[35]

An entry-level critical care nurse should be able to safely manage most routine critical care patients. Critical care nurses who function at the advanced level have expanded knowledge that enable them to focus on more complex concepts and provide care to the more complicated patients.

TIP: The attorney should obtain information about the critical care experience of the nurse assigned to care for the patient. Ask if the nurse is cross-trained to work in other areas of nursing. If the nurse's experience is outside of critical care, inquire about the orientation the nurse received prior to working in critical care. Determine if

anyone was assigned to assist the non-critical care nurse with some of the patient care responsibilities. Request information on what nursing tasks were delegated to a UAP.

The master's-prepared critical care clinical nurse specialist (CNS) provides leadership in patient care. This specialist also functions as a liaison between the physicians and nurses, teaches classes, conducts research, collaborates with families, and at times follows the patient from admission to discharge. Making daily rounds, conducting weekly interdisciplinary patient conferences, and being accessible to the staff nurses, the CNS is a valuable member of the critical care team.

The nurse practitioner (NP) is another member of the critical care team. A critical care pediatric NP, for example, could complete the admission history and physical, write admission orders, conduct certain invasive procedures, make daily rounds, and also serve as a liaison between physicians and nurses. Critical care case managers are valuable in ICUs affected by managed care contracts. Despite having multiple members of the critical care clinical team, mistakes may go undetected if members do not communicate as a healthcare team.

D. Certification

Nurse managers may require their staff to maintain membership in a critical care nursing association and provide proof of specialty certification after two or more years of practice. Additional information on certification is included in Chapter 6, *The Foundations of Nursing Practice*, in Volume I.

E. Continuing Education

The critical care environment and professional organizations provide formal and informal opportunities for education.[36] Formal classes as well as bedside teaching continue for as long as the nurse practices in critical care. Attendance at critical care inservice programs and conferences is expected, so the critical care nurse can stay abreast of current trends and new knowledge.

TIP: Meticulous and detailed records should be maintained by the nurses and the hospitals as proof of all educational achievements. This information is discoverable and may be used to show that the nurse assigned to an acutely ill patient lacked advanced learning through formal classes, certification, and inservice attendance.

Physicians and other staff are expected to participate in nursing education. Many hospitals have hired unit instructors, clinical nurse specialists, or educators for staff development, although these positions continue to be in jeopardy as hospitals downsize professional staff for budgetary reasons.[37]

After a period of time working in critical care, the nurse is expected to complete additional courses to demonstrate advanced competency. Competence with the intra-aortic balloon pump, the Ventricular Assist Device (VAD), IV conscious sedation, advanced trauma life support (ATLS), or pediatric advanced life support (PALS) are examples of advanced practice. These devices and courses are described in more detail in Chapter 17, *Emergency Nursing Malpractice*.[38]

4.5 Standards of Care

In 1969, the American Association of Critical Care Nurses (AACN) was established to improve nursing care of the critically ill by education of critical care nurses. In 1981, AACN published the first edition of the *Standards for Nursing Care of the Critically Ill*, which has since been revised and updated. This important publication established an explicit set of expectations related to the process by which critical care nurses provided care and controlled the critical care environment. Current information on the organization, standards, and publications can be found on its website.[39]

Through the leadership of its members, the AACN has made a significant contribution to the development and publication of standards such as those found in the *Core Curriculum for Critical Care Nursing, AACN Standards for Nursing Care of the Critically Ill, AACN Outcome Standards for Nursing Care of the Critically Ill*, and numerous other publications. Since 1976, the AACN has also offered the certification examination in critical care nursing. The national association and state chapters offer a wealth of educational opportunities to promote the care of critically ill patients and their families.[40]

In clinical practice, the critical care nurse, like all professional nurses, utilizes the nursing process in the delivery of patient care. In addition, the standards developed by leaders within the profession reflect appropriate care delivery for specific patient situations and can be found in the AACN publications listed previously. Standards of nursing care that impact critical care nursing include not only those developed by the AACN, but also those established by the American Nurses Association, community/regional standards, hospital/medical center standards, unit practice standards/policies, precedent court cases, specialty organization standards, and certification in a specialty area. Current textbooks and nursing literature in critical care nursing are also sources of standards that may apply to a specific case.[41] Critical care

nurses are expected to periodically read and refer to their hospital's policies and procedure manual and individual unit protocols, whether on paper or electronically, and to update their practice using current evidence from nursing research.

TIP: In examining standards of care for legal cases, nursing experts may find discrepancies between hospital policy and procedures and unit protocols, particularly if they have not been updated recently, and existing standards of care from the AACN, the literature, or new research.

In addition to the standards promulgated by the AACN, the State Department of Health may have standards that proscribe practice for nurses in the critical care units. These standards may be obtained by contacting the agency for the particular state.[42] Another source of standards is The Joint Commission and these are available at its website (www.jointcommission.org).

4.6 Sources of Liability

Some of the most frequent sources of liability for the critical care nurse are explored in this section. Information is included on future trends, which are shifting the focus of liability and may form the basis for litigation in the future.[43]

A. Airway Maintenance

Nurses are taught that one of the most critical of all nursing activities is to maintain the ABCs: airway, breathing, and circulation. Patients will die if these three essential functions are not maintained.

TIP: Patients experiencing impaired airways make up a large percentage of patients in critical care areas.

Hypoxemia (insufficient oxygen in the blood) resulting in the need for oxygen or a ventilator can have many causes. Lung disorders may include chronic disease, chest trauma, surgery, infection, aspiration, clots in the lungs, or complete respiratory failure. Airway management involves pulmonary assessment (listening to the lungs), chest physiotherapy, managing chest tubes, ventilatory support, and weaning procedures. Because many ICU patients receive multiple drug therapies, including narcotics, protocols that serve as guidelines should be available for nurses who suspect clinically significant opioid-induced respiratory depression.[44] Essential to any critical care nursing assessment is the ability to recognize abnormalities in arterial blood gases (ABGs), and to apply this analysis in evaluating the most complex and involved patients. By quickly being able to interpret ABGs, the critical care nurse may prevent a critical situation from becoming worse.[45]

1. Paralysis of the diaphragm with neuromuscular blocking agents

The advancement in the delivery of mechanical ventilation for respiratory support to patients with respiratory failure has driven the need to address the most effective neuromuscular junction blocking drugs (NMBDs). NMBDs are chemical agents that interfere with the transmission or reception of impulses from the motor nerves to skeletal muscles. By effectively blocking the neurotransmitter acetylcholine at the postjunctional membrane, these agents can be used to induce muscle relaxation and respiratory paralysis. For example, NMBDs are administered for general anesthesia by anesthesiologists in the operating room (OR) to mechanically control breathing during surgery. The clinical application of neuromuscular blocking agents has moved from the OR to the ICU to facilitate mechanical ventilation for selected patients.[46]

The increasing use of neuromuscular blocking agents in the ICU requires familiarity with their basic pharmacologic properties, as well as an appreciation of potential problems associated with chronic neuromuscular blockade.[47] The most common uses include:

- enhancement of mechanical ventilation
- reduction of increased intracranial pressure (ICP)
- decrease in oxygen consumption
- reduction of metabolic energy expenditures
- inducement of muscle relaxation for patients undergoing endotracheal (ET) intubation [48]

The patient may experience fear and anxiety because NMBDs paralyze the diaphragm. Therefore, sedation and supportive care must accompany neuromuscular blockade. Sedation has been identified as a priority issue by the AACN and The Joint Commission. Indications for sedation range from treatment for anxiety and agitation to abolishing asynchrony with the ventilator ("bucking" the ventilator or breathing that is not synchronous with the rate of the machine).[49]

Succinylcholine is a commonly used, ultra-short-acting neuromuscular blocking agent; others include Pavulon, Norcuron, and Tracium. The depth of paralysis desired should be delineated by the prescribing physician. Standing orders may be written to indicate the end-point desired, for example 1) no evidence of any spontaneous body movement; 2) body movement acceptable, but no evidence of spontaneous respirations; or 3) movement acceptable, no evidence of ventilatory asynchrony.[50]

Peripheral nerve stimulation monitoring is imperative in critical care patients to limit the risk of overdose with neuromuscular blocking agents and prolonged block beyond the prescribed time period. Peripheral nerve monitoring is mandatory whenever obliteration of spontaneous movement is the therapeutic goal for a patient receiving a neuromuscular blocking agent.[51] This prevents accidental administration of surplus drug beyond the smallest amount to achieve the desired outcome.[52]

The attorney may see the abbreviation TOF on medical records of patients on ventilators. Train of four (TOF) stimulation is a very simple technique for monitoring patients receiving neuromuscular blocking agents. Two small electrodes are attached to the ulnar nerve on the wrist. Using a small handheld stimulator, the nurse can activate four electrical stimuli that have the potential to produce four thumb movements. Paralyzed patients will not elicit a twitch, indicating they are not responding to the stimuli.[53]

TIP: Failure to closely monitor and manage patients with neuromuscular blocking agents can result in devastating consequences, for example, prolonged muscle weakness or paralysis, an inability to wean the patient from mechanical ventilation, or accidental extubation.

Because an awake patient must also be sedated when paralyzed with neuromuscular blocking agents, there is increased risk of ventilator incidents. The patient is incapable of communication due to the presence of the endotracheal tube in the mouth or nose. Sedated paralyzed patients are unable to move their hands to activate a call bell or signal for a nurse. They cannot verbally call for help, make any movements to reattach their breathing tubing, cough to clear their airway, or express pain and discomfort. The accidental removal of the patient from the ventilator (extubation) can result in the patient's death. These cases warrant careful evaluation of the nursing care and the measures taken to prevent this catastrophe. Respiratory therapists (RT) share responsibility with the nurse in monitoring and managing the mechanically ventilated patient. Charting by the RT is separate from nursing notes and includes forms that document the ventilator settings, maintenance of the equipment, RT visits, and other documentation (e.g., pulmonary assessment and suctioning).[54]

2. Suctioning

Maintenance of an airway is also dependent on the nurse clearing secretions from the airway. Tracheal suctioning through an endotracheal (ET) or tracheal tube is a common nursing procedure. Complications of tracheal suctioning may cause hypoxemia (decreased oxygen in the blood), cardiac dysrhythmias (irregular heartbeat), bronchospasm (closing of the airways of the lung), tracheal trauma, and infection. Obstructed airways with mucus plugs; accidental or unintentional extubation (patient withdrawing the tube, the tube being expelled due to inadequate taping, or forceful coughing causing the tube to become dislodged); and equipment failure can occur in intensive care units. Agitation and sedation may contribute to self-extubation, and restraints may not prevent unplanned extubation. Extra vigilance in turning and caring for the intubated patient is required. Awake and alert patients who self-extubate often suffer no consequences and do not require reintubation. Unplanned extubation in the awake, alert patient may not necessarily result in an adverse outcome or require reintubation, whereas the patient who is not awake and alert may suffer cardiac and or respiratory arrest, resulting in brain damage from lack of oxygen or even death. Jury verdict review and analysis-type publications are replete with examples of patients who suffered a dislodged or blocked airway, often with devastating loss of oxygen. The following case illustrates a failure to respond to a clogged tracheostomy tube:[55]

> On July 29, 1996, plaintiff Lydia Martel, a 56-year-old woman, unemployed at the time, was admitted to defendant Brooklyn Hospital Center. Brought into the emergency room for an asthma attack, she was intubated, placed on a ventilator, and given asthma medications. The plaintiff came under the care of Dr. Marlene Schwartz, a pulmonologist and critical care specialist. She was then transferred to the intensive care unit on the ventilator and was medically paralyzed and sedated because she was fighting the endotracheal tube. At 6:00 A.M. on July 31, 1996, the plaintiff suffered an episode of bradycardia and cyanosis, which was attributed to mucus plugs obstructing her airways. She responded to suctioning and the administration of 100 percent oxygen. X-rays revealed atelectasis consistent with additional mucus plugs; however, no additional care was implemented as a result of this episode. On August 1, 1996 at 8:00 A.M., the plaintiff's heart rate increased from 100 beats per minute (bpm) to 150 bpm, and although the nursing staff noted this change, a physician was not called to evaluate the plaintiff's status. At 8:38 P.M., Lydia Martel's daughter came to the ICU to visit her mother and found her purple in color and not breathing. The plaintiff's daughter called for help and a code was called for respiratory and cardiac arrest. The arrest was attributed to mucus plugs obstructing the oxygen flow to the plaintiff's lungs. Oxygen saturation levels via pulse oximeter were not documented during this time. The plaintiff was resuscitated, but she suffered anoxic encephalopathy, resulting in brain damage. She is in a persistent vegetative state. The plaintiff has exhibited no meaningful level of awareness or consciousness since the cardiac arrest. She will require constant skilled nursing care for the remainder of her life. The plaintiff claimed defendant Schwartz departed from accepted medical standards in failing to perform a bronchial lavage through a bronchoscope or by catheter on July 31, 1996, which would have loosened and removed the mucus plugs from Martel's lungs and protected her from pulmonary obstruction. The plaintiff further contended the hospital personnel failed to call for an evaluation of the patient at 8:00 A.M. on August 1, 1996, when her heart rate increased from 100 bpm to 150 bpm, a known sign of oxygen deprivation. The plaintiff claimed hospital personnel also failed to timely respond to the patient's respiratory arrest at 8:38 A.M., allowing oxygen deprivation for a prolonged period of time. The plaintiff claimed these departures were substantial factors in causing anoxic encephalopathy, brain damage, and the resultant vegetative state. The defendant hospital argued that the nursing staff acted appropriately in evaluating and suctioning the patient, that the staff responded to the respiratory and cardiac arrest in a medically correct and timely manner, and that the plaintiff's brain damage was an unavoidable complication of her severe asthma. Defendant Schwartz claimed a bronchoscopy and bronchial lavage were not indicated because the mucus plugs were located in the bronchioles and in the peripheral areas of the lungs, and were therefore not amendable to that type of treatment. Schwartz argued that even if the bronchial lavage had been performed, it would not have altered the plaintiff's course. The case subsequently settled for an undisclosed amount.[56]

3. Ventilation without intubation

Noninvasive positive pressure ventilation (NPPV) is a technique that improves gas exchange by keeping the alveoli (air sacs) open with positive pressure, typically done through a nasal mask. This technology is increasingly being used for patients with chronic obstructive pulmonary disease and sleep disorders such as sleep apnea.[57] Though ventilation without intubation decreases dependency needs compared to conventional mechanical ventilation, the critical care nurse needs to closely monitor the patient so that the mask is not removed. All patients should be connected to a pulse oximeter, and ABGs should be closely monitored for acute respiratory failure, especially during the first few hours of treatment.[58]

4. Weaning from the ventilator

Weaning patients from ventilatory support requires a multidisciplinary team approach to include the nurse, respiratory therapist, pulmonologist, and others (e.g., infection control specialist, trauma surgeon, or thoracic surgeon). The weaning process consists of trials to evaluate progress towards planned extubation. Efforts to speed up the weaning process allow for earlier discharge from the ICU. Nurses are responsible for accurately monitoring adequate oxygen saturation levels so the weaning process from a ventilator is safely accomplished and complications are avoided.[59]

Critical care nurses are responsible for maintaining emergency equipment in good working order. Hospitals maintain policies that define the contents of code carts and designate responsible parties for restocking after use and periodic maintenance checks. Some nurses check the code cart after each shift; others do it every 24 hours; and some exchange the cart with pharmacy after use, depending on the nursing unit. Many carts have a flexible or secured lock that alerts the nurse at a glance that the cart has been restocked, exchanged, or opened.[60]

TIP: In cases where policies or procedures on code cart checks may apply, plaintiff's counsel should request such policies or procedures during the discovery phase.

Correct equipment must be stocked and easily obtainable to be able to reintubate a patient in an emergency situation. Failure to adequately stock equipment may be difficult to detect when reviewing malpractice cases. Often the healthcare professionals attribute a poor outcome during a resuscitation effort to the patient's underlying medical problem.[61]

TIP: Risk managers and counsel for both sides must rely on the willingness of the healthcare professionals to come forward. These individuals are often the only ones who can volunteer information about performance or equipment issues that may have affected the success of the resuscitation.

---

5. Ventilator-associated pneumonia

Ventilator-associated pneumonia (VAP) has been recognized as a major complication occurring in patients receiving mechanical ventilation in critical care units. Research has demonstrated that VAP rates can be reduced by meticulous and consistent oral care.[62] The AACN has published best practices and the Centers for Disease Control and Prevention has developed guidelines for care. These should be incorporated in some way into the protocols for nursing care in a critical care unit. Nurses must document compliance with the evidence-based practice protocols, with the goal of reducing rates of VAP.

B. Consent

The second major liability issue to be discussed is the nurse's role in obtaining informed consent. Due to emergency admissions, where in some cases not even the individual's name is known, informed consent may not be obtained prior to emergency resuscitation or before instituting life-saving measures. In these situations when the patient is unable to give consent, or when there are no relatives or next of kin, critical care nurses are allowed to make exceptions for informed consent. In all other situations, hospital, state, and federal guidelines for informed consent for competent adults, incompetent adults, and minors must be followed. In addition, patient rights must be honored: 1) right to refuse treatment; 2) right to die; 3) right to information; 4) right to privacy; and 5) right to confidentiality.[63]

Informed consent is a legal and ethical concept that requires the physician, or other healthcare provider, to supply the patient sufficient information to make an intelligent, informed decision about a proposed treatment or procedure and the potential risks.[64] A nurse's failure to question whether the patient is receiving adequate information may be a violation of the Nurse Practice Act.[65] Consent for research, and human experimentation, and the Patient's Bill of Rights include strict guidelines to prevent misuse of human rights.[66] The standard of care requires that the nurse (a) participate as a witness in the signing of a consent form, and (b) ensure the patient is fully competent to sign. State laws, The Joint Commission standards, and the American Hospital Association Bill of Rights for Patients have included provision for ensuring the communication needs of the culturally and ethnically diverse patients are met, if they do not speak or understand English.[67] The nurse should alert the treating clinician that a signed consent form is required for a specific test or procedure, and that the signature is dated to legally comply within the given number of days or hours.[68]

A Floridian man was hospitalized in a burn unit after he sustained burns to his face and neck. The burn surgeon was informed that the critical care nurses were encountering many mucus plugs when they suctioned out his endotracheal tube. The surgeon, who planned to perform a minor surgical procedure to release tendons on the man's hands, decided to do a bronchoscopy while the patient was in the OR. Although the surgeon made this decision at 6:30 A.M. and the man's wife was at his bedside in the critical care unit, none of the medical team approached the wife to obtain consent for the bronchoscopy. The patient was taken to the operating room at 9 A.M. The operating room nurses noted the absence of consent for the bronchoscopy but did not discuss this issue with the surgical team. When the man's endotracheal tube was removed from his throat, his airway was obliterated due to internal swelling. It took several minutes to perform an emergency tracheostomy, and the delay resulted in brain damage.

The plaintiff filed a suit against the medical team in the operating room and the operating room nurses. The surgeon argued during his deposition that he did not need to obtain informed consent because the bronchoscopy was done as an emergency procedure and was so covered by the hospital's policies. He stated that even if the operating room nurse had informed him that the consent was absent, he would have done the procedure anyway. The plaintiff argued that had he known of the risks of the bronchoscopy, he would not have agreed to have the procedure done. He also maintained it was not an emergency procedure since the decision was made almost two and one-half hours before the plaintiff was taken to the OR. The critical care nurses were named in the suit. The plaintiff argued that the nurse who sent the patient to the OR from the ICU bore some responsibility to ensure that consent for the bronchoscopy was on the chart. The case was settled out of court for $700,000, with contributions from the hospital and physicians (unpublished settlement).

C. Advance Directives and Organ Procurement

Since the implementation of advance directives, the critical care nurse must be aware of the patient's wishes for a "do not resuscitate" (DNR) status and specific written orders on the chart to be followed for medical treatment or conversely for the withholding of treatment.

TIP: Failure to comply with advance directives could result in the nurse being held liable.

Advance directives should be addressed when the patient is admitted. Often on admission the critically ill patient cannot establish her desired advance directives because she is not awake, alert, or competent. If the critical care nurse suspects the patient may be incapable of making her own decisions, this issue should be brought to the physician's attention.[69] The social services representative or others should attempt to contact the family or significant others to learn of a patient's living will or legal papers regarding advance directives. Information should be placed in the chart and the physician should write orders expressing the patient's decision to prevent any miscommunication. Critical care nurses may be faced with family members who oppose the patient's directives.[70] In fact, some healthcare providers adhere to erroneous beliefs that they will be subject to a negligence or wrongful death action if they do not follow the wishes of the family.[71] Failure to adhere to the patient's decision can bring charges of battery as illustrated by the following case:

> Mr. Winter had a discussion with his physician before being admitted to the hospital and wished to be a "No Code Blue." When he suffered ventricular fibrillation, the nurse resuscitated him by shocking his heart with an electric current. The family filed suit against the hospital for "wrongful life, battery and negligence." The court held that if the patient's instructions specifically precluded the treatment given, the nurse committed a battery on the patient. The court was not prepared to recognize the "wrongful life claim." Therefore, the court of appeals affirmed the judgment of the lower court in part, reversed it in part, and remanded the case for trial.[72]

According to the United Network for Organ Sharing website (www.unos.org), over 107,000 individuals in this country desperately await replacement organs. Decisions regarding organ donation are frequently made in the critical care setting, because the majority of potential donors die here. Caring for patients in a "suspended state of being" who are potential organ donors is an integral part of ICU care. A timely organ donation process may depend on the ICU nurse working with the family and following the hospital's guidelines to keep the dying patient's organs viable while avoiding legal issues of do not resuscitate (DNR) orders and advance directives, withdrawal of care, and withholding food and fluids. The critical care nurse must be familiar with the "Uniform Anatomical Gift Act of 1968" which states in part that, "[a]ny individual of sound mind and 18 years of age or more may give all or any part of his body, with the gift to take effect upon his death." Critical care nurses are required to ask about organ donation whenever a death is imminent and the patient is a possible donor (usually a young, healthy person who suffered a sudden irreversible catastrophe). With the shortage of available organs, the continual improvement in transplantation techniques, and the long list of patients waiting for suitable organs, attorneys may find themselves in the midst of ethical and legal dilemmas surrounding issues of organ procurement.[73]

D. Pressure Ulcers

The cost of pressure ulcers, both in terms of money and human suffering, is great. The prevalence of pressure ulcers, according to some studies, is greater in critically ill patients; therefore, prevention should be a top nursing care priority. One key factor in the development of pressure ulcers appears to be the patient's poor ability to sense and respond meaningfully to pain and discomfort. A variety of additional compromising conditions add to the risk of pressure ulcer development (e.g., decreased mobility, moisture, poor nutrition, hypotension, sepsis, or low cardiac output). Early and routine assessment of risk factors and thorough skin inspection are critical for prevention and maintenance. The most common sites for pressure ulcers continue to be the sacrum or coccyx, and the heels. Preventing pressure ulcers should be a top nursing care priority because of their high prevalence in critically ill patients. Frequent repositioning and the use of positioning devices to relieve pressure are important, but these actions and devices do not relieve the critical care nurse of the responsibility for ongoing, systematic assessment of the risk for pressure ulcers and for skin inspection.[74] Please refer to Chapter 25, *Wounds*, for additional information.

E. Falls and Use of Restraints

Patient falls from bed are a source of constant concern to hospital and nursing service administrators. Between 1995 and 1998, patient falls were among the top ten sentinel events—incidents that cause or create the potential for serious patient injury or death—reported to The Joint Commission.[75]

Most hospitals have a "Fall Risk" section on the admission nursing database that requires the nurse to assess the patient's risk for falling. The patient, therefore, is evaluated at admission for risk factors.[76] These include the risk factors in Figure 4.1.

Critical care environments with 24-hour lighting, constant noise of monitoring equipment, telephones ringing, alarms going off, and code blue emergencies create sensory overload in acutely ill patients. Couple this with side effects

Age: patients over 60 may be at greater risk

History: history of transient ischemic attacks (TIAs), CVA (strokes), "dizzy spells" and past history of falling

Cognition: patient's complaint of confusion, hallucinating, sundowning, disoriented

Seizures: taking seizure medication

Visually impaired: bump into things

Hearing impaired: do not have their hearing aid

Substance abuse: elevated blood alcohol or drug levels

Motor deficits: impaired gait, use assistive devices, weak and frail

Postoperative: may be under the influence of anesthesia or medications

Postural hypotension: syncope attacks when getting out of bed or standing

Attitude: overly independent and refuse to ask for assistance, especially at night to use the bathroom or bedside commode

Figure 4.1 *Risk factors for falls*

of their illness or surgery, medications, and sleep deprivation, and patients may become agitated and confused, climbing over the side rails to get out of bed. This is sometimes called "ICU psychosis." These multiple factors place the ICU patient at risk and require greater vigilance by the critical care nurse for fall prevention. Most patient falls occur during the first week of hospitalization due to the patient's unfamiliarity with the environment.[77] The location of falls, noted in order of decreasing frequency, includes the bedside, chair, corridor, dayroom, and bathroom.[78] Time of day is critical with the highest incidence of falls in patients over the age of 75 occurring between 6:00-10:00 A.M. and 4:00-8:00 P.M.[79] Neurosurgical patients with cognitive impairment, such as head trauma or traumatic brain injury (TBI), require extra supervision as they recover and become agitated and restless. They are at risk for seizure activity and may exhibit unexpected behavior. When the skull is not intact, the soft brain tissue underneath is unprotected. Small children and those recovering from cranial surgery may be required to wear a protective head covering, such as a helmet, until the cranial bone heals.[80]

Although physical restraints used to be quite prevalent in the acute care setting, restraints have come under new scrutiny with less use of restraints based on new hospital policies. Soft wrist restraints are still commonly used to prevent self-extubation. The Joint Commission revised restraint standards for hospitals.[81] Hospital policies, procedures, and protocols must clearly address (1) preventive strategies and effective alternatives to restraint use; (2) early identification of potential harmful patient behaviors that may necessitate the use of restraints; (3) proper use of restraints; and (4) ongoing staff orientation and education. An effective restraint reduction program is built on creative, innovative substitutes for restraints, rather than merely removing the restraints and abandoning the patient to his own unassisted autonomy.[82] Nursing interventions to reduce falls focus on proper attendance with frequent observation, toileting routines involving offering patients a bedpan to prevent bladder distension, using family members or a sitter for restless or agitated patients, and not leaving the patient unattended in a risky situation (e.g., to answer the phone, another call light, or a patient alarm).

TIP: A review of the hospital policies regarding fall assessment, identification of at-risk patients, fall prevention, and restraints can determine nursing negligence. Newer technology is replacing older beds with movement sensing devices that can alert the nursing staff of a patient's attempt to exit the bed. Some institutions are requiring bed alarms on all patient beds after 7 P.M.

The following case illustrates a situation where alarms on the bed either failed to activate or were not utilized by the nursing staff:

> A 74-year-old woman was admitted for brain surgery, and was transferred to the intensive care unit for pulmonary distress, requiring continuous ventilatory support. She was ordered to have complete bed rest, oxygen, intravenous medications, a Foley catheter, and monitoring. Several days after the surgery, her family found her on the floor. No alarms were noted to be activated. The plaintiff later was discovered to have a fractured hip. The plaintiff contended her fall was caused by the failure of the hospital nurses to follow hospital safety procedures, and that the painful fracture went undiagnosed for five hours. The defendant admitted the fall precautions were not followed, but denied any causative link between the conduct of its staff and the plaintiff's injuries. The jury found the defendant to be negligent, but that the negligence was not the cause of the patient's injuries. A defense verdict was returned. *Travous Farroqu v. North-*

ridge Hospital Center, Los Angeles County, (CA) Superior Court, Case No. Lco29-237.[83]

More information on the use of fall prevention and liability issues can be found in Chapter 7, *Medical Surgical Malpractice Issues.*

F. Response to Alarms and Changes in Condition

In a busy ICU, alarms go off so frequently that nurses can become desensitized and may not race to the bedside every time an alarm sounds. The syndrome has been dubbed "alarm fatigue" and is currently under study.[84] The Joint Commission noted that 65 percent of recent sentinel events involving ventilator-related deaths were due to malfunction or misuse of an alarm, or an inadequate alarm.[85] Nurses use judgment in deciding which alarms to respond to quickly. In some cases, the nurse simply checks the monitor first, realizing that a lead may be loose, the patient is turning over in bed, or someone is with the patient and forgot to silence the alarm. Increasing the sensitivity to irregular heart rhythms presents a design trade-off between sensitivity and specificity. If the telemetry system's sensitivity to arrhythmic events is increased, that is, abnormal heart rhythms trigger an alarm, then it may possibly desensitize the critical care nurse's surveillance to all alarms.[86]

Critical care policy usually states that the patient alarms are never to be turned off. Most monitoring systems or ventilators have the capacity to temporarily silence the alarm for 15 seconds or so without terminating the system, or disconnecting the monitoring equipment. It is usually a very intricate procedure to turn off an alarm—a safety feature intentionally built into the system to help prevent casual dismissal of alarms.

TIP: When a patient is transported to and from the ICU for diagnostic studies or procedures, the monitor may not be reconnected or alarms may not be reset appropriately. Patients should be transported with a portable monitor and an ICU nurse.

The alarm parameters are the upper and lower values that trigger the alarm. For example, the order may state to set the heart rate (HR) sensor to alarm above 120 beats per minute or below 50 bpm. The Joint Commission issued in September 2004 a set of goals and requirements to improve the effectiveness of clinical alarm systems. Policies and procedures should address the alarm set-up (especially high and low limits of physiological monitoring, such as heart rate and blood pressure), and should be consistently implemented in critical care units.[87] The rule is, always look at the patient first, then the equipment for disconnections or mechanical problems, and never turn off an alarm. Some newer equipment emits different sounds for different problems, such as one tone for loose or removed leads and another for physiological changes in the patient. This helps address the complacency that nurses may develop in response to repeated non-urgent alarm triggering.

TIP: Question nurses about the practice of turning off alarms. Examine hospital policies on the use of alarms. Information that an alarm was turned off in a specific situation may be located in the incident report.

Reaction time is important in responding to an alarm. Nurses should always notify another nurse when leaving the unit or when she will be unable to immediately respond to a patient's alarm.[88] In the event of a cardiac arrest, the cardiac rhythm strips, code sheet, code team members' progress note entries, nursing notes, flow sheets, and medication administration time should all reflect the exact time the code was called and the response time of the resuscitation efforts. Discrepancies lead to suspicion and warrant close scrutiny. The use of different clocks by different personnel compounds the problem of evaluating the response time.

TIP: Standard ACLS protocols can be used to compare the patient's resuscitation records to the existing ACLS standard of care. Just as healthcare professionals can discount false alarms and fail to investigate true alarms, they also can be misled by equipment that provides a falsely reassuring pattern.[89]

This was a factor in a California case involving a 53-year-old New York man. The patient was on the Pritikin program when he suddenly collapsed. He was successfully resuscitated and rushed to Cedars Sinai Medical Center where a defibrillator was surgically implanted into his chest. Following surgery, he was placed in the intensive care unit where an experienced critical care nurse and a cardiology fellow monitored his condition. At 9:30 P.M., the patient began experiencing serious clinical changes that did not respond to treatment, although the monitoring equipment for his blood circulation indicated that his pulmonary artery occlusion pressure (PAOP) or the capillary pressure in the left atrium of the heart measured by a special catheter that wedges a tiny balloon in the most distal portion of the pulmonary artery. Cardiac output

(the volume of blood expelled by the ventricles of the heart) and cardiac index (a measure of the cardiac output of a patient per square meter of body surface) were all normal. At 11:45 P.M., the nurse phoned the cardiac surgeon, who said he would be coming to the hospital in one hour to do a lung transplant and would see the patient then. The patient had bright red blood in the drainage tubes and quickly became comatose at 12:30 A.M. The surgical code team was called. The patient's chest was opened in the ICU. A tiny hole in the aorta was discovered, and subsequently compressed, stopping the bleeding. The patient remained comatose after surgery and was soon brain dead.

The plaintiff named both the hospital and the cardiac surgeon as defendants. It was the plaintiff's position that beginning around 9:30 P.M. there was steady leakage from the defect in the aorta, culminating in the dramatic hemorrhage at 12:30 A.M. It was contended that the nurse and the cardiology fellow paid more attention to the reassuring numbers on the equipment than to the clinical appearance of the patient. The jury was out for six days after a 21-day trial. The $884,000 verdict was awarded by a vote of nine to three. Only the hospital was found liable. Interviews with jurors after the trial revealed that they accepted the proposition that the nurse and cardiac fellow were distracted from the patient's clinical deterioration by the favorable electronic monitoring data. The jury felt that something more aggressive should have been done by at least 11:30 P.M. Had adequate information been given to the cardiac surgeon at that time, he would have returned to the hospital to carry out the necessary emergency surgery.[90]

Clinical nursing judgment requires not only the collection of hemodynamic data, and an ongoing evaluation of the trends of that data, but also a comparison of these trends with early subtle changes, subjective complaints, and the patient's overall appearance. Failure to do so results in nursing the equipment, not the patient.

Equipment used in critical care settings is highly sophisticated. Delicate electronic components can be misused or fail. When a piece of equipment is associated with patient injury, consider the role of the machine, if any, in the injury sustained by the plaintiff. Invasive lines, monitoring equipment and intravenous infusion pumps have come under closer scrutiny lately, and must be equipped with safety features specific to each type of machine. Skill in using machinery correctly, and in troubleshooting, is a prerequisite to critical care nursing and is a shared responsibility with support departments. Larger hospitals employ biomedical technicians skilled in diagnosing and repairing medical equipment.

TIP: The biomedical department is responsible for using a log to document periodic checks of equipment. This information can be obtained through discovery.

Some equipment is maintained by other departments such as Central Supply. Interrogatory questions can focus on the responsibilities of various departments for equipment maintenance.

Hospitals that suspect or prove a patient has been injured by a piece of equipment are required to report this to the Food and Drug Administration (FDA) under the provisions of the Safe Medical Devices Act of 1990. The Safe Medical Devices Act requires hospitals, nursing homes, ambulatory surgery centers, and outpatient treatment centers to report information that reasonably suggests a device has or may have caused or contributed to the death, reportable illness, or reportable injury of a patient of the facility. A reportable illness or injury:

- is life threatening,
- results in permanent or serious impairment of a body function or permanent or serious change to a body structure, or
- necessitates medical or surgical intervention to preclude permanent or serious impairment of a body function or permanent or serious damage to a body structure.[91]

G. Nursing Research

Another area of potential liability for critical care nurses involves using patients for medical or nursing research. Critical care research standards are designed to protect the patient and to eliminate any possible abuse. Critical care nurses should be well informed of all research being conducted on their patient population. Human subjects must give informed consent. Nurses and doctors are responsible for conducting research in strict adherence with the study guidelines approved by the research department and human rights committee or institutional review board (IRB). Nurses involved with a research protocol must complete the Human Subjects Certification Program offered by the federal government and institutions involved with funded research. Nurses asked to administer drugs should only do so after knowing the legal implications of such an act. Experimental drugs are those not fully approved by the FDA. Before administering experimental drugs the critical care nurse should:

1. know the drug's approval status,
2. be assured by the physician that proper informed consent has been obtained,
3. be assured by the principal investigator (PI) that the study has been approved, and
4. know that the subject has been provided the mandated requirements from the IRB.

Research and ethics committees are responsible for the approval and supervision of institutional medical research.[92]

TIP: Policies and procedures on the performance of research on patients can be obtained from the hospital. The American Hospital Association Patient Bill of Rights should be used as evidence of the consent for research.

4.7 Trends that Influence the Liability of Critical Care Nurses
A. Aging of America

America is changing from a nation of youth to a nation of grandparents, as evidenced by the rapid increase in numbers of the old and very old (those over age 85). It has been estimated that although the elderly comprise only 12 percent of the U.S. population, they use approximately one-third of U.S. healthcare dollars and up to 20 percent of ICU daily costs.[93] The twenty-first century continues to demand a cadre of critical care nurses to care for this aging population, and the need is ever growing.

B. Increased Reliance on Computers

As discussed in Chapter 7, *Nursing Documentation,* in Volume I, computers are increasingly being used to document the delivery of nursing care. Most critical care technology incorporates computer technology, such as dysrhythmia detection, infusion pumps, and pulse oximetry. Bedside and handheld computers in a variety of forms automatically document and store data such as continuous blood pressure, temperature, pulse, respirations, intake, output, intracranial pressures, and other patient parameters directly from the bedside to monitors at the nurses station. Documentation from the handheld computers at the bedside is downloaded every two hours, building a paperless chart. Information about the patient is immediately available to all healthcare providers by the click of a computer mouse, and available for access anywhere in the hospital. Computer programs assist clinicians in decision-making based on immediate analysis of the data.

Fewer errors occur as the same computer information can be automatically accessed and acted upon by all departments instantly. Poor handwriting by healthcare providers will be a problem of the past when computerized documentation is fully implemented. Through modems, physicians may view critical care data from their offices or living rooms. Critical care nurses must continue to update their computer literacy skills to collaborate with other healthcare providers and improve their practices. Virtual reality will allow critical care nurses to acquire new skills and to practice with new equipment without actually involving a real patient.

C. Nursing in the Telemedicine Setting

Telemedicine is becoming a viable alternative for the delivery of critical care in understaffed units.[94] Remote access to experts greatly expands the capability of critical care units. Telemedicine has long been a component of medicine, but until recently it was confined to niche areas. Defined as information-sharing between at least two physically and geographically disparate sites for educational or health purposes, some form of telemedicine has been used in the past.[95] Given the current shortage of intensivists, and physicians specially trained and certified in critical care medicine, telemedicine provides patients with consultation by intensivists who may be off-site and involved with the care of several patients concurrently. A team of intensivists can monitor more than 150 patients at several locations simultaneously. Known as enhanced ICU (eICU), the hundred-plus hospitals involved are using technology developed by a Baltimore-based company. Video cameras allow patient visualization, and computers transmit medical records, x-rays, monitoring information, and lab results to the offsite intensivist. Newer technology even allows the intensivist to use robotic arms to perform a physical examination. Aside from the inherent problems involved in using computer technology, eICUs, or virtual ICUs as they are also known, can provide an extra set of eyes to monitor patients. One important legal implication of this technology is the assignment of responsibility for monitoring the patient among those on- and off-site. Meticulous documentation is still a necessity, but computer technology may be playing a much greater role in accomplishing the task. A backup system to compile documentation during system downtime must be built into any computerized application.

D. Use of Unlicensed Assistive Personnel

Critical care nurses can expect to take on expanded roles while delegating more nonclinical support tasks, and using unlicensed assistive personnel (UAP) for patient care. The critical care nurse must delegate effectively with the increased use of UAPs. Certain institutional and critical care requirements should be established before UAPs are incorporated into the critical care setting. Responsibility for patient care does not diminish by delegation, but rather becomes a shared responsibility.

The AACN recommends the critical care nurse assess the individual patient and the task before delegating.[96] For additional information on this topic, see Chapter 7, *Medical Surgical Malpractice Issues,* in this Volume, and Chapter 8, *Inside the Healthcare Environment*, in Volume I.

E. Managed Care

Managed care controls which patients get an ICU bed. Pre-approved diagnostic tests, treatments, and medications complete the plan of care in a managed care environment. Managed care impacts critical care in an attempt to maximize cost-effectiveness, decrease length of stay, and promote early discharge. Managed care depends on a planned approach to hospital care that includes the critical care units and is outcome oriented in a specific time frame. Utilizing the collaborative model, case management is usually coordinated by a registered nurse who assumes primary responsibility and accountability for the patient management. Collaboration with critical care nurses reinforces adherence to the expected patient goals during the critical care aspect of hospitalization. Daily follow-up of patients in the ICU or CCU by an assigned nurse case manager determines any variances from the established plan. The case manager independently, or with collaboration, analyzes the case to determine whether physiologic variances of the patient, failure of the provider, or the managed system of care contributed to an unexpected outcome.[97]

TIP: A critical care case manager may document on the medical record. Look for the name of a nurse followed by the abbreviation CM (case manager). Information about variances from the plan of care may be considered privileged.

F. ICU Occupancy

As ICUs have proliferated, their charges have risen to 20 percent of total hospital charges. Ideally, only patients who benefit from ICU care should receive it. In the present climate, the lack of data identifying who most benefits from critical care prevents physicians from allocating resources on a selective basis. One study found that surgical ICU patients with a length of stay greater than ten days have a high mortality rate and consume a major part of resources. Those patients with a length of stay longer than 30 days had minimal functional recovery.[98] Stricter criteria for ICU admission may be based on findings such as these. The criteria for admission to a critical care unit may become so restrictive that borderline patients, who in the past were admitted and recovered, may in the future be denied access to these hospital resources.[99]

TIP: Attorneys should carefully evaluate these criteria when acutely ill plaintiffs have not been treated in the ICU or when ICU admission was not granted.

G. Cost Containment in ICU

Cost constraints affect decisions on the acquisition of everything from new technology to staffing and unit-based lab testing. The family, which has been relegated to spending most of the time in waiting rooms, will become part of the care team, learning how to manage the patient for whom they will be responsible in the home in only a few days after ICU discharge.[100] The current trend towards earlier patient discharge has already shifted the care burden from the ICU to home care agencies and the family.

Federal legislation and regulation may create a regionalized system of Critical Care Centers of Excellence to provide high-quality patient care in an efficient and cost-effective manner. These future changes will have profound ethical and legal ramifications. The existing laws, standards of care, Nurse Practice Acts, and the way we think about critical care nursing are changing. To do no harm in caring for patients with life-threatening illnesses will be a greater challenge in the future than ever imagined. Progress and plans for the future of critical care must incorporate built-in measures that eliminate or limit litigious actions.[101]

H. Admission and Discharge to the Critical Care Unit

As beds become more difficult to obtain in critical care units, strict guidelines must be enforced for admission and discharge to critical care units. Availability of staff and beds are the two most limiting factors. When a critically ill patient cannot be admitted to a critical care unit due to a shortage of beds or staff, the patient may be held in the emergency department or postanesthesia care unit until a bed becomes available. The patient must receive the same intensive level of care as would be provided in the ICU. The unit's medical director makes the final admission/discharge decision. The nurse's documentation and opinions carry weight during the process of assigning beds. Bed rounds are usually performed each day to allow for discussion between the medical director and charge nurse to decide who is to be transferred and who is to be admitted. The following scenarios give rise to patient care dilemmas:

- a shortage of critical care nurses that will affect patient safety and violate nurse-patient ratios,
- a limited number of available beds,
- reductions or unit closing due to financial constraints,
- an unexpected influx of patients from natural or human-caused disasters, or
- the inappropriate use of critical care for terminally ill or hospice patients.[102]

Administrative policies provide written guidelines for admission and discharge that protect the patient from an untimely or unsafe discharge. Alternative arrangements should be in place for emergencies, that is, the use of postanesthesia care units (recovery room) or an on-call staff. Inappropriate discharge to a non-acute nursing unit not equipped to manage the patient is a dangerous alternative. The following criteria are examples of how one hospital defined the requirements to be admitted or discharged from a neurological intensive care unit.[103]

Admission criteria for a neurological intensive care unit (NICU):

1. Prospective patients needing assessment at least every two hours; patients may be admitted directly from the operating room.
2. Patients needing neurologic assessment more frequently than every two hours.
3. Patients with uncontrolled seizures requiring assessment at least every hour.
4. Patients needing monitoring or treatment unavailable in general care areas (EEG, invasive monitoring, drug infusion, mechanical ventilation, and so on).
5. Overflow from intensive care areas; these patients may not always have neurologic diseases—if not, we try to accept more stable patients.[104]

Discharge criteria from this NICU to a general floor include:

- There is no neurologic change for 24 hours; seizures are controlled with medicine; metabolic homeostasis is present; intravascular volume is adequate; there is no life-threatening arrhythmia or hemodynamic instability; respiratory status is stable; and assessments are required every four hours or more frequently. If the patient is not a candidate for the general nursing floor or ward, different criteria are used for transfer to an intermediate or step-down nursing unit as listed below:

- There is no life-threatening arrhythmia or hemodynamic instability; respiratory status is
stable but requires ventilatory support or frequent respiratory treatment; intracranial monitoring is discontinued.[105]

The practice of "pulling" or "floating" a non-critical
care nurse to an intensive care unit is also fraught with problems. The inexperienced nurse who is unable to use the essential equipment jeopardizes the patient and hospital.

TIP: A critically ill patient should receive the same level
of care, whether it is provided by a critical care nurse or
a closely supervised non-critical care nurse.

Many units manage this concern by assigning an experienced critical care nurse to oversee the non-critical care
nurse and to take responsibility for the observations that require critical care training. Often facilities will train a core
group of nurses so they will have the skills to work in critical care units as needed.[106]

4.8 Screening Critical Care Cases

The patient's medical records in critical care document the
minute-to-minute or hour-to-hour patient observations and
interventions by the critical care nurse. Documentation enables the physician and other members of the treating team
to evaluate and plan the patient's care. The chart serves as the
means of communication to ensure continuity of care among
the caregivers. This is particularly important in critical care
where the number of specialists, interns, residents, and attending physicians is typically higher than for other units.[107]

There is great variability in critical care charting, ranging from the nurse recording almost everything about the
patient, known as narrative charting, to recording by exception, where only abnormal findings are documented. The
American Association of Critical Care Nurses states that
documentation should:

1. be accurate (use factual observations),
2. be timely (notations and events must be timed),
3. reflect patient status and unusual events,
4. reflect omission of care and rationale,
5. reflect that physician was informed of unusual/
   adverse situations, and nature of physician's response,
6. be legible,
7. reflect method of patient admission, his/her condition on admission, discharge planning, and condition on discharge, and

8. reflect use of the nursing process on a continuing
   basis throughout the hospitalization.[108]

The lack of standardization concerning vital information to be collected is an important risk management and
quality assurance issue in critical care units across the country. Even within units, opinions differ as to what information
should be collected. Flow sheets with areas for checking off
items or providing a brief entry have streamlined nursing
documentation in critical care units. All nursing personnel
are expected to know and follow the guidelines for correctly
completing the flow sheets. Logically, request for production should include a copy of all institutional policies related
to documentation in the critical care setting.

When reviewing flow sheets, the attorney should be
aware that commonly these documents consist of several
pages linked together as one unit. There may not be a place
for the date and time on each page, posing special challenges
to the copying services and medical records departments. It
is wise to request to see the original document to reconstruct
accurate dates and times of documentation.

TIP: One of the easiest ways to see if a page has been
omitted when a critical care flow sheet was copied is
to remove the flow sheet section from the medical records package and to study the order of the pages. Each
flow sheet page may not necessarily be dated. Therefore,
once the pattern is detected, missing pages will be evident.

The attorney may encounter a variety of terms, which
describe the severity of the patient's condition. The Acute
Physiologic and Chronic Health Evaluation (APACHE) system is unique to critical care. An abbreviated form known
as APACHE II was originally developed after research by
Knaus and colleagues.[109] The system is easy to use and incorporates the admission score or the worst score for each
parameter over 24 hours as the documented patient score.
For trauma patients, the Glasgow Coma Scale (GCS), along
with the Trauma Severity Index, are commonly used to assess the integrity of the nervous system following head injuries. The Trauma Severity Index is discussed in more detail
in Chapter 17, *Emergency Nursing Malpractice.*

Proximate cause can be difficult to prove when a patient
is critically ill. The patient's underlying medical problems,
except in obvious cases of nursing malpractice, may have
more to do with a bad outcome than nursing actions or inactions. For example, consider an older diabetic patient who
smokes two packs of cigarettes a day, is grossly overweight,
is non-compliant with anti-hypertensive medications and

insulin, and leads a sedentary lifestyle. This individual consumes alcohol on a daily basis and fails to keep scheduled clinic appointments. When he blames the healthcare team for a poor response following hospitalization for a cerebrovascular accident (CVA), the attorney must consider contributory negligence.[110]

The question of damages must be addressed as attorneys are increasingly faced with plaintiffs who were critically ill elderly patients at the time of the alleged malpractice. The factors that boost economic damages, such as lost wages and dependents, are missing in the elderly population. It is easy for families to attribute an unexpected poor outcome to the medical problems of the elderly patient. When healthcare professionals are forthcoming about a medical mishap that injured a patient, the family of an elderly patient may be less likely to bring suit than if the injured patient were younger and healthier.[111] Please refer to Chapter 5, *Medical Errors: Roots of Litigation*, in Volume I, for more on this topic.

The collegial relationship between doctors and nurses in critical care units tends to promote mutual respect. This frequently results in physicians responding quickly when critical care nurses contact them about a change in the patient's condition. Unlike many medical surgical nursing units visited once a day by the patient's physician, the patients in critical care units are often seen by several physicians during 24 hours. Thus the nursing expert witness retained to defend a critical care nurse may argue that the physicians were aware of significant changes in the patient's status. However, reporting important changes to a resident, for example, and allowing a patient's condition to deteriorate over time without insisting the resident contact the attending physician, is below the standard of care. In a teaching hospital, with medical students and residents, critical care nurses have a duty to the patient that requires going through the designated steps that guarantee physician notification.[112]

4.9 Summary

With the growing demand for critical care beds, downsizing of hospital staff, and cost-containment of expensive critical care nursing, there exists a need for legal and ethical decision making regarding patients' lengths of stay, admission and discharge criteria, purchasing and use of technology, nurse-patient ratio, use of unlicensed assistive personnel, safety and environmental standards, and physician coverage. Each of these issues has the potential to create litigious outcomes.[113]

Critical care nurses who do not provide nursing care according to doctors' orders, their hospital policy and procedures, or prevailing national standards should be held accountable for their actions. Although unjustified lawsuits are occasionally filed, poor nursing care that causes serious injury and death constitutes nursing malpractice. While critical care nurses face terrific challenges in the twenty-first century, such as ever-changing technology, sicker patients, more patients, while supervising lesser-trained, unlicensed workers, the focus must still be on basic nursing care principles.

Life often teeters on the fragile edge in the ICU, making it easier to blame death or long-term injury on a nursing or medical action occurring in that setting. It is important for the legal team to carefully evaluate all of the information in the medical record, previous medical records, office visits, accident reports, and any other information before pursuing litigation. This evaluation, because it is very technical, is best achieved by a nurse.

Endnotes

1. Lynaugh, J. et al., *Critical Care Nursing: A History.* Philadelphia: University of Pennsylvania Press, 1998.

2. Hyman, S. A., V. Williams, and R. J. Maciunas, "Neurosurgical Intensive Care Unit Organization and Function," *Journal of Neurosurgical Anesthesia* 5, no. 2 (1993): 71–80.

3. Sole, M. L., D. G. Klein, and M. J. Moseley, *Introduction to Critical Care Nursing.* Fifth edition. Philadelphia: W. B. Saunders Co., 2008.

4. American Association of Critical-Care Nurses, *Scope and Practice for Nursing Care of the Critically Ill Patient and Family.* Aliso Viejo, California: AACN, 1997.

5. Urden, L. D., K. M. Stacy, and M. E. Lough, *Thelan's Critical Care Nursing: Diagnosis and Management.* Sixth edition. St. Louis: Mosby, 2009.

6. See note 3.

7. See note 2.

8. Kirchhoff, K. and N. Dahl, "American Association of Critical Care Nurses' National Survey of Facilities and Units Providing Critical Care," *American Journal of Critical Care* 15, no. 1 (2006): 13–27.

9. Knaus, W. A., E. A. Draper, and D. P. Wagner et al., "An Evaluation of Outcome From Intensive Care in Major Medical Centers," *Annals of Internal Medicine* (1986): 410–418.

10. Baggs, J. G. and M. Schmitt, "ICU nurse-physician collaboration: Working together," *Society of Critical Care Medicine, 24th Educational and Scientific Symposium,* San Francisco, January 31–February 4, 1995.

11. Barker, E., "Critical Care Malpractice Issues," in *Nursing Malpractice*, ed. P. Iyer. Tucson, Arizona: Lawyers and Judges Publishing Co., 1996.

12. Rosenthal, G., D. Harper, and L. Quinn et al., "Severity-adjusted Mortality and Length of Stay in Teaching and Non-teaching Hospitals," *JAMA* 276 (1996): 322.

13. *Id.*

14. Springhouse. *Nurses' Legal Handbook*. Fifth edition, 2004.

15. *Id.*

16. *Id.*

17. See note 11.

18. See note 14.

19. Laska, L. (ed.), "Woman Bleeds to Death from Retroperitoneal Hemorrhage Following Angiogram," *Medical Malpractice Verdicts, Settlements and Experts* (September 2003): 17.

20. See note 11.

21. *Id.*

22. *Id.*

23. *Id.*

24. *Id.*

25. *Id.*

26. *Id.*

27. *Id.*

28. Dorman, T., P. Angood, D. Angus, and T. Clemmer et al., "Guidelines for Critical Care Medical Training and Continuing Medical Education," *Critical Care Medicine*, 32, no. 1 (2004): 263–272.

29. *Id.*

30. www.JointCommission.org/accreditd+organizatioons/ ambulatory+care/sentinel+events/set+ventilators/, Accessed 6/24/10.

31. Meyer, R., Wang, S., Li, X., Thomsom, D., and L. O'Brien-Pallas, "Evaluation of a Patient Care Delivery Model: Patient Outcomes in Acute Cardiac Care," *Journal of Nursing Scholarship* 41, no. 4 (2009): 399-410.

32. *Id.*

33. Feutz-Harter, S., "Standards of Care and Staffing," *Nursing and the Law*, Sixth edition, 63–73, 1997.

34. Moniz, D. M., "Too Few Staff, Too Much Risk," *RN* 61, no. 12 (1998): 63.

35. See note 11.

36. American Association of Critical-Care Nurses, *Mission, Vision and Values. Policy Statement*. Aliso Viejo, California: AACN, 2002.

37. See note 11.

38. *Id.*

39. www.aacn.org, Accessed 3/13/10.

40. See note 11.

41. *Id.*

42. *Id.*

43. *Id.*

44. Pasero, C., "Reversing Respiratory Depression with Naloxone," *American Journal of Nursing* 100, no. 2 (2000): 26.

45. Dickman, M., "ABG's As Easy As 1, 2, 3," *Advance for Respiratory Care Practitioners* (May 6, 2002): 24–25.

46. See note 11.

47. Jaber, S., Jung, B., Corne, P., et al. "An Intervention to Decrease Complications Related to Endotracheal Intubation in the Intensive Care Unit: A Prospective, Multiple-Center Study," *Intensive Care Medicine* (2010) 36:248-255.

48. See note 11.

49. *Id.*

50. *Id.*

51. *Id.*

52. Herbstreit, F., Peters, J., Eikermann, M., "Impaired Upper Airway Integrity by Residual Neuromuscular Blockade," *Anesthesiology* 110, no. 6 (2009): 1255-1260.

53. See note 11.

54. See note 47.

55. See note 11.

56. Laska, L. (ed.), "Failure to Appropriately Treat Status Asthmaticus—Failure to Respond to Respiratory Arrest—Anoxic Brain Damage Resulting in Permanent Vegetative State," *Medical Malpractice Verdicts, Settlements & Experts* (March 2003): 17.

57. Maggiore, S., Richard, J., Abroug, F., Diehl, J., et al. "A Multicenter, Randomized Trial of Noninvasive Ventilation with Helium-Oxygen Mixture in Exacerbations of Chronic Obstructive Lung Disease," *Critical Care Medicine* 38, no. 1 (2010): 145-151.

58. Ferreira, J., Chipman, D., Hill, N., Kacmarek, R., Bilevel vs ICU Ventilators Providing Noninvasive Ventilation: Effect of System Leaks," *Chest* 136, no. 2 (2009): 308-318.

59. See note 11.

60. *Id.*

61. *Id.*

62. Feider, L., Mitchell, P., Bridges, E., "Oral Care Practices for Orally Intubated Critically Ill Adults," *American Journal of Critical Care* 19, no. 2. (2010): 175-183.

63. See note 11.

64. Patton, M., "The Standards for Disclosure of Risk in Informed Consent," *Journal of Legal Nurse Consulting* 11, no. 1 (2000): 17–19.

65. *Id.*

66. Polit, D. and C. Beck, *Essentials of Nursing Research.* 7th ed. Philadelphia: Lippincott, Williams and Wilkins, 2009.

67. Springhouse. *Nurses' Legal Handbook.* Fifth edition, 2004.

68. See note 11.

69. Kirsch, N., "The Multidisciplinary Team: End-of-Life Ethical Decisions," *Topics in Geriatric Rehabilitation* 25, no. 4. (2009): 292-306.

70. Meehan, K., "Advance Directives: The Clinical Nurse Specialist as a Change Agent," *Clinical Nurse Specialist* 23, no. 5. (2009): 258-264.

71. *Id.*

72. *Id.*

73. *Id.*

74. Kaitani, T, Tokunaga, K., Matsui, N., Sanada, H., "Risk Factors Related to the Development of Pressure Ulcers in the Critical Care Setting," *Journal of Clinical Nursing* 19, (2010): 414-421.

75. www.JointCommission.org/NR/rdonlyres/67297896-4EI6-4BB7-BFOF-5DA4A87B02F2101SC_STATS--trends.year.pdf. Accessed 6/24/2010.

76. See note 11.

77. Capezuti, E., Wagner, L., Brush, B., et al., "Consequences of an Intervention to Reduce Restrictive Side Rail Use in Nursing Homes," *Journal of the American Geriatric Society* 55, no. 1 (2007): 334–341.

78. *Id.*

79. Keefe, S., "Fall Prevention," *Advance for Nurses* (April 4, 2005): 40–41.

80. See note 11.

81. See note 75.

82. Wilson, E., "Physical Restraint of Elderly Patients in Critical Care," *Critical Care Nursing Clinics of North America* 8, no. 1 (1996): 61–70.

83. Laska, L. (ed.), "Woman Suffers Broken Hip After Bed Alarms Either Failed to Activate or Were Not Used," *Medical Malpractice Verdicts, Settlements & Experts* (June 1998).

84. Graham, K. and Cvach, M., "Monitor Alarm Fatigue: Standardizing Use of Physiological Monitors and Decreasing Nuisance Alarms," *American Journal of Critical Care* 19, no. 1 (2010): 28–34.

85. *Id.*

86. See note 11.

87. *Id.*

88. *Id.*

89. Feutz, S., "Misleading Instruments Lead to Verdict Against Hospital," *Journal of Nursing Law* 1, no. 4 (1994): 50–52.

90. See note 11.

91. See note 5.

92. See note 66.

93. McGuire, A. and V. Serra, "The Cost of Care," *International Health* 27, no. 1 (2005): 45–46.

94. www.aacnboldvoicesonline.org Tele-ICUs Offer Potential to Improve Patient Care. Accessed 6/24/10.

95. Lilly, C., Thomas, E., "Tele-ICU: Experience to Date," *Journal of Intensive Care Medicine* 25 no. 1 (2010): 16–22.

96. Bittner, N. and Gravlin, G., "Critical Thinking, Delegation, and Missed Care in Nursing Practice," *Journal of Nursing Administration* 39, no. 3 (2009): 142-146.

97. See note 11.

98. Iwashyna, T., Kramer, A., Kahn, J., "Intensive Care Unit Occupancy and Patient Outcomes," *Critical Care Medicine* 37 no. 5 (2009): 1545-1557 .

99. See note 11.

100. *Id.*

101. *Id.*

102. *Id.*

103. *Id.*

104. *Id.*

105. See note 4.

106. See note 11.

107. *Id.*

108. Alspach, J.G. (ed.), *Core Curriculum for Critical Care Nursing*. Fourth edition. Philadelphia: W. B. Saunders, 2006.

109. Knaus, W. A., E. A. Draper, and D. P. Wagner et al. "APACHE II: A Severity of Disease Classification System," *Critical Care Medicine* 13, no. 6 (1985): 818–29.

110. See note 11.

111. *Id.*

112. *Id.*

113. *Id.*

Additional Reading

Heart and Lung: The Journal of Acute and Critical Care. http://journals.elsevierhealth.com/home

Chapter 5

Perioperative Nursing Malpractice Issues

Jo Ann Pietro, JD, RN and Dianna McCorkle, BSN, RN, CNOR

Synopsis
5.1 Introduction
5.2 Perioperative Standard of Care
5.3 Perioperative Roles and Responsibilities
    A. The Circulating Nurse
    B. The Registered Nurse First Assistant (RNFA)
    C. Scrub Nurse or Technician
    D. Surgical Counts
    E. Handoff
5.4 Legal Theories
    A. Historical Development of Perioperative Legal Theories
    B. Specific Legal Theories
        1. The captain of the ship doctrine
        2. Borrowed servant doctrine
        3. Vicarious liability
        4. Res ipsa loquitur
        5. Informed consent
        6. Abandonment
5.5 Nursing Errors
    A. Retained Foreign Objects
    B. Sentinel Events: Wrong Site Surgery, Medication Errors, and
       Surgical Fires
    C. Medication Errors
    D. Injury From Equipment
        1. Overview
        2. Burns
            a. Thermal burns
            b. Chemical burns
            c. Surgical fires
    E. Handoff Communication
    F. Chain of Command
5.6 Postanesthesia Care Unit Liability Issues
    A. Overview
    B. Sources of Injury
        1. Lack of oxygen
        2. Nerve damage from restraints or bandages
        3. Cardiac dysrhythmias
    C. Handoff
5.7 Ambulatory Surgery
    A. Preoperative Instructions
    B. Preoperative Assessment
    C. Patient Monitoring
    D. Medication Errors
    E. Discharge Planning and Criteria
    F. Falls
    G. Follow-Up Telephone Calls
5.8 Screening the Perioperative Case
5.9 Risk Management Hints
5.10 Summary

Endnotes
Additional Reading
Table of Cases
Appendices

5.1 Introduction

In the years since the prior edition of this book, perioperative nursing has continued to evolve in its professional role, further establishing the unique nature of this nursing specialty. Perioperative nurses can now be found working in hospital surgical suites, free-standing same day surgery centers, endoscopy suites, radiology centers, as well as physician-based office practices.

Perioperative nurses function in a highly collaborative environment interfacing with healthcare professionals, such as the surgeon, radiologist, anesthesiologist, nurse anesthetist, physician assistants, Registered Nurse First Assistants (RNFA), and many others. The stereotypical idea of the Operating Room Nurse as a nurse limited to caring for a patient within the confines of the operating room has greatly shifted into a more dynamic, involved process. Today, caring for the surgical patient can take place with a preoperative interview either by telephone or direct interview, or in the physician's office, patient care unit, or preoperative holding area. The process of caring for the patient continues during the intraoperative phase until the completion of surgery. Perioperative nursing care continues through the recovery phases in the postanesthesia care unit (PACU), patient care units (in a hospital), physician offices, patient discharge units, patient's home, and both telephone and written patient questionnaires and surveys.

This chapter clearly outlines perioperative malpractice to include incidents that occur in a hospital operating room, a same day surgery center or in a recovery room. As perioperative nursing expands into newer venues, so does perioperative malpractice. The historical background and landmark cases involving perioperative malpractice provide an excellent foundation and wealth of information for legal professionals.

All perioperative settings are engulfed in similar sights and sounds. The operating room is staffed with specially trained technicians, nurses, and doctors. The surgical team wears scrubs, shoe coverings, paper hats, gloves, and disposable face masks. The day-to-day surgical environment can range from very noisy to extreme quiet depending on the surgical procedures performed. The constant recirculated cool air, the high level of hygiene, the tension austere, even severe furnishings, the intense organization, the need to account for all equipment and supplies, the increase of technology and equipment, and restricted access are common to all perioperative facilities. Foreign to the general nursing population, these are the familiar work surroundings for the perioperative nurse. While the attorney can never expect to feel as comfortable in this setting as does the nurse, the information in this chapter provides insights for attorneys in evaluating the conduct of these specialized nurses.

TIP: Attorneys who evaluate perioperative malpractice claims must be sensitive to the everyday atmosphere in which perioperative nurses work. This knowledge can be used when deposing or interviewing defendants.

The definition of perioperative nursing is "the practice of nursing directed toward patients undergoing operative or other invasive procedures."[1] A perioperative nurse is defined as "the registered nurse who, using the nursing process, develops a plan of nursing care and then coordinates and delivers care to patients undergoing operative or other invasive procedures."[2] Refer to Figure 5.1 for an overview of the perioperative roles.

5.2 Perioperative Standard of Care

The Association of Operating Room Nurses (AORN) is the professional organization representing approximately 41,000 perioperative nurses in the United States and abroad. The Association was formed between 1949 and 1954 in New York City by a group of OR Nursing supervisors. Today, AORN is recognized as the principal organization for perioperative nurses. Yearly, AORN issues its *Standards, Recommended Practices and Guidelines*, which serves to guide the perioperative nurse caring for the surgical patient.

Circulating nurses: nurses in the operating room who remain outside the sterile field. This nurse provides necessary equipment and medications to the surgeon, scrub nurse, and anesthesiologist. The nurse is backup support to the operating room team. According to TJC standards, the circulating nurse must be a registered nurse.

Scrub nurses: nurses in the operating room who remain in the sterile field. The nurse hands equipment and medications to the surgeon. This individual may be a registered nurse, licensed practical nurse, or a scrub technician.

Registered Nurse First Assistant (RNFA): perioperative nurses who through specialized training work in collaboration with the surgeon and healthcare team members. The RNFA functions as a full assistant to the surgeon and does not work as a scrub nurse.

Recovery room nurses or post anesthesia care nurses: nurses in the recovery room. These nurses care for the patient in the immediate postoperative phase by monitoring and evaluating patients until they are fully reactive. Most of the nurses are registered nurses. A few licensed practical nurses may also be used in PACU.

Same day surgery nurses: nurses who function in a same day surgery unit. They may care for the patient before, during, and after surgery.

Unlicensed Assistive Personnel: personnel who function in the operating room in various job assignments. Some UAPs assist in direct patient care activities depending upon the level of education and training and demonstrated competency. Examples of this position held in the operating room can include: operating room technician (ORT), anesthesia technician, orderly, or aide.

Figure 5.1 Perioperative Nursing Practice Roles

To determine whether nursing malpractice has occurred, the attorney must first understand the requisite nursing standards of care. The perioperative nurse is not held to a higher standard of care, notwithstanding the greater acuity level in these settings. Because surgical patients are medicated, anesthetized, or recovering from anesthesia, they are more vulnerable and consequently depend more on the nurse to safeguard them than do other patients. Anesthetized patients are unable to alert the nurse if they are experiencing difficulty. In addition, the sophisticated equipment and drugs used during surgery, such as drills, saws, cautery and laparoscopic equipment, anesthesia gases, and possible toxic drugs, present greater opportunities for injury. This combination of factors makes the perioperative setting particularly dangerous, requiring the use of additional precautions to protect patients.

Even in this setting of heightened danger, the perioperative nurse is still held to the standard of care required of the reasonably prudent nurse acting in similar circumstances. The comparison to the reasonably prudent nurse may appear to place an increased burden on the perioperative nurse. However, this perception is incorrect. For example, if a new surgical procedure is being performed, the circumstances dictate the employment of more safeguards than in a routine surgery. Standards of care for the perioperative nurse can be found in the source materials shown in Figure 5.2.

1. The American Nurses Association—www.ana.org
2. The Association of Operating Room Nurses—www.aorn.org
3. The American Society of PeriAnesthesia Nurses—www.aspan.org
4. Individual State Board of Nursing (i.e., Nurse Practice Act)—www.njsana.org/practice/npa
5. The Joint Commission—www.jointcommission.org
6. Federal and State statutes
7. www.findlaw.com
8. State Department of health rules and regulations which affect hospital standards
9. Current nursing literature
10. Current generally accepted nursing practices in perioperative settings

Figure 5.2 Sources of the Standard of Care with Website Addresses for Perioperative Nursing

TIP: The legal standard mandates nothing more than an evaluation of the nurse's conduct against how a reasonably prudent nurse would have acted in similar circumstances.

5.3 Perioperative Roles and Responsibilities

The perioperative nurse's duties begin when the patient enters the operating room holding area and end when the patient and the patient's care are transferred to the PACU nurse. If an operating room nurse is responsible for patient recovery, the responsibility ends when the patient is discharged from the PACU. Once the patient is in the holding area prior to surgery, the operating room nurse must first assess that all the preoperative requirements have been met. These include:

- Checking proper identification of the patient
- Verifying the surgical procedure and surgical site as applicable
- Locating a signed, dated, witnessed consent form in the patient's chart from the patient, or guardian if a minor
- Reviewing the chart to determine whether the patient has received the prescribed preoperative tests (blood, electrocardiogram [EKG], chest x-ray, and so on)
- Reviewing the chart to determine whether the patient underwent a timely preoperative clearance physical
- Administrating any preoperative medications

An essential nursing responsibility is to ascertain if the patient is wearing an identification band and the correct information regarding the intended surgery is documented properly in the chart. In rare, but sometimes catastrophic, situations the wrong patient has been taken into the operating room and subjected to surgery intended for another patient. Proper identification of the patient is paramount. It is also mandatory that laboratory blood work-up be performed; however, if it was not obtained or if the values are abnormal, the nurse must bring this to the physician's attention.

Before transporting the patient to the operating room, the nurse ensures the necessary equipment and medications are available to proceed with the intended surgical procedure. The nurse should be sure to document any equipment checks, if performed. Surgeons' preference cards list and detail the operating surgeon's specific needs. This card is utilized by the nurse to prepare for surgery. Preference cards are updated routinely to reflect the changing needs and requirements of the surgeon. Once the operating room nurse has ensured the room and personnel are present and ready, the next responsibility is to provide safe transportation within the operating room suite by using side rails and stretcher straps (if equipped). The patient is safely transferred to the operating room bed and is properly positioned for surgery. At this time and prior to beginning surgery, a "time out" verification is performed in the operating room. Time out verification is part of a three-tiered approach developed by The Joint Commission in 2003. Time out verification has been refined and enhanced over the years. It continues to be a Joint Commission mandate. This verification is the final process of a three-part approach as delineated in The Joint Commission Universal Protocol for Preventing Wrong Site, Wrong Procedure, Wrong Person Surgery. The protocol specifically addresses the implementation of a pre-procedure verification, the identification by marking the surgical site, and a time out prior to beginning surgery to validate all elements of the preoperative phase.

All members of the surgical team involved in providing direct patient care must ensure they are about to perform surgery on the correct patient, identify the correct surgery, correct the surgical site as applicable (right and left distinction), and confirm the correct level, as in spinal surgery or multiple surgeries on the same limb such as fingers or toes. The members of the surgical team include the anesthesiologist, anesthesia residents or a certified registered nurse anesthetist, surgeon, surgical resident, RNFA (Registered Nurse First Assistant) working with a surgeon, the circulating nurse, and scrub technician or scrub nurse. Any conflicts or discrepancies during the time out must be resolved prior to commencing anesthesia.

TIP: It is the shared responsibility of all surgical team members to participate in the performance of the time out verification. A designated member of the surgical team shall initiate the time out verification. Documentation should reflect that a time out has been performed.

A. The Circulating Nurse

The operating room nurse remains with the patient during the induction phase of anesthesia to assist the anesthesiologist or nurse anesthetist as required. When the surgery begins and throughout the course of surgery, the circulating nurse monitors the patient, charts the administration of medication, and observes the patient's response to the medication and procedure. The circulating nurse is responsible for various activities and as such remains unsterile so that he can be free to move about the operating room while surgery is in progress. If additional supplies are required, the circulator is able to procure and deliver such supplies to the scrub technician or nurse working within the sterile field. The circulating nurse and the anesthesiologist work together to provide safe patient care throughout the surgical experience. The circulating nurse remains available to the anesthesia provider for any assistance she may require during surgery.

B. The Registered Nurse First Assistant (RNFA)

The RNFA works with the surgeon in the performance of surgical patient care. Some of the functions of the RNFA may include performing preoperative patient evaluation, collaborating with other healthcare members regarding the patient's plan of care, and writing preoperative orders. In the operating room, the RNFA functions as the first assistant, similar in scope of duties of a first assistant surgeon, which include handling or cutting tissues, using medical devices, providing exposure for the surgeon, and providing hemostasis (minimizing blood loss through the use of cautery equipment and suturing). Postoperatively, the RNFA may write postoperative orders or operative notes according to established hospital protocol. The RNFA may participate on postoperative rounds and assist with patient discharge planning. When an Operating Room Nurse has pursued the necessary education to become a RNFA, specific liability issues arise. To avoid liability, a hospital that utilizes RNFAs must in conjunction with hospital legal counsel review the state's Nurse Practice Act for guidance on the use of RNFAs. Hospitals should establish policies for RNFAs based on the state's Nurse Practice Act as well as guidelines of professional organizations such as the AORN. Policies should clearly delineate the knowledge and skills as well as a credentialing process for RNFAs. The hospital should review its surgical consent to include the use of RNFAs. Refer to the individual state Nurse Practice Act when researching the scope of responsibility of the RNFA as well as state statutes, regulations, and hospital policies and guidelines.

C. Scrub Nurse or Technician

It is the scrub nurse or technician's duty to assist the surgeon by providing the correct surgical instruments or medication when requested. The scrub nurse or scrub technician is often referred to as working in the "sterile field." The scrub role requires the nurse or technician to perform a surgical scrub, and don a surgical gown and sterile gloves over the surgical attire worn in the operating room. In that sterile field immediately surrounding the patient are sterile supplies, instruments, and sterile drapes that isolate only the part of the body to have the intended surgery. It is the responsibility of the scrub person to assist the surgeon or surgical team within that sterile field as well as maintain a sterile field working collaboratively with the circulating nurse.

D. Surgical Counts

One of the most important duties in the operating room is the performance of surgical counts. Surgical counts include but are not limited to an accounting of surgical instrumentation, sharps (scalpels, needles), laparotomy pads, x-ray detectable sponges, and miscellaneous items. Surgical counts are initiated by the scrub technician or nurse and circulating nurse before a surgical procedure commences. The purpose of the initial count is to establish a baseline accounting of all instruments, sharps, sponges, and miscellaneous items prior to commencing a surgical procedure. Counts continue throughout the surgical procedure as items are added to the surgical field to replenish supplies such as laparotomy sponges, sutures, and so on. Reflecting the collaborative atmosphere in the operating room, surgical counts are then performed:

- before closure of a cavity within a cavity (e.g., a cesarean section would require an incision into the uterus)
- before wound closure commences
- at skin closure or end of the procedure
- at a time of permanent relief assignment of either the scrub technician or the circulating nurse

At the time of closure of a surgical procedure, the call for the surgical count can be initiated by the surgeon, the circulating nurse or scrub technician. It is important the individual assigned to the scrub role is aware of the number of sponges in use at all times. Having an accurate accounting facilitates a smooth count at the end of surgery and at the time of relief. Counts are performed by the circulating nurse and scrub technician or nurse together. There are many accountable items used in the course of a surgical procedure that must be visually and audibly accounted for prior to the close of a surgical procedure. The accounting of these items is documented on a count sheet, which may or may not be part of the perioperative nurses record. The operating surgeon also visually inspects and removes with his or her hand any sponges or other items to ensure these items have not been left in the patient as the surgical counts begin. The surgeon then commences closure as the closing count progresses. Once the initial closing count has been established as correct, the surgeon is verbally advised of the correct count by the circulating nurse. The surgeon continues with wound closure. In the event of an incorrect count, the surgeon is immediately notified by the circulating nurse. The

wound closure should stop until all efforts have been made to find and account for the missing item. If the item cannot be located, an x-ray should be taken to locate needles, metal instruments, or sponges that have a radio-opaque thread or strip.

During the normal course of a work day in the operating room, the relief of the circulating nurses and scrub technicians occurs routinely for a break, lunch relief, or a shift change. When a circulating nurse or scrub technician or nurse is assigned for a break or lunch relief, a surgical count is performed. The name of relief personnel and outgoing staff is documented on the perioperative record. The time of the relief should reflect both incoming and outgoing nursing staff.

Technical aids are available to assist the operating room team in the effort to prevent the retention of sponges, gauze towels, and laparotomy pads. These include the use of radio frequency (RF) detectable sponge systems, radio frequency identification (RFID) detectable sponge systems, and barcoded sponge systems.[3] All of these aids augment the manual count; however, they do not replace it. The RF detection system can detect a sponge that is embedded with an RF tag that is somewhere inside a body cavity. A wand or an antenna is utilized to detect the embedded sponge. The RFID and the RF systems operate in similar manners. Both systems aid in the early identification of a retained sponge.[4,5] These technologies can prevent the need for an additional surgery and eliminate or reduce the need for an intra-operative x-ray to detect a missing sponge. Another available detection system is that of bar-coding of sponges. This technology came on the scene in early 2006 and has detected more counting discrepancies involving sponges than the traditional counting method.[6] However, bar-coding will not detect misplaced or retained sponges, and scanning a cavity for a bar-coded labeled sponge that is covered in blood has proved to be difficult.[7] The counting process is one that is dependent on human performance in a complex medical environment. The retained foreign object risk can be reduced by a multifaceted and multidisciplined approach which mandates strict adherence to standardized counting process, consistent and methodical wound exploration before closing, attention to human factors contributing to error, and the use of available assistive technology.

TIP: Each institution has policies and procedures outlining the performance of surgical counts. These policies may be found in the operating room policy and procedure manuals. Policy and procedure for an incorrect count should also be outlined in the operating room policy and procedure manual.

E. Handoff

Once the surgery is completed, and the anesthesia provider has determined the patient has met the criteria for transfer, the patient is safely transported via stretcher from the operating room, accompanied by the anesthesia provider and the circulating nurse, to the recovery room. A handoff report is given to the PACU nurse by the circulating nurse as well as the anesthesiologist. At this time any pertinent information regarding the patient's physiological status, the surgical procedure performed, and any other information is reported to the PACU nurse. After the handoff report is given, the PACU nurse assumes the responsibility for patient care. The PACU nurse must assess the patient in the immediate postoperative phase until fully conscious. This nurse also monitors the patient's airway and evaluates hemodynamic stability. Finally, it is the PACU nurse who provides instructions when the patient is discharged to home, such as occurs in same day surgery units.

5.4 Legal Theories

Time-honored legal concepts are applicable in perioperative malpractice cases, particularly theories of vicarious liability, including the captain of the ship doctrine, the borrowed servant doctrine, and respondeat superior. The theory of *res ipsa loquitur* is also often applicable. If one of these legal theories is not applicable because of the particular facts of the case, the general standard for determining malpractice is employed: duty, breach of duty, proximate cause, and damages. The legal theories of informed consent and abandonment sometimes come into play in perioperative nurse malpractice cases. These legal theories and their effects on nursing malpractice are explained in Section 5.4.B.

A. Historical Development of Perioperative Legal Theories

The legal responsibility to provide safe and appropriate care to a patient is not new. As early as 400 B.C. the Code of Hammurabi provided the following law: "If a physician make a large incision with the operating knife, and kill him, or open a tumor with the operating knife, and cut out the eye, his hands shall be cut off."[8] Today's plaintiffs and their attorneys are interested in monetary awards if a surgical error occurs.

For a substantial period of time in the adjudication of medical malpractice, nurses were not named as defendants because the law did not acknowledge their role as healthcare providers. Nurses were perceived as the handmaidens or servants of the physicians, not as independent practitioners. The law was limited to deciding whether the hospital or the doctor would be held liable for errors made by nurses. This judicial approach created a significant impediment to the recognition of nursing as an independent profession. Hospitals were also shielded from liability under the concept of charitable immunity, which was rooted in the historical fact that hospitals were originally established to provide care for the poor. Accordingly, the courts often sought to shift responsibility to the physicians because the injured patients would have no source from which to recover for their injuries. Hospitals were protected by their immunity.

With the advent of health insurance and governmental reimbursement for health services in the 1950s, hospitals were transformed into business entities. It was slowly recognized that hospitals no longer required protection from lawsuits. There were no longer valid reasons to treat hospitals differently from any other business. The hospital, as employer, is responsible for the negligent acts of its employees. Our courts began to denounce charitable immunity as a defense that prevented recovery for damages caused by the malpractice of hospital employees. See *Darling v. Charleston Community Memorial Hospital*, 33 Ill. 2d 326, 211 N.E.2d 253, 14 A.L.R. 869 (1965), cert. denied, 383 U.S. 946 (1966); *Flagiello v. Pennsylvania Hospital*, 417 Pa. 486, 208 A.2d 193 (1965); *Helms v. Williams*, 166 S.E.2d 852 (N.C. 1969). (Cases cited in this chapter are listed in the table of cases at the end of the chapter.) Many hospitals still enjoy the protection of charitable immunity in that hospitals have a cap or dollar limit which the plaintiff can recover in a malpractice case. In 1972, health care shifted ever so slightly in the patient's favor with the advent of the Patient's Bill of Rights, which sets forth basic entitlements regarding care and treatment.

TIP: While total immunity is no longer prevalent, in some states the healthcare entity still has some statutory protection.

Often there is a statutory limit placed on liability. These limits or caps currently range from $20,000 to $250,000. (See the Massachusetts statute M.G.L.A. 231 and the New Jersey Statute N.J.S.A. 2A:53A-8.) If the entity has immunity or a cap on its liability, the plaintiff may circumvent it by suing an individual nurse employee. Once an employee is sued, the cap still remains for the entity. However, the employer's insurance for the employee becomes available, which is not subject to a statutory limit. Accordingly, nurses represent an alternate source of recovery.

TIP: Before suing a healthcare entity, be it a hospital or same day surgery center often owned by a hospital, the plaintiff's attorney must research the jurisdiction's laws on immunity.

The shifts in the healthcare industry have brought changes for the registered nurse. The nurse's independent professional role has been established. With ever increasing frequency, nurses are being named as individual defendants in malpractice suits. Professional autonomy has brought accountability for any negligence committed and has also brought financial accountability and the need for malpractice insurance. Nurses are worthy defendants because their insurance policies are available to compensate the injured patient. The prudent registered nurse is one who purchases her own malpractice insurance.

TIP: Nursing is now recognized by law as a profession with its own legally imposed standards of care and personal liability.

B. Specific Legal Theories

This subsection of the chapter defines the legal theories used in nursing malpractice cases. The origins of each theory are traced and illustrated with case law. Theories to be discussed include:

- Captain of the ship
- Borrowed servant
- Vicarious liability
- *Res ipsa loquitur*
- Informed consent
- Abandonment

1. The captain of the ship doctrine

The captain of the ship doctrine imputes liability to the surgeon for the negligent acts of others. The rationale is that the surgeon is in charge of the operating room team just as a captain is in charge of the ship. The surgeon directs and controls the other perioperative healthcare providers. In applying the doctrine, it must be determined if the healthcare provider was a servant of the surgeon in the sense that this provider was subject to the surgeon's control.

TIP: The legal elements that comprise control are: (1) the surgeon directs the manner in which the specific task is to be performed; and (2) the task is performed in furtherance of the surgeon's business.

As nursing and medicine have evolved, each of the healthcare providers present in the perioperative setting has acquired professional autonomy and hence responsibility for certain defined duties. Providers are held to the individual standards of care of their particular professions. As a result of these developments, the captain of the ship doctrine appears to be falling into disuse. It is used in only a few states. Usually it is applied when there is an overlap of responsibility between the surgeon and the nurse. The nurse may actually perform negligently, but it is the surgeon's responsibility to check that this act was properly performed. The courts will impute liability to the surgeon on the basis that the surgeon cannot abdicate this responsibility.

The seminal case on the captain of the ship doctrine was *McConnell v. Williams*, 361 Pa. 355, 65 A.2d 243 (1949), in which malpractice occurred during a surgical procedure. The surgeon was deemed captain of the ship and held vicariously liable for the nurse's and the anesthesiologist's acts of negligence. The doctrine has flourished in Pennsylvania. Not only have the Pennsylvania courts found surgeons responsible for the actions of the operating room nurse and the anesthesiologist, but they have also deemed them responsible for the negligent actions of residents, nurse anesthetists, interns, and hospital blood bank employees.

In *Yorston v. Pennell,* 153 A.2d 255 (Pa. 1969), the surgeon was held liable for the negligent act of a surgical resident in performing surgery along with a junior intern and a nurse anesthetist. The case involved a failure to communicate knowledge of the patient's allergy to penicillin. Liability was imputed to the surgeon because the surgeon had the choice to perform the surgery but instead delegated it to a resident. The resident became the agent of the surgeon. Thus, the surgeon could not avoid the duty owed to his patient.

In *Rockwell v. Stone*, 404 Pa. 561, 173 A.2d 48 (1961), the chief surgeon was found liable for the negligence of an anesthesiologist who administered an injection at the surgeon's direct order. The court determined that the issue of agency was one for the jury to decide. If the jury found that an agency relationship existed, the surgeon was to be held liable under the doctrine of respondeat superior.

In the case of *Mazer v. Lipshcutz*, 327 F.2d 43 (3d Cir. 1964), a gall bladder surgical patient was given the wrong blood, resulting in the patient's death. Although the surgeon was not involved in the selection of the incorrect blood, the case was remanded by the circuit court with instruction for a new trial on the liability of the surgeon under the captain of the ship doctrine.

TIP: As healthcare services and technology have expanded over time, so has the autonomy of individual healthcare providers whose roles have become more precisely defined with specialization. Recognizing these factors, not all jurisdictions give credence to the captain of the ship doctrine in the perioperative setting.

In contrast to the cases cited above, in 1977, the Texas Supreme Court decided *Sparger v. Worley Hospital, Inc.*, 547 S.W.2d 582 (Tex. 1977). In this case, the court criticized and refused to apply the captain of the ship doctrine. Suit was brought by a patient for injuries sustained as a result of a retained foreign body. In rejecting the captain of the ship doctrine, the court noted that the mere presence of the surgeon in the operating room was insufficient to impute the negligence of others to him. The court in *Sparger* held that liability for the negligent acts of hospital employees would be imposed on the surgeons only if: (1) the surgeon was directing their actions instead of the hospital, under the borrowed servant doctrine; (2) the surgeon had authorized other healthcare providers to perform an act in his stead, as his agent under respondeat superior; or (3) the other providers were actively the surgeon's employees.

Even after the precise analysis set forth in *Sparger*, the captain of the ship doctrine has continued to be applied in certain jurisdictions. The Pennsylvania courts were undeterred in using the doctrine. In 1978, a surgeon was held liable for the death of a patient caused by the anesthesiologist because the surgeon had the authority to countermand the anesthesiologist's actions. *Schneider v. Albert Einstein Medical Center*, 390 A.2d 1271 (Pa. 1978). The doctrine was recognized but not applied in *Adams v. Leindholdt*, 579 P.2d 618 (Colo. 1978) when hospital operating room personnel caused injury to a patient's extremity. Massachusetts has also embraced the doctrine. A Massachusetts court has held that a surgeon is liable for the negligence of those assisting under his direction or control. *Regula v. Bettigole*, 425 N.E.2d 768 (Mass. App. 1981). Although the doctrine is still in use, it is applied in a limited number of jurisdictions. The viability of this doctrine is dubious, at best, in today's healthcare system. Each perioperative healthcare provider is considered a professional with responsibility and hence accountability for specified tasks and individual actions.

2. Borrowed servant doctrine

The borrowed servant doctrine is another legal theory that imputes the negligence of one healthcare provider to another. The courts have used this doctrine to impute the negligence of the nurse to the surgeon through the fictional creation of an employer and employee relationship. This doctrine is based on the reasoning that the employer (surgeon) has used the person's services and has exercised complete control and supervision over the person during this situation.

TIP: A borrowed servant is a person actually employed by one employer, but for a limited time or purpose this person is considered to be the employee of another employer.

The operating room nurses and technicians are the employees of the hospital, but have often been found to be the borrowed servants of the surgeon during an operation. If the surgeon exercises sufficient control over the operating room staff, the doctrine of borrowed servant may apply. The surgeon becomes vicariously liable for the nurse's or technician's conduct as her servant who has been borrowed from the hospital for the period of the operation when this servant was under the surgeon's complete control and supervision.

This doctrine has been applied in varied situations but it is most often used in surgical malpractice cases. Sometimes the nurse is found to be the employee of both the hospital and the surgeon, depending on the extent to which the surgeon has exercised control over the nurse and has thereby supplanted the hospital as the nurse's employer.

In other cases, the nurse's negligent act has been considered administrative in nature (e.g., see *Benedict v. Bondi*, below). When this occurs the nurse's actions are the sole responsibility of the hospital and the nurse is not the borrowed servant of the surgeon. In other situations, the nurse's actions are considered to be solely within the nurse's professional responsibility and here the doctrine is similarly not applied. Some states do not recognize the borrowed servant doctrine at all. Attorneys should research the laws of the state in which they practice to determine whether this doctrine applies and, if so, in what situations.

Benedict v. Bondi, 122, A.2d 209 (Pa. 1956) is an example of when a distinction was made between the nurse's administrative functions, for which the nurse was not considered the borrowed servant of the surgeon, and the nurse's functions during the operation as a servant. The court reasoned that the nurse is the employee of only the hospital when performing such administrative acts as placing clean sheets on the operating table, preparing gowns, gloves, and sterile drapes, sterilizing instruments for the operation, ensuring the instruments are properly positioned for availability during the operation, and positioning the patient on the operating table.

Conversely, if the nurse performs acts at the direction of the surgeon, the nurse becomes the surgeon's borrowed servant. In *Benedict*, the court found that the nurse's incorrect placement of a hot water bottle while the patient was on the operating room table was a medical duty for which the nurse was the borrowed servant of the surgeon. The cases that distinguish between administrative and medical functions are discussed in more detail in Section 5.4.B.3, *Vicarious liability*.

The economics of bringing a lawsuit against a hospital have influenced the naming of defendants. Case law in some states has determined the surgeon and the hospital are joint employers of nurses. In the past, hospitals generally had a charitable immunity from liability, or the dollar amount of recovery against the hospital was limited. These providers generally have overlapping and joint duties and responsibilities in the perioperative setting.

Until recently, nurses had limited malpractice insurance through the hospital and little if any personal malpractice insurance. Accordingly, if the jury found negligence and the injuries were extensive, the plaintiff would have no deep pocket from which to be compensated. To rectify this injustice the courts fashioned the borrowed servant doctrine to extend liability to the surgeon.

TIP: The borrowed servant doctrine applies when the surgeon had direction and control over the nurse who committed the negligent act.

The difficulty the courts have had with the borrowed servant doctrine relates to identifying those situations in which the surgeon had sufficient direction and control to justify imputing liability to the doctor for the nurse's negligent act. For example, simply because a surgeon orders the nurse, who is a hospital employee, to administer a certain medication does not necessarily make the surgeon liable for the nurse's negligent administration of that medication. *Miller v. Hood*, 536 S.W.2d 278 (Tex. 1976). Similarly, in *Sesselman v. Muhlenberg Hospital*, 124 N.J. Super. 285, 306 A.2d 474 (1973), the patient was injured as a result of the negligent administration of anesthesia by a certified registered nurse anesthetist. The court found that the nurse anesthetist was not an agent of the surgeon simply because she received instructions from him. The key to understanding these cases appears to be that the physician did not directly supervise the nurse's actual administration of the medication or anesthesia and the nurse had her own professional responsibility to perform these acts correctly.

However, in other cases this same analysis was equally applicable and yet the surgeon was found responsible for the nurse's actions under the borrowed servant theory. In *Willinger v. Catholic Medical Center of Southwestern Penn.*, 362 A.2d 280 (Pa. Sup. Ct. 1976), a certified nurse anesthetist administered an overdose of anesthesia while the surgeon was out of the operating room. The surgeon was still held responsible under this theory, although the captain of the ship theory is probably a more rational justification for this result.

Similarly, in *Pecks v. Charles B. Towns Hospital*, 275 App. Div. 302, 89 N.Y.2d 190 (1949), a physician was held liable for the nurse's error in administering the wrong blood to a patient. The court held that this task was medical in nature and that the nurse was acting on behalf of the surgeon. The rationale underlying this decision is that once the nurse is as-

signed by the hospital to assist the surgeon, the nurse is then under the surgeon's supervision during the operation. Consequently, the surgeon was responsible for all the nurse's actions, even though he was not personally watching or directing them when the nurse committed the negligent act. *Synnott v. Midway Hospital*, 287 Minn. 270, 178 N.W.2d 211 (1970).

Another example of this analysis is a case that involved a surgeon who ordered the operating room nurse to remove rings from laparotomy pads but did not supervise the actual removal. The surgeon was still held responsible under the borrowed servant theory. *Martin v. Perth Amboy General Hospital*, 104 N.J. Super. 333, 250 A.2d 40 (1969). The nurse's negligence was imputed to the surgeon because the nurse was acting as his agent, as his borrowed servant from the hospital. In a sense, she was removing the rings instead of the surgeon doing it himself. Here again the captain of the ship theory would be equally applicable to achieve the same result.

TIP: In some situations the nurse is held to be a joint servant or employee of both the surgeon and the hospital.

Sometimes a nurse may act simultaneously under the supervision of the surgeon and under the hospital's accepted procedures. In *City of Somerset v. Hart*, 549 S.W.2d 814 (Ky. 1977), a scalpel blade was left in a patient but, under the hospital's policy, it was the operating room staff's job to count the blades. The court found the nurse to be a joint servant of the surgeon and the hospital. These conflicting decisions can be reconciled by considering that there are three different theories of responsibility being put forth. Various courts have come to different conclusions as to which theory should be given predominance. See Figure 5.3.

---

1. The nurse has a professional responsibility to correctly perform a nursing or medical task, without direct supervision by the surgeon, once the nurse has been ordered to carry out such a task by the surgeon.
2. The surgeon is responsible for the actions of the entire surgical team because of supervisory authority over all of them.
3. The hospital also has overall responsibility for the actions of its staff in the regular performance of their duties, particularly when these duties are performed in accordance with the hospital's policies and procedures.

Figure 5.3 Three Theories of Responsibility Under the Borrowed Servant Doctrine

The standard of care for nursing has become more precisely defined with the development of professional practice parameters for nurses and, as a result, the borrowed servant doctrine is declining in use. At the present time, most often the nurse is held responsible for negligence under professional standards. The hospital is held liable under the theory of respondeat superior, as the nurse's employer. The surgeon is no longer being found to be a nurse's employer.

3. Vicarious liability

Before addressing the subject of vicarious liability, certain words having legal significance must be understood. The law provides that when a principal confers such authority, she also must assume the liability for any improper acts by her agent that occur in the course of the agent's exercise of the authority conferred. This liability, which is imputed to the principal for acts of her agent, is generally known as vicarious liability. The type of vicarious liability prevalent in the perioperative setting is known as respondeat superior in that the "superior," that is, the employer hospital or physician, is responsible for the actions of subordinate employees. (Other forms of such liability are discussed in subsequent sections.)

TIP: When one person authorizes another to act or speak on his behalf or to represent his interests, the person granting this authority is known as the principal and the person receiving it is the agent.

Under respondeat superior in the employment setting of a hospital, the employer is liable for negligent acts of the employee committed during the course of employment. By comparison, the physician is most often an independent contractor, except for an intern, resident, or house physician directly engaged by the hospital. Hospitals have different legal responsibilities for the improper acts of physicians, as independent contractors. However, this subject is beyond the scope of this treatise.

TIP: Although nurses are independent practitioners, with individual liability and responsibility, they are almost always employees.

Hospitals are deemed responsible for the negligent actions of their nurse employees in general, including when they are functioning in the perioperative setting. Examples include imposing liability on the hospital when the nurse improperly positions a patient, uses monitors or cautery equipment, assesses a patient's condition, administers medication, or counts instruments. Therefore, whenever the perioperative nurse is an employee of the hospital, the hospital is also held liable for any negligent acts by the nurse under the theory of respondeat superior.

In *Leonard v. Watsonville Community Hospital,* 47 Cal.2d 509, 305 P.2d 36 (1956), a Kelly clamp was left inside the plaintiff's abdomen. The patient sued the hospital, the surgeon, and the operating room nurses. The trial court dismissed the nurses and the hospital from the case. The plaintiff won on appeal by demonstrating that the Kelly clamp was provided by the hospital, that it was the nurse's job to hand the instrument to the surgeon, and that the hospital had no policy for counting the instruments used in surgery but had one for counting sponges and needles. Similarly, in *Koepel v. St. Joseph Hospital and Medical Center,* 8 Mich. App. 609, 155 N.W.2d 199, rev'd on other grounds, 381 Mich. 440, 163 N.W.2d 222 (1968), it was determined that the defendant hospital was liable for the negligent act of its operating room nurse, who had improperly restrained the plaintiff's arm.

In some situations the hospital is not held vicariously liable for its nurse employees. In this situation, the surgeon is held liable under the doctrine of respondeat superior because the operating room personnel are under the surgeon's complete control and supervision. Even though the operating room personnel are still employees of the hospital, they are deemed to have been borrowed by the surgeon because they were operating under her direct and specific control and supervision while the surgery was ongoing.

TIP: When nurses in the operating room are under the direct supervision of the surgeon and their negligent acts are due to direct orders from the surgeon, the hospital may not be held liable for the nurses' actions.

The law of vicarious liability in the operating room has undergone significant changes over the last 40 years. Before 1957, the courts focused on whether the negligent acts of the nurse were "administrative" or "medical" in nature. If they were the former, the hospital was responsible as the principal under respondeat superior. If they were the latter, the surgeon was responsible under the same theory. In *Schloendorff,* the nurse prepared the patient for surgery. The court ruled that she was acting at the direction of the surgeon, not the hospital, because she was performing a medical function related to the surgery. In this case, the surgeon removed an organ without proper consent. The surgeon, not the hospital, was held responsible for the nurse's negligence. *Schloendorff v. Society of New York Hospital,* 211 N.Y. 25, 103 N.E. 92 (1914).

TIP: Basing liability on whether the conduct was "administrative" or "medical" is known as the *Schloendorff* rule.

In subsequent years, problems arose with the *Schloendorff* rule in that it often caused unfair results. For example, a nurse was found to be negligent in placing hot water bottles on a patient after surgery and after the surgeon had left the operating room. Moreover, the surgeon had not ordered application of the bottles. After the patient sustained burns, the surgeon was held responsible for the nurse's negligence because her actions were considered "medical" and hence under the surgeon's supervision rather than "administrative" in nature under the hospital's control. *McGuinn v. Knickenbocker Hospital*, 89 N.Y.S. 2d 32, aff'd 276 App. Div. 1079, 97 N.Y.S. 2d 186, aff'd 302 N.Y. 633, 97 N.E.2d 760 (1949).

In another situation when the surgeon was not present, the nurse's improper action of administering blood to the wrong patient was deemed to be an administrative act, thereby rendering the hospital responsible. The decision was based on the rationale that the nurse had negligently performed the administrative act of reading the hospital's documentation on which patient to transfuse. *Necolayff v. Genesee Hospital*, 296 N.Y. 936; 73 N.E.2d 117 (1947). Giving a transfusion is clearly a medical act. This case is an example of the inconsistent decisions reached when applying the *Schloendorff* rule.

Finally, in 1957, the law changed with the decision in *Bing v. Thunig*, 2 N.Y.2d 656 (1957). In this case the nurses applied Zephiran, a flammable alcohol-based antiseptic, to a patient's back. Some of the antiseptic spilled onto the bed linens but the nurses did not change the linens. Subsequently the surgeon arrived. Not knowing that the bed linen was soiled with Zephiran, he applied an electric cautery to the patient who was then burned when the linen caught fire. In deciding whether the hospital or the surgeon would be held responsible for the nurses' negligence, the court stated that it would not apply the medical-versus-administrative analysis of *Schloendorff*. Instead, the court applied the principle of respondeat superior. The court focused its analysis on the question of under whose direction and control the nurses were working at the time of their negligence. Since the surgeon was not present at that time and had not given an order for the application of Zephiran, the court concluded that the hospital was responsible. The *Bing* decision was a turning point in judicial thinking about medical malpractice. After *Bing*, the focus of the courts' analysis on whether a function was medical or administrative began to diminish. These changes have continued through today. As a result, the legal analysis used in *Bing* to determine which providers are culpable has become the predominate approach.

TIP: Although some states continue to apply the *Schloendorff* rule, the Bing court instantly recognized and discussed the changes in the healthcare industry that necessitated new legal thinking about which healthcare providers should be held responsible for a particular act of malpractice.

The court also acknowledged that under the law, as it then existed, surgeons were often saddled with culpability, not because of any fair application of the administrative-versus-medical analysis, but rather because of a hospital's charitable immunity. Such immunity often left the injured patient without any compensation for an injury if the hospital, instead of the surgeon, was found responsible for the negligence of the operating room staff. Hence, the surgeon was often held responsible even when the negligence was really not of the surgeon's doing, in that the surgeon neither personally performed the negligent act nor directed another member of the surgical team to perform a task.

By 1957, hospitals were no longer functioning solely for the purpose of providing charity care, but were operating as private businesses. Thus, there was no reason to continue shielding them from liability. It was no longer appropriate to fictionally create an employer/employee relationship between the surgeon and the nurse when the nurse's terms and conditions of employment were within the hospital's total control. For all of these reasons the *Bing* court applied the theory of respondeat superior to determine whether the surgeon or the hospital, in addition to the nurse, should be held responsible for the nurse's malpractice.

TIP: Respondeat superior is the prominent theory employed by the courts for determining whether a surgeon or hospital is responsible for the perioperative nurse's negligence.

4. Res ipsa loquitur

The theory of *res ipsa loquitur*, or "the thing speaks for itself," is commonly used in perioperative malpractice cases where the facts so obviously bespeak of negligence that an expert witness is not necessary to establish what occurred. Moreover, the plaintiff only needs to demonstrate injury and does not need to prove a specific omission or standard of care. Examples of when this theory is used are shown in Figure 5.4. All of these factual scenarios lend themselves to the use of this theory.

- Retention of a foreign body such as a sponge
- A fall off a stretcher
- A patient injured from an object that falls off a cabinet
- Burns from an anesthesia fire or from faulty equipment

Figure 5.4 *Examples of Res Ipsa Loquitur*

1. The injury is such that it does not ordinarily occur in the absence of negligence.
2. The instrumentality that caused the plaintiff's injury was under the exclusive control of the defendant.
3. The plaintiff did not contribute to the injury.

Figure 5.5 *Elements which Establish Res Ipsa Loquitur*

TIP: If the court agrees with the plaintiff's attorney that res ipsa loquitur is applicable, then not only does the plaintiff not need an expert witness to establish that malpractice has occurred, but the burden of proof also shifts to the defendant to prove that the standard of care was not breached.

The elements shown in Figure 5.5 must exist for *res ipsa loquitur* to be applicable. These elements can easily be established in any of the factual scenarios described above. The theory of *res ipsa loquitur* has existed for centuries in our legal system. The enormous changes in health care over the last several decades have had a significant effect on the development of new legal theories of malpractice. This has resulted in the abandonment of other theories that simply no longer work because of these changes. One exception is *res ipsa loquitur*. It is today as relevant to certain claims of perioperative malpractice as it was 50 years ago.

A classic example of a res ipsa case involves a retained sponge. A sponge is not left in a patient after surgery unless the scrub nurse or the circulating nurse failed to correctly count them and the surgeon failed to properly check the surgical site before it was closed. The instrumentality that caused the injury, the sponge, is clearly in the control of the operating room personnel and the surgeon. The anesthetized patient obviously could not have contributed to the injury. United States courts are replete with such cases. The plaintiff prevails at trial or is paid a settlement in the overwhelming majority of the cases. In *McQuilla v. Maryview Medical Center, Anonymous Vascular Surgeon,* Portsmouth (Va) Circuit Court, Case No. CL03-2441,[7] the plaintiff underwent an aorto-bifemoral bypass graft surgery during which the defendant surgeon and circulating nurse failed to account for a surgical towel used to pack the bowel. Six months later, the patient's stomach became distended. After an x-ray revealed a mass, exploratory surgery was performed and the towel was removed. The hospital denied responsibility and argued it was the doctor's responsibility. The doctor claimed he shared responsibility with the nurses. According to published accounts, the jury returned a verdict in favor of the plaintiff for $1.2 million. Of particular note in this case was the surgical towel. A surgical towel, or commonly referred to as a huck towel, is often used to protect the abdominal walls when using large abdominal retractors. These towels are not x-ray detectable; nevertheless, the surgical team (surgeon, circulating nurse, and scrub nurse or technician) has the responsibility to account for these towels if they are used in the abdominal cavity.

In cases where the defendant nurses prevail, a sound and sufficient medical rationale is necessary to defeat plaintiff's claim. In *Paterson v. Good Samaritan Hospital and William Tesauro, M.D., Nassau County (New York) Supreme Court, Index No. 8944/95,* the plaintiff underwent an emergency cesarean section because of placenta accreta and severe bleeding. It was determined that a laparotomy pad and ring had been left inside her and were subsequently removed during a second surgery the same day as her cesarean section. Plaintiff claimed damages which consisted of digestive problems and pain. The nurses averred that they had alerted the surgeon to the potential of a missing pad and ring. Dr. Tesauro countered that it was his opinion that the plaintiff was about to exsanguinate and it was more important to control her bleeding than to search for the missing pad. This lawsuit went to trial. The hospital and the nurses were dismissed at the end of plaintiff's case and the jury returned a no cause in favor of the surgeon.

Ybarra v. Spangard, 146 P.2d 982, aff'd 154 P.2d 687 (CA 1944), was the first malpractice case in which this theory of law was successfully employed. The plaintiff underwent an appendectomy but sustained a pressure injury of his right arm. The plaintiff was not able to identify the specific act or the particular defendant that had caused his injury. The defendant nurses, surgeons, and anesthesiologist argued that *res ipsa loquitur* could not be applied when there were several defendants, when a division of responsibility as to the cause of injury was not established, when the injury could be from separate acts of one or more persons, or when there were several instrumentalities that could have been the offending agent.

The court refused to accept the defendants' arguments and ruled it was unreasonable to require an unconscious plaintiff to identify any one person or instrumentality that caused his injury. The court stated: "Where a plaintiff received unusual injuries while unconscious and in the course of medical treatment, all those defendants who had any control over his body or the instrumentalities which might have caused the injuries may properly be called upon to meet the inference of negligence by giving an explanation of their conduct."

Similarly, *res ipsa loquitur* has been used in cases where an operating room patient received burns. Electrical burns can occur because of faulty cautery or cardiac monitors. Anesthesia gases and certain topical anesthetics are flammable and may burn patients. Hot intravenous bags, heating pads, or medicated solutions may result in burns, especially when applied to a semiconscious or unconscious patient unable to complain about being burned.

In *Christina Wilkins and Kathryn Hager, a minor v. Mercy Hospital and Donald Beasely,* Canyon County (Id) District Court, Case No. 01-04218, the plaintiff, age six, underwent surgery by defendant Beasely. During the operation, a nurse used hot water to heat a nasal splint. The hot water caused burn injuries to the plaintiff's neck and upper chest. The hospital settled for an undisclosed amount and a defense verdict was returned for the surgeon.[10]

Res ipsa loquitur is also used in situations where tourniquets are negligently used, restraining devices are improperly placed, or when improper positioning of the patient has occurred. These errors can result in brachial, thoracic, or peroneal nerve palsies. Relying upon *res ipsa loquitur*, a plaintiff prevailed on a claim of gangrenous sores which resulted from too tightly placed straps. *Palmer v. Clarkside Hospital*, 213 Miss. 601, 57 So. 2d 473 (1952). A plaintiff similarly prevailed in a case in which the operating room nurses were found to have improperly positioned a patient for surgery, causing the patient to suffer nerve palsy. *Jones v. Harrisburg Polyclinic Hospital*, 437 A.2d 134 (Pa. 1981).

After a properly performed dilatation and curettage procedure, the stable patient was being transferred from the operating room table to a stretcher for transport to the recovery room. The stretcher tilted, causing the patient to fall to the floor, causing injury. The plaintiff did not offer any proofs as to what was wrong with the stretcher and relied upon *res ipsa loquitur*. The plaintiff sued the hospital, the operating room nursing staff, and the anesthesiologist. The plaintiff prevailed against the hospital and was awarded $15,000. *Fisher v. Barnert Hospital* et al., New Jersey Superior Court, Bergen County, Docket Number BER-L-13127-90, unreported decision.

Res ipsa loquitur was used in the landmark New Jersey case, *Anderson v. Somberg*, 67 N.J. 291, 338 A.2d 1, cert denied, 423 U.S. 929 (1975). During a laminectomy, a small piece of metal broke from a rongeur being used by the surgeon. Medical complications ensued, necessitating a second surgery. The plaintiff suffered severe and permanent injuries. The plaintiff sued the manufacturer and the seller of the rongeur, the surgeon, the nurses, and the hospital. The plaintiff had a number of experts theorizing as to the negligence of each defendant. However, the plaintiff could not definitely prove whose negligence proximately caused the plaintiff's injury. The plaintiff successfully argued that he did not know which defendant caused his injuries because he was anesthetized, but obviously someone had done something wrong. The plaintiff used a *res ipsa loquitur* theory to recover his damages. However, in this case, the doctrine was expanded. The burden of proof was shifted to the defendants. They were required to rebut the inference of negligence because the court determined they were more likely to possess knowledge of the cause of the accident. Also, the jury was instructed that the occurrence indicated liability on the part of one or more of the defendants. Although there are not many claims in which the *Anderson v. Somberg* theory would apply, it will obviate the plaintiff's burden of proving which party in a multiple-defendant situation is the offending wrongdoer.

The *Anderson v. Somberg* decision highlights how difficult it is to defend against a claim which relies on *res ipsa loquitur*. However, good nursing documentation can aid the nurse's defense. Documentation can help to demonstrate that the nurse exercised due care, followed hospital policy, or properly performed the required task at issue. Institutions should have policies on nursing documentation requirements. Checklists can be helpful in documenting that proper care was taken in providing patient services. Exculpation is also possible, of course, if through expert testimony the nurse defendant can prove the nurse was not negligent. With expert testimony, the nurse can refute the inference of negligence raised by the theory of *res ipsa loquitur*. The plaintiff's attorney should consider retaining an expert witness in a res ipsa case in anticipation of the defense using an expert witness. Without an expert witness, the plaintiff's attorney will have difficulty rebutting the position of the defense's expert.

The plaintiff's attorney should also try to anticipate the defense's strategy in a res ipsa case. For example, consider a situation in which the plaintiff loses a tooth during intubation by a nurse anesthetist. The defense may attempt to assert that poor oral care by the plaintiff resulted in loose teeth, and, therefore, the plaintiff was contributorily negligent.

Before naming a nurse or hospital as a defendant in a res ipsa case, the plaintiff's attorney should clearly determine that the nurse or technician was responsible for providing the care that allegedly injured the patient.

5. Informed consent

It is not the nurse, but the physician, who is responsible for informing a patient about the risks, benefits, and alternatives to a particular procedure. The physician has the obligation to obtain the signed consent as demonstrated by case law: *Cooper v. Roberts*, 220 Pa. Super. 260, 286 A.2d 647 (1971); *Logesky v. Sheptak*, 12 Pitt. S.C. J. 67 (Allegheny Co. 1973); *Harimish v. Children's Hospital Medical Center*, 387 Mass. 152, 439 N.E.2d 240 (1982); *Ackerman v. Lerwick*, 676 S.W.2d 318 (Mo. App. 1984); *Truman v. Thomas*, 27 Cal.3d 285 (1982).

TIP: The execution of an informed consent form is always required if a patient is to undergo an invasive or surgical procedure.

Before the surgery, the operating room nurse has the duty to make sure a signed, dated, and witnessed consent is in the patient's chart pursuant to the institution's policy. A potential source of liability involving informed consent occurs when the surgeon decides to add another procedure without obtaining informed consent. In non-emergency situations, the surgeon is expected to obtain informed consent from the patient. Nurses in the surgical suite are often placed in the position of acting as a patient advocate to protect the patient's right to an informed consent. Operating room policy and procedure manuals have policies on informed consent that can be obtained through discovery.

Neither the nurse nor the hospital has a duty to inform a patient of the risks associated with a surgical procedure. Nor do they have to explain the nature of a test or surgery. A hospital has no affirmative duty to ensure that a patient is provided with an informed consent even for an unusual surgery.

In a New York case, it was found that the hospital had no obligation to advise a patient about a rare surgery known as a spinal jack. *Fiorentino v. Wanger*, 227 N.E.2d 296 (1967) rev'd 262 App. Div. 2d 693, 272 N.Y.S. 2d 557 (1966). Also, a Missouri appellate court has ruled that a hospital is under no duty to obtain the patient's informed consent. Rather, it was the physician's obligation to provide the necessary information about a procedure to the patient even when the nurse was the one who actually presented the consent form to the patient for signature. *Roberson v. Menorah*, 588 S.W.2d 134 (Mo. App. 1979). Also see *Ackerman v. Le-*

rwick, 676 S.W.2d 318 (Mo. App. 1984); *Cooper v. Curry*, 589 P.2d 201 (N.M. 1978).

In *Beck v. Lovelle*, So. 2d 245 (La. App. 1978), the court concluded that even if the nurse obtained the signed consent it was still the physician's duty to give the patient sufficient information about the procedure and possible associated risks. In *Beck*, the plaintiff's obstetrician believed that his patient desired a tubal ligation and after a cesarean section was performed, the obstetrician was going to perform the tubal. The nurse pointed out that there was no duly executed consent for that procedure. The obstetrician then ordered the nurse to leave the operating room to obtain the husband's consent, which the nurse did. The surgery was performed and the woman sued her obstetrician, the hospital, and the nurse. The nurse was not found negligent because she had properly identified the lack of consent and brought it to the doctor's attention. The nurse's role in obtaining a signed consent form from the husband was done under the direction of the physician, thereby absolving the nurse of liability.

In another case, two hospital-employed nurses presented and obtained the patient's signature on a consent form for an arteriogram. They did not explain the procedure nor did they know if it had been explained by the doctor. The patient became paralyzed during the test. The patient sued the doctor, the nurses, and the hospital. The nurses and the hospital were exonerated, but the doctor was held liable for $200,000 in damages. *Tropp v. Cayson*, 471 So. 2d 375 (Miss. 1985).

Relatively few cases actually involve the perioperative nurse in the informed consent process. However, it is becoming an area of concern, especially with the increase of same day surgical procedures. If the same day surgical staff nurse is asked to witness a patient's consent for surgery he can witness the patient's signature as long as the nurse is not scheduled to participate in the surgery. Staff directly involved with a patient's surgery should not witness signatures on consents. Institutions should write policies governing signed consents. Procedures also should be devised on what the nurses should do when the consent is for a different procedure than what was planned, when the consent is insufficient, or when no consent was obtained. Nurses are expected to follow their institution's policy when a problem arises or ask the surgeon for instructions to avoid personal liability.

6. Abandonment

Abandonment is a theory of negligence that may apply in the perioperative setting but is not often used when suing nurses. Nurses have relationships with patients just as physicians do. In the operating room, the relationship begins when the patient enters the holding area and ends when the patient is properly transferred to the recovery room nurse. In the PACU, the relationship begins upon admission and ends once the patient is discharged. Traditionally, only physicians have been charged with abandonment of patients. However, this theory can be used against the nurse who deserts a patient.

In *Czubinsky v. Doctors Hospital*, 188 Cal. Rptr. 685, 139 Cal. App. 3d 361 (1983), a circulating nurse was determined to have abandoned her patient. At the end of an uneventful ovarian cystectomy, the surgeon left the operating room. The circulating nurse also left at the instruction of the surgeon. However, she advised the surgeon that she did not agree with his instruction because she had not finished her duties and knew that the patient was in a critical postoperative period. After they left, the patient arrested with only the anesthesiologist and scrub technician present. The technician then left to call for assistance, leaving the anesthesiologist alone to handle the emergency.

The court in *Czubinsky* took notice of the hospital's policy that stated that the circulating nurse must be present during the entire procedure to assist the anesthesiologist. The patient's expert testified that a cardiac arrest is to be anticipated and procedures should be in place to promptly recognize and deal with a code. It was determined that the nurse's absence was the proximate cause of the plaintiff's brain damage. The surgeon was also negligent in directing that the circulating nurse leave the operating room.

The nurse's negligence was not excused by the fact that she was following the surgeon's directions. The court held her liable on the theory that it was her personal, professional responsibility not to abandon her patient.

TIP: The nurse's abandonment may be the proximate cause of an injury if it is concluded that had the nurse been present, the instability would have been promptly recognized and quick intervention would have prevented the harm.

Accordingly, this case demonstrates that nurses cannot blindly follow instructions from surgeons and be protected from liability on the theory that they were only following orders from their superiors. Nurses have their own professional responsibilities independent of the physician. Therefore, the nurse should first advise the physician if the nurse believes that the doctor's directions may result in nursing malpractice and then, if necessary, take whatever appropriate actions are needed to avoid committing malpractice.

1. Inaccurate counts of instruments and sponges
2. Negligent use of cautery equipment or monitoring devices
3. Improper positioning of the patient for surgery resulting in nerve damage
4. Lost specimen samples
5. Incorrect monitoring of hemodynamic stability during surgery
6. Improper administration of medication
7. Inadequate safeguarding of the patient
8. Failure to properly identify the patient and the planned surgery

Injuries that may occur in the operating room may include:

1. Injury during transfer to and from the operating room and post anesthesia care unit
2. Burns
3. Injury from malfunctioning surgical tool
4. Respiratory or cardiac arrest
5. Nerve damage
6. Requirement for second operation to remove retained instrument or sponge

Figure 5.6 Examples of Perioperative Errors and Injuries

5.5 Nursing Errors

The most common forms of perioperative negligence are listed in Figure 5.6. Injuries range from a bruise to death. They can include burns, nerve damage, infections, the development of adhesions, the need to reoperate, allergic reactions, hemorrhage, fractures, hemodynamic instability, brain damage, and cardiac arrest.

It is often difficult to determine which perioperative provider was negligent because technicians, nurses, and doctors function as a team. The roles and responsibilities of the providers can be identical or overlapping. In evaluating which provider may have been negligent, the attorney must review the surgical, anesthesiology and nursing standards of care, and the institution's job descriptions and its perioperative policies and procedures. In this review, the attorney and the expert witness should be mindful that hospital policies are often at variance with those of a same day surgery center. Generally, the nurse has a more expanded role in a same day surgery center or small hospital where fewer personnel are available. Accordingly, the perioperative nurse's culpability for malpractice depends upon the scope of functions and responsibilities assigned by the particular institution.

Specific perioperative nursing malpractice issues are discussed next. These include:

- Retained foreign objects
- Failure to identify the patient or the planned surgery
- Medication errors
- Injury from equipment

A. Retained Foreign Objects

A retained foreign object is the most common basis for a malpractice claim against the operating room staff. Objects routinely used in operations that may be improperly retained include needles, sponges, laparotomy pads, and medical instruments such as Kelly clamps, hemostats, or scissors. Foreign objects left behind subsequent to surgery can be left in any part of the body but most frequently they are left in the abdominal cavity and thorax.[11] A case-control study of retained foreign objects reveals that sponges are most frequently retained, followed by instruments.[12] The National Quality Forum considers a retained object to be a serious preventable event.[13] The Centers for Medicare & Medicaid Services has taken the position that retention of a foreign object is considered to be a hospital-acquired condition for which reimbursement will not be provided.[14] Further, The Joint Commission has taken the position that the unintended retention of a foreign object is considered to be a sentinel event.[15] Cases of a retained foreign object are usually brought under the *res ipsa loquitur* theory. Interestingly, despite a clear deviation from the standard of care and damages, just as many cases have found the nurse liable as not liable when this occurs. The inconsistent results depend on how the court analyzes the facts.

In a case in which the surgeon was found solely liable for a hemostat that was left inside a patient, the court concluded that the surgeon was the only one responsible for counting the instruments. Hence, he had exclusive liability. *Masse v. Mueller*, 218 N.W.2d 514 (Wisc. 1974).

In *Nicholson v. Sisters of Charity of Providence*, 463 P.2d 861 (Or. 1970), a pin was left in the plaintiff's abdomen. Although it was the nurses' job to count the pins, the facts revealed that the surgeon was in complete charge of the surgery. Therefore, the surgeon was found responsible and not the nurses. In another case, retained sponges following a hysterectomy caused a strangulated hernia that necessitated a further surgery. Over 200 sponges were used in this

complicated, lengthy surgery. The sponge count was solely the responsibility of the nursing staff. Toward the end of the surgery, the circulating nurse left the operating room, leaving the scrub technician alone. The entire operating room nursing staff was found liable and the jury rendered a verdict of $600,000. *Kitchen v. Minelli* et al., Case No. 83/12424 (Pa. 1990) (unpublished decision). In *Ramone v. Mani*, 535 S.W.2d 654 (Tex. Civ App. 1975), it was established that the nurses were trained and directed by the hospital as to the procedures to follow in counting sponges. Thus, the hospital and not the surgeon was held liable for the improper sponge count resulting in a $20,000 verdict.

Yet in another similar case, the surgeon had delegated the task of counting the sponges to the nurses. Accordingly, it was concluded that there was liability on all parties for the patient's second surgery to remove the sponge. Also see *Rudeck v. Wright*, 709 P.2d 621 (Mont. 1985). In another case, the surgeon similarly delegated the counting task and yet the opposite conclusion was reached. The results in these types of cases are fact specific. In *Rogers v. Duke*, 766 S.W.2d 547 (Tex. 1989), only the operating room nursing staff was held liable for the incorrect count and retention of a lap pad. The court determined that the counting of sponges was an administrative task that was the responsibility of the hospital's staff. Similarly, in *Danks v. Maher*, 177 So. 2d 412 (La. App. 1965), the court found the counting of sponges to be an administrative act. Thus, the nurses and the hospital, not the surgeon, were deemed liable. To the same effect see *Grant v. Touro Infirmary*, 207 So. 2d 235 (La. App.), affirmed in part and reversed in part on other grounds, 223 So. 2d 148 (La. 1968).

In the case of *Savage v. Three Rivers Medical Center*, Lawrence County (KY) Circuit Court, Case No. 06-0051, plaintiff succeeded in obtaining a $861,178 verdict against the hospital for a retained sponge. The surgeon settled before trial for an undisclosed amount. The sponge was left during a hysterectomy that occurred in December 2001. Despite complaints of abdominal pain post surgery, a diagnosis of a retained sponge was not made until April 2005. The retained sponge was surgically removed along with a portion of the small bowel.

In other retained foreign object cases, the surgeons similarly claimed they relied upon the operating room nursing staff. It was the staff who performed the counts and who reported incorrectly. Yet, some courts have refused to relieve the surgeons of liability. See *Tutton v. Patterson*, 714 S.W.2d 268 (Tex. 1986); *Powell v. Mullins*, 479, So. 2d 1119 (Ala. 1985); *Burke v. Washington Hospital Center*, 154 U.S. App D.C. 253, 475 F.2d 364; (9th Cir. 1992).

Conversely, in *VanHook v. Anderson*, 824 P.2d 509 (Wash. 1992), a different outcome resulted. In that case, the surgeon was unsure if he had left a sponge in the patient. When the surgeon checked with the nurses before closing the surgical site, they reported the count as correct. The court held that there was insufficient evidence to demonstrate that the surgeon exercised the requisite control over the nurses. Although the nurses were deemed negligent the surgeon was not held vicariously liable.

In earlier cases when sponges were left in patients, the surgeons were held accountable for the nurses' negligence in reporting incorrect counts. The hospitals were initially dismissed as defendants. However, on appeal the decisions were reversed and remanded to the trial courts to ascertain whether the nurses were agents of the hospitals or the surgeons. *Wilson v. Lee Memorial Hospital*, 65 So. 2d 40 (Fla. 1953); *Buzan v. Mercy Hospital, Inc.*, 203 So. 2d 11, 29 A.L.R.3d 1059 (Fla. App. 1967).

TIP: The key to understanding seemingly conflicting decisions is to determine how independently the nurse functioned during the operation.

If the nurse followed a hospital's standard operating procedure in conducting the count, without any direct involvement by the surgeon, the nurse and hospital are definitely liable. The surgeon may also be liable on the theory that the doctor was in overall charge and therefore responsible for all the actions of the entire operating room team: the captain of the ship doctrine.

TIP: When a nurse has followed a hospital's standard operating procedure in conducting a count, the surgeon will most often be absolved of liability because of lack of direct involvement in the negligent act of counting the sponges or instruments after their use.

If the surgeon is personally involved in directing the nurse's count, and the nurse is simply following the doctor's orders without independent decision making, it is likely the nurse will be absolved of liability. The surgeon will be held solely responsible. Nevertheless, defendants have prevailed in some retained foreign object cases, although this is not common. In *Stephen Pratte v. Terrie Smidt, R.N. et al.*, Suffolk County (Mass.) Superior Court, Case No. SUCV94-05147, the plaintiff underwent cardiac surgery for an electrical conduction disturbance of the heart. The surgeons were assisted by several surgical nurses. Two weeks after the surgery it was determined a metal suture needle had been left inside the plaintiff's pericardial sac. As a result of the retained needle the plaintiff developed additional cardiac problems necessitating two surgeries. The plaintiff did not

sue all of the nurses and the surgeons. The defendants admitted liability, but claimed that the mistake may have been made by the surgeons or the other nurse, that the error did not constitute negligence and the plaintiff's problems were related to his underlying condition. In this case the jury returned a verdict in favor of the defendants.

TIP: Liability is easily established through the theory of res ipsa loquitur: that a foreign object was retained bespeaks of negligence without the need for other evidence or expert testimony.

Defending the retained object case on liability is almost impossible. The only real defense available to the nurse is to completely shift liability to the surgeon on the theory that the nurse acted at the doctor's direct orders. Absent this defense, it is very difficult for the nurse to avoid culpability. The attorney should obtain the incident report associated with a retained object. The nurse may have documented that the surgeon was advised of a missing object. If the surgeon denies a request for an x-ray, it can be argued that the nurse could not have done anything else. If the nurse performed the counts and accounted for all instruments and sponges but a foreign body was still left inside the patient, then the nurse was negligent. If no count was performed but something was left in a patient, the nurse is again negligent. If the institution has no policy requiring a count, it can be held liable because the absence of such a policy is below the accepted industry standards. However, this situation does not absolve the nurse of liability. The attorney can also attempt to defend this type of case based on the requirements of proximate cause and damages. With regard to proximate cause, the defense has to show that plaintiff's pain and suffering is unrelated to the retention of the foreign object. However, this is a rare occurrence.

TIP: In most cases, the only plausible defense is to defeat the plaintiff on the claim of damages.

The *New England Journal of Medicine* reported that there were approximately 1,500 medical errors in 2003 that involved surgical team members accidentally leaving a surgical tool or sponge inside a patient. Some facilities conduct general surveillance using a routine postoperative screening x-ray but many do not. However, x-ray detection of sponges and needles can be difficult due to size or location of the objects. Instruments that are made of stainless steel are most likely to be successfully detected. Moreover, sponges that can become twisted or folded become compacted and are not readily detectable. Cima et al. demonstrated that in 34 cases of an actual retained foreign object in which the count was correct, 20 (60 percent) of the retained foreign objects were detected on a postoperative high-resolution radiograph survey film. In 68 events of near misses and actual retained foreign objects, 46 (67 percent) had intraoperative radiographs performed. In 18 incidents in which a retained foreign object was eventually detected, intraoperative radiographs identified 12 of those objects. The authors of the study offer that given the unreliability of portable intraoperative radiographs, postoperative survey radiographs should be performed with dedicated high resolution radiograph equipment in a dedicated imaging area. Kaiser et al. demonstrated that in 3 of 29 (10 percent) cases in which intraoperative radiographs were taken to detect radiopaque sponges, the radiograph was falsely negative. Poor quality radiographs, multiple foreign objects in the field, and failure to communicate the purpose of the radiograph to the interpreting radiologist were cited as factors involved. Gawande et al. have recommended radiographic screening at the end of cases involving an emergent procedure, unexpected change in procedure, or high patient body fat content.

It can take years before the patient begins to exhibit symptoms of the retained foreign object. The longer a surgical sponge remains in the human body, the greater the potential for harm. A retained surgical sponge left inside the body can result in infected abscesses or injury to an internal organ. Sepsis, nerve damage, bowel perforation, internal bleeding, organ damage and blood clots may also result. The surgery to remove a foreign object can be costly and painful for the patient. Death may also occur as a result of a retained foreign object.

On some occasions the plaintiff may sustain no injury as a result of having a retained sponge or instrument. Some gauze pads are insignificant in size. They are as small as two inches by two inches and may cause the patient no harm. Surgical instruments or devices such as screws and plates used in orthopedic surgery are sterile and comprised of inert metals. No tissue will adhere to them and no infection will result. The plaintiff may not require surgical intervention for removal, thus has no injury. This again is a rare situation because the plaintiff can assert emotional distress, anxiety, or some other psychological injury. The bottom line in avoiding this type of liability is for nurses to:

1. strictly follow the hospital's procedures on surgical counts;
2. properly document that these procedures were followed during the surgery; and
3. advise the surgeon of the results of counts and obtain agreement to these results. Such actions mini-

mize the potential for a retained object and may shift the focus of liability from the nurse to the surgeon if negligence nevertheless occurs.

B. Sentinel Events: Wrong Site Surgery, Medication Errors, and Surgical Fires

The Joint Commission has defined a sentinel event as an unexpected occurrence involving death or serious physical or psychological injury or the risk thereof.[16] Serious injury involves the loss of a limb or function. Sentinel events specific to the operating room are wrong site, wrong procedure, wrong patient surgery, medication errors, and surgical fires. The Joint Commission has developed National Patient Safety Goals that address specific sentinel events with safety goals to prevent the re-occurrence of a sentinel event. Refer to Chapter 4, *Patient Safety Initiatives*, in Volume I, for information on the history of the National Patient Safety Goals. The Universal Protocol for wrong site, wrong procedure, wrong patient surgery is a three-tiered approach to addressing this sentinel event.

The Joint Commission undertook a detailed review of wrong site surgery; the study was completed in 1998. It was determined that wrong site surgery was most common during orthopedic procedures, followed by urological, and then neurosurgical cases. The Joint Commission made the following recommendations for reducing the risk of wrong site surgery:

1. Clearly mark the operative site and involve the patient in the marking process to enhance the reliability.
2. Verify the surgical site with the patient.
3. Require an oral verification of the correct site in the operating room by each member of the surgical team.
4. Develop a verification checklist that includes all documents referencing the intended surgery and site (including the medical record, radiographic studies and their reports, the informed consent document, the operating room record, and the anesthesia record), and direct observation of the marked operative site on the patient.
5. The surgeon should be personally involved in obtaining the informed consent.
6. Ensure thorough ongoing monitoring that verification procedures are followed for high-risk procedures.

Wrong site surgery, in summary, broadly defines all surgical procedures performed on the wrong patient, wrong body part, wrong side, or wrong level of a correctly identified anatomical site. Many safeguards prevent an operation on the wrong site. The confusion between the right and left side of the body is responsible for many of these errors. The nurse in the holding room is responsible for reviewing the consent form and verifying with the patient the site to be operated on. However, at this point the patient may be sedated and not reliable. For this reason, surgeons now initial the correct surgical site with ink before the surgery when the patient is alert and can verify the correct site. Some patients mark their own site for the benefit of the doctor. Prior to starting the planned surgery, the surgeon, anesthesiologist, perioperative nurse, and scrub nurse or technician share responsibility for the correct identification of the surgical patient, surgical procedure, and surgical site.

TIP: Operations performed on the wrong site are difficult to defend. Settlements are almost always negotiated because juries find these mistakes to be incomprehensible errors.

In *Haile v. Sutherland*, 598 N.W. 2d 424 (Minn, 1999), the plaintiff was scheduled for the removal of a left axillary mass and a left chest lipomatous mass. After the surgery it was discovered the surgeon had instead removed benign tissue from her left breast. The plaintiff's damages are obvious. The surgeon claimed the incorrect surgery was undertaken because the nurses had improperly draped the surgical site. The nurses and the surgeon had the combined obligation to properly locate, drape, and palpate a precise area of the plaintiff's left chest region to ensure the correct surgery was performed. After a series of legal maneuvers the case was resolved, but the court did not address the issue of improper draping. This case is another example of potential liability for operating room nurses.

The attorney should carefully review the medical record to determine at what point the healthcare professionals recognized the wrong site was being operated on. A mistake detected early in the procedure may result in no lasting damages, depending on the operation. This outcome also permits the defense expert to argue the "so what" defense because there was no injury to the patient. However, the plaintiff can counter by emphasizing an incision was made, tissue pulled apart, scar tissue created, and so on.

Since the initial 1998 review of 15 wrong site surgeries by The Joint Commission, a subsequent Sentinel Event Report was issued in 2001. The report cited the number of wrong site surgery cases had increased from the initial 15 reported cases to 150 cases. The root cause analysis of these cases identified several causes including a breakdown of communication among surgical team members, as well as policy, staffing, and organizational issues.

In response to the increasing numbers of wrong site surgery cases, The Joint Commission further implemented a "time out" procedure in addition to the previous patient safety guidelines. The time out is used as an active form of communication in the operating room to verify the correct patient and correct surgical procedure. These approaches are all active forms of communication that involve verbal verification with the patient or responsible adult, and ensure the surgical team verbally verifies the correct patient, surgery, site, and procedure before commencing the actual surgery.

Several states, such as New York, New Jersey, Connecticut, Minnesota and Pennsylvania have gathered medical data and statistics and have made that information available to the public. Included in the reportings are data related to perioperative cases. The Pennsylvania Patient Safety Reporting System, along with reportings related to multiple different surgeries released figures on the numbers of people injured, disfigured or killed as a result of fires that occurred during surgery. The numbers are significant. Operating room fires are believed to affect between 550 and 650 patients per year.[17] While the number is small, given that there are approximately 50 million surgeries performed in the United States annually, the consequences for the individuals concerned can be life-altering and can result in disabilities and disfigurations. Moreover, one to two patients die every year as a result of OR fires. The head and neck are the most vulnerable body areas due to the significant exposure to oxygen, and flammable materials like hair. About 65 percent of surgical fires take place inside a patient's airway, or in the upper body, while only a quarter happen elsewhere. Electrosurgical tools are responsible for approximately 70 percent of fires, and 2 percent are caused by light sources, burrs or defibrillators, and hot wires. Approximately 10 percent are ignited by lasers.[18]

C. Medication Errors

Medication safety in the operating room has come under scrutiny due to serious and tragic errors resulting in permanent disability or death. Many medications used in the operating room must be removed from their original containers to be delivered to the sterile field to be administered by the operating surgeon. The transfer of medications is performed by the circulating nurse. Once placed on the sterile field, these medications or other solutions are placed in sterile containers or syringes. As part of The Joint Commission National Patient Safety Goals the following measures are required:

1. Containers, syringes must be labeled at the sterile field even if only one medication is placed on the sterile field.
2. Labels include the name, strength, date, and initials of the person preparing the medication.
3. Labels are to be verified verbally and visually by two qualified individuals.
4. No more than one medication or solution is labeled at one time.
5. Original medication/solution containers remain available for reference in the perioperative area until the conclusion of the surgery.
6. Any medications or solutions found unlabeled are promptly discarded.
7. At change of shift or break relief, all medications both on and off the sterile field are actively reviewed by the entering and exiting personnel.

There is a significant potential for inflicting serious injury from a medication error in the operating room. There is a heightened risk of using the wrong solution if it is not correctly identified or labeled. The surgeon relies on the scrub and circulating nurses for preparing the correct solutions. In an Alabama case, the surgeon requested a local anesthetic, Marcaine. Marcaine comes with and without epinephrine. Although the surgeon requested Marcaine without epinephrine, the circulating nurse mistakenly retrieved the Marcaine with epinephrine. The circulating nurse called out "Marcaine plain" and held out the wrong vial for the scrub nurse. Neither the scrub nurse nor the circulating nurse rechecked the label on the vial before the solution was withdrawn into a syringe and injected into the patient's feet. The plaintiff alleged that she developed complications from the epinephrine, and sued the hospital, as the employer of the scrub and the circulating nurses, and also sued the surgeon. In this case there were two alleged violations of the standard of care: the use of the wrong anesthetic and the inappropriate use of a licensed practical nurse as a circulating nurse. The jury found the hospital was liable for the nurses' negligence but found the surgeon not negligent. The patient made a motion for a new trial, arguing that because the nurse was negligent, the surgeon must also be liable under the doctrine of agency. The patient argued that because the hospital had loaned the employee to the surgeon, the surgeon should be vicariously liable for the nurses' actions. The trial judge agreed and granted a new trial.

When the surgeon appealed, the Alabama Supreme Court reversed the order for a new trial and ordered that the original jury's decision be reinstated. The decision was based in part on the undisputed fact that the circulating nurse was a LPN rather than a RN; The Joint Commission standards require that a RN act as a circulator. The court concluded it was possible and permissible for the jury to consider these facts as negating any argument that agency doctrine should apply because the "hospital had obviously provided someone who was not as qualified or experienced as the surgeon was entitled to have."[19] In *Pamela Colvin v. Robert Wood Johnson Medical Center et al.*, Middlesex County (N.J.), the plaintiff underwent a cervical biopsy. Before the surgery she had a preoperative wash of the surgical site with acetic acid. Instead of the wash being a 3 percent solution, it was 100 percent. Plaintiff sustained burns, scarring, and psychological trauma. During trial the hospital, a nurse, a pharmacist, and a pharmacist technician settled for $100,000. The jury returned a verdict of $500,000. Unfortunately, this type of error is made periodically in other operating rooms resulting in significant burns and scars.

D. Injury From Equipment

1. Overview

Today's operating room is vastly different from that of ten years ago. Changes in operative techniques including the use of laparoscopic surgery, laser surgery, microsurgery, and vascular surgery have increased the complexity of the equipment that must be prepared, provided, and used. The hospital has an obligation to conduct itself reasonably in the selection, the provision and maintenance of equipment and supplies. The perioperative nurse has the obligation to conduct herself reasonably when obtaining, providing, and using equipment.

TIP: Prior to use in a planned surgery, the operating room nurse is responsible for ensuring equipment has been inspected by the biomedical department. A visual inspection should be performed to ascertain the biomedical department's inspection sticker(s) on equipment with the date of inspection and date of upcoming inspection. The circulating nurse is responsible for checking the integrity of plugs, electric cords, and switches to ensure they are in working order.

The use of videography adds a potential source of discovery. In some instances operating room nurses have been asked to turn off the recording device when the surgeon encountered a particularly difficult part of the operation. The videotape should be retained and treated as part of the medical record. Fewer surgeries are being recorded because surgeons have become sensitive to the fact that a videotape can be used against them.

There are more equipment-related malpractice cases as a result of technological advances. The parties may find that not only is theory of malpractice applicable but so is the theory of product liability. With the theory of product liability comes the standard of strict liability, which may automatically impute liability to the maker of the equipment because of a manufacturing or design defect. The manufacturer may attempt to shift the alleged negligence to the users of the equipment.

Some states have enacted laws that provide immunity to healthcare providers if there is a clear product defect (see NJSA 2A: 58C-11c). Courts are beginning to recognize that healthcare providers should not be accountable if they unknowingly use a defective device. Pennsylvania has no statutory immunity, but its courts have afforded protection to the healthcare providers. In *Cafazzo v. Central Medical Health Services*, 660 A.2d 521 (Pa. 1995), which involved a mandibular prosthesis, it was determined that hospitals and doctors could not be held strictly liable for defects in prosthetic medical equipment. It is believed that this trend of legal exoneration will be followed in other states as these types of cases come before the courts.

If there is no wrongdoing on the part of the manufacturer, some courts are placing more responsibilities on the operating room nurse. In a case in which the plaintiff underwent a cervical diskectomy and fusion, the surgeon elected not to use bone harvested from the plaintiff or the bone bank, but rather used an artificial material which later proved to be inadequate because it failed to provide sufficient stability, thus necessitating a second surgery. The court determined the hospital was negligent because the nurse ordered the material at the request of the surgeon without review by a manager. The product literature specifically stated that this material was not be used in spinal surgeries. *Hall v. Arthur*, 141 F.3d 844 (8th Cir. 1998).

An injury related to the use of sophisticated equipment in the operating room occurred in a case in which the plaintiff died during a hysteroscopy when gas was pumped into her through the exhaust line. Although the manufacturer was sued, the jury found negligence on the hospital, nurses, and surgeon and awarded $2 million. It was revealed the defendant nurses had not attended any hospital-held inservice on this machine and had no previous experience with it at the time of the plaintiff's surgery. Moreover, their nursing supervisor was unaware of their lack of experience. *Chin v. St. Barnabas Medical Center*, 711 A.2d 352 (N.J. Super. A.D. 1998).

In this situation and others similar, the introduction of new medical equipment while providing safe patient care can be augmented with an on-site representative from the medical equipment manufacturer. The manufacturer's representative possesses specific knowledge regarding the use of the medical equipment and can interact with the surgeon during the surgical procedure and with the circulating nurse in setting up the new equipment.

TIP: Informed consent requires the patient be aware of the presence of a medical representative during surgery. The medical representative may not perform the duties of a scrub nurse, technician or a circulating nurse.

---

2. Burns

Burns resulting from heat or chemicals are one of the most common injuries occurring in the perioperative setting. However, this injury is preventable if healthcare providers exercise due caution.

a. Thermal burns

Thermal burns may occur from improper use and grounding of electrocauterizing machines and the application of warming pads or hot solution bags. In a New Jersey case that was settled, the anesthesiologist asked the OR nurse to give him an IV bag to use to position the patient's shoulders for a tonsillectomy. The bag's purpose was to hyperextend the plaintiff's neck to facilitate the surgery. The nurse took a hot bag from a warming closet and placed it under the patient's back. The plaintiff was lying on a sheet, under which was the IV bag. Under the bag was a warming blanket set at 102°F. The procedure lasted approximately 30 minutes. In the post anesthesia care unit, the plaintiff complained of pain in her back. The nurses discovered an IV bag-shaped burn on the patient's shoulders. The hospital made a payment on behalf of the nurse. *Cennamo v. St. Barnabas*, unpublished opinion.

A three-month-old infant was burned in Kansas when the child was placed on a heating pad during hernia surgery. Even though the heating pad contained a warning against the use of the pad on an infant, or a sleeping or unconscious person, the circulating nurse set up the pad at the request of the anesthesiologist. The child sustained second- and third-degree burns of his buttocks. The burns were not detected until the child's mother changed his diaper at home a few hours after surgery. The defendants admitted liability. The District Court, Sedgwick County, found in favor of the plaintiffs and awarded damages of approximately $400,000. When the defendants appealed, the Supreme Court of Kansas affirmed the judgment of the lower court and held that the award was not excessive. Before the trial, the defendants sought to exclude from evidence the heating pad and an enlargement of the warning as irrelevant to the issue of damages. The trial judge denied this motion. The appellate court affirmed and held that the determination of relevancy was a matter of logic and experience and not a matter of law.[20]

Clearly in this case the nature of the warning on the heating pad had a high degree of relevance to the liability issues. However, the operating room nurse is still responsible for warning the surgeon when hazardous situations are encountered. "Failure to assess and to take immediate action, when necessary—whether to stop a surgeon from using a malfunctioning power tool, for instance, or to speak up about some problem with anesthesia is the cause of many a lawsuit."[21]

TIP: Most electrosurgical generators today have intricate safety features that reduce the risk of burns.

Patients are not only injured by simple devices such as heating pads or solutions that are improperly prepared at excessive temperatures, but they can be injured from high-tech electrocautery devices. Advances in minimally invasive surgery have enabled patients to undergo surgical procedures, previously performed through an incision, using a laparoscope. Cautery employed in minimally invasive surgery exposes patients to the risk of burns to the bowel, vessels, organs, and other structures during laparoscopic abdominal and pelvic surgeries. This type of injury may go unnoticed because the injury is out of the surgeon's operating field of vision. Stray electrosurgical burns are caused by stray energy. Stray energy can be the result of instrument insulation failure, capacitive coupling, and direct coupling.[22] The mechanism of these failures result in intra-abdominal burns.

The active electrode is an instrument that introduces the electro-surgical current into the patient's abdomen. The end of the electrode can be a blade, hook, ball, loop, or needle. Active electrode instruments used in laparoscopic surgery are long (almost 14 inches in length) and have a protective insulating material covering the shaft of the instrument. Insulation damage, hairline cracks, and fractures provide an alternate path for electric current to flow into the patient's abdomen. The resulting burns are instantaneous and cause severe injury due to the concentrated energy. The temperature at the end of the active electrode is approximately 700°C.

Paradoxically, the smaller the hole or fracture in the insulation the greater the burn at the non-targeted tissue site. Insulation defects can occur before or during a procedure. Defects occurring before a procedure can occur as a result of handling during reprocessing when sharp instruments in the tray come in contact with each other. The insulation contact with other sharp instruments damages the insulating sheath, and exposure to the high temperature (270°F) during sterilization can weaken the insulation sheath.

During a procedure, defects can occur due to the stress of high voltage electrical currents passing through the operative instrument. Damage to the insulator of the instrument can occur if it comes in contact with another sharp-edged instrument such as a trocar.

During laparoscopy, the surgeon's field of vision is small and limited to about a 1.5 inch magnified operating field leaving the remainder of the active electrode (14 inches), trocar, and trocar cannula outside of the operative field of vision. Stray energy from insulation failure can occur anywhere along the length of the active electrode thereby causing burns to non-target tissue.

Prompt diagnosis is difficult in same day surgery because many patients are discharged home on the day of surgery. Several days may pass before a patient notifies her physician of a complaint. In the initial postoperative period at home, the symptoms of a burn may mimic the normal postoperative symptoms of laparoscopy, which include pain and a generalized ill feeling.

A bowel perforation from an electrosurgical burn causes the intestinal contents to leak into the abdominal cavity. This causes a bacterial infection known as fecal peritonitis, a condition that requires further surgery and aggressive postoperative antibiotic therapy. Patients who survive these burns often suffer severe emotional, financial, and long-lasting physical complications. In some instances of bowel injury, necrosis (tissue death) may occur, thus requiring surgical removal of the necrotic bowel with a subsequent temporary or permanent colostomy.

Most hospitals do not have a policy or procedure for inspecting and testing laparoscopic equipment either in the perioperative or biomedical department. Nor is there a mechanism in place to track use of non-disposable equipment or perform routine checks to ensure instrument integrity. It is very difficult to rely on a visual inspection, because some holes are pinpoint in size and cannot be detected by the naked eye. Nondisposable and single use active electrodes can have defects that may be beyond the surgeon's view. In one instance a patient underwent a laparoscopic monopolar electrosurgery to dissect pelvic adhesions. It was believed her surgery had gone well and she was discharged home that same day. Seven days later she was diagnosed with peritonitis related to bowel injury due to burns that had occurred during the initial surgery. A jury awarded her $500,000 for her ordeal. *Karl v. Armstrong*, No. 92-7084 (Hillsborough County, Fla. 1997).

TIP: Since 1999, AORN has addressed the use of active electrode monitoring in its standards. AORN reflects the current scientific data in support of its position regarding the use of active-electrode monitoring and has cited the current scientific information and research in its *Standards, Practices and Guidelines* publication.

In 2005 and 2006, *Standards, Recommended Practices and Guidelines* addressed the use of active electrode monitoring and specifically states: "Use of active electrode monitoring devices minimizes the risks of undetected insulation failure, direct coupling and capacitive coupling injuries."[23]

b. Chemical burns

Chemical burns may result from antiseptic solutions or the use of highly concentrated caustic chemicals such as high level disinfectants. In *Van Hyning v. Hamilton Hospital*, the jury returned a $1 million verdict when a man's penis was burned. During laser surgery to remove genital warts, the operating room nurse provided the surgeon with a solution of 99 percent acetic acid instead of the 5 percent solution normally used to color the warts before removal. The plaintiff claimed he suffered severe burning and bleeding during sexual intercourse. The hospital was unable to explain how pure acid had been removed from the pharmacy. The hospital was found to be 50 percent responsible with the balance of the liability assigned to a doctor and a nurse.

c. Surgical fires

In 2003, The Joint Commission released a sentinel event alert concerning surgical fires. The report cited from ECRI research that the most common causes of a surgical fire were by an electrosurgical unit (68 percent) and lasers (13 percent). The most common locations for a surgical fire were an airway (34 percent), fires to the head and face (28 percent), and other sites inside or outside the patient's body (38 percent). An oxygen-enriched atmosphere (OEA) was a contributing factor in 74 percent of these fires. The Joint Commission added surgical fire prevention to the 2005 National Patient Safety Goals. Surgical fires in the operating room result in serious injury and sometimes death. The unique environment of the operating room factors into the risk of fire. Commonly referred to as the fire triad, the environmental factors that contribute to a surgical fire are an oxygen source, a fuel source, and an ignition source. These three factors are in great abundance in the operating room. Safety guidelines for all personnel working in the operating room include education and training to the above factors and response procedures in the event of a surgical fire. A proactive approach and safe practice by anesthesia, surgery, and nursing is critical in controlling each specific side of the triad, thus avoiding a surgical fire.

One of the most horrific operating room fires occurred in 1990 when a 26-year-old Los Angeles woman died as a result of burns sustained from the surgical drapes which had caught on fire. The surgical drapes caused a thick smoke to form around the operating room and staff members could not put out the fire.

An 81-year-old man died as a result of flash fire during the placement of a breathing tube ignited by an electrosurgical unit. The deceased man incurred burns to his mouth and trachea. The case settled for $450,000.[24]

E. Handoff Communication

Patients entering the hospital may be transferred to many different areas during one hospital stay. A surgical patient may be cared for in the preoperative unit, the operating room, post anesthesia care unit, a surgical intensive care unit, or a postoperative surgical unit. Communication as an ongoing process is critical to optimum patient care. The "handoff communication" to another provider is significant. Failure to provide sufficient data can result in injury to the patient. The handoff communication is so critical that it is one of The Joint Commission's National Patient Safety Goals that began in 2006 and continues to the present.

In the operating room, a nurse may be relieved, such as for a break, lunch, or change of shift: a handoff communication is performed. For a break, the circulating nurse provides a report to her relief nurse. This report should briefly detail the necessary information regarding the patient and the surgery being performed. Surgical counts are reviewed to provide the relief nurse with an account of what items are currently in use. In the event additional items are requested, the relief nurse documents added items to the surgical field. Upon the return of the circulating nurse, the relief nurse provides a report summarizing patient care as well as items added and documented to the surgical field during the relief. During other relief periods, such as lunch or change of shift, the relief report is more detailed and can include patient history, intraoperative patient care, surgical progress, and an instrument, sponge, needle, and sharps count.

Upon completion of surgery, the patient is transported to the PACU by the anesthesia provider and circulating nurse. Upon admission to the PACU, a detailed report is given to the PACU nurse by the circulating nurse regarding the patient, any pertinent medical history, the surgical procedure performed, medications given in the operating room, blood loss, urinary output if monitored via catheter, and applicable implants (i.e., a pacemaker). The anesthesiologist provides a report to the PACU nurse regarding the type of anesthesia given, medications given relative to pain management postoperatively, fluid intake, blood loss, urinary drainage if monitored in surgery, blood pressure status, and any other anesthesia-related pertinent data.

F. Chain of Command

The nurse's duty to intervene or initiate the chain of command is a most sensitive issue, yet reflects significant concerns in the area of perioperative malpractice. Chain of command has been defined as "a specific course of action involving administrative and clinical lines of authority established to ensure effective conflict resolution in patient care situations."[25]

Because of differences of opinion and differences in professional knowledge and skills, patient care conflict issues can arise between physicians and nurses. The physician bears the responsibility for medical decision making. Nurses are professionally accountable for their own actions and have a duty to intervene when medical care does not appear to meet the standard of care. Failure to invoke the chain of command can constitute a breach of duty with a subsequent harm to the patient and a legal action of negligence. Nursing and other healthcare team members have a duty of care that includes patient advocacy.

The purpose for a chain of command policy is to ensure the following:

- resolve a conflict involving patient care
- clarify a care management plan
- obtain necessary patient care intervention
- provide for patient advocacy within the institution
- support patient safety by maintaining a standard of care
- support risk management by reducing liability exposures

It is essential the perioperative suite has clearly defined patient care and safety policies with proper enforcement under a chain of command policy.

A variety of situations in the perioperative area necessitate the use of a chain of command policy, including the procedures for skin preps and limitation of fire risk when using flammable prep solutions, trial of new equipment, and incorrect counts. A circulating nurse may disagree with the operating surgeon regarding the use of flammable skin prep in a certain situation. If the surgeon insists on using the flammable agent and the nurse forsees a risk of harm to the patient and no resolution, the chain of command should be invoked. Incorrect counts should always invoke a chain of command when the lost item (sponge, instrument, sharp)

cannot be found. If the operating surgeon continues with closure, invoking the chain of command results in acquiring additional assistance and supervisory expertise to avoid conflict and effect safe patient care according to operating room policy and procedure.

In PACU, invoking the chain of command for a patient for a deteriorating condition such as postoperative blood loss or airway management problems is appropriate when the surgeon, anesthesiologist, or attending physician cannot be reached. It can be intimidating for the staff nurse who has to deal with surgical department policies and procedures. However, the nurse needs to be mindful of the duty of safe care owed to the patient. Sound department policies and education to all members of the surgical staff will aid in fostering a professional atmosphere conducive to safe patient care and can prevent situations that place patients at risk of injury. The perioperative nurse must document events as they occur. Important considerations when using the chain of command are:

- recording events in a clear and objective manner with specific facts and time of entry
- listing the names of people notified and times of contact
- refraining from character or personal attacks or finger pointing

---

TIP: Absence of a written chain of command policy does not mitigate the nurse's responsibility to recognize problems and take appropriate action to prevent patient injury.

Refer to Chapter 1, *The Roots of Patient Injury,* in Volume I, for a discussion on the role of communication in medical errors.

5.6 Postanesthesia Care Unit Liability Issues
A. Overview

This section addresses liability issues in the critical period when the patient is recovering from anesthesia. The chapter concludes with a discussion of same day surgery areas. In general, most of the injuries patients sustain relate to the failure of basics of nursing care:

- Failure to assess and observe, and reach appropriate diagnoses
- Failure to communicate important changes in the patient's condition
- Failure to initiate timely, pertinent interventions

The patient in the post anesthesia care unit (PACU) is at high risk for injury when any of the three basic nursing responsibilities is not performed correctly. Anesthesia prevents the patient from alerting the nurse or anyone else to complications.

The PACU is an intense environment. Post anesthesia nurses often complain of sensory overload. Beeping monitors, windowless rooms, surgical garb and dim lighting contribute to the stress of working in the unit. The flow of patients is often unpredictable. A number of operations may complete simultaneously, bringing an influx of patients all at once. Unstable, critically ill postoperative patients may be brought into the PACU rather than being transported directly to the intensive care unit. The PACU nurse possesses specialized knowledge regarding anesthetic agents and techniques, complications associated with anesthesia, and the interventions to prevent and treat complications.[26]

The requirement for frequent monitoring of vital signs and the patient's status can strain the capabilities of the PACU nurse when the usual complement of nurses is reduced. Staffing levels drop during breaks and meal times, and when post anesthesia care nurses take patients back to the medical surgical, pediatric, or critical care units. A plaintiff's attorney should investigate the staffing protocols of the hospital when a PACU injury is sustained.

B. Sources of Injury

A variety of errors can occur in the PACU (Figure 5.7). This subsection addresses a few of the most serious types of injuries that can result from deviations from the standard of care in the PACU. Patients recovering from anesthesia require careful assessment of their status when they arrive in the PACU, throughout the stay, and at the time of discharge. Refer to Appendix 5.1 for a summary of the care of a woman who died in the same day surgery area, and Appendix 5.2 for the report of the plaintiff's recovery room nursing expert.

A standardized tool called the Aldrete score (Figure 5.8) is used by many facilities to systematically assess patients. Lack of monitoring at critical times can result in brain damage from lack of oxygen, nerve damage from restraints, or death from cardiac arrest.

1. Lack of oxygen

The lack of oxygen resulting in respiratory compromise is probably the greatest risk associated with general anesthesia. Oxygen deprivation can be caused by a mechanical obstruction, intravenous and inhaled anesthetic agents, muscle relaxants or narcotics, pain, and even surgery itself.

- Administration of blood to the wrong patient
- Medication errors
- Injection injuries
- Failure to detect hypoxia
- Failure to inform the physician of clinically significant changes in the patient's condition
- Failure to monitor
- Injury from equipment
- Failure to detect a change in the patient's condition during transport to the postoperative bed
- Falls
- Negligent supervision of others

Figure 5.7 Examples of Negligent Acts in PACU

Post Anesthesia Recovery Aldrete Score

Able to move four extremities voluntarily or on command	=2
Able to move two extremities voluntarily or on command	=1
Able to move 0 extremities voluntarily or on command	=0
Able to deep breath and adequate exchange	=2
Dyspnea or limited breathing	=1
Apneic	=0
Bp ± 20 percent preop systolic level	=2
Bp ± 20-50 percent preop systolic level	=1
Bp ± 50 percent preop systolic level, children under 10, apical pulse	=0
Awake, coherent	=2
Arousable on calling	=1
Not responding	=0
Normal skin color	=2
Pale dusky blotchy skin	=1
Cyanotic	=0

Figure 5.8 Aldrete Score

The nurse is expected to monitor the patient for signs of respiratory problems and to prevent these complications from occurring. The standard of care requires that the post anesthesia care nurse count and record the respiratory rate at frequent intervals.

In a 1979 case, a teacher underwent surgery to correct a tear duct obstruction. Afterward, he experienced spatial disorientation, loss of visual fields, and memory problems. He was fired from his job a year later because memory loss was causing performance problems. When a neurologist diagnosed brain damage, he filed suit against the PACU nurses. His expert witness neurologist alleged the medication given to counteract the anesthesia was insufficient and a protracted period of hypoxia following surgery probably caused the patient's condition.

Examination of the medical record showed that nurses noted on the chart the patient was "doing well" and there were no apparent complications. They did not record the respirations despite the fact there was a place for them on the chart. The defendants argued it was standard policy to count and observe respirations of a patient in the recovery room and to administer oxygen if needed. However, the nurses argued that such information was not charted unless something unusual was observed. The plaintiff's expert witness countered that it was poor practice not to chart respirations after the patient was given such a massive dose of narcotics. The court held there was sufficient evidence for a jury to find (1) that the nurse anesthetist had given both an excessive dose of narcotics and an inadequate dose of medication to reverse the narcotic effects, (2) that her actions could have decreased the respiratory rate and depth enough to prevent an adequate supply of oxygen from reaching the brain, and (3) that the problems would have been discovered and treated had the recovery room nurses properly monitored the patient's respirations. *Wagner v. Kaiser Foundation Hospitals*, 589 P.2d 1106 (Or. 1979) (Cushing, 1982). The absence of recorded respirations was a critical factor that complicated the defense of this case. The plaintiff was able to prevail by using indirect and circumstantial evidence to imply that the injury was due to the absence of monitoring.

Chapter 28, *Medication Errors*, discusses the effects of narcotics on the respiratory rate. Narcotics are given with great frequency in the PACU. It is common for the nurses to administer small, frequent doses of Morphine and Demerol as patients emerge from anesthesia and become aware of pain.

A California woman claimed nurses in the recovery room were negligent in monitoring her. The 41-year-old unemployed plaintiff underwent an uncomplicated hyster-ectomy. Narcotics and a sedative were given to her in the recovery room. She stopped breathing for several minutes without any of the staff noticing, and incurred permanent brain damage. In the suit, the plaintiff claimed the nurses negligently failed to monitor her condition. A $1.44 million settlement was reached.[27]

In a similar case, a New Jersey nurse was held negligent for the failure to monitor the patient, even though she asked another nurse to observe the patient while she was out of the recovery room. The anesthesiologist was exonerated. The 27-year-old patient, Mr. Eyoma, was taken to the PACU after an uneventful gall bladder operation. He suffered from respiratory depression and died after being in a coma for a year. A misunderstanding contributed to his damages. The anesthesiologist testified that the patient's respirations were 12 per minute when he arrived in the PACU (normal respiratory rate is 16 to 20). Knowing the patient had received Sufenta, which can depress respirations, the anesthesiologist testified that he told the PACU nurse "please watch him." He further testified that he knew Sufenta can have a delayed effect of suppressing respirations and, in his judgment, there was no need to administer any drugs to reverse the anesthetic agents.

The defendant nurse testified that just after the anesthesiologist left she asked another nurse to monitor the patient, and then went out of the PACU to care for another patient. She also testified she did not get a verbal response or any acknowledgment from the other nurse. When she returned to the PACU no one was near the patient. His respirations were down to eight per minute. For some inexplicable reason, when the anesthesiologist returned to the PACU and asked about the patient's condition, the nurse said he was fine. However, the anesthesiologist found him in respiratory arrest. Despite the resuscitation efforts, the patient was without spontaneous respirations for 20 minutes.

In the ensuing suit, the anesthesiologist and the PACU nurse were named as defendants. An anesthesiologist testified to the deviations from the standard of care of the anesthesiologist. The defense nurse expert witness testified about the anesthesiologist's conduct, alleging he should have administered Narcan to reverse the respiratory effects. The nursing expert witness also said the anesthesiologist improperly delegated the monitoring duty to the PACU nurses. The defense expert physicians said the sole cause of the respiratory arrest was the improper monitoring by the PACU nurse and that such monitoring was the nurse's responsibility. The nurse was criticized for leaving the patient without receiving verification from the second nurse that monitoring of the patient would continue in her absence. This may have been seen as abandonment by the jury. The court said the facts could support a finding of liability against the anesthesiologist for not telling the nurse the name of the narcotic agent given in the OR and not observing the patient long enough after the transfer to the PACU. The jury exonerated the physician and held the nurse 100 percent liable for failure to monitor, failure to detect the patient had stopped breathing, and failure to get him the necessary medical attention in time.[28]

In this case, the defendant nurse was charged with failure to perform all three of the basic nursing responsibilities mentioned earlier in this section of the chapter:

1. Failure to assess and observe, and reach appropriate diagnoses
2. Failure to communicate important changes in the patient's condition
3. Failure to initiate timely pertinent interventions

Continuous pulse oximetry is common in the PACU. Alarms can be set on these machines to alert the nurse to a drop in oxygen saturation level. Readings below 90 percent usually warrant notification of the anesthesiologist. It is unknown if pulse oximetry equipment was attached to Mr. Eyoma. Had it been present, this catastrophe may have been avoided. Cases involving a drop in oxygen saturation may occur because of a lack of proper monitoring, a failure to set alarms, or a product failure. The attorney involved in litigating this type of case should review the literature for the standard of care at the time of the incident. The PACU's policies on the use of pulse oximetry should be obtained as well.

Eyoma is also instructive because the jury awarded $17,500 to the estate for loss of enjoyment of life, $25,000 to children, and no damages to the patient's mother. The nurse appealed and the estate, mother, and children cross-appealed. The Superior Court of New Jersey, Appellate Division, ruled that the verdict finding the nurse 100 percent liable was sound and that a new trial was not required as to liability. It held that even though the victim was unconscious and unable to appreciate his incapacitation for the last year of his life, the court properly permitted recovery of hedonic damages. The court ruled that the jury award of $17,500 was insufficient to compensate the decedent's estate for over one year of lost wages and total physical impairment and disability without considering the loss of enjoyment of life's pleasures. A new trial was to be held on all damages to avoid manifest injustice. *Eyoma v. Falco*, 247 N.J. Super. 435, 589 A.2d 653 (1991).

Another case demonstrated the dire consequences of the PACU staff's failure to promptly recognize an airway problem and have treatment instituted. The plaintiff died because of those omissions. Two hours after completion of a carotid endarterectomy, the plaintiff began to complain of throat burning. It is alleged the nurses delayed in communicating that information to the physicians, who in turn failed to timely diagnose and treat the cause of her problem, which was incisional bleeding. The plaintiff suffered a respiratory arrest, and cardiac resuscitation was unsuccessful. *Michael Apuzzo, individually and as Administrator Ad Prosequendum of the Estate of Marian Apuzzo, deceased v. Robert Wood Johnson Hospital et al.*, Middlesex County, New Jersey, Docket No. MID-L-9565-94.

2. Nerve damage from restraints or bandages

As the anesthesia wears off, a brief period of delirium may occur. This is called "emergence delirium" and is accompanied by thrashing and restlessness. PACU nurses are expected to protect the patient from injury by using padded side rails and close observation. The use of restraints has the potential for increasing anxiety, psychosis, and inflicting injury as the following case shows.

A six-year-old child who had undergone eye surgery was trying to reach the bandages on her eyes during her stay in the PACU. The PACU nurse applied restraints. During this time the child's mother, who was at the child's side, informed the nurse that her daughter complained that the restraints hurt her arms and that they were checked infrequently. Eighteen hours later, when the restraints were removed, there was damage to the girl's left arm. The court held that the nurses were negligent for failing to prevent the child from struggling against the restraints. The nurse's decision to put restraints on this patient was not criticized but rather the inadequate degree of observation over the restrained patient.[29]

In *Kober v. Hackensack Hospital et al.*, Bergen County, New Jersey, Docket No. BER-L12459-95, the plaintiff, a known diabetic, underwent a lifesaving cardiac bypass surgery. While in PACU she began to complain of pain in her bandaged leg where the saphenous vein had been harvested. Subsequently, she developed a neuropathy and had difficulty walking. It is alleged the nurse and the physician failed to appreciate the significance of her complaints given her underlying diabetic condition. The defendants contended that her complaints did not go unrecognized and that her injury was due to her diabetes and not because of a too tightly wrapped bandage. The plaintiff voluntarily dismissed the case on the eve of trial.

3. Cardiac dysrhythmias

Several inhaled anesthetics can cause irregular heartbeats or a decrease or increase in the heart rate. Cardiac monitoring is a routine part of post anesthesia care nursing. Chapter 4, *Critical Care Malpractice Issues*, contains a discussion on the risks associated with turning off alarms on cardiac monitors.

TIP: The temptation to turn off alarms exists in the PACU and may be associated with a failure to detect a clinically significant change in the patient.

Patients reacting from anesthesia are also prone to hypotension (low blood pressure) from pain medication, anesthesia, bleeding, or improper positioning. Hypertension (high blood pressure) may result from too much fluid, pain, or preexisting cardiac conditions. Treatment of dysrhythmias begins with determining and removing any source of problem. Antidysrhythmic drugs, resuscitation equipment, and monitoring equipment should be immediately available.[30]

In *Arachikavitz v. Akron General Hospital*, the plaintiff, age 43, underwent an emergent appendectomy in December 2001. Post emergency surgery, the plaintiff was taken to the PACU for postoperative care and subsequently moved to a surgical bed in the hospital. The following morning the patient was found unresponsive with irreversible brain damage and in a persistent, vegetative state. The plaintiff claimed he was suffering from a sleep apnea and was moved prematurely. The defendant physicians argued the patient suffered from a postoperative septic shock due to his appendicitis, and his injuries were not related to the anesthesia. The defendants further argued the nursing staff moved the patient without the approval of the physicians. A confidential settlement was reached with the hospital along with a $4 million verdict.[31]

In *Treinas v. Deepdale General Hospital*, the PACU nurses refused to give a potent medication to correct a patient's high blood pressure because they felt they could not provide appropriate monitoring. Treinas was brought into the hospital for repair of a torn Achilles tendon. Although he was given antihypertensive medication before and during surgery, his blood pressure remained high. The physician ordered the nurses to administer Nipride but the nurses refused, citing hospital policy that prohibited administering this drug to patients outside of the ICU.

The physician then ordered the patient to be transferred to ICU. During the one-hour wait for a bed, the patient received other medications that marginally reduced his high blood pressure. Once in ICU he received Nipride but it failed to control his high blood pressure. He developed respiratory distress, was put on a ventilator, and died 16 hours after reaching ICU. An autopsy report attributed his death to an undiagnosed tumor and heart failure. The patient's wife sued the hospital for medical malpractice. When the hospital filed a motion for summary judgment, it was denied. The hospital appealed this decision. The appellate court reviewed an affidavit prepared by a physician who opined that the refusal to administer Nipride and the delay in transferring the patient did not contribute to the patient's death. On the basis of this affidavit, the court ruled that the nurses acted appropriately in refusing to administer a drug in violation of hospital policy. The hospital's motion for summary judgment was granted. *Treinas v. Deepdale General Hospital*, 570 N.Y.S.2d 185 (1991).[32]

A California judge ordered a $20.2 million settlement, an exorbitant award for injuries related to a cardiac arrest followed by survival in a brain damaged state. In *Jose Pepe DeSoto for Denise DeSoto v. Regents, University of California, UC Irvine Medical Center*, Orange County, California, Superior Court, the plaintiff underwent reattachment of two fingers that had been amputated in an automobile accident. After 30 minutes in PACU she arrested and was resuscitated into a permanent vegetative state. It was determined the cardiac arrest resulted from a breathing tube clogged with mucus.

The PACU is rich with potential for injury to patients. Lack of knowledge, attention lapses, inadequate staffing, and equipment failures can contribute to patient injury. The damages are often significant and proximate cause is usually not difficult to prove.

C. Handoff

When a patient is released by the anesthesiologist to be transferred from the PACU to a medical surgical unit, an initial report is telephoned by the PACU nurse caring for the patient to the unit. The individual receiving the initial call may be a staff nurse, or unit charge nurse. Generally, the initial report alerts the unit of the imminent transfer from the PACU and should include the name of the patient, a brief report of the patient's surgical and postoperative status, and any special needs required in the patient room, such as oxygen therapy and special medical equipment, for example, fracture frames that are to be attached to the bed.

Upon arrival to the unit, the PACU nurse assists with the transfer of the patient from the stretcher to the bed with the unit nurse assigned to the patient. Upon completion of patient transfer, a detailed report is given to the nurse assigned to the patient that should include:

- the patient's medical history
- allergies
- medications used prior to surgery

- surgical procedure performed
- estimated blood loss, fluid intake and output, drainage tubes
- medications given in the operating room and the PACU
- respiratory status, blood pressure, and cardiac status
- level of consciousness
- any nausea or vomiting postoperatively
- neurological status (for patients with a regional block such as an epidural)
- management of pain in PACU
- color of skin and nail beds and capillary refill for patients with casts

The unit nurse should be informed of the presence of a patient controlled analgesia pump (PCA pump), the pain medication used in the pump, as well as the dose and frequency. Family members may be present at the time the patient is admitted to the surgical or short stay unit. The patient's condition and any equipment used in the care of the patient should be explained to the family members by the surgical unit nurse. Special instructions must be given to family members of the patient with a PCA pump. Family members should be instructed that a PCA pump is strictly for the patient to control his own pain and no one should push the button for the patient as it can have serious outcomes for the patient.

In a 2006 case, *Flowers v. HCA Health Services of Tenn.*, involving a PCA pump, a patient was found to be unresponsive on her second hospital day post kidney stone surgery. She was unable to be resuscitated and pronounced dead. Postmortem, a lethal level of morphine was found in her bloodstream. The patient died from a morphine overdose, which the court ruled could not have happened without negligence on the part of the caregivers.

TIP: The PCA pump has several error issues, such as PCA by proxy (a nurse or family member presses the button to deliver pain medication); improper patient selection: infants, children, and cognitively impaired adults; and inadequate patient monitoring. Patient education, drug mix-ups, device design flaws, and inadequate staff training are also identified as factors that affect PCA pump use.

5.7 Ambulatory Surgery

The rapidly increasing number of surgical procedures performed in an outpatient/ambulatory surgery unit has increased and so has the liability exposure for perioperative nursing. Outpatient surgery centers afford patients the op-

portunity to undergo surgical procedures in a non-hospital setting which is a smaller setting. Generally perceived by patients to be more intimate, friendly, and less cumbersome to negotiate, outpatient surgery centers' popularity and patient volume continues to grow and prosper. The number of visits to a freestanding outpatient surgery center is estimated to have increased nationally by 300 percent from 1996 to 2006. By 2006, it was estimated that 57.1 million procedures were performed during 34.7 million ambulatory surgical center visits.[33] Additionally, surgical knowledge is ever advancing, and with it the complexity of surgical cases. As well, the surgeries are being performed on patients that have more complex medical pictures. Outpatient surgery centers are now beginning to take on more complex surgeries and patients.[34]

Preoperative patient teaching is a highly effective nursing function that has significant benefits to all patients but in particular outpatient surgery patients. The benefits of patient education include a speedy recovery, relief of anxiety, increase of self-esteem by increasing self-efficacy, reduced cost of hospitalization, prevented complaints about care, and decreased perceived immediate and residual pain.[35] Preoperative education for families of a patient undergoing surgery reduces or alleviates anxiety, reduces hospital costs, hastens the return of normal family functioning, increases self-esteem, and develops support for the caregiver's efforts. It is expected that outpatient surgeries will only increase. However, with shorter hospital stays, patient teaching has become a greater challenge for perioperative nurses.

Patients (and families and caregivers) must be adequately prepared to assume responsibility for postdischarge care. Decisions must be made on what the patient needs to know to ensure preparedness for surgery, facilitate patient cooperation, and provide for self-care at home. Perioperative nurses need to provide preoperative instruction, postoperative assessment, and preparation for discharge. Perioperative nurses working in a same day surgery setting are expected to be extra vigilant in their preoperative assessments.

A. Preoperative Instructions

The preadmission testing nurse is typically the individual who begins the data-gathering process when the patient comes in for the required blood work or EKG several days before surgery. The preadmission testing nurse usually provides instructions on the surgical routine and the behavior expected of the patient, for example, not eating or drinking after midnight before the surgery.

Oral instructions may be supplemented or replaced with written instructions and should cover the time the patient is expected to arrive at the same day surgery suite, the expected length of surgery, limitations on food intake, how to accommodate essential medications that cannot be missed such as antiseizure medications, pain management after discharge, and the requirement to have a responsible adult take the patient home and stay with the patient for 24 hours after surgery.

TIP: Failure to provide instructions or ascertain that the patient understands the instructions can contribute to patient injury.

The standard of care requires that a registered nurse, rather than a licensed practical nurse, obtain the initial assessment information when the patient arrives in the same day surgery center on the day of the procedure. Critical information about the patient's health status should be brought to the attention of the surgeon or anesthesiologist. For example, some patients have a family history of a rare but often fatal condition known as malignant hyperthermia. This condition may manifest itself during or after surgery. The anesthesiologist and same day surgery nurse should ask about a history of this condition.

B. Preoperative Assessment

The healthcare professionals working in the same day surgery area have a right to expect reasonable cooperation from the surgical patient. A patient may refuse to give personal information because:

1. too many healthcare providers have been collecting the same data,
2. the patient does not understand the significance of providing certain information, or
3. the patient is suspicious or secretive about sharing personal information.

In the following case the lack of knowledge about a patient's cardiac disease was a factor in her brain damage. A woman from Kentucky went into a cardiac arrest during a breast biopsy and suffered brain damage. The outcome might have been avoided had the surgeon known the patient was suffering from a potassium deficiency. When Mrs. Clark was admitted to the hospital she informed the nurse that she was using Lasix, a drug used to reduce high blood pressure. The nurse charted this in the medications section of her chart. The attending physicians indicated they never saw this note when they obtained a preoperative history from Mrs. Clark the night

before surgery. A third physician testified that this form was not on Mrs. Clark's chart when it went to the operating room. During surgery Mrs. Clark suffered a cardiac arrest. The jury entered a verdict in favor of the defendants. The plaintiff appealed.

On appeal the defendants won again. The court said "for her own safety a patient must exercise ordinary care to give an accurate history to her treating physician." One of the physicians testified that he asked Mrs. Clark whether she had been taking any medications and she denied she had. She also specifically denied she had heart disease. The court said there was evidence she misled her physician about her condition.[36]

In this case, the patient understood the importance of volunteering the information, when the nurse asked her, that she was taking Lasix. For some inexplicable reason she did not share the same information with the physician. A second curious factor in this case is why the physicians did not read the nursing admission assessment. The plaintiff's attorney may find it beneficial to cross-examine the surgeon on the purpose of nursing documentation. Juries are usually not sympathetic when a doctor admits to not reading nursing documentation. It is easy for the plaintiff's attorney to stress the reason why the nurse documents in the medical record and how critical information can affect the patient's outcome.

TIP: When the patient fails to communicate important health information or cooperate, the nurse should note this and notify the physician if necessary. A patient may be unable to provide important history information because of:

1. decreased or altered level of consciousness,
2. severe pain or fear,
3. certain psychiatric disturbances,
4. a language barrier, or
5. disorientation.

When this occurs, the nurse is obligated to attempt to gather the information from other sources and should clearly document any difficulties in communicating with the patient.

C. Patient Monitoring

Patient monitoring is very similar to the care rendered in an in-hospital acute care setting. However, more emphasis in a team approach to patient care is placed upon the family or caregiver as well as healthcare professionals. The candidate for elective surgery in the ambulatory setting is defined by the patient's overall health, the type of surgical procedure, and the anesthesia provided.

There are different types of anesthesia that the patient and the anesthesiologist discuss and agree upon during a preoperative anesthesia evaluation. Anesthesia can be in the form of a local anesthetic, intravenous sedation, or a general anesthesia. As with any surgical procedure, the patient must have the required preoperative laboratory and diagnostic tests prior to surgery. Certain risk factors for ambulatory surgery patients include:

- heart disease, such as congestive heart failure or prior heart attack
- respiratory diseases, such as emphysema or asthma
- any communicable disease, such as tuberculosis
- diabetes
- obesity
- steroid therapy
- alcohol, drug abuse, or both
- psychiatric illness, psychotropic drug therapy
- extreme age, history of latex allergy
- history of malignant hyperthermia, personal or family member
- inadequate home resources for postoperative care

These risk factors need to be evaluated in order to obtain a more comprehensive preoperative evaluation, order the appropriate laboratory or diagnostic studies, plan for any special needs during surgery, and arrange as necessary any home care needs for the postoperative period to avoid unanticipated complications.

On the day of surgery, the preoperative nurse evaluates the patient on admission. After the patient check-in process and initial chart review is completed, patient monitoring is initiated. This patient monitoring includes:

- obtaining vital signs
- determining the NPO status
- administering any medications ordered and observing for reactions
- assessing the patient comfort and/or pain levels preoperatively
- providing emotional support for family member or caregiver and patient

In addition to current prescription medications taken by the patient, herbal remedies have often been overlooked by patients when gathering medical information. Viewed as a "natural product," patients may forget to inform the nurse or anesthesia provider regarding the use of these products. Patients need to be queried regarding the use of herbal products, due to their increased usage. Some herbal products can significantly change the patient's heart, blood pressure, bleeding properties and can interact with anesthesia.

In the ambulatory care setting, perioperative nursing encompasses the entire surgical experience, from admission through the discharge process. In the ambulatory surgery unit, this includes the postoperative care of the patient. The American Society for PeriAnesthesia Nurses (ASPAN) addresses the postoperative care and divides the care into three subgroups:

- Phase I—equipped similarly to a traditional hospital PACU: staff and personnel are equipped and trained to respond and prevent complications resulting from anesthesia or surgery. There is close monitoring of patient vital signs, response to anesthesia, respiratory status, fluid intake and output, observation for postoperative surgical bleeding, nausea, vomiting, and so on. Patients must meet the discharge criteria of Phase I PACU before transitioning to Phase II.[37] The criteria for patient transition is:
    - airway patency, respiratory function, and oxygen saturation
    - stability of vital signs including temperature
    - level of consciousness and muscular strength
    - mobility
    - patency of tubes, drains, catheters, intravenous lines
    - condition of dressing or surgical site
    - skin color and condition
    - intake and output
    - comfort
    - anxiety
    - interaction with family, caregiver, or parent
    - numerical score (if used)

- Phase II—can be in some institutions located within a Phase I PACU. Phase II PACU is often a separate area where patients are physically moved into a more comfortable setting using recliners for patient comfort. Discharge from Phase II is defined as "adequate recovery from anesthesia, not from the surgical procedure." These criteria include:
    - adequate respiratory function
    - stability of vital signs
    - resolution of hypothermia

- level of consciousness and muscular strength
- ability to ambulate consistent with preoperative baseline
- ability to swallow
- minimal nausea and vomiting
- skin color and condition
- condition of surgical site
- adequate pain control
- adequate neuron-vascular status of an operative extremity
- ability to void
- physical, emotional, psychological factors[38]

Refer to Appendix 5.3 for an expert witness report involving a case of failure to monitor in the same day surgery area.

- Phase III—is an extended recovery period for patients who do not meet the criteria for discharge from Phase II and the ambulatory surgery unit. Those patients who do not meet the criteria are usually patients who have experienced unexpected complex postoperative care (postoperative nausea, vomiting and/or pain control), unexpected surgical complications, or problems related to the family or caregiver in the home environment. When it is determined that a patient requires an extended or overnight stay, the ambulatory surgery facility must coordinate the transfer and follow-up care with the receiving facility or overnight hospital unit. A copy of the patient record, discharge summary, and notes must accompany the patient to the receiving facility. A verbal report to the receiving facility or unit should be provided at the time of discharge from the ambulatory surgery unit.[39]

TIP: Recent developments in anesthetic agents have allowed patients to awaken from anesthesia more quickly, thus bypassing the more acute settings of the Phase I PACU and recovering from their anesthesia in Phase II. It is important to understand that the phases of postoperative recovery are distinct levels of nursing care, monitoring and assessment for the surgical patient in the postoperative period.

D. Medication Errors

Preoperative and postoperative medications are given in the same day surgery suite. Potential for administering the wrong medication exists in this area. In a New Jersey case, a nurse in a preoperative same day surgery area administered eye drops not ordered by the physician. The patient was to have eye surgery without dilation before surgery. Because of an error in communication and the nurse's assumption that the patient was to have her eye dilated, the nurse administered dilating drops. She wrote the medication as if it were a telephone order, although there was no communication between her and the surgeon before she began giving the patient the eye drops. When the surgeon discovered the error he attempted to reverse the dilation, then performed the surgery. The patient claimed she did not have a good result from the surgery and sued the surgeon, who in turn attributed the poor result to the preoperative dilation. The case was settled with contributions from the surgeon and nurse. *DeSouza v. Wunsh*, unpublished decision.

E. Discharge Planning and Criteria

Discharge planning is often considered a postoperative activity that occurs at the time of discharge. However a good assessment of the patient's needs at the time of discharge is best performed during the preoperative phase. Discharge planning is defined as "preparing for moving the patient from one level of care to another within or outside the current health agency."[40] The perioperative nurse can make a significant contribution to the discharge process through implementation of a discharge plan early in the preoperative phase. Whether a patient will be discharged to the home or remain within the hospital, the perioperative nurse may serve as a liaison between the family and essential hospital personnel, such as social services to assist the patient and family. Many facilities address the issue of stability of the patient at the time of discharge by specifying criteria that must be met before the patient leaves.

Most hospitals use the Aldrete system, which was discussed earlier in this section. In the ambulatory surgery setting, the Aldrete scoring system was modified in 1995 in response to the trends in day surgery patient care. The Aldrete score remains essentially unchanged with the exception of a substitution for color index with SaO2 (oxygen saturation) and the addition of five criteria to meet the discharge requirements from an ambulatory surgery unit. The modified Aldrete, which was explained earlier, is used to meet discharge criteria from the ambulatory surgery setting.

Additionally, professional organizations, such as the American Society of Anesthesiologists and the American Society of PeriAnesthesia Nurses, have promulgated standards relating to the discharge of a patient. It is left to the nurse caring for the patient to determine if the patient is stable enough to be discharged. Examples of discharge criteria are shown in Figure 5.8. Strict, clear-cut criteria must be in place and adhered to before permitting the patient to leave. Patient care in the PACU should meet the ASPAN standards of care as well as any specific department discharge policies to avoid an adverse event.

As part of the discharge process, nurses often give written instructions because many patients are unable to recall facts about the follow-up instructions they were given. The patient or responsible adult must sign the written instructions to verify understanding. The patient is discharged with a responsible adult to accompany her home. A follow-up phone call to the patient at home is customary and provides additional feedback from the patient and family member or caregiver to the nurse regarding their surgical experience.

Of concern to ambulatory surgery units is the issue of patients leaving a same day surgery post procedure unit without a responsible adult to drive the patient home. In *Young v. Gastro-Intestinal Center Inc.*, the Supreme Court of Arkansas CV-2002-7057, on appeal reversed and affirmed the Appellees. It was determined that when a patient is admitted through an office for a diagnostic or surgical procedure, the patient is informed that arrangements for a responsible driver must be made prior to admission for the intended procedure or surgery. The surgical provider, for example, the surgical center or diagnostic center, relies on the patient's statements that transportation has been arranged.

In *Young v. Gastro-Intestinal Center*, the patient was scheduled for and underwent a colonoscopy. Preoperatively he told the staff that he had a friend to drive him home. Postoperatively it was learned there was no friend to accompany the patient home and in fact the patient had every intention of driving himself. The patient was repeatedly advised to remain the required length of time for recovery or to wait until someone could drive him home. The patient refused. Young signed an AMA (against medical advice) release form before he left. The patient, as it was later learned, went on to another medical appointment. Returning home from the second medical appointment, Young was involved in a one car crash resulting in his death several months later. It was determined in both the trial court and court of appeals, the nurse had neither the right nor a legal duty to impose physical restrictions, personally drive him home, retain his car keys, or physically restrain him. In the Arkansas Court of Appeals findings, it was determined the nurse on duty went above and beyond what was expected or reasonably required as a standard of care. The patient was not discharged but left against medical advice. Short of physical restraint, there was no duty to the patient beyond the preoperative guidelines of having a driver take the patient home at the time of discharge. The patient was aware of this requirement preoperatively. He informed the center there were arrangements for a driver when there were none.

Accordingly, in the PACU, as in other areas of nursing, proper documentation is required. Good charting can be the key to a nurse successfully prevailing in a lawsuit either by having the case dismissed or by winning at the time of trial. The following case typifies how documentation can be a nurse's best defense.

In *Guido & Elvira Guerriero v. C. Silverman, M.D. et al.*, Essex County, N.J., Docket No. ESX-L-2653-92, the plaintiff underwent an outpatient cataract removal. The ambulatory care nurse carefully instructed the plaintiff to call his physician with any problems related to his eye. The nurse checked off the appropriate boxes on the discharge instruction sheet and gave the plaintiff a copy of it. The plaintiff developed eye pain but delayed in contacting his physician. By the time plaintiff was seen by the ophthalmologist, he had a severe infection and lost his vision in one eye. One of the plaintiff's claims of negligence was that he had not been informed of the signs and symptoms of infection. However, the nurse was able to demonstrate that instructions had been provided. This case was dismissed without payment to the plaintiffs.

TIP: Analysis of documentation becomes critical when there are allegations that the patient experienced complications after discharge. This is particularly true when there may have been evidence that signs and symptoms of the complications would have shown up while the patient was in the same day surgery suite. Review the medical record for a copy of the written instructions.

F. Falls

Several discharge criteria come into play in determining the patient's readiness for discharge from the same day surgery unit. The patient's blood pressure should be near preoperative values. The patient should be able to walk without assistive devices (if done preoperatively), tolerate liquids, and urinate. Dressings should be evaluated for postoperative bleeding. Patients should be assisted to the bathroom as the lingering effects of anesthesia can make the patient dizzy and prone to falls. The nurse is expected to make an assessment of the patient's condition and exercise judgment as to whether it is necessary to stay in the bathroom with the patient. See Figure 5.9.

- Orientation
- Pain
- Nausea and Vomiting
- Surgical Bleeding
- Circulation and Sensation
- Vital signs
- Ambulation
- Oral Intake
- Voiding

Figure 5.9 Discharge Criteria from the Same Day PACU

G. Follow-Up Telephone Calls

It is common practice for the same day surgery nurse to contact the patient following discharge to ascertain the patient's status and obtain the patient's opinion of the services performed by the same day surgery nurses. The nurse is in an excellent position to identify postoperative complications and provide advice on the course of action the patient should take. The chart should reflect the substance of any conversation in which advice is given. The risks of providing advice over the telephone without seeing the patient are the same inherent in any type of "telephone medicine." Nurses routinely encourage the patient to contact the surgeon when symptoms warrant medical attention. Such symptoms can include postoperative pain, fever, chills, or unexpected bleeding from the surgical site. The medical record should be carefully reviewed for evidence of complaints solicited from the patient and instructions, particularly when there is a possibility the patient chose to ignore the guidance provided by the nurse.

TIP: Follow-up phone calls are usually documented in the medical record and reflect the postoperative patient information collected at the time of the call.

5.8 Screening the Perioperative Case

Many liability risks face the surgical nurse and the rest of the perioperative team. The attorney evaluating cases of injuries occurring in the surgical suite needs to consider the roles and responsibilities of all concerned. Policies and procedures offer detailed information on the standard of care for the operating room nurse. It is essential that they be reviewed as the case proceeds.

Review of perioperative nursing documentation should be compared with the standards of the Association of Operating Room Nurses. This organization has specific criteria for the information that nurses should document. For postoperative documentation, refer to American Society of Peri-Anesthesia Nursing standards. The typical forms generated in the surgical suite are listed in Chapter 7, *Nursing Documentation,* in Volume I. In general, nurses are expected to document at every step in the preoperative, intraoperative, and postoperative phases. The medical record should reveal the information shown in Figure 5.10. In most perioperative cases, since the nurse's contact with the patient is brief, the defendants have no memory of the events and rely on the medical record. However, if sufficient charting is present, either by way of a written narrative note or the use of a checklist form, a plaintiff's attorney should carefully evaluate the viability of the claim.

As previously discussed, the handoff communication is an active form of communication among caregivers that occurs from the operating room to the recovery room; from surgeon or anesthesiologist to nurse or operating room nurse to PACU nurse. The primary objective of the handoff communication is to provide accurate, up-to-date information regarding the patient: his care and treatment rendered, current condition, and any recent or anticipated changes in the patient condition. Handoffs occur at nursing shift changes, physicians transferring complete responsibility to another physician, or staff leaving a unit for a short time with a relief present to assume temporary responsibility.

5.9 Risk Management Hints

At a minimum, the nurse should always follow the institution's policies and exercise diligence in caring for the perioperative patient. If there is no hospital policy on a particular function, then the institution should be encouraged to write one. Professional associations, such as the American Nurses Association or the Operating Room Nurses Association, have prepared standardized nursing policies. An institution can adopt these policies in whole or with minor changes to adapt them to circumstances unique to a particular institution.

Institutions have a duty to conduct their operations in accordance with currently accepted standards of the relevant profession. A hospital's failure to adopt and follow a policy of the Operating Room Nurse Association or the American Society of PeriAnesthesia Nurses can be considered, by itself, an act of negligence in some situations. In *Tralette v. French Hospital,* 180 Cal. Rptr. 152 (Cal. App. 1982), the court held that the hospital had a legal duty to devise an adequate operating room sponge accounting procedure. This ruling meant it was negligent for the hospital not to have a written policy.

Policies are accepted statements on how services should be provided to optimize patient safety. If it can be proven the nurse adhered to the institution's policy and that this policy is consistent with current industry standards, the probability of nursing malpractice is greatly reduced. Reliance on a written policy is one of the best defenses in a *res ipsa loquitur* case.

TIP: Injury to patients from malpractice can be prevented especially through the development of policies for repetitive perioperative tasks.

Protocols for surgical clearance are imperative. This includes guidelines to ensure that perioperative standing orders are met: for example, the patient received the correct preoperative medications in proper dosages, the informed consent was signed, blood work was completed and the values were within acceptable ranges, and the order for no food or drink was observed.

Preoperative
- The steps taken to prepare the patient for surgery (preoperative checklist) which is supposed to ensure all the ordered tests are completed and interpreted before surgery.

Holding area
The holding room nurse's observations, which include:
- greeting and initiating patient check in procedures
- placement of identification band
- reviewing the consent and validating the surgical procedure with the patient (site, limb, etc.)
- review of ordered preoperative tests
- documenting the placement of an intravenous access if performed in the holding area.
- preoperative vital signs
- medications administered (e.g., eye drops, IV antibiotics) and documented on the preoperative assessment form

Operating room
- The patient's skin condition on arrival and discharge from the operating room (particularly in relation to the grounding pad site)
- The location of the grounding pad, the lot number and expiration date of the grounding pad, the specific machine number used, and settings used with the electrocautery machine
- The patient's mental, physical, and emotional status on arrival to the operating room
- Positioning and padding used during surgery
- The type of temperature control blanket and the temperature settings used
- Insertion of intravenous devices, urinary catheters, drains, packings and dressings
- Medications administered by the operating room nurse
- Sites of cardiac monitors
- The use of a tourniquet cuff, and the times the cuff was inflated and deflated
- The instrument, needle, and sponge counts
- The types of implants used, the serial numbers and sizes
- The classification of the wound—clean, contaminated and so on

- The time of the patient's arrival and departure
- The names of the persons who accompanied the patient to the PACU
- The names of the scrub and circulating nurses
- The times and names of the individuals who relieved the scrub and circulating nurses for breaks
- Estimated blood loss and urinary output, if applicable

Post anesthesia care unit
- The time of the patient's arrival and departure
- The patient's vital signs
- Location and condition of the dressing or cast
- Medications administered and the patient's response
- Pain assessment
- Pulse oximetry readings
- Urinary output
- Time of extubation
- Intravenous fluids administered
- The patient's status on admission and discharge as measured against standardized criteria (Aldrete score)
- The name of the nurse who receives report on the patient, if the patient is being transferred to an inpatient unit

Same day surgery
- Preoperative history, physical assessment
- The patient's mental and emotional status before surgery
- Verification that the patient did not eat or drink before surgery
- Allergies
- Vital signs before surgery
- Treatments performed in the preoperative area
- Perioperative documentation, as described above
- Postoperative assessment, as described above
- The patient's compliance with discharge criteria
- The postoperative phone call, including the patient's status and advice given

Figure 5.10 Perioperative Nursing Documentation Responsibilities

The Joint Commission reviewed 64 cases related to operative and postoperative complications: 84 percent resulted in death and 16 percent resulted in serious injury. However, the cases did not include those directly related to medication errors or administration of anesthesia. Fifty-eight percent of the complications occurred during the postoperative procedure period, 23 percent during the intraoperative phase, 13 percent during post anesthesia recovery, and 6 percent during anesthesia induction. Recommendations of risk-reduction strategies are as follows:

- Improving staff orientation and training
- Educating and counseling physicians
- Expanding on-call coverage, especially in radiology
- Standardizing procedures across settings of care
- Revising the credentialing and privileging procedures
- Clearly defining expected channels of communication
- Revising the competency evaluation process
- Monitoring consistency of compliance with procedures
- Implementing a teleradiology program
- Improving communication between the various healthcare disciplines[41]

Based on numerous reported cases of malpractice, there are several areas where the need for detailed policies is particularly acute. Foremost is a comprehensive policy on informed consent. Other areas where written, standardized policies are critical include sponge and instrument counting, patient monitoring with various devices, such as cardiac monitoring during procedures, and documentation of medication administration. Policies and job descriptions that specify the member of the team responsible for a given task are helpful in extricating nurses from lawsuits in which the entire surgical team is sued. Appropriate patient discharge criteria need to be standardized through written policies that include discharge instructions for the patient. After everything else has been considered, proper documentation is still the nurse's best defense.

TIP: The operating room nursing staff should have written policies to follow in situations where a patient is already medicated and the consent is found to be defective or deficient.

5.10 Summary

The vast majority of patients undergo the perioperative experience without sustaining a complication. However, if an injury occurs in this clinical practice area it is usually one that can lead to significant damages. Litigating perioperative cases can be complicated by the multiple overlapping responsibilities of the surgical team. These cases constitute a complex area of medical malpractice. The attorney needs to exercise caution and have the requisite knowledge when delving in this arena. Yet, it can be a worthy endeavor because it offers the plaintiff's attorney the opportunity to access several deep pockets as a source of recovery for the injured client. It also provides the defense attorney with unique and creative avenues of defense.

Endnotes

1. Association of Operating Room Nurses, *Standards, Recommended Practices and Guidelines,* pg. 7, AORN Publications, Denver, Colorado, 2005.

2. *Id.,* p. 15.

3. ECRI Institute. Radio-frequency surgical sponge detection: a new way to lower the odds of leaving a sponge (and similar items) in patients [evaluation]. *Health Devices* 37, no.7 (2008 Jul): 193-202.

4. *Id.*

5. Regenbogen, S.E., Greenberg, C.C., Resch, S.C., et al. Prevention of retained surgical sponges: A decision-analytic model predicting relative cost-effectiveness. *Surgery* 145, no. 5 (2009 May): 527-35.

6. Greenberg, C.C., Diaz-Flores, R., Lipsitz, S.R., et al. Bar-coding surgical sponges to improve safety: A randomized controlled trial. *Ann Surg* 247, no. 4 (2008 Apr): 612-6.

7. See note 3.

8. Guthrie and Rhodes, "The History of Medicine and Surgery, The Ancient Middle East and Egypt," The New Encyclopedia Britannica, Vol. 23, 775. Chicago: Encyclopedia Britannica, Inc., 2005.

9. Laska L. (ed.), "Surgical towel left in aorto-bifemoral bypass graft surgery patient," *Medical Malpractice Verdicts, Settlements and Experts* (December 2004): 41.

10. Laska, L. (ed.), "Burns to neck and chest of girl from hot water used to heat nasal splint," *Medical Malpractice Verdicts, Settlements and Experts* (May 2005): 46.

11. Lincourt, A.E., Harrell A, Cristiano J, et al. Retained foreign bodies after surgery. *J Surg Res* 138, no. 2, (2007 Apr): 170-4.

12. Gawande A.A., Studdert, D.M., Orav, E.J., et al. Risk factors for retained foreign bodies after surgery. *N Eng J Med* 348, no. 3 (2003 Jan 16): 229-35.

13. Centers for Medicare & Medicaid Services. Hospital-acquired condition (present on admission indicator) [online]. 2009 Feb 19 [cited 2009 Mar 11]. Available from Internet: http://www.cms.hhs.gov/HospitalAcq-Cond/ 06_Hospital-Acquired_Conditions.asp, accessed 7/12/10.

14. National Quality Forum. *Serious reportable events in healthcare 2006 update: a consensus report.* Washington (DC): National Quality Forum; 2007.

15. The Joint Commission. Joint Commission fact sheet. Facts about the sentinel event policy [online]. 2008 Mar 20 [cited 2009 Mar 11]. Available from: http://www. jointcommission.org/AboutUs/Fact_Sheets/sep_facts. htm. accessed 7/14/10.

16. www.jointcommission.org/SentinelEvents/Policyand-Procedures/se_pp.htm, *Sentinel Event Policy and Procedures*. Updated June 2005, accessed 714/10.

17. Pennsylvania Patient Safety Reporting System, www. patientsafetyauthority.org, accessed 7/14/10.

18. September 25, 2008, On Fire in the OR: Hundreds are Hurt Every Year (MSNBC: Fires in the Operating Room).

19. Murphy, E., "Liability for incorrect intraoperative medications," *AORN Journal* (November 1989): 1106.

20. Tammelleo, A. (ed.), "Infant severely burned by heating pad," Regan Report on Nursing Law (October 1987): 2.

21. Kapsar, P., "Risks of surgery: Some are the nurse'," *RN* (November 1989): 71.

22. Odell, R. C., "Pearls, pitfalls and advancements in the delivery of electrosurgical energy during laparoscopy," *Problems in General Surgery* 19, no. 2 (2002): 5–17.

23. Association of Operating Room Nurses, *Standards, Recommended Practices and Guidelines, RP: Minimally Invasive Surgery, RP III,* 507. Denver, Colorado: AORN Publications, 2006.

24. Laska, L. (ed.), "Flash fire During Surgery—Death- $450,000 Massachusetts Settlement," *Medical Malpractice Verdicts, Settlements and Experts* (July 2005): 41.

25. Davis, P. D., "The Nurse's Duty to Intervene-Initiating the Chain of Command, What You Should Know: Practice Guidelines," www.thedoctors.com/risk/general/practiceguidelines/j4242.asp, September 2003, accessed 6/20/10.

26. Kuc, J. and Pietro, J., "Safe discharge from the PACU and ambulatory care setting," *Journal of Nursing Law* 6, no. 2 (August 1999): 7–14.

27. Laska, L. (ed.), "Woman claims negligent monitoring in recovery room after pain killers administered caused brain damage," Medical Malpractice Verdicts, Settlements and Experts (December 2004): 28.

28. Cushing, M., "Back to (PACU) Basics," *American Journal of Nursing* (July 1992): 21.

29. Creighton, M., "Recovery Room Nurses: Legal Implications," *Nursing Management* (January 1987): 22.

30. Odom, J., "Postoperative Patient Care and Pain Management," In *Care of the Patient in Surgery*, Twelfth edition, by Rothrock J. Alexander, 253–279. St. Louis: Mosby, 2003.

31. Laska, L. (ed.), "Failure to properly monitor following appendectomy," *Medical Malpractice Verdicts, Settlements & Experts* (April 2006): 3.

32. "Following hospital policy: a legal risk?" *Nursing* 94 (May 1994): 26.

33. 28 Pa. Code § 551.3 [online]. [cited 25 Feb 2009] Available from: http://www.pacode.com/secure/data/028/ chapter551/s551.3.html, accessed 7/14/10.

34. Cullen, A.J., Hall, M.J., Golosinsky, A. Ambulatory surgery in the United States, 2006. National Health Statistics Reports. No. 11. Hyattsville (MD): National Center for Health Statistics; 2009.

35. Fox, V. J., "Patient Education and Discharge Planning," In *Care of the Patient in Surgery*, Twelfth edition, by Rothrock J. Alexander, 297–327. St. Louis: Mosby, 2003.

36. Regan, W., "Nursing care data sheets," *Regan Report on Nursing Law* 1 (February 1980).

37. McEwan, D. R. J., "Patient Education and Discharge Planning," In *Care of the Patient in Surgery*, Twelfth edition, by Rothrock J. Alexander, 1201–1204. St. Louis: Mosby, 2003.

38. Redmond, M. C., "Post Anesthesia Assessment Phase II," In *PeriAnesthesia Nursing Core Curriculum, Pre-operative, Phase I and Phase II PACU Nursing*, by Quinn and Shick, 1246. St. Louis: Saunders, 2004.

39. *Id.*

40. See note 35.

41. www.jointcommission.org/sentinelevents/sentine-leventalert/sea_12.htm, *Operative and Postoperative Complications: Post Anesthesia Assessment Phase II Lessons for the Future*, Issue 12, February 4, 2004, accessed 7/14/10.

Additional Reading

The Joint Commission, (www.theJointCommisssion.org) *National Patient Safety Goals,* 2006-2009 and pending 2010 goals, accessed 6/20/10.

Institute For Safe Medication Practices, www.ismp.org/newsletters/acutecare/articles/20030710.asp?ptr=y, Safety Issues with Patient Controlled Analgesia-Part I-How errors occur, accessed 6/20/10.

Table of Cases

Ackerman v. Lerwick, 676 S.W.2d 318 (Mo. App. 1984)

Adams v. Leindholdt, 579 P.2d 618 (Colo. 1978)

Anderson v. Somberg, 67 N.J. 291, 338 A.2d 1, cert denied, 423 U.S. 929 (1975)

Beck v. Lovelle, So. 2d 245 (La. App. 1978)

Benedict v. Bondi, 122, A.2d 209 (Pa. 1956)

Bing v. Thunig, 2 N.Y.2d 656 (1957)

Burke v. Washington Hospital Center, 154 U.S. App. D.C. 253, 475 F.2d 364 (9th Cir. 1992)

Buzan v. Mercy Hospital, Inc., 203 So. 2d 11, 29 A.L.R.3d 1059 (Fla. App. 1967)

Cafazzo v. Central Medical Health Services, 660 A.2d 521 (Pa. 1995)

Cennamo v. St. Barnabas, unpublished opinion.

Chin v. St. Barnabas Medical Center, 711 A.2d 352 (N.J. Super. A.D. 1998)

City of Somerset v. Hart, 549 S.W.2d 814 (Ky. 1977)

Cooper v. Curry, 589 P.2d 201 (N.M. 1978)

Cooper v. Roberts, 220 Pa. Super. 260, 286 A.2d 647 (1971)

Czubinsky v. Doctors Hospital, 188 Cal. Rptr. 685, 139 Cal. App. 3d 361 (1983)

Danks v. Maher, 177 So. 2d 412 (La. App. 1965)

Darling v. Charleston Community Memorial Hospital, 33 Ill.2d 326, 211 N.E.2d 253, 14 A.L.R. 869 (1965), cert. denied, 383 U.S. 946 (1966)

DeSouza v. Wunsh, unpublished decision.

Eyoma v. Falco, 247 N.J. Super. 435, 589 A.2d 653 (1991)

Fiorentino v. Wanger, 227 N.E.2d 296 (1967), 262 App. Div. 2d 693, 272 N.Y.S. 2d 557 (1966)

Fisher v. Barnert Hospital, et al., New Jersey Superior Court, Bergen County, Docket Number BER-L-13127-90, unreported decision.

Flagiello v. Pennsylvania Hospital, 417 Pa. 486, 208 A.2d 193 (1965)

Florence Marie McWilliams v. Valley Medical Center, d/b/a/ Santa Clara County.

Flowers v. HCA Health Services of Tenn., 2006, WL 627183 (Tenn. App., March 14, 2006)

Grant v. Touro Infirmary, 207 So. 2d 235 (La. App.), aff'd in part and rev'd in part on other grounds, 223 So. 2d 148 (La. 1968)

Guido & Elvira Guerriero v. C. Silverman, M.D. et al., Essex County, N.J., Docket No. ESX-L2653-92

Haile v. Sutherland, 598 N.W.2d 424 (Minn, 1999)

Hall v. Arthur, 141 F.3d 844 (8th Cir. 1998)

Harimish v. Children's Hospital Medical Center, 387 Mass. 152, 439 N.E.2d 240 (1982)

Helms v. Williams, 166 S.E.2d 852 (N.C. 1969)

Jones v. Harrisburg Polyclinic Hospital, 437 A.2d 134 (Pa. 1981)

Jose Pepe DeSoto for Denise DeSoto v. Regents, University of California, UC Irvine Medical Center, Orange County, California, Superior Court

Karl v. Armstrong, No. 92-7084 (Hillsborough County, Fla. 1997)

Kitchen v. Minelli et al., Case No. 83/12424 (Pa. 1990)

Koepel v. St. Joseph Hospital and Medical Center, 8 Mich. App. 609, 155 N.W.2d 199, rev'd on other grounds 381 Mich. 440, 163 N.W.2d 222 (1968)

Leonard v. Watsonville Community Hospital, 47 Cal.2d 509, 305 P.2d 36 (1956)

Logesky v. Sheptak, 12 Pitt. S.C. J. 67 (Allegheny Co. 1973)

Martin v. Perth Amboy General Hospital, 104 N.J. Super. 335, 250 A.2d 40 (1969)

Masse v. Mueller, 218 N.W.2d 514 (Wisc. 1974)

Mazer v. Lipshcutz, 327 F.2d 43 (3rd Cir. 1964)

McConnell v. Williams, 361 Pa. 355, 65 A.2d 243 (1949)

McGuinn v. Knickenbocker Hospital, 89 N.Y.S.2d 32, aff'd 276 App. Div. 1079, 97 N.Y.S.2d 186, aff'd 302 N.Y. 633, 97 N.E.2d 760 (1949)

Miller v. Hood, 536 S.W.2d 278 (Tex. 1976)

Moore v. Halifax Hospital, 202 So. 2d 568 (Fla. 1967)

Necolayff v. Genesee Hospital, 296 N.Y. 936 73 N.E.2d 117

Nicholson v. Sister of Charity of Providence, 463 P.2d 861 (Or.)

Palmer v. Clarkside Hospital, 213 Miss. 601, 57 So. 2d 473 (1952)

Pamela Colvin v. Robert Wood Johnson Medical Center et al.

Paterson v. Good Samaritan Hospital and William Tesauro, M.D., Nassau County (New York) Supreme Court, Index No. 8944/95

Pecks v. Charles B. Towns Hospital, 275 App. Div. 302, 89 N.Y.2d 190

Powell v. Mullins, 479 So. 2d 1119 (Ala. 1985)

Ramone v. Mani, 535 S.W.2d 654 (Tex. Civ. App.)

Regula v. Bettigole, 425 N.E.2d 768 (Mass. App. Ct. 1981)

Riase v. Wood, 540 So. 2d 646 (Ala. 1988)

Roberson v. Menorah, 588 S.W.2d 134 (Mo. App. 79)

Rockwell v. Stone, 404 Pa. 561, 173 A.2d 48 (1961)

Rogers v. Duke, 766 S.W.2d 547 (Tex. 1989)

Rudeck v. Wright, 709 P.2d 621 (Mont. 1985)

Savage v. Three Rivers Medical Center, Lawrence County (KY) Circuit Court, Case No. 06-0051

Schloendorff v. Society of New York Hospital, 211 N.Y. 25, 103 N.E. 92 (1914)

Schmidt v. Gibbs, 807 S.W.2d 928 (Ark. 1991)

Schneider v. Albert Einstein Medical Center, 390 A.2d 1271 (Pa. S.Ct. 1978)

Sesselman v. Muhlenberg Hospital, 124 N.J. Super 285, 306 A.2d 474 (1973)

Smelko v. Brinton, 740 P.2d 591 (Kan. 1987)

Sparger v. Worley Hospital, Inc., 547 S.W.2d 582 (Tex. 1977)

Stears v. Park Avenue Hospital, Cal. Super. Ct. Los Angeles Co. Docket No. EAC 9578, May 1973, Citation 27:161, September 15, 1973

Synnott v. Midway Hospital, 287 Minn. 270, 178 N.W.2d 211

Tralette v. French Hospital, 180 Cal. Rptr. 152 (Cal. App. 1982)

Treinas v. Deepdale General Hospital, 570 N.Y.S.2d 185 (1991)

Tropp v. Cayson, 471 So. 2d 375 (Miss. 1985)

Truman v. Thomas, 27 Cal.3d 285 (1982)

Tutton v. Patterson, 714 S.W.2d 268 (Tex. 1986)

VanHook v. Anderson, 824 P.2d 509 (Wash. 1992)

Van Hyning v. Hamilton Hospital, Mercer County (New Jersey) Superior Court

Wagner v. Kaiser Foundation Hospitals, 589 P.2d 1106 (Or. 1979)

Willinger v. Catholic Medical Center of Southwestern Penn., 362 A.2d 280 (Pa. Sup. Ct. 1976)

Wilson v. Lee Memorial Hospital, 65 So. 2d 40 (Fla. 1953)

Ybarra v. Spangard, 146 P.2d 982 (Cal. 1944) aff'd 154 P.2d 687

Yorston v. Pennell, 153 A.2d 255 (Pa. 1969)

Young v. Gastrointestinal Center Inc. (Ark. 2005 No. CV-2002-7057)

Appendix 5.1
Summary of Same Day Surgery Death Case

The patient was a 38-year-old woman admitted to the hospital for an operative laparoscopy. Her chief complaints were chronic pelvic pain, dysmenorrheal (painful menstruation), and infertility.

The patient's vital signs before surgery were blood pressure 100/76, pulse 73, temperature 96, and oxygen saturation 98 percent. Surgery was performed at 9:10 A.M. on 8/25/99 by Dr. S and Dr. V. A sales representative from the manufacturer was present in the operating room.

Dr. S made an infra-umbilical incision and inserted a Verres needle. A syringe was used to confirm the location of the Verres needle. The abdomen was filled with 3 liters of carbon dioxide gas. The incision was enlarged, and a 10/11 mm bladed trocar was inserted. The laparoscope with the attached camera was threaded through the trocar. Two additional 5 mm trocars were then inserted under direct visualization. Dr. V came to the operating room to assist in the surgery.

During the one and one-half hour long surgery, adhesions were lysed (cut) and chromotubation was used. The operative report notes that "Indigo carmine and normal saline with some blood was aspirated." The trocar sites were checked but no further investigation was performed as to the source of the bleeding.

At 10:40 A.M., the surgery was complete. The patient left the operating room for the post anesthesia recovery unit (PACU). Throughout the surgery the vital signs were continuously monitored. Upon discharge from the operating room, the blood pressure was 120/60 and the pulse was 80. Upon arrival at the PACU, the blood pressure was 138/68 and the patient's pulse was 135. Her respiratory rate was 28. She was unconscious with an oral airway in place. Oxygen was administered by face mask at 6 liters with an oxygen saturation of 96 percent. A cardiac monitor showed she was in a sinus tachycardia with a heart rate ranging from 128-138 beats per minute. The patient was medicated with a total of 10 mg of Morphine and 4 mg of Zofran.

The patient's blood pressure showed a consistent drop in the PACU and her pulse consistently rose. The last blood pressure reading was 105/60 at 11:05 A.M. The next blood pressure reading was due at 11:20 A.M. but was not taken. The pulse at 11:20 A.M. was 138.

There were no vital signs taken from that point on. At noon, the patient arrived at the same day surgery unit. Repeat vital signs were not taken. The values recorded on the same day surgery unit are identical to the last values taken in the PACU.)

The nursing notes written between 12:40 P.M. and 2:35 P.M. state the patient was resting comfortably or asleep. According to the nursing notes, on one occasion, her perineal pad was checked for bleeding (at 1:10 P.M.), and her abdominal band aides were checked at 1:35 P.M. At 2:35 P.M., the patient was found unresponsive, pale, and not breathing. A resuscitation effort occurred and was unsuccessful in reviving the patient. She was pronounced dead at 3:35 P.M.

An autopsy performed the following day revealed 900 cc of blood in the abdomen with blood clots. A perforation of the inferior vena cava was noted. There were two mesenteric perforations. The cause of death was determined to be "acute internal hemorrhage due to perforation of the inferior vena cava during a laparoscopic procedure."

Appendix 5.2
Plaintiff Recovery Room Nursing Expert's Report

As requested, I have reviewed the following materials related to the above captioned file:

- Affidavit of Merit of PK
- Amended Complaint
- Same Day Surgery Record of Henry—dated 1/11/05
- Autopsy and Toxicology Report of Mrs. Henry—dated 1/12/05
- ASPAN Standards—dated 2004
- Minor Medical Center's Answers to Interrogatories
- Minor Medical Center's Nursing Standards of Care Same Day Surgery, Exhibit P-2
- Minor Medical Center's Supplemental Answers to Interrogatories
- Minor Medical Center's PACU Guidelines and Policies, Exhibit P-2
- Minor Medical Center's Discharge/Transfer Policies of PACU, Exhibit P-2
- Minor Medical Center's Admission Policies of the PACU, Exhibit P-4
- Minor Medical Center's PACU Delivery of Care Method, Exhibit P-5
- Minor Medical Center's Nursing Direction Policy of the PACU
- Anesthesia Order Sheet, Exhibit P-6
- Nurse U's C.V., Exhibit P-1
- Same Day Surgery Post-Operative Nursing Assessment, Exhibit P-8
- PACU Nursing Record, Exhibit P-7
- Attorney's Request for Hospital Records Correspondence, Exhibit P-9, dated 1/19/05
- Nurse U's Answers to Interrogatories
- Transcript of Testimony of Nurse U
- Minor Medical Center's Credentials Manual of the Medical Staff
- Minor Medical Center's Criteria for Granting Privileges for Procedures which Require Specific Training and Experience
- Minor Medical Center's Rules and Regulations of the Medical Staff
- Plaintiff's Expert Report of Dr. P—dated 12/7/05

Mrs. Henry was 38 years old at the time of this occurrence, when she was admitted to Minor Medical Center with the diagnosis of pelvic pain. According to the medical record, Mrs. Henry was taken to the Operating Room on January 11, 2005 for a diagnostic laparoscopy, chromotubation and possible laparotomy. The surgical procedure was completed and Mrs. Henry was taken to the Post Anesthesia Care Unit (PACU) accompanied by Anesthesiologist, Dr. Y. After approximately 45 minutes in the PACU, Mrs. Henry was transferred to the Same Day Surgery Unit (SDS) where she became unresponsive, with no pulse or spontaneous respirations noted. Resuscitation was unsuccessful and Dr. N pronounced her dead at 3:35 P.M.

Nurse U received Mrs. Henry in the PACU at 10:40 A.M., according to the medical record. Upon admission to the PACU, Nurse U performed and documented her initial assessment including airway patency, vital signs, surgical site, positioning, intake and output, and pain assessment. Mrs. Henry was noted to be unconscious with an oral airway in place upon admission. Oxygen was administered via a simple facemask at 6 liters with a saturation of 96 percent. The cardiac monitor indicated Mrs. Henry to be in a sinus tachycardia with a heart rate of 135/bpm. An IV of Ringers Lactate was infusing via the left antecubital space.

Throughout her PACU stay, Mrs. Henry remained tachycardic with a heart rate ranging from 128-138/bpm. Her blood pressure (BP) ranged from 138/68 upon admission to 105/60 at 11:05 A.M. Nurse U failed to take a BP at 11:20 A.M., immediately prior to discharge. She was medicated with a total of 10 mg of Morphine Sulfate and 4 mg of Zofran. According to the medical record, Mrs. Henry was discharged to the SDS unit at 11:25 A.M. Mrs. Henry was received in SDS at 12:00 P.M. Her whereabouts was unknown for 35 minutes.

Opinion

After careful review of the medical record, I am of the professional nursing opinion that Nurse U deviated from accepted standards of nursing practice in her care of Mrs. Henry.

Nurse U was the admitting nurse and the primary nurse following Mrs. Henry throughout her PACU stay, according to the medical record and her deposition (p.63). She received the patient from Dr. Y supine with the head of bed elevated 20 degrees. She was unresponsive with an oral airway in place. Appropriate monitoring equipment, such as a cardiac monitor, blood pressure cuff, pulse oximeter and tympanic thermometer were available but not completely and timely used in monitoring Mrs. Henry in the PACU. At 10:40 A.M., Mrs. Henry's initial vital signs were taken, recorded and communicated to Dr. Y as stated in Nurse U's deposition (p. 65). The patient's skin was warm and dry and she had three abdominal band aids in place, according to the medical record.

The Post Anesthesia Care Unit Guidelines and Policies of Minor Medical Center state, "Vital signs, including temperature, shall be checked every 15 minutes and properly recorded." The Admission Policies of the PACU #5 state, "An anesthesiologist shall remain in the PACU at least until the patient's vital signs including blood pressure, heart rate, respirations and pulse oximetry are recorded. Vital signs will be continually monitored and charted minimally every 15 minutes until discharge. Unstable patients will be monitored as their status requires."

According to Nurse U, Dr. Y in accordance with the policy, remained in the PACU during the time Mrs. Henry's vital signs were taken (p. 65). In accordance with the policy, Dr. Y left the PACU after the transfer of care to Nurse U and initial vital signs were taken and recorded (p.65). However, Nurse U deviated from these guidelines when she failed to take and record Mrs. Henry's BP at 11:20 A.M.

Nurse U also failed to take and record Mrs. Henry's temperature throughout her entire PACU stay except for the initial temperature taken upon admission at 10:40 A.M. In reviewing the vital signs recorded on the PACU Nursing Record, there is a dangerous trend in her pulse and BP that should have alerted Nurse U that Mrs. Henry may be experiencing hypovolemia. Although Mrs. Henry's BP was returning to her pre-operative level, the recorded BPs continued to show a decrease in value. Along with this decreasing BP, Mrs. Henry remained tachycardic.

In her deposition (p. 127-128), Nurse U states that she questioned Dr. Y initially about Mrs. Henry's tachycardia; however she never addressed the continued tachycardia or decreasing BP with Dr. Y or any other physician. When Nurse U expressed initial concerns in regard to Mrs. Henry's tachycardia, she stated in her deposition (p. 162) that "Dr. Y reported the patient was probably anxious, there was no decrease in her heart rate." Nurse U should have investigated alternative reasons for the continued tachycardia.

Number 7 in the Post Anesthesia Care Unit Guidelines and Policies states: "The patient should meet discharge criteria before transfer from the PACU." In Minor Medical Center's Discharge/Transfer Policies of PACU, criteria for discharge include stable BP and stable cardiac rate and rhythm as two parameters needed to achieve discharge criteria. In light of the decreasing BP, failure to take BP reading at 11:05 A.M., failure to take a temperature at 10:55 A.M.,

11:05 A.M. and 11:20 A.M., and continued tachycardia, it is my professional nursing opinion that Mrs. Henry had not stabilized and therefore did not meet discharge criteria. Notwithstanding, Nurse U states in her deposition (p. 117-122) that Mrs. Henry met discharge criteria at 11:25 A.M. and she accompanied her back to the SDS. According to the medical record, Mrs. Henry arrived back at SDS at noon. There was a 35 minute period, during which Mrs. Henry's whereabouts is unknown.

Nurse U was responsible for the total patient care of Mrs. Henry while in the PACU. According to Minor Medical Center's policy, Delivery of Care Method, total care is described as "carrying out all aspects of the nursing process, including assessment. It also implies the use of relevant standards, medication administration, documentation, interaction with physicians, charge nurse and patient's family as indicated." Nurse U deviated from this policy by failing to completely and timely assess Mrs. Henry's vital signs and communicate with the anesthesiologist and/or surgeon regarding Mrs. Henry's vital signs as stated in her deposition (p. 162-168). She failed to document any nursing interventions performed in response to Mrs. Henry's hemodynamic status, for example but not limited to, assessment of the surgical site, communication with physicians or fluid boluses.

The 2004 Standards of Nursing Practice set forth by the American Society of PeriAnesthesia Nurses includes in Resource 4 the data required for initial, ongoing and discharge assessments. The ongoing assessment should include, but not be limited to monitoring, maintaining and/or improving circulatory function, monitoring of surgical site and documenting nursing actions and/or interventions with outcomes. For reasons previously stated, it is my professional nursing opinion that Nurse U failed to provide these standards of nursing practice to Mrs. Henry.

Summary

I reiterate my professional nursing opinion; Nurse U deviated from the accepted standards of nursing practice. As a PACU nurse, Nurse U failed to recognize and interpret signs of hypovolemia as an indication of the possibility of acute blood loss. She failed to appropriately and timely monitor Mrs. Henry in accordance with the PACU policies as they existed. My opinion is based upon careful review of the medical record and all documents provided to me.

Thank you for the opportunity to consult on this case. If further information becomes available, I reserve my right to amend my report.

Appendix 5.3
Plaintiff's Same Day Surgery Nursing Expert's Report

Dear _____,

Thank you for forwarding material relating to this case. I have reviewed this material:

- Complaint
- Office records of Dr. S
- Admission to Minor Medical Center 1/11/05
- Autopsy and Death Certificate
- Deposition of MC
- Second amended complaint and jury demand
- Plaintiff's answers to interrogatories
- Plaintiff's answers to supplemental interrogatories
- Answers to interrogatories of Dr. S.
- Answers to interrogatories of Dr. V.
- Answers to interrogatories of Minor Medical Center
- Answers to interrogatories of Nurse R. RN
- Answers to interrogatories of Nurse D. RN
- Answers to interrogatories of Nurse B. RN
- Answers to interrogatories of Nurse U. RN
- Answers to interrogatories of R. M CST
- Answers to interrogatories of Nurse Z. RN
- Answers to interrogatories of Nurse S. RN
- Answers to interrogatories of Nurse T. RN
- Minor Medical Center's supplemental answers to interrogatories
- Surgical Manufacturer and MC's answers to interrogatories
- Surgical Manufacturer, Inc and MC's supplemental answers to interrogatories
- Surgical Manufacturer product literature
- Surgical Manufacturer product inquiry verification report
- Surgical Manufacturer analysis report
- Surgical Manufacturer Med Watch Report
- Defense report of defense surgeon expert
- Deposition of Nurse T.
- Deposition of P. Henry
- Deposition of C. W.
- Deposition of B. N.
- Deposition of Nurse Z
- Deposition of Nurse R.
- Deposition of Nurse U

Summary of Medical Facts

J. Henry was a 38-year-old woman who was being treated by Dr. S. She was admitted to Minor Medical Center on 1/11/05 for a diagnostic laparoscopy. That day, the patient had a laparoscopy with dye injection and lysis of adhesions. This information was available to both the post anesthesia care unit (PACU) nurse and the same day surgery (SDS) nurse.

The PACU nurse, Nurse U, documented three blood pressures between 10:40 A.M. and 11:20 A.M.

- 10:40 Blood pressure: 138/68, pulse 135, respirations 28, temperature 96.7
- 10:55 Blood pressure: 110/62, pulse 128, respirations 24
- 11:05 Blood pressure 105/60, pulse 138, respirations 20
- 11:20 No blood pressure taken, pulse 138, respirations 20

There were no further vital signs taken in the recovery room. The patient was transferred to Same Day Surgery Unit either at 11:25 A.M., according to the PACU notes of Nurse U, or 12:00 P.M., according to the notes of Nurse R. The nursing notes of Nurse Z, timed as being written between 12:40 P.M. and 2:35 P.M., state that the patient was resting comfortably or was asleep. According to the nursing notes, on one occasion, her perineal pad was checked for bleeding (at 1:10 P.M.) and on one occasion, her abdominal band-aids were checked (at 1:35 P.M.). Mr. Henry was at his wife's bedside from about 11:25 P.M. to the time of her arrest. He left from 1:00 P.M. to 1:10 P.M. for a break, and otherwise was in the room. According to the testimony of Mr. Henry, no nurses entered his wife's room during this time frame, except for one occasion about 20 minutes after he arrived. At that time, J. Henry was complaining of feeling cold, and the nurse was informed.

At 2:35 P.M., the patient was found unresponsive, pale, and not breathing. A resuscitation effort occurred and was unsuccessful in reviving the patient.

Standard of care

The deviations from the standard of care in Mrs. Henry's care occurred because of a failure to follow professional standards of care from the American Society of PeriAnesthesia Nurses (ASPAN) and the State Division of Health Facilities Evaluation and Licensing.

ASPAN Standards

Mrs. J. Henry was a vulnerable patient who had just undergone a surgical procedure. The Standards of Perianesthesia Nursing Practice 2004 cover care provided in the Post Anesthesia Care Unit and the Same Day Surgery Unit (Phase II and III). These standards, published by the American Society of PeriAnesthesia Nurses, state:

> Our unique knowledge base regarding anesthetic agents and techniques, the physiological and psychological bodily responses to these intrusions, vulnerability of patients subjected to anesthesia and medical interventions regarding anesthesia is coupled with all the principles of medical surgical nursing. Basic life-sustaining needs are of the highest priority, and constant vigilance is required because the perianesthesia needs of the patients are neither minimal nor episodic.

There are two ASPAN standards that are most applicable to the analysis of the care provided to J. Henry. The first is the one that describes responsibilities for assessment.

Assessment

Standard VII, Assessment

Standard: Perianesthesia nursing practice includes the systematic and continuous assessment of the patient's condition. The nurse assures that the data are collected, documented, and communicated. The professional nurse analyzes the data to determine appropriate nursing interventions.

Rationale: Assessment and data collection provide a clinical and legal basis for nursing actions and accountability.

Each of the ASPAN standards is further delineated by structure, process and outcome criteria.

Standard VII, Assessment, Structure Criteria:

1. Specific admission protocols and guidelines are identified for all perianesthesia care settings. These guidelines will address general, local, and regional anesthesia, special procedures, infectious and critical care patients.
2. Unit policies define the components and frequency of nursing assessment.
3. A mechanism exists to set patient care priorities based on the uniqueness of each patient.
4. A mechanism exists to assure that assessment data are available to all appropriate health care providers.

Standard VII, Assessment, Process Criteria

1. The professional nurse assures that all admissions are identified as appropriate and evaluated based on written guidelines.
2. The professional nurse performs the initial assessments and assures a systematic and pertinent collection of data.
3. The professional nurse differentiates the severity of patient problems and prioritizes patient care, designating an appropriate acuity level.
4. The professional nurse reviews all available patient care documentation, revises the data as appropriate and shares information with other health care team members.

Standard VII, Assessment, Outcome Criteria

1. Inappropriate admissions are identified through Quality Improvement program.
2. Assessment and data analysis are documented and based on reliable data and are consistent with accepted practice.
3. Written evidence of nursing assessment and plan of care is available for every patient.
4. Usage of Nursing Diagnosis is at the discretion of individual units.

The Standards of Perianesthesia Nursing Practice 2004 also identify the data required for initial, ongoing and discharge assessment. In Phase II, where Nurse R and Nurse Z delivered their care, the initial assessment of the patient was to include documentation of:

> integration of data received at transfer of care, vital signs (respiratory rate and status, blood pressure, pulse, temperature), level of consciousness, position of patient, patient safety needs, condition and color of skin, neurovascular assessment, as applicable, condition of dressings, drains and tubes, as applicable, muscular response and strength, fluid therapy, location of lines, condition of IV sites, type and amount of fluid infusing, level of physical and emotional comfort, numerical score, if used.

The ongoing assessment was to include:

> identification of the patient and name family normally uses, monitor, maintain and/or improve respiratory and circulatory functions, promote and maintain physical and emotional comfort, monitor surgical/procedural site, interpret and document data obtained

during assessment, administer analgesics and other medications as ordered, record results, provide maximum degree of privacy, provide for safety and confidentiality of information and records, encourage fluids by mouth as indicated, ambulate with assistance, position the patient gradually from a supine to fowlers position, ask patient to urinate prior to discharge, if indicated, review discharge planning with patient, family/accompanying responsible adult as appropriate, provide written home care instructions, and provide follow-up for extended care as indicated. A follow-up phone call to evaluate status is to be performed.

There was no assessment of the patient for 35 minutes (between 11:25 A.M. and 12 P.M.) when the patient was either left in the PACU or left in the Same Day Surgery Unit without attention.

Nurse R did not perform an independent assessment of the patient's vital signs. Instead, the nurse wrote down the patient's blood pressure as 105/60 (a value obtained 55 minutes earlier.) The temperature was recorded as 96.7, a value obtained one hour and 20 minutes earlier at 10:40 A.M. The pulse was recorded as 138 and the respirations as 20, values obtained 40 minutes earlier.

This practice by Nurse R failed to conform to the national standard of care defined by ASPAN. It was not her practice to perform an assessment of the patient's vital signs on admission to the Same Day Surgery Unit. Instead, she followed a misleading practice of documenting vital signs obtained in another unit at a different time, and documented these on the medical record as if these vital signs were obtained on the Same Day Surgery Unit.

There is a discrepancy in testimony as to whether Nurse T assumed responsibility for the patient before Nurse Z took over, or if she was not involved in the patient's care after surgery. Nurse T would have been obligated according to ASPAN standards to perform an independent assessment of the patient's vital signs. If Nurse T gave Nurse Z report on the patient and did not tell her that the vital signs recorded at noon were actually at least 40 minutes to 1 hour 20 minutes old, that was a deviation from the standard of care.

Evaluation

The second ASPAN standard that applies to Mrs. Henry's care refers to evaluation.

Standard IX, Evaluation

Standard: The professional nurse continuously measures the patient's progress toward the desired outcomes and revises the plan of care and interventions as necessary.

Rationale: Evaluation of the health status of the patient is done to determine the effectiveness of nursing interventions so that the plan of care may be continued, or altered.

Standard IX, Evaluation, Structure Criteria

1. Written guidelines are established to assure that nursing actions are analyzed and evaluated.
2. A mechanism exists for consultation to assist the nurse in evaluating the effectiveness on interventions.
3. Written guidelines are established for discharge of the patient from Phase I, II and III.

Standard IX, Evaluation, Process Criteria

1. When interventions are not effective, the professional nurse revises the plan of care.
2. The professional nurse consults and/or collaborates with peers, physicians, and other resources when evaluating the effectiveness of interventions.
3. Nursing staff utilizes guidelines for discharge.

Standard IX, Evaluation, Outcome Criteria

1. Documentation reflects current data and is recorded and used to measure progress toward goal achievement.
2. Consultation is documented as appropriate.
3. Documentation reflects that the patient was appropriately discharged.

Nurse Z did not follow any practice for routine assessment of vital signs throughout the course of the patients stay in the Same Day Surgery Unit. This is particularly striking because the discharge criteria on the nursing documentation form states that the vital signs must be stable. Since there was no specific practice to take the vital signs on admission to the unit and no specific practice to take them during the stay on the unit, the ability to evaluate the patient's achievement of stable vital signs was limited at best.

The Same Day Surgery form used by Minor Medical Center specified the discharge criteria: vital signs stable, retaining fluids/food, nausea/vomiting minimal, absence of respiratory distress, able to ambulate (with appliance as ordered), alert, and voided/if ordered. These discharge criteria are appropriate and conform to the standard of care. The medical record of J. Henry contains no documentation that efforts were made to evaluate this patient's progress towards the goal of discharging her. There is no indication that she was offered fluids, that her need to urinate was questioned, that she was evaluated for pain, that there was an attempt to get her out of bed to walk to the bathroom, or that her lack of progress in waking up was ever questioned. Mr. Henry testified that these interventions were not performed. The responsibility for evaluating Mrs. Henry fell on Nurse Z. The failure to evaluate the patient's status relative to progress towards discharge was a deviation from the standard of care.

State Division of Health Facilities Evaluation and Licensing N.J.A.C. 8:43G-18.5 Nursing care patient services

e) Each patient shall receive nursing care that is organized around ongoing, patient-specific care planning and is consistent with medical care planning. The planning shall include setting measurable goals with the patient and family to the extent possible. This planning, nursing interventions, and patient responses shall be documented in the medical record as defined by hospital policy.

Mrs. Henry had a pattern of declining blood pressure in the PACU. Her pulse was also rapid. According to the testimony of Nurse U, she told Nurse R that the patient's heart rate was a little high and that her heart rate merited watching. Neither Nurse R, Nurse Z, nor Nurse T did any monitoring of the rapid heart rate. The reasonably prudent same day surgery nurse who receives the patient from the PACU is expected to look at the vital signs taken by the nurse who cared for the patient before her arrival on the SDS Unit. The reasonably prudent nurse is expected to recognize the need to obtain a set of vital signs when the patient arrives in the SDS Unit, and to continue to monitor vital signs until they are stable.

The hospital's statement that nursing care was to be individualized, systematic and continuous defines the responsibility to look at the patient and obtain basic information such as vital signs. When asked about the frequency of taking vital signs in the SDS Unit, Nurse W testified that nurses were to use nursing judgment based on their assessment of the patient. In addition to the dropping blood pressure and rapid pulse rate seen in the PACU, Mrs. Henry was showing other signs of bleeding. Her husband testified that she was pale, cold and had abdominal distention. The medical record does not reflect that Nurse Z made these critical assessments.

All nurses deposed agreed that monitoring vital signs takes a few minutes, and that the equipment needed to perform this essential skill was readily available on the nursing unit. Nurse N testified that it is important for a patient who had just had surgery two or three hours before, that a nurse takes vital signs (page 24 of her deposition.)

Nurse R and/or Nurse T deviated from the standard of care by not evaluating the patient's condition upon arrival or until she was relieved by Nurse Z. She failed to take vital signs, note the patient's pallor and cold temperature, particularly in light of the pattern of vital signs in the PACU.

If Mr. Henry's testimony is correct, Nurse Z failed to evaluate the condition of the patient during the two hours the patient was under her care. She failed to note the significance of pallor, abdominal distention, and complaints of being cold, which should have been alarming coupled with a history of declining blood pressure and increasing pulse. She failed to take vital signs or evaluate the patient's lack of progress towards achieving the discharge criteria.

With a reasonable degree of nursing probability, the deviations from the standard of care of these nurses contributed to the chain of events that culminated in the death of J. Henry.

Very truly,

_____

Chapter 6

Psychiatric Nursing Liability

Linda Esposito, PhD, MPH, MSN, APRN-BC and Wanda K. Mohr, PhD, RN, FAAN

Synopsis
6.1 Introduction
6.2 Medical Ethics
6.3 Nurse Practice Acts and Standards of Practice
6.4 The Expanding Role of Nursing
6.5 Obligations of Psychiatric Nurses Under Standards
6.6 Violations of Nursing Practice Standards
    A. Boundaries and Boundary Violations
    B. Violations of Confidentiality
    C. Failures of Assessment, Evaluation, and Documentation
    D. Failure to Provide for Safety
6.7 Liability Risk Related to Psychopharmacology
6.8 The Conundrum of Whistle-blowing
6.9 Rights of Patients Receiving Psychiatric Nursing Care
    A. Freedom from Unreasonable Restriction
    B. Informed Consent
    C. Substituted Consent
    D. Privileged Communication
    E. Evolving Legal Rights
    F. Right to Treatment
    G. Right to Treatment in the Least Restrictive Environment
    H. Seclusion and Restraint
    I. Right to Refuse Treatment
    J. Right to Aftercare
6.10 Legal Issues and Special Patient Populations
6.11 Nursing Ethics in Community Mental Health
6.12 Conclusion
Endnotes

6.1 Introduction

Malpractice payments made by nurses have increased by 63 percent.[1] These figures represent a fraction of the cases that may have been brought against nurses and an award was not made. In addition to potential harm to individuals entrusted into the nurses' care, being named in a malpractice suit is an overwhelming experience that can have financial and professional altering effects. Psychiatric-mental health nurses are accountable for their services they perform or fail to perform. Concepts regarding standard of care arise which are not often clear. It is an area that is continuously evolving which charges the professional to seek continued education. In addition, courts may rule on a plaintiff's behalf based on the *gold standard* of what a reasonably prudent nurse would deliver in a similar situation. This may be a challenge to

determine. Based upon the legal literature, malpractice exists when the action of the psychiatric-mental health nurse results in direct damage to the patient. The elements of malpractice are the four Ds: Dereliction (or deviation) from Duty Directly causing Damages.[2]

- "The clinician had a *Duty of providing reasonable care* to the patient.
- There was a *Dereliction of that duty*, when judged by the standard of the average, prudent practitioner.
- The patient sustained *Damage, a compensable injury or harm*.
- The damage was a *Direct result* of the clinician's failure to exercise a reasonable standard of care."[3]

As the psychiatric-mental health nurse's role expands, increased responsibility and accountability clearly result. Assessments, treatment plans, and interventions must be carried out in a professional, competent manner. Development of measurable outcomes is a crucial activity that assists in verifying treatment efficacy and can inform the treatment plan with required changes that should be made. Working in a multidisciplinary environment and/or seeking collateral information assists in achieving the provision of quality care. While doing so, psychiatric-mental health nurses can ensure their practice meets professional standards, legal mandates, and ethical guidelines. Prescribing psychotropic medications especially in pediatric patients has increased due to advances in psychopharmacology. Also, treating special populations such as children and adolescents has additional unique standards of care specifically formulated to protect these vulnerable populations (i.e., parental consent, child assent, confidentiality issues). Liability for suicide, informed consent and the duty to protect are a few examples of the psychiatric-mental health nurse's responsibilities. Furthermore, it is essential for the psychiatric-mental health nurse to be aware of ethical principles and how to reduce the risk of malpractice.

The goal of this chapter is to discuss and raise the psychiatric-mental health practitioner's awareness of important practice issues and responsibilities within their scope of rendering care. The following information should not be viewed as conclusive. Additional reading and continued education is recommended regarding standards of practice, ethical principles, and legal concerns.

6.2 Medical Ethics

Psychiatric-mental health nursing practice is guided by standards of care, scope of practice guidelines, nursing ethics, and bioethics. To ensure ethical care is rendered, the American Medical Association adopted its first code of ethics in 1847. There are six values that apply to medical ethics:[4]

1. Autonomy—the patient has a right to refuse or choose their treatment.
2. Beneficence—the practitioner should act in the best interest of the patient.
3. Non-Malfeasance—a paramount concept in the provision of care is to do no harm
4. Justice—concerns the distribution of scarce health resources, the decision of who gets what treatment, and if care is rendered to all in a fair and equal manner.
5. Dignity—the patient has a right to dignity.
6. Truthfulness and honesty—involves informed consent.

These values are basic to the principles of ethical professional care. Along with the American Nurses Association's ethical principles, an additional resource for the psychiatric-mental health nurse is the American Psychiatric Association publication of *The Principles of Medical Ethics with Annotations Especially Applicable to Psychiatry*.[5] Here the ethical principles are further delineated to reflect the actions of the practitioner specifically applicable to psychiatry.

6.3 Nurse Practice Acts and Standards of Practice

When considering whether care rendered to the patient is within the standard practice of care, a general principle applies pertaining to the rendering of adequate care to a patient by a "typical" psychiatric nurse. Determinants of standard of care include court opinions, hospital policies and procedures, psychiatric literature, and state and federal guidelines.[6]

The following are examples of standard of care questions that frequently arise in malpractice:[7]

- Was the diagnosis correct and how was the diagnosis made?
- Was reasonable care taken in making the diagnosis: did the nurse spend enough time examining the patient? Were appropriate tests ordered? Were necessary consultations requested and performed?
- Was a reasonable treatment plan created and explained to the patient?
- Were the risks and benefits of the proposed treatment modalities explained to the patient?
- Did appropriate follow-up occur? Specifically, were follow-up visits scheduled in a timely fashion? Did the nurse determine the patient's response to treatment? Did the nurse check to see whether adverse effects had developed? Was consultation obtained on complicated matters?

Providing care that is evidence-based is a standard of care for the psychiatric nurse.

Utilizing data from psychiatric texts, journals, and articles to assist the rendering of care to patients is an important aspect of developing treatment plans and formulating a diagnosis.

The Nurse Practice Act in each state defines the practice of nursing, describes its scope, and identifies its limits within that state. For example, the Pennsylvania Nurse Practice Act defines itself as:

An act relating to the practice of professional nursing; providing for the licensing of nurses and for the revocation and suspension of such licenses, subject to appeal, and for their reinstatement; providing for the renewal of such licenses; regulating nursing in general; prescribing penalties and repealing certain laws. (Tit. amended Dec. 17, 1959, P.L.1888, No.689)

Although Nurse Practice Acts differ according to state, the definition of professional nursing in the Pennsylvania Code is similar to that in most states:

The "Practice of Professional Nursing" means diagnosing and treating human responses to actual or potential health problems through such services as case finding, health teaching, health counseling, and provision of care supportive to or restorative of life and well-being, and executing medical regimens as prescribed by a licensed physician or dentist.

Standards of nursing practice are written documents that outline minimum expectations for safe nursing care. They are used to guide and evaluate nursing care, and the courts look to standards of practice for guidance when malpractice cases are deliberated. Failure to meet these standards may result in action against the nurse's license even if no actual patient injury resulted. Some states have written generic standards of practice for nurses at all levels (from vocational through advanced practice). Nursing specialties and subspecialties have also articulated the standards of practice that are specific to their field. The current Psychiatric Mental Health Nursing standards were published by The American Nurses Association in 1990 and can be purchased through their website (www.nursingworld.org).

6.4 The Expanding Role of Nursing

Nursing is expanding its scope and roles as a result of increasing nursing education, health access needs in communities, and the strong political activities of nursing organizations. New challenges, responsibilities, and opportunities are created out of the expanding scope of practice. Advanced nurse practitioners have prescriptive authority in every state and receive third-party reimbursement from private insurers and Medicaid reimbursement in many states.

The 2000 edition of *Scope and Standards of Psychiatric-Mental Health Nursing Practice* describes psychiatric-mental health nursing as "the diagnosis and treatment of human responses to actual or potential mental health problems."[8,9]

Psychiatric-mental health nurses are educated and prepared to practice their specialty at both the basic and advanced levels. Nurses who have completed a nursing program and have passed their state's licensing examination, practice at the basic level. Those who have received at least a master's degree in nursing, practice at the advanced level as clinical nurse specialists or nurse practitioners.

The most basic level of practice includes nurses educated at a:

- Three-year diploma program typically administered in hospitals;
- Two to three-year associate's degree program usually offered at community colleges;
- Four-year baccalaureate degree program offered at senior colleges and universities.

Graduates of all three programs sit for the same NCLEX-RN licensing examination. Despite the differing educational requirements, there is little practical difference in their scope of practice. At this basic level of practice, psychiatric-mental health nurses promote and encourage the maintenance of health and prevention of disorder, assess biopsychosocial functioning, serve as case managers, design therapeutic environments, and promote self-care activities including medication and symptom management. These nurses also administer medications and employ complementary interventions such as teaching relaxation techniques. They educate patients and families about health, illness, and treatment, provide supportive counseling, intervene in crises, and promote psychiatric rehabilitation.[10,11]

The advanced practice nurse (APN) is an umbrella term given to a registered nurse (RN) who has met advanced educational and clinical practice requirements beyond the two to four years of basic nursing education required of all RNs. There are two types of advanced practice nurses: nurse practitioners and clinical nurse specialists. Some states, such as New Jersey, do not recognize any difference between the two, choosing instead to call both "Advanced Practice Nurses." At the advanced level of practice, psychiatric-mental health nurses deliver comprehensive primary mental healthcare services to patients. These functions include health teaching and screening, performing preventive interventions, and evaluating and managing persons with mental illnesses. Advanced practice nurses also manage mental illnesses which includes formulating diagnoses; ordering and interpreting laboratory tests; prescribing and managing psychopharmacologic medications; conducting individual, family, and group therapies; and facilitating psychiatric rehabilitation.[12,13]

In most psychiatric care settings, nurses are members of an interdisciplinary team. These teams function collaboratively to provide comprehensive care that may include general medical care, substance abuse services, psychotherapy, medication management, access to entitlements, and other needed therapies or assistance. Each team member brings her specialized knowledge to treatment. Team members might include psychologists, psychiatrists, psychiatric nurses, dieticians, social workers, and paraprofessionals such as lay volunteers and former patients. The team also includes the patients and their families.

6.5 Obligations of Psychiatric Nurses Under Standards

Psychiatric-mental health nurses are charged with the responsibility to practice within the standards of practice. Failure to follow standards of care, including failure to complete an assessment and develop a treatment plan, using a variation in standard procedures and failure to follow a physician's verbal or written orders, is one major category of negligence that results in malpractice litigation.[14] Informed by state practice acts, nurses are guided to ensure that their practice remains within the limits of these state practice acts. Furthermore, nurses are held accountable to practice within the limits of their own competency, professional code of ethics and professional practice standards. Clearly, it is important that the nurse is familiar with these standards and maintains updated knowledge of regulatory, standards and policy revisions.

Nurses form therapeutic relationships with patients to gain an understanding of their needs for care. Awareness of their own behavior and of the patient's needs allow a professional to focus on the person or persons receiving care, and to accurately evaluate the outcomes of care. Interactions in nurse-patient relationships are characterized by trust, respect, intimacy, and power. All nurses must appreciate these foundations underlying their relationships with patients, and execute their professional actions and behaviors accordingly. The obligation to maintain standards of professional competence and ethics always lies with the nurse, whatever the context and nature of the nurse-patient relationship.

Practice standards are always evolving to keep pace with the rapid changes occurring in the healthcare sector. Nursing organizations constantly monitor the practice standards to ensure they fit with the reality of the workplace and continue to safeguard the public. Nurses have many obligations that fall under their practice standards. These obligations are contained in the *Scope and Standards of Psychiatric Mental Health Nursing Practice* as published by the American Nurses Association, the American Psychiatric Nurses Association, and the International Society of Psychiatric Mental Health Nurses.[15,16]

6.6 Violations of Nursing Practice Standards
A. Boundaries and Boundary Violations
The term boundary includes the notion of limits or lines or borders.[17] Professional requirements for practice are met when nurses demonstrate their knowledge, skills, and attitudes of therapeutic behavior that are outlined in the practice standards and competencies. Professional boundaries separate therapeutic behavior of nurses from any behavior which, well intentioned or not, could lessen the benefit of care to patients, families, and communities. Professional boundaries can be thought of as limits to the nurse-patient relationship that allow for a safe, therapeutic connection between the professional and patient. Laws create some boundaries, and other limits are set by licensing agencies. Still other expectations of conduct are established by the professional. Boundaries are important for professional nurses to maintain because there is an unequal relationship between the patient and the nurse. Patients, particularly psychiatric patients, are vulnerable on the basis of disability, impairment, repeated encounters with societal stigma, and need for positive regard.

Table 6.1

A Continuum of Nurse Behavior with Patients, Patients, Families and Communities

Under Involvement	Professional Behavior	Over Involvement
(Distant) (e.g., neglect of patient needs)	(Therapeutic)	(Boundary Violation) (e.g., romantic or sexual relationship with patient)

The continuum illustrated in Table 6.1 provides a picture of therapeutic versus non-therapeutic behavior in the nurse-patient relationship. The continuum places under-involvement at one extreme of behavior and over-involvement at the other. At the center of the continuum, professional behavior represents therapeutic interactions between professionals and patients. Ideally the majority of interactions occur within the middle range of the continuum.

Nurses must maintain boundaries in therapeutic relationships with patients. Interpersonal boundaries protect patients from emotional harm that would impede their recovery. They must be initiated when the patient begins treatment and continue throughout treatment and, for the most part, continue even after the therapeutic relationship has ended. During treatment, providers must conduct interactions with patients within appropriate guidelines and focus on the patient's growth and movement toward wellness. Members of the healthcare team must recognize that stepping outside the boundaries of their professional roles can compromise a patient's recovery.

Boundary violations are usually insidious in their development. Initially a provider may be unaware the relationship is drifting from therapeutic interactions into a friendship or social relationship. As this relationship changes, the judgment of the healthcare provider becomes clouded, and the therapeutic needs of the patient slip from focus. An example of a boundary violation is discussed below:

During a psychiatric-mental health rotation of several weeks, a student nurse was assigned to work with an inpatient sex offender. Toward the end of the rotation, the student shared with the instructor that the patient asked the student to contact him after she completed the rotation. The student explained that she had developed feelings of friendship toward the patient and felt sorry for him. The instructor reminded the student of the policy stating that students could have no contact with patients after the rotation had been completed. The instructor counseled the student explaining why continued contact would be detrimental to the patient's recovery. Three months later, however, the agency informed the instructor that the student was both calling and writing to the patient. The patient insisted that the student was stalking and harassing him, although she denied this, and filed criminal charges against her. She was dismissed from the program.

In another example, a nurse maintained a therapeutic relationship with a patient during a lengthy hospitalization. Once the patient was discharged, however, the nurse entered into an intimate relationship with the patient. The relationship ended six months later, at the nurse's instigation. Following this event, the patient became extremely depressed and suicidal, and needed to be readmitted to the hospital.

Boundary violations are a kind of abuse because they involve a misuse of power. Abuse can be defined as misusing power or betraying of trust, respect, or intimacy between the nurse and the patient, which the nurse or others know may cause, or could be reasonably expected to cause, physical or emotional harm to a patient. This includes neglect or physical, verbal, emotional, sexual, or financial harm. Forms of abuse that constitute boundary violations are illustrated in Figure 6.1, adapted from Bernstein and Hartsell.[18]

Physical Abuse: involves touching or exhibiting behaviors towards patients of a nature that may be reasonably perceived by the patients, nurses, or others to be violent or to inflict physical harm. Examples include, but are not limited to: hitting, scratching, pushing, kicking, using force, biting, pinching, slapping, shaking, and/or handling a patient in a rough manner. (See Sections 6.9.A and 6.9.H on restraints).

Verbal Abuse: communication of an abusive nature. This includes behavior or remarks towards patients that may be reasonably perceived by the patient, nurse, or other to be: demeaning, seductive, exploitive, insulting, derogatory, and/or humiliating.

Emotional Abuse: involves using verbal and non-verbal behaviors that demonstrate disrespect for the patient and that are reasonably perceived by the patient, nurses, or others to be emotionally harmful. Such behaviors might include, but are not limited to: sarcasm, intimidation, teasing or taunting, retaliation, inappropriate posturing or gestures, insensitivity to the patient's culture, race, religious practices, economic status, or education, insensitivity to the patient's preferences with respect to sex and family dynamics, and consciously deciding to withhold information that could contribute to the patient's well-being.

Sexual Abuse: involves touching patients in a manner that may be reasonably perceived by the patient, nurses, or others to be of a sexual nature. It also includes initiating, encouraging, or engaging in sexual intercourse or other forms of physical sexual contact with patients. The consequences of sexual relationships with professionals can be long term for patients.

Financial Abuse: involves taking actions with or without the informed consent of a patient that results in monetary, personal, or other material benefit, gain, or profit to the nurse, or in monetary or personal material loss for the patient. Such behaviors include, but are not limited to: borrowing money or property from a patient; misappropriation or misuse of money or property, withholding of finances through trickery or theft, forced sale of house or possessions, forced change of will, influence, pressure, or coercion to obtain the patient's money or property, abuse of trusteeship, of bank accounts, of power of attorney, or of guardianship.

Neglect: involves exhibiting behaviors toward patients that may be reasonably perceived by the patient, nurses, or others to be a breach of the professional's duty to care. Neglect occurs when nurses fail to meet the basic needs of patients who are unable to meet them themselves. Such behaviors include, but are not limited to, deliberate withholding of basic necessities or care, such as clothing, food, fluid, needed aids of equipment, and medication. Neglect also occurs through inappropriate activities such as withholding communication, confining, isolating or ignoring the patient, denying the patient care, or denying the patient privileges.

Figure 6.1 *Forms of Abuse. Adapted from Bernstein, BE and Hartsell, TL. Portable Lawyer for Mental Health Professionals. New York: John Wiley's Sons, 2004*

Twenty-five states have passed laws prohibiting sexual relations between patients and mental health professionals, and the mental health literature is replete with articles on sexual contact and sexual boundary violations.[19] But it has relatively little to say about non-sexual violation of boundaries. A search for "boundary violations" resulted in only 21 cases, the oldest of which was in 1995, indicating that case law has not caught up with professional ethical codes.

B. Violations of Confidentiality

It is a professional and an ethical duty to use knowledge gained about patients only for the enhancement of their care and not for other purposes, such as gossip, personal gain, or curiosity. Nurses must maintain the confidentiality of verbal and written information. Preserving confidentiality is especially important in the care of patients with mental illnesses. All healthcare professionals, particularly in mental health, have a strict obligation to maintain the confidentiality of information revealed by a patient in the course of treatment. The exception to this is when a patient reveals intent to harm themselves, another, or intent to commit a crime.

Healthcare practitioners must maintain a delicate balance. With managed care companies as the payers for behavioral health services in many cases, providers (hospitals, nurses, social workers, physicians) must provide clinical information to the managed care company case manager to justify admission and continued treatment of patients. Thus, healthcare providers must obtain "fiscal informed consent" from the patient or family.[20] Nurses are responsible for knowing the legal requirements regarding clinical confidentiality and the requirements of managed care companies to be informed of the patient's clinical condition for reimbursement.

The Health Insurance Portability and Accountability Act (HIPAA) of 1996 outlines appropriate use and disclosure of the health information of patients, identifies patients' privacy rights, requires certain privacy practices of healthcare providers, and requires the development and implementation of administrative, technical, and physical safeguards to ensure the security of patients' health information. HIPAA's Final Rule (45 C.F.R. Parts 160 and 164),[21] which became effective October 15, 2002, provides standards for the privacy of individually identifiable health information. Under this privacy rule, healthcare providers and others must guard against the misuse of any patient's identifiable health information. The rule also limits sharing such information and affords significant new rights to enable patients to understand and to control the use and disclosure of their health information. Refer to Frank-Stromberg et al.[22] for additional information about HIPAA.

The case below describes a violation of confidentiality:

Mr. S, who had been a patient for over two years at a psychiatric clinic, robbed a bank and that same afternoon made an appointment to be seen in the clinic the next day. Upon arrival to his appointment he was exceedingly agitated and told the nurse that he had done something stupid for which he would go to jail. Further he stated that he had taken an overdose of his psychotropic medications. The nurse construed this to mean he had made a suicide attempt. Mr. S showed her a handgun he was carrying, but said it was not the weapon he had used in the robbery. He said he had used a toy gun in the commission of that crime. She inquired if the handgun was loaded, and asked him to unload it and place it in her desk drawer, which she then locked. She then advised him to go to the ED to be seen for his overdose and she called 911 for transport. As part of its protocol, the ambulance company called the police. When they arrived at the clinic, the nurse gave them the gun.

Mr. S was taken to the hospital. In the course of further investigation, the nurse told the police he had committed a robbery the day before and Mr. S was arrested at the hospital the following day. A suit was filed by the patient claiming the nurse violated his right to confidentiality. The Supreme Court of Massachusetts ruled against the nurse, noting that once the gun was locked in her desk drawer, there was no further threat of harm. The nurse could have given the gun to the police, but since it was not used in the commission of a crime, she could not identify or reveal anything else about its circumstances. The court noted that it is strictly confidential information when a patient reveals during the course of treatment that he or she has committed a crime (with the exceptions noted in which professionals have a duty to warn) and that it is unprofessional for a healthcare provider to report it to anyone, including law enforcement.[23]

C. Failures of Assessment, Evaluation, and Documentation

Every nurse is obliged to give patients appropriate care and interventions based on careful assessments that are relevant to meet patients' needs given the current state of knowledge. This care should be provided in an effective manner given the state of knowledge, and nurses are presumed to be competent to fulfill this responsibility. Patients have a right to receive nursing that includes a careful assessment for biological, functional, psychosocial, environmental, cultural, spiritual, developmental, self-care, nutritional risk, education, abuse/neglect risk, potential for violence against self or others, and discharge care needs. Nurses are also obliged to develop a plan of care that prescribes individualized interventions to attain expected outcomes and reflects recognized standards of care and practice. They should also reassess the plan of care and revise it based on this reassessment data.

Accrediting agencies such as The Joint Commission[24] and federal and state regulations require each patient to have a medical record. Documentation may be in the form of narrative notes, SOAP notes (recording information by subjective data, objective data, assessment, and plan), or clinical pathways. Medical records may be kept manually or electronically. Medical records are legal documents. All nursing notes and progress records should reflect descriptive, nonjudgmental, and objective statements. Attorneys should be aware that significant data should include current observations of the patient through the use of the nurse's critical assessment, an accurate report of verbal exchanges with patients, and a description of the patient outcomes of the care provided. The medical record is the best source of legal protection in a malpractice suit.[25] Attorneys who represent plaintiffs or defendants should request copies of the entire medical record and retain medical and nursing experts to assist in their analysis of the significance of the information provided therein.

Verbal communication should be straightforward, forthright, descriptive, without opinion, and limited to those involved in the patient's care and treatment. For each patient, personalized descriptions (as opposed to professional pronouncements) should be presented. The record should contain examples in the patient's own words and narratives to the extent that is possible insofar as showing that the patient is informed, gives consent, and is actively engaged in his treatment. Comprehensive medical histories and physical assessments should be conducted and recorded. Psychiatric patients, like other patients, often have chronic comorbid medical conditions. They frequently do not attend to their healthcare needs, and the medications they take often are responsible for their developing chronic medical conditions, such as hypertension, hypercholesterolemia, and diabetes. A lack of attention to details can often have negative consequences for patients as the case example below illustrates:

Eddie Jeremiah (not his real name) was a 16-year-old African American youth admitted to The Pines, a well-known psychiatric institution, from a local medical center emergency room where he had been taken by his mother after a two week history of idiosyncratic behavior following a closed head injury

that he sustained in an auto accident. On the way to the emergency department Eddie tried to leap out of the car, but was restrained by his older brother. In the emergency department he was examined by the intern on duty, given antipsychotic medication, diagnosed with schizophrenia, and referred to The Pines for treatment.

His condition deteriorated while at The Pines, and he was continued on his antipsychotic medication which was incrementally increased every three to four days. Eddie was placed in seclusion for 21 days and monitored on a one-to-one basis by the staff. During this time he exhibited rigidity, unstable vital signs, difficulty swallowing, uncoordination, ataxia, and confusion. On day 15 he became hypertensive, febrile, and agitated. The medical consultant ordered a beta blocker to treat his hypertension, but because of his continued agitation and confusion, he was not actually physically evaluated by a medical physician. He was given a benzodiazepine to treat his agitation, following which he fell and dislocated his shoulder. The dislocation was not documented until seven days later following his transfer to the medical center.

On day 21, Eddie's physical condition deteriorated to the point that it seemed prudent to transfer him back to the medical center. Upon his arrival, he was evaluated by the senior medical resident who suspected that the serious and life-threatening condition neuroleptic malignant syndrome (NMS) led to his antipsychotic medication. The medical resident discontinued the antipsychotic and drew the appropriate blood tests, which determined that Eddie had a CPK (enzyme that is elevated during this condition) that was 7000 (normal: 30-174). Treatment for NMS was initiated, but unsuccessful. Eddie's sensorium never cleared and he began to have uncontrollable seizures. He died five days later. A lawsuit ensued against The Pines, and its treating physicians and nurses.

The nurse expert retained by the plaintiff wrote the report, quoted in part in Figure 6.2. The case was settled out of court. It illustrates not only a lack of attention to detail, but also a lack of competence, poor data gathering, and substandard documentation. It also sadly illustrates that these medical professionals failed to connect the dots with regard to assessing, reassessing, and evaluating the lack of progress that characterized this patient's course. It also illustrates a degree of abuse insofar as it is not permissible (therapeutically and legally) to seclude people for that length of time.

Mr. Jeremiah was ill-served by all of the professionals caring for him at The Pines, and specifically the nursing caring fell well below the standards of care as articulated by the American Nurses Association Standards of Psychiatric and Mental Health Nursing Practice. In addition, the nurses failed in their ethical obligations to Mr. Jeremiah in a number of areas, specifically violating at least two of the principles as articulated in the American Nurses Association Code of Ethics (ANA, 1985) that was operational at the time of Mr. Jeremiah's hospitalization. Moreover, the nurses did not live up to the standard of what would be expected of a reasonably prudent professional nurse in the same circumstances.

The ANA Standards of Psychiatric and Mental Health Nursing Practice Standard I states that "the psychiatric mental health nurse collects health data." The rationale for this standard is that comprehensive assessment of the client and relevant systems enable the psychiatric mental health nurse to make clinically sound judgments and plan appropriate interventions with clients. The nurses involved in Mr. Jeremiah's care failed to properly assess his condition and in some instances did not appear to know what they were observing. An example of this is contained in a note (02.17.year) that reads "patient having trouble swallowing, no signs of EPS." Indeed, dysphagia is a sign of EPS, as well as an indicator of NMS. Another example of failure to collect health data is the issue of the flow sheets from seclusion. Mr. Jeremiah seems to have been in seclusion during most of his stay at The Pines. There is no concrete, operational indication as to the necessity for seclusion. What little there is has to do with his "disorientation" and "confusion." There are two issues here. Disorientation/confusion is not a cardinal symptom of schizophrenia. While people with schizophrenia have been known to become confused, it is not typical of them to remain confused. Psychiatric nurses should know this and the nurses caring for him should have questioned it and documented their concerns. The second issue has to do with his being in seclusion despite their documenting his disorientation. The two do not necessarily compute. Removing a patient from his environment and placing him in an environment devoid of reality-based environmental stimuli should have served to increase his disorientation rather than decrease it.

The nurses repeatedly failed in their own institution's protocols for gathering data (i.e., vital signs) during patient seclusion. They failed to obtain vital signs until quite late in his tenure at the facility. They documented that Mr. Jeremiah was ataxic and indeed that he had fallen and yet they administered Ativan to him. The reasonably prudent nurse would know that ataxia is a contraindication to administering a benzodiazepine. Indeed it would increase his ataxia and put him at increased risk for more falls. These are only a few examples of substandard care under Standard I.

The ANA Standards of Psychiatric and Mental Health Nursing Practice Standard II states that "the psychiatric mental health nurse analyzes the assessment data in determining the diagnosis." The rationale for this standard is that the basis for providing psychiatric mental health nursing care is the recognition and identification of patterns of response to actual or potential psychiatric illnesses and mental health problems. The nurses involved in the care of Mr. Jeremiah failed to recognize several key signs that indicated that his diagnosis and treatment was not adequate. They also failed to recognize his developing neuroleptic malignant syndrome. Nurses are taught to make observations in the interest of treatment and treatment modification, and to analyze and synthesize data. These nurses did none of those. They duly checked off their flow sheets but they made the most cursory observations and I did not see any note that indicated to me that they were doing in-depth holistic assessments. They seemed to be operating by rote and stimulus response type thinking, rather than on intelligent and thoughtful assessment. Nurses are also taught to make observations with the goal of avoiding potential problems. The reasonably prudent nurse would have observed that this patient's symptoms were unrelenting despite neuroleptics (a sign of potential NMS), that he was exquisitely sensitive to neuroleptics (again a sign of potential NMS), and that he was disoriented (a sign of improper diagnosis). While there is ample room to lay the responsibility for this tragic misadventure at the foot of his physicians, nurses are also expected to be accountable for their professional practice and judgment, and to advocate for their patients, especially in the event that those patients are being subjected to incompetent care. There is nothing in the chart to indicate that any nurse took a strong stand with respect to Mr. Jeremiah's deteriorating condition. Again, these are just a few areas in which the nurses were in violation of Standard II.

On the matter of violation of the ANA Code of Ethics, the following principles were violated by Mr. Jeremiah's nurses:

- The nurse acts to safeguard the client and the public when health care and safety are affected by incompetent, unethical, or illegal practice by any person. (Not done.)
- The nurse maintains competency in nursing. (Competence in psychiatric mental health nursing was lacking in this case.)

Figure 6.2 *Portion of Expert Witness Report*

With respect to treatment planning, all patient plans should be individually developed and involve engagement of the patient, measurable objectives connected to signs and symptoms, and periodic evaluation. This implies there should be a clear justification for the use of one form of treatment versus another. Linking interventions and treatment to signs and symptoms is an indication that thoughtful and precise treatment planning has taken place. Interventions and treatments are bound to fail when they are not developed on the basis of individuals' development and are sensitive to their various cognitive, social, and emotional domains and needs. The reality of individual assessment and treatment is often an unrealized ideal. The use of checklists, structured interviews, and standardized treatment plans and evaluation instruments, though efficient, runs the risk of practitioners building assessments and asking questions devoid of context, thereby omitting many important portions of clinical reality. However, they are a reality of current practice.[26] At the very least, patient assessments should include an elaboration of the categories contained under "safety" such as suicidal, homicidal, other self-harm, ideation of harm to others, or verbalizations of harm to others.

D. Failure to Provide for Safety

A common issue in malpractice litigation is failure to document an adequate suicide assessment. The health and safety of patients are the primary foci for nursing assessment and intervention. This assessment includes specific attention to patients' rights and best interests. When patients threaten self-injury or suicide, nurses and other healthcare professionals are obliged to keep them safe from harm. In today's managed care environment, people admitted to an acute inpatient psychiatric unit are often dangers to themselves or others. Nurses working in these facilities (as well as outpatient facilities) often deal with a range of suicidal and other self-harm behaviors such as threats of suicide, suicide attempts, suicidal ideation, high-risk behaviors, and, sometimes, successful suicide. There is a range of warning signs patients may exhibit in relation to suicidal thinking, feelings, and behavior. Most authors agree that risk factors for patients more likely to commit suicide are:

- male gender
- white
- single (never married, divorced, widowed)
- history of substance abuse
- hopelessness
- social isolation
- previous suicide attempt

Up to half of suicides among patients with schizophrenia occur during the person's inpatient hospitalization.[27] Thus, nurses and other mental health professionals are obliged to have knowledge of these risk factors and warning signs, and a repertoire of skills in this area so they can respond effectively when confronted with these situations. Establishing rapport and therapeutic alliance, special observation, and due diligence are only three tools in the mental health professional's armamentarium in providing for safety from self-harm.[28] The case below illustrates the positions the courts have taken on the responsibility of mental health practitioners and the safety of their patients:

A 36-year-old mother of two young children hung herself two days before her appointment with her mental health practitioner. Her husband filed a lawsuit alleging the professional, who recognized that his wife's condition required weekly (rather than monthly) management, abandoned her. The suit alleged that the practitioner failed to take steps to protect her from suicide and that this failure was a proximate cause of her death. After the mental health practitioner sought to have a civil suit dismissed on the basis that to reveal her suicidal ideation would breach confidentiality, the New Jersey Superior Court's Appellate Division refused to dismiss and concluded: "We do not necessarily disagree with defendant's contention that what Mrs. Marshall revealed to the doctor and what all of Mrs. Marshall's close relatives observed did not indicate that Mrs. Marshall's suicide was imminent. What concerns us is the absence of any observations by defendant just prior to the suicide." Even though defendant recognized that Mrs. Marshall's condition required weekly monitoring, the defendant failed to treat Mrs. Marshall weekly and instead scheduled an appointment almost one month after his initial session with the patient. If defendant had been following Mrs. Marshall on a weekly basis, as he himself found was necessary, then the immediacy of Mrs. Marshall's suicidal intentions might have been perceived by him and defendant may have incurred a duty to 'warn and protect' under the statute. Assuming the truth of plaintiff's proofs, therefore, it was defendant's own negligence that possibly prevented recognition of an imminent suicide threat. Thus, defendant's lack-of-imminence argument is analogous to the 'ostrich defense,' which is often rejected in federal criminal cases. E.g., *U.S. v. Williams*, 202 F.3d 959, 963 n.1 (7th

Cir. 2000) (defendant 'may not escape liability by shutting his eyes for fear of what he would learn' and later plead ignorance).

Under these circumstances, we conclude that N.J.S.A. 2A:62A-16 does not bar plaintiff's negligence action. A jury should assess whether defendant's conduct met the accepted standard of care, and if not, whether the deviation was a proximate cause of Mrs. Marshall's suicide."[29]

When a patient threatens violence to another person, the responsible mental healthcare professional faces a decision with potential clinical, ethical, and legal consequences. The clinician must first decide whether there is a realistic risk of violence or whether the patient is expressing fantasies or just blowing off steam. Clinical assessments of dangerousness should be regarded as assessments of risk, rather than as predictions of violence. No violence risk assessment in the chart is a common issue in malpractice litigation. As we are not able to predict with certainty or near certainty whether or not a person will be violent, an assessment should seek to describe the individual with a full clinical and behavioral description. Whenever possible, the individual should be assessed in an ongoing manner, rather than just once. The probability of future dangerous behavior can be related to the similarity of the person's current situation to situations in which they were violent in the past.

As in suicidality, a prior history of violent behavior is the single best predictor of future violence. After careful assessment of the potential for violence, clinicians can make an informed estimate on whether or not a threat exists. If violence is unlikely, then the legal and ethical duties are simple and the clinician should maintain the patient's confidentiality and continue the evaluation or treatment as clinically indicated. However, new legal duties may arise if the clinician concludes that potential violence is an issue. Potential conflict can develop between the duty to protect and the duty to maintain confidentiality. The duty to protect may involve warning a third party or initiating involuntary hospitalization of the patient, both of which breach confidentiality. Generally, mental health practitioners have a duty to warn third persons of patients' dangerous propensities when they have communicated serious threats of physical violence against reasonably identifiable victims. They should follow the precedents set under the *Tarasoff* decision in which the California Supreme Court held that a therapist bears a duty to use reasonable care to give threatened persons such warnings as are essential to avert foreseeable danger arising from a patient's condition.[30]

Several courts have discussed the foreseeability component of the duty to warn and have imposed upon mental health professionals an affirmative duty to investigate the possibility of dangerousness. In *Bradley Center Inc. v. Wessner*, a private hospital was held liable for failing to pursue "further attempts to evaluate in a more intensive fashion the inside deterioration" of a patient who, while released on a one day pass, murdered his ex-wife.[31] In *Hedlund v. Superior Court of Orange County*, a California court recognized that the duty to warn is "inextricably interwoven with the diagnostic function," and that "the duty imposed on the therapist is first to diagnose or recognize the danger posed by the patient."[32] Under these cases, the mental health professional has a duty to take some initiative in determining a patient's dangerousness even in the absence of a verbalization. As the following case illustrates:

> A mental health practitioner evaluated a man with chronic schizophrenia, spending five minutes with the patient and failing to review past records that showed a history of substance abuse, violence, and noncompliance with medication.[33] Beyond that, the facts are in dispute. The parents alleged that they told the clinician their son carried around pictures of decapitated animals; that they feared their son was a lethal threat; and that they never turned their backs on him. They further alleged they begged to have their son hospitalized, but were told their son was harmless. The son was sent home with a prescription he refused to take. Two days later, without provocation, he severely beat his stepfather, causing brain damage and precipitating a myocardial infarction. The parents sued, alleging breach of the duty to protect. On appeal to Arizona's Supreme Court, the court held there was a duty to protect in this case and the plaintiffs were foreseeable victims.

It seems prudent at this point to address the issue of contracting for safety. There is a certain amount of intuitive appeal to believing that a clinician or an institution should have a contract for safety (CFS) in the patient record in order to diminish liability should a tragedy, such as suicide or homicidal behavior, occur. Indeed, nurses and physicians often contract for safety and as recently as four years ago[34] contracting for patient safety was being promoted in the nursing literature as an intervention. Some facilities and mental health systems actually make it a policy to seek a safety contract with any patient who mentions suicide or threatens violent behavior. There is no empirical evidence that CFS has any effect on patient behavior, and certainly it does not have the force of law behind it. Indeed, a CFS may render staff less vigilant and may distract them from more comprehensive and individualized assessment. Reid asserts that relying on a CFS is foolish and may lead to legal entanglements and charges of negligence.[35,36]

Safety of hospitalized patients is the responsibility of staff and the institution in regards to policy and surveillance and enforcement. Failure to protect an inpatient from being sexually assaulted by another inpatient is a common issue in malpractice litigation.

> The plaintiff, age 14, was admitted to a psychiatric ward in October 2005. The plaintiff suffered depression. The plaintiff claimed that a 22-year-old male patient came into her room uninvited and raped her. The plaintiff alleged inadequate monitoring by the hospital's staff. The plaintiff claimed she had been in the hospital for less than 12 hours when the incident occurred and that she did not know her assailant. The plaintiff maintained that the attack aggravated her preexisting bipolar disorder and anxiety disorder and caused post-traumatic stress. The hospital denied any negligence. The assailant was found guilty of the criminal charges brought in the matter and is now registered as a sex offender. According to a published account a $1.2 million settlement was reached.

Additional areas documented in the literature that are common issues in malpractice litigation are[37]

1.   Failure to protect third parties. In the inpatient setting an example may be that a dangerous patient escapes from the hospital and the family is not notified. In an outpatient setting, duty to warn others of homicidal ideations or threats was not conducted.
2.   Protecting and releasing information. Confidential information released about the patient requires an authorization by the patient.
3.   Failure to obtain informed consent; side effects of medication were not discussed.
4.   Inappropriate relationship with patient; therapist had sexual relationship with patient.
5.   Medication. Women treated with medication which may cause birth defects are not evaluated for pregnancy prior to initiation of medication.
6.   Negligent discharge. Patient discharged while still suicidal; and abandonment; therapist terminated treatment without referral when patient failed to pay bill.

6.7 Liability Risk Related to Psychopharmacology

Prescribing psychotropic medications to patients is an expanded responsibility of the advanced practice nurse. Advances in psychopharmacology and advances in treatment have increased the use of psychotropic medications in all populations, along with medical malpractice litigation. Use of these medications in the pediatric population has been controversial. Concerns exist regarding the off-label use of psychotropic medications voiced by consumers and by experts.[38] Adverse drug events (ADEs) are a focus of attention by the patient safety movement in an effort to decrease medical errors.

Medical malpractice actions involving psychopharmacology usually allege negligence in prescribing, administering and monitoring medication(s), and/or failure to obtain informed consent or adequate informed consent.[39] Allegations about negligent prescribing encompass the adequacy of assessment/evaluation of the patients, diagnostic formulations, and the decisions regarding medication(s).

Off-label prescribing is a widespread and well-accepted part of medical practice and is not, in and of itself, a professional liability risk. Off-label uses range from the clearly controversial to those considered the established standard of care. Typical off-label uses include prescribing for a condition not indicated on the FDA-approved labeling, and prescribing at a different dosage than indicated or a different patient population.

These are common sources of liability when prescribing a medication:

1.   the diagnosis of the psychiatric disorder;
2.   the adoption of an appropriate rationale for drug therapy;
3.   the choice of a particular drug;
4.   assessment of past history of medication responses;
5.   ruling out co-existing medical conditions;
6.   obtaining informed consent;
7.   administration of medication regarding appropriate dose and route;
8.   prescribing multiple medications;
9.   monitoring the therapeutic effect and side effects;
10. ceasing the medication when a therapeutic effect has been achieved or maintaining long-term medication at the lowest effective dosage.[40]

Documenting that the patient (or in the case of the pediatric population, the guardian) has been educated on the risk-benefit of starting medication, how the medication will affect the patient, side effects of the medication and ensuring proper monitoring when initiating or changing medications are within basic standards of practice. An assessment and documentation of patients who could possibly be pregnant or become pregnant should be done. Emphasizing precautions he should take while on psychotropic medications is an additional safeguard for the patient's well-being.

6.8 The Conundrum of Whistle-blowing

The duty to report and warn warrants a discussion of the precarious nature in which nurses may find themselves when they attempt to assure the safety of patients by blowing the whistle on dangerous practices. The term whistleblower refers to any employee who reports dangerous, unethical, illegal, or incompetent acts to appropriate agencies outside the employer's facility. On the basis of this definition, the decision to blow the whistle to external authorities is a potentially risky endeavor fraught with moral conflicts and professional and personal risks. As numerous whistle-blowing cases demonstrate, there are no definitive answers to whether a given act results in the desired outcome until the consequences of the action can be evaluated.[41,42] Hindsight is often credited with 20-20 vision, but in reality it may or may not provide the insights necessary to protect the public welfare or future whistleblowers from retaliation.

The nursing profession's goals, values, and ethics teach that nurses are patient advocates. Advocacy is a pervasive theme throughout the profession and is a core element of nursing education. Statutory protections for the whistleblower fail to provide the comprehensive protection needed for professionals and the clients they serve. If the organization views whistleblowers as troublemakers who should be punished for violating organizational norms of silence, then even the most comprehensive legislation is inadequate to protect whistleblowers from personal and professional risks. The political structure and power dynamics of corrupt organizations may find a way around these safeguards even when structural mechanisms are in place (e.g., ethics committees, misconduct committees, institutional review boards [IRBs]).

Lennane conducted a survey of whistleblowers from various occupations who had exposed corruption or danger to the public.[43] All subjects (N=35) in this non-random sample suffered adverse consequences. For 20 of the subjects, victimization started after the first internal complaint. Retaliation took many forms including dismissal, demotion, resignation, or early retirement due to illnesses associated with victimization. Twenty-nine subjects had stress-related symptoms, 15 were started on long-term treatment with medication, 17 considered suicide, 30 reported adverse effects on their children, and almost half of the subjects reported reductions in income of 75 percent. The nursing profession is particularly vulnerable to retaliation if misconduct is reported. In a predominantly female profession, employed primarily in hospital settings where they are paid by the institution, nurses have a variety of potentially conflicting loyalties: to the patient, the physician, the institution, society at large, and to themselves. When unethical or illegal conduct is reported through appropriate channels and nothing is done, the nurse is forced to choose between ignoring the situation and doing nothing, or ultimately finding it necessary to hire an attorney for legal representation. Given their economic situation vis-à-vis the institutions they are up against, one might well ask how many nurses are willing to take this risk.

6.9 Rights of Patients Receiving Psychiatric Nursing Care

An important issue in psychiatric-mental health nursing care is recognizing the basic rights of patients. This issue is particularly relevant because treatment of patients with mental illnesses tends to be more coercive, less voluntary, and less open to public awareness and scrutiny than is the treatment and hospitalization of patients with other disorders.

A. Freedom from Unreasonable Restriction

When patients with psychiatric disorders enter a hospital, they may lose their freedom of independence: they will be unable to schedule their time, as well as choose and control their activities of daily living (ADLs). If also adjudicated incompetent, patients lose the freedom to manage financial and legal affairs and make many important decisions. Because of the loss of these important freedoms, the courts and advocates of patients with psychiatric disorders closely guard and value the rights these patients retain. Some of these rights include the right to communicate with an attorney, the right to send and receive mail without censorship, the right to have visitors, the right to the basic necessities of life, and the right to safety from harm during hospitalization.

Certainly, treatment issues sometimes arise that call for limitations on visitors. Patients may participate in a behavior modification treatment program that requires the earning of tokens to secure certain privileges or articles. Despite such limitations, patients still retain the right to challenge such restrictions, and treatment facilities may have to prove the value or necessity of such abridgments to rights. Unreasonable and capricious restrictions used as punishment of the kind that took place during the for-profit hospital scandals of the 1980s are a violation of patient rights and cannot be tolerated.[44]

Restraints and seclusion are considered a form of restriction. The application of restraints and the use of seclusion are considered high-risk treatment modalities because they are dangerous interventions that can result in injury or even death.[45] From a legal standpoint they are also high-risk because patients may perceive such methods as a form of punishment, and these modalities greatly inhibit the patient's right to freedom. Therefore, accrediting agencies and governmental entities require policies and procedures to govern these practices. Many states have developed statutes to define the use of restraints and seclusion within psychiatric facilities, and the federal government (Centers for Medicare and Medicaid Services) has issued strict guidelines for their use in facilities that receive federal funds as third-party reimbursement. The Joint Commission has revised the standards guiding the use of restraints and seclusion several times since 1996. These standards guide the application of restraints or initiation of seclusion, monitoring of the patient while these methods are imposed, and assessment for continuing need of the restraints or seclusion. The standards also specifically require the leaders of the organization to limit the use of restraints and seclusion to clinically justified situations.[46]

Patients have limited rights to be paid for work within long-term residential institutions. Forced or even voluntary labor by patients without payment violates the principles of law in our society.

Nursing has long espoused that one of its important roles in the healthcare system is to act as a patient advocate. Discussing rights within treatment teams, including these rights in the nursing care plan, and ensuring that procedures for rights protection are included in facility and unit policies and procedures, are nursing activities that fulfill the patient advocate role. One important resource that should be accessible to nursing is ongoing legal advice and consultation in the area of patient rights.

B. Informed Consent

Informed consent is consent that a recipient of health care gives to treating providers in an interaction (or series of interactions) that enables her to understand a proposed treatment or procedure, including the way the treatment or procedure will be administered, the prognosis if the treatment or procedure is given, side effects, risks, possible consequences of refusing the treatment or procedure, and other alternatives.[47]

All patients have the right to give informed consent before healthcare professionals perform interventions. The administration of healthcare treatments or procedures without a patient's informed consent can result in legal action on the patient's part against the primary provider and the healthcare agency. The patient will prevail in such a lawsuit, alleging battery (touching another without permission) if it can be proven that he did not consent to the procedure.[48]

Consent is an absolute defense against battery, which is the reason informed consent is imperative in healthcare situations. In the case of *Canterbury v. Spence* (1972), the court said the patient could truly be informed only if the primary provider shared with the patient all things that the patient "would find significant" in deciding whether to permit or participate in a particular treatment regimen. Informed consent requires that healthcare professionals give the patient adequate and accurate knowledge and information.[49] It mandates that the patient have the legal capacity to give consent and give it voluntarily.

As a broad mandate for informed consent, Congress passed the Patient Self-Determination Act (PSDA), which became effective December 1, 1991. The PSDA requires healthcare facilities to provide clear written information for every patient concerning her legal rights to make healthcare decisions, including the right to accept or refuse treatment.

Informed consent also protects patients from being subjected to experimental treatments and research projects without their knowledge and agreement. Because of the complexity of informed consent issues with patients who have psychiatric disorders, institutions with programs that involve research or experimental treatment approaches must have institutional review boards to evaluate such projects and programs and to approve or disapprove them based on strict patient protection criteria. Human subjects committees usually view favorably research approaches that entail no undue risks to patients, have strong expectations of benefit, and allow patients to withdraw from the project at any time, provided that patients give voluntary consent to participate.

C. Substituted Consent

When a patient cannot give informed consent, healthcare providers must obtain substituted consent for necessary treatments or procedures. Substituted consent is authorization that another person gives on behalf of a patient who needs a procedure or treatment but cannot provide such consent independently. The appointment of a healthcare proxy is one example of the concept of substituted consent.

Substituted consent can come from a court-appointed guardian or in some instances from the patient's next of kin. If the patient has not previously been adjudicated incompetent and if the law so permits and no next of kin are available to give substituted consent, the healthcare agency may initiate a court proceeding to appoint a guardian to enable professionals to carry out the procedure or treatment. In an emergency, the patient in danger of harming self or others can be given medication or be restrained or secluded without consent.

Nurses and other healthcare providers must know the statutory requirements for obtaining substituted consent. In their role as patient advocates, nurses also must know whether a patient has been adjudicated incompetent and whether consent from a next of kin or guardian is a legally acceptable substitution.

D. Privileged Communication

Privileged communication is provided by statute in each state. These statutes delineate which categories of professionals are given the legal privilege to withhold conversations and communications. Although statutes differ among states, they customarily provide this privilege to physicians, attorneys, clergy, and in some states, psychologists, nurses, and other healthcare providers. Psychiatric nurses should be aware of statutorily privileged communication; and if the nursing privilege is limited or nonexistent, they should be aware of what boundaries to set in therapeutic interviews. In the absence of statutory privileges for nurses, the nurse may be required to repeat communications between the nurse and patient in court through the subpoena process. Therefore, nurses should not encourage patients to share sensitive or incriminating data. They should limit therapeutic communication to that required by the treatment plan.

Some cases have involved the issue of the identification of the appropriate circumstances that warrant breach of the confidential relationship with a patient. As discussed in a previous section, a leading case in this area is *Tarasoff v. Board of Regents of University of California*, which held that therapists may have a duty to protect a person threatened by a patient.[50] Courts have held that, although the duty of confidentiality between patient and therapist should be recognized, a higher duty to protect the public safety intervenes and supersedes the duty of confidentiality. Currently there are no nursing cases regarding this point, but nurses must be aware that threats against other people cannot be ignored or unattended, especially when there is some reasonable opportunity for the patient to follow through on these threats.

Other types of situations in which a breach of confidentiality may be required by law of all health professionals include allegations of child abuse, threats of suicide, and allegations of sexual misconduct made against a therapist.

E. Evolving Legal Rights

United States laws constitute the system of binding rules of action or conduct that govern the behavior of people with respect to their relationships with their government and with others. In general, laws reflect the moral values and beliefs of a given population and are intended to reflect the popular belief about the "rightness" or "wrongness" of particular acts. Although guided by ethical principles, which are foundational, laws change and evolve to reflect the changing values and beliefs of society.[51] Examples of areas affected by recent changes in the law include fetal tissue use, abortion, confidentiality for patients with AIDS, the expanded role of nurses and prescriptive privileges, as well as others. Nurses should be familiar with the law and legal system to make informed choices and to ensure their practices are consistent under the legal system. Unfortunately, most education programs do not contain significant content with regard to the legal contexts of nursing practice.

1. Right to treatment

The idea that patients with psychiatric illnesses have a legally actionable right to psychiatric treatment began to develop in the late 1960s and culminated in the early 1970s in the circuit court case of *Wyatt v. Stickney* (1971).[52] The case provided innovative statements about the rights of civilly committed patients with mental illnesses in state hospitals. The court stated that such patients do have certain treatment rights, which include the following:

- Treatment must give some realistic opportunity for improvement or cure.
- Custodial care is insufficient to meet treatment requirements.
- A lack of funding does not excuse the state from treatment responsibilities.
- Commitment without treatment violates the due process rights of patients.

Perhaps the most important pronouncement in this case concerns the three determinants for the adequacy of treatment: a humane environment, a qualified staff in adequate numbers, and individualized treatment plans. This case gave the nation guidance about treatment rights; however, the Supreme Court did not review it. The Supreme Court decision on *O'Connor v. Donaldson* is commonly thought to be the leading case for the right to treatment.[53] The decision states, however, that no state can confine a person with mental illness in a state hospital who is not a threat to self or others if he can survive safely in the community alone or with the help of willing, responsible family members or friends.

2. Right to treatment in the least restrictive environment

Courts have given guidance to the mental health system on many matters, including standards about the settings in which treatment should occur. As early as 1969, in *Covington v. Harris*, the court held that a person treated involuntarily should receive such treatment in a setting that is least restrictive to liberty but will still meet treatment needs. Least restrictive environments can be community resources instead of hospitalization, open units instead of locked units, or outpatient or home care instead of inpatient care.[54] Nurses must constantly assess a patient's condition and status for initiating more or less restrictive treatment alternatives based on the patient's evolving needs.

3. Seclusion and restraint

Until recently, seclusion and restraint have been an assumed part of the psychiatric nurses intervention armamentarium. However, in recent years reports of serious adverse effects (including death) have been published resulting from seclusion and restraint prompting critical examination of their utility.[55] A Cochrane review on the efficacy of seclusion and restraint yielded 35 articles, none of which met the minimum inclusion criteria for research.[56] Because of safety concerns and lack of evidence of their efficacy, the federal government has passed legislation to limit the use of these coercive techniques. The Patient's Rights Conditions of Participation for hospitals (psychiatric, short-term, rehabilitation, long-term, children's, and alcohol-drug hospitals) participating in Medicare and Medicaid provides that patients "have the right to be free from seclusion and restraints, of any form, imposed as a means of coercion, discipline, convenience, or retaliation by staff." The Rule defines restraints to include physical and mechanical restraints and drugs "used to control behavior or to restrict the patient's freedom of movement" if that drug is not a standard treatment for the patient's medical or psychiatric condition. See the CMS website for additional reading.[57] Nurses are obliged to be aware of these rules and regulations and can be held legally responsible if they are violated.

4. Right to refuse treatment

The doctrine of informed consent implies that patients have the right to choose or refuse medical and health treatment. Certainly, healthcare providers, through interpersonal relationships and patient education, may try to convince patients about the need for certain treatments. Only in rare or life-threatening instances, however, will courts intervene in treatment decisions.

5. Right to aftercare

Care in the community following psychiatric hospitalization is needed to prevent readmission and to ensure the rehabilitation of former inpatients. There is no absolute legal right at this time to aftercare programs unless state statutes provide such a right. It is conceivable that case laws may evolve to mandate aftercare services as a right of patients with mental disorders.

In conjunction with other members of the interdisciplinary team, nurses plan for aftercare treatment. As knowledgeable and responsible professionals they should see (to a reasonable degree) that patients with psychiatric illnesses have access to adequate aftercare services. These services include outpatient counseling, home care, medication follow-up, vocational placement, and sheltered living environments. Nurses also have an obligation to help patients and their families adhere to treatment plans. Mentally ill patients, especially those who are physically compromised, are treated with various lifestyle modifications including weight loss and diet adjustment, smoking cessation, exercise, stress reduction, and drugs. Nurses should assess the patient and identify potentials for non-compliance. They should be aware of cultural and psychosocial factors, illiteracy, age, and other barriers to compliance. Involving patients in their own care is essential and involving family members, especially in terms of educating and strategizing with them in the care of their loved one, is essential to success as medication adherence and self-care can be serious challenges for the mentally ill. As always, nurses should document carefully the kind of discharge plan, arrangements, and education that has been provided.

6.10 Legal Issues and Special Patient Populations

A special population of psychiatric patients includes the minor or juvenile. Until recently, parents or guardians had an almost absolute privilege to admit their minor children younger than 18 years for mental health treatment. State recognition of some rights of more mature children (12 to 18 years old) to protest such treatment, however, has eroded this absolute right.

In 1979, the U.S. Supreme Court, in *Parham v. J. R.*, gave a more definite standard for juvenile admissions, to which state statutes and hospital policy should conform.[58] The Supreme Court held that parents can authorize the admission of juveniles, yet some neutral fact finder should determine whether statutory requirements for admission are satisfied. Furthermore, an adversarial hearing for admission is not required, nor does due process require that the fact finder be legally trained or be a hearing officer. By ruling in this way, the Court balanced the competing interests of the rights of parents and guardians to control the lives of their children with the right of children to due process before their liberty is limited.

Psychiatric-mental health nurses need to be mindful of these procedural protections for the benefit of their juvenile patients. Limiting hospitalization to statutory requirements is an important advocacy activity for pediatric patients with mental illness.

In the case of private practice, psychiatric-mental health nurses should obtain the necessary consent to treat from parents of juvenile patients. In the case of joint custody divorced parents, both parents are required to sign consent to treat. In addition, obtaining assent from the juvenile is recommended.

6.11 Nursing Ethics in Community Mental Health

Working with patients in community mental health affords nurses the opportunity to practice at a greater level of autonomy than nurses who work in mental health facilities. As the level of autonomy rises, however, so do the levels of responsibility and accountability. Community mental health nurses are not only responsible for working with patients, families, and multidisciplinary treatment teams, but also with public and private agencies and the community at large.

Community mental health nurses must comprehend how, out of necessity, legislation and policies establish boundaries for ethical decision making. In the community, nurses frequently encounter patient care situations surrounded by ambiguities. For example, questions that may be asked include: what are the nurse's responsibilities if a patient living in the community with schizophrenia chooses to stop taking her medication? A nurse who believes that a patient's autonomy outweighs all other ethical principles may believe the patient has a right to make that choice and decide not to intervene. This nursing decision may mean the nurse is placing both the patient's life at risk and the community's safety in jeopardy. Generally, however, the interest of the community overrides the interest of the patient.

6.12 Conclusion

This chapter has discussed a number of issues pertinent to the nursing care of psychiatric patients. Among the important points included are that boundaries are essential in therapeutic relationships, and nurses must evaluate and maintain the boundaries in the nurse-patient relationship. Psychiatric nurses are independent professionals and are held to an expert standard of practice. Moreover, failure to meet the standard of care that results in an injury to a patient makes the nurse liable for nursing negligence or malpractice. To provide legally acceptable nursing care in psychiatric-mental health settings, nurses and all mental health professionals must be informed about a variety of legal issues, including

patient rights, and nurses must take responsibility, along with other health team members, to see that patient rights are protected. Nurses also have the responsibility to understand legal issues and to follow the law in providing care to the psychiatric client. Nurses must learn to value, respect, and seek out knowledge about laws, legislation, and the legal processes that regulate, impede, and facilitate professional nursing practice. Being aware of such standards, staying informed about new and changing legislation that affects clinical practice, and understanding proposed and past legislation affecting mental health care, psychiatric mental health nurses can provide quality care that safeguards the rights and safety of patients.

Endnotes

1. Croke, E.M., "Nurses, negligence, and malpractice." *American Journal of Nursing*. 103, no. 9 (2003): 54-63.

2. Rodgers C., (2009) "Keys to avoiding malpractice: Standard of care in psychiatric practice." *Psychiatric times*, Vol. 26 No. 12, Forensic Psychiatry. pg 1-3. http://www.pschiatrictimes.com/display/article/10168/1491873. Accessed 6/1/2010.

3. Ash, P. and Nurcombe, B. "Malpractice and professional liability." In *Lewis's Child and Adolescent Psychiatry*. 4th edition, pg.1018. Philadelphia, PA: Lippincott Williams and Wilkins, 2007.

4. Bewuchamp, T., and Childress, J. *Principles of Biomedical Ethics*. New York: Oxford University Press 2001.

5. American Psychiatric Association, *The Principles of Medical Ethics*. Arlington, VA: American Psychiatric Association, 2009.

6. See note 2.

7. See note 2.

8. American Nurses Association, *Code of ethics for nurses with interpretive statements*. Washington, D.C.: American Nurses Publishing, 2001.

9. American Nurses Association, *Scope and standards of psychiatric-mental health nursing practice*. Washington, D.C.: American Nurses Publishing, 2000.

10. See note 1.

11. See note 2.

12. See note 1.

13. See note 2.

14. See note 1.

15. See note 1.

16. See note 2.

17. Radden J., "Boundary violation ethics: Some conceptual clarifications," *Journal of the American Academy of Psychiatry & the Law* 29, no. 3 (2001): 319–26.

18. Bernstein, B. E. and T. L. Hartsell, *Portable Lawyer for Mental Health Professionals.* New York: John Wiley's Sons, 2004.

19. Miller, R. D. and G. J. Maier, "Nonsexual boundary violations: Sauce for the gander," *Journal of Psychiatry & Law* 30, no. 3 (2002): 309–329.

20. Dasco, S. and C. Dasco, *Managed care answer book.* New York: Panel Publishers, 1995.

21. HIPAA Final Rule, 45 C.F.R. Parts 160 & 164, 2002.

22. Frank-Stromborg, M. Burns, B. Morgan, and D. Bromme Sierens, "HIPAA," In *Medical Legal Aspects of Medical Records, Second Edition*, eds. P. Iyer and B. Levin. Tucson, AZ: Lawyers & Judges Publishing Co., 2010.

23. *Commonwealth v. Brandwein* 760 N.E. 2d 724 (Mass., 2002).

24. Joint Commission on the Accreditation of Healthcare Organizations. *Comprehensive Accreditation Manual for Hospitals.* Oakbrook Terrace, IL, 2006.

25. Etzioni, A., "Medical records. Enhancing privacy, preserving the common good," *Hastings Center Report* 29, no. 2 (1999): 14–23.

26. Olson, J. N. and W. K. Mohr, "The Lost Art of Accuracy: A Contextual Approach to Assessment," *Journal of Psychosocial Nursing and Mental Health Services* 40, no. 10 (2002): 38–45.

27. Molbert, B. and J. C. Beck, "Assessing Violence in Patients: Legal Implications," *Psychiatric Times* 20, no. 1 (2003).

28. McCleary, R., K. Chew, J. J. Hellsten, and M. Flunn-Bransford, "Age-and Sex-Specific Cycles in United States Suicides, 1973–1985," *American Journal of Public Health* 81 (1991): 1494–97.

29. *Marshall v. Klebanov*, No. A-2237-03T5 (N.J. Super. Ct. App. Div. June 22, 2005)—DEx 98913.

30. *Tarasoff v. Board of Regents of University of California*, 592 P.S. 553 (1974).

31. *Bradley Center Inc. v. Wessner*, 161 Ga. App. 576, 287 A.W. 2s 716, 723.

32. *Hedlund v. Superior Court of Orange County*, 34 Cal. 3d 695, 669 P. 2d 41, 45, 1983.

33. *Hamman v. County of Maricopa*, 775 P.2d 1122 (Ariz. 1989).

34. Kelly, K. T. and M. P. Knudson, "Are No-Suicide Contracts Effective in Preventing Suicide in Suicidal Patients Seen by Primary Care Physicians?" *Archives of Family Medicine* 9 (2000): 1119–1121.

35. Reid, W. H., "Promises, promises: Don't rely on patients' no-suicide/no-violence 'contracts'," *Journal of Practical Psychiatry and Behavioral Health* 4 (1998): 316–318.

36. Reid, W. H., "Contracting for safety redux," *Journal of Psychiatric Practice* 11, no. 1 (2005): 54–57.

37. See note 3, pg 1022.

38. Melonas, JM. (2005) "Preventing and reducing professional liability risk related to psychopharmacology. *Psychiatric Times*. 23 (14):1. http//www.psychiatrictimes.com/display/article/10168/48416. Accessed 6/2/2010.

39. See note 38, pg 2-4.

40. See note 3, pg 1027.

41. Witt, P., "Notes of a Whistleblower," *American Journal of Nursing* 83 (1983): 1649–1651.

42. Zorn, E., "Whistle-blower Saved Lives, Lost Everything Else," *Chicago Tribune* (June 21, 1987): 1, 2.

43. Lennane, J. K. "Whistleblowing: A Health Issue," *British Medical Journal* 307 (1993): 667–70.

44. Mohr, W. K., "The private psychiatric hospital scandal: A critical social approach," *Archives of Psychiatric Nursing* 8, no. 1 (1994): 4–8.

45. Mohr, W. K., T. A. Petti, and B. D. Mohr, "Adverse effects associated with the use of physical restraints," *Canadian Journal of Psychiatry* 48 (2003): 330–337.

46. See note 16.

47. Rossoff, A. J., *Informed Consent: A Guide for Healthcare Remedies*. Rockville, Maryland: Aspen Systems, 1981.

48. Prosser, W., *Cases and Materials on Torts*. New York: Foundation Press, 1991.

49. *Canterbury v. Spence*, 464 F.2d 772 (1972).

50. Kapp, M. B., *Our Hands Are Tied: Legal Tensions and Medical Ethics*. Westburn, Connecticut: Auburn House Press, 1998.

51. *Id.*

52. *Wyatt v. Stickney*, 325 F. Supp. 781 (1971).

53. *O'Connor v. Donaldson*, 422 U.S. 563 (1975).

54. *Covington v. Harris*, 419 F.2d 617 (1969).

55. Sailas, E. and M. Fenton, "Seclusion and restraint for people with serious mental illnesses," *The Cochrane Library* 2. Chichester, U.K.: John Wiley and Sons, 2005.

56. See note 33.

57. http://www.cms.hhs.gov/cop/2b.asp. *CMS Interpretative Guidelines for Hospital Conditions of Participation for Patients' Rights*. Accessed 7/9/10.

58. See note 17.

Chapter 7

Medical Surgical Malpractice Issues

Marlene Roman, MSN, RN, ARNP, CMSRN and Beth Cohen, MSN, RNC, ARNP

Synopsis
7.1 Introduction
7.2 Medical Surgical Units
    A. Description of Units
    B. Outpatient Surgical Patients
    C. Patient Status Types
        1. Inpatient status
        2. Observation status
        3. Outpatient in a bed
7.3 Staffing
    A. Composition of Staff
        1. Unlicensed assistive personnel
        2. Supplemental staff
        3. Advanced practice nurses
    B. Scheduling
    C. Assignments
        1. Assessment skills
        2. Competency
        3. Delegation
        4. Ratios
7.4 Nursing Practice
    A. Standard of Care
    B. Evidence-Based Practice (EBP)
7.5 Factors That Contribute to Malpractice Claims
    A. Staffing Issues
        1. Nurse-patient ratios
        2. Nursing delegation
        3. Non-direct patient care activities
        4. Special staffing considerations
    B. Patient and Family Issues
        1. Customer service
        2. Unrealistic expectations
        3. Undermining patient confidence
7.6 The Noncompliant Patient
    A. Noncompliance with Medical and Nursing Interventions
    B. Leaving Against Medical Advice (AMA) or Elopement
        1. Refusal to discuss with physician
        2. Documentation
    C. Presence of Unauthorized Items at the Bedside (Contraband)
        1. Personal items
        2. Forbidden substances or items
        3. Tampering with medical equipment
7.7 Special Populations
    A. Frail Elderly
    B. Physically and Mentally Challenged
    C. Non-English Speaking or Low Literacy
    D. Patient at Risk for Withdrawal
        1. Patient denial
        2. Early recognition of withdrawal

7.8 Standards of Care
    A. Absence or Outdated Standards of Care
    B. Deviations from Standard of Care
        1. Failure to monitor
        2. Failure to assess
        3. Failure to rescue
        4. Failure to communicate
            a. Failure to report abnormal lab results
            b. Failure to report changes in patient condition
            c. Faulty communication system
        5. Failure to follow or question physician's orders
        6. Intravenous complications
            a. IV insertion and maintenance
            b. Vesicants
            c. Infusion pumps
7.9 Provision of Inadequate Care
    A. Failure to Listen and Respond
    B. Prevention of Aspiration
    C. Failure to Adequately Monitor Respiratory Status of a Postoperative Patient
    D. Multiple Failures
    E. Stability at Discharge
7.10 Summary
Endnotes
Additional Readings

7.1 Introduction

This chapter focuses on the malpractice issues that commonly occur in nursing units designated as medical surgical. Patients are generally over the age of 18 with medical or surgical conditions, or a combination of both. With today's emphasis on cost containment and the promotion of outpatient care, patients actually admitted to the hospital as inpatients are often sicker than in the past, and sometimes leave with minimal improvement. The trend towards outpatient care and surgery has resulted in both fewer admissions to medical surgical units with more acute illnesses and enormous pressures to quickly discharge patients to less expensive alternatives. Additionally, hardships have been imposed on patients and their families because of the need to travel to receive care, especially in rural areas. The burden has been placed on the patient and family or significant other to continue the care at home or in a subacute care setting.

7.2 Medical Surgical Units
A. Description of Units

The term "nursing unit" is the accepted term to describe an inpatient hospital unit. The term "ward" is no longer used. Depending on the size of the hospital, a medical surgical unit consists of varying mixtures of patients with a medical or surgical condition, or both. Some hospitals have pure medical and pure surgical units. Others create a mixture of each type of patient. In large enough hospitals, it is common to group patients according to clinical conditions. Patients with respiratory conditions may be on one unit, and patients with abdominal conditions may be on another.

TIP: The largest number of beds in a general hospital is usually devoted to the care of medical surgical patients.

A telemetry unit is one in which a patient's heart rate and rhythm may be continuously monitored. These patients may have known cardiac conditions or be at risk for developing an arrhythmia. Monitoring may be done by the nurse assigned to the patient or a monitor technician. Monitor technicians are unlicensed although required to complete a course of study which focuses on identification of rhythms, including arrhythmias, which require immediate attention. Their responsibilities include monitoring many patients at one time, usually at a central station. They may also be responsible for monitoring patients off the unit. Some hospitals utilize remote monitoring in which the patient is housed on one unit and the monitoring equipment and technician are housed on another unit.

Life-threatening arrhythmias could go undetected, resulting in untimely death and potential litigation. The risk is highest if a patient with actual or potential risk of cardiac arrhythmia is not assigned to a telemetry unit. Timely communication of arrhythmias to the appropriate healthcare provider is essential. The American College of Cardiologists (ACC) guidelines recommend that "adequate human surveillance must be available 24 hours a day by staff qualified in electrocardiogram (EKG) recognition." The ACC also recommends there be adequate numbers of trained personnel to respond to and treat life-threatening arrhythmias.[1] Regardless of the use of a monitor technician, it is the responsibility of the nurse to know the patient's cardiac status and to communicate changes to the appropriate physician in a timely manner. Standards of care require setting appropriate parameters on alarms and responding to warning alarms. Refer to Chapter 4, *Critical Care Malpractice Issues*, in this Volume, and Chapter 4, *Patient Safety Initiatives*, in Volume I, for more information.

The plaintiff, a cardiologist, had under his care a 54-year-old male being monitored in the telemetry unit of the defendant hospital. According to the plaintiff, he left orders for nurses to contact him if the patient developed heart irregularity or pressure in the chest. The patient died of a ruptured aortic aneurysm. The plaintiff claimed that when nurses noted symptoms in the patient they did not contact him. When the patient's family filed a malpractice suit, the hospital and nurses settled for $250,000. The jury found against the cardiologist for $662,000. The cardiologist filed suit for contribution. He asserted that if the nurses had not been negligent the patient would not have died. According to Metro Verdicts Monthly, the jury found in favor of the plaintiff for $331,000.[2]

TIP: A job description indicating the qualifications of telemetry nurses and monitor technicians should be obtained when a case involves telemetry care.

B. Outpatient Surgical Patients

The tremendous push to perform more surgery on an outpatient basis has reduced the number of patients who require overnight admission for postoperative care. The typical outpatient presents to the hospital for same-day surgery the morning of the surgery, goes to the operating room from a specialized intake area, and after monitoring in the post anesthesia care unit, is discharged to home. Surgical patients requiring continued hospitalization postoperatively tend to have complicated medical problems, major operations, a prolonged recovery from the anesthesia, or a complication during anesthesia or surgery, all of which put them at a higher risk. These patients are designated as short stay or 23-hour patients. If they require a longer stay, they need to be "rolled over" into a full admission status.

C. Patient Status Types

All patients are assigned a patient status upon use of a hospital service. The terminology of status types may vary from hospital to hospital.

1. Inpatient status

An acute level of service or a complex surgery or procedure is one that requires an overnight stay. The length of stay (LOS) is typically more than 24 hours. Documentation should be present to support the severity of the signs and symptoms and intensity of services. Examples of service may include cardiac monitoring and neurological checks every four hours.

2. Observation status

Observation status patients require monitoring to evaluate an outpatient condition or to determine the need for possible inpatient admission. This is similar to a short-stay or 23-hour admission. The LOS usually does not exceed 24 hours. Examples of service may include a work-up or treatment for asthma or syncope (fainting). Other examples might include postoperative complications such as vomiting or inability to void.

3. Outpatient in a bed

A patient who has had an outpatient invasive diagnostic or surgical procedure or same-day therapeutic procedure who requires continued observation/monitoring may be placed on an inpatient unit. These patients are typically discharged in less than 24 hours, often as soon as four hours. Examples of procedures may include invasive radiology procedures, such as an angiogram, endoscopy, a blood transfusion, and a cardiac catheterization.

7.3 Staffing
A. Composition of Staff

Nurses who work on medical surgical units range from the new graduate to the highly experienced nurse. Entry level education for registered nurses (RN) includes diploma, associate's degree (AD), and bachelor of science (BSN). The licensed practical nurse (LPN) preparation usually ranges from approximately 18 to 24 months and is often offered at either a technical school or community college. Education for the nursing assistant or patient care attendant (NA or PCA) varies from a hospital-based course to a three to six month program offered at a technical school.

Historically, staffing on a medical surgical unit consisted of a combination of RNs, LPNs, and unlicensed assistive personnel (UAP), such as a NA or PCA, a nurse manager, and unit secretary. Current studies have shown that more favorable patient outcomes can be expected when the staffing mix favors RNs over LPNs. Many hospitals are moving in this direction.[3]

In recent years, care delivery has shifted to a patient-focused model where the number of people performing services has been minimized. Therefore, nursing personnel have picked up duties formerly done by others, such as the intravenous (IV) team and phlebotomists for blood drawing. Refer to Chapter 8, *Inside the Healthcare Environment*, in Volume I, for additional information on staffing models.

TIP: Staffing levels are established by hospital policy and influenced by the standards of the State Department of Health and The Joint Commission. Staffing sheets, which record the name of the nurses on duty, and computer listings of the number of patients on each shift are usually retained in the hospital and can be obtained during discovery. Additionally, many hospitals classify patients' acuity on a daily basis. Since this is done at a set time, changes in condition may not be reflected on the document.

---

1. Unlicensed assistive personnel

Unlicensed assistive personnel (UAP), such as nurse's aides and technicians, supplement the number of registered nurses and licensed practical nurses. The ANA defines them as "individuals who are trained to function in an assistive role to the registered professional nurse in the provision of patient/client care activities as delegated by and under the supervision of the registered professional nurse."[4] Duties may include bathing, feeding, and transporting patients, distributing snacks to patients, as well as cleaning incontinent patients. Many hospitals have made sweeping changes in how health care is delivered, financed, and organized. One trend in care delivery is to have the UAP performing an electrocardiogram (EKG), a phlebotomy, and bedside glucose testing. Refer to Chapter 2, *Where Have All the Nurses Gone?*, in Volume I, for more information.

2. Supplemental staff

When there is a need to supplement regularly employed nursing staff, many hospitals contract with outside agencies. Contracts encompass nurses hired on a per shift basis or longer term. These nurses are often referred to as agency nurses or travelers. Another option for staffing is to use "pool" or per diem nurses. These are hospital employees who work on an as-needed basis and usually agree to work a set of number of shifts per month. Pool staff is preferred over agency nurses because pool staff typically participates in a hospital orientation, and thus these individuals are more familiar with the facility and hospital policies. Refer to Chapter 2, *Where Have All the Nurses Gone?*, in Volume I, for more information.

3. Advanced practice nurses

Advanced practice nurses, such as clinical nurse specialists and nurse practitioners, are commonly found on some medical surgical units. The level of expertise demonstrated by the APN has been shown to increase the satisfaction with care and the quality of care, as these nurses provide support for the medical surgical staff nurses when they are challenged by particularly complex patients. The services they can provide, both as teacher and practitioner, have been shown to be valuable in improving the quality of nursing care. The educational preparation, certification requirements, and licensure vary from state to state.

B. Scheduling

In the recent past, many hospitals scheduled staff to work eight-hour shifts. Often, the nurse was hired to work rotating shifts with alternating weekends. Today, more flexibility in scheduling often no longer necessitates rotating shifts. Also, shifts now may vary from eight to ten or twelve hour shifts per week or a combination thereof, such as two eight-hour shifts and two twelve-hour shifts per week. Often, overtime is requested when staff is in short supply. Several states have enacted legislation barring mandatory overtime. Recommendations were made for a maximum amount of hours that could be worked per week. Many hospitals have written policies specific to these recommendations. Yet, many hospitals enforce mandatory overtime when staffing is needed.

TIP: It is common to find inexperienced nurses in larger proportions on the medical surgical unit than in any other clinical area. Based on staffing needs, it is not unusual for an inexperienced or new graduate nurse to be hired for the off-shift where there are fewer resources to draw from.

C. Assignments

1. Assessment skills

Assessment skills are important for the medical surgical nurse. The medical surgical patient relies on the skills of the nurse to detect subtle changes in the patient's condition, which are clinically important. The medical surgical nurse is expected to observe clinically significant changes in a patient's skin color, level of consciousness, significant laboratory results, and responses to treatments and activity.

TIP: The experience and skill level of each nurse is considered when making the assignment. Often, assignments are created by assigning a block of rooms rather than properly matching the patient's care requirements with the skill level of the nurse.

---

2. Competency

Healthcare facilities are accountable for documenting competency assessment and maintenance. There should be documentation that staff members have adequate knowledge and skills to perform their designated job responsibilities. The Joint Commission requires the competence of all staff members be assessed, maintained, demonstrated, and improved upon on an ongoing basis. Most hospitals provide an orientation period which consists of a combination of classroom education and nursing unit experiences. During this period, initial orientation and role-specific competencies are assessed and documented. Hospital policies vary but most evaluate the newly hired staff nurse at three months and then annually.

3. Delegation

Delegation is the transfer of responsibility for the performance of a task from one individual to another while retaining accountability for the outcome.[5] Factors involved in delegation include knowing the skill level and capability of the person being delegated to as well as the needs of the patient. Potential liability is created when hospitals use agency, travel, or pool personnel. It is difficult for the person delegating to be assured of the competency and skill level of staff infrequently assigned to his unit. This may also be an issue when staff float to another unit. Examples of delegation include the making of the shift assignment and conferring responsibility of care for a group of patients to a specific nurse. Another example would be delegation of a specific task to be completed by a UAP. In this case, the responsibility for the correct and timely completion of the task lies with the licensed nurse. The lack of knowledge or inadequate supervision of the unlicensed aide may contribute to the delayed recognition and response to a serious change in a patient's condition.

TIP: The RN and/or LPN can be held accountable if she does not delegate appropriate tasks to the UAP.

---

4. Ratios

With insurers and managed care organizations attempting to cut down on reimbursements, hospitals are forced to implement measures to cut costs. One of the largest costs to hospitals is nursing staff. Many hospitals have downsized their nursing staffs, and replaced them with unlicensed assistive personnel. Nearly all hospitals use some form of statistical staffing formula to determine the number of nurses needed. These formulas often do not incorporate many factors that directly impact the amount of nursing care needed. As previously mentioned, classification systems for patient acuity reflect one point in time and often do not capture or anticipate sudden changes, such as unexpected discharges, emergency surgery, or change in patient condition. The American Nurses Association (ANA) has long been involved in increasing the public's awareness of this issue, and has been instrumental in introducing legislation in many states that would mandate minimum staffing ratios. California became the first state to enact this legislation in October

1999. In 1999, the ANA released Principles for Nurse Staffing, which outlines some minimum requirements in realistic evaluations of staffing patterns. In 2005, the ANA published the "Utilization Guide for the ANA Principles for Nurse Staffing." These principles highlight the importance of adequate staffing. "Adequate nurse staffing is critical to the delivery of quality patient care."[6] Refer to Chapter 2, *Where Have All the Nurses Gone?*, in Volume I, for additional information on staffing.

7.4 Nursing Practice
A. Standard of Care

Standards of care describe a competent level of nursing care as demonstrated by the nursing process, involving assessment, diagnosis, outcomes identification, planning, implementation, and evaluation. The nursing process encompasses all significant actions taken by medical surgical nurses in providing care to all clients, and forms the foundation of clinical decision-making.[7]

The standard of care is an issue of fact for the jury to decide. Except in an unusual case, this standard is determined based on expert testimony. In addition, professional publications and literature help establish the standard of care. The American Nurses Association and the Academy of Medical Surgical Nurses publishes standards of care for the medical surgical nurse. There are established peer-reviewed journals, such as *MedSurg Nursing,* which focus on the needs and interests of the medical surgical nurse. There are other journals routinely used, but some are not peer-reviewed. *MedSurg Nursing* has been identified as one of the top 20 nursing publications devoted to publishing research utilization articles.[8] Hospital-specific policies, procedures, and protocol governing practice are considered standards of care. These standards of care should be written utilizing evidence-based best practice. Nursing personnel must be educated to these standards of care, and held accountable for adherence to them; and to this end, these standards must be accessible for nursing staff at all times.

B. Evidence-Based Practice (EBP)

"Several definitions of EBP are provided in the literature, and they generally have a common core: well-designed research + clinical expertise + patient concerns and preferences = EBP."[9] The Agency for Healthcare Research and Quality (AHRQ) developed a national network of evidence-based practice centers. These centers are responsible for performing systematic reviews of research literature, synthesizing the studies, and rating the quality of the research. Conclusions are then reached on what constitutes best evidence to date. The conscientious nurse can then make explicit and judicious use of current best evidence when making decisions about the provision of health care. Refer to Chapter 6, *The Foundations of Nursing Practice*, in Volume I, for more information on evidence-based nursing.

7.5 Factors That Contribute to Malpractice Claims

There are several factors on the typical medical surgical unit that promote an environment fostering malpractice claims. These include: staffing issues, customer service and satisfaction issues, priorities and time management issues, and deviations from the standard of care.

A. Staffing Issues

There are many staffing-related issues that could be a factor in a malpractice claim. The largest budget item for a hospital is the nursing staff, especially salaries for the registered nurse. Hospitals' response to a reduction in reimbursement from insurers and managed care organizations has been to downsize nursing staff, especially the registered nurse, in order to cut costs. Registered nurses are often replaced by licensed practical nurses or unlicensed assistive personnel.

1. Nurse-patient ratios

Nationally, there is a slow trend toward legislating nurse to patient ratios. It has been documented that the general public's caregiver preference is a registered nurse. Therefore, several factors should be reviewed, such as what is the normal staffing pattern, what is the normal nurse patient ratio, and what is the community standard? When a nurse is responsible for the direct care of a higher number of patients, the nurse will spend less time with any individual patient. This increases the potential for having a dissatisfied patient as well as missing the subtle signs and symptoms of clinical deterioration.

TIP: The patient care assignment for a particular shift, which lists the patients assigned to each nurse, is typically not kept; however, a listing of the rooms assigned to each nurse may be kept as well as a listing of admissions, transfers, and discharges.

2. Nursing delegation

Delegating on the typical medical surgical nursing unit can be seen as two separate processes. One process involves creating a patient care assignment for each staff nurse. Some institutions give licensed practical nurses (LPNs) their own team of patients to provide direct patient care, and often have a registered nurse (RN) oversee the care delivered. The second process involves the delegation of individual tasks by the nurse to other team members, such as the un-licensed assistive personnel (UAP). In both processes, "the nurse has the responsibility and accountability to delegate or not delegate direct patient care assignments or tasks."[10] Factors that influence this decision include the complexity of the patient's condition or task, the potential for harm, the competency of the healthcare provider, and the necessary critical thinking skills. "In the context of delegation, accountability means bearing responsibility for both the action and inaction of yourself and those to whom you delegate tasks."[11] The Academy of Medical Surgical Nurses' position statement "Unlicensed Assistive Personnel" suggests the following factors be considered before delegating patient care activities to the UAP: "assessment of the patient's condition; complexity of the patient's condition; complexity of the technology and procedures performed; predictability of patient outcomes; level of preparation and education of the UAP; competency of the UAP; ratio of medical surgical RNs to UAP based on patient need; amount of supervision the medical surgical RN is able to provide; and the hospital's position description and approved job duties of the UAP."[12] In reverse, a person who accepts a task or assignment knowing that she is not competent and does not communicate this or seek assistance, is also held accountable. This is another source of potential litigation.

As discussed above, the nurse may be liable for the acts of unlicensed assistive personnel. In the case cited, the nurse had a duty to know the aide's skill level. The instructions given to the aide were less than clear and concise. The nurse was responsible to see that instructions were understood and followed. The aide was an employee of a home health agency, and not the hospital.

A patient was admitted to relieve pressure on her brain by the placement of a ventricular shunt. She suffered from hypertrophic encephalitis, which can cause pressure from excessive fluid buildup within the brain. The shunt would allow drainage of the excess fluid, relieving the pressure on the brain. Postoperatively, she did exhibit some signs of complications. The surgeon ordered a CT scan of the head, which showed no signs of abnormalities. The surgeon, realizing that some of the symptoms could be expected following brain surgery, ordered the patient be kept under observation. The patient's family members stayed with her throughout the day and evening. For the night shift, a "sitter" was hired to watch over the patient. This was an employee of a home health agency, not the hospital. Her specific instructions were to watch over the pa-

tient and report any changes or abnormalities to the nurse. The night nurse did her routine assessments and neurological checks on the patient. No part of the assessments showed abnormalities. When she questioned the home health employee on the patient's condition, her response was "fine." During the night, the patient got up to go to the bathroom twice. On the second trip, the aide noticed she was having difficulty standing. She hit the call bell, which was answered by two nursing assistants. After the patient was placed back in bed, she soon fell asleep. No mention was made to either the family or the nurse of the patient's new symptoms.

That morning, when the surgeon made rounds, he noted symptoms of a stroke or seizure. Testing verified his suspicions. The patient was taken back to surgery, where the shunt was removed and replaced by an alternative drainage system. The patient, as a result of the complications, spent weeks in intensive care and several extra months in the hospital.

The family sued the hospital, nurse, physician, and home health agency for negligence. The initial trial found for the defendants. On appeal, in which only the home health agency was named, the court of appeals readily reversed the opinion of the lower court, and held that the home health aide had a duty to report any abnormal changes. The amount of the judgment was not reported. *Milazzo v. Olsten Home Health Care, Inc.*, 962 S.W. 2d 151 TX (1998).[13] One needs to question the appropriateness of leaving an aide with a patient requiring complex care.

3. Non-direct patient care activities

There are various non-direct patient care activities that pull the nurse away from the bedside. This decreased time at the bedside has a direct implication for a nurse's ability to identify subtle clues that may lead to negative patient outcomes. With the shift in the skill mix of the nursing staff, the RN has acquired more supervisory responsibilities. As a result, RNs spend less time at the bedside. Non-bedside responsibilities include:

- documenting
- transcribing orders
- answering telephone calls
- transporting patients
- attending committee meetings
- collecting data
- reviewing medical records

- obtaining supplies and medications
- attending inservices
- looking up results of lab work and procedures
- locating physicians, case managers, and social workers
- teaching students
- placing telephone calls for patient-related needs

All are time-consuming, although necessary, and take the nurse away from the patient's bedside. Many of these non-bedside responsibilities may create conditions that lead to nursing errors. For instance, a patient did not receive a blood transfusion or medication because the order was not transcribed either correctly or in a timely manner, or it was missed altogether.

4. Special staffing considerations

Special staffing considerations which may impact malpractice nursing claims include the use of foreign-trained nurses. While basic training may differ from United States-trained nurses, they are required to pass the same RN licensure exam. Training may not be a factor in a malpractice case: miscommunication, written and verbal, may contribute. When a hospital utilizes agency nurses or supplemental staff, a copy of licensure and BLS certification must be sent by the agency and kept on file. The hospital must provide an orientation to the hospital and the unit the nurse will be working on. These nurses must be assigned to units that meet their educational and training level; that is, a medical surgical nurse should not be assigned to a critical care unit.

Some hospitals cap the amount of overtime an individual is able to work. However, many nurses "moonlight" at other facilities. A nurse working three 12-hour shifts has four other days to work additional shifts at other facilities. Not only are they possibly working when exhausted, but there is the potential for not correctly identifying institutional policies. Refer to Chapter 2, *Where Have All the Nurses Gone?*, in Volume I, for more information.

B. Patient and Family Issues

1. Customer service

It has become the norm for medical-surgical nursing units to measure or evaluate customer satisfaction. "Measurement of patient satisfaction stands poised to play an increasingly important role in the growing push toward accountability among healthcare providers."[14] "Press Ganey, the hospital industry's leading independent vendor of patient satisfaction measurement and improvement services, believes that more satisfied patients are less likely to file

medical malpractice lawsuits." In general, a dissatisfied patient will share complaints with more people than a satisfied patient will share a positive experience. A patient who has heard the complaints and is admitted to the same facility may have preconceived notions about the quality of care to be received while hospitalized. That patient is more likely to be critical or find fault with the care delivered.

2. Unrealistic expectations

Patients' unrealistic expectations can contribute to dissatisfaction and result in consultation with a plaintiff's attorney. This is even more so with all of the medical television shows. What a person often views on television is not realistic, yet the patient and family come to the hospital with the notion that real life is similar to what they see on television. There is often a disparity between the amount of attention a patient expects to receive on a medical surgical unit and the amount of care actually provided. Flexible open visiting hours on these units mean that family members can arrive earlier than in the past and spend more time with the patient at the bedside. While this can be beneficial for the patient because family members may attend to some of his needs, it is not always welcomed by nurses. Family may be viewed more as a nuisance if they continually interrupt the work of the nurse to ask a question, ask for attention or complain of lack of attention. Nurses working near or at capacity may not appear to be uniformly friendly to family members who come to the nurses' desk demanding attention for the patient. There are many instances when the patient is content with the amount of attention and care received, but the family is dissatisfied.

3. Undermining patient confidence

Medical surgical staff members tend to forget that everything said may be overheard. This can occur at the nurses' station, especially at night, in the elevators, and in the hallways. Often what is considered playful banter by staff may be highly offensive to patients and family members. Discussions about the degree of short-handedness, use of staffing, or lack thereof, as an excuse for deficient or poor care, and other such overt conduct can undermine the patient's expectations and increase the likelihood of suit in the event of a bad outcome. Plaintiff's attorneys screening nursing malpractice cases hear stories of inattentive and rude nurses who respond in an unthinking manner to a family member. When an unexpected negative outcome occurs and there is friction between the family or patient and the nursing staff, it is difficult to differentiate between malpractice and discourteous care. The caregiver's attitude is a key factor in patient satisfaction and confidence in the care received.

7.6 The Noncompliant Patient

Several types of patient conduct should act as red flags for plaintiff's attorneys because certain actions on the part of the patient or family can injure and sour a potentially good plaintiff case by providing a strong argument for contributory or comparative negligence. "Potentially contributing patient acts" (PCPA) is a risk management term for patient behaviors that may contribute to an injury, the extent of damages experienced, or the failure to respond to medical and nursing care. Juries are unsympathetic towards patients who do not follow the instructions of physicians and nurses.

TIP: PCPA are usually well documented in the medical record. There may be progress notes or a problem list written by healthcare professionals detailing evidence of patient behavior that contributed to the injury.

Examples of PCPA are described below.

A. Noncompliance with Medical and Nursing Interventions

Although patients have the right to refuse medical and nursing care, ignoring these instructions may result in harm to the patient.

TIP: The nursing problem list and/or progress notes may contain descriptions of behavior that contradicts the instructions given to the patient. Nurses routinely document noncompliant behavior problems.

B. Leaving Against Medical Advice (AMA) or Elopement

A mentally competent and lucid patient has the right to leave the hospital and cannot be forced to stay. All hospitals should have specific policies dealing with these situations and all staff members should be familiar with them. Some hospitals track the number of AMAs to determine what the causes are for the patient leaving. When a patient announces a plan to leave the hospital, most policies state that the nurse should notify the nursing supervisor and the patient's physician after determining, if possible, the patient's reason for leaving. The physician is responsible for informing the patient of the risk of refusing further treatment. The risks of leaving should be specific. The patient must be informed the condition might worsen and, if it is applicable, death may result. Most authorities agree the patient should be told she is welcome to return to the hospital if a change of mind occurs. A nurse should never tell the patient the hospital refuses to readmit the patient or that the physician will not provide further care if the patient signs out AMA. The mental status and

the discussion with the patient of the risks and benefits of various courses of action should be documented in detail.

1. Refusal to discuss with physician

If the patient announces an intention to leave but is unwilling to wait for the physician to be contacted, the nurse should make every attempt to encourage the patient to delay the departure until the physician is reached. If the patient refuses to wait, the nurse documents the patient's refusal to discuss the issue with the physician.

TIP: The nurse is required to inform the physician the patient has left the hospital against medical advice. This notification is documented in the patient's medical record.

2. Documentation

The patient is asked to sign a release form indicating he understands the risk of signing out AMA. The medical record should reflect that the nurse documented the circumstances of the patient's desire to leave AMA, the assessment of mental status, the actions taken, and the time the patient left. Most hospitals have a policy to address AMA. An occurrence report is usually filed with the risk manager.

When a patient is at risk for elopement, hospital personnel must ensure the safety of the patient from elopement. Some hospitals communicate to the hospital community about a patient at risk for leaving the hospital.

TIP: Some hospitals have policies that address utilizing sitters at the bedside of patients at risk for elopement. This is especially true if the patient is unable to make decisions about care, such as with an Alzheimer's patient.

In some instances, there is no prior indication for the risk of elopement. If a patient is missing, nurses attempt to locate the patient as quickly as possible. Nursing policy usually requires notification of the supervisor, the physician, hospital security and the police, if indicated. When a hospitalized patient is discovered missing, the consequences may be serious depending on the condition of the patient. Contributing to the harm of the patient may be severe weather conditions, traffic patterns in the local area, unfamiliarity with the area, lack of funds, and inappropriate attire. If the patient is agitated and violent, others could be harmed. The police are notified if the patient is at risk for self-harm, may harm others, or has left the facility with a medical device in place, such as a central intravenous catheter. Refer to Chizek for additional information about elopement.[15]

C. Presence of Unauthorized Items at the Bedside (Contraband)

1. Personal items

Unauthorized items or contraband may take many forms. Most items brought in by patients or family members and friends are checked by the biomedical department before use in the hospital. Heating pads, hair dryers, computers, and electric razors often fit into this category. Injuries which arise from the unauthorized use of such items are unlikely to result in significant liability, provided hospital policy is followed and the patient or family members are instructed about the policy.

2. Forbidden substances or items

Possession of alcoholic beverages, illegal drugs, or tobacco (in smoke-free hospitals) is forbidden. Many hospitals have policies allowing smoking in certain areas by specific patients, often by physician order only. Forbidden items include guns, knives, and pepper-spray. If there is reasonable suspicion the patient is in possession of any of these substances or items, the nurse should notify hospital protective services (security). Most hospitals have a policy allowing the patient's belongings to be searched and for these items to be removed. Most of these policies include contacting the police department when appropriate. When appropriate, these substances should be removed and returned upon discharge or sent home with family members.

3. Tampering with medical equipment

At times patients or visitors manipulate equipment, without understanding the consequences. The nurse may observe or there may be indications that medical equipment has been tampered with, such as a change in the IV flow rate, a traction device removed, adjusted monitoring equipment, or manipulation of biomedical equipment. The nurse should assess whether this was innocent, such as the family increasing the oxygen delivered to help the patient breathe better, or intentional, such as increasing the drip rate on a continuous morphine infusion. The nursing documentation should describe what the nurse did about the problem, such as instructing the patient and visitor not to touch the equipment or notifying the physician of the problem. Nurses should continually assess for repeated behavior or new occurrences.

7.7 Special Populations
A. Frail Elderly
The graying of America has impacted the nursing profession greatly in the last few decades. Defined in terms of chrono-

logical age, the elderly include individuals 65 years of age or older. The fact that medical surgical nurses see greater numbers of older adults in their practice should come as no surprise when demographic data are taken into account. The standard of care requires medical surgical nurses to be aware of normal aging and risks in old age to deliver gerontological care competently. Age-related changes create a unique set of norms by which assessment data must be interpreted. To assure a high standard of care when working with the elderly, the nurse must be aware there are unique risks of illness and injury, altered presentations of symptoms and responses to therapy, and more complex psychosocial variables to address. HR.01.05.03 of *The Joint Commission Accreditation Manual* (2010)[16] states the staff are expected to participate in ongoing education and training that is specific to the needs of the patient populaiton served by the hospital. Common sources of litigation involving geriatric patients involve injuries sustained secondary to a fall, development of pressure ulcers, and adverse reactions to medications. It is important for the medical surgical nurse to obtain a thorough history to identify pre-existing conditions and medications that affect the course of the hospitalization. If the patient is transferred from another level of care, such as an assisted living facility (ALF) or skilled nursing facility (SNF), the hospital staff should make every attempt to obtain these records. The risk associated with medication use is heightened because of the elderly's altered metabolism, detoxification and excretion of medications, combined with the interactions from multiple drugs consumed (polypharmacy). The nurse should differentiate normal aging changes from pathology and assess present physical findings in comparison to prior level of functioning on admission.

B. Physically and Mentally Challenged
The term "disability" is defined per the Americans with Disability Act as an individual with a physical or mental impairment that substantially limits one or more of the major life activities of such individual.[17] Persons with disabilities present a challenge for medical-surgical nurses. Physically disabled patients may include, but are not limited to, those who require special adaptive equipment, such as: wheelchairs, walkers, or prosthetic devices. In addition, patients who are morbidly obese or partially or fully paralyzed may be considered physically disabled. Often overlooked are patients with hearing and vision impairment. Although most hospitals have communication assistive devices, such as telephone amplification or large print educational materials, these often go unused.

Patients who are mentally disabled are those who have lack of understanding or insight, such as a patient with dementia or mental retardation. There may be a tendency for nurses to infantilize them. Nurses may make assumptions about their education level and assume they know nothing about their illness. Nurses decide who has the right to give consent for treatment and procedures. Assumptions made about the presence and severity of pain is complicated by the difficulty of verifying information.

C. Non-English Speaking or Low Literacy

Because of the difficulty communicating, medical surgical nurses are challenged by patients who are non-English speaking or have low literacy. Written materials such as patient education and discharge paperwork are geared toward low literacy levels and may be available in multiple languages. However, consent forms are not written at a low literacy level. Consent forms may be available in the most common languages found in the community. A greater challenge for medical surgical nurses is verbal communication. Due to patient confidentiality requirements, as outlined in the Health Insurance Portability and Accountability Act,[18] the patient's friends or family members as interpreters may not be used because of the revelation of private medical information. Furthermore, the translation of medical information by an untrained interpreter may be incorrectly communicated. Another challenge of communication is the identification of which patients need language interpreters. The question arises when the patient or the person giving historical medical information speaks broken English or is using hand gestures to answer questions or give a history. Whenever the nurse has any doubt regarding information being given or received, a translator must be used to ensure that all information is correct.

In the following case, healthcare personnel failed to meet the responsibility of obtaining a translator and the judge found in favor of the plaintiff:

> The plaintiff's week-old daughter was brought by ambulance to the emergency room of the defendant hospital's pediatric facility. The infant was accompanied by her mother and her uncle. The triage nurse took a history from the uncle, who conveyed information using what she referred to as "broken English" and hand signs.
>
> At one point the uncle demonstrated to the nurse that he had tapped on the infant's chest, but when asked if the child had stopped breathing, he answered, "No, no, I don't know." A translator was never requested by the nurse, who believed that the report and statements from the EMT's, combined with information from the uncle, was sufficient. A

first-year pediatrics resident who later obtained a history felt that a translator was not required, but documented that the history was "limited by language."

> The infant was soon discharged, but within hours she stopped breathing. After four days on life support, she died.
>
> The plaintiffs claimed that death was due to an apneic event triggered by acute tracheobronchitis and bronchiolitis consistent with respiratory syncytial viral infection (RSV). The plaintiffs maintained that a detailed, accurate history was not obtained; as a result, the defendants failed to recognize that the baby had experienced a life-threatening initial apneic event at home. The plaintiffs charged that it was the duty of the hospital personnel to determine whether an interpreter was needed and that translation services should have been provided if there was any doubt. The matter was tried before a judge, who found in favor of the plaintiffs and awarded them $400,000.[19]

TIP: Translation is required to be done by trained medical interpreters who have been deemed competent in the language they are translating.

D. Patient at Risk for Withdrawal

There is often a misunderstanding by the healthcare providers and patients that a patient addicted to drugs or alcohol will undergo detoxification while in the hospital. These patients are admitted to a medical-surgical unit for an acute problem. The staff in a medical surgical setting should not try to cure the patient of alcohol or drug addiction, or rehabilitate her. The goal is to prevent the complications that are a consequence of the patient's addiction, manage comfort, and optimize outcomes. Detoxification should occur in a setting where the healthcare personnel have been specifically educated to detoxify a patient safely.

Withdrawing from either alcohol or drug abuse increases morbidity and mortality. This population is at risk for injury, persistent altered mentation, seizures, coma, and death. Symptoms of intoxication or withdrawal can be mistaken for other medical diagnoses. For instance, a patient with bloodshot eyes, lack of coordination, and slurred speech could be suffering from subdural hematoma. Patients who have impending withdrawal from alcohol or drugs and are undergoing surgery with general anesthesia have a greater risk than the general population of regurgitation and/or aspiration of stomach contents.

1. Patient denial

Caring for patients addicted to alcohol or pharmaceutical substances may pose specific liability risks for the medical surgical nurse. Patients frequently deny any form of addiction, even when faced with substantial evidence of the abuse. They may fear legal repercussions, denial of benefits by insurance entities, involvement of social agencies, such as Children's Services, loss of employment, or social stigmatization. The latter fear may be heightened in a patient whose reputation is essential to his livelihood.

2. Early recognition of withdrawal

Patients may be dependent on one or more addictive drugs. Withdrawal symptoms range from generalized malaise to acute paranoia to severe seizure activity, depending on prior drug use or degree of dependency. These patients have a higher potential for elopement, injury to self or others, or leaving against medical advice. In the face of the patient's denial of usage, it is difficult to predict the type of withdrawal symptoms the patient may experience or the time frame in which to expect the onset. The standard of care requires that the medical surgical nurse be able to assess for signs and symptoms of withdrawal. Early recognition is imperative and should begin during the admission process. The nurse is expected to act as a collaborative member of the interdisciplinary team by consulting with the appropriate members. The management of withdrawal symptoms requires a team approach, including use of medications to minimize and prevent delirium tremens (either alcohol or drug-related).

TIP: Many hospitals utilize a screening tool upon admission to determine risk of withdrawal. Once the patient is identified as at risk, many hospitals use a standardized assessment tool, such as the Clinical Institute Withdrawal Assessment (CIWA), to determine level of severity of withdrawal.

Chronic alcoholics are often either evasive or untruthful when asked to provide information on the amount of alcohol routinely consumed. In fact, an old adage states that whatever the patient admits to consuming should be doubled. Experienced nurses learn to recognize subtle signs of alcohol abuse and monitor for signs of alcohol withdrawal, which usually become evident in two to three days after abstinence begins. Prevention of withdrawal (delirium tremens or DTs) is preferable to managing the alcoholic patient actively going through DTs.

The patient's hallucinations and unpredictable violence poses a hazard to the patient, as the following case shows: The plaintiff's husband was admitted to the St. Elizabeth Hospital for treatment of a gastrointestinal disorder. The man, age 45, was an alcoholic and was supposed to be watched for alcohol withdrawal symptoms. The plaintiff claimed that the nurse on duty the day the patient died was unaware of these precautions. When his family members reported that the man was nervous and agitated, the nurse allegedly promised to check on him but never did. The man later broke through a window and plunged seven floors to his death. The defense claimed the man jumped from the window so soon after the family reported his distress that the nurse's response time was reasonable. According to published accounts, a $1.3 million verdict was returned. Post-trial motions were pending. *Martinez v. St. Elizabeth Hospital*, Union County (NJ) Superior Court.[20]

Critical information about the potential for DTs must be passed on in the change-of-shift report, documented in the medical record and included in the plan of care. Even if this information is not passed on in report, the nurse assigned to the patient is accountable for knowing the past medical history and critically thinking of the effect it may have on the current diagnosis, as well as potential problems during the current hospital stay. According to the defense expert witness in this case,[21] while the patient was anxious, he did not exhibit any signs of alcohol withdrawal before he went out the window. His prior psychiatric background was not revealed to the nurses. The defense expert witness failed to take into consideration that anxiety is one of the autonomic symptoms of alcohol withdrawal. Another consideration is the fact that a symptom was reported to the nurse, who then failed to respond to the family's request.

7.8 Standards of Care
A. Absence or Outdated Standards of Care

Standards of care may be computerized or in a paper manual. If computerized, the hospital should have policies stating how staff can access them when the computer is down. These need to be readily accessible to staff. Often hard copies are kept in specific locations in the hospital. Are these areas accessible to the evening/night staff? For example, if the paper manual is kept in nursing administration, it is usually the nursing supervisor who has access.

In the ever-changing world of health care, it is impossible to have a policy and/or procedure to address every eventuality when caring for a patient. Many hospitals designate an additional reference, such as a nursing textbook, to augment their own policies and procedures. These textbooks are often outdated and need to be replaced with the current edition. In the absence of any referenced policy or procedure, nursing personnel need to rely on the community standard, which is what the reasonable and prudent nurse would do given the same set of circumstances in a similar setting in the community. In other words, the nurse should seek counsel from senior nurses on the unit or notify the supervisor.

The Joint Commission requires an annual review of patient care policies. Many hospitals have a committee designated to review and revise their policy and procedure manuals. The purpose of this review is to ensure that evidence-based best practice is incorporated into their policies and procedures. Attorneys need to be aware of the possible problematic areas in the process used to review, revise, and distribute policies. A common process is: a committee reviews and revises a policy; the policy is sent for retyping with changes; the policy is proofread and forwarded for signature to the appropriate person, such as the Chief Nursing Officer; and the policy is sent for copying and distribution or posted on the computer. Oftentimes, the policy is placed in the manual or posted on the computer without communication to the nursing staff. Staff need to be made aware of revisions and/or new policies in order to utilize them. The revised policy may not have been distributed at the time of the litigious event even though the date may reflect it was in effect. Refer to Chapter 8, *Inside the Healthcare Environment*, in Volume I, for more information on this topic.

TIP: Once suit is filed, policies and procedures in effect at the time of the incident should be sent with the medical record for the expert witness to review.

B. Deviations from Standard of Care

The next section of this chapter deals with common deviations from the standard of care. Most, if not all, hospitals have policies and procedures to define the assessment and reassessment requirements. In some instances, the policy is very specific, such as monitoring and assessing a post-operative patient, a patient receiving a blood transfusion, or a patient receiving patient-controlled analgesia. The medical surgical nurse sets priorities to determine what needs to be done now, what can be delegated to someone else, and what can wait. Patients may not receive needed care if an error is made in setting priorities.

In general, deviations from the standard of care fall under the following broad categories: failure to monitor, failure to assess, failure to rescue, failure to communicate, and failure to follow or question physician's orders. Many times, one or more deviations from the standard of care can be detected by the expert witness; however, one of them tends to be the determinant factor in a lawsuit. Common deviations are discussed and illustrated with cases.

1. Failure to monitor

Failure to monitor can mean one of two things: failing to monitor the patient or failing to monitor the person to whom a responsibility was delegated.

TIP: The state Nurse Practice Act identifies what is within the scope of practice for the RN and LPN.

In the case example that follows, failure to monitor vital signs as well as failure to monitor the LPN assigned to collect the data is illustrated. The frequency and lack of vital signs was an important issue. There is no mention of the RN monitoring the LPN's care.

A 75-year-old patient was admitted for revision of a total right hip prosthesis and died post-operatively. The surgery lasted seven hours, was extensive and included an osteotomy of the femur. Upon his transfer to the post anesthesia care unit (PACU), his vital signs became unstable and his blood pressure dropped dramatically. The anesthesiologist contacted the orthopedic surgeon. After intravenous fluids were given, the patient's blood pressure immediately stabilized. When the patient was transferred to the medical surgical unit, he was assessed by a licensed practical nurse.

His vital signs were not checked by the nurses on the medical surgical unit for the rest of the day. The nursing staff later found the patient in cardiac arrest. Although resuscitation restored the patient's heartbeat, he suffered brain damage and died two days later. The plaintiff argued the nurses deviated from the standard of care by failing to appropriately assess the decedent's vital signs upon arrival to the medical surgical unit; failing to appropriately assess signs and symptoms of hypovolemia (inadequate fluid volume), a well-known post-operative complication of orthopedic surgery; and failing to contact the physician for appropriate interventions. The plaintiff also argued the hypovolemia led to hypovolemic shock, which led to the cardiac arrest and death. They argued that if the nurses had not given substandard care, the decedent would have been diagnosed with hypovolemia, which could have been treated with additional IV fluids and blood transfusions.

The defendant doctors stated that the patient's blood pressure did not vary substantially from his normal blood pressure, especially after the extensive surgery and the fluid loss. They opined that the patient suffered from disseminated intravascular coagulopathy (DIC) caused by a combination of the extensive surgery and the autotransfusion of his own blood through a sulcotrans device; that the sulcotrans caused an allergic reaction; and that nothing could have been done to reverse the disseminated intravascular coagulopathy. The parties settled for $350,000.[22]

It would be prudent for an initial head-to-toe assessment on a fresh post-operative patient to be done by a RN. Care could then be delegated to the LPN with the understanding that the LPN will report any changes from the baseline assessment to the RN, and conversely that the RN will periodically request that information from the LPN. Aside from the failure to adequately monitor the patient's vital signs post-operatively, there is also the issue of inappropriate placement of the patient. Because the patient had complications post-operatively in the PACU regarding his blood pressure, placement would have been more appropriate on a unit that had a higher level of care, such as a telemetry unit where the patient could have been monitored more closely.

2. Failure to assess

Nurses as well as physicians are responsible for the performance and documentation of a physical assessment of their patients. Assessments can be head-to-toe or a focused assessment, which involves one organ or body system. A full head-to-toe assessment is often more detailed than a nurse would perform on a patient admitted to the hospital. A nursing physical assessment normally has the nurse assess body systems, such as neurological, cardiac, respiratory, gastrointestinal, genitourinary, integumentary, and musculoskeletal. Skills required to do a head-to-toe assessment include inspection, auscultation, palpation, and percussion. Inspection always comes first and requires a visual assessment of the body. Auscultation follows and requires the healthcare professional to listen to sounds produced by the body, usually through the use of a stethoscope. Palpation uses sense of touch to assess factors such as temperature, texture, moisture, location and size of organs, swelling (edema), presence

or absence of pulse, and presence of masses. It also assesses for presence of tenderness. An example would be assessing for appendicitis where the clinician will depress the area over the appendix and briskly release. This will elicit rebound tenderness in the presence of appendicitis. Percussion is rarely done by nursing. It involves the tapping of areas on the body to elicit a sound that indicates presence of fluid or air. A nurse's assessment of a patient often begins with a set of vital signs. These include temperature, blood pressure, pulse, and respirations. It may also include pulse oximetry to determine level of oxygenation. Initial assessment includes a general survey by observing the patient's initial appearance, behavior, and orientation, which includes level of consciousness. Often the completion of a physical assessment is guided by a pre-printed assessment form that goes through each of the body systems. These forms will identify parameters for normal findings.

The following case example illustrates several deviations from the standard of care, including the failure to monitor vital signs and urinary output, and match the physical assessment and laboratory results with the deterioration of the patient's clinical status. Additionally, the surgeon further breached the standard of care by improperly using a gastrostomy tube.

The plaintiff's decedent, a 53-year-old retired resident of Prince George's County, Maryland, had elective bariatric surgery for weight control performed five years after retirement by the defendant surgeon at the defendant hospital. Despite advertising the use of National Institute of Health (NIH) approved procedures, and obtaining the plaintiff's consent, the defendant performed a modification of the Fobi pouch—a surgical technique currently being considered by NIH, but not yet approved. Postoperatively, the plaintiff's decedent was allowed to languish in a dangerous hypotensive state with no urine output for over eight hours. By the morning of post-op day one, the decedent was in renal and respiratory failure. By post-op day two, the decedent had spiking fevers and lab results consistent with an intra-abdominal leak. By post-op day four, the decedent showed clear signs and symptoms of sepsis. The hospital intensivist suggested at several points, beginning on post-op day one, that the symptoms indicated an infection located in the abdominal area. The surgeon could have at that time utilized a tubogram which would indicate a leak in the bypassed section of the stomach, but rather relied on an upper GI film series. This series failed to detect leaks in the bypassed gastric remnant, or around the gastrostomy tube site. The surgeon was faced with undeniable evidence of a leak when stool began to ooze from the incision site. The plaintiff indicated a gastrostomy tube was not indicated in a first-time bariatric surgery patient. The decedent remained in intensive care for two and one-half months and endured five subsequent surgeries before she expired in another hospital. The plaintiff contended that the hospital breached the standard of care by not properly notifying the physician when the decedent remained in a hypotensive state with no urine output. The defendant surgeon breached the standard of care by improper use and placement of a gastrostomy tube, failure to perform a proper post-operative assessment, failure to timely recognize the signs and symptoms of a gastric leak, and failure to remove the necrotized stomach tissue, which was the obvious source of the decedent's sepsis. The plaintiff claimed the decedent's gastric leak could have been timely and easily diagnosed by ordering a tubogram. The defendants denied all of the plaintiff's allegations and claimed they acted within the standard of care. A confidential settlement was reached.[23]

The documented standards of care in a hospital setting refer to the hospital's policy and procedure manuals, which are usually under the auspices of nursing. The standard from which the physician deviated regarding the use of a gastroscopy tube would be documented in the medical literature.

3. Failure to rescue

"Failure to rescue occurs when early signs and symptoms a) fail to be recognized and acted upon, b) are recognized and interventions start too late or not at all, and c) are recognized and treatment initiated without patient response."[24] "Although failure to rescue is based on the premise that many deaths in hospitals are preventable, failure to rescue does not necessarily imply wrong-doing."[25] The following case shows how failure to recognize and intervene led to the patient suffering a hypoxic brain injury:

The plaintiff, age 44, suffered a hypoxic brain injury when nurses and a respiratory therapist failed to intervene when his condition worsened. After nurses testified they knew the plaintiff was facing foreseeable respiratory arrest, but did not call a code or summon a doctor until the plaintiff actually went into cardio-respiratory arrest, the trial

court granted summary judgment to the plaintiff on the claim that nursing negligence caused the injury. The physician was given summary judgment. The hospital's chief nursing officer also testified the hospital placed untrained and incompetent nurses at the bedside who could not provide even the basic minimum care. According to Texas Reporter, an $18,418,490 verdict was returned, which included $11.4 million in punitive damages. The jury's decisions on the verdict form resulted in the punitive damages being unrestricted by a cap.[26]

"It is important for the medical surgical nurse to anticipate the unexpected, recognize the problem, and intervene before it's too late. Once problems are recognized, resources must be mobilized to correct a deteriorating condition. Staff nurses must feel empowered to make the decision to intervene early and not wait for the absence of pulse or respirations."[27] In view of the chief nursing officer's statement above, there is a question of whether or not the experience and skill level of each nurse was considered when assigning this patient.

In 1999, the Institute for Healthcare Improvement (IHI) launched the 100,000 Lives Campaign. The 3,100 hospitals that participated in this initiative saved an estimated 122,000 lives in 18 months. One of the goals of this campaign included implementing changes in care that were proven to prevent avoidable deaths. With such a great success, the IHI initiated a new campaign in 2006 to protect patients from five million incidents of medical harm over the following two years. Part of the original initiative was the formation of a rapid response team, which is a group of clinicians who bring critical care expertise to the patient anywhere it is needed. Several key roles include assessing and stabilizing the patient's condition and organizing information communicated to the physician to determine interventions and possible patient relocation to a higher level of care. The medical surgical nurse would be able to use the rapid response team to assist in assessing and intervening as necessary. Refer to Chapter 4, *Patient Safety Initiatives,* in Volume I, for more information on the 5 Million Lives Campaign, which followed the 100,000 Lives Campaign.

The National Patient Safety Goal (NPSG) #16, which was written by The Joint Commission in 2009, was to "Improve the Recognition and Response to Changes in the Patient's Condition." NPSG 16.01.01 required that hospitals select a method for staff to request additional assistance from a specially trained individual when the patient's condition appeared to be worsening. It also stated that the hospital should encourage the patient and family to seek assistance when the patient's condition worsened. In 2010, NPSG #16 was retired and the elements of this goal were moved to other areas of The Joint Commission survey. Although it is not an active NPSG, it is embedded in other areas of the survey and, therefore, continues to be assessed by The Joint Commission. Hospitals responded to this requirement by forming Rapid Response Teams (RRT). While members of the team vary, members usually include an ICU nurse, respiratory therapist, and a physician. A rapid response is usually identified as a special "code." This is initiated by telephone with a call overhead announcing the rapid response. The bedside nurse is expected to take the patient's vital signs, complete a focused assessment and be prepared to report findings to the team upon arrival. The team then guides any further assessments and interventions for the patient.

The following case study is an example of a failure to rescue, in which both the patient and the nurses would have benefited from the use of a Rapid Response Team.

A 49-year-old female with a six-month history of headache was diagnosed with a colloid cyst. A frontal craniotomy was performed without incident. The patient had an uneventful ICU stay with the exception of two grand mal seizures within the first 24 hours post surgery. The patient was transferred to a med-surg telemetry unit on post-operative day 6. She was alert and oriented, and moving all extremities. She was ordered to have neurological checks every four hours by the nursing staff. The neuro checks in ICU were all within normal limits. On post-operative day 7 (the day after arrival to the med-surg telemetry unit), the patient was confused and disoriented to place and time with a pain level of 0/10 on a 0-10 scale. On post-operative days 8 and 9, the patient was noted to be following commands. She was using all four extremities and was alert and oriented to person, place and time. She was ambulating with a slightly unsteady gait. She occasionally gave inappropriate answers to questions. Her pain level was a 0/10. On post-operative day 10, the surgeon charted, "Patient most likely to be discharged tomorrow." The nurses notes state the patient was oriented only to person, was unsteady on her feet, and pain 0/10. Neuro checks continued every four hours. At 12:00 A.M. midnight, the patient was noted to be confused, and disoriented to person, time and place. Blood pressure was 146/69, heart rate 85, respiratory rate 20, pain level 9/10, and the patient complained of a headache. The nurse gave the patient two tablets of

Codeine 30mg as previously ordered and returned to reassess the patient's pain. The patient stated a pain rating of 0/10. On post-operative day 12 at 7:38 A.M., the patient was found unresponsive. No vital signs or neuro checks were documented since noon the day before. A code blue was called but the patient died.

In this case study, there were many opportunities for the nurses to call the physician or surgeon to inform them of the changes in the patient's neurological status. Yet, this was never done. If a Rapid Response Team had been in notified, the nurses could have called the team for assistance when the neuro checks indicated a negative change. The nurses in this example "failed to rescue" the patient even though there were many indications of a deteriorating condition. On post-operative day 7, the patient was noted to be confused; on days 8 and 9, the patient had a gait disturbance and although technically oriented to person, place and time, the patient often gave inappropriate answers. When the patient suddenly had pain which she did not have previously, the nurse medicated her without performing a thorough assessment. Had the nurse reported the changes or called a rapid response at any of these times, the neurological changes could have been reported and acted upon and her death could have been avoided.

4. Failure to communicate

Timely and appropriate communication among healthcare providers is the key to optimal patient care. In this age of technology, our communication processes include computer-generated reports, fax machines, and cell phones. All have their own inherent problems, such as the computer going off-line. Human error, the complexities of verbal and written communication, and system issues often lead to failure to communicate important information. As described in Chapter 4, *Patient Safety Initiatives,* in Volume I, The Joint Commission introduced the National Patient Safety Goals several years ago. The purpose of these goals is to promote specific improvements in patient safety. The goals highlight problematic areas in health care and describe evidence and expert-based solutions to these problems. One of the goals is "to improve the effectiveness of communication among caregivers."[28] The following cases will illustrate various types of failure to communicate.

a. Failure to report abnormal lab results

Today's healthcare environment includes the performance of multiple diagnostic tests to rule out or confirm medical diagnoses. Most hospitals have a system to notify the nurse of critically abnormal lab results. This notification may take the form of a phone call from the laboratory technician, a message through the computer system, or a fax of the result sent from the lab to the nursing unit, or a combination of the above.

The following is an example of a notification which did not take place and was not documented as having taken place, with the result that the patient's diabetes went undiagnosed and untreated until too late:

> The plaintiff's decedent went to the hospital complaining of a spider bite. She was suspected of having diabetes and was asked by the treating physician and nurse if she was diabetic, which she denied. The woman had been diagnosed as diabetic eight years earlier but thought she was "cured." The decedent had an elevated white blood cell count and an ongoing infection at the time of admission. Blood work that was ordered for the morning after admission indicated a glucose level of 403 (normal for this lab is 80-120; reference numbers vary from lab to lab). The laboratory had the results just before 4 P.M. on the day after admission. The results were transmitted to the hospital by an outside laboratory shortly after 6:15 P.M. Neither the treating physician or the nurses looked at the results until the next morning, at which time the patient was in a ketoacidotic coma. She soon died.

> The plaintiff claimed the defendants failed to diagnose and treat the diabetes. The laboratory's policies and procedures provided for phoning the results of lab work with critically abnormal results, which the lab tech said he did, although he could not identify the person who answered nor to whom the results were transmitted. All other defendants denied receiving a call from the lab but confirmed the lab was supposed to call with the results of "panic values" (critically abnormal lab values). The nurses did not obtain the lab results from the teletype machine, because the teletype was supposed to contain only routine lab results unless a call was placed to the nurses. The treating physician testified he did not check the teletype machine, because it was the nurse's job to do so. A $455,000 settlement was reached. Of this amount, the nurses and hospital paid all but $105,000.[29]

In this case it would be difficult for the nurses to explain the reason for failing to check the teletype machine for lab results from approximately 6:15 P.M. until the follow-

ing morning. Aside from relying only on a lab-documented result, the nurses were obligated to perform clinical assessments of the patient. As the patient's level of consciousness was changing, the nurse was responsible for reporting this to the physician, regardless of receiving the lab value result. The nurses should have done point of care testing using either a glucometer or urine dipstick, both of which would have shown a high glucose level.

TIP: Under ordinary circumstances, laboratory personnel document the name of the person who was informed of the abnormal results. These are recorded on a log in the lab. The nurse will record abnormal results and notification of the physician in the medical record. Computerized lab results are placed in the medical record too.

In the following case, nurses were aware of the abnormal lab results but failed to communicate either the lab results or the patient's condition to the physician:

> A 43-year-old man was admitted to the defendant hospital with abdominal pain that was timely diagnosed as pancreatitis. Over the next 24 hours his condition deteriorated. The plaintiffs alleged the patient was not sufficiently hydrated to manage his pancreatitis, and that his nurses failed to monitor and communicate the patient's condition and test results to the treating physicians. At 5 A.M., the day after admission, the patient's lab results showed a serious aberration of lab values. Those results were reported to nurses at 10 A.M. The nurses faxed the lab results to the treating physician's office at noon where they sat for a period of time. A message was left with the physician to call the nursing unit regarding the results. The medical record did not reflect this information. The patient's condition seriously deteriorated throughout the day, and at 6 P.M., a "code blue" was called. Massive fluid resuscitation began. The patient was resuscitated, but subsequently developed necrotizing pancreatitis, and was transferred to another hospital where he died several weeks later. The defendant physicians contended the nurses failed to communicate the patient's abnormal lab results and deteriorating condition to them, and the initial orders were adequate for treatment of pancreatitis. The defendant hospital contended this was a physician's problem and the responsibility for treatment should not have been placed on the nurses. The demand by the plaintiff was $160,000 in medicals and lost in-

come of $1 million. The actual verdict was $4.5 million.[30]

TIP: The medical surgical nurse is expected to be aware of critical, abnormal lab values and take appropriate action.

The nurse and physician share the responsibility of following up on abnormal lab results. The nurse is expected to inform the physician of such results upon receipt. The clinical consequences of failure to take action on a panic value can be severe, as evidenced in this case. An appropriate chain-of-command process must be in place and communicated properly to nurses, physicians, and anyone else involved with the process. If the procedures are not clearly written or not covered thoroughly in orientation, problems can occur. Employees need to feel confident the hospital administration supports the chain-of-command and are backed up when they use it properly. It appears the nurse in this case had sufficient reason to go up the chain-of-command in light of the physician's lack of response.[31]

b. Failure to report changes in patient condition

Often, the nurse is the first to recognize when a patient's clinical condition has changed. The changes may range from very subtle to profound. The nurse's primary obligations are to safeguard the patient, notify the physician, and document observations and actions taken.

On May 3, 1998, the plaintiff, a 60-year-old man, was admitted to Sherman Hospital with complaints of back, neck, shoulder, and chest pain. At 11:30 A.M. on May 5, the plaintiff developed partial numbness of his hands and had to be catheterized due to urinary retention. At noon, the plaintiff reported to the bedside nurse he was unable to feed himself at lunch because his arms were too weak. The nurse fed him his entire lunch and noted his condition in his medical chart, but failed to notify any physician of the patient's complaints or changes. At 2:00 P.M., the patient reported to the nurse he was unable to move his arms or legs and the numbness now involved his entire hands. The nurse noted his complaints in detail in the chart, but again failed to report this to any physician. At 5:15 P.M., a neurologist came in to see the patient on a routine consult that had been requested at 11:30 A.M. by the defendant orthopedic specialist, Dr. Kogan. The neurologist was surprised to find

the patient was quadriplegic, and complete spinal cord compression was diagnosed on the basis of clear clinical signs. Because of the plaintiff's large size (350 pounds), he could not fit into the MRI scan machine at Sherman Hospital. He was transferred to Northwestern Memorial, arriving at 10:15 P.M., after which he was diagnosed with a massive herniation of the C5-6 disc. He underwent discectomy and decompression surgery on May 6 at 7:15 A.M. However, the plaintiff was left with permanent quadriparesis/quadriplegia, without functional use of any of his extremities. He is now completely bedridden and requires a feeding tube. The plaintiff contended the hospital was negligent because its nurse failed to notify any physician of the patient's deteriorating neurological status, and that urinary catheterization was done without a physician's order—which are both deviations from accepted standards of nursing practice. The hospital claimed Dr. Kogan ordered the catheterization, which he denied. This issue was important because if Dr. Kogan knew of the catheterization and the patient's inability to urinate, he would be required to order an emergency neurological consultation rather than a routine consult. Defense for the hospital asserted the plaintiff's symptoms between 11:30 A.M. and 5:15 P.M. were nothing more than a continuation of earlier problems with his use of his upper extremities that had been reported to his internist at 8:30 A.M. that morning, and the plaintiff's outcome would have been the same even if he had been seen by a doctor earlier because his spinal cord was already irreversibly damaged. Defense for the hospital also argued the plaintiff, age 65 at the time of trial, had a life expectancy of only four to six more years due to his pre-existing morbid obesity, diabetes, and hypertension. According to the Cook County Jury Verdict Reporter, the jury awarded a total verdict of $22,353,000 against Sherman Hospital, but returned a defense verdict for Dr. Kogan.[32]

As evidenced in the above case, the nurse assessed the patient and documented the change in patient condition but failed to notify the physician of these changes. Nurses are the patient's last line of defense, and, as such, have the duty to protect the patient.

In another case, the nurses failed to notify the physician of an abnormal excessive urinary output, which resulted in the patient's death.

The plaintiff's decedent, age 54, was admitted to the hospital in June 2006 for treatment of low blood sodium. The decedent had diabetes insipidus, a deficiency in regulating urine output, which can lead to dehydration and increased serum sodium. On the third day of admission the decedent's husband found her comatose and non-responsive. She died three weeks later. The plaintiff claimed that on the second day of admission the decedent had urinated more than ten liters of fluid over a 16-hour period, leading to dehydration, brain damage and her death. The plaintiffs also claimed that the nurses failed to inform doctors of the excessive urination and that the woman's condition was not adequately monitored. The defendants claimed that a consulting endocrinologist, Dr. Shapiro, was solely responsible for the care and treatment decisions leading to the woman's death. The defendant physician, Dr. Mehta, also claimed that the hospital's nursing staff did not inform him of any change in the decedent's condition. According to a published account Christos was found 40 percent negligent and Shapiro was found 60 percent at fault. Dr. Mehta was not found negligent. The jury awarded $1,478,949 and after the reduction for Dr. Shapiro's negligence, they recovered $591,581 from the hospital.[33]

In the following case, the nurses documented changes in the patient's condition but failed to notify the physician:

Our client was an active 69-year-old female that went to a Central Florida hospital complaining of severe neck pain. She was admitted and was undergoing extensive evaluations to determine the source of her problems. Two days later hospital employees were charting that she was having neurological deficits but failed to report these critical findings to the doctors. When the deficits were noted by the doctors the next day, she was then diagnosed with a cervical spinal epidural abscess. The delay in diagnosis closed a window of opportunity for surgery that would likely have cured the problem with little residual effect. Our client is now left with irreversible paraplegia. The hospital claimed that the findings that were charted were not significant and, further, that surgery would not have made a difference. This confidential settlement will provide our client with funding for medical and attendant care for her lifetime. $2,500,000 confidential settlement.[34]

c. Faulty communication system

In the following case, the nursing staff communicated the change in patient condition to the surgeon's nurses. The nursing staff assumed the information given to these professionals would be relayed to the surgeon.

On October 29, 2002, the plaintiff's decedent Vicki Bramlett, age 36, a state prison guard in Lubbock, underwent a laparoscopically assisted vaginal hysterectomy by gynecologist Benny P. Phillips, a partner in Lubbock Gynecologic Oncology Associates. Bramlett had a history of pain and endometriosis. After being transferred from the recovery room to the floor, Bramlett had a very low urinary output, which can indicate internal bleeding. At 5:35 P.M., Phillips had his nurses call the hospital's nurses and order the following tests: a stat fluid challenge over the next 30 to 60 minutes and a stat H & H. (A fluid challenge measures urinary output, and H&H stands for hemoglobin and hematocrit.) The hospital nurses were instructed to call back with the results in about one hour.

At 6:30 P.M., the hospital nurses called Phillips' nurses and said Bramlett's hemoglobin had dropped from 15.7 to 9.8, which represented a 40 percent decrease in blood volume, and she had failed the fluid challenge. Phillips was in surgery, and his nurses left a voicemail on his cell phone at 6:43 P.M. Shortly after 7 P.M., Phillips finished his surgery, but was running late for an appointment with his personal trainer and did not check his voicemail. At about 7:45 P.M., Bramlett had no blood pressure. The hospital called Phillips' nurses, who reached him on his cell phone, but Bramlett who had 4,000 milliliters of blood in her abdomen, vomited and aspirated. She suffered a hypoxic brain injury and organ damage, and a few days later, was removed from life support. Bramlett's family sued Phillips for negligence and malice and sued Lubbock Gynecologic Oncology Associates LLP on a theory of vicarious liability. The plaintiffs also sued the hospital, which settled in 2003 for a confidential amount. At trial, the plaintiffs argued Phillips was more at fault than the hospital. The plaintiffs alleged Phillips failed to monitor or follow up in time regarding the H&H and fluid challenge of a patient whom he suspected was bleeding. According to the plaintiffs, he could have gone to Bramlett's room after getting out of surgery, or he could have gone on to his appointment and called the hospital, or he could have checked his voicemail, but he did none of these things, even though he knew it takes only 30 minutes to an hour to get H&H results back. The plaintiffs also argued the chain of communication between Phillips and the hospital nurses was faulty, and the hospital nurses' communications had to go through as many as six steps before reaching the doctor. The defense argued the hospital nurses negligently failed to monitor Bramlett properly throughout the afternoon, take her blood pressure every two hours as ordered, and report changes in her status. The jury found Phillips 75 percent negligent and the hospital 25 percent negligent. The jury also found malice by Phillips. The plaintiffs' damages were $14 million, including $3 million in punitives against Phillips.[35]

In this case, the nursing staff relayed the change in patient condition to a healthcare professional, assuming this information would be relayed to the surgeon. This does not take away the responsibility of communicating patient status from the nurse caring for the patient. It is the responsibility of the nurse to ensure the physician gets the message. As the patient continued to decline, the nursing staff should have made subsequent calls to the surgeon. A lack of response should have prompted the nursing staff to contact the nursing supervisor.

TIP: A nurse should invoke the chain-of-command when, in the judgment of a competent and prudent nurse, the patient's condition requires a physician's prompt attention or intervention and the physician has not responded.

---

5. Failure to follow or question physician's orders

Physician orders are given to medical surgical nurses in a number of ways. They can be written down by the physician, entered into the computer, given over the phone as a telephone order, or stated in person to the nurse as a verbal order. The nurse is expected to review all physician orders. Any orders that seem to be inappropriate or incorrect need to be questioned by the nurse. Illegible orders need to be clarified with the physician, not with another peer. The Joint Commission, as part of its National Patient Safety Goals, has published a list of Do Not Use Abbreviations to prevent medical errors. In addition, there is now a standard for anyone taking a telephone order to read back the order to ensure it was heard and documented correctly. Verbal orders are only to be used in an emergency situation since the physician

is on site and should either write or enter the order directly into the medical record. With the ability to have computerized physician order entry (CPOE) from remote locations, in the future there should less need to utilize telephone orders. Liability regarding physician's orders usually falls within two categories: failure to follow physician orders and failure to question physician orders.

It is the nurse's responsibility to be aware of all orders including pre-printed or handwritten orders. The nurse was still responsible for questioning that no pre-operative antibiotic was ordered. A call should have been placed to the surgeon asking about an order for pre-operative antibiotics.

A 41-year-old woman was scheduled for a total vaginal hysterectomy and bladder suspension, to be performed at the defendant hospital. The gynecological surgeon who was to perform the hysterectomy prepared handwritten orders for hospital nurses relative to the patient's care. Those orders said nothing about the administration of prophylactic antibiotics the day before surgery. The surgeries were performed without apparent incident, but seven days later, the patient was back in the hospital with a potentially life-threatening pelvic abscess infection. She underwent a laparotomy, and ultimately recovered. However, she was left with physical difficulties including bowel problems and aggravation of her pre-existing insulin-dependent diabetes. She also claimed she had been suffering from post-traumatic stress since the surgery. She sued the hospital for failing to give her prophylactic antibiotics. The operating surgeon testified he had a standing order that antibiotics be given one hour before every surgery, and he expected those orders to be followed. According to Alabama Jury Verdict Reporter, a jury verdict for the plaintiff resulted in a $765,000 judgment.[36]

Another example of a nurse not questioning the physician's orders is cited below:

The patient was admitted to the hospital for an elective biopsy of right lung masses, which were found to be benign. She had an epidural catheter placed by anesthesia personnel for postoperative pain control. She was transported to the floor after being released from the recovery room. That evening she complained of some nausea and a headache. The defendant doctor prescribed Demerol. However, the anesthesiologist's preprinted orders stated, "No narcotics, sedatives, or other respiratory depressants to be given during infusion of epidural medication and for 12 hours after medication is discontinued." At 10:30 P.M., the nurse administered Demerol to the patient. At 10:55 P.M., the patient was allegedly found to be unresponsive. The surgical team was called and arrest protocols were undertaken. She was intubated, placed on a mechanical ventilator, and subsequently taken to the ICU where further resuscitation measures were done. Later, cerebral brain flow studies showed no ongoing cerebral function. She was determined to have suffered brain death. She died immediately after cessation of life support. The jury awarded $3.8 million. Negligence was admitted ten days before trial. *Porter v. Summa Health System et al., Summit County (OH) Common Pleas Court*, Case No. 98-03-0937.[37]

The nurse needs to be aware of current orders on the chart, as well as the hospital-specific policy. The nurse should have questioned the Demerol order, because the telephone call communicated a headache and nausea and did not include increased pain level. The order from the anesthesiologist specifically stated no narcotics, sedatives, or other respiratory depressants. The nurse was unfamiliar with the pre-printed order set for epidural analgesia and with the potential interaction between the Demerol and the epidural medication.

In the following example, the nurses did not follow the physician's order which resulted in a negative outcome:

The plaintiff, age 67, underwent a non-nerve sparing radical retropubic prostatectomy in August 2003 at the defendant hospital. Three days later the plaintiff was discharged. The next day he was seen by the physician who assisted in the surgery for complaints of bloating and constipation. He did not have a fever, nausea, vomiting or chills. He had normal bowel sounds; his urine was clear and he had passed a small amount of stool the day before. The next day the plaintiff went to the defendant's emergency room because he still felt bloated and constipated. He was diagnosed with a postoperative ileus and admitted to the hospital. One of the admitting orders was "Fleets enema—if okay with Dr. Rives." A nurse administered an enema without contacting Dr. Rives. The plaintiff then developed a fistula between the rectum and bladder. This required a diverting loop sigmoid colostomy for 11 months,

surgical insertion of a suprapubic catheter, a direct vision internal urethrotomy, surgical repair of the fistula with harvesting of tissue from his scrotum and implantation of an artificial urinary sphincter in his scrotum due to incontinence caused during the fistula repair. The plaintiff alleged negligence in the failure to call Dr. Rives before administering the enema, which perforated the rectal wall, causing the fistula. The hospital admitted negligence but maintained that the fistula was a complication of surgery which the enema uncovered, rather than caused, and argued that the surgeons inadvertently weakened the rectal wall during surgery. The hospital also contended that the incidence of developing a fistula following prostate surgery was very low. According to Illinois Jury Verdict Reporter a $2,378,258 verdict was returned.[38]

6. Intravenous complications

Potential complications may be associated with the insertion of an intravenous access device as well as the administration of fluids. In recent years there has been a move away from intravenous therapy teams. These teams were usually made up of specifically trained nurses whose main responsibility was inserting peripheral intravenous lines and peripherally inserted central catheters (PICCs), and assessing these insertion sites during rounds. Although use of such teams has been associated with high quality of care and decreased complications, many hospitals have eliminated these teams to save money. In hospitals that have deleted the IV team, current practice requires the patient's bedside nurse to be responsible for peripheral IV insertion and maintenance. Placement of a PICC is most often done by a radiologist, surgeon, or outside agency nurse because training is extensive and requires frequent use of the skill. Other central lines (tunneled, port, percutaneous) are placed by either a surgeon or radiologist. Although not universal, many states require a LPN to complete an intravenous course to be able to insert and maintain peripheral and central IVs.

The following case illustrates the successful claim of a plaintiff who lost her finger after an alleged arterial injury:

An 84-year-old plaintiff was admitted to the hospital for severe bronchitis and claimed a licensed vocational nurse, in the presence of a registered nurse, introduced an intravenous needle into an artery in the right arm rather than into a vein. Shortly thereafter, when an antibiotic was administered, the plaintiff sustained a severe reaction. She alleged a vascular injury, which subsequently required amputation of her right little finger. There was an inability to use the right hand and emotional distress caused by its deformed appearance. She continued to experience pain and an unpleasant sensation in the hand. The case was settled for $162,460. *Goldie Chambers v. Cedars-Sinai Medical Center, Los Angeles* (CA) Superior Court, Case No. BC 078 638.[39]

The RN and LPN needed to be more aware of vascular anatomy. When the artery was accessed, the device should have been immediately removed. An artery will pulsate and the color of the blood is usually bright red.

The plaintiff, age 55, underwent an endoscopy at the defendant hospital. Prior to the procedure, a nurse started an IV line for saline using a 22-gauge IV catheter. Although the endoscopy was uneventful, following the procedure, the plaintiff was treated for a neuroma on the radial sensory nerve. Surgical removal was required. Notwithstanding the surgery, the plaintiff continued to complain of impaired function in the wrist. The plaintiff claimed improper venipuncture technique by the defendant's nurses caused the neuroma. The hospital conceded that the plaintiff suffered injury, but claimed the injury was a known complication and not the result of negligence. According to Jury Verdicts Ohio a defense verdict was returned.[40]

Even when site selection and materials are correct, an unexpected outcome can still occur. A negative outcome may be an inherent risk of the procedure itself and not negligence on the part of the provider.

a. IV insertion and maintenance

Hospitals are usually very careful to spell out the procedure for insertion of intravenous needles and catheters. Nurses are expected to select an appropriate site and size needle based on an assessment of the patient's condition and the nature of the therapy that will be administered. For example, transfusion of blood requires a larger needle than infusion of standard intravenous fluids. On the other hand, elderly people, who usually have more fragile veins, need the smallest gauge catheter suitable for the fluids to be administered. Policies also exist on how frequently the IV site should be assessed. These policies should also address how often the IV dressing and tubing should be changed, how often the insertion site should be rotated, and how the tubing, insertion site, and IV fluids are labeled. Often these policies

are written to reflect recommendations from the Center for Disease Control and/or the Infusion Nurses Society. The assessment of the site and the insertion of a new intravenous device are documented in the medical chart. Medical surgical charts frequently contain this information on a flow sheet.

b. Vesicants

Some intravenous medications are known to be vesicants, meaning a solution or medication that causes the formation of blisters, with subsequent sloughing (shedding) of tissues occurring from tissue necrosis (death).[41] These types of fluids—such as dopamine hydrochloride, norepinephrine, high concentrations of potassium chloride or sodium bicarbonate, and most of the cancer-fighting drugs, to name a few—should not be infused into smaller vessels, such as those in the hand or in veins lying over moving joints, such as the wrist or inner part of the elbow. Some facilities require these fluids only be administered through a central venous catheter, though even this does not guarantee the fluids will not extravasate (go into the tissues). The unrecognized infiltration of this type of caustic medication can cause a great deal of tissue damage. Nurses are expected to follow policies on checking the site, questioning the patient about the presence of pain, and looking for swelling and redness.

A 47-year-old disabled man who suffers from diabetes and chronic pancreatitis, has been awarded $1.5 million settlement for pain and suffering in his medical malpractice suit. Johnnie Jackson was admitted to Coffee Regional Medical Center in Douglas, Georgia, on April 30, 2005, seeking treatment for complications from his pancreatic disease. According to court documents, a nurse inserted an IV containing Phenergan, an anti-nausea drug, and Demerol, a painkiller, into Jackson's right wrist at about 6:30 P.M. that evening. When his condition was checked an hour or so later everything appeared to be alright. However, at about 3 A.M. May 1, the site of the insertion was "painful and swollen" and the needle was removed 45 minutes later. Roughly nine hours later, when Jackson's doctor finally checked in on Jackson, the physician discovered that the drugs had leaked into Jackson's surrounding tissue. The physician elevated Jackson's hand but the pain continued. On the afternoon of May 2, Jackson was transported to the South Georgia Medical Center in Valdosta where an Orthopedic surgeon performed surgery on his wrist but was unable to save the thumb. Jackson spent another 24 days in the Valdosta facility where he underwent "multiple additional surgeries to save his hand" according to a complaint Shamp filed in 2007, naming Coffee Regional and five nurses as defendants, asserting that the nurses had allowed the drugs to infiltrate the tissue surrounding the IV needle. There was $1.5 million awarded. [42]

c. Infusion pumps

Medical surgical nurses are expected to operate and troubleshoot problems with infusion pumps. There are multiple types of infusion pumps, such as those designed to deliver intravenous fluids and medications and those specifically designed to deliver narcotic pain medications (patient-controlled analgesia and epidural infusions). These devices are equipped with an alarm which signals the end of infusion, or when a problem arises such as air in the IV line or an occlusion. Unfortunately, some of the medical-surgical units are designed with long corridors, which can place the nurse out of earshot of alarms. One of the past National Patient Safety Goals outlined by The Joint Commission was that the effectiveness of clinical alarms be improved.[43] This National Patient Safety Goal has since been retired, meaning it is not scored during a survey but it is still required that clinical alarms be in place. Hospitals have responded by testing the alarm on the pumps and putting into place a method to ensure the audibility of alarms throughout the unit.

TIP: Attorneys may want to obtain records from maintenance or the biomedical engineering department to see how often the alarm systems are checked, if they are checked.

While devices are designed to detect increases in pressure in the IV line, infusion pumps may continue to pump fluid into a patient even if the needle has slipped out of a vein, in some cases. The amount of fluid that may continue to infuse outside of the vein will be influenced by several factors, such as the sensitivity of the pump, the viscosity of the fluid, or the condition of the tissue surrounding the vein. The alarms are designed to sound based on resistance at the IV insertion site. Patients with poor tissue elasticity, such as the elderly, may have a large amount of fluid infuse into the surrounding tissue before triggering the alarm on the infusion pump. Unconditional reliance on the pump may result in a nurse overlooking a complication associated with the pump. More information on intravenous-related injuries is contained in Chapter 24, *Intravenous Therapy Malpractice.*

7.9 Provision of Inadequate Care

The cases that follow include situations in which nurses either refused to take a patient's complaints seriously or failed to make a basic observation. They indicate the importance of listening and observing carefully. Failure to do so is difficult, if not impossible, to justify. Patient advocacy is the heart of nursing.

A. Failure to Listen and Respond

Willie Brown was injured while working at the Broadmoor Animal Hospital and admitted to Southern Baptist Hospital in June 1989 for treatment of a severely infected finger. On June 30, a student extern from Northeastern Louisiana University working under the supervision of an SBH pharmacist, allegedly prepared a defective Bunnell's solution that was administered to Brown's surgical wound. The solution was dripped into the gauze of Brown's dressing from approximately 12:30 P.M. on June 30 until 10:00 A.M. the following day. Throughout the evening, Brown complained to the nurse of a burning sensation in his hand, but his complaints went unheeded. When his bandages were removed on July 1, it was discovered Brown had suffered second and third degree burns to his right ring finger and extensive chemical burns to his hand, wrist, and forearm. As a result of the burns, he underwent six additional surgeries, which included amputation of his right ring finger and several skin grafts. The verdict and judgment was for the plaintiff in the amount of $1,009,344, subject to the statutory cap of the Malpractice Liability for State Services Act. This was affirmed as modified on appeal to the Court of Appeal of Louisiana, Third Circuit (See: 715 So.2d 439). *Willie Brown v. Southern Baptist Hospital et al., Civil District Court*, Parish of New Orleans (LA), Case No. 90-2364 and 90-10341.[44]

In the following case, several nurses failed to take note of a large discrepancy in the amount of fluid being infused as an irrigation compared to the amount of fluid draining from the site:

A 34-year-old man went to a physician after being bitten by a cat on his index finger. He was admitted to St. Francis Medical Center for an incision and drainage procedure. During the surgery a catheter was sutured into the index finger. The incision was closed with another rubber drainage tube coming out the bottom of the site. Through this drainage system he had a continuous infusion of irrigation fluids started. Over the next 21 hours the infusion did not drain properly, and began to infiltrate the patient's hand. When his bandages were removed the following day, his hand was severely swollen and blistered. He subsequently developed reflex sympathetic dystrophy (RSD). He sued the hospital and physician, alleging the infiltration caused the RSD. He claimed the hospital failed to alert the physician to his worsening condition in a timely manner and also failed to discontinue the irrigation. The patient alleged the physician failed to respond after he was finally contacted by the hospital's nurses. The hospital and the physician denied the infiltration caused the patient's RSD. The jury awarded $662,000, with 40 percent allocated to the hospital and 60 percent to the physician. *Roberts v. St. Francis Medical Center and Tobin*, Cape Girardeau County (MO) Circuit Court, Case No. CV693-1257CC.[45]

B. Prevention of Aspiration

The medical surgical nurse is expected to use assessment skills to determine potential risks in a patient's condition. Monitoring can then be done appropriately as an ongoing part of daily care. The results of this assessment may warrant intervention, such as contacting the physician and instituting protective mechanisms to prevent harm to the patient. Aspiration precautions include having the patient sitting upright while eating or if complaining of nausea or vomiting, making dietary modifications, repositioning the head during swallowing, and providing patient/family education. The nurse should position a patient with the head of the bed elevated and the patient rolled to one side if sedated or otherwise not alert enough to turn her head if vomiting occurs.

A wide variety of patients are at risk for aspiration including those who are obese, have decreased reflexes, have lost muscle strength, and have decreased mental status. A patient at risk can be identified objectively by having a video swallow performed by a speech therapist. When a patient is identified, dietary modifications as well as patient education are ordered. A patient can aspirate via oral route or from regurgitated contents from the stomach. Prevention is the best approach to avoid the deadly consequences of this process.

In the following case, the nurse's failure to recognize the risk of aspiration based on the patient's history, failure to implement aspiration precautions, as well as failure to make changes in the plan of care once the patient's condition deteriorated were essential issues:

In February 1999, the decedent underwent successful cardiac bypass surgery. However, during the post-surgical recovery he developed dysphagia (inability to swallow) from prolonged intubation such that food and/or liquid aspirated into the lungs. The decedent had a known preexisting history of gastroesophageal reflux. Healthcare providers placed a food tube into the decedent's stomach for the purpose of feeding him without the necessity of swallowing. However, the food tube was placed directly into the stomach in an area which permitted regurgitation of food and liquids up to the esophagus and into the plaintiff's decent lungs. As a result, food that passed into the tube came up through the esophagus, choked the patient, and then passed into the lungs—creating crisis and asphyxiation. In fact, medical records documented the decedent's coughing up blue dye, which had been added to the tube feedings precisely to detect such a dangerous reflux pattern. However, the defendants failed to properly move the tube to the jejunum, which would have safely permitted passage of the nutritional support without regurgitation or aspiration. Subsequently, the decedent was transferred to the defendant hospital where a diagnosis of GERD (gastroesophageal reflux disease) was made. The plaintiff claimed employees of the defendant hospital failed to move the tube, and failed to take any other action necessary to intervene and to prevent reflux, regurgitation, choking, and aspiration. On March 2, 1999, the decedent aspirated materials into his lungs and suffered cardio-respiratory arrest and could not be resuscitated. The decedent died at age 73, leaving a widow and three adult children. The defendants denied all allegations of negligence, causation, and harm, contending the food tube was properly placed and did not require revision. They also argued moving the tube would not have prevented the decedent's aspiration, and argued that the patient died from a primary cardiac arrest from precious heart damage. They also denied the aspiration had occurred—particularly since there was no evidence of food aspiration at the time of attempted resuscitation. This matter was settled for $800,000.[46]

In another case, the plaintiff underwent a discectomy surgery in May 1997. Nearly two years later, when he was seen at Huntsville Hospital January 13, 1999, it was suspected the herniation had recurred, and a diagnostic lumbar myelogram was performed. Following the procedure, the 31-year-old patient was taken to the radiology nursing area, where initially his vital signs seemed normal at 10:30 A.M. Forty-five minutes later, the patient took lunch. One hour later, he complained of back pain. The attending nurse, Shirley Sanderson, administered Demerol to the patient.

Over the next two hours, the nurse checked the patient at regular intervals. Also important, the patient's wife left the clinical area to have lunch. Before leaving, she advised the nurse her husband was suffering from nausea, possibly secondary to the Demerol. The wife remembered asking the nurse to "keep an eye" on her husband. By 2:30 P.M., the patient was in severe crisis. Upon her return from lunch, his wife discovered her husband unconscious. Nurse Sanderson arrived and learned he was not breathing and he had no pulse. A Code was called and CPR was initiated, but was unsuccessful. The patient's airway became obstructed when he vomited. His estate alleged negligence by the hospital, linking that error to the cause of death.

Particularly, the error focused on the use of Demerol, which inhibited the decedent's ability to protect his airway. The plaintiff alleged that close monitoring was required during use of a sedating narcotic medication, in order to insure against airway obstruction. The process of the Code resuscitation attempt was also faulted, since no suction machine was immediately available.

Huntsville Hospital argued Sanderson's care and monitoring of the patient was proper. Noting she checked him at regular intervals, it was suggested he was discovered soon after his airway had become obstructed. Then, once he was discovered, a Code and CPR were properly and immediately begun. Causation issues were also raised, with the hospital maintaining that other drugs in the patient's system would have affected his response to an obstructed airway. According to the Alabama Jury Verdict Reporter, the jury returned a defense verdict.[47]

C. Failure to Adequately Monitor Respiratory Status of a Postoperative Patient

Monitoring the respiratory status in the postoperative patient is one of the crucial nursing responsibilities. Although a pulse oximeter is utilized to evaluate the oxygen level in the patient's blood, it is not the gold standard to use in respiratory assessment since its values can be altered by poor perfusion and dark nail bed pigmentation. Pulse oximetry also gives oxygenation level only, not carbon dioxide levels. Pulse oximetry is a good monitoring tool, but when abnormal readings are noted, a more thorough assessment is warranted. If the patient's clinical picture suggests respiratory distress, even in the presence of a normal oximetry reading, further assessment is necessary. Hypoxemia, a condition in which the blood's level of oxygenation becomes dangerously low, can be difficult to detect. When there is a concern, the gold standard is to obtain an arterial blood gas. Compromised respiratory status can result in severe hypoxemia in a relatively short period of time.

Those patients most at risk include postoperative patients, especially those recovering from abdominal, cardiothoracic, and orthopedic surgeries, patients with underlying cardiovascular disease or cerebral ischemia, obese patients, patients with a history of smoking, patients with sleep apnea, and those receiving opiates (by any route) for pain relief. In addition, patients with pre-existing respiratory problems such as chronic obstructive pulmonary disease (COPD), asthma, and pneumonia are at risk.[48]

Frequency of vital signs is usually every 15 minutes for four measurements, every 30 minutes for two measurements, every hour for four measurements, then routine per unit. Established post-operative monitoring practices need to be followed in the absence of written protocol or specific physician orders. Any variation of what is expected or normal in the post-operative course, such as loss of pulses after vascular surgery, needs to be reported to the physician. Nursing may always exceed the required monitoring frequency but must minimally adhere to written protocol or physician orders.

TIP: Many facilities have a post-operative protocol which outlines the routine care a post-operative patient should receive within the first 24 to 48 hours. These protocols identify the frequency of monitoring, including vital signs, pain level, output, and respiratory status.

The failure to assess respiratory status can result in a delay in diagnosis of a problem, as the following case illustrates:

A 73-year-old woman underwent an elective left hip hemiarthroplasty (hip replacement). She is survived by two adult nieces, both of whom are Intensive Care nurses. They alleged that the patient was released prematurely from the Post Anesthesia

Care Unit, and that she was, in fact, unresponsive. Subsequent pulse oximetry readings showed a finding of 57 percent (normal is 95-100 percent). They further alleged various floor nurses and the surgeon failed to take action to address the hypoxemia despite repeated requests from the nieces.

The defense contended the patient was not unresponsive on dismissal from the Post Anesthesia Care Unit, and the pulse oximetry reading was an error. An autopsy revealed the patient had expired due to a cerebral fat emboli, and, based on this, the defense further contended earlier use of supplemental oxygen would not have affected the outcome. A defense verdict was returned. *Estate of Genevieve Young, deceased v. Resurrection Hospital, Dr. Harbans Mavi,* Cook County (IL) Circuit Court, Case No. 95L-15459.[49]

In the presence of an abnormal pulse oximetry reading, further assessment should be done, including an arterial blood analysis. This should be correlated with the patient's clinical picture. In this instance, however, cause of death was a cerebral fat emboli making respiratory interventions a moot point.

D. Multiple Failures

Nursing is not a profession merely of technical skills. Caring for a patient requires the ability to critically think through all actions. Critical thinking involves taking all the information on hand and looking at it proactively and troubleshooting a potential future event before it happens. The nurse and physician share the responsibility of following up on abnormal assessments.

The following case demonstrates more than one instance of failure to critically think—for example, the patient in this case was discharged with a temperature of 100.9°F. Later in her readmission, the patient was having diarrhea and receiving insulin therapy, both of which are known to decrease potassium levels. This is even more important in a person who has a history of low potassium. In both these examples, the nurse with good critical thinking skills would have acted upon this information.

The 68-year-old housewife stepped on a nail at her home. She was initially treated conservatively with a tetanus shot by her family physician, with orders to report any changes or worsening. This same physician had been treating her for years for a chronically low potassium level. Two days later the pain was worse. She was evaluated by an orthopedist,

who diagnosed infection in the "third metatarsal head." She was admitted to the hospital for antibiotic therapy and surgical drainage of the wound. She was given potassium preoperatively after a lab test showed a low level. On the third and fourth day of her hospitalization, she experienced nausea and vomiting. Her potassium level dropped to 2.7 (normal is 3.5 to 5.0). On the sixth day she was dismissed to go home by the orthopedist, who claimed her temperature was normal at the time of discharge. The next day she returned to her family physician with complaints of continued pain, swelling, and fever. She was immediately readmitted. Her medications were changed from the Ciprofloxin she was sent home on to IV Gentamycin and Piperacillin. She was seen the next day by an infectious disease specialist, who found she had been dismissed two days previously with a temperature of 100.9°F. The next day she was found to have a slightly elevated blood glucose level, and insulin therapy was initiated. She began having diarrhea that afternoon. The next day her family physician noted she was very tired and nauseated. Insulin therapy was continued, but she remained very weak. No electrolytes had been ordered, which would have shown a potassium level. That afternoon her temperature began to climb over 100°F, and her blood pressure dropped to 85/52 at 4:00 P.M., but no physician was notified of the change in her condition. At 8:50 P.M. she went into cardiac arrest, and was resuscitated. At 9:34 P.M. her potassium level was found to be 2.4. The next day she was seen by a critical care specialist, who opined the low potassium level was secondary to her recent diarrhea and insulin therapy, and was likely the cause of the cardiac arrest. She died four days later.

The plaintiffs alleged that the respondents failed to properly manage and evaluate the decedent's potassium level, the drop in which caused her arrest and ultimate death; that the decedent's health before the hospitalization was good; that her weakness and lethargy which came shortly after her water loss were clear signs of electrolyte imbalance with a potassium deficiency; and that the decedent's prior medical records revealed a longstanding history of potassium imbalance which was only sporadically managed by her family physician. Defendants contended the medical care given the decedent was at all times within the standard of care, and her doctors had no reason to suspect a low potassium level. The jury returned a verdict of $250,000. *Jose Montes et al. v. Kaiser Foundation Hospital et al.*, Los Angeles County (CA) Superior Court.[50]

A nurse has the duty to question a discharge when an abnormal finding, such as an elevated temperature, is present. Further, in this case, the patient's blood pressure dropped to 85/52, indicating a change in condition and requiring the physician be notified. It is incumbent upon the nurse to know the patient's medical history. In this case, the patient had a history of low potassium levels. If the nurse had been aware or had critically thought about the consequence of having diarrhea and administering insulin on the potassium level, the physician would have been notified and the nurse would have monitored for potential arrhythmias related to low potassium level.

E. Stability at Discharge

Today's cost-conscious healthcare environment has led to great pressure to rapidly discharge patients from medical surgical units. This phenomena is cynically referred to as "quicker and sicker," because it forces nurses to begin planning the patient's discharge even before the patient is diagnosed. Nurses, social workers, and others are required to identify discharge needs as soon as the patient enters the medical surgical unit. For example, the nurse and other hospital staff members are expected to inquire about the patient's living situation and the availability of someone to provide home care after discharge if there is an anticipated need. If the patient will need ongoing care at home, referrals to home care agencies early in the admission are expected.

To complicate matters further, at times a patient is unable to leave immediately after dismissal due to many factors, such as transportation or lack of necessary equipment at home. Until the patient physically leaves the hospital, the staff is still responsible for monitoring the patient. The oncoming shift may not receive a report on the patient. The patient normally has all of the required paperwork and is awaiting a ride home. The patient should not be officially discharged until he leaves the unit.

One of the critical liability issues surrounding the discharge of the patient is the stability of the patient at the time of discharge. The nurse is obligated to inform the physician of any factors that might affect the planned discharge.

The following case illustrates what can happen if the nurse fails to inform the physician of significant changes in the patient's status, which may warrant further investigation before discharge:

The plaintiff was discharged from the defendant hospital the day after reconstructive surgery for a sprained ankle that would not heal properly. The plaintiff alleged she complained prior to dismissal that the cast was too tight. There was no documentation in the record of this complaint. Later that evening she returned to the defendant hospital complaining of severe pain in the ankle and foot. It was determined she was suffering from compartment syndrome in her right leg as a result of the cast being too tight. The plaintiff claimed superficial peroneal nerve damage from the compartment syndrome caused a permanent foot drop injury.

The defendants contended the syndrome developed after her release, and the hospital records indicated she had very little pain at discharge. According to published accounts, the $1.2 million verdict found the hospital 99 percent liable, and the surgeon 1 percent liable. *Pakech v. Children's Hospital of Philadelphia*, Philadelphia County (PA) Court of Common Pleas.[51]

Both nurses and doctors can be lulled into overlooking clinical changes in a patient who has been cleared for discharge. At times, a discharge order is written and discharge paperwork is completed and signed by nurse and patient, but the patient may not physically leave the unit. This may be due to circumstances beyond the control of the patient. An example would be lack of or timely arrival of a ride home. In cases such as this, the nurse has a responsibility to continue to monitor the patient until the patient has physically left the unit. This would include calling the physician if a change in status was noted. The discharge order can always be cancelled.

7.10 Summary

There are many factors that contribute to poor patient outcome on the medical surgical units. Many of the cases cited in this text are due to errors in either nursing or physician care, but poor patient outcomes may also result from patient conduct.

As detailed at the beginning of the chapter, the medical surgical patient is at risk of receiving inadequate or inappropriate care. The high demands on the attention of the nurse, coupled with staffing crises, create an environment that leaves many nurses feeling frustrated over not being able to provide the kind of care they wish to give. "Human beings, in all lines of work, make errors. When agreement has been reached to pursue a course of medical treatment, patients should have the assurance that it will proceed correctly and safely so they have the best chance possible of achieving the desired outcome."[52] Today's medical surgical nurse needs to stay current with rapidly changing technology and to maintain a broad base of knowledge in order to effectively care for the acutely ill patient in the hospital. Documentation of nursing care is paramount to show that proper care was given in accordance with policies and procedures and the prevailing standard of care. Documentation must also show compliance with or questioning of physician orders. Additionally, potentially contributory patient acts that result in patient self-injury must be documented. With the increased emphasis on cost-effective managed care, the difficulties for medical surgical nurses to provide adequate care will increase, because they will be expected to do more with advanced technology, more acutely ill patients, and a shorter length of hospitalization, but with less resources and staff.

Endnotes

1. Jaffe, A., J. Atkins, and Fields, "Position statement: recommended guidelines for in-hospital cardiac monitoring for detection of arrhythmia," *Journal American College Cardiologists* 18 (1991): 431–433.

2. Laska, L. (ed.), "Cardiologist claims nurses failed to contact him despite orders to do so should heart irregularity or pressure in chest develop," *Medical Malpractice Verdicts, Settlements, and Experts* 9, no. 2 (February 2006): 25.

3. Aiken, L., S. Clarke, D. Sloane, J. Sochalski, and J. Silber, "Hospital nurse staffing and patient mortality, nurse burnout, and job dissatisfaction," *JAMA* 288, no. 16 (2002): pgs. 1987–1993.

4. Kido, V., "The UAP dilemma," *Nursing Management* 32, no. 11 (2001): 27–29.

5. American Nurses Association. (2005). ANA Principles for Delegation. Retrieved 6/20/10: www.safestaffing-saveslives.org/WhatisSafeStaffing/SafeStaffingPrinciples/PrinciplesforDelegationhtml.aspx#Definitions.

6. American Nurses Association. (2005). Utilization Guide for the ANA Principles for Nurse Staffing. Retrieved 6/20/10: www.safestaffingsaveslives.org/WhatisSafe-Staffing/SafeStaffingPrinciples/UtilizationGuide.aspx.

7. Academy of Medical Surgical Nurses (AMSN), S*cope and Standards of Medical-Surgical Nursing Practice*, Fourth edition. Pitman, New Jersey: Anthony J. Jannetti, Inc., 2007.

8. Estabrooks, C., C. Winther, and L. Derksen, "Mapping the field: A bibliometric analysis of the research utilization literature in nursing," *Nursing Research* 53, no. 5 (2004): 293–303.

9. Baigis, J. and A. Huges, "Evidence-based practice," J*ournal of the Association of Nurses in Aids Care* 12, supplement (2001): 9–18.

10. See note 4.

11. Fisher, M., "Do your nurses delegate effectively?" *Nursing Management*, 30, no. 5 (1999): 23–26.

12. Academy of Medical Surgical Nurses (AMSN), "AMSN official position statement on: Unlicensed assistive personnel (UAP)," www.medsurgnurse.org. Retrieved June 10, 2010.

13. Varga, K., "Nurse required to be in two places at one time," Nurses Protection Group at http://www.npg.com/npg/case0222.htm. February 1998.

14. Guadagnino, C., "Role of patient satisfaction," *Physician's News Digest*. Site: www.physiciannews.com. Retrieved September 6, 2005.

15. Chizek, M., "Elopement," In *Nursing Home Litigation: Investigation and Case Preparation*, Second Edition, ed. P. Iyer. Tucson, Arizona: Lawyers and Judges Publishing Co., 2006.

16. *CAMH Refreshed Core, The* Joint Commission, *January 2010*.

17. The Americans with Disabilities Act of 1990, as amended. www.ada.gov/pubs/ada.htm, accessed June 20, 2010.

18. Roman, M., "HIPAA: The essentials," *MedSurg Matters* 14, no. 2 (2005): 3–4.

19. Laska, L. (ed.), "Interpreter needed to take infant's history," *Medical Malpractice, Verdicts, Settlements and Experts*. Retrieved from www.clinicianreviews.com/index.asp?page=8_13544.xml, accessed 02/25/11.

20. Laska, L. (ed.), "Man suffering from alcohol withdrawal during hospitalization for gastrointestinal disorder jumps from window to death," *Medical Malpractice, Verdicts, Settlements and Experts* 9, no. 2 (February 1993): 25.

21. Reynolds, K., W. Wheeler, and P. Iyer, "Medical Surgical Malpractice Issues," In *Nursing Malpractice*, ed. P. Iyer. Tucson, Arizona: Lawyers and Judges Publishing Co., 2001.

22. Laska, L. (ed.), "Hip replacement surgery—fluid loss—failure to assess vital signs," *Medical Malpractice Verdicts, Settlements and Experts* 11, no. 7 (July 1995): 22.

23. Laska, L. (ed.), "Anonymous-53-year-old woman deceased v. anonymous surgeon," *Medical Malpractice Verdicts, Settlements and Experts* (April 2003).

24. Ashcraft, A., "Differentiating between pre-arrest and failure-to-rescue," *MedSurg Nursing Journal* 13, no. 4 (2004): 211–215.

25. Clarke, S. and L. Aiken, "Failure to rescue: Needless deaths are prime examples of the need for more nurses at the bedside," *American Journal of Nursing* 103, no. 1 (2003): 42–47.

26. Laska, L. (ed.), "Failure to intervene during worsening of respiratory condition," *Medical Malpractice Verdicts, Settlements and Experts* (May 2005).

27. See note 23.

28. The Joint Commission, 2010 *National Patient Safety Goals*. http://www.JointCommission.org/ Patient-Safety/NationalPatientSafetyGoals/ Retrieved June 20, 2010.

29. Laska, L. (ed.), "Woman with spider bite denies being diabetic and glucose level results not properly reported from lab or noted by nurses," *Medical Malpractice Verdicts, Settlements, and Experts* 10, no. 12 (December 1994): 25.

30. Balck, B., "Nurses failed to communicate abnormal results," *Healthcare*, Arch Insurance Group. Site: http://www.archinsurance.com/product.asp?id=healthcareriskmanagment&t=E. June 2004.

31. *Id.*

32. Laska, L. (ed.), "Hospital allows patient to develop quadriplegia," *Medical Malpractice Verdicts, Settlements, and Experts* (May 2003).

33. Laska, L. (ed.), "Failure to properly monitor woman's urine output blamed for dehydration and increased serum sodium—Death-$591,581 net verdict in Texas, *Medical Malpractice Verdicts, Settlements and Experts* Nov 2009.

34. Medical Malpractice – Hospital – Paraplegia. $2,500,000.00 confidential settlement, www.bnflaw.com/verdicts.asp. Retrieved June 20, 2010.

35. Verdict Search, "Hospital nurses had trouble reaching doctor about bleed," www.verdictsearch.com/jv3_news/newsletter/nat/091405/1.jsp. 2005. Retrieved September 2005.

36. Laska, L. (ed.), "Failure to administer prophylactic antibiotics before hysterectomy leads to pelvic abscess necessitating a laparotomy for an Alabama woman," *Medical Malpractice Verdicts, Settlements and Experts* (December 2003).

37. "Medical malpractice—improper medication," *Ohio Lawyers Weekly-Verdicts and Settlements* 3 O.L.W.441. (May 1999).

38. Laska, L. (ed), "Hospital's nurse administers fleet enema to man with post-surgery ileus following prostatectomy without following order to call surgeon for permission, first—fistula develops, necessitating extended treatment and surgeries—hospital admits negligence in administering enema, but claims fistula was from earlier surgery—$2.3 million Illinois verdict, *Medical Malpractice Verdicts, Settlements and Experts* (March 2009).

39. Laska, L. (ed.), "Woman claims I.V. inserted into artery," *Medical Malpractice Verdicts, Settlements, and Experts* 10, no. 11 (November 1994): 23.

40. Laska, L. (ed.), "Venipuncture for IV for surgery blamed for neuroma on radial sensory nerve," *Medical Malpractice Verdicts, Settlements and Experts* (April 2005).

41. *Mosby's Dictionary of Medicine, Nursing and Health Professions,, 8th* edition. St. Louis: Mosby Co., 2009.

42. $1.5 Million Awarded in Medical Malpractice Lawsuit. Atlanta, GA. APR-14-10: www.lawyersandsettlements.com/case/medical-malpractice-lawsuit-personal-injury. Retrieved 6/21/10.

43. See note 28.

44. Morelaw. *Willie Brown v. Southern Baptist Hospital et al*. Morelaw at http://www.morelaw.com/verdicts. April 1998.

45. "Hand infiltration yields $662,000 verdict," *Healthcare Risk Management's Legal Review & Commentary, Supplement*. January 1998.

46. Laska, L. (ed.), "Estate of anonymous 73-year-old man, deceased v. anonymous hospital, et al.," *Medical Malpractice Verdicts, Settlements and Experts* (September 2003).

47. Laska, L. (ed.), "Man Dies Following Lumbar Myelogram Due to Blocked Airway Caused by Vomitus," *Medical Malpractice Verdicts, Settlements & Experts*. http://www.nso.com/case/cases_area_index.php?id=88&area=Med/Surg. June 2003. Retrieved March 2006.

48. Eichhorn, J., "Recognizing and preventing hypoxemic injury risk on the general care floor," *ASHRM Journal* (Winter 2003): 17–22.

49. Laska, L. (ed.), "Nurses' failure to diagnose post-operative hypoxia results in death," *Medical Malpractice Verdicts, Settlements and Experts* 16, no. 2 (February 2000): 27.

50. Laska, L. (ed.), "Failure to properly manage complications from foot injury blamed for cardiac arrest," *Medical Malpractice Verdicts, Settlements and Experts* 13, no. 6 (June 1997): 22.

51. Laska, L. (ed.), "Patient's leg cast too tight—compartment syndrome develops permanent foot drop," *Medical Malpractice Verdicts, Settlements and Experts* 13, no. 10 (October 1997): 36.

52. Kohn, L., J. Corrigan, and M. Donaldson (eds.), *To Err is Human: Building a Safer Health System*. Washington, D.C.: National Academy Press. 2000.

Additional Readings

2010 Hospital Accreditation Standards, Joint Commission Resources, 2009.

Bartzak, P. "Professional Work Ethic: Strategies To Motivate Bedside Nurses To Deliver High Quality Patient care," MEDSURG Nursing, vol. 19, No. 12, March/April 2010, pages 85-89.

Institute of Medicine, " 5 Million Lives Campaign," www.ihi.org/IHI/Programs/Campaign/Campaign.htm?TabID=1. 2008. Retrieved June 20, 2010

Thornlow, D. "Increased Risk For Patient Safety Incidents in Hospitalized Older Adults," *MEDSURG Nursing*, vol. 18, No. 5, Sept./Oct. 2009, pages 287-291.

United States Department of Health and Human Services, Agency for Healthcare Research and Quality—AHRQ PSnet, Patient Safety Network. http://psnet.ahrq.gov.

Chapter 8

Respiratory Malpractice

Hilary J. Flanders, MPH, RN-BC, RRT

Synopsis
8.1 Introduction
8.2 Types of Patients Who May Require Respiratory Care
8.3 Professionals Who Provide Respiratory Care in the United States
   A. Physicians
   B. Respiratory Therapists
   C. Nurses
   D. EMTs/Paramedics
   E. Others
8.4 Malpractice in the Respiratory Care Setting
8.5 Overview of the Respiratory Care System
8.6 Principles of Gas Exchange and Circulation
8.7 Clinical Issues
   A. History and Physical
   B. Common Symptoms/Chief Complaints
      1. Cough
      2. Hemoptysis
      3. Chest pain
      4. Dyspnea
   C. Common Lung Conditions/Complications and Management Techniques
      1. Pneumothorax
      2. Pleural Effusion
8.8 Respiratory Equipment and Medications
   A. Oxygen Therapy
   B. Artificial Airways and Airway Management
      1. Endotracheal tube
      2. Tracheostomy tube
      3. Purpose of bag valve mask
      4. Guidelines for endotracheal suctioning
   C. Mechanical Ventilation
      1. General principles
      2. Ventilator modes and settings
   D. Respiratory Medications
      1. Bronchodilators
         a. Beta-adrenergic agonists
         b. Anticholinergics
         c. Methylxanthine derivatives
      2. Anti-inflammatory medications
         a. Steroids
      3. Intravenous (IV) and oral
      4. Inhaled
      5. Nasal
         a. Leukotriene D4 receptor antagonists
         b. Mast cell stabilizers
      6. Antibiotics
8.9 Diagnostic Tests
   A. Imaging Studies
   B. Bronchoscopy
   C. Laboratory Studies
      1. Arterial blood gas (ABG)
      2. Microbiology
         a. Sputum culture and sensitivity, and Gram stain
         b. Cytology
         c. Acid-fast bacillus (AFB) test
   D. Pulse Oximetry
   E. Pulmonary Function Testing
      1. Spirometry
      2. Peak flow meter
8.10 Respiratory Diseases and Management Techniques
   A. Pneumonia
   B. Asthma
   C. Chronic Obstructive Pulmonary Disease (COPD)
   D. Lung Cancer
   E. Tuberculosis
   F. Pulmonary Fibrosis
   G. Pulmonary Hypertension
8.11 Summary
Endnotes
Additional Information

8.1 Introduction

Respiratory diseases are common in the United States today. They may be acute or chronic in nature, and they "rank among the highest in prevalence, incidence, morbidity and mortality, and resource utilization of all diseases in the United States."[1] Respiratory illnesses may be life-threatening, requiring complex professional medical treatment. This chapter covers some relevant respiratory concepts, symptoms, diseases, equipment, diagnostic tools, treatments, and documentation guidelines. In addition, it provides examples of medical, nursing, and respiratory therapy malpractice cases that have occurred, or could potentially occur in the respiratory care setting.

8.2 Types of Patients Who May Require Respiratory Care

Difficulty breathing is considered one of the most frightening experiences a human being can face. People of all ages may encounter respiratory problems at some point in their lives. Examples include tiny neonates who are born prematurely, children with asthma, adults with lung cancer, and elderly patients with emphysema. At all ages, individuals may experience serious trauma or surgery which interferes with respiratory function. Attorneys may be involved in litigating cases involving patients who suffer fractured ribs or crushing chest injuries as a result of a personal injury, for example. A critically ill patient may be placed on a ventilator. Additionally, litigation may center on respiratory injury caused by healthcare providers. For example, tube feeding solution may improperly infuse into the lung instead of the stomach; a patient may inhale vomitus; or an anesthesiologist may improperly intubate a patient, resulting in brain damage due to lack of oxygen.

8.3 Professionals Who Provide Respiratory Care in the United States

Physicians, respiratory therapists, nurses, EMTs/paramedics and others provide care for respiratory patients. Many of these healthcare professionals have the education and expertise to treat patients with respiratory dysfunction. In most situations, respiratory care is delivered by an interdisciplinary team including several of these provider types.

A. Physicians

Physicians are responsible for diagnosing illnesses as well as prescribing and administering treatment(s) for patients who are sick or injured. Doctors who routinely treat respiratory patients include (but are not limited to) general and family practitioners, general internists, pulmonologists, thoracic surgeons, anesthesiologists, emergency physicians, otolaryngologists, pediatricians, and neonatologists. Some of these physicians have extensive training and experience in meeting the complex needs of respiratory patients, but some do not.

B. Respiratory Therapists

The level of responsibility and the amount of knowledge and expertise necessary to be a respiratory therapist has increased and evolved over the years.[2] Respiratory therapists are part of an interdisciplinary team that cares for respiratory patients. They evaluate and treat patients with respiratory dysfunction under the general supervision of a physician. Evaluation includes taking a patient's history, performing a physical examination, and performing relevant diagnostic testing.

TIP: Treatment(s) may include providing oxygen, aerosolized medications, mechanical ventilation, and even cardiopulmonary resuscitation (CPR).

Regular assessments of their patients are performed, and respiratory equipment is checked and maintained.

The minimal educational requirement for becoming a respiratory therapist is usually an associate's degree, although bachelor's and master's programs also exist. Two levels of certification are available from the National Board of Respiratory Care: Certified Respiratory Therapists (CRTs) are entry level practitioners, and Registered Respiratory Therapists (RRTs) are advanced practitioners.[3] Medical records may contain either of these two designations.

C. Nurses

Registered nurses (RNs) coordinate the care of patients. They establish care plans for individuals with respiratory disease, and evaluate their progress. Tasks that a RN may perform include "administering medication, including careful checking of dosages and avoiding interactions; starting, maintaining, and discontinuing intravenous (IV) lines for fluid, medication, blood, and blood products; administering therapies and treatments; observing the patient and recording those observations; and consulting with physicians and other health care clinicians."[4] Nurses perform diagnostic testing and participate in the analysis of results. They educate patients about their conditions, and provide support and advice to patients and family members as needed.[5]

RNs are typically educated via diploma, associate's degree, or bachelor's degree programs. Nurses who care for respiratory patients work in a variety of settings including: physician offices, emergency rooms, medical/surgical floors, operating rooms, intensive care units, home care companies, rehabilitation centers, as well as many other possible locations. While most nurses are prepared to manage most aspects of chronic respiratory care, some have additional specialized training and experience in providing respiratory care in acute or emergency situations.

D. EMTs/Paramedics

EMTs and paramedics are first responders to medical emergencies. They are usually sent to the scene of an emergency via a 911 dispatcher where they frequently assist firefighters and police officers. EMTs and paramedics assess the condition of the patient(s) involved and attempt to determine the cause of the emergency. In addition, any underlying medical problems and/or medications that a patient has taken must be determined if at all possible. Under formal medical protocols and direction, they provide appropriate emergency care while transporting the patient to a medical facility to receive further care. Emergency care, even outside the hospital setting, is provided under the direction of an emergency physician.[6]

EMTs may have any of three levels of certification: "EMT-Basic, EMT-Intermediate, and EMT-Paramedic."[7]

Tasks that each level of practitioner is permitted to execute vary by state. It can take 1-2 years of training to achieve the highest level, EMT-Paramedic, and students can receive an associate's degree at this point in many college-based programs. In addition to the academic program, paramedics must have an extensive amount of clinical/field experience and pass a certification examination.[8]

EMTs and paramedics administer oxygen and provide CPR as needed. Paramedics may administer some emergency medications, and may perform endotracheal intubation when a patient cannot breathe.

E. Others

There are other medical professionals who care for respiratory patients. These include (but are not limited to) physical therapists, occupational therapists, recreation therapists, and speech-language pathologists.

TIP: In clinical settings, various technicians and personal care aides also provide hands-on care to respiratory patients under the direction of a physician or nurse.

8.4 Malpractice in the Respiratory Care Setting

As with other healthcare specialties, there are four basic components needed to establish malpractice:

1. There must be a relationship between the patient and the nurse, physician, respiratory therapist or paramedic. If a medical professional becomes involved in any aspect of a patient's care, then a *duty* to that patient exists.

2. The extent or scope of *duty* that the clinician owes to the patient must be determined. Often expert witnesses are used for this purpose.

3. There must be evidence of a deviation from standard practice. An acceptable level of practice can be defined as "care that would have been provided by the ordinarily prudent"[9] clinician under similar circumstances.

4. Finally, the departure from acceptable care practices must have caused harm to the patient.[10]

Standards of care relevant to malpractice cases are often confirmed by standards recommended by professional societies and organizations. Examples include guidelines suggested by the Respiratory Nursing Society, the American Lung Association, the American Association for Respiratory Care, the American Thoracic Society, and the American College of Chest Physicians. In addition, standards can be ascertained from reputable medical journals and textbooks, manufacturer's instructions for equipment, and hospital policies.[11]

When attempting to establish a deviation from accepted standards of care, lawyers utilize medical documents and testimony of staff members. Causation can be proven via the testimony of expert witnesses and the use of medical literature.[12]

One example of malpractice that a clinician may encounter involves providing medical care without proper training or education.[13] In other words, if a nurse who has worked on a psychiatry floor for 20 years is "floated" to the cardio-thoracic ICU, and a patient is harmed, this may result in an allegation of malpractice.

If a clinician is compelled by a facility to take care of an unreasonable amount of patients at the same time, and patient(s) are harmed, this could lead to a malpractice claim. Clinicians must understand that providing care that is below accepted standards, for any reason, may provide grounds for professional malpractice claims.[14]

When an action is obviously negligent, the legal doctrine that applies is *res ipsa loquitur*, which translates to "the thing speaks for itself." For instance, if a respiratory therapist assembles ventilator tubing improperly, and a patient does not receive enough oxygen as a result, then the basis for a malpractice claim is clear.[15]

8.5 Overview of the Respiratory Care System

People have two lungs which are situated within the chest cavity. Air is inhaled into the lungs and carbon dioxide is exhaled out of the lungs via tubes known as the trachea, the right mainstem bronchus, and the left mainstem bronchus.[16] The pleura are smooth, filmy sheets of tissue. A layer of pleura lines the interior of the chest cavity, and the other coats the exterior of the lung. In the pleural space, between the pleura, a small amount of fluid is secreted. This liquid helps the pleura slide smoothly past one another when the lungs inhale and exhale. The two pleural layers "provide low friction surfaces to enable the lungs to expand and contract easily with as little friction as possible."[17]

When we take a breath, air is inhaled through the mouth or nose, passes through the pharynx and larynx, flows down the trachea, and enters the lungs via a bifurcation that divides into the right and left mainstem bronchi. Further subdivision of the airway occurs, which leads to smaller and smaller branches ending in a tiny sac called the alveolus.[18] Gas exchange takes place at these alveoli—oxygen is taken up by the blood in exchange for carbon dioxide, which is subsequently exhaled. The ribs are bones that keep the wall of the chest rigid. Intercostal muscles (between the ribs) move the ribs up and back enabling the lungs to inflate and deflate during inspiration and expiration. The primary muscle used for breathing, however, is the diaphragm. The diaphragm moves downward and allows the lungs to fill with air. It moves back in an upward direction when one exhales.[19] See Figure 8.1.

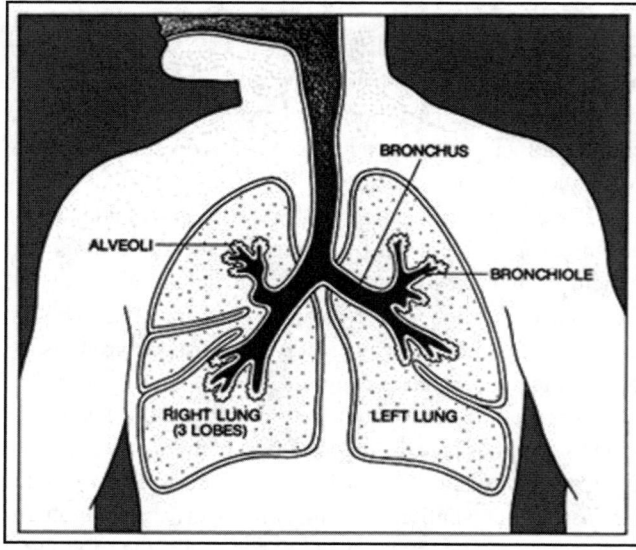

Figure 8.1

8.6 Principles of Gas Exchange and Circulation

Cells (and therefore tissue) within the human body will die if they are not properly oxygenated. The lungs absorb oxygen from air (which contains 21 percent oxygen), and excrete carbon dioxide out of the body. This occurs when "carbon dioxide diffuses across the alveolar wall from the respiratory capillaries into the alveoli and is exhaled."[20] Oxygen is circulated throughout the body via red blood cells. It has an affinity for the hemoglobin within these cells, and readily attaches to it. Oxygenated blood comes from the lungs via the pulmonary veins to the left atrium and ventricle to the aorta. The aorta pumps this oxygen-rich blood to the rest of the body where it is absorbed.

When the body's cells deplete the oxygen from the blood, the blood travels back toward the heart through the peripheral veins. Then, by way of the vena cava and the pulmonary arteries, the deoxygenated blood flows through the right atrium and ventricle, and back out to the lungs. From there, the cycle starts again.[21]

8.7 Clinical Issues
A. History and Physical

Clinicians caring for respiratory patients are expected to take an accurate patient history, perform a thorough physical exam, and document these processes accurately and completely. In routine situations, the patient's medical chart is reviewed for information regarding the patient's current illness, past medical problems, lifestyle, individual habits, environmental and occupational history.[22] The patient's smoking history is documented in "pack years." A person who smoked one pack of cigarettes a day for 20 years would have a 20 pack year history of smoking, as would a patient who smoked two packs a day for ten years. Obviously, in emergency situations, such information may not be available.

If possible, the patient should be interviewed. The patient's identity should be verified. The reason for seeking medical care and the history of the current illness should be confirmed and documented. Changes in orientation level, cough (including type and amount of sputum), changes in breathing pattern, and any type of chest pain should be described. In some circumstances, a family member may provide this information, and the clinician would record the source of the information.[23]

During the physical exam, the respiratory clinician inspects, palpates (feels with hands), percusses (taps over the skin's surface to assess internal structures), and auscultates (listens to, usually with a stethoscope) the patient. Abnormal findings would be recorded, including adventitious breath sounds (such as crackles or wheezes), asymmetrical chest expansion, accessory muscle use (use of additional muscles to help with inspiratory and expiratory efforts), lower extremity edema, distention of the jugular vein, cyanosis (bluish tissue discoloration), and clubbing (enlargement of the tips of the digits).[24]

Vital signs, including temperature, heart rate, blood pressure, respiratory rate, and oxygen saturation, are taken and recorded. Appropriate laboratory work, imaging studies, and pulmonary function testing should be ordered and, when available, documented and reviewed.[25]

B. Common Symptoms/Chief Complaints

The respiratory clinician is responsible for assessing patients thoroughly and documenting findings carefully. The following are key symptoms to be noted as part of the formal history and physical evaluation for each patient.

1. Cough

Coughing is a protective response that guards against aspiration, and/or a way to clear secretions in the lungs (i.e. sputum). Coughing is often the first symptom seen in asthma, postnasal drip, pneumonia, bronchitis, lung cancer and tuberculosis.[26]

A patient's cough "should, at least initially, be described as to severity, length, frequency, inciting factors (if known), relationships to body position, smoking, known allergens or other inciting factors, past attempts (successful or not successful) at therapy, and type and volume of sputum production."[27] Sputum characteristics are often indicative of particular diagnoses.

In addition, the time of day that the cough occurs, and whether the patient experiences pain with the cough, are significant.[28] It would be appropriate for a respiratory clinician to take a detailed history, examine the chest, take a chest x-ray, and measure the function of the lungs.[29]

An Illinois plaintiff alleged the decedent, age 63, went to an internist many times for complaints of coughing. Seasonal allergies were diagnosed and over-the-counter medication was recommended. In 2000, after the decedent coughed up blood, she complained to the internist she felt tired and suffered from body aches and shortness of breath. The internist recommended a stress test, which was normal, and then began treating the patient for asthma. Her symptoms worsened. In 2002, she went to an emergency room and underwent a chest x-ray, which revealed Stage IV lung cancer with metastasis. She died of her disease; the plaintiff alleged a delay in diagnosis of lung cancer. A $1.05 million settlement was reached.[30]

2. Hemoptysis

Hemoptysis is coughing up blood. Common diagnoses associated with this symptom include tuberculosis, lung cancer, pulmonary emboli, bronchiectasis, pneumonia, and acute tracheobronchitis, although sometimes there is no overt explanation for it.[31,32] Sputum that is streaked with blood should be sent to the laboratory and tested for tuberculosis, other infection, and neoplastic cells.[33]

3. Chest pain

There are several types of chest pain that a patient can experience. The first is angina pectoris, which is chest pain or tightness generated from ischemia (reduced blood flow) to the coronary arteries. Radiation of the pain to the shoulders, neck and left arm often occurs. If the pain cannot be relieved by rest and is accompanied by sweating, nausea and vomiting, this strongly suggests that the patient is having a myocardial infarction (heart attack).[34]

Pleuritic chest pain, or pleurisy, is caused when the pleura become inflamed and rub against one another. The resulting pain "is often sharp, gnawing, nonradiating, localized, and worsened by deep breathing or coughing."[35] Pleurisy is commonly found with pneumonia, as well as other pulmonary disorders.[36]

In cases of chest wall pain, the chest itself hurts, and can be palpated from the exterior of the chest. Possible causes include rib fractures, costochondritis (inflammation of the cartilage of the ribcage), and herpes zoster (shingles).[37]

TIP: It is important to determine the cause of chest pain. If the pain is related to cardiac function, this could be an emergency situation.

When a patient has chest pain, the clinician should take vital signs (temperature, heart rate, blood pressure, respiratory rate, and oxygen saturation, if possible), listen to the lungs and heart, and look for swelling of the ankles (which might indicate heart, liver, or renal failure). If cardiac problems are known or suspected, a resting EKG should be done, and a cardiac stress test should be considered. A chest x-ray may be warranted, particularly if the patient is having pleuritic chest pain and feeling ill. If the x-ray is within normal limits and it is suspected that the patient has a pulmonary embolus (a sudden blockage in an artery of the lung), then further imaging techniques (such as a CT scan) will be necessary to know how to proceed with care.[38]

A 55-year-old Florida man went to the ER and complained of chest pain, sweating, nausea, and increased discomfort when taking deep breaths. The nurse triaging the patient found his (abnormal) vital signs to be as follows: pulse 104, blood pressure 135/109, and respiratory rate of 24. The plaintiff maintained that the triage nurse told her that paperwork needed to be completed before the patient could be seen by a physician. Approximately ten minutes after the decedent arrived in the ER, he collapsed and became pulseless. CPR was performed for approximately 15 minutes, and he was defibrillated once. Ultimately his vital signs stabilized. However, per echocardiogram, his heart was pumping inadequately. The decedent underwent heart catheterization, angioplasty, and had at least one stent placed. The patient did not regain consciousness after the procedure. EEG results indicated that the patient was brain dead. He eventually died. The plaintiff claimed that the decedent was not triaged in a timely manner. She also alleged that a protocol for chest pain was not initiated in a timely manner (including the use of oxygen, and the placement of an IV line). The plaintiff further maintained that the defendant did not respond properly to the cardiac emergency, and that the ER was inadequately staffed. The jury returned a verdict for the defense.[39]

4. Dyspnea

Dyspnea is defined as "air hunger resulting in labored or difficult breathing, normal when caused by vigorous work or athletic activity."[40] There are many possible pulmonary and cardiac reasons for this shortness of breath.[41]

An Ohio woman with a history of right leg pain and shortness of breath was diagnosed with possible pulmonary embolism, pneumonia or fluid overload. She was sent to the hospital and admitted. The physician ordered stat blood work and diagnostic testing, but there was a delay in treatment. The patient died. No autopsy was initially done, but the body was later exhumed. The cause of death was a saddle pulmonary embolism. The decedent's sister worked in the defendant's office and obtained a copy of the records without the knowledge of the defendant. After suit was filed, the defendant's records were provided during discovery; they differed from the original which had been given to the sister. The defendant had added that on the second office visit he tested for a Homan's sign and also tested for calf tenderness, both of which alleged tests were negative. These entries were added after the death and at least six weeks after the office visit. The defendant also made alterations to the first office visit records as well as the hospital records. The defendant denied liability. A $5.85 million settlement was reached.[42]

The clinician should take a detailed history of the patient with unexplained dyspnea. In addition, the clinician should evaluate that patient's lungs and heart, assess vital signs, and look for swelling of the ankles. Pulmonary function tests may also be helpful in the diagnostic process. Other useful tests may include a chest x-ray, EKG and echocardiogram (a type of cardiac ultrasound), oximetry, blood tests, and a CT scan.[43]

Dyspnea can be associated with abnormal breath sounds, such as stridor and wheezes. Stridor may occur if a patient's upper airways become obstructed. Stridor is usually characterized by a loud, high-pitched inspiratory noise that is often audible without a stethoscope. Stridor may occur with laryngeal edema (swelling), cancer of the bronchus, or tracheal stenosis (narrowing of the trachea).[44]

Wheezes are high-pitched, musical noises that are typically more evident during the expiratory phase. They occur when airways narrow and the patient's airflow becomes turbulent. Wheezing is common in chronic bronchitis, asthma, and left-sided heart failure.[45]

C. Common Lung Conditions/Complications and Management Techniques

1. Pneumothorax

Pneumothorax is the collapse of a lung, either partially or completely, because of the escape of air into the space between the pleura, which deflates the lung. It is often abbreviated as PTX. It can occur from a variety of causes including trauma, insertion of central (venous) lines, chest compressions, mechanical ventilation, cystic fibrosis, asthma, and lung biopsies. Occasionally, it happens spontaneously.[46]

The affected patient is short of breath and has chest pain on the side of the chest where the pneumothorax has occurred. The respiratory clinician would find the patient's breath sounds to be diminished, and observe decreased chest movement, of the affected side. With percussion (a tapping technique used by clinicians), a hyperresonant note (loud and low-pitched) may also be present. A pneumothorax can be definitively diagnosed by a chest x-ray.[47]

A chest tube was inserted into a New York woman with a pneumothorax 13 hours after her condition was diagnosed. The procedure caused episodes of oxygen desaturation. The plaintiff subsequently underwent two other re-inflation procedures. Several days later she was awakened from a medically induced coma; she was blind. Plaintiffs alleged the blindness was caused by a failure to timely treat the pneumothorax. A $9.1 million settlement was achieved.[48]

Small pneumothoraces may resolve on their own. Current medical literature indicates that patients with small pneumothoraces should still be observed in the hospital. Patients with larger pneumothoraces should have a chest tube inserted to reinflate the lung.[49] Very specific guidelines exist for physicians and nurse practitioners who insert chest tubes. Failure to insert the tube properly can jeopardize the patient. Errors can be made by inexperienced clinicians and improper techniques can result in the chest tube being inserted into the wrong space.[50]

2. Pleural Effusion

A pleural effusion is the accumulation of fluid between the pleura. This fluid may consist of transudate (extravascular fluid), pus from an infection, blood, or chyle (lymphatic fluid). Circulatory and inflammatory disorders are typically the causes. Examples include trauma, infection, or malignancy.[51]

Clinicians may establish the likelihood of this problem by taking a history, doing a physical examination, and analyzing imaging studies. Confirmation of the presence of a pleural effusion can be made by thoracentesis (a needle puncture into the pleural space to drain fluid). Appropriate treatments include performing a thoracentesis, inserting a chest tube, resolving the underlying disorder, or allowing the fluid to absorb back into the lymph vessels.[52]

A 60-year-old Michigan woman had a cardiac bypass procedure. She was discharged from the hospital seven days later. She went to her cardiologist's office for a follow-up visit one week after she was discharged. She informed the cardiologist that she was having shortness of breath. After another four days, she began having increased shortness of breath, and was brought to the hospital. She was treated by an ER physician (who did consult with the cardiologist). A large left-sided pleural effusion was visible via chest radiograph. The patient was admitted to the hospital, but waited in the facility's hallway for several hours. Heparin and nitroglycerin paste were administered. Her heart stopped 20 minutes after the medications were started. The resuscitation efforts were successful, but her brain was severely damaged, leaving her in a permanent vegetative state. The plaintiff alleged that the cardiologist should have obtained a chest x-ray during the follow-up visit. The plaintiff maintained that the ER doctor should have immediately done a thoracentesis to treat the pleural effusion, and should have diagnosed ischemia. In addition, the plaintiff claimed that the patient's condition required oxygen therapy which she did not initially receive. The parties involved agreed upon a settlement of $1,498,000 (the cardiac physician was excused before the settlement occurred).[53]

8.8 Respiratory Equipment and Medications
A. Oxygen Therapy

Oxygen therapy is necessary when there is evidence or suspicion of acute hypoxemia (low level of oxygen in the blood). Increasing the amount of oxygen in the alveoli can help diffuse more oxygen into the circulatory system.[54] Oxygen therapy is intended to alleviate hypoxemia by increasing tension in the alveoli and increasing the oxygen being transferred to the blood. This relieves labored breathing, and decreases the stress on the heart muscle.[55]

Symptoms of hypoxemia include elevated heart and/or respiratory rate, increased depth of breathing, diaphoresis (sweating), accessory muscle use, cyanosis (blue/gray discoloration of tissue), and/or mental confusion. Depending on the underlying cause of hypoxemia, the clinician will need to choose the appropriate amount of oxygen to administer, and titrate as needed.[56] See Figure 8.2.

Nasal cannulae are plastic tubes that are attached to an oxygen source. They have two prongs that rest in the nostrils, and are capable of delivering supplemental oxygen concentrations of up to approximately 40 percent (depending on the flow rate of oxygen and ventilatory pattern). The medical record often contains the abbreviation NC for nasal cannula. Most patients tolerate this therapy well and find it reasonably comfortable.[57]

However, there are risks of scarring with the use of cannulae.

A California infant was awarded $385,000 after he underwent several plastic surgeries to correct scarring from a nasal cannula. The plaintiffs alleged the staff at the hospital at which he was born taped the tubing of the nasal cannula on his face too tightly, causing severe pressure necrosis.[58]

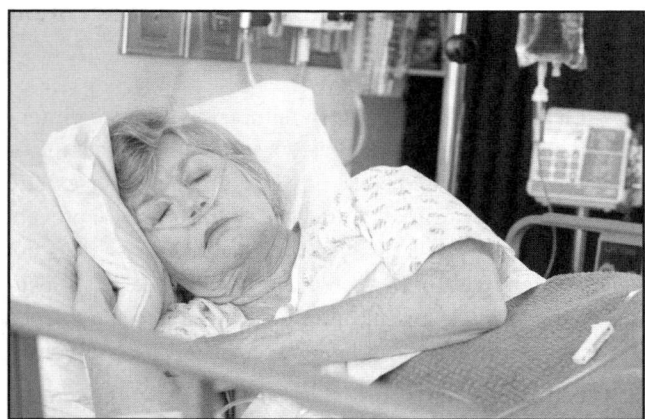

Figure 8.2

Simple masks are made of plastic and are placed over the patient's nose and mouth. A tube at the bottom of the mask is attached to an oxygen source. This mask can provide oxygen concentrations of approximately 55 percent.[59] Patients often find oxygen masks to be uncomfortable, and they can interfere with dietary intake.[60]

Venturi masks provide the patient with various oxygen concentrations. They can deliver oxygen concentrations from 24-50 percent, depending on how the clinician adjusts the device. They are also made of plastic and go over the patient's nose and mouth.[61]

Partial rebreather and nonrebreather masks provide higher concentrations of oxygen, and are needed for patients with more severe hypoxemia. Partial rebreathers can provide less than or equal to 60 percent, and nonrebreathers provide approximately 100 percent oxygen. There are other oxygen therapy devices that can provide 100 percent oxygen, such as mechanical ventilators and tracheostomy masks.[62]

The medical record often contains abbreviations for these pieces of equipment. For example, a partial rebreather mask is often charted as PRB, and a nonrebreather mask as NRB. See Figure 8.3.

Risks associated with oxygen therapy include oxygen toxicity, hypoventilation in patients with chronic obstructive pulmonary disease (see Section 8.7), constriction of the vasculature in the lungs and kidneys, development of retrolental fibroplasia (fibrous tissue behind the lenses of the eyes), and flammability of the gas itself. Fires in the operating room may be associated with the use of oxygen and a spark from electrocautery. Clinicians should only use as much oxygen as the patient needs, and should monitor oxygen saturations and arterial blood gases to titrate oxygen appropriately. (See Section 8.6.) COPD patients on oxygen should be monitored closely. In addition, patients on oxygen should not smoke, as this may start a fire.[63]

B. Artificial Airways and Airway Management

1. Endotracheal tube

If a patient is in respiratory failure, medical professionals (i.e., physicians, paramedics, some respiratory therapists, nurse anesthetists, and some advanced practice nurses) are qualified to perform endotracheal intubation to prevent damage from hypoxia (a situation where the body does not have enough oxygen).[64] An endotracheal tube (ETT) is usually made of malleable plastic. It is passed into the trachea via the mouth or nose utilizing specialized tools (such as laryngoscope and Magill forceps). See Figure 8.4.

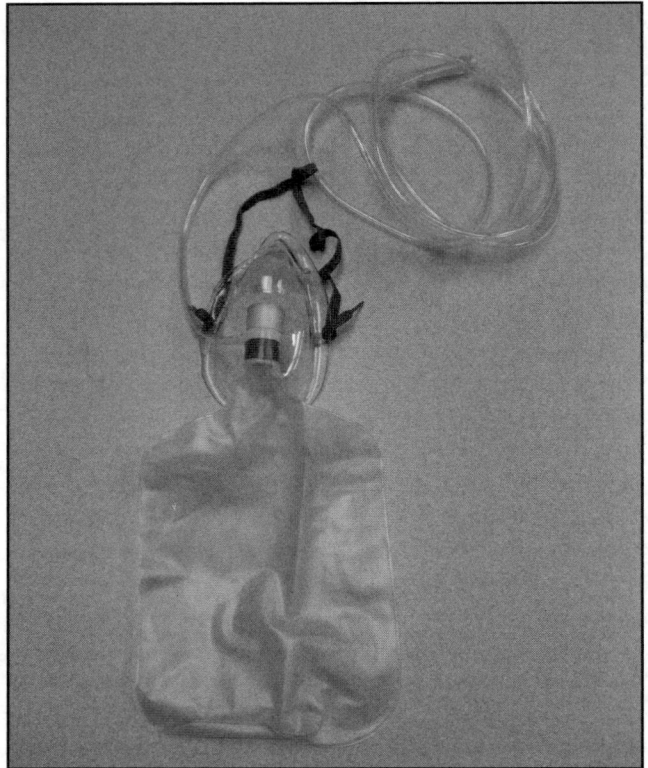

Figure 8.3

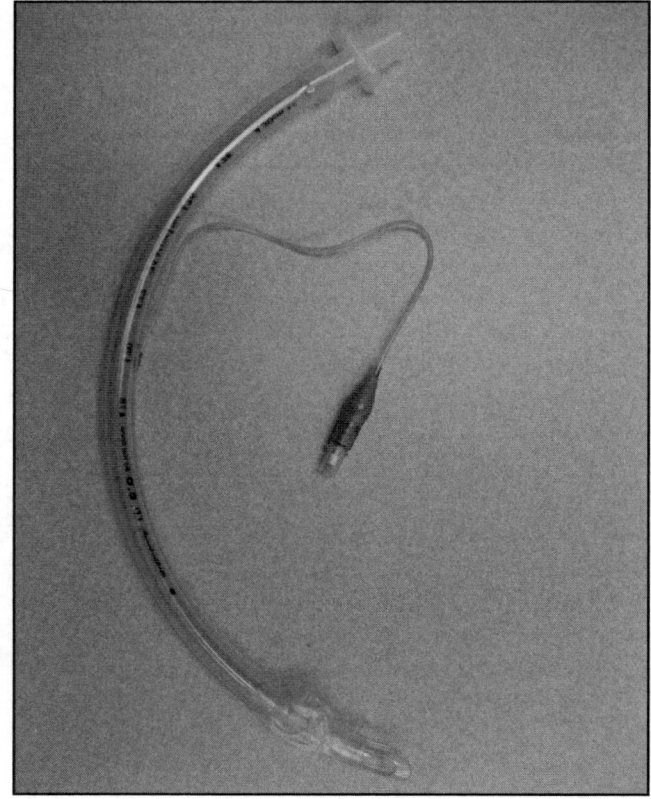

Figure 8.4

The patient can be ventilated and oxygenated via this ETT. The size of the tube is determined by the size, weight, gender and anatomy of the patient. The patient will be unable to speak because the ETT goes through the vocal cords. The steps of this invasive procedure include pre-oxygenating the patient with 100 percent oxygen, administering a sedative and a paralyzing drug, applying pressure to the cricoid area on the neck (to prevent the tube from entering the esophagus, as well as to prevent vomiting and aspiration into the lungs), inserting the ETT, and confirming placement of the tube.[65] Proper tube placement is indicated by observing bilateral chest excursion, listening with a stethoscope for bilateral breath sounds, using a CO_2 detector to make sure that this gas is being exhaled, and checking for oximetry readings between 98 and 100 percent. In addition, the clinician should listen over the stomach with a stethoscope to make sure that no air flow noises are evident. Definitive confirmation of tube placement is made by a chest x-ray.[66]

There are many possible complications from this procedure. During endotracheal intubation, there can be physical trauma to the tissue, perforation of the airway, injury to the spinal cord, spasms of the bronchi and bronchioles, spasms of the larynx, hemodynamic instability, increased intraocular or intracranial pressure, improper esophageal intubation as well as many other possible problems. After the ETT is confirmed to be in the proper place, the patient may have issues with airway obstruction, mucous plugs, aspiration of fluid into the lungs, pneumothorax, dislodgement, or disconnection of the tube. When the patient is extubated (the ETT is removed), laryngeal swelling, aspiration of fluid from the mouth or stomach, or cuff malfunction may occur. After extubation, the patient may experience additional difficulties. These may include, but are not limited to, hoarseness, laryngeal swelling, throat pain, vocal cord dysfunction, tracheal stenosis (narrowing of the trachea), tracheomalacia (tracheal collapse), and nerve injury.[67]

A New Jersey mother delivered her baby via cesarean section because the position of the fetus was unclear. At the time of birth, the baby was not able to breathe. Intubation of the infant took greater than ten minutes. The mother claimed that this delay in treatment caused brain injury. The child in question is currently non-verbal and unable to walk. The mother alleged that the obstetrician was responsible for a delay in the delivery, and that the pediatrician was responsible for a delay in intubation. The defendants stated that the child suffers from an unrelated neuromuscular or genetic disorder. A settlement of $4.5 million was negotiated.[68]

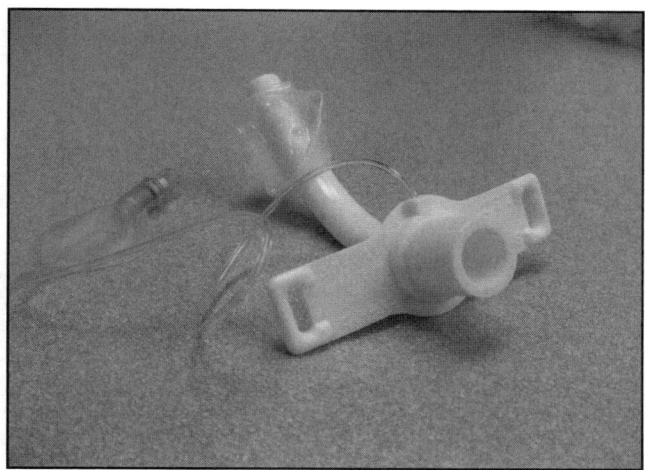

Figure 8.5

2. Tracheostomy tube

A tracheostomy involves an artificial airway surgically placed in the trachea. This artificial airway, called a tracheostomy tube, is made of hard plastic or metal, and comes in various shapes and sizes. Some have cuffs and some do not. See Figure 8.5.

A tracheostomy is indicated when long-term airway management becomes necessary. For instance, it may be required if a patient is in a coma or needs to be on a ventilator for an extended period of time. Additional indications might be to circumvent a blockage of the upper airway, to improve pulmonary toilet (the removal of phlegm), and to reduce the risk of aspirating oral secretions or stomach contents into the lungs.[69]

Traditionally, tracheostomies have been performed in the operating room, but they may also be inserted percutaneously (through the skin) as a bedside procedure. If possible, the procedure should be discussed with the patient and/or family preoperatively. Therefore, consent can be given, and questions and concerns can be addressed.[70]

TIP: After the tracheostomy tube is placed, the patient should be closely monitored for increased respiratory secretions, oxygen saturation, work of breathing, and cyanosis (a blue hue to the skin that is a result of hypoxia). Vital signs, anxiety level, condition of the surgical site, and signs and symptoms of infection should also be assessed.[71]

Clinicians should be on the lookout for a large amount of bleeding, or persistent oozing of blood after a tracheostomy. A little bleeding postoperatively is considered normal. Bleeding may indicate that a blood vessel is damaged and needs further attention from a surgeon. If an artery is involved, this problem can be deadly.[72]

To prevent obstruction, healthcare providers need to suction a tracheostomy tube when the patient cannot clear secretions. (See Section 8.5.B.4.) In addition, the air that the patient breathes through the tube should be warmed and humidified, and the patient should be properly hydrated.[73]

A 40-year-old man was in motorcycle accident. The accident caused injury to his brain. After a few weeks, the patient was transferred from the hospital to a rehabilitation facility. The medical professionals at the rehab facility restrained the plaintiff's chest and extremities to prevent him from removing his feeding tube and his tracheostomy tube. A patient observer (or sitter) was also placed in his room 24 hours/day to prevent the pulling of tubes. At one point, the patient observer noted that the plaintiff had difficulty breathing. The patient observer pressed the call light to summon help—a nurse arrived after a number of minutes. The nurse attempted to suction the patient's tracheostomy tube, and found that it was obstructed by a mucus plug. She asked for the help of a nearby medical resident, and the resident also was unable to clear the airway. Finally, the staff physician for the unit was notified, and an emergency code team was paged. When the staff physician arrived, the patient was cyanotic. He attempted to use a manual resuscitator ("Ambu" bag) on the patient, but was unsuccessful. The emergency code team arrived quickly, and documentation indicated that the patient's ability to breathe was restored in ten minutes. The plaintiff's family was notified that the plaintiff was in a persistent vegetative state, however they declined the removal of support. Over time, the plaintiff ultimately did make some recovery. He could recognize people and speak, but was unable to walk. He had persistent pain, and issues with memory loss. The plaintiff alleged that the mucus plug in the tracheostomy tube could have been removed sooner if the emergency code team was paged earlier. The plaintiff also maintained that the medical resident should have either replaced the entire tracheostomy tube, or removed the inner cannula in order to alleviate the blockage. The defendants claimed that they responded within an appropriate amount

of time with appropriate procedures. They also claimed that the plaintiff's lingering problems are due to the original accident, and not the hypoxic event. A verdict of $2,109,716.75 was awarded.[74]

The tracheostomy tube may become dislodged inadvertently. If this happens within one or two days postoperatively, it is considered an emergency because the surgical tract has not matured. The complete formation of this tract takes approximately five to seven days, and surgical sutures should stay in place at least this long. Accidental dislodgement of the tube may occur via a forceful cough, excessive or careless handling of the tube (by the clinician or the patient), or suctioning.[75]

Methods of preventing dislodgement include the proper use of cloth ties that secure the tube, and patient/family education about tracheostomy care. If the patient is depressed, anxious, or agitated, then the need for medications for these conditions should be evaluated.[76]

Occasionally, subcutaneous emphysema may occur when a tracheostomy tube is placed. This is caused by air that is inadvertently introduced into the tissue in the neck or chest. It bulges the skin, and produces crepitus (an odd, crackling sound and sensation) with palpation. Subcutaneous emphysema is often disturbing to the patient and visitors.[77]

Further complications include tracheal stenosis and tracheomalacia. In addition, a tracheoesophageal fistula could occur from excessive cuff pressure (greater than 25 cm H_2O). This fistula is a communication between the esophagus and the trachea that is a result of tracheal erosion. It causes air to go into the stomach, which predisposes that patient for aspiration of stomach contents, which can cause a pneumonia. The cuff pressure should be assessed per the institution's policy to prevent significant damage to the airway. This task is usually performed by the respiratory therapist.[78]

A speaking valve (made by the Passy-Muir company, and often abbreviated in medical charts as PMV) can be fitted to a tracheostomy tube in order to enable audible speech. Regaining the ability to speak is often an important part of recovery for patients with tracheostomies, but PMVs can be dangerous for patients who are severely unstable, unconscious, have significant airway obstruction, have copious secretions, are at a high risk for aspiration, or cannot tolerate deflation of the cuff.[79] If a clinician applies the PMV to a patient's tracheostomy tube without deflating the cuff, the patient will be unable to breathe properly. This mistake could result in the patient's suffocation.

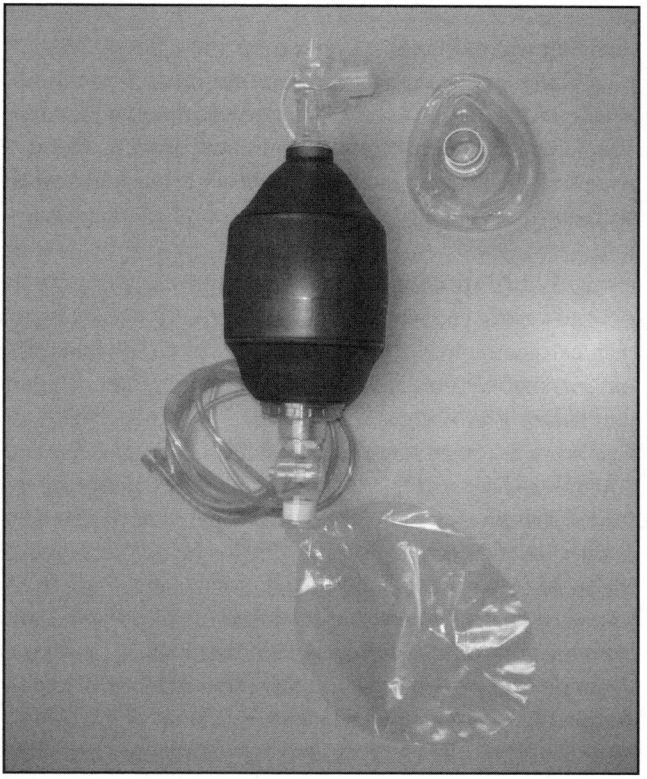

Figure 8.6

3. Purpose of bag valve mask

The bag valve mask (or "Ambu" bag) is used during resuscitation of patients with nonexistent or inadequate respirations. It is attached to a source of 100 percent oxygen, and applied to the patient's airway. If the patient has an ETT or a tracheostomy tube in place, the bag is attached directly to the artificial airway and squeezed repeatedly to ventilate the patient. If the patient has no artificial airway, then a face mask is attached to the bag and placed over the patient's nose and mouth. Two clinicians may need to perform this task jointly to get an adequate seal when the bag is squeezed. Patients with artificial airways that require extended support will need to transition to mechanical ventilation as soon as possible.

There have been incidents where clinicians failed to attach the "Ambu" bag to an oxygen source during a respiratory emergency. This error could cause extreme hypoxia and potentially thwart a resuscitation effort. See Figure 8.6.

4. Guidelines for endotracheal suctioning

When a patient with an artificial airway has secretions that cannot be expectorated (coughed up), the healthcare professional may need to perform endotracheal suctioning. Guidelines for this invasive procedure include: pre-oxygenating with 100 percent oxygen for more than 30 seconds,

hyperventilation by bag valve mask or ventilator (optional), and utilizing pulse oximetry (in the hospital setting). Actual suctioning occurs when the suction catheter is inserted into the patient's trachea and negative pressure is applied as the catheter is pulled out of the airway. Sterile technique should be used by the clinician.[80]

The amount of negative pressure should be the lowest that effectively removes the secretions. Each suctioning pass should not exceed 15 seconds. After patients are suctioned, they should again receive 100 percent oxygen, this time for a minute or longer. They may also be hyperventilated. The clinician should monitor the patient for negative reactions to the intervention, and repeat as often as needed to maintain a patent airway.[81]

Possible complications associated with endotracheal suctioning include respiratory arrest, cardiac arrest, hemodynamic instability, increased intracranial pressure, pulmonary bleeding or hemorrhaging, infection, atelectasis (deflation of the alveoli), hypoxia, and constriction of the airways. Failure to pre-oxygenate the patient prior to suctioning increases the likelihood of hypoxia. Blood-tinged secretions documented in medical records are sometimes associated with tissue damage from suction-related trauma. Despite these potential hazards, there are very few contraindications to the procedure, as a patent airway is necessary for survival.[82]

C. Mechanical Ventilation

1. General principles

Mechanical ventilators are used in acute care hospitals, rehabilitation hospitals, long-term and home care settings.[83] Acute goals of providing mechanical ventilation include improving gas exchange in critically ill patients, as well as easing labored respirations. Examples of patients who would require the use of a ventilator might be those in respiratory failure, those with neurological dysfunction, or those who are comatose. Mechanical ventilation can be categorized as invasive and noninvasive.[84]

A District of Columbia case involved a 27-year-old quadriplegic who required the use of a ventilator at night. He was arrested for possession of marijuana and placed in jail. The medical staff at the jail did not provide a ventilator for him. On his first day in jail he suffered a respiratory crisis and was taken to the hospital, where he was seen by Dr. V. He initially planned to admit the patient and place him on a ventilator, but after speaking with the medical staff at the jail, he was released back there with a prescription for oxygen by nasal canula. On the fourth day, the patient suffered another respiratory crisis and was returned to the hospital. This time he was seen by Dr. I. Despite a PCO2 reading of 56, he was not placed on a ventilator. He gradually declined and died five hours later. None of the defendants seriously alleged the death was from any cause not related to negligence. All defendants paid a total of $4.6 million.[85]

Classic, invasive mechanical ventilators push air into the lungs via an artificial airway to facilitate breathing. Positive pressure techniques are divided into volume-control and pressure-control modes. Volume-control modes provide an exact volume with each breath, but the pressures exerted on the lungs may vary. Pressure-control modes provide an exact pressure, but the volumes are variable.[86]

Complications of conventional mechanical ventilation include injury to the alveoli from barotrauma (damage from high pressures) and volutrauma (damage from large volumes). In addition, it may cause a patient to have a pneumothorax, arrhythmias, decreased perfusion (blood flow) in the kidneys, or reduced urine production.[87]

Noninvasive mechanical ventilation utilizes either positive pressure or negative pressure. In noninvasive positive pressure ventilation (NPPV), air is introduced via a full face mask, nasal mask, or plastic mouthpiece to apply pressure to the airway. This modality is used for the same purpose as conventional mechanical ventilation. However, patients who are reluctant to be intubated may opt for ventilators that provide NPPV.[88]

Complications of NPPV may include necrotic areas on the face from chafing of the mask, aspiration, distention of the stomach, dry mucous membranes, eye infections, and lack of ability to remove secretions effectively. A properly fitting mask is essential when using NPPV to prevent air leakage and protect against skin damage and eye damage.[89]

Noninvasive negative pressure techniques physically manipulate the outside of the chest to improve ventilation. They are useful for patients with chronic respiratory or neuromuscular conditions. Negative pressure can help correct elevated hypercapnia (elevated CO_2 levels in the blood) and hypoxemia, and reduce the incidence of respiratory failure. Examples of devices that provide noninvasive mechanical ventilation include the iron lung, the chest cuirass, and the poncho. These devices can be problematic if the patient has claustrophobia, if the patient cannot stay supine, or if the airway becomes obstructed. In addition, if the patient's abdomen or chest are covered (as with the chest cuirass), clinicians do not have direct access to the patient for assessment and treatment purposes.[90]

Clinicians should be extremely careful with the use of sedation in patients on any noninvasive ventilator. The risks associated with oversedation (aspiration, low blood pressure, and inadequate breathing) need to be weighed against the risks of anxiety and ventilator asynchrony.[91]

2. Ventilator modes and settings

Most patients who require traditional, invasive mechanical ventilation receive assist-control (A/C), intermittent mandatory ventilation (IMV), and/or pressure-support ventilation (PSV).[92] In assist-control, the ventilator delivers a set volume or pressure at an established frequency and flow rate. The patients are able to initiate extra breaths as needed, but they remain at the same volume or pressure no matter how many are triggered.[93]

IMV features a fixed frequency of breaths along with a set volume or pressure, but the patient is allowed to have spontaneous respirations between mandatory ventilator breaths.[94] This mode is usually synchronized (SIMV) to prevent disruption of the patient's own breathing effort.[95]

PSV is indicated when a low level of pressure is needed to enhance each spontaneous respiration. The pressure level selected depends on the patient's respiratory rate.[96] The patient is essentially breathing on his own; however the ventilator provides a boost to the patient's inspiratory phase. This mode is contraindicated if spontaneous respirations are inadequate or absent.[97]

Another common mode of ventilation is continuous positive airway pressure (CPAP). In this mode, positive end expiratory pressure (PEEP) is applied continuously to increase pressure on the airways and alveoli, but additional ventilatory support is not provided. Clearly, this mode is also not appropriate if the patient's spontaneous respiratory effort is poor.[98]

Common ventilator settings include the respiratory rate, tidal volume, minute volume, inspiratory flow rate, sensitivity, PEEP, and oxygen concentration . Audible alarms are set on the ventilator to warn clinicians of issues like apnea (lack of breathing), high pressure, and a disconnected ventilator. See Table 8.1.

Physicians do not typically order specific alarm settings for ventilators. The alarm levels are usually chosen and adjusted by the respiratory therapist, according to hospital policy and clinical judgment. If the alarms are improperly set by the therapist, harm to the patient might occur. For example, if the high pressure limit is set to high (in a volume-control mode), too much pressure could be applied to the lungs, and barotrauma could occur.

Table 8.1
Examples of Common Ventilator Settings with Definitions

Setting	Definition
Respiratory Rate	# of breaths provided by a ventilator in one minute
Tidal Volume	Amount (volume) of gas a ventilator provides in a single breath
Minute Volume	Respiratory Rate x Tidal Volume
Inspiratory Flow Rate	Rate or speed that gas is pushed through the ventilator circuit into the lungs
Sensitivity	Amount of inspiratory force necessary for the patient to trigger a breath from the ventilator
PEEP	Positive end expiratory pressure (helps improve gas exchange by maintaining pressure continuously in the airway and keeping alveoli open)
Fractional Inspired Oxygen (FIO_2)	Percent oxygen provided by the ventilator (21%-100%)

Occasionally, the patient will fight or "buck" the ventilator, which is usually caused by "a mismatch between the patient and ventilator inspiratory and expiratory times."[99] It is often distressful for the patient. Choosing the correct ventilator modes and settings, the right amount of sedation, and an appropriate pain control regimen should reduce the incidence or severity of this problem.

D. Respiratory Medications

In the U.S., "30% of all medical malpractice cases involve medication-related injuries."[100] Use of the incorrect drug, dose, or route may injure a patient, and subsequently lead to legal action. In addition, clinicians must monitor for toxicity and side effects.[101] See Chapter 5, *Medical Errors: Root of Litigation,* in Volume I, for more information.

1. Bronchodilators

Bronchodilators are medications that help relieve bronchoconstriction (narrowing of the airway). Categories of bronchodilator medications include Beta-adrenergic agonists, anticholinergics, and methylxanthine derivatives.[102]

a. Beta-adrenergic agonists

One class of bronchodilators, the beta-adrenergic agonists, functions by relaxing the smooth muscles of the small airways. The short acting Beta2-agonists, such as albuterol or levalbuterol, are considered rescue medications for asthmatics. Patients with COPD (see Section 8.7) are usually prescribed a more routine maintenance schedule for these drugs.[103] Asthmatics that use their rescue medication more often than twice per week should have a steroid added to their regimen.[104]

Long acting Beta2-agonists, such as formoterol or salmeterol, are used as maintenance medications for COPD and asthma patients. They are also prescribed for individuals who have exercise-induced asthma or nocturnal asthma. These medications should not be confused with rescue therapy drugs, and a rescue inhaler should also be prescribed.[105]

Possible side effects of Beta2-agonist bronchodilators include palpitations, tachycardia (rapid heart rate), anxiety, and tremors. Allergic reactions to inhaled aerosols have been reported among people who have sensitivity to peanuts or soybeans.[106]

b. Anticholinergics

Another class of bronchodilators is the anticholinergic class. They function by reducing the secretion of mucus and relaxing the smooth muscles, particularly in the large airways. The short-acting anticholinergic medication, ipratropium bromide, is also considered a rescue inhaler. However, its effect occurs in about 15 minutes rather than just minutes required for Beta2-agonists. Albuterol and ipratropium bromide are frequently given together to maximize the bronchodilator effect.[107]

Long-acting anticholinergics, such as tiotropium, are used for maintenance of COPD patients with the expectation of reducing exercise intolerance over time. Again, a rescue inhaler should also be prescribed for the patient to provide prompt relief if needed. Possible side effects of anticholinergics include nervousness, dry mouth, cough, and unpleasant taste.[108]

Inhaled medications must be delivered correctly to be effective. Clinicians are responsible for instructing patients how to use their metered dose inhalers or nebulizers properly and for monitoring their compliance over time.[109] See Figures 8.7 and 8.8.

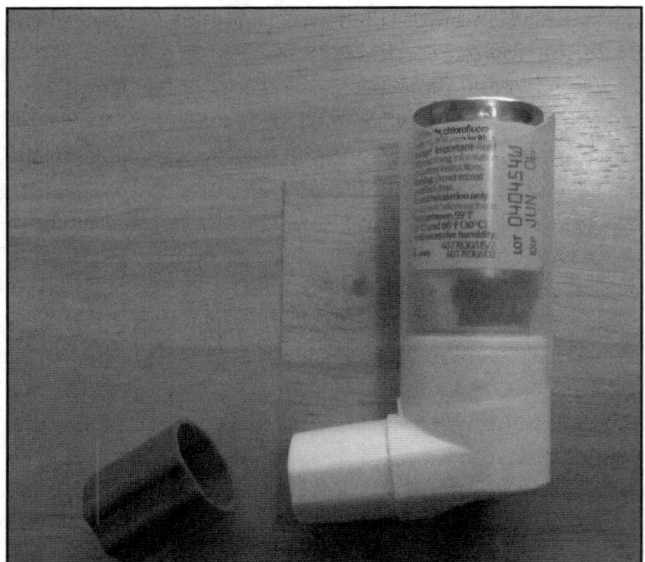

Figure 8.7

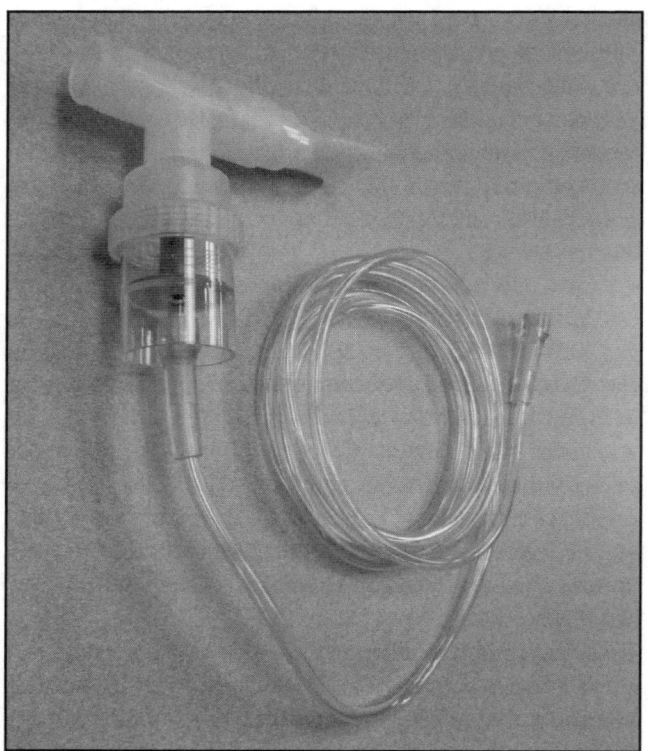

Figure 8.8

c. Methylxanthine derivatives

Theophylline is not used very much in current practice. This medication (which comes in the oral or IV form) can have more serious side effects than other bronchodilators, including seizures and death. It has many food and drug interactions, and blood levels need to be monitored closely.[110]

2. Anti-inflammatory medications
a. Steroids

TIP: Corticosteroids are the most powerful anti-inflammatory medications available today.[111] Steroids are frequently administered via the intravenous (IV), oral, inhaled, or nasal routes.

---

3. Intravenous (IV) and oral

IV and oral steroids can be used to battle inflammatory respiratory conditions like asthma. Examples include hydrocortisone and methylprednisolone. These medications are not designed to be used for long periods of time, and need to be tapered down slowly.[112,113]

Possible side effects of IV and oral steroid use depend on the dose and duration of use. They include high blood sugar, impaired healing, fluid retention, mood swings, electrolyte imbalances, osteoporosis, headache, blurred vision, and eye problems. If oral steroids are rapidly withdrawn, an insufficiency of the adrenal gland may occur. Symptoms of this insufficiency include fever, nausea, dyspnea, joint soreness, fatigue, muscle weakness, anorexia, dizziness, and fainting.[114]

4. Inhaled

Inhaled steroids can be used for ongoing treatment of inflammatory respiratory conditions. Examples include beclamethasone, budesonide, fluticasone, flunisolide, and triamcinolone.[115]

Since they are inhaled and not taken orally, any side effects experienced are localized. Possible side effects include coughing, hoarseness, and oral yeast infections. The patient should be advised to rinse the mouth after using these products to prevent or reduce these effects.[116]

5. Nasal

Like inhaled steroids, some of the same steroids may be used nasally for ongoing treatment, and side effects are not typically systemic. Side effects may include headache, epitaxis (nosebleeds), dryness and nasal irritation.[117]

a. Leukotriene D4 receptor antagonists

Leukotrienes cause bronchoconstriction, and can also trigger inflammation and edema. Zafirlukast and Montelukast block leukotrienes. They are used to control symptoms of persistent severe asthma, or to help wean the dose of oral corticosteroids. Montelukast can also be used to treat allergic rhinitis (irritation of the nasal passages) or sinusitis.[118]

Gastrointestinal discomfort and dizziness are possible side effects of leukotriene D4 receptor antagonists. In addition, these medications can elevate the enzymes of the liver, so liver function tests should be performed regularly. This drug is not effective for emergency use.[119]

b. Mast cell stabilizers

These medications (cromolyn sodium and nedocromil sodium) are used to prevent bronchoconstriction when used prior to contact with an identified trigger. The inflammatory responses from allergens and exercise are inhibited by these inhaled medications. Possible side effects include nasal irritation, and a foul taste in the mouth. This medication may be taken on a regular schedule for mild asthma, or 20 to 30 minutes prior to exercise for those with exercise-induced asthma.[120]

6. Antibiotics

Antibiotics are commonly used to treat respiratory infections. They may be administered via the oral, inhaled, or IV route.[121] Amoxicillin and Vancomycin are examples.

Possible side effects of antibiotics are skin rashes, nausea, vomiting, diarrhea, as well as allergic responses. Vaginal or oral candidiasis (yeast infection) may occur when a patient is on antibiotic treatment. Severe, persistent diarrhea from *Clostridium difficile* may be caused by antibiotic therapy.[122]

The misuse and overuse of antibiotics promotes drug-resistant bacteria. Improper use of these medications may include treating infections that are not caused by bacteria, using too many antibiotics simultaneously, failing to change from IV to oral medication when appropriate, failing to take an accurate history of the patient's allergies, and failing to anticipate possible drug-drug interactions.[123]

8.9 Diagnostic Tests
A. Imaging Studies

Imaging studies that are commonly used in respiratory care may include the chest x-ray, the CT scan of the chest, and the MRI of the chest. Proper interpretation and handling of films is essential. See Figure 8.9.

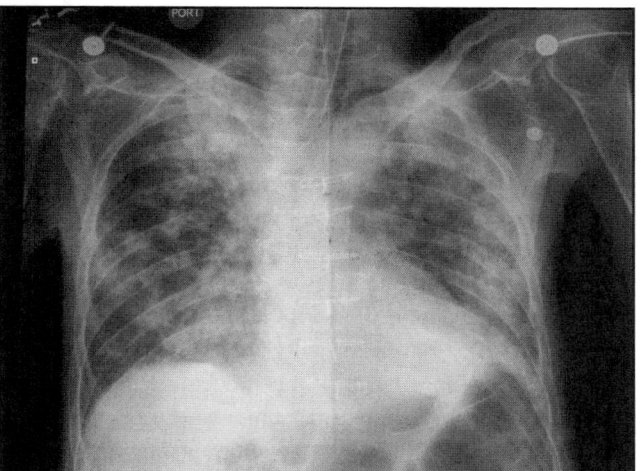

Figure 8.9

A Massachusetts case involved a patient who had a 30-year history of smoking. In 2001, he went to the defendant, a family physician, with respiratory complaints. A nodule in the upper lobe of the lung was seen on CT scan. The defendant misplaced the results of the scan and the patient was not informed of the findings. The next year the patient developed pneumonia. During treatment of his pneumonia, x-rays revealed changes in the lower lymph areas. Another CT scan was not performed until December 2003. This revealed a mass in the right lobe. The patient was then diagnosed with stage IV lung cancer; he died five months later. The plaintiff claimed the defendant was negligent in failing to inform the decedent of the result of the 2001 CT scan and in failing to advise the decedent to follow up within three months of that scan. The plaintiff claimed that an earlier diagnosis would have resulted in a better prognosis. The defendant claimed that an earlier diagnosis would not have changed the outcome. A $650,000 settlement was reached.[124]

B. Bronchoscopy

Physicians use bronchoscopes for diagnostic and therapeutic purposes. They are manufactured in a rigid model, and also in a bendable fiber-optic design. This tool allows the clinician to visualize the airways for irregularities, to biopsy tissue from suspicious lesions, to aspirate sputum to send for microbiological analysis, and to visualize the larynx. In addition, bronchoscopy can be used to clear tenacious secretions, to remove foreign materials from the tracheobronchial tree, and to staunch bleeding in the bronchi.[125]

The first step in the procedure is to topically anesthetize the back of the patient's throat. Then, the bronchoscope is advanced through the mouth or nose (or artificial airway) and into the lower airways via the trachea. If necessary, bronchial washings can be collected and lung tissue can be biopsied. Also, excessive secretions can be removed via aspiration.[126]

The patient should have nothing to eat or drink for eight or more hours prior to the procedure to inhibit aspiration of stomach contents into the lungs. After the procedure, the patient should not eat or drink until the anesthetic has subsided and the gag reflex returns, usually at least two hours.[127]

Possible complications of this procedure include throat pain, laryngospasm (muscular contraction of the vocal cords), aspiration of fluid into the lungs, and hemorrhaging. Clinicians should monitor for airway obstruction or bloody sputum after a bronchoscopy is performed.[128] Some facilities provide a form with a preprinted drawing of the lungs to facilitate the documentation of the findings of the test.

C. Laboratory Studies

1. Arterial blood gas (ABG)

The management of the arterial blood gas (ABG) is critical to clinicians who care for patients with respiratory disorders. This test is often ordered when a patient has signs and symptoms of respiratory dysfunction. Clinicians must have specialized training to develop the expertise required to collect, analyze, and interpret the results of this blood test.[129]

From this one lab test, clinicians are able to determine patients' acid-base level (pH), how well they are ventilating ($PaCO_2$), and how well they are oxygenating (PaO_2). They are able to determine whether an abnormal status is caused by an acute or a chronic problem, whether the patient's blood is acidic or alkaline, whether the patient has a metabolic or a respiratory condition, and whether the blood is carrying enough oxygen. Normal value ranges for an ABG are as follows: pH = 7.35–7.45; $PaCO_2$ (partial pressure of carbon dioxide) = 35-45 torr; PaO_2 (partial pressure of oxygen) = 80-100 torr; HCO_3 (bicarbonate) = 22-26 mEq/L; and SaO2 (arterial oxygenation) = > 95%.[130]

TIP: In order to collect an ABG, a trained medical professional (usually a respiratory therapist) must insert a needle into one of the patient's arteries and withdraw a blood sample.

Recommended sites for the puncture are the radial artery (preferred), brachial artery, and femoral artery. The puncture site must be cleaned with an antimicrobial solution. If the radial artery (in the wrist) is the target, then an Allen's test should be performed to make sure there is collateral circulation to the hand from the ulnar artery. An ABG may be done if the Allen's test is found to be within normal limits, the patient is free of severe bleeding disorders, and she does not have an AV fistula (a surgically created hemodialysis access port) above the intended puncture site. Possible complications include bleeding, hematoma and arterial occlusion (blockage).[131] In some circumstances, an indwelling arterial line may be placed to monitor hemodynamic status (heart rate and blood pressure), and make obtaining the blood sample easier and less painful.

If a healthcare provider attempting to draw an ABG inserts the needle improperly and hits a nerve instead of the radial artery, and the patient sustains nerve damage, then there may possibly be grounds for a malpractice suit. If an arterial occlusion were to occur from a poorly executed arterial stick, the patient could suffer from a significant reduction in the blood flow to the hand (causing severe injury). This could also result in a strong malpractice case.

2. Microbiology
a. Sputum culture and sensitivity, and Gram stain

If pulmonary infection is suspected, the physician may order a sputum culture and sensitivity (C&S) and possibly a Gram stain. The sputum is collected from the patient via deliberate coughing, suctioning or bronchoscopy and sent to the microbiology lab. The C&S detects the existence of bacteria, and can determine which anti-infective medications are effective to eradicate the infectious organism(s). The Gram stain detects the presence of and identifies the characteristics of Gram negative and Gram positive bacteria.[132]

b. Cytology

Cytology is a sputum diagnostic test that detects the existence of cancerous cells. If malignant cells are found, further diagnostic workup and/or treatment will most likely be necessary.[133]

c. Acid-fast bacillus (AFB) test

This diagnostic test detects the existence of acid-fast bacilli, which indicates the presence of mycobacteria. Usually, when this test is ordered the physician is attempting to determine if the patient has tuberculosis (TB). Often, serial specimens are sent for analysis.[134]

D. Pulse Oximetry

Pulse oximeters are used to monitor oxygen saturation. They are noninvasive monitors that indirectly measure arterial oxygenation (SaO_2). The invention of this technology has reduced the number of invasive ABGs necessary for respiratory patients.[135]

A sensor is placed on a patient's finger, earlobe, toe or forehead. This sensor points light at red and infrared wavelengths through the pulsing capillaries under the skin. It measures the percentage of oxygen absorbed by the hemoglobin in the blood. A normal SpO_2 range for a healthy individual breathing room air is 97-99 percent. However, levels as low as 95 percent are considered acceptable by many experts, with even lower acceptable ranges depending on the patient's condition. The monitors and sensor probes come in multiple shapes and sizes.[136] See Figure 8.10.

Indications for continuous pulse oximetry monitoring include patients with unpredictable airways or lung disorders, patients undergoing invasive diagnostic tests (such as bronchoscopy), critical care or respiratory patients who need to be transported, perioperative patients, and those receiving hemodialysis. Spot-checks should be ordered when a patient is on long-term oxygen therapy, or on a chronic mechanical ventilator with a tracheostomy in place.[137]

A 22-year-old California man sustained a head injury when he fell from a truck. He had a surgical procedure to reduce pressure on his brain. He was then taken to another hospital's ICU. Over time, his condition improved—he could answer questions and tolerated some oral nutrition. He did, however, continue to require mechanical ventilation, and his upper extremities were restrained. Approximately three weeks after he arrived, his ICU nurse was summoned to another room to handle an issue with an intravenous line. The plaintiff's artificial airway plugged when the nurse was out of the room. His pulse oximeter alarmed, which indicated he had low levels of oxygen in his blood. Additional alarms could be heard when his pulse rate decreased. A code was called several minutes later. Resuscitation efforts were successful; however MRIs showed evidence of brain injury due to severe hypoxia. The plaintiff remains unresponsive. The plaintiff claimed that the defendant was negligent in failing to monitor and react to alarms. The defendant alleged that brain damage from the original accident was serious, and that the plaintiff would have had a limited recovery even if the hypoxic event did not occur. A settlement of $4.25 million was attained with the defendant hospital, and $500,000 with the nurse.[138]

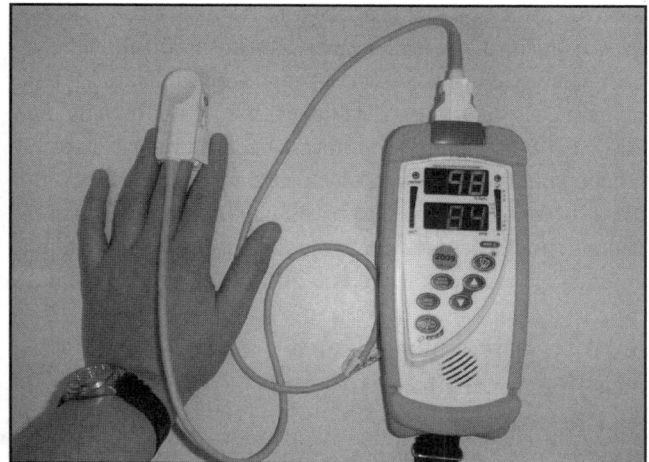

Figure 8.10

E. Pulmonary Function Testing

Pulmonary function testing (PFT) is the use of breathing tests to determine the presence and degree of respiratory dysfunction a patient may have. Progression of overall disease can be tracked over time. In addition, PFTs are often ordered preoperatively to evaluate a patient's risk of respiratory complications after the surgery.[139]

1. Spirometry

Specific lung volumes are measured using an apparatus called a spirometer. Those trained in pulmonary function testing (frequently respiratory therapists) perform the tests and compare them to predicted values for the patient's height, weight, and gender. See the AARC Clinical Practice Guidelines for additional details.[140]

The National Lung Health Education Program has recommended that smokers over the age of 45, as well as patients who present with wheezing, dyspnea with exertion, increased mucus production, or a persistent cough receive spirometry. The use of spirometry to evaluate asthmatics has been recommended by the National Asthma Education Program for almost 20 years.[141]

In fact, experts in the field of pulmonology believe that spirometry should always be used in patients who have symptoms consistent with respiratory disease. This simple test "is key to monitoring responses to therapy."[142]

2. Peak flow meter

Peak expiratory flow is the measurement of a patient's greatest expiratory flow effort after pulling in as much air as possible. A small plastic meter (peak flow meter) is used. It is recommended that asthmatics measure this flow rate on a daily basis and adjust their medication accordingly. Studies have indicated that using a peak flow meter as indicated reduces visits to the ER and prevents hospitalization.[143]

Although it varies according to height and age, the range of normal values for this test are approximately 380-700 mL. If the patient (or clinician) notes a reduction of 20-50 percent in peak flow, rescue medications are indicated. If the airflow is compromised by 50 percent or more, then the patient should be emergently evaluated by a clinician, and emergency treatment should be initiated.[144]

8.10 Respiratory Diseases and Management Techniques

A. Pneumonia

Pneumonia is inflammation in the lungs caused by an infectious agent, such as bacteria, fungi, and viruses. This inflammation causes the airways to become flooded with fluid which thickens, consolidates and interferes with the lung's function, reduces lung volumes, and causes difficulty breathing.[145]

A patient with pneumonia usually presents with a productive cough (sometimes hemoptysis) and a fever. Pleuritic chest pain and breathlessness may be present, and the patient appears extremely ill, often with an elevated heart rate and respiratory rate. The patient may be struggling to breathe. In severe situations, cyanosis may be present, as well as accessory muscle use and decreased chest excursion over affected areas. Percussion will produce a decreased resonance over regions of consolidation. Crackles may be heard by the clinician, which indicate excessive sputum production, and a friction rub may be present if the pleura are inflamed.[146]

The white blood cell count (WBC) will be elevated if the infectious agent is bacterial, but will remain normal if nonbacterial. Chest x-rays vary with the severity of disease. They show zones of increased opacities (white areas) which represent areas of consolidation. ABGs frequently indicate alkalosis of a respiratory nature, and hypoxemia. Sputum cultures are sent to the microbiology lab to determine which pathogen is causing the pneumonia. Sensitivity testing detects which antibiotics can successfully treat the infection.[147]

Treatment of pneumonia may be given in outpatient or acute care settings depending on the severity. If the patient has hypoxemia, oxygen therapy may be required. Increased humidity in inspired air can help loosen thick sputum. The appropriate anti-infective medication should be started as soon as possible to treat the infection, and supportive measures (such as intravenous fluid) provided as needed.[148]

B. Asthma

Asthma refers to reversible bronchospasm and swelling of the mucosa complicated by increased pulmonary secretions.

The airways become obstructed. Some types of asthma have specific triggers, such as exercise or allergens, and others have no evident cause.[149]

Symptoms vary from mild wheezes to status asthmaticus, a potentially fatal situation where an asthma attack is resistant to standard treatment.[150] Asthmatic patients complain of episodic chest pain/tightness, breathlessness, wheezing, and coughing. Between asthma flare-ups, patients may have no difficulty breathing. However, the pattern of symptoms can change throughout a patient's lifetime, and needs to be tracked and monitored in collaboration with medical professionals.[151]

It is sometimes difficult for physicians to diagnose asthma because symptoms vary, and it can easily be confused with other pulmonary disorders. The provider should conduct a detailed interview about current and past symptoms (and triggers), and a physical examination should be performed. Pulmonary function tests such as spirometry and peak flow measurement may be ordered (see Section 8.6.E).[152]

Treatment of asthma may include maintenance medications, rescue medications (see Section 8.5.D), and allergy medications. The correct treatment regimen is dependent on many factors, and may need to be adjusted over time.[153]

C. Chronic Obstructive Pulmonary Disease (COPD)

COPD, which is both incurable and progressive, consists of lung disorders that cause damage from airway obstruction. Most of the time COPD is caused by long-term smoking, but it is occasionally caused by a genetic problem. Two primary examples are chronic bronchitis and emphysema. Some people suffer from both of these types of COPD.[154]

Chronic bronchitis can be described as a condition where a long-term cough causes the airways to become inflamed. The airways narrow, and excess mucous is produced, which causes obstruction of airflow.[155] Emphysema is a condition where the alveoli are progressively destroyed, usually by smoking. Air flow becomes limited when exhaling.[156]

Treatment by a pulmonologist may be recommended if COPD is suspected by a primary care physician. Diagnostic tests may include a chest x-ray, CT scan, spirometry, sputum analysis, and ABG. Non-surgical treatments may include smoking cessation, oxygen therapy, bronchodilators, antibiotics and steroids. Surgical options include wedge resection or lung transplant.[157]

Acute exacerbations (flare-ups) of COPD may cause respiratory failure if not treated promptly. The hospital setting may be warranted to provide additional oxygen, medication and close monitoring.[158]

D. Lung Cancer

Lung cancer causes more fatalities in the United States than prostate, colon, breast and lymph cancers collectively. Approximately 90 percent of patients with lung cancer are (or were) smokers. Other risks for lung cancer include exposure to radon, asbestos, and secondhand smoke. In addition, gender, familial history, and alcohol consumption may play a role.[159] The cells that make up the lining of the lung become damaged. Initially, the body can repair itself, but with extensive exposure increased damage allows various types of cancer to develop. In the early stages of lung cancer, there are usually no symptoms noted. In late stages, a patient may complain of a persistent cough, hoarseness, wheezing, breathlessness, chest pain, or hemoptysis.[160]

TIP: Diagnostic tools used when lung cancer is suspected include chest x-rays, CT scans, sputum analysis, and tissue biopsies. Physicians use staging to define the degree of cancer a patient has. Bone scans, MRI, or positron emission testing (PET) may be used to assist with accurate staging.[161]

Complications from lung cancer may include pleural effusion, metastasis (spreading to other places in the body), and death. The diagnosis is grave, but new treatments targeting specific malignant cells are showing some success in extending life. Early detection improves the chance of survival.[162]

Treatments may include chemotherapy, radiation, surgery, targeted drug therapy (drugs that target cancer cell abnormalities), investigational medications, palliative care or a combination of any of the above. Oncologists, physicians who treat cancer patients, will help the patient decide which therapeutic direction to take.[163]

E. Tuberculosis

Tuberculosis (TB) refers to bacterial infection with an organism called *Mycobacterium tuberculosis*. It is passed from host to host via tiny droplets that are expelled when a contagious person speaks, spits, coughs, sneezes, sings or laughs. TB most often affects the lungs, but it can also attack the kidneys, brain or spine.[164]

Although it was once thought to be eradicated in the United States, TB has resurfaced with more drug-resistant, lethal strains. The United States has toughened laws that permit TB patients to be detained, quarantined, and isolated if necessary.[165]

Certain people are at a higher risk for contracting TB than others. Examples include those who are immunocompromised (such as those with HIV infection), substance abusers, healthcare workers, the impoverished, the homeless, and immigrants.[166]

Symptoms of TB include fatigue, fever, chills, poor appetite, weight loss, persistent cough, hemoptysis, and chest pain. Diagnostic testing for TB includes simple Mantoux skin tests and/or more sophisticated blood tests. If evidence of TB is found, further tests such as chest x-rays, CT scans, and/or sputum cultures may be done. Patients may be referred to a pulmonologist (lung doctor) or an infectious disease physician for further care.[167]

If a radiologist misinterprets a chest x-ray as being normal, and it is later determined to suggest active tuberculosis, then there may be grounds for a malpractice case. Furthermore, if a radiologist misreads a radiograph of a patient with active TB, and the patient infects another human being, the radiologist could theoretically be liable for the infection of the third-party.[168]

Complications of TB may include damage to lung tissue, pain, joint damage, and meningitis. Treatments primarily include medication therapy. However, anti-tuberculosis drugs need to be taken for anywhere from six months to two years.[169]

Physicians need to prescribe an appropriate medication regimen based on the patient's age, medical history, and the area of the body affected by TB. In addition, the type of TB (latent versus active) and the level of drug resistance need to be considered. Liver toxicity can be a significant problem with these medications, so acetaminophen and alcohol should be avoided during treatment, and liver function should be monitored closely.[170]

F. Pulmonary Fibrosis

Pulmonary fibrosis is a progressive disease where the tissue of the lungs becomes scarred. It is thought to be brought about by repetitive injury to the alveoli and the spaces between them. This eventually scars the tissue and causes stiffness of the lungs, which results in difficulty breathing.[171]

Possible causes of this type of damage include radiation and chemotherapy, occupational/environmental factors, some medications, gastrointestinal reflux disease (GERD), infections, and autoimmune disorders. Sometimes, the etiology is never determined.[172]

Symptoms include a nonproductive cough, dyspnea, fatigue, aching joints and muscles as well as weight loss. The symptoms progressively worsen until the patient becomes breathless while doing basic activities of daily living. Common complications include hypoxemia, elevated blood pressure in the lungs (pulmonary hypertension), heart failure and respiratory failure.[173]

Diagnostic tests include chest x-rays, specialized highly sensitive CT scans, pulmonary function tests, exercise stress tests and oximetry. Many times, definitive diagnosis with pulmonary fibrosis requires a lung biopsy.[174]

Treatment is fairly limited. It includes medicating with combinations of immunosuppressants and providing oxygen therapy. If these do not provide relief, a lung transplant may become the only remaining option.[175]

G. Pulmonary Hypertension

Pulmonary hypertension is a progressive illness where small blood vessels in the lungs narrow or become blocked. Blood flow is impeded in the lungs, which increases the pressure in the pulmonary arteries. As pressure increases in the pulmonary arteries, the heart must pump harder to push blood through the lungs. This causes the muscle of the heart to grow weaker, sometimes leading to complete heart failure.[176]

Symptoms include fatigue, dyspnea, dizziness, syncope (fainting), chest pain, swelling in the lower extremities, cyanosis, and rapid heart rate. Complications include heart failure, irregular heart rhythms, bleeding into the lungs, and blood clots in the lungs.[177]

Diagnostic testing may include an echocardiogram (which allows the physician to visualize the heart using sound waves), pulmonary function testing, a specialized scan that measures the perfusion (blood flow) in the lungs, a CT scan, a MRI, and a lung biopsy. Cardiac catheterization, a procedure where a tube is threaded through the right side of the heart and pulmonary artery, might be recommended to measure pressures and determine which drugs work best on the patient's heart.[178]

Treatment for pulmonary hypertension can be complex. Many medications help reduce the effects of the disease, such as epoprostenol and sildenafil. The right combination for each patient will need to be determined by the physician.[179]

Oxygen therapy often becomes necessary for these patients. Occasionally, lung and heart transplants may be appropriate options for patients with pulmonary hypertension.[180]

8.11 Summary

It is important to recognize that complications and negative outcomes are not usually caused by negligence in the healthcare setting. A medical malpractice claim can only be established if a patient receives substandard care that directly results in harm.[181]

The skilled care required by respiratory patients is highly complex and often of an emergency nature. The factors presented in this chapter illustrate the significant level of education and experience required to manage a wide variety of urgent and challenging circumstances. Respiratory clinicians are expected to have the advanced practice abilities to respond quickly and correctly in the areas of assessment, diagnosis, mechanical assistance, pharmacological treatment, and stabilization of critical medical situations.

Endnotes

1. Geiger-Bronsky, M. and Wilson, D.J. *Respiratory Nursing, A Core Curriculum.* p. 590. New York: Springer Publishing Company, 2008.

2. Kacmarek, R.M. et al. *The Essentials of Respiratory Care.* Fourth Edition. p. xi. St. Louis, Missouri: Elsevier Mosby, 2005.

3. http://www.bls.gov/oco/pdf/ocos084.pdf.

4. http://www.bls.gov/oco/pdf/ocos083.pdf.

5. *Id.*

6. http://www.bls.gov/oco/pdf/ocos101.pdf.

7. *Id.*

8. *Id.*

9. Giordano, K. "Examining nursing malpractice: a defense attorney's perspective." *Critical Care Nurse.* April 2003, Volume 23(2), p. 104.

10. *Id.*

6. Johnson, N.M. *Respiratory Disorders—(Medico-legal practitioner series).* p. 22. London: Cavendish Publishing Limited, 1999.

7. Johnson, N.M. *Respiratory Disorders—(Medico-legal practitioner series).* p. 24. London: Cavendish Publishing Limited, 1999.

8. *Id.*

11. Clark, A.P. and Garry, M.B. "Legal Implications of Standards of Care." *Dimensions of Critical Care Nursing.* March-April 1991, Volume 10(2), p. 101.

12. *Id.*

13. Carrol, C. *Legal Issues and Ethical Dilemmas in Respiratory Care.* p. 26. Philadelphia: F.A. Davis Company, 1996.

14. *Id.*

15. *Id.*

16. Johnson, N.M. *Respiratory Disorders—(Medico-legal practitioner series)*. p. 22. London: Cavendish Publishing Limited, 1999.

17. *Id.*

18. Johnson, N.M. *Respiratory Disorders—(Medico-legal practitioner series)*. p. 23. London: Cavendish Publishing Limited, 1999.

19. See note 7.

20. Johnson, N.M. *Respiratory Disorders—(Medico-legal practitioner series)*. p. 25. London: Cavendish Publishing Limited, 1999.

21. *Id.*

22. Kacmarek, R.M. et al. *The Essentials of Respiratory Care*. Fourth Edition. p. 325-336. St. Louis, Missouri: Elsevier Mosby, 2005.

23. *Id.*

24. *Id.*

25. *Id.*

26. Barnes, T.A. *Core textbook of Respiratory Care Practice*. Second Edition. p. 6. St. Louis, Missouri: Mosby-Year Book, Inc., 1994.

27. *Id.*

28. Johnson, N.M. *Respiratory Disorders—(Medico-legal practitioner series)*. p. 45. London: Cavendish Publishing Limited, 1999.

29. Johnson, N.M. *Respiratory Disorders—(Medico-legal practitioner series)*. p. 46. London: Cavendish Publishing Limited, 1999.

30. Laska, L. (Ed.) "Failure to diagnose lung cancer," Medical Malpractice Verdicts, Settlements, and Experts, May 2008, p. 27.

31. Barnes, T.A. *Core textbook of Respiratory Care Practice*. Second Edition. p. 9. St. Louis, Missouri: Mosby-Year Book, Inc., 1994.

32. Johnson, N.M. *Respiratory Disorders—(Medico-legal practitioner series)*. p. 46-48. London: Cavendish Publishing Limited, 1999.

33. Barnes, T.A. *Core textbook of Respiratory Care Practice*. Second Edition. p. 9. St. Louis, Missouri: Mosby-Year Book, Inc., 1994.

34. Johnson, N.M. *Respiratory Disorders—(Medico-legal practitioner series)*. p. 57. London: Cavendish Publishing Limited, 1999.

35. Barnes, T.A. *Core textbook of Respiratory Care Practice*. Second Edition. p. 9. St. Louis, Missouri: Mosby-Year Book, Inc., 1994.

36. Johnson, N.M. *Respiratory Disorders—(Medico-legal practitioner series)*. p. 58. London: Cavendish Publishing Limited, 1999.

37. Barnes, T.A. *Core textbook of Respiratory Care Practice*. Second Edition. p. 9. St. Louis, Missouri: Mosby-Year Book, Inc., 1994.

38. Johnson, N.M. *Respiratory Disorders—(Medico-legal practitioner series)*. p. 58-59. London: Cavendish Publishing Limited, 1999.

39. Laska, L. (Editor), "Failure to timely triage and treat man with chest pain—cardiac arrest ten minute after arrival," *Medical Malpractice Verdicts, Settlements, and Experts*, October 2009, page 16.

40. Wilkins, R.L. and Dexter, J.R. *Respiratory Disease, Principles of Patient Care*. p. 395. Philadelphia, PA: F.A. Davis Company, 1993.

41. Johnson, N.M. *Respiratory Disorders—(Medico-legal practitioner series)*. p. 52-53. London: Cavendish Publishing Limited, 1999.

42. Laska, L. (Ed.), "Failure to timely treat woman with pain in leg and shortness of breath," Medical Malpractice Verdicts, Settlements, and Experts, May 2008, p. 26.

43. Johnson, N.M. *Respiratory Disorders—(Medico-legal practitioner series)*. p. 53-56. London: Cavendish Publishing Limited, 1999.

44. Johnson, N.M. *Respiratory Disorders—(Medico-legal practitioner series)*. p. 56-57. London: Cavendish Publishing Limited, 1999.

45. *Id.*

46. Johnson, N.M. *Respiratory Disorders—(Medico-legal practitioner series).* p. 177-178. London: Cavendish Publishing Limited, 1999.

47. Johnson, N.M. *Respiratory Disorders—(Medico-legal practitioner series).* p. 178-179. London: Cavendish Publishing Limited, 1999.

48. Laska, L. (Ed.), "Failure to timely diagnose and treat pneumothorax in woman with severe asthma attack," Medical Malpractice Verdicts, Settlements, and Experts, December 2008, p. 22.

49. Baumann, M.H. et al. "Management of Spontaneous Pneumothorax—An American College of Chest Physicians Delphi Consensus Statement." *Chest.* February 2001, 119(2). p. 590-602.

50. Johnson, N.M. *Respiratory Disorders—(Medico-legal practitioner series).* p. 181-183. London: Cavendish Publishing Limited, 1999.

51. Kacmarek, R.M. et al. *The Essentials of Respiratory Care.* Fourth Edition. p. 399-400. St. Louis, Missouri: Elsevier Mosby, 2005.

52. *Id.*

53. Laska, L. (Editor), "Failure to recognize and treat pleural effusion in woman prior to arrest—brain damage and vegetative state," *Medical Malpractice Verdicts, Settlements, and Experts*, December 2009, page 4.

54. Kacmarek, R.M. et al. *The Essentials of Respiratory Care.* Fourth Edition. p. 608. St. Louis, Missouri: Elsevier Mosby, 2005.

55. Singh, C.P. et al. "Oxygen Therapy." *Journal, Indian Academy of Clinical Medicine.* July-September 2001, 2(3), p. 178-184.

56. DiPietro, J.S. and Mustard, M.N. *Clinical Guide for Respiratory Care Practitioners.* Norwalk, CT: Appleton & Lange, 1987, p. 64-68.

57. Singh, C.P. et al. "Oxygen Therapy." *Journal, Indian Academy of Clinical Medicine.* July-September 2001, 2(3), p. 178-184.

58. Laska, L. (Ed.), "Nasal cannula used for newborn with breathing difficulties secured with tape," Medical Malpractice Verdicts, Settlements, and Experts, July 2008, p. 28.

59. DiPietro, J.S. and Mustard, M.N. *Clinical Guide for Respiratory Care Practitioners.* Norwalk, CT: Appleton & Lange, 1987, p. 64-68.

60. Singh, C.P. et al. "Oxygen Therapy." *Journal, Indian Academy of Clinical Medicine.* July-September 2001, 2(3), p. 178-184.

61. DiPietro, J.S. and Mustard, M.N. *Clinical Guide for Respiratory Care Practitioners.* Norwalk, CT: Appleton & Lange, 1987, p. 64-68.

62. *Id.*

63. *Id.*

64. Jagim, M. "Airway Management, Rapid-sequence intubation in trauma patients." *AJN.* October 2003, 103(10), p. 32-35.

65. *Id.*

66. *Id.*

67. Divatia, J.V. and Bhowmick, K. "Complications of Endotracheal Intubation and other Airway Management Procedures." *Indian Journal of Anaesthesia.* August 2005, 49(4), p. 308-318.

68. Laska, L. (Editor), "Delay in performing Cesarian section and delay in intubation a birth blamed for brain damage, *Medical Malpractice Verdicts, Settlements, and Experts*, April 2009, page 38.

69. Geiger-Bronsky, M. and Wilson, D.J. *Respiratory Nursing, A Core Curriculum.* p. 525. New York: Springer Publishing Company, 2008.

70. Geiger-Bronsky, M. and Wilson, D.J. *Respiratory Nursing, A Core Curriculum.* p. 526. New York: Springer Publishing Company, 2008.

71. *Id.*

72. Geiger-Bronsky, M. and Wilson, D.J. *Respiratory Nursing, A Core Curriculum.* p. 526-527. New York: Springer Publishing Company, 2008.

73. *Id.*

74. Laska, L. (Editor), "Failure to timely clear tracheostomy tube for man recovering from brain injury in motorcycle collision—man has unexpected recovery," *Medical Malpractice Verdicts, Settlements, and Experts*, October 2009, page 18.

75. Geiger-Bronsky, M. and Wilson, D.J. *Respiratory Nursing, A Core Curriculum.* p. 527-528. New York: Springer Publishing Company, 2008.

76. *Id.*

77. *Id.*

78. Geiger-Bronsky, M. and Wilson, D.J. *Respiratory Nursing, A Core Curriculum.* p. 528-530. New York: Springer Publishing Company, 2008.

79. http://www.passy-muir.com/ceu/pdfs/ACourseMaterial.pdf.

80. Branson, R.D., et al. "AARC Clinical Practice Guideline, Endotracheal Suctioning of Mechanically Ventilated Adults and Children with Artificial Airways." *Respiratory Care.* May 1993, 38(5), p. 500-504.

81. *Id.*

82. *Id.*

83. Geiger-Bronsky, M. and Wilson, D.J. *Respiratory Nursing, A Core Curriculum.* p. 498. New York: Springer Publishing Company, 2008.

84. Tobin, M.J. "Advances in Mechanical Ventilation." *New England Journal of Medicine.* June 28, 2001, 344(26), p. 1986-1996.

85. Laska, L. (Ed.), "Failure to provide quadriplegic with ventilator during short jail stay," Medical Malpractice Verdicts, Settlements, and Experts, June 2009, p. 21.

86. Geiger-Bronsky, M. and Wilson, D.J. *Respiratory Nursing, A Core Curriculum.* p. 497. New York: Springer Publishing Company, 2008.

87. Geiger-Bronsky, M. and Wilson, D.J. *Respiratory Nursing, A Core Curriculum.* p. 518. New York: Springer Publishing Company, 2008.

88. Geiger-Bronsky, M. and Wilson, D.J. *Respiratory Nursing, A Core Curriculum.* p. 499-500. New York: Springer Publishing Company, 2008.

89. Geiger-Bronsky, M. and Wilson, D.J. *Respiratory Nursing, A Core Curriculum.* p. 501. New York: Springer Publishing Company, 2008.

90. Geiger-Bronsky, M. and Wilson, D.J. *Respiratory Nursing, A Core Curriculum.* p. 498-499. New York: Springer Publishing Company, 2008.

91. Gay, P.C. "Complications of Noninvasive Ventilation in Acute Care." *Respiratory Care.* February 2009, 54(2), p. 246-257.

92. Tobin, M.J. "Advances in Mechanical Ventilation." *New England Journal of Medicine.* June 28, 2001, 344(26), p. 1986-1996.

93. Geiger-Bronsky, M. and Wilson, D.J. *Respiratory Nursing, A Core Curriculum.* p. 503. New York: Springer Publishing Company, 2008.

94. Tobin, M.J. "Advances in Mechanical Ventilation." *New England Journal of Medicine.* June 28, 2001, 344(26), p. 1986-1996.

95. Geiger-Bronsky, M. and Wilson, D.J. *Respiratory Nursing, A Core Curriculum.* p. 503. New York: Springer Publishing Company, 2008.

96. Tobin, M.J. "Advances in Mechanical Ventilation." *New England Journal of Medicine.* June 28, 2001, 344(26), p. 1986-1996.

97. Geiger-Bronsky, M. and Wilson, D.J. *Respiratory Nursing, A Core Curriculum.* p. 504. New York: Springer Publishing Company, 2008.

98. *Id.*

99. Thille, A.W. et al. "Patient-ventilator asynchrony during assisted mechanical ventilation." *Intensive Care Med.* August 2006, 32, p. 1515.

100. Giordano, K. "Examining nursing malpractice: a defense attorney's perspective." *Critical Care Nurse.* April 2003, Volume 23(2), p. 104-105.

101. *Id.*

102. Geiger-Bronsky, M. and Wilson, D.J. *Respiratory Nursing, A Core Curriculum.* p. 475-495. New York: Springer Publishing Company, 2008.

103. *Id.*

104. *Id.*

105. *Id.*

106. *Id.*

107. *Id.*

108. *Id.*

109. *Id.*

110. *Id.*

111. *Id.*

112. *Id.*

113. Becker, J.M. et al. "Oral versus intravenous corticosteroids in children hospitalized with asthma." *Journal of Allergy and Clinical Immunology.* Volume 103(4), p. 586-590.

114. Geiger-Bronsky, M. and Wilson, D.J. *Respiratory Nursing, A Core Curriculum.* p. 475-495. New York: Springer Publishing Company, 2008.

115. *Id.*

116. *Id.*

117. *Id.*

118. *Id.*

119. *Id.*

120. *Id.*

121. *Id.*

122. *Id.*

123. *Id.*

124. Laska, L. (Ed.), "Misplacement of CAT scan report showing nodule in upper lobe of lung results in delay in diagnosis of lung cancer," Medical Malpractice Verdicts, Settlements, and Experts, February 2008, p. 22.

125. Geiger-Bronsky, M. and Wilson, D.J. *Respiratory Nursing, A Core Curriculum.* p. 86-87. New York: Springer Publishing Company, 2008.

126. *Id.*

127. *Id.*

128. *Id.*

129. DiPietro, J.S. and Mustard, M.N. *Clinical Guide for Respiratory Care Practitioners.* p. 22-25. Norwalk, CT: Appleton & Lange, 1987.

130. *Id.*

131. Geiger-Bronsky, M. and Wilson, D.J. *Respiratory Nursing, A Core Curriculum.* p. 84-85. New York: Springer Publishing Company, 2008.

132. Geiger-Bronsky, M. and Wilson, D.J. *Respiratory Nursing, A Core Curriculum.* p. 92-93. New York: Springer Publishing Company, 2008.

133. *Id.*

134. *Id.*

135. Valdez-Lowe, C. et al. "Pulse Oximetry in Adults." *AJN.* June 2009, 109(6), p. 52-60.

136. *Id.*

137. *Id.*

138. Laska, L. (Editor), "Man in ICU following brain surgery required due to falling off truck suffers airway obstruction while nurse is with another patient—delayed response to alarms," *Medical Malpractice Verdicts, Settlements, and Experts*, May 2009, page 19-20.

139. Geiger-Bronsky, M. and Wilson, D.J. *Respiratory Nursing, A Core Curriculum.* p. 77-78. New York: Springer Publishing Company, 2008.

140. Kacmarek, R.M. et al. *The Essentials of Respiratory Care.* Fourth Edition. p. 344-349. St. Louis, Missouri: Elsevier Mosby, 2005.

141. Petty, T.L. "How To Blow Your Defense." *Chest.* November 2002, Volume 122 (5), p. 1868-1869.

142. *Id.*

143. Geiger-Bronsky, M. and Wilson, D.J. *Respiratory Nursing, A Core Curriculum.* p. 570-571. New York: Springer Publishing Company, 2008.

144. *Id.*

145. Wilkins, R.L. and Dexter, J.R. *Respiratory Disease, Principles of Patient Care.* p. 269-275. Philadelphia, PA: F.A. Davis Company, 1993.

146. *Id.*

147. *Id.*

148. *Id.*

149. Wilkins, R.L. and Dexter, J.R. *Respiratory Disease, Principles of Patient Care.* p. 15-20. Philadelphia, PA: F.A. Davis Company, 1993.

150. *Id.*

151. *Id.*

152. http://www.mayoclinic.com/health/asthma/DS00021/METHOD=print&DSECTION=all.

153. *Id.*

154. http://www.mayoclinic.com/health/copd/DS00916/METHOD=print.

155. *Id.*

156. http://www.mayoclinic.com/health/emphysema/DS00296.

157. http://www.mayoclinic.com/health/copd/DS00916/METHOD=print.

158. *Id.*

159. http://www.mayoclinic.com/health/lung-cancer/DS00038/METHOD=print.

160. *Id.*

161. *Id.*

162. *Id.*

163. *Id.*

164. http://mayoclinic.com/health/tuberculosis/DS00372/METHOD=print.

165. Berlin, L. "Tuberculosis: Resurgent Disease, Renewed Liability." *American Journal of Roentgenology.* June 2008, Volume 190, p. 1438-1444.

166. http://mayoclinic.com/health/tuberculosis/DS00372/METHOD=print.

167. *Id.*

168. Berlin, L. "Tuberculosis: Resurgent Disease, Renewed Liability." *American Journal of Roentgenology.* June 2008, Volume 190, p. 1442.

169. *Id.*

170. *Id.*

171. http://www.mayoclinic.com/health/pulmonary-fibrosis/DS00927/METHOD=print&DSECTION=all.

172. *Id.*

173. *Id.*

174. *Id.*

175. *Id.*

176. http://www.mayoclinic.com/health/pulmonary-hypertension/DS00430/METHOD=print&DSECTION=all.

177. *Id.*

178. *Id.*

179. *Id.*

180. *Id.*

181. Giordano, K. "Examining nursing malpractice: a defense attorney's perspective." *Critical Care Nurse.* April 2003, Volume 23(2), p. 104-105.

Additional Information

American Association for Respiratory Care (AARC) guidelines on their website

Respiratory Nursing Society's Scope & Standards (sent to ANA for approval in 08/09)

Chapter 9

Orthopaedic Nursing Malpractice Issues

Barbara J. Levin, BSN, RN, ONC, LNCC and Nancy E. Mooney, MA, RNC, ONC

Synopsis
9.1 Introduction
   A. National Association of Orthopaedic Nurses
   B. Sentinel Event Alert
9.2 Basic Assessment of the Orthopaedic Patient
   A. Neurovascular Assessment
   B. Spinal Assessment
9.3 Back Pain
   A. Risk Factors
   B. Sciatica
   C. Disc Herniations
   D. Caude Equine
9.4 Fractures
   A. Open Versus Closed Fractures
   B. Imaging
   C. Modalities of Immobilization
      1. Casts
      2. Cast-brace
      3. Traction
      4. External fixation
9.5 Complications
   A. Compartment Syndrome
   B. Bone Union Problems
   C. Cast Syndrome
   D. Limb Length Discrepancies
   E. Osteomyelitis
   F. Foot Drop
   G. Deep Vein Thrombosis
   H. Pulmonary Emboli
   I. Fat Embolus Syndrome
9.6 Discharge Planning for the Orthopaedic Patient
9.7 Conclusion
Endnotes

9.1 Introduction

Orthopaedics is the specialty of healthcare professionals who care for individuals with musculoskeletal injuries and disorders across the lifespan. From the neonate with congenital disorders through the frail elderly person suffering a hip fracture, orthopaedic caregivers restore motion and function and help individuals get back to their optimal level of functioning. Salmond reports that the burden of musculoskeletal disease in the United States is profound. Musculoskeletal injuries are a major cause of morbidity and have a substantial effect on health and quality of life. They are the most reported chronic impairment and the number one reason for visits to physicians, accounting for more than 131 million visits to healthcare providers with 7.3 million musculoskeletal procedures performed annually.[1] Orthopaedic injuries commonly occur in a variety of personal injury accidents, from falls to motor vehicle accidents.

Musculoskeletal disorders are the most frequent causes of severe long-term pain and physical disability, affecting hundreds of millions of people around the world. The extent of the problem and its burden on patients and society can be understood from some examples:

1. Joint diseases account for half of all chronic conditions in people age 65 and over.
2. Back pain is the second leading cause of sick leave.
3. Fractures related to osteoporosis have almost doubled in number in the last decade; it is estimated 40 percent of all women over 50 years old will suffer from an osteoporotic fracture.
4. The severe injuries caused by traffic accidents and war produce a tremendous demand for preventive and restorative help. Developing countries spend much money on trauma-related care.
5. Crippling diseases and deformities continue to deprive many children of their normal development.

The impact from such bone and joint disorders on the individual, society, and healthcare and social systems led to an initiative beginning with an inaugural Consensus Meeting held in Lund, Sweden in April 1998 and culminating in a proposal for the Decade of the Bone and Joint from 2000-2010.[2] The President of the United States proclaimed the Bone and Joint decade to continue through 2011. The Decade of the Bone and Joint raises awareness of the following:

*   suffering and costs to society associated with musculoskeletal disorders such as joint diseases, osteoporosis, and spinal disorders,

- severe trauma to the extremities and crippling diseases and deformities in children, and
- the resources presently available and the need to advance this through research.

No single organization can accomplish the desired benefits for the patient. The Bone and Joint Decade is a multidisciplinary initiative involving everyone concerned with care including communities, patients, healthcare providers, and researchers. The goals of the Decade will be achieved by

1. raising awareness of the growing burden of musculoskeletal disorders on society,
2. empowering patients to participate in their own care,
3. promoting cost-effective prevention and treatment, and
4. advancing understanding of musculoskeletal disorders through research to improve prevention and treatment.

Given the pervasiveness of orthopaedic problems, it is evident that nurses in many settings interact with patients with disorders of the bone. Nurses are charged with preventing orthopaedic injuries such as fractures, as well as treating patients with injuries in every setting where health care is delivered. Nurses may be involved in assisting the patient from the moment of injury and throughout the care. Nursing liability results from negligence associated with orthopaedic trauma. It can arise at any point in the patient's recovery.

A. National Association of Orthopaedic Nurses

The National Association of Orthopaedic Nurses (NAON), founded in 1980, is a professional organization devoted to promoting the specialty of orthopaedic nursing. Its mission statement is "to advance the quality of musculoskeletal health care by promoting excellence in research, education, and nursing practice."[3]

The following is the philosophy of NAON:

The National Association of Orthopaedic Nurses believes the specialty of orthopaedic nursing should set forth the highest standards of nursing practice for optimum patient care. We believe in the concept of man as a total being having physical, psychological, social, emotional, and spiritual needs. The orthopaedic nurse in cooperation with the patient and other members of the health team utilizes this concept of man to assess, plan, imple-

ment, and evaluate a plan of patient care. This nursing process is essential to assure that each patient achieves the highest possible level of health. We are committed to the advancement of the profession of nursing. We believe that educational programs that foster personal and professional growth will develop competence and excellence in nursing practice for the orthopaedic nurse. We support and encourage research and advanced clinical practice as the foundation for expertise in nursing practice.[4]

B. Sentinel Event Alert

The Institute of Medicine study was the first on medical errors to become widely available to the public. This study highlights the death rate from medical errors, which is one of the top ten causes of death in the United States. Data from The Joint Commission Sentinel Event Alert provide a more complete picture of the types of medical errors occurring in this nation's hospitals. The Alert describes 19 major events, six of which are relevant to orthopaedic surgery:

- Medication errors (11.4 percent)
- Operative or postoperative complications (12.8 percent)
- Wrong-site surgery (11.9 percent)
- Delay in diagnosis (6 percent)
- Patient falls; leg length issues (4.7 percent)
- Transfusion errors (2.7 percent)[5]

TIP: It has been suggested the adverse event numbers are vastly underreported since the hospitals rely on voluntary reporting of adverse events.

As a result of this and other studies, healthcare facilities are implementing a variety of measures to decrease incidents. For example, Joint Commission recommends all surgical cases have a "time out" before the procedure begins. This is a time in which the surgical teams pauses and identifies the patient, procedure, and site. For additional information on this topic refer to Chapter 5, *Perioperative Nursing Malpractice Issues,* in this Volume, and Chapter 4, *Patient Safety Initiatives,* in Volume I. The American Academy of Orthopaedic Surgeons' (AAOS) "Sign Your Site" initiative is another example. Wrong-site surgery is considered by The Joint Commission as a sentinel event. The root cause analysis identified several contributing factors, which included breakdown of communication among the patient, physician, and members of the surgical team. Other cited areas included lack of a system to mark the surgical site, absence of a preoperative checklist, and an incomplete preoperative assessment. The root cause analysis further determined that pertinent information was at times unavailable in the operating room (e.g., patient records, imaging studies), distraction factors were present (e.g., late starts), and staffing issues existed as causal factors. To combat this problem, Joint Commission mirrors the recommendations of the "sign your site" program, including that the surgical site be identified, that a verification checklist be used, and that oral identification of the patient's identity, the surgical sites, and the scheduled procedure be obtained.[6]

9.2 Basic Assessment of the Orthopaedic Patient

A. Neurovascular Assessment

The neurovascular assessment is the foundation of orthopaedic nursing practice. The failure to perform an adequate neurovascular assessment can result in devastating injuries caused by delay in recognition of a complication.

TIP: Neurovascular assessment includes:

- Color—pink, white, gray, black—capillary refill. What is the capillary refill time? (The ideal capillary refill is less than three seconds. It is measured by the time it takes for color to be restored to a nailbed after pressing on it, then releasing the pressure.)
- Sensation—Does the extremity have intact sensation? Are there any areas with decreased sensation?
- Movement—Is the patient able to move the extremity? Is the patient able to plantarflex (depress the foot as though pressing on a gas pedal) and dorsiflex the foot (move the foot toward the head—upwards)? Is the patient able to lift or move the entire extremity?
- Temperature—Is the extremity warm, cool, cold? The nurse should compare both extremities.
- Swelling—Is swelling noted in the extremity? Fingers, toes? The nurse should compare this to the unaffected extremity and monitor any changes.

Healthcare providers must have baseline assessments for comparisons to be made postoperatively and post-injury. When an attorney or legal nurse consultant reviews the orthopaedic client's medical records, he is expected to find that neurovascular assessments have been performed and documented as this is critical for this patient population. (Refer to Figure 9.1 and Figure 9.2.) These include evaluation of the color, sensation, and movement of the extremity. In addition, pulses should be evaluated and documented. This baseline assessment also includes a comparison of one side to the opposite side. The patient is at risk for neurovascular dysfunction after an orthopaedic injury or procedure. All changes in the vascular and neurological integrity, as well as

the pain status should be assessed at regular intervals, and changes should be reported to healthcare providers. (Refer to Figure 9.3 and Figure 9.4.)

TIP: When reviewing orthopaedic care rendered to children, remember that they are not like adults. Consider the developmental levels for children, which will assist in understanding the degree of comprehension. The various levels assist in guiding the attorney or legal nurse consultant in understanding if the child is able to articulate or communicate her needs.

B. Spinal Assessment

Patients with spine disorders can present many ways. The patient may have a congenital defect such as scoliosis or kyphosis, or an acute strain such as an acute onset of low back pain. All patients with spine disorders are evaluated for neurological impairment including the following:

- numbness,
- pain,
- motor function,
- spasm, and
- bowel and bladder symptoms.

A careful history of what provokes and improves the symptoms must be elicited and documented in the medical record. In general, these disorders are treated non-surgically, despite the fact they often involve much pain for the patient.

The following case describes the importance of monitoring and communicating changes in neurovascular assessments to the surgeon:

The plaintiff, a 69-year-old man, was being evaluated and treated for back pain and had a laminectomy with a bone graft and hardware insertion. A few years later, the plaintiff was admitted to the hospital for a decompression and removal of the hardware. Immediately following the operation, he was able to move all four extremities. At 2:10 P.M., the plaintiff was transferred to the orthopaedic unit where the nurse noted on her admission assessment the patient complaints of numbness and pain in both feet. Throughout the afternoon and night shifts, this patient complained of pain and numbness in both feet. He began developing weakness in his legs as well as burning, tingling, and severe pain. The nursing staff did not contact the physician regarding these adverse changes. Early the next morning, the physician examined the patient and confirmed the patient was unable to move his legs. Emergency surgery was performed, at which time cauda equina was diagnosed secondary to spinal cord compression from a hematoma. After ten days in the hospital this patient was transferred to rehabilitation for aggressive therapy. His functional status at the time of discharge home revealed reduced strength in his lower extremities, lack of perianal and genital sensation, low muscle tone, and bilateral absence of ankle reflexes. Long-term complications also include recurrent urinary tract infections from the self-catheterization needed to empty the bladder. He continues suffering from intractable pain and is on numerous medications including narcotics. This case settled for $1.36 million (unpublished settlement).

The nursing process was not followed in this case. The nursing staff noted the changes in the neurovascular status and documented these changes but they failed to appreciate their importance and communicate them to the orthopaedic surgeon. If the nursing staff had communicated the changes immediately, urgent evaluation and treatment could have been provided by the orthopaedic surgeons, thus preventing the permanent injuries sustained.[7]

9.3 Back Pain

Many people visit their physicians and the emergency room with complaints of back pain. Most patient episodes are self-limited and successfully resolve without specific therapy. In 2002, there were approximately 15 million office visits for this complaint.[8]

Neurovascular Scale—Lower Extremity

Vascular Assessment: Dorsalis Pedis/Posterior Tibial

Capillary Refill Temperatur	Nail Bed Color	Pulses	Skin
2+ = Brisk	p = Pink	N = Normal/Palpable	W = Warm
1+ = Diminished	Pa = Pale	Ab = Absent	Cl = Cool
0 = No Refill	C = Cyanotic	D = Doppler	Cd = Cold

Neurological Assessment

Nerve	Movement	Sensibility
Tibial	Plantarflexion	Sole of foot
Peroneal	Dorsiflexion	Dorsal space great toe
Femoral	Straight leg raise	Anterior thigh

Movement
N = Normal
D = Diminished
Ab = Absent

Sensibility
* = Normal
Nu = Numbness
T = Tingling
D = Diminished (paresthesia)
Ab = Absent

Assess the extremity for sensation, motion, and vascular status.

Figure 9.1 Neurovascular Scale – Lower Extremity. *Reprinted with permission by the National Association of Orthopaedic Nurses. All rights reserved.*

Normal Range of Motion (Shown in Degrees)

Cervical Spine
Flexion: 80-90
Extension: 70
Side flexion: 20-45
Rotation: 70-90

Thoracic Spine
Forward flexion: 20-45
Extension: 25-45
Side flexion: 20-40
Rotation: 35-50
Costovertebral expansion*
Rib Motion*

Lumbar Spine
Forward flexion: 40-60
Extension: 20-35
Side flexion: 15-20
Rotation: 3-18

Shoulder
Elevation through abduction: 170-180
Elevation through forward flexion:
        160-180
Lateral rotation: 80-90
Medial rotation: 60-100
Extension: 50-60
Adduction: 50-75
Horizontal adduction and abduction:
        130
Circumduction: 200

Elbow
Flexion: 140-150
Extension: 0-10
Supination (forearm): 90
Pronation (forearm): 80-90

Wrist
Abduction (radial deviation): 15
Adduction (ulnar deviation): 30-40
Flexion: 80-90
Extension: 70-90
Pronation: (forearm): 85-90
Supination (forearm): 85-90

Hip
Flexion: 110-120
Extension: 10-15
Abduction: 30-50
Adduction: 30
Lateral rotation: 40-60
Medial rotation: 30-40

Knee
Flexion: 0-135
Extension: 0-15
Medial Rotation (tibia
        on femur): 20-30
Lateral Rotation (tibia
        on femur): 30-40

Ankle
Plantar flexion: 50
Dorsiflexion: 20
Supination: 45-60
Pronation: 15-30

*Maneuvers other than measuring arcs of motion are used for assessment in these instances.

Figure 9.2 Normal Range of Motion (Shown in Degrees). Reprinted from Orthopaedic Nursing, Maher et al. p. 199, Copyright 2002, with permission from Elsevier.

Indicators of Neurovascular Compromise

Compare one extremity to the other:
1. Circulation
   A. Color: Pale/Blanched, White or Cyanotic/Blue
   B. Temperature: Cool, Cold, Hot
   C. Capillary refill: More than 3 seconds
       i. Pulses: 0 = absent; 1 = weak/thready
       ii. Tissue turgor: hollow/prunelike or tense/distended
2. Motion
   A. Weak
   B. Limp
   C. Paralysis
3. Sensation
   A. Paresthesia
       i. Reduced sensory
   B. Pain out of proportion
   C. Pain on passive stretch
   D. Lack of feeling

Figure 9.3 Indicators of Neurovascular Compromise

Grading Muscle Strength—Lovett Scale

0	Zero (0)	No palpable contraction of muscle
1	Trace (T)	Palpable contraction of muscle; no joint motion
2	Poor (P)	Complete ROM with gravity eliminated
3	Fair (F)	Complete ROM against gravity; no added resistance
4	Good (G)	Complete ROM against gravity; some added resistance
5	Normal (N)	Complete ROM against gravity with full resistance

Figure 9.4 Grading Muscle Strength—Lovett Scale. Reprinted from Orthopaedic Nursing, Maher et al. 200, Copyright 2002, with permission from Elsevier.

While the total costs of low back pain in the United States exceed $100 billion per year, 75 percent of the total costs are attributable to fewer than 5 percent of the patients with low back pain.[9] Back pain is the leading cause of work-related disability and a lead contributor for missed work.

The spine is a flexible support located in the center of the body, and the segments fit together like a puzzle. There are 33 vertebrae which are subdivided into sections of seven cervical (C1-C7), 12 thoracic (T1-T12), five lumbar (L1-L5), five sacral (S1-S5, fused), and four coccyxgeal (tailbone, fused) vertebrae.

Back pain impacts lifestyle and quality of life and when these are in jeopardy, the search for treatment begins.

A. Risk Factors

- Smoking
- Obesity
- Physically strenuous work or exercise
- Sedentary work
- Poor physical condition
- Weight gain during pregnancy
- Poor posture
- Aging
- Build up of scar tissue from previous injuries
- Injury or trauma
- Degenerative conditions
- Osteoporosis or other bone diseases
- Viral conditions
- Congenital anomalies
- Irritations to joints or discs
- Disc injury such as disc tear or a herniation (the disc slips)
- Scoliosis abnormal curvature usually seen in children but may develop in the older population who have arthritis
- Spinal stenosis (space around the spinal cord narrows)[10]

TIP: When evaluating the medical records, it is important to evaluate if there are signs of a systemic disease. Is there evidence of a neurologic compromise such as a change in color or sensation or movement? Is there psychological stress which may contribute to the patient's pain?

Back pain may be described as dull or sharp pain, stabbing pain, achy or crampy. When reviewing the medical records, determine if the pain is constant or intermittent, if it improves or worsens with rest or activities or if the pain travels. Do the symptoms get worse during examination and palpation of the area?

A focused history and examination include determining the location, duration, and severity of the pain. A few questions to determine include: Are there exacerbating features? Is there an underlying cause? Please review Chapter 26, *Falls and Their Consequences*, to review additional information regarding spine injuries.

B. Sciatica

Sciatica is a nerve root irritation, which results in pain. Typically, this pain is felt from the low back and radiates down the thigh to the knee. The sciatic nerve begins in the lumbar spine area and extends through the buttocks. The most frequent cause is a herniated disc, which places pressure on the nerve causing irritation and oftentimes is at the L5-S1 nerve roots. Other causes include irritation of the nerve from tumors, adjacent bone, bleeding, infections, spinal stenosis, and trauma as examples.

Sciatica may cause pain (mild or sharp), a burning sensation, weakness, numbness or tingling with or without radiation down the leg. Mild sciatica usually goes away with time.

C. Disc Herniations

The spine, as described prior, is comprised of bones (vertebrae), which are cushioned by small oval disks. The annulus is the tough outer cover of the disk, and the soft inner layer is known as the nucleus. When a disk herniation occurs, a portion of the nucleus pushes through a tear in the annulus into the spinal canal. This can irritate a nerve and cause pain. Additionally, this can develop into numbness and weakness, and further cause numbness and weakness in the back or arms or legs.

The lumbar spine, which is commonly referred to as the lower back, is a common area for lumbar disc herniation. While many of these herniations do not cause significant symptoms, others require a range of conservative treatment through surgical intervention. Conservative treatment includes medications, exercises or physical therapy and possibly steroid injections. Surgical intervention has been found less effective in the group of patients who present with mild symptoms. The patients who report serious neurologic symptoms had a better response to surgery compared to nonsurgical treatment.[11] A nursing malpractice suit may involve an allegation of a disc herniation caused by a severe fall.

The following case is an example of the nurses' delay in communicating a change in neurovascular assessment, which resulted in paralysis.

A 57-year-old had a bilateral decompressed laminectomy for a pre-existing neck injury. Postoperatively he remained hospitalized for a week unable to move his legs. Emergency surgery was performed and revealed a small hematoma, which was impinging on the spinal cord. The plaintiff remained paralyzed from T8 (thoracic level 8) vertebra down. The plaintiff alleged he began experiencing difficulty moving his legs and had other symptoms of spinal cord progression on the day prior to the emergency surgery and the nurses failed to contact the physicians. There was a $1.5 million settlement.[12]

D. Caude Equine

While many patients are successfully treated at their physician office or even in the emergency room, others require an evaluation by either a neurosurgeon or an orthopaedic surgeon. Cauda equine syndrome is a rare disorder affecting the bundle of nerve roots (cauda equine) which is located at the lower end of the spinal cord and is a surgical emergency. If these patients do not get emergent attention, then permanent paralysis, impaired bowel or bladder control, and loss of sexual sensation can result.

Symptoms include:

- Bladder and/or bowel dysfunction (especially urinary retention), causing retained waste or incontinence.
- Severe or progressive problems in the lower extremities, including loss of or altered sensation between the legs, over the buttocks, the inner thighs and back of the legs (saddle area), area around the rectum, and feet/heels.
- Pain, numbness, or weakness spreading to one or both legs that may cause the person to stumble or have difficulty getting up from a chair.[13]
- Suspected spinal cord compression—Acute neurologic deficits may be present with cancer patients. Emergent evaluation is needed. The surgeon determines if surgical decompression or radiation therapy is needed.
- Progressive or severe neurologic deficit.

A nursing malpractice suit may be filed when warning signs of spinal compression are not detected or reported by a nurse to the appropriate physician.

TIP: Algorithms for approach to the patient with back pain have been developed by the American College of Physicians and the American Pain Society.

9.4 Fractures

"In the United States, approximately 5.6 million fractures occur yearly. Of these fractures, 10 percent have delayed healing. Of this 10 percent, 150,000 to 200,000 nonunions occur. Three percent of these involve long bone fractures."[14] Ten percent of fractures require secondary corrective surgical procedures due to some variant of healing post fracture or fusion. Discussion of delayed union and nonunions continues later in this chapter.

A. Open Versus Closed Fractures

A fracture is generally defined as a break or disruption in any part of the bone. Unlike other anatomical parts, such as heart tissue, bone heals. Fractures are generally classified as open (the bone is broken and has pierced the skin) or closed (the skin is intact). Fractures are confirmed by x-ray; the first nursing responsibility for patients with a fracture is to keep the site as clean as possible and immobilize the extremity to prevent further injury. Figure 9.5 is the classification of fracture by configuration.

There are many classification systems for grading the seriousness of fractures; the Gustilo and Anderson System is as follows:

- Grade I open fractures are described as having associated open wounds less than 1 cm with minimal soft tissue injury and a clean wound bed; these open fractures are generally thought to result from a sharp spike of bone penetrating the skin from inside to out.

- Grade II injuries have an open wound greater than 1 cm in length with a moderate associated soft tissue injury and with a moderately contaminated wound bed.

- Grade III open fractures generally have wounds greater than 10 cm in length; these injuries are further subdivided into:
  - Type A—with minimal stripping of the soft tissues surrounding the bone.
  - Type B—with extensive soft tissue stripping probably requiring a soft tissue flap to close or cover the wound.
  - Type C—with an associated major vascular injury.

Fractures can also be characterized by the type of fracture line. The type of fracture dictates the kind of pain the person will have, although it is safe to say most fractures are painful and require immediate medical attention. Figure 9.6 is a photo of an open grade 1 femur fracture. Figure

Fracture	Structure Involved
Transchondral	Involves cartilaginous surface of bone
Chondral	Surface of cartilage disturbed/torn
Osteochondral	Both bone and cartilage fractured
Closed	Bone does not communicate with skin surface
Open	Bone has protruded to surface of skin
Complete	Both cortical surfaces disrupted
Incomplete	Break in cortex does not extend through bone
Avulsion	Tearing soft tissue attachment from the bone
Comminuted	Greater than two fracture fragments
Impacted	Wedged/compacted bone fragments
Joint involvement	
• Intra-articular	Fracture extending into the joint
• Intracapsular	Fracture within joint capsule
• Extracapsular	Fracture extends outside capsule
• Supracondylar	Above condyle(s)
Types: transverse, oblique, spiral	

Figure 9.5 *Classification of Fracture by Configuration. Reprinted with permission by the National Association of Orthopaedic Nurses. All rights reserved.*

9.7 is the x-ray of the open grade 1 femur fracture. Figure 9.8 is a photo of the irrigation and debridement procedure performed in the operating room to cleanse the open femur fracture. Figure 9.9 is a x-ray of the ORIF (open reduction internal fixation) hardware used to fix the fracture.

There are a multitude of descriptions of fractures related to anatomic part, given that the human skeleton has 206 bones. In the forearm and wrist, there are 12 separate possible fractures, each named for a distinct part of the forearm and wrist. Some are common (Colles' fracture, which is a distal radial head fracture, resulting from a fall on an outstretched hand) and some very rare (Essex-Lopresti, which is another radial head fracture, with a distal radioulnar dislocation, resulting from perhaps a similar fall, but landing in a different direction).

It is easy to see, when considering the mechanism of injury that fractures cause pain. Fractures are caused by direct force, as in a crush injury, and so forth. Some are the result of intrinsic factors, such as energy-absorbing capacity, elasticity, fatigue, strength, size, and density. Within the nursing malpractice context, fractures may result from falls

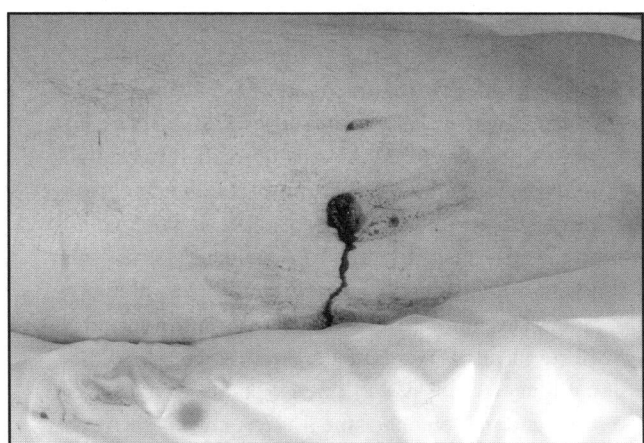

Figure 9.6 Open Grade I Femur Fracture

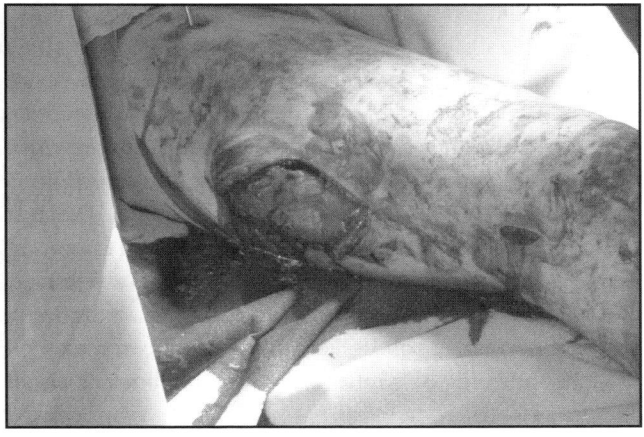

Figure 9.8 Photo of Irrigation and Debridement in the Operating Room

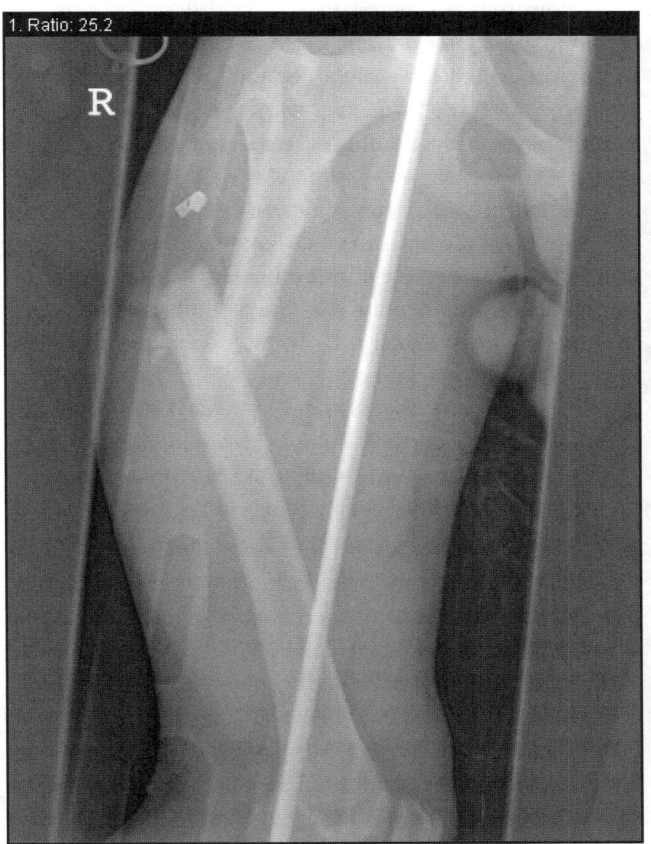

Figure 9.7 X-ray of an Open Grade One Femur Fracture

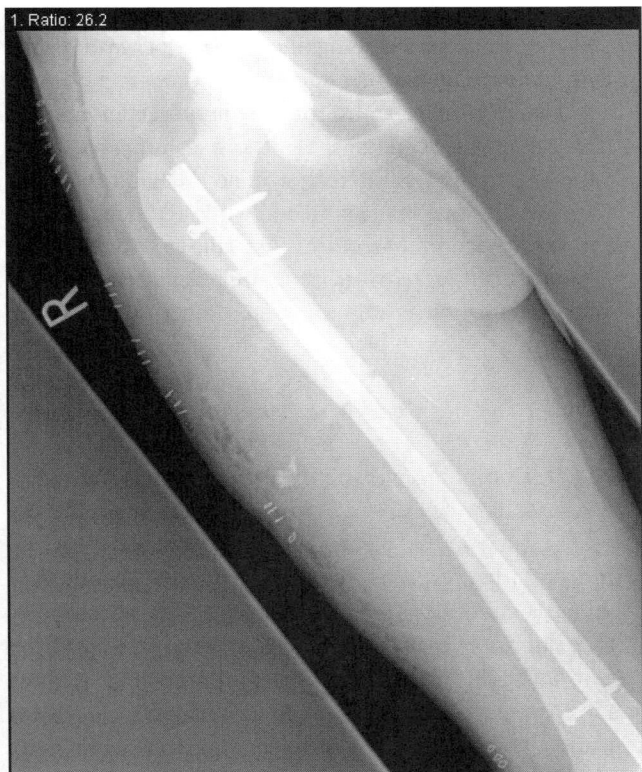

Figure 9.9 X-ray of ORIF (Open Reduction Internal Fixation) Hardware

resulting from failure to monitor or from being dropped by staff during transfer. Fractures of the hip, spine, and skull, in particular, can create devastating injuries.

Rarely do fracture injuries involve only bones without other associated injury. For example, a person who has been involved in a fall could easily have a fracture that impacts soft tissue, nerves, muscle, vessels, and tendons. Movement causes further pain, which is why patients with suspected fractures are kept in one place until the extremity can be immobilized with a splint. Fractures themselves are painful, but the concomitant soft tissue damage can be excruciating.

The following case reflects the potential impact of concomitant soft tissue damage:

> A 37-year-old man was injured when he slipped on ice in a shopping center parking lot. He alleged the icy patch was the result of overnight hosing in the loading dock area and that the parking lot was improperly maintained. He suffered multiple fractures to his right ankle and a torn meniscus. After undergoing four operations, he is now suffering from traumatic arthritis and likely will need ankle fusion surgery. He is no longer able to work as a delivery person but is employed in light construction. He had to give up his work as a volunteer firefighter and his position as a drummer in a band. This case settled for $425,000.[15]

A thorough neurovascular assessment can inform the clinician of the degree to which soft tissue and nerves are damaged. Depending on where the fracture is located, the bone shards can cause other damage to the body. Nerves can be severed in the mechanism of injury and clots can form from a fracture and cause pulmonary emboli. Unless bleeding is controlled, internal hemorrhage is a possibility if, for example, a fracture happens near an organ such as the spleen. Nurses have an important role in preventing fractures and the associated complications. They also provide patient education on fracture healing by encouraging a healthy diet and proper weight bearing (as ordered). Figure 9.10 shows the biologic and biomechanical inhibitors and stimulators associated with bone healing.

TIP: Soft tissue injury can cause swelling to the area, so documentation of the degree of swelling, along with a neurovascular assessment, is important.

The following case reflects the importance of a neurovascular assessment:

A ten-year-old girl, Maura, was riding her bicycle when she was thrown off the bike after hitting a pothole. Maura was transported emergently to the hospital where she was diagnosed with an open left radius/ulna fracture. She was immediately brought to the operating room for an irrigation and debridement. Postoperatively, a plaster cast was applied to her entire arm—wrist to shoulder. Maura complained and cried about the pain during the evening. The nurse assumed Maura's pain was in her lower arm. A postoperative assessment revealed capillary refill less than three seconds, intact sensation, and movement of the fingers. During the night shift, Maura's fingers swelled. Maura continued to complain of the pain. The nurse administered pain medication as ordered and elevated the hand onto pillows. By the morning, Dr. S evaluated Maura and found her cast "tight" on the proximal end of the cast—which was just below the shoulder. Additionally, Maura's fingers were more swollen and dusky. The cast was promptly removed and Dr. S diagnosed Maura with compartment syndrome. Dr. S assessed the pressures in Maura's arm and noted them to be elevated. Dr. S brought Maura to the operating room where he did a fasciotomy (release of the muscle compartments). The child required three additional trips to the operating room because of an extensive amount of necrotic tissue. Dr. S documented in the medical record, "I should have been contacted yesterday afternoon when Maura began with her pain complaints." This case settled for an undisclosed amount just after the depositions were taken (unpublished settlement).

It should never be assumed a patient's pain is actually in the location of the surgery. It is vital each nurse ask the patient for the location and intensity of the pain. The nurses did not communicate the noted changes to the physician. The physician testified that if he had been informed the day prior, he could have prevented the following sequelae.

TIP: The nurse should assess the edges of the cast to note smoothness, rough areas, or breaks in the integrity of the cast. A skin check is also done to see if there are areas of abrasions, redness, or swelling.

Bones have an amazing, and in some ways unique, characteristic: healing occurs through regeneration of tissue rather than scar tissue formation. For example, if a person has a heart attack, there is death to the tissue that does not regener-

Biologic and Biomechanical Inhibitors and Stimulators Associated With Bone Healing			
Inhibitors	**Associated Factors**	**Stimulators**	**Associated Factors**
Cigarette smoking	Nicotine causes vasoconstriction of microcirculation and inhibits angiogenesis.	Mechanical and electromagnetic forces	Satisfactory reduction of fracture; early mobilization; micromovement about fracture
Comorbid medical conditions, e.g., diabetes mellitus	Microvascular disease; peripheral vascular disease; prolonged hyperglycemia	Good vasculature supply; angiogenesis about site of healing bone	Collateral circulation
Nutritional status; excessive alcohol intake	Malnutrition; poor dietary intake of essential nutrients, vitamins/minerals	Sufficient essential nutrient and micronutrient intake	Antioxidant intake
Pharmacotherapy	Steroids, antiinflammatories (COX-1/COX-2); antineoplastics; bisphosphonates	COX-2; polypeptide skeletal growth factors: IGF, fibroblast growth factor, heparin binding growth factor; platelet derived growth factor (PDGF); Cytokines—ILs, TNF, BMP, colony stimulating factor (CSF); and statins and leptins	Systemic regulators, local activity modulated by alteration in synthesis, activation, receptor-binding, and other binding proteins
Rheumatoid arthritis and other autoimmune diseases	Autoantibodies and associated immunocompetence	Electromagnetic stimulation	Proper placement of pads, wires, and coils about bone healing site
Irradiation of soft tissues, bone, and organ structures	Excessive heterotrophic ossification about fracture or traumatized soft tissues	Genetic determinants	African American bone density greater vs. Caucasian and Asian; genetic and ethnocultural influences related to healing wounds and fractures
Hypogonadism; hypothyroidism, parathyroidism, and other endocrine disorders	Primary and secondary osteoporosis; menopause and andropause	Ankylosing spondyloarthropathies (pathologic conditions)	Increased bone density seen in osteopetrosis (marble bone disease); Albers-Schonberg disease; osteopoikilosis; the sclerotic phase of Paget's disease
Other associated factors: patient age, sex, and neurovascular injury about site of bone healing; patients' functional level; amount of soft tissue injury about site of bone injury	Older persons with comorbid medical conditions, the young, and the infirm	Age and general health status prior to bone injury	Healthy, nutritionally sound, active individuals who do not smoke or drink alcohol excessively tend to heal better

Figure 9.10 *Biologic and Biomechanical Inhibitors and Stimulators Associated with Bone Healing. Reprinted with permission by the National Association of Orthopaedic Nurses. All rights reserved.*

ate. Bone can heal if given the appropriate circulation to the fracture site and adequate immobilization. See Figure 9.10 for biologic and biomechanic inhibitors and stimulators associated with bone healing. Bone is dynamic tissue and can be classified as either cancellous (spongy) or cortical (compact). There are several factors that influence healing of fractures:

- the location of the fracture (did the bone have a good blood supply at the end of the bones?)
- immobilization
- the extent of the soft tissue damage
- the weight-bearing status of the bone

If the fracture is clean and set properly with either surgical repair or casting, the fracture will heal. Predisposing health issues can impair or delay the healing process; this topic is discussed later in the chapter.

B. Imaging

Radiographic studies are important early tools in the assessment of the orthopaedic patient, especially a trauma patient. Protocols generally require an x-ray of the cervical spine, chest, and pelvis on any patient with severe trauma. Care must be taken to prevent patients from moving until x-ray confirmation is completed. Nurses play an important role in reinforcing this with patients, families, and well-meaning witnesses at accident scenes. Cervical collars placed on the neck of a patient with a potential spine fracture must not be removed by a nurse without an order from a physician. X-rays are generally taken in two perpendicular planes to reduce the risk of a missed associated injury. See Figure 9.11 for views for x-rays. These are AP (anterior posterior) and lateral views of the femur, patella, tibia. Please refer to Figure 9.12 regarding x-ray projections, positioning and pathology. Also refer to Figure 9.13, radiographic classification of lower extremity fractures.

C. Modalities of Immobilization

1. Casts

The primary principle in fracture treatment is immobilizing the fracture in a manner that promotes healing, minimizes pain, and keeps the patient as mobile as possible. In general, a fracture is immobilized above and below the fracture site. For example, the cast on a fractured tibia would incorporate the ankle and the knee to prevent motion in the fracture. Casting is one mechanism of immobilization. A cast is an immobilizing device made up of layers of plaster or fiberglass (water-activated polyurethane resin) bandages molded to the body part that it encases. There are five purposes of casts:

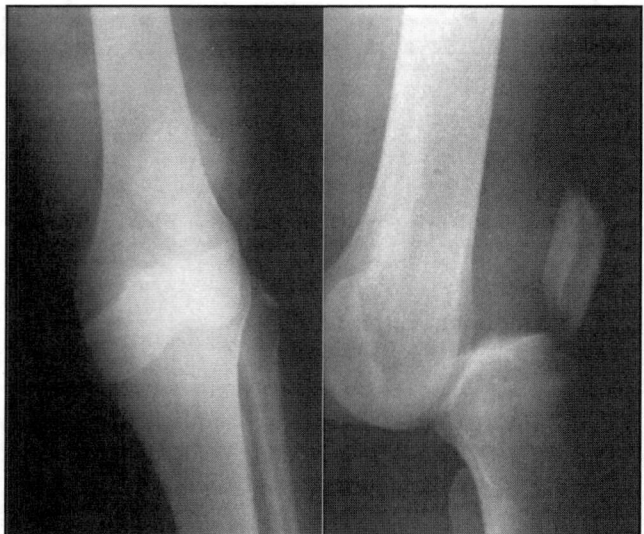

Figure 9.11 Views for X-rays—Anterior/Posterior (left); Lateral (right)

1. To immobilize and hold bone fragments in reduction
2. To apply uniform compression of soft tissues
3. To promote early mobilization
4. To correct and prevent deformities
5. To support and stabilize weak joints

Casts are categorized as short arm, short leg, long arm, and long leg, depending on the fracture. While they are heavy, they do provide comfort to individuals while the fracture heals. The healthcare provider can monitor the fracture healing through an x-ray of the extremity. Bone healing can be seen through a plaster cast. Casts are worn for four to eight weeks, depending on the healing process of the individual and the degree of the injury.

Complications can arise with casts if they are not monitored closely. Neurovascular compromise can occur due to positioning of the extremity or the pressure of the cast or splint applied. Pressure of the cast on neurovascular and bony structures can cause nerve palsies, pressure ulcers, and necrosis. These complications imply that the extremity is numb: has the feeling of "pins and needles" and is not only painful but also not functional. This might happen when something is put into the cast. A well-meaning adult might want to scratch an itch in the cast, and put a wire hanger in the cast that cannot be removed. Children are notorious for inserting small toys, pencils, or whatever will fit into a cast. The item can cause pressure and pain to the patient if not found in a timely manner. Part of the routine care of a patient with a cast is to educate the patient (and parents of the child patient) not to put anything down the cast.

		X-Ray Projections, Positioning, and Pathology		
Area	Projection	Patient Position	Radiographic Objective	Pathology Demonstrated
Hip	A-P (anterior-posterior)	Patient is supine with hips and knees extended and great toes touching medially.	To visualize the proximal femur and hemipelvis.	Fractures of the femoral head, neck, and intertrochanteric area.
	Lateral	Patient is supine with affected hip flexed 45 degrees and abducted 45 degrees.	To visualize the femoral head, neck, and hip joint space.	Fractures of the femoral head, neck, and intertrochanteric area.
		If a fracture of the hip is highly suspected, the affected hip is NOT manipulated. The opposite hip is flexed and a "shoot through" lateral view is taken.		
Femur	A-P	Patient is supine with hips and knees extended and great toes touching medially.	To visualize the entire femur, hip, and knee from A-P position.	Fractures of the femur.
	Lateral	Patient is lying in a lateral position with the area of interest closest to the table. The hip is in a true lateral position with the knee flexed. The opposite leg is extended and positioned posteriorly.	To visualize the entire femur, hip, and knee from lateral position.	Fractures of the femur.
		If a fracture of the femur is highly suspected, the affected hip is NOT manipulated. A "cross-table" lateral view is taken of the affected femur. This view very rarely will show the hip joint.		
Knee	A-P	Patient is supine with both hips and knees extended and great toes touching.	To visualize the distal femur, proximal tibia, and fibula from A-P position. The patella is identified anterior to the distal femur.	Fractures of the distal femur, proximal tibia, fibula, and patella.
	Lateral	Patient is lying in a lateral position with affected knee closest to the table and flexed about 30 degrees. The opposite hip is flexed and propped into position anterior to the affected knee.	To visualize the distal femur, proximal tibia, and fibula from lateral position. The patella is identified anterior to the distal femur.	Fractures of the patella, distal femur with intercondylar eminences, and tibial plateaus.
	P-A (posterior-anterior)	Patient is prone on the table with knees extended.	To visualize the knee, especially patella which is seen slightly superior and anterior to the knee joint. View of choice for suspected patella fracture.	Fractures of the patella, especially fractures of distal femur and proximal tibia and fibula.
	Internal oblique	Patient is supine with hips and knees extended. The foot of the affected leg is internally rotated 45 degrees.	To visualize the fibular head and its articulation with the tibia.	Fractures of the lateral tibial plateau, fibular head, and posterior lateral femoral condyle.
			To visualize the lateral tibial plateau and lateral femoral condyles.	

Figure 9.12 *X-ray Projections, Positioning and Pathology. Reprinted with permission by the National Association of Orthopaedic Nurses. All rights reserved.*

Fracture Area	Name of Classification	Radiographic Description	Possible Studies Indicated
Femoral neck	Garden's classification of femoral neck fractures (Garden, 1974).	**Stage I** – Fracture is incomplete or impacted. Bone trabeculation may remain intact within the inferior neck. **Stage II** – Complete fracture through the femoral neck without displacement. Trabeculation is disrupted by the fracture line but alignment is maintained. **Stage III** – Complete fracture through the femoral neck with partial displacement. **Stage IV** – Complete fracture with severe displacement of fracture fragments.	A-P of the pelvis for hips and a cross-table lateral of the injured hip. (An internal rotation A-P view may be valuable). MRI may be indicated for symptomatic hip with negative radiologic findings. The literature has indicated that MRI has identified fractures of the femoral neck within 24 hours of injury when plain films did not reveal this fracture (Koval & Zucherman, 1994).
Intertrochanteric	Evans' classification of intertrochanteric fractures (Evans, 1949).	**Type I** – The fracture line extends from the less trochanter superiorly and laterally in the direction of the greater trochanter. **Type II** – The fracture line extends from the lesser trochanter obliquely in an inferior direction.	A-P of the pelvis for hips and a cross-table lateral of the affected hip.
Subtrochanteric	Seinsheimer's classification of subtrochanteric fractures (Seinsheimer, 1978).	**Type I** – Nondisplaced fractures or with less than 2 mm of fracture fragment displacement. **Type II** – Two-part fracture. **Type IIA** – Transverse femoral fracture. **Type IIB** – Spiral fracture with the lesser trochanter attached to the proximal fracture fragment. **Type IIC** – Spiral fracture with the lesser trochanter attached to the distal fragment. **Type III** – Three-part fracture. **Type IIIA** – Spiral fracture with the lesser trochanter attached to the third fragment which also has an inferior spike of cortex. **Type IIIB** – Spiral fracture of the proximal femur with a third butterfly fragment. **Type IV** – Comminuted fracture with four or more fragments. **Type V** – Subtrochanteric-intertrochanteric fracture; any subtrochanteric fracture that extends through the greater trochanter.	A-P of the pelvis for hips and lateral of the affected hip.
Femoral shaft	Winquist's classification of comminution (Winquist & Hansen, 1980).	**Type I** – Minimal or no comminution at fracture site. **Type IIA** – A fragment is at the fracture site, but at least 50% of the circumference of the cortices of the two major fracture fragments is comminuted. **Type III** – 50%-100% of circumference of the two major fracture fragments is comminuted. **Type IV** – Fracture fragments have no cortical contact.	A-P and lateral of entire femur. X-ray evaluation of the hip for fractures of the femoral neck. X-ray evaluation of the femur distal to the fracture including the knee.
Supracondylar and intercondylar fractures	AO/ASIF classification of supracondylar femoral fractures (Ferkel et al., 1989).	**Type A** – A displaced fracture in the distal femoral metaphysis that does not involve the articulating surface of the distal femur. **Type B** – A minimally displaced or undisplaced fracture through the articulating surface of the distal femur. **Type C** – A comminuted intra-articular fracture of the distal femur.	A-P and lateral films including the hip. Tunnel x-ray view clearly shows the intercondylar region. Tomograms and CT scans demonstrate the position and placement of the fracture. Oblique views.
Tibial plateau	Moore's classification of fracture - dislocations of the knee (Moore, 1981).	**Type I** – The fracture line splits through the center of the intercondylar notch. **Type II** – The fracture line separates the entire intercondylar notch and a medial or lateral plateau from the tibia metaphysis. **Type III** – A portion of the rim of the medial or lateral plateau is completely avulsed. **Type IV** – A four-part fracture usually consisting of the medial plateau, the lateral plateau, the intercondylar notch, and the tibial metaphysis.	A-P and lateral views of the knee. If no fractures seen, oblique, tangential, or tunnel views may be required. MRI or isotope bone scan may be done to pinpoint the area of the fracture. Tomograms or computed tomograms may be used for depressed or displaced fracture measurements of the tibial plateau.
Patella	Described by radiologic appearance of fracture (Rockwood, Green, & Bucholz, 1991, p. 1765).	**Undisplaced** – Fracture line may be in any direction, but there is no separation of the fracture fragments. **Transverse** – Fracture line runs horizontally through the patella. Most common patella fracture. **Lower or upper pole** – Fracture of the most proximal or most distal 15%-20% of the patella. **Comminuted, undisplaced** – More than two fracture fragments that are in anatomic position. **Comminuted, displaced** – More than two fracture fragments that are out of place.	P-A and lateral and sunrise views. Arthrography studies or MRI may be used to identify marginal fractures or osteochondral fragments. Arthroscopy may be indicated for visualization of osteochondral fracture.

Figure 9.13 *Radiographic Classification of Lower Extremity Fractures. Reprinted with permission by the National Association of Orthopaedic Nurses. All rights reserved.*

Fracture Area	Name of Classification	Radiographic Description	Possible Studies Indicated
Patella		**Vertical (marginal)** – Longitudinal fracture through the patella that is usually the result of direct trauma. **Osteochondral** – Fracture from the articulating surface of the patella. May be associated with subluxation or dislocation of patella.	
Tibial shaft	Jonner's and Wruhs' classification of tibial shaft fractures (Johner & Wruhs, 1983).	**Type A** - "Simple" fractures induced by torsion or bending with spiral, oblique, or transverse patterns. **Type B** - "Butterfly" comminuted fractures induced by torsion or bending and compression. **Type C** - "Comminuted" multiple fracture fragments, usually induced by torsion, four-point bending, or crushing.	A-P and lateral views of the entire tibia and fibula, including the knee and ankle.
Distal tibia	Bourne's classification of pylon fractures (Bourne, 1989).	**Type I** - Undisplaced fractures of the distal tibia extending into the tibial plafond. **Type II** - Moderate comminution of distal tibia with moderate incongruity of articular surface. **Type III** - Grossly comminuted distal tibia with incongruity of articular surface.	A-P, lateral, and mortise views of the ankle. A-P and lateral tomography and CT to evaluate complex or comminuted fracture patterns. MRI is especially useful when plain films are negative.
Malleoli	A-O classification of malleolar fractures (Muller, Nazarian, & Koch, 1988).	**Type A** - Fracture of the fibula below the syndesmosis. **Type A1** - Isolated. **Type A2** - With a fracture of the medial malleolus. **Type A3** - With a posteromedial fracture. **Type B** - Fracture of the fibula at the level of the syndesmosis. **Type B1** - Isolated. **Type B2** - With a medial lesion (malleolus or ligament). **Type B3** - With a medial lesion and fracture of posterolateral tibia. **Type C** - Fracture of the fibula above the syndesmosis. **Type C1** - Diaphyseal fracture of the fibula, simple. **Type C2** - Comminuted fracture of the distal fibular diaphysis. **Type C3** - Fracture of the proximal fibula.	A-P, lateral, and mortise views of the ankle. Oblique views of the ankle.
Neck of the talus	Hawkins' classification of talar neck fractures (Hawkins, 1970)	**Type I** - Nondisplaced vertical fracture of the talar neck. **Type II** - Displaced fracture of the talar neck with subluxation or dislocation of the subtalar joint. **Type III** - Displaced fracture of the talar neck with dislocation of the body of the talus from the subtalar and ankle joints.	A-P, lateral, and mortise views. Tomography may be used to evaluate complex fracture patterns if CT is not available. CT demonstrates in detail the fracture patterns of comminuted, complex fractures. Provide multiplane imaging. MRI allows multiplane imaging without radiation. Especially valuable for evaluating osteochondral lesions of the talus when plain x-rays are negative. Bone scans are primarily used in evaluating osteochondral fractures and stress fractures.
Calcaneus	Essex-Lopresti's classification of calcaneal fractures (Essex-Lopresti, 1952). Sangeorzan's classification of navicular fractures (Sangeorzan, Benirschke, Mosca, Mayo, & Hanson, 1989).	**Extra-articular** – Fractures of the anterior process tuberosity, medial process, sustentaculum tali, and body. **Intra-articular** – Nondisplaced fractures, fractures of the tongue, joint depression, and comminuted fractures.	Lateral of the heel and A-P of the foot. Comparison views of the opposite heel. Axial view of the calcaneus best shows the tuberosity, body, and posterior facet. Oblique views of the calcaneus to subtalar joint involvement. CT scanning will identify displacement and comminution.
Navicular		**Type I** - A coronal place fracture with no angulation of the forefoot. **Type II** - Fracture line is plantar medial to dorsal lateral and forefoot is displaced laterally. **Type III** - Comminuted fracture with the forefoot laterally displaced.	A-P, lateral, and oblique views of the foot. Comparison views of the opposite foot. Magnification views. Bone scans, especially for stress fractures. CT to evaluate intra-articular fractures.

Figure 9.13 *Radiographic Classification of Lower Extremity Fractures. Reprinted with permission by the National Association of Orthopaedic Nurses. All rights reserved. (continued)*

Nurses are the primary users of medical devices in the direct care of patients in the acute care settings. They are responsible for understanding the rationale for the equipment as well as utilizing the equipment properly. Essential nursing knowledge about these devices is comprehensive and includes:

- understanding the patient problem requiring use of the device,
- demonstrating technical competence with the equipment,
- correlating data received from the devices with the patient's condition,
- selecting appropriate interventions based on the data,
- understanding how to intervene if malfunction occurs, and
- implementing safety precautions for both patient and nurse.[16]

The following is a case example:

The plaintiff was a 21-year-old male involved in a high-velocity motor vehicle accident. He sustained a right tibia and fibula fracture. The patient went to the operating room for an open reduction internal fixation procedure and was admitted to the orthopaedic floor. The admitting nurse documented that there was a minimal amount of swelling noted to the right toes and that the right foot had "pink warm toes with intact sensation." Further the nurse noted she could insert her fingers under the lip of the cast and feel a dorsalis pedis pulse. The nurse gatched (lifted the foot of) the bed and placed the right leg on two pillows. During this time, this patient rated his pain as a 5 out of 10 as he was using the Dilaudid PCA (patient-controlled analgesia pump) which was set at 0.8 cc every ten minutes with no basal rate. (The patient was not getting a continuous infusion of Dilaudid.) Two hours later, the nurse noted an increase in swelling of the toes and foot along with complaints of 10 out of 10 pain. This nurse contacted the anesthesiologist who ordered an increase in the PCA Dilaudid pump settings 1.2 cc every ten minutes with a basal dosage of 0.5 cc. Additionally, the patient was given Toradol 30 mg IV every six hours. Ice was applied to the toes and foot. The next nursing shift began at 7 P.M. and the nurse assessed the patient at 11 P.M. The patient

was "writhing in bed with 10/10 pain. He complained of numbness and tingling of his foot and an inability to move the swollen toes." The nurse was unable to assess the pulse as the space under the lip of the cast was swollen. This nurse administered a bolus of Dilaudid and administered the next dose of Toradol early. (The medication was not due until midnight.) This nurse phoned the anesthesiologist and explained that the patient was agitated and was experiencing difficulty sleeping. A sleeping medication was ordered as well as a bolus of Dilaudid. The orthopaedic resident evaluated the patient at 5 A.M. and found the patient without sensation to the foot. He determined there was so much swelling that this caused a compartment syndrome. Promptly, the orthopaedic resident removed the tight cast, evaluated the compartment pressures, phoned the orthopaedic surgeon and returned the patient to the operating room for a fasciotomy. The compartment pressures in all compartments were elevated. The anterior and lateral compartments were noted to be grey and dusky. This patient returned to the operating room for additional irrigation and debridements of the necrotic muscle and tissue. There was a confidential settlement. (Unpublished settlement.)

The nursing staff should have followed the nursing process by communicating these significant changes to the orthopaedic surgeon. While some facilities use the anesthesiology team to monitor and maintain pain control post surgery, it is important for the nursing staff to communicate adverse findings to the orthopaedic surgeon. In this case, the nurses on staff testified that they were unaware "tight casts could cause compartment syndrome." Also, the nurses explained that they were unaware the "extremity could swell so much." It is imperative nurses caring for orthopaedic patients understand the mechanisms of fractures and the application of casts.

2. Cast-Brace

Cast-braces are based on the concept that some weight bearing will assist the fracture in healing. These devices are a combination of a cast and a hinged brace, which promotes the formation of bone and provides a distribution of forces across the fracture site, promoting healing. They are usually applied once the initial edema and pain have subsided and there is evidence of fracture stability. The principle with cast-braces is to promote early motion of joints and ambulation.

3. Traction

There are essentially three kinds of traction—skin, skeletal, and manual, as defined below. Traction is a force applied to a specific direction. Six purposes of traction are:

1. To reduce and immobilize a fracture
2. To regain normal length and alignment of an injured extremity
3. To lessen or eliminate muscle spasm
4. To prevent deformity
5. To allow patients freedom to do some activities in bed
6. To reduce pain

Manual traction is used to reduce fractures prior to treatment or immobilization. A dislocated shoulder is sometimes reduced with manual traction. The healthcare provider pulls on the individual's arm, hopefully causing traction to return the shoulder to its normal anatomy. This type of injury happens with pitching, when the shoulder becomes separated due to the thrusting motion.

Skin traction is used for short-term traction to exert a small amount of traction on a fractured extremity. Patients who have hip fractures often have skin traction (called Buck's traction) while they await surgical repair. Skin traction provides temporary comfort to patients and can be removed and reapplied periodically. No more than five to eight pounds of traction are generally used with skin traction. This type of traction is also used on children, but the weight is less. Skin traction can cause skin blisters and necrosis (tissue death). The skin in the traction must be inspected periodically for any untoward reaction.

Skeletal traction is a force applied to a body part through fixation directly into or through bone by means of a metal pin or screw. This is rarely used now as technology has shown that taking patients to the operating room and fixating their fracture gets them up earlier, preventing many of the complications such as pneumonia, pressure ulcers, pulmonary embolism, renal calculi, foot drop, and so forth.

The following case demonstrates how the nurse's lack of knowledge caused a below-the-knee amputation.

Mrs. W was a 76-year-old woman admitted to the community hospital with a right femoral neck fracture dislocation. Due to Mrs. W's extensive cardiac history, it was determined she would require a full medical work up prior to bringing her to the operating room. She was then placed in five pounds of Buck's traction and admitted to a medical surgical floor. The patient was assigned to a new graduate nurse who thought this traction should not be removed. The nurse communicated with the other shifts: "Do not remove this Buck's traction." Additionally, the nurse thought she was to add five pound of weights per day. By the fifth day, it was noted by the orthopaedic surgeon that the patient had 25 pounds of weights on her leg and was appearing "lopsided in the bed." Over the course of the five days, Mrs. W complained of right leg pain and was regularly medicated. Mrs. W went to the operating room on the fifth day. The Buck's boot was removed; the surgeon and nurses noted there was necrotic skin and muscle on the heel of the right foot that continued posteriorly to the knee area. The Buck's boot was "so tight that there were marks into Mrs. W's skin which were actually pulling off the skin." After extensive surgeries, Mrs. W's right leg was amputated.

This new graduate nurse did not follow the nursing process by identifying the exact location, intensity, and duration of the pain of which Mrs. W complained. Also, the nurse failed to perform regular neurovascular assessments. Buck's traction can be loosened for skin assessment and care. The nurse explained that "she felt knowledgeable about the use of Buck's traction since she had worked with it once before." The nurse manager's files revealed the following: "This nurse needs a mentor since she does not ask questions." This case settled for an unpublished amount.

4. External fixation

External fixation is a method of fracture immobilization in which a system of percutaneous pins or wires is connected to a rigid external frame. It can be constructed in many different configurations and permits three plane corrections of deformities. It might be used in an open fracture, in which there is a high risk for infection. Fractures of the pelvis, fingers, and limbs are the most common sites stabilized by external fixators.

Pin tract infections may be complications of an external fixator. The risk of infection increases the longer the fixator is in place. Generally, the longer the fixator is in place, the higher the probability the pins can loosen. Loose pins must be reported to the physician and in some cases removed so that the pin tract infection does not lead to osteomyelitis, a serious bone infection. The medical literature does not support any one method of pin care treatment.[17] Please review Figure 9.14 for NAON evidence-based pin site care recommendations.

NAON Evidence-Based Pin Site Care Recommendations (2004)

1. Pins located in areas with considerable soft tissue should be considered at greater risk for infection.

2. At sites with mechanically stable bone-pin interfaces, pin site care should be done on a daily or weekly basis (after the first 48-72 hours).

3. Chlorhexidine 2mg/ml solution may be the most effective cleansing solution for pin site care.

4. Patients and/or their families should be taught pin site care before discharge from the hospital. They should be required to demonstrate whatever care needs to be done and should be provided with written instructions that includes signs and symptoms of infection.

Figure 9.14 *NAON Evidence-Based Pin Site Care Recommendations. Reprinted with permission by the National Association of Orthopaedic Nurses. All rights reserved.*

The fixator is applied under general anesthesia, and there is pain associated with the surgery. In the first few weeks of having the fixator, the patient experiences pain and needs to be medicated. Fixators may be worn for up to one year or until the pain subsides.

9.5 Complications

Prevention of complications is a hallmark of orthopaedic care. The team works hard to get orthopaedic patients mobile and ambulating, to prevent some of the complications of orthopaedic injuries. The hazards of immobility are fairly clear—staying in bed leads to pneumonia, pressure ulcers, weakness, urinary retention, increased heart rate, and so forth. Almost every system in the body has increased stress when one is immobile, leading often to pain. For example, pressure ulcers from staying in one position too long are painful and often preventable conditions. The major goal of the orthopaedic community is to prevent these complications. Some of the complications related to orthopaedic conditions are:

- Compartment syndrome
- Bone union problems
- Cast syndrome
- Limb length discrepancy
- Osteomyelitis
- Foot drop
- Deep vein thrombosis (DVT)
- Pulmonary embolism (PE)
- Fat Embolism Syndrome (FES)

Each of these complications is explained below.

A. Compartment Syndrome

Compartment syndrome is a true orthopaedic emergency. Progressive pressure within a confined space compromises the circulation and the function of tissues within that space. A compartment is enveloped by tough, inelastic fascial tissue, and when swelling of the muscles occurs, the fascia does not expand. Compartment syndrome can happen in either the upper or lower extremity, and the onset can be as short as two hours to as much as six days after an injury or incident.[18] There are three types of compartment syndrome:

- Acute—most prevalent, generally happens within a week (often sooner) after traumatic, high-energy injuries. Typical sites are fractures of the tibia, supracondylar humerus, and forearm. These areas have a relatively small amount of space for swelling.
- Chronic—due to exertion from exercise. Generally bilateral, leads to great pain, which is relieved once the individual rests.
- Crush syndrome—a manifestation of prolonged muscle compression and compartment syndrome. This is also referred to as rhabdomyolysis and is seen more in major traumatic injuries.

Refer to Figure 9.15 for potential causes of acute compartment syndrome.

TIP: It is important the nurse document the sequence of events when compartment syndrome is suspected, using correct times in the order the events occurred. Prompt diagnosis and treatment are vitally important. Appropriate neurovascular assessment must be carried out.

There are 46 anatomic compartments within the body, 36 of which are located in the extremities.[19] Muscle compartments of the leg are the most frequently involved, including the anterior, lateral, superficial posterior, and deep posterior.[20]

Potential Causes of Acute Compartment Syndrome

√   Fractures
√   Direct compartment trauma
•   Surgery
•   Venomous bites
•   Crush wounds
•   Postischemic swelling
•   Electrical injuries
√   Edema formation
•   Prolonged tourniquet time
•   Vascular obstruction
•   Thermal injuries
•   Excessive use
√   Coagulopathies resulting in bleeding into a
    compartment
•   Anticoagulant therapy
•   Hemophilia
√   Other causes
•   Constrictive dressings
•   Gas gangrene
•   Use of pneumatic antishock garments
•   Intravenous infiltration
•   Drug overdose

Figure 9.15 *Potential Causes of Acute Compartment Syndrome. Reprinted with permission by the National Association of Orthopaedic Nurses. All rights reserved.*

Nursing management of this condition requires the nurse pay attention to the patient's symptoms and report them. Orthopaedic nurses generally are the first to suspect compartment syndrome and need to be vigilant in both reporting and documenting findings. The symptoms are generally described as the six "P"s:

•   Pain—specifically progressive, intense pain not relieved with analgesia. The nurse must be attentive to this, and not judge the patient as a problem or label the patient as drug seeking. Pain on passive motion is likely due to muscle ischemia. The patient complains more if the provider dorsiflexes the foot or toes.
•   Paresthesia—the sensory component of the peripheral nerve becomes progressively ischemic; the patient will experience numbness and tingling.
•   Pallor—capillary refill is greater than 3 seconds.
•   Paralysis—a decrease in the blood supply to the muscles leads to progressive paralysis.

•   Pulselessness—a late, and the least-reliable, sign.
•   Pressure—an elevated pressure in a compartment.

Nurses who suspect compartment syndrome must call the physician immediately and loosen any dressing or confining material. A cast cutter should be available in case the provider chooses to remove the cast. There is a lack of consensus as to whether elevating the extremity increases the pressure to the compartment or further impedes circulation.

The diagnosis of compartment syndrome can be measured by an intracompartmental pressure monitor, which measures the pressure in the individual compartments. Normal pressure is 0-10 mm HG. Pressures above 30 mm HG are critical.

Treatment includes a fasciotomy done emergently in the operating room. This surgery relieves pressure by opening the skin and fascia surrounding the swollen compartment. Surgeons thoroughly evaluate the compartmental contents for signs of ischemia, or frank necrosis once the fascia is released. The released fascia and skin are not closed with sutures but are left open, and a bulky dressing is applied after the fasciotomy.

The extremity can be elevated to the heart level but not above. Additionally, ice packs should be avoided as this can constrict the blood vessels thus decreasing the blood flow to the area.

These patients often return to the operating room a few days later for an irrigation and debridement. Decision making at this time includes whether or not the wound should be closed or remain open. Sometimes wounds may remain open until the swelling decreases. Physicians determine if skin grafting is needed to cover the wound. Muscle flaps may be necessary if the wound is more extensive.

There can be medical-legal aspects relative to the diagnosis of compartment syndrome. Some clinical variables are associated with monetary recovery for the plaintiff.[21]

•   Physician documentation of abnormal finding on neurological examination but no action taken.
•   Poor physician communication.
•   Increased number of cardinal signs (pain, pallor, pulselessness, paralysis, or pain with passive stretching).
•   Increased time to fasciotomy—this was the most prominent risk factor for an indemnity payment.[22]

The following is an example of a delay in diagnosis of compartment syndrome:

Mr. V was a 58-year-old man admitted to the hospital for a left total knee replacement. Postoperatively he was placed on a CPM (continuous passive motion machine), which gently flexes and extends the leg. He arrived at the nursing unit at 7:15 P.M. It was the change in shift, and the 7 A.M.–7 P.M. nurse made the patient comfortable but did not formally admit the patient. The 7 P.M.–7 A.M. nurse was informed of Mr. V's arrival and did not evaluate the patient until 10:40 P.M. When the night nurse saw the patient, he complained of 10/10 (a pain scale of 0-10) pain. The night nurse increased Mr. V's PCA (patient-controlled anesthesia) Morphine and returned at midnight. Mr. V complained of 10/10 pain and numbness and tingling. Vital signs were taken—blood pressure 188/90 (the patient's baseline was 134/68), heart rate 110 (the patient's baseline was 80), respiratory rate 20, and temperature 100.4°F. The nurse reviewed the physician orders and again increased the PCA Morphine dose. By 2 A.M., Mr. V explained that his pain was 6/10, yet he had increased numbness and tingling. The nurse touched his foot and noted that it was cool. The nurse placed a blanket on the foot. By 5:30 A.M., the patient explained that "his leg was sleeping." The nurse touched the leg and noted that Mr. V did not have any sensation. She informed her charge nurse, who stated "the orthopaedic surgeon will be in soon and you can inform him then." The orthopaedic surgeon arrived at 7:20 A.M. and evaluated the patient. The orthopaedic surgeon was surprised to find Mr. V's leg wrapped in a blanket and the CPM machine on. He removed the blanket to find a discolored, mottled, cold, pulseless foot. Compartment pressures were measured—anterior 110; lateral 78; posterior 62, deep posterior 60. Mr. V was brought to the operating room immediately and a fasciotomy was done. Extensive necrotic muscle was noted.

Mr. V. required 12 surgeries and developed osteomyelitis. He was treated with long-term intravenous antibiotics and eventually had an above-the-knee-amputation. This case settled for a confidential amount. (Unpublished settlement.)

The medical records revealed there were neurovascular assessments performed initially in the recovery room but not on the floor. The last neurovascular assessment was documented at 5:10 P.M. The nursing staff failed to follow the physician orders of regularly performing neurovascular assessments. There were several objective factors that warranted communication to the orthopaedic surgeon: an elevation in the baseline vital signs; increase in pain unrelieved by the increased doses of PCA Morphine; and changes in assessment, i.e., a cold, mottled foot, numbness and tingling, and then a "sleeping leg." This nurse failed to advocate for her patient and failed to use the chain of command by recognizing the abnormal assessment and communicating the findings to the physician and nursing supervisor. As a result of this case, the hospital performed a "needs assessment" of its staff and determined that the facility needed to develop an educational plan for its staff. Every staff member on this unit attended inservices on "caring for the orthopaedic patient."

B. Bone Union Problems

Bone healing occurs in five phases—hematoma formation, granulation, callus formation, consolidation, and remodeling. It is beyond the scope of this chapter to discuss these; however, reasons bone may not have healed properly are addressed.

The following clinical complications (delayed union, nonunion, and malunion) are not always preventable. Nurses can assist patients by ensuring the patient eats properly and is as mobile as is prescribed.

1. Delayed union—bone takes longer to heal than average for the type of fracture. This occurs most commonly in the tibia and fibula, and the scaphoid. There is a continuation or increase in bone pain beyond a reasonable healing time. The healing has slowed but not completely stopped.
2. Nonunion—fractured bone fails to unite, causing pain at the fracture site. Nonunion relates to healing that has not taken place in four to six months.
3. Malunion—the fracture heals, but not in alignment, causing a deformity of the bone.

Causes of these altered healing processes include:

*   infection
*   inadequate fracture mobilization
*   inadequate blood supply to the fracture site
*   uncontrolled repetitive stress on the fracture site[23]

The following diagnostic tests may be utilized:

- Serial x-rays (to view callus formation)
- CT scans
- MRI

Figure 9.16 portrays a delayed union of a fracture. There are a variety of interventions used to aid the delayed union or nonunion. These include:

- bone grafting
- internal fixation
- external fixation
- electrical bone stimulation

The following case example portrays the education a legal nurse consultant provides:

Ms. T was a 27-year-old morbidly overweight smoker and regular intravenous drug user. She was also a diabetic involved in a pedestrian versus car accident. She had several orthopaedic injuries including an open left tibia and fibula fracture. The decision was made to amputate above the left knee after several hospitalizations and numerous surgeries. Ms. T heard from a neighbor that "she should not have needed her leg amputated—after all she just broke her leg." She sought the services of a plaintiff's attorney, who hired a legal nurse consultant (Levin) to review the medical records. It was determined Ms. T was having nonunions and malunions with her fracture healing. She developed osteomyelitis and was treated with months of intravenous antibiotics. Ms. T was noncompliant with her care and continued ambulating on her left leg despite being educated on "non-weight bearing status." This contributed to the delays in healing. Ms. T continued smoking and using IV drugs, which also exacerbated the poor healing. She was predisposed to difficulties with healing as she was a diabetic. The attorney and legal nurse educated Ms. T about her health issues and contributory factors. The attorney did not accept Ms. T's case.

C. Cast Syndrome

Cast syndrome (superior mesenteric artery syndrome) is a rare and potentially fatal sequellae of body cast application. It is thought to be caused by a hyperextension of the spine resulting in a lumbar lordosis, leading to compression of the third portion of the duodenum between the superior mesenteric artery and the aorta, posteriorly.

Symptoms include abdominal pain, distention, and vomiting. While a rare complication, it happens in children following body cast application after Harrington rod insertion for scoliosis. The treatment includes decompressing the abdomen and bowel with a nasogastric tube, and feeding the patient intravenously for three to four days.

Vigilant assessment of the patient's intake (fluid and food) and listening to the abdomen with a stethoscope for the presence of bowel sounds will prevent further progression of cast syndrome.

D. Limb Length Discrepancies

Limb length discrepancy may result from a severe fracture. A difference in length between the two upper extremities or the two lower ones can exist. The lower extremities are more problematic, as a change in the angle of the pelvis causes pain to the hips and knees from constant limping. The etiology of the discrepancy can be congenital, vascular, neurological, or due to a tumor, infection, or fracture.[24]

TIP: Leg length discrepancy can cause an abnormal gait, possible back pain, and degenerative joint disease. It can be a potential complication postoperatively due to infection, muscle weakness, neurovascular insufficiency, or peroneal nerve injury. This can be remedied by the patient wearing a shoe lift or an orthosis to compensate for the discrepancy.

In general, limb length discrepancies less than 2 cm warrant no treatment. Bone age is performed at the time of the limb length discovery to predict the remaining growth. The physician will discuss treatment options with the patient which may include limb lengthening on the affected side or limb shortening on the opposite side.

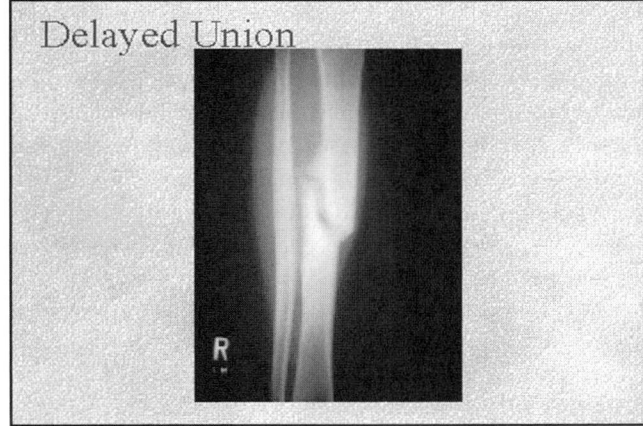

Figure 9.16 Delayed Union of a Fracture

E. Osteomyelitis

Osteomyelitis is a severe pyogenic infection of the bone and surrounding tissues that requires immediate treatment. Pyogenic means it is infected, or septic, and pus-producing. This infection is transmitted in one of three ways:

1. Through the bloodstream
2. Through an adjacent soft tissue injury
3. By direct introduction of the causative microorganism into the bone

Osteomyelitis occurs in neonates, children, and adults for different reasons. In children under the age of three, the causative organism is Haemophilus influenza, and over age five, the causative organism is generally Staphylococcus aureus. These patients often undergo surgical intervention, long-term intravenous antibiotics (four to eight weeks), and have wounds that are painful, non-healing, and often draining. There may also be tenderness to the area, as well as muscle spasm. Osteomyelitis is a late complication of a stage IV sacral pressure ulcer, when the tissue damage invades the bone. It is difficult to eradicate and can necessitate weeks of intravenous antibiotics, and sometimes aggressive surgery to trim off the bone.

Prevention is of paramount importance. All healthcare workers, the patient, and the family are encouraged to use good handwashing techniques as well as infection control principles when working with any patient who has an orthopaedic injury. Unfortunately, this can be a long-term problem, involving impaired mobility, pain, impaired skin integrity, depression, and fear.

F. Foot Drop

Foot drop is a disorder of the distal aspect of a lower extremity. This impairment is a malfunction of either a peripheral nerve or a part of the central nervous system. For example, a patient developed foot drop after receiving as many as 60 intramuscular injections in her buttocks. A large collection of blood resulted from these injections due to the blood thinners being administered to the patient. The nurses did not question the use of intramuscular medication, which was contraindicated. This case was settled.

Foot drop is also known as peroneal nerve disorder or palsy. The peroneal nerve is a section of the sciatic nerve; pressure on the peroneal nerve can cause foot drop. The peroneal nerve can be injured during surgery (for example, total hip arthroplasty or disc injuries) or with prolonged bed rest since it is located superficially near the side of the knee.

The following is an example of a peroneal nerve palsy complication which occurred after a total knee replacement:

Mrs. Hirsch, a 67-year-old woman, had a left total knee replacement. After surgery, she was placed in the CPM (continuous passive motion machine) range 0-30 degrees and gradually increased to 60 degrees. The physician requested the patient use the machine two hours at a time for a total of three times daily. The nursing staff kept the patient in the machine for 18 hours. The patient complained of pain to the left lateral aspect of her leg. The physician assessed Mrs. Hirsch the next morning and noted a red mark to the left leg. The knob of the CPM machine was pressing on the peroneal nerve area and caused a permanent foot drop. This case settled for a confidential amount.

Foot drop results in lifestyle changes. Simple things like driving become challenging, as patients no longer have the ability to move the foot up and down—it is generally in a drooping position. Patients can wear a brace to bring the foot into a normal or neutral position, but this is a serious life-changing event. The brace does not improve nor cure the functional impairment.

G. Deep Vein Thrombosis

Patients who have orthopaedic surgery or any kind of trauma are at high risk for deep vein thrombosis (DVT). A thrombosis is a blood clot, and much like the fat emboli, it travels through the bloodstream to the lung, causing a pulmonary embolus. Awareness is heightened with hip and knee surgical patients as they have an increase risk of developing a deep vein thrombosis.

Dr. Robert Virchow, a nineteenth century pathologist, was the first person to recognize that blood clots on the pulmonary artery begin as venous thrombi elsewhere. He stated, "The detachment of larger or smaller fragments from the end of the softening thrombus which are carried along by the current of blood and driven into remote vessels gives rise to the very frequent process on which I have bestowed the name Embolia." This was the beginning of Virchow's triad which includes:

- hypercoagulability,
- stasis, and
- injury to the wall vessel[25]

Figure 9.17 demonstrates risk factors for development of deep vein thrombosis. Early ambulation and mobility are key in prevention of DVT. There are several modalities to prevent DVT, with little consensus in the medical community as to the best course of prevention and treatment. Generally, the medications used are aspirin, Coumadin, or low molecular heparin. The surgeon decides the treatment modality. Several issues contribute to the preference—what the surgeon is accustomed to using, what has worked for him in the past, patient selection and compliance, and the home care situation of the patient. For example, if the patient takes Coumadin, he needs blood drawn daily to determine blood level. This may be impractical for some patients. Other patients are taught to do self injection of low molecular heparin and need their blood drawn weekly. The discharge plan for the patient must consider several factors.

Mechanical devices, such as antiembolic stockings (like elastic bandage quality); sequential compression devices which help pump blood in the veins back up to the heart; and foot pumps, which do the same thing, are used while the patient is in bed. Once the patient is up and walking, the foot pumps and sequential compression devices are usually discontinued. The antiembolic stockings may still be worn, but their efficacy in returning blood to the heart is limited at that point.

Deep vein thromboses can be painful. Warm, moist heat and elevation of the extremity and analgesics are usually prescribed by the physician.

Nursing liability is associated with:

- failure to follow physician orders to ambulate the patient
- failure to report signs of a deep vein thrombosis
- failure to implement orders for anti-thrombotic measures
- medication errors resulting in under or over coagulation

H. Pulmonary Emboli

Pulmonary embolism refers to the obstruction of one or more pulmonary arteries by a thrombus (clot) most often originating in the deep veins of the legs or the right side of the heart. There are many risk factors associated with pulmonary emboli:

- Immobilization
- Obesity
- Varicose veins
- Trauma
- Pelvic fractures
- Lower extremity (especially hip fractures)
- History of thromboembolic disease
- Pregnancy
- Postoperative patients
- Elderly patients

Risk Factors for the Development Of Deep Vein Thrombosis

- Obesity
- Age (greater than 60)
- History of cardiac disease (atrial fibrillation, rheumatic heart disease, hypertension, myocardial infarction, or congestive heart failure)
- Cigarette smoking
- Use of oral contraceptives
- Immobility
- Chronic pulmonary disease
- Carcinoma
- Varicose veins
- Prior deep vein thrombosis or pulmonary embolism
- Trauma or surgery involving pelvis, hip, or knee (especially hip fractures)

Figure 9.17 *Risk Factors for the Development of Deep Vein Thrombosis. Reprinted with permission by the National Association of Orthopaedic Nurses. All rights reserved.*

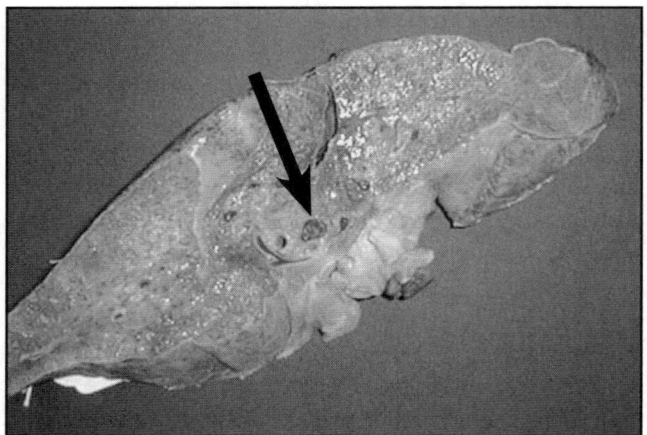

Figure 9.18 *A Fatal Pulmonary Embolism*

Figure 9.18 shows a fatal pulmonary embolism in the middle of the lung.

These patients suffer chest pain, difficulty in breathing, and a tremendous amount of apprehension. Some patients report a feeling of impending doom. This too is considered an orthopaedic emergency and requires critical intervention. Sculco and colleagues[26] report that the fatality rate for post-operative-related pulmonary embolus can be lowered to less than 0.1 percent if the following three things are done:

1. Collective use of predeposited autologous blood
2. Expeditious operative technique, getting patients to the operating room more quickly to avoid clots forming while immobile
3. Early mobilization after surgery

Nursing liability is associated with failure to:

- recognize sudden changes in a patient's condition
- administer anticoagulants as ordered
- report abnormal clotting times or symptoms of a pulmonary embolus to the prescriber

I. Fat Embolus Syndrome

Fat embolism occurs after trauma or long bone fractures and is a major cause of morbidity and mortality. Fat emboli are small collections of fat globules that travel from the marrow of the bone through the bloodstream to the patient's lung.

Restlessness, anxiety, confusion, irritability, and disorientation may be the first signs of fat embolism syndrome. It is important for nurses caring for trauma patients, especially those with long bone fractures such as the femur, to notice the signs of restlessness and irritability; sometimes they are confused with pain. In about 50 percent of the patients, petechiae (tiny hemorrhages in the skin) will be found. Young

adults (ages 20 to 30) and older adults (ages 60 to 70) with multiple fractures, long bone fractures, or pelvic fractures are particularly susceptible to development of fat emboli.

The exact mechanism of how this occurs is not well understood. The mortality rate ranges from 5 to 15 percent.[27] The patient is acutely ill, has difficulty breathing, and can possibly die. Treatment is generally preventative—stabilizing fractures as soon as possible. Primary supportive interventions include oxygen therapy (intubation if necessary), fluid volume replacement, airway management, and although controversial, steroid therapy. Oftentimes this patient population is transferred to the intensive care unit setting.

9.6 Discharge Planning for the Orthopaedic Patient

Discharge planning should begin upon admission. Many hospitals have nursing case managers who facilitate the discharge plans. Case management (done to promote quality cost effective outcomes) is a collaborative process of assessment of, planning of, facilitation of, and advocacy for options and services to meet an individual's healthcare needs through communication and available resources.[28] Patients are being discharged from the hospital at earlier stages of recovery. Some patients are transferred to rehabilitation centers while others are being discharged home. Some patient conditions require more acute and intense nursing care. The case manager or nursing staff collaboratively identify services needed by the patient. The discharge process is important to the patient's recovery because this is when the nurse and the case manager educate the patient and the family about the discharge plan. Patients need education and directions to adequately care for themselves after discharge. Proper discharge planning significantly reduces complications and enhances patient recovery.

The discharge plan for home may include:

- Prescriptions for medications with education
- Equipment—such as a cane, walker, or crutches
- Follow-up appointments
- Visiting nurses care
- Physical therapy, occupational therapy, or both
- Education on topics such as signs and symptoms of infections
- Suggestions for when to contact the physician

If the patient is being discharged with anticoagulation, the patient needs information about the medication and adverse effects. If the patient is being discharged with injection anticoagulation, it is vital the patient be educated on the use and delivery of the medication. Proper technique and return demonstration are important. Nursing liability is associated with failing to provide discharge instructions, giving incorrect advice, failing to make appropriate referrals, and failing to evaluate comprehension of patient education.

9.7 Conclusion

While the musculoskeletal system is complex, it has the amazing capacity to heal. Fractures can heal, and with careful medical management and nursing care, patients can get back to their optimal level of functioning. Orthopaedic healthcare providers have the privilege to work with patients across the lifespan and help them to get to a functional level.

Complications do occur, but the focus of both medical care and nursing care is prevention of these complications. As both pharmaceutics and technology improve, orthopaedic care, along with early ambulation, outcomes will improve.

Endnotes

1. Salmond, S., "Orthopaedic Wellness," In *Orthopaedic Nursing*, Third edition, eds. A. Maher, S. Salmond, and T. Pellino. Philadelphia: W. B. Saunders, 2002.

2. United States Bone and Joint Decade. http://www.us-bjd.org/patients_public/index.cfm.

3. http://www.orthonurse.org.

4. http://www.orthonurse.org/about/mission.cfm.

5. Joint Commission on Accreditation of Healthcare Organizations. *Ambulatory Care sentinel event statistics.* June 24, 2003. www.jointcommission.org.

6. Wong, D., J. Herndon, and T. Canale. "Medical Errors in Orthopaedics: Practical Pointers for Prevention," *American Journal Bone Joint Surgery* 84-A, no. 11 (November 2002): 2097–2100.

7. Laska, L. (ed.), "Failure of Nursing Staff to Timely Notify Surgeon Regarding Adverse Back-Surgery Sensation and Pain Symptoms—Cauda Equina Syndrome From Hematoma Causes Permanent Neurologic Deficits—1.36 million settlement in North Carolina," *Medical Malpractice Verdicts, Settlements and Experts* (June 2002).

8. Deyo, Ram Mirza, SK, Martin, BI. Back pain prevalence and visit rates: estimates from U.S. national surveys, 2002, Spine 2006; 31:2724.

9. Katz, JN. Lumbar disc disorders and low back pain: socioeconomic factors and consequences. J. Bone Joint Surg AM 2006; 88 Suppl 2:21.

10. "Lower Back Pain Fact Sheet. nih.gov." http://www.ninds.nih.gov/disorders/backpain/detail_backpain.htm. Retrieved 20010-May 20.

11. Contemporary Management of Symptomatic Lumbar Disc Herniations, Orthopaedic Clinics of North America 2010 (41) p. 222

12. Laska, L. (Editor), "Failure to Report Symptoms of Spinal Cord Compression Timely Blamed for Paralysis," *Medical Malpractice Verdicts, Settlements, and Experts*, February 2009, page 18.

13. Caude Equine Syndrome. http://orthoinfo.aaos.org/topic.cfm?topic=A00362. accessed 2010, May 23.

14. Williamson, V., *Management of Lower Extremity Fractures*, 421. Pitman, New Jersey: Anthony Janetti, 1998.

15. Mooney, N. E., "Pain and Suffering in Orthopaedics," In Patricia W. Iyer (ed), *Medical Legal Aspects of Suffering,* Tucson, Arizona: Lawyers and Judges Publishing Co., 2003.

16. Phieffer, L. S. and J. A. Goulet, "Delayed unions of the tibia," *The Journal of Bone and Joint Surgery* 88-A, no. 1 (2006): 205–216.

17. McConnell, E. A., "How and what staff nurses learn about the medical devices they use in direct patient care," *Research in Nursing Health* 18 (1995): 165–171.

18. Holmes, S. B. and S. J. Brown, "Skeletal pin site care: National Association of Orthopaedic Nurses guidelines for orthopaedic nursing," *Orthopaedic Nursing* 24, no. 2 (March-April 2005): 99–107.

19. Levin, B. and N. Morris, *NAON Core Curriculum of Orthopaedic Nursing,* Complications, 2006.

20. *Id.*

21. Bhattacharya, T. and M. Vrahas, "The Medical-Legal Aspects of Compartment Syndrome," *The Orthopaedic Forum* 86-A, no. 4 (April 2004): 864–868.

22. *Id.*

23. Levin, B. and N. Morris. *NAON Core Curriculum of Orthopaedic Nursing*, Complications, 2006.

24. Child, S., "Stimulators of Bone Healing," *Orthopaedic Nursing* (November-December 2003): 421–428.

25. Follman, D. and A. Maher, "Assessment of the Musculoskeletal System," in *Orthopaedic Nursing*, by A. Maher, S. Salmond, and T. A. Pellino, 159. Philadelphia: W. B. Saunders, 1994.

26. Dalen, J., "Pulmonary Embolism: What Have We Learned Since Virchow?" *Chest* 4 (October 2002).

27. Sculco, T. P., C. W. Colwell, V. D. Pellegrini, G. H. Westrich, and F. Bottner, "Prophylaxis against Venous Thromboembolic Disease in patients having total hip or total knee arthroplasty," *Journal of Bone and Joint Surgery* 2, no. 84 (March 2002): 466–477.

28. CMSA guidelines, http://www.CMSA.com.

Chapter 10

Subacute and Long-Term Care Nursing Malpractice Issues

Patricia W. Iyer, MSN, RN, LNCC, Gloria Blackmon, BSN, RN, LNHA, and
Georgette Bieber, RNC, LNCC[1]

Synopsis
10.1 Introduction
10.2 Subacute Care
10.3 Overview of Long-Term Care
    A. Settings and Populations
    B. Roles and Responsibilities in Long-Term Care
        1. Medical Director
        2. Director of Nursing (DON)
        3. Registered Nurse
        4. Licensed Practical Nurse
        5. Certified Nurses Aide
    C. Vulnerabilities Due to Sensory Changes
        1. Visual changes and the elderly
        2. Hearing changes and the elderly
        3. Taste changes and the elderly
        4. Sense of smell changes and the elderly
        5. Sensation, skin and tissue changes and the elderly
        6. Balance and dexterity changes and the elderly
    D. Dementia
10.4 Staffing and Retention
    A. Staffing
    B. Retention
10.5 Litigation Trends
10.6 Compliance with the Standard of Care
    A. State, Federal, and Professional Standards
    B. Surveys of Facilities
10.7 Review of the Nursing Home Clinical Record
    A. Minimum Data Set
    B. Resident Assessment Protocol
    C. Resource Utilization Groups
    D. Quarterly and Annual Reassessments
    E. The MDS and Change of Condition
10.8 Liability Issues
    A. Assessment and Care Planning Process
    B. Falls
    C. Side Rail Use
    D. Burns
    E. Abuse, Neglect, and Assaults of Residents
        1. Abuse
        2. Neglect
        3. Assaults by residents
        4. Sexual assaults
    F. Pressure Ulcers
        1. Regulations
        2. Case

        3. Controversies
            a. Licensed practical nursing role
            b. Prescriptive privileges
            c. Avoidable versus unavoidable
            d. Arterial or venous
            e. Terminal ulcer or substandard care
        4. Products
    G. Wandering and Elopements Resulting in Injury
        1. Liability risks associated with wandering
        2. Cases relating to injury caused by wandering
    H. Failure to Recognize a Change in Condition
    I. Medication Errors
10.9 Defense of the Long-Term Care Case
    A. Overview
    B. Defense Theories
        1. Right to refuse care
        2. Preexisting illness or disputing the proximate cause
        3. The injury was not foreseeable
        4. The standards of care were followed
10.10 Summary
Endnotes
Additional Reading

10.1 Introduction

Although long-term care used to refer only to nursing home care, today it is delivered in a variety of settings. Long-term care may take place in assisted living or in other types of creative programs that utilize a continuum of care for the older adult, in addition to an individual's own home. The type of care provided in long-term care has changed. In addition to custodial care, many nursing homes are now providing subacute care and rehabilitation services.

According to the American Association of Retired People (AARP), which collected information in 2009 about the growing older population, there are ten key findings that affect provision of long-term care services:

1.   The population age 85 or old—the age group that is most likely to need long-term care services—is growing at a dramatic rate.

2. The older population is more racially and ethnically diverse than ever before.

3. The older population is financially and socially diverse.

4. Family caregivers are the main providers of long term care services in all states.

5. Older people with disabilities have a growing array of service options, but the services are costly and can deplete life savings of older households.

6. Nursing facility residents, beds, and occupancy rates have remained nearly constant over the last five years, despite an increase in older population.

7. The bulk of Medicaid long term care dollars go to nursing homes rather than home and community-based services.

8. The number of older people and adults with physical disabilities receiving Medicaid-funded home and community-based services has increased over the past five years.

9. Long term care spending is not the primary cause of Medicaid spending growth.

10. On average, Medicaid dollars can support nearly three older people and adults with physical disabilities in home and community-based settings for every person in a nursing facility.

Clearly, the nursing home care is expensive and the quality of care delivered in long-term care and subacute beds affects a large portion of the population either directly (as patients) or indirectly (as relatives of patients). With the aging of the baby boomers, it can be anticipated that this level of care will become a more important factor in health care.[2]

Nursing home cases are litigated by medical malpractice attorneys, nursing home litigation attorneys, and elder law attorneys. Nursing home litigation cases require specialized knowledge, as well as a considerable investment of time and financial resources.[3] This chapter touches on an area of liability that has grown since the previous edition of this text: nursing home care.

10.2 Subacute Care

Subacute care, also called postacute care, is simultaneously a new and an old concept. It is new in the hospital setting, but has long been provided in the long-term care facility as "skilled nursing." Subacute care in hospitals sprang up as a result of the push that began in the early 1980s to discharge patients more quickly from hospitals. This led to the "quicker and sicker" phenomenon: discharging a patient after a short time in the hospital, which results in a patient going home ill and potentially being readmitted to the hospital in

a relatively short period of time. This created a demand for a setting that could provide care when the patient's needs are too complex to be managed at home or in a traditional long-term care setting which provides supportive care only. Examples of the type of patients cared for in a subacute care setting are shown in Figure 10.1.

TIP: Subacute care may be provided either in a hospital in beds that have been converted to subacute status, or in a nursing home staffed with a sufficient number of registered nurses who have been prepared to care for patients with higher requirements for nursing care.

Little has been written in the risk management literature on the risks associated with subacute care. The risks associated with providing subacute care affect hospitals, long-term care facilities and long-term care hospitals. These risks center primarily on the ability of the facility to provide the appropriate level of care with staff who have been educated to manage the complex needs of the residents. Patients in subacute care units tend to be younger than those in usual long-term care units. Many subacute units refer to their clients as "patients" since they are being treated and are expected to be discharged as opposed to the long-term clients who live in the facility. Injurious falls are a common source of injury. An award could therefore be higher because of the economic losses sustained by an employed individual or one with responsibilities for dependent children.

- Postoperative
- Chemotherapy
- Total parenteral nutrition
- Complex wounds
- Intravenous therapy
- Dialysis
- Tube feedings through the nose or stomach
- Recovery from stroke
- Rehabilitation after an amputation
- Work conditioning
- Pain management
- Long-term ventilator therapy
- Head injuries
- Hospice care for terminally ill patients
- AIDS
- Need for suctioning through the nose, mouth or tracheostomy

Figure 10.1 Types of Patient Conditions and Treatments that are Appropriate for Subacute Care

TIP: Hospitals can incur liability risks by failing to recognize the type of nursing care that is required by the subacute patient and by staffing a subacute nursing unit with an insufficient number of trained staff. Registered nurses are essential for guiding the care provided by licensed practical nurses and unlicensed assistive personnel.

There are a relatively small number of acute long-term care hospitals (LTACH) or designated sections of general acute-care hospitals known and licensed as long-term care hospitals. These hospitals provide long-term subacute care, are exempt from the DRGs (diagnostic related groupings), and have an average length of stay over 25 days.[4] In most states LTACHs are required to meet the acute-care hospital regulations of the state in which they are located as well as the Medicare and Medicaid certification requirements. These hospitals generally specialize in some type of subacute care such as ventilator care or wound care.

Attracted initially by the economics of the reimbursement for subacute care, owners of long-term care facilities have been in the subacute care market for many years. Depending on the state nomenclature, subacute units or post-acute units are sometimes called skilled nursing units. In order to successfully and safely provide safe nursing care, the subacute care nursing staff must be able to manage the technology and multiple medical problems of residents in these types of units.

Sources of liability for subacute care in the long-term care facility are shown in Figure 10.2. Long-term care facilities that have converted some of their beds to subacute ones is increasingly recognizing the added risks associated with providing the higher level of care required by these residents. Staff nurses who provide subacute care need a blend of acute care and long-term care skills. Since a physician is not always on the premises of a subacute care unit, the nurses need excellent physical assessment skills, the ability to prevent and recognize complications, and good clinical judgment concerning when to contact the physician. Many long-term care facilities are hiring nurses from the acute care arena and teaching them how to function in a long-term care setting. The nurses learn how to involve the patient and family in care planning, perform the extensive documentation required in long-term care, and act more independently without an on-site physician. The addition of advanced practice nurses and physicians assistants has enhanced the long-term care facility's ability to provide the additional medical management needed in the subacute setting. The line that divides subacute care and acute care will continue to blur as subacute care becomes more and more acute.

1. Lack of physicians on site to manage medical problems as they arise
2. Inadequate education of the staff to care for patients with subacute needs
3. Failure to establish standards of care for the subacute patient
4. Lack of appropriate specialized equipment such as machinery, suction and oxygen built into the wall
5. Accepting a patient with a higher level of nursing care need than can be accommodated in the facility
6. Failure to respond to an emergency situation
7. Medication and treatment errors
8. Lack of appropriate observation of residents
9. Failure to institute a falls prevention program
10. Failure to question inappropriate medical orders

Figure 10.2 *Sources of Liability for Subacute Care Provided in Nursing Homes*

TIP: The attorney who is researching subacute care cases may not find it easy to locate cases labeled as "subacute care." As subacute care units become more widespread, the case law will begin to identify cases as having occurred in a subacute care unit. The case write up may refer to a short-term stay for rehabilitation care.

10.3 Overview of Long-Term Care
A. Settings and Populations

In addition to community-based programs that provide care for a specific population of individuals, long-term care settings consist of "rest homes," assisted-living facilities, nursing homes (also called nursing facilities), and long-term care hospitals. The continuing care retirement community (CCRC) combines independent living with other levels of care (usually assisted living and nursing home) and offers the older adult the opportunity to age in place and stay within the same community as her medical and nursing needs change. Those living in long-term care facilities are called "residents" to emphasize that the facility is their home and to foster the community relationship. The vast majority of residents who are admitted for true long-term care are elderly. Thus, in addition to the admitting diagnoses, the defining difference between subacute and long-term care is often the age of the individual.

Although long-term care facilities provide mainly custodial care, as opposed to the care provided in acute and subacute units, there has been a notable change in the nature of the residents who are admitted to long-term care. Because medical science has been able to add years to life, the residents of today's nursing home are older and have more chronic diseases than their counterparts of 20 years ago. They are living long enough to become demented and to develop the debilitating effects of degenerative diseases. While people used to come to long-term care facilities for residential and personal care, today the majority of residents require assistance in many of their activities of daily living (ADLs) and a large percentage are incontinent.[5] This change in resident population, along with increasing regulations and declining reimbursement, has presented major challenges for staff in long-term care.

Simultaneously, nursing homes are caring for younger people who have chronic problems requiring short- and long-term rehabilitation or other special needs such as tube feeding.[6]

A growing number of progressive homes strive to create a nursing home environment that honors residents' wishes and dignity through elimination of restrictive visiting hours, and provision of opposite sex roommates and individualized care. Many such settings have residents living in households or neighborhoods that have 10 to 30 people, their own communal kitchen and living room, and not in rooms lined up in hospital-like corridors anchored to nursing stations. Residents often wake up when they wish and have a breakfast made to order. Residents are active participants in their care. Consistency in assignments enables staff to detect subtle changes, which may result in prevention of pressure ulcers, weight loss and falls.[7]

B. Roles and Responsibilities in Long-Term Care

The majority of lawsuits are generated either from issues regarding care and treatment provided in the long-term care/ subacute facilities or from the assisted living settings. The roles and responsibilities of particular individuals providing care in the long-term subacute care setting are clearly outlined in the federal regulations under Title 42: Public Health Part 483: Requirements for States and Long-Term Care Facilities, Subpart B: Requirements for Long-Term Care Facilities. The roles and responsibilities of particular individuals providing care in an assisted living setting are different in each state.

1. Medical Director

The facility must have a licensed physician who serves as the medical director to coordinate medical care in the facility and provide clinical guidance and oversight regarding the implementation of resident care policies. The medical director collaborates with the facility leadership, staff, and other practitioners and consultants to help develop, implement, and evaluate resident care policies and procedures. The policies and procedures must reflect current standards of practice and help the facility identify, evaluate and address/resolve medical and clinical concerns and issues.

2. Director of Nursing (DON)

The facility should have a full-time director of nursing or nursing administrator who is a registered professional nurse licensed in that particular state and has supervisory experience in the provision of care to long-term care residents. The DON supervises all nursing personnel. The DON may serve as a charge nurse only when the facility has an average daily occupancy of 60 or fewer residents in order to be able to provide the oversight of resident care and services necessary to attain or maintain the highest level of physical, mental, and psychosocial well-being of each resident as determined by resident assessments and individual plans of care.

3. Registered Nurse

The registered nurse (RN) renders professional nursing care to the residents. It is the duty of the registered nurse to follow facility policies and procedures in the implementation of treatment orders, in the assessment of resident treatment needs, and in the development and implementation of the resident's plan of care that is based on the assessment. The registered nurse is responsible for the maintenance of the resident's medical record and to communicate with the other members of the interdisciplinary team in conjunction with participation in the supervision of all care provided to the residents.

4. Licensed Practical Nurse

The licensed practical nurse (LPN) renders nursing care to the residents and outnumbers the registered nurses in most facilities. It is the duty of a licensed practical nurse to follow facility policies and procedures in the implementation of treatment orders, to provide residents' treatment needs and to take the appropriate action regarding the implementation of the specific interventions as outlined in the resident's plan of care. The licensed practical nurse is responsible for maintaining the resident's medical record and communicating with the other members of the interdisciplinary team in conjunction with participation in the supervision of all care provided to the residents. Licensed practical nurses can participate in the assessment process of residents by gathering and documenting data in the medical record; however, the registered nurse is responsible for correlating the data with the clinical information and perform the assessment.

5. Certified Nurses Aide

The certified nurse aide (CNA) provides nursing or nursing-related services to residents in a facility. The nursing aide must be competent and is required to complete a training program with a competency evaluation as approved by the particular state within four months of hire as a full-time employee. The certified nurse aides provide most of the hands-on care provided in long-term care facilities. The written information regarding each resident's particular needs should be available to the nurse's aide via the resident's plan of care or on some type of individualized and updated worksheet.

C. Vulnerabilities Due to Sensory Changes

In order to identify the liability risks in long-term care, it is important to understand the profile of typical long-term care residents as they progress through the normal aging process. The elderly are at high risk for impairment of the senses, which puts them at risk for injury.

1. Visual changes and the elderly

The attorney reviewing medical records of residents will occasionally encounter chart entries that describe the person as "legally blind." Legal blindness is defined as corrected visual acuity in the better eye of 20/200 or worse or as vision restricted to 20 diopters in its widest diameter.[8] Individuals with limited vision may be able to count fingers in front of their eyes, detect hand motion, or detect light. The individual who is functionally blind has no light perception. Three percent of persons over the age of 85 in the United States are legally blind; approximately 25 percent of nursing home residents are legally blind. Blindness is caused by diabetes, glaucoma, hypertension, trauma, and arteriosclerosis. Decreased ability to accommodate is often the first visual change, which affects the ability to focus clearly over distances or to read and then see clearly at a distance. People experiencing this problem need prescription changes or "longer arms" to be able to read. A smaller pupil requires more light. An older person needs approximately three times as much light as a 20-year-old needs. Moving out of a darkened room into bright light causes difficulty because the older eye adapts more slowly to changes in illumination.[9] Visual changes such as this increase the risk of injury.

Color and depth perception are affected by the normal yellowing of the lens of the eye. This affects the ability to judge distances. Reds, oranges, and yellows are easier for the elder to distinguish than blues and greens. Pinks and beiges may be difficult to distinguish. Elders need strong, bright contrasting colors. They may be unable to follow simple color codes.

The four most common eye diseases in the elderly age 75 to 85 in nursing homes are:

- Cataracts: 46 percent
- Age-related macular degeneration: 28 percent
- Open angle glaucoma: 7.2 percent
- Diabetic retinopathy: 7 percent[10]

The elderly are prone to the development of cataracts, a problem that is easily corrected by surgery if recognized by the nursing home healthcare personnel. A cataract causes an increase in lens opacity which creates glare sensitivity and reduces visual acuity. The elder is also at risk for macular degeneration, which consists of deterioration in the back of the eye caused by hardening of the arteries, resulting in a loss of central vision. The easiest way to realize how this affects the vision of an elder is to imagine wearing a pair of glasses with a black dot covering the center of each lens. Peripheral vision remains intact. Increased intraocular pressure results from an obstruction in ocular drainage and is detectable with a tonometry reading. Uncorrected acute glaucoma can lead to blindness.

Many nursing home residents are diabetic. The likelihood and severity of diabetic retinopathy increases with the duration of diabetes. Juvenile or Type I diabetes is often diagnosed in childhood, whereas Type II or adult onset diabetes is usually diagnosed in middle to older age. Retinopathy is likely to be worse if blood sugar is poorly controlled. Almost all diabetics with the disease for more than 30 years will show visual changes. Diabetic retinopathy is caused by damage to the blood vessels in the retina. Non-proliferative retinopathy is characterized by blood vessels that leak fluid into the retina, blurring vision. Proliferative retinopathy, which occurs at later stages, is marked by growth of new fragile blood vessels that easily bleed, causing loss of vision and scarring. Diabetes is a growing problem in the United States.

Patients with Alzheimer's disease have visuospatial abnormalities, and the inability to distinguish moving objects clearly. The resident may be easily startled by these experiences, resulting in loss of balance and falling.

Homonymous hemianopia (ho-mon-e-mus hemee-an-oopea) may result from a stroke or a head injury that damages the optic nerve. This is defined as blindness in the same (left or right) visual field of each eye. Hemineglect may occur, resulting in inattention to one side of the body—dangling an arm out of a wheelchair, failing to shave one side of the face, ignoring spilled food on one side, and so on.

Visual problems, which affect the quality of the nursing home resident's life as well as create safety risks, may be treatable. Treatable causes of visual changes are listed below:

- Conjunctivitis
- Cataracts
- Retinal bleeding
- Retinal tear
- Entropia
- Extropia
- Dry eyes
- Migraine
- Bacterial corneal ulcers
- Herpes simplex
- Sinusitis
- Brain tumor
- Hyperthyroidism

Vision difficulties may produce these behaviors:[11]

- Coordination difficulties (buttoning, finding food on a plate)
- Tunnel vision (positioning of objects seemingly ignored)
- Visual hallucinations—rapidly move at edge of vision field
- Squinting
- Color selection—bright over dull colored objects
- Depth perception problems—spilling food or drink
- Inability to copy words or numbers
- Difficulty distinguishing an object from its background

Nursing staff are expected to recognize the visual changes associated with aging and provide adaptive measures for the nursing home environment:[12]

- Use nightlights in bathroom and bedroom.
- Avoid cluttered environment.
- Avoid highly buffed floors that reflect overhead light with glare.
- Provide large print room door tags with the resident's name and room number.
- Use a high contrast color on the edges of steps.
- Keep clothes and objects in the resident's room in the same positions.
- Keep food and utensils in the same places on the tray.

- Create lighting within the facility that is consistent, evenly distributed, and of adequate intensity.
- Place fluorescent or brightly colored tape around outlets, light switches, and doorknobs.
- Provide cups and glasses with contrasting rims.
- Place light objects on dark surfaces and vice versa.

Adaptive equipment useful for residents includes:[13]

- Magnifying glasses
- Large print books, telephone books, and newspapers
- Magnifying television screen systems
- Talking books
- Computer-operated voice synthesizers that read from books
- Audiotape cassettes for correspondence
- Radio stations with special programming for the visually impaired
- Self-threading needles
- Adaptive clothing-zippers, Velcro openers, large buttons
- Braille watches, talking clocks
- Adapted games
- Telephone adaptations for the visual impaired—giant button adapters or call makers
- Braille or other coded markings at entrances to commonly used rooms

Nurses should:

- Monitor for signs and symptoms of dry eyes.
- Mark resident's glasses with the resident's name.
- Encourage routine annual eye exams.
- Provide eyeglasses or recognize need for change in prescription.
- Inquire about eye pain.
- Report signs of eye infections.
- Keep commonly used objects within reach of resident so searching and stretching to reach something will not be needed.
- Provide a safe environment.

2. Hearing changes and the elderly

Hearing loss is a silent and often overlooked disability that can dramatically affect the quality of one's life and increase risk of harm. Of people over 65 years of age, between 28 and 55 percent may have some degree of hearing impairment. Among those older than 80, 66 percent may have impaired hearing. In addition, an estimated 90 percent of institutionalized persons have hearing problems.[14] The inability to hear high pitched consonants (f, s, sk, l, sh) is the first impairment; it may occur gradually and not be noticed. The earlier the problem is detected and a hearing aid is put into use, the greater the possibility of compensating for the loss.

Treatable causes of hearing loss include:

- build up of ear wax,
- foreign bodies,
- ear infection, and
- hypothyroidism.

Preventable causes of hearing loss include ototoxicity from:

- aminoglycoside antibiotics (the "mycins": Gentamycin, Vancomycin, and so on)
- nonsteroidal anti-inflammatory drugs
- salicylates (aspirin)
- Quinine
- Quinidine
- Lasix
- topical ear antibiotics

Nurses should observe for clues indicating hearing loss such as:

- the resident asking people to repeat statements
- moving the head to the right or left in an attempt to better understand what is being said
- social withdrawal
- increasing the radio or television volume to a high level in order to be hear it
- inappropriate responses to conversation

Nurses should question whether inappropriate responses or inability to follow directions are due to hearing loss versus dementia.

Nurses should report signs of decreased hearing so interventions may be considered: hearing aid, cleaning wax out of ear, use of amplifying devices on TV or phones.

Physicians may order Debrox for three days and then flush the ears to remove wax.

Physicians should periodically order therapeutic blood levels of the "mycin" medications to ensure that ototoxicity does not occur.

Nurses should be alert to signs of hearing loss when residents are taking ototoxic medications.[15]

3. Taste changes and the elderly

Taste buds and flavor identification decline with age. Taste buds decline to one-sixth of a 20-year-old by the late seventies. Gum disease, poor teeth, and periodontal disease reduce appetite.[16] Causes of taste changes or appetite include:

- Depression
- Medications especially antibiotics
- Nebulizer therapy
- Gastric reflux
- Thrush (common after antibiotic therapy)
- Cancer
- Bell's palsy
- Head trauma
- Hepatic disease
- Renal disease
- Zinc deficiency
- Hypothyroidism
- Diabetes
- Local radiation therapy
- Laryngectomy
- Smoking
- Vitamin D deficiency
- Dentures[17]

Medications, including the following, can cause taste changes:

- Dilantin
- Carbamazepine/Tegretol
- Lithium
- Ampicillin
- Tetracycline
- Metronidazole/Flagyl
- Aminoglycosides
- Fluroquinolones
- Marcolides
- Antihypertensives
- ACE inhibitors—Lotensin, Capoten, Vasotec, Monopril, Prinivil, Univase, Accupril, Aceon, Altace, and Mavik
- Calcium channel blockers—Norvasc, Plendil, Cardene, Procardia, Cardif, Nimotop, Calan, Isopitin
- Anti-gout medications—Allopurinol, Colchicines[18]

Taste difficulties may produce these behaviors:[19]

- Loss of or increased appetite—lost appetite because the resident cannot taste; increased food intake to achieve some taste, resulting in weight changes
- Metallic taste in the mouth
- Statements about food—complaints about bitter or sour flavors
- Questions—mistaken identity of foods
- Tongue coating
- Excessive seasoning—increased sugar and salt usage

4. Sense of smell changes and the elderly

The sense of smell declines much more significantly with age than does the sense of taste. The age-related changes in the ability to recognize odors may result in the elderly person not being able to recognize when food is not edible or when natural gas is escaping in the kitchen. Since much of the sensory stimulus that is perceived as taste is actually smell, the inability to smell results in a loss of taste.

Diseases that can affect the sense of smell include:[20]

- Alzheimer's disease
- Sinusitis
- Hypothyroidism
- Diabetes
- Head trauma
- Parkinson's disease
- Asthma
- Viral infections
- Laryngectomy

Medications that affect smell include:[21]

- Calcium channel blockers
- Antithyroid agents
- Opiates
- Amphetamines
- Nasal decongestants
- Zinc nasal spray

Other factors that affect smell include:[22]

- Flu
- Colds
- Smoking
- Nasal obstructions and discharges
- Nose bleeds
- Allergies

The nursing home staff, in recognition of the factors that affect taste and smell, should:

- Oversee hygiene to ensure residents who are able are cleaning themselves and bathe people who cannot.
- Make meals appealing through variety in color, texture, and contents.
- Provide mouth care before meals, particularly breakfast.
- Review medications that may influence sense of taste and appetite.
- Observe for dental needs, as manifested by a bad mouth odor that may affect taste.
- Alter the dining room environment if needed, to make it pleasant.
- Provide increased spices in food to compensate for declining taste buds and smell.
- Not administer medication during meal time unless specifically ordered with meals.
- Provide an opportunity to rinse the mouth with water if a poorly tasting medication must be given with food.
- Not administer respiratory treatments for a half hour before or after meals.

5. Sensation, skin and tissue changes and the elderly

Altered sensation may result from spinal cord injuries, demyelinating neurological impairment due to stroke or multiple sclerosis, peripheral vascular disease, peripheral arterial disease and diabetes. It is common for those with advanced diabetes to lack sensation on the soles of the feet, resulting in unnoticed lesions that may progress to ulcers without the awareness of the resident. Nurses are aware of the need to perform foot inspections of diabetic residents. Many of the age-related skin changes are due to sun exposure. Age-related skin changes include:

- Loss of muscle tone
- Thinning of skin, which (is) can be accelerated by the prolonged use of steroids
- Decrease in nerve endings, particularly in the fingers
- Decreased perception of hot and cold [23]
- Loss of leg hair, a sign of circulatory impairment
- Loss of subcutaneous fat
- Dry, flaky, itchy skin
- Loss of elasticity due to loss of the fibrous connective layer.

Interventions for a potential for altered skin integrity include:

- Avoid pressure.
- Apply moisturizer routinely especially after bathing.
- Provide perineal care after each incontinent episode.
- Encourage resident to wear long sleeves if prone to skin tears.
- Keep nails trimmed.
- Float heels off bed if unable to self position.
- Use body supports for positioning.
- Avoid trauma such as contusions, skin tears.
- Safeguard skin from burns.

The elderly may have an unfulfilled need to be touched. Nursing home staff should to be aware of the need to:

- Provide touch in socially acceptable and sensitive ways.
- Provide rocking chairs as an alternative to those who are not receiving enough touching.
- Recognize that behavior may change if the resident is not being touched enough, and that the resident may seek touch.
- Recognize that the resident who has vision and hearing impairments may find touching even more important. This individual will need to hold onto furniture or hand rails when walking.
- Not wear gloves when transferring or dressing unless exposed to body fluids.

6. Balance and dexterity changes and the elderly

Loss of spatial perception and muscle tone may result in a shuffling gait, leaning forward when walking, and stiffness of the joints. Both men and women may develop a bent-over posture from loss of bone in the spine. In extreme cases, the individual has difficulty raising his head to look up or eat unassisted. Limitations in balance place the resident at high risk for falls as well as weight loss. Changes in dexterity lead to difficulty opening jars, grasping small items, using buttons and zippers, and holding food items without spilling. People with arthritic hands have even greater difficulty with these tasks.

D. Dementia

Most nursing homes have a very high percentage of confused elderly residents. Currently 4 million Americans suffer from Alzheimer's disease (AD), the most common form of dementia. Due to the steady increase in average lifespan over the last 100 years, more people are at risk for developing AD in the future, and many of these individuals will require care in long-term care facilities. AD is an irreversible, progressive brain disorder that gradually destroys a person's emotional and cognitive abilities, such as the ability to carry out daily activities, communicate, make judgments, learn, and reason. Affected people experience changes in behavior including paranoia, hallucinations, wandering, or sleep disturbances.[24] The classic symptoms of Alzheimer's disease include progressive deterioration of memory and judgment, difficulties finding the right words, and impaired motor functioning including the ability to eat and swallow. Depression is more common in the early stages of the disease. Mild depression affects 30 percent of Alzheimer's residents, whereas severe depression occurs in 10 percent of Alzheimer's residents. Psychosis (delusions, hallucinations, paranoia) occurs in one-third to one-half of residents with Alzheimer's and is seen more commonly in advanced stages of Alzheimer's disease. [25]

According to the Alzheimer's Association, a staging framework based on a system developed by Barry Reisberg, M.D., Clinical Director of the New York University School of Medicine's Silberstein Aging and Dementia Research Center, outlines key symptoms characterizing seven stages ranging from unimpaired function to very severe cognitive decline. This framework, found at www.alz.org/AboutAD/Stages.asp (Table 10.1), corresponds to the widely used concepts of mild, moderate, moderately severe, and severe Alzheimer's disease. It also demonstrates which stages fall within the more general divisions of early-stage, mid-stage, and late-stage categories. However, it is noted that not all individuals will have all symptoms in each stage or experience each stage as the disease process can vary in each person.

The inability to protect the resident from harm is frequently the reason why family members bring the resident to a long-term care facility for care. Home safety problems associated with this disease include the risk of fires, unsafe driving, wandering out of the house, falls, physical violence, and cuts from unsafe use of sharp objects. Fire safety is a concern because persons with this diagnosis often forget that they are cooking and leave pots on the stove or forget to turn off burners. With the exception of unsafe driving, the resident in a long-term care facility can fall victim to any of the same types of safety hazards.

Nurses who work with Alzheimer's residents spend much of their time

- Monitoring behaviors and response to psychotropic medications,

Table 10.1
Stages of Alzheimer's Disease

Stage 1: No impairment (normal function)
Unimpaired individuals experience no memory problems and none are evident to a healthcare professional during a medical interview.

Stage 2: Very mild cognitive decline (may be normal age-related changes or earliest signs of Alzheimer's disease)
Individuals may feel as if they have memory lapses, especially in forgetting familiar words or names or the location of keys, eyeglasses or other everyday objects. But these problems are not evident during a medical examination or apparent to friends, family or co-workers.

Stage 3: Mild cognitive decline
Early-stage Alzheimer's can be diagnosed in some, but not all, individuals with these symptoms.
Friends, family or co-workers begin to notice deficiencies. Problems with memory or concentration may be measurable in clinical testing or discernible during a detailed medical interview. Common difficulties include:
- Word- or name-finding problems noticeable to family or close associates
- Decreased ability to remember names when introduced to new people
- Performance issues in social or work settings noticeable to family, friends or co-workers
- Reading a passage and retaining little material
- Losing or misplacing a valuable object
- Decline in ability to plan or organize

Stage 4: Moderate cognitive decline (Mild or early-stage Alzheimer's disease)
At this stage, a careful medical interview detects clear-cut deficiencies in the following areas:
- Decreased knowledge of recent occasions or current events
- Impaired ability to perform challenging mental arithmetic—for example, to count backward from 100 by 7s
- Decreased capacity to perform complex tasks, such as marketing, planning dinner for guests or paying bills and managing finances
- Reduced memory of personal history
- The affected individual may seem subdued and withdrawn, especially in socially or mentally challenging situations

Stage 5: Moderately severe cognitive decline (Moderate or mid-stage Alzheimer's disease)
Major gaps in memory and deficits in cognitive function emerge. Some assistance with day-to-day activities becomes essential. At this stage, individuals may:
- Be unable during a medical interview to recall such important details as their current address, their telephone number or the name of the college or high school from which they graduated
- Become confused about where they are or about the date, day of the week, or season
- Have trouble with less challenging mental arithmetic; for example, counting backward from 40 by 4s or from 20 by 2s
- Need help choosing proper clothing for the season or the occasion
- Usually retain substantial knowledge about themselves and know their own name and the names of their spouse or children
- Usually require no assistance with eating or using the toilet

continued on next page...

Table 10.1
Stages of Alzheimer's Disease (continued)

Stage 6: Severe cognitive decline (Moderately severe or mid-stage Alzheimer's disease)
Memory difficulties continue to worsen, significant personality changes may emerge and affected individuals need extensive help with customary daily activities. At this stage, individuals may:

- Lose most awareness of recent experiences and events as well as of their surroundings
- Recollect their personal history imperfectly, although they generally recall their own name
- Occasionally forget the name of their spouse or primary caregiver but generally can distinguish familiar from unfamiliar faces
- Need help getting dressed properly; without supervision, may make such errors as putting pajamas over daytime clothes or shoes on wrong feet
- Experience disruption of their normal sleep/waking cycle
- Need help with handling details of toileting (flushing toilet, wiping and disposing of tissue properly)
- Have increasing episodes of urinary or fecal incontinence
- Experience significant personality changes and behavioral symptoms, including suspiciousness and delusions (for example, believing that their caregiver is an impostor); hallucinations (seeing or hearing things that are not really there); or compulsive, repetitive behaviors such as hand-wringing or tissue shredding
- Tend to wander and become lost

Stage 7: Very severe cognitive decline (Severe or late-stage Alzheimer's disease)
This is the final stage of the disease when individuals lose the ability to respond to their environment, the ability to speak and, ultimately, the ability to control movement.

- Frequently individuals lose their capacity for recognizable speech, although words or phrases may occasionally be uttered
- Individuals need help with eating and toileting and there is general incontinence of urine
- Individuals lose the ability to walk without assistance, then the ability to sit without support, the ability to smile, and the ability to hold their head up. Reflexes become abnormal and muscles grow rigid. Swallowing is impaired.

- Providing cognitively appropriate activities,
- Managing continence programs,
- Monitoring meal intake and weight,
- Educating staff and families ,
- Managing aggressive behaviors,
- Treating depression,
- Controlling the behavior of those with hallucinations, delusions, and illusions,
- Minimizing injury from inappropriate social behaviors,
- Providing distraction for repetitive behaviors, phrases, and movements,
- Interpreting reality,
- Managing basic needs,
- Maintaining normalcy and managing behavior disturbances,
- Managing sleep disturbances,
- Minimizing injury from sundowning,
- Providing a safe environment for the wanderer, and
- Identifying and controlling causes of agitation.

A prime issue is protecting the resident from hazards. Special care units for Alzheimer's residents are being designed and used in long-term care facilities to provide the specialized services needed by these residents. The physical environment is specifically designed to make the unit safe, attractive, and well organized. Special care units for residents with Alzheimer's are now specifically regulated in a number of states which includes training for their specialized care staff.

Federal regulations provide that the "resident has the right to be free from any physical or chemical restraints imposed for the purposes of discipline or convenience, and not required to treat the resident's medical symptoms."[26] Chemical restraint may erode a resident's autonomy, lessen consciousness of self and surrounding environment, contribute to functional decline, and increase fall risk. Other consequences include agitation, gait disturbance, memory impairment, sedation withdrawal, movement disorders, and orthostatic/postural hypotension.[27] Many facilities require the use of assessment forms to document the behavior that would justify the use of medication for behavior control.

TIP: All medications prescribed in nursing faculties must have a reason for use and this must be documented in the resident's record.[28]

10.4 Staffing and Retention
A. Staffing

Given the challenging nature of working with geriatric and long-term care residents, this area of nursing creates both rewards and difficulties. Nurses who are drawn to long-term relationships are attracted to long-term care. The joys associated with receiving consistent assignments, getting to know families, and protecting vulnerable residents appeal to many nurses. The difficulties associated with working with demented residents affects recruitment and retention. Low staffing is one factor that leads to liability concerns in the long-term care facility. The workload is heavy; the population is vulnerable; and the direct care is primarily provided by nurse's aides or assistants. The day shift nurses typically supervise three to five nursing assistants. Each assistant is assigned to care for six to ten residents. This means that each registered nurse is responsible for supervising the care of 18 to 50 residents in an eight-hour shift. This is in sharp contrast with the smaller number of patients for which a nurse is responsible in a hospital, which rarely exceeds 15. (See Chapter 2, *Where Have All the Nurses Gone?*, in Volume I, for more information on staffing.)

Long-term care staffing has a direct relationship to Medicare and Medicaid reimbursement rates as labor is the largest expense of any facility. Nursing assistants are the frontline workers in nursing homes and provide most of the direct care to residents. The majority of these workers are female, have a high school diploma, and become certified by completing a federally required 75-hour course that includes a 16-hour practicum. These employees perform demanding work, usually for very low pay. Frequently their role in resident care is not recognized or rewarded. Often these individuals are poorly prepared for the realities and demands of their job and turnover rates can be as high as 100 percent.[29] Many factors have combined to create what is now recognized to be a critical nursing shortage. Among others, more employment opportunities for women, better health care, and a growing elderly population have contributed to this shortage. The shortage has had a major impact on all areas of long-term care and is particularly evident in America's nursing homes where factors such as salaries, job image, workload, advancement opportunities, and inadequate reimbursement from Medicare and Medicaid contribute to the problem.[30]

The majority of nurses who work in long-term care are Licensed Practical Nurses (LPNs). These nurses complete a one-year training program and, along with the Certified Nursing Assistant (CNA), must work under the supervision of a Registered Nurse (RN). The RN may be educated at the diploma, associate's, or baccalaureate degree level and often functions in a supervisory capacity within the nursing home. The nursing shortage has affected all levels of nursing staff and has limited the guidance and supervision that an experienced RN can provide to the LPNs and CNAs.

Insufficient staffing leads to staff burnout and attrition, and, in worst-case scenarios, may contribute to resident abuse. Low staffing jeopardizes quality of care and can affect the ability of the facility to continue operating. Deficiencies identified during the annual state survey can result in monetary penalties and closure of beds, and can compromise a facility's reputation, thus having an adverse impact on census.[31]

Several studies have demonstrated a relationship between staffing levels, in the nursing home, and the quality of care that the residents receive. An analysis completed by the Center for Medicare and Medicaid Services (CMS) in 2000 and reported to Congress in 2002 concluded that providing less than two hours of CNA care per resident per day substantially increased the risk of hospitalization, pressure ulcer development, weight loss, and functional decline. CMS also conducted a time and motion study, during which they reviewed the time required to implement five daily care services that correlated to positive outcomes. Based on the time necessary to perform these activities, the reviewers determined that a resident of average acuity would require 2.9 hours of CNA time per day. Additionally, as part of this same study, CMS identified preferred staffing levels for RNs and LPNs to be 0.45 and 1.0 hours, respectively, per resident per day.

The results of the study, using a subset of the data, showed that increasing RN time by 30-40 minutes per resident per day would result in an increased use of oral nutritional supplements and a decrease in the following:

- Pressure ulcer development
- Urinary tract infections

- Weight loss
- Loss of ADL functioning
- Hospital deaths[32]

Although the investigators recognized that increasing RN hours to the recommended levels would be costly, they estimated that this expense would be more than offset by the dollars saved in pressure ulcer treatment and hospitalizations alone. Interestingly, the study concluded that adding LPN and CNA hours had a positive effect only on the development of pressure ulcers.

Consumer groups have also demanded improved staffing and quality of care in nursing homes. A variety of legislation and regulation has been introduced in response to these concerns. President Bush and President Obama recognized the critical need to provide education for nursing training and signed funding acts. The Medicare and Medicaid Quality Improvement Act and the Nursing Home Quality Protection Act (2001) were instrumental in ensuring that all staff in nursing homes completed criminal background checks prior to employment. There have also been attempts, at both the state and federal levels of government, to establish minimum staffing levels.

Low staffing in the nursing home is often difficult to identify. While there are federal staffing regulations for LTC, these requirements are vague and it is left to the states to define appropriate staffing levels. For example, the Omnibus Reconciliation Act of 1987 (OBRA) states that "…nursing services must be sufficient to meet resident care needs." The law also obliges each nursing home to have a RN Director of Nursing; a RN on duty eight hours a day, seven days a week; and a licensed nurse on duty at all times. The Medicare and Medicaid regulations require nursing facilities to provide nursing services that "…meet professional standards to attain and maintain the highest practicable physical, mental and psycho-social well-being of each resident." In January 2003, the federal government mandated that all nursing homes post daily staffing numbers in an area that would be visible to both residents and visitors.

The federal requirement to post staffing data includes the language that the Medicare- and Medicaid-certified facilities must post daily for each shift the current number of licensed and unlicensed nursing staff directly responsible for resident care in the facility. The language "direct care" eliminates time spent on collecting data for the minimum data set or attending team meetings. Data includes the number of residents on each unit and the total number of nursing hours for each staffing category.

All states must conform to federal staffing laws, but may also require additional conditions for licensure within the state. In some states, the staffing requirements are based only on resident census; in others the regulations may also take into account the case mix of the residents.[33] Many states, including those that already have staffing requirements, are considering legislation that would mandate specific staffing ratios for both nurses and nursing assistants. These ratios were initially proposed by the National Citizens Coalition for Nursing Home Reform (NCCNHR) and have been endorsed by the prestigious Hartford Institute for Geriatrics.

While the idea of mandating higher staffing in long-term care appears to have merit, this cannot be accomplished unless attention is given to those factors that are responsible for the current staffing crisis. Long-term care has an image problem. Isolated events paint a picture of nursing home staff as uncaring and, in some cases, abusive. Hospital nursing is perceived to be more glamorous while long-term care nursing is often viewed as distasteful, custodial care of confused older individuals. Workloads are heavy; reimbursement systems force salaries that are below those paid by hospitals; and schedules are often inflexible. Regulations instituted to prevent Medicare fraud have resulted in an overwhelming amount of paperwork, preventing the nurses from working with the residents and overseeing the care provided by other levels of staff. Compounding the problem is the fact that nursing homes often suffer from lack of managerial and clinical resources. Many managers are under-prepared educationally for the roles they have assumed. They are ill-equipped to mentor staff or to effectively communicate their needs to those in the organization who control the resources.

Unfortunately, low staffing breeds low staffing. As staff shortages become more evident, workloads increase, and people become overwhelmed and leave. Turnover is costly to the nursing home. New staff must be oriented and trained before they are permitted to work. In the meantime, their position is filled by staff who are working overtime or by temporary workers. In addition to the financial implications, a high turnover rate affects the morale of both staff and residents and interrupts the continuity of care that residents and families have come to value. Nursing home litigation is often initiated because of clinical issues such as pressure ulcers, medication errors, or falls when, in reality, the root cause of these may be understaffing. Without specific staffing requirements that are relevant to the number and types of residents in the home, it falls to the administration of the nursing home to define and provide adequate staffing. With cuts in reimbursement—coupled with dramatic increases in the costs of salaries, benefits, and liability insurance—the nursing home administrator faces a monumental challenge in attempting to meet the quality of care and quality of life needs of the nursing home resident.

B. Retention

Attention to recruitment and retention has occurred in part due to the increasing awareness of the high costs of turnover, including orientation and training of new employees, coupled with shrinking reimbursement. Beyond the financial implications, a high turnover rate affects the morale of residents and staff. In order to solve this problem, nursing home managers and administrators must focus on hiring the right people and retaining them. Although there is no prescribed formula to do this, adequate compensation and benefit packages and the use of creative scheduling have been effective in attracting and retaining staff. Many facilities are restructuring the nursing home environment to create neighborhoods within the facility to ensure consistency of staffing and greater knowledge of and involvement with a core of residents. Improving the image of long-term care by stressing the advantages of working in this setting would assist in recruitment efforts. Some settings are implementing flexible scheduling, providing tuition to help certified nursing assistants enter nursing school, empowering staff, and stressing the emotional rewards of working with residents and their families.

10.5 Litigation Trends

Liability risks are growing in long-term care. There is an increased awareness across society of medical errors and their effects. Gibson and Singh discussed the issue from the layperson's perspective in *Wall of Silence*.[34] Bewley wrote *Killer Cure*[35] to inform the public of the gaps in health care that put them at risk while King shared the story of how a medical error killed her child, and the crusade she started to make medical care safe.[36] Drs. Wachter and Shojania provided an insider's view of medical errors in *Internal Bleeding*.[37] While not directed specifically at the issue of nursing home quality of care, publication of this information increases the public's awareness of the risks of health care. Each text offers suggestions for making health care safer and more responsive.

From a societal perspective, awareness of the risk of exposing a loved one to substandard nursing home care can foster a family's sense of helplessness and guilt. The inability to protect the patient from harm is frequently the reason family members reach the decision to bring a family member to a long-term care facility. When a loved one is injured within a nursing home, there is a tendency for the family to want answers and to assign blame.

TIP: The concept that the elderly are "not worth much" when calculating damages is fading.

Despite recent changes in several states resulting in cap limits, there continues to be some large verdicts and settlements regarding nursing home cases. Since the late 1990s, the public has displayed a growing intolerance for general neglect and abuse from trained caregivers and the corporate greed exhibited by long-term facility owners. Often, experienced plaintiffs' firms are now being contacted by firms unfamiliar with the intricacies of nursing homes cases to jointly work a case in order to become more proficient in this area of the law. Substandard or negligent care that in the past would have gone unnoticed is increasingly giving rise to lawsuits.

TIP: Punitive damage awards are becoming more commonplace in suits involving the elderly.

In a highly unusual step for such a case, a Philadelphia jury leveled $5 million in punitive damages against Jeanes Hospital and a Wyncote nursing home in the death of a man who developed ultimately fatal pressure ulcers while at both facilities. The damages—$1.5 million against Jeanes and $3.5 million against the Hillcrest Convalescent Home—came two weeks after the same Common Pleas Court jury awarded $1 million in compensatory damages in the case. The damages were awarded to the widow of Joe N. Blango, who died of pressure ulcers in 2008, two years after being discharged from Jeanes Hospital in the city's Fox Chase section.

While compensatory damages are not unexpected in such cases, punitive damages are, according to lawyer Robert L. Sachs, who handles nursing-home cases and serves as liaison to the Philadelphia court for other nursing-home litigators. "To my knowledge, this is the first nursing-home case to go to the jury on punitive damages in Philadelphia," said Sachs, who was not involved in the Blango case. Rebecca Harmon, a spokeswoman for Temple University Health System, which owns Jeanes, said Temple would appeal the verdict. "There is not one shred of evidence to support any liability in this case as it relates to Jeanes Hospital, and the contemplation of punitive damages is simply inexplicable," she said in an e-mail. "We're very proud of the high-quality care provided to patients each and every day at Jeanes Hospital."

Steven R. Maher, who represented Blango's widow, said that in his 25 years of handling such cases, this was only the second time a jury had awarded punitive damages. One reason, he said, was the high standards required to permit punitive damages to be considered. A jury must find that a facility had engaged in "outrageous and reckless conduct," he said. Blango went to Jeanes on May 21, 2006, after suffering weakness and confusion. He was 74 at the time and was thought to have suffered a stroke. According to Maher, doctors at Jeanes failed to properly diagnose that Blango was suffering from a urinary-tract infection that, as a result, worsened and left him susceptible to the pressure ulcers that ultimately killed him.

After about a week at Jeanes, Blango was transferred to Hillcrest, where he stayed two weeks until his condition worsened and he was returned to Jeanes. He was released to go home after three days. Maher contended that workers at Jeanes and Hillcrest allowed the pressure ulcers to fester and Blango to go malnourished to the point that he lost 28 pounds. After he returned home, Blango was cared for by his wife, Shirley, before dying from the pressure ulcers two years later. "This verdict sends a message," Maher said, "that this type of care is unacceptable and will not be tolerated."[38]

10.6 Compliance with the Standard of Care

A. State, Federal, and Professional Standards

Both the state licensing agency and the Centers for Medicare and Medicaid Services (CMS) are responsible for surveying nursing facilities, long-term care hospitals, and rehabilitation hospitals. Assisted living facilities are state-regulated, some by the state health department and some by the social services department. Regulations can be obtained from these organizations to screen the potential nursing malpractice case and to build a strong risk management program or defend the claim. The American Nurses Association publishes standards of gerontological nursing, which are updated periodically.[39] Some facilities opt to become certified by The Joint Commission and are judged by the long-term care standards of that organization.

The Omnibus Budget Reconciliation Act (OBRA), which was enacted in 1987 and phased in over the following three years, was the government's attempt to improve the quality of care delivered in nursing homes. OBRA regulates the way nursing homes deliver care, provide staff, train nursing assistants, monitor the quality of care that is provided, and protect the resident's rights. Facilities that do not comply with the regulations can be fined, and payment for

Medicare and Medicaid services withheld based on the severity of the findings. Since its inception, the survey process has updated to meet the needs of the industry and ensure the foundation of the original tenets of OBRA is addressed. For example, in July 1995, a new federal survey process went into effect which intensified the sanctioning and fining system.

To obtain the regulations and F-tags, contact the American Health Care Association, which publishes *The Long Term Care Survey* for purchase.[40] Many attorneys and nursing home administrators refer to this book as the "Watermelon Book," a reference to its cover. It contains a vast array of regulations, protocols, forms, and survey procedures with guidance to surveyors who inspect nursing homes that receive federal funding. The regulations are referred to as F-tags, which are published in the Federal Register.

Nursing home plaintiff's attorney David Cohen identified the top 11 F-tags from a liability perspective:

1. Pressure sores (F-tag 314)
2. Comprehensive care plans (F-tag 279)
3. Sufficient nursing staff (F-tag 353)
4. Medical directors responsible for all clinical care (F-tag 501)
5. Urinary incontinence (F-tag 315)
6. Range of motion (F-tag 317)
7. Restraints (F-tag 222)
8. Nutrition (F-tag 325)
9. Hydration (F-tag 327)
10. Abuse (F-tag 223)
11. Quality of care (F-tag 309)[41]

In July 1999, the CMS survey process was retooled and became based on 24 "quality indicators." The 24 quality indicators, or QIs, listed in Figure 10.3 were developed by CMS to promote consistent and unified assessment of quality care across facilities.[42] The data submitted by the facility in its minimum data set (MDS) is used by CMS to construct a facility profile and individual resident profiles. The profiles are based on the 24 QI variables. Facilities are surveyed annually, at a minimum, by state agencies on how they use the QIs in the quality assurance program.[43] The facility profile is then compared to a statewide peer group. The surveyor uses the profiles to focus the survey on identified potential problems. In addition, special survey procedures apply to any resident whose QI report shows significant weight loss, dehydration, pressure ulcers, or fecal impaction. There are also survey procedures for review of staffing levels, medication therapy, and fraud and abuse prevention.

Accidents

1. **Incidence of new fractures**—residents who have had a hip fracture or other fracture that is new since the last assessment
2. **Prevalence of falls**—residents who have experienced a fall within the time frame of the most recent assessment (past 30 days)

Behavior and emotional patterns

3. **Behavioral symptoms affecting others; high risk and low risk**—residents who have displayed behaviors, such as verbal or physical abuse or socially inappropriate and disruptive behavior affecting others on the most recent assessment. Behavior has to occur at least once in the assessment period of seven days.
4. **Symptoms of depression**—residents who have a sad mood and have two or more symptoms of functional depression such as negative statements exhibited up to five days or more per week, agitation or withdrawal exhibited up to five days or more per week, waking with an unpleasant mood five days or more per week.
5. **Symptoms of depression without antidepressant therapy**—symptoms of depression are defined using same criteria as in previous QI, but no antidepressant therapy was provided.

Clinical management

6. **Use of nine or more medications**—residents who received nine or more different medications on most recent assessment

Cognitive patterns

7. **Incidence of cognitive impairment**—residents who are not cognitively impaired in the previous assessment but who are cognitively impaired in their most recent assessment. Cognitive impairment is defined as having impaired decision-making abilities and short term memory problems.

Figure 10.3 *CMS Quality Indicators by Domain Used with Data from MDS 2.0 to Obtain Facility and Individual Resident Profiles. (Source: CMS Publication 7 (OBRA), State Operations Manual, Transmittal 10, Exhibit 270, July, 1999)*

Data about nursing homes is available in the form of a facility quality indicator profile report. The report identifies each quality indicator, the facility percentage, and how the facility compares to others in the state. High percentile ranking does not necessarily indicate a lack of quality, but should be used by the facility as a signal for improvement. In some cases, a high percentile score may be a result of admission policies or care specialization rather than an indicator of poor care.[44] For example, a facility that specializes in wound care and healing complex pressure ulcers will have a higher percentile ranking in QI 24.

In 2002, CMS began a new national program called the Nursing Home Quality Initiative (NHQI). CMS expanded the original quality indicators to include pain and quality measures for the short-stay and post-acute population. Quality Measures/Quality Indicators are listed in Figure 10.4. The goals of the NHQI are twofold: to provide consumers with an additional source of information about the quality of nursing home care and to provide data, clinical resources, and quality improvement materials to providers in their ongoing quality improvement activities.

The survey process is once again in the process of being overhauled with the rollout of the Quality Indicator Survey (QIS). On May 16, 2008, the CMS dispensed a memo updating state survey directors.[45] The major difference in this survey process is that it utilizes a computer-based software application to drive the process and MDS-submitted information along with resident and family interviews. There has been some concern by both facilities and surveyors regarding the outcomes, but since the early inception of the quality assessment began in 1993, major data collection and research has been conducted through the initial pilot and demonstration states to ensure that this is a more outcome-based review. An evaluation of the outcomes can be viewed on the CMS website.[46]

Measure ID	Domain/Measure description
Accidents	
1.1	Incidence of new fractures
1.2	Prevalence of falls
Behavior/ Emotional Patterns	
2.1	Residents who have become more depressed or anxious
2.2	Prevalence of behavior symptoms affecting others: Overall
2.2-HI	Prevalence of behavior symptoms affecting others: High Risk
2.2-LO	Prevalence of behavior symptoms affecting others: Low Risk
2.3	Prevalence of symptoms of depression without antidepressant therapy
Clinical management	
3.1	Use of nine or more medications
Cognitive patterns	
4.1	Incidence of cognitive impairment
Elimination and incontinence	
5.1	Low-risk residents who lost control of their bowels or bladder
5.2	Residents who have/had a catheter inserted and left in their bladder
5.3	Prevalence of occasional or frequent bladder or bowel incontinence without a toileting plan
5.4	Prevalence of fecal impaction*
Infection control	
6.1	Residents with a urinary tract infection
Nutrition/Eating	
7.1	Residents who lose too much weight
7.2	Prevalence of tube feeding
7.3	Prevalence of dehydration*
Pain Management	
8.1	Residents who have moderate to severe pain

Figure 10.4 *Facility Quality Measures/Indicators Chronic Care Measures*

Physical functioning

9.1   Residents whose need for help with daily activities has increased
9.2   Residents who spend most of their time in bed or in a chair
9.3   Residents whose ability to move in and around their room got worse
9.4   Incidents of decline in range of motion

Psychotropic drug use

10.1   Prevalence of antipsychotic use, in the absence of psychotic or related
                 conditions: Overall
10.1-HI   Prevalence of antipsychotic use, in the absence of psychotic or related
                 conditions: High Risk
10.1-LO   Prevalence of antipsychotic use, in the absence of psychotic or related
                 conditions: Low Risk
10.2   Prevalence of antianxiety/hypnotic use
10.3   Prevalence of hypnotic use > 2 times in last week

Quality of life

11.1   Residents who were physically restrained
11.2   Prevalence of little or no activity

Skin care

12.1   High-risk residents with pressure ulcers*
12.2   Low-risk residents with pressure ulcers*

Post-Acute Care Measures

13.1   Short-stay residents with delirium
13.2   Short-stay residents who had moderate to severe pain
13.3   Short-stay residents with pressure ulcers

* These are sentinel events to be thoroughly investigated by surveyors. Sentinel means that they signal the
need for an investigation.

Figure 10.4 Facility Quality Measures/Indicators Chronic Care Measures (continued)

Now that the survey is driven by the software program, some providers feel more confident that they will not be victims of surveyor bias or vindictiveness because the software program does not carry emotion. On the other hand, because there will be more interviews of facility residents and staff, some facilities are expanding resident satisfaction and customer service efforts. This new process has not yet reached all states as not all surveyors have been trained. Although there are differences in how the information is collected and the on-site survey is conducted, adherence to the OBRA Federal Regulations remains intact.

National Nursing Home Quality, LLC won the contract from CMS to train surveyors and providers on the QIS process. According to their website, a total of 3,245 QIS surveys have been conducted as of December 29, 2009.[47]

Facilities are also required to self report certain occurrences to the Department of Health or its equivalent within certain timeframes. Each state and the District of Columbia have a list of the occurrences and the timelines of when it is to be reported.[48] The failure to do so may result in a citation.

TIP: A current Quality Measures/Indicators Report can be obtained from the facility or the state office of the department of health. Some facilities may archive former reports. A subset of ten quality measures are posted on the Nursing Home Compare website, a CMS-developed Internet search tool to allow state and national comparisons between nursing facilities. The actual results of the latest annual survey with any deficiencies including the scope and severity can be obtained online by using the Nursing Home Compare on www.medicare.gov

B. Surveys of Facilities

A variety of federal, state, and local organizations are actively involved in monitoring the quality of care provided by long-term care agencies. The results of the routine surveys by the state licensing agency are published and are available to the public and attorneys. It is possible that a facility may be surveyed by both the state and the federal government within two weeks after receiving a complaint, although some state licensing agencies are so backed up with complaints that it may take longer to send a surveyor to the facility to investigate the complaint. The findings of these surveys are admissible in malpractice claims if related to the issue.

TIP: Families or attorneys with a concern about the care a resident has received may request that the state department of health make a specific trip to the facility to investigate the nursing care.

The Office of Ombudsman, one of which is located in every state, may also be involved in investigating complaints about care the elderly may receive and may have prepared a report which is obtainable by the family or their attorney.

There are three common ways to access survey findings regarding facility surveys. The facility is required to have the survey results in an accessible place to the residents and public. Therefore, one can simply go to the facility and read the most current review. A copy of the results can be requested from the governing body that surveys long term care facilities in that state, for example the Department of Health. Lastly, information can be accessed through the www.medicare.gov website. Once at the website, click on "Compare Nursing Homes in Your Area" and follow the steps to locate the facility or facilities in question. Survey information can also be accessed through reporting resources such as www.memberofthefamily.net or www.healthgrades.com for a fee.

Readers interested in obtaining this information should know the CMS website will not give the actual specifics of the deficiencies but rather which regulation was violated and the level of severity received. Also, on this website, the reader will have access to the Five Star Rating System. Five Stars is the most favorable. However, there are some limitations on the use of this system, and those key points are explained on the website. Visiting the facility will also allow the reader to see what specific action or inaction occurred that contributed to the cited deficiencies.

10.7 Review of the Nursing Home Clinical Record

The documentation in the medical record is a key consideration when screening a potential malpractice case. Nursing home charts may be voluminous if the resident has been at the facility for a year or more. The first step in evaluating a claim is to organize the medical record into subsections based on the type of documentation. Each subsection should be organized in chronological order with the oldest document on the top of the stack. Preprinted index tabs are useful for identifying the components of the chart. Refer to Table 10.2 for a suggested organization of sections.

TIP: Color photocopies of the medical record may be useful if tampering with records is suspected, and are easier to read than black and white photocopies. It is rarely necessary for the attorney to incur the expense of obtaining color photocopies presuit, as the attorney may decide to not take the case.

Long-term nurses commonly identify the burdensome requirements for documentation that govern the charting in nursing homes. Documentation requirements in nursing homes are intensifying with the higher admission and discharge rates and the requirements of regulatory agencies. The limited number of professional nurses employed by nursing homes results in an increased amount of time being spent by each nurse on documentation and consequently less time spent with the resident. The American Nurses Association defines this problem as rooted in the conscientious nature of nursing. This is due in part to the emphasis put on documentation in nursing education, and to institutional and regulatory requirements. But as the documentation burden increases, nurses report that documentation comes at the expense of direct patient care, compromising the quality of patient care that documentation is supposed to ensure.[49]

Table 10.2

Nursing Home Record Organization

Patient Name: _____   Admission Date(s): _____

	Present	N/A	Missing	Need
(Before first section):				
Certification letter				
Face sheet				
Admission Records:				
Discharge summary				
Admitting record				
Admission notice				
Patient transfer form				
History and Physical:				
History and physical record				
Physician's Orders:				
Physicians' handwritten or typed order form				
Telephone orders				
Progress Notes:				
Physicians' annual care and discharge plan				
Special review, multidisciplinary care/ discharge plan				
Multidisciplinary care plan, interim problems				
Physician progress notes				
Multidisciplinary progress notes				
Multidisciplinary team conference attendance record				
Consultations i.e. Podiatrist, Pharmacist, Dental, others				
Nurses Notes:				
Agency-specific admission form				
Minimum Data Set				
State-specific admission form				
RAPs (resident assessment protocols)				
Nursing care plan				
Health care plan				
Graphic chart				
Vital sign sheet				
Narrative notes				

continued on next page…

Table 10.2 (continued)

	Present	N/A	Missing	Need
At risk for pressure ulcer form				
Medication and Treatment:				
Medication charts				
Treatment charts				
Other flow sheets (weights)				
Lab and Special Report:				
Lab work				
Blood transfusion				
Portable x-ray				
Rehab and Therapy:				
Activities assessment and records				
Physical therapy assessment and records				
Occupational therapy assessment and records				
Speech and language assessment and records				
Dietary:				
Nutritional assessment				
Progress notes				
Social Services:				
Social services assessment				
Patient's/Resident's social history				
Advanced directives				
Discharge Planning				
Miscellaneous Records:				
DNR documentation				
Certification and Re-certification				
Abnormal involuntary movement scale (AIMS)				
Acknowledgement form				
Designated representative form				
Advanced directives form				
Self Administration of medication				
Restraints consents/releases				
Billing Information				

Daily nurses' notes are uncommon in long-term care after the first few weeks after admission: flow sheets document treatments, ADL care, medications, and recording of weights and vital signs. OBRA regulations state that a resident must be seen by a physician once every 30 days for the first 90 days after admission, and at least once every 60 days thereafter, unless the nurse notifies the physician of a problem that requires a visit. An advanced practice nurse (APN) or physician assistant (PA) may provide every other visit after the first 90 days. Therefore physician's progress notes are infrequently written. Many facilities have moved to computer documentation of physician's orders, resulting in orders that are printed every 30 to 60 days and signed by the doctor, APN or PA. There are more nursing facilities embracing technology and the electronic health record. The most common application enables electronic documentation by CNAs, using such systems as CareTracker and Point-ClickCare. The reader may need to request software user guidelines to determine if documentation is complete and accurate.

A. Minimum Data Set

There are a few forms of documentation that are unique to nursing homes. To provide the minimum standard of care throughout the country, it was determined that a minimum set of data had to be collected in a standardized way. A standardized assessment tool called the Minimum Data Set (MDS 3.0) is used nationwide. It is a multi-page collection (including the face sheet) of resident information. There are items regarding demographic, physical, mental, and psychosocial function information. The resident's status is assessed over the previous seven days. The MDS must be completed by day 14 of the resident's admission to the long-term care facility. For reimbursement, a resident receiving Medicare benefits will have a preliminary MDS completed on day five for Resource Utilization Groups (RUGs) payment. Nurses, physicians, social workers, recreational therapists, the dietician, and other involved professionals participate in the completion of the MDS.

All nursing facilities participating in Medicare or Medicaid programs are required to conduct, initially and periodically, a comprehensive assessment of a resident's needs, using a state-specified resident assessment instrument (RAI).[50] The RAI includes both the MDS and utilization guidelines including the Resident Assessment Protocols (RAPs). This assessment instrument provides a comprehensive, accurate, standardized, and reproducible assessment of each resident's ability to perform daily life functions; it also identifies significant impairments in each resident's functional capacity. The federal requirement also mandates facilities to encode

and electronically transmit the MDS data from the facility to CMS through the state agency MDS database.[51] A number of systems and monitoring protocols that use MDS data have been developed and implemented, such as 1) SNF prospective payment system (PPS) for calculating reimbursement, 2) nursing facility quality of care monitoring, and 3) the public reporting of nursing facility quality of care.

The intent of the federal requirement is to provide the facility with ongoing assessment information of a resident's strengths and problems. It forms the basis for an individualized care plan that helps the resident attain the highest practicable physical, mental, and psychosocial functioning. The new 3.0 MDS has a new resident interview process; five-day look-back periods; new measurements and staging for pressure ulcers and pain; changes to RUGs; and shorter submission guidelines.[52] The 3.0 MDS was implemented on October 1, 2010. The updated information about the tool, its enhancements and manual are located on the CMS website.[53]

B. Resident Assessment Protocol

Once the MDS is completed, a second unique form is used. This is called the Resident Assessment Protocol (RAP). It is a decision tree based on the data collected in the MDS. For example, if certain items are flagged on the MDS, they are later studied as RAPs. The RAPs are utilized to identify possible causes and risk factors for each problem area, and provide guidance for further assessment and determination that a plan of care may need to be developed to address each problem area. The facility is required to document, on the RAP's summary form, the decisions made during this process as to whether or not to proceed to care planning. This process of identifying problems must be completed within 14 days after admission to the facility.

CMS requirements specify that an interdisciplinary care plan must be developed within seven days after completion of the MDS. The care plan should identify the resident's major problems, based on the MDS and RAP and include interventions designed to support the resident and prevent injury. There is no standardized care plan format. The most common method for developing the care plan is within the context of a team meeting with professionals in several disciplines participating in the process.

RAP guidelines are not meant to be prescriptive nor meant to replace the clinical judgment of the facility's staff as long as there is evidence of underlying rationale for the care plan. The team may decide that additional matters that were not identified through the MDS and RAP system should be included in the care plan.

C. Resource Utilization Groups

The Balanced Budget Act of 1997 included the implementation of a Medicare Prospective Payment System (PPS) for skilled nursing facilities certified for Medicare and Medicaid.[54] CMS's method for calculating reimbursement shifted from the DRG method of calculating the reimbursement for acute hospitals to a Resource Utilization Group (RUG) method. Reimbursement under the RUG system is based on a resident classification system which captures the staff resources expended in resident care. Some residents require total assistance with their activities of daily living (ADLs) and have complex nursing needs. Other residents may require less assistance with ADLs, but require other services such as rehabilitation or restorative nursing services.[55] The MDS data is used to define RUG-III groups that form a hierarchy from the greatest to the least resources used. Providing more specialized nursing care, licensed therapies, more restorative nursing, and so on, is more costly and is reimbursed at a higher level. RUGs determine Medicare payment and in some states, Medicaid payment.

The RUG-III classification system has eight major classification groups. The eight groups are further divided by the intensity of the resident's activities of daily living (ADL) needs, making a total of 53 RUGs. Nine payment categories have been added to the RUGs system. Residents receiving both rehabilitation and extensive nursing services will now qualify for one of the new RUGs.[56] (See Figure 10.5.)

MAJOR RUG-III GROUP	CHARACTERISTICS ASSOCIATED WITH MAJOR RUG-III GROUP
Rehabilitation Plus Extensive Services	Residents receiving physical, speech, or occupational therapy AND receiving IV feeding or medications, suctioning, tracheostomy care, or ventilator/respirator.
Rehabilitation	Residents receiving physical, speech, or occupational therapy.
Extensive Services	Residents receiving complex clinical care or with complex clinical needs such as IV feeding or medications, suctioning, tracheostomy care, ventilator/respirator and comorbidities that make the resident eligible for other RUG categories.
Special Care	Residents receiving complex clinical care or with serious medical conditions such as multiple sclerosis, quadriplegia, cerebral palsy, respiratory therapy, ulcers, stage III or IV pressure ulcers, radiation, surgical wounds or open lesions, tube feeding and aphasia, fever with dehydration, pneumonia, vomiting, weight loss or tube feeding.
Clinically Complex	Residents receiving complex clinical care or with conditions requiring skilled nursing management and interventions for conditions and treatments such as burns, coma, septicemia, pneumonia, foot infections or wounds, internal bleeding, dehydration, tube feeding, oxygen, transfusions, hemiplegia, chemotherapy, dialysis, physician visits/order changes.
Impaired Cognition	Residents having cognitive impairment in decision-making, recall and short-term memory. (Score on MDS 3.0 cognitive performance scale >=3.)
Behavior Problems	Residents displaying behavior such as wandering, verbally or physically abusive or socially inappropriate, or who experience hallucinations or delusions.
Reduced Physical Function	Residents whose needs are primarily for activities of daily living and general supervision.

Figure 10.5 Eight Major RUG-III Classification Groups

D. Quarterly and Annual Reassessments

The standard of care requires that staff members systematically monitor resident status between annual assessments. A quarterly MDS review is also required. The quarterly review focuses the assessment on a particular subset of MDS items to enable staff to detect gradual changes in resident status. This subset has been defined by CMS as a minimum quarterly assessment. This core of critical indicators helps staff track residents' decline or improvement. The quarterly review also determines whether the care plan needs to be revised. A facility is not obliged to use the CMS quarterly review form as long as the core items are exactly the same and the form has been approved by the state agency. An identifiable summary of the resident's status must be documented. The resident and the plan of care must be reviewed at least every 90 days and revised as necessary to suit the resident's needs. The care plan does not have to be rewritten each time, but instead can demonstrate the continuity of care and progression of resident status. At a minimum, each resident's chart will have two comprehensive minimum data sets and three quarterly reviews for any given 12-month period.

E. The MDS and Change of Condition

Should a significant change in resident status be identified, either through the quarterly review process or at any other time, a comprehensive MDS assessment needs to be conducted and the care plan revised. Before the completion of a new MDS, a suspected significant change should be documented in the progress notes. The resident's responses and all interventions must be carefully documented. A significant change means a major decline or improvement in the resident's status that will not typically resolve itself without further interventions, including disease-related interventions, by staff. The significant change has an impact on more than one area of the resident's health status, and the existing care plan no longer matches the current needs of the resident. The following are examples of decline or improvement in health status: changes in incontinence patterns; changes in ADL functioning; emergence of a pressure ulcer at Stage II or higher when no ulcers were previously present at Stage II or higher; an unplanned 5 percent weight loss in the last 30 days; changes in behavior or mood; a new condition or disease which renders the resident clinically unstable. Refer to Blackmon, Iyer, Tobias, and Thomas[57] for more information about long term care records.

10.8 Liability Issues

A. Assessment and Care Planning Process

In addition to the mandated federal assessments, there also must be evidence of assessment and care planning to meet the needs of newly admitted residents. The facility's staff is expected to provide for the resident's safety based on this initial assessment. A number of lawsuits have risen out of injuries sustained by residents before the comprehensive MDS is completed. The adjustment to a new environment can create or increase the resident's confusion and risk for falls. Thus, the period of adjustment to the facility is associated with an increased risk for injury.

TIP: Deviations from the standard of care can occur when the nursing staff fails to accurately assess the resident's needs, fails to identify nursing diagnosis, or fails to implement a plan of care to address the resident's needs.

The resident, family, and nurse's aides all play an integral role in the comprehensive assessment and care planning process. Communication between licensed nursing personnel and nursing assistants is critical since the nurse's aides provide the majority of direct personal care to residents. A study conducted of three Midwestern nursing homes noted that the care planning process differed despite common MDS systems.[58] Across these facilities, reliance of the MDS coordinator on verbal input from key direct care staff varied considerably. In two of the facilities a number of interviewed CNAs felt left out of the care planning process. After MDS and care plan review, changes in care plans were communicated to charge nurses, who then updated the relevant data into the documents that guided daily care, including end-of-shift reports. Staff attitudes about the documents used to link assessments and care planning to the delivery of care seemed to vary. A significant number of staff interviewed stated they knew what to do without having to refer to care plans, assignment guides, or even end-of-shift reports. The authors concluded that the preference of staff for informal communication and reluctance of certified nursing assistants to use written media diminished the effectiveness of the nursing process.

The care plan must be updated based on changes in the resident's condition.

In an Illinois case, a blind, paranoid schizophrenic man was placed on a unit with door alarms and windows that could be opened 8.125 inches. The resident managed to get the window open and fall to the ground. The plaintiff claimed the decedent was trying to elope from the facility and did not realize he was on the fifth floor. The plaintiff claimed negligence in the assessment of the decedent as an elopement risk, particularly given his prior window climbing behavior at the facility. A $1 million verdict was returned against the facility.[59]

The next section of the chapter provides a discussion of the liability issues of falls, burns, abuse, neglect, assaults, pressure ulcers, wandering, and failure to recognize a change in condition.

B. Falls

Falls and fall-related injuries are common liability concerns in nursing homes. Injurious falls may result in fractures of major bones, including the hip, arm, pelvis, and skull; paralysis from spinal cord injury; or decline or death from intracranial bleeding. Coumadin, a commonly used anticoagulant for atrial fibrillation, worsens the injuries from falls. The incidence of falls in nursing homes is 1.6 falls per bed per year.[60] A fall can set in motion a spiraling series of events, starting with a fracture in a relatively mobile person. This resident, after surgical repair, becomes more immobile and is at risk for pneumonia, pressure ulcers, depression, and incontinence.

At one time, the use of restraints was routine and unquestioned as the way to keep residents safe from falls. Reports of asphyxiation from restraints led to a re-examination of the use of these devices. As described in Miceli, Capezuti, Lawson and Iyer[61] awareness of the hazards of restraints was increased in the late 1980s. Research on the hazards of restraints, arguments against the ethics of tying down residents, and restrictions on the use of restraints culminated in the passage of OBRA. The 1987 Omnibus Budget Reconciliation Act (OBRA) and guidelines from the Centers for Medicare and Medicaid Services address the use of restraints. They require Medicare-skilled nursing facilities and Medicaid nursing facilities to promote an environment free of restraints.

Recognition has been increasing that the very devices that were designed to prevent injury have actually promoted injury in some residents. For example, side rails have been associated with injury to residents as they increase the distance to the floor when a resident climbs over them.[62]

Although directed by OBRA in 1990 to reduce and eliminate the use of physical and chemical restraints the subject still stirs up debate and there is noncompliance with the guideline. Careful and diligent assessment of staff attitudes, family fears, and physician awareness of regulations often must be overcome to keep a resident from being "tied down" just because it seems safer. Physical restraints include the use of side rails, geriatric chairs (referred to as Geri-chairs), belts, lap trays, and chest vests (often called a Posey, after the manufacturer). Use of homemade devices, such as gauze bandages and sheets, is considered below the standard of care. Leather restraints cannot be used in a nursing home. Some of the commonly used safety devices include: alarms for the bed and chair, low beds (except for residents with hip replacements), bedside floor mats (some are alarmed), self-release seat belts (some are alarmed) and tray tables.

Chemical restraints include the use of sedation to reduce violent, disruptive, or unsafe behavior. Justifications for the use of restraints include the desire to prevent falls; to prevent residents from removing tubes inserted into various veins, arteries, and body openings; and to control violent residents. Before a physical or chemical restraint can be used, the interdisciplinary team must develop a plan, and an order must be issued from the attending physician. Active falls-prevention and restraint-reduction programs must be in effect in every nursing facility.

A woman who weighed 63.9 pounds was admitted to a health care center for a short term rehabilitation stay to regain weight and strength. Five hours after admission she sought assistance to go to the bathroom. When no one came she attempted to get out of bed by herself and fell, breaking her shoulder and hip. Plaintiff alleged she was not adequately assessed for her fall risk. Although there was a written "Fall Risk Assessment" in the records, the plaintiff maintained that this appeared to have been completed after the fall, not in any initial admission assessment. A Connecticut jury returned a $1.5 million pain and suffering award, and also awarded about $46,000 for medical and funeral expenses. The jury assessed 5.9 percent fault to the decedent, resulting in a net award of about $1.4 million.[63]

A variety of devices and adaptations to the environment have been developed in recent years. Long-term care facilities have been even more active than hospitals in the use of strategies to prevent falls and lessen reliance on restraints. Much effort has been made to educate nurses about restraints and to change attitudes about their use.[64] Another challenge is getting nursing staff to follow the safety protocols, including frequent monitoring of residents at high risk for falling.

TIP: All falls are not preventable. Once a resident is identified as a fall risk the facility should document the implementation of the least restrictive safety device or devices in the care plan. If the resident falls, the care plan should be revised immediately to include the new interventions.

- Using non-skid footwear
- Placing the mattress on the floor
- Keeping brakes locked on beds
- Creating a toileting schedule
- Providing hip protector pads
- Keeping the environment uncluttered
- Using chair and bed alarms
- Evaluating medication regimen to determine if any of the drugs have side effects that may contribute to falls, such as dizziness or drops in blood pressure upon standing
- Providing physical therapy to strengthen muscles and improve balance
- Providing assistive devices such as walkers
- Defining how many people it takes to safely transfer the resident
- Using safe transfer techniques
- Properly caring for the equipment used to transfer residents, such as Hoyer lifts
- Providing supervision of residents, such as when they are in day rooms or dining rooms
- Keeping the floor dry
- Providing appropriate illumination, particularly for residents with visual changes
- Providing eye examinations and prescription changes for residents who need them

Figure 10.6 Measures to Reduce Risk of Falls

Nursing standards require identifying the resident who is at risk for falls and implementing least restrictive measures to protect the resident. Some of these measures are shown in Figure 10.6.

TIP: The standard of care on the use of restraints was changed so drastically that attorneys should no longer automatically evaluate a case assuming that the resident should have been restrained in order to prevent a fall. Rather, the standard of care incorporates the use of alternative approaches to avoid injury to the resident.

Cases involving hip fractures are the most problematic in terms of damages. Fall cases are viewed by some attorneys as one of the most defensible types of allegations. The nursing home has an obligation to provide the least restric-

tive environment and to permit the resident to have some mobility. The first fall is usually the easiest to defend. A resident with no prior history of falling, who is not at risk for falls, and with no documented change in status, may suddenly fall. A resident who falls out of a Hoyer lift might have contributed to the fall by unexpectedly moving, causing the Hoyer lift to topple. The circumstances of the fall have to be carefully examined, as well as all of the supporting documentation such as care plans, interdisciplinary team meetings, incident reports, and therapy and nursing notes.

C. Side Rail Use

Injuries from side rails and death by strangulation are still occurring in long-term care facilities. By nature of the setting, the resident population has high-risk characteristics of confusion, lack of functional control of limbs, anxiousness, and restlessness. Therefore, this population requires great caution and proper planning to decrease the risk of side rail injuries and asphyxiation.

In 1995, the FDA distributed an alert regarding Entrapment Hazards with Hospital Bed Side Rails which was applicable to nursing homes recommending actions to prevent incidents from occurring. A recent report from the FDA noted that between 1985 and January 1, 2006 there were 413 deaths and 120 injuries from the use of side rails. The commonality is that from the initial alert in 1995 to the present, most of the injuries and deaths affect the elderly.[65]

The Safe Medical Devices Act of 1990 requires hospitals, long-term care facilities, and others to report to the FDA any deaths, serious illnesses, and injuries associated with the use of medical devices, including side rails. Seven zones of entrapment are:

- Within the rail
- Between the top of the compressed mattress and the bottom of the rail between rail supports
- Between the rail and the mattress
- Between the top of the compressed mattress and the bottom of the rail at the end of the rail
- Between split bedrails
- Between the end of the rail and the side edge of the head or footboard
- Between the head or footboard and the end of the mattress[66]

According to OBRA guidelines, side rails are considered a restraint unless being used by the resident for positioning or as an enabler. If a resident wants the rails up for personal comfort level, the hazards are to be explained and an appropriate consent and order obtained. The appropriate assessments and orders must be initiated even if the resident wants the rails for positioning.[67]

The facility has a duty to ensure all resident beds are safe and mechanically intact, which includes wheels with locking mechanisms to prevent the bed from moving when residents get up or lay down and when receiving care and assistance from caregivers. In addition, long-term care staff should recognize individuals who are at risk and through the interdisciplinary process, develop the appropriate plan of care.

TIP: Nursing facilities should have a system in place to check all beds routinely for gaps between the mattress, frame, and side rail. Most facilities only use half rails.

Whenever the facilities are getting new replacement mattresses, ordering new side rails, or even interchanging mattresses, beds, and side rails, the manufacturer information should be readily available to maintenance, housekeeping, and nursing staff to ensure that different products can be used together. Staff should know where to obtain bumpers, wedges, and so on, applicable to the equipment in the facility, and how to apply them correctly to ensure the safety of the resident.

Staff must also continually review the propriety of the use of bed rail orders. As a resident becomes more confused and weaker from a disease process or acute illness, what was safe before may no longer be so; this resident requires a different intervention, and a conference with the resident (if possible), family, and physician should be scheduled. Facilities should be on high alert for any behaviors or sentinel events that demonstrate increased risk and act upon them immediately.

TIP: An intervention is required once a facility staff is aware that a resident has slid down in the bed, been found with an extremity caught in the rail, been found to hold her face close to the rail, or been found wedged between the mattress and rail.

D. Burns

Burn injuries to individuals over the age of 60 occur with a frequency that is out of proportion to that of all other ages except the very young. Elderly victims experience higher morbidity and mortality from burn injuries than any other age group. The majority of these injuries are preventable. The elderly are at particular risk for burns because of the factors listed below:

- Decreased perception of hot liquids due to decreased circulation

- Sensory impairment (smell, sight, hearing), which diminishes awareness of heat

- Cognitive impairment, which decreases awareness of being burned and also places the patients in high-risk situations

- Delayed reaction time and impaired mobility, which prevents the elderly from getting away from the source of heat

Burns involving 20-30 percent of the resident's body surface are lethal to 50 percent of people over the age of 60. Individuals with burns that cover more than 40 percent of their body surface, or cover 20 percent and are combined with smoke inhalation, have the poorest prognosis for survival. This is particularly true if the individual has preexisting cardiac or pulmonary conditions. The long-term care facility is obligated to provide care to reduce the risk of burn. State regulations may dictate bath and shower water temperature. If such regulations exist, it is difficult for the nursing home to argue that it was unaware of the state requirements. If not, counsel can rely on the doctrine of *res ipsa loquitor* to draw the inference that absent the defendant facility's negligence, the resident's burns could not have occurred.[68]

An Oregon nursing home resident was wheelchair-bound and taking medication that left his skin sensitive to the sun. The plaintiff claimed that the staff of the defendant nursing home left him in the sun, causing him to become sunburned and dehydrated. The plaintiff suffered skin ulcers with necrosis, as well as the dehydration. He recovered. A $50,000 settlement was reached.[69]

TIP: Facilities that allow residents to smoke must use great caution, develop an individualized care plan to address smoking safety for the resident, and adhere to the Life Safety Code and facility policies.

Fires in nursing homes may be more common than realized. Data show that an average of 2,300 of the country's approximately 16,300 nursing homes reported a structural fire each year from 1994 to 1999, and that there was an average of five fire-related nursing home deaths nationwide annually. Cooking and laundry dryers represent the leading causes of fires, but resident deaths were chiefly associated with smoking, primarily in their rooms.[70] Unfortunately, not all facilities have automatic sprinkler systems in place. Some facilities receive waivers due to building age and construction requirements in place at the time of construction. After the devastating fires in Hartford, Connecticut, and Nashville,

Tennessee, that resulted in 31 deaths, a Government Accountability Office (GAO) report was requested. It was published July 16, 2004 and discussed the need to reevaluate allowing older facilities to operate without sprinklers, and the retrofitting of older buildings with fire-safety systems.[71] In the wake of the Nashville fire, Tennessee required all nursing homes and assisted living facilities to have sprinkler systems.

Liability issues arise when confused, frail individuals are permitted to smoke while unattended. Poor hand dexterity may result in dropping lighted cigarettes. Visitors must be instructed to not give cigarettes to residents who are irresponsible in their smoking habits. With an increasing number of states passing laws requiring public places to be smoke free, there should be less indoor smoking.

E. Abuse, Neglect, and Assaults of Residents

Legal and medical definitions of abuse are very broad. Every state determines what acts of mistreatment are considered criminal, fraudulent and substandard, or civilly negligent. Periodically allegations of abuse or neglect are raised as part of a claim against a facility. At times, the acts rise to the criminal level.

A federal grand jury indicted American Healthcare Management Inc, its chief executive officer and three nursing homes for a conspiracy related to the failure of care and abuse of elderly residents. Prosecutors said that several residents of the three nursing homes suffered from dehydration and malnutrition, went for extended periods of time without bathing, and developed pressure ulcers that would have been preventable with proper care. The main reason for the failures was a lack of staff. The felony counts included conspiracy to defraud the United States, false statements involving a healthcare benefit program, healthcare fraud, and payment to non-licensed physicians.[72]

Evidence mounts that assaults, homicide and rapes of patients/residents are growing. The Joint Commission's Sentinel Event Database includes a category of assault, rape and homicide (combined) with 256 reports since 1995—numbers that are believed to be significantly below the actual number of incidents due to the belief that there is significant underreporting of violent crimes in healthcare institutions. While not an accurate measure of incidence, it is noteworthy that the assault, rape and homicide category of sentinel events is consistently among the top ten types of sentinel events reported to The Joint Commission. Since 2004, the Sentinel Event Database indicates significant increases in reports of assault, rape and homicide. The Joint Commission issued a June 3, 2010 Sentinel Event Alert—"Preventing Violence in the Health Care Setting."[73]

TIP: Few issues raise more emotional responses in the care of the elderly than the concerns about abuse and neglect. Settlements, as seen in this section of the chapter, are often out of proportion to the injuries sustained when residents are beaten by the nursing staff.

---

1. Abuse

Abuse can be intentional or accidental. Intentional abuse is a conscious, deliberate act geared to inflict financial, physical, or emotional harm.

Financial abuse may be manifested by unusual or inappropriate activity in bank accounts, signatures on checks that do not resemble the adult's signature, and recent changes in power of attorney or a creation of a will. There may be missing checks or money or unexplained decreases in bank accounts, missing personal belongings and deliberate isolation of a family member or the caregiver.[74]

Physical abuse is detected by observing for signs of bruises, welts, cuts or wounds, cigarette or rope burn marks, or blood on the adult that he may not be able to explain. The physically abused adult may have injuries that have been neglected, poor skin condition or hygiene and loss of weight. Injuries may be hidden by clothing.[75]

Emotional abuse may result in helplessness, withdrawn behavior, hesitation to talk openly, anxiety, trembling, clinging of fearfulness. The adult may blame herself for the current situation.[76]

Accidental abuse can occur because of lack of knowledge, inexperience, or lack of desire or ability to provide proper care.[77]

Nursing home residents are particularly at risk for abuse and neglect for a number of reasons. First, they typically have a number of chronic conditions that lead to limitations in physical functioning. Thus, they are dependent on others for assistance with activities of daily living. More than two-thirds of nursing home residents have significant cognitive impairment, due to diseases such as Alzheimer's or dementia. Finally, many residents do not have regular contact with family or friends outside of the nursing home. These resident characteristics, along with challenging behaviors, place residents at greater risk of both abuse and neglect.

Although there has been only minimal research on the causes of abuse and neglect in long-term care settings, various studies and surveys have concluded that there are three factors that cause or significantly contribute to abuse and neglect in nursing homes:

- staffing shortages that cause neglect and create stressful working conditions in which abuse is more likely to occur;
- staff burn-out, often a product of staffing shortages, mandatory overtime, and the fact that many staff must work two jobs to survive financially; and
- poor staff training, particularly about the impact of dementia and how to interpret and manage challenging behaviors among residents.

The Joint Commission identified factors that contribute to staff abuse of patients. The stressful environment together with failure to recognize and respond to warning signs such as behavioral changes, mental health issues, personal crises, drug or alcohol use, and disciplinary action or termination, can elevate the risk of a staff member becoming violent towards a patient. Though it is a less common scenario, health care workers who deliberately harm patients by either assaulting them or administering un-prescribed medications or treatments, present a considerable threat to institutions, even when the patient is unable to identify the responsible person. These situations point directly to the critical role human resources departments have in developing and following through on hiring, firing and disciplinary practices (which should be supported by management), and in performing thorough criminal background checks on all new hires.[78]

A South Carolina CNA comments on this problem: "Oh, yeah, I've seen abuse. Things like rough handling, pinching, pulling too hard on a resident to make them do what you want. Slapping, that too. People get so tired, working mandatory overtime, short-staffed. It's not an excuse, but it makes it so hard to respond right."[79] Poor staff training is the third likely cause or contributing factor for abuse and neglect in nursing homes. Direct care staff is not adequately trained in handling a resident with challenging behaviors, such as resisting care or ADL assistance or physical aggression. In general, staff members who are adequately trained on the neurological changes associated with dementia and on how to interpret and manage challenging behaviors are more likely to use a non-confrontational and accommodating approach to dealing with these behaviors.

The Omnibus Budget Reconciliation Act of 1987 (OBRA 87) gave residents of nursing homes for the first time the right to be free from verbal, sexual, physical, and mental abuse, corporal punishment, and involuntary seclusion.[80] Abuse is further defined as the willful infliction of injury, unreasonable intimidation, or punishment resulting in physical harm, pain, or mental anguish.[81] It also includes the deprivation by an individual, including a caregiver, of goods or services that causes physical harm, or pain or mental anguish.

Nursing home abuse cases are one of the more complex areas of nursing malpractice. Abuse cases may be difficult to detect and to prove. The true incidence of abuse is unknown. Residents and the long-term care staff may deny that mistreatment is occurring. The victim may be overwhelmed, embarrassed, or physically unable to ask for help. Denial is common among victims, perpetrators, and even the medical staff.[82] Bruises may be covered by clothing and thus out of the sight of even regular visitors. The cognitively impaired resident may be unable to communicate that physical abuse is occurring. In many cases, residents must rely on observant staff members who are able to detect abuse or neglect and are willing to report it, often at risk to their jobs. CMS regulations require the nursing home to report the abuse to the state department of health and to such other agencies as required by state law.

TIP: The federal law that mandates that all nursing homes investigate and report allegations of abuse is 42 CFR§ 483.13 [c] (2-4).

The Office of Adult Protective Services, the Office of the Ombudsman, and law enforcement agencies may become involved when suspected cases of abuse are uncovered. The facility that fails to report abuse or covers it up can be cited for deficiencies, fined, and required to develop a corrective plan.

A 71-year-old California nursing home resident's family noticed bruises on her arms, legs and face. The woman was unable to speak due to a stroke. The family complained to management, but claimed there was no investigation. After complaints for more than a year from the plaintiff's family and a family of another resident across the hall, the plaintiff's family installed a hidden camera in her room. The recording showed an employee slapping the plaintiff, pulling her by her hair, roughly handling her neck and hands, and treating her violently in a shower seat. The plaintiffs alleged elder abuse, negligence and breach of the patient's bill of rights. The jury awarded $7.75 million, including $3 million in punitive damages against the employee and the owner of the facility, and $2 million against the facility. Jurors apportioned fault 40 percent to the facility, 40 percent to the employee and 20 percent against the owner of the facility.[83]

2. Neglect

The nursing home staff can also be guilty of neglect. Neglect is the refusal or failure to fulfill a caretaking obligation; examples include abandonment, denial of food, clothing, or medical assistance, or withholding of medications or assistive devices. Neglect may be detected by seeing a resident in an unsafe or unclean living environment, rashes, sores or lice on the body, inadequate clothing for the weather, malnourishment or dehydration. The person looks unkempt.[84]

In a number of studies CNAs explained why staffing shortages caused or contributed to abuse and neglect. First, the CNAs noted that when they were short staffed there was no way to meet all of the residents' needs. The first things to be neglected were usually range of motion exercises and other types of restorative nursing care, keeping residents hydrated, and giving residents the necessary time and assistance with eating. Short staffing typically means that a CNA is asked or required to work all or part of a second shift, leading to exhaustion and worn tempers. Other times, short staffing means a CNA might have more than 60 residents to care for on the day shift. During night shifts, a single CNA might have 30 or more residents to care for. A comment from a Florida CNA reveals the depth of the problem. "The worst thing (about being a CNA) is the sense of powerlessness. To see residents suffering, but you've got 15 on your hands, and can't get to a resident. You tell the charge nurse what going on; she just looks at you like you're a fool, says nothing she can do. Yeah, it's that hopelessness of not being able to make a difference."[85]

TIP: Like abuse, neglect may be difficult to uncover. Residents are by definition often frail. Death from neglect may be easily overlooked or attributed to natural causes or changes associated with aging.

Verdicts or settlements for neglect cases also yield substantial award. The damages are relatively severe and often result in death. The neglect cases range from infections to murder. Punitive damages may be assessed if the nursing home failed to investigate the employee prior to offering that person a job. In one of the typical cases, a resident developed pressure ulcers allegedly because of negligent nursing care.

A Virginia nursing home resident developed several pressure ulcers, malnutrition, dehydration, and septic shock. She died from gangrene of both feet. The plaintiff claimed inadequate staffing levels allowed the decedent to lie in her own feces and develop dehydration and malnutrition. This was inexcusable because the resident was tube fed. The plaintiff claimed the decedent was not repositioned regularly, which caused additional pressure ulcers. The plaintiff also claimed that extra protein was not administered to avoid skin breakdown and promote healing. The plaintiff also claimed the business model for the facility was based more on profitability than patient care. Arbitration resulted in an award of $2.777 million.[86]

Many family members are heavily involved in feeding the long-term care resident. Meal times are brief and there are often not enough nursing staff to provide full attention to the needs of the resident, as a study performed by Tickle and Hull[87] found in a three-month observation in a nursing home. The investigators noted that family members spoke repeatedly about the need to help with feeding and to supervise meals. The investigators quoted several family members who emphasized the need to come for each meal, to ensure that their loved one was receiving proper nutrition. The families expressed empathy for the staff and repeatedly said the nurses and aides had to work too hard or did not have enough help. Interestingly, the staff of this particular nursing home projected an attitude of amused acceptance and tolerance of the families. This was in spite of the fact that family members were performing tasks such as feeding or walking the resident, which the staff would have to do themselves if the family member was not present. The staff seemed to view the family as an interruption in their work. The observers noted that the family member was considered to be someone the staff had to tolerate and believed that the family member had no contribution to make to the resident's care. It is easy to see how this attitude could lead to a breakdown in communication between the staff and the family, dissatisfaction, and a lawsuit if the resident experienced an injury in the facility.

3. Assaults by residents

Workplace violence is not the first thought that comes to mind when one thinks of a nursing home. It is primary to ensure that residents are not abused by staff, but what is also significant regarding this subject is that staff members are often abused mentally and physically by the residents. Workplace violence is one of the most complex and dangerous occupational hazards facing nurses working in today's healthcare environment. The complexities arise, in part, from a healthcare culture resistant to the notion that healthcare providers are at risk for patient-related violence combined with complacency that violence (if it exists) "is part of the job."[88]

Mixing the young, mentally ill patients; homeless people; or those with criminal backgrounds with vulnerable nursing residents is a recipe for trouble. The nursing home industry points to the costs and practicality of attempting to perform background checks on prospective residents to ban convicted sex offenders.[89] While the nursing home population continues to be what is considered the traditional elderly client, there are younger disabled residents with criminal backgrounds present in facilities.

The causes of assaultive behavior can be classified as:

1. Resident-initiated, such as medication reactions, mental illness, dementia, poor impulse control or a prior history of violence.
2. Environmentally induced, by things such as noise, bright lighting, temperature extremes, high activity levels, and crowding.
3. Staff-initiated, such as inadequate or poorly prepared staff, rigid routines, poor relationships between staff and residents.[90]

In 2002, the Indiana Alzheimer's Association convened a Working Group of consumers, long-term care professionals, and state agencies to complete a study of aggressive and potentially harmful behavior among long-term care residents pursuant to Senate Concurrent Resolution 18. A summary of findings presented by the Group to the Governor's Task Force on Alzheimer's Disease and Related Senile Dementia follow. Data is limited on the incidence and degree of harm caused by resident aggression. While the Working Group initially focused on aggressive behavior among nursing home residents toward other residents—as charged—it found in literature and practice at least equal concern about aggressive behavior of residents toward staff and family members in a variety of settings including home care, assisted living, adult day care, and so on. The problem of aggressive behavior concerns not only family members of victims, but also family members caring for aggressive loved ones, direct care staff, and administrators subject to liability and occupational health and safety (OSHA) issues. Moreover, while the Working Group initially focused on aggressive behavior among nursing home residents with Alzheimer's disease and other forms of dementia—as charged—it eventually recognized that aggressive behavior is a problem among a larger pool of nursing home residents, including residents with mental illness, co-occurring mental illness and dementia, physical health problems such as urinary tract infections, pain, and a history of violent or criminal behavior. Indeed the aggressive Evansville nursing home resident that prompted this study had a violent criminal history as well as alcohol-related dementia. Refer to Figure 10.7 for some of the conclusions of this study.

Understanding of the causes of disruptive behavior can only result in increased awareness and improved nursing home practices. Liability issues center around whether the behavior was foreseeable and could have been prevented.

In *Jean Conford, Individually and as a Representative of the Estate of Lucille Parrish et al. v. W.T. Manor*, Lucille Parrish, age 86, was a resident of a nursing home. A fellow resident entered her room at approximately 1:30 A.M. and proceeded to pull her from the bed. During the struggle, Parrish became disrobed. As a result of the struggle and because of her thin skin, she lost a majority of her skin on her right arm. Parrish died 27 days later on May 29,

---

Studies indicate that aggressive behavior is associated with a variety of factors related to residents, including but not limited to dementia:

- Previous history of violence/criminal record
- Untreated pain or other discomfort
- Medical conditions, such as urinary tract infections
- Depression, other mental illness, co-occurring disorders
- Males
- Mid to late stage Alzheimer's disease
- Other forms of dementia not related to Alzheimer's, such as head injury and alcoholism (younger and stronger residents with other dementias sometimes are placed in special care units for behavior management)
- Provocation by other residents and caregivers, often during assistance with activities of daily living (ADLs)

Figure 10.7 From 2002 Alzheimer's Association and Working Group Study Governor's Task Force on Alzheimer's Disease and Related Senile Dementia

2000, due to system failure as a result of the trauma she sustained. The male resident had a history of wandering, psychotic behavior, and mistaking his male roommate for his wife. There were prior episodes where he tried to pull his roommate out of his bed. The plaintiffs, the surviving adult children of Lucille Parrish, alleged inadequate staff and supervision. The nursing home contended the incident was unforeseeable and that they were not able to predict the resident's behavior. They had already increased his Haldol, which they claimed always calmed him down. Before trial, after the jury had already been picked, the defendants agreed to settle with the plaintiffs for $3 million plus court costs of $5,313.50.[91]

Clearly, in this case there is the question of whether the attack was foreseeable and therefore preventable. The questions raised by this case, as in any such assault case, involve what the facility did to prevent these injuries. The medical record must reflect the interventions that were carried out to manage the resident with violent tendencies.

The liability issues associated with the problems of the violent resident are complex. As described in Section 10.8.B, *Falls*, of this chapter, the use of physical and chemical restraints is actively discouraged. Because of these trends, the assaultive resident cannot be locked up or chemically restrained to the point of being nonfunctional. The staff of the long-term care facility has to walk a fine line between protecting the rights of the residents and protecting the rights of the combative individual. Nursing facilities must do a thorough job in obtaining the history and identifying the needs of potential residents who are admitted to their facilities. However, this can be a challenge and may not immediately signal red flags but still result in horrific outcomes.

The protection of residents from an assaultive resident is a difficult clinical issue. It requires the staff to identify the resident as a possible abuser, recognize the triggers that bring about assaultive behavior, and modify the environment. Refer to Figure 10.8 for examples of strategies nursing home staff may use to deal with aggressive behaviors. The nursing staff should be empowered through education and training to manage the stressors of this work environment. They should have policies in place to address this facet of care: facility physicians and the administration should actively address potential and actual behavioral problem residents so that an appropriate care plan and staffing can be put into place to thwart foreseeable incidents.

TIP: Once a resident is admitted to a facility it is very difficult to effect a transfer to a psychiatric facility as there are very few who accept gero-psych residents for a long-term stay. Most often the resident with serious behavior issues only receives emergency psychiatric treatment for 7–10 days and is transferred back to the nursing home.

- Reducing noise levels by turning down the volume on the television
- Eliminating the public address system
- Restricting shouting or loud talking by the staff members
- Removing pictures and mirrors and replacing them with carpet remnants
- Restricting unnecessary traffic
- Performing noisy activities in more remote areas
- Carefully monitoring TV to eliminate violent movies
- Playing relaxing music
- Forming small dining groups rather than eating in a large dining room
- Improving staffing so there will be optimal supervision of cognitively impaired residents and prompt attention to basic needs
- Maintaining calmness on the part of staff
- Avoiding arguing with the individual
- Looking for understandable patterns for the behavior
- Being consistent in routine and caregivers
- Ignoring angry behavior is distracting and support do not work
- Watching for signs of frustration
- Trying to soothe and redirect the resident

Figure 10.8 *Strategies to Reduce Aggressive Behaviors: Modified from J. Nelson, "The influence of environmental factors in incidents of disruptive behavior,"* Journal of Gerontological Nursing *21, No. 5 (May 1995): 19–24 and "Managing challenging behaviors in dementia patients,"* The Gerontological Nursing Counseling Points *(February 2006): 5.*

- Lack of a strong support system
- Generational beliefs about sexual abuse may increase feelings of shame and guilt
- Abuse may exacerbate an existing illness
- Longer recovery time dealing with abuse
- Increased chance of sustaining serious injury
- Increased vaginal or anal tearing and bruising that may never fully heal
- Brittle pelvis or hip bones can be broken by friction or weight
- Increased risk of infections
- STDs

Figure 10.9 How is Sexual Abuse Different for Elders? (http://www.aging.state.pa.us/aging/lib/aging/3-Final_pdf) pages 4-5 accessed 05/23/06.

4. Sexual assaults

The data is only beginning to emerge for this population, but it is known that cases of sexual assault go unreported. The real extent of elder sexual abuse remains unknown.[92] The importance of diligence of staff in identifying, reporting, and preventing occurrences cannot be understated. The nursing home population is very vulnerable for several reasons. Refer to Figure 10.9. A resident is dependent upon staff. Cognitive or functional impairment can result in a resident not being able to voice what happened or appropriately describe what occurred. Sadly, some residents mistake abusive caregivers for visitors—including a family member such as their husband or wife, or a suitor; they mistake the abuse for affection.

A mentally disabled Virginia man was sexually assaulted by a CNA who was hired at the facility despite the fact that he had five assault and battery convictions. This CNA also sexually assaulted another mentally impaired resident. The employee was suspended for two weeks but then rehired. The employee was the only employee in the building from 5 P.M. to 11 P.M. The employee sodomized the plaintiff repeatedly, permanently damaging his sphincter muscle in his rectum. This caused the plaintiff to require adult diapers. The plaintiff's physician testified the injury was caused by penile penetration and is not surgically correctable. The owner of the facility had known the employee for 24 years, knew he was gay and that he had been in numerous fights with his gay lover, resulting in injuries to the partner. A $750,000 verdict was reached, which included $250,000 in punitive damages.[93]

As many residents are cognitively impaired and unable to communicate what has occurred, nurses are expected to make careful observations, document behavior, and report any suspicions of sexual abuse to authorities and to the family. Changes may be manifested in sleeping or eating patterns, reactions to a certain person, or withdrawal from contact. The nursing home should have protocols regarding the collection and preservation of evidence such as bed linens and the patient's clothing. When a cognitively intact resident discloses that a sexual assault has occurred, she is often not believed, and therefore the incident is not reported to the police. One prevalent misconception about rape is that it is sexually motivated. In American culture, older people tend not to be considered attractive, so many people will ignore or disbelieve an older woman who says she has been sexually assaulted.[94] The police are expected to involve a Sexual Assault Nurse Examiner (SANE), if available, to use the rape kit to provide evidence to the police.

TIP: Sexual assault cases pose proof issues. Many cognitively impaired residents cannot describe what happened. It may be impossible in some cases to determine the identity of the assailant.

F. Pressure Ulcers

Frail elderly residents of a nursing home are at risk for the development of pressure ulcers. They typically have multiple risk factors, including thinner skin, less lean muscle mass, immobility, incontinence, malnutrition, or dehydration. Research has shown that a significant number of pressure ulcers develop within the first four weeks after a resident is admitted to a facility.[95] Attuned to the liability issues associated with the development of pressure ulcers, nursing staff are aware of the need to document the condition of the resident's skin on admission to the facility. In addition to identifying the presence of pressure ulcers at the time of admission, the admission assessment identifies at-risk residents and areas of skin that are at risk for breakdown. At-risk residents need to be identified and interventions implemented promptly.

TIP: When reviewing a claim involving the development of pressure ulcers, carefully scrutinize the admission assessment sheet to see if the condition of the skin on admission was documented. Ask for any photographs of the resident's pressure ulcer that may have been taken over the course of the admission. Vivid photographs can have a substantial emotional effect and may be a pivotal factor in settling a case.

---

1. Regulations

In November 2004, The Centers for Medicare and Medicaid Services issued guidance to surveyors involved in visiting nursing homes.[96] The pressure ulcer federal regulatory requirement 42 CFR 483.25 (c) includes some key changes, which are summarized below. One of the authors (PI) of this chapter has added some comments in parentheses. Attorneys, expert witnesses, risk managers, and legal nurse consultants who evaluate pressure ulcer cases are urged to review the complete document for all of the pertinent points. The document concludes with a protocol for surveyors to use to evaluate a pressure ulcer development in a facility. It serves also as a blueprint for evaluating liability.

- At the time of the assessment and diagnosis, the clinician is expected to document the clinical basis of the ulcer (e.g., underlying condition contributing to the ulceration, ulcer edges and wound bed, location, shape, condition of surrounding tissues) which permit differentiating the ulcer type, especially if the ulcer has characteristics consistent with a pressure ulcer, but is determined not to be one. (Look at the initial admission assessment or wound care sheet, if the facility uses one, for the status of skin on admission. It is helpful to set up a table to track each site of breakdown, noting stage, dimensions, drainage, and so on.)

- Unavoidable pressure ulcers are defined for the first time. "An unavoidable pressure ulcer occurs when the facility staff evaluated the resident's clinical condition and pressure ulcer risk factors, defined and implemented interventions that are consistent with resident needs, goals, and recognized standards of practice, monitored and evaluated the impact of interventions, and revised the approaches as appropriate." (Documentation in the medical record should support that all of these components were carried out. Be aware that documentation

may not reflect actual care. One study indicated that while nurses may be charting that turning is being done every two hours, the actual care provided is much less. A study of 16 California long-term care facilities demonstrated that repositioning was documented as being done every two hours in 95 percent of at risk residents, but were actually being turned every three hours in only 23 percent of residents at risk, as measured by a wireless movement monitor.)[97]

- The staff should perform a complete assessment in order to effectively prevent pressure ulcers and to identify the resident with pressure ulcers. An admission assessment helps to identify the resident at risk of developing a pressure ulcer or one who entered with pre-existing signs. These are defined as a very dark area that is surrounded by profound redness, swelling, or hardness. This suggests that deep tissue damage has already occurred. (The records of the facility that sent the resident to the nursing home may need to be examined to see if the appropriate standard of care was delivered. The nursing home can be expected to argue that the staff inherited the problem from another facility such as a hospital. Current theory is that a stage I always understates the underlying damage. The skin is the last tissue to show ischemic injury. Deep tissue injury may have begun at another facility, and become evident on admission to the nursing home.)

- It may be harder to identify redness in a resident with darkly pigmented skin. Other signs should be sought, such as bogginess, hardness, coolness, increased warmth, or skin discoloration. (Look for documentation that the staff noted these signs. A 2004 study found that black nursing home residents are significantly more likely to develop pressure ulcers than white residents are. The authors concluded that the black residents had a greater need for help in performing activities of daily living, a pressure ulcer on admission, fecal incontinence, or both fecal and urinary incontinence, dementia and Medicaid coverage. The researchers also hypothesized that caregivers might have a harder time detecting early-stage pressure ulcers on dark skin. The study included only data on pressure ulcers at stage II or worse. Underdetection of stage I ulcers could have resulted in a greater number of ulcers progressing to stage II in those residents.)[98]

- A resident with a pressure ulcer who continues to lose weight either needs more calories or correction, where possible, of conditions that are creating a hypermetabolic state. Continuing weight loss and failure of a pressure ulcer to heal despite reasonable efforts to improve caloric intake may indicate that the resident is in a multi-system failure or an end-stage or end-of-life condition warranting additional assessment of the resident's overall condition. (Some residents have terminal illnesses, such as undiagnosed cancer, which causes uncontrollable weight loss. A medical expert should review the records for signs that might be consistent with undiagnosed malignancies, such as unexplained bleeding, or for statements in physician progress notes indicating that the family or patient declined investigation of suspicious signs and symptoms.)

- It is critical that each resident at risk for hydration deficits or imbalance, including the resident with a pressure ulcer or at risk of developing an ulcer, be identified and that hydration needs are addressed. (Documentation about fluid intake should be reviewed. Evaluate laboratory results for evidence of dehydration such as electrolyte abnormalities, dry mucous membranes, and so on.)

- Some studies have found that fecal incontinence may pose a greater threat to skin integrity than urine, most likely due to bile acids and enzymes in feces. (Review the medical record to determine if the resident was incontinent of bowel and bladder. Family statements or testimony may indicate that the resident was often found in soiled sheets or with feces caked to the skin.)

- The care plan for a resident who is reclining and dependent on staff for repositioning should address position changes to maintain the resident's skin integrity. This may include repositioning at least every two hours or more frequently depending on the resident's condition and tolerance of the tissue load (pressure). (Residents on tube feedings are maintained with the head of the bed elevated to reduce the risk of aspiration. This puts pressure on the sacral area. Protective mattresses are important aides in reducing pressure.)

- Wheelchairs are often used for transporting residents, but they may severely limit repositioning options and increase the risk of pressure ulcer development. Wheelchairs with sling seats may not be optimal for prolonged sitting during activities or meals. Available modifications to the seating can provide a more stable surface and better pressure reduction. (Look for evidence that protective seat cushions were provided by physical or occupational therapy. Review the medical record to determine, if possible, how long the resident was sitting in a wheelchair each day.)

- The resident's heels and elbows are particularly vulnerable to pressure due to their little surface area. It is important to pay particular attention to reducing the pressure on these areas. (The medical record should include documentation of the use of heel protectors and elevation of the heels while in bed. Heel protectors alone are not as effective as eliminating pressure through elevation.)

- Staff should remain alert on a daily basis to potential changes in the skin condition. A resident who complains of pain or burning at a site where there has been pressure should be evaluated. (Evidence shows that residents with dementia are able to accurately report pain, and that pressure ulcers are painful in all stages.)

- Components of assessment of an ulcer include:
  - Differentiate the type of ulcer
  - Use pressure redistribution measures
  - Determine the ulcer's stage
  - Describe and monitor the ulcer's characteristics
  - Monitor the progress towards healing
  - Monitor for potential complications
  - Determine if the ulcer is infected
  - Assess nutritional status
  - Notify family
  - Assess, treat, and monitor pain, if present
  - Monitor dressings and treatments

With each dressing change or at least weekly (and more often when indicated by wound complications or changes in wound characteristics), an evaluation of the pressure ulcer wound should be documented. At a minimum, documentation should include the date observed and:

- Location and staging
- Size, depth, presence, location, and extent of any undermining or tunneling/sinus tract
- Exudate: color, odor and approximate amount
- Pain, if present: nature, frequency (episodic or continuous)
- Wound bed: color, type of tissue, evidence of healing (granulation tissue) or necrosis (slough or eschar)
- Description of wound edges and surrounding tissue (rolled edges, redness, hardness/induration, maceration)

- Resident's nutritional status including the acceptance of dietary or nutritional supplements as ordered

Based on F-314, there are five key parameters that any skin assessment performed in a long-term care facility should address:

- Temperature
- Turgor
- Moisture
- Integrity
- Color[99]

- If the ulcer fails to show some evidence of healing within two to four weeks, the ulcer and the resident's overall condition should be reassessed. (Evaluate the plan of care and determine if a wound care team was involved. Were treatments appropriate to the stage of the ulcer? Was a dietician involved? Were treatments administered as ordered or were ones missed?)
- If photographs are used, they should be taken in compliance with a protocol that addresses frequency, consistent distance from the wound, type of equipment used, means to assure digital images are accurate and not modified, inclusion of the resident identification/ulcer location/dates, and so on within the photographic images, and parameters for comparison. (Some facilities are using the additional precaution of photographing all pressure ulcers found at the time of admission. The photographs and documentation establish a baseline to evaluate changes in skin integrity. Some defense attorneys are discouraging the use of photographs. Most defense attorneys do not like facility staff to take photographs because they provide graphic demonstration of the injury. The National Pressure Ulcer Advisory Panel (NPUAP) and the Wound, Ostomy, and Continence Nurses Society (WOCN) neither recommend nor discourage the use of photography as a documentation tool for pressure ulcers. Photography poses both advantages and drawbacks. Both NPAUP and WOCN recommend that organizations have written guidelines about if and when photography is to be used.[100])

Pressure ulcer cases can horrify a jury, making these cases high risk for the defense. Careful investigation of the medical record, photographs, and family statements about care can be helpful in determining if the standard of care was followed.

2. Case

In the following case, the plaintiff contended that the nursing home failed to provide the proper standard of care and supervision to a resident who developed severe pressure ulcers and ended up with a diverting colostomy.

The 75-year-old nursing home resident suffered from dementia. He developed pressure ulcers which necessitated several hospital admissions. The pressure ulcers eventually became infected. The decedent's treatment included the creation of a diverting colostomy. When the decedent was transferred to another nursing home, he was found to have more than 20 pressure ulcers. The man's infection spread and he died. The plaintiffs claimed that his death was due to infected pressure ulcers caused by inadequate treatment at the defendant nursing home. The defendant nursing home claimed that the hospital's staff had been negligent in its treatment of the pressure ulcers. The defendant also claimed the pressure ulcers were unavoidable due to the decedent's confinement to bed. The hospital claimed the nursing home staff had provided inadequate treatment. A jury returned a finding of negligence against the nursing home, awarded $18.75 million, which included $15 million in punitive damages. The estate's recovery was reduced under a high/low agreement to $750,000.[101]

This case illustrates that the development of pressure ulcers can lead to illness, long periods of treatment, death, and liability.

3. Controversies

Several factors unique to working and caring for high risk residents affect the determination of liability and damages.

a. Licensed practical nursing role

As mentioned earlier in the chapter, licensed practical nurses outnumber registered nurses in long term care facilities and oversee the care delivered by CNAs. Licensed practical nurses are not licensed to independently perform assessments. However, institutions may have evolved practices delegating wound assessment responsibility to these staff members. Clinicians can expose themselves to legal action by accepting responsibilities exceeding their scope of practice. Likewise, facilities may be found liable for routinely requiring such actions of their staff.[102] Ideally, a well educated wound care team, or registered nurses who have been kept current with staging guidelines will perform the assessments.

b. Prescriptive privileges

Intuitional practices need to be evaluated to ensure they are in compliance with prescribing regulations. If a wound is debrided using an enzymatic debriding agent, a healthcare provider with prescriptive privileges such as a physician, nurse practitioner, or physician assistant, must sign the order. These agents are pharmaceuticals. Some facilities have evolved standing orders that incorporate enzymatic debriding agents that nurses can implement without a provider's signature. Such a practice would be outside compliance with prescribing laws.[103]

c. Avoidable versus unavoidable

CMS has targeted pressure ulcers, in part, because of the high cost associated with caring for them. In fiscal year 2007 alone, there were 257,412 Medicare beneficiaries with pressure ulcers, for which the average DRG payment per case was $43,180.[104] The net cost of caring for pressure ulcers is estimated at $11 billion per year.[105] CMS treats hospitals and long term care facilities differently related to the development of pressure ulcers. CMS has acknowledged that in long term care pressure ulcers can be avoidable or unavoidable. Facilities may receive civil monetary penalties, deficiencies, and even loss of license for the facility and inability to receive Medicare payments. In acute care, CMS states pressure ulcers are reasonably preventable. Facilities are denied reimbursement for care for the development of a stage III or IV ulcer.[106]

Determination of whether a pressure ulcer is avoidable or unavoidable heavily depends on analysis of the medical record. Thorough documentation must be balanced by the demands of patient care.

d. Arterial or venous

Differentiating between venous or arterial ulcers and pressure ulcers drives both treatment and evaluation of liability. Blame is attached to the development of pressure ulcers in a way that is not associated with venous or arterial ulcers. An algorithm helps to guide the clinician in deriving the correct diagnosis.

- Where is the wound? If it is on a lower extremity, it could be either a vascular or a pressure ulcer.
- Is there vascular insufficiency? A blockage in an artery may signify peripheral vascular disease.

- If there is vascular insufficiency, is there gangrene? If yes, this is an arterial ulcer.
- If there is no vascular insufficiency, is the resident a diabetic? If yes, is this an area of repetitive trauma, such as to the bottom of the feet? If yes, it is a diabetic ulcer.
- If the patient is not diabetic, are there signs of venous stasis disease in the legs? If yes, this is a venous stasis ulcer.
- If there are no signs of venous stasis, is the ulcer on a bony prominence? If yes, this is a pressure ulcer.[107]

e. Terminal ulcer or substandard care

Karen Lou Kennedy-Evans first described what became known as the Kennedy Terminal Ulcer in 1989. This is a subgroup of pressure ulcers that some individuals develop as they are dying. They are usually shaped like a pear, butterfly, or horseshoe, and are located predominantly on the coccyx or sacrum (but have been reported in other anatomical areas.) The ulcers are a variety of colors including red, yellow or black, are sudden in onset, typically deteriorate rapidly, and usually indicate that death is imminent. An expert panel, called Skin Changes at Life's End (SCALE) evaluated the concept of unavoidable pressure ulcers at end of life. They reached consensus on ten points. Three of these are:

- Physiological changes that occur as a result of the dying process (days to weeks) may affect the skin and soft tissues and may manifest as observable (objective) changes in skin color, turgor, or integrity, or as subjective symptoms such as localized pain. These changes can be unavoidable and may occur with the application of appropriate interventions that meet or exceed the standard of care.
- Skin changes at life's end are a reflection of compromised skin (reduced soft tissue perfusion, decreased tolerance to external insults, and impaired removal of metabolic wastes).
- Risk factors, symptoms and signs associated with SCALE have not been fully elucidated, but may include:
  - Weakness and progressive limitation of mobility
  - Suboptimal nutrition including loss of appetite, weight loss, cachexia and wasting, low serum albumin/pre-albumin, and low hemoglobin as well as dehydration
  - Diminished tissue perfusion, impaired skin oxygenation, decreased local skin tempera-

ture, mottled discoloration, and skin necrosis

- Loss of skin integrity from any of a number of factors including equipment or devices, incontinence, chemical irritants, chronic exposure to body fluids, skin tears, pressure, shear, friction, and infections[108]

4. Products

There exists a plethora of products on the market to prevent and treat pressure ulcers. The manufacturers of products have to prove their products are safe, but there is no requirement to complete efficacy studies prior to releasing the product to the market. Pressure ulcers are best treated by relieving pressure and maintaining a moist environment. Hydrocolloid dressings have been found to be superior to saline soaked dressings. Hydrocolloids do not allow bacteria to penetrate the wound and protect it from incontinence. Research shows that the following treatments are not effective: honey, sugar, skin equivalents, antacids, zinc paste, gold leaf, aluminum foil, topical insulin, cytozime factors, and sulfa silvadene. Oral zinc has not shown to improve healing, but higher protein in the diet is effective. Outcome studies show ulcers heal faster with debridement. Heel ulcers are exceptions. They should not be debrided or covered with moist dressings. Pressure reduction boots should be used.[109] Refer to the updated National Pressure Ulcer Advisory Panel (www.npuap.org) for the most recent guidelines for pressure ulcer prevention and treatment issued in 2009.

Accurate staging of pressure ulcers provides the data needed to determine if the wound is responding to treatment or if the plan of care should be altered. The nursing home typically uses one flow sheet to document the weekly skin assessments, including details about the pressure ulcer, and another flow sheet to document the implementation of the treatments designed to help the pressure ulcer heal.

According to the updated interpretive guidelines, nursing homes are required to document that the resident was assessed for pressure ulcer pain regardless of what the stage of the pressure ulcer is, and pain management must be addressed through the care planning process and treated accordingly. Refer to Chapter 25, *Wounds*, for additional information on this topic.

TIP: The easiest pressure ulcer case to defend is that of a pre-existing wound that heals within the nursing home.

G. Wandering and Elopements Resulting in Injury

Clinicians are imprecise in using the term wandering. To some it means a propensity to elope from the unit or fa-

cility. To others it signifies the ambulation patterns of persons with way-finding problems. The term can also apply to the frequent and repetitive activity of cognitively impaired persons, considered remnants of earlier habits and preferences.[110]

Research continues in earnest to evaluate patterns and interventions and effectiveness of interventions to keep residents safe while not circumventing their freedom while wandering. Often nursing staff will use wandering and elopement interchangeably. However elopements, which involve purposeful and repeated attempts of a resident to leave the facility, are more difficult to control than random wandering into stairwells or other potentially unsafe areas.[111]

TIP: Wandering poses a significant liability risk when the resident sustains injury or escapes from the facility undetected.

---

1. Liability risks associated with wandering

The wanderer poses a risk because he can be so intent on the act of wandering that dangerous elements in the environment will not be recognized. Wanderers often will take a cue from their environments. For example, if a resident sees a coffee pot, the resident may pick up the coffee pot and wander to search for a cup. This could result in a burn or shattered glass if the resident dropped the coffee pot, creating a wet surface which could increase the risk for a slip and fall.

Falls and fractures are also consequences of wandering behavior. A resident may wander into equipment, other residents, or walk-in closets. Those who elope may fall due to inclement weather, surface changes, fatigue, and muscle weaknesses. Falls and the possibility of elopement are high during the first 72 hours of admission for ambulatory residents and wheelchair residents who are able to self-propel. This is because their environment is new and the need to find "home" or something that they recognize as home. Families are encouraged to bring items to personalize the resident's room to make the transition easier. The risk of falling increases in relation to the cognitive impairment of the wanderer. Those who wander tend to burn off more calories than the more sedentary residents. Often this type of resident will not sit down to eat a meal but "eat on the run," and is therefore at risk for weight loss. The wanderer also is sometimes the victim of verbal and physical abuse from peers because of entering other resident's rooms and rummaging through, touching, or picking up possessions that belong to others.

To ensure the safety of residents who wander and have the desire to leave the facility, the long-term care staff must be vigilant in their observation efforts. When new staff

- Place stop signs at exit doors
- Put black carpet or paint at exit doors (some residents perceive this as a black hole)
- Encourage families to rotate their visiting schedules to provide the resident with more company
- Place the resident in an accelerated activities therapy plan
- Increase scheduled exercise programs
- Redirect the resident
- Provide staff education regarding alarm use and interventions
- Educate family members not to open doors for residents to outdoors or parking lots
- Create enclosed courtyards
- Ensure that all, not just nursing, staff are aware of who are the wanderers and "potential for elopement" residents
- Schedule direct observation of high risk residents when alternatives fail
- Provide calming music therapy
- Be sure the resident is wearing identification
- Encourage daily exercise to reduce excess energy and promote sleep
- Keep a current photograph of the resident on hand in case the person becomes lost
- Ensure the resident's physical needs are met
- Assess the resident for signs of illness or pain

Figure 10.10 Helpful Tips for Wandering and Elopement, modified in part from "Challenging behaviors in dementia patients," Gerontological Nursing Counseling Points, pg. 8, February 2006

members are hired or agency staff is employed, it is very useful for the charge nurse to go over who is at risk. Often facilities will also have a notebook for the receptionist to assist in identifying those residents.

Electronic monitoring systems can be placed on all doors of egress; these sound when a resident attempts to leave. These systems are becoming more advanced as technology advances. There are some systems that can be coded with the resident's wrist or ankle bracelet which allows the long-term staff to know exactly who was near a door, opened a door, or possibly eloped. The benefit of these systems is clear, but some of the more sophisticated systems are expensive. There is also the occasional resident who does not like the bracelet on and will focus a great deal of effort in getting free from it, which can result in skin tears. The clinical record should reflect an interdisciplinary approach to the strategies to protect the resident and the results. Refer to Figure 10.10 for examples of useful strategies for dealing with wandering.

TIP: Any time the long-term care facility staff cannot locate a resident, it has to be assumed the resident has eloped. This should result in an immediate search of the facility's interior and grounds.

2. Cases relating to injury caused by wandering

This case is an example of multiple failures:

A Massachusetts nursing home resident with dementia was a known escape risk, as he had a high activity level and had made 16 previous attempts, three of them successful. He was in a secure Alzheimer's unit, which was locked with a punch code pad. He entered the code to the elevator, took the elevator to the first floor, and walked through the reception area and out the front door. He fell down an embankment and was found by a security guard from a neighboring building. He suffered hypothermia and a fractured hip which required surgery. His health declined and he died. The plaintiff alleged negligence in failing to change the keypad code on a weekly basis and failure to implement a system of guards to prevent escape. A $325,000 settlement was reached.[112]

It is clear from a review of the above case that unmonitored wandering and actual elopement can result in death or injury by a variety of environmental conditions that are hazardous to residents. The facility should have a system in place to evaluate those who are at risk for both of these behaviors and plan their care, activities, and environment accordingly. Should an Alzheimer's resident successfully elope from a residential facility, one of the issues in the case is likely to be whether the home was an appropriate setting and whether safeguards had been instituted to prevent elopement or to monitor the wandering. There would also be a focus on whether the search for the missing resident was conducted timely and thoroughly, and whether the appropriate parties were notified (family, physician, administration, police department).

Refer to Iyer[113] for additional information on nursing home liability issues.

H. Failure to Recognize a Change in Condition

As discussed in other chapters, there is often a fine line between medical and nursing diagnoses. The nurse practicing in a long-term care facility is placed in a position of making clinical judgments without a physician readily at hand. The long-term care nurse has the option of sending the resident to the emergency room of the local hospital for an evaluation if warranted. Many long-term care nurses welcome the opportunity to exercise their nursing judgment and autonomy. This is a source of satisfaction, but is also a source of liability when the nurse's clinical judgment is absent or incorrect. The following cases illustrate the consequences of not keeping the physician informed of changes in the resident's condition.

A Colorado man was discharged from a rehabilitation facility after a history of pulmonary emboli that developed after a back injury. He was on Coumadin and other anticoagulants. He also had stage III lung cancer. When his wife picked him up at discharge he was perspiring, clammy, short of breath and somewhat incoherent. The wife claimed that several licensed practical nurses were told of her concerns but none of them assessed him. The nurses insisted the decedent's condition was related to a urinary tract infection. Paramedics were called and the decedent was transported to a hospital, where he died six hours later of a myocardial infarction. The plaintiff claimed that the facility, which used more licensed practical nurses than registered nurses, failed to have a higher quality of care that was required for medically complex patients such as the decedent. The plaintiff claimed the nursing staff missed obvious signs and symptoms of the heart attack and were negligent in failing to assess the decedent after his wife asked for help. The plaintiff also claimed that the decedent's blood work drawn on the day of his discharge, showed no infection,

but did show critically elevated enzymes, indicating a heart attack. The plaintiff claimed the lab results were received more than an hour prior to his discharge, but the information on the abnormal values was not relayed to him, his wife, or the paramedics. A jury awarded $450,000. [114]

The American Medical Directors Association developed a clinical practice guideline to highlight acute changes of condition. These are defined as a sudden, clinically important deviation from a patient's baseline in physical, cognitive, behavioral, or functional domains. "Clinically important" means a deviation that, without intervention, may result in complications or death. One of the primary goals is to avoid transferring the resident, when possible, to the hospital, where care is costly, disruptive, and exposes the resident to risks of hospital-acquired complications.[115] Many conditions may be safely managed in the nursing home.

Family members who see an acute change in the condition of their loved one may pressure the nursing staff or physician to transfer the resident to the hospital. It is more likely that the facility will be faulted for keeping a resident at the nursing home who appears to need a higher level of care than for sending the resident to the hospital. Nurses may initiate a transfer to the hospital if they are unable to reach the physician and believe the resident needs acute care. A physician may send the resident to the hospital because of the financial disincentives to provide acute care while the resident is kept at the nursing home.

I. Medication Errors

Chapter 28, *Medication Errors*, provides details regarding medication errors in many settings of nursing care delivery. The elderly are at particular risk for medication errors due to the number of medications prescribed to them, as well as their decreased ability to tolerate excessive doses. Pharmacist William Simonson[116] focused on other potential sources of injury: excessive doses, excessive duration, inadequate monitoring, inadequate indications for use, and adverse reactions necessitating dose reduction or discontinuation. Excessive doses may occur when the prescriber does not "start low and go slow" or slowly increase the dosage of a medication. Age-related changes reduce the elder's ability to metabolize medications. Excessive duration of treatment involves not stopping a medication when it has lost its effectiveness due to chronic administration. Such categories of medications include sedatives, antibiotics, and certain medications that control behavior related to dementia.

Inadequate monitoring refers to failure to evaluate the impact of a medication on the elder. For example, an elder may become excessively sedated from a sleeping medication, or suffer kidney or liver damage from a mediation such as Lipitor or certain antibiotics. The indication for prescribing a medication must be substantiated in the medical record. Inadequate indications for use may be alleged when a resident receives psychotropic medications to control behavioral issues which are no longer present. Adverse drug reactions may have life-threatening effects. It is important for nursing home staff to detect and respond to signs of medication reactions.[117]

TIP: Defendants involving a case of medication error may include facility administrator, director of nursing, nursing staff, consultant pharmacist, nurse practitioners, attending physician, and the medical director.[118]

In an Arizona case, a woman was admitted to the hospital for treatment of sciatic pain after a fall. Fifteen milligrams of Morphine Sulfate Controlled Release (MS Contin) twice a day, was prescribed. Shortly before the patient was transferred to a skilled nursing facility, the dose of MS Contin was increased to 30 mg. The hospital's case manager recorded the increase of MS Contin to 30 mg twice a day without striking out the previous order for 15 mg. The patient received 45 mg of Morphine twice a day and died from acute Morphine intoxication. The nursing home settled and the plaintiff recovered $600,000 from the hospital where the order originated.[119]

10.9 Defense of the Long-Term Care Case
A. Overview

There are several obstacles in defending claims in long-term care. Long-term care facility records are quite voluminous and have contents unlike the traditional hospital record. Licensed nurse charting is often not completed on a daily basis if the resident is not receiving skilled Medicare services or has had no changes. This type of record often details only incidents, or change, with nothing in between. This can look suspicious to an outsider not familiar with the differences. In addition, the volume of the records lends itself to showcasing other types of errors or documentation issues that while not central to claim issue, reflects poorly on the facility and staff. Staff members are often shocked and dismayed when a lawsuit is brought by the family. This is especially the case when they thought there had been positive communication and the family was satisfied with the care. The staff needs much support from the counsel and risk manager of the facility.[120] Another obstacle to rapid resolution of claims is de-

lay in the defense team's capability to initiate and organize strategy.[121] The staff should not automatically think the lawsuit is a "done deal."

B. Defense Theories

There are several viable ways to defend a claim against a long-term care facility. Theories are illustrated with recent cases. These theories include invoking the right to refuse care, disputing the proximate cause of the injury, asserting that the injury was not foreseeable, and asserting that the standards of care were followed.

1. Right to refuse care

The resident has the right to refuse care if she is competent. The evaluation of competence has important implications with the aging of the long-term care population and the influx of long-term psychiatric residents into long-term care facilities. Residents are considered incompetent to make medical decisions when they are unable to understand information about their medical condition and its implications or when they are unable to communicate their decisions even though they understand.[122] Evaluation of the resident's clinical record should reveal objective data to assist in determining competency.

One of the basic rights of the nursing home resident is the right to define advance directives which specify the care the resident wishes to receive in the event of a sudden illness or a cardiac arrest. The long-term care facility is expected to keep this information on file and to respect the wishes of the resident.

2. Preexisting illness or disputing the proximate cause

The presence of pre-existing illness provides a strong defense on proximate cause when the plaintiff is attempting to link the injuries to the damages. As a general rule, people in nursing homes are not healthy. The defense can and will offer experts to say that even with the best of care, the same injury would have occurred.[123]

3. The injury was not foreseeable

The successful prevention of injury can flow from the healthcare professional's ability to recognize signs of an impending problem. Residents can do unpredictable things.

4. The standards of care were followed

Review of the medical record as well as strong testimony from the defendants can be instrumental in convincing a jury that the appropriate standards of care were followed. A bad result does not mean that bad care was given. See Iyer for several chapters on the defense perspective on nursing home litigation.[124]

10.10 Summary

The spread of litigation into long-term care can be attractive to plaintiff's attorneys. The early '90s provided encouragement to pursue these types of cases with landmark jury verdicts. Baby boomers and potential residents have become savvier regarding long-term care, resident's rights, what nursing home care is, what it offers, and what to do when they do not receive what was promised. This area will remain in the spotlight. The existence of well-defined clinical standards and state and federal regulations can be used to screen as well as defend cases involving subacute and long-term care. The standards and regulations can also be incorporated by the long-term care facilities into their policies, procedures, and risk management programs.

Endnotes

1. The authors appreciate the contributions of Joanne Kelsey BSN RN LNHA and Kathleen Tully MSN NP LNHA to previous editions of this chapter.

2. Houser, A., Fox-Grage, W., and Gibson, M. *Across the States 2009: Profiles of Long Term Care and Independent Living*, Washington, DC, AARP, 2009.

3. Braun, J. and Iyer, P. "Nursing Home Litigation and the Elder Law Attorneys," *Elder Law Handbook*, 4th Edition, Ohio State Bar Association, 2010, 299-328.

4. See 42 C.F.R. 412.23(e).

5. Sahyoun, N., L. Pratt, H. Lentzner, A. Dey, and K. Robinson, "The changing profile of nursing home residents 1985–1997," *The Aging Trends* 3, no. 4 (2001).

6. Cowles, L., "Nurturing field," *Advance for Nurses, Pennsylvania, New Jersey, Delaware*, 41–42, 2006.

7. Baldauf, S. "These Nursing Homes Care About Their Elderly Charges," *US News and World Report*, February 5, 2010.

8. Ouslander, J., D. Osterweil, and J. Morley, *Medical Care in the Nursing Home*, Second Edition, New York: McGraw Hill, 1997.

9. Stanley, M. and P. Beare, *Gerontological Nursing*, Philadelphia: F. A. Davis Company, 1995.

10. Forciea, M.A. and R. Lavizzo-Mourey, *Geriatric Secrets, Questions you will be asked*, Philadelphia: Hanley and Belfus, 1996.

11. Adapted from *Sensitizing People to the Processes of Aging: The In Service Educator's Guide* by M. Ernst and H. Shore. Dallas Geriatric Research Institute, 1977. Distributed by: Judith L. Warren, PhD, Extension Program Leader and Professor and Extension Gerontology Specialist, Family Development and Resource Management, Texas Cooperative Extension, Texas A&M University, College Station, Texas. 1995.

12. See note 8.

13. Id.

14. See note 9.

15. Id.

16. See note 11.

17. See note 10.

18. Id.

19. See note 11.

20. See note 10.

21. Id.

22. Id.

23. See note 9.

24. "Managing challenging behaviors in dementia patients," *Gerontological Nursing Counseling Points* (February 2006): 4–14.

25. Tueth, M., "How to manage depression and psychosis in Alzheimer's disease," *Geriatrics* 50, no. 1 (January 1995): 43–49.

26. See 42 C.F.R 483.13 (a).

27. See note 3.

28. Simonson, W. Unnecessary drugs in nursing facilities, *Journal of Legal Nurse Consulting*, Spring 2009, Vol. 20, No. 2, 13.

29. "The nurse staffing crisis in nursing homes: a consensus statement," National Citizens Coalition for Nursing Home Reform, 2001.

30. *Id.*

31. "New report puts nurse staffing at top of survey list," *Long-Term Care Survey Alert* 3, no. 8 (2000): 73.

32. Horn, S., P. Buerhaus, N. Bergstrom, and R. Smout, "RN Staffing Time and Outcomes of Long-Stay Nursing Homes Residents," *American Journal of Nursing* 105, no. 11 (November 2005): 58–69.

33. Black, K., B. Ormond, and J. Tilly, "State-initiated nursing home nurse staffing ratios: annotated review of the literature," U.S. Department of Health and Human Services, 2003.

34. Gibson, R. and J. Singh, *Wall of Silence,* Washington, D.C.: Lifeline Press, 2003.

35. Bewley, E. *Killer Cure*, Indianapolis, Dog Ear Publishing, 2010.

36. King, S. *Josie's Story*, New York, Atlantic Monthly Press, 2009.

37. Wachter, R. and K. Shojania, *Internal Bleeding*, New York: Rugged Land, 2004.

38. http://www.philly.com/inquirer/breaking/business_breaking/20100317_Unusual_damages_set_in_Phila__bedsores_case.html," accessed 5/1/10.

39. *Scope and Standards of Gerontological Nursing Practice,* Second edition. ANA, 2001.

40. *American Health Care Association, Long Term Care Binder and Quarterly Updates, March 2009.*

41. Cohen, D. "Mark your Nursing Home Case with F-tags," *TRIAL*, August 2009, 44-47

42. "Quality Indicators," *Gerontological Nursing Counseling Points* (September 2005): 4–14.

43. *Id.*

44. *Id.*

45. http://www.cms.hhs.gov/surveycertificationgeninfo/downloads/SCLetter08-21.pdf.

46. http://www.cms.hhs.gov/CertificationandComplianc/Downloads/QISExecSummary.pdf.

47. http://nursinghomequality.com.

48. http://www.nj.gov/health/forms/aas-45.pdf.

49. *Principles for Documentation*, American Nurses Association, 2005.

50. See 42 C.F.R 483.20(b).

51. *Resident Assessment Instrument, MDS 2.0 Comprehensive User Guide*, Quality Measures/Quality Indicators, revised November 2005.

52. http://www.healthtech.net/documents/MDS%203.0%20Looking%20Ahead.pdf.

53. http://www.cms.hhs.gov/Nursinghomequalityinits/25_NHQIMDS30.asp.

54. Federal Register Vol. 63, No. 91, May 12, 1998, Final Rule.

55. See note 51.

56. *Id.*

57. Blackmon, G., Iyer, P., Tobias, A. and Thomas, J. "Long Term Care Records," in Iyer, P. and Levin. B. (Eds.) *Medical Legal Aspects of Medical Records*, Second Edition, Tucosn, AZ: Lawyers and Judges Publishing Company, 2010.

58. Taunton, R. L., D. L. Swagerty, B. Smith, J. A. Lasseter, and R. H. Lee, "Care Planning for Nursing Home Residents: Incorporating the Minimum Data Set Requirements into Practice," *Journal of Gerontological Nursing* 30, no. 12 (2004): 40–49.

59. Laska, L. (ed.), "Blind, paranoid schizophrenic man managed to get out of window which could open only a little bit more than eight inches," *Medical Malpractice Verdicts, Settlements, and Experts* (January 2010), 23-24.

60. Rubinstein, L. and K. Josephson, "Falls and fall-related injuries," In *Medical Legal Aspects of Long Term Care*, ed. J. Levin. Tucson, Arizona: Lawyers and Judges Publishing Co., 2002.

61. Miceli, D., Capezuti, E., Lawson, W., and Iyer, P., *Falls Handbook: Clinical and Medical-Legal Perspectives of Falls Across the Lifespan*, Flemington, NJ, Med League, 2007.

62. Capezuti E., W. Lawson, M. Hammer, and J. Melone. "Falls and Restraints Liability Issues," in *Nursing Home Litigation: Investigation and Case Preparation*, Second Edition, ed. P. Iyer. Tucson, Arizona: Lawyers and Judges Publishing Co., 2006.

63. Laska, L. (ed.), "Extremely thin woman falls getting out of bed after no response to call for assistance to bathroom," *Medical Malpractice Verdicts, Settlements, and Experts* (October 2009), 27.

64. Lamb, K., A. Minnick, and L. Mion, L. et al., "Help the healthcare team release its hold on restraints," *Nursing Management* 30, no. 12 (December 1999): 19–23.

65. http://www.abanet.org/tips/publicservice/bedrail.pdf.

66. Braun, J. and E. Capezuti, "Bedrail entrapment: Is your facility safe?" www.nursinghomesmagazine.com (November 2004): 56–61.

67. See 42 C.F.R. 483.25(h).

68. See note 3.

69. Laska, L. (Ed), "Wheelchair-bound man taking medication which makes him sensitive to sun left in sun, causing sunburn and dehydration," *Medical Malpractice Verdicts, Settlements, and Experts,* (May 2010), 25.

70. Braun, J. "Fire safety: is your facility legal?" www.nursinghomesmagazine.com, pgs 38-49, September 2004.

71. Blackmon, G., "Smoking Presents 'Catch 22,' *LNC Resource* 2, no. 3 (March 2005).

72. "Nursing home managers indicted for patient abuse, Medicare/Medicaid fraud" www.ksdk.com/news_article_aspx?sotryid=87943.

73. "Preventing violence in the healthcare setting," Sentinel Event Alert, 6/3/10, www.jointcommission.org/SentinelEvents/SentinelEvent Alert/sea_45.htm, accessed 6/6/10.

74. Warren, L. "Recognizing the Signs of Elder Abuse," *Elder Law Handbook*, Ohio State Bar Association, 2010334-338.

75. *Id.*

76. *Id.*

77. See note 73.

78. Paris, B., "Elder abuse and neglect: how to recognize warning signs and intervene," *Geriatrics* 50, no. 4 (April 1995): 4–51.

79. *Elder Abuse In Residential Long-Term Care Facilities: What Is Known About Prevalence, Causes, and Prevention Testimony Before the U.S. Senate Committee on Finance*, Catherine Hawes, PhD Professor Department of Health Policy and Management, School of Rural Public Health, Texas A&M University System Health Science Center, College Station, Texas. June 18, 2002.

80. See 42 CFR§483.13.

81. See 42 CFR 488.301.

82. Levine, J., "Elder neglect and abuse: a primer for primary care physicians," *Geriatrics* 58, no. 10 (October 2003): 37–44.

83. Laska, L. (Ed), "Abuse of woman at facility not investigated by facility despite a year of complaints," *Medical Malpractice Verdicts, Settlements, and Experts*, (March 2010), 22.

84. See note 73.

85. See note 77.

86. Laska, L. (Ed), Failure to properly care for woman blamed for the development of additional pressure sores, malnutrition and septic shock, *Medical Malpractice Verdicts, Settlements, and Experts*, January 2010, 24.

87. Tickle, E. and K. Hull, "Family members' roles in long-term care," *MEDSURG Nursing* 4, no. 8 (August 1995): 35–40.

88. McPhaul, K. and J. Lipscomb, "Workplace Violence in Health Care: Recognized but not Regulated" *Online Journal of Issues in Nursing* 9, no. 3, manuscript 6 (September 30, 2004). Available: www.nursingworld.org/ojin/topic25/tpc25_6.htm.

89. Tooher, N., "Rising nursing home violence spurs increase in lawsuits," *Lawyers Weekly USA* (May 9, 2005).

90. Chou, K., M. Kaas, and M. Richie, "Assaultive behavior in geriatric patients," *Journal of Gerontological Nursing* 21, no. 11 (November 1996): 21–34.

91. Laska, L. (Ed.), "Woman in nursing home assaulted by fellow resident," *Medical Malpractice Verdicts, Settlements and Experts* (March 2003): 28.

92. Burgess, A., K. Brown, K. Bell, L. Ledray, and J. Poarch, "Sexual abuse of older adults," *American Journal of Nursing* 105, no. 10 (October 2005): 66–71.

93. Laska, L. (Ed.), "Mentally retarded man sodomized by Certified Nursing Assistant Known by Assisted Living Facility Owner to have Assault and Battery Convictions," *Medical Malpractice Verdicts, Settlements and Experts* (August 2009): 29.

94. See note 92.

95. Bergstrom, N., B. Braden, B. Kemp, M. Champagne, and E. Ruby, "Predicting Pressure Ulcer Risk: A Multistate Study of the Predictive Validity of the Braden Scale," *Nursing Research* 47, no. 5 (1998): 261–269.

96. This revision can be found at http://www.cms.hhs.gov/manuals/pm_trans/R4SOM.pdf.

97. Bates-Jensen, B. M., M. Cadogan, D. Osterweil, L. Levy-Storms, J. Jorge, N. Al-Samarrai, V. Grbic, and J. F. Schnelle. "The Minimum Data Set pressure ulcer indicator: does it reflect differences in care processes related to pressure ulcer prevention and treatment in nursing homes?" *Journal of the American Geriatrics Society* 51, no. 9 (2003): 1203–12.

98. Baumgarten, M. et al., "Pressure ulcers and race in nursing homes," *Journal of American Geriatric Society* 52, no. 8 (2004): 1293–1298.

99. Centers for Medicare and Medicaid Services. Tag F314. Available at http://www.cms.hhs.gov/transmittals/downloads/R2250MA.pdf.

100. International Expert Wound Care Advisory Panel, Legal Issues in the Care of Pressure Ulcer Patients: Key Concepts for Healthcare Providers, June 22, 2009.

101. Laska, L. (Ed.), "Development of multiple bedsores blamed for death," *Medical Malpractice Verdicts, Settlements and Experts* (March 2010): 22.

102. See note 100.

103. *Id.*

104. Centers for Medicare and Medicaid Services. Medicare Program: Proposed changes to the hospital inpatient prospective payment systems and Fiscal Year 2009 rates. Available at http://edocket.access.gpo.gov/2008/pdf/08-1135.pdf, accessed 6/6/10.

105. Reddy, M, Gill, S, Rochon, P., "Preventing pressure ulcers: a systematic review." *JAMA*, 2006: 296:974-984.

106. See note 100.

107. Dr. D. Thomas, *Wound Care*, American Medical Directors Association, March 16, 2006.

108. Skin Changes at Life's End (SCALE) Expert Panel, *Final Consensus Statement*, 10/1/09.

109. See note 107.

110. Szwabo, P. and G. T. Grossberg (eds.), *Problem Behaviors in Long-Term Care: Recognition, Diagnosis, and Treatment,* New York: Springer Publishing Co., 1993.

111. Weinberg, A. D., *Risk Management in Long-Term Care,* New York: Springer Publishing Company, 1998.

112. Laska, L. (Ed.), "Man with history of elopement leaves secure Alzheimer's unit," *Medical Malpractice Verdicts, Settlements and Experts* (September 2009): 28.

113. Iyer, P. (ed.), *Nursing Home Litigation: Investigation and Case Preparation,* Second Edition. Tucson, Arizona: Lawyers and Judges Publishing Co., 2006.

114. Laska, L. (Ed.), "Nurses at rehabilitation facility fail to assess man with perspiration, clammy and short of breath," *Medical Malpractice Verdicts, Settlements and Experts* (May 2010): 23-24.

115. *Acute Change of Condition in the Long-Term Care Setting,* American Medical Directors Association, 2003 at page 1.

116. See note 28.

117. *Id.*

118. *Id.*

119. Laska, L. (Ed.), "Failure to check prescription for Morphine at time of admissions man with perspiration, clammy and short of breath," *Medical Malpractice Verdicts, Settlements and Experts* (January 2009): 23-24.

120. Brown, S., "Continuing care facilities," *Journal of Healthcare Risk Management* (Winter 1994): 43-44.

121. Myers, S., "A practical guide to the defense," In *Nursing Home Litigation: Investigation and Case Preparation,* Second Edition, ed. P. Iyer. Tucson, Arizona: Lawyers and Judges Publishing Co., 2006.

122. Rouse, R., "Living wills in the long term care facility." *Journal of Long Term Care Administration* 16, no. 3 (Summer 1988): 14–19.

123. See note 41.

124. See note 113.

Additional Reading

Bendix, J. "Exploiting the elderly," *RN,* March 2009, 42-46.

Mason, D. "Contrasts in long-term care," *AJN,* January 2009, 50-51.

Chapter 11

Assisted Living Liability

Sean Doolan, Esq. and Monica Kenny, Esq.

Synopsis
11.1 Introduction
    A. Overview of the Assisted Living Industry
    B. Definitions
    C. Role of the Wellness Nurse
    D. Statutory and Regulatory Protections of Residents
        1. Assisted Living Reform Act of New York: Pub Health
            Law Article 46-B
        2. Florida Statute: Pub Health Law Title 29, Chapter 400
        3. The Joint Commission
        4. Elder abuse reporting laws
        5. Common law standard of care if statutes and regulations
            are absent
        6. How to locate the applicable statutory scheme in your
            state
11.2 Admission and Discharge Considerations
    A. Admission Criteria
    B. Discharge Criteria
    C. The Admission Agreement
        1. Liability and the admission agreements
            a. Individual Service Plan
            b. Resident's rights
        2. Managed risk agreements
    D. Rules, Regulations and Statutory Authority
    E. Family Dynamics
11.3 Typical Assisted Living Facility Case Allegations
    A. Elopement
    B. Falls
    C. Wound Care
    D. Medication Errors
    E. Physical Abuse
        1. Physical assault
        2. Sexual assault
        3. Verbal/psychological abuse
    F. Failure to Supervise
    G. Wrongful Admission/Discharge/Retention
    H. Drug Diversion
11.4 Theories of Liability
    A. Common Law Negligence
    B. Statutory Violations
    C. Wrongful Death
    D. Consumer Fraud
    E. Breach of Contract
    F. Premises Liability
11.5 Who are the Defendants?
11.6 Marketing
11.7 Staffing
    A. Rules, Regulations and Statutory Authority
    B. Appropriate Staffing Levels
11.8 Dementia/Alzheimer's Units
    A. Rules, Regulations and Statutory Authority
    B. Inadequate Care for Alzheimer's or Dementia Residents
    C. Staffing
    D. Building Design and Layout
11.9 Summary
Endnotes

11.1 Introduction

This chapter gives a brief overview of the liability from a defense and plaintiff's prospective of nurses with respect to assisted living facility litigation. Furthermore, the material reviews some of the complexities of assisted living facility litigation including typical case scenarios, statutory schemes, the role of a wellness nurse and admission and discharge criteria in an assisted living facility. The attorney currently handling nursing home abuse and neglect cases will see many similarities between prosecution and defense of assisted living facility cases. While the authors are plaintiff's attorneys, every effort will be made to give a balanced overview of litigation in assisted living facility cases.

A. Overview of the Assisted Living Industry

The nation's population of persons 65 years of age or older increased by 12 percent between 1990 and 2000.[1] As of the 2000 census, there were approximately 35 million people 65 years of age or older.[2] These numbers represent only those actually counted in the census, not necessarily the actual number. Additionally, the percent increase was the highest in the age group of 85 years or older, which increased by 38 percent.[3]

Residential healthcare facilities are the most rapidly growing form of senior housing since the 1990s.[4] These facilities are referred to by a variety of names across the states, including assisted living facilities, personal care homes, domiciliary care homes, adult congregate living facilities, adult care homes, and shelter care homes.[5] This growth is attributed to both of the preferences of the elderly and their families and of public policy aimed at reducing nursing home use.[6] According to a National Institute of Justice study, it is estimated that there are approximately 50,000 facilities nationwide housing a mainly older population with approximately 900,000 to 1 million beds, contrasted with about 17,000 nursing homes with 1.6 million beds.[7]

Residential healthcare facilities (referred to collectively as "assisted living facilities") are becoming increasingly popular with the elderly. They provide a comfortable middle ground for housing once an elderly person is no longer able to safely live alone. Some factors contributing to the popularity and growth of the assisted living industry include:

- the aging of the American population;
- the need of seniors requiring assistance with activities of daily living;
- the continued increase in the number of seniors living alone;
- divorce;
- the role of women as workforce members, making them unavailable to be caretakers; and
- the philosophy of "aging in place."

The philosophy of "aging in place" is a goal in the assisted living arena today. The idea is to accommodate a resident's changing needs and preferences to allow the resident to remain in the particular setting as long as possible. For example, a resident may be admitted with mild dementia but with the ability to tend to the activities of daily living with little or no assistance. However, over time, the resident's dementia may worsen requiring assistance with the activities of daily living. If the assisted living facility is designed with aging in place in mind, the resident may not need to be moved to another facility, but can remain at that facility in a different area offering the services necessary.

Additionally, the increased net worth of seniors may prevent individuals from qualifying for public assistance for alternative housing options. Our nation is constantly looking for less expensive methods of health care for seniors as well as other individuals. A resident in an assisted living facility is more likely to privately pay for the services, with no financial assistance from the government for the cost of the facility. This is a relief to the Medicare and Medicaid systems.[8]

Assisted living facilities offer services such as meals, laundry, housekeeping, community activities and 24-hour staff. However, assisted living facilities do not inhibit a resident's daily activities in the same way a nursing home does. In a nursing home, a resident would typically not have the ability to leave the facility unattended. In an assisted living facility, the resident could leave as long as the facility was not concerned about the resident's ability to do so.

B. Definitions

An elderly person in need of day-to-day care has several housing alternatives available, depending on location, such as an independent living apartment, adult home, assisted living facility or a nursing home. The differences among these housing alternatives can vary widely.

Although there is no universal definition for an assisted living facility, some states have defined these facilities statutorily. Generally, an assisted living facility provides assistance with certain activities of daily living for seniors that need some help, but not 24 hour a day care. Either the assisted living facility or the resident can contract with outside agencies, such as home healthcare agencies, to provide additional services to residents.[9] These services can include such things as 24 hour supervision or medication administration. The general philosophy of an assisted living facility is to allow aging while preserving the resident's autonomy, independence and freedom of choice as long as possible.

Adult care facilities, sometimes considered as part of a state's statutory scheme regarding assisted living facilities, provide services to adults who, although not requiring continual medical or nursing care, are by reason of physical or other limitations, unable or substantially unable to live independently.[10] These facilities function as a family type home or residence and provide care either temporarily or long term.

Nursing homes provide the highest level of services available to seniors outside of a hospital. These facilities offer 24 hour a day care by medical professionals, including certified nursing assistants, registered and licensed practical nurses, therapists and physicians.[11] However, the resident's schedule and activities are much more rigid in a nursing home compared to an assisted living facility.

Assisted living facilities offer a variety of services depending on the facility. Many will provide such things as an emergency response system, round-the-clock security, transportation and community services. However, a nursing home will offer more services including call-bell response, health services, periodic monitoring and skilled nursing care. These services are usually unavailable in the assisted living facility setting.[12] Additionally, nursing homes are usually much more equipped to properly care for those residents suffering from Alzheimer's disease or dementia. The federal and state government strictly regulate nursing homes, but there are no federal regulations for assisted living facilities and only some states have enacted statutes or regulations for assisted living facilities.

C. Role of the Wellness Nurse

Generally, a wellness nurse in an assisted living facility will have such duties as assessing residents, supervising certified nursing assistants (CNAs) and sustaining relations with residents and their families. A wellness nurse may also be involved in the development and implementation of the Wellness Program for the facility.

A wellness nurse, typically an LPN or RN, supervises the administration of medications and monthly checks for weight and vital signs. Though the wellness nurse in a facility may hold a different title, the important thing is to look for a licensed nurse in the facility.

TIP: An attorney's investigation should focus on what the wellness nurse is required to provide for, has done for, and knows about the resident. The attorney should discuss with the client the interaction between the resident or the resident's personal representative and the wellness nurse and request copies of any correspondence between them.

Nurses, like physicians, take an oath of service. Instead of the Hippocratic Oath of physicians, nurses take the Florence Nightingale Pledge. Each nurse solemnly pledges, "Before God and in the presence of this assembly, to pass my life in purity and to practice my profession faithfully. I will abstain from whatever is deleterious and mischievous, and will not take or knowingly administer any harmful drug. I will do all in my power to maintain and elevate the standard of my profession, and will hold in confidence all personal matters committed to my keeping and all family affairs coming to my knowledge in the practice of my calling. With loyalty will I endeavor to aid the physician in his work, and *devote myself to the welfare of those committed to my care.*" (emphasis added) As with the Hippocratic Oath for physicians, this Pledge can be used as a standard by which nurses must comply.

A plaintiff's attorney should consider naming the wellness nurse as a defendant if the investigation reveals that the wellness nurse owed the resident a duty of care and breached that duty. Often, the wellness nurse is involved in the initial assessment, any reassessments and the monitoring of the resident's medical condition on a regular basis. Carefully review any statutes or regulations applicable to assisted living facilities in the jurisdiction to see if there are any requirements for the wellness nurse. There are, of course, pros and cons to naming the wellness nurse as an individual defendant.[13]

TIP: During the initial investigation, the attorney should attempt to find out from the family or other witnesses what records the wellness nurse or the facility maintained with respect to the resident. Unfortunately, the ju-

---

risdiction may not require the facility to maintain many records, if any. The plaintiff's attorney should consider bringing a pre-suit motion to preserve those records, if available in the jurisdiction.

Another important area to investigate is the interactions the wellness nurse had with any home healthcare agency or physician that provided healthcare to the resident. Some facilities will maintain they were mere landlords and that the home healthcare agency was responsible for any healthcare needs of the resident. However, at the same time, some of the facility's employees—the wellness nurse, the director, or some other employee—will have attended the regular care plan meetings held by the home healthcare agency with respect to the resident. Additionally, research whether the wellness nurse had access to the resident's medical records or one-to-one contact with any treating physician.

TIP: Remember to research if the resident contracted with a home healthcare agency for nursing services. Investigate if that agency breached its duty of care to the resident; if so, the plaintiff's attorney should consider naming the agency and the individual nurses.

D. Statutory and Regulatory Protections of Residents

As of 2011, there were no federal statutes or regulations that apply to assisted living facilities. Therefore, when litigating an assisted living facility case, the lawyer must look elsewhere for either statutory and regulatory mandates or common-law standards of care.

Some states have chosen to regulate assisted living facilities. These statutes are likely to provide both minimum resident's rights and responsibilities of the facility.

1. Assisted Living Reform Act of New York: Pub Health Law Article 46-B

As an example of recent legislation regarding assisted living facilities, New York passed the Assisted Living Reform Act (ALRA) in 2004.[14] One of the main components of that Act centers on the definition of an "assisted living facility" and the requirements of a facility defined as such.[15] An assisted living facility is defined as "an entity which provides or arranges for housing, on-site monitoring, and personal care services and/or home care services (either directly or indirectly) in a home-like setting to five or more adult residents unrelated to the assisted living provider."[16] If a facility meets the definition of assisted living set forth in the Act, it must obtain licensure through the state.[17] In order to do so, the facility must meet certain criteria and be in good standing with the Department of Health.[18] Operating an assisted living facility without the proper licensure is deemed a Class A misdemeanor in New York.[19]

In addition to simply defining assisted living facilities, the ALRA regulates many, if not all, of the facilities that have come to be known as "look-alike" or "scofflaw" facilities. These are facilities operating in a manner as to arguably keep them outside of the regulation of the state, yet who market themselves as providing "assisted living" or "assisted living services."

Probably the most significant part of the ALRA is the enumeration of certain rights for each assisted living facility resident. These rights include the right to be fully informed of his medical condition and the right to all information necessary to make an informed decision to enter the assisted living facility.

2. Florida Statute: Pub Health Law Title 29, Chapter 400

Florida regulates assisted living facilities through its Pub. Health Law Title 29, Chapter 400. This Chapter is very similar to the New York ALRA. Florida's Chapter 400 defines assisted living facilities as a "building or buildings, section or distinct part of a building, private home, boarding home, home for the aged, or other residential facility, whether operated for profit or not, which undertakes through its ownership or management to provide housing, meals, and one or more personal services for a period exceeding 24 hours to one or more adults who are not relatives of the owner or administrator."[20] Personal services are defined as "direct physical assistance with or supervision of the activities of daily living and the self-administration of medication and other similar services," but do not include the provision of medical, nursing, dental, or mental health services. Florida's statute also gives residents certain rights that a facility cannot violate including, but not limited to, the right to live in a safe and decent environment and the right to present grievances to the regulatory agency.[21]

Unlike New York, Florida has a specific statute regarding punitive damages in a civil action against an assisted living facility. Punitive damages are allowed in a case of intentional misconduct or gross negligence. If the plaintiff is able to prove this, an award of punitive damages may not exceed the larger of three times the amount of compensatory damages award or $1 million. In the event the jury or judge finds the facility acted unreasonably for financial gain, the amount can grow to four times the compensatory damages award or $4 million. A finding of specific intent to harm the resident makes the cap on punitive damages inapplicable.

All awards of punitive damages are split equally between the plaintiff and the Quality of Long Term Care Facility Improvement Trust Fund.

TIP: Most states will give their Department of Health the responsibility of promulgating regulations and inspecting assisted living facilities to ensure compliance. Any statute granting this authority will generally spell out the definition of assisted living and give the regulatory authority to the Department of Health. The Department is likely to regulate such things as the environmental conditions, building safety and specific rights to make complaints against the facility.

---

3. The Joint Commission

The Joint Commission was founded in 1951 to act as an independent accrediting body for hospitals nationwide. As such, The Joint Commission currently accredits nearly 80 percent of U.S. hospitals. The accreditation process focuses on what the institution is doing right and how it can improve its performance, as contrasted with a state regulatory agency oversight which focuses on what the institution is doing wrong and exacting punishments for the same. The Joint Commission sets standards for assisted living facilities.

The attorney should determine whether the facility being investigated has Joint Commission accreditation. Most accredited facilities advertise they have Joint Commission approval or use The Joint Commission logo on their letterheads. Accreditation can be verified by looking in Quality Check which appears on The Joint Commission website.[22] Quality Check allows anyone to search for accredited organizations by city, state or type of setting.

The 2005 Joint Commission standards include chapters entitled *Consumer Protection, Rights and Ethics, Continuum of Services, Assessment* and *Reassessment, Resident Services, Resident Education, Health and Wellness Promotion, Improving Performance, Leadership, Managing the Environment, Managing Human Resources, Managing Information, and Infection Control*. There is no hard copy of the 2006 Joint Commission Accreditation Manual for Assisted Living (AMAL) as there is for hospitals; rather, the standards will be posted on The Joint Commission's website.[23]

Although there is a survey process, the authors' overview of the website and a telephone conversation with a Joint Commission representative indicate that the results of these survey reports and statements of deficiencies by an assisted living facility are not published for public review. The website does reflect a facility's approval for accreditation.

TIP: If The Joint Commission accredits the assisted living facility, review The Joint Commission's standards, which provide a standard of care.

As discussed in Chapter 4, *Patient Safety Initiatives*, in Volume I, The Joint Commission issues National Patient Safety Goals and Recommendations each year, the purpose of which is to prevent specific types of errors.[24] Carefully review these goals to see if any relate to the injury the resident sustained. If so, inquire as to whether that facility followed the recommendations of The Joint Commission.

TIP: When deposing the operators of the facilities that do not have Joint Commission accreditation, the plaintiff's attorney should ask whether they considered seeking Joint Commission accreditation approval and, if not, why. Inquire if they are familiar with the standards. Even if a facility does not have accreditation, the standards may be used as a guideline when questioning those in charge of the facility.

The Joint Commission has a toll free hotline available 24 hours a day, seven days a week, at 800-994-6610, to handle complaints relating to quality care issues within the scope of Joint Commission standards. It is suggested that the resident or the resident's family file a complaint with The Joint Commission. Carefully review any complaint your client or other individual has filed. It is also important to review prior complaints filed against the facility to see if there were any substantiated complaints similar to the resident's.

Effective January 1, 2006, due to a lack of interest, there will be no new assisted living facilities accredited by The Joint Commission. It is unfortunate that assisted living facilities have not had more interest in the accreditation process. Check with The Joint Commission to see if the assisted living facility was accredited prior to January 1, 2006. If so, and if any cause of action was accrued while the facility was accredited, the standards of The Joint Commission may be applicable.

TIP: An attorney should be undeterred by statutory vagueness with respect to assisted living facilities. Assisted living facilities are responsible for complying with the community's standards of care notwithstanding vague statutes and regulations.[25]

4. Elder abuse reporting laws

Every state has enacted statutes that authorize the development of adult protective services agencies. Typically, these agencies establish an investigation and reporting sys-

tem for allegations of abuse against elderly persons. Check with the local agency involved for any statutory authority that may be present within the agency.

Elder abuse reporting laws vary widely from state to state. The following factors will vary from state to state:

- age and circumstances of the victim
- the definition of abuse
- types of abuse and/or neglect
- the classification of civil or criminal violations
- reporting requirements
- remedies for the abuse

Additionally, every state has passed the Long Term Care Ombudsman Program, responsible for advocating on behalf of residents in long-term care facilities. Ombudsmen are usually granted full and unencumbered access to all facilities, residents and resident records with or without notice to the facility. Contact the Ombudsman responsible for the particular assisted living facility.

In the event a plaintiff's attorney believes the abuse or neglect the client suffered deserves official investigation, she should advise the client to contact local law enforcement officials. Some cases can rise to a criminal violation such as assault, battery, or even sexual assault or rape.

Inquire into whether or not the assisted living facility reported the incident to the police or the Board of Nursing. If an assisted living facility reports an employee to criminal authorities, the insurance company may have a basis to disclaim coverage for that employee's actions leading to the report. The authors are aware of a case in which a nurse removed a resident's bed alarm; later, the resident fell out of bed, suffered a fractured hip and subsequently died. The facility reported this nurse to authorities and he plead guilty to assault. The insurance company, in that case, denied coverage for the nurse's intentional criminal actions.

TIP: Use a Freedom of Information Law (FOIL) Request to gather any information the police may have on the particular case. Request any information about the resident, facility and employees. Also, inquire if the Board of Nursing has taken disciplinary action against the nurse.

5. Common law standard of care if statutes and regulations are absent

Whether or not the jurisdiction provides either statutes or regulations for assisted living facilities, the attorney should look to the common law. The common law will likely supplement and explain the statutes and/or regulations and may set forth the standard of care for these facilities.

TIP: There are many standards of care that arise in an assisted living facility context. For example, a physician is held to a different standard of care as a registered nurse. An attorney should be aware of each applicable standard of care.

Even if the facility is not regulated, employees of the facility may be licensed in some respect through the state. Registered Nurses and Certified Nursing Assistants are required to be licensed. Look to the regulations applicable to each of those licenses. The licensure requirements will be useful in determining whether the employees were qualified for the positions they held.

The profession of nursing has its own standards of care. In the event the assisted living facility provides nursing and/or medical services, an expert witness or legal nurse consultant should review these standards to determine whether or not they were followed in the particular case. If they were not, there may be a viable argument that the injury to the client would not have occurred if the employees had conformed to the standard of care in their profession.

6. How to locate the applicable statutory scheme in your state

In 2003, the National Center for Assisted Living released its "Assisted Living State Regulatory Review: 2003."[26] This publication lists each state's regulatory agency and contact information. For example, Alabama's assisted living facilities are regulated by the Alabama Department of Public Health; Delaware has a Long Term Care Division of its Department of Health and Social Services responsible for assisted living facilities.[27] Look at the American Assisted Living Nurses Association's website for information on how to locate the applicable statutes and agencies.[28]

TIP: Some states have not officially regulated assisted living facilities. If the applicable state has not, look to national organizations to which the facility may belong, as those organizations may require compliance with its minimum guidelines for membership.

11.2 Admission and Discharge Considerations

Profit is the driving force behind the negligent admission and discharge of assisted living facility residents. When facilities have empty beds, profits can easily cloud the judgment of the assisted living facility's staff. Liability is often found when profits become more important than the health, welfare and safety of the assisted living facility residents. This theme of profits over people should be explored in ev-

ery case from both plaintiff and defense perspectives. The plaintiff's attorney can use this as a central theme of the case while the defense attorney should know if the assisted living facility is vulnerable to that theme.

A. Admission Criteria

There is no uniformity in the admission/discharge criteria among the states. Medicare and Medicaid laws are the only federal regulations that govern the assisted living industry. The applicability of these laws to assisted living facilities is limited. Most jurisdictions have enacted their own statutes and/or regulations that cover the admission process. A careful review of the same will assist you in determining the standard of care and whether there has been a breach of the standard of care. Some states have delineated criteria and prerequisites for admission to an assisted living facility.

In the event that the state has no statutory scheme to cover the admission process, look to the common law to determine if there is liability. Under the common law, the nursing process of assessment, diagnosis, planning, implementation and evaluation is applicable in assisted living facilities. Consult Chapter 1, *The Roots of Patient Injury*, in Volume I, for an explanation of the nursing process. Under the common practice, an assisted living facility should not accept a patient whose needs it cannot meet.[29]

It is important to gather all of the admission documents when determining if there is liability. Many jurisdictions require an admission agreement and specify some of the information it must contain. For example, every New York assisted living facility admission must include a residency agreement and an individualized service plan. The resident agreement must include the admission criteria for that facility, among other information.[30] In New York, the individualized service plan must be developed with the resident's physician and in accordance with the medical, nutritional, functional, cognitive and other needs of the resident.[31]

Most assisted living facilities use a licensed practical nurse or a registered nurse to oversee the admission process. Unfortunately, the admitting nurse often has the conflicting responsibility of making sure all the beds are filled but at the same time only admitting those residents that meet the facility's admission criteria. There may be liability when a nurse accepts residents whose needs exceed that which the facility is capable of meeting or legally permitted to provide.

The admitting nurse will often perform an assessment to determine if a resident is appropriate for the facility. Review a copy of the assessment form as well as the admission agreement. Read the admission agreement, admission policy and advertising materials of the facility to establish a breach in the standard of care. A nurse expert would be most helpful in reviewing these documents.

B. Discharge Criteria

When an assisted living facility can no longer meet a resident's needs, or when the law and regulations require it, a resident must be moved or discharged to a different level of care. In the authors' practice, more often than not, the liability in these cases centers on the failure to discharge a resident whose needs the facility can no longer meet. For example, a resident admitted with the beginning stages of Alzheimer's could worsen in her condition, elope from the facility and be harmed.

Carefully review the state's statutory and regulatory scheme as it relates to discharge criteria. Again, as discussed in more detail later, states regulating the admission of residents will likely have rules affecting the discharge of residents. If the state does not have a statutory or regulatory scheme, look to the common law standard. Once again, consulting with a nurse expert will help you in determining the standard of care.

In determining whether a resident should have been discharged earlier, examine the statutory or regulatory scheme in the state as it relates to assessing residents. For example, in New York the individualized service plan must be reviewed and revised as frequently as necessary to reflect changes in the resident's needs but not less frequently than once every six months.[32] If a facility's staff does not routinely assess its residents, it may open itself up to liability.

In many facilities a registered nurse is responsible for overall management of a resident's care, which includes routine assessments. Accordingly, a registered nurse in regular contact with residents of assisted living facilities has the responsibility of assessing residents to determine whether they need a higher level of care.

The authors encountered an unlicensed assisted living facility that took the position that it was a mere landlord and owed no duty to the residents. However, the facility had a registered nurse on staff that claimed herself as such to the residents and their families. On a resident's intake, the nurse gave the resident, and the facility, her business card with her name and "RN." She was referred to as the Wellness Director in the facility, and the facility's marketing materials indicated it had a registered nurse on staff. Further, she kept a log of the residents' unusual activities and reported them to the families. The theory is that she was acting in the capacity of a nurse and, accordingly, should be held to that standard of care.

In reviewing the case to determine liability for failure to timely discharge a resident, review all of the assessments and the resident's primary care physician's records, not just the admission assessment.

TIP: It is vital to utilize a nurse expert in evaluating these documents to determine liability.

C. The Admission Agreement

When evaluating the merits of the case, the plaintiff's attorney should secure a copy of any agreement the resident or facility signed prior to meeting with the family. In an assisting living case, various contractual agreements may have been signed, such as an admission agreement, resident rights agreement, Medicare/Medicaid forms, among others. The assisted living facility may have medical records in its possession with respect to the resident.

TIP: A defense attorney should secure the original records regarding the resident as soon as possible. This helps to avoid contamination of the records. However, if there are medical records included in the resident's file, the attorney should comply with HIPAA requirements in obtaining the medical record.

---

1. Liability and the admission agreements

Admission agreements may be a binding contract that specifies the financial obligations of the family as well as the services the facility will provide. These agreements could give rise to a breach of contract action, discussed in more detail later.

Often the agreement will specify:

- name, address and telephone number of the facility;
- the owner and operator of the facility;
- the name of an individual who can accept legal service for the facility;
- a statement of the licensure status of the facility and any home healthcare or personal care service agency that is under an agreement with the facility;
- the effective period of the residency agreement;
- the name of the resident's representatives; and
- a statement of the resident's rights.

The facility may also attempt to limit its liability in the admission agreement. In one such case with which the authors are familiar, the admission agreement was labeled a "lease" and included a clause, attempting to limit the facility's liability to only damages caused by the facility's gross negligence. Another means to limit the facility's liability is with the use of arbitration agreements. If there is an arbitration agreement, determine if it applies to the case.

Many states have regulations addressing what must be contained in the admission agreement. For example, in New York each resident entering into an assisted living facility must enter into a written residency agreement.[33] The minimum requirements for the residency agreement include:

- name, address and telephone number of the facility;
- owner of the facility;
- operator of the facility;
- name of an individual that can accept legal service for the facility;
- a statement of the licensure status of the facility and any home healthcare or personal care service agency that is under an agreement with the facility;
- effective period of the residency agreement; and
- name of the resident's representatives.

The agreement must also set forth what services will be provided to the resident and the monetary rate as well as additional services available for an extra cost, either directly from the facility or through an arrangement with another agency. The name of any agency under contract with the facility must also be disclosed. Criteria used for admission and retention of a resident must be set forth as well as the procedures and standards for termination, discharge or transfer of a resident.[34] The facility must disclose to the resident:

- the state of licensure;
- any ownership interest the facility has in excess of 10 percent in a company that is providing through the facility care, materials, equipment, or other services to the residents;
- any ownership those entities may have in the facility;
- the resident's ability to receive services from other entities and from his choice of physicians;
- the availability of public funds for payment;
- the Department of Health's toll free telephone number for complaints; and
- the availability of an Ombudsman and her telephone number.[35]

Many states will require that a copy of the residency agreement be given to the resident, the resident's personal representative and legal representative, if any. Furthermore, residency agreements must be kept on file for a specified period of time after the termination of the residency.

a. Individual Service Plan

Some states require an assisted living facility to prepare and implement an Individual Service Plan (ISP), which is a multidisciplinary care plan. Usually, the ISP will be developed with the resident, resident's representative, assisted living operator, home care services agency, and resident's physician. The ISP should be developed in accordance with the medical, functional, cognitive and other needs of the resident; it should include the services to be provided to the resident and by whom they will be provided. The ISP should be reviewed and revised as frequently as necessary to reflect changes in the resident's needs, usually not less than biannually.

b. Resident's rights

The rights of assisted living facility residents may be delineated in the residency agreement or statutes and regulations. Some states afford such resident rights as voluntary participation, informed consent, protection against coercion to work in the facility and security for the resident's personal possessions stored by the facility. Residents can also be guaranteed the right to be fully informed of their medical conditions and proposed treatment and to refuse treatment or medications. Additionally, residents are usually granted the right to advance notice of any fee increase. A written statement of the resident's statutory rights should be given to the resident and posted in a public area of the facility.

Furthermore, every resident should have the right to receive courteous, fair, and respectful care and treatment from the facility and receive adequate and appropriate assistance with daily living activities as needed. This is just a sample and is not an exhaustive list of the rights enumerated throughout the states. Penalties for violations of these rights should be fully researched.

The attorney should request a copy of the resident's rights from the assisted living facility. These may be found in the marketing materials or admission records. These rights may also be located in the jurisdiction's statutes or regulations. These rights may impose an affirmative duty upon the nurse in an assisted living facility context and create liability.

2. Managed risk agreements

Managed risk agreements[36] are widely used in the assisted living facility arena. These agreements attempt to balance the choice and independence of the resident with the health and safety of the resident and other residents in the facility. Usually, these agreements are made when the resident's decisions create a safety risk for himself or other residents. The facility and the resident attempt to respect the interests of each other and come to an agreement as to the liability of each party.

Some states have chosen to regulate these agreements. New Jersey requires that the assisted living facility staff identify the cause of its concern for the resident's safety, discuss this concern with the resident, negotiate a managed risk agreement that minimizes any such risk, offer possible alternatives and document this process or lack of agreement as well as the decisions reached.[37] Other states have regulated managed risk agreements by allowing facilities and residents to agree on sharing responsibility for making and implementing decisions affecting the scope and quantity of services provided by the facility.[38]

In any case, the attorney should inquire as to whether a managed risk agreement was in place between the resident and the assisted living facility and, if so, review that agreement carefully. These are contracts; so, even if there are provisions that purport to limit the facility's liability, contractual defenses may be available to your client.

D. Rules, Regulations and Statutory Authority

If a state has any statutory or regulatory direction for the admission and discharge of residents in assisted living facilities, an attorney should review these carefully. Any violation of these directions could be strong evidence of negligence on the facility's part.

Some states have delineated criteria and prerequisites for admission to an assisted living facility. These criteria could include limiting the seriousness of the residents' medical condition; requiring a home healthcare agency's or doctor's certification that the individual is a proper candidate for an assisted living facility; or requiring an evaluation of the potential resident by the assisted living facility.[39] If a state has regulated the admission of residents to assisted living facilities, those regulations should include some requirement on the facility's capability of meeting the resident's needs.

The responsibility of promulgating these statutes or regulations can reside in the legislature or agency of the state or with local authorities. An attorney should review all applicable statutes, agency regulations and even local laws and zoning regulations. Zoning ordinances may set forth useful regulations such as how many persons can reside in one housing development or what permits or licensing an assisted living facility must have to operate in that local jurisdiction. Keep in mind that if an agency has been given the responsibility of inspecting assisted living facilities, that agency may have also been granted regulatory authority. Conduct a review of the agency's regulations.

States regulating the admission of residents will likely have regulations affecting the discharge of residents, such as setting forth the situations in which a resident could rightfully terminate the agreement with the assisted living facility or when a facility must discharge a resident because the resident is no longer suitable for an assisted living facility.

As with admission criteria, discharge criteria may be set forth in statutes, regulations or local laws. Therefore, an attorney must review all possible areas where these regulations may be found. Additionally, an attorney should review the agreement between the resident and the assisted living facility, which may identify additional criteria for discharge or contain provisions that would imply additional admission criteria. Advertising materials from the facility, described in more detail below, should be reviewed carefully for any assertion by the facility of its admission or discharge criteria. The attorney should be alert to the possibility that finances may have kept the resident in an unsafe situation within an assisted living facility. The administrators may be reluctant to give up the income generated by the resident's stay. On the other hand, the resident may insist on remaining in the assisted living facility when a nursing home is the more appropriate setting. Many assisted living facility residents want to retain their independence as long as possible, even if that means taking risks.

An attorney may also review guidelines of state agencies or private entities. While these guidelines may not have the force and effect of law, deviation from them can be used as evidence of negligence on the part of the assisted living facility if those guidelines are generally accepted in the industry. For example, there are several organizations devoted to the assisted living industry such as Assisted Living Federation of America[40] and Senior Solutions of America.[41] Browsing through these organizations' publications may uncover suggested and generally accepted guidelines. Even if they are not generally accepted, the particular facility may be a member of that organization. Membership may require an assisted living facility to provide the minimum level of services the organization suggests, in a way analogous to The Joint Commission for hospitals.

As the demand for residential care facilities (RCFs) grows and there is increased regulation, it is expected that there will be a corresponding increase in unlicensed facilities. These cases can be very difficult to investigate. The state government agencies are reluctant to take action because they have very little leverage over these facilities. State agencies also have limited resources to pursue claims against unlicensed facilities. Additionally, these facilities typically do not maintain records or insurance.

E. Family Dynamics

The plaintiff's attorney needs a clear understanding of the family dynamics when selecting assisted living facility cases. Ask the following questions about the relationship between the caller and the resident:

- Was the caller involved in the resident's life?
- Did she visit?
- Is she familiar with the resident's medical conditions?
- Does she have healthcare proxy or power of attorney if the resident is still alive?
- If she was not involved and the victim is deceased, was anyone else involved?
- May the attorney speak with this person?

TIP: If the family was uninvolved and did not visit, the plaintiff's attorney should be certain he wants to handle the case. Would the jury care more about the victim than the family did? This is possible if the injury was egregious enough.

Find out as much as possible about the family dynamics. Ask if all the siblings are on friendly terms with each other. Is the spouse alive? If there is no spouse, does the potential client understand that she will have to share the settlement with her siblings? The attorney may hear, "But my brother was not involved; he never visited; why should he get anything?" The attorney should resolve this issue early and tell the potential client the case cannot be taken without resolution of this issue. This dynamic is present in many cases. It might be helpful to meet all potential family members who can legally pursue the intestate's claim, if applicable. Select the most compelling, reliable, and knowledgeable individual to act as the estate representative.

TIP: An efficient way of finding out the family dynamics is to ask the caller the names and addresses of all siblings. If there is a family split, the caller will likely say something to the effect of "I have no idea about my brother; I haven't spoken to him in years" or "Well, the last I knew my sister was in prison somewhere."

11.3 Typical Assisted Living Facility Case Allegations

TIP: In all case allegations, it is a good practice to secure copies of any police reports or 911 tapes made as a result of the particular case.

A. Elopement

There is a significant difference between wandering and elopement. A resident wanders by entering or leaving an area without permission. He is typically not seeking an exit from the facility. On the other hand, a resident is seeking to exit the facility if he elopes. Wandering behavior should be interpreted as a prelude to elopement. Elopement is a common scenario in an assisted living facility, as the resident will be seeking to leave.

In January 2005, a Missouri case involving elopement settled through mediation for $1 million. The plaintiff decedent, age 80, was diagnosed with dementia, major depression, and a history of wandering, and was admitted to an assisted living facility. In December 2001, the resident walked out of the front door and was struck by a car, sustaining severe injuries. The resident died two months later. The plaintiff claimed that the alarm system was not turned on and that the facility had no written procedures or guidelines in place to train personnel on the assessment of residents or the use of door alarms.[42]

A common defense in elopement cases is that the resident could rightfully come and go as he pleased. When investigating this defense, the attorney should carefully review the records to determine whether the facility was on notice that the resident was an elopement risk, either through an assessment or some other means. She should look for records kept by the facility of unusual behavior, wandering or attempted elopement. For example, in a recent case the authors handled, the facility kept a communication log to record unusual incidents, which documented a resident's attempts at eloping from the facility. The facility was given a letter from the resident's neurologist that the resident should be placed in a secure environment due to her deteriorating condition. The previous behavior and the notice from the resident's neurologist gave the facility a duty to discharge this resident to a more secure environment.

The attorney should also interview the resident's family in elopement cases. Inquiry should be made into whether or not the family advised the facility of any unusual behaviors the family had witnessed in the resident.

B. Falls

Resident falls are becoming increasingly common in assisted living facilities. Residents enter an assisted living facility primarily because they need assistance with activities of daily living. As residency time increases, needs will likely increase, including assistance in ambulating. In the event a facility does not recognize this need or does not adequately provide it, a resident's risk of falling increases. Unattended items, such as lunch or cleaning carts, may pose a significant threat to residents ambulating through hallways.

In a recent Nevada case involving a group home and a home healthcare agency, the resident fell from bed and suffered a fractured hip. The plaintiff contended that the defendants should have provided safety measures including side rails, floors mat, and/or hip protection. The defendants argued that the plaintiff's fall could not have been prevented and that there was a duty on the part of the defendants not to use side rails. The parties settled the matter for $423,000, with $388,000 being paid by the group home.[43]

In a recent New York case, the resident suffered from a fall down a flight of stairs during an unannounced fire drill. The resident was a recent admission and the facility was advised on admission that the resident had previously experienced a fire in her home. The resident was advised by staff to remain seated in the common area and wait for staff to return to assist her down the stairs during the evacuation. The resident later left without supervision and assistance due to her fears and fell down the stairs suffering injury. The plaintiff was able to defeat the defendants' motion for summary judgment with respect to a claim that there was insufficient supervision, instruction and evacuation planning.

If the case involves a fall from a resident's bed, an attorney should investigate the level of care the assisted living facility gave with respect to activities inside the resident's individual room. Did the facility check on residents at night; did the facility assess residents for the risk of falling from bed; or did the facility offer side rails as an option for residents?

C. Wound Care

Pressure ulcers are less frequent in assisted living facilities than nursing homes. It is expected that pressure ulcer cases will increase as more people enter assisted living facilities. The usual liability theory would state that the resident was unsuitable for an assisted living facility and should have had a higher level of care, such as a nursing home. The typical assisted living resident, upon admission, is ambulatory and does not develop pressure ulcers as a result. However, as time progresses, the resident's health declines and he may

become unable to ambulate, significantly increasing the risk of pressure ulcers.

Some assisted living facilities are not transferring these residents to a facility that can provide a higher level of care. Review of local laws and regulations should help in determining whether or not the facility has specific admission and retention standards. There may be a violation of standards if the facility retains a resident beyond the time it can properly care for her. The attorney should investigate the resident's health at the time of admission, looking for such things as the risk of pressure ulcers or dehydration. In most cases, liability can be determined by the state's admissions criteria. For example, Virginia regulations prohibit assisted living facilities from admitting or retaining residents who have stage III or stage IV pressure ulcers. Other states have similar regulations, while others are still developing them.

It is important in a pressure ulcer case to locate each healthcare provider who had contact with the client since the date of admission. Typically, the assisted living facility will have a contract with a home healthcare agency to meet all of the residents' needs. This healthcare provider is both a potential defendant and another insurance policy. This is particularly helpful if an unlicensed assisted living facility contracts with a licensed home healthcare agency.

In *Sander v. Mendosa,* Fla., Dade County Cir. Ct., No. 01-30436 (CA13), June 8, 2004, T. Patrick Ford, Jr., Esq. sued both the unlicensed owner/operator of the assisted living facility and the licensed home healthcare agency for severely neglecting a resident resulting in horrific pressure ulcers. While his client prevailed against both defendants, only the licensed home healthcare agency had insurance that has paid on the judgment.

In a case in California, a quadriplegic man redeveloped prior pressure ulcers. The plaintiff contended that the defendant facility failed to properly care for his pressure ulcers, notify his physician of his condition, and adequately chart his condition. The defendant argued the decedent's death was unavoidable as the result of his various medical conditions and that he outlived 95 percent of his peers with similar medical conditions. The jury returned a verdict of $2 million, which was subsequently reduced to $500,000 on the basis that the decedent's deterioration could not have been prevented.[44]

In a New York case, the resident was admitted to an adult home with mild dementia and a previous stroke. At the time of admission, the facility required a 24-hour home healthcare aide as a condition of his admission. The facility then advised that there was an immigrant family residing in the adult home and one member of the family was a home health aide. The resident was told he must pay that individual in cash each week for the services she was to render. The resident later suffered further strokes, which caused the resident to become wheelchair bound and dependent on the aide for lifting, changing, and other activities of daily living. The resident then developed Stage IV sacral pressure ulcers. The facility's defense is that they had no knowledge that the resident was no longer walking, they had no duty to inquire as to his health status, that they were mere landlords, and the resident arranged for the services of the home health aide independently.

Because assisted living cases will typically involve neglect over an extended period of time, which can be viewed as abuse, the local law enforcement agency may be interested in prosecuting. Reporting injuries to law enforcement should be explored.

D. Medication Errors

According to a recent study conducted by *USA Today,* more than one in five of the assisted living facilities inspected in several states were cited for at least one significant violation with respect to medications. Several violations were repeatedly cited:

- over- or under-medication
- improperly labeling medications
- failing to properly train staff in dispensing medications
- failing to have prescriptions refilled on time
- failing to ensure residents were taking the medication as prescribed

The study also indicated that a 2002 survey by the National Academy for State Health Policy found that nearly half of the 34 states responding to the survey identified medication errors as some of the most often cited violations.[45]

The attorney should determine if medication errors occurred in every case. Medication errors can lead to many other problems within an assisted living facility. For example, a resident could fall if he were given too much or too little of a prescribed medication. The medication may affect the resident's balance or focus, causing him or her to

be unsteady on his or her feet. If a resident is given too much Coumadin, a blood thinner, the resident may suffer from injuries or fatal internal bleeding.

For example, in California, a medication error was partially to blame for a 43-year-old mentally ill man's attempted suicide. The plaintiff alleged that the resident's attempted suicide was the result of a combination of failure to give prescribed medications, properly monitor the resident, and restrict access to the facility's roof, leading to bilateral tibia and fibula fractures and a fractured hip. The defendant maintained that the resident refused his medication. The verdict in this case was returned in the amount of $1.5 million, the defendants being held 70 percent at fault.[46]

A common defense in medication error cases is that the resident refused prescribed medications. If there is such a defense, the attorney should investigate the competency of the resident, what efforts were made by the facility to encourage the resident to take the medications, if the facility advised the resident of the ramifications of failing to take the medications and whether or not the resident's treating physician was advised of the resident's refusal.

A medical expert or legal nurse consultant should review all prescribed medications as well as all administered medications. These should be examined for the correct application of medications according to the resident's mental capabilities. Often a resident will be suffering from dementia without diagnosis; therefore, the medication prescribed is not treating the dementia or its symptoms. This can lead to poor quality of care.[47]

TIP: Finding an expert in an assisted living facility case can be difficult. The first step should be to speak with the attorney's legal nurse consultant to see if she has, or knows someone with, the requisite experience. An Internet or publication search can be helpful in locating expert witnesses or authors in the field. Of course, it is possible to contact professional expert witness location companies as well as litigation groups.[48]

The critical question is whether the resident has the capacity to self-administer medications. If the resident suffers from cognitive deficits, the facility must diligently assess and reassess the resident's ability to self-administer. The initial assessment is rarely incorrect. The more common scenario is the failure to reassess the resident's ability after a decline in mental capacity. Because medication errors can lead to serious harm if a resident is not reassessed, the nurse may be liable for any resulting harm.

> In one medication error case, the plaintiff suffered from an overdose of heart medication after the medications were negligently left in her room. By all accounts, the plaintiff was competent but due to macular degeneration, she was unable to visibly distinguish between her heart medication and her pain medication. As a result, she was totally dependent on the assisted living facility to "set up" her medications. After the facility set up her medications, she would self-administer those medications at the nursing station. On one evening, her heart medication was negligently delivered to her room, which she then took believing that it was her pain medication. As a result, she suffered from confusion, disorientation, decreased muscle strength, lethargy, renal failure, and bradycardia. The case ultimately settled for $95,000.[49]

TIP: Know the distinction between administering and dispensing medications. Dispensing can be as simple as placing medications in a container for the resident to take on his own. Administering medications involves giving the medications directly to the resident or even placing them in his mouth.

Under most statutory schemes, a nurse's aide can dispense medications but cannot administer them. The attorney should check the state's statutory scheme to determine who can administer medications.

Depending on the state, there may or may not be regulations on who can administer medications. Some states require a trained professional (such as a RN or a LPN) administer any medication. Other states allow nonprofessionals to administer medications under the supervision of the wellness nurse. Still others allow nonprofessionals to administer medication without supervision.

In the event of a medication error, look to the facility's practice. Who was given the authority to administer medications; did that person actually administer them? Then check the state's regulations. Was the person with medication administration authority authorized by the state to do so?

TIP: The attorney handling a medication error case should demand the facility's policies and procedures on medication administration.

E. Physical Abuse

Physical abuse including such things as physical assault, sexual assault, or verbal and psychological abuse, in assisted living facilities are prevalent. Liability for such abuse is typically established by the admission and retention criteria if the assailant is another resident. If the assailant is an employee, liability is established by the failure of the facility to screen its employees—proper background checks, criminal history checks, reference checks, sexual offender registry, and so on. Another growing problem is the admission of sex offenders to assisted living facilities. The facility may also have inadequate staffing, leading to a failure of the facility to supervise not only the victim but also the assailant.

> In an Illinois case, an assisted living facility resident was severely assaulted by another resident. Discovery revealed that the defendant's program director had assured the victim's family that the assailant would have one-on-one supervision, which did not occur. *Kosac v. REM* Indiana, Lake County (IN) Superior Court, Case No. 45D10-0201-PC-00006.

If the client is a victim of a potential sexual or physical abuse case or suspicious death, there may be a law enforcement investigation. These reports provide immediate, front-line investigation of such incidents, which serve as valuable discovery tools in the case. Law enforcement agencies are sometimes eager to discuss an abuse case with a plaintiff's attorney and offer "off the record" comments about what they have found. Check the state's sex offender registration to determine if the assailant was a registered sex offender.

1. Physical assault

As mentioned above, a physical assault on a resident can be by either a staff member or another resident. The Administration on Aging, in its instructions to Long-Term Care Ombudsmen, defined physical abuse as "willful infliction of injury, unreasonable confinement, intimidation or cruel punishment with resulting physical harm, pain or mental anguish or deprivation…of goods or services that are necessary to avoid physical harm, mental anguish, or mental illness."

> An 83-year-old veteran died in a Pennsylvania assisted living facility specializing in Alzheimer's/dementia care. A nurse from the facility had listed the cause of death as "failure to thrive" yet the owner of the funeral home found a 1 foot by 1 foot bruise along the resident's side and called

the county coroner. Ultimately there was a murder conviction and 30 year prison sentence for a staff member who had kicked the resident because the resident had soiled his bed.

2. Sexual assault

In a New York case that the authors handled, a certified nurse aide raped a 90-year-old demented resident at a long term care facility. The resident told a staff member that she had been raped and the facility conducted an investigation. The aide's sperm was recovered from the resident's vagina and the aide acknowledged his guilt. He was prosecuted and convicted of the charge. The facility released a press release applauding itself for taking such quick action and suggesting that it had done an adequate investigation because as a part of the hiring process the aide had passed a drug test and the New York State Nurse Aide Registry indicated that he did not have a criminal history. There are two obvious defenses to this case. First, that the facility is not responsible for the intentional criminal conduct of it employees and second, that the resident did not suffer any actual pain and suffering because she suffered from dementia.

As to the first defense, the case investigation revealed that the aide had in fact been fingerprinted at the time he was hired but that the facility had failed to follow through and obtain the results of the fingerprint search. Had the facility followed through on those results, it would have discovered that he had a prior felony conviction. As to the second defense, the resident's pain and suffering was established through the resident's family as well as through medical experts and the resident's medical records.

TIP: If the resident is cognitively impaired, it may be difficult proving pain and suffering as a result of sexual abuse. Interview family and review the records for changes in behavior after the assault to determine if they are related to the sexual assault.

In a Florida case, a 28-year-old disabled schizophrenic man was living in an assisted living facility and alleged his roommate and another resident sexually abused him over a three-month period. The defendant denied any sexual abuse. The jury returned a verdict for the plaintiff in the amount of $540,000.[50]

3. Verbal/psychological abuse

In a study of a random sample of more than 1,100 staff in 512 assisted living facilities in ten states, 15 percent of the staff reported witnessing other staff engage in verbal abuse or forms of punishment such as withholding food, excessive use of physical restraints, or isolating difficult residents.[51] There may be no physical harm in a case of psychological or emotional abuse which may make these cases difficult to bring since most states do not have resident's rights statutes.

F. Failure to Supervise

A failure to supervise allegation will likely be made in all liability cases with an assisted living facility. An investigation will frequently uncover inadequate staffing. Staffing shortages and insufficient training are not exclusive to nursing homes; they place the elderly at risk in assisted living facilities as well. For example, Arizona state regulators imposed a $3,000 fine for inadequate staffing in a facility that left a resident unconscious in the hot sun, resulting in the death of that resident from heat exposure.[52] Such a fine is inadequate for such gross neglect.

A *USA Today* investigation revealed that nearly one in five assisted living facilities was cited for at least one staffing violation, ranging from too few employees to the lack of a certified facility manager. In some cases, residents fended for themselves because no caregivers were on site. More than one in four facilities were cited for training violations, such as failing to ensure employees had adequate instruction in first aid, emergency procedures and resident rights. It is estimated the actual violations are significantly higher because of weak regulatory oversight.[53]

Some facilities' employees lack basic first aid and CPR training. A Florida resident was found choking on food, but when the residents called for assistance from the employee on duty, she did not have the required training in first aid and CPR. A resident had to contact emergency personnel.[54]

Unlike nursing homes with a federal regulatory scheme, assisted living facilities are exclusively regulated, if at all, by each state. As a result, national uniform staffing standards have not been developed. Many employees of assisted living facilities need not be licensed. In a nursing home, a licensed certified nurse assistant's median salary is $8.61 per hour according to a 2003-2004 report by the National Center for Assisted Living. In assisted living facilities, unlicensed caregivers earn even less.[55]

In a New York case, the resident was admitted to an assisted living facility that had an additional license from the state for "enriched housing," or additional services allowing for aging in place. The resident's dementia had progressed to the point that her physician advised the facility that she needed to be transferred to the more secure area of the facility designed for dementia and Alzheimer's patients. The facility instead placed the resident in that area during the day and then returned the resident to her assisted living apartment at the end of the day. The day of the injury the resident was returned to her room at the end of the day in an agitated state. Due to a staff member not reporting to work, the 3:00 A.M. check was not completed. The resident was found on her kitchen floor laying in feces and blood, with swollen eyes and blood coming from the side of her mouth. The resident died from the injuries she received. In this case, the facility was unable to move the resident to the dementia unit in their facility. However, the facility could have assisted in transferring the resident to a different facility with the proper supervision and assistance for that resident.

In an outrageous example of incompetence, a resident was choking on food in an assisted living facility. The attendant was stopped from calling 911 by another attendant because it was the facility's policy to contact the administrator before doing so. This case is an example of both inadequate training and supervision.[56]

G. Wrongful Admission/Discharge/Retention

As discussed in Section 11.2 above, when a potential resident first comes to an assisted living facility for potential admission, an evaluation is necessary to see if the resident is in fact able to live in such a setting safely. This evaluation should be ongoing throughout the resident's placement in such a facility. However, there are incidents where such is not done, or is done incorrectly, and resident are either admitted to or retained in a level of assisted living that is not consistent with their needs.

With the increasing desire to age in place, many residents are seeking admission to an assisted living setting that will allow for them to remain in the same facility when their needs increase. However, if a facility does not properly manage what level of care is necessary for the resident, a resident may be retained in an area of the facility that cannot provide the level of assistance required for that resident. This is a delicate balancing act between providing the least restrictive environment with the level of care that is needed to meet the needs of the resident.

Additionally, the fact that residents of assisted living facilities are primarily private paying, an assisted living facility has a desire to keep as many residents as possible at one time. Empty beds do not garner monthly income. This could cloud a facility's judgment when deciding to recommend discharge from the assisted living facility into a nursing home for instance.

> In a case in New York, a resident was transferred from a nursing home to a hospital. At the time of discharge from the hospital, he was admitted to an adult home. While a resident of the adult home, the resident suffered a fall that was not properly treated and he died shortly thereafter. The plaintiff brought an action against the adult home and the treating physician alleging, inter alia, wrongful admission to the adult home. The plaintiff asserted that the resident was in need of a higher level of care than an adult home. Summary judgment was granted to the adult home based on the defense that they relied on the treating physician's expertise in recommending an adult home setting.

TIP: This case illustrates the difference between the standard of care in adult homes, assisted living facilities, and nursing homes. Be sure to know which standard of care is placed on the particular facility in your state.

H. Drug Diversion

These cases involve scenarios in which the staff of an assisted living facility has diverted medications, usually for pain, from residents. In one case, a nurse removed the medication from a Fentanyl patch by syringe. In another case, a nurse substituted water for morphine in capsules. In yet another case, a resident's pain medications were taken by a nurse and the records were falsified to reflect that the resident had received his medications.

11.4 Theories of Liability

In an assisted living facility case, it is advisable to name all parties as defendants. In many cases, an assisted living facility will be owned by one entity, but operated by another entity. Additionally, the facility may be managed by yet another entity and receive medical services from a home healthcare agency.

If the facility is licensed through the state, an attorney should do a search of the department or agency responsible for such licensure to investigate what entity is on file as operating the particular facility. It is also advisable to do a full title search into the property itself. As noted above, it is not uncommon for the property to be owned by an entity or person other than the operator of the facility. If it is later determined that the property owner has no management or operating authority over the facility, that entity can be released from the lawsuit.

A. Common Law Negligence

The plaintiff's attorney should assert a common law cause of action for negligence in every assisted living facility case. However, be careful in pleading this cause of action. If the attorney alleges breaches in medical or nursing standards of care, she will likely face a motion to dismiss on the grounds the case is medical malpractice and not negligence. There is no reason to allege breaches of medical or nursing standards of care since assisted living facilities are not providing medical care. Instead, cite the state statutes or regulations as the standard of care and the facility's failure to comply as a breach of that standard of care.

One of the benefits of pleading common law negligence is that the attorney will not be subject to medical malpractice damage caps or limitations on attorney fees. Typically, a negligence cause of action has a longer statute of limitations and does not have the other restrictions of a medical malpractice case.

TIP: Quality assurance privileges should not apply since assisted living facilities are not providing health care.

B. Statutory Violations

In the event the jurisdiction provides for civil remedies for violations of statutes or regulations, a cause of action should be pleaded for violation of those statutes. The most common example is an intentional tort. Some states statutorily provide for civil remedies for violations of statutes or regulations with respect to assisted living facilities. These statutes can be analogized to a state regulation that gives nursing home residents a private cause of action for any violation of their rights.

TIP: In a state that regulates assisted living facilities in the same or similar manner as nursing homes, the attorney should submit a Freedom of Information Law (FOIL) request to the agency with the responsibility to oversee the facilities. In the event there was a reporting requirement involved in the case, the agency may have records relating to the incident itself.

C. Wrongful Death

The challenge in a wrongful death case can be causally relating the death to an injury. If a resident falls, breaks her hip, and dies three months later, it may be difficult to causally relate the death to the fracture, although there was a steady decline in health. Discuss this in depth with the medical expert. Be mindful that the statute of limitations is likely shorter than a common law negligence statute of limitations.

Damages in a wrongful death case may be limited to economic loss such as lost wages, funeral expenses, medical bills and loss of financial support. Therefore, the damages under this cause of action may be limited, as the resident will not likely have many economic damages.

D. Consumer Fraud

Residents injured in assisted living facilities should consider theories other than those typically found in tort actions. While the care in an assisted living facility may involve breaches of professional standards, there may be a cause of action under the state's Consumer Protection Act. When considering a consumer protection claim, plead the specific representations the facility has made in an attempt to procure the resident and indicate how those representations induced reliance by the resident and his family.

For example, in a recent New York case, the facility advertised itself as an assisted living facility with 24-hour staff. The family of the resident, relying on those assertions, did not move the resident to a nursing home. However, when the resident later eloped from the facility and died from exposure, the facility claimed it was simply a landlord with no responsibility for the resident's safety.

TIP: Look carefully at consumer protection statutes in the jurisdiction. Some states allow for treble or punitive damages in certain consumer fraud scenarios.

E. Breach of Contract

Upon admission, prospective residents sign a contract or lease. As stated above, carefully review this contract for such clauses as arbitration agreements, waivers of liability and limitations on damages. The theory of a breach of contract cause of action in an assisted living facility will hinge on the facility's failure to fulfill its duty to provide the contracted-for services. The challenge to this cause of action is determining the damages caused by the breach. One aspect of damages could be to claim all monies paid to the facility, particularly if the client is a private payer. In other cases, the plaintiff's attorney may be able to recover for failure to provide contracted services, even though the failure did not cause physical injury. For example, if the facility agreed to perform all laundry services for the resident and failed to do so, the resident may have contracted with an outside agency for this service. Damages would be easily determined by the cost of the outside service.

Although parties do not normally assert causes of action for breach of contract in a personal injury claim, this strategy should not be overlooked with an assisted living facility. The injured party or family may be paying the facility out of personal funds. The attorney may consider a cause of action for breach of contract to return said funds. One advantage to pursuing a claim for breach of contract is that it extends the statute of limitations in many states.[57] The cause of action usually occurs when the breach occurs regardless of the aggrieved party's lack of knowledge of the breach.

In a case in New York, the plaintiff brought a separate cause of action for breach of contract because the facility had increased the monthly rate without proper notice pursuant to the agreement between the resident and the facility. The plaintiff provided a letter from the facility that advised the resident of an increase in the monthly rate effective as of the date of the letter. The defendant moved for summary judgment on this claim, as well as others. The court found that there was a triable issue of fact to be decided and denied the defendant's request for summary judgment on that claim.

The contract may also contain express and implied warranties. If the facility expressly states it is equipped to care for certain residents, such as those suffering from Alzheimer's, the family may have relied on those written representations. If the facility represents that it is specifically qualified to perform work or its services are of a particular character, that may give rise to an implied warranty. An implied warranty is not created by an express agreement but rather implied by actions of the parties. For example, in most states, a landlord of a residential rental unit is subject to an implied warranty of habitability.

TIP: A breach of contract cause of action can also be used to illustrate a course of conduct of the defendant in violating the rights of the resident.

F. Premises Liability

The facility owner and groundskeepers' employer should be named as defendants in a premises liability claim. The facility may have a contract with a company for all maintenance required. In most states, these companies will be brought in as a third party defendant as they do not have a direct contractual relationship with the client. As previously stated, assisted living facilities are consistently arguing they have no duty to the resident other than that of landlord. In the event a facility is successful in arguing this defense to the court, a resident's complaint will not be entirely dismissed if a cause of action has been pleaded in premises liability. Even a landlord has liability for those common areas under his control.

TIP: Find out who owns and maintains the facility and the grounds when the case involves a fall or a wandering injury.

11.5 Who are the Defendants?

In every assisted living facility case, the plaintiff's attorney should consider naming the owner of the property and building as well as the operator of the business. Both the plaintiff's and defendant's attorney should know the "corporate story." For liability and tax reasons, a multitude of corporations are often involved in owning, operating, and managing an assisted living facility. It is important the attorney know the relationships among one another and with the assisted living facility. Any relationship between these corporations and the home healthcare agency should also be explored.

TIP: An attorney should consider deposing the administrator of the facility first to determine the corporate structure. The attorney should ask questions to identify the organizational tree and chain of command.

The plaintiff's attorney should consider naming any home healthcare agency that does business with the target assisted living facility and client. There may be a basis for liability even if contact with the resident is minimal and limited to something as minor as dispensing medications. If the home healthcare agency is responsible for reporting healthcare changes to the facility or family, and such changes require a higher level of care for the resident, failure to report and act may lead to liability for the home healthcare agency. The considerations for naming a home healthcare agency nurse as a defendant are similar to those for naming the wellness nurse of the assisted living facility. Naming these entities gives an additional defendant a possible additional insurance policy. However, there are drawbacks to naming these entities as defendants, as they now have the ability to point fingers and confuse the jury. If a jury finds the wellness nurse deviated from the scope of her employment, the assisted living facility's insurance company may disclaim coverage for any verdict. Also note another law firm will likely be involved in discovery and scheduling. However, there are cases wherein naming the home health care agency and the wellness nurse is worth the extra work and risk.

On the other hand, a plaintiff's attorney may begin a suit by naming the facility owner, assisted living facility operator and home healthcare agency. After entering into the discovery phase and conducting the first depositions, it may be that the facility was managed by yet another entity, which the attorney may name as well. In this case, it would be more beneficial to the plaintiff to identify all of these entities as defendants than incurring the problems created by doing so. However, the wellness nurse might not be individually named if she was acting within the scope of her employment. To add her as a defendant would only cloud the issues.

The defense attorney must determine the identity of the client. In many assisted living cases, as noted above, there are several defendants named including individual employees of the assisted living facility. Conflicts of interest can arise in such cases and the defense attorney must be astutely aware of these.

11.6 Marketing

Because assisted living facilities are marketing-driven businesses, there should be a wealth of information regarding the specific facility. The attorney should look for any "puffery" and slick advertising on the facility's website, in brochures and other advertisements. All of these materials are designed to sell the facility to potential residents and their families, many of which may have been provided to the family at the time of admission. Review this information carefully as it may contain representations by the facility that give rise to the standard of care, establish a breach of contract claim, or develop a consumer protection claim.

TIP: See whether the facility advertised that it had a registered nurse on site. Some facilities have even advertised they have a registered nurse on site 24 hours a day. Any advertising of a registered nurse on-site should be explored in depositions.

If the target assisted living facility has Joint Commission accreditation, carefully review how it promoted that. A facility that receives Joint Commission accreditation is provided with a publicity package to celebrate its accreditation, which includes sample news releases, logos and other promotional materials.

11.7 Staffing
A. Rules, Regulations and Statutory Authority

Unfortunately, the federal government has not enacted legislation regarding assisted living facilities. Therefore, an attorney must look to state laws and regulations that address levels of staffing needed for each assisted living facility. Any such regulation should be in the form of setting forth the minimum staff-to-resident ratio, requiring certain training for

staff or requiring certain trained staff to be available to the residents at set time intervals. A state might require that an assisted living facility provide for the services of a physician on a regular basis or require a contract with a physician on call in the event of an emergency, regulations similar to those required of nursing homes, yet not as demanding because the level of care needed for assisted living facility residents is not as great as that needed for nursing home residents.

TIP: If the case involves a staffing issue, look to the marketing materials for any assertion by the assisted living facility with respect to staff levels, training, qualifications or availability. If the facility did not have the staffing it advertised, there may be an additional cause of action for consumer fraud.

In dealing with assisted living facility cases, the authors have noticed that staffing problems frequently include the staff's qualifications, training and number. However, other staffing issues might include the failure to properly screen staff members. Many states require background checks for prospective employees of these facilities, but that does not mean everything about the prospective employee is checked prior to employment. Some states do not require a facility to inquire about out-of-state convictions. These authors recommend all states require a complete background check on prospective employees to ensure there are no unacceptable staff members in these facilities.

TIP: An attorney should investigate whether the wellness nurse had responsibility for determining the facility's policies and procedures with respect to the level, qualifications and training of the facility's staff. This may lead to the discovery of inappropriate determinations on the part of the wellness nurse or the facility's failure to follow its own policies and procedures.

B. Appropriate Staffing Levels

Staffing can create major concerns in assisted living facilities. These concerns include both the lack of appropriate staffing levels as well as the level of staff training. As in nursing homes, assisted living facilities suffer from high staff turnover and low salary rates.[58]

Training for staff members is usually limited, maybe because it is believed there are insufficient reasons for providing training. The level of care provided in assisted living facilities is much lower than in nursing homes. There may be a lack of financial resources to provide such training. Either way, there is often an insufficient amount of training for the staff in these facilities.

A comprehensive study found that more than 99.5 percent of the staff in RCFs identified resource constraints as the most significant challenge they faced.[59] There are many factors that lead to inadequate resources in RCFs. First, generally there is no federal funding for RCFs. Second, the industry is growing at such a rapid pace that state regulating industries are having a difficult time keeping pace. Third, the RCF industry has aggressively resisted efforts to enhance regulations.[60] Fourth, at the present time, states are financially strapped because of the recession. Fifth, most states did not specify minimum staffing levels in RCFs.

When an 85-year-old man in a Florida assisted living facility was found by other residents choking on food, gasping for breath and turning blue, the only staff member on duty lacked the appropriate training to assist him. Or consider the case of a woman in a Minnesota facility who died as a result of a medication error because when she suddenly became disoriented, the facility failed to contact a physician for over a month. The medication error eventually caused her to suffer severe drug withdrawal, causing her death.[61]

11.8 Dementia/Alzheimer's Units
A. Rules, Regulations and Statutory Authority

The selection and retention of adequately trained staff to care for residents with dementia or Alzheimer's disease is essential to the resident's quality of life and safety, especially in assisted living facilities. These facilities are typically not as highly staffed as nursing homes because the residents do not need the level of care nursing home residents require. However, if an assisted living facility chooses to offer accommodations for dementia or Alzheimer's disease residents, the staff level must be appropriate and properly qualified. The facility must provide for residents' safety with proper design, appropriate activities and proper admission and discharge criteria.

Attorneys should review all possible areas of regulation of dementia or Alzheimer's units within assisted living facilities. Many states that regulate assisted living facilities will further regulate facilities that offer accommodations to these residents. For example, New York's Assisted Living Reform Act requires an assisted living facility to obtain an additional license before it may accommodate these residents.[62] Remember to review statutes, agency regulations, local laws, ordinances and generally accepted guidelines.

B. Inadequate Care for Alzheimer's or Dementia Residents

A recent study indicated two-thirds of residents in randomly selected assisted living facilities in central Maryland suffered from dementia.[63] Of those, approximately one-half were adequately evaluated and treated. This study also revealed that over 25 percent of the residents suffered from other psychiatric disorders with similarly low rates of treatment.[64]

Another study revealed that of seven assisted living facilities in the Omaha, Nebraska, area, more than half of the total residents studied had cognitive deficits.[65]

C. Staffing

Reviewed data suggests that assisted living facility staffs are ill-equipped to manage mental or psychological disorders such as Alzheimer's disease or dementia.[66] Assisted living facilities may not adequately train their staff as a result of a misguided belief that there is not the same need for this training as in a nursing home. A facility may not expend its financial resources to train staff if the number of residents with cognitive deficits is relatively low.

TIP: Always demand the facility's policies and procedures with respect to staffing levels as well as staff training.

Many states have little or no requirements with respect to staffing in Alzheimer's or dementia units within assisted living facilities, with the following states having none: Arizona, Connecticut, District of Columbia, Georgia, Hawaii, Maryland, New Hampshire, New Jersey and Wyoming.[67] Anyone interested in the state's requirements need to inquire with the regulating body.

D. Building Design and Layout

The design and layout of an Alzheimer's or dementia unit is extremely important for the residents' safety, security and autonomy. Design and layout should allow for the maximum amount of personal autonomy while still adequately protecting the residents' safety and security.

Those who suffer from Alzheimer's and dementia are often confused as to time and place. The design and layout of the units must help reduce or eliminate this confusion. These units should have simple signs in contrasting colors at eye level to help residents comprehend them. Entries to the resident's rooms should be personalized in order to facilitate easy distinction among rooms. Creating regular schedules for activities to be held in the same place will help avoid confusion. A facility should also make regular destinations such as the dining or activities room easily visible and recognizable.[68]

Because of the level of confusion in Alzheimer's and dementia patients, security of the unit is also a concern. A facility must determine the level of security needed for its residents. Security measures such as automatic locks on exit doors or a wander guard system should be considered and implemented as needed. Assisted living facilities may not have the authority to lock down the building as a nursing home may, but it may be advisable to have a person at the exit door who can keep track of who comes and goes.[69]

Additionally, audio stimulation should be minimized as much as possible. Public address systems and overhead music should be avoided. Also, incidental noises from ice machines, or kitchen appliances should be reduced. Doing these simple things will decrease the amount of auditory stimulation and allow the residents to focus. The same should be done with visual stimulation such as lighting. Keep glare from windows down by using carpeting or glare-resistant televisions. Lighting should be as even as possible, avoiding pools of light and dark.[70]

11.9 Summary

There are many areas to consider when an issue arises with assisted living facilities and the nursing practice. Because assisted living is such a growing field and the elderly population is growing, it is expected there will soon be more states regulating this area.

Nurses play vital roles within these facilities and must be held accountable for their responsibilities. An attorney prosecuting or defending a case against an assisted living facility must be astutely aware of the jurisdiction's statutes, regulations and rules, if any, regarding assisted living facilities. The nurse working in the assisted living facility field must also be well-informed of these to ensure the facility's compliance. If there are no such statutes, regulations, or rules, the community's standard of care must be met, if not surpassed.

Endnotes

1. U.S. Census Bureau, Profiles of General Demographic Characteristics, 2000, http://www.census.gov/prod/cen2000/dp1/2khus.pdf, last visited September 21, 2005.

2. *Id.*

3. *Id.*

4. Detecting, Addressing and Preventing Elder Abuse in Residential Care Facilities, report to the National Institute of Justice U.S. Department of Justice Bethany L. Bakces, M.P.H., M.S.W., C.H.E.S. Social Science Analyst and Project Officer Texas A&M Health Science Center School of Rural Public Health.

5. *Id.*

6. *Id.*

7. *Id.*

8. See note 1.

9. These services can include such things as 24-hour supervision or medication administration.

10. NY Social Services Law Section 2(21).

11. Strong Health, Types of Long Term Care Facilities, http://www.stronghealth.com/services/seniors/caring/typesoflongtermcare.cfm, last visited September 21, 2005.

12. http://www.carepathways.com, last visited September 21, 2005.

13. See Section 11.6 for further discussion.

14. Codified at NY Pub. Health Law Art. 46-B. This Act became effective on February 23, 2005.

15. *Id.*

16. NY Pub. Health Law§ 4651(1).

17. NY Pub. Health Law§ 4652.

18. NY Pub. Health Law§ 4656.

19. *Id.*

20. Personal services are defined as "direct physical assistance with or supervision of the activities of daily living and the self-administration of medication and other similar services," but do not include the provision of medical, nursing, dental or mental health services.

21. Fla. Stat.§ 400.428.

22. Joint Commission on Accreditation of Healthcare Organization, http://www.jointcommission.org, last visited March 21, 2010.

23. *Id.*

24. *Id.* You can find the National Patient Safety Goals under the "Patient Safety" menu.

25. Braun, J.D. and A. Julie, *Assisted Living: Law and Advocacy*, ElderLaw Portfolio Series, Portfolio 24, 2005.

26. http://www.ncal.org/about/2003_reg_review.pdf. Last visited November 27, 2005.

27. *Id.*

28. http://www.alnursing.org. Last visited December 5, 2005.

29. Jeffrey J. Downey, Esq. *Trial Magazine* (August 2004).

30. NY Pub. Health Law§ 4658.

31. NY Pub. Health Law§ 4659.

32. New York Pub Health Law§ 4659(5).

33. NY Pub. Health Law§ 4658.

34. *Id.*

35. *Id.*

36. These agreements are also known as "Shared Risk Agreements" or "Negotiated Risk Agreements."

37. United States Department of Health & Human Services, http://aspe.hhs.gov/daltcp/reports/98state1.htm#negotiated, last visited September 29, 2005.

38. *Id.* discussing Ohio regulations.

39. Depending on the state's statutory scheme, this evaluation may be conducted by a nurse, a physician or the director or administrator of the assisted living facility.

40. More information on the Assisted Living Federation of America can be found on its website at http://www.alfa.org.

41. More information on Senior Solutions of America, Inc. can be found on its website at http://www.aging-parents-and-elder-care.com/Pages/Assisted_Living_and_Other.html.

42. Laska, L. (ed.), "Resident wanders from facility and is struck by vehicle on highway," *Medical Malpractice Verdicts, Settlements, and Experts* (January 2005): 27.

43. Laska, L. (ed.), "Elderly man falls from bed in Nevada group home and breaks hip," *Medical Malpractice Verdicts, Settlements, and Experts* (August 2004): 28.

44. Laska, L. (ed.), "Failure to attend to pressure sores and declining condition," *Medical Malpractice Verdicts, Settlements, and Experts* (September 2005): 32.

45. *USA Today* reviewed inspection records for the period of 2000 through 2002 for the states of Alabama, Arizona, Colorado, Florida, Indiana, New York and Texas. This report can be found at http://www.usatoday.com/money/industries/health/2004-05-24-assisted-living-cover_x.htm, last visited September 22, 2005.

46. Laska, L. (ed.), "Schizophrenic suffers multiple fractures in suicide attempt," *Medical Malpractice Verdicts, Settlements, and Experts* (August 2004): 27.

47. Agsalsa, S., Study Shows Inadequate Psychiatric Care in Assisted Living Facilities, November 10, 2004, http://www.eurekalert.org/pub_releases/2004-11/bpl-ssi111004.php, last visited September 22, 2005.

48. Also, contact the National Center for Assisted Living. This organization's mission is to promote "successful nursing practice in assisted living facilities" to benefit nurses and residents. This organization currently working with nursing and assisted living experts to establish the first assisted living nurse certification program, to certify nurses specifically in the assisted living facility field.

49. Laska, L. (ed.), "Failure to carefully supervise partially blind patient's medication intake," *Medical Malpractice Verdicts, Settlements, and Experts* (March 2004): 46.

50. Laska, L. (ed.), "Disabled man suffers sexual assault in assisted living facility," *Medical Malpractice Verdicts, Settlements, and Experts* (February 2004): 28.

51. See note 4.

52. Her body temperature was 108 degrees when found.

53. See note 42.

54. Problems with Staffing, Training Can Cost Lives, USA TODAY, May 26, 2004, http://www.usatoday.com/money/industries/health/2004-05-26-assisted-day2_x.htm, last visited September 22, 2005.

55. *Id.*, citing Report by the National Center for Assisted Living 2003-2004.

56. Laska, L. (ed.), "Choking death while assisted living center's staff tried to contact administrator for OK to call 911," *Medical Malpractice Verdicts, Settlements, and Experts* (February 2004): 31.

57. For example, in New York, the Statute of Limitations for Breach of Contract is six years, as opposed to three years for negligence.

58. Wright, PhD, B. *An Overview of Assisted Living: 2004*, Public Policy Institute, AARP, October 2004.

59. See note 4.

60. See the New York Case of Matter of Empire State Assoc. of Assisted Living, Inc. et al., 26 Misc. 3d 340 (Sup. Ct., Albany County, 2009).

61. See note 21.

62. See note 21.

63. See note 21.

64. See note 21.

65. See note 21.

66. See note 21.

67. http://www.alz.org/Health/Care/design.asp. Last visited November 27, 2005.

68. *Id.*

69. *Id.*

70. NY Pub. Health Law§4654, 4655.

Chapter 12

Legal Issues in School Nursing Practice

Marian Nowak, RN, MSN, MEd, MPH

Synopsis
12.1 Introduction
12.2 What is School Nursing?
    A. Why We Need School Nurses
    B. School Nurse Functions
    C. School Nurse Certification
    D. School Nurse Organizations
12.3 Nursing Assessments
    A. History and Physicals
    B. Employee Health
    C. Workers' Compensation
    D. Scoliosis Screening
    E. Blood Pressure Screening
    F. Audiometric Screening
    G. Vision Screening
    H. Treating Sick and Injured
    I. Immunizations
12.4 Special Issues
    A. Substance Abuse
    B. Child Abuse
    C. Emergency Care
12.5 Disabilities
    A. Disabilities Act
    B. Students with HIV
    C. Students with Attention Deficit Disorder
12.6 Medications in Schools
    A. General Concepts
    B. Oral Medication
    C. Over the Counter Medications
    D. Antibiotics
    E. Stimulants
    F. Injectable Medication
    G. Medication Records
12.7 School Medical Records
    A. General Considerations
    B. Best Evidence Rules
12.8 Staffing Issues
    A. General Considerations
    B. Recommended Ratios
    C. Safe Staffing
12.9 Codes of Ethics
    A. School Nursing Code of Ethics
        1. Client Care
        2. Professional Competency
        3. Professional Responsibilities
    B. Nursing Code of Ethics
12.10 Spiritual Health in School Health Services
    A. Religious Rights in Public Schools
    B. Legal Implications of Refusing Rights
12.11 Summary
Endnotes

12.1 Introduction

School nurses have been helping children in schools since 1903. Years ago the school nurse was a public health nurse who was mainly responsible for preventing the spread of infections and for giving immunizations. Today the school nurse has many professional functions and is an integral part of a child's educational team.[1] School nursing is defined as a specialized practice of professional nursing that advances the well-being and academic success of students. Nurses assist students in every level of growth and development.[2]

12.2 What is School Nursing?

School nursing is a specialized practice that promotes student health necessary to achieve lifelong academic achievement. School nurses facilitate positive student responses to normal development; promote health and safety; intervene with actual and potential health problems; provide case management services; and actively collaborate with others to build student and family capacity for adaptation, self-management, self-advocacy, and learning.[3] After the child's home, school represents the second most influential environment in a child's life. As school nurses work in the community to enhance the educational environment, they insure children's health needs are met. School nurses must consider both individual needs and population needs when planning health-related services.

A. Why We Need School Nurses

Nurses in schools help children fully benefit from their educational program. The nurse coordinates care with outside medical agencies and consults with school staff on medical issues. School nurses must provide varied and often complex nursing services. Although school health services may vary from state to state, 89 percent of the states have at least one school-based health center and 77 percent of schools have either a part-time or full-time school nurse.[4]

TIP: The school nurse is the only medical expert available within this setting to help children who may become injured or ill during the school day.

B. School Nurse Functions

According to the National Association of School Nurses (NASN), the school nurse has eight main functions within the school:

1. *Provide direct health care to students and staff.* The school nurse provides care to students and staff who have been injured or who have acute illnesses. Care may involve treatment of health problems within the scope of nursing practice, communication with parents about treatment, and referral to other providers.

2. *Provide leadership for health services.* In addition to providing health services directly, as the health care expert within the school, the school nurse assesses the overall system of care. This leadership role includes developing a plan for responding to emergencies or disasters, and training staff as deemed necessary or to fulfill code requirements.

3. *Provide screening and referral for health conditions.* The nurse plays a role in addressing potential health problems that are barriers to learning or symptoms of underlying medical conditions. Screening activities may include vision, hearing, body mass index (BMI), or other screening. Screenings should be performed as designated by law or on factors such as the need for testing in a given population aggregate, test validity, program cost-effectiveness, and the availability of resources.

4. *Promote a healthy school environment.* The school nurse provides for the physical and emotional safety of the school community. The school nurse monitors immunizations, teaches about bloodborne pathogens, and attends to school environments. The nurse may offer an assessment of playground safety, indoor air quality, emotional environment (violence activities), or a review of patterns of illness or injury.

5. *Promote health.* The school nurse disseminates health education, develops health education curricula, and encourages comprehensive, sequential, and age-appropriate health-related information. The nurse is a member of the coordinated school health team that promotes the health and well-be-

ing of school members through collaborative efforts.

6. *Serve in a leadership role for school health policies and programs.* As the healthcare expert within the school system, the school nurse takes a leadership role in the development and evaluation of school health policies. Additionally the nurse often participates in measuring health service outcomes or research.

7. *Serve as a liaison between school and community.* The nurse works as coordinator of personnel, family, community, and healthcare providers in delivering continuity of care. He or she participates as the health expert on Individualized Education Plans and Americans with Disabilities Act Section 504 teams. How the nurse fulfills these functions is listed in Table 12.1, which also depicts some common daily tasks.[5]

C. School Nurse Certification

In order to work in public schools, all nurses must obtain additional education and certification from the Department of Education. School nurses may receive certification in their individual states to allow them to practice in their state or they may take a national certification test sponsored by the National Association of School Nurses that permits them to work in any area of the U.S. To maintain nursing licenses and certifications, nurses are required to engage in approved continuing education programs. For example in New Jersey, school nurses must obtain 100 hours per five years of continuing education offered by a New Jersey Department of Education approved provider. In addition, the New Jersey Board of Nursing requires 15 hours per year of approved professional continuing education credits in order to maintain a nursing license.

TIP: Since school nurses are not allowed to prescribe medical treatments, they work under the supervision of a school doctor often referred to as a Medical Inspector.

The school Medical Inspector approves protocols for the overall school health services programs and acts as a consultant to the school administration on medical matters. Individual states adopt laws to regulate the practice of nursing in schools. However, all federal laws apply in a school setting. In all states nurses must be registered professional nurses to practice in a school setting.

Table 12.1
Tasks of The School Nurse

Professional Role	Implementation
Perform Health Assessment	Physical assessment, interview, and discussion with key individuals.
Treat School Day Injuries	Protocols approved by a medical provider that is consistent with national standards of care.
Treat School Day Illness	Protocols approved by the school physician that is consistent with national standards of care.
Dispense Prescription Medications	With a legally acceptable prescription that includes name of the medication, dose, route, and how often it is to be dispensed.
Dispense Emergency Medications	With a legally acceptable prescription that includes name of the medication, dose, route, and under what conditions the medication is to be administered.
Provide Emergency Assistance	Identifies critical health issues and arranges for immediate transportation of medical emergencies that occur during the school day.
Provide Emergency Injections	With a legally acceptable prescription that includes name of the medication, dose, route, and under what conditions the medication is to be administered. Examples include injectable medications such as glucagon injections for diabetic patients and epinephrine injections for those suffering from a severe allergic reaction known as anaphylaxis.
Develop Individualized Health Plans	Develops plans to foster student achievement during the school day and to provide for medical needs while in school.
Develop Emergency Health Plans	Develops plans to foster student achievement during the school day and to provide for medical needs should an emergency situation occur. Students in most need of emergency plans include children with asthma, severe allergic reactions, and those who have diabetes type I, due to the increased risk of developing emergent health problems.
Collaborate/ Coordinate Care of Students with Other Organizations	Coordinates care with medical, social, and community agencies. Examples may include: coordination of immunizations with the Department of Health Clinic, making referrals to mental health agencies, coordinating care with clinics, hospitals or primary care provider.
Monitor Immunizations	Provides for community protection of communicable diseases by monitoring and assisting parents to procure proper immunizations at correct intervals. Recommends exclusion of students who do not comply with immunization statutes.
Track Communicable Disease Trends	Monitors communicable disease trends and general morbidity trends by collecting statistics on the school population and reporting the same to public health authorities.
Provide or Recommend Tuberculosis Testing	Follows recommendations of the CDC for tuberculosis testing in communities.
Provide Screening Tests	Checks for undetected health issues such as hearing, vision, growth and development, or nutritional issues. The nurse will often use vision testing equipment, certified audiometers, BMI rates, and other assessment tools.
Provide Care of Special Needs Students	Follows Section 504 of the Americans with Disabilities Act statutes by making provisions for the individualized needs of disabled students.
Promote a Healthy School Environment	Teaches principles of wellness to those in the school environment. This may include inservice education for teachers, assembly programs, special events, or clubs.
Maintain Records and Reports	State and local records and mandated reports are completed by school nurses. Some reports require statistical data collection and others are for the purpose of the individual student health record. Confidentiality of all health records must be maintained.
Advocate for Students	Meets with others to plan and establish an integrated program that meets students' health needs.

Certification of nurses ensures that standards of nursing practice are promoted in this setting. The components of the nursing process are applied in the school nursing setting. Within this process the ANA and NASN establish standard practices for nurses such as elements of nursing assessment, diagnosis, and outcomes. The standards for functioning in a school are further defined by standing orders, protocols, and job descriptions that are approved by the board of education.

TIP: Standards of care are available on the National Association of School Nurses' website at www.nasn.org. Search under the heading of position papers and standards of care. Also ask to review the School Health Services Handbook found in each school district for district-specific policies.

D. School Nurse Organizations

School nurse associations are organized on the county, state, and national levels. The national organization is the National Association of School Nurses and is the leading professional association for school health services. Members of NASN are eligible to take advantage of many professional resources for school nursing policy, advocacy, research, and continuing education. Over 14,000 nurses in the U.S. benefit from the largest organization devoted exclusively to the specialty of school nursing.[6] There are many other nursing and community health focused organizations which can serve as a resource to school nurses. These organizations include The American Nurses Association, the National Association of Pediatric Nursing, the American Public Health Association, and the American Association for Health Education.

12.3 Nursing Assessments
A. History and Physicals

Health histories contain information about the individual's past and current medical conditions, and physicals include examinations to identify physical symptoms. In a school setting, histories and physicals are recorded in the student's medical record and they may vary from state to state. Physical examinations are recommended for school age children at various intervals.

The history is the first step in the assessment process. Collecting data from the family, physician, and student, when appropriate, is essential. Physical assessment data may include a combination of screening tests and observed physical elements (e.g., heart rate, respiratory rate, blood pressure, pain assessment, hearing tests, vision testing, etc.). A nursing diagnosis is a method of organizing and summarizing nursing data to define the student's health. By col-

lecting this information the nurse then can set goals of care and plan nursing interventions. The goals of care are broad-based statements that address the educational relevancy of the individualized healthcare plan. Nursing interventions are actions taken to achieve a desired health outcome. Once developed, the plans are then placed in a document called an individual care plan. Evaluation of the plan involves the annual review of the plan or adjustments as the child's health status changes.[7]

B. Employee Health

The school nurse provides care to staff who have been injured or who have an acute illness. Care may involve treatment of health problems within the scope of nursing practice, communication with employees for treatment, and referral to other providers. The school nurse uses the nursing process to assess, diagnose, plan, implement, and evaluate care for students (and employees) with chronic health conditions. Often the school nurse advises the employee on proper medication administration and the performance of health care procedures that are within the scope of nursing practice and are ordered by an appropriately licensed healthcare provider. The school nurse also assists faculty and staff in monitoring chronic health conditions. As the scope of nursing practice expands to utilize the increasingly complex technology needed to provide up-to-date care for clients, the school nurse's body of knowledge grows through personal professional development.[8]

C. Workers' Compensation

Depending on state requirements some nurses may have responsibilities for employee related injuries. If an employee is injured during work hours and her employer abides by workers' compensation programs, the nurse is often the first agent to assess and evaluate the employee injury. The nurse is not only responsible for taking appropriate action in such cases, she is also responsible for giving feedback on the overall school district's plan to protect its employees. School nurses must follow the standard of care in rendering first aid to employees. School employees are protected under PEOSHA regulations. This means employees must be protected from known work hazards including toxic and hazardous substances. Regulations of OSHA and PEOSHA of the U.S. Department of Labor, Health, and Safety Administration provide schools with detailed information on employee rights. Two significant federal regulations that relate to school environments include federal regulations of Occupational Exposure to Bloodborne Pathogens and Hazard Communications Rule.[9] Often school nurses offer information and classes pertaining to these topics to school district employees.

D. Scoliosis Screening

Scoliosis screening tests as well as intervals of testing are dictated by state department of education law. Scoliosis is defined as a curvature of the spine and causes a sideways curve of the backbone, or spine. These curves are often S- or C-shaped. Scoliosis is most common in late childhood and the early teens, when children grow fast. Girls are more likely to have it than boys, and it can run in families. Symptoms include leaning to one side and having uneven shoulders and hips. The curve might be temporary and it might be due to muscle spasms, inflammation, or having different leg lengths. People with mild scoliosis might only need to wear braces.[10]

There are three general causes of scoliosis:

- Congenital (present at birth) is caused by the malformation of the spine bones (vertebrae) or fused ribs during fetal development.
- Neuromuscular scoliosis is caused by poor muscle control, weakness, or paralysis due to disorders like cerebral palsy, muscular dystrophy, spina bifida or polio.
- Idiopathic scoliosis in adolescents is the most common type, and the cause is unknown.[11]

Screening for proper alignment of the spine is often performed by school nurses.

TIP: School nurses who fail to detect scoliosis may have deviated from the standard of care.

Screening in schools is important because early interventions can prevent further complications of spinal deformities. Schools generally screen males and females separately. Student privacy should be protected by allowing students to enter the testing area one by one. Once identified as having a potential problem, the nurse then refers the child for further evaluation. The evaluation may include spine x-rays and at times an MRI.[12] Treatment depends on the cause, the size and location of the curve, and predicted growth.[13–15]

E. Blood Pressure Screening

Blood pressure screening intervals and testing are dictated by state department of education law. Standards for blood pressure screening can be found at the National Heart, Lung, and Blood Institute National Blood Pressure Control Committee. It is important to keep in mind that different ages have different blood pressure ranges. While high blood pressure (hypertension) is far more common among adults, the rate among children in the United States is on the rise. Left un-

treated, high blood pressure can eventually lead to damage to the heart, brain, kidneys, and eyes. If identified early through screening, children can be treated and lead a normal life.

TIP: Information on childhood hypertension is available at: www.nhlbi.nih.gov and www.kidshealth.org.

F. Audiometric Screening

Audiometric or hearing screening is dictated by state department of education law. In some states a speech therapist administers the hearing tests for school age students. Since good hearing is essential to language development, loss of hearing has serious implications for children audiologically.[16]

It has long been recognized that hearing loss and auditory processing disorders (APD) affect a child's ability to learn language and achieve academically. The effects of hearing loss vary depending on several factors, including the nature and degree of impairment. It is essential that children with hearing loss or APD receive comprehensive audiologyc services. All children could benefit from audiology services to assist in the development of listening skills and provisions of measures to prevent hearing impairment.[17]

Federal legislation defines the responsibilities of public education for children with disabilities (PL 93-112, Rehabilitation Act of 1973, Section 504, 1973; PL 100-407, Technology Related Assistance for Individuals with Disabilities Act, 1988; PL 101-336, Americans with Disabilities Act of 1990; and PL 101-497, Individuals with Disabilities Education Act [IDEA 97]). Together these legislative mandates require access to a free, appropriate public education (FAPE) for all children with disabilities. Other mandates and provisions, such as universal newborn hearing screening; Medicaid's Early and Periodic Screening; diagnostic and treatment programs; and state and local audiology screening programs, help to ensure that children with hearing loss are identified and that appropriate referrals and services are provided.[18]

The role of the audiologist in the school is defined in IDEA regulations, Part B, which applies to children ages three to 21. These regulations define audiology as follows:

1. Identification of children with hearing loss;
2. Determination of the range, nature, and degree of hearing loss, including referral for medical or other professional attention for the habilitation of hearing;
3. Provision of habilitative activities, such as language habilitation, auditory training, speech reading (lip-reading), hearing evaluation, and speech conservation;

4. Creation and administration of programs for prevention of hearing loss;

5. Counseling and guidance of children, parents, and teachers regarding hearing loss; and

6. Determining children's needs for group and individual amplification, selecting and fitting an appropriate aid, and evaluating the effectiveness of amplification. (34 CFR §300.24(b)(1)

The regulations (34 CFR §300.303) also require that "Each public agency shall ensure that the hearing aids worn in school by children with hearing impairments, including deafness, are functioning properly." IDEA also indicates that when developing an IEP, the team must "consider whether the child requires assistive technology devices and services." (34 CFR §300.46(a)(2)(v)).[19] When a child is identified as having a potential hearing problem, the nurse should notify the parentS and recommend a follow-up hearing evaluation.

G. Vision Screening

Vision screening is dictated by individual state department of education administrative codes. Mandates generally specify intervals of screening. Vision screening in schools involves the detection and referral for treatment of commonly occurring visual anomalies.[20] "Commonly occurring" is defined as a condition whose prevalence is 1 percent or greater of a potentially affected population. Early detection of a vision problem can have educational and behavioral benefits, and certainly has quality of life benefits. School vision screening is distinct from school vision assessment, which is conducted when a teacher or parent refers a child to the nurse because of a suspected visual problem. Assessment is more comprehensive than screening and the nurse considers all available data in formulating a nursing diagnosis.[21]

Traditional school vision screening has focused on the examination of *distance vision* in order to detect myopia, the most common of visual disorders, and to a lesser extent, high astigmatism. Screenings of other visual functions in school, specifically *near vision, binocular vision, and color vision*, are inconsistent across the states. Ophthalmology and optometry consultants to NASN's current publication on vision screening strongly support the school screening of near vision in young children.

Specific aspects of the nursing role may include:

- Employ the most accurate yet practical techniques, equipment, and tests for the age group.
- Consider the higher probability of issues among children with certain chronic, genetic, and congen-

ital conditions, lower socioeconomic backgrounds, or parents or siblings with an identified vision problem.

- Assist families in understanding their children's conditions and the referral process.
- Encourage the examination of a child's eyes by an eye professional at least once in a child's school life.
- Establish vision screening programs for early childhood and vulnerable groups.[22]

H. Treating Sick and Injured

The school nurse is responsible for treating the sick and injured during the school day.

TIP: One of the greatest potential sources of liability involves the school nurse's role in treating the sick and injured during the school day.

The nurse follows standing orders or protocols established by the school physician and standards of care set by professional nursing organizations. When children are injured during the school day the nurse will generate an incident report that defines the conditions of the event, nursing assessment, interventions, and notification of the appropriate person. Notification may include the parents or guardian and the school doctor. Notification of the parents may be written or verbal. The timing and type of notification depends on the severity of the injury. In some instances the nurse simply sends a note home with the student and in other instances the nurse may call the parent to offer needed information about the injury and about home care measures. If the injury is serious children are often transported to the emergency department accompanied by the school nurse.

Head injuries are of particular concern in a school setting because of their potential for seriousness. The assessment of the student includes a detailed history and physical assessment. The nurse will check for signs and symptoms of increased intracranial pressure (ICP). If the injury appears minor and there are no signs of ICP, the nurse will have the student return for a reevaluation later in the school day. Many nurses give students written head injury information for their parents. In scenarios involving serious head injuries, the nurse will arrange for an immediate emergency medical evaluation.

A college soccer player fell on the field during a game and was accidentally kicked in the head. He went to the school nurse's office, where he was examined by the school nurse and a sports medicine physician. He received instructions to go to an emergency room if he noticed any changes. Within a day, he became lethargic and his roommate suggested he go to an emergency department. He declined. A day later he was unarousable and was taken to the hospital, where he was diagnosed with an intracerebral bleed. He suffered permanent cognitive deficits. He sued the school nurse and sports medicine physician. After the plaintiff completed his case at trial, the defense made a motion to dismiss the case. The judge carefully asked the family if they were aware of an offer to settle the case and if they had made a decision about accepting it. The family insisted they were not going to accept the settlement and wanted the trial to proceed. The judge then granted the motion to dismiss. (Unpublished New Jersey case.)

While attending to children with chronic illness, nurses develop an individualized healthcare plan. However, in many instances the nursing measures are considered episodic or emergency care measures. The range of school health services varies by school district. The following health services are the minimum recommended by the American Academy of Pediatrics:

- Assessment of health complaints
- Medication administration
- Care of students with special healthcare needs
- A system for managing emergencies and urgent situations.
- Mandated health screening programs
- Verification of immunizations
- Infectious disease reporting
- Identification and management of students' chronic healthcare needs that affect educational achievement[23]

I. Immunizations

All states require immunizations of children as part of a communicable disease management program and schools generally assign the responsibilities of communicable disease management to school nurses. Immunizations (vaccinations) are responsible for the control of many infectious diseases that were once common in the country and therefore immunizations of school age children are mandated. Vaccines have reduced, and in some cases eliminated, diseases that routinely killed or disabled many infants, children, teenagers, and adults. However, the viruses and bacteria that cause vaccine-preventable disease and death still exist and can be passed on to unvaccinated people. In addition, vaccine-preventable diseases have a costly impact on Americans, resulting in lost work time for parents, doctor's visits, hospitalizations, and premature deaths.[24]

The immunizations requirements vary from state to state and for each county. The requirements for state immunizations can be found by contacting the local department of health.

TIP: For general immunization information and for schedules of immunizations recommended by the Centers for Disease Control and Prevention log on to: www.cdc.gov/immunizations.

Immunization requirements many change depending on epidemiologic data that evaluate disease trends. It is the responsibility of the school nurse to track immunizations and to recommend exclusion from school if children do not have appropriate immunizations. Schools must be consistent in their application of exclusions and readmission to avoid claims of discrimination or harassment.[25]

12.4 Special Issues
A. Substance Abuse

Since 1975, the Monitoring the Future (MTF) survey has measured drug, alcohol, and cigarette use, and related attitudes among adolescent students nationwide. The MTF survey is funded by the National Institute of Drug Abuse and is conducted by the University of Michigan's Institute for Social Research. In the 35th annual study, conducted during 2009, the most positive result indicated that cigarette smoking is at its lowest point in history. These findings are particularly noteworthy since tobacco addiction is one of the leading preventable contributors to many of our nation's health problems. However, substance abuse among teens is still of great concern to schools. The non-medical use of prescription drugs is on the rise among 12th graders. Use of Vicodin and OxyContin increased during the last five years among tenth graders, and remained unchanged among 8th and twelfth graders. Nearly one in ten high school seniors reported past-year non-medical use of Vicodin, and one in 20 abused OxyContin.[26]

Since the school nurse is responsible for health assessment of students, he is often asked to evaluate students who are thought to be under the influence of a dangerous substance. The nurse determines if the student must be transported to the emergency department for treatment, and some states require substance testing. Opponents claim this may be an infringement of civil rights. Some schools avoid substance testing due to the cost of testing.[27] Many schools have student assistance programs and employ a specialist in counseling these children, and in some states this is required under education law. The substance abuse counselor is under the direction of the administration, and relevant information may be shared in order to plan an effective program. Information of a confidential nature may not be shared.[28]

Some states require schools to provide screening of students who are believed to be under the influence of a dangerous substance. Most states have provisions to ensure educational services are provided when a student is in a substance abuse treatment program. In *Field v. Haddonfield Board of Education* (1991), a court ruled that drug treatment was not a related service. Thus, a school is not required to provide treatment. Since substance abuse is considered to be a disability, children treated for this are provided assistance under Individuals with Disability Act (IDEA) provisions.[29] All schools in the U.S. are permitted to perform random drug testing on athletes. Since it is thought that substances may affect the performance of sports participants, the right for schools to promote random drug testing has been upheld in the U.S. Supreme Court.[30]

B. Child Abuse

Child abuse or neglect is a reportable offense in all 50 states. Reporting does not require permission from the child or school administration. Professionals are required to provide a report to the appropriate child protection agency, and if suspected child abuse is not reported there can be penalties. In 1974 the Federal Child Abuse Prevention and Treatment Act was passed, and it was amended in 1992.

According to this Act, school district policies should clearly define roles and responsibilities of the school employees as related to suspected child abuse. Not only are nurses required to report such suspected cases, the entire school staff is required to do the same. Nurses are required to comply with professional standards of practice when assessing a child, and providing objective detailed documentation is a safeguard for both the student and staff. School staff must know the warning signs and how to document the abuse. Documentation is critical and will allow accurate recall of the incident; however, taking photographs of physical findings is generally not the responsibility of the school.[31]

When a school nurse suspects a child's health is impaired due to a lack of medical follow up or a parent's refusal to seek appropriate medical care, the nurse is required to notify Child Protective Services (e.g., Division of Youth and Family Services, DYFS) or police under state neglect statutes. "As agents of the state the authorities may limit parental refusal of medical treatment for their children based on legal interests of the state regarding the following: preservation of life, protection of minor dependents, prevention of irrational self-destruction, maintenance of the ethical integrity of health professionals, and protection of the public's health." In some circumstances a court order may be obtained to override parental denial of treatment.[32]

C. Emergency Care

Emergency care in schools involves not only the care of emergent conditions such as asthma, anaphylactic reactions, and serious fractures (compound complex fractures), it also addresses the need for a school to be prepared for the possibility of a mass casualty incident such as a shooting or terrorist attack. All schools are required to have emergency plans. The nurse is often involved in designing the emergency plan and acts as a key member in the emergency crisis team. School nurses identify potential risks and measure the effectiveness of emergency training. They have information about children with special healthcare needs and, as licensed healthcare professionals, they respond to serious adverse events that threaten the health, safety, or well-being of a school population.[33]

Despite the extreme scenarios that may occur, school crisis plans are developed as a response to all types of emergencies. In schools, emergencies can stem from a gas leak, weather, a nearby fire, or school violence.[34]

TIP: The U.S. Department of Education's "Practical Information on Crisis Planning: a Guide for Schools and Communities" is available at: www.ed.gov/admins/lead/safety/emergencyplan/crisisplanning.pdf.

12.5 Disabilities
A. Disabilities Act
The Education for All Handicapped Children Act of 1975 (EHA) established national standards for a free and appropriate education for children with disabilities. In subsequent legislation the IDEA continued to support and develop standards. In 2004, revisions to the IDEA included nursing services as one of the related services that a student with a disability is entitled to receive in order to participate in educational programming. These services require the nurse to provide individualized care for the medically involved students. In addition, the Rehabilitation Act of 1973 (section 504) and subsequent revisions require any school program that receives federal aid to make reasonable accommodations. These reasonable accommodations include, but are not limited to, nursing services such as medication administration, glucose monitoring, insulin administration, and health-related procedures.[35]

Section 504 of the American with Disabilities Act states that no qualified individual with a disability in the United States shall be excluded from, denied the benefits of, or be subjected to discrimination under any program or activity that either receives federal financial assistance or is conducted by any executive agency or the United States Postal Service." Since all public schools receive federal funds they must abide by these laws.

Each federal agency has its own set of section 504 regulations that apply to its programs. Agencies that provide federal financial assistance also have section 504 regulations covering entities that receive federal aid. Requirements common to these regulations include reasonable accommodation for employees with disabilities, program accessibility, effective communication with people who have hearing or vision disabilities, and accessible new construction and alterations. Each agency is responsible for enforcing its own regulations. Section 504 may also be enforced through private lawsuits. It is not necessary to file a complaint with a federal agency or to receive a right-to-sue letter before going to court.[36]

Under this Act schools must provide:

1. Qualified interpreters, note takers, transcription services, written materials, telephone handset amplifiers, assistive listening devices, assistive listening systems, telephones compatible with hearing aids, closed caption decoders, open and closed captioning, telecommunications devices for deaf persons (TDD's), videotext displays, or other effective methods of making aurally delivered materials available to individuals with hearing impairments;

2. Qualified readers, taped texts, audio recordings, Braille materials, large print materials, or other effective methods of making visually delivered materials available to individuals with visual impairments;

3. Acquisition or modification of equipment or devices; and

4. Other similar services and actions.[37]

Nurses may assist the school team in procuring these student services by contacting appropriate social service and medical rehabilitation agencies. In addition they may develop plans to ensure a physical disability does not hinder the student's ability to navigate the school, and accommodate for physical disabilities.

TIP: Information and 504 complaints should be addressed to:

U.S. Department of Justice
Civil Rights Division
950 Pennsylvania Avenue, N.W.
Disability Rights Section—NYAV
Washington, DC 20530
www.ada.gov
Voice: 800-514-0301, TTY: 800-514-0383

B. Students with HIV

Student with HIV have the right to continue school with reasonable accommodations. In many instances students may want this diagnosis to be kept confidential. The nurse is responsible for constructing a plan to allow for the medical accommodations of the student while maintaining the confidentiality requirements. The school nurse should also function in an advocacy role should the diagnosis be revealed.

TIP: State and federal laws "protect the confidentiality of HIV-related information, the rights and obligations of people with HIV with respect to disclosure of their HIV status in various settings, the importance of privacy and confidentiality guarantees to health care and prevention programs, and possible legal actions when an unauthorized disclosure of an individual's HIV-related information occurs."[38]

"Under anti-discrimination laws such as the ADA, particularly as amended in 2008, the fact of a disability, including those such as early HIV disease with no visible manifestations, is the basis for protection from discrimination against those who are living with a disability."[39]

C. Students with Attention Deficit Disorder

Under section 504 of the ADA and IDEA, public schools have an obligation to provide appropriate supportive services for students who have been diagnosed with ADD. Section 504 applications in these cases are closely related to any other student who may need accommodations for special medical needs. Under these regulations schools must make an effort to identify children with disabilities. Once identified, the school must make both educational and medical accommodations. As an ethical matter, school nurses support and advocate for students who have this disability. It is important for families and school staff to advocate for children with ADD. The nurse often serves as a resource to the family, student, and administration.[40]

12.6 Medications in Schools
A. General Concepts

Increased in-patient safety is a concern among all nursing sectors. When workloads are too heavy, safety can easily become compromised in any nursing setting.[41] In a school setting, the nurse is often the one to intercept the errors made by the physician and pharmacist. Special attention should be given to medication administration practices since medication adherence issues, the potential for errors and the potential for abuse exist in any school setting. The school nurse has the responsibility to follow all standard medication practices to insure the safety of school age children.

Table 12.2
Categories of Controlled Substances

Category	Use
I	Experimental
II	No Refills
III	Refilled up to 5-6 times
IV	Refilled up 5-6 times
V	Restricted to the extent of non-regulated drugs

Medications in schools are to be administered by qualified persons, or in some circumstances students may self-administer medication. Certain medications that have a potential for abuse are more vigorously guarded. Controlled substances are medications such as stimulants and depressants (narcotics and some sedatives) that have the potential for abuse and are subject to requirements of the Comprehensive Drug Abuse Prevention and Control Act of 1971. In order to control the use of medications, controlled substances are divided into five categories as listed in Table 12.2.[42]

B. Oral Medication

Only when absolutely necessary should medication be prescribed for administration during school hours. When it is necessary, the parents or legal guardians must obtain direction for the same from a licensed physician or advanced practice nurse. Medication must be kept in a secure place. The security of the storage place will vary depending on the type of medication involved. Controlled drugs require a locked storage area in accordance with the Minimum Storage Requirements for Narcotic Substances Guidelines (Department of Health and Human Services).[43]

In some states diabetic injections, epinephrine injections, and asthma inhalers may be self-administered by students if they have permission from their parent and the prescribing physician. Sometimes, a parent may ask that prescribed medication be administered at school (or a variation in dosage of a medication) on an "as needed" (or prn) basis. This is appropriate only in very rare situations where it is necessary to maintain the child in school despite complex medical problems.[44] Particular attention should be given to asthma inhaler medication since it is considered an emergency medication. With proper documentation and education on self-administration, children are allowed to self-administer their medication during the school day. In instances where the school nurse is administering the inhaler medication, care should be given to establish the storage of this medication in a location that is readily assessible to the asthmatic student. When a school accepts responsibility for the administration of medication to students, the school will owe a duty of care to those students to ensure that reasonable care is taken. The duty is to ensure, in the absence of the parent/legal guardian, that the student is given the correct dosage of the correct medication at the correct time, according to prescribed instructions.[45]

In some states, a teacher authorized by the principal may accept responsibility to give medication to a student under certain circumstances such as after-school activities or excursions. In these instances parents/guardians must provide the school with a written statement of their request along with a written approval by the prescribing physician. Staff members retain the right to refuse to administer medication if they feel uncomfortable or unqualified. In an emergency, staff may have an obligation to attempt to administer medication, even though they may not feel qualified. Some states have regulations requiring school nurses to attend trips or excursions in order to administer medication.

TIP: Regulations governing medication administration in schools are defined by state department of education rules and regulations.

C. Over the Counter Medications

Non-prescribed oral medication (such as analgesics and over-the-counter medication) should not be administered by teachers or other members of the school staff. It is not recommended that school staff administer cold remedies, analgesics, or another medication that can be bought without a prescription.

Students in schools often take over the counter medications for minor ailments. In some instances children should not be given medications in schools. Students experiencing fever, severe headache, earache, or toothache may have symptoms of conditions that require further investigation by the appropriate health practitioner.[46]

D. Antibiotics

Most antibiotics can be prescribed to be administered before and after school hours. In the event that these medications must be given during school hours, the regulations of all prescription medications must be followed, parental guardian permission must be obtained, the medicine must be in the original container, and the container must be properly labeled.

TIP: It is of particular importance that no dosages of this medication are missed in order to keep blood levels of the medication consistent. Failure to give the medication as prescribed may cause the student to begin another regimen of the medication, thus delaying the effectiveness of the treatment regimen.[47]

E. Stimulants

Students should be closely supervised when taking stimulant medication. School nurses often develop a system to ensure that medication is given correctly. This should include plans for after-school activities and other excursions. The nurse should be aware that medications should be administered in a private location to prevent teasing by other children. The same regulations as with all medications brought to school apply. In some instances parents ask for two containers to enhance accuracy and ease of medication delivery.[48]

Since stimulants have a potential for abuse, careful handling of this medication is imperative. Many school policies require nurses to count these medications in the presence of the parent and co-sign medication forms which list the exact number of doses received by the school and date the medication was received.

F. Injectable Medication

Non-medical staff in schools should not routinely administer injections. Non-medical staff can administer injections only in an emergency where no other medical assistance can be obtained within the required time span. The most likely instance will be the administration of adrenalin for severe allergic (anaphylactic) reactions.

When administration of an injection during school hours is necessary, agreements of parent/guardian, the prescribing physician, and school personnel are documented in a written school day plan. Medication storage and labeling must be maintained. Used syringes should be placed in a disposable container (e.g. "sharps" disposal container). The Environmental Protection Agency and Department of Health and Human Services have very specific guidelines for regulated medical waste.

Should a student or staff member suffer a puncture wound from a discarded syringe, the bloodborne pathogen procedures must be followed. This regulation is designed to protect individuals from microscopic organisms. If exposed, an immediate medical evaluation is recommended.[49]

TIP: Bloodborne pathogens are of concern any time staff may have contact with blood. Information about employee and student rights on exposure to bloodborne pathogens is available at: www.osha.gov/SLTC/bloodbornepathogens/index.html

G. Medication Records

Records of medication administration should be kept, and each entry on the record should be completed by the person administering the medication. The information should contain:

- Student name
- Medication name
- Dosage
- Time of medication
- Method (i.e., oral, inhaled, injected)
- Name of person giving the medication

The school must develop systems for recordkeeping that maintain and respect confidentiality of student medications. In the case of HIV it is illegal to keep records relating to a person's HIV status unless:

- Information is coded for privacy (i.e., identity of the person is not apparent).
- Records are protected by safeguards against loss, unauthorized access, use, modification, or disclosure.
- Limited access is maintained.
- HIV/AIDS related records should be secure and stored separately if possible.
- Records/documents are destroyed when they are no longer required.[50]

12.7 School Medical Records
A. General Considerations

The Family Educational Rights and Privacy Act (FERPA), also known as the Buckley Amendment, concerns both access to and privacy of school records. FERPA applies to educational agencies and institutions that receive funds under programs administered by the Secretary of Education. The types of records covered include all educational records that contain information directly related to a specific student. Under FERPA, parents/guardians (applies to students under 18 years) have the following rights:

1. To see the educational records that the institution is keeping on the student.
2. To seek amendment of those records.
3. To have some control over the disclosure of information from her records.
4. To file a complaint with the FERPA Office in Washington, DC, for failure of the school to comply with the law.[51]

Under FERPA (34C.F.R.99.3R4), confidential information is forbidden to be disclosed except with written permission from the parent/guardian. This includes the release, transfer, or other communication of personally identifiable information contained in educational records. Oral, written, faxed or electronic information is protected under this law.

School and medical records are accessible to parents within a reasonable period of time but in no case more than 45 days. Under IDEA the access must be provided to parents prior to any IEP meeting or special education as well as a due process hearing.[52]

B. Best Evidence Rules

Best evidence refers to the authentication of medical and school records. Records should be protected from alteration and should not be written over. Most evidence law is based on proper records. Therefore the ability to document accurately is imperative. If records cannot be authenticated the evidence provided by them is weakened and may be discredited in court.[53]

Many schools throughout the country are phasing in a "real-time" computerized documentation system that improves the accuracy of records and will automatically record the time of entry. To provide for confidential records, safeguards to unauthorized access to student information, lock out systems, firewalls and "anti-hacking" programs should be considered.

12.8 Staffing Issues
A. General Considerations

There is a difference between medical services and nursing services in a school setting. The school nurse plays a vital role in expanding health services; however, he may not function as a replacement for a medical provider. Although school nurses care for sick and injured on a daily basis their care is governed by written orders of the school physician. Other tasks such as participating in screening tests, monitoring immunization, and maintaining state reports are governed by statutes. These statutes also require nurses to develop individual health plans for chronically ill children and for those with conditions that require emergency plans, provisions for multiple disabilities, and children needing epinephrine administration.[54] The delivery of these services becomes a formidable task when nurses are expected to service large patient populations. Some school nurses have patient populations in excess of 1,000 patients. Patient safety is a critical issue given that death from adverse events is now the sixth or eighth leading cause of death in America.[55]

Market forces have not resolved the issue of patient safety and quality of care related to nurse staffing. The

American Nurses Association has developed strategies to assure sufficient staffing. These strategies include: hospitals to be held accountable for nurse staffing plans and mandated nurse to patient ratios through legislation. Accountability and mandated ratios are strategies that have also been recommended by state and national nursing organizations; however these recommendations have not been enforced through legislation.[56]

B. Recommended Ratios

Determination of staffing for school nurses is generally a local function.[57] Thus caseload assignments vary greatly. Historically the federal government and National Association of School Nurses have recommended a nurse-to-student ratio of one nurse to 750 students.[58] In a special education population there is a recommended ratio of one nurse to 125 students, and the corollary of this is to staff one nurse to 500 students given a combined student population. According to Selekman and Guilday a task-oriented role definition no longer describes the impact nurses have on individuals as well as communities.[59]

In recent years there has been a trend to include more students with multiple learning and medical needs in a general school setting. With the inclusion of medically involved students, school nurses are faced with providing care on multiple levels. A ratio of one RN to hundreds of students in a given patient population presents a nursing challenge. Nurses in schools are expected to have input on mental and physical health issues as well as physical health challenges, for each student. School nurses are required by the scope of nursing practice to provide education and counseling to their clients. The nurse, along with psychologists, counselors, social workers, and other support staff, is part of the mental health treatment team.[60]

C. Safe Staffing

Staffing is left to the individual districts. Boards of education must provide adequate staffing within the confines of the budget. Due to budgetary constraints administrators often do not provide for adequate staffing. With overwhelming responsibilities, the school nurse often finds herself multitasking. Distractions while administerng medication pose a safety issue in a school setting. School nurses are often faced with simultaneous multiple medical situations where they must set priorities among equally pressing medical needs.

A recent news article reported on a school nurse who became distracted while administering Ritalin resulting in an overdose and subsequent death of a child. More students missed getting medication, got the wrong dose, or had some other medication-related error while in school in 2005-2006 than in recent years. Some researchers attribute the increased medication administration incidents to district cutbacks in nursing and health services.[61]

12.9 Codes of Ethics
A. School Nursing Code of Ethics
The School Nurse Code of Ethics as developed by the National Association of School Nurses contains information on school nursing code of ethics. The preamble acknowledges laws and conditions of ethical conduct.

1. Client Care
The school nurse is an advocate for students, families, and members of the school community.

2. Professional Competency
The school nurse maintains the highest level of competency by enhancing professional knowledge and skills, and by collaborating with peers, other health professionals and community agencies while adhering to the standards of school nursing practice.

3. Professional Responsibilities
The school nurse participates in the profession's efforts to advance the standards of practice, expand the body of knowledge through nursing research, and improve conditions of employment.[62]

TIP: For more information on the school nurses code of ethics and interpretative statements access www.nasn.org.

B. Nursing Code of Ethics
The nursing code of ethics sets standards for nurses in the United States. It serves as a framework for professional nursing practice and addresses many professional functions as well as ethical issues. The nursing code of ethics is promulgated by the American Nurses Association and has nine provisions.[63] The code can be viewed in its entirety at the American Nurses Association website: www.nursingworld.org.

12.10 Spiritual Health in School Health Services
A. Religious Rights in Public Schools
As patient advocates, nurses ensure all aspects of the human condition are preserved. One way a nurse may support the spiritual development of children is by including religious preferences in the overall nursing care plan. Nurses often educate children, parents, and school staff about religious rights in public school settings.

School staff members sometimes think schools must be "God-free zones." This is not true as "parents have a constitutional right to direct and control the upbringing of their children, and laws or governmental actions that unreasonably infringe upon the rights of parents to raise and educate their children according to their own values are constitutionally suspected." The Rutherford Institute responds to over one thousand requests for assistance annually from parents whose rights were placed in jeopardy.[64]

The Department of Education's guidance states:

> The Supreme Court has repeatedly held that the First Amendment requires public school officials to be neutral in their treatment of religion, showing neither favoritism toward nor hostility against religious expression such as prayer. Accordingly, the First Amendment forbids religious activity that is sponsored by the government but protects religious activity that is initiated by private individuals, and the line between government-sponsored and privately initiated religious expression is vital to a proper understanding of the First Amendment's scope.[65]

Rather than requiring school officials to censor students' religious speech, under most circumstances, the First Amendment forbids such censorship. The Supreme Court has consistently held that school officials may not impose restrictions to freedoms.[66]

B. Legal Implications of Refusing Rights
The easiest way to avoid legal issues when a student wishes to engage in religious expression is to issue a simple disclaimer, putting the community on notice that the student's expression is just that—the expression of a student. It must be clear that the information is not an announcement of the official view of the school or its administration. This will achieve several goals of protection of free speech rights of religious students and avoid misunderstandings that might lead to lawsuits based on the Establishment Clause.[67]

Some legal points that educators must keep in mind:

- A neutral stand towards religion in accordance with the first amendment's Establishment Clause must be observed. It has government neutrality toward religion as its central demand. When student expression is at issue, it is important to simply refrain from imposing restrictions on religious expression that are not imposed on secular expression.

- Knowledge of the Department of Education's Guidance on Constitutionally Protected Prayer in Public Schools is necessary: despite the limited scope of its title, this document contains a wealth of information for educators including their legal duties toward religious expressions of students.
- One must determine if the school falls under the Equal Access Act: If the school is a public, federally funded secondary school, it is covered by the Equal Access Act if school officials maintain a "limited open forum."[68]

12.11 Summary

The school nurse carries a heavy responsibility for the health of students, staff, educators, and even visitors to the school. He must be current in the theory and practice of nursing, vigilant for emergencies and the unexpected event, and ever ready to teach or advocate for his clients. Practice, education, and administration are all contained within the scope of school nursing.

Endnotes

1. Nowak, M. (2009) E-board Web, Hammonton Public School District cited from Urbanti, D., Steel, P., Harteer, B.J., Harrell, D. (1996). The Evolution of the School Nurse Practitioner. *Journal of School Nursing.* (2) 6-9. http://ncbi8.nlm.gov/pubmed/8704386, accessed 6/20/10.

2. National Association of School Nurses. *Definition of School Nursing.* Silver Spring, MD: National Association of School Nurses Position Paper (April 16, 2007). www.nasn.org, accessed 4/30/10.

3. *Id.*

4. Nies, A. and McEwen, M. *Community and Public Health Nursing.* (4th ed.) St. Louis, Missouri: Elsevier-Saunders, 2007. (p.606-618).

5. See note 2.

6. Selekman, J. and Wolfe, L. *School Nursing Certification Review. Membership Statement.* NASA 8484 Georgia Ave Suite 420 Silver Spring, MD.

7. Arnold, M. and Silkworth, C. *The School Nurse's Source Book of Individualized Healthcare Plans*, Vol. 2. North Branch, MN: Sunrise River Press, 2006.

8. See note 2.

9. Schwab, N. and Gelfman, M. *Legal Issues for School Health Services.* North Branch, MN: Sunrise River Press, 2001.

10. Medequist, D. J., "Surgical treatment of congenital scoliosis." *Orthop Clin North Am.* 2007; 38(4):497-509. http://nlm.nih.gov/medlineplus/Scoliosis, accessed 6/20/10.

11. Lonner, B. S., "Emerging minimally invasive technologies for the management of scoliosis." Orthop Clin North Am. 2007; 38(3): 431-440. http://nih.gov/medlineplus/Scoliosis, accessed 6/20/10.

12. Zieve, D. and Kaneshiro, N. *Scoliosis Surgery.* (2009). http://nlm.nih.gov/medlineplus/ency/article/007383. htm, accessed 6/20/10.

13. Medline Plus. Scoliosis Information Sheet (2009). http://www.nlm.nih.gov/medlineplus/scoliosis.html, accessed 6/20/10.

14. *Id.*

15. *Id.*

16. Selekman, J. *School Nursing: A Comprehensive Text.* Philadelphia: F. A. Davis Co. 2006.

17. ASHA. Guidelines for Audiometric Services in and for Schools. ASHA information sheet, 2006. www.asha. org/docs/html/GL2002-00005.html, accessed 6/20/10.

18. American Speech, Language, and Hearing Association. 2006. http://www.asha.org/docs/html/GL2002-00005. html#sec1, accessed 6/20/10.

19. *Id.*

20. See note 16.

21. National Association of School Nurses. (2006). Position Statement: School Vision Screening. http://www. nasn.org, accessed 6/20/10.

22. Common Vision Defects Factsheet (2009). http://firstoptic.co.uk/common%20vision%20defects.htm, accessed 6/20/10.

23. See note 21.

24. American Academy of Pediatrics. (2008) *School Health Policy and Practice Manual.* Vol. 121, (5) 1053.

25. National Association of School Nurses. (2006). Position Statement: Immunizations. http://www.nasn.org, accessed 6/20/10.

26. See note 9.

27. *Id.*

28. National Institutes of Drug Abuse (2009). NIDA Info Facts: High School and Youth Trends. http://www.drugabuse.gov/infofacts/HSYouthtrends.html, accessed 6/20/10.

29. Yamaguchi, R., McPherson, S. and Twemlow, S., "Relationship between student illicit drug use and school drug testing policies." *Journal of School Health* 73, no. 4 (2003): 159-164.

30. See note 9.

31. *Id.*

32. See note 16.

33. See note 9.

34. *Id.*

35. Grant, T. W., "Bring your first aid kit: An unannounced mock drill. "*Journal of School Nursing* 18, no.3 (2002):174–178.

36. Mortin, A., (2006). In Case of Emergency: School Crisis Plans. Homepage article. http://www.education.com/magazine/article/School_Crisis_Plans, accessed 6/20/10.

37. National Association of School Nurses. (2005). Position Statement: NASA School Health Nursing Services Role in Health Care Section 504 of the Rehabilitation Act of 1973. http://www.nasn.org/Default.aspx?tabid=280, accessed 6/20/10.

38. U.S. Department of Education. *Americans with Disabilities Act of 1990*, Subpart A—General § 35.104 Definitions. http://www2.ed.gov/policy/rights/reg/ocr/edlite-28cfr35.html, accessed 6/20/10.

39. *Id.*

40. Center for HIV Law and Policy. (2009) http://www.hivlawandpolicy.org/resource_categories/index/?ResourceCategory.=3, accessed 6/20/10.

41. See note 9.

42. *Id.*

43. Stokowski, L. (2004). "Trends in Nursing: 2004 and Beyond." *Topics in Advanced Practice Nursing e Journal.* http://www.medscape.com/viewarticle/46671, accessed 6/20/10.

44. See note 9.

45. Department of Education Medication Administration in Schools (2008). http://www.education.tas.gov.au/school/health/students_health_care_requirements/medication, accessed 6/20/10.

46. *Id.*

47. *Id.*

48. *Id.*

49. *Id.*

50. *Id.*

51. *Id.*

52. *Id.*

53. Brandeberg, M. Office of General Council, Citadel Military College of North Carolina. FERPA Fact Sheet. (2010). http://www.citadel.edu/publicsafety/studentrecords.html, accessed 6/20/10.

54. See note 9.

55. *Id.*

56. National Association of School Nurses. (2006). Position Statement: Medical Services vs. Health Services in the School Setting. http://www.nasn.org/Default.aspx?tabid=229, accessed 6/20/10.

57. See note 43.

58. Taliaferno, V., (2005) Where are the school nurses? Report for NASN, http://www.nassnc.org/files/pdf/NASN_Newsletter_031.pdf, accessed 6/20/10.

59. Selekman, J. and Guilday, J. Identification of Desired Outcomes for School Nursing Practice. *Journal of School Nursing* 19 (2003): 344-350.

60. N.J. Department of Education School Health Services Programs. NJ Department of Education 2004.Workshop Document.

61. Hetzer, A. (Aug. 3, 2006). Medication Errors at Schools on the Rise. Milwaukee Journal Sentinel http://www.accessmylibrary.com/coms2/summary.accessed 6/20/10.

62. National Association of School Nurses. (2002). *Code of Ethics: With interpretive statements for the school nurse* Brochure.

63. *Nursing Code of Ethics.* (2009). ANA http://www.nursingworld.org, accessed 6/20/10.

64. The Rutherford Institute Report. (2009). *Parent Rights.* http://www.rutherford.org/Issues/ParentsRights.asp, accessed 6/20/10.

65. *Id.*

66. Whitehead, J. Inside the Schoolhouse Gates. (2005). www.rutherford.org/articles_db/legal_features.asp?article_id=120, accessed 6/20/10.

67. *Id.*

68. *Mergens, supra*; *Lamb's Chapel v. Center Moriches Union Free Sch. Dist.*, 508 U.S. 384 (1993); *Good News Club v. Milford Central Sch. Dist.*, 533 U.S. 98 (2001). As cited in Whitehead, J. (2005). Inside The Schoolhouse Gates. The Rutherford Institute Inside Guide. http://www.rutherford.org/pdf/publicschoolreport.pdf, accessed 6/20/10.

Chapter 13

Managed Care Liability

Peter A. Kolbert, Esq. and John C. Webber, Esq.

Synopsis
13.1 Introduction
13.2 Definitions
    A. MCO
    B. HMO
    C. PPO
13.3 Purpose of Laws/Policy Considerations
    A. HMO Act of 1973
    B. ERISA (Employment Retirement Income Security Act of 1974)
        1. Standing under ERISA
        2. Statute of limitations for ERISA claims
        3. Venue for ERISA claims
        4. ERISA decisions
        5. *Aetna v. Davila* and *Cigna v. Calad*
13.4 Litigation Permitted Under ERISA
13.5 Conclusion
Endnotes

13.1 Introduction

This chapter discusses the current statutory framework that governs the liability of managed care organizations (MCOs) for medical negligence and denial of treatment decisions. It is intended to provide the reader with insight into ERISA, the protections it affords HMOs, and the remedies that are available to an aggrieved party seeking compensation. The chapter also presents recent Supreme Court decisions as well as available statutory remedies.

The traditional model of a patient, doctor, and nurse working in concert to decide a patient's course of medical treatment is one that has been mostly relinquished to nostalgia in today's healthcare environment. With the rise of MCOs, health maintenance organizations (HMOs), and preferred provider organizations (PPOs), most Americans— more than 170 million patients by most estimates—find that their medical decisions are directed, at least in part, by what their managed care company will approve. Moreover, in this new healthcare environment, the role of the family nurse practitioner, registered nurse, and the certified nurse's assistant is becoming more essential and integral.

What happens when medical care turns sour? What if a MCO denies coverage of a proposed medical procedure or test that has been recommended by a physician, nurse practitioner, or nurse midwife? Can a patient add the HMO or PPO as a party to a malpractice claim? As a defendant in a malpractice claim, can a nurse practitioner or a nurse midwife commence a third-party action against the patient's health insurance provider if the provider limited the amount of time that the patient could be in the hospital, or advised that they would only pay for certain prescriptions or permit certain tests? As discussed below, the answer—with very few exceptions—is generally no!

Patients and medical professionals rationally believe that a health insurance provider is an integral part of the process of delivering health care. Given its central role in so many decisions, a patient's HMO certainly would appear to be a proper party to any potential malpractice litigation. However, the federal law that governs managed care organizations, and the Supreme Court's interpretation of that law, has greatly insulated managed care companies from exposure to, or liability arising from, medical malpractice claims.

State law generally governs liability arising out of the delivery of health care. Thus, the potential liability of a medical provider, such as a doctor or nurse, generally is founded upon state common law, or state statutory schemes.[1] However, this is not the case when the potential defendant is a managed care organization, health maintenance organization, or preferred provider organization. When defending or seeking to prosecute these entities for the denial of medical benefits, or for the resultant injuries, one must be prepared to navigate a federal statutory scheme and, most importantly, the United States Supreme Court decisions interpreting that scheme. This chapter outlines the major issues and several recent Supreme Court decisions governing this area.

13.2 Definitions

Within the area of managed health care there are several acronyms and terms commonly used, and a general knowledge of them is central to understanding the issues involved in any discussion of managed care liability.

A. MCO

> **TIP:** MCO is a broad term and encompasses many different types of organizations, payment mechanisms, review mechanisms, and collaborations, which includes HMOs and PPOs.

The most important feature of a managed care organization is that it puts in place systems and procedures to control the cost of health care. These systems and procedures usually include reviewing the medical necessity of care, incentives to use certain designated medical providers, and case management. Managed care is sometimes used as a general term for the activity of organizing doctors, hospitals, and other providers into groups in order to enhance the quality and cost-effectiveness of health care. Typical of a managed care organization is that one organization manages the risk, contracts with providers, handles the processing of claims and is paid for by employers. A managed care organization acts as a "go-between" for payers and providers and patients.

B. HMO

> **TIP:** HMOs offer prepaid, comprehensive health coverage for both hospital and physician services.

The HMO is paid monthly premiums by employers, insurance companies, government agencies, and other groups representing covered lives. The HMO must meet the specifications of the 1973 HMO Act as well as many rules and regulations required at the state level. There are four traditional models: group model, individual practice association, network model, and staff model. A HMO contracts with healthcare providers (e.g., physicians, hospitals, and other health professionals). The members of a HMO are required to use participating or approved providers for all health services, and generally all services must meet further approval by the HMO through its utilization program. Members are enrolled for a defined period of time. HMOs are the most restrictive form of managed care benefit plans because they restrict the procedures, providers, and benefits.

C. PPO

> **TIP:** A PPO is a combination of hospitals, physicians, and even nurse practitioners and midwives who agree to render particular services to a group of people, perhaps under contract with a private insurer.

A PPO is a healthcare delivery system where the providers of medical care contract to provide services to members at discounted fees. Members may seek care from non-participating providers but generally are financially penalized for doing so by the loss of the discount and subjection to co-payments and deductibles. The services may be furnished at discounted rates, and the insured population may incur out-of-pocket expenses for covered services received outside the PPO, if the outside charge exceeds the PPO payment rate. PPOs are a common method of managing care while still paying for services through an indemnity plan. Most PPO plans are point-of-service plans, in that they will pay a higher percentage for care provided by providers in the network. Many insurers will offer PPOs as well as HMOs. Generally, PPOs offer more choices for the patient and provide higher reimbursement to the providers.

13.3 Purpose of Laws/Policy Considerations
A. HMO Act of 1973

The HMO Act of 1973[2] provided grants and loans to provide, start, or expand a health maintenance organization (HMO); removed certain state restrictions for federally qualified HMOs; and required employers with 25 or more employees to offer federally certified HMO options alongside traditional indemnity insurance upon request (the dual choice provision). This gave HMOs a competitive advantage over traditional insurance programs. The Act solidified the term HMO and gave HMOs greater access to employer-based markets, providing for their rapid expansion.

B. ERISA (Employment Retirement Income Security Act of 1974)

ERISA is an acronym for the Employment Retirement Income Security Act of 1974.[3] This statute was put into place by Congress with the "primary focus of guaranteeing uniform regulation of pension benefits to preserve the economic advantages of large multi-state corporations."[4] According to Justice Clarence Thomas of the United States Supreme Court, "Congress enacted ERISA to protect…the interests of participants in employee benefit plans and their beneficiaries by setting out substantive regulatory requirements for employee benefit plans and to provide for appropriate remedies, sanctions, and ready access to the Federal Court. The purpose of ERISA includes expansive preemption provisions…which are intended to insure that employee benefit plan regulation would be 'exclusively a federal concern.'"[5]

In order to accomplish this goal, section 514(A) of ERISA provides that it "shall supersede any and all State laws insofar they 'relate to' an employee benefit plan.…In turn all state laws that 'relate to' an employee welfare benefit plan, including common law or state statutory rights of employees seeking to recover plan benefits, are preempted by ERISA."[6] Importantly, ERISA provides that if treatment is wrongfully denied, the MCO can be liable for the cost of the treatment it failed to provide. Neither ERISA nor the case law interpreting it provides for, with few exceptions, any measure of damages beyond this.

TIP: ERISA applies to self-funded private employment plans, not those insured by an outside insurance company.

Section 510 of ERISA provides that it is unlawful to discharge, discipline, or discriminate against a participant or beneficiary for exercising any right to which that person is entitled under the provisions of an employee benefit plan, or interfering with the benefits to which such participant may become entitled under the plan. Despite its broad language, Section 510 does not prohibit an employer from modifying the terms of an employee benefit plan where the effect of such modification is to discriminate against participants with specific illnesses. Accordingly, while employers are prohibited from discharging employees to avoid paying benefits, they are permitted to reduce or terminate non-vested benefits simply by modifying the terms of the plan. An appropriate vehicle to address an employee's claim that an employer improperly reduced benefits for a specific illness, such as AIDS, may be found under the Americans with Disabilities Act.[7] The Act also prohibits the "threat of the use of force…to…attempt to restrain, coerce, or intimidate any participant or beneficiary for the purpose of interfering with or preventing the exercise of any right to which he is or may become entitled under the plan."

1. Standing under ERISA

Section 502(a) of ERISA sets out who has standing to bring an action under the Act. It states that a "civil action may be brought…by a participant or beneficiary to recover benefits due to him under the terms of his plan, to enforce his rights under the terms of the plan, or to clarify his rights to future benefits under the terms of the plan."

2. Statute of limitations for ERISA claims

There is no federally mandated statute of limitations for ERISA claims, since ERISA's civil enforcement provisions do not contain a statute of limitations. Therefore, courts look to the most analogous state limitations period in determining the appropriate statute of limitations to apply.[8] The one exception is for breach of fiduciary duty claims, in which the statute of limitations is six years from the date of the last action that constituted a breach, or six years from the latest date the fiduciary could have cured a breach of omission. If the claimant had actual knowledge of the breach, the statute of limitations runs three years from the date the claimant had actual knowledge.

In at least two cases, *Santino v. Provident Life and Accident Ins. Co.*,[9] and *Alcorn v. Raytheon Co.*,[10] courts have held that an ERISA plan's internal deadline for filing suit for denied benefits supersedes the state statute of limitations, since contract law allows parties to shorten statutes of limitation. As such, practitioners considering an action must first look to the terms of the plan, and then to the applicable statute of limitations in the local jurisdiction.

3. Venue for ERISA claims

Claims brought under ERISA have federal court jurisdiction. As such any party considering an action against a HMO must be prepared to prosecute its claim in federal court. Claims brought in state court may be removed by the managed care organization to federal court.

4. ERISA decisions

The focus of this chapter concerns the current state of the law regarding managed care organizations' liability for the delivery of health care. The Supreme Court's recent decision in *Aetna Health, Inc. v. Davila* and *CIGNA Healthcare of Texas v. Calad*[11] (discussed below) is the road map that all practitioners must follow. However, a brief discussion of some earlier Supreme Court decisions surrounding ERISA will give the reader some helpful insight.

Early Supreme Court decisions on the liability of MCOs focused on the preemption provision of ERISA, and overwhelmingly found that federal law (ERISA) preempted most state statutes that "related to" any employee benefit plan.[12] However, as managed care became an increasingly significant factor in American life, the Supreme Court issued several decisions that identified certain state laws that were not preempted by ERISA.

In *New York State Conference of Blue Cross & Blue Shield Plans v. Travelers*,[13] the Court upheld a New York State law that imposed surcharges on patients covered by HMOs. The HMOs had argued that any law affecting them was preempted. However, the Supreme Court did not agree. The court reasoned that the surcharges, and the statutory scheme on which they were based, were distinguishable from other laws it had found to be preempted by ERISA because the surcharges did not restrict the decision making and management of the plan administrators. The charges only affected the plan's cost and not the benefits it would provide. The decision hinged upon the interpretation of the "relate to" phrase found in ERISA.

Five years later, the Supreme Court, in *Pegram v. Herdrich*[14] ("*Pegram*"), issued a decision that many felt was a chink in the armor of ERISA preemption. In *Pegram* the high court confronted the issue of whether treatment decisions made by physician employees of an ERISA HMO were protected by ERISA preemption from negligence claims flowing from their treatment decisions. The plaintiff, Cynthia Herdrich, initially sued her health plan in state court, under Illinois law, for offering financial rewards to physicians to limit care. A HMO enrollee, Herdrich also sued her HMO and one of its doctors in state court for medical malpractice and fraud, alleging the doctor delayed confirmatory tests for eight days so as to have them done more cost-effectively within the network. Herdrich suffered a ruptured appendix during the waiting period. She alleged the delay was malpractice, which had exacerbated her condition and caused her pain and suffering. The Supreme Court found the medical malpractice claim was not preempted by ERISA, and the patient got a damage award of $35,000. But the fraud and fiduciary duty claim, based upon the doctor's and the HMO's failure to reveal the incentives for physicians to use in-network care, was dismissed. The Supreme Court held in this case, because the HMO was making mixed decisions regarding eligibility and treatment, that ERISA did not cover these "mixed" decisions. The Supreme Court decided that gate-keeping HMO physicians' cost-control efforts were "mixed" medical and administrative activity, and decided that these mixed determinations should never be subject to ERISA's fiduciary duty to act solely in the interest of plan participants and beneficiaries.

The Court found that mixed eligibility and treatment decisions that may be made by HMO doctors are not fiduciary acts under ERISA because Congress never intended for the common law trustee fiduciary standard to apply to such decisions. This could be read as a suggestion that both "mixed eligibility decisions" (which the Court says involve pure "eligibility decisions"; that is, whether the plan covers the requested benefit) and "treatment decisions" about "the appropriate medical response" are subject to state malpractice law.

The Court in *Pegram* said:

These decisions are often practically inextricable one from another....This is so not merely because; under a scheme like [the defendants'], treatment and eligibility decisions are made by the same person, the treating physician. It is so because a great many and possibly most coverage questions are not simple yes-or-no questions, like whether appendicitis is a covered condition (when there is no dispute that a patient has appendicitis), or whether acupuncture is a covered procedure for pain relief (when the claim of pain is unchallenged). The more common coverage question is a when-and-how question. Although coverage for many conditions will be clear and various treatment options will be indisputably compensable, physicians still must decide what to do in particular cases. The issue may be, say, whether one treatment option is so superior to another under the circumstances, and needed so promptly, that a decision to proceed with it would meet the medical necessity requirement that conditions the HMO's obligation to provide or pay for that particular procedure at that time in that case.[15]

However, the Court did state that exposing HMOs to financial liability for their physicians' mixed eligibility and treatment decisions, on a fiduciary theory, would have an adverse impact on those HMOs providing medical care for profit. Fiduciary duties under the common law and under ERISA "characteristically attach to decisions about managing assets and distributing property to beneficiaries." If HMO doctors, or nurse practitioners for that matter, were ERISA fiduciaries, they could never make a legal decision. "Since inducement to rationed care goes to the very point of any HMO scheme, and rationing necessarily raises some risks while reducing others," fiduciary principles are inapplicable. The Court decided that no fiduciary breach action could be brought under ERISA because, in part, such action would be a "mere replication of state malpractice actions with HMO defendants."

Subsequently, in *Rush Prudential v. Moran* ("*Rush*"),[16] the Court held that an Illinois law, which allowed a right to an independent medical review if a MCO denied a benefit, was not preempted by ERISA. Certainly attorneys viewed the *Pegram* and *Rush* decisions as possibly changing the ERISA preemption landscape and giving rise to the possibility that MCOs might be liable when their decisions contributed to an adverse result.

Demonstrating the friction that has always existed between states' rights and federal authority, several states passed laws that opened up MCOs to potential liability for coverage decisions. However, as is discussed below, the United States Supreme Court decision in *Aetna Health, Inc. v. Davila* and *CIGNA Healthcare of Texas v. Calad*—two companion cases decided together in 2004—put a halt to the gradual erosion of the ERISA preemption and changed the ERISA landscape dramatically.

5. *Aetna v. Davila* and *Cigna v. Calad*

In response to ERISA's prohibition against compensatory and punitive damages, several states enacted Healthcare Liability statutes that were intended to serve as a remedy to patients who were negligently denied care, and harmed as a result thereof. One such statute was the Texas Health Care Liability Act (THCLA) of 1997.[17] This Texas statute authorized an action in State court and permitted the recovery of compensatory damages. Thereafter, relying upon the act that had been put into law by the state legislature, two plaintiffs (Juan Davila and Ruby Calad) brought claims against their respective carriers under THCLA in Texas state court. A discussion of each case now follows.

Juan Davila sought damages from Aetna for its denial of his claim for a prescription for Vioxx, a prescription medication for arthritis pain. Aetna denied the claim and advised Davila that Naprosyn was the proper medication, and that Vioxx was not within his benefits. Davila took the Naprosyn but allegedly suffered complications from the Naprosyn, which required extensive treatment. He filed suit in Texas state court against Aetna pursuant to THCLA.

Ruby Calad was discharged from a hospital following surgery when CIGNA Healthcare, her managed care organization, advised that her condition did not meet her plan's criteria for prolonged hospitalizations. This discharge allegedly resulted in her suffering complications. Like Juan Davila, Ruby Calad brought suit against her managed care organization, CIGNA, in Texas state court pursuant to THCLA, seeking compensatory damages for her pain and suffering.

Both of these lawsuits were removed to federal court by the defendants under ERISA. The United States District Court in Texas then dismissed the cases when the plaintiffs refused to drop their claims under THCLA. However, on appeal the 5th Circuit reinstated the claims. An appeal—you might call it a "Texas standoff"—ensued, and the cases, now joined, went to the United States Supreme Court. The principal issue was whether ERISA preemption precluded Davila's and Calad's state law claims under THCLA, and limited recovery, if successful, to the cost of the denied treatment, or whether they were, if successful, entitled to compensatory damages under the Texas statutory scheme.

On June 21, 2004, the Supreme Court issued its decision in the companion cases of *Aetna Health, Inc. v. Davila* and *CIGNA Healthcare of Texas v. Calad.*[18] According to the New England Journal of Medicine, the 9-0 decision "effectively immunized managed-care organizations (MCOs) from liability for negligent decisions about the care of patients in private employer-sponsored health plans."[19]

The Supreme Court's interpretation of ERISA eliminated any potential liability for claims relating to pain and suf-

fering, lost wages, or medical specials. Following the *Calad* and *Davila* decision, the liability of a MCO for their decisions is, for the most part, limited to the cost of the treatment denied, rather than any compensation for any injuries flowing from such denial. The Supreme Court concluded that, absent Congressional intervention, MCOs are not liable to patients, or medical providers, for anything beyond contractual benefits. The Court in issuing its decision stated:

> It is clear…that [the plaintiffs] complain only of denials of coverage promised under the terms of ERISA-regulated employee benefit plans.…[A] managed care entity could not be subject to liability under the [state statute] if it denied coverage for any treatment not covered by the health care plan that it was administering. Thus, interpretation of the terms of [the plaintiffs'] benefit plan forms an essential part of their [state law] claim and…liability would exist here only because of [the HMO's] administration of ERISA-regulated benefit plans. [Their] potential liability under the [state statute] in these cases, then, derives entirely from the particular rights and obligations established by the benefit plan.[20]

The Supreme Court concluded that the plaintiffs in *Davila* and *Calad* were seeking redress "only about denials of coverage" and not about medical treatment decisions that were made by the MCOs. This was a critical distinction, as it separated the cases at issue from the court's earlier decision in *Pegram*, discussed below. In doing so, the Court treated the mixed decisions opinion in *Pegram* narrowly, applying it only when there is not an independent physician involved in the medical decision process. At length the court pointed out how *Pegram* involved a situation where the "plaintiff's treating physician was also the person charged with administering plaintiff's benefits; it was she who decided whether certain treatment decisions were covered."[21] The court then identified that in the case at bar petitioners are not respondents treating physicians, and the decisions at issue are pure eligibility decisions.

In her concurring opinion, Justice Ginsburg stated that the decision was the only one that could be reached due to the statute's plain language. She observed that a "regulatory vacuum" existed and that "virtually all state law remedies are preempted but very few federal substitutes are provided." At the same time she stated that she joined "the rising judicial chorus urging that Congress and [this] Court revisit what is an unjust and increasingly tangled ERISA regime."[22]

Following the *Calad* and *Davila* decisions, it is safe to say that the liability for a MCO's denial of coverage is limited to the cost of the treatment denied, rather than any compensation for any injuries flowing from such denial.

13.4 Litigation Permitted Under ERISA

TIP: The ERISA preemption issue is so critical because there is no alternative to entirely compensate a patient who may have been injured by a decision made by a MCO.

ERISA's intent was to provide participants and beneficiaries access to federal courts to protect their interests in employee benefit plans. Because of the pronouncement by the Supreme Court in *Davalia* and *Calad*, ERISA now offers only limited remedies to potential plaintiffs who are denied benefits and suffer an adverse result as a consequence.[23]

Following the Supreme Court's decision in *Calad* and *Davila*, state statutory schemes, designed to provide patients with a remedy for injuries flowing from a denial of benefits by a HMO, will fall to the wayside. In fact, in *Vytra Healthcare v. Cicio*[24] and *CIGNA HealthCare of Florida v. Land*,[25] the Court vacated decisions by the U.S. Courts of Appeals for the Second Circuit and Eleventh Circuit, in which those courts had found that state law medical malpractice claims were not preempted by ERISA, and remanded the decisions for further consideration in light of its ruling in *Calad* and *Davila*.

The lower courts have followed the Supreme Court's direction and have interpreted ERISA strictly. For example, the Fifth Circuit cited the *Calad* and *Davila* decisions, finding that claims under state law could not proceed and were "completely preempted by ERISA" in *Mayeaux v. Louisiana Health Service and Indemnity Co.*[26] Similarly, the Third Circuit, in *Barber v. UNUM Life Ins. Co. of Am.*,[27] found that Pennsylvania's bad faith claims were preempted.

TIP: Currently there are essentially only two areas of permissible litigation against HMOs by which a prospective litigant (plan member or beneficiary) can seek damages exceeding the limited defined scope of recovery permissible under ERISA. The first is for actions against those plans that are not covered by ERISA. The second involves the "mixed eligibility and treatment decisions" exception from the court's *Pegram* decision.

If ERISA were simply an alternate legal scheme to fully compensate injured patients, the preemption issue would not be so critical. As currently interpreted by the Court, however, ERISA offers only very limited remedies. Section 502(a) (3) authorizes a plan participant or beneficiary

to "obtain…appropriate equitable relief…to redress…violations [of ERISA] or…to enforce [ERISA] or the terms of the plan." The Court's remedy jurisprudence has turned on the interpretation of the words "appropriate equitable relief." The Court has read these words narrowly to mean that an injured patient is entitled to compensation solely for the erroneously denied benefit, not for other injuries resulting from the denied benefit. Of course, this severely limits the amount of recoverable damages.

There have been several other theories proposed, as ways around the ERISA preemption, to possibly target a MCO for its denial of coverage decisions. These alternative avenues include state law-based claims for breach of contract;[28] breach of good faith;[29] breach of fiduciary duty;[30] respondeat superior;[31] ostensible agency;[32] and even civil RICO claims.[33] However, to date none of these avenues have been used to successfully overcome the ERISA preemption nor have any resulted in monetary damage awards for the plaintiff.

Under Section 502(a) (3), a participant in a MCO can seek to recover the "appropriate equitable relief…to redress…violations [of ERISA] or…to enforce [ERISA] or the terms of the plan." However, the courts, following the instruction of the Supreme Court, have read these words narrowly and determined that an injured patient is entitled to compensation solely for the erroneously denied benefit, not for other injuries resulting from the denied benefit. So a patient could receive compensation for a MCO denying a MRI (the cost of the MRI), but not for the cancer that a MRI would have uncovered.

In addition to awarding benefits due, courts may also issue declaratory or injunctive orders requiring the payment of future benefits under either or both § 502(a)(1)(B) or the authorization for equitable relief in § 502(a)(3). However, monetary or damage remedies are not available on these claims.

13.5 Conclusion

As the landscape of ERISA litigation stands now, a plan member can recover the cost of the services, treatment, or medications denied, but will not be awarded any compensation for conditions or suffering that resulted from such denial. A plan member can also seek injunctive relief against a MCO to compel it to provide treatment after an initial denial. But the ability to receive compensatory damages for any injuries suffered will remain unattainable, until or unless Congress follows the suggestion of Justice Ginsburg, in her *Davila* concurring opinion, and modifies the ERISA legislation to address this issue. The exception to this rule is limited to the Supreme Court's "mixed eligibility and treatment decisions" exception from the *Pegram* case and to plans that do not fall under the ERISA scheme.

Endnotes

1. For example, in New York State, malpractice claims are a creature of common law. However, all wrongful death actions are prescribed by the Estates Powers and Trust Law ("EPTL").

2. 42 U.S.C, §6A (XI).

3. 29 USC§ 1132.

4. See, "Managed Care Liability, ERISA Preemption, and State 'Right to Sue' legislation in *Aetna Health, Inc. v. Davila.* James W. Kim, Loyola University," *Chicago Law School Journal* 36 (2004): 651–652.

5. *Aetna Health Inc. v. Davila*, 542 U.S. 200 at 208, 2004.

6. See Gossbart, D., S. Davis, S and W. Neggers, "Managed Care Liability," in *Nursing Malpractice*, Second edition, ed. P. Iyer. Tucson, Arizona: Lawyers and Judges Publishing Co., 2001.

7. 42 U.S.C. § 12101–12213.

8. *Johnson v. State Mut. Life Assurance Co. of America*, 942 F.2d 1260, 1261-1262 (8th Cir. 1991).

9. 2001 WL 1628316 (6th Cir., Dec. 21, 2001).

10. 2001 WL 1604084 (D. Mass., Nov. 21, 2001).

11. 42 U.S. 2000 (2004).

12. See, *Alessi v. Raybestos-Manhattan,* 451 U.S. 504 (1981); *Shaw v. Delta Airlines,* 463 U.S. 85 (1983); *FMC Corp. v. Holliday,* 498 U.S. 52 (1990). In each of these matters, ERISA preempted state laws that impacted on the administration of employee benefit plans.

13. 514 U.S. 645 (1995).

14. 530 U.S. 211 (2000).

15. 530 U.S. 211 at 228 (2000).

16. 536 U.S. 355 (2002).

17. Tex Civ. Prac. & Rem. Code Ann Sec. 88.002 (Vernon Supp. 2004). Similar statutes were passed in Arizona, California, Georgia, Louisiana, Maine, New Jersey, North Carolina, Oklahoma, Oregon, Washington, and West Virginia.

18. 542 U.S. 2000 (2004).

19. Mariner, W., "The Supreme Court's limitation of managed-care liability," The New England Journal of Medicine 351, no. 13 (September 23, 2004): 1347–1352.

20. *Aetna Health Inc. v. Davila,* 542 U.S. 200, 213 (2004).

21. *Id*. at 218.

22. *Id*. at 222.

23. *Davila* does not impact ERISA-exempt policies, such as private personal plans and those held by government employees. People insured under these plans can still obtain full compensation for the injuries caused by a HMO's wrongful denial of benefits.

24. 124 S. Ct. 2902 (2004).

25. 124 S. Ct. 2903 (2004).

26. 2004 U.S. App. Lexis 13685 (5th Cir. July 1, 2004).

27. 383 F.3d 134 (3d Cir. 2004).

28. *Barber v. UNUM Life Insur. Co. of America*, 383 F.3d 134 (3d Cir. 2004).

29. *Id.*

30. *Knieriem v. Group Health Plan, Inc.,* 434 F.3d 1058, 1059 (8th Cir. 2006).

31. *Woods v. Southern Co.,* 396 F. Supp. 2d 1351 (D. Ga. 2005).

32. *Krasny v. Waser,* 147 F. Supp. 2d 1300 (D. Fla. 2001).

33. *Caffey v. Mansur Group, Inc.,* 67 Fed. Appx. 370 (7th Cir. 2003).

Chapter 14

Dialysis Therapy Malpractice

Kelly L. Dyar, RN, CNN

Synopsis
14.1 Introduction
   A. History of Dialysis
   B. Chronic Kidney Disease
   C. End Stage Renal Disease
   D. Acute Renal Failure
14.2 Types of Dialysis Therapies
   A. Hemodialysis
   B. Peritoneal Dialysis
   C. Self-Care
14.3 Equipment for Hemodialysis
   A. Water Systems
      1. Reverse osmosis systems
      2. Deionization tanks
   B. Components
      1. Patients and their access
      2. Blood pump
      3. Dialyzers
      4. Anticoagulation
      5. Dialysate delivery system
      6. Dialysate
      7. Monitoring systems
         a. Arterial pressure monitor
         b. Venous pressure monitor
         c. Air detector
         d. Dialysate circuit monitors
14.4 Vascular Access
   A. Fistula
   B. Arteriovenous Graft
   C. Central Venous Catheters
      1. Perm-cath
      2. Vas-cath
14.5 Treatment Delivery
   A. Pre-Dialysis
      1. Pre-Dialysis assessment
   B. During Treatment
   C. Post Treatment
   D. Documentation
14.6 Legal Issues
   A. Scope of Practice
   B. Standards of Care
   C. Standards of Professional Performance
   D. Policies and Procedures
      1. Physician orders
   E. Informed Consent
   F. Guidelines for Care
      1. Universal guidelines
         a. Anemia
         b. Bone metabolism and disease
         c. Fluid balance and congestive heart failure
      2. Infection control
      3. Vascular access
      4. Treatment-related complications
         a. Dialysis disequilibrium
         b. Air embolism
         c. Exsanguination
      5. Equipment-related complications
         a. Hemolysis
         b. Pyrogenic reactions
         c. Dialyzer reactions
14.7 Summary
Endnotes

14.1 Introduction

Dialysis is a procedure provided to patients who no longer have adequate kidney function. Each person has two kidneys and can function with as little as ten percent still working without requiring dialysis therapy. Dialysis is a therapeutic procedure, not a curative process. While it does replace some functions of native kidneys, it does not replace all, nor does it restore kidney function.

A. History of Dialysis

Dialysis was first named in 1861 by Thomas Graham. Almost 80 years later Willem Kolff designed the first artificial kidney, using it for patients with acute kidney failure. In 1956 Dr. Kolff designed a disposable dialyzer that began to be mass-produced by Travenol. Up until this point dialysis was reserved for acutely ill patients, but in 1959 an external shunt was developed by Quinton-Scribner, and in the United States home dialysis began. The 1960s proved to be a decade of rapid advancement as the first hollow fiber artificial kidney, like those in use today, was developed and tested.[1]

With the passing by Congress of the Medicare ESRD Act in 1972 dialysis went from limited availability to a widely available therapy. With the passing of this act Congress granted Medicare coverage to any United States citizen who met the requirements to receive Medicare, regardless of their age. Dialysis went from being a very expensive procedure with little oversight to being regulated by the federal government through Medicare. Following this, even more rapid advancement occurred with dialyzers that processed patient blood more efficiently and decreased treatment length and frequency. In the 1980s peritoneal dialysis became more common, allowing even more flexibility for patients.

In the current era dialysis continues to move forward with improved vascular access and more efficient equipment. Home dialysis therapy is increasing. Nocturnal dialysis, or dialysis done at night, is also increasing, allowing patients to work before coming to their clinic in the late evening. Some patients now dialyze at home six days per week with a slower and longer treatment with decreased side-effects and comorbidities seen in standard hemodialysis treatments.

B. Chronic Kidney Disease

Chronic kidney disease (CKD) is best defined by the Kidney Disease Outcome Quality Initiative (KDOQI) guidelines, which are published by the National Kidney Foundation. The timeline stated in the definition is that the damage or abnormality must have been present for three months or more with structural or functional abnormality present, with or without a decrease in the glomerular filtration rate. Glomerular filtration rate is the rate at which the kidney removes waste products, specifically creatinine. This abnormality is seen either by a pathologic abnormality, or by markers of kidney damage such as abnormal blood, urine, or imaging tests. It also can be defined as a glomerular filtration rate (GFR) of less than 60 for at least three months.[2] Typical blood tests for measuring kidney function are blood urea nitrogen (BUN), creatinine, urine collection for 24 hours, as well as other lab tests. BUN is a waste product that is produced when protein is digested and broken down for the body to use. Creatinine is a waste product of a person's own body protein, specifically muscle, and it is produced as the body breaks down and rebuilds muscle tissue. Both are removed from the body only by the kidneys, so they are the most reliable markers of kidney function. Because BUN is a byproduct of protein that is ingested, it can vary from day to day depending upon foods consumed. Creatinine is considered to be the more reliable and stable indicator as it is not affected as much by protein that is ingested.

Chronic kidney disease is now stratified into five different stages, with the lower numbers signifying a lesser degree of damage to the kidney. Any person who has a GFR of 60 or less is diagnosed with chronic kidney disease, even if no kidney damage is present. Upon diagnosis of CKD, KDOQI recommends that patients be staged, and then referrals to a nephrologist and/or vascular surgeon be made as appropriate based upon the current guidelines.[3] Research has shown that early referral can have a positive impact upon patient outcomes. Patients typically do not need chronic, maintenance dialysis therapy until their GFR drops to 15 or less. Diabetic patients are typically started on dialysis with a GFR of 15, while non-diabetics are started at a GFR of around 10. Patients who require dialysis therapy are diagnosed as CKD stage 5, also known as end stage renal disease (ESRD). Occasionally someone who is lower than stage 5 may require dialysis therapy, especially during acute illnesses. When this occurs it may be diagnosed as acute on chronic kidney failure. Many times dialysis will only be temporary, but further kidney damage typically occurs, hastening progression through the states. Sometimes the damage done may be too significant, and the patient may rapidly progress to the final stage as a result of a significant acute illness, or exposure to some toxic substance.

C. End Stage Renal Disease

As noted above, this is the fifth and final stage of CKD. It is at this point that a patient can no longer survive without maintenance dialysis. Dialysis therapy is not intended to repair or correct damage to a patient's kidneys. Once ESRD is diagnosed the patient's kidney damage is too severe, and chronic dialysis therapy must be started. Beyond being the main organ that excretes wastes and excess fluid, the kidneys also have some endocrine, or hormone, activity as well. Healthy kidneys secrete erythropoietin, which is a hormone that tells the bone marrow to produce red blood cells; therefore damaged kidneys do not secrete this hormone, leading to anemia. Vitamin D is also affected by kidney damage, leading to bone disease in dialysis patients if left untreated. Another function of healthy kidneys is regulation of blood pressure, through fluid removal, salt balance in the body, and production of renin. When kidneys fail many side effects can occur, from waste product build-up, excess fluid leading to swelling and increased blood pressure, anemia, brittle bones, and finally, severely elevated blood pressure. While some of these can be addressed through dialysis therapy, the remainder cannot.

In healthy kidneys the microscopic glomerulus and nephron selectively remove waste products, electrolytes (such as sodium, potassium, calcium, magnesium, and phosphorus), fluid, and other substances. They have an amazing ability to know what to excrete, and what to hold on to. When kidneys fail they lose the ability to remove waste products, extra fluid, and in some cases electrolytes as well. When excess fluid builds up in someone, rather than being removed through urine, swelling, elevated blood pressure, fluid in the lungs, and congestive heart failure can occur. When BUN and creatinine build up it can lead to confusion, nausea, vomiting, anorexia, and even mental fatigue or encephalopathy. As electrolytes build up, muscle twitches, weakness, irritability, and even irregular heart rhythms can also occur. In order to prevent these dangerous events, dialysis must be initiated and continued. Because this is a chronic condition that will not improve or be repaired, dialysis therapy must be ongoing, and patients must adhere to a special diet designed to slow or prevent the buildup of fluid, waste products, and electrolytes.

D. Acute Renal Failure

Acute renal failure can occur separate from, or in conjunction with, chronic kidney disease. Many times it occurs as a result of multisystem organ failure and will be seen in an acute care, or hospital setting. Sometimes it will be documented as "acute on chronic" kidney failure, which is when someone with decreased kidney function suffers some type of acute illness, such as an acute case of the flu, and becomes even more ill. Depending upon the degree of kidney function prior to the acute illness or injury, this may be reversed with careful monitoring and treatment. Other times the insult to the already weak kidneys is too great and kidney function is diminished to the point that chronic dialysis is required.

In other situations acute renal failure may be the result of an acute illness or injury. Some causes can be drug overdose or suicide attempts, severe injuries from accidents and/or crush injuries, or following major infections or injuries. Acute dialysis is often provided following drug overdoses to help in removing harmful chemicals or drugs, or to balance electrolytes and acid balance in the patient's blood, and not necessarily because the kidneys have failed. Acute dialysis is completed the same as chronic dialysis; however the nurse and physician must consider incorporating interventions that will continue to preserve the patient's kidneys with the hopes that the kidney damage will not be permanent.

14.2 Types of Dialysis Therapies
A. Hemodialysis

Hemodialysis is the most prevalent type of dialysis therapy provided to patients with kidney failure. It is most often provided in an outpatient dialysis facility. In hemodialysis blood is removed from the patient and moved through an artificial kidney, known as a dialyzer, in order to cleanse the blood of waste products, excess minerals and electrolytes, and excess fluid. In order to perform a hemodialysis treatment the patient's blood must be removed from their body. The blood is obtained by use of a vascular access. For this process there must be two connections, one called arterial that pulls blood from the body, and the other called venous and is the route by which blood is returned to the body. This is happening concurrently, so the blood is not removed from the body, cleansed and then returned, but rather is a continual circuit with removal and return occurring simultaneously. In hemodialysis blood lines are connected to the dialyzer and are on the dialysis machine, and the flow of blood is controlled by a blood pump on the machine. The speed of the blood pump is ordered by the physician and programmed by the nurse or technician.

Most blood lines and dialyzers hold a combined volume of approximately 250 to 300 cc of blood, which would be approximate to one unit of blood. Most patients can tolerate this amount of blood outside their body as it is continuously being pulled out and returned. As the blood is being moved through the dialysis circuit, pressures within the circuit are continuously being monitored by the dialysis machine. The arterial pressure is important to monitor as it tells you the quality, or speed, of blood flow as it is being pulled from the patient. This is typically measured before the blood enters the blood pump, so since it is a "pulling" reading it is read in negative numbers. The closer the number is to zero the better the blood flow, and the more negative the number the poorer the flow is. The opposite is true of the venous pressure. This is a measure of the resistance that is met in returning the blood back to the patient. Several things work together to give this number. First is the rate of the blood pump speed which varies from 300 to 500, depending upon the patient. The higher the blood flow the higher the venous pressure will be. Another factor in venous pressure is the size of the fistula needle that is used for the treatment. Sizes range from a small 17 gauge up to a large 14 gauge needle. The smaller the needle size the higher the venous pressure reading will be as there is greater resistance to push the blood through a smaller needle into the patient. A third factor in venous pressure is the quality of needle placement. If the needle is inserted, or cannulated, well into the patient's access and floats in the middle of the diameter of the access then the pressure will be lower as it will have less resistance. If the needle placement is questionable and the needle tip is close to the side of the access the venous pressure can be higher. It is important to note that the actual pressure within the patient's access is often very low, so the venous pressure is not affected much by the actual pressure within the patient's dialysis access. The actual venous pressure reading is primarily due to the force required to push the blood through the blood lines and needle.

Hemodialysis treatments in a chronic outpatient facility are usually performed three times per week, and treatment length can vary from as little as two hours to as long as five hours. Treatment length is based upon several factors, including patient size, dialyzer size, and finally the quality of blood flow from the patient's vascular access.

- Larger patient size = more waste products = longer treatment length
- Larger dialyzer size = faster removal of waste products = shorter treatment length
- Higher blood flow = faster removal of waste products = shorter treatment length

In hemodialysis the patient's blood flows through the blood lines by being pumped by the blood pump, which forces it through the dialyzer. The dialyzer has thousands of small straw-like tubes, called fibers, which have a selectively permeable membrane. The portion of the circuit that holds the blood, including the dialyzer fibers, is called the blood compartment. The outside of the fibers are surrounded by a special fluid, and this part is known as the dialysate compartment.

TIP: Selectively permeable means that only certain molecules will be allowed to pass through the membrane.

What passes through is based upon molecular size. The dialyzer fibers have pores large enough to allow waste products and electrolytes to pass through, but too large to allow blood proteins to pass through.

Dialysis happens through osmosis, diffusion, and ultrafiltration. These are chemical terms that describe how solids and water move. Osmosis is the movement of water, and diffusion is the movement of solids. In diffusion solids move from a higher concentration level to a lower concentration level. This is accomplished by use of a fluid mixture called dialysate. There is no urea or creatinine in the dialysate fluid, and since these are elevated in a kidney failure patient's blood these solids will flow out of the patient's blood and into the dialysate, where it will be removed from the patient and washed away. The dialysate has varying levels of electrolytes such as: potassium (K), sodium (Na), calcium (Ca), magnesium (Mg), and also glucose. This is based upon the doctor's order, which is based upon the patient's usual blood work results for these levels. Because persons with kidney failure cannot efficiently remove potassium with their failed kidneys it tends to build up in their blood, so a lower potassium level is used in the dialysate to help remove excess potassium from their blood.

TIP: A normal blood potassium level is 3.5 meQ to 5.3 meQ. A typical dialysate level of potassium will be 2.0 meQ to 4.0 meQ, depending on the patient's blood level, medical history, and medications.

Fluid is removed through both osmosis and ultrafiltration. Osmosis is the movement of water across a membrane that is permeable to water. Water will move from an area of lower solid levels to an area of higher solid level. This is done in order to dilute the level of solids on the other side of the membrane. A very simple example of this in nature is what happens when sugar is placed on sliced strawberries. The sugar level outside the strawberries is higher than the sugar level in the strawberry cells, so water leaves the cells of the strawberry in an attempt to dilute the high sugar concentration outside of the strawberries. The result is the very sweet juice that is a combination of water from the strawberries and the sugar. This happens in dialysis, but not to a large degree in hemodialysis. Primarily in hemodialysis fluid is removed due to ultrafiltration. This is when a pressure gradient is present between the blood compartment and the dialysate compartment. It is controlled by the dialysis machine itself through hydraulic (water) pressure. There is a small amount of positive pressure in the blood compartment of the dialyzer that pushes water through the membranes of the dialyzer fibers, forcing extra water to leave the patient's blood stream to be discarded. Most of the pressure exerted to move water out of a patient's blood is a negative, or pulling, pressure that is applied by the machine to the blood compartment. This pressure "sucks" fluid out of the patient's blood so that it can be removed and discarded. Once the fluid and waste products are removed the dialysate is considered "spent" and is flushed by the machine through a drain hose and carried away to the sewer system.

In an outpatient dialysis facility patients will dialyze in a community setting, meaning they will be in a large treatment room with several other machines and patients. Staff to patient ratios can vary depending upon state regulations and company policies. In an outpatient facility there will be a mix of unlicensed patient care technicians (PCTs), LPN/LVNs, and RNs. Usual staff assignments will assign either a PCT or LPN direct care of the patient including accessing the vascular access, initiation and termination of treatment, and monitoring the patient while the treatment is delivered. LPNs might do a pre- or post-dialysis assessment on a patient as well, depending on state nursing board rules, but they may not perform an annual patient assessment. An RN may also provide direct care in a patient assignment, but most commonly they will be assigned as charge nurse and will perform patient assessments, administer medications, and supervise the overall care delivery. An RN is also required by federal regulations to complete initial and updated patient history and assessments as well as patient care plans.

Some benefits of hemodialysis therapy include constant staff monitoring, interaction with staff and other patients, and also not having to worry about self-care. Disadvantages of hemodialysis include the fact that it is a chronic ongoing treatment, dependence upon staff members for care, loss of control and independence, and also the restrictions that a three times per week therapy places upon a patient. There are also very strict dietary restrictions and fluid restrictions since the blood is only cleansed three times per week and buildup of wastes and fluid must be minimized between treatments. Travel and vacations are difficult to plan as treatment in the destination city must be made. Schedules in outpatient clinics also make it very difficult to work a typical schedule as the majority of clinics are only open during the day. Some clinics are now offering nocturnal, or nighttime, dialysis therapy. In this type facility patients will come to the clinic after their work day, around 7 or 8 P.M. They will dialyze at night, often while they sleep, and then will go home following their treatment.

B. Peritoneal Dialysis

In peritoneal dialysis (PD) a synthetic tube is surgically inserted into a patient's abdomen. Specifically it is placed into the peritoneal membrane, which is a thin membrane that surrounds and lines the abdominal cavity. It has many folds as it surrounds the abdominal organs such as the stomach, liver, spleen, and intestines. The kidneys lie outside and behind the peritoneal sac, so they are described as being retroperitoneal (behind the peritoneum). The membrane is so thin and large that the surface area of the membrane is roughly equal to each person's body size. It is very porous as it has millions of tiny pores or openings that selectively allow waste products and fluid to pass through the capillaries and into the peritoneal opening. This happens by osmosis and diffusion, just as in hemodialysis; but in peritoneal dialysis it is occurring with the body's own membrane, not an artificial one.

With peritoneal dialysis there must be fluid introduced into the peritoneal cavity in order for dialysis to occur. The patient makes a clean connection to a bag filled with sterile fluid and allows the fluid to flow into their peritoneal cavity through the tube that was surgically placed. The fluid is known as dialysate and is much like the dialysate used for hemodialysis. It does not have any urea or creatinine in it, and levels of other electrolytes are very low to aid in diffusion. The fluid will stay in their abdomen for the length of time prescribed by the physician. During this time, known as dwell time, waste products will diffuse out of their blood and into the sterile dialysate. Excess electrolytes and minerals will also move into the fluid. Osmosis will also occur

while the fluid dwells in the cavity, and this will be controlled by the amount of dextrose, or sugar, that is in the fluid. Peritoneal dialysate fluid will range from a very low dextrose concentration of 1.5%, a mid-range of 2.5%, and a high percentage of 4.25%. Again looking at the example of sugared strawberries, the higher the amount of dextrose in the fluid, the more water will be removed from the patient. After the amount of time prescribed by the physician, the patient will again connect to tubing and will drain out the dialysate fluid, which will carry with it the waste products, excess electrolytes and minerals, and the extra fluid removed from the patient during the procedure. This connecting, filling, and draining can take place manually every four to six hours with the patient connecting to a new bag and tubing set each time. This is known as CAPD, which stands for Continuous Ambulatory Peritoneal Dialysis. It also can happen with use of a machine, known as a cycler. This is typically known as CCPD, which means Continuous Cycling Peritoneal Dialysis, and is usually the more common type of PD that is done today. With this therapy a patient will place several bags of PD fluid on the machine, called a cycler, and connect the tubing set to the fluid bags and the machine. The patient will then connect to the tubing once, usually at bedtime. They will be connected to the machine for eight to ten hours and the machine will drain out the old fluid, fill with fresh fluid, allow the fluid to dwell, and then after the prescribed amount of time drain and fill again. This will happen with multiple cycles throughout the treatment, usually while the patient sleeps. The spent fluid either flows from the machine tubing to a drain such as their bathtub or sink drain, or it collects in a large bag. When the therapy is over the patient will disconnect and the tubing and fluid removed from the patient is discarded.

Unlike hemodialysis this type of dialysis is typically performed at home, and is a daily therapy, which is why it is referred to as continuous. Patients on PD will have fluid in the abdomen for the majority of the day. In some rare cases a patient may have a few "dry" hours each day, but for the most part they will always have dialysis fluid in the peritoneal cavity. Patients who perform this type of treatment will be trained in this procedure by a nurse when they start on dialysis. A family member or partner may also be trained to assist them, or in some cases if the patient is unable to perform the therapy themselves the family member will do all the steps. Once the patient has been fully trained she will have the necessary supplies delivered to her home and will do all the treatment at home. Once to twice each month she will return to the clinic for blood work and a clinic visit where her home records will be reviewed and she will be assessed for compliance and tolerance of PD. Usually they will see the nurse, doctor, social worker and dietician for review and follow up. Many patients prefer this type of therapy because their diet is not very restricted and they are much more independent.

Benefits of PD include more independence and control over their own care, more autonomy to make some treatment decisions at home, a liberalized diet and fluid limitation, and ability to travel easier. Patients generally report feeling better since the daily therapy is much more like what healthy kidneys provides. Disadvantages are the fact that it is a daily therapy that must be done on an ongoing basis with no break for the patient or caregiver. Supplies must be stored appropriately and can take up a large amount of space. Finally, while most patients enjoy the freedom and independence that comes with self-care, some do report that it is a burden to know they are fully responsible for their own care at all times.

C. Self-Care

Self-care in dialysis therapy is a growing trend. This can range from peritoneal dialysis, or it can be self-care in a chronic hemodialysis facility, and even self-care hemodialysis at home. Today's patients are demanding that they be more involved in their care, and as younger patients who are still working are being stricken with kidney failure they are seeking ways to receive dialysis care that will allow them to remain productive and continue full-time employment.

Peritoneal dialysis is the most common self-care modality and was discussed earlier. In this therapy patients are trained to perform their own PD at home and return to the clinic periodically for follow-up visits. Patients are trained to take care of the PD tube that is surgically implanted all the way through monitoring their fluid intake and daily weights to decide which type of PD fluid to use to remove the amount of fluid they have gained.

Staff-assisted hemodialysis is in-center hemodialysis in which the patient performs some of the care under the supervision of the staff members. This can be as simple as patients weighing themselves independently and reporting their weight to the staff, or it can be as complex as all the steps for the treatment under the supervision and with the assistance of staff members. Some patients only obtain their vital signs and report them to staff; others obtain them and make treatment decisions, such as how much fluid to remove during the treatment. Other patients cleanse their access site and place their fistula needles without assistance, and some remove their dialysis needles.

TIP: If a patient is performing any self-care they should be fully trained and the training should be documented in the medical record.

Documentation of patient training should be in the patient's medical record to show that the patient has been trained in recognized standards and facility policies. Any tasks the patient performs should be documented each treatment in the patient's medical record so that patient self-care can be separated from staff-delivered care. If a patient deviates from set facility policies and standards this should also be documented, including patient refusal to adhere to policies. If the patient is not following facility policies then re-education and training should be documented, including soliciting reasons why patients may feel they need to deviate from how they have been trained. After re-training, if a patient continues to refuse to follow policies or continues to perform the steps differently from how he was instructed then the physician should be notified and the refusal should be documented. The physician will need to be consulted as to whether or not it is an acceptable deviation from standards and procedures and whether or not the patient will be allowed to continue with self-care delivery.

Home hemodialysis is the final type of self-care. In this therapy the patient does her hemodialysis therapy at home. The patient and a care partner are trained in performing hemodialysis on the equipment they will use at home. New equipment is much smaller and is portable, allowing patients much more mobility. The patient or partner will perform all the steps in the dialysis treatment, from preparation of the dialysis machine to accessing the vascular access, to actual performance of the treatment itself. All of this is done in the patient's home. Much like PD, the patient will return to the dialysis clinic for periodic follow-up visits. In this type of self-care the patient may follow a conventional three times per week schedule much like in-center hemodialysis, but some patients are dialyzing four to six times per week. Treatments may be delivered just like in-center dialysis with high blood flows and shorter treatment lengths; however new research is showing that longer treatments with slower blood flows delivered several (four to six) days per week are much less taxing to patients and has fewer side effects for the patient. In this type of therapy, the patient sets her own dialysis schedule and chooses what days and times to perform the treatment. The patient is typically given parameters for how many days per week she can dialyze, and also how many days she can go without performing a treatment. Some flexibility in treatment length is also allowed, but in general patients are expected to follow their doctor's prescribed treatment parameters. For the most part patients are on their own while dialyzing at home; however a staff member in these programs must be on-call at all times in the event a patient experiences mechanical problems with her equipment, or has a treatment delivery problem that needs help from a staff member to troubleshoot. A few dialysis clinics that provide home hemodialysis have the ability to monitor the patient treatments electronically, and any machine readings and alarms are relayed electronically to the clinic. In the event of a life-threatening alarm or vital sign reading, protocols are in place for staff actions, including initiating EMS response if the patient does not respond to contact attempts. However, this is not the most typical setting, due to staff expense and the restrictions it places on patients who can only dialyze during hours that the monitoring staff is scheduled. Benefits of home hemodialysis are very similar to PD in that the diet is typically more liberal and travel and flexibility with scheduling exist. Disadvantages and restrictions on this type of therapy are also similar to PD, but an added component is the requirement of a partner to be present during dialysis. This restricts some patients from being able to perform it as some complications of hemodialysis can be life-threatening. For this reason a home hemodialysis patient is usually required to have a trained partner who can respond in the event of such a complication, and this partner must be present at all times when the patient is dialyzing.

14.3 Equipment for Hemodialysis
A. Water Systems

In hemodialysis, water is required to mix with the dialysate solution, which is highly concentrated. The water is mixed with the concentrated solution prior to flowing past the patient's blood in the dialyzer. Dialysate flows can range from a slow 500 cc per minute to a rapid 800 cc per minute.

TIP: In a three-hour dialysis treatment with a dialysate flow of 800 cc the patient will be exposed to 144,000 cc of water during the treatment. This translates to 144 liters, or 36 gallons of water in one treatment. In one week of three treatments the patient with the same treatment time would be exposed to 432 liters, or 108 gallons of water.

Due to the high exposure of hemodialysis patients to water it is understandable that the water must be purified to remove any dangerous or toxic contaminants. Water is purified through either a reverse osmosis machine, or a deionization tank. Some chemical components that could be present in water include calcium, fluoride, chlorine and chloramines, and aluminum. Pesticides and organics can be present as well. Organic matter would include bacteria or viruses. Because water sources vary from location to location, the contaminants can vary as well. For this reason water must be purified to remove the majority of potential contaminants and organic materials. In addition, water must

be tested periodically in order to ascertain if the water treatment is sufficiently removing anything that could possibly be dangerous to a patient.

TIP: The American Association for Medical Instrumentation (AAMI) sets the maximum allowable levels of chemical contaminants that can be found in water used for hemodialysis. Acceptable levels for microbial content are also set. AAMI also sets expected testing frequency for chemical components and bacterial components.

Pre-treatment systems are usually present before a water purification system. These are usually done to protect the water system itself, or to remove contaminants that cannot be removed by the water purification system. One pre-treatment step would be a sediment filter. This is a large tank that is used to remove large particulate matter from the incoming water. The next step may be a water softener. This step is used to prevent hard water from entering the water purification system as hard water can damage it and decrease the ability to purify water. Next in the pre-treatment is a carbon filter. This is a required step as it removes chlorine and chloramines from the pre-treated water. If chlorine remains in the water before it enters the water purifier it can damage reverse osmosis membranes, and it can be dangerous to patients. Chlorine is usually added to water as a microbial agent to kill potentially harmful bacteria in the water. If it comes into contact with patient blood it can cause severe damage to red blood cells causing a dangerous anemia. If a deionization system is used and chloramines are not removed it can combine with the resin in deionization tanks causing nitrosamines to be formed, and these are carcinogenic.

1. Reverse osmosis systems

Reverse osmosis (RO) systems are the primary water purification system used in dialysis facilities. Osmosis is the movement of water from an area of low solid concentration to an area of high solid concentration. Typically this happens to dilute a large amount of solids. In a reverse osmosis machine the opposite occurs. Inside the machine are very thin membranes that very easily allow water to pass through, but will reject over 90 percent of bacteria, particles, and other contaminants. The machine motor puts pressure on the water forcing it to move across the membranes while not allowing solids to pass through. The purified water then flows to the patient's dialysis machines through a series of pipes. A reverse osmosis machine should be monitored for water quality both through measuring the amount of solids dissolved in the product water as well as periodic sampling for solids and bacteria. This machine is also usually the last step in the process before the water flows to patients. Occasionally following the RO machine you will find an ultraviolet filter that also is used to destroy any bacteria or virus that makes it through the RO membranes. RO machines are disinfected on a periodic basis to prevent bacterial growth.

TIP: A storage tank may be found immediately following an RO machine or water system. This is used to store water, especially in larger clinics, as an RO machine cannot produce enough water at high flow times of the day. Any water storage tank is a potential site for bacteria to grow and must be disinfected periodically as well.

---

2. Deionization tanks

Deionization (DI) tanks have resins that can remove up to 99 percent of ions such as calcium, copper, fluoride, nitrates, sulfates, sodium, and zinc. These produce water that is relatively free of these chemical components, but cannot remove bacteria. These tanks work by the minerals being "stuck" to the resin in the tank; however the resin has limited capability for this. For this reason the resin can become "exhausted" quickly, which means that it has no more ability to remove these contaminants. Water quality from a deionization tank must be monitored constantly. If a tank becomes exhausted and it goes undetected then contaminants can flow to patients. In many facilities in which incoming water quality is very poor a series of DI tanks may be found before an RO machine. Occasionally DI tanks are used when an RO machine breaks down and water must still be produced for patient use. In an acute in-patient dialysis facility a DI tank may be the only water purification system in use.

TIP: Because a DI tank does not remove bacteria there is a big risk for bacterial contamination, both in the tank itself and in the plumbing that carries treated water to patients.

B. Components

Hemodialysis machines are manufactured by many different companies. The majority are produced for use in chronic outpatient dialysis facilities. While there may be additional options added by each manufacturer, the main components are discussed here. Each will be discussed in detail.

TIP: While dialysis machines are highly complicated machines with computer systems for monitoring patients, monitoring and continual assessment of patients by a person is the most critical part of dialysis treatment delivery.

---

1. Patients and their access

The first component of hemodialysis systems is patients and vascular access. This will be discussed in detail later.

2. Blood pump

This is a mechanical pump that turns continuously during the dialysis treatment. The purpose is to pull blood from the patient's dialysis access, push it through the dialyzer, and return the blood back to the patient. Blood pumps have rollers that rotate and compress the blood tubing against the wall of the blood pump compartment. The blood tubing has a blood pump segment that is slightly larger in diameter than the remainder of the dialysis tubing, and the blood pump is calibrated for the size of this tubing. Using this calibration the machine knows how many rotations per minute of the blood pump are required to deliver the programmed blood flow rate. If there is high pressure after the blood pump it can cause blood to flow backward into the blood pump segment, reducing the actual delivered blood flow rate. If blood flow before the blood pump is obstructed the blood compartment pressure will decrease. This pressure is read through a pre-pump arterial pressure monitor, and should be monitored throughout the treatment. Because it is before the blood pump you are getting a measure of the blood flow from the dialysis access, and it is a negative, or pulling, pressure.

TIP: Pre-blood pump arterial pressure should be less than or equal to -250 mmHg.

If the pressure becomes more negative it indicates poor blood flow coming from the patient's dialysis access. If it becomes more negative than -250, then red blood cell damage could occur. If red blood cells are damaged it can lead to a life-threatening anemia and risk of cardiac arrest from the release of potassium from the damaged red blood cells.

3. Dialyzers

Dialyzers are also manufactured by multiple different companies. The most typical dialyzer is made of multiple tiny fibers that blood will flow through. Dialyzers are selected based upon their size and ability to remove both waste products and excess fluid from the blood. Blood tubing is connected to both ends of a dialyzer, and blood flows from the top of the dialyzer and out the bottom of the dialyzer. Dialysate is delivered to the dialyzer by two hoses that are also connected to the dialyzer. Dialysate flows opposite to the blood flow, so it flows from the bottom of the dialyzer to the top. This helps the removal of waste products to occur faster.

4. Anticoagulation

When blood comes into contact with foreign surfaces or air it sets off a chain reaction that causes the blood to begin to clot. Blood lines and dialyzers would be foreign surfaces, so there is an increased risk of blood clotting during a dialysis treatment. If there is significant clotting during the dialysis treatment, the dialyzer or blood lines could become clotted. Blood that is clotted cannot be returned back to a patient, so clotting during the dialysis treatments can lead to the risk of anemia from having to discard clotted blood. Measures are taken to prevent this anticoagulation. The first measure is to maximize the blood flow to the highest rate safe for the patient. Typical blood flow rates will be 400 to 500. A faster blood flow rate helps decrease the blood from being sluggish as slow-flowing blood has a higher risk of clotting. The second measure is to administer an anticoagulant to help prevent clotting. The typical anticoagulant is heparin. This is injected into the patient prior to the dialysis treatment and helps the blood to not clot during the dialysis treatment. In some treatments heparin is also administered throughout the dialysis treatment. In some cases a patient cannot receive heparin, so a final measure to help prevent clotting is periodic administration of normal saline (0.9 percent) IV fluid, which helps flush the circuit to prevent clotting.

5. Dialysate delivery system

This is part of the internal workings of the machine and is not seen. There is a proportioning pump that mixes the dialysis solution with water to make the final dialysate that is delivered to the dialyzer. Typically this is inside the machine with a very small pump, but in some dialysis facilities it may be a large tank that mixes the dialysate and delivers it to each machine in the final concentration.

6. Dialysate

The dialysate is the solution that is delivered to the dialyzer in order to clean the blood. The major component is water which is mixed with the dialysis fluid. There are two different dialysis fluids that are used. The first is usually referred to as "acid" since it is an acidic, concentrated solution that is mixed with the purified water. The dialysis fluid comes in either large barrels stored in tanks in the dialysis facility, gallon jugs, or in powdered form that is mixed in the dialysis facility with water before being delivered to the machine. Dialysate contains sodium, potassium, magnesium, calcium, chloride, and glucose. There is also a buffer solution called bicarbonate. Bicarbonate is the second solution mixed with the water to make the final dialysate that is delivered to the patient. Bicarbonate comes either in a liquid form or powdered form. The powder is mixed with water for the correct dilution ratio. The machine pulls the acidified and bicarbonate solutions into the machine where the proportioning pump mixes it with the purified water before delivering it to the patient.

TIP: Any staff that is mixing acid or bicarbonate dialysate from dry powders must be trained and demonstrate competency to perform this task. Documentation of such training and competency should be in the employee's personnel record.

Most dialysis facilities set a standard dialysate formulation. The majority of the dialysate used will be this specific mix, and the most common dialysate will have a potassium level of 2.0. Lab values for individual patients may indicate that the patient needs a higher potassium level, or he may need a higher calcium level. This can be done by adding a packet of potassium chloride or calcium chloride to the patient's dialysate to increase the potassium or calcium level. This should be done only to individual jugs of acid concentrate.

TIP: Because potassium or calcium packets are considered to be a medication they should be added to the dialysate concentrate only by a licensed nurse.

---

7. Monitoring systems

The dialysis machine would be very dangerous if it did not have systems in place to monitor the function. For this reason there are several monitors in place that are programmed to alarm if there are deviations from the normal settings.

a. Arterial pressure monitor

This monitor is typically before the blood pump and is in place to monitor the pressure between the patient and blood pump. It can be used as an indicator of how good the flow from the dialysis access to the machine is. The pressure reading will be shown as a negative reading since it is a pulling pressure that pulls blood from the patient. The pressure is translated to a monitor and provides a reading that can be visualized. It is displayed on a gauge, which is either a video display or a LED readout. This reading is monitored by upper and lower limits that can be set either manually or automatically by the machine. The spread of the upper and lower limits is typically 30 to 50 points above and below the actual reading. The limits are set to help protect the patient, as both an audible and visible alarm will be triggered if the actual pressure reading goes above or below the set limits. When the alarm is triggered it will stop the blood pump as well to protect the patient. If an alarm is triggered it will require intervention by the caregiver, which will include manually resetting the machine to resume blood flow and continue the dialysis treatment.[4]

TIP: If an arterial pressure alarm is triggered a dialysis caregiver should assess the patient's access and blood lines to determine the cause for the alarm before resetting the machine.

Some reasons for the alarm to go low, or more negative, include the patient's blood pressure drops, the bloodline is occluded or kinked slowing the flow, or the dialysis access is not giving good blood flow either because of an insufficiency of flow through the dialysis access, or because the needle placement is providing insufficient blood flow. Some reasons for the alarm to go high, or become less negative, include: the arterial bloodline separates from the dialysis access or needle, saline IV fluid is infused, an air leak prior to the blood pump occurs, or the blood pump speed is decreased manually.

b. Venous pressure monitor

This pressure monitor measures the pressure between the dialyzer and the patient as the blood is returned to the patient. The monitor portion of the tubing is typically held in an air detector, which will be discussed later. The reading for this will be displayed in the same fashion as the arterial pressure in a display on the machine. Alarm limits are set above and below the actual reading. This monitor reading is usually a positive reading. The reading will sometimes increase throughout the treatment as the blood has fluid removed from it and becomes thicker, as the thickening blood resists flow more. In the event of a high or low venous pressure alarm several things occur simultaneously. First, an audible and visual alarm is given, usually a continuous beeping that must be manually addressed by pressing a button in order to silence the alarm. The second response by the machine is to stop the blood pump, which prevents injury to the patient by continuing to pump blood. Next the venous line clamp closes to prevent blood from being able to leak out of the blood lines via gravity in the event of needle dislodgement. The machine cannot and will not resume the treatment and restart the blood pump until a staff member takes action and presses a second button which resets the machine. When action is taken and corrections made the staff member can press a reset button that will open the venous line clamp and restart the blood pump, allowing the treatment to resume.

TIP: In the event of a venous pressure alarm it is imperative that the bloodlines and patient access be assessed before correcting and resetting the dialysis machine.[5] If a low venous pressure alarm was triggered due to a line disconnect or needle dislodgement patient blood loss can occur rapidly if the machine is reset and restarted without correcting the problem.

Some causes of a low venous pressure alarm can include separation of a blood line from the patient's dialysis access, a leak in the blood circuit, a decrease in the blood pump speed, the blood line between the dialyzer and monitor being occluded decreasing the amount of blood coming out of the dialyzer, or a clotted dialyzer that does not allow any blood through. Causes of high venous pressure can include the bloodline being occluded or kinked between the monitor and the patient, poor positioning or infiltration of the venous dialysis needle, or a clot in the venous pressure monitor itself.[6]

c. Air detector

The air detector picks up on air bubbles or foam in the venous blood line. It monitors for this through the use of light that is transmitted through the venous blood chamber. This is usually automatically set by the dialysis machine when blood is sensed in the bloodlines. However, it must be manually engaged by placing the venous chamber into the air detector monitor, and by placing the venous return line into the line clamp device. A key partner of the air detector is the venous line clamp. This is always located downstream of the venous chamber as it is in place to prevent any air from reaching the patient once it is detected. When the air detector is triggered it stops the blood pump, closes the venous line clamp, and triggers a visible and audible alarm. These alarms must be manually addressed and reset before the blood pump will resume and dialysis will restart. While the closing of the venous line clamp is automatic, the blood line must be manually inserted into the line clamp so that the line can be clamped in the event air is detected.

d. Dialysate circuit monitors

Dialysate circuit monitors are in place to monitor the quality and safety of the dialysate that is being delivered to the patient. The first monitor is for dialysate conductivity. This is basically the amount of electricity that the dialysate can conduct, which is a measure of whether or not the mineral composition is correct. The reading is usually displayed on the face of the machine, but in some cases it is only read manually. Even when the machine displays the conductivity it must be verified manually with a sample of dialysate and conductivity meter. The monitor sets upper and lower limits, and if the conductivity increases or decreases outside the set limits an audible and visual alarm will be triggered and the flow of dialysate will stop to protect the patient. This alarm can be triggered if the concentration of the dialysate and water is incorrect. A low alarm would be caused by too much water, too little dialysate solution, or having only one of the two required dialysis solutions present. A high alarm would be caused by too little water or too much dialysis solution.

Dialysate temperature is also monitored. There is a thermostat in the machine that controls the heating of the dialysate. The range is usually preset by the manufacturer, although some machines allow for very small manipulations of the delivered temperature. An alarm can be caused if the heater malfunctions or power supply is interrupted.

Blood leak monitors are also present to pick up on any red blood cells present in the dialysate. The dialyzer membranes do not allow blood to actually pass through them, so any red blood cells present on the dialysate side of the dialysis system indicates that a fiber in the dialyzer has ruptured. When a blood leak is detected the machine will give an audible and visible alarm, stop the blood pump, and also stop the flow of dialysate. Special strips can be used to test the dialysate leaving the machine to see if any blood cells are present indicating the blood fibers have ruptured. If they have and corrections are not made the patient can lose blood causing anemia, or the patient can become infected from the unsterile dialysate fluid flowing into the blood compartment. If a genuine blood leak is determined the treatment must be stopped and resumed with a new circuit and dialyzer, without returning the blood to the patient. Blood leaks are rare and can be caused by poor handling of the dialyzer, excessive fluid removal rates, or manufacturer defect. Manufacturer defect could be the cause if more than one patient using the same lot number of dialyzer had a blood leak.

14.4 Vascular Access

Access to the patient's blood is a definite requirement in order for a hemodialysis treatment to take place, so a vascular access must be placed. There are three main types that will be discussed.

A. Fistula

A fistula is considered to be the gold standard for hemodialysis vascular access. This is considered a native dialysis access as it is made from the patient's own blood vessels. It is simply the surgical connection between an artery and vein. When the surgical connection is made the arterial blood which is under very high pressure is diverted into the vein, which has very loose and elastic walls. This high pressure causes the vein to enlarge and the walls to thicken. This makes it large enough to tolerate placement of very large dialysis needles for the treatment. This is considered to be the gold standard because there is reduced risk of complications as it is created from the patient's own blood vessels, which decreases the body's reaction to it. Benefits of a fistula include reduced rate of clotting and infection, safer than an external access such as a catheter, less risk of reaction to synthetic materials, longer lasting than other dialysis access types, and better and quicker healing from needle placement. Disadvantages include the fact that it can take up to three months or longer before a fistula has matured enough to be used. It is more difficult surgically to create than other access types, and it is also more difficult to cannulate, or place needles, than a graft.

Complications seen with fistulas include poor blood flow causing the fistula to fail to develop, stenosis (or narrowing) of the fistula interrupting or blocking blood flow through the fistula, clotting or thrombosis of the fistula, infection, cardiac failure from the fistula drawing the blood away from the heart and through the fistula, or steal syndrome in which there is not enough blood flowing to the hand. Fistulas also can fail due to poor cannulation techniques.

B. Arteriovenous Graft

A graft is synthetic tubing that is surgically placed between an artery and a vein. It is surgically connected on one end to an artery, the blood flows through it, and the other end is connected surgically to a vein where the blood flows back into the vein and into circulation. Needles are placed into the synthetic portion of the graft to obtain blood for the dialysis treatment. A graft is usually indicated for a patient who has circulatory problems or has had repeated failures of a fistula. Advantages of a graft are that it can be used very soon after placement, with some new types being approved for needle placement and dialysis within 24 hours after surgery. It provides a larger area to place needles making cannulation much easier. The size of the graft as well as the flow of blood through a graft does not depend on a vein to mature. In some cases if the blood flow is very good through the graft it will actually cause the vein that it flows into to begin dilating, creating a fistula that can possibly be used later if needed. There is a higher incidence of complications with dialysis grafts compared to fistulas. Several of these are related to the fact that it is a synthetic object placed into the body, which reacts to its presence. Grafts clot more frequently, and often are more difficult to declot. There is a higher rate of infection, as well as possibility of allergic reactions to the graft material. Many grafts require some type of intervention or surgical revision within about a year to 18 months. Actual puncture sites into the graft never really heal, they just seal over. Repeatedly placing needles into the same place over and over can actually damage the graft.

Complications of grafts are similar to a fistula. The first complication that can be seen is clotting, or thrombosis, of the access. This can be because of stenosis, or narrowing, of either the inflow or outflow part of the graft. Thrombosis can also occur if the patient has a sudden and prolonged drop in her blood pressure, compression of the graft by holding pressure too long or sleeping on the graft arm, or even by the patient carrying heavy objects such as purses or backpacks. Pseudo-aneurysm, or false aneurysm, is another complication, which means the graft has unusually dilated in one portion due to repeated sticks in the same area. This causes a weakening of the graft and can become a surgical emergency. An accidental traumatic fistula can be caused by someone placing a needle through both walls of the graft material and puncturing another artery or vein that runs close to the graft. Infection is another complication, and this can be due to poor aseptic technique prior to needle placement, bacteria traveling from another infected site on the patient, or from poor personal hygiene and care of the access. Steal syndrome occurs more often in grafts than fistulas as they are generally larger in diameter. Blood is diverted upward through the graft and back towards the heart rather than flowing to the hand or foot on the affected limb. This causes pain and coldness of the affected extremity. Poor cannulation techniques also can have a negative impact on a patient's graft causing failure.

In a case published in *The Ohio Trial Reported* (#137269) a patient alleged that he suffered severe hand and arm injury due to placement of a dialysis needle. The plaintiff alleged that the technician punctured the left median nerve causing permanent loss of sensation and loss of function in several digits of his left hand. The plaintiff alleged the defendant was negligent in failing to meet the standard of care. The defendant claimed the event did not occur and that there was no record of the event. The defendant argued that the injury was due to hematoma formation following infiltration during dialysis on a separate occasion. The jury deliberated for approximately one-half day before deciding for the plaintiff.

Infiltration is the leakage of blood out of a dialysis access and into the surrounding tissues. A hematoma is a large collection of blood in an organ or tissues. A hematoma can cause pain during formation and until it is resolved by being absorbed back into the body. However, once resolved the pain usually resolves and most are not severe enough to cause permanent nerve damage.

C. Central Venous Catheters

This section includes two main groups of catheter types. One is indicated for temporary and very short term use, while the other has a longer application. Catheters are surgically placed either in the operating room, radiology suite, or at the patient's bedside, depending upon the type of catheter. Most are made of rigid material and are divided into two lumens surrounded by one synthetic tube. The majority of the catheter is implanted and cannot be seen; however two ports or tubes with clamps can be seen outside the patient's body. One of the ports is used to pull blood from the patient; the other is used to return blood. There are many different manufacturers, and this text does not attempt to discuss each one, but rather to generalize based upon the intent of use.

1. Perm-cath

This is a dual-lumen catheter that is indicated for use of three weeks or longer and is typically placed for usage in the outpatient setting for chronic hemodialysis. These catheters are usually lumped together and called Perm-cath as they are intended for longer usage. These are typically placed surgically as they have cuffs on them that are located below the level of the skin. The cuffs cause a local reaction and the skin attempts to grow into the cuff, helping create a barrier against infection, and also helping to make them more stable and secure. The catheter is placed into a large vein, usually the internal jugular vein. This is used when someone is new to dialysis and is waiting either to have his permanent access placed, or the patient has had one placed and is waiting for it to mature. In some cases it is the access of last resort when all fistula or graft sites have been exhausted. Occasionally it is placed at patient preference when the patient refuses a fistula or graft to avoid needle placement. The advantages of a perm-cath include that fact that it can be used immediately after placement once a chest x-ray has been obtained to confirm placement. The material used for a Perm-cath is softer than other central venous catheters, so it is more acceptable for long-term placement. It is anchored in place by the cuffs, and this helps decrease infection risk. Also it has an insertion site on the chest wall, but the longest part of the catheter is actually tunneled under the skin before the catheter actually is inserted into the vein. This tunneling also helps to minimize infection. It is not without disadvantages, however, because despite the protections in place catheters are highly susceptible to infection. This is partially due to the fact that it inserts into a large vessel, but also can be linked to poor hygiene, patients bathing against medical advice, and breaks in aseptic technique within the dialysis facility when providing dressing changes. Dressing changes can be uncomfortable for patients, especially if chest hairs are pulled, which can also increase infection risk. There is also a very high risk of narrowing of the vein that the catheter is inserted in, which can cause immediate and long-term problems.

Complications of a Perm-cath include hemothorax (blood in the chest cavity) or pneumothorax (air in the chest cavity). Both of these can be life-threatening and require immediate intervention. An artery or vein can be punctured during placement, causing blood loss. Internal tissues, such as lung tissue, trachea, or even the heart muscle, can suffer damage. The catheter can break off causing it to embolize, or travel through the blood stream. Irregular heart rhythms can occur as well. Other complications that can occur after placement include an air embolism, infection, septicemia, clotting, stenosis or narrowing of the blood vessel, or catheter malposition.

2. Vas-cath

This term is usually reserved for a temporary catheter that is placed for hemodialysis access. These are usually shorter in length than Perm-caths and can be placed at the bedside. The structure of them is the same, and they are typically used in emergent situations when dialysis needs to occur quickly. It is usually reserved for in-patient care. This catheter is usually recommended to be used for less than three weeks, and while it is most often seen in acute situations for new dialysis patients, a vas-cath may be placed when a chronic dialysis patient needs surgery on her fistula or graft due to clotting or infection but must be dialyzed immediately. Most advantages of this catheter are the same as for perm-caths, but have the added benefit of being able to be placed blindly at the bedside and used right away. A chest x-ray should always be performed following placement to verify that the tip is in the correct position. Disadvantages are similar as well. How long this type of catheter can be left in place varies depending upon the placement site. A vas-cath placed into the internal jugular vein (on the side of the neck) can be in place for up to three weeks. There is less risk of puncturing a lung with this placement, and the risk of causing stenosis is lower as well. If the site is the femoral vein (in the groin) then the infection rate increases, so it can only be in place for a few days, usually less than one week. This site is used often in extreme emergencies because placement is very easy and it does not require x-ray placement verification before use. This is very uncomfort-

able, however, for patients as they must lie still and blood flows are often dependent upon the patient's position. In some cases placement into the subclavian vein (exits on the chest wall under the clavicle) is required. This site can be left in place for several weeks, but is least preferred as there is a very high risk of complications. Complications for a vas-cath are similar to those of a Perm-cath.

In a case originally published in *The Georgia Trial Reports* (#131106), a medical malpractice wrongful death claim was filed by the estate of a dialysis patient. It was alleged that she died due to a delay in treatment of complications from the placement of a dialysis catheter. She had catheter placement and then returned to the dialysis center where dialysis treatment was stopped prematurely due to physical distress. She was transported to the hospital where she died with bleeding in the lung area. The surgeon, in addition to the dialysis clinic, was named as a defendant. The plaintiff alleged the decedent's death resulted from complications with placement of the catheter and the delayed treatment by both her physician and the dialysis center. The plaintiff alleged that the surgeon punctured the lung four times in placing the catheter which resulted in a hemopneumothorax. The plaintiff claimed the surgeon was aware when he released her to return to the dialysis clinic and that he failed to notify the clinic of the complication. Further they argued that the nurse at the clinic released the decedent to be taken to the hospital by her sons after she went into distress. The plaintiff's expert stated that the standard of care required the dialysis clinic to call for emergency transport and that the decedent's internal bleeding was aggravated by blood thinner administered for dialysis. There was an hour delay from the time she was taken off dialysis to the time her sons arrived to take her to the emergency room. Defendants contended proper monitoring and that prompt non-emergent transport was arranged and that patient symptoms did not warrant emergent transport. Verdict was for the defense.

One key responsibility of a nurse following placement of any type of dialysis catheter is to ask for a specific order to use the catheter prior to actually starting dialysis treatment. In addition, the nurse may ask for a copy of the radiology report and review it as well. If the nurse has any concerns or questions about the catheter being in proper placement it is appropriate to contact the physician and ask that the x-ray be reviewed. Given the possible complications from catheter placement the nurse should be vigilant for any signs of complications following placement.

14.5 Treatment Delivery

Actual treatment delivery is where the majority of staff time is spent. This involves setting up for the treatment, initiating the treatment, monitoring during the treatment, and ending the treatment.

A. Pre-Dialysis

This includes preparation for the dialysis treatment and involves not just setting up the dialysis machine but performing safety checks on the water system and the dialysis machine. Water checks are usually required prior to patient treatments starting for the day, and are required at periodic intervals depending upon the type of water system and the facility policy. Dialyzers are prepared according to manufacturer instructions and facility policies. Dialyzers and blood lines should always be prepared in an aseptic manner to prevent infection.

TIP: Dialysis is not a sterile procedure; it is considered to be clean, or aseptic.

TIP: Some dialysis facilities practice dialyzer reuse.

In dialyzer reuse a dialyzer is assigned to one patient. Following the dialysis treatment the dialyzer is capped and returned to the reuse room where it is aseptically cleaned and sterilized to be used again. Reuse has several advantages and some disadvantages. If the patient participates in reuse he is required to be educated on reuse and must give informed consent prior to dialyzers being reused. There are also strict labeling guidelines that must be followed as well as strict regulations for checking that the dialyzer is being used on the correct patient, and that the sterilant is fully removed prior to starting the dialysis treatment.

Saline IV fluid is usually used to fill the dialyzer and blood lines before the treatment to remove any air or particles that might be in them before use. The dialysate compartment of the dialyzer is filled with dialysate as well. If the patient is on reuse the dialyzer must be checked by two people for absence of sterilant before treatment can begin, and patient identity must be verified and match the labeling on the dialyzer.

TIP: Checking for negative dialyzer sterilant and for correct patient ID is always documented on the patient's dialysis flow sheet.

The dialysis machine and water systems must be free of any type of chemical or cleanser, and the temperature of the dialysate as well as the conductivity must be within limits. Conductivity should be verified with a manual meter before the treatment begins. Alarm tests are standard practice for all dialysis machines, and should be done prior to starting treatment. At minimum they must be performed at the beginning of the day, but some machines and facility policies require them to be tested before each dialysis treatment. Dialyzers are typically recirculated after set up, which means that the saline solution and dialysate are continually flowing by means of the blood pump. Dialyzers must continue to recirculate until the dialysis treatment begins.

1. Pre-Dialysis assessment

It is during this assessment, completed before dialysis begins, that the patient's current status is determined and the treatment plan is formed. This should include at minimum:

- Weight, along with comparison to the prior treatment and to the ordered dry weight
- Vital signs, including heart rate, blood pressure, respiratory rate, and temperature
- Evaluation of fluid status by checking for signs of edema (swelling), and possibly assessment of jugular vein distention
- Mental status
- Ambulation and any gait changes or changes in mobility
- Peripheral pulses, especially in the access extremity
- Auscultation (listening with a stethoscope) of heart sounds for rate, rhythm, and quality
- Auscultation of breath sounds for any wheezes or sounds of fluid in the lungs
- Skin changes
- Assessment of the patient's vascular access
- Any gastrointestinal complaints, including appetite, presence of nausea, vomiting, diarrhea, or heartburn
- Headaches, muscle cramping, difficulty breathing, chest pain, fever, bleeding, or any other new or different symptoms[7]

This portion of the treatment gives the nurse a great deal of information. All the data gathered is compared to prior treatment information, watching for any trends. While the treatment should closely follow the doctor's orders, most dialysis facilities have protocols in place that allow for some nursing judgments to be made. An example of this would be if a patient has been reaching her dry weight but complains of shortness of breath, then the dry weight could be challenged to remove extra fluid in case the patient has lost body weight and is building up fluid. Another example would be if a patient reports a fall at home, the nurse may decrease or hold her anticoagulation (heparin) until the doctor is notified to prevent bleeding due to the fall. This information also should be used to make recommendations for dialysis order changes; or if abnormal information is gathered the physician may need to be notified prior to starting the dialysis treatment.

The dialysis access will also be prepared based upon facility protocol. It is recommended that if the patient has a graft or fistula that the access be cleansed with antibacterial soap prior to the staff member cleaning the access for needle placement.

TIP: The patient should be instructed on cleaning his access site with soap and water when arriving at the dialysis facility. If the patient cannot clean his own arm then a staff member should clean it with soap and water.

After the access is washed it should be cleansed with the solution required by the facility policy. In most cases this will be 70 percent alcohol followed by a povidone-iodine (Betadine) solution. Each needle insertion site should be cleansed in a circular motion starting in the middle and working out in widening circles. If the patient uses a catheter the ports are usually soaked in a solution chosen by the facility.

TIP: Because of the high risk of infection it is imperative that aseptic procedures be followed in cleansing the dialysis access prior to use.

Following cleansing of the access the treatment is initiated by first accessing the vascular access. If it is a graft or fistula, this is done by placing two large bore needles, usually ranging from 17 to 14 gauge. If the patient uses a catheter it is opened by attaching syringes to each port and drawing out the solution used to keep the catheter from clotting. If the patient receives anticoagulation it is administered prior to the treatment as well. Any labs are drawn at this time before anticoagulation and before starting the treatment. The blood lines are connected to the patient's vascular access and the blood pump is started. The dialysis access should always be secured well. Dialysis needles should be taped in a chevron or butterfly type pattern to secure them and prevent them from becoming dislodged during treatment.[8]

TIP: Procedures for connecting the bloodlines and starting the blood pump can vary. Review of this policy is always important.

B. During Treatment

After connection to the bloodlines the patient's ordered blood flow should be set, along with all alarms and dialysate flow rate. During the treatment the patient should be monitored throughout the treatment. This includes obtaining blood pressure and pulse as well as any other applicable vital sign depending upon patient condition; monitoring the dialysis machine readings for blood flow, dialysate flow, venous and arterial pressures, and transmembrane pressure; removing ultrafiltration rate and amount; and completing any other parameters required by the dialysis facility policy. The majority of these will be documented on the flow sheet; however their absence from the flow sheet does not preclude monitoring them. The patient should also be assessed for how she is tolerating and responding to the treatment. The patient should be spoken to and assessed with each vital sign check. Timing and frequency of these assessments varies from facility to facility, so policy for this is important as well. All of the readings as well as assessment of the patient's tolerance of the treatment should be documented. Any unusual complaints or problems should be documented.

Dialysis is typically discontinued at the end of the prescribed treatment time by returning the patient's blood using saline. All parameters on the machine are documented, specifically how much fluid was removed during the treatment. The patient's blood is usually returned at a low blood pump speed.

TIP: Any anticoagulation being delivered via an infusion pump should be stopped prior to the end of the dialysis treatment to prevent excessive bleeding after needle removal. Depending upon how easily the patient clots, it may be turned off 30 minutes to one hour before the end of the treatment. If the patient uses a catheter it may be left on until the end of treatment.

C. Post Treatment

Following the dialysis treatment another set of vital signs is obtained and is compared to the pre-dialysis readings. This includes weight, heart rate, blood pressure, respiratory rate, and temperature. The heart and lungs should again be auscultated for any changes. The dialysis needles are removed and pressure is held either by the patient or a staff member until bleeding stops. A clean bandage is then applied to the needle insertion site for discharge home. If the patient has a catheter it is usually flushed with saline solution, and a diluted heparin solution is inserted to remain until the next treatment to prevent clotting of the catheter. The patient is again assessed for mental status as well as any complaints, including new signs or symptoms that need intervention. The patient's general condition and how he departs from the facility (i.e., walking, wheelchair, etc.) are noted and documented. All information gathered before, during, and after the treatment should be reviewed and interpreted to determine if further intervention or teaching should occur.

D. Documentation

Each aspect of the dialysis treatment should be documented, including patient information, vital signs, treatment orders and parameters, and patient response to treatment. Primarily the staff will document on a flow sheet; however they may document in progress notes or care plans as well. Documentation is heavily regulated by CMS and state regulations, so it is important to be familiar with each individual state regulation. A nursing history and assessment is required to be completed within 30 days of the patient's admission to the facility, 90 days after the first assessment, and then yearly thereafter. Care plans are also required to be completed periodically and offer further information on the status and condition of patients. Documentation should include evaluation of the patient and her response to the dialysis treatment, not just the machine readings.[9]

14.6 Legal Issues

In many situations the question will be whether or not the care was delivered in a manner that meets the current standard of care for dialysis therapy. The physician orders the dialysis treatment in an outpatient dialysis setting through standard orders that are applied for each dialysis treatment. In an acute or in-patient dialysis situation, the orders may be written individually for each dialysis treatment. Orders from other practitioners, such as an infectious disease physician, may also need to be considered for a dialysis treatment. An example would be if an antibiotic needs to be administered with a dialysis treatment. It is the responsibility of the nurse to safely deliver the dialysis treatment in compliance with physician orders, facility policy, and currently accepted standard of care. In many cases the nurse may not be the one who is actually providing the care, but rather is supervising the delivery of care by an LPN/LVN, or by a patient care technician (PCT).

A. Scope of Practice

The American Nephrology Nurses' Association (ANNA) has published its Scope of Practice for Nephrology Nursing.[10] ANNA states that the purpose for its scope of practice is to "describe for the public and the profession the nature of this specialty's nursing practice." Nephrology nurses apply the nursing process in their delivery of care, whether they are providing hands-on care or simply directing the care of this population of patients. ANNA further sets two categories of nurse providers in this specialty: the nephrology nursing generalist and the nephrology nursing specialist. The generalist is a registered nurse with either a baccalaureate, associate's, or diploma in nursing education. Further this nurse has additional education in nephrology nursing practice and demonstrates clinical expertise by obtaining certification as a nephrology nurse (CNN). ANNA further states within the scope of practice that the nurse's practice is guided by the Standards of Clinical Practice for Nephrology Nursing. The nurse will utilize the nursing process, provide healthcare education specific to nephrology, and collaborate with a multidisciplinary team and other professionals or agencies to assure high quality care. Further, the nephrology nurse generalist recognizes, values, utilizes, and participates in research activities and integrates knowledge and technical skills specific to nephrology care. Finally, the nurse will participate in a comprehensive quality assurance program. Nephrology nurses may be integrators of care, or providers of care. The nephrology nurse coordinates services, prepares and monitors patients, evaluates responses to care, collaborates with patients and family members in setting goals, develops and implements the plan of care to achieve the set goals, and evaluates the effectiveness of the plan by examining outcomes.

The nephrology nursing specialist is an advanced practice nurse who has expertise in nephrology care and has a minimum of a master's degree in nursing or a nursing-related field. Refer to ANNA's Scope of Practice for specifics regarding this role.[11]

B. Standards of Care

The American Nephrology Nurses' Association is nationally recognized as a nursing organization that has established the scope of practice, competencies, and educational requirements for delivery of nephrology care, including the delivery of dialysis treatments. ANNA has published the *Nephrology Nursing Standards of Practice and Guidelines for Care*. The most recent edition was published in 2005 and has been used at trial to establish if the standard of care has been met. The standards follow the American Nurses Association (ANA 2004) statement that "Standards are authoritative statements by which the nursing profession describes the responsibilities for which its practitioners are accountable." These standards provide the broad foundation for practice and help build the framework as well. Guidelines are defined by ANNA as "systematically developed statements that address the care of specific patient populations or phenomena and are based upon the best available scientific evidence and/or expert opinion."[12] The most recent edition includes recommendations from the National Kidney Foundation Kidney Disease Outcome Quality Initiate (K/DOQI). ANNA divides their text into Standards of Care and Nephrology Nursing Guidelines for Care. Standards of Care addresses broad, generalized topics of assessment, diagnosis, outcome identification, planning, implementation, coordination of care, health teaching and health promotion, consultation, prescriptive authority and treatment, and evaluation. ANNA goes further to address Standards of Professional Performance. These include quality of practice, education, professional practice evaluation, collegiality, collaboration, ethics, research, resource utilization, and leadership.

The National Kidney Foundation also has clinical practice guidelines. These are titled Kidney Disease Outcome Quality Initiative (KDOQI) and are evidence-based guidelines for clinical practice. They can be found at www.kidney.org/professionals/kdoqi/guidelines_commentaries.cfm. These guidelines are reviewed frequently by experts in the field and are based upon the current literature and research. These are much more broad than ANNA's publication and do not speak specifically for nephrology nursing care. These are referred to often by regulatory agencies in reviewing dialysis care delivery.[13]

A more recent body that has published guidelines for dialysis care is Kidney Disease: Improving Global Outcomes (KDIGO). This is an independent foundation focused on improving the care and outcomes of kidney disease patients globally. This foundation was formed in 2003 and is managed by the National Kidney Foundation. Several of their guidelines would be applicable in nephrology nursing; however as they are newer guidelines their use in trial may not have been fully established. These guidelines can be found at www.kdigo.org.

The Centers for Disease Control and Prevention has published information in regards to preventing transmission of infection among hemodialysis patients. These can be viewed at www.cdc.gov/mmwr/preview/mmwrhtml/rr5005a1.htm.[14]

The Centers for Medicare and Medicaid Services (CMS) also regulates provision of dialysis care through Conditions for Coverage. The conditions for coverage are very broad and speak to everything from facility governance to infection control. These can be found at www.cms.gov/cfcsandcops/13_esrd.asp#topofpage.[15]

C. Standards of Professional Performance

Each state has a Board of Nursing which sets that state's minimum requirements for licensure of qualified registered nurses. Each hiring facility has the responsibility of providing nurses that are able to provide competent care to its patients. Each nurse should have documentation of his current nursing license as well as an evaluation of his competency to provide dialysis-specific skills. Further, federal regulations as set forth by the Centers for Medicare and Medicaid Services (CMS) require current certification in cardiopulmonary resuscitation (CPR). Some states may also require that a nurse be certified in advanced cardiac life support (ACLS).

TIP: Personnel files should include documentation of orientation programs, a competency or skills checklist that is updated annually, and inservice education documentation. Some states also require that each nurse maintain clinical competency by obtaining continuing education (CEU) credits to renew her license.

Registered nurses are responsible for the coordination of care. This means they may be supervising other registered nurses, LPN/LVNs, patient care technicians, and other unlicensed caregivers. Each state also sets forth the minimum requirements for LPN/LVNs. Each facility should verify competency of these nurses as well. The final group of workers that typically provide direct patient care to dialysis patients are unlicensed patient care technicians.

The CMS conditions for coverage speak to minimum qualifications for dialysis personnel. First, 494.140 defines personnel qualifications:[16]

- A nurse manager must be employed and be a full-time employee who is also a registered nurse. Further this nurse must have at least 12 months of experience in clinical nursing and have an additional six months of experience in providing nursing care to patients on maintenance dialysis.
- A charge nurse responsible for each shift must be a RN, LPN, or LVN who meets the minimum requirements for the state in which he is employed. This nurse must also have at least 12 months experience in providing nursing care which includes three months of experience in dialysis care. If the nurse is an LPN or LVN he must work under the supervision of a registered nurse.
- Staff nurses can be employed and are defined as nurses who provide care and treatment to patients and must be either a RN or LPN meeting the practice requirements of the state in which they are employed.

TIP: In addition to setting minimum qualifications for nurses, CMS regulations state that each patient must be fully visible throughout the entire dialysis treatment.

Staffing ratios must be such that every patient can be viewed at all times. While CMS does not set specific staff to patient ratios, some states do. For example, the State of Georgia requires that each facility have a RN on duty any time patients are in the facility, even if they are in the waiting area and not undergoing treatment. One nurse is required for each ten patients, so the first nurse must be a RN. Each additional ten patients dialyzing require another licensed staff member which may be either a RN or a LPN. So for 20 patients dialyzing there must be two nurses.

- Patient care technicians must meet all applicable state requirements for education, training, credentialing, competency, standards of practice, certification, and licensure in the state in which they are employed as a dialysis technician. PCTs must also have a high school diploma or equivalency, and have completed a training program approved by the governing body and medical director of the facility. The training program is completed under the direction of a RN. In addition, a PCT must be certified under a state certification program or a national commercially available certification program. All patient care technicians employed on or before October 14, 2008 must be certified within 18 months of this date. Newly employed PCTs must become certified within 18 months of being hired as a dialysis PCT.[17]

TIP: Some states require licensure for patient care technicians in addition to the certification that is required by CMS regulations.

- Water treatment technicians must complete a training program that has been approved by the medical director and governing body.

TIP: Some states have set more stringent guidelines for personnel qualification requirements. Each state's regulations must be reviewed as well.

D. Policies and Procedures

Each facility should have in place policies and procedures which set forth the expected care delivery. All facility staff should have access to these for review and reference. They should be reviewed and approved annually by the medical director and governing body and should cover all care delivered within the facility. Documentation of staff training in all policies and procedures should be present. The policies and procedures should be in compliance with national standards and appropriate federal, state, and local regulations.

1. Physician orders

Policies and procedures will set forth how physician orders can be given. A nurse has a responsibility to determine if an order is appropriate and to question or clarify an order that seems inappropriate. For example, if a physician orders for a nurse to remove 5 liters of fluid from a patient who has low blood pressure, this could result in the patient going into shock and could be contraindicated. The nurse has a responsibility to question or clarify this order. Each state sets forth how physician orders can be written or given to a licensed nurse. If a physician is on site and has access to the patient's medical record the order should be written by the physician to help reduce the risk of errors due to transcription. A verbal order, which is where the physician verbally and face to face with the nurse gives the order, is only acceptable in an emergency situation such as a cardiac arrest or when the physician is performing a procedure and is in sterile attire. A verbal order should always be read back to the physician prior to carrying out the order. A telephone order can be given over the phone when the physician is not present in the dialysis unit. This order also should be read back and verified to the physician prior to implementing the order.

TIP: Many dialysis facilities now have electronic ordering systems and the physician can electronically enter orders on an Internet site for the dialysis clinic to put into place. Physicians can also review and sign their orders electronically. Each facility, based upon state and federal guidelines, sets the policy for how quickly a physician must review and sign all orders.

E. Informed Consent

Performing a dialysis treatment is an invasive procedure, and therefore it requires informed consent. All patients have the right to accept or refuse treatment without the threat of retribution. Informed consent should include the therapy name, a description of the therapy, the risks of therapy, alternative therapies available, and the consequences of refusing therapy. Each state may have additional requirements. If the patient will participate in dialyzer reuse he must give separate informed consent for this as well. The CMS guidelines also list other specific requirements for patient notification, such as patient rights and responsibilities, facility rules, and how to report a grievance.

F. Guidelines for Care

ANNA defines these as "systematically developed statements that address the care of specific patient populations or phenomena and are based on the best available scientific evidence and/or expert opinion."

1. Universal guidelines

These guidelines speak to categories of care of the dialysis patient that are not directly related to treatment delivery. While there is potential for nursing negligence or malpractice in these areas, they are not typical areas found in cases. A full listing can be found in ANNA's *Nephrology Nursing Standards of Practice and Guidelines for Care*.[18] Those that a nurse is most often active in are listed here along with potential areas for nursing malpractice.

a. Anemia

A hormone, erythropoietin, is produced by healthy kidneys and tells the bone marrow to produce red blood cells. Damaged kidneys do not make this hormone in sufficient quantities; therefore dialysis patients suffer from chronic anemia. Patients on hemodialysis also lose a small quantity of blood with each dialysis treatment, increasing their risk for anemia. A nurse has a responsibility to assess a patient for signs and symptoms of anemia including reviewing lab tests that impact anemia.

The patient also should be assessed for causes of anemia, rather than just attribute anemia to dialysis or end stage renal disease. The patient should also be assessed for her understanding of anemia, including symptoms to report such as increasing shortness of breath, chest pain, vomiting blood and tarry stools which indicate bleeding in the gastrointestinal tract. The nurse will collaborate with the physician to utilize an anemia management protocol which should be inclusive of laboratory studies and medication management. Epogen is the trade name for synthetic erythropoietin and can be administered either intravenously or subcutaneously. Because dialysis patients can also be deficient in iron, which can worsen their anemia, iron supplementation may be necessary. Several iron preparations are available and are given intravenously during dialysis treatments.

TIP: Severe anaphylactic reactions have been reported with use of intravenous iron preparations. The current medications available do not have as high a risk of these reactions; however careful administration procedures and policies need to be followed. Facility policy as well as the medication package insert should be reviewed if a medication reaction is suspected.

The nurse will administer medications as prescribed and monitor response to the medications, reporting to the physician any concerns, including failure to respond as expected. Most dialysis facilities will have an anemia management protocol to guide and direct the management of patient anemia. Some protocols are titled guidelines. A nurse should be trained in use of the protocol or guidelines. Typically a nurse can use the protocol to enter a dosage change in the patient's medical record as a medication order, or order appropriate laboratory studies. If the nurse feels that the patient needs to be managed outside of the protocol the physician should be contacted and consulted. Areas to evaluate carefully are how efficiently laboratory studies are reviewed and evaluated for appropriate dosage changes.

TIP: Any nurse who is assigned the responsibility of anemia management should receive full training and education in this. Personnel records should reflect this training. Protocols and/or guidelines must be reviewed and approved by the medical director and the governing body of the dialysis facility.

b. Bone metabolism and disease

Dialysis patients are at severe risk for bone disease. This is a result of the failed kidneys being unable to excrete excess phosphorus. Calcium and phosphorus are closely tied to each other. When the phosphorus level rises the body tries to lower it by pulling calcium from the bones. Dialysis does not effectively remove phosphorus from the blood, and phosphorus is found in most food sources. Dialysis patients are given a phosphorus restricted diet and are prescribed medications to take with food that bind to the phosphorus, keeping it in the gut rather than being absorbed into the blood stream. The diet is very difficult to follow, and the medications must be taken with every meal and are large and difficult to swallow. These lead to very low patient compliance with diet and medication adherence. As a result, many dialysis patients struggle with high phosphorus levels that lead to their body leaching calcium from the bones, leading to weak and brittle bones. This places dialysis patients at increased risk of fracture. A result of a high phosphorus level is the patient secreting parathyroid hormone in increasing amounts, which worsens the pulling of calcium from the bones. As the phosphorus level increases, it can bind in the blood with the calcium and form small deposits in the soft tissues of the body. This can cause sores that progress to gangrene, and interruption of blood flow to other organs such as the intestine or heart. For these reasons management of patient calcium, phosphorus, and parathyroid hormone levels is crucial.

Nurses have a responsibility to complete a fall risk assessment and to assess the patient for their ability to ambulate. Interventions should be made to protect the patient from falling at all times due to the significant risk of fracture from any fall or injury. Bone pain, joint pain or swelling, history of falls, and signs of soft tissue or skin injury should be evaluated routinely. The patient should be educated on the risk factors for renal bone disease, including medication and diet compliance. The nurse must collaborate with the physician and the dietitian to plan appropriate therapy. Several medications are on the market that are administered by IV during dialysis treatments to help decrease parathyroid hormone levels, and these should be administered as ordered. These are often known as Vitamin D analogs. If the nurse identifies that the patient has limited financial resources for food or medications, the social worker should be consulted to evaluate resources that can assist. The patient should be taught signs and symptoms of renal bone disease as well as the need to follow the diet and medications as prescribed.

TIP: Most facilities have protocols or guidelines for bone parameter management. In many facilities these are managed by the dietitian; however the nurse should always have input into this as well.

The nurse, or dietitian, should be trained in bone and mineral metabolism and management prior to administering a protocol. Evidence of this training should be present in personnel files, and any protocol should be reviewed by the governing body and approved by the medical director.

c. Fluid balance and congestive heart failure

Because dialysis patients rely upon dialysis for removal of extra fluid, it is imperative that care be given to adequate fluid removal with each dialysis treatment. The nurse should assess the patient for signs of excess fluid as described in pre-dialysis assessment. The nurse should review any applicable laboratory or x-ray studies, especially any chest x-rays for evidence of excess fluid in the patient's lungs. Fluid building up in a patient's lungs is one of the key reasons that a full lung assessment should be done before and after each dialysis treatment. The nurse has a responsibility to collaborate with the physician if an assessment of excess fluid is made. Each patient has a dry weight set by the physician, but nursing judgment can be used if more or less fluid needs to be removed. Removal of too much fluid carries with it the risk of low blood pressure or shock and also risk of clotting the patient's dialysis access. Failing to remove enough fluid has the risk of congestive heart failure or pulmonary edema, both of which are considered medical emergencies and can

be life threatening. The nurse should monitor the patient's response to fluid removal and be prepared to increase or decrease fluid removal as needed and indicated. The patient should be instructed on signs of increasing fluid status, such as shortness of breath, chest pain, fatigue, and swelling or edema. Low blood pressure, chest pain, or muscle cramps can occur if too much fluid is removed.

TIP: Each dialysis facility should have a maximum fluid removal amount specified.

Removing more fluid than this set limit requires an individual physician order. Each facility also should have a maximum UF (ultrafiltration/fluid removal) rate. Exceeding this rate requires a physician order. Each dialyzer also has a maximum safe UF rate, so package inserts should be reviewed for this information.

2. Infection control

Dialysis facilities have great potential to be breeding grounds for infection. Bloodborne pathogens are any microorganism present in blood or body fluids that has the potential to cause disease or illness. These represent great risk for both patients and staff of dialysis facilities. Patients and staff should be protected from the spread of bacterial, viral, and fungal infections at all times. OSHA has regulations regarding healthcare workers that must be followed at all times. The CDC also has published information in regards to preventing transmission of infection among hemodialysis patients. These can be viewed at www.cdc.gov/mmwr/preview/mmwrhtml/rr5005a1.htm.[19]

Dialysis patients have lower immunity and are at higher risk of infection. Bacterial infections present a significant risk, especially with the rise of multi-drug resistant organisms. The majority of bacterial infections that originate in dialysis facilities are related to the dialysis access. For this reason it is imperative that aseptic techniques be followed in preparing the patient's dialysis access. Patients should be assessed for signs of infection with every dialysis treatment, and they should be asked questions regarding fevers, pain, redness, or drainage if infection is suspected. The nurse should intervene by collecting appropriate lab studies, including blood or wound cultures. The physician should be notified as soon as infection symptoms are noted or identified, as even minimal delays can be disastrous. Antibiotics should be administered as ordered; or if the patient will take oral antibiotics at home the patient should be instructed on dosing and regimens and evaluated for compliance. Care should be taken to prevent the spread of infection among patients.

TIP: All staff should be instructed on infection control techniques, and an infection control policy should be in place.

Infection control policies should include when and how a patient should be isolated in the event of an infection that has potential to be transmitted to other patients. Documentation of staff infection control training should be evident in the training records. Each dialysis facility is required by CMS conditions for coverage to track and evaluate infection episodes. Quality assurance records should reflect such tracking and review.

Dialysis patients are also at increased risk of acquiring Hepatitis B or Hepatitis C. The obvious desired patient outcome is that the patient will remain negative for both Hepatitis B and Hepatitis C. Patients can be screened for Hepatitis B with both the antigen, which indicates the patient is contagious, and antibodies, which give immunity. Hepatitis C screening is only available for antibodies. Presence of these indicates infection with Hepatitis C. If patients are found to have no immunity to Hepatitis B they should be offered vaccination. Patients do have the right to refuse vaccination; however they should be educated on the risks of Hepatitis B if they do not gain immunity through vaccination. There is no vaccine for Hepatitis C. CMS requires isolating patients who are positive for Hepatitis B, so they must be dialyzed in a dedicated area with dedicated equipment that is reserved for Hepatitis B positive patients only.

HIV is also a risk for patients on dialysis due to the large risk of exposure to blood and/or body fluids in a dialysis environment. OSHA recommends following universal precautions at all times when the potential for splashing with blood or body fluids is present. Patients with HIV are not required to be isolated during dialysis.

TIP: Patients who are positive for Hepatitis B, Hepatitis C, or HIV should not participate in dialysis reuse programs. CMS and CDC offer guidelines for frequency and type of testing to screen for Hepatitis B and C.

Tuberculosis is also a risk for dialysis patients due to the communal environment. Patients must be screened for tuberculosis upon admission to a dialysis facility and annually thereafter. Patients should also be screened for risk factors for tuberculosis. If tuberculosis is suspected, or if a patient has a positive skin test, the patient's physician and the medical director should be notified. Further notification may be required based upon local health department regulations. Respiratory isolation is usually required for patients with active tuberculosis; however this requires a special negative pressure isolation room, which most dialysis facilities do not have. Therefore patients with active respiratory tuberculosis will likely be admitted to the hospital for dialysis until they are considered cleared or no longer contagious.

3. Vascular access

This is an area that has given rise to many legal cases. The patient's vascular access is his lifeline. Without access for dialysis treatments, the dialysis patient's life is at risk. The main goal is for the patient's access to provide adequate blood flow to achieve the dialysis prescription, the patient to be free of complications, and the patient to understand his vascular access. The dialysis access should be fully evaluated and assessed prior to each dialysis treatment. It is imperative that it be evaluated for any signs of infection such as redness, swelling, warmth, tenderness or pain. Such signs or symptoms should be reported to the physician prior to using the dialysis access. If the patient uses a dialysis catheter, the dressing should be removed and site care provided, along with assessment of the site prior to initiating the treatment. The reason for this is due to the possibility of holes developing in the plastic tubing. Some holes are located in the tubing, which is covered by the dressing, and failing to remove the dressing to examine the entire catheter can lead to blood loss, air embolism, or risk of infection. Further, some holes can develop in the catheter below the level of the skin, so careful assessment when flushing the catheter prior to dialysis treatment is required. Another example would be if an exit site infection is present and the dressing is not removed until later in the dialysis treatment. Several antibiotics can be administered during dialysis, but one (Vancomycin) requires at least 90 minutes for administration. Removing the dressing late in the treatment and finding signs of infection could possibly not allow for time for administration of antibiotics before the treatment ends. But most importantly, the standard of care requires a full assessment of the access prior to initiation of the dialysis treatment, and if the catheter dressing is not removed before the treatment then neither the access nor the patient have been fully assessed. While the patient's access should be evaluated prior to treatment, this assessment should also include the access extremity for any signs of blood flow changes or nerve pain. This would include observing for presence of pulses, swelling, color and temperature, changes in sensation, limitation of movement, and so on.

TIP: In the event of signs of infection of a graft of fistula the access should not be cannulated.

In some cases the physician may order that the dialysis treatment proceed, but the nurse has the responsibility to accurately and correctly convey the severity of the infection to the physician. The nurse should document all the information given to the physician, and should also document all instructions and orders received from the physician.

TIP: Physicians should be notified of any signs or symptoms of access infection as soon as such signs are noted.

A delay in notification of an infection or starting treatment in an infected access has the potential to be disastrous. Access infections, because of the quantity of blood that flows through a dialysis access, can quickly develop further into bacteremia, or blood infection, if not treated. Failure to quickly treat can lead to loss of the dialysis access, requiring another procedure or surgery for placement of a new access. In addition, an infected access can become weakened by the infection causing a higher risk of access rupture, which can lead to exsanguinations.

The patient should be assessed for any difficulty with cannulation or any pain from placement of needles. Needles should always be taped securely to prevent them from being dislodged. All connections to the access should remain visible and secure. Any signs of infiltration or hematomas should be observed, and interventions made immediately upon noting their presence. Any difficulty in achieving or maintaining the prescribed blood flow should be evaluated and the physician should be notified. Any bleeding or oozing from the dialysis vascular access site should be addressed immediately. Routine bleeding should be reported to the physician. Any pain, increased temperature, or air or foam in the dialysis lines should be addressed.

Other possible complications are as follows:

- Infiltration is blood that has leaked into the tissues around the dialysis access, usually a result of poor needle placement.

In most cases the needle should be removed, then ice applied to decrease blood from leaking into the surrounding tissues. Heat can be applied after the first 24 hours. The patient should be taught follow-up care for the infiltrated access at home, including how to apply ice and heat, and signs and symptoms of infection.

TIP: Infiltration is most often a result of poor needle position or placement as the needle as punctured through the dialysis access.

An immature fistula is also at risk to infiltrate as it cannot tolerate the high pressures applied by the dialysis flow. The dialysis staff has a duty to report to the nephrologist or vascular surgeon if they feel an access is not ready to have needles placed. Most dialysis clinics have a policy in place for how many times one staff member can attempt to stick a patient before she must obtain help. Two to three unsuccessful attempts should be reported to the physician prior to continuing.

- Bleeding from the sites can occur during treatment or afterward when needles have been removed. During dialysis the staff can attempt to cushion and pad the site with gauze to try to stop the bleeding, but most cases will require the needle to be removed. Pressure should be held until bleeding stops. This is true following dialysis as well. Needles are removed and pressure is held until bleeding stops. If bleeding is excessive or continues for more than the amount of time specified by the unit policy, the physician should be notified. Patients can be taught to hold pressure on their access following treatment; however patients should be assessed for suitability for this. Under no circumstances should a patient ever be discharged home with active bleeding. Patients should be assessed each treatment for any bleeding at home between treatments, and this should be reported to the nephrologist and the vascular surgeon. Patients also should not be discharged home with the gauze used to hold pressure after treatment, but should have a clean bandage applied prior to discharge home.
- Clotting of the dialysis access requires medical intervention. Care in the facility to prevent this includes holding pressure tightly enough to stop bleeding without interrupting the flow of blood through the access, and not allowing the patient to become hypotensive. Failure to quickly and adequately intervene with hypotension can lead to a clotted access.

TIP: Dialysis accesses should be assessed for flow prior to treatment. This is done by feeling for the thrill, which is a purring type feeling, and listening for the bruit, which is a whooshing sound. If both the thrill and bruit are absent, the access should not be cannulated.

---

4. Treatment-related complications

This list is not exhaustive; however it covers the majority of complications that occur during dialysis treatments.

a. Dialysis disequilibrium

This is a neurological side effect of dialysis treatment. Blood urea nitrogen (BUN) is one of the waste products that builds up in the blood of a dialysis patient. It also builds up in the spinal fluid and brain tissue. When a patient has a very high level of BUN it is quickly removed from the blood, but more slowly removed from the brain tissue. It draws water towards it, so when the BUN level remains high in the brain tissue, water will flow into the brain causing edema of the brain. This causes sudden and severe symptoms such as headache, nausea, vomiting, restlessness, low blood pressure, changes in mental status, seizures, coma, and even death. It is a rare complication that usually occurs only in acute dialysis patients that are new on dialysis, or in patients who have missed several treatments and have a very high level of BUN in their blood. However, it can occur with any patient, so signs and symptoms need to be monitored closely. This can be prevented with very short and slow dialysis treatments with low blood and dialysate flows, such as 250 blood flow and 500 dialysate flow. Some medications, such as mannitol, can also be administered to help pull fluid from the brain tissue to help prevent swelling. A high dialysate sodium level can also help prevent this from occurring. If signs or symptoms become present, treatment should be terminated immediately and the physician notified.

TIP: Any patient who misses several dialysis treatments is at increased risk of disequilibrium syndrome. In this event the physician should be notified to decide if it is safe to dialyze the patient in the outpatient facility or if he requires hospital admission.

---

b. Air embolism

Air embolism is the introduction of air into the patient's bloodstream, usually via the dialysis access. Because the patient is connected to dialysis tubing with multiple potential routes of entry for air this presents a very large risk. This can be caused by a defective or unarmed air detector, or an unarmed or malfunctioning venous line clamp. Any loose connection in the circuit is a potential portal of entry for air. Signs and symptoms include seeing air in the blood circuit, chest pain, shortness of breath, coughing, cyanosis (blue tinge to lips or fingers), visual changes, confusion, coma, paralysis, or death. Air embolism is preventable with careful set-up and proper use of the protective equipment. The air detector and line clamp should always be armed and in use through all parts of the treatment, including treatment termination. All connections should be secure and checked to make sure they are tight enough. The blood lines should be monitored along with the patient to make sure that no leaks or air are noted at any point. Treatment and intervention should be delivered immediately if air embolism is suspected. This includes stopping the blood pump to stop infusing air immediately. The patient should be placed on her left side in Trendelenberg position (with the head very low and feet in the air). This position traps the air in the right ventricle of the heart preventing it from progressing to the lungs. Oxygen should be started immediately, and vital signs should be monitored continuously. If pulse oximetry (oxygen blood level) is available this should be implemented as well. The physician should be notified immediately, and in most cases initiating EMS is warranted as well.

c. Exsanguination

This is also known as bleeding out, or fatal hypovolemia due to excessive blood loss. Exsanguination can occur from accidental or traumatic separation of blood lines, dislodgement of needles from the access site, rupture of a graft or fistula, separation of a cap from a dialysis catheter, and rarely from the dialyzer blood membrane rupturing. The source of bleeding is typically obvious. Early patient signs can be dizziness, shortness of breath, and chest pain from rapid onset low blood pressure due to blood loss. Failure to address or recognize the blood loss can quickly lead to shock, convulsions, or cardiac or respiratory arrest leading to death. Blood loss is preventable in most circumstances. All bloodlines and access connections should be secure and visible at all times. Connections should be Luer-lock and tightly connected. Needles should be taped securely with a butterfly or chevron pattern so they cannot move easily.[20] All catheters should be capped and secured; clamps for the ports should be closed prior to discharge home. Blood lines should be in the blood pump properly to prevent shredding of the tubing, and the dialysate blood leak detector should be operational and functioning. In the event of blood loss the blood pump should be turned off and a clamp placed to prevent further blood loss. Any bleeding sites on the patient should be immediately secured and pressure-held to stop bleeding. The nurse should evaluate if it is safe to return any blood to the patient from the blood lines; if it is safe the blood should be returned as quickly as possible. Saline IV fluid should be administered as quickly as is safe to increase the patient's circulating blood volume. Oxygen should be administered as well. EMS should be initiated for transport to the hospital, and the physician should be notified. Blood products should be administered as ordered and appropriate. Other preventative measures include the nurse monitoring the patient and the machine rather than just writing down the machine reading with each vital sign check. The patient should be fully assessed with each reading. Also, since a venous needle dislodgement or line separation can cause the venous pressure to drop rapidly, the nurse should evaluate the venous blood line and the patient's access prior to silencing the alarm and resetting the machine to resume treatment. In the event of a needle dislodgement or line separation, if the machine is reset without correcting the cause of the alarm then the patient can continue to lose blood. If the arterial needle dislodges or becomes disconnected the arterial pressure will become less negative, again triggering an arterial pressure alarm. Again, the patient and the lines should be assessed prior to resuming treatment. Failure to do so can result in either more blood loss, or air entering the blood circuit with the possibility of air embolism.

TIP: Patients should be educated on keeping their access and blood lines visible at all times. This should be monitored and documented with each vital sign check.

Patients tend to be very cold during dialysis treatment and prefer to be fully covered with a blanket. Education should be given to patients, and this education should be documented in the medical record. Patients share responsibility for making sure their access is visible at all times; however even if they are covered up the nurse has the responsibility to uncover the access and blood lines to make sure that the access is secure and free of complications.

In a case published in *The National Jury Verdict Review and Analysis* (#8388) the family of a 74-year old diabetic with history of chronic kidney failure brought suit against the dialysis center where their mother had been a patient. The allegation was that dialysis protocol was disregarded and the patient's catheter became disconnected from the bloodlines resulting in hemorrhage of a significant amount of blood that resulted in permanent brain damage. The plaintiff alleged that their mother was left alone while receiving dialysis and that the catheter site was obstructed by clothing. Early in treatment the catheter became disconnected and massive bleeding onto the floor was not noticed until she became unconscious and fell from her chair to the floor. The defendant center failed to initiate timely resuscitative measures. She was resuscitated by paramedics but she had suffered irreversible brain damage. Eventually she was treated in an extended care facility but succumbed to a blood infection that was fatal. The plaintiffs alleged negligence, and breach of proper procedures with regard to the observation, monitoring and care

of dialysis patients. The defendants contended that they attended to the patient as soon as the nature of her condition was noticed and maintained that the plaintiff's death was not causally related. The matter was resolved prior to trial.

Dialysis catheters connect to the dialysis tubing with a Luer-lock connection. This is a threaded connection, so when it is fully engaged it is almost impossible to break the connection without unscrewing the two parts of the connection. Accidental disconnection of bloodlines from a dialysis would likely be related to an incomplete connection at the time of treatment initiation.

5. Equipment-related complications

Because of the complexity of the dialysis equipment and the complexity of the dialysis circuit, there is potential for complications arising from either source. For this reason careful preparation and monitoring is required at all times. While this section is not all-inclusive, it does cover the greatest potentials of risk to the patient.

a. Hemolysis

This is the destruction of red blood cells (RBC). While a very small amount of hemolysis occurs from mechanical damage to the RBCs as they travel through the dialysis circuit, this amount is negligible and poses no threat to patients. In the extreme cases of hemolysis discussed here, the destruction of the RBCs causes a sudden and severe anemia due to the decrease of circulating RBCs. Since the RBCs carry oxygen through the body, suddenly decreasing the quantity and quality of RBCs causes the patient to become hypoxic, or without oxygen. Another problem that arises with sudden hemolysis is the release of potassium that is stored inside the RBC. Small amounts of hemolysis release potassium as well, but the dialysis machine can remove this easily. In extreme cases with large amounts of hemolysis the potassium cannot be removed quickly enough, causing the patient to receive a large infusion of potassium from her own blood returning to her body from the dialysis machine. Elevated levels of potassium can cause interruption of muscle contractions, including the heart. Left untreated this can lead to cardiac arrest. Because of the risk of death, staff must always monitor for hemolysis. Signs and symptoms of hemolysis are basically the same, regardless of the cause.

While hemolysis can occur in one patient, the majority of causes can impact the entire facility, so any time more than one patient complains of the following symptoms simultaneously or very close together it is imperative to consider if a problem with water or dialysate supply has occurred. Signs and symptoms include chest pain, shortness of breath, and low blood pressure. The classic symptom is seen in the dialysis blood lines. Typically the blood is a dark red or burgundy color, but in hemolysis the rupture of the RBCs lightens the blood so that it takes on a more clear appearance that is often described as being like cherry soda. The patient may also complain of burning at the venous needle or catheter site; he may complain of feeling hot if the dialysate temperature is too high. In addition, irregular heartbeats may be noted, and lab studies would reveal a decrease in the hemoglobin and hematocrit and an increase in the potassium level.

Causes of hemolysis are as follows:

- Dialysate solution that is either hypotonic or hypertonic. Dialysate should mimic the chemical composition of the blood in regards to the amount of sodium that it holds. If the sodium level of the dialysate is too high or too low the RBCs will be destroyed, causing hemolysis. This can be due either to improper mixing of the dialysate or bicarbonate solutions, improper dilution of the dialysate inside the machine, or failure of the dialysate meter to give an accurate reading. Dialysate solutions come in individual gallon jugs, large 55 gallon drums, or a dry powder that must be mixed. The risk of improper mixing of the dialysate solutions is the biggest risk as there is more room for human error. Dialysate conductivity is checked by the dialysis machine with an internal meter, but it should be checked with an independent meter before each and every dialysis treatment, and it should be repeated if the dialysate is changed during the treatment for any reason. The independent meter should be checked against a standard solution every day before use, and these checks should be recorded in a quality control log. Employees should be trained and demonstrate competency in performing quality control checks and conductivity checks on the dialysis machine. Employees who prepare dialysate solution by mixing a dry powder with purified water should be trained and demonstrate competency in this preparation. Several checks are required on the solutions before they are allowed to flow to the dialysis stations, and logs are required for this as well.

- Another cause of hemolysis is the administration of hypertonic or hypotonic solutions to the patient. Concentrated sodium chloride solutions are occasionally ordered for the treatment of low blood pressure or muscle cramps caused by fluid removal during dialysis. Administering the concentrated hypertonic solution pulls fluid from the tissue and into the bloodstream relieving the low blood pressure and cramps. The solution is usually given in 5 to 10 cc bolus injections, and should be administered very slowly. Sterile water is hypotonic and can also cause destruction of RBCs. Sterile water should never be injected into a patient directly. It is used to mix and reconstitute dry medications, such as antibiotics, to prepare them for injection; but, again, it should never be injected directly into a patient.

- Hemolysis can also occur if the dialysate is overheated. This would occur if the dialysis heater malfunctions *and* the dialysate temperature monitor fails. This would be very rare as it would require two portions of the machine's protections to fail simultaneously.

- Hemolysis can also occur if there is very high negative pressure in the dialysis circuit. This can be due to the pre-pump arterial pressure being very negative, usually > -250 without intervention. This negative pressure can cause the cells to rupture, causing hemolysis.

- Another source of hemolysis is the presence of chemicals in the dialyzer or blood lines, or chemicals in the water. Presence of solutions to sterilize the dialyzer after manufacture or chemicals used to reprocess dialyzers for reuse can cause hemolysis. Copper piping or nitrates in well water can be a cause, but these are very rare and usually not seen, as PVC piping is typically used and well water is a very rare source of water for dialysis facilities. If hemolysis occurs in a home setting with well water in use, this could be a potential risk. The main source of hemolysis in the water would be a break-through of chlorine or chloramines into the dialysis water supply. These are used to kill bacteria in the water and are placed in city water supplies. Because all city water has chlorine or chloramines, the water is required to be checked prior to dialysis treatments, and at multiple points throughout the day. Each facility has its own policy for frequency of testing, and it should be strictly followed. The policy should be in compliance with the recommendations as set by the American Association for Medical Instrumentation (AAMI). Employees who perform testing on the water should be trained and demonstrate competency in performing this task. Most policies require that a licensed person verify the readings for chlorine/chloramines, and this should include the nurse verifying the results, not just signing that the testing was done. Another potential source of exposure to chlorine is through bleach used to clean dialysis machines and supplies. Dialysate containers and wands used for connections are typically cleaned and disinfected with a diluted bleach solution. It is imperative that such containers are rinsed free of bleach, and that testing is done to determine the absence of bleach before they are used again. Machines are sterilized and disinfected on routine schedules, either with bleach or another chemical. Both have the possibility of causing patient reactions if not fully rinsed from the machine prior to use. Again, testing must be done prior to patient treatment to determine if all bleach or sterilant has been fully removed from the machine. Documentation of a negative result is required. If a dialyzer has been reprocessed and had a chemical sterilant placed for reuse, two people must verify that the sterilant has been fully removed from the dialyzer before use. This must be done while the patient is sitting in the dialysis chair, with the patient also verifying the absence of sterilant if the patient has adequate vision to read the testing strip. If the dialysis clinic uses paper charting then two signatures indicating negative sterilant should be present, ideally with one of them being the patient. Computer charting would require two staff members to verify the absence of a chemical. It would be important to note the time stamp of this testing documentation in computer charting to verify that the time stamp indicates the testing was completed prior to the initiation of treatment.

TIP: Because testing for chlorine/chloramines and dialyzer sterilizing chemical require reading of the color changes on the testing equipment, any employee who performs this testing must be given a test for color-blindness.

If an employee is color-blind to any degree she should not be performing these tests. A color blind employee can obtain the samples for testing and can perform the test, but other staff members must read and document the results.

The majority of causes of hemolysis can be prevented through careful preparation and testing of equipment and supplies, but careful monitoring and carrying out preventa-tive steps will limit the risk of hemolysis. Rapid intervention in the event of hemolysis will decrease the risk to patients. Prevention includes proper checking of all systems and water supply prior to and during patient treatments. Regular preventative maintenance on machines per manufacturer's guidelines is needed to make sure all machine components are functioning properly. Hypertonic saline solutions to treat low blood pressure should be administered slowly, and can be diluted with normal saline before administration to help prevent hemolysis. Checking medications labels in accordance with the five rights of medication administration can make sure that sterile water is not administered inadvertently. Pre-pump arterial pressures should be monitored frequently, and adjustments made if the pressure exceeds -250. Any copper piping should be removed and replaced, and charcoal filtration of the water supply should be done to remove chlorine and chloramines. Verification and documentation of absence of chemicals should be performed prior to every dialysis treatment. The patient bloodlines should be assessed for color and clarity with every vital sign check to make sure there have been no changes that could indicate hemolysis.

Rapid intervention is key if hemolysis is suspected. If it is suspected, dialysis should be stopped immediately without returning the blood to the patient. Blood should not be returned because it could contain the offending agent, and reinfusion of the patient's blood could worsen the situation. Also, the amount of potassium in the blood could be harmful to the patient; and as the bloodlines hold one unit or less, the loss of this small amount of blood is not as detrimental as continuing to expose the patient to the offending agent. Vital signs should be monitored continuously, and if cardiac monitoring is available this should initiated. Oxygen should be administered, and lab studies for hemoglobin, hematocrit, and electrolytes should be drawn. Normal saline can be used to replace the volume of blood lost or to treat low blood pressure. The physician should be notified, and EMS initiated if indicated. In most cases the bloodlines should be saved for testing to determine the source of the hemolysis. If the hemolysis is isolated to one patient most testing will include only this patient. The machine in use should be pulled from use and tagged as out of service until the biomedical technician can perform a full check on the machine. If the suspected agent is the bloodlines, then the entire lot of bloodlines should be checked. Samples of dialysate may be tested as well. If the hemolysis is more widespread and includes more than one patient, then full testing of all machines, bloodlines, and water delivery systems may need to be done.

In August 1987 an outpatient dialysis center made changes to its water system but did not change the pre-treatment portion that would remove chlorine and chloramines from the water supply. During the following three weeks at least 100 patients were exposed to chloramines-contaminated dialysate. At least 41 patients required transfusions to treat hemolytic anemia. There were no deaths, but between the months of October 1987 and March 1988 there were 12 patient deaths, which was an increase over the facility's usual death rates.[21] Following this, the FDA issued a safety alert to all dialysis facilities.[22]

Water must be tested for chlorine and chloramines prior to each dialysis shift. Each facility should have in place policies and procedures for testing the water, and a protocol to follow if the chlorine level is above the acceptable maximum level. Any staff member who performs water testing should be trained, and documentation of training should be present.

In May 1998 at least 30 patients in three states developed hemolysis while dialyzing in outpatient facilities, with two patient deaths resulting. Investigation implicated bloodlines that had a narrowing of the aperture through which blood flowed during treatment. This caused mechanical hemolysis as the blood cells were damaged as they moved past the narrowing. On May 25, 1998 the manufacturer issued a voluntary recall of specific lots. On June 10, 1998 two additional deaths were reported and the recall was expanded. The CDC asked that any episode of hemolysis using the affected brand of blood tubing be reported. In July 2009 following an inspection of a plant in Italy that manufactures the same blood tubing affected in 1998, a warning letter was issued by the FDA. Failure to test the device was noted. The warning letter comments on failure to report to the FDA that the manufacturer became aware of a device having caused or contributed to a death from mechanical hemolysis. This cites that the patient suffered hemolysis that required treatment with antibiotics and transfusion of six units of blood cells; however the patient continued to suffer hemolysis, ultimately leading to death (FDA).[23]

b. Pyrogenic reactions

This complication is caused by exposure to infectious agents. This can be from an infection that the patient has acquired or as a result of pyrogens in the dialysis system. Pyrogen simply means fever causing. While bacteria can be present in the dialysis system, the most common offender is known as endotoxin. This is a byproduct of bacteria breakdown and is highly toxic to humans. It can be found in the dialysate, reprocessed dialyzers, or the water circuit supplying the dialysis machines. Signs and symptoms can include the patient feeling suddenly cold after dialysis starts, shaking chills with temperature elevations, fever, and low blood pressure. If the fever is a result of pyrogens from the dialysis system the symptoms usually begin within the first hour of dialysis treatment.

Prevention begins with proper water treatment, including proper techniques for cleaning and disinfecting the water system, dialyzers, and equipment. The frequency of water system and dialysis machine disinfection is defined in policy and procedures, usually based upon manufacturer recommendations. Water systems are required to be cultured and tested on periodic bases to determine if any bacterial growth is present. Machines and any water storage tanks or dialysate mixing tanks must be cultured. The American Association for Medical Instrumentation sets the limits for bacterial growth and sets recommendations for actions when bacterial growth is present. The amount of time the disinfectant must be present is defined as well. Dialyzers that have been reprocessed have a minimum amount of time the disinfectant must be present before they can be used, and there is an expiration date based upon the type of sterilant used. Dialysate solutions have expiration times as well, so it is imperative that all open solution containers be labeled with the date and time they were opened. All concentrate containers must be cleaned and disinfected properly to prevent bacterial growth.

Treatment includes assessing for the source of the infection. If it is limited to one patient then, following intervention with the patient, the machine should be pulled for culturing. The bloodlines and dialyzer must be saved for culturing. The patient should have blood cultures drawn; however blood cultures are typically negative in pyrogen reactions because the offending agent is the byproduct of bacteria breakdown, so no live bacteria is present to grow in the culture. A positive blood culture usually indicates that either the patient presented with infection, or that there was a gross contamination of the supplies while preparing the dialysis machine. Another cause of positive blood cultures in a reprocessed dialyzer can be that the dialyzer was not reprocessed adequately, leading to bacterial growth. Water should be cultured before it enters the dialysis machine and at points throughout the entire water system, especially if more than one patient is affected. This will help identify the actual site of bacterial or endotoxin colonization. Dialysate from the containers or supply should be cultured, along with a sample from the dialyzer. Blood from the dialyzer and the blood tubing should be collected for culture. Medications to reduce a fever should be administered, along with any indicated antibiotics as ordered. The physician will be notified, and if necessary the patient should be transferred to the hospital for treatment.

c. Dialyzer reactions

A reaction to a dialyzer can occur because the dialyzer is a synthetic material. Typically reactions occur early in the onset of treatment, and the risk of reaction is elevated with use of a new dialyzer. Reactions can be either due to first use syndrome, or anaphylactic. In a first use syndrome the body's immune system is activated by exposure to the dialyzer membrane. This usually occurs with cellulose-based membranes. Signs and symptoms occur usually within the first 15 minutes of treatment, and are seen as back pain, chest pain, and low blood pressure. These reactions can be prevented by using a synthetic membrane, or by performing dialyzer reuse. Treatment is based upon the symptoms and includes stopping the dialysis treatment without returning the blood, and infusing normal saline for blood pressure support. Anaphylactic reactions are life-threatening reactions. The patient can be hypersensitive to either the dialyzer or sterilant. It is more likely to occur with dialyzers made with Cuprophane® membranes, which are rare. Some patients who are taking ACE inhibitor blood pressure medications can react more often with some dialyzer membranes. This can also occur with some medications, most often with iron preparations. Signs and symptoms include acute constriction of the bronchioles seen as severe wheezing, shortness of breath, feeling uneasy, agitation and chest tightness, coughing, itching, facial swelling or flushing, and low blood pressure or elevated blood pressure. This also usually occurs within the first 15 minutes of treatment or administration of the offending medication. If the dialyzer is suspected, treatment should be stopped without return of the blood to the patient. If a medication is suspected and there has been enough time for the medication to completely be returned to the patient then treatment can be stopped and the blood returned to the patient. If the reaction is due to a continuing infusion of a medication, such as an antibiotic, then the medication infusion should be stopped. Epinephrine or IV Solu-Cortef for anaphylaxis may be indicated. Benadryl can be administered as well, and oxygen for respiratory support. Administration of IV fluid to support blood pressure may be warranted. The physician should be notified and any allergies documented in the patient's medical record.

In *John Ross v. Nebraska Medical Center*, the decedent went for a regular outpatient hemodialysis treatment. Briefly after the treatment started he experienced shortness of breath, lost consciousness, and went into cardiac arrest. Emergency measures were started, including transport to the hospital where vital signs were reestablished; however he remained in a coma for approximately ten days before he died. The plaintiff claimed the decedent had a dialyzer reaction and that the clinic staff was negligent in failing to perform a proper examination prior to administering dialysis. The plaintiff also claimed failure to properly respond to the allergic reaction when it developed. The defendants denied negligence and noted the decedent was an asthmatic whose inhaler was empty when symptoms first appeared. The verdict was for the defense.[24]

In this case details reported are scant, but an allegation of failure to properly assess the decedent was made. This could possibly include failure to properly identify the dialyzer prior to dialysis treatment. If the dialyzer were a reprocessed dialyzer, the assessment should include determining that all the sterilant has been removed from the dialyzer prior to start of treatment. Review of the medical records for the start of symptoms and when the first intervention was made would be appropriate. It would also be important to review what measures were taken, and at what time, in regards to recognizing and treating a suspected allergic reaction of any type.

14.7 Summary

It is clear that great potential for dialysis malpractice cases exists. Complications from dialysis treatments, while not unexpected given the nature of dialysis, can be reduced and avoided by careful treatment preparation and delivery, as well as with close monitoring of patient response to dialysis care. Quick intervention in the event of a complication can reduce the risk of injury a patient may sustain. Standards of care can be easily identified in malpractice cases. Documentation in dialysis facilities may be weak due to the rote and routine nature of dialysis care. Careful evaluation of documentation is required.

Endnotes

1. American Nephrology Nurses' Association. *Core curriculum for nephrology nurses* Lancaster, L. (ed.). Fourth Edition. Pitman, NJ: Anthony J. Jannetti, Inc., 2001. P. 257-258.

2. National Kidney Foundation. "Kidney Disease Outcomes Quality Initiative Guidelines and Commentaries, 2006" http://www.kidney.org/professionals/KDOQI/guidelines_ckd/toc.htm.

3. *Id.*

4. Waeleghem, J.V., et al., "Venous needle dislodgement: How to minimize the risks," *Journal of Renal Care*, 2008. p. 166.

5. *Id.*

6. See note 1, p. 273.

7. American Nephrology Nurses' Association. *Nephrology nursing standards of practice and guidelines for care*, Fifth Edition. Pitman, MJ: Anthony J. Jannetti, Inc., 2005. p. 275.

8. See note 4. p. 164-164.

9. Federal Register Vol. 73, No. 73/Tuesday, April 15, 2008/Rules and Regulations p. 20482 to 20483.

10. See note 7. p. 3-4.

11. *Id.* p. 4.

12. *Id.* p. 7-16.

13. See note 2.

14. Centers for Disease Control and Prevention. "Recommendations for preventing transmission of infections among chronic hemodialysis patients." *MMWR* (April 27, 2001).

15. Federal Register Vol. 73, No. 73/Tuesday, April 15, 2008/Rules and Regulations p. 20482 to 20483.

16. *Id.*

17. *Id.*

18. See note 10. p. 33-51.

19. See note 14.

20. See note 4. p. 165.

21. Arduino, M.J., "CDC investigation of noninfectious outbreaks of adverse events in hemodialysis facilities, 1979-1999," *Seminars in Dialysis*, March – April (2000). p. 87.

22. U.S. Food and Drug Administration. "FDA safety alert: Chloramine contamination of hemodialysis water supplies," February 19, 1988.

23. U.S. Food and Drug Administration. "Warning letter to Gambro Daseo S.p.A. Bloodline Division," July 2, 2009.

24. Laska, L. (ed), "Failure to properly examine man prior to dialysis and failure to respond to distress during dialysis," *Medical Malpractice Verdicts, Settlements and Experts*, October, 2009, p. 21.

Chapter 15

Home Healthcare Nursing Malpractice Issues

Nanette Sulik, MSN, RN, CSN, Valerie V. Parisi, RN, CRRN, CLCP, Barbara Mladenetz Weber Berry, MSN, RN, and Mindy Cohen, RN, MSN

Synopsis
15.1 Introduction
15.2 What Is Home Care?
15.3 Range of Services Offered in the Home Care Setting
    A. Providers
    B. Settings
    C. Types of Care
    D. Scope of Practice
    E. Managed Care Issues
15.4 Home Care Standards
    A. American Nurses Association: Scope and Standards of Home
        Health Nursing Practice
    B. Specialty Nursing Standards
    C. Agency-Defined Standards
    D. Centers for Medicare and Medicaid Services (CMS)
    E. Agency for Healthcare Research and Quality (AHRQ)
    F. The Joint Commission
        1. Employee hiring
        2. Employee competence
        3. Employee education
        4. Patient care
        5. Leadership
        6. Ethical issues
    G. Payors
15.5 Anatomy of the Home Care Record
    A. Admission
    B. Assessment
    C. Plan of Treatment and Physician's Orders
    D. Nursing Care Plan
    E. Progress Notes
    F. Flow Sheets
    G. Medication Administration Record (MAR)
    H. Therapies
    I. Case Management
    J. Laboratory Results
    K. Miscellaneous
    L. OASIS
15.6 Risks in Home Care
    A. Inadequate Communication Between Nurses
    B. Inadequate Planning and Care Implementation Among
        Disciplines
    C. Imprecise Communication Between the Physician and Nurse
    D. Improper Provision of Specialized Services
    E. Inadequate Coordination Among Providers of Care
    F. Potential for Staff Dishonesty
    G. Patient Safety
    H. Failure to Recognize Changes in the Patient's Condition
    I. Patient Abandonment

15.7 Defense Strategies
    A. Documentation
    B. Standard of Care Issues
    C. Noncompliance
    D. Agency Issues
15.8 Case Studies
    A. Home Care Negligence Case Study 1
    B. Home Care Negligence Case Study 2
    C. Home Care Negligence Case Study 3
    D. Home Care Negligence Case Study 4
15.9 Case Screening
    A. Appropriateness of the Care
    B. Liability of the Agency
        1. Hiring and employee competence
        2. Employee supervision functions
        3. Clinical case supervision
        4. Compliance with local and national standards
    C. Identification of Potential Defendants
        1. The home care agency
        2. Other agencies
        3. Payors
    D. Recommendations for Reviewing the Home Care Record
15.10 Summary
Endnotes

15.1 Introduction

Home healthcare nursing is as old as nursing itself, yet in the age of shortened hospital stays and managed care, more patients are dependent on care in the home. Patients are now discharged home from the hospital "sicker and quicker," and demographically, with the baby boomer generation reaching retirement, many of these patients have risks from advancing age and chronic disease. This results in the need for experienced nurses with clinical proficiency to provide expert nursing care. The advent of mandatory OASIS (Outcome and Assessment Information Set) data collection requirements (for determination of reimbursement and quality measures) in 1999 has added more pressures to overburdened nurses. Home care nursing is challenged to continue providing quality service with increasingly limited resources. These new pressures have caused greater concern about quality care and patient safety as more and more patients receive care at home.

Visiting nurse agencies (VNAs) have been around since the 1800s, providing care for those at home during the tuberculosis epidemic. Modern home care was born with the advent of Medicare in the 1960s. A system was established for intermittent, skilled nursing visits specific to a diagnosis or condition. These visits were usually in response to discharge from the hospital after a diagnosis of diabetes or stroke. The 1980s brought more changes as DRGs (diagnosis-related groups) determined the number of days that a Medicare patient could stay in the hospital. At the same time, high-tech pediatric home care has become available to high-risk infants, as well as antenatal care and monitoring to manage high risk pregnancies. Greater home patient acuity is due to earlier discharge from the hospital, additional sick patients at home, and the introduction of high-tech procedures such as IV infusion, total parenteral nutrition, dialysis, and ventilators at home. The use of this equipment in the home carries greater risks of injury to patients in an environment without the resources of a hospital and imposes increased responsibility upon home care nurses for patient and family education.

Home care became a growth industry through the 1980s and 1990s. The VNAs were joined by private agencies in providing high-tech care at home. Patients preferred to be at home, surrounded by loved ones. Home management presented a monetary savings compared to the cost of hospitalization. Hospice programs flourished as terminally ill patients chose to die at home rather than in an impersonal hospital setting. Home care agencies expanded to operate their own medical equipment divisions and pharmacies, thus widening the services they could provide. Home care was a win-win situation for both patients and the healthcare system.

In the 1990s many home healthcare agencies struggled to survive investigations of fraud, abuse, and cuts in funding at a time when the chronically ill, disabled, and elderly required services more than ever. With tighter control of healthcare spending, the Medicare program continues to limit reimbursement, and agencies are faced with curtailing benefits to ensure long-term survival. This current practice environment has led to nurses working with larger caseloads, leading to a greater potential for error.

Home care nursing is conducted under a diverse set of circumstances. This chapter outlines types of home healthcare; clinical and administrative standards of home care; theories of liability in home care, including case samples to illustrate those areas of liability; and common defenses, including documentation issues in home care today. Guidelines for effective case screening are provided. This chapter also assists the attorney in locating important documents in the chart that will illustrate whether or not home care standards have been violated. The role of the changing practice

milieu is also explained in the context of how this environment contributes to nursing liability.

15.2 What Is Home Care?

Home care has broad applications. It implies "care service" in the home setting and could refer to professional or non-professional services. Professionals may include registered and licensed practical nurses; physical, speech, respiratory and occupational therapists; social workers; nutritionists; and spiritual counselors. Paraprofessionals are primarily home health aides and therapy assistants; the latter are authorized in some states to work in home care under the supervision of professional therapists.

There is also a distinction within the industry that separates certified and non-certified agencies. A certified organization has the ability to obtain reimbursement from Medicare, the federally sponsored healthcare program for citizens aged 65 years and older. These agencies may bill their regional Medicare insurance intermediary directly for services they provide to clients. This privilege does not come easily. Medicare-certified agencies are heavily regulated and must meet the federal government's "Conditions of Participation" for the Medicare program and state requirements for licensure as home health agencies. Many voluntarily meet national accreditation standards with either The Joint Commission or Community Health Accreditation Programs (CHAP). Medicare services are intermittent or brief in duration and generally eligible to the client who demonstrates a potential for rehabilitation. A chronic condition usually does not support eligibility for Medicare services. Hospice care is the exception to this rule. Clients may elect to participate in the Medicare hospice benefit if they have less than six months of life expectancy and are no longer seeking curative treatment.

Non-certified agencies are less regulated. Each state determines the type of license they need for operation. For some states, a license through the state's department of consumer affairs is required to provide healthcare staffing. These agencies may provide nurses or aides to perform brief, intermittent visits to the home or private duty arrangements where a client may secure round-the-clock assistance. They charge the insurance company or the client privately, but are unable to bill Medicare.

TIP: There are also home health staffing registries that may operate with a business license and merely link a clinician with a client for a finder's fee and waive responsibility for the actions of the clinician. These agencies should at minimum screen staff for current licensure, require a criminal background check, and malpractice insurance if applicable.

Table 15.1
Continuum of Home Healthcare Services

Chronic	Acute	Specialty	High Technological
• Live-In Aides	• Skilled Nursing	• Palliative and Hospice Care	• Infusion Therapy
• Personal Care	• Rehabilitation	• Traditional	• Antibiotics
• Companions	• Physical Therapy	• Pediatric	• Chemotherapy
• Homemakers	• Occupational Therapy	• Inpatient/Respite	• Hydration
• Adult Day Care	• Speech Therapy	• Bereavement	• Pain Management
• Case Management	• Restorative Nursing	• Pediatrics and Neonatal	• Enteral Feedings
	• Medical Social Work	• High Risk Antepartum	• Ventilator Care
	• Home Health Aides	• Private Duty Nursing	• Telemonitoring (Pacemaker)
	• Nutrition	• Mental Health	• Apnea Monitoring
	• Laboratory Tests (in home)	• Continence Programs	• Photo Therapy
	• Medical Supplies and Equipment	• Wound Care	• Cardiac Monitoring
	• Central Intake and Case Management		• EKGs
			• X-Rays
			• Respiratory Therapy

Nearly 25 percent of home care agencies are voluntary non-profit, 65 percent are proprietary and 10 percent are government-based.[1]

There is a range of services included under the umbrella of home care. Table 15.1, *Continuum of Home Healthcare Services*, depicts five main categories in this area of specialization: chronic, outreach/preventative, acute, specialty, and high technological care. Within each domain, the potential for litigation exists, an example of which is provided in each category.

- A client receiving *chronic* care may sue because a live-in aide was negligent in fulfilling his duties and caused the client to sustain a fall resulting in injury.
- An *acute* care client may pursue litigation because a home physical therapist neglected to follow protocol prescribed by the orthopedic physician resulting in further injury.
- A *specialty* care client resorts to legal action because the visiting nurse did not meet the standards of care for a wound procedure or failed to report a significant change to a physician. The client's condition deteriorated as a result of this negligence.
- Finally, a client requiring *high technological* home health services may seek legal recourse for an infection at the site of infusion therapy, acquired as a result of the nurse's poor technique.

The environment differentiates this specialty from others in health care. Providing services in a client's home is much different than in an institutional setting. It is unlikely there will be other healthcare staff present as witnesses. Joint visits are made, but that is the exception. The importance of documentation is paramount. The chart is the core piece of evidence that demonstrates the clinicians' actions.

This chapter emphasizes the importance of documentation in home care and how the legal professional may analyze the areas commonly demonstrating documentation deficiencies.

Home care is a non-dominant sector of the healthcare arena; however, industry trends show that more consumers are choosing home care.

Home health spending growth is projected to climb 7.8 percentage points in 2014, making it the fastest-growing service in health care. This increase is chiefly driven by faster growth in Medicaid spending on this sector. Medicare spending for home health increased 6.8 percent in 2010. Total growth is expected to average 7.6 percent per year from 2007 through 2016, with the strongest growth coming from Medicaid. These accelerations reflect states' continuing efforts to use home health care and home and community-based services to provide long-term care to Medicaid recipients as substitutes for traditional institutional services.[2]

Today, an individual requiring several weeks of intravenous therapy could more easily be treated at home instead of the hospital, with less cost and less risk of exposure to infectious organisms. As the population ages, health issues increase which impact the need for home care services. Although home care is not an area of highest risk, with increased growth, lawsuits will rise concomitantly. The following section details the range of services provided in the home care setting today.

15.3 Range of Services Offered in the Home Care Setting
A. Providers

The diversity of home care providers, settings and services has increased dramatically in recent years. Home care providers may include the companion, aide, licensed practical nurse, registered nurse, physician, medical equipment supplier, pharmacist, rehabilitation therapist (physical, occupational and speech therapists), social worker, psychologist, nutritionist, case manager and insurance carrier. Below is a discussion of several roles unique to home care providers.

1. Companion: provides basic housekeeping and companionship services to the patient intended to maintain a healthy, orderly living environment.

2. Home health aide: assists patients with routine activities of daily living (feeding, personal hygiene, dressing, mobility) under the direct supervision of a licensed registered nurse, social worker or physical therapist. These duties are considered custodial—not skilled—care. Under the Medicare program, a patient requiring skilled nursing care is eligible for a home health aide who works under the direct supervision of the licensed registered nurse to perform unskilled services. The home health agency should define, in writing, any treatments the aide may administer. These responsibilities must conform to the scope of practice for an aide. The agency cannot ask the aide to perform functions only registered nurses are permitted to do (e.g., catheterize a patient). Common aide duties include taking the patient's temperature, pulse and respiratory rate. In some states, home health aides cannot take a patient's blood pressure. Examples of additional responsibilities may include bathing, dressing, feeding, caring for the bladder catheter and certain equipment in the home and using a Hoyer lift (used to move large or difficult-to-move patients from one location to another). Certified home health aides receive formal training and evaluation in safe performance of these skills.

TIP: The companion does not perform duties or procedures associated with personal care. The home health aide does not administer medication. Limitations on the duties of the home health aide are defined by each state's Nurse Practice Act.

---

3. Generalist and specialist nurses: provide care in the home and responsibilities include patient teaching, physical assessment, formulating and performing activities within the nursing care plan, collaborating with other disciplines, monitoring use of equipment and supervising ancillary personnel such as home health aides or licensed practical nurses.

The specialist nurse works as a consultant to the generalist in developing the care plan for certain patient populations. An example of this is the use of an enterostomal therapy nurse to work with the primary care nurse in developing wound care strategies. Another example is the use of oncology and cardiac teams to develop clinical pathways and consult with the generalist staff in providing care to patients with those diagnoses. Specialist nurses have relevant clinical experience in their specialty as well as certifications in their field.

4. Rehabilitation therapist: serves in one of two capacities. The therapist may perform an initial evaluation and develop a home program implemented by the patient, family, or nursing staff. Under this scenario, periodic evaluation by the therapist may be needed. Alternately, the patient may require ongoing therapy from a rehabilitation specialist for a given period of time. A supplemental home program may be given depending on the patient's need. In cases where rehabilitation therapy is needed, but skilled nursing is not required, the therapist can also supervise services of a certified home health aide.

5. Clinical supervisor: is a registered nurse responsible for assessing, planning, organizing, directing, coordinating, and evaluating the care of patients. For example, when a patient is going to have a peripheral intravenous line (in the arm) changed to a central line (into a major vein in the chest), the clinical supervisor may call a meeting with the patient, family, nurse, medical equipment company, and pharmacist to prepare for changes necessary for a smooth transition. Additionally, the clinical supervisor is usually responsible for orienting, supervising, and evaluating employees providing home care services to patients.

6. Case manager: is usually a registered nurse (but can also be a physical therapist or social worker if skilled nursing is not indicated) responsible for coordinating care within the agency and between providers. In some agencies, a clinical supervisor may assume this role. The case manager is usually responsible for interacting with the patient's insurance carrier.

7. Physician: must order and review the plan of care and certify that it is appropriate and current based on assessment data provided by the case manager.

8. Payor or insurance provider: is a significant player in the patient care team. Initial, ongoing, or additional reimbursement for services must be approved by the payor.

B. Settings

The home healthcare setting is usually the patient's house. However, the recent proliferation of alternative living arrangements broadens the location of the home. Home care may be provided in any location in which a patient resides, which includes a community living house, a vacation home, or an assisted living facility. Some home health agencies subcontract nursing aides to assisted living and long-term-care facilities.

C. Types of Care

Home care services range from simple assistance with household or personal care to complex technical care. Patients across the lifespan can be cared for in their homes. Jaundiced infants are discharged from the hospital and given phototherapy at home. A high-risk obstetric patient can be managed at home with uterine monitoring. Dialysis, chemotherapy, mental health visits or hospice care at end of life can all be performed at home. Ventilators, cardiac monitors, infusion pumps, oxygen tanks and compressors, and pulse oximeters (oxygen monitoring) are just a few pieces of technical equipment used in providing home care services.

The two predominant methods for providing home care are visits and shifts. A visit is when a provider goes to the patient's home for a brief period to perform an assessment, provide patient education or administer a treatment. Shifts are 4 to 12 hour periods when a clinical staff member (RN, LPN, home health aide) provides care to a patient in the home. Patients cared for on shifts are typically those on ventilators or those with significant neurological or respiratory needs. Increasingly, home health aides work shifts for home care patients with simpler needs, such as a patient recovering from a total joint replacement procedure. Home care in shifts is provided to both children and adults.

D. Scope of Practice

Contracting refers to any working agreement that is renegotiable. The client signs a contract with the agency to accept treatment prior to opening the case. Contracting allows the client and family to participate with the healthcare team to set goals. This facilitates the effectiveness of treatment plans and the promotion of self-care. See Table 15.2 for scope of practice by discipline.

E. Managed Care Issues

Medicare-certified home healthcare agencies, in order to remain competitive when payments by Medicare have been decreased, may cut back on full-time nursing staff leaving patients in the care of per diem staff or may rotate staff to provide coverage. Per diem staff are not full-time employees, and may or may not see the same patients each time they work. The nurse's care can be fragmented if she does not know the patient. Managed care has also brought about changes resulting in fewer nursing visits. This leaves the home health nurse and agency vulnerable to closing a case too soon if the payor refuses reimbursement. This can place the nurse in the predicament of either risking patient abandonment, or losing compensation every time the required nursing care is denied payment. Some agencies may choose to offer non-reimbursed visits for the purpose of decreasing liability. Example: the HMO declines to authorize additional visits for wound care. The agency may elect to make additional non-reimbursed visits in order to teach wound care, signs and symptoms of infection, when to call the physician, and so on, especially if appealing the HMO to change an initial decision.

Agencies are also vulnerable to difficulty finding qualified nursing assistants and home health aides to care for increasingly fragile, elderly, and disabled populations. These trends leave less-qualified staff personnel caring for more complex patients.

A discussion of Medicare and the Centers for Medicare and Medicaid Services would be incomplete without mentioning the effects of prospective payment on the reimbursement of home care services for Medicare-certified agencies. Payments are based on diagnosis-related groupings, just as hospitals are reimbursed. This requires home care nurses to more accurately collect data to reflect patient acuity. Home care nurses currently use a tool called OASIS to document and code all patient care data so the proper reimbursement is received. This form is a standardized comprehensive assessment tool required by CMS. OASIS is discussed further in this chapter.

TIP: Since the OASIS form is used for initial patient assessments and ongoing periodic documentation of the patient care plan, the attorney may want to request it because it provides data-driven quality indicators of the care received and assessments performed.

Table 15.2
Responsibilities of Each Discipline

- **Nursing:** Practice responsibilities of the home care nurse include direct and indirect care. Direct care includes physical aspects of nursing care and personal interactions. Skilled nursing care is covered by Medicare and other third-party payers. Examples of skilled nursing services include: assessing and evaluating a client's health condition; administering treatments, rehabilitative exercises, medication administration and teaching, catheter insertion, colostomy irrigation, and wound care. Direct care also includes teaching the client and family to safely give general care, treatments, therapies, and medications when indicated.
  Indirect care activities are those that a nurse does on behalf of clients to coordinate care. Examples include: documentation of care, consulting with other nurses and health care providers, and multidisciplinary care conferences.

- **Medicine:** Physician practice responsibilities in home care are to order care. Every client under Medicare home care programs must be under the current care of a doctor of medicine, podiatry, or osteopathy. The physician must certify that a medical problem exists and certify a plan of treatment for the home health agency before care is provided to the client. The plan must be re-certified periodically and notification of changes in condition must be promptly responded to.

- **Respiratory Therapy:** The respiratory therapist (RT) supervises the initiation of oxygen therapy and ventilators as ordered, assesses respiratory status and response to treatment, and educates patients, families and other caregivers on safe use and care of equipment.

- **Physical Therapy:** The physical therapist (PT) provides treatment to restore and maintain strength and function for clients in the home and educates patients and caregivers on safety to prevent further injury.

- **Occupational Therapy:** The occupational therapist (OT) teaches clients to develop and maintain the abilities to perform activities of daily living in their home. The focus of treatment mainly involves the client's upper extremities to restore muscle strength and mobility and achieve an optimal level of functioning.

- **Speech Therapy:** The speech pathologist or speech therapist (ST) works to assist people with communication problems related to speech, language, or hearing.

- **Social Work:** Social workers assist clients and families to deal with social, emotional, and environmental factors that adversely affect their well-being by identifying and referring clients to appropriate community resources.

- **Certified Home Health Aide:** The certified home health aide assists clients who have lost some independence in activities of daily living by assisting with personal hygiene and activities. Additional duties may include light housekeeping, laundry, meal preparation, and shopping. The home health nurse or physical therapist directly supervises the home health aide.

- **Homemakers and Companions:** Homemakers or companions are not trained in assisting clients with personal care, but can assist with home management tasks such as housekeeping, shopping, laundry, and meal preparation.

1. Knowledge of Medicare and managed care rules
2. Interpersonal skills
3. Flexibility
4. Reliable car
5. Case management skills
6. Clinical skills and judgment
7. Self-directed
8. Desire to learn new skills
9. Knowledge and acceptance of cultural differences
10. Sense of humor
11. Assessment skill competence

Figure 15.1 Attributes of the Effective Home Healthcare Nurse

15.4 Home Care Standards

A. American Nurses Association: Scope and Standards of Home Health Nursing Practice

Various standards affect home health care. The American Nurses Association initially developed standards for home healthcare nurses most recently revised in 1999. A typical home care nurse is considered a "jack-of-all-trades." In an average day, the home care nurse can see six patients, ranging from those with terminal cancer to an infected diabetic foot ulcer. To provide safe and effective care, the home care nurse should have the attributes shown in Figure 15.1.

B. Specialty Nursing Standards

Specialist nurses must operate within the standards of their specialty. A specialist nurse in the home care setting would be held to a higher standard due to advanced clinical expertise and certifications. These standards are defined by the certifying specialty nursing organizations. An example of specialty standards would be the standards of the Intravenous Nursing Society, which are comprehensive and apply to home infusion therapy. Peripherally inserted central catheter (PICC) lines are used in the home care setting for the administration of medications such as antibiotics, chemotherapy, and cardiac drugs. A patient at home on a dobutamine (IV cardiac drug) drip should be cared for by a nurse with a critical care certification. Enterostomal therapy nurses are certified and have had advanced courses in the care of wounds and ostomies. A nurse on the high-risk infant care team doing developmental assessments might be a pediatric nurse practitioner. All standards of these sub-specialties would apply to care provided in the home.

C. Agency-Defined Standards

Individual agencies may also have their own standards as evidenced by such documentation as disease-specific clinical pathways, nursing care plans, and policies and procedures. These plans specify the assessment measures the nurse must perform in the home and the teaching that should be provided. For example, blood pressure measurements in three planes (sitting, in both arms, and standing) are expected on admission and in two planes (sitting and standing) on all cardiovascular patients to look for orthostatic changes in blood pressure which could result in dizziness and falls. Random blood sugar measurements are expected to be performed on diabetic patients. Teaching about each disease process is outlined in the plan and checked off when accomplished, with documentation of the patient's understanding and return demonstration of those instructions. Individual agency standards are developed in response to all licensing, regulatory, and accrediting bodies.

D. Centers for Medicare and Medicaid Services (CMS)

Generalist nurses practice under their state Nurse Practice Act as well as Centers for Medicare and Medicaid Services and ANA guidelines. An example of CMS guidelines is the requirement for an in-home plan by the skilled nurse to direct the actions of the aide in personal care duties. The RN (or in some cases, the therapist) must make an on-site visit no less than every two weeks to a patient receiving home health aide services. Another CMS guideline is the requirement for communication between the RN and other team members such as the physical therapist, occupational therapist, speech therapist, and social worker to ensure their efforts are coordinated effectively and to support the objectives outlined in the standard of care.

   CMS guidelines are the gold standard that many insurance providers require of participating agencies. The Centers for Medicare and Medicaid Services defines skilled nursing services as those reasonable and necessary to the treatment of the beneficiary's illness or injury and requiring the skills of a registered nurse, or licensed practical nurse supervised by a registered nurse.[3] The patient must be homebound, and the service must be intermittent and limited by the number of hours and length of time the care can be delivered. Examples of skilled nursing care include skilled assessment and observation, Foley catheter care, tube feedings, wound care, management of the skilled nursing care plan, and patient teaching activities. Skilled nursing care does not include pouring medications, homemaker services, and personal care. Medicare does not reimburse for continuous nursing care over a 24-hour period. In 2006, Medicare funded 37 percent of home care expenditures, and Medicaid funded 19 percent; together they covered 56 percent of all home care costs.[4]

E. Agency for Healthcare Research and Quality (AHRQ)

In addition to CMS, the federal government, through the Agency for Healthcare Research and Quality, has developed standards that affect home care, including guidelines for acute pain, cancer pain, and the treatment and prevention of pressure ulcers.

TIP: The federal government has developed many policies affecting home health care. A good place to search for these policies is at the National Guidelines Clearinghouse found at www.guidelines.gov.

F. The Joint Commission

The Joint Commission (formerly the Joint Commission on Accreditation of Healthcare Organizations) offers accreditation to home care agencies on a voluntary basis. Although accreditation is a voluntary process, it is industry practice to achieve this accreditation. There are over 6,000 accredited home care agencies in the United States.

The following general standards are common industry practices in home care and are in compliance with The Joint Commission standards. This review is not exhaustive, but rather highlights those areas at greatest risk for litigation. "Employee" refers to the individuals providing care to the patients of an agency, regardless of whether they are employees or subcontractors.

1. Employee hiring

a.	Although not all states require a criminal background check and child-abuse clearance, it is quickly becoming a common industry practice to perform these screenings on all employees, particularly unlicensed personnel. The employee must sign an authorization form allowing the agency to perform these investigations. In some states, a criminal background check is required for home health aide certification or licensing of RNs and LPNs.

TIP: Criminal clearance investigations have been in effect in other industries for quite some time. The tests are inexpensive and easy to perform.

b.	Agencies should obtain auto insurance information and Department of Motor Vehicle reports on all employees with driving responsibilities.

c.	It is common to verify the accuracy of information on the employment application, and that all licenses of licensed personnel are current and active.

2. Employee competence

a.	The job description defines the employee qualifications, duties, and health status of all levels of staff.

b.	Expected staff competencies are defined for all levels of clinical staff.

c.	Complete personnel files are maintained on all employees. Employee health files are kept separately from the general personnel file.

d.	The agency must maintain an adequate number of trained staff to meet the needs of the patients served.

e.	Appropriately trained supervisors must be available to supervise patients and employees. For example, an agency that serves high-risk obstetrics patients cannot use a cardiac nurse supervisor in the obstetrics program.

f.	Staff supervision and evaluation must include periodic evaluation of the employees while they are providing care in the patient's home.

g.	An agency must have a mechanism in place for evaluating employees subcontracted from another agency. An appropriate individual must conduct the evaluation. For example, when an agency subcontracts with physical therapists but does not have a physical therapy supervisor on staff, arrangements must be made to have one available for staff consultation and evaluation.

h.	On-call supervision must be available to staff after regular business hours.

i.	Employee review of policies, procedures and skills; and assessment of employee competence is conducted upon hiring, upon completion of orientation, and periodically according to agency policy.

j.	All employees are oriented to the agency, to their employee job description, and to each patient's care to whom they are assigned.

k.	The agency must verify current status of licenses.

3. Employee education

Employees should receive education on the following subjects:

a.	**Patient populations served**. It is essential the nursing staff keep current in their knowledge related to the patients for whom they provide care. Examples include disease management, medications and their side effects, and special needs related to the patient's age.

b. **Medical equipment**. Nurses must be prepared to manage all medical equipment in the home. Additionally, nurses must be able to use their knowledge to teach patients and their family members how to use the equipment safely. For each piece of equipment, the following issues should be covered in employee education: operation, electrical safety, mechanical safety, troubleshooting, maintenance, fire hazards, and infection control issues. Whenever new equipment is introduced, all nurses responsible for using the equipment should receive appropriate training. Once a nurse has been taught and supervised in how to use a piece of equipment, the home care nurse and supervisor should document what was taught and observed, followed by signatures of both.

c. **Home safety**. Lifting and transfer techniques and fire, electrical, and personal safety (e.g., traveling into unsafe neighborhoods) should be reviewed periodically.

d. **Infection control**. Managing and preventing infections is the responsibility of all home care nursing staff. It is the agency's task to educate staff on the storage and handling of body substances or hazardous waste, prevent the spread of infectious diseases, and report patient or employee infections.

e. **Reporting incidents**. Incident reporting is one important aspect of the home care performance improvement program (quality assurance). Nursing staff need to understand what the agency defines as an incident and how incidents are reported and documented. Accidents, injuries, and falls are typical examples of reportable incidents. Concerns regarding child or elder abuse are reportable to authorities.

4. Patient care

a. Patients are admitted based on admission criteria.

b. Assessments are performed on admission (within an agency-defined time frame) and reassessments are performed periodically as needed or as required by CMS.

c. Nurses are expected to identify special circumstances that trigger specific assessments, such as nutrition or pain, or reassessments, such as a change in the patient's physical or mental status.

d. Nurses perform care according to the physician's orders and accepted plans of care and standards.

e. Agencies must maintain an on-call system for patient emergencies.

f. Clinical consultation and supervision is available 24 hours a day for all home care providers.

g. The standard of care requires nurses to determine the patient's ability and willingness to provide self-care and the family's ability and willingness to assist.

h. Nurses will determine the patient's and family's ability and willingness to learn and will provide education accordingly.

i. All care rendered will require obtaining informed consent as well as special procedures which require their own consent (e.g., IV placement, indwelling catheter, and dialysis). As such, it is prudent for the nurse to document a discussion with the patient of the risks, benefits, and alternatives, as well as the right to refuse the treatment.

j. Home nurses need to recognize symptoms indicating possible abuse and neglect in patients of all ages and respond appropriately.

k. Nurses must be competent in the operation and troubleshooting of required equipment. The nurse should assure that the patient and family are adequately trained to manage patient equipment in the home.

l. Immediate replacement of malfunctioning rental equipment must be made available by the home care or durable medical equipment company. Many home care patients have their own medical equipment for use in their home. When this is the case, either the agency or patient must maintain a service contract with an equipment supplier to provide routine maintenance (according to manufacturer guidelines) and replacement if needed.

m. Standards of care require nurses to follow infection control procedures.

n. The agency is expected to verify licensure of the physicians managing their patients.

o. Agency policies must identify the time frame within which physicians must sign verbal orders.

p. Home care nurses must effectively communicate with all team members (e.g., physician, rehabilitation therapist, case manager).

q. The agency is expected to maintain a list of appropriate community resources and make these available to staff and patients when needed.

r. A mechanism is in place to exchange relevant information with appropriate individuals when a patient is referred, transferred, or discharged.

s. The agency and its employees must maintain the patient medical record.

5. Leadership

a. The agency must comply with local, state, and national regulatory agencies (Food and Drug Administration/FDA, Department of Transportation/DOT, Centers for Medicare and Medicaid Services/CMS, and Occupational Health and Safety Administration/OSHA), and so on.

b. Standards of care require the agency to plan, implement, and evaluate an agency-wide quality improvement program.

c. The agency is to maintain contractual agreements.

d. The home care nurse implements emergency-preparedness and fire-protection plans for the office location and the patient's home.

e. The home care agency implements a system for reporting, investigating, and responding to all incidents.

f. Sentinel events are identified, reported, analyzed immediately, and prevented. Examples of a sentinel event might include a feeding pump failure, which results in rapid infusion of fluids and death of a patient or a foot soak that results in burns to the patient's feet.

TIP: A sentinel event is an unexpected occurrence involving death or serious physical or psychological injury, or the risk thereof. "Serious injury" refers to the loss of limb or function. "The risk thereof" includes any variation for which a recurrence would carry a significant chance of a serious, adverse outcome.

---

6. Ethical issues

a. The statement of client rights and responsibilities must be signed by the patient on admission to the agency.

b. The agency should have policies on advance directives, withdrawing or withholding medical treatment, and "do not resuscitate" instructions.

c. Agencies should have an ethics committee available to assist patients and staff in the resolution of ethical issues (e.g., withdrawing medical treatment).

d. Clinical decisions should be based on identified patient needs regardless of compensation or financial risk to the agency.

e. Agencies must have a mechanism in place for decision making if an external source (e.g., payor or physician) denies payment or treatment.

f. Staff must maintain patient confidentiality.

g. The staff must encourage the active involvement of patients and their families in the patient's care as a patient safety strategy.

h. The home care agency will define and communicate the means by which patients and their families can report concerns about safety, and encourage them to do so. (This is a 2009 Joint Commission National Patient Safety Goal.)

See Figure 15.2 for homecare safety goals. (Refer to Chapter 4, *Patient Safety Initiatives*, in Volume I, for additional information on these goals.)

G. Payors

Payors or insurance carriers also use standards to determine "medical necessity" and what is reimbursable under a given plan. These are usually developed by medical directors on staff at the insurance company. It is often very difficult to acquire the written practice guidelines or standards used by payors to reimburse expenses for care. Case managers are usually the first-line workers at the insurance company to define covered expenses against standard care for a given problem or diagnosis. The medical director reviews all case manager decisions when these are challenged.

15.5 Anatomy of the Home Care Record

The medical record in home care is as diverse as the many types of agencies performing home health services. A certified agency must conform to federal, state, and accreditation, if chosen, standards. The home care medical record is organized by section, similar to the hospital record, although some documents will differ. All original records are kept at the agency's office. While each agency's records may be organized slightly differently, below is a description of general sections of a chart and the documents to be found in each section.

TIP: Every certified home health agency must periodically complete a standardized assessment tool, OASIS, on all Medicare and Medicaid clients.

A. Admission

Admission records include the referral form, all insurance documents including OASIS, the consent for treatment, advance directives, client rights and responsibilities, and discharge summary. The referral form can be a wonderful source of information for plaintiff and defense attorneys. It will contain information shared between the discharging institution and home care agency. This information describes

- *Reading back verbal orders.* When a physician gives a verbal order to a home healthcare provider, having that provider read it back will give both parties a chance to confirm accuracy.
- *Standardizing abbreviations* and avoiding those on the Do Not Use list such as cc or µg.
- *Correctly identifying the patient* and any specimen container in the patient's presence.
- Establishing and monitoring the timeliness of *reporting and receipt of critical tests* and critical results and values by the responsible licensed caregiver.
- *Monitoring anticoagulation therapy,* which poses risks to patients and often leads to adverse drug events due to complex dosing, requisite follow-up monitoring, and inconsistent [patient] compliance. The use of standardized practices for anticoagulation therapy that include [patient] involvement can reduce the risk of adverse drug events.
- Complying with the WHO or CDC *hand hygiene guidelines* and other best practices or evidence-based guidelines will reduce the transmission of infectious agents.
- *Evaluating the [patient's] risk for falls* and take action to reduce the risk of falling as well as the risk of injury, should a fall occur.
- *Reconciling prescriptions across the continuum of care,* so providers, patients, and their families have an accurate list of current medications. Communicate any changes to the patient's other providers.
- Identifying medications with look-alike and sound-alike names.
- Using a *standardized approach when handing off care* for a patient to another provider that ensures all pertinent information is relayed and allows sufficient time for the new caregiver to ask questions.[5]

Figure 15.2 2009 National Patient Safety Goals for Home Health Care to improve patient safety and communication among caregivers in a home health situation.

the patient's condition at the time of discharge from a hospital, which can then be compared with his condition while receiving home care. A Joint Commission National Patient Safety Goal focuses on the need to maintain an accurate list of medications across the continuum of care. This includes ensuring that current information about medications is reconciled and documented on admission of the patient to the home care agency.

B. Assessment

Initial nursing assessment forms along with reassessment forms will be found in this section. The initial nursing assessment provides the baseline for comparisons over time. If a patient has been injured while in the care of another agency, or prior to the home care referral, this form will help the attorney determine if the patient's condition worsened under the care of the home care nurse. There is more detailed information regarding the mandatory OASIS assessment later in this section.

C. Plan of Treatment and Physician's Orders

The plan of treatment (POT) outlines all care the patient is to receive. This document contains the physician's orders, similar to the section of orders in a hospital chart. It is renewed every 60 days. Updated POTs include any revisions to patient care (e.g., changes in medications or therapies) since the last POT. In addition to the POT, this section will also include subsequent physician's orders. In the home care setting, many physicians' orders will be verbal orders written down by a nurse since there is no physician in the home. The physician must sign all verbal orders within a specified period of time, often depending on the payor. This section of the record is particularly important in a case involving a lack of communication between a home healthcare nurse and the patient's physician.

D. Nursing Care Plan

This document may also be known as a plan of care or clinical pathway. The nursing care plan identifies nursing diagnoses or a patient's problem list, outlines the patient's goals (or expected outcomes), and defines treatments and education designed to help the patient meet these goals. This document is designed to be a road map that the patient follows on the road to recovery. The plan or pathway should be disease- or problem-specific. It is based on physician's orders, accepted standards of care for the patient's problem or diagnoses, as well as assessment and reassessment data. Revisions in the plan of care must be made as the patient's condition changes.

E. Progress Notes

Progress notes include the summary nursing notes and a record of communications with physicians, other team members, and family members. This section will likely contain detailed notes about what happened if an injury occurred in the home. The agency's follow-up or investigation may be documented.

F. Flow Sheets

Examples of documents found in the flow sheets include documentation of care provided by the home health aide, vital signs, intake and output, calorie counts, wound observations, treatment records, and equipment maintenance and cleaning records. Flow sheets can be critical in establishing the patient's condition on a daily basis and demonstrating whether care was provided as ordered.

G. Medication Administration Record (MAR)

MARs document the time, dosage, and route of administration of all medications given to a patient. Education provided to the patient regarding her medications must also be documented.

H. Therapies

Documentation of all allied health providers are found in the therapies section. These include physical therapists, occupational therapists, speech therapists, social services, nutritionists, and so forth. The notes of these professionals supplement the nursing documentation about the patient's condition, and any injuries the patient suffers during physical therapy should be documented in this section.

I. Case Management

Documentation related to coordination of care is included in the case management section. Case management is the process of assuring the patient's care is appropriate, effective, free from duplication, and appropriately communicated among members of the healthcare team. Examples include communication with the patient's physician, insurance company or other agencies involved in a given patient's care. Documentation of care conferences and family meetings may also be found in this section.

J. Laboratory Results

Some agencies may receive notification of laboratory results. These documents will be kept in a separate section in the medical record and may become important in cases when long-term use of medications such as Coumadin (blood thinner) should be monitored with blood tests.

K. Miscellaneous

The miscellaneous section may include documentation of orientation of new personnel to the patient's care or infection reports. Additional records may include a home chart or communication log. Almost all charting is now done electronically, however if a paper system is still being used, the following applies. Certain records may be kept in the patient's home for shift cases or cases in which nurses or home health aides are providing regularly scheduled care. These records may be copies or originals and would include the care plan, progress notes, treatment flow sheets, and medication records, to name a few. If the home chart is made up of original records, the agency will have a regular time period, usually one month, when the chart is thinned (removal of original records from the home chart to the permanent record maintained in the office). If an incident in the home results in injury or death, the records in the home care chart should be quickly obtained and secured. It may contain the only documentation that led up to the incident. Both the home care agency and the attorneys should be fully aware of the location of these records.

TIP: Keeping electronic records current and accessible to other disciplines, or keeping duplicate records in the home and matching originals in the office facilitates accurate communication between agency personnel (such as the clinical supervisor) and the staff member providing care in the home.

The home communication log is not kept as an official part of the medical record, but is used to facilitate communication between the different staff members involved in a patient's care and between the family and staff. Examples of information kept in this log include copies of a home exercise program developed by the physical therapist, a description of how the patient managed over the weekend when no nurses were present, or a brief report of a visit to the doctor.

L. OASIS

OASIS consists of 90 mandated questions. These responses are transmitted to the state health department and then forwarded to Medicare for benchmarking purposes. Benchmarking is a quality tool used to measure and compare the performance of home care agencies. In addition to including the client's diagnoses and surgeries, this document is an evaluation of the client's living arrangement, supportive assistance required, activities of daily living, body systems and wounds, and medications.

The data derived from OASIS drive the care plan that is the guide for the clinician. Some agencies use clinical intervention tools, such as care paths or maps, which match the client's diagnosis and specify care measures for each visit. Many agencies are automating their records; staff work with laptops in the patient's home. This helps streamline the documentation process but carries its own pitfalls. The interaction between the home care staff and patient can become impersonal if the nurse focuses more on the computer than the patient. The attorney should ask for paper copies of any computer documents prepared by the home care nurse, including the OASIS data set.

15.6 Risks in Home Care

Home healthcare nursing offers unique challenges for the nursing professional. These challenges can be quite daunting for the former acute care nurse now working in the home care setting. Home healthcare nurses must be able to function autonomously and often have to expeditiously make decisions about patient care. They need to know when and where they can get help in patient care situations in which they are alone in the home with a patient and family. Unlike the hospital setting, help is not down the hall.

Home care nurses are guests in their patients' homes. Safety concerns and other patient care issues must be balanced against lifestyle, cultural preferences, and customs. What is ideal in the hospital may be unobtainable and unrealistic in the home setting. The need for sterility for a Foley catheter insertion in the hospital setting is replaced with the use of clean technique in a home. The nurse may be faced with the need to set up a medication schedule for an isolated elderly patient who cannot remember whether she ate today or not. These challenges require an experienced home healthcare nurse with top-notch assessment skills and clinical expertise. This section discusses risks in home healthcare nursing and potential areas of liability in this practice environment.

A. Inadequate Communication Between Nurses

Agencies offering home health services typically provide care 24 hours per day, seven days a week.

TIP: Unless a client secures a "live-in" arrangement, there will always be the transition of care from one nurse to another. Complete documentation to transfer vital information is essential as a safeguard to risk management concerns. The transfer of information is referred to as the "handoff" and is coming under scrutiny by the patient safety movement as it relates to maintaining safety.

Most home health agencies utilize their weekday staff to case manage the clients. Evenings, nights, and weekends are considered after-hours. These shifts are managed by a staff which usually does not work the traditional shift of daytime hours, Monday through Friday. Because of this situation, the potential exists for information to "fall through the cracks," and this is often the basis for a litigious situation.

An attorney reviewing a home health chart should note the days of the week and time of the visits. Assess the continuity of care by noting the different nurses involved on a case. The greater the number of staff involved, the higher the probability there could be a lack of coordination among them. Home care agencies should have an established protocol to assure that staff responsible after-hours and weekends are documenting their assessments, and communicating necessary information to the day staff.

Weekends and evening/night after-hours are sometimes high-risk shifts, and this is magnified because some of the nurses working these times may be per diem employees. If they work only occasionally, they may not be present enough to command a thorough knowledge of the agency's practices. While the status of per diem itself does not indicate less than optimum functioning of a nurse, some professionals consider them the weaker links in the system.

Both per diem and full-time staff nurses are not expected to take an assignment without familiarizing themselves with it. Proper supervision must be given to new staff to ensure they can perform the expected nursing procedures safely. Periodic field evaluations must be done at least every year, after it is determined the staff has met basic competencies. If a nurse has been requested to see a patient with a tracheostomy, for example, and he has not cared for such a patient before, it would be unsafe for a visit to be made without orientation and backup. Home care agencies must maintain procedure checklists to demonstrate that nurses are safely performing that procedure. It is the responsibility of both the nurse and supervisor to know what constitutes an appropriate assignment for that nurse. At the same time, nurses caught in an unfamiliar and potentially dangerous clinical situation in a patient's home must immediately contact their supervisor, who may be able to meet them there to provide assistance as well as needed expertise. All nurses must be comfortable with what to do in an emergency and be prepared to act. This means they must be competent to provide emergency basic life support and demonstrate the ability to follow agency policies and procedures for each emergency that may arise. Examples of situations requiring prompt response include: a patient having a seizure or an unstable blood sugar level, or an infant having continued episodes of apnea. A home care nurse accepting an assignment must be prepared at all times to deal with a worst-case scenario.

Improper screening of employees is also an area of liability. Earlier in the chapter, Joint Commission standards for employee hiring were listed. Sadly, some staff members have committed criminal offenses, including rape and murder. In many of those cases, criminal background checks were not conducted. Each new hire should be carefully evaluated for clinical expertise and the ability to function independently. Many agencies have prospective nurses make a home visit with an experienced nurse within the agency. This gives each the opportunity, albeit limited, to see how the new nurse functions in the home environment and interacts with patients and families in that setting. All home care agencies must be sure the new hire can provide evidence of appropriate nursing licensure, CPR certification, a driver's license, a background check, and malpractice insurance if appropriate.

B. Inadequate Planning and Care Implementation Among Disciplines

In addition to multiple nurses servicing a client, there is a second element that contributes to risks in home care. The disciplines represented in most home care agencies include nursing, physical, speech and occupational therapies, respiratory therapy, social work, nutrition, and home health aide services. Some clients require more than one discipline to provide all the necessary care. For example, a client who has sustained a stroke would have most or even all of the aforementioned disciplines provide home visiting.

It is imperative in this situation that there is internal coordination of these disciplines, and typically, it is the nurse who acts as the case manager. The goals of the nurse must be known by the therapist, and vice versa. The home health aide must be instructed by the professional disciplines in the unique aspects of client care. Home care agencies should have policies on "coordination of services." A timely transfer of information among disciplines is essential. An example of how poor interdisciplinary communication may lead to litigation is described:

> A client's family was instructed to use a transfer board to move the client from the bed to a chair. The physical therapist taught the client and family how to do this safely. However, the therapist did not share (either verbally or in writing) this information with the nurse and the home health aide. The aide, unaware of the transfer board teaching, independently struggled with the client while performing a transfer, and the client was hurt in the process.

In this scenario, the physical therapist should have communicated to the nurse and aide the goal of having the client and family successfully use a transfer board. In addition, the therapist should have made a joint visit with the home health aide to demonstrate the correct procedure and observe that the aide was capable of doing this independently.

C. Imprecise Communication Between the Physician and Nurse

A third potential risk area in the home healthcare environment is the method in which information is transmitted. Previously addressed was the need for communication to be documented and shared among disciplines. A serious concern is the exactness and specificity of the communication, including the physician's orders for care. In a home health agency, it is typical to have an intake nurse, or a department in a large organization, responsible for receiving client referrals for service. These referrals may come from doctors, staff within hospitals, and possibly the families or clients themselves who are seeking assistance.

TIP: Transmission of accurate information from intake to the clinician in the home providing care is a critical area for potential liability.

There is usually an intake form, typically labeled a referral and treatment plan that elicits demographic data, recent medical information that includes dates of hospitalizations, diagnoses, surgeries, and specific physician orders including medications and visits prescribed for all home health disciplines, including their frequency. This is often faxed to a home health agency to initiate services prior to the receipt of the original copy. The exactness of the order prescribed by the physician cannot be underestimated. It is expected that, upon patient admission, the home care nurse will check the intake form against discharge instructions from the hospital; call the physician to confirm initial orders; and clarify any discrepancies between the intake sheet and the hospital discharge orders. Joint Commission published the 2009 Home Care National Patient Safety Goals with the goals of improving the accuracy of patient identification, improving the effectiveness of communication among caregivers, improving the safety of using medications, reducing the risk of healthcare associated infections, and accurately and completely reconciling medications across the continuum of care.[6] These standards will improve communication among healthcare professionals as the patient transitions from hospital to home care, thus improving patient safety.

The home care nurse is expected to promptly report serious changes in the patient's condition to the physician. The nurse should have the clinical judgment to recognize those changes that require immediate response. The discovery of a patient with abnormal breath sounds requires a phone call from the home at the time of the visit, not the next day. Every effort is expected to be made to contact the physician, including paging or using the answering service. The patient should not be left alone until the problem has been resolved through communication with the physician. In extreme cases, the nurse may need to call an ambulance and wait until it arrives. In these days of cell phones, it is easier to get a physician to call back while the nurse is still at the home visit, but the nurse must be prepared for how to proceed if response is delayed. The conversation with the physician and what was reported should be documented. Changes in orders should be recorded on a verbal order sheet, read back and confirmed for accuracy.

D. Improper Provision of Specialized Services

A fourth area of potential risk within home health agencies is the movement toward specialized services. The emphasis on maintaining patients after earlier hospital discharge has brought more advanced technological services to the home setting. Providing intravenous nutrition or medications (infusion therapy) and monitoring for preterm (early) labor are common examples of this trend. The home health agency touting an ability to deliver specialized services is in demand by insurance companies trying to reduce costly hospitalizations. However, an agency desiring to promote itself as specializing in certain areas must demonstrate that staff have the required training and continuing education to perform these skills. Staff must receive a baseline of competency testing to ascertain these clinical skills, and this should be repeated annually. Specialized services often involve specialized equipment. Inadequately trained nurses may be ineffective in problem solving when intervention is required. Offering specialty services requires that the agency maintain a staff capable of delivering this level of service whenever the need arises. After-hours and weekend shifts present challenges in ensuring staff coverage in most home health agencies. Providing a specialized infusion therapy nurse at that time can be difficult. An agency cannot accept responsibility for a client and admit the case if it has specialty staff limited to only certain hours.

Infusion therapy may involve monitoring blood levels to determine that the client is receiving the therapeutic benefits. Some medications may be toxic if the patient's liver or kidney functioning is abnormal. It is the specialty nurse's responsibility to ensure appropriate diagnostic studies have been ordered and results have been called to the physician in a timely manner.

E. Inadequate Coordination Among Providers of Care

The fifth and most complex risk for home heath agencies is their relationship to other entities servicing the client. The home healthcare agency infrequently stands alone as the sole provider of services. It often coordinates with other organizations on behalf of meeting a client's needs. The home health agency providing the intermittent services of the nurse, home health aide, therapist, nutritionist, or social worker may interface with other organizations. A joint effort may involve the collaboration between an infusion company that independently provides drugs and a specialized staff of intravenous nurses, and the home health agency, both engaged in home visits to service the client. The infusion company may be contracted by the insurance company for the specialty service of infusion therapy, but the home care agency is performing other skilled services the client requires.

Although the home health nurse functions as the case manager for a client and coordinates all the care (therapies, social work, nutrition, and aides) provided internally through the home care agency, communication and cooperation with other external providers are often critical components in attaining client goals. Social service organizations often provide assistance to home health care. Both work autonomously, yet collaborate for the client's welfare.

The most common example of external agency coordination occurs with a Medicare-certified home health agency that supplies the client's skilled care and minimal aide services, and a homemaker company providing a supplement to the Medicare services. This supplement can be paid for privately or perhaps subsidized by welfare.

Some welfare programs offer consumer choice options allowing the client to receive monies to independently hire aide services or obtain an aide through a staffing firm. Many clients choose to hire their own aides.

TIP: Hiring a private aide has a greater potential for liability due to the lack of checks and balances on the independently hired aide. It is anticipated legal actions will increase with the growth of these programs.

F. Potential for Staff Dishonesty

An acknowledged fact of life within the home care industry is the risk associated with unscrupulous staff that takes advantage of the independent environment of home care. Deceitful behaviors can range from failure to report a client's deteriorating condition to fraudulent notes or timesheets and theft.

It is unusual for one employee of the agency to be the sole provider of care to a client. Typically, routine checks and balances are established or clinicians relieve staff for each other's absences. It is expected that each practitioner will review the previous clinician's notes and compare present findings to the former report. Any significant discrepancy or negative progression in a client's condition warrants consultation with a supervisor. Management oversight should mitigate the possibility of any clinician concealing an adverse event. Agencies are required to have corporate compliance plans as part of their employee training requirements. Staff should be educated regarding the serious consequences of dishonest behavior as well as the draconian measures the government initiates against agencies that have committed fraud. Refer to Chapter 27, *Significance of Healthcare Fraud in Nursing*, for more information on this subject.

G. Patient Safety

The home care nurse is responsible for maintaining a safe and clean environment. This can be a challenge if the patient lives in a dirty and cluttered home. If the patient is unable to maintain a safe home because of age, disability or lack of family and neighborhood supports, a social work referral should be obtained to investigate community resources for that patient. Teaching must be directed at proper handling of wound-care supplies and other medical equipment and at proper disposal of soiled dressings. The patient must be taught proper handwashing technique. There should be documentation that these instructions were given and universal precautions were maintained. In the case of infectious diseases such as AIDS or MRSA (methicillin-resistant staphylococcus aureus) in a wound, evidence should be documented of precautions taken and teaching directed at protecting both the patient and community.

The home healthcare nurse on initial assessment should check the home for safety hazards such as throw rugs, clut-ter, electrical hazards, smoking in the home with oxygen use, and potential for bathroom falls due to lack of rubber mats and other safety equipment. The patient should be instructed in these hazards and how to correct them; this should be documented.

Any signs of inability to safely perform activities of daily living such as bathing or cooking should be documented with appropriate referrals for occupational therapy, a home health aide, and physical therapy. The home care nurse is responsible for ensuring the patient or caregiver can use all medical equipment safely and knows who to call in case of a malfunction. This is especially important in the case of oxygen or apnea monitor use. The home care nurse must also document that the patient has been taught how to call 911 and knows how to reach the home care agency after hours.

TIP: Dirty homes or unsafe neighborhoods exist in both the inner city and rural areas. The nurse can be a catalyst for making referrals to appropriate city inspection agencies. Social services should be involved for assistance with referrals and placement if needed. Agencies must have clear policies for the use of security personnel, as needed, in housing projects and unsafe neighborhoods.

Medication safety is of utmost importance in the home. Upon admission, the home care nurse should document all the medications the patient is taking and compare them to the discharge orders. The physician should be notified of any medication discrepancies within 24 hours of opening the case. The 2009 Home Care National Patient Safety Goals, published by The Joint Commission, recommends implementing a process for obtaining and documenting a complete list of the patient's current medications upon the patient's entry to the organization and with the involvement of the patient. This process includes a comparison of the listed medications to those ordered for the patient while under the care of the organization. A complete list of the patient's medications is communicated to the next provider of service when a patient is transferred to another setting, service, practitioner, or level of care within or outside the organization.[7] Proper administration, including timing and introduction to the purpose for all medications should be taught on the first visit, with subsequent instruction on purpose, side effects, and safety measures. An exception would be insulin and not only the administration, but purpose, side effects, safety, signs of hyper and hypo-glycemia, and use of blood glucose monitor if ordered should be taught at the initial visit. The home care visit pattern must reflect the appropriate intensity until the patient can demonstrate independence with these instructions.

The patient or caregiver should be encouraged to discard medications no longer in use so the patient does not take them by mistake. If nurses do this without permission, this is taking away the patient's property and risking a charge of theft. The patient can request that nurses discard, but in that case the nurses are facilitating the patient's request. If the patient refuses to discard, old prescriptions should be stored far away from the current dosages to prevent administration errors. This is particularly important when the patient is taking the same medication but in a different dosage. For example, a congestive heart failure patient may have been taking 0.25 mg of Lanoxin before hospitalization but now be on 0.125 mg of the same drug. Continuing on the old regimen could result in digoxin toxicity, which is potentially fatal. Of particular concern are patients on Coumadin or other anticoagulants (often referred to as blood thinners). It is imperative the home healthcare nurse instruct the patient in signs and symptoms of bleeding and bruising, and foods that can interfere with absorption. Prothrombin time/international normalized ratio (PT/INR) testing must be scheduled as ordered to ensure the blood does not become too thin. Patients who live alone and cannot be trusted to count their own pills on a daily basis should be given seven-day medication boxes and visited daily to ensure they can safely use this system.

Another difficult situation is posed when the non-compliant client's actions place him at risk. In this scenario, the agency may be liable if there is no documentation that supports the agency's concern and attempt to remedy the matter. An example of non-compliance may be a client who is at risk of falling and refuses to obtain rails in the home and wear an emergency activation device. The home health agency clinician recognizes that without these assistive devices, this client is unsafe for home care. Therefore, the best strategy is to develop an agreement with the client that specifies her adherence to certain conditions (obtaining rails on the stairs and in the bathroom and wearing a "help signal" device) as a prerequisite for services to continue. Both the agency representative and the client sign this contract, and it is advisable the clinician and a manager deliver this to the home and discuss the matter.

If the client refuses to cooperate with this proposed agreement, or denies there is a problem, a certified letter to the client, physician, and family is necessary. It should outline that the client, family, and physician have been previously advised about the safety risk the client faces and that no action has been taken to remedy the situation. Since agency policies mandate a safe environment for the delivery of client care, the agency must terminate services when this condition is not met (Figure 15.3).

Safe use of technological equipment is also an area of concern. More patients are now being sent home on ventilators or with peripherally inserted central catheter (PICC) lines. The patient or caregiver must be trained in what to do in the event of equipment malfunction, including how to get in touch with the agency and emergency care. The nurse responding to a call concerning equipment malfunction must be able to troubleshoot the equipment and decide what emergency measures should be instituted. The nurse must also be able to recognize signs of complications such as infected PICC lines requiring immediate medical attention. All instructions to the patient and caregiver must be documented as well as their responses to teaching and ability to give a return demonstration. The home care visit pattern must reflect the appropriate intensity until the patient can demonstrate independence with these instructions.

H. Failure to Recognize Changes in the Patient's Condition

The home healthcare nurse is responsible for assessing the patient's health status on each visit. All home care agencies have assessment sheets that must be completed at each visit. Vital signs and other assessment data such as weight, random blood sugar, breath sounds, a narrative of the patient's condition, and wound-care measurements will be on this sheet. The home healthcare nurse must know what constitutes a change in condition that requires reporting to the physician. The patient's physician relies on the home care nurse to be the physician's "eyes and ears."

When the attorney looks at the assessment sheet it is essential to observe whether each area is completed. The home care nurse should complete a total patient assessment and ensure each area on the sheet is completed. Blood pressure should be taken both sitting and standing in cardiovascular patients. Edema or swelling as well as measurements of the lower extremities should be documented at each visit. Errors in this area can occur when a home care nurse is dealing with an unfamiliar diagnosis or condition. It is imperative the nurse contact specialty resource personnel within the agency or a supervisor when dealing with an unfamiliar clinical situation. Before the visit, if a nurse feels the condition is not one he can care for safely, arrangements should be made for a joint visit with a supervisor or other experienced staff who can instruct in the condition or procedure. For instance, a nurse who has not changed a tracheostomy tube in some time may want backup.

I. Patient Abandonment

The current managed care environment, with the emphasis on fewer patient visits and cost containment, leaves the

Notification of Safety Problem

Date

Dear Client:

This letter is to notify you that our Agency is being prevented from providing effective home health services in your home. In order to provide these services, we must be assured of our clinicians' safety in the home and the client's cooperation in allowing our personnel to perform their duties in a safe environment. This has not been our experience in your case.

We would like to be of service to you and have discussed this matter with your physician. However, unless the following circumstances are remedied immediately, we will have to cease providing our services in your home:

(Identification of caregiver safety issues that must be corrected.)

I understand that the Agency requires that I (or my responsible caregiver) correct the safety issue described above, as a condition to receiving future services from it.

_____
Client/Responsible Caregiver Signature

_____
Agency Representative Signature

If you would like to discuss this matter further, please contact the Director of Patient Care Services.

Sincerely,

Executive Director

C: Client's Physician
       Family Member (if applicable)

Figure 15.3 *Notification of Safety Problem Letter*

**Notification of Termination of Care
within 30 Days**

Date

Dear Client:

Our Agency's professional practice policies specify that when a client is physically and/or mentally unable to care for himself/herself, there must be a responsible primary caregiver who is capable of assuring 24-hours a day responsibility for the client. This is essential for the client to be eligible for continued services.

Your medical condition requires that you have 24-hours per day supervised care and we have discussed this with your physician. This letter is to notify you that your needs exceed the scope of intermittent home health care offered by this Agency and we must terminate services to you within 30 days of this letter which is _____.

Since we are interested in helping you obtain adequate care for your situation, we strongly recommend that you seek placement in a supervised facility, such as a nursing home. Our social work staff has presented information to you regarding long-term-care arrangements and we would facilitate a transfer to such a facility for you. We have advised your physician of our recommendation and the potential termination of Agency services.

We are concerned for your safety, and hope that you will seek alternate living arrangements as soon as possible.

Sincerely,

Executive Director

C: Client's Physician
       Family Member (if applicable)

Figure 15.4 *Notification of Termination of Care Letter*

home care nurse open to allegations of abandonment. The risk of patient abandonment can also occur with Medicare beneficiaries when services are stopped because of patient noncompliance. Though this is an acceptable reason to terminate services, the nurse must make sure sufficient steps have been taken to ensure the patient has not been abandoned.

Upon receiving a referral, a home care nurse will go to the home to do an initial nursing assessment. No patient-nurse relationship is established until the nurse, based on assessment findings, opens the case to service. If the nurse finds no need for skilled nursing or finds a patently unsafe environment such as an elderly, demented patient living alone in filthy conditions, she will not open the case to service; therefore, no relationship will be established. In the case of an unsafe situation, the hospital, physician, and appropriate government agencies should be contacted. Once this is done the nurse is under no obligation to open that case. There has been no abandonment.

Once the case is open, however, a patient-nurse relationship exists. A home care nurse may need to discontinue care to a patient who is noncompliant, such as refusing to take medication or make a follow-up appointment with a physician. Care must be taken to ensure the patient is not unilaterally discharged with short notice. The patient and his physician must be made aware of the reason for the discharge. Another situation can occur when skilled care has ended and only custodial care is needed. An example of this would be a wound-care patient whose wounds have healed but who still requires home health aide assistance because of deconditioning. All efforts must be made to transfer care to other sources, such as private pay or county agencies on aging, so patient safety is not threatened. The goal of home care is to work toward independence at discharge. Family members must be taught patient care from the beginning so they can take over as soon as possible. Sometimes, unsafe patient situations exist as a client deteriorates while living alone with no willing caregiver. The client resistive to leaving the home creates problems for the home health agency. The agency must send the client, family, and physician a letter outlining why the patient is no longer a candidate for home care and review the efforts made to assist them with alternative plans. The letter concludes with a date that will officially terminate the client from services. A minimum notification of two weeks is essential, but 30 days is desirable. A sample of this letter is provided in Figure 15.4. A common example of this problem arises when a client requires more than intermittent care and needs a live-in caregiver to remain safely in her home.

There are times when the agency cannot grant a two-week notice prior to discharging a client. This is usually a scenario that puts the agency at risk due to a safety concern in the client's environment that jeopardizes the organization's staff. In this situation, the client and family are advised of the risk and asked to remedy the situation immediately. The physician is also apprised of the matter (Figure 15.5). If the family and patient do not comply, a final visit is made that prepares the client for discharge, and arrangements to obtain follow-up care are documented.

Termination of Services Letter

Date

Dear Client:

We have previously advised you and your physician of certain conditions in your home which have prevented our Agency from providing safe and effective home health services to you. We can only service clients if the home environment is safe for them. The client safety issues in your home have not been remedied in spite of our request to do so.

Since Agency policies mandate a safe environment for the delivery of client care, the Agency must terminate services when this condition is not met. Therefore, we are hereby notifying you that effective _____ we will no longer provide services in your home.

Should you wish to obtain health services elsewhere, we would attempt to try to facilitate this. Please let us know if you want to pursue other arrangements for care.

Very truly yours,

Executive Director

C: Client's Physician
      Family Member (if applicable)

Figure 15.5 Termination of Services Letter

Managed care and prospective payment has made patient abandonment more likely. After the initial nursing assessment, in the case of a managed care plan, the home care nurse will call a precertification nurse at the agency with a report. This precertification nurse will then call the insurance case manager with this report and request authorization. Thus, the information goes through at least three nurses before a decision is made. Unless all involved have excellent communication skills, much can be lost in translation. After the insurance case manager has been contacted, a certain number of visits will be authorized. If that number is not enough, it is the nurse's responsibility to be an advocate for the patient and request more visits. With the proper documentation and communication skills, these are usually approved. If the nurse fails to do this, there is a risk for abandonment of the patient.

Medicare patients must be discharged once they no longer meet the Medicare homebound eligibility requirements for home visits. When the patient is no longer homebound she is expected to seek care as needed at the office of her primary care provider, or in the case of rehabilitation, at a rehabilitation center. This change in status and referral back to the primary provider as the case manager should be documented.

TIP: If there is a question of whether the patient was properly discharged, review the discharge summary and instructions. The reason for the discharge should be documented along with notification of physician and family. There should be documentation of the patient's ability to verbalize knowledge of appropriate signs and symptoms, and demonstrate the knowledge and skills needed to treat healthcare problems. There should also be documentation of the patient's current ability to perform activities of daily living.

15.7 Defense Strategies
A. Documentation

The key to any defense of a home healthcare negligence case is documentation. The nurse may be the only other person in the home, except the patient, at the time of the alleged incident. No one else may have been present to back up the nurse's events. Good documentation done in a factual, accurate, complete, and timely manner can go a long way in providing a defense. The attorney investigating a home healthcare case should consider these discovery tips:

1. Ask for the nursing progress notes, initial nursing assessment notes, plan of care, medication administration record, and OASIS forms.

2. Look for internal communication logs for communication with physicians, the nursing supervisor, and the precertification nurse for approval of more visits.

3. Look for physical assessment and vital signs at each visit. Look for the narrative note to reflect untoward findings even if a Charting By Exception system is used. (Refer to Chapter 7, *Nursing Documentation*, in Volume I, for an explanation of this charting system.)

4. Look for home health aide records and evidence of RN supervision every two weeks.

5. Look for patient teaching and documentation of a return demonstration or verbal understanding of the instructions.

6. Look for signs of patient noncompliance.

TIP: Many home care nurses are using laptops in the field with the notes computer-generated. No matter what method is used, variances, problems, and patient and caregiver responses to the care and instruction given must be documented.

B. Standard of Care Issues

Defense of a home health claim often rests on an analysis of standards of care. The attorney, legal nurse consultant, and nursing expert witness will be asking these questions: Did the nurse follow the accepted standard of care? Did the nurse use the chain of command when confronted with an unfamiliar situation? Was the physician contacted in a timely manner? Were proper emergency measures taken?

TIP: In any case of home healthcare liability, documentation of communication with the physician; nursing interventions; the use of the chain of command; and specialty resources within the agency should be reviewed. Look for communication logs, which should have dates and times of calls to the physician, the nursing supervisor, the precertification nurse, and other professionals. These can support or refute the nurse's report of events.

Did the nurse document what happened so that events are clear? Again, the record will speak volumes in providing a defense. Figure 15.6 offers tips for providers to reduce liability risk.

The nurse's adherence to the agency's own policies and procedures is also important. It is essential to obtain the specific policies and procedures for the issues in question. For example, if the lawsuit seeks damages from skin breakdown, see if a risk assessment tool was used and preventive mea-

In most cases, at least one of the following is at the heart of a malpractice claim:

- *Malpractice itself.*
- *Poor communication with patients:* involve them in treatment decisions and discuss with them who will provide hands-on care, whether the patient will be able to participate in his or her care, and what to do and who to call if problems arise.
- *Poor communication with other providers:* request that the hospitalists caring for their patients inform them if those patients will receive home care and that the hospitalists provide them with copies of orders and care plans.
- *Lack of follow-up:* to be effective, plans for follow-up need to be agreed on and in place before action is required. When working with patients who are receiving home health care, the primary care physician, as well as the home health agency staff and any specialists the patient is seeing, should receive in a timely manner: test and lab results; notification and review of critical test results; notice of telephone calls from the patient, family, or caregiver; and notification of missed or cancelled appointments. Discuss who will have follow-up responsibility for patient test or lab results, who should answer questions the patient and family may have, and who will be responsible for after-hours call coverage should a question or problem arise.
- *Failure to receive informed consent.*
- *Poor documentation:* providers can do certain things to reduce their exposure to risk. Good communication, follow-up, and documentation on their part can go a long way toward reducing their chances of being sued.
- *Communicating openly* with patients, their families, and home healthcare providers; following up to make sure tests are administered and results are acted upon; and thoroughly documenting communications, orders for care, and results of tests are some of the best ways to reduce malpractice risk.[8]

Figure 15.6 Tips for providers to reduce risk of liability

sures were taken. Look for adherence to wound care policies and referral to the wound care specialist. Again, look for documentation of notification of the physician and adherence to the physician's orders.

TIP: Policy and procedure manuals are kept in the office and some but not all agencies may provide each nurse with a smaller version called a field manual. With the increased use of laptops, policies may be accessible by this means or can be accessed with a call to the supervisor.

C. Noncompliance

An example of noncompliance might be a case of a patient with a draining wound which leads to infection. The patient may allege negligence by the home care staff, yet the record may reflect daily wound assessment, with notification of the physician regarding wound status. Further investigation could reveal the patient refused to see the physician and only did so two to three days later at the nurse's urging. This nurse has followed the standard of care by continued assessment, notification of the physician of changes in the patient condition, instruction of the patient and family in the need for medical follow-up, and subsequent documentation of their refusal to follow these instructions.

In the case of a patient with the infected wound, the attorney should look for signs of the patient's noncompliance. Did the patient refuse to turn himself? Did the caregivers refuse to change or reinforce a saturated dressing despite well-documented instruction to the family?

In other cases, failure to take medication properly despite instruction or refusal to follow up with the physician provides a defense, if the nurse has made every effort to teach the patient and family and they refuse to follow through. Look at interactions with the physician. Has the physician responded to the nurse's phone calls and taken appropriate action? Did the nurse have to call repeatedly to get a physician to respond?

D. Agency Issues

In the case of agency liability, the strongest defense will be the maintenance of employee records demonstrating competence and continuing education in accordance with the agency's standards. Employee screening policies such as criminal background checks and references are also important. Maintaining clear policies and procedures in line with current nursing practice and exhibiting a chain of command will demonstrate agency competency.

15.8 Case Studies

Now that elements of home care practice, theories of nursing liability and potential defense strategies have been examined, Sections 15.8 and 15.9 illustrate complete analyses of hypothetical and actual home care cases and how to screen malpractice cases.

A. Home Care Negligence Case Study 1

Nursing negligence caused the plaintiff to suffer second degree burns on his legs when a home health nurse negligently allowed his shower water to get too hot. The plaintiff is paraplegic and needs assistance in and out of the shower which includes the duty to set the water temperature, especially due to a lack of feeling in his legs.

As a result the plaintiff was treated for his burns and endured several infections through the burns causing a significant impact on his health. A significant settlement was secured for the plaintiff just a few weeks before trial and after the insurance company consistently refused to settle the case. The company claimed the plaintiff burned himself for monetary gain and that he lacked feeling in his legs and therefore suffered only a little.

The medical expert was highly critical of the procedure the home health nurse followed and her lack of oversight during the shower preparation process. The grueling discovery process finally revealed enough evidence to show that despite any desperate claims of self infliction of the wounds, there was so much evidence of negligence established that they had to settle or risk a potential multimillion dollar verdict after a trial.[9]

B. Home Care Negligence Case Study 2

The plaintiff's decedent suffered from Duchenne muscular dystrophy and was nearly paralyzed and required continuous mechanical ventilation. Advantage Nursing Services was under contract to provide the decedent with 24-hour home care. In late January 2002 the decedent's ventilation tube became disconnected while the LPN on duty was asleep in another room. When the LPN awoke she heard the alarm, but by the time she reached the decedent he was unconscious and had no pulse.

The plaintiff claimed that the LPN had not been trained to effectively administer CPR to an intubated patient and that the LPN was negligent in falling asleep. The plaintiff also claimed that Advantage's hiring practices were insufficient in that there was no investigation of applicants' self-reported qualifications and experience. The defendant argued that there was an orientation and preceptorship in place. The defendant also argued that the death was due to the decedent's medical condition, and was not related to the LPN sleeping on the job, or inadequate administration of CPR. According to a published account a $579,000 settlement was reached.[10]

C. Home Care Negligence Case Study 3

The plaintiff, age 85, was diagnosed with terminal cancer in 2004. Her doctor ordered hospice care. She was moved to Hospice House where care was provided by employees of Visiting Nurse Association. She remained under the care of the Visiting Nurse Association employees for 23 days until her death in July 2004. The plaintiff alleged negligence in the failure of the Visiting Nurse Association and Hospice House to disclose that they were not licensed to provide hospice care. The plaintiff claimed that the care plan outlined by the decedent's doctor was not followed in that the decedent was not given a narcotic patch during the last five days of her life, but was given oral narcotic medications instead. The plaintiff claimed that most of the oral medication drooled out of the decedent's mouth. The plaintiff maintained that the nurse stated that it would be a waste to provide the narcotic patch to someone so near death. According to Nebraska Verdicts and Settlements a $12,500 verdict for pain and suffering was returned. The plaintiff appealed the dismissal of the misrepresentation claims. The Nebraska Supreme Court upheld the verdict.[11]

D. Home Care Negligence Case Study 4

In this case example, a healthy child born in an Illinois hospital had a different blood type than his mother. A sample of blood was obtained from him at birth to determine if this would be a problem. However, the defendant doctor who obtained the blood did not have it tested immediately, and within three days, the newborn suffered brain damage (bilirubin encephalopathy) as a result of blood incompatibility; he died at the age of 16 days. The plaintiff alleged several defendant doctors and a home healthcare agency were negligent for failing to perform the testing in a timely manner, despite the mother's efforts to have it done. The home care nurse was responsible for ensuring the test was done in a timely manner and results were obtained immediately and called to the physician. The defendants denied any negligence and claimed the infant's death was due to sudden infant death syndrome, rather than any act of omission on their part. The jury returned a $30 million verdict to the plaintiff.[12]

1. Was the care provided appropriate?
2. How liable is the agency?
3. Who are the potential defendants?

Figure 15.7 *Case Screening Questions*

Records to Request

1. Table of contents from all clinical and operational policy and procedure manuals
2. Patient education materials (list or related to patient problems and diagnoses)
3. Job descriptions
4. Personnel files: application and screening tools, employee orientation and periodic performance evaluations, continuing education records, current licensure
5. Personnel medical files: these are kept separately from the non-medical employee information
6. Patient satisfaction survey results
7. Patient complaint log
8. Performance improvement reports (indicate priority areas being reviewed by the agency)
9. Incident reports and related investigational documentation
10. Home care medical record
11. Records from other agencies providing services to the patient
12. Contracts between agencies and other agencies, payors, and independent contractors

Figure 15.8 *Records to Request when Reviewing a Home Care Case for Negligence*

15.9 Case Screening

This section explores several questions to assist in determining whether negligence occurred. Under each question is a discussion of pertinent issues and recommended sources of information to use in analyzing a case. Examples from claims and cases will illustrate various points. See Figures 15.7 and 15.8 for specific case screening questions and records to request when reviewing a home care case for negligence.

Documentation of Appropriateness of Care

1. Physician orders
2. Plan of treatment, nursing care plan, and clinical pathway
3. Patient rights and responsibilities
4. Standards of care for the home care nurse
5. Clinical policies and procedures
6. Advance directives; consent forms
7. "Do not resuscitate" orders
8. Documentation of assessment, care and education provided, and patient's response to treatment
9. Communication with the physician
10. Job descriptions

Figure 15.9 *Documentation that Permits Analysis of the Appropriateness of Care*

A. Appropriateness of the Care

The essential elements of this question revolve around the following analysis: First, determine if the problem was new or ongoing. Was it recognized, communicated to appropriate individuals, and treated in a timely manner? Was the care based on agency policy, professional standards, physician's orders, and so forth? Second, are patient safety issues involved in the case? In the first case example, a patient sustained burns due to failure to monitor shower temperature. In this example, patient safety was not protected.

A third element to consider is whether the correct provider performed the care in question. For example, during a seizure, a patient fell out of his chair and broke his hip. The aide appropriately called 911 and the home care office. Upon investigating, it became clear the aide had been giving the patient his antacid instead of his anti-seizure pill. In this scenario, administering medication is not the role of the aide but that of a licensed nurse.

Sources of information useful in assessing appropriateness of care can be found in Figure 15.9.

B. Liability of the Agency

1. Hiring and employee competence

Several questions should be explored regarding employee competence. First, was the information on the employment application verified before hiring (i.e., did the agency determine that the employee's work history and experience were accurate)? Was there an adequate background check (criminal or child abuse clearance, Department of

Motor Vehicles) on the employee before hiring? Did the agency act appropriately if negative background information was discovered after hiring the employee? The agency has a duty to discharge an employee once an unfit history becomes known.

Was the care provider oriented to agency policies and procedures, roles and responsibilities, and each assignment? If the home care provider documented care according to agency policies and procedures and accepted industry standards, a claim is less likely to hold up in a court of law. Consider the homebound patient who begged a nurse to take him for a drive. The nurse, wanting to be helpful to her patient, honored the request. While driving, they were in an auto accident causing minor injuries to both. In addition to the personal injury claim, the patient sought to bring a negligence claim against the nurse and the home care agency. According to agency policy, nurses are not allowed to transport patients under any circumstances. This issue was addressed at orientation to the agency and during the annual safety inservice training. There was documentation in the nurse's continuing education file she was aware of this policy. Furthermore, the personnel file was current and indicated this nurse was an excellent employee. The nurse stated in her deposition she was not following any directive from the patient's plan of care or the home care agency; she was just trying to be helpful to the patient, and was aware this action went against agency policy. The negligence claim against the agency was dropped.

2. Employee supervision functions

Employee supervision is an important area to assess. Supervision should be reviewed in two aspects. One is the ongoing supervision and evaluation of the employee in question. The second issue relates to the management of the incident if supervision was or should have been directly involved. Medicare regulations require home health aides to be supervised every two weeks. Non-Medicare agencies must set and comply with state licensing regulations and their own standards for supervising aides. The frequency of supervising visits depends on the patient's status as well as other variables.

3. Clinical case supervision

Cases properly organized and coordinated by the clinical supervisor facilitate the nurse's ability to practice within acceptable standards of care. Clinical case supervision involves admitting appropriate patients, assuring appropriate staff is assigned to care for them, making changes to the patient's care process as needed, communicating with appropriate team members based on patient care needs, and assuring consultation is available to staff at all times.

TIP: An attorney reviewing a home health record should look for the use of clinical supervision, consultation, or referral to a clinical specialist. The lack of this care when the patient's condition warrants it may indicate the agency did not possess the appropriate clinical personnel to care for the patient.

4. Compliance with local and national standards

The agency should be functioning in accordance with state licensing laws and related regulatory agencies, such as OSHA and Department of Transportation (DOT). For example, home medical equipment companies must follow strict DOT regulations governing the transportation and handling of oxygen.

Sources of information to assist in the analysis of the above issues include:

- policies and procedures related to hiring practices,
- competence evaluation,
- supervision of staff,
- how staff assignments are made,
- employee orientation and continuing education records,
- employee evaluations, and
- documentation of supervisory visits or phone calls to the patient and the family.

C. Identification of Potential Defendants

Naming the responsible parties is a critical element in every lawsuit. A thorough review of the medical records usually reveals the clinicians who may have liability in a claim. In addition to the direct care providers, the liability of other individuals or entities should be explored by both plaintiff and defense counsel.

TIP: Defendants in a claim may include individuals or other entities in addition to the direct care provider. These may include supervisory or administrative personnel, the agency itself, subcontracted agencies, or other organizations also providing care to the patient, parent organizations, or insurance companies.

1. The home care agency

In reviewing the agency's liability, determine if the care provider was properly hired, oriented, trained, supervised, and evaluated.

2. Other agencies

There are two essential elements to review related to other agencies as potential defendants in a home care case.

First, examine the relationship between the direct home care provider and the agency. If the direct provider is an employee of Agency B being subcontracted to Agency A, and is negligent toward a patient of Agency A, then Agency B may be another defendant. The contract between the two agencies will identify which agency is responsible for such functions as training, orientation to cases, and evaluations. It may be necessary to review the providers' personnel files from each agency, the interagency contract, and policies and procedures from both agencies.

It is important to know if the agency is freestanding or responsible to another entity. Where are policies set: at the individual branch site or from the affiliated hospital or a corporate office? If the agency is part of a chain, have similar cases been filed elsewhere in the organization?

TIP: Insurance companies may incur liability by their lack of authorization for the provision of home care services or in standards included in their contract with a home care agency.

---

3. Payors

Payors should also be identified in the assessment of the defendants of a home care negligence claim. Many insurance plans today are "managed," even if they are not HMOs. It is, therefore, important to review the case manager's notes in addition to the nurses' progress notes. The case manager's documentation will note discussions with the insurer related to authorization for continued and additional services.

Consider the 50-year-old gentleman who was authorized to receive four post-open-heart-surgery nursing visits for assessment and patient education. At the fourth visit, the chest wound was still draining. Two days later, he returned to the hospital with a wound infection, which required surgical drainage and intravenous antibiotics. How adequate was the assessment data documented by the nurse in the patient's record? Did the documentation support the need for additional visits? Did the home care nurse request additional visits of the case manager? Did the agency's case manager request additional visits of the insurance company? Were the visits approved by the insurance company and was the nurse scheduled to visit the patient the day after he was hospitalized? Were additional visits not approved? A thorough analysis is necessary to define where, if any, liability exists. Sources of information related to this aspect of case screening are shown in Figure 15.10.

Identifying Potential Defendants

1. Contract agreements with other agencies and with the insurance carrier
2. The agency's tables of organization and by-laws
3. Franchise agreements
4. Policies and procedures for all related agencies
5. Personnel files from all related agencies
6. The patient's health insurance contracts
7. Nursing progress notes and documentation related to communication with the agency's supervisor or case manager and the physician
8. Documentation of patient care conferences
9. Case management documentation of interactions with insurers

Figure 15.10 Sources of Information Useful in Identifying Potential Defendants

D. Recommendations for Reviewing the Home Care Record

The final segment of this chapter outlines the process of reviewing the home care record and describes the information a legal professional would require in order to fully understand the accountability of the agency.

First, determine what type of home care agency is involved in the lawsuit. Is it certified or not? The answer to this question will alert the reviewer to the regulations that must be adhered to by the organization.

Secondly, ask who was billed for the service(s) the client received. Even in non-certified agencies, if contracts are held with the state for Medicaid (indigent) services, then the organization must meet the criteria of that particular program.

Thirdly, ascertain if multiple agencies are involved with the case. Sometimes the client does not understand the professional's versus non-professional's role and misdirects her accusation.

Finally, ask questions about what internal policies and procedures the agency would follow in regards to the incident that led to legal action. For example, if the wound care ordered by the physician was specified as "per agency protocol," determine exactly what this written procedure includes.

The medical record created by a home health agency can be overwhelming. Most organizations have adopted standard forms to help clinicians address all the critical issues. The industry admits it is the most paper-intense specialty in health care. All of this magnifies the task of reviewing a home care record.

To initiate a home care chart review, a basic approach is recommended:

- Ask if the record includes all previous admissions to the organization or only the episode in question.
- Divide the papers into categories, if the chart is not already sectioned.
- Isolate physician orders, beginning with the most current.
- Separate treatment notes by discipline: nursing, therapies (physical, occupational, speech), aides, and allied health (social work and nutrition).
- Identify all admitting information, including the referral form and any documents received from the referring physician or institution.
- Check if the patient or family signed agency consent forms.
- Classify all billing and insurance information together.

Aside from the documents in the record, the legal reviewer may wish to see an occurrence report that described the incident. Typically, these are maintained by the quality assurance or risk management departments.

It may be helpful to view agency records on continuing education of staff to determine if clinicians are kept current on procedures. This is especially true if the legal issue involved a task that is a basic skill set that would constitute a standard of practice. For example, if a client was injured while a home health aide was performing a transfer, ask when was the last inservice provided by the agency offered to teach transfer techniques.

Finally, consider utilizing the skills of expert nurse witnesses. These individuals can contribute their years of experience and education in quickly assessing the merit of a case.

15.10 Summary

This chapter is an overview of the potential areas of nursing negligence in the home healthcare arena. Home care is a booming field that provides cost-effective care to our most fragile citizens: infants, the disabled, and the elderly. The need for competent, experienced nurses in home care has never been higher because of earlier hospital discharge

of sicker patients and the use of more technologically advanced care in the home setting. Sound standards and practice guidelines provide a framework within which safe quality home care can be provided. At the same time, changes in reimbursement have affected the skill-level of care being provided in the home. These trends unfortunately portend more lawsuits in this important area of nursing. Agencies now and in the future will need to strive for excellence to keep up with the demands of the home care patient populations while struggling to survive in a competitive market.

Endnotes

1. Centers for Medicare & Medicaid Services (CMS), Data Compendium, (pdf: 07pg57a) http://www.cms. gov/DataCompendium/17_2007DataCompendium. asp#TopOfPage, Accessed 4/21/10.

2. Poisal JA, Truffer C, Smith S, Sisko A, Cowan C, Keehan S, Dickensheets B. "Health spending projections through 2016: modest changes obscure part D's impact," *Health Aff* (Millwood). 2007, Mar-Apr;26(2): w242-53. Epub 2007 Feb 21. National Health Statistics Group, Office of the Actuary, Centers for Medicare and Medicaid Services, Baltimore, Maryland, USA. DNHS@cms.hhs.gov PMID: 17314105 [PubMed—indexed for MEDLINE], Accessed 4/21/10.

3. Center for Medicare and Medicaid Services—http:// www.cms.gov, Accessed: 4/21/10.

4. Centers for Medicare & Medicaid Services, Office of the Actuary, National Health Care Expenditures Historical and Projections: 1965-2019 http://www.cms.gov/ NationalHealthExpendData/03_NationalHealthAccountsProjected.asp#TopOfPage, Accessed 4/21/10.

5. Joint Commission National Patient Safety Goals. www. jointcommission.org/PatientSafety/NationalPatientSafetyGoals/09_ome_npsgs.htm. Accessed: 4/21/10.

6. *Id.*

7. *Id.*

8. Velasco, C., "Reducing Malpractice Risk for Physicians Providing Home Care," *Medicine, Law, and Policy (October 2008)* http://www.minnesotamedicine.com/ PastIssues/October2008/tabid/2685/Default.aspx, Accessed: 4/21/10.

9. Nursing Malpractice Case—Home Health Care Nurse Negligently Burns Paraplegic's Legs in Shower—Settlement 1 Week before Trial by Benjamin J. Sansone. http://www.missouriinjurylawblog.com/2007/07/nursing_malpractice_case_-_home_health_care_nurse_negligently_burns_parpelegics_legs_in_shower_-_90000_settlement_before_trial_-_daniels_v_allen_and_cap_inc.html Posted On: July 18, 2007, Accessed 4/21/10.

10. Laska L. (ed.), "Death after ventilation tube becomes disconnected while home health nurse is asleep" *Medical Malpractice Verdicts, Settlements and Experts* (November 2009): 21.

11. Laska L. (ed.), "Failure of hospice nurse to give woman narcotic patch during last days of life" *Medical Malpractice Verdicts, Settlements and Experts* (December 2009): 18.

12. Laska L. (ed.), "Failure to test Bilirubin of newborn leads to brain damage and death," *Medical Malpractice Verdicts, Settlements and Experts* (August 2004): 25.

Chapter 16

Emergency Medical Services

Mary Fakes, RN, MSN and Scott Mullins, AAS, EMT-P

Synopsis
16.1 Introduction
16.2 History and Development of EMS Systems
16.3 Types of Services
    A. First Responders
    B. Basic Life Support Transport
    C. Advanced Life Support Transport
    D. Ambulance Districts
    E. Fire Protection Districts
    F. Hospital-Based Programs
    G. Private Services
    H. Air Medical Ambulance Transport
    I. Other Types of Services
    J. Non-medical Transport Services
16.4 EMS Certifications
16.5 Types of Patient Transports
    A. Emergency Transport
    B. Facility-to-Facility Transports
    C. Facility to Home or Nursing Home
16.6 Transport and Crew Responsibilities
    A. Patient Safety
    B. Life-Threatening Transport
    C. Urgent Transports
    D. Routine Transports
    E. Patient Restraints
16.7 Medical Direction
16.8 Documentation
    A. T-Bone
    B. Head On
    C. Rear End
    D. CID
    E. C-Collar
    F. KED
    G. Traction Splint
    H. PASG or MAST
    I. Backboard
    J. Level of Orientation
    K. Multiple Systems Trauma
    L. Single System Trauma
    M. Seat Belt and Airbag
    N. Trauma Center
    O. Car Versus Pedestrian
    P. Star Pattern on the Windshield
    Q. Passenger Numbering
    R. Car Pillars
16.9 Refusal of Care
16.10 Do Not Resuscitate
16.11 Controlled Substances
16.12 Communications
16.13 Termination of Resuscitation in the Field
16.14 Summary
Endnotes

16.1 Introduction

Emergency Medical Services (EMS) is the system in place that responds to pre-hospital incidents of injury and illness. This system includes dispatchers, first responders, emergency medical technicians, paramedics, nurses, physicians, and the equipment and training to accomplish their missions.

16.2 History and Development of EMS Systems

The early organized care of the sick and injured began during the late 1700s when Napoleon Bonaparte appointed Baron Dominique-Jean Larrey to institute a medical patient care system for the French Army.[1] This decision was made after discovering that wounded soldiers left on the field for several days had an increase in complications as well as suffering. By 1797, Baron Larrey had developed a system that sent trained medical personnel to the wounded soldiers on the battlefield. This benefited Napoleon's conquest efforts. The special carriage designed by Baron Larrey that allowed the medical personnel to access the wounded became known as ambulance volante, or flying ambulance.[2] The concept of removing the sick, injured, and dead from battlefields existed in some form since the early Greek and Roman times; it was Baron Larrey who put some organization to the system.

TIP: Baron Larrey is considered the "father of emergency medical services" due to all of the precepts of emergency medical care that are still used today: 1) rapid access by trained personnel to the patient and 2) treatment in the field and stabilization of the patient with 3) rapid transportation back to the medical facility, while 4) providing medical care en route.[3]

The utilization of EMS systems has not always been smooth in the United States. During the Civil War, both sides suffered in their abilities to manage the care of the wounded soldiers in the field. McSwain notes that during the Second Battle of Bull Run in August 1862, on the Yankee side alone, 3,000 wounded lay in the field of Bull Run for three days and 600 lay there for a week.[4]

The Geneva Convention of 1864 recommended that hospitals, the sick and wounded, and personnel involved in medical care and ambulances were to be considered neutral. Furthermore, safe passage was to be provided for all involved in the medical care of the sick and wounded.

By 1865, the first ambulance service was started in the United States in Cincinnati at Cincinnati General Hospital.[5] Other services followed across the country. The original method of notifying the need for EMS services involved the hospital running a bess, which triggered a weight to fall, lighting the gas lamp which woke the physician and driver.[6] This system also caused the harness and saddle to drop from the ceiling onto the horse and the stable doors to open.

Modern Emergency Medical Services (EMS) has its roots in the 1960s following the 1966 publication of the National Academy of Science's "White Paper" entitled *Accidental Death and Disability: The Neglected Disease of Modern Society*.[7-8] This paper brought to light the deficiencies in providing pre-hospital and emergency care in the country. The federal government and its leadership began to organize EMS and trauma care. Prior to 1966, there were unregulated and disconnected methods for people to receive care before they arrived at the hospital. In many places, the local funeral home was the only resource that could transport to the hospital a person lying down.

Funeral homes were still the only methods of emergent transportation for the sick and injured in some areas of the country as late as 1975, even within 30 miles of a metropolitan area such as St. Louis, Missouri.[9] Care rendered at the time was limited to placing the sick or injured person on a stretcher and perhaps delivering oxygen as the care and transport were being managed by a funeral director, embalmer, or other unlicensed funeral home staff member.

Further expansion of the EMS movement occurred in 1966 when individual states gained authority to set the standards, implement programs, and regulate EMS through the 1966 Highway Safety Act.[10] Subsequent federal and state initiatives were responsible for the refinement and improvement of the care rendered to citizens during the next two decades after the "White Paper." That document suggested that the quality of pre-hospital care was an important determinant of survival from sudden injury. This recognition stimulated the development of federal funding through the Highway Safety Act of 1966. Subsequent to the enactment of the law, education was determined to be the most appropriate response. Funds started to be allocated to develop a National Standard Curriculum (NSC) for emergency medical technicians. It took five years for the contractor to deliver the first NSC in response to model legislation recommended by the National Highway Transportation Safety Administration (NHTSA). Many states adopted the NSC in the form of either law or rules. The curriculum and the scope of practice became intertwined. In 1973, Congress passed the Emergency Medical Services Systems Act (P.L. 93-142).[11] This law provided grants and other funding mechanisms to establish regional EMS systems including training and manpower. Additionally, the National Highway Transportation Safety Administration (NHTSA) created a curriculum that evolved into the current 40-hour First Responder Program developed primarily for police officers. The first meeting of the National Registry of Emergency Medical Technicians (NREMT) took place in 1970 to provide uniform standards for credentialing ambulance attendants.[12] In 1975, the American Medical Association first recognized the EMT-Paramedic as an allied health occupation.[13] NHTSA published the "EMS Agenda for the Future" as a guide for the continued advancement of EMS.[14]

Further expansion of pre-hospital transportation of patients to include routine use of air transport began in 1972. St. Anthony's Hospital (Denver, Colorado) and Loma Linda Hospital (California) established the first hospital-based helicopter air medical programs in the United States. The models were based on the first documented success of civilian air transport of patients in the 1960s when the Scottish Air Ambulance System began moving patients from outer islands to the mainland.[15]

16.3 Types of Services
A. First Responders
Resources to provide a local ambulance service are limited in many locations. Rural areas tend to have services that are responsible for large geographical areas so that they are fiscally capable of providing any level of service. Volunteer fire departments and ambulance squads are usually the first responders in these areas. There is a wide range of training for first responders. They may have only an American Red Cross First Aid Class as their education. In 1970, NHTSA created the 40-hour First Responder Course that became the standard of education for first responders.[16] First responders may not document much about their activities at an accident scene as there is little within their curriculum that deals with documentation.

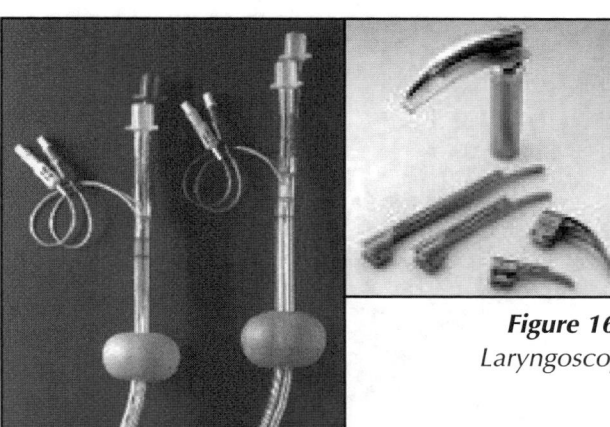

Figure 16.2
Laryngoscope

Figure 16.1 *Combitube*

Rural locations are not the only places where first responders offer services. In urban and suburban locations, many fire departments and police departments respond to emergency calls but do not transport the patient. The education level of the personnel can range from basic to advanced life support. These organizations benefit from the direction of physicians.

TIP: The documentation provided by the first responders often does not arrive with the patient to the hospital but follows later. Many states require first responders to submit documentation if they are under the direction of a physician and are licensed by the state.

B. Basic Life Support Transport

The least educated level of transport ambulance service is basic life support or emergency medical technician (EMT) level. In many states, this level of service provider is referred to as an Emergency Medical Technician—Basic (EMT-B). All states, based on the Department of Transportation guidelines, license or regulate ambulance services that transport people. Basic life support ambulances are staffed with a crew of at least one basic EMT and possibly a first-responder-trained driver. State statutes vary on the minimum training level of the ambulance crew. EMT-Bs can provide oxygen therapy, automatic defibrillation, spinal immobilization, splinting, and insertion of a multilumen airway such as the Combitube® (Figure 16.1).[17] They generally cannot administer IV fluids or medications. In addition, an EMT-B generally cannot utilize a laryngoscope, which is an illuminating instrument inserted into the pharynx to permit visualization of the pharynx and larynx to place an endotracheal tube or breathing tube[18] (refer to Figure 16.2). They are not educated to perform complex diagnostics such

as electrocardiography (EKG). Because of limited funding and the cost of education and advanced equipment, basic life support ambulance services are the only services available in many parts of the country. Since these services are licensed and regulated by the state, documentation standards for basic life support ambulance services varies state to state.

C. Advanced Life Support Transport

The highest level of education within the National Standard Curriculum (NSC) is advanced life support (ALS) or EMT-Paramedic.[19] Emergency services are provided under the direct supervision of a physician medical director and include invasive and pharmacological therapies for injuries or illnesses. Some of these therapies include manual defibrillation, electrocardiography, endotracheal intubation, intravenous fluid therapy, and the administration of medications. Since these services involve advanced therapies, they also have requirements for comprehensive documentation. These services are almost always involved in a form of quality review, which includes a review of the documentation, by their physician medical director. The ambulance crew for advanced life support service is composed of at least one paramedic who has the education and skills to perform the advanced procedures listed above. The paramedic's documentation is more detailed than that of the EMT-B and includes a thorough systems assessment, similar to that seen in nursing assessments documented on the patient care report.

Pre-hospital emergency or transport nursing requires the RN to have knowledge in a wide variety of patient care areas that he may encounter. The nursing process model is the basis for which nurses provide care. The concepts used in this model are assessment, diagnosis, outcome identification, planning, implementation, and evaluation.[20] The nurse bases care on the entire patient including the family and the patient's environment; this is what makes the nurse unique from other pre-hospital care providers. Transport nursing requires additional education, with some states requiring nurses to have concurrent licensure or certification as an emergency medical technician (EMT) or emergency medical technician-paramedic (EMT-P) before practicing in the pre-hospital arena.[21]

D. Ambulance Districts

Ambulance districts are political subdivisions created to provide a tax support for the provision of emergency medical services. Ambulance districts have broad legal powers to provide ambulance service. Typically an elected board of directors has statutory authority to levy taxes, impose fees for service, enter into contracts for services, enact ordinances, purchase equipment, hire staff, and provide for the administration and successful provision of the ambulance service. The ambulance district has much the same authority as a county level subdivision of government, although its sole function is the provision of ambulance service.

E. Fire Protection Districts

Fire protection districts are political subdivisions legally empowered to offer emergency medical services as well as fire protection services. These tax-supported entities have less power than ambulance districts for providing emergency medical services. While they also have an elected board of directors and the authority to do many of the same activities as an ambulance district, their primary function is to provide fire protection services. In some states fire protection districts can provide only first responder and emergency transports and no other services. Medical records generated during transportation of a patient need to be obtained directly from the fire protection district.

F. Hospital-Based Programs

Many areas have hospital-based EMS services that transport both emergency and non-emergency patients. These services may have more requirements for documentation than public entity services because they have to meet both state and hospital regulations. There may be circumstances in which hospital-based systems are held accountable for more than the normal EMS regulations because the system is hospital-based. An example is that the hospital-based ambulance follows stricter Consolidated Omnibus Budget Reconciliation Act of 1985 (COBRA) regulations since it is an actual service performed by the hospital.[22] The hospital-based service is required to comply with any and all Medicare program regulations as they apply to the hospital's responsibility in treating individuals with emergency medical conditions under the provisions of the Emergency Medical Treatment and Labor Act (EMTALA).[23,24] The hospital-based service is the entity responsible for keeping the medical records of patients transported by them.

G. Private Services

There are many localities that contract with private businesses to meet the needs of their area for ambulance services. Most of these companies bid on the emergency contracts in order to provide non-emergency services, which are certainly more profitable than the emergency services. For example, non-emergency services include transporting patients to their homes or nursing homes. The difference in for-profit versus not-for-profit may cause some documentation issues. Generally these documentation issues have to do with their billing practices such as Medicare billing.

Figure 16.3 Air Medical Ambulance (Helicopter)

Figure 16.4 Air Medical Ambulance (Airplanes)

H. Air Medical Ambulance Transport

The concept of civilian air transport is based on the success of military air evacuation in the Korean and Vietnam wars.[25] Civilian transport began in the 1970s, and in the beginning the focus was on moving patients to trauma centers.[26] Most air ambulance services (Figure 16.3) are either private business ventures or affiliated with a major hospital group or trauma center. These services can be either rotary winged (helicopter) or fixed wing (airplane). Helicopter services provide time-critical transport either from facility to facility or from the primary scene to a specialty resource center such as a tertiary care facility or a specialized trauma hospital. Fixed wing services (Figure 16.4) move patients over long distances from facility to facility. These services must comply with federal government regulations of the Federal Aviation Administration (FAA) and state regulations.[27] In addition, air medical ambulances may voluntarily be accredited by the Commission on Accreditation of Medical Transport Systems (CAMTS).[28] Due to the significant health issues of patients being transported, there is a greater need for in-depth documentation. In addition to emergency transports, there are a variety of specialized transport situations in which higher level staffing—critical care nurses, respiratory therapists, and even physicians—is needed. This results in a higher level of treatment as well as increased documentation requirements. These entities maintain medical records for patients they transport. There may be additional requirements if the transport crosses state boundaries. Specialized equipment such as newborn isolettes and intra-aortic balloon pumps (IABP), among others, may be used on these flights, based on the patient's condition and the necessity for the transport. There are unique aspects of care that need consideration when caring for patients during air transport such as the impact that the aircraft's vibration has on the patient, hypoxia, and hypothermia.[29]

I. Other Types of Services

There are locations in the United States where ambulance service is provided by a volunteer organization that charges fees for service and bills insurance and Medicare. Since these are licensed by the state they must adhere to the same documentation rules as tax-supported, hospital-based, or private ambulance services. There may be no living facilities for the staff of these services. They may respond from their homes to the ambulance garage to pick up the vehicle and travel to the scene. There can be significant delays in the crew's response when this is the situation. Additionally the crews are "on the clock" from the time they are dispatched, so if there is an accident or incident in their personal vehicles before they get to the ambulance then they might be covered by worker's compensation or even the service's liability insurance. These situations certainly require additional documentation that would be utilized during litigation.

J. Non-medical Transport Services

The non-medical transport services have become big business due to Medicare billing affecting the marketplace. These services transport passengers who have conditions that preclude them from using a normal car or van. This category includes wheelchair patients and others who must be transported lying down. There are few regulations since these passengers do not have a medical condition that requires care from the driver, or attendant if there is one. The only necessary documentation is a certification by the patient's physician that the patient does not need medical treatment or monitoring during the transport. One of the main issues with these services is that the transferring facility and the receiving facility must agree on the transfer and have a physician certify that no medical care is needed. Many laws do not identify the people being transferred by these services as "patients" but rather as "passengers."

TIP: The federal government's reimbursement program requires significant justification for the use of an ambulance for routine transfers, so these cost-effective services are becoming much more popular.

16.4 EMS Certifications

Pre-hospital and EMS professionals are often mandated by state law or medical direction to maintain certain credentials beyond their basic licensure. In some states, maintaining certain certifications is necessary in order to re-license. Some of the common certifications or credentials may include:

- Basic Life Support Healthcare Provider (BLS),
- Advanced Cardiac Life Support (ACLS),
- Advanced Cardiac Life Support Experienced Provider (ACLS-EP),
- Pediatric Advanced Life Support (PALS),
- Pre-hospital Trauma Life Support (PHTLS),
- Certification in Emergency Nursing (CEN®),
- Certification in Flight Nursing (CFRN), and
- Certified Flight Paramedic (FP-C).

The BLS Healthcare Provider Course teaches cardiopulmonary resuscitation (CPR) skills (including providing ventilation with a barrier device, a bag-mask device, and oxygen) for helping victims of all ages; use of an automated external defibrillator (AED); and relief of foreign-body airway obstruction (FBAO).[30] It is intended for participants who provide heath care to patients in a wide variety of settings, including pre-hospital and in-hospital settings. The participant of this program receives a course completion card upon successful completion of a written examination and practical skills.

First responders are often credentialed in a Heartsaver Automated External Defibrillator (AED) course.[31] Heartsaver AED, a comprehensive course for the First Responder, is designed to teach CPR; use of an automated external defibrillator (AED); and relief of foreign-body airway obstruction to all lay rescuers, particularly those expected to respond to emergencies in the workplace. It is specifically designed for lay rescuers who are required to obtain a course completion card documenting completion of a CPR AED course.

The ACLS Provider Course offers the knowledge and skills needed to evaluate and manage the first ten minutes of an adult ventricular fibrillation/ventricular tachycardia (VF/VT) arrest.[32] Providers are expected to learn to manage ten core ACLS cases:

- A respiratory emergency;
- Four types of cardiac arrest:

1. simple VF/VT,
2. complex VF/VT,
3. PEA (pulseless electrical activity), and
4. asystole (no heart rate); and
*   Five types of prearrest emergencies:
    1. bradycardia (slow heart rate),
    2. stable tachycardia,
    3. unstable tachycardia (rapid heart rate),
    4. acute coronary syndromes, and
    5. stroke.

The course is 8 to 16 hours in length. It is intended for healthcare professionals that staff emergency, intensive care, or critical care departments and is intended for emergency medical providers such as physicians, nurses, emergency technicians, paramedics, respiratory therapists and other professionals who may respond to a cardiovascular emergency. The participant of this program receives a course completion card upon successful completion of a written examination and practical skills. The card expires two years from the date of course completion.

The American Heart Association (AHA) developed a program for healthcare professionals who previously completed the ACLS Provider course and were looking for increased information and challenges.[33] The ACLS-EP course provides greater complexity and variety to the ACLS cases. The course is a ten-hour class that allows the participant to renew the ACLS provider status, and covers four additional skills/discussion stations. The advanced material includes toxicology, environmental emergencies, electrolyte imbalances, and complicated myocardial infarction management. The course is specifically designed for the paramedic who practices in high run volume departments or works for critical care companies such as air medical transport agencies. Physicians and critical care and emergency department nurses can also benefit from the material. Like all other AHA programs, the participant receives a course completion card upon successful completion of a written examination and practical skills. The card is valid until two years from the date of course completion.

The intended audience for a PALS course is pediatricians, house staff, emergency physicians, family physicians, nurses, paramedics, respiratory therapists, as well as pre-hospital professionals who are responsible for the well-being of infants and children.[34] The goal of the PALS program is to provide the participant with the information needed to recognize pediatric patients at risk for cardiopulmonary arrest. The course teaches strategies to prevent the arrest. There is a didactic portion to the program as well as multiple skills stations for the participants to practice the cognitive and psychomotor skills needed to resuscitate and stabilize pediatric patients in respiratory failure, shock, or cardiopulmonary arrest.

The Pre-hospital Trauma Life Support (PHTLS) course is a continuing education program created to provide EMS education in the handling of trauma patients.[35] The program is designed to enhance and increase knowledge and skill in delivering critical care in the pre-hospital environment.[36] The program includes identification of the mechanism of injury, recognition of life-threatening injuries, and content about the related pathophysiology as well as how to assess and manage trauma patients. The course was developed by the National Association of Emergency Medical Technicians (NAEMT) and the American College of Surgeons Committee on Trauma. It also yields a certification card upon successful completion of a written and practical examination. Basic Trauma Life Support (BTLS) programs have varying degrees of credentialing from the basic for the EMT-B or First Responder to the advanced for the paramedic or other advanced provider.[37] While similar in course content, the BTLS programs are credentialed through BTLS International and offer course certification cards.

The Critical Care Emergency Medical Transport Program^{SM} (CCEMTP) is designed to prepare nurses and paramedics to function effectively as members of a transport team.[38,39] The intensive program works to bridge the gap between pre-hospital and hospital care and transport for the team members. The program includes information on the special needs of the critically ill during transport and how to maintain the stability of hospital equipment and procedures during transport.[40] The program typically includes two weeks of classroom instruction and can include an optional 32- to 40-hour clinical component. The program offers a three-year certification through the University of Maryland, Baltimore.

In July 1980 the Board of Certification began offering an examination in Emergency Nursing.[41] Upon successful completion of this examination the Registered Nurse (RN) is then designated as a Certified Emergency Nurse, or CEN®.[42] In July 1993 a collaboration between the National Flight Nurses Association, now known as the Air and Surface Transport Nurses Association (ASTNA) and the Board of Certification for Emergency Nursing (BCEN) offered the first CFRN examination for RNs.[43] Certification is the process of offering a method in which there is a means to measure competencies in the areas of emergency and transport nursing.[44] The Board for Critical Care Transport Paramedic Certification (BCCTPC) oversees the examination for Certified Flight Paramedic (FP-C), which was first administered in 2000.[45]

There are a number of other programs that specialize in educating pre-hospital and hospital professionals about specific patient populations such as burn victims, and pediatric, obstetrical, and geriatric patients. A key to understanding the certification or credential is to look to the credentialing organization and determine the history of the organization and the requirements for instructor status. In addition, prerequisites for the program can give a clue as to the level of difficulty of the program. The more pre-course requirements there are, the greater level of information is provided and tested during the course.

16.5 Types of Patient Transports

Practicing pre-hospital care requires that the healthcare professional possess knowledge in all areas of patient care that he may encounter. The patient population can vary from geriatric to neonate emergencies as well as anything from medical, surgical, traumatic, psychological, infectious disease, or hazardous material exposures. The nature of the emergency, injury, or illness can be classified from minor to life-threatening.

There are three basic types of patient transports:

- from the scene of the accident or illness to the hospital,
- from one medical facility to another medical facility, and
- from the medical facility to a patient's residence or long-term care facility.

A. Emergency Transport

When a person has an injury or illness and cannot travel to her primary physician (if she has one), she calls for transport by an ambulance. A variety of providers offer this service. Public providers or private companies respond to these calls for assistance. Once a provider responds to a call, a legal duty to the caller is established. Dispatchers may also engage in directing treatment over the phone if they are trained and have the capability to do so. The documentation necessary for this type of transport should be comprehensive enough to accommodate the dispatch instructions if they are used, and the first responders' treatments if they are not involved in transport.

These reports should include the location description where the patient was picked up. An address or facility name is usually used. There should be sufficient patient identification information including home address, phone number, social security number or driver's license number if available, and the patient's date of birth. Some demographic information is generally used for statistical purposes. Response times should be noted, although some of the times in rural services may not be completed until the crew returns to the base so it may not be included in the patient care report that is left with the patient. The reason for the transport should be noted even if the actual provider impression is different. There are times that the patient verbalizes only one complaint. This should be thoroughly documented in addition to the actual physical assessment findings of the responding crew members. The assessment findings may differ from the complaints offered by the patient. For example, the patient may describe burning pain in the center of his chest as indigestion. The alert EMS crew would be assessing for signs of a heart attack and documenting color, pulse rate, intensity of pain, and so on. In this instance, clear documentation should state what was verbalized versus what were the actual physical findings by the EMS crew. Once the patient is being transported and treated, there should be significant detailed documentation on the patient assessment including:

- vital signs such as pulse, respiratory status, and blood pressure,
- level of consciousness, and
- signs and symptoms of injury or illness.

The time the assessment was made should be recorded. Once the assessment is complete, there should be documentation of all therapies performed on the patient including status before and after each therapy. The more invasive the therapy, the more detailed the documentation must be.

TIP: If the pre-hospital care professional places an endotracheal tube in the patient there must be a detailed assessment of the patient's respiratory and neurological status prior to and after the intubation. This should include verification of proper tube placement, and the methods by which it was verified. The tube must be confirmed to be in place by several methods such as direct auscultation, end-tidal CO_2 monitoring, esophageal detector devices, or pulse oximetry.[46,47] There should be documentation of the respiratory status after the intubation and what steps were taken to maintain correct tube placement during transport.

Narrative documentation that supplements and supports all non-narrative documentation of assessments and therapies (on flow sheets) performed during the transport should be completed. Any difficulties, incidents, or other factors encountered during the transport should be documented. The record needs to include a statement describing the condition of the patient when he arrived at the receiving facility and the name or signature of the person that received the patient report and took over the patient's care.

EMS professionals are expected to follow the appropriate standards of care. Careful stabilization of a potentially spinal-injured patient is essential, as was the issue in the following case:

James T. Edwards v. Hillsborough County involved James T. Edwards, who was then 29 years old and had suffered repetitive falls resulting in a head injury. 911 was called and the 911 operator advised that Mr. Edwards be relocated, so he was placed into a chair. At that time, Mr. Edwards was able to move his arms and legs. Hillsborough County EMS responded, and the EMS run sheet documented the history that the patient fell down. EMS personnel grasped Mr. Edwards by the arms and legs and carried him with his body drooped in a "U" shaped position, then placed him on the stretcher for transfer to the emergency room. Upon arrival in the emergency room, Mr. Edwards was placed in a Philadelphia collar. The medical record documents that the patient was not previously immobilized, and no purposeful movement in the upper extremities or lower extremities was present; also priapism was noted. X-rays revealed subluxation of C6-C7 with spinal cord compromise. The plaintiff claimed the EMS paramedics failed to stabilize and immobilize Mr. Edwards' neck, head, or spine prior to initiating movement or transport. The paramedics testified that head, neck, and back immobilization equipment was available to them, yet they did not follow the Hillsborough County protocol for patient transport, and they acknowledged failing to immobilize Mr. Edwards' neck and spine in any manner. The protocol also mandated that patients such as Mr. Edwards be transported to a trauma center. Mr. Edwards was instead transported by EMS to a local community hospital ill-equipped to handle emergency care of his serious neurological injuries. The defendant initially disputed liability and advanced arguments that the plaintiff's condition was a proximate result of the falls that he sustained, and not the result of negligence of the Hillsborough County paramedics. However, ultimately this action was resolved in a $2.4 million settlement, with the assistance of a claims bill passed by the Florida Legislature.[48]

In the case of *James T. Edwards v. Hillsborough County*, the plaintiff claimed that the EMS providers failed to stabilize and immobilize Mr. Edwards, who fell and subsequently had documented abrasions and edema to the cranial area, with a Glasgow Coma Score of 9, indicating a moderate head or brain injury. There are several areas that can be addressed. Mr. Edwards was involved in a fall, and he had motion of all four extremities upon the arrival of the EMS crew and documented head injuries. EMS has the duty to perform an examination sufficient enough to discover the presence of life-threatening conditions, even when the patient's initial presentation does not make him appear to be critically ill. In addition, the patient must be protected from further harm until a thorough medical evaluation can take place in a controlled environment, such as an emergency department, to rule out injuries such as spinal damage. High levels of suspicion should be maintained for neck injuries from falls. The adult skull weighs more than 17 pounds and rests on a small segment of the cervical spine, similar to a bowling ball on a broomstick handle.[49] Sudden deceleration such as from a fall can generate sufficient force to fracture or dislocate the vertebrae.[50] Spinal cord injuries should be assumed to be present until they are ruled out medically.

The duty to render appropriate care for potential spinal cord injuries was ignored. The treatment is the same regardless of where the potential spinal cord injuries are located. The skill of spinal immobilization from a seated position, such as the position in which Mr. Edwards was found, is a testable station during the National Registry of Emergency Medical Technicians' licensure examination.[51] The emergency personnel should have performed assessment pre- and post-immobilization of sensory and motor function in all four extremities if the patient was responsive. Internal policies and procedures in this case were not followed as the patient was carried by the arms and legs and no spinal precautions were initiated until the patient arrived without movement at the community hospital. In addition, had the EMS agency's protocols been followed, the patient would have initially been transported to a tertiary care facility where a higher level of care could have been rendered to minimize or eliminate potential long-term neurological deficits.

In this incident the EMS professionals failed to provide the level of care that was required for Mr. Edwards. Through this breach of duty Mr. Edwards was physically harmed. Prior to the treatment rendered by the EMS personnel, Mr. Edwards was able to move all extremities. After treatment his condition significantly deteriorated.

B. Facility-to-Facility Transports

The transfer from one facility to another can be made in two situations. First, when a patient has a need that cannot be fulfilled at the facility, there must be a transport to a facility that can meet that need.[52] In this instance a physician deems that the medical benefits of the transfer outweigh the risk of the transfer. The second occurs when the patient requests a transfer to another facility.[53] These transports can be either emergent or non-emergent. In preparation for transfer, the referring facility 1) must continue to provide care up to its level of capabilities until the transport crew assumes care and 2) must assure that qualified staff with all necessary equipment to care for the patient while en route to the receiving facility is available.[54]

The state-mandated documentation is still required. This pre-hospital care report (PCR) documentation varies, from standardized trip sheets that are computerized and sent into the state for review to handwritten documentation. There may be additional records including a physician statement that the transfer is medically necessary and an acknowledgement by the receiving facility that it will accept the patient. The same documentation of assessments, signs and symptoms of injury or illness, therapies, changes in patient status, and a detailed narrative should be completed. Additionally, there may be records transferred from the sending facility to the receiving facility. In the following case, the plaintiff alleged that key documents indicating pain medication given to the patient were not sent with him:

> In *Bryan McMullen v. Sherif T. Elamir, MD*, a Texas man who suffered a hip dislocation went to the hospital, where he was first given pain medication. He claimed that after he was transported to another hospital, the defendant doctor gave him inadequate pain medication, resulting in several hours of pain and suffering. The defendant argued that the patient's medication record did not arrive with him from the transferring hospital, and that once it did, the medications were adjusted appropriately. According to East Texas Trial Reports, the plaintiff reached a settlement with the ambulance company. The jury verdict was for the defendant doctor.[55]

There are facility-to-facility transfers in which the patient requires specialized care that is not within the scope of practice of the EMS crew. When this is the case, a healthcare provider such as a registered nurse, respiratory therapist, or even a physician may accompany the patient. In these situations, the documentation of the EMS crew might not be as detailed as that of the higher level provider because the crew is just operating the conveyance and not specifically performing primary care for the patient. Most often, the EMS patient care records refer the reader to the documentation of the healthcare provider who accompanied the patient and performed the assessments and treatments. A healthcare provider at the receiving facility may be asked to sign a form indicating transfer of responsibility (Figure 16.5). In compliance with the Healthcare Information Portability and Accountability Act (HIPAA), the patient may be given a copy of the squad's privacy statement (Figure 16.6).

Alarm Number ________ Date ________ **Eureka Fire Protection District** Patient Name ____________________

No ECG Strip Attached

No ECG Strip Attached

I have received the transfer of care of the above named patient on this date from the Eureka Fire Protection District personnel and have received a report on the patient's condition, assessment, and therapies rendered to this patient by the Eureka Fire Protection District personnel.

Care Transferred To:

Signature ____________________

I have received a copy of the Private Health Information Policy of the Eureka Fire Protection District.

Patient Signature ____________________

Figure 16.5 Care Transferal Form – (ECG strip)

Eureka Fire Protection District

Eureka, Missouri

Privacy Policy

THIS NOTICE DESCRIBES HOW MEDICAL IN-FORMATION ABOUT YOU MAY BE USED AND DISCLOSED AND HOW YOU CAN GET ACCESS TO THIS INFORMATION. PLEASE REVIEW IT CAREFULLY.

Purpose of this Notice: Eureka Fire Protection District is required by law to maintain the privacy of certain confidential health care information, known as Protected Health Information or PHI, and to provide you with a notice of our legal duties and privacy practices with respect to your PHI. This Notice describes your legal rights, advises you of our privacy practices, and lets you know how Eureka Fire Protection District is permitted to use and disclose PHI about you.
Eureka Fire Protection District is also required to abide by the terms of the version of this Notice currently in effect. In most situations we may use this information as described in this Notice without your permission, but there are some situations where we may use it only after we obtain your written authorization, if we are required by law to do so.

Uses and Disclosures of PHI: Eureka Fire Protection District may use PHI for the purposes of

treatment, payment, and health care operations, in most cases without your written permission. Examples of our use of your PHI:
For treatment. This includes such things as verbal and written information that we obtain about you and use pertaining to your medical condition and treatment provided to you by us and other medical personnel (including doctors and nurses who give orders to allow us to provide treatment to you). It also includes information we give to other health care personnel to whom we transfer your care and treatment, and includes transfer of PHI via radio or telephone to the hospital or dispatch center as well as providing the hospital with a copy of the written record we create in the course of providing you with treatment and transport.
For payment. This includes any activities we must undertake in order to get reimbursed for the services we provide to you, including such things as organizing your PHI and submitting bills to insurance companies (either directly or through a third party billing company), management of billed claims for services rendered, medical necessity determinations and reviews, utilization review, and collection of outstanding accounts.
For health care operations. This includes quality assurance activities, licensing, and training programs to ensure that our personnel meet our standards of care and follow established policies and procedures, obtaining legal and financial services, conducting business planning, processing grievances and complaints, creating reports that do not individually identify you for data collection purposes.
Reminders for Information on Other Services. We may also contact you to provide you with other information about alternative services we provide or other health-related benefits and services that may be of interest to you.

Use and Disclosure of PHI Without Your Authorization. Eureka Fire Protection District is permitted to use PHI without your written authorization, or opportunity to object in certain situations, including:
For Eureka Fire Protection District's use in treating you or in obtaining payment for services provided to you or in other health care operations;

Figure 16.6 Privacy Policy – Eureka, Missouri

For the treatment activities of another health care provider;

To another health care provider or entity for the payment activities of the provider or entity that receives the information (such as your hospital or insurance company);

To another health care provider (such as the hospital to which you are transported) for the health care operations activities of the entity that receives the information as long as the entity receiving the information has or has had a relationship with you and the PHI pertains to that relationship;

For health care fraud and abuse detection or for activities related to compliance with the law;

To a family member, other relative, or close personal friend or other individual involved in your care if we obtain your verbal agreement to do so or if we give you an opportunity to object to such a disclosure and you do not raise an objection. We may also disclose health information to your family, relatives, or friends if we infer from the circumstances that you would not object. For example, we may assume you agree to our disclosure of your personal health information to your spouse when your spouse has called the ambulance for you. In situations where you are not capable of objecting (because you are not present or due to your incapacity or medical emergency), we may, in our professional judgment, determine that a disclosure to your family member, relative, or friend is in your best interest. In that situation, we will disclose only health information relevant to that person's involvement in your care. For example, we may inform the person who accompanied you in the ambulance that you have certain symptoms and we may give that person an update on your vital signs and treatment that is being administered by our ambulance crew;

To a public health authority in certain situations (such as reporting a birth, death or disease as required by law, as part of a public health investigation, to report child or adult abuse or neglect or domestic violence, to report adverse events such as product defects, or to notify a person about exposure to a possible communicable disease as required by law;

For health oversight activities including audits or government investigations, inspections, disciplinary proceedings, and other administrative or judicial actions undertaken by the government (or their contractors) by law to oversee the health care system;

For judicial and administrative proceedings as required by a court or administrative order, or in some cases in response to a subpoena or other legal process;

For law enforcement activities in limited situations, such as when there is a warrant for the request, or when the information is needed to locate a suspect or stop a crime;

For military, national defense and security and other special government functions;

To avert a serious threat to the health and safety of a person or the public at large;

For workers' compensation purposes, and in compliance with workers' compensation laws;

To coroners, medical examiners, and funeral directors for identifying a deceased person, determining cause of death, or carrying on their duties as authorized by law;

If you are an organ donor, we may release health information to organizations that handle organ procurement or organ, eye or tissue transplantation or to an organ donation bank, as necessary to facilitate organ donation and transplantation;

For research projects, but this will be subject to strict oversight and approvals and health information will be released only when there is a minimal risk to your privacy and adequate safeguards are in place in accordance with the law;

We may use or disclose health information about you in a way that does not personally identify you or reveal who you are.

Any other use or disclosure of PHI, other than those listed above will only be made with your written authorization, (the authorization must specifically identify the information we seek to use or disclose, as well as when and how we seek to use or disclose it). You may revoke your authorization at any time, in writing, except to the extent that we have already used or disclosed medical information in reliance on that authorization.

Patient Rights: As a patient, you have a number of

Figure 16.6 *Privacy Policy – Eureka, Missouri (continued)*

rights with respect to the protection of your PHI, including:

The right to access, copy or inspect your PHI. This means you may come to our offices and inspect and copy most of the medical information about you that we maintain. We will normally provide you with access to this information within 30 days of your request. We may also charge you a reasonable fee for you to copy any medical information that you have the right to access. In limited circumstances, we may deny you access to your medical information, and you may appeal certain types of denials.

We have available forms to request access to your PHI and we will provide a written response if we deny you access and let you know your appeal rights. If you wish to inspect and copy your medical information, you should contact the privacy officer listed at the end of this Notice.

The right to amend your PHI. You have the right to ask us to amend written medical information that we may have about you. We will generally amend your information within 60 days of your request and will notify you when we have amended the information. We are permitted by law to deny your request to amend your medical information only in certain circumstances, like when we believe the information you have asked us to amend is correct. If you wish to request that we amend the medical information that we have about you, you should contact the privacy officer listed at the end of this Notice.

The right to request an accounting of our use and disclosure of your PHI. You may request an accounting from us of certain disclosures of your medical information that we have made in the last six years prior to the date of your request. We are not required to give you an accounting of information we have used or disclosed for purposes of treatment, payment or health care operations, or when we share your health information with our business associates, like our billing company or a medical facility from/to which we have transported you.

We are also not required to give you an accounting of our uses of protected health information for which you have already given us written autho-

rization. If you wish to request an accounting of the medical information about you that we have used or disclosed that is not exempted from the accounting requirement, you should contact the privacy officer listed at the end of this Notice.

The right to request that we restrict the uses and disclosures of your PHI. You have the right to request that we restrict how we use and disclose your medical information that we have about you for treatment, payment or health care operations, or to restrict the information that is provided to family, friends and other individuals involved in your health care. But if you request a restriction and the information you asked us to restrict is needed to provide you with emergency treatment, then we may use the PHI or disclose the PHI to a health care provider to provide you with emergency treatment. Eureka Fire Protection District is not required to agree to any restrictions you request, but any restrictions agreed to by Eureka Fire Protection District are binding on Eureka Fire Protection District.

Internet, Electronic Mail, and the Right to Obtain Copy of Paper Notice on Request. If we maintain a web site, we will prominently post a copy of this Notice on our web site and make the Notice available electronically through the web site. If you allow us, we will forward you this Notice by electronic mail instead of on paper and you may always request a paper copy of the Notice.

Revisions to the Notice: Eureka Fire Protection District reserves the right to change the terms of this Notice at any time, and the changes will be effective immediately and will apply to all protected health information that we maintain. Any material changes to the Notice will be promptly posted in our facilities and posted to our web site, if we maintain one. You can get a copy of the latest version of this Notice by contacting the Privacy Officer identified below.

Your Legal Rights and Complaints: You also have the right to complain to us, or to the Secretary of the United States Department of Health and Human Services if you believe your privacy rights have been violated. You will not be retaliated against in any way for filing a complaint with us or to the government. Should you have any questions,

Figure 16.6 Privacy Policy – Eureka, Missouri *(continued)*

comments or complaints you may direct all inquiries to the privacy officer listed at the end of this Notice. Individuals will not be retaliated against for filing a complaint.

Effective Date of the Notice: October 1, 2003
Eureka Fire Protection District
Notice of Privacy Practices

IMPORTANT: THIS NOTICE DESCRIBES HOW MEDICAL INFORMATION ABOUT YOU MAY BE USED AND DISCLOSED AND HOW YOU CAN GET ACCESS TO THIS INFORMATION. PLEASE REVIEW IT CAREFULLY.

As an essential part of our commitment to you, Eureka Fire Protection District maintains the privacy of certain confidential health care information about you, known as Protected Health Information or PHI. We are required by law to protect your health care information and to provide you with the attached Notice of Privacy Practices.

The Notice outlines our legal duties and privacy practices respect to your PHI. It not only describes our privacy practices and your legal rights, but lets you know, among other things, how Eureka Fire Protection District is permitted to use and disclose PHI about you, how you can access and copy that information, how you may request amendment of that information, and how you may request restrictions on our use and disclosure of your PHI.

Eureka Fire Protection District is also required to abide by the terms of the version of this Notice currently in effect. In most situations we may use this information as described in this Notice without your permission, but there are some situations where we may use it only after we obtain your written authorization, if we are required by law to do so.

We respect your privacy, and treat all health care information about our patients with care under strict policies of confidentiality that all of our staff are committed to following at all times.

PLEASE READ THE DETAILED NOTICE. IF YOU HAVE ANY QUESTIONS ABOUT IT, PLEASE CONTACT OUR PRIVACY OFFICER.

Figure 16.6 *Privacy Policy – Eureka, Missouri (continued)*

C. Facility to Home or Nursing Home

There may be a need to return a discharged patient to his home for further convalescence or to a rehabilitation or nursing facility. Commonly these patients cannot be transported other than with an ambulance. The state defines documentation for these transports. The patient condition that requires ambulance transfer—as well as initial assessment of the patient including basic vital signs—should be documented on the report. Details of the patient's condition on arrival at the receiving facility or the patient's home should be documented as well as reassessment of the patient as needed. There may be no one at the home to receive the patient. EMS crews should document if the patient is received at his home by someone or if the patient is left alone (Figure 16.7).

A routine transportation from a hospital to a home can turn into a medical emergency, as the following case describes:

> In *Narcisa Flores, Individually and on Behalf of the Estate of Ricardo A. Flores, Cynthia A. Flores and Graciela Flores v. USA, Audie Murphy Veterans Hospital and the Department of Veterans Affairs*, the plaintiff decedent, Ricardo A. Flores, a 63-year-old insulin-dependent diabetic and paraplegic, died after suffering cardiorespiratory arrest on a 270-mile trip from a VA hospital in San Antonio, Texas, to his home in Hidalgo County. He had consumed only about 74 percent of his breakfast on the day of discharge, and his blood sugar level before departure was less than 73. When the VA ambulance in which he was being transported was about 193 miles south of San Antonio, he suffered cardiopulmonary arrest. The VA attendants called the local sheriff's department for assistance and began cardiopulmonary and mouth-to-mouth resuscitation. A commercial ambulance arrived and its personnel checked his blood sugar level, which was dangerously low at 29. One ampule of 50-percent dextrose was administered. His heartbeat and respiration resumed, but he was unresponsive. An air-ambulance arrived and took him to a hospital in Edinburg, Texas, where he was found to be acidotic and to have suffered extensive oxygen deprivation affecting his brain and neurologic stability. The plaintiffs alleged that the VA ambulance was negligently ill-equipped, since it had no glucometer, no 50-percent dextrose solution, no intravenous kit, no intravenous solutions, no heart monitor, and no oxygen mask. The plaintiffs further alleged that Flores was in a hypoglycemic condition when he left the hospital. The defense maintained that although the patient's blood sugar was low, his condition technically was not hypoglycemic. The plaintiffs further alleged that Flores was prone to esophageal spasms and choking. The defense maintained that he had complained only of swallowing problems, and that the results of a recent barium swallow were normal. The plaintiffs further alleged that the stretcher provided for the decedent could not be raised to allow him to sit upright to eat. The defense maintained that the stretcher could be and was raised, allowing the patient to sit upright and eat normally. The plaintiffs alleged that Flores ate nothing on this trip. The defense countered in maintaining that he ate a sandwich and drank fluids. The plaintiffs further alleged that Flores was not given his noon meal before this trip. The defense maintained that he was. The plaintiffs further alleged that hospital protocol required Flores to be transported in a commercial ambulance. The defendants denied such a protocol existed. The plaintiffs further alleged the hospital was negligent for administering insulin before the trip, and for not monitoring his blood sugar levels during the trip. The defendants denied negligence and claimed that Flores was negligent for not eating all of his breakfast or lunch, and for refusing additional nourishment when the ambulance stopped at a convenience store. Besides negligence and wrongful death, the plaintiffs alleged negligent hiring, negligent entrustment, and gross negligence. The plaintiffs sued the federal government, the hospital, and the Department of Veterans Affairs under the Federal Tort Claims Act. According to the Texas Blue Sheet, after the judge found the hospital 65 percent liable and Flores 35 percent negligent, the plaintiffs were awarded $1.3 million ($130,000 to the estate for conscious pain and suffering, $650,000 to the widow for mental anguish and loss of companionship and society). A final judgment for $845,000 was entered. The plaintiffs thereafter settled for $740,000, avoiding any appeal. The judge found that, although the VA employees transporting Flores responded correctly to the medical emergency, Flores' previously designated, standing "Do Not Resuscitate" order affected his care subsequent to the initial cardiopulmonary arrest.[56]

In this case, the documentation generated by the ambulance attendants would have been crucial. The food con-

RUN REPORT # 999999

Date of Run 08 01 2004
Mo Day Century Year

999999

Vehicle ID # 44 17

Ambulance Service #
AAA AMBULANCE SERVICE
Ambulance Service Name

PATIENT INFORMATION
Doe John A
Last Name First Name M.I.
123 MAIN ST. Eureka
Street, Route, etc. City
St. Louis MO 63025
County State Zip

Date of Birth 09 25 19 52
Month Day Century Year

RACE: [1] Black [2✓] White [3] Hispanic [4] Other

SEX: (1) Male [2] Female

LOCATION OF PICKUP
Hometown Hospital
Name of Hospital, Nursing Home, Clinic, or Street, Route, Highway #
Eureka St Louis MO 63025
City County State Zip

PATIENT DESTINATION
123 Main St.
Eureka Name of Hospital, Nursing Home, Clinic, Ambulance Service, Home, etc. MO
City State

NARRATIVE
Routine Transfer of Patient from Hospital to Home After MI

Vitals 128/74 Pulse 80 Resp 18 Clear and Present in all Fields

Pt Arrived at His Residence with no Changes and Care Turned over to His Wife

ACTUAL MILEAGE TO SCENE: _____ MILEAGE FROM SCENE TO DESTINATION: 18

TYPE OF RUN

TO SCENE
[1] Emergency response requested
[2✓] Non-emergency response (routine)

FROM SCENE
[01] Life threatening, transported
[02] Urgent, transported
[03✓] Routine, transported
[04] Dry run, no transport

TIMES
Call Received 0900
Unit Dispatched 0901
Unit En Route 0902
Arrive Location 0922
Depart Location 0935
Arrive Destination 0955

PLACE OF INCIDENT
[0] Home
[1] Farm
[2] Mine/Quarry
[3] Industrial Place
[4] Recreation/Sport
[5] Street or Highway
[6] Public Building
[7✓] Residential Institution (hospital)
[8] Other
[9] Unspecified

LICENSE NO.
Driver B 1 2 3 4 5
Att. #1 P 1 2 3 4 5
Att. #2

VITAL SIGNS
Systolic Blood Pressure 128
Respiratory Rate 18
Glasgow Coma Score 15

PROTECTIVE EQUIPMENT
[1] None [6] Belt & Bag
[2] Unknown [7] Helmet
[3] Seat Belt [8] Other
[4] Child Seat [9✓] Not Applicable
[5] Air Bag

FACTORS AFFECTING EMS
[01] Adverse weather
[02] Adverse road conditions
[03] Vehicle problems
[04] Unsafe scene
[05] Language barrier
[06] Extrication >20 minutes
[07] Hazardous materials
[08] Crowd control
[09] Med. control failure
[10] Other
[11✓] Not applicable

TREATMENT AUTHORIZATION
[1] On-line (radio/telephone)
[2] On-scene
[3] Protocol
[4] Written orders (patient specific)
[5] Orders refused
[6] Unknown
[7✓] Not applicable

TRAUMA ASSESSMENT

	Amputation	Burn	Crush	Dislocation/FX	Blunt	Gunshot	Laceration	Puncture/Stab	Pain	Soft Tissue
Head	00	10	20	30	40	50	60	70	80	90
Face/Eye/Ear	01	11	21	31	41	51	61	71	81	91
Neck	02	12	22	32	42	52	62	72	82	92
Spine	03	13	23	33	43	53	63	73	83	93
Thorax	04	14	24	34	44	54	64	74	84	94
Abdomen/Pelvic Contents	05	15	25	■	45	55	65	75	85	95
Upper Arm/Shoulder	06	16	26	36	46	56	66	76	86	96
Lower Arm/Hand/Elbow	07	17	27	37	47	57	67	77	87	97
Upper Leg/Hip	08	18	28	38	48	58	68	78	88	98
Lower Leg/Foot/Knee	09	19	29	39	49	59	69	79	89	99

Cause of Injury 312

ILLNESS ASSESSMENT
[01] Abdominal pain/problems
[02] Airway obstruction
[03] Allergic reaction
[04] Altered level consciousness
[05] Behavioral/psychiatric
[06] Cardiac arrest
[07] Cardiac rhythm disturbance
[08] Chest pain/discomfort
[09] Diabetic symptoms
[10] Hyperthermia
[11] Hypothermia
[12] Hypovolemia/shock
[13] Inhalation injury (toxic gas)
[14] Poisoning/drug ingestions
[15] Pregnancy/O.B. delivery
[16] Respiratory arrest
[17] Respiratory distress
[18] Seizure
[19] Smoke inhalation
[20] Stroke/CVA
[21] Syncope/fainting
[22] Vaginal hemorrhage
[23] Other _____
[24] Unknown
[25✓] Not applicable

DESTINATION DETERMINATION
[01] Closest facility (none below)
[02] Patient/family choice
[03] Patient physician choice
[04] Managed care
[05] Law enforcement choice
[06] Protocol
[07] Specialty resource center
[08] On-line medical direction
[09] Diversion
(name of hospital diverted from)
[10] Other
[11] Unknown
[12✓] Not applicable

TREATMENT

D	Att.		D	Att.		D	Att.		D	Att.	
01	02	Bag mask/Demand valve	19	20	Drug administered	39	40	I.V. administered # ___	59	60	Oxygen by mask ___ lpm
03	04	Bleeding controlled	21	22	Endotracheal intubation	41	42	I.V. failed # ___	61	62	P.C.P.D. applied
05	06	Blood specimen drawn	25	26	Other airway	43	44	I.V. maintained	63	64	Pulse oximetry
07	08	C.P.R.	27	28	EKG monitor	47	48	Intraosseous infusion # ___	65	66	Spinal immobilization
09	10	Cardiac pacing	29	30	Extremity splint	53	54	N.G. tube	69	70	Suction airway
13	14	Cricothyrotomy	31	32	Extrication ___ time	55	56	O.B. delivery	71	72	Thoracentesis
15	16	Defibrillation ___ watts/sec. # ___ attempts	35	36	Glucose test ___ mg/dl	57	58	Oxygen by cannula ___ lpm	75	76✓	Other V.S. TRANSPORT

MO 580-0597 (R1-99) **MISSOURI AMBULANCE REPORTING SYSTEM** White/AMBULANCE SERVICE Canary/HOSPITAL-PATIENT COPY

Figure 16.7 Routine Transfer Home

sumed on the trip, as well as the patient's refusal of food from a convenience store, should have been documented. As noted, the judge did not find any liability on behalf of the ambulance crew.

16.6 Transport and Crew Responsibilities
A. Patient Safety

EMS professionals are responsible for a wide range of activities during patient care and transport. The key to a successful transport is the assurance of the safety of the crew and the patient. It is not possible to help the patient if the EMS crew is injured before care can be rendered, so the first area of responsibility is to keep them safe.[57] Though typically emergency scenes are usually safe, they can also be unpredictable and care must be taken at all times to ensure everyone's safety. Surveying the scene and determining safety is imperative; this means both at the scene as well as at the referring facility it is one of the first steps a pre-hospital professional takes as part of the care of the patient.[58] In order to assure crew and patient safety, potentially unsafe situations or violent patients need to be identified as early as possible.

The driver of an emergency vehicle is expected to use care when rushing to an accident scene. In the following case, the driver's actions were found to be the cause of injuries to the ambulance's passenger and the driver of a tractor-trailer:

> This was a consolidated action stemming from the collision between an ambulance in emergency mode and a tractor-trailer. The plaintiffs were a paramedic who was riding in the back of the ambulance as well as the driver of the tractor-trailer. The defendants included the driver of the ambulance, Lima Fire Company, Middletown Township, the driver of the tractor-trailer, and his employer. The ambulance entered an intersection on a red light without due caution, causing the accident. The ambulance driver maintained he entered the intersection under lights and siren and the truck driver failed to yield the right of way to the emergency vehicle. Injuries included a hip dislocation, a lumbar disc herniation, fractured ribs and sternum, and a fractured thoracic vertebra.
>
> While the jury was deliberating, the plaintiff paramedic, Crist, settled with the defendant ambulance company for $75,000, and his claim against the tractor-trailer driver and owner went to verdict. The jury deliberated for several hours over a two-day period before finding the defendant ambulance

driver/fire company/township 95 percent negligent and the defendant tractor-trailer driver/employer 5 percent negligent. The plaintiff paramedic, Crist, was awarded $1,774,900 in damages. The plaintiff truck driver, Hoover, was awarded $753,850, which was reduced by his apportionment of comparative negligence. The plaintiffs' recovery against the defendant township/fire company/ambulance driver was capped at $500,000 per state statute. The case settled after the verdict for a confidential sum.[59]

The same hazards that are present for the EMS provider are present for the patient and bystanders at an accident scene. The EMS professionals must be concerned with their own safety as well as the safety of those in their care and in the immediate area of the response scene.

TIP: Incidents that affect patient safety must be documented on the patient care report. These can include motor vehicle crashes, patient handling accidents, or medication or treatment errors, even if the crew utilizes all safety equipment while transporting the patient.

It is a troubling fact that emergency crews attempting to help others are sometimes risking their own lives. There have been several instances in which EMS crews have been shot, wounded, or killed while doing their job. In February 2004, a lieutenant with the Lexington Kentucky Fire Department was shot and killed after she responded to a call for help. In Kansas City, Missouri, a paramedic was shot when a sniper opened fire on emergency crews at the scene of a house explosion.[60] Any situation that imperils the EMS crew needs to be fully described and documented in the crew's report. A major cause of EMS crew injuries and deaths are vehicle accidents.

B. Life-Threatening Transport

The most crucial ambulance transport is reserved for those patients who would die without the initial stabilizing treatment and rapid transport to an appropriate facility. These transports range from 4 percent of the patients transported as reported by the Eureka Missouri Fire Protection District to as much as 60 percent of the total ambulance transports in the City of New York.[61,62] The patients who are transported when they have a life-threatening illness also need the most interventions by the crew. There needs to be a greater detailed documentation since they require more treatments. These are the patients who would die if interventions were not provided by the EMS crews. Medication therapies to counteract allergic reactions, IV therapy for trauma patients,

```
Service No  189049            OUT OF HOSPITAL CARE REPORT        Unit No.  2417
Inci# 04-9999999   Pt# 0001       License Manager              Alarm Date 08/01/2004
FDID# 09518
```

```
Incident No 04-9999999   Onset Date   / /      Onset Time          Location Type
   Crash No              Trauma ID           911 Used 2 E911        5 Street or Highway
                                                                  Response Code to Scene
Scene Address                              Station 1    Shift N      1 Emergency
I 44 EAST BOUND & ANTIRE RD /EUREKA, MO 63025                     Highest Experience Level at Scene
                                                                    3 Paramedic/Firefighter
Township EU      District 02      County STLCO  Census 2215.00    Lights & Siren to Scene?
Mutual Aid None                   Occupancy                         4 Emergent, with lights or siren
```

Patient # 000001 Name DOE, JOHN A	Times	Response Analysis
Address 123 MAIN ST	Dispatch Notified 09:00:00	Dispatch 00:00:00
Rm Phone	Unit Notified 09:00:00	En Route 00:02:00
City Eureka St MO Zip 63025	Unit Enroute 09:02:00	To Scene 00:03:00
Race White Gender M DOB {09/25/1951} Age 52 yrs 10 mos	Arrived Scene 09:05:00	To Pt/Vict 00:00:00
SSN 111-11-1111 Primary Physician	Arrived Pt/Vict 09:05:00	On Scene 00:10:00
Dispatched For MVC	Enroute to Dest 09:15:00	Transport 00:20:00
Type of Service 1 Emergency Response Requested	Arrived Dest 09:35:00	Tot Resp Time 01:00:00
Chief Complaint		Out of Srv 01:15:00
Provider Impression T22 MVC, driver	Cleared 10:00:00	
Tx Authorization 1 On-line	Back in Service 10:15:00	ALS Response
Injury Sustained? Yes		Total Miles
Injury Intent 3 Unintentional	ALS Arrival	Loaded Miles 18.00
Mechanism of Injury NA Not Applicable		
Human Factors Affecting Care		

Patient Prior Medical History	Factors Affecting EMS Care	Prior EMS Care Given	Safety Equipt Worn by Patient
13 None	11 Not Applicable		1 None

Injury/Illness Detail

Type	Area	Severity	Primary Symptom	Job Rel?

Basic Vitals

Time	LOC	Airway	Resp Rythm-Effort/Qlty	Pulse Rythm/Quality	Skin	Cap Refill	Bleeding	Pupils-L/R	Posture
09:06:00	V	Head Tilt -		Regul-Thready	Normal	2 secs	Hemorrhage	1 / 1	Supine
09:16:00	V	Head Tilt -		Regul-Thready	Normal	2 secs	Hemorrhage	1 / 1	Supine
09:26:00	V	Head Tilt -		Regul-Thready	Normal	2 secs	Hemorrhage	1 / 1	Supine

Secondary Vitals

Time	Pulse	Resp	Temp	BP	Pa02	Skin Appearance	Eye/Mtr/Vrbl		GCS	RTS	Cardiac
09:06:00	110	12	Unk	90/60	92mmHg	Moist/Diaphoretic	4 6 4		14	12	Sinus Rhythm
09:16:00	100	Unk	N/A	100/0*	98mmHg	Moist/Diaphoretic	4 6 4		14	99	Sinus Rhythm
09:26:00	94	Unk	N/A	110/0*	98mmHg	Moist/Diaphoretic	4 6 4		14	99	Sinus Rhythm

* Denotes Blood Pressure Reading by Palpation or Doppler

Procedures Performed
F - Procedure Failed

Time	Procedure	Notes	Staff Id	Attempts
09:06:00	P02 Bag mask/Demand valve		241060	1
09:06:00	P04 Bleeding controlled		241060	1
09:06:00	P76 Assessment, Vital Signs, Transp		241060	1
09:07:00	P68 Spinal immobilization		241060	1
09:07:00	P64 Pulse oximetry		241060	1
09:08:00	P40 IV administered	X 2 R AND L AC 500 CC BOLUS EACH 14 GA ANGIOCATH	241060	1
09:09:00	P70 Suction airway		241060	1
09:10:00	P22 Oral or Nasal tracheal Intubati	7.5 MM TUBE CLEAR LUNG SOUNDS R ABSENT LEFT 22 CM	241060	1
09:12:00	P72 Thoracentesis	NEEDLE DECOMPRESSION LEFT CHEST GOOD LUNG SOUNDS A	241060	1

```
08/04/2004      08:49                                            Page   1
```

Figure 16.8 *Out of Hospital License Manager (MVC Computer Rollover)*

```
Service No  189049                OUT OF HOSPITAL CARE REPORT              Unit No.  2417
Inci# 04-9999999   Pt# 0001            License Manager                     Alarm Date 08/01/2004
FDID# 09518
```

Exposure Precautions Taken		Medications Administered			
Staff Member	Precaution Type	Time	Medication	Staff Id	Dosage
241052 Steve Mann	02 Gloves				
241060 Scott Mullins	02 Gloves				

Disposition

```
Transported to  D30 Not Listed            Dest Determined by  07 Specialty Resource Center
Mode of Transport  01 Ground              Diverted To
Agency Tiered With                        Patient Disposition  01 Life threatening, transported
Lights/Siren from Scene?  Emergent, with lights or siren    Pulse on Transfer    NA Not Applicable
```

Insurance

Type	Policy #	Group #	Insured Name

Patient Narrative

RESPONDED FOR A MVC. ON SCENE EXTRICATED 52 Y/O MALE PATIENT UNRESTRAINED DRIVER OF A ROLLOVER HIGH SPEED MVC. PATIENT RESPONDS TO VERBAL STIMULI PATIENT SNORING RESP 12 PER MINUTE. AIRWAY OPENED WITH JAW THRUST. PATIENT EXTRICATED TO BACKBOARD WITH FULL SPINAL IMMOBILIZATION. ENROUTE ORAL AIRWAY INSERTED. MEDICAL CONTROL CONTACTED WITH REPORT AND RECEIVED ORDERS FOR INTUBATION AND IV FLUID BOLUS. PAT IENT INTUBATED AS ABOVE. LUNG SOUNDS ABSENT LEFT SIDE. NEEDLE DECOMPRESSION COMPLETED TO PATIENT LEFT CHEST. GOOD LUNG SOUNDS ALL FIELDS. VITALS ASSESSED AS ABOVE. SECONDARY SURVEY PATIENT HAS MULTIPE LACERATIONS AND ABRASIONS TO HEAD CHEST AND LOWER EXTREMITIES. POSSIBLE BILATERAL FEMUR FRACTURES. IV'S ESTABLISHED AS ABOVE VITALS REASSESSED. PATIENT VENTILATED 20 X PER MINUTE WITH 100% O2. ARRIVED AT TRAUMA CENTER AND TURNED OVER CARE TO TRAUMA TEAM IN ROOM 4

Officer/Member Making

```
Signature_____        Signature_____
Officer Name  Mullins, Scott         08/04/2004   Member Name Mullins, Scott            08/04/2004


Signature_____
Attending Physician
```

Figure 16.8 Out of Hospital License Manager (MVC Computer Rollover) (continued)

and advanced airway management procedures are all examples of therapies utilized for patients with life threats. See Figure 16.8 for a patient care report example.

C. Urgent Transports

The vast majority of emergency transports are urgent in nature but not life-threatening. These make up from 96 percent of patients transported in the Eureka Fire Protection District to only 40 percent of the total ambulance transports in the City of New York.[63,64] While not as treatment-intensive as life-threatening transports, many treatments are performed for these patients, requiring thorough documentation. There needs to be adequate documentation since treatments are performed. Examples of urgently transported patients might include a patient with a fractured ankle from a skiing accident to a person who suffers from dehydration while working outside on a very hot day. Figure 16.9 is an example of an urgent transport patient care report.

D. Routine Transports

When patients are transported from facility to facility for routine appointments or therapy, the documentation needed is significantly less than if treatments are being performed on the patient. Often patients need to go to another facility for a diagnostic test or outpatient procedure. Skilled nursing facilities may have to send residents to get x-rays, CT scans, MRIs or other diagnostic procedures if the resident cannot travel by car or van. In this situation the ambulance is just conveying the resident. The crews are simply monitoring the resident's status and not providing treatments or other therapies.

TIP: Routine transport documentation tends to be brief and concise because the crews are observing, but not treating the patient.

E. Patient Restraints

Transportation of patients adds an additional consideration of operational safety. In most ground- and fixed-wing transport vehicles the patient is isolated from the vehicle's operator by either distance or physical barriers.[65] Based on the type of aircraft, the patient may be lying directly next to the pilot in a helicopter. It is imperative to recognize the potential threat to the operation of the aircraft.

The Commission for Accreditation of Medical Transport Systems requires that each entity have a policy to address both physical and chemical restraints for combative patients.[66,67] Therefore, patient restraints are sometimes utilized for the safety of the patient and the crew. Patients prone to violence or who cannot follow commands may need to be restrained. Pre-hospital providers do not routinely use medications to restrain patients. However, during routine transports pre-medication may be used when the physician determines that it is most appropriate. If this approach is used there must be documentation accompanying the patient that includes the medication used, the dose, and specific instructions on emergency procedures.

Physical restraints are common tools used by ambulance crews under strict medical direction. Most medical directors have established criteria for physical restraint use and the documentation that must be completed. Patients needing to be physically restrained are those that pose a safety threat to themselves or others due to intoxication, mental disorders, or other physiological criteria. Physically restraining a patient is not undertaken lightly. Often additional crew members are brought for support for the patient that has to be restrained. The rear of the ambulance is not without its share of potential weapons (Figure 16.10). During transport an unrestrained patient with violent intent can create a perilous situation for the crew.

16.7 Medical Direction

Every pre-hospital provider must be supervised by a medical director. This physician assumes the ultimate responsibility of the medical direction, or the oversight of the patient care aspects of the EMS system. What this means varies greatly among states and medical directors. Most medical direction involves standing orders or protocols that the crew can follow when the patient meets the criteria established in that protocol.[68] The EMS professional is operating as a designated agent of the physician.[69] The EMS professional has the authority to give medications and provide emergency care as an actual extension of the medical director's license to practice medicine, even though the physician may not even be in verbal contact with the responding unit when care is rendered.

EMS systems have developed standing orders because physicians cannot be at every scene response. These policies and procedures are approved by the medical director and authorize the EMS professional to perform particular tasks or skills based on certain situations.[70] An example of a standing order may be to administer oxygen to a patient who is in congestive heart failure without waiting to speak to a physician in the medical control emergency department (Figure 16.11).

```
Service No  189049                OUT OF HOSPITAL CARE REPORT            Unit No.  2417
Inci#  04-9999999   Pt#  0001          License Manager                  Alarm Date 08/01/2004
FDID#  09518
```

```
Incident No  04-9999999   Onset Date   / /      Onset Time              Location Type
   Crash No              Trauma ID          911 Used 2  E911             0 Home
                                                                       Response Code to Scene
Scene Address                            Station 1      Shift N            1 Emergency
123 MAIN ST /Eureka, MO 63025                                          Highest Experience Level at Scene
                                                                          3 Paramedic/Firefighter
Township EU      District 02       County STLCO  Census 2215.00        Lights & Siren to Scene?
Mutual Aid None                         Occupancy                         4 Emergent, with lights or siren
```

	Times	Response Analysis
Patient # 000001 Name DOE, JOHN A	Dispatch Notified 09:00:00	Dispatch 00:00:00
Address 123 MAIN ST	Unit Notified 09:00:00	En Route 00:02:00
Rm Phone		To Scene 00:03:00
City Eureka St MO Zip 63025	Unit Enroute 09:02:00	To Pt/Vict 00:00:00
Race White Gender M DOB {09/25/1951} Age 52 yrs 10 mos	Arrived Scene 09:05:00	On Scene 00:15:00
SSN 111-11-1111 Primary Physician	Arrived Pt/Vict 09:05:00	Transport 00:20:00
Dispatched For CHEST PAIN	Enroute to Dest 09:20:00	Tot Resp Time 01:00:00
Type of Service 1 Emergency Response Requested	Arrived Dest 09:40:00	Out of Srv 01:15:00
Chief Complaint		
Provider Impression M08 Chest Pain/Discomfort	Cleared 10:00:00	ALS Response
Tx Authorization 1 On-line	Back in Service 10:15:00	
Injury Sustained? No		Total Miles
Injury Intent 3 Unintentional	ALS Arrival	
Mechanism of Injury NA Not Applicable		Loaded Miles 18.00
Human Factors Affecting Care		

```
Patient Prior Medical History   Factors Affecting EMS Care   Prior EMS Care Given       Safety Equipt Worn by Patient
13 None                         11 Not Applicable                                        9 Not Applicable
```

Injury/Illness Detail

Type	Area	Severity	Primary Symptom	Job Rel?

Basic Vitals

Time	LOC	Airway	Resp Rythm-Effort/Qlty	Pulse Rythm/Quality	Skin	Cap Refill	Bleeding	Pupils-L/R	Posture
09:08:00	A	Patent			Normal	N/A	None	1 / 1	Supine
09:12:00	A	Patent			Normal	N/A	None	1 / 1	Supine
09:20:00	A	Patent			Normal	N/A	None	1 / 1	Supine
09:30:00	A	Patent			Normal	N/A	None	1 / 1	Supine
09:35:00	A	Patent			Normal	N/A	None	1 / 1	Supine

Secondary Vitals

Time	Pulse	Resp	Temp	BP	PaO2	Skin Appearance	Eye/Mtr/Vrbl			GCS	RTS	Cardiac
09:08:00	80	18	N/A	146/84	98mmHg	Normal	4	6	5	15	12	Sinus Rhythm
09:12:00	76	16	N/A	146/84	99mmHg	Normal	4	6	5	15	12	Sinus Rhythm
09:20:00	76	16	N/A	140/80	99mmHg	Normal	4	6	5	15	12	Sinus Rhythm
09:30:00	78	16	N/A	142/82	99mmHg	Normal	4	6	5	15	12	Sinus Rhythm
09:35:00	78	16	N/A	142/80	99mmHg	Normal	4	6	5	15	12	Sinus Rhythm

```
08/04/2004        07:37                                                          Page    1
```

Figure 16.9 *Out of Hospital License Manager (Computerized) – Five Vital Signs*

```
Service No  189049              OUT OF HOSPITAL CARE REPORT           Unit No.  2417
Inci# 04-9999999   Pt# 0001            License Manager                Alarm Date 08/01/2004
FDID# 09518
```

* Denotes Blood Pressure Reading by Palpation or Doppler

Procedures Performed

P - Procedure Failed

Time	Procedure	Notes	Staff Id	Attempts
09:10:00	P64 Pulse oximetry		241060	1
09:10:00	P28 EKG monitor	SINUS RHYTHM	241060	1
09:10:00	P76 Assessment, Vital Signs, Transp		241060	1
09:11:00	P60 Oxygen by mask	15 LPM NRB	241060	1
09:14:00	P40 IV administered	NS 1000 ML, TKO RATE 18 GA 1 1/4" LEFT AC	241060	1

Exposure Precautions Taken

Staff Member	Precaution Type
241052 Steve Mann	02 Gloves
241060 Scott Mullins	02 Gloves

Medications Administered

Time	Medication	Staff Id	Dosage
09:14:00	19 Normal Saline	241060	
09:15:00	34 Baby Aspirin	241060	325 Milligram
09:18:00	18 Nitroglycerin	241060	0.04 Milligra
09:23:00	18 Nitroglycerin	241060	0.04 Milligra
09:23:00	18 Nitroglycerin	241060	0.04 Milligra
09:32:00	16 Morphine	241060	2 Milligrams

Disposition

```
Transported to  D30 Not Listed              Dest Determined by  02 Patient/Family Choice
Mode of Transport  01 Ground                Diverted To
Agency Tiered With                          Patient Disposition 02 Urgent, transported
Lights/Siren from Scene?  Emergent, with lights or siren    Pulse on Transfer   NA Not Applicable
```

Insurance

Type	Policy #	Group #	Insured Name

Patient Narrative

RESPONDED TO A RESIDENCE FOR A PATIENT WITH A CC OF CHEST PAIN. ON SCENE PATIENT IS A 52 Y/O MALE C/AX3 WITH COMPLAINT OF SUB STERNAL CHEST PAIN AN 8 ON A 1-10 SCALE. ASSESSED VITALS AS ABOVE. PLACED PATIENT ON O2 15 LPM PER NRB MASK. ATTACHED ECG MONITOR SHOWING SINUS RHYTHM. CONTACTED MEDICAL CONTROL ENROUTE WITH REPORT. RECEIVED ORDERS FOR IV NS TKO, ASPIRIN 325 MG PO, NITRO .04 MG X 3 Q 5 MINUTES BASED ON PAIN. IF PATIENT NOT PAIN FREE AFTER NITRO MORPHINE SULFATE 2 MG EVERY 5 MINUTES UNTIL PATIENT PAIN FREE. IV ESTABLISHED AND ASPIRIN ADMINISTERED, NITRO ADMINISTERED. VITALS REASSESSED AS ABOVE. PAIN NOW A 6. SECOND NITRO GIVEN AFTER 5 MINUTES PAIN NOW A 4 THIRD NITRO GIVEN AFTER 5 MINUTES PAIN NOW A 2. VITALS REASSESSED AS ABOVE. MORPHINE 2 MG GIVEN IV PUSH AFTER FIVE MINUTES PATIENT NOW PAIN FREE. ARRIVED AT HOSPITAL AND TURNED OVER CARE OF PATIENT TO ER NURSE IN ROOM 4

Officer/Member Making

```
Signature_____     Signature_____
Officer Name   Mullins, Scott        08/04/2004   Member Name Mullins, Scott       08/04/2004


Signature_____
Attending Physician
```

```
08/04/2004        07:37                                                          Page    2
```

Figure 16.9 *Out of Hospital License Manager (Computerized) – Five Vital Signs (continued)*

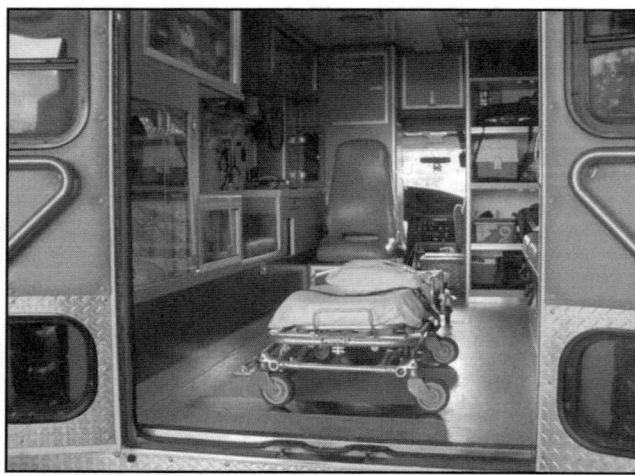

Figure 16.10 *Ambulance*

A medical director may provide direct supervision via radio or telephone for more complex cases and rely less on standing orders. There are almost always certain procedures or situations where the medical director will require contact. These can include:

- the administration of narcotic medications,
- refusal of care,
- do not resuscitate documents, and
- major invasive skills, including
  - endotracheal intubation,
  - surgical cricothyrotomy (allows rapid entrance into the airway for temporary ventilation and oxygenation of patients for whom the airway control is not possible by other methods), and
- pericardiocentesis (insertion of a large hollow needle into the pericardial sac surrounding the heart to remove accumulated fluid), to name a few.[71,72]

POLICY AND PROCEDURE MANUAL FOR PRE-HOSPITAL EMS
Office of Paramedic Education

CATEGORY:	Prehospital Patient Care
TITLE:	Adult Cardiac Emergencies—Congestive Heart Failure

Characterized by respiratory distress, basilar crackles (rales), jugular vein distension and possible peripheral edema.

1. Establish and maintain an airway; administer oxygen at 12-15 liters per minute if tolerated well by the patient. Assist ventilations as necessary.
2. Obtain vital signs and a brief history, noting the onset of dyspnea, any associated chest pain, and any prescribed medications the patient is taking. Place the patient on a cardiac, oxygen saturation, and CO2 monitor (if available).
3. Sit the patient upright and let his legs dangle.
4. Contact medical control with patient report and request orders. If, for whatever reason, contact with medical control cannot be established, prehospital emergency health care, professionals may continue as follows:
   a. Establish an IV line of Normal Saline at a TKO rate.
5. Medical Control may give further orders including:
   a. Nitroglycerin tablet(s) sublingually if BP>100mm Hg. systolic or Nitrolingual spray sublingually
   b. Furosemide (Lasix) 40 mg. IV push
   c. Morphine Sulfate 2-4 mg. IV push
   d. Patients with CHF should never receive albuterol
   e. Transport the patient to the hosptial in an upright position. Monitor vital signs, respiratory status and cardiac rhythm en route.

Effective Date: October 1, 1993 Revision Date: August 12, 1999

Figure 16.11 *Examples of a Pre-hospital Policy*

These situations tend to have greater liability associated with them, so the situation warrants medical direction and detailed documentation.

Medical directors also are involved with the educational aspect of the pre-hospital provider's work. Continuing education is a requirement for all EMS providers. The medical director must ensure quality of care by conducting evaluation of selected calls, and reviewing the EMTs' and paramedics' skills to assure that the patient is getting the best treatment possible. Much of the review and follow-up is based on the documentation provided by the EMS professional.

16.8 Documentation

TIP: There are multiple methods of documentation in use in the pre-hospital arena. The most common are the traditional paper-based records. Recently, electronic formats are becoming more prevalent.

No matter what format is used, there are several items that should be documented in the patient care report. There should be as much patient identification information as possible. The patient's name, address, date of birth, social security number, telephone number, and insurance information should be noted. The scene of the incident or where patient contact was first made should be noted, as well as the date. Specific times including when the call was received by the dispatcher, when the units were dispatched, when the units responded, when they arrived at the scene, when they departed the scene for the hospital, and when they arrived at the hospital should be documented. Additionally, the time the crew was available or returned to service should be noted. These times can establish the time frame that the patient was experiencing the injury or illness. Comparison can be made with the recorded progress of the patient in the emergency department. For instance, if a patient was exhibiting the signs and symptoms of a stroke and was being transported from a rural facility, she might not be a candidate for specific therapies due to the time of transport. Initial patient assessment findings, as well as continuing assessments, should be noted, especially after therapies. There should be a pre- and post-therapy assessment. Routine assessments should be based on the patient's condition. Assessments are documented closer together for the more serious patients and further apart for the less serious patients. All therapies should be thoroughly documented. Changes in patient status should be noted as the transport takes place. Patient medical history, medications, and allergies should be documented as well. The identity of the person accepting the patient should also be documented. A rule of thumb is that the care of the patient should never be turned over to a person of lesser experience or licensure than the EMS provider. Most patients are relinquished to a nurse or a physician in the emergency department.

Specific protocols and therapies may direct documentation. The issues of patient restraint and refusal of care are of particular importance for detailed documentation, and are detailed further in the chapter.

Abbreviations are frequently utilized for the sake of expediency when completing patient care reports. Often these abbreviations take the form of a kind of shorthand and are not recognized except by the writer. Since this would prove to be impossible to interpret by anyone other than the writer, many medical direction physicians publish approved abbreviations within their protocols and standing orders. Appendix A of this textbook includes abbreviations that are often noted in EMS records.

In addition to abbreviations, there are also many terms that are used to describe the kinematics or mechanism of the injury by the EMS provider. These descriptions are important in that they lead the healthcare providers to suspect occult or hidden injuries based on the mechanism of injury. For example, an adult jumps from a window and lands on his feet. He then complains of bilateral heel pain. A corresponding lumbar injury should be suspected until proven otherwise due to the mechanism of injury. An appropriate description of the events surrounding the injury should be thoroughly documented. Commonly used terms are described below.

A. T-Bone

A T-bone is a description of a side-impact collision when one vehicle impacts a second vehicle directly on the side (Figure 16.12). The EMS record may include a description of the number of inches or feet of intrusion. This term refers to how far the car was dented in by the second vehicle. The medical record of the person sitting next to the side of the car that was hit may describe injuries on the side of the body next to the damaged portion of the car. Additionally, the individual may be thrown into other portions of the interior of the car, sustaining injuries on other parts of the body.

B. Head On

This term is a description used to describe a motor vehicle crash where one vehicle impacts another vehicle front to front (Figure 16.13). When this occurs the individual is pushed forward and backward by the impact. Intrusion of the engine into the passenger compartment may result in crushing of extremities or the chest from impact with the steering wheel. The medical record may describe bruising on the chest or knees. The patient's head may strike the windshield. The seat or seat belt may be broken and the airbag activated.

Figure 16.12 T-bone Damage

Figure 16.13 Head-on Damage

Figure 16.14 Rear-end Hit

C. Rear End

This occurs when one vehicle strikes another from the rear (Figure 16.14). This type of impact may result in acceleration or deceleration injuries. Complaints of neck, low-back, and head injuries are commonly documented. This type of injury may also result in breaking of the seat or seat belt.

D. CID

A cervical immobilization device (CID) is used to maintain stabilization of the cervical spine on patients in which the mechanism of injury leads one to suspect a cervical spine injury (Figure 16.15).

E. C-Collar

A cervical collar (c-collar) is a device used to assist in the maintenance of stabilization of the cervical spine on patients where there is mechanism to suspect a cervical spine injury. Hard cervical collars are typically applied when trauma to the cervical spine is likely (Figure 16.16).

F. KED

A Kendrick Extrication Device (KED) is a tool used to help extricate victims of motor vehicle accidents (Figure 16.17). The medical record may document the amount of time it took to extricate the patient from the vehicle. Documentation of extrication time is imperative in pre-hospital records. Based on the accepted theory that there is a "Golden Hour" for a serious trauma patient to begin definitive treatment (surgical), the documentation of the time of extrication becomes crucial for the patient care report.[73] Extended extrication times greatly reduce the pre-hospital provider's ability to deliver a trauma patient to a trauma center for definitive care within the "Golden Hour." Many studies have shown that there is a greatly increased mortality rate if the serious trauma patient does not receive definitive care within the "Golden Hour."[74] Extended extrication during cold weather may result in dramatic lowering of the patient's body temperature that needs to be treated with warming blankets in the emergency department.

G. Traction Splint

Traction splints are designed for use with patients that have upper leg fractures. They have a variety of names and manufacturers and are often referred to by the manufacturer's name, such as Hare® Traction Splint or Segar® splints. The concept behind the traction splint is to place traction on the leg to stabilize the fractures, minimize further injury, and decrease bleeding (Figure 16.18).

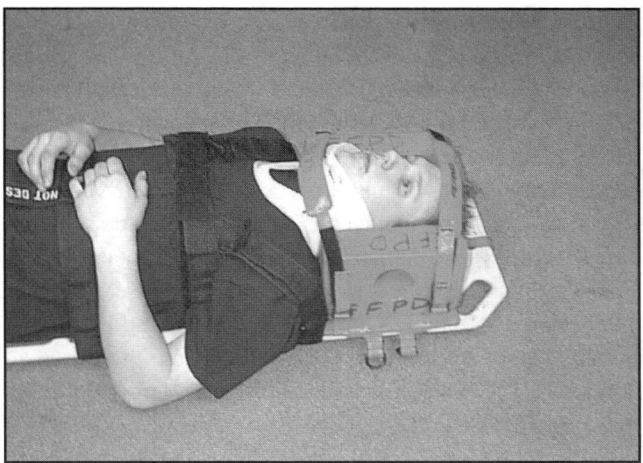

Figure 16.15 *Cervical Immobilization Device (CID)*

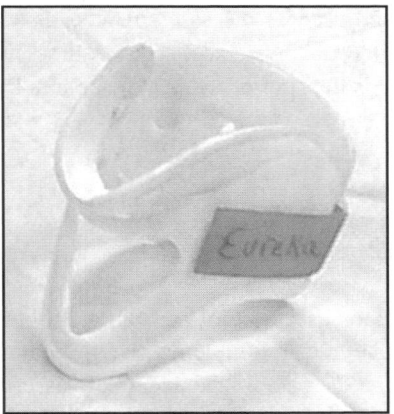

Figure 16.16 *Hard Cervical Collar*

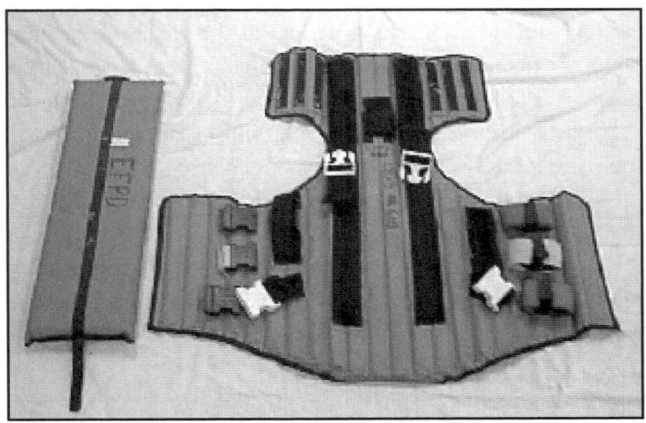

Figure 16.17 *Kendrick Extrication Device (KED)*

H. PASG or MAST

Pneumatic Anti Shock Garment and Medical Anti Shock Trousers are devices designed to improve blood pressure for patients that have multiple system trauma. There are significant research controversies with these devices (Figure 16.19).[75]

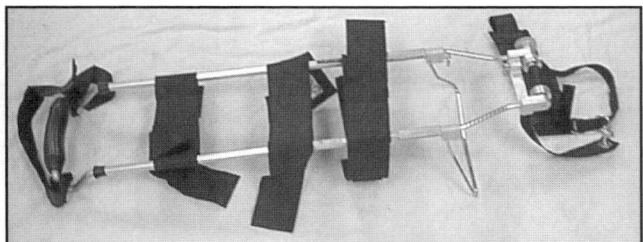

Figure 16.18 *Traction Splint*

Figure 16.19 *Anti-Shock Trousers*

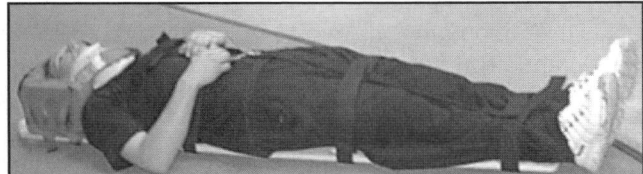

Figure 16.20 *Backboard*

I. Backboard

A backboard (bb)/rigid board is designed for use in spinal immobilization procedures (Figure 16.20). The management for a suspected unstable spine such as injuries sustained from a fall or motor vehicle crash is to immobilize the patient in a supine position on a rigid longboard in a neutral inline position. This neutral inline immobilization position should include the head, neck, torso, and pelvis to prevent any further movement of the suspected unstable spine that could result in damage to the spinal cord.[76] Spinal immobilization follows the principles of fracture management of immobilization to the joint above and below the suspected injury. Since the anatomy of the spinal column and the interaction caused by forces affect other parts of the body attached to it, the principle of immobilization extends from the head to the legs.[77]

The Glasgow Coma Scale is scored between 3 and 15, with 3 being the worst and 15 the best. It is composed of three parameters: Best Eye Response, Best Verbal Response, and Best Motor Response, as given below:

Best Eye Response. (4)
1. No eye opening.
2. Eye opening to pain.
3. Eye opening to verbal command.
4. Eyes open spontaneously.

Best Verbal Response. (5)
1. No verbal response.
2. Incomprehensible sounds.
3. Inappropriate words.
4. Confused.
5. Orientated.

Best Motor Response. (6)
1. No motor response.
2. Extension to pain.
3. Flexion to pain.
4. Withdrawal from pain.
5. Localising pain.
6. Obeys commands.

Note that the phrase "GCS of 11" is essentially meaningless, and it is important to break the figure down into its components, such as E3V3M5 = GCS 11.

A Coma Score of 13 or higher correlates with a mild brain injury, 9 to 12 is a moderate injury and 8 or less a severe brain injury.

Teasdale G., Jennett B., LANCET (ii) 81-83, 1974.
http://www.trauma.org/scores/gcs.html

Figure 16.21 Glasgow Coma Scale

J. Level of Orientation

The EMS squad typically documents the status of the patient on its arrival and during transport. A&Ox3 means that the patient was alert, and knew who she was, where she was, and the date. A&Ox4 means that the patient was oriented x3 and remembered events leading up to the arrival of the squad, such as how the accident occurred. In addition, the patient could provide her name, time, and place. Some squad members use the term CA&Ox3 for conscious, alert, and oriented. A patient who has suffered a head injury and possible concussion might be asked to name the president as a method of evaluating confusion. Loss of consciousness may be documented as "+ LOC."

The Glasgow Coma Scale (GCS) is a frequently used method of evaluating the patient's level of responsiveness. Figure 16.21 depicts this scale. Internationally the GCS is recognized as the method used in the assessment of head injury severity and degree of coma.[78,79] The overall score ranges from 3 to 15 and is the sum of the best responses in three categories:

- eye opening,
- motor response, and
- verbal response.

The ability to score or use the tool appropriately has enabled providers to make meaningful comparisons among a series of assessments on the patient and accurately assess his level of injuries.[80]

Scene behavior is an area of documentation that serves as a mental or neurological status baseline for later care and comparison. Many times a patient at the scene of an incident may display behaviors that change prior to arrival at the hospital. Pre-hospital providers should accurately describe behaviors observed on the scene, and document these on the patient care report. Often treatments rendered by these providers may improve or alter the patient's behaviors once treatment has begun.

Documentation of the level of a patient's responsiveness can be crucial in establishing pain and suffering, as the following case illustrates:

> In this action, the plaintiff contended that the defendant landlord of an apartment building negligently permitted a discarded couch to remain in the lobby for a three-day period, notwithstanding provisions in the code requiring that the lobby be used for ingress and egress only. The plaintiff contended that the extended presence of the couch in the lobby permitted an unidentified arsonist to start a fire that re-

sulted in the death of the 23-year-old decedent, who was sleeping in a third-story apartment when the fire started. The decedent had attempted to escape down the stairs and suffered extensive third degree burns and smoke inhalation, which the plaintiff contended caused severe pain for at least 20 minutes. They contended that the decedent suffered third degree burns over most of his body and would have presented one of his acquaintances to testify that the decedent was crying out for his mother as he was being brought to the ambulance. The defendant denied that this testimony was accurate. The defendants contended that because of the administration of extensive amounts of pain medication once the decedent was placed in the ambulance, it was clear that he could not experience pain. The plaintiff would have maintained that although the hospital records did not reflect overt signs of consciousness, the ambulance records revealed that the decedent was uncontrollable as he was being taken from the building. The plaintiff's forensic pathologist would have contented that in view of the severe nature of the burn injuries, it was highly likely that the decedent continued to experience some level of pain and suffering for the 20 to 30 minutes before he expired. The case settled prior to trial for $600,000 with the landlord paying $500,000 and the architect $100,000. The plaintiff, who would have argued that the pain medication would not prevent the decedent from experiencing some level of pain from the severe burn injuries, also would have argued that irrespective of this issue, the records supported the plaintiff's claims that the decedent was in severe pain when taken from the building.[81]

In this case, the EMS records would have been used to document the level of awareness.

K. Multiple Systems Trauma

A patient described as having suffered multiple systems trauma experiences trauma that affects more than one organ system in the body. Generally, this is a more severely traumatized patient. Figure 16.22 describes procedures used by EMS to treat this patient.

POLICY AND PROCEDURE MANUAL FOR PRE-HOSPITAL EMS
Office of Paramedic Education

CATEGORY: Prehospital Patient Care
TITLE: Trauma—Multiple System Trauma (MST)

1. Treatment of the MST patient in the field should be aimed at securing an airway, oxygenation, ventilation, treating life-threatening injuries and transporting.
2. Rapidly assess and extricate the patient utilizing PHTLS/BTLS techniques. Standing orders may be utilized to begin ALS care—see section 800.100.
3. Begin transport of the patient as soon as possible to the closest appropriate hospital as indicated by medical direction or section 300.300—Triage and Transport—Trauma Patients.
4. Use of air medical services may be considered when appropriate. See section 300.600.
5. Consider PASG for control of blood loss, management of pelvic fractures, or long transport times with the unstable MST patient. PASG is contraindicated in patients with pulmonary edema, traumatic diaphragmatic herniation, or known hemorrhage above the diaphragm. Inflate with order from Medical Direction if the patient is hypotensive (BP<90 mm Hg).
6. Unless the patient is entangled in wreckage and extrication is required, IV LINES SHOULD BE STARTED ENROUTE TO THE HOSPITAL. LR or NS are the fluids of choice and should be started with 14 or 16 gauge catheters. One IV line is indicated in a patient who is normotensive. Two IV lines should be established in the hypotensive patient.
7. Complete stabilization of the patient in the field is not essential. Continue stabilization enroute to the hospital. Delays at the scene may cause harm!
8. Notify medical direction of the potential for a serious trauma patient as soon as possible to expedite activation of the appropriate resource.

Figure 16.22 *Policy and Procedure—Multiple System Trauma*

L. Single System Trauma

This term is used to identify a patient who experiences trauma that affects only one organ system in the body. For example, a patient who has fractured her arm has suffered an orthopaedic injury. A single system trauma patient usually has less severe injuries.

M. Seat Belt and Airbag

The squad may comment on whether the seat belt of the victim was broken during the impact. Seat belt abrasions may be seen on the patient's neck, chest, or abdomen. The squad may document that the airbag was deployed. Airbag injuries to the face may be noted.

N. Trauma Center

A trauma center is a hospital with resources kept readily available to treat the most severely traumatized patients. These resources include:

- a team of emergency room personnel specially trained in the management of the trauma patient,
- trauma surgeons,
- available operating room staff and equipment, and
- physicians in specialties such as vascular, neurological, and orthopaedic surgery.

Many states regulate the designation of a trauma center based on these resources. Emergency department records of trauma centers are often structured to permit documentation of when each of the trauma personnel was notified of the arrival of the trauma victim. It is common for the EMS squad to call the hospital prior to its arrival. This notification permits the emergency department to begin the process of alerting the trauma team to the patient's impending arrival.

O. Car Versus Pedestrian

The EMS record may identify the mechanism of injury. Car versus pedestrian refers to a car striking a pedestrian. Other common terms are car versus tree, bus versus pedestrian, car versus bike, and so on. This term is often carried over to the emergency department records.

P. Star Pattern on the Windshield

A star pattern is a distinctive pattern of breakage created when an object strikes the windshield during a vehicle collision. It resembles a starburst pattern. EMS records containing this phrase identify that a victim's head struck the windshield. This impact creates the potential for a head or spinal injury.

Q. Passenger Numbering

Generally passengers are numbered across the front seat from left to right, then the rear seat left to right, and so on. Not all reports are numbered in this fashion or numbered at all.

R. Car Pillars

The car pillars are the posts that join the roof to the body of the vehicle. They are labeled from front to back—A, B, C and so on—and either driver side or passenger side.

16.9 Refusal of Care

EMS services do not transport every patient they encounter. Patients have the ability to refuse care if they are competent adults. Generally these patients are involved in a minor incident that does not potentially have serious consequences, such as the minor motor vehicle crash (MVC) where there is not a serious mechanism of injury (the fender bender in a parking lot) (Figure 16.23). A minor laceration or minor illness for which the patient can see his private physician is an example of a situation that may warrant refusal of care. Most physicians providing medical direction require direct overview of the refusal with contact by phone or radio so that the physician can evaluate the assessment by the field personnel and determine if the patient should be advised to be treated or transported. There should be complete documentation to outline the reason for the call and the assessment findings. The reason for treatment refusal and the evidence that the patient understands the risks of refusing treatment should be recorded. The patient may be asked to sign a form indicating refusal of treatment (Figure 16.24). Such a form was crucial in mounting a successful defense in the following New York case:

> In *Patricia Dunham, Adminx. of the Estate of Bobby A. Dunham, deceased, et al. v. City of New York et al.*, the plaintiff called 911 in the early morning in March 1997. Her 51-year-old husband had been suffering from severe headaches for two hours. Emergency medical services personnel arrived six minutes later and found the decedent's blood pressure to be moderately elevated, but an otherwise normal examination was obtained. The decedent and the plaintiff signed a document indicating that he had refused transportation to a hospital. Twenty-one hours later the decedent experienced a seizure-like episode. He was taken to a hospital and diagnosed with a ruptured cerebral aneurysm. He died the next day. The plaintiff claimed that the emergency services personnel had discouraged the decedent from going to the hospital. The defendants denied this and contended that the decedent expressed a desire to stay home. According to a published account, a defense verdict was returned.[82]

```
Service No  189049              OUT OF HOSPITAL CARE REPORT          Unit No.  2417
Inci#  04-9999999   Pt#  0001         License Manager                Alarm Date 08/01/2004
FDID#  09518
```

```
Incident No 04-9999999  Onset Date  / /    Onset Time          Location Type
  Crash No            Trauma ID       911 Used  2  E911         5 Street or Highway
                                                                Response Code to Scene
Scene Address                        Station 1    Shift N         1 Emergency
131 EUREKA TOWNE CENTER DR /EUREKA, MO 63025                    Highest Experience Level at Scene
                                                                 3 Paramedic/Firefighter
Township EU     District 02     County STLCO  Census 2215.00    Lights & Siren to Scene?
Mutual Aid None                     Occupancy                     4 Emergent, with lights or siren
```

Patient # 000001 Name DOE, JOHN A	Times	Response Analysis
Address 123 MAIN ST	Dispatch Notified 09:00:00	Dispatch 00:00:00
Rm Phone	Unit Notified 09:00:00	En Route 00:02:00
City Eureka St MO Zip 63025	Unit Enroute 09:02:00	To Scene 00:03:00
Race White Gender M DOB [09/25/1951] Age 52 yrs 10 mos	Arrived Scene 09:05:00	To Pt/Vict 00:00:00
SSN 111-11-1111 Primary Physician	Arrived Pt/Vict 09:05:00	On Scene
Dispatched For MVC	Enroute to Dest	Transport
Type of Service 1 Emergency Response Requested		Tot Resp Time 01:00:00
Chief Complaint	Arrived Dest	
Provider Impression T22 MVC, driver		Out of Srv 01:15:00
Tx Authorization 1 On-line	Cleared 10:00:00	ALS Response
Injury Sustained? Yes	Back in Service 10:15:00	Total Miles
Injury Intent 3 Unintentional		
Mechanism of Injury NA Not Applicable	ALS Arrival	Loaded Miles 18.00
Human Factors Affecting Care		

```
Patient Prior Medical History   Factors Affecting EMS Care   Prior EMS Care Given   Safety Equipt Worn by Patient
13 None                         11 Not Applicable                                   6  Belt & Bag
```

Injury/Illness Detail

Type	Area	Severity	Primary Symptom	Job Rel?

Basic Vitals

Time	LOC	Airway	Resp Rythm-Effort/Qlty	Pulse Rythm/Quality	Skin	Cap Refill	Bleeding	Pupils-L/R	Posture
09:06:00	A	Patent			Normal	0 secs	None	1 / 1	Supine

Secondary Vitals

Time	Pulse	Resp	Temp	BP	PaO2	Skin Appearance	Eye/Mtr/Vrbl			GCS	RTS	Cardiac
09:06:00	76	16	0.00	132/74	0mmHg	Normal	4	6	5	15	12	Sinus Rhythm

```
                    * Denotes Blood Pressure Reading by Palpation or Doppler
```

Procedures Performed

```
                                                                    P - Procedure Failed
```

Time	Procedure	Notes	Staff Id	Attempts
09:06:00	P76 Assessment, Vital Signs, Transp		241060	1

Exposure Precautions Taken / Medications Administered

Staff Member	Precaution Type	Time	Medication	Staff Id	Dosage
241052 Steve Mann	02 Gloves				
241060 Scott Mullins	02 Gloves				

Disposition

```
Transported to NA Not Transported        Dest Determined by  12 Not Applicable
Mode of Transport  01 Ground             Diverted To
Agency Tiered With                       Patient Disposition  04 Dry Run No Transport
Lights/Siren from Scene?  Emergent, with lights or siren   Pulse on Transfer   NA Not Applicable
```

Insurance

Type	Policy #	Group #	Insured Name

Patient Narrative

```
RESPONDED FOR A MVC.  ON SCENE MINOR MVC NO DAMAGE TO VEHICLE.  PATIENT 52 Y/O M THAT REFUSES TREATMENT OR TRANSPORT.
NO APPARENT INJURIES.  VITALS ASSESSED AND MEDICAL CONTROL CONTACTED FOR REFUSAL APPROVAL, APPROVED
```

```
08/04/2004      09:00                                                Page    1
```

Figure 16.23 *Out of Hospital License Manager – Refuses Treatment*

```
Service No  189049              OUT OF HOSPITAL CARE REPORT        Unit No.  2417
Inci# 04-9999999   Pt# 0001           License Manager             Alarm Date 08/01/2004
FDID# 09518
                              Officer/Member Making
_____

Signature_____      Signature_____
Officer Name  Mullins, Scott      08/04/2004  Member Name Mullins, Scott       08/04/2004


Signature_____
Attending Physician
```

```
08/04/2004      09:00                                        Page    2
```

Figure 16.23 *Out of Hospital License Manager – Refuses Treatment (continued)*

Eureka Fire Protection District

Refusal of Treatment and / or Medical Care

ADDRESS _____

CITY _____ STATE _____ ZIP CODE _____ PHONE (___) _____

D.O.B. _____ B/P _____ PULSE _____ RESP _____

INJURY OR ILLNESS _____

MEDICAL CONTROL # _____ DR. _____ NAME OF EMT OR EMT-P _____ LIC. # _____

 I hereby voluntarily acknowledge and state that I have been advised by the above named Emergency Medical Technician, or Paramedic, regarding the state of my present physical condition in that I have been advised that my medical condition warrants transportation by ambulance service.

 I hereby voluntarily refuse said ambulance transportation as recommended by the aforementioned Emergency Medical Technician, or Paramedic and I do hereby for myself, my heirs, executors, administrators and assigns forever release and fully discharge said Emergency Medical Technician, Paramedic, or Physician Medical Control harmless in regard to my decision to refuse ambulance vehicle transportation. I also acknowledge that I have been provided with a copy of the Private Health Information Policy of the Eureka Fire Protection District.

————————————————————
PATIENT
————————————————————
WITNESS
————————————————————
WITNESS

Figure 16.24 *Refusal of Treatment/Medical Care*

16.10 Do Not Resuscitate

Many people are concerned with the possibility of their health deteriorating to the point of becoming a burden to their loved ones. People with terminal illnesses may elect to prepare documents that outline what the healthcare providers should do in the event of a serious life-threatening event. Many decide to have the providers forego heroic measures for resuscitation. Many elect that nothing be done. Generally there is a physician statement that the plan of care has been discussed with the patient and the patient's immediate family, and then the document is notarized. Figure 16.25 is an example of a protocol that directs how the EMS crews should respond to do not resuscitate orders. Frequently, the EMS crews must follow the patient's wishes even at the direct disregard of the family members who are present and are requesting treatment for the patient. The need for complete documentation on the report is vital to rebut the possible litigation from family members in the future. A copy of the do not resuscitate order is a helpful addition to the report.

16.11 Controlled Substances

Some of the most effective treatments accomplished in the pre-hospital setting utilize controlled substances as medications. The Controlled Substances Act (CSA), Title II of the Comprehensive Drug Abuse Prevention and Control Act of 1970, is the legal foundation of the government's fight against the abuse of drugs and other substances.[83,84] There are five schedules of controlled substances: schedules I, II, III, IV, and V (see Figure 16.26). EMS providers are authorized to use medications in schedules II, III, IV, and V. Morphine and Demerol are Schedule II medications and Valium and Versed are Schedule IV medications. State agencies also regulate the use of these medications.

TIP: The basis for documentation pertaining to controlled substances can be divided into two areas: storage and administration.

POLICY AND PROCEDURE MANUAL FOR PRE-HOSPITAL EMS
Office of Paramedic Education

CATEGORY:	Prehospital Patient Care
TITLE:	Miscellaneous—Do Not Resuscitate Orders

This policy is written in accordance with MO 19 CSR 30-40, effective February 26, 1995 and it's subsequent interpretation by the Bureau of EMS and their legal council on November 11, 1995 entitled Procedures for Outside the Hospital Do Not Resuscitate (DNR) Request. Requests are orders by a patient's physician to refrain from initiating cardiopulmonary resuscitative measures in the event of cardiac or respiratory arrest. **DNR Requests are compatible with maximal therapeutic care and the patient may receive vigorous support (i.e. airway, IVs, drugs) up until the point of cardiac or respiratory arrest.**

Fire and EMS service administrators are encouraged to notify long term care facilities of the presence of this form so that it may be completed for those patients wishing not to be resuscitated. It shall be made clear to these facilities that this DNR Request form is the most easily recognized and honored in the prehospital setting.

Prehospital emergency care providers shall honor the DNR Request form when properly executed and presented. Procedures for acceptance of DNR request forms include:

1. If the validity of the DNR form is questioned, resuscitation should begin and medical control shall be contacted immediately to determine whether the DNR order is to be honored.
2. The DNR Request form shall be signed and dated by the patient or their legal representative and witnessed and signed by the patient's physician.
3. The revocation provision shall remain unsigned in order for the DNR Request Form to remain in effect.
4. The DNR Request forms shall be with the patient at the time of the prehospital care provider's arrival.
5. Medical control shall be contacted and informed of the presence of the DNR form.
6. If the DNR request is presented after basic life support / advanced life support procedures are implemented, the prehospital care provider shall consult with medical control prior to termination of resusitation efforts.
7. The prehospital care provider shall assist appropriate agencies in documentation of the existence of the DNR request form on the provider's patient care report form.
8. The DNR request form shall remain with the patient.
9. The patient has a right at any time to rescind the DNR request form.
10. The primary obligation of the EMS crew shall be resuscitation, not verification of DNR documents.

Figure 16.25 *Policy and Procedure – Do Not Resuscitate Orders*

U.S. SCHEDULE OF CONTROLLED SUBSTANCES
Under the Jurisdiction of the Federal Controlled Substances Act

Schedule I

These substances have a high potential for abuse and do not have a currently accepted medical use. Examples include: LSD, heroin, mescaline, peyote. They are not obtainable by prescription but may be legally procured for research, study, or institutional use.

Schedule II

These substances have a high abuse potential and a high liability for significant or severe physical or psychological dependence. A non-renewal prescription is required to obtain these substances. Examples include: opium derivatives, other opioids, short acting-acting barbiturates, secobarbital, morphine, meperidine, cocaine, and amphetamines.

Schedule III

The potential for abuse is less than Schedule I or II drugs with a moderate to low physical dependence but a high psychological dependence. This includes certain stimulants and depressants that have not previously been included in the schedules and preparations containing limited amounts of certain opioids. Prescriptions are required for these scheduled drugs and are refillable up to five times within six months if indicated by the physician. Examples include: chlorphentermine, glutethimide, mazindol, paregoric, phendimetrazine.

Schedule IV

This classification has a lower potential for abuse than the previous schedule and prescriptions are required. Examples include certain types of tranquilizers or psychotropics, chloral hydrate, valium, Phenobarbital, meprobamate.

Schedule V

This schedule includes drugs with less potential for abuse than previous schedule. Preparations contain limited quantities of the prescribed narcotics and are generally intended for use as an antitussive (cough) or antidiarrheal medication. The medication may be distributed without a prescription provided that certain criteria are met such as it is distributed by a pharmacist to some one over the age of 18 years and a record of the distribution is kept alone and other specific criteria are met.

Figure 16.26 U.S. Schedule of Controlled Substances

Storage documentation focuses on a two-person inventory system when the control of the medications changes hands at shift change. Security for storage almost always consists of a dual locking storage facility on the ambulance or at the squad's building. A physical inventory is documented any time the storage cabinet is opened. An example of an inventory document is shown in Table 16.1. Another type of storage documentation consists of the base supply storage. Usually two people check the inventory on a periodic basis and when the medicines need to be replenished, issued to ambulances after administration.

Administration documentation includes the information on the patient care record and on the medication storage documents. The following information is recorded:

- the alarm number,
- patient name,
- date,
- time of administration,
- prescribing physician's name and, if possible, signature,
- medication name and dosage and any amount wasted.

Table 16.2 is an example of the form for medication administration.

16.12 Communications

Even with standing orders and protocols, there is a very real need for the pre-hospital providers to be able to effectively and efficiently communicate with their medical control (director) physician. Unusual patient presentations, certain procedures, refusal of care, and termination of resuscitation efforts in the field are all situations that require physician oversight. For years, radio communication was the prime method of the EMTs' and paramedics' contact with the hospital. With the advancement of technology, the cell phone is now the primary means of communication. Advanced diagnostics such as 12 lead electrocardiography are now routinely transmitted via cell phone to the receiving facility. Much of the communication between the pre-hospital providers and the hospital is recorded in the event that an incident later requires review. This is typically done by the hospital.

16.13 Termination of Resuscitation in the Field

There are certain situations in which a patient will not respond to heroic resuscitative efforts. Many EMS services medical directors will allow, after consultation with the physician, termination of the resuscitation effort without transporting the patient to the hospital. In certain cardiac rhythms such as asystole (a cardiac rhythm associated with no discernable electrical activity on the ECG and often referred to as "flat line"), there is little to be gained from transporting the patient to the hospital only to be pronounced dead shortly after arrival.[85,86] The documentation required for these cases is directed by medical direction protocols (Figure 16.27) and includes all of the patient care interventions, the orders from the medical control physician, the situation surrounding the call for assistance, and an electrocardiogram of the patient's rhythm.

Cummins notes that asystole rarely is associated with a positive outcome. After a thorough assessment of the patient, efforts should be directed at assisting the family and friends that may be present in understanding the situation and why prolonged efforts are unnecessary, futile, often unethical, and ultimately dehumanizing, if not demeaning.[87]

16.14 Summary

The assessment, management, and transportation of the critically ill and injured is a highly stressful activity for the professionals involved in this area of medicine. The scope of practice varies from state to state as well as from agency to agency. In one area EMTs may be able to perform certain basic procedures and levels of care while in another the same procedure is out of their specified scope of practice. Verification of specific laws or policies governing the level of licensure of the pre-hospital professional is necessary to thoroughly understand their responsibilities and limitations while rendering aid to the sick and injured. Review of the EMT professionals' documentation will yield valuable information about the status of the patient at the scene and en route to the hospital.

Table 16.1: Daily Controlled Substance Inventory

Eureka Fire Protection District   # 211A R7/04

DAILY CONTROLLED SUBSTANCE INVENTORY

UNIT NUMBER 2417   This form must be changed monthly.   MONTH   YR

DATE	TIME	DEMEROL	MORPHINE	VALIUM	VERSED	TAG #	ONCOMING SIGN	OFFGOING SIGN

SEE REVERSE SIDE FOR ADDITIONAL DOCUMENT REQUIREMENTS

Table 16.2: Medical Control Report

Eureka Fire Protection District   # 211B R7/04

CONTROLLED SUBSTANCE USAGE RECORD

TICKET#	DRUG/DOSE	WASTE	TOTAL	SIGNATURE	SIGNATURE	PATIENT NAME	PHYS NAME	DATE	TIME	COMMENTS

DRUG REPLACEMENT

DATE	TIME	DRUG	AMOUNT	BY WHOM

TAG REPLACEMENT

DATE	TIME	OLD TAG#	NEW TAG#	# KEYS PRESENT	SIGNATURE	SIGNATURE	REASON FOR USE

POLICY AND PROCEDURE MANUAL FOR PRE-HOSPITAL EMS
Office of Paramedic Education

CATEGORY:	Prehospital Patient Care
TITLE:	Miscellaneous—Termination of Resuscitation in the Field

Purpose

Studies have shown that patients in asystole or pulseless electrical activity (PEA) who do not respond to Advanced Cardiac Life Support procedures within 15 to 20 minutes will not survive in the Emergency Department. Continued resuscitation efforts are traumatic to the patient, patient's families, costly, and hazardous to the EMS crew transporting the patient. This policy is intended as a guideline with the clear understanding that the medical control physician must have the latitude to make decisions based on the patient's best interest.

Procedure

1. Assess Airway, Breathing, Circulation (ABCs).
2. If breathing and pulse are absent, begin basic life support (BLS) and Advanced Cardiac Life Support (ACLS) procedures. Factors that may influence this step would be clear evidence that a patient would refuse ACLS efforts (i.e. a declaration of intent) or a clear indication of futility (i.e. a terminal illness or verifiable absence of breathing and cardiac output for longer than 15 minutes).
3. ACLS protocols should be followed for approximately 20 minutes by ACLS providers or by online medical control.
4. If during the resuscitation effort:
    a. there is no return of a palpable pulse greater than 60 for five minutes and
    b. the patient shows no continued neurological activity (i.e. motor response, eye opening or spontaneous respirations {not agonal}) and
    c. the patient remains in asystole or pulseless electrical activity, the paramedic should notify the online medical control physician. A decision will be jointly made as to terminating resuscitation efforts in the field.
5. Arrests in trauma, drownings, poisonings, hypothermia, hyperthermia, and children are excluded from this policy and will have resuscitation efforts continued and be transported. Patients in refractory ventricular fibrillation or refractory ventricular tachycardia will also be transported.
6. As a general rule, all patients age 18 and younger who present or progress to cardiopulmonary arrest will be resuscitated and transported.
7. If the resuscitation effort has been terminated, the paramedic will have the responsibility of informing the family that the patient has been declared dead by the medical control physician. If the family has questions about the decision, they will be referred to the medical control physician.
8. After the resuscitation effort has been terminated and the family informed, the paramedic will inform the law enforcement agency having jurisdiction (if they are not already present on the scene) that a death has occurred. The paramedic shall remain on the scene until law enforcement officers arrive on the scene. The paramedic will then determine the appropriateness of leaving the scene based on an assessment of the family's needs at that point.
9. If there is any doubt in the paramedic's mind about termination of the resuscitation efforts in the field, full resuscitation efforts should continue while the patient is transported to the appropriate emergency department.
10. When resuscitation efforts are terminated in the field, a copy of the Patient Care Report Form for that patient is to be forwarded to the Coordinator of the Office of Paramedic Education within 72 hours of the call. The report and radio/telephone report will be reviewed by the Coordinator of Paramedic Education and the EMS Medical Director. At a minimum, the narrative should include the details of the resuscitation efforts including any and all interventions performed (IV, drugs, intubation). Further, documentation of the reasons the resuscitation was terminated should also be documented (history of cancer, extensive down time, etc.)

Figure 16.27 *Policy and Procedure – Termination of Resuscitation in the Field*

Endnotes

1. McSwain, Jr., N., *Short History of EMS,* www.Fire-house.com. 2004, accessed 7/10/10.

2. *Id.*

3. *Id.*

4. *Id.*

5. *Id.*

6. *Id.*

7. *Id.*

8. Santa Barbara Public Health Department, *Emergency Medical Services History.*

9. Lemme Funeral Home records, 1995.

10. See note 9.

11. *National EMS Research Agenda.* National Highway Transportation Safety Administration, 2001.

12. National Registry of Emergency Medical Technicians. *History of the NREMT.*

13. *National EMS Research Agenda.* National Highway Transportation Safety Administration. *History of EMS Research,* 2001.

14. *Id.*

15. *Id.*

16. *Id.*

17. Limmer, D. and M. O'Keefe, *Emergency Care, Tenth* edition. Upper Saddle River, New Jersey: Pearson Prentice Hall, 2005.

18. *Id.*

19. *Emergency Medical Technician Paramedic: National Standard Curriculum (EMT-P).* National Highway Transportation Safety Administration. www.nhtsa.dot.gov, accessed 7/10/10.

20. Holleran, R., *Emergency & Transport Nursing Examination Review.* St. Louis: Mosby, 2005.

21. *Id.*

22. Federal Register, Part II, Department of Health and Human Services, Centers for Medicare and Medicaid Services, 42 CFR Parts 413, 482, and 489. http://www.medlaw.com. 2003, accessed 7/10/10.

23. *Id.*

24. Leaver, M., "EMTALA—at last," *Healthcare Review* 16, no. 10 (2003): 15.

25. Thomas, S., F. Cheema, S. Wedel, and D. Thomas, "Trauma Helicopter Emergency Medical Services Transport: Annotated Review of Selected Outcomes-Related Literature," *Pre-hospital Emergency Care* 6, no. 3 (2002): 359.

26. *Id.*

27. FAA Regulations. http://www.faa.gov/avr/afs/faa/8400/8400_vol3/3_001_03.html.

28. ARCH Air Medical Service, Inc. CAMTS. http://www.archairmedical.com/About_us.html.

29. Topley, D., J. Schmelz, J. Henkenius-Kirschbaum, and K. Horvath, "Critical Care Nursing Expertise During Air Transport," *Military Medicine* 168, no. 10 (2003): 822–826.

30. American Heart Association. http://www.american-heart.org, accessed 7/10/10.

31. *Id.*

32. *Id.*

33. *Id.*

34. *Id.*

35. Basic Trauma Life Support International. http://www.btls.org, accessed 7/10/10.

36. *Id.*

37. See note 37.

38. Centers for Emergency Medicine. http://www.centerem.net/education/CCEMTP.htm.

39. UMBC-Emergency Medicine. http://ehs.umbc.edu, accessed 7/10/10.

40. See note 40.

41. See note 21.

42. *Id.*

43. *Id.*

44. *Id.*

45. *Id.*

46. Cummins, R. (ed.), ACLS Provider Manual. Dallas: American Heart Association, http://www.heart.org/HEARTORG/CPRAndECC/HealthcareTraining/AdvancedCardiovascularLifeSupportACLS/The-Handbook-of-Emergency-Cardiovascular-Care-for-Healthcare-Providers_UCM_308747_Article.jsp, accessed 7/10/10.

47. Wang, H., R. Domeier, D. Kupas, M. Greenwood, and R. O'Connor, "Recommended Guidelines for Uniform Reporting of Data from Out-of-Hospital Airway Management: Position statement of the National Association of EMS Physicians," *Pre-hospital Emergency Care Philadelphia* (January-March 2004).

48. Laska, L. (ed.), "Failure to properly stabilize and support head injury patient results in permanent quadriplegia," *Medical Malpractice Verdicts, Settlements & Experts* (October 2003): 16–17.

49. See note 18.

50. *Id.*

51. National Registry of Emergency Medical Technicians. The Nation's EMS Certification. Exam Coordinators Documents. http://nremt.org/downloads/spinalimmoblizationseated.pdf.

52. Oman, K., J. Koziol-McLain, and L. Scheetz, *Emergency Nursing Secrets*. Philadelphia: Hanley & Belfus, Inc., 2001.

53. *Id.*

54. *Id.*

55. Laska, L. (ed.), "Texas man claims he was given inadequate pain medication for hip dislocation," *Medical Malpractice Verdicts, Settlements & Experts* (April 2003): 26–27.

56. Laska, L. (ed.), "Hypoglycemic paraplegic suffers cardiopulmonary arrest and death after 270-mile ambulance trip," *Medical Malpractice Verdicts, Settlements & Experts* (May 2003): 16–17.

57. See note 18.

58. See note 21.

59. Kessler, B. and C. Harvey, (eds.), "$2,528,750 combined verdict," *Jury Verdict Review & Analysis* (July 2004): 22.

60. www.Firehouse.com. "Worst Nightmare: Domestic Dispute Call Turns to Tragedy," Retrieved from http://cms.firehouse.com/content/article/article,jsp?id+26153&sectionID=17and.

61. Eureka Fire Protection District, Response Report. Eureka, Missouri, 2003.

62. City of New York Fire Department, Statistics. http://www.nyc.gov/html/fdny/pdf/stats/ems_cwsum_cy03.pdf.

63. *Id.*

64. *Id.*

65. Sheldon, P. and M. Day, "Sedation Issues in Transportation of Acutely and Critically Ill Patients," *Critical Care Nursing Clinics of North America* 17, no. 3 (2005): 205–250.

66. *Id.*

67. *Accreditation Standards of the Commission on Accreditation of Medical Transport Systems,* Sixth edition. Anderson, South Carolina: Commission on Accreditation of Medical Transport Systems, 2004.

68. Day, M., "Transport of the Critically Ill: The Northwest MedStar Experience," *Critical Care Nursing Clinics of North America* 17, no. 2 (2005): 183–190.

69. See note 18.

70. *Id.*

71. See note 47.

72. Desai, K., "Pericardiocentesis," *eMedicine* (April 2002).

73. *Id.*

74. *Id.*

75. Mercy Memorial Hospital. MAST. http://www.mercymemorial.org/EMS/mast.htm, accessed 7/10/10.

76. McSwain, N. (ed.), *PHTLS Basic and Advanced Prehospital Trauma Life Support,* Fifth edition St. Louis: Mosby, 2003.

77. *Id.*

78. *Id.*

79. McQuillan, K., Flynn Makic, M.B., and E. Whalen, *Trauma Nursing From Resuscitation Through Rehabilitation,* 4th edition. Philadelphia: W. B. Saunders Co., 2009.

80. *Id.*

81. Kessler, B. and C. Harvey, "$600,000 Recovery—defendant landlord allows discarded couch to remain in lobby for three days." *Jury Verdict Review & Analysis* (March 2004): 10.

82. Laska, L. (ed.), "Plaintiff claims emergency medical services personnel discouraged transport to hospital," *Medical Malpractice Verdicts, Settlements, & Experts* (December 2004): 15.

83. U.S. Drug Enforcement Administration. Controlled Substances Act. http://www.usdoj.gov/dea/agency/csa.htm, accessed 7/10/10.

84. Shannon, M., B. A. Wilson, and C. Stang. Upper Saddle River, New Jersey: Pearson Education, Inc., 2003.

85. Caggiano, R., "Asystole." *eMedicine* (November 2004).

86. See note 47.

87. *Id.*

Chapter 17

Emergency Nursing Malpractice*

Christine B. Macaulay, MSN, RN, CEN, Tammy Murphy, ASN, RN, CAP III and
Donna Hunter-Adkins, BSN, RN, CEN, CCM, CRRN, CLCP, LNCC

Synopsis
17.1 The Nature of Emergency Care
  A. Expectations of the ED Nurse
    1. Multiple roles
    2. Practice settings
  B. Patient Expectations
  C. Impact of Overcrowding
  D. Strategies for Overcrowding
    1. Diverting patients
    2. Staff composition
    3. Pressures on nurses
    4. Patient safety initiatives
17.2 Importance of Standards of Care in Litigation
  A. Early Standards of Care in the ED
  B. Basic Life Support, Advanced Life Support, and Beyond
  C. Early Trauma Standards
  D. Current Emergency Department Standards of Care
  E. Standards Directly Affecting Emergency Nursing
    1. American Nurses Association
    2. Emergency Nursing Association
      a. ENA assessment standard
      b. ENA diagnosis standard
      c. ENA outcome identification standard
      d. ENA planning standard
      e. ENA implementation standard
      f. ENA evaluation standard
      g. ENA education standard
      h. ENA performance appraisal standard
      i. ENA collaboration standard
      j. ENA resource utilization standard
    3. Scope and standards of pediatric nursing
    4. Scope and standards of medical surgical nursing standards
    5. Scope and standards of gerontological nursing practice
    6. Infusion nursing standards of practice
17.3 Qualifications of ED Nurses
  A. Additional Trauma Criteria
  B. Qualifications of the Triage Nurse
17.4 Entering the System: Initial Emergency Management
  A. First Responders' Care: Good Samaritans and EMS
  B. Flight Transport Teams
  C. Pre-Hospital Records
  D. Monitor Printouts
  E. Liability Questions Regarding Pre-Hospital Care

17.5 Emergency Department Nursing Practice in Action
  A. Triage
    1. Importance of triage
    2. Triage classifications
      a. Emergency Severity Index (ESI)
    3. Components of the triage system
    4. Pitfalls of triage
    5. Telephone advice
    6. Performance standards for the triage nurse
    7. Cases involving telephone advice
    8. Case of inappropriate triage classification
    9. Case of failure to properly triage child and begin antibiotics in a timely manner for meningitis
    10. Failure to timely assess man with chest pain—man dies an hour after leaving
    11. Case involving delay
    12. Case involving delay in CT scan, head injury, partial paralysis
  B. Treatment
    1. Assignment to treatment area
    2. Purpose
  C. Trauma Patients
  D. Cases Involving Treatment Area Assessment
    1. Patient in police custody denied medical screening: medical and nursing negligence alleged
    2. Failure to validate triage nurse's assessment
    3. Failure to properly assess trauma patient
    4. Failure to assess, report, and advocate
17.6 Diagnosis, Expected Outcome, and Care Planning
  A. Nursing Diagnosis: NANDA
  B. Expected Outcomes
  C. Care Planning
  D. Cases Involving Nursing Diagnosis and Planning
    1. Failure to anticipate and plan for potential problems
    2. Failure to anticipate safety needs of patient
    3. Failure to care for a belligerent patient
17.7 Implementation
  A. Competencies Required of Emergency Nurses
  B. Selected Competencies
    1. Care of the admitted patient
    2. Cervical and spinal immobilization
    3. Sedation in the emergency department
    4. Emergency equipment
    5. Pain management in the emergency department

---

*A special thank you to the authors who contributed to previous editions of this chapter:
Mary Kathryn Saville BSN, RN, MBA, CEN, LNCC, and Ellen Barker MSN, RN, CNRN

6. Cases involving implementation
    a. Failure to implement spinal precautions
    b. Failure to properly position patient for spinal tap, failure to properly resuscitate or monitor
    c. Failure to obtain health history results in heart failure
    d. Medication errors
17.8 Evaluation
  A. Importance of Evaluation
  B. Cases Involving Evaluation
    1. Failure to evaluate
    2. Failure to report chest pain
    3. Failure to detect critical changes
    4. Failure to evaluate and communicate lack of response to interventions
    5. Failure to properly report EKG showing myocardial infarction—delay in treatment blamed for death
    6. Failure to perform adequate testing for illness in asplenic man—death
    7. Failure to properly communicate regarding positive culture for bacteria in blood
17.9 Patient Education
  A. Consequences of Improper Patient Education
  B. Expected Outcome of Patient Education
  C. Cases Involving Patient Education
    1. Defense verdict related to discharge instructions
    2. Improper discharge instructions
17.10 Patient Advocacy
  A. Role of Nurse as Patient Advocate
  B. Selected Aspects of Advocacy
    1. Safeguarding life in the ED: chain of command and inappropriate or unclear medical orders
    2. Consent issues
      a. ED treatment
      b. Refusal of tests, treatment, admission, medications
      c. Assault and battery by ED staff
      d. Advance directives in the ED
      e. Health Care Proxies and what they allow
    3. Requests for additional staff
    4. Use of the recently dead for practicing procedures
    5. Failure to safeguard life at transfer or discharge
      a. Dumping
      b. Stranded patients and families
      c. Failure to safeguard life after discharge: callbacks
      d. Interpreters
  C. Cases Involving Patient Advocacy
    1. Obstruction of care
    2. Failure to safeguard life in the ED
      a. Failure to activate the chain of command
      b. Failure to insist on appropriate care
      c. Failure to recognize signs and symptoms of a myocardial infarction
    3. Dumping
      a. Infant not admitted to hospital
      b. Transfer of stable patient
      c. Transfer of unstable patient
      d. Transfer of Vicodin-overdose patient while unstable—death
      e. Failure to transfer as ordered, blame for death from abdominal aneurysm
      f. Pregnant patient
      g. HMO dumping
    4. Failure to safeguard life at discharge: failure to notify patient of abnormal test results
    5. Failure of hospital personnel to obtain interpreters for family of infant
17.11 Screening the Emergency Record for Nursing Negligence
  A. General Comments
  B. Elements of Nursing Negligence Cases
    1. Duty
    2. Breach of duty/negligence
    3. Damages
    4. Causation
  C. The Emergency Department Chart
  D. Documentation Red Flags for Nursing Liability
  E. What to Look for in the Medical Record
  F. Documents to Obtain in Evaluating Liability
17.12 Defenses
  A. Withholding Information
  B. Leaving Against Medical Advice
17.13 Summary
Endnotes
Additional Reading

17.1 The Nature of Emergency Care

This chapter:

1. provides an overview of emergency care standards as they relate to the hospital emergency department (ED);

2. provides ED nursing standards of care including position statements;

3. outlines seven areas of liability faced by emergency nurses;

4. presents case examples involving nursing liability;

5. describes screening principles in evaluation of emergency records for nursing negligence with special emphasis on

   a. damages and causation,

   b. components of ED medical records,

   c. relevant evidence in ED records and other hospital documents, and

   d. red flags in nursing documentation;

6. presents common defense positions for ED nursing practice;

7. presents issues related to emergency medical treatment and Active Labor Act (EMTALA); and

8. discusses Computerized Physician Order Entry (CPOE).

The information presented in this chapter aims to familiarize attorneys, healthcare system quality improvement leaders and risk managers with expected standards of practice in emergency department (ED) nursing in order to determine the application of legal principles to negligence claims. Detailed legal discussions and citations will not be presented, although pertinent case examples will be. This chapter develops theories of emergency nursing negligence in correlation with nursing standards for Assessment, Diagnosis and Care Planning, Implementation, Evaluation, Patient Education, and Advocacy. Unlike many areas of nursing practice, the pace and stress of emergency nursing, combined with the urgent issues of the patient population, leave very little room for error and a great deal of opportunity for catastrophic outcomes.

Emergency care delivery systems continues to experience increasing demands both from internal and external forces which, if not systematically and effectively responded to, lead to poor patient outcomes. Research studies completed by organizations such as the Institute of Medicine (IOM) and Health Grades document thousands of patient medical errors every year that were preventable causing significant harm or death to patients due to lack of adherence to known safe practice standards.[1] An example of this is when steps in handoffs of care are not followed, leading to errors in medication administration or omission of care. The results of several published reports tie ED overcrowding to delayed treatment and lack of treatment.[2] During the period of 1993 to 2003 a study completed by the National Hospital Ambulatory Medical Care Survey was reported by the Center for Disease Control. The survey showed a 26 percent increase in emergency department visits. At the same time the number of emergency departments decreased by 12.3 percent. The mean wait to see a physician is 46.5 minutes. On average, patients spent 3.2 hours in the ED.[3] The volume of visits continues to increase despite the efforts of healthcare administrators in the 1990s to redirect visits to out-of-hospital care sites. That was a time when managed care initiatives provided great incentives for not admitting patients and getting permission to see patients in the ED. Reasons for an ED visit are many, from the various trauma events—such as motor vehicle crashes, domestic violence crimes, gunshot wounds, and alcohol- and drug-related accidents—to the issues related to access to care.[4] Some of the reasons for overcrowding are due to decreased capacity, increased acuity, nursing shortage, physician shortage, ancillary service delays, reduced access to subspecialty care services, language and cultural barriers, reduced access to primary care services and increased complexity of diseases and associated evaluations.[5] A higher unemployment rate often means loss of medical insurance, resulting in people postponing routine medical care until illnesses reach an acute stage.

These issues have exponentially increased workloads for emergency department personnel. Predictions in the late '80s and early '90s that emergency departments would shrink in size due to the positive effects of managed care plans failed to be realized. Instead more healthcare facilities are experiencing the opposite: extreme overload and not enough beds or personnel to handle the increasing demand.

There are several groups of patients that present a challenge to the emergency room nurse:

- The homeless—discharging this population presents the nurse with challenges
- Non-English speaking
- Hearing or sight impaired
- Patients who have substance abuse issues
- Patients who have multiple comorbidities
- Pediatric patients
- Suicide risk patients
- The geriatric population
- Patients at risk of fall or bed entrapment
- Patients who present to the ED frequently
- Patients who have eating disorders, either morbidly obese or significantly underweight
- Patients with same sex orientation
- Patients in police custody
- Pregnant patients

There are a variety of factors leading to litigation in the emergency department. These include:

- Technology: Emergency departments have implemented many new technologies to support documentation, monitoring, patient tracking, and communication as well as safety systems. With any new system or equipment there comes required training and competency validation with continuous monitoring for that staff using the technology effectively. In a case involving the allegation of improper use of equipment or durable medical supplies, the nurse should be able to document that she has had adequate training in this area. Detailed records of each staff member's education should be maintained per hospital policy. The hospital should also maintain a log of equipment maintenance as failure of the equipment is sometimes the proximate cause of patient injury or death. Pulse oximetry is an example of this. There are cases in which nurses or unlicensed assistive personnel have frequently turned off alarms due to "alarm fatigue," which resulted in missing signs that the patient was not being oxygenated. Some of these cases have resulted in very large judgments for the patient's estates. Machinery and equipment do not substitute for the competent nurse using her knowledge, experience, and education to assess the patient within expected standards.
- Pharmacology: This is a multi-factorial issue. Each year new medications are added to the hospital formulary. The use of poly-pharmacy by many patients, especially the geriatric population is also an-

other area of high risk. Due to the episodic and urgent nature of care of the patient in the emergency department, it is incumbent upon the ED nurse to follow standards in taking the patient's history with regard to the use of medication which assists the provider in medication reconciliation. The nurse should be careful to assess the patient's history of taking any over-the-counter medications. The patient should also be asked about use of herbal or holistic medications, including drinks such as teas, coffees, nutrition "shakes" and ointments or pastes. Each patient should be asked about use of illicit drugs. The emergency department record should also document the medications the patients are instructed to be taking on discharge from the emergency department for the patient and primary care providers.

- Overcrowding, including boarding in the emergency department: The current healthcare crisis and the economic crunch have had a domino effect on the entire health system, with the ED bearing the brunt. Boarding patients in the ED (holding them until a bed is ready) requires policies and procedures specific to this patient population to assure they receive the required standard of care.

- Staffing shortage: The shortage of registered nurses and experienced nurses is ongoing. This is due partly to the fact that there is a shortage of nurse educators, thus limiting the supply of nurses entering the profession at the same time that the baby boomer nurses are retiring. The staff shortage becomes a critical factor when hospitals are challenged to do more with less, sometimes by reducing the numbers of registered nurses. This becomes a significant factor in the risk for malpractice and negligence in the emergency department. Key to many medical errors is the fact that orientation and annual competencies are not effectively met. Refer to Chapter 2, *Where Have All the Nurses Gone?*, in Volume I.

A. Expectations of the ED Nurse

An emergency nurse needs to act with a high degree of nursing autonomy and have the ability to initiate appropriate independent and interdependent care with limited direction while at the same time informing and educating the patient and family on the plan of care. As a professional nurse, each emergency nurse is expected to modify practice based on assessment of the patient's learning needs, standards of care, evidence of best practices, healthcare system policies and

the patient's individual needs. As the profession of emergency nursing continues to evolve with advances in technology and science, regulatory demands, evidence of best practices and healthcare reform, professional nurses are expected to practice collaboratively while delivering competent, timely and compassionate patient care. The nurse's primary commitment is to the patient.

TIP: Nurses are licensed by the state Board of Nursing in the state they practice and accountable to state boards of nursing to comply with the scope of practice they provide as well as the standards set by their nursing specialty organization. Therefore, emergency nurses are legally and professionally responsible for the nursing care they deliver.

Key elements of practice for emergency nurses are their accountability for care coordination as described in the Emergency Nurses Association (ENA) position statement, "Autonomous Emergency Nursing Practice." ENA defines the nurse's role as "autonomous" with an independent nursing scope of practice as related to care provided in partnership with the ED attending. Interdependent practice among emergency nursing, medicine, and other healthcare disciplines is the standard, with the goal of providing efficient, safe, and timely care. Professional nurses have accountability and responsibility to the patient for collaborative practice, compliance with their specialty standards, coordination of care with physicians and accountability for their own actions. Nurses' performance is expected to be evaluated regularly by a supervising RN for effectiveness and compliance with all current standards of care through outcome of care analysis.

1. Multiple roles

The emergency nurse's role is derived from basic nursing skills which encompass direct competent patient care, collaboration with other healthcare professionals and the patients' families, and advocacy, education, and promotion of health and safety.

- Patient Care—Emergency nurses care for patients and families in hospital emergency departments, ambulances, helicopters, urgent care centers, cruise ships, sports arenas, industry, government, and anywhere someone may have a medical emergency or where medical advances or injury prevention is a concern.
- Education—Emergency nurses provide education to the public through programs to promote well-

ness and prevent injuries, such as alcohol awareness, child passenger safety, gun safety, bicycle and helmet safety, and domestic violence prevention.

- Leadership and Research—Emergency nurses also may work as administrators, managers, and researchers who work to improve emergency health care.

2. Practice Settings

Emergency nurses may practice in one or more of the following areas:

- Emergency Departments
- Hospitals
- Healthcare Administration
- Education
- Research
- Urgent Care Centers
- Schools of Nursing/Universities/Colleges
- EMS/Pre-hospital Transport
- Ambulances
- Helicopters
- Airplanes
- Poison Control Centers
- Telephone Triage
- Military
- Medical Equipment, Resources, and Pharmaceutical Companies
- Crisis Intervention Centers
- Prisons/Correctional Facilities
- Research Institutes
- Government/State EMS Offices/Boards of Nursing
- Community
- Cruise Ships
- Sporting Events and Concerts
- Camps
- Special Events
- Travel Facilities

B. Patient Expectations

Non-critically ill patients using the ED as their primary care provider compete with critically ill or critically injured patients for time, space, and expertise of ED staff. The public expects that a patient should be promptly seen no matter what the complaint. Some EDs have tried staffing "fast tracks" to offset the bottlenecking of the main ED and to use as a marketing tool; they soon realized that reaching the promised time goals—of how long until a patient should be seen and treated—is not always feasible in such an unpredictable environment. Television shows and movies often use the ED as a backdrop to a story and portray events in EDs for the entertainment value rather than reality. This may be patients' only knowledge of emergency care until their first experience in an ED.

The public's expectations are quite often based on perceptions of what an ED visit should be rather than what the standard of care is. Family doctors often contribute to the expectations of patients by sending their patients to the ED when they cannot attend to them. The patient arrives with an expectation that, since their physician called ahead to notify the ED that they were sending the patient in for evaluation, they will be taken quickly into the treatment area. They expect to see the ED physician within a few minutes of arrival no matter what the nature of their visit. In addition, women with complications of labor arrive through the ED needing to be taken up to the labor and delivery suite. Protocols must be in place for the various symptoms of this population for the safety of the mother and baby. Some conditions require immediate physician assessment and treatment to ensure that the most desirable outcomes of care are met for both mother and baby.

C. Impact of Overcrowding

The United States Government Accountability Office (GAO) completed a report in 2009 on emergency department overcrowding. The findings from the GAO report support previous data that crowded conditions in emergency departments continues at alarming rates and often results in undesirable patient care outcomes. The GAO report reviewed 197 articles from 2003, reviewed national data and interviewed content experts and research organizations. The reasons for emergency department overcrowding are summarized in Figure 17.1.

- Boarding of admitted patients due to lack of access to inpatient beds
- Lack of access to primary care provider
- Increasing acuity of patients
- Difficulty transferring, admitting, or discharging psychiatric patients
- Aging population
- Staff shortages
- Shortage to on call specialist
- Hospital processes and financial factors

Figure 17.1 Causes of Emergency Department Overcrowding (U.S. Government Accountability Office Report 2009). See Endnote 4.

Poor outcomes related to ED overcrowding are:

1. delays in treatment for seriously ill or injured patients,
2. miscommunication between professionals because of increased volume,
3. increased mortality,
4. increased wait time to see the physician,
5. enhanced potential for errors,
6. violence,
7. ambulance diversion forcing EMS crews to "shop around town" for an ED that will accept critical patients,
8. negative effect on teaching missions in academic medical center, and
9. prolonged pain and suffering[6]

Changes in healthcare reform have not yet demonstrated positive impact on the working conditions in emergency departments. ED staff report daily challenges of under staffing, poorly oriented or educated staff, use of unlicensed assistive personnel (UAP) and lapses in human performance leading to preventable errors in patient care. Staff in EDs are constantly hurrying to catch up with new learning requirements, regulatory changes, shrinking healthcare resources, and an aging population and workforce. This requires constant vigilance of emergency department and health system leadership to respond to changing demands effectively and to budget time for staff learning. The recognized goal to prevent patient care errors by requiring staff to practice safety behaviors is the standard and should be clearly evident in documentation, staff behavior and self-reports.

The need to properly educate staff is key to setting the stage for safe care delivery. All too often this is short changed due to budget and human resource issues. In addition, appropriate supervision, monitoring outcomes of care, and an effective quality program continue to be the minimum requirements for any emergency department wishing to maintain the standard of care. Emergency care is difficult to manage due to the very nature of its business: salvaging the outcomes of physical or mental trauma, and acute or chronic illnesses, or at least mitigating suffering, 24 hours daily, seven days a week at unpredictable moments. Couple these elements with growing reports of patient care errors and growing patient expectations, and we can see the perfect storm leading to undesirable patient care outcomes.

D. Strategies for Overcrowding

1. Diverting patients

"Diverting" is one procedure commonly used by ED staff to offset high volume. This practice has evolved as a risk notification tool to let ambulance companies know that the ED has reached maximum capacity for safely caring for its patients. This does not mean the ED can deny the transport if there is no other safe option that is close enough. If the pre-hospital crew determines the transport must go to the hospital on divert, the hospital must accept the patient at least for the medical screening. Quite often, surrounding EDs in the geographic area quickly become overwhelmed and also go on divert. Diverting ambulances due to an overwhelmed ED has become a source of conflict among staff, ambulance crews, nearby emergency departments, physicians whose patients get diverted to another hospital, and administrators who see diversion of patients as lost revenue. Emergency physician directors have lost their contracts with hospitals based on not complying with the administrators' policies of not diverting patients. As a result of poor outcomes for patients, the EMTALA regulations broadened to areas outside of the ED with standards concerning accepting, treating, transferring, and diverting patients.

Additionally, amendments to the EMTALA obligations continue to change as cases are reviewed and comments accepted. Expected improvements around this critical access issue were promoted by studies done by the Institute of Medicine and the Centers for Disease Control and Prevention setting the new standards for access to care. Quality improvement initiatives in many emergency departments have led hospitals to avoid diverting by working with institutional internal and external partners. Strategic direction and support of senior management is directly correlated to outcomes of this standard and is considered essential in changing negative outcomes of diversion to positive outcomes. Many healthcare systems have set the standard of no diversion and worked on improving interdepartmental cooperation by eliminating the "silo mentality," resulting in positive patient care outcomes.[7] Please refer to Figure 17.2 as an example.

2. Staff composition

Hospitals have attempted to hire unlicensed assistive personnel (UAP) to perform nursing functions to meet cost constraints and staffing shortages. This remains an area of concern and is error prone. Some EDs train UAPs to perform activities such as paperwork, vital signs, phlebotomy, and vein catheterization with the goal of freeing up RNs to concentrate on the critical thinking and complex skills needed to provide safe care for their patients. Problems with using UAPs arise due to the lack of role clarity and scope of practice, coupled with lack of required supervision.

TIP: Cases continue to be brought to trial due to preventable errors when UAPs work outside their scope of practice. This is often seen during patient encounters such as the triage process, handoffs, transport, or when a higher level clinical person is needed to perform an assessment but is unavailable, resulting in harm to a patient.

Often a patient can wait in the ED for prolonged periods (greater that 12 hours) to get a bed on the inpatient unit, which may also be overcrowded or short staffed. Medication and treatment errors can be more common during this waiting period. Holding the patient in the ED for long periods creates opportunities for human errors to occur and is not the best practice when adequate skilled staff and equipment are not available. The best models of care have systems to expedite transfer of care to the inpatient care units as soon as possible while providing the necessary standards of care and equipment in the ED until transfer can take place.[8,9]

Examples of poor supervision of UAPs and inadequate staff knowledge are documented in cases of:

- patient strangulation after a patient was placed in a bed with the wrong size mattress,

- lack of monitoring patients during medication administration and handoffs of care,

- intoxicated patients who suffer harm after eloping from the emergency department when adequate monitoring was not in place, and

- a patient burned when a UAP applied a hot microwaved cloth on a child's arm to prep for IV insertion causing burns that required surgery. All preventable events if the proper systems, staff and competencies had been in place.[10]

Some health systems cross-train intensive care unit (ICU) nurses to support care in the ED during high volume periods or during understaffed shifts. Another method used to effectively cover high volume times or uncovered shifts is paying RNs to be on call for each shift.[11] These solutions are not problematic when they are systematically planned and implemented to assure that floating or covering staff have the necessary knowledge and skills to care for the patients to whom they are assigned. The problem is that healthcare systems short-cut the training and competency validation needed for staff to assume roles in the emergency department. The emergency departments must have a systems management approach to meet the required outcomes needed for the standard of care. Records must be maintained to document the appropriate education and competency evaluations that are met for each staff providing care in the emergency department.

Color Codes for Management System Status Indicators	
Condition Code	**Diversion Criterion**
GREEN (Open) Open/Accepting	When the hospital is able to accept incoming ambulance patients based upon regional point-of-entry plans.
YELLOW (Cautionary) ED Full	When all of the emergency department's regular beds are occupied and hallway and/or alternative space is being utilized to treat emergency department patients.
No CCU	When a hospital has no availability of critical care beds (ICU/CCU) and the emergency department is boarding critical care patients, but the emergency department is still capable of treating stable non-critical cases.
No CS	When a hospital has no CT Scan capability.
No Maternity	When a hospital which normally accepts maternity patients has no ability to accept maternity patients in the labor and delivery unit.
RED (Diversion) Ambulance Diversion	When the hospital's emergency department has reached the point of emergency department saturation (as defined above) and has made the decision to redirect incoming ambulance traffic.
BLACK (Closed) Closed	When it is unsafe to deliver an incoming patient regardless of the patient's condition to a hospital. Examples: fires; flooding, threats, biological or chemical contamination.

Figure 17.2 *Massachusetts Ambulance Diversion Policy*

The National Council of State Boards of Nursing has set standards for the nurse in the delegation of unlicensed assistive personnel. Authority to delegate varies from state to state; therefore, the jurisdiction's statutes and regulations must be checked in each state. The American College of Emergency Physicians' report in 1999 raised questions about the role of emergency medical technicians (EMTs) and paramedics working in emergency departments. The Emergency Nurses Association (ENA) Position Statement, The Use of Non-Registered Nurse (Non-RN) Caregivers in Emergency Care Setting, identifies role confusion in the use of the non-RN staff in the emergency setting. Non-RN caregivers include licensed practical nurses (LPN), licensed vocational nurses (LVN), and UAP.

TIP: Certified nursing assistants (CNA), orderlies, technicians, emergency medical technicians (EMT), paramedics, and nursing students in externship programs are UAPs.

The ENA supports the state practice acts of registered nurses in not delegating professional duties to non-RN personnel. Professional nursing duties include nursing assessment, nursing diagnosis, outcome identification, planning, implementation, and use of professional judgment; these responsibilities must remain the role of the professional nurse. Tasks delegated to a UAP cannot be re-delegated by unlicensed assistive staff. The licensed registered nurse determines and is accountable for the appropriateness of the delegated nursing task. Inappropriate delegation by the nurse, or unauthorized performance of a nursing task by assistive personnel, can lead to negative patient outcomes.

The highest clinical level of nurses who work in the emergency department is that of advanced practice registered nurses (APNs). These include the clinical nurse specialist (CNS) and the nurse practitioner (NP). The use of the NP to support the medical screening and treatment of the less-ill patients presenting to the emergency department has grown over the last ten years. The NP works in urgent treatment centers and the main emergency department. According to malpractice insurers, malpractice suits for NPs are rising in number and increasing in severity. Once sheltered by physicians and their insurance policies, nurses are now on their own in many cases.

Nurse leaders of advanced practice nurses convened a meeting in Washington, DC, in 2005 to discuss the issues.[12,13] The following are key points:

- Approximately 20-30 percent of nurse practitioner care is delivered by phone, exposing APNs to a liability they might not have previously considered.

- Courts must establish what is reasonable for a prudent APN. They establish "reasonable" by looking at policies and procedures, the literature existing at the time of the event, and then at national standards and causation: Was the action or inaction caused by the advanced nurse practitioner?

- APNs named in lawsuits can consider calling The American Association of Nurse Attorneys for counsel or advice even if they are covered under their employers' malpractice policies. Nurse attorneys might have a better grasp of the legalities involved with nursing practice.

- Advanced practice nurses should ask to see their employer's malpractice policies to make sure they are named in the documents. They should consider having their own policies as well, especially if they moonlight.

- Advanced practice nurses who practice with a physician who is under- or uninsured might become the deep pocket defendant—the one who is covered for the highest amount and, therefore, is more attractive to name in a lawsuit.

3. Pressures on nurses

Nurses are not merely on the front line in this drama; they are the front line in ED care. Nursing presence in this arena extends the arms of the medical staff and complements hospital resources so that more patients can be processed faster and, theoretically, more economically. Nurses have a statutory obligation to make critical decisions based on a large body of education. Without full authority to treat and prescribe, ED nurses are expected to accurately assess patients presenting with clinical symptoms needing immediate/emergent and urgent medical care as well as those with non-urgent symptoms that can wait to be seen.

TIP: ED nurses are expected to facilitate each patient's care.

The American Nurses Association (ANA) reviewed the state of EDs nationwide in 2001 and found that ambulance diversion and the shortage of critical care nurses placed EDs nationwide in crisis. The ANA's second look at the state of the ED in 2006 found that ED crowding had not improved. In 2006, the increased workload, and pressure to see patients faster, added to the already difficult recruitment of nurses to the emergency department. Many emergency departments accept new graduates, float nurses, and agency nurses, often from outside the United States, to help fill the gaps in staffing.[14]

Yet staffing issues add to nurses' stress since new hires may not be fully educated to the department, local, and national standards of emergency nursing care when assigned to provide care for a shift. A new graduate usually requires a minimum of 12 to 16 weeks orientation and should not be used in the triage role until he has at least six months to one year of ED experience. The triage nurse is required to be one of the most expert nurses in the ED.[15] However, sometimes the nurse is not adequately trained and formally checked off on all the competencies needed as a triage nurse before assigned the role. In an attempt to facilitate care in an increasingly overwhelmed system, producing at times angry patients and families, hospital administration and management have focused on "customer satisfaction" rather than system issues leading to safety and satisfaction outcomes. By virtue of their front-line position, advocacy role, and presence at the bedside, nurses are most often remembered by the angry patient or family, and are frequently blamed by the public for inadequate system designs in the ED. They also can be the key to preventing errors and overcoming barriers caused by poor systems if they maintain the patient as their focus and remain accountable for their own professional growth throughout their career.[16] Additionally, since emergency departments are not profit centers, they are often last to be considered during budget allocations, as many other "product lines" compete for ever-diminishing hospital resources. This often leads to gaps in maintaining standards of care. Advocating for patient safety is at times a difficult responsibility for nurses, but it must remain at the center of their daily practice as their role requires.

Regardless of staffing shortages or waiting rooms full of anxious patients and families, the ED nurse often spends extra time and effort on certain patients who may require additional support, such as the intoxicated, psychotic, violent, hearing impaired or blind patient, or patients with language barriers, just to name a few.

ENA standards and state standards guide nursing actions for the care of patients presenting to the ED who may be victims of abuse. Some larger EDs have teams to support these additional needs, but the nurse must facilitate all of the patient's care needs. The staff is obligated to follow standards of care as well as state and hospital reporting regulations.

Professional nurses who enter the realm of emergency care today accepts the challenge of upholding well-established clinical and statutory standards in the face of tremendous, sometimes overwhelming, obstacles—including those presented by the hospitals for which they work. These standards protect a vulnerable public from the "system problems" of health care just as manufacturing standards and product liability laws protect unsuspecting consumers from design defects in cars, airplanes, or other products.

4. Patient safety initiatives

Health care is shifting to building safer health systems by adopting some initiatives similar to the airline industry. These initiatives create blame-free environments when errors occur.[17] The intent is to encourage front-line staff to identify areas that may cause negative outcomes for patients and to redesign improved care. The paradigm is shifting but requires full commitment from senior leadership and health system boards to contribute the needed human and physical resources. This is no longer seen as optional but a characteristic of safe health systems. More information can be found on The Joint Commission (TJC) website (www.jointcommission.org).

A performance improvement project in 2002 at nine teaching and general hospital emergency departments demonstrated the effectiveness of team training in the emergency department. The evaluation used teamwork strategies utilized in the aviation industry to improve safety. The results of the prospective multi-center study showed significant improvements in patient care and a decrease in error rates in the ED as a result of adapting the aviation safety model to the ED. Attention to team training, standard team operating rules, plans of care, standardized communication, and improved processes led to safe and effective care in the ED.[18]

National Patient Safety Goals are set each year by The Joint Commission for high-risk, error-prone care events. The safety goals are derived from reported errors in many health systems. Identifying patients at risk of suicide was first added to the inpatient side and is now required in the outpatient setting. The standards are based on evidence from research and past events, with expert consensus. Many of the goals are related to gaps in communication and poor processes related to patient care such as proper patient identification.

TIP: Emergency departments are particularly vulnerable to communication gaps.[19]

It has long been recognized that the ED environment is high risk and must have strategic initiatives with good elements of safe design to support the required standards of care. In order to meet the current standards in the complex ED environment, each emergency department must provide competency-based orientation programs, an active quality improvement program, and competency assessment on an ongoing basis for all staff—continuous learning and training that empower all staff to advocate and assert a position on behalf of the patient.[20]

Evidence of the nursing staff's intent to provide quality care can be articulated by their knowledge of ED standards of care and by their records. The records include not only the patient's medical records but also the staff's orientation records, continuing education records, policies and procedures, staffing records, registration logs, triage logs, and records of wait times. Hospital emergency departments not monitoring wait times are not looking for opportunities to improve their system for safe care. Emergency department staff who demonstrate knowledge of the standards through accurate records, policies, programs, and compliance in using the standards, provide the minimum emergency care environment required today.

Many hospital administrators have moved away from only non-clinical leadership possessing the authority for strategic planning. The current management models include top leaders with a mix of clinical and management expertise to support effective, safe, and successful planning with goal setting focused on safe care in order to actualize what has been learned from evidence. The emphasis on patient safety can no longer be just a slogan. It must be evident at all levels of the organization with the bedside staff being key to success. The medical team model of practice described earlier is an essential standard that can provide safe care in the complex environment of the emergency department no matter how large or small. The goal of safety, which is embedded in today's health system language, has moved from a slogan to an internal initiative witnessed by each professional's behavior and accountability to engage in purposeful and cooperative care at every point during the patient's care. Health systems have turned to the nuclear and aviation industry to learn how to manage and maintain safe care environments. This should be evident in all emergency department policies, procedures and staff practice.

17.2 Importance of Standards of Care in Litigation

It may appear unnecessary to some litigation practitioners to discover which of the many complicated clinical standards apply to their client's case. It may be tedious to translate those standards into appropriate legal terminology to construct either a claim or defense. Care standards provide the basis from which successful attorneys on either side of a case design their strategies. They also establish the foundation for expert witnesses' opinions about whether negligence occurred. Medical and legal literature consistently report instances in which entire cases are argued before juries and won, only to be reversed by the court because the plaintiff failed to introduce expert testimony regarding the standard of care. Thus failure to identify and litigate medical neg-

ligence cases according to this fundamental concept could result in legal negligence claims.

TIP: *Healthcare Standards* is a valuable publication for researching standards and is a comprehensive guide to organizations that set practice standards for healthcare specialties. It lists the publications produced by each organization and provides addresses, phone and fax numbers, e-mail addresses, and websites.[21]

A. Early Standards of Care in the ED

In the past, patients admitted to the ED were evaluated and treated individually, according to the dictates of their private physicians or the opinions of treatment teams on duty for that particular shift. Evidenced-based research or expert consensus has standardized treatment in emergency departments, for patients suffering from trauma, chest pain, or stroke, to name a few. Measurement of treatment outcomes has focused on how quickly medication is started to treat patients presenting with chest pain. Studies have evaluated "door to needle time" for drugs like TPA. Decreased wait time for evaluation, diagnosis, and treatment has improved patient outcomes. Registered nurses are the first to assess patients in the emergency department, and they play a key role in best patient outcomes; therefore, many standards have evolved relating to the orientation of nursing staff, ongoing education, and competency assessment of nurses. As the number of ED patients increased, guidelines were developed to organize vast amounts of information about specific emergency disease states, forming reliable treatment protocols. Protocols on how to treat particular conditions evolved as a way to manage patients efficiently while maintaining patient safety.[22]

The role of the triage nurse expanded in response to evidence-based practice, and expert consensus led to the use of specific criteria to categorize each patient's severity of illness upon presenting to the ED. Protocols and guidelines enable the nurse to provide an acceptable minimum standard of care for each patient no matter how busy the emergency department. These standards also provide guidance on reassessment of patients within certain time frames while they remain in the waiting room or main ED prior to seeing the physician.[23]

B. Basic Life Support, Advanced Life Support, and Beyond

In 1966, the National Research Council Conference on CPR (cardiopulmonary resuscitation) recommended that healthcare providers be trained in Basic Life Support using techniques of external chest compression and ventilation (or forcing air into the victim's mouth). Early guidelines emanated from the American Heart Association. In 1979, an American Heart Association conference established standards and guidelines for CPR and emergency cardiac care. The following year, deliberations and recommendations of the conference were published in *Journal of the American Medical Association*. Basic Life Support expanded to include removing an obstruction from an airway (Heimlich's maneuver). After the techniques of Basic Life Support were established, an Advanced Life Support (ALS) course evolved. Advanced Life Support focuses on the use of medications and procedures such as intubation to augment chest compressions and ventilation.[24]

TIP: Recommendations on how best to resuscitate a patient are called algorithms; these are taught in Advanced Life Support courses. These are readily available in the medical literature and can be reviewed and compared with healthcare professionals' actions during resuscitation.

Organizations involved in establishing the standards for these courses include the American Heart Association, the American Society of Anesthesiologists, and the American College of Emergency Physicians, the Red Cross, and the American Medical Association.

The American College of Surgeons assumed a leadership role in recognizing that trauma is a surgical disease. An American College of Surgeon's committee worked to establish standards for the care of the trauma patient, which led to the development of the Advanced Trauma Life Support (ATLS) course. Protocols from the ATLS course serve as excellent guidelines to manage head and spine injuries and can be found in course manuals from the American College of Surgeons.

In 1983, during a national conference on pediatric resuscitation, participants stated that courses in neonatal and pediatric advanced life support were urgently needed. Three years later, the Pediatric Advanced Life Support (PALS) course was developed and made available by the American Heart Association and the American Academy of Pediatrics.

Pre-hospital providers (rescue squads, paramedics, emergency medical technicians) recognized that the care provided by the "first responders" was often fragmented and needed a single focus. (The first people to offer rescue assistance at the scene are "first responders." These may include good samaritan laypersons or fully trained Emergency Medical Technicians.) The Pre-Hospital Trauma Life Support (PHTLC) course was finalized in 1984 and was taught

nationwide to provide standardization and quality assurance for the trauma patient.

Development of standards and courses to educate healthcare providers in CPR and ALS (Advanced Life Support) has had an enormous impact on emergency care. Research-based techniques taught in these courses have provided both lay rescuers and healthcare professionals with tools that save lives. CPR has shown, through research and training, that lives can be saved. If performed improperly, cracked ribs, rib separations, or damage to the internal organs can occur. This training is widely available and is a standard for all healthcare workers.[25]

By the 1980s, healthcare personnel had accepted the use of written guidelines but recognized that ED systems had different capacities to deliver care based on medical and nursing expertise, and on available technology. Interdisciplinary committees were established among providers to modify guidelines so that minimum levels of care could be defined for specific types of hospitals, for example, teaching hospitals as opposed to small rural or community hospitals with limited resources. Such guidelines promote standards of care by delineating the limits of care possible within facilities and by establishing criteria in which emergency patients should be transferred to centers where necessary technology can be deployed.

Guidelines create a framework for evaluating the details of a specific plaintiff's case despite accompanying disclaimers that the information should be construed as a suggestion (implying voluntary compliance) rather than a standard (which implies mandatory adherence). Debates arise as to whether a hospital's standards, protocols, or algorithms may be considered legal evidence of the accepted standard of care at the time the events in question occurred. The answer will depend on the rules of evidence governing learned treatises in the jurisdiction and the testimony of expert witnesses at trial.[26] The Additional Reading section at the end of this chapter contains excellent information on the use of protocols and guidelines in medical negligence claims.

C. Early Trauma Standards

Patients who have sustained serious injury require rapid transportation to the nearest trauma center. The Federal Emergency Services Act of 1972 was important legislation specific to the care of a trauma patient. This led to the establishment of over 300 Emergency Medical Services regions in the United States and the current Level I (most intensive care can be provided), II, or III (least intensive care is available) designations. Many states linked this Act with the Highway Safety Act of 1966 and provided funds to upgrade pre-hospital care, train EMTs and paramedics, and purchase communication and patient care equipment.[27]

The Joint Commission also developed quality assurance standards for trauma patients in 1989. Other professional organizations that have developed standards for trauma care facilities include the American Society of Testing Materials, American College of Emergency Physicians, and the American Academy of Pediatrics. Figure 17.3 lists names and websites for organizations that develop trauma and other clinical practice standards affecting emergency nursing.[28]

In addition to trauma guidelines established by medical and nursing organizations, states enact their own trauma standards. These may be similar to or more stringent than guidelines established for Trauma Center Accreditation. For example, the Pennsylvania Trauma Systems Foundation was established under the authority granted by the Pennsylvania General Assembly in the EMS Act of 1985-45. The Act required that the foundation establish standards for the operation of trauma centers in the Commonwealth, adopting "at a minimum, the current guidelines for trauma centers as defined by the American College of Surgeons (ACS) for Level I or Level II trauma centers."[29]

Special hospital forms and flow sheets were designed to collect specific data for head and spine injury to reflect these standards while enabling the treating ED team to detect early trends or changes in patient status. Neurological deficits or complications must be identified and treated early for the best outcome. Early treatment for neurological problems can prevent devastating complications, such as increased intracranial pressure and cerebral herniation.

D. Current Emergency Department Standards of Care

Standards and guidelines continue to be used by emergency department staff to develop appropriate patient care systems, measure quality, and improve ED nursing practice. Demonstrated competence in meeting standards of care is the basis of performance appraisal and promotion as well as accreditation by TJC and other agencies.

Every medical specialty and age group is represented in the ED population; therefore, standards governing the management of each apply to care provided in the ED and are investigated in pursuit of negligence claims. In addition to specialty standards, emergency care organizations develop treatment paradigms that guide the course of diagnosis and management in the ED. Many non-nursing organizations develop standards that impact ED nursing practice. Because emergency nurses are charged with patient advocacy, they must be familiar with standards outside of their own practice in order to identify deviations and safeguard patients.

The emergency department policy and procedure manuals cover key procedures and well as hospital-specific

Medical
American Academy of Pediatrics (www.aap.org)
American Board of Emergency Medicine
       (www.abem.org)
American College of Emergency Physicians
       (www.acep.org)
American Academy of Orthopaedic Surgeons
       (www.aaos.org)
American College of Radiologists (www.acr.org)
American College of Surgeons (www.facs.org)
American Heart Association (www.amhrt.org)
American Society of Anesthesiologists (www.asahq.org)
American Trauma Society (www.amtrauma.org)
Brain Trauma Foundation (www.aitken.org)
Centers for Disease Control and Prevention
       (www.cdc.gov)

Nursing
American Nurses Association (www.ana.org)
Emergency Nurses Association (www.ena.org)
National Flight Nurses Association (www.nfna.org)

Hospital
American Hospital Association (www.aha.org)
Bylaws
Job descriptions
Performance review and advancement criteria
Policy and procedure manuals
Protocols

Regulatory and Government
American Academy of Physician Assistants
       (www.aapa.org)
American Association of Medical Assistants
       (www.aama-ntl.org)
Emergency Medical Service Regulations
       (see also ACEP)
EMTALA/COBRA
       (www.acutecare.com/emtala.htm)
       (www.medicine.com/emerg/topic)
       (www.svmic.com)
       (www.ama-assn.org)
       (www.emtala.com/emtala/regs.txt)
       (www.medlaw.com/sitegide.htm)
HCFA—Health Care Financing Administration
       (www.hcfa.gov)
TJC—The Joint Commission
       (www.jointcommission.org)
Nurse Practice Acts (www.ncsbn.org)
OSHA—Occupational Safety and Health
       Administration (www.osha.gov)
State Practice Acts for Medicine (www.docboard.org)

Figure 17.3 Sources of Standards Affecting Emergency Nursing Practice

policies which guide patient care. The Joint Commission accreditation manual includes: assessment of the emergency department patient, patient identification, pain assessment, assistance with procedures, patient safety issues, staff competency, and infection control. Other policies typically include:

- Triage
- Assessment of the ED patient
- Patients at risk of suicide
- Patients brought in by police
- Victims of violent crimes
- Reporting alleged abuse
- Patient identification
- Standards of care
- Monitoring of patient
- Blood transfusions
- Care of the dying patient
- Organ/tissue/eye donation
- Sedation
- EMTALA guidelines
- Medication management
- Bioterrorism: emergency department triage protocol
- Managing emergency department excess volume
- Emergency department diversion
- Workplace violence prevention plan
- Position descriptions, performance evaluations, skill competencies
- Fall risk assessment standard
- Bed entrapment safety
- Safety rounds

Protocols are a set of steps which aid in the diagnosis and treatment of particular types of patients. This greatly reduces delays and improves overall patient treatment times as well as patient flow through the ED. These protocols require staff compliance as approved by hospital administration and the emergency department nursing and physician directors. Some of the protocols that should be available for staff access and use in the health system policy manual are:

- Pain management
- Fever control
- Pediatric fever control
- Adult abdominal pain
- Chest pain
- Dyspnea in the absence of chest pain
- Extremity injury
- Lacerations

- Suspected urinary tract infection in an adult
- Pharangitis
- Reassessment of a patient in the waiting area (long waits)
- Risk of suicide

TIP: The protocols may vary by health system but should be available for staff education and reference with integrated regulatory standards as well as evidence-based practice standard.

E. Standards Directly Affecting Emergency Nursing

1. American Nurses Association

Nursing: Scope and Standards of Practice by the American Nurses Association (ANA) defines practice standards for professional nursing.[30] The Emergency Nurses Association formally acknowledges and supports these standards. In addition to defining those elements of the nursing process which comprise the standards of care (assessment, diagnosis, outcome identification, planning, implementation, and evaluation), the ANA provides the following standards of professional performance: quality of care, performance appraisal, education, collegiality, ethics, collaboration, research, and resource utilization.

Nurse Practice Acts in each state echo the ANA standards. Depending on case details, nurses face disciplinary action from their state nursing boards for failure to literally and figuratively place themselves between their patients and all conditions that could be foreseen as detrimental. Attorneys evaluating medical records for nursing negligence are therefore advised to become familiar with state statutes defining professional nursing standards, continuing education requirements, disciplinary action rules, and descriptions of specific types of professional misconduct published within state nursing practice acts.

2. Emergency Nursing Association

ENA believes that the scope of nursing practice and the standards of nursing care within emergency care settings are defined generally by professional nursing and by state boards of nursing, and specifically by the ENA as defined in the ENA Standards of Emergency Practice, the ENA Scope of Practice, and the ENA Core Curriculum.

In 1983, the ENA developed practice standards of care for all professional nurses in the emergency setting. These remain the foundation for clinical emergency nursing practice today. The ENA publishes texts and position statements that can be ordered through its website. The ENA sets specific parameters regarding ED nursing function which address:

1. placing patients in the appropriate treatment area,
2. having the patient evaluated by a nurse,
3. complying with current standards of care,
4. collaborating about care with the ED physician,
5. evaluating effectiveness of nursing and medical interventions,
6. planning for patient transfer or discharge from the ED,
7. coordinating patient admission to the hospital, and
8. educating the patient and others about illness or injury and about discharge instructions.

At all junctures of patient contact, the ED nurse is expected to accurately document the patient's understanding of events as well as the nurse's communication of pertinent changes to appropriate personnel.[31]

American Nurses Association standards are utilized as the foundation for the development of emergency nursing specialty standards. The first ENA standards were developed in 1983. The Emergency Nursing Standards of Clinical Nursing Practice list the ANA standards for reference along with the Emergency Nursing Association specialty measurement criteria which applies to the emergency nurse. These specialty standards and measurement criteria define how an emergency nurse should perform at the competent and excellent levels.

a. **Competent Level**: Each standard identifies the levels of performance the emergency nurse, or an institution, should consider in establishing goals for the nurse's professional practice. Competent emergency nursing is demonstrated by sound clinical judgment in autonomous practice.

b. **Excellent Level**: This is practice that surpasses the competent level and contributes to the growth of emergency nursing practice. Excellent nursing practice may be demonstrated by expert clinical nurses or advanced practice registered nurses.

TIP: Triage does not take the place of the required medical screening exam by a qualified physician/ provider. Triage simply determines the order a patient may be seen by the physician/provider. The patient priority of care may be re–triaged by the emergency treatment room staff based on ED physician direction.

---

a. ENA assessment standard
The ENA 1999 Standards are:

i. Triage assessment
The emergency nurse triages each patient and determines the priority of care based on physical, developmental, and psychosocial needs, as well as factors influencing access to health care and patient flow through the emergency care system. Safe, effective and efficient triage can only be performed by a registered professional nurse who is educated in the principles of triage and who has a minimum of six months experience in emergency nursing.

ii. Treatment area assessment
The emergency nurse initiates accurate and ongoing assessment of physical and psychosocial concerns of patients within the emergency care system.

iii. ENA diagnosis standard
The emergency nurse analyzes assessment data to formulate nursing diagnosis and identify collaborative problems for each patient and/or family.

iv. ENA outcome identification standard
The emergency nurse identifies expected outcomes individualized to the emergency patient based on assessment, nursing diagnosis, collaborative problems, and/or medical diagnosis.

v. ENA planning standard
The emergency nurse formulates a plan of care with the emergency patient and/or family based on:

- assessment;
- nursing diagnosis;
- collaborative problems;
- identified outcomes; and
- medical diagnosis, within the nurse's legal scope of practice.

vi. ENA implementation standard
The emergency nurse implements a plan of care based on:

- assessment and reassessment,
- nursing diagnoses and/or collaborative problems, and
- outcome identification.

vii. ENA evaluation standard

The emergency nurse evaluates and modifies the plan of care based on observable patient responses and attainment of expected outcomes.

viii. ENA education standard

The emergency nurse recognizes self-learning needs and opportunities and is accountable for maximizing professional development and optimal emergency nursing practice.

ix. ENA performance appraisal standard

The emergency nurse adheres to established standards of practice, including activities and behaviors that characterize professional status.

x. ENA collaboration standard

The emergency nurse ensures open and timely communication with emergency patients, significant others and other healthcare providers through professional collaboration.

xi. ENA resource utilization standard

The emergency nurse collaborates with other healthcare providers to deliver patient-centered care in a manner consistent with safe, efficient, and cost-effective resource utilization

---

TIP: Emergency nurses are required to have the education, knowledge and application skills to care for all ages of patients. This requires that they know and adhere to multiple specialty nursing standards.

A list of nursing specialties and standards of care regarding emergency nursing are listed below. Websites are also listed for further reference.

3. Scope and standards of pediatric nursing

The American Nurses Association (ANA) and the Society of Pediatric Nurses (SPN) jointly published on the Scope and Standards of Pediatric Clinical Nursing Practice in 1996. These standards focused on professional performance and standards of nursing care for the pediatric nurse. There are two levels of pediatric nursing: basic and advanced.

4. Scope and standards of medical surgical nursing standards

Academy of Medical-Surgical Nurses (AMSN) are nurses who care for adult patients in many settings, such as inpatient care units, clinics, HMOs, ambulatory care units, home health care, long-term care, skilled nursing homes, urgent care centers, surgical centers, and universities, just to name a few. Medical-surgical must keep up with advances in technology as their colleagues in intensive care do. The medical surgical nurse can manage several patients, new admits and discharged patients throughout the day. They must juggle their assignments so they can do assessments; administer care, treatments, medications, teaching, patient care coordination and documentation along with effective handoffs of care.

5. Scope and standards of gerontological nursing practice

These scopes and standards apply to gerontological nursing in clinical practice across all settings, from institutions and ambulatory care centers to alternative living and home care in the community. These standards apply to all professional nurses. The gerontological standards contain specific criteria for defining expectations and competent care associated with the basic and advanced clinical practice of gerontological nursing. As in pediatric nursing, gerontological nursing has two levels of nursing practice: basic and advanced practice.

6. Infusion nursing standards of practice

The standards reflect a broad emphasis on infusion not just infusion therapy. The ultimate goal of these standards is patient protection. The goal for these standards is to protect and preserve the patient's right to safe, quality care and protect the nurse who administers infusion therapy. The autonomy, accountability and responsibilities for these nurses are defined.

The infusion nurse specialist is a registered nurse who, through study, supervised practice, and validation of competency, has acquired knowledge and developed skills necessary for the practice of infusion nursing. The infusion nurse's practice settings are diverse, and patient care services may overlap into many settings. Infusion nurses are accountable for adherence to the current standards regardless of practice setting. When emergency nurses perform infusion therapy they too must comply with these standards.

Extravasations and nerve damage are some of the foremost injuries leading to legal action against emergency department nurses. Some of the largest verdicts in the United States have been awarded for extravasation cases. Staying educated in the nerve anatomy of the extremities and IV drug administration warnings is one of the top priorities for the emergency nurse. Refer to Chapter 24, *Intravenous Therapy Malpractice,* for more information. Figure 17.4 is a sample of an infusion injury.

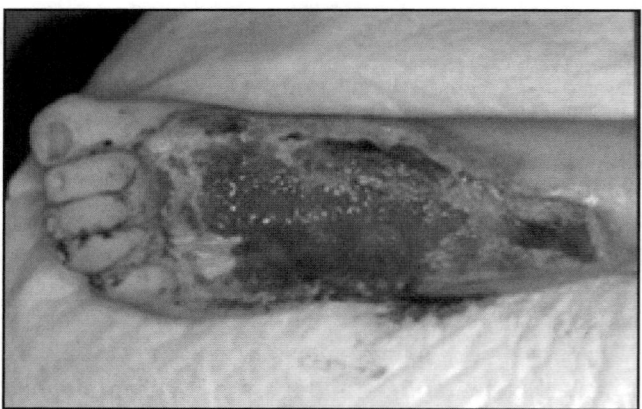

Figure.17.4 *Example of Injury from Improper management of IV site*

- Timely notifying the physician of presenting patient acuity, changes in the patient's condition or lack of response to interventions
- Reporting information to the physician from lab reports, x-rays, family or consulting physicians
- Reporting condition and care provided before transfer out of the ED to the critical care unit, general care floor, operating room, or outside facility—including return to the nursing home, rehabilitation center, psychiatric facility, jail, or transfer hospital
- Keeping family informed of critical condition and changes, and allowing them to see the patient (if the suit includes claims for intentional infliction of emotional distress
- Lack of safe and effective handoffs of care

Figure 17.5 *Communication Issues in ED Nursing Litigation*

17.3 Qualifications of ED Nurses

Emergency nurses must have good assessment skills and the ability to prioritize and communicate clearly to other members of the healthcare team. These skills result from acquisition of professional knowledge and from clinical practice. The skills needed can range from pediatric assessment and treatment, trauma of all types, cardiac symptoms in various age groups, pregnant women with fetus development from weeks to months, and geriatric patients who are poor historians to patients with disabilities or language barriers. Figure 17.5 presents communication themes commonly cited in ED nursing litigation.

All nurses must have valid licenses in order to legally practice in any state. In addition, the specialized nature of emergency nursing demands competence and performance of a multitude of procedures and knowledge of a wide variety of disease states encompassing the entire lifespan. Therefore, as early as 1994 the ENA adopted the position that ED nurses should attain the Certified Emergency Nurse (CEN) credential as a way to assure the public "that the professional nurse has attained a level of knowledge necessary to provide care at a competent level."[32] The Nursing Credentialing Research Coalition (NCRC) demonstrated that specialty certification such as the CEN decreases practice errors and adverse events by nurses.[33]

TIP: Documentation verifying that an employee was oriented to the ED and all the roles performed in the ED such as triage, education, competency validation records, and performance reviews for nurses can be obtained from the hospital through discovery. Ask about skill updates through hospital evaluation activities, journal readings, continuing education inside and outside of the hospital, and certifications in interrogatories and depositions. Check with state nursing boards as well as hospital records about currency of required continuing education.

The ENA includes the following among its minimum criteria for qualification to practice ED nursing:[34]

- Appropriate orientation to the ED including to the role of triage nurse.
- Demonstrated knowledge and skill for stabilization and treatment of emergency patients.
- Basic Life Support (BLS) status.
- Advanced Life Support (ALS) and/or Pediatric Advanced Life Support (PALS) provider status, as appropriate.
- Certification in Emergency Nursing (CEN).
- Trauma Nursing Core Course (TNCC) provider status.
- Emergency Nursing Pediatric Course (ENPC) provider status.

As discussed, professional, regulatory, and accrediting agencies require certification status and competency verification of ED nurses as well as their employers. Healthcare institutions must not only screen prospective ED staff for appropriate qualifications but also provide necessary training to ensure safe, consistent care. Emergency department nurses, and employing hospitals, assume liability risk if staff are not properly oriented and staff skills are not up to date. The ED nurse's personnel records, including performance appraisals, should contain up-to-date certifications and evidence of participation in educational opportunities that enhance emergency nursing knowledge and information. Lack of skills, out-of-date certifications, and failure to maintain current clinical knowledge can be cited as contributing factors to negligent patient management. The ED nurse may have current knowledge of evidence-based protocols for treating commonly seen conditions.

TIP: Chest pain, stroke, and spinal trauma have very specific treatment protocols found effective through research-based evidence which provides best outcomes for patients. For more detail, the reader is referred to the standards for each of these conditions.[35]

A. Additional Trauma Criteria

The ENA sets the Trauma Nurse Core Course (Provider) as the minimal trauma education standard because it contains the identified body of essential trauma nursing knowledge.[36] Other criteria for trauma nurses or their employing institutions include eight hours per year of continuing education, proficiency in trauma-associated equipment, documentation using a trauma flow sheet, certification in ALS for 75 percent of staff, certification as CEN by the ENA for a minimum of 50 percent of staff, and proof of adequately trained staff to perform cardiac, trauma, or burn resuscitation (including pediatric) 24 hours per day, 365 days per year. Figure 17.6 offers websites with standards for emergency nurses.

The requirements in Figure 17.7 standardizes and summarizes the knowledge base required by any ED nurse concerning trauma standards of care for the general population. Additionally, they establish standards by which ED nurses can be held liable. The fulfillment of practice standards also establishes that an ED nurse is able to recognize deviations by physicians from expected treatment, further implicating ED nurses who fail to serve as patient advocates.

B. Qualifications of the Triage Nurse

Triage comes from the French word *trier* (sorting or choosing). Triage is a concept for mass medical care in disasters and military actions (combats) and was adapted for application in healthcare settings. In emergency departments, triage refers to the function of immediate assessment of patients as they encounter the emergency department and the assignment of patients to pre-established categories or classifications of urgency of need. The primary goal of triage is to determine which patients require prompt care and which patients can wait without a threat to life or limb. The

---

Professional Nursing Associations That Provide Specialty Standards

- Emergency Nurses Association (ENA) (www.ENA.org)
- Academy of Medical-Surgical Nurses (AMSN) (www.AMSN.org)
- Society of Pediatric Nursing (www.spn.org)
- National Gerontological Nursing Association (www.NGNA.org)
- Infusion Nursing Association (www.INS.org)
- Clinical and Lab Standards Institute (www.CLSI.org)
- American Academy of Ambulatory Care Nursing (www.AAACN.org)
- American Psychiatric Nurses Association (www.APNA.org)
- Joint Commission of Accreditation Hospital Organization (www.jointcommission.org)
- www.nursesbooks.org

Figure 17.6 *Professional Nursing Standards web sites*

Examples of some requirements for ED trauma nursing staff

- A minimum of two RNs per shift who actively function in trauma resuscitation and who have completed the trauma nurse course.
- The patient classification system utilized by the institution should define the severity of injury/illness of the patient or the workload of the nurse which will indicate the number of nursing staff needed to adequately provide patient care.
- All RNs functioning in this department shall be credentialed in trauma nursing within one year of assignment to the department. Those RNs who were assigned to the department prior to trauma center accreditation must be credentialed in trauma nursing within two years of that accreditation. Evidence of ongoing skills proficiency, e.g., clinical competence, must be maintained.

Figure 17.7 *Some Requirements for ED Trauma Nursing Staff*

philosophy of doing the most good for the most number of people is an underlying goal of emergency care. Triage at mass casualty incidents differs greatly from that of hospitals because the very seriously ill or injured patients who may not survive are passed over in priority to salvage those who have a better chance of survival.

The emergency department patient is greeted by a registered nurse who performs an assessment, assigns a category of urgency, and initiates a plan of care and some diagnostic or therapeutic intervention by protocols. In essence, the nurse is utilizing the nursing process, a systematic way of providing care for patients.

The ENA recommends the following qualifications of staff assigned to perform triage: licensed as RNs in the state they are performing triage, at least six months of ED experience, and completion of a competency-based triage program evidenced by education records. These records must include a skills checklist documenting the orientee's successful performance of the skills required to safely triage patients; this must be checked off by an experienced preceptor.

Other personal characteristics include effective communication with patients, families, and staff; and the ability to accurately use the nursing process in decision making to assess, plan, and achieve required patient care outcomes. All staff who work in the ED must have Basic Life Support (BLS); after one year they should also be certified in Advanced Life Support (ALS). Advanced trauma life support (ATLS) may also be required depending on the trauma designation of the emergency department. All nurses in the emergency department should become certified in emergency nursing (CEN) after two years. In addition to the broad knowledge base and training afforded by professional nursing education and licensure, maturity, keen clinical judgment, and critical decision-making skills are essential for the triage nurse to differentiate rapidly between emergency and non-emergency patient conditions without the benefit of detailed information.

Assigning the proper triage category is critical to the outcome of care of ED patients. The effectiveness of the triage nurse's assessment can be measured by comparing the initial assessment to the final diagnosis. Nurse managers have an obligation to monitor the competency of their staff on an ongoing basis. The key is to avoid under-triaging patients, which is a golden rule of triage assessment: "If in doubt of severity then increase the triage category." The skill of assigning the proper triage category is often underestimated and is the root cause of delays in care, permanent disability, or death. Detailed education, attention to ongoing competency, and excellent interpersonal skills are required to determine if a nurse is making the best clinical

judgment in assigning a triage category or implementing an intervention. Some organizations fall short in providing this standard, leading to legal actions after patients experience untoward events. The value of a systematic approach to the role of the triage nurse and ongoing monitoring of competency of all staff who perform the triage role cannot be overemphasized.[37]

EMTALA regulations require a timely medical screening by a physician or, if approved in the hospital bylaws, an advanced practice nurse. The triage nurse's assessment does not qualify for the medical screening requirement under EMTALA but can directly impact compliance with the EMTALA standards by under-triaging the patient, leading to delays in the medical screening.[38]

17.4 Entering the System: Initial Emergency Management
A. First Responders' Care: Good Samaritans and EMS

The initial care of a patient in the ED begins before the patient is transported to the hospital. The first people to reach an injured or ill patient may vary from untrained Good Samaritans to a fully equipped ambulance. The concept of trauma as a national disease led to the founding of the Emergency Medical Services (EMS) system. Public, private, or hospital-based ambulance or helicopter teams may be the first trained professionals to assess and treat the patient. The ambulance dispatched to assist the patient may be equipped with only basic supplies or may be a mobile intensive care unit containing equipment needed to provide advanced life support. It is therefore essential for the attorney to review documentation of patient care from the moment the call was first received via the emergency medical system to evaluate for appropriate timely rescue at the scene. Medical records generated by first responders may not be part of the patient's hospital record and must often be requested separately.

TIP: Patients brought in by pre-hospital emergency personnel require a face-to-face report. This report is required to be documented on a report sheet and a copy is left with the receiving hospital.

The "duty" to the patient begins when the call for help is received by the EMS dispatcher. Calls to the 911 line or its equivalent are often recorded. The tape may be obtained, if the attorney acts quickly, usually within a week after the call was made. Unfortunately, the attorney often becomes involved in the case after this tape is destroyed.

The role of EMS is to provide care to people before they arrive at a healthcare facility. The capabilities, skills, and knowledge of paramedics and emergency medical technicians (EMTs) vary a great deal. The advent of communication equipment that allows transmission of vital data about the patient to a physician in an emergency department has the potential for improving patient outcomes. EMS personnel and paramedics transfer their care duties over to the receiving hospital through a formal process of report and physical movement to a location in the ED. In most states they are not allowed to perform as paramedics in the acute care environment. The EMTALA regulations apply to patients who have an emergency and are within 250 yards of the hospital.[39]

B. Flight Transport Teams

Air medical services have grown considerably and have contributed to reduced out-of-hospital time with on-the-scene and en-route care by flight nurses. Shortened helicopter transport time with skilled flight nurses is dramatically changing the mortality and morbidity of the trauma population. This is contributing to a new standard of care of timeliness and a level of care that includes rapid on-the-scene assessment and transportation of trauma patients.

C. Pre-Hospital Records

Written records, such as police, paramedic, or ambulance reports include:

- the time the call was initially received,
- the time emergency help arrived at the scene,
- assessments and treatments provided at the scene,
- initial description of mechanism of injury,
- statements made by the injured person,
- behavior of the injured patient en route to the hospital, and
- time of arrival at the ED.

TIP: The credentials of the "first responders" (e.g., fire and rescue with BLS, paramedics with ATLS) should be sought during discovery if this is important to the case. The certifications of these individuals will not be apparent from the record; i.e., EMTs do not normally sign their name with their certifications of BLS, ATLS, and so on. Refer to Chapter 16, *Emergency Medical Services*, for additional information on the responsibilities of these care providers.

D. Monitor Printouts

Whether by ground or air ambulance travel, patients are transported from the injury scene to the ED, with sophisticated monitoring equipment capable of tracking temperature, pulse, respiration, blood pressure, oxygen saturation, heart rhythm, and sometimes 12-lead EKG tracings. Printouts from ambulance equipment are not usually included in the hospital ED record, but are part of pre-hospital records. It is necessary to request these directly from the transport company.

If automatic early defibrillation (AED) equipment was used to create a shockable rhythm in a patient who was unconscious, pulseless, and apneic, a printout should be attached to the chart. The early defibrillation program has a data management component that can later be downloaded via a computer that has a memory module to record all events, e.g., the patient's cardiac rhythm, rate, pattern, and definitive care before, during, and after interventions at the scene. Unlike human interventions in the field, the defibrillator cannot "shock" someone unless the patient needs it. The voice module even talks to the treating team with statements like "check pulse" and "stand back to shock." Request the full printout from the rescue team if this information is missing.

E. Liability Questions Regarding Pre-Hospital Care

While the scope of this chapter concerns standards of care and negligence issues arising in the course of ED treatment, the following questions should be considered in the course of evaluating liability:

1. Did the individuals who provided pre-hospital care have immunity from legal claims under Good Samaritan laws?
2. Was there an unnecessary delay of the first responders in arriving at the scene that jeopardized the patient's chance for survival? What caused the delay?
3. Did emergency first aid at the scene, whether BLS, advanced life support (ALS), or advanced trauma life support (ATLS) fall below the standard of care and result in harm to the victim? Of special interest are improperly placed endotracheal tubes, dropping the patient, not immobilizing the trauma patient's spine, and excessive attempts at IV access that delayed arrival to ED and interfered with IV access in the department.
4. Was the victim transported to an inappropriate emergency facility? What was the reason for the transport? Can this be shown to be detrimental to the patient receiving appropriate, timely care?
5. Did a nurse's performance as part of the transport team meet the standard of care during the pre-hospital period?

17.5 Emergency Department Nursing Practice in Action

A. Triage

1. Importance of triage

Preparations are made for treatment once the emergency facility receives notification of a patient's arrival. ED personnel are expected to document communication that occurred with the first responders. This should show that accurate information was relayed from the first responders (often referred to as "the field") to the receiving institution so that they may prepare for the patient. The ED nurse is usually the first healthcare professional to see the patient when she arrives. Triage is the process by which the nurse makes a professional judgment about the severity of the patient's condition based on critical thinking and knowledge. The nurse determines where the patient is placed in the treatment area and how quickly the ED physician ranks the patient severity of symptoms to expedite the care of the sickest patients.

TIP: Since patients often rate the quality of their ED stay by how long it takes for a physician to see them, some EDs are using doctors to perform triage.

---

2. Triage classifications

Triage is a process of rapidly sorting or classifying patients according to the need for emergency treatment and potential for further injury. Some hospitals use three levels: emergent (first priority), urgent (second priority), and non-urgent (lowest priority). Most use a four-level system to identify the sicker, more urgent patients sooner.[40] Based on the services available, the ED nurse may use five triage categories, which will be discussed.

TIP: Ask for the hospital's triage policy and triage guidelines used in the ED. Ask for the policy regarding the qualifications of the triage nurse and compare with the credentials of the nurse who performed the triage.

---

a. Emergency Severity Index (ESI)

Research has documented a five-tier system as more effective in the triage of patients and is recommended by the ENA and ACEP. Dr. Richard Wuerz and David Eitel developed the ESI in 1998 and pilot testing yielded favorable results. The ESI Triage Group was formed and the Agency for Healthcare Research and Quality awarded them a grant to carry out further development of the ESI, Version 4.

A well-implemented ESI program can help hospital emergency departments rapidly identify patients in need of immediate attention, and determine which patients could safely and more efficiently be seen in a fast-track or urgent care rather than the main emergency department. The mission of developing the ESI, Version 4 is to improve the quality, efficiency and effectiveness of health care for all Americans.

Inclusion of resource needs in the triage rating is a unique feature of the ESI in comparison with other triage systems. Acuity is determined by the stability of vital functions and potential for life, limb, or organ threat. The triage nurse estimates resource needs based on previous experience with patients presenting with similar injuries or complaints. *Resource needs* are defined as the number of resources a patient is expected to consume in order for a disposition decision to be reached. Once trained to use the algorithm, the triage nurse will be able to rapidly and accurately triage patients into one of five explicitly defined and mutually exclusive levels. The ESI provides emergency departments with a reliable triage system.

Triage with the ESI algorithm requires the experienced ED nurse to start at the top of the algorithm. The actual ESI algorithm is described in detail below. The algorithm uses four decision points (A, B, C, and D) to sort patients into one of the five triage levels. See Figure 17.8. With practice, the triage nurse will be able to rapidly move from one ESI decision point to the next. Following implementation of this system, it is important that the triage nurses continue to be cautious when assigning triage acuity ratings. Whether the emergency department uses the ESI level system or another five-level system, staff need to know and comply with the guidelines using their clinical judgment and current evidence-based practice to assign a score. Any under triage and deviation from the algorithm could result in an undesired outcome for the patient, leaving the triage nurse liable.

TIP: The triage nurse has the responsibility for making rapid decisions based on a speedy but accurate assessment of each patient who presents. When the flow of patients and services pivots around decisions made by the emergency triage nurse, any departure from the standard of care can cause serious problems for all other members of the emergency team. The most important aspect to consider in the triage process is to determine who provided care, was it within his scope of practice and was the triage nurse directly supervising unlicensed assistive personnel (UAP).

TIP: For more information on ESI visit www.ahrq.gov/research/esi.

The five-tier system decreases the ambiguity of who are the most acute patients.[41] Hospitals have used the three-

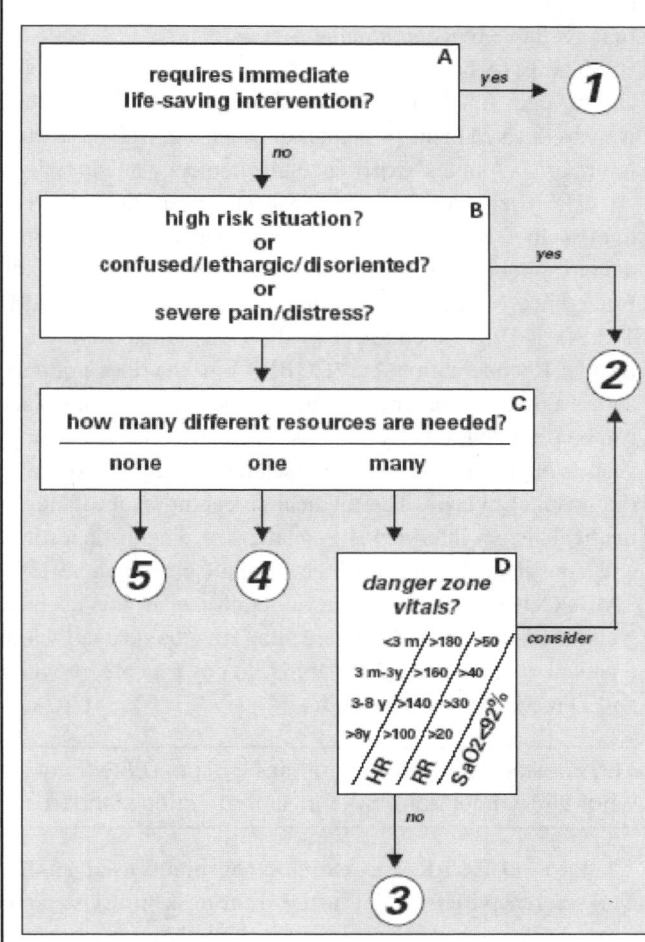

A. Immediate life-saving intervention required: airway, emergency medications, or other hemodynamic interventions (IV, supplemental O2, monitor, ECG or labs DO NOT count); and/or any of the following clinical conditions: intubated, apneic, pulseless, severe respiratory distress, SPO2<90, acute mental status changes, or unresponsive.

Unresponsiveness is defined as a patient that is either:
1. Nonverbal and not following commands (acutely).
2. Requires noxious stimulus (P or U on AVPU) scale.

B. High risk situation is a patient you would put in your last open bed.

Severe pain/distress is determined by clinical observation and/or patient rating of greater than or equal to 7 on 0-10 pain scale.

C. Resources: Count the number of different types of resources, not the individual tests or x-rays (examples: CBC, electrolytes and coags equals one resource; CBC plus chest x-ray equals two resources).

D. Danger Zone Vital Signs. Consider uptriage to ESI 2 if any vital sign criterion is exceeded.

Pediatric Fever Considerations:
1. 1 to 28 days of age: assign at least ESI 2 if temp >38.0 C (100.4F)
2. 1-3 months of age: consider assigning ESI 2 if temp >38.0 C (100.4F)
3. 3 months to 3 yrs of age: consider assigning ESI 3 if: temp >39.0 C (102.2 F), or incomplete immunizations, or no obvious source of fever.

©ESI Triage Research Team, 2004 (Refer to teaching materials for further clarification)
©ESI Triage Research Team, 2004. Reproduced with permission.

Figure 17.8

tier triage system for years to differentiate true emergencies from non-urgent cases. The problem with the three-tier system is that most ED patients fall in the urgent middle category, leaving the chance for a less experienced triage nurse to use clinical judgment which in the past has proven faulty.

Long waits frustrate patients who present to an ED with a "non-urgent" or "referred by their physician" category. At times these patients decide they do not want to wait any longer. In the case where the patient wants to leave, the nurse should make sure the doctor is aware and the patient should be informed of the risk. Documentation of the event should be recorded on the patient medical record. A patient's signature of understanding the risk of leaving must be obtained when possible. Patients leaving before being seen by the physician are often classified as "left without being seen" (LWBS) or "left without being treated" (LWT). When there is no response to the triage nurse's attempt to locate a patient, the nurse would document the number of times "called with no answer."

For patients who are seen by the doctor and then choose to leave before a diagnosis is confirmed, documentation should include:

1. the patient was offered a leaving against medical advice (AMA) form with explanation of risk of leaving,
2. the staff made an effort to have the patient sign it and the patient either signed it or refused to do so,
3. the patient was given an explanation that leaving without treatment was not in the patient's best interest, and
4. a record was generated with the above information along with the signature of two witnesses.

If a patient returns after leaving, a new chart or medical record must be created. This chart documents the patient return time, her condition at time of return presentation, and a new triage assessment determining actual physical and mental status at the time of return.

3. Components of the triage system

A well-developed triage system now has at least four categories to help discriminate between patient needs that fall under the urgent category in a tier system. The common goal of an effective triage system is rapid identification of patients with life-threatening conditions.[42] Also important are:

*   trained experienced personnel who can accurately assess patients presenting with a variety of complex problems and record the pertinent data on the medical record,
*   a communications systems for reporting patient information to specific personnel,
*   a method of prioritizing patients according to acute care levels while in the ED,
*   doctors who can timely complete physical examinations on all patients, and
*   a quality monitoring committee assigned to evaluate the time patients spend in the ED and work with staff on improving the outcomes.

The triage system should be in place 24 hours a day. Effective triage occurs within two to five minutes of arrival. It is important to realize that there is a designated area in which triage is conducted for patients arriving at the ED by private transport or who, though transported by ambulance, are deemed stable enough to go to the waiting area first. A registered nurse performs the triage process for every patient; the process is expected to occur upon arrival of the first available registered nurse.

The ENA believes "safe, effective, and efficient triage can be performed only by a registered professional nurse who is educated in the principles of triage and who has a minimum of six months' experience in emergency nursing."[43]

The triage assessment involves determining the patient's chief complaint, taking vital signs, and collecting data to support triage decisions. Under the provisions of the Emergency Medical Treatment and Active Labor Act (EMTALA), a 1985 amendment to the Consolidated Omnibus Budget Reconciliation Act (COBRA), triage does not constitute a medical screening exam. A medical screening exam can be provided only by a licensed independent practitioner such as physician, dentist, or nurse practitioner as allowed in the hospital bylaws. The medical screening exam includes medical history interview, physical exam, diagnostic testing, and consultation with pertinent on-call physicians.[44] EMTALA/COBRA are discussed in detail later in this chapter. Neither triage nor medical screening may be delayed while a patient is questioned about ability to pay for care, or while an ED record is being created.

TIP: Substandard hospital policies will not protect nurses who fail to meet national and state practice standards.

Prior to COBRA, community hospitals used an ED clerk or receptionist to sit at the front desk to register patients, collect personal data, and make judgments concerning when to call a nurse. Patients with serious problems were left to wait hours before being evaluated by healthcare professionals. Health systems with a focus on patient safety not only have a RN triage all patients 24 hours a day, seven days a week, but also monitor the effectiveness of their process. The standard now requires a RN with experience and training to safeguard from past errors of improper triage and delays in appropriate treatment which have led to poor or even fatal patient outcomes.

TIP: Unlicensed assistive personnel (UAP) or clerks who collect health insurance information should not delay or interfere with the triage process, which is essential in quickly identifying at-risk patients and assigning a triage severity category for communication to the ED team. The goal is to appropriately prioritize each patient. The first duty to the patient is to prevent delay in the treatment of the emergency. Also of importance no matter what triage system is in place is to ask who is providing the assessment and if the unlicensed staff are within their scope of practice according to state and institution policies.

The ED chart should reflect both a triage classification and reassessments based on the patient's condition. The triage nurse will reassess waiting patients for a medical screening every 15 to 60 minutes, depending on the severity of the illness or injury, until the patient is placed in a treatment bed.[45]

TIP: The ED record should display the patient's triage category on the first nursing assessment note. Look for this at the top of the page containing nursing documentation. Some hospitals have a separate page labeled "triage note." Many hospitals have moved to an electronic triage record which forces an assignment of the triage level of acuity/category after the nurse completes the assessment of the patient's presenting symptoms.

Figure 17.9 lists key areas of liability associated with triage. Review Figure 17.10 for possible outcomes related to triage assessment. Triage liability risks increase when:

- patients are not being evaluated by registered nurses on arrival,
- nurses and physicians fail to perform appropriate assessments and serious conditions are missed,
- inadequate information about the patient's complaint is gathered,
- incomplete information is provided to patients about the expected wait, the results of tests, and the expected treatment, or
- delays in assessment, including the medical screening, occur.

In addition to assessing patients and assigning a category of priority, the triage nurse is responsible for public relations. The nurse must remain calm while supporting anxious and sometimes angry patients and visitors who are tired of waiting, and keeping unruly children under control. Triage nurses regulate visiting; crowd control; and patient, family, and staff safety while in the waiting room. Most triage desks or rooms have an emergency buzzer to immediately summon security. Metal detectors and competent security officers are becoming more commonplace in some hospitals. Violence directed to ED staff is taking a toll on the health and coping skills of staff who work in this potentially dangerous area.

4. Pitfalls of triage

Common pitfalls of triage in emergency nursing are as follows:

- Listening to the complaint without taking a closer look. The assessment should include objective data

---

- Failure to timely triage, initiate treatment, or notify physician of patient emergent symptom
- Inadequate or incomplete triage assessment
- Failure to reassess patient every 15 to 60 minutes while the patient is waiting to be placed in treatment area
- Failure to provide assistance to a triage nurse when indicated by overwhelming numbers of patients (charge nurse) or when requested by a triage nurse
- Failure to recognize age-specific or disease-specific urgent symptoms
- Under triage—classification not accurate according to standards, patient symptoms or risk

Figure 17.9 ED Nursing Liability Associated with Triage

- Disability or death caused by delay in triage
- Disability or death from refusing treatment in ED
- Disability or death caused by inappropriate triage classification and delayed placement in the treatment area or placement in the wrong area, such as the nonurgent section when the patient is having a heart attack

Figure 17.10 Possible Outcomes Related to Triage Assessment

synthesis and that of the presenting complaint (subjective data). For example, did the nurse actually touch the patient who was complaining of a fever? Did the nurse listen to breath sounds of the patient who was complaining of difficulty breathing?

- Forgetting that some patients exaggerate and others minimize. Consider that patients may not be capable of accurately describing an injury or illness. Be cognizant that some report very little while others embellish. The nurse has to be very good at listening and developing interview tactics.
- Becoming overwhelmed by an increased number of patients and depersonalizing individual assessment. The nurse who finds herself in this category is more likely to one day be overwhelmed by a legal summons to explain why a nursing diagnosis was missed. It is very important for staff to recognize this danger and be proactive in preventing or mitigating this scenario.

- Losing objectivity. Occasionally, the triage nurse probes and tests a patient to determine the true urgency of the presenting complaint. This is done in an attempt to rule out more serious clinical pictures and to reduce the volume of patients requiring immediate intervention. This is a dangerous pitfall. The nurse may fail to collect objective data and process it, and instead becomes a gatekeeper for the emergency department.

- Overlooking less-urgent or less-serious injuries and illnesses. A too-narrow focus on the presenting complaint can be misleading. It is appropriate to focus on the most immediate need for intervention. However, the patient may need eventual attention to a lesser problem. One of the authors (CM) has seen many patients whose lives were saved by very good emergency trauma care; months or even years later an injury that was never diagnosed was finally evaluated and treated. In addition to the misery suffered by the patients, this issue has serious legal implications as the defense will deny responsibility if there is no notation made of additional subjective or objective complaints.

- Becoming isolated and over-stressed may lead to errors in triage and assessment. The responsibility and pace of the triage nurse is stressful. The nurse often feels overburdened and separated from the rest of the emergency team. It is helpful to rotate roles in the ER so that all professional nurses become skilled in triage and the other areas of emergency care (trauma and pediatric and adult medicine).

- Allowing visitors to overwhelm the department. This can take away from the assessments of incoming patients.

- Being indecisive, leading to serious or disastrous triage mistakes. This problem may be addressed by algorithms, decision trees, protocols, classification systems, and quality assurance reviews.

- Failing to sort patients appropriately resulting in the extreme risk of sending some to clinics or other facilities. Other patients may flood the treatment area when they could safely wait their turn.

- Jumping to conclusions leading to a wrong triage decision and a bad outcome for the patient. If a patient presents with lethargy, slurred speech, and staggered gait, the nurse should not assume that the patient is a chemical (drugs or alcohol) abuser. Unequal pupils may be due to a glass eye, not a neurological emergency. Psychotic behavior can be

the result of a drug reaction or hypoglycemia. It is important to avoid the bias that can be developed with years of service in this area.

- Failing to properly assess a patient who is intoxicated leading to a delay in diagnosing medical problems.

- Transporting a patient to jail who then suffers medical complications related to undiagnosed head injury, inability to clear his airway, or another problem.

5. Telephone advice

In addition to triaging patients in the waiting room, the triage nurse often is placed in the role of performing telephone triage. It is common for patients and their families to contact the local emergency department for advice in managing everything from the birth of a baby to a patient who has had a cardiac arrest and is lying dead on the floor. Many times the ED is so hectic that no nurse is available specifically to address phone concerns of the public. Accountability for telephone advice rests on any nurse who provides it. Most hospitals follow the rule of no telephone advice with the exception of advising to go to the nearest ED or call 911.

The act of providing health care via telephone to an unseen patient is fraught with potential for miscommunication and incomplete or inaccurate advice because a nurse is relying on a layperson's evaluation of the clinical picture. The ENA published a position statement revising its previous stand against telephone triage. The ENA recognizes that sophisticated telephone triage programs provide quality healthcare assessment. It is deemed essential that these established programs provide:[46]

- experienced professional registered nurses with specialized education in triage,
- telephone assessment,
- communication and documentation skills,
- mandatory continuing education and clearly defined protocols,
- policies and procedures, and
- a continuous quality improvement program.

All hospital EDs approving telephone triage should have written telephone triage protocols addressing the following:

- Documentation of calls.
- Guidelines, algorithms, or checklists of questions to ask the caller.

- Standardized forms to record responses and directives given to the caller (e.g., call 911, bring the person to the ED, or take the person to a doctor's office or clinic).

For protection from liability, nurses are typically instructed by their employers to 1) direct the patient to come to the ED to be evaluated in person regardless of the stated concern or 2) call 911 for emergency assistance. Depending on the circumstances it may be advisable for the triage nurse to record the advice provided over the phone or that the patient was advised to come to the ED.

The following case is an example of nurses failing to give correct advice in handling a phone call:

The woman was pregnant with her fourth child. Each of her previous pregnancies had resulted in cesarean section delivery. Within one week she had presented to the ED on three occasions, believing she was in labor. Each time she was reassured that she was not. When she returned home after the last ED visit, she started to have vaginal bleeding. She called the ED of a different hospital and spoke with a nurse. This nurse, before giving advice, spoke to her supervisor. Both nurses agreed that it was okay for the patient to stay at home and wait for the bleeding to stop. The bleeding did not stop. She called her physician who also told her to stay at home. Later that day she reported to the ED. During the cesarean section it was determined that she had ruptured her uterus along an old incision line. The baby had already experienced serious brain damage from lack of oxygen.

The court findings include the following:

- The nurses were negligent.
- The nurses failed to make a correct assessment; they believed the patient was only having some minor spotting from the vaginal exam.
- The nurses did not listen to the patient's description of her complaints or explore the full history of the situation.
- The nurses' advice to remain home and wait and see was completely incorrect.
- This negligence was a direct cause of the child being born with brain damage.
- The court also found that the physician was negligent. However, the negligence did not relieve the hospital of legal responsibility for the nurses'

conduct. The patient herself was also negligent to some extent. (Unreported case.)

Nurses are accountable for knowing the standards of care for each population presenting to the emergency department or calling for advice. Many hospitals have written policies with the standards of care defined for pregnant women accessing the emergency department to prevent just such events discussed in the above case.

TIP: It is unlikely that any type of medical record will be generated when the ED nurse provides telephone advice. Some hospitals have policies regarding telephone advice which most often require no advice with the exception of going to the nearest ED. It may be difficult to establish what was said to the plaintiff since these conversations are rarely documented. Telephone advice cases may be difficult to litigate and may rest on the credibility of the plaintiff and defendants.

If the nurse provides advice over the phone, the advice must conform to the standard of care. The caller may need instructions on seizure management, poison control remedies, bleeding control measures, or childbirth before emergency medical services arrives or before the patient can reach the ED. The nurse must be careful not to engage in the unauthorized practice of medicine or to exceed the scope of nursing practice. Even though the patient is not on the premises of the hospital when the call is made, the telephone nurse has a duty to provide accurate information when giving advice.[47] Refer to Chapter 18, *Telephone Triage,* for more detail on this topic.

6. Performance standards for the triage nurse

According to the Emergency Nurses Association, the triage nurse performs the following:

- Immediately and rapidly assesses patient on presentation to the ED. Triage staffing is based on the volume and acuity of patient presenting.
- Documents the patient's complaint, past medical history, vital signs including pain assessment, allergies, medications, and other pertinent information.
- Determines patient priority and the appropriate location for further evaluation.
- Administers first aid and other triage nursing interventions.
- Continuously monitors and documents reassessments based on the patient's presenting symptoms

until the patient is brought into the treatment area of the ED.

- Keeps the family and significant others informed of the patient's status and progress while the patient is in the ED.[48]

7. Cases involving telephone advice

A six-month-old clinic patient diagnosed with an upper respiratory infection (URI) developed new problems one evening. His mother called the managed care organization's emergency after-hours telephone line when her son's temperature reached 104°F. He was vomiting, moaning, having difficulty breathing, and not moving normally. The nurse receiving the call had not been properly oriented to her duties and was working without a written or computerized protocol for fever in infants. She told the mother to give the child a tepid bath. She failed to report all of the child's symptoms to the on-call pediatrician, who decided it was not an emergency and instructed the nurse to have the mother take the child to a hospital over 40 miles away. The mother had to call that facility for directions, then contact her husband at work and wait for him to drive home to transport them. Ten miles from their destination the child went into cardiac arrest. Even though he was resuscitated at a closer facility, he had suffered such profound tissue ischemia that his hands required amputation at the wrist and his legs required amputation at the knees. Because there was no record or protocol which supported the nurse's version of her phone discussion, the jury returned a verdict of more than $45 million for the plaintiffs. On appeal, the case settled for an undisclosed amount.[49]

A 46-year-old man was seen in the ED for acute onset of flank pain and fever. His history included mild, diet-controlled diabetes, and his blood glucose was recorded as 253. Based on a diagnosis of kidney infection, intravenous antibiotics were administered, after which the patient stated he felt much improved. He was discharged with a Bactrim (antibiotic) prescription and instructions to phone the ED if his condition worsened. Six hours later he became diaphoretic, feverish, and lethargic, and family members phoned the ED as instructed. They were told by the defendant nurse that he was simply reacting to the medication. When he lost con-

sciousness, paramedics were called to the home, and he was admitted to the hospital with a fever of 107°F, hypotension, and shortness of breath due to septic shock. He died the following day, never having regained consciousness. On autopsy, it was determined that he had acute supportive prostatitis. No kidney infection was found. The case settled prior to the trial.[50]

8. Case of inappropriate triage classification

A 33-year-old woman presented to the defendant ED complaining of radiating chest pain, nausea, and indigestion, classic symptoms of myocardial infarction (heart attack). Her blood pressure was significantly elevated at the triage desk. The triage nurse, however, assigned a Priority II triage classification and sent the patient to the waiting room. The patient waited for more than 50 minutes. She was discovered in the restroom in cardiac arrest, and resuscitation efforts were unsuccessful. The plaintiff argued that the standard of care for the decedent's symptoms included an immediate EKG and cardiac enzyme measurement, continuous cardiac monitoring, and emergent physician evaluation. There was a high probability the patient would have survived if the standard had been met. Through successful motions to compel, the plaintiff obtained the hospital's emergency room rules and regulations, which stipulated that chest pain patients are to be assigned Priority I, and should be immediately evaluated and continuously observed. The hospital's policies provided that Priority II patients were to be reassessed by triage personnel every 30 minutes. These internal documents demonstrated that the hospital failed to comply with its own standards. The defense claimed that its failure to render prompt care was unavoidable because all monitored ED beds were full; however, the plaintiff presented well-established procedures implemented by hospitals in the event of overcrowding: floating personnel from other units to the ED, calling in additional ED staff, moving admitted patients to their assigned beds quickly to free ED beds, and diverting non-emergent ambulance traffic to other hospitals. The plaintiff's decedent did not have a strong earning history, but economic loss projections ranged from $300,000 to $400,000 based on the replacement value of services provided to her husband and three minor children. Despite 1994 legislation which created a $280,000 cap on non-economic damages, the plaintiff was able to settle for $850,000 based on compelling arguments that the cap does not apply to death cases or cases involving non-negligent plaintiffs. Additionally, the plaintiff was exploring negligence claims for the hospital's failure to equip the restroom with a help button or other safety device that might have allowed the decedent to summon aid. The negligence claim would not have been subject to the cap on non-economic damages.[51]

9. Case of failure to properly triage child and begin antibiotics in a timely manner for meningitis

The decedent age four, was brought to the emergency department with an upper respiratory infection for two days, and had complaints of headaches, fever, vomiting, lethargy, stiff neck and photophobia. The child was triaged as emergent, not critical. The child was not seen by the emergency department doctor for two hours. Eventually the child was diagnosed with meningitis or sepsis and then the workup was ordered. There was a delay in ordering the antibiotics and another delay in administering these stat medications which were ordered as a result of the blood tests which indicated a systemic infection. There was another delay in administering them for almost an hour after they were ordered. There was a lumbar puncture which revealed clear cerebrospinal fluid and this shot out under high pressure into the doctor's chest indicating increased intracranial pressure. Cultures later confirmed pneumococcal bacterial meningitis. The child's care was transferred to another emergency room doctor, who ordered a pediatric consult. The child suffered brain herniation and died in the early morning hours the following day.

Plaintiff claims: The defendant hospital failed to have the child assessed by a qualified triage technician, who in turn missed the stiff neck and photophobia and failed to appreciate the significance of lethargy, causing the assessment of an inappropriate acuity rating with a delay in diagnosis and treatment. Also the emergency department doctor failed to order antibiotics and failed to address signs of increased intracranial pressure. The

nurses delayed administering the antibiotics once they were ordered.

Verdict: A $250,000 settlement was reached with the consulting pediatrician. There was a $7 million verdict against all the defendants.[52]

10. Failure to timely assess man with chest pain—man dies an hour after leaving

The 43-year-old decedent entered into the hospital's emergency department suffering from chest pains. While waiting either 45 minutes or 2.5 hours (accounts vary on time) to be seen by the physician, the decedent stepped outside for a cigarette. He had not been triaged or treated. The decedent began to feel better and decided to go home. Within one hour, the decedent died from a heart attack. Fault was assessed 30 percent to the hospital, 30 percent to the physician, and the remaining 40 percent to the decedent. According to published account a $1,535,500 verdict was awarded to the plaintiffs.[53]

11. Case involving delay

The plaintiff mother had a normal pregnancy with her second child, but about a week before her due date she began having contractions. The plaintiff and her husband arrived at the defendant's hospital emergency department around 6:10 P.M. on January 6, 2001. The couple had timed her contractions at two minutes apart as they were driving to the hospital. The plaintiff was taken to the obstetrics department around 7:00 P.M. and a fetal monitor showed a fetal heart rate of 70 to 80 beats per minute. An emergency cesarean section was performed, resulting in delivery at 7:26 P.M. The newborn needed resuscitation and was put on a heart lung machine. Five days later the newborn died. The plaintiff claimed the delay in being seen resulted in a delay in delivery, which led to the infant's death. The hospital contended the plaintiffs should have called their obstetrician instead of going to the emergency department. The plaintiffs contended, however, that the hospital had given them a book during neonatal classes instructing them to go to the hospital immediately if there were any problems. The hospital stated the child would have died anyway. There was a $3.5 million verdict.[54]

12. Case involving delay in CT scan, head injury, partial paralysis

The plaintiff, a 62-year-old, fell down a flight of stairs and sustained a head injury. She was transported by ambulance to the hospital and during transport the ambulance crew noted slurring of speech, amnesia and disorientation. A CT scan was ordered upon arrival at the hospital which revealed an uncal herniation of the brain stem. After being at the hospital for one hour, the patient became comatose, was resuscitated and underwent brain surgery. There was a large parietal lobe hematoma found. The patient suffered partial paralysis. She is confined to a wheelchair and has a speech impairment. The allegations included the hospital staff's failure to promptly assess her and delay in doing a CT scan. There was a $10.7 million verdict.[55]

B. Treatment

1. Assignment to treatment area

Whether by triage placement or EMS arrival, patients are ultimately sent to the treatment area according to the nature and severity of their symptoms as judged by ED nurses. In the treatment area, patients spend on average six hours undergoing tests and interventions prior to when one of three treatment decisions is made:

1. The patient will be treated and discharged.
2. The patient will be transferred to another hospital for more advanced treatment unavailable by the initial facility.
3. The patient will be admitted to the hospital.

Initial placement in the treatment area has great impact on the order in which patients are seen. However, once the triage nurse transfers care to the primary nurse in the ED treatment area, it is the responsibility of the nurse assuming care to closely observe the patient and to expedite care when circumstances warrant. Thus, it takes highly developed professional skills to function effectively. In addition to specific skills and education pertaining to emergency care, ED nurses must have a broad knowledge base of diseases and human behavior across the age spectrum from infancy to geriatrics and be adept at recognizing abnormalities. They must be able to quickly recognize the need for assistance and for specialty intervention, and have excellent teamwork skills. Despite immense pressure and stress from crisis conditions in the department, ED nurses must be able to manage care

of their assigned patients such that critical patients can be timely transported to the operating room or specialized care units without compromising care of the remaining patients as well as the patients they are transferring. Safe handoffs—the need to properly communicate all patient-specific information related to care and treatment—have been identified as a TJC National Patient Safety Goal. The ED has many points of handoff and therefore must be extremely diligent in maintaining the patient safety standards.[56]

2. Purpose

Verification of triage assessment and discernment of changes in condition are mandatory upon the patient's placement in the ED treatment area: appropriate interventions cannot be initiated otherwise. It is not feasible for the triage nurse to conduct assessment to the degree of detail provided in the treatment area, where more time and more privacy allow in-depth personal questions. It is also not feasible for the triage nurse to simultaneously work in the treatment area. Each separate role requires the nurse's full attention.

Further, it is common for patients who arrive by ambulance to bypass the designated, or ambulatory, triage section and enter the ED directly. In this instance, the RN who greets the patient makes a rapid decision about acuity and placement in the treatment area, thus performing triage. Some ambulance patients may be deemed stable enough to send to the ambulatory triage area for further processing. Often they are assigned a general, minor, critical, or emergent care bed directly from the ambulance carrier. Unless this treatment area nurse accompanies the patient to an assigned bed and assumes responsibility for care, her initial findings are not documented. Problems arise when the ED staff fails to inform a busy nurse that a new patient has been assigned or fails to communicate initial observations to the nurse responsible for care management of a newly placed patient.

Nurses who provide direct patient care within the ED are called primary nurses, assigned nurses, or treatment area nurses. They are accountable to expand upon the baseline assessment performed by a triage nurse. See Figure 17.11 for components of the initial ED nursing assessment. Primary and secondary assessments are major components of the nurse's responsibility. The primary assessment identifies life- or limb-threatening conditions for immediate management (e.g., airway, breathing, circulation, disability, and neurological status).

TIP: Refer to standard nursing textbooks for a detailed nursing history and assessment. The attorney will find the standards to be invaluable in learning about the components of a physical assessment.

Airway: The ED nurse should determine airway patency and the patient's ability to speak, and should note hoarseness, or stridor (noisy breathing).

Breathing: The ED nurse documents rate, depth and pattern of respirations; cyanosis (blue color of the lips or fingernails), dyspnea (difficulty breathing), listens to the lungs for abnormal breath sounds; observes how the chest moves during breathing and the patient's effort to breathe or restlessness. If pulse oximetry or arterial blood gases are indicated the ED nurse analyzes the results. (Pulse oximetry is a technique used to measure the oxygen concentration of the blood, most commonly by placing a clip over a finger. The clip is attached to a wire which is connected to a machine. The patient's oxygen level appears within seconds on the machine. Arterial blood gases are analyzed from a blood sample that is obtained from an artery.)

Circulation: The ED nurse determines heart rate, pattern, dysrhythmias (abnormal heart rhythms), radial (in the wrist) or peripheral pulses (in the arms or legs), capillary refill (which is evaluated by pressing on the fingernail, then releasing the pressure to see how quickly the fingernail resumes normal color), skin color, level of consciousness, blood pressure, and frank or occult (hidden) bleeding.

Disability: A neurologic assessment is indicated if the patient displays signs of a decreased level of consciousness. The nurse performs a Glasgow Coma Score and checks the pupils for shape, size and response to light.

Expose: The ED nurse should completely undress or cut away all clothing for exposure to assess general appearance, and areas of trauma, burns, wounds, bleeding and bruising. The temperature is recorded and the patient covered with warm blankets. The ED temperature can be adjusted to accommodate the patient's low or high temperature. Respect for privacy and dignity is maintained and the patient covered except for periods of assessment.

Figure 17.11 A Quick Guide to Emergency Department Nursing Assessment

A: Allergies
M: Medications patient is currently taking
P: Past illnesses
L: Last meal (in case anesthesia is needed for surgery)
E: The event or the environment surrounding the injury

Figure 17.12 Assessment Based on AMPLE

The secondary survey is used for management after resuscitation and includes a head-to-toe assessment for identification of acute and potential problems for nursing diagnosis and care planning. ED nurses must be experienced in physical assessment skills for all age groups to quickly detect findings that are within normal limits of a patient of the same age and general condition. Additional assessments will depend largely on the patient's most pressing complaints and symptoms. Figure 17.12 highlights information elicited through the AMPLE algorithm. The nurse should question friends or relatives about the patient's prior medical history when the patient is unable to provide information.

The ENA holds ED nurses responsible for the development and use of routine protocols and procedures for assessment, identification, and referral of survivors of domestic violence, and for mandatory healthcare provider education about domestic violence.

ED nurses must take time to interact with, and carefully assess, each patient brought into the treatment area in order to detect subtle clues indicative of chemical dependence or abuse. Anecdotes describing how life-threatening injuries or medical problems were simply "missed" by ED staff because of a patient's obvious intoxication or stupor are disturbingly common, for instance, the "town drunk" who was not drunk at all but was dying of diabetic ketoacidosis, or the "drunk kid" who additionally had been hit on the back of the head and was actually in a coma, not merely "passed out" or "sleeping it off." The ED patient who smells of alcohol or appears to be intoxicated is entitled to the same quality of care as other patients. Though difficult behavior may present obstacles to assessment, suspicion of drug or alcohol abuse should alert the nurse that serious underlying causes for the patient's actions may be masked.[57] The intoxicated patient who is a frequent visitor of the emergency department presents liability associated with making accurate assessments. Head injuries may be overlooked and dismissed, but the plaintiff has a legal advantage in the long run because assessment standards require the nurse to anticipate this potential and protect such a patient.

Failure to perform a complete assessment can too easily lead to overlooking critical injuries or failing to detect serious health risks. This will implicate the ED nurse as well as the physician in the event of patient harm.

C. Trauma Patients

Transport-related injuries are by far the leading cause of death and disability from injury. Injury (motor vehicle crashes, homicide, suicide, and drowning) exceeds all other causes of death combined in children between the ages of one and nineteen years. It accounts for 65 percent of all deaths in children under 19 years of age.[58]

TIP: Patients must be exposed by removing all clothing to allow accurate assessment: look for evidence of this in nursing documentation.

Trauma patients are given two types of scores within five to ten minutes of arrival: the Glasgow Coma Score (GCS) (Figure 17.13) and the Trauma Score (Figure 17.14). The GCS is a quick method of assessing the degree of consciousness or coma. The nurse determines the patient's ability to open his eyes, and to provide a verbal and motor response. The item scores are combined to provide a score which ranges from 3 to 15. A deep coma is scored three points, while full consciousness with no deficits receives a GCS of 15. If nervous system symptoms and changes in the level of consciousness (LOC) are apparent, the GCS and neurological assessment must be repeated and documented periodically according to the patient's condition. The Total Trauma Score combines the Glasgow Coma Score with physiologic parameters to indicate injury severity and prognosis.

Figure 17.15 lists key areas of liability associated with assessment; Figure 17.16 presents types of damages related to ED treatment assessment.

TIP: Plaintiff's attorneys should be aware of a potential client's Total Trauma Score, as it will figure powerfully in defense; no matter how tragic the death, it will be difficult to establish blame with ED personnel when the patient's chances of survival were, for example, only 25 percent at best. Generally, the higher the Glasgow Coma Score the better the prognosis. Conversely, failure to provide the opportunity for survival available from a trauma center could result in a powerful plaintiff's verdict. The developers of the revised trauma score and the American College of Surgeons Committee on Trauma recommends that any patient with a GCS less than 13, systolic blood pressure less than 90, respiratory rate greater than 29 or less than ten, or total revised trauma score of 11 or less be sent to a trauma center.

Eye opening	
Spontaneously	4
In response to voice	3
In response to pain	2
No response	1

Best verbal response	
Oriented to person, place, time	5
Confused, speaks but disoriented	4
Inappropriate but comprehensible words	3
Incomprehensible sounds but no words spoken	2
None	1

Best motor response	
Obeys command to move	6
Localizes painful stimulus	5
Withdraws from painful stimulus	4
Flexion, abnormal decorticate posturing	3
Extension, abnormal decerebrate posturing	2
No movement or posturing	1

Total possible points	3–15

Interpretation of scores	
Major Head Injury	≤ 8
Moderate Head Injury	9–12
Minor Head Injury	13–15

The highest score obtainable for the Glasgow Coma Scale is 15; lowest is 3.

Figure 17.13 *Glasgow Coma Scale*

D. Cases Involving Treatment Area Assessment

1. Patient in police custody denied medical screening: medical and nursing negligence alleged

The day before Mr. Gooch was stopped by the West Virginia State Police for erratic driving, he was treated with an antibiotic injection and Vitamin B12 for severe bronchitis by his family doctor. The trooper observed that Mr. Gooch got out on the wrong side of his car. He vomited and urinated on himself, and had slurred speech, and balance and coordination difficulties. Assuming Mr. Gooch was drunk, the trooper issued a field sobriety test, which he failed. Although Mr. Gooch informed the trooper that he had not been drinking, rather that he was on medication, the trooper ar-

Area of measurement	Value
Systolic blood pressure (mmHg)	
> 89	4
76–89	3
50–75	2
1–49	1
0	0
Respiratory rate (spontaneous, patient-initiated inspirations/minute)	
10–29	4
>29	3
6– 9	2
1– 5	1
none	0
Glasgow Coma Scale score	
13–15	4
9–12	3
6– 8	2
4–5	1
3	0
Total Possible Points	**0–12**

Selected survival probabilities based on revised trauma scores:

12	99.5%
10	87.9%
8	66.7%
6	63.0%
3–4	33.3%
2	28.6%
0	3.7%

Figure 17.14 Revised Trauma Score

- Inadequate initial assessment—missed incorrect placement of endotracheal tube; missed head injury; missed pneumothorax; missed myocardial infarction, cerebral vascular accident, diabetic crisis, infection, and so forth
- Failure to recognize seriousness of condition
- Failure to identify potential disease states correlating with presenting complaints, mechanism of injury, or prehospital or family reports
- Failure to recognize patient's competency or incompetency
- Failure to recognize impairment from substance abuse, head injury, neurologic disease (acute or chronic), psychotic state, developmental abnormalities, age, or acute stress reaction
- Failure to recognize danger to patient from abuse, neglect, or domestic violence
- Failure to recognize potential for self-harm or harm to others

Figure 17.15 Assessment-Related Basis of ED Nursing Liability

- Disability or death resulting from failure to accurately assess and recognize seriousness of condition
- Disability or death resulting from failure to accurately assess and detect changes in condition
- Disability or death resulting from failure to accurately assess and recognize lack of response to interventions
- Injury, suffering or death resulting from treatment omissions or delays due to incompetent or impaired state of patient from substance abuse, head injury, neurologic disease, psychotic state, developmental abnormalities, age, acute stress reaction
- Death or disability for failure to administer emergency interventions when patient's incompetency is not recognized and incompetent patient refuses treatment (drug overdose or suicide attempt)
- Death or disability by allowing return to dangerous environment or caregivers

Figure 17.16 Possible Outcomes Related to ED Treatment Area Assessment

rested him for driving under the influence. Mr. Gooch was taken to a local ED for blood alcohol and drug testing. He was not triaged by staff. No ED chart was made for him, but his name was entered on the ED log book. Mr. Gooch's blood was drawn and given to the trooper, and he was incarcerated until the next day. After he drove away from the jail and stopped miles down the road, he was clearly in distress. He was transported to another hospital, where he was admitted. He died two days later of streptococcal pneumonia. His blood test from the first hospital was negative for blood alcohol. The decedent's wife brought suit against the hospital for failing to recognize his medical condition while he was undergoing blood alcohol testing. The plaintiff's medical expert testified that "It is foreseeable that some individuals brought in by the police may be ill, rather than intoxicated. Failure to have a policy requiring a medical check in the face of this is negligence....Further, regardless of whether an individual is chemically under the influence or ill, he needs to be medically evaluated to determine whether or not he is capable of safely surviving incarceration or whether he is well enough to leave the hospital for any reason. This medical exam was not accomplished in this case, and is below the standard of care." Defense prevailed by establishing that "the entry of Mr. Gooch's name in the Emergency Room log is not evidence that a contractual relationship existed" and that the hospital had no knowledge, from either Mr. Gooch or the trooper, that Mr. Gooch had claimed he was ill and not under the influence of drugs or alcohol. The first hospital successfully refuted that they knew or should have known that Mr. Gooch was ill. The conclusion was that "it is a good idea to offer any person brought to the ED by a police officer the medical screening examination and stabilizing treatment required by COBRA/EMTALA."[59]

Please see Figure 17.17 for more information.

2. Failure to validate triage nurse's assessment

A 15-year-old male was brought to the ED by his mother three hours after having been assaulted by three men. Included in his injury description were blows to the head, pain in the right temple area, and dizziness without loss of consciousness, all indicating considerable force directed toward the brain. A triage note mentioned a history of a blood clotting disorder which the nurse maintained at trial was learned later. The patient's blood pressure was slightly elevated, and he vomited, both of which indicate possible intracranial pressure. Despite known potential of brain injury, which would be increased in the presence of a blood clotting disorder, there was no documentation of an assessment by the treatment area nurse or of communication with the ED. Only a jaw x-ray was ordered, which was

- Provides evidence of the nurse's recognition of the patient's condition
- Illustrates the nurse's anticipation of potential health problems
- Demonstrates appropriateness of care
- Establishes the minimum standard of care for the clinical scenario

Figure 17.17 *Relevance of Nursing Diagnosis to ED Nursing Liability*

negative except for impacted wisdom teeth, resulting in the patient being discharged with referral to a dentist. Discharge instructions written by the ED physician and delivered by the treatment area nurse directed the patient return to the ED if "vomiting or severe headache should occur." The fact that these were presenting symptoms was never addressed. That night the plaintiff was unable to be aroused from sleep and was unresponsive when EMS arrived to his home. He was diagnosed with a subdural hematoma and his history of hemophilia was finally acknowledged. An emergency craniotomy, to evacuate the blood on his brain, was performed and a tracheostomy for long-term ventilator breathing support. He had a permanent neurological impairment, and the origin of injury was the right temple area which was his initial complaint. A $3.25 million settlement was reached.[60]

3. Failure to properly assess trauma patient

A 68-year-old man had been seen in the defendant ED after slipping on ice. His chest x-ray was incorrectly interpreted by the ED doctor as negative and he was diagnosed with bruised ribs and discharged home. Five days later he returned complaining of severe pain, and had an oxygen saturation of 85 percent (normal is 95-100 percent). Despite his known history, which now included multiple rib fractures diagnosed by the radiologist from his original chest x-ray and a bruised heart muscle, the patient waited more than 24 hours in the ED to be seen and admitted to the ICU. By this time, multiple pulmonary emboli developed causing an anoxic brain injury and stroke. The jury determined that the first ED physician to see the patient was not liable, and the second ED physician was 10 percent liable. The hospital, through its nurses, was assessed 75 percent liability of $1.1 million.[61]

4. Failure to assess, report, and advocate

Nurses must monitor their patients competently, and promptly and effectively communicate changes in status to the physician. This is one of the most frequent breaches seen in nursing care that ends up in litigation.

A 75-year-old woman was admitted to the emergency department with a headache and right arm weakness. The physician wrote an order to admit her to the neurological unit, but she was not admitted until three hours later. There was a call placed to one physician yet was returned by another 1.5 hours later. The physician ordered medications for the blood pressure and nausea. Three hours later, the nurses called a physician to report neurological changes and elevated blood pressure. The physician ordered an emergency CT scan which revealed a massive brain hemorrhage. The patient had surgery three hours later but did not recover. She later died in a hospice.

The Court of Appeals of Texas ruled that the medical expert retained by the plaintiff's family correctly stated the legal standard of care for nurses in this situation and stated how the nurses' negligence in departing from the standard of care was the legal cause of the patient's death. The court faulted the nurses because they "meekly accepted inadequate responses of Dr. [X] and Dr. [Y] with no further calls to physicians until the patient was in extremis."

A physician who is not actually present has no way to appreciate the magnitude of the downward neurological changes a patient is experiencing unless the nurses fully communicate and insist upon prompt evaluation of the patient's changing status.

Additional points made by the court include the following:

- Cerebral hemorrhage requires prompt medical intervention.
- When a patient with acute neurological process is ordered to be admitted to an intensive care setting, that transfer cannot be delayed. Delay in transfer can mean critical delay in treatment.
- The nurses must correctly assess the patient's changing neurological status.
- Failure of the nurses to advocate for their patient and to insist upon prompt medical evaluation, including a brain CT scan, can delay proper diagnosis and treatment.

The court accepted the expert's opinion that this patient's death would have been avoided with proper management of her case by the hospital's nurses. A bleeding lesion in the brain requires prompt cessation of Coumadin (a blood thinner medication), which the patient had been taking and required fresh frozen plasma to reverse the Coumadin. A prompt brain CT scan to locate and evaluate the lesion for medical treatment should have been done. Delay in this life-saving treatment was linked directly to inadequate nursing care.[62]

17.6 Diagnosis, Expected Outcome, and Care Planning
A. Nursing Diagnosis: NANDA

The lay public, including the legal community, is often not aware of the complexities of clinical nursing practice, and the distinct responsibilities for which nurses are licensed. Among these is the requirement that nurses assign their own diagnoses after assessment of each patient.

In 1982, the North American Nursing Diagnosis Association (NANDA) was developed to establish nursing diagnosis classifications so that nurses would have standardized terminology to meet the needs of their profession and their patients. Nursing Interventions Classifications (NIC) was created to assist nurses in documenting their care and to facilitate nursing knowledge growth through evaluation of patient outcomes.[63] NANDA has now become an international group that works to classify nursing diagnosis, and to review and accept new diagnoses as needed. The ENA has integrated this process in its standards to define measurement criteria for ED nurses. The Nursing Process in an emergency department is a systematic collection of data which is focused on any area or system found to be abnormal or injured. To meet the ENA Standard of Assessment and Diagnosis, the staff collects subjective data on the chief complaint; history of present illness; medical-surgical history; and psychosocial history including use of alcohol and recreational drugs, before moving to an objective assessment. The objective assessment includes vital signs, pain assessment, weight in children, and a physical exam related to the presenting complaint. The nurse identifies the actual and potential problems or nursing diagnosis based on pertinent data collected in the focused assessment.[64]

Nursing interventions originate from nursing diagnosis. If accurate and complete assessment is the foundation of appropriate nursing care, it follows that accurate nursing leads to appropriate nursing actions, called "interventions or the plan of care." If clinical information is not appreciated for its potential impact on the patient, negative outcomes often occur. The nursing interventions, both collaborative and independent, are patient centered with specific goals to be reached.

ED physicians, out-staffed at least 3:1 and often as much as 7:1 by ED nurses, rely heavily on nursing expertise to provide them up-to-the-minute information about patients in the department so that priority cases receive timely, effective care. While the physicians attend to medical decisions, ED nurses formulate care plans—often abbreviated in the ED setting but with broad strokes, evident in their documentation. Each plan is specific to individual patients' diagnoses, and determines the nature and frequency of patient contact. This is called the care plan specific to the nursing process.

B. Expected Outcomes

Once a nursing diagnosis is established, standardized outcomes define desired physical and psychosocial outcomes that measure the success of each intervention delivered. Expected outcomes provide standards for ED nursing care by establishing what, and how often, to monitor for specific conditions. The evaluation of intervention outcomes also guides the nurse and physician in continued care needs of the patient. According to the ENA, each patient's expected outcomes are to be based on evaluation of the assessment, nursing diagnoses, collaborative problems, and reevaluation if positive outcomes are not met. ENA also notes that the social, psychological, and environmental factors for a patient may be difficult to collect at times, but must be recognized as critical to a complete nursing plan of care. It emphasizes that including this data into the overall plan may make the critical difference regarding appropriate treatment and realistic follow-up expectations.[65]

C. Care Planning

The ENA requires emergency nurses to formulate for each patient a plan of care that is "systematic and consistent with safe, effective, and fiscally responsible patient care."[66] Figure 17.18 presents planning criteria used by the ENA, of interest to attorneys. The absence of evidence of such planning can complicate the defense of the case in the event that patient records are evaluated for nursing negligence.

Protocols and hospital policies are available to guide nurse care planning for a variety of emergency situations, such as trauma, stroke, heart attack, cardiac/respiratory resuscitation, blood administration, conscious sedation, and patients requiring restraint. Flow sheets usually exist to allow efficient documentation of assessment, interventions, and evaluations of such patients. The nurse is expected to challenge, and report if necessary, ED staff—including physicians—who fail to follow established ED protocols.

Care planning includes more than awareness of the need to monitor a patient's vital signs; it also involves awareness of threats to patient safety and includes planning to prevent

---

The care plan

- is "based on current scientific knowledge, recognizing diversity, that addresses nursing diagnosis and/or collaborative problems"
- is developed in collaboration with "patient, family, and appropriate health care providers"
- "identifies priorities for nursing actions, patient goals, and patient outcomes"
- "addresses environmental, physical, developmental, and psychosocial stressors"
- "incorporates teaching and learning principles…based on identified learning needs and developmental level"
- "communicates the plan…to other health care providers, the patient and…family to ensure continuity of care"
- "utilizes Nursing Interventions Classification (NIC)…as appropriate"

Figure 17.18 Selected ENA Care Planning Criteria of Interest (ENA, 1999)

harm of, and protect patient safety for, an incapacitated individual in the context of a nurse-patient/client relationship. It also should describe strategies and alternatives to attain the expected outcomes. These include planning that is based on each patient's "characteristics or situation; age, culturally appropriate, environmentally sensitive" and include the patient and family in planning.[67] Planning is fundamental to patient safety. Failure to plan could result in an unmonitored or unsupervised patient vomiting, then aspirating because nurses failed to anticipate this obvious potential danger in an unconscious, intoxicated, or overmedicated patient. The standard of care requires positioning the patient on her side, elevating the head of the stretcher to protect the face from vomitus, or timely obtaining an order to insert a NG tube when indicated. Patient safety and maintaining a safe environment are primary nursing responsibilities and cannot be delegated.[68]

Planning includes anticipation of potential injuries in the ED such as falls from a stretcher or assaults by other patients, as was the case in *Freeman v. St. Clare's Hospital Center*:

A female patient with multiple limbs restrained was not monitored according to restraint policy, which requires evaluation every 15 minutes. Additional safety measures were not planned despite the presence of another ED patient who was known to be aggressive. The hospital was held liable for failing to make reasonable plans to protect this restrained patient when she was injured during an attempted rape in the ED.[69]

TIP: When a patient sustains injury while admitted to the ED, litigation outcome hinges on documentation that ED nurses followed appropriate standards to protect the patient from injury. Example: fall risk assessment criteria and TJC standard.

Planning criteria require ED nurses to anticipate danger by a patient to self or others before allowing that individual to drive a car, or even to be discharged from the ED. For example, a hospital, through its ED nurses, can be held liable for injuries to the patient as well as to her victims if an inebriated, sedated, suicidal, or homicidal patient is allowed to drive a car away from the ED, because nurses have a duty to plan for patient safety at discharge as well as during the ED admission. If a nurse is unable to talk an impaired patient into making alternative plans for a ride, it is necessary to communicate with any of the following for further instructions: family, physicians, social services, hospital administration, or the local police department. If necessary, security personnel must be deployed to restrain the patient if this is the only way to prevent unsafe behavior.

In the obvious absence of planning, courts have rendered opinions that the duty to prevent self-inflicted harm arises when there is a foreseeable risk that the patient's condition includes the danger of injury to self. Doctors and nurses both have a respective responsibility to treat patients for mental disorders and associated symptoms such as suicidal or other self-harmful acts. ED nurses are found negligent for failure to observe sufficiently or to monitor properly: a result of poor planning. A mentally ill or impaired patient will not be held responsible for self-inflicted injuries after coming under the care of professional nurses and physicians who have been properly advised of the patient's condition.[70]

Figure 17.19 lists key areas of liability associated with nursing diagnosis and planning; Figure 17.20 presents types of damages related to nursing diagnosis and planning.

D. Cases Involving Nursing Diagnosis and Planning

1. Failure to anticipate and plan for potential problems

A 43-year-old diabetic patient was injured driving his pickup truck into a cement signpost while in-

- Failure to establish a nursing diagnosis consistent with clinical presentation
- Failure to anticipate potential complications associated with clinical presentation and to plan appropriately
- Failure to identify contraindications to ordered medications, including drug interactions with the patient's routine medications
- Failure to plan for patient care needs by appropriately classifying acuity level
- Failure to anticipate patient care needs, and plan consultations with appropriate specialty units when additional expertise is indicated (such as labor and delivery, psychiatry, neonatal intensive care)
- Failure to
  - anticipate and address patient safety needs within the hospital setting, including ancillary departments (CT Scanning, Radiology, Angiography)
  - anticipate and plan for danger from other patients and staff (violence, irresponsible smokers, theft)
  - anticipate danger to the patient from himself and develop a preventive care plan (suicidal, confused, distraught, intoxicated, addicted, psychotic, immobilized, restrained, seizure)
  - diagnose and plan for protecting the patient from child or elder abuse, domestic violence
  - anticipate environmental hazards and develop a preventive care plan (wet floors, electrical hazards, chemical spills, biohazards, falls, fire)

Figure 17.19 Basis of ED Nursing Liability Associated with Diagnosis and Planning

toxicated. He bled to death after a timely transport to an ED where he went undiagnosed and untreated by the ED physician and nurse for over three hours. The ED nurse was found liable for failure to respond to the patient's rapid pulse and low blood pressure, failure to take frequent vital signs, failure to monitor the patient closely, and failure to call the patient's wife for his medical history before he died. The attending physician acknowledged that medical history by an intoxicated patient is unreli-

- Falls from a stretcher or examination with no risk assessment,
- Injury or loss of life resulting from lack of restraints after the nurse fails to recognize the potential for violence or self-harm
- Injuries caused by lack of patient supervision, like bed entrapment
- Self-injury of a psychiatric patient who was not placed in a protective ED environment
- Aspiration from feeding a patient scheduled for surgery who is not allowed to eat or drink, or one who is too lethargic to swallow

Figure 17.20 Harm Related to Nursing Diagnosis and Planning in the ED

able. Plaintiff argued that the patient's intoxication made the need for a trauma evaluation even more urgent. A $2 million settlement was reached during mediation.[71]

2. Failure to anticipate safety needs of patient

Giuditta Tobia, an 85-year-old female, was admitted to Cooper Hospital ED in New Jersey. A fourth-year medical student obtained her history. While waiting for an x-ray, Mrs. Tobia told the medical student that she needed to use the bathroom. Because she "seemed reasonably alert and competent," he assisted her to sit on the side of the stretcher and lowered the rails. She was left unattended on the stretcher. The patient claimed that the student failed to lock the wheels, which caused her to fall as she tried to jump or slide to get down. Nurses assisting her after she fell placed her in a wheelchair rather than a backboard, causing her hip fracture to dislocate. Mrs. Tobia asserted that the student breached ED policy that "any patient not being attended, or directly supervised or observed, either by a nurse or doctor, shall be secured by having safety rails raised on the stretcher...especially when handling patients who have symptoms of alcohol, drug ingestion, are unconscious, confused, or elderly." The jury found Mrs. Tobia 100 percent at fault. On appeal, the Supreme Court of New Jersey held that when a health professional's duty includes the duty to exercise reasonable care to prevent a patient from engaging in self-damaging conduct, the healthcare professional may not as-

sert contributory negligence as a defense to a claim arising from a patient's self-inflicted injury.[72]

3. Failure to care for a belligerent patient

It can be a challenge for a nurse to care for a belligerent patient who may not be aware of her surroundings. This is not an uncommon scenario for the emergency department nurse. These situations are fraught with hazard for both the patient and caregivers.

When the patient was brought to the emergency room on Sunday at 10:00 A.M., he had a blood alcohol level twice the legal limit for driving. On Saturday night, while extremely intoxicated and under the influence of marijuana, he had put his arm through a glass window while fighting with a friend. He sustained severe lacerations as well as a possible closed-head injury. In the emergency department, the patient was belligerent and uncooperative. He was using foul language and racial slurs. The patient had to be moved to the isolation room which had its own video surveillance system. After he began removing the bandages from his lacerated arms he was placed in six-point restraints on a gurney. When the patient began spitting, a biohazard hood was placed over his head and taped in place by a hospital nurse. After he calmed down late Sunday afternoon, his injured hands were carefully sutured by a hand surgeon and a head CT scan was done (it was negative).

The court ruled the following:
The hospital had a legal duty to care for him despite his belligerence. Consent to treatment is not required in a medical emergency. A medical emergency exists when the patient needs care but is not mentally competent to make an informed judgment for his own well-being. Every person is entitled to proper medical care and humane treatment even if his own conduct makes it more difficult. Hospital personnel are entitled to take reasonable measures to facilitate care, to protect patients from self-destructive acts, and to treat a patient without fear of injury. There was no evidence of any intent by the hospital's personnel to harm the patient, only to restrain him for his own safety so that he could be treated.

The patient himself had no memory of the events in the emergency department. The only evidence was the testimony of hospital personnel and the hospital's security videotapes. The Chief Judge of the U.S. District Court for the Western District of Kentucky reviewed the testimony and the videotapes carefully before rendering an opinion. The lawsuit was thrown out.[73]

The following is another case example. The Court of Appeals in Louisiana viewed an episode of combativeness as a patient's medical emergency rather than a patient's defiance of caregivers' authority.

Trained paramedics had sheriff's deputies handcuff and shackle a patient having a seizure in a restaurant in the community. The patient had a long history of seizure disorder, information that could have been obtained from his family member who was with him.

The court, after upholding the jury's verdict of negligence, conceded the patient was partially at fault for not taking his Dilantin. The court reduced the $800,000 plus the verdict of negligence to $50,000 plus medical expenses.[74]

Additional points by the court include the following: The standard of care with combative patients is to be mindful that the patient has a medical condition which accounts for his combativeness. In the interests of safety, only soft restraints are appropriate, such as the methods hospitals and nursing homes commonly use to keep patients from crawling out of bed or dislodging their IV tubes. The court noted that there are a variety of options for ensuring patient safety during a combative episode. Bandages, ace bandages, blankets, sheets, towels, and gauze or leather straps can be used as appropriate alternatives to the methods and devices commonly used to keep nursing home patients secure in their beds.

During a combative episode it is mandatory for the nurse to protect the head and airway while the patient is manually and physically restrained. There must be an attempt to find the medical cause of the patient's behavior and to determine the patient's medical history if not already known to the patient's caregivers.[75]

TIP: All measures to ensure patient safety should be clearly and thoroughly documented in the nurse's notes. One ED injury case was successfully defended because ED nursing notes indicated that certain safety measures (locked bed wheels, raised side rails, and call bell within reach) were in place and were sufficient for an alert, oriented patient who did not require constant observation.[76]

17.7 Implementation
A. Competencies Required of Emergency Nurses

In addition to skills generally expected of nurses—such as administration of medications and blood, IV insertion, placement of nasogastric tubes and indwelling bladder catheters, dressing changes and sterile technique—ED nurses must master a large number of complex procedures. Performance errors in any of these can result in serious harm to patients. Some of these are listed in Figure 17.21.

B. Selected Competencies

1. Care of the admitted patient

ED nurses whose patients are waiting for admission to a critical care bed are expected to provide the same standard of care the patient would receive in the critical care unit. This means that nurses should be using cardiac monitors, continuing to evaluate and document the patient's condition, and administering treatments and medications as ordered. When there are extensive waits for a critical care bed, emergency department nurses become involved in serving meals, giving baths, starting nursing care plans, and other activities associated with hospitalized patients. Failure to implement orders such as administering antibiotics can not only increase a patient's hospital length of stay, but may allow serious infections to become unmanageable. This may play a significant role in negligence claims.

2. Cervical and spinal immobilization

Suspected spinal cord injuries require strict immobilization of the head, neck, and back until fracture of any vertebral structure is ruled out. Catastrophic outcomes occur when nurses allow patients who have potential cervical or spinal injuries to move about or to remove their cervical collars. Cervical collars are usually placed by the pre-hospital team, but it is the responsibility of the first ED nurse encountering such patients to ensure protection of the spinal column. Soft cervical collars have limited use in acute trauma. A hard cervical collar provides a much greater level of protection. When the mechanism of injury suggests even a remote possibility of spinal trauma in a patient arriving by ambulance or by private transport, the ED nurse must anticipate, plan, and implement immobilization immediately by placing the patient flat on a stretcher with a hard cervical collar properly applied. The nurse must also educate both the patient and family about the importance of not sitting up or moving the head. In a patient who is unable to cooperate with such instructions (e.g., head trauma, intoxicated patients) it may be necessary to apply protective restraints to

- Arterial blood gas collection
- Assessment of age-appropriate behavior across the life continuum (infant–elder)
- Assisting with application of casts and splints
- Assisting with burr hole placement (holes drilled in skull to relieve pressure)
- Assisting with pacer insertion and open heart massage
- Basic EKG screening
- Use of blood or fluid warming equipment
- Care of amputated body parts for possible reattachment
- Central IV line and arterial line insertion and management
- Cervical and spinal immobilization—basic and advanced (skull tongs, beds)
- Chest tube assembly and assistance with insertion
- Collection of forensic samples and preservation of chain of custody: rape, gunpowder, blood alcohol, weapons
- Conscious sedation: adult and pediatric
- Crash cart equipment use: adult and pediatric
- Decontamination procedures for chemical accident victims
- Diagnostic peritoneal lavage
- Emergency medications: dosages, routes, techniques—adult and pediatric
- Emergency cricoidectomy (external opening of trachea for airway by incision at throat)
- Experience, skill in all specialties (addiction, ambulatory care, general surgery, medical, obstetrics, pediatric psychiatric, trauma) and the ability to consult appropriate management and clinical personnel to deliver care
- Fluid resuscitation
- Gastric lavage—for overdose, decompression, stomach content evacuation or to control bleeding
- Initial burn care
- Intracranial pressure monitoring
- Intubation equipment use and assessment for proper intubation
- Lethal heart rhythm recognition
- Monitoring equipment
- Patient restraint
- Spinal tap and lumbar puncture—patient position, setup, specimen management
- Suction techniques—endotracheal, nasopharyngeal, oropharyngeal
- Suture kit—setup and removal of sutures
- Warming devices—heating blankets, heat lamps, heat packs or cloths

Figure 17.21 Skills Required of ED Nurses

protect the spine, including taping the patient's head to the stretcher. According to standards of care, all interventions for potential spinal cord trauma must be documented in the ED record. Frequent evaluation and documentation of motor and sensory function are also essential to track development or progression of symptoms or deficits. Hospital documents should contain the following:

- ED spinal cord injury protocols.
- Established referral system to the nearest regional spine center.
- Policies and procedures covering cervical collar selection and application.
- Policies and procedures covering cervical and spinal immobilization and removal of devices.
- Staff orientation and competency verification of proficiency in spinal cord injury assessment and prevention.

3. Sedation in the emergency department

Many times it is necessary to sedate patients in the ED so that essential care can be delivered. Examples of such instances include cardioversion (shocking a conscious patient), intubating for mechanical ventilation, setting broken bones, and suturing very anxious patients or children with complex lacerations when a trip to the operating room is not indicated. Medications to sufficiently sedate such patients to allow the procedure to be performed place the patient at high risk for complications such as

- Decreased breathing,
- Respiratory arrest,
- Vomiting,
- Inhalation of foreign material due to diminished gag reflex,
- Abnormal heart rhythms, and
- Drug reactions.

Specially trained nurses and one-to-one patient monitoring are required to ensure patient safety. The ENA position, or standard, is that the institution must establish an educational and competency validation mechanism before allowing nurses to manage patients receiving sedation. Further, hospitals must provide adequate staffing and written guidelines for safe patient monitoring and drug administration, as well as protocols for dealing with potential complications. Lastly, there must be clear criteria determining when a patient may be safely discharged after sedation.[77]

4. Emergency equipment

ED nurses start every shift by documenting that appropriate emergency equipment is available and in excellent working order (pulse oximetry, crash carts with pediatric and adult defibrillators, intubation tools, trauma stretchers, and many routine supplies and medications). Nurses need to verify that alarms work properly upon assuming care of their patients on monitoring equipment. The Joint Commission has identified that the ability to hear alarms in a unit is a National Patient Safety Goal.[78]

It is perplexing, however, and alarming when nurses totally ignore a system that is helpful and lifesaving. Perhaps due to fatigue and sensory overload, it has been noted that nurses have disconnected alarm systems. This is very risky business for any nurse. Equally risky is relying on monitors and alarms without actually assessing the patient, as one court has opined. In addition, there are cases where the alarms have been turned off only to have the staff miss a patient symptom of respiratory distress resulting in death.

A son, his wife, and his children raced over to the local emergency room after being advised that the son's mother had been taken there after complaining of chest pain and shortness of breath while playing bingo in a church social hall. The nursing staff advised the family that their mother was not there. They returned to the church where it was confirmed that the mother had, indeed, been transported to the ER. They returned to the hospital ER where they searched each individual cubicle. The son found his mother in a cubicle, sitting alone without oxygen or a heart monitor. He asked someone to come help her. His mother complained of indigestion-type chest pain. He tried to help her to the bathroom but she collapsed, unconscious. He ran out screaming for help. The mother could not be revived even with a full code. She was pronounced dead one hour and 15 minutes after the paramedics' record noted she had arrived at the hospital emergency room.

Additional points include the following:
A discrepancy between the paramedics' record of the time of the arrival and the time originally noted in the hospital records was apparently eliminated by alteration of the records by the hospital emergency room nurses. The nursing staff placed the patient in a room by herself. They did not continue the oxygen that had been started by the paramedics. The nurses did not even check and reassess the patient. The family sued the hospital for medical malpractice and wrongful death.

The court ruling:
The jury entered a verdict of no liability in favor of the defendant hospital, which the lower judge threw out in favor of a substantial judgment for damages in favor of the family. The Louisiana Court of Appeal upheld the verdict but reduced it by 10 percent as it felt that there was just a 90 percent likelihood the patient would have come out of the hospital alive even without any negligence by the nursing staff.[79]

Other findings include:
The patient should have been placed and kept on a cardiac monitor. A cardiac monitor should be watched by a competent person, either by staying with the patient continuously or by continuously monitoring the patient's status by remote telemetry at a central location. Alarms on a monitor can be set to sound for changes in the patient's cardiac status, but the court did not approve of the use of alarms as a substitute for continuous close monitoring of a cardiac patient.

TIP: Crash cart (aka Code Cart) checklists are routinely examined for accreditation purposes by TJC and states' department of health, so they are filed and preserved. Depending on case specifics, the attorney may find them central to successful outcomes, especially when a clear pattern of failure to ensure proper equipment can be demonstrated.

Emergency personnel must be trained, and maintain their competency, in the use of lifesaving medical devices such as defibrillators. This equipment must be kept in clean, operating order and should be regularly checked for accuracy. A maintenance log should be kept. Additionally, when using this device, the individual should adhere to published and respected guidelines, such as those promulgated by the AHA ACLS (Advanced Cardiac Life Support) standards. Nurses are responsible for preventing the use of defective equipment and for correctly using available equipment. Manufacturers, bioengineering departments, and nursing staff share responsibility for keeping technological equipment free from malfunctions that could endanger patients.[80]

TIP: Since nurses are the staff most familiar with the equipment and are the principal users, they are most likely prone to be named as negligent should a bad outcome occur.

Cardiac monitors, either stationary or portable, defibrillators, resuscitation devices, infusion pumps, various measuring devices, and life-support systems represent prime sources of negligence claims. Under the Safe Medical Devices Act (SMDA), hospitals are required to report to the FDA—and, in some cases, to the manufacturer—equipment problems that result in serious injury, illness, or death. These reports are available to attorneys through the Freedom of Information Act.

The following is an example of failure to follow protocols for EMTs:

Fifty-one-year-old Clayton Wilson suffered a heart attack at his home in the early morning hours of November 20, 1997. An EMT and a paramedic, both employed by the Dickson County Ambulance Service in Tennessee, responded to the 911 call. Upon their arrival, Mr. Wilson was breathing; chest compressions had been started by the wife. While at the home, the patient was allegedly pink and warm. The crew did not take a defibrillator/monitor into the house. He was placed on oxygen and carried by stretcher to the ambulance. Attempts to start an IV by the EMT were unsuccessful. The paramedic was working with the airway. Upon the arrival to the hospital, the patient was documented as being "deeply cyanotic and blue."

The EMT documented his account of the medical service rendered to Mr. Wilson. He stated that he knew the care was deficient but he was relying upon the advanced training of the paramedic. This document was heavily relied upon by the court. The paramedic admitted he did not take a defibrillator/monitor into the house. Plaintiff's expert Dr. Smith (ER physician) testified that the paramedic failed to use the defibrillator, failed to intubate Mr. Wilson, failed to call the emergency room, and so on. He further opined that he believed that Mr. Wilson had a 60-70 percent chance of survival had the defibrillator been used.

Court ruling: The Judgment was for $385,000 for value of his life and $500,000 for loss of consortium. Due to statutory limitations, the total award was reduced to $500,000. The monetary award was affirmed by the Appellate Court.[81]

Figure 17.22 lists key areas of liability associated with implementation, while Figure 17.23 presents types of damages related to implementation.

5. Pain management in the emergency department

Perhaps one of the most common errors in nursing and medical care is that of undertreating or failing to treat pain. Many caregivers have their own ideas about pain and, unfortunately, force their views onto patients. This area continues to be ripe for litigation despite TJC guidelines relating to pain management. Failure to identify and intervene on behalf of a patient who is in pain may expose the nurse to litigation as a result of practicing nursing below the standard of care. Obstacles to pain management include the inability to communicate pain rating, competing priorities of care, lack of documentation, and practitioners' lack of knowledge.

The need to prioritize oxygenation and circulatory needs outweighs the administration of analgesics and sedative medication in the emergency department. After the initial resuscitation efforts, maintaining pain management should be a priority in overall management of the patient. Undertreated pain has a negative effect on many organ systems.

As in all areas of nursing practice, nurses in the ED are responsible for properly assessing their patient and then applying the nursing process. The nursing process was first defined in 1973 in the American Nurses Association standards. They are updated periodically with the most recent revision in 2004.[82] All nurses are held accountable to these practice standards, including the steps of the nursing process and standards of professional performance, which describe a competent level of behavior in the professional nurse's role.

There must be written evidence of the nursing process in every patient contact. Documentation requirements include assessment, diagnosis, planning, implementation, and evaluation. These process steps are the foundation of professional nursing care and professional conduct.

The agents of pain may be:

- Biological factors
- Chemical agents
- Physical factors
- Psychological factors

Research indicates that there are no objective identifiers of pain. Pain is always subjective in nature and the nurse may utilize certain standards in order to gauge intensity and severity of pain. However, not all patients react the same way to unpleasant sensory and emotional experience associated with actual or potential tissue damage. Stoic patients may simply suffer in silence. The nurse should utilize and chart the nursing process when caring for a patient who is experiencing pain.

- Medication errors—wrong dose, wrong drug, wrong patient, wrong route, wrong time, or omission of a dose
- Failure to adhere to national standards of care for given clinical condition—including when hospital policies are outdated
- Improper administration of blood products
  - wrong patient
  - wrong blood type
  - wrong rate
  - improper equipment
  - failure to note adverse reaction
- Using faulty equipment or not having equipment or supplies readily available
- Failure to use or assemble critical care equipment competently—chest tube, intubation, suction, defibrillator, cervical collar, splints, casts, restraints
- Failure to maintain spinal and cervical immobilization
- Failure to perform CPR properly
- Failure to maintain adequate airway
- Fluid overload or inadequate fluid or blood product replacement
- Needle or sharp-instrument injury
- Failure to recognize and remove a constrictive dressing, cast, or limb restraint
- Improper tube insertions into body orifices, such as the bladder, stomach, or respiratory tract
- Improper insertion of IM or IV needles resulting in nerve injury or infection
- Failure to timely and correctly carry out the physician's orders
- Performing treatments or care outside of the state practice act
- Failure to document
- Destruction of medical records

Figure 17.22 Basis of ED Nursing Liability Associated with Implementation

- Abscess from a needle stick
- Blood or blood product reactions due to incorrect blood type
- Brain injury from lack of oxygen due to misplaced endotracheal tube
- Disability or death from failure to implement a physician's oral or written orders
- Disability or death from failure to promptly report patient's condition to medical staff
- Disability or death from failure to notify the physician of critical test results
- Disability or death from failure to notify the physician of significant changes in the patient's condition
- Disability or death from failure to notify the ED physician of delayed response from the consulting or attending physician or delayed diagnostic tests
- Disability or death from receiving medications twice or an overdose because the first dose was not documented
- Disability or death related to delay in admission or transfer
- Drug reactions due to medication errors
- Fluid overload resulting in increased intracranial pressure or congestive heart failure
- Hypovolemia from failure to properly administer and monitor patient's IV fluid intake
- Injury to a body part or strangulation resulting from improper use of restraints
- Infections due to contamination during invasive procedures
- Infected sutures caused by failure to completely remove sutures
- Organ damage from insertion of tubes, such as a nasogastric tube or an indwelling urinary catheter.
- Sciatic nerve injury from improper technique during IM injection
- Tissue injury from IV infiltration
- Tissue necrosis or damage from a constrictive dressing, cast, splint, or restraint

Figure 17.23 Examples of Harm Related to Implementation in the ED

Documentation of follow up to ensure that nursing measures such as distraction, medication, and so on have alleviated the pain or distress is required as part of the nursing intervention and assessment for effectiveness. Nurses should not simply be content to "look in on" a patient who has been medicated. The patient should be thoroughly assessed and reevaluated serially in order to determine the efficacy of the treatment as well as other untoward or undesirable effects. The use of a "pain scale" which is required by standards should be documented and the time should be noted. All emergency departments should utilize some type of professionally designed scale that is appropriate to the age population. The nurse must evaluate the assessment of pain and individualize the care. For example, there may be a language barrier, thus preventing the patient from understanding the inquiries of the nurse. In this case, it may be necessary to call for a translator. Consider also the patient who cannot speak due to the placement of an endotracheal tube. Alternatively, a "face scale" or other standardized scale for this population should be used to determine the intensity of the pain. There are many scales designed specifically for children and non-speaking patients; and African-American and Hispanic scales have also been developed. Each patient should be assessed on a regular basis utilizing an appropriate and consistent standardized tool. The nurse is expected to collect subjective and objective data used to implement and evaluate care. See Figure 17.24.

- Subjective data may be obtained by verbal or coded communication of pain descriptors and a self-description of pain.

The nurse may utilize a common mnemonic ("PQRST") as a systematic way to obtain information about pain from adults.

P   (Provoke): What provokes the pain? What makes it better? What are positions of comfort and discomfort?

Q   (Quality or Character): What type of pain is it (burning, tight, crushing, tearing, pressure)?

R   (Radiation): Where does the pain start? Where does it go? The patient is asked to point with one finger to where the pain is the most uncomfortable.

S   (Severity): How severe is the pain on a scale of 0 to 10 (0 representing no pain and 10 representing the worst pain)?

T   (Time): When did the pain start? How long did it last? What time did the intensity change?

Objective data that may be obtained in assessing for pain include:

- Failure to draw conclusions from abnormalities in blood pressure, heart rate, cardiac rhythm, oxygen saturation, temperature—in ED and during diagnostic testing outside department as appropriate
- Failure to reassess appropriately based on condition
- Failure to recognize and report lack of response to interventions (pain, temperature/blood pressure/pulse/breathing, bleeding, urinary output, oxygen saturation, blood gases, intracranial pressure, pupil response, level of consciousness, blood glucose and other chemistries, movement, position)

Figure 17.24 *Basis of ED Nursing Liability Associated with Evaluation*

- Guarding behavior (i.e., protective).
- Self-focusing behavior.
- Narrowed focus (altered time perception, withdrawal from social contact, impaired thought process, irritability, anxiety).
- Distraction behavior (moaning, crying, pacing, seeking out other people or activities, restlessness).
- Facial mask of pain (eyes lackluster, "beaten look," fixed or scattered movement, grimace).
- Alteration in muscle tone, which may span from listless to rigid.
- Autonomic responses not seen in chronic, stable pain (e.g., diaphoresis, blood pressure and pulse rate change, papillary dilation, increased or decreased respirations).
- Sleep disturbance.

Failure to exercise the degree of care that a nurse of similar training or prudence would exercise under the same circumstances is considered the basis of nursing negligence. See Figure 17.25.

In addition to following facility guidelines for identifying and managing pain, the nurse is expected to adhere to published guidelines for the management of pain. The U.S. Department of Health and Human Services, through the Agency for HealthCare Research and Quality (AHRQ), published guidelines that describe practices that offer clinicians standards to pain assessment and management for clinical practice.[83] TJC also has standards of care for pain assessment and effective management.[84]

- Death or disability resulting from failure to reassess patient and detect problems
- Death or disability resulting from failure to timely detect medication/transfusion error or other complications of treatment

Figure 17.25 *Examples of Types of Patient Harm in the ED Related to Evaluation*

6. Cases involving implementation
a. Failure to implement spinal precautions

The plaintiff arrived by private vehicle transport by co-workers after sustaining a large cut on his head. He walked into the ED without assistance, where he spent four hours. Cervical spine x-rays were inconclusive of spinal fracture because the entire cervical spine was not visualized, only to C-5. His head was sutured and he was preparing for discharge when he developed complete paralysis. A cervical collar was never applied. After transfer to a different facility, it was discovered that he had a dislocation at C6-7. Because he suffered only bruises to the spinal cord, he regained most of the use of his arms and legs and his ability to walk. The case settled for $900,000 before trial.[85]

b. Failure to properly position patient for spinal tap, failure to properly resuscitate or monitor

The plaintiff, an eight-month-old boy, presented to the defendant ED for evaluation of ear infection and fever. While assisting an intern performing a spinal tap, an ED nurse held the child improperly, causing his neck to hyperflex and closing his trachea for approximately three minutes. Cardiac arrest due to oxygen deprivation resulted. Plaintiff further alleged that, after instigating this crisis, ED staff failed to properly resuscitate and monitor the patient. The child suffered brain damage with quadriplegia and total blindness, requiring tube feedings and total care. The jury verdict was for $27.57 million.[86]

c. Failure to obtain health history results in heart failure

A 24-year-old man presented to the emergency room with severe chest pain. His vital signs were as follows: blood pressure 132/88, pulse 126 beats per minute, temperature 99 degrees, and oxygen saturation 99 percent on room air. He appeared otherwise healthy and described no recent illnesses or previous history of similar chest discomfort. The emergency room was busy that evening, and the triage staff member thought the patient was stable and triaged him to the waiting room. Two hours after the initial triage, the patient returned to the triage officer complaining of severe pain, requesting to be seen immediately. The staff member told the relatives that the department was busy and that he would be seen as quickly as possible after those patients with more serious illness were seen first. Shortly thereafter, the patient collapsed in the waiting room. Advanced cardiopulmonary resuscitation was required to revive the patient. The patient suffered a severe myocardial infarction. A toxicological analysis revealed large quantities of cocaine in his system. He later admitted to smoking larger amounts of the drug at a party earlier that evening but thought it had nothing to do with his symptoms and did not offer the information. The patient recovered but suffered from significant heart failure.[87]

d. Medication errors
i. Injection injury

The plaintiff, an adult female, sought a tetanus shot for an infected toe at defendant ED. The shot was improperly given in her hip, damaging the sciatic nerve and causing immediate pain. An implanted stimulator, which must be replaced every three years, was required for pain control. The jury verdict was $1.7 million.[88]

ii. Wrong patient

A 63-year-old woman presented to the ED with weakness and possible seizures. Laboratory results for another patient were placed on her chart, resulting in her receiving eight units of intravenous insulin. She was not diabetic. She developed extremely low blood sugar, severe anxiety, and flaccid paralysis, and died less than 12 hours after admission. The jury awarded her estate $100,000.[89]

17.8 Evaluation
A. Importance of Evaluation

Building upon initial assessments by the triage nurse and treatment area nursing staff while incorporating physician history and physical data, ED nurses closely monitor patients to determine whether their condition is deteriorating or whether interventions are successful at stabilization. This process, referred to as evaluation, allows nurses to timely identify changes that warrant communication with physicians and further orders.

Failure to evaluate and communicate vital signs and mental status or to evaluate and report other significant information (such as test results, family input, consulting physician orders) delays or impedes diagnosis and treatment. Abdominal trauma, compartment syndrome, drug overdose/reaction, head injury, heart attack, and shock (hypovolemic, septic, neurogenic, anaphylactic, and cardiogenic) are only a few examples of situations that mandate frequent nursing evaluation. Early signs of life-and-limb-threatening complications may be missed during the initial work-up, so it is the nurse's consistent evaluation and communication that makes it possible for treating physicians to initiate therapy before damage becomes irreversible. The ENA standard for evaluation requires modification of care plans "based on evaluation of observable patient responses and attainment of expected outcomes." Documentation that the patient was "continually evaluated" is required to meet this standard of care.[90]

B. Cases Involving Evaluation

1. Failure to evaluate

An 18-year-old high school student walked to a hospital ED in New Jersey after falling from the hood of a moving car while "car surfing" and suffering loss of consciousness. An x-ray revealed a skull fracture. Six hours after arrival, he lapsed into a coma and suffered permanent brain damage because his epidural hematoma and resultant increased intracranial pressure went unnoticed. After initial assessment, there was no record that the patient was evaluated by a nurse, or that his condition was communicated to the ED physician. Although not the only cause of damages, nursing failure to evaluate or communicate critical changes affected medical intervention: neither a computerized tomography (CT) nor a neurological consultation was ordered until the patient became comatose. The case settled for $1.25 million.[91]

2. Failure to report chest pain

The decedent was 46 years old when he presented to defendant ED for evaluation of a syncopal episode. His history included a normal treadmill EKG during a workup for epigastric pain, but heavy smoking and significant obesity were indicative of increased risk for heart attack. While in the ED, he experienced chest pain with radiation to his left arm, which the ED physician interpreted as normal. He was fitted with a Holter monitor (a continuous EKG machine) and discharged. One hour later, he suffered a fatal heart attack, which was recorded by the Holter monitor. It was learned in discovery that this patient had experienced a second episode of chest pain radiating to his left arm shortly before discharge that the ED nurse had failed to evaluate or to report to the ED physician. The case settled for $350,000.[92]

3. Failure to detect critical changes

A 54-year-old diabetic presented to the defendant ED complaining of weakness. Her serum glucose was noted to be 407, but she was not provided insulin or therapy to prevent complications of diabetes. Instead, she was administered intravenous sugar water. Despite a laboratory test, which showed that her blood sugar increased to 555 and that her arterial blood gases were abnormal, the sugar infusion was continued over the next 33 hours. She developed ketoacidosis, went into cardiac arrest, and died. Appropriate nursing evaluation and communication of critical changes in vital signs, cardiac rhythms, and mental status as well as laboratory values would have resulted in discontinuing the sugar infusion, administration of appropriate intravenous fluids, and insulin. The case settled for $1.45 million.[93]

4. Failure to evaluate and communicate lack of response to interventions

The plaintiff was admitted through the ED for observation of chest pain. It was later determined that he experienced a heart attack either just prior to or during the night of admission, but the only treatment rendered was pain medication. Upon evaluation by physicians the following morning, he was taken for emergency angioplasty. There was no evidence of nursing evaluation of patient status, or of communication with physicians about patient status, from the time of admission until medical rounds. The nurse and hospital settled for a confidential amount before trial.[94]

5. Failure to properly report EKG showing myocardial infarction—delay in treatment blamed for death

The plaintiff's decedent, age 47, had a history of diabetes and hypertension. She was hospitalized with chest pain after preaching her first sermon at her church. An EKG was performed within ten minutes of her arrival, which was interpreted as an acute, evolving myocardial infarction. The technician who performed the test simply placed the EKG in the chart without notifying the nurses. The EKG was discovered an hour later by a physician, just before the decedent went into cardiac arrest. Resuscitation was largely unsuccessful and the decedent was transferred to another hospital, where attempts to unblock the artery were unsuccessful. The decedent lapsed into a coma and remained in a "locked-in" state until her death 20 months later. The plaintiff faulted the hospital on the ground that the EKG technician had an obligation to notify either the doctors or the nurses of the results. The technician had died by the time the suit was filed. The hospital admitted that at the time of the incident no policy was in place for the treatment of patients with chest pain. The plaintiff also faulted the physician, claiming there was an affirmative obligation to look for the EKG within 10 to 15 minutes and that it was negligence to wait 29 minutes after the cardiac arrest to use electroshock. The defense claimed that the decedent was suffering from a massive heart attack at the time of her arrival at the hospital and that the outcome would not have been significantly different regardless of the treatment given. According to a published account a $2 million settlement was reached.[95]

6. Failure to perform adequate testing for illness in asplenic man-death

The plaintiff's decedent, age 59, had a surgical history of splenectomy from several years earlier. He came to the emergency department with body aches and a fever—of 24 hours duration—which ibuprofen had not resolved. His temperature was 103.6°F, and his blood pressure and heart rate were elevated. The triage nurse noted the splenectomy. The defendant physician found no infection, but he did not order laboratory or other diagnostic tests. Viral syndrome was diagnosed; Tylenol and two li-

ters of lactated ringers were ordered. Over the next one and one-half hours, the decedent's fever moderated; his heart rate decreased; and his blood pressure normalized. He was discharged with instructions to drink plenty of fluids and to take Tylenol and Motrin. He was found unresponsive at home later that day. The decedent was pronounced dead on arrival at the emergency department 12 hours after discharge. An autopsy attributed the death to sepsis secondary to streptococcus pneumonia in an asplenic patient. The plaintiff claimed that immediate treatment with intravenous empiric anti-microbial agents and a septic workup should have been performed to determine whether the symptoms were due to pathogens known to predispose asplenic patients to post-splenectomy sepsis. The physician claimed she did not know the decedent was asplenic and denied knowing that the splenectomy predisposed him to systemic infection. According to the published account, an $850,000 settlement was reached.[96]

7. Failure to properly communicate regarding positive culture for bacteria in blood

The plaintiff, age 56, went to the emergency department of a hospital due to severe headaches and neck pain. The defendant emergency department physician worked him up for meningitis and took blood samples for a culture to determine if there was bacteria in the blood. He was discharged early on the following day. The lab technician claimed he told the physician that the cultures were positive for bacteria. The physician denied ever receiving the information, and no action was taken on the positive blood cultures. About 20 days later the plaintiff underwent a two-level fusion of the cervical spine due to bone destruction and an abscess resulting from streptococcus viridians cervical osteomyelitis. The plaintiff is no longer able to work as a commercial pilot. The plaintiff claimed that if proper treatment had been given with antibiotics the fusion would not have been necessary. According to Florida Jury Verdict Report confidential settlements were reached with the hospital and the physician.[97]

TIP: Nurses have a duty to report abnormal vital signs, symptoms, and lab results.[98]

17.9 Patient Education

Patient and family education during the ED stay and at discharge are important ED nursing responsibilities. A study showed that older adults constitute 20 percent of the ED population, and of these, 40 percent received at least one new medication to add to an already complex regimen. The study concluded by demonstrating that ED care increased the need for "effective medication teaching, counseling, and follow-up for older adult ED patients."[99] Most emergency departments use computer-generated or pre-printed instruction sheets to explain aftercare for common conditions such as fever, head injury, sprains, and wound care, but the nurse must individualize this information. Figure 17.26 presents some essential elements of discharge instructions.

While the ED physician is responsible for much of the content of discharge instructions, ED nurses are responsible for delivering the information. By virtue of this role and the fact that the ED nurse is the last professional in contact with the patient, ED nurses are also accountable to ascertain whether patients and caretakers comprehend what they are being told and if they are capable of carrying out instructions. In the process of providing such a vital service, ED nurses are uniquely positioned to determine whether the patient is truly stable for discharge. Therefore, ED nursing notes form the basis for evaluating negligence in this area. The patient, family, or both should be asked to sign the discharge instruction sheet to ensure that the instructions have been given and comprehended. When the patient is under police custody, the officers responsible for the patient should sign the discharge instruction sheet and carry out the follow-up care.

TIP: Even when a patient leaves the ED against medical advice (AMA), the nurse has a duty to give discharge instructions and document patient comprehension and actions taken.

A. Consequences of Improper Patient Education

Discharge policies should be strictly enforced in the interests of patients and professionals alike. Failure to include appropriate instructions may result in:

- Return ED visits.
- Delay in recognition of complications.
- Hospital admission resulting from serious complications.
- Legal action if patients have to be treated in another facility where they learn that their condition was misdiagnosed or improperly treated.

B. Expected Outcome of Patient Education

An expected outcome for ED discharge instructions should include statements such as:

- The patient demonstrates the knowledge of, or has skill in, activities designed to restore, or promote and maintain, health status; and
- the patient verbalizes knowledge of available follow-up resources.

- Emergency facility name, phone number and date.
- Patient's name, medical record number, and signature (or signature of caregiver).
- Witness signature.
- General instructions related to chief complaint or discharge diagnosis, or both, including symptoms that would indicate a need to return to the emergency department.
  - For lacerations, include signs of infection as well as dates and times to return for wound checks and suture removal. Specify frequency of dressing changes and ointments to be applied, and to keep dressings clean and dry.
  - For broken bones and sprains, specify intermittent application of ice or heat, and for how many days it is to be used. Also instruct on proper use of ace bandages, crutches.
- Individualized instructions related to specific injuries such as head injury, postsedation precautions, outpatient diagnostic tests
- Names of medications prescribed in the emergency department, with appropriate precautions such as "no alcohol, driving or operating equipment while on _____." This may require drug teaching sheets.
- Follow-up physician, with phone number and time period for contact.
- Specific number of days of time off work and date allowed to return.
- Qualifying statement about ED treatment as first aid care, the need for ongoing care by a physician, and the importance of reading and following instructions provided.

Figure 17.26 Essential Elements of Discharge Instructions (Sadler, 1999)

Figure 17.27 lists key areas of liability associated with patient education; Figure 17.28 presents types of damages related to patient education.

C. Cases Involving Patient Education

1. Defense verdict related to discharge instructions

The plaintiff, a 26-year-old salesman, went to the ED with complaints of abdominal pain and vomiting, where he was diagnosed with possible gastritis or gastroenteritis. He was given oral and written instructions to see either his own doctor or a referred doctor within two days. He did not follow these instructions but returned to the ED six days later with a perforated appendix complicated by gangrene. Emergency appendectomy with partial colon resection, primary anastomosis, and small bowel resection were required. The plaintiff claimed that his printed instructions were outdated and inadequate and that he neither understood nor recalled the verbal instructions because he was under the influence of Demerol at discharge. ED documentation enabled the defense to show that the patient was alert and oriented at discharge, and that he signed discharge instructions clearly advising him to seek medical follow up within two days.[100]

- Failure to adequately prepare the patient and family for high-risk procedures before obtaining consent.
- Failure to provide appropriate discharge instructions such that the patient or family is aware of symptoms indicating need to return to ED, the time frame for follow up with referrals, proper use and side effects of prescribed medications, appropriate activity level and diet, and specific care in detail, such as wound care, suture removal, use of ice packs or heat.

Figure 17.27 Basis of ED Nursing Liability Associated with Patient Education

---

- Disability or death from failure to adequately instruct patient or family at discharge
- Worsening of condition due to delayed recognition of complications

---

Figure 17.28 Types of Harm in the ED Related to Patient Education

2. Improper discharge instructions

A man who injured his right ring finger playing softball was treated in defendant ED for sprain injury. At discharge he was given a phone number to call "if the finger did not get better." No information was provided about the risk of soft tissue, nerve, or tendon injury that could require surgery, and no specific instructions were given describing symptoms indicating the need for immediate medical care. The patient waited 17 days before deciding he could not tolerate his lack of progress. Unfortunately, the surgery he required could only have been performed within seven to ten days of injury, and he was left unable to move or flex his finger. The defense claimed that verbal instructions were provided, informing the plaintiff that he had a tendon injury and should contact an orthopaedist within one to two days. The jury verdict awarded the plaintiff $110,000.[101]

17.10 Patient Advocacy
A. Role of Nurse as Patient Advocate
The requirement that nurses function as advocates for their patients derives in part from the ANA Code of Ethics for Nurses with Interpretive Statements: "The nurse promotes, advocates for and strives to protect the health, safety, and rights of the patient in an ethical manner."[102] This is further specified in Measurement Criteria, the key indicators of competent practice for each standard.[103]

Unlike planning, implementation, or other nursing process negligence theories that address conduct directly related to the nurse-patient relationship, advocacy issues concern acts by which nurses passively subject a patient to danger by failing to intervene between the patient and other parties, including family, organizational, and medical entities. Figure 17.29 lists four advocacy liability areas encountered in ED nursing practice. Selected aspects are discussed in greater detail in the following section.

B. Selected Aspects of Advocacy

1. Safeguarding life in the ED: chain of command and inappropriate or unclear medical orders

Because of their specialized knowledge and presence at the bedside, nurses are usually able to recognize inappropriate medical and nursing care and to intervene in time to prevent harm. Therefore, in the presence of unsafe care, nurses are responsible for acting on behalf of vulnerable patients, even though nurses do not make medical diagnoses or prescribe treatment. Sometimes simply notifying the charge nurse is sufficient to ensure that standards are met. Other times it entails activating the "chain of command," involving charge nurse, nursing supervisor, hospital administrator, risk management, department chief, and medical chief of staff. Nurses who fail to intervene become liable as though they had directly participated in the negligent acts.

TIP: Further documentation of nursing requirements to act as patient advocates may be discovered in hospital policies to that effect.

---

1. Obstruction of care
- Denying access to system, including
  - Turning away EMS
  - Refusal to allow patients to register for care
- Judgmental attitude resulting in misrepresentation of complaints to medical and nursing staff or inappropriate placement in treatment area

2. Failure to safeguard life in the ED
- Failure to properly supervise staff
  - Failing to place the charge nurse over all ED personnel
  - Failing to place each RN over all personnel in contact with assigned patients, including students, lab, x-ray, respiratory, EMT, physician assistants
  - Hospital failing to establish qualifications, verify absence of criminal backgrounds, licensure status and competence of all staff
- Failure to request additional staff when acuity indicates
- Failure to obtain appropriate consents
- Failure to honor advance directives
- Failure to recognize or honor religious preferences
- Failure to question inappropriate or unclear medical orders
- Failure to activate the chain of command in the presence of unsafe medical or nursing care
- Breach of confidentiality
- Failure to provide opportunity for autopsy or organ donation after death in the ED; conversely to prevent autopsy or organ donation against rightful wishes of family or patient; for second opinion when the patient or family requests it; for further information from MD when requested
- Failure to properly identify the body after death, resulting in misplacement, improper cremation, or violation of the family's or patient's burial rights
- Loss of the patient's personal items, such as dentures, prosthetic devices, clothes, jewelry, money, or body parts

3. Failure to safeguard life at transfer or discharge
- Inappropriate or improper transfer or discharge of an unstable patient: dumping
- Allowing victims of child abuse, elder abuse, domestic violence, or rape to leave with suspected perpetrators
- Failure to report suspected patient, child, or elder abuse
- Discharging impaired patients without safe transportation or proper clothing
- Discharging impoverished patients without medication when it is clear they will be unable to get prescriptions filled

4. Failure to safeguard life after discharge
- Failure to contact the patient about abnormal findings for follow-up
- Failure to contact the patient to urgently return to ED for further treatment/testing based on critical test result

Figure 17.29 Basis of ED Nursing Liability Associated with Patient Advocacy Role, Depending on Hospital Policy or State Law

Consider the implications of this court of appeals finding: "The rule that nurses are obligated to follow the attending physician's instruction is subject to several exceptions. Where an emergency arises, it is of course incumbent upon the nurses…to exercise their own judgment.…Also, a nurse is not obligated to follow orders that are obviously negligent. Furthermore, the fact that a nurse follows hospital or physician orders does not relieve the nurse of the duty to use reasonable care." In the past ED nurses were advised that this heralded an era when it may not be sufficient for the emergency nurse to just bring relevant information and questions to the emergency physician.

One opportunity for patient advocacy would involve a physician who resists transferring a severely burned patient to a regional burn center or a seriously ill infant to a pediatric hospital. The ED nurse who knows that the hospital is not equipped to manage burns or children would question the decision to admit the patient and notify the charge nurse, who would proceed up the chain of command as indicated until a satisfactory result is obtained for the patient.

TIP: Advocacy care is not always documented in the ED record. Rather, it may be contained in ED internal communications and administrative records, or incident reports. Or, it may be discovered during depositions.

---

2. Consent issues
a. ED treatment

Generally, patients sign treatment consents after the triage evaluation and during the process of registration, while the ED chart is being generated. Both triage and registration processes are pre-empted in life-threatening situations such as major trauma, cardiac arrest, respiratory arrest, seizure, severe bleeding, industrial chemical accidents, unconscious children, overdoses, and psychiatric emergencies. In these instances patients are rushed to the treatment area through triage or they arrive by air or ambulance transport. Pre-hospital providers notify ED staff of their imminent arrival, and clinical information is provided so that urgent care can begin the moment the patient enters the ED. "Paperwork" takes a back seat to patient care, and though documentation standards remain in effect, flow of care is much sketchier and consent forms are not obtained.

The act of going to an ED during an emergency generally implies consent for treatment. Courts have ruled that life-threatening conditions requiring immediate treatment permit consent to be implied. In this type of ED admission, documentation that a medical emergency existed, that withholding treatment threatened the patient's life, and that there was insufficient time to obtain informed consent should be clear. Additionally it should be recorded that ED staff made every attempt to locate next of kin, parents of a minor, or significant others, for consent.

b. Refusal of tests, treatment, admission, medications

Courts apply informed consent standards to refusal of care cases. The nurse and physician responsible for warning the patient of the risks of refusing treatment should carefully document this advice, in addition to the circumstances of patient departure. Patients who walk out of the ED without letting anyone know they are leaving are referred to as "absent without notification" (AWON). When ED nurses are unable to find a patient who has been registered, they must document what was known about the person's mental and medical status. The medical record is to be saved and should contain an explanation about why it was not possible to warn the patient about the risks of leaving without treatment.

c. Assault and battery by ED staff

In cases where consent was unclear or the clinical scenario was not sufficient for implied consent, charges of unauthorized patient contact by the nurse (assault and battery) can be made. Case 249 Mass. 456 [1999] reversed vindication for ED staff who forcibly restrained and intubated a 29-year-old asthmatic woman against her and her family's objections after she refused treatment and tried to leave. Defendant argued that the patient's blood gas results proved she was not competent to refuse the life-saving treatment offered, and that her sister did not have the knowledge to refuse for her. The case was remanded to Superior Court for a new trial.[104] Emergency circumstances, often complicated by stress, intoxication, and fear, greatly cloud the ability of ED staff to determine whether a patient retains "decision-making capacity." Components of this ability include knowledge of the options, awareness of the consequences of each option, and appreciation of personal costs or benefits of choices.[105]

d. Advance directives in the ED

Terminally ill patients are not the only population to which ED nurses are accountable for failure to respect end-of-life decisions. Healthy individuals, aware of the possibility of serious traumatic injuries that would deprive them of their rights to refuse treatment, now prepare "living wills" to avert discomfort from being kept alive in a "vegetative state" while their families languish emotionally and financially. The ED is often the arena where such issues must be confronted.

e. Healthcare proxies and what they allow

The health care proxy is a simple legal document that allows a person to name someone he knows and trusts to make healthcare decisions for him, if for any reason and at any time he becomes unable to make or communicate those decisions. It is an important document because it concerns not only the choice made about health care, but also the relationships patients have with their physician, family and others who may be involved in the patient's care. The laws vary state to state and the patient should be well educated in his state's law. If the patient names an agent, this person will make decisions about the patient's health care *only* when the patient is, for some reason, unable to do so. The agent can act for the patient if he is in a coma, temporarily unconscious, or has some other condition in which he cannot communicate healthcare decisions. In some states the law is that the agent named, cannot act for the patient until the doctor determines, in writing, that the patient lacks the ability to make healthcare decisions. This is known as the proxy being *invoked*.

3. Requests for additional staff

Under the best of circumstances, it is difficult to maintain adequate staffing in any ED because it can transform from empty to overflowing in minutes. When a full ED is composed of simple cases, there is little difficulty managing care, but when the patient mix contains trauma, heart attack, unconscious victims from any cause (brain injury, drug overdose, and stroke) or psychotic patients, the challenge is great. ED nurses must accompany such patients wherever they go out of the department and must provide virtually constant monitoring in the ED. Other patients in the department at the same time may require intensive screening and intervention related to domestic violence or teaching about newly prescribed medications. According to the editor of the *Journal of Emergency Nursing*, ED nurses across the country are frustrated, their managers are resigning, and the number of emergency departments that are chronically short-staffed is growing.[106]

Staff nurses are expected to keep nursing management apprised when additional staff is needed and to prioritize by providing care to the sickest patients first. Nursing supervisors should assist in finding additional staff when indicated and may also participate in patient care. Frequent evaluation and meticulous documentation of all patients is expected, regardless of how busy the nurses may be.[107]

4. Use of the recently dead for practicing procedures

Patients pronounced dead on arrival (DOA) or who expire in the ED are used in some facilities for staff to practice

invasive procedure skills such as central line or chest tube insertion, intubation, and pericardiocentesis.[108] The ENA agrees with the need to teach and practice these and additional skills including:

*   cricothyrotomy,
*   cross-clamping of the aorta,
*   intraosseous needle insertion, and
*   liver biopsy.

The ENA emphasizes that some form of consent must be obtained from patient or family and that the individual practicing must have a legitimate need to master the skill.[109]

ED consent forms must provide the opportunity for patients to elect "informed refusal" of procedures and treatments with respect for living wills or religious affiliations preventing certain interventions such as blood transfusions.

5. Failure to safeguard life at transfer or discharge
a. Dumping
i. EMTALA/COBRA

Patients are protected at arrival, transfer and discharge from the ED through the federal law known as the Emergency Medical Treatment and Active Labor Act (EMTALA), also known as the anti-dumping act, was enacted in 1986. EMTALA is an amendment to COBRA, EMTALA was expanded in 1989 to extend transfer liability to on-call physicians and to require written informed consent prior to transfer. Additional amendments have been published in 2000, 2003 and 2008. The Centers for Medicare and Medicaid Services regulates compliance with EMTALA.[110] Figure 17.30 summarizes protections under COBRA/EMTALA last updated as of July 16, 2010.

The Act dictates that a patient who "comes to the emergency department" be thoroughly evaluated and any emergency condition stabilized prior to discharge or transfer. It establishes strict standards for transfer to other facilities to ensure patient safety. EMTALA was passed in response to widespread publicity in the late 1970s and early 1980s that uninsured patients were being transferred to "charity" or "county" hospitals in the midst of medical emergencies so that for-profit facilities could avoid costs associated with their care.

In addition to general guidelines furnished by EMTALA, four punishable violations are identified:

*   Signing a transfer certificate when the physician knew, or should have known, that the benefits did not outweigh the risk.

- All patients who come to the ED must be screened for an emergency medical condition before a decision to discharge or transfer the patient can be made. An emergency medical condition is defined as one manifesting acute symptoms of sufficient severity, including pain (and, as of July 7, 1994, this applies to psychiatric patients), such that an absence of immediate medical attention could result in:
  - placing the person in serious jeopardy
  - serious impairment or dysfunction to body functions or organs
  - posing a threat to the health and safety of a pregnant woman or unborn child
- According to the 1995 Guidelines, "Come to the ED" means "if an individual arrives at a hospital and is not technically in the ED, but on the premises (including the parking lot, sidewalk, driveway)—[note also on a helicopter pad, in a hospital-owned ambulance, or an ambulance dock, in a labor and delivery department] and requests medical care, he or she is entitled to a medical screening examination." It is expected that EMTALA also applies to a "noncontiguous or off-campus hospital-owned facility that operates under the hospital's provider number."[1]
- The screening exam must be detailed enough to accomplish the objective of revealing an emergency medical condition. It should include "an appropriate medical history and physical examination, appropriate diagnostic testing, consulting with pertinent on-call physicians or other health care providers, and reassessing the patient prior to discharge or transfer." This remains an ongoing process until it has been determined that the patient is stabilized and discharged or transferred. The process must be clearly and completely documented in the patient's medical records."[2]
- Persons deemed qualified to perform medical screenings (physicians, nurse practitioners, physician's assistants) must be designated in a policy approved by the hospital's board of directors or governing body. Duties to be performed must be specified and must be within the scope of practice for these individuals. This disqualifies nurses and nurse practitioners in some states.
- Hospital protocols regarding medical screening must be followed for all patients with similar complaints, without regard to the patient's ability to pay or participation in managed care programs.

- If an emergency medical condition exists, the patient must receive stabilizing treatment as needed, including evaluation by a physician.
- The patient cannot be in active labor at the time of transfer. Active labor is defined as imminent delivery coupled with inadequate time to transfer the patient or a threat to the safety of the mother or child if transfer occurs.
- The patient must be stabilized before transfer. The physician makes a determination that to a reasonable degree of medical probability there will be no material deterioration of the patient's condition as a result of or during the transfer. Stabilization may include any of the following: establishing and assuring an adequate airway and breathing, controlling hemorrhage, stabilizing fractures, establishing intravenous lines for fluid administration, replacing lost fluids and blood, and determining that the patient's vital signs and urine output are sufficient to sustain life.
- Transfer is defined as movement of the patient, at the recommendation of a hospital employee, within the hospital, to another hospital, or discharge from the hospital.
- An unstable patient may be transferred if the patient or physician requests it because the medical benefits outweigh the increased risk of transfer.
- A stable patient can be transferred if the appropriate facility agrees to accept the patient. The receiving facility must have adequate space and qualified personnel to take care of the patient.
- The sending hospital must document that a responsible person at the receiving hospital has agreed to accept the patient, that clinical information has been communicated, that appropriate medical and diagnostic information is transferred along with the patient to the receiving facility, and that an appropriate vehicle is used for the transfers.

(COBRA/EMTALA interpretive guidelines are available online at www.medlaw.com.)

1. Mannino, A. "EMTALA and you: beyond the legalese," ENA Government Services online, www.ena.org/services/govt/emtala/article3.htm. February 2000.
2. Smith, W., "EMTALA—What is an 'appropriate medical screening examination?'" ENA Government Services online, www.ena.org/services/govt/emtala/article2.htm, February 2000.

Figure 17.30 Current Interpretation of EMTALA/COBRA Amendments

- Misrepresentation of a patient's condition or any other information on the transfer certificate.
- Failure of the medical facility to provide treatment within its capacity to stabilize the patient before transfer.
- Failure of an on-call physician to appear within a reasonable time when notified by an ED that her services were required.

EMTALA does not require a finding of negligence before concluding that a hospital or physician is in violation of the law. In fact, courts have interpreted that the Act was not designed to ensure accurate diagnosis for each presenting ED patient. Its sole purpose was to provide a federal course of action for failure to:

- Determine whether an emergency medical condition exists.
- Stabilize and appropriately transfer patients with an existing medical emergency who are unable to pay for their health care.

Debates about what constitutes an "emergency condition" and "stabilization"—even "hospital property"—have contributed to the body of law in the aftermath of this legislation. Health Care Financing Administration (HCFA) guidelines, effective July 14, 1998, provided uniformity in EMTALA interpretation concerning treatment of managed care enrollees who present to the ED. These are summarized in Figure 17.31.

EMTALA extends to persons who may have been denied medical screening due to "improper motives" such as drunkenness, race, political affiliation, psychiatric illness, or AIDS.[111] Thus, all emergency patients, regardless of complaint or financial resources, are provided screening and stabilization or transfer under the Act.

TIP: Hospitals may not always create a medical record for all patients who present for treatment. Request the triage sign-in log to determine whether a patient attempted to register for ED care.

EMTALA states that an unstable patient cannot be sent home or to another facility unless the circumstances of the patient leaving the hospital meet the Act's rigorous level test for an appropriate transfer.

The following are case examples:

Case #1:
The patient was taken by ambulance to the emergency department after a prescription-drug over-

dose. On admission, he was disoriented, hallucinating, and out of control. After evaluation by the ER physician, the patient was admitted to the ICU where he was assigned one-to-one monitoring by a nurse. The nurse was thorough in her assessment, including a risk for pressure ulcers. The patient asked to make a phone call. The nurse allowed him to do so after disconnecting his IV and monitors. The patient left the hospital after calling someone to pick him up. He was subsequently arrested while apparently still under the influence.

The court ruled this patient got an appropriate medical screening examination and received substantial efforts to stabilize his medical condition. His hospital care also fulfilled the common-law standard of care. That is, he had no grounds to sue the hospital or his caregivers for malpractice.

Additional points made by the court:

- A hospital cannot force a patient who comes in as an emergency to leave before the patient has been examined and stabilized.

- A hospital may not refuse to screen and stabilize a managed care enrollee, even if the plan refuses to authorize or pay for the visit.
- A managed care plan may not refuse to screen, stabilize or appropriately transfer patients not enrolled in their plan who seek ED care in its hospital if it receives Medicare reimbursements.
- Hospitals and managed care plans may not request or require authorization before providing a medical screening exam, even if the plan requires preauthorization for payment.
- After it has been appropriately determined that there is no medical emergency or that a patient has been stabilized, EMTALA no longer applies. The hospital may seek prior authorization for further services. A hospital may follow registration procedures for patients with emergency medical conditions and request insurance information as long as it does not delay screening or treatment.

Fiesta, J. "No dumping: ED transfer risk," Nursing Management 30, no. 10 (January 1999): 10.

Figure 17.31 *EMTALA Requirements for Managed Care Enrollees who Present for ED Treatment (Fiesta, 1999)*

- However, a patient who wants to leave voluntarily against medical advice can and must be allowed to go. What this patient did after he left is not the hospital's fault.[112]

Case #2:

After experiencing episodes of syncope, the patient was taken to the hospital emergency department by ambulance. According to the court record, she had also been falling and had poorly controlled high blood pressure. After three hours of close observation, her blood pressure had dropped from 200/100 to 133/91, and a physician ordered her to be discharged. She was instructed to stop taking her Atenolol and to follow up in her primary-care physician's office. He also cautioned her to get in the habit of sitting on the side of the bed for five minutes before trying to stand up. It took more than two hours after the physician discharged her for an ambulance to arrive to take her home. During that time she twice fell off the bed where she was sitting. The nurse took her blood pressure both times, got readings of 180/110 and 170/100, but did not notify the physician. The patient left and then came back to the hospital two days later. She had a stroke. She had to undergo comprehensive rehab for the sequelae of her stroke and now has significant residual functional limitations.

This patient sued the hospital for violation of EMTALA and in the same lawsuit sued the two physicians and the nurse for common-law medical malpractice.

The hospital asked the U.S. District Court for the District of New Jersey for a preliminary ruling whether this case comes under EMTALA. The court ruled that is does. The court has not yet ruled on the malpractice allegations filed against the nurse, the physicians, and the hospital as the nurse's employer.[113]

Another provision of EMTALA relevant to ED nursing concerns the patient in active labor. While it is preferable for babies to be born in a sterile environment such as a labor and delivery unit, women are not able to control the arrival of their infants. Every ED must be prepared (through staff education, equipment availability, and screening competence) for emergency delivery to determine whether a delivery is imminent. Consequences to the infant as well as the mother from lack of preparedness or refusal to accept via ambulance are inexcusable from regulatory as well as ethical perspectives.

Enforcement of EMTALA is provided through regional Health Care Financing Administration (HCFA) offices. Complaints ultimately come to HCFA from physicians, patients, EMS, routine site visits, newspaper articles, peer review organization screens, state agencies, and receiving hospitals, which must report possible COBRA violations within 72 hours or face financial penalties as well. Penalties against medical or nursing staff who refuse to transfer unstable patients or who report violations of EMTALA are prohibited.[114] Credible allegations are investigated through an unannounced focused survey by state licensing officials.

If a violation is found, a Civil Monetary Penalty (CMP) is levied by the Office of the Inspector General. Sanctions can be stiff and are not covered by malpractice insurance: the hospital, physician, or both can be fined $50,000 and can be excluded from Medicare participation through loss of certification. The largest hospital CMP on record is $150,000.[115]

In addition to federal accountability for EMTALA violations, hospitals may face civil lawsuits by persons who believe that ED staff caused them harm in the course of EMTALA infractions. Legal remedy is available not only to indigent or uninsured patients but to any individual who believes medical screening and stabilization was denied them prior to discharge or transfer. Managed care organizations, physicians, and nurses are essentially protected from being individually sued under EMTALA[116]; however, ED nurses and physicians are the vehicles through which hospitals are frequently found culpable.

Federal courts have consistently ruled that EMTALA does not replace state tort claims of medical negligence. EMTALA violations are increasingly incorporated into medical malpractice case law, as evidenced by *Power v. Arlington Hospital Association*: the court concluded that, because the Virginia Medical Malpractice Act applies to any tort based on healthcare services rendered by a healthcare provider and EMTALA claims arise in the course of patient treatment, that the Virginia Medical Malpractice Act applies to EMTALA claims. This decision caused the cap on damages against hospitals provided by Virginia law to be applicable to EMTALA claims. In other malpractice cases it is possible for courts to discard all state laws and find state limitations on damage awards unacceptable, as was the case with Florida in *Cooper v. Gulf Breeze Hospital, Inc.*[117]

EMTALA sanctions could affect settlement of negligence claims, enhance the legitimacy of damages, or influence jury awards. EMTALA has additional implications for ED cases because patients may recover personal injury damages if, after discharge or transfer to another facility, their condition worsened. The patient is only obliged to show that her condition was not "stabilized" at the time of departure.

ED nursing conduct, including documentation, plays a pivotal role in the outcome of such lawsuits.

To prevail in an action based on EMTALA the plaintiff must prove that the hospital had actual knowledge of an emergency, failed to stabilize before transfer or discharge, and failed to follow established procedures. To defend against claims related to transfers, appropriate staff must have obtained a signed consent showing that a competent patient either elected or refused transfer after being fully informed of both benefits and risks. The Act excuses hospitals, and indirectly physicians, from their duty to stabilize or transfer where the offer was made but refused by the patient, as long as the patient was properly evaluated prior to the transfer. Hospitals and providers must also be able to produce evidence that their standards regarding discharge and transfer are applied uniformly to all patients without regard to funding.

Once a patient is determined to not have an emergency medical condition requiring stabilization or to not be in active labor, EMTALA no longer applies: non-emergency patients may be discharged or transferred based on financial considerations.

ii. Transfer requirements under EMTALA

Figure 17.32 itemizes EMTALA requirements for transfer of patients. ED nurses should be thoroughly familiar with the risks associated with inappropriate transfers and are obligated as advocates to protect the patient from them. Instances occur in which ED nurses work in concert with ED physicians against "economic transfers" by primary care doctors who want their patients transferred to preferred hospitals with equal or less capability, in spite of standards that require observation admission to the initial facility for at least 24 hours to stabilize the patient. To protect the hospital from liability, ED nurses should verify and document justification for transfer. They should be insistent that informed consent or treatment refusal documents be obtained. In the event of attempted inappropriate transfers the ED nurse has a duty to activate the chain of command and to involve hospital administration.

Despite federal efforts over the past ten years to protect a uniquely American right to medical care when in critical condition regardless of payment issues, patient dumping continues. ED nurses are accountable for participation in patient dumping because employing hospitals are fined according to their conduct. As patient advocates they must be familiar with EMTALA provisions and must consult appropriate management staff before discharging patients when a potential EMTALA violation exists.

- A physician must provide written certification of the need to transfer, though a qualified medical person designated by hospital bylaws, rules or regulations may sign as long as a physician has been consulted and there is agreement to transfer.[1]
- The patient or family must provide informed consent to the transfer.
- The receiving facility must have available space and qualified personnel to provide appropriate medical treatment, and agree to accept the patient. The law now mandates that hospitals with specialized units (burn units, neonatal intensive care units and trauma centers) accept transfer patients needing such care.[2]
- The transferring hospital must forward appropriate medical records of examination and treatment.
- Transfer must be effected through qualified personnel, equipment and vehicle as indicated by condition of the patient, and any other requirements as the Secretary of Health and Human Services may find necessary.[3]

1. Huntington, E. "New EMTALA regulations: issues and answers for emergency department—nurses," Journal of Nursing Law 2, no. 2 (1995): 27–33.
2. Fiesta, J. "No dumping: ED transfer risk," Nursing Management 30, no. 10 (January 1999): 10.
3. Hollowell, E. and H. Bloch, "Coproviders and institutional practice," In Legal Medicine, Third edition, edited by S. Sanbar. St. Louis: Mosby, 1995.

Figure 17.32 *Transfer requirements under EMTALA*

iii. Proper transport of unstable patients is not dumping

Because persons transported by non-hospital means are not considered the hospital's responsibility until arrival, EMTALA allows denial of patients when the ED is on diversionary status unless the ambulance transports the patient regardless of dispatcher instructions.

A hospital may transfer acutely ill patients for other than economic motives when the patient's condition requires care beyond the capabilities of the ED or of the initial hospital. ED physicians have protocols for immediate communication with and transfer to appropriate facilities. The initial ED staff is responsible for stabilizing patients and moving them as rapidly as possible by the best mode of travel possible with a qualified transport team. Often ED nurses from the sending ED accompany the patient to the receiving facility and may provide care during the trip. In such cases, the nurse remains responsible and accountable until the patient is officially received at the second facility. In some areas, the receiving hospital may have its own transport team to send for the patient.

TIP: Identification of the nurse responsible for the patient during transport can become a significant legal issue if the patient develops complications during transport and the treatment provided is substandard. The attorney will need to make a determination as to exactly which nurse is responsible for the patient, particularly if the referral ED hospital team or transport nurse takes over patient care at the original ED. Is the initial receiving ED nurse totally responsible until the patient is discharged or is the care provided jointly? Exactly which nurse is legally responsible for the patient may be a source of dispute. Jurisdictional matters come into play if the incident occurred during flight.

---

iv. Required transport documents

Figure 17.33 presents a checklist of documents the ED nurse should have verified to be contained in the patient's medical record prior to transfer to another. Continuity of care depends on both written and verbal communication, and errors or miscommunication impact patient care during transfer as at any other time. Fax transmissions are part of the medical record and should be included when copies of the patient's chart are requested. ED nurses who have been delegated decision-making responsibility regarding patient transfers should have specific guidelines or protocols that require supervisor, hospital administrator, and physician collaboration.

TIP: If a physician is not physically present to provide written certification, qualified ED staff may obtain a verbal transfer order from a physician. Eventually, that physician must countersign the written certification.

---

b. Stranded patients and families

As with unprotected children, spouses, and elderly, impaired patients and the severely impoverished require nursing advocacy. Recently, due to consolidation of technology into tertiary care centers, patients are often stranded in unfamiliar neighborhoods, cities, even other states due to diversion and transfers away from local hospitals. Such circumstances can result in patients being discharged from the ED with no clothing or transportation home—or even the means to contact family for assistance. Likewise, persons impaired

- Receiving hospital has agreed to accept the patient
- A registered nurse or physician at the receiving hospital has been given a complete report on the patient, including history, chief complaint, course of care in the transferring ED, test results, vital signs, destination of the patient (ED or specific unit), plan of care and admitting physician's name
- Physician certification that transfer is necessary
- Medical certification that, based on the information available at time of transfer, the anticipated medical benefits outweighed any increased risks of transfer
- The patient or family's written request or consent to be transferred after being informed of the specific risks involved and of the hospital's obligations under EMTALA
- Accepting physician has been notified of transfer and will assume care
- Appropriate transportation with personnel qualified to provide appropriate level of care
- Copies of all evaluation and treatment records, lab studies with results, consultations, and patient's medical condition at time of transfer
- Copies of x-ray and CT films
- Valuables, dentures, eyeglasses and other personal items are accounted for and given to the transport team or family

Figure 17.33 Essential Transfer Documentation

by substance abuse, victims of violence, head injury, psychiatric conditions, and developmental delays may find themselves stranded or vulnerable. Uninsured and severely impoverished patients may be discharged with instructions for medications, equipment, and specialized care that they have no hope of obtaining without financial assistance or social service intervention. ED nurses are responsible for ensuring the safety of such individuals after the ED has rendered care. Liability for harm rests with the nurse who discharged the patient.

c. Failure to safeguard life after discharge: callbacks

Nationwide, the number of ED malpractice suits citing failure to contact patients about abnormal diagnostic studies has increased.[118] It is an established ED standard of care to contact all patients who left the ED triage or treatment areas without notifying staff or who left against medical advice (AMA). Additionally, current standards compel follow-up contact with all patients evaluated and discharged from the ED with head injuries, chest pain, suicidal or homicidal potential, and all whose diagnostic tests return abnormal results. These attempts must be documented in the ED record, including dates and times of each call and any phone number dialed. A registered letter must be sent to the address provided by the patient if the patient needs to be informed of a potentially serious medical problem and cannot be reached by phone. Protocols directing these efforts are imperative and must specify time frames, usually no longer than three days after discharge, within which ED staff must make contact. Additionally, copies of the positive test result are to be faxed to the primary physician listed by the patient upon ED registration, with a note that efforts to reach the patient have been unsuccessful. These, too, must be documented in the ED chart generated on the relevant date. Figure 17.34 presents types of damages related to patient advocacy.

d. Interpreters

The patients have rights to an interpreter. Staff should know how to access intepretors. See Figure 17.35 for an example of a Patient's Bill of Rights.

C. Cases Involving Patient Advocacy

1. Obstruction of care

The decedent, a 23-year-old unemployed male, was taken by his family to the defendant ED for weakness, fever, dry mouth, and frequent urination. He was grossly obese and required a wheelchair to get into the hospital. Both triage and emergency treatment were denied for seven hours, though the patient had signed the triage log requesting to be seen. Eventually the family decided to leave. The following morning the patient lapsed into unconsciousness and was transported to another hospital where he died of previously undiagnosed diabetes. The case settled for $245,000.[119]

2. Failure to safeguard life in the ED
a. Failure to activate the chain of command

A 52-year-old man with Down's syndrome was an unrestrained passenger traveling with his sister when her car was totaled in a severe collision. The patient struck his head on the windshield with suf-

- Death or disability for failing to activate the chain of command to ensure appropriate patient care when the physician's competence, qualification, or appropriateness is questioned
- Disability or death for failure to receive appropriate treatment due to inadequate staffing and failure to call for backup or notify supervisor
- Disability or death from loss of opportunity to give informed consent, to obtain second opinion, or to further consult with an M.D.
- Disability or death from permitting an incompetent patient to walk out of the ED and become injured
- Disability or death from transporting a patient in unstable condition (dumping)
- Emotional distress from collection of blood alcohol or other specimens against the patient's objections
- Emotional distress resulting from receiving blood or other ED treatments that are against a patient's religious beliefs or practices
- Family pain and suffering due to misplacement of body, improper cremation, denial of the family's or patient's burial rights
- Financial loss and family pain and suffering due to the loss of the patient's personal items and belongings
- Lost opportunity for organ donation or autopsy
- Pain, suffering and economic loss caused by intubation and mechanical ventilation or other "heroics" while disregarding the patient's advance directives
- Pain and suffering of a terminally ill patient who refuses heroic life-saving measures and is denied pain control interventions
- Patient or child abuse from the failure to report suspected patient abuse and discharging the injured patient to the abuser

Figure 17.34 Harm Related to Failure to Act as Patient Advocate in the ED

Office of Civil Rights

Title VI, Civil Rights Act of 1964 prohibits exclusion from services and discrimination on grounds of race, color or national origin. This extends to people with non-English or Limited English Proficiency. The federal Americans with Disabilities Act and Article 114 of the Massachusetts Constitution extend those rights to Deaf and Hard of Hearing people.

The law varies state to state, below is an example of Massachusetts State Law in part:

Massachusetts General Laws, Chapter 111, Section 25J and Chapter 123, Section 23 A, state that acute care hospitals must provide adult competent medical interpreters, face to face or over the phone, at no cost to all non English speaking and limited English proficient patients seeking care or treatment in emergency departments or acute psychiatry units. This law should apply to all patient care areas.

Patients have the right to:

- Request a medical interpreter anytime, even if they speak limited English.
- Use or refuse the medical interpreter, face to face or over the phone.
- If the patient agrees to the use of an interpreter, the nurse must document that one was used and the name of the interpreter each and every time a communication is used with the patient.
- If the patient refuses an interpreter, a refusal form must be signed by the patient, but they must understand what they are signing. It is in the best interest of the patient that an interpreter is present during this refusal.

Helping patients exercise their right ensures:

- safe care
- effective communication
- understanding of medical information
- compliance with follow up treatment
- cooperation
- satisfaction

Figure 17.35 Patient's Bill of Rights

ficient force to cause a non-displaced nasal fracture and multiple facial lacerations. At the scene and throughout his ED admission he continued to yell, "I can't move!" He was immobilized appropriately by EMS and taken to defendant ED, where he was examined by an inexperienced ED physician four months out of his residency. The patient complained that every place the doctor touched him was painful. Cervical x-rays revealed extensive narrowing of the spinal cord at C3-C4 and C4-C5. The radiologist relayed his concerns that this patient had a higher predisposition for spinal cord injury, which he suspected. The ED physician dismissed these findings. Six hours later, he discharged the patient despite continued declarations that he could not move. The ED nurse did not challenge the discharge order and activate the chain of command to ensure appropriate consult with a neurosurgeon. The ambulance person who took the patient home was a 30-year EMS veteran who testified that at no time did the patient move his arms or his head, and that he was unable to assist paramedics in moving from ED stretcher to ambulance or from ambulance stretcher to his own bed. The next morning the plaintiff was unable to lift his head or sit up. He was still crying that he could not move. He was subsequently diagnosed with spinal cord compression requiring surgery. He suffered permanent paralysis and now requires 24-hour care to eat, dress, bathe, and manage his basic needs. The case settled for $1.3 million.[120]

b. Failure to insist on appropriate care

The decedent was 62 years old when he presented to the defendant ED with complaints of pressure-like chest pain, shortness of breath, and weakness. Six months previously he had been diagnosed at this ED for myocardial infarction and flown to Duke, where he successfully underwent cardiac catheterization. This time he waited two hours in the waiting room and four more hours in the treatment area before evaluation by a physician's assistant. Despite his history and symptoms the physician's assistant spent only seven minutes with the patient and discharged the patient with a diagnosis of gastritis, a prescription for Zantac, and instructions to buy Gas-X. The patient died of cardiac complications on the way home. ED nurses would have had the opportunity to intercede on behalf of the patient to prevent his death. The case settled for $1.025 million.[121]

c. Failure to recognize signs and symptoms of a myocardial infarction

A 38-year-old female presented to the emergency department at 3:35 A.M. complaining of a cough and chest pains. Seven minutes later she was seen by the triage nurse who made note of the fact that she smoked a pack of cigarettes per day. The nurse failed to note there was a positive history of coronary artery disease. The patient was seen 30 minutes later by a nurse who assessed her but did not place her on a cardiac monitor.

The ER physician saw her at 5:07 A.M. and ordered an EKG and cardiac enzymes. The EKG, done at 5:25 A.M., was read by the same ER physician as "worrisome" just before he turned her care over to the day shift physician coming on duty. A nitroglycerine drip was started at 5:40 A.M. and was effective by 6:15 A.M. in reducing her chest pain from level eight (0-10 scale) to level one. Subsequent data revealed marked ST segment elevation in the lateral leads compared to the earlier EKG; the second set of lab tests revealed markedly elevated cardiac enzymes. The patient was sent for a CT scan with a cardiac monitor without a registered nurse certified in Advanced Cardiac Life Support (ACLS). She vomited twice between 9:10 and 10:30 A.M. for which she was given intravenous Phenergan with a saline bolus. A cardiologist happened to be reviewing EKGs in the ER and at 11:10 A.M. determined he should evaluate the patient. At 12:05 P.M., the cardiologist did an angiogram which revealed 100 percent occlusion of the left anterior descending coronary artery. Despite having a balloon angioplasty, the patient now has significantly impaired cardiac function and may require a transplant.

The Court of Appeals of Texas analyzed the allegations raised in the patient's suit against the hospital and the physicians by reviewing the accepted national standard of care for emergency room nurses caring for patients with signs and symptoms of acute myocardial infarction.

The court findings:

- A hospital is required to have a clinical pathway for nurses to follow.

- The standard of care for emergency room nursing includes the ability to quickly recognize patients with signs and symptoms of acute myocardial infarction and to take action. The medical goal is to administer thrombolytic drugs or perform a coronary angioplasty within 60 minutes to minimize long-term ischemic damage to the heart.[122]

3. Dumping
a. Infant not admitted to hospital

City fire department paramedics were treating an infant in cardiac arrest when they contacted University of Chicago Hospital's (UCH) telemetry system. Only five minutes from the infant's home, the nurse instructed the paramedics to transport to another hospital because their pediatric ICU was full. The child later died. The court held that since their telemetry system was distinct from UCH's ED, the hospital did not violate EMTALA. However, in a footnote the court added that it would reconsider if evidence existed that a hospital used its telemetry system as part of "a scheme to dump patients." *Johnson v. University of Chicago.*[123]

b. Transfer of stable patient

In Puerto Rico, an ED patient was immediately seen by a physician based on her presenting symptoms, and was diagnosed with acute appendicitis. Because she did not have medical insurance and could not pay privately, she was transferred under medical orders to a public hospital where she arrived three hours later. During subsequent emergency surgery, her right ureter was cut and she suffered complications. The court ruled that the first hospital had not violated EMTALA because the patient was stable when transferred. *Torres Nieves v. Hospital Metropolitano,* 1998.[124]

c. Transfer of unstable patient

The plaintiff's attorneys in the following New Mexico case proved that the patient was negligently dumped because of her inability to pay for medical care:

On January 22, 1988 at 9:30 P.M., the plaintiff, age 52, walked into Heights General Hospital complaining of a splitting headache and tingling in her fingers. These symptoms were consistent with the beginning of a stroke. The emergency room physician called the physician consultant, who said that the plaintiff needed immediate surgery. However, Heights General Hospital sent her to University Hospital shortly before midnight while she was in an unstable condition. She was not operated on until February 2, at which point she was paralyzed on one side and had lost certain brain functions. The plaintiff claimed she was negligently treated and should have been operated on sooner, and claimed she was "dumped" by Heights General Hospital and transferred to University Hospital because of her inability to pay for medical attention. The defendants denied negligence generally. A $1.7 million verdict was returned.[125]

d. Transfer of Vicodin-overdose patient while unstable—death

The plaintiff's decedent was taken to the emergency department by ambulance. The admitting diagnosis was unintentional Vicodin overdose. During the next several hours the attending doctors and nurses noted that the decedent was disoriented, did not understand instructions, was not alert, and was both incoherent and tachycardic. Following treatment for hypokalemia, low blood potassium, a decision was made to transfer her non-emergently to a second hospital. Two EMTs agreed to transport the decedent, even though she was not stable. Upon arrival at the second hospital the decedent was lifeless, with no pulse or respirations. Resuscitation attempts were not successful. The plaintiff alleged negligence in transferring the decedent because she was not stable. This Texas case was settled confidentially. EMTALA regulations would also come into this case for proper transfer obligations for all parties involved.[126]

e. Failure to transfer as ordered, blame for death from abdominal aneurysm

According to the plaintiff, the defendant hospital failed to transfer the decedent, age 64, to an out-of-state hospital pursuant to a physician's order in December 2000. The plaintiff claimed the decedent died as a result of the lack of a transfer and no surgery to repair the thoraco-abdominal aneurysm. The defense denied any legal duty to pay or guarantee payment for the out-of-state flight. The defendant also asserted that its social worker acted properly in attempting to coordinate the timely flight and secure payment from the decedent's military health insurance. According to Florida Jury Verdict Reporter a defense verdict was returned.

f. Pregnant patient

A pregnant patient arrived at the defendant ED at 3:10 A.M. She was assessed by the ED nurses to be "dilated at 4 cm with seventy percent effacement and bulging membranes at -2 station." This assessment was telephoned to a general practitioner on call and to an unidentified doctor at a specialized center. Instructions were given to transfer the patient on her left side. Ambulance staff were hesitant to accept the patient, realizing that hospital guidelines prohibited transfer of a woman in labor at 4 cm dilation, but the ED nurse directed them to "put the patient in the ambulance, turn on the lights and sirens and GO." The patient was not reassessed prior to transfer. En route, her membranes ruptured, so the ambulance pulled off the road and arranged a "Life Flight" to the receiving hospital. Before the Life Flight arrived, one of the EMTs decided to tear open the amniotic sac because the patient was having contractions and the baby was not descending into the birth canal. Minutes later, the patient's cervix suddenly clamped down around the baby's neck causing the baby to become cyanotic (blue), suffocate, and die. The parents brought suit against both hospitals, the doctor and ED nurses, as well as the EMTs. The plaintiff asserted that the failure of the nurses to use tangible equipment in assessing, recording, and communicating the status of the patient's labor and the well-being of the fetus resulted in death. Additionally, the court found that the ED nurses, who were employees of a government facility, had not established, as a matter of law, that they were performing duties different from nurses engaged in a similar practice in the private sector or exercising a function unique to government.[127]

g. HMO dumping

Mr. Smith experienced chest pain at home and called 911, after which he was transported by EMS to the closest hospital. His physician was actually on staff at a different facility. Mr. Smith's EKG and cardiac enzymes were normal and his chest pain atypical but suggestive of new onset angina. The ED physician recommended admission to a monitored bed at the hospital. The patient and his wife agreed to admission but worried about coverage by their managed health plan, and insisted that the ED physician call their primary doctor before they proceed. While the patient's wife attempted unsuccessfully to determine whether their plan would pay for admission to the initial hospital, the ED physician and the patient's primary doctor argued about whether it was "safe" to transfer a patient with chest pain that might be cardiac. The primary physician, who had not personally examined the patient, argued that Mr. Smith would be accompanied by paramedics and that the plan hospital was only 20 minutes away. He then got on the phone with the patient's wife and told her it was unlikely that her husband had a heart attack, that admission would only be a precaution, and that he would prefer to care for the patient at his own hospital. He expressed doubt that the insurance company would approve admission to the initial facility because the patient was medically stable. She agreed to transfer her husband. Despite restating his position and his continued unease, the ED physician went along with this transfer and agreed it is "probably OK." No refusal of treatment or AMA forms were obtained, although an ED nurse recommended that these be filled out. Transfer forms were completed by the ED physician, but there was no documentation that the patient and his wife were warned of the potential for complications during transport such as dysrhythmia, disability, or death. Appropriate transfer procedure occurred regarding ED-to-ED medical and nursing communication and record copying. Just prior to departure, Mr. Smith again experienced chest pain. The ED nurse provided the standard of care in following standing orders for nitroglycerin and getting the physician to the bedside. Again, the ED physician allowed the transfer to occur. The primary physician's partner, now on call, did not know the patient and also questioned the plan to transfer a possible cardiac patient, but did not disrupt the plan. En route, Mr. Smith suffered a full-blown heart attack with complications. The receiving hospital ED reported an EMTALA violation and the family sued the ED physician, the initial hospital, the primary physician, and his partner who had the last opportunity to prevent the transfer.

The initial hospital was in clear violation of EMTALA because both nursing and medical ED staff documented the patient's unstable condition and then did not protect him by refusing to transfer or by implementing full treatment for chest pain of possible cardiac origin. There was no documenta-

tion that the patient was not documented as having refused recommended treatment, nor was he advised of the risks of transfer. The ED physician may not be sued under EMTALA but will be for medical negligence by way of knowingly allowing a foreseeable event to occur. Allowing the primary care physician who had not examined the patient to convince him against his better judgment will not mitigate the outcome against the ED physician.[128]

From the nursing standpoint, ED nurses could be named in both EMTALA and tort actions against the employing hospital for failure to activate the chain of command on behalf of this patient. Nurses who participated in the transfer could be sued directly.

4. Failure to safeguard life at discharge: failure to notify patient of abnormal test results

A 26-year-old woman arrived at the ED after fainting and hitting her head. Paramedics who transported the patient reported that she was awake and alert when they arrived, and had experienced a sharp abdominal pain just before passing out. Her vital signs remained stable. Additional information gathered by the nurse included that the patient was sexually active and had two menstrual periods in the preceding week, the latest beginning one day before the syncopal episode. A small amount of blood was noted in her vagina on pelvic exam, but was otherwise unremarkable. Discharge instructions signed by the patient included a statement that she would be contacted if the pregnancy test obtained in the ED was positive. Before leaving the ED, the patient provided an address and phone number where she could be reached. Later that afternoon, the lab reported her pregnancy test as positive. Four weeks after this ED visit, the patient contacted hospital administration to demand a monetary settlement and threatened to sue: she had just spent three weeks in another hospital for hypovolemia and ectopic pregnancy. The hospital's risk manager, ED medical director, and nurse manager discovered no documentation of any attempts to contact this patient by phone or letter. The involved ED nurse recalled several attempts to reach the patient by phone without success, but there was no proof of her efforts. She admitted that she did not send a letter. The hospital's insurance company determined it had no way to defend a lawsuit, and the decision was made to negotiate a settlement of six figures.[129]

5. Failure of hospital personnel to obtain interpreters for family of infant

The plaintiffs' week-old infant daughter was taken to the emergency department pediatric facility via ambulance. This hospital serves an ethnically diverse population, many of whom speak limited or no English. The infant's mother and uncle were with the patient; the triage nurse took the history from the uncle, who conveyed information using "broken English" and hand signs or gestures. At some point the uncle demonstrated to the nurse that he had tapped on the infant's chest, but when asked if the child had stopped breathing he stated, "No, no, I don't know." A translator was never requested by the nurse, she believed that the EMT's and the uncle's information was sufficient. A pediatric resident later obtained a history and felt that the translator was not required, but documented that the history was "limited by language." The infant was discharged, but within hours stopped breathing and after four days on life support, she died.

Plaintiff Claims: The death was due to an apneic event triggered by acute tracheobronchitis and bronchiolitis consistent with RSV (respiratory syncytial virus infection) and that the infant suffered an initial apneic event at home. They claimed it was the duty of the hospital staff to determine when an interpreter is needed and that the translation service was required if there was any doubt. The staff failed to obtain a detailed and accurate history, which caused the failure to recognize that the baby had experienced a life-threatening event at home prior to arriving at the hospital. They also argued that admission to the hospital was warranted for observation of the infant, and the failure to hospitalize the infant lead to her death. There was a verdict for $400,000.[130]

17.11 Screening the Emergency Record for Nursing Negligence

In the ED setting, it is difficult for a physician to be liable without implicating ED nurses because of the latter's duty as patient advocates when the physician is not providing appropriate or timely care. As the legal community appreciates the legal ramifications of this, nurses will be included more

fully in claims. For present purposes, nursing negligence will be the primary focus.

A. General Comments

In evaluating the merits of a case, it is important that attorneys look past catastrophic outcomes for breaches in standards of care. The ED is a stage where inevitable human tragedies play out their final scenes, and every untimely or unexpected death does not implicate healthcare providers. Examples are dissecting aortic aneurysm, raging infection, and traumatic arrest, where rapid diagnosis and medical technology may be powerless to prevent death.

Therefore, though it may seem basic to some readers to review the basic elements of negligence theory, litigation experience has shown that millions of unproductive litigation hours and dollars have been spent on cases when the end result was truly determined before the patient arrived at the ED. Simplicity is elegance—and has more jury appeal.

B. Elements of Nursing Negligence Cases

1. Duty
Duty is implied for ED nurses at the moment the patient arrives.

2. Breach of duty/negligence
In order to learn whether negligence occurred, standards of care must be known well enough to apply them to a specific case. ED nurses can be held to the clinical specialty standards appropriate to a patient's diagnosis, the emergency care standards, nursing and state statutes, TJC standards, EMTALA regulations, as well as hospital standards defined by policy, procedure, protocol, and job description.

TIP: An expert, consulting or testifying, should be involved early in the evaluation for merit, as he is invaluable in finding red flags. The attorney should also expect all expert witnesses reviewing an emergency case to identify appropriate standards. Standards change over time, so those in force at the time of the alleged malpractice case must be used. This is one reason why it is strategically important for experts to have been clinically active at the time an alleged incident occurred.

---

3. Damages
Sadly, substandard treatment frequently occurs in the ED as a result of staff knowledge gaps, stress levels, patient acuity, and other factors discussed previously. For a patient or family members to prevail through the courts, however, there must be some measurable negative outcome. Common

types of damages resulting from negligent ED nursing care have been presented earlier in the chapter.

4. Causation

It is essential to determine the likelihood that negligence on the part of ED nursing actually caused or contributed to the catastrophic outcome. It is woefully easy to get caught up in the tragedy of the outcome or the emotional state of plaintiffs, and overlook this element of liability.

A 25-month-old girl developed such severe diarrhea that her mother began to notice dark stains with a red halo on her underpants. Concerned that it might be blood, she took her to their local ED, where the physician was unconcerned because the child was well-hydrated. He ordered a stool culture and discharged her with instructions for a clear liquid diet. For the remainder of the day, the child continued to have bloody diarrhea, so her mother took her to a different ED. There, her hemoglobin was noted to be 3.5 grams below acceptable limits, while her hematocrit was 17.4 points below lower normal, indicating bleeding. The pediatrician on call was not the child's regular doctor. Rather than admit her and notify her personal physician, he sent the child home with instructions to schedule an appointment the next morning (Monday). On Monday, the girl was sicker. The stool culture results that had been due Sunday were still not available, so the mother drove to the hospital herself to obtain them before calling the ED-referred pediatrician. Calling his office as instructed, she was informed that he was gone for the day and that no appointments were available until Tuesday morning. By mid-Monday, the child was listless and would not drink or eat. At 3:30 P.M. she lost consciousness, then required CPR. After eight long and gruesome hours, she died in a tertiary care center. The plaintiff position was that a series of atrocious ED nursing and medical breaches in the standard of care resulted in missed diagnosis, lack of proper treatment, and extreme suffering for this child and her single mother. With the defense claiming that a bacterial infection essentially doomed the child from the onset, causation was the linchpin of the case. The autopsy exposed the primary cause of death as hemorrhagic colitis caused by bacteria—but one that is rarely fatal in the United States because it is treated quickly and effectively, as opposed to other countries where it is fatal about 50 percent of the

time. The original stool culture performed 36 hours before the child lost consciousness revealed this too. The case settled through mediation and the issue of proximate cause was never resolved.[131]

TIP: Autopsy findings are very helpful in determining the severity of underlying disease that resulted in death. If results cannot definitively establish what caused an untimely death—the disease or the healthcare providers—they can dramatically influence settlement.

Determining the exact time a patient actually entered the system, became unresponsive, or received treatments is fundamental to case outcome. Hospital records will contain the time of the following events: the patient registered to be seen, the triage nurse evaluation was conducted, the clerk entered the patient into the system, any unresponsiveness of patient and staff actions, the doctor was informed of and subsequently examined the patient, the tests were ordered, and the tests were actually conducted.

TIP: The attorney should not be intimidated by forms. A properly prepared chronology will reconstruct events in a manageable format that will illuminate any inconsistencies in documentation as well as treatment times.

C. The Emergency Department Chart

The medical record generated in an ED can vary from a one-page document to several pages. EDs are moving to an electronic method of documenting to improve documentation legibility and revenue, and decrease errors in communication. Some facilities use pre-printed templates for each diagnosis to drive appropriate documentation. Typically the record contains the following information:

1. Basic information about the patient, such as name, address, insurance information, employer, age, presenting complaint (this information is usually entered by a clerk using a computer), and time of arrival. Collection of this demographic data should not delay the triage assessment. In fact many hospitals only allow a mini-registration to support EMTALA regulation.

2. Nursing triage documentation at a minimum includes: time seen, triage category, patient complaint and pertinent history, nursing assessment performed by the triage nurse including onset and character of symptoms, age-appropriate pain assessment on all patients, vital signs including pain assessment, patient's allergies and last known teta-

nus injection, medication history, weight and private physician's name.

3. The history and physical (H&P) completed by the physician with the time it was performed. (This may be dictated as a separate page.)

4. Standard tests which can be checked off or circled, such as x-rays and blood work. (Often the results are written next to the test, using symbols such as - for negative and + for positive.)

5. Medical diagnosis and disposition (admit, discharge, transfer) with times for each.

6. Nursing assessment and treatment records, which includes chronological information about treatments that were performed, medicines administered and additional assessments completed while the patient remained in the ED waiting for a bed on the inpatient floor or disposition.

7. Trauma flow sheets.

8. The results of diagnostic blood work, urine tests, x-rays, CT scans, and so on.

9. Consent for treatment.

10. A copy of the discharge instructions signed by the patient (which should be in the patient's primary language).

D. Documentation Red Flags for Nursing Liability

The medical record is the fundamental source of proof for claims of nursing negligence. Presence or absence of ED documentation reveals volumes about each patient's experience. Documentation must indicate to a qualified reviewer that nurses provided care appropriate to clinical symptoms and foreseeable complications, including adequate monitoring to prevent negative outcomes. ED nurses are required to document observations about population-specific (pediatric, elderly) and disease-appropriate (psychiatric, developmentally delayed, neurologically impaired) behavior as well as signs of distress.

E. What to Look for in the Medical Record

Look at the information recorded by the triage nurse and the triage category assigned to the patient when evaluating nursing documentation. There should be congruence between the severity of the patient's condition and the category. For example, a patient complaining of chest pain would receive the highest priority, whereas a patient who has had a cold for three days would be classified as least urgent. Look for evidence that the patient was periodically assessed while in the ED. A long gap between assessments is a red flag and may indicate that the patient was overlooked. If the patient

was restrained, evaluate the record for evidence that the circulation was periodically checked and the patient's elimination needs were attended to. Look for indications that the nurse informed the physician of significant changes in the patient's condition.

The following case portrays the failure to assess and triage properly:

A patient came to the emergency room with abdominal pain. He had been discharged from the same hospital a day earlier after a lengthy stay. A peritoneal catheter was removed just before his discharge from the hospital. A nurse assessed him in the ER. His vital signs were elevated. He was placed in an examining room to be evaluated by the physician. The physician had not arrived by 90 minutes by which time the patient had suffered cardiac arrest. He could not be resuscitated. The autopsy revealed the cause of death as a massive intraperitoneal hemorrhage.[132]

The following is the court ruling:
According to the Appellate Court of Connecticut, it was wrong not to have quickly and correctly assessed this patient so that he would be taken immediately to surgery. However, the family's negligence lawsuit against the hospital did not succeed. The family's expert medical witness was not a surgeon, and was not qualified to testify that a successful surgical outcome would have been more likely than not.

The following is another example of how the triage nurse failed the family:

The baby had been discharged the day before from the NICU when the parents brought him back to the ER. They told the nurse that the baby had turned blue at home, was limp, and had not had a bowel movement. His eyes had also rolled back into his head. The parents said they were following instructions to bring the baby back at once if there was a change. From the court records, it appeared that there was a struggle in the ER between the highly emotional and agitated parents and the ER triage nurse. The parents wanted the baby seen immediately by a physician and the triage nurse insisted that the parents fill out certain forms. After a cursory examination of the baby, the nurse informed the parents that the baby was fine. She then repeatedly reassured them their baby was fine, apparently in order to calm the parents and stop their demanding behavior. She classified the baby as semi-urgent under the hospital's classification scheme, which meant that the baby would require medical intervention within eight hours, but did not have an immediately life-threatening condition. The nurse told the parents to wait and the physician would be with them shortly. However, based on the nurse's reassurances concerning the baby's condition, the parents left after only a few minutes. They did not see the ER physician. The baby died several hours later.

The court ruling is as follows.
The court faulted the triage nurse in several respects. She did not take a complete history and did not correctly assess the gravity and immediacy of the baby's condition. The nurse did not bring the baby to the physician's immediate attention, as she should have.

Most importantly, the nurse falsely reassured the parents the baby was alright and was not in need of immediate medical attention. This was done primarily to control and defuse the parent's behavior. The court blamed the parents' leaving the hospital on the nurse's false reassurances and held the hospital liable for payment of substantial legal damages for the nurse's actions. The parents were not to blame for leaving against medical advice. The hospital was ordered to pay nearly $2 million for negligence.[133]

TIP: Review the nurses notes for information about the time other healthcare professionals performed care. This information, for example, could identify the time the anesthesiologist attempted to intubate the patient and record how many attempts were made before the tube was actually secured. In contrast, the anesthesiologist's entry may only record that the patient was intubated at a given time. If hypoxia was later determined to have occurred, the nurse's documentation could be invaluable in determining the possible sources of any negligence.

Accurate chronological documentation is essential for the treating team to evaluate the patient's response for continuing resuscitative efforts, for treatment, and for comparison of trends as the patient's condition worsens or improves. The nurse's notes should also contain entries concerning personnel who participated in the patient's care and the treatment provided, with the exact time.

- Absence of efforts to contact discharged patients with significant test results
- Absence of chain of command activation when appropriate
- Absence of circulation and perfusion monitoring in affected limbs before and after splinting, casting, suturing, medical or protective restraint
- Absence of sterile technique maintained during invasive procedures such as IV insertion, Foley catheter insertion, arterial blood gas collection, chest tube placement, central line insertion, diagnostic peritoneal lavage, suturing, and so on
- Absence of nursing entries that important information was communicated
- Absence of the patient's signature on AMA, transfer, treatment refusal forms and consents without corresponding explanation in nursing notes.
- Absence of reevaluation of abnormal assessment findings upon return to department from testing (x-ray, CT scan, angiography, ultrasound) or before discharge, transfer or admission
- Absence of vital sign and cardiac monitoring
- Brief entries that "do not say anything" about the patient's physical condition, only fill up space
- Cursory assessments
- Discrepancies between medical and nursing charges to the patient and charted interventions
- Discrepancies between recorded observations of nurses and physicians, or between nursing notes of nurses caring for the patient in question
- Discrepancies in times between nursing and other records, for example, times of arrival, triage, placement in the treatment area, MD evaluation, ordered tests, completed tests, leaving department for tests, returning to ED, consultant notification, of attempts to reach consulting physicians, arrival of consultant or admitting physicians, implementation of orders, MD notification of problems, of disposition, time the patient actually left ED (for OR, transfer, admission, discharge), discharge instructions being provided, duration of teaching, of family notifications and attempts to notify family, law enforcement, and so on
- Evidence of missing pages or altered records
- Failure to document safety measures including: requests for assistance with critical patients; assignment of staff to observe appropriate patients; requests that family remain with patient at all times; curtain or door to patient room open at all times; side rails, bed locks, call bells
- Long gaps between assessments
- Sloppy, illegible entries

Figure 17.36 *Red Flags in ED Nursing Documentation. From Kightlinger, R., "Sloppy records: the kiss of death for a malpractice defense," Medical Economics 76, no. 11 (June 1999): 166.*

Lack of documentation complicates litigation. Information and actions not charted can be established at the time of trial if nurses can identify standards of practice that allowed charting by exception or ED routine care that every patient with a given condition would have received.

Nurses are required to document comments from patients leaving against medical advice, refusing treatment, and verbalizing threats toward staff or others. If patients refuse to sign appropriate documents, nurses must describe such behavior and have their statements witnessed in the medical record. Figure 17.36 suggests red flag areas for nursing documentation.

The Ohio Court of Appeals ruled in 2004 that nurses have no legal duty to attempt to stop an individual who refuses treatment being offered and leaves. A nurse would commit a civil medical battery, opening the possibility of a civil lawsuit, by attempting to force an individual to remain and accept treatment.

The patient was admitted to the first hospital with complaints of inability to walk or stand, inability to talk and slurred speech, decreased mental state, chest heaviness, dizziness, aches in her joints, numbness and tingling in her hands, low grade fever, tachycardia, agitation, and irritability. After four days of observation and treatment, the physician decided to move her to the hospital's mental health unit for a psychiatric evaluation. The patient and her sister did not agree with the plan and left. Two hours later, they were at another hospital emergency room. The second hospital got the records from the first hospital and ran additional tests. The tests showed she had low lymphocyte, red blood cell, hemoglobin, and hematocrit levels along with elevated sedimentation rate, creatinine kinase, and alkaline phosphate. After almost a day in the second hospital's emergency room, the physician informed her of his intent to admit her to the hospital's mental health unit. The patient and her sister were upset with this decision and went home. Two days later the patient was dead. The medical examiner's autopsy established meningoencephalitis as the cause of death. The patient's family filed a complex medical malpractice lawsuit against both hospitals, six physicians, and one nurse.

The following is the court's ruling:
The second hospital was dismissed from the suit based on a finding of no legal liability. There was no legal liability by its ED nurses for failing to in-

tervene to stop this patient from leaving against medical advice. The nurses had no legal duty to stop the patient. The hospital could have faced civil liability for medical battery, that is, unauthorized treatment, if the nurses had forcibly intervened.[134]

F. Documents to Obtain in Evaluating Liability

A request for medical records requires the hospital to copy all sides of ED documents. The spaces for entries are often small and cramped, making these records very difficult to reproduce. ED nursing records requested should include the triage note, electronic patient tracking reports, ED registration logs, computerized physician order entry records, admission logs, consultations, and orientation and competency records for each role the staff has performed and policies and procedures related to the case. It may be necessary to obtain the original chart and make enlargements of the records in order to decipher them. Newer electronic recordkeeping will eliminate these problems.

TIP: EDs must maintain a log of all patients seen in the ED, including the time they entered and left and the diagnosis. The attorney who suspects that a patient did not receive appropriate care because the ED was very busy that day should ask for the ED log. The facility can redact the names of all patients except the one involved in the suit. The staffing sheet for the day in question can also be requested.

Figure 17.37 lists important documents to obtain in evaluating ED cases for nursing negligence.

17.12 Defenses

Figure 17.38 presents defense positions used by ED nurses who are sued for negligence.

A. Withholding Information

An alert, oriented, and coherent woman arrived by ambulance complaining of right foot pain for the previous three hours. She denied trauma but told the triage nurse she had fallen twice that morning because of weakness. She also complained of pain in her left lower abdomen. The nurse noted that the abdomen was soft. The patient was rated as non-emergent, appropriate for patients with suspected sprained ankle. The ED physician examined the patient less than 15 minutes after her arrival and noted she was in no apparent distress, although she

- AMA forms
- Autopsy reports
- Coroner reports
- Death certificates
- Discharge instructions
- EMS and flight ambulance records
- Final laboratory and toxicology reports
- Incident reports
- Operative and procedure consents
- Patient registration forms
- Performance reviews
- Police reports
- Refusal of treatment forms
- Staff credential, competency education, orientation and performance review records
- Staffing sheets
- Telephone triage records
- Transfer consents
- Triage patient log
- Policy on Fall Risk Assessment and actions to be taken
- Policy on preventing bed entrapment
- Suicide risk assessment and interventions

Figure 17.37 *Important Documents to Obtain in Evaluating ED Nursing Negligence*

1. "Captain of the ship" supervision by physicians
2. Nurses cannot be held to medical standard of care when it is beyond their scope of practice
3. Relied on expertise of attending, consulting, or ED physicians
4. Unforeseeable complication according to nursing expertise
5. Unforeseeable complication based on presenting symptoms and history
6. Outcome was a natural consequence of presenting condition
7. Living will preempted family demands
8. Contributory/comparative negligence

- Withheld information
- Left against medical advice (AMA) or absent without notification (AWON)
- Refused tests, treatment, admission or medications
- Patient competent to use reasonable care to avoid injury
- Noncompliance—incompetent, unimpaired patients only
  - In ED
    - Refusal to follow staff instructions after discharge
    - Failure to follow discharge instructions such as wound care
    - Failure to return for specific symptoms or follow up as instructed
    - Failure to contact referral or primary physician

Figure 17.38 *Defense Positions for ED Nurses*

now complained of pain in her shoulder as well as her right foot and left abdomen. He obtained a history that she was a brittle, insulin-dependent diabetic. It was decided to admit the patient for observation and, as she had no local physician, an on-call doctor evaluated her at 11:05. He obtained a family history of heart-related deaths. At 11:15, two and one-half hours after she arrived, a family member phoned to inform ED staff that the patient had a history of heart problems characterized by pain in her shoulder. She was confirmed as having a heart attack and treatment was initiated. She died hours later. The defense prevailed.[135]

B. Leaving Against Medical Advice

A woman arrived at the ED of DeKalb General Hospital at approximately 11:25 A.M. and was seen by the triage nurse, who took her history, made an assessment, and took her vital signs (blood pressure, temperature, pulse, respiration). Her vital signs were slightly elevated but within normal limits. She denied pain and gave a history that after eating the day before and the day of the ED visit, she experienced a burning pain in her chest radiating to her right side. She also reported that after the pain subsided, she needed to have a bowel movement. The triage nurse classified the woman as having a non-life-threatening illness, or a Category Two, and told her that it would be a long wait since the ED was very busy. After the patient waited four and one-half hours, a social services representative explained that the doctor would see her next. The patient, however, stated that she "had waited too long" and left, stating that she would see her own doctor in the morning. The next day she did not see her own physician and went to work instead. She died two days later. The patient's personal representative brought suit against the hospital, alleging that the ED nurse's act of classifying the patient as a Category Two resulted in the patient's death. The hospital responded by moving for summary judgment which was granted by the DeKalb Superior Court. The decision was appealed by the patient's representative. The Court of Appeals of Georgia affirmed the judgment of the lower court and held that the patient's voluntary termination of her relationship with the ED effectively severed any causal relationship between the triage nurse's decision and the patient's death. She left the hospital as the doctor was ready to see her, under her own power and in no apparent distress. She went to work under her own power and in no apparent distress.[136]

The triage nurse was deemed to have met the standard of care by obtaining a history, completing an assessment, and collecting and recording vital signs. Based on these findings, the nurse categorized the client and explained the long wait. Additional issues in evaluation of this case include documentation of continued assessments during the four-hour wait, of attempts by the triage nurse to persuade the patient to remain for evaluation, and of patient signature on an AMA (Against Medical Advice) form.

17.13 Summary

Complex factors discussed in detail in this chapter combine to make the ED setting a high-risk environment for both patients and the healthcare personnel from the standpoint of professional liability. Personal stress and physical danger increase the likelihood of distraction for nurses in this often overwhelming hard-to-manage care area. However, maintaining high performance standards, supervising greater numbers of unlicensed assistive personnel, and advocating the best care for patients, remain the minimum standard of care. Statutory requirements that nurses act as patient advocates will result in pressure on ED nurses to increase dramatically over the foreseeable future.

TIP: Common emergency room errors. The following represent over 50 percent of emergency-room-related malpractice suits:
- Failure to properly triage
- Failure to assess
- Failure to diagnose
- Delayed diagnosis
- Misdiagnosis

Other common mistakes:[137]
- Anesthesia malpractice (includes conscious sedation)
- Failure to adequately and thoroughly test
- Failure to administer the proper medication
- Surgical errors
- Failure to adequately supervise unlicensed assistive personnel
- Failure to obtain, communicate laboratory tests
- Failure to adequately handoff care
- Contaminated blood transfusions

Common conditions that are involved in mistakes:
- Heart attack (failure to follow established evidence-based guidelines and inadequate triage assessment)
- Brain aneurysm (failure to recognize symptoms and/or implement timely treatment with appropriate personnel)
- Stroke (failure to identify at triage and implement established guidelines and/or implement appropriate diagnostic testing and timely interventions)
- Appendicitis (failure to identify risk at triage and improper discharge without proper diagnostic testing)
- Pulmonary embolism (inadequate triage or failure to recognize symptoms and institute timely diagnostic testing and interventions)
- Failure to follow the chain of command
- Failure to recognize age-specific abnormal assessments

ED nursing practice includes higher levels of autonomy and advanced training which permits ED nurses to actually prevent damage arising through medical negligence. Missed opportunities by ED nurses to advocate appropriate patient care will be recognized as nursing negligence. Potential plaintiffs appealing to law firms for redress will find attorneys who, due to the extent of malpractice coverage carried by ED nurses, will direct more lawsuits at individual nurses as well as their employing facilities.

Successful attorneys handling ED malpractice claims against physicians and hospitals must be familiar with standards of ED nursing practice taught in nursing educational programs, hospital orientation, and policy manuals, and espoused by ED nursing leadership. They will systematically apply these standards to hold the healthcare system accountable through individual nurses. Discrepancies between standards of practice and reality will be balanced in court without regard to environmental factors that interfere with nursing performance such as administrative efforts to control healthcare costs or workplace stressors.

These standards will remain the yardstick by which ED nursing practice will be judged when things go wrong in the ED—legally, as well as professionally. It behooves the legal community to learn and to apply them as it requires the ED nurses to uphold them.

Endnotes

1. Institute of Medicine. Hospital-based emergency care: At the breaking point. 2006. http://books.nap.edu/openbook.php?record-id=ocr.pg 129,130,132. Accessed May 4, 2010.

2. Pines JM, Hollander JE, Emergency department crowding is associated with poor care for patients with severe pain . *Ann. Emerg Med.* 2008; 51(1):1-5.

3. Pines JM, Localio AR, Hollander JE, et al. The Impact of emergency department crowding measures on time to antibiotics for patients with community-acquired pneumonia. *Ann. Emerg Med.* 2007; 50(5):510-6.

4. United States Government Accountability Office(GAO) 2009 Report: Hospital emergency departments, Crowding continues to occur, and some patients wait longer than recommended time frames Retrieved July 14, 2010 from http://www.gao.gov/new.items/d09347.pdf.

5. American Academy of Pediatrics: *Overcrowding Crisis in our nation's emergency departments: is our safety net unraveling? Retrieved July 11, 2010 from http://pediatrics.aappublications.org/cgi/cotent/full/114/3/878.*

6. Derlet, R., and J. Richards, "Overcrowding in the nation's emergency departments: complex causes and disturbing effects," *Annals of Emergency Medicine* 5, no. 1 (January 2000): 63.

7. Twanmoh J.R.,:*When overcrowding paralyzes an emergency department.* Retrieved July 11, 2010,http://www.managedcaremag.com/archives/0606/0606.peer_ER.pdf.

8. AHRQ Patient Safety Initiative: *Chapter 2. Efforts to reduce medical errors:AHRQ's response to senate committee on appropriations questions.*Retrieved July 11, 2010, from http://www.ahrq.gov/pscongrpt/psini2.htm.

9. New Jersey Department of Health and Senior Services: *Patient Safety Reporting Initiative Updates – February 2006.* Retrieved July 11, 2010, from http://www.state.nj.us/health/ps/documents/feb2006_newsletter.pdf.

10. Alfred S, *Dangers of microwave heated compresses* Archives Internal Medicine *2004* Vol. 164,1242-1243.

11. Flynn, M., McKeown, M. *Nursing staffing levels revisited: a consideration of key issues in nurse staffing levels and skill mix research, Journal* of Nursing Management, (2009) 17 (6), 759-769.

12. Emergency Nurses Association, "Role of delegation by the emergency nurse in clinical practice settings," ENA Position Statement, 1998.

13. Trossman, S., "A state of emergency, nurses continue to contend with crowded EDs," *The American Nurse,* American Nurses Association, (January-February 2006).

14. *Id.*

15. Emergency Nurses Association, *Triage: Meeting the challenge.* Des Plaines, Illinois, 1997.

16. Emergency Nurses Association Nursing, *Core Curriculum* Fifth edition. Philadelphia: Saunders, 2007.

17. Nance J., *Why hospitals should fly the ultimate flight plan to patient safety and quality care,* Second River Healthcare Press, Bozeman ,Mt. 2008

18. *Institute of Medicine, Keeping patients safe, transforming the work environment of nurses, 2003.*

19. "Error reduction and performance improvement in emergency department through formal teamwork training: evaluation results from Med Teams Project." *Health Service Research* 37 (December 2002): 1553.

20. ANA, "Certified nurses report fewer adverse events: survey links certification with improved health care," *The American Nurse* (January-February 2000).

21. ECRI, *Healthcare Standards,* Plymouth Meeting, Pennsylvania, www.ecri.org 2006.

22. Emergency Nurses Association, *Standards of emergency nursing practice,* Sixth edition. Des Plaines, Illinois, 2007.

23. *Id.*

24. American Heart Association. Advanced Cardiovascular Life Support (ACLS) ,updated June 2010, Retrieved July 11, 2010. http://www.heart.org/HEARTORG/CPRandECC/HealtcareTraining/AdvancedcardiovascularlifesupportACLS.

25. *Id.*

26. George, J. and M. Quattrone, "Nurse-physician communication breakdown: is it a basis for nurse liability?" *Journal of Emergency Nursing* 22, no. 2 (April 1996): 144.

27. Champion, H., "Trauma care in the new millennium: emerging technology for vehicular safety and emergency response to roadway crashes," *Surgical Clinics of North America* 79, no. 6 (December 1999): 1229.

28. Emergency Nurses Association. *Trauma Nursing Core Course Provider Manual,* Fifth edition. Des Plaines, Illinois, 2000.

29. Pennsylvania Trauma Systems Foundation online *Trauma Hospitals,* http://www.ptsf.org/hospitals.htm.

30. Emergency Nurses Association, *Emergency Nurses Association Scope of Emergency Nursing Practice.* Retrieved on July 11, 2010. http://www.ena.org/IQSIP/NursingPractice/scopes/Documents.ScopeEmNP.

31. See note 16.

32. See note 22.

33. See note 16.

34. Emergency Nurse Association: *standards of emergency nursing practice,* Des Plaines, Ill, 1999, The Association

35. See note 22.

36. See note 31.

37. See note 14.

38. See note 16.

39. Mitchner, J. and C. Yeh, "The emergency medical treatment and active labor act: What nurses need to know," *Nursing Clinics of North America* 37, no. 1 (2002): 19–34.

40. CMS online, *EMTALA,* http://www.cms.hhs.gov/EMTALA.

41. See note 15.

42. Chick, S. et al., *Pairing Emergency severity Index 5-Level Triage Data With computer Aided System Design to Improve Emergency Department Access and Throughput.* Proceedings of the 2003 Winter Simulation conference, http://www.informs-cs.org/wsc03papers/249.pdf.

43. Gilboy, N., D. A. Travers, and R. C. Wuerz, "Reevaluating triage in the new millennium: A comprehensive look at the need for standardization and quality," *Journal of Emergency Nursing* 25, no. 6 (1999): 468–73.

44. See note 15, 16.

45. Emergency Nurses Association: *Emergency Nurses Association position statement: telephone advice.* Retrieved July11,2010,from http://www.ena.org/telephone_advice-ena_PS.pdf.

46. Smith, W., "EMTALA—What is an 'appropriate medical screening examination?'" ENA Government Services online, www.ena.org/services/govt/emtala/article2.htm, February 2000.

47. See note 16.

48. Emergency Nurses Association. "Telephone advice," *ENA Position Statement,* 2001.

49. See note 16.

50. McMichael, M., "Dialing for dollars? The risks of telephone triage nursing," *Journal of Legal Nurse Consulting* 9, no. 1 (January 1998): 16.

51. Laska, L., "Premature discharge from emergency room blamed for death of diabetic," *Medical Malpractice Verdicts, Settlements & Experts* (July 1998).

52. Laska, L., "Failure to properly triage child and timely begin antibiotics for meningitis death—$7 million verdict," *Malpractice Verdicts, Settlements & Experts* (Febuary 2009): 12.

53. Laska, L., Failure to timely assess a man with chest pains-man dies a hour after leaving the hospital-1,5 million gross verdict in Kentucky *Malpractice Verdicts, Settlements & Experts* (July 2008): 11.

54. Laska, L., Hospital makes woman in labor wait 30 minutes in the emergency department while clerk tries to find out who ordered a pizza—placental abruption results in death of an infant," *Malpractice Verdicts, Settlements & Experts* (October 2004).

55. Laska, L., Failure to perform immediate CT scan—woman with head injury from fall on stairs suffers partial paralysis due to uncal herniation to brain stem *Malpractice Verdicts, Settlements & Experts* (June 2009): 12.

56. The-Joint-Commission-National-Patient-Safety-Goals-2010.Retrieved-July-2010 http://www.jointcommission.org/General Public/NPSG/10 npsgs.htm.

57. Emergency Nurses Associations Position statement Medical Evaluation of Suspected Intoxicated and Psychiatric Patients. Retrieved July 12, 2010 from http://www.ena.org/sitecollectiondocuments.

58. *Emergency Nurses Association Core Curriculum for Pediatric Emergency Nursing*. Sudbury, Massachusetts: Jones and Bartlett Publishers, 2003.

59. Pennsylvania Trauma Systems Foundation accessed, http://www.ptsf.org/hospitals.htm, June 2006.

60. George, J. and M. Quattrone, "Persons brought to the ED by police: are they patients?" *Journal of Emergency Nursing* 23, no. 4 (August 1997): 354.

61. Laska, L., "Failure to diagnose subdural hematoma in teenager with clotting problems," *Medical Malpractice Verdicts, Settlements & Experts* (January 1999): 12.

62. Laska, L., "Failure to diagnose rib fractures," *Medical Malpractice Verdicts, Settlements & Experts* (August 1998): 23.

63. *Tovar v. Methodist Healthcare*.S.W. 3d, 2005 WL 3079074 (Tex. App., November 16, 2005), (As reported in *Legal Eagle Eye Newsletter* 13, no. 12.) December 2005.

64. NANDA Basics, www.nanda.org/html/plan04.html (accessed 2006).

65. See note 14.

66. *Id.*

67. *Id.*

68. American Nurses Association Nursing scope and standards, 2004.

69. See note 14.

70. Sedlak, S. K., "Hypothermia in trauma: the nurse's role in recognition, prevention and management," *International Journal of Trauma Nursing* 1, no. 1 (1995): 19–26.

71. Tammelleo, A. "'Duty to protect' is bar to contributory negligence defense," *Regan Report on Nursing Law* 35, no. 4 (September 1994): 4.

72. Laska. L., "Intoxicated man becomes unconscious in wreck," *Medical Malpractice Verdicts, Settlements and Experts* 19 (July 1995).

73. *Tobia v. Cooper Medical Center*, 643 A. 2d 1—NJ, 1994.

74. Legal questions, Nursing 1995, 25(2), 77, 1995.

75. *Rathey v. Priority EMS, Inc.* So.2d, 2005 WL 174566 (LA App., Jan 12, 2005). Also reported in *Legal Eagle Eye Newsletter* 13 (March 2005).

76. See note 54.

77. 677 So2d 568 (La. App. Ct., 1996).

78. Emergency Nurses Association (ENA), *Joint statement by ENA and the American College of Emergency Physicians (ACEP) on the delivery of agents for procedural sedation and analgesia by emergency nurses*, March 2005.

79. See note 53.

80. *Gordon v. Willis Knighton Medical Center*, 661 So. 2d 991, (La., App., 1995).

81. See note 19.

82. See note 28.

83. AHRQ Clinical Practice Guidelines online accessed, 2006. http://www.ahrq.gov/clinic/cpgonline.htm#Products.

84. See note 53.

85. Laska, L. "Missed diagnosis of C6-7 dislocation," *Medical Malpractice Verdicts, Settlements and Experts* (May 1999).

86. Laska, L. "Negligently performed spinal tap results in child's asphyxiation," *Medical Malpractice Verdicts, Settlements and Experts* (October 1997).

87. Stearns, D. "Emergency Department Records," In *Medical Legal Aspects of Medical Records*, eds. P. Iyer, B. Levin, and M. A. Shea, 446. Tucson, Arizona: Lawyers and Judges Publishing Co., 2006.

88. Laska, L., "Tetanus shot in hip blamed for injury to sciatic nerve with pain," Medical Malpractice Verdicts Settlements & Experts 14, no. 6 (June 1998): 15.

89. Laska, L., "Administration of insulin to non-diabetic blamed for death," *Medical Malpractice Verdicts, Settlements and Experts* (May 1999).

90. See note 14.

91. Laska, L., "1.25 million settlement in New Jersey," *Medical Malpractice Verdicts Settlements and Experts* (November 1994).

92. Laska, L., "Failure to admit man with chest pan and history of syncope," *Medical Malpractice Verdicts, Settlements and Experts* (March 1998).

93. Laska, L., "Failure to provide proper IV fluids to diabetic, leading to ketoacidodsis and death," *Medical Malpractice Verdicts, Settlements and Experts* (May 1998).

94. Laska, L., "Heart attack-plaintiff claims hospital treated chest pain with medication only," *Medical Malpractice Verdicts, Settlements and Experts* (July 1998).

95. Unknown North Carolina venue.

96. Laska, L., "Failure to Perform Adequate Testing for Illness in Asplenic Man—Death," *Medical Malpractice Verdicts, Settlements and Experts* (March 1998).

97. Confidential Florida Jury verdict.

98. Sheehy, S., "A duty to follow up on laboratory reports," *Journal of Emergency Nursing* 26, no. 1 (February 2000): 56.

99. Hayes, K., "Adding medications in the emergency department: effect on knowledge of medications on older adults," *Journal of Emergency Nursing* (June 1999).

100. Laska. L., "Man diagnosed with perforated appendix after discharge from ED," *Medical Malpractice Verdicts, Settlements & Experts* (January 1998).

101. Laska, L., "Man with injured finger not given proper discharge instructions," *Medical Malpractice Verdicts, Settlements & Experts* (June 1998).

102. *ANA Code of Ethics for Nurses with Interpretive Statements,* American Nurses Association, 2001.

103. See note 28.

104. Sheehy, S. and J. George, "Emergency consent: how would you act?" *Journal of Emergency Nursing* (October 1999).

105. See note 14.

106. See note 7.

107. *ENA Crowding in the emergency department.* ENA Position Statement, 2005.

108. Denny, C., "Practicing procedures on the recently dead," *Journal of Emergency Medicine* (November-December 1999).

109. Mantini, S., "What's EMTALA, and what are the implications," ENA Government Services online, www.ena.org/services/govt/emtala/article1htm. 2000.

110. *Id.*

111. *Id.*

112. *Johnson v. Health Central Hospital.*, 2006 WL 709320 (M.D) Fla., March 20, 2006. (Also reported in *Legal Eagle Eye Newsletter* 15, no. 5), May 2006.

113. United States District Court, New Jersey, June 29, 2005. Also reported in *Legal Eagle Eye Newsletter* 13, no. 8 (August 2005).

114. See note 109.

115. American College of Emergency Physicians' (ACEP) EMTALA, www.acep.org/webportal/PatientsConsumers/critissues/UninsuredUnderinsured/emtala.htm, 2006.

116. *Id.*

117. Wigder, H. and J. Moffatt, *Standards of Care in Emergency Medicine*, Gaithersburg, Maryland: Aspen Publishers, December 1999.

118. Sheehy, S., "A duty to follow up on laboratory reports," *Journal of Emergency Nursing* 26, no. 1 (February 2000): 56.

119. Laska, L., "Administration of insulin to non-diabetic blamed for death" *Medical Malpractice Verdicts, Settlements & Experts* 15, no. 5 (May 1999): 15.

120. Laska, L., "Failure to perform neurological exam," *Medical Malpractice Verdicts Settlements & Experts* 14, no. 7 (July 1998): 17.

121. Laska, L., "Man presents to ED with chest pains—physician's assistant diagnoses gastritis and discharges," *Medical Malpractice Verdicts, Settlements & Experts* 15, no. 10 (October 1998): 16.

122. As reported in *Legal Eagle Eye Newsletter* 13, no. 9, (September 2005).

123. Fiesta, J., "No dumping: ED transfer risk," *Nursing Management* 30, no. 1 (January 1999): 10.

124. *Id.*

125. Laska, L., "Woman having stroke claims hospital transferred her to other hospital because of inability to pay," *Medical Malpractice Verdicts, Settlements, and Experts* 28 (August 1994).

126. EMTALA.com, The 2003 Final regulations online www.emtala.com/2003regs.htm.

127. Tammelleo, J., "Nurse orders labor patient moved—death results," *Regan Report on Nursing Law* 34, no. 9 (February 1994): 1.

128. See note 117.

129. See note 119.

130. Laska, L., "Failure of Hospital Personnel to Obtain Interpreters for Family if Infant Brought to Emergency Room," Emergency Medicine, Medical Malpractice Verdicts, Settlements & Experts (July 2009).

131. Heydlauff, A., "A case study: the death of a 2-year-old and causation in medical malpractice," *Journal of Legal Nurse Consulting* 7, no. 2 (April 1996): 12.

132. *Wallace v. Saint Francis Hospital and Medical Center*, 688 A 2d 352 Conn. App., 1997.

133. *South Fulton Medical Center, Inc. v. Poe*, 480 S.E. 2d 40 Ga. App, 1996.

134. *Griffith v. University Hosp.*, 2004 WL 2847850 (Ohio App., December 9, 2004. Also reported in *Legal Eagle Eye Newsletter* 13, no. 2 (February 2005).

135. *Scott v. Hutchinson Hospital*, 959 F. Supp. 1351, 1997.

136. Tammelleo, A., "Duty to protect is bar to contributory negligence defense," *Regan Report on Nursing Law* 35, no. 4 (September 1994): 4.

137. http://atlanta10.cityspur.com.2009 (accessed 6-25-10).

Additional Reading

Emergency Nurses Association, *Holding patients in the emergency department.* ENA Position Statement, 2006.

Health Grades online posting April 20, 2009 "How safe is your hospital" http://www.healthgrades.com/cms/newsletters/hg-advisor/How-Safe-is-Your-Hospital.aspx?cid=44760

Iyer, P. and N. Camp, *Nursing Documentation: A Nursing Process Approach,* Fourth edition. Flemington, New Jersey: Med League Support Services, 2004.

Sadler, M. (1999). Emergency care documentation. In: Iyer, P. and Camp, N. (1999). *Nursing Documentation: A Nursing Process Approach, Third Edition.* St. Louis, MO: Mosby, 201.

Chapter 18

Telephone Triage:
A Primer for Lawyers and LNCs

Carol Rutenberg, RN-BC, C-TNP, MNSc, M. Elizabeth Greenberg, RN-BC, C-TNP, PhD, Trish Councell, BSN RN, and Austin A. Evans, Esq.

Synopsis
18.1 Introduction
18.2 Background
   A. Telephone Triage as a Sign of the Times
   B. The Origins of Telephone Triage
   C. Telephone Triage Defined
18.3 Telephone Triage Practice Settings
   A. Call Centers and Other Formal Telephone Triage Services
   B. Doctors Offices and Clinics
   C. Other Settings
18.4 Standards Directing the Practice of Telephone Triage
   A. Basic Standards of Nursing Practice
   B. Nursing Process
   C. Professional, Regulatory, and Accreditation Standards
      1. Staffing
      2. Multitasking/working with interruptions
      3. Access
      4. Call flow
      5. Recommendation of medications
      6. Decision support tools
      7. Documentation
      8. Initial call considerations
18.5 Areas of Concern/Controversy
   A. Telephone Triage as Professional Nursing Practice
   B. The Role of Decision Support Tools
   C. Interstate Practice
18.6 The Practice of Telephone Triage
   A. Elements of Negligence in the Context of Telephone Triage
      1. Duty
      2. Breach
      3. Causation
      4. Damages
18.7 Common Pitfalls in Telephone Triage Nursing Practice
   A. Failure to Adequately Assess
      1. Jumping to conclusion
      2. Stereotyping the patient
      3. Accepting the patient's self-diagnosis
      4. Failure to speak to the patient
      5. Fatigue and haste
      6. Knowledge deficit
   B. Practice Errors
      1. Failure to *listen* and *think*
      2. Failure to use critical thinking and exercise clinical judgment
      3. Failure to err on the side of caution
      4. Failure to anticipate worst possible
      5. Failure to use decision support tools
      6. Overreliance on decision support tools
      7. Failure to facilitate continuity of care
      8. Failure to advocate for the patient
      9. Fear of being "wrong"
      10. Failure to document pertinent negatives
      11. Functioning outside scope of practice
   C. Organizational System Failure
      1. Delay in care related to inadequate staffing or poor call flow design
      2. Initial triage by unqualified personnel
      3. Multitasked telephone triage nurses
      4. Failure to provide guidance documents
      5. Failure to collaborate with the provider
      6. Failure to provide specialized training to triage nurses
      7. Requiring RNs to practice outside their state(s) of licensure
18.8 Conclusion
Endnotes

18.1 Introduction

The growing presence and sophistication of telecommunications technology has set the stage for delivery of patient care over distance. Care delivered via telecommunications technology represents telehealth. The practice of telehealth is manifested in a multitude of forms, many using some type of telecommunications technology beyond the telephone. However, the most prevalent, and arguably the practice that carries the greatest potential for risk, is telephone triage. Telephone triage is the practice of nursing over the telephone. More specifically, telephone triage can be described as an encounter with a patient/caller in which a specially trained, experienced registered nurse, utilizing the nursing process and guided by medically approved decision support tools (protocols) and clinical judgment, determines the nature and urgency of the patient's problem and her associated needs.[1] The desired outcome of the call is patient support, collaborative planning, and referral to the appropriate level of care, within the context of the patient's needs and preferences.[2] The plan of care is individualized and includes advice, patient education, attention to continuity of care, and follow-up as necessary to assure a safe outcome. Additionally, well-documented organizational outcomes of telephone triage include patient satisfaction, improved quality of life, and cost-effectiveness.

TIP: The most common settings in which telephone triage is practiced are formal call centers and doctors' offices or clinics. However, telephone triage is practiced in virtually any setting in which a patient can access a nurse by telephone. The key to success in telephone triage is having nurses with an understanding of the practice who are adequately trained and functioning within an organization that recognizes and facilitates the practice of effective telephone triage.

This chapter describes telephone triage and outlines the prevailing standards and organizational elements necessary to support the delivery of safe, effective care over the telephone. Nursing skills integral to the practice of telephone triage will be discussed in general terms. Telephone triage and the associated legal and risk management principles is the focus of this chapter.

18.2 Background
A. Telephone Triage as a Sign of the Times
As the provision of health care has transitioned from inpatient to outpatient settings, technology and methods of delivery have evolved as well. Due to various societal and economic forces, the delivery of care via telecommunications technology is ubiquitous in the American healthcare arena. Telehealth technology (including telephones, Internet, and a wide variety of remote monitoring devices) is being utilized in patient management with ever-increasing frequency.

Telehealth services are offered by a variety of healthcare professions including medicine, nursing, pharmacy, dentistry, mental health, emergency services and others. Telehealth is "the delivery, management, and coordination of health services that integrate electronic information and telecommunications technologies to increase access, improve outcomes, and contain or reduce costs of health care."[3] Various types of telecommunications technology are utilized to provide remote monitoring, evaluation, consultation, and treatment of patients in rural areas, correctional facilities, rehabilitation centers, and other non-traditional settings as well as at home. Programs for the elderly and disabled utilize telecommunications technology to provide routine monitoring services, and the telephone provides a primary means of

two-way communication between healthcare professionals and their patients.

B. The Origins of Telephone Triage
In the mid 1980s, telephone triage was identified as an effective demand management strategy, utilized by health maintenance organizations (HMOs) and other healthcare organizations in an effort to hold down costs. It was believed that if registered nurses (RNs) were employed to assess patients over the telephone, they would be able to determine which patients could be managed safely at home and which patients required a higher level of care. The goal was to eliminate unnecessary emergency department visits, anticipating that cost savings would result. Unfortunately, this approach potentially delayed care, increasing the likelihood of unfavorable outcomes, and telephone triage initially came to be perceived as a barrier to care.

Over time, societal and economic forces fueled by the growing presence of and reliance on telecommunications technology, led to the acknowledgment of telephone triage as a legitimate type of nurse/patient interaction with its goal being safe, effective, and efficient care. Telephone triage provided a means for nurses to assist patients in identifying the nature and urgency of their healthcare needs and to develop an appropriate plan of care. Health education, including home care advice or referral to the appropriate level of care, is often regarded as a desirable endpoint of telephone triage. In order to accomplish this goal, the nurse must identify the patient's needs preferences, and barriers to care, providing support and collaboration in development of a plan of care that is acceptable to and in the best interest of the patient.

C. Telephone Triage Defined
The National Council of State Boards of Nursing (NCSBN) has defined telenursing as the practice of nursing over distance using telecommunications technology.[4]

The American Academy of Ambulatory Care Nursing (AAACN) has provided the primary guidance for this practice, having defined telehealth nursing, telephone nursing, and telephone triage.[5]

Telehealth Nursing
"The delivery, management, and coordination of care and services provided via telecommunications technology within the domain of nursing."

Telephone Nursing
"All care and services within the scope of nursing practice that are delivered over the telephone. Tele-

phone nursing is a component of telehealth nursing practice restricted to the telephone."

Telephone Triage
"An interactive process between nurse and client that occurs over the telephone and involves identifying the nature and urgency of client health care needs and determining the appropriate disposition. Telephone triage is a component of telephone nursing practice that focuses on assessment, prioritization, and referral to the appropriate level of care."

Telehealth nursing is an umbrella under which many types of nursing reside. Care provided using remote monitoring devices, care provided via the Internet, and utilization of other forms of telecommunications technology in the provision of nursing care is telehealth nursing. Telephone nursing, a component of telehealth nursing includes disease management (such as congestive heart failure monitoring), behavioral modification (such as smoking cessation), and basic communication with the patient including such functions as reporting test results.

This chapter specifically addresses telephone triage instead of the larger practice areas of telehealth nursing or telephone nursing. The reason for this focus is twofold. First, regardless of the purpose of the telephone encounter, once the patient presents a symptom for consideration, the nurse must determine the nature and urgency of the patient's problem; the encounter then meets the definition of telephone triage. Second, due to the extremely complex nature of telephone triage, it is the arguably the most sophisticated and high-risk form of nursing care provided in the ambulatory care setting today.

TIP: Although telephone triage is an integral part of nursing in the 21st century, it is largely misunderstood as a practice and unrecognized as a significant form of patient care delivery.

18.3 Telephone Triage Practice Settings

Telephone triage is growing in both prevalence and importance in our society. In its most visible form, telephone triage services are provided in call centers which might be owned and operated by hospitals or healthcare systems, third-party payers, or businesses as proprietary ventures. Call centers may be large or small, formal or relatively informal, and automated to a greater or lesser extent. Many telephone triage services are gradually moving toward a virtual call center model, with nurses taking calls remotely from home.

A. Call Centers and Other Formal Telephone Triage Services

Hospital-based call centers, initially conceived in many cases as marketing tools, offer a valuable service to the communities they serve. Patients, who lack a relationship with a primary care provider and thus rely on the emergency department (ED) for primary care, may access a nurse and receive healthcare advice over the phone. Unfortunately, as the healthcare economy has dictated the need to decrease organizational costs, many of these programs have been phased out. Where they have survived, they often offer myriad services to the hospital and its patient base, including the provision of triage services to the community and after-hours services to patients of physicians or clinics affiliated with the hospital or healthcare system.

Third-party payers such as insurance companies or HMOs also continue to staff call centers in order to control cost and improve the health of their members. Government agencies such as those associated with the Department of Defense (Army, Navy, Air Force) or the Veterans Administration provide telephone triage call centers for their beneficiaries.

Finally, telephone triage services are provided by a wide variety of independent proprietary ventures that contract with physicians, physician groups, employers, and other organizations. These telephone triage services are provided in order to reduce the after-hours burden on practicing physicians and to provide nursing support to patients in need of health care or advice.

B. Doctors Offices and Clinics

In many doctors' offices and clinics, patients are screened by receptionists, medical assistants, or other unlicensed personnel who take messages and convey them to the physician. These personnel are often utilized to provide telephone advice or to make appointments when they are deemed necessary. In addition to unlicensed personnel, LPNs or LVNs are often utilized in the management of patients over the telephone. However, due to the assessment skills and independent clinical judgment necessary to perform this function, telephone triage is generally considered to be outside the scope of practice of anyone other than a registered nurse. Telephone triage has been recognized as professional nursing practice, and with increasing frequency, registered nurses are being employed in the role of telephone triage nurse.

C. Other Settings

In addition to call centers and doctors' offices, telephone triage services are provided in a full range of other healthcare settings, each with their own unique objectives. Home health programs employ telephone triage nurses to assess patients and determine the need for a home visit or other intervention in an effort to satisfy their imperative to reduce acute care rehospitalization. Student health centers provide telephone triage services to students, their mission being to reduce the impact of acute illness on their student population, helping them stay fit to attend class and reducing the potential for the spread of disease in their relatively close community. Correctional facilities utilize telephone triage nurses to assess the acute healthcare needs of inmates and sometimes to provide remote care to those who are incarcerated.

Mental health professionals assess established patients who are in crisis or screen new patients for organic disease prior to admitting them to a mental health service. Nurses responsible for the care of the mentally and developmentally disabled population who reside at home or in group homes provide direction and assistance over the telephone to families, caregivers, and the patients themselves when circumstances warrant. Some urgent care centers (UCC) and emergency departments (ED) provide telephone triage services to patients who are unsure whether to seek care at their facility. Even inpatient nurses often find themselves receiving calls from patients who have recently been discharged from the hospital and have questions regarding their care at home.

18.4 Standards Directing the Practice of Telephone Triage

Over time, standards have been developed to direct the practice of telehealth nursing. These include basic standards of nursing practice as well as those promulgated by professional organizations such as the AAACN. Various federal and state regulatory standards exist to protect the patient and several accrediting bodies have standards that directly or indirectly impact care delivered over the telephone. Finally, organizational standards or policies exist to standardize and direct practice within a specific setting.

A. Basic Standards of Nursing Practice

Although utilization of various technologies has become an integral element of nursing practice, controversy has existed regarding whether nurse-patient interactions utilizing telecommunications technology indeed constitute the practice of nursing. In answer to this question, the American Nurses Association (ANA) identifies nursing issues related to the practice of telephone triage.[6] This issue was addressed definitively by the NCSBN in their position paper, *Telenursing: A Challenge to Regulation*. This document states, "The NCSBN recognizes nursing practice provided by electronic means as the practice of nursing" and asserts that "it is regu-

lated by the boards of nursing."[7] This landmark document established telehealth nursing as professional nursing, aligning it from a regulatory perspective with other types of nursing practice.

B. Nursing Process

The nursing process provides the basis and structure for the practice of nursing, even over the telephone.[8] Although decision support tools and the use of telecommunications technology have become central elements in the practice of telephone triage, the five steps of the nursing process should be utilized and documented in each patient encounter and are described below.

1. *Assessment:* The telephone triage nurse must be able to assess the patient without seeing them or touching them. Due to the challenging nature of patient assessment over the phone, and the fact that nurses must make sophisticated decisions with limited sensory input, special skills must be employed to assure an appropriate assessment and delivery of safe, effective care. For example, rather than listening to a patient's lungs with a stethoscope or evaluating a patient's color, the nurse must listen to the patient's breathing and assess for cyanosis and retractions via expert interviewing techniques in order to assess their respiratory status.

2. *Diagnosis:* Although telephone triage nurses do not make medical diagnoses, they think diagnostically, considering a wide range of possible causes of the patient's symptoms. Telephone triage nurses must think "outside the box," avoiding accepting patient self-diagnosis, stereotyping the patient, or assuming the most common cause of the complaint in order to decrease the likelihood that a high risk, but unexpected problem might be missed. In addition to determination of the patient's physical problem, the nurse must identify knowledge deficits and other patient needs that must be addressed in order for the patient to experience a desirable outcome.

3. *Planning:* In developing a plan of care, the nurse must collaborate with the patient and their family in order to identify the most appropriate approach and to increase the likelihood of compliance. Collaboration with other members of the healthcare team, including but not limited to the physician, is often necessary as well. The telephone triage nurse must consider multiple factors including a number of patient variables such as motivation, age, baseline health, and other factors that might influence the

patient disposition. Other variables such as time of day and distance from care may influence decision making as well as the availability of transportation and other resources impacting their ability to carry out the plan of care.

4. *Intervention:* Due to the remote nature of the practice, telephone triage nurses cannot provide care directly to the patient and therefore must depend on others to provide the necessary care. Attention should be given to continuity of care and communication of appropriate information to those who will be caring for the patient, be it the emergency department staff, the patient's physician, or the patient or their family.

5. *Evaluation:* The last step in the nursing process requires the professional nurse to evaluate the outcome of the previous steps, assuring development of a plan that will alert the nurse if the patient is unable to carry out the plan of care or if the patient's condition does not improve. Often it is sufficient to instruct the patient to call back if they do not get better, but at times, the responsibility for follow-up must rest with the nurse or other members of the healthcare team.

C. Professional, Regulatory, and Accreditation Standards

1. *Professional Standards:* The AAACN has developed Telehealth Nursing Practice Administration and Practice Standards which were initially published in 1999. These standards provide general guidance and are universally applicable in ambulatory care settings. The Emergency Nurses Association (ENA) has also developed a Position Statement regarding telephone advice.[9] Standards addressing ambulatory care nursing and other publications of the AAACN also provide professional guidance to the telephone triage nurse, as do various American Nurses Association (ANA) publications. Although guidance documents specific to telephone triage are not plentiful, nursing standards and other publications are applicable to telephone triage as with other forms of nursing.

2. *Certification:* National certification, validating skills and knowledge in a specialty practice area, was available in telephone nursing practice from 2001-2007 and is now only available for renewal via maintenance activities based on continuing education. Telephone triage nurses may seek board certification as an Ambulatory Care Nurse, sponsored by the American Nurses Credentialing Center (ANCC). This certification represents expert knowledge regarding telephone triage and other areas of ambulatory care nursing.

3. *Regulatory Standards:* Primary regulation is provided by the State Boards of Nursing, but states such as California have also passed legislation addressing the delivery of telehealth services. It is likely that other states will follow suit in the coming years. At present, approximately one-third of the Boards of Nursing have developed written policies in the form of Position Statements, Declaratory Rulings, FAQs, and other documents which address various facets of the practice of telephone triage. Specific elements of telephone triage and scope of practice are discussed later in this chapter (See Section 18.5.C, *Interstate Practice*).

   Also of regulatory concern is the Health Insurance Portability and Accountability Act (HIPAA) which provides protection for patient healthcare information. While the nature of telephone communication poses potential challenges in assuring the identity of the person to whom the nurse is speaking, reasonable judgment should be exercised and efforts to comply with HIPAA should not impede care. Coordination of services often involves contact with a variety of resources including the patient's family, day care centers, school nurses, emergency departments, pharmacies, and other healthcare providers or organizations. While safeguarding protected healthcare information should be a priority, it should not interfere with the delivery of safe and effective care to the patient.

4. *Accreditation:* Multiple forms of accreditation are available to healthcare organizations. Some of the most common accrediting bodies include The Joint Commission (TJC), the National Committee for Quality Assurance (NCQA), and the Accreditation Association for Ambulatory Health Care (AAAHC). The American Accreditation Healthcare Commission, formally known as the Utilization Review Accreditation Commission (URAC), accredits call centers on a voluntary basis and includes criteria which address staffing, use of decision support tools, documentation, quality management, call metrics such as average speed of answer, and other program elements

5. *Organizational Standards and Program Development*

Although the theoretical basis for telephone triage nursing provides a consistent structure for practice,[10] wide variability exists among organizational approaches to telephone triage. In spite of the ubiquitous nature of telephone triage, it is frequently misunderstood or underestimated in its ability to impact care. Although telephone triage has been shown to be an effective means of quality care,[11,12] if done improperly, it can have devastating effects. Several "rules" of practice ("standards" deliberately not used here) have evolved, many of which are based on conventional wisdom that is not supported in fact. Unfortunately, care delivered on this basis may fall short of the standard of care.

Call centers, in their efforts to standardize practice, have often inadvertently prescribed practices, such as strict adherence to decision support tools, which minimize the role of nursing judgment. Conversely, less formal settings such as doctors' offices and clinics often underestimate the potential significance of this practice, and offer little guidance to nurses who are responsible for the provision of telephone triage services.

The reality of safe and effective nursing care delivery over the telephone lies somewhere in the often yet uncharted area between extreme formalization and an almost complete lack of structure and direction. Program elements that represent best practices provide support to avoid either of the previously described extremes and improve the overall quality of care delivered over the telephone. Policies that address program design issues such as staffing, access, call flow, appropriate use of decision support tools, collaborative practice, and documentation help assure the delivery of safe and effective care. Extensive experience with telephone triage nurses and organizations providing these services has led to the following principles of practice.

1. Staffing

RNs have the minimum education, knowledge and skills necessary to perform telephone triage, due to the complex nature of patient management over the telephone. This position is supported by both professional and regulatory standards. Nurses providing telephone triage services must possess a specialized skill set and demonstrated competency in critical thinking and the assessment of patients over the telephone. In addition, as prescribed by the AAACN Standards, adequate staffing, which considers the complexity and needs of the caller, must be available.[13]

2. Multitasking/working with interruptions

There is a growing body of evidence that shows that interruptions during the performance of complex cognitive functions decreases effectiveness and can lead to mistakes.[14,15] It is therefore highly desirable for telephone triage nurses to be dedicated to the telephone rather than being multitasked.

3. Access

Nurses consider the availability of resources and access to care in formulating triage recommendations.[16,17] When nurses lack appointments or are discouraged from utilizing the emergency department in the interest of cost containment, poor outcomes may result. Nurses must be permitted and empowered to facilitate appropriate care for the patient in order to assure quality care.

4. Call flow

How the calls are answered and routed and by whom can have a significant impact on the quality of the overall encounter. Generally speaking, when nurses are able to take calls live, or to handle the patient's concerns with one call management, the patient's needs are best served. However, in many settings, due to fiscal constraints and real or perceived customer preferences, calls are "front-ended" by clerical personnel and routed to nurses in accordance with written guidelines or operator judgment. In these cases, it is critical that the organization recognize that this initial screening by unlicensed personnel represents first level triage which is best performed by the telephone triage nurse.

5. Recommendation of medications

Policies regarding recommendation of medications over the telephone by RNs must be explicit, usually guided by medically approved decision support tools, and consistent with the scope of practice in the relevant jurisdiction. See Section 18.5.C for further discussion.

6. Decision support tools

Use of decision support tools, also called protocols, guidelines, and sometimes standing orders, represent the standard of care. Nurses who are functioning in organizations that have not selected, approved, and made these tools available are at increased risk of overlooking a significant finding. Conversely, forced compliance resulting in misuse of decision support tools can interfere with critical thinking and potentially result in less optimal outcomes.[18,19]

7. Documentation

Development of a documentation template is advisable because it provides guidance and structure to nurses who are assessing patients over the telephone. A well-designed documentation tool provides the nurse with a blueprint for patient assessment but should ideally not be overly prescriptive, thereby potentially limiting nursing judgment. Charting by exception, or failure to document the pertinent negatives, poses a problem. In order to enhance communication among members of the healthcare team, documentation should be complete, descriptive of the conversation, and reflective of critical thinking. And in the event of a lawsuit, if it is not written, it is difficult (if not impossible) to prove that it was discussed. Similarly, there exists a perception that recording calls affords extra protection in the event of litigation. In fact, it is not unusual for the recording and the written record to have significant differences for reasons that are not well understood. Recorded calls are excellent for coaching and quality assurance activities. Quality assurance efforts should not only reflect compliance with policy but they should also measure evidence of use of the nursing process, which "provides the basis and structure for the practice of professional nursing and is used consistently with all telehealth nursing encounters."[20]

8. Initial call considerations

At the onset of a phone call a callback telephone number should be obtained in case the call is disconnected. Should the call be disconnected the nurse should make a reasonable effort to call the patient back. It is also important to know where the patient is physically located, not just a home address.

The necessity for informed consent is as important in telephone triage as it is in face-to-face care. If the patient initiated the call, consent to participate in the call can be implied.

With the exception of an emergency situation, the nurse should speak directly with the patient or obtain consent from the patient to speak to somebody else.

The patient's expectation of privacy should also be no different than any other type of healthcare encounter. When calls are monitored or recorded the patient should be made aware of this before the interview begins. The patient can make an informed decision to proceed with the call.

18.5 Areas of Concern/Controversy

As telephone triage has evolved, areas of controversy have emerged. Key among these areas of concern are questions such as who is qualified to perform telephone triage and what is the appropriate use of decision support tools. Interstate practice poses additional challenges and will be discussed more fully in Section 18.5.C.

A. Telephone Triage as Professional Nursing Practice

Due to lack of understanding of the practice of telephone triage and various organizational constraints, it has not been unusual in the past for organizations to opt to assign telephone responsibilities to unlicensed personnel, reserving their licensed staff for the provision of "direct patient care." This approach reflects the belief that personnel such as appointment clerks, receptionists and medical assistants or other unlicensed assistive personnel (UAP) are capable of appropriately managing telephone encounters based on common sense, experience, or written or unwritten guidelines.

This notion dismisses the reality that telephone triage and other types of telephone encounters require careful patient assessment in order to accurately determine the exact nature of the call. Frequently these unlicensed personnel are placed in the role of "message taker," serving as the conduit for information sharing between the patient and the provider. Often these unlicensed personnel are provided with "protocols" or "red flag lists" intended to guide them in the collection of patient information or identification of life-threatening emergencies.

TIP: The argument proffered in support of data collection by unlicensed personnel is that the provider, not the clerk or medical assistant, is making the ultimate decision. The fallacy in this thinking is belief that identification of patient complaints is straightforward and can be reduced to a series of prescribed questions and answers. The process used in telephone nursing practice, regardless of the setting, follows a predictable course with consistent cognitive tasks being performed sequentially and/or simultaneously.[21]

Telephone triage requires interpretation from the moment the phone is answered until the call is disconnected and beyond. Because of this, telephone triage in practice is ideally restricted to RNs with experience and specialized training.

Medical assistants and other UAP who provide telephone triage services are doing so under the supervision of the physician as "captain of the ship." In these cases, it is critical that they limit their functions to collection of data. Furthermore, the physician assumes responsibility for making decisions based on data collected by others who might not have the knowledge or clinical judgment to collect complete and accurate data. It is important to recognize that patients are not always willing or able to articulate the exact nature of their problem. Because the practice of telephone triage demands interpretation based on critical thinking and clinical judgment it should not be expected of clerical and unlicensed personnel. For example, a patient who is having a myocardial infarction might complain of "indigestion," "bursitis," or a "toothache."

Critical thinking is necessary to enable the nurse to look beyond the spoken word to listen for factors of clinical significance such as breathlessness and level of concern or distress reflected in the patient's voice. Additionally, when RNs interact with a patient they must do more than "take a message," looking beyond the spoken complaint to consider other, more life-threatening possibilities. Often nurses must analyze or synthesize raw data provided by the patient and consider that information in the context of the whole. For example, even for a patient with a previous history of gastroesophageal reflux disease, indigestion must be carefully evaluated to rule out a possible cardiac event.

While LPNs or LVNs might seem like a lower cost alternative to RNs, their scope of practice generally precludes them from being able to perform telephone triage. The definition of licensed practical or vocational nursing varies slightly from state to state and the wording of their scope of practice varies as well. However the scope of practice of LPNs and LVNs does not generally include independent assessment of complex or unpredictable problems. As with medical assistants, it is not uncommon for organizations to utilize LPNs and LVNs as message takers or to permit them to manage patients "per written protocols." However due to the interpretive nature of telephone triage, it is outside the scope of practice of LPNs and LVNs. Therefore performance of telephone triage by under qualified personnel carries a risk of significant legal exposure.

RNs are licensed to function autonomously and are ideally suited for the role of telephone triage. RNs are skilled in complex cognitive functions including critical thinking and clinical judgment, which are essential to the provision of safe and effective care. The RN's scope of practice permits (requires) independent assessment, diagnosis of urgency and patient needs, development of a plan of care, and evaluation of all nurse-patient encounters. The involvement of RNs in the ambulatory care setting has been shown to improve the quality of care and cost effectiveness of care rendered.[22] Due to their professional expertise, RNs are able to address multiple areas of concern for the patient, collaborating with other disciplines and involving the physician as appropriate and necessary. RNs possess the education and level of licensure needed to provide safe and effective telephone triage services.

B. The Role of Decision Support Tools

Traditionally, decision support tools have been used in formalized telephone triage settings. In the past, attempts have been made to distinguish among protocols, guidelines, algorithms, and in some cases, standing orders. However, semantic differences aside, they are all tools designed to support the nurse's decision making.

Decision support tools provide guidance to the nurse in assessing the patient, diagnosing urgency, and developing a disposition. Some decision support tools also include additional information which helps standardize practice within an organization such as recommendation of over-the-counter medications and other interventions.

One area of concern is the extent to which it is appropriate and necessary for RNs to rely on decision support tools in their delivery of care over the telephone. One school of thought asserts that use of medically approved decision support tools will improve quality and limit the nurse's potential liability in decision making. In conjunction with this belief, many telephone triage nurses and administrators believe that if a nurse deviates from a decision support tool and has a bad outcome, they "won't have a leg to stand on in court." However, this notion belies the fact that registered nurses are licensed to utilize independent nursing judgment in application of the nursing process (assessment, diagnosis, plan, intervention and evaluation). It has been shown that nurses who have access to decision support tools are less likely to use the nursing process than nurses who do not.[23] Either way, RNs are accountable for their actions regardless of the information contained in the decision support tool. In fact, whether the nurse strictly adheres to the decision support tool or not, in the event of a bad outcome, if there is inadequate evidence of critical thinking or sound clinical judgment, the nurse will be in a position that is difficult to defend.

TIP: The nurse must consider the context such as time of day, distance from care, and available resources as well as specific patient characteristics such as age, recent illness, and comorbidities, factors that might not be addressed in the decision support tool. Thus, after considering all available information, the nurse's judgment might suggest an action that is different than the one recommended in the protocol or guideline. For this reason, nurses should be allowed to deviate from decision support tools if there is a compelling reason to do so.

However, while most organizations will allow nurses to upgrade the disposition, or recommend a higher level of care, many prohibit downgrading, or sending patients to a lower level of care. Organizations that have policies which allow nurses to downgrade dispositions vary on whether they require nurses to collaborate with a provider prior to deviation or if they are allowed to act independently. However, the ultimate responsibility for decision making rests with the nurse regardless of organizational policy or the content of the decision support tools. If nurses are not allowed to deviate from the decision support tool when necessary to support the best care for their patients, the knowledge, experience and judgment of the nurse are underutilized and the organization, the nurse and ultimately the patient may pay the price. While decision support tools are important adjuncts to the practice of telephone triage, they are not decision *making* tools and should never supersede the clinical judgment of the RN.[24–26]

C. Interstate Practice

The use of telecommunications technology has removed or made invisible the geographical barriers that previously identified the particular jurisdiction in which care was being delivered. This has posed challenges to the State Boards of Nursing which exist to regulate nursing and define scope of nursing practice. One of the primary challenges associated with telephone triage is the question of where nursing is taking place when nurses and patients communicate over the telephone. The majority of the State Boards of Nursing believe that the locus of responsibility rests with the state in which the patient is located, but this is not universally true as a handful of states feel that the opposite is true. This area of controversy is addressed further in Section 18.4, *Standard Directing the Practice of Telephone Triage.*

In 1997 the NCSBN unanimously approved an interstate compact which supported mutual recognition of nurse licensure.[27] This bill, now referred to as the Nurse Licensure Compact (NLC), was first signed into law in Utah in 1998, and within the next 12 years, almost one-half of the states followed suit. States that have adopted the NLC have agreed to recognize the licenses of nurses who reside in other Compact states, but no provision has been made for nurses in non-Compact states. Given the current situation, no nurse can be assured that the patient is calling from a state which licenses or recognizes the license of the nurse.

Licensure is not the only area of concern related to interstate practice. Because there are 50 states, there are 50 Nurse Practice Acts and thus 50 different sets of rules. Each state has its own definition of registered nursing as well as different rules and regulations governing the practice of nursing in their state. Some states have declaratory rulings, position statements, frequently asked questions (FAQs) or other guidance documents providing various forms of direction. Nurses who provide care to patients in multiple jurisdictions need to be aware of differences in policies or interpretations among the involved states.

Another area of concern relates to differing guidance regarding recommendation of medications by telephone triage nurses. Some states consider the recommendation of over-the-counter (OTC) medications as being within the scope of practice of the registered nurse. Other states say that nurses may recommend OTC medications only as directed by medically approved decision support tools, while still other states regard this practice as being outside the scope of practice of RNs under any circumstances. Similar controversy exists relative to renewal of existing prescriptions or recommendation of new legend (prescription) drugs based on a signed, medically approved decision support tool. While some states have provided written guidance regarding these issues, others have not.

Likewise, variation exists in the definitions of registered nursing and licensed practical or vocational nursing of each state. While all states clearly regard telephone triage as being within the scope of practice of the registered nurse, the majority of the Boards of Nursing regard telephone triage as being outside the scope of practice of LPNs or LVNs. In some cases, LPNs and LVNs are permitted to collect information from the patient under the supervision of a nurse or a physician. However, because of the unpredictable nature of telephone triage, even under supervision, LPNs and LVNs may not perform telephone triage because it requires independent assessment, diagnosis of urgency, formulation of a plan of care and evaluation of the interaction, which is not within the scope of practice of LPNs or LVNs.

The role and importance of decision support tools also varies from state to state. Some states specify that use of decision support tools is an essential element of care while other states are not prescriptive with standards that specifically speak to the provision of care over the telephone.

18.6 The Practice of Telephone Triage

Although telephone triage has been regarded by many as a specialty for several years, it is becoming increasingly apparent that having the ability to provide safe, effective, professional care to patients and their families is a skill that all nurses must have, especially those who work in ambulatory care. Just as other forms of technology have shaped the way we deliver care to our patients (consider the impact of the cardiac monitor), the basic principles of nursing have remained unchanged. In many cases, telephone triage has morphed into a practice that is centered around use of decision support software and "appropriate" utilization of healthcare resources rather than focused on the patient. In some cases employers may impose time limits on how much time a nurse may spend on a phone call, potentially resulting in haste that leads to less optimal outcomes.

Quality assurance activities frequently measure productivity rather than the quality of nursing practice. Value is often placed on efficiency and compliance with the "rules" established by the organization to dictate the nature of the nurse's actions. And unfortunately, in some cases, the patient has been lost in the process.

Largely because of the growing complexity of care being delivered in ambulatory care settings, patients and their families often find themselves in a quandary about what care to seek and from whom.

TIP: American healthcare consumers are in need of an advocate to help them navigate this complicated environment and to coordinate the resources involved in their care. Registered nurses, by virtue of their education, licensure, and professional scope or code, are ideally suited to meet this need.

In conjunction with other responsibilities of the ambulatory care nurse, the role of telephone triage is rapidly evolving and assuming greater significance in the healthcare landscape, especially as our population is living longer and with more chronic illnesses that require care outside the hospital.

Ostensibly, the purpose of telephone triage is to determine the nature and urgency of the patient's problem and to make an appropriate disposition. However, in order to provide individualized care that meets the needs of the patient and their family, telephone triage nurses must develop a plan of care within the context of the patient's life situation and with regard for her preferences and available resources.

The telephone triage call first requires a "gathering information" phase in which data is gathered and context is established. A variety of factors may impact decision making. For example, factors such as the patient's baseline health status including preexisting conditions, extremes of age, distance from care, and the ability to understand and follow directions given may impact the nature of the call. Next, and actually often simultaneously, "processing" occurs during which the nurse verifies the reason for the call, determines the nature of the patient's problem, and makes decisions about what needs to be done. The "output" of the call may be a recommended disposition, or the nurse may provide patients with collaboration and support in their own decision making. Often, especially when the patient is very sick, the caller already knows the desired disposition but is calling the nurse for collaboration or support in carrying out the indicated disposition, such as returning to the office or emergency department for evaluation. A key element of this process is the fact that interpretation must occur *every step*

of the way, making it clear that this process falls within the domain of the registered nurse who is trained and licensed to perform critical thinking and exercise clinical judgment during all phases of the process.[28,29]

Patients rely on the nurse to give them sound advice and will generally follow instructions explicitly as they understand them. For this reason, telephone triage nurses must be extremely cautious in assessing their patients, diagnosing urgency and identifying patient needs, developing a plan of care that assures continuity and evaluating the effectiveness of their actions. Failure to do so can have devastating effects.

TIP: Although sound application of clinical judgment and basic nursing principles are essential, it has been observed that when bad outcomes occur, it is often related to flaws in program design rather than lack of knowledge or skill on the part of the nurse.

Organizations that have not adequately addressed program design elements that create an environment that supports success are more likely to have unfavorable outcomes. Specifically, in situations in which nurses must perform telephone triage with multiple interruptions, lack of decision support tools (or policies discouraging their appropriate use), inadequate access to appointments and other resources, or an organizational culture that fails to recognize and reward the use of clinical judgment create an environment in which the nurse must be hypervigilant in order to avoid mistakes. In these situations, critiquing a nurse's performance is almost like "armchair quarterbacking" within a system that is destined to fail. While nurses are always accountable for their actions, the ability of the nurse to provide safe and effective care can be significantly confounded if the system is broken.

A. Elements of Negligence in the Context of Telephone Triage

Although litigation related to telephone triage is becoming more and more common, few cases will be found in the law literature. This is most likely because cases involving telephone triage misadventures are attributed to other problems such as delay in care or failure to diagnose. Telephone triage cases are also frequently settled out of court. Often the care delivered in these cases has fallen short of the standard of care or the documentation has been insufficient to support a successful defense.

1. Duty

When the nurse picks up the phone, a relationship is established with the patient by virtue of the fact that the nurse made himself available to provide care to the patient. The nurse then has a duty to provide care that is consistent with the standard of care, regardless of whether the patient is actually enrolled in or eligible for those services.

Patients, especially the very sick ones, often know the appropriate or desired disposition before they contact the nurse. While recommendation of a disposition might appear to be the desired output of a telephone triage encounter, it is likely that support, collaboration and other activities directed at facilitation of that disposition are more meaningful outputs. In other words, a primary role of the nurse is often to validate the patient's concern and essentially give the patient "permission" to do what they feel is appropriate.

2. Breach

Occasionally, patients are unable to adequately articulate their concerns, and negative outcomes are the result of nurses discouraging patients from following their own instincts. A good rule of thumb would be that patients who are concerned and wish to be seen should be seen. Due to potential risk associated with inadequate communication, the ultimate decision regarding disposition should be in the hands of the patient. A caveat to this statement would be the patient who chooses not to follow the recommendations of the nurse in a life-threatening situation. In these cases, it might be appropriate for the nurse to take actions to force a disposition such as calling 911 for a patient over that patient's protest.

TIP: Before acquiescing to the wishes of a patient who is refusing care, the nurse must (to the best of her ability) feel confident that the patient is competent to refuse care and fully understands the anticipated consequences of his actions. The nurse has the responsibility to be certain that she has taken all reasonable actions of a prudent nurse in the same or similar situation, and documentation of what the nurse told the patient and the patient's response should be extensive.

---

3. Causation

While it is not the job of the telephone triage nurse to formulate a medical diagnosis or to prescribe a medical plan of care, causation, if proven, will often be related to delay in care caused by the nurse's failure to accurately and promptly recognize potentially life, limb or vision threatening conditions. This is often related to failure to perform an adequate assessment or failure to use critical thinking and to exercise sound clinical judgment. Knowledge deficit could also be a source of error, but appropriate use of decision support tools should minimize this potential. Failure to provide complete and ac-

curate instructions to the patient and take steps to assure continuity of care can also be a source of bad outcomes. Finally, organizational design elements related to call flow can be a significant cause of delay in care. Although it is "only a phone call," the improper actions of the telephone triage nurse can result in bad outcomes up to and including death.

4. Damages

Damages are assessed on a case-by-case basis and awarded on the specifics and merit of each case. The damages sustained by the patient and his family often occur due to delay in care or failure to diagnose related to improper actions on the part of the nurse.

18.7 Common Pitfalls in Telephone Triage Nursing Practice

There are a number of common pitfalls which might contribute to bad outcomes, and knowledge of these practice errors should be in the minimum skill set of a nurse performing telephone triage. These pitfalls can generally be divided into failure to adequately assess, telephone triage practice errors and organizational system problems.

A. Failure to Adequately Assess

A complete and accurate patient assessment is fundamental to any effective telephone triage encounter. A number of practice errors are products of incomplete assessment and should be avoided.

1. Jumping to conclusion

Jumping to a conclusion about the cause or nature of the patient's problem can lead to disaster. For example, just because a patient has been diagnosed with chronic sinusitis in the past does not guarantee that her headache today is a product of her chronic sinusitis.

2. Stereotyping the patient

Stereotyping patients can cause nurses to limit their thinking and short-circuit an adequate assessment. For example, generalizations, such as the notion that a patient is too young (or too old) to be pregnant, or that young women do not have heart attacks or strokes are a common cause of oversights in patient assessment. Additionally, failure to adequately assess frequent or repeat callers can lead to missed cues. These patients are often well-known to the staff and thus their assessment might be curtailed by assumptions regarding the nature of their problem. All patients should be thoroughly assessed each time they call in order to identify unexpected problems. Failure to look beyond the obvious can be deadly.

3. Accepting the patient's self-diagnosis

Although patients are frequently correct in their assumptions about the cause of their symptoms, they have a limited knowledge of the possibilities and thus might attribute their symptoms to a condition with which they are familiar, throwing the nurse off course. Patients are often adept at describing symptoms consistent with their presumed diagnosis and inadvertently failing to report others that they believe to be of little significance. This may be one of the most dangerous pitfalls because unless the nurse is on guard, it is easy to overlook an inaccurate patient self-diagnosis. The ready access to sophisticated medical information over the Internet has increased the possibility of a seemingly well-informed patient to miss the mark. Regardless of the patient's explanation of the problem, it is the responsibility of the nurse, not the patient, to know what information the nurse reasonably needs to make an informed professional assessment leading to an accurate conclusion.

4. Failure to speak to the patient

Nurses should make it a point to speak to the patient, even if it is only to assess the patient's respiratory status as in the case of a non-verbal patient such as an infant, a patient who is mentally disabled, one suffering from dementia, or even a patient who is comatose. This contact provides the nurse with important information such as the patient's respiratory status, their level of consciousness and their apparent degree of distress. There is also information that only the patient knows and thus an assessment through a third party can be misleading. While the family member can often provide valuable information, failure to speak directly to the patient can result in the nurse making decisions on incomplete or inaccurate information. For example, comments such as "wife states patient doesn't have any suicidal ideation" must be verified with the patient.

5. Fatigue and haste

Fatigue and haste can lead to errors in nursing judgment and errors of omission, and must be avoided with telephone triage. While it is common for the nurse to have several calls waiting, the nurse must spend enough time on each call to perform a thorough assessment and develop a plan of care appropriate for each patient. Rushing through a call or fatigue caused by failure to take breaks can significantly impact the quality of the call. The nurse whose judgment is impaired due to fatigue or who is rushing to get to the next caller is more likely to overlook something of significance. Conversely, the nurse who does not feel time pressure or is not overcome by fatigue is better able to recognize implicit or subtle cues and avoid errors in nursing judgment.

6. Knowledge deficit

Regardless of their knowledge, experience or expertise, knowledge deficits can lead to incomplete assessment or cause the nurse to draw the wrong conclusion. Decision support tools are important adjuncts to the telephone triage process and can significantly enhance the quality of the information gathering. Decision support tools, used as checklists, will decrease the likelihood of something important being overlooked. The prudent nurse will also utilize decision support tools as study guides to aid in increasing his knowledge base.

B. Practice Errors

Success in telephone triage requires application of general principles of nursing over the telephone. However, there are a number of rules of thumb that decrease the likelihood of bad outcomes.

1. Failure to *listen* and *think*

Nurses who are rushed, distracted, or otherwise unable to focus clearly on the call can overlook critical pieces of information that would lead to the correct disposition. Preoccupation with the computer can in and of itself provide enough distraction to cause a nurse who is not listening carefully to miss a critical comment by the patient. Stereotyping the patient, jumping to conclusions or otherwise failing to focus on what the caller has to say can lead to negative outcomes. Likewise, failing to recognize the potential for a serious problem to be understated by the patient can lead to missed cues. Admittedly, the quality of the telephone triage encounter is partially dependent on the quality and veracity of advice provided by the caller. However, the nurse must listen *actively,* assuring the accuracy of her assessment. It is the responsibility of the nurse, not the patient, to know what elements must be assessed in order for the nurse to accurately identify the nature and urgency of the problem and develop an appropriate plan of care.

2. Failure to use critical thinking and exercise clinical judgment

Telephone triage nurses must do more than *listen*; they must *hear*. Nurses are knowledge workers and telephone triage is a cognitive process. Failure to exercise clinical judgment can cause nurses to overlook the true nature of the patient's problem. Because of the potential complexity of telephone triage encounters, even calls which appear to be routine may result in bad outcomes if the nurse fails to apply critical thinking to look beyond the obvious.

3. Failure to err on the side of caution

Due to the potential ambiguity of the telephone triage encounter and because the nurse is basing decisions on information that has not been confirmed by inspection or other objective information, it is necessary for the nurse to err on the side of caution. A rule of thumb is if the nurse (or the patient) is concerned, or if there is any question about disposition, the patient should probably be seen promptly. The adage is, "if in doubt, send them out."

4. Failure to anticipate worst possible

In the face to face setting, nurses and physicians are taught to rule out the most common problems before looking for the worst possible. Likewise, over the telephone, patients' symptoms are more likely to represent common problems than unusual, unexpected, or potentially life-threatening problems. However, although many nurses are "most common thinkers" (due to education and experience), it is not good practice to immediately assume the most common cause of the symptoms. It has been said that "if you don't find it often, you often don't find it." Telephone triage nurses must discipline themselves to look for the worst case scenarios first, and after ruling them out, proceed to the less life-threatening causes of the problem.

5. Failure to use decision support tools

Decision support tools supplement knowledge deficits, serve as reminders, and provide the nurse with a checklist of questions to consider, given the patient's presenting problem. Consistent use of decision support tools during a telephone encounter decreases the likelihood that the nurse will overlook important information during the patient assessment. When decision support tools are available, it is not uncommon for nurses to refer to them only when they are uncertain about the nature of the problem or the desired course of action. Unfortunately, as with any checklist, the tools are only effective if they are actually used.

6. Overreliance on decision support tools

As discussed previously, overreliance on decision support tools can be just as problematic as failure to refer to them. Policies that prohibit the nurse from deviating from the decision support tool limit the role of nursing judgment and may lead to less favorable outcomes. In order to appropriately individualize the care for each patient, the nurse must consider patient preference as well as contextual factors like time of day, distance from care, and specific patient characteristics. Individualizing care to meet the patient's needs requires critical thinking, clinical judgment, and col-laboration with the patient. Thus these tools should be used for decision *support,* not decision *making.*

7. Failure to facilitate continuity of care

In reality, given the physical distance between the nurse and the patient, telephone triage nurses are unable to do anything *to* or *for* the patient. Instead, the role of the nurse is to share information and coordinate services so that someone else can take the appropriate action *to* or *for* the patient. The role of the telephone triage nurse might be patient education so the patient and her family can provide the care. Or the nurse might refer the patient to the appropriate level of care so that another healthcare professional is able to provide the necessary care. If the nurse makes the referral without sharing the relevant information with the individuals who will actually provide the care, it is roughly equivalent to a quarterback throwing a pass without advising the receiver that he would be doing so. While telephone triage is episodic, continuity of care is critical to safe and effective healthcare management. It is desirable for the nurse to follow up if it is foreseeable that the patient will not be willing or able to carry out the plan of care and if the risk to the patient is significant.

8. Failure to advocate for the patient

Often, patients who seek advice over the phone are unable to advocate for themselves or navigate the complex healthcare milieu in which they must access care. Nurses are patient advocates and there is probably no other setting in which patient advocacy takes on greater significance than in the telephone triage setting. Telephone triage nurses must be prepared to work within a challenging healthcare system to assist the patient in acquiring necessary care. This requires knowledge of available services and how to access them. In some cases, nurses must be prepared to act on the patient's behalf. Patients who are incompetent or otherwise unable to act in their own best interest or patients who do not understand the consequences of their actions should not be allowed to refuse care if by so doing they are putting the life, limb or vision of themselves or another at risk.

9. Fear of being wrong

Closely tied to but often in direct conflict with the responsibility for patient advocacy is the nurse's reluctance to overreact and to recommend care that is beyond what is actually necessary. In other words, the nurse is afraid of being wrong. In making telephone triage dispositions, there are generally two ways that the nurse can be wrong. First, the nurse can err by failing to refer patients to their provider or emergency department when they are indeed sick enough for the referral. Obviously, no nurse wants to be wrong under those circumstances. However, it is also possible for the nurse's actions to *appear* to be wrong if he sends a patient to the doctor's office or emergency department when, in retrospect, the patient did not need that level of care. Nurses' concerns about being criticized or second guessed for erring on the side of caution (a key element of safe telephone triage) can dissuade them from taking more aggressive action which might be in the best interest of the patient. This is particularly the case when the appropriate disposition would be to send the patient to the emergency department (ED) when he has already been evaluated in the ED earlier that day. Often, especially with patients who are experiencing a significant problem, the patient knows the appropriate disposition before he calls the nurse, and the most meaningful actions of the nurse will be the provision of support or collaborative decision making.[30] In order to provide safe care, the effective telephone triage nurse understands that she can never be wrong if she refers the patient for evaluation. She can only be wrong if she does not.

10. Failure to document pertinent negatives

A disturbing trend, precipitated in large part by the design of decision support software, has been for telephone triage nurses to document only the positive findings, implying or leaving it to the reader to assume that other pertinent findings were negative. Because it is not always appropriate to ask every question listed in a decision support tool, assumption that the nurse asked every question is not always reasonable. Additionally, while it is indisputable that the medical record is a legal document, it is more importantly a communication tool. Through the medical record, the telephone triage nurse relates patient findings, the nurse's thought process, and the nature of the telephone triage encounter to other members of the healthcare team. Therefore, it is particularly important that the nurse's documentation be detailed, accurate, and reflective of critical thinking.

11. Functioning outside scope of practice

Telephone triage requires a significant amount of independent clinical judgment and therefore, nurses must take care to not overstep their own scope of practice. While rules vary from state to state regarding what is within the scope of practice for RNs and LPNs or LVNs, the basic definitions of registered nursing and licensed practical or vocational nursing provide insight into what is appropriately within the role of each level of licensure. Registered nurses performing telephone triage must be certain that they are not making medical diagnoses, nor prescribing or recommending medications unless they are competent to do so; the action is consistent with organizational policy, and the function is permitted (or not prohibited) by the rules and regulations promulgated by the State Board(s) of Nursing.

C. Organizational System Failure

In many cases, poor patient outcomes may be the result of inadequate program design or lack of clear supportive direction from the organization. Even the best nurse can be "set up to fail" in the context of a poorly designed system. In fact, many of the previously described practice errors may be caused or exacerbated by organizational issues.

1. Delay in care related to inadequate staffing or poor call flow design

Inadequate staff or inappropriate staff utilization can be a contributing factor in delayed call return. In addition to providing adequate staff, organizations should develop policies regarding how various types of calls are routed and how quickly calls will be returned. For example, failure to return calls regarding acute symptoms in a timely fashion may result in a significant delay in care. Likewise, use of voicemail that is not checked routinely may also result in delayed call return. Additionally, allowing calls regarding acute symptoms to wait until the next day (or later) to be returned is taking an unnecessary risk. Policies should exist regarding call return which detail time frames that are both safe and achievable, and ideally those expectations should be communicated to the caller.

2. Initial triage by unqualified personnel

In many organizations, clerical personnel are utilized to answer the call, collect the initial information from the caller including the nature of the call, and then route the caller to the appropriate person or department. While this *seems* to make sense, in fact, systems such as these place an unlicensed person in a position to identify high-risk callers. Although this is most often accomplished through use of a list of high risk complaints, or a "red flag" list, use of these lists requires some degree of interpretation, placing the intake personnel in a position to determine urgency. In other words, they are doing first level triage. Organizations that use this approach often argue that the clerk is only taking a message to be managed later by the nurse. However, due to the patient's potential inability or unwillingness to disclose the nature and urgency of their problem, or the clerical personnel's inability to recognize key findings, the nature and urgency of the call can be underestimated, resulting in a delay in care.[31]

3. Multitasked telephone triage nurses

Performing telephone triage or other nursing functions when multitasked can lead to loss of concentration and increased errors.[32,33] The ideal telephone triage situation is one in which a nurse is dedicated to the telephone and thus not interrupted or distracted by other responsibilities. A multitasked nurse is a prime candidate to overlook a subtle cue mentioned in passing or to fail to recognize the significance of an unusual finding. While the organization has a responsibility to avoid asking nurses to perform multiple tasks at the same time, the professional nurse has the responsibility to assure that each patient is getting the nurse's undivided attention.

4. Failure to provide guidance documents

Organizational direction is necessary to ensure quality care. Written policies should exist to standardize practice and facilitate intra-organizational communication. Decision support tools should also be provided under the auspices of the organization. These tools must be reviewed by nurses and physicians and approved by the medical, administrative, and nursing directors. These tools provide guidance to telephone triage nurses, decrease ambiguity in decision making, standardize practice, and supplement knowledge deficits, further decreasing the likelihood of variability in the quality of call management. However, as previously noted, while they should be available and their use mandatory, nurses should be allowed to exercise clinical judgment in application of these tools, resulting in plans that are appropriately individualized for each patient. Documentation templates also improve consistency and completeness in documentation, helping the nurse organize the information for more effective communication with other members of the healthcare team.

5. Failure to collaborate with the provider

The triage nurse should communicate relevant caller information to the patient's provider. Communication facilitates continuity of care and supports follow up as appropriate and necessary. Although telephone triage is within the independent scope of practice of registered nurses, provider involvement can enhance the quality of advice given to the patient in circumstances in which medical care is part of the plan. Additionally, physicians have a right and a responsibility to know what is going on with their patients. While telephone triage is nursing practice, patient management is a team effort.

6. Failure to provide specialized training to triage nurses

Although telephone triage is not a specialty per se, it does require a specialized skill set as described in general terms above. Nurses who provide telephone triage services should have the training and experience necessary to appropriately recognize the potential significance of each patient encounter and to provide the care as needed. While not every RN is necessarily qualified to practice telephone triage, those who undertake to do so must have the requisite knowledge, experience and specialized training to assure that the care they deliver is safe, effective, and consistent with organizational policy and meets the standard of care.

7. Requiring RNs to practice outside their state(s) of licensure

Due to consistent adoption of the Nurse Licensure Compact, discussed previously in this chapter, nurses often inadvertently take calls from patients located outside of their jurisdiction. While this is unavoidable in many circumstances, such as patients on vacation who are calling on their local cell phone, organizations who have formal relationships with patients or healthcare providers in other states should assure that they are not asking their nurses to knowingly and deliberately disregard the requirements for interstate practice. While this is a complex issue which will probably not be resolved in the near future, efforts to ignore this problem, hoping it will go away, serve to put the organization, the telephone triage nurses and the patients they serve at risk.

Case Example:
Persistent atypical headache (formal call center with decision support tools)

One case involved a middle-aged female patient who called her telephone triage nurse complaining of a headache accompanied by unusual neurological symptoms. The patient had already been evaluated in the emergency department earlier that day, but the patient continued to be extremely concerned and called the telephone triage nurse for advice. It was apparent from the patient's comments that she was seeking "permission" to return to the emergency department or otherwise to obtain a same day evaluation by a neurologist. The telephone triage nurse methodically reviewed multiple decision support tools including headache, sinus symptoms and even urinary symptoms but was unable to find a clear-cut recommendation to refer the patient for prompt evaluation. The nurse advised the patient to be seen again the next day if her symptoms did not resolve, but unfortunately the patient died the next morning while dressing to return to the emergency department.

This case is an example of overreliance on decision support tools and failure to err on the side of caution in a situation that defied common logic. Although the nurse consulted multiple decision support tools, none of which clearly indicated need for an immediate evaluation, the nature of the patient's complaints was unusual and failed to fit any predictable pattern. In order to increase patient safety, when patients are extremely concerned, the nurse should be concerned. Even obscure or unexpected symptoms should be taken seriously and carefully evaluated.

Case Example:
Pediatric patient with "funny" breathing (doctor's office with no formal program)
A two-year-old was seen by his pediatrician and diagnosed with tonsillitis. The mother called later that day complaining that she was "concerned about his breathing." A multitasking office nurse returned the call an hour later advising the mother that the office was closing and that she could take her son to the urgent care center or emergency department if he got worse. The initial documentation was scant and even the full page late entry failed to reflect an adequate assessment or any evidence of critical thinking. The child died later that night related to respiratory difficulties.

Multiple clinical errors were made in this situation including failure to perform an adequate assessment, failure to utilize critical thinking, failure to err on the side of caution and failure to create adequate documentation of the call. Additionally, the situation was further complicated by the organizational failure to develop and implement policies regarding the practice of telephone triage, including failure to provide decision support tools and failure to provide specially trained staff to provide this service. It is also likely that the fact that the nurse was multitasked contributed significantly to the nurse's poor performance.

Case Example:
Same-day surgery post-op complication
A patient who had an appendectomy in outpatient surgery called later in the day complaining of increasing pain and vomiting. Although the patient also complained of weakness and significant fatigue, the nurse apparently made the assumption

that these symptoms were related to her surgery earlier that day and discounted the significance of the complaints. The patient had, in fact, ruptured her appendiceal stump and was leaking fecal material into her peritoneum. The patient later died of peritonitis and other complications related to her surgery.

The nurse had a decision support tool that included the words "weakness" and "fatigue" as red flags, but she failed to utilize it appropriately. This case is an example of the nurse jumping to a conclusion about the cause of the patient's complaints and, once again, failing to err on the side of caution. Although pain and vomiting are frequent complaints following abdominal surgery, the telephone triage nurse must "look outside the box" in order to identify unanticipated complications.

18.8 Conclusion

Telephone triage is professional nursing practice. Done right it can make a tremendous difference in the quality of the patient's healthcare experience and can literally save lives; but done wrong it can have devastating effects. The nurse who undertakes to provide care to patients over the telephone must practice in a manner that assures patient safety and facilitates desirable outcomes. Focus on process (rather than outcomes) is likely to assure care that minimizes the potential for harm. Experienced nurses with specialized training, practicing in the context of a well-designed program, increases the potential for favorable outcomes and decreases the likelihood of liability related to the practice of nursing over the phone.

Endnotes

1. Rutenberg, C. (2009). *Telephone Triage Policy Manual.* Telephone Triage Consulting, Inc. Hot Springs, AR.

2. Greenberg, M.E. (2009). A comprehensive model of the process of telephone nursing. *Journal of Advanced Nursing, 65*(12), 2621-2629.

3. American Academy of Ambulatory Care Nursing (2007). *Telehealth Nursing Practice Administration and Practice Standards.*(4th ed.). Pitman, NJ: Anthony J. Jannetti. p. 22.

4. National Council of State Boards of Nursing, (1997). Telenursing: A challenge to regulation. *National Council, Position Paper.*

5. See note 3.

6. American Nurses Association (1996). *Telehealth: Issues for nursing*. Author: American Nurses Association, Inc. www.nursingworld.org retrieved 5/6/10.

7. See note 4.

8. See note 3.

9. Emergency Nurses Association (2001). Emergency nurses association position statement: Telephone advice. Chicago: Emergency Nurses Association. www.ena.org/about/position.

10. See note 2.

11. Lattimer V., George S., Thompson F., Thomas E., Mullee M., Turnbull J., Smith H., Moore M., Bond H. and Glasper A. (1998). Safety and effectiveness of nurse telephone consultation in out of hours primary care: randomised controlled trial. *British Medical Journal 317*(7165), 1054–1059.

12. International Council of Nurses (2008). International Nurses Day Kit. Delivering quality, serving communities: nurses leading primary health care. Retrieved from http://www.icn.ch/indkit2008.pdf on 14 October 2008.

13. See note 3.

14. Kalisch, B.J. (2010). Interruptions and multitasking in nursing care. *Joint Commission Journal on Quality and Patient Safety 36*(3), 126-132.

15. D'Ausilio, R. (2009). The pitfalls of call center multitasking. *Medical Call Center News, AnswerStat* magazine, September 2009, Issue 3, 1-2. http://www.medicalcallcenternews.com/issue/09/09.pdf retrieved 4/15/10.

16. Edwards, B. (1994). Telephone triage: How experienced nurses reach decisions. *Journal of Advanced Nursing, 19*, 717-724.

17. Wahlberg A.C., Cedersund E. and Wredling R. (2003) Telephone nurses' experience of problems with telephone advice in Sweden. *Journal of Clinical Nursing 12*(1), 37–45.

18. Greatbatch, D., Hanlon, G., Goode, J., O'Caithain, A., Strangleman, T., Luff, D. (2005). Telephone triage, expert systems and clinical expertise. *Sociology of Health & Illness, 27*(6), 802-30.

19. Valanis, B., Moscato, S., Tanner, C., Shapiro, S., Izumi, S., David, M., Mayo, A. (2003). Making it work: organization and processes of telephone nursing advice services. *Journal of Nursing Administration, 33*(4), 216-23.

20. See note 3.

21. See note 2.

22. Swan, B. A., Conway-Phillips, R., and Griffin, K. F. (2006). Demonstrating the value of the RN in ambulatory care. *Nursing Economic$, 24*(6), 315-322.

23. Mayo, A., Chang, B., Omery, A. (2002). Use of protocols and guidelines by telephone nurses. *Clinical Nursing Research. 11*(2), 204-219.

24. See note 5.

25. See note 13.

26. Wilson Rl, Hubert J, (2002). Resurfacing the care in nursing by telephone: Lessons from ambulatory oncology. *Nursing Outlook, 50*, 160-4.

27. National Council of State Boards of Nursing (1998). *Nurse licensure compact*. Chicago: National Council of State Boards of Nursing.

28. See note 2.

29. O'Cathain A, Nicholl J, Sampson F, Walters S, McDonnell A, Munro J (2004). Do different types of nurses give different triage decisions in NHS Direct? A mixed methods study. *Journal of Health Services Research & Policy, 9*(4), 226-233.

30. See note 2.

31. Klasner A, King W, Crews T, Monroe K (2006). Accuracy and response time when clerks are used for telephone triage. *Clinical Pediatrics 45*, 267-269.*Health Services Research & Policy, 9*(4), 226-233.

32. See note 9.

33. See note 10.

Part II:
Advanced Roles

Chapter 19

Nurse Practitioner Liability Issues

Patricia Goode, RN, ANP/FNP

Synopsis
19.1 Introduction
19.2 Defining the Nurse Practitioner's Role
    A. Definition
    B. Functions of the Nurse Practitioner
19.3 Nurse Practitioner Requirements
    A. Nursing License
    B. Educational Requirements for Nurse Practitioners
    C. Certification
19.4 Legal Regulation of Nurse Practitioners
    A. Federal Regulation
    B. State Regulation
    C. State Boards of Nursing
    D. Judicial Opinion
    E. Healthcare Facilities
19.5 Scope of Practice
    A. Nurse Practitioner Functions
    B. Overlapping Areas of Function
19.6 Nurse Practitioner Standards of Care
19.7 Legal Issues for Nurse Practitioners
    A. Practice Expansion
    B. Collaborative Practice
    C. Prescriptive Authority
    D. Documentation
19.8 Areas of Nurse Practitioner Litigation
    A. Diagnosis
    B. Treatment
    C. Referrals and Consultations
19.9 Summary
Endnotes

19.1 Introduction

The nurse practitioner is at the center of a paradigm shift in health care today. As the role of the nurse practitioner has continued to grow and expand, autonomy of the practice of advanced nursing has placed nurse practitioners in positions of increased responsibility, and thus increased liability for the decisions they make and the care they render to patients.

Nurse practitioners now provide health care throughout the entire spectrum of primary and specialty practice arenas. Figure 19.1 lists the areas of nurse practitioner practice that are certified by the American Nurses Credentialing Center. Nurse practitioners may hold one or more certifications and are expected to keep current within their practice areas through continued education and ongoing clinical involvement in their specialties. They must have a thorough understanding of the standards of care and the regulatory and legal obligations of their practice area. In this chapter we explore the role of the nurse practitioner in the healthcare community; the regulations of nurse practitioner practice; the changing roles, tasks, and autonomy of the nurse practitioner; and areas of potential litigation against nurse practitioners.

TIP: Over the past ten years, liability claims have increased against nurse practitioners.

In the past, nurse practitioners' liability was limited because nurse practitioners functioned under the direct authority of a physician. Thus, their involvement in a liability claim was typically secondary to the primary claim against the physician. The view of the nurse practitioner as a primary target of litigation shifted as federal, state, and regulatory agencies legislated increasing levels of autonomy for the nurse practitioner as an independent healthcare provider. All levels of regulatory, judicial, and credentialing agencies continue to struggle with identifying areas of overlapping responsibilities between advanced practice nursing and medicine.

- School/College
- Geriatric
- Adult
- Neonatal
- Pediatric
- Family
- Women's Health
- Psychiatric/Mental

Figure 19.1 Nurse Practitioner Certifications

- State Nurse Practice Acts
- American Nurses Associations
- Nurse Practitioner Associations
- Joint Commission
- Medicare
- Medicaid
- Professional Textbooks

Figure 19.2 *Standards of Care Resources*

Familiarity with the state Nurse Practice Act is the most important legal and regulatory component when evaluating the level of nurse practitioner liability in a given situation. Subsequently, a review of the standards of care for nurse practitioner actions and decision making should be undertaken. Figure 19.2 lists resources for reviewing standards of care for nurse practitioners. This chapter provides more specific information about the role of the nurse practitioner and the nurse practitioner's professional responsibilities within the healthcare community.

19.2 Defining the Nurse Practitioner's Role
A. Definition
The nurse practitioner is a registered nurse who has completed advanced academic education and has developed clinical experience and expertise. The nurse practitioner's education and clinical experience qualifies him to diagnose, treat, and manage most common acute and chronic illnesses, functioning as an independent practitioner or in collaboration with a physician. The term advanced practice nurse (APN) is applied to any nurse who has advanced nursing education or has a master's degree in a particular clinical specialty. Advanced practice nurses can include clinical nurse specialists (CNS), nurse practitioners (NPs), certified nurse midwives (CNM), and nurse anesthetists (CNAs). Nurse practitioners' practice includes all nursing functions as well as functions and tasks that previously were provided only by physicians.

B. Functions of the Nurse Practitioner
According to the American Association of Colleges of Nursing,[1] nurse practitioners provide comprehensive care within an area of specialization and can:

- evaluate an individual's health by taking a complete history, and ordering and interpreting results from appropriate laboratory and diagnostic tests and procedures.
- diagnose health and medical conditions by reviewing available health information and applying ad-

vanced clinical decision-making processes.
- manage health problems by developing an individual plan of care, prescribing treatments and medications, obtaining consultations and referrals, and coordinating healthcare services.
- promote health by ordering health screenings, prescribing preventive therapies such as diet, exercise, and vaccinations, and teaching and counseling families and individuals.
- collaborate with patients, families, and other healthcare providers. A nurse practitioner can serve as a patient's primary care provider and is able to provide the coordination and management of care required in various healthcare delivery systems including medical home, accountable organizations, transitional care, and so on.

19.3 Nurse Practitioner Requirements
A. Nursing License
All nurse practitioners must possess a current nursing license. Requirements for a nursing license are determined by state laws, and are generally governed by the state Board of Nursing.

B. Educational Requirements for Nurse Practitioners
In 1994, the American Association of Colleges of Nursing recommended that all advanced practice nurses, including nurse practitioners, be master's degree prepared to be eligible for nurse practitioner certification.[2] Beginning in January 1999, the Health Care Finance Administration (HCFA) released regulations requiring nurse practitioners to be master's degree prepared for reimbursement. Most nurse practitioner associations also require nurse practitioners to be master's degree prepared.

C. Certification
Nurse practitioner certification can be obtained from credentialing bodies such as the American Nurses Credentialing Center (ANCC), which is part of the American Nurses Association (ANA). Credentialing is determined by standards that are set by the ANA and other professional organizations, along with successful completion of a written examination. Minimum clinical practice requirements are also set by these credentialing agencies.

19.4 Legal Regulation of Nurse Practitioners
Regulation of nurse practitioner practice is primarily through the state rules and regulations as specified in the state Nurse

Practice Acts. However, there are three sources of law that dictate nurse practitioner practice:

- Statutory law, which includes federal laws passed by Congress (including Medicare and Medicaid) and state laws, which include the Nurse Practice Acts.
- Administrative law, which includes federal agencies, or boards and commissions legislated by Congress and the states. State Boards of Nursing and the Centers for Medicare and Medicaid Services (CMS) under the U.S. Department of Health and Human Services are considered under the administrative law.
- Judicial law, which includes court cases and the opinions rendered in these cases. The rapidly expanding roles of the nurse practitioner, and the legislative guideline revisions that are constantly under review, make it imperative for nurse practitioners to keep abreast of the most current scope of practice in their particular specialty and within the state in which they practice. These rapid changes have also presented many challenges as the scope of practice issues may not be as clearly defined in many instances, and may vary state by state.[3]

A. Federal Regulation

There are four regulatory bodies involved with nurse practitioner practice. These include the United States Congress, the Drug Enforcement Agency (DEA), the Food and Drug Administration (FDA), and the Centers of Medicare and Medicaid Services under the Department of Health and Human Services (CMS).

B. State Regulation

A state's Nurse Practice Act broadly defines the legal scope of practice in each state. Regulations vary state by state in their clarity and specificity. In some states, advanced nursing practice is defined by exception, and in other states, the scope of practice is defined by the physicians with whom the nurse practitioner works. Amendments are added to the Nurse Practice Act as the state legislature considers the evolving nurse practitioner scope of practice.

C. State Boards of Nursing

The state boards of nursing are given their authority under the state Nurse Practice Act, and their main function is to set policy, procedure and regulation of nursing licenses. The Board of Nursing mission is to safeguard the public health and welfare and to protect citizens from unauthorized, un-

qualified nurses. They are authorized to enforce the rules and regulations of the nursing profession and establish requirements for obtaining an advanced practice nursing license.[4] The Board of Nursing is authorized to discipline nurses who violate the Nurse Practice Act or other regulations as set forth by the board. If questions arise concerning a particular nurse practitioner action, contacting the state Board of Nursing will provide the most information concerning the scope of practice.

D. Judicial Opinion

Previously reviewed cases concerning nurse practitioner actions and decisions within the judicial system will also provide a foundation for legislative and regulatory bodies to make decisions, provide discipline, and add amendments to the existing Nurse Practice Act. As litigation involving nurse practitioners increases, this becomes an increasingly important source of information.

E. Healthcare Facilities

Healthcare facilities where nurse practitioners function will set practice boundaries through the use of policies, procedures, facility credentialing, and practice guidelines. These guidelines should be obtained from the facility in any litigation involving a nurse practitioner.

19.5 Scope of Practice

Nurse practitioner scope of practice is essential information in any potential allegations or liability case review. Scope of practice information helps juries, judges, and expert witnesses decide whether the nurse practitioner breached the standards of a "reasonable and prudent nurse practitioner in the same or similar situation."[5]

A. Nurse Practitioner Functions

Individual nurse practitioner scope of practice is based on level of education, past experience and the level of agreed upon collaboration with physicians and other healthcare providers. When evaluating a nurse practitioner scope of practice, it is sometimes necessary to review both the Nurse Practice Act and the Medical Practice Act to find more specific restriction and definitions of nursing practice versus medical practice. In some states the Medical Practice Act is much more clearly defined than other healthcare practitioner practice acts.

TIP: Physician and nurse practitioner roles overlap in many areas, yet practitioners are held to the standards of their respective practice codes.

B. Overlapping Areas of Function

Many of the functions that were exclusively performed by physicians in the past are now accepted functions of the nurse practitioner. Some of the areas of overlapping function include evaluation of disease states, diagnosis of disease, and medical treatment of diseases. Prescriptive privileges, and now in many states, the prescription of controlled substances, are routine nurse practitioner functions. Generally, any task or function delegated by the physician to the nurse practitioner has been accepted by both state practice boards and judiciary bodies as within nurse practitioner scope of practice.

Liability and litigation questions concerning overlapping functions are generally answered by the state Nurse Practice Act and the state Medical Practice Act. Clarifying these overlapping responsibilities in the work setting is generally accomplished by written collaborated agreements. These agreements provide both providers with legal protection and establish a consensus between interdisciplinary health providers.

19.6 Nurse Practitioner Standards of Care

Standards of care are authoritative statements that the profession of nursing uses to define the responsibilities for which practitioners are held accountable. These statements provide direction for nursing practice and are based on the values and priorities of the profession. Nurse practitioner actions can be evaluated within this framework, thus providing the public with accountability measurements.

Standards of practice for nurse practitioners are included in the state nursing practice acts. Other resources for standards of care include professional associations, healthcare agency policy and procedures, professional journals and textbooks, court cases, and job descriptions.

The American Nurses Association (ANA) has always been a leader in providing standards of nursing practice. Practice standards for specialty nurses and advanced practice nurses are defined by the ANA. Federal agencies and other organizations have also established practice guidelines and standards of care. These include Medicare and Medicaid, and The Joint Commission.

Beginning in 1993, the American Association of Nurse Practitioners developed standards of care that identify specific nurse practitioner qualifications, the process of patient care, nurse practitioner work environment, collaborative practice responsibilities, documentation, patient advocacy, quality assurance, research, and supportive professional roles.

19.7 Legal Issues for Nurse Practitioners
A. Practice Expansion

The rapidly changing role responsibilities of the nurse practitioner have caused increased recognition of the overlapping functions of the nurse practice and the physician. These changes demand increased legal accountability for the actions of the nurse practitioner, and the outcomes under the care of the nurse practitioner. As professional education, experience, and the scope of practice expand, the risk of liability and the number of law suits against nurse practitioners will increase.

B. Collaborative Practice

In some states there are no requirements for physician involvement in nurse practitioner practice. However, in the majority of states, there is required "supervision" or "collaborative" physician involvement.[6] Written protocols, consisting of mutually agreed upon medical guidelines that define individual as well as shared responsibilities between the physician and the nurse practitioner are required by many states.

TIP: Collaborative practice between physicians and nurse practitioners is defined by states and varies widely.

Written protocols are considered a standard of care because they provide a minimum level of safe practice under specific situations. As nurse practitioner practice evolves, the state legislatures continue to address a number of scope of practice and collaborative issues.

Collaborative practice is defined on three different levels:

* Federal
* State
* Institution, or individual nurse practitioner practice guidelines

The federal definition of collaborative practice before 1998 was defined as "mandated supervision by a physician." With the introduction of the Medicare Reform Act of 1997, the collaborative practice definition was relegated to the state Nurse Practice Acts.[7] At the state level, collaborative practice is defined state by state within the Nurse Practice Act. Collaborative practice is a mutually agreed upon outline with a physician or a physician group that defines the scope of practice necessary to manage patient care. Nurse practitioners are held responsible for the patient care they provide, but the collaborative agreement provides the overall medical direction of care so that there is a continuum of medical and nursing care for each patient. The collaborative agreement is based upon accepted medical and nursing standards of care. It is also in agreement with any federal or state regulations and statutes governing medical and nursing practice, as well as the prescription of drugs. States requiring collaborative practice agreements require that the agreement be in writing.

Practice guidelines, which are written agreements between the nurse practitioner and the physicians working in a practice setting, include appropriate consultation and referral procedures, and protocols for resolving conflicts about patient care within that practice. They are discoverable documents.

C. Prescriptive Authority

Increasing numbers of states are legislating prescriptive authority for advanced practice nurses. The intent of the legislation is to increase access to care and to utilize advanced practice nurses to their full capability as accessible full service providers.

Each individual state specifies the requirements a nurse must meet in order to qualify for this aspect of practice. In general, state Nurse Practice Acts grant prescriptive authority to nurses who provide evidence of advanced educational preparation, proof of certification from a nationally recognized certifying body, specific numbers of recently acquired hours of pharmacology preparation, and evidence of continuing education in the pharmaco-therapeutics related to the nurse's specialty area of practice.

Most prescriptive authority acts require the nurse practitioner to have a collaborative or supervisory agreement with a physician to prescribe. These state laws also specify which scheduled drugs the nurse practitioner can prescribe. Therefore every nurse practitioner must be familiar with the prescriptive laws in the state where she practices. When nurse practitioners prescribe medications, they are responsible to determine if the correct diagnosis has been reached, and that the choice of drug is the best for that particular patient.

TIP: It is the responsibility of the nurse practitioner to be aware of the regulations governing prescriptive authority in the respective state and to comply with these regulations.

D. Documentation

To be in compliance with federal and state laws and regulations, the care rendered to patients must be thoroughly documented. If the care given to patients is not documented, the court and expert witnesses may assume it was not done.

Documented opinions, treatments, decisions, and referrals are much more solid evidence than oral testimony. Standards of nurse practitioners' documentation include written history and physicals, differential diagnosis, treatment plans, and patient education.

Documentation of care also includes any written materials given to the patient, the patient's acknowledgment of understanding of potential risks and benefits, results of noncompliance with medications and treatments, and confirmation that the patient is aware of when to call the practitioner, and when to follow-up.

With the recent introduction in many states of mandated computerized medical records, there are new concerns about accuracy of documentation, organization of patient data, timeliness of documentation, and patient data privacy. The premise of patient confidentiality within the healthcare system applies to all types of documentation systems. Computerized medical records, however, increase the risk of widespread breaches in confidentiality as opposed to paper charting.

There are various laws protecting medical record privacy.[8] The federal Privacy Act of 1974 protects the confidentiality of medical records in veterans' hospitals. The Health Insurance Portability and Accountability Act (HIPAA) passed by Congress in 1996, sets the standard for the electronic transfer of health data. The HIPAA Privacy Rule was issued on April 14, 2003. This rule was formulated by the U.S. Department of Health and Human Service (HHS) to further address growing public concerns about privacy and security of health information. All businesses and health plans were required to be in compliance by April 14, 2004. Each state is free to amend or adopt laws that further protect medical record privacy. State laws concerning medical information privacy can be found at www.hpi.georgetown.edu/privacy/records.html. An accounting of disclosures of health information is required by HIPAA. Audits of information are typically available for the prior six years, although there are exceptions to this accounting process.

Those individuals who see medical records for treatment, payment, and healthcare operations are not required to submit an accounting of disclosures. It is important to note that HIPAA only applies to three specific entities: healthcare providers, health plans, and healthcare clearing houses. Many other entities that may have access to medical information are not covered by HIPAA regulations. These may include:

- Agencies that deliver Social Security and welfare benefits
- Workers' compensation

- Life insurance companies
- Auto insurance companies
- Those who conduct healthcare surveys
- Health screening such as at healthcare fairs, shopping centers, pharmacies, and malls
- Law enforcement agencies
- Researchers who obtain data from healthcare providers
- School nurse visits

19.8 Areas of Nurse Practitioner Litigation

Malpractice claims made against nurse practitioners have been steadily rising. The National Practitioner Data Bank 2004-2008 documents the increasing judgments and settlements against nurse practitioners. These increases have been brought about by several factors, including current tort law, the insurance market, social tendencies, and the expanding scope and autonomy of nurse practitioner practice, thus placing them in a more litigious position. States ranking highest in nurse practitioner litigation include Florida, California, New York, Massachusetts, and Pennsylvania.

In order of frequency of claims, the following allegations made against nurse practitioners include: 1) Failure to diagnose; 2) Failure to treat or monitor; and 3) Improper management or performance.

A. Diagnosis

Areas of nurse practitioner litigation related to diagnosis include failure to diagnose, delay in diagnosis, and failure to obtain appropriate tests (see Figure 19.3). The common complaints given by patients leading to the highest number of litigations include:

- Breast lump, nipple discharge, breast rash, enlarged lymph nodes
- Chest pain or shoulder pain in a smoker
- Chest, jaw, or neck pain in an adult
- Lower abdominal pain

---

1. Breast cancer 33.5%
2. Lung cancer 16.9%
3. Myocardial infarction 13.1%
4. Appendicitis 10.3%
5. Rectal cancer 9.7%

Source: CNA Health Profession Nurse Practitioner Claims Analysis 2008

Figure 19.3 Most Frequently Missed Diagnoses

The following case points out the importance of careful assessment of patient concerns, and proper and timely actions or referrals to resolve the issues:

In an anonymously reported Massachusetts case, a patient sued four defendants—two primary care physicians, a dermatopathologist and a nurse practitioner for failure to diagnose malignant melanoma. After she had already been to the two primary care physicians and the dermatopathologist, the patient saw the NP and said that her mole had been biopsied two years earlier and that it was normal. The patient requested the mole be removed, but the NP told her that before she could be sent to anyone for removal, the NP would have to get the biopsy report and medical records from the original primary care physician. The NP noted in her records that the mole was a typical dysplastic and suggested that the plaintiff wear sunscreen, but did not tell the plaintiff that the mole could be cancerous or precancerous. The case was settled at mediation for $675,000.[9]

In this situation, the nurse practitioner noted clearly in the patient record that the mole was *not* normal, and in fact *dysplastic,* and yet there was no biopsy appointment made either in the office or with a dermatology specialist. While it is appropriate to get prior patient records, obtaining those records should not have delayed appropriate action by the nurse practitioner.

The nurse practitioner also did not document in the patient record whether there was any discussion of the type of skin lesion present or the potential risk involved with this type of skin lesion. It is therefore assumed that no discussion of this type took place.

The plaintiff, age 47, was injured in a traumatic incident that took place in a gym. He went to the defendant nurse practitioner for seven months following this incident. During that time the plaintiff claimed that the defendant failed to diagnose bilateral distal biceps tendon ruptures or refer the plaintiff to an orthopedic surgeon.

By the time the plaintiff went to a surgeon the tendons could be neither retracted nor re-attached. Grafting and muscle reattachment were performed at the Mayo Clinic. The defendant argued that as nurse practitioner, she had no responsibility, while the plaintiff argued that a nurse practitioner is authorized to diagnose and treat patients.

The supervising physician reached a confidential settlement prior to trial, according to Florida Jury Verdict Reporter. A jury found for the plaintiff, finding 50 percent negligence by the defendant and 50 percent negligence by the physician (the jury was not informed of the settlement). Damages of $1,848,068.50 were assessed. This resulted in a $970,000 judgment.[10]

In this case the nurse practitioner failed to make the appropriate diagnostic and patient management decisions in a timely fashion. X-rays, MRIs and orthopedic referral should have been made within time intervals that meet the standards of care for this type of injury. Careful documentation of each visit and the discussions between the nurse practitioner and the patient, including missed appointments and follow-ups would be important in evaluating negligence in this case.

B. Treatment

Nurse practitioner litigation regarding patient treatment typically involves the following areas:

1. Failure to treat symptoms in accordance with established standards
2. Improper patient care management
3. Delay in treatment or care
4. Improper treatment related to patient complaints

Errors in choosing or writing prescriptions accounted for the majority of allegations related to medications. Other areas frequently found in litigation include failing to properly discontinue medications, administering the wrong medication, and ordering incompatible or contraindicated medications.

C. Referrals and Consultations

According to the Nurse Service Organization, the highest *severity* of litigation occurs when there is failure of the advanced practice nurse to obtain appropriate physician consultation or referral. Referral and consultation with a physician is appropriate when the needs of the patient exceed the nurse practitioner's education, certification and experience. A low threshold for consultation and referral are supported by all nurse practitioner associations and organizations.

Legislation included in the Nurse Practice Act and the Medical Practice Act of each state outlines appropriate physician referral and consultation. Facility-specific protocols also further define appropriate referral guidelines between the nurse practitioner and the physician staff, including specialists.

There is no restrictive language in the Nurse Practice Acts that limits the ability of the nurse practitioner to directly refer to a specialist physician; however local facility policy and procedures may be more restrictive. The following case demonstrates the responsibilities of the NP:

The plaintiff's decedent, age 19, went to the defendant family practice physician and nurse practitioner beginning in February 2000 with complaints related to her nose and sinuses. The defendants maintained that the symptoms were consistent with allergies. The decedent was prescribed Amoxicillin at her first presentation. A second course of antibiotics was prescribed ten days later. In August 2000, the decedent complained of nosebleeds and was diagnosed with sinusitis with nosebleeds. The teenager had begun complaining of persistent daily frontal headaches, loss of sense of smell, difficulty breathing and frequent nosebleeds, but the medical records did not document these symptoms.

In September 2000, the decedent was seen by the nurse practitioner who diagnosed allergic rhinitis and prescribed Allegra and saline nasal spray. The decedent was seen by the nurse again in October and November, at which point the decedent had an enlarged lymph node.

In March 2001, the decedent saw a covering doctor and noted that her right nostril was blocked. The covering physician asked her to see her regular physician, at which time she was referred to an ENT. At that visit the diagnosis of a mass was immediately made.

In April 2001, the decedent underwent endoscopic surgery. An MRI in May showed the tumor to extend intracranially. The decedent subsequently underwent craniofacial resection and postoperative radiation therapy. Despite aggressive treatment the cancer recurred and she died in December 2001.

The plaintiffs claimed that the decedent should have been referred to a specialist at least seven months before her diagnosis.

The defendants claimed that the decedent had generalized complaints consistent with allergic rhinitis and that sinonasal cancers were rare. The defendant also claimed that the specific tumor type was notoriously aggressive and that a seven-month delay would not have changed the outcome.

According to a published account a $1.5 million settlement was reached.[11]

Unfortunately, many nurse practitioners will recognize how this scenario could play out in day to day practice. In many instances, patients are seen for acute or urgent visits where only one complaint is addressed. There was a six-month interval between the first and second visit, not a particularly worrisome interval for sinus complaints. However, the additional complaints of headache, loss of smell, difficulty breathing and nosebleeds demonstrate a progression of symptoms, which the nurse practitioner may not have realized if the prior patient visit was not reviewed with an eye for establishing a pattern to the complaints or worsening complex of symptoms.

The next three visits were noted to be only one month apart, with an enlarged lymph node appearing nine months after the initial visit. In retrospect a worsening progression can be clearly established.

One way to avoid this kind of outcome is to review previous visits related to the presenting complaint, noting any pattern or progression of complaints. Obtaining a sinus x-ray or CT scan of the sinuses should be instituted whenever a pattern or progression of symptoms is noted, or if the patient does not respond to therapy and frequently returns to the office. Referral to a specialist should also be initiated at that time.

Documenting all of the specific complaints offered by the patient will help avoid any missed information that will assist in timely diagnosis and treatment. Scheduling follow-up appointments and documenting missed appointments will demonstrate efforts to resolve patient complaints and illnesses.

19.9 Summary

The challenges of the current healthcare system to meet the medical needs of the population have moved the nurse practitioner into a position of prominence as healthcare providers. Increasing numbers of nurse practitioners are functioning as independent practitioners and are providing an ever-widening scope of services to patients.

Along with the increased responsibility for patient care management, there exists the potential for increased allegations of negligence or malpractice. Familiarity with nurse practitioner education, licensure, credentialing, scope of practice, and standards of care will enable a thorough evaluation of cases involving advanced practice nurses.

Endnotes

1. *AACN Position Statement*. Updated January 1998.

2. American Association of Colleges of Nursing (1996) *The Essentials of Master's Education for Advanced Practice Nursing* Washington, D.C.

3. *Nurse Practitioner Legal References*. Ch. 1 Springhouse, PA.

4. National Council of State Boards of Nursing.

5. West's Encyclopedia of American Law.

6. Buppert, C., *The Nurse Practitioner Business Practice & Legal Guide*. Aspen Publishers, Inc., 1999.

7. American Academy of Nurse Practitioners, *Standards of Practice*. Washington, D.C. 1993.

8. HIPAA Privacy Rule and Public Health (April 2003) 52: 1-12.

9. http://www.nso.com/case-studies/casestudy-index.jsp NSO Legal Case Study April 2005.

10. http://www.nso.com/case-studies/article/112.jsp   NSO Legal Case Study April 2005.

11. http://www.nso.com/case-studies/article/241.jsp   NSO Case Study September 2008.

Chapter 20

Nurse Anesthesia Malpractice Issues

F. David Rodden, CRNA, MSN, MS*

Synopsis
20.1 Introduction
20.2 Overview of Anesthesia Care in Relation to Malpractice Allegations
    A. General Anesthesia
    B. Regional Anesthesia
        1. Spinal anesthesia
        2. Epidural anesthesia
        3. Brachial plexus block
        4. Intravenous regional anesthesia (IVRA or Bier block)
        5. (Individual) nerve blocks
    C. Monitored Anesthesia Care (also known as MAC, local/MAC, or local/standby)
20.3 Common Potential Sources of Liability
    A. Statistical Trends in Anesthesia Malpractice Claims
    B. Airway and Breathing Problems
    C. Inadequate Circulation
    D. Production Pressure
20.4 Analysis of Malpractice Claims
    A. Preanesthetic Assessment
    B. Planning Among Anesthesia Provider, Surgeon, and Patient
    C. Induction and Maintenance of General Anesthesia
    D. Patient Monitoring
        1. Frequency of monitoring parameters
        2. Monitoring fluid status
    E. Providing Safe Emergence at the Proper Time
    F. Postanesthesia Care
    G. Fast-Tracking
    H. Postanesthesia Surveillance
    I. Products Used in Anesthesia
        1. The anesthesia machine
        2. Monitors used in anesthesia
        3. Medications
20.5 Safety in the Operating Room
    A. Positioning
    B. Eye Protection
    C. Thermal Considerations
20.6 Anesthetizing Locations
    A. Hospital and Medical Center Operating Room
    B. Labor and Delivery Unit
    C. Ambulatory Surgery Center (ASC)
    D. Office-Based Anesthesia
    E. Remote Anesthetizing Locations
20.7 Anesthesia Policies
    A. Departmental Manuals and Documents
    B. Institutional Policies and Procedures

20.8 Analysis of the Medical Record
    A. Preanesthetic Evaluation and Informed Consent
    B. Physical Status Classification (ASA Class)
    C. Emotional and Psychological Status
    D. Anesthesia Record
    E. Automated Anesthesia Records (AAR)
    F. Postanesthesia Evaluation
20.9 Potential Defenses
20.10 Identifying Potential Defendants
    A. Anesthesiologists
    B. Certified Registered Nurse Anesthetists (CRNAs)
        1. Nurse anesthesia education
        2. Continuing education and practice requirements for CRNAs
        3. American Association of Nurse Anesthetists (AANA) membership and organization
        4. The Professional Practice Manual for the Certified Registered Nurse Anesthetist
    C. Other Less Common Anesthesia Providers
20.11 Anesthesia Outcomes
20.12 Supervisory Issues for CRNAs
20.13 Unique Aspects of Anesthesia Care
20.14 Human Error, Crisis Management, and Anesthesia Practice
20.15 Summary
Endnotes
New Publications for Consideration
Acknowledgments

20.1 Introduction

The practice of anesthesia has the objectives of 1) rendering the patient insensible to pain and stress; 2) supporting and enabling the surgeon or procedurist in the necessary intervention; and 3) preserving patient safety. These three objectives can be met under almost all circumstances, but occasionally compromises may be necessary. A variety of circumstances, including emergent or unexpected problems, patient morbidity and comorbidity, and the complexity of the case may create a situation in which all objectives cannot be fully achieved.

The value of proper planning and communication in creating a safe and successful anesthetic cannot be overstated, including obtaining informed consent. Urgent medical necessity may not allow for optimum planning and commu-

*The author appreciates the contributions of Deborah Dlugose, RN, CCRN, CRNA, to previous editions of this chapter.

nication, and the urgency must be documented effectively for proper retrospective evaluation.

The objectives of various anesthesia providers are the same. Patient morbidity and mortality may occur even when anesthesia and surgical performance meet the standards of care. The difficulty in analyzing anesthesia-related claims lies in the complicated nature of anesthesia delivery to patients with diverse physiology, pathophysiology, and comorbidity. The goals of this chapter are to describe:

- the role of the anesthesia provider in health care.
- the anesthetic techniques employed in meeting the anesthetic objectives, including associated equipment and medications.
- the process utilized to meet anesthesia objectives.
- the reasonable and expected standard of care in providing anesthesia.
- how anesthesia objectives may not be met.
- how to identify when the standard of care in meeting anesthesia objectives has not been met.

Dornette lists the following ten factors inherent to the practice of anesthesia, predisposing to injury and subsequent litigation:

1. dosages of agents producing general anesthesia are typically more than 50 percent of the lethal dose
2. general anesthetic agents deprive patients of protective reflexes, setting the stage for airway obstruction, aspiration of vomitus and other foreign materials, and related complications
3. airway management problems are not uncommon; the anatomic configuration of many patients prevents direct laryngoscopy (visualization of the vocal cords) making intubation of the trachea difficult, and thus predisposing to airway obstruction and hypoxia
4. most general anesthetics, and all paralytics (muscle relaxants), obliterate or suppress spontaneous respiratory activity
5. general anesthetic agents, in a dose-dependent fashion, adversely affect sympathetic nervous system activity, vasomotor tone, and myocardial function, especially in patients receiving antihypertensive medications, and potentiate the risks of hypotension, myocardial depression, and circulatory arrest
6. some types of regional anesthesia, notably epidural techniques, may result in cardiovascular collapse due to toxic reaction to local anesthetic (inadvertent vascular injection), or unintended "total spinal" anesthesia

7. attempts to produce spinal anesthesia may result in high or total spinal, or produce spinal nerve or spinal cord injury, with attendant sensory and motor loss that may be permanent
8. modern techniques of invasive monitoring may be mandated by standards of care, but possess the potential (albeit small) for fatal complications
9. short-term involvement by anesthesia providers, coupled with substantial fees for service, is more likely to result in litigation, than would be the case if the patient-provider relationship was more extended
10. modern health care is delivered by a team, so any injury will usually result in the naming of all parties on the record, regardless of the relationship to actual injury.[1]

Dramatic improvements in anesthesia safety have occurred in the last 20 years.[2] Anesthesia-related mortality rates, in healthy patients, are vanishingly small, on the order of 1:300,000 or less.[3] Anesthesia agents and techniques have improved; however, great credit goes to developers of technology for monitoring of arterial oxygenation (SaO_2 or SpO_2) and end-tidal (exhaled) carbon dioxide ($ETCO_2$). These technologies have become a standard of care. Failure to utilize standard technology or respond to data provided by standard technology constitutes negligence.

Anesthesia practitioners saw a progressive decline in professional liability insurance rates subsequent to the above technologies.[4] As of 1999, the number of claims had stabilized but claim costs had increased.[5] The author's informal review of reported anesthesia related cases over the last two years revealed mostly defense verdicts, except where failure of airway management occurred, and in this area there was a preponderance of large settlements or findings for the plaintiff.

The anesthesia community's interest in patient safety and prevention of malpractice claims has been reflected in the development and ongoing support of closed claim studies by both the American Society of Anesthesiologists (ASA) and the American Association of Nurse Anesthetists (AANA). The ASA (since 1984) and the AANA (since 1985)[6] have analyzed closed claims to identify important areas for risk management. These activities have led to the development of educational programs, clinical algorithms, and the promotion of standards of care.[7] Publications such as the Anesthesia Patient Safety Foundation Newsletter and Current Reviews in Nurse Anesthesia focus on issues of patient safety.

The anesthesia provider must be aware of what is reasonable and possible and must be willing to apply a new approach when clinical evidence and patient satisfaction justify it. When the surgical approach changes, the anesthetic approach may need to change as well, but patient safety must remain a priority.

Anesthesia poses risks to the patient that become obvious as he reads the consent form. Dental injury is the most common anesthesia-related injury, while the most serious injuries are those related to airway management.[8] Difficult intubation, unrecognized esophageal intubation, and unrecognized anesthesia circuit disconnection have all resulted in catastrophic patient injuries. Some common liability issues are presented in this chapter, but patient variability coupled with unique surgical and medical situations can create an almost infinite number of risks and problems. An adverse outcome may occur without negligence. (An adverse outcome may occur even when the standard of care has been met.)

TIP: Anesthesia-related case analysis requires examination of contributing factors:

- patient factors (unusual anatomy, allergies, preexisting pathology)
- surgical factors (surgical approach, surgical error, blood loss)
- anesthesia process (planning and choice of anesthesia technique, clinical delivery of the plan, problems with ventilation, oxygenation, perfusion, anesthesia errors such as wrong syringe or failure to respond to alarms, failure to properly transfer patient care responsibilities)
- system factors (equipment problems, support services, staffing, human issues)

Hopefully this chapter is viewed as a tool for legal nurse consultants, attorneys, paralegals, and interested anesthesia providers who wish to explore, from a new perspective, the practice of anesthesia and its associated malpractice issues and challenges.

20.2 Overview of Anesthesia Care in Relation to Malpractice Allegations

The advances in blood transfusion, antibiotics, and anesthesia are as responsible for the success of modern surgical care as the practice of surgery itself. Surgery was both brutal and primitive before dentist W.T.G. Morton successfully demonstrated the effectiveness of ether as an anesthetic in 1846.[9] In the year following, John Snow refined the crude device Morton had invented to better control the delivery of the ether to the patient, dramatically reducing anesthetic failures. Dentists and nurse anesthetists were the first practitio-

ners of modern anesthesia and in the U.S. predated the medical specialty of anesthesia.[10] Nurse Alice Macgaw became a specialist in anesthesia and used psychological preparation to reduce the anesthetic requirement.[11] Ralph Milton Waters, M.D. was appointed the world's first university Professor of Anesthesiology at the University of Wisconsin in 1933.[12]

In the early twentieth century, surgeons recruited nurses to provide anesthesia, replacing medical students whose attention and interests were often directed toward the surgery and not anesthetic management. Nurses were identified as capable, detail-oriented caregivers who would reliably focus on the patient's condition and deliver safe anesthesia care.[13] Certified Registered Nurse Anesthetists (CRNAs) are directly responsible for more than 60 percent of the anesthetics administered in the United States each year. In rural areas more than 90 percent of anesthetics are delivered by CRNAs.

The first responsibility of the anesthesia provider is patient safety. The standard of anesthesia care is the same regardless of discipline. The ASA and AANA have similar standards of care. The anesthesia community in the United States consists of two major sets of providers: physician anesthesiologists and CRNAs. Other groups providing a much smaller percentage of anesthesia care include dentists and oral surgeons, podiatrists, and anesthesiologist assistants (AAs). Surgeons administering field infiltration with local anesthesia are also providing anesthesia care. CRNAs may provide anesthesia independent of other anesthesia providers (as is often the case in rural areas) or may work in a team setting with physician anesthesiologists, receiving medical direction from a physician anesthesiologist, or medical supervision from either the anesthesiologist or collaborating surgeon. Many factors influence CRNA practice, including federal Medicare reimbursement guidelines, state practice statutes established by boards of medicine and nursing, and hospital anesthesia department guidelines and regulations. This chapter focuses on CRNA-administered anesthesia, but practically speaking, it is difficult to focus only on CRNA-delivered care because that care may be provided in a team setting with a physician anesthesiologist. Analysis of care provided by the team requires careful consideration of the level of control exerted by each provider. It is a major challenge to define practice relationships and each individual's participation in critical events that result in litigation.

TIP: In anesthesia team practice, the role of each provider must be identified, including actions that may have contributed to adverse outcomes or prevented injury.

Anesthesia practice includes a variety of anesthesia techniques, which are utilized separately or in combination to produce better outcomes with less risk of side effects. Many anesthesia providers began their training with a warning that anesthetic agents are poisons that need to be administered in a careful and considered manner. To ensure the intended procedure is carried out, the CRNA may utilize a variety of anesthetic agents and adjuncts to produce sedation, unconsciousness, senselessness, and immobility. The CRNA must provide constant monitoring and the necessary support to maintain physiologic processes that were attenuated or temporarily abolished by the anesthetic agents and techniques. The vigilance provided by the CRNA is required not only to protect the patient from the noxious effects of the surgery, but also from the anesthetic agents and techniques themselves.

The CRNA routinely provides rapid intervention to induce and maintain the anesthetic state, and facilitate emergence and recovery from anesthesia when the anesthetic state is no longer required. The CRNA variously responds to changes in vital signs, airway problems, blood and fluid loss, and infrequently, allergic reactions and anaphylaxis. Underlying medical conditions may precipitate serious problems during anesthesia or may serve as complicating factors when crisis occurs.

Multitasking is frequently required of the CRNA, who is routinely depended upon to reassess the patient during surgery, prioritize needs and treatments, and provide any necessary care, including massive blood and blood product transfusion, and cardiopulmonary resuscitation. Proficiency in the interpretation of information from invasive monitoring devices and in the application of Basic and Advanced Life Support is a requirement of the CRNA.

Anesthesia may be delivered using a variety of techniques or modalities, each offering advantages, difficulties, and risks. A technique may be preferred or precluded by the surgery, patient condition, or patient preference or deferral. The following subsections describe common methods of providing anesthesia as well as complications and possible untoward outcomes.

A. General Anesthesia

General anesthesia refers to rendering the patient unconscious and unresponsive to the painful stimulus of the surgery. It may be delivered via the respiratory tract with a combination of inhaled agents using a mask, laryngeal mask airway (LMA), or endotracheal tube. It may also be delivered by providing an infusion of hypnotic, analgesic, and possibly paralytic drugs through the intravenous line. The patient may be allowed to breathe spontaneously or be mechanically ventilated. Modern anesthesia machines include a ventilator that may or may not, at the discretion of the

CRNA, be included in the anesthesia circuit. Ventilator settings accommodate patients with significant lung pathologies.

Supplemental oxygen is always administered, usually between 30 and 100 percent of the total gas administered. The abbreviation FiO_2, indicating fraction of inspired oxygen, is commonly used. The atmosphere at sea level provides 21 percent oxygen. A potent, inhaled anesthetic (commonly sevoflurane, desflurane, or isoflurane) is added to the gas supplied. Halothane is still used, but the other older agents have largely fallen out of favor due to adverse effects and slower onset and resolution of effects. All potent, inhaled agents except halothane are of the chemical class of ethers. Each potent, inhaled agent is delivered via its own dedicated vaporizer in an amount that is a very small percentage of the total volume of gas administered to the patient.

Nitrous oxide may be used with oxygen and can double the potency of the ether. The potency of the specific agent is defined by the minimal alveolar concentration (MAC), and generally can be considered as the lower range of dosage that maintains unconsciousness and unresponsiveness (immobility) to the surgical stimulus. For example, the MAC of isoflurane is 1.15 volume percent when used alone with oxygen, but drops to 0.55 volume percent when used with a combination of 50 percent oxygen and 50 percent nitrous oxide. Using less than MAC makes it more likely the patient will not remain unconscious throughout surgery, but patient movement usually alerts the anesthesia provider that more anesthesia is needed before the patient awakens.

Adding a muscle relaxant—a neuromuscular blocking agent (NMBA), like vecuronium—to the anesthetic increases the risk of patient awareness, because the patient may be awake but unable to move. Many surgical procedures, however, require paralysis, and the risk of unintended patient awareness is greater.

Sedatives, narcotics, and NMBAs all are utilized with general anesthesia and usually improve the quality of the anesthetic, but also pose the risks of postoperative somnolence, respiratory depression, and residual weakness and airway obstruction, respectively. Postoperative nausea and vomiting, with its concurrent risk of aspiration, also represent a concern for the anesthesia provider.

TIP: The four priorities of anesthesia: airway, airway, airway, and airway!

Hypoxemia (decreased blood oxygen) and hypercarbia (increased blood carbon dioxide) may result from initial failure to secure the airway, unrecognized esophageal intubation, or loss of airway control. Evidence of hypoxemia or hypercarbia may fuel negligence actions. With the advent of pulse oximetry and end-tidal CO_2 monitoring as standard monitoring technology, however, the incidence of these problems has decreased.[14]

Aspiration of gastric contents is one of the greatest concerns of the anesthesia provider, as it should have been in the following case:

> In *Luellen Makeny, Admr. v. James W. Parisian, M.D.*, Fairfax County, Virginia, Circuit Court, case N. L1358397, a verdict of $966,397 was awarded as a result of aspiration of stomach acids and death. The fatality was blamed on the failure of the anesthesiologist, who did not appropriately apply cricoid pressure to his patient during induction of anesthesia, despite a history of gastric reflux and obesity.[15]

TIP: Other problems occurring with general anesthesia include hypertension and hypotension, tachycardia and bradycardia, postoperative nausea and vomiting, postoperative respiratory depression, and airway obstruction. These problems are encountered no matter how expert and vigilant the anesthesia provider.

Chart review should focus on the anesthesia provider's timely measures to resolve these problems. Careful preoperative assessment leads to appropriate planning to reduce the chance for surprise and untoward events during anesthesia care. Appropriate planning and execution of an anesthetic care plan cannot reduce risks to zero. Evaluation of cases should focus on steps taken to minimize patient risk.

Genetically transmitted problems, such as malignant hyperthermia (MH), may not be identified preoperatively. Malignant hyperthermia occurs in humans only with the anesthetic triggers of potent inhalation agents like halothane, ethrane, isoflurane, desflurane, and sevoflurane or the depolarizing neuromuscular blocking agent succinylcholine. Avoiding these triggers requires a special anesthetic care plan and the CRNA's prior knowledge of a family history of this genetically transmitted trait. The patient may be unaware of a family history of this problem, and the CRNA must focus on rapid identification and aggressive treatment of this potentially fatal crisis. MH may occur early in the case, near the end of the case, or postoperatively even as much as 24 hours after the conclusion of the procedure.

Mortality of MH was previously as high as 90 percent, but with early diagnosis and appropriate and aggressive treatment it is now less than 10 percent. Emphasis is now on early markers, including muscle rigidity, tachycardia, and

increased end-tidal CO_2 in addition to temperature monitoring and standard use of end-tidal CO_2 monitors, as a result of the research and educational efforts of the Malignant Hyperthermia Association of the United States (MHAUS).[16] The association of MH with muscular dystrophy has greatly decreased the use of the trigger drug succinylcholine and has virtually eliminated its use in pediatric cases. MHAUS conducts a registry for North America.[17]

B. Regional Anesthesia

Regional anesthesia utilizes a local anesthetic to prevent pain impulse through the affected nerves. The patient may remain awake, but not have any sensation associated with the surgical procedure until the local anesthetic effect has worn off. The ability to move the anesthetized limb may also be affected. Full recovery of sensation and movement may not occur until several hours after the surgery depending on its duration and the type and amount of local anesthetic injected.

Spinal and epidural anesthesia are the most commonly utilized regional anesthetic techniques, causing anesthesia by administering local anesthetic into the cerebrospinal fluid (CSF) as in spinal anesthesia, or just outside the dura mater in the epidural space as in epidural anesthesia. Various nerve blocks have been utilized to anesthetize an arm, a leg, a digit, the vocal cords, the eye, or a portion of the face or mouth. Sterile technique is important in the practice of regional anesthesia, especially when local anesthetic is injected near the spinal cord.

Regional anesthetic techniques are successful less than 100 percent of the time; the rate of failure of spinal anesthesia is variously reported as 4 to 13 percent, and usually attributed to technical failure. There are reports of resistance to local anesthetic effect. Onset of desired effect may not occur for five to ten minutes, and the effect may not last long enough for the surgeon to complete the procedure if surgical difficulties are encountered. If the patient experiences pain, it may be necessary to change to general anesthesia.[18] These factors must be addressed prior to obtaining consent. Patient refusal is an absolute contraindication to regional anesthesia. Antithrombotic (inhibition of platelets) and anticoagulant (inhibition of blood clot formation) therapies, as well as coagulopathy (disorder of blood clot formation), are contraindications to regional anesthesia. Recommendations from the American College of Chest Surgeons include progressively greater levels and longer duration of thromboprophylaxis, raising concerns among anesthesia providers about risk of spinal hematoma associated with neuraxial anesthesia. If not diagnosed quickly, with equally quick neurosurgical intervention, spinal hematoma is likely to cause irreversible neurologic deficit.[19] Regional anesthesia is typically combined with sedation for optimum patient satisfaction.

TIP: Breaches of sterility are difficult to prove unless another healthcare provider observed contamination of the gloves, field, or needle, and documented the event.

The attorney may need to depose other healthcare providers present when regional anesthesia was administered to seek observations of breaks in aseptic technique. This may be difficult to ascertain because the anesthesia providers may have proceeded quickly while others present were likely to be involved in independent responsibilities.

1. Spinal anesthesia

Spinal anesthesia involves injection of a local anesthetic drug and sometimes a small dose of narcotic—Fentanyl or preservative-free morphine—into the cerebrospinal fluid of the subarachnoid space via a specialized small gauge needle advanced between lumbar vertebrae, below the first and second lumbar vertebrae. Nerves leaving the spinal cord around and below the area of the spinal anesthetic are blocked, with resultant loss of lower body blood vessel tone, and loss of sensory and motor function.

The level and spread of the block depends on the dose administered, the type of solution (hyperbaric or hypobaric), and the positioning of the patient immediately after the block. A saddle block is a low-level spinal anesthetic mixed with a hyperbaric solution and placed with the patient in a sitting position to facilitate anesthesia of the perineal area. This method may be used during labor. The patient must be monitored carefully, with frequent measurement of blood pressure. Blood pressure typically drops significantly and almost immediately after administration of the local anesthetic. Rapid treatment with vasopressor drugs and intravenous fluids is required with a significant drop in pressure. If the level of block rises higher than desired and anticipated, severe hypotension and respiratory arrest may occur. Cardiac arrest may also occur, as in the following case:

Shortly after he was administered a spinal anesthetic for a transurethral prostatectomy, a 64-year-old patient suffered severe hypotension and subsequent cardiac arrest. Although toxicological evidence showed the patient had received an overdose of the local anesthetic in the spinal block, the jury focused on the anesthesia provider's slow recognition and treatment of the crisis, awarding a verdict of $1.2 million against the anesthesiologist and $150,000 against the hospital. *Isaiah Doss v. Dr. Noel G. Al-*

cantara, Bethany Hospital, Cook County Illinois Circuit Court, Case No. 95L-6747.[20]

TIP: Similar events can happen with appropriate doses. Antihypertensive medications and relative hypovolemia can decrease blood pressure. Very low blood pressure may result in poor perfusion of the respiratory centers in the brain stem, and respiratory arrest may follow. Heavy sedation, especially with propofol and Fentanyl, further increases risk. Therefore, the anesthesia provider must be vigilant and prepared for emergency management of airway, breathing, and circulation. Constant monitoring is essential.

Injuries to nerves may occur, especially if local anesthetic is injected directly into a nerve root or the spinal cord itself. Regional anesthetic complications may include transient neurologic syndrome (TNS) or, rarely, permanent sequelae related to destruction of neurologic structures, as likely occurred in the following case:

In *York v. Raouf El-Ganzouri*, a patient was administered a combined spinal-epidural anesthetic prior to a total knee arthroplasty (replacement). During the administration of the spinal-epidural by the attending anesthesiologist the plaintiff patient was twice heard to scream out with cramping of the right thigh and swelling of the right calf. Plaintiff argued the defendant doctor entered the epidural space and the intrathecal (subarachnoid space) above intervertebral space L1-2 (where the spinal cord ends), directly piercing the spinal cord and irreversibly injuring spinal cord nerve fibers. The anesthetic effect occurred shortly thereafter and the patient underwent the planned procedure. Following surgery plaintiff could not move his right leg. Additionally, he suffered loss of bowel and bladder control, as well as sexual dysfunction. Defendant argued the spinal cord injury resulted from spinal cord infarction secondary to a drop in blood pressure during the surgery, when the resident anesthesiologist was providing the anesthesia care. Defendant further maintained that when the plaintiff was heard to complain of pain, he withdrew the needle and reinserted it before administering local anesthetic. Judgment in the amount of $12,598,591 was upheld for plaintiff by the Appellate Court of Illinois after appeal by defendants.[21] *York v. Raouf El-Ganzouri*, 353 Ill. App. 3d 1, 817 N.E. 2d 1179, No.1-03-0222, 1-03-0259(cons.), (2004).

2. Epidural anesthesia

Epidural anesthesia involves the use of a syringe and large bore needle to find the epidural space (which lies just outside the dura mater) and subsequent placement of a catheter into the epidural space, through which anesthetic drugs may be intermittently or continuously injected to establish anesthesia and pain relief. Depending on the dose and concentration of local anesthetic drug, an epidural anesthetic may be primarily analgesic, as used for labor and vaginal delivery, or it may be used to provide complete surgical anesthesia, as in cesarean section and lower extremity peripheral vascular procedures.

Doses and volumes that establish epidural anesthesia are much larger than those used in spinal or intrathecal anesthesia. Unintentional injection of an epidural dose of local anesthetic into the subarachnoid space can produce a high spinal cardiac arrest, as was previously described. It is possible to inadvertently place an epidural catheter into an epidural vein; subsequent injection of local anesthetic into the epidural vein and general circulation may produce local anesthetic toxicity, seizures, and cardiac arrest. As with spinal anesthesia, initiation of epidural anesthesia is followed by a decrease in blood pressure. The decrease in blood pressure occurs quickly but is not usually as dramatic as with spinal anesthesia. Treatment with a vasopressor drug and additional intravenous fluid may be necessary.

The local anesthetic bupivicaine is especially cardiotoxic. The use of small test doses and titration of doses reduces, but does not eliminate, risk. An epidural catheter may migrate into an epidural vein or through the dura into the subarachnoid space, and so it is appropriate to aspirate the catheter (pull back the plunger on the syringe) for the presence of blood and cerebrospinal fluid each time prior to dosing—injecting—the catheter. The newer bupivicaine analog drugs l-bupivicaine and ropivicaine are available. These drugs are at least theoretically safer than bupivicaine, but are also much more expensive, and as a result of the additional cost have not attained great popularity or usage. Use of the readily available fat emulsion Intralipid has been effective in the rescue of patients suffering from accidental intravenous injection of bupivicaine.[22] Epidural placement of dilute local anesthetics and narcotics at the lumbar or higher thoracic level of the spinal column may be chosen to provide postoperative pain relief for certain abdominal or intrathoracic surgeries. Continuous lumbar epidural infusions are routinely used for relief of the pain of labor. Monitoring the epidural infusion and its effects and keeping the epidural catheter securely in the epidural space are responsibilities shared by CRNAs and staff nurses caring for that patient. Occurrence of complicating side effects does not indicate negligence; negligence occurs when providers fail to monitor carefully and react quickly and appropriately when complications occur.

A middle-aged woman received epidural analgesia postoperatively after total knee replacement. She contended that she continued to receive epidurally administered medication for two and one-half days even though she suffered increasing neurologic deficits in her legs and feet. A $5 million settlement resulted. *Bothe et al. v. DeLaCruz et al.*, Lee County Illinois, Circuit Court Case No. 95L 18.[23]

Although regional anesthesia is frequently used in obstetric patients for a variety of advantages, the anatomic and physiologic changes of pregnancy also create extra risks for the mother and baby that must be considered by the anesthesia provider during planning and administration. Case review and questioning of the anesthesia provider should focus on the provider's awareness of the implications of pregnancy that would influence the planning and administration of an anesthetic to the pregnant patient. The AANA Professional Practice Manual for the Certified Registered Nurse Anesthetist[24] includes standards for providing obstetric anesthesia and analgesia, and is a helpful resource when preparing a direct examination or cross-examination of the CRNA.

3. Brachial plexus block

Sometimes referred to as an axillary block, this regional technique provides anesthesia of the arm by injection of local anesthetic into the nerve sheath of the brachial plexus, which provides sensory and motor function for the arm. The brachial plexus may be approached by several alternative routes, with the needle placed at axillary, infraclavicular, supraclavicular, or interscalene locations.

The various approaches to brachial plexus block offer advantages and disadvantages. With traditional approaches, failure of the block to provide adequate anesthesia occurs from 10 to 40 percent of the time, and may require either the addition of heavy sedation with local infiltration of local anesthetic or conversion to general anesthesia. Training and experience in the use of a nerve stimulator as the technique for locating the nerve plexus have decreased failure rates to less than 2 percent; supplementary nerve blocks may need to be performed in about 20 percent of cases where the nerve stimulator is used.[25]

TIP: Regional anesthetic techniques have a significant failure rate, and requirement to convert to general anesthesia is not evidence of either negligence or malpractice. Requirement for sedation does not indicate a failed block, but in fact produces better patient satisfaction.

4. Intravenous regional anesthesia (IVRA or Bier block)

Intravenous regional anesthesia (Bier block, named for its developer) is an alternate method of providing anesthesia for the arm. This approach involves placing a dual tourniquet on the upper arm, wrapping the elevated arm tightly to reduce its blood volume, inflating the proximal cuff to a pressure well above blood pressure, and injecting a large amount of dilute local anesthetic, literally flooding the arm with the drug. The primary disadvantage of this technique is its relatively short period of effectiveness. There is a real danger of local anesthetic toxicity if the tourniquet is accidentally deflated in the first minutes of the case; local anesthetic toxicity with seizures and respiratory arrest are managed by the vigilant and well-prepared anesthesia provider.

TIP: Accidental early tourniquet deflation is not, in and of itself, evidence of negligence. Risk of complications and the reasonable alternatives to the approach should be addressed during the obtaining of informed consent. However, failure to check the function of anesthesia equipment and the lack of evidence of certification and maintenance of equipment by the department or institution may provide an impetus for litigation.

---

5. (Individual) nerve blocks

Individual nerve blocks may be placed to anesthetize other smaller structures, such as feet, digits, eyes, or specific areas of tissue (skin, fascia, and muscle). Any of these techniques may be complicated by untoward reactions to medications, including the possibility of intravenous injection of large amounts of potentially toxic local anesthetic into the bloodstream. It is always possible that injury to adjacent structures may occur. Proper technique does not necessarily prevent injury. Epinephrine even in very low concentrations should never be used for digital or penile blocks. Discussion of risks is part of the initial anesthesia process.

C. Monitored Anesthesia Care (also known as MAC, Local/MAC, or Local/Standby)

Monitored anesthesia care typically includes intravenous sedation and analgesia. It may be accompanied by infiltration with local anesthetic of an area of the body by the surgeon or other procedurist. Sedation and analgesia are a continuum,[26] described as follows: As the patient is initially given sedation, she will usually be able to respond to verbal commands with little change in cardiovascular function. This is referred to as "minimal sedation" and provides anxiolysis (reduction of anxiety).

As more sedation and the analgesia are administered the patent will respond to verbal commands only after tactile stimulation, with maintenance of airway, spontaneous ventilation, and cardiovascular function. This is called "moderate sedation/analgesia" and provides conscious sedation.

Additional administration of sedation and analgesia will result in a depressed state of consciousness during which the patient cannot be easily aroused, but may respond purposefully following repeated or painful stimuli; the ability to maintain ventilatory function may be impaired, and it may be necessary for the CRNA to utilize a chin lift or jaw thrust to maintain the airway. Cardiovascular function is usually preserved. This state is referred to as "deep sedation/analgesia."

Further administration of sedation and analgesia may result in unresponsiveness to even painful stimuli. The ability to independently maintain ventilation is frequently impaired; there may be a need for assistance in maintaining the airway, and spontaneous ventilation may be so depressed that positive pressure ventilation is required. Cardiovascular function may also be impaired at this point. This is the state of "general anesthesia."

Sedation and analgesia are ideally titrated to a level of consciousness that allows for patient maintenance of airway and breathing and response to commands, while the surgeon infiltrates the area of surgery with local anesthetic, or the procedurist (gastroenterologist, radiologist, pulmonologist, or cardiologist) begins the procedure. Too much sedation or analgesia may result in unconsciousness and loss of airway due to anatomic airway obstruction.

Historically this technique (sometimes called "vocal local") utilized a benzodiazepine sedative (e.g., valium or versed) and a narcotic (e.g., demerol, morphine, or Fentanyl), and reassurance as the surgeon administered the local anesthetic. Additional doses of sedative, analgesic, and local anesthetic were frequently administered, especially if the procedure took longer than anticipated.

With the advent and increasing use of propofol, used with or without a sedative and narcotic, it has become common practice for patients to be more heavily sedated (to unconsciousness) for cases that were previously done with the patient mildly sedated or awake. With this practice the anesthesia provider may need to support the airway with a chin lift or jaw thrust maneuver, providing adequate oxygenation and ventilation. With this more aggressive approach, the anesthesia provider incurs greater active responsibility for patient safety, and it can be argued that in fact the technique is really a variant of general anesthesia. The rapid onset and metabolism of propofol has made this approach possible, and has become the norm rather than the exception in some settings. Additional safety has been added by real-time monitoring of oxygenation and end-tidal CO_2. In the 1990s, however, litigation for injuries occurring during MAC increased significantly from 1.9 percent of claims in the 1980s to 6.0 percent of claims in the 1990s. There was also a greater proportion of permanent injuries—30 percent—and a lower proportion of temporary injuries compared to general and regional anesthesia.[27]

Because the airway can be lost quickly when using propofol, the provider should effectively establish and maintain the airway and provide adequate ventilation. The AANA-ASA Joint Statement Regarding Propofol Administration,[28] issued April 14, 2004, emphasizes the importance of the administrator of the sedation being trained in the administration of general anesthesia, and not otherwise involved in the procedure. This joint statement was in response to a Joint Statement of a Working Group from the American College of Gastroenterology, the American Gastroenterologic Association, and the American Society of Gastrointestinal Endoscopy, published on March 8, 2004, and a subsequent joint position statement from the Society of Gastroendoscopy Nurses and Associates and the American Society of Gastrointestinal Endoscopists, which includes the position that "the routine assistance of an anesthesiologist/anesthetist for average risk patients undergoing standard upper and lower endoscopic procedures is not warranted."[29]

The June 2009 death of pop icon Michael Jackson as he was being sedated with propofol by a cardiologist will hopefully make clear the very real dangers of propofol in the hands of non-anesthesia personnel. A problem unique to propofol is its egg/soy emulsion. Due to the highly lipid nature of propofol it requires an equally lipid emulsion in which to dissolve. This necessary emulsion is essentially equal to the petri dish as a medium in which to grow bacteria. Propofol should be drawn up in a syringe using sterile technique, and the syringe must be discarded after no more than 12 hours. Many practitioners discard syringes and opened bottles after six hours. Use of a contaminated syringe of propofol may result in bacteremia. Patient mortality due to overwhelming and unremitting infection has been directly attributed to use of contaminated propofol syringes.

TIP: Any intervention, procedure, or treatment should be undertaken only if there is a plan for and an ability to deal with known complications that may occur.

A 47-year-old male underwent removal of a mole under local anesthesia and MAC. His medical history included multiple sclerosis, chest wall deformity, and current upper respiratory infection. During the procedure he received midazolam and alfentanil, resulting in respiratory distress. Treatment consisted of intubation, mechanical ventilation, and admission to the intensive care unit. Sixteen hours later the patient pulled out his endotracheal tube, resulting in death from respiratory failure. The jury awarded the patient's family $100,000. Estate of *Joe McCoy, deceased v. S. Sychay, M.D., Floramado Li-cando, M.D., and Sacred Heart Hospital,* Cook County (Illinois) Circuit Court, Case No. 93L-4810.

This case was described in AANA's Newsletter for CRNAs (Quality Review in Anesthesia)[30] with emphasis on the following:

1. Exercise extreme caution in the administration of potent drugs during monitored anesthesia care, especially in high-risk patients.
2. The surgeon should consider very carefully the necessity of allowing a high-risk patient with upper respiratory infection to undergo surgery; the anesthesia provider should advise that the case be postponed until the infection is treated.

In some circumstances, usually involving very ill patients, the CRNA's role involves only monitoring the patient and providing oxygen, without giving additional medications that might compromise physiologic stability. The surgeon administers local anesthesia, usually an infiltration of the surgical field, and performs a minimally invasive procedure. The CRNA is prepared to intervene if the patient's condition becomes unstable, as evidenced by hypoventilation, hypoxemia, or extremes of heart rate and blood pressure.

The standard of care for anesthesia applies in these cases as it does for all others. Emergency plans and appropriate equipment for maintaining the patient's airway, breathing, and circulation in the event of local anesthetic toxicity, or other untoward events associated with local anesthesia, must be in place whenever any local anesthetic is administered. The CRNA is responsible for monitoring the patient for the effects (or lack of effect) of any local anesthetic administration, as well as keeping a running tally of the amount of local anesthetic administered.

Each local anesthetic has a therapeutic and toxic range, published in package inserts as well as in anesthesia texts. When the surgeon or other procedurist administers local anesthetic, it is the anesthesia provider's responsibility to clearly communicate the point at which it is unwise to administer additional local anesthetic. Local anesthetic may be mixed with epinephrine or be commercially prepared in a solution with epinephrine. Epinephrine increases the duration of the local anesthetic and increases the maximum dose of local anesthetic. Epinephrine may produce cardiovascular effects (such as tachycardia, hypertension, and chest pain) that require immediate treatment by the CRNA and preclude further use of the epinephrine solution.

20.3 Common Potential Sources of Liability

The most frequent and costly allegations against nurse anesthetists insured by a major insurer of healthcare providers are listed in Figure 20.1. These statistics are consistent with the anesthesia literature and reports of verdicts and settlements. Common themes and terminology emerge, often associated with the "ABCs" of patient care: airway, breathing, and circulation. See Figure 20.1.[31]

The ten most frequent allegations against CRNAs insured by St. Paul during 1994-1998 included:

	% of total claims	average cost in dollars
dental injury	16.7	2,200
baby-related	9.6	55,400
adverse reactions	9.3	93,500
death-related	7	49,100
cardiac arrest	5.7	126,500
oxygen supply/hypoxia	5.7	159,000
patient monitoring	5.0	91,800
equipment-related	4.2	11,700
nerve-related	4.0	34,400
intubation/throat-related	3.3	58,700

The ten most costly allegations (in descending order) against CRNAs insured by St. Paul during 1994-1998 were:

	% of total claims	average cost in dollars
oxygen supply/hypoxia	5.7	159,000
aspiration	2.3	130,700
cardiac arrest	5.7	126,500
eye-related	2.2	112,000
adverse reaction	9.3	93,500
patient monitoring	5.0	91,800
intubation/throat-related	3.3	58,700
arm/shoulder-related	1.4	57,400
baby-related	9.6	55,400
death-related	7.0	49,100

Professional liability premiums for nurse anesthetists decreased on average by 39 percent; comparing 1988 data from St. Paul Fire and Marine Insurance with 2004.

Figure 20.1 St. Paul Insurance Report on Nurse Anesthesia, 1994-1998. CNA data. Source: AANA. Quality of Care in Anesthesia. AANA Publishing, 2004.

A. Statistical Trends in Anesthesia Malpractice Claims

The number of claims against anesthesia providers has decreased in this new century, while average severity of claims and cost of settlements have increased. Claims for severe patient injury, including permanent brain damage and death, are decreasing. Claims for inadequate ventilation and oxygenation are also decreasing, while the incidence of difficult intubation leading to serious injury or death is relatively stable. Also relatively stable are claims related to cardiovascular- and respiratory-damaging events.[32,33]

St. Paul, the largest malpractice insurance carrier in 2000, has withdrawn entirely from the malpractice insurance arena, as have six of the previous top ten writers of medical malpractice insurance. The malpractice insurance business is volatile and unpredictable and is influenced by factors other than malpractice claims and payouts. In the period from 1994 to 2000 competition between providers prevented rate increases. Several new millennium influences impacted heavily on malpractice rates, including the economy, stock market, and events influencing these, most notably the September 11, 2001 terrorist attacks. Insurers must respond to all influences, with distribution of costs affecting all rates. Rates are set by predictions and not necessarily by previous losses.[34] As of this writing, federal tort reform has not occurred, and juries are influenced by the media in their expectations and judgments, with an ever-increasing cost to healthcare providers as claims are defended and resolved.[35] The mean medical malpractice payment made due to anesthesia malpractice by nurses in the United States was $527,821, from 44 payment reports of nurse anesthetists.[36]

B. Airway and Breathing Problems

Airway maintenance is the number one concern in anesthesia; consider that it may only take two to three minutes for respiratory arrest to produce brain injury and irreversible cardiac arrest. The anesthetized patient will likely require some airway support, if not the placement of an airway adjunct. The anesthetized and paralyzed patient absolutely requires airway control with ventilatory support. Failure to maintain the airway and adequately support ventilation will result in failure of oxygen delivery to the tissues and failure of elimination of carbon dioxide, with progressive tissue and blood acidosis. Failure to rapidly restore adequate airway and ventilation will quickly result in tissue injury and death. Hypoxia (low O_2) or hypercapnia (high CO_2) will compromise the heart, with a resultant slowing of the heartbeat. Cardiac arrest will quickly follow. Very ill patients have much less tolerance for hypoxia and hypercapnia. Cases of unexplained cardiac arrest during anesthesia may have been related to an unappreciated episode of loss of airway or ventilatory failure. Newer technologies such as the glidescope, fiberoptic endoscope, and intubating laryngeal mask airway provide options in the management of the difficult airway.

TIP: Bradycardia (slow heart rate) is usually a late sign when related to hypoxia and hypercapnia. Use of atropine to cause an increase in heart rate is inappropriate unless accompanied by measures to improve ventilation.

Loss of airway control may arise from a variety of situations including unanticipated difficult tracheal intubation; unrecognized esophageal intubation; obstruction of the airway by factors such as laryngospasm, edema, tumor, vomitus, or foreign body; and failure to perform emergency tracheostomy when conventional, less invasive maneuvers have failed. Clinical and legal literature includes many case reports of this type of event.

Anesthesia has become safer since the development of pulse oximetry and end-tidal carbon dioxide monitoring in the 1980s, and the inclusion of these monitors as standard of care shortly thereafter. Pulse oximetry and capnography provide real-time evidence of oxygenation and ventilation. Pulse oximetry uses a probe placed on a finger or thumb or a sensor placed on the bridge of the nose or ear lobe, to determine oxygen saturation of hemoglobin. An oxygen saturation value and a pulse oximetry waveform are produced. Capnography utilizes a sample of exhaled gas to generate a waveform of, and value for, exhaled CO_2. Exhaled gas can be sampled from the anesthesia circuit tubing or from a probe placed in one nare in a patient receiving supplemental oxygen through a nasal cannula or face mask. Oxygen nasal cannulas with a sampling port for CO_2 are used by some CRNAs.

Lack of adequate oxygen saturation or exhaled CO_2 should generate immediate action by the CRNA. Preset and adjustable alarms give immediate notice of loss of waveform or abnormal values.

TIP: During review of records and deposition, it is useful to determine if alarms for pulse oximetry or capnography were utilized or silenced. It is also important to determine if a precordial or esophageal stethoscope was utilized by the CRNA.

Lack of end-tidal CO_2 indicates ventilation is not occurring or circulation is not present. Movement of the chest wall by itself does not confirm the presence of ventilation, but the presence of an end-tidal CO_2 waveform in addition to chest wall movement confirms ventilation. If true cardiac arrest has occurred, no end-tidal waveform will be present even if ventilation is supported. Aerobic metabolism (metabolism utilizing oxygen) must be occurring for CO_2 to be produced. Appearance of CO_2 on the end-tidal CO_2 monitor during a resuscitation attempt is evidence of return of circulation and some degree of aerobic metabolism.

TIP: The most common cause of a large drop in end-tidal CO_2 in a mechanically ventilated patient is a large decrease in blood pressure and cardiac output.

Failure of monitors to provide reassuring data requires the CRNA to conclude that the problem lies with the patient. Quick assessment and intervention is essential in preventing patient injury.

Plans involving an anesthesia team's implementation of the difficult airway algorithm should be in place and familiar to anesthesia providers. The ASA introduced the *Difficult Airway Algorithm* in 1993 and updated it in 2002.[37] This algorithm focuses on preanesthetic identification of potentially difficult airways, preparation of equipment and personnel to provide the best plan to secure the airway, and alternative plans should the initial attempts fail.

By 1997, use of the *Difficult Airway Algorithm* was considered a standard of care as reported in Anesthesia Malpractice Prevention.[38] In 1999, the State of New Jersey amended its regulations to include a mandatory requirement for a difficult airway cart for every anesthesia department.[39]

The *Difficult Airway Algorithm* defines the standard of care for management of the difficult airway but does not guarantee success. The anesthesia provider must be prepared to perform emergency cricothyrotomy and use jet ventilation if other measures to ventilate the patient have failed. Anesthesia providers expect to meet the standard of care, but that never guarantees a successful outcome; hence, the importance of informed consent. Consult the *Difficult Airway Algorithm* from *ASA Practice Guidelines for Management of the Difficult Airway.*[40]

Even when a patent airway is established and effective ventilation is provided, hypoxemia may exist. Any of a number of factors may be responsible for hypoxemia. Pulmonary factors include hypoventilation, atelectasis, ventilation-perfusion mismatch, and lung edema.

Cardiac factors would include decreased cardiac output due to hypovolemia, heart failure, tachy- or bradyarrhythmias, or the effects of medication, either anesthetic agents or routine patient medication. Preexisting conditions like chronic obstructive pulmonary disease or cardiomyopathy can contribute to hypoxemia.

TIP: Positioning of the patient for surgery can have dramatic adverse effects on oxygen saturation, especially in the very ill and morbidly obese.

Low oxygen saturation requires immediate attention. Oxygen saturation is represented as a percentage and refers to the measured amount of oxygen carried by the oxygen-carrier hemoglobin compared with the total possible amount of oxygen that could be carried, multiplied by 100 to give a percentage. Increasing the amount of administered oxygen (FiO_2 is the fraction of inspired gas that is oxygen or the percent oxygen) is the acceptable initial intervention, but the anesthesia provider must attempt to ascertain and correct the problem. Failure to respond to information supplied by standard monitors can lead to devastating consequences. The anesthesia provider must not only be vigilant but also act quickly to determine the source of the problem and correct it.

It is important that the relationship between hypoxemia and hypoventilation be understood. With anesthesia the most common cause of hypoxemia is hypoventilation. Almost all anesthetic agents and adjuncts cause hypoventilation and, secondarily, hypoxemia. This relationship exists even when the airway is secured with an endotracheal tube, unless the patient is also properly mechanically ventilated.

Hypoventilation can initially be masked by administering supplemental oxygen, which can give the CRNA a false sense of security. If hypoventilation worsens, the continued administration of supplemental oxygen will not prevent hypoxemia. At this point, reserve of oxygen in the lungs and blood has been exhausted, and a rapid and continuous decrease in oxygen saturation will occur.

TIP: All hypoxemia is not under control of the anesthesia provider. Bronchospasm, pneumothorax, air and pulmonary embolism, and heart failure may occur despite the best anesthesia care plan and perfect execution of that plan. These events offer a defense against a malpractice claim when the standard of care is properly met.

Inability of the anesthesia provider to correct hypoxemia is a crisis best resolved by communicating with the surgeon and seeking additional help from an anesthesiologist or other immediately available anesthesia provider. Prolonged severe hypoxemia can lead to cardiac arrest and brain injury.

TIP: Pulse oximeters—"sat monitors"—change pitch with changing oxygen saturation values. The pitch is highest at 100 percent saturation; the pitch decreases as saturation decreases, so the astute, experienced anesthesia provider will never turn off the pulse oximeter tone.

C. Inadequate Circulation

Hypovolemia is the most common circulatory problem associated with anesthesia. Decreased blood volume initially manifests as increased heart rate, low blood pressure, decreased cardiac output, and decreased urine output. Decreased blood flow to tissues results in lack of oxygen and nutrient delivery, and decreased elimination of waste. Blood pH may decrease, causing metabolic acidosis, but this value is not routinely measured. Blood pH represents the acidity or alkalinity of the blood, and is tightly regulated by the body. Severe acidosis, as represented by a lower-than-normal pH, can decrease the blood pressure and cardiac output dramatically.

General anesthesia attenuates the brain stem and sympathetic nervous system response to hypovolemia. Intravenous sedation, especially heavy sedation, may create a similar effect. Spinal and epidural regional anesthesia may cause hypotension by blocking sympathetic outflow from the spinal cord, preventing lower body blood vessels from constricting appropriately to support venous return, cardiac output, and blood pressure. (A large fluid "preload" is typically given prior to administration of spinal and epidural anesthesia.)

The nothing-by-mouth status of the patient presenting for surgery may result in hypovolemia. Bowel preps administered prior to bowel surgery and colonoscopy exacerbate dehydration and hypovolemia. Typical deficits can be one to two liters of fluid.

TIP: The CRNA expert witness should review the medical record for preoperative orders, intake and output totals, and preoperative blood pressure and heart rate.

The surgical procedure causes hypovolemia in two basic ways: blood loss and insensible loss. Blood loss can be occult if the blood is not suctioned from the surgical field or if the rate of suctioning lags the rate of blood loss. Blood loss is almost always underestimated. One large surgical sponge fully saturated with blood represents 250 ml of whole blood. The surgical procedure itself may make estimation of fluid and blood loss difficult and complicated.[41] Hypotension and tachycardia must never be ignored, especially during prolonged surgery.

TIP: An excellent review and list of guidelines and recommendations for the clinical use of blood was published in *Update in Anesthesia*.[42]

Insensible loss is loss that is not apparent by clinical measurement and cannot be visualized. It occurs when the protective layer of skin is breached and unprotected tissue is exposed to a cool, dry atmosphere—typical of the OR. Exposing bowel or lung to the atmosphere can easily result in 500 ml of fluid loss per hour. The anesthetized patient ventilated with the anesthesia circuit and machine can also lose several hundred milliliters of fluid during a long case by breathing cool dry gases: oxygen, nitrous oxide, and medical air. Fluid shifts from blood vessels to tissue, subsequent to surgical trauma, can create significant hypovolemia.

TIP: Measuring hourly urine output is a simple method of determining adequacy of cardiac output, vascular volume, and kidney perfusion. A urine output between 0.5-1 ml per kg of body weight per hour is acceptable. Review records for urine output measurements, and correlate findings with heart rate and blood pressure.

Persistent low pressure that does not respond to basic measures such as increased fluid administration and vasopressors, indicates a need by anesthesia to search for other causes, such as heart failure. Failure to successfully treat hypotension may result in inadequate perfusion of vital organs, severe metabolic acidosis, and worsening hypotension and poor perfusion—a vicious cycle leading to cardiac arrest.

The causes of hypotension include, but are not limited to, failing heart muscle, myocardial infarction, pericardial tamponade, anaphylactic or anaphylactoid reaction, tension pneumothorax, pulmonary embolus, sepsis, and injury to major blood vessels. When the CRNA is unable to resolve the problem, he should communicate with the surgeon and call for consultation and help if physical assistance is required. Appropriate consultation is a standard of care.[43] The attorney and expert witness should review the medical records, especially the anesthesia record, to determine if the CRNA identified the existence of the problem, provided appropriate and timely supportive care, and searched for causes, including utilization of consultation. Documentation of identification of a problem and attempts to correct it are paramount to a defensible claim.

TIP: Prolonged use of phenylephrine, or other vasopressor (drug that supports blood pressure), may signify an undiagnosed problem, and under-perfusion of vital organs. Adequate urine output of at least 0.5-1.0 ml per kg of body weight per hour is some assurance of adequate perfusion. The urinary catheter has been called the "poor man's" cardiac output monitor.

In one case, settled immediately prior to court, prolonged and excessive blood loss should have been anticipated but was not prepared for. The patient had one peripheral intravenous line. Surgical misadventure contributed significantly to blood loss; surgical residents operated independently for a number of hours while the attending surgeon performed surgery on a different patient. The patient was positioned prone, which was hemodynamically disadvantageous and made emergent placement of a central venous line almost impossible. A second peripheral intravenous line could not be placed. The required blood and blood products could not be administered rapidly enough to prevent intraoperative cardiac arrest. Cardiac arrest occurred only after continuous ongoing blood loss, hypotension, and tachycardia, treated repeatedly with the vasopressor phenylephrine. The supervising anesthesiologist was not present to assist the CRNA in the vital administration of fluids, blood, and blood products. The CRNA did not request help. (Unpublished case, settled.)

TIP: When significant blood loss is expected it is vital to place two "large bore" intravenous lines for administration of adequate fluids and blood products. When fluid and blood resuscitation are required the CRNA must obtain assistance to manage the patient.

During the past decade the number of claims against anesthesia providers for postoperative loss of vision has increased. Among other causes, perioperative ischemic optic neuropathy (PION) has received attention in the medical literature, particularly related to cardiac surgery, nasal, head, or neck surgery, and extensive spinal fusion procedures. Most patients were male and over 50 years of age on average. Cases were long and involved administration of large amounts of fluid and blood. Some observers linked the problem to more conservative transfusion practices (related to the risk of transfusion-transmitted diseases such as AIDS and hepatitis) that allow the patient to be anemic for longer periods of time.[44]

The technique of deliberate intraoperative hypotension, used to limit intraoperative blood loss, has been cited as a possible causative factor in PION. Prone and head-down (Trendelenburg) positions have also been implicated. Articles in widely read anesthesia publications have alerted anesthesia practitioners to the problem.[45,46] The ASA has established a Closed Claims Study, has established a postoperative visual loss registry, and continues to study the problem of postoperative vision loss.

Technological advances in surgery have created new mechanisms for physiologic crisis. Laparoscopic surgery continues to have new applications, utilizing the technique of insufflation of gas into body cavities for both diagnostic and therapeutic procedures. Sharp, hollow trocars are introduced through skin, muscle, and fascia. Pressurized gas expands body cavities and allows surgeons to see and operate their instruments. Puncture of organs and blood vessels may occur unnoticed, only to be discovered postoperatively. Sudden and massive bleeding may require an immediate major incision and opening of a body cavity. Insufflation of gases under pressure may create gas emboli which enter the bloodstream. These gas bubbles travel to the heart and may, if enough volume exists, coalesce to form a large bubble, settling under the pulmonic valve of the heart to block the flow of blood and causing cardiovascular collapse.

In a California case, alteration of a pressure relief valve on an insufflator used for arthroscopic knee surgery forced gases under high pressure to travel through the patient's tissues, where compression of the heart and lungs caused cardiopulmonary arrest. The patient remained in a persistent vegetative state after being resuscitated. A net verdict of $7.1 million was reported. Analysis of the case focused on the anesthesiologist's action in monitoring, assessing, and intervening. Interestingly, an 11-minute discrepancy existed between his description of events and the nursing notes. *Leal v. Golden*, No. VC 004-018 (Los Angeles County, California, May 18, 1994).[47]

TIP: Monitoring of end-tidal CO_2 provides rapid evidence of cardiovascular collapse, which may occur with a large gas embolus.

The end-tidal CO_2 value drops precipitously toward zero, reflecting the failure of venous blood to reach the lungs. This coincides with a rapid drop in blood pressure to near zero, and loss of the pulse oximeter waveform. Loss of the end-tidal waveform and pulse oximeter waveform will occur almost immediately, but blood pressure may not be measured more frequently than every five minutes. End-tidal CO_2 values should be recorded on the anesthesia record when general anesthesia is administered, and obtaining these values is advisable for any anesthetic involving deep sedation.

D. Production Pressure

Organizational factors in the anesthesia and surgery environment may foster human error. Production pressure is a concept that continues to be examined for its contribution to adverse outcomes as cost constraints affect clinical practice.

In a 1998 ASA survey,[48] "production pressure" ranked second only to "difficult airway" as an important safety issue. Anesthesiologists revealed they frequently felt pressured to proceed with cases despite inadequate preoperative data and evaluation, and in the presence of contraindications to surgery. Anesthesiologists felt overt pressure from surgeons not to cancel or delay cases even when warranted, and to hasten anesthetic procedures. Nearly half of respondents had witnessed production pressures resulting in what were classified as unsafe actions by fellow anesthesiologists. Fear of losing future income or work from surgeons was identified as a factor influencing practice.[49]

Production pressure may increase communication failures between the anesthesiologist and surgeon; CRNA and physician supervisor; trainee and faculty; and OR nurse and CRNA. Failure to communicate vital information correctly may be directly or indirectly related to an adverse event.[50]

The obligation to be prepared for a crisis is clearly recognized by anesthesia professional organizations. Inadequate crisis management and lack of team preparation may worsen the outcome in an unforeseeable situation. The defense of the CRNA may focus on the lack of foreseeability and appropriate crisis management, despite a poor outcome.

TIP: Unstable patients should not be transported from the OR because of production pressure.

20.4 Analysis of Malpractice Claims
A. Preanesthetic Assessment

Preanesthetic assessment and documentation of physical status are the first steps in the delivery of anesthesia care. The patient interview, involving obtaining a history and eliciting a chief complaint, and physical examination are completed in this period. Where the patient is a poor historian or unable to communicate effectively, relatives or caregivers may be required to provide needed information. When possible, complete medical records should be made available for review by the anesthesia provider, especially if the patient has a complicated physical status or a previous difficult perioperative course. The CRNA's review of medical records supplies information about history and physical examination, as well as patient pathology, medications, and procedures previously performed. The CRNA is responsible for directing the procurement of the records. Old anesthesia records may shed light on problems encountered with previous anesthetic intervention. It is not uncommon for a patient with an extended hospital stay to have a "thinned" chart, and almost inevitably the archived portion of the chart includes the anesthesia records from previous cases. Therefore it is helpful for the CRNA to request the entire medical record from the medical records department.

It is particularly important for the anesthetist to inquire about serious problems such as airway difficulty or hemodynamic instability with prior anesthetics. All laboratory results as well as other pertinent tests ordered—such as EKG, stress test, pulmonary function tests, and chest x-rays—should be available to, and reviewed by, the anesthesia provider prior to formulating and executing the anesthesia plan.

TIP: It is inappropriate to proceed with the anesthetic and procedure if results from necessary tests, ordered by the anesthesia provider, are not yet available.

Review of medications must include use of herbal and over-the-counter (OTC) remedies, which may have serious effects when combined with anesthetic agents. CRNAs must query patients about use of herbal vitamins and supplements, teas, foods, remedies, as well as any OTC medications. Surveys estimate that 22-32 percent of patients having surgery use herbal medicines.[51] Carol Norred, a CRNA PhD student, conducted a study titled *Use of Contemporary and Alternative Medicines by Surgical Patients*. She reported more than half of the 500 patients surveyed consumed one or more types of alternative medicines during a two-week period prior to surgery.[52] Patients may not think of these as medications and not understand their significance. The ASA and AANA recommend stopping all such products at least two weeks before surgery. Patients who deliberately conceal the use of such substances and are subsequently injured during the perioperative period by the interaction between the substance or substances and the anesthesia and surgery assume at least some responsibility for their injury.

All patients must be questioned about a family history of serious problems with anesthesia. Malignant hyperthermia and atypical pseudocholinesterase enzyme are two genetically transmitted conditions that may result in serious anesthetic problems if not previously identified. Malignant hyperthermia (MH) is a potentially fatal metabolic disease triggered by certain anesthetic agents (inhaled agents excluding nitrous oxide and succinylcholine) in genetically sensitive individuals. MH can be avoided by using alternative anesthetic techniques that omit triggering agents.

Atypical pseudocholinesterase is a genetically transmitted reduction of the enzyme that metabolizes succinylcholine, a depolarizing neuromuscular blocking agent used primarily to facilitate placing an endotracheal tube in the trachea. The atypical form of the enzyme is unable to rapidly metabolize succinylcholine in the usual three to five minutes; depending on the atypical form it may take 30 minutes to as much as three to five hours. Since there is no antidote or "reversal" of this effect, the affected patient must remain on a mechanical ventilator until the effects of succinylcholine wear off by metabolism of the drug, and the patient's strength returns.

Consultation with other healthcare providers (pulmonologists, cardiologists, endocrinologists, nephrologists, neurologists) may be necessary to ensure patients with significant systemic disease are in optimum condition for the perioperative stresses of anesthesia and surgery. Consultation should occur early enough that appropriate measures can be taken to optimize the patient's condition. Consultation should be formal and specific to the patient's needs. Determination of anesthetic technique and intraoperative management remains the purview of the anesthesia provider.[53]

TIP: Consultation may be limited or impossible if the patient's condition is life threatening. In some circumstances it is appropriate to recommend transfer of the patient to another facility where more specialized care is available, if there is sufficient time for transport.

Inadequate preoperative evaluation is a common theme in many cases in which other allegations are made. For example, in *Baker v. Doctor's Hospital*, No. 91-CV-2271, Court of Common Pleas, Stark County, Ohio, May 10, 1993, the patient required emergency surgery for left hemothorax after administration of heparin for prevention of pulmonary embolus after a first surgery. The 63-year-old patient had several serious medical problems, including a very recent cardiopulmonary arrest. The CRNA received an oral report preoperatively from the anesthesiologist and the senior surgical resident. He did not review the medical records thoroughly and did not have a full appreciation of the severity of the patient's status. The CRNA's management included techniques and doses inappropriate for the critically ill patient. The anesthesiologist did not remain with the patient in this difficult situation, and the CRNA did not seek help from the anesthesiologist. The patient claimed awareness and pain during the procedure, resulting in post-traumatic stress disorder. Although a defense verdict was returned, another jury might have viewed the evidence differently.[54]

In *Franklin v. Gupta*, the morbidly obese patient Franklin, also with severe COPD (emphysema),

was scheduled for a carpal tunnel release. Suffering from severe chronic obstructive pulmonary disease, the patient was seen prior to surgery by the supervising anesthesiologist, but no note was made or instructions given to the CRNA or other anesthesiologist regarding the patient or the anesthetic plan. The CRNA saw the patient preoperatively the next morning, classified the patient as ASA III (a patient with a severe system disorder, which may restrict the patient's activities), and planned to administer a brachial plexus block via axillary approach as opposed to general anesthesia, which would have been inadvisable due to the patient's lung disease. Despite the patient's severe dyspnea at rest, no arterial blood gas specimen was drawn to determine the patient's degree of instability. The patient was administered Fentanyl, in divided doses, 150 mcgs (3 ml) of Fentanyl (an extremely potent narcotic), and placed in a supine position on the operating room table (a position in which it is difficult for a very obese patient to breathe). The patient was then administered a brachial plexus block via an axillary approach which was "patchy" (not completely effective). The CRNA desired to repeat the block, but the surgeon requested the patient immediately be given general anesthesia. To resolve the situation, the CRNA left the patient in the care of another CRNA and left the operating room to discuss the case with the anesthesiologist, who had originally seen the patient and was contemporaneously caring for another patient and unable to attend to Franklin.

Upon returning to the operating room, the original CRNA found the relieving CRNA ventilating Franklin. In the original CRNA's absence, the patient had become cyanotic and developed complete cardiac arrest. The CRNA had ventilated the patient, given atropine to restore a cardiac rhythm, and inserted an endotracheal tube in order to place the patient on a ventilator. The surgery was cancelled, and the patient was transferred to the intensive care unit.

A jury entered judgment in favor of the surgeon, but rendered a verdict for $375,000 against the hospital, nurse anesthetist, and anesthesiologist. The Maryland Appellate Court held that the patient-plaintiff proved an injury caused by negligence of the CRNA and the anesthesiologist. Considering the patient's delicate physical and mental condition, coupled with the contested nature, extent, and proximate cause of the patient's injury (post-traumatic complaints), the Appellate Court declined to hold that the trial court had abused its discretion by finding the jury's verdict unreasonable. Specifically, the anesthesiologist was negligent in failing to instruct the CRNA in regard to the anesthetic plan and not being available to attend to his patient. Similarly, the CRNA did not appreciate the degree of disability of the patient, manifest in the classification of plaintiff as an ASA III instead of ASA IV (patient with life-threatening disorder). The CRNA negligently administered a large dose of Fentanyl to a supine, morbidly obese patient. *Franklin v. Gupta* 567 A.2d 524, 81 Md. App. 345, No. 940, (1990).[55]

Note: See Section 20.8.B for explanation of ASA classification.

TIP: The anesthetic plan must be thoroughly documented, with data that supports the appropriateness of the plan, and must be explained to the patient in sufficient detail that the benefits and risks are understood by the patient. Any patient may need general anesthesia if the original and different plan fails or cannot be executed properly.

A thorough preanesthetic evaluation of a patient scheduled for surgery and requiring anesthesia must be performed, and must document the patient's readiness for anesthesia. Suboptimal medical condition must be addressed before elective procedures. The responsible anesthesia provider must determine, with or without the help of consultants, patient readiness.

> In *Kornak v. Anesco et al.* the decedent was scheduled for implantation of a pacemaker to treat complications related to a congenital heart defect. The decedent traveled from Illinois to Florida where pacemaker implantation surgery was to be performed by Dr. Charles Byrd. The decedent was admitted to the hospital one day prior to the surgery, and developd an accumulation of fluid in the lungs overnight. He was evaluated by the anesthesiologist Mina Akhnoukh, and subsequently received anesthesia for the planned surgery by Dr. Stephanie Otmezguine. The patient suffered respiratory failure and died two weeks later. Dr. Byrd settled prior to trial. Plantiff claimed surgery should have been delayed while fluid was cleared from dece-

dent's lungs. Defendants claimed no responsibility for the decision to perform surgery, but only to prevent pain during surgery. *Martha Kornak, indiv. and as PR of the estate of James Kornak and his survivors v. Anesco North Broward LLC, Mina Akhnoukh, M.D. et al.,* Broward County (Fl) Circuit Court, Case No. 03-022761.[56] Original verdict of $4,504,000 was reduced to $2,207,000.

If an anesthesiologist is supervising a CRNA, it must be noted as part of the written anesthesia plan, and the supervising anesthesiologist must be available to supervise and provide necessary assistance to the CRNA. When the anesthesia provider sees the patient, it should be made clear to the patient the extent of the provider's involvement.[57] Medicare guidelines stipulate the type and degree of involvement of the anesthesiologist and surgeon in the reimbursed case. See Section 20.12 in this chapter for an explanation of Medicare requirements for medical supervision and medical direction.

B. Planning Among Anesthesia Provider, Surgeon, and Patient

Each surgery has its own unique anesthetic requirements. Surgery on limbs and digits are amenable to regional techniques, as are vascular procedures on the lower extremities, and genito-urinary procedures. Intracranial procedures, thoracic surgery, cardiac surgery, intra-abdominal procedures, and orthopedic procedures on the spine typically require general anesthesia with an endotracheal tube.

Some procedures require specialized anesthetic techniques: for example, removing a tumor-containing lobe of one lung requires the use of a double-lumen endotracheal tube to isolate breathing to the other lung while the surgeon works. A fiberoptic bronchoscope is used to determine correct position of the double lumen tube. Special procedures and equipment may require additional training and special skills, as well as additional staff.

> In Michigan, brain injury from intraoperative lack of oxygen resulted in a $869,999 settlement. The 16-year-old plaintiff had a history of sickle cell disease with left lower lobe pneumonia. Subsequent sickle cell crisis, anemia and collapsed lung resulted in plaintiff being taken to surgery by the defendants. An attempt was made intraoperatively to place a double lumen endotracheal tube during surgery. The plaintiff suffered cardiopulmonary arrest and hypoxic brain injury during surgery, required resuscitation, was placed on a ventila-

tor after surgery, and remained in a coma for the following several weeks. Plaintiff was eventually discharged to a rehabilitation facility, undergoing extensive speech, physical and vocational rehabilitation therapy lasting two months. Plaintiff's brain injury resulted in dystonia and ataxia, necessitating assistance with daily functions. Cognitive-linguistic and expression deficits also persisted. Plaintiff maintained failure to establish and maintain double lumen tube endobronchial intubation, and failure to adequately maintain ventilation and oxygenation, with defendants denying any negligence. The settlement included $54,500 for the plaintiff's mother. *Jacqueline Henderson, Indiv. and as n/f of S.H. v. Edward R. Sparrow Hospital, Sparrow Health System, Physician Anesthesia Service, P.C. et al.*, Ingham County (MI) Circuit Court, Case No. 04-1382-NH.[58]

Surgeon and patient preference may play a role in the choice of anesthetic technique; this is appropriate if patient safety is not to be compromised. Many patients refuse regional anesthesia, even when it is in their best interest, due to fear of being paralyzed or feeling pain; and, of course, that choice is also a right. This may increase the patient's anesthetic risk. For example, the patient with severe pulmonary and cardiovascular disease who is scheduled for a femoral-popliteal bypass is best served by an epidural technique. If the patient insists on "going to sleep," despite recommendations against that technique, the risk is increased. This should be clearly explained to the patient and documented in the medical records, on the consent form or preanesthetic evaluation form.

The purpose of informed consent is just that: to inform the patient of the choices and the risks and benefits so the best personal choice can be made. The anesthetic pre-evaluation, discussion with surgeon and consultants, formulation of an anesthesia plan, and obtaining of the informed consent are all part of the process of providing anesthesia care. It is easier and more effective for all concerned to allow adequate time to plan elective procedures with the participation of all parties. By respecting the importance of the process, the best plan can be made by the anesthesia provider with the support of the surgeon and the patient's full participation and understanding of the benefits and risks of the anesthesia plan and technique. The informed consent for anesthesia and surgery implies communication between all parties. Appropriate and adequate communication must occur for successful outcomes. Failure of communication puts all parties at risk.

In a $2.9 million Missouri settlement the 50-year-old plaintiff suffered from a recurrent history of papillomas (wart-like tumors) of the throat. The plaintiff saw a new surgeon due to a change in health insurance. The new surgeon discovered that the regrowth of the papillomas almost completely obstructed the plaintiff's airway. The new surgeon scheduled the plaintiff for surgery, but never communicated the plaintiff's history and new findings.

The anesthesiologist never assessed the extent of the plaintiff's airway compromise, or the location of the tumors. Anesthesia was induced and the plaintiff paralyzed, but the anesthesiologist was then unable to place the endotracheal tube. Attempts to contact the surgeon were initially unsuccessful because the surgeon was outside the operating room making a personal phone call. By the time the surgeon was contacted, and emergency surgical airway (tracheostomy) secured, the plaintiff was profoundly brain injured. Ultimately the brain injury resulted in the plaintiff being unable to walk, talk, eat, or care for himself. *Anonymous Man v. Anonymous Surgeon, Anonymous Hospital and Anonymous Anesthesiologist*, Warren County (MO) Circuit Court.[59]

TIP: Informed consent by the patient should be documented. Written notes that accompany the consent form should support the process and may provide defensibility against subsequent claims. Such notes should clarify and elucidate risk. Many cases exist in which the patient claims no explanation of risks was provided even when a signed and witnessed consent form was part of the medical record.

It should be stressed to the patient that no technique is without risk. The option of not having anesthesia should be presented where it is possible, such as natural childbirth versus epidural analgesia for labor.

In a Pennsylvania case the 24-year-old plaintiff-patient charged the CRNA with negligent administration of an epidural for labor. Plaintiff was full term and in the second stage of labor. She had a previous history of epidural anesthesia for labor as well as a history of back pain. Plaintiff claimed the insertion of the epidural catheter was difficult and protracted. She also argued her labor pain was severe, and she was not presented with the option of not having the epidural. The expert witness for the plaintiff, an anesthesiologist with a pain practice, argued that the abnormal EMG as well as the lesser degree of skill possessed by a CRNA, as compared with a physician, made it likely the injury resulted from negligent care. Review of the medical record by the CRNA expert witness revealed a relatively quick procedure, without evidence of difficulty or complication. The CRNA could not remember giving the patient the option of not having the epidural. The consent for anesthesia had been obtained by the anesthesiologist prior to the actual administration of the epidural. The anesthesia record was concise, easy to read, and included necessary documentation of technique and time. Jury found for the defendant after a short period of deliberation. *Allison Bennington v. Albert Einstein Medical Center.* Philadelphia County, Court of Common Pleas #010404378. (Unpublished case.)

A CRNA administered epidural anesthesia for cesarean section to a 29-year-old woman whose labor had failed to progress. Shortly after incision the patient complained of pain. Defendant-CRNA stated she gave patient-plaintiff the option of being put to sleep with a general anesthetic. The patient declined this option, and the CRNA administered a narcotic, a tranquilizer, and nitrous oxide. Alleging a general anesthetic was not offered, patient-plaintiff maintained she suffered severe posttraumatic stress disorder. The husband also claimed he suffered this disorder because he witnessed his wife's pain in the delivery room. A defense verdict was returned. *Karen and David D'Agostino v. Swedish Hospital Medical Center et al., King County* (Washington) Superior Court, Case No.92-2-10525-0.[60]

Like most malpractice cases, the pertinent issue involved credibility: to avoid liability and refute plaintiff's claim, defendant-CRNA had to prove the option of general anesthesia was declined.

TIP: Regional anesthesia does not have a 100 percent success rate, even with the most experienced and skilled practitioners. Guarantees should never be made to the patient regarding outcome. Resorting to general anesthesia is always a possibility when any other technique is chosen. Attorneys should carefully review consent forms, preanesthetic evaluations, and anesthesia records for evidence of alternatives to the selected technique.

Planning between the CRNA and the surgeon or other procedurist includes the ordering of appropriate medications. Preoperative medications are usually ordered. This would include antibiotics as well as routine medications. Most routine medications are continued and taken with small sips of water on the morning of surgery. Exceptions to this rule include diuretics, antithrombotics, and anticoagulants. Drugs such as aspirin, plavix, and warfarin may need to be discontinued several days to a week before surgery. It may be dangerous to discontinue some drugs. Beta blockers, calcium antagonists, antihypertensives, and steroids should not be discontinued before surgery. Diabetic patients may require a special plan, and consultation with the endocrinologist may be helpful.

TIP: An anesthetic concern arises if a regional technique such as a spinal or epidural is chosen. Failure of the patient to discontinue an antithrombotic or anticoagulant medication in sufficient time to allow the return of normal platelet function and coagulation precludes the use of regional techniques. Refer to The American Society of Regional Anesthesia and Pain Medicine for delineation of risks and consensus recommendations, available online.[61] These recommendations were established at The Second ASRA Consensus Conference on Neuraxial Anesthesia and Anticoagulation in 2002.

Knowledge of nothing-by-mouth (NPO or nil per os) status is critical. Aspiration of gastric contents may be life threatening; the inflammatory response to gastric acid causes a diffusion barrier to oxygen that may require postoperative mechanical ventilation. The term "full stomach" describes a patient at high risk for aspiration. The ASA has published guidelines—not standards—based on meta-analysis of available data, which indicate that fasting from clear liquids for at least six hours after meals is advisable in healthy patients.[62] Ingestion of alcoholic beverages or fatty foods necessitates a longer period of fasting, although "hard and fast" guidelines are not available.

Patients with a full stomach (severe diabetes, scleroderma, post-gastric bypass, morbid obesity, severe pain, hiatal hernia, bowel obstruction, nasogastric tube, opioid use, upper GI bleeding, and pregnancy) require special preparation with medication and anesthetic technique. Patients with gastric esophageal reflux disease (GERD), dysphagia (difficulty swallowing), and gastroparesis (slow passage of food and liquid through the GI tract) should be evaluated on a case-by-case basis. In these patients, the traditional requirement for eight hours of fasting may be advisable, although research data is lacking. Use of histamine-2 blockers and agents to promote gastric motility may be useful, although not standard.

Aspiration is considered largely preventable with the use of certain techniques. Certain medications may also help protect the patient against aspiration or minimize the effects of aspiration should it occur.

Clear oral and written instructions on fasting must be given to patients well before surgery, and patients must be questioned regarding NPO status immediately prior to the anesthetic. A sip of water with medications taken the morning of surgery is considered acceptable. Elective surgery should be postponed if the patient has not followed NPO instructions. In this circumstance the surgery is commonly rescheduled for later in the day, when the patient is six to eight hours NPO.

Careful documentation offers some defense against liability for the consequences of aspiration. With any anesthetic technique in which the patient has lost airway reflexes, aspiration must be considered, even if no aspiration was observed. Rapid sequence induction (RSI) with cricoid pressure (pressure on the cricoid ring of the trachea to occlude the esophagus), and the placement of an endotracheal tube is the "gold standard" for definitive airway protection against aspiration. Awake intubation is a lesser-used alternative.

TIP: In cases involving aspiration of gastric contents, the analysis should focus on risk identification and the use of medication and maneuvers to prevent it.

The risk of aspiration cannot be completely eliminated. Any anesthetic and surgery may result in patient unconsciousness and loss of protective reflexes. Surgery planned as "straight local" (without anesthesia care) can suddenly become complicated and require anesthesia, and this puts the patient who is not NPO at serious risk. When anesthesia is consulted urgently in a case previously scheduled "straight local," there is some defense should aspiration occur. In emergent situations when the surgeon determines the risk of postponing surgery outweighs the risk of aspiration, the CRNA must plan techniques that reduce the risks as much as possible.

In *BB v. BW, CRNA, TT, MD*, No. 33-C2-93-000666 (Kanabec County, Minnesota, 1994) a 64-year-old woman required general anesthesia for repair of an incarcerated ventral hernia. She aspirated gastric contents at induction of general anesthesia and died one month later. The plaintiffs alleged the CRNA failed to take extra precautions necessary

to protect the patient who was at high risk for aspiration (because of obesity, symptoms of bowel obstruction, or narcotic medication). The plaintiff further maintained that the CRNA did not leave the patient supine during induction (versus head up), did not apply cricoid pressure, and did not administer a non-depolarizer prior to succinylcholine. Additionally, plaintiff alleged the CRNA conducted the extubation before the patient was sufficiently awake and failed to analyze blood gases when oxygen saturation fell to 92 percent. A $210,000 settlement was reached.[63]

C. Induction and Maintenance of General Anesthesia

Specific management of general anesthesia varies widely. CRNAs have preferred combinations of drugs and doses, as well as the timing of their administration. These combinations of drugs, doses, and even the timing are tailored to the individual patient and surgical procedure. Nevertheless, common features can be observed, and considerations for safety should be apparent in the management of the anesthetic.

TIP: Considerations for the safe use of the general anesthetic should be identified as a case is reviewed. Standards published by professional anesthesia organizations provide guidelines for management of a specific technique. These guidelines should be utilized by the expert witnesses in the analysis of a case.

Preoperative preparation includes confirmation of readiness and proper function of all equipment and supplies. Checklists should be utilized to assure complete preparedness. These checklists have been compared to preflight checklists used by pilots. The Food and Drug Administration has published an anesthesia machine checklist.[64] Intravenous and other necessary lines—arterial lines, central venous lines, and occasionally epidural catheters—may be started in a preoperative holding area. Sedation is frequently administered at this time, and the patient subsequently must be carefully and continuously monitored. The patient is then transported to the operating room, moved to the operating table, and positioned. A headrest may be used, and arm boards support the arms, or the arms are tucked at the patient's side. Electrocardiograph leads, blood pressure, and pulse oximetry monitors are placed, with the initiation of their use. Additional monitoring may also be initiated at this time, such as pulmonary artery catheter for pulmonary artery waveforms, peripheral nerve stimulator, and bispectral analysis monitor (BIS monitor for determining anesthetic depth).

TIP: If many hours or days have passed since the preanesthesia evaluation was conducted, it is necessary to document that the patient's condition is unchanged, or conversely, what significant change has occurred. It then becomes the judgment of the CRNA how to proceed, and this must be documented.

The anesthetic induction takes place after the patient is positioned on the operating room table, monitors are placed, and baseline vital signs are obtained. This includes administration of 100 percent oxygen, called preoxygenation or denitrogenation, and additional sedation and narcotics as deemed necessary by the anesthesia provider. A hypnotic (e.g., propofol, pentothal, or etomidate) is administered to induce "sleep," and the airway is managed by an anesthesia mask, a laryngeal mask airway, or an endotracheal tube. If the patient is to be intubated using an endotracheal tube, a neuromuscular blocking agent (e.g., succinylcholine, rocuronium, vecuronium) is typically utilized after the anesthesia provider confirms the ability to ventilate (breathe for) the patient via mask.

TIP: It is important to determine the ability to ventilate a patient before the patient is paralyzed. (The term "muscle relaxant" is generally used in place of the correct "neuromuscular blocking agent" when describing the use of paralytic agents.)

Ventilation is omitted if the patient is not NPO, or has significant likelihood of gastric contents, but pressure is applied to the cricoid cartilage until appropriate endotracheal tube position is confirmed by identification of CO_2 and auscultation of breath sounds over both lungs.

Managing the airway is an essential part of general anesthesia, and at this point difficulty may arise. "Can't ventilate, can't intubate (CVCI)," or "lost the airway" are critical phrases representing the situation in which the anesthetized patient cannot be ventilated by facemask, laryngeal mask airway, endotracheal tube, or any other method.

Emergency cricothyrotomy is the last resort. Difficult anatomy is the most common cause of this crisis. In most, but not all, cases the "difficult airway" can be identified during the preanesthetic evaluation, either by patient history or physical exam. There are several rating methods for predicting the ease or difficulty of placing an endotracheal tube, the most utilized being the Mallampatti scale, but it has been criticized as having low sensitivity and specificity.[65] The

ASA Difficult Airway Algorithm should be used when difficulty is encountered, with results documented in the medical record. Multiple attempts at intubation are more likely to result in death. The laryngeal mask airway should be utilized as a bridging measure to manage the airway, and usually works well even for patients who are difficult to intubate.[66] Most recently the use of video laryngoscopy is advocated for any anticipated difficult intubation.

In an Illinois case the 61-year-old plaintiff was admitted for hip replacement. Due to a previous bad experience with insertion of a breathing tube for general anesthesia, the plaintiff requested a spinal anesthetic. When the anesthesiologist had difficulty inserting the spinal needle into the intrathecal space, he proceeded with general anesthesia. After putting the patient to sleep and giving paralytic drugs the anesthesiologist was unable to insert the breathing tube. He planned on ventilating by mask, but another defendant anesthesiologist decided to try to intubate the patient, again without success. After a third anesthesiologist tried to intubate the plaintiff, she went into cardiac arrest, due to the anesthesiologists' inability to ventilate. Multiple attempts at intubation had caused massive swelling of airway tissues, making mask ventilation impossible. Eventually the plaintiff was resuscitated, but the cardiac arrest caused severe brain damage, She died three weeks later. Plaintiff argued that if she had been allowed to awaken after the initial attempts at intubation she would have survived, and that defendants were responsible for effectively ventilating and oxygenating her while waiting for the surgeon to perform an emergency tracheostomy. A $10,500,000 verdict was returned against the defendant anesthesiologists and their employer. The first anesthesiologisst settled for $975,000 just prior to trial.[67] *Estate of Nellie Hood, deceased v. Dr. Mario F. Magleo, Dr. Ruperto U. Buscaino, Noel G. Alcantara, M.D., S.C., Holy Cross Hospital,* Cook County (IL) Circuit Court, Case No. 05L-5414.

Failure to manage the airway is likely to be catastrophic for all associated with the event, as is evident by the large settlements and judgments meted out for this occurrence. Under the best circumstances there is about a two to three minute window of opportunity for the anesthesia provider to initiate effective ventilation for the non-breathing patient. Cyanosis is a late sign of difficulty, as is progressive bradycardia. Severely anemic patients will not become cyanotic.

An anaphylactic or anaphylactoid reaction to any drug administered in the perioperative period may occur, even with the best assessment, planning, and execution of the anesthetic, and loss of airway may suddenly occur due to swelling of tissues in the airway. Rapid and appropriate response is lifesaving.

TIP: Analysis of cases where airway problems occurred should include review of the medical record for pre-anesthetic airway evaluation, early calls for airway assistance, and utilization of the difficult airway cart and algorithm. Evidence of surgical intervention, where appropriate, should also be sought.

Although the above script for induction is usually followed, patients with airway risks should receive special care. Rapid sequence intubation (RSI) with cricoid pressure is appropriate for patients with a full stomach. In this circumstance, or if the patient is a difficult airway, an awake intubation using a fiberoptic intubating endoscope may be undertaken. An awake intubation preserves the patient's reflexes and ability to breath.

The administration of general anesthesia to children who are NPO may be undertaken by allowing the child to breathe oxygen, nitrous oxide, and an inhaled anesthetic—halothane or sevoflurane, but not isoflurane or desflurane. After the child loses consciousness, the intravenous catheter can be placed and drugs administered intravenously. An intravenous induction will, alternatively, be done if the child cooperates and an intravenous catheter can be placed prior to taking the child to the operating room. For elective cases, eutectic mixture of local anesthetics (EMLA) cream may be applied approximately 45 minutes prior to the case for a painless intravenous catheter insertion. An oral preparation of the sedative midazolam may also be given to children at this time.

There has been a trend toward regionalization of pediatric anesthesia care, although burgeoning ambulatory surgery centers have funneled cases from hospitals and medical centers. Pediatric anesthesia morbidity, historically, has been about 35 percent, compared with 17 percent for adults. One-third of children over five years experience postoperative nausea and vomiting, about double the rate experienced by adults.[68]

The highest rate of complications, including cardiac arrests, occurred in children less than one year old. Age was not a predictor, only ASA classification of 3-5. Medication-related causes of arrest have decreased. The use of sevoflurane has increased, and the use of halothane has decreased. Sevoflurane has more favorable pharmacodynamic and pharmacokinetic profiles than halothane. Succinylcholine use has decreased dramatically, leaving hyperkalemia from massive blood transfusion as a cause of cardiac arrest in children. The possibility of undiagnosed muscular dystrophy in children has generally precluded the use of succinylcholine. Cardiovascular causes of arrest have increased slightly.[69]

Maintaining proper depth of anesthesia during the procedure is both an art and a science, with the goals of hypnosis, analgesia, and amnesia. The anesthesia provider titrates inhaled and injected medications, based on monitoring traditional vital signs, arterial oxygen saturation, end-tidal CO_2, and exhaled anesthetic gases. A balance must be achieved between adequate anesthesia and patient safety. Too much anesthesia can result in inadequate tissue perfusion and gas exchange. Too little anesthesia may result in patient movement, awareness, and poor conditions for both surgeon and patient. The procedure and surgeon may require neuromuscular blockade. The anesthesia provider then administers a paralyzing agent and monitors patient response to the paralytic using the peripheral nerve stimulator.

There are other special techniques and considerations that vary with the type of surgical procedure. Some examples are:

1. obstetrical anesthesia, involving the considerations of protecting the fetus and limiting uterine relaxation and blood loss;
2. deliberate hypotensive technique to limit blood loss during intracranial procedures, spine procedures, and plastic and reconstructive surgery;
3. brain protection with barbiturates for neurosurgical procedures and for vascular procedures where complete circulatory arrest must be utilized (repair of aneurysm of the ascending aorta);
4. major vascular procedures such as repair of abdominal aortic aneurysm may require a dopamine infusion for reno-vascular protection;
5. pulmonary artery pressure, thermodilution, and transesophageal echocardiographic monitoring for open heart and major vascular procedures, and for severely compromised cardiac patients having non-cardiac surgery; and
6. epidural catheters utilized to supplement general anesthesia intraoperatively, and to provide for postoperative pain relief.

TIP: The primary consideration for CRNAs is maintaining patient safety while providing optimal surgical conditions and patient satisfaction. Planning and communication are necessary for the best outcomes. The CRNA makes judgments throughout the case based on issues of patient comfort and safety, as well as surgeon preference.

D. Patient Monitoring

The primary monitors are the senses of the CRNA. Early CRNAs utilized the five senses to monitor patients, with considerable safety. Introduction of new technologies has improved patient safety, but it is apparent that when monitors are utilized inappropriately and the senses are not applied to patient monitoring, the patient may be irreversibly injured.

Reviews of recent "anesthetic disasters" reveal similarities. Three cases were reported in which patients suffered either severe brain damage or death. The common elements were inactivation of pulse oximeter, end-tidal CO_2, and ventilator low pressure monitor alarms, and preoccupation by the anesthesia provider that caused the provider to leave the patient's head for an extended amount of time. Only upon the provider's return to the patient's head was it apparent ventilation had been interrupted. Lack of focused vigilance, a primary requisite for patient safety, was evident in these cases.[70]

TIP: Review of anesthetic disasters should include, in the discovery phase, questions about monitor alarms and activities which may have taken the provider away from the patient's head.

The process of monitoring includes a vigilant mindset and is a loop among patient, monitors, and provider. Both the ASA and AANA publish monitoring standards, which are refined as new modalities are added and improved. The standards establish the standard of care by which CRNAs are judged. Introduction of a new modality presents a challenge for attorneys reviewing a case. A period of time elapses before a modality becomes a standard of care, but when the monitor significantly contributes to patient safety, as supported by clinical studies and its acceptance in the professional community, it becomes a standard of care.[71] In 1996, the FDA approved the use of the Bispectral Index (BIS) Monitor for measuring the hypnotic component of the anesthetic. Bispectral Electroencephalographic Monitoring is a method of EEG monitoring and processing through the use of an algorithm. BIS monitoring demonstrates an increasing degree of coherence of EEG frequency bands as sleep occurs and deepens, and represents this coherence as a score of awareness on a scale of 0-100: 100 is "wide awake," between 40 and 60 represents sleep (as might occur using a hypnotic agent such as propofol), and 0 represents an isoelectric EEG (as might occur in a patient with a barbiturate-induced coma or brain death). BIS values of 40-60 represent adequate hypnosis for general anesthesia and the ability to recover to consciousness quickly.

A potential benefit with the use of the BIS monitor includes improved titration of hypnotic medications, thus reducing the incidence of underdosing and overdosing, which may occur when individual patient variability is coupled with the wide variety of events that are part of surgical and anesthetic practice. Increased appreciation of the patient's anesthetic state allows for better assurance of adequate anesthetic depth, as well as more rapid emergence from anesthesia, which has implications for improved, more cost-effective patient care.

Perhaps the major advantage offered by the BIS monitor is reduced risk of awareness during anesthesia. Recent publicity in the mass media about awareness under anesthesia has increased public concern, as well as increased interest in technology designed to reduce awareness risk. The simplistic viewpoint that a monitor will eliminate risk is inconsistent with the complex nature of the problem. Although lack of vigilance may be responsible for some cases of awareness, a variety of other factors may be responsible, such as type of surgery, medications, and anesthetic techniques. Awareness is more common in trauma surgery, open-heart surgery, and cesarean sections (where concern for fetal well-being may influence choice and dose of medications).[72]

Awareness as an anesthetic problem was reviewed by Sigalovsky,[73] who cites the incidence of 0.18 percent in patients receiving muscle relaxants, and at 0.10 percent for patients not receiving that class of drugs. Litwiller[74] addressed the problem of expectation, supporting the anesthesia community's continued reliance on sound clinical studies to further define the problem and its solution rather than succumb to lay media pressure to define a new and decidedly expensive standard of care. In response to additional research and public concern, the ASA introduced a Practice Advisory for Intraoperative Awareness and Brain Function Monitoring. The anesthesia provider is encouraged to carefully consider the use of brain function monitors in patients at high risk for intraoperative awareness.[75] It may be that the courts will define the new standard in a future trial case, as occurred in a 1987 case:

> The District Court of Columbia Appellate Court affirmed that failure to monitor end-tidal CO_2 contributed to the patient's death (i.e., unrecognized esophageal intubation), and that a prudent hospital should have purchased and required the use of a monitoring device which had previously been rec-

ommended by the ASA (1985) and in the Harvard monitoring standards (also 1985). *Washington v. Washington Hospital Center*, 579 A.2d 177 (D.C. App.1990).[76]

TIP: Development of new monitoring techniques extends the senses and capabilities of the anesthesia provider but does not reduce the responsibilities of the vigilant, artful provider of anesthesia care.

---

1. Frequency of monitoring parameters

There are two factors to consider: frequency of monitoring and frequency of recording. Real-time monitors like EKG, SaO_2, end-tidal CO_2, and inhaled and exhaled gas concentration (Fi/Fe) monitors (system of anesthesia and respiratory analysis) provide continuous information, with numeric information and as a waveform, which may be valuable in identifying problems and aiding diagnosis.

Non-invasive blood pressures are taken as often as every minute or as infrequently as every five minutes, based on the stability of the patient per the judgment of the CRNA. These values are recorded on the anesthesia record as frequently as every five minutes (heart rate and blood pressure) or as infrequently as every 15 minutes (temperature, end-tidal CO_2, SpO_2, Fi/Fe anesthetic gases, ventilator settings, urine output, estimated blood loss).

Response to the peripheral nerve stimulator (PNS) is also recorded to document degree of neuromuscular blockade when neuromuscular blockers are given. Parameters such as central venous pressure, pulmonary artery pressure and cardiac output are recorded in similar fashion. Time is plotted on the horizontal axis, and measurements and values are plotted beneath the appropriate times.

2. Monitoring fluid status

The CRNA is responsible for tracking blood loss and communicating losses to other members of the surgical team, especially informing them of changes in the patient's condition. Monitoring changes in fluid status is essential to maintaining normal vascular volumes, supporting perfusion of vital organs. Failure to replace lost volume can injure vital organs such as the brain, heart, kidney, liver, spinal cord, and the optic nerve.

Insensible fluid loss and fluid shifts cannot be directly measured, but must be estimated and considered as fluids are replaced. Urine output and concentration direct the CRNA in determining the amount and rate of fluid replacement. Blood pressure and heart rate initially change very little as fluid deficit accrues, and the CRNA must estimate, using other values, the amount of fluid replacement required.

TIP: There is no scientific rationale for stimulating the kidneys with a dose of Lasix. Lasix merely prevents plasma previously filtered by the kidneys from being reabsorbed in the tubules.

The type of surgery scheduled is predictive of blood loss. Planning for anesthesia includes anticipating fluid and blood requirements, and intravenous access must be sufficient to deliver large amounts of fluid in a relatively short period of time. Short, large bore catheters provide fast rates of flow. Flow is proportional to radius to the fourth power, so a slightly larger intravenous catheter allows for much more flow. It is difficult to start a large bore intravenous line in a patient who has already become dehydrated and anemic. In some cases the arms may be tucked and not accessible to the CRNA.

Blood loss can be measured directly in canisters, but may need to be estimated from surgical sponges and accumulation on drapes, gowns, and even the OR floor. Loss of blood, and concomitant loss of oxygen-carrying capacity may be so great as to cause severe tachycardia and ECG changes. This typically happens only when the patient has previously lost large amounts of blood preoperatively, which may occur in patients with ruptured aortic aneurysms, or ectopic pregnancies and trauma.

Less often, fluid overload and electrolyte imbalance may result when irrigation fluids are used by surgeons during urinary tract procedures and diagnostic laparoscopies. Patients with renal insufficiency and failure may come to the OR with excess volume. These situations may be further complicated if the patient's heart is unable to tolerate the increased amount of circulating volume.

TIP: Case analysis should identify the rationale for the fluid and blood administration. It is more effective to utilize an expert to dissect the intricacies of the anesthesia record.

Markarian points out that the anesthesia record provides a great deal of information, but also recognizes the impossibility of charting everything that is seen, felt, heard, and measured.[77] Records should ideally be contemporaneous, but during induction, emergence, and unstable periods, this rarely happens. The electronic record helps, but does not completely resolve this problem.[78]

E. Providing Safe Emergence at the Proper Time

The timing of emergence from general anesthesia is an art. Patient variability plays a role in timing the emergence.

Intravenous and inhaled anesthetics are discontinued near the end of the case, as judged by the skill, knowledge, and experience of the CRNA, so that the hypnotic effects may wear off. Inhaled agents are exhaled, while injected agents are redistributed from the brain and metabolized by enzyme systems of the liver, kidneys, adrenals, and blood.

The effects of neuromuscular blocking agents are reversed, with the dose of the reversal agents guided by use of the peripheral nerve stimulator. It may not be possible to fully reverse the effects of the paralyzing agent if the dose was too large or administered too near the end of the case. It may also be necessary to reverse the effects of narcotics and sedatives, although this is done infrequently.

Administration of reversal agents does not guarantee full return of physiologic function. The CRNA administers 100 percent oxygen as the patient fully emerges and is extubated, providing some degree of oxygen reserve should the patient have an airway, breathing, or circulation problem at this crucial time. Vigilance must be maintained for the rare situations in which the reversal is not sustained.

TIP: Use of the peripheral nerve stimulator is a standard of care when the patient has been given neuromuscular blocking agents. The emergence from anesthesia is considered so important that Centers for Medicare and Medicaid Services' regulations demand the physical presence of the medically directing anesthesiologist during emergence.

Most patients undergo tracheal extubation in the operating room, although there are circumstances in which it is inappropriate to do so. These patients remain intubated in the recovery room and may require mechanical ventilation. Unanticipated changes in airway, breathing, or circulation require the patient remain in the OR until stabilized.

In *Green v. Schoum* the plaintiff's 63-year-old decedent was taken to the emergency room where he was diagnosed with a perforation of a viscous organ and pneumoperitoneum. He was then taken to the operating room where general anesthesia was induced, with requisite placement of an endotracheal tube. During the subsequent surgery the anesthesiologist removed the endotracheal tube. The decedent stopped breathing and suffered brain damage. He never regained consciousness, dying 11 months after the surgery. Plaintiff alleged that the endotracheal tube was removed prematurely, and that if necessary a tracheostomy or cricothyroidotomy should have been performed to restore

the airway. Defendant claimed decedent demonstrated the ability to breathe without the endotracheal tube. Claims against the surgeon and hospital were dropped. A $2 million settlement with the anesthesiologist was reached.[79] *Dagmar Green, as Guardian for Her Husband Irving Green, etc. v. Steven Schoum, M.D. et al., Island Medical Pain Management Services, P.C., Atlantic Medical Anesthesia Associates, P.C., Burton Glass, M.D. et al.,* Nassau County (NY) Supreme Court, Index No. 4593/04.

Emergence from anesthesia has been compared with landing an airplane. It is a dynamic period of return of reflexes and awareness, and requires the complete attention of the CRNA. Blood pressure and heart rate may vary widely during this time, despite the best efforts of the CRNA, and may require treatment so a normal physiologic state may be preserved.

In *Bainhauer, Jr. v. Lehigh Valley Hospital* a dose of the antiemetic drug droperidol, was administered to the plaintiff-patient by the CRNA at the end of a parathyroidectomy procedure. Droperidol is known to cause hypotension. The blood pressure was recorded as being low at the time of administration. The plaintiff, known to have a preoperative diagnosis of essential hypertension, subsequently manifested signs of a stroke. Plaintiff argued that the droperidol should not have been administered since he was hypotensive at the time of administration. Also at issue was the intraoperative use of the vasopressor phenylephrine. As documented in the notes of the resident who had assisted the surgeon, this was administered by the anesthesiologist. It was maintained by plaintiff that the defendants had failed to provide proper follow-up care after his surgery, when he was suffering from hypotension. The jury found no negligence on the part of defendants (i.e., hospital, physician, nurses). Plaintiff-patient appealed. The Superior Court of Pennsylvania vacated the trial court's decision and the case was remanded for a new trial. *Bainhauer v. Lehigh Valley Hospital*, 834 A.2d 1146, 2003 PA Super. 338, No. 3461 EDA 2002, (2003).[80]

F. Postanesthesia Care

When the CRNA is satisfied the patient is stable, transfer to the postanesthesia care unit (PACU) is initiated. Transfer technique requires careful assessment of the patient's stability before the move as well as consideration of the need for supplemental oxygen and monitoring in route. Adequate manpower is required for movement of the patient from the OR table to the stretcher. In some settings, critically ill or unstable patients are transferred directly to the intensive care unit (ICU). Direct transfer to the ICU may also occur if the PACU is closed nights and weekends. The same standards apply for postanesthesia care, whether it is delivered in the PACU or the ICU.

TIP: Transfer of the patient is under the direct control and authority of the anesthesia providers. It is inappropriate for this authority to be usurped by another healthcare provider. It is likewise inappropriate to delegate the responsibility to non-anesthesia personnel.

The PACU is a critical care unit with special standards of its own. The American Society of Peri Anesthesia Nurses (ASPAN) publishes guidelines and standards for postanesthesia nursing care. Postanesthesia care is also addressed by the AANA and ASA.

Postanesthesia nurses function as members of the anesthesia care team, although their chain of command may be derived through either the director of perioperative nursing or the director of anesthesia. CRNAs are required to provide a detailed report of the patient's condition, anesthetic and surgical course, anesthesia techniques, intraoperative medications, and history. CRNAs must ensure the stability of the patient before releasing him to the PACU nurse. All postoperative orders should be clarified before the CRNA releases the patient to PACU or ICU care. This importantly includes postoperative pain orders. Pain is the fifth vital sign. The patient may be on the pain service of the anesthesia department; if such is the case, all pain and sedation orders will be coming from anesthesia.

TIP: The anesthesia provider should never release a patient to the care of non-anesthesia personnel if those personnel are not fully capable of caring for the patient.

Availability of anesthesia providers to provide routine and emergency care in the PACU should be clearly defined to ensure that any deterioration in the status of the PACU patient is immediately addressed. A patient with an airway or ventilatory problem may need to be urgently intubated. Surgeons direct some aspects of PACU nursing care, especially those related to postoperative monitoring of bleeding, extremity pulses, and wound care. Anesthesia and surgery cooperate in management of surgical complications involving or affecting the airway. In these cases, the patient may

need to be emergently reintubated and returned to the OR for definitive surgical care. (See Chapter 5, *Perioperative Nursing Malpractice Issues*, for more information on the responsibilities of the PACU nurse.)

A 29-year-old plaintiff's decedent underwent a partial thyroidectomy. A neck hematoma developed shortly after surgery, but went undiagnosed for several hours. Massive internal and external swelling of neck caused airway compromise and breathing difficulty, and at that time the anesthesiologist was called to the decedent's bed. The defendant anesthesiologist believed that intubation would be difficult or impossible due to the swelling, and decided to wait for the surgeon's arrival. (The surgeon had been called when the hematoma had been identified.) Respiratory arrest occurred before the surgeon arrived, and the anesthesiologist attempted to intubate the decedent but was unsuccessful. Death occurred secondary to hypoxia and brain injury. Plaintiff claimed intubation should have been attempted immediately. Defendant argued that he had acted reasonably, and that neck hematoma was a surgical complication requiring surgical treatment. A defense verdict was returned.[81] *Shawna M. Core et al. v. Anonymous Anesthesiology Defendants.* Fairfax County (VA) Circuit court, Case No. 2007-13185.

TIP: The process of transport of the patient to the PACU, and subsequent release of care to the PACU nurse, can be complicated by unexpected patient deterioration. Communication of essential information may be missed during this period. Case analysis should examine whether problems were anticipated and if measures were taken to deal with these problems.

After the patient meets discharge criteria showing recovery from the immediate effects of anesthesia, her care is released to the surgeon for transfer to the appropriate nursing unit, ICU, or same-day unit to home. These patient movements are primarily driven by written protocol and discharge criteria. Policies for discharge criteria and assumption of patient responsibility are described in PACU policies, obtainable in discovery.

G. Fast-Tracking

Fast-tracking is a developing set of anesthesia techniques aimed at speeding recovery from anesthesia as well as improving outcomes, with the overall goal of reducing healthcare costs. Clinical use of newer agents with rapid onset and fast emergence may result in a patient who is able to bypass the PACU and go directly to a nursing unit or a step-down PACU—commonly called Phase II—before being discharged home. Fast-tracking has been aided by the development of minimally invasive surgery.[82]

Postoperative complications such as pain, shivering, nausea, and vomiting can limit the success of fast-tracking, as can the selection of patients with complicated medical problems. Over-aggressive fast-tracking reduces the quality of patient care and increases liability. Fast-tracking is also being applied to post-cardiac surgery patients, with earlier extubation and shorter lengths of stay than conventional postoperative courses.[83]

Changes in medications and techniques which contribute to the success of a fast-track program must be part of a carefully planned program, with close surveillance of patients and outcomes. Use of newer hypnotic and inhalation agents has been studied in the ambulatory surgery setting. Gupta et al. looked at recovery from propofol, isoflurane, sevoflurane, and desflurane. No agent was at a significant disadvantage in terms of time to eye-opening and following commands. Propofol reduced the incidence of nausea and vomiting, compared with the other agents. Nausea and vomiting have a cost in terms of increased recovery time due to delayed discharge.[84] Fast-tracking may not reduce nursing workload after ambulatory surgery.[85]

H. Postanesthesia Surveillance

Postanesthesia follow-up, assessment, and intervention are integral parts of care on the anesthesia continuum. Patients should be visited—or telephoned if rapidly discharged from the hospital—to assess for postanesthesia complications. A variety of minor complications are common: sore throat, fatigue, mild headache, and muscle aches. Serious sequelae such as neurologic changes, heart failure, pneumonia, atelectasis, and myocardial ischemia should be documented and appropriate interventions implemented.

Anesthesia providers should address serious anesthetic complications with a follow-up letter to the patient. Complications triggering a follow-up letter might include airway difficulty, anaphylactic reactions, or unusual responses to medications, knowledge of which might have profound and positive influence on future anesthetic care. A standard template should be developed to reduce confusion, improve compliance, and enable all affected patients to receive full benefit. Patients should be advised of the importance of transmitting such information to future anesthesia providers. The attorney should ask the patient if she has ever received such a letter.

I. Products Used in Anesthesia

Adverse outcomes may be related to products used in the care of the patient. Administration of anesthesia involves multiple monitors, disposable and reusable products, and medications, all of which have a potential for causing harm to the patient. Decisions to use the many products utilized in the OR are usually made independently of the CRNA, and most are cost-driven.

Whenever a new product, medication, or piece of equipment is introduced, risk increases due to unfamiliarity, confusion, and hesitation. For example, inability to successfully prime unfamiliar intravenous pump tubing and set up the intravenous pump delays treatment, causes stress to the CRNA, and may result in an unintended dose of medication or fluid to be delivered to the patient. The process may be successful but could distract the CRNA, preventing or delaying that provider from making an important observation or initiating necessary treatment.

Whether a hospital or anesthesia department is liable for misadventure of an employed CRNA utilizing a newly introduced product may be a theoretical issue, given that the user of any equipment needs to read the package insert or other information, instructions, and warnings, and utilize the product only in a way intended by the manufacturer. However, if the equipment was evaluated and selected by the employer, and the CRNA obligated to use it, then it could be argued that both the CRNA and employer are potentially liable.

The Anesthesia Patient Safety Foundation (APSF) publishes research and clinical updates on anesthesia-related products. Both the AANA and ASA address safety issues as part of their overriding objectives. Experimental products can only be utilized after giving specific informed consent and after the institutional review board (IRB) of the institution has given approval for all facets of product use.

TIP: In a product liability suit, the reviewing attorneys should determine whether the employed anesthesia provider had opportunity to review product information prior to use, received education on the intended application, and was cautioned about risks and benefits. The question might be asked, "Was there a reasonable alternative to using that product?"

---

1. The anesthesia machine

The anesthesia machine is a complex, multi-functional apparatus which delivers medical-quality "fresh gases"—oxygen, nitrous oxide, air—that can carry potent, volatile, anesthetic inhalation agents—isoflurane, halothane, desflurane, or sevoflurane—to the patient. Metered amounts of the fresh gases are diverted through a calibrated vaporizer and pick up precise volumes of the inhaled anesthetic agent. The combination of fresh gas and inhaled anesthetic are delivered to the patient through a breathing circuit connected to any of several airway devices—mask, endotracheal tube, laryngeal mask airway, tracheostomy tube—and deliver the selected gases to the patient's airway, lungs, bloodstream, and eventually the brain to provide general anesthesia.

The fresh gas and inhaled agent mixture can be delivered to the lungs by the patient's own spontaneous breathing. The CRNA may also assist ventilation by squeezing the anesthesia (breathing) bag to deliver the agent; completely control breathing by ventilating at a rate greater than the patient's; or control ventilation automatically by switching an integral mechanical ventilator into the breathing circuit. Controlled mechanical ventilation may be facilitated by narcotics and neuromuscular blocking agents, and frees the CRNA's hands. The ventilator settings of tidal volume, rate of breathing, and rate of gas flow are set and adjusted by the anesthesia provider based on the patient's body habitus, physiologic condition, anesthetic objective, and surgical necessity. Typically, the ventilator is not used at the beginning and end of a case, but saves labor and provides stability during the surgery, which may last many hours.

The latest standards for anesthesia machines and workstations come from the American Society for Testing and Materials.[86] Anesthesia machines and monitors manufactured before promulgation of the 2000 standards likely do not meet all requirements. The institution and anesthesia provider department are responsible for examining and certifying the safety of the machine and monitors, in conjunction with the biomedical department or designee. Many hospitals contract the testing and maintenance of the machine to an outside service. It has been proposed that anesthesia machines incorporating ventilators with hanging bellows should be replaced.

TIP: When machine malfunction is suspected as causing or contributing to injury, the attorney should review department policies for preventive maintenance and repair, as well as all documentation associated with this process.

Fresh gases are piped in from large tanks located on the hospital premises, with small backup tanks attached to the anesthesia machine. The inhaled agents are contained in small but sufficient amounts in the machine's agent-specific vaporizers. The accumulation of CO_2 in the breathing circuit is prevented by the inclusion of canisters of soda lime or baralyme which neutralize the CO_2 in an exothermic re-

action. The breathing circuit of the anesthesia machine is called the circle-system because it recirculates exhaled gases thus allowing low flow of fresh gases, conserving patient heat, humidity, and the cost of the inhaled agent.

A self-inflating resuscitation bag ("ambu bag") must be present in the rare case of machine failure or loss of gas pressure. Anesthesia machines have become increasingly complex but also have more safety features added to prevent an operating situation that is potentially unsafe for the patient.

Integrated monitors with built-in adjustable alarms that intercommunicate make the machine system more flexible and adjustable, but with more potential for distraction. The CRNA must monitor the patient directly with the help of the anesthesia machine and monitors, but the CRNA must also program and monitor the machine. It is not responsible for the CRNA to deliver anesthesia on "auto-pilot" (not paying attention to the machine and monitors, but instead relying on alarms).

2. Monitors used in anesthesia

The CRNA is the primary monitor, using the senses to observe color, temperature, breathing, and pulse. Ideally a monitor should have no risk of injury to the patient and reliably provide valid information. Monitors provide information that needs interpretation, and therefore do not lessen the responsibility of the anesthesia provider. Standard monitors are not invasive, have no significant risk, and thus do not require special informed consent. Standard monitoring includes precordial or esophageal stethoscope, blood pressure, electrocardiograph (ECG), pulse oximeter, temperature, end-tidal CO_2, and oxygen percentage (when an anesthesia machine is utilized).

Invasive monitoring techniques have significant risk, and a consideration of risk versus benefit must be judged before use and should be accompanied by special consent. Typically this special consent can be added to the anesthesia consent form as a note documenting the communication with the patient. Invasive monitoring in anesthesia practice includes intra-arterial pressure monitoring, central venous pressure monitoring, and pulmonary artery pressure monitoring (giving the anesthetist the ability to measure cardiac output and derive hemodynamic values that are otherwise unavailable). The main risk associated with invasive monitoring is injury to blood vessels and adjacent structures. Specific injuries related to central vein cannulation, and known to cause death, include perforation of the heart with pericardial tamponade, catheter, or wire embolism, and injuries to veins and arteries other than the pulmonary artery.[87] Inadvertent placement of a catheter or introducer into an artery rather than vein continues to be a life-threatening problem. Two approaches have been recommended: 1) use portable two-dimensional ultrasound devices, and 2) identify the vessel as artery or vein via transduction of the vessel pressure waveform. Doppler technology helps to better identify blood vessels and adjacent structures, and more efficiently and safely place central venous catheters and introducers. Injury and fatality rates have decreased since 1990, as compared with the two previous decades.[88]

Breath sounds and heart sounds can be monitored using a basic stethoscope or the anesthesia precordial stethoscope. The precordial stethoscope consists of a weighted bell connected to a fitted earpiece with a length of flexible rubber tubing. The provider can listen to breath sounds and heart tones continuously throughout the case, which is the traditional care model. It is estimated less than half of the anesthesia provider population regularly utilizes a precordial stethoscope in practice. Adding a self-contained sphygmomanometer allows blood pressure to be taken. Use of an adjustable, automatic oscillometric blood pressure monitor is now a practical standard.

An ECG monitor with five leads enables continuous monitoring for heart rate and rhythm as well as for myocardial ischemia and injury, and has the ability to generate a rhythm strip for analysis. A three-lead ECG can be used for patients with minimal ischemic or dysrhythmic risk.

An oxygen analyzer is considered by some authorities as the most important monitor because it prevents a hypoxic mixture of gases from being delivered to the patient. An in-circuit monitor for oxygen concentration should include a low percentage threshold alarm.

Pressure and volume monitors in the breathing circuit prevent barotrauma injuries, as well as breathing circuit disconnections and low volume situations that could be fatal if undetected. Ventilation should be monitored continuously with any anesthesia technique, including sedation technique. Any technique requiring artificial airway support requires continuous monitoring of end-tidal CO_2.

The end-tidal CO_2 monitor samples gases from the breathing circuit, face mask, or nasal cannula to create a waveform and present a value of CO_2 on the monitor. The presence of a waveform with significant sustained value reassures the anesthesia provider that ventilation is taking place. The end-tidal value, derived from the plateau of the end-tidal waveform, correlates most closely with the arterial CO_2 in the awake, non-sedated patient, and correlates to a lesser degree in the sedated, anesthetized patient. The degree of divergence of the end-tidal CO_2 and arterial CO_2 values may depend as much on blood pressure and cardiac output as on respiratory function, provided ventilation ex-

ists. Interpretation of any end-tidal value is essential for safe anesthesia care.[89]

Pulse oximetry (oxygen saturation) values, usually abbreviated as SpO_2 or SaO_2, are obtained via a sensor placed on a thumb or finger and are accompanied by an arterial waveform. Special adhesive, disposable sensors are available for application to the bridge of the nose, ear lobe, or digit. Continuous "real-time" monitoring of arterial oxygenation is essential for safe anesthesia care. Interpretation of values is usually unnecessary, but artifact may be produced by movement, electrical interference, and intravenous injection of various dyes for diagnostic purposes. Sustained SaO_2 values below 50, although not reliable, are valid when accompanied by the arterial waveform, in the sense that the patient needs immediate evaluation and intervention. The basic risk associated with pulse oximetry occurs when the patient, with a finger or thumb sensor, is emerging from anesthesia and attempts to rub an eye; corneal abrasions have resulted in this way and would be considered *res ipsa loquitur*.

Temperature monitoring is accomplished with either a temperature strip or an esophageal stethoscope. The temperature strip offers no risk other than inaccuracy. The esophageal stethoscope, utilized only with general endotracheal tube anesthesia (GETA), creates a minor risk of injury to the lips of laceration or abrasion, or rarely, perforation of the esophagus. Unintended placement of the esophageal stethoscope into the trachea has occurred and may result in delivery of inadequate tidal volumes due to rupture or displacement of the endotracheal tube cuff. Proximity of the esophageal stethoscope to the endotracheal tube may result in falsely low temperature readings, due to the cooling effect of unwarmed anesthetic gases.[90]

Systemic arterial "lines," used to continuously and accurately measure blood pressure, present significant risk of nerve and vascular injury. Thrombosis of the artery, with loss of blood supply to the extremity, is possible. Radial artery catheter placement is safer than brachial artery or femoral artery placement, due to the normal large collateral circulation offered by the ulnar artery, but the modified Allen's test used to establish collateral ulnar flow adequacy is not a reliable indicator.[91] The value of continuous arterial pressure monitoring is related both to the procedure as well as the patient's morbidity, and is a judgment in most cases. Technology includes special catheter over needle devices, fluid-filled transducer systems, transducer cables, and the pressure monitor which is generally a modality available with anesthesia monitoring systems. Equipment failure is rare.

Monitoring of central venous and pulmonary artery pressures may be indicated for patients with serious cardiopulmonary dysfunction, and for patients undergoing major cardiovascular procedures. As with systemic arterial pressure monitoring, there is significant risk, including accidental carotid artery injury, air embolus, infection, pulmonary artery rupture, cardiac rhythm disturbances, and cardiac conduction block.[92]

Pulmonary artery monitoring offers the ability to measure cardiac output and derive values for resistance, improving the anesthesia provider's ability to optimize cardiac output and systemic blood flow. A central vein, usually either the internal jugular via the neck, or subclavian vein via the chest, must be cannulated (catheterized) to allow passage of the pulmonary artery catheter through the heart to the lung. As with systemic pressure monitoring, special technology is involved, and invasive pressure monitoring has a cost of time as well as risk. Production pressure may impact the decision to include invasive monitoring of systemic and central pressures and cardiac output. Patients may arrive in the OR with other invasive monitoring devices in place, such as epidural or ventricular catheters for monitoring intracranial pressures. These devices create additional responsibility for the anesthesia provider and can provide benefit or serve as a distraction, especially when a problem exists prior to the patient's arrival in the OR. Review of all perioperative records is necessary when a problem with an invasive monitor inserted prior to arrival in the OR is suspected.

Anesthesia providers may also be required to access a central vein for intravenous feedings. Such was the case of *L.B. v. Dr. Deborah Johnson et al.*, Trempealeau County (WI).[93] The 74-year-old plaintiff fell at home, rupturing her spleen. After emergency surgery, she suffered complications necessitating removal of part of her intestines, and she needed intravenous feedings through a central vein catheter. The defendant anesthesiologist used the internal jugular approach, but inadvertently placed the large catheter into the adjacent carotid artery without recognizing the error. The subsequent confirmatory x-ray revealed an abnormality, and a later x-ray was recommended by the consulting radiologist. In dispute was whether this finding and recommendation was adequately communicated to the anesthesiologist. No lateral x-ray or other confirmatory tests were done to show proper position of the catheter. Intravenous feedings were begun and the highly lipid and concentrated feeding solution circulated to the brain and caused several small strokes, ultimately leaving her left side partially paralyzed. With preexisting crippling rheumatoid arthritis, and then paralyzed, plaintiff needed admission to a nursing home for long term care. A

verdict was returned for $1,123,448, with the anesthesiologist totally at fault.

3. Medications

The selection of anesthetic agents and anesthesia adjuncts from the many available for administration is an important aspect of anesthesia care. These agents and adjuncts are administered through multiple routes: inhaled via mask, laryngeal mask airway, or endotracheal tube; injected intravenously (most common route); injected subcutaneously (infiltration of tissue for placement of peripheral intravenous and central venous catheters, intra-arterial lines, epidural catheters, and subarachnoid space intrathecal (spinal) injection); transdermally (nitropaste, scopolamine, narcotics); and sublingually (nitroglycerin).

General knowledge of pharmacodynamic and pharmacokinetic principles, specific knowledge of the pharmacodynamics and pharmacokinetics of the specific drugs used, and the interactions with other specific anesthetic and non-anesthetic medication used, is essential for safe, effective anesthesia. Knowledge of the patient's health status and the surgical plan is equally important because these affect choice of technique, selection of agents, and consideration for doses and titration.[94]

In *Roberts v. Cox*, an infant scheduled for tympanoplasties, adenoidectomy, and maxillary sinus drainage underwent a mask induction with oxygen, nitrous oxide, and halothane. *Roberts v. Cox*, 669 So.2d 63 (LA App. 1996). After two unsuccessful attempts to place an intravenous line, the infant was administered 30 mg of succinylcholine intramuscularly to facilitate placement of the endotracheal tube. Following a straightforward intubation, with visual, auscultatory, and end-tidal CO_2 confirmation of proper endotracheal tube placement, the surgeon turned the infant's head to begin the tympanoplasty. The patient then went into asystolic cardiac arrest. CPR was initiated, and epinephrine and atropine were administered through the endotracheal tube (consistent with Pediatric Advance Life Support guidelines), with tube position again being confirmed. The infant was successfully resuscitated, but subsequently suffered some temporary developmental setbacks. The surgery was rescheduled and completed without incident the following year. The child subsequently was diagnosed with Becker's muscular dystrophy. The infant's family filed a negligence action against the anesthesiologist, claiming that an improper and negligent esophageal intubation was performed. The family maintained the case should have been postponed until an intravenous line was started. Defendant argued the cause of the arrest was a hyperkalemic response to succinylcholine, common in patients with muscular dystrophy, and that starting a case without an intravenous line did not fall below the standard of care. Multiple expert witnesses supported the anesthesiologist in his decisions. A verdict was entered in favor of defendant, within both the lower and appellate courts. Affirming the judgment for the defendants, the Louisiana Appellate Court held that the anesthesiologist could not be accountable for knowledge of a diagnosis that had not yet been made.[95] Today a different verdict would likely occur, with the anesthesia community feeling that succinylcholine should be avoided in this age group.

After the introduction of the non-depolarizing neuromuscular blocking agent rocuronium (which can be used in place of the depolarizing neuromuscular blocking agent succinylcholine, and does not cause release of potassium from the cells) it has become inappropriate to administer succinylcholine to children because of the possibility of undiagnosed muscular dystrophy. Pediatricians are urged to screen their patients for the presence of occult myopathy.[96] A possible exception to the exclusion of succinylcholine in the unscreened child might be a life-threatening laryngospasm requiring immediate neuromuscular blockade.

In a New Jersey case a 43-year-old man fell 15 feet from a ladder and suffered a fractured spine. He was in the intensive care unit and mechanically ventilated for three days. After being taken off ventilatory support and extubated, the patient had difficulty breathing. The physician subsequently considered reintubating the patient, but held off, hoping for improvement in the patient's breathing. Anticipating the patient would be reintubated, the ICU nurse filled a syringe with succinylcholine, a medication used to paralyze the patient for intubation. The syringe was not labeled. The patient was not reintubated. When the doctor ordered morphine for pain the nurse mistakenly gave the succinylcholine. The patient stopped breathing, could not be reintubated, and died. The case settled for $1.5 million. *Estate of Rabatin v. Barrter.*[97]

This case illustrates the importance of exercising care in the selection, labeling, and delivery of intravenous (IV) fluids and medications. Administration of a blood product requires double-checks and signatures for patient identity by bracelet and the blood product's label to reduce the chance of transfusion reaction due to clerical error. Please refer to Figure 20.2 to appreciate the scope of pharmacologic agents available to anesthetists.

20.5 Safety in the Operating Room
A. Positioning

Positioning the patient safely is a responsibility jointly shared by the anesthesia and surgical teams.[98] In cases involving positioning injury, mechanisms of injury may be obscure,[99] or may occur without any apparent etiology. Thompson and Lui discuss the possibility of preexisting subclinical (without symptom or sign) neuropathies that may contribute to an injury. The *ASA Closed Claim Study*[100] describes distinctive features of ulnar nerve injury cases: less than 10 percent of cases showed an evident mechanism for nerve injury, and 27 percent had ulnar nerve injury despite the use of protective padding. These features suggest that unrecognized mechanisms of ulnar nerve damage may exist. Since 75 percent of ulnar nerve injury claims are filed by males it is possible that the male body has an anatomic predisposition to ulnar injury. Brachial plexus and lumbosacral nerve injury claims show a preponderance of female plaintiffs.[101] Thus, it may be difficult to prove causation, resulting in many of these cases using the principle of *res ipsa loquitur*, with variable success, as described by Dornette.[102] Perioperative peripheral nerve injuries are the second most common cause of professional liability (after death) among anesthesiologists in the ASA closed claims database.[103]

Anesthesia documentation includes descriptions of positioning and other protective actions. Pressure points should be identified and protected with foam padding or gel pads. Body position should be maintained in natural and neutral alignment. The chin of the patient should be in line with the sternum, and the neck should not be excessively flexed or extended. It is best, especially with procedures at or near the axilla, to ask the patient preoperatively to assume the position necessary for the surgery to determine if that position causes discomfort. If so, the surgeon needs to work with the CRNA to find a position that will not cause a stretch injury to the brachial plexus. This is always a risk when the arm is abducted dramatically (arm above shoulder).

TIP: Neuromuscular blocking agents increase the risk of nerve, muscle, and joint injury because the protective stretch reflex is interrupted by muscle paralysis. Attorneys reviewing cases involving nerve or musculoskeletal injury should carefully review the anesthesia record to determine drug selection.

Medical Gases:
- Oxygen (used by itself, or in conjuction with nitrous oxide or air)
- Nitrous oxide (used in conjunction with oxygen to reduce requirement for inhaled anesthetics)
- Air (used in conjunction with oxygen to reduce risk of atelectasis and fire)

Inhaled Anesthetics (produce and maintain general anesthesia):
- Desflurane (quick onset and offset)
- Enflurane (rarely used today)
- Halothane (much less commonly used today)
- Isoflurane (useful and safe in all applications)
- Sevoflurane (most commonly used inhaled anesthetic, especially valuable for mask induction for pediatric patients)

Hypnotic Anesthetics (induce general anesthesia; propofol can provide maintenance of sleep; ketamine provides analgesia):
- Propofol
- Thiopental
- Ketamine
- Etomidate

Local Anesthetics (block sensory, muscle, and autonomic nerve function):
- Lidocaine
- Bupivicaine (cardiotoxicity with accidental intravenous injection)
- Levobupivicaine (less cardiotoxic alternative to bupivicaine)
- Tetracaine
- Chloroprocaine
- Mepivicaine
- Ropivicaine (less cardiotoxic alternative to bupivicaine)
- Eutectic Mixture of Local Anesthetics (EMLA) (cream applied to skin provides local anesthesia for inserting intravenous catheters)

Local Anesthetic Adjuncts (mixed with local anesthetics to increase duration or density of local anesthetic block):
- Epinephrine
- Phenylephrine
- Clonidine

Narcotic (Opioid) Agonist Adjuncts (provide potent to profound analgesia):
- Fentanyl (most commonly used narcotic in anesthesia practice)
- Alfentanil
- Sufentanil

- Remifentanil (extremely short-acting narcotic)
- Morphine
- Demerol

Narcotic (Opioid) Partial Agonist Adjuncts (provide potent, but limited analgesia):
- Butorphanol
- Nalbuphine

Narcotic (Opioid) Antagonist (to reverse the effects of narcotics):
- Naloxone

Benzodiazepine Sedatives (sedation, anxiolysis, possibly amnesia):
- Midazolam (most commonly used benzodiazepine in anesthesia practice)
- Diazepam
- Lorazepam

Benzodiazepine Antagonist (to reverse the effects of benzodiazepine sedatives):
- Flumazenil

Neuromuscular Blocking Agents (NMBAs) (provide paralysis of skeletal muscle but not smooth muscle—sometimes inappropriately called muscle relaxants):
- Depolarizing neuromuscular blocker:
    - Succinylcholine (depolarizing neuromuscular blockade; becoming much less utilized)
- Non-depolarizing neuromuscular blockers:
    - d-tubocurarine
    - Pancuronium
    - Atracurium
    - cis-Atracurium
    - Mivacurium
    - Rocuronium
    - Vecuronium

Anticholinesterases (to reverse the effects of NMBAs; must be administered concurrently with either glycopyrrolate or atropine to prevent bradycardia and other severe side effects of anticholinesterases):
- Neostigmine
- Edrophonium
- Pyridostigmine

Antisialogogues/Antimuscarinics (drying agents for oral secretions; prevents severe side effects of anticholinesterases; increase inappropriately slow heart rate):
- Atropine
- Glycopyrrolate

Figure 20.2 Anesthetic Agents and Adjuncts in Current Usage

Antiemetics (used to minimize incidence of, or stop, vomiting):
- Droperidol (associated cardiac side effects have reduced usage)
- Ondansetron
- Dolasetron
- Metoclopramide
- Promethazine (intravenous use has resulted in ischemia, necrosis, and loss of limb when intravenous catheter is outside the lumen of the vein)
- Benzquinamide
- Decadron
- Scopolamine

Aspiration Prophylaxis (drugs used to minimize risk of aspiration of gastric contents):
- Histamine Blocking Agents (reduce secretion of gastric acid):
  - Cimetidine
  - Ranitidine
  - Famotidine
- Gastrokinetic Agent (increase speed of gastric emptying):
  - Metoclopramide

Non-particulate Antacid (raises pH of gastric contents):
- Sodium citrate

Cardiovascular Medications:
- To raise blood pressure:
  - Ephedrine
  - Phenylephrine
  - Dopamine
  - Norepinephrine
- To increase heart rate (treatment of bradycardia and hypotension):
  - Atropine
  - Glycopyrrolate
- To decrease blood pressure:
  - Esmolol
  - Labetolol
  - Hydralazine
  - Nitroprusside
  - Nitroglycerin
  - Diltiazem
  - Nifedipine
- To decrease heart rate and control tachydys-rhythmias:
  - Esmolol
  - Labelolol
  - Diltiazem

Bronchodilators (to treat bronchoconstriction):
- Albuterol inhaler
- Ipratroprium inhaler
- Levalbuterol inhaler
- Aminophylline infusion

Steroids (to reduce inflammation):
- Decadron (also used as prophylaxis for post-operative nausea and vomiting, aka PONV)
- Solu-cortef
- Solu-medrol

Non-steroidal anti-inflammatory (NSAID):
- Ketorolac

Oxytoxics (to cause tonic uterine contraction):
- Oxytocin

Anticoagulant (slows intrinsic pathway of coagulation cascade):
- Heparin

Heparin-reversal (binds heparin molecule):
- Protamine

Intravenously Administered Fluids:
- Crystalloids
- Lactated Ringer's
- Dextrose 5% in Lactated Ringer's
- 0.9% NaCl
- Colloids
- 5% albumin
- 25% albumin
- heta-starch

Blood Products:
- Whole Blood (rarely used)
- Packed Red Blood Cells
- Fresh Frozen Plasma
- Platelets

Medications Used in Emergency and Resuscitation:
- Epinephrine
- Sodium Bicarbonate
- Lidocaine
- Procainamide
- Adenosine
- Magnesium Sulfate
- Isoproterenol
- Dopamine
- Dobutamine
- Calcium Chloride

Medication for Malignant Hyperthermia:
- Dantrolene

Treatment of Local Anesthetic Toxicity:
- Intralipid

Figure 20.2 *Anesthetic Agents and Adjuncts in Current Usage (continued)*

Positioning devices may also be involved in injuries. Devices that support the patient's extremities may be improperly placed or may slip into a dangerous position after initial correct positioning, thus resulting in nerve injury. The typical OR table has removable arm boards attached to provide safe positioning for the arms of the supine patient. The angle of the upper arm relative to the torso should be maintained at less than 90° in order to prevent stretch injury to the brachial plexus. Because arm boards have adjustable locking mechanisms, the position of the arm board may shift during the procedure and cause a stretch injury. Monitoring patient position is the duty of the anesthesia provider, frequently a daunting task. Surgeons may inadvertently lean on patients during surgery, and the anesthetist must be vigilant to detect this and instruct the surgeon to remove the pressure on the patient. Surgical instruments are infrequently placed on the drapes covering the patient's face, and the anesthetist must insist that the instrument in question be moved to a safe position.

The prone position offers risk to the patient in multiple ways. It is common to induce general anesthesia on the patient stretcher located alongside the OR table. Once the induction is completed, with endotracheal tube properly positioned and secured, orogastric (OG) or nasogastric (NG) tube, and esophageal stethoscope placed, and eyes appropriately protected, the patient is log-rolled to a prone position on the OR table. The head and extremities must be protected and supported; the move needs careful orchestration (directed by the CRNA in most cases), with proper planning and preparation, and enough staff to comfortably support the patient's weight. The head is supported in a special foam pillow designed to provide space for the eyes, nose, mouth, and endotracheal tube.[104] (A special commercially available device called the Prone View utilizes a mirror to allow continuous visualization of the nose and eyes. A generous foam pad provides cushioning, and the endotracheal tube is free of constriction and bending.) The neck should not be excessively flexed or extended.

The female chest needs rolls placed longitudinally under the sternum and supporting the torso, preventing lateral traction on the breasts, and with two longitudinally placed rolls under the hips to support the pelvis. The male patient needs careful support and positioning to protect the external genitalia, with the torso and pelvis supported with longitudinally placed rolls. The arms may be supported on well-padded arm boards. It may be necessary with older patients and with certain procedures to tuck the arms along the torso, which makes it difficult to access the arms for repositioning of blood pressure cuff or pulse oximeter probe during the surgery. Intravenous access must be established, secured carefully, and determined to be adequate before the patient is rolled to a prone position. Once the arms are positioned and tucked, with draw or folded sheets, proper function of monitors and intravenous line should again be checked before the patient is draped.

Anticipatory padding and checking of pressure and support points prior to beginning the case are essential. Accessible limbs, joints, and head position should be monitored by all members of the team, especially during long surgeries, perhaps with slight periodic changes in position to reduce the chance of injury.[105] The prone position makes the patient more susceptible to hypotension, probably due to venous pooling in the lower extremities.[106] Ventilation is aided by support to the torso and pelvis, but still may be more problematic than if the same patient were supine. At the conclusion of the case the patient is log-rolled back to the stretcher with the same care and attention, and all pressure points can be checked for possible injury.

TIP: Documentation should include protective aspects of positioning the unconscious patient. This information may be found in both the anesthesia record and the perioperative nursing notes.

Patients who undergo vaginal, perineal, or rectal procedures are likely to be placed in the lithotomy position with legs supported by stirrups. Several stirrup styles are available for surgical preferences. Care in positioning and ongoing monitoring of the patient's leg position is mandatory. The perioperative nurses usually position the legs, with final approval from the surgeon. The CRNA's vantage point from the head of the table gives another angle from which to identify potential risk for pressure or stretch. The patient in lithotomy position is at increased risk for sciatic nerve and common peroneal nerve injury.

Patients placed in a lateral (side-lying) position must be stabilized in the correct position. Soft positioning mats (called "bean bags") are evacuated by suction to hold the patient in the desired lateral position. Dangerous pressure points on the edge of the mat require attention. Other padded post devices, mayo stands, folded blankets, and adhesive tape variously maintain the desired position and protect the patient's upper arm. An axillary roll, typically a one liter IV bag wrapped in a hand towel and placed under the upper torso, helps support the patient's weight and takes pressure off the shoulder, reducing risk of brachial plexus stretch injury and preserving circulation to the down arm. Circulation of the down arm must be monitored.

TIP: The anesthetist must ensure the IV bag is at room temperature. Patients have been burned by the use of hot IV bags that were inside or lying on top of a sterilizer.

Multi-jointed OR tables allow a wide range of positions. The CRNA generally controls movement and positioning of the table, in cooperation with the needs of the surgeon and the assistance of perioperative personnel. When any segment of the table is being moved, care must be taken that the table joint does not endanger any part of the patient's body. Amputated fingers have been reported, associated with raising the foot of the OR table at the end of a case requiring the lithotomy position. Specialized OR tables are also utilized. Orthopaedic surgeons use a fracture table to allow access for the C-shaped fluoroscopy unit, which is necessary for proper reduction of femur-neck fractures. Urologists use a cystoscopy table with x-ray capability. The obstetrical delivery table also has its own unique features, which facilitate access to the perineum. Each table offers unique advantages and associated risk. Knowledge of table limitations, especially associated with patient weight, is important in order to reduce table instability and patient falls.

Perhaps the greatest risk to the patient during positioning and repositioning is unintentional malposition of the endotracheal tube, including accidental extubation. Trendelenburg (head down) position tends to move the endotracheal tube deeper into the trachea and may result in right endobronchial intubation with ventilation of only the right lung. Reverse Trendelenburg (head up) position tends to move the tube out of the trachea, with the risk of extubation. Confirming and reconfirming endotracheal tube position is a necessary and repetitive task of the anesthesia provider. Additional risk exists in pediatric and neonatal patients when an uncuffed endotracheal is utilized. Laryngeal mask airways have proved very safe, but additional risk for loss of airway exists when the lateral position is required.

A $2.2 million verdict was returned against an Illinois anesthesiologist after a 35-year-old woman suffered hypoxia, cardiac arrest, brain damage, and ultimately death as a result of accidental extubation during repositioning from supine to lithotomy position. A five-minute period of asystole occurred. The defendant argued that severe bronchospasm made ventilation almost impossible. *Estate of Kathleen Stunkel, deceased v. Dr. Victor Lichtenburg, D.O., Park Ridge Anesthesiology Associates, Ltd., Advocate Health and Hospitals Corp., d/b/a Lutheran General Hospital*, Cook County (IL) Circuit Court, Case No. 05L-66.[107]

B. Eye Protection

Tear production diminishes greatly during anesthesia, and eyes must be protected from drying by taping them closed or using sterile eye ointment. If the surgical position places the eyes at extra risk for pressure, techniques to minimize the risk must be utilized and documented. The options for eye protection include eye pads and protective goggles. Eye goggles are useful for protecting patients' eyes from inadvertent trauma in surgeries like shoulder arthroscopy. In certain YAG laser-surgery procedures eye protection for both patient and personnel is mandated in order to prevent retinal damage from stray and misdirected laser beams.

C. Thermal Considerations

Temperature support is an important aspect of anesthesia care. General anesthesia resets the hypothalamic thermostat to a lower setting. Without special measures body temperature will fall and a metabolic challenge to the body is created. This challenge is evident at the end of the anesthetic, when the patient emerges with the thermostat reset to normal. Shivering ensues, and cardiac output and ventilation must increase to support the restoration of normal body temperature. Very young and old patients do not tolerate the effects of intraoperative hypothermia well, become acidotic and display cardiovascular and respiratory depression.[108]

During very long procedures, especially those with large amounts of fluid and blood loss, body temperature may fall dramatically. Lowered body temperature decreases metabolism and prolongs drug effects, as well as causing abnormal coagulation. Urologic procedures involving large amounts of ambient (room) temperature irrigation can cause body temperature decreases of five degrees in two hours.

Traditional approaches to temperature maintenance and restoration have been associated with problems. Warming blankets utilizing water may cause thermal burns if the patient is not covered with a thin blanket. Heated IV bags placed over the groin and axilla are unsafe; wrapping the bag with a hand towel still leaves open the possibility of accidentally uncovered hot plastic directly contacting the patient's skin and causing a severe burn.

Placing IV bags and bottles in a poorly regulated fluid or blanket warmer exposes the patient to another thermal risk; overheated intravenous and irrigating fluids are especially hazardous, as water can contain a tremendous amount of thermal injury. Adding a heater-humidifier to the anesthesia breathing circuit exposes the patient to infection, overhydration, and burns of the airway.

Fluid warmers and convection-forced air-disposable heating blankets (Bair huggers) control and maintain body temperature in the normal range, with low risk of injury.

Cases are reported in which thermal burn was suffered by the patients when the heater unit hose was placed under a blanket and allowed to blow heated air directly on the patient's skin, rather than being properly utilized in conjunction with the disposable blanket. A warming device should never be used over the lower extremities when a vascular procedure involving arterial clamps is being performed or when lower extremity perfusion is markedly compromised. Warming devices may malfunction and overheat, but modern devices have safety mechanisms including thermostats and are safe when properly maintained.

TIP: Administration of two liters of room temperature IV solution—a conservative amount of fluid for most major cases—can decrease patient core temperature by up to two degrees. Attorneys reviewing anesthesia and perioperative nursing records should look for documentation regarding use of warming devices, amount of intravenous fluid administration, and amount of surgical irrigation.

20.6 Anesthetizing Locations
A. Hospital and Medical Center Operating Room

The operating room usually consists of a receiving or holding area, a collection of suites or rooms where the procedures are carried out, associated substerile rooms, a recovery room (or PACU), and support areas including anesthesia and surgical supply rooms and carts, "dirty" rooms for equipment to be cleaned, and sterilizing rooms where equipment needed immediately by the surgeon may be sterilized. The patient is met by perioperative staff in the holding area, and checked in to ensure all documentation and consents are present and complete.

Anesthesia personnel also meet the patient and conduct the preanesthesia evaluation, including obtaining informed consent if these completed documents are not already in the medical record. A brief interview should be conducted even if the patient has already been seen to determine if any significant changes have occurred or if the patient is NPO. The intravenous line and sometimes other lines and catheters are placed at this time. Oxygen, suction, monitors, resuscitation equipment, medications, and supplies should be readily available, usually on a resuscitation cart. There are reports of young, healthy patients suffering vasovagal syncopy—unconsciousness associated with slowing of the heart and low blood pressure—and even cardiac standstill when personnel are attempting to start an intravenous line.

The holding area is typically a very busy environment, with many individuals involved with, and communicating about, the patient's readiness for the procedure. Patients who need sedation and cannot be immediately taken to the OR should be monitored and receive supplemental oxygen.

When the patient is taken to the OR another checklist is conducted to provide assurance that the patient is truly ready for the procedure. A "timeout" is conducted, during which all personnel concur regarding consented procedure and operative site, including laterality. This "timeout" is presently being emphasized by TJC. (The author is aware of an interscalene block, not without risk, having been performed on the wrong side of the neck of a patient scheduled for carotid endarterectomy. The "timeout" had not yet been conducted. The patient suffered no harm, but the risk associated with two procedures is at least twice that associated with "getting it right the first time." Errors of this kind are obviously indefensible.) Refer to Chapter 4, *Patient Safety Initiatives*, in Volume I, and Chapter 5, *Perioperative Nursing Malpractice Issues*, in this volume, for additional information on "timeout."

The 39-year-old plaintiff initiated an action against the surgeon and CRNA after the surgeon performed open carpal tunnel release instead of the previously scheduled release of a trigger finger, for which the diagnosis was made and the consent was obtained. The correct procedure was performed the following day. The plaintiff claimed the incorrect surgery resulted in scarring and diminished use of his fingers, and faulted both the surgeon and the CRNA for not consulting plaintiff's chart prior to surgery. The Tennessee Jury Verdict Reporter noted a defense verdict for the CRNA and a confidential settlement with the surgeon. *Roy Jones v. Sonny Roberson*, CRNA, Shelby County (TN) Circuit Court, Case No. CT-000847-01.[109]

Following the end of a procedure, when extubated and stable, the patient is transported to the PACU or ICU. The PACU is adjacent to the OR, and stable patients are often taken to the PACU without oxygen and monitoring equipment, a judgment call by the anesthesia provider. However, the patient is at risk of "desaturating" during the short trip, and most ORs provide stretchers with oxygen tanks underneath, which encourages routine use.

In the majority of urban ORs the CRNAs are providing the constant anesthesia care of the patient; the anesthesiologists are present in the area of the OR and available to the CRNA for assistance and consultation if summoned. In a rural setting the CRNA may be providing the total anesthesia service. CRNAs provide most rural anesthesia in the United States.

TIP: Attorneys may acquire useful information during deposition by inquiring about the timeline and procedure in the OR. The perioperative record provides documentation of major events and should agree with the anesthesia record.

B. Labor and Delivery Unit

Anesthesia has historically occupied a role in obstetrical care since John Snow provided chloroform anesthesia to Queen Victoria in the nineteenth century. A variety of techniques are utilized in labor and delivery, including intravenous analgesia and epidural analgesia for labor and vaginal delivery. Epidural anesthesia, intrathecal anesthesia, and general anesthesia are used for cesarean section. A specialized knowledge base recognizing the requirements of both mother and baby, with an understanding of fetal blood supply, is vital for the anesthesia provider in this area.

The labor and delivery unit is one of a few places where family members may be present during surgery and anesthesia. Although efforts are made to shield the family from the sights associated with surgery of the abdomen, inadvertent glimpses may cause distress to family members. The CRNA and the labor and delivery nurse have the responsibility for the family member.

Delivery of the baby, especially when the baby requires resuscitation, is an additional element of concern. A second anesthesia provider may be necessary to help the pediatrician with resuscitation of a premature neonate. Postoperatively, the new mother may be on an anesthesia pain service, which may be staffed by both CRNAs and anesthesiologists.

Laboring patients and postoperative patients may have epidural catheters, with continuous analgesic infusions of dilute local anesthetic and small amounts of narcotic. Protocols exist for activities such as rebolusing epidural catheters and changing epidural syringes. These protocols may be different in various areas of the country and different from hospital to hospital in the same area. State nursing boards address these activities. A dialogue between the Association of Women's Health, Obstetric, and Neonatal Nurses (AWHONN) and the Society for Obstetric Anesthesia and Perinatology (SOAP) speaks to responsibilities regarding epidural infusions. (See newsletters from respective organizations.)

In *Kelly v. Adams*, a 20-year-old laboring woman (deceased at the time of the trial) was receiving epidural analgesia. She was found unresponsive 20 minutes after a continuous epidural infusion was started. Plaintiff contended the defendant anesthesiologist and CRNA failed to recognize that the catheter was inadvertently placed in the sub-

arachnoid (spinal) space rather than in the epidural space. Plaintiff also alleged the expectant mother's vital signs were not properly monitored. The baby was delivered by emergency cesarean section with the mother in extremis. The mother subsequently died. A verdict of $2.3 million was returned, with 51 percent of fault assigned to the anesthesiologist, 49 percent to the CRNA, and 1 percent to the hospital. The hospital provided a confidential settlement before trial. *Kelly v. Adams*, Case No. 98-00752, 780 S0. 2d 67 (Fla. App. 2000).[110]

The anatomic and physiologic changes that occur during pregnancy create an increased risk to the parturient, should she need general anesthesia. The primary risks are "full stomach" (high risk of aspiration) and higher likelihood of difficult or impossible tracheal intubation. Thorough preanesthetic assessment of the parturient, including airway assessment, the availability of the difficult airway cart, and consideration of awake intubation (preserving reflexes and protection of the airway in case of vomiting) with fiberoptic scope should a difficult airway be predicted, are reasonable measures that should routinely be taken.

The *ASA Closed Claim Study* shows a reduction in the percentage of claims for maternal death and neonatal brain damage, attributed to the greater use of regional anesthesia for cesarean sections, but a large proportion of claims for more minor maternal injuries, including headache, back pain, pain during anesthesia, and emotional distress. Thirty-six percent of minor claims involved emotional distress, compared with 7 percent of the minor, non-maternal claims over the same period. It has been proposed that at least some claims may be due to unrealistic expectations and dissatisfaction with care.[111,112]

In *Glassman v. Costello* the patient had a spinal anesthetic and was prepared for cesarean section. When the incision was made the patient complained of pain and requested that the surgeon stop, stating "I can feel that." The patient was preoxygenated and given curare, pentothal, and succinylcholine. The patient was ventilated but could not be intubated. The surgeon was instructed to continue with the surgery and "take the baby." The CRNA stated that he informed the surgeon at this time that the patient was not intubated. The CRNA attempted to ventilate with the mask and then, after administering more succinylcholine, attempted reintubation but had difficulty with "airway resistance." The surgeon noted dark blood in the surgical field, and pulse oximeter tones revealed a very low oxygen saturation. This indicated that ventilation and oxygenation were grossly inadequate. The surgeon stated he only knew of the failed intubation at the point where he noticed dark blood in the field. The endotracheal tube was removed and ventilation was again attempted using the mask, with the oxygen saturation going up and down several more times. Additional help arrived, but the patient could not be intubated and died shortly thereafter. The Kansas Supreme Court held the surgeon liable for the actions of his team. Further, the Appellee-obstetrician was found to have a duty of care regarding administration of anesthesia by a member of his medical team. More specifically, he had a responsibility not to proceed with surgery until the endotracheal tube was placed and airway protection and ventilatory capability were assured. *Glassman v. Costello*, 267 Kan. 509, 98 P. 2d 1050, No. 78,905 (1999).[113]

TIP: Responsibilities for neonatal resuscitation are assigned to other non-anesthesia providers (pediatrician, neonatologist, house physician), although AANA guidelines recognize certain situations in which the CRNA may participate.[114] (See Chapter 2, *Neonatal Nursing Malpractice Issues*, for additional information.)

C. Ambulatory Surgery Center (ASC)

More than 60 percent of all surgical procedures are performed in surgicenters. Experts predict this will continue to rise.[115] Driven by cost constraints, physician dissatisfaction with the traditional hospital OR, and patient preference, these centers have replaced the hospital as the usual site for routine procedures. Centers for same-day surgery are highly regulated. They are accredited by the American Association of Ambulatory Surgery Centers (AAASC) and TJC, and inspected and credentialed for Medicare and Medicaid by the Centers for Medicare and Medicaid Services (CMS).

The standard of care for anesthesia providers remains the same as for traditional hospital-based anesthesia, even though these centers do not have the advantages of full hospital support. Since isolation from resources may have great implications in an emergency situation, these centers must have well-defined protocols for response that include a pathway for transfer to a hospital providing emergency care. The ambulatory surgery center is designed to stabilize the patient in the emergent situation and to rapidly transport that patient to the hospital or medical center for definitive care of the emergency.

Other liabilities are associated with the ASC. Thorough preanesthesia evaluation and planning are essential. Patients screened by telephone, or during referral by the surgeon, may not be well prepared for anesthesia and surgery when a complicating medical condition is discovered, and immediate availability of consultants, laboratory, and radiology may be limited. Postponing the case in this situation may be best, but because the surgeon and patient have both planned this procedure there may be pressure to proceed despite the reticence and concern of the CRNA.

D. Office-Based Anesthesia

Approximately 10 million surgical procedures were performed in physicians' offices in 2005, about twice as many as in 1995. Roughly 10 percent of all surgeries are performed in physicians' offices.[116] Most states do not have regulations regarding facility accreditation for office procedures, although the AANA (2002) and the ASA (1999)[117] have published standards for office-based practice, which are designed to "promote a common base for the delivery of quality patient care in the office-based setting."[118] The AANA standards are congruent with Standards of Nurse Anesthesia Practice.[119] Anesthesia providers working in an office-based setting should, as part of their professional responsibilities:

- Confirm that the surgeon has the appropriate credentials to perform the surgery.
- Determine the need for accreditation of an anesthetizing site.
- Develop or confirm appropriate emergency protocols.
- Provide supervision of recovery of patients after anesthesia.
- Gather quality-improvement data.[120]
- Ensure availability of emergency equipment, in working order.
- Provide for patient safety, delivering anesthesia care that conforms to the standard of care.

E. Remote Anesthetizing Locations

Nurse anesthetists may also provide care within the hospital in locations physically remote from the OR. All anesthetizing locations within a facility must meet established standards of care regarding monitoring and safety, with reasonable adjustments made for environmental hazards such as radiation. These remote sites include diagnostic and therapeutic locations such as radiology, magnetic resonance imaging (MRI), radiation therapy specialty departments such as interventional neuroradiology, mobile lithotripter, cardiac catheterization lab, and electrophysiology laboratories where patients undergoing certain procedures receive sedation or general anesthesia. Nerve blocks and other regional anesthesia techniques are provided by CRNAs in some pain clinics, and CRNAs serve as integral members of acute pain management services. Psychiatric patients receive a brief general anesthetic for electroconvulsive therapy (ECT), often at locations remote from the anesthesia department.

Ultra-rapid drug detoxification (UROD) programs are utilizing anesthesia providers to provide deep sedation and general anesthesia for their patients. Many risks of traditional withdrawal cold turkey therapy, including the most dramatic symptoms, are avoided by UROD. However, these patients require comprehensive workup and extensive follow-up as well as a four to five hour anesthetic and treatment process. Liability issues include risks of drug interactions, informed consent, and premature patient discharge.[121] Insurance companies may not pay for these programs, on the basis of their experimental nature.

CRNAs should be knowledgeable regarding their own safety, especially in regards to radiation exposure. Guidelines for protection and the monitoring of exposure should be in place and observed. If the anesthesia provider must be physically remote from the patient due to radiation risk, provisions for remote monitoring must be made, including all required anesthesia monitors. Each anesthetizing location has special needs, with special risks to both patient and anesthesia provider. An orientation is important in reducing risk in these areas.[122]

TIP: Review of cases involving a remote anesthetizing location should include in the focus provision for all standards of monitoring and equipment availability.

20.7 Anesthesia Policies

Anesthesia departments maintain policy and procedure manuals consistent with institutional requirements, state regulations, and accreditation requirements. Both departmental and institutional manuals may be obtained as part of discovery. Analysis of requirements listed in manuals may provide key information for either plaintiff or defendant, showing breach of standards, or bolstering the defense if standards were defined and met.

A. Departmental Manuals and Documents

Departmental policy and procedure manuals should reflect current standards and practice guidelines. Practice guidelines and standards are published by the AANA and ASA, and these standards and guidelines are reflected in The Joint Commission requirements for accreditation. State boards of nursing and medicine promulgate requirements for licensure and practice.

Manuals must set protocols for equipment maintenance and documentation. Following any critical incident, the role of equipment should be examined, although human error is more likely than equipment failure to be involved in critical incidents, patient injury, or death. Unfamiliarity with equipment may lead to misuse. Review of equipment checkout lists may reveal a problem with a particular piece of equipment or reveal the equipment checkout is not being carried out on a regular basis by a particular anesthesia provider. Ongoing records of maintenance and service of all anesthesia-related equipment should be kept by the department.

Some equipment problems may reflect a pattern of failure due to design or manufacturing fault. Department manuals should include the procedure to report malfunctions to the Medical Device Problem Reporting System of the U.S. Food and Drug Administration.[123]

Inadequate maintenance of the anesthesia workstation puts the patient at risk. A vaporizer calibration problem or a sticking vaporizer valve may contribute to patient awareness.[124]

Complete anesthesia workstation checkout is done every morning or before the first case of the day. CO_2 absorbent canisters should be changed on a regular basis. It is the accepted practice to check only the low-pressure breathing circuit with subsequent cases. Suction apparatus should be checked before each case. Anesthesia machines should be turned off when not in use. Continuous flow of fresh gas through a vaporizer can dry out the CO_2 absorbent, contributing to production of toxic products and increasing the risk of combustion of the dry absorbent.[125,126] (Refer to Figure 20.3.)

TIP: Anesthesia workstation checkout lists, as well as preventative maintenance and vaporizer calibration records, should be obtained and reviewed by attorneys when there is suspicion that an equipment problem contributed to injury.

B. Institutional Policies and Procedures

Facility policy and procedure manuals also include processes and procedures for credentialing anesthesia providers as well as determining clinical privileges.[127] CRNAs, as dependent practitioners, often function with high levels of autonomy. This may create challenges as a case is reviewed and litigated. State and federal governments may be involved in setting certain policies and procedures that influence the practice of anesthesia in the facility. Scope of practice is variously controlled by state boards of nursing and medicine.[128] The Joint Commission has general guidelines with regular updates that must be incorporated into each department's manuals and policies.

Departmental manuals and policies should include such topics as:

- Organizational elements and specification of responsibilities
- Orientation and competency procedure for new personnel
- Continuing education requirements
- Mechanisms for evaluating personnel
- Disaster plans and protocols
- Quality assurance activities of the department
- Practice tips and suggested courses of action for particular circumstances
- Preanesthetic evaluation
- Immediate preinduction reevaluation
- Discharge of the patient from the PACU
- Recording of all pertinent events during anesthesia
- Recording of postanesthesia visits
- Guidelines for role of anesthesia services to hospital infection control
- Recommendations for preanesthetic apparatus checkout
- Guidelines for environmental safety
- Procedure for treatment of cardiac and respiratory arrest
- Procedure for management of malignant hyperthermia
- Procedure for reporting problems with drugs and medical devices: *Medwatch Online Voluntary Reporting Form 3500A*
- Procedure for reporting sentinel events

Figure 20.3 *Topics Usually Addressed in Anesthesia Department Manuals*

20.8 Analysis of the Medical Record

Anesthesia documentation has developed along with the specialty. Anesthesia records are as detailed as any medical or nursing documentation. Unfortunately, when critical events resulting in litigation occur, attention to contemporaneous documentation may not be possible. This situation creates tremendous challenges in recreating events. It may be difficult to capture, especially on a timeline, exactly what transpired, and details may be lost to memory. Discovery will then, by necessity, involve multiple depositions to accurately capture the entire sequence. It is helpful if anesthesia providers write a post-crisis note as an addendum, although this may be viewed as one way to "sanitize" the crisis.

Three forms constitute mandatory documentation for anesthesia care:

- preanesthetic evaluation and informed consent (these may be separate documents)
- anesthesia record
- postanesthesia note

A. Preanesthetic Evaluation and Informed Consent

The preanesthesia evaluation form provides the basis for, and development of, the anesthetic plan. It is also the basis for the process of securing informed consent from the patient. It should include the chief complaint, health and anesthesia history, and a focused physical exam, related to both anesthesia and the planned surgery. Relevant diagnostic and laboratory information should also be recorded or attached. A standardized preprinted form should be used and updated as necessary by the anesthesia department. See Figures 20.4 and 20.5.

The value of a Preanesthetic and Preprocedure Assessment Clinic (PPAC) has been demonstrated. The clinics are staffed variously by CRNAs, anesthesiologists, and other advanced practice nurses. Coordination of activities, including preadmission testing, may be expedited by non-anesthetists. Fewer cancellations of surgery and fewer unnecessary consultations occur when anesthesia is consulted by the primary physician six or more days before elective surgery.[129]

An emergency situation may make it difficult or impossible to obtain informed consent. This provides some degree of protection for the anesthesiologists or nurse anesthetist, as long as the surgeon documents the dire necessity for surgery.

It may be useful and appropriate to obtain specific consent for placement of invasive catheters which have intrinsic risk (arterial catheter, pulmonary artery catheter, epidural catheter, Cordis central vein catheter), with at minimum a note in the medical record or addendum to the anesthesia consent form.

B. Physical Status Classification (ASA Class)

The ASA physical status classification is an important element of preanesthetic assessment and documentation. The American Society of Anesthesiologists developed this five-category physical status classification to improve communication between providers of health care and to allow statistical development of patient data by assigning a numerical value to patient health. The ASA classification is now a standard among anesthesia providers and perioperative personnel in the U.S.

Objectives of preanesthesia evaluation include:

1. Determination of patient's fitness to undergo surgery and anesthesia.
2. Planning for precautions and special considerations.
3. Identification of need for additional testing and/or consultation.
4. Identification of allergic and adverse reaction history.
5. Identification of patient's NPO status: provide instruction if part of re-admission preanesthetic evaluation.
6. Development of a rapport with patient in order to establish trust and ease anxiety, which facilitates the informed consent process, with discussion of benefits and risks of each alternative, recommendation of best option for patient, and discussion regarding patient preference.

Elements of preanesthesia evaluation:

1. Chart review.
2. Patient interview.
3. Patient physical exam.
4. Formulation of anesthesia plan.
5. Obtaining informed consent.

Essential documentation includes:

1. Prior surgeries and anesthetics, including complications.
2. Complications of anesthesia in blood relatives (seeking information about genetically transmitted problems such as malignant hyperthermia, atypical pseudocholinesterase, muscular dystrophy).
3. Review of systems (cardiovascular, respiratory, gastrointestinal, neurological, genitourinary, endocrine, musculoskeletal).
4. Exercise tolerance and normal activity.
5. History of present illness and its treatment; history of previous illness and its treatment.
6. When the patient was last seen by a physician, and for what reason.
7. Current medication use, including prescriptions, over-the-counter drugs, herbal medications and supplements including vitamins.
8. Social history, including use of tobacco, alcohol, and recreational drugs, as well as cessation of same.
9. Allergies to medications, foods, latex, and other environmental substances.
10. Focused physical assessment must include:
    • airway adequacy, difficulty, or problem

• dental status
• body habitus, including height and weight
• cardiovascular system including heart sounds
• pulmonary system including lung sounds
• examination specific to patient's condition or planned procedure, including any planned regional anesthetic technique

Diagnostic findings that must be documented:

• ECG
• echocardiogram
• results of stress test
• chest x-ray
• pulmonary function tests
• laboratory values and reports including acknowledgement of abnormalities and action taken regarding abnormal values

Additional points

1. The extent of a surgical procedure influences the need for routine testing. The ASA (2002) produced a preoperative testing advisory, outlining available studies and giving details regarding the medical consultant's opinions on the value of various diagnostic tests.[120] This advisory includes a review of the consultant's assessment and recommendations. (A consultant does not "clear" the patient for surgery or recommend the anesthetic technique, but rather comments from the specialist's perspective about the patient's readiness for surgery, i.e., does the patient have a reversible process that should be treated prior to surgery? The anesthesia provider remains the anesthesia expert.) The medical consultant is typically a specialist in internal medicine, with or without a sub-specialty.
2. Assignment of ASA Physical Status Classification. (This does not, by itself, quantify risk or predict outcome.)
3. Formulation of an anesthesia plan, the benefits and risks of which are discussed with the patient and are acceptable. Reasonable alternatives to that plan must be presented and discussed. Non-physicians should discuss plan with the supervising physician (surgeon). Note: If an anesthesiologist is involved, the plan should be discussed with and agreed upon by both anesthesiologist and surgeon.
4. Pre-induction evaluation to assess for interim changes, if preanesthetic evaluation took place earlier.

Figure 20.4 *Components of the Preanesthetic Evaluation*

PRE-OPERATIVE ANESTHESIA SUMMARY	Date		OR #	

Kennedy Surgical Center
Washington Township

Pre-Operative Diagnosis

Operation Proposed

Type of Anesthesia Discussed with Patient	Consent	ASA Status	NPO AFTER
		1 2 3	

Height	Weight	Allergies	☐ Yes ☐ NO	Surgeon

HISTORY FROM:
☐ PATIENT   ☐ PARENT GUARDIAN
☐ PARENT   ☐ SIGNIFICANT OTHER
☐ COMMUNICATION/LANGUAGE PROBLEM

ALLERGIES	Y	N
MEDS		
FOODS		
LATEX		

Previous Surgery and Anesthesia

Anesthetic Related Complications
in any Family Member?   ☐ Yes
☐ No

Problems

Medication (including herbal supplements)

DENTITION ☐ Natural ☐ Missing Teeth ☐ Loose Teeth ☐ Chipped Teeth
☐ Dentures Removed ☐ Yes ☐ No ☐ Capped/Bonded Teeth

AIRWAY	Neck Mobility	Jaw Mobility	Uvula Visible	Hyoid to Mandible Distance	AIRWAY CLASS	Anticipate Good Airway?
	☐ Good	☐ Good	☐ Yes	☐ Adequate		☐ Yes
	☐ Fair	☐ Fair	☐ No	☐ Marginal	1 2 3 4	☐ No
	☐ Poor	☐ Poor		☐ Inadequate		☐ Questionable

RESPIRATORY	YES	NO
ASTHMA		
BRONCHITIS		
COPD		
TOBACCO USE		

_____ PACKS/DAY FOR _____ YEARS

CARDIOVASCULAR	YES	NO
ANGINA		
CHF		
HTN		
MI		

HEPATO/GASTROINTESTINAL	YES	NO
ETHANOL USE Frequency_____		
STREET DRUGS Frequency_____		
HEPATITIS		
REFLUX		

NEURO/MUSCULOSKELETAL	YES	NO
CVA		
TIA		
SEIZURE HISTORY		

ENDOCRINE	YES	NO
DM		
HYPO/HYPERTHYROID		

HEME/ONC	YES	NO

RENAL	YES	NO

OTHER

UCG	☐ NEGATIVE	☐ POSITIVE

ECG

NPO AFTER: _____

MEDICATIONS TAKEN TODAY

POST ANESTHESIA EVALUATION
COMPLICATIONS   ☐ YES   ☐ NO
COMMENTS

DOS Pre-Anesthesia Review
I have reviewed the pre op evaluation and examined the patient.
The patient is ready for the scheduled procedure.

_____
ANESTHESIOLOGIST SIGNATURE   DATE

_____
ANESTHESIOLOGIST SIGNATURE   DATE

Figure 20.5 *Anesthesia assessment. Reprinted with permission.*

Physical status is classified as one of five categories, with ASA-I indicating a healthy patient and ASA-V indicating a moribund patient not expected to live beyond 24 hours. ASA-VI has recently been added to indicate a brain-dead patient awaiting an organ procurement procedure.

Assignment of ASA classification is somewhat subjective and not predictive of anesthetic or surgical risk. It is a relative value scale. Different anesthesia providers may rate a patient differently, but with a difference of one class. A patient may be variously rated as ASA-II or ASA-III. An ASA-IV or ASA-V rating is rarely debated. If the procedure is declared as an emergency, an E is added to the classification; for example ASA-IIE, for a patient with mild asthma and acute appendicitis.

The ASA developed the Physical Status rating in 1963 to classify the patient in terms of health and not in terms of anesthetic or surgical risk. It is now almost universally used, as well as misused (if construed as a predictor of operative risk) in the U.S.[130] (See Figure 20.6.)

C. Emotional and Psychological Status

There is no system commonly utilized by anesthesia for evaluating the patient's emotional and psychological status. Often it is not mentioned at all in the patient's evaluation, yet it may be a contributing factor in litigation.[131] Undergoing anesthesia is one of the ultimate loss of control situations a person may experience. Patients must trust strangers with their vital body functions. Patients who express severe anxiety or predictions of doom require extra counseling and confirmation of their preparation for the procedure. This may entail meeting with the surgeon again as well as ensuring all questions and concerns have been addressed to the patient's satisfaction. This must be included in the medical record.

The serious nature of anesthesia must never be minimized to the patient. "There are no minor anesthetics."[132] Poor communication or apparent lack of concern for the patient or the family by anesthesia providers may contribute to the patient seeking legal counsel following an adverse outcome. This aspect may be magnified by the anesthesia provider's less conspicuous role and more limited nature of contact with patient and family. The gravity of any situation must be conveyed by the CRNA to the family.[133]

Failure to provide all elements of informed consent may contribute to a plaintiff's action. It is a standard of care for CRNAs to obtain informed consent and document it in the medical record. This consent may be a note, but it is now common to utilize separate consent forms for surgery and anesthesia.

[Authors' note: This classification was deliberately simplified by the ASA to reduce confusion and eliminate misuse of the system.]

ASA Physical Status Classification System (2002)
P1—A normal, healthy patient
P2—A patient with mild systemic disease
P3—A patient with severe systemic disease
P4—A patient with severe systemic disease that is a constant threat to life
P5—A moribund patient who is not expected to survive without the operation
P6—A declared brain-dead patient whose organs are being removed for donor purposes

These definitions appear in each annual edition of the ASA Relative Value Guide. There is no additional information that will help you further define these categories.

Figure 20.6 *ASA Physical Status Classification. Reprinted with permission of the American Society of Anesthesiologists: 520 N. Northwest Highway, Park Ridge, IL 60068-2573.*

The author was a material witness in a case in which a gastroenterologist was charged with failing to provide information necessary for obtaining informed consent. The plaintiff sustained a colon perforation during the colonoscopy. Perforation of the colon is a known complication and was listed on the colonoscopy consent form, which the plaintiff signed. Recall of the plaintiff was very vivid and positive in regard to the process of giving informed consent for anesthesia. Both plaintiff and defense used the informed consent obtained by the anesthesia provider to argue their position. It is important to note that the anesthesia provider was not named by the plaintiff as a defendant in the action.

A 57-year-old female had an exploratory laparotomy for abdominal pain. Plaintiff subsequently suffered hoarseness resulting from dislocation of a laryngeal arytenoid cartilage. This allegedly occurred as the CRNA intubated the patient's trachea during the induction of general anesthesia. Defendant denied any negligence. Jury Verdict Reporting Service cited a defense verdict. *Barbara A. Clancy v. Northwest Anesthesia , L.C., Mike Mueller*, St. Louis County (Mo) Circuit Court Case No

02CC0003607.[134] (Injury to vocal cords is a known, although rare, complication of tracheal intubation. It is usually listed on the anesthesia consent form.)

Simpson and Blumenreich suggest identifying on the consent form all persons present and listening to the discussion regarding the consent. It is suggested the patient may be anxious and incapable of remembering the discussion regarding anesthesia consent.[135] The possibility of retrograde amnesia from midazolam exists, if midazolam is given shortly after the consent is obtained.

D. Anesthesia Record

The second part of the essential anesthesia documentation is the anesthesia record. The anesthesia record is one of the most difficult documents for non-anesthesia providers to interpret. The document is a recording of pertinent information, on a timeline, describing the anesthetic course. The response to anesthetic agents and adjuncts can usually be deduced from the record, or there may be a specific notation of a requirement for, or response to, the medication.

Evaluating the anesthesia record and correlating it with events described in the notes of other practitioners present in the room is an essential part of case analysis. As was mentioned previously, the expert witness for anesthesia is a valuable resource in this regard. Nevertheless, the process is challenging, as each provider documents information specific to her own sphere of responsibility and may not reflect the patient's condition at that particular time. For example, estimated blood loss may only be recorded at the conclusion of the case, but bleeding early in the case may account for most of the total and may be responsible for an unanticipated and sudden drop in blood pressure. The documentation surrounding such an occurrence may be lacking, although that occurrence is not unusual.

Poor record design and failure to document all information may result in gaps in information. Uncharted data may have great importance when the case is being reconstructed. The anesthesia record is notable for large amounts of complex information recorded in small spaces, using graphic recording techniques, abbreviations, and symbols that may not be standardized. Charts must be reviewed in context, rather than dissected with elements analyzed independently.

Difficulty in interpreting the anesthesia record may be reduced by employing a mnemonic to extract major elements that should appear on the anesthesia record. Using a functional approach to record interpretation will uncover clinical priority setting: "Describe the problem the anesthesia provider was concerned about at that particular time." It is helpful when analyzing the record to recreate the chart identifying each of the categories listed in the following mnemonic. Attempt to extract information from the graphic record on monitoring, anesthesia techniques, identification of problems encountered by the provider, interventions, and patient response to the interventions. Refer to Figure 20.7.

Although the format of the anesthesia record is designed to handle many parameters and pieces of information, it is impossible to record every aspect of the anesthetic course. While vital signs are typically recorded every five minutes, they may be monitored more frequently. Blood pressure determinations recorded every five minutes may reflect an "average pressure" from measures obtained at two or three minute intervals, or even more frequently when a patient is unstable. The chart reflects the trend. Five minutes is considered the maximum interval between measurement and recording of monitored parameters. A longer period of time may be acceptable in certain non-operative settings, such as for patients with laboring epidural catheters, but only after the catheter has been placed, bolused, and the continuous infusion started. At least three successive stable vital signs are initially recorded by anesthesia; and when the patient is considered stable by the CRNA and labor and delivery nurse, the patient is monitored by the nurse at 15-minute intervals.

Parallel to the graphic recording of vital signs is another graph which shows agents, medications, and fluids delivered. This design allows temporal correlation of medication effects and results of interventions. The anesthesia record incorporates significant events that are noted with remarks indicated by numbered notes placed on the graph, by traditional anesthesia symbols, or by specific times. Abbreviations are more local than universal. Refer to Figure 20.8.

Events such as induction, intubation, local anesthetic infiltration, incision, conclusion of procedure, extubation, transfer to PACU, and transfer of patient responsibilities to PACU personnel are considered significant. Other events specific to a procedure, an anesthetic technique, or an individual case may also be charted. Although charged with the duty to document significant events, CRNAs demonstrate a wide range of opinions as to what is significant enough to record. AANA guidelines provide detailed descriptions of minimum expectations for anesthesia records.

Legibility problems are due to both poor handwriting and poor design of forms, which may leave too little room for the large amount of necessary information. Many forms are inconsistent with the size of normal handwriting. The trend toward checklists diminishes the amount of handwriting but sometimes has the disadvantage of not being timed. It is also easy to make errors on checklists, as they are often completed quickly and in a cursory manner.

[Use the mnemonic: A-B-C-C-D-E-F (note the two C's) And L-L-M-N-O-P-Q-R-S-T-T (note two L's and two T's)]

A for Airway

- Did the patient maintain his own airway, or was an airway device of some type utilized?
- What evidence is there that the airway was maintained?
- Were there signs of unrelieved airway obstruction?
- What problems or difficulties associated with airway maintenance were encountered?
- How were the difficulties handled?
- When were the airway devices placed?
- What was the rationale for use of adjuncts?

B for Breathing

- What parameters are documented to show that ventilation existed?
- What evidence was there for oxygenation?
- What was the respiratory rate?
- Were respirations spontaneous, assisted, or controlled?
- What was the quality of breath sounds?
- How were breath sounds assessed: by using an esophageal stethoscope or precordial stethoscope?
- Was there evidence of abnormality in lung function? How was this assessed? Were breath sounds normal or adventitious? (Wheezing? Rales? Rhonchi? Reduced or absent breath sounds?) Were peak inspiratory pressures normal or high?
- What concentration of oxygen was being delivered at any given time during the case? How was this documented?
- How were breathing abnormalities treated? What was the response?

C for Circulation

- What parameters are documented regarding cardiovascular function?
- How was circulation assessed: by palpation of pulses, stethoscope or pulse oximeter? Was blood pressure taken by non-invasive monitor, arterial line, manual sphygmomanometry?
- What did the EKG reveal? (Heart rate normal, fast or slow?) What was the rhythm? (Regular, irregular, ectopic beats or pauses?) Were there ST-T wave changes indicating ischemia or injury?
- What actions were taken for these abnormal findings?
- What were the results of those interventions?
- Do the vital signs make sense when correlated with medications administered and special or unusual surgical events?

C also stands for Consciousness

- What was the patient's level of consciousness at any given moment?
- Was this the expected or desired level of consciousness?
- What interventions were made to change the patient's level of consciousness?
- Were there any unusual presentations of patient's level of consciousness? (Was there a stormy induction, slow emergence, awakening during surgery? Difficulty anesthetizing the patient?) Was there evidence of seizure activity?

D for Drugs

- What agents were used to provide the elements of general anesthesia? What agent or agents were used for hypnosis? (For analgesia? For amnesia? For neuromuscular blockade?)
- How were these agents administered? (In one dose or divided doses? Over what period of time?) Did the desired result occur with each administered drug? Did any undesired results occur? What actions were taken? What was the result?

E for Elimination

- What body fluids were lost or not replaced? Was there preoperative dehydration from NPO status, or from blood loss? What was the hourly urine output? What was the total urine output? (GI fluids suctioned or drained?) Did abnormal fluid collection from body cavities occur?
- How was fluid balance assessed? Were there unanticipated fluid losses?

Figure 20.7 Aid to Interpreting the Anesthesia Record

- Did the patient's vital signs correlate appropriately with documented fluid balance?

F for Fluid Input
- How were lost body fluids replaced? What solutions were given and in what amounts? Over what period of time?
- How was fluid/blood replacement determined? (Theoretical calculations from formulas?) Did the anesthesia provider monitor urine output, CVP, PA pressure?
- What evidence shows that fluid balance was adequate?
- Was there surgical irrigation, and if so how much?
- Was there evidence of overhydration? How and when did this manifest itself? How was it treated? What was the response to treatment?
- Was there a history of renal insufficiency, renal failure, heart failure, or pulmonary fluid accumulation? Was this acknowledged by the anesthesia provider? What evidence is there for the management of this patient's special needs?

L for Level of Anesthesia
- What evidence is there that the patient under general anesthesia was adequately anesthetized?
- Is there any evidence of patient awareness? Did anesthesia suspect intraoperative awareness as it occurred, or only learn of it postoperatively?
- With regional anesthesia, what dermatone or anatomic landmarks defined the sensory blockade? Was the level appropriate? Was the blockade spotty or dense?
- Were there any complications associated with the level of sensory blockade, such as pain, hypotension, or unconsciousness?
- Did the patient ultimately require general anesthesia, if not originally provided for?

L for Laboratory Studies
- Was blood for any lab studies drawn intraoperatively?
- What was the indication?

- What were the results?
- What interventions were made based on the results of those studies?
- Were there any delays in obtaining results? What was the effect of any delay?

M for Machine and Equipment
- What type of anesthesia machine was used?
- Is there evidence of preinduction checkout?
- Did O_2 and N_2O tanks have adequate pressure?
- Was emergency equipment available such as Bag-valve-mask, emergency medications drawn up, emergency airway cart available as well as crash cart and defibrillator?
- Were appropriate monitors being used? Did they function effectively? Were alarms activated or disabled?
- Was there any intraoperative machine or equipment malfunction? How was this handled?

N for Neuromuscular Blockade
- Were neuromuscular blocking agents used to provide intraoperative paralysis? Which drugs were used, and in what doses?
- How was the depth of the neuromuscular blockade monitored?
- Was the neuromuscular blocking agent reversed?
- What evidence was there that adequate neuromuscular function had returned?
- Was the response to the neuromuscular blocking agent abnormal?
- Was the response to the reversal agent unusual?
- What action was taken to deal with the unusual response? What was the response to the action?

O for Ocular
- How were the patient's eyes protected?
- Was there increased risk to the eyes, related to pressure or the prone position?
- Extensive spinal procedure?
- Hypotensive technique?

Figure 20.7 Aid to Interpreting the Anesthesia Record *(continued)*

- Was there use of laser beam? (Surgery on face, neck or head?)

P for Position
- What were the details of patient positioning?
- Who participated in positioning the patient?
- Were pressure points identified and padded?
- How were surgical needs related to positioning?
- How were patient factors related to positioning? Did the patient have joint problems, back, neck, or shoulder pain?
- Was there a history of previous nerve or musculoskeletal injury or condition? (Gravid uterus?)
- Was there evidence of ongoing surveillance of position, including respect for normal anatomic position?
- Was neuromuscular blockade utilized?

Q for Quality (Performance) Improvement
- How is anesthesia documentation utilized in a quality improvement program?
- Was this particular record used in a quality (performance) improvement meeting?

R for Room
- Where was the anesthesia delivered? (In the OR, Radiology, Labor and Delivery, or a remote location?)
- What unique considerations were identified in the anesthetizing location? Was the anesthetist in a remote location from patient?
- Did video monitoring of patient in a scanner by anesthesia occur? Was this an option?
- Was there evidence of the anesthetizing location being unprepared for emergency situations?

S for Surgery
- Were surgical needs or requests from surgeon identified?
- How were unique surgical conditions handled and documented?
  - Did the surgery involve the use of tourniquet?

- Cross-clamp of vessels?
- Cardiopulmonary bypass (extracorporeal circulation)?
- Cardiovascular standstill?
- Lasers?
- Special monitoring?
- Multiple providers?
- Deliberate hypotension?
- Double-lumen tubes?
- Adjunctive medications?
- Frequent laboratory studies?
- Were any unusual surgical events mentioned? Compare the anesthesia record with surgeons' notes and perioperative nurses' notes.
- What were the responses to surgical stimuli and maneuvers?
- Was there a dramatic change in vital signs?
- Was there patient movement during surgery?

T for Temperature
- Was temperature monitored? If so, by what method?
- What values were obtained? How were they interpreted?
- Were any warming devices used?
  - Fluid warmer?
  - Warming mat or blanket?
  - Heater-humidifier in breathing circuit
  - Warming lights?
  - Blanket or plastic wraps?
  - Convective warming blanket?
- Were any cooling devices utilized?
- Were problems found related to these devices?
- Was there evidence of thermal injury?

T for Times
- How are times documented on chart?
- Do event times correlate with those of the surgeon and perioperative nurse?
- Are event times rounded off to "five-minute" numbers?
- Does this create any inconsistency in interpreting events?

Figure 20.7 *Aid to Interpreting the Anesthesia Record (continued)*

ANESTHESIA RECORD

Date _____ OR # _____

Kennedy Surgical Center
Washington Township

Pre-Operative Diagnosis

Operation Proposed

Type of Anesthesia Discussed with Patient | Consent | ASA Status 1 2 3 | NPO AFTER

Height | Weight | Allergies □ Yes □ NO | Surgeon

	Time																						TOTALS

GASES
Oxygen (L/min)
□ N₂O (L/min)
□ Air (L/min)

IV MEDS

Antibiotics _____ Dose _____ mgs / IV Time _____
_____ _____ mgs / IV _____

FLUIDS

SYMBOLS
KEY B.P.
V | X
Λ T
Pulse •
Spontaneous Resp.
Assisted Resp. Δ
Controlled Resp. ▽

MONITORS
Ekg
% O₂ Inspired (FO₂)
O₂ Saturation (SaO₂)
End Tidal CO₂
Temp: □ C □ F
Position

IMMEDIATE
PRE-INDUCTION
REVIEW □

INCLUDES:
PT. ID
CHART REVIEW
NPO STATUS
PERMITS
VS
ALLERGIES

200
180
160
140
120
100
80
60
40
20

RECOVERY
Time _____

□ Phase I
□ Phase II
Fast Track Score _____
B/P _____
HR _____
S_pO₂ _____
RR _____
□ Stable
□ Awake
□ Drowsy

VENT
Tidal Volume
Resp. Rate
Peak Presure
PEEP

PATIENT SAFETY	MONITORS AND EQUIPMENT	ANESTHETIC TECHNIQUE	AIRWAY MANAGEMENT
□ Anes. Machine # _____ □ Safety Belt On □ Axilary Roll □ Armboard Restraints □ Arms Tucked □ Pressure points checked and padded □ Eye Care: □ Ointment □ Saline □ Taped □ Pads □ Goggles	□ Steth □ Precord □ Esoph □ Non-Invasive B/P □ Left □ Right □ Continuous EKG □ Oxygen Sensor □ Pulse Oximeter □ Gas Analyzer □ End Tidal CO₂ □ Nerve Stimulator □ Temp. _____ □ Bair Hugger □ IV(s) _____	General: □ Pre-Oxgenation □ Rapid Sequence □ Cricold Pressure □ Intravenous □ Inhalation Regional: □ Spinal □ Epidural M.A.C. □	Intubation: □ Oral □ Rae □ Nasal □ Tube Size _____ □ Blade _____ □ Glidescope □ Secured at _____ □ Breath Sounds _____ □ ETCO₂ LMA □ Size _____	□ Uncuffed, leaks at _____ cm H₂O □ Cuffed □ Min. occ. pres. □ Air □ NS Airway: □ Oral □ Nasal Circuit: □ Circle □ NRB □ Mask Case □ Nasal Cannula □ Via Tracheostom □ Simple O₂ mask

	START	STOP	REMARKS _____
Anesthesia			_____
Procedure			_____
CRNA			_____
ANESTHESIOLOGIST			_____

Post-Op Diag: _____ | Procedure: _____

Figure 20.8 Reprinted with permission.

Documentation that cannot be included on a standard anesthesia record may require extra description in the progress notes of the medical record. The obligation to record significant events is not diminished by inadequate design of a chosen anesthesia record form. However, the CRNA's first responsibility is to safe patient care. A skimpy record does not necessarily prove poor care was provided, but it does not support that good (standard) care was rendered. A detailed record also does not prove good care was given. Failure to provide complete, accurate documentation of anesthesia care constitutes a deviation from the standard of care. Standard VI of Scope and Standards for Nurse Anesthesia Practice states: "There shall be complete, accurate, and timely documentation of pertinent information on the patient's medical record."[136]

In *Bentley v. Langley, Fleming, Rouse, and Lenoir County Memorial Hospital,* the patient was undergoing a laminectomy in the prone position when the CRNA informed the surgeon the patient was in cardiac arrest. As the anesthesiologist was called, the patient was rolled to a supine position. The patient was resuscitated by the CRNA, the anesthesiologist (who had arrived quickly), and the surgeon. The patient suffered massive brain injury and died a short time afterward, even though the resuscitation took place quickly, according to documentation. The CRNA testified there was no warning or change from a stable condition before the patient's heart stopped, and there was documentation supporting that assertion. Summary judgment for the defendants was reversed upon appeal, with the court finding issues of material fact as to 1) whether the CRNA negligently failed to monitor the patient, 2) whether the defendant surgeon and defendant anesthesiologist were negligent in failing to adequately supervise the CRNA, and 3) whether the defendant surgeon and defendant anesthesiologist were negligent in the supervision of the defendant CRNA. *Bentley v. Langley*, 296 N.C. 735, 254 S.E. 2d 176, No. 788SC87, (1979).[137]

TIP: The anesthesia record can be viewed as a vigilance tool. Its preprinted format reminds the provider to check and document all important parameters.

E. Automated Anesthesia Records (AAR)

AAR are utilized and advocated by some departments, but are not widely utilized. Information from electronic monitors is automatically transmitted to a computer whose print-out is formatted similar to a traditional anesthesia record. A keyboard is employed by anesthesia providers to input information such as drug dosages, specific events such as induction and emergence, and placement of invasive lines, as well as any atypical or untoward occurrences or observations. The keyboard function allows providers to edit portions of the record. Voice recognition has been applied in some systems.

There are multiple advantages to an automated system: less paperwork for the provider, more accurate recording of measurements, data, and information, and a legible, consistent format. The automated anesthesia record is, or can be, part of a larger data collection and analysis system termed the automated information management system (AIMS). The digital database lends itself to statistical analysis and can be easily applied to the functions of billing, quality assurance, supervision, teaching, and research.

Researchers have demonstrated the impossibility of recording by hand all of the data presented to the anesthesia provider by modern monitoring systems, or even recognizing the rate of change of the data being presented.[138] The differences between handwritten records and those produced by an automated system are statistically significant and at times clinically significant.[139] It has even been demonstrated that recording intervals of one minute may not be sufficient to demonstrate the true physiologic changes that occur during anesthesia and surgery.[140]

The author conducted research (master's thesis, unpublished, 1989) using a non-invasive and continuous monitor of blood pressure and heart rate, and demonstrated statistically and clinically significant differences between two- and ten-minute recording intervals of blood pressure from a continuous record of patients undergoing general anesthesia and electro-convulsive therapy (ECT). Blood pressures were much higher than predicted by experienced staff.

AAR have some drawbacks. Interference with electronic signals (artifacts) may require editing by the CRNA. The most striking example of this problem occurs during the surgeon's use of electrocautery to cut tissues and stop bleeding. The ECG signal is lost during this time, resulting in erroneous heart rate recording, possible erroneous recording of heart arrhythmia, and triggering of alarms. The provider must then manually indicate the presence of electronically generated artifacts. Other artifacts may be present on the record without being recognized and identified by the CRNA.

These drawbacks may be outweighed by the advantages of more accurate recording and significant time savings. CRNAs have had the experience of documenting values only to find that the just-recorded value has changed, sometimes significantly. It has been estimated that between 15 and 20 percent of a provider's time is spent documenting and recording events and data, and it has been argued that relieving the provider of a task will allow for more supervisory and cognitive activity, thus preventing a crisis situation.[141] If a crisis occurs, automatic recording will allow the provider to focus on the patient, and postanesthesia evaluation of crisis management will be more objective and instructive.

Electronic objectivity also reduces the human tendency to "smooth" the vital signs. (To "smooth" the data is to edit it to appear more favorable or to guess at vital signs rather than record the displayed value.) The possibility of tampering with AAR is always present, despite built-in security safeguards. Computer system failures may obliterate the record completely. It remains to be seen whether a computerized record will carry more value as evidence in a negligence action. Gibbs predicted that as technology improves, so will the accuracy, reliability, and security of automated record systems; it will then be possible to determine who participated and what took place in each episode of patient care.[142]

Even without the fully computerized AAR, monitors utilized in current anesthesia delivery systems include a printout function that allows a paper record of the automatic recording of vital signs and other measured and recorded important anesthesia parameters. Even stand-alone noninvasive blood pressure monitors and ECG monitors have store and print functions.

> In *Becker v. Plemmons*, the non-invasive blood pressure monitor printout showed a five-minute period when the patient had no recordable blood pressure or heart rate. The CRNA delayed another five minutes before calling a "code." *Becker v. Plemmons*, 598 N.E. 2d 564, Ind. App (Aug 31, 1992).[143]

TIP: Requests for records should include any printout information not normally placed into the medical records that may have been saved from a crisis event (e.g., ECG strips, non-invasive blood pressure monitor records).

F. Postanesthesia Evaluation

The postanesthesia evaluation is the last of the three essential anesthesia documentation forms. Discharge from the PACU requires either a note from an anesthesia provider or the PACU RN's use of strict PACU discharge criteria. (Some healthcare facilities require that a physician anesthesiologist discharge the patient from the PACU.) The medical record should include a note from the CRNA, indicating the

patient was evaluated to identify possible anesthesia-related problems identified intraoperatively or postoperatively. The visit by the CRNA, upon which the postanesthesia note is predicated, provides an opportunity to review the anesthetic course with the patient. This visit is particularly important if there were any problems, such as a difficult intubation, possibly associated with the anesthesia that should be communicated to future anesthesia providers. The timing of the visit may be dictated by the healthcare facility policy. It is commonplace for the CRNA to visit an inpatient within 24 hours after surgery and anesthesia. The policy for postanesthesia visits is obtainable through discovery.

Addressing perianesthetic problems at a postanesthesia visit is sound risk management technique. Information should be provided to the patient and the family throughout the perianesthetic period, beginning with a preanesthesia visit and continuing until postanesthesia surveillance ends.

Fear of anesthesia, coupled with a lack of true understanding, can be overcome by continuous open and honest communication between the CRNA and patient. The low visibility of the CRNA, who may only see the patient for several minutes prior to induction of anesthesia, may promote questions from the family and patient. Ignorance regarding accessibility of the CRNA to answer questions and discuss care may create distrust of anesthesia providers. The patient's perception of, rather than the reality of, anesthesia provider accessibility is important. This is especially true if there were problems with anesthesia or problems erroneously attributed to anesthesia by another healthcare provider.

20.9 Potential Defenses

Analysis of a case involving a claim against anesthesia care can be complex and challenging, even to an experienced attorney. Case review should include a determination of whether the CRNA anticipated difficulty after conducting the preanesthetic assessment. The attorney should attempt to determine if the CRNA formulated a plan that afforded patient safety. Evidence of utilization of emergency backup plans should also be sought. Given the lack of complete understanding of physiologic factors that influence physiologic behavior under anesthesia, it is not surprising that no plan can absolutely guarantee safety. Gaba refers to the lack of a "schematic" for each patient.[144] Multiple factors, many of which are not under the control of the CRNA, can influence outcomes after crisis.

Unexpected reaction to medication can occur, as may surgical events such as uncontrolled bleeding. Consider that an anaphylactoid reaction to a drug administered to a patient during anesthesia can result in morbidity or mortality, even if appropriate and timely treatment and support are followed. Consider that inadvertent laceration of the aorta during the repair of an aortic aneurysm may result in immediate blood loss of 50 percent of the circulating volume, and adequate blood replacement (the responsibility of the anesthesia provider) may not be possible even with several large bore intravenous lines in place. In either of the above situations, vital organs may suffer damage even if the anesthesia response is rapid and accurate.

Medical crises such as myocardial infarction, stroke, or pulmonary embolus may occur coincidentally, without apparent link to anesthetic or surgical events. Patients with unknown histories of drug abuse, undiagnosed tumors, or unknown medical conditions may develop serious symptoms and deterioration of vital signs. In these crisis situations, where unknown factors are at play, the provider can only react to events, working to sustain the patient's airway, breathing, and circulation.

Identifying elements beyond the CRNA's control may provide a defense. Examination of the CRNA's response to unexpected events may also provide a defense. If the actions fell within an appropriately applied protocol for the emergency then negligence has not occurred. Patients who have given informed consent for anesthesia have been made aware that some risk is associated with every procedure and anesthetic technique and that unanticipated events may take place, with serious consequences. At the same time, protocols and guidelines (for example, Advanced Cardiac Life Support) that protect the patient must be followed, and anesthesia care encompasses crisis management as standard care.

Expert witnesses give opinions in a case regarding the appropriateness of care rendered by an anesthesia provider. The likelihood that opinions will agree is unlikely, given that in many cases both plaintiff and defendant have an expert testifying on their behalf.

Expert witness opinion in medical malpractice has been identified as based on implicit assessment or unstated opinion. This differs from opinion based on criteria specified and stated before assessment. In one study, pairs of anesthesiologist-reviewers independently assessed the appropriateness of care in anesthesia malpractice claims. With the study methods controlling for bias, reviewers agreed on 62 percent of claims and disagreed on 38 percent. There was agreement that care was appropriate in 27 percent of cases and substandard in 32 percent.[145]

20.10 Identifying Potential Defendants

Anesthesia care in the United States is most commonly delivered by physician anesthesiologists (approximately 35 percent) and certified registered nurse anesthetists (approxi-

mately 65 percent). Small groups of other healthcare providers may provide anesthesia services, usually under limited circumstances, as described later.

TIP: Other participants in anesthesia care may need to be identified, especially in teaching institutions where student nurse anesthetists, resident physicians, and medical students may be present. This information may sometimes be found in the perioperative record, which lists all personnel in the OR for that case, kept by the operating room circulating nurse. Tasks performed by learners require supervision by licensed personnel.

A. Anesthesiologists

Anesthesiologists are physicians whose specialty has been defined by their professional society as a discipline within the practice of medicine specializing in the medical management of patients who are rendered unconscious or insensible to pain and emotional stress during surgical, obstetrical, and other medical procedures. The anesthesiologist provides preoperative, intraoperative, and postoperative evaluation and treatment of these patients. The anesthesiologist, like other anesthesia providers, is responsible for the protection of life functions and vital organs under the stress of anesthetic, surgical, and other medical procedures. The anesthesiologist is specially trained for, and may specialize in, the management of problems in pain relief. Anesthesiologists may be responsible for critical care units, and especially the management of pulmonary problems. Anesthesiologists are trained and proficient in cardiopulmonary resuscitation.

As a physician specialty, anesthesiology developed formally between World War I and World War II. Before that time nurse anesthetists administered most anesthetics, although many individual physicians made great contributions to the specialty. The American Society of Anesthesiologists (ASA) was founded in 1937 and now has more than 37,000 members. The ASA publishes standards, practice guidelines, and statements as well as other pertinent documents. About 90 percent of anesthesiologist members of the ASA are board-certified diplomats of the ASA.

The Joint Commission promulgates standards for surgical and anesthesia services. These standards do not require an anesthesiologist on staff. The guidelines define leadership responsibilities, service lines, and the need for defining the qualifications and competence of staff.[146]

The physician supervising anesthesia services must be qualified to assume professional, organizational, and administrative responsibility for the quality of anesthesia service. There is no Joint Commission reference to a supervising anesthesiologist.[147]

State medical and nursing boards and The Joint Commission guidelines may be very different regarding requirements for supervision of CRNAs. Many states do not require anesthesiologist supervision of CRNAs. If CRNAs are considered by the state nursing board to be licensed, independent practitioners, they may independently provide anesthesia services, working collaboratively with the "operating practitioner" or a "qualified physician." The operating practitioner can be a doctor of medicine, a doctor of osteopathy, a dentist, an oral surgeon, or a podiatrist. The "qualified physician" is not necessarily an anesthesiologist, but must have appropriate training, experience, or privileges.[148] The ability of the CRNA to practice independently of physician anesthesiologists is crucial in areas that are medically underserved. Residents of these areas might otherwise be denied access to crucial healthcare services.

A New Jersey decision, however, demonstrates the influence of regulatory boards on the autonomous practice of a non-physician licensed practitioner. It effectively created a requirement specifying anesthesiologist supervision, rather than physician supervision, of general and regional anesthetic administration by CRNAs.

In New Jersey State Association of Nurse Anesthetists, v. New Jersey State Board of Medical Examiners, the Supreme Court opted not to intervene in the promulgation of restrictive practice regulations. *New Jersey State Association of Nurse Anesthetists v. New Jersey State Board of Medical Examiners*, Docket No. A-2729-02T2, 372 N.J. Super. 554; 859 A.2d 1239; 2004 N.J. Super. The Supreme Court's decision was influenced by several premises, including the tradition of granting administrative agencies (such as the Board of Medical Examiners, or BME) "wide latitude" in exercising "discretion and authority in meeting their statutory objectives," and the notion that the BME is not regulating the nursing profession but rather the physicians who offer anesthesia in an office setting. While Appellant-NJANA argued that the BME had not demonstrated a need for physician anesthesiologist supervision on the basis of safety, respondent (BME) argued that it did not need to wait for statistics documenting unsafe conditions in order to exercise its authority to take measures to protect patient safety. The decision came despite the Appellant-NJANA reference to the United States Department of Health and Human Services stating it "cannot agree that anesthesia administration is the practice of medicine and therefore can only be done

after medical school training." 66 Fed. Reg.[4674 at] 4680 (January 18, 2001).[149,150]

The responsibility for anesthesia services was the threshold issue in a Texas case:

In *Denton v. LaCroix*, a 31-year-old woman received epidural anesthesia for labor, with another dose of local anesthetic administered by a CRNA in preparation for a cesarean section. No anesthesiologist was present. The patient subsequently developed respiratory distress, and the CRNA called twice for the anesthesiologist without a response. She then called a resuscitation code, to which an emergency physician responded, but that physician was unable to successfully manage the crisis. A pediatrician who had also responded took charge. The patient suffered hypoxic brain damage before being resuscitated. At the trial, the anesthesiologist group claimed the understanding that obstetricians were responsible for anesthesia services if no anesthesiologist was present. The obstetricians testified they had never agreed to assume responsibility for anesthesia service, and they were in any event not qualified to do so. Hospital policy required that an anesthesiologist conduct a preoperative evaluation, obtain informed consent, and remain physically present or immediately available. The CRNA, however, testified she was unaware of this policy. The chairman of the anesthesiology department testified he had been warning the hospital administrator about similar violations of the policy for the previous four years, without effect. His memo to the hospital administrator on this subject was admitted into evidence. A judgment against the defendant hospital and its corporate owner was entered for $8.7 million.[151] The judgment was affirmed by the Texas Appellate Court, with evidence sufficient to support the jury's finding against the hospital based on a theory of direct corporate liability, notwithstanding the jury's failure to find the treating physicians and nurse anesthetist negligent. *Denton v. LaCroix*, 947 S.W. 2d 941 (Tex. App. 1997), No. 92-40026-362.[152]

B. Certified Registered Nurse Anesthetists (CRNAs)

CRNAs are registered nurses who have been formally educated in, and have demonstrated competence to practice, nurse anesthesia. Nurse anesthesia is recognized as a specialty within the profession of nursing. As independently licensed health professionals, CRNAs are responsible and accountable for their respective practices.[153] Nurse anesthetists have been providing anesthesia for more than 100 years. Bankert has admirably chronicled the history and development of the profession.[154]

The legal basis for CRNA practice has been summarized by Mannino,[155] by Jenny and Shotten in Dornette,[156] and by Blumenreich.[157] Whether or not anesthesia practice is necessarily the practice of medicine has been, and continues to be, disputed. Several landmark court cases have established that anesthesia is not the practice of medicine but rather the practice of nursing when it is practiced by nurses.

In *Chalmers-Francis v. Nelson*, the California Supreme Court reasoned that anesthesia as practiced by nurses under the immediate supervision and direction of a surgeon does not involve diagnosis or prescription within the meaning of the Medical Practice Act. The court further concluded that Nurse Dagmar Nelson was merely carrying out the physician's order and ruling that anesthesia as practiced by the nurse anesthetist was within the scope of nursing practice. *Chalmers-Francis v. Nelson* 6 Cal. 2d 402, 57 P.2d 1313 (1936).[158]

Malpractice payouts in cases involving CRNAs must be reported to the National Practitioner Data Bank (NPDB).[159] At this point, attorneys do not have access to NPDB information about specific individuals unless they can prove the employer failed to query the NPDB about malpractice claims every two years. The NPDB was not thought by Congress to be a complete source of adverse action information on healthcare providers and practitioners. Thusly, in 1996 the Health Insurance Portability and Accountability Act was enacted as Public Law 104-19, Section 221(a). The Act directed the Secretary of Health and Human Services to create the Health Integrity and Protection Data Bank (HIPDB), designed to combat fraud and abuse in the healthcare delivery system and provide a resource to help state and federal agencies determine if the providers they plan to employ were ethically and professionally competent.

Since 1999, federal and state government agencies and health plans are required to report to the HIPDB all final adverse actions taken against any licensed or certified physician, dentist, or nurse, as well as any other healthcare provider, supplier, or practitioner. Eligible users can submit a query to the HIPDB, including practitioners who wish to review any possible information entered about them. Each data bank communicates information to the other regarding healthcare providers.

CRNA practice typically involves four general categories: preanesthetic assessment, evaluation, and preparation; induction, maintenance, and emergence from anesthesia; postanesthesia care; and perianesthetic clinical support. The AANA publishes the Scope and Standards for Nurse Anesthesia Practice that offer guidance for CRNAs and healthcare institutions regarding the scope of nurse anesthesia practice. The scope of practice of the CRNA addresses the responsibilities associated with anesthesia practice and is performed in collaboration with other qualified healthcare providers. Collaboration involves two or more parties working together, each contributing her respective area of expertise.

The practice of anesthesia is a recognized specialty in both nursing and medicine. Anesthesiology is the art and science of rendering a patient insensible to pain by the administration of anesthetic agents and related drugs and procedures. Anesthesia and anesthesia-related care represents those services that anesthesia professionals provide upon request, assignment, and referral by the patient's physician or other healthcare provider authorized by law, most often to facilitate diagnostic, therapeutic, and surgical procedures. In other instances, the referral or request for consultation or assistance may be for management of pain associated with obstetrical labor and delivery, management of acute and chronic ventilatory problems, or the management of acute and chronic pain through the performance of selected diagnostic and therapeutic blocks or other forms of pain management. CRNAs practice according to their expertise, state statutes, and institutional policy. In some states including New Jersey a CRNA is considered an advanced practice nurse (APN), and must be licensed as such.

1. Nurse anesthesia education

Courses for nurse anesthesia training were developed during the first half of the twentieth century. The American Association of Nurse Anesthetists (originally named the National Association of Nurse Anesthetists) first met in 1931 with development of standards for nurse anesthesia training as one of its goals. There are over 108 accredited nurse anesthesia educational programs graduating more than 1,000 graduate registered nurse anesthetists annually. These graduates sit for a certifying exam after successful completion of all program and certification candidate requirements.

Beginning in 1998, all CRNA programs were required by the Council on Accreditation of Nurse Anesthesia Educational Programs to be in a graduate framework. Programs are a minimum of 24 months in length (most are 27 to 28 months in length). Entry level nurse anesthesia practice requires a master's degree; the majority of programs grant a master of science in nursing (MSN) degree. Many experienced CRNAs have only registered nursing diplomas and certificates of successful completion of nurse anesthesia programs, and continue to be eligible to practice.

TIP: The CRNA is the only anesthesia provider to be required to pass a certification examination in anesthesia in order to practice.

---

2. Continuing education and practice requirements for CRNAs

To continue practice, a CRNA must earn 40 continuing education credits (CEs) within each two-year accreditation cycle, provide evidence of active CRNA practice, maintain the registered nurse licensure, and verify the absence of mental, physical, or other problems that might interfere with practice.

3. American Association of Nurse Anesthetists (AANA) membership and organization

As of 2009 there were more than 39,000 practicing CRNA members of the AANA. The AANA utilizes an administrative staff and four separate and functionally independent councils to direct its professional activities and manage its services. The AANA promotes and coordinates continuing education activities and membership services, and publishes practice standards, guidelines, and interpretive and position statements. These publications are essential for legal cases involving CRNA practice. (The standards for CRNA practice are listed in Figure 20.9.)

4. The Professional Practice Manual for the Certified Registered Nurse Anesthetist

This manual is published by the American Association of Nurse Anesthetists. It is a frequently updated and comprehensive collection of standards, guidelines, position and interpretive statements, and advisory documents that can be used by attorneys and expert witnesses to help in the review of cases involving CRNAs. CRNAs should be familiar with the contents of this manual as a basis for their practice. Further discussion of many of these topics is included in *A Professional Study and Resource Guide for the CRNA* (2005), AANA Publishing, Inc.

C. Other Less Common Anesthesia Providers

There are, as of 2010, seven master's level programs, 24 months in length, for the education and training of anesthesiologist assistants (AAs). These programs are accredited by the Commission on Accreditation of Allied Health Educa-

---

The American Association of Nurse Anesthetists (AANA) promulgates Standards for Nurse Anesthesia Practice. These standards can be found in Section II of the *Professional Practice Manual for the Certified Registered Nurse Anesthetist,* as well as on the AANA website (AANA.com). The standards are designed to assist in evaluation of quality of anesthesia care, promote development of practice quality, communicate standards and expectations for anesthesia care to the public, and preserve and support patient rights.

- Standard I addresses the requirement for preanesthesia assessment.
- Standard II describes the requirement for obtaining from the patient informed consent for anesthesia care.
- Standard III identifies the requirement for a specific plan of anesthesia care for each patient.
- Standard IV describes the process of implementation, continuous assessment, and adjustment of the anesthesia care plan in response to patient response to anesthetic and surgical implementation, in order to maintain safe physiologic condition.
- Standard V identifies specific requirements for monitoring the patient receiving anesthesia care.
- Standard VI describes the requirement for comprehensive and accurate documentation of anesthesia care.
- Standard VII delineates the requirement and process for transfer of care that assures continuity and safety.
- Standard VIII identifies the institution-specific requirement for checking readiness of anesthesia delivery and monitoring systems utilized, and identifes minimum standards for systems which monitor the performance of anesthesia delivery equipment.
- Standard IX delineates the requirement for institutional infection control precautions.
- Standard X describes requirements for ongoing review and evaluation of anesthesia care.
- Standard XI describes the requirement for ethical practice, especially in preservation of patient rights.

Figure 20.9 Examples of Standards of Care for Certified Registered Nurse Anesthetist

tion Programs (CAAHEP). There is no prerequisite healthcare experience, but rather a required baccalaureate degree in a life science. Students may take a postgraduate certifying examination administered by the National Commission for Certification of Anesthesiologist Assistants. AAs only practice in a limited number of states. Currently about 600 AAs are working in about one-third of the states. Physician assistants (PAs) may practice in the specialty of anesthesia by obtaining postgraduate education and training in anesthesia, including completing a program for anesthesiologist assistants. These providers function only under the direction of a physician anesthesiologist. Anesthesiologist assistants are unable to practice without the presence and direction of anesthesiologists. This practice arrangement is called medical direction. (The term "direct medical supervision" has also been used in the context of AA practice.)

Anesthesia care may also be given by oral surgeons and dentists as providers or as team members. Podiatrists may also function as anesthesia providers in a more limited capacity. For many years some obstetricians administered regional anesthesia for labor and delivery, although this practice is now rare. Many local anesthetic infiltrations are performed by surgeons and other interventionists (radiologists, cardiologists, plastic and cosmetic surgeons, and so on) for minor procedures in a wide variety of settings. Any administration of a local anesthetic can result in serious adverse effects and an immediate need for emergency cardiopulmonary support, including Basic and Advanced Life Support. Standards for delivery of anesthesia care have become progressively more rigorous in all respects, including credentialing, technical aspects of delivery, monitoring, and emergency preparedness.[160,161]

Other healthcare providers may have a bearing on elements of cases involving anesthesia care. Preoperative medical consultants, surgeons, perioperative nurses, and postanesthesia nurses work with anesthesia providers at various points along the anesthesia care continuum. These other practitioners may share responsibility, even though it may be more limited, with anesthesia providers.

Non-anesthesia consultants may become problematic when they advise anesthesia providers on the technique, agent, or dosage, effectively usurping anesthesia authority and negating anesthesia expertise. Anesthesia provider requests for consultation should have the objective of determining patient readiness for anesthesia and surgery and determining a "tune-up" strategy for optimizing patient condition if necessary. Proper planning by anesthesia should allow adequate time for communication, with a written report of consultation placed on the chart. Patients must be advised prior to consultation that assistance is being sought, and it must be understood that they have a right to approve or disapprove of any planned consultation.[162]

20.11 Anesthesia Outcomes

Studies have not demonstrated that there is a significant difference in anesthesia outcome among categories of providers. From a statistical viewpoint, patient outcomes are similar, regardless of whether the anesthesia is provided by CRNAs or anesthesiologists.[163] Smith et al. reviewed available published studies on the influence of anesthesia provider on patient safety. They concluded that, due to confounding variables and the dearth of high-level primary evidence, it was impossible to draw a conclusion relating patient safety to anesthesia provider type.[164] The issue of outcome statistics is still being debated by the ASA and AANA.[165,166] The CDC initially considered studying the issue but concluded that mortality[167] and morbidity in anesthesia are too low to justify an expansive (and expensive) project. The ASA encouraged a definitive study of the issue, but agreed with the Pine[168] study in suggesting the best outcomes might occur with collaboration between the CRNA and anesthesiologist. Blumenreich has pointed out that most complications, especially the catastrophic ones, occur as a result of a lack of vigilance, and so education beyond a certain point could not be expected to make a difference in outcomes.[169] CRNAs and anesthesiologists may work together in anesthesia care teams, or each may practice without the other, depending on the institution and on state regulations.

TIP: One of the first outcome studies was conducted by nurse anesthetist Alice Macgaw, who recorded 14,000 anesthetics had occurred without a fatality.

20.12 Supervisory Issues for CRNAs

More than 27 million anesthetics are administered in the United States each year, and 65 percent are directly administered by CRNAs. CRNAs administer anesthesia for all types of surgical cases, from the simplest to the most complex. In two-thirds of all rural hospitals, CRNAs are the sole providers of anesthesia services.

CRNAs serve as academic and clinical faculty in educational programs for student nurse anesthetists. They also participate in anesthesia education for other health professionals such as residents and dentists. CRNAs are competent to provide expert testimony, as described by Blumenreich.[170,171] Practice arrangements for CRNAs vary widely. CRNAs may work in many possible types of practice within the specialty of anesthesia care. These may include such arrangements as hospital employee; teaching hospital employee; medical center employee; anesthesiology group employee; in private practice, as partner or employee of a CRNA group, employing a physician anesthesiologist; in individual private practice; and locum tenens, on temporary assignments of varying length, with employment obtained through an agency.

Nurse anesthesia has a long history of providing quality anesthesia care and is recognized as a well-established nursing specialty practice, preceding formal regulation by states.[172,173] This regulatory process "ratified existing practice rather than reshaping the parameters of the profession."[174] Institutional policies may play a larger role in defining individual and local CRNA practice, particularly in areas such as the delivery of regional anesthesia. Some institutions prohibit CRNAs from providing regional anesthesia.

As licensed independent practitioners, CRNAs may be authorized—through the granting of clinical privileges—to deliver anesthesia care, in conformity with TJC standards. CRNA practice is not a medically delegated act, unless specifically defined as such by state nursing boards or institutional policy. CRNAs collaborate with other qualified and legally authorized healthcare providers in their delivery of anesthesia services.[175]

Long-standing debate continues about the issue of supervision of CRNA practice. ASA promotes the idea that CRNAs require anesthesiologist supervision in order to provide safe, quality care.[176] The AANA opposes this viewpoint as well as statutory or regulatory proposals which require such arrangements.

Turf wars have been fought in multiple states, with varying outcomes. Texas Senate Bill 673, the Omnibus Health Care Bill, defines the conditions under which a CRNA may deliver anesthesia and allows full utilization of the services and skills of CRNAs. In New Jersey, as previously discussed, CRNAs providing general or regional anesthesia must be supervised by an anesthesiologist. In most states, however, there are no requirements for anesthesiologist presence, except as described in institutional policies. More detail about governmental and non-governmental regulation of CRNA practice is provided in *A Professional Study and Resource Guide for the CRNA* (2005).

The responsibility for anesthesia falls to the anesthesia provider and not the surgeon, unless the surgeon chooses to control the specific anesthetic interventions, such as technique, drug, or dosage. The issue of responsibility is related to the degree of control exercised by the surgeon over the anesthesia provider and not to the specific professional identity (CRNA, MD, or DO) of the provider.[177]

TIP: Cases involving issues of supervision are strongly influenced by the individual considerations of the case, more so than any regulation, guideline, or protocol.

Practice arrangements are likely to be defined from an administrative viewpoint as well as from a clinical perspective. For instance, in some institutions CRNAs are employed by the hospital but their day-to-day clinical practice involves medical supervision by a group of private practice anesthesiologists. Practice arrangements may raise such questions as:

1. Who is an agent of whom?
2. Who exercises control and supervision?
3. What effects result from two professions?

Both Peters and Dornette summarize elements of this issue. Issues of negligence involving CRNA practice are often complicated by questions of control and supervision.[178,179] Identity and proximity of the supervisor are important elements, as described by Schaikewitz.[180]

TIP: It is important to determine whether the supervisor was present during crucial periods of the anesthetic.

Institutional or departmental policy may address the level of supervision for a particular anesthesia department. Wide variability exists in the actual practice patterns when such policies exist. It has been pointed out that policies requiring physician anesthesiologist supervision may actually create a liability risk, especially when such policies are not followed. These policies may also prevent access to care when they are restrictive of CRNA practice. Issues of reimbursement may drive supervision requirements. Medicare guidelines stipulate requirements for physician supervision and medical direction of CRNAs providing anesthesia care.

In *Battaglia v. Jones*, a 40-year-old married man with two children was undergoing a knee arthroscopy when he suffered cardiac arrest. He was resuscitated but had suffered massive brain damage and died several weeks later. Review of the evidence showed that the anesthesiologist had met with, and obtained consent from, the patient. The anesthesiologist represented that she would provide for the anesthesia. A CRNA subsequently provided the anesthesia, with the supervising anesthesiologist leaving the room after surgery began. Evidence and expert opinion indicated that the right main bronchus was intubated, resulting in ventilation of primarily one lung, and that an esophageal stethoscope was place incorrectly into the left lung, further diminishing ventilation of that lung. During the case the patient developed a progressive bradycardia, or slowing of the heart, culminating in complete cardiac arrest.

There was an alleged 17-minute delay between the last documented heart rate and notification of the OR team that the plaintiff had no pulse and was in cardiac arrest. No alarms sounded, and expert witnesses concluded that either the alarms were turned off or the alarm limits were set too broadly to be useful. The surgeon noticed the CRNA working under the drapes separating the surgical field from the anesthetist, and at that point the CRNA stated that the plaintiff was having ventilation problems. The surgeon immediately withdrew the instruments and uncovered the plaintiff, who was grossly cyanotic. The anesthesiologist was summoned, and resuscitation of the plaintiff began.

There was an estimated 10 to 14 minute delay by the CRNA in identifying the cardiac arrest. An expert witness stated that a one-minute delay in notifying the team would constitute negligence. The autopsy showed that death was due to brain damage from a lack of oxygen. Important findings were related to the negligent and incompetent care rendered to the plaintiff by the CRNA, the failure of the anesthesiologist obtaining consent in notifying the plaintiff that the CRNA would be giving the anesthesia, and the failure to adequately supervise that CRNA. Additionally identified was the joint responsibility of the supervising anesthesiologist group in not identifying the incompetence of the CRNA and allowing her to render substandard care to plaintiff.

Other members of the anesthesiology group had disagreed with vicarious liability theories that held them jointly responsible in the death of the plaintiff, and appealed the original decision as related to their responsibility. The Texas Appellate Court affirmed. *Battaglia v. Jones*, 93 S.W. 3d 132, (Tx App.Ct., 2002), No. 14-00-00428-CV.[181]

When there is no statutory requirement for the presence of an anesthesiologist, questions invariably arise about the liability of healthcare providers, such as surgeons who work with nurse anesthetists, theoretically supervising and operating at the same time. Vicarious liability has been assigned to surgeons working with CRNAs under four theories of liability:

1. The *captain of the ship* doctrine automatically deems the surgeon legally responsible for acts of negligence by his assistants, including perioperative nurses and CRNAs. This is rarely applied today unless it is apparent the surgeon exercised control over the CRNA's actions. If the surgeon specifically dictates anesthesia technique, drug selection, or drug dose, then liability may be assumed under this theory of supervision.

2. The *borrowed servant* doctrine holds the surgeon responsible for the CRNA's actions (even though the CRNA may not be in the surgeon's employ) because he actually uses or controls the CRNA's services.

3. The theory of *respondeat superior* holds the surgeon responsible for the acts of his employees or those he controls.

4. The theory of *negligent supervision* holds the surgeon responsible for controlling the actions of the CRNA (and other nurses in the OR).[182]

The distinctions among the above theories are not always obvious, as a review of common law interpretations and decisions will reveal.

In *Harris v. Miller* a nurse anesthetist was working with an orthopedic surgeon on a patient for a lumbar laminectomy. No anesthesiologist was present at the small hospital. The hospital manual stated the CRNA worked under the direction of the surgeon. The CRNA's preoperative evaluation failed to note the patient's enlarged heart, and no ECG was ordered despite a history of mild obesity and high blood pressure. The CRNA failed to check for bilateral breath sounds after the patient was placed in a prone position for surgery. Postoperative x-ray revealed right main stem bronchus intubation, leaving the left lung unventilated. During the procedure, the patient's vital signs became unstable, but the nurse anesthetist did not inform the surgeon. The surgeon was trying to control ongoing surgical bleeding and did not inquire about the patient's vital signs, although he did request a blood transfusion. Approximately three hours into the surgery the CRNA informed the surgeon the patient had no blood pressure or pulse, at which point the surgeon ordered discontinuation of the anesthetic. One-hundred percent oxygen was given to the patient. By the time the patient was turned back to a supine position and resuscitated he had sustained permanent brain damage. The North Carolina Supreme Court held that the surgeon did have control over the actions of the anesthetist, as shown when he began to direct the resuscitation, and that he could be held vicariously liable for the anesthetist's negligence. Several experts also testified the surgeon should have remained informed about the patient's vital signs in light of the surgical bleeding. *Harris v. Miller*, 438 s.e. 2d 731 (N.C. 1994).[183]

State regulations vary widely in the amount and type of supervision required of physicians overseeing the anesthesia care from CRNAs delivered to the physician's patients. In 1997 the Health Care Financing Administration (HCFA) (now the Centers for Medicare and Medicaid Services, or CMS), proposed a rule that would remove the federal Medicare requirement and defer to state law on the issue of physician supervision of CRNAs. In 2001 this proposal was effectively withdrawn, leaving states with the option of eliminating the requirement of physician supervision for CRNAs. As of 2010, 14 states had "opted out" of the requirement for physician supervision of CRNAs. Residents of "rural" states may be denied access to anesthesia services if physician supervision is required, given that almost all anesthesia services are provided by CRNAs, without anesthesiologist availability, and in the case of emergencies without any physician supervision.

California's Governor Arnold Schwarzenneger recently made the decision to opt out of the Medicare provision requiring physician supervision of CRNAs. On February 3, 2010 the California Medical Association and the California Society of Anesthesiologists filed suit to block Governor Schwarzenneger's decision, on the broad issue of patient safety.[184] The AANA and California Association of Nurse Anesthetists argue that CRNAs provide safe care, and the issue is patient access to emergency care, especially in rural areas.

TIP: Attorneys reviewing cases involving CRNA care may need to review CMS regulations for reimbursement, determining physician anesthesiologist involvement (medical direction versus medical supervision). The following must also be reviewed: state medical and nursing statutes and regulations, hospital guidelines, departmental policies and procedures, and any submission of reimbursement documentation. If private insurance is a sole or secondary provider, insurance bills, guidelines, and documentation should also be reviewed.

For a case to be considered medically directed, an anesthesiologist must be present during critical points in the procedure and be immediately available for diagnosis and treatment of emergencies. Medically directed anesthesia services are performed by a CRNA or an AA, and require that the anesthesiologist:

1. perform preanesthesia examination and evaluation;
2. prescribe the anesthesia plan;
3. personally participate in the most demanding procedures of the anesthesia plan, including induction and emergence, if applicable;
4. monitor at frequent intervals the course of anesthesia administered;
5. remain physically present and available for immediate diagnosis and treatment of emergencies; and
6. order postanesthesia care.

Medically supervised anesthesia services are performed by a CRNA and supervised by the attending physician. When a CRNA is medically supervised, the attending physician must:

1. review and verify the preanesthesia evaluation performed by the CRNA;
2. review the anesthesia plan, including medication;
3. review and comment during preanesthesia care;
4. review and comment during postanesthesia care.[185,186]

TIP: Anesthesiologist assistants must perform services under the medical direction of an anesthesiologist. Therefore, by definition, anesthesiologist assistants may not perform "medically supervised" anesthesia services.[187] The term "direct supervision" is used by the American Society of Anesthesiologists, and in Anesthesiologist Assistant licensure language (www.anesthesiaassistant.com/AnesthesiologistAssistantLegislation.html), and specifies that the supervising anesthesiologist be immediately present within the anesthetizing area. Medical direction requires more intensive involvement by the anesthesiologist. See requirements for medical direction by the anesthesiologist (immediately above).

In a case settled in Michigan for $3,045,000 the plaintiff was admitted to the hospital for a low anterior colon resection. A thoracic epidural catheter was placed for postoperative pain management. The plaintiff was taken to the OR by the defendant anesthesiologist assistant who, without approval of the anesthesiologist, activated the epidural with 5 ml of 2 percent lidocaine with epinephrine. The defendant AA then induced general anesthesia with the anesthesiologist in attendance. Shortly after the induction the anesthesiologist left to care for another patient. The patient became hypotensive and bradycardic, and then develop pulseless electrical activity (ECG rhythm in the absence of a pulse). The plaintiff was successfully resuscitated following cardiac arrest, but was disabled due to hypoxic ischemic injury. Plaintiff maintained hypotension resulted from epidural administration of local anesthetic in presence of bowel preparation-induced volume depletion, and that AA was slow to call the anesthesiologist to return to the OR for assistance in treating the hypotension. Defendants claimed it was appropriate for AA to treat the blood pressure without immediately calling the anesthesiologist, and that hypotension was due to an allergic response to the induction medications. *Anonymous Woman v. Anonymous Anesthesia Assistant, Anonymous Anesthesiologist and Anonymous Hospital*, unknown Michigan venue.[188]

Issues of direction of the AA by the anesthesiologist are at the heart of this occurrence, and speak to the absence of medical direction, or direct supervision necessary for the practice of the anesthesiologist assistant.

20.13 Unique Aspects of Anesthesia Care

Some unique aspects of anesthesia care deserve comment. The qualified anesthesia provider must remain with the anesthetized patient at all times, unless relieved by another qualified provider, who receives a status report and is prepared to function effectively in the role of the previous provider. Relief names and times must be clearly indicated on the anesthesia record. Fatigue, boredom, and sleep deprivation have all been addressed in the anesthesia literature. A heavy and prolonged workload, frequently occurring with night and weekend call, may contribute to error. Studies have established that 24 hours of continuous wakefulness impairs psychomotor equivalent to a blood alcohol level of 0.1 percent, which is above the legal limit for driving in all states. Regular breaks and meals for the CRNA are important for patient welfare. Studies have shown that personnel "changes" during anesthesia are useful in the discovery of errors and problems that need resolution.[190]

Anesthesia practice is an area of high risk for substance abuse because of high stress levels, fatigue, periods of boredom, respect not equivalent to responsibility, and easy accessibility to and knowledge of controlled substances.[191] Although awareness and education of anesthesia providers has increased regarding this serious occupational risk, it is still a factor potentially contributing to adverse outcomes. Prevention and early identification of chemical dependency have been identified as important elements of departmental function leading to increased patient safety.[192,193] The discovery that a defendant is a substance abuser may have a profound effect on a medical malpractice case.

20.14 Human Error, Crisis Management, and Anesthesia Practice

Several authors have described similarities between anesthesia care and aviation. The role of human error has been identified in both the aviation industry and in anesthesia practice.[194] Anesthesia care and commercial aviation share the following factors:

- safety as a primary concern;
- complex, dynamic events which may arise from circumstances beyond the control of the provider or pilot;
- special characteristics of the process;
- blending of technical and intellectual dexterity, with multiple levels of mental activity;
- standard, complicated "workstations" with alarms and backup systems;
- checklist procedures;
- data acquisition and storage (aviation "black box");
- repetitive tasks, boredom, and fatigue, with an occasional sudden need to act quickly to avoid disaster; and
- ongoing education and training.

Gaba's work suggests following the aviation industry's model of crew resource management (CRM) in anesthesia care, using:

- prioritization of tasks;
- distribution of workload;
- communication;
- mobilization and use of all available resources;
- monitoring and cross-checking.[195]

Simulators have been used in the aviation industry for training, evaluation, and reorientation. Anesthesia simulators are now utilized at a number of training facilities, and computer simulation software is now widely available and increasingly utilized in the anesthesia community.[196] Increases in performance have been measured in studies utilizing simulators for medical and anesthesia training.[197]

Perhaps the insurance industry could promote the formalized use of simulators by discounting premiums for participating departments and institutions. Examination of the anesthesia providers' actions from the point of view of crisis management may provide a defense, or may show evidence of being unprepared. Since it is impossible to anticipate every possible event in anesthesia, reconstruction of events and activities should focus on reasonable anticipation and preparation as well as appropriate intervention and ongoing assessment. While high levels of uncertainty and time pressures during physiologic crisis require preparedness, events may occur so rapidly that adverse outcomes may result despite the CRNA's correct and defensible actions.

The complex nature of decision making in anesthesia has been explored in Gaba's work on modes of error, which provides insight into the "tightly-coupled physiologic systems" that are part and parcel of anesthetic mishap.[198,199] In spite of "tightly-coupled" physiologic systems, rarely does a single error lead to an adverse outcome. A "cascade of events" leads to the crisis and adverse outcome.[200] Inaction in the face of physiologic warnings (low blood pressure, decreased oxygen saturation, rapid heart rate, and the like), or clinging to a historically unsuccessful approach in treating a problem are characteristic behaviors associated with the adverse outcome.[201]

While retrospective analysis may indicate that a different management would have been the best course, it is important to remember that abstract thinking does not, nor can it be expected to, occur during the crisis.[202] In any event, as Gaba points out, the human body does not come with a "schematic," and so a wide range of responses must be expected; and while a good plan is necessary, changes or adjustments in plan are commonplace.[203]

TIP: Depositions may need to be taken from many personnel in order to identify when and how decisions were made during the crisis, and to reconstruct chronologically the events leading up to the crisis.

Gaba also points out that organizational factors may contribute to the occurrence of human error.[204] In the mid-1990s the anesthesia literature began to address problems associated with production pressure,[205] and these pressures have increased due to healthcare reforms that mandated cost-effective practice with shrinking anesthesia and surgical reimbursement.[206] An APSF survey,[207] referred to previously, listed production pressure as the number two concern of anesthesia providers, with difficult airway management as the number one risk. Public concerns regarding medical mistakes, including medication errors and anesthesia awareness will continue to push the anesthesia community

towards more circumspect practice. TJC has introduced requirements for analysis of sentinel events, and continuous activity in regards to performance improvement has put the anesthesia community on notice.

20.15 Summary

Anesthesia practice is characterized by paradoxes. It is a highly technical specialty, and yet it cuts across all healthcare specialties, involving patients with a wide variety of medical, surgical, therapeutic, and diagnostic requirements. The anesthesia specialist must be a generalist as well as a specialist. Psychomotor skills for invasive techniques must be coupled with a large body of theoretical knowledge and combined with judgment and decision-making skills.

Anesthesia has been described as "hours of boredom, interrupted by moments of sheer terror." Delivery of anesthesia is the maintenance of life and health while simultaneously administering potentially lethal medications that interrupt life-supporting reflexes. CRNAs use technologically advanced delivery and monitoring systems simultaneously with the five senses and "common sense" to make expert decisions.[208]

In this context, anesthesia practice offers unique challenges in its analysis. CRNAs practice with high levels of competence and autonomy, but share responsibility with other independent practitioners in a complex and dynamic environment. Many outside influences impact CRNA practice, but individual anesthesia providers retain the obligation to function at or above the standard of care. Analysis of cases involving CRNAs requires an understanding of the basic clinical principles of anesthesia safety as well as the ability to delineate legal responsibility for anesthesia care and the adverse outcome.

Endnotes

1. Dornette, W., (ed.) *Legal Issues in Anesthesia Practice*, vii–viii. Philadelphia: F. A. Davis, 1991.

2. Simpson, J., "Understanding malpractice litigation." In *Professional Aspects of Nurse Anesthesia Practice*, eds. S. D. Foster and L. M. Jordan. Philadelphia: F. A. Davis, 1994.

3. Macready, N. (ed.), "Medical errors: an anesthesia success story," *Anesthesia Malpractice Prevention* 5, no. 2 (2000): 9–16.

4. Eichorn, J. and Hassan, Zaki-Udin. Anesthesia, perioperative mortality, and predictors of adverse outcomes. In Complications of Anesthesiology, eds. E. Lobato, N. Gravenstein, and R. Kirby. Philadelphia: Lippincott, Williams&Wilkins, 2008.

5. St. Paul Medical Services. *Nurse Anesthesia Update*, 3–7, 1999.

6. *Id.*

7. Cheney, F., "The American Society of Anesthesiologists' Closed Claims Project: What we have learned, how it has affected patients, and how it will affect practice in the future?" *Anesthesiology* 91, no. 2 (1999): 552–556.

8. Caplan, R., "The ASA Closed Claims Project: Lessons Learned. 50th Annual Refresher Course Lectures and Clinical Update Program," *American Society of Anesthesiologists* 121 (1999): 1–7.

9. Waters, R. M., "John Snow, First Anesthetist," *Bios* 25, no. 136, 40–45.

10. Boulton, T. B. "Ralph Waters' Visit to Great Britain in 1936," asahq.org/Newsletters/2001/09_01/boulton. htm, accessed 5/17/10.

11. *Id.*

12. Thatcher, V., *History of Anesthesia with Emphasis on the Nurse Specialist,* 88. Philadelphia: Lippincott, 1953.

13. Bankert, M., *Watchful Care: A History of America's Nurse Anesthetists*. New York: Continuum Publishing Company, 1989.

14. Peterson, G. N., et al., "Management of the difficult airway: a closed claims analysis," *Anesthesiology* 103, no. 1 (July 2005: 33–39).

15. Laska, L. (ed.), "Aspiration of stomach acids and death blamed on negligent anesthesiologist," *Medical Malpractice Verdicts, Settlements, and Experts* (July 1998): 4.

16. www.mhaus.org, accessed 5/17/06.

17. www.mhreg.org, accessed 5/17/06.

18. Horlocker, T. T. et al., "The second ASRA consensus conference on neuraxial anesthesia and anticoagulation," *Regional Anesthesia and Pain Management* 28 (2003): 172–197.

19. Horlocker, T. T., "New Guidelines for Antithrombotic Therapy: Making Blood Thinner Than Water," *ASA Newsletter*. www.asahq.org/Newsletters/2005/05-05/ Horlocker05_05.html, accessed 5/17/10.

20. MacReady, N. (ed.), "Was anesthesiologist responsible for man's hypotensive crisis, death?" *Anesthesia Malpractice Prevention* 4, no. 12 (December 1994): 92–94.

21. *York v. Roof El-Ganzouri.* www.state.il.us/court/ opinion/appellatecourt/2004/1stdistrict/september/ html/1030222.htm

22. ASRA Practice Advisory on Local Anesthetic Systemic Toxicity. Neal et al. *Regional Anesthesia and Pain Medicine.* March/April 2010. Volume 35, Issue 2, pp 152-161.

23. Laska, L. (ed.), "$5 million Illinois settlement for woman kept on epidural anesthesia too long following knee-replacement surgery," *Medical Malpractice Verdicts, Settlements, and Experts* (May 1998): 2.

24. American Association of Nurse Anesthetists. *Professional Practice Manual for the Certified Registered Nurse Anesthetist*. Park Ridge, Illinois, 2005.

25. Perris, T. M. and J. M. Watt, "The road to success: A review of 1000 axillary brachial plexus blocks," *Anesthesia* (2003): 58.

26. American Society of Anesthesiologists, "Continuum of Depth of Sedation; Definition of General Anesthesia and Levels of Sedation/Analgesia," (Approved by ASA House of Delegates on October 13, 1999, and amended on October 27, 2004). www.asahq.org/Sedation, accessed 5/17/10.

27. Domino, K. B., "Trends in Anesthesia Litigation in the 1990's: Monitored Anesthesia Care," *ASA Newsletter* (June 1997) 67, no. 6. www. asahq.org/Newsletters, accessed 5/17/10.

28. AANA-ASA "Joint Statement Regarding Propofol Administration." www.asahq.org/news/propofol statement.htm, accessed 5/17/10.

29. "Position Statement: ASGE/SGNA Role of GI Registered Nurses in the Management of Patients Undergoing Sedated Procedures," www.sgna.org/Resources/ statements/jointstatement.cfm. 2004, accessed 5/17/10.

30. *American Association of Nurse Anesthetists Newsletter.* Quality Review in Anesthesia 2, no. 6 (January-February 2000): 3.

31. See note 4 at 7.

32. See note 6.

33. Cheney, F., 'Changing Trends in Anesthesia-Related Death and Permanent Brain Damage," *ASA Newsletter* 66, no. 6 (June 2002).

34. *Id.*

35. *Id.*

36. United States Department of Health and Human Services. *2003 Annual Report*, National Practitioner Data Bank.

37. "American Society of Anesthesiologists Task Force on Difficult Airway Management. Practice Guidelines for Management of the Difficult Airway." 2002 www.asahq/difficult airway algorithm, accessed 5/17/10.

38. Macready, N., (ed.), "Plan strategy for difficult extubations; algorithm is considered standard of care," *Anesthesia Malpractice Prevention* 2, no. 11 (November 1997): 81–84.

39. Moss, E., "NJ State safety regulations now include airway cart," *Anesthesia Patient Safety Foundation Newsletter* (Spring 1999): 4.

40. See note 37.

41. McCullough, T. C. et al., "Estimated blood loss underestimates calculated blood loss during radical retropubic prostatectomy," *Urologica Internationale* 72, no. 1 (2004): 13–16.

42. Cherian, M. N. and J. C. Emmanuel, "Clinical Use of Blood," *Update in Anaesthesia* 14, article 6 (2002).

43. See note 1.

44. Roth, S., "Postoperative Vision Loss," In *Miller's Anesthesia*, Sixth edition. Philadelphia: Elsevier, 2005.

45. Williams, E., et al., "Postoperative ischemic optic neuropathy," *Anesthesia and Analgesia* 80 (May 1995): 1018–1029.

46. Lofsky, A. and M. Gorney, "Induced hypotension tied to possible vision impairments," *Anesthesia Patient Safety Foundation Newsletter* 13, no. 2 (Summer 1998).

47. Schaikewitz, P., "Failure to notice gas accumulation costs anesthesiologist $7 million plus," *Anesthesia Malpractice Protector* 6, no. 12 (December 1994): 133–135.

48. Stoelting, R. K., "APSF Survey Results Identify Safety Priorities. Airway Still Number 1," www.apsf.org/resource_center/newsletter/1999/spring/05apsf survey.htm, accessed 5/17/10.

49. Gaba D. M., S. K. Howard, and B. Jump, "Production pressure in the work environment. California anesthesiologists' attitudes and experiences," *Anesthesiology 81*, no. 2 (August 1994): 4880–5000.

50. *Id.*

51. Ang-Lee, M., C. Yuan, and J. Moss, "Complementary and Alternative Therapies," *Miller's Anesthesia,* Sixth edition. Philadelphia: Elsevier, 2005.

52. "Possible Risks to Surgical Patients Who Use Complementary/Alternative Medicines," www.anesthesiapatientsafety.com/patients/med/CAM.asp, accessed 5/17/10.

53. Rozien, M. F. and L. A. Fleisher, "Anesthetic Implications of Concurrent Diseases," *Miller's Anesthesia*, Sixth edition. Philadelphia: Elsevier, 2005.

54. Lewyn, M., "Anesthetized patient claims pain and awareness, sues anesthesia team," *Anesthesia Malpractice Protector* 6, no. 3 (1994) 25–29.

55. *Franklin v. Gupta* 567 A. 2d 524, 81 Md. App. 345, No. 940. Lexis 2, January 3, 1990. www.lexis-nexis.com, accessed 5/21/10.

56. Laska, L. (ed.) "Man Dies After Undergoing Pacemaker Surgery Despite Fluid in Lungs." *Medical Malpractice Verdicts, Settlements, and Experts.* (May 2009): 4.

57. See note 1.

58. Laska L. (ed.), Brain Injury from lack of oxygenation during surgery for collapsed lung in teenager—$869,999 Michigan settlement. *Medical Malpractice Verdicts, Settlements, and Experts.* (June 2009): 3.

59. Laska, L. (ed.), "Man With Papillomas in Throat Unable to be Intubated Becausee Anesthesiologist Didn't Check Condition." *Medical Malpractice Verdicts, Settlements, and Experts* (September 2009): 45.

60. Laska, L. (ed.), "Epidural anesthesia for cesarean section inadequate," *Medical Malpractice Verdicts, Settlements, and Experts* (October 1994): 38.

61. American Society of Regional Anesthesia. "Regional Anesthesia in the Anticoagulated Patient: Defining the Risks (The Second ASRA Consensus Conference on Neuraxial Anesthesia and Anticoagulation)," www.asra.com/consensus_statements/RAPM-Anticoagulation.pdf, accessed 5/17/10.

62. American Society of Anesthesiologists. "Practice Guidelines for Preoperative Fasting and the Use of Pharmacologic Agents to Reduce the Risk of Pulmonary Aspiration: Application to Healthy Patients Undergoing Elective Procedures," www.asahq.org/publicationsAndServices/NPO.pdf, accessed 4/12/06.

63. Schaikewitz, P., "Respiratory distress settlement incurs $210,000 settlement," *Anesthesia Malpractice Protector* 6, no. 8 (August 1994): 91–92.

64. U.S. Food and Drug Administration, "Anesthesia apparatus checkout recommendations," http://www.fda.gov/cdrh/humfac/anesckot.pdf., accessed 5/17/10.

65. Rose, D. K. and M. M. Cohen, "The airway: problems and predictions in 18,500 patients," *Canadian Journal of Anaesthesia* 41 (1994): 372.

66. See note 35.

67. Laska, L. (ed.) "Failure to Achieve Intubation of Woman for Surgery." *Medical Malpractice Verdicts, Settlements, and Experts.* (April 2009): 5.

68. Cohen, M. M., C. B. Cameron, and P. G. Duncan, "Pediatric anesthesia morbidity and mortality in the perioperative period," *Anesthesia and Analgesia* 70, no. 2 (February 1990) 160–67.

69. Morray, J. P. and S. M. Bhananker, "Recent findings from pediatric perioperative cardiac arrest (POCA) registry," *ASA Newsletter* 69 (June 2005).

70. Lofsky, A. S. "Turn your alarms on!" *Anesthesia Patient Safety Foundation Newsletter* (Winter 2004).

71. See note 1.

72. American Society of Anesthesiologists, "Practice Advisory for Intraoperative Awareness and Brain Function Monitoring," Approved by ASA House of Delegates, October 2005. www.asahq.org/news/AwareAdvisory-FinalOct05.pdf, accessed 5/17/10.

73. Sigalovsky, N., "Awareness under general anesthesia," *AANA Journal* (October 2003): 71.

74. Litwiller, R., "Awareness under general anesthesia and ASA." *ASA Newsletter* (January 2004).

75. See note 72.

76. See note 1.

77. See note 1.

78. Gaba, D., K. Fish, and S. Howard, *Crisis Management in Anesthesia.* New York: Churchill Livingstone, 1994.

79. Laska, L. (ed.) "Premature Extubation Blamed for Brain Damage and Death." *Medical Malpractice, Verdicts, Settlements, and Experts.* (May 2009): 3.

80. *Bainhauer v. Lehigh Valley Hospital*, 834 A. 2d 1146, 2003 PA Super. 338, No. 3461 EDA 2002 (2003). http://www.thefreelibrary.com/Was+contraindicated+neosynephrine+cause+of+stroke+during..._a0114783138. Accessed 5/23/10

81. Laska, L. (ed.) "Failure to Attempt Intubation for Woman with Neck Hematoma Following Thyroidectomy." *Medical Malpractice, Verdicts, Settlements, and Experts.* (June 2009): 3.

82. Dreyfuss, J., "Fast track anesthesia: emerging issues and opportunities," *Anesthesiology News,* Special Supplement (June 1999).

83. London, M., et al., "Fast tracking into the new millennium: an evolving paradigm," *Anesthesiology* 4, no. 1 (October 1999).

84. Gupta, A., et al. "Comparison of Recovery Profile After Ambulatory Anesthesia with Propofol, Isoflurane, Sevoflurane and Desflurane," *Anesthesia and Analgesia* (2004): 98.

85. Song, D. et al., "Fast-tracking (bypassing the PACU) does not reduce nursing workload after ambulatory surgery," *British Journal of Anaesthesia* 93, no. 6 (2003).

86. American Society for Testing and Materials (ASTM): "Standard Specifications for Particular Requirements for Anesthesia Workstations and Their Components" (ASTM F1850-00.) West Conshohocken, Pennsylvania: American Society for Testing and Materials, 2000.

87. *Id.*

88. Bowdle, T. M., "Central line complications from the ASA closed claims project: An update," *ASA Newsletter* 6 (June 2002).

89. *Id.*

90. Lake, C. L., R. Hines, C. Blitt, and D. Lake, *Clinical Monitoring.* Philadelphia: W. B. Saunders, 2001.

91. *Id.*

92. *Id.*

93. Laska, L. (ed.) "Failure to Properly Place Central Line for Intravenous Feedings." *Medical Malpractice Verdicts, Settlements, and Experts.* (January 2009): 3.

94. Stoelting, R. K. (ed.), *Pharmacology and Physiology in Anesthetic Practice,* Fourth edition. Philadelphia: Lippincott Williams & Wilkins, 2006.

95. *Roberts v. Cox,* 669 S0. 2d 63 (LA App. 1996). Lexis 324. www.lexis-nexis.com, accessed 5/23/10

96. Larach, M. G., H. Rosenberg, G. A. Gronert, and G. C. Allen, "Hyperkalemic cardiac arrest during anesthesia in infants and children with occult myopathies," *Clinical Pediatrics* 36, no. 1 (January 1997).

97. "Syringe Swap," *New Jersey Law Journal* 12 (January 24, 2000).

98. Martin, J. T. and M. A. Warner (eds.), *Positioning in Anesthesia and Surgery,* Third edition. Philadelphia: W. B. Saunders, 1997.

99. Thompson, G. and A. Lui, "Perioperative Nerve Injury,"In *Anesthesia and Perioperative Complications,* eds. J. Benumof and L. Saidman. St. Louis: Mosby Year Book, 1992.

100. Caplan, R., "The ASA Closed Claims Project: Lessons Learned," 50th Annual Refresher Course Lectures and Clinical Update Program, *American Society of Anesthesiologists* 121 (1999): 1–7.

101. *Id.*

102. See note 1.

103. Cheney, F.W. Domino, K.B., Caplan, R.A., et.al. Nerve injury asssociated with anesthesia: A closed claims analysis. *Anesthesiology.* 1990; 90:1062.

104. Faust, R. J., R. F. Cuchiara, and P. S. Bechtle, "Patient Positioning," *Miller's Anesthesia,* Sixth edition. Philadelphia: Elsevier, 2005.

105. See note 98.

106. Id.

107. Laska, L. (ed.) "Failure to Recognize Extubation Blamed for Asystole and Death." Medical Malpractice Verdicts, Settlements, and Experts. (October 2009): 4.

108. Sessler, D. I., "Temperature Monitoring," *Miller's Anesthesia,* Sixth edition. Philadelphia: Elsevier, 2005.

109. Laska, L. (ed.), "Carpal Tunnel Surgery Performed Instead of Trigger Finger Release," *Medical Malpractice Verdicts, Settlements, and Experts* (April 2005): 3.

110. Laska, L. (ed.), "Epidural anesthesia goes into subarachnoid space in woman in labor," *Medical Malpractice Verdicts, Settlements, and Experts* (August 1999): 3.

111. Chadwick, H. S. "Editorial. Obstetrics anesthesia: medical risks in the USA," *Minerva Anesthesiologica* (2005): 71.

112. Davies, J. M., "Obstetric anesthesia closed claims. Trends over last three decades," *ASA Newsletter* (2004): 68.

113. *Glassman v. Costello,* 267 Kan. 509, 98 P. 2d 1050, No. 78,905, (1999). Lexis 390. www.lexis-nexis.com, accessed 5/23/10

114. American Association of Nurse Anesthetists. Standards and Guidelines, "Guidelines for the Management of the Obstetrical Patient for the Certified Registered Nurse Anesthetist," *Professional Practice Manual for the Certified Registered Nurse Anesthetist.* Park Ridge, Illinois: AANA Publishing, 2003.

115. www.emedicinehealth.com/outpatient_surgery/article_em.htm, accessed 5/17/10

116. Koch, M. E., S. Dayan, and D. Barinholtz, "Office-based anesthesia: An overview," *Anesthesiology Clinics of North America* 21 (2003): 417.

117. ASA Guidelines for Office-Based Anesthesia. www.asahq.org/publicationsandServices/standards/12.pdf, accessed 5/17/10.

118. American Association of Nurse Anesthetists. Standards and Guidelines, "Standards for Office Based Anesthesia," *Professional Practice Manual for the Certified Registered Nurse Anesthetist.* Park Ridge, Illinois, AANA Publishing, 2005.

119. American Association of Nurse Anesthetists, "Scope and Standards for Nurse Anesthesia Practice," *Professional Practice Manual for the Certified Registered Nurse Anesthetist*. Park Ridge, Illinois, AANA Publishing, 2005.

120. Twersky, R., "Take on new responsibilities," *Anesthesia Malpractice Prevention* 2, no. 9 (September 1997): 69.

121. Walman, A., "Risks in ultrarapid drug detox," *Anesthesia Malpractice Prevention* 4, no. 9 (November 1999): 65– 72

122. Stenrud, P. E., "Anesthesia at Remote Locations," *Miller's Anesthesia*. Philadelphia: Elsevier, 2005.

123. U.S. Food and Drug Administration. Center for Devices and Radiologic Health. www.fda.gov/opacom/more-choices/fdaforms/fdaforms.html, accessed 5/17/10.

124. Dorsch, J. A. *Understanding Anesthesia Equipment*, Fourth edition. Philadelphia: Lippincott Williams & Wilkins, 1999.

125. *Id.*

126. Carbon Dioxide Absorbent Dessication Safety Conference. *APSF Newsletter.* www.apsf.org/resource_center/newsletter/2005/summer/01co2.htm, accessed 5/17/10.

127. Learman, J., "Credentialing and Privileging in Clinical Practice," In *A Professional Study and Resource Guide for the CRNA*, eds. S. D. Foster and M. Faut-Callahan, American Association of Nurse Anesthetists. Park Ridge, Illinois: AANA Publishing, 2001.

128. Tobin, M. H., "State Governmental Regulation of Nurse Anesthesia Practice," In *A Professional Resource and Study Guide for the CRNA*, eds. S. Foster and M. Faut-Callahan, 111–131. Park Ridge, Illinois: AANA Publishing, 2001.

129. Rozien, M. F., "Preoperative Evaluation," *Miller's Anesthesia*. Philadelphia: Elsevier, 2005.

130. "ASA Physical Status Classification." Asahq.org/clinical/physicalstatushtm, accessed 5/17/10.

131. Simpson, J. A. and G. A. Blumenreich, "Understanding Malpractice Litigation," In *A Professional Study and Resource Guide for the CRNA*, eds. S. Foster and M. Faut-Callahan, 89–109. Park Ridge, Illinois: AANA Publishing, 2001.

132. Walman, A., "Informed consent in anesthesiology: What is it?" *Anesthesia Malpractice Provider* 6, no. 11 (November 1994): 126–128.

133. See note 122.

134. Laska, L., (ed.), "Improper Intubation for Laparotomy Blamed for Arytenoid Dislocation of Larynx and Hoarseness," *Medical Malpractice Verdicts, Settlements, and Experts,* (March 2005): 3.

135. See note 122.

136. See note 110.

137. *Bentley v. Langley*, 296 N.C. 735, 254 S.E. 2d 176, No. 788SC87, (1979). Lexis 2332. www.lexis-nexis.com, accessed 5/23/10

138. Reich, D. L. et al., "Arterial Blood Pressure and Heart Rate Discrepancies Between Handwritten and Computerized Anesthesia Records," *Anesthesia and Analgesia* (2000): 91.

139. Greorini, P., A. Gallina, and M. Caporaloni, "Comparison of One Minute Versus Five Minute Sampling Rate of Physiologic Data," *The Internet Journal of Anesthesiology* 1, no. 4 (1997). www.ispub.com/journal/the_internet_journal_of_anesthesiology/archive/volume_1_number_4_1.html, accessed 5/17/10.

140. *Id.*

141. Gaba, D. M., M. Fish, and S. Howard, *Crisis Management in Anesthesiology*. New York: Churchill Livingstone, 1994.

142. Gibbs, R., "The present and future medicolegal importance of record keeping in anesthesia and intensive care: the case for automation," *Journal of Clinical Monitoring* 5, no. 4 (October 1989): 251–255.

143. Lewyn, M., "CRNA held liable for patient's death during elective surgery," *Anesthesia Malpractice Protector* 6, no. 3 (March 1994) 31–32.

144. See note 141.

145. Posner, K. L. et al., "Variation in Expert Opinion in Medical Malpractice Review," *Anesthesiology* 85, no. 5 (November 1995).

146. The Joint Commission Standard LD.3.70. www.jointcommission.org.

147. Blumenreich, G. A., "Anesthesia and JCAHO," www. aana.com/Resources.aspx?id=2396. accessed 5/17/10.

148. *Id.*

149. *Id.*

150. 66. Fed. Reg. [4676 at] 4680 (January 18, 2001).

151. Schaikewitz, P., "Unavailability of anesthesiologist leads to patient's brain damage," *Anesthesia Malpractice Protector* 7, no. 1 (1995): 1–4.

152. *Id.*

153. See note 119.

154. Bankert, M., *Watchful Care: A history of America's Nurse Anesthetists.* New York: Continuum Publishing Company, 1989.

155. Mannino, M., *The Nurse Anesthetist and the Law.* New York: Grune & Stratton, 1982.

156. Jenny, S. and M. Shotten, "The legal status of the nurse anesthetist," In *Legal Issues in Anesthesia Practice,* ed. W. H. L. Dornette. Philadelphia: F.A. Davis, 1991.

157. Blumenreich, G. A., "The U.S. Legal System and Issues Affecting Clinical Practice," In *A Professional Study and Resource Guide for the CRNA,* eds. S. Foster and L. Jordan, 203–223. Philadelphia: F. A. Davis,1994.

158. *Id.*

159. Garde, J., "Keeping in balance with the National Practitioner Data Bank," *CRNA Forum* 7, no. 1 (1991).

160. Jordan, L., "Qualifications and capabilities of the certified registered nurse anesthetist," In *Professional Aspects of Nurse Anesthesia Practice,* eds. S. Foster and L. Jordan, 3–10. Philadelphia: F.A. Davis, 1994.

161. Tunajek, S., "Standards of Care in Anesthesia Practice," In *A Professional Study and Resource Guide for the CRNA,* eds. S. Foster and M. Faut-Callahan, 255–285. Park Ridge, Illinois: AANA Publishing, 2001.

162. See note 1.

163. Zambricki, C. S., "'Anesthesia providers, patient outcomes, and costs: The AANA responds to the Abenstein and Warner article in the June 1996 Anesthesia and Analgesia," *AANA Journal* (1996): 64.

164. Smith, A.F., Kane, M., Milne R., Comparative Effectiveness and Safety of Physician and Nurse Anaesthetists: A Narrative Systematic Review. *British Journal of Anaesthesia.* 93: 540, 2004.

165. Warner, M. A., "The Continuing Saga of Surgical Mortality and Anesthesia Providers," www.asahq. org/Newsletters/2003/07_03/warner.html, accessed 5/17/10.

166. Silber, J. H. et al., "Hospital and Patient Characteristics Associated with Death After Surgery. A Study of Adverse Occurrence and Failure to Rescue," *Medical Care* 30 (1992): 615.

167. American Association of Nurse Anesthetists. *Quality of Care in Anesthesia. Synopsis of Published Information Comparing Certified Registered Nurse Anesthetist and Anesthesiologist Patient Outcomes.* Park Ridge, Illinois, 2004.

168. Pine, M., K. D. Holt, and Y. B. Lou, "Surgical Mortality and Type of Anesthesia Provider," *AANA Journal* (2003): 71.

169. See note 163.

170. See note 157.

171. Blumenreich, G. A., "The CRNA as an expert witness," *Journal of the American Association of Nurse Anesthetists* 62, no. 2 (1995): 85–87.

172. See note 11.

173. See note 12.

174. See note 128.

175. See note 159.

176. American Society of Anesthesiologists. *ASA Standards, Guidelines, and Statements.* Park Ridge, Illinois: American Society of Anesthesiologists, October 1992.

177. See note 1.

178. Peters, Fineberg, Kroll, and Collins. *Anesthesiology and the Law.* Ann Arbor, Michigan: Health Administration Press, School of Public Health, 1983.

179. See note 1.

180. See note 152.

181. *Battaglia v. Jones*, 93 S.W. 3d 132, (Tx App. Ct., 2002), No. 14-00-00428-CV. Lexis 2938. www.lexis-nexis.com,accessed 5/23/10

182. See note 1.

183. See note 131.

184. www.ama-assn.org/amednews/2010/02/22/prsa0222. htm, accessed 5/17/10.

185. Schaikewitz, P., "Physician can be held liable for nurse anesthetist's negligence," *Anesthesia Malpractice Protector* 6, no. 6 (June 1994): 91–92.

186. "Nurse Anesthetist and Anesthesiologist Assistant Services Handbook Sections," Wisconsin Medicaid and Badgercare Nurse Anesthestist and Anesthesiologist Assistant Services Handbook. www.dhfs.state.wi.us/ Medicaid2/handbook/nurse-anes/text/services.htm, accessed 5/18/06.

187. Broadston, L. S., "Reimbursement for Anesthesia Services," In *Professional Resource Guide for the CRNA*, eds. S. Foster and M. Faut-Callahan, 287–312. Park Ridge, Illinois: AANA Publishing, 2001.

188. Laska, L. (ed.) "Administration of Lidocaine With Epinephrine Through Epidural Prior to Colon Surgery Blamed for Hypotension." *Medical Malpractice Verdicts, Settlements, and Experts.* (January 2010): 3.

189. Howard, S., "Fatigue and the Practice of Anesthesiology," www.apsf.org/resource_center/newsletter/2005/ spring/01fatigue.htm, accessed 5/17/10.

190. Dawson, D. and K. Reid, "Fatigue, alcohol, and performance impairment," Scientific Correspondence, *Nature* (1997): 338.

191. Chopra, V. and J. Bovil, "Improving Anesthesia Safety," In *Hazards and Complications of Anesthesia*, Second Edition, eds. T. Taylor and E. Major. New York: Churchill Livingstone, 1993.

192. Quinlan, D., "Peer Assistance, Part 1 and Part 2," In *A Professional Study and Resource Guide for the CRNA*, eds. S. Foster and M. Faut-Callahan, 425–486. Park Ridge, Illinois: AANA Publishing, 2001.

193. Polk, S. L., "Substance Abuse in Anesthesia: patient safety among issues," *Anesthesia Patient Safety Foundation Newsletter* 8, no. 1 (1991): 1–2.

194. See note 141.

195. *Id.*

196. Nyssen, A. et al., "A Comparison of the Training Value of Two Types of Anesthesia Simulators: Computer Screen-Based and Mannequin-Based Simulators," *Anesthesia and Analgesia* (2002): 94.

197. Schwid, H. A., "Anesthesia simulator improves performance in mannequin-based simulator," *Teaching and Learning in Medicine* (2001): 13.

198. Gaba, D. L., "Human error in anesthetic mishaps," *International Anesthesiology Clinics* 27, no. 3 (Fall 1989).

199. See note 141.

200. *Id.*

201. *Id.*

202. Gaba, D. L., S. K. Howard, and S. D. Small, "Situational awareness in anesthesiology," *Human Factors* (1995): 37.

203. See note 141.

204. *Id.*

205. Pierce, Jr., E., "Safety, status, future explored by directors," *Anesthesia Patient Safety Foundation Newsletter* 8, no. 1 (1998): 1–2.

206. Gravenstein, J., "Will cost containment decrease safety?" *Anesthesia Patient Safety Foundation* 10, no. 3 (1995): 25–29.

207. See note 49.

208. Hetrick, W., "Vigilance revisited," *American Society of Anesthesiologists Newsletter* 59, no. 10 (1995): 10–11.

New Publications for Consideration

Gaba, D. L., *Crisis Management in Anesthesiology, Second Edition*. Churchill Livingstone. (Due April 2012).

Lobato, E.B., Gravenstein, N., and Kirby, R. R. *Complications in Anesthesia, Fourth Edition*. Lippincott Williams & Wilkins. (2007)

Nagelhout, J. J. and K. L. Plaus, *Nurse Anesthesia*. Fourth Edition. Saunders Elsevier. (2009)

Acknowledgments

My everlasting gratitude and thanks to D. Catrina Sparacio RN, BSN, JD, and Fran Elliot, RN, PhD, APN, for their invaluable assistance and continued encouragement in editing this chapter. Thanks to Deborah Dlugose, former chapter author, for foundational work in this area. (Special thanks to my wife Julie for putting up with me while I worked on this chapter, and helping me with some of the most tedious aspects of the revision.)

Your friend,
Dave Rodden

Chapter 21

Midwifery Malpractice and Litigation

Elaine K. Diegmann, CNM, ND, FACNM

Synopsis
21.1 Growth of Nurse Midwifery in the United States
21.2 The American College of Nurse Midwives (ACNM)—The National Organization
    A. Accreditation
    B. Core Competencies
    C. Certification
    D. Standards for Midwifery Practice
    E. Ethics
    F. Total Quality Management
    G. Licensure
    H. ACNM Insurance Services
21.3 Foundations of Practice
    A. State Entry into Practice
    B. Regulatory Boards
    C. Prescriptive Privileges
    D. Collaborative Practices
    E. Vicarious Liability
    F. Standards and Scope of Practice
    G. Job Description
    H. Proper Orientation
    I. Facility Policies and Procedures
21.4 Sources of Liability
    A. Control of Risk
    B. Prevention
        1. Fetal assessment and fetal heart rate interpretation
        2. Shoulder dystocia
        3. Resuscitation efforts
        4. Diagnostic errors
        5. VBAC (vaginal birth after cesarean)
        6. Testing measures
        7. Laceration repair and healing
    C. Additional Sources of Liability
        1. Inappropriate use of oxytocin
        2. Fetal death
        3. Failure to notify the physician in a timely fashion
    D. Why People Sue
    E. Education
21.5 Case Presentations
    A. Shoulder Dystocia
    B. Interpretation of a Fetal Heart Tracing
    C. Physician Consultation
21.6 Crucial Questions Following Untoward Events
21.7 Risk Reduction
    A. Clinical Guidelines
    B. Current Practice
    C. Philosophy of Care
    D. Credentialing
    E. Students in the Clinical Setting
21.8 Summary
Endnotes

21.1 Growth of Nurse Midwifery in the United States

The word midwife is derived from *mid,* which means "with," and *wif,* which is translated as "a woman."[1] The translation is literally "with woman," and the simplest definition of the term midwife is "women assisting women to give birth."

Midwifery is often described as the second oldest profession for women brought about by the first. Midwives are even mentioned in the Old Testament of the Bible. In the Book of Exodus, Pharaoh commanded the midwives to kill all the sons born to Hebrew women. They disobeyed, stating that the Hebrew women delivered before the midwife could arrive and carry out the order.

The following are some interesting facts about midwives:

- The first law to regulate midwifery was passed in Germany in 1452.
- In Britain, an instructional manual dates back to 1671.
- In France, evidence of formal education can be traced to the 1500s.
- Midwives came over on the Mayflower and there is documentation that one baby was born at sea.
- Granny midwives came on the slave ships to the colonies in the New World.
- Southern plantations used slave midwives to birth the plantation's mistresses and slaves.
- In Europe, midwives were and continue to be the main attendants of mothers at birth.

In the colonial United States, midwives were responsible for the care of most pregnant women. Preparation of the midwives occurred locally and in unregulated schools that were built on the apprenticeship model with no academic achievement required. In the late 1800s, the best trained midwives were part of the Mormon community which had relocated to Utah.

At the beginning of the twentieth century in the United States, no one can be certain how many babies were born to women attended by midwives. However, at this time there was a beginning trend for physicians to attend births as the financial status of families improved. The place of birth began to shift to the hospital, leaving the midwives to care for the poor women in their homes.

The Flexner Report of 1910 exposed the poor quality of the medical schools and recommended closure of all medical schools and reorganization according to the standard set by Johns Hopkins Medical School. No such report paralleled the need to improve the midwifery preparation. As the medical schools were undergoing positive change, most midwifery schools were closing.[2]

During the early twentieth century it was discovered that the status of maternal and child health in the United States remained poor. In 1912, the Children's Bureau was established to collect statistics on infant mortality rates in the United States. The data revealed that the United States' mortality rates were higher that most rates in Europe. This trend continues to the present day.

Maternal mortality rates were also high, and most deaths were due to puerperal fever, commonly known as "childbed fever." It was easy to insinuate that the midwives were responsible even though puerperal fever deaths were higher in hospitals. This observation, noted by Dr. Ignaz Semmelweis in the 1880s, led to his discovery of the cause of puerperal fever. He observed that not only was the number of deaths higher in hospitals but it also was higher in wards run by physicians than those run by the midwives. Simple handwashing in an antiseptic was the difference in technique noted between the two areas. These findings were ignored.

The campaign against midwives continued, emphasizing that the midwives were untrained and incompetent; that pregnancy was a disease condition which required the care of highly trained medical personnel; and that the activities of the midwives were preventing the progress of medical obstetrics. One of the leading obstetricians of the day, Dr. J. Whitridge Williams, recommended that medical education be improved to educate more physicians and nurses to make the midwife unnecessary. Another well-known physician, Dr. Joseph DeLee, stated that pregnancy and birth were not normal but pathological; therefore, midwives should not even be mentioned as possible providers. There were some attempts by states to license, regulate, and educate midwives. By 1930, only ten states did not require midwives to register, but formal education was not emphasized, so the "grammy" uneducated midwife continued to fade into history.[3]

A new idea of professional midwifery was being born, as formalized training was being attempted. In 1912, the Belleville Hospital in New York opened the "first publicly funded" midwifery training school. In 1914, at a meeting of the National Public Health Nursing Organization, Dr. Frederick Taussig introduced the idea of "nurse midwives." This model provided additional education for nurses. With the enactment of the Sheppard-Towner Maternity and Infancy Protection Act in 1921, the recommendation came to train people to improve maternal and child health. To this end, articles appeared suggesting the educating of nurses to be midwives.

The nurse midwife was introduced to the United States in 1925 by Mary Breckinridge who brought British nurse midwives to Kentucky and established the Frontier Nursing Service (FNS). Breckinridge had discovered the concept of the British nurse midwife while serving with the Red Cross in France. In 1923, on her return to the United States, she went to rural Kentucky to learn about the health problems of the people. She knew that the nurse midwife was the answer to these problems, and in the same year, she went to England to become a nurse midwife. On her return, she established the FNS, which still exists today. She developed practice protocols for nurse midwives and physicians to work together to meet the healthcare needs of the surrounding communities. She established home birth services which improved maternal and infant outcomes. She spearheaded the opening of a hospital in Hyden, Kentucky to serve the local residents.[4]

The Maternity Center Association (MCA), incorporated in 1918, opened health centers in New York City in which public health nurses worked with physicians. MCA recognized the need to educate nurses to become midwives. In 1930, a group of MCA members of the Board of Directors and Mary Breckinridge incorporated as The Association for the Promotion and Standardization of Midwifery. The association opened the Lobenstine Clinic for patient care services, and in 1931 opened the first school for nurse midwives, The Lobenstine Midwifery School.[5]

TIP: There are now 38 nurse midwifery education programs including two direct-entry education programs across the United States with over 11,000 certified nurse midwives and certified midwives practicing and attending approximately 11.2 percent of the births in this country.

The following definitions will help the reader understand the role of the professional certified nurse midwife

(CNM) and certified midwife (CM), and what constitutes the practice of midwifery in the twenty-first century.

- The Certified Nurse Midwife (CNM) is an individual educated in the two disciplines of nursing and midwifery, who possesses evidence of certification according to the requirements of the American College of Nurse Midwives.

- A Certified Midwife (CM) is an individual educated in the discipline of midwifery, who possesses evidence of certification according to the requirements of the American College of Nurse Midwives.

- Midwifery practice as conducted by CNMs and CMs is the independent management of women's health care, focusing particularly on pregnancy, childbirth, the postpartum period, care of the newborn, and the family planning and gynecological needs of women. The Certified Nurse Midwife and Certified Midwife practice within a healthcare system that provides for consultation, collaborative management or referral as indicated by the health status of the client. Certified Nurse Midwives and Certified Midwives practice in accordance with the Standards for the Practice of Nurse Midwifery, as defined by the American College of Nurse Midwives.[6]

21.2 The American College of Nurse Midwives (ACNM)—The National Organization

The first American nurse midwifery organization was the Kentucky State Association of Midwives in 1929. It was not until 1952 that the American Nurses Association (ANA) and the National League for Nursing (NLN) were formed. Many nurse midwives were members of these organizations. Wanting recognition, Sister Theophane Shoemaker wrote to these organizations asking for a special section for the nurse midwives. They were refused because the nursing organizations felt that midwifery was really the practice of medicine. Twenty nurse midwives attending an ANA convention in 1954 formed a Committee on Organization. In May 1955, this committee voted to form The American College of Nurse Midwifery. The new organization set goals to develop standards for education and practice, assist in the development of nurse midwifery services, and approve nurse midwifery education programs. In 1968, the American College of Nurse Midwifery merged with the Kentucky American Association of Nurse Midwives and changed its name to the American College of Nurse Midwives (ACNM). The

ACNM has set the standard for educational programs for nurse midwives since 1962 and for alternative-entry midwives since 1994. The organization has assured the clinical safety of entry level practice by several mechanisms.

A. Accreditation
The Accreditation Commission of Midwifery Education (ACME) is responsible for reviewing the quality and content of all midwifery educational programs. Each program is evaluated by the same standards, which insure the same quality of education for every program. The ACME is recognized by the United States Department of Education.

B. Core Competencies
The ACNM developed "The Core Competencies for Basic Midwifery Practice" which describes the fundamental knowledge, skills, and behaviors expected of every new practitioner.

TIP: The curriculum of every educational program accredited by the ACME incorporates the entry-level competencies of the core competencies, which insures consistency in the quality of the graduate regardless of the nature of the exit credential earned.[7]

C. Certification
The American Midwifery Certification Board (AMCB) is responsible for another mechanism to insure consistency and competency for practice. The AMCB administers the National Certification Examination which every graduate must pass in order to become licensed to practice in each state. This division is a member of the National Organization of Certifying Agencies and is certified by the National Commission for Certifying Agencies. Since 1996, certification has been time limited and was valid for eight years. Certification was maintained by one of the following two options:

Option 1: AMCB Certificate Maintenance Module Method
Three maintenance modules must be completed during the eight-year certification cycle.

Option 2: Reexamination Method
The current AMCB Certification Examination must be retaken no sooner than the seventh year of the current eight-year certification cycle.

Prior to 1996, certification was granted for a lifetime. All nurse midwives certified prior to 1996 were encouraged to enroll in the Continuing Competence Assessment mechanism (CCA). Each cycle was five years in length, and the enrollee had to accumulate 50 credit hours within that timeframe and send the documentation to the ACNM. This mechanism provided a way to maintain currency in practice. Beginning in 2010, the certification of all practicing midwives regardless of their year of certification was time limited and was valid for a period of five years. The two options stated above will remain valid methods of recertification with the following revisions:

Option 1: AMCB Certificate Maintenance Module Method
Three maintenance modules must be completed during the five-year certification cycle.

Option 2: Reexamination Method
The current AMCB Certification Examination must be retaken no sooner than the fourth year of the current five-year cycle.

D. Standards for Midwifery Practice
The ACNM promulgates the Standards for the Practice of Midwifery which defines the scope of practice. Every midwife regardless of practice site or exit degree earned is held to the same standards. These standards support the "degree of care a reasonably prudent person with the same qualifications should exercise under the same or similar circumstances."[8]

E. Ethics
A code of ethics sets forth values, principles, and standards to which professionals aspire and by which their actions are judged. The ACNM developed The Code of Ethics to set the moral obligations to which all certified nurse midwives and certified midwives should adhere to in their professional roles.[9]

F. Total Quality Management
The ACNM, recognizing that a profession that does not oversee itself will find itself policed by others, organized the National Quality Management Committee to assist members to develop and implement quality management programs in their practices which should include peer review and quality assessment.

G. Licensure
Every new midwifery graduate who completes an ACME accredited educational program and passes the AMCB National Certification Examination must become licensed in the state in which she will practice. In some states CEUs are required to maintain licensure. In such states the midwife will be individually responsible for meeting that requirement.

H. ACNM Insurance Services
The ACNM has been involved in providing insurance coverage for its members since the early eighties. The ACNM does not own an insurance company but it endorses a specific policy. In 2003, ACNM engaged the Contemporary Insurance Services to provide coverage for the membership. Part of this service is a proactive risk management program which helps members avoid litigation or be prepared to defend against claims.[10]

21.3 Foundations of Practice
A. State Entry into Practice
Nurse midwives are licensed as advanced practice nurses in 37 states. Five states have their own practice laws, and, therefore, set the licensure requirements specifically for the practice of midwifery. The remaining states are licensed by Boards of Medical Examiners, as in New Jersey, or by State Departments of Health.

B. Regulatory Boards
The regulatory boards promulgate rules which set the limits for midwifery practice in the state. Clinical guidelines are developed based on the regulations and set the scope of practice in the practice sites. Regulations differ from state to state. Some states still have supervisory language which requires that midwives must practice under the supervision of the physician. This usually means that patients are admitted under the physician's name, and all orders and progress notes must be countersigned within 24 hours. The supervisory language may extend to the need for notification or consultation for each patient, regardless of risk status, managed by the nurse midwife.

C. Prescriptive Privileges
Most states have passed legislation granting nurse midwives prescriptive privileges issued and monitored by their licensing boards. The more progressive states have also added the right to prescribe controlled dangerous substances.

D. Collaborative Practices
Collaborative practice means that the relationship format is developed jointly by the nurse midwife and the physician. Collaborative practice models allow for a variety of contact categories that range from informal working associations to very structured arrangements.[11] Collaborative agreements

must include how and when consultation, collaborative management, and referral will be conducted. The midwife should be able to explain the terms of the collaborative agreement under which she practiced and whether a physician was consulted according to the terms of the agreement. Refer to Figure 21.1 for an outline of the essential components of a collaborative agreement. The collaborative agreement may address the same scope of practice as the clinical guidelines.

I.   Introduction
    A. Names of physician(s) and midwives who will enter into this agreement.
    B. The nature and scope of the practice and institution(s) in which the practitioners will hold privileges.
    C. The regulatory body and source of regulations governing practice.
II.   Categories of patients for independent midwifery management.
III. Risk categories that require consultation or collaboration.
IV. Problems that require transfer.
V.   Specific skills that the midwife may perform.
VI. Special procedures for which the midwife may have additional preparation.
VII. A special section for the intrapartum procedures because of the litigious nature of the event.
VIII. Prescriptive privileges and general categories of medication which the midwife may prescribe.

These categories are guidelines to provide assistance in reviewing practice plans.

Figure 21.1 *General Components of a Collaborative Practice Plan*

The clinical practice guidelines usually set the scope of practice for midwifery care based on the state regulations or statutes. Hospital bylaws, site of birth, and health and liability insurance contracts may also affect the scope of midwifery practice within the state. These entities may set stricter guidelines for midwifery practice but such guidelines may not exceed the scope of practice promulgated by state regulation or statute.[12]

E. Vicarious Liability

Physicians are always concerned with the degree of responsibility for the practice decisions of the midwife and the possibility of increased liability in any claims filed against the midwife. The physician is subject to increased liability only if the midwife is an employee of the physician. If a collaborative agreement exists, the degree of liability depends on the terms of the agreement and documentation of the actions resulting in the claim. If the patient's care requires collaboration, consultation, or referral, a plan must be clearly documented as to the management plan and the role of all the practitioners involved in the care.[13]

> In *Shannen Est, inf. by her m/n/g Myrtha Voley v. Long Island College Hospital, Ramin Ahmadi, Paul Kastell, Charlotte Ledoux, Deborah Paley, Sally Urang, and Robyn Heath,* the 30-year-old mother was admitted to the hospital in early labor. She had a history of two previous cesarean sections due to failure to progress in one birth, and fetal distress in another. The plaintiff complained she was not seen by an obstetrician from the time she arrived at the hospital until after the infant was delivered 18 hours later by nurse midwives. Nurses' notes indicated "doctor aware" of the mother's status and progress. The infant was born with Apgars of 4 at one minute and 6 at ten minutes. The cord pH was 7.14, indicating acidosis, and the plaintiff claimed this was related to meconium aspiration. The plaintiff contended that if an obstetrician had been in attendance, the physician would have noted the long labor, history of two previous cesareans, intrapartum fever, and meconium, and would have ordered a fetal scalp sampling. She also contended that acidosis would have been detected earlier and a cesarean would have been timely performed. The child, age three at the time of settlement, has cerebral palsy and spastic quadriparesis. A $2.85 million settlement was reached. The settlement was on behalf of the hospital and nurse midwives in equal portions. The physicians were released without payment.[14]

F. Standards and Scope of Practice

The midwife should be familiar with the standards of midwifery practice discussed earlier in this chapter and should develop clinical guidelines based on them. Attorneys investigating claims should obtain the clinical guidelines. Copies of these documents should be available in every site in which the midwife provides care. Hospitals, especially those that have more than one midwifery practice providing services, may also have clinical guidelines which usually set a general scope of practice to which all midwives who hold privileges in that institution must adhere. How the scope of practice is delineated is essential in establishing deviations. One of the most common problems identified following a poor outcome is that the midwife was functioning outside of the scope of practice without proper notification of the collaborating physician.

G. Job Description

The job description describes the expected functions of the midwife within the practice. This document should be available and will clarify the practice model in the practice site. The description may vary from site to site. The job description specifically delineates the scope of practice and line of command; states the qualifications to meet the responsibilities of the job; addresses the time commitments in the office and hospital; and outlines the additional responsibilities of the position such as first assisting during surgery.

H. Proper Orientation

Any midwife accepting a position should be oriented to the site, the channels of collaboration, consultation, and referral. There should be a formal orientation with a specific timeframe depending on the experience of the midwife. This information should be available and requested during the investigatory phase of any untoward event.

I. Facility Policies and Procedures

The policies and procedures of the institution and clinical guidelines that dictate practice may be more restrictive but not more expansive than the national standards and state regulations. Language in these documents may restrict admission and discharge privileges of the midwife and require specific physician supervision. It is important to establish if the midwifery involvement was in accord with the institution policies and midwifery guidelines. The failure of a midwife to be present during labor was an issue in the following case:

> In this Ohio case, the plaintiff mother went to the defendant hospital for delivery of her first child. The defendant midwife had primary responsibility for her care. The mother was placed on a fetal monitor and Pitocin was administered. Fetal monitoring tracing was reassuring for 48 hours. During that time the defendant midwife was present on only one occasion, even though hospital policy required examination every 24 hours and even more

frequently with the administration of Pitocin. Approximately two hours before actual delivery time the fetal monitor strip began to manifest changes which raised concern. The nurses also lost the fetal heart tone and were actually monitoring the maternal heart rate. When the nurses located the fetal heart rate, a sinusoidal pattern was noted. It was not addressed for 40 minutes. When the midwife delivered the child, it was lifeless and could not be resuscitated. The pathology examination of the placenta revealed an abruption. The plaintiff claimed the midwife was required to be present during labor by hospital policy. The defense claimed the baby died due to a viral syndrome. A $875,000 settlement was reached.[15]

21.4 Sources of Liability

Midwives and all practitioners must always be prepared for the untoward event. Documentation is paramount in all aspects of practice. Proof of competency and current certification must be producible.

A. Control of Risk

In today's liability climate, strategies must be developed to improve patient safety and limit risk. Risk management has had to become proactive in planning for error prevention. Attention is focused on the structures and processes of providing care.[16] The ACNM developed measures to reduce risk and improve midwifery practice by benchmarking or measuring one's processes and outcomes against the "best practice." The ACNM is encouraging current practices to include benchmarking in quality improvement programs for clinical practice. "Benchmarking is the process of comparing one's practice to the best in the field to identify the operational and clinical practices that lead to the best outcomes, including increased customer satisfaction, increased effectiveness, and increased efficiency."[17]

B. Prevention

TIP: Closed claims analysis is one methodology which can be used to identify risks in clinical practice. This method can set the parameters for preventive action that may potentially minimize future errors.

Closed claims analysis can be used to identify negative practice patterns that can compromise patient safety and to alert practitioners about potential risks in their practices and suggest corrective actions.[18] Insurance companies use closed claims to identify practice issues. Since the threat of litigation faces every midwife in practice today, the ACNM formed a proactive risk management division. One of the objectives of the division is to monitor claims in order to identify the most common areas for litigation and to educate midwives to decrease their risk.

A closed claims analysis was conducted by the ACNM. Sixty-five cases from 22 states were reviewed. All the cases were from 1982 to 2001. The analysis identified seven categories which represent the most common problems named in malpractice claims. They are presented below in order of prevalence. A more recent analysis has been done but the results have not been published as yet. The seven categories identified in the initial review remain the most common problems named in malpractice claims and in a similar order of prevalence.

1. Fetal assessment and fetal heart rate interpretation

Electronic fetal monitoring is used almost universally in the United States today regardless of the risk status of the mother; it represents the most widely used technology during labor. The monitor records the fetal heart rate baseline, the variability of the baseline, the presence of accelerations and the absence of decelerations either by external assessment through a small device placed on the maternal abdomen or by internal assessment by attaching an electrode to the fetal scalp. The normal heart rate for the fetus is 110-160 beats per minute. In the reassuring fetal heart rate, the variability or fluctuations of the rate range from an increase of 5 to 25 beats per minute. Accelerations which are defined as up to 15 beats per minute increase above the fetal heart rate are good indicators of the fetal status.[19]

The major factors in fetal heart monitoring cases involved a delay in calling the collaborating physician; discrepancies and delay in making appropriate management decisions; delay in timely resuscitative efforts; inappropriate continuation of induction with Pitocin; and ineffective fetal monitoring during second stage.

In this Massachusetts case, the plaintiff alleged a delay in responding to fetal distress, leading to brain damage from the umbilical cord around the infant's neck. The 15-year-old mother chose her obstetrical practice because it offered certified nurse midwives as well as obstetricians. After rupture of the membranes, light green meconium was seen, indicating some stress on the fetus. The midwife started Pitocin. When the woman was almost completely dilated, the labor nurse allowed her to start pushing.

The pushing efforts resulted in dramatic changes on the fetal heart monitor. Neither the midwife nor the labor nurse called a physician to evaluate the plaintiff or the fetal heart monitor. The midwife was then called out of the room to attend to another patient, while during the next hour the plaintiff was pushing and the fetal heart rates showed decelerations, decreased variability, and eventually tachycardia. After ten minutes of tachycardia, the labor nurse called the midwife back into the room. She returned to the room 20 minutes later, and the baby was delivered 12 minutes later through thick meconium. The baby's umbilical cord was wrapped tightly around her neck and had to be cut before she could be delivered from her mother. The baby suffered permanent brain damage and is unable to walk or talk. Mediation resulted in a $5.5 million settlement.[20]

Misinterpretations and mismanagement of EFM tracings are some of the most prevalent reasons for obstetrical litigation after the birth of neurologically impaired infants. The medical literature does not support intrapartum events as the primary cause of adverse neurological outcomes. Permanent neurological damage in the newborn attributable to intrapartum asphyxia is about 1.6 per 10,000 births.[21] Other causes such as antenatal insult, prematurity, or infection have been shown to be the more common cause of cerebral palsy with incidences up to 25 percent and above.

In the last decade, two task forces have convened to address the problem of neonatal encephalopathy and cerebral palsy and both published criteria to assist in establishing the intrapartum period as the causal event. The International Cerebral Palsy Taskforce published its criteria in 1999, and the American College of Obstetricians and Gynecologists Taskforce on Neonatal Encephalopathy and Cerebral Palsy published its criteria in 2003.[22]

The claims are frequently related to failure to recognize non-reassuring fetal heart tracings, and to take the appropriate action or to notify the physician in a timely manner. This is an area of liability for both midwives and labor and delivery nurses.

TIP: Recent studies have been able to establish an association between fetal heart patterns and compromised fetal outcomes in the presence of specific fetal tracing patterns which indicate that the fetus is not able to compensate.

The fetal tracing patterns may include:

- minimal or absent variability for an hour or more not due to a known cause such as maternal medication
- recurrent late decelerations or repetitive severe variable decelerations with decreased or minimal variability
- persistent tachycardia (fetal heart rate above 170) or bradycardia (fetal heart rate under 100 for ten or more minutes) with minimal or absent variability

The following case is a good example:

The plaintiff mother was expecting her first child. At 38 weeks gestation the mother called the midwifery service reporting that she did not feel well and that her baby was not moving as much. The responding defendant midwife addressed the mother's complaints of cough, bud did not address the decreased fetal movement. Two days later the mother went to a hospital with complaints of decreased fetal movement. The defendant registered nurse placed the mother on a fetal monitor and immediately noted decelerations and absence of accelerations. This registered nurse and the defendant student nurse midwife were the caregivers for the mother up to delivery and they took no steps to improve blood flow and oxygen to the baby. The supervising certified nurse midwife was contacted at some point before delivery and informed of the non-reassuring appearance of the fetal heart rate pattern. The midwife did not come to the hospital. The attending obstetrician was on the premises, but was unaware that the midwife with the patient was a student and claimed no responsibility to supervise the student midwife. After about an hour and one-half the obstetrician ordered a biophysical profile, which resulted in a score of 2/10, which the plaintiff claimed required an immediate cesarean section. Consent for a cesarean section was not obtained for another hour and the anesthesiologist was not informed that the procedure needed to be done emergently. The mother was not taken to the operating room until three hours after the completion of the biophysical profile. The baby was delivered by cesarean section about 41 minutes later. At delivery the newborn's heart rate was 20; he was floppy and was not breathing. Cord pH levels of 7.02 and 7.04 indicated acidosis. Apgar scores

were three and seven. The infant had hypocalcemia, thrombocytopenia and hematuria. He was diagnosed with hypoxic ischemic encephalopathy, cerebral palsy and global developmental delay. The child cannot walk or speak. He cannot hold his head up or sit unattended. He is fed with a gastrostomy tube. The plaintiffs claimed that the defendants were negligent in failing to properly respond to the obvious signs of fetal compromise. The defendants denied any negligence. A $3.5 million settlement was reached.[23]

The most consistent finding in compromised infants is the decreasing, minimal, or absent variability which accompanies the decelerations and shifts in the fetal heart baseline. The fetus does have compensatory mechanisms to prevent hypoxia (decreased level of oxygen in tissue) unless the fetus or placental functions are compromised. Variability in heart function indicates that the central nervous system of the fetus is intact and the compensatory mechanism is able to adapt to maintain fetal well-being. The midwife, the physician, and the labor and delivery nurse have to be able to recognize when the variability sharply differs from established criteria and act in an appropriate, timely manner. Failure to use consistent accurate nomenclature in describing events has added to this misconception.[24]

In 2008 the NICHD (National Institute of Child Health & Human Development), ACOG (American College of Obstetricians and Gynecologists), and SMFM (Society for Maternal-Fetal Medicine) partnered in a workshop to revisit the definitions and terminology utilized to describe fetal heart patterns in order to standardize definitions. It was concluded that congruence in operating definitions would decrease individualized interpretation of fetal heart tracings and increase evidence-based clinical management during the intrapartum period. A most recognized change is the replacement of the term "hyperstimulation" in regard to the frequency of uterine contractions to tachysystole. Tachysystole is defined as five or more contractions in a 10-minute period over 30 minutes.[25]

A Cook County (IL) Circuit Court case involved a woman was admitted to the hospital for induction of labor. That morning, the fetal monitoring tracing was reassuring and oxytocin was initiated. By early afternoon, contraction patterns demonstrated hyperstimulation, with prolonged decelerations. The nurses did not intervene or alert the physician. Oxytocin was continued and increased. By 1 P.M., the fetal monitoring strip showed late decelerations, rising baseline, diminished variability, and lack of accelerations. Oxytocin was continued even though the patient was experiencing extensive contractions. This deteriorating pattern continued until 11:17 P.M. when the doctor left the room to attend to two other deliveries. At this point, contraction patterns showed a marked decrease in baseline, severe decelerations, and absent variability. The nurse continued the oxytocin at more than 24 mU. Upon her return to the delivery room shortly after midnight, the doctor noted a nonreassuring fetal tracing.

At delivery the infant's Apgar scores were 2, 4, and 5. Initial cord blood was 6.98. She was diagnosed with hypoxic ischemic encephalopathy and remained in the NICU for one month. She is severely neurologically impaired and nonambulatory, and cannot communicate. She resides in a nursing home where she is fed with a stomach tube. The mother contended that neither the physician nor the nurse provided adequate interventions. Denying negligence, the defendants argued there was no approximate cause for the infant's condition and claimed the injury occurred during the last few minutes before delivery. The case was settled for $21.5 million.[26]

2. Shoulder dystocia

Shoulder dystocia is an acute obstetrical emergency which is not predictable since almost 50 percent occur in average size infants (7-8 lbs). In the study cited above, failure to arrange for a timely consultation if shoulder dystocia is anticipated was the primary factor in malpractice claims, followed by excessive traction during the birth; incomplete documentation of time and events; inappropriate use of vacuum extraction by the nurse midwife; and use of fundal pressure.

Shoulder dystocia can be defined, as the presentation is cephalic and the head has been born but the shoulders cannot be delivered by the usual methods.[27] Risk factors which have been identified include obesity, diabetes, prior birth complicated by shoulder dystocia, and macrosomia. Prolonged first and second stages of labor and the use of instrumentation in vaginal birth are two of the most common risk factors that present in the intrapartum period. None of these risk factors alone is more accurate in predicting shoulder dystocia. It is the combination of factors that has a higher predictive value. The combination of macrosomia and prolonged labor that needs instrumentation to execute the birth is known as the "Grief Equation" for provider and family. This combina-

tion can cause up to 23 percent of shoulder dystocia cases. Perhaps a more predictive factor for shoulder dystocia may be a disproportion between the body and the head. Shoulder dystocia occurs more frequently when the truncal measurement exceeds the head measurement.[28] Another approach to defining shoulder dystocia is to measure the total time after the birth of the head from neck to completion of the birth. Shoulder dystocia is defined as neck to completion of birth interval of greater than 60 seconds with the necessity to use maneuvers to complete the birth.[29]

In this Washington case, the plaintiff used the services of a group of midwives. Her prenatal course was unremarkable until an ultrasound showed that her baby had an estimated fetal weight of 4,691 grams (10 lbs, 4 ounces), which was greater than the 90th percentile for 38.9 weeks. Although the mother had conversations with the nurse midwives after this test, she was not advised about the extent of the risk of shoulder dystocia, nor was the option of cesarean section ever presented. Approximately three weeks later, the mother's membranes spontaneously ruptured. The mother's second stage of labor was abnormally long. When the mother was exhausted from pushing and experiencing minimal progress, the midwife contacted an obstetrician on call, who told the midwife to keep doing more of the same, and who never bothered to see or examine the mother. The infant was too high to allow forceps or vacuum-assisted delivery. No preparations were made for a cesarean section. The baby's head was seen by 7:51 A.M., and the obstetrician arrived at 8:46 A.M. By 8:54 A.M., the fetal head was out, but the obstruction was unable to delivery the infant for the next ten minutes because of shoulder dystocia. Another obstetrician ultimately delivered the baby in one or two minutes. The baby was born without heart rate or respiratory effort, and was weighed at 11 lbs, 2 ounces. It was determined that he had suffered profound asphyxia caused by the shoulder dystocia. The case settled for $5.5 million before any expert depositions were taken.[30]

The first responsibility of the nurse midwife is to recognize that the birth will not occur by the usual methods. The turtle sign in which the fetal head recoils against the perineum is the first clue. The nurse midwife should start the clock, which means to begin to record the time interval until completion of the birth, and call for help. The management plan must orchestrate delivery with a decreased amount of traction by increasing pelvic dimensions to disimpact the shoulders or decrease the shoulder dimensions. The standard of care requires the nurse midwife to stop maternal pushing and attempt birth with downward traction on the head. Simultaneously the infant respiratory tract must be cleared; the hand should be passed along the anterior and then the posterior aspect of the baby to rule out fetal tumor or anomaly or nuchal cord; the maternal bladder should be emptied; and an episiotomy should be cut or enlarged if necessary. Next, the nurse midwife begins a series of maneuvers. There is no specific management plan or sequence of maneuvers that has proven to be superior, and resolution often depends on the clinical skills and acumen of the clinician. The two most agreed upon maneuvers are the McRoberts position and suprapubic pressure.

The McRoberts position sharply flexes the knees against the maternal chest with the legs at an outward angle. The mother will need assistance in positioning the legs and keeping them in the proper position. The McRoberts position straightens the lumbar curve and increases posterior room by straightening the exit angle. If the birth cannot be executed, then suprapubic pressure should be used. To be effective the clinician must determine the position of the shoulders in order to instruct the assistant to push the shoulders in the right direction. While the mother is still maintained in the McRoberts position, the hand of the assistant, which is placed externally just above the symphysis pubis, puts pressure on the fetal anterior shoulder and pushes it toward the chest while pushing down toward the sacrum to dislodge the shoulder. Successful execution of the birth will occur 40 or more percent of the time if using the McRoberts alone, and 81 or more percent of the time when used in combination with suprapubic pressure.[31]

If the birth has not been completed, a series of rotational maneuvers should be used. Any particular sequence has not proven more successful than another. The Rubin maneuver places the clinician's hand on the posterior surface of the anterior shoulder, adducts and rotates the anterior shoulder to the oblique angle. This maneuver has been described in the literature as the rotation of the anterior shoulder in adduction 180 degrees to the posterior pelvis.[32] The Woods Screw maneuver rotates the posterior shoulder in abduction to the anterior pelvis. This maneuver can be repeated to produce a corkscrew effect by bringing the posterior shoulder anterior again.[33]

If the birth has still not been successfully completed, delivery of the fetal posterior arm is the next maneuver. This maneuver requires that the clinician's entire hand be placed in the posterior vagina. Then the clinician moves down the fetal posterior arm until the elbow is reached; places the thumb in the antecubital fossa pressing inward to cause the elbow to bend; moves up the forearm and grabs the fetal hand; brings the hand outward across the chest; and sweeps the hand across the face. Other maneuvers are discussed in the literature such as fracture of the clavicle or the Zavanelli maneuver which requires the replacement of the fetal head back in the vagina and the performance of a cesarean section.[34]

Gentle pressure or traction is part of the normal birth mechanism. Excessive prolonged traction on the head with an impacted shoulder can contribute to brachial plexus injuries. Increasing amounts of force seem to be applied to the fetal head as the degree of difficulty of the birth increases. In a study by Allen et al., the amount of pressure applied to the fetal head was measured using Newton's unit of measure (0.22 lbs of force per unit). The study found that the peak force with a spontaneous birth was 47N; with a difficult birth it was 69N; and with a birth complicated by shoulder dystocia resulting in clavicular fractures and brachial plexus damage it was 100N. The faster the force was applied, the more prone the fetus was to injury. So in conclusion, pressure or traction on the fetal head must be applied slowly, gradually, and uniformly as long as there is movement of the anterior shoulder under the symphysis.[35]

The nurse midwife's documentation of all aspects of management in shoulder dystocia is crucial to the nurse midwife. The documentation should begin at the admission of the patient by addressing the assessment of the estimated fetal weight (EFW) by ultrasound or Leopold's maneuvers (abdominal palpation); and by determining pelvic adequacy by clinical pelvimetry (measurement of the maternal pelvis manually through the vagina). When risk factors are identified that suggest an increased risk for shoulder dystocia, the collaborating physician should be consulted and the plan of management discussed with the woman and family. There should be documentation that the obstetric team, including pediatrics and anesthesia, was prepared. Once shoulder dystocia has occurred, documentation of time and every step and maneuver is the best defense.

Simulation and practice drills for the obstetric emergency involving shoulder dystocia have been identified in the literature as making a difference in the coordinated function of the people involved in managing shoulder dystocia and the outcome. A study involving six United Kingdom hospitals was done utilizing simulation drills for the management of shoulder dystocia. Post drills, the participants were able to successfully resolve the shoulder dystocia and execute the birth 83.3 percent of the time as opposed to 42.9 percent pretraining. Since the outcomes after shoulder dystocia are most often the result of inappropriate clinical management, regularly scheduled training/simulation drills which teach coordinated team efforts may improve outcomes.[36]

The following case illustrates the issue of shoulder dystocia and birth injury:

The plaintiff mother, age 26, delivered her second child. Dr. Kim was the attending obstetrician who performed the delivery. Shoulder dystocia occurred during delivery and nursing assistance was called. Dr. Kim delivered the infant within three minutes with the use of McRoberts maneuver and suprapubic pressure. The newborn was born with a hypotonic left arm. She was diagnosed with a brachial plexus injury which was treated with therapy and a tendon transfer procedure. The plaintiff alleged that Dr. Kim applied excessive traction during the delivery, the hospital had insufficient nursing personnel in the delivery room, the nurses failed to properly place the mother in the McRoberts position and an unidentified nurse improperly applied fundal pressure rather than suprapubic pressure. The defendants claimed that the proper maneuvers were used, including gentle downward traction. The defendants also claimed that the hospital notes indicated that the fetus was in the right oblique anterior presentation with the shoulder dystocia involving the right shoulder, but the injury was to the left brachial plexus. The defendants maintained that any downward traction would not have caused injury to the left shoulder. The plaintiff countered that Dr. Kim had turned the baby's head so as to impact the left shoulder on the mother's pubic symphysis and making the left shoulder anterior at the time of delivery. According to Cook County Jury Verdict Reporter a defense verdict was returned. The plaintiff had entered a high/low agreement with Dr. Kim for $800,000/$100,000, so the plaintiff was to receive $100,000. [37]

3. Resuscitation efforts

Neonatal resuscitation supplies the external support and intervention that is necessary to insure that the neonate makes a successful transition to extrauterine life. The primary problem in resuscitative efforts in the cases analyzed as part of the ACNM study was a delay in initiating resuscitation, followed by failure to call the appropriate resuscitative team in a timely fashion.

A 27-year-old primigravida was admitted in active labor. She was full term and had had a nor-

mal pregnancy. Labor progressed and during the deceleration of the first stage of labor occasional variable decelerations were identified. External resuscitative measures were instituted successfully. During pushing in the second stage of labor, the variable decelerations became deep and repetitive. The midwife called the collaborating physician to the hospital to expedite the birth. The midwife also requested that Pediatrics (Peds) be notified because the hospital did not have 24-hour in-house Peds coverage. The physician managed the birth and used a vacuum extractor to complete the birth in an expeditious manner. There was a tight nuchal cord twice around the neck which required cutting before the birth could be completed. The baby was delivered limp, cyanotic with no spontaneous respirations. The nurse received the baby since Peds was not present. They attempted to initiate resuscitative efforts. The suction did not work; the ventilation bag was the wrong model for the wall suction; and the mask was the wrong size. Attempts were made by the physician to perform manual CPR while the nurse hunted for working equipment. The infant was unable to be resuscitated and expired. It was disclosed in deposition that Peds were never called. The midwife, physician, the nurses and the hospital were named in the suit. The midwife and the physician were eventually dismissed. The plaintiff primarily blamed the nurses and the hospital for failing to notify the Peds and for not having working equipment on the unit. The nurses were further blamed for not checking the equipment on a regular basis to insure its working condition. The case was settled out of court for $1.2 million. (Unpublished case.)

4. Diagnostic errors

Failure to recognize preeclampsia in a timely manner was the most common allegation in the ACNM study, followed by subsequent development of HELLP (Hemolysis-Elevated Liver enzymes-Lowered Platelets) syndrome, and placenta abruption secondary to preeclampsia. Preeclampsia is a pregnancy-specific syndrome. It is characterized by elevated blood pressure, proteinuria, and elevated liver profile. As the syndrome becomes more severe, the HELLP syndrome can result which increases maternal and perinatal morbidity. The diagnosis of eclampsia is made when the mother develops convulsions. The continued elevation of the blood pressure can cause placenta abruption which is defined as premature intrauterine separation of the placenta.[38]

Nurse midwives manage the prenatal as well as labor and delivery phase of obstetrical care. The failure to diagnose complications and to consult appropriately can result in liability at any stage in this process as the following cases illustrate:

The plaintiff, who was 35.5 weeks into her second pregnancy, awoke with a headache in January 2002. She thought it was a migraine and took her usual home remedies. She awoke again two hours later and continued to have a dull headache. She called her obstetrician's office that afternoon and was told to come to the office for a check of her blood pressure. When she arrived around 3:00 P.M. she still had a headache. Her blood pressure was 174/74. Lab studies revealed protein in the urine as well as a rise in the uric acid. The plaintiff was also extremely swollen and hyperreflexic. The plaintiff claimed that these symptoms were consistent with severe preeclampsia, while the defendant found them consistent with mild preeclampsia, particularly with the plaintiff stating that the headache was in line with prior migraines. The defendant also claimed that two subsequent blood pressure readings were lower and that none of the blood pressure readings were high enough to cause her to sustain a bleed which would cross the blood brain barrier.

The plaintiff claimed that she had hypercarbia due to the medications, which lowered the autoregulatory capability and increased the risk of bleed from an otherwise low blood pressure. The defendant gave the plaintiff more medication for migraine without success in relieving the headache. A plan was developed to wait until morning to do a test to assess the development of the baby's lungs and the plaintiff was placed in a darkened room with orders for her vital signs to be checked every four hours. The headache continued and began to radiate to the back of her head. Demerol was ordered and administered. An hour later the plaintiff reported improvement. A blood pressure reading taken at that time was elevated, which was attributed to the movement of the plaintiff's arm. Two subsequent blood pressures taken a few minutes later showed that the blood pressure lowered. The defendant checked the plaintiff an hour after that and she appeared to be sleeping soundly. Ten minutes later, the defendant went into the room and was not able to arouse her. Narcan was administered for a presumed narcotic cause of the lack of responsiveness. An emergency cesarean section delivery was performed and the baby was born healthy.

The plaintiff was then taken emergently to another hospital where blood was drained from her brain caused by a stroke. She remained in a semicomatose state and was eventually transferred to a rehabilitation facility where she remained for about six months. During that time she had a shunt placed in her head, which ultimately became infected and required several procedures to clear the infection and replace the shunt. The plaintiff suffered numerous physical injuries and cognitive deficits. She walks with a brace and has a pronounced limp. Her vision has been affected, preventing her from driving at night or during inclement weather. She also has severe memory lapses. The plaintiff claimed that severe preeclampsia should have been diagnosed and that the delivery should have been performed immediately. The plaintiff also contended that she should have been more closely monitored. A $6.4 million verdict was returned.[39]

The plaintiff went to the emergency room in August 2004 with abdominal pain and vomiting during pregnancy at 27 weeks gestation. Emergency room physicians diagnosed gastritis and reflux and gave her Maalox. She initially improved. The 27-year-old woman subsequently vomited. An abdominal ultrasound and blood tests were ordered, which showed elevated liver enzymes. Emergency room physician Dr. Koto called defendant Dr. Chams and informed her of the plaintiff's symptoms and lab results. Dr. Chams' practice had been the plaintiff's prenatal care provider for about three weeks. The next emergency room physician to take over the plaintiff's care, Dr. Himmelman, also called Dr. Albert Chams regarding normal ultrasound results and elevated liver enzymes. The plaintiff was then sent for a non-stress test, which was normal and reported to Dr. Chams. The plaintiff was then discharged. The plaintiff returned to the emergency room with abdominal pain two days later, at which time blood work resulted in a diagnosis of HELLP syndrome. The defendants were called and Dr. Chams performed an emergency cesarean section delivery. The newborn sustained profound brain damage and required 24 hour care until her death in July 2007. The plaintiff mother developed a large liver hematoma which was treated conservatively and took over three years to resolve. The plaintiffs claimed that the HELLP syndrome should have been diagnosed at the time of the first presentation. The defendants claimed that the blood work was not reported to them and that the emergency room physicians missed the abnormal lab results due to shift change. The defendants also claimed that the plaintiff's presentation was atypical for HELLP syndrome and that the infant would have had significant disabilities if delivered at that time due to prematurity. According to Cook County Jury Verdict Reporter, a $1.5 million settlement was reached with the emergency room physicians and the hospital. A jury returned a $6,171,119 verdict against the remaining defendants. Post-trial motions were pending.[40]

5. VBAC (vaginal birth after cesarean)

The common factor in cases involving VBAC was the lack of physician involvement in management decisions.

Uterine rupture during a trial of labor in patients who have had a previous cesarean section has gained publicity in the press and literature since the article published in the *New England Journal of Medicine*.[41] Today most physicians will not do VBACs themselves or serve as a collaborating physician for nurse midwives who want to attempt one. The use of prostaglandins or Cytotec in cervical ripening should not be part of the management of the VBAC patient, and Pitocin should only be used when the physician is in the hospital since the incidence of uterine rupture increases with the induction of labor by pharmacological measures. The nurse midwife working in an environment that still supports the trial of labor must be very careful to keep within the scope of practice; to give informed consent to the patient; and to have the physician in-house and well-informed. Since uterine rupture can occur at any time with or without a uterine scar, the midwife must be knowledgeable about the signs of uterine rupture and be able execute the resolution of the emergency with a favorable outcome. The documentation of the timing of the recognition of the rupture, the notification of the physician and the activation of the medical team will be the midwife's best defense. Uterine rupture can be life-threatening to mother and baby.

An NIH Consensus Development Conference on Vaginal Birth After Cesarean: New Insights was convened in March, 2010 and resulted in a Panel Statement regarding VBAC (Vaginal Birth After Cesarean). The statement was developed to give practitioners and consumers the most current data on VBAC to assist them in decisions regarding the option. The conclusions of the panel is that trial of labor after cesarean is a viable option for women provided they meet certain criteria and have been given informed consent regarding the risks and benefits of vaginal birth after cesarean and elective repeat cesarean section. Providing the woman desires a VBAC; has a documented low transverse operative scar; does not have medical problems which may affect her or her baby and providing her caregiver supports VBAC as a reasonable option and can do the birth in a hospital in which the appropriate support team is readily available, a trial of labor can be a safe option for mother and baby. Since emerging literature is reporting an increase in the maternal death rate in the United States due to the increasing number of cesarean sections, a trial and labor and vaginal birth after cesarean will be offered to women as part of current practice and supported by the healthcare community.[42]

In a Virginia case, the plaintiff mother went into labor in March 1997. A previous pregnancy had resulted in a cesarean section delivery. Labor was managed by a nurse midwife employed by the defendant. Pitocin was used during labor and after this the plaintiff's labor contraction pattern demonstrated an increased resting tone, indicating uterine stress. The plaintiff claimed that the nurse midwife never contacted the obstetrician about this. The uterus ruptured, resulting in a drop in the fetal heart rate. A cesarean section delivery was performed 30 minutes later. The baby suffered brain injury and was diagnosed with cerebral palsy. According to a published account a $939,000 verdict was retuned.[43]

6. Testing measures

In the ACNM study, the issues related to fetal or maternal testing identified were failure to perform the necessary testing, misinterpretation of results, or failure to notify the patient of the test results.

The plaintiff mother's obstetrician/gynecologist, Dr. Kaufman, ordered blood tests, including one for cystic fibrosis, in January 2004. Laboratory Corp. of America claimed that it did not receive a request for the cystic fibrosis test. Dr. Kaufman and his colleague, Dr. Andrew Sun, did not realize until the plaintiff was born in September 2004 with cystic fibrosis that the test had not been performed.

The plaintiff alleged negligence in failing to properly test for the cystic fibrosis gene. The plaintiff claimed that the proper testing would have revealed that both the mother and father were carriers of the cystic fibrosis gene, which would have led to an amniocentesis and a termination of the pregnancy. The defendants claimed that the mother decided that she did not want to be screened for carrier status and told them after the birth that she would not have terminated the pregnancy even if she had been told that the baby had cystic fibrosis. The laboratory claimed that it had conducted the tests ordered by the physicians. According to a published account a $2 million settlement was reached.[44]

7. Laceration repair and healing

Common allegations involving obstetrical tears included failure to diagnose the appropriate degree of laceration; the structures involved; and the development of complications such as dehiscence (wound pulling apart), recto-vagina fistula (formation of passage between vagina and rectum), and incontinence.[45]

Lacerations are defined as:

- First degree which involves skin and fascia.
- Second degree which involves skin, fascia, and perineal muscles.
- Third degree which involves skin, fascia, perineal muscles, and the rectal sphincter muscle.
- Fourth degree which involves skin, fascia, perineal muscles, the rectal sphincter muscle, and rectal lumen.

The fourth degree laceration is the most problematic since it involves an extensive repair with proper approximation of the muscles and structures affected. Dehiscence (breakdown of the repair) can occur more frequently. When the breakdown involves the rectal lumen repair, a recto-vaginal fistula can develop, which is a direct opening from the rectum to the vagina allowing feces to leak from the vagina.

The plaintiff mother, age 37, delivered a son. The delivery was managed by defendant Dr. Fong, a resident, and defendant Dr. Roshan, an obstetrician. Labor had been induced, which was followed by an increase in the heart rate of both the mother and the fetus. The mother's temperature also rose. The physicians opined that the mother could have chorioamnionitis and a forceps delivery

was decided upon. During the delivery the mother sustained a fourth-degree laceration of her vagina which extended to her rectum. Dr. Fong repaired the laceration, but the mother claimed that the repair was not effective. The mother claimed that she suffers permanent residual incontinence as a result. The plaintiff also claimed that the child suffered from cerebral palsy as a result of injury during delivery. The defendants claimed that the mother had a good recovery and that the child did not have brain injury. The defendants claimed that the child has tibial torsion and is pigeon-toed which caused his gait problems. According to a published account a $19.65 million verdict was returned. The mother was awarded $11,965,000 and the child was awarded $7,650,000.[46]

C. Additional Sources of Liability

There are other actions or situations which result in outcomes that expose the midwife to potential liability and can result in malpractice claims. Three frequently named situations are discussed below.

1. Inappropriate use of oxytocin

There are clear indications for the use of oxytocin for induction of labor: nonreassuring fetal antepartal testing, preeclampsia, oligohydramnios (low volume of amniotic fluid), maternal diabetes, history of fetal demise at term, intrauterine growth restricted fetus, and so on.[47] The standard of care does not support the administration of oxytocin with arrest of labor either in the first or second stage;

- in the presence of a undocumented or classical uterine scar;
- with uterine hyperstimulation with a low cervical uterine scar;
- in the presence of fetal compromise; and
- without continuous surveillance of the status of the mother and fetus.

The incidence of untoward outcomes increases when the nurse midwife deviates from the accepted uses of oxytocin. Even the appropriate use of oxytocin without a uterine scar does not guarantee a safe outcome. It is important to understand the use and action of oxytocin. It has demonstrated safe successful use in reducing uterine atony and initiating or augmenting uterine contractions. One common problem arises when the midwife fails to recognize a tachysystole-hyperstimulation pattern that can lead to fetal compromise and uterine rupture, as illustrated:

The plaintiff, age 18, went into labor and was admitted to St. John's Regional Medical Center for the delivery of her first child. Family practice physician Dr. Jules Merenda was managing the delivery. After two hours of lack of progress Dr. Merenda consulted with obstetrician/gynecologist Dr. Mirela Cemaianu, who ordered Pitocin to augment uterine contractions. The Pitocin was started at a low dose and increased by a small amount after 20 minutes in accordance with protocol. After 50 minutes of Pitocin treatment failing to induce progress, Dr. Merenda ordered a cesarean section. Dr. Cemaianu declined to come in and perform the surgery, so it was performed by Afshan Ghiai, a physician provided by the plaintiff's prenatal clinic. A healthy baby girl was delivered without any complications being noted. The plaintiff suffered persistent low blood pressure and Dr. Ghiai performed an exploratory laparotomy and discovered a five centimeter laceration in the posterior aspect of the uterus. Dr. Ghiai attempted to repair the laceration, but was unsuccessful. A total hysterectomy was performed, which included the removal of one ovary.

The plaintiff claimed that Drs. Merenda and Cemaianu were negligent in using Pitocin because her uterus was already hyperstimulated. The plaintiff alleged negligence by the nurses in increasing the Pitocin dosage when contractions were so close together. The plaintiff additionally contended that she was instructed to push too long before a cesarean section was ordered which, along with the uterine hyperstimulation caused a spontaneous rupture of the uterus. The plaintiff also alleged negligence by Dr. Ghiai in failing to discover the uterine rupture while performing the cesarean section and in failing to repair it during the exploratory laparotomy. The plaintiff also maintained that the nurses failed to call Dr. Ghiai timely when her blood pressure began to drop. The defendants contended that the three and one-half hours of pushing was reasonable, as well as the use of Pitocin. The defendants also claimed that the uterine laceration was an undiscovered extension of the incision made during the cesarean section, not a spontaneous rupture. Dr. Ghiai also alleged that she was entitled to be considered a Good Samaritan because she was not on call at the time of the cesarean section and came in to perform the surgery because she felt it was urgently needed. Dr. Ghiai also denied any negligence in failing to see the rupture during the

cesarean section due to the posterior aspect of the uterus. After a bench trial a $261,501.57 verdict was returned against Dr. Ghiai. A defense judgment was entered as to all the other defendants.[48]

2. Fetal death

Fetal death can occur without apparent cause, but it is beyond the scope of this chapter to address these issues. Fetal death most often results from midwife failure, physician failure, and system failure which refers to a multifaceted breakdown that includes institutional problems such as missing or malfunctioning medical equipment; failure to perform procedures in a timely fashion; lack of properly trained personnel; and so on. Any of the reasons discussed in this section can cause fetal death which for the most part could have been prevented with proper surveillance, consultation, and action.

3. Failure to notify the physician in a timely fashion

Competent and timely consultation must be a priority for the midwife. Failure to notify the collaborating physician is a major omission across the spectrum of deviations from the standard of midwifery care. When the midwife does not incorporate the appropriate involvement of the physician in patient management situations that have deviated from normal, the midwife is vulnerable to liability. This constitutes functioning outside of the scope of midwifery practice and the standard of care. In the following Massachusetts case, the plaintiff alleged the midwife failed to involve the physician in a timely manner:

The plaintiff mother was admitted to the hospital in labor at full term with the nurse midwife assuming her care around 8 A.M. After an unremarkable fist stage labor, the mother began the second stage at 12:30 P.M. She began to push. The defendant midwife did not record any observations on the progress of the entire second stage of labor. Ten minutes into the second stage, the external fetal monitor began to record several episodes of slow heart rate and fetal heart rate decelerations, which persisted. The nurse midwife did not place an internal fetal scalp electrode in order to more accurately assess fetal well-being. She claimed that at several points during the labor she consulted the covering obstetrician, but did not turn the case over to this individual. The infant was delivered vaginally at 3:08 P.M. with a cord blood pH of 7.04. His Apgar scores were 3/4/5, and he was suffering from prenatal depression, poor perfusion, poor blood pressure, and respiratory distress. He developed seizures and developmental delays. Plaintiff contended that the defendant was negligent when she failed to turn the patient over to a physician for management, which the standard of care mandated should have included a timely cesarean delivery. The defendant contended that she acted in accordance with the standard of care at all times, and the outcome would have been no different with an earlier delivery. The case settled for $925,000.[49]

D. Why People Sue

There are a variety of factors that influence a parent's decision to bring an obstetrical lawsuit against a midwife. Some people sue not so much because of the outcome but how the case was handled. Claims may arise from communication breakdown with the patient and family. Often families feel that no one cared enough to be available to answer questions and to provide support for grieving families.[50] In a survey published in the *Journal of the American Medical Association*, the most common reason was lack of informed consent: not preparing the family about the possibility of problems or injury to the infant. Money for long-term care for a compromised child was another reason why families sue.[51] Refer to Chapter 5, *Medical Errors: Roots of Litigation*, in Volume I, for another perspective on this topic.

E. Education

One of the allegations in a claim against a nurse midwife may be a lack of preparation or ongoing education specific to the midwife's role. Part of the discovery process may involve a request for production of evidence of training about the clinical issues associated with the outcome.

Ongoing education should be part of any risk management plan. Practitioners should be reminded of the importance of communication. Review sessions should be held on how to initiate consultation, collaboration, and referral. Terms to describe fetal heart patterns must be agreed upon and used by all members of the healthcare team in any given situation. Periodic update classes on fetal monitoring strips are a good risk management tool.

Some institutions are investigating having emergent drills on an ongoing basis similar to neonatal resuscitation and basic life support classes offered in the hospitals. Shoulder dystocia drills are most often used. For example, Baystate Medical Center in Massachusetts developed a set of skills and sequence of maneuvers to be used when a shoulder dystocia occurs. This training is institution-specific and is required of all practitioners. However, any institution can develop a drill or training to keep its staff prepared for emergencies.

21.5 Case Presentations
A. Shoulder Dystocia

A 17-year-old woman having her first baby (G1 P0000), with a gestational age of 41 weeks, was admitted for induction following a biophysical profile of 6/8 with oligohydramnios (decreased fluid). The estimated fetal weight by ultrasound was 8 lbs. The patient's prenatal course was uneventful with the exception of a 77-lb weight gain.

The glucola screen was normal. Her weight was recorded as 317 lbs at the time of her admission. The patient was admitted at 3 P.M. The pelvic assessment was: cervix 1 cm dilated, 80 percent effaced or thinned and the presenting part -1 station which refers to the descent of the presenting part through the pelvic diameters. The contractions had started spontaneously and were 7-8 minutes apart.

The following is the sequence of events:

7:45 P.M.—Pelvic exam unchanged. AROM (artificial rupture of membranes) fluid clear.
Augmentation with Pitocin.

11:15 P.M.—Pelvic exam unchanged with contractions every 3-4 minutes.

2:30 A.M.—Pelvic exam cx (cervix) 3 cms/80% effaced /-1 station—contractions unchanged

5:10 A.M.—4 cms/80%/-1 station—contractions unchanged

8:30 A.M.—5 cms/80% effaced/-1 station—contractions unchanged

1:00 P.M.—5-6 cms/80% effaced/-1 station with molding (overriding of the fetal skull bones). Midwife consulted with physician.
Plan: Reevaluate in 2 hrs. The midwife turns the patient over to medical management and remains in a supportive role. The midwife is uncomfortable with the lack of progress and molding and estimates the baby to be bigger than ultrasound estimate.

2:30 P.M.—Physician evaluation: 8 cms/100/-1 station

7:15 P.M.—Fully and pushing

8:13 P.M.—Temp 101, FH 180s continues to push

9:10 P.M.—Physician decides to expedite delivery and use forceps. The patient is transferred to delivery room. Simpson forceps were applied x 2 unsuccessful.

10:00 P.M.—Vacuum applied x 3. Episiotomy cut on 3rd application. Head delivered very slowly. Shoulders were transverse. Could be minimally rotated. McRoberts unsuccessful and posterior arm could not be delivered. The clavicle could not be broken.

10:13 P.M.—Stat cesarean section called. Zavanelli done.

10:18 P.M.—Male infant with meconium stained amniotic fluid delivered. Apgars 0/0/2 at one, five, and ten minutes. Full resuscitation for 7 minutes. Infant on assisted ventilation, pupils fixed. No purposeful movements. Seizures since birth. Birth weight 11 lbs, 2 ozs. The infant examination revealed bilateral occipital bone fractures with severe displacement of all the cranial sutures. Life support was discontinued after one month.

This case was a true disaster. The obese mother initially had gained an excessive amount during the pregnancy. The ultrasound was inaccurate in estimating the fetal weight which is not unusual considering the maternal weight. At 41 weeks with an unfavorable BPP, the admission was appropriate. At 7:45 P.M., the plan to rupture the membranes and start Pitocin was appropriate at the time. At 1 P.M., the consultation was necessary since the patient was in a protracted labor pattern with molding of the fetal head. The midwife was exercising good judgment in turning the patient over to medical management. The patient had been in labor with augmentation for almost 24 hours. According to the midwife's assessment of the fetal weight with Leopold's maneuvers, the baby was much larger than the ultrasound estimate.

The patient was pushing without progress for two hours. This was an arrest of the second stage, and instead of calling for a cesarean section, the physician decided to do an instrument vaginal birth. With a failed application of forceps, the safe management decision would have been to call for the section at this time. The use of the vacuum was unsafe management. Since the forceps had failed, to repeat the process with another instrument was malpractice. The fetal head was literally "pulled apart" and the occipital fractures were probably caused by the head being pulled between the ischial spines of the pelvis. The maneuvers attempted were ineffective since the shoulders were wedged in the transverse position. The only maneuver left was the Zavanelli but it was useless since the infant had already been fatally damaged. However, it had to be used in order to extract the infant by the only means possible.

The parents sued. The midwife was dismissed from the case since her management and decision to transfer the patient was in accord with the scope of midwifery practice. The physician was held liable for failing to recognize an arrest of labor, not calling for a cesarean section, and inappropriate use of instruments in the attempt at a vaginal birth. The money settlement was low since the infant had died.

B. Interpretation of a Fetal Heart Tracing

A 25-year-old woman who was having her second baby (G2 P1001), gestation age at 40 weeks, was admitted in active labor. The vaginal exam revealed the patient to be 7 cms/80% effaced/-1 station. The fetal heart was 120 with no decelerations and positive variability. The patient was expeditiously admitted by the nurse and midwife. The prenatal course was normal. The assessment on the labor unit was normal.

The midwife ruptured membranes and the fluid was "blood-tinged" according to the midwife. Fetal heart pattern remained at 120 with variability. The patient felt the urge to push and the birth was gently executed. The infant was born macerated and stillborn. The midwife, the nurse, and the family were in shock. It was obvious that the infant had been dead at least 24 hours.

What happened? The patient arrived in active labor and everyone was concentrating on getting her ready for a safe delivery. Upon questioning the midwife and staff at a peer review meeting, it was determined that the blood-tinged fluid was really a "port wine" color specifically seen in stillborns. The significance was not recognized because the fetal heart looked reassuring. When the fetal heart strips were reviewed, the maternal pulse was recorded at 120 in the record. It was the maternal pulse that was recording as the fetal heart rate. No one had evaluated the maternal vital signs as they prepared for the imminent birth. Even having recognized the similarity of the recording to the maternal pulse, the providers might not have made the connection since the tracing was very deceiving. Looking at the tracing and knowing the outcome made the interpretation easier. The outcome would not have changed, but had the midwife been more observant, the fetal demise might have been recognized and the patient would have at least been prepared for the outcome. The midwife and the midwifery service supported the patient and family during their hospital stay and were available for questions. Contact with the patient was continued at home and the midwife involved went to the funeral. The family did not sue.

C. Physician Consultation

A 30-year-old G4 P3003 (having her fourth baby) at 40 weeks was admitted in active labor. She was 5 cms/80%/-3 station. The FH was reassuring. The fetal weight was estimated to be a pound heavier than any previous baby. The prenatal course was uneventful. The midwife was at the bedside supporting the patient. The course of labor was slow and the midwife recorded molding of the fetal head and advancing descent. The patient was complaining of severe pain in the suprapubic area and received medication with little relief. The contraction pattern was showing hyperstimulation even without Pitocin. The patient had a protracted pattern of dilation and became fully dilated eight hours after admission. The patient continued to complain of the pain in the suprapubic area especially while pushing.

The patient continued to push for over two hours when she had a severe pain in the pubic area with sudden relief. The fetal heart became bradycardic and the contraction pattern could not be determined. The patient was turned to the left side and given oxygen. The collaborating physician was called immediately, and she came in a short period of time. The patient was prepared for the cesarean section while the physician was on her way. When the abdominal incision was made, the infant was found in the abdomen and the uterus had ruptured. The resuscitative efforts were not successful and the infant was pronounced dead. The couple sued and was awarded a settlement which would have been higher had the infant survived. (Unpublished case.)

This case is a good example of a uterine rupture without a uterine scar in a spontaneous labor. The midwife was in attendance and very supportive. She knew that the baby was larger, but felt that the patient could push the baby out with encouragement. She was not concerned with the length of the second stage and did not consider the severe suprapubic pain to be abnormal. Often suprapubic pain can be a sign of cephalopelvic disproportion as the fetal head attempts to mold to accommodate the pelvis; it can also be a sign of possible impending uterine rupture. Even upon review of the contraction pattern during the deposition, the midwife did not recognize that there was tachysystole-hyperstimulation pattern. She never considered a uterine rupture and was shocked at the need for the cesarean section. She called the physician because of the fetal bradycardia. The physician should have been called in earlier to evaluate the patient for the protracted labor and unusual pain in the suprapubic area. The midwife was the primary defendant in the claim, and the physician was dismissed from the case because she had not been advised of the patient's admission or informed of the labor progress.

21.6 Crucial Questions Following Untoward Events

The following questions should be asked by the clinician, the institution, and certainly the attorneys who will be investigating events:

1. Could the injury have been prevented? Was the management reasonable, evidence-based, and consistent with the clinical guidelines of the practice?
2. Was the provider's conduct consistent with the reasonable conduct of other providers in the profession? Did the provider function within the scope of practice and adhere to current care standards? Was the collaborating physician informed in a timely fashion?
3. Was the documentation detailed and descriptive? Were dates and times recorded accurately? Were the sequence and description of the event consistent? Was the patient given informed consent? What particular actions were utilized to correct or complete the process?

21.7 Risk Reduction

To reduce risk the nurse midwife must take responsibility for all decisions in the delivery of patient care and should be able to identify a safe management plan for the actions taken. The care must be consistent with acceptable current evidence-based practice. In the investigation of any claim, identification of the decision-making process and the management plan can make a difference in the outcome of the allegations. In a case resulting in a neonatal demise, the nurse midwife was dismissed from the case because she documented the presence of thick meconium upon rupture of the membranes and the onset of deep variable decelerations immediately after the rupture. She wrote that she applied an internal electrode to the fetal scalp and started an amnioinfusion as corrective measures. She included in the plan the notification of her collaborating physician and the neonatal resuscitation team. The physician came in a timely fashion and assumed management which included the birth. The neonatal team arrived without a neonatalogist and the equipment was not functioning which resulted in a failed resuscitation and the demise of the infant. The nurse midwife was functioning within her scope of practice by recognizing the problem, instituting the proper corrective measures, and notifying the proper members of the team. The hospital and the physician were held responsible.

A. Clinical Guidelines

Clinical (practice) guidelines are important because they establish the scope of midwifery practice. State regulations address the clinical guidelines and include mechanisms for consultation, collaboration, and referral and set the scope of practice within the state (refer to Section 21.3.B, *Regulatory Boards*). Standard V of the *Standards for the Practice of Midwifery* addresses written clinical guidelines and the parameters for the scope of midwifery care. Care given must be consistent with the interventions written in the clinical guidelines. All members of the practice must agree upon these guidelines. Care provided must reflect the scope of care as defined by the state regulatory body and the ACNM, and must be in accord with current practice. All definitions and terminology written in the guidelines should be consistent and used by everyone in the practice to insure congruency in documentation. There are many practice types in midwifery: a single or several midwives in private practice; large midwifery services in medical centers working with a variety of residents and attending physicians; and home birth or birth center midwives. Regardless of the type and site of practice, the midwife functions according to the ACNM standards of practice and under the same state regulations.

B. Current Practice

Evidence-based practice is a growing paradigm in today's practice climate. Care decisions must have supportive evidence in the literature through research to defend its use before instituting it into practice. Practice guidelines should be based on current evidence as well. Midwives must be familiar with the U.S. Preventative Services Task Force Grading and Recommendation System which can assist clinicians in determining the effectiveness of clinical research. Research is rated for its research design and study population. Most peer-reviewed journals use this grading system to rate the articles published to help readers make appropriate conclusions regarding the research and its possible inclusion into practice. Refer to Chapter 6, *The Foundations of Nursing Practice*, in Volume I, for additional information on evidence-based practice.

C. Philosophy of Care

Every practice should have a philosophy of care. Every clinician in the practice should share the philosophy especially in the areas of intervention and use of technology. In nurse midwifery practices the practice philosophy must be congruent with the philosophy of the ACNM. The ACNM philosophy was revised in 2004 and can be found on the ACNM website (www.midwife.org).

D. Credentialing

Midwives must hold privileges in the healthcare institutions in which they practice. These privileges should delineate the scope of midwifery practice in the state. The credentialing process should be granted through the medical staff office by the same process as physician credentialing. It is essential for midwifery privileges to include reference to the independent practice within a healthcare system with appropriate collaboration, consultation, and referral, and should include admission and discharge privileges. Physicians are responsible for their own actions and decisions from the point of contact with the midwife concerning the patient's progress or condition. This delineation of responsibility is important during the process of establishing or disproving proximate cause of injury.

TIP: The ability to admit and discharge places the responsibility of care decisions and outcomes on the nurse midwife.

E. Students in the Clinical Setting

Most midwifery students are baccalaureate-prepared nurses who want to expand their scope of practice. They are enrolled in graduate certificate or master's programs which are usually one to two years in length for full-time study. The student midwife must be supervised primarily by certified nurse midwives. There is no mandated ratio of students to preceptors, but it is usually one to one. The academic faculty teaches the didactic portion of the curriculum in the educational program and the preceptor is the clinical faculty person responsible for teaching and supervising in the clinical area. In a few programs, the academic faculty also acts as preceptors since they run full scope nurse midwifery faculty practices.

Students must carry liability insurance during their clinical experiences. They may be required to purchase individual liability insurance or the institution may have a self insurance plan under which all employees, faculty, and students are covered.

The agreement established with the clinical site must clearly state the responsibilities of all concerned parties: the student, the clinical site, the preceptor, the academic faculty, the institution. The agreement must be kept current with periodic review. The preceptor should always be physically present at the site even though the student may be managing the patient. There should be no reason why a student would ever be left alone at the site.

21.8 Summary

Often in health care, especially in the specialty of obstetrics, litigation is unavoidable and untoward events can occur at any time. If the compliance and competency of the midwife can be verified, the investigative process will be more efficient and complete. The checklist of items in Figure 21.2 will assist in establishing the knowledge base and the behavior of the midwife during the event.

Competence
- Did the midwife function within the scope of practice?
- Did she have written clinical guidelines?
- Did her practice reflect the midwifery regulations set forth by the state regulatory body?

Compassion
- Did the midwife communicate with the family and support the grieving process?
- Was the midwife available to the family to answer questions?

Consultation
- Was the consulting physician involved appropriately and in a timely fashion?
- Did the collaborative agreement or clinical guidelines delineate the risk factors that required physician involvement?

Charting
- Was the documentation clear and concise?
- Were the events in sequence?
- Was the timeline well documented?
- Was the involvement and role of the physician(s) and support staff well delineated?

Currency in practice
- Can the midwife provide proof of current certification and some type of continuing competency assessment documentation?
- Does the midwife hold current privileges and did she function in accordance with the delineation of her privileges?

Continuing education
- Can the midwife provide proof of attendance at approved relevant continuing education programs on a yearly basis?

Figure 21.2 *List of Items to Assist in Establishing the Knowledge Base and the Behavior of the Midwife During the Untoward Event*

Endnotes

1. Rooks, J., *Midwifery and Childbirth in America*. Philadelphia: Temple University, 1997.

2. *Id.*

3. *Id.*

4. *Id.*

5. *Id.*

6. *Definition of a Certified Nurse Midwife,* ACNM Position Paper, Silver Springs, Maryland, 2001.

7. *Core Competencies for Basic Midwifery Practice,* ACNM, Silver Springs, Maryland. 2003. Available: www.midwife.org. Accessed 6/23/10.

8. *Standards for Midwifery Practice,* ACNM, Silver Springs, Maryland. 2003. Available: www.midwife. org.

9. *Code of Ethics of the American College of Nurse Midwives,* ACNM, Silver Springs, Maryland. 2003. Available: www.midwife.org. Accessed 6/23/10.

10. *Professional Liability Resource Packet,* ACNM, Silver Springs, Maryland. 2002.

11. Tharpe, N., *Clinical Practice Guidelines for Midwifery and Women's Health*. Midwife Publications, 2004.

12. *Id.*

13. Jenkins, S. M., "The myth of vicarious liability: impact on barriers to nurse midwifery practice," *Journal of Nurse Midwifery* (1994).

14. Laska, L. (ed.), "Failure to perform timely cesarean section," *Medical Malpractice Verdicts, Settlements, and Experts* (March 2003), 36.

15. Laska, L. (ed.), "Failure to properly monitor fetal heartbeat," *Medical Malpractice Verdicts, Settlements, and Experts* (May 2005), 28.

16. Angelini, D. et al., "Liability and risk management issues in midwifery," *Journal of Midwifery and Women's Health* (November-December 2005): 453.

17. Collins-Fulea, C. et al., "The American College of Nurse Midwives benchmarking project," *Journal of Midwifery and Women's Health* (November-December 2005): 461–471.

18. Angelini, D. et al., "Closed claims analysis medical malpractice cases involving nurse midwives," *Journal of Midwifery and Women's Health* (November-December 2005): 454–460.

19. Varney, H. et al., *Varney's Midwifery.* Massachusetts: Jones and Bartlett Publishers, 2004.

20. Laska, L. (ed.), "Failure to timely respond to fetal distress," *Medical Malpractice Verdicts, Settlements, and Experts* (August 2004), 29.

21. Fahey, J. et al., "Intrauterine asphyxia: Clinical implications for providers of intrapartum care," *Journal of Midwifery and Women's Health* (November-December 2005): 498–506.

22. *Id.*

23. *Id.*

24. Oxorn, H., *Human Labor & Birth.* New York: McGraw-Hill, 1986.

25. Macones, G. et al., "The 2008 National Institute of Child Health and Human Development workshop report," (September 2008).

26. "Oxytocin was increased despite ominous signs," *OBG Management* (August 2006).

27. Cohen, B. et al., "The incidence and severity of shoulder dystocia correlates with a sonographic measurements of asymmetry in patients with diabetes," *American Journal of Perinatalogy* (1999).

28. Spong, C. et al., "An objective definition of shoulder dystocia: prolonged head to body delivery interval and/or the use of ancillary obstetric maneuvers," *Obstetrics & Gynecology* (1995).

29. *Id.*

30. Laska, L. (ed.), "Failure to perform medically appropriate cesarean causes infant brain damage," *Medical Malpractice Verdicts, Settlements, and Experts* (August 2003) 37.

31. Jevitt, M., "Shoulder dystocia: Etiology, common risk factors, and management," Journal of Midwifery and Women's Health (November-December 2005): 485–497.

32. Naef, R. et al., "Guidelines for the management of shoulder dystocia," *Journal of Perinatology* (1994): 435–441.

33. See note 24.

34. Cunningham, F. et al., *Williams Obstetrics*, Twenty-first edition. New York: McGraw-Hill, 2001.

35. Allen, R. et al., "Risk factors for shoulder dystocia: an engineering study of clinician-applied force," *Obstetrics & Gynecology* (1991).

36. Crofts, J., F., et al., "Observations from 450 shoulder dsytocia simulations," *Obstetrics & Gynecology* (October 2008).

37. Laska, L. (ed), "Improper management of shoulder dystocia blamed for brachial plexus injury"*Medical Malpractice Verdicts, Settlements, and Experts* (May 2009) 35.

38. See note 19.

39. Laska, L. (ed), "Failure to diagnose severe preeclampsia and timely perform delivery" *Medical Malpractice Verdicts, Settlements, and Experts* (May 2009) 32.

40. Laska, L. (ed), "Failure to diagnose HELLP syndrome in pregnant woman." *Medical Malpractice Verdicts, Settlements, and Experts* (September 2009) 29.

41. Lydon-Rochelle, M. et al., "Risk of uterine rupture during labor among women with a prior cesarean section," *N New England of Medicine* (July 2001): 3-8.

42. NIH consensus development conference, "Vaginal birth after cesarean: new insights," (March 8-9, 2010).

43. Laska, L. (ed), "Failure of midwife to properly manage vaginal birth after cesarean." *Medical Malpractice Verdicts, Settlements, and Experts* (October 2009) 28.

44. Laska, L. (ed), "Failure to see that testing for cystic fibrosis is done" *Medical Malpractice Verdicts, Settlements, and Experts* (July 2009) 33.

45. See note 19.

46. Laska, L. (ed), "Woman claims permanent incontinence from laceration during delivery" *Medical Malpractice Verdicts, Settlements, and Experts* (January 2009) 34.

47. See note 19.

48. Laska, L. (ed), "Woman requires hysterectomy following cesarean section," *Medical Malpractice Verdicts, Settlements, and Experts* (January 2009) 35.

49. Laska, L. (ed), "Midwife delivers infant with developmental delays, "*Medical Malpractice Verdicts, Settlements, and Experts (*April 2004) 48.

50. Holder, W., "Shark proof your practice," *Lifelines* (October 1997).

51. *Id.*

Part III:

Causes of Action

Chapter 22

Preventing Healthcare-Acquired Conditions Means Never Having to Say You're Sorry

Carol Ann Armenti, MA, JD

Synopsis
22.1 Introduction
22.2 The Healthcare Climate Begs Change
22.3 Financial Climate Motivates
22.4 Payment Implications
22.5 DRA Revisited
22.6 Unintended Consequences
    A. Medicare Fraud
    B. Inequity of Loss
    C. Lack of Patient Care
    D. Increased Testing, Increased Harm, Increased Costs
    E. Medical Malpractice
    F. State and Private Pay Non-Reimbursement
    G. Patient Protocols
22.7 Documentation Implications
    A. Medical
        1. Facilities affected and POA reporting requirements
        2. Record and coding requirements
    B. Legal
        1. Never events
        2. HAC events
        3. Burdens of production and persuasion
22.8 Summary
Endnotes

22.1 Introduction

Discussion of the inevitable lag between legislative rhetoric and practical implication is lost in the language of healthcare reform. Only now are we beginning to realize the impact of changes required by the Deficit Reduction Act of 2005, legislation which implicitly mandated fiscal economies. The Act directed the Centers for Medicare and Medicaid Services (CMS) to identify high volume procedures which result in adverse events and are reasonably preventable through the use of evidence-based guidelines. The goal of this directive was to reduce the financial burden of Medicare by adopting a non-reimbursement policy for the treatment of the presumptively preventable adverse events. But implementation of policy inevitably results in intended and unintended consequences long after public posturing dims from memory.

22.2 The Healthcare Climate Begs Change

It is more than a decade since the release of the seminal Institute of Medicine (IOM) report on the topic of medical error.[1] Consumers Union, through its Safe Patient Project, released the inflammatory *To Err is Human – To Delay Is Deadly*.[2] The article purports to describe the failure of the United States to improve the fatally flawed system of health care, identified in the IOM report, by instituting changes reflected in its recommendations.

The Consumers Union commentary seeks to take advantage of the ten-year anniversary of the IOM report by capitalizing both on its title, *To Err Is Human: Building a Safer Health System*, and the political climate, in which healthcare reform is a topic of daily discussion. The report posits:

> Today our country has an opportunity for dramatic changes to our fragmented healthcare system. Health reform to ensure that all Americans have access to high quality health care should also include significant and active mandates to reduce medical harm.[3]

Indeed, it does appear that little progress has been made since 1999, when the IOM cited the findings of the Harvard Practice Study performed in the 1980s, which found that as many as 98,000 deaths occurred annually due to medical error. A more recent, related report by the IOM found that at least 1.5 million *preventable* medication errors occurred annually.[4] The federal and state governments responded swiftly to the loss of health care resulting from the loss of employment-related medical insurance during the current unemployment crisis. The response is limited to subsidizing COBRA benefits for an extended period for employees of large employers, and a patchwork of state-subsidized COBRA-like plans for employees of small employers.[5] While the initial IOM report initiated a flurry of activity under the Clinton Administration to address preventable medical error, the government was not galvanized into concrete responses, proposing only cosmetic change by creating a task force to address the issue.[6]

It may be true that a swift response was not imminent; it is also true that a lumbering response was initiated. Money, not medical harm, makes the world go 'round. Perhaps flush financial times under the Clinton Administration worked against change. In financially flourishing time, the estimated $29 billion a year cost of medical error to the United States economy was simply insufficient impetus to reform.

Conversely the current, undisputedly broken economy engenders change. Though it may be characterized properly as a sluggish response, the federal government responded to its healthcare economic loss in the Deficit Reduction Act of 2005 (DRA).[7] The DRA notes the escalating cost of healthcare services, recognizing the financial waste inherent in a poorly performing healthcare system, and responds by requiring the Secretary of Health and Human Services (HHS) to identify high cost or high volume conditions that could reasonably be prevented through the application of evidence-based guidelines.[8]

The DRA vindicated this nation's medical malpractice attorneys, whose actions on behalf of their clients injured by medical error are often characterized as frivolous. Despite data which suggest that only a small fraction of patients sustaining injury by medical negligence file suit, medical malpractice attorneys are routinely maligned as ambulance chasers, rather than lauded as sympathetic Davids willing to fight healthcare Goliaths to redress the suffering of their clients.[9]

There is little question that government interest in medical error is economic rather than benevolent for even the legislative language of medical malpractice speaks, not to the injuries caused to the patient, but to the government's budget. When the New Jersey Legislature enacted "The Patients First Act," ironically, it spoke not to the rights of the patients, but to medical malpractice insurance.[10] "The State's healthcare system and its residents' access to healthcare providers are threatened by a dramatic escalation in medical malpractice liability insurance premiums, which is creating a crisis of affordability in the purchase of necessary liability for our healthcare providers...."[11] Apparently the New Jersey Legislature found the appropriate response to escalating premiums was not to prevent harm but to reform tort liability.[12] The Legislature took the position that tort reform ensures "that healthcare services continue to be available and accessible to residents of the State and to enhance patient safety at healthcare facilities."[13]

New Jersey is not alone in passage of tort reform legislation, which responds to patients suffering medical harm by increasing the burden on plaintiffs' bar, thereby protecting physicians from suit. While obvious financial self-preservation motivates much of the tort reform rhetoric instigated by healthcare providers and insurers, patient advocates who sometimes speak the language of tort reform may be motivated by other self-interests.

With a myopia driven by the personal pain of the patient, or the patient's family members, patient advocates lobby for reforms which will promote emotional healing.[14] Advocates may attempt to teach physicians to feign sympathy in exchange for release-exacted transparency by assuaging their hearts. Transparency rarely requires additional *quid pro quo*. In such scenarios medical error may be admitted and specious regrets conveyed, but no commitment to prevent further occurrence of the medical error results.

It is against this backdrop of competing interests, and crisis and response, that the legislative requirements of the DRA must be viewed.

22.3 Financial Climate Motivates

In response to the requirements of the DRA, HHS devised a list of candidate conditions for inclusion in the Hospital Inpatient Prospective Payment System (IPPS) regulations.[15] The DRA requires HHS to identify at least two conditions that are

- high cost or high volume or both,
- resulting in the assignment of a case to a diagnostic-related group (DRG) that has a higher payment when present as a secondary diagnosis, and
- could reasonably have been prevented through the application of evidence-based guidelines.[16]

TIP: The identified conditions came to be known as Hospital Acquired Conditions, or HACs.

"Medicare's IPPS encourages hospitals to treat patients efficiently." The lead sentence HHS chose to introduce the proposed HAC regulation offers insight into the purpose of the legislation.[17] There is no suggestion that a benevolent government is identifying preventable conditions to protect its people from unnecessary suffering. There is only the suggestion that prudent reimbursement policy motivates hospitals to efficiently treat patients.

In its description of the legislative mandate, the Federal Register describes a cost savings which is realized by denying Medicare payment for the HAC. Implementation of the new rule requires hospitals to diagnose a primary condition, consistent with the current rule. The hospital must then report a secondary diagnosis, if one exists, present on admission (POA). Medicare will deny reimbursement for the higher charges if, at the time of billing, the hospital requests payment for a condition, which was not POA, and the charges are greater than those which would have been incurred based on the original diagnosis.

To implement the new regulation, public input was sought regarding conditions preventable with evidence-based guidelines.[18] These comments were summarized in the final rule.[19] Both the Centers for Medicare and Medicaid Services and the Center for Disease Control and Prevention (CDC) reviewed candidate conditions. The following list was considered for inclusion:

- surgical site infections
- ventilator-associated pneumonias
- catheter-associated bloodstream infections
- pressure ulcers
- hospital falls
- septicemia
- vascular catheter-associated infections
- Clostridium difficile-associated disease
- Methicillin-Resistant Staphylococcus Aureus (MRSA)
- providing incompatible blood products
- surgical air embolism
- retained surgical foreign object
- wrong surgery/wrong body part

Both the CDC and CMS selected the HACs after the close of public comment based on adherence to the high cost, high volume, preventable condition criteria required by the DRA. Public comment was again sought on the published final rule, which included the candidate conditions.[20] The agencies selected seven HACs for inclusion.

1. foreign object retained after surgery
2. air embolism after surgery
3. blood incompatibility
4. advanced pressure ulcers (bedsores)
5. falls and trauma
6. vascular and urinary catheter-associated infections
7. surgical site infection after coronary bypass graft (CABG)

In April 2008, an augmented list of HACs was published in the IPPS FY 2009.[21] The candidates in this iteration included:

- surgical site infection following elective procedures
- Legionnaires' disease
- glycemic (blood sugar) control
- iatrogenic pneumothorax (medically induced collapsed lung)
- deep vein thrombosis/clot (DVT)
- Staphylococcus aureus septicemia (blood infection)
- Clostridium difficile-associated disease.

Following the appropriate comment period, CMS announced the selection of DVT and glycemic control from the proposed additional list for HAC inclusion.

22.4 Payment Implications

A Diagnosis-related group (DRG) is a system of classification of hospital cases.[22] This system, developed for Medicare and first used in the State of New Jersey, consigns cases to groups expected to have similar hospital resource use. These groups are based on International Classification of Diseases (ICD) diagnoses, weighted for procedure, sex, age, and the presence of complications.

The Health Care Financing Administration, formerly known as HCFA, supported the development of the DRG system. HCFA, now CMS, intended to use the DRGs to form a prospective payment system. The prior payment was based purely on cost, and subject to the vagaries of idiosyncratic hospital billing. A DRG-based system of payment offered the ability to normalize expense and better project hospital costs. For example, each DRG anticipates a length of stay and certain procedures, represented by Current Procedural Terminology (CPT) codes. These CPT codes, developed by the American Medical Association, are a systematic listing of procedures and services performed by physicians.[23]

Within each DRG, a case may include a secondary condition. These are assigned as:

- a complicating condition (CC),
- a major complicating condition (MCC), or
- a composite complicating and major complicating condition (CC/MCC).

TIP: If, when a case is billed, an acquired condition is listed POA, then Medicare will continue to assign a discharge to a higher payment rate. If the acquired condition was not POA, Medicare denies payment for the higher, complication-related reimbursement rate.[24]

The DRA provides that Medicare deny payment for cases in which a HAC results in the assignment of a case to a DRG that has a higher payment when present as a secondary diagnosis.[25] The regulations require Medicare to pay as though the secondary diagnosis were not present. For example, an elderly man is admitted to the intensive care unit after developing pneumonia. Prolonged immobility results in a sacral pressure ulcer which progresses to Stage IV (the worst stage). The patient then requires a skin flap procedure to cover the hole on his sacrum. The result is reimbursement to the facility for the care associated with the pneumonia, but not for the pressure ulcer.

Payment implications began on October 1, 2008 for the conditions identified in both the IPPS FY (fiscal year) 2008 and 2009 final rule. For discharges occurring after that date, there is no reimbursement for charges associated with the HACs. Balance billing is prohibited; that is, hospitals may not bill patients for the unreimbursed charges.[26]

A comprehensive diagnosis, indicating both a primary condition and secondary complications, is critical to hospital reimbursement. Hospitals are denied full reimbursement for its services if it fails to either properly diagnose or note the full diagnosis on admission. Consider this scenario: A patient is admitted to the hospital from a nursing home. She complains of pain in her right hip on admission, but the physician fails to order an x-ray. She slips in her urine on the second day. A fractured hip is diagnosed on x-ray. Though the fracture may well have been present on admission, the hospital is unable to prove that the fracture did not occur at its facility and it is denied reimbursement for the necessary reparative surgery. It is assumed that if treatment is needed for a HAC, which was not noted as being present on admission, the condition was preventable through proper implementation of science-based guidelines, and the treatment is not reimbursed.

22.5 DRA Revisited

The Social Security Act, as amended pursuant to the DRA, requires the HHS Secretary to carry out the requirements of the DRA.[27] Though the Social Security Act mandates the initial selection of HACs, it permits subsequent additions as long as these subsequent lists contain at least two conditions. It also anticipates the expansion of the principles behind the hospital inpatient healthcare-associated conditions payment provision to the outpatient prospective payments system (OPPS).[28]

The implication is clear. Anticipating success in cost containment in the inpatient setting, the principles resulting in HAC prospective billing will migrate to outpatient settings. Indeed, on December 18, 2008, during a CMS Listening Session entitled, "Hospital Outpatient Healthcare-Asso-

ciated Conditions," Carol Bazel, MD and Heather Hostetler, JD, both of CMS, presented on the topic.[29]

Rather than lead with the cost savings associated with the HAC model, Bazel emphasized the intent of CMS "to drive quality improvement, value, and patient safety in the HOP (hospital outpatient) setting."[30] Note that "patient safety" now achieves at least afterthought status. Bazel reported that the Outpatient Prospective Payment System was the target of forthcoming regulation. DRGs apply only to hospitals. Ambulatory Payment Classification Groups (APC), which apply in outpatient settings, replace DRGs as the source of OPPS billing data. Other indicators must be developed for the OPPS program because APCs lack the POA data critical to DRG billing.

TIP: Possible hospital outpatient HACs have been identified, notwithstanding the difficulty in capturing accurate data. These include conditions which occur in both inpatient and outpatient settings, such as retention of foreign surgical objects, air embolisms, and falls. Other potential hospital outpatient HACs are conditions relating to surgical procedures, infections relating to hospital outpatient care, and medication errors.[31]

As the application of the principles behind HAC non-reimbursement migrates from inpatient to outpatient, it is reasonable to conjecture a further migration to physician settings. Such an evolution is particularly intriguing because there is no requirement that United States physicians practice evidence-based medicine. Health maintenance organizations (HMOs) routinely deny physician reimbursement for procedures identified by CPTs, which are not generally associated with the appropriate diagnostic code. But payment is not denied for actual treatment of a condition, regardless of whether the condition was the result of less than optimal care by the physician. Requiring physicians to practice evidence-based medicine on pain of non-reimbursement represents both a revelation and revolution in medical care.

22.6 Unintended Consequences

The Deficit Reduction Act intends to contain costs by denying Medicare reimbursement for care which harms the patient. Its effect is to punish poor recordkeeping and failure to abide by evidence-based medicine. The DRA also heralds unintended consequences, some more foreseeable than others, as described below.

A. Medicare Fraud

Recollect that by rule, CMS deliberately selected conditions that frequently occur. Thus, the hospital cost for treating unreimbursed HACs may be exorbitant. This lack of reimbursement creates a powerful incentive for hospitals to code creatively, recapturing lost billables. Realistically, at least some of the costs CMS hopes to save through denial of reimbursement will be lost to Medicare fraud, a flourishing industry currently estimated by the Government Accounting Office at billions of dollars annually.[32] Indirect costs will be lost to increased Department of Justice investigation and prosecution, though the federal government potentially recoups some of these costs through fines imposed on the less skilled frauds which are detected.

B. Inequity of Loss

The current non-reimbursement of HACs refers only to hospitals. But care at hospitals is not provided by staff alone. Healthcare providers such as surgeons have privileges to provide services on site; certain subspecialties such as anesthesiology or pathology are typically provided by onsite subcontracted physician groups.

The current rule does not contemplate the following scenario: a surgeon, who is not on staff, provides services at a hospital and leaves a foreign object in the patient—an HAC. A subsequent non-staff surgeon removes the object, which is identified when the patient develops septicemia. Medicare Part B (physician coverage) pays both the surgeon responsible for the HAC, and the surgeon remediating the HAC. Medicare Part A (hospital coverage) denies payment to the hospital for the higher level of patient care necessitated by treatment for the septicemia resulting from the HAC. Hospital staff may or may not have been able to prevent the condition.

C. Lack of Patient Care

Faced with no way to recoup payment for the treatment of HACs, hospitals may discharge patients prematurely, potentially increasing the harm to the unnecessarily injured patient. Consider the plight of the discharged patient who seeks care for the treatment of an HAC. If the patient presents at the hospital that provided the original care, which resulted in the current HAC, there is a question as to whether the hospital may now code the condition POA, in order to obtain reimbursement. Hospitals may be reluctant to admit a patient for which reimbursement may be an issue. If the patient presents at a different hospital, there may be no doubt the subsequent hospital will be paid. Merely inconveniencing the patient by redirecting admission to a different hospital resolves payment issues, and defeats the purpose of the regulation.

D. Increased Testing, Increased Harm, Increased Costs

Admission tests may become more rigorous as hospitals adopt policies designed to avoid absorbing costs for treating HACs with which the patient initially presents, but which the attending physician fails to document as POA. This results in increased costs for testing, potentially shifting Medicare A (hospital) costs to Medicare B (physician) costs. Inherent in increased patient testing is increased harm to the patient related to the additional testing. This leads to further increased costs to treat the harm caused by the increased admission testing.

E. Medical Malpractice

CMS assembled its HAC list, relying on evidence-based guidelines, consistent with its imprimatur that conditions be preventable. An increase in the sheer number of HAC-based medical malpractice lawsuits is virtually assured, resulting in a transfer of the costs of HACs from CMS coffers to the state civil courts.

TIP: Medical malpractice attorneys may assert that evidence-based standards legislatively recognized by a federal agency are entitled to judicial notice. This could lead to the assumption that HACs are presumptively negligent, relieving plaintiffs of their burden to prove negligence and shifting the burden to defendants to rebut that presumption.

F. State and Private Pay Non-Reimbursement

Healthcare insurance coverage is most often provided through three avenues: Medicare, Medicaid and HMOs. As the national healthcare insurer, Medicare sets the standard by which all other healthcare entities reimburse. Medicaid is a program adopted in each state, which receives federal funds to insure the indigent. CMS actively encouraged the state Medicaid programs to adopt its Medicare payment policies. HMOs, which are state-licensed private companies, are not subject to Medicare payment practices. Cutting short the debate as to whether private companies would adopt HAC non-reimbursement policy, some states swiftly enacted legislation prohibiting HMOs from reimbursing HAC events.[33]

G. Patient Protocols

HACs by definition presume the failure of the hospital to prevent the occurrence of certain conditions. However, some HACs such as falls, DVT, and blood sugar control, can be influenced by patient behavior. For example, it is common practice for a hospital to require bedridden patients to wear elastic stockings. If the patient refuses or removes the stockings, and a DVT develops, Medicare penalizes the hospital by non-reimbursement for the care required to remediate the DVT. Patients may expect their activities to be more closely monitored. Conceivably, hospitals may ask non-compliant patients to be financially responsible for care necessitated by a condition caused by their own actions against medical advice.

22.7 Documentation Implications
A. Medical

The HAC non-reimbursement scheme turns on the POA indicators recorded in the hospital medical records.

1. Facilities affected and POA reporting requirements

CMS requires hospitals to submit POA information on diagnoses for all inpatient discharges on or after October 1, 2008. CMS returns all claims submitted for payment not containing proper POA indicators to the provider for correction and resubmission. Note, however, that the POA reporting requirement applies only to designated hospitals, and a variety of facilities are exempt from the reporting requirement. Refer to Figure 22.1 for a list of hospitals currently exempt from the POA indicator requirement. All facilities not on the exemption list must comply with the reporting requirement; this discussion refers only to affected institutions.

Following is a summary of the general POA reporting requirements:

- The POA indicator is required for all claims involving Medicare inpatient admissions.
- POA is defined as present at the time the order for inpatient admission occurs. Conditions that develop during an outpatient encounter, including emergency department, observation, or outpatient surgery, are considered POA.
- A POA indicator is assigned to principal and secondary diagnoses.
- Issues related to inconsistent, missing, conflicting, or unclear documentation must be resolved by the provider.
- If a condition would not be coded and reported based on Uniform Hospital Discharge Data Set definitions and current official coding guidelines, then the POA indicator is not reported.
- CMS does not require a POA indicator for the external cause of injury code unless it is reported as "other diagnosis."[34]

- Critical Access Hospitals
- Federally Qualified Health Centers
- Long-Term Care Hospitals
- Religious Non-Medical Health Care Institutions
- Maryland Waiver Hospitals
- Inpatient Psychiatric Hospitals
- Cancer Hospitals
- Inpatient Rehabilitation Facilities
- Children's Inpatient Facilities
- Veterans Administration/Department of Defense Hospitals
- Rural Health Clinics

Figure 22.1 *Facilities exempt from POA reporting requirements.*

2. Record and coding requirements

Federal regulations require hospitals to maintain accurately written and promptly completed medical records. The medical record must contain information justifying admission and supporting the diagnosis.[35]

TIP: The hospital is required by regulation to include in the final medical record all complications, hospital-acquired infections and unfavorable reactions to drugs and anesthesia.[36] Because Medicare denies payment requests for the treatment of conditions on the HAC list when they appear as secondary diagnoses, it is critical that these conditions be documented as POA, if possible.[37] If they are not documented POA, CMS denies reimbursement for treatment.

Since the inception of the HAC policy, procedure dictates that the hospital record created on admission for each patient includes the presence or absence of HACs. It is incumbent upon the attending physician, or "any qualified healthcare practitioner who is legally accountable for establishing the patient's diagnosis," to determine whether a condition is POA, or whether the presence of a condition cannot be determined based on clinical judgment.[38] HAC policy permits the attending physician more documentation choices than merely the presence or absence of a HAC. Figure 22.2 represents the range of responses permitted in the initial admission record. The final record must be completed within 30 days following discharge.[39]

Code	Reason for Code
Y	Diagnosis was present at time of inpatient admission. CMS will pay the CC/MCC DRG for those selected HACs that are coded as "Y" for the POA Indicator.
N	Diagnosis was not present at time of inpatient admission. CMS will not pay the CC/MCC DRG for those selected HACs that are coded as "N" for the POA Indicator.
U	Documentation insufficient to determine if the condition was present at the time of inpatient admission. CMS will not pay the CC/MCC DRG for those selected HACs that are coded as "U" for the POA Indicator.
W	Clinically undetermined. Provider unable to clinically determine whether the condition was present at the time of inpatient admission. CMS will pay the CC/MCC DRG for those selected HACs that are coded as "W" for the POA Indicator.
1	Unreported/Not used. Exempt from POA reporting. This code is equivalent to a blank on the UB-04; however, it was determined that blanks are undesirable when submitting these data via the 4010A. CMS will not pay the CC/MCC DRG for those selected HACs that are coded as "1" for the POA Indicator. The "1" POA Indicator should not be applied to any codes on the HAC list. For a complete list of codes on the POA exempt list, see page 110 of the Official Coding Guidelines for ICD-9-CM. http://www.cdc.gov/nchs/datawh/ftpserv/ftpicd9/icdguide08.pdf

Figure 22.2 CMS POA indicator reporting options, description and payment.

CMS set forth the ICD-9-CM Codes, which are not reimbursable if not POA. Refer to Figure 22.3 for the list of offending codes designated in 2008. The appearance of any of the codes on the table in the final bill, not documented POA, triggers non-payment for the service. In the words of CMS, "The importance of consistent, complete documentation in the medical record cannot be overemphasized." All issues relating to inconsistent, missing, conflicting, or unclear documentation must be resolved by the provider.[40] Providers must be careful when adding late entries that belatedly allege a condition was present on admission. Those who scrutinize the chart may challenge such entries and seek confirming data.

B. Legal

The recently adopted HAC regulations create both challenges and opportunities for attorneys. While general or in-house hospital counsel brace themselves for a potential assault to the client revenue stream, they devise prophylactic strategies to guard against new medical malpractice vulnerabilities. Counsel with personal injury practices, including medical malpractice, expectantly await their state's first precedent-setting case determining whether an HAC constitutes negligence. According to the 10th annual Hospital Professional Liability and Physician Liability Benchmark Analysis, the number of hospital professional liability claims is increasing and is expected to increase by 1 percent per year. The study, released by Aon Corp. and the American Society for Healthcare Risk Management, both based in Chicago, polled more than 1,500 facilities to examine trends in claims and loss costs related to hospital and physician professional liability. The study attributes the rise in claims to the economic downturn, less public sympathy toward healthcare providers, and a 2008 rule that prevents the Baltimore-based Centers for Medicare and Medicaid Services from reimbursing hospitals for certain errors known as "never events" because they are considered preventable and should never happen.[41] Inquiry into the genesis of "never events," as distinguished from HACs, as well as examining the legal standards controlling personal injury suits, is an invaluable exercise for both the plaintiff's and defendant's bars.

1. Never events

A never event is a medical error so egregious that it should never occur. The term never event entered colloquial use after the National Quality Forum (NQF), a private organization with membership including the American Medical Association, published a list of 27 serious, preventable adverse healthcare events in 2002.[42] The list consists of such "adverse" events as operating on the wrong patient or body part, and retaining a foreign object after surgery. To be considered for inclusion on the list, a clearly identifiable and measureable event must be serious and adverse, indicative of a problem in a healthare facility's safety system and important for public accountability.[43]

TIP: In 2003, Minnesota became the first state to pass legislation requiring reporting of every never event.[44]

HAC	CC/MCC (ICD-9-CM Codes)
Foreign Object Retained After Surgery	998.4 (CC) 998.7 (CC)
Air Embolism	999.1 (MCC)
Blood Incompatibility	999.6 (CC)
Pressure Ulcer Stages III and IV	707.23 (MCC) 707.24 (MCC)
Falls and Trauma: • Fracture • Dislocation • Intracranial Injury • Crushing Injury • Burn • Electric Shock	Codes within these ranges on the CC/MCC list: 800-829 830-839 850-854 925-929 940-949 991-994
Catheter-Associated Urinary Tract Infection (UTI)	996.64 (CC) Also excludes the following from acting as a CC/MCC: 112.2 (CC) 590.10 (CC) 590.11 (MCC) 590.2 (MCC) 590.3 (CC) 590.80 (CC) 590.81 (CC) 595.0 (CC) 597.0 (CC) 599.0 (CC)
Vascular Catheter-Associated Infection	999.31 (CC)
Manifestations of Poor Glycemic Control • Diabetic Ketoacidosis • Nonketotic Hyperosmolar Coma • Hypoglycemic Coma • Secondary Diabetes with Ketoacidosis • Secondary Diabetes with Hyperosmolarity	250.10-250.13 (MCC) 250.20-250.23 (MCC) 251.0 (CC) 249.10-249.11 (MCC) 249.20-249.21 (MCC)
Surgical Site Infection, Mediastinitis, Following Coronary Artery Bypass Graft (CABG)	519.2 (MCC) And one of the following procedure codes: 36.10-36.19

Figure 22.3 *HACs and related codes.*

In 2004, HealthPartners, then one of the largest healthcare insurers in Minnesota, announced non-reimbursement for never event-associated procedures. The Minnesota Medical Association criticized the legislation as "simplistic" and "not evidence-based." Remarkably, Bernard Emkes, former president of the Indiana State Medical Association, declared that not all the charges surrounding a medical mishap should be absorbed, especially if the patient received good care before the adverse event.[45]

Also in 2004, New Jersey enacted legislation requiring hospitals to report serious, preventable adverse events to the state and the patient's family. That same year, Connecticut adopted a list of reportable events in the context of in-patient and outpatient care. In 2005, Illinois mandated hospitals and ambulatory surgery centers (in-patient and outpatient care) report its state-specific list of never events.

In 2006, shortly after the release of the second NQF never event list, the Leapfrog Group, a Washington D.C.-based coalition of the nation's largest corporations and public agencies, advocated the adoption of policies prohibiting billing the victims of never events for the costs of care. The Leapfrog Group aspires to "reduce preventable medical mistakes and improve the quality and affordability of health care." Leapfrog also encourages healthcare providers to publicly report quality and outcomes to enable consumers and purchasing organizations to make informed healthcare choices.[46]

The pedigree of never events is the public and corporate sense that no reasonable person could argue that the wrong leg of a patient could be amputated in a healthcare facility that employs sound medical procedures. Whether an adverse result can be deemed a never event wholly depends upon the year and location in which the event occurred.

2. HAC events

Unlike never events, HACs are products of federal legislation, and are regulatory-process derived. HACs are high volume, *reasonably* preventable conditions which should not occur in a hospital employing evidence-based guidelines. HACs were not born primarily of public outrage over preventable medical error, but from the need for value-based care in a time of escalating healthcare costs in a budget-strapped economy.

To the legal profession, the intrinsic value of HACs is evidentiary. The central question is not whether the inflammatory label of "never event" or the wonderfully evocative acronym HAC must be used to describe a serious adverse outcome. The question is whether qualifying for either list changes the nature of impending litigation.

3. Burdens of production and persuasion

All personal injury lawsuits require a showing that the negligence of the defendant caused damages to the plaintiff. An exception to this rule is the assertion of strict liability, in which the simple occurrence of an event bespeaks negligence as a matter of law. When alleging strict liability, the plaintiff is relieved of the burden of producing evidence showing negligence occurred. It is enough to show that an event, which damaged plaintiff, occurred, and that the defendant bore responsibility for the event.

Professor D. Michael Risinger considered whether the effect of HAC legislation is to create a regimen of strict non-reimbursement, regardless of whether an event resulted from negligence. Some would say commission of a HAC would constitute negligence as a matter of law. He concludes that it does not, pointing to the list based in financial public policy, rather than liability.[47] He then considered whether the inclusion of an event on the list effectively shifts the burdens of both production and persuasion from the plaintiff to the defendant. He believes a court could do this, but only if it were convinced that the administrative investigation had been a full one. Such an investigation must establish that an extensive record of good evidence exists that the HACs were not only contracted almost exclusively in hospitals, but also that proper care could usually have prevented them. Thus, a court could rule that plaintiff need not show negligence, but plead *res ipsa loquitur*, shifting the burdens both of production and persuasion to the defendant to show that an event occurred despite its non-negligence. That is, the defendant took due care and yet still the HAC occurred. He suspects that this will not be the case, but admits its possibility.

Lastly, Risinger considered the issue of admissibility. He believes that the HAC classification may be relevant to the issue of causation. Arguably, the list falls under the public records hearsay exception, which applies to findings of a public official based on an investigation of acts, conditions or events. Therefore, though not necessarily available as a burden-shifting device, inclusion of an adverse event on the list might be introduced as persuasive of negligence to the trier of fact, be it judge or jury. The mere occurrence of a HAC supports plaintiff's allegation that the adverse event occurred because the actions the hospital took or failed to take were not within the standard of care. This is because a government agency concluded that a HAC ordinarily does not occur if a hospital follows evidence-based guidelines.

22.8 Summary

The Deficit Reduction Act of 2005 mandated value-based medicine for programs operating under the auspices of the Centers for Medicare and Medicaid Services. The Act authorized Health and Senior Services, which directs CMS programs, to establish programs to implement its directive. CMS, in conjunction with the CDC, selected high volume procedures with established evidence-based guidelines designed ordinarily to prevent specific adverse events. When the specified adverse events occur in a hospital setting, and the events were not present on admission, CMS withholds reimbursement for treatment. It is incumbent upon the hospital to resolve any problems with non-reimbursement. The non-reimbursement policy became effective in October 2008. The HAC policy principles migrated to outpatient facilities in 2009, and will affect physician practices sometime thereafter. Though intended to reap financial savings for government reimbursed care, the effects of HAC policy are far-reaching, influencing private health insurance reimbursement, patient care and medical malpractice litigation.

The greatest potential benefit of the implementation of this policy is increased patient safety. Nearly a million lives have been lost to medical error since the publication of the IOM report. Ultimately, the families of those lost, and the families of those whose lives yet may be saved, will not care if financial motivation drove a change in public policy. A different outcome will be enough. Apologies will not be necessary.

Endnotes

1. Kohn LT, Corrigan JM, Donaldson M, eds. *To Err Is Human: Building a Safer Health System.* Washington, DC: Institute of Medicine, 1999.

2. To Delay Is Deadly Executive Summary. http://cu.convio.net/site/PageServer?pagename=spp. (Accessed 5/22/09).

3. *Id.* at 3.

4. Aspden P, Wolcott J, Bootman JL, Cronenwett LR, eds. Committee on Identifying and Preventing Medication Errors: *Preventing Medication Errors: Quality Chasm Series.* Institute of Medicine of the National Academies. Washington, National Academy Press, 2006.

5. American Recovery and Reinvestment Act, Pub. L. 111-5.

6. "Clinton orders task force to seek reduction in medical errors," CNN.com, 12/7/99. http://archives.cnn.com/1999/HELTH/12/07/medical.errors.01/index.html. (Accessed 5/18/09).

7. Deficit Reduction Act of 2005, Pub. L. 109-171.

8. Armenti, C. "Three Little Words Change Everything: Medicare Non-Reimbursement Policy." *LSNJ Report.* September 2008.

9. Studdert, David M. et al. "Claims, Errors, and Compensation Payments in Medical Malpractice Litigation," *N Engl J Med.* May 2006, 354:2024-33.

10. N.J.S.A. 2A:53A-38, et seq.

11. N.J.S.A. 2A:53A-38(b).

12. Brown, A. "New Jersey Medical Malpractice Law," New Jersey Institute for Continuing Legal Education. 2005.

13. N.J.S.A. 2A:53A-38(f).

14. American Tort Reform Association, Medical Liability Reform, http://www.atra.org/issues/index.php?issue=7338. (Accessed 5/22/09).

15. Changes to the Hospital Inpatient Prospective Payment Systems and Fiscal year 2008 Rates, 72 FR 47130, 47200-217.

16. Pub. L. 109-171, §5001(c).

17. This public relations spin occurred in August 2008, when the CMS Office of Public Affairs announced "Medicare Takes New Steps to Help Make Your Hospital Stay Safer," http://www.cms.hhs.gov/apps/media/press/factsheet.asp. (Accessed 9/11/09).

18. Pub. L. 109-171, §5001(c).

19. 71 FR 48051-53.

20. 42 CFR 411, et seq.

21. 72 FR 24716.

22. Medicare Claims Processing Manual, Rev. 1780, 07/24/09, available at http://www.cms.hhs.gov/manuals/downloads/clm104c03.pdf. (Accessed 9/11/09).

23. Current Procedural Terminology, Standard Edition. American Medical Association. 2000.

24. 73 FR 48471.

25. http://www.cms.hhs.gov/HospitalAcqCond/01_Overview.asp. (Accessed 5/25/09).

26. http://www.cms.hhs.gov/apps/media/press/factsheet. asp. (Accessed 10/5/09).

27. 42 USCA §1395ww(3).

28. 73 FR 41416.

29. 73 FR 64618.

30. 73 FR 68781-68781.

31. http://www.cms.hhs.gov/HospitalOutpatientPPS. (Accessed 5/25/09).

32. www.gao.gov/press/fradunet2009mar30.pdf.(Accessed 5/25/09).

33. NJ Pub. L. 2009, c.122.

34. www.cms.hhs.gov/HospitalAcqCond   (Accessed 7/25/09).

35. 42 C.F.R. §482.24(c).

36. 45 C.F.R. §482.24(c)(2)(4).

37. www.cms.hhs.gov/HospitalAcqCond/01_Overview. asp. (Accessed 5/25/09).

38. *Id.*

39. 42 C.F.R. §482.24(c), et seq.

40. *Id.*

41. http://www.businessinsurance.com/article/20091020/ NEWS/910209990 (Accessed 11/7/09).

42. www.cms.hhs.gov/apps/media/press/release. asp?Counter=1863. (Accessed 5/25/09).

43. www.qualityforum.org/projects/sre2006.aspx.   (Accessed 9/13/09).

44. www.ama-assn.org/amednews/2006/12/18/bisc1218. htm. (Accessed 5/25/09).

45. www.qualityforum.org/projects/sre2006.aspx.   (Accessed 5/25/09).

46. www.leapfroggroup.org/home. (Accessed 5/25/09).

47. Private communication, dated May 28, 2009, between the author and D. Michael Risinger, Professor of Evidence, Seton Hall University School of Law.

Chapter 23

Infections in Hospitals and Nursing Homes

Ginny Lee, MBA/HCM, MSN, RN, Luke Curtis, MD, MS, CIH,
Jacqueline Vance, RNC, CDONA/LTC, and Lorraine M. Harkavy, RN, MS

Synopsis
23.1 Introduction
23.2 Susceptibility Factors for Infection among Hospitalized Patients and Nursing Home Residents
23.3 Barriers to the Optimal Management of Infections in Hospitals and Nursing Homes
    A. Hospitals
    B. Nursing Homes
23.4 Common Types of Infections in Healthcare Facilities
    A. Urinary Tract Infections (UTI)
        1. Endemics
        2. Prevention
    B. Lower Respiratory Tract Infections or Pneumonia
        1. Prevention
        2. Risk factors
    C. Surgical Site Infections (SSI)
        1. Risk factors
        2. Prevention
    D. Catheter (CVC) Associated Blood Stream Infections (BSI)
        1. Risk factors
        2. Prevention
23.5 Special Organisms: MRSA, VRE, VISA/VRSA
    A. MRSA and VISA/VRSA
    B. VRE
23.6 Antibiotic Use
23.7 Nursing Home Infections
    A. Urinary Tract Infections
    B. Respiratory Tract Infections
    C. Gastrointestinal Infections
    D. Skin Infections
23.8 Infection Control Programs
23.9 Hospital Federal Regulations and Accreditation
    A. Regulatory Requirements
    B. Joint Commission on Accreditation of Healthcare Organizations
23.10 Components of a Hospital Infection Control Program
    A. Surveillance of Infections (HAI)
    B. Isolation of Patients with Infectious Diseases
    C. Hand Hygiene
    D. Development and Implementation of Standards of Practice (SOP)
    E. Training and Education for Staff
    F. Occupational Health Program
    G. Environmental Services, Including Laundry
23.11 Nursing Home Infection Control
    A. Federal Regulations
    B. Elements of Comprehensive Institutional Infection Control Programs

    C. Immunization Programs
    D. The Importance of Following a Care Process
        1. Recognition
        2. Assessment
        3. Treatment
        4. Monitoring
23.12 Liability Associated with Transmittal of Infections in Long-Term Care
    A. Recommended Precautions
    B. Standard Precautions versus Contact Precautions
    C. Employee Health
    D. Environmental Decontamination
    E. Liability Associated with the Delay in Recognition of Infections
    F. Liability Associated with the Delay in Treatment or Transfer to the Hospital
        1. Decision to transfer
        2. Decision on treatment measures in palliative care
        3. Neglect
23.13 Antibiotic-Resistant Infections and Antibiotic Use
23.14 Summary
Endnotes

23.1 Introduction

It is important when considering litigation to understand the unique risk factors that increase the incidence of patients developing infections and the system barriers specific in the healthcare setting. The demographics for the patient in acute care differ from those in the long-term care facility, yet there are commonalities. Many patients with acute illnesses are elderly with frail, age-related immunosuppression, placing them at risk for infection. In hospitals, there is a widespread age range of patients, from neonates through the elderly. The acutely ill patient presents with comorbid conditions—including traumatic injuries and immunosuppressive diseases requiring the need for critical care. This increases the risk of acquiring a healthcare-associated infection.

Acute care infection, commonly known as healthcare-acquired infections (HAI) or nosocomial infections, statistics are compelling, as it has been estimated that more than 2.5 million HAIs occur each year contributing to or directly causing death in 250,000 patients.[1] HAIs in hospitalized patients vary between 5 and 15 percent.[2] Of these, many occur in patients who are critically ill, have traumatic injuries, had extensive medical procedures or major surgical operations, or are highly immunocompromised. HAIs can lead to complications in 25-33 percent of those patients admitted to intensive care units.[3] The added cost of HAIs has been estimated to be $4.5 billion annually.[4] Roberts et al. estimated the average cost of a healthcare-acquired infection to be $15,275.[5] The cost of these infections is $30.5 billion based upon 2 million HAIs annually, a substantial investment when one considers it has been estimated that 35 percent of these may be preventable.[6] The Centers for Disease Control and Prevention further divides the occurrence of infections by type including, "The frequency of HAIs varies by location. Currently, urinary tract infections comprise the highest percentage (34%) of HAIs followed by surgical site infections (17%), bloodstream infections (14%), and pneumonia (13%). In addition to the substantial human suffering exacted by HAIs, the financial burden attributable to these infections is staggering. It is estimated that HAIs incur an estimated $28 to $33 billion in excess healthcare costs each year."[7] These four categories account for three quarters of all HAIs.

TIP: Estimates of the true impact of HAIs may be misleading. First, patients have very short stays in hospitals even when experiencing serious illness or surgery. Once discharged, these patients may be lost to the system, developing a hospital-associated infection that goes undetected by current epidemiological methods. Second, a once dominant HAI, MRSA, is now found openly in the community making it difficult to distinguish between hospital-acquired and community-acquired infection identifying primary exposure. Finally, some states have mandatory reporting of HAIs, but currently this is sparse. There is current legislation to make all hospital acquired infections reportable to DHS and Hospital Compare.

Over 1.6 million to 3.8 million infections occur annually in long-term care (LTC) facilities in the United States, or approximately one to two infections per resident each year.[8] Richards estimates that infections may cause as many as 388,000 deaths in long-term care patients each year. Infections account for up to half of all transfers from long-term care facilities to hospitals, resulting in an estimated 150,000 to 300,000 hospital admissions annually.[9]

Infections are a common and significant source of morbidity and mortality among residents of LTC facilities[10] as well as hospitalized patients. It is essential to understand the elements of an infection control program, the federal regula-

tions, and the accepted process for recognizing and managing infections. The goal of this chapter is to address the subject of infections in hospitals and LTC facilities and guide the attorney or legal nurse consultant through the challenging material.

23.2 Susceptibility Factors for Infection among Hospitalized Patients and Nursing Home Residents

The infectious disease process is a combination of three primary factors: the host, the environment, and pathogenic microorganisms. People acquire infections through this process. The interplay between the elements of the infectious disease process is necessary for an infection to occur. Each element plays a role, though not all must be of equal significance.

Host factors that contribute to the occurrence of infections include:

- Immune suppression such as in hematopoietic stem cell transplant patients;
- Age—both the very young, such as the premature newborn, and the elderly (over 85 years) have age-related immune defervesence (the immune system is weakened);
- Underlying chronic disease states such as diabetes, or acquired immune deficiency syndrome (AIDS); and
- Malnutrition—which is very common in elderly patients in hospitals and extended care facilities. One review of five published studies reported that severe protein-calorie malnutrition was found in 42 to 91 percent of hospitalized patients over the age of 65.[11] Various studies have reported that malnourished patients are as much as five times as likely to contract a hospital-acquired infection as compared to a well-nourished patient.[12]

Many of these host factors cannot be controlled or changed. The patient presents with factors which increase the likelihood of acquiring a healthcare-acquired infection.[13]

The environment plays a role in the occurrence of infectious disease. Contributing factors include the structural environment and the living environment, that is, other humans and the patient. Included in these categories is medical equipment especially that which interrupts the normal host defense mechanisms such as the skin, mucus membranes of the nose and other parts of the respiratory system, and perineal area. Medical devices include, for example, vascular access devices, endoscopes, and bladder catheters. These devices often are lifesaving and have increased medical diagnostic capabilities, but they also pose a risk to the patient by bypassing the host's anatomical barriers including skin and mucous membranes. The decontamination of medical equipment differs from that appropriate for the structural environment. This is discussed later in this chapter.

Microorganisms cause infections including HAIs. Bacteria, viruses, and fungi are ubiquitous and can be found in dust, in soil, and on surfaces, and are ever-present in humans. Many of these are normal flora living in and on the body. The host's underlying health or disease, previous contact with specific microorganisms, experience of a traumatic injury, history of antibiotic use, and other factors play a role in whether the person becomes infected.[14] The hospital poses a somewhat unique environment in that many organisms are increasingly resistant to the antibiotics frequently used to treat infectious diseases. Emerging pathogens continue to cause serious infections. Examples of these resistant and emerging infectious agents include:

- Methicillin-resistant Staphylococcus aureus,
- Vancomycin-resistant Staphylococcus aureus,
- Acinetobacter baumannii,
- Vancomycin-resistant Enterococci,
- Streptococcus pneumoniae, and others.

While these are primarily found in acute care settings, there is continued recognition that these organisms can be found in other healthcare arenas such as long-term care, day care centers, same day surgery centers, ambulatory clinics, emergent care centers, dialysis centers, as well as the general community. See Section 23.5 for additional discussion of these organisms.

The interplay between the host and the microbial population determines the likelihood of an infection. There are endogenous organisms (the patient's own organisms), and exogenous organisms (the flora of others or the environment). Virulence factors—such as the ability of a disease-causing microorganism to invade the host while not being contained by the body's defenses, resulting in severe disease—and pathogenicity (disease-causing) factors result in infection of the host. Microorganisms thrive in the environment and the human body, some more likely to cause disease than others. Sterilization is the only known way to completely eliminate or eradicate microorganisms and is limited in its application to medical equipment and surgical instruments.

TIP: The immune system is an essential part of the host's reaction to invading microorganisms.

A thorough discussion of the immune system is beyond the scope of this chapter; however, the immune system is made up of several components. The immune system goes into action when the body is insulted by invading microorganisms, which are recognized as foreign antigens or proteins. The immune system includes both specific and nonspecific defenses. Examples of nonspecific defenses are intact skin, tearing of the eyes, proteins within the mouth that are capable of killing bacteria, and the acid of the stomach. Specific defenses include the cell-mediated immune system—which consists of T lymphocytes—and humeral-mediated immunity, which consists of B lymphocytes.

Unfortunately, despite best efforts of the quality control staff, many hospital-acquired infections cannot be prevented. In a litigious society the first inclination is to lay blame. Whether infections in nursing home residents are a source of liability is a very challenging question, as several considerations relevant to prevention of infection differ in LTC populations than in acute care.[15] The frail elderly have traits that make them susceptible to infections.

For most LTC residents, the facility is their home, a place where many people experience infections. Therefore, one must ask several questions when considering litigation:

- To what degree are unusual measures appropriate or realistic to prevent the usual infections in this setting?
- When is it reasonable to limit mobility or social interaction of persons in their usual residence to prevent transmission of infection?
- Could this infection have been prevented if reasonable measures were put into place?

LTC residents are often functionally impaired, with incontinence, poor function mobility, or impaired mental status. Impaired functional status can result in admission to long-term care facilities and is a risk factor for infection. Risk factors of poor function and multiple chronic illnesses are not modifiable and thus lead to infection. To quote Nicolle, "If the major predictors of infection in LTC facilities are poor functional status and co-existing chronic illness, and these conditions cannot be altered, to what extent is it realistic to anticipate that endemic infections can be prevented in such residents? In addition, with the number and severity of existing conditions, how much illness or death is attributable to infections per se, rather than to underlying chronic disease?"[16]

TIP: The attorney and legal nurse consultant should be aware that non-modifiable conditions of LTC facility residents make them prone to common infections, and it is almost impossible to blame a person or a process for this occurring. Therefore, it can be problematic when assessing the impact of an infection on a patient. The attorney and expert witnesses should focus on whether the infection was recognized, assessed, treated, and monitored in a timely fashion.

23.3 Barriers to the Optimal Management of Infections in Hospitals and Nursing Homes

A. Hospitals

Hospitals and nursing homes provide barriers to the optimum management of infections. Many hospitals may not analyze their own laboratory tests and thus the facility may "outsource" these services by sending the specimen to the laboratory. There can be a delay in obtaining the laboratory results when outsourcing specimens. "Stat" laboratory results may not be obtainable. The laboratory plays a pivotal role in determining the causal microorganisms; thus ready access is vital to diagnosis and treatment. While bacterial culture results are usually available within about 48 hours, gram stains can be done and read in a matter of minutes. This provides acute care infection control efforts with more rapid results. Gram staining, however, does not provide definitive results. The final culture needs to be reviewed, and if necessary a change in treatment may be initiated.

Often treatment is initiated based on the usual causal organisms. Therefore treatment may be based on empirical data. Once these culture results are available and reviewed by the physician, a treatment plan will be reevaluated. Some organisms are resistant to certain antibiotics. If organisms are resistant to the antibiotic used as treatment, a change in antibiotic is indicated.

TIP: Resistance is defined as when the antibiotic does not slow or kill the organism. When an organism is sensitive to an antibiotic, this organism will be affected by the antibiotic.

Accommodations can be made for those patients who require isolation in the hospital setting. A hospital stay is recognized as temporary, which makes it possible to confine patients to their rooms when controlling communicable diseases. Even hospitals have to face the necessity of the infected patient leaving the room for therapy, diagnostic tests, and surgery. In some instances patients may leave to visit other patients, go to the lounge, or even the cafeteria. Thus,

patient transport to other locations complicates the ability to control infections.

Another barrier includes the costs of medical care, which have risen at the same time payments for care provided have declined. Coincidentally, patients in hospitals today tend to be much sicker; and people living longer increases subjection to chronic diseases, often requiring more sophisticated and costly care. This conundrum demands greater resource availability, yet less is available.

Staffing for most infection control departments is limited and can be another major barrier to fighting infections. For years the infection control community has unsuccessfully attempted to identify the proper infection control specialists and epidemiologist-to-patient ratio, as health care is in constant flux. The original standard proposed by the CDC was one full-time ICP for every 250 occupied beds.[17] This is considered no longer relevant to modern hospitals. A description of the role of the infection control professional is found in Section 23.10 of this chapter.

The art and science of acute care infection control is far more complex than it was in the 1960s, even when taking into account that era's hospital-acquired infections of penicillinase-producing staphylococci. Intensive care units did not exist in most hospitals then. Hospitals now have numerous intensive care units filled with critically ill susceptible patients. Patients are living longer and acquiring diseases or treatments that diminish the effectiveness of the immune system. Sophisticated medical diagnostic techniques and interventions are double edged as they may save and prolong life but not without risk of adverse consequences such as infections. Antibiotics are lifesaving and at the same time lead to the development of microbial resistance to these drugs.

TIP: The infection control specialist has the responsibility to review, comprehend, and develop standards of practice to respond to regulations and standards with implications for infection control and disease prevention in employees. This specialist oftentimes collaborates with an infection control team and other disciplines.

B. Nursing Homes

The differences between acute care and LTC facilities affect the recognition and treatment of infections. For most residents in long-term facilities, the facility is now their home, where they will live out the rest of their lives. It is important to recognize that wherever a person resides, he is at risk for infections. Laboratories are usually not "in house" in LTC facilities.[18] In a hospital, microbiology laboratories are more commonly available on site. Invasive techniques—such as a bronchosopy or biopsy—for obtaining cultures are also readily available. The acute care hospital is better staffed and special isolation precautions are applied for short periods of time. LTC facility residents may carry resistant organisms and now are accommodated for longer periods of time with less staff. Diagnostic tests are not easily obtained in LTC because they may require the patient to be transferred out for the test. While there are mobile diagnostic testing services, not all facilities have access to them and there is a wait time for those services. While a stat blood test or a reading of a chest x-ray may take less than one hour in a hospital, it can take many hours to get the results back to a LTC facility.

Furthermore, setting up an infection control program in LTC is not problem-free. For example, there are residents who are carriers. They are colonized or not clinically infected with a resistant organism such as Methicillin-resistant Staphylococcus aureus (MRSA) or Vancomycin-resistant enterococcus (VRE). The presence of carriers creates a conflict between two principles of nursing home practice: maintaining a safe environment and maximizing independent function. Long-term care facility personnel are often faced with difficult decisions that balance infection control and quality of life. Such decisions include providing extra supervision for residents who need assistance in hygiene when out of their room so that they can maintain the social activity that is necessary to their quality of life; the facility staff should know when to restrict their mobility to ensure the safety of the other residents and staff. Once a person is colonized, she remains so for the remainder of her life. Obviously, it would be cruel to restrict people to isolation for the remainder of their lives just because they may need assistance in hygiene when out of their room.

23.4 Common Types of Infections in Healthcare Facilities

Infections occur in hospitalized patients and nursing home residents. There are some quantitative and qualitative differences in these two populations, therefore requiring separate discussions of each. While there are many different possible infections that can occur affecting all body systems, there are several that are most common. Urinary tract infections are the most common in both groups. Other infections are more likely to be seen in one type of care environment. The hospitalized patient may acquire a bloodstream infection due to the higher likelihood of having an intravascular medical device as a treatment modality or a surgical site infection, because even minor surgical procedures are rarely done in nursing homes. Lower respiratory infections occur in inpatient care environments, and the hospitalized patient is more likely to need a ventilator, which may increase the risk of infection.

The National Nosocomial Infection Surveillance System (NNIS) provides the most complete data on hospital-acquired infections. The NNIS data is based on reported surveillance data from nearly 300 participating hospitals. In 2005, NNIS was officially changed to National Healthcare Safety Network (NHSN). The NHSN is a voluntary online reporting system that is managed by the Division of Healthcare Quality Promotion (DHQP). The CDC supports more than 2,100 hospitals in 21 states that use the NHSN system of reporting.

The most common causal association of hospital-acquired infections includes the use of medical devices. Most urinary tract infections are related to urinary tract instrumentation, especially indwelling catheters (range 3.0-6.7 UTIs for every 1,000 catheter days). The occurrence of pneumonia is primarily ventilator associated (range 2.9-15.2 pneumonias every 1,000 ventilator days). Blood stream infections occur in patients with central line catheters (range 2.7-7.4 every 1,000 central line days of use). There are other risk factors, not the least of which is the surgical procedure itself, especially in patients who have wounds that are already contaminated as a result of traumatic injury or if there is spillage into the abdominal cavity from the bowels.[19]

Due to the rising number of patients requiring dialysis for the treatment of chronic renal failure associated with hypertension or diabetes, and other clinical manifestations, dialysis centers have found themselves in the predicament of reporting their infections. A large majority of dialysis patients are covered by Medicaid and/or Medicare, and infections related to the deliverance of care are mandated to be reported to CMS and the local Quality Improvement Organization (QIO) for the region.

The four major sites of hospital-acquired infection include:

- Urinary tract infections (UTI),
- Lower respiratory infections, specifically pneumonia (PNEU),
- Surgical site infections (SSIs), and
- Bloodstream infections (BSIs).

Most hospitals today use the Centers for Disease Control and Prevention (CDC) definitions and criteria for determining the presence of infection. These definitions were developed by the CDC to provide consistency and comparability amongst those hospitals that use the definitions in their surveillance program to identify the occurrence of hospital-acquired infections. This is discussed further in Section 23.10.

A. Urinary Tract Infections (UTI)

Several definitions for urinary tract infections are dependent on the patient's presentation and age. This section focuses on the symptomatic urinary tract infection. The determination of the occurrence is based on the presence of signs or symptoms including a fever of greater than or equal to 100.4°F, urgency, frequency, dysuria or suprapubic tenderness, and a positive urine culture finding of greater than or equal to 100,000 microorganisms/cm[3].[20]

Urinary tract infections are the most common type of nosocomial infection[21] and have been estimated to account for 40 percent of all nosocomial infections.[22] Laupland et al. studied the acquisition of UTIs in intensive care unit patients. The incidence of ICU-acquired UTI was 9.6/1,000 ICU days. Factors associated with the occurrence included:

- The female patient,
- Admission to a medical ICU, and
- The non-cardiovascular surgical patient.[23]

UTIs are usually the result of urinary tract instrumentation due primarily to indwelling catheters. Causative microorganisms most commonly include: *E. coli, Enterococci,* and *Staphylococci.* Less common causes include *Klebsiella, Enterobacter, Proteus,* and even *Corynebacteria,* yeasts, and fungi. Many of these organisms come from the patient's own flora, which primarily reside in the bowel. The organisms get into the bladder through several routes. The infecting organisms gain entry to the bladder by traveling up the outside of an indwelling catheter which is introduced at the time of catheterization, or through intraluminal ascent from the catheter drainage collection bag. Contaminating microorganisms can gain access to the bladder if the catheter-drainage bag junction is opened.[24] Urinary tract infections can be associated with increased morbidity and even death.[25] Complications from UTIs include blood stream infections and sepsis. The rates of nosocomial bacteremia range from 1.3-14.5 cases for every 1,000 hospital admissions.[26] UTIs can lead to other serious complications including infection of male genitalia, endocarditis, osteomyelitis, septic arthritis, and meningitis.

1. Endemics

Endemics are most often related to the use of catheters. These endemics can be widespread and involve many patients. The causative organisms often are resistant to the usual antibiotics, leaving less choice for treatment or the need to use more broad spectrum drugs, which can lead to further infectious complications or development of resistant organisms. Factors contributing to outbreaks of hospital-ac-

quired urinary infections include bladder catheters, contaminated antiseptics used for irrigation of catheters, transmission on the hands of healthcare workers, improper handling or sharing amongst patients of urine collection or measuring devices and urometers, and environmental contamination.[27]

2. Prevention

The Centers for Disease Control and Prevention has published guidelines for the prevention of catheter-associated infections. An important tool of primary prevention is to avoid the use of catheters if at all possible. If catheters must be used, removal as soon as these devices are no longer necessary is advocated. The CDC has published guidelines to establish the necessity and when catheters are not a necessity.

Lengthy use of indwelling catheters increases the likelihood of infections with over 20 percent of catheterized patients acquiring a catheter-associated infection. The recommended prevention methods[28] requires healthcare providers to:

- use sterile aseptic technique during catheter insertion;
- maintain a closed sterile drainage system;
- avoid routine catheter irrigation as this requires opening the system which leads to likely microbial contamination and the possibility that the irrigant solution may be contaminated;
- maintain unobstructed urinary flow;
- keep the catheter drainage system lower than the level of the patient's bladder to prevent backflow of urine from the drainage bag;
- collect specimen through needle aspiration to avoid opening the catheter-tubing juncture; and
- change the catheter only as indicated and not on a routine arbitrary schedule.

Healthcare providers are responsible for the care of patients with catheters and need to follow the above recommended methods. Nurses and physicians are to be cognizant of overall patient conditions, as this affects the likelihood that patients may get a UTI. Proper fluid intake is important for cellular metabolism and maintenance of urine flow through the bladder. However, staff are to be mindful of conditions in which fluid intake needs to be restricted, avoiding procedures that have been shown to be ineffective in preventing UTI, such as treating colonization of the meatus or using antibiotics for patients with asymptomatic bacteruria, that is, the presence of bacteria in the urine without signs of infection. The Joanna Briggs Institute researches and condenses the latest findings for the establishment of evidenced based practice (EBP). According to the Joanna Briggs Institute (JBI),[29] the use of silver alloy-coated or antibiotic impregnated catheters decreases the risk of short-term urinary catheter use. Prophylactic antibiotics also help to reduce UTIs in short-term catheter use. JBI also reports that daily hygiene with normal tap water is sufficient in perineal care. Perineal hygiene is important especially in patients who have diarrhea. Staff personnel must review culture results and report unusual microorganisms including if these are resistant to antibiotics. However, the single most effective deterrent of UTIs is mandatory staff education.

TIP: In determining possible negligence, the attorney or legal nurse consultant should review the personal hygiene the patient received while being catheterized. Did the facility follow EBP and the recommendations of the CDC? Does the documentation include changes in urine color, odor, etc.? Did the facility follow their own policy and procedure for catheterization and care?

B. Lower Respiratory Tract Infections or Pneumonia

Hospital-acquired pneumonia is the most difficult infection to diagnose. There are numerous descriptions of the disease in medical literature. The most common presentation includes fever, cough, and purulent sputum. Radiological studies are needed to further characterize the illness. A progressive pulmonary infiltrate is one cardinal sign. Routinely collected cultures of sputum, blood, and tracheal aspirates are nonspecific and may not be helpful either for the diagnosis or in the selection of treatment choices. The CDC noted in its overview of nosocomial pneumonia that the "gold standard" was to collect sputum specimen through bronchoscopy in order to obtain sputum from deep within the lung to better identify causative organisms. The most common causative organisms are *Pseudomonas aeruginosa, Proteus, Acinetobacter,* and *Staphylococcus aureus.* Most of these organisms arise from patients' own oropharyngeal flora.

Hospital-acquired pneumonia accounts for about 1 percent of all hospital-acquired infections and 27 percent of intensive-care-acquired infections.[30] This causes morbidity and death, which adds to the cost of health care.[31] Patients most at risk for pneumonia are those with burns, traumatic injuries, serious conditions, chronic or underlying diseases, prolonged hospitalization, aspiration, and prior treatment with antibiotics.[32] Patients who had thoracic or abdominal surgery are also at increased risk of nosocomial pneumonia. The lynchpin for all of these conditions related to the occurrence of pneumonia is universally associated with mechanical ventilation and endotracheal intubation. Therefore, the focus of hospital-acquired pneumonia is ventilator-associated pneumonia (VAP). Seven percent of intensive care unit patients develop pneumonia. Seventy-five percent of these were VAP.

TIP: Patients with VAP remain hospitalized for four to seventeen days longer than intensive care unit patients who do not acquire VAP.[33]

---

1. Prevention

Prevention of VAP is difficult due to the source of microorganisms and the underlying illnesses of susceptible patients. These patients are among the most seriously compromised and require ventilator-assisted respiration often for prolonged time periods. The CDC Guideline for Prevention of Healthcare-Associated Pneumonia (2003) lists several measures to prevent VAP. These include:

- Provide staff education about pneumonia, and infection control practices; "ensure worker competency" in the implementation of these.
- Conduct epidemiological surveillance to identify ICU patients at risk of VAP, and the causative microorganisms and their susceptibility patterns. The data should also identify effective prevention methods. Surveillance information should be given to direct patient caregivers for development of preventive intervention strategies.
- Maintain, clean and sterilize respiratory equipment properly to reduce contamination with microorganisms.
- Reduce the opportunity for person-to-person transmission of causative organisms. Standard Precautions include proper hand hygiene, and use of personal protective equipment (PPE) to protect both patients and healthcare workers from contamination.
- Strictly follow proper procedures during patient suctioning and tracheostomy care.
- Modify host risk factors when possible. Examples include proper immunizations such as influenza and pneumococcal vaccinations as needed; prevent aspiration by proper positioning.
- Pay careful attention to minimize aspiration associated with enteral feedings, prevention of oropharyngeal colonization in specific patient groups undergoing cardiac surgery, and use of H2-blockers, sucralare or antacids to reduce gastric colonization in patients receiving ventilatory-assisted respiratory care.[34]

The CDC also recommends the following in the prevention of ventilator-associated pneumonia:

- Keep the head of the patient's bed raised between 30 and 45 degrees unless other medical conditions do not allow this to occur.
- Check the patient's ability to breathe on his own every day so that the patient can be taken off of the ventilator as soon as possible.
- Clean their hands with soap and water or an alcohol-based hand rub before and after touching the patient or the ventilator.
- Clean the inside of the patient's mouth on a regular basis.
- Clean or replace equipment between uses on different patients.[35]

Ventilator-associated pneumonia is not the only cause of HAI pneumonia. Lengthy hospitalizations, comorbidities, immunosuppression and prolonged surgical procedures requiring general anesthesia increase the risk of hospital-acquired pneumonia. Post-operative and sedentary patients should be instructed on actions that decrease the occurrence of hospital-associated pneumonia, including: turn, cough and deep breathing, proper use of incentive spirometer, and prompt mobilization of the patient as soon as deemed safe.

Hand hygiene, including glove use and appropriate personal protective equipment, will minimize the likelihood of transferring hospital infectious agents to patients. Intensive care units commonly have waterless hand cleansers and gloves readily available at bedside.

The JBI published the following EBP guidelines for VAP:

- It is recommended, if possible, that intubation and reintubation be avoided.
- Orotracheal intubation and orogastric tubes should be preferred over nasotracheal intubation and nasogastric tubes to reduce the risk of VAP.
- The continuous aspiration of sub-glottic secretions is suggested to reduce the risk of early-onset VAP (Grade B).
- The endotracheal tube cuff pressure is recommended to be maintained at greater than 20 cm H_2O to prevent leakage of bacterial pathogens around the cuff into the lower respiratory tract.
- Patients are recommended to be kept in the semi-recumbent position (30–45 degrees).
- It is suggested that contaminated condensate should be carefully emptied from ventilator circuits, and condensate should be prevented from entering either the endotracheal tube or inline medication nebulizers.
- Intensive insulin therapy is recommended to maintain serum glucose levels between 80 and 110 mg/dl in ICU patients with diabetes and to prevent VAP.[36]

2. Risk factors

The most common risk factors include prolonged intubation greater than 48 hours, chronic respiratory disease, prolonged sedation, and comorbidities. Nursing staffs recognize the risk factors for hospital-acquired pneumonia and there are a variety of interventions that may reduce the occurrence of pneumonia. These include elevating the patient's head and upper torso to minimize secretions going into the lungs, suctioning oral secretions, turning patients, performing chest physiotherapy, and using more solid foods to minimize fluids being aspirated. Also, the standard of care requires avoiding sedatives, which affect the ability to swallow. All of these measures must be consistent with the treatment plan, as some may not be instituted if inappropriate for the patient.

Proper maintenance of respiratory equipment is important. Condensation can collect in the corrugated tubing and should be disposed of properly so as not to allow back flow toward the patient. Ventilatory accessories should be maintained correctly and recommended change times are to be followed.

C. Surgical Site Infections (SSI)

Surgical site infections are the direct result of surgical intervention, regardless of the body system involved. Infections can occur as superficial wound infections, as deep tissue infections, or in the organ space. The CDC defines these infections as those which occur within 30 days after the operative procedure if no implant is left in place or within one year if implants are inserted into the body during the procedure. Implants include "non-human derived implanted foreign bodies such as prosthetic heart valves, non-human vascular grafts, mechanical heart, or hip prosthesis that is permanently placed in a patient during surgery."[37] Signs of SSIs include purulent drainage (pus), fever, wound dehiscence (splitting open along suture lines), or abscess at the wound site. Other signs include swelling at the incision site, heat, and erythema (redness).

TIP: There are an estimated 27 million surgical procedures performed each year in the United States. Surgical site infections account for about 16 percent of HAIs, making them the third most common nosocomial infection.[38]

Table 23.1
**Microorganisms Isolated from Surgical Site Infections,
NNIS data for the years 1990-1996***

Microorganism	Percent Infections
Staphylococcus aureus	20
Coagulase-negative staphylococci	14
Enterococcus spp.	12
Pseudomonas aeruginosa	8
Enterobacter spp	7
Proteus mirabilis	3
Klebsiella pneumoniae	3
Other streptococci species	3
Candida albicans	3

*Adapted from NNIS.

A landmark study conducted by Cruse and Foord demonstrated the seriousness of this complication. Patient stays were extended by as much as ten or more days, which increased costs of care.[39] SSIs continue to occur as patients have aged and technology has developed. This may be attributed to many of the risk factors presented earlier in this chapter including the emergence of multiple-drug resistant microorganisms. Patient characteristics that have been suggested as predetermining the odds for an infection include smoking, chronic diseases particularly diabetes, use of steroids, poor nutrition, and obesity.

The most common causative organisms and the frequency these are isolated according to NNIS data are listed in Table 23.1. Many of these are organisms from patients' own flora.

1. Risk factors

Some risk factors for SSI, though not all, can be mitigated by properly preparing the patient for surgery and limiting exposure to the hospital organisms. Prolonged preoperative hospital stay prior to surgery seems to be an independent risk factor for SSI, although it is not well understood as to how this factors into infection occurrence. Preoperative shaving greatly increases the likelihood of infection, and numerous studies have borne this out. In Seropian and Reynolds and other landmark studies, patients who had a pre-operative shave with a razor had a significantly greater chance of infection than those that had hair removed using a depilatory.[40]

The length of the surgical procedure influences the occurrence of SSI. Studies have shown that surgical procedures lasting longer than two hours are more commonly associated with infection. This may be related to the patient char-

acteristics, the type of surgery, or if the procedure involves contaminated wounds (e.g., those with spillage from the gut or open traumatic wounds). Other factors associated with SSIs include the presence of a remote infection at the time of surgery, drains left in the surgical wound in order to drain fluid away from the surgical site (use of sterile closed suction drainage minimizes this risk), and surgical technique.

2. Prevention

Surveillance of SSI has proven effective in bringing attention to this problem. (Surveillance is an epidemiological method used by hospital-based infection control professionals.) Cruse and Foord showed that simply giving infection rates to the surgeons resulted in a reduction in SSI rate. This has been demonstrated repeatedly ever since.[41] Surgical infection surveillance includes capturing the data accurately, using specified criteria for determining the presence of an infection, and ensuring nonjudgmental, anonymous reporting of infection rates to surgeons.

Roberts v. Lowry, 673 So. 2d 1323 (La. App., 1996).
The patient's finger was amputated in an accident with farm machinery. He wrapped his hand and arm in his shirt, picked up his finger, and got a ride to the hospital emergency room. At the hospital, according to the record in the Court of Appeal of Louisiana, the ER physician cleaned and debrided the wound and called in an orthopedic surgeon to re-attach the finger. The court accepted the patient's testimony that before the initial cleansing and debriding in the emergency room, the ER nurses cut back the patient's shirt to the elbow and did not completely clean the hand itself or the arm.

Instead, the court ruled, to prevent infection the patient's shirt should have been removed and his whole hand and arm carefully washed, prepped for surgery and covered with sterile drapes, before the wound was cleansed and debrided by the ER physician.

The re-attachment surgery seemed to have gone well, but infection set in. A physician who treated the patient with antibiotics for the infection testified the infection was related to *Clostridium*. The court accepted expert testimony linking the *Clostridium* infection to a lapse in aseptic technique by the ER nurses and physician, rather than a lapse in sterile technique during the finger re-attachment procedure.

The patient had more surgeries after the re-attachment. A hand specialist finally restored full use of the finger and hand by removing adhesions and scar tissue from around a nerve. Nevertheless, the patient sued the hospital where he got his emergency care and the ER physician for negligence over the infection caused in the ER and the resulting need for additional surgeries. He won a large verdict for damages which was upheld on appeal.[42]

TIP: The CDC "Guideline for Prevention of Surgical Site Infection, 1999"[43] is a comprehensive review of recommended methods for reducing the occurrence of SSI. The recommendations are divided into four categories: preoperative, intraoperative, postoperative, and surveillance. The reader is referred to this document for a complete description of these methods. The document can be found at www.cdc.gov/ncidod/hip.

The JBI has provided EBP before, during and after surgical procedures to reduce the occurrence surgical site infections.

Preoperatively, these include management of surgical personnel, mechanically environment control, and management of operating room surfaces. Examples of EBP[44] include:

Management of Surgical Personnel

- Surgical staff should be educated and encouraged to report promptly to their supervisor when they have signs and symptoms of an infectious illness. (Level IV)
- Surgical staff should receive hepatitis B vaccination at the exposure to bloodborne pathogens unless medically contraindicated. (Level IV)
- General traffic in and out of the operating room/ theatre should be reduced as far as possible. (Level IV)

Mechanical Environmental Control

- Normal skin flora of surgical staff and patients cause more than half of all infections following clean surgery. (Level IV)
- Conventional plenum ventilation with filtered air, using filters with an efficiency of 80-95 percent to remove airborne particles more than 5μm is used in most modern operating rooms/theatres. (Level IV)
- A laminar air-flow system with high-efficiency particulate air (HEPA) filters can remove airborne particles of 0.3μm and above with 99.97 percent efficiency, and are generally used for orthopaedic and implant surgery. (Level IV)

- 20 air changes per hour to obtain 50-150 colony forming units/m^3 of air is the recommended bacterial threshold in most countries. (Level IV)
- It is reported by several studies that improvements in airflow and ultraviolet lighting reduce not only bacterial counts but also rates of surgical site infection (SSI). (Level IV)

Management of Operating Room Surfaces

- Operating room surfaces (tables, floors, walls, etc.) have rarely been shown to be the source of surgical infection for patients. (Level IV)
- Operating room surfaces that are visibly soiled or contaminated with potentially infectious material should be cleaned before the next procedure. (Level IV)
- Routine cleaning of all operating room surfaces are important to return the operating room to a clean state after each procedure. (Level IV)

Intraoperatively, the JBI[45] recommends the following:

Surgical Hand Scrubs

- Surgical hand scrubs are to remove debris and transient microorganisms from the nails, hands and forearms, reduce the resident microbial count to a minimum and inhibit rapid rebound growth of microorganisms.
- Skin integrity is important to prevent surgical site infections (SSI); therefore, hands and forearms should be free of open lesions and breaks in cuticles. (Level IV)
- Fingernails should be kept short, clean and healthy. (Level IV)
- Artificial nails should not be worn. Rings, watches and bracelets should be removed before performing hand scrubs. (Level IV)

Skin Preparation

- Many reports have confirmed that most SSI are from normal skin flora (coagulase-negative Staphylococcus nonaures). (Level IV)
- The surgical site should be assessed before skin preparation. Skin assessment should focus on the presence of moles, warts, rashes and other skin conditions. (Level IV)
- The following are some special precautions for skin preparation: (Level IV)
  - Preparing areas with high microbial counts;
  - Isolating colostomy sites, covering with an antiseptic-soaked sponge and preparing them;

- Using normal saline to prepare burned, denuded or traumatized skin;
- Avoiding the use of chlorhexidine gluconate and/or alcohol based products on mucous membranes;
- Allowing sufficient contact time for antiseptics before applying sterile drapes;
- Allowing sufficient time for complete evaporation of flammable agents;
- Documenting patient skin preparation in the patient record.

Antibiotic Administration

- Antibiotics should be administered so that the bactericidal concentration is present in the tissues at the time of incision. (Level IV)
- Re-administration of antibiotics should be performed every half-life of the antibiotic so that the bactericidal concentrations are maintained in the tissues while the incision remains open. (Level IV)

Normothermia Management

- Maintenance of normothermia during the perioperative period reduces the risk for SSI. (Level IV)
- Monitoring body temperature with an esophageal probe or bladder probe is recommended. (Level IV)

Glycemic Control

- In patients undergoing heart surgery, increased intraoperative blood glucose is associated with increased complications, including post-operative infection. (Level IV)
- Intraoperative infusions of glucose, insulin and potassium (GIK) in heart surgery have not demonstrated convincing benefits in multiple randomized trials. (Level IV)[46]

Post-operative treatments will vary based on the type of organism that has manifested within the wound. Prompt identification of the surgical site infection based on physical assessment of the wound, obtaining a wound culture and starting treatment immediately can improve the outcome of the surgical site infection.

D. Catheter (CVC) Associated Blood Stream Infections (BSI)

1. Risk factors

The NHSN definitions for blood stream infection differentiate clinical sepsis from laboratory-confirmed BSI.

A laboratory-confirmed BSI is one in which a pathogen is cultured from the patient's blood and is not related to an infection at another body site. The septic patient presents with clinical signs or symptoms such as fever, hypotension, or oliguria (scant urine production). The physician must institute treatment appropriate for sepsis. Catheter-related BSI is considered when the patient presents with symptoms related to the catheter findings, i.e., microorganisms found on the catheter are the same as those cultured from the patient's blood.

Catheter-associated blood stream infections (BSI) are seen throughout the inpatient hospital setting as well as in other healthcare venues. Both peripheral venous catheters and central venous catheters (CVC) are implicated, but the central line catheter is most commonly associated with BSI. These infections considerably add to morbidity mortality and increased hospital length of stay. In addition, the financial burden is significant. It has been estimated that death from CVC-related BSIs is as high as 25 percent. The estimated cost for care of these patients in the United States is $2.3 billion annually.[47]

The risk of acquiring a catheter-related infection is multifactorial and contributes to the possibility of infection development. The following are risk factors:

- Underlying disease (i.e., cancer),
- Severity and type of illness (i.e., burns),
- Immunosuppression,
- Multiple traumas,
- The conditions under which the catheter is placed (i.e., emergency vs. elective placement),
- Techniques used during catheter placement (i.e., sterile technique vs. clean), and
- The type of catheter inserted.

The most common organisms linked to catheter BSIs are common skin organisms that contaminate the catheter at the insertion site. These include coagulase-negative *Staphylococcus* and *Staphylococcus aureus*. Other infecting organisms are *enterococcus*, *Escherichia coli*, *Enterobacter* especially *Pseudomonas aeruginosa*, *Klebsiella pneumoniae*, and Candida species.

Markabani v. Prasad, 2007 WL 1227709 (Mich. App., April 26, 2007). The patient was a 27-year-old auto mechanic who was burned on his face, neck and hands when gasoline he spilled on himself accidentally ignited. He went to the intensive-care burn unit at the hospital after skin graft surgery for third-degree burns on the back of his hand. His temperature spiked and his white blood count became elevated. These signs are not uncommon after skin graft surgery. Later, however, a blood culture linked the infection to Enterobacter cloacae, which most likely entered his system through an IV insertion site. The Court of Appeals of Michigan accepted the testimony of two nursing experts who testified for the patient in his lawsuit against the hospital in reaching the decision he had grounds for his case.

An IV inserted outside the hospital has to be removed right away, once a new IV has been started, and that was not done in this case. The EMT's IV was left in the patient for an extended period of time. IVs started in the hospital have to be rotated every 72 to 96 hours to prevent infection. The patient had to have the pus-filled basilic vein removed from his forearm and after the surgery was left with reflex sympathetic dystrophy in the underlying ulnar nerve.[48]

2. Prevention

Minimizing the occurrence of catheter-related BSIs is a multi-step process. Meticulous care of the catheter and sterile technique during insertion are the mainstays of good practice in the handling of these devices. The CDC's "Guidelines for the Prevention of Intravascular Catheter-Related Infections"[49] include the following recommendations:

1. Educate healthcare workers about appropriate use and proper procedures for insertion and maintenance of intravascular catheters and proper procedures. Periodic evaluation of competence and knowledge regarding central line catheters use and care is suggested.
2. Ensure appropriate nurse to patient ratio to allow for adequate staff to be able to provide needed line care.
3. Monitor catheter sites for indications of BSI or local infection.
4. Maintain hand hygiene procedures prior to contact with the central catheter using either antiseptic soap and water or waterless alcohol-based products.
5. Use only aseptic technique during insertion and care of the central line catheters. This includes donning sterile gloves during insertion of central line catheters.
6. Catheter site care includes proper skin antisepsis prior to insertion and during dressing changes. Use either sterile gauze or transparent dressings to cover the catheter site as needed. Dressings are to be changed at least weekly.
7. Use an insertion site with the least likely risk for complications.
8. Promptly discontinue catheters no longer indicated for patient care, and use clinical judgment in determining need of catheter replacement.

A complete list of all of CDC's catheter recommendations can be found in the reference.

The JBI lists the following EBP for central line care:

- Use guide wire assisted catheter exchange to replace a malfunctioning catheter. (Grade A)
- Administration sets in continuous use need not be replaced more frequently than at 72 hour intervals unless they become disconnected or a central venous access device is replaced. (Grade A)
- Routine administrations of intranasal or systemic antimicrobials before insertion or during the use of a central venous access are not recommended to prevent catheter colonization or bloodstream infection. (Grade A)
- Antibiotic lock technique is recommended to reduce catheter-related bacteremia. (Grade B)
- Needle-free devices can minimize the risk of contamination and reduce the incidence of sharps injuries and the potential for the transmission of bloodborne pathogens to healthcare workers. (Grade B)
- Patients should be educated in the care of their catheters. (Grade B)
- A specialist team is recommended to reduce infection rates. (Grade B)
- Transparent dressings should be changed every seven days or sooner if they are no longer intact or moisture collects under the dressing. (Grade B)
- A gauze dressing needs to be assessed daily and changed with inspection of the insertion site or when the dressing becomes damp, loosened or soiled. A gauze dressing should be replaced by a transparent dressing as soon as possible. (Grade B)
- Sterile normal saline for injection should be used to flush and lock catheter lumens that are in frequent use. (Grade A)
- A pulsated flushing technique (1 ml at a time) by maintaining positive pressure is recommended to create turbulence within the catheter lumen, removing debris from the catheter wall. (Grade B)[50]

23.5 Special Organisms: MRSA, VRE, VISA/VRSA

Since the serendipitous discovery of penicillin, microorganisms have been identified as antibiotic resistant. In the 1950s, resistance rose to crisis proportions and continues today. Antibiotics are often called "miracle drugs." We recognize the limitation of these drugs, though still effective in many instances; microorganisms are often resistant to the intended drug mechanisms of action. A few microorganisms are recognized as being particularly troublesome, including:

- Methicillin-resistant *Staphylococcus aureus* (MRSA),
- Vancomycin Intermediate reaction *Staphylococcus aureus* (VISA),
- Vancomycin-resistant *Staphylococcus aureus*, and
- Vancomycin-resistant Enterococcus (VRE).

This section briefly discusses these pathogens. Both MRSA and VISA are *Staphylococci*. In the past several decades, MRSA has caused hospital-acquired infections particularly among immunocompromised and critically ill patients. A recent study noted that elderly persons were highly likely to be carriers of MRSA at the time they were admitted to a hospital.[51]

A. MRSA and VISA/VRSA

The occurrence of MRSA among all hospitals raised to 29 percent between 1975 and 1991.[52] The authors report that the percentage of MRSA ranged from 15 percent in hospitals with less than 200 beds to 38 percent in hospitals with greater than 500 beds. Emori and Gaynes[53] suggested that control "measures were either applied or followed inconsistently or may be ineffective" and they called for a reevaluation of how MRSA is handled.

MRSA is now established in inpatient acute care facilities and causes bloodstream, respiratory, wound, skin, and surgical infections, among others. The critically ill and immunocompromised patients are at the greatest risk of infection; however, no patient is completely protected. Staff at hospitals can acquire and become carriers of MRSA, and on rare occasions have been epidemiologically implicated in transmitting the organism to patients, albeit unknowingly. Recommendations regarding these transmissions have been published.[54]

The appearance of VISA followed the resistance of *Staphylococcus aureus* to the standard therapies. As the commonly used and formerly effective drugs including Penicillin and the semi synthetic pencillinase-resistant antimicrobials

of methicillin, oxacillin and nafcillin were no longer effective it became common practice to prescribe vancomycin for the treatment of MRSA infections and for empiric treatment of infections that were commonly caused by MRSA.[55] The effectiveness of vancomycin against staphylococci was diminished. In 1996 the first known case was reported. The occurrence of VISA is a worldwide problem with cases being reported from the United States, Europe, and Asia. Two cases of Vancomycin-resistant *Staphylococcus aureus* were reported in 2002. Vancomycin is not an effective treatment for VRSA, leading to less treatment options for infections caused by this organism.

Preventing the spread of these organisms should be of high priority as treatment options are limited. Infection control measures include:[56]

- Alert system for laboratory notification to infection control and clinical staff when the organism is identified in specimen.
- Patients should be isolated in a private room and placed on Contact Precautions.
- When possible dedicate equipment and caretaker staff in order to minimize the possibility of the organism being transmitted to others.
- Educating the staff and volunteers and visitors to the importance of proper hand hygiene, environmental cleanliness, device decontamination, and other control measures.
- If possible, minimize the number of persons who have direct contact with the patient.
- When necessary to transfer patients notify the receiving unit or facility that the patient has the organism; also notify it of the status of treatment and control measures in place.
- Assess the efficacy of the control systems in place.

Interrupting transmission of MRSA and VISA/VRSA relies on diligent application of the aforementioned and many of the same principles already elucidated in this chapter. In addition, the reader is referred to the next section on VRE for other control recommendations.

B. VRE

Vancomycin-resistant enterococcus was first detected in 1986. This organism is now prevalent in most hospitals in the United States, where the vancomycin-resistant gene can be transferred to other microorganisms. This can result in spread to many patients. The two species of enterococcus most commonly resistant are *E. faecalis* and *E. faecium* (VRFE).

TIP: The mortality rate from VRFE is over 39 percent.[57]

VRE causes infections in multiple body sites including the bloodstream, wounds, and urinary tract. Enterococci are normal body flora found in the gastrointestinal tract and are naturally resistant to many antibiotics other than vancomycin. Vancomycin is often used to treat organisms that are resistant to other antibiotics. The available treatment options are reduced if resistance develops. Colonization with VRE, once established, may be indefinite leaving the colonized patient and others at risk of possible infection.[58] It is important to note that resistant organisms are no more lethal than their nonresistant counterparts, except that they are difficult to treat.[59] However, a high prevalence of colonization with resistant organisms does not appear to increase facility infection rates or necessarily lead to excess illness or death.

Controlling the spread of VRE is necessary to minimize those at risk. There are four areas of control, which are the standards of care in treating these high-risk patients:

- Prudent and appropriate use of vancomycin (i.e., limit the use of this antibiotic to those circumstances known to be effective).
- Educational programs for staff. These need to be tailored to the specific audience for which intended. For example, physicians need a greater appreciation of the ultimate outcomes of inappropriate prescriptions and use of vancomycin, and to recognize the need to not use this drug in cases of colonization but to "save" it for treatment interventions.
- Infection control measures should be implemented. These include appropriate use of isolation for colonized or infected patients, and proper hand decontamination before and after touching patients and contaminated surfaces.
- Detection and reporting of the occurrence of VRE are essential to identify and control the spread. Recognition of the occurrence of VRE allows for proper implementation of control measures including epidemiologic studies to determine those at greatest risk, and measures most effective in minimizing the occurrence of these infections. These may include prompt notification of staff caring for VRE patients. Control measures during current and future hospitalizations of colonized patients and establishment of a monitoring system should be organized.

23.6 Antibiotic Use

Antibiotic use has been both lauded and vilified in the lay and medical literature as well as the media. While antibiotics are lifesaving drugs, overuse can result in the development of multidrug resistant organisms. This leads to the failure of these drugs to "cure" infections caused by these "super-bugs," as some have been labeled. The physician walks a fine line when deciding whether or not to prescribe antibiotics. Often decisions to treat are made empirically before the culture result is known, or in some cases even if the patient is infected. The standard of care requires nurses to question orders for antibiotics to which the patient is allergic, or if the accepted dosage range is exceeded, administer the antibiotics as soon as they are available from the pharmacy, administer the antibiotics according to the frequency and doses specified by the prescriber, and promptly act if an allergic or anaphylactic reaction is observed. Refer to Chapter 28, *Medication Errors*, for more on this topic.

Some hospitals have instituted formulary programs in which some antibiotics are restricted. Others have removed certain antibiotics from the pharmacies. Some now require an infectious disease consult prior to dispensing certain antibiotics. The CDC promotes "12 Steps to Prevent Antimicrobial Resistance among Hospitalized Adults."[60] These are grouped into several categories: prevent infection, diagnose and treat infection effectively, use antimicrobials wisely, and prevent transmission.

23.7 Nursing Home Infections

According to data from the Centers for Disease Control and Prevention, the most common infections among LTC residents are urinary tract infections, lower respiratory tract infections, soft tissue infections, and gastroenteritis. With the frequent transfer of residents between the hospital and LTC facility, there has been an increase in antibiotic-resistant microorganism infections observed in LTC facilities. Another infection seen frequently in LTC is *Clostridium difficile* diarrhea. Tuberculosis remains a problem although it is less frequent. Pneumonia is the only infection in this setting that is often fatal.[61]

TIP: When reviewing records, it is important to know the difference between colonization versus true infection.

A. Urinary Tract Infections

Colonization is the presence, growth, and multiplication of the organism in one or more body sites without observable clinical symptoms. A carrier refers to an individual who is colonized. Colonization can occur on the skin surface, a wound, a pressure ulcer, in the sputum, or in the urine. An infection is a condition where the bacteria invades a body site, multiplies in the tissue, and causes clinical manifestations of disease, such as fever, a wound with pus, respiratory illness or symptoms, or other signs of inflammation (warmth, redness, swelling). Infection is usually confirmed by positive cultures from sites such as blood, urine, sputum, or wound. Risk factors for UTI in the elderly include:

- atrophic urethritis (age-associated inflammation of the urethra)
- atrophic vaginitis (age-associated inflammation of the vagina)
- prostate enlargement
- catheter use (indwelling vs. condom catheter)
- chronic bacterial prostatitis (chronic prostate inflammation)
- GU (genitourinary) abnormalities (e.g., vesicorectal fistula)
- GU calculi
- urinary diversion procedures (e.g., ileal bladder diversion)
- urethral strictures[62]

Some additional elements, recognizable on an admission assessment, indicate risk factors for infection. Urinary tract infections (UTIs) are the most common bacterial infection among the elderly. While most patients are asymptomatic (show no symptoms), the prevalence rates of bacteriuria (having bacteria in the urine shown by a positive culture but is not a UTI) are 25 to 50 percent.[63]

UTIs occur frequently in the elderly because there are a number of suspected risk factors unique to the elder population. These risk factors include alterations in urinary tract structure and limited functional status, which impairs mobility, hygiene, and toileting.[64] Some suspected factors have been proven, such as neurogenic bladder. While associations with UTIs have been recognized with age, menopause, instrumentation, and a history of a recent urinary tract infection, diet does not seem to increase the risk.

Bacteriuria is common in LTC. Elders who live in LTC facilities have a high prevalence of asymptomatic bacteriuria. With the presence of neurogenic bladder, the prevalence of asymptomatic bacteriuria is even higher, averaging 25 to 50 percent in women and 15 to 40 percent in men. There is an unfortunate tendency to manage LTC patients who present with a positive urine cultures as having UTIs. The American Medical Directors Association's (AMDA)

"Urinary Incontinence Clinical Practice Guideline"[65] states that bacteriuria should not be treated in the absence of symptoms. Nevertheless, bacteriuria is often treated in the presence of new behavioral disturbances in dementia patients. Asymptomatic bacteriuria (the presence of bacteria and a positive urine culture which is not related to a disease state) is not related to mental status or behavioral changes. Practitioners should make the correct decision to not treat asymptomatic bacteriuria. Bacteriuria alone does not cause chronic genitourinary tract symptoms. Mortality for elderly persons with asymptomatic bacteriuria is similar to that for elderly persons without asymptomatic bacteriuria. Unfortunately, bacteriuria is too often treated and one of the most common reasons for prescribing antimicrobial therapy in long-term care facilities.[66] This contributes to excess antimicrobial use and worsens the problem of antimicrobial resistance.

TIP: According to the evidence-based data, it is actually better not to treat asymptomatic bacteruria.

In untreated asymptomatic bacteriuria, the organisms (especially E. coli) lose their virulence and become susceptible to the bactericidal effect of normal human plasma. Large amounts of bacteria in the urine may therefore protect against symptomatic bacteriuria caused by more powerful strains.[67] Diagnosing a symptomatic infection can be challenging in the elderly, since it requires clinical findings to differentiate asymptomatic bacteriuria from a UTI. The usual symptoms that may occur in the younger population—difficult or painful urination, urinary frequency, incontinence of recent onset, and flank pain—may not necessarily be present in the elder population. Fever, which is a common sign and symptom in many infections, may not necessarily present in the elderly.[68] Therefore, diagnosis of a UTI requires consideration of clinical symptoms, comorbidities, and the severity of the presentation of the illness.[69] For example, confusion and delirium may be attributed to a severe UTI. Moreover, frail elderly persons with multiple comorbidities and a complicated UTI may have an atypical or subtle presentation of infection, which may include a change in appetite or agitation. Also, an elder with urinary incontinence with a UTI may experience an increase in the number of episodes of incontinence.[70] Attempting to assess for pain (a marker for symptomatic UTI) in patients with dementia increases the challenge as some 67 percent of residents in LTC facilities have some level of dementia.

Some physicians use the McGeer & MSHD definitions for LTC nosocomial infections for diagnosing a symptomatic UTI.[71]

TIP: To meet the criteria for a suspected UTI, three of the following must be met: fever (greater than 38°C or 100.4°F) or chills, new or increased burning pain on urination, new flank or suprapubic pain or tenderness, changes in character of urine, and worsening mental function. If the patient has an indwelling urinary catheter, the criteria for a suspected UTI needs two of the following: fever (greater than 38°C or 100.4°F) or chills, new flank or suprapubic pain or tenderness, changes in character of urine, and worsening mental function.

In June 2005, the Centers for Medicare and Medicaid revised the OBRA regulations to focus on urinary incontinence and use of Foley catheters. The new F-315 tag states, "A resident who enters the facility without an indwelling catheter is not catheterized unless the resident's clinical condition demonstrates that catheterization was necessary. A resident who is incontinent of bladder receives appropriate treatment and services to prevent urinary tract infections and to restore as much normal bladder function as possible. The explanations for the surveyors of long-term care facilities focus on the resident's choices, end of life, and advance directives." Surveyors determine if these items were considered when reviewing the plan of care. [72]

Cultures must be appropriately collected by nursing staff in order to obtain valid results. It is best to collect urine specimens at the end of the night shift when there is a minimum of four hours of urine in the bladder. Specimens should be refrigerated and tested within four hours of collection. Although nitrate dipstick tests may be used, they are not sensitive enough to diagnose urinary tract infections in high-risk patients. [73]

B. Respiratory Tract Infections

Influenza and pneumonia are serious respiratory infections in the LTC setting. The most common outbreak of respiratory infection is caused by influenza A. [74]

The elderly, especially those with chronic health problems, are much more likely to develop serious complications after an influenza infection. According to the Centers for Medicare and Medicaid Services (CMS) publication "Pneumonia Project Overview," [75] pneumonia and influenza are among the six leading causes of death in the United States and 90 percent of those deaths occur in the over-65-year-old population. LTC facilities should have policies and procedures in place to vaccinate staff, residents, and new admissions, and recognize clinical symptoms of influenza. Only about 20-25 percent of employees in nursing homes receive the pneumonia vaccine. Many distrust the vaccine, fear needles, or fear becoming ill. The unvaccinated employees represent a major reservoir for introducing flu into a nursing home. [76] Reimbursement for the influenza and pneumococcal vaccines should not be a hindrance for vaccinating LTC residents. Since 1993, Medicare Part B has covered the administration of the vaccines. CMS recommends that facilities use standing orders for annual flu vaccinations and vaccination of new admissions during the flu season. Jennifer O'Hagan, CMS/CDC Standing Orders Project Coordinator, explained that since influenza and pneumococcal vaccines remain underutilized in institutional settings such as LTC facilities, scientific evidence shows that standing order programs for adults can help address the problem of missed opportunities for immunization. [77]

TIP: Though the typical symptoms of pneumonia in the younger population are a sudden onset of fever accompanied by pain in the upper back and extremities, headache, chills, and a cough, LTC residents may only show a decreased or absent appetite, confusion, shortness of breath, and lethargy. Therefore, LTC facility staff should be alert for these nonspecific symptoms, especially when influenza has been reported in the community.

Nursing-home-acquired pneumonia is a common condition among nursing home residents and a leading cause of morbidity and mortality. The immense problem of pneumonia in the long-term care setting can be attributed to several risk factors, such as old age, poor hygiene, lack of vaccinations, and poor infection control practices. Added to this complex issue is the increasing resistance of organisms to antibiotics. [78] Pneumonia can lead to delirium, functional decline, and development of new pressure ulcers. Pneumonia can be part of a chain of complications that occur: a fractured hip leading to immobility, then pneumonia.

The standard of care requires the long-term care nurse to report signs of pneumonia to the resident's physician. The decision to admit the resident to the hospital is controversial, as the medical literature does not support the premise that patients have better outcomes when they are hospitalized for pneumonia. [79] Pneumonia can be one of many illnesses that affect a resident. The following case includes allegations of inadequate care, which resulted in pneumonia, among other conditions:

In the *Estate of Jennie Sanford v. William E. Campbell, Senior Care Consultants, Inc.*, on May 13, 1997, Jennie Sanford was admitted to a Senior Care Center. Ms. Sanford's admitting diagnosis included Parkinson's disease, dementia, non-insulin dependent diabetes mellitus, anemia, and hypovolemia. While under defendants' care, Ms. Sanford acquired malnutrition and dehydration, recurrent urinary tract infections, and chest congestion. The plaintiff claimed the defendants did not adequately assess her mother until an assessment was requested by Ms. Fink on February 5, 1998. On February 11, 1998, Ms. Sanford was hospitalized for bronchial pneumonia, malnutrition, dehydration, urinary tract infection, and toxic encephalopathy. Ms. Sanford's condition worsened and she died February 18, 1998. The plaintiff alleged the defendants primarily failed to provide necessary medical care and failed to provide appropriate monitoring. The defendants argued that Ms. Sanford died from respiratory pulmonary edema, not due to any negligence. According to a published account, this action settled for $150,000.[80]

C. Gastrointestinal Infections

Gastroenteritis is a common gastrointestinal infection. A case of gastroenteritis is defined as a person with diarrhea or vomiting. Diarrhea is defined as two or more loose stools per day or an unexplained increase in the number of bowel movements.[81] Endemics of gastroenteritis occur frequently in LTC facilities. Usually *Clostridium difficile* (*C. difficile*), *Salmonella*, or *Shigella* (which are bacteria) is seen in this setting manifesting as diarrhea. *C. difficile* is the most frequent etiologic agent for healthcare-associated diarrhea.[82] Stool cultures and *C. difficile* toxin assays should be obtained to confirm this type of infection.

In the October 1998 issue of *Emerging Infectious Diseases*,[83] *C. difficile* was reported to have been responsible for a large number of hospitalizations and deaths.

Clinical features of *C. difficile* include:

- watery diarrhea,
- fever,
- loss of appetite,
- nausea, and
- abdominal pain or tenderness.

TIP: Attorneys or expert witnesses should review the medical records to evaluate if the LTC facility staff considered the diagnosis of *C. difficile* in elderly residents with those symptoms, particularly those who recently received antibiotics, were hospitalized, or were institutionalized.

This disease is most often transmitted via the hands of healthcare personnel who have had contact with contaminated feces or environmental surfaces. Therefore, if the resident has this infection and was not recently on antibiotics or hospitalized, this infection may be traced to compromised care.

Once a stool culture is collected, the resident will usually test positive for both the organism and its toxin, if *C. difficile* is present. If the resident was on antibiotics, it is important to evaluate if these were discontinued as this is the common medical practice. If the resident's antibiotic was not discontinued, check if the physician has documented in the medical record that the benefit of continuing the antibiotic outweighs the risk of discontinuing it.

Contact precautions are recommended only if the resident has diarrhea. A patient on contact isolation is in an isolated room where staff wear gowns and gloves. Staff wash their hands prior to and after caring for this patient. The gown and gloves prevent the germs from getting on the staff clothing. The gown and gloves are removed prior to departing the patient room. Facility policies should ensure adequate environmental and medical device cleaning and disinfection, especially for items likely to be contaminated with feces.

The peritonitis that can result from a misplaced tube is not really a GI infection. Percutaneous gastrostomy (PEG) tubes provide nutrition to residents who are unable to swallow. One end of the tube is in the stomach, and the other end protrudes from the abdominal wall. The tube can become displaced out of the stomach, requiring reinsertion. These tubes may be associated with catastrophic infection if tube feeding solution is instilled into the abdominal cavity instead of into the stomach. A misplaced PEG tube led to a lawsuit after a child died.

In *Alfred Johnson et al. v. Kindred Healthcare Operating*, a ten-year-old minor plaintiff suffered from Olivoponto Cerebellar Degeneration, and was placed in the defendant nursing home for full-time care. He was unable to speak or walk, but recognized his parents whenever they would visit him. He had been fitted with a Flex-Flo gastrostomy tube, which was periodically replaced by the defendant nursing home's staff. On April 16, 2000, a LPN replaced the minor plaintiff's feeding tube without being supervised by a RN. She noted in her log that the tube was reinserted with some resistance. Five hours later, the minor plaintiff was found to be unresponsive and was rushed to the hospital. The minor plaintiff became febrile, hypotensive, and tachycardic. A CT scan revealed the feeding tube had perforated his stomach. The perforation was repaired, but the plaintiff suffered massive sepsis (infection), leading to global organ failure. The minor plaintiff was diagnosed with septic peritonitis, anemia, and adult respiratory distress syndrome. He was placed on a ventilator and died of sepsis in May 2000. The plaintiff was prepared to present evidence from the Department of Family Services survey. This report proved the defendant nursing home had previously made errors in feeding tube placement and had not properly trained its staff in this procedure. The case was settled for $775,000, according to published accounts.[84]

The goal of prevention and treatment of intestinal infections is to promote healthy bacterial flora in the gut. Avoiding excessive use of antibiotics can promote normal bacterial flora in the gut and reduce risk of *Closteridium difficile* and other infections. Use of probiotic bacteria such as *Lactobacillus* and *Bifidobacterium* and probiotic yeasts such as *Saccharomyces boulardii* have been shown to significantly reduce infections of *C. difficile* and VRE in hospitalized patients[85–87] Such probiotic bacteria can be given orally to patients or in enteral feeds to tube-fed patients.

Viable spores of intestinal pathogens are often found on the hands of healthcare providers. For example, one study reported that viable *Closteridium difficile* spores were collected on the hands of 59 percent of healthcare providers.[88] Frequent handwashing by hospital personnel has been associated with significantly lower rates of nosocomial *Closteridium difficile* infections.[89] Bathing patients regularly and regular cleaning of bedding and room surfaces can also reduce risk of hospital-acquired intestinal infections.

Closteridium difficile is spore forming bacteria which is resistant to many antibiotics. *C. difficile* may be killed by bleach, but may not always be killed with alcohol or detergent-based cleaning solutions.[90]

D. Skin Infections

Two types of soft tissue infections are common in LTC facility settings: infected pressure ulcers and scabies. It is difficult to establish the source of infection for pressure ulcers because the exudates (material these ulcers are coated with) usually contain colonized bacteria. Therefore, cultures are not reliable for determining the causative bacteria and should not be used by legal professionals to evaluate damages. However, if cellulitis is present (abnormal redness of the skin, swelling, warmth, and streaking along the lymph nodes), a culture of the wound may be warranted. Infected pressure ulcers commonly pose liability risks.

AMDA has developed two guidelines for the treatment of pressure ulcers: "Pressure Ulcers"[91] and "Pressure Ulcer Therapy Companion."[92] These guidelines provide recommendations for treatment of infected pressure ulcers. Since many wounds drain and have exudates, infection control practices related to the wound care warrant the use of contact precautions. The colonization of wounds is normal and therefore can be handled with standard precautions. The use of standard precautions, supplemented by contact precautions in accordance with established protocols, remains an important principle or means of infection control with pressure ulcer infections.

Scabies is a major problem in LTC facilities, particularly among residents who are debilitated and require extensive hands-on care. Scabies is transmitted by contact with the organism, usually person to person, or through contact with infected clothing or linen. A fact sheet issued by the CDC describes the signs and symptoms of scabies as pimple-like irritations, burrows, or rash of the skin which are seen on the webbing between the fingers; the skin folds on the wrist, elbows, or knees; the penis; the breasts; or the shoulder blades.

TIP: Scabies causes intense itching, especially at night, manifesting sores caused by scratching. These sores can sometimes become infected with bacteria.

Once scabies is suspected, the residents and staff on the unit where the case was found should be examined for signs and symptoms. An outbreak of scabies (when a facility experiences two or more concurrent cases of scabies affecting residents or staff members) should be reported to the medical director and the local health department. Two or more consecutive cases of scabies occurring within four to six weeks of each other should also be considered an outbreak. While outbreak reporting guidelines are made on a state-by-state level, four to six weeks is the national average. Prior to the application of scabicides, facility personnel should use contact precautions when caring for infested residents as this decreases the risk of transmission to employees and other residents. Additionally, specific environmental treatments need to be applied.

There are many published recommendations for the treatment and prevention of scabies, but the CDC provides the following recommendations:

- Application of recommended topical scabicides, such as permethrin cream and crotamiton cream, is suggested. Lindane cream has been used, but according to a CDC report, resistance and adverse effects from lindane have been reported.
- Identification of exposed personnel.

- Initiation of prophylactic scabicide treatment to personnel exposed to scabies.
- Exclusion of personnel with confirmed scabies from the care of residents until they have received appropriate treatment and have been effectively treated.[93]

23.8 Infection Control Programs

Hospitals have a longer history of modern dedicated infection control programs than the long-term care industry. Though historically infection control efforts can be traced back to biblical times, modern day infection control programs in hospitals began in earnest in the early 1960s. Much of this occurred in reaction to the scourge of *Staphylococcus aureus* infections in surgical patients and newborns in the 1950s. It was realized that control efforts were needed and hospitals formed infection control committees. The role of infection control practitioners was a natural evolution from these, with the committees appointing individuals, most notably experienced nurses, to develop and oversee programs to better understand and attempt to control hospital-acquired infections. Today, every hospital in the United States has implemented an infection control program. Many publications and training programs now exist to help the infection control professionals in their efforts to implement a quality infection control program within their institutions.

While there are many similarities between hospital and long-term care infection control programs, some significant differences exist. This is due to the variations in the extent of hospital patient acuity, the diverse departments in the hospital setting, and the sheer number of patients and staff requiring oversight. The hospital infection control program is discussed separately in Section 23.10 of this chapter.

An increasing number of LTC facilities have developed infection control programs within the last 20 years. A major contribution was the publication of guidelines by the Association for Professionals in Infection Control and Epidemiology (APIC) in 1991. These were updated in 1997 as the Society for Healthcare Epidemiologists of America (SHEA)-APIC position paper on infection prevention and control in long-term care facilities.[94] This important document reviews infections in such facilities and makes specific recommendations for a feasible and relevant control program.

Bolieu v. Sisters of Providence in Washington, 953 P. 2d 1233 (Alaska, 1998). The nursing home's infection control nurse sent several nursing assistants to a dermatologist for skin lesions. The dermatologist concluded they had contracted staph infections while bathing and taking blood pressures from nursing home residents with staph infections.

The nursing assistants were given worker's compensation time loss and medical expense payments, as their staph infections were deemed an on-the-job occupational occurrence.

Some of the nursing assistants' spouses contracted staph infections of their own and sued the nursing home, pointing to the link to their spouses' jobs established by the treating dermatologist. The Supreme Court of Alaska upheld the spouses' right to sue the nursing home. It overturned a lower court's decision to throw out the whole case without giving the spouses their day in court.

The Supreme Court of Alaska recognized that potential sources of staph infection are widespread. When the spouses went back to the lower court to have their day in court, they would have to prove conclusively their own skin problems came from the nursing home via their spouses' exposure on the job.

The court faulted the nursing home, first of all, for inadequate infection control measures which allowed residents to contract staph infections and for those infections to spread among residents and to staff.

The court did not delve into the specifics of infection control in a nursing home, that subject being covered extensively by federal and state regulations and accreditation standards.

The specific issue in the case was whether a healthcare facility's responsibility for infection control inside its walls creates a legal responsibility extending outside those walls to family members of its caregiving staff. The court said caregivers' family members do have the right to sue, assuming they can produce solid proof that a lapse in infection control practices within the facility has had the effect of infecting them with a contagious disease.

The court also ruled that when a caregiving staff member contracts a contagious infection on the job the facility must warn the staff member of the risk of spreading it to family members, and the facility must provide instructions geared to the specific infectious agent on how spread of that agent to family members can be avoided.[95]

23.9 Hospital Federal Regulations and Accreditation

There are two primary organizations responsible for regulating hospitals. The Centers for Medicare and Medicaid Services (CMS) has the responsibility of overseeing acute care hospitals. The Joint Commission (TJC), a private standard-setting organization, which has been granted deemed status by CMS, is the primary source of hospital accreditation. These two will be reviewed together as these are inextricably intertwined through the deemed status process. CMS recognizes TJC accreditation as proof that hospitals satisfy CMS regulations.

A. Regulatory Requirements

While the regulations governing hospitals and the accreditation standards are not exactly comparable there is sufficient commonality in their respective requirements. CMS regulations are called Conditions of Participation (COPs). COPs encompass a set of regulations setting minimum health and safety standards for hospitals. Hospital accreditation by TJC is automatically "deemed" to meet health and safety requirements for participation in federal government payment programs of Medicare and Medicaid. However, in 2008, due to the pressures of the American Hospital Association, CMS approved an additional accrediting organization, the National Integrated Accreditation for Healthcare Organizations (NIAHO) is a program offered by DNV Healthcare Inc.

The COP encompassing infection control is CMS Standard §482.42.[96] The hospital must provide a sanitary environment to avoid source and transmission of infections and communicable diseases, and there must be an active program for the prevention, control, and investigation of infections and communicable diseases of patients and personnel. CMS provides "Interpretive Guidelines"[97] to further elucidate these requirements. The guidelines include the processes that must be in place to demonstrate conformance with the regulations. These are:

- definition of healthcare-associated infections and communicable diseases (CDs);
- measure for identifying, investigating, and reporting HAIs and CDs;
- provision of a safe environment consistent with recognized infection control precautions;
- isolation procedures and policies for infected and immunocompromised patients and use and description of Standard Precautions as a means to minimize infection transmission and to protect patients and healthcare workers;
- methods of monitoring and evaluating aseptic practices;
- procedures for hand hygiene, respiratory protection, sterilization and disinfection of environmental and medical equipment and surfaces, housekeep-

ing techniques, care of textiles such as bed linens, waste disposal, handling of contaminated sharp instruments such as needles and scalpels, and physical separation of clean from dirty areas, equipment and supplies;
- authority statements disclosing lines of responsibility and rights of individuals to instigate infections of apparent cross transmission, disease exposure and control measures as needed to protect the hospital population;
- training and orientation of hospital staff to all applicable aspects of the infection control and prevention program;
- standards for evaluating the effectiveness of infection control and prevention measures; and
- procedures for reporting of communicable diseases as specified by local, state or federal agencies.

B. Joint Commission on Accreditation of Healthcare Organizations

The Joint Commission is a private organization that sets guidelines and standards for facilities regarding safe and effective patient care. Many payers for hospital reimbursement require accreditation from The Joint Commission. The Joint Commission boosted its recognition for infection control when it made it a separate standard in the 1970s. Although The Joint Commission writes and enforces its own standards, there are many similarities to those required by CMS. The Joint Commission standards include such requirements as minimization of risk for developing infections through the establishment of a hospital-wide infection control program. On a continuing basis, the infection control program needs to identify risks that increase the likelihood of acquisition and transmission of infectious agents. Based on these risks, the hospital must prioritize and set goals for preventing HAIs, implement the strategies to minimize HAIs, evaluate the effectiveness of the infection control interventions, and redesign these to increase their effectiveness, as needed. Other standards include appropriate staffing to meet these challenges, departmental cooperation for putting in place appropriate infection control measures throughout the hospital, and emergency management activities to respond to unusual events such as bioterrorism or pandemics (epidemic over a wide geographic area affecting a large portion of the population).

23.10 Components of a Hospital Infection Control Program

Infection control programs are an integral part of modern healthcare institutions. These are most effective when the program is integrated throughout the entire hospital community. Each department, beginning with administrators and managers, plays a key role in preventing the transmission of infectious diseases. The infection control professional, with the guidance of the infection control committee, orchestrates the program but cannot keep the program afloat without support and cooperation at every level.

Most hospitals publish standards of practice in a single document usually titled *Infection Control Manual* or some variation on the theme. This document must be readily accessible through either print- or web-based programs. While it is standard to have written standard operating procedures (SOPs), the format varies from institution to institution.

The professional staff responsible for program management includes infection control practitioners, hospital epidemiologists, infection control or quality improvement committees, and administrative officers. Many departments contribute to the control of infections in a supportive role. These include pharmacy, laboratory, environmental, and maintenance services. Central supply personnel, those who are responsible for decontamination and sterilization of surgical instruments and other devices, also play an important role. Key players are the clinical, direct care staff of nurses, doctors, and therapists.

The infection control practitioner has the primary responsibility for the day-to-day program activities. Voluntary professional and practice standards have been delineated in a published article.[98] The publication notes that the standards define the "profession's accountability to the public" and the healthcare consumer. These standards "describe a level of individual competence in the professional role." While infection control professionals have always recognized the importance of gaining the public trust and responsibly carrying out duties, these published standards allow the professionals as well as others to better understand the responsibilities of individual practitioners.

A. Surveillance of Infections (HAI)

Surveillance, that is, finding and documenting the occurrence of infections, was established as a core element of infection control programs in the 1960s. The Center for Disease Control, as it was called in that era, published guidelines that provided the criteria for determining the presence of a HAI.[99] Over the years, these have been consistently refined and can be found on the CDC website (www.cdc.gov) or in numerous medical publications. Surveillance is based on the epidemiological principle for identifying cases and the factors that influence the associated cause and the mechanisms to prevent the occurrence. Using surveillance principles to identify cases of HAIs is an example of a premiere quality

initiative and is the foundation for a quality infection control program. All accreditation and regulations governing hospitals require an active surveillance program.

The underlying purpose of surveillance is to reduce infection rates, establish baseline rates of infection occurrence in the affected population, identify outbreaks, and evaluate control measures and be in compliance with regulations and accreditation requirements. An established surveillance program should contain several components. A basic one includes codified definitions of HAI. The most commonly adopted are based on those used in the NNIS program. Other expected parts of a quality infection control program include:

- collecting data by trained personnel who know how to interpret and review patient medical records;
- evaluating signs and symptoms in order to determine the true occurrence of a HAI;
- detailing policies for the specifics of the surveillance program;
- identifying staff responsible for carrying out these standards: data analysis, distribution and reporting; and
- identifying measures to mitigate the occurrence of infections and the effectiveness of these measures.

Recently another use of surveillance data has emerged: the demand by consumers and payers for data on the occurrence of healthcare-acquired infections. While the infection control community endorses openness, there are concerns. Public reporting of infection data must be based on reliable scientific principles. This requires comparative patient populations; effective and accurate case-finding methods; and validation of data. Misuse and misunderstanding of the data will lead to unreliable conclusions that can result in bad decisions. A document, prepared by the CDC advisory committee, on public reporting can be found in the endnotes[100] or at www.cdc.gov/ncidod/hip/HICPAC/Hicpac.htm.

B. Isolation of Patients with Infectious Diseases

Isolation of patients with transmissible infectious diseases is an essential component of a quality infection control program. Most hospitals use the CDC Guideline for Isolation Precautions in Hospitals,[101] as the basis for their protocols outlining the isolation standards of practice. Hospital staff are encouraged to adapt the CDC guideline according to the specific needs of the patient population cared for in their institution. Therefore, a review of specific hospital requirements may differ to some degree from those put forth by the CDC. However, every hospital should have well-documented isolation policies. These should be based on the mechanisms of disease transmission and the acuity and characteristics of the patient population served. The basic foundation of prevention of disease transmission should incorporate both standard precautions, whenever handling blood or body fluids, or contaminated items, regardless of whether a patient is diagnosed with an infectious disease. The additions of transmission-based precautions are recommended if there is a communicable disease.

C. Hand Hygiene

The single most important and effective means for preventing infections is proper hand hygiene. Unfortunately this is a challenge for healthcare staff because of the demands of constant patient care. The advent and scientifically proven value of waterless alcohol-based hand gels, foams, and liquids has added a powerful weapon to the arsenal of effective hand hygiene products. In 2002, the Guideline for Hand Hygiene in Health-Care Settings was published in *Morbidity and Mortality Weekly Report*.[102] This document serves as the foundation for the hand hygiene program for many hospitals. The minimum program specifications include indications for hand hygiene and cleansing, surgical hand antisepsis guidelines, the rationale by which hand hygiene products are selected, educational programs, and administrative support for the program.

D. Development and Implementation of Standards of Practice (SOP)

All infection control programs are based on written, documented standards of practice (SOPs). These are tailored to the specific institution for which they are written. SOPs, also called policies and procedures, provide information for minimizing the transmission of disease. Every department within the facility plays an important role in controlling and preventing disease. This includes management and administrative personnel who provide support for the program, direct patient caregivers who are at the bedside, professional staff providing services such as the pharmacy and laboratory, as well as the support staff responsible for maintaining and cleaning the facility.

Policies and procedures should have information describing:

- the goals and objectives of the program,
- how the program is managed,
- who is responsible for implementing the program,
- each department's responsibilities and how these will be carried out,

- the continuous quality improvement protocols,
- communicable disease reporting systems,
- isolation protocols,
- environmental procedures for housekeeping and laundry,
- building maintenance and air handling systems,
- sterilization and disinfection protocols and descriptions,
- reuse of devices including those that may be intended for single patient use,
- visitor and volunteer policies,
- sterilization and disinfection, and
- handling of biohazardous and other medical waste.

E. Training and Education for Staff

Essential components of quality infection control and prevention programs include training and education programs. Education programs keep staff abreast of the latest scientific findings; impart information concerning regulations and guidelines; review hospital policies; and present new initiatives. One of the most important aspects includes informing the staff about infection rates, types of infections, and unusual and emerging microorganisms and how they can implement procedures and practical measures that prevent infections and transmission of communicable diseases. It is important for the staff to keep updated with the regulations and requirements as mandated by various local (rare), state, and government regulatory agencies.

Annually, staff should receive infection control education. Certainly, more frequently attended programs are preferable. The most effective education programs incorporate both didactic and hands-on learning opportunities. These programs must also be customized to the specific audience for which they are intended. Misunderstandings and mistakes can occur by using the same teaching techniques for audiences with different characteristics. The presenter is to provide training for staff with diverse backgrounds, varying levels of education, and language abilities. Information needs to be job-specific, though some topics such as hand hygiene should be presented to all staff with the lesson plan tailored to the specific audience.

F. Occupational Health Program

A major aspect of a quality infection control and prevention program includes a comprehensive occupational health program. This serves both the staff and the patient population. There are many occupational health issues intertwined with outcomes that may affect the occurrence of disease in patients, and vice versa. Some diseases can be transferred from or to healthcare workers, like varicella zoster (more commonly known as chicken pox or shingles); human immunodeficiency viral infections, which can be transmitted through contact with contaminated body fluids or blood; respiratory illnesses such as tuberculosis; and others. These exposures can occur to patients as well as staff. The infection control program, in concert with the employee health department, works toward minimizing the occurrence of these transmissions and prevention of secondary transmissions to others.

G. Environmental Services, Including Laundry

Environmental services, commonly called housekeeping services, are an essential component of an infection control program. In addition to cleaning the hospital, this department also has responsibility for medical waste management. Keeping the hospital clean is both an infection control and an aesthetic endeavor. The accumulation of soils especially body fluids and other contaminants pose a potential infection control risk. Environmental services staff needs to be trained in cleaning methods and decontamination principles. Blood and other regulated body fluids spills are to be disinfected prior to removal. Staff needs to be apprised of special precautions to take to protect themselves and others. While it appears obvious, the environment is not always given the attention needed, which can result in undue risk of exposure to contaminants and can play a significant role in the transmission of infectious agents.

Although soiled hospital textiles have long been known to harbor microorganisms, there have been rare circumstances in which these have contributed to transmission of an infection. Regardless, it is prudent to handle soiled linen with due care. Used laundry is to be contained at the site of collection, that is, where it was used. Commonly, either plastic or cloth bags are used. These are then delivered directly to the laundry room, or temporarily stored in a soiled utility area until being retrieved by housekeeping staff. Many hospitals work with contract laundry services rather than process their own; however, the basic tenets of proper washing, drying, handling, and distributing hold true regardless. Soiled laundry is to be kept apart from clean. Staff are to be properly dressed (gowns, gloves, face shields or masks) when handling soiled laundry, and hand hygiene is an essential component whenever working with soiled laundry and before handling clean linens.

Oversight for medical waste handling is under individual state regulatory agencies. The Federal EPA has deferred to the states on this issue. Each of the 50 states has developed waste regulations. Primarily, waste management regulation focuses on the type and amount of medical waste and if it is contaminated with blood or body fluids.

23.11 Nursing Home Infection Control
A. Federal Regulations

All skilled nursing facilities are required by the Omnibus Budget Reconciliation Act of 1987 (OBRA '87) to have an infection control program. CMS implements this federal law by publishing requirements for LTC facilities applying to accept Medicare or Medicaid patients. Federal regulations require every LTC facility to establish an infection control program to investigate, control, and prevent infections within the facility. Although current federal regulations do not require facilities to have an infection control committee, some states do.[103] Therefore, it is important to check the applicable state regulations.

In the State Operations Manual, there is specific language under F-tag 441[104] that defines what the federal government looks for in facility infection control. These regulations state, "The intent of this regulation is to assure that the facility has an infection control program which is effective for investigating, controlling, and preventing infections,"[105] and, "The facility must establish and maintain an infection control program designed to provide a safe, sanitary, and comfortable environment and to help prevent the development and transmission of disease and infection."[106]

These published guidelines on infection control include definitions of infection, risk assessment, outbreak control, antibiotic monitoring, and assessment of compliance with policies and procedures. Federal regulations also require facilities to maintain written records of incidents and corrective actions related to infections. These records should document the following:

- identity of the infected resident,
- date of the infection,
- causative agent, and
- site of the infection.

B. Elements of Comprehensive Institutional Infection Control Programs

The American Medical Directors Association's (AMDA's) *Common Infections in the Long Term Care Setting* clinical practice guideline is an important document for an attorney's library.[107] The AMDA guideline explains that a facility's infection control program should have processes and policies in place for surveillance, disease reporting and monitoring, standard and contact precautions, isolation procedures, outbreak control, immunizations, and resident and employee health programs. It shows how the program's components should include systems and processes to recognize, track, and monitor infections and include a systematic approach to preventing infections.

AMDA emphasizes that an effective infection control program needs to be interdisciplinary and be overseen by the medical director. The primary members of the program include the medical director, administrator, and director of nursing; these members are familiar with federal, state, and local regulations that address or impact infection control in LTC. The secondary members include employees from the nursing, housekeeping, and dietary departments. The infection control team must also define the infection control problem if it exists.

It is important to note that the differences between acute care and LTC facilities affect the development and management of infection control. Generally, long-term care facilities have fewer resources. Part-time employees or employees with many other responsibilities are often responsible for infection control, and the secretarial and computer resources may be limited. The educational level of the staff is often lower than in acute care facilities. LTC facilities are primarily staffed with licensed practical nurses (LPNs) and certified nursing assistants (CNAs), with a low ratio of registered nurses. Failure to have an effective infection control program was an allegation in a Texas case.

> In *Clara Thacker et al. v. Senior Living Properties*, the plaintiff's decedent was an 87-year-old nursing home resident who was admitted to the defendant nursing home on September 17, 1998. She suffered from a variety of problems, including peripheral vascular disease, osteoporosis, kyphoscoliosis, depression, hypothyroidism, anxiety disorder, and a history of a bleeding ulcer. While living at the nursing home, the decedent developed multiple pressure ulcers that became infected. She also experienced repeated episodes of malnutrition and dehydration. The claim asserted the nursing home was understaffed, and that it had neglected to meet the decedent's basic needs. The suit also asserted that the nursing home lacked a sufficient infection control program. Several of the nursing home staff members were named defendants. The defense stated that the nursing home was properly staffed, and that the decedent's injuries were an unavoidable consequence of her advanced age and medical condition. According to published accounts, the case settled for $1.6 million.[108]

C. Immunization Programs

To increase the number of long-term care patients who are vaccinated against influenza, CMS recommends that facilities use standing orders for annual flu vaccinations and for new admissions during the flu season.[109] AMDA recommends implementing an immunization program for all facility residents.[110] Influenza vaccine is advised yearly for all residents. Although vaccinations are somewhat less effective in the elderly than in younger people, it has been estimated to reduce the risk of influenza-related hospitalization and death in older people by up to 70 percent.[111]

The indications for revaccination with pneumococcal vaccine are controversial. The American College of Physicians recommends revaccination after six years for older patients who received the pneumococcal vaccine before age 65. However, insufficient data are currently available on the value of revaccination every six years in healthy elderly persons.[112] The pneumococcal vaccine may be given safely with influenza vaccine, using a different deltoid for each injection.[113]

D. The Importance of Following a Care Process

The Society for Healthcare Epidemiology of America, Inc.-Association for Professional in Infection Control and Epidemiology (SHEA-APIC) infection control guidelines are evidence based.[114] Recommendations are characterized as A (having good evidence to support the recommendation), B (moderate evidence to support a recommendation), and C (poor evidence to support the recommendation). The quality of evidence is designated as follows: I (at least one randomized controlled trial), II (at least one well-designed clinical trial without randomization), or III (opinions of respected authorities). The infrequency of evidence designations in the guidelines demonstrates the limitations of available research.

TIP: AMDA's guidelines are accepted as the "best practice" for the LTC setting as they are created from evidence- and consensus-based opinion. These clinical practice guidelines are tools to guide care decisions.

These guidelines were developed by "hands-on" interdisciplinary workgroups using a process that combined evidence- and consensus-based thinking specifically for the LTC setting. Each guideline is a starting place that guides the care team through a process of addressing the particular condition in a patient. (Each guideline is presented in a user-friendly format and contains an introduction explaining the purpose, development process, and terminology; a step-by-step narrative text that covers definition, recognition, diagnosis, treatment, and monitoring of the condition discussed; and an algorithm that summarizes the steps involved in addressing the condition.) Because frail elderly patients have an above-average risk of death and complications from an infectious disease, prompt recognition, assessment, and treatment of infections are imperative.[115]

The care process consists of four stages:

- recognition (who is at risk or has an infection),
- assessment (root cause analysis—the reason the patient is at risk for an infection; the location, cause, and type of infection are identified),
- treatment (based on the findings of the assessment), and
- monitoring (evaluating the effectiveness of the treatment to determine if the treatment needs to be changed).

TIP: All nursing staff should be trained to identify and report conditions that put a resident at high risk for infection. Since the elderly do not present with the same signs and symptoms as younger adults, this may create a challenge.

---

1. Recognition

Clinically infected elder adults in LTC facilities will often have a change of mental status, a decline in physical function, or other nonspecific symptoms such as a new episode of incontinence, falling, or lethargy. The presence of a fever may also be a sign of infection. While fever in a younger adult is recognized as 100°F or above orally, this may not be indicative of a fever in an elderly person. It is suggested that the presence of fever in LTC facility residents is a two-degree increase over the upper limit of their usual baseline temperature.[116]

TIP: When evaluating medical records, the attorney and legal nurse consultant should inquire if the facility has a consistent, evidence-based process to detect the possible presence of infections, and learn how the information is gathered, analyzed, and acted upon.

The American Medical Directors Association recommends the following steps:[117]

- **Step 1**. Does the patient have a change of condition that suggests the presence of an infection? Infection may present with localized symptoms or with generalized, nonspecific symptoms.
- **Step 2**. Is the patient at risk for developing an infection? A major risk factor for infection is being a patient in a long-term care facility or a hospital.

2. Assessment

When evaluating a medical record, look for verification of an infection. There is a process to characterize details of signs and symptoms related to a current infection, and the etiology of any infection is investigated, clarified, or both. The steps under this stage, recommended by the American Medical Directors Association, are as follows.

- **Step 3**. Perform a history and physical examination and order appropriate laboratory tests. Diagnostic testing and other elements of an appropriate evaluation should be done promptly in all patients where an infection is suspected. However, if an advance directive exists or family or patient wishes limit such, those directives must be honored. AMDA states, "The purpose of the work-up is to identify the cause and determine the severity of the infection."
- **Step 4**. Assess whether the patient's condition warrants transfer to a hospital. AMDA states, "Hospitalization of long-term care patients should be avoided to the extent possible. In addition to cost considerations, patients generally benefit from treatment in familiar surroundings." Hospitalization can increase discomfort and confusion among the elderly. Hospitalization is also associated with an increased risk of deconditioning, pressure ulcers, and colonization with resistant organisms.[118]

Bentley et al. suggest that transfer to a hospital may be appropriate when any of the following conditions exist:

A. the patient is clinically unstable and the patient or family desires aggressive intervention, or
B. critical diagnostic tests are not available in the facility, and the scope or intensity of the required treatment is beyond the facility's capacity to provide or specific infection-control measures are not available in the facility.[119]

Complications such as renal obstruction, pyelonephritis, sepsis, unstable pulse or blood pressure, or serious illness combined with uncertain diagnosis may warrant a hospital transfer in patients with a urinary tract infection.[120]

- **Step 5**. Assess whether the patient's condition warrants implementation of heightened infection control precautions.

3. Treatment

TIP: There should be a documented rationale for the recommended intervention or interventions. Check that there is a care plan in place that has relevant details of the care of the individual and includes treatment of the infection. Most importantly, look for evidence that the care plan is implemented as written, or documentation explains why the plan was not followed.

The steps under this stage recommended by AMDA are defined below.

- **Step 6**. Treat the symptoms of infection. Tailor treatment to the patient's symptoms to the extent possible. Infection is a catabolic state and infected patients may be at risk of weight loss. Look for careful monitoring of the resident's nutritional status and an initiation of nutritional interventions, unless the resident's advance directives state otherwise.

In *Anonymous Plaintiff v. Anonymous Nursing Home*, on August 7, 2000, the plaintiff's decedent became a resident of the defendant nursing home. She was 81 years old and recovering from a broken hip. Her health history included high blood pressure (hypertension), diabetes, and previously a mild stroke. At the time of her nursing home admission, she had a 3 x 3 cm superficial decubitus ulcer on her coccyx. From August 7, 2000 to August 28, 2000, the decubitus ulcer increased in size and severity. Records from August 28 reveal that the wound had grown to approximately 12 cm in diameter, and contained necrotic tissue, was foul-smelling, and oozing blood. The wound was documented as a Stage IV decubitus ulcer. It was also noted that the patient had become lethargic, less responsive, and was complaining of severe pain. Her urine was cloudy and foul-smelling, and reportedly went untreated. On August 28, the plaintiff's decedent was transferred from the nursing home to a local hospital to rule out sepsis. Hospital records revealed the patient had an underlying infection either due to the decubitus ulcer or her urinary tract. Upon her transfer to the hospital, nursing admission procedures found her urinary catheter was clogged and her urine was infected. On August 29, the patient's condition was grave and her decubitus ulcer required debridement to

the bone by a surgeon. On August 30, the patient was designated "comfort measures only." On August 30, she died, with cause of death documented as urosepsis. The decedent's family alleged the defendant nursing home was negligent and personnel failed to appropriately and adequately monitor, provide care for, and treat their mother, thereby causing her wrongful death. Allegations included failure to provide effective treatment in the presence of an infected Stage IV pressure ulcer, failure to request an appropriate wound care consultation, failure to order or request labs in order to monitor nutrition and hydration, failure to document her daily temperatures, failure to measure intake or output during the infectious process, failure to provide antibiotic treatment despite ongoing signs of infection in the wound and in her urine, and failure to provide adequate medication to alleviate the plaintiff's ongoing pain. The family also alleged the decedent's call button was periodically placed out of her reach. The nursing home denied these allegations and asserted that they provided adequate care and treatment to the plaintiff's decedent. The parties mutually agreed mediation, which resulted in a final settlement of $250,000 prior to case filing, according to a published account.[121]

- **Step 7.** Prescribe appropriate antibiotic therapy. AMDA states that "Treatment with antibiotics is appropriate when the practitioner determines on the basis of an evaluation that the most likely cause of the patient's symptoms is a bacterial infection." It is important for the practitioner to consider the patient's overall condition, prognosis, advance directives, and expressed patient or family preferences when determining whether to proceed with antibiotic treatment. Elderly LTC patients are at increased risk of drug-related adverse effects because of the physiologic effects of aging, the use of multiple medications, and the presence of comorbid conditions. In addition to the adverse effects associated with antibiotics themselves, adding antibiotics increases the potential for harmful drug interactions.

4. Monitoring

The patient should be periodically reassessed until the infection is resolved. The interventions are adjusted based on the patient reassessments, which include monitoring for complications. AMDA recommends the next step.

- **Step 8.** Monitor the patient's progress. The resident with an infection should be closely monitored. A nurse should evaluate the patient with an infection at least once during every shift while the patient is unstable or significantly symptomatic and should document relevant findings in the patient's medical record. The evaluation should include the patient's overall condition. The practitioner should be notified promptly if the patient's condition worsens.

TIP: It takes at least three days for antibiotics to show effectiveness. Symptoms and abnormal test results related to an infection do not necessarily resolve quickly.

- **Steps 9-11.** Provide direction guidance for facility infection control.
- **Step 12.** Monitor the management of infections in the facility. Federal regulations require long-term care facilities to maintain a log of infections and a record of every patient who is treated for an infection.

23.12 Liability Associated with Transmittal of Infections in Long-Term Care

A. Recommended Precautions

Federal regulations state that facilities "must require staff to wash their hands after each direct resident contact for which handwashing is indicated by accepted professional practice."[122] The attorney should check that the facility has clear policies and procedures for handwashing and evidence, such as audits, that they are being followed. Outbreaks of gastroenteritis and the spread of *C. difficile* diarrhea are often transmitted from staff.

B. Standard Precautions versus Contact Precautions

The CDC instructs that infection control precautions are divided into two groups: standard and contact. The term "universal precautions" was dropped from the CDC lexicon several years ago, although it may still be used in some facilities. Standard precautions are designed to be used for all patients to reduce the risk of transmission of infectious agents. Standard precautions emphasize handwashing, gloves (when touching body fluids), masks, eye protection, and gowns (when splashing of body fluids is likely).[123]

For patients with certain infections, contact precautions should be used in conjunction with the standard precautions. Contact precautions should be used for patients with documented or suspected transmissible infectious diseases.

Transmission-based precautions include precautions for airborne infections (spread by means of droplets) and infections spread by person-to-person contact.[124]

It is important to understand that although the CDC guideline was developed for hospitals, some of its recommendations are applicable to LTC facilities. Each facility is expected to adapt the aspects of the CDC guidelines that apply to its needs.[125] As stated earlier, isolation of patients with infections is problematic in most LTC facilities as private rooms are rarely available and isolating residents for a long period of time is not conducive to a good quality of life.

There is no evidence that the use of stringent isolation precautions decreases illness or death from antibiotic-resistant organisms in LTC facilities.[126] Stringent isolation precautions are necessary only when there is a high risk that colonized patients will transmit the infection to others (e.g., MRSA-infected patients who have draining skin wounds that cannot be covered).[127]

C. Employee Health

Facilities are required to prevent employees with transmissible infectious diseases from direct patient contact. Additionally, employees with draining skin wounds should not have contact with patients' food. However, federal regulations do not require that employees with communicable health conditions be excluded from work.[128] AMDA advocates that facilities offer, and strongly encourage all employees to obtain, annual influenza vaccinations. In some states, such as Arkansas, all LTC employees for whom vaccination is not contraindicated are required to receive annual influenza vaccinations.

D. Environmental Decontamination

Policies and procedures are recommended for cleaning and disinfecting; environmental health department employees must know the difference. Cleaners reduce the number of infectious agents present, but do not kill them. Only disinfectants containing active ingredients such as quaternary ammonium chloride or bleach are capable of killing infectious agents.[129] It is recommended that facilities use both a cleaning product and a disinfectant or a combination cleaner and disinfectant at all times. All frequently touched surfaces (e.g., hand rails, bed rails, doorknobs, faucet handles, bedside commodes) and equipment (e.g., walkers, wheelchairs) should be routinely decontaminated. Whirlpools have also been known to be a source of contamination.[130,131] Environmental health department staff should carefully follow manufacturers' recommendations for the use and dilution of disinfectants. Without proper cleaning and disinfecting, outbreaks and the transmission of infections can occur.

E. Liability Associated with the Delay in Recognition of Infections

As many as one-third of elderly patients with acute infections may not have a fever.[132] For this reason, in the long-term care setting, absence of a fever should not be considered an adequate reason to rule out the presence of infection if other indicators are present. Acute infection, among other possibilities, should be considered any time a frail elderly patient experiences an acute change in condition, regardless of whether a fever is present. Just as infection may be present in the frail elderly without fever, the presence of a fever does not always indicate infection.[133]

There are condition changes and common symptoms that may indicate infection in a nursing home. If these conditions or symptoms are present, an assessment to discover the cause would be indicated. Furthermore, there are common components of an initial nursing assessment of a suspected infection and there are usual elements of work-up that would be done by a practitioner for the most common categories of infections.

F. Liability Associated with the Delay in Treatment or Transfer to the Hospital

Delays in treatment may occur in a hospital when the antibiotic comes from the pharmacy and is not administered for several hours. There are progressive infections, which require stat medication administration. The physician order should be flagged or marked as having a stat order. There are a variety of documentation practices and this chapter will not address this topic. Communication is the key to timely delivery of this medication. The physician or the unit secretary communicates with the nurse to inform her about this stat order. The nurse can phone the pharmacy to request immediate delivery of the medication.

Delivery of medications varies among facilities. This may include the hospital personnel or pharmacy technician that delivers the medication to the unit. Some facilities have a tube system where the medication is inserted into a canister, which travels through the hospital walls and arrives at its predialed destination for a timely delivery. The nurse must then retrieve the medication from the canister.

1. Decision to transfer

Most practitioners agree that a resident's quality of life is improved by treating within the LTC facility if at all possible and avoiding transfer to a hospital. However, there are times when hospitalization should be considered. Bentley suggests that transfer to a hospital may be appropriate when any of the following conditions exist:

- the patient is clinically unstable and the patient or family desires aggressive intervention,
- critical diagnostic tests are not available in the facility,
- the intensity of the required treatment are beyond the facility's capacity to provide, or
- specific infection control measures are not available in the facility.[134]

2. Decision on treatment measures in palliative care

It is ethically acceptable not to offer antibiotic treatment to a patient who is receiving palliative or end-of-life care.[135] However, an antibiotic may be prescribed to a patient who has a bacterial infection and who receives palliative or end-of-life care for two reasons:

1. to relieve the patient's discomfort, or
2. to protect the health of others in the facility.

3. Neglect

Failure to diagnose and treat infections can be a source of liability. The nursing staff is responsible for reporting signs of infection to the attending physician, who is expected to make decisions regarding treatment of the infection. The following case provides a description of a man who suffered from several infections:

In *Eugene Perry, Sr., James Howard Perry, Mary Perry, Michael David Perry, Harriet Perry Smith, Wilma Perry-Wallace, Joann Owens and Connie Waters v. Sun Healthcare Group, Inc.,* beginning in April 2000, the plaintiff's 83-year-old decedent, Eugene Perry, became totally dependent for assistance with physical care, activities of daily living, and supervision, as a result of multi-system failures including advanced lung disease. He was ventilator-dependent and required nasogastric tube feedings for nutrition. On June 23, 2001, the decedent was admitted to the Sunbridge Healthcare and Rehabilitation-Palomares skilled nursing facility. On July 1, he was discharged to an acute hospital and did not return. On November 11, 2001, he died at another skilled nursing facility. The plaintiff, as surviving family members, sued Sun Healthcare Group Inc., Irvine, and associated companies, alleging some 11 causes of action. Primary complaints were medical negligence, wrongful death, elder abuse, unfair business practices and injunctive relief, as well as other ancillary causes of action. The plaintiffs contended the defendants neglected the decedent's care that he developed ulcerative sores, severe infections, a foul-smelling discharge from his tracheostomy, maggot infestations in various parts of his body that were so severe that his breathing was blocked, and related medical conditions such that he died as a direct and proximate result. The plaintiffs established evidence that the defendants' actions amounted to reckless and malicious intent within the meaning of Welfare and Institutions Code 15657—the Elder Abuse Statute—and therefore justified the imposition of punitive damages. The jury returned an initial award of $500,000 in noneconomic damages on the elder abuse cause, but found for the defense on the wrongful death action.[136]

23.13 Antibiotic-Resistant Infections and Antibiotic Use

LTC facility residents are at risk for antimicrobial drug-resistant microorganisms including Methicillin-resistant Staphylococcus Aureus and Vancomycin-resistant Enterococcus (VRE). The frequent movement of residents between hospitals and LTC facilities most likely assists in the transfer of these organisms. Because of the frequent interchange of patients between hospitals and nursing homes, infections caused by antimicrobial drug-resistant bacteria will continue to emerge in geriatric populations.

Although often essential for the treatment of infected patients, antibiotics are associated with adverse side effects, unnecessary healthcare costs, and the development of resistance. Antibiotic use puts pressure on bacterial flora, which leads to resistant organisms. On the other hand, in serious infections, failure to prescribe adequate antibiotics can be associated with lethal outcomes. Choosing the right antibiotic can be challenging as the practitioner often encounters serious infections in need of quick antibiotic treatment in a setting where drug-resistant organisms are often prevalent.[137]

Reducing the inappropriate use of antibiotics requires a facility-wide approach. AMDA advises practitioners to consider the following factors when selecting an antibiotic:

- the severity of the patient's illness and the stability of his condition,
- the patient's medical history and coexisting conditions,
- the patient's known drug allergies, if any, and history of adverse drug reactions,
- the risk of interactions with other medications the patient is taking,

- the nature and location of the infection,
- the drug's cost and availability on a formulary, if relevant,
- the ease of administering the drug (e.g., single daily dose vs. multiple doses), and
- culture and sensitivity data.

While experts agree that more research is needed, important strides have been made in establishing guidelines for recognizing the importance of antibiotic resistance, and defining the appropriate use of antibiotics in the long-term care setting. (See, for example, the National Guideline Clearinghouse, www.guideline.gov.) AMDA recommends these guidelines be adapted, as appropriate, in facilities and communicated to clinical staff.[138]

Inappropriate antibiotic use can affect the success or failure of an infection control program. Reviewing the use of antibiotics encourages appropriate prescription of these medications and may limit the development of antibiotic-resistant organisms within the facility.

23.14 Summary

Hospitalized patients present with numerous risk factors for infection. Infection control programs work diligently with hospital staff, support service personnel, administration and management, and physicians with an overarching effort toward minimizing the occurrence of healthcare-associated infections. Many infections simply cannot be prevented regardless of laudable efforts on the part of staff. One needs to judge hospitals on whether or not failures contributed to infectious adverse outcomes or if there simply was nothing that would have prevented these. A thorough review of the presence and implementation of a quality infection control program is a good place to start.

As a group, nursing home residents exhibit all the risk factors for infections associated with the elder population. Therefore, infections occur commonly in this setting. Concentration should therefore not rely heavily on whether the infection occurs, but rather if the facility had processes in place for prompt recognition and management of infections and if those processes were in fact followed.

Endnotes

1. Emori, T. G. and R. P. Gaynes, "An overview of nosocomial infections, including the role of the microbiology laboratory," *Clinical Microbiology Reviews* (1993): 428–442.

2. *Id.*

3. Roberts, R. R., R. D. Scott II, and R. Cordel et al., "The use of economic modeling to determine the hospital costs associated with nosocomial infections," *Clinical Infectious Diseases* 36 (2003): 1424–1432.

4. *Id.*

5. Eggimann, P. and D. Pittet, "Infection control in the ICU," *Chest* 120 (2001): 2059–2093.

6. *Id.*

7. Centers for Disease Control and Prevention, "Public health focus: surveillance, prevention, and control of nosocomial infections," *MMWR* 41 (1992): 783–787.

8. Richards, C., "Infections in residents of long-term care facilities: an agenda for research, report of an expert panel," *Journal of the American Geriatrics Society* 50 (2002): 570–576.

9. *Id.*

10. Vance, J. and K. M. Wilson, "Getting a handle on infection control in long-term care," *Caring for the Ages* 2, no. 9 (September 2001): 22–27. Columbia, Maryland: American Medical Directors Association.

11. Kubrak C Jensen L. Malnutrition in Acute Care Patients; a Narrative Review. *International Journal of Nursing Studies* 2007; 44:1036-54.

12. Schneider SSM, Veyres P, Pivot X, et al. Malnutrition is an independent risk factor associated with nosocomial infections. *British Journal of Nutrition* 2004; 92:105-11.

13. Hamer, D. and M. Barza, "Prevention of Hospital Acquired Pneumonia in Critically ill patients," *Antimicrobial Agents and Chemotherapy* 7 (1993): 931–938.

14. Isenberg, H. D. and R. F. D'Amato, "Indigenous and pathogenic microorganisms of humans," In *Manual of clinical microbiology*, eds. P. R. Murray, E. J. Baron, and M. A. Pfaller et al., Washington, D.C.: ASM Press, 1995.

15. Smith, P. W. and P. G. Rusnak, "Infection prevention and control in the long-term care facility," *Infection Control and Hospital Epidemiology* 18 (1997): 831–849.

16. Nicolle, L. E., "Preventing infections in non-hospital settings: long-term care," *Emerging Infectious Diseases* 7, no. 2 (March-April 2001): 205–207.

17. Eichoff, T. C., P. S. Brachman, and J. V. Bennett et al., "Surveillance of nosocomial infection in community hospitals, I: surveillance methods, effectiveness and initial results," *Journal of Infectious Diseases* 120 (1969): 1305–1317.

18. Nicolle, L. E., D. Bentley, R. Garibaldi, E. Neuhaus, and P. Smith, SHEA Long-term Care Committee, "Antimicrobial use in long-term care facilities," *Infection Control and Hospital Epidemiology* 17 (1996): 119–128.

19. Mangram, A. J., T. C. Horan, and M. L. Pearson et al., "Guideline for prevention of surgical site infection," *Infection Control and Hospital Epidemiology* 20 (1999): 247–278.

20. Burke, J. P. and D. K. Riley, "Nosocomial urinary tract infection," In *Hospital epidemiology and infection control*, ed. C. G. Mayhall, 139–153. Baltimore: Williams & Wilkens, 1996.

21. Horan, T. C. and R. P. Gaynes, "Surveillance of nosocomial infections," In *Hospital Epidemiology and Infection Control*, Third edition, ed. C. G. Mayhall, 1659–1702, Philadelphia: Lippincott Williams & Wilkins, 2004.

22. Platt, R., B. F. Polk, and B. Murdock et al., "Mortality associated with nosocomial urinary tract infection," *New England Journal* 307 (1982): 637–642.

23. Haley, R. W., D. H. Culver, and J. W. White et al., "The nationwide nosocomial infection rate: A need for vital statistics," *American Journal of Epidemiology* 121 (1985): 159–167.

24. Laupland, K. B., S. M. Bagshaw, and D. B. Gregson et al., "Intensive care unit-acquired urinary tract infections in a regional critical care system," *Critical Care* 9 (2005): R60-65.

25. Wong, E. and T. M. Hooton, "Guideline for prevention of catheter-associated urinary tract infections," *American Journal of Infection Control* 11 (1985): 28–33.

26. See note 22.

27. Pittet, D. and R. Wenzel, "Nosocomial bloodstream infections: Secular trends in rates, mortality, and contribution to total hospital deaths," *Archives of Internal Medicine* 155 (1995): 1177–1184.

28. Denton, M. and K. Kerr, "Microbiological and clinical aspects of infection associated with Stemotrophomonas maltophilia," *Clinical Microbiology Reviews* 11 (1998): 57–80.

29. Center for Disease Control. Guideline for Prevention of Catheter-associated Urinary Tract Infections, 2009.

30. *Id.*

31. Hamer, D. H. and M. Barza, "Prevention of hospital-acquired pneumonia in critically ill patients," *Antimicrobial Agents and Chemotherapy* 37 (1993): 931–938.

32. Carstens, J. (2009). Urethral Catheter (Indwelling Short-Term): Urinary Tract Infection Prevention. *Evidence Summaries - Joanna Briggs Institute.* Retrieved May 31, 2010, from Evidence-Based Resources from the Joanna Briggs Institute. (Document ID: 1857331641).

33. Tablan, O. C. et al, Centers for Disease Control and Prevention, "Guideline for prevention of healthcare-associated pneumonia," 2003. Recommendation of the CDC and the healthcare infection control practices advisory committee. *MMWR* 53(RR03):1–36, 2003. http://www.cdc.gov/mmwR/preview/mmwrhtml/rr5303a1.htm

34. See note 31.

35. *Id.*

36. Xue, Y. (2008). Ventilator-Associated Pneumonia: Prevention. *Evidence Summaries - Joanna Briggs Institute.* Retrieved May 31, 2010, from Evidence-Based Resources from the Joanna Briggs Institute. (Document ID: 1602371281).

37. Alp, E., M. Guven, and O. Yildiz et al., "Incidence, risk factors and mortality of nosocomial pneumonia in intensive care units: a prospective study," *Annals of Clinical Microbiology and Antimicrobials* 3 (2004): 17–27.

38. Center for Disease Control. National Health Safety Network. http://www.cdc.gov/nhsn/wcOverviewNHSN.html

39. Center for Disease Control. Ventilator-Associated Pneumonia: Resources for Patients and Healthcare Providers. http://www.cdc.gov/ncidod/dhqp/dpac_ventilate.html

40. Seropian, R. and B. M. Reynolds, "Wound infections after preoperative depilatory versus razor preparation," *American Journal of Surgery* 121 (1971): 251–54.

41. Cruse, P. J. and R. Foord, "The epidemiology of wound infection: a 10 year prospective study of 62,939 wounds," *Surgical Clinics of North America* 60 (1980): 27–40.

42. Legal Eye Newsletter for the Nursing Profession. September 1996.

43. Center for Disease Control. 1999. Guideline for Surgical Site Infections.

44. Xue, Y. (2009). Surgical site infection: Pre-Anaesthesia and Intraoperative during surgery. *Evidence Summaries - Joanna Briggs Institute.* Retrieved June 1, 2010, from Evidence-Based Resources from the Joanna Briggs Institute. (Document ID: 1737376831).

45. Xue, Y. (2009). Surgical Site Infection: Operating room/theatre environment controls. *Evidence Summaries - Joanna Briggs Institute.* Retrieved June 1, 2010, from Evidence-Based Resources from the Joanna Briggs Institute. (Document ID: 1771791321).

46. Xue, Y. (2009). Surgical Site Infection: Preoperative Evaluation & Preventive Measures. *Evidence Summaries - Joanna Briggs Institute.* Retrieved June 1, 2010, from Evidence-Based Resources from the Joanna Briggs Institute. (Document ID: 1737376841).

47. O'Grady, N. P., M. Alexander, and E. P. Dellinger et al., "Guidelines for the prevention of intravascular catheter-related infections," *MMWR*, Recommendations and Reports 51 (RR10):1–26, 2002.

48. Legal Eye Newsletter for the Nursing Profession. June 2007.

49. Center for Disease Control. Guidelines for the Prevention of Intravascular Catheter Infections.

50. Xue, Y. (2009). Central Venous Catheter (CVC): Dressing and Flushing. *Evidence Summaries - Joanna Briggs Institute.* Retrieved June 1, 2010, from Evidence-Based Resources from the Joanna Briggs Institute. (Document ID: 1737391651).

51. Lucet, J. C., K. Grent, and L. A. Armand-Lefevre et al., "High prevalence of carriage of Methicillin Resistant Staphylococcus aureus at hospital admission in elderly patients: Implications for infection Control Strategies," *Infection Control and Hospital Epidemiology* 26 (2005): 121–126.

52. Yokoe, D. S., "Epidemiology and prevention of nosocomial infections." In *Infectious Diseases*, eds. S. Gorbach, J. Bartlett, and N. Blacklow. Philadelphia: Lippincott, Williams and Wilkins, 2004.

53. See note 1.

54. Kerstein, M., M. Flower, and L. M. Harkavy et al., "Surveillance for postoperative wound infections: practical aspects," *The American Surgeon* (1978): 210–214.

55. See note 51.

56. *Id.*

57. See note 52.

58. American Medical Directors Association, *Common infections in the long term care setting. Clinical Practice Guideline.* Columbia, Maryland, 2004.

59. Center for Disease Control, "Interim guidelines for prevention and control of staphylococcal infection associate with reduced susceptibility to vancomycin," *Morbidity and Mortality Weekly Report* 46 (1997): 628–636.

60. Center for Disease Control. "12 Steps to Prevent Antimicrobial Resistance Among Hospitalized Adults," www.cdc.gov/drugresistance/healthcare/ha/12steps_HA.htm.

61. Naughton, B. *Optimizing the management of pneumonia in the long term care setting,* AMDA conference, March 2006.

62. Nicolle, L. E., "Urinary tract infections in geriatric and institutionalized patients," *Current Opinion in Urology* 12, no. 1 (January 2002): 51–55.

63. "Urinary tract infections," In *Geriatrics at Your Fingertips*, eds. D. Beuben, K. Herr, J. Pacala, J. Potter, T. Semla, and G. Small, 70–73. New York: American Geriatrics Society, 2000.

64. *Id.*

65. American Medical Directors Association. *Urinary incontinence clinical practice guideline.* Columbia, Maryland, 2005.

66. *AMDA Conference - Management of Urinary Infections in the Nursing Home: Little Consensus, Much Controversy,* Hosam Kamel, Maryland, CMD, March 2006.

67. See note 65.

68. *Id.*

69. *Id.*

70. *Id.*

71. McGreer A, Campbell B, Emori TG, et al. Definitions of infection for surveillance in long-term care facilities. Am J Infect Control. 1991; 19(1):1-7.

72. Center for Medicare and Medicaid Services (CMS). Survey and certification (S & C) group. Delay in effective date for revisions of appendix PP, state operations manual (SOM), surveyor guidance for Urinary Incontinence and Catheters (Tag F315). CMS S & C Publication No. S&C-05-23. Available at: www.cms.hhs.gov/medicaid/survey-cert/sc0523.pdf.

73. See note 64.

74. Gammack, J. K. "Use and management of chronic urinary catheters in long-term care: much controversy, little consensus," *Journal of the American Medical Directors Association* 3 (2002): 162–168.

75. Pneumonia Project Overview. http://www.national-pneumonia.org/PNEProjectOverview103102.pdf.

76. *Id.*

77. Shefer, A., McKibben, L., Bardenheier, B., Bratzler, D., Roberts, H. March 2005. Characteristics of long-term care facilities associated with standing order programs to deliver influenza and pneumococcal vaccinations to residents in 13 states. Journal of the American Medical Directors Association - March 2005 (Vol. 6, Issue 2, Pages 97-104, DOI: 10.1016/j.jamda.2004.12.020)

78. Tablan, O. C. et al, Centers for Disease Control and Prevention, "Guideline for prevention of healthcare-associated pneumonia," 2003. Recommendation of the CDC and the healthcare infection control practices advisory committee. *MMWR* 53(RR03):1–36, 2003. http://www.cdc.gov/mmwR/preview/mmwrhtml/rr5303a1.htm

79. Hamer, D. H. and M. Barza, "Prevention of hospital-acquired pneumonia in critically ill patients," *Antimicrobial Agents and Chemotherapy* 37 (1993): 931–938.

80. Laska, L. (ed.), "Failure to properly monitor and assess nursing home resident," *Medical Malpractice Verdicts, Settlements, and Experts* (August 2001): 39.

81. Frost, F., G. F. Craun, and R. L. Calderon, "Increasing hospitalization and death possibly due to clostridium difficile diarrheal disease," *Emerging Infectious Diseases* 4, no. 4 (October-December 1998): 619–625.

82. *Id.*

83. *Id.*

84. Laska, L. (ed.), "Feeding tube replacement for minor perforates stomach," *Medical Malpractice Verdicts, Settlements, and Experts* (July 2004): 26.

85. McFarland L. Meta-analysis of probiotics for the prevention of antibiotic associated diarrhea and the treatment of Clostridium difficile disease. *American Journal of Gastroenterology* 2006; 101:812.

86. Hickson M, D'Souza AL, Muthu N. Use of probiotic Lactobacillus preparation to prevent diarrhea associated with antibiotics: Randomised double blind controlled trial. *British Medical Journal* 2007 335:80-4.

87. American Medical Directors Association, *Multidisciplinary medication management toolkit*, Chapter 10. Columbia, Maryland, 2003.

88. Schroeder MS. *Closteridium difficile-* associated diarrhea. *American Family Physician* 2005; 71(5):921-8.

89. Stone SP, Beric V, Quick A, Balestrini AA, Kibler CC. The effect of enhanced infection-control policy on the incidence of *Closteridium difficile* infection and methacillin-resistant Staphylococcus aureus colonization in acute elderly medical patients. *Age and Ageing* 1998; 27(5):561-8.

90. See note 88.

91. American Medical Directors Association, *Pressure ulcers: Clinical practice guideline*. Columbia, Maryland, 1996.

92. American Medical Directors Association, *Pressure ulcer therapy companion*. Columbia, Maryland, 1999.

93. http://www.cdc.gov/ncidod/dpd/parasites/scabies/factsht_scabies.htm.

94. Horan-Murphy, E., B. Barnard, and C. Chenoweth et al. "APIC/CHICA-Canada infection control and epidemiology: Professional and practice standards," *American Journal of Infection Control* 27 (1999): 47–51.

95. Legal Eye Newsletter for the Nursing Profession. July 1998.

96. Center for Medicare and Medicaid Services. CMS Standard §482.42. http://www.access.gpo.gov/nara/cfr/waisidx_04/42cfr482_04.html

97. CMS Interpretive Guidelines. www.apic.org/Content/.../CMS/Interp_Guidelines.pdf

98. Centers for Disease Control and Prevention Healthcare Infection Control Practices Advisory Committee (HICPAC), *Draft guideline for environmental infection control in healthcare facilities*, 2001.

99. Garner, J. S., J. V. Bennett, and W. E. Scheckler et al., "Surveillance of nosocomial infections," In *Proceedings of the International Conference on Nosocomial Infections*, eds. P. S. Eickhoff and T. C. Eickhoff. Chicago: American Hospital Association, 1971.

100. See note 98.

101. Center for Disease Control. Guideline for Isolation Precautions.

102. Centers for Disease Control and Prevention, "Guideline for hand hygiene in health-care settings: Recommendations of the healthcare infection control practices advisory committee and the HICPAC/SHEA/APIC/IDSA Hand Hygiene Task Force," *MMWR* 51, no. RR-16 (2002): 1–63.

103. Federal Nursing Home Reform Act of 1987. OMNIBUS Budget Reconciliation Act of 1987. www.ssa.gov/OP_Home/comp2/F100-203.htm

104. Interpretive Guidance at FTag441.www.cms.gov/surveycertificationgeninfo/pmsr/itemdetail.asp?itemid=cms1228778.

105. *Id.*

106. *Id.*

107. American Medical Directors Association, *Common infections in the long term care setting. Clinical Practice Guideline*. Columbia, Maryland, 2004

108. Laska, L. (ed.), "Nursing home resident suffers pressure sores and malnutrition from neglect," *Medical Malpractice Verdicts, Settlements, and Experts* (August 2004).

109. McKibben, L., T. Horan, and J. I. Tokars et al., "Guidance on public reporting of healthcare-associated infections: Recommendations of the Healthcare Infection Control Practices Advisory Committee," *American Journal of Infection Control* 33 (2005): 217–226.

110. Poland, G. A., A. M. Shefer, and M. McCauley et al., "Standards for adult immunization practices," *American Journal of Preventive Medicine* 25, no. 2 (2003): 144–150.

111. *Id.*

112. *Id.*

113. *Id.*

114. See note 102.

115. Bentley, D. W., S. Bradley, and K. High, K. et al., "Practice guideline for evaluation of fever and infection in long-term care facilities," Guidelines from the Infectious Diseases Society of America. *Journal of the American Medical Directors Association* 2, no. 5 (September-October 2001): 246–258.

116. *Id.*

117. See note 107.

118. *Id.*

119. *Id.*

120. "Urinary tract infections," In *Geriatrics at Your Fingertips*, eds. D. Beuben, K. Herr, J. Pacala, J. Potter, T. Semla, and G. Small, 70–73. New York: American Geriatrics Society, 2000.

121. Laska, L. (ed.), "Nursing home resident suffers pressure sores and malnutrition from neglect," *Medical Malpractice Verdicts, Settlements, and Experts* (August 2004).

122. See note 102.

123. *Id.*

124. *Id.*

125. *Id.*

126. *Id.*

127. *Id.*

128. See note 110.

129. See note 107.

130. Berrouane, Y. F., L. A. McNutt, B. J. Buschelman, P. R. Rhomberg, M. D. Sanford, R. J. Hollis, M. A. Pfaller, and L. A. Herwaldt, "Outbreak of severe pseudomonas infections caused by a contaminated drain in a whirlpool bathtub," *Clinical Infectious Diseases,* (nas aeruginosa i6), 1331–1337. Epub, December 31, 2000.

131. Hollyoak, V., P. Boyd, and R. Freeman, "Whirlpool baths in nursing homes: use, maintenance, and contamination with pseudomonas aeruginosa," *Commun Dis Rep CDR* Rev. 5, 7, R102-104 (June 23, 1995).

132. See note 115.

133. See note 115.

134. *Id.*

135. *Id.*

136. Laska L. (ed.), "Negligent care of disabled bedridden eight-three year old patient," *Medical Malpractice Verdicts, Settlements, and Experts* (August 2003): 34–35.

137. Nicolle, L. E., L. J. Strausbaugh, and R. A. Garibaldi, "Infections and antibiotic resistance in nursing homes," *Clinical Microbiology Reviews 9 (1996): 1–17*

138. Naughton, B. *Optimizing the management of pneumonia in the long term care setting,* AMDA conference, March 2006.

Chapter 24

Intravenous Therapy Malpractice

Susan Masoorli, RN

Synopsis
24.1 Introduction
24.2 Peripheral Vascular Access Devices
    A. Butterfly
    B. Catheter
        1. Catheter over-the-needle device
        2. Catheter insertion documentation
        3. Midline catheter
        4. Midline catheter documentation
    C. Insertion Site Selection
    D. Gauge Selection
24.3 Central Venous Access Devices
    A. Non-Tunneled Central Venous Catheters
    B. Tunneled Catheters
    C. Peripherally Inserted Central Catheters (PICC)
    D. Implanted Ports
24.4 Site Assessment Documentation
24.5 Legal Issues
    A. Vascular Access Organizations
    B. Standard of Care Issues
        1. Clinical competency
        2. Policies and procedures
        3. Informed consent
        4. Number of attempts
        5. The use of armboards
        6. Appropriate infusion solutions and medications
        7. Documentation guidelines
24.6 Vascular Access Device Complications
    A. Peripheral Access Devices
        1. Nerve injury
        2. Infiltration
        3. Extravasation
    B. Central Venous Catheter Complications
        1. Catheter malposition
        2. Catheter malfunction
        3. Air embolism
        4. IV catheter-related sepsis/infection
24.7 Clinical and Liability Issues
24.8 Conclusion
Endnotes

24.1 Introduction

Peripherally inserted central catheters (PICC lines), central venous catheters (CVCs), implanted ports, tunneled catheters, triple lumen catheters, midlines and peripheral intravenous (IV) catheters are all types of devices used to access the vascular system (veins) for the infusion of medications and solutions. People who enter the healthcare system have a high probability of having one of these devices inserted for IV therapy. Even though the practice of accessing veins was developed in the 1600s, research and production of new improved and safer devices has escalated dramatically within the past ten years. There are over 500 million peripheral catheters and 5 million central venous catheters inserted annually in the United States.[1] IV catheters are inserted in hospitals, long-term care and rehabilitation facilities, patient homes, physician offices, occupational health, work sites and schools. Clinicians must act as patient advocates and a firewall to prevent bad practices from occurring. The Institute for Healthcare Improvement (IHI) and The Joint Commission on the Accreditation of Healthcare Organizations give permission to all healthcare workers to stop poor bedside practices such as breaking sterile technique during a central venous catheter insertion. In addition Medicare and various insurance agencies have elected not to reimburse hospitals for vascular access infections that occur during a hospital admission. Infections and many other vascular access and IV therapy complications are preventable. The dramatic increase in the number of infusion therapy malpractice cases is due directly to the lack of competently trained healthcare providers inserting and monitoring the various types of vascular access devices and IV therapies. Physicians, RNs, LPNs, medical technicians, radiologic technologists and emergency medical personnel are among the many healthcare providers who insert intravenous devices. However, their training is limited or non-existent. Today, with the focus on patient safety and improved patient satisfaction, better education of healthcare providers is needed.

24.2 Peripheral Vascular Access Devices

Peripheral veins can be accessed for the infusion of fluids and medications or the withdrawal of blood. Peripheral veins are defined as the superficial veins of the upper extremities and lower extremities in neonates. Medical records should include a notation about the type of device that was used to start intravenous fluids. There are three types of peripheral intravenous devices: short stainless steel needles, midline catheters and catheter over-the-needle devices.[2]

A. Butterfly

A short stainless steel needle is commonly called a *butterfly* and has a beveled or slanted tip and integral plastic extension tubing. These devices are currently used on a very limited basis, due to the high risk of infusion-related complications.[3] The advantage for using this type of device is that it is easier to insert and a visible flash of blood will be detected in the plastic extension tubing, which signifies that the needle tip is seated within the blood vessel. However, the sharp beveled tip of the needle remains in the vein. If the vein moves, or the needle moves within the vein, the risk of vein puncture is substantial. Vein puncture will result in the leakage of blood into the tissue, causing a hematoma (bruise) to form or the leakage of medications and solutions into the tissue (infiltration). If the drugs have the potential to burn the tissue (extravasation), resulting tissue and muscle injury can occur. In the recent past, clinicians involved in short-term procedures requiring the injection of medications, such as in the radiology department for the injection of contrast agents, often selected this type of device. Stainless steel needles are not the device of choice for any type of infusion, for any duration of time. These devices are primarily used for withdrawing blood for analysis.

TIP: These devices are particularly dangerous in the pediatric and geriatric populations, since their veins may be fragile and prone to needle puncture.[4]

B. Catheter

1. Catheter over-the-needle device

The most appropriate peripheral venous access device for routine IV therapy is the catheter over-the-needle device which is defined as a catheter that is less than or equal to 3 inches in length. There are many brands on the market, but all have the same design elements. There are more steps involved in accessing a vein using an IV catheter as opposed to a stainless steel needle. However, once the catheter is positioned properly within the vein, the risk of IV-related complications is significantly reduced. Catheter over-the-needle devices are two-piece devices: a catheter and a needle. The plastic catheter sits over the beveled needle. When the needle enters the vein, a flash of blood will be visible in the flash back chamber. The beveled needle is removed and the plastic catheter is fully advanced into the vein. Today, most catheters are designed to soften and mold to the contours of the vein after the needle is removed, thereby reducing the incidence

of vein puncture and irritation. According to the Infusion Nurses Society (INS) Standards of Practice, short peripheral access devices should be rotated to a new vein site every 72 hours.[5] However, the Centers for Disease Control and Prevention (CDC) Intravascular Guideline recommends peripheral IV devices be rotated every 72-96 hours.[6] It is a federal law passed in 2001 that all IV catheters must have a needle safety device to prevent contaminated needlestick injury.

2. Catheter insertion documentation

There are specific documentation requirements for the insertion of vascular access devices.[7] The documentation for peripheral catheters should include

- date and time of insertion,
- type of device,
- length of IV catheter,
- gauge of IV catheter,
- anatomical name of the accessed vein,
- number of attempts,
- patient tolerance of the procedure, and
- signature of person inserting the device.

A correctly written example of documentation following a catheter insertion is shown below.

Sample Note
Date/Time
#22-gauge one inch Braun Introcan inserted into left mid cephalic vein on first attempt.
1000ml NSS infusing by gravity at 100ml/hr. Patient states "I did not feel the stick at all."
—H. Bradley, RN

TIP: The current INS Standards of Practice state that all peripheral intravenous devices should be rotated every 72 hours or upon suspected complication or therapy completion. The longer the same peripheral device remains in place, the higher the complication rate.

All intravenous device insertions and site rotations should be documented on the infusion therapy flow sheet or the nurses' progress notes. The documentation should also include an assessment of the condition of the site from where the catheter was removed and the reason the intravenous device was removed. This information should be recorded in the nurse's progress notes.

3. Midline catheter

A midline catheter is defined as a peripheral catheter

that is between 3–8 inches in length.[8] Specially trained nurses can insert this device at the bedside. An introducer needle is inserted into a vein slightly above the antecubital fossa (inner aspect of the elbow) into the basilic or cephalic vein. The catheter is advanced through the introducer needle to below the shoulder in the axillary vein. The introducer needle is then removed, leaving the catheter in place. According to the INS Standards of Practice, midline catheters can remain in place for up to four weeks.[9] Review of the literature shows there is evidence of higher risk of venous thrombosis (blood clot) with this catheter type. Many hospitals restrict or prohibit the use of midline catheters because of the complication. Only medications approved for peripheral IV catheters can be infused through midline catheters.

4. Midline catheter documentation

The documentation for midline catheters should include

- date and time of insertion,
- type of device,
- anatomical name of the access vein,
- gauge of device,
- length of catheter,
- external length of catheter,
- number of attempts,
- patient tolerance of procedure, and
- signature of person inserting the device.

A correctly written example of documentation prepared after a midline catheter insertion is shown below.

Sample Note
Date/Time
A 20-gauge BD midline catheter inserted into right basilic vein, one inch above the antecubital fossa on the first attempt. 2cm of catheter is external. Patient states "My elbow is a little sore."
—B. Waters, RN

This is required documentation content by the Infusion Nurses Society. In most cases, the documentation of the insertion of an intravenous access device is found in the medical or nursing progress notes. However, the procedure may be documented on the intravenous flow sheet. In specialty areas, such as the emergency room and outpatient surgery, there are often specified areas on the nursing assessment forms to document the insertion of the intravenous device.

C. Insertion Site Selection

The INS Standards of Practice state that areas of joint flexion,

such as the wrist area and the antecubital fossa (elbow area), should be avoided as insertion sites,[10] as this increases the risk of complications due to joint movement. The best location for the insertion of peripheral IV devices is in the forearm. The cephalic and basilic veins are straight and large in diameter. Refer to Figure 24.1. These should be the first choices. The metacarpal veins on the back of the hand are the first choice only when the patient is scheduled for surgery. Anesthesia providers must have access to the IV site to inject additional medications as well as to assess the IV site during the intraoperative procedure. The Standards also state that the IV devices should not be inserted into the legs of adult patients as this increases the risk of thrombophlebitis which is the inflammation of the vein with a clot formation.[11] This can result from slower blood flow through the veins in the lower extremities due to an increased number of large semilunar valves. Arms of patients with impaired drainage due to axillary lymph node removal related to metastatic breast cancer or head and neck cancer should not be used for peripheral IV insertions. The impaired drainage of fluid from the arm can cause swelling to occur (lymphedema) making assessment of the IV site for complications more difficult. Arms of patients with functioning AV shunts or fistula for dialysis should also be avoided because the venous anatomy may be compromised.

The preservation of peripheral veins in patients with chronic kidney disease who may need hemodialysis in the future has taken on a new sense of urgency. Patients with chronic kidney disease, Stage 3 or greater, or a serum creatinine level greater than 2.0 mg/dl may need a fistula for hemodialysis. It is the position of the Association for Vascular Access (AVA)[12] and the American Society of Diagnostic & Interventional Nephrology (ASDIN) that the veins in the forearm should be preserved for future fistula placement. The primary sites for peripheral IV access in these patients are the metacarpal veins in the hands. This practice should continue only if the vein is appropriate and safe for catheter cannulation and IV infusion.

D. Gauge Selection

The clinician who inserts a peripheral IV catheter is responsible for assessing the diameter and condition of the vein. The vein should be straight, smooth, soft and pliable for approximately 1 inch in length. Hard and sclerosed (scarred) veins are often seen in the IV drug abuser population. The diameter of the catheter should be 50 percent of the diameter of the vein, which will allow for blood to flow around the IV catheter. This acts as a cushion to prevent the IV catheter from rubbing and irritating the vein lining (causing phlebitis).[13] The higher the number of the catheter gauge, the smaller the diameter of the catheter. A 24-gauge catheter is very small in diameter, and is appropriate for neonatal, pediatric and geriatric patients. A 22-gauge catheter is appropriate for most adult IV infusions. A 20-gauge catheter is most appropriate for adult blood transfusions and minor surgery. However, in adult patients with poor peripheral vein access, a 22-gauge catheter can be used for blood transfusions.[14] An 18-gauge catheter is appropriate for trauma patients and operations with a high risk for large amounts of blood loss. Large bore 16- and 14-gauge catheters are most appropriate for major trauma and major surgeries. The selection of the appropriate gauge peripheral IV catheter is the responsibility of the clinician inserting the device. The IV insertion documentation should always include the size and length of the catheter used.

TIP: The IV insertion documentation should always include the anatomical name of the accessed vein, as well as the size and length of the catheter used.

24.3 Central Venous Access Devices

Central venous catheters (CVC) are defined as catheters whose tips rest in the vena cava.[15] The superior vena cava (SVC) is the largest vein in the body and sits in the center of the chest just above the heart.[16] The inferior vena cava (IVC) can be accessed by inserting a catheter into the femoral vein in the groin area. Both the SVC and IVC drain blood into the right atrium of the heart. Because the rate of blood flow in these veins is substantial, they are the safest locations for all CVC catheter tips.[17]

A. Non-Tunneled Central Venous Catheters

Non-tunneled central venous catheters were the first type of centrally placed catheters and to this day have the highest complication and fatality rate when not properly inserted and monitored. Currently physicians and specially trained nurses can insert these catheters at the bedside, in the oper-

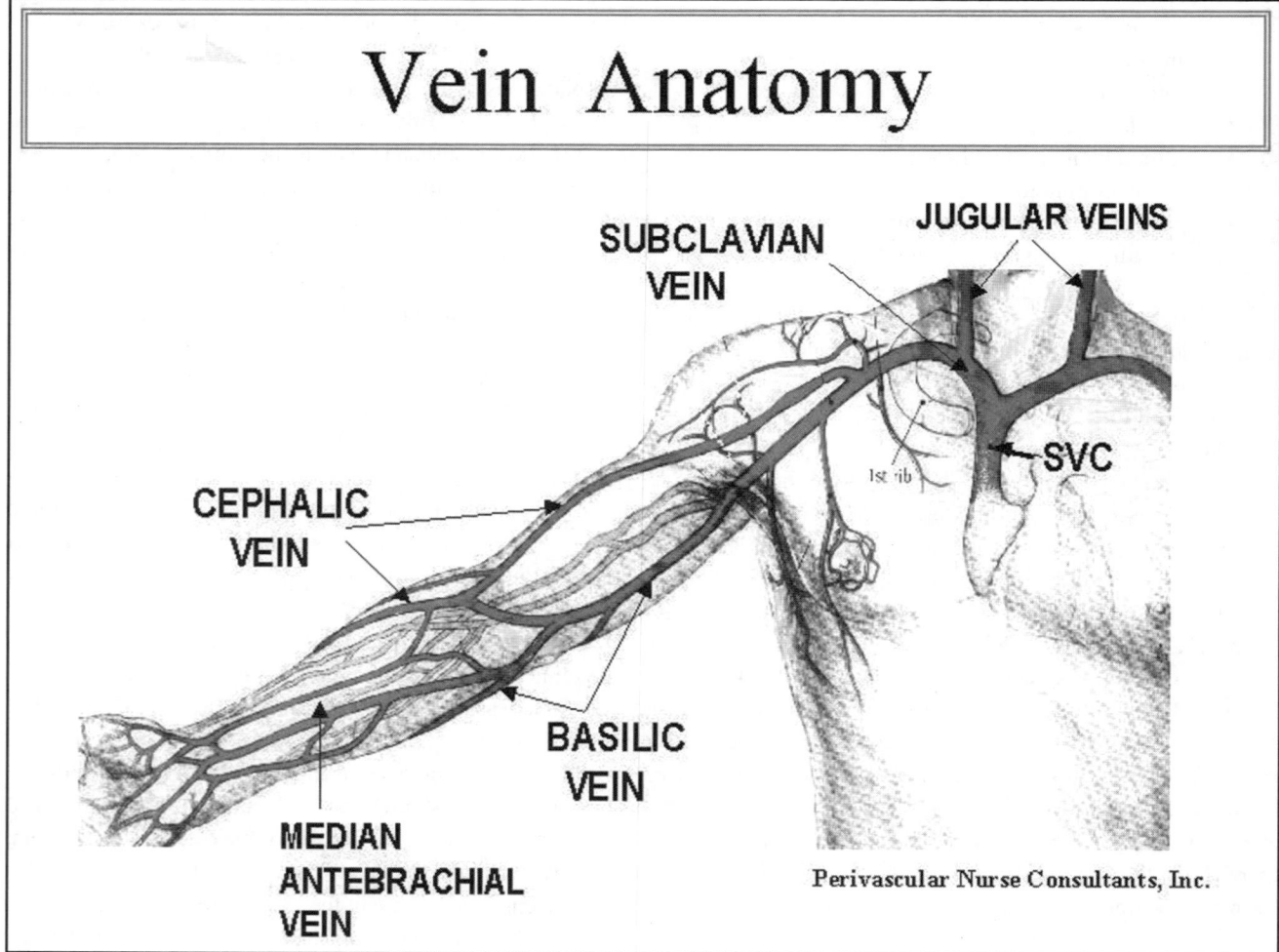

Figure 24.1 Veins of Arm and Chest

ating room, or in interventional radiology. It is highly recommended that these catheters be inserted using ultrasound for vein visualization. Using the old "landmark system" is a deviation from the standard of care.[18] The catheters are inserted into the subclavian or internal jugular vein. The subclavian vein is located under the collar bone, whereas the jugular vein is located on the side of the neck. A large-bore needle is inserted into the vein, and a 6–8 inch long catheter is advanced through the needle with the catheter tip resting in the superior vena cava. This catheter is associated with high infection rates (sepsis), pneumothorax (lung puncture and collapse), and the entry of air into the venous system (air embolism). This catheter has the highest mortality rate related to these complications. This type of catheter can be inserted relatively quickly into critically ill patients who need large vein access for rapid infusions and multiple life-saving drugs, such as in cardiac arrests and major trauma.[19]

The attorney, paralegal, legal nurse consultant, or expert witness (reviewer) should be able to locate the insertion site by review of the medical record. The name of this catheter type is often abbreviated as CVP for central venous pressure catheter or TLC for triple lumen catheter or SC for subclavian catheter. It is the standard of care that all types of central venous catheters require a chest x-ray post insertion to determine catheter tip placement in the SVC.[20] Some facilities require signing of an informed consent for the performance of catheter insertion. Physicians rarely document any information related to the catheter insertion, other than "catheter inserted."

B. Tunneled Catheters

TIP: Tunneled catheter brand names include Hickman and Broviac.

Tunneled catheters are durable and are considered to be among the safest of central venous catheters. These catheters are generally inserted by physicians in the operating room under anesthesia.[21] As with non-tunneled catheters, the subclavian or jugular vein is accessed, and the catheter is advanced into the superior vena cava. However, from the catheter insertion site below the collar bone to the nipple point on the chest, a blunt-tipped introducer is advanced under the skin creating a subcutaneous tunnel through which the catheter is advanced. The catheter will exit somewhere on the patient's chest. All tunneled catheters have an attached cotton cuff which sits within the tunnel. Scar tissue will grow around the cuff in about ten days after catheter insertion.[22] The cotton cuff has two functions: to anchor the catheter in place and to prevent bacteria from migrating up the tunnel and into

the venous system. This catheter was initially designed for transplant patients who were severely immunocompromised and at extreme risk for infection. This catheter is often used in patients requiring long-term daily infusions, such as Total Parenteral Nutrition (TPN), for the rest of their lives.[23]

Many clinicians are under the misconception that *Groshong* denotes a specific type of catheter. The term denotes a unique catheter tip design, which is available on all types of central venous catheters. Open-tipped catheters are catheters with straight cut tips, where all IV solutions exit the catheter at the distal tip. Groshong-tipped catheters have a black plug which covers the catheter tip. A three-way slit valve is on the distal side of the catheter, which allows the valve to open by pressure and permits the IV solutions/medications to enter the venous system. When negative pressure is applied by pulling back on a syringe plunger to withdraw blood, the valve opens inward and allows the removal of blood.[24] When the catheter is not being used, the valve remains in a closed position inhibiting the reflux of blood or air into the catheter and entering the bloodstream, which could be a potentially fatal situation. Groshong-tipped central venous catheters are in limited use and are usually utilized based on the inserter's catheter preference.

C. Peripherally Inserted Central Catheters (PICC)

Peripherally inserted central catheters (PICC) are the newest central venous catheters. They were used initially in the neonatal population but now are exceedingly popular in the adult population and are primarily used for long-term IV antibiotics. However, PICC catheters have been used successfully for hydration, chemotherapy, and parenteral nutrition. These are the longest central venous catheters, approximately 25 inches in length. Specially trained nurses, physicians, and radiologists can insert these catheters at the bedside. A large vein is accessed just above the antecubital fossa usually the basilic or brachial veins.[25] The catheter is advanced up the arm into the subclavian vein which is located under the collar bone and down into the superior vena cava. The catheter tip rests just above the heart or at the atrial/caval junction. These catheters have a low incidence of catheter-related complications when inserted and monitored properly and are often used in home care where patients or caregivers are instructed to self-administer their intravenous medications.[26] It is the standard of care and the recommendation of the AVA, The Joint Commission and CDC that all central venous catheters including PICC lines, be inserted using ultrasound to locate the vein, to assess the condition of the vein and to assess adjacent structures in order to minimize insertion-related complications such as arterial puncture and nerve injury.[27] The documentation for PICC insertion should include:

- date and time of insertion,
- catheter gauge, brand and lot number,
- anatomical name of the access vein,
- type of introducer used,
- if a guidewire was used,
- total measured length of catheter,
- external length of catheter,
- radiographic confirmation of anatomical location of catheter tip,
- patient response to procedure, and
- signature of person inserting the device.

Sample Note
Date/Time
4 Fr Bard Per-Q-Cath, lot #5064, with guidewire inserted into left basilic vein via 20-gauge microintroducer with ultrasound. Catheter measured 50cm total length with 1cm remaining external. Patient states "My arm feels fine." Patient sent to x-ray for confirmation of tip placement.
—S. Huang, RN

Date/Time
Catheter tip confirmed in superior vena cava. Verbal report obtained from Dr. Smith. Will use catheter for 8:00 P.M. dose.
—M. Alvarez, RN

D. Implanted Ports

TIP: Implanted ports are devices that are totally under the skin and are inserted by physicians in the operating room or by interventional radiology.

A subcutaneous skin pocket is made on the chest, and the port housing, with a self-sealing silicone gel center, is placed into the pocket and sutured to the chest wall.[28] The catheter is inserted into the subclavian or jugular vein and advanced with the final catheter tip placement in the superior vena cava. The port pocket is then sutured closed once the catheter tip is correctly placed. The advantage of this device is that because the port is totally under the skin, there is little or no care in between usage of the port. The clinician will feel the metal back of the port and obtain a 3-ml blood return when ports are properly accessed.[29] In order to use ports, a special non-coring Huber needle is pushed through the skin and into the port. These needles are available in various gauges and lengths. These devices are the catheters of choice for oncology patients who require long-term intermittent chemotherapy infusions. Ports can remain in place for many years and have

a low complication rate when properly inserted and monitored. Insertion documentation is commonly located on the surgical operative report. Verification of catheter tip placement is on the chest x-ray or fluoroscopy report. Ports can be inserted into veins, arteries, the liver, spinal column, pleural space and abdominal cavities for the infusion of IV fluids or the withdrawal of bodily fluids such as ascites.

24.4 Site Assessment Documentation

TIP: All peripheral and central catheters can be disconnected from a continuous IV fluid source. A resealable end cap is attached to the catheter hub. This may be documented as a saline lock (SL), intermittent lock (IL), and by the other terms as well. This device is part of routine nursing practice that limits unnecessary IV fluids and allows for greater patient mobility.

The frequency of assessing and monitoring the intravenous puncture site is dependent on many factors, including the age of the patient, the type of medications/solutions infused, the IV flow rate and the type of vascular access device. Pediatric and geriatric patients require more frequent vascular access device assessment because of the fragility of their veins.[30] Vesicant medications/solutions (drugs with the potential to burn the skin and tissue if they leak out of the vein and into the surrounding tissue) require more frequent monitoring to prevent serious injury.[31]

Examples of vesicant drugs are:

- sodium bicarbonate,
- calcium chloride,
- calcium gluconate,
- concentrated potassium chloride solutions,
- adriamycin,
- dilantin, and
- phenergan.

Examples of non-vesicant drugs are:

- ancef,
- cipro,
- heparin,
- sodium chloride, and
- penicillin.

Peripheral intravenous access devices inserted into small veins are more prone to puncture the vein as compared to catheters inserted into the larger veins of the forearm. Non-vesicant pediatric infusions should be assessed hourly at a minimum. The insertion site of vesicant pediatric infusion should be assessed every 30 minutes at a minimum. Adult non-vesicant solutions should be assessed every four hours and vesicant infusions every hour at a minimum. Institutional policies should stipulate the frequency of catheter site assessment and documentation requirements. Many hospital policies state that IV sites should be assessed every shift (a shift can be 8, 10 or 12 hours). Assessing the IV site every 8-12 hours is not sufficient to prevent serious IV-related complications from developing and it is a deviation from the standard of nursing care. The assessment of a vascular access device should include the condition of the skin at the catheter insertion site, the surrounding skin area, the flow rate, adverse reactions to medications and solutions, and any infusion-related complications.[32] The assessment should be documented in the nurses' progress note flow sheets, on the intravenous flow sheet on the medication administration record (MAR), or on the treatment administration record (TAR). Facility policy may specify other locations.

24.5 Legal Issues

The question in many IV therapy malpractice cases is, "Was the right catheter inserted into the patient?" The physician orders the IV medication or solution on the physician order sheet. In most cases, the type of access device is not specified by the physician. The nurse reviews the IV orders and determines if a peripheral access device is appropriate based on the type of therapy, length of therapy, and the condition of the veins in the patient's arms. If the patient is not a candidate for a peripheral access device, the nurse notifies the physician and asks that a central vascular access device be inserted. It is the nurse's responsibility to infuse safely the medications/solutions through the appropriate intravenous device. There are many algorithms available on the Internet to assist in proper vascular access device selection for specific patients. (See www.accessabilitybybard.co.uk.)

A. Vascular Access Organizations

TIP: There are several sources of standards of care for infusion therapy.

The Infusion Nurses Society (INS) is a nationally recognized nursing organization that has established the scope of practice, competencies, and educational requirements for the administration of infusion therapy. The organization publishes Standards of Nursing Practice which are applicable to all nurses in all settings who administer any type of infusion therapy. Standards have been published in 1981, 1990, 1998, 2000 and 2006. Currently a committee has been created to review and update the Standards for publication in 2011. These Standards have been used at trial to establish if the standard of nursing care has been met.

The Oncology Nurses Society (ONS), a nationally recognized nursing organization, published *Vascular Access Device Guidelines* in 1996 and 2004. They also published *Chemotherapy and Biotherapy Guidelines and Recommendations for Practice* in 2000 and 2009. These guidelines provide information to healthcare professionals who specialize in the care of cancer patients and infusion related therapies such as blood transfusions and intravenous chemotherapy. The guidelines are very broad and non-binding and are meant to assist the clinician with proper infusion techniques.

The Association for Vascular Access (AVA), formerly known as NAVAN, is a nationally recognized multidisciplinary organization composed of physicians, nurses, pharmacists, and catheter manufacturers who specialize in vascular access. The organization has published position papers on specific issues such as catheter tip position and internal jugular PICC lines.

The Society of Interventional Radiologists (SIR) is a nationally recognized organization composed of physicians, nurse practitioners, and physician assistants who insert vascular access devices in the radiology department. The organization publishes guidelines for practice and has developed a comprehensive curriculum for training clinicians on the appropriate procedures for insertion of vascular access devices. In addition to the publications of the aforementioned organizations, a literature search can be performed to find evidence-based research and a review of published data to support vascular access device related issues.

The Centers for Disease Control & Prevention (CDC) published *Guidelines for Prevention of Intravascular Device Related Infections* in 1996 and 2002. Currently, a committee has been convened to update these Guidelines. With over 500,000 reported catheter-related blood stream infections each year, the government is very concerned about the cost to both patients and the healthcare system. This document addresses infection-related issues for all indwelling catheters, including peripheral and central venous access devices. CDC's information is meant to be used in establishing institutional policies and procedures. The CDC discourages routine site rotation for central venous catheters. The organization states that central venous catheters should be removed when therapy is complete or when there is evidence of a catheter-related complication.

The Food and Drug Administration (FDA) is required to review manufacturer's data for marketing a new catheter. In addition, the FDA must review the product information sheet and directions for use before the product can be marketed.

MedWatch, which is a mandatory reporting service for catheter-related adverse reactions, can be helpful when tracking a history of problems for a specific vascular access device, medication, or infusion equipment such as IV pumps.

Still, with all these organizations providing vascular access device information, standard of care issues can be difficult to identify. Many routine practices associated with the insertion, care, and maintenance of vascular access devices have not been validated by evidence-based research.

B. Standard of Care Issues

1. Clinical competency

Every state has a Board of Nursing whose main responsibility is to license qualified nurses. It is the responsibility of the hiring facility to provide competent qualified nurses to care for their patients. INS and Joint Commission also recommend validation of competency for nursing procedures as deemed necessary by the facility.[33] Nurses who are required to administer intravenous chemotherapy are expected to have documented training on chemotherapeutic agents, mode of action, infusion techniques and adverse reactions.

TIP: Hospital personnel files should include complete program outlines of orientation programs, validated competencies, and inservice continuing education programs which were attended by the nurses. Providing incompetent nurses to deliver infusion therapy is a deviation of the standard of care.

2. Policies and procedures

All regulating bodies, including the state Boards of Nursing, The Joint Commission, and the Infusion Nurses Society, require that nurses have access to current institutional policies and procedures. Many hospitals and other healthcare facilities provide updated nursing policies and procedures in each nursing unit on computers for easy access. These policies should be reviewed annually and approved by an organizational committee. The manual should include the institution's procedures for insertion, care, and maintenance for all vascular access devices, infusion therapies, and infusion related equipment. The manual should provide information to the staff on when, where, and how to document pertinent patient events. There must be an order by a physician for a nurse to initiate infusion therapy. The order should include the therapy, rate of flow, dose, frequency and the signature of the physician. However, it is the responsibility of the nurse to use critical thinking skills to determine if the order is appropriate and if the vascular access device is appropriate for the ordered therapy.

3. Informed consent

All patients have the right to accept or refuse treatment without the threat of retribution. Informed consent should include a description of the vascular access device, a description of the insertion procedure and identification of probable complications, and vascular access device options if applicable. Signed consent forms are most commonly used for insertion of central venous pressure catheters, tunneled catheters, implanted ports, and PICC lines. Identification and description of the consent process in the progress notes is also acceptable.

4. Number of attempts

TIP: The INS Standards of Practice stipulates that only two attempts per practitioner should be made when inserting a vascular access device, but does not limit the number of attempting practitioners.[34]

In some cases patients who have been repeatedly punctured trying to access their veins have successfully sued for assault. The staff's inability to carry out treatment may have significant adverse clinical results.

In a recent South Dakota case, a two-year-old child was admitted to the hospital with severe dehydration. The same nurse attempted unsuccessfully to insert a peripheral IV catheter 16 times. The child was unable to receive fluids, sustained a cardiac arrest and died. The result was an out of court settlement with the hospital for substantial damages (unpublished settlement).

5. The use of armboards

Armboards can be used to stabilize an area of joint flexion (wrist and elbow) to prevent the catheter from moving. Roller bandage should not be used to anchor or secure the extremity to the armboard as this will prevent assessment of the IV site.[35] The use of armboards and their removal should be documented in the nurse's progress notes. Hospitals should have written policies which describe the appropriate use of armboards. If armboards are used, nursing assessment and documentation should include the color and temperature of the skin. The nurse must check the nail beds for color and capillary refill which denotes how well the blood is circulating to the hand. Armboards should be applied in a manner that allows for unimpeded visualization of the IV site.[36]

6. Appropriate infusion solutions and medications

According to the INS Standards of Practice the following IV solutions/medications are not appropriate for infusion into peripheral veins through peripheral IV catheters and midline catheters:[37]

- Continuous vesicant infusions such as Dopamine and many chemotherapy drugs.
- Total Parenteral Nutrition (TPN); reviewers (expert witnesses, risk managers, legal nurse consultants, and attorneys) should look on the TPN order sheet to determine the glucose (sugar) and amino acid (protein) concentration. The sugar concentration should not exceed 10 percent and the protein should not exceed 5 percent. This is an issue in many neonatal IV extravasation malpractice cases.
- Drug pH; the pH of the drug should not exceed 9 or go below 5. A commonly infused antibiotic, Vancomycin, has a pH of 2.4 and should be infused through a central venous catheter.
- Drugs with an osmolality greater than 600 mOsm/L.

It is the responsibility of the nurse to determine that the ordered drug is appropriate for the type and location of the IV device that the patient has in place. Infusing caustic drugs through small veins can result in permanent vein damage and is a deviation from the standard of care.

7. Documentation guidelines

The INS Standards state that nursing documentation should contain complete information regarding infusion therapy and vascular access in the permanent medical record. The documentation should include factors relating to assessment, intervention and the patient's response to the intervention. When multiple catheter devices or multiple catheter lumens are being used, documentation should indicate what fluids and medications are being infused through each pathway. There is an increasing number of computer-based nursing documentation programs being used by healthcare facilities. In most cases these programs are inadequate and insufficient. A check-off box once every 8-12 hours is an incomplete assessment. Phrases such as "IV infusing well," "no redness or swelling noted," "dressing dry and intact" and "site WNL" are insufficient. Nurses should document their observation of peripheral and central venous catheter sites. Nursing documentation, and the lack thereof, is a major contributing factor in many nursing malpractice cases.

24.6 Vascular Access Device Complications

This section discusses the most common complications related to peripheral and central venous catheters which result in malpractice claims.

A. Peripheral Access Devices

1. Nerve injury

Nerve injuries related to peripheral IV device insertion and phlebotomy have been reported in the medical literature since the late 1990s. A neuroma (scar tissue on the nerve) can form on the surface of the nerve when the needle makes contact with the nerve. Permanent progressive nerve injury can be the result when the nerve fibers are cut with an IV needle.[38]

Needle injury to the radial nerve during peripheral vascular access device insertion is a common needle insertion injury which can result in Reflex Sympathetic Dystrophy (RSD) which has been renamed Complex Regional Pain Syndrome (CRPS).[39] This can be a permanent, progressive, painful disability. Needle injury to the median nerve in the antecubital fossa (inner elbow) during a blood drawing procedure can result in this injury. Important issues related to nerve injuries are the angle of the needle during the insertion procedure and how far the needle is initially inserted. The higher the angle, the higher the risk for nerve contact. The maximum angulation of the needle during insertion should be 0-15 degrees. Only the tip of the needle should be inserted initially to minimize nerve contact. The distal one-third of the cephalic vein, just above the thumb, should be avoided because the radial nerve is superficial in this area. The inner aspect of the wrist above the palm of the hand should also be avoided, as the median nerve is superficial in this area.[40] Injury to the distal median nerve can result in carpal tunnel syndrome. When the needle makes contact with the nerve, the patient will complain of an immediate "electric shock" sensation down the arm into the fingertips and/or numbness or tingling. Ulnar nerve injury has been reported with the improper insertion technique of a PICC line. This procedure should be performed using ultrasound to identify and locate the vein and the nerve, which will reduce the opportunity to contact the nerve.[41] The appropriate intervention is to remove the needle immediately. Documentation of the adverse event should be found in the progress notes, on an unusual occurrence form or a variance report.

The expertise of the phlebotomist/nurse was an issue in the following cases:

> The plaintiff, age 17, went to a Foundation Hospital in February 2006 for a routine venipuncture. The plaintiff claimed that the angle used by the phlebotomist to insert the needle was inappropriate, causing a deep needle stick to the right median nerve in the right cubital fossa. The plaintiff claimed that she suffered complex regional pain syndrome with extreme

burning pain in the right arm and hand, swelling of the right arm and hand, right arm discoloration, stiffness to the joints in the right arm, uncontrollable muscle spasms in the right arm and an overall lack of strength. The plaintiff underwent some physical therapy for the arm, but was unable to continue it due to pain. The plaintiff claimed that she was told that she would require surgery with a dorsal column stimulator to send electric impulses into her right arm to alleviate the pain. The defendant maintained that any injury which the plaintiff sustained should have resolved within a year. According to published account an arbitrator awarded $959,700.[42]

The deviation from the standard of care was the angle of the needle during the blood drawing procedure. The higher the angle, the more opportunity to hit the median nerve. This was a deciding factor determined by the jury to have caused the injury.

The plaintiff was admitted to the cardiac care unit of Medical South in February 2003. Her physicians ordered periodic blood tests. Over the next three days the plaintiff's right arm began to swell and become painful and numb. A vascular surgeon was called for a consult. He initiated conservative treatment. The next day surgery was performed which revealed a hematoma in her right arm caused by a breach of a vein or artery which had occurred during a blood draw. The defendant claimed that there was no negligence and that the surgeon should have performed surgery earlier. According to a verdict reporting source a $3 million verdict was returned for the plaintiff and her husband was awarded $500,000 for lost consortium. A confidential post-trial settlement was reached.[43]

The lack of proper assessment of the IV site and the lack of documentation were the deviations from the standards of care in this case.

2. Infiltration

Infiltration occurs when the vascular access device punctures the vein and non-vesicant solutions or medications enter the surrounding tissue.[44] The main symptoms of infiltration are swelling and coolness around the IV site. The IV site is cool because the IV fluids that are leaking under the skin are not body temperature. Nurses are required to assess the IV site by palpation and visualization through the intact transparent IV dressing.[45] At the first sign of an infil-

tration, the infusion should be stopped and the IV device removed. The most important issue related to infiltration malpractice cases is the amount of IV fluid in the tissue. *Small* infiltrations are not always preventable. *Large* infiltrations are preventable with frequent and proper IV site assessment. Nurses should measure and document the size of the swollen area.[46] The routine application of warm or cold compresses to the infiltrated site and/or elevation of the affected extremity without a physician order are a deviation from the standard of nursing care. Ongoing, frequent assessment of the IV site for skin changes is required. In the event of a large infiltration, the physician should be notified immediately if the patient complains of numbness and tingling within the swollen area. This is a symptom of a nerve compression injury which can result in compartment syndrome. If not treated appropriately a surgical fasciotomy (opening the skin to relieve pressure within the tissue) may be required to prevent permanent nerve injury.[47]

In the following case, the lack of site assessment and size of the infiltration were the two issues at trial:

The plaintiff, age 43, was diagnosed with nasal airway obstruction, and surgery was recommended for the nose. Before the surgery, performed in June 1996, an IV line was placed on the top of the plaintiff's right hand near her wrist for administration of anesthesia and fluids. The plaintiff began to feel severe pain in the hand and arm where the IV had been placed and was fully awake and in pain for the entire surgery. The IV line placement was not checked during the surgery. At the end of the surgery the plaintiff was unable to move her right arm due to massive swelling. In the recovery room the patient's hand and arm were elevated and warm compresses were applied. The plaintiff suffered infiltration of the IV into the tissue of the arm, instead of the circulatory system. The arm was painful and swollen for several weeks after surgery. Two years after the procedure the plaintiff underwent two surgeries to recompress the radial and ulnar nerves. The plaintiff was left with large scars. The plaintiff also claimed that she continued to experience stiffness, loss of mobility and range of motion, burning, throbbing, aching and general pain in the right arm and hand. The nurse anesthetist claimed that it was the anesthesiologist who started the IV. The anesthesiologist claimed that his only contact with the plaintiff was when he examined her in the recovery room. According to published accounts a $500,000 settlement was reached.[48]

3. Extravasation

Extravasation occurs when the vascular access device punctures the vein and vesicant solution enters the tissue. A vesicant is a medication/solution that is capable of burning the skin and surrounding tissue.[49] The most important identifiable symptoms of extravasation are swelling and coolness around the IV site. Patients may or may not complain of burning or stinging during the extravasation. Extravasation may result in blisters, blackening of the skin, and eventually skin loss and can cause significant tissue, muscle and nerve injuries requiring skin debridements, skin grafting, and in many cases amputation. Extravasation is significantly more damaging to the skin, muscle and nerves than infiltration. Nurses who infuse vesicants must be extra vigilant when assessing the IV site for the earliest possible symptoms of extravasation. There are many recommendations for antidotes to reverse adverse tissue effects; however, there is no research data that validates the use of these antidotes.[50]

TIP: Prevention is the best treatment for extravasation.

Non-chemotherapy vesicants are administered by nurses on a daily basis. These can include IV solutions that contain calcium, magnesium and concentrated potassium chloride. There are no antidotes for these extravasations. In addition, there are chemotherapy drugs that are very dangerous vesicants, including anthracyclines such as Adriamycin. New on the market is an FDA-approved drug to reverse the tissue damage associated with anthracycline extravasations. Totect has been proven to reverse the tissue damage associated with anthracycline extravasations.[51] However, it must be infused as soon as possible and within six hours of the extravasation event. This is the only FDA-approved drug which will reverse potential tissue damage related to anthracycline extravasations. For all other chemotherapy vesicant extravasations, prevention is the best treatment, since there are no reliable treatments.[52]

In the following case, site assessment was the main issue at trial:

> The plaintiff, age 55, was hospitalized in April 2003. The plaintiff claimed that the ICU nurse was negligent in failing to timely assess the IV site, initiate the appropriate intervention and call a physician about the development of an IV extravasation of calcium gluconate. This caused severe pain, swelling and dark nail beds. The plaintiff also claimed that the orthopedic hand specialist physicians were negligent in failing to diagnose and treat an unrecognized forearm compartment syndrome and in failing to timely diagnose and treat a recognized hand

compartment syndrome within the six-hour window of opportunity to re-establish blood flow before the tissue in the arm and hand died. The plaintiff's right arm and hand lost circulation for eight and one-half hours, became necrotic, died and ultimately required a mid-forearm amputation. According to a published account a $450,000 verdict was returned.[53]

The compartment syndrome was a result of a large amount of IV fluid in the tissue. The calcium burned the tissue in the arm which resulted in the amputation. The jury found negligence in all counts.

TIP: The key clinical issue for infiltration and extravasation is the amount of solution in the tissue.

> In the following case, the plaintiff, a 34-year-old man working as a child care provider, was a cancer treatment patient at the defendant's hospital. While receiving IV treatment involving ABVD chemotherapy, there was an extravasation that went unappreciated during the full administration of the treatment, despite the plaintiff raising specific complaints regarding pain and discomfort. As a consequence, the claimant developed a 5-by-5 centimeter dark tender area over the dorsum area of the hand, hypersensitivity, limited motion of the right finger, a "swan neck" deformity of the small finger and some Reflex Sympathetic Dystrophy with chronic pain, all of which are deemed to be permanent. The defense alleged the IV was properly administered, and that the area of injury was not at the site of the IV. This case proceeded to trial, where the jury awarded the plaintiff $322,000.[54]

TIP: Removal of the access device, immediate physician notification, appropriate nursing interventions and surgical intervention should be documented along with the patient's complaints in the progress notes. Many of these patients require extensive follow-up care with orthopedists, vascular surgeons, and plastic surgeons to treat the damaged areas.[55]

B. Central Venous Catheter Complications

1. Catheter malposition

TIP: All central venous catheter tip locations must be verified by radiologic confirmation in the superior vena cava prior to use.

The standard of care for infusing through any type of central venous catheter is to verify the location of the catheter tip radiographically by chest x-ray prior to use. The positions of INS, ONS, SIR, AVA, and the FDA are that correct catheter tip location is in the superior vena cava (SVC). Optimal tip location is the distal one-third of the SVC or the atrial caval junction.[56] When catheter tips rest in other venous locations, such as the subclavian or the brachiocephalic vein, the incidence of thrombus (clot) formation and vein perforation increases exponentially. The only exception is for hemodialysis catheters, which can reside in the right atrium of the heart because of the required high pressures during the dialysis procedure. Nurses who infuse through central venous catheters must have x-ray confirmation of tip placement prior to use. If the catheter tip is not in the SVC, the catheter should not be used for any infusion of any type for any duration of time. The result of infusing through malpositioned catheters can be permanent injury and in many cases has resulted in patient fatalities.[57] The best tip location is in the SVC, which is straight for approximately three inches in the center of the chest allowing the catheter to rest inside the vein without making contact with the vein wall. Blood flows through the SVC at a rate of 2000 mls/minute which allows for maximum dilution of the medication/solution with blood, eliminating complications such as vein irritation and perforation. Hospitals should have specific policies stating that central venous catheters require radiographic confirmation of the catheter tip in the SVC immediately after catheter insertion. The catheter cannot be used for any infusion until x-ray confirmation is obtained.[58]

In the following case the initial x-ray report showed the catheter tip in the wrong place:

> The plaintiff, an 11-month-old girl, developed respiratory distress after cardiac catheterization. Upon admission to the recovery area, the child had an elevated heart rate and respiratory rate. Her lower extremity pulses were diminished, indicating poor perfusion. Four days later, the cardiologist placed a central venous catheter in the patient jugular vein. An x-ray report indicated that the tip of the catheter appeared to pass into the right atrium of the heart, and to lie a little beyond the margin of the heart. The plaintiffs contended that the cardiologist rendered substandard care when he failed to adjust the position of the catheter before it was used to infuse IV fluids. The next day the child suffered cardiorespiratory arrest and, despite respiratory efforts, died. X-ray of the lungs showed that the IV fluid completely filled the right lung.

> Autopsy revealed that the jugular catheter was outside the vein, in the neck passing through parietal pleura into the right pleural cavity. The defendants claimed they provided proper care. The case settled for $2.4 million.[59]

If the doctors and nurses had verified correct catheter tip placement prior to infusing the catheter the child would not have died.

The next case resulted in a substantial settlement during trial. The events were marked by physician miscommunication.

> The decedent was admitted to the hospital by defendant Dr. Mac with a presumed diagnosis of Crohn's disease. Defendant ordered a central venous catheter for the purpose of infusing IV fluids and total parenteral nutrition, which was performed by defendant Dr. Z, a general surgeon. Dr. Z positioned the catheter in the right atrium of the decedent's heart. Dr. Z allegedly discovered the catheter was incorrectly positioned in the decedent's heart after reviewing the chest x-ray films, but the plaintiffs claimed Dr. Z left the catheter in decedent's heart and ordered it could be utilized in that position. Plaintiffs also alleged Dr. Z was negligent in failing to withdraw the catheter from the right atrium into the superior vena cava and failing to inform decedent and Dr. Mac that the catheter was in a position that could result in perforation of the heart and a cardiac tamponade. Dr. Z admitted he fell below the standard of care when he left the catheter in the decedent's heart. Plaintiffs alleged Dr. Mac, a gastroenterologist, discovered the catheter was positioned in the decedent's heart but did not reposition it or request that Dr. Z reposition it. Dr. Mac left town for a medical conference without informing the on-call physician, defendant Dr. H, of the misplaced central venous catheter, which was infusing IV fluids and TPN. Dr. Mac denied liability and claimed that reliance on Dr. Z to place the catheter properly was appropriate and the standard of care did not require a gastroenterologist to know it was dangerous to leave the catheter in the patient's heart.

> The decedent awoke in the night with complaints of chest pain, chest tightness, and a blood pressure of 68/44. Hospital nurses contacted Dr. H, who believed the decedent was having either a cardiac event or pulmonary embolism and ordered diagnostic tests. Decedent's condition continued to

deteriorate over the next hour and ten minutes until a code was called. Plaintiffs claimed that the catheter perforated decedent's heart and deposited TPN in the pericardial sac, which caused an acute cardiac tamponade. The defense claimed that cardiac tamponade was not the cause of death. A defense expert admitted that the catheter perforated the decedent's heart and deposited TPN in her pericardial sac, which caused a fatal arrhythmia. S Health Systems settled prior to trial for a confidential amount. During trial, the matter settled for $1.2 million (unpublished verdict).

2. Catheter malfunction

TIP: The only reliable method to determine if the central venous catheter is still in a vein and is functioning properly is to aspirate (withdraw) 3 mls of blood prior to each infusion.

Lack of a substantial 3 ml free flowing blood return is indicative of a catheter malfunction.[60] Lack of blood return could be the result of a catheter tip outside the vein, causing the intravenous fluid to enter the chest cavity, or of a catheter that has broken inside the patient. However, the most common reason for lack of blood is the presence of a fibrin sheath completely encapsulating the outer catheter surface as well as the catheter tip. Symptoms include the ability to infuse solution/medications without resistance, but little or no blood can be aspirated from the catheter. Evidence-based research has proved that all central venous catheters will become encapsulated in a fibrin sheath within ten days of the catheter insertion.[61] This appears to be the body's protective mechanism against the foreign body catheter. The fibrin sheath will continue to grow if not removed on a timely basis. If no blood return is obtained, a physician's order for the instillation of Cathflo (Alteplase) should be obtained. Cathflo is the only FDA-approved drug for catheter clearance. This procedure is painless to the patient and has few associated risks. Infusing through a fibrin-sheathed catheter increases significantly the risk of blockage of the vein with a blood clot, thrombus formation, and extravasation. Salvaging the catheter, as opposed to catheter removal, is the appropriate intervention.

Nurses do not always document that they have verified proper functioning of the central line prior to medication administration. They may testify that this is their normal routine. In the following case, the nurse was asked to explain the term "no blood return." The nurse assigned a benign meaning to the term. However, "no blood return" was inter-

preted to mean that the device was not functioning properly. Major clinical damages resulted from this incident.

The plaintiff, age 69, had cancer in her right breast and went to an oncology clinic for chemotherapy. She underwent two treatment sessions through an intravenous needle positioned into an access port surgically implanted above her left healthy breast. During the third session, the chemotherapy drug Adriamycin leaked out of the port and into the left breast tissue. As a result, the healthy breast became necrotic and the plaintiff required a mastectomy and breast reconstruction. The plaintiff claimed that the needle was improperly positioned during the third treatment session, causing it to become dislodged. The plaintiff also claimed that the nurses had failed to properly monitor her, which allowed a full bag of Adriamycin to be administered into the healthy breast tissue. According to a published account a $500,000 verdict was awarded.[62]

Mrs. P was diagnosed with non-Hodgkin's lymphoma. She was to receive six cycles of Adriamycin, Oncovin, and Cytoxan in an outpatient facility. Prior to her first cycle she received an implanted port. On cycle one, two, and three the nurse noted a positive blood return, and the chemotherapy was infused without incident. The fourth cycle documentation noted that no blood return was obtained, but the port flushed easily and the chemotherapy was infused. The fifth cycle documentation revealed "Mediport accessed with 20-gauge huber needle, no blood return—flushes freely. Pre meds given. Adriamycin 85 mgms in 50 cc's over 15 minutes—halfway through infusion patient complained of discomfort. Area appeared swollen, ice applied. Dr. notified."

Mrs. P returned to the clinic two days later with her chest and breast swollen, red, hard, and blistered. There was a large infected cavity. A large area of slough encompassed the entire breast and nipple. Follow-up with a surgeon resulted in a mastectomy due to the extreme amount of tissue damage.

The nurse testified that "no blood return" means that there is a fibrin sheath on the end of the catheter—but this was normal and to be expected. It was not an indication that the port was malfunctioning. The jury awarded $1 million to the plaintiff (unpublished settlement).

Confirmation of the central venous catheter tip location can be found on chest x-ray or fluoroscopy reports. Once tip placement has been confirmed, the location should be recorded on the Medication Administration Record (MAR). A physician's order "OK to use" does not provide the anatomical location of the catheter tip and is an invalid order. Central venous catheters used in hospitals, home care, long-term care, outpatient facilities, and so on must follow the same rules. Nurses should document in the progress notes the presence and amount of blood flow obtained prior to each infusion. Using central venous catheters without verifying a blood return is a gross deviation from the standard of care.[63]

3. Air embolism

Air embolism may cause anoxic encephalopathy; it is defined as the presence of air within the vascular system. The exact amount of air required to cause damage or death is controversial. However, most experts agree that a minimum of 15 mls (1/2 ounce) of air bolus can result in transient or permanent neurologic deficits. Minor to major strokes, permanent vegetative states and fatalities have been reported to be caused by intravascular air embolism.[64]

How does air enter the vascular system? There must be a direct or indirect opening into the vascular system. This can occur when the IV catheter is removed at the completion of the therapy or the catheter is accidentally pulled out by the patient. The direct opening into the vascular/venous system must be above the level of the heart while the patient simultaneously changes her intrathoracic pressure (chest pressure). This is done by crying, laughing, sneezing, coughing, yelling, vomiting, deep breathing, and so on. The change in chest pressure will allow air to enter the vascular/venous system through the catheter exit site. Seconds is all the time needed for air in the vascular system to enter the right ventricle, causing an "air lock."[65] The air will prevent any blood from entering the pulmonary circulation and/or will cause a displacement of blood to the brain. This will result in a drop in blood pressure, a rapid pulse rate and confusion followed by lack of consciousness and possibly death. Subclavian and in particular jugular vein access sites and catheters are high risk for air embolism because they are located above heart level. Physicians and nurses who insert these catheters should be cognizant of risk of air embolism during the insertion procedure. It is especially important to prevent air from entering the vascular system when the wire is removed from the introducer needle before the catheter is inserted. Many catheter manufacturers discuss this risk in the FDA-approved product and insertion procedure information included on all product trays.[66]

Healthcare providers who care for patients with subclavian or jugular vein catheters also need to understand the risk of air embolism. Air can enter the vascular system when the IV tubing is changed, when catheter end caps are changed and when the catheter is discontinued or removed. Any time the catheter is opened to air, the nurse should instruct the patient on the Valsalva maneuver. The patient takes a deep breath and holds it, while the IV tubing/cap is changed. This maneuver stabilizes the intrathoracic chest pressure and prevents air from entering the open catheter. The Joint Commission and INS recommend that only Leurloc connections (screw-on) be used to prevent accidental IV tubing/cap disconnection.[67]

When the central venous catheter is removed, application of a gel-based ointment (Neosporin, triple antibiotic, etc.) should be applied liberally to the venous opening, followed by a transparent dressing. The gel-based ointment will prevent air from entering the venous system. The INS Standards state that the catheter exit site should be assessed every 24 hours until the site is epithelialized (scab formation). The scab will prevent air from entering the vascular system and then the dressing can be removed.[68]

What should the healthcare provider do if air embolism is suspected? Immediately stop further air from entering the vascular system by pinching the open IV catheter or covering the opening to the vascular system. Once this is accomplished, turn the patient on her left side, place her in the Trendelenburg position (head down, feet up) and notify the physician. The positioning will allow the air to rise to the top of the right ventricle and permit the blood to flow into the pulmonary circulation. A surgeon can use CT scans to visualize the air and can employ intracardiac needles to remove the air.[69]

With the increase in the number of jugular vein catheter sites, the number of air embolism cases is increasing. Air embolism in peripheral IV catheters is rare because the vein opening is below heart level. Most peripheral IV air embolism cases are due to pumped or injected air into the venous system. As of October 1, 2008, Medicare has classified IV catheter-related air embolism as a "never" event. Medicare reported 45 air embolism cases in 2006. Medicare, as well as many other insurance companies, will not reimburse hospitals for the treatment of air embolism. Air embolism can be difficult to diagnose and almost impossible to treat with success. Education of the healthcare providers is essential for the safety of the patients.

From a legal perspective, hospitals should have a central venous catheter removal policy and procedures, which details the application of ointment to prevent air embolism. Only physicians and trained registered nurses can remove central venous catheters. There should be documentation in the nurses' personnel files that their competency has been validated and they are permitted to remove central venous catheters.

In the following case the defendant hospital admitted that the nurses did not follow hospital policy:

The plaintiff, age 51, was admitted to the hospital in September 2003 for revision of an implantable morphine pump used to control pain. Prior to the plaintiff's discharge, the defendant nurse removed the right subclavian central venous catheter. After removal of the central venous catheter, the plaintiff sustained a stroke. The plaintiff claimed the removal of the catheter, while the plaintiff was seated in an upright position, caused an air embolism which resulted in a right frontal lobe infarction. Prior to the trial, the defendants admitted negligence in the training of its nurse, violation of policy and procedures regarding removal of the IV catheter and negligence by the nurse in removal of the IV catheter. The defendants did not admit that removal of the IV catheter was the legal cause of the stroke and argued that the blood clot was due to a dilated cardiomyopathy. According to Florida Jury Verdict Reporter a $3,826,991 verdict was returned.[70]

On September 13, 2000, CF was born with a cardiac murmur and was transferred to a hospital to be worked up for his cardiac defect. After the work-up it was determined he had a significant cardiac anomaly which would require a total of three surgeries early in his lifetime. On September 22, 2000, he was taken to surgery for the first of three operations. As the anesthesiologist gave medication through an umbilical venous catheter line, CF dropped in blood pressure and went into an arrest. The cardiac surgeon was called to the operating room. Upon her arrival, she noted air bubbles in the IV line. Open cardiac massage was performed. However, the infant died on the table. The cardiac surgeon noted when performing the open cardiac massage that the heart was filled with air. Likewise, an autopsy indicated that the cause of death was due to air embolism. The likely scenario was that the IV line was not purged of air. There were three health care providers involved with the setup and the control of the intravenous line. All blamed each other. The plaintiff's expert indicated the entire anesthesia team was responsible for the mistake. The plaintiff's cardiolo-

gist, however, indicated that the plaintiff had an impaired life expectancy, and that each one of the three early surgeries carried a significant risk of mortality and morbidity. According to a published account, the case was settled prior to trial for $325,000.[71]

One of the main issues of this case was that the nurses did not follow hospital policies and procedures.

4. IV catheter-related sepsis/infection

Each year many thousands of catheter-related infections are reported. According to the CDC, catheter-related bloodstream infections are the eighth leading cause of death in the United States. Staph epidermidis, an organism commonly found on the skin, is most often the source of the infection.[72] Using sterile technique, cleansing the skin properly with Chlorhexidine prior to catheter insertion and using maximum barrier precautions (sterile draping the patient from head to foot) will significantly reduce the incidence of infection.[73] Catheter-related infections have been litigated with minimal success even when the patient dies. There are many extenuating circumstances which may have contributed to the infection; however, it is difficult to prove in a court of law that there was a deviation from the standard of care. Important evidence of infection such as sudden temperature elevations, positive catheter tip cultures and positive blood cultures should be documented in the patient's record.[74]

In the following case the peripheral IV catheter remained in place for five days, which is longer than the three day standard of care:

The plaintiff, a 48-year-old woman, suffering from chronic Hepatitis C, was released from the hospital with instructions to a home health care agency to provide her with a hep-lock IV therapy of saline solution for five days. The home health care nurses left the IV in longer than reasonable, failed to recognize symptoms of infection, and failed to timely return to effectively monitor the patient's IV site after conclusion of the treatment. The plaintiff's arm was so severely infected with a staphylococcus infection that the cephalic vein had to be removed from the wrist to several inches above the elbow. After two surgeries attempting to remove scar tissue from the radial, nerve, without reduction in severe pain, the patient opted for dissection of the nerve to alleviate the pain. This procedure resulted in residual numbness at the nerve distribution. Reflex Sympathetic Dystrophy developed in the arm and this was treated by placement of a spinal cord stimulator that the patient will require for the remainder of her life. The jury rendered a verdict in the amount of $2,383,181 for the injured plaintiff and $75,000 for the spouse.[75]

The plaintiff, age 36, was treated for a headache at Mercy Hospital in October 2000. While there, the plaintiff received intravenous medications and fluids through an IV placed in her wrist. Prior to discharge four days later the IV catheter was removed and her wrist was warm compressed. The plaintiff, however, complained of wrist pain where the IV had been. The plaintiff was again admitted to the hospital with pain, swelling and discoloration in her right hand and forearm. Dr. N diagnosed the plaintiff with cellulitis and consulted Dr. Z, a vascular surgeon. Later that day the plaintiff was transported to University Hospital, where she underwent emergency compartment syndrome surgery. Dr. C, an orthopedic surgeon, was called to attend to the plaintiff, but reportedly refused to do so. The plaintiff alleged negligence in the failure to diagnose and treat the wrist pain during the initial hospitalization. The plaintiff alleged negligence in failing to properly treat the cellulitis. The plaintiff claimed that she suffered extreme pain and suffering, scarring, embarrassment, emotional distress and limitation on the use of her wrist. The defendants denied negligence and claimed that the plaintiff had suffered a known complication. According to Trial Reporter a defense verdict was returned.[76]

Even though the plaintiff obviously had an injury related to the IV device, the jury felt there were no deviations in the standard of care.

24.7 Clinical and Liability Issues

The areas of intravenous infusion therapy and peripheral and central venous catheters are fraught with areas of nursing malpractice. High-risk areas of nursing liability are:

1. Not rotating peripheral IV catheters every 72 hours to prevent complications and to maintain vein health.
2. Not removing peripheral IV catheters at the first sign of an IV complication.
3. Inserting peripheral IV catheters into the wrist above the thumb, the inner aspect of wrist above the palm, the antecubital fossa and the ankle area specifically in neonates. These areas are high risk

for nerve injury, infiltration and extravasation.
4. Not assessing the IV site at appropriate intervals leading to the advancement of non-serious complications to very serious complications.
5. Not describing what the IV site looks like when the IV device is removed.
6. Not verifying the anatomical location of all central venous catheter tips. Using central venous catheters with tips outside the vena cava have led to serious complications including patient death.
7. Not obtaining a 3 ml blood return on all central venous catheters. Without a blood return there is no proof that the catheter is still in the vein and functioning properly.
8. Not applying an air occlusive dressing when a central venous catheter is removed intentionally or accidentally.
9. Not documenting a complete assessment of the catheter site (no check marks).
10. Not notifying the physician in a timely manner when the patient presents with early signs of IV-related complications.

The above listed areas are deviations from the standard of nursing care when caring for patients with venous catheters. Nurses who follow the standards of nursing practice and the standards of nursing care have a very good chance of winning their cases. However, if it can be proven that the injury sustained by the plaintiff was a direct cause of not following the nursing standards, then a plaintiff verdict is likely.

24.8 Conclusion

The number of infusion and vascular access device malpractice cases has increased dramatically over the past five years. Many vascular access injuries result in serious tissue damage and sometimes the demise of the patient. Standards of care and standards of practice issues can easily be identified in many malpractice cases. Hopefully, the number of malpractice cases will increase the awareness of healthcare professionals to the seriousness of the injuries that can result from negligent vascular access device insertion and care.

Endnotes

1. Centers for Disease Control and Prevention. "Guidelines for Prevention of Intravascular Catheter Related Infections." *MMWR*. August 9, 2002.

2. Plumer, A.L. *Principles and Practice of Intravenous Therapy, Seventh Edition*, Philadelphia PA., Lippincott, Williams and Wilkins 2007.

3. *Id.*

4. Schelper, R. "The Aging Venous *System." Journal of Vascular Access.* Fall 2003, p. 8-10.

5. *Infusion Nursing Standards of Practice.* INS, 10 Fawcett Street, Cambridge, MA 02138, November 2006.

6. *See* note 1.

7. *See* note 5.

8. *See* note 2.

9. *See* note 5.

10. *Id.*

11. *Id.*

12. "NAVAN Position Statement." *Journal of Vascular Access Devices,* Summer 1998 p. 9-11.

13. Terry. J. et al. *Intravenous Therapy Clinical Principles and Practice, Third Edition* Philadelphia, PA: W.B. Saunders Company 2009.

14. Acquillo, G. "Blood Transfusion Flow Rates.*" Journal of the Association of Vascular Access* Winter 2007 Vol. 12, No. 4.

15. Vesely, T. et al. "The Diverse and Conflicting Standards and Practice in Infusion Therapy." *Journal of Vascular Access Devices.* Fall 2002.

16. Ray, C., *Central Venous Access,* Philadelphia, PA, Lippincott Williams & Wilkins 2001.

17. *Id.*

18. Wise, M. et al. "Catheter Tip Position: A Sign of Things to Come." *JVAD,* Summer 2001.

19. *IV Therapy Made Incredibly Easy,* Lippincott, Williams & Wilkins, Philadelphia, PA 2006.

20. Sorrell, D. *Access Device Guidelines: Recommendations for Nursing Practice & Education* Pittsburgh, PA, Oncology Nurses Society 2004.

21. *See* note 16.

22. *See* note 1.

23. Wilson, S. *Vascular Access: Principles and Practice, Fourth Edition.* Mosby—St. Louis, MO. 2002.

24. Phillips, L. *Manual of IV Therapeutics, Fourth Edition,* FA Davis, Philadelphia, PA 2005.

25. *Id.*

26. *See* note 2.

27. *See* note 1.

28. *See* note 23.

29. *See* note 2.

30. Masoorli, S. "Pediatric Infusion Therapy: Small Children at High Risk." *Journal of the Association for Vascular Access,* Fall 2003, p. 42-43.

31. *See* note 5.

32. *Id.*

33. *See* note 24.

34. *See* note 5.

35. *Id.*

36. *Id.*

37. *Id.*

38. Schull, P. *IV Drug Handbook.* McGraw-Hill, New York, 2009.

39. Horowitz, S. "Venipuncture-Induced Causalgia: Anatomic Relations of Upper Extremity Superficial Veins and Nerves, and Clinical Consideration.*" Transfusion,* September 2000, Vol. 40.

40. Masoorli, S. "Nerve Injuries Related to Vascular Access Insertion and Assessment." *Journal of Infusion Nursing,* November / December 2007: Vol. 30 No. 6.

41. *See* note 39.

42. Laska, L. "Teenager Claims Venipuncture Caused Median Nerve Injury With CRPS." *Medical Malpractice Verdicts, Settlements and Experts.* March 2009 p. 26.

43. Laska, L. "Women Claims Blood Draw Caused Hematoma and Swelling in Arm." *Medical Malpractice Verdicts Settlements and Experts.* January 2010, p. 17.

44. Fabian, B. "Intravenous Complications: Infiltration," *Journal of Infusion Nursing,* July/August 2000.

45. *See* note 5.

46. Masoorli, S. "Legal Issues Related to Vascular Access Devices and Infusion Therapy." *Journal of Infusion Therapy,* May/June 2005: Vol. 28 No. 38.

47. *See* note 40.

48. Laska. L. "IV Infiltration (Extravasation) Causes Arm Injuries and Need for Multiple Surgeries." *Medical Malpractice Verdicts, Settlements and Experts.* November 2004, p. 2.

49. *See* note 5.

50. *Id.*

51. Oncology Nurses Society *Chemotherapy and Biotherapy Guidelines and Recommendations for Practice, Third Edition* 2009.

52. *Id.*

53. Laska, L. "Failure to Timely Inform Physician of IV Infiltration (Extravasation)." *Medical Malpractice Verdicts, Settlements and Experts.* July 2007, p. 20.

54. Laska, L. "Extravasation from IV Results in Pain, Deformity of Finger and RSD." *Medical Malpractice Verdicts, Settlements and Experts.* April 2006, p. 25.

55. *See* note 5.

56. *See* note 15, 23.

57. *See* note 54.

58. *See* note 5, 15, 24.

59. Laska, L. "Death of 11-Month Old Girl Following Cardiac Catheterization Blamed on Misplaced Central Venous Line." *Medical Malpractice Verdicts, Settlements and Experts.* September 2002, p. 5 and 6.

60. *See* note 15, 45.

61. *Id.*

62. Laska, L. "Adriamycin Leaked During Chemotherapy Treatment Causing Need for Mastectomy." *Medical Malpractice Verdicts, Settlements and Experts.* May 2009, p. 37.

63. *See* note 4.

64. Froede, R. *Handbook of Forensic Pathology, Second Edition,* Northfield, IL, 2003.

65. Hadaway, L. "Air Embolus" *Nursing 2002,* October 2002.

66. *See* note 62.

67. *See* note 5.

68. *Id.*

69. *See* note 62.

70. Laska, L. "Air Embolism from Inappropriate Removal of (CVC) IV Line Blamed for Stroke." *Medical Malpractice Verdicts, Settlements and Experts.* June 2007, p. 17.

71. Laska, L. "Air in Unpurged IV Line Results in Embolus and Wrongful Death of Infant." *Medical Malpractice Verdicts Settlements and Experts.* November 2003, p. 26.

72. *See* note 1.

73. Hatler, C. et al. "Walk the Walk to Reduce Catheter – Related Blood Stream Infections" *American Nurse Today.* January 2010: Vol. 5 No. 1.

74. *Id.*

75. *Id.*

76. Laska, L. "Home Healthcare Service Causes Serious Infection in Arm." *Medical Malpractice Verdicts, Settlements and Experts.* September 2001, p. 24.

77. Laska, L. "Failure to Diagnose and Properly Treat Cellulitis Caused by IV in Wrist." *Medical Malpractice Verdicts Settlements and Experts,* May 2009, p. 10.

Chapter 25

Wounds

Martie Hawkins, RN-BC, BSN, CWOCN, CCM

Synopsis

25.1 Introduction
25.2 Definitions
    A. Traumatic Wounds
    B. Surgical Wounds
    C. Chronic Wounds
    D. Burn Wounds
    E. Arterial Insufficiency Ulcers
    F. Venous Stasis Ulcers
    G. Neuropathic (Diabetic) Ulcers
    H. Pressure Ulcers
    I. Terminal Ulcers
25.3 Assessment of Wounds
25.4 Disease Burden
25.5 Skin Assessment
    A. Descriptive Characteristics
    B. Measurements
25.6 Characteristics of Wounds and Ulcers
    A. Documenting
        1. Tunneling
        2. Undermining
        3. Edges
        4. Wound bed
        5. Periwound skin
        6. Drainage (exudate)
    B. Staging
        1. Stage I
        2. Stage II
        3. Stage III
        4. Stage IV
        5. Unstageable
        6. Suspected deep tissue injury—depth unknown
    C. Causative Factors
        1. Pressure
        2. Shearing
        3. Friction
        4. Chemical breakdown
    D. Assessment
    E. Early Skin Damage
        1. Blanchable
        2. Nonblanchable
    F. Avoidable Versus Unavoidable Ulcers
        1. Unavoidable pressure ulcers
        2. Avoidable pressure ulcers
        3. Refusals
    G. Photography
    H. Pressure Ulcer Risk-Screening Tools
        1. Braden Scale
        2. Norton scale

        3. PUSH tool
25.7 Burns
    A. Classification of Burn Injuries
        1. First-degree burns
        2. Second-degree burns (partial thickness)
        3. Second-degree burns (deep partial thickness)
        4. Third-degree burns (full thickness)
        5. Fourth-degree burns (destruction of muscle and bone)
    B. Transfer of Burn Patients
25.8 Other Ulcers
    A. Arterial Ulcers
    B. Venous Ulcers
25.9 Plan of Care
25.10 Pain
25.11 Major Comorbid Conditions
    A. Systemic Conditions
    B. Tissue Perfusion
    C. Anemia
    D. Edema
    E. Moisture
    F. Incontinence
    G. Nutritional Status
        1. Protein calorie malnutrition (PCM)
        2. Lab values
        3. Pressure ulcers and nutrition
        4. Weight
    H. Obesity
    I. Diabetes
    J. Infection
    K. Infection and Pressure Ulcers
    L. Steroids
    M. Aging
    N. Immunocompromised
    O. Stress
25.12 Contributing Comorbid Factors
25.13 Wounds, Pressure Ulcers, and Legal Implications
    A. Chronic Wounds
    B. Treatment Plan
25.14 Aggressive Wound Care Management
    A. Goals of Healing
    B. Cleansing
    C. Debridement
        1. Autolytic
        2. Mechanical
        3. Chemical
        4. Surgical
        5. Maggot debridement
    D. Appropriate Dressing
    E. Wound Care Specialist

F. Interventions for Prevention
G. Support Surfaces, and Pressure Reduction and Relief
   1. Bedbound
   2. Chairbound
   3. Elevate heels
   4. Pillow positioning
   5. Mobility and activity
H. Education of the Patient, Caregiver, and Significant Other
25.15 Sources of Standards of Care
   A. AHCPR Guidelines
   B. NPUAP
   C. Literature
25.16 Medical Record
25.17 Summary
Endnotes
Additional Reading

25.1 Introduction

A wound is defined as a disruption in the normal condition and function of body tissue. Origins for wounds are:

- Trauma
- Surgery
- Chronic wounds
- Burns
- Arterial insufficiency
- Venous insufficiency
- Neuropathic (diabetic) ulcers
- Pressure ulcers
- Terminal ulcers

The characteristics and legal implications of these types of wounds are discussed in this chapter. It is common for potential plaintiffs to approach an attorney after a pressure ulcer developed in a hospital, subacute care, rehab care, long-term care facility and even in-home care. Attorneys are also approached with questionable non-healing surgical wounds or wounds that have developed complications in healing. Many people equate pressure ulcers with neglect. This chapter explores the causes of pressure ulcers, as well as other skin disruptions, and defines the prevention and treatment. This information is designed to assist the reader in understanding this complex area of nursing practice so that cases with merit are resolved and non-meritorious claims are rejected.

25.2 Definitions
A. Traumatic Wounds

A traumatic wound is an unintentional wound caused as a result of trauma (e.g., shallow abrasion, scratch, fall, or injury from accidents). Traumatic wounds may be partial thickness (shallow) or full thickness (deep wounds).

B. Surgical Wounds

Surgical wounds are intentionally created and are usually acute wounds which are well-approximated by the surgeon. They are closed wounds and heal by primary intention (sutured shut). Wounds left open after surgery heal by secondary intention (scar tissue formation) and usually are related to a complicating factor that prevents closure of the wound during surgery or complications that happen after surgery (e.g., infection or contamination, dehiscence or opening up of the wound).

C. Chronic Wounds

Chronic wounds have an underlying pathological process that makes the wound non-healing by producing repeated and prolonged insults to the tissues causing a chronic condition. "A chronic wound is a manifestation of one or more underlying conditions. Included are wounds with the following etiologies: pressure, venous, arterial, diabetic, ischemic, non-healing surgical, cancer, end-of-life, and mixed etiologies."[1]

D. Burn Wounds

Burn wounds are unique; they are not treated like other wounds. They are dynamic and can evolve into deeper injuries over time, depending on the initial injury, treatment, and subsequent environmental insults.

- First-degree burns are localized injury or superficial tissue destruction involving the epidermis.
- Second-degree burns are superficial partial thickness tissue destruction involving the epidermis and dermis. Deep partial thickness burns may involve the dermis, leaving only skin appendages.
- Third-degree burns (full thickness) involve the epidermis, dermis, and underlying subcutaneous tissue. Third-degree burns may extend to subcutaneous tissue, muscle, or bone.
- Fourth-degree burns involve both skin and underlying structures, such as muscle and bone. The tissue is dead metabolically with full-thickness skin loss with eschar (charred tissue).

E. Arterial Insufficiency Ulcers

Arterial insufficiency ulcers are formed due to blockage of an artery, leading to inadequate circulation to the lower extremity. These are sometimes confused with pressure ulcers. They characteristically involve appendages like toes.

F. Venous Stasis Ulcers

Venous stasis ulcers result from chronic venous insufficiency secondary to venous hypertension. They are often located on legs, below the knee.

G. Neuropathic (Diabetic) Ulcers

Diabetics often suffer from poor circulation and are prone to ulcers on the leg or foot due to vascular and neurological complications. The blood vessels become smaller, causing poor circulation and insufficient oxygen to the lower extremities. Minor trauma such as tight-fitting shoes or a scratch can cause a wound.

H. Pressure Ulcers

Pressure ulcers can be caused by many factors: pressure, shearing forces, friction forces, and moisture. Pressure-related skin breakdown is localized injury to the skin caused by the compression of soft tissue between the underlying surface and a bony prominence. The pressure causes cellular death deep at the bone and extends up to the skin surface. A number of contributing or confusing factors are also associated with pressure ulcers.[2]

I. Terminal Ulcers

Critical illness and severe medical stress on the body can cause failure of the skin, which is the largest organ of the body. The major organs are the first to receive the oxygen and nutrients needed to keep them working and the amount left for the skin is minimal. Like other organ systems, skin can experience severe duress during a critical or chronic illness. In many instances, the skin will fail along with other organ systems. Terminal ulcers occur in people who have several medical illnesses or are critically ill as they approach the end of life. The development of full-thickness pressure ulcers (skin failure) are found in the critically and chronically ill. If all preventive measures are being done, the terminal ulcer would be considered a comorbid pathologic process rather than a simple "failure to turn," as is often alleged. Data reveal that ultimate resolution of skin failure in the presence of such a disease burden is difficult at best.[3] It is considered an unavoidable skin breakdown or skin failure and "typically appears as pear-shaped, red/yellow/black, similar in appearance to an abrasion, and tend to occur suddenly in the sacral/coccoygeal region not long before death."[4]

25.3 Assessment of Wounds

The initial assessment takes into account the immediate and emerging needs of the patient, and considers all comorbid (co-existing) conditions. The initial assessment helps the nursing staff determine the components of the individualized care plan and establishes the necessary interventions and goals for that particular patient. "The goal of assessment is to determine the appropriate care, treatment, and services to meet a patient's initial needs as well as his or her changing needs while in that particular setting. Identifying and delivering appropriate care, treatment, and services depends on three processes:

1. Collecting data about each patient's health history, physical, functional, and psychosocial status, and needs as appropriate to the setting and circumstances
2. Analyzing data to produce information about patients' needs for care, treatment, and services and to identify the need for additional data
3. Making care, treatment and service decisions based on information developed, about each patient's needs and his or her response to care, treatment, and service."[5]

Each admission assessment is conducted by qualified staff within a time frame specified by the policies and procedures of that particular facility, and by state and federal regulations. The assessments are defined by the facility, and individualized to meet each patient's needs, and address the needs of a special population.[6] Federal regulations in the nursing facility state that "upon a resident's admission, a facility must have written physician orders providing essential care, consistent with the resident's current mental and physical status."[7]

TIP: A complete admission assessment presents a picture of the patient at admission, the characteristics of any existing skin breakdown and any skin abnormalities, and his current treatment.

A thorough assessment from top to toe should be done with notations of any abnormalities, including skin breakdowns (whether pressure related or not), wounds, and incision lines. This assessment also indicates comorbid problems that complicate the ability to heal any wounds or skin breakdown. The nursing assessment must include a system's assessment, which includes: cardiovascular, respiratory, mental, emotional, mobility, nutritional, neurological, integumentary, integrity, gastrointestinal, and genitourinary. If a breakdown is present, identification of the origin and contributing factors is necessary to prevent further breakdown or a worsening of the area. Reassessment should be done with a change in condition at well-established intervals. This helps the nurse assess the medical condition at that point in time.

Assessments must:

- be timely and appropriate,
- include a head to toe visual assessment,
- include all the body systems,
- thoroughly document each component,
- be done by a registered nurse,
- identify risk factors, and
- be used to define the nursing diagnoses for the nursing care plan.

The total assessment is important. Included items are:

1. physician admission assessment
2. nursing admission assessment and medical history
3. height and weight
4. health history
5. allergies
6. substance use
7. home medications
8. abuse and neglect screening
9. skin assessment (with descriptive characteristics)
10. lifting and movement assessment
11. mobility, functional status
12. mental, emotional status
13. pain—acute and chronic
14. fall risk assessment
15. special precautions initiated at admission
16. standing orders for specialty services (nursing orders)
17. any advance standing orders from the physician upon admission

The initial assessment takes into account the immediate and emerging needs, and considers all comorbid conditions. It helps staff determine the components of the individualized care plan and establishes the necessary interventions and goals for the particular individual.

25.4 Disease Burden

Greg Brown's research[8] on pressure ulcers documents:

The major diagnoses for all patients who developed pressure ulcers were: a history of cerebrovascular accident (18.4 percent), diabetes of any type (13.6 percent), cancer of any type (12.8 percent), and coronary artery disease (11.2 percent). Most patients (63.5 percent) had more than one major diagnosis adding to their disease burden. Diabetes of any type, congestive heart failure, and ethanol

abuse were more prevalent in the living group by a few percentage points. Chronic obstructive pulmonary disease, renal failure of any type, and cancer of any type were more prevalent in the deceased group, also by only a few percentage points. The average age of patients at ulcer onset was higher for the deceased group with the exception of the long-term care setting. In this setting, persons who died were an average of 1.6 years younger than the living group.

25.5 Skin Assessment

Skin assessment should be done on a regular basis in order to plan preventive interventions, evaluate treatment effects, and communicate with other caregivers. Careful identification of a patient most likely to develop pressure ulcers allows for quick intervention and effective use of available resources such as staff time and equipment. More diligent reassessment and revising of the care plan and treatment plan is necessary if there is deterioration of the medical condition or skin breakdown.

The Agency for Health Research and Quality (AHRQ), formerly the AHCPR, recommends that assessments be done for skin breakdown development on admission to a facility, then reassessed periodically.[9] Nurses in acute care should regularly reassess every 24 to 48 hours or if there is a change in the individual's condition. Long-term care nurses assess the resident's skin on admission and weekly for the first four weeks and then at least monthly to quarterly or whenever there is a condition change.[10] Skin condition should be assessed on bath days by the bath aide and reported to the nurse if any abnormal findings. Home-care clients should have skin assessments done with each nursing visit and by the bath aide if one is involved. Any changes should be reported to the family and physician, followed by documentation of this notification.

Many different types of nursing documentation forms exist to assess the skin surface. Some forms have a body diagram on them, some have check-off boxes, and some ask the nurse to write a narrative. The break in skin integrity (whether wound, incision, scars, bruises, ulcers, skin tears, burns, and scabs) should be described on this form or in the admission assessment.

A. Descriptive Characteristics

The characteristics of each particular break in skin integrity (i.e., site, stage, size, drainage, periwound skin, and interventions) should be documented. It is important that if prior treatment was being done the treating physician or wound clinic be contacted for directions for continued care.

B. Measurements

Measuring and recording the size of skin breakdown upon admission help clinicians develop the goals of care and care plan because large, deep wounds take more time to heal than small, shallow wounds. The standard of care requires regular wound measurements to help clinicians decide whether their plan of care is effective.

TIP: Measurements are recorded in centimeters. The conversion equation is 2.54 cm equals 1 inch. Tape measurements or tracings are most often used to measure wound size. Both measuring and tracing methods have advantages and disadvantages and their accuracy depends largely on the ability of the individual doing the measuring.

Any visible wound or skin breakdown (pressure ulcer, skin tear, burn), even if all that is can been seen is a wound bed that is 100 percent covered with non-viable tissue (slough/eschar), needs to be measured. Length is the longest length measured from the head to toe direction. The longest width is measured at the widest width perpendicular (at a 90 degree angle) to the length from side to side. See Figure 25.1 for a deep tissue injury.

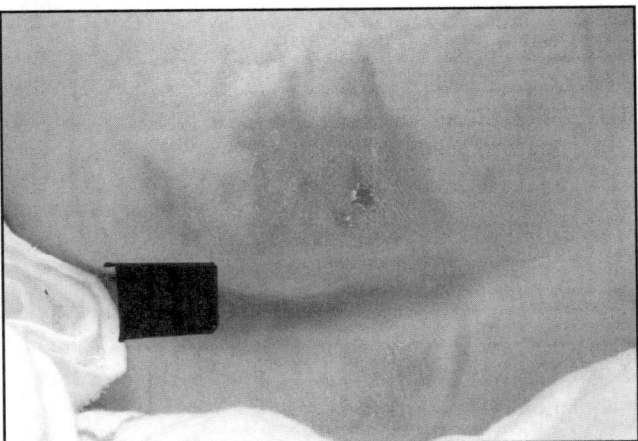

Figure 25.1 Deep Tissue Injury

25.6 Characteristics of Wounds and Ulcers
A. Documenting

Measuring and recording the size of a wound upon admission helps the nurse develop the care plan, treatment, and goals to be accomplished. Regular wound measurements at least once a week, or more often with changes in the wound, help nurses decide whether their plan of care is effective. Objective measurement and thorough documentation of the progress is important. Documentation of the length, width, depth, absence or presence of cellulitis, and amount and character of drainage must be performed at least weekly.[11]

Documenting the location of the skin breakdown includes recording the anatomical location and measurements of the breakdown. Measurements should be dated and in centimeters. Use of inches or objects (nickel, quarter, baseball, orange, and grapefruit) for comparison is not an acceptable way of measuring. The documentation of measurements informs the physician, nurse, and other medical personnel of the width (from side to side at the widest point), length (measured at the longest point), and depth of the breakdown at a particular point in time. Depth is measured from the viable surface to the deepest portion of the skin breakdown or ulcer base.

Digital cameras are often used but there exists a liability issue with its potential for image alteration and enhancement.[12]

TIP: If the base of the wound, the true depth, cannot be determined, the area cannot be staged.

Only pressure-related wounds are staged; surgical, traumatic, skin tears, arterial, venous, and diabetic ulcers are not staged. Pressure-related wounds can be a shallow stage II or III with granulation tissue, black necrotic tissue, or yellow slough tissue covering the base of the wound. The nurse must be able to see the base of the wound, the true depth, in order to stage it. Many times the depth of the ulcer is not documented, which is incomplete documentation of the skin breakdown.

1. Tunneling

Tunneling is tracts limited to a small edge of the ulcer or in the wound bed and extend in one direction. See Figures 25.2 and 25.3 for tunneling.

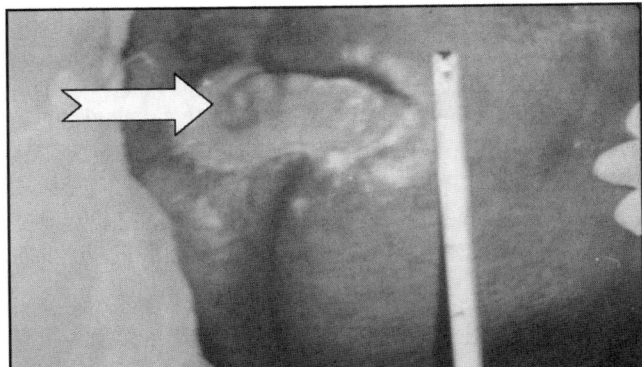

Figure 25.2 Tunneling and Granulation Tissue

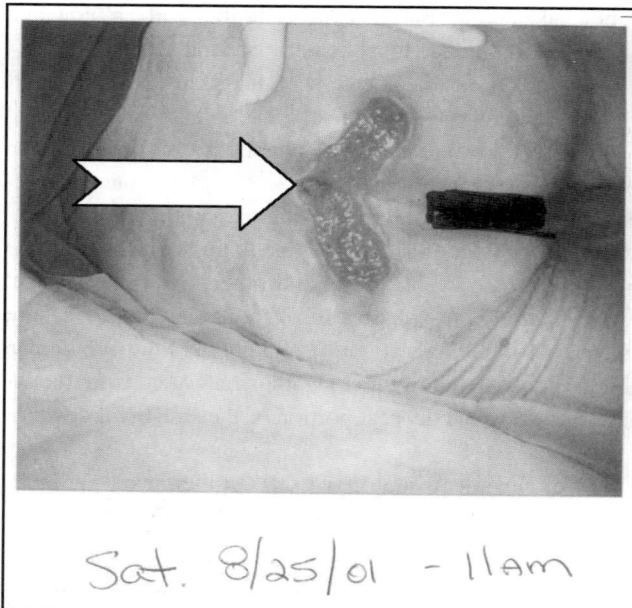

Sat. 8/25/01 - 11am

Figure 25.3 *Tunneling and Granulation Tissue*

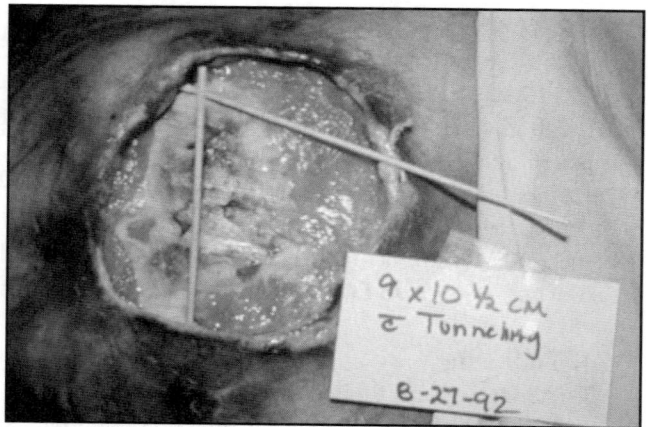

9 x 10 ½ cm
c̄ Tunneling

8-27-92

Figure 25.4 *Undermining and Rolled Edges*

2. Undermining

Undermining, or rimming, may be found along the edges of the wound, which indicates tissue destruction around a wound's edges. It results in a wound bed that extends under intact skin. Undermining should be carefully measured and probed to determine how far it extends under intact skin. It is important for the nurse to measure all undermining and tracts to show progress in wound healing and effectiveness of the dressing.[13] See Figure 25.4 for undermining.

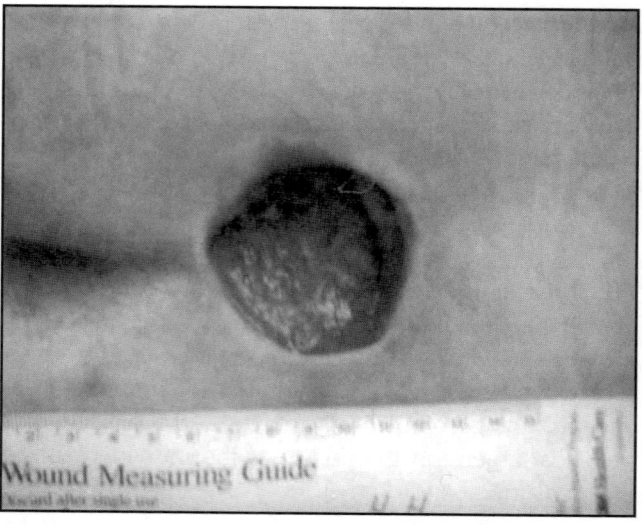

Figure 25.5 *Granulation Tissue*

3. Edges

Smooth edges of a wound indicate normal healing. Healing happens with contraction from the edges and granulation from the base. A rolled edge indicates the wound is old and probably chronic in nature. The edges have healed and will have to be stimulated to continue healing. This is done with surgical removal of the edge (curetting the edge) or with the use of silver nitrate. See Figure 25.4 for rolled edges.

4. Wound bed

Granulation tissue is healthy healing tissue of the wound bed and presents as a beefy red tissue. With each weekly measurement there should be a decrease in the size of the wound as it contracts and fills in. If the wound bed appears a pale pink to pale red or has no decrease in the size over several weeks, clinicians should suspect an underlying infection and appropriate diagnostic testing (wound culture, x-rays, CAT scan, MRI) should be done. See Figure 25.5 for granulation tissue.

Slough is non-viable (devitalized) tissue that appears to be white, pale yellow to dark yellow, tan, gray or green in coloring with either a wet or dry appearance. Pink granulation buds may appear through the yellow slough. It may be very adherent (almost leathery-like) or loose and stringy in appearance. Slough provides a good medium for bacteria to grow in. This tissue needs to be debrided (cut off) for granulation to take place. See Figure 25.6 for slough and black necrotic tissue.

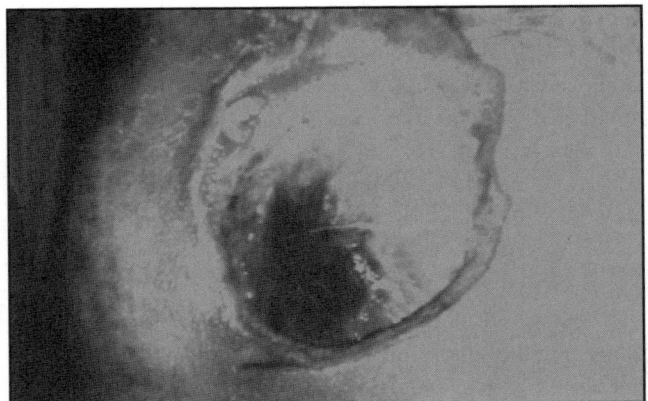

Figure 25.6 Yellow Slough and Black Eschar

Eschar is non-viable tissue that can be wet or dry in appearance and ranges in color from gray, brown, or green, to dark red and black. The eschar tissue can be loose or firmly adherent, hard, soft, dry or wet. It contains necrotic (non-viable) cells and debris and forms a medium for bacterial growth. Diagnostic testing needs to be done on the circulation if eschar dries and hardens on evaluation, and is located on the feet, heels, ankles, or leg. If poor circulation is apparent, debridement would be contraindicated. "Heel ulcers with dry eschar may not need debridement (either mechanically or chemically) unless the ulcer is associated with signs of infection such as edema, erythema, fluctuance, or drainage."[14] The eschar is hiding deeper damage if it is soft and boggy. If redness is apparent around the eschar, infection should be suspected and appropriate treatment started. Granulation will not happen as long as eschar remains in the wound bed. See Figure 25.7 for eschar.

5. Periwound skin

Periwound skin consists of the skin immediately surrounding the skin breakdown for approximately 4 cm. This skin should be dry and have normal coloration for that person.[15] Problems exist when the peri-ulcer skin appears soggy or macerated, seen as white areas surrounding the wound (Figure 25.8) with breaks in the skin, and has redness and drainage. In lighter skin pigmentation, inflammation appears bright red or dark red and "angry" looking, which may indicate infection or possible more skin breakdown under the intact skin. Individuals with dark skin tones may develop a deepening of color or a purple hue to skin color. The majority of documentation may not address the periwound skin condition (see Figure 25.9 for inflamed periwound skin) but should describe abnormalities, and appropriate treatment should be started to promote healing.

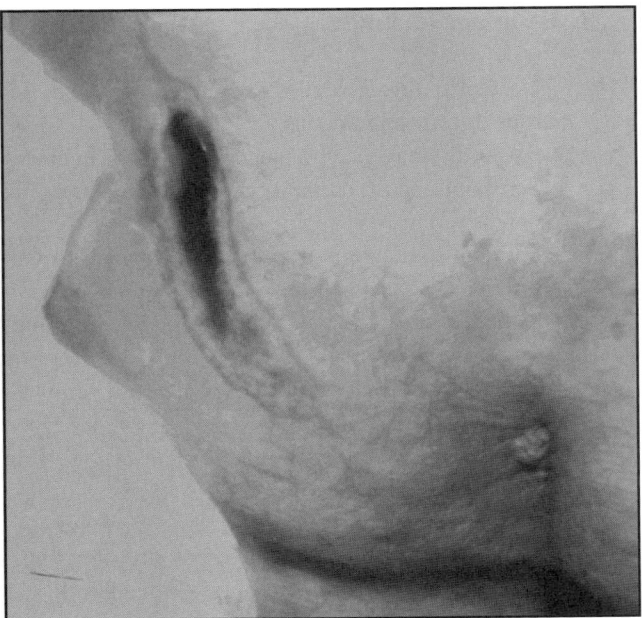

Figure 25.7 Black Eschar

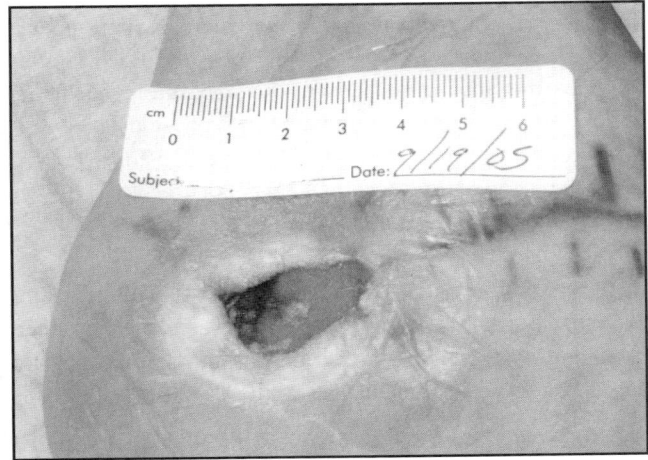

Figure 25.8 Maceration around Wound

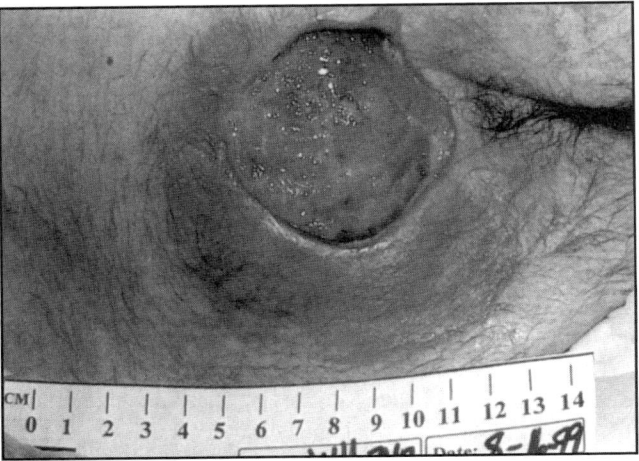

Figure 25.9 Inflamed Periwound Skin

6. Drainage (exudate)

- Normal drainage (exudate) is documented as serous or serosanguineous.
- Serous drainage is thin, watery, and clear in color.
- Serosanguineous drainage is thin, watery, and pink to pale red in color.
- Purulent drainage is thin or thick, opaque to yellow, green, tan, or brown in color and is accompanied by an offensive odor, which generally indicates infection.
- Foul purulent drainage is thick, opaque or yellow to green in color, and has an offensive odor, described as pungent, strong, foul, fecal, or musty. Infection may be suspected if odor is present and diagnostic testing needs to be done. (However, some odor is normal with the use of hydrocolloid dressings, [Duoderm]; occlusive dressings, [Tegaderm]; and the wound VAC dressings.)

Drainage measurement should be found in documentation as none, scant, small amount, medium amount, moderate, large amount, or saturating the dressing. Each facility provides the appropriate descriptive measurements in its policy and procedures. Certain dressings provide a means of measurements (e.g., wound manager pouch, ostomy pouches, or the wound VAC dressing canisters).

B. Staging

In February 2007, the four stages of pressure ulcers were expanded to include definitions for unstageable and deep tissue injury (DTI). Staging definitions and descriptions are based largely on visible changes to the skin/tissues.[16]

1. Stage I

Stage I pressure ulcers are observable non-blanchable erythema (persistent redness) of intact skin. Redness remains even when all pressure is relieved from the area. Darkly pigmented skin may not have visible blanching; its color may differ from the surrounding skin.[17] The skin is reddened, warm, and has edema and hardness. In comparison to adjacent or opposite areas on the body other signs may include changes in one or more of the following: skin temperature (warmth or coolness), tissue consistency (firm or boggy feel), and sensation (pain, itching). A stage I wound may indicate "at-risk" persons (a heralding sign of risk).[18]

2. Stage II

Stage II pressure ulcers consist of a partial thickness skin loss involving the epidermal, the dermis, or both layers of the skin. It is a superficial break in the skin integrity with or without drainage, is painful, is reddened and appears as an abrasion, "intact or open/ruptured serum-filled"[19] blister, or shallow crater. Presents as a shiny or dry shallow ulcer without slough or bruising. This stage should not be used to describe skin tears, tape burns, perineal dermatitis, maceration or excoriation. "Bruising" indicates suspected deep tissue injury.[20]

3. Stage III

A stage III ulcer is a full-thickness skin loss involving damage to the subcutaneous tissue that may extend down to, but not through underlying fascia. Subcutaneous fat may be visible but bone, tendon or muscle are not exposed.[21] It is a deep crater with or without undermining and tunneling of adjacent tissue. The depth of a stage III pressure ulcer varies by anatomical location. The bridge of the nose, ear, occiput and malleolus do not have subcutaneous tissue, and stage III ulcers can be shallow. In contrast, areas of significant adipose tissue can develop extremely deep stage III pressure ulcers. Bone/tendon is not visible or directly palpable.[22]

4. Stage IV

A stage IV pressure ulcer is a full-thickness skin loss with extensive destruction. Damage may involve muscle, bone, or supporting structures. There is tissue necrosis and serious damage to tissues. Undermining (tissue destruction underlying intact skin along the wound margins) and sinus tracts/tunneling (course or pathway that can extend in any direction from the wound and results in dead space with potential for abscess formation) also may be present.[23] The depth of a stage IV pressure ulcer varies by anatomical location. The bridge of the nose, ear, occiput and malleolus do not have subcutaneous tissue and these ulcers can be shallow. Stage IV ulcers can extended into muscle or supporting structures (e.g., fascia, tendon or joint capsule) making osteomyelitis possible. Exposed bone or tendon is visible or directly palpable.[24]

5. Unstageable

An unstageable pressure ulcer is a full thickness tissue loss whose wound base is completely covered with necrotic tissue or slough (non-viable tissue). The base of the pressure ulcer is completely obscured and must be observed in order to measure the depth of the ulcer and stage it. Figures 25.10 through 25.13 show staging. Figure 25.14 depicts an ulcer that cannot be staged due to the presence of eschar covering the base of the sore. Until enough slough and/or eschar is removed to expose the base of the wound, the true depth, and the stage, cannot be determined. Stable (dry, adherent, intact without erythema or fluctuance) eschar on the heels serves as "the body's natural (biological) cover" and should not be removed.[25]

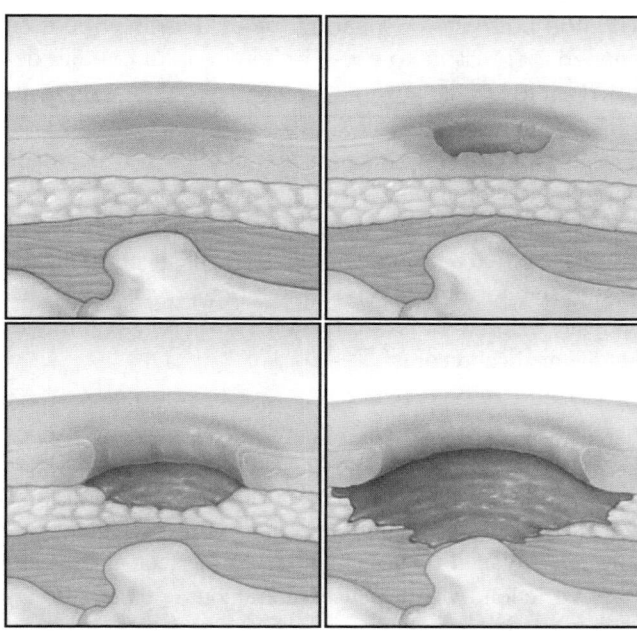

Figure 25.10 (top left) Pressure Ulcer Stage I. **Figure 25.11** (top right) Pressure Ulcer Stage II. **Figure 25.12** (bottom left) Pressure Ulcer Stage III. **Figure 25.13** (bottom right) Pressure Ulcer Stage IV. Figures courtesy of KCI.

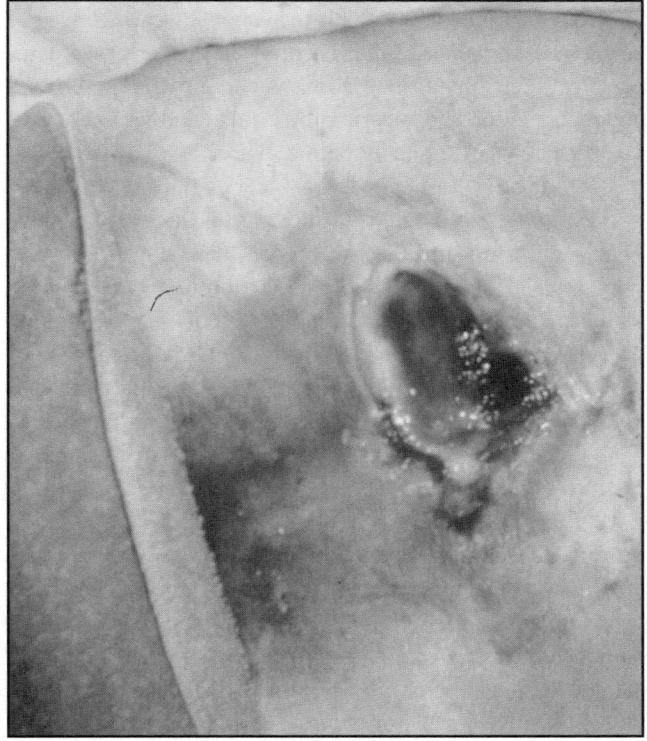

Figure 25.14 Unstageable Pressure Ulcer

6. Suspected deep tissue injury—depth unknown

Deep tissue injury should be suspected when there is a purple or maroon localized area of discolored intact skin or blood-filled blister due to damage of underlying soft tissue from pressure or shear. The area may be preceded by tissue that is painful, firm, mushy, boggy, warmer or cooler as compared to adjacent tissue. Deep tissue injury may be difficult to detect in individuals with dark skin tones. Evolution may include a thin blister over a dark wound bed. The wound may further evolve and become covered by thin eschar. Evolution may be rapid, exposing additional layers of tissue even with optimal treatment.[26] See Figure 25.14 for an example of deep tissue injury.

C. Causative Factors

1. Pressure

The main factors that contribute to the development of pressure ulcers are pressure, shearing forces, friction, and moisture. Pressure and time are involved in the formation of pressure ulcers. Soft tissue becomes compressed between a bony prominence such as the bed or chair and the amount of time compressed without relief leads to the death of cells closest to the bony prominence. This begins the formation of deep damage starting at the bone and extending upward through the tissues until it shows up as a reddened or discolored area. Damage continues to happen if pressure is maintained. More tissue is destroyed because of the relationship between unrelieved pressure and the amount of time involved.

Any device can lead to a pressure-related skin breakdown, and assessment needs to be done beneath and around the device. Such potential devices could be: oxygen tubing (look behind the ears), face masks, trach ties (look behind the neck and under the ties); IVs, monitoring devices, NG and feeding tubes (check the nares and if the tube brace is too tight on the abdomen); splints, braces, CPM (continuous passive motion) devices, traction (check the heels), neck collars, urinary catheters and fecal catheters; foot-drop boots (multi-podus) and heel protectors, and under support stockings.

Nursing should be involved in the education of patients, family, and caregivers about pressure ulcer prevention and treatment. Topics that should be addressed are:

1. Etiology and risk of pressure ulcers.
2. Risk factors of the patient for pressure ulcers.
3. Appropriate skin assessments.
4. Development of an individualized plan of care for prevention.

5. Development of an individualized plan of treatment.

6. Implementation of the plan of care.

7. Demonstration of proper positioning to relieve pressure.

8. Instruction in documenting.

9. Instruction in proper hygiene.

10. Instruction in adequate nutrition and hydration.

11. Managing urinary and fecal incontinence.

12. Instruction in the damages of shearing and friction issues.

13. Use of appropriate positioning devices and foam padding.

14. Use of lifting devices such as draw sheets or a trapeze.

15. Instruction in trying to prevent contractures.

16. Avoidance of donut pillows to relieve pressure. This causes an abnormal distribution of pressure around the ulcer. The donut pillow can be inflated too much, making it too hard; or it can be too soft, allowing the patient to touch the surface of the bed or chair, causing pressure to the damaged skin.

17. Avoidance of massage of reddened areas over bony prominences.

18. Repositioning on a regular basis when in bed or when out of bed in a chair.

19. If there is a new onset of pain, or change in the drainage or size of the wound, notify the healthcare provider or physician.

2. Shearing

Shear force is another factor that contributes to the mechanical destruction of tissue. It is a mechanical force parallel rather than perpendicular to an area of tissue. Because the skin does not move freely, the primary effect of shearing occurs at the deeper fascial level of the tissues overlying the bony prominence, mainly the coccyx and sacral areas. The blood vessels and tissues attached in the bone area are pulled in one direction because of body weight, while the surface tissues stick to the sheets and remain stationary. The body skeleton actually slides downward inside the skin. Puckering of the skin may be noticed in the gluteal area. Blood vessels can become either obstructed and torn or stretched. This is most likely to happen when patients are dragged along the surface of the sheets during repositioning or are placed in high Fowler's position and slide down in the bed (or the nursing staff lifts the patient under the arms to reposition up in the bed causing the skin to rub on the sheets instead of using a lift sheet). Other high-risk patients are those who are agitated or spastic.

TIP: The presence of shearing forces deceases the time needed for pressure to cause ischemia or for cellular destruction to occur.

To avoid shearing forces, the head of the bed should be raised to no more than a 30° angle, except for short periods during eating. Documentation must verify that the height of the bed is raised above 30° as relative to medical conditions (e.g., respiratory conditions or aspiration precautions). This documentation must be verified on a regular basis throughout the medical records.

3. Friction

Friction is another factor causing mechanical destruction of the epidermal outer layer of the skin. Pressure over stretched tissues is several times more damaging than pressure over relaxed tissues. Rubbing of the feet or buttocks causes friction, which reduces the amount of pressure required for pressure ulcers to form. Moisture from perspiration or excrement leads to maceration, which increases friction and weakens the skin, setting the patient up for skin breakdown.

Friction commonly occurs in patients unable to lift themselves sufficiently for repositioning. If a patient is scooted across the bed linen, the outer protective layer of skin may be rubbed away. This mechanical wearing away of surface tissue increases the potential for deeper tissue damage. The skeleton moves forward due to gravitational forces and then friction and shearing forces act together to contribute to necrosis of tissue in the sacral area.

A patient who depends on others for care may need two caregivers to assist with moving up in bed. The caregivers will use a lift sheet to prevent the body from dragging. Nurses are expected to protect elbows and heels if the patient is exposed to friction. Socks, elbow protectors, and transparent dressings are effective. The nursing standard of care involves the use of lift sheets to move the patient to keep from pulling or dragging the patient across the sheets. Heavy-duty Hoyer lifts are available to assist with movement of obese patients.

In the past, nursing schools taught that massaging bony prominences or reddened areas would increase oxygen flow to the areas to prevent skin breakdown. Current literature warns against massaging as it can cause redden fragile cells damage, thus increasing the area of damage. It is contraindicated. Nursing experts still occasionally see medical records with notes by nurses who massaged bony prominences or reddened areas.

4. Chemical breakdown

Chemical breakdown results from the interaction of both urine and stool on the epidermal protective layer of the skin. The skin breakdown usually starts as reddened excoriated skin. Add to this redness the forces of friction, shearing, and pressure, and the skin will continue to breakdown with deeper damage.

Protection of the skin is an important part of nursing care. This is accomplished with the use of scheduled toileting, frequent cleansing of the perineal and buttock areas, frequent changing of absorbent pads and diapers, and use of protective ointment applied to the skin after each incontinent episode. Moisturizing dry skin helps keep it supple and prevents cracking of the skin which allows microorganisms into the skin. The skin of diabetic and dialysis patients must be carefully inspected because it becomes very dry. The AHRQ has developed guidelines that advocate the use of protectant moisture barriers.[27] Research and literature supports the ability of these products to protect the skin and maintain skin integrity. The goal is to keep the area clean, dry, and protective from the harmful effects of incontinence.[28]

D. Assessment

A complete patient history and wound assessment findings are the foundation for developing the patient care plan. A thorough patient assessment from top to toe should be done with notations of any treatments being done and any abnormalities, including all skin breakdowns, whether pressure related or not. These treatments need to be verified with the treating physician for continuation of the same treatment if appropriate. Also the nurse is expected to document whether this skin care constitutes a surgical or non-surgical wound, and whether it is chronic or acute in nature.

TIP: Realistic and clearly defined goals of care are particularly important when managing patients with chronic wounds because they often have a number of comorbid conditions that may affect the healing process or plan of care.

The assessment of an individual with a pressure ulcer is the basis for planning treatment, evaluating treatment effects, and communicating with other caregivers. Pressure ulcers should be assessed at least weekly, but deterioration either in a patient's overall condition or in the pressure ulcer itself mandates more immediate reassessment of the treatment plan. A clean pressure ulcer with adequate interventions and blood supply should show evidence of healing within two to four weeks. Failure to do so should prompt a reevaluation of the plan of care, an evaluation of adherence to the plan, and a pos-

sible modification of the treatment plan.[29] Treatment needs of a pressure ulcer change over time, in terms of both healing and deterioration. Treatment strategies should be continuously reevaluated based on the current status of the ulcer.[30]

The nursing documentation should include an assessment including the descriptive wound characteristics listed below. These variables determine the goals of care, the care and treatment plan, and the prognosis for healing:

1. Location (use anatomical location on the body),
2. Depth (is measured perpendicular to deepest point),
3. Size (surface area and shape in centimeters),
4. Exudates (type, quantity, and characteristics),
5. Necrotic tissue characteristics (e.g., dry, wet, yellow, grey, brown, black),
6. Sinus tracts, undermining or tunneling,
7. Granulation tissue and/or epithelialization. Epithelialization is a fundamental process whereby dead or damaged tissue is replaced by new and healthy cells. Epithelial cells from the wound edges migrate across the wound bed from both sides in order to seal the wound and give it a protective covering,[31] and
8. Surrounding tissue, erythema (persistent redness), edema, and induration.[32] Induration is a slight swelling at the wound edge, and if redness and warmth is present, may indicate underlying infection or more tissue damage.[33]

The surrounding peri-skin provides information about the status of the wound and the result of treatment. Normal skin color should surround the wound bed. If this area appears reddened or darker in color it may indicate undermining of the ulcer. This should be examined and possible changes in treatment should occur.

E. Early Skin Damage

Individuals debilitated or at extremely high risk for pressure ulcers may exhibit nonblanchable tissue changes in less than two hours. Nonblanchable erythema is more serious than blanchable erythema.

1. Blanchable

Blanchable erythema, the earliest sign of ischemia (lack of blood flow of nutrients and oxygen to tissues, which results in cellular death), appears as a pink to red area of skin. In light-skinned individuals, compressing the reddened area causes the color to blanch or turn white. When compression is removed, redness reappears immediately. When the pressure that caused the blanchable erythema is removed, the tissue should resume its normal color within 24 hours.[34]

2. Nonblanchable

The color intensity of nonblanchable erythema is greater than in blanchable erythema. The color of nonblanchable erythema does not fade when compressed by the finger. A decrease in capillary flow leads to ischemia and increased capillary permeability. Abnormal reactive hyperemia (hyperemia is the normal reactive vasodilation of the tissues in response to pressure and is characterized by bright red, blanchable area) vasodilation is the body's normal response to repair cell damage by prolonged ischemia. This is a stage I reddened area of the skin and if pressure is relieved on a continuous basis, it can be reversed. If a reddened area is found over a bony prominence, the nurse should relieve all pressure to the area for 30 minutes. If the redness does not resolve, a diagnosis of a stage I pressure ulcer may be documented. Literature verifies this 30-minute rule. Figures 25.15 through 25.18 provide examples of the main pressure points over bony prominences.

F. Avoidable Versus Unavoidable Ulcers

1. Unavoidable pressure ulcers

The new Federal Regulations for Long Term Care 483.25 (c) defines "unavoidable pressure ulcers." The facility must provide all preventive interventions and document the use of the interventions consistently and appropriate to the resident. If this is done, the pressure ulcer is considered unavoidable if the resident developed a pressure ulcer. These interventions must be individualized, implemented, monitored, and revised as appropriate. Changes in condition must be recognized, evaluated, reported to the practitioner, (physician, nurse practitioner, physician assistant), and addressed.

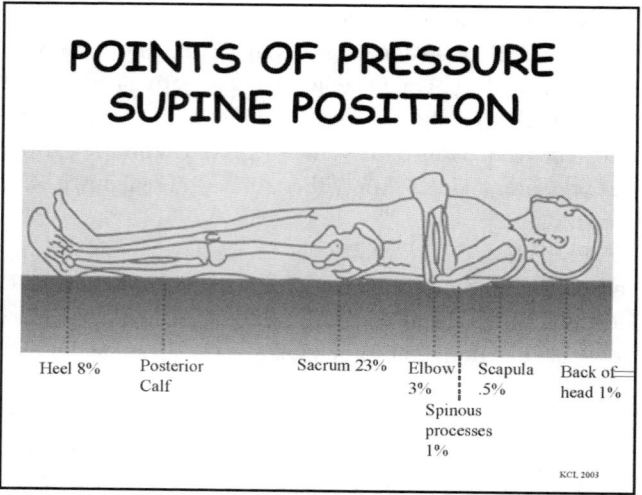

Figure 25.16 *Points of Pressure in Supine Position with Main Percentages of Skin Breakdown, courtesy of KCI*

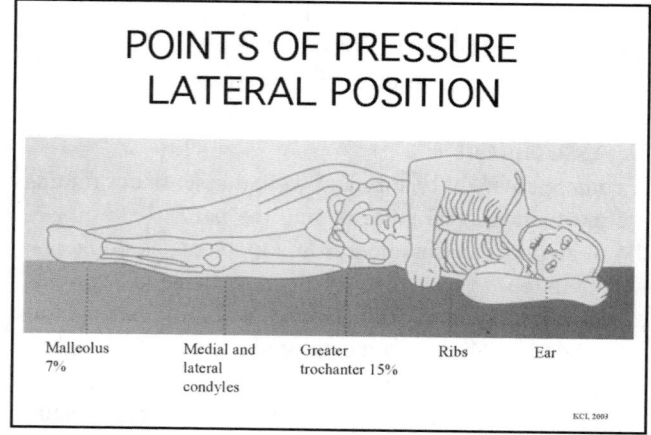

Figure 25.17 *Points of Pressure in Lateral Position with Main Percentages of Skin Breakdown, courtesy of KCI*

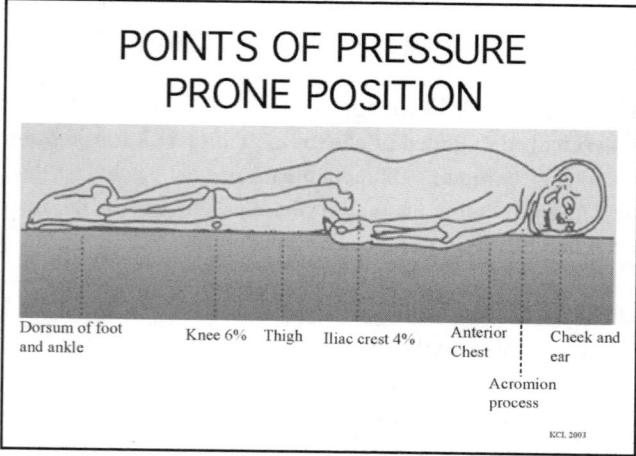

Figure 25.15 *Points of Pressure in Prone Position with Main Percentages of Skin Breakdown, courtesy of KCI*

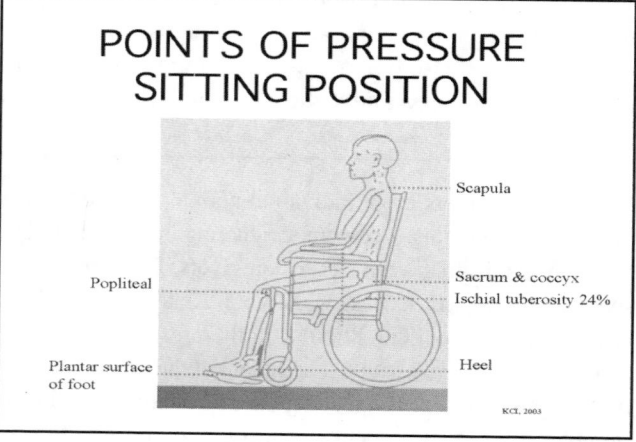

Figure 25.18 *Points of Pressure in Sitting Position with Main Percentages of Skin Breakdown, courtesy of KCI*

2. Avoidable pressure ulcers

Avoidable pressure ulcers develop because the facility did not do one or more of the following interventions. These interventions must be individualized, implemented, monitored, and revised as appropriate for each resident. The facility must assess for pressure ulcer risk factors, plan individualized interventions, implement interventions consistently, monitor and evaluate the effect of the interventions, and revise interventions as appropriate.[35]

3. Refusals

Individuals in all care settings (acute care, subacute care, long term care, rehab care, assisted living and home care) have the right to make "informed decisions" and decide their own plan of care. These rights include the right to be non-compliant with pressure ulcer prevention and the treatment plan. Individuals can refuse some or all aspects of their care. A pressure ulcer may be unavoidable if the individual refuses to adhere to the recommended prevention interventions in spite of pressure ulcer prevention education. Of course, documentation in the nursing record confirms that the education happened repeatedly and documents the non-compliance of the individual. The defense will use the documentation to prove the patient was aware of the risk of non-adherence to the preventive plan of care.

A nurse confronted by a patient who refuses care should document:

1. The nurse's evaluation of the basis for refusal
2. How the nurse identified potential alternatives
3. Which potential alternatives the nurse instituted
4. That the nurse evaluated the effectiveness of the potential alternatives
5. What was tried, how often, and the outcome, and notification to the physician and family of refusals

One such case occurred in a nursing home where a resident with untreatable painful spinal meningitis refused treatment, turning and even nutrition related to severe pain. She had failed treatment for this condition several times. She did not want to be "snowed" with pain medication and the nursing staff worked with her to meet her needs with minimal pain. The family and physician were aware of the resident's wishes and were kept updated regularly. The nursing staff documented education to the resident on a regular basis, documented 490 times in her medical record refusals to eat, be turned, be bathed and cooperate with the nursing staff. The staff went as far as moving the television set from one side of the room to the other side of the room so the resident would turn to the other side. She did develop pressure-related skin breakdown from lying in one position all the time. Resident decided to refuse all treatments and soon expired. The family sued the nursing home for pressure ulcer skin breakdown. Defense used the documentation to prove that the patient was competent and had the right to decide her own plan of care and her own wishes.

G. Photography

Some facilities or clinics include photographs as part of the admission process to document the status of the skin upon admission or as an adjunct to treatment documentation. Photographs are taken of every bruise and skin breakdown and photographs are repeated weekly to document healing progress or deterioration. The AHRQ Guidelines suggests pressure ulcers be assessed and documented at least weekly unless there is a change in the condition of the breakdown.[36] Assessment of the peri-ulcer skin provides information about the risk of the ulcer or skin breakdown increasing in size. Protocols must be established and followed by each facility or home health agency.

TIP: Consistent methodology in obtaining the photograph is essential if photographs are used in pressure ulcer assessing.

Pictures must be taken the same distance from the wound bed and at the same angle. Documenting the distance from which the photograph was taken is extremely important, because different distances may distort the true size of the pressure ulcer.[37] The NPUAP[38] strongly encourages that the protocol include a means for client identification (initials—no names), date and time marking, measurements of the ulcer, and linear measurement scale next to the wound (i.e., 10 cm strip of paper tape) in each frame. The photographs become part of the medical record. HIPAA regulations require that every individual or her power of attorney sign an authorization form giving permission for the photographs.

The photographs present a good determination of the rate of healing or deterioration from the changes in measurements. The visual record becomes a communication tool between all specialties especially when the dressings are unable to be removed at the time of physician visits; home care shows the physician the visual records when the patient is unable to make physician visits.

Digital cameras are often used but there exists a liability issue with their potential for image alteration and enhancement. There must be certification by the facility that the pictures have not been altered. There should be standard guidelines established by the facility. Protocols should include: informed consent, control timing of photographs, criteria about who can take the photographs, type of camera being used, consistency in photographing the wounds, patient identification, date identification, identification of wound and information about maintenance of photographs.[39]

TIP: Defense attorneys and clinicians have discouraged taking photographs of deteriorating wounds. They are aware of the likelihood the photos will be used in the event of litigation to descriptively portray a wound. Clear photographs of large pressure ulcers are usually repulsive, especially to a non-medical person.

H. Pressure Ulcer Risk-Screening Tools

Pressure ulcer screening tools vary in terms of cost, ease of use, time required to do the screening, reliability, and predictive validity. It is important to note that depending on the severity of illness and comorbidities, less pressure may be required to obstruct capillary blood flow and cause skin breakdown. Pressure ulcers can develop within two to six hours.

TIP: The key to preventing pressure ulcers is to promptly identify at-risk individuals so preventive measures may occur.

Risk assessment has become part of the standard healthcare practice. Most external agencies that review or accredit healthcare facilities require that risk assessment and related protocols be used.[40] The AHRQ Panel Guidelines[41] recommends an assessment for pressure ulcer risk be done using a valid and reliable evidence-based assessment tool (e.g., Norton and Braden Scales).

Literature and research studies have documented that with the use of formal pressure ulcer risk assessment implementation and preventive protocols, pressure ulcer incidence and prevalence dropped by 60 percent.[42] The facility and staff become more aware of clients at risk for skin breakdown and preventive protocols are initiated. Recommended intervals for assessing pressure ulcer risk are based on the stability of the patient's condition, the severity of illness, and the clinical setting. Acute care clients should be assessed on admission, then at least every 48 hours or with changes in condition. Long-term care clients should be assessed on admission, every 48 hours for the first week, weekly for the first month, and monthly to quarterly thereafter, or whenever the health condition changes. Home health clients should be assessed on admission and at each visit.[43]

1. Braden Scale

The Braden Scale is among the most widely used tools for predicting the development of pressure ulcers.[44] It is widely used by all types of facilities and home care as a screening tool for initial assessment and reassessment of clients at risk worldwide. This tool consists of six subscales that evaluate sensory perception, activity level, mobility, nutrition status, and current exposure to moisture, friction, and shearing forces. Each risk area is assigned a score ranging from one (highly impaired) to three/four (no impairment). All risk area scores are added and the total overall risk ranging from 6 to 23 is determined. The lower the Braden Score, the lower functioning level, and therefore the higher level of risk of developing pressure ulcers.[45]

Dr. Braden[46] has tested the complete tool for reliability and validity. Accurate use of the Braden Scale facilitates prevention by distinguishing individuals at risk for pressure ulcers. The scale is available for no charge at www.braden-scale.com/images/bradenscale.pdf. Dr. Braden has provided information about preventive interventions to accompany her scale to assist with the prevention of skin breakdown.

2. Norton scale

This rating scale consists of five parameters: physical condition, mental status, activity, mobility, and incontinence. Each category is rated on a scale of one to four and the sum of the ratings yields a score. A score of 16 or less indicates increased risk for pressure ulcer development. A lower score indicates increasing risk of skin breakdown. Norton found a relationship between the scores of elderly patients and the incidence of pressure ulcers.

3. PUSH tool

The PUSH tool does not represent a comprehensive pressure ulcer assessment. The pressure ulcer is assessed and scored on the three elements in the tool:

1. length times width
2. exudate amount
3. tissue type

This tool monitors the healing of the ulcer only. The clinician must look at all other comorbid conditions of the patient plus other risks for skin breakdown.

25.7 Burns

Burns may result from nursing negligence. Mechanisms of injury may occur in a number of ways. The American Burn Association has established policies and procedures about the triage and treatment of burns. Burn wounds are a unique type of wound and are not treated like other wounds. Each burn patient, each burn wound on a given patient, and each patient's clinical status differs from all others.[47] Nurses who treat burns should attend a certification course on burns that prepares them to triage, treat, and provide appropriate transfers. Nurses must be aware of causation of burns in the normal hospital setting (e.g., heating pads, operating room grounding pads, allergic reactions to chemicals causing sloughing of the skin and tape burns). Once discovered, such wounds must be reported to the appropriate department and causation must be investigated. The following are examples of burns that have been sustained while a patient was under the care of a nurse:

- A quadriplegic man was scalded when a nursing home aide added coffee urn water to his tub.
- A woman in a nursing home rolled into a hot radiator and was in this position undetected for one hour.
- A woman was unsupervised while smoking in her home. Her clothes caught fire, resulting in burns.
- An elderly woman in a nursing home was burned on her buttocks when the heating pad was turned up too high.
- A man in a nursing home was smoking unsupervised and set his bed and himself on fire, resulting in double amputation and death.
- A woman in the hospital spilled hot tea water on her lap, resulting in burns to her thighs and perineal area.
- A strong acidic solution was handed to a surgeon by an OR nurse instead of the 3 percent that was to be used. Severe genital burns resulted.
- An infant was burned by a diaper heated in the microwave.
- A man was burned under the electrocautery grounding pad during surgery because of improper placement of the pad with a wrinkle in it, letting some drainage under the pad.
- A woman was burned by an electrocautery grounding pad applied on top of the anti-embolism stocking.
- A man was burned in surgery under the electrocautery grounding pad because it was placed over an open skin tear area on the buttock.
- An infant's arm was burned by a light used to illuminate her veins.
- A nursing home resident was left unattended in the hot sun and developed a severe sunburn.

The American Burn Association, which establishes policies and procedures about the triage and treatment of burns, is constantly investigating new ways of treatment. Burn wounds are unique and are not treated like other wounds. They are dynamic and can evolve into deeper injuries over time, depending on the initial injury, treatment, and subsequent environmental insults. A burn is defined as an injury to the skin or other organic tissue caused by thermal or acute trauma. It occurs when some or all of the cells in the skin or other tissues are destroyed by hot liquids (scalds), hot solids (contact burns), or flames (flame burns).[48]

TIP: Tissue injury beneath the nonviable tissue can continue to develop because of additional heat and inflammation. The underlying damage of tissue can either deteriorate with necrosis of the tissue or begin to heal over a period of time.

Treatment needs to be individualized for each patient because of other comorbid problems. The depth of the heat injury depends on the length of time of heat exposure and the penetration depth of that heat. Wet heat (scald) travels more rapidly into tissue than dry heat (flame) because water conducts heat 100 times greater than air.[49]

Important facts about burns include:

- Most people are killed by cardiac arrest.
- Electrical shock may result in unconsciousness and orthopedic injuries.
- The wound is difficult to assess—most of the damage is beneath the skin.
- Fluid resuscitation is difficult—clinicians cannot rely on the burn size.

A. Classification of Burn Injuries

1. First-degree burns

First-degree burns are superficial tissue destructions involving only the epidermis. Key points are:

- There may be local pain and erythema (redness); blisters are absent for about 24 hours.
- The burns may be dry and without blisters.
- There is minimal or no edema.
- The burn area blanches with fingertip pressure and refills when pressure is removed.
- There may be mild to absent systemic response.
- The burn may need no treatment except in large burns of infants or the elderly.

- The burn heals in three to five days with peeling but no scarring; it may discolor.
- Treatment consists of topical agents: lotions, emollients.
- Examples of first-degree burns are sunburn and flash flame.

2. Second-degree burns (partial thickness)

This burn is superficial partial thickness tissue destruction involving the epidermis and portions of the dermis. Key points are:

- The second-degree burn is red to pale ivory.
- The burn is mottled with pink, red, white, tan areas.
- The burn is moist in appearance.
- Tactile and pain sensors are intact.
- There may be large moist blisters that will increase in size.
- The burn blanches with fingertip pressure and refills when pressure removed.
- The area may be very painful.
- The burn heals in 10 to 21 days with variable amounts of scarring.
- The burn may convert to full thickness and require grafting.
- Treatment is performed with topical agents: Bacitracin, Xeroform.
- Examples of causes of second-degree burns are contact with hot liquids or solids; flash flame to clothing; direct flame; chemicals; and ultraviolet light.

3. Second-degree burns (deep partial thickness)

Deep partial thickness burns may involve the entire dermis, leaving only skin appendages. Key points are:

- Deep partial thickness burns are clinically indistinguishable from full-thickness burns at time of admission.
- Epidermis and some dermis are destroyed.
- There may be a mottled appearance with large areas of waxy white appearance.
- The skin surface is dry.
- The burn will heal spontaneously in about 30 days; current therapy includes excision and skin grafting.
- Hair follicles remain intact—hair will regrow.

- Cause considerable scar formation—hypertrophic scarring is common and joint function is usually impaired.[50]
- Deep partial thickness burn results from contact with hot liquids or solids; flash flame to clothing; direct flame; chemicals; and ultraviolet light.

In partial thickness burns, the viable tissue beneath the layer of necrosis is still injured—known as the "zone of injury"—and can become nonviable over time depending on the degree of injury and subsequent insults, such as infection.[51]

4. Third-degree burns (full thickness)

Third-degree burns involve the epidermis, dermis, and often injure underlying subcutaneous adipose tissue layer. These burns:

- may extend to subcutaneous tissue, muscle, or bone
- appear white, cherry red, dark tan, or black; may or may not contain a deep blister; may contain visible thrombosed veins (because of destruction of skin elasticity)
- are dry with leathery eschar
- have charred vessels visible under eschar
- may include thick-walled blisters that do not increase in size
- do not blanch with pressure
- result in destruction of elasticity of dermis, giving the wound a dry, hard, leathery appearance
- are accompanied by marked edema and decreased elasticity, which may necessitate escharotomies of circumferential burns
- are painless to touch
- have no healing potential
- require excision and grafting, depending on extent and location
- may require amputation
- potential threat of wound sepsis
- are treated with Silvadene, Sulfamylon
- come from contact with hot liquids or solids, flame, or chemicals or electrical contact

---

TIP: Burned skin (third-degree) becomes tough, dry, and leathery and loses its elasticity. Because of this restriction the patient is unable to breathe appropriately. Incisions made along the skin allow the tissue to expand and decrease pressure on the underlying structures. Escharotomies are performed anywhere on the body where the burn surface or swelling interferes with circulation.

A full-thickness burn results in complete destruction of the epidermis and dermis, leaving no residual epidermal cells to promote granulation. Initially, the dead avascular burn tissue (eschar) appears waxy white in color. If the burn produces char or extends into the adipose layer due to prolonged contact with a flame source, a leathery brown or black appearance can be seen, along with surface coagulation veins.

Early surgical debridement of the damaged tissue is important and is typically followed by closure of the area with skin grafting or skin substitute such as Dermagraft-TC, synthetic grafts, cultured epithelial autograft (CEA), including Integra and BioBrane. Deep burn wounds are typically surgically excised and closed with a skin graft or skin substitute early in their course.

5. Fourth-degree burns (destruction of muscle and bone)

Fourth-degree burns are the most severe burn injuries and involve both skin and underlying structures, such as muscle and bone. The tissue is dead metabolically with full-thickness skin loss with eschar (charred tissue). Once the charred tissue is removed it becomes an open wound prone to infection with plasma (fluid) loss and heat loss. This burn goes through all the layers of the skin and down into the muscle and bone and there are serious complications and harm to the body structure. Fourth-degree burns demand immediate emergency attention in a burn center.

TIP: Appropriate burn wound care may necessitate multiple treatment modalities, each with varying sequencing, for different parts of a burn wound depending on the burn depth of each injured part.[52]

B. Transfer of Burn Patients

Burn patients who should be transferred to a certified burn center are those who have:

1. Partial thickness burns greater than 10 percent of total body surface area (TBSA)
2. Burns that involve the face, hands, feet, genitalia, perineum, or major joints
3. Third-degree burns in any age group
4. Electrical burns, including lightning injury
5. Chemical burns
6. Inhalation injury
7. Pre-existing medical disorders that could complicate management, prolong recovery, or affect mortality (diabetes mellitus, obesity, hypertension and cardiovascular disease)
8. Burns and concomitant trauma (such as fractures)

in which the burn injury poses the greatest risk of morbidity or mortality.

9. Pediatric burns in hospitals without qualified personnel or equipment for the care of children.
10. Special social, emotional, or long-term rehabilitation interventions.[53]

25.8 Other Ulcers

It is important to differentiate the types of ulcers that exist in order to prescribe timely and appropriate treatment. The ulcer type must be diagnosed and appropriate diagnostic testing done. Delay in treatment, misdiagnosis of the ulcer, and inappropriate treatment can result in deterioration of the ulcers, resulting in non-healing ulcers or amputation.

A. Arterial Ulcers

Assessment is important for signs and symptoms of arterial disease when complaints are made of foot pain or calf muscle pain. Risk factors for atherosclerotic arterial occlusive disease and arterial insufficiency ulcers are diabetes, smoking, advanced age, hyperlipidemia, and hypertension. Diagnosis is typically corroborated by noninvasive tests, but angiography may be required. The underlying cause needs to be investigated. Liability becomes apparent when lack of diagnostic testing occurs and appropriate treatment does not happen in a timely manner. The cause must be treated (e.g., bypass grafting or balloon angioplasty). The person is at risk for deterioration of diabetic-related arterial ulcers with necrosis and possible amputation. Treatment of arterial leg ulcers is directed towards correcting the poor arterial blood supply; for example, by surgically correcting arterial blockages, and by supporting ulcer healing using topical agents (medicines in cream or ointment) and wound dressings. The nursing admission assessment should document signs and symptoms of circulation problems and any history that involves impairment of circulation (e.g., diabetes, arteriosclerosis, prior arterial surgery, and edema). It is important that documentation includes pulses, circulation, or sensation of the lower extremity. There must be good communication between nurses and the physician when such signs and symptoms of circulation problems exist.

B. Venous Ulcers

Vascular compromise of the lower leg can result in ischemia of the tissues, which results in tissue breakdown, necrosis, and loss of limb. The most common healing processes are multi-layer compression dressings and/or a zinc oxide impregnated dressing, which provides improved circulation and a moist wound environment. Congestive heart failure is a risk because of pushing fluid upwards in the body related to improper compression wrapping of the lower legs. Controlling edema (swelling) and venous hypertension is important. The goal of treatment is to prevent superinfection by use of topicals and frequent dressing changes. The healthcare team promotes healing by debridement, use of growth factors, grafts, and a maintenance program for edema control. Consistent good compression (through compression stockings, circ-aids, sequential compression dressings, ace wraps, tubigrip and thrombo embolic device stockings) is the most important part of treatment. Non-diagnosed edema and treatment may cause this compromise and result in non-healing ulcers and osteomyelitis. Prompt assessment and reassessment and reporting to the physician of the edema and increasing pain should trigger diagnostic studies and result in salvage of the limb by a revascularization procedure.

TIP: Vascular diseases (arterial and venous), which impair tissue perfusion and oxygenation, need to be corrected by surgery or managed carefully to assist in healing.

Please see Table 25.1 for a comparison of arterial, venous, and neuropathic ulcers. Diabetics are prone to neuropathic ulcers, which are caused by lack of sensation to the feet and reduced circulation.

25.9 Plan of Care

Based on the immediate medical conditions and comorbid conditions that exist, the standard of care requires that a plan of care be developed by the nursing staff and all involved specialties. This care plan should be revisited and revised as wounds, ulcers, and the medical condition change throughout the patient's stay in the acute or long-term care setting.

TIP: Assessment of the individual should be done every shift, or more often as the condition warrants. The care plan should be changed appropriately.

Formulation of the care plan should be completed within 24 hours in an acute care setting and within seven days in the long-term care setting. The goal of developing a comprehensive plan of care is to provide individualized care in the setting based on the specific medical needs. The comprehensive individualized care plan must address all elements identified through the comprehensive assessment when admitted to the facility. Care is planned and provided in an interdisciplinary, collaborative manner by all specialties (nursing, certified nursing assistants, physical therapy, occupational therapy, speech therapy, dieticians, and so on). Please refer to Chapter 6, *The Foundations of Nursing Practice*, in Volume I, for additional information.

Effective prevention and treatment are based upon consistently providing such routine interventions and individu-

alized interventions as

1. turning more frequently than every two hours,
2. blood sugar testing,
3. supplemental protein foods,
4. intake and output records when appropriate,
5. protective ointments with individuals in diapers,
6. elevating the heels off of the mattress, and
7. elevating the head of the bed above 30° because of severe respiratory conditions or aspiration precautions.

If the care plan becomes obsolete, the patient/resident is not being taken care of appropriately and in a timely manner.

TIP: Patients deserve care that respects their choices, supports their participation in the care provided, and recognizes their right to achieve personal health goals.

The Federal Regulations in the Nursing Facility states that "each resident must receive and the facility must provide the necessary care and services to attain or maintain the highest practicable physical, mental, and psychosocial well-being, in accordance with the comprehensive assessment and plan of care."[54]

25.10 Pain

All clients must be assessed for pain related to the wound or its treatment. Assessment tools may be found in the acute pain management guidelines (policy and procedures) of the facility.

TIP: Caregivers should not assume pain does not exist because an individual cannot express or respond to it.

A majority of patients with wounds or ulcers experience pain both at rest and at dressing change; pain varies in intensity from mild to excruciating. A new onset of pain or increase in pain may indicate "infection, underlying tissue destruction that is not visible, or vascular insufficiency."[55] A ten-point pain scale, with ten being severe, should be used to assess the pain level. This should be evaluated with every shift assessment, and if a change in condition occurs, the cause must be treated. Federal Regulations in the Nursing Facility requires that every patient's pain be measured regularly from the time the patient is admitted and that proper pain relief is administered. Interventions need to be taken to alleviate the cause or causes of pain on a regular basis.[56] Pain that interferes with movement and affects mood or nutritional intake may contribute to immobility and add to the potential for developing a pressure ulcer or to the potential for delayed wound healing or non-healing of an existing ulcer.[57]

Table 25.1
Comparison of Arterial, Venous and Neuropathic Ulcers

Type	Definition	Location	Symptoms	Characteristics
1. Arterial	Ulcer due to blockage of arteries leading to inadequate circulation to the lower extremity	This type of ulcer is usually located on the feet, often on the heels, tips of toes, and between the toes where the toes rub against one another. They occur commonly in the nail bed if the toenail cuts into the nail bed.	Patients with arterial circulation problems complain of severe pain described as burning, cramping or aching. Pain is relieved by dependency of the limb or dangling it over the side of the bed. When the legs are in a dependent position they become red related to the position and this redness disappears when the leg is elevated. The ulcer has very little bleeding.	The ulcer appears with well-defined edges—a punched out look. The wound base appears pale and dry. The wound base color can be yellow, brown, gray or black. It may have swelling and redness around the ulcer base on the good skin.
2. Venous	Chronic venous insufficiency ulcers are caused by venous hypertension in the lower extremity. Venous hypertension is most commonly the result of dysfunctional values that do not allow the upward flow of blood in the lower veins of the legs.	The ulcers are found in the gator (sock) region of the leg—proximal to the malleolus, the lateral lower leg, the gator sock area.	The pain is described as dull, aching heaviness and many times continues after the ulcer has healed. The pain is relieved by elevation of the legs. The ulcer has a large amount of drainage. Other characteristics are: yellow slough (necrotic tissue), redness, inflammation, slough tissue, edema and odor.	It appears as a shallow irregular shaped ulcer with a granulating (red) wound base, irregular stasis dermatitis, and hyperpigmentation (hemosiderin staining). Palpable pedal and/or posterior pedal and/or posterior tibial pulses are present. It has a large amount of drainage and odor.
3. Neuropathic	Diabetics have a decrease in the size of the blood vessels causing poor circulation (poor blood supply) to the extremities. They are prone to ulcers on the leg or foot, due to vascular and neurological complications. Tissue hypoxia and infection play major roles in healing failure. Anyone with impaired sensation of the feet can also be prone to ulcerations.	Over time because of the lack of sensation diabetics develop abnormal pressure points that become prone to ulcers. Ulcers on the leg or foot, due to vascular and neurological complications. Usually related to minor trauma. Dryness of the foot leads to foot calluses and cracks in the skin surface.	Diabetics are well known to develop severe neuropathies (impaired protective sensation) of the feet and may extend up the lower legs sometimes as high as the knees. Pain present depends on the severity of the neuropathy. Pain quality is described as "pins and needles," tingling, numbness and burning sensation and itching.	Ulcerations of the soles of the feet (plantar area) usually under metatarsal heads are the frequent locations. Ulcers are very slow healing or non-healing. It is very common to have osteomyelitis (infection of the bone). Ulcers may appear pink/red in color or brown/black. Surrounding tissue of ulcer is often calloused.

25.11 Major Comorbid Conditions
A. Systemic Conditions

Any systemic condition that adversely affects health status can negatively alter healing. Renal and hepatic disease, malignancy, and sepsis are among these conditions. In addition to systemic factors, local factors such as wound bed desiccation (drying of the wound bed), hypothermia, and heavy bacterial colonization can affect the repair process.[58]

B. Tissue Perfusion

Chronic tissue hypoxia has been associated with impaired collagen synthesis and reduced tissue resistance to infection.[59] Decreased oxygenation of the blood and tissue perfusion status is often related to a delay or deterioration in healing repair. Oxygen is critical to the healing process and fuels the cellular functions essential to both repair and the healing process.

TIP: Untreated anemia, edema, abnormal lab values, or dehydration mean less oxygen to the cells for cellular repair and healing.

Interventions to support healing must address both tissue perfusion and oxygenation. Cigarette smoking is particularly deleterious to healing because it affects perfusion and oxygenation.[60] Patient education promotes the decrease or cessation of smoking because smoking decreases the oxygen content of the red blood cells. Smoking is linked to greater risk of cardiovascular disease, respiratory related diseases, and poor healing. Quitting smoking has proven health benefits, even at a late age. When an older person quits smoking, circulation improves immediately, and the lungs begin to repair damage. Some surgeons will not operate until the individual has stopped smoking for three to four weeks before elective surgery. One vascular surgeon will not treat vascular or arterial ulcers unless the client agrees to stop smoking.

C. Anemia

Anemia is also a contributing factor in determining whether cellular hypoxia (lack of oxygen) and cellular death will occur. Cellular survival is threatened when there is a decrease in the red blood cells, which carry oxygen and nutrients to the cells of the body. Cellular metabolism is restricted further in anemia. Well-hydrated and nourished tissue is viable and helps prevent against the adverse effects of comorbidities.[61]

D. Edema

Edema of varying degrees is undoubtedly a contributing factor of skin breakdown. An increased amount of interstitial fluid widens the distance from the capillary to the cell. Decreased cellular oxygen and nutrient delivery to the cells intensify metabolic wastes which increases bacterial colonization, raising osmotic pressure and cell dehydration because of the inability to delivery oxygen and nutrients to the cell. The cells become fragile and more susceptible to minimal trauma, which results in skin breakdown/pressure injury and cellular death.[62]

E. Moisture

Constant exposure to wetness can waterlog or macerate the skin. Moisture is absorbed into the epidermis and it becomes soft, fragile, and susceptible to breakdown. Excessive moisture may be the result of perspiration, gastrostomy tube drainage, drainage, soaking the skin during bathing, and fecal or urinary incontinence.

TIP: Maceration is a contributing factor in the etiology of skin breakdown primarily because the excessive moisture softens the tough epidermis layer.

Once macerated, the epidermis (the tough outer protective layer of skin) is easily eroded. Tissue becomes fragile. Moist skin is five times as likely to become damaged or ulcerated as dry skin. Moist skin increases the risk of friction as the patient is moved across the surface of the bed linen.

F. Incontinence

Fecal incontinence exposes the skin to bacteria in the stool and adds to the risk of infection. If the patient is incontinent of both urine and stool, the urea from the urine reacts chemically with the stool and causes further damage.[63] It is important the nurses use absorptive underpads or briefs as appropriate to wick the moisture away from the skin surface. Regular changing should occur with incontinent patients. The care plan for a patient with a risk of moisture related to incontinence should have goals designed to reduce the contact of moisture with the skin. It is important to determine the cause of incontinence and investigate. Frequent causes of incontinence include infection, impaction, antibiotic administration, infrequent toileting, and intolerance of tube feedings.[64]

TIP: Fecal incontinence provides an environment where physical and chemical trauma compromise tissue integrity and increase the chance of developing reddened, excoriated skin.

Skin breakdown develops because of the weakening of the protective tough epidermis layer of the skin. With added friction, shearing, and pressure, the skin continues to break-down, developing into pressure ulcers.

G. Nutritional Status

Nutritional status is critical to wound repair. Nutrients provide the raw materials needed for the multitude of cellular activities that constitute wound healing. Initial nutritional assessment and continued management are essential to any successful treatment program. Prevention and early intervention are instrumental in caring for patients nutritionally at risk. Sufficient nutrition is important to maintain the body in positive nitrogen balance to increase wound healing. Compromised nutritional status such as unintentional weight loss, under nutrition, protein energy malnutrition and dehydration deficits are know risk factors for pressure ulcer development. Other risk factors which are nutrition related are: low body mass index, reduced food intake and impaired ability to eat independently.[65]

TIP: Adequate nutrition is critical in maintaining a competent immune system and therefore prevents infection.

Protein, calories, vitamin C, vitamin A, and zinc are important elements to supplement and monitor; the amino acids arginine and glutamine may also be important to supplement.[66] Every effort should be made to prepare palatable meals served in an environment conducive to eating. Special care must be taken to make pureed and mechanically altered diets attractive. Food molds and special preparation techniques are crucial in improving the visual appeal of these modified texture diets. Menus also should be individualized, culturally appropriate, and varied to optimize intake and avoid flavor fatigue.

Medical nutritional supplements can be incorporated into the plan of care if oral intake is still below desired levels after all practical issues have been addressed.[67] Similarly, adding an appropriate amount of powdered protein supplement can augment the nutritional value of cereal and similar foods.

1. Protein calorie malnutrition (PCM)

Protein calorie malnutrition is common among patients subjected to catabolic stress as the result of wounds, burns, injuries, surgery, sepsis, or certain chronic diseases (e.g., cancer). Such catabolic stimuli may be particularly hazardous if the nutritional status is already compromised by inadequate intake.[68]

TIP: Patients with burns, wounds, or infection who are adequately nourished at the time of their injury may nevertheless develop protein-calorie malnutrition.

Injury causes an increased metabolic rate, which results in an increase in caloric need. The degree of hypermetabolism is directly related to the severity of injury. The caloric needs are increased and, simultaneously, protein needs are increased disproportionally.[69] Protein is abnormally diverted into energy generating metabolic pathways. Such a sustained catabolic stimulus can lead to the depletion of lean body mass (LBM) and profound unintentional weight loss. Mortality is high in patients who have sustained LBM losses of about 30 percent. Pressure ulcers are common,[70] as the following case shows:

The plaintiff entered a nursing home with deconditioning and weakness, known pressure ulcer of the left buttock (stage II), incontinence of bowel and bladder, history of weight loss, foley catheter and totally dependent on the nursing staff and agents to take care of her daily needs including hydration and nutrition. Facility medical records contain a documentation form to record the percentage consumed at each meal and any refusals of food. Upon review of the medical records less than 50 percent of the meal percentage was documented, refusals were documented but no documentation appeared about offering substitutions for refusal of food/fluid. Labs done showed a gradual deterioration and her protein stores and gradual decrease in her weight (three different times it was recorded during her residency significant weight loss of 9 percent in 90 days, 5.6 percent in 30 days and 7.9 percent in 90 days). During her residency she continued with pressure related skin breakdown of bilateral heels, right buttock, coccyx, left buttock and elbow. Many studies cite a strong link between deteriorating nutritional status, weight loss, decreased protein stores and the development and healing of skin breakdown. In relation to nutrition deficits plaintiff's attorneys alleged that the facility failed to document the intake/output of nutrition on a resident who was dependent upon the staff, reassess Mrs. F's nutritional status when significant changes in status occurred, provide adequate nutritional care to facilitate the prevention and healing of skin breakdown, offer supplements when the resident had documented poor intake, offer substitutes of equal food when refusals happened, weigh the patient on a regular basis when reported weight loss, failure of the certified dietician manager and certified registered dietician to address and respond in a timely manner to decrease in weight and skin breakdown development progressions.

Nutritional interventions should ensure adequate caloric intake to address malnutrition, including the removal of nonessential dietary restrictions and medications, treatment of the cause of anorexia when known, supplementation with calories and protein, and consideration of enteral feeding when appropriate.[71] Often with chronic wounds, a secondary insult occurs and causes the metabolic needs to rise. This can be seen during infection in chronic wounds.

For patients with functional gastrointestinal systems, the final option in treating involuntary weight loss is tube feedings. Placement of a feeding tube may be considered as a last resort (as explained below) to supply adequate nutrition. It is important to discuss this option early in the treatment of involuntary weight loss and PCM (protein calorie malnutrition) to allow the patient and family adequate time to consider it. All discussions should be documented in the patient record. The use of enteral and parenteral nutritional support should always be considered when the patient is unable to meet nutritional needs because of the inability to chew or swallow, thus decreasing the absorption of nutrients.[72]

Tube feedings are important for maintaining the nutritional status of a patient, yet someone must be evaluating and documenting adequate, appropriate, and timely nutritional assessments and ensure the tube feedings are done correctly. Weighing the patient is an important part of the nutritional assess and should be done on the same scales and with the same chair (if needed) each time. The following case demonstrates the failure to do this:

> The patient was an 81-year-old with the diagnosis of unstable angina. Her past medical history included hypertension, hyperlipidemia, diabetes, seizures, and Parkinson's disease. Clinical nutrition notes documented the patient weighed 189 pounds on February 28, and 165 pounds on March 8. A suggested goal rate of Glucerna was 65 cc/hr. On March 11, there was no reported tube-feeding intolerance; the tube feeding was running at 30 cc/hr. Per the nurse the patient was taking the tube feeding with low residuals. On March 15, the tube feeding was only at 45 cc/hr and weight was documented as 168 pounds. On March 19, the tube feeding continued at 45 cc/hr. On March 22, the tube feeding remained at 45 cc/hr (71 percent of caloric needs) and the patient was unable to take clear liquids. The physician requested further nutritional assessment and consideration of a PEG tube on March 27. On March 28, the clinical nutrition notes indicated the patient was eating poorly and

her albumin continued to be low. After hospitalization for surgery and return to the nursing facility on April 22 documentation verified the patient's weight at 147.9 pounds. Deviations from the acceptable standard of care caused and/or contributed to damages suffered, including but not limited to malnutrition and a stage IV ulcer on the left heel and the bridge of the nose. (The settlement was undisclosed.)

2. Lab values

Persons at risk for malnutrition need to have a nutritional assessment on admission to a nursing home. The assessment should be repeated at least every month unless there is a deterioration in condition. "No laboratory test can specifically determine an individual's nutritional status. Serum albumin, prealbumin and other lab values may be useful to help establish overall prognosis but may not correlate well with clinical observation of nutritional status."[73] Multiple factors decrease albumin levels (which have historically been used widely in practice) as an indicator of visceral protein status. Decreased albumin levels may happen even when protein intake is appropriate and adequate. Multiple factors that affect the albumin levels could be: infection, acute stress, surgery, cortisone excess, hydration status.

Inadequate intake of protein causes the body to break down muscles (catabolism) to obtain enough amino acids for the continuing synthesis of serum albumin. Thus albumin levels do not drop in fasting states or in malnutrition until the condition is severe. Protein requirements may be greatly increased during stress, infection, or injury. Although albumin normally has a long half-life, the serum albumin may fall within three to five days in a critically ill client. The degree of decrease reflects the severity of the illness.

Prealbumin is a sensitive indicator of recent changes in catabolism because of its short half-life of only 1.9 days. Low levels of prealbumin signify the need for a comprehensive nutritional evaluation.

TIP: Current weight and calorie counts may help determine therapy needed to restore and maintain nutritional balance.

Prealbumin responds quickly to refeeding. Prealbumin concentrations of 18 to 45 mg/dL are within normal limits. Values of 10 to 18 mg/dL are indicative of mild depletion. Moderate depletion is considered to be values of 5 to 9 mg/dL, and less than 5 mg/dL is indicative of severe PCM (protein calorie malnutrition) which can be life-threatening. Concurrent corticosteroid treatment or renal insufficiency can falsely elevate prealbumin. It is important to also do daily food and fluid intake, daily weights and frequent reviews of nutrition interventions.

3. Pressure ulcers and nutrition

Many studies cite a strong link between deteriorating nutritional status and the lack of development and healing of skin breakdown. Nutritional status should be screened and assessed at admission, with each condition change, and when progress towards healing is not observed.

1. Refer all individuals with a pressure ulcer to the dietician for early assessment of and intervention for nutritional problems.
2. Assess weight status for each individual to determine weight history and significant weight loss from usual body weight.
3. Assess the individual's ability to eat independently.
4. Assess the adequacy of total nutrient intake (food, fluid, oral supplements, enteral/parenteral feedings).[74]

TIP: The goal of nutritional intervention is to optimize the environment for healing by providing adequate nutrients, to fuel healing and to maintain body weight.

Studies abound on how the absence of specific qualities of nutrients and protein affect the overall condition of the patient and potential for skin breakdown and healing. Nutritional support is important, and literature indicates that protein above and beyond the normal range is necessary to help the body with stress of severe skin breakdown and infection.

When the nutritional assessment confirms the individual is malnourished, the first interventions consist of assisted oral feeding and oral supplements. Nutritional support (usually tube feedings) should be used to place the patient into positive nitrogen balance if dietary intake continues to be inadequate, impractical, or impossible. A second assessment should be done within three days to determine whether intake goals have been achieved. If intake is still inadequate, tube feeding should be initiated to achieve a positive nitrogen balance. The goal is to create an environment that enhances soft tissue viability and promotes healing of the pressure ulcer.[75]

TIP: Involuntary weight loss can be either an insidious process that gradually happens over time or a sudden dramatic decrease in body weight.

Typically, the loss of body weight is accompanied by PCM, making this a critical problem. Certain patients are especially prone to PCM, such as those experiencing a catabolic state due to a wound, burn, sepsis, fever, major surgery, or other catabolic condition. Immunocompromise from cancer, certain oncologic therapies, or HIV infection also leaves patients at risk for PCM, again because immunocompromise is conducive to a net catabolic or hypermetabolic state, which means the patient burns calories by breaking down muscle mass.

Patients with various diagnoses are predisposed to or at high risk for developing PCM. Among them are patients with diseases or conditions that force the body into a state of hypercatabolism or hypermetabolism. Diagnoses in this category include wounds, burns, sepsis, major surgery, cancer, pulmonary disease, or any major traumatic injury. These conditions put stress on the body, thereby greatly increasing nutrient needs. Protein calorie malnutrition:

*   decreases immune response
*   decreases angiogenesis
*   decreases collagen synthesis
*   decreases epidermal migration
*   decreases tensile strength
*   alters the immune response
*   alters the inflammatory reaction
*   alters tissue regeneration
*   places the patient at risk for development of pressure ulcers
*   places the patient at risk for delayed healing of pressure ulcers

The following case alleges that inadequate care resulted in malnutrition, dehydration, and pressure ulcers:

A young man with severe cognitive impairments resided at a long-term care facility and was totally dependent on the nursing home staff which included all ADLs, nutrition and turning/repositioning. His needs were supposed to be anticipated by the nursing home staff. He resided at this nursing home for two months during which time he became severely malnourished and dehydrated and developed a very extensive stage IV pressure ulcer on his sacrum. His sacral bone was exposed and the ulcer was infected. His overall condition rapidly deteriorated and he was hospitalized in critical condition. He eventually died from complications related to his injury. Plaintiffs alleged that "under the Nursing Home Care Act, the nursing home was obligated to provide the adequate care needed to prevent Mr. X's condition from deteriorating." They had an obligation to communicate that they could not provide the care Mr. X needed because of his cognitive and behavioral deficits to his family and transfer him to a facility that could accommodate his needs. The facility and physician agreed to pay $700,000 to the family.[76]

4. Weight

Baseline admission weight should be done for individuals:

- with pressure ulcers
- with unplanned weight loss or gain
- who are 10 percent below their ideal body weight
- with an admission diagnosis of malnutrition or dehydration
- who leave more than 50 percent of their food uneaten at most meals
- on parenteral and enteral nutrition.
- on dialysis
- with poorly controlled diabetics
- receiving drug therapy that may contribute to nutritional deficiencies

---

TIP: Clinical conditions (e.g., refusal to eat, advanced disease, burns, chemotherapy, and so on) may impede the maintenance of acceptable nutrition.

Individuals at risk for nutritional problems should be weighed weekly. With the onset of illness, the connection between changes in admission weight and present weight provides a valuable index of nutritional assessment. If weight loss persists even after all practical, environmental, and dietary interventions have been tried and documented, it may be appropriate to consider pharmacologic interventions.

Involuntary weight loss correlates with:

- pressure ulcer occurrence
- infections
- loss of muscle, mobility
- decreased albumin, prealbumin
- increased mortality rates
- decreased immunity

Liability issues specific to nurses and nutrition issues may consist of:

- failure to provide a nutritional care plan with timely and appropriate nutritional interventions for a patient with poor nutritional intake.
- failure by the facility and its agents to accurately assess nutritional intake, fluid intake, and protein and caloric needs.
- failure to monitor and record: food intake daily on a resident at risk for nutrition or hydration problems related to chronic pain; use of narcotics; and care plan documentation requiring intake and output (I&O) records.
- failure of the hospital and its staff to reassess nutritional status when significant changes in status occur, such as decreased albumin, decreased prealbumin, decreased oral intake, and NPO (nothing by mouth) for several days.
- failure to keep I&O records documented with a resident who has skin breakdown, decreased intake, foley catheter, and constipation problems.
- failure to document the I&O of nutrition and hydration on a patient dependent on the staff of the hospital to provide extra protein and vitamins to assist in the healing process of her beginning skin breakdown.
- failure to provide adequate nutritional care to facilitate the prevention and healing of skin breakdown.
- failure to prevent weight loss.
- failure to inform the family in a timely manner of changes in the condition or refusal of the resident to eat.
- failure of the nursing staff, certified dietician manager, and certified registered dietician to address and respond in a timely manner to declines in nutritional intake, declines in albumin levels, and skin breakdown development progression.
- failure to include the clinical and laboratory evidence in the overall assessment and plan of care in a timely manner, which would additionally demonstrate the patient was at risk for deterioration of her skin breakdown and poor healing.
- failure to address anemia in a patient and take appropriate actions with appropriate dietary care plan.

H. Obesity

Wound healing problems may develop because of several obesity-related issues, because obese individuals often have concomitant medical problems. They tend to develop wound infections and dehiscence (separation of wound edges) at a rate greater than non-obese patients.

Comorbid medical problems that place them more at risk of pressure ulcers and non-healing are diabetes, hypertension, poor oxygenation related to pulmonary restrictive disease, poor circulation because fat tissue is not well perfused, delayed healing, proneness to infections, and malnourishment related to obesity. Poor tissue perfusion, tension to the wound edges, intra-abdominal pressure, inadequate oxygenation and protein malnutrition contribute to surgical complications and overall skin breakdown problems. Mobility also may be a problem in the obese, and pneumonia or deep venous thrombosis may occur secondary to immobility.

TIP: Obese individuals are prone to pressure ulcers related to unknown pressure distribution patterns and may develop pressure ulcers in abnormal areas (e.g., under the abdominal apron, under the breasts, between the fat rolls of the abdomen, sides, back, and between the buttocks) because of the weight of the skin.

It is not unusual to find pressure-related skin injury in atypical places in obese patients. Pressures within a deep skin fold are sufficient to cause this type of damage in the immobile patient. Pressure exerted over soft tissue for an extended period of time creates pressure necrosis. "Bottoming out" in bed causes pressure on the buttocks area from the bedsprings. "Bottoming out" is determined by placing the caregiver's hand with palm side up under the mattress overlay or seat cushion below the pressure ulcer skin breakdown area or under a bony prominence (which is a high risk for skin breakdown). If the caregiver can feel the patient's body through the mattress or chair cushion, the appropriate amount of pressure-reducing surface is not being used. A thicker or different type of support surface should be provided.

Bariatric (obese) individuals need to have special bariatric equipment fitted to the individual from the time of admission. It is important that the bed can support the weight of the patient and that the wheelchair/bedside chair is wide enough for them. The bed must be sufficiently wide enough to allow the individual to turn and long enough to keep the feet from touching the bottom of the bed.

The facility must also provide other bariatric equipment such as overhead trapezes on beds, walkers, and commodes.

Good skin assessments need to be done regularly, especially between the skin folds. Assistance is usually necessary in order to assess the skin folds and under the pannis areas.[77]

TIP: Calorie needs for healing are directly related to weight, so obese patients need increased calories for maintenance than with persons of normal weight.[78]

Liability issues specific to nurses and obesity issues may consist of:

- failure to provide properly sized equipment for an obese patient.
- failure to turn an obese patient regularly to relieve abnormal pressure to pressure points, as evidenced by documentation: "unable to position patient in bed due to size."
- failure to move the patient in bed appropriately as evidenced by documentation ("pulled up in bed"), which results in friction and shearing damage to the skin.
- failure to document regular skin assessments every shift as the hospital documentation and policies require. This may be evidenced by documentation: "skin intact as best can be assessed."
- failure to document intake and output on a patient with feeding tube and Foley catheter.
- failure to institute a plan of care and interventions necessary to prevent pressure ulcers with an obese patient.
- failure to use "team effort" by the healthcare staff in caring for an obese patient. This is evidenced by documentation that there was a lack of adequate staff to assist with turning of this patient.
- failure to document daily hygiene and personal care and assess the skin condition at the same time.
- failure to reflect in the nursing documentation consistently and repeatedly all necessary nursing interventions to prevent and minimize life-threatening complications in an acutely ill obese patient.
- failure on the part of the facility's administration to provide sufficient resources to care for an obese patient.
- failure to have the nursing staff educated and properly trained in the positioning of an obese patient dependent on the staff for all movement.
- failure to provide on admission nutritional assessment and reassessment to assist the dietician in determining the ongoing needs of an obese patient.
- failure to provide optimal nutritional support to meet the metabolic needs of the critically ill patient. The goal is not to place an obese patient on a weight reduction diet but rather optimize the environment of healing by providing adequate nutrients to fuel healing and maintain body weight.

- failure to assess and provide preventive measures to abnormal pressure areas on the obese patient such as within the skin folds and under the abdominal apron to make sure skin breakdown does not happen.

- failure to provide necessary care to an obese patient regarding documentation of inability to turn, lift or transfer the obese patient.

- failure to appreciate the significance of nutritional evaluation and laboratory investigation of the nutritional status of the critically ill patient.

I. Diabetes

Diabetics are well-known for poor healing of any type of break in skin integrity whether a wound or pressure-related skin breakdown. Blood vessels decrease in size with diabetes, causing poor blood supply circulation to the extremities and causing proneness to ulcers on the leg or foot due to vascular and neurological complications.

Nursing responsibilities include:

- performing good skin assessments,
- documenting all suspected areas (e.g., callous areas on the feet, fissures of the heels, reddened areas, abnormal bone formation and abnormal walking),
- monitoring of the glucose levels,
- documenting blood glucose levels accurately and promptly, and
- reporting unstable glucose levels and poor nutritional intake to the physician.

Communication between the nurses and physician is important so that immediate testing and evaluation can be done when the diabetic is at risk for complications. The physician needs to be informed of any vascular changes to the lower legs and feet, or refusals of the patient to take insulin.

In the elderly, diabetic complications may be untypical, mistaken for other medical problems or overshadowed by other illnesses. Management should include frequent blood glucose monitoring during an illness, with infection, or during times of high stress; management should also maintain adequate fluid and nutritional intake and communicate with the physician any changes in the patient's overall condition.[79]

An aggressive multidisciplinary approach is needed with the management of neuropathic (diabetic) wounds. The diabetic foot is especially vulnerable to amputation because of the frequent complications of peripheral neuropathy, infection, and peripheral vascular disease. This triad leads to

ulceration, infection, and finally gangrene and amputation. Once ulcers have developed it is important the healthcare team provide timely, appropriate, and consistent treatment to prevent more serious complications such as loss of digits or loss of limb. It is important that diabetics maintain strict stable glucose levels during periods of healing. High glucose levels alter leukocyte function and increase the risk of infection. If infection is present antibiotic treatment must be delivered with appropriate topical wound care. Diagnostic testing includes transcutaneous oxygen measurements, pulse examinations, and peripheral vascular evaluation.

Adjunctive hyperbaric oxygen treatments can be used in combination with revascularization. Measurements for appropriate orthotics help restore normal lifestyle while protecting from pressure-related ulcers on an insensate foot, which has no sensation of pain or discomfort and is sometimes reported as numbness of the feet.

Liability issues specific to nurses and diabetic issues may consist of:

- failure of the hospital and its agents to accurately assess nutritional, fluid, protein, and kcal needs and intakes of a diabetic patient.

- failure to provide an effective and complete nutritional care plan with timely appropriate nutritional interventions for a diabetic patient with poor intake.

- failure to monitor and maintain adequate and appropriate glucose levels in a resident with unstable diabetes, which could lead to complications, skin breakdown, and poor healing.

- failure to document continuous teaching and education on diabetes to the patient and family.

- failure to record and report to the physician unstable glucose monitoring.

- failure to include the clinical and lab evidence in the overall assessment and plan of care, which would demonstrate the patient was at risk for deterioration of skin breakdown and poor healing.

- failure to test a non-healing ulcer of the foot to determine if osteomyelitis is involved.

- failure to consult a wound care specialist to provide aggressive wound care for a patient with diabetic ulcers with necrotic tissue.

- failure to assess and treat circulation problems in a diabetic.

Delay in treatment of circulation problems with a diabetic can have a negative outcome as seen in the following case:

A 73-year-old female plaintiff was admitted to a nursing home with diabetes, electrolyte imbalance, hypertension, transient ischemic attack, and altered mental status. She was dependent on the facility for all care. Preventive interventions such as repositioning and elevating the heels were rarely documented. Her blood sugars were unstable, causing visits to the hospital, a lethargic condition, and poor healing. The resident had lower extremities cool to the touch; an absence of hair with dry, shiny skin; and faint pulses shortly after admission. She developed diminished pedal pulses, redness, edema, and cold feet. These signs and symptoms of peripheral vascular disease were not acted upon in this diabetic patient. The resident developed a diabetic ulcer of the foot. On September 5, a physician consult reported diabetic ulcers, severe contractures of legs and feet, discoloration of skin, an ulcer on the foot, and coolness of temperature. The physician's report states she had peripheral vascular disease in both feet with poor blood flow to the digital areas. The physician documented that care had to be given to treat the diabetic ulcer due to poor circulation.

On September 27, the nurses documented a weekly skin assessment: "Left great toe with dark black gangrene; left medial foot 3 x 3 no depth, no drainage; left lateral foot and 2 areas are now dark eccomotic. No palpable pedal pulse entire leg warm to touch." This information was placed in the problem book for the physician to assess. Fifteen days later, surgery was done because the deteriorating foot was starting to endanger her life. The plaintiff settlement amount is unknown.

Severe neuropathies (impaired protective sensation) may develop in diabetics. Neuropathies are known to occur in the feet and extend up the lower legs, sometimes as high as the knees. Diabetic ulcers can remain undetected for long periods of time because of the lack of pain sensation; some diabetics do not realize they have a break in skin integrity until the drainage is found on socks; by then, the damage is serious and infection is present.

TIP: It is important diabetics maintain strict stable glucose levels during periods of healing. High glucose levels alter leukocyte function and increase the risk of infection.

The vascular diseases (arterial and venous) that impair tissue perfusion and oxygenation need to be corrected by surgery or managed carefully to assist in healing. Diabetics must perform good skin checks on a regular daily basis and always wear foot covering such as a shoe to reduce repetitive trauma. It is strongly recommended they see a diabetic foot specialist to have regular checkups for corrective fitted shoes to relieve pressure points on their feet. Diabetics develop abnormal pressure points of the feet that become prone to ulcers because of the lack of sensation. Once ulcers are found it is important that timely, appropriate, and consistent treatment happen to prevent more serious complications such as loss of digits or loss of limb.

J. Infection

Infection is present when microorganisms invade the tissue and is another major complication that affects wound healing. Bioburden is the metabolic stress imposed by bacteria on a wound. All wounds are colonized but rarely are the bacteria present on the wound surface the same as the microorganisms responsible for wound infections. Infection disrupts the inflammatory phase of the healing cascade. It distracts the immune system. The normal immune response is interrupted and the body must spend more energy to fight the microorganisms. Infection is defined as the "presence of colonized bacterial growth greater than 100,000 or greater microorganisms 10 per gram of tissue if it extends into healthy surrounding tissue."[80] Typical signs and symptoms of infections are: purulent exudate, odor, erythema, induration, warmth, tenderness, edema, pain, fever and elevated white cell count. However, clinical signs of infection may not be present, especially in the immuno-compromised patient or the patient with poor perfusion.[81]

TIP: Cellulitis (inflammation marked by warmth and redness of the skin) must be addressed by the use of dressings, antibiotics, or surgery. Increased drainage or purulent drainage may be a sign of infection and must be investigated.

Fungus around a wound is often the result of cellulitis. It is easy to recognize and has a classic rash pattern and a yeast smell. It should be treated with a topical antifungal agent and sometimes systematic intravenous or oral antifungal treatment.[82]

Advancing infections are accompanied by an elevated white blood cell count and body temperature signs of a systemic infection. Other assessment criteria should be considered: delayed healing of a wound, discoloration, friable granulation tissue (bleeds too easily), unexpected pain or tenderness, pocketing of fluid at the base of the wound, abnormal smell, and wound breakdown.[83] Diabetics may not exhibit early signs of infection because of their medical condition. When signs are recognized the infection is often more intense than initially believed.

K. Infection and Pressure Ulcers

Odor and abnormal drainage indicate infection in pressure ulcers and need to be addressed appropriately. A wound infection prolongs the inflammatory phase, delays collagen synthesis, prevents epithelialization, and increases the production of pro-inflammatory cytokines, which may lead to additional tissue destruction. Infection is a common cause of wound chronicity and requires prompt aggressive treatment. Prompt surgical debridement of all infected and necrotic tissue is essential.

All pressure ulcers are contaminated and colonized with bacteria. An infection consists of growth of organisms with reaction from the wound such as erythema, edema, temperature change, drainage change, odor, and possibly complaints of pain. Dirty wounds and ulcers regularly contain dead cells, debris, and old wound drainage which act as a medium for the growth of bacteria. If wounds are not properly cleansed and regularly monitored, contamination can eventually lead to infection. Systemic infection related to an infected wound may sometimes be confirmed by a positive blood culture.[84]

Nurses are expected to describe infection signs and symptoms when documenting about the wound. The periulcer skin may appear as red, swollen and angry looking with warmth and induration. There may be a change in the color, volume, odor, and consistency of the drainage. Granulation tissue may appear as pale red or pale pink in color. Clinical signs may include fever; increase in white blood cells; spontaneous dehiscence; delayed healing with no improvement in two weeks in a clean ulcer; friable (easily disrupted) granulation tissue; tenderness to the surrounding skin; complaints of an increase in pain or new onset of pain; a positive tissue biopsy (also known as a punch biopsy: uses an instrument that punches the skin and removes a piece of tissue to document the presence of wound infection);[85] and sudden high glucose levels in a diabetic patient.

The AHCPR Guidelines published in 1994 recommend that if a pressure ulcer does not exhibit signs of healing with topical antibiotics within a two-week time period, the wound be cultured using a tissue biopsy. This is more definitive than a swab culture.[86]

TIP: Prompt removal of nonviable tissue prevents the growth of bacteria. It is important to recognize the signs of contamination and infection in pressure ulcers.

L. Steroids

Administration of corticosteroids during periods of stress affects many processes of wound healing. Steroids suppress and disrupt the inflammation phase. There is decreased healing and new skin formation. High levels of cortisol or steroids inhibit leukocyte and macrophage migration, which increases the wound's vulnerability to infection. Vitamin A and anabolic steroids can partially counteract the negative effects of cortiocosteroids.[87]

M. Aging

The aging process causes many changes in the skin and underlying tissues and makes patients more susceptible to injury, more prone to breaks in their skin integrity, and poor healers. Comorbid conditions and multiple medication use in the aging slows healing. See Table 25.2 for the changes in skin associated with aging.

N. Immunocompromised

Immunocompromised disease states (evidenced by chemotherapy or HIV infection) can severely impair the patient's ability to adequately continue with the healing phase.

TIP: Any disease process or medication that suppresses the immune system can alter healing. Connective tissue and inflammatory diseases—such as lupus, rheumatoid arthritis, Behcet's syndrome, scleroderma, and cryoglobulinemia—can severely impair wound healing as well as the treatment of wounds.[88]

O. Stress

The goal of psychosocial management is to create an environment conducive to patient adherence to the present ulcer treatment plan.[89] Stress is a potential cofactor in impaired healing. The proposed mechanism is through stimulation of the sympathetic nervous system, with the outflow of vasoactive substances and subsequent vasoconstriction. The major stressors usually are depression, change of lifestyle, disfigurement of the body, mental anguish, confusion, dependent on others to meet wants and needs, pain, psychological stress; some patients undergo a major lifestyle change and develop suicidal thoughts and actions.

TIP: Both psychological and physiological stress have been implicated as potential cofactors in skin breakdown and impaired wound healing.

Table 25.2

The aging person has many skin texture changes which consist of:

Decrease in:	Increase in:
• Tensile strength • Sweat gland output • New skin formation • Elasticity • Turgor • Dermis and subcutaneous tissue • Healing (delayed)	• Capillary fragility • Subcutaneous hemorrhages • Wrinkling/sagging of the skin • Sensitivity • Pigmentation • Thinness of the skin (tissue paper)

Factors that make individuals even more high risk for skin breakdown:

- Poor healing and pressure ulcers
- Abnormal lab values of hypotension
- Cardiac disease malignancy
- Circulation problems medications
- Decreased functional ability oxygen use
- Diaper use, dialysis pain
- Foley catheter
- Respiratory disease
- HTN
- Smoking
- Hydration
- Systemic conditions
- Impaired/decreased mobility
- Thyroid problems
- Tube-feeds

Additional risks:

- Over age 70
- Diastolic blood pressure less than 60
- Increased (body) temperature
- Prolonged time in operating room
- Current intake of protein
- Cardiovascular disease
- Oxygen intake
- Healed pressure ulcer areas
- Multi-system organ failure
- End-of-life condition
- Refusing care and treatment

Figure 25.19 Risk Factors for Skin Breakdown

25.12 Contributing Comorbid Factors

Factors which make the individual even more high risk for skin breakdown and pressure ulcers are shown in Figure 25.19. Summaries of a medical malpractice case highlight the main opinions of the expert reviewing the case and acknowledge the existence of comorbid conditions:

The defendants and their employees owed Mr. W and other residents a variety of duties under federal statutes and regulations, state statutes and regulations, and the common law. At all times mentioned herein, defendants had a duty to provide for the safety of residents, particularly residents who were impaired and in need of special precautions for their safety, by providing each resident with adequate supervision, assistance, nutrition and nursing and medical intervention to prevent injury or deterioration of his health, to provide curative and restorative care as needed and as prescribed by physicians and to have a system in place that would deliver such care in an efficient manner.

During the time Mr. W was under the care of HS employees; they knew and had reason to know that Mr. W was an incapacitated and vulnerable adult related to his multiple comorbid conditions. Among the duties defendants and their employees owed to Mr. W was the duty to provide reasonable and appropriate healthcare services in accordance with the recognized standard of care.

They owed to Mr. W the duty to protect him from nutritional problems, infections and pressure ulcers, and to competently help him recover from same. They owed the duty to provide adequate staff to monitor his condition and to adequately train, motivate, and supervise that staff in performing assessments or planning for his care and safety needs.

During the times Mr. W was a resident at HS, acting through its agents and employees, the facility failed to exercise the degree of care, skill and learning expected of reasonable healthcare providers in the professions or classes to which they belong within the state acting in the same or similar circumstances.

The above-described breaches, abuse and neglect resulted in part from a lack of supervision, planning and training by the governing authority over defendants and their administrators.

As a further proximate result of the failure of defendants, as alleged above plaintiff suffered deterioration of the skin breakdown, multiple hospitalizations, surgery, need for continued nursing care, incurred medical costs, anguish, stress, shock and mental suffering.

The following case illustrates that pre-existing conditions can be used as a defense against the formation of pressure ulcers:

The plaintiff's decedent, age 72, was a patient at the defendant hospital November 18 to December 27, 2002. He was placed in restraints on November 27 and remained in them until his death. The plaintiff claimed the defendant's nurses failed to turn, inspect, and properly care for the decedent, so that he developed a sacral decubitus ulcer and died. The plaintiff also claimed nurses failed to follow the wound care protocol. The defendant claimed death resulted from pre-existing medication conditions, including diabetes, peripheral vascular disease, congestive heart failure, chronic obstructive pulmonary disease, and a 50-year history of cigarette smoking. According to Texas Reporter a defense verdict was returned.[90]

25.13 Wounds, Pressure Ulcers, and Legal Implications

An attorney may be handling a case that alleges nurses were responsible for causing a wound. These wounds vary in degree of severity from abrasions to major skin, organ, or bone injury with resulting surgery and lengthy hospital stays. The treatment and the plan of care is physician directed. Nurses may also bear liability if they fail to provide the ordered treatment.

A. Chronic Wounds

As with many chronic diseases, a chronic wound requires intervention by multiple healthcare disciplines to address the many conditions and comorbidities that impact wound healing.[91] The cause of the chronicity needs to be investigated. Diagnostic testing such as CAT scan, MRI, bone scan, cultures, and ankle-brachial index (ABI) should be done to diagnose causative factors. Multidisciplinary treatment should be used with these individuals. Treatment to eliminate causative factors is imperative. The major question is, why won't this wound heal?

B. Treatment Plan

If there is a disagreement with the treatment plan, the nurse needs to discuss with the primary physician or surgeon the

recommendations for treatments. If the nurse still disagrees with the treatment plan, the chain of command at the facility needs to be used. Nurses caring for patients and residents should promptly report to the primary treating physician or surgeon any change in the clinical condition of the individual and document it completely in the medical records. This documentation includes the name of the person informed of the concern, the discussion, and any orders received. Family members also need to be notified of changes in the family member's condition.

25.14 Aggressive Wound Care Management
A. Goals of Healing

The goals of healing stage I or stage II ulcers are to provide all preventive interventions possible to restore them to their original intact skin integrity and prevent skin breakdown progression to stage III and stage IV. It is more economical to provide preventative measures in the beginning than to heal stage III and stage IV ulcers. The goal of topical wound management is to optimize the microenvironment of the wound. This includes cleansing, debriding necrotic tissue, and applying an appropriate wound cover. Evaluation and reevaluation of the ulcers must be continued with aggressive changes in the topical therapy if the present therapy is not showing improvement and the ulcers continue to deteriorate.

B. Cleansing

Wound cleansing is the first step in the wound assessment process. The ulcer needs to be cleansed to remove debris and drainage from the wound bed so the base of the wound can be assessed. The major purpose of cleaning the wound is to decrease its bioburden and facilitate healing.[92] Normal saline is used when no germicidal action is required. Saline solution should also be used as a rinse after other solutions are used to irrigate the wound. Different microbial cleansers are on the market for wound cleansing (e.g., Saf-Clens, Shur-Clens, and MicroKlenz).

C. Debridement

An essential component of wound bed preparation is debridement of the devitalized tissue to expose healthy tissue so healing can take place. Debridement is an invasive procedure and requires special training and knowledge of viable and nonviable skin. Debridement of any tissue by medical personnel other than a physician requires a physician's order. The standard of care is to have a course in debridement; this should be part of the medical personnel's job description (wound ostomy continence nurse [WOCN], physical therapist), acknowledging that their profession is able to do this.

TIP: Moist nonviable tissue supports the growth of pathological organisms. The removal of nonviable tissue alters the healing of the wound.

Debridement stimulates healing by removing necrotic (nonviable) tissue that impedes healing and often hides underlying damage to the tissues. Moist necrotic tissue is yellow, gray, brown, or tan in color; dry necrotic tissue is thick, hard, leathery, and brown or black. Debridement can be done using a variety of methods: autolytic, mechanical, chemical, surgical, and the use of medically sterile maggots.

1. Autolytic

Autolytic debridement uses semi-occlusive moisture retention dressings (transparent dressing or hydrocolloid) over the wound to allow the natural wound fluids to soften the eschar. This type of debridement is slow, requiring multiple dressing changes and irrigations of the wound to remove the necrotic debris. This is usually pain free and puts very little stress on the patient. This is not appropriate for infected wounds or those with deep cavities.

2. Mechanical

Mechanical debridement uses irrigation fluids delivered by physical therapists or nurses trained in pulsed lavage or whirlpool to remove nonviable tissue of the wound. Foreign particles and necrotic debris are flushed out of the wound. This does not harm healthy tissue growth.

Wet to dry dressings are considered mechanical debridement because of the drying of the gauze onto the tissue and removal of the gauze, which removes both viable and nonviable tissue. This method is not recommended because of the damage to viable tissue. This type of debridement causes pain in the patient.

3. Chemical

Prescription medication is placed on the wound bed and a dressing is applied. Medications (e.g., Collagenese Santyl) dissolve the nonviable tissue in the wound bed. Some enzymes are selective and only recognize devitalized tissue. The nurse protects the periwound tissue with a skin protectant ointment or skin protective wipe. The action of the enzymes is aimed specifically at necrotic and nonviable tissue. It should be used for limited amounts of time only. When the wound is clear of necrotic (nonviable) tissue, a reassessment must be performed and another wound management plan implemented.

4. Surgical

Surgical debridement involves the use of a scalpel, scissors, or other sharp instrument to remove necrotic or nonviable tissue from the wound bed. This is the most rapid form of debridement and the preferred way for wounds with large amounts of thick, adherent eschar and devitalized tissue. Sharp debridement is preferred with life-threatening cellulitis or sepsis. These types of wounds would be debrided in the operating room or in a special procedures room. This type of surgical debridement may be contraindicated for some patients related to loss of blood or being unable to undergo anesthesia.[93]

TIP: Nonviable tissue must be removed in order to promote new tissue growth.

---

5. Maggot debridement

On January 12, 2004, the FDA gave permission for use of maggots for "debriding non-healing necrotic skin and soft-tissue wounds, including pressure ulcers, venous tissue ulcers, neuropathic foot ulcers, and non-healing traumatic or post surgical wounds." Maggot therapy has been reported to be beneficial for debridement of necrotic tissue, killing infection in the wound and helping promote wound healing because of the stimulation of granulation tissue, epithelial cell proliferation, and tissue oxygenation. Medical maggots are obtainable through BioTherapeutics, Education & Research Foundation at University of California, Irvine.[94] Patients who do not consent or who are uncomfortable with maggot debridement should be educated about other debridement methods. It is important to ensure the patient, family, and staff that measures will be taken to prevent the maggots from getting into the environment. A special wound dressing is designed to keep the maggots where they belong. This dressing is changed every 48 hours with removal of the maggots and irrigation of the wound. Patients may report a tingling or other sensation. Many times one treatment completely debrides the wound.[95]

D. Appropriate Dressing

Adequate and appropriate treatment of a beginning skin breakdown is imperative. A lesion appearing to be a superficial ulceration may be only the tip of the iceberg. There may be penetration deep into the tissue with necrotic and devitalized tissue not readily apparent. If the skin is intact, pressure relief is important to allow the tissues to heal. A break in skin integrity must be addressed. The 2009 European Pressure Ulcer Advisory Panel and National Pressure Ulcer Advisory Panel have summarized evidence-based guidelines on pressure ulcer prevention and treatment and state, "A two-week period is recommended for evaluating progress toward healing. However, weekly assessments provide an opportunity for the health care professional to detect early complications and the need for changes in the treatment plan."[96]

TIP: It is important to maintain a moist wound healing environment. Removal of any nonviable tissue is imperative because it fosters the growth of bacterial organisms and provides a medium for infection.

Appropriate topical dressing selection needs to consider the following characteristics of the wound: cause of the skin breakdown, anatomical location, extent of the wound, condition of the wound bed (whether granulating tissue or nonviable tissue), wound size, amount and type of drainage, condition of periwound skin, any diagnosis of infection, presence of any undermining, presence of any tunneling or tracts, and presence of pain. The primary dressing is placed directly on the wound bed and should be kept sterile to prevent contamination of the wound by outside sources. The cover dressing is in contact with the outside environment and held in place by application of different types of tape, Montgomery straps, or adhesive cover dressings. Education on different dressings is necessary for their appropriate facilitation of wound healing. Reassessment of the treatment should occur every two to three days; if there is no change in the condition of the skin breakdown after 10 to 15 days, the treatment plan must be revised and a different treatment used. No one dressing can be used on all stages of skin breakdown.

E. Wound Care Specialist

The expertise of a wound care specialist assists and directs the nursing staff with the measures necessary to prevent or minimize the loss of skin integrity. A wound care specialist provides support in the areas of education, research, and patient care. This individual recommends and initiates preventative therapy, and continuously reassesses and adds therapies as needed.

The WOCN has a bachelor's degree, attends a certified course, and specializes in wounds, ostomies, and continence. This specialist can sit for a certification in wounds, ostomies, and continence, which is renewed every five years. The certification test assures patients and the general public that the nurse has the theoretical knowledge for a specific area of practice. Basic concepts are tested during the certification process in a specialty nursing practice and can be considered expert knowledge.

Many facilities—acute care, long-term care, rehab care, and home care—employ WOCNs full-time or on a consult-

ing basis. Some facilities send nurses to wound courses and seminars and use them as their wound care nurses who do all dressing changes on wounds, ulcers, and skin breakdowns.

In many facilities the WOCN is consulted by use of a physician's order or through established triggers on the admission assessment. Home-care settings must have a physician's order to consult the WOCN. The WOCN evaluates the patient, determines a plan of care, and confers with the physician. Prevention or treatment orders from the physician are written by the WOCN. The patient's case manager, WOCN, physician, or primary nursing staff determine revisits in order to evaluate resolving or deterioration of the wounds. The WOCN's documentation can be found in the physician's progress notes, nurses' progress notes, or on special WOCN documentation records.

WOCN may also be found in outpatient wound clinics where they work with interdisciplinary teams to provide comprehensive wound treatment programs. Outpatient wound clinics vary in scope and availability of advanced wound care diagnostics, dressings, protocols, and ownership.[97] Literature supports the use of a multidisciplinary team approach in dealing with the non-healing or chronic wound. Clinics provide adjunctive wound care and do not take over the primary care provider's role. They work closely with the nursing facility, home care, and family to coordinate treatment and improve patient outcomes. WOCNs assess the patients, offer recommendations for treatment to the primary physician or wound clinic physician, and perform treatment dressing changes.

F. Interventions for Prevention

Most pressure ulcers can be prevented, and stage I pressure ulcers can be resolved and need not worsen under most circumstances. However, even the most vigilant nursing care may not prevent the development and worsening of ulcers in very high-risk individuals. In those cases, intensive therapy must be aimed at reducing risk factors, at preventative measures, and at treatment. Preventing pressure ulcers is imperative when the overall goal is to cure an illness, rehabilitate the individual, or help the individual live optimally with a chronic illness.[98]

The following case illustrates a high-risk individual for whom the hospital documented appropriate and timely care being given; her pressure ulcers deteriorated in spite of this care:

A 95-year-old female was admitted to Memorial Medical Center with complaints from the family of not swallowing for the past two weeks. She had stopped talking the day of admission and was moaning all night. The emergency department documented that the patient was extremely emaciated; staff was unable to draw labs because of dehydration. There were coarse rhonchi throughout the lungs, contractures of all extremities, and decubiti present. The primary diagnoses consisted of acute but ill-defined cerebrovascular disease; pneumonia due to inhalation of food or vomitus; volume depletion disorder (dehydration); urinary tract infection; dysphasia (difficulty in swallowing); contractures; possible cerebral vascular accident (CVA); diabetes mellitus; essential hypertension; abnormal hemodynamics; anemia; emaciation; poor intake; age-related changes; and other conditions of underweight (weight 70 pounds). The medical record verifies the physician orders, nursing notes, progress notes, diagnostic testing reports, respiratory treatment notes, IV treatment notes, medication administration records, speech therapy evaluation notes, dietician evaluation notes, physical therapy and occupational evaluation notes, case management and specialty physician consults for respiratory, internal medicine, and wound care. Because of her overall medical conditions and comorbidities this patient was not a victim of medical or nursing neglect based on the documentation reviewed. The patient had a history of pressure ulcers before she entered the hospital and it is documented she had pressure ulcers when admitted. These were treated appropriately and timely by the staff and in spite of their vigilant nursing care more pressure ulcers developed and deteriorated during her residency at Memorial Medical Center. This case had no merit against Memorial Medical Center.

G. Support Surfaces, and Pressure Reduction and Relief

Pressure reduction devices should be used on the bed and chair with a patient at risk for skin breakdown. Preventive measures can prevent or minimize skin breakdown. A turning or repositioning schedule should also be used and individualized according to the patient's overall condition.

Support surfaces must be selected by a clinician familiar with the therapeutic benefits associated with each product. These considerations are increased support area, low moisture retention, reduced heat accumulation, shear reduction, pressure reduction, pressure relief, and cost per day to the facility. Some facilities have purchased mattress replacement systems or mattress overlays. These are cleansed by housekeeping departments and may be reused for patients.

TIP: It is important to remember that support surfaces are only one component of a comprehensive plan. Support surfaces alone neither prevent nor heal pressure ulcers. They are to be used as part of a total program of prevention and treatment.[99]

The type of mattress overlay or specialty bed will depend on resources available to the facility. Policy and procedures of the facility will document the process for obtaining the correct type of support surface related to the patient's condition. A majority of support surfaces is available on a rental basis and has contracts with bed companies that allow special pricing.

No support surface can be used for all types of patients, nor does does evidence show that one support surface consistently performs better than others. Any individual at risk for developing pressure ulcers should be placed on a pressure-relieving and pressure-reducing surface to relieve pressure points of the body. The patient's individual medical condition dictates the support surface to be used; surfaces may change as the medical condition changes. Refer to Figure 25.20 for a summary of bed surfaces.

TIP: A pressure relief or pressure reduction surface is an adjunct and does not replace the need for regular repositioning.

Support surfaces halt the progression of pressure ulcers, assist with pain relief, and improve pulmonary status. They consist of a pressure relieving surface that "distributes the body weight over a large area."[100]

1. Bedbound

Repositioning, a long-accepted way to avoid pressure ulcers, is still vitally important. The primary risk factors for skin breakdown and pressure ulcers are immobility, impaired physical mobility, and limited activity levels. The shifting of body weight should be carefully documented, as should the use of a special bed or other device. The nurse should reposition the bedbound patient every two hours to change the pressure points on the body. Turning frequency should be based on the characteristics of the support surface and the individual's response. Some patients are too unstable to turn, so it is necessary to turn the patient more slowly or in small increments, to assist with stabilization of vital signs. Small shifts in the body position change the pressure points on the bed and should be used in those individuals who cannot tolerate frequent major shifts in body position.[101] The patient should be instructed on regular changing of position if he is able to reposition himself. The nurse should document the education and acknowledgment by the patient of the importance of position changes.

This list is not inclusive of the many types available but provides some of the familiar names.

1. Mattresses: Non-powered
These non-powered mattresses are placed directly on or integrated into a semi-electric or total electric hospital bed frame. Air, fluid, foam, gel, water or a combination may be used to distribute pressure and reduce friction and shear. Patients with stage II, III, or IV pressure ulcers or post-operative myocutaneous flaps or skin grafts will benefit from them (www.woundsource.com).
  A. **Bariatric:** Cam Tec 4000 Series Bariatric Bed, Geo Mattress Atlas, Low Profile FlairAir, Top Gard Pressure Reduction Mattress;
  B. **500 plus or more capacity:** 6303 H, Atmos Air, Barri-Float, Cam Tec 4000 Series Bariatric Bed, Comfort Flair, Geo-Mattress Atlas, Multi Density, RIK Fluid, Tempur-Med, Ultra-Form Plus Bariatric;
  C. **Combination Product:** Comforma 9000, Gel-Pro Sleep System, Medline Nylex II, Multi Density Support Surface, Pre-Vent Series, Prism, Ultra Form Elite, Waffle M.R.S.;
  D. **Foam Product:** Comfortline, Cam Tec 4000, Conforma 9000, Critical Care Heel East, First Wave, Geo-Mattress, Infection Control Pressure Reduction Isoflex, Medline Nylex, Multi Density, NatureSleep, NWC, Pre-Vent, PrimeAire, Prism, Q-Star, Spectrum, TheraRest, UltraForm;
  E. **Gel Product:** 6303 H, Gel-Pro Sleep System, Isoflex.

2. Mattresses: Powered
Powered mattresses are placed directly on or integrated into a semi-electric or total electric hospital bed frame. Alternating pressure, low air loss or powered flotation without air loss is used. An air pump or blower provides either sequential inflation and deflation or a low interface pressure throughout and designed to reduce friction and shear. These are recommended for patients with stage II, III, or IV pressure ulcers or post-operative myocutaneous flaps or skin grafts.
  A. **Bariatric:** Rem-Air XL, BariSelect, Big Turn, Flexicair Eclipse, Mighty Air, Plexus, Sapphire, Stage IV Millennium Plus, Synergy Air, Tempur-Air;;
  B. **500 pounds or more capacity:** DFS-3, Rem-Air XL, BariSelect Birg Tuen, Flexicair Eclipse, Mighty Air, Pegasus Airwave, Plexus, Power-Pro Elite, PressureGuard Easy Air, Sapphire 11005A, Stage IV 2000, Stage IV Millennium 3, Synergy Air Elite, Tempur-Air;
  C. **Alternating Pressure:** Alpha Active, Sentry 1200, Big Turn, Mighty Air, Plexus Air Express, Sof-Matt, Symmetric Aire Plus, Synergy Air Elite

3. Overlays: Non-Powered
Non-powered overlays are placed directly over a mattress. They have a base thickness of two to five inches and utilize air, foam, gel, water or other materials. Depending upon their composition they may help reduce friction and shear. These are recommended for patients with limited mobility, major risk factors or any stage pressure ulcer.
  A. **Bariatric:** Gel Cell Plus, ROHO Dry Floatation, Sof-Care;
  B. **350 pounds or more capacity:** Bye-Bye Decubiti Mattress, Gel Cell Plus, Gel-Pro, RIK Fluid Overlay, ROHO Dry Floatation, Sof-Care, StarrMatt, Stat H20, Waffle
  C. **Combination Product:** Gel-eeze, Gel Cell Plus, Gel-Pro Sleep Mat, Soft-Care II, UltraForm;
  D. **Foam:** Gel-eeze, Channel Foam, Conforma, Convoluted Foam, Gel Cell Plus, Gel-pro Sleep Mat, Geo-Matt, NatureSleep, NWC 400, Premium Convoluted Bed Pad, T-Foam, Triad, Ultra-form;
  E. **Gel:** Gel-eeze, Gel Cell Plus, Gel-Pro, Medline Gel, NWC 400, Stat H20, T-Gel;
  F. **Static Air:** Aero-Flow II, Bye-Bye Decubiti, Carelite II, Deluxe Air, MedRite Static Air, PRODIGY, Sapphire OZ, Sof-Care II, StarMatt, Stat-Air, Waffle Static Air;
  G. **Water:** Medline Water Overlay, Stat H20/State-Gel

Figure 25.20 Types of Beds. The WoundSource website for support surfaces is: www.woundsource.com/product-category/support-surfaces.

---

4. Overlays: Powered

These are powdered overlays placed directly over a mattress. The inflated cell height measures three and one-half inches or greater and utilizes low air loss or powered flotation without air loss or alternating pressure. These are recommended for patients with limited mobility, major risk factors or any stage pressure ulcer

4a. Bariatric: Air Maxxis, First Step Select Heavy Duty, SPR Plus III;

4b. 350 pounds or more capacity: Air Maxxis, autoexcel, First Step Select, James Air, Pro 2000, SOR Plus III, Synergy Air, Wolkner Turning System;

4c. Additional names: Accucair Continuous airflow, Beta Bed, Aero-Pulse, Air Maxxis, Air Pro Elite, Autoexcel, First Step, JamesAir, Medline MedTech 5000, Paradise Pump, Plexus, Pro 2000, Rapid-air, Sapphire 150, Silkair, SPR Plus III, Synergy Air, Volkner

5. Beds: Powered and Air-Fluidized

These beds are semi-electric or completely electric hospital beds with a full integrated powered mattress that is an air-fluidized support surface. The total height of the mattress is three inches or greater and designed to reduce friction and shear. It employs the circulation of filtered air through silicone-coated ceramic beads, creating the characteristics of fluid. These are recommended for patients with stage III and IV pressure ulcers or post-operative myocutaneous flaps or skin grafts.

A. Bariatric: Contoura 1080, Bari Maxx II, BariAir, Barikare, Magnum II Bariatric, Maxxis, TotalCare Bariatric, Tri Flex II (www.woundsource.com);

B. 500 pounds and plus capacity: Contoura 1080, Bari Maxx II, BariAir, Barikare, Magnum II, Maxxis, TotalCare, Tri Flex II (www.woundsource.com);

C. Chair Conversion: Contoura 560, Minuet 2, TotalCare, Bari Maxx II, BariAir, Barikare, Magnum II, Maxxis 300/400, Therapulse, TotalCare Bariatric, VersaCare (www.woundsource.com);D. Additional names: Clinitron, PrimeAire, Fluid Air Elite, KinAir III, TotalCare Short Stay, TotalCare with Treatment, ZoneAire

Figure 25.20 *Types of Beds. The WoundSource website for support surfaces is: www.woundsource.com/product-category/support-surfaces (continued).*

A written individually tailored repositioning schedule needs to be developed for all at-risk patients who can be turned. A repositioning schedule must be implemented and performed at least every two hours when in bed (as promulgated by the AHCPR Guidelines and literature review). Review of the documentation of a patient's record ensures these schedules were followed. Repositioning schedules reduce the time factor—the duration of pressure exerted on the skin. It is important the nurse indicate the side turned on to verify that different positions are being used, especially if pressure ulcers are present. Many types of documentation can be used to verify the turning and repositioning of patients. These schedules are usually documented every two hours but may need to be individualized depending upon the overall condition of the patient. Some facilities have the documentation on a separate flow-sheet, where the side turned on is indicated; other records may be found in the treatment records, nursing notes, or certified nursing assistant records. If documented by nursing that the patient is "self-turn" then be certain that the patient is actually turning herself.

The standard of care of a prudent nurse is to assess the patient's skin and reposition the patient to relieve pressure areas on a regular basis. Literature reflects that when a patient becomes bedbound or chairbound and develops difficulty repositioning, the nurse must be more diligent with interventions and with the documentation of such repositioning.

2. Chairbound

A chairbound patient should be repositioned every 15 to 30 minutes depending on the condition of the patient. Patients should have a cushion in the wheelchair to relieve pressure, whether skin breakdown is apparent or not. Chair cushions may be provided or purchased by the facility while the patient is a resident in the facility. Some wheelchair cushions must be custom-made to fit the deformities of the back or buttocks.

The wheelchair seat is a sling-type seat without padding; pressure-reducing devices such as those made of foam, gel, air, or a combination thereof are important. Pressure must be relieved when sitting for any length of time. Individuals should be taught how to shift their weight in the chair or wheelchair every 15 to 30 minutes. Care plans should reflect the necessity of shifting weight off of pressure points. Caregivers and patients should be educated on the importance of weight shifting if the patient is unable to do so independently.

A patient who has a pressure ulcer on a sitting surface should avoid sitting for any length of time. Sitting should be allowed for limited amounts of time, usually only for meals and then back to bed.

3. Elevate heels

The heels of bedbound patients unable to reposition themselves must be elevated from the bed surface. Heels have the full weight of the leg on only a very small surface area in contact with the bed mattress. The first signs and symptoms of skin breakdown of the heels are complaints of pain, redness, or mushy (soft) tissue. Heel boots provide the best way to elevate heels from the bed. They need to be removed twice daily to check for reddened areas. Pillows may be used to elevate heels but one needs to observe often for misplacement by the patient.

4. Pillow positioning

Pillows can pad bony prominences to relieve pressure to those areas. Nurses are expected to place pillows between the patient's knees when in the side-lying position to avoid skin-on-skin contact. Pillows may be placed along the back to prevent the patient from turning. Pillows also needed to pad the ankles from the bed surface.

5. Mobility and activity

If mobility problems exist, the physical therapist and occupational therapist must evaluate the patient and establish a plan of treatment to increase mobility and activity as tolerated. Physical therapy, occupational therapy, and restorative nursing (therapy provided by specially trained nursing or ancillary staff) should work with patients of limited mobility and activity to continue with exercises such as passive range of motion, active range of motion, dining with assistance, or stand-by prompting. It is important to prevent contractures related to nonuse of affected limbs. Contractures develop whenever a limb or joint is not moved regularly through its full range of motion. The muscles shorten and the limb is unable to straighten out, causing abnormal pressure points, thus another risk for skin breakdown.

H. Education of the Patient, Caregiver, and Significant Other

The medical records must consistently reflect the education of the client, caregiver, and significant other about the medical conditions, treatment, and plan of care. Education programs should be updated as the medical condition of the patient changes.[102]

TIP: Education is the means by which current knowledge about pressure ulcers can be turned into effective strategies for prevention and treatment.

The nursing standard of care requires designing, developing, and implementing educational programs for patients, caregivers, and healthcare providers that reflect the continuum of care. Programs should be structured, comprehensive, and provide an organized approach to prevention. The faculty should provide effective treatment protocols that promote healing as well as prevention. All instructions and information should be given in appropriate language and appropriate age level understanding. Nurses are expected to involve the patient and caregiver, when possible, in pressure ulcer treatment and prevention strategies and options. Nurses include information on pain, discomfort, possible outcomes, and duration of treatment, if known.

Some individuals are visual learners; demonstrations and return demonstrations are the way they remember things. Others learn with written material or videotapes. The nurses must find the appropriate teaching method and regularly repeat instructions.

The nursing standard of care requires documenting instructions about all interventions and treatments, and recording the demonstrations of dressing changes or treatments by caregivers and their reactions. The medical records should contain documentation about what was taught, what the patient said, and what the nurse assessed on each interaction.

25.15 Sources of Standards of Care
A. AHCPR Guidelines

The Agency for Health Care Policy and Research (AHCPR) was established in December 1989 under Public Law 1010-239 to enhance the quality and effectiveness of healthcare services and access to these services. The AHCPR Guidelines was formed in May 1992 and printed in 1994 by the Agency for Health Care Policy and Research (AHCPR), now known as Agency for Health Care Research and Quality (AHRQ). The Guidelines was developed by a panel of experts and is based on the best available scientific evidence and clinical expertise. It offers a comprehensive program for prevention and treatment of pressure ulcers. The recommendations are intended for clinicians who examine and treat individuals in all healthcare settings. AHCPR carries out its mission by conducting and supporting general health services research, including medical effectiveness research.

The website (www.ahrq.gov) contains the Guidelines, and a hard copy may be ordered online.

TIP: The Guidelines provides the healthcare community with current practice parameters based on expert opinion and synthesis of scientific evidence.

The Joint Commission (TJC) recommends use of the AHRQ clinical practice guidelines. The Centers for Medicare and Medicaid Services are using the guidelines to create policy and reimbursement criteria and to direct the federal and state survey process of long-term care facilities. Many hospitals and nursing homes incorporate the AHRQ Pressure Ulcer Guidelines in their policies and procedures for pressure ulcer prevention and treatment.

The European Pressure Ulcer Advisory Panel (EPUAP) and National Pressure Ulcer Advisory Panel (NPUAP) met together over four years and developed updated evidence-based guidelines on pressure ulcer prevention and treatment. This was published in 2009 and replaces the 1994 guidelines. It provides detailed analysis and discussion of available research, critical evaluation of the assumptions and knowledge of the field, and a description of the methodology used to develop guidelines. The goal of this international collaboration was to develop evidence-based recommendations for the prevention and treatment of pressure ulcers that can be used throughout the world. The guidelines are available through the NPUAP website (www.npuap.org).[103]

B. NPUAP

The National Pressure Ulcer Advisory Panel (NPUAP) is an independent, not-for-profit professional organization dedicated to the prevention and management of pressure ulcers. Formed in 1987, the NPUAP Board of Directors is composed of leading experts from different healthcare disciplines—all of whom share a commitment to the prevention and management of pressure ulcers. The NPUAP serves as a resource to healthcare professionals, government, the public and healthcare agencies. It welcomes and encourages the participation of those interested in pressure ulcer issues through utilization of NPUAP educational materials, participation at national conferences, and support of NPUAP efforts in education, public policy, and research. The web address is www.npuap.org.

TIP: The goal of the NPUAP is to assist healthcare professionals in reducing the incidence and prevalence of pressure ulcers.

C. Literature

Large amounts of literature exist about the prevention and treatment options available for wounds and pressure ulcers. This literature is always supported by evidence-based research and verifies the different preventative and treatment options. All medical supply companies have researched their products for effectiveness and can provide literature on case studies and controlled studies on their products.

25.16 Medical Record

The medical record is defined as the historical archive of everything of relevance that occurs to the patient. Hospital policies and procedures are explicit about what needs to be documented regarding skin and wound care. The medical record must document anything significant relating to the history and care of the patient from admission to discharge.

TIP: The medical record must tell the story of the patient's residency in the facility from admission until discharge.

Professional responsibility and accountability are among the most important reasons for accurate documentation. Documentation of skin care is part of the nurse's overall responsibility for patient care. The clinical record facilitates care, enhances continuity of care, and helps coordinate the treatment and evaluation of the patient. The American Nurses Association emphasized the role of documentation by stating:

> The nurse is responsible for data collection and assessment of health status of the client; determination of the nursing care plan directed toward designed goals; evaluation of the effectiveness of nursing care in achieving the goals of care; and subsequent reassessment and revision of the nursing care plan.[104]

TIP: Documentation must clearly communicate a nurse's judgment and evaluation of the patient's status. The nurse's ability to affect patient outcomes must be demonstrated in practice and in charting.

Documentation is a nursing obligation. The medical records verify that nurses assessed and communicated, planned and collaborated, implemented, and then evaluated the care provided and reported important findings to the physician as often as necessary. Appropriate and timely charting facilitates communication and helps determine the need for different types of interventions as the patient's or resident's condition changes. Physicians rely on the nursing staff to inform them of changes in the patient's or resident's condition. The nursing staff and ancillary personnel care for the patient 24 hours a day and should be continuously reassessing and evaluating the patient. They are the eyes and ears of the physician; updates to the physician or staff must be appropriate and timely. Documentation should reflect date and time of the phone call, the person involved in the discussion, the subject of the discussion, and the outcome of the discussion (new orders, no orders, continue same treatment). In the following case the lack of assessment, documentation, and communication was a factor in the settlement for the plaintiff.

An 82-year-old male entered the nursing home because his wife could no longer care for him. He was admitted September 23 with diagnoses of CVA and aphasia. Comorbid medical conditions included immobility, impaired range of motion, and inability to transfer independently. The plaintiff was incontinent of bowel and bladder and dependent on staff for all activities of daily living. He was able to move his left side, had stiffness of the right extremities, and his skin was not reddened. No documentation existed of beginning skin breakdown of the heel. It was documented as soft, mushy, and later as a stage IV pressure ulcer. Skin assessments were documented two times at the nursing home. Documentation did not exist of preventive measures such as protection of bony prominences, padding of the heels, heel protectors, or use of pillows to bridge the heels off of the bed.

The March 11th documentation stated the resident had a necrotic heel ulcer, stage IV with black necrotic tissue, but the nurse was unable to see the wound base. The plaintiff was admitted to a hospital March 21 with diagnoses of right heel gangrene, severe right-sided weakness, and severe contracted right fingers. Upon examination in the ER, the physician removed the necrotic tissue from the right heel and maggots (these were not medically placed maggots) fell out from the ulcer. The plaintiff also had several ulcers on his scrotum.

Plaintiff's attorneys alleged the resident suffered from painful pressure ulcer necrosis, infestation of his wounds with maggots, infection, hospitalization, surgeries, pain and suffering, lack of quality of life, and subsequent amputation and death. Plaintiff settlement amount was undisclosed.

Documentation is also used for reimbursement purposes. If no proof (e.g., nursing notes, treatment sheets) exists in the medical record of the use of certain products (e.g., wound management pouch, wound VAC dressings) no reimbursement will be made to the hospital by insurance companies if that particular chart is audited.

Nurses must document clinically valid reasons why certain interventions were not appropriate or feasible (i.e., unable to turn to left side related to contractures, head of bed elevated related to respiratory condition, or head of bed elevated one hour before and after eating related to aspiration precautions).

Sloppy recordkeeping presents a picture of unprofessional and suspect care. Nursing notes written four to ten days after the date are suspected of being doctored. Filling in blanks on a physician order sheet using two different pens and two different handwritings presents doubts on who wrote the orders or when they were written.

The omission of significant information in the medical record has serious consequences. Failure to document raises the question of whether the nurse provided the required care. Dubious documentation related to wound care can consist of:

- Gaps in documentation (missing days)
- Repetitive and rote (same note written verbatim whenever a particular nurse charts)
- Inconsistencies within the chart (no pressure ulcers documented by one nurse, pressure ulcers documented the previous shift)
- Too good to be true (documentation of patient eating 100 percent of every meal yet losing weight)
- Documentation and intake and output records were perfect, but nursing notes document poor hydration, poor intake
- Poorly kept erratic records (I&Os ordered by physician but the records are incomplete and missing different shifts of reporting)
- Contradictions between departments (nursing documents the patient is able to turn self, physical therapy documents (on the same day) patient is too weak to turn—maximum assist)
- Orders not carried out (physician orders wound care specialist—five days later wound care specialist visits patient or resident)
- Problems not reported to MD (no documentation of informing physician of stage II skin breakdown until five days later when a picture was taken of the area)

- MD fails to respond when notified (repeated notes in the chart, "1st call to MD, 2nd call to MD, 3rd call to MD, finally the MD returns my call")
- Records changed or falsified (wound care specialist note written in detail one month after her visit documenting the noncompliance of the patient—date was crossed through and another date one month later was written in)

TIP: Written documentation reflects that the nurse was appropriately monitoring and communicating the patient's progress (or lack thereof) to the whole medical team.

One such case where documentation was important dealt with the care and treatment of Mrs. B. Packing material was found deep within Mrs. B's lumbar wound causing extensive infection and the need for medical care, treatment and additional surgery. From the medical records, it appears that the placement of the packing material was performed either in the Medical Center operating room or during home wound care provided by X Home Care. Plaintiff's attorneys allege that both the facility and home care agency are part of the lawsuit related to the documentation found or not found in the medical record. The facility or the home care both failed to determine the number/location of any and all packing material placed in the wound, they failed to document the number/location of any and all packing material, and they failed to determine the continued presence of any such "packing material" at any level/depth in the wound.

25.17 Summary

Once the individual risk factors for a patient have been assessed and identified, nurses are responsible for outlining a plan of care and formulating the interventions that will prevent and minimize the complications that undoubtedly accompany the risk to skin integrity. The focus, of course, is on prevention.

TIP: Literature indicates prevention is less expensive than treatment. The cost of prevention increases as the patient's risk level increases.

It is not just pressure alone but the many comorbid conditions that affect the patient's healing. The cost, in human suffering and money, of chronic wounds, infected wounds, or pressure ulcers remains an important issue in health care.

Endnotes

1. Van Rijswijk, L. "The fundamentals of wound assessment," *Ostomy/Wound Management* 42, no. 7 (August 1996): 42.

2. National Pressure Ulcer Advisory Panel (NPUAP) Black et al., Pressure Ulcer Stages Revised—Updated Staging System, NPUAP, 2007.

3. Brown, G., "Long-term outcomes of full-thickness pressure ulcers: healing and mortality," *Ostomy Wound Management* 49, no. 10 (October 2003): 48.

4. Schank, J., "Kennedy Terminal Ulcer: the "Ah-Ha!" Moment and Diagnosis, *Ostomy Wound Management* (September 2009): 40.

5. *Hospital Accreditation Standards,* Joint Accreditation of Healthcare Organizations, 163–164, 2006.

6. *Id.* at 64.

7. Synopsis of Federal Regulations in the Nursing Facility, CFR 483, 1–24, 2000.

8. See note 3 at 46.

9. Agency for Health Care Policy and Research, U.S. Department of Health & Human Services, *Clinical Practice Guidelines Number 3 Pressure Ulcers in Adults: Prediction and Prevention,* 3. Rockville, Maryland, December 1994.

10. Braden, B. and J. Maklebust, "Preventing Pressure Ulcers with the Braden Scale," *American Journal of Nursing* 105, no. 6 (June 2005): 72.

11. Brem, H. and C. Lyder, "Protocol for the successful treatment of pressure ulcers," *The American Journal of Surgery,* supplement (July 2004): 125.

12. (WOCN Position Paper—Photography in Wound Documentation, 2004).

13. Hess, C. *Wound Care,* Second edition, 97. Springhouse, 1997.

14. Dimant, J., "Implementing Pressure Ulcer Prevention and Treatment Programs: Using ADA Clinical Practice Guidelines," *JAMDA* 2 (2001): 322.

15. Bryant, R. (ed.), *Acute and Chronic Wounds: Nursing management*, Second edition, 98. Mosby, 2000.

16. See note 2 at 1.

17. Id at 7.

18. Id at 1.

19. Id at 7.

20. Id at 7.

21. Id at 8.

22. Id at 8.

23. Milne, C., D. Dubuc, and L. Scheetz, *Wound, Ostomy, and Continence Nursing Secrets,* 40. Philadelphia: Hanley and Belfus, Inc., 2003.

24. See note 2 at 8.

25. Id at 8.

26. Id at 8.

27. See note 9 at 3–4.

28. Clever, K., G. Smith, C. Bowser, and K. Monroe, "Evaluating the Efficacy of a Uniquely   Delivered Skin Protectant and Its effect on the Formation of Sacral/Buttock Pressure   Ulcers," *Ostomy Wound Management* 48, no. 12 (December 2002): 61.

29. Agency for Health Care Policy and Research, U.S. Department of Health & Human Services, *Clinical Practice Guidelines Number 15 Treatment of Pressure Ulcers,* 26. Rockville, Maryland, December 1994.

30. European Pressure Ulcer Advisory Panel (EPUAP) and National Pressure Ulcer Advisory Panel (NPUAP), International Guidelines—Treatment of Pressure Ulcers: Quick Reference Guide, 2009, 11.

31. Maklebust, J. and M. Sieggreen, *Pressure Ulcers Guidelines for Prevention and Nursing Management,* Third edition, 10–75. Springhouse, 2001.

32. See note 14 at 319.

33. See note 23 at 46.

34. See note 31.

35. Federal Regulations in the Nursing Facility. (November 2004) F309—CFR483.25.

36. See note 29 at 25.

37. Lyder, C., "Pressure Ulcer Prevention and Management," *JAMA* 289, no. 2 (January 2003): 224.

38. *NPUAP FAQ: Photography for pressure ulcer documentation,* 1–4. Restón, Virginia, 2003.

39. WOCN Postiion Paper—Photography in Wound Documentation 2004—1.

40. See note 10 at 70–72.

41. See note 9 at 14.

42. Maklebust, J., M. Sieggreen, D. Sidor, M. Gerlach, C. Bauer, and C. Anderson, "Computer-based Testing of the Braden Scale for Predicting Pressure Sore Risk," *Ostomy/Wound Management* 51, no. 4 (April 2005): 40–52.

43. See note 10 at 70–72.

44. Ayello, E., "Predicting Pressure Ulcer Sore Risk," *Best Practices in Nursing Care to Older Adults* 1, no. 5 (July 1999).

45. See note 10.

46. See note 10.

47. American Burn Association White Paper, "*Surgical Management of the Burn Wound and Use of Skin Substitutes,*" American Burn Association, 2009, 8.

48. Id at 2.

49. DeSanti, I., "Pathophysiology and Current Management of Burn Injury," Advances in Skin & Wound Care (July-August 2005): 323–332.

50. See note 47 at 6.

51. See note 49.

52. See 47 at 10.

53. *Standards of Care—Burns,* Salt Lake City, Utah: American Burn Association and Intermountain Burn Center, 2003.

54. See note 7.

55. See note 13 at 102.

56. See note 15 at 34–37.

57. Fleck, C., "No Pain, No Gain? Addressing Pain in Patient with Wounds," Presentation, NorthWest WOCN Conference, Post Falls, Idaho, 1–12, September 2005.

58. See note 15 at 34–37, 41–44.

59. Id at 47.

60. *Id.*

61. Kosiak, M., "Etiology and Pathology of Ischemic Ulcers," *Archives of Physical Medicine & Rehabilitation* (February 1959): 62–66.

62. *Id.*

63. Maklebust, J. and M. Sieggreen, "Pressure Ulcers: Update on Prevention and Management," *RN Magazine* (December 1991).

64. NPUAP, Dorner, et al., "The Role of Nutrition in Pressure Ulcer Prevention and Treatment: National Pressure Ulcer Advisory Panel White Paper," 2009 NPUAP 1-15.

65. Id at 10.

66. See note 15 at 41–44.

67. *Id.*

68. Collins, N., "Assessment and Treatment of Involuntary Weight Loss and Protein—Calorie Malnutrition," *Advances in Skin & Wound Care* 13, supplement 1 (May-June 2000): 4–10.

69. See note 15 at 49.

70. DeSanti, L., "Involuntary Weight Loss and the Non-healing Wound," *Advances in Skin & Wound Care* (May/June 2000): 11–20.

71. See note 37 at 225.

72. See note 29.

73. NPUAP White Paper—Nutrition 2009 (1-4).

74. See note 30 at 12.

75. Levin & Perconti (ed.). *Client Tell—The Newsletter For and About the People We Serve, Fall 2009, 4.*

76. European Pressure Ulcer Advisory Panel and National Pressure Ulcer Advisory Panel. Treatment of pressure ulcers: Quick Reference Guide. Washington DC: National Pressure Ulcer Advisory Panel; 2009 25.

77. *Id.*

78. See note at 65.

79. Burggraf, V. and R. Barry, *Gerontological Nursing Current Practice and Research,* 57. Thorofare, New Jersey, 1996.

80. Matson, S. *Wound care management.* Lecture to Legal Nurse Association of Orlando Conference, 4. Orlando, Florida, May 1999.

81. Wound Ostomy Continence Nurses Society Guidance on Oasis-C Integumentary items—Glossary, (December 2009) at 7.

82. See note at 11 at 14S.

83. See note 1 at 40–52.

84. See note at 10.

85. See note 29 at 59–60.

86. *Id.*

87. See note 15 at 36.

88. Worley, J., "Why Won't This Wound Heal? Factors Affecting Wound Repair," *Dermatology Nursing* (August 2004): 360.

89. See note 29 at 31.

90. Laska, L. (ed.), "Failure to properly turn patient in restraints" *Medical Malpractice Verdicts, Settlements and Experts* (May 2005): 19.

91. See note 1 at 50.

92. Salcido, R., "Pressure Ulcers and Wound Care," *eMedicine*—www.emedicine.com, (August 2005): 1–41.

93. Ayello, E. and J. Cuddigan, "Debridement: Controlling the Necrotic/Cellular Burden," *Advances in Skin & Wound Care* 17, no. 2 (March 2004): 67.

94. Sherman, R., "Bio-Therapeutics—Maggot Debridement," Presentation, NorthWest WOCN Conference, 1. Post Falls, Idaho, September 2005.

95. See 23 at 62–63.

96. See note 76 at 11.

97. Id note 94 at 266.

98. See note 9 at 2.

99. See note 30 at 16.

100. American Medical Directors Association (AMDA) and the American Health Care Association,8 *National Guideline Clearinghouse Pressure Ulcers,* 1-16. 2004.

101. See note 76 at 21.

102. See note 30 at 78.

103. See note 76 at 1.

104. American Nurses Association, *Nursing: Scope and Standards of Practice,* 104–107. 2004.

Additional Reading

American Burn Association White Paper, *"Surgical Management of the Burn Wound and Use of Skin Substitutes,"* American Burn Association, 2009 1-49.

Castle, S., "Controversies in skin trauma," in *Medical Legal Aspects of Medical Records*, Second Edition, eds. P. Iyer, B. Levin, Tucson, Arizona: Lawyers and Judges Publishing Co., 2010.

Dorner, B., M. Posthauer, and D. Thomas, "The Role of Nutrition in Pressure Ulcer Prevention and Treatment: National Pressure Ulcer Advisory Panel White Paper" *Nutrition White Paper* (2009 NPUAP) 1-15.

Dunleavy, K, "Putting a dent in pressure ulcer rates," *Nursing 2008*, January 2008, 20-21

European Pressure Ulcer Advisory Panel (EPUAP) and National Pressure Ulcer Advisory Panel (NPUAP), International Guidelines—Treatment of Pressure Ulcers: Quick Reference Guide, 2009 1-48.

Iyer, P. (ed.), *Nursing Home Litigation: Investigation and Case Preparation.* Tucson, Arizona: Lawyers & Judges Publishing Co., 2006.

Iyer, P. and N. Camp, *Nursing Documentation, A Nursing Process Approach,* Fourth edition. Flemington, New Jersey: Med League Support Services, 2004. www.medleague.com

Jazarowski, K., "Wounds and burns," In *Medical Legal Aspects of Pain and Suffering*, ed. P. Iyer. Tucson, Arizona: Lawyers and Judges Publishing Co., 2003.

Jazarowski, K. "Skin trauma," In *Medical Legal Aspects of Medical Records*, Second Edition, eds. P. Iyer, B. Levin, Tucson, Arizona: Lawyers and Judges Publishing Co., 2010.

Jazarowski, K. and S. Castle, "Skin trauma," In *Nursing Home Litigation: Investigation and Case Preparation*, Second edition, ed. P. Iyer. Tucson, Arizona: Lawyers and Judges Publishing Co., 2006.

Kayser-Jones, J, Beard, R. and Sharpp, T. "Dying with a Stage IV pressure ulcer," *AJN,* January 2009, 40-48

Kinetic Concepts, Inc., *Pictures of Pressure Ulcers,* http://www.kci1.com/education/webed/adpu/adpu1.swf.

Lyder, C., R. Shannon, O. Empleo-Grazier, D. McGeHee, and C. A. White, "Comprehensive Program to Prevent Pressure Ulcers in Long Term Care: Exploring Costs and Outcomes," *Ostomy Wound Management* 48, no. 4 (2002): 52–62.

Stechmiller, J, L Cowan, J Whitney, L. Philips, R Asiam, A Barbul, F Gottrup, L. Gould, M. Robson, G Rodeheaver, D. Thomas, and N. Stotts, "Guidelines for the prevention of pressure ulcers," *Wound Repair and Regeneration* (2008) 16 151-168.

Zulkowski, K. and Gray-Leach, K, "Staging pressure ulcers: What's the buzz in wound care? *AJN,* January 2009, 109 (1), 27-30.

Appendix 25.1
Websites for Wounds, Skin Breakdown, Pressure Ulcers

- Agency for Healthcare Research and Quality: www.ahrq.gov

- American Academy of Wound Management: www.aawm.org

- American Geriatrics Society: www.americangeriatrics.org

- American Nursing Association: www.nursingworld.org

- American Professional Wound Care Association: www.apwca.org

- Joint Commission: www.jointcommission.org

- Kinetic Concepts, Inc. (KCI): www.kci1.com

- Kinetic Concepts, Inc. (KCI) Pictures of Pressure Ulcer Stages: www.kci1.com/education/webed/adpu/adpu1.swf

- Lund & Browder Chart—(Rule of Nines): www.sunmed.org/burns.html

- National Pressure Ulcer Advisory Panel: www.npuap.org

- Pressure Ulcers in Adults: Prediction and Prevention—Clinical Practice Guideline Number 3—AHCPR Pub. No. 92-0047: May 1992: www.ncbi.nlm.nih.gov/books/bv.fcgi?rid=hstat2.chapter.4409

- Pressure Ulcers, Surgical Treatment and Principles: www.emedicine.com

- Preventing Pressure Ulcers: A Patient's Guide, Consumer Guidelines Number 15—AHCPR Pub. No. 92-0048: www.ncbi.nlm.nih.gov/books/bv.fcgi?rid=hstat2.chapter.9527

- Treating Pressure Sores—Consumer Guide Number 15 AHCPR Publication No. 95-0654: December 1994: www.ncbi.nlm.nih.gov/books/bv.fcgi?rid=hstat2.chapter.9615

- Wound Care Institute: www.woundcare.org

- Wound Ostomy and Continence Nurses Society (WOCN): www.wocn.org

- Wound Product Source Book: www.woundsource.com

Chapter 26

Falls and Their Consequences

Barbara J. Levin, BSN, RN, ONC, LNCC, Kelly Shanley, MSN, RN, and Elizabeth Hill, PhD, RN, PLNC

Synopsis
26.1 Overview of Falls
26.2 Definition of a Fall
    A. Fall Rates
    B. Age of Those Who Fall
26.3 Serious Reportable Events
    A. Medicare
    B. Increased Length of Stay and Costs
26.4 Assessment of Fall Risk
    A. Intrinsic and Extrinsic Factors
    B. Risk Factors
26.5 Fall Prevention Programs
    A. Interventions for Fall Prevention in the Hospital Setting
    B. Environmental Interventions for Fall Prevention in the Home Setting
    C. Restraints
    D. Hourly Rounding
26.6 Complications of Falls
    A. Describe Types of Injuries Related to Falls
    B. Types of Fractures
        1. Radius fracture
        2. Tibial fractures
        3. Hip fractures
        4. Spinal injuries
    C. Head Injury
        1. Cerebral contusions
        2. Diffuse axonal injury
        3. Intracranial hemorrhage
        4. Subdural hematoma
        5. Epidural hematoma
        6. Intracerebral hemorrhage
    D. Complications from the Injuries
    E. Ambulation Difficulties
    F. Repeat Falls
    G. Delirium
    H. Increased Length of Stay
    I. Fear of Falling
26.7 After the Fall
    A. Evaluation
    B. Incident Reports
26.8 Litigation with Falls
26.9 Conclusion
Endnotes

26.1 Overview of Falls

"It takes a child one year to acquire independent movement and ten years to acquire independent mobility. An older person can lose both in a day," Bernard Isaacs, The Challenge of the Geriatric Medicine.

"Falls are the leading cause of fatal and nonfatal injuries in people 65 years-old and older in the United States."[1] They can play a catastrophic role in this population. Approximately 90 percent of hip fractures in this population result from a fall from the standing position. Significant morbidity can occur, not directly due to a fall but rather the resultant complications.[2] The Centers for Disease Control and Prevention (CDC), the National Quality Forum (NQF), the Institute for Clinical Systems Improvement (ICSI), the Agency for Healthcare Research and Quality (AHRQ), the National Institute of Health (NIH), and The Joint Commission (TJC), report that patient falls are the most common adverse event in hospitalized patients in the United States.[3-6]

Patient falls are a nursing-sensitive outcome used to measure quality of care in various healthcare facilities nationwide. The need for reporting falls data to the Department of Health and Human Services indicates the seriousness of patient falls within the healthcare industry. The availability of local, regional, and national data creates the ability to benchmark and use patient falls as a measure of quality of care for the consumer.[7] Patient falls data provide opportunities to assess how the ever-changing healthcare setting affects patient safety.[8] Falls data provide healthcare organizations with outcome metrics and opportunities for process improvement around quality of patient care.

The information presented in this chapter is designed to provide the nurse, attorney, nurse attorney, and legal nurse consultant with information about patient falls. Insight is provided to answer questions such as: when do patient falls occur, how do they occur and what are healthcare facilities doing to protect the patient? The goal is for our readers to become familiar with information related to patient falls and to use the knowledge gained to assist in understanding medical records.

This chapter also includes the regulatory and agency guidelines which must be followed. The financial implications of patient falls with injury are addressed from both the patient's and the organization's perspective. A plan for the assessment of patient fall risk and implementation of hospital-wide fall prevention initiatives are detailed. Particulars of the most common injuries resulting from patient falls in the hospital are another valuable aspect included in this chapter.

26.2 Definition of a Fall

A single definition of a patient fall has not been universally determined and accepted within the healthcare arena. Therefore, data collected have been found to be underreported, skewed, and misinterpreted.[9] The lack of a universally accepted definition may also present difficulties within legal cases involving patient falls. Defining a fall and characterizing the type of fall must be considered and determined to ensure validity of data collected on falls.

The Institute of Clinical System Improvement provided these examples of fall definitions:

a) "an event that a patient came to rest on the floor, ground, or lower level;

b) unintentionally coming to the ground or lower level other than as a consequence of a violent blow, loss of consciousness, or sudden onset of paralysis as in a stroke or epileptic seizure;

c) a sudden, unintentional change in position causing a patient to land at a lower level, on an object, the floor, ground, or other surface. Included are slips, trips, and falling into other people, being lowered, or loss of balance, and legs giving way. If patients are found on the ground, it should be determined there was a fall, unless they are cognitively impaired and indicate they purposely put themselves there;

d) a sudden unintentional change in position causing the patient to land at a lower level other than as a consequence of a violent blow, loss of consciousness, or sudden onset of paralysis as in a stroke or epileptic seizure, or overwhelming external force."[10]

According to the National Database of Nursing Quality Indicators (NDNQI), endorsed by the NQF and The Joint Commission, a fall is "an unplanned descent to the floor (or extension of the floor, e.g., trash can or other equipment) with or without injury to the patient." An assisted fall is a fall in which any staff member (whether nursing service employee or not) was with the patient *and* attempted to minimize the impact of the fall by easing the patient's descent to the floor or in some manner attempting to break the patient's fall. Assisting the patient back into bed or chair *after* a fall is not considered an assisted fall. A fall that is reported to have been assisted by a family member or visitor also does not count as an assisted fall.[11]

TIP: Since TJC National Patient Safety Goals were implemented in 2005, fall reduction has been a focus, and is now incorporated in the provision of care chapter of the 2010 Accreditation Manual for Hospitals.[12]

Each healthcare facility accredited by TJC, that receives Medicare or Medicaid reimbursements, is required to have a fall prevention program in effect with continuous monitoring of the effectiveness. Additionally, each organization must define a fall with careful consideration of state and federal laws. State legislature has encouraged local disclosure of nursing-sensitive indicators, including patient falls with injury, which are used by the public to make educated decisions on where to pursue health care. The data also encourages healthcare facilities to be accountable for patient outcomes.

The American Nurses Association, the originators of the nursing-sensitive indicators, is also prompting legislation to mandate reporting of the quality indicators to the public through the Nationwide States Legislative Agenda.[13] Regulations and statutes across the country in states such as Florida, Colorado, Maine, Connecticut, Rhode Island, and Texas have passed legislation requiring data collection and a reporting agency or quality council to aggregate data for best practice. Most of these indicators include patient falls. Other states such as Maryland, South Dakota, Georgia, Washington, and Pennsylvania introduced legislation for reporting and collecting outcomes data on medical errors and adverse events.

In a classic paper, Morse and others reported that falls in some patients are preventable.[14] They defined an "anticipated physiological fall" as a fall that occurs in patients who are identified as "fall prone" based on a risk assessment. Study findings indicate that most fallers (78 percent) could be assessed at risk because of physiologic risk factors. An example would be an individual who has a history of falling, impaired gait, comorbidities, or cognitive impairment. Physiologic reasons, which are not predictable, account for 8 percent of patient falls. Examples would include a medical occurrence such as syncope, seizure, or cerebral vascular accident (CVA) or stroke. "Accidental" patient falls only account for 14 percent of falls. Morse described "accidental" as caused by the patient slipping, tripping, or experiencing a fall due to some other environmental issue. Finally, an important consideration made by Morse et al. was that more than half of all second falls occurred under circumstances similar to the first fall.[15]

The preventability of falls has also been discussed by various healthcare quality organizations. The Centers for Medicare and Medicaid (CMS) created the list of "never events," which were deemed "reasonably preventable" and adopted by the NQF, which by law must be measured.[16] Unfortunately, there is no clear explanation as to what "reasonably preventable" means in the statute from CMS. The intended rationale for creating the list of "never events" was to increase hospital awareness of quality care and prevent hospital acquired conditions.[17] "Reasonably preventable" is determined by the coded data for each patient at the time of discharge. These codes refer to primary and secondary diagnoses which are disease-related. CMS determines the potential of fall risk by using the code system to establish the presence of comorbidities, diseases that place patients at higher risk for falls. More discussion of patient falls is warranted as they are the most common "never" or "serious reportable" events.

A. Fall Rates

Fall rates are calculated based on staff-reported incidents and calculated as the number of patient falls divided by the number of patient days multiplied by 1,000. Acute care facility-wide fall rates average 3.73 per 1,000 patient days and vary based on nursing unit-type.[18] For organizations who participate in the National Database of Nursing Quality Indicators (NDNQI), quarterly benchmarks for fall rates are available for comparison by unit type (such as medical, surgical, ICU, rehabilitation, etc.), hospital size, and status as an academic medical center, teaching facility, or non-teaching facility.[19]

The current data on fall rates in hospitals has not been compiled on a national level. Massachusetts, however, recently publicly reported average rates of 3.57 falls/1,000 patient days in hospitals of 200-299 beds, and 4.76 falls/1,000 patient days in hospitals over 500 beds.[20] Injuries from falls were 0.96/1,000 patient days overall and 0.64/1,000 patient days, respectively, on medical units. The National Health Service of the United Kingdom reports an average fall rate of 4.8 falls/1,000 patient days nationwide.[21]

B. Age of Those Who Fall

CMS houses one of the largest administrative databases for health services and patient information that was traditionally collected for billing and reimbursement purposes. As such, the CMS data was never intended for use in quality assurance.[22] The CDC, however, provides greater insight related to the scope of falls occurring in the United States, but not specific to hospitals like the data from CMS.

TIP: In 2007, falls were the leading cause of nonfatal unintentional injuries in the United States, including all races, sex, age groups (except ages 15-24) and dispositions. In the 65 or older age group, 64.4 percent or 2,113,114 of unintentional injuries result from falls. In the 55-64 age groups, 35.9 percent or 724,735 of unintentional injuries are fall-related.[23,24] Research has determined that those who are falling in acute care settings include the 65 year-old and older population, as this group has the highest fall rate.

26.3 Serious Reportable Events
A. Medicare

Patient falls are the most common adverse event occurring in United States hospitals today. This Serious Reportable Event (SRE) is defined as a death, serious injury or disability associated with a fall while being cared for in a healthcare facility.[25-29] As of October 1, 2008, Medicare, the government's health program available to people 65 and older, stopped reimbursing hospitals for SREs or a hospital acquired condition (HAC).[30,31] The rationale for this decision is based upon the increased cost and length of stay for patients who were seriously injured or disabled due to the perceived "preventability" of a patient fall.[32-35]

B. Increased Length of Stay and Costs

Some studies suggest that as many of 30 percent of falls result in a serious injury requiring an increased length of stay, and increase in the cost of hospitalization.[36,37] Fall injuries account for 6 percent of medical expenses among those 65 and older. The United States spends more than $20 billion annually for the treatment of injuries to older people after falls. The majority of the cost is for hip fracture care, which averaged $37,000 per patient in 2006. The Centers for Disease Control and Prevention (CDC) estimates that by the year 2020, the annual and indirect cost of fall injuries is expected to reach $54.9 billion (in 2007 dollars).[38] The cost is measured by the increase in resource allocation, increased length of stay, and increased referrals to rehabilitation or nursing home care.

The financial implications for hospitals are substantial when a patient fall with injury occurs. Because reimbursement for the Medicare patient is now limited, the financial responsibility must be absorbed by the facility. Additionally, injury is an important source of liability for hospitals. Thus, the ability to identify and prevent patient falls is not only a safety issue, but a financial issue.

26.4 Assessment of Fall Risk
A. Intrinsic and Extrinsic Factors

When reviewing the medical record of a person who sustained a fall, it is important to understand fall risk. The first step in any fall prevention and management program is the assessment of fall risk. While there are many risk factors for falls that are well documented in the literature and a variety of fall risk assessments used, there are two major types of factors that can put a patient at risk for falls. These include intrinsic and extrinsic risk factors. Intrinsic risk factors are also known as "person factors" which include things such as changes in cognition or incontinence that might result from disease/illness. Extrinsic risk factors are also known as environmental factors, and are external to the person such as tubes/drains and floor surfaces.

Most falls are complex in nature resulting from a combination of factors.[39] As such, the inclusion of both personal and environmental factors are critical to the assessment of fall risk for patients in any healthcare setting.[40]

B. Risk Factors

In a hospital setting some of the most common risk factors that should be included in the assessment of fall risk include:

- History of previous falls (in the past three months)
- Medications (benzodiazipines, antidepressants, and antiarrhythmics)
- Incontinence (bowel or bladder)
- Leg weakness
- Unsteady gait
- Poor balance
- Mental status change (confusion, disorientation, and altered level of consciousness)
- Orthostatic hypotension

In addition, environmental factors that should be considered when assessing fall risk in hospital settings include:

- Presence of objects that might tether the patient such as IV tubes and drains
- Use of assistive devices when walking
- Wet or slippery floor surfaces

An example of an environmental issue occurred in the following case of a 59-year-old woman who was hospitalized and while walking to the bathroom slipped and fell on an unknown liquid on the floor. The woman suffered injuries to the left ankle and foot, and the mid and lower back. She claimed the defendant's employees allowed the substance to be on the floor and failed to warn her of its presence. The defendant claimed that the plaintiff was the cause of the injuries because she failed to be watchful of her surroundings and use reasonable care. The defendant also claimed the plaintiff had been informed not to walk unassisted. There was a defense verdict.[41]

The following is another example of an extrinsic factor contributing to a fall:

Mr. S underwent a heart valve repair surgery, and requested assistance ambulating to the bathroom. There was no response to his request and he walked to the bathroom unassisted. On his way back to bed, he placed his hand on the bed while getting into bed and the bed moved. He fell to the floor and fractured his left hip. Surgical intervention was done and, postoperatively, his condition deteriorated. He experienced delirium, loss of appetite, retention of fluids, pressure ulcers and infection. Mr. S died from the complications of the fall, which included respiratory failure due to pneumonia. The plaintiffs claimed Mr. S was not provided proper assistance to safely ambulate to the bathroom. Additionally they claimed the hospital did not have adequate nursing staff, failed to lock the brakes on the bed or inspect the bed to make sure the brakes operated properly, and had not properly monitored Mr. S. The defendant claimed the decedent got out of bed despite instructions not to do so and comparative negligence in causing his own injuries. There was a $125,000 settlement reached.[42]

TIP: In a fall, more active people are more likely to be exposed to high-intensity forces of impact, whereas the risk of injury in those who are less active depends more upon their susceptibility (fragile bones).

The reviewer of medical records should evaluate the fall risk assessment and obtain information about the facility's falls management program. The falls management program needs to adequately capture risk factors relevant to the patient care population of the healthcare institution. A standardized assessment of fall risk should be completed upon admission to establish a baseline and approximately every 12 hours thereafter as an example. In an acute care setting a variety of tools exist for the assessment of fall risk. One of the most current and frequently used tools in hospital settings both nationally and internationally is The Johns Hopkins Fall Risk Assessment Tool (Figure 26.1).

THE JOHNS HOPKINS FALL RISK ASSESSMENT TOOL

FALL RISK FACTOR CATEGORY

Scoring not completed for the following reason(s) (check any that apply):

☐ Complete paralysis, or completely immobilized. Implement basic safety (low fall risk) interventions.

☐ Patient has a history of more than one fall within 6 months before admission. Implement high fall risk interventions throughout hospitalization.

☐ Patient has experienced a fall during this hospitalization. Implement high fall risk interventions throughout hospitalization.

☐ Patient is deemed high fall-risk per protocol (e.g. seizure precautions). Implement high fall-risk interventions per protocol.

COMPLETE THE FOLLOWING AND CALCULATE FALL RISK SCORE.	POINTS
AGE (**SINGLE**-SELECT) ☐ 60 – 69 years (**1 point**) ☐ 70 – 79 years (**2 points**) ☐ ≥ 80 years (**3 points**)	
FALL HISTORY (**SINGLE**-SELECT) ☐ One fall within 6 months before admission (**5 points**)	
ELIMINATION, BOWEL AND URINE (**SINGLE**-SELECT) ☐ Incontinence (**2 points**) ☐ Urgency or frequency (**2 points**) ☐ Urgency/frequency and incontinence (**4 points**)	
MEDICATIONS: INCLUDES PCA/OPIATES, ANTI-CONVULSANTS, ANTI-HYPERTENSIVES, DIURETICS, HYPNOTICS, LAXATIVES, SEDATIVES, AND PSYCHOTROPICS (**SINGLE**-SELECT) ☐ On 1 high fall risk drug (**3 point**) ☐ On 2 or more high fall risk drugs (**5 points**) ☐ Sedated procedure within past 24 hours (**7 points**)	
PATIENT CARE EQUIPMENT: ANY EQUIPMENT THAT TETHERS PATIENT, E.G., IV INFUSION, CHEST TUBE, INDWELLING CATHETERS, SCDS, ETC) (**SINGLE**-SELECT) ☐ One present (**1 point**) ☐ Two present (**2 points**) ☐ 3 or more present (**3 points**)	
MOBILITY (**MULTI**-SELECT, CHOOSE ALL THAT APPLY AND ADD POINTS TOGETHER) ☐ Requires assistance or supervision for mobility, transfer, or ambulation (2 points) ☐ Unsteady gait (**2 points**) ☐ Visual or auditory impairment affecting mobility (**2 points**)	
COGNITION (**MULTI**-SELECT, CHOOSE ALL THAT APPLY AND ADD POINTS TOGETHER) ☐ Altered awareness of immediate physical environment (1 point) ☐ Impulsive (2 points) ☐ Lack of understanding of one's physical and cognitive limitations (4 points)	
*MODERATE RISK = 6-13 TOTAL POINTS, HIGH RISK > 13 TOTAL POINTS TOTAL POINTS	

Figure 26.1 *Johns Hopkins Fall Risk Assessment Tool*

The Johns Hopkins Fall Risk Assessment Tool is a seven-item tool appropriate for use in the acute care setting that provides a quick snapshot of overall fall risk. The tool can be completed easily and quickly (within about five minutes) by the nurse assigned to care for the patient. The items included on the tool include the influence of advanced age, fall history, specific medication classes, patient care equipment that tethers, mobility, and cognitive and elimination functions.[43] Upon completion of the tool an overall summary score is calculated; the higher the score the greater the patient's risk of falling. From this score a level of risk is determined as low, moderate or high. Based upon the patient's score at any particular point in time, interventions can be selected from each of the three columns of the list of recommended fall-prevention strategies (Figure 26.2) to target patient-specific risk factors.

TIP: Obtain the falls management protocol for the facility when reviewing a case and note the risk areas. Some facilities identify risk for falls or no risk for falls. Other facilities determine the level of risk—"low, moderate or high risk" followed by an action plan for each level of risk.

The following is an example of an inadequate risk assessment:

A woman was involved in a minor automobile accident and fractured three ribs. She had difficulty breathing as well as a decreased appetite and became extremely thin, weighing only half her normal weight at 63.9 pounds. She was evaluated at her local hospital and was referred to a rehabilitation center for a short-term stay to regain weight and strength. Five hours after admission, she sought assistance to the bathroom. When no one arrived, she attempted to get out of bed independently and fell. She sustained a fractured shoulder and hip. Emergency surgery was done on her hip and she died while in the intensive care unit. The claims against the rehabilitation facility included failure to adequately assess the decedent's fall risk. There was a written "Fall Risk Assessment" within the medical records but it was determined that it was completed after the fall, not in the initial admission assessment. Other allegations included the decedent was placed in a different bed after the fall, which had rails on it. The original bed lacked a bed

alarm to alert the staff of any attempt to get out of bed. The defendant claimed that the decedent had been told not to leave the bed without assistance. The defendant also explained the decedent had a life expectancy of only six months to a year at the time of admission. The jury assessed 5.9 percent fault to the decedent, resulting in a net award of $1.4 million to the plaintiff.[44]

In summary, when reviewing a fall-related injury/death case, it is critical to evaluate whether a standardized method or assessment of fall risk was completed and updated on a routine basis and if the tool was properly scored. Each facility determines the frequency with which fall assessments are completed; for instance at Johns Hopkins Hospital where patient acuity tends to be high, fall risk assessments are performed every 12 hours. Many other facilities perform their fall risk assessments every 24 hours unless there is a change in condition warranting more frequent assessments. Discrepancies may be identified between how items within the fall risk tool are scored and documentation in other areas of the medical record. Identification of such discrepancies warrants careful review.

26.5 Fall Prevention Programs
A. Interventions for Fall Prevention in the Hospital Setting

A falls management protocol is a two-step process that includes identification of patient risk factors through meticulous fall risk assessment and then implementation of appropriate follow-up interventions. As such, when reviewing a fall-related injury/death case, it is critical that risks be identified, but more importantly that interventions were implemented for prevention. Many interventions are actually quite simple and involve manipulation of the environment by the nurse in order to allow patient needs to be safely met. A few examples include moving a high fall-risk patient to a room near the nurses' station and keeping frequently used items such as the call bell, tissues and water close to the patient to prevent reaching. Another intervention that can be implemented to effectively meet the needs of patients is hourly rounds which has been shown to reduce patient falls in hospital settings.[45] Other changes that nursing staff can readily make within the care environment to promote patient safety are to keep beds in the lowest position with brakes applied when unattended. Similarly, safety locks should be employed on patient wheelchairs.

The Johns Hopkins Hospital Nursing Practice and Organization Manual Volume II	Policy Number	328
	Effective Date	6/1/07
Subject	Page	1 of 7
FALL RISK ASSESMENT, PREVENTION AND MANAGEMENT, ADULT APPENDIX B: FALL PREVENTION INTERVENTIONS	Supersedes	11/1/06

Appendix B:
Fall Prevention Intervention Guidelines by Risk Category

LOW FALL RISK	MODERATE FALL RISK	HIGH FALL RISK
Fall risk score: 0-5 points	Fall risk score: 6-13 points Color code: YELLOW	Fall risk score: >13 points Color code: RED
Maintain safe unit environment, including: <ul><li>Remove excess equipment/ supplies/furniture from rooms and hallways.</li><li>Coil and secure excess electrical and telephone wires.</li><li>Clean all spills in patient room or in hallway immediately. Place signage to indicate wet floor danger.</li><li>Restrict window openings</li></ul> The following are examples of basic safety interventions: <ul><li>Orient patient to surroundings, including bathroom location, use of bed, and location of call light.</li><li>Keep bed in lowest position during use unless impractical (as in ICU nursing or specialty beds)</li><li>Keep top two side rails up (excludes box beds). In ICUs, keep all side rails up.</li><li>Secure locks on beds, stretchers, and wheelchairs.</li><li>Keep floors clutter/obstacle free (with attention to path between bed and bathroom/commode)</li><li>Place call light and frequently needed objects within patient reach. Answer call light promptly.</li><li>Encourage patients/families to call for assistance when needed.</li><li>Display special instructions for vision and hearing.</li><li>Assure adequate lighting, especially at night.</li><li>Use properly fitting nonskid footwear</li></ul>	<ul><li>Institute flagging system: yellow card outside room and yellow sticker on medical record, Hill ROM flag (if available), assignment board/ electronic board.</li></ul> Implement measures listed under low fall risk and: <ul><li>Monitor and assist patient in following daily schedules</li><li>Supervise and/or assist bedside sitting, personal hygiene, and toileting as appropriate.</li><li>Reorient confused patients as necessary</li><li>Establish elimination schedule, including use of bedside commode, if appropriate.</li></ul> Evaluate need for: <ul><li>PT consult if patient has a history of fall and/or mobility impairment.</li><li>OT consult</li><li>Slip resistant chair mat (do <u>not</u> use in shower chair)</li><li>Activation of bed/chair alarm.</li><li>*Use of seat belt, when in wheelchair.</li></ul> * See Med/Surg Restraint Policy	<ul><li>Institute flagging system: red card outside room and red sticker on medical record, assignment board/electronic board; Hill ROM flag, if available</li></ul> Implement measures listed under low/moderate risk and: <ul><li>Remain with patient while toileting</li><li>Observe q 60 minutes unless patient is on activated bed or chair alarm.</li><li>If patient requires an air overlay, use side rail protectors.</li><li>When necessary, transport throughout hospital with assistance of staff or trained caregivers. Consider alternatives, e.g., bedside procedure. Notify receiving area of high fall risk.</li></ul> Evaluate need for the following : <ul><li>Moving patient to room with best visual access to nursing station</li><li>Activated bed/chair alarm</li><li>Low bed</li><li>Protective devices, e.g. hipsters, helmets</li><li>24 hour supervision/sitter</li><li>Physical restraint / enclosed bed (only with authorized prescriber order).</li></ul>

Figure 26.2 Recommended Fall-prevention Strategies

The risk factors within the environment are often more easily remedied by the nurse, while interventions for personal risk factors can be more complex. However, in order to best prevent falls, a comprehensive interdisciplinary intervention program that addresses patient-specific risk factors in a targeted way is most effective.[46] For example, a patient with delirium who is acutely confused needs to have a thorough diagnostic work-up by the physician with a goal of identification of the underlying cause. In addition to the physician, a pharmacist might be very helpful in such a case to assess the potential of drug-to-drug interactions or medication-related sources of acute confusion. At the point at which the acute confusion is identified and while the underlying reason for it is being examined, the nurse plays a critical role in the minute-to-minute management of the patient's safety. Some of the interventions mentioned above for the environment, particularly moving the patient to a room near the nurses' station and performing frequent (minimum of hourly) nursing rounds to assess current orientation and needs are important. Bed and chair alarms are other devices that should be explored for patients with impulsive behavior or who forget to use call bells to ring for assistance. If after exhausting all of these interventions, the patient still remains at high-risk for falling, a 24-hour sitter should be considered.

Some facilities begin discharge teaching in a pre-admission clinic for scheduled procedures. One New England area hospital uses this opportunity to evaluate the patient population for fall risk. The total knee and total hip replacement population is evaluated by physical therapy and has the option to sign a contract addressing fall prevention safety. This individualized attention to safety needs is addressed prior to admission and alerts patients to their personal role in fall prevention.

An important part of planning for discharge or transition to home or another care facility includes providing patient and family education related to fall prevention and promoting a safe environment. This is especially important for patients who remain at risk for falls upon their discharge, in particular for older adults as approximately 33 percent residing in the community experience at least one fall each year, according to the American Academy of Orthopaedic Surgeons.

B. Environmental Interventions for Fall Prevention in the Home Setting

- Keep walking paths free of clutter and obstacles (e.g., newspaper, throw rugs and cords)
- Maintain adequate lighting in all areas especially in stairways

- Locate assistive devices (e.g., walkers and devices) within reach
- Ensure certain walking devices are used properly and consistently; consult physical therapy as needed
- Repair uneven or loose floor/stairway surfaces
- Ensure floor surfaces are clean and that spills/wet areas are promptly addressed
- Procure and utilize devices such as long-handled grabbers to prevent reaching or stooping
- Place frequently used items nearby or within reach
- Install handrails on stairs and steps
- Install grab bars in the bathtub or shower and by the toilet
- Remove cords or wires on the floor
- Eliminate chairs that are too low to sit in and get easily out of
- Avoid floor wax
- Ensure that the telephone can be reached from the floor

In addition to these environmental interventions, assessments of other fall risk factors by the multidisciplinary care team are an important part of discharge planning and follow-up care. For example, a review of the patient's medications by a pharmacist in particular for high-risk classes of medication, polypharmacy as well as nursing assessments for postural hypotension (drops in blood pressure with position changes). These assessments can lead to medication adjustments and changes during hospitalization that should be followed-up after discharge by the patient's primary care physician. Other important evaluations might include assessments of leg strength, gait and balance with inpatient treatment and possibly referrals for outpatient physical therapy. The social worker will play a key role in planning for and orchestrating multidisciplinary referrals.

C. Restraints

Restraints are physical and chemical restrictors of movement administered or applied by a nurse. During the last two decades, federal and accrediting agencies have worked to reduce or eliminate the use of restraints in patient care environments. Facilities failing to comply with guidelines for appropriate restraint use may face citations and fines imposed by state quality assurance boards and/or the Centers for Medicare and Medicaid Services (CMS). CMS is the federal organization that certifies all Medicare and Medicaid participating hospitals and other facilities where health services are provided. Guidelines for restraint use are included in the CMS final rule on patient's rights.[47]

The two basic types of restraints are physical and chemical. A physical restraint is a manual method or mechanical or physical device such as material or equipment attached or adjacent to the patient's body with a goal of restricting movement or access to the body that a patient cannot readily remove.[48] Physical restraints include limb (i.e., wrist or ankle), jacket or vest, and side rails (all four side rails up). A chemical restraint is a medication that is unnecessary for the treatment of medical symptoms but used rather for the convenience of staff.[49] Restraints have been used with the intent of preventing harm or injury to a patient, nurse, or others; however, there are inherent risks of restraint use that have been recognized by the healthcare community. Over time one large misconception that physical restraints prevent injurious falls has been disproven. In fact, several studies have shown that fall-related injuries have actually increased with restraint use.[50-52] The harms associated with physical restraints range from minor ones to death. Well-documented negative outcomes of physical restraints involve many body systems and include: mental status changes, difficulty breathing, pneumonia, impaired hydration and nutrition, aspiration, strangulation, compromised circulation, impaired skin/tissue integrity (i.e., redness, skin tears, abrasions, pressure ulcers), incontinence, entrapment, muscle atrophy, reduced bone mass, contracture, fractures and death. In light of the many negative consequences that could result from the use of physical restraints, a logical conclusion is that they might actually do more harm than good for patient safety.

TIP: Review the facility policy on fall prevention as well as the restraint policy. When reviewing the medical records, determine which restraint-free measures were warranted and which ones were actually employed.

TIP: Documentation within the medical record related to restraint use should include:
- Verification that the patient was reoriented and all care-related interventions explained
- Consideration of movement of the patient's room closer to the nurse's station
- Use of bed/chair alarms or pressure sensor mats as appropriate
- Use of 24-hour sitter as needed

Keeping all four side-rails up on a bed requires a physician order because this is considered a physical restraint. Like any physical restraint, the benefits and the risks of the use of all four side rails should be carefully weighed prior to their use. According to the United States Food and Drug Administration (FDA) today there are approximately 2.5 million nursing home and hospital beds.[53] The U.S. FDA requires reporting of incidents involving beds with side rails. There were 772 incidents of patients being trapped, caught, entangled or strangled with patient outcomes ranging from death (460 patients) to no injury (176 patients) reported to the FDA from 1985 through 2008.[54]

Research has also demonstrated a link between falls and the use of side rails.[55,56] Similar to other forms of physical restraints attempting to escape the bed, and in this case navigating the side rails, is a time when injurious falls occur.

TIP: Reasons patients attempt to get out of bed may be purposeful such as to use the toilet which is a high-risk time for falls.[57]

D. Hourly Rounding

Some facilities have implemented "hourly rounding" to attend to basic needs, promote patient safety and prevent falls.[58] Simple questions commonly asked of the patient include: "Do you need anything? Would you like something to eat or drink? Do you need to go to the bathroom?" The nursing staff ensures that commonly used items such as the telephone are within easy reach for the patient. Additionally, the nursing staff must make certain that the call bell is within the patient's reach. For confused patients, the nursing staff reorients or reminds the patient of his name, location, time, reason for the hospitalization and plan of care. All patients are encouraged to ask questions.

TIP: Some facilities require staff to document that rounds were performed. These documents may or may not be kept within the medical record. The facility may keep the documents for all patients on a particular unit together.

26.6 Complications of Falls

A variety of complications can result from a fall. These complications have a direct effect on morbidity and mortality after a fall. While the list is lengthy, this chapter will focus on a few highlighted areas.

A. Describe Types of Injuries Related to Falls

"Patient falls are the most common adverse events reported in hospitals."[59] The best way to deal with complications is to prevent them from happening. About 30 percent of falls result in injury, and 4 to 6 percent of them result in serious injury.[60] While hospital falls affect both young and old patients, many of them occur when the patient is alone or involved in elimination-related activities.[61]

In the United States, rates of fall-related fractures among older adults are more than twice as high for women as for men. Falls can result in significant consequences such as injuries, which in turn lead to disability, loss of independent living, pain and reduced quality of life. Injuries from falls include contusions, abrasions, facial injuries, fractured bones, head injuries, and even death. Older adults sustain more injuries of the head, thorax and lower limb/pelvis, while the younger population more frequently sustains abdomen and upper limb injuries.[62]

Older adults have higher rates of injury after a fall because of their age and increased bone fragility making fractures more likely to occur.[63] This population warrants an evaluation for osteoporosis which is a decrease in bone density which decreases overall bone strength. A history of a fracture is an important risk factor for subsequent fractures.

Falls continue to be the leading cause of traumatic brain injury (TBI) and contribute substantially to morbidity and mortality in older adults. TBI may be an overlooked diagnosis as they can be caused by a bump or a blow to the head. In 2005, "Half of unintentional fall deaths and 8% of hospitalizations for nonfatal falls were attributable to TBI."[64,65] This data includes falls which occur in the home environment and are not specific to falls within the hospital.[66,67]

TIP: More than a third of inpatient falls result in one or more injuries.[68] Most of the injuries are minor, yet 3 percent of all falls result in fractures.

TIP: In order to determine potential causes of a fall, careful attention needs to be paid to this important clinical problem. Falls may go unrecognized or unreported for a variety of reasons:

- There is no recognized injury by the staff or the patient at the time of the fall.
- The patient does not mention the incident to the healthcare provider.
- The patient has not been asked about her fall history.
- The patient believes that falls are part of the aging process.
- The staff fear negative ramifications when working in a punitive culture.

B. Types of Fractures

1. Radius fracture

The distal radius fracture is the most common fracture site in the upper extremity. Hand and forearm fractures often result when one outstretches the arms with the wrist in extension to decrease the impact of the fall. The younger population is more prone to fractures from high-energy trauma such as that sustained during sports while fractures in the older population are frequently the result of low-energy trauma related to osteoporotic bones. Distal radius fractures correlate with a higher risk of hip fractures in men, while spinal compression fractures correlate more closely with being a woman. Figures 26.3 through 26.5 show open radius fractures and the surgical treatment.

TIP: When reviewing medical records of an individual who has sustained a radius fracture, it is important to note the assessment of neurovascular status, including motor and sensory function of the median, radial, and ulnar nerves. The patient who has acute median nerve compression often has a change in sensation in the thumb and index fingers.

Mr. Flanagan was an alert and oriented 72 year-old man who had a left total knee replacement. On postoperative day four he was preparing to be transferred to a rehabilitation center. He wanted to use the bathroom and got out of bed on his own. He forgot that he was wearing bilateral sequential compression devices (SCDs or pneumoboots) and upon standing fell forward. The tubing of the device was connected to the machine on the bed. He sustained bilateral radius fractures and required two additional surgeries. He remained in the hospital an additional six days.

Acute management of distal radius fractures is warranted to prevent emergent complications such as significant nerve injury or vascular compromise. Open fractures or compartment syndrome require emergent intervention. Please refer to Chapter 9, *Orthopaedic Nursing Malpractice Issues*, for more information.

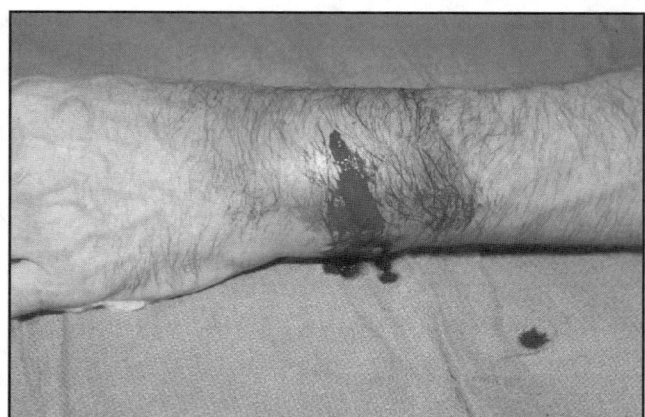

Figure 26.3 *Complex Open Distal Radius Fracture—Open Fracture*

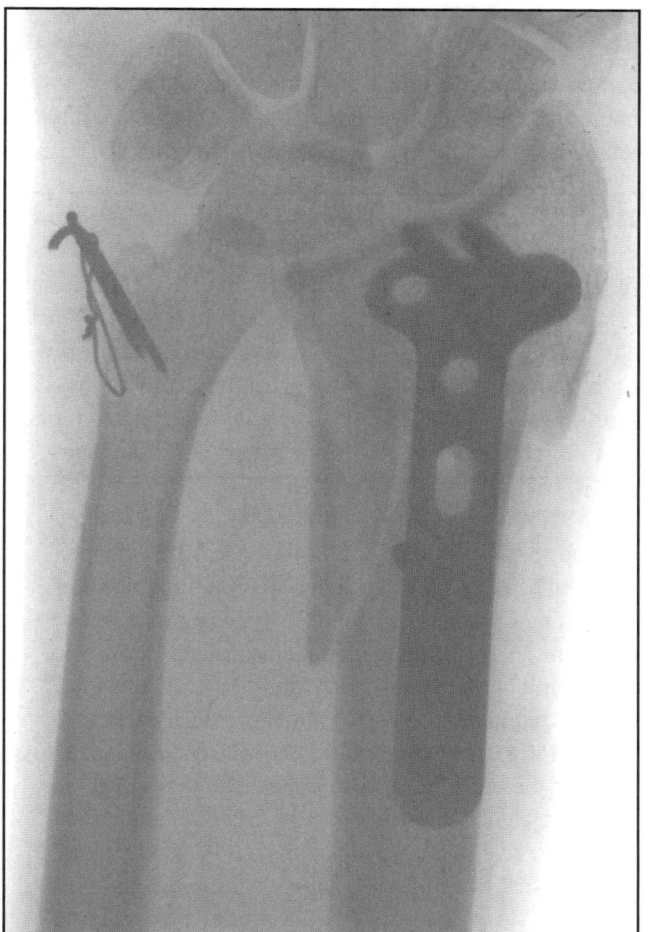

Figure 26.4 *Surgical intervention for the open radius fracture*

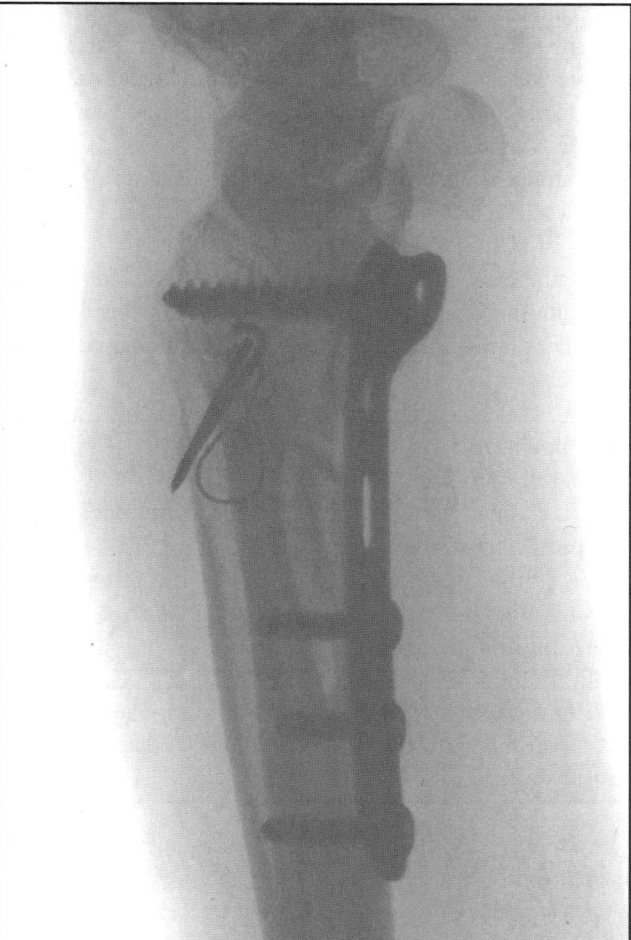

Figure 26.5 *Another view of the surgical treatment*

Many older adults are best served by conservative fracture management and rehabilitation designed to maximize function, despite the presence of significant deformity. Osteoporosis contributes to fracture instability, which complicates the management of fractures in older adults.

2. Tibial fractures

The tibia is the major weight-bearing bone of the lower leg. When patients fall, significant direct trauma including hyperextension injuries and twisting motions may result in tibial fractures. A knee effusion or localized swelling and tenderness over the bone may be present. Lacerations and contusions (bruises) may also be present. When reviewing the medical record, note if any healthcare provider noted an open fracture. Patients who are diagnosed with an open fracture typically go to the operating room for surgical intervention such as an irrigation, debridement and administration of antibiotics. Patients who develop vascular injury or suspected compartment syndrome require an immediate orthopedic evaluation. The treatment plan for tibial fractures may include splinting, elevation, or operative intervention dependent upon the specific type of fracture and whether the fracture is displaced (out of alignment) or non-displaced. Please refer to Chapter 9, *Orthopaedic Nursing Malpractice Issues,* to review more on this topic.

3. Hip fractures

Hip fractures are the most frequent type of fall-related fractures. Ninety percent of the 380,000 hip fractures treated annually occur as a result of a fall.[69] Most people who sustain hip fractures are unable to stand and ambulate following the injury. Hip fractures can be a devastating injury as they are a major source of morbidity and mortality in the older adult population.[70] Patients who have sustained a hip fracture are at an increased risk of a second hip fracture.[71] Due to their higher rates of osteoporosis, approximately 76 percent of all hip fractures occur in women.[72]

The term hip fracture is a general term; however, there are specific types of hip fractures. Intracapsular include femoral neck fractures and femoral head fractures. Extracapsular include intertrochanteric fractures and subtrochanteric fractures.

Intracapsular fractures have a higher rate of non-union and these fractures are more likely to develop avascular necrosis of the femoral head due to the tenuous blood supply to the area. Subtrochanteric fractures are often treated with intramedullary rods or nails. The risk of this approach is implant failure due to the stress placed on that part of the femur.

TIP: Mechanisms of hip fracture:
- A fall onto the lateral hip
- Twisting mechanism in which the patient's foot is planted and the body rotates
- A sudden spontaneous fracture, which then causes the fall
- A pathologic fracture

TIP: Approximately one-half of older patients are unable to regain their ability to live independently after an injurious fall.[73]

The primary goal of fracture management is to return the patient to the prior level of function. Treatment often includes surgical intervention followed by early mobilization. At times non-operative management or conservative management is the preferred method and historically this has resulted in an unacceptable rate of morbidity and mortality, and malunion and nonunion of the bones. The later method may be used if an individual's health history is extensive which may place them at a very high-risk of mortality from anesthesia or the surgery. This method may also be selected if an older adult with dementia was non-ambulatory prior to surgery and expresses minimal subjective or objective pain. This group still requires mobilization to help prevent them from developing complications related to prolonged bed rest such as pneumonia, risk for decubitus ulcers, deep vein thrombosis, and urinary tract infections.

Surgical intervention is usually done within 24–48 hours post-injury. The surgeon reviews the radiology studies and health in order to decide upon the type of surgery needed. Types of surgical intervention include: open reduction internal fixation (ORIF), hemiarthroplasty or total hip replacement. Delays may occur when medical clearance is needed for patients with comorbid conditions such as cardiac, pulmonary and fluid and electrolyte imbalances, which may need treatment prior to surgery.

Postoperative management focuses on early mobilization, as this will help reduce the incidence of the previously mentioned complications. All patients should receive 24–48 hours of antibiotic coverage, which are usually written as total doses of antibiotics to be administered by the surgeon.

TIP: Outcomes of patients after hip fractures include: 25 percent make a full recovery; 40 percent will require nursing home admission; 50 percent will be dependent upon a cane or a walker; and 24 percent of those over age 50 will die in one year.[74] The rationale that only 25 percent of hip fracture patients make a full recovery is due to the deconditioning that occurs during recuperation which contributes to poor functional outcomes.

Mrs. A was a 78-year-old woman who was admitted to the hospital with a diagnosis of "syncope." Her health history included a stroke and she was taking Coumadin, which is an anticoagulant (blood thinner) medication. The medical team performed an initial assessment, admitted her to the hospital, and requested a telemetry monitor. The nursing staff performed the initial assessment and determined she was a risk for falls. During the late evening, Mrs. A attempted to climb out of bed on two separate occasions. The nursing staff reoriented her and assisted her back to bed. Three hours later the nursing staff heard a cry and responded to Mrs. A's room where she was found on the floor near the bathroom. She was diagnosed with a right hip fracture and a subdural hematoma. Mrs. A required additional surgeries and she died 12 days later. Upon review of the medical record, it was determined there were no interventions or plan of care defined within the record for the prevention of falls. Additionally, the nursing staff never used the bed alarms, which were part of every bed, on this patient. This case settled on behalf of the plaintiff/decedent for a confidential amount.

4. Spinal injuries

Spinal injuries can result from falls; thus a full assessment is critical after a fall to determine if there are injuries to the spinal cord. The spine consists of 33 vertebrae: 7 cervical, 12 thoracic, 5 lumbar, 5 sacral and 4 coccygeal. The vertebral column provides the body's basic structural support and protects the spinal cord. The cervical spine is the most commonly injured part of the spinal column due to its exposed location and its inherent flexibility. The thoracic spine is rigidly flexed and a great amount of force is needed to damage this area of a healthy adult. For older adults with osteoporosis or bone disease, minor trauma may be sufficient to cause a compression fracture.

The thoracolumbar area is the second most commonly injured region. The spine changes from a kyphotic to a lordotic curve. Of all the thoracolumbar spine injuries, 90 percent of fractures occurred between T11-L4. Since the spinal canal is relatively wide at this level, thoracolumbar injuries rarely result in complete cord lesions.[75]

The thoracic and lumbar areas have a three-column scheme. These columns are anterior, middle, and posterior. The location and extent of the fracture can determine the stability and instability of the spine.

Spinal column injury may result in spinal cord trauma through a number of mechanisms:[76]

- Transection: Penetrating or massive blunt trauma resulting in spinal column injury that may tear part of the spinal cord; less severe trauma may have similar neurologic effects by displacing bony fragments into the spinal canal or through disk herniation.
- Compression: Wedge, or anterior, compression fractures account for 50 to 70 percent of all thoracolumbar fractures.[77] Often simple wedge fractures cause no neurologic impairment.
- Burst fractures: The burst fractures account for approximately 14 percent of all thoracolumbar injuries.[78] Compressive forces fracture the vertebral endplate then pressure the nucleus pulposa upon the vertebral body. The bony fragments can retropulse into the spinal canal. All burst fractures should be considered unstable because neurologic deficits are seen in 42 to 58 percent of patients.[79]
- Contusion: Contusions of the spinal cord can occur from bony dislocation, subluxations, or fracture fragments.
- Vascular injury: Primary vascular damage to the spinal cord should be suspected when there is a discrepancy between a clinically apparent neurologic deficit and the known level of the spinal column injury.

If a patient is diagnosed with a spinal cord injury, the treatment plan includes an immediate surgical consultation. If there are no physicians with an expertise in orthopedics of the spine for consult available onsite, then the facility arranges an immediate transfer to a hospital that can render care for the injury. The treatment plan may include any of the following: surgical intervention, steroid administration, or application of a halo device (this may be used for the cervical or upper thoracic fractures).

C. Head Injury

The most important consideration in any head injury is whether or not the patient has sustained a brain injury. If a patient had previously been oriented and has experienced a fall with noted confusion or behavioral disturbances then they should be assessed for a head injury.

Across all age groups, a traumatic brain injury also known as TBI is often caused by a fall (35 percent).[80] TBI occurs when an external force injures the brain. Falls cause more than half of all TBIs among children aged 0-14 years compared to approximately 60 percent among adults aged 65 years and older.[81] Types of injuries include cerebral contusions, diffuse axonal injury, intracranial hemorrhage, subdural hematoma, epidural hematoma, and intracerebral hemorrhage.

1. Cerebral contusions

Cerebral contusions are considered a more severe injury in which the brain is bruised.

2. Diffuse axonal injury

Diffuse axonal injury is caused by the brain moving back and forth in the skull. This type of injury is not a result of a blow to the head and can be seen with patients who have fallen, or have been involved in a vehicle crash, or with shaken baby syndrome. When the brain moves back and forth a shearing of the brain cells and cell death occurs, causing swelling in the brain. The swelling increases pressure and causes a decrease in blood flow to the brain which can result in additional injury. Recovery is dependent upon the location and severity of the axonal injury.

3. Intracranial hemorrhage

An intracranial hemorrhage is a hematoma (collection of blood) which develops within the closed cranium and is considered the most serious of all brain injuries. There are a variety of causes which include: TBI, falls, abnormalities of blood vessels such as an aneurysm or vascular malformation, and high blood pressure. The bleeding or the swelling increases the pressure on the brain tissues and can quickly destroy it.

TIP: Additional factors, which increase the risk of a bleed, include:
- Bleeding disorders
- Brain tumors
- Liver disease
- Use of aspirin or blood thinners (anticoagulant medications such as Coumadin, heparin)

Recovery is dependent on the severity and location of the bleed.

4. Subdural hematoma

This is usually the result of a serious head injury. When this occurs acutely, the blood fills the brain quickly and compresses the brain tissue causing a brain injury and possibly even death. Subdural hematomas can also result from minor injury. For example, in the older population these may initially go undiagnosed due to there being a slow bleed.

5. Epidural hematoma

An epidural hematoma results after a head injury and is considered extradural because the blood collects in the space between the skull and the dura (which surrounds the spinal cord and keeps in the cerebrospinal fluid). The cause may be attributed to a skull fracture which causes a rupture or laceration of the artery which is located between the dura and the skull. A typical pattern of symptoms includes loss of consciousness followed by alertness and loss of consciousness again; however, this presentation of symptoms may not occur in every patient. An epidural hematoma is an emergent situation and requires immediate care.

6. Intracerebral hemorrhage

An intracerebral hemorrhage occurs when a diseased blood vessel within the brain bursts and bleeds into the brain. The most common cause is hypertension. This type of brain injury occurs infrequently with patients who fall.

TIP: Determine if the patient was taking any blood thinners such as Aspirin, Coumadin, heparin or any others which can increase the risk for and severity of a bleed.

Recovery from a brain injury depends upon both the location and severity of the injury. For example, some patients may have only a headache while the more severely injured may require a ventilator because the injury has affected the respiratory center and they are unable to breathe.

D. Complications from the Injuries

When falls result in fractures of hips or femurs, during periods of immobility following surgical correction of these fractures, there is a risk of venous thromboembolism (VTE). A VTE includes two types of complications: a deep vein thrombosis (DVT) and a pulmonary embolism (PE) in which components of the blood such as red blood cells, fibrin, leukocytes and platelets form a mass or a clot within a vein. While a DVT is most common in the leg veins, a PE results when a portion of the clot or thrombus detaches

from the vein wall, travels to the lungs, and lodges within the pulmonary arteries. Complications from this include pulmonary infarction, atelectasis, right ventricular failure and even death. Refer to Chapter 9, *Orthopaedic Nursing Malpractice Issues,* for additional information. There are several other complications which can occur as a result of immobility including: decubitus ulcers, orthostatic intolerance (drop in blood pressure of more than 20 mmHG or a rise in heart rate to more than 120 bpm), musculoskeletal disuse, and constipation as examples.

TIP: When reviewing the medical records, determine if measures were implemented to prevent a VTE. These measures include: sequential compression device (SCD), TED stockings, blood thinner medications such as aspirin or Coumadin or unfractionated or low molecular weight heparin, early ambulation, frequent plantarflexion and dorsiflexion exercises (foot pumps), and deep breathing exercises.

During recovery after surgical correction of a fracture, older adults in particular are at an increased risk of pneumonia due to pulmonary secretion stasis. Aspiration plays a key role in hospital-acquired pneumonia. Preventive measures include early ambulation/mobilization, incentive spirometry, and chest physical therapy. Support measures may be implemented upon diagnosis and include supplemental oxygen, antibiotics, nutritional support and evaluation, and chest physical therapy.

TIP: There are patients who may be at risk for aspiration pneumonia. These patients may experience difficulties managing their own secretions. Within the medical record, there may be a note stating the patient coughs or chokes with every bite or even a drink of liquid. These patients usually have a dietitian or even a speech pathology consult. Swallowing studies may have been done with evaluation of the results of these studies. Recommendations may include the patient having a special diet, which includes liquids that are thickened to a specific consistency.

TIP After a fall there is a stronger relationship between the patient's comorbidities and the risk of death following a fall in the older person.[82]

E. Ambulation Difficulties

Patients who have sustained falls may have difficulties ambulating post fall due to discomfort of the injured area. Ambulation difficulties are not limited to patients with abrasions, contusions, fractures, and head injuries. The cause of the fall should be investigated to prevent falls from occurring in the future.

TIP: Determine the reason why the patient fell. The causes are often multifactorial including:
- Weakness
- Environmental (includes wet floor, object on floor)
- Cognitive impairment
- Balance and/or gait
- Dizziness
- Age
- Orthostatic hypotension
- Visual impairment
- Limitations with ADLs (activities of daily living)
- Footwear (barefoot, stocking feet, shoes with slippery bottoms including high heels)
- Acute medical illness (i.e., infection)
- Alcohol or drug consumption or withdrawal

TIP: After determining the cause of the fall, it is helpful to review nursing as well as physical therapy notes as these provide a rich source of information. The patient may need an assistive device such as a walker, a cane or even crutches to assist with ambulation. Patients who already have assistive devices should be assessed for proper use; for example, the tips of canes or walkers may not be making adequate contact with the ground.

F. Repeat Falls

The patient who falls is at a much higher risk of falling again than one who has never experienced a fall. Thus, determining the etiology of the initial fall is critical to the prevention of future falls. Important things to consider when attempting to determine the etiology of the fall include:

- Were measures taken to prevent the patient from falling again?
- If the patient has a balance or gait problem, is he being evaluated by the physical or occupational therapist?
- Is the patient being offered an assistive device?
- Is the patient alert and oriented to person, place and time?
- If the patient is confused, is he being reoriented? Is he able to understand and follows directions?
- Has the medical record noted the patient has been classified as a fall risk?
- When was the most recent time the patient's risk for falls was reevaluated prior to the fall?

- If the patient is noted to be at risk for falls, has this also been addressed in the plan of care?

G. Delirium

"Delirium is an abrupt onset of a cluster of fluctuating, transient changes and disturbances in consciousness, cognition, and perception in medically ill patients."[83] This may occur as a result of head trauma, intoxication of a variety of medications, infectious processes, and other health-related factors.

H. Increased Length of Stay

Patients aged 65 years or older had a lengthier hospital stay, higher admission to long-term care facilities, and higher mortality than younger age groups. "Hip fracture was also an independent factor associated with the three adverse outcomes."[84]

I. Fear of Falling

Fear of falling, also known as post-fall anxiety syndrome, is a well-recognized syndrome in older adults. This fear may result in the person self-limiting their activities. Fear of falling can also contribute to individuals reducing their mobility and physical fitness, resulting in deconditioning which places them at even a greater risk for a fall.[85] Persons experiencing this fear may alter their gait after a fall by taking small steps also known as "baby steps."

26.7 After the Fall
A. Evaluation

Fall response and evaluation are both important aspects of post-fall care in healthcare facilities. The hospital fall prevention plan should include a mechanism for patient evaluation post-fall and data collection of the fall required by TJC and CMS.[86,87] The patient's condition is the first priority. Once the patient is evaluated and stable, documentation of the event should follow hospital policy and procedure in the medical record. Specific guidelines and regulatory requirements vary from state-to-state, thus the author of the documentation must understand the hospital policy to decrease liability. Medical record documentation of the event and incident reporting are two separate and different means to communicate the event. Information such as the examination and brief physical assessment to evaluate for injury, including an assessment for orientation and postural blood pressure change are important elements for inclusion in the medical record documentation. The healthcare personnel should document an objective description of how the patient was found, including attention to detail but without assumptions of how or why the patient fell, a description of the fall from the patient if able, the location, and whether the fall was witnessed or unwitnessed.

The following is an example of a comprehensive nursing note after a fall.

> At 8:30 P.M., Mr. Brown, a 77-year-old man who was post total hip replacement, was found on the floor next to the bathroom in his room. He stated, "I know I should have used the call light to request assistance but I thought I could do this on my own. I did not wear slippers and slid on the floor." "My left leg hurts." He was alert and oriented times three. This patient denies hitting his head and explained he injured his left leg when he fell forward. There are no open areas noted. His vital signs are temperature 98.8; heart rate 74 regular; blood pressure 138/74; respiratory rate 18; oxygen saturation 98% on room air. He was assisted back to bed with a three-person assist. Dr. Jones was called and came to evaluate the patient. Physician orders have been written and include x-rays of the left leg. The charge nurse was informed. At 9:45 P.M., the x-rays were done and the report confirms a left tibia fracture. Dr. Jones informed nursing that this patient should not eat anything after midnight (NPO) since he would go for surgical correction in the operating room in the morning. The call bell was at his side and this patient has been reminded to use the call bell to request assistance. Hourly rounds and safety rounds done.

The following is an example of an incomplete note after a fall:

> Patient fell on the floor and complained of pain. X-rays done.

TIP: It is important to note the mental status of the person who fell. Determine if the patient was able to use a call bell for assistance and if the call bell was in an easy to reach location.

TIP: After a fall occurs, the nursing care plan should be reviewed by the nursing staff and additional updated interventions should be implemented as appropriate.

B. Incident Reports

Patient falls are the most common adverse events reported in hospitals that represent nearly 40 percent of inpatient incident reports.[88] In some states, incident reports are not discoverable unless a nurse writes "incident report filed"

within the medical record. The incident reporting system in some facilities may be electronic and include an automatic delivery of the report to the risk management department. If not, a standardized written report should be filed. Incident reporting is a detailed account of many aspects of a fall collected for process improvement and liability purposes. A detailed description of the fall should be documented from both the patient's perspective and the staff's perspective. The names of witnesses and nursing staff involved, the location of the fall, use of restraining and medical devices (IV pole or walker) and the events preceding the fall should be included in the report.[89] The injury and seriousness of the patient's condition determine next steps. If the event includes a serious reportable event or death, as described earlier, reporting to the state's department of public health may be required by law. Additionally, other entities such as the Board of Registration in Medicine or others may have been informed if the event is reported as a serious reportable event (SRE).

TIP: Try to obtain the incident report. Determine the mental status of the patient who fell. Was the patient aware of the actions that led to the fall? Was the patient using an assistive device such as a walker or a cane? Compare the patient's physical abilities to the physical or occupational therapy notes. This is one area within the medical record that reveals the amount of assistance needed by the patient. Note the consistency of documentation of the patient's mental status and physical status surrounding the time of the "fall."

26.8 Litigation with Falls

Patient falls occurring in the hospital setting are categorized as falls with and without injury. Falls with injury resulting in fractures, dislocations, intracranial injuries, and crushing injuries are considered a hospital-acquired condition (HAC) and serious reportable event (SRE).[90] A review of the medical record by an experienced legal nurse consultant or attorney may raise the question of negligence as the facts of the fall are discovered. Requests for additional information may reveal a deviation in the standard of care when the hospital's policy and procedures for fall prevention have not been followed by the employees of the organization. Documentation should be scrutinized for discrepancies such as failure to recognize and document when a patient is at risk and failure to implement fall prevention interventions when a patient is at risk.[91] Additionally, some patients are not compliant with the nurse or staff's requests to call for help when getting up. Solid documentation of attempts the patient made and the corrective action taken to prevent falls may substantiate the goal of patient safety and reduce exposure to litigation.

When a patient fall does occur, adherence to the hospital's policies and procedures for patient care and documentation of the patient's condition is necessary. Failure to recognize injury due to the fall may result in litigation. Failure to recognize and treat injuries after a fall and failure to note a change in patient condition are possible areas a sharp legal nurse consultant or attorney may identify as contributing factors to the patient's injury and resultant damages.

If the elements of negligence are met, the issue of hospital and individual liability may be pursued. The plaintiff may view the injuries as occurring from a "never event" which in of itself is negligence. Furthermore, plaintiffs may indicate that there is negligence because the patient experienced a HAC; someone did not recognize a risk for fall. Is there a "duty" to the patient to ensure that a HAC does not occur? Because CMS and other private insurance companies are not paying for some HACs, does this translate to practice that is substandard, and bad care that consumers do not have to pay for?

Are regulations and standards from CMS and TJC admissible in court? The CMS safety regulations do not define standards of care; rather their original purpose was for billing and reimbursement. In theory, federal reimbursement rules should not impact the legal determination of hospital or individual liability. The reality is that plaintiff's attorneys may persuasively argue that if the federal government calls HACs substandard care, so should the jury.

Consideration of liability risks around patient safety prompts hospitals and healthcare providers to be more vigilant in documentation. The paper and electronic medical records provide caregivers with tools to document care; however, they may be too cumbersome for some. The caregiver must have knowledge of which aspect of care is electronic and which is paper to adequately document care rendered, therefore a review of the medical records is necessary to obtain all information documented for patient care and safety.

In summary, nursing liability surrounding a patient fall may fit into one or more of these allegations:

- Failure to identify the patient as being at risk for falls
- Failure to periodically reevaluate the patient's risk for falls
- Failure to reassign a new risk for falls following a fall
- Failure to identify an individualized plan of care for a patient at risk for falls
- Failure to instruct the patient to call for help, if able, when ambulating
- Failure to provide the appropriate degree of monitoring for a patient at risk for falls

- Failure to supply the appropriate amount of assistance when ambulating or transferring a patient
- Failure to use available interventions such as safety straps in the OR, lifting systems, floor mats, one to one sitters, bed alarms, lockable windows, and Wanderguards
- Failure to properly assess a patient who has fallen
- Failure to detect signs of injury
- Failure to notify a physician (and in some settings, the family and regulatory agencies) of the fall
- Failure to recognize and report signs of deterioration after a fall
- Concealing evidence of a fall

26.9 Conclusion

Falls are a widespread safety concern affecting all age groups, across both public and private locations as well as community and healthcare settings. The younger population tends to have high velocity falls while the older population more commonly sustains falls from their own height. Fall prevention in the inpatient setting requires an interdisciplinary team and multifaceted approach. Patient safety in hospitals has the attention of accreditation agencies, public health organizations, private insurance companies, and the government. Reducing the rate of falls within healthcare settings requires strong management and administrative commitment to support, analyze, create, and maintain a data-driven fall prevention program. Additionally, enthusiastic and engaged staff with vigilance in patient care, monitoring and teaching patients/families, and reducing risk factors is needed.

As CMS reimbursement for "preventable conditions" decreases, with private insurance companies soon to follow, our focus on patient safety and fall reduction correlates directly with the need for delivery of cost-effective care in the hospital environment.[92] In summary, hospitals of the future will be faced with financial challenges in many areas, one of which is the implementation of fall prevention programs to promote quality outcomes management and allow for maximum reimbursement.

Endnotes

1. AAOS Fall Prevention Facts http://orthoinfo.aaos.org/topic.cfm?tpoic=A00101.

2. Baumgaertner, MR, Higgins, TF. Femoral Neck Fractures. *Rockwood and Green's Fractures in Adults,* Bucholz, RW, Heckman, JD, Rockwood, CA, Green, DP (Eds), Lippincott Williams & Wilkins, Philadelphia (2002), p. 1579.

3. Agostini JV, Baker DI, Bogardus ST. *Making Health Care Safer: A Critical Analysis of Patient Safety Practices. (AHRQ Publication No. 01-E058).* Rockville, MD: Agency for Healthcare Research and Quality, 2001, File Inventory, Evidence Report/Technology Assessment Number 43; Prevention of Falls in Hospitalized and Institutionalized Older People; Chapter 26, pp. 281–299.

4. Center for Disease Control and Prevention. Falls Among Older Adults: An Overview. Retrieved from http://www.cdc.gov/ncipc/factsheets/adultfalls.htm.

5. Institute of Clinical System Improvement. Health Care Protocol: Prevention of Falls. March, 2008. Retrieved from: http://www.icsi.org/falls__acute_care___prevention_of__protocol_/falls__acute_care___prevention_of__protocol__24255.html.

6. Shorr, R., Mion, L., Chandler, M., Rosenblatt, L., Lynch, D., Kessler, L. 2008. Improving the Capture of Fall Events in Hospitals: Combining a Service for Evaluating Inpatient Falls with an Incident Report System. J Am Geriatric Society. Retrieved from Pubmed: PMCID: PMC2361382. NIHMSID: NIHMS37976.

7. Institute of Clinical System Improvement. Health Care Protocol: Prevention of Falls. March, 2008. Retrieved from http://www.icsi.org/falls__acute_care___prevention_of__protocol_/falls__acute_care___prevention_of__protocol__24255.html.

8. Dunton, N., Gajewski, B., Taunton, R.L., and Moore, J. Nurse staffing and patient falls on acute care hospital units. *Nursing Outlook*, (2004), 52(1), 53-59.

9. Hill-Westmoreland, E. E., and Gruber-Baldini, A. L., Falls Documentation in Nursing Homes: Agreement of the Minimum Data Set with Chart Abstractions of Medical and Nursing Documentation. *Journal of the American Geriatric Society*, (2005), 53(2), 268-273.

10. 2006 National Patient Safety Goals. Joint Commission on Accreditation of Healthcare Organizations [online]. [Accessed August 4, 2006]. Available at: http://www.jointcommission.org/PatientSafety/NationalPatientSafetyGoals.

11. American Nurse Association. (2008). Nursing Quality Indicators. Retrieved May, 2, 2010 from: http://www.nursingworld.org/MainMenuCategories/ANAPoliticalPower/State/StateLegislativeAgenda/NursingQualityIndicators.

12. Joint Commission. 2010. Joint Commission Requirements. Retrieved May 2, 2010 from http://www.jointcommission.org/Standards/Requirements.

13. American Nurse Association. (2008). Nursing Quality Indicators. Retrieved May, 2, 2010 from: http://www.nursingworld.org/MainMenuCategories/ANAPoliticalPower/State/StateLegislativeAgenda/NursingQualityIndicators.

14. Morse, J.M., Tylko, S.J., and Dixon, H.A. Characteristics of the fall-prone patient. *Gerontologist*, (1987), 27(4), 516-522.

15. Morse, J.M., Tylko, S.J., and Dixon, H.A. Characteristics of the Fall-prone Patient. *Gerontologist*, (1987). 27(4), p. 516-522.

16. Humphreys, G. *Bulletin of the World Health Organization*, (2009) March; 87(3).

17. *Id.*

18. Dunton, N., Gajewski, B., Taunton, R.L., and Moore, J. Nurse Staffing and Patient Falls on Acute Care Hospital Units. *Nursing Outlook*, (2004), 52(1), p. 53-59.

19. The Joint Commission. 2010. National Quality Forum (NQF) Endorsed Nursing-Sensitive Care Performance Measures. *Implementation Guide for the National Quality Forum (NQF) Endorsed Nursing-Sensitive Care Performance Measures.* Retrieved from http://www.jointcommission.org/PerformanceMeasurement/MeasureReserveLibrary/nqf_nursing.htm.

20. National Quality Forum (NQF). Safe Practices for Better Healthcare–2009 Update: A Consensus Report. Washington, DC: NQF; 2009.

21. *Id.*

22. Aydin, C., Burnes Bolton, L., Donaldson, N., Storer Brown, D., Buffum, M., Elashoff, J., Sandhu,M. Creating and analyzing a statewide nursing quality measurement database. *Journal of Nursing Scholarship*, (2004), 36(4), p. 371-378.

23. Center for Disease Control and Prevention. Falls Among Older Adults: An Overview. Retrieved from http://www.cdc.gov/ncipc/factsheets/adultfalls.htm.

24. National Center for Injury Prevention and Control, Centers for Disease Control and Prevention (producer). [2010, May,1].Available from: URL: http://www.cdc.gov/injury/wisqars.

25. Dunton, N., Gajewski, B., Taunton, R.L., and Moore, J. Nurse staffing and patient falls on acute care hospital units. *Nursing Outlook*, (2004), 52(1), 53-59.

26. Agostini JV, Baker DI, Bogardus ST. *Making Health Care Safer: A Critical Analysis of Patient Safety Practices. (AHRQ Publication No. 01-E058).* Rockville, MD: Agency for Healthcare Research and Quality, 2001, File Inventory, Evidence Report/Technology Assessment Number 43; Prevention of Falls in Hospitalized and Institutionalized Older People; Chapter 26, pp. 281–299.

27. Center for Disease Control and Prevention. Falls Among Older Adults: An Overview. Retrieved from http://www.cdc.gov/ncipc/factsheets/adultfalls.htm.

28. Institute of Clinical System Improvement. Health Care Protocol: Prevention of Falls. March, 2008. Retrieved from http://www.icsi.org/falls__acute_care___prevention_of__protocol_/falls__acute_care___prevention_of__protocol__24255.html.

29. Shorr, R., Mion, L., Chandler, M., Rosenblatt, L., Lynch, D., Kessler, L. 2008. Improving the Capture of Fall Events in Hospitals: Combining a Service for Evaluating Inpatient Falls with an Incident Report System. J Am Geriatric Society. Retrieved from Pubmed: PMCID: PMC2361382. NIHMSID: NIHMS37976.

30. Humphreys, G. *Bulletin of the World Health Organization*, (March 2009); 87(3).

31. McAllister, S. *APR DRG Weighs and the relationship to patient falls. Nursing Economics*, 2009, 27(2) p. 119-123.

32. Bemis-Dougherty, A., Delaune, M. Reducing Patient Falls in Inpatient Settings. *Physical Therapy*, May 2008, p. 36-42.

33. Humphreys, G. *Bulletin of the World Health Organization*, (March 2009); 87(3).

34. McAllister, S. *APR DRG Weighs and the relationship to patient falls. Nursing Economics*, 2009, 27(2), p. 119-123.

35. Spetz, J., Jacobs, J., Halter, C. Cost effectiveness of a medical vigilance system to reduce patient falls. *Nursing Economics*, (2007), 25(6), p. 333-352.

36. *Id.*

37. Dunton, N., Gajewski, B., Taunton, R.L., and Moore, J. Nurse staffing and patient falls on acute care hospital units. Nursing Outlook, (2004). 52(1), 53-59.

38. AAOS Fall Prevention Facts http://orthoinfo.aaos.org/topic.cfm?tpoic=A00101.

39. Tideiksaar, R. Falling in old age: Prevention and management. (2nd ed.) New York: Springer, (1997).

40. Hill, E. E., Nguyen, T. H., Shaha, M., Wenzel, J. A., DeForge, B. R., and Spellbring, A. M. Person-environment interactions contributing to nursing home resident falls. *Res.Gerontol.Nurs.*, (2009), 2(4), 287-296.

41. Laska, L. (Editor), "Woman Falls Going to the Bathroom Due to Substance on the Floor – Ankle, Foot and Back Injuries," *Medical Malpractice Verdicts, Settlements, and Experts,* November 2009, p. 19.

42. Laska, L. (Editor), "Man Gets Out Of Bed Alone After Nurse Fails To Respond to request for Assistance to Bathroom-Fall When Bed Moves as He Returns to bed-Fractured Hip with Decline and Death," *Medical Malpractice Verdicts, Settlements, and Experts,* November 2009, p. 17.

43. Poe, S. S., Cvach, M., Dawson, P. B., Straus, H., and Hill, E. E. (2007). The Johns Hopkins Fall Risk Assessment Tool: postimplementation evaluation. *J.Nurs.Care Qual.*, 22(4), p. 293-298.

44. Laska, L. (Editor), "Extremely Thin Woman Falls Getting Out of Bed After No Response to Call for Assistance to Bathroom-Death After Surgery for Hip Fracture," *Medical Malpractice Verdicts, Settlements, and Experts*, October 2009, p. 27

45. Meade, C. M., Bursell, A. L., and Ketelsen, L. Effects of nursing rounds: on patients' call light use, satisfaction, and safety. *Am.J.Nurs.*, (2006). 106(9), p. 58-70.

46. Hill-Westmoreland, E. E., Soeken, K., and Spellbring, A. M. A meta-analysis of fall prevention programs for the elderly: how effective are they? *Nurs.Res.*, (2002). 51(1), p. 1-8.

47. Centers for Medicare & Medicaid Services, & Department of Health and Human Services. (2006). Medicare and Medicaid programs; hospital conditions of participation: patients' rights. Final rule. Fed.Regist., 71(236), 71377-71428.

48. *Id.*

49. *Id.*

50. Capezuti, E., Evans, L., Strumpf, N., and Maislin, G. Physical restraint use and falls in nursing home residents. *Journal of the American Geriatrics Society*, (1996). 44(6), p. 627-633.

51. Capezuti, E., Strumpf, N. E., Evans, L. K., Grisso, J. A., and Maislin, G. The relationship between physical restraint removal and falls and injuries among nursing home residents. *J.Gerontol.A Biol.Sci.Med.Sci.*, (1998). 53(1), M47-M52.

52. Tinetti, M. E., Liu, W. L., and Ginter, S. F. Mechanical restraint use and fall-related injuries among residents of skilled nursing facilities. *Ann.Intern.Med.*, (1992) 116(5), p. 369-374.

53. U.S.Department of Health& Human Services, and U.S.Food and Drug Administration. (2010). *Hospital beds*. Retrieved from: http://www.fda.gov/MedicalDevices/ProductsandMedicalProcedures/GeneralHospitalDevicesandSupplies/HospitalBeds/default.htm.

54. U.S.Department of Health& Human Services, and U.S.Food and Drug Administration. (2010). *Hospital beds*. Retrieved from: http://www.fda.gov/MedicalDevices/ProductsandMedicalProcedures/GeneralHospitalDevicesandSupplies/HospitalBeds/default.htm.

55. Capezuti, E., Talerico, K. A., Cochran, I., Becker, H., Strumpf, N., and Evans, L. Individualized interventions to prevent bed-related falls and reduce siderail use. *J.Gerontol.Nurs.*, (1999). 25(11), p. 26-34.

56. Capezuti, E., Maislin, G., Strumpf, N., and Evans, L. K. Side rail use and bed-related fall outcomes among nursing home residents. *Journal of the American Geriatrics Society*, (2002). 50(1), p. 90-96.

57. Hill, E. E., Nguyen, T. H., Shaha, M., Wenzel, J. A., DeForge, B. R., and Spellbring, A. M. Person-environment interactions contributing to nursing home resident falls. *Res.Gerontol.Nurs.*, (2009). 2(4), p.287-296.

58. Meade, C. M., Bursell, A. L., and Ketelsen, L. Effects of nursing rounds: on patients' call light use, satisfaction, and safety. *Am.J.Nurs.*, (2006). 106(9), p. 58-70.

59. Terrell, K, Weaver, C. ED Patient Falls and Resulting Injuries, *Journal of Emergency Nursing*, (March 2009), Vol. 35 (2), p. 89.

60. http://www.ahrq.gov/research/nov04/1104RA4.htm accessed 3/6/09.

61. *Id.*

62. Bergeron, E., Clement, J. A Simple Fall in the Elderly: Not So Simple, *The Journal of Trauma: Injury, Infection and Critical Care.* (February 2006), Vol. 60(2), p. 268-273.

63. http://www.cdc.gov/HomeandRecreationalSafety/Falls/adultfalls.html.

64. Thomas, KE, Stevens, JA. Fall-related traumatic brain injury deaths and hospitalizations among older adults-United States in 2005, *Journal of Safety Research* (2008), 39, p. 269-272.

65. Messinger-Rapport, B. Falls in the Nursing Home: A Collaborative Approach, *Nurs Clin North America,* (2009), 44, p.187.

66. Thomas, KE, Stevens, JA. Fall-related traumatic brain injury deaths and hospitalizations among older adults-United States, *Journal of Safety Research*, (2008), 39, p. 269-272.

67. Messinger-Rapport, B. Falls in the Nursing Home: A Collaborative Approach, *Nurs Clin North America,* (2009) 44, p.187.

68. Journal of Emergency Nursing, "ED Patient Falls and Resulting Injuries," Terrell, K, Weaver, C. Vol. 35 (2), March 2009, p. 89.

69. Fall prevention facts 2009 http://orthoinfo.aaos.org/topic.cfm?topic=A00101.

70. Centers for Disease Control and Prevention: http://www.cdc.gov/TraumaticBrainInjury/causes.html.

71. Berry, SD, Samelson, EJ, Hannan, MT, et al. Second Hip Fracture in older men and women: the Framingham Study. *Arch Intern Med* (2007); 167:1971.

72. National Center for Health Statistics, Trends in Health and Aging. http://www.cdc.gov/nchs/agingact.htm.

73. Thomas, KE, Stevens, JA. Fall-related traumatic brain injury deaths and hospitalizations among older adults-United States in 2005, *Journal of Safety Research*, (2008), 39, p. 269-272.

74. Falls and Hip Fractures http://orthoinfo.aaos.org/topic.cfm?topic=A00121&return_link=0.

75. Savitsky, E., Votey, S. Emergency department approach to acute thoracolumbar spine injury. *J. Emergency Med,* (1997); 15:49.

76. Guthkelch, AN, Fleischer, AS. Patterns of cervical spine injury and their associated lesions. *West J. Med* (1987); p. 147-428.

77. Holmes, JF, Miller, PQ. Epidemiology of thoracolumbar spine injury in blunt trauma. *Acad Emerg Med* (2001); 8:866.

78. *Id.*

79. *Id.*

80. Centers for Disease Control and Prevention: http://www.cdc.gov/TraumaticBrainInjury/causes.html.

81. Centers for Disease Control and Prevention http://www.cdc.gov/HomeandRecreationalSafety/Falls/fallcost.html.

82. http://www.cdc.gov/HomeandRecreationalSafety/Falls/adultfalls.html.

83. Morris, N. and Levin, B. Complications, *Core Curriculum for Orthopaedic Nursing*, 6th edition, 2007, p. 177.

84. Bergeron, E., Clement, J. A Simple Fall in the Elderly: Not So Simple, *The Journal of Trauma: Injury, Infection and Critical Care*. (February 2006), Vol. 60(2), p. 268-273.

85. Messinger-Rapport, B. Falls in the Nursing Home: A Collaborative Approach, *Nurs Clin North America*, (2009), 44, p. 187.

86. 2006 National Patient Safety Goals. Joint Commission on Accreditation of Healthcare Organizations [online]. [Accessed August 4, 2006]. Available at: http://www.jointcommission.org/PatientSafety/NationalPatientSafetyGoals.

87. National Quality Forum (NQF). Safe Practices for Better Healthcare–2009 Update: A Consensus Report. Washington, DC: NQF; 2009.

88. Schwendimann R. Buhler H. Falls and Consequent Injuries in Hospitalized patients: effects of an interdisciplinary falls prevention program. *BMC Health Services*, (2006), 6:69.

89. Shorr, R., Mion, L., Chandler, M., Rosenblatt, L., Lynch, D., Kessler, L. 2008. Improving the Capture of Fall Events in Hospitals: Combining a Service for Evaluating Inpatient Falls with an Incident Report System. J Am Geriatric Society. Retrieved from Pubmed: PMCID: PMC2361382. NIHMSID: NIHMS37976.

90. Joint Commission. 2010. Joint Commission Requirements. Retrieved May 2, 2010 from http://www.jointcommission.org/Standards/Requirements.

91. Aiken, T. *Legal, ethical, and Political Issues in Nursing*. (2nd ed.). Philadelphia: F. A. Davis (2004). p. 157.

92. Humphreys, G. *Bulletin of the World Health Organization*, March 2009; 87(3).

Chapter 27

Significance of Healthcare Fraud in Nursing

Rose Clifford, RN, Agnes Grogan, BS, RN, and Mary Leverock, RN, BSN, QAUR

Synopsis
27.1 Introduction
27.2 The Nature of Reimbursement
    A. Types of Insurance
    B. Relevance of Coding
    C. Physician's CPT Codes
    D. ICD-9 Codes
    E. HCPCS
    F. Elements of Reimbursement
27.3 Understanding Healthcare Fraud
    A. Fraud versus Abuse
    B. Potential Fraudulent Circumstances
    C. Types of Providers at Risk
    D. Why Does Fraud Occur?
27.4 Types of Healthcare Fraud
    A. Understanding the Types of Healthcare Fraud
    B. Different Types of Healthcare Fraud Affecting Nursing
        1. False claims
        2. Self-referrals
        3. Kickbacks
    C. Types of Fraud Schemes Occurring in Nursing Specialties
        1. Nursing specialty areas most prone to healthcare fraud
            a. Pre-hospital and emergency nursing practice
            b. Mental health nursing practice
            c. Long-term care nursing practice
            d. Home health care nursing practice
            e. Hospice nursing practice
            f. Managed care nursing practice
            g. Renal dialysis nursing practice
        2. Non-nursing specialty areas prone to healthcare fraud
            a. Pharmaceutical sales and clinical research
            b. Physician practice
        3. Administrative level or nurse owners of healthcare entities
            a. Hospitals
            b. Nursing registry
            c. Durable medical equipment
         4. Nursing specialty areas less prone to healthcare fraud
        5. Advanced practice nurses
27.5 How Healthcare Fraud Differs from Nursing Malpractice
    A. How Nursing Contributes to Healthcare Fraud
    B. The Effects of Healthcare Fraud in Medical or Nursing
        Malpractice
27.6 Nursing Involvement in Whistleblower Cases
    A. What is Qui Tam?
    B. Duty to Disclose
    C. What to Do with Evidence of Healthcare Fraud
27.7 Consequences of Healthcare Fraud for the Nurse
    A. What Are the Consequences?
    B. Civil Monetary Penalties

C. Exclusion from Federal Programs
27.8 Summary
Endnotes
Additional Reading

27.1 Introduction

Common issues regarding nursing malpractice are not the only avenues through which a nurse could face liability. Nurses are at greater risk for unknowingly becoming involved in healthcare fraud, particularly in some specialty areas, simply through the everyday process of delivering nursing care, during the normal course of their duties, and inadvertently through the systems required to carry out, document, and deliver such care.

In 2004, healthcare expenditures were estimated at $2.1 trillion, which represented 15.5 percent of the Gross Domestic Product. The Centers for Medicare and Medicaid Services (CMS) estimates that by the year 2012, total healthcare spending will exceed $3.1 trillion.[1]

Healthcare fraud is a huge problem costing billions of dollars a year for American taxpayers. Detection remains a top priority for the Department of Justice and the Office of the Attorney General; the latter works closely with federal, state, and local law enforcement to investigate and prosecute Medicare and Medicaid fraud.

Healthcare fraud occurs when an individual or a healthcare provider intentionally deceives others to gain some kind of unauthorized benefit for the individual or entity. It most frequently appears in the form of fraudulent Medicare or Medicaid billing for services never rendered or for services reimbursed at higher rates than were actually charged. Healthcare fraud is not just financial. Of greater importance is the serious adverse effect it has on the quality of patient care. Most healthcare professionals (including nurses) are hard-working, honest individuals sincerely interested in helping patients get better.

The documentation of patient care delivery through the nursing process and the actual writing of the nursing notes directly correlates to the appropriateness of the claims submitted for payment. Patient eligibility for payment is determined through documentation. Nursing documentation identifies the patient's need and is the evidence that justifies the billing for the delivery of such services.

Nurses become involved with healthcare fraud in part because they are extremely busy giving patient care. They are not privy to the upper management decisions or to the underlying intent of their facilities. Often they are patient focused and unfamiliar with federal and state rules and regulations governing the prevention of healthcare fraud or the government programs under which they work. As a result, nurses follow board decisions; administrative directives; instructions from their nursing supervisor; and physician orders without realizing the potential adverse outcome related to healthcare fraud.

TIP: Healthcare fraud and abuse is not always evident in nursing practice. Sometimes an honest nurse giving direct patient care stumbles upon it. Healthcare fraud and abuse cost the taxpayers of America billions of dollars in Medicare and Medicaid revenue, monies that would otherwise go to providing care for the elderly or qualified beneficiaries. Nursing is directly affected by hospital systems of documentation and their policies that require one style of documentation over another. Many nurses do not realize how their work can result in their direct involvement in healthcare fraud or abuse allegations. Even the nursing action of taking a physician's telephone orders can involve covert fraud schemes.

One first needs some understanding of various reimbursement processes to comprehend how a nurse may become involved in healthcare fraud. A brief explanation of types of insurance coverage and various coding systems used to submit billing claims is offered in the following paragraphs.

27.2 The Nature of Reimbursement
A. Types of Insurance
Medicare is a federal government program that provides health insurance to people over age 65 and to some people under age 65 with disabilities. Reimbursement by Medicare depends on whether the insured was hospitalized or an outpatient. Coverage includes:

- Part A—Hospital Insurance: Inpatient hospital care, skilled nursing facility care, and some home health care. It has an annual deductible and copayments. Most people pay no monthly premium.
- Part B—Medical Insurance: Doctor visits, but not routine exams, medically necessary medical sup-

plies and equipment, physical and occupational therapy, outpatient mental health services, and other outpatient hospital services. It has a premium that is deducted from Social Security, Civil Service, or Railroad Retirement pension benefits. There is also an annual deductible and a copayment of 20 percent of approved charges.

Medicaid is a federally funded government program that provides medical benefits to low-income people who have no medical insurance or inadequate medical insurance. Although the federal government establishes general guidelines for the program, the Medicaid program requirements are actually established by each state. Workers' compensation reimburses for care provided to an injured worker. States have regulations and fee schedules that explain what and how they will reimburse providers. Private insurers reimburse according to insurance policies obtained by the patient, either through the employer or directly from the insurance entity.

B. Relevance of Coding
Healthcare insurers process billions of claims for payment each year in the United States. Standardized coding systems are essential for Medicare and other health insurance programs to ensure these claims are processed in an orderly and consistent manner.

Medical procedure codes that accurately describe healthcare services rendered and diagnosis codes that indicate why services were provided, when entered into provider information systems, can drive Medicare billing and quality assurance, statistical reporting, and even care management. Further, proper coding is critical as it affords the means for providers to receive their correct reimbursement from Medicare, Medicaid, or a private insurer. If incorrect codes are used, the claim may be overpaid or, in some rare instances, may be underpaid.[2]

The following paragraphs provide a brief explanation of these systems.

C. Physician's CPT Codes
Current Procedural Terminology (CPT) is a uniform coding system consisting of descriptive terms and identifying codes for reporting medical services and procedures. It is the most widely accepted medical nomenclature for billing to the public and private health insurance programs. The American Medical Association (AMA) developed it in 1966. The AMA also has a system for periodic updating to keep pace with changes in our medical environment as new procedures are developed. In 2000, the CPT code set was designated by the

Department of Health and Human Services as the national coding standard for physician and other healthcare professional services and procedures under the Health Insurance Portability and Accountability Act (HIPAA). The CPT code set will need to be used for all financial and administrative healthcare transactions sent electronically.[3]

The CPT codes are republished and updated annually by the AMA and are available in the fall of each year preceding their effective date to allow for implementation. Providers are responsible for using correct and current codes on their billing forms. Failure to do so can result in delay, or even denial, of payment.

D. ICD-9 Codes

The International Classification of Diseases and Clinical Modification (ICD-9-CM) lists diagnoses equated with a three-digit number that may or may not be modified further for accuracy and specificity. It is used to code and classify morbidity (disease) data from inpatient and outpatient records, physicians' office records, and most statistical surveys. In 1988, the Medicare Catastrophic Coverage Act mandated the reporting of ICD-9-CM diagnosis codes on Medicare claims. Private insurance carriers adopted similar diagnosis coding requirements. In 1992, the World Health Organization (WHO) completed work on the tenth revision, which has a new title: the International Statistical Classification of Diseases and Related Health Problems and a new alphanumeric coding system. It is expected that the change from ICD-9-CM to the National Center for Health Statistics' (NCHS) ICD-10-CM and the HCFA's ICD-10-PCS (Procedural Coding System) will be adopted and implemented in the future.

Medical coders translate written diagnoses into numeric and alphanumeric codes. HCFA provides specific guidelines to aid in standardizing coding practices across the United States. Many times claims are disallowed when a HCFA-1500 form (used to submit Medicare Part B claims) has an ICD-9 code that refers to a diagnosis that is not applicable and for which there should be no financial obligation. Further, if the CPT codes on the HCFA-1500 form relate to services not usually associated with the ICD-9 diagnosis, the claim may be denied or payment delayed pending additional documentation.

E. HCPCS

HCPCS stands for HCFA Common Procedure Coding System. The HCPCS is divided into two principal subsystems, referred to as level I and level II of the HCPCS. Level I of the HCPCS is comprised of CPT (Current Procedural Terminology), discussed earlier. Level I of the HCPCS, the CPT

codes, does not include codes needed to separately report medical items or services regularly billed by suppliers other than physicians.

Level II of the HCPCS is a standardized coding system used primarily to identify products, supplies, and services not included in the CPT codes, such as ambulance services and durable medical equipment (prosthetics, orthotics and supplies [DMEPOS]) when used outside a physician's office. Because Medicare and other insurers cover a variety of services, supplies, and equipment not identified by CPT codes, the level II HCPCS codes were established for submitting claims for these items. The development and use of level II of the HCPCS began in the 1980s. Level II codes are also referred to as alphanumeric codes because they consist of a single alphabetical letter followed by four numeric digits, while CPT codes are identified using five numeric digits.

F. Elements of Reimbursement

Individual providers, such as physicians, chiropractors, and physical therapists, submit their claims to Medicare, Medicaid, and certain private insurers on forms that request procedural and diagnostic codes. These codes tell the payer what service was provided and whether the service is usually associated with the diagnostic code billed. For example, if the diagnostic code indicated the patient had anemia, a procedural code for mechanical traction services would be questionable. The insurance entity assigns payment based on the codes indicated on the claim form, either through a set fee schedule or based on a contractual discount or other arrangement.

Individual providers receive their payment from worker's compensation according to various state fee schedules and regulations. Worker's compensation in some states also determines payment for an inpatient hospitalization according to diagnostic codes. Private insurers reimburse hospitals according to individual policies or in accordance with various contractual arrangements between the facility and the payer.

Medicare and Medicaid reimburse healthcare facilities and providers according to several coding methodologies:

- Acute care facility: If the patient was in a hospital, the hospital assigns a DRG (Diagnosis-Related Group) code. Medicare designates pre-set amounts for the DRG payment, whether the patient is in the hospital for one day or four days. The only way the payment is altered is through the use of outliers—facts that lengthen the hospital stay.
- Skilled nursing facility: If the patient had a stay in a skilled nursing facility, the reimbursement is

prospective, and like DRGs, is based on a RUG (resource utilization group) code. Determining a patient's RUG is like taking a snapshot of care needs over a period of time. This picture is used to predict future care needs for which a prospective rate is set. Patients are classified into one of 44 resource utilization groups based on the combined responses to MDS questions. RUGs categorize patients according to the amount of staff time required to care for them, and each RUG has an associated per diem or daily rate.

- Ambulatory surgery center: Care provided on an outpatient basis at an approved Ambulatory Surgery Center (ASC) is also paid on a prospective basis. For the services to be reimbursed by Medicare, they must meet criteria specified in §416.65 and are published by CMS in the Federal Register. The ASC is reimbursed according to a prospectively determined standard overhead amount per procedure.

27.3 Understanding Healthcare Fraud

Over the years, institutions and individual providers have discovered and implemented schemes to defraud the government—federal or state—and private insurers through submission of fraudulent claims. While it is true that not all claims are intentionally fraudulent, they can be considered abusive in certain respects.

A. Fraud versus Abuse

TIP: Fraud is an intentional deception or misrepresentation that could result in the payment of some unauthorized benefit. Abuse involves actions inconsistent with sound medical, business, or fiscal practices. Abuse directly or indirectly results in higher costs to the Medicare program through improper payments that are not medically necessary.

The primary difference between fraud and abuse is a person's intent. Did the person know she was committing a crime? Fraud and abuse both have the same effect. Medicare fraud steals valuable resources from the Medicare Trust Fund that would otherwise provide benefits to Medicare beneficiaries.[4]

B. Potential Fraudulent Circumstances

Nurses are at particular risk for becoming involved with healthcare fraud because their work (carrying out of physician orders, nursing notes, and assessments):

- directly correlates to claims submitted for payment,
- determines a patient's qualification or eligibility for healthcare programs and services, and
- documents the level of service needed to continue to receive such care.

Administrative level or nurse owners of healthcare entities (e.g., staffing agencies, home health agencies, assisted living facilities, equipment companies, and ambulance companies) may, out of ignorance, denial, or greed, expose their professional licenses to sanctions. Furthermore, nurses employed in settings such as skilled nursing facilities, home health agencies, ambulatory surgery centers, and other areas are at risk. Their documentation relating to the level of care provided, the length of time involved in care, and supplies used may inadvertently expose them to allegations of fraud.

C. Types of Providers at Risk

All providers who carry out any type of healthcare service either directly or indirectly can be the targets or perpetrators of fraud and abuse. From individuals to institutional providers, healthcare consumers may be lured into fraudulent schemes through telemarketing and other promotional activities or contracts. Anyone who submits a claim for payment is at risk if the claim was inappropriately completed. The federal government has the authority to investigate a claim's validity. If the investigation determines that a claim has fault, whether from an inadvertent mistake or outright fraud, criminal and civil sanctions can be imposed.[5]

D. Why Does Fraud Occur?

Healthcare fraud can occur for various reasons. The most common are the desire for free, easy money and greed. Common reasons also include:

- no single payer source,
- complicated, complex, intertwined set of billing rules and regulations,
- consequences and penalties are less than for felony crimes such as murder or running drugs, and
- the risks do not outweigh the potential benefits of huge financial gain, and violators do not think they are going to get caught.

For most nurses, other common reasons are attributed to:

- a need to maintain employment within a particular organization,
- a desire to please an employer,

- inadequate instruction relating to coding issues,
- facility protocol for charging of supplies,
- understaffing that results in meager and poor documentation of care, if any,
- designed charge sheets and documentation forms, and
- following supervisor's instruction in completing documentation.

27.4 Types of Healthcare Fraud
A. Understanding the Types of Healthcare Fraud

Healthcare fraud generally involves inappropriate billing for services never provided. Healthcare abuse occurs when healthcare providers provide medically unnecessary services or services that fall below the standard of care without intentionally meaning to defraud.

TIP: Healthcare fraud is not an honest mistake by a provider. It is not an unexpectedly high hospital bill, nor is it a separate billing charge for radiology services or anesthesia services. It may not even be a higher reimbursement rate on the Medicare Summary Notice (MSN) received by the beneficiary. Healthcare fraud is a deliberate intent to defraud. It is a pattern of illegal practice and not a one-time clerical mistake or billing error.

Carolyn Buppert, a nurse practitioner and attorney out of Annapolis, Maryland, noted in a 2001 article *Avoiding Medicare Fraud*:

Mistakes, errors, misunderstanding of the rules, or negligence is not fraud. If mistakes, however, occur with such frequency and in such a pattern that an investigator and prosecutor suspect that the provider knows that the claims are false, has recklessly disregarded the rules, or has deliberately stayed in ignorance of the rules, an FBI investigation may be initiated.

Investigators consider the following factors in determining whether mistakes are honest: (1) Were the mistakes always in favor of the provider? (2) What would an objective observer think about these mistakes? (3) Could the mistake have resulted from a differing but reasonable interpretation of the rules?[6]

A nurse may come across healthcare fraud schemes in any area of nursing practice, but some areas are more prone to fraud than others. High-risk areas include:

- pre-hospital (ambulance companies),
- hospitals,
- long-term care nursing facilities (nursing homes, skilled nursing facilities, and rehabilitation facilities),
- physician practices,
- home health,
- durable medical equipment companies,
- hospice agencies,
- laboratories, and
- mental health centers.

Many diverse healthcare fraud schemes are perpetrated by unscrupulous providers who target these areas. Reimbursement rules are different for each provider and for Medicare; Medicaid; TriCare, which was formerly known as CHAMPUS (Civil Health and Medical Program of the Uniformed Services); and private insurance companies. The rules and regulations are complicated, are vague, and often change over time. In addition, the reimbursement rules are not usually consistent with licensure rules or with accreditation requirements, which can be confusing, making detection of healthcare fraud more difficult.

Some of the most common healthcare fraud schemes are as follows:

- Falsely claiming medical necessity for services that are not medically necessary
- Billing for services never provided
- Billing for higher reimbursement when low reimbursement service is more appropriate (upcoding)
- Billing for medical equipment or supplies not ordered, needed, or received
- Billing related services as if they were provided separately (unbundling)
- Double billing for the same services
- Billing for DME home medical equipment after it has been picked up
- Billing for medical services or supplies no longer medically necessary
- Billing for non-covered supplies
- Using someone's Medicare number other than the beneficiary receiving the care
- Soliciting, offering, or receiving any bribes, rebates, kickbacks, or remuneration of any kind (payment, fee, salary, wage, compensation, recompense, pay, reward, return, stipend, or reimbursement) for referrals or influencing the provision of healthcare
- Not charging the 20 percent copayment for Medicare-reimbursable services

- Billing for experimental medical services not approved by Medicare
- Billing inappropriate procedural codes and/or diagnostic codes (i.e., screening versus diagnostic codes)
- Fraudulent cost reporting by institutional providers

B. Different Types of Healthcare Fraud Affecting Nursing

Three major areas of healthcare fraud affect nurses directly. These are situations in which a nurse may be involved knowingly or unknowingly:

1. false claims,
2. self-referrals, and
3. kickbacks.

1. False claims

The primary federal statutes that define how the government determines responsibility and liability for healthcare fraud is the False Claims Act. Statute 42 U.S.C. Section 1320a-7b, False Claims (criminal and civil), prohibits anyone including nurses from knowingly and willfully making or causing to be made a false statement or misrepresentation of material fact on any claim to the United States or any state agency for health program payment. This includes claims for medical items or services based on a billing code a person "knows or should know" will result in greater payment than the services actually provided or a claim for medical items or services a person "knows or should know" is not medically necessary.

The federal civil False Claims Act defines the standard of "should know" as "acting in deliberate ignorance or with reckless disregard of the truth or falsity of the information submitted." Specific proof of intent to defraud is not required. Federal prosecutors use the civil False Claims Act as the most powerful tool in fighting healthcare fraud against the Medicare and Medicaid programs. Federal and state prosecutors argue that continuously billing for services for which the intermediaries and carriers repeatedly deny meets this standard of "should know."

The federal civil False Claims Act also broadened the interpretation of its terminology "not provided as claimed." It was expanded to include:

engaging in a pattern or practice of presenting or causing to be presented a claim for an item or service that is based on a code that the person knows or should know will result in a greater payment to the person than the code the person knows or should know is applicable to the item or service actually provided.[7]

Key federal civil false claim statutes are found in 31 U.S.C. Sections 3729-3733. A person is liable who knowingly presents or causes to be presented to the government a false or fraudulent claim for payment or approval of use of a "false" record to obtain payment. The "knowingly" standard in essence means the individual has actual knowledge of the information, acts in deliberate ignorance of the falsity or truth of the information, or acts in reckless disregard of the veracity of the information.

The following is a healthcare fraud case involving billing for substandard care with nurses falsifying charts:

Advocates sued Albuquerque-based Sun Healthcare Group and others in federal court claiming the nursing home companies collected government payments for substandard care. Brought under the federal False Claims Act, the lawsuit claims the nursing home operators failed to provide the level of care required by Medicare and Medicaid, then falsified records to show otherwise. The falsified records were then used to obtain reimbursement from the government healthcare programs, the lawsuit says. In addition to Sun, defendants included Integrated Health Services of Owings Mills, Maryland, and Crestwood Hospitals. The lawsuit deals with the care at Crestwood nursing homes in California over several years. Integrated Health Services managed Crestwood homes for about two years ending in 1996, according to the lawsuit. Sun took over management of some of the homes in 1996 and acquired about a dozen Crestwood homes in 1997, the lawsuit says.

The lawsuit was filed in January 1997 by advocates for nursing home residents. The advocates are suing on behalf of themselves as well as for the U.S. government on what is known as qui tam, or whistleblower, litigation. The lawsuit alleges the defendants had a practice of not employing enough staff to maintain the quality of care required to participate in Medicare and Medicaid. As a result, some nursing home residents suffered dehydration, malnutrition, mental and social isolation, urinary infections, pressure ulcers and other problems. 'Defendants' conduct was the result of corporate-imposed budget constraints to maximize their profits and to allow their CEO to receive large compensations,' the lawsuit says.

As part of the lawsuit, three former employees at Crestwood homes have filed affidavits that records were falsified. One ex-worker said she and other nurses falsified patient charts to cover up that medications were not given as ordered by physicians. The lawsuit says the defendants filed false claims to obtain more than $50 million a year in reimbursement from Medicare and Medicaid.[8]

2. Self-referrals

Self-referral regulations have evolved over time. A 1989 study by the Health and Human Services (HHS) Inspector General reported that physicians with financial interest (they owned or invested in independent clinical laboratories) referred Medicare patients for 45 percent more laboratory services than physicians without financial interests. The Institute of Medicine (IOM) reported ethical concerns about physician self-referrals in a 1986 study. The first law to place limits on self-referral was part of the Omnibus Budget Reconciliation Act (OBRA) of 1989 and became effective January 1, 1992. Between 1991 and 1992, the American Medical Association (AMA) became involved with the ethical issue of physicians referring patients to facilities in which they had a financial interest.

TIP: In 1992, the AMA House of Delegates voted that in most instances self-referral is unethical. OBRA of 1993 expanded the self-referral ban to include ten additional health services. These are referred to as designated health services.

---

3. Kickbacks

A kickback is any formal or informal arrangement between two parties involving one healthcare provider's offer to pay for Medicare business referrals from a second party. Kickback arrangements can be between two healthcare providers such as a physician and a hospital or a hospital and a home health agency. In nursing it could involve a nurse practitioner who refers to a physician or a nurse who goes through a physician's office records to refer patients to one home health agency. In short, a kickback is the acceptance of kickbacks, bribes, or rebates in any form in exchange for referrals. State and federal law prohibits payments to individuals who refer patients to a particular hospital, doctor, or home health agency. Kickbacks unfairly generate added business.

The Department of Health and Human Services, Office of Inspector General (OIG) interprets the anti-kickback statute to apply to anyone who knowingly and willfully solicits, receives, offers, or pays remuneration in cash or in kind to induce or in return for:

- Referring an individual to a person or entity for the furnishing, or arranging for the furnishing, of any item or service or service payable under the Medicare or Medicaid programs; or
- Purchasing, leasing or ordering, or arranging for or recommending the purchasing, leasing or ordering of any good, facility, service or item payable under the Medicare or Medicaid programs.

It is often hard to identify a kickback. Many times it is a silent or verbal agreement with an unwritten understanding to refer patients or patient information (protected health information). At other times contracts may actually be the foundation of a kickback scheme. Sometimes, a one-time offer leads to a constant understanding and stream of referrals that seemed harmless at first. Healthcare contracting is very complex, and the fact that a contract has been prepared by an attorney does not necessarily mean the arrangement is in full compliance with all anti-kickback provisions of the law.

Although the term "kickback" brings to mind the exchange of money, this is not always the case. Nurses may receive kickbacks as non-cash items such as:

- receiving a free day at the spa,
- being able to rent facilities or space below fair market value or for free (may be most applicable to nurses with a Medicare or Medicaid provider number because that number can generate money),
- receiving free supplies (any type),
- receiving expensive reference books,
- staffing a nurse in a physician's office when the nurse is paid by another entity (may be most applicable to specialty nurses such as obstetrics or in assisted living facilities),
- a discount or rebate,
- obtaining items of value for which no payment is expected (a cell phone, laptop, car rental, a free meal, a free place to stay).

Each situation must be reviewed on a case-by-case basis, as what may appear to be under conditions of employment could actually be a valid arrangement.

TIP: Kickbacks in the medical arena result in distorted medical decision making, increased costs, and unfair competition to honest competitors. It often results in the provision of unneeded services or over-utilization of services, which further drains the government insurance system.

Most nurses can be peripherally involved without full knowledge of the arrangement as they are often not a part of the decision-making arrangements. The quality of patient care is jeopardized when kickbacks encourage physicians to order or delay services or supplies based on profit rather than patient needs or medical necessity such as in managed care arrangements. Healthcare providers found guilty of kickbacks face criminal investigation, prison time, civil monetary penalties, and exclusion from the Medicare program.

Some examples of kickbacks include:

- Providing hospitals or nursing homes with discharge planners or home healthcare coordinators as a way of gaining referrals.
- Inappropriately paying for referrals to gain Medicare patients.
- Paying physicians for each plan of care certified on behalf of the home health agency verifying medical necessity and homebound status.
- Giving anything free or paying Medicare beneficiaries to either switch home health agencies or to receive care at a specific clinic.
- Nurses referring patients to pharmaceutical and durable medical equipment.

The following healthcare fraud case is an example of a nurse referring patients and receiving kickbacks:

An Indiana pharmaceutical and Durable Medical Equipment company inflated the cost of the drugs provided to Medicaid beneficiaries and paid kickbacks to nurses for referring patients to the company. They gained $2 million from these fraudulent activities.[9]

C. Types of Fraud Schemes Occurring in Nursing Specialties

Healthcare providers and the corporate entities that own them sometimes lose sight of the reason why they are in business: to provide quality patient care with sound business principles. In today's market, the financial success of the corporate entity becomes more important than the delivery of good patient care. For some, true corporate values have changed by focusing only on profit. The race for high profits has led to some highly dysfunctional and unethical practices in patient care and billing. This corporate mentality has created hectic practice environments with high patient ratios, low staffing, higher patient acuity, and shorter patient stays. In the midst of this, nurses are expected to provide quality patient care.

Medicare coverage issues are very complicated and often not well understood by the majority of nurses. They involve fundamentals of billing, coding, and finance, knowledge not usually necessary in performing patient care duties. Many times this makes recognizing healthcare fraud difficult. Most nurses are unaware of the billing aspects of patient care or how their practice environments, their nursing actions, and their documentation methods may contribute to healthcare fraud.

1. Nursing specialty areas most prone to healthcare fraud
a. Pre-hospital and emergency nursing practice

In the pre-hospital setting, Medicare pays for ambulance services when a Medicare beneficiary must be taken to a hospital or skilled nursing facility and transportation by any other means would endanger the beneficiary's life. Medicare pays for the ambulance mileage to the nearest qualified hospital or skilled nursing facility. Medicare does not pay for ambulance transport to a physician's office, clinic, or to the emergency room where the sole purpose is to walk through the emergency room to the professional office building to see the beneficiary's physician.

Medicaid pays for ambulance services when a physician certifies the medical necessity such as from the hospital to the beneficiary's residence upon discharge from an inpatient stay. Medicaid does not pay for ambulance services to a hospital or other facility for outpatient services or to or from a physician's office or clinic.

Pre-hospital healthcare fraud schemes include:

- Billing for Advanced Life Support (ALS) services when no oxygen was administered and only Basic Life Support (BLS) services were provided.
- Falsifying documentation to indicate the need for ALS.
- Billing for individual ambulance service when in reality multiple patients were picked up simultaneously and transported to the multiple sites or to the emergency room only to have the patients walk through the emergency room to their physician offices.
- Falsifying patient documentation to substantiate medical need to transport via ambulance from an in-hospital admission to the beneficiary's home.
- Billing for more mileage than actually traveled for patient transport.
- Billing ambulance transport as medically necessary for ambulatory dialysis patients to and from the dialysis center.

- Billing for emergency transport of non-emergency ambulatory beneficiaries.

The following healthcare fraud cases are examples of improper billing for emergency transport of non-emergency ambulatory beneficiaries:

On May 29, 1997, St. Joseph's Medical Center, a Baltimore-area hospital in the District of Maryland, agreed to pay the United States $564,000 to settle FCA allegations that it improperly billed the Medicare program for ambulance transportation of patients. From 1992 to 1995, Medicare paid St. Joseph's $188,000 for 159 claims for ambulance transportation of patients actually transported by hospital gurney for diagnostic services to offices located within or near the hospital complex. St. Joseph's also entered into a compliance agreement with the HHS-OIG.

On June 27, 1997, American Ambulance & Oxygen, in the District of Maryland, agreed to pay the United States $1.45 million to resolve allegations it violated the False Claims Act (FCA) in transporting Medicare patients for routine medical office visits. The Medicare beneficiaries were ambulatory and did not qualify for ambulance transportation.

On February 27, 1998, in the Southern District of Mississippi, the owners of Gieger Transfer Services, an ambulance company, were sentenced to 80 months in prison and ordered to pay restitution of $228,917 and a $12,500 fine. The defendants billed Medicare $400 per ambulance trip, claiming that patients taken on non-emergency ambulance trips were "bed confined" when, in fact, many could walk and had no need for ambulance transportation. A substantial portion of the money paid to the United States under the agreement was derived from the forced sale of beachfront properties purchased by the owners following the sale of their company in September 1997. The forced sale of the properties resulted from a $2.25 million civil settlement with the owners and the company formerly owned by them.[10]

Both criminal and civil Medicare fraud charges were filed. Criminal fraud charges usually result in prison time while civil fraud charges result in monetary penalties. The beachfront properties were purchased with money received through fraudulently billed ambulance services. Part of the civil settlement agreement was the forced sale of the beachfront properties in order to pay back Medicare.

Note this fraudulent scheme:

In 1992, the Giegers founded Gieger Transfer Service, Inc./Gieger Ambulance Service (GAS) to transport both emergency and non-emergency patients. GAS expanded rapidly and by the time the company was sold in 1997, GAS operated over 40 ambulances in 12 counties in rural Southeastern Mississippi. GAS transported a large number of Medicare patients. After 1993, GAS filed electronic reimbursement requests with Medicare. GAS's initial attempts to obtain reimbursement from Medicare did not go smoothly. In response to this problem, the Giegers began misrepresenting to Medicare that all of GAS's non-emergency transports were for "bed-confined" patients. Consistent with this billing practice, the Giegers instructed their paramedics and emergency medical technicians not to use the word "ambulatory" on the patient transport reports.[11]

Emergency room healthcare fraud schemes include:

- Billing patient stays as "observation—23 hour stays" rather than admitting as an inpatient. Observation stays are reimbursed at a higher rate through Medicare Part B than the inpatient DRG rate
- Double billing visits
- Billing a higher level of treatment than provided
- Billing for services not rendered such as violations of the Emergency Treatment and Active Labor Act (patient dumping)

The following healthcare fraud case is an example of double billing patient stays as "observation stays":

The Sun-Sentinel reported on February 14, 2005 that "Cleveland Clinic Florida has repaid the U.S. government $2.75 million to settle accusations that the hospital routinely overbilled Medicare from 1993 to 2001," federal prosecutors said. "The hospital had been overcharging Medicare for 'observation' of patients during normal recovery from minor surgery and emergency room visits," said Marcos Daniel Jimenez, U.S. Attorney for South Florida. Under federal rules, the service is supposed to be included in billing for the care given.[12,13]

The following healthcare fraud case is an example of billing a higher level of treatment than what was provided. On April 6, 2000, in testimony before the House Committee on Commerce, Subcommittee on Oversight and Investigations Regarding Medicare and Third-Party Billing, companies acknowledged fraudulent billing. These are excerpts from a Statement of Lewis Morris Assistant Inspector General for Legal Affairs, Office of Inspector General, and U.S. Department of Health and Human Services:

Perhaps the most alarming example of the systematic abuse of the Federal healthcare programs by a third-party billing company can be found in the recent case of Emergency Physician Billing Services, Inc. (EPBS). At the time of the investigation, EPBS provided coding, billing and collections services for emergency physician groups in over 100 emergency departments in as many as 33 states. Based upon allegations presented by a qui tam relator, the United States charged that EPBS and its principle owner, Dr. J.D. McKean, routinely billed Federal and state healthcare programs for higher level of treatment than was provided or supported by medical record documentation.

EPBS was paid based on a percentage of revenues either billed or recovered, depending on the client. EPBS coders received a base pay with bonuses based on the number of charts processed and were required to process 40 emergency room medical charts per hour [40 x 8 = 320 per day], or the equivalent of a chart every 90 seconds. By contrast, a competitor of EPBS requires 120 charts per day. The EPBS coders were able to meet these quotas by taking short-cuts and disregarding information in the chart. As the trial court noted, no coder at EPBS ever attended training or any other informational meeting regarding emergency department coding other than in-house EPBS training and no coder ever contacted a physician with questions regarding a chart.

After a trial in which the United States District Court for the Western District of Oklahoma found EPBS and Dr. McKean liable under the FCA, the defendants agreed to pay $15.5 million to resolve their civil and administrative monetary liabilities. In addition, Dr. McKean agreed to be excluded from participation in the federal healthcare programs for 15 years. Currently, the government is pursuing physician groups that benefited from EPBS's fraudulent practices.[14]

The following healthcare fraud case is an example of billing for services not provided:

A registered nurse in the Emergency Department at Evans Army Community Hospital at Fort Carson Army Base in Colorado was sentenced to 60 months in prison for tampering with a consumer product that affected interstate commerce. On 300 occasions, the defendant gained access to sterile syringes containing Morphine and Demerol meant for patients in the emergency room. The defendant withdrew the contents of those syringes into another syringe for self use. The defendant would then refill the syringes with saline, Nubain, or Phenergan and return them to the emergency room's medication distribution system for future patient use. The refilled syringes were later used to treat emergency room patients.[15]

Refer to Chapter 16, *Emergency Medical Services*, and Chapter 17, *Emergency Nursing Malpractice*, for more information on care issues in these settings.

b. Mental health nursing practice

The field of psychiatric nursing or mental health nursing has long been an area in which fraud and abuse have occurred. It was one of the first areas investigated for fraud. Mentally ill patients are easy, vulnerable targets for abuse and exploitation by the complex nature of the disease. Many have been abandoned by their friends and families. They often do not have the awareness or mental capacity to understand their illness, much less their Medicare or Medicaid benefits. Some have trusted counselors, yet many remain at risk for financial fraud and abuse by the very healthcare providers they know and trust.

Psychiatric nursing environments encompass acute inpatient hospitals as well as outpatient facilities, forensic treatment programs, adolescent treatment programs, and juvenile sex offender programs.

TIP: The stigma of having a mental illness alone may prevent patients from questioning their providers or their benefits. It is very important for the mental health nurse to be aware of any potential healthcare fraud or abuse schemes and take measures to protect patients and report suspicions to the appropriate entity.

Mental health fraud schemes:

- billing for unlicensed personnel to administer care to patients as though they were licensed

- billing for inappropriate or non-covered services
- billing social gatherings as individual psychiatric therapy or group sessions as individual counseling sessions
- billing for substandard care
- billing for care while holding the patient against his will

According to a study of New York Stock Exchange listed healthcare service companies: "Tenet Healthcare settled 700 lawsuits filed by former patients in Texas accusing them of holding the patients in psychiatric hospitals against their will until their insurance was used up. Tenet paid a $100 million settlement."[16]

The following healthcare fraud case is an example of substandard care:

A mentally ill patient with no health insurance was kept in Florida Medical Center's psychiatric emergency room for three days before being seen by a psychiatrist, and was asked 12 times to sign a form that would allow the hospital to transfer him somewhere else, according to records released Wednesday by state investigators...." In a letter sent to the hospital's chief executive officer, Aurelio Fernandez, DCF administrators said the Tenet-owned hospital is under investigation for Medicare and Medicaid fraud, violation of patients' civil rights, abusing the Baker Act, and "unacceptable clinical practices."[17]

The following healthcare fraud case is an example of billing for unlicensed personnel as though they were licensed:

On March 19, 1997, a Georgia psychiatrist and his associates were charged with conspiracy, mail fraud, wire fraud, dispensation of controlled substances, and money laundering in the Southern District of Georgia. The defendants conspired to defraud CHAMPUS, Medicare, and Medicaid by employing unlicensed and unqualified therapists to provide mental health services to Georgia and Florida beneficiaries and then bill the government programs as if the psychiatrist had provided the services himself.[18]

TIP: The attorney or nurse reviewing potential fraud in the mental health environment needs to determine whether or not the mental health nurse was aware or peripherally involved in the fraudulent schemes that perpetrate and affect mental health nursing practice. Look closely for group therapy sessions that involve some sort of recreational activity or component, mental health clients who cannot communicate, and the use of unlicensed personnel providing services that a licensed person should be offering.

Please see Chapter 6, *Psychiatric Nursing Liability*, for more insights on the concerns in this setting.

c. Long-term care nursing practice

The nurse-to-patient ratio in long-term care facilities is much lower than in acute care facilities such as hospitals. The minimum standard depends on the federal and state guidelines, the type of long-term care facility (such as skilled facility versus non-skilled facility), and sometimes patient acuity levels. At a bare minimum in some states, it can be as low as one nurse to 60 patients (residents) seven days a week during daylight hours. Facility residences are either elderly or persons with disabilities. The residents, like mental health patients, are mentally incapacitated and often unaware of their surroundings or the services that they receive. If they are mentally unaware, they seldom participate in the decision-making process regarding their care and treatment. Frequently, there is little oversight of the care rendered or the supplies needed. When there are minimum nurse-to-patient ratios, the nurse and the bedside nursing staff are extremely busy and may not be well versed in nursing facility fraud or long-term care scams to defraud Medicare or Medicaid. Often, fear of retaliation against the nurse or the resident may prevent individual reporting of suspected fraud or abuse perpetrated by long-term care administration, doctors, co-workers, or other providers.

The basis for fraud actions taken against long-term care facilities is the federal regulations for long-term care facilities that state "each resident must receive and the facility must provide the necessary care and services to attain or maintain the highest practicable physical, mental and psychosocial well-being, in accordance with the comprehensive assessment and plan of care."[19]

Long-term care nursing facility fraud schemes include the following:

- billing for substandard care as though it were quality of care service
- allowing patients to suffer from pressure ulcers, malnutrition, dehydration, or abuse
- failing to provide care covered by contract and deliberate understaffing

- falsifying records to justify inappropriate billing
- billing for unnecessary services from which the patient will not benefit (e.g., psychiatric therapy to Alzheimer's patient or patient in a coma)
- providing group therapy for medically unnecessary physical therapy, occupational therapy, or speech therapy while billing for individual therapy sessions
- billing for gang visits by physicians (ophthalmologist, podiatrist) or other healthcare professionals (physical, occupational, or speech therapists) who bill services for all residents as individual services whether seen or not
- billing social activities as psychotherapy
- up-coding: billing for supplies more expensive that the ones actually provided
- billing for care not provided (drug diversion)
- billing Medicare Part B for medical supplies that are not covered under Part A and not provided to the patient
- billing for patient supplies that have been created from stockpiles
- misrepresenting diagnoses on billing in order to obtain pay (e.g., routine foot care for toenail clipping, comprehensive eye exams when lower level eye exams were performed, falsifying documentation to justify need for cataract surgery, billing acupuncture as physical therapy)
- falsely inflating the level of patient care (the RUG)

The following healthcare fraud case is an example of up-coding, which is billing for supplies that are more expensive than the ones actually provided:

On March 10, 1997, a Kissimmee, Florida man who supplied diapers to nursing home patients and then billed Medicare for prosthetic devices was sentenced in the District of Kansas to ten years in federal prison for receiving more than $47 million in Medicare reimbursements for false claims he submitted. The case was investigated jointly in the District of Kansas and the Middle District of Florida. In Kansas, the Medicare carrier discovered that Ben Carroll, who operated under various business names (Bulldog Medical, MLC Geriatrics), had received over $2.3 million by submitting false claims. In order to deceive Medicare carriers, Carroll instructed employees to refer to and bill the non-reimbursable diapers as "Urinary Collec-

tion Devices," a reimbursable catheter. Carroll obtained the diapers for 30-40 cents each, then billed Medicare for the catheter product, which Medicare reimbursed at $7-$8.45 each. After the Kansas Medicare carrier stopped paying his claims, Carroll continued his scheme in Florida. He conspired with a nursing home chain by entering into an agreement whereby the nursing home chain would receive a "packaging" fee for packaging incontinence products, including the non-reimbursable diaper. The packaging fee was, in actuality, a kickback Carroll paid for the purpose of ensuring that the nursing home chain would distribute the incontinence products to its homes, thus allowing Carroll to continue his false billing scheme. On September 18, 1996, Carroll pled guilty to mail fraud one week before trial was to begin in the Kansas case, and agreed to plead guilty to Florida charges which, at that time, had not been filed. Carroll pled guilty to one count of conspiracy to commit mail fraud on November 18, 1996, in the Middle District of Florida. For purposes of sentencing, the Florida case was transferred to the District of Kansas. In addition to serving a ten year sentence, he agreed to forfeit $32 million in funds derived from his scheme to defraud Medicare.[20]

A July 14, 2000, press release from the Office of New York State Attorney General Eliot Spitzer is a healthcare fraud example of billing for care not provided—drug diversion:

Attorney General Eliot Spitzer announced that a nurse's aide at a Rochester-area nursing home has admitted to removing powerful narcotic patches from three terminally ill patients earlier this year. The patients had been prescribed the patches for pain management. The aide stole the patches for her own use and either left the patients with no patch or replaced the stolen patches with patches she previously used and were no longer effective. In one instance, the pain medication patch had been removed the day before the patient died of cancer. Maryann Saxe, a nurse's aide formerly employed at Westgate Nursing Home, appeared before Gates Town Court Judge John Rivoli and plead guilty as charged to two counts of Willful Violation of Health Laws and two counts of Petit Larceny. The Judge ordered Saxe, who was presently enrolled in a drug treatment program, to continue treatment.

'Every day patients in nursing homes put their lives and trust in the hands of healthcare professionals,' said Spitzer. 'For this employee to betray her sworn duty by stealing the medication of dying patients is cruel, offensive, and inexcusable. This conviction sends a clear message to all healthcare workers that my Medicaid Fraud Control Unit will aggressively prosecute those who mistreat patients in their care.'

On February 4, Saxe physically abused a 79-year-old male patient, suffering from Parkinson's disease, by removing a prescribed duragesic patch containing the pain-relief medication Fentanyl from his body, causing a skin burn. Six days later, Saxe removed a second Fentanyl patch from the patient's body.

On February 16, Saxe removed a Fentanyl patch from the body of an 87-year-old female patient suffering from strokes and a hip fracture, and one from the body of a 55-year-old female patient suffering from rectal cancer. As a result of the unauthorized removal of the patches, Saxe caused the three patients substantial pain and discomfort.

Saxe, a former registered nurse who surrendered her license in September after being charged administratively with stealing medication prescribed for a patient, worked as a nurse's aide at Westgate Nursing Home, located at 525 Beahan Road in Gates, from January to February 17, 2000.[21]

According to the Department of Justice Healthcare Fraud and Abuse Annual Report for Fiscal Year 2004, Medicare sometimes pays twice for the same service: once to a skilled nursing facility under Medicare Part A and again to an outside supplier under Medicare Part B. Not all facilities and suppliers have established adequate controls to prevent improper billing for Part B services included in the Part A payment rate. As a result, the HHS/OIG identified $108.3 million in improper payments to Medicare Part B suppliers during 1999 and 2000. It recommended that CMS recover the improper payments and instruct its Medicare contractors to establish and enhance billing controls.[22]

The attorney paralegal and legal nurse consultant must be aware of the potential for any of the above scams occurring within long-term care facilities. Foresight is needed to anticipate the potential problems with stockpiling supplies or saving unused components of supplies for central supply to repackage and again bill Medicare or Medicaid. Two very important events that nurses may see are services be-ing provided to patients who will not benefit from such services like psychotherapy sessions to a coma or Alzheimer's patient. The second event is the possibility that the patient files are easily accessed by individuals other than the medical practitioners and nurses taking care of the patients, such as individuals from durable medical equipment companies. Chapter 10, *Subacute and Long-Term Care Nursing Malpractice Issues*, details the major nursing liability concerns in long-term care.

d. Home health care nursing practice

Home health nurses are becoming more aware, through publicity about cases being prosecuted, of the fraudulent schemes affecting their nursing practice. Some home health agency owners or consultants are nurses. Beneficiaries are eligible to receive home health services when they are certified by a physician as being homebound. Medicare considers a beneficiary homebound if she is normally unable to leave home or if leaving home requires a considerable and taxing effort to do so. A beneficiary may leave home on a short-term basis to seek medical treatment or infrequently for non-medical reasons such as going to the hair salon or going to a religious service and still be considered homebound. Nurses working in the home health environment are more aware of their patients' abilities to get around and whether or not they are truly homebound and qualified to receive reimbursable services.

Home healthcare fraud schemes include:

- falsifying certification of homebound status,
- billing for beneficiaries who are not homebound,
- illegally recruiting beneficiaries to receive home health visits who are not homebound,
- offering anything free such as groceries, transportation, or milk in exchange for a person's Medicare number,
- offering enticements to switch home health agencies,
- offering kickbacks to hospitals or physician for patient referrals,
- offering physicians cash for signing treatment plans for ineligible patients,
- having financial ties to durable medical equipment companies,
- home health agencies licensed to provide durable medical equipment (DME) by state Medicaid programs improperly billing for DME (some registered nurses provide home care to their relatives and bill them as home health visits),
- billing for more home health visits than provided,

- billing housekeeping or custodial services as skilled nursing visits or therapy services,
- billing for phantom patients,
- billing for services not rendered,
- billing for services to patients who are not eligible,
- billing for unnecessary services,
- billing for professional beneficiaries,
- billing for services at a site other than where the home care was provided,
- billing for home care chart review when the documentation does not support the reimbursement,
- double billing for services not rendered.

In these types of cases, the attorney must be able to identify beneficiaries who are not truly homebound but are receiving home care resulting in payment. Home health nurses may be told to instruct their patients to limit their normal activities outside the home while receiving home healthcare so they do not appear to be too active to qualify for homebound status. Additionally, the attorney needs to know

- if the nurses, at the direction of their supervisors or home health agency owners, are being pressured, enticed, or instructed to talk any of their patients into accepting unneeded items or services,
- if the nurses encouraged or instructed the home health aides to tell the patients that the home health aides can do their shopping, housekeeping, or meal preparation, or
- if the home health nurses instructed the home health aides to continue to provide aide services when the patients no longer receive or require skilled nursing services or therapy services.

The following is a fraud case centered on billing for services not rendered:

Maryland Attorney General J. Joseph Curran, Jr. announced today that Registered Nurse Dolores E. Scott...pled guilty in Baltimore County Circuit Court to one count of felony Medicaid Fraud pursuant to a plea agreement. The statement of facts read into the record and agreed to by Scott established that she caused the Maryland Medical Assistance program to pay $133,992 to her employer, Comprehensive Nursing Services, Inc., for in-home nursing care that she had not actually provided to her patient (Anthony). Scott herself realized approximately $90,000 in income from this scheme.

Between June 20, 2002 and August 1, 2004 Scott submitted falsified time slips to her employer, Comprehensive Nursing Services Inc., that overstated the hours of care that she had provided to her patient, Anthony. Scott would have accurate time slips signed by one of Anthony's parents and then altered the slips before turning them in to Comprehensive. Maryland Medical Assistance paid the going rate of $28.20 to Comprehensive for each false hour billed and Comprehensive in turn paid Scott $19 per hour. Comprehensive Nursing Services Inc., which was not involved in the scheme, discovered the scam in early August of 2004 because of duplicate hours on the time slips of Scott and another nurse who also took care of Anthony. At that time, Comprehensive Nursing Services Inc. reported it to the Medicaid program.

Scott's sentencing has been scheduled. The maximum penalty for Medicaid fraud is five years incarceration and a fine of $100,000. Pursuant to the plea agreement the state will recommend a split sentence of three years incarceration with part of the sentence to be suspended and part to be served. The state will also recommend a period of five years probation and restitution in the amount of $133,000.[23]

This case was prosecuted by the Medicaid Fraud Control Unit of the Attorney General's Office, which has statewide authority to prosecute cases of Medicaid fraud.

The following healthcare fraud is a case example of a home health nurse double billing for services, billing services not rendered, and falsifying nursing notes:

Attorney General Eliot Spitzer announced today that a Rocky Point registered nurse, who was paid to provide home healthcare to a severely disabled young girl, was sentenced to perform 840 hours of community service and five years probation for her role in stealing more than $58,000 from New York taxpayers by billing Medicaid for services she never provided or had previously been paid for.

Registered Nurse Trudy Vosper, 65, of Rocky Point, was sentenced on January 27, 2006, by Suffolk County Court Judge C. Randall Hinrichs following her guilty plea in November of 2005, to the felony crime of Grand Larceny in the Third Degree. In addition, Vosper was ordered to pay restitution to the state in the amount of $58,337. Vosper will also be referred to the State Education Department's Office of the Professions for a review of her nursing license. Vosper admitted that between October 1, 1998, and December 31, 2003, she was assigned to care for the disabled daughter of co-defendant Yolande Mezil-Thomas, who was approved to receive 19 hours of skilled home-care nursing services a day, seven days a week. Vosper, with Mezil-Thomas's assistance, submitted numerous claims to Medicaid in which she knowingly overstated the extent of home care services provided to Mezil-Thomas's child, including times when Vosper was out of town in Florida, Pennsylvania and elsewhere, as well as during times when she was receiving massage therapy. After payment came from New York State, Vosper and Mezil-Thomas shared over $35,000 in fraudulent Medicaid proceeds. In attempting to cover up the fraud, Vosper also made false entries in her daily nursing notes.

In addition, Vosper admitted to stealing an additional $22,000 from Medicaid by submitting claims to Medicaid which represented that the child had no other insurance, when the girl was in fact insured by the private insurance carrier Health Insurance Plan of New York (HIP). By doing this, Vosper succeeded in being paid twice for the same services.

The patient at the center of this fraud has been a Medicaid recipient since her premature birth nine years ago and required extensive skilled nursing care. "When a Medicaid provider commits fraud they are stealing from a program designed to assist those truly in need and presenting the taxpayers with a bogus bill," said Spitzer. "Those who criminally game and manipulate the system will be prosecuted and punished." Attorney General Spitzer thanked the Suffolk County office of the Department of Social Services and the Health Insurance Plan of New York for their assistance and cooperation during the course of the investigation.

Special Assistant Attorney General Lara Merchan of the Medicaid Fraud Unit's Long Island Regional Office prosecuted the case. Assisting in the investigation were Special Investigator Dawn Scandaliato and Special Auditor Investigator Mary Ann Carney.[24]

Chapter 15, *Home Healthcare Nursing Malpractice Issues,* offers more information on services provided at home.

e. Hospice nursing practice

The nurse's emphasis in hospice care is to make the remaining days of the terminally ill patient more comfortable and meaningful. The nurse supports the patient and family through the final stages of dying. Medicare eligibility, Medicaid rules, or financial billing is not the uppermost priority in the care and treatment of a dying patient. As a result, patients and frontline nurses do not always understand or focus on Medicare and Medicaid eligibility requirements or the specific billing rules. In addition, in the final stages of dying the beneficiaries are not cognitively aware of services they are or are not being provided. Even if hospice fraud is suspected, the patient and family are leery of reporting, fearful of retaliation from the agency, staff, or prescribing physician; interrupting hospice services; or causing pain to their dying family member or themselves.

TIP: To be eligible for hospice care the beneficiary must be terminally ill. Medicare defines terminally ill as having six months or less to live.

The beneficiary becomes eligible for Medicare hospice benefits when he is diagnosed with an irreversible disease in the terminal process and he is certified by the treating physician and the hospice medical director as being terminally ill with six months or less to live. The beneficiary must then sign a statement choosing hospice benefits instead of regular Medicare coverage. The hospice care must be provided by a Medicare-approved hospice agency. Hospice benefits include:

- Medicare coverage for doctors,
- nursing care,
- DME,
- medical supplies,
- palliative medications for symptom control and pain relief,
- short-term hospital care,
- respite care,
- home health aide,
- homemaker services,
- physical therapy,
- occupational therapy,
- speech therapy,
- dietary counseling,
- beneficiary and family grief counseling, and
- social services.

Hospice coverage does not pay for any treatment to cure the terminal illness. However, the beneficiary may choose at any time to quit hospice care and return to his regular treating physician or health plan. Hospice fraud schemes include:

- double billing Medicare and Medicaid for hospice services,
- billing hospice services under the spouse's beneficiary number—dipping into the spouse's lifetime credit for hospice care in order to obtain more coverage, and
- billing hospice services for non-terminal diagnosis, and certifying non-terminal patients for hospice care.

The following healthcare fraud cases are examples of billing hospice services for non-terminal diagnoses:

Visiting Nurses Association Hospice in Rockford, Illinois was investigated for Medicare abuse. The problem included patients who were diagnosed with a terminal illness but lived longer than seven months. June Gibbs-Brown, Inspector General, stated, "we found a high percentage of people that were being entered into the hospice program, and they didn't have an ailment that they would expect not to live more than six months…30 providers were decertified."

A nationwide fraud investigation called Operation Restore Trust was begun. Twelve hospices in five states—Florida, California, Texas, New York, and Illinois—were audited. The audit found that in cases where patients lived longer than seven months, two-thirds of the records did not justify a terminally ill diagnosis; therefore, the patients should not have been certified for hospice care. As a result, the hospices were asked to pay back $83 million in Medicare payments.[25]

f. Managed care nursing practice

"The false claims issues in Medicare run directly at cross-purposes with what the managed care motivations, incentives and orientations are in providing services," said Alice G. Gosfield, JD, former president of the National Health Lawyers Association.[26] As a result, physicians, their mid-level providers, their nurses, and their support staff are at risk of doing something adverse to the intent of the Medicare rules and regulations. According to Gosfield, managed care strategies and fraud and abuse problems intersect in several places: mid-level providers, such as nurse practitioners and physician assistants, are used to doing some of what the physician normally does. In 1997, Congress authorized payments to nurse practitioners for Medicare-provided services. They are reimbursed at 85 percent of the physician fee schedule. Problems arise when the nurse practitioner visit is billed at the physician level fee. Another area of concern is the physician's independent contractor status and where the service was performed: in the physician's office or in a managed care clinic. It also centers on the location of the physician's office: attached to a hospital or clinic or at an independent office building. Where the office visit was performed dictates who can bill for the physician's services: the clinic or the doctor. Also, problems arise when Medicare is billed for a physician office visit when the service technically took place in a hospital outpatient or a managed care setting.[27]

According to the Attorney General of Virginia, Robert F. McDonnell:

Managed care presents different fraud issues. Whereas in standard healthcare reimbursement situations, the fraud is characterized by overbilling, a managed care environment creates an incentive to deny care to patients/consumers. This means that while a fee has been paid by the managed care organization (MCO) to the doctor for covered services, the services are denied or cut back for other than sound medical reasons. This not only defrauds the insurance company, but also compromises patient health.

Fraud in MCOs also arises in enrollment practices whereby healthy patients are "recruited" to join certain MCOs in a practice known as "cherry picking." Often, they are paid in some fashion for their enrollment.[28]

As the population ages and more baby boomers join federally funded managed care plans, detecting managed care fraud will become a growing future challenge. According to the Department of Justice Healthcare Fraud Report Fiscal Year 1997:

In managed care arrangements, the fraud prevention and detection effort is primarily concerned with ensuring that the full quality of care and range of services that providers contract to provide are actually delivered. Proper contracting provisions, quality assurance mechanisms and post-care audits are required to ensure that providers comply with the care requirements and are accountable for their activities.[29]

Nurses working in managed care environments or with physicians involved in managed care may see some of the following fraud schemes. They most likely will not have been privy to the managed care organization's corporate decisions that brought about these schemes. Managed care fraud schemes include:

- Managed care underutilization issues: failure to provide the patient with needed services
- Kickbacks

The following healthcare fraud case is an example of kickbacks in a managed care setting:

Schering Sales Corporation, a sales and marketing subsidiary of drug manufacturer Schering-Plough Corporation, plead guilty and paid a $52.5 million fine on charges that it paid a health maintenance organization (HMO) a kickback to induce the HMO to keep Schering's drug, Claritin, on its formulary (a list of drugs that the HMO covers for its beneficiaries). Schering-Plough also settled its FCA liability and paid the United States, 50 state Medicaid programs, and certain Public Health Service (PHS) entities, approximately $293 million for failing to report the company's true best price for Claritin to the Medicaid programs. At the same time, Schering-Plough entered into a Corporate Integrity Agreement, or CIA with the HHS/OIG to correct its government pricing and Medicaid rebate reporting failures.[30]

Refer to Chapter 13, *Managed Care Liability*, for additional perspectives on this aspect of health care.

g. Renal dialysis nursing practice

Renal dialysis nursing is another area in which fraud is potentially high. These cases usually involve billing for unnecessary services, payment of kickbacks, and inappropriate ambulance transport of non-bedridden dialysis patients. One such case involved Fresenius Medical Care North America, Inc., the world's largest provider of renal dialysis products and services. It agreed to pay the U.S. government $486 million to resolve a sweeping healthcare fraud investigation of their subsidiary, National Medical Care, Inc., for submitting unnecessary claims.[31]

Another healthcare fraud case was in Pennsylvania involving a company providing end-stage renal disease (ESRD) services through a network of subsidiary corporations it had acquired. It agreed to pay the government $16.5 million to resolve allegations of false Medicare claims submitted by one of the subsidiaries. The claims arose from the sale of Medicare-reimbursable noninvasive diagnostic tests between 1992 and 1995. The subsidiary companies provided financial inducements to primary care physicians and to renal dialysis facilities in exchange for the referral of patients for diagnostic testing. As a result, a percentage of the tests performed by the subsidiaries were medically unnecessary. The final settlement resolved three different qui tam lawsuits which had been brought against the subsidiaries and/or the parent company.[32]

2. Non-nursing specialty areas prone to healthcare fraud

There are some non-specialty areas of nursing where one might find healthcare fraud. Nurses may or may not be directly involved. They include pharmaceutical sales, clinical research, and physician practice.

According to Tax Payers Against Fraud the following fraud case occurred:

In 1995, Eli Lilly agreed to pay $36 million to settle a False Claims Act lawsuit that charged the company with illegally marketing and promoting Evista, an osteoporosis drug, for off-label purposes. The suit charged that in 1998 the company promoted Evista for the prevention and reduction of breast cancer and cardiovascular disease.[33]

a. Pharmaceutical sales and clinical research

Pharmaceutical fraud includes other schemes such as false prescriptions, pharmaceutical distribution fraud, misbranded pharmaceutical fraud, and pharmaceutical company fraud which includes how pharmaceuticals are marketed. An example of pharmaceutical company fraud is the following:

Pfizer, a division of the Warner-Lambert Company, paid $430 million in fines and settled its FCA liability for illegal marketing conduct and fraudulent promotion of the drug Neurontin for uses not approved by the U.S. Food and Drug Administration (FDA). Neurontin was approved by the FDA in December 1993 solely for adjunctive or supplemental anti-seizure use by epilepsy patients. Under the provisions of the Federal Food, Drug and Cosmetic Act, 21 U.S.C.§ 301, et seq., a company must specify the intended uses of a product in its new drug application to FDA. Once approved, the drug may not be marketed or promoted for so-called off-label uses—any use not specified in an application and approved by FDA. However, Warner-Lambert's strategic marketing plans, as well as other evidence, showed that the company aggressively marketed Neurontin to treat a wide array of ailments for which the drug was not approved. The company promoted Neurontin for the treatment of various pain disorders, Amyotrophic Lateral Sclerosis (ALS, a degenerative nerve disease commonly referred to as Lou Gehrig's Disease), attention deficit disorder, migraine, drug and alcohol withdrawal seizures, and restless leg syndrome.[34]

In the previously described Schering-Plough case, in the late 1990s, Claritin was Schering's best-selling drug. Claritin was substantially more expensive, however, than its biggest competitor, Allegra. When one of Schering's best customers demanded a price reduction in Claritin—because it cost the HMO millions of additional dollars a year to purchase Claritin instead of Allegra—Schering refused, in part, because it knew that it then would have to lower the Claritin price for the Medicaid programs. Under the Medicaid Drug Rebate Statute, drug manufacturers are required to report their "best prices" to the federal government and to pay quarterly rebates to Medicaid to ensure that the nation's insurance program for the poor receives the benefit of favorable drug prices offered to other large purchasers of drugs. As a participant in the Medicaid Rebate Program, Schering was required to report its "best price" and to pay rebates on Claritin. Similarly, under the provisions of the PHS drug pricing program, Schering was required to charge PHS entities such as AIDS drug programs and community health centers a discounted price, based in part on the Medicaid price.

After the HMO removed Claritin from its formulary, Schering offered to make up the difference in price between Claritin and Allegra by offering the HMO a $10 million package of added value, in lieu of an actual price reduction on Claritin. The United States alleged that, as part of this "value added" package, Schering offered to provide $3 million worth of deeply discounted Claritin Reditabs, health management services at far below fair market value and an interest free loan in the form of prepaid rebates. Schering also offered to pay an annual fee of 2 percent of the annual gross sales of Schering drugs to the HMO, or approximately $2.4 million, disguised as a "data fee" in order to give the appearance that the fee was a fair market value transaction rather than a hidden inducement to the HMO to keep Claritin on its formulary.

Schering also provided to another HMO a risk share arrangement in which Schering covered a portion of the managed care customer's respiratory drug costs, provided deep discounts on other Schering products, provided payment and services for Internet development, and provided an interest-free loan in the form of prepaid rebates. Because of Schering's failure to account for these discounts in its reported best price for Claritin, the Medicaid program and PHS entities paid far more for Claritin from 1998-2002 than Schering's two managed care customers.[35]

Healthcare fraud has been evident in clinical research (clinical trials):

> On September 15, 1998, in the Central District of California, the owner and president of American Pharmaceutical Research (APR) were sentenced to 15 months in jail for conspiring to make false statements within the jurisdiction of the Food and Drug Administration (FDA). This case arose out of a FDA audit during which time it was learned that APR, which hired itself out to pharmaceutical companies to conduct clinical drug trial on human subjects, falsified drug study data that was being submitted to the FDA and failed to comply regularly with required drug testing and procedures.[36]

b. Physician practice

Physician practice settings can be a highly rewarding area of nursing practice or they can be very difficult depending on the individual physician's personality and method of practice and style of communication. Most nurses generally have faith in the physicians for whom they work. There is usually a long-standing, close-working relationship and an extended bond of trust. A vast majority of physicians are good practitioners and provide quality care to their patients in a compassionate and earnest way. In accordance with the manner in which they practice, they are even more honest when submitting their billing claims—accurately representing the care rendered. But without a good practice manager or office nurse, physicians are frequently overwhelmed by attempts to comply with Medicare and Medicaid rules, regulations, and requirements. Compliance can easily become a problem and get out of control in a busy practice of medicine. Sometimes, physicians knowingly fail to comply. Occasionally, the physician's unpleasant personality causes his office staff to report suspicions of wrongdoing. With sufficient evidence physicians can be investigated for any of the following schemes of fraud:

- billing services for phantom patients
- billing for nursing home visits that were never made
- billing for comprehensive physical examinations for only visiting nursing home patients or when a partial or no exam occurred
- billing for gang visits as individual visits where the physician never rendered the service, rendered only some of the visits, or rendered unnecessary services
- falsifying medical records to document the provision of nonexistent services or up-coding services
- accepting a fee for home health, hospice, hospital, or nursing home referrals
- receiving money to certify medical necessity for each patient's plan of care on behalf of a home health agency, nursing home, or hospice agency
- paying beneficiaries each time they receive treatment in a specific clinic
- falsifying Certificates of Medical Necessity
- physician sharing of beneficiaries, patient lists, and referrals
- sending recruiters to find beneficiaries to entice them into having a medical examination
- giving beneficiaries free gifts in exchange for the use of their Medicare numbers
- psychiatrists conducting group therapy sessions in long-term care facilities and then billing for individual sessions
- billing non-covered services as covered services
- unbundling services
- billing for unnecessary procedures
- allowing home health agency nurses or discharge planners to review office patient records, pulling beneficiary names, numbers, and private health information in order to make agency referrals
- billing for daily hospital visits when service was not provided
- billing physician extender (nurse practitioner, physician assistant) visits as though they were physician services
- billing for prescribing pharmaceutical samples
- accepting remuneration for patient referrals
- billing for unapproved use of a drug
- billing for administration of diluted medications such as oncology drugs

TIP: According to a 2005 FBI report the most significant trends observed in recent healthcare fraud cases included the willingness of medical professionals to risk patient harm in their schemes. Current fraud schemes consist of traditional schemes that involve fraudulent billing, but also incorporate unnecessary surgeries, diluted cancer drugs, and fraudulent lab tests.[37]

The following healthcare fraud case is an example of a physician accepting pay for patient referrals to the hospital:

On October 25, 2005, Tax Payers Against Fraud reported that a Tennessee hospital, Erlanger Medical Center, agreed to pay a $40 million fine in connection with kickback and false billing charges brought by the U.S. Justice Department. Federal officials contended they had $120 million in valid claims against Erlanger, which was paying physicians to refer patients to the hospital. The case was brought by a whistleblower under the False Claims Act.[38]

The following case is about an oncologist administering diluted cancer drugs:

A Crossville, Tennessee, oncologist blamed her nurses, her busy schedule and complicated billing procedures as she was sentenced to 15 years in prison after shortchanging her patients of chemotherapy drugs. The family members of cancer patients under her care asked the judge to give Dr. Young Moon a maximum sentence and said her greed was the reason she shorted their loved ones of life-saving medications.

Moon was convicted in December on three counts of healthcare fraud and one count of lying to federal authorities about the scheme. The doctor was accused of under dosing patients from 1999 until early 2002....In addition to the prison sentence, Moon was ordered to pay $432,238 in restitution for the money she defrauded from Medicare, TennCare and BlueCross BlueShield of Tennessee. Part of that, $271,000, she was ordered to pay as soon as her Crossville home is sold, the judge said. Moon said she will appeal.

The doctor accepted responsibility for being a poor manager, for her busy schedule and her failure to properly supervise her nurses....Although Moon could have faced up to 35 years in prison for her conviction, the judge decided her sentence should fall between 15 and 19 years....Once she is out of prison, she will have to serve two years under supervised release, which is like probation. While under supervised release, the doctor is barred from working in the healthcare profession, the judge ordered.

Assistant U.S. Attorney Samuel G. Williamson had asked the judge for the upper part of the range, saying Moon neither showed remorse nor took responsibility for her actions. Her deeds included shorting at least 75 patients of their cancer drugs with the intent to defraud insurance companies of nearly $1.3 million, Assistant U.S. Attorney Ellen Bowden McIntyre said.[39]

3. Administrative level or nurse owners of healthcare entities
a. Hospitals

Most nurses involved in direct patient care who have no financial or administrative duties will most likely not be involved in implementing or recognizing suspicious fraudulent schemes within their hospitals. Patients receive so many services in the hospital during a short period of time—at a time that they are not at their cognitive best either due to their illness, injury, pain, or the effects of receiving their medications—that they are often unaware of their services. Medicare rules for reimbursement of hospital care are intricate and complex, allowing for fraudulent schemes to go unnoticed. Hospital fraud schemes include:

- misrepresenting or billing an up-coded diagnosis in order to receive a higher reimbursement such as billing for pneumonia when the beneficiary had a cold (some DRGs reimburse at a higher rate)
- billing patient stays as "observation stays—23 hour stays" for three to four days rather than admitting as an inpatient. Observation stays are reimbursed as a percentage of the charge through Medicare Part B which is usually a higher rate than what the regular inpatient DRG rate would have been
- billing for more services than what were actually provided such as billing multiple physical therapy visits when there were less documented or billing for more x-rays taken than what was done
- billing for unnecessary procedures such as unnecessary invasive procedures, surgeries, or medical procedures
- hospitals paying kickbacks and illegal remuneration to physicians for patient referrals
- billing outpatient services as though they were inpatient services; it is to the facility's financial benefit to discharge the patient on paper but not in reality and to either bill for both services or begin billing for outpatient services

- hospitals accepting kickbacks for referring patients to one home health agency
- posting inappropriate date of discharge
- double billing services

The following healthcare fraud case is an example of billing for unnecessary surgical procedures:

On the eve of a criminal fraud trial scheduled to start November 22, Tenet Healthcare Corporation had reached a $32.5 million global settlement for a variety of charges involving its Redding, California, Medical Center which was allegedly performing unnecessary heart surgeries on healthy patients in order to bill Medicare, Medicaid, TriCare, and private insurance carriers.[40]

The *Los Angeles Times* reported in August 2003 that Tenet Healthcare, the second largest for-profit hospital chain in the nation, agreed to pay $54 million to settle allegations that two physicians at Tenet-owned Redding Medical Center in California participated in a "scheme to cause patients to undergo unnecessary invasive coronary procedures," such as artery bypass and heart valve replacement surgeries in order to defraud Medicare. This is the largest settlement recovered from a hospital in a case related to alleged unnecessary surgeries or other medical services.[41]

The following healthcare fraud case is an example of a hospital paying kickbacks for patient referrals. In September 2003, the U.S. Department of Justice (DOJ) concluded:

This was "the most comprehensive healthcare fraud investigation ever undertaken" by the agency with $1.7 billion recovered from HCA, Inc. for submitting false claims to Medicare and Medicaid. The settlements were made in order to bring an end to the government's cases against them. It resolved allegations of overpayment of claims arising from HCA's cost reporting practices and submitting false statements, and it effectively resolved suits alleging that HCA hospitals engaged in paying out kickbacks and other illegal remuneration to physicians in exchange for patient referrals.[42]

The following healthcare fraud case shows double billing of outpatient services and inpatient services:

A Miami hospital will pay $16.8 million to settle a whistleblower suit filed by a former Florida Medicaid employee charging that it double-billed Medicaid. Both Jackson Memorial Hospital and its outpatient clinics billed Medicaid under their respective provider numbers for the same covered service. The former employee (whistleblower) who filed the case will collect about $1.4 million.[43]

b. Nursing registry

Nurses are often owners of nursing registries or staffing agencies. The following healthcare fraud case involves nursing registry fraud:

In Maryland, a registered nurse pled guilty to operating a scheme to defraud area nursing homes by making false representations to the nursing homes that the defendant provided them with state-licensed and certified employees from the defendant's healthcare staffing company. The nurse's company had provided temporary nursing staff to nursing homes, hospitals, patients' homes and doctors' offices, including licensed practical nurses (LPNs), registered nurses (RNs), certified nursing assistants (CNAs), and geriatric nursing assistants (GNAs). Under Maryland law, the company was required to verify the licensure and status of the LPNs, RNs, and GNAs before dispatching these workers to healthcare facilities to render temporary nursing support. In fact, many of the licenses the company provided to its client nursing homes were falsified, altered or forged. When law enforcement agents executed search warrants at the defendant's home and business, they found more than 60 "cut and paste" documents containing the names of several of the company's employees that had been altered, blocked out or "corrected" with white-out to make the documents appear as bona fide licensing and certification documents from the State of Maryland.[44]

Other areas such as home health agencies, assisted living facilities and rehabilitation facilities are owned, administrated or operated by nurse executives. Refer to Chapter 11, *Assisted Living Liability*, for more on the topic of appropriateness of care.

c. Durable medical equipment

Durable medical equipment (DME) is equipment appropriate to use in the home and prescribed by the attending physician who certifies that it is medically necessary to the individual who is ill or injured in order to perform activities of daily living. DME includes items such as a cane, walker, or wheelchair. It is items used repeatedly and generally not useful to another individual who is not ill. Common DME fraud schemes include:

- dishonestly obtaining or buying Medicare Health Insurance Claim Numbers to fraudulently bill Medicare. Some DME companies offer free services in exchange for a Medicare number or call appearing to conduct a survey and ask for a Medicare number.
- hospitals allowing DME companies to provide discharge planners employed by the DME companies. The discharge planner works in the hospital to assist the patient with discharge plans, making sure that every item is ordered whether or not it is medically necessary and that it is ordered from the DME company.
- physicians ordering unnecessary equipment and/or supplies the beneficiary never uses.
- billing for female urinary collection devices for incontinence but in reality providing adult diapers. The urinary devices cost Medicare $9 per device. Adult diapers cost 26 cents each. Billings to Medicare have been as high as $5,200 per month per patient.
- billing repeatedly for unnecessary surgical dressings that are either contraindicated or not proportionate to the actual wound size or number.
- billing for enteral or parenteral supplies when the beneficiary was given free cases of milk supplements or groceries.
- owning or having an arrangement with a laboratory that falsifies oximetry tests to certify the need for home oxygen therapy.
- using diagnosis codes that do not reflect the true condition of the patient in order to bill higher-end medical supplies such as oxygen concentrators.
- using another beneficiary's Medicare number to get supplies or equipment for an individual.
- supplying and billing for unauthorized or prescribed medical equipment that is medically unnecessary such as lymphedema pumps.
- ordering and billing for excess repair for equipment.

When reviewing any case that involves the recommendation of medical equipment, an attorney, legal nurse consultant, or paralegal must be aware of durable medical equipment companies that use telemarketing schemes to obtain Medicare numbers, offer anything free in exchange for patient information, or offer free services to their patients and then bill Medicare or other insurers for services that are not ordered, not medically necessary, and not provided.

4. Nursing specialty areas less prone to healthcare fraud

There are some nursing specialty areas less likely to be involved in healthcare fraud schemes: critical care, medical surgical, obstetrical, orthopaedics, and pediatrics. Obstetrical and pediatric patients are not likely qualified Medicare beneficiaries. There is still the issue of quality of care for critical care, medical surgical, or orthopaedics. Billing Medicare for substandard care such as what is seen in medical negligence cases is actionable under the False Claims Act. This is an avenue available to the U.S. Attorney General.

5. Advanced practice nurses

Advanced practice nurses are at a higher risk of being involved or uncovering some type of healthcare fraud either within their practice or in connection with the hospitals or physicians with whom they are affiliated. Advanced practice nurses include advanced nurse practitioners, certified registered nurse anesthetists, and midwives. With each of these practice areas there is a greater opportunity for the nurse to function as an independent contractor. These nurses are considered mid-level providers and carry out some of the routine functions of the physicians. Some mid-level providers carry their own patient load and have admitting privileges to hospitals. Their provision of care is overseen either by a physician or in affiliation with a physician. In those situations, the advanced practice nurse has more control over her billing and the services rendered.

Buppert suggests the following:

In 1997, Congress authorized payments to nurse practitioners (NPs) for Medicare-provided services. NP services are now reimbursed at 85 percent of the physician fee schedule. As this source of reimbursement was realized, so was a new area of liability for NPs. Failure to follow billing rules can result in payment denial, repayment of fees already paid, mandated educational activities, fines, fraud prosecution, loss of Medicare billing ability and loss of employment. Appropriate billing entails adhering to guidelines for selecting procedure codes and proper medical documentation.[45]

Buppert describes some high-risk situations for nurse practitioners:

Government auditors and investigators focus on provider documentation. Failure to document medical necessity of hospital days and failure to document services furnished and billed are one focus of fraud initiatives. Auditors look for false claims that (1) misrepresent the actual provider, (2) misrepresent the service provided, or (3) misrepresent the diagnosis in order to receive increased fees. A misrepresentation is proved when a provider fails to support bills with adequate medical record documentation. Initially, poor documentation is punished by denial of payment.[46]

In some situations, the advanced practice nurses are employed by the hospital, physician entity, or a healthcare company. In those instances, they may have little control over the actual billing of their services other than reporting their hours and documenting the care they have rendered.

Karin Bierstein, a practice management coordinator, noted the following:

In *United States v. Erickson*, Bruce L. Erickson, M.D., and co-defendant Great Falls Eye Surgery Center were convicted by a jury of knowingly and willfully overbilling Medicare and Medicaid patients. Dr. Erickson, who had lost privileges at a local hospital, was a 50 percent owner of the eye surgery center. The center had started operations in 1989 and had first come to the attention of the Healthcare Financing Administration (HCFA) in 1990. The HCFA agent who investigated the center's billing practices in 1991 found that the center routinely charged Medicare for overlapping nurse anesthetist services, billing as many as 27 hours for the services of a single nurse anesthetist in a ten-hour workday. In 1992, the center had changed the way it billed Medicare after consulting with another eye surgery institution in Utah. The new system recorded continuous back-to-back blocks of nurse anesthetist services, with the anesthesia time for one patient beginning immediately after the anesthesia time for another patient had ended. This suggested to the HCFA agent that the billing periods must include pre- and/or postoperative stretches of time when the nurse anesthetist was away from the patient. Apparently, the defendants acknowledged that the patients were not continuously attended, since they chose to challenge the Medicare regulation stating that "time units involve the continuous actual presence of the physician..." as being unconstitutionally vague. The Court of Appeals disagreed, however. It found that both on its face and as commonly understood by other providers: "the regulation clearly limits CRNA [certified registered nurse anesthetist] reimbursement to periods when the CRNA is actually with and looking after the patient. The regulation requires 'personal attendance' that is said to cease when the patient is placed in the care of another."[47]

27.5 How Healthcare Fraud Differs from Nursing Malpractice

TIP: Nursing malpractice is a standard of care issue. A breach of the nursing standard results in an injury to a patient. It is usually unintentional. Healthcare fraud is primarily a financial issue. It is an intentional act that may or may not affect patient care, but results in inappropriate financial gain to an individual or entity that may result in patient injury.

There is a difference between nursing malpractice and healthcare fraud. Sometimes they coexist. A Medicare patient develops a pressure ulcer (bedsore) during a hospital stay or nursing home stay and it is proven the pressure ulcer clearly developed as a result of nursing malpractice. The service was billed to Medicare. The submission of billing for services rendered could be found to be fraud under the False Claims Act where substandard care is billed as though it were appropriate care.

A. How Nursing Contributes to Healthcare Fraud

Nurses unknowingly contribute to healthcare fraud by being uninformed about the specifics of what constitutes healthcare fraud and abuse. Often they are busy providing direct patient care and are unaware of the rationale for what they are being asked to do by their employers and supervisors. For example, many nurses are naive as to how their documentation may lead to suspicious situations of fraud, which are susceptible to criminal and civil investigations.

When Medicare dictates specific requirements for eligibility, nurses working in those particular areas need to know and understand the rules. For example, home health patients must be homebound; otherwise home visits or any fictitious documentation to substantiate homebound status in order for the home health agency to support their billing practice is fraud. Any documentation made for the sole purpose of substantiating a bill is fraud especially if the nurse is justifying the process in his mind. Requests appear innocent on the surface. Nursing supervisors and physician employers have asked nurses to add to, rewrite, or destroy an original note for the purposes of quality assurance. Suggestions of using more compliant language or a suggested wordlist have been encouraged to make sure the nurse's documentation is in compliance and supportive of the bill being submitted. Frequently the nurse is only trying to do her job and please the employer. Appearing as a team player is usually beneficial to the nurse. Changing a few notes here and there seems innocuous. If the nurse is helping the doctor submit a claim for a higher level of service than the service actually provided, the nurse should know that is fraud. Department pizza parties or rewards of any kind for completing or passing documentation inspection should be further investigated.

Advanced practice nurses such as certified registered nurse anesthetics (CRNA), advanced registered nurse practitioners (ARNP), and nurse midwives may apply for their unique provider identification number (UPIN) and submit claims to Medicare and Medicaid. It is very important these nurses understand how that number is used and can be abused without their knowledge. Those nurses must take special precautions to protect their number. Unprotected access to the UPIN can open the door to fraudulent use of the number.

B. The Effects of Healthcare Fraud in Medical or Nursing Malpractice

---

TIP: Plaintiff's attorneys can strengthen their malpractice cases by proving that the care billed for either was never rendered or was below the standard of care. In most states this factor alone raises the issue of punitive damages; and if the failure to provide care can be raised, the federal FCA can be invoked.

A plaintiff can take the case issues from a single patient-care issue to a facility-provider issue by identifying fraudulent billing practices and showing a systemic focus on financial gain rather than on quality patient care. In addition, defendants who are fraudulently billing for non-rendered care can be identified. An itemized (line item) billing review can identify such billing issues, on which counsel may focus. These include inappropriate treatments, substandard care, excessive facility fees, and excessive professional fees above the usual and customary. Exposure of improper billing practices can be a great incentive to negotiate or settle. Also, it can expand the case from a malpractice case to a false claims *qui tam* relator case, adding dollar value to the malpractice damages aspect. Such facts discovered to have occurred before the sentinel event of the malpractice case add fuel to the fire for the plaintiff's attorney. However, if these facts are revealed in discovery, the downside is slowing the discovery process by taking the case from civil tort action to a federal criminal or federal civil action.

TIP: Conversely, defense attorneys may want to consider the fraudulent billing aspect as a basis for early settlement or negotiations. They may want to limit the possible exposure of their clients to federal or state fraud investigations by early detection of billing practices or quality of care issues, which may put the healthcare provider at greater risk.

Procuring a corporate counsel (healthcare law attorney) to bring in independent billing auditors may be a wise choice. Further, the defense counsel may want to control damage awards when fraudulent charges are identified for services not rendered, or for services not rendered as billed, or for services provided that were not medically necessary. The greatest benefit is that the substantiation of proper billing practices strengthens the defense of any malpractice case.

27.6 Nursing Involvement in Whistleblower Cases

The number of healthcare qui tam cases grew from 17 in fiscal year 1992, to 269 in fiscal year 2004. *Qui tam* is a Latin abbreviation for "*qui tam pro domino rege quam pro sic ipso in hoc parte sequitur*," meaning who as well for the king as for himself sues in this matter. Any individual (relator) may file a qui tam action. When a qui tam action is brought to the attention of the government, the government has an initial 60-day time frame to investigate and decide if it wants to litigate the case or not. The government may decline to intervene and the relator may then find an attorney to file the case. Under the statute, individual relators are rewarded a percentage of the money the government recovers as a direct result of their whistleblower lawsuit. The percentage depends on how much the relator and his attorneys contributed to the case. The percentage ranges from 15 to 30 percent of the total recovery. In addition, the False Claims Act allows for the recovery of attorney fees and costs. This encourages private law firms to invest their resources to fight healthcare fraud on the government's behalf. If the U.S. Attorney's Office joins the whistleblower lawsuit then they take the lead in the investigation and prosecution: as a result the whistleblower award is reduced by 15 to 25 percent.

The widespread publicity of the monetary successes for some relators has resulted in an explosion of qui tam lawsuits. Relators in the *United States v. NMC Homecare Inc.*, D-Mass, received $65.8 million from the civil money penalty. Since the False Claims Act was amended, the federal government has recovered more than $17 billion.

The False Claims Act is the government's single most powerful tool in the fight against healthcare fraud. The qui tam provisions, which allow whistleblowers to file False Claims Act lawsuits, are the real means to the success of the Act.

In fiscal year 2004, $82.8 million in funds were awarded to private persons who filed suits on behalf of the federal government under the qui tam provisions of the False Claims Act, 31 U.S.C.§ 3730(b).[48]

A. What is Qui Tam?

A qui tam action occurs when an individual, called a relator, alleges that someone (an entity or person) has submitted false claims and files a complaint with the U.S. Attorney's office. The relator must be the first to file as the original source of the information. Some healthcare providers will self-disclose to reduce their exposure and to put the best spin on a difficult situation, particularly when the possibility of a qui tam action looms. Filing a qui tam is possible because of the False Claims Act (FCA). Although there are many critics of the FCA, Senator Charles E. Grassley (R-Iowa) is not one of them. Referencing the $489 million settlement in criminal and civil penalties paid by Fresenius Medical Care North America, Sen. Grassley said this settlement "proves the merits of the law beyond any reasonable doubt [that] the FCA is the government's most effective tool against fraud."

B. Duty to Disclose

Anyone, such as an individual, a patient, a patient's family member, or an employee, who has reason to believe fraud and abuse has occurred may file a qui tam. Any individual considering filing such an action may want to consult with a reputable attorney. Some attorneys are now specializing in qui tam cases on a contingency fee basis. These attorneys can be located on the Internet as well as through advertisements in local or national trade publications. Developing a legal practice focused on qui tam cases can take time to build. As with other types of legal intervention, a qui tam case may drag on in the legal system for years.

In many hospitals and other institutions there is a tendency to think that nothing needs to be done when billing mistakes are made in the institution's favor. But that decision is a risky one if it involves Medicare or any other federal health insurance funds. Failing to report Medicare billing errors to the federal government can adversely affect healthcare providers and their employees in two ways: 1) they could be prosecuted for criminal violations, which could result in prison time as well as fines, and 2) they could be sued for treble damages by whistleblowers and the government.

Several years ago, the government began to use a little-known provision of the Social Security Act to discourage healthcare fraud. The "duty to disclose" provision of the 1977 amendments to the law [42 USC sec. 1320-7b (a) 3] makes concealing from the government or failing to report Medicare overpayments a felony.[49]

Under the "duty to disclose" provision, healthcare providers and others who conceal or fail to disclose that they have received larger payments than they are entitled to are guilty of a felony and could be imprisoned for up to five years and fined up to $25,000. Their employees, including auditors, who conceal these overpayments, may be guilty of a misdemeanor and subject to fines.

C. What to Do with Evidence of Healthcare Fraud

When an individual has evidence of an entity (e.g., company, corporation, physician group, hospital, nursing home, home health agency) or person (e.g., nurse, physician, dentist, ARNP, CRNA) submitting improper or "false claims," the individual may file a complaint with the U.S. Attorney. To start a cause of action under the False Claims Act, a qui tam plaintiff may allege the defendant either:

1. knowingly presented or caused to be presented, to an officer or employee of the United States government…a false or fraudulent claim for payment or approval;
2. knowingly made, used, or caused to be made or used, a false record or statement to get a false or fraudulent claim paid by the government; or
3. conspired to defraud the government by getting a false or fraudulent claim allowed or paid.[50]

The False Claims Act, 31 U.S.C.§ 3729(a) (1)–(3). 31 U.S.C.§ 3729(a) (4)–(7) sets forth several other theories that may be applicable in specific circumstances.

The Act is intended to encourage individuals with first-hand knowledge of fraudulent activity to come forth to report and stop Medicare fraud. The whistleblowers statute allows individuals with direct knowledge of any individual, entity, or activity of taking federal money under false or fictitious pretenses (such as false claims of providing appropriate and safe nursing care and receiving federal monies for the submitted claim) to report it.

The following are common healthcare fraud schemes that have been successfully prosecuted on the basis of qui tam relator information:

- billing for prescribed brand-name drugs when generic drugs are actually provided
- billing for a series of tests when a single test was ordered (known as unbundling)

- billing for services, procedures, or supplies that were not provided
- misrepresenting or up-coding services (billing less expensive procedures as more expensive procedures)
- billing for services performed by a lesser-qualified person or unlicensed person, e.g., billing a doctor's rates for work that was actually conducted by a physician assistant, nurse, or resident intern
- misrepresenting the charges for services, procedures, or supplies provided
- engaging in fraud in cost reporting (inclusion of unrelated expenses)
- paying prohibited kickbacks for patient referrals that result in the government funding medically unnecessary services and equipment
- falsely inflating the number of hours nurses spend caring for patients or submitting
- submitting false nurse sign-in sheets, time cards, and other fabricated documents to support bills

The following healthcare fraud case is an example of a registered nurse turned whistleblower who alleged cost reporting fraud:

Washington, D.C.—The San Diego Hospital Association and one of its facilities, Sharp Memorial Hospital, have agreed to pay the United States $6.2 million to settle allegations that Sharp submitted false claims by fraudulently misstating organ acquisition costs on the hospital's Medicare reports for 1991 through 1999. The alleged misrepresented costs include employee salaries, medical director fees, laboratory costs and square footage that were not incurred or used for organ acquisition activities and thus did not qualify for reimbursement under Medicare regulations as organ acquisition costs.

The allegations arose from a lawsuit filed by Judith A. King under the qui tam or whistleblower provisions of the False Claims Act, which allow a private person to sue on behalf of the United States and share in any recovery. King, a heart transplant coordinator at Sharp Memorial, will receive $1.2 million of the settlement proceeds.

The case is entitled *United States and State of California ex rel. Judith A. King v. San Diego Hospital Association*, Civil No., 00-CV-0848-BTM (RBB) (S.D. Cal. filed Apr. 26, 2000).[51]

Nurses who blow the whistle on their employers run the risk of retaliation. Some are protected by the False Claims

Act while others are not. As a result many states have introduced state legislation to help protect the nurse:

> Nurses who report cases of patient neglect or abuse know that doing so is a risky proposition. They immediately put their credibility and medical knowledge on the line and may face serious backlash from their superiors. Absent federal whistleblower legislation, many states have written their own statutes protecting nurses from possible retaliation from an employer.
>
> If you were to put a human face on the need for whistleblower protection, that face just might belong to Mary Hochman. A respected and experienced convalescent home nurse, Hochman committed suicide rather than continue to face the fury directed at her by her supervisors after she reported to state regulators cases of patient neglect and abuse in the Santa Barbara nursing home where she worked.
>
> Hochman had reported that a nurse's aide hit an 81-year-old patient who suffered from dementia. Her employer allegedly told her to cover up the information, and when she refused to participate in the cover up, Hochman's supervisors targeted her for retaliation.
>
> The following states—as a result of the cooperation between state legislatures and state nursing associations—have enacted whistleblower legislation since 1998: Alaska, Arkansas, California, Colorado, Connecticut, Florida, Illinois, Kentucky, Minnesota, Missouri, New Jersey, North Dakota, Texas, Utah, Washington and Wisconsin.[52]

Some states have enacted State False Claims Acts. They include California, Delaware, Florida, Hawaii, Illinois, Louisiana, Massachusetts, Nevada, Tennessee, Texas and the District of Columbia. Whistleblowers in those states can recover money from the healthcare entities for retaliating against the nurse for reporting.

27.7 Consequences of Healthcare Fraud for the Nurse

The U.S. General Accounting Office has reported that billions of Medicare dollars are lost each year to Medicare fraud and abuse. To every taxpayer it means higher healthcare costs and lower available coverage. To beneficiaries it means greater financial hardship and ultimately the loss of much-needed services.

A. What Are the Consequences?

Failure to follow Medicare billing rules can result in payment denial, repayment of fees already paid, mandated educational activities, fines, fraud prosecution, loss of the ability to bill Medicare, and loss of employment. Persons convicted of healthcare fraud may be sentenced to prison time in addition to having to pay restitution and civil monetary penalties. They may also be excluded from federal and state government programs for a number of years. Licensed professionals may lose their professional license practices either temporarily or permanently.

B. Civil Monetary Penalties

The government is serious about punishing providers at the civil or criminal level for submitting false claims. New regulations in 1999 raised the ante for civil monetary penalty (CMP) from $2,000 to $10,000 per false claim.

C. Exclusion from Federal Programs

For Medicare, Medicaid, and other government programs, the Office of Inspector General (OIG) can exclude a healthcare provider from participating in any government program. This is true even when the U.S. Attorney's Office declines to prosecute a case. This exclusion is designated for a number of years. This means that for any services performed or ordered by an excluded individual, the government has a right to deny payment.

The OIG has a mandated duty to exclude all persons or entities from participation in any federal healthcare program, including Medicare and Medicaid, when the person or entity has been "convicted of program-related crimes, crimes related to patient abuse or neglect, felony convictions for defrauding other healthcare programs and felony convictions for the illegal manufacture or distribution of controlled substances." Exclusion is a matter of discretion when applied to medical professionals who have lost a license due to performance of professional duties, competence, financial integrity or for providing substandard or unnecessary services.

An excluded nurse cannot perform any service or receive any payment for such services if any part of the payment is generated from a government program. If an institution's payroll is dependent on funding from the government, an excluded individual cannot be hired in any capacity. For example, the excluded nurse could not be hired in a secretarial position for a participating Medicare or Medicaid healthcare provider. U.S. Attorney of the Western District of Missouri, Bradley J. Schlozman indicated the following:

> Under federal law, healthcare providers who have been criminally convicted of healthcare offenses,

including fraud and patient abuse, can be excluded from participating in the Medicare and Medicaid programs. This means that the healthcare provider cannot bill or receive payments from those programs. There are currently over 15,000 healthcare providers and entities excluded from participating in government healthcare programs.[53]

TIP: Information on exclusions is available at www.hhs.gov.

27.8 Summary

It is in everyone's best interest to report suspected incidences of healthcare fraud against Medicare, Medicaid, TriCare, and private insurers. Healthcare fraud increases everyone's cost for health care and exposes more and more patients to substandard quality care. Detecting and controlling healthcare fraud will improve patient care by stopping those providers who continue to put patients at risk with unnecessary life-threatening procedures for the sake of personal financial gain.

Endnotes

1. U.S. Department of Justice Federal Bureau of Investigations Financial Crimes Section Criminal Investigative Division Financial Crimes Report to the Public 2005. Available at http://www.fbi.gov/publications/financial/fes_report052005/fcs_report 7 of 32, retrieved 5/3/06.

2. Bureau of National Affairs, Inc., Special Report I, Vol. 6, No. 7, 276–279.

3. American Medical Association, Fourth edition, CPT 2006.

4. California Health Advocates, retrieved 3/7/05.

5. Federal Fraud Enforcement—Physician Compliance, http://www.ama-assn.org/ama/pub/category/4598.

6. Buppert, C., "Nurse Practitioner: Avoiding Medicare Fraud, part 1." LookSmart, January 2001. 2 of 4. Available at http://www.findarticles.com/p/articles/mi_qa3958/is_200101/ai_n89, retrieved 4/23/06.

7. Clifford, R. and M. Leverock, "Investigation of Billing Fraud," In *Nursing Home Litigation: Investigation and Case Preparation,* Second Edition, ed. P. Iyer. Tucson, Arizona: Lawyers and Judges Publishing Co., 2006.

8. Integrated Health Services and Fraud, "Patient Advocates Sue Firms Over Care Quality: Troubled Times in Nursing Homes." *Albuquerque Journal* (August 3, 1999).

9. Murphy, T., "Strengthening Medicaid: reducing waste, fraud and abuse," Available at murphy.house.gov/UploadedFiles/HealthCareFYI_27.pdf, retrieved 4/23/06.

10. USDOJ: Deputy Attorney General: Publications and Documents—Healthcare Fraud Report Fiscal Year 1998. Available at http://www.usdoj.gov/dag/pubdoc/health98.htm, retrieved 5/3/06.

11. Veritus Medicare VMS—Ambulance Services. Available at www.veritusmedicare.com/provider/fraud/ambulance_services.html, retrieved 4/23/06.

12. Health Fraud News. May 5, 2006. Available at http://www.healthfraudnews.org/?cat=148, retrieved 5/5/06.

13. FY 2005 False Claims Act Settlements. Taxpayers Against Fraud. Available at http://www.taf.org/total2005.htm, retrieved 5/5/06.

14. Morris, L., *Assistant Inspector General for Legal Affairs, OIG, before the house committee on commerce, subcommittee on oversight and investigations, regarding Medicare and third-party billing companies.* April 6, 2000. Available at http://www.hhs.gov/oig/testimony/00406fin.htm and http://www.aaem.org/openbooks/morris.shtml, retrieved 4/23/06.

15. Department of Health and Human Services and the Department of Justice Healthcare Fraud and Abuse Control Program Annual Report For FY 2004, September 2005. Available at http://oig.hhs.gov/publications/docs/hcfac/hcfacreport2004.htm, 12 of 26, retrieved 5/3/06.

16. Jackson, L. M., *Efforts to Combat Healthcare Fraud: A Study of NYSE Listed Healthcare Service Companies* (The paper was completed under the supervision of Dr. Mary Ellen Oliverio, Professor of Accounting, Lubin School of Business, Pace University), 1999.

17. Mental Health John Little. Health Fraud News. Available at http://www.healthfraudnews.org/?cat=120 , retrieved 4/23/06.

18. USDOJ: Deputy Attorney General: Publications and Documents—Healthcare Fraud Report Fiscal Year 1997. Available at http://www.usdoj.gov/dag/pubdoc/health97.htm, 20 of 26, retrieved 5/2/06.

19. Social Security Act 42 CFR 483.25 Quality of Care.

20. See note 18 at 26 of 26.

21. "Nurse's Aide Admits to Stealing Narcotic Patches from Dying Patients at Monroe County Nursing Home." New

York State Office of Attorney General News. Available at http://www.oag.state.ny.us/press/2000/jul/jul14a_00.html, 1 of 2, retrieved 5/3/06.

22. See note 15 at 15 of 26.

23. Maryland Attorney General—News Release: Registered Nurse Pleads Guilty to Felony Medicaid Fraud Charge. March 15, 2006. Available at http://www.oag.state.md.us/Press/2006/031506.htm, retrieved 4/23/06.

24. Registered nurse sentenced in Long Island home care scam. Available at http://www.oag.state.ny.us/press/2006/feb/feb02a_06.html, 4/2/06, press release, retrieved 4/23/06.

25. Online NewsHour, "Correct Care? Are some of the providers fudging the rules?" Elizabeth Brackett reports on federal investigations into Hospice Fraud—June 19, 1997, transcript: ONLINE FOCUS. Available at http://www.pbs.org/newshour/bb/health/june97/hospice_6-19.html, retrieved 4/23/06.

26. Gesensway, D., "Managed care vs. Medicare fraud and abuse laws," *ACP Observer* (May 1996). Available at http://www.acponline.org/journals/news/may96/fraud.htm, retrieved 4/23/06.

27. *Id.*

28. McDonnell, Robert F., Virginia Medicaid Fraud Control Unit (MFCU). Available at http://www.oag.state.va.us/Protecting/mfcu/mfcu.htm, retrieved 4/23/06.

29. See note 18.

30. About the Healthcare Fraud Unit—Fraud Unit, Federal Bureau of Investigation Oct 25, 2004. Available at http://fbi.gov/hq/cid/fc/hcf/about/hcf_about.htm, retrieved 4/23/06.

31. See note 15 at 6 of 26.

32. The Department of Health and Human Services and The Department of Justice Healthcare Fraud and Abuse Control Program Annual Report For Fiscal Year 1999, January 2000. Available at http://www.usdoj.gov/dag/pubdoc/hipaa99ar21.htm, retrieved 5/3/06.

33. Taxpayers Against Fraud Education Fund. The False Claims Act Legal Center. Available at http://www.taf.org, retrieved 4/23/06.

34. See note 15 at 5 of 26.

35. *Id.* at 6 of 26.

36. USDOJ: Deputy Attorney General: Publications and Documents—Healthcare Fraud Report Fiscal Year 1998. Available at http://www.usdoj.gov/dag/pubdoc/health98.htm 12 of 20, retrieved 5/3/06.

37. U.S. Department of Justice Federal Bureau of Investigations Financial Crimes Section Criminal Investigative Division Financial Crimes Report to the Public 2005. Available at http://www.fbi.gov/publications/financial/fes_report052005/fcs_report, retrieved 5/3/06.

38. Taxpayers Against Fraud Education Fund. The False Claims Act Legal Center, Redding Hospital Reaches Global Settlement on Heart Surgery Frauds. August 7, 2003. Available at http://www.taf.org, retrieved 5/3/06.

39. De la Cruz, B., "Doctor gets 15 years in fraud Cancer patients got diluted doses." *The Tennesseean Newspaper* (4/25/06). Available at http://www.tennessean.com/apps/pbcs.dll/article?AID=/20060425/, retrieved 4/27/06.

40. Redding Hospital Reaches Global Settlement on Heart Surgery Frauds. Taxpayers Against Fraud Education Fund, The False Claims Act Legal Center. Available at http://www.taf.org, retrieved 5/3/06.

41. Kaiser Daily Health Policy Report (11/1/02). *Los Angeles Times* (8/7/03), retrieved 4/23/06.

42. "Historic settlement nets United States $1.7 billion," *Andrews Online* (9/5/03), retrieved 4/23/06.

43. "Official blows the whistle on provider." *Hospital compliance wire* (7/22/03). Available at http://www.eliresearch.com/specialty/hospital_liability_litigation.html, retrieved 4/23/06.

44. See note 15 at 11 of 26.

45. Buppert, Carolyn, "Nurse Practitioner: Avoiding Medicare Fraud, part 1," *LookSmart*, January 2001. 1 of 4. Available at http://www.findarticles.com/p/articles/mi_qa3958/is_200101/ai_n89, retrieved 4/23/06.

46. *Id.* at 2 of 4.

47. Bierstein, K., "Ophthalmologist Convicted of Fraudulent Billing, Sentenced to Prison Time," American Society of Anesthesiologists, August 1996 Newsletter Article. Available at http://www.asahq.org/Newsletters/1996/08_96/practice.htm1, 2 of 4, retrieved 4/23/06.

48. See note 15 at 3 of 26.

49. Social Security Act, 42 USC sec. 1320-7b (a) 3.

50. False Claims Act, 31 U.S.C.§ 3729(a)(1)–(3). 31 U.S.C.§ 3729(a)(4)–(7).

51. "San Diego Hospital to Pay U.S. $6.2 Million to Settle False Claims Allegations," Press release from the U.S. Department of Justice, Thursday March 6, 2003. Available at http://www.usdoj.gov, retrieved 5/29/06.

52. "Spotlight on nurses 2001 Legislation Helps Nurses 'Blow the Whistle' on Patient Neglect and Abuse," *NurseZone*. Available at http://www.nursezone.com/include/PrintArticle.asp?articleid=5892, 1 of 3, retrieved 5/29/06.

53. Slozman, B. J., *U.S. Attorney/Western District of Missouri. Healthcare Fraud Unit.* Available at http://www.usdoj.gov/usao/mow/units/health.html, retrieved 5/3/06.

Additional Reading

Alabama PSC task order: summary of PSC task order scope of work. Centers for Medicare & Medicaid Services. Available at www.cms.hhs.gov/providers/psc/Alabama.asp.

Barewell, B., "Lorain nurse convicted of Medicaid fraud," *Morning Journal*. Available at www.morningjournal.com.

CERT documentation request letters. Centers for Medicare & Medicaid Services. Available at www.cms.hhs.gov/providers/psc/CERTletters.asp.

Clinic owner and nurse sentenced. Health Fraud News. May 19, 2005. Available at http://www.healthfraudnews.org.

CMS DAVE website homepage. Centers for Medicare & Medicaid Services. Available at www.cms.hhs.gov/providers/psc/DAVE/Homepage.ASP.

CMS Manual System: Pub. 100-04 Medicare claims processing. Transmittal 209. Available at http://www.gamedicare.com/provider/NewCMSTransmits/CR%203333%20SNF%20.

Coalition against insurance fraud. Available at http://www.insurancefraud.org.

Comprehensive error rate testing (CERT) program. Centers for Medicare & Medicaid Services. Available at www.cms.hhs.gov/providers/psc/CERT.asp.

CPT process—how a code becomes a code. American Medical Association. Available at www.ama-assn.org/ama/pub/category/print/3882.html.

Data assessment and verification project. Centers for Medicare & Medicaid Services. Available at http://www.cms.hhs.gov/providers/psc/DAVE/background.asp.

Dave beta test summary. Centers for Medicare & Medicaid services. Available at www.cms.hhs.gov/providers/psc/DAVE/beta.asp.

Dolan, M., "Doctor accused of insurance fraud," *Baltimore Sun* (November 22, 2005). Available at www.baltimoresun.com/news/health/bal-md.doctor22nov22,1,136951.story?coll=bal-health-headli.

Federal fraud enforcement—physician compliance. American Medical Association. Available at www.ama-assn.org/ama/pub/category/4598.html.

Felony warrant issued in case investigated by MFCU. Health Fraud News. February 17, 2005. Available at http://www.healthfraudnews.org.

Fundamentals of reimbursement: what every graduating resident should know before starting practice. ACEP Reimbursement Committee.

Gainsharing arrangements. American Medical Association. Available at http://www.ama-assn.org/ama/pub/category/print/15238.html.

Healthcare fraud and abuse. American Medical Association. Available at http://www.ama-assn.org/ama/pub/category/4598.html.

Hewitt, A. S., "Attorney arrested in connection with large auto insurance fraud ring," Available at www.insurancefraud.com

Homecare nurse charged with fraud. *Health Fraud News* July 2, 2005. Available at http://www.healthfraudnews.org.

"Home health agency accused of 10,000 hours of fraudulent billing," *Health Fraud News* February 11, 2005. Available at http://www.healthfraudnews.org.

Illinois/Indiana/Kentucky PSC Task Order: Summary of PSC task order scope of work. Centers for Medicare & Medicaid services. Available at www.cms.hhs.gov/providers/psc/IllinoisIndianaKentucky.asp.

"Imposter LPN pleads guilty," *Health Fraud News* July 11, 2005. Available at http://www.healthfraudnews.org.

"Joint federal-Oregon investigations leads to criminal charges and $2.4m in restitution and fines," *Health Fraud News* March 2, 2005. Available at http://www. healthfraudnews.org.

Legislative news. *Insurance Fraud Weekly ePort.* November 18, 2005. Available at http://www.insurancefraud. org/legnews.htm.

Long term care hospital study bed sore patient billing investigation PSC task order. Centers for Medicare & Medicaid services. Available at www.cms.hhs.gov/providers/psc/LTC.asp.

"LPN convicted of grand larceny," *Health Fraud News* May 25, 2005. Available at www.healthfraudnews.org.

"LPN testifies concerning survey deceptions," *Health Fraud News* August 2, 2005. Available at http://www.healthfraudnews.org.

The Medicare integrity program—program safeguard contractors (PSCs). Centers for Medicare & Medicaid Services. Available at http://www.cms.hhs.gov/PROVIDERS/PSC/PSCWEBP2.ASP.

Medicare Learning Network (Medlearn) consolidated billing for skilled nursing facility (SNF). Centers for Medicare & Medicaid Services. Available at www.cms.hhs. gov/medlearn/snfcode.asp.

Meyer, J. A., Fighting Medicare fraud: more bang for the federal buck. Prepared for taxpayers against fraud education fund, April 22. Available at http://www.taf.org/meyerreport.htm.

"Mother and daughter plead guilty," *Health Fraud News* July 27, 2005. Available at http://www.healthfraudnews.org.

New York State Assembly Bill Summary A08107. November 25, 2005. Available at http://www.assembly.state. ny.us/leg/?bn=A08107.

Non-physician practitioner questions and answers. Medlearn Matters: Information for Medicare providers. Medlearn Matters Number: SE0418.

"Nurse and home health company indicted," *Health Fraud News* March 19, 2005. Available at http://www.healthfraudnews.org.

"Nurse indicted for alleged sexual abuse," *Health Fraud News* (August 13, 2005). Available at http://www. healthfraudnews.org.

"Nurse indicted for inflating hours," *Health Fraud News* April 20, 2005. Available at http://www.healthfraudnews.org.

"Nurse jailed for care not provided," *Health Fraud News* June 23, 2005. Available at http://www.healthfraudnews.org.

"Nurse pleads guilty in human growth hormone scheme," *Health Fraud News* March 26, 2005. Available at http://www.healthfraudnews.org.

"Nurse testifies of staffing records falsification," *Health Fraud News* July 26, 2005. Available at http://www. healthfraudnews.org.

"Nurse turns self in to investigators," *Health Fraud News* June 22, 2005. Available at http://www.healthfraudnews.org.

Nursing homes overview. Adventis. Available at http:// www.longtermcarelink.net/reference/ref_number_or_ nh_beds.htm.

Office of Inspector General Work Plan. Department of health & human services. Fiscal year 2006.

PSCs by state. Centers for Medicare & Medicaid Services. Available at www.cms.hhs.gov/PROVIDERS/PSC/ map.asp.

PSC task orders. Centers for Medicare & Medicaid Services. Available at http://www.cms.hhs.gov/PROVIDERS/PSC/PSC%20Task%20Orders.asp.

"RN impostor sentenced," *Health Fraud News* April 19, 2005. Available at http://www.healthfraudnews.org.

Statistics. The False Claims Act Legal Center. Available at http://www.taf.org/statistics.htm.

Tackett, Eric, "Understanding CPT codes," *SIU Awareness* Winter 2005.

Two nursing home caretakers plead guilty, surrender licenses. Health Fraud News. April 16, 2005. Available at http://www.healthfraudnews.org.

Using long-term care MDS data: patient days and case mix. Health services research and evaluation American healthcare association. Available at www.ahca.org.

Chapter 28

Medication Errors

Patricia W. Iyer, MSN, RN, LNCC, James O'Donnell, PharmD, FCP, ABCP, and David Benjamin, PhD, FCP, FCLM

Synopsis
28.1 Introduction
28.2 Detection of Errors
    A. Concealment of Errors
    B. Observation
    C. Subtherapeutic Levels or Exaggerated Levels of Medications
    D. Antidotes
    E. Statements in the Progress Notes/Discharge Summary
28.3 Investigating the Claim
    A. Establishing the Details Regarding the Error
        1. What medication was involved?
        2. What type of error was made?
        3. What caused the error?
    B. Screening the Client
    C. Use an Intake Sheet
    D. Obtaining Medical Records
    E. Mitigation of Damages
    F. Physician Factors that Affect Medication Error Cases
    G. Attorney Factors that Affect Medication Error Cases
    H. Identifying the Defenses
28.4 Factors that Contribute to Errors
    A. System Factors
        1. Research and education
        2. Nursing administration
        3. Staffing issues
        4. Shift change
        5. Medication errors across a continuum
        6. Computer- and technology-related errors
        7. Medication reconciliation
    B. Individual Factors
        1. Psychological aspects of human error: mistakes and slips
        2. Inexperience, ignorance (knowledge deficit), inattention
        3. Violations of policies, procedures, or protocols
        4. Failure to educate patient on importance of home monitoring
28.5 Ordering Stage Errors
    A. The Order-Entry Process
    B. Hazards Associated with the Ordering Stage
        1. Handwriting, stray marks and letters
        2. Unapproved abbreviations
        3. Telephone and verbal orders
        4. Not using critical thinking
28.6 Transcription Stage Errors
28.7 Dispensing Stage Errors
    A. Wrong Drug
    B. Wrong Drug Strength
    C. Wrong Directions

    D. Lack of Drug Review
28.8 Administration Stage Errors
    A. The Five Rights
        1. Right drug
        2. Right patient
        3. Right dose
        4. Right route
        5. Right time
    B. Examples of When the Five Rights Go Wrong
        1. Wrong drug
        2. Wrong patient
        3. Wrong dose
        4. Wrong route
        5. Wrong time
    C. Additional Types of Medication Errors
        1. Omitted dose
        2. Duplicate dose
        3. Unordered drug error
28.9 High-Risk Medications
    A. Insulin
    B. Opiates
    C. PCA (Patient Controlled Analgesia)
    D. Coumadin and Heparin
    E. Cancer Drugs
    F. Methotrexate
28.10 High-Risk Populations
    A. Pediatrics
    B. Elderly
    C. Allergic versus Intolerant
    D. Critically Ill Patient
    E. Patients Assigned to Student Nurses
28.11 Litigation of the Medication Error Claim
    A. Useful Discovery Items
    B. Types of Experts Needed
    C. When Early Settlement is Advised
28.12 Summary
Endnotes

28.1 Introduction

Medication errors affect patients in all aspects of health care. One out of five drugs administered in hospitals and skilled nursing facilities is in error and 34 percent of preventable adverse drug events can be traced back to the administration process.[1,2] Perhaps the most difficult aspect of discussing this topic is that no one seems to know the true scope of the problem. Vast differences are seen depending on the methodologies used to measure rates. One group of researchers compared three methods: process observation, chart review, and incident reporting and found 11.7 percent dosing errors by the observer method compared with 0.7 percent error rate from chart review and less than 0.2 percent rate (only one case) using incident reports. Further, they observed a fairly high rate of false negatives and false positives as compared to an expert research pharmacist. This same group estimates one in five doses results in an error.[3]

The true numbers of medication errors are unknown, either because of lack of awareness that an error has occurred, dismissal of the error as unimportant to report because the patient was not harmed, or fear of reporting an error because of possible reprisals.

Drug mishaps are nothing new. In fact, studies dating back several years[4] show that about 2 percent of hospital patients experience preventable adverse drug events, although the majority are not fatal. Medication error has been cited as the cause of death for one out of every 131 outpatient deaths and one in 854 inpatient deaths. After being read a common definition of a medical error, about one in three people (34 percent) say they, or a family member, have experienced one at some point in their life. This includes 21 percent of all Americans who say that a medical error caused "serious health consequences," such as death (8 percent), long-term disability (11 percent), or severe pain (16 percent).[5]

Approximately 50 percent of people with chronic conditions experience a medical error in either their own care or that of a family member. This is far more than those without a chronic illness (30 percent).[6] Studies from Canada, New Zealand, Denmark, Australia, and the United Kingdom show that approximately 10 percent of all patients in acute care settings experience significant injury from medical care.[7] A Danish study performed through direct observation, unannounced control visits, and chart reviews detected 1,065 errors in 2,467 opportunities for errors, or 43 percent. The frequency of medication errors was:

1. Ordering: 39 percent
2. Transcribing: 56 percent
3. Dispensing: 4 percent
4. Administering: 41 percent
5. Discharge summaries: 76 percent[8]

MEDMARX, a voluntary, Internet-accessible system for reporting medication errors, was being used by more than 775 hospitals and healthcare systems as of 2003. In the five-year period of 1999-2003, a total of 580,759 errors were reported, although 98 percent did not result in patient harm.[9]

The Institute of Medicine estimated that medication errors injure 1.5 million people and cost billions of dollars annually.[10] Healthcare facilities supplement data about voluntarily reported errors by computer detection of errors, chart reviews, observational studies, and other ways to generate a more accurate picture of the kinds of errors that take place. Computer alerts note when a medication error may have occurred by identifying orders for antidotes used to treat medication errors. Certain significant laboratory results may reveal subtherapeutic or toxic levels of medications.[11]

The Harvard Medical Practice Study, which was based on review of New York patients' medical records, is perhaps the most well-known example of the use of chart review to detect medical errors. Of 30,000 records examined, the investigators found that 1 percent of the patients had experienced errors that caused injury. This study was based on 1980s records and published in the 1990s.[12] It revealed that most (56.8 percent) adverse events that occur to hospitalized patients result in no or minor impairment, with complete recovery in one month. Twenty-two percent of these adverse events were caused by negligence. Another 13.7 percent of the adverse events led to disabilities that lasted more than one month but less than six months. However, 2.6 percent of adverse events resulted in permanent, total disability, with one-third of these caused by negligence. While 13.6 percent of the adverse events resulted in the death of the patient, half of these deaths were caused by negligence.

TIP: The study focused on the negligence of physicians and nurses, and should be read by attorneys who handle malpractice cases.

Although healthcare providers were somewhat aware of the results of the Harvard Medical Practice study, the press remained uninformed. When the study was described in an Institute of Medicine report published in 1999, the public first learned that 44,000–98,000 people die each year as a result of medical errors. The actual numbers are unknown, as the Harvard Practice Study relied on examination of hospital charts. The investigators did not review physician office records, nursing home records, or clinic records, or detect unrecorded errors. HealthGrades announced in July 2004 that as many as 195,000 people could be dying in U.S. hospitals because of easily preventable errors. Their findings were based on three years of Medicare data in all 50 states and Washington, DC.

28.2 Detection of Errors
A. Concealment of Errors
Methods of detecting medication errors reveal widely varying results. Some medication errors are not reported be-

cause they are not noticed by the person who made them. Accurate information regarding errors relies on voluntary reporting of errors by those who make or observe them. A study reported in June 2005 revealed that many nurses, physicians, and pharmacists fear punitive action would be taken by their licensing boards in the wake of a medication error, whether it was a near miss or a fatal error with many system-based causes. Fear of punishment from licensing boards may greatly contribute to underreporting of medication errors. Thirty percent of all respondent nurses felt they would receive a verbal or written reprimand, or be required to undergo education, even if the error never reached the patient. Refer to *ISMP Survey on State Licensing Boards Response to Medical Error* for details of the results at www.ismp. org/s/survey200502R.asp.[13] A 2008 survey of nurses about medication errors included a question, "During my nursing career, I failed to report one or more medication errors because I thought reporting an error might be personally or professionally damaging." Thirty-seven percent of nurses answered "true." This answer may reflect nurses' concerns about working in an environment that punishes nurses and others for making medication errors.[14]

B. Observation

While chart review may detect errors in medication orders, observational studies are considered to be more valid in detecting errors in dispensing or administering medications. Observation was proven to be most effective in detecting errors made when 2,556 doses of medications were administered. Using a combination of incident report review, chart review, and direct observation at 36 hospitals and skilled nursing facilities in Colorado and Georgia, observers detected 300 of 457 pharmacist-confirmed errors. This represented an error rate of 11.7 percent. Only 17 errors were detected by chart review (0.7 percent error rate) and one error was detected by incident report review (0.04 percent error rate). All errors detected involved the same 2,556 doses.[15]

C. Subtherapeutic Levels or Exaggerated Levels of Medications

Drug levels are infrequently tested in hospital and other organized healthcare settings (nursing homes, home health care), with the exception of drugs classified as "narrow therapeutic windows," such as Digoxin, Phenytoin, Gentamicin and other aminoglycosides, and Vancomycin. With these drugs, the drug levels are routinely ordered as part of a therapeutic drug monitoring effort (TDM), usually coordinated by the pharmacist in the institution.

TIP: If a medication error is suspected with one of these medications, the attorney or expert should closely examine the physicians' or pharmacists' notes to determine if blood levels were ordered, if appropriate clinical laboratory testing was ordered, if the frequency and timing of the testing was appropriate, and then examine and interpret what levels were reported. Were the levels subtherapeutic, therapeutic, or toxic?

If a drug overdose is suspected clinically, the physician might order a toxicology level on the blood or other fluids of the patient (or decedent), as well as the contents of any drug administration delivery systems (syringes, syringe pumps, IV bags, and so on) to determine the identity and concentration of any suspected substances. This is particularly important in death investigations. If a suspect drug or medication is unknown to the medical examiner, it is unlikely an analysis for its identity and concentration will be performed, and therefore, it will be missed—if it is early enough in the case investigation, the sample may still be stored at the medical examiner's office or at some off-site toxicology laboratory, which, contrary to most hospital clinical labs, maintains samples for at least six months, or longer if requested.

TIP: Consult with a pharmacologist or toxicologist to determine the potential for identification of toxic substances stored in biological fluids taken during an acute event or postmortem. Many attorneys petition the court to order preservation of any existing biological fluid specimens for future forensic evaluations.

D. Antidotes

Computerized surveillance may also play a role in uncovering certain errors. Medication errors involving narcotics may be detected by searching for Narcan (naloxone) orders for patients (Narcan reverses narcotics overdoses). Several hospital computerized medication order-entry systems have the potential for identifying adverse drug events.[16] Benadryl (diphenhydramine) is another sentinel antidote ordered "stat," the drug of choice for allergic reactions. The order may not say, "patient has a rash," but the order of an antihistamine is the classic first-line response for a drug allergic reaction. The next line of severity includes corticosteroids (Solu Medrol or Hydrocortisone), which mitigate the inflammatory response, and sympathomimetics like Adrenalin (epinephrine) used to stimulate cardiovascular function and overcome pulmonary toxicity. Orders for any of these critical intervention drugs are strong evidence that a drug reaction has occurred, and dictates a very thorough review of the medical records, or later in discovery, interrogatories, or questions to treaters involved in the care of the patient.[17]

E. Statements in the Progress Notes/Discharge Summary

As discussed in Chapter 5, *Medical Errors: Roots of Litigation,* in Volume I, healthcare providers have an ethical and regulatory requirement to disclose errors. Yet this is not always done. The 2008 medication errors study cited above[18] asked respondents to respond to the question, "When I make a mistake, I fully disclose the error to the patient or family member." Twenty-seven percent answered, "always," 49 percent answered "sometimes" and 25 percent answered "never." The authors of the study suggested that the nurses' behavior was affected by the stigma associated with disclosing an error, a lack of disclosure policy or certain organizational constraints. For example, a policy that requires managers to disclose errors impedes self-disclosure.

Discussions or notations of drug reactions are not always recorded in progress notes by attending physicians, and are rarely documented in the discharge summary. Even when the discharge summary or operative notes are made after an adverse event or death, notes about the drug event are frequently absent.

28.3 Investigating the Claim

The first thing to establish is what happened to the patient as a result of the medication error. Table 28.1 identifies different categories of errors, according to the National Coordinating Council for Medication Error Reporting and Prevention. It is unlikely a plaintiff's attorney is willing to assume responsibility for reporting a medication error that could be categorized as A-D. Category E errors may be questionable depending on the amount of time the patient was temporarily affected as a result of the error. Category F errors may not be deemed serious enough to institute a suit. The administration of a medication to which the patient had a known allergy may have resulted in a trip to the emergency department and an overnight admission, but no lasting damages. Category G, H, and I medication errors may result in the patient or family seeking the services of a plaintiff's attorney.

A. Establishing the Details Regarding the Error

The attorney or legal nurse consultant involved in the screening of the case must analyze the client's understanding of what occurred. The following questions should be asked:

1. What medication was involved?
2. What type of error was made?
3. What caused the error?

1. What medication was involved?

High-risk medications include chemotherapeutic drugs, opioids (narcotics), and anticoagulants (blood thinners), hormones, and cardiovascular agents. The medications most frequently involved in Category E-I errors are shown in Table 28.2. Medication information may be obtained by reading the *Physician's Desk Reference*, a nursing drug book produced by one of the major nursing publishers, or by performing an Internet search for the drug literature provided by the manufacturer.

Table 28.1

Error Category	Result of Error
A	Circumstances or events with the capacity to cause error
B	An error occurred by the error did not reach the patient
C	An error occurred that reached the patient but did not cause patient harm
D	An error occurred that reached the patient and required monitoring to confirm that it resulted in no harm to the patient and/or required intervention to preclude harm
E	An error occurred that may have contributed to or resulted in temporary harm to the patient and required intervention
F	An error occurred that may have contributed to or resulted in temporary harm to the patient and required initial or prolonged hospitalization
G	An error occurred that may have contributed to or resulted in permanent patient harm
H	An error occurred that required intervention necessary to sustain life
I	An error occurred that may have contributed to or resulted in the patient's death

Reprinted with permission of USP. Hicks, R., Santell, J, Cousins, D. and Williams, R., MEDMARX 5th Anniversary Data Report: A Chartbook of 2003 Findings and Trends 1999-2003, Rockville, MD: USP Center for the Advancement of Patient Safety, 2004.

Table 28.2
Most commonly reported products involved in medication errors in 2003

Name of medication and action	Number of errors in MEDMARX data from 10 percent of U.S. hospitals	Percentage
Insulin* (controls blood sugar)	362	8.7
Morphine* (pain reliever)	218	5.3
Heparin* (thins blood)	160	3.9
Potassium chloride* (electrolyte necessary for cardiac functioning)	122	2.9
Warfarin/Coumadin* (thins blood)	109	2.6
Fentanyl* (fast acting pain reliever)	108	2.6
Hydromorphone/Dilaudid* (pain reliever)	94	2.3
Vancomycin* (antibiotic)	75	1.8
Furosemide/Lasix (reduces blood pressure by increasing urination)	64	1.5
Meperidine/Demerol* (pain reliever)	55	1.3
Enoxaparin/Lovenox* (thins blood)	53	1.3
Lorazepam/Ativan (sedative)	52	1.3
Ceftriaxone/Rocephin (broad spectrum antibiotic)	44	1.1
Dopamine* (increases blood pressure)	44	1.1
Diltiazem/Cardizem (anti-anginal)	40	1.0

* Denotes high-risk medication.
Reprinted with permission of USP. Hicks, R., Santell, J, Cousins, D. and Williams, R., MEDMARX 5th Anniversary Data Report: A Chartbook of 2003 Findings and Trends 1999-2003, Rockville, MD: USP Center for the Advancement of Patient Safety, 2004.

2. What type of error was made?

The error may have occurred at any of the steps from prescription to administration. The error could have been made by a prescriber (physician, physician's assistant, nurse practitioner), a dispenser (pharmacist or pharmacy technician), or someone who administered the medication (physician, nurse, medical assistant, or medication aide).

TIP: According to the data analyzed and reported by MEDMARX, the four most common types of errors were omission, improper dose/quantity, prescribing error and unauthorized drug given to the patient.[19]

---

3. What caused the error?

It may be unclear at the screening stage what caused the error. Sometimes the patient or family was given an explanation of the cause. The five most common causes of medication errors are performance deficits, not following procedures or protocols, inaccurate or omitted transcription of information, incorrect computer entry, and documentation errors. Healthcare providers cited the top five contributing

factors to errors as distractions, workload increases, inexperienced staff, insufficient staffing, and shift change.[20] Causes of the errors are explored as discovery proceeds. Refer to Section 28.5 for more information on causes of errors.

B. Screening the Client

Make note of the initial impression of the potential client. Is the client able to answer questions clearly? Does the client seem to be exaggerating? Is he believable? Does the information provided sound reliable, or does the story seem too fantastic to be true? Carefully observe the nonverbal body language of the client. Read the narrative of the patient. Does it have a ring of truth? The wilder the narrative, the less likely there is a case. Is the person simply angry over the way he was treated? Attorneys generally avoid a client with an extensive criminal record or a prisoner who complains about the quality of medical care. These folks are notoriously poor witnesses. If a patient is admitted to a facility who is heavily intoxicated or in a drug-induced condition and then suffers from a medication error, he typically makes an unsympathetic plaintiff.

C. Use an Intake Sheet

The law firm intake or client interview sheet is an important form. Not only does it give the attorney vital, personal information on the client in the case, but a properly prepared intake sheet will allow the attorney to secure information for discovery requests. Also, intake questions and questionnaires may be the single best source to jog the client's memory so that facts which may otherwise be forgotten are revealed.

D. Obtaining Medical Records

In an effort to avoid alerting the medical records department or risk manager to a potential suit, many plaintiff's attorneys request that the client obtain a copy of the medical record to screen a potential nursing malpractice case. Some attorneys ask a physician to obtain the record on behalf of the client, for the same reason. Medical records departments often notify their risk manager when a record request comes from a plaintiff's attorney's office. The healthcare professionals involved in the care of the patient may be informed of this request and, therefore, may take this opportunity to review the medical record. Refer to Chapter 7, *Nursing Documentation*, in Volume I, for more information.

Some attorneys prefer to obtain the records rather than ask the client to do so to ensure the records needed to properly evaluate the case are obtained. It is essential to have the client sign medical authorizations to send out HIPAA-compliant requests for copies of any medical reports and information needed to fully evaluate the case. Many attorneys request a second copy of the medical record before the case goes to trial. This enables the attorney to detect changes made in the medical record after the initiation of a lawsuit. Although this type of tampering with the record is rare, it can have a profound impact on a malpractice case.

The basic information needed to obtain medical records includes:

1. Name of patient upon entry to the facility
2. Date of birth
3. Social Security number
4. Dates of treatment or admission
5. Inpatient treatment versus outpatient treatment in the ER, clinic, and so on
6. Physician's name and address[21]

TIP: A full certified copy of the medical record is needed to review a medication error case. Although a record is sent to the attorney or insurance carrier with the letter from the medical records department stating that it is a certified copy, this does not mean that both sides of

every page have been properly copied. It is not unusual for a medical records clerk or an employee of a copying service to fail to turn over a page, or omit some of the pages of a multi-page flow sheet.

The attorney and paralegal should expect that an expert witness or a legal nurse consultant reviewing the medical records will draw these omissions to the attention of the attorney. A nurse is in a better position to spot the omissions than an attorney or a paralegal because the nurse understands how the typical record is maintained and organized. Once the medical records are obtained, further investigation of the claim proceeds. The factors below are important to both the plaintiff and defense attorney.

E. Mitigation of Damages

The value of a claim is always affected by the question of damages.

1. How was the plaintiff's health prior to the medication error?
2. Did the plaintiff have any chronic conditions?
3. Was the plaintiff employed before the medication error?
4. Is there any evidence the plaintiff made disability claims, or received work excuses or releases prior to or at the time of the medication error?
5. Has the plaintiff had any diagnostic testing prior to the medication error that documents preexisting injuries?
6. What medications was the plaintiff taking before the medication error?
7. Did the plaintiff report involvement in other medication errors or injuries either before or after the current medication error?
8. Did the plaintiff fail to seek follow-up medical care?
9. Are there any potentially damaging statements in the medical records about the plaintiff?
10. Are there inconsistencies in the medical records?
11. What comments about how the medication error occurred were recorded in the medical records?
12. Are there discrepancies about how the medication error happened?
13. Is there evidence the patient withheld information from the treating doctor?
14. Has the patient refused to have certain diagnostic tests performed? What is the explanation for the refusal?
15. Was the plaintiff compliant with medical treatment?

16. Did the plaintiff take the medications as prescribed?
17. Did the patient keep the appointments?

F. Physician Factors that Affect Medication Error Cases

1. Does the patient's treating doctor support the medical diagnosis with a description of the patient's symptoms?
2. Are the facts in the history correct?
3. How often did the doctor see the patient after the injury?

G. Attorney Factors that Affect Medication Error Cases

1. Who did the plaintiff contact first after the medication error? Was it the plaintiff's attorney or a physician?
2. Did the plaintiff contact the plaintiff's attorney before contacting a doctor after the medication error?
3. Do the doctor's records state the patient was referred by the plaintiff's attorney?
4. Do the doctor's medical records contain any references to phone calls with the plaintiff's attorney?
5. Do the doctor's records contain any implications that the plaintiff's attorney is directing the patient's care?
6. Do the doctor's records contain any implications that the plaintiff's attorney has requested a revision of a report to favor the plaintiff?
7. Does the plaintiff's attorney's name appear on the medical billing?

H. Identifying the Defenses

The most obvious way to defend a medication error case is to dispute damages. A Category A-F error that does not result in permanent injury has limited or no damages, permitting the defense attorney to use the "so what?" defense. Another commonly used defense is to point to the known risks associated with taking a medication. A side effect may be the necessary price the patient has to pay for taking the medication, but side effects signal a need to discontinue the medication. Decreased hearing as a side effect of certain antibiotics signifies a need to stop the medication. Questions then arise concerning how quickly the complication or adverse reaction was recognized. Was it immediate or did the doctor or nurse practitioner miss the diagnosis?

Medication errors may occur when a critically ill patient is under the care of healthcare providers. Two of the high-risk medications, Dopamine and Ativan, are typically used in the critical care unit. A complicated case involving a patient with a long list of underlying problems permits the defense to point out that the causation of death is in question. Invariably, the alleged malpractice becomes inexplicably tied to the underlying disease processes from which the patient suffers. The seriousness of the underlying medical problem often makes proving causation more difficult.

Novel or sophisticated medical issues intertwined with a medication error may make a case defensible. If the alleged malpractice involves an emerging area of medicine, plaintiff's attorneys may be less inclined to pursue the case. It will make obtaining competent experts much more difficult since there probably are only a select few individuals competent to testify on the case. The jury may be sympathetic towards medical pioneers trying new techniques.

28.4 Factors that Contribute to Errors

From a nursing systems perspective, there are both system and individual factors that contribute to errors.

A. System Factors

The medication administration system is a complex one with multiple opportunities for errors. Reduction of medication errors is dependent on developing a culture of safety. As discussed in Chapter 5, *Medical Errors: Roots of Litigation*, in Volume I, a fatal medication error at Johns Hopkins University Medical Center involving an 18-month-old girl resulted in huge changes to the patient safety program. The original "Comprehensive Unit Based Safety Program (CUSP)" consisted of eight steps.

1. Assessment of the culture of safety
2. Education in the science of safety
3. Staff identification of safety concerns
4. Senior executives adopting a unit
5. Improvements implemented from safety concerns
6. Efforts documented and analyzed
7. Results shared
8. Culture reassessment[22]

1. Research and education

As discussed in Chapter 6, *The Foundations of Nursing Practice*, in Volume I, research studies that advance nursing's knowledge of evidence-based best practices are not easily or quickly transferred to the clinical setting. It can take years for recommendations based on solid research to be integrated into nursing educational programs and memorialized in current clinical policies and procedures. Faculty at nursing schools may not understand or have enough time to teach students about new and evolving technologies and their impact on medication administration. Busy medical surgical units in hospitals, where students typically spend a significant amount of their clinical time, are complex environments in which to teach medication administration.

2. Nursing administration

Although The Joint Commission stresses the need for the same quality of care to be delivered throughout an organization, there is often lack of standardization of policies. For example, IV conscious sedation may be delivered in the operating room, emergency department, or endoscopy area, among other sites. The degree of monitoring and assessment for complications should be identical wherever this procedure is performed. If policies for this procedure were developed by anesthesiologists without nursing input or without regard to best practices, potential for error may occur.

Nursing administration may also be implicated in setting up an environment for errors by:

1.   not providing sufficient nursing staff,
2.   not acknowledging the importance of adequate safeguards to provide patient safety,
3.   not remaining current in best practices,
4.   not involving bedside nurses in decision making about implementing new technologies,
5.   not changing practices that drain nursing time away from the bedside,
6.   not planning how to address patient safety when technology fails to work,
7.   not helping other healthcare departments communicate with nursing about patient safety issues, and
8.   not detecting methods nurses are using to work around or sabotage safeguards.

Although individuals perform work and provide services, it is best to think of them as part of a system, and a system is more than the sum of its parts. There are a multitude of interactions and interrelationships in the system involved in providing medications to patients. Lucien Leape, M.D., one of the authors of the Harvard Practice Study, has estimated that up to 20 steps are involved with the prescribing, transcribing, dispensing, and administrating process in a paper-based (non-computerized) hospital setting. With so many interim steps to traverse, it is no wonder errors occur. Contrast that scenario to one in which a physician writes a prescription for a patient in an outpatient setting. The patient takes the prescription to the pharmacy and the pharmacist fills it. Simplicity supports safety. The fewer steps involved in the process, the lower the likelihood for error.[23] The challenge is to examine which steps are necessary, eliminate unnecessary and error-prone steps if possible, and build quality assurance and safety nets to detect mistakes before they become medication errors.

3. Staffing issues

Staffing issues never seem to be solved. It is clear that if resources, professional staff (pharmacists and nurses), and support staff (technicians, nursing assistants or nursing aids) are unavailable, the existing staff will be stretched beyond limits, which creates a dangerous situation. Stopgap measures of voluntary or mandatory overtime, with staff routinely working double shifts, solve the immediate staffing issue, but create an increased error-prone environment by introducing fatigue and sleep-deprivation issues.

Another staffing issue that can increase the risk of errors is the use of temporary, or "agency," employees. Nurses without orientation to or experience in the system are less invested and cannot be expected to get up to speed in a setting that normally provides weeks to months for new employee orientation. This staffing issue is confounded by institutions that rely heavily on temporary employees—who are at an increased risk of errors—rather than invest in regular employees. The agency employee will probably cost more in wages and agency fees than a regular employee, but there are no long-term employee costs or benefit costs, as with a regular employee. This is not unique to health care. It is prevalent throughout many industries, for the same reasons.

4. Shift change

"It fell through the cracks" is a common explanation for an omission. For example, the order for heparin for the newly admitted stroke patient was received at 2:30 P.M. The order did not have the patient's weight, which is required for calculating the dose of heparin based on an agreed-upon protocol. The day pharmacist called the day nurse, who agreed to get the weight and call back the pharmacist. The day nurse did not get the weight and went home at 3:30 P.M. The day pharmacist did not hear from the nurse, left the order in the pending orders box, and went home at 4 P.M. Neither the nurses nor the pharmacist on subsequent shifts raised questions about the lack of clarification and the absence of a heparin dose for the patient. The order was discovered "overlooked" 16 hours after it was written; a weight was obtained; the doses prepared; and the first dose was administered to the patient 28 hours after the order was written. His condition severely deteriorated, and he suffered an acute massive stroke. In this case, the order "fell through the cracks," which is not uncommon at shift changes. The patient did not recover from the stroke—he died. The family sued, claiming the nurses and pharmacists departed from the standard of care by not providing timely medication subsequent to the physician's orders. While there were experts who provided opinions that the delay in administration of the heparin did not contribute to the stroke, the delayed order subjected the hospital and its employees to litigation (unpublished case).

TIP: The facility should have a clear communication method for resolution of orders, and make sure any unresolved matters at shift change are endorsed to the next shift, which can resolve it and provide timely services.

Staff on a nursing unit of a major teaching hospital recognized that handoffs and medication administration occurred at change of shift, resulting in nurses who felt harried. To avoid the bottleneck that occurred at that time, the nurses changed the morning medication administration time from 8 A.M. to 10 A.M. This increased the amount of time nurses had for direct patient care.[24]

5. Medication errors across a continuum

Failure to monitor in the outpatient setting has a different appearance. A typical scenario may look like this:

A patient is transferred to a nursing home. The nurse filling out the list of medications the patient was receiving in the hospital makes transcription errors, omitting two medications and recording an incorrect dose of a third medication. The nurse in the nursing home accepted this list as accurate and transcribed it onto the physician order sheet. The physician in the nursing home signed off on the orders, assuming they were accurate. This is an all-too-common situation. To avoid medication errors of this type, TJC has listed among its 2006 National Patient Safety Goals the need to "Reconcile Medication Across a Continuum of Care." This means that a TJC-accredited facility must ensure that upon admission and upon discharge that the changes in a patient's medication regimen are "reconciled" (listed) and that changes in medications and dosages are correctly recorded and implemented.

Some hospitals utilize nurses or pharmacists to call patients after discharge to verify that new prescriptions have been filled and that the patient is taking his/her medications according to the most recent orders of the prescribing physician. The Visiting Nurse Association (VNA) and other home health nursing agencies can also play a valuable role in helping to ensure that newly prescribed medications are taken as directed.[25]

6. Computer- and technology-related errors

Table 28.3 shows the results of studies conducted by the Agency for Healthcare Research and Quality (AHRQ) to determine at what stage in the Medication Use Process (MUP) errors occurred. Up to 68 percent of errors occurred during the prescribing/ordering phase. Twenty-five to 38 percent of errors occurred during administration, followed by transcription errors and pharmacy dispensing errors.[26,27]

TIP: Avoiding medication errors requires communication of the right drug, right dose, right route, and right frequency of administration from one healthcare professional to another.

Illegible medication orders, look-alike drug names, and confusion of brand and generic names lead to medication errors.[28] When an error is made in the prescribing/ordering phase of the process, it can permeate the MUP and result in an adverse experience for the patient. Much attention has been given to instituting new practices for prescribing, such as Computerized Physician Order-Entry (CPOE), because of the prevalence of errors during the prescribing/ordering phase of the MUP. One study showed that in the hospital setting, CPOE decreased serious medication errors by 55 percent and potential Adverse Drug Events (ADEs) by 84 percent.[29]

Table 28.3
**Occurrence of Medication Errors
in Studies of Hospitalized Patients**

Physician ordering	39-49 percent
Nursing administration	26-38 percent
Transcription	11-12 percent
Pharmacy dispensing	11-14 percent

Modified from: Bates, D. W., D. L. Boyle, and N. Laird, et al., "Incidence of Adverse Drug Events and Potential Adverse Drug Events," *JAMA* 274, no. 1 (1995): 29–34.
Leape, L. L., D. W. Bates, and D. J. Cullen, et al., "Systems Analysis of Adverse Drug Events," *JAMA* 274, no. 1 (1995): 35–43.

Computerized systems are defined as computer programs that maintain patient drug profiles and generate prescription-fill or dispensing lists. They may also interface with laboratory and other hospital departments. Computerization assists in the initial monitoring of a patient's drug therapy and decreases the chance of drug interactions. Most systems used today have built-in programs to detect potential drug interactions. Computerization decreases the likelihood of drug sensitivities (allergies) and therapeutic duplications of medications going unnoticed, and warns of high or low dose alerts. Some systems include drug/disease contraindications. These enhancements improve medication safety and documentation. Technological advances are heralded as safety benefits for patients and potential cost and resource savers for institutions. However, the nurse should be aware that with any system, errors can creep in. Factors associated with medication errors, such as inexperience, distractions, and lack of knowledge, apply to computer and other technology-related errors.

CPOE eliminates transcription and interpretation of the handwriting of the prescriber, but other types of error can be introduced.

> For example, a hospital that printed computer-generated medication administration records (MAR) for distribution to patient care units discovered a flaw the hard way. NovoLog Mix 70/30 (insulin aspart protamine, insulin aspart), 10 units by subcutaneous injection before breakfast, was prescribed for a patient with diabetes. The hospital used insulin pens to improve the safety and efficacy of insulin delivery, so the order was entered into the pharmacy computer as "insulin aspart prot: insulin aspart (NovoLog flex pen 70/30) 10 unit SUBCUT ACBRKFST." Because the computerized MAR allowed a limited number of characters per field, this order was truncated and appeared as "NovoLog FlexPen 70." After the patient received 70 units of NovoLog and became hypoglycemic, the error was noticed two days later when a more experienced nurse questioned the high dosage. The hospital has since changed its MAR profile for NovoLog Mix 70/30 FlexPen.[30]

Another such incident affected a rehabilitation institute patient who was being treated for HIV. The resident physician intended to select azidothymidine (an antiviral used early in the AIDS epidemic), but somehow selected azathioprine (the drug listed just above azidothymidine on the computer screen). Azathioprine is an immunosuppressant. When the order was entered into the computer, it was noted by the pharmacist who provided daily doses. The computer created a MAR (medication administration record) used to chart the administration of the incorrect azathioprine (an immunosuppressant in an immunosuppressed patient). The MAR was also available to the patient's physicians. The patient received the wrong drug for seven days; he did not receive his azidothymidine for that period as well. On discovery of the error, HIV specialists assessed the effect of the wrong drug and not receiving the correct drug. A lawsuit was filed against the hospital. There was no question of liability; it was admitted. The only question was of causation. Did the consequences of the error harm the patient? The hospital settled the case early in the litigation. This is called the parallax error. All pharmacists and nurses are taught that when pouring a liquid in a measuring container, the measurement read will differ according to the angle of view. This is called parallax. In this case, the resident physician saw the aziothymidine, but selected the line above it.

Further system failures followed. The pharmacist should have realized that an HIV patient, already immunosuppressed, should not receive an immunosuppressant. The pharmacist should be assessing the reason for prescribing. The nurses should be making similar assessments. The physician resident should have noticed the error when he viewed the MAR on daily rounds.

Many facilities use computerized medication carts (Pyxis and others) to reduce medication errors and improve efficiency. In these systems, the patient's medication record is stored on a computer built into the medication cart. The nurse presses a button to select the medication required for the patient. The computer identifies the exact bin number and drawer for each medication. The drawer containing the medication opens so the nurse can remove the dose, similar to a vending machine. The system is designed to reduce the chance the nurse will administer the wrong medication. Experts in safe medication practices[31] point out potential sources of error with this system:

1. A nurse can retrieve a drug from an automated medication cart before a pharmacist screens the order for allergies or double-checks the dose.
2. Some computerized medication carts are poorly designed, allowing a drug to easily drop into the wrong slot. Some medication carts are stocked haphazardly. For example, a baby received an adult concentration of Digoxin (which slows the heart rate) because the adult and pediatric strengths of the medication were side-by-side in the cart. Filling several medication orders at once from a

computerized cart further adds to the potential for medication mix-ups.

3. If the bins are filled with the wrong drug by the pharmacy employee, usually a technician, the wrong drug can be dispensed, leading to an error. This is the type of error that permitted actor Dennis Quaid's twins to receive highly concentrated heparin instead of the low dose heparin flush.

4. Not all drugs can be accommodated in the automatic-dispensing system, especially refrigerated drugs. Lack of inclusion in the system causes the system to revert to the antiquated "Floor Stock System," a system cluttered with flaws and prone to error that led to a strong movement in hospitals 30 years ago to initiate unit dose dispensing.

The following case provides an example of how the Pyxis system failed, and how classic errors led to brain damage in one patient.

A 46-year-old patient went to the emergency department of a suburban Chicago hospital complaining of severe gastric distress following dinner at a Mexican restaurant. The ED physician prescribed Pepcid (famotidine). Pepcid requires refrigeration. Since the Pyxis machine does not accommodate refrigerated storage, any medications requiring refrigeration are stored in a medication refrigerator. Pepcid vials are small, 2 ml, with a small, blue label. They were stored in an organizer tray on one of the ED medication refrigerator shelves. The nurse mistakenly selected Pavulon (pancuronium, Organon), which paralyzes the diaphragm, instead of Pepcid, and administered the Pavulon intravenously. Ten minutes later, the patient's husband called out for help, "my wife stopped breathing," after she let out a loud gasp. The ED resident quickly recognized the potential problem, asked to see the vial of Pepcid, and discovered that Pavulon was mistakenly given. The patient was emergently intubated with difficulty, and it was estimated that she was "down" for 10 to 15 minutes (inadequate or no breathing). She was resuscitated; however, she was seriously brain damaged, requiring specialized care. This is a classic case of "confirmation bias." The nurse saw Pepcid in her mind's eye when she took the vial out of the refrigerator. She saw it when she drew the medication out of the vial with the syringe, and she thought she was administering it when she administered the drug intravenously. The case went to

trial. Liability was admitted; the only fight was how much the hospital had to pay. The jury returned a verdict of $6 million (unpublished case).

TIP: Nurses must avoid at-risk behaviors related to technology, such as overriding alerts and using workarounds. For example, nurses who use barcoding technology have been known to photocopy a patient's ID band and place the copy on a clipboard to scan the bar code, instead of scanning at the bedside. In fact, 32 percent of nurses answered "sometimes" to the question, "When working with mediation administration technologies, I bypass or work around built in safety features." Bypassing safeguards can have particularly devastating outcomes in critical situations.[32]

---

7. Medication reconciliation

The Joint Commission added medication reconciliation to the National Patient Safety Goals in 2005. The wording on this goal has since been modified because of the difficulty of implementing it. The goal focuses on the need to ensure that the healthcare providers have an accurate list of the medications a patient is taking. This is particularly important at admission, transfer, and discharge from a facility. Reconciling medications is complicated by:

- A patient who cannot recall medications taken at home, or family and friends who cannot provide the information for a patient unable to do so
- Involvement of many physicians in the care of a patient
- An incomplete medication list
- Staff who are unfamiliar with the medications
- A patient who is not taking the medications as prescribed
- Clinicians who do not allow enough time to interview a patient about the medications
- A patient who takes an extensive list of medications
- Errors that are made in recording
- Orders that are miscommunicated or incomplete
- Confusion about when and who performs medication reconciliation[33]

B. Individual Factors

1. Psychological aspects of human error: mistakes and slips

Cognitive psychologists and human-factors specialists have been concerned with the biology, psychology, and sociology of errors for decades. They have learned a great deal about why people make errors and how to prevent them by developing models of human cognition and studying complex environments such as airplane cockpits and nuclear power plant control rooms. Most mental functioning is automatic, effortless, and rapid. We do not have to "think" to eat or to drive a car to work. This automatic mode is unconscious, rapid, and effortless; like the new microprocessors, it occurs in parallel-processing mode. While our minds are under "intentional control," we have to pay attention only when there is a change.[34] Psychologists consider an error a disorder of intentional acts, and they distinguish between errors in planning an act and errors in its execution. If a prior intention to reach a specified goal leads to action, and the action leads to the goal, then all is well. A mistake occurs if the plan of action contains some flaw (for example, planning to give a medicine to a child, but failing to realize the child requires a different dose than an adult). A "slip" or "lapse" occurs in carrying out the action. A slip is a form of human error defined to be "the performance of an action that was not what was intended." A slip of the pen, when a nurse intends to write chlorpromazine but distractedly writes chlorpropamide, is an example. Lapses are covert slips, particularly errors of memory. Slips and lapses are errors due to failures of skill: picking the wrong medicine or administering the medicine to the wrong Mr. Brown when two patients have the same surname.

Slips are errors that occur when an individual is functioning in the automatic mode. They usually result from distractions or failure to pay attention at critical moments. A common error mechanism is loss of activation, in which attention is distracted and a thought process is lost.[35] Slips can occur at the point in which an intention to act is formed if the situation that demands action is misclassified, and thus the wrong schema is chosen. A prescriber who habitually orders meperidine 100 mg as a postoperative analgesic might specify the dosage of morphine as 100 mg as the result of such an error. Errors in carrying out the sequence of events specified in the schema, such as omitting or duplicating some steps, are a further important class of slips. An example would be when a nurse, having already added 20 mEq of potassium chloride to a bag of infusion fluid, forgets having done so and adds an additional 20 mEq of potassium chloride. There can also be faults in activation of the schema that lead to slips. For example, when several things are happening at the same time, two schemata can become confused. A verbal slip that illustrates this is when a person may be thinking of both "closed" and "shut," but says "clut."

Slips and lapses are distinguished from mistakes. Mistakes can be subdivided into those due to lack of expertise (knowledge-based errors), when there is ignorance of the rule required and thus a need to plan an action from first principles; and those due to failure of expertise (rule-based errors), when rules are applied inappropriately.

Psychological factors include other activity (being busy and distracted) as well as emotional states such as boredom, frustration, fear, anxiety, and anger. All lead to preoccupations that divert attention. Psychological factors, though considered internal or endogenous, may be triggered by external factors, such as overwork, interpersonal relations, and other forms of stress. Environmental factors, such as noise, heat, visual stimuli, and motion, can divert attention and lead to slips.[36]

2. Inexperience, ignorance (knowledge deficit), inattention

Lesar, Lomaestro and Pohl[37] reported on an analysis of data from a nine-year study of medication prescribing errors in a teaching hospital. Antibiotics were most often involved in a prescribing error. One-third of the errors were overdoses of antibiotics, with the rest of the errors defined as underdoses (26.3 percent) or allergy to the antibiotic (22.3 percent). The authors concluded that 30-50 percent of all adverse drug events were preventable. The following factors were cited as contributing to prescribing errors:

1. Increased workload
2. Intensity of care
3. Inadequate prescriber knowledge of medications and drug therapies
4. Inadequate performance in managing drug therapy

Ensuring appropriate medication use is a complex process that requires knowledge of drugs, timely access to accurate and complete patient information, and a series of interrelated decisions over a period of time. In a study conducted by Lesar,[38] the most common factors associated with errors were decline in renal or hepatic function requiring alteration of drug therapy (13.9 percent); patient history of allergy to the same medication class (12.1 percent); using the wrong drug name, dosage form, or abbreviation (11.4 percent for both brand and generic name orders); incorrect dosage calculations (11.1 percent); and atypical or unusual and critical dosage frequency considerations (10.18 percent). The most common groups of factors associated with errors were those related to knowledge and application of knowledge regarding drug therapy (30 percent); knowledge and use of knowledge regarding patient factors that affect drug therapy (29.2 percent); and nomenclature: incorrect drug name, dosage form, or abbreviations (13.4 percent).[39]

3. Violations of policies, procedures, or protocols

A policy is a statement of the goal of the process, the intention of what is done; a protocol or procedure is a checklist of how the act is accomplished, how the service is provided, and who provides the service. Procedures and protocols are carefully written by accomplished practitioners across multidisciplinary lines to provide checks and balances so that medication errors of all types—slips, mistakes, inexperience, inattention, ignorance, commission, and omission with respect to prescribing, dispensing, and administration—can be avoided. Established policies and procedures provide a roadmap for patient safety; all healthcare workers should be knowledgeable of the relevant policies and procedures in the institution, and quality assurance efforts should include monitoring compliance with policy and procedures.

A reproduction (with permission) of a recent case provides a poignant example of the serious consequences of failure to follow procedure. This case also demonstrates a system failure:

The following case involves a patient who received intrathecal Vincristine. He did not die, but was permanently paralyzed as a result of this medical error. This case provides a good study of systems design, of the value of systems, and of what happens when the system breaks down (i.e., when the system is not followed).

This patient, a 69-year-old farmer, was scheduled to complete a successful methotrexate/Vincristine treatment for lymphoma at a major university medical center. His prognosis was good. He was planning on retiring soon, and knew that he would be the primary caregiver for his wife, who was beginning to show signs of Alzheimer's disease. His children had grown up and moved away.

One fateful day in May 2000, he arrived at the oncology clinic for his scheduled methotrexate intrathecal and Vincristine intravenous treatment. Because the intrathecal injection must be performed under guided fluoroscopy, the oncologist reserved a radiology suite. No nurse was available to accompany or assist the oncologist who was to administer the injection. The oncologist, not wanting to miss the appointment, stopped at the clinic pharmacy and asked the pharmacist for the "methotrexate and flush (preservative-free NaCl)." The syringes for both the Vincristine IV and the methotrexate intrathecal had already been prepared. The staff pharmacist on duty in the clinic pharmacy

asked the oncologist: "Would you like the complete order?" The oncologist confirmed, and the pharmacist proceeded to place both the Vincristine and the methotrexate syringes in the container, which the oncologist then took to the radiology suite. There the oncologist injected what he knew was methotrexate, followed by the Vincristine syringe (which he assumed was preservative-free NaCl).

The patient was taken back to the clinic where, he believed, he would receive the intravenous Vincristine, but the Vincristine could not be found. A call to the pharmacy led to the discovery that the Vincristine had been given to the oncologist who immediately went to Radiology and retrieved the discarded syringes from the sharps container. To his horror, he realized the Vincristine had mistakenly been administered intrathecally in place of the saline flush.

Physicians immediately conducted an emergency spinal-fluid dialysis/replacement, saving the patient's life. Sadly, the patient was completely paralyzed below the nipple line of his body. The oncologist, devastated over the event, quickly settled with the patient for $500,000.

Had the system been followed, this accident probably never would have occurred. First, a nurse should have accompanied the oncologist, who while engaged in a delicate intrathecal injection, did not read the label of the syringe he was administering. Next, the pharmacy department had a policy in place for utilizing the Vincristine manufacturer's syringe label, which read "FATAL IF GIVEN INTRATHECALLY. FOR INTRAVENOUS USE ONLY," and the red-bordered syringe overwrap that warned: "FATAL IF GIVEN INTRATHECALLY. FOR IV USE ONLY. DO NOT REMOVE COVERING UNTIL MOMENT OF INJECTION." The oncology clinic pharmacy manager decided these were unnecessary for adult patients, because the oncology-clinic staff was competent and well-informed. The staff pharmacist, who knew about the policy in the main hospital's sterile-products-compounding room, followed this unofficial exemption. That same staff pharmacist, given a verbal order for the "methotrexate and the flush" gave both the methotrexate and the Vincristine to the physician, thereby violating another system rule: never to place the methotrexate and Vincristine in the same container. Since many staff pharmacists rotated through the oncology-clinic pharmacy, it was common knowledge that the precautionary syringe label and overwrap were not being used.

A lawsuit was brought against the university hospital, staff pharmacist, oncology clinic pharmacy manager, and director of pharmacy. The lawsuit alleged the "Hospital and its employees failed to properly promulgate and enforce appropriate policies, procedures, and protocols relating to the ordering, packaging, delivery, dispensing, and administration of Vincristine; that the Hospital and its employees failed to properly train and supervise employees, and that those failures were substantial factors in causing the plaintiffs' injuries and damages." The lawyers for the hospital and the pharmacists argued it was the oncologist who was to blame, and the pharmacists and the university were not negligent. While the oncologist was admittedly negligent, an overriding theme of the litigation was that this was a system failure—that if adequate system controls had been in place and enforced, the accident would not have happened. One of the authors (JOD) consulted on and testified in this case. In his testimony, he described both the patient and the oncologist as victims of this system failure.

Although a good system was in place, the system had been violated in several instances. There was no nurse to accompany the oncologist. The pharmacist provided Vincristine in place of the saline flush, did not question the systems violation (not using the syringe label and overwrap), and provided both drugs in the same container. The pharmacy clinic manager violated the system policy and the manufacturer's precautionary labeling. The director of pharmacy allowed an environment in which a manager could change or elect not to follow policies. Another important systems violation was that the safety policies were exempted with the *assumption* of a competent and informed staff.

This was an unnecessary error. After protracted mediation and settlement negotiations, an additional $1.6 million was added to the settlement package—thus providing a $2.1 million settlement, which would almost cover all future medical expenses and economic losses. Some other provision would have to be made for care of the patient's frail wife, whose Alzheimer's disease had advanced.[40]

4. Failure to educate patient on importance of home monitoring

A significant problem can occur if patients are inadequately informed of required follow-up care for outpatients after discharge from the hospital. One such example related to Coumadin (warfarin sodium, a blood thinner). Even under the best of circumstances, one out of ten patients has problems with Coumadin. An absolute essential for monitoring the efficacy and safety of Coumadin is outpatient INR (International Normalized Ratio for prothrombin time, a measure of the degree of blood thinning). The INR must be maintained in a certain range. If it is too low, the patient risks clotting. If it is too high, the patient risks bleeding. Arrangements must be made for outpatient laboratory testing for INRs. An assessment must be made of the patient's understanding of the need for:

1. testing,
2. the scheduling for the testing,
3. an understanding of the signs and symptoms of Coumadin toxicity, and
4. immediate contact with the physician.

Failure to provide such necessary educational information can result in serious morbidity or mortality. This educational need is critical with more complex therapies provided to patients at home, coupled with early discharge from the hospital. In addition to teaching, nurses follow up with the patient in the form of reminders of treatment schedules, and confirm testing has occurred as an additional method of providing the safest ambulatory treatment to patients on critical drug therapies.

28.5 Ordering Stage Errors

The potential for medication errors by nurses begins when the healthcare provider orders a medication. Medications may be ordered by physicians, nurse practitioners, physician assistants, and pharmacists in many states. For simplicity, the term "healthcare provider" is used to refer to the individual prescribing the medication.

A. The Order-Entry Process

TIP: Each medication order must consist of these components: name of the medication, dose, route, and frequency.

The order for the medication can be brought to the nurse's attention in a number of ways. It may be handwritten onto the order sheet that is part of the patient's medical record or entered into a computer system. Handwritten orders are transcribed, or copied, onto the medication administration record (MAR) by either a unit secretary or nurse. Many agencies require the registered nurse to review the unit secretary's transcription for accuracy. The unit secretary usually does not need a medical background to be qualified for the job. Computer order-entry by physicians may result in the order being communicated electronically to the pharmacy for filling and dispensing to the nursing unit, with addition of the medication to the computerized medication-administration record.

TIP: Many unit secretaries are in nursing school, so it is important to inquire about the background of this individual if appropriate to the case.

Table 28.4
Examples of Look Alike Drug Names

Acetohexamide	Acetazolamide
Advair	Advicor
Amaryl	Reminyl
Avinza	Evista
Celebrex	Celexa
Chlorpromazine	Chlorpropamide
Cisplatin	Carboplatin
Clonidine	Klonopin
Diabeta	Zebeta
Diflucan	Diprivan
Epinephrine	Ephedrine
Fentanyl	Sufentanil
Hespan	Heparin
Humulin	Humalog
Hydromorphone	Morphine
Lamisil	Lamictal
Lente	Lantus
Leukaran	Leucovorin Calcium
Novolin	Novolog
Prilosec	Prozac
Primacor	Primaxin
Protonix	Protomine
Retrovir	Ritonavir
Serzone	Seroquel
Taxol	Taxotere
Vincristine	Vinblastine
Xanax	Zantac
Zyprexa	Zyrtec
Zyrtec	Zantac

B. Hazards Associated with the Ordering Stage

There are many hazards associated with order entry. Some are specific to handwritten orders, while others may occur even with computerized order entry.

1. Handwriting, stray marks and letters

A recent report by the Committee on the Quality of Health Care in America has drawn attention to the prevalence of errors in day-to-day medical care delivery, with a major source attributable to illegible, poorly written, or difficult to interpret prescriptions.[41]

Stray marks, such as initials, check marks, or letters indicating transcription of the order has occurred may lead to a misinterpretation of an order. For example, some facilities use letters such as "M" to indicate the order was placed on the medication administration record, "K" to state it was up on a kardex or "O" to indicate it was ordered. Accupril was interpreted as Monopril in one setting because a unit secretary placed an "M" in front of the order to note it was transcribed onto the MAR.[42]

Many drugs have similar appearing names. Refer to Table 28.4 for examples. Nurses are expected to match the patient's diagnosis with the drug before transcription of the order and administration of the medication. Drugs with look-alike names may be used for very different purposes.[43] Refer to Figure 28.1 for an example of a handwritten prescription. The physician intended to prescribe Tenormin. The prescription was filled as Femara, and administered to the patient. This female hormone was contraindicated given her history of uterine cancer.

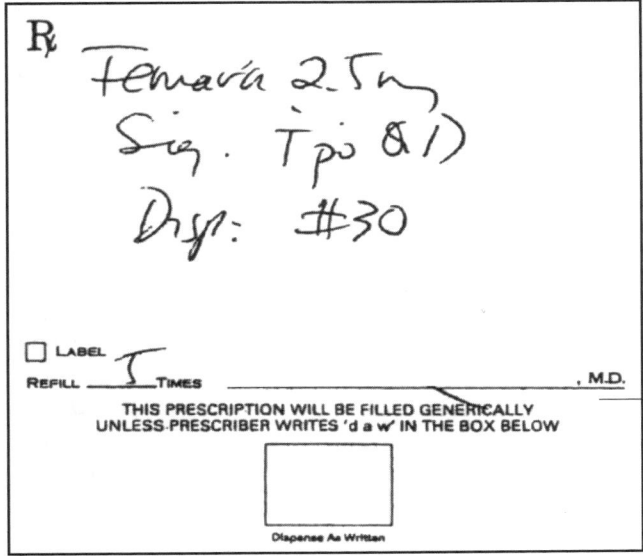

Figure 28.1 Example of Misinterpreted Prescription

While computerized prescribing systems might cut the quantity and severity of medication ordering errors, they cannot eliminate them completely. It is still possible for a prescriber to enter an order into the wrong electronic record. Not all the performance problems defined in the study below are alleviated by an electronic prescribing system.

A study performed to assess medical students' and housestaffs' knowledge, attitudes, and behaviors regarding safe prescribing used anonymous, self-administered questionnaires about safe prescribing. Of 175 respondents, results indicated they did the following:

1. Checked prescribing information before prescribing new drugs: 89 percent
2. Checked for drug allergies: 59 percent
3. Checked for renal impairment: 56 percent
4. Checked for potential drug to drug interactions: 30 percent

The authors of the study concluded that routine use of safe medication-prescribing behaviors were poor. Contributing factors may have been inadequate training and a culture that did not support safe prescribing.[44] A study of U.S. hospitals that switched from using doctors' handwritten prescriptions to computerized drug ordering systems had a 66 percent drop in medication errors. Illegible handwriting on prescriptions and transcription mistakes causes as many as 61 percent of medication errors.[45]

2. Unapproved abbreviations

Potential for error occurs when the healthcare provider uses a confusing abbreviation. This issue has been highlighted in recent years with The Joint Commission's requirement to avoid dangerous abbreviations. Healthcare providers are expected not to use U for units; IU for international units. The "u" abbreviation has been mistaken for zero, causing ten-fold overdoses to be administered. Other dangerous abbreviations include QD, Q.D., qd, or q.d. for every day; QOD, Q.O.D., qod, q.o.d. for every other day; trailing zeros for X.0 mg; and MS or MS04 for morphine; or MgS04 for magnesium sulfate.[46] See the TJC website for strategies used by facilities to eliminate dangerous abbreviations.[47] Implementation of this goal requires healthcare organizations to revise existing medical record forms. Specialized order sheets might include these abbreviations. Any transcription or interpretation error involving a zero or a decimal point means the patient could potentially receive at least ten times more medication than indicated, or only one-tenth of the ordered dose.

TIP: Ask the hospital to provide the approved list of abbreviations, and ask if they have a list of unauthorized abbreviations.

Abbreviations contribute to or cause many errors. Reports of such errors have been published routinely. The abbreviation "TAB," meant to signify "triple antibiotic" (a name for a hospital sterile topical antibiotic mixture), caused patients to have their wounds irrigated with a diet soda. A prescription could be written with directions as follows: "OD OD OD" to mean one drop in the right eye once daily! Abbreviations should not be used for drug names because they are particularly dangerous. The writer may, through mental error, confuse two abbreviations and use the wrong one. Similarly, the reader may attribute the wrong meaning to an abbreviation. To further compound the problem, some drug name abbreviations have multiple meanings (ASA can stand for aspirin or aluminum subacetate).

Changing behavior associated with the use of dangerous abbreviations includes modification of prescriber order forms, use of computer order entry, education, one on one counseling, and use of slogans and posters.

3. Telephone and verbal orders

Misunderstandings or documentation of wrong orders are prevalent when orders are received orally or by phone. Telephone orders may be taken in noisy, distracting environments. Accents and healthcare workers for whom English is a second language may add to confusion in interpreting verbal orders. Most agencies discourage verbal orders in circumstances other than emergencies. Every facility should have well-known and enforced policies that specify the criteria for dictating and accepting oral and phone orders. The Joint Commission brought this issue to the forefront when it was included as one of the 2006 Patient Safety Goals. The second Patient Safety Goal states the commitment to improve the effectiveness of communication among caregivers. The accredited facilities must implement a process for taking oral or telephone orders that require a verification "read-back" of the complete order by the person receiving the order. Simply repeating back the order is not sufficient. Whenever possible, the receiver of the order should write down the complete order or enter it into a computer, then read it back, and receive confirmation from the individual who gave the order. This goal applies to all oral and telephone orders.[48] Refer to Chapter 4, *Patient Safety Initiatives*, in Volume I, for more information on National Patient Safety Goals.

There are many assonant medications. For example Celexa (citalopram) and Cerebyx (fosphenytoin) sound alike.

Xanax, used to treat anxiety, may be confused with Zantac, the histamine blocker that treats ulcers. Enjuvia, which is estrogen, may be confused with Januvia, which treats diabetes. Patients frequently mistake these two names. A nurse who cannot clearly interpret a spoken order should ask the speaker to repeat the name of the drug and the dosage. The nurse should also ask the prescriber to spell the name of the drug.

When taking a spoken order, the nurse should ask for the drug's indication. The Institute for Safe Medications Practices recommends including indications in written orders as well. Nurses should ask the prescriber to countersign the spoken order within 24 hours. Other patient safety recommendations include use of remote computerized order entry, which allows the prescriber to access the medical record and enter orders electronically, and use of fax machines to fax in orders.

4. Not using critical thinking

Nurses are expected to recognize and question inappropriate medication orders. Examples include inappropriate drugs, dosages, routes, frequencies, and interactions. Drug to drug interactions may result in visually noticeable or chemical incompatibilities. A nurse who questions an order would ordinarily discuss the concerns with the prescriber. If a satisfactory resolution to the concern is not achieved, the nurse is expected to consult with the nurse's direct supervisor, and allow the supervisor to continue up the chain of command until the concern is resolved.

28.6 Transcription Stage Errors

Transcription errors occur when information is incorrectly transcribed from a medication order to a medication administration record. Errors may be made in the name of the medication, the frequency, dosage, route or identity of the patient. The following is a case that illustrates the harm that can come when a pharmacist or another healthcare professional fails to maintain a "holistic" point of view when evaluating a patient's medications:

This case involves a lawsuit waged by the family of a 90-year-old woman who had a thyroidectomy and had been taking levothyroxine sodium (Levoxyl) for several years. She was a patient at a nursing home in the area and, subsequent to a transient ischemic attack (TIA), was admitted to a local tertiary-care hospital for treatment. Hospital staff noted the patient's thyroidectomy history and continued her Levoxyl therapy. When the patient was transferred to her new nursing home, staff prepared a discharge summary along with a copy

of the electronic medication administration record (MAR). For some reason, the patient's medication list was transcribed by hand and sent with the patient (instead of the hospital printing and sending the electronic MAR). Somehow, the Levoxyl was omitted from the patient transfer form. The nursing home's attending physician did not notice the thyroidectomy history or Levoxyl therapy, despite the fact that both were mentioned several times in the medical records that accompanied the patient

The attending physician wrote admitting orders using the handwritten medication list. Consequently, the Levoxyl was never ordered or administered to the patient. About two weeks after the patient's admittance to the nursing home, a consultant pharmacist visited the nursing home to perform the monthly medication reviews. This pharmacist signed the medication order sheet, certifying the patient's chart had been reviewed at the facility by the pharmacy consultant. Like the doctor, the pharmacist failed to detect the patient's history of thyroidectomy, hypothyroidism, or Levoxyl therapy. The consultant pharmacist's defense was that the standard of care did not require a review of the patient's chart, just the medication orders. This expert (JOD) disagreed, and testified that the consultant pharmacist deviated from the standard of care by not reviewing the chart.

After approximately nine weeks without thyroid medication, the patient's condition deteriorated. She was urgently transferred back to the hospital in a myxedema coma (severe acute hypothyroidism). The Levoxyl omission was discovered during a resident physician's review of her chart. Despite the subsequent reinstitution of the thyroid medication, the patient died a week later.

The hospital and the attending physician at the nursing home were sued. All parties contributed to a settlement.

28.7 Dispensing Stage Errors

The following discussion focuses on pharmacists and provides specific examples. The reader will recognize that the general factors leading to errors are also specific factors in the pharmacist's arena. Nurses play a role in dispensing errors when they do not recognize the wrong medication or strength of medication has been dispensed, or become involved in the dispensing function.

Pharmacists have an independent duty to protect their patients from harm, and must consult with prescribing physicians in a positive way so mistakes and misunderstandings are avoided or corrected. Pharmacists are increasingly becoming the target of malpractice litigation. This phenomenon has resulted in the development of strategies to reduce the risks of medication errors, as well as to manage pharmacist liability.[49]

Pharmacists Mutual (see Figure 28.2) has identified the most common categories of errors and omissions most responsible for claims against pharmacists for malpractice. They are, in order of frequency:

1. Wrong drug
2. Wrong strength of drug
3. Wrong directions
4. Lack of drug review (which can result in allergies or contraindicated combinations of drugs being administered)
5. Failure to properly counsel patients on medication usage
6. Non-bodily injury
7. Other (miscellaneous)

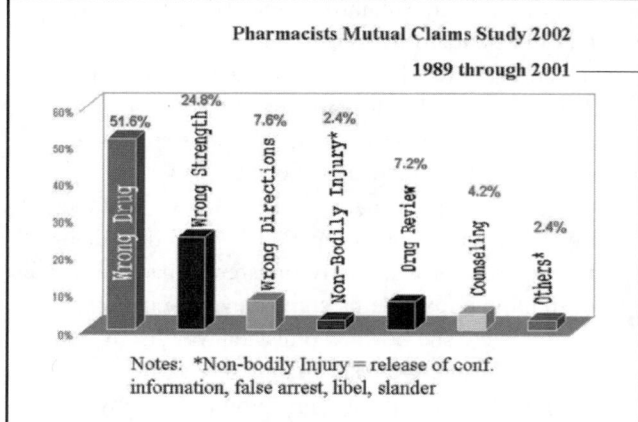

Figure 28.2 *Pharmacists Mutual Claims Study 2002. Reprinted with Permission: www.pharmacistsmutual.com*

A. Wrong Drug

Since 1990, the number of "wrong drugs" administered has remained relatively consistent, although the reasons for these errors appear varied. In one case, the pharmacist took a prescription for Digoxin over the phone from a doctor's office. The pharmacist prepared the label, counted the correct drug into the tray, and poured it into the bottle. As he placed the bottle next to the completed label, the phone rang again, with a request for warfarin. The pharmacist filled the prescription for warfarin in the same manner, but somehow, the two labels were mixed up. The warfarin bottle received the Digoxin label and was given to the wrong patient.

In another case, a technician simply took the wrong bottle from the shelf. If a busy pharmacist does not catch the error when performing her check, or does not check the technician's work, the results can be serious.

Distractions in the pharmacy are another common and unavoidable part of every workday. Label switches can result due to "multi–tasking" or filling multiple prescriptions for a single patient. A patient may have a prescription for Coumadin (warfarin) once a day and Lasix (Furosemide) twice a day. If the labels are switched, and the patient ends up taking Coumadin twice a day, he may suffer a serious hemorrhage from the Coumadin and congestive heart failure from undertreatment of the Lasix.

Sometimes drug names look alike. Prescriptions for Navane can be mistaken for Norvasc, Prilosec for Prozac, Lasix for Losec. Interestingly, the Lasix/Losec error precipitated a name change by the Losec manufacturer (it was renamed Prilosec). After that, Prilosec and Prozac were mistakenly dispensed in place of one another. This problem occurs so frequently that a special committee of the United States Pharmacopeia (USP) has been formed to look at the selection of new drug names. There is an evolving science in understanding and preventing this error of fine distinction.

The physicians' handwriting is another cause of pharmacist error. Often the subject of jokes, the typical physician's scrawl presents the most dangerous type of pharmacist error. An increased use of electronic prescribing would help obviate such interpretative errors between physician and pharmacist.

B. Wrong Drug Strength

The second largest category of claims (24.4 percent) shown in the Pharmacists Mutual Study is wrong strength. A common example would be receiving a prescription for Digoxin 0.125 mg, and filling it in error with Digoxin 0.25 mg. Misplacement of a decimal point is a very common way these errors occur. Another error is picking up the wrong bottle when filling the prescription. Perhaps the drug is correct, but the dosage is wrong. Depending upon the drug prescribed, the results of selecting the wrong strength can be dangerous, even fatal. Another common outcome is a lack of efficacy. A too low dose of an anticoagulant (such as Coumadin) being administered could fail to prevent a fatal clot. Even old, familiar drugs are subject to this error. Drugs filled most frequently are involved in more errors, simply as a matter of incidence. For example, Haldol is used for senile dementia. It would be unusual for Haldol 5 mg to be prescribed for an ambulatory elderly patient. A more common dosage is 0.5 mg. The drugs with the greatest numbers of available dosage forms offer the greatest probability for a dosage error. The drugs that can cause the most toxicity will result in claims. These drugs have the lowest "therapeutic index": the relationship between a therapeutic level and toxic level is small. If the patient suffers from damage or an adverse effect—even if the patient only has to present to an emergency room—this can result in a cause of action against the pharmacist and pharmacy.

C. Wrong Directions

At 7.8 percent of all claims, "wrong directions" represents a significant number reported in the Pharmacists Mutual Study. These cases involve incorrect directions in the computer. In one case, a pharmacist entered a new prescription for birth control tablets into the computer and inadvertently typed, "Take two tablets daily." For nine months, this patient refilled her birth control prescription every 15 days while following the erroneous label directions, without anyone at the pharmacy noticing the discrepancy. The most dangerous "wrong directions" claims are for children's prescriptions, especially children under the age of six.

To avoid labeling the prescription with the wrong directions, pharmacists should always check the label directions against the hard copy prescription. Another good practice is for the pharmacist to follow a standard procedure of removing the prescription from the bag as she counsels each patient. The pharmacist should read the written directions to the patient and ask, "How did your doctor explain you were to take this medication?" The pharmacist can use similar words to determine whether the patient understands what the directions mean. The pharmacist should ask the patient to repeat the directions on the prescription. This serves two purposes: it allows the pharmacist to double-check the label directions, and, by removing the prescription from the bag, it creates the appearance of a professional service rather than the mere sale of a "commodity" in a sack.

D. Lack of Drug Review

OBRA-90 (Omnibus Budget Reconciliation Act) requires pharmacists to review all prescriptions prior to filling them and check for interactions, allergies, and a list of other potential problems. Especially because pharmacy technicians are increasingly used to reduce the pharmacist's workload, this area of claims—previously almost unheard of—now represents over 9 percent of all claims.

Drug review was first described in The Standard of Practice of the Profession of Pharmacy.[50] The American Pharmaceutical Association (APHA), in concert with the American Association of Colleges of Pharmacy (AACP), defined standards of practice for the profession of pharmacy. Many or all of the requirements eventually legislated and mandated by the OBRA were components of the standards of practice. OBRA requires medication profiles, as well as review for therapeutic duplication, allergy, cross sensitivity, drug disease, and contraindications. Failure to provide meaningful patient drug review has resulted in claims and lawsuits that plead error of omission.

28.8 Administration Stage Errors

Following the five rights is drilled into nurses. This helps to prevent errors, but errors may still occur even if all five rights are followed. For example, a physician or other prescriber may order a medication on the wrong medical record. Or a therapeutic value too high to safely administer a medication may be incorrectly reported for the wrong patient.[51]

A. The Five Rights

A number of serious reported medication errors have resulted in fatal overdoses. As with most such errors, more than one safeguard within the medication administration system either failed or simply was not in place. Medication errors are preventable. Nurses are taught the "five rights" of medication administration in nursing school.

1. Right drug

The nurse is expected to question any unclear order or one that seems inappropriate. As part of the medication-administration process, the nurse must read labels and obtain information from authoritative sources (references, pharmacy consultation) about correct drug usage when encountering unfamiliar drugs. Many nurses were taught to read the order for the medication three times: when first reviewing the medications to be administered to the patient, when removing the medication from the drug cart drawer, and just before administering it to the patient.

2. Right patient

The nurse must check the patient's identification band to make sure the name on the medication administration record (MAR) matches the identification band. When the identification band has been removed for any reason, such as swelling in the arm due to an intravenous infiltration, the nurse is responsible for ensuring another identification band is applied to the patient. When medications are labeled with the patient's name, the nurse should check the medication package to ensure a match. As described in Chapter 4, *Patient Safety Initiatives*, in Volume I, Joint Commission National Patient Safety Goals stress the importance of using patient identifiers to correctly confirm the patient's identity. The use of bar codes on medication packages and patient identification bands helps to reduce the risk of administering the medication to the wrong patient.

3. Right dose

The third "right" requires the nurse to understand all abbreviations and measurements used at the facility. When confronted with a questionable dose, the nurse must consult authoritative sources to verify the dose is correct. Errors in dosage may occur if calculations are performed incorrectly. A wrong dose error typically occurs when the patient receives an amount of medicine greater or less than the amount ordered.

4. Right route

The nurse is expected to administer the medication according to the route specified in the order. Some medications can only be given intramuscularly, and not intravenously or orally. Nurses are taught how to administer injections using recommended sites and to document the site of the injection on the MAR. A good nursing library contains several well-illustrated basic textbooks that describe the techniques for proper administration of injections.

Injectable drug errors surpass those for other methods of administration, accounting for about two-thirds of administration mistakes. The risk of error increases with the need to perform steps to prepare the medication, such as changing the drug concentration, having to perform several steps to prepare the medication, or readying the drug outside of the pharmacy. Lack of labeling of the syringe also greatly increases the risk of a mix up.[52]

5. Right time

Pharmacology courses in nursing school teach nurses the expected frequency of certain categories of medications. For example, most antibiotics are given more than one time a day to maintain a consistent blood level.

B. Examples of When the Five Rights Go Wrong

Many medication errors clearly fall within the scope of the five rights of medication administration. This section of the chapter presents information on cases involving deviations from the five rights. Review of published reports of settlements and verdicts is useful for locating expert witnesses and networking with attorneys who have been involved in similar cases.

1. Wrong drug

Misinterpretation of a prescriber's handwriting, a dispensing error, or selecting the wrong drug from the supply can result in administration of the incorrect drug. Responses to a 2004 survey of 1,600 hospitals showed that less than half (41 percent) always label containers (including syringes, ba-

sins, and other vessels used to store drugs) in the sterile field of an operating room, physician's office, cardiac catheterization suite, endoscopy or radiology suite, and other areas. An alarming 18 percent did not label medications and solutions on the sterile field at all, and other 42 percent reported inconsistent labeling of solutions. A 2006 Joint Commission National Patient Safety Goal now highlights the need to label all drugs and solutions in perioperative and procedural settings.[53]

Look alike sound alike (LASA) medication errors are known sources of error. Pharmaceutical companies, pharmacies, and healthcare providers are increasingly using "tall man" lettering to reduce the risk of mixing up similar sounding medications. The FDA has approved tall man letters for list of generic drugs, and patient safety groups such as the Institute for Prevention of Medication Errors has singled out others. For example, the FDA approved tall man lettering for PredniSONE and prenisoLONE, for DOBUTamine and DOPamine and chlorproMAZINE and chlorproPAMIDE. Tall man letters should be used on computer-generated pharmacy labels, pharmacy computer drug selection screens, shelf labels, automated dispensing cabinet screens, computer generated medication administration records, and preprinted order sheets.[54] Additionally, the standard of care requires the nurse to understand the purpose of each medication before it is administered. Most LASA drugs are used for different purposes.[55]

2. Wrong patient

The MARs for two infants were mixed up, resulting in administration of SYNAGIS (palivizumab), used to prevent respiratory syncytial virus, to the wrong child. The infants were side-by-side in isolettes, and both their MARs were on the counter between the two isolettes. Coincidentally, both infants had the same first name along with very similar hospital identification numbers. The nurse failed to notice she was referring to the wrong MAR and administered a dose of Synagis to the wrong infant.[56] Clearly, the nurse did not check the newborn's identification band before administering the medication intended for another. As noted in Chapter 4, *Patient Safety Initiatives,* in Volume I, prudent nursing practice involves the use of two identifiers to verify patient identity before medication administration. The room number may not be used as one of the identifiers.

3. Wrong dose

The miscalculation of a dosage is a common source of error in both the prescription and administration of medications. Lesar reports that errors in the use of dosage equations account for more than 15 percent of all medication prescribing errors. These types of errors have significant potential for producing adverse events. Children are at particular risk for this error as the broad range of sizes and ages require individualized calculation of dosages.[57] Wrong doses of medication may be administered, leading to overdose or underdose. Additionally, incorrectly mixing a medication with the wrong volume of diluent may result in an overdose or underdose.

> A 47-year-old woman undergoing an outpatient endoscopic lithotripsy procedure for removal of a kidney stone was involved in a procedure that took over six hours. She died 12 hours later from fluid overload caused by absorption of the irrigating fluid used, and by the resulting low sodium, high potassium, pulmonary edema, general tissue edema, acidosis, renal failure, and other conditions. The plaintiffs claimed the defendants committed numerous acts of malpractice related to the irrigating fluid used, including the use of distilled water rather than saline, failure to keep track of the volume of irrigating fluid used, and failure to verify that adequate drainage of the bladder was taking place. The parties settled for a confidential amount following mediation.[58]

4. Wrong route

Wrong route errors occur when the correct form of drug is administered, but in the incorrect site on the patient's body, such as ear drops administered in the eye or intramuscular (IM) injections given intravenously (IV). In one case, a liquid diet that should have been given through a tube into the patient's stomach was by mistake administered intravenously. In another case, Maalox was administered into an intravenous line instead of through a tube inserted into the stomach.

In some instances, medications meant to be applied on the skin (topically) have been injected into the body. Refer to Chapter 4, *Patient Safety Initiatives,* in Volume I, for more information on the National Patient Safety Goals, which address the labeling of solutions.

Listing topical medications on the MAR, even when they are technically part of a treatment plan, can help avoid error. Clear labeling of all medications and double-checking labels before use are also important. Keeping treatment solutions on the bedside table increases the likelihood of staff error and may be dangerous if they are within a patient's reach. Many institutions use large, brightly colored or luminescent stickers and labels that read, "For topical use only."

5. Wrong time

Administering the medication before it is due or delays in the administration of medications are considered wrong time errors. Some medications must be given at specific times to maintain an appropriate blood level. Timing of meals or other medications may also affect the therapeutic impact of a medication. The following case illustrates the potential consequences of this occurrence:

> When one patient arrived at an emergency department with a fever of 103.2 degrees, low blood pressure, weakness, dizziness, and chills, she was diagnosed with a kidney infection. She was transferred to a second hospital without having received any antibiotics. The physician ordered antibiotics to be given at 2 P.M., but these were not administered. Around 5 P.M., the patient was admitted to a nursing unit, accompanied by a dose of antibiotics. Medical records did not document that this dose was quickly administered. At 8 P.M., the first dose of antibiotics was given to the patient. By 1 A.M., the patient's condition deteriorated and she was transferred to the intensive care unit in septic shock. She suffered a cardiac arrest within seven hours and died. Plaintiff's experts were critical of the nurses and physicians for the delay in administration of antibiotics. The defense argued that the infecting organism was so virulent that no treatment would have saved her life. The case was settled for $2.1 million.[59]

C. Additional Types of Medication Errors

This section provides more information on other types of medication errors. Examples of cases involving these types of errors are included.

1. Omitted dose

An omission error takes place when a patient has not received her medication by the time the next dose is due. When a dose is not administered, the usual practice is for the nurse to put his initials in the box for the designated dose. The nurse draws a circle around the initials to indicate the dose was omitted. Following this, the nurse documents the reason for the omitted dose on the medication administration record or on the medical record. The nurse may fail to administer a medication for a variety of reasons. These may include any of the following:

1. The medication order was not transcribed onto the medication record.

2. The medication was not available in the nursing unit at the time it was to be given.

3. The patient was not in the nursing unit at the time the medication was to be given.

4. More than one medication administration record was in use. When the nurse was administering medications, the second sheet was overlooked.

5. When the nurse was preparing the medications for the patient, one or more of the medications was overlooked.

6. The medication was administered to another patient in error.

7. The medication record was recopied when all of the spaces were used up and in the recopying process the medication was not copied onto the new record.

Other than when the patient or the medication was not available at the specified time, the remaining reasons for omissions of a medication constitute errors. Omission errors may be difficult for the attorney to detect if the nurse covered up the omission and signed the medication administration record to indicate the dose was given. If the drug was one for which therapeutic blood levels can be checked, consistent omissions of the medication would result in subnormal blood levels. Refer to the expert witness report in Appendix 28.1 for an example of the consequences of an omitted dose.

2. Duplicate dose

A duplicate dose may be administered to a patient if a nurse does not follow the procedures for documenting a medication dose, and a second nurse comes along and administers the medication. For example, the following situation resulted in a duplicate dose:

A nursing home patient died of an overdose of Fentanyl. When the decedent was taken to a hospital, she had three patches of Fentanyl on her back for treatment of rheumatoid arthritis. Proof showed that each patch contained Fentanyl, which is considered to be 50 to 100 times stronger than Morphine. The jury returned a $1 million verdict.[60]

3. Unordered drug error

An unordered drug error occurs when a patient receives a medication for which the physician did not write an order. Some authors refer to this as an unauthorized drug error. This category includes outcomes that result when a nurse

switches medications for two patients; each patient is the victim of an unordered drug error (as well as an omission).

A Texan woman who had a previous cesarean section was pregnant, and in the defendant hospital for labor and delivery. Pitocin was started. While in labor, the woman's uterus ruptured and the baby was found to have been without oxygen for an indeterminate amount of time. The plaintiffs claimed the hospital, doctors, and nurses were negligent in giving Pitocin to the patient. The doctor claimed he did not remember ordering the Pitocin, and he did not believe he would have ordered it under the circumstances. The jury found the doctor not negligent, but the hospital negligent. They awarded the plaintiff $1,587,000 in damages.[61]

28.9 High-Risk Medications

The Joint Commission (TJC) has identified high-risk sentinel medications. Even though the original list was compiled in 1999, the same drugs continue to be problematic. This fact in itself certainly demonstrates the failure of educators, regulators, and legislators to effectively rectify the problems associated with getting information about drugs to the prescriber. TJC's high alert medications include:

1. Insulin
2. Opiates/PCA (patient-controlled analgesia)
3. Concentrated solutions of potassium chloride (KCl) and potassium phosphate
4. IV anticoagulants (heparin)
5. Sodium chloride (NaCl) solutions above 0.9 percent
6. Intrathecal administration of chemotherapy by the wrong route[62]

Extensive discussions in earlier sections of the chapter have addressed the anticoagulants warfarin (Coumadin) and heparin (which would include low molecular weight heparins Lovenox, Organon, and Fragmin). Additional discussion follows, with several case examples. Drugs are high risk if they have a low therapeutic index, or are intrinsically toxic. The therapeutic index is defined as the ratio of the toxic dose to the therapeutic dose. Such low therapeutic index drugs provide little margin for overdose. Intrinsically toxic drugs include narcotics, anticoagulants, digitalis, and chemotherapy. Table 28.5 provides a list of common high-risk drugs, based on their pharmacologic properties.

Table 28.5
Identifying High-Risk Drugs

Characteristic	Prototypes
Narrow Therapeutic Index (NTI)	Digoxin, anticoagulants
Inherent Undesirable Effect(s)	Steroids, chemotherapy antibiotics/allergy
Class of Drugs Which Shares Toxicity	NSAIDs*, ACEIs**
Narcotics—Patient Controlled Analgesia	Morphine, all opiates
Newly-Approved Drugs	Temofloxacin (unknown safety profiles)
"Off-Label" Uses of Drugs	Fen-Phen
Pharmacokinetic Drug Interactions	SSRIs*** (Zoloft, Paxil, Prozac)
Direct-to-Consumer Promoted	Add-a-med

Modified from Benjamin DM and O'Donnell JT. "Medication Errors," In Sandbar S, Ed. Legal Medicine. American College of Legal Medicine. Schaumburg, IL 2006.
*NSAID NonSteroidal Anti-inflammatory Drug
**ACEI Angiotension Converting Enzyme Inhibitor
***SSRI Selective Serotonin Reuptake Inhibitor

A. Insulin

Insulin is the mainstay for treatment of virtually all type-I and many type-II diabetic patients. Frequently, hospitalized non-diabetic patients who have elevated glucose readings due to high glucose intravenous solutions are subject to insulin errors in the ordering of insulin, interpretation of the order, or preparation of the insulin injection, which can have disastrous consequences. Some agencies and institutions require a nurse preparing to give an insulin injection to have another nurse review the order and the prepared syringe to verify the correct dose has been drawn up. Insulin is ordered in units. The prescriber should spell out the word "units" and not abbreviate it. The dosage may be misunderstood if the order contains the symbol "U," which has been confused for a "0." Some of the most serious errors are due to misinterpretations of abbreviations used in medical writing in patient charts. A slash mark (/) has been mistaken for a "1," causing a patient to receive a 100-unit overdose of NPH insulin when the slash was used to separate an order for two insulin doses: 6 units regular insulin/20 units NPH insulin.[63]

The primary risk associated with insulin therapy is hypoglycemia. While insulin is used to lower blood sugar in hyperglycemia (overly high blood sugar), those who have normal levels and hyperglycemia who have their blood-sugar levels lowered accidentally face morbidity and mortality of hypoglycemia.[64] Since the brain depends on glucose as its primary fuel, hypoglycemia, or low blood-glucose level, has a marked impact on brain metabolism. Alterations of brain function are responsible for the characteristic symptoms of hypoglycemia. As glucose levels fall, prodromal signs and symptoms may appear. Such manifestations include hunger, salivation, an overall ill-at-ease feeling, or even nausea. Hypoglycemia may lead to convulsions resulting in brain damage, as well as in serious musculoskeletal injuries. The essential biochemical event is a blood sugar level of less than 25–30 mg/100 ml, lasting one to two hours, and leading to exhaustion of the store of cerebral glucose and glycogen. Within this brief span of time, as cerebral oxidation proceeds without exogenous glucose, the structural component of neurons are metabolized and irreversible damage occurs. The cerebral cortex suffers major damage; cortical nerve cells degenerate and are replaced by micogliacytes and astrocytes.[65]

In a Minnesota case, the plaintiff was admitted to the hospital for treatment of shoulder pain. Her blood sugar was to be monitored and maintained through insulin administration by hospital staff. Within five hours of admission, the plaintiff was overdosed with insulin. She suffered severe hypoglycemia, which resulted in severe brain damage. She was placed on life support, but this was removed after one week. A $675,000 settlement was reached in this case involving a 64-year-old, wheelchair-bound woman.[66]

Nursing responsibilities include accurate transcription of insulin orders, questioning inappropriate doses, inaccurately drawing up insulin in the correct number of units, and observing patients for signs and symptoms of hypo- or hyperglycemia.

B. Opiates

The opiate drug class—morphine, Demerol, and Dilaudid—consists of high risk drugs. Morphine is the opiate against which all others are measured. Fentanyl patches contribute to medication errors and fatalities. There have been over 100 deaths attributed to the use of Fentanyl patches because of inappropriate prescription to opioid-naive patients (those without a tolerance), or incorrect use or disposal. Opiates depress respiratory drive even at therapeutic doses; therein lays the risk. The patient may not know breathing is impaired. A sleeping patient is at greater risk. Opiates given with other central nervous system depressants (phenothiazines, benzodiazepines) further increase the risk.[67]

In a Minnesota case, the plaintiff's decedent went to the hospital because of a two-day history of abdominal pain. An epidural catheter was placed for pain control after surgery for his intra-abdominal abscess. The infusion was initially ordered at 2 mcg/ml to be infused at a rate of 10 ml per hour. This resulted in an hourly dose of 20 mcg per hour. Around noon the next day a nurse wrote a telephone order from the defendant doctor for a dose change in the Fentanyl infusion. The order was to increase the dose of Fentanyl in the epidural infusion to 10 mcg/ml to run at the same rate as before. This resulted in an hourly dose of 100 mcg/hour of Fentanyl. This new infusion began around 2 P.M. When the nurses checked the decedent around 4:30 A.M. the next day, he had no pulse and was not breathing. A code was called and resuscitation begun, which was unsuccessful. An autopsy revealed that the decedent had a blood level of Fentanyl that was 13 mg/ml. The plaintiff claimed the defendants were negligent in ordering and administering an excessive dose of Fentanyl and in failing to properly assess and monitor changes in the decedent's condition. A confidential settlement was reached.[68]

Nursing responsibilities include preparing and administering correct doses of narcotics, questioning inappropriate doses, withholding opiates from a patient when such medications are contraindicated, and observing for and intervening when respiratory depression is noted.

C. PCA (Patient Controlled Analgesia)

PCA became popular in the late 1980s, and today is the standard and most frequent method for administering opiates for acute pain, in the hospital and sometimes at home. The Institute for Safe Medication Practices has identified safety issues with PCA. PCA has considerable potential to improve pain management by allowing patients to self-administer more frequent, but smaller, doses of pain medications. Safe use of PCA requires proper patient selection, education, and monitoring.[69] The ISMP performed a review of actual errors involving PCA therapy, including cases reported voluntarily by healthcare practitioners to the USP-ISMP Medication Errors Reporting Program and those solicited by ISMP for the project. Some of the most serious errors occurred because the basic premise of PCA was violated. PCA is to be con-

trolled by the patient only. A patient already sedated by an opiate or opioid pain medication will not activate the PCA pump to deliver another dose. This built-in safeguard protects the patient from overdose. However, family members and nurses have innocently pushed the button for patients, hoping to keep them comfortable. The well-intentioned "PCA by proxy" has led to oversedation, respiratory depression, and even death.

Other factors leading to PCA errors include:

1. Improper patient selection
2. Product mix-up, wrong drug, or wrong concentration
3. Inadequate patient education
4. Ineffective monitoring of the patient's vital signs
5. Insufficient staff training
6. Practice-related problems (inaccurate programming, incorrect transcription of orders, compounding errors, similar to the routine medication error factors discussed earlier in the chapter)
7. Prescribing errors
8. Design flaws in the PCA pumps[70]

Nursing responsibilities for the use of PCA pumps include the need to:

1. Question the use of the PCA pump in patients with sleep apnea, obstructed airways, or the inability to self-medicate
2. Correctly program the pump
3. Accurately record the amount of opiate received by the patient per shift
4. Observe the patient at ordered intervals and more frequently
5. Accurately count respiratory rate
6. Report changes in patient condition
7. Provide patient education about the use of the pump and the need to avoid medication by proxy

It is common for facilities to use a sedation scale as follows:

S: Asleep
1: Awake and alert, no action needed
2: Slightly drowsy, no action needed
3: Frequently drowsy, drifts off during conversations, requires action, decrease dose of sedating medication
4: Somnolent, minimal or no response to physical stimulation, unacceptable. Stop opioid, consider

administering naloxone (to counter effects of opioids)[71]

Increasingly, patient safety advocates are recommending:

1. Avoidance of a continuous infusion of the pain-relieving medication for someone who does not have a tolerance of the medication
2. Awareness of the higher risk for oversedation patient profile—a diagnosis of sleep apnea, older than 65, morbid obesity, and receiving a continuous basal infusion
3. Use of standard medication concentrations
4. Use of standard order sets
5. Use of prefilled syringes and bags
6. Avoidance of using PCA pumps with infants, young children, confused older adults, and those taking drugs that potentiate the effects of the opioids
7. Annual verification of competency of staff
8. Frequent monitoring and reassessment of pain levels
9. Use of pulse oximetry and capnography for early detection of oversedation[72]

D. Coumadin and Heparin

Another class of high-risk drugs includes Coumadin and heparin, both anticoagulants. Patients who need anticoagulants are at risk for clotting, with complications of deep vein thromboses, pulmonary embolism, coronary thrombosis, and cerebral thrombosis. Other thrombotic conditions can affect any part of the vasculature. With too much anticoagulation, however, the patient may bleed internally and risk grave results, including death. After several well-publicized heparin overdoses drew attention to confusion in labeling heparin, the manufacturers of this drug made changes in the labels. The following is a case report related to heparin:

A 53-year-old man entered the hospital for femoral bypass surgery. Before his surgical procedure, an inadequate preoperative cardiac workup was performed. Twenty hours after the uneventful surgery, the patient's hemoglobin and hematocrit were low, indicative for possible bleeding. After the surgery, the doctor ordered 7,500 units of heparin to be administered over a 24 hour period or 2,500 units every eight hours continuously. One hour after the order was written, the nursing staff misread the instructions. Instead of administering 2,500 units of heparin, they administered 25,000 units of heparin. This caused the patient to continuously bleed, his

urine output to decline to zero, and his heart rate to increase to over 130. Consultations with a nephrologist and cardiologist were ordered to see if they could determine the cause of the continuing abdominal pain and the renal failure. At no time did the doctor believe his orders were not followed with respect to heparin administration. Finally, about eight hours after the first heparin infusion, the patient was taken back to surgery for an exploratory laparotomy. However, a nurse again prepared him with an additional (negligently misinterpreted) 25,000 units of heparin. Profound and serious bleeding was apparent, but the physician team had no idea what was causing the bleeding. The patient died from a coronary thrombus. The plaintiff claimed the cause of death was the failure to adequately perform a preoperative cardiac workup, as well as the negligent administration of toxic levels of heparin. The defendant hospital admitted liability regarding the actions of the nurse, but denied the actions of the nurse had anything to do with the patient's death. The matter settled for $2.5 million after the jury was selected. *Marie Lenoure, Special Administrator for the Estate of Victor LePore v. Oak Pak Hospital*, Cook County (IL)[73]

Trauma complicates the risks associated with giving Coumadin, heparin, and other medications which prolong clotting time. Nursing responsibilities include questioning whether anticoagulants should be continued after trauma, increasing the risk of bleeding.

In an Alabama case, the plaintiff's decedent previously suffered a stroke and was on Coumadin therapy. She suffered a fall in her home and was admitted to the defendant hospital. The nurse assigned to watch for changes in the decedent's physical presentation did not inform the doctor the decedent was lethargic and manifested changes in her blood pressure, heart rate, and respiration. The physician released the decedent to return home. The next day, the patient fell into a coma, and was readmitted to the hospital. She died several days later from a subdural hematoma. The plaintiff claimed the hospital's staff failed to obtain copies of the decedent's coagulation studies, investigate the history of Coumadin therapy, order a CT scan, order a blood test, report the changes in physical condition, and obtain a neurological consultation. The defendants claimed there was no negligence and that the decedent would not have survived even if surgery was performed. A $2.5 million verdict was returned.[74]

E. Cancer Drugs

Antineoplastics always occupy the list fo dangerous drugs, but not due to the inherent toxicity associated with these cancer chemotherapy drugs, for it is extremely rare for litigation to arise following routine chemotherapy, despite frequent devastating toxicity associated with it. Drugs that extravasate into the tissues can cause extensive damage. (Refer to Chapter 24, *Intravenous Therapy Malpractice*, for more information.) Litigation arises when mistakes are made (the wrong dose, frequency, or route of administration), often with devastating results. For example, one of the authors (PI) summarized medical records to explain pain and suffering after inadvertent administration of Vincristine into the spinal fluid. Vinca alkaloids destroy the central nervous system. In a case described in 2009, a 25-year-old woman received vindesine in the spinal fluid and died. Patient safety advocates recommend that vinca alkaloids such as vincristine, vinblastine, vindestine, and vinorelbine never be kept in the same treatment room as intrathecal (into the spinal fluid) medications.[75] The following case report is another example of a chemotherapy error:

> The plaintiff's decedent, a 54-year-old man, was diagnosed with cancer of the tongue. The treatment plan included surgery, radiation therapy and chemotherapy. The patient was admitted to the hospital for 5 FU after treatment with Cisplatin. The 5 FU was given by bolus instead of continuous infusion. When switching from continuous infusion to a bolus, the dose needs to be significantly reduced. In the decedent's case, the dosage was never decreased during the five-day course, so he received 1,500 mg per day. He suffered from a very low platelet count, low red blood cell count, sepsis, acidosis, and died. The plaintiffs claimed the defendant's negligent administration of the wrong dosage of 5 FU caused the death. The defense admitted liability for settlement discussion purposes only, but also claimed the decedent's life expectancy was less than five years. The case settled for $1,358,000.[76]

F. Methotrexate

Methotrexate is used for chemotherapy, to treat arthritis, or dissolve ectopic pregnancies and other conditions. It has complicated dosing schedules and potential for toxicity due to potentially confusing frequencies. It is commonly indicated for weekly dosing and has been involved in several severe and fatal reactions as a result of being dispensed erroneously as daily doses.

> The plaintiff's decedent, age 85, broke her arm shoveling snow in her driveway. She was admitted to a nursing home for a temporary stay. Her physician wrote a prescription for methotrexate for her rheumatoid arthritis to be given once per week. The nurse transcribed the order incorrectly, resulting in the woman receiving that drug every day. After 17 days the woman died from the overdose of the medication. The plaintiff alleged negligence in the nurse transcribing the order incorrectly, the doctor signing the order without reading the nurse's note and in the pharmacy failing to discover the dosage error. A $1 million settlement was reached.[77]

Because of the number of fatalities from errors with oral methotrexate, clinicians should consider it a "high-alert" medication. As such, there are several measures that can reduce the risk of an error when oral methotrexate is prescribed:

1. Build alerts in electronic prescribing systems and pharmacy computers to warn clinicians whenever doses of oral methotrexate have been entered (and to remind staff to check the indication with the patient in a retail setting). Configure the systems to avoid defaulting to a daily dosing schedule.

2. Have a pharmacist conduct a prospective drug-utilization review before dispensing oral methotrexate to determine its indication for use, verify proper dosing, confirm the correct dosing schedule on medication administration records and prescription labels, ensure staff and patient education, and promote appropriate monitoring of the patient.

3. Establish a system that ensures outpatients receive counseling when picking up new prescriptions and refills (e.g., mark the bag with a red flag to alert clerical staff that counseling is required).

4. Provide patients with clear written instructions that name a specific day of the week for taking the tablet(s). When possible, avoid choosing Monday since it could be misread as "morning." Prepare instructions in large print to assist elderly patients with poor eyesight.

5. Advise patients to contact their physician if they miss a dose. Tell them a flare-up of the disease is unlikely with one missed dose.

6. Ensure written drug information leaflets are given to patients and they contain clear advice about the weekly dosage schedule, not a daily dosage schedule.

7. Explain to patients that taking extra doses is dangerous. Encourage feedback to ensure the patient understands the weekly dosing schedule and that the medication should not be used as needed for symptom control.

8. Solicit help from a responsible caregiver if the patient appears to have cognitive or severe sensory difficulties.

9. Prescribe the drug as a dose pack (e.g., Rheumatrex by Lederle), which helps reinforce the weekly dosing schedule.

The expert witness report located in Appendix 28.2 provides an example of a report which addresses the liability associated with failing to recognize an inappropriate order for Methotrexate. The report, at the attorney's request, also describes the impact on the patient.

One of the recommended ways to reduce high risk drug errors is to have another practitioner do an independent double check of the medication. According to the 2008 Medication Error survey,[78] only 58 percent of the respondents always had someone else do a double check. Thirty-seven percent sometimes requested this and 5 percent never did. When compared to 2002, there was an 11 percent increase in nurses who never used a double check system, while the percent of nurses who always requested a double check remained constant.

28.10 High-Risk Populations

The effects of medication errors can range from insignificant to deadly. Failure to monitor levels of certain medications can result in either toxic responses from levels too high or a lack of therapeutic effect from levels too low. A vulnerable patient may receive the wrong medication, dose, or route of administration, or not receive the medication at all. Interactions between medications can result in toxic effects or one medication making another ineffective.

A. Pediatrics

Children are at particular risk of medication errors for a number of reasons. Unlike adults, they cannot question an unfamiliar medication or provide details of medical conditions which stimulate a healthcare professional to question the appropriateness of a medication order. All of the child's systems function closer to their maximum capacity than an adult's in order to meet metabolic demands. In the face of

illness, metabolic demands are increased even more, especially with fever, infection, injuries, or burns. Although children generally have healthy hearts and lungs that allow them to compensate for deficits, their immature systems have fewer reserves when stressed, leading to the possibility of rapid decompensation.[79] A medication error taxes a child's already limited ability to respond to physiological stresses. Additionally, children are at risk for medication errors due to the:

1. Different and changing drug dosages needed to treat children of different ages and sizes

2. Need for calculating individualized doses based on the patient's age, weight, body surface, and clinical condition

3. Lack of available dosage forms and concentrations appropriate for administration to neonates, infants, and children

4. Need for precise dose measurement and appropriate drug delivery systems

5. Lack of published information or Food and Drug Administration-approved labeling regarding dosing, safety, efficacy, and clinical use of drugs in the pediatric population[80]

6. Differences in responses to medications than how healthy adults react

7. Need for stocking more than one concentration of a medication

B. Elderly

Medication errors affect elderly individuals in all healthcare settings. Risk factors that put the elderly at especially high-risk for adverse medication outcomes include:

1. age-related decline in liver and kidney function,

2. greater sensitivity to the effects of medications,

3. reduced ability to tolerate usual adult doses,

4. multiple chronic diseases requiring multiple chronic medications, and

5. under-representation of the elderly in clinical trials.[81]

Medications control the symptoms of the elderly, prevent complications of disease, improve the quality of the frail senior's life, and maintain or improve physiological status.[82] Polypharmacy, or the prescribing of several medications at the same time, is common among the elderly. The more medications a resident is taking, the greater the chance of interactions, and the greater the risk of errors. Medicaid data for one state showed that during a 30-day period, 68 percent of long-term care residents had received nine or more prescription drugs, and 32 percent had received 20 or more prescription drugs.[83]

An Atlanta Legal Aid Society, Inc. study found that 21 percent of nursing home residents interviewed said they had been given the wrong medications, but 38 percent said the error was corrected when they pointed it out to the nurse. Fourteen percent said they actually ingested the wrong medication.[84]

A study of adverse drug events, some of which are due to medication errors, revealed the most common causes of prescribing errors in nursing homes. These were wrong dose (63 percent), failure to consider drug interaction (22 percent), and wrong choice of a drug (9 percent). Physicians also failed to order monitoring associated with the medication (83 percent) and did not respond to signs and symptoms of drug toxicity or to laboratory evidence of drug toxicity (41 percent).[85]

C. Allergic versus Intolerant

Perhaps the most preventable, and certainly among the most lethal, of medication errors is the administration of a drug for which the patient has an allergic history. Every patient should be asked: "Are you allergic to aspirin, iodine, sulfa, or penicillin? Have you ever had an allergic reaction to any drug?" Some patients do not consider over-the-counter medications as drugs, so the nurse must ask the question. Data about allergies should be documented on the front of the chart, on the patient's history and physical, on the nursing admission sheet, and on the medication administration record. Some facilities even include information about allergies on the patient's identification band, on the wall above the hospital bed, and on every physician order sheet.

Many patients report having allergic reactions to medications. However, on closer questioning, it can be determined they had nausea, vomiting, or diarrhea, not an allergy in a true immunologic sense. These symptoms are more accurately termed an intolerance, which would not preclude subsequent administration. The patient should be warned about the possibility of these symptoms and how to combat them, such as taking with food to avoid an upset stomach, and so on. The nurse is expected to question the patient who reports an allergy to a medication to find out what occurred. Nurses are expected to question an order that directs the nurse to administer a medication to which the patient is allergic, and to be able to identify drugs related to the one in question. If the patient says she is allergic to penicillin, the nurse would question an order for Ampicillin. A patient allergic to steroids should not be given Prednisone, Cortisone, or any of the many forms of steroids.

A New York woman's allergy to steroids was manifested by becoming psychotic. Before and after surgery on her shoulder for a displaced fracture of the surgical neck of the right humerus, she was given steroids to treat an asthmatic condition. The steroids were administered first in the form of Solu-Cortef, an intravenous form of hydrocortisone, followed by prednisone, an oral form. Following several doses of steroids, she became psychotic and was seen wandering around the hospital unit from room to room. In her confusion, she would not keep her sling on the operated arm. The inability to keep her arm immobilized resulted in damage to the surgical site. After the steroids stopped, she became alert and oriented. When she returned to the hospital a month later to redo the surgery on her shoulder, she reported an allergy to prednisone, but the nurse who obtained that information did not ask her what type of allergic reaction she had. She was again given Solu-Cortef, despite the notation on the order sheet that she was allergic to prednisone. The plaintiff's nurse expert witness (PI) was prepared to testify that the nurse should have recognized Solu-Cortef and prednisone as steroids and questioned this order. The order was filled by the night nursing supervisor, who also did not note the allergy. Again, following the Solu-Cortef administration, the plaintiff became confused, was seen banging on the hospital window with the arm that had been operated on, convinced her grandchildren were playing in the trees outside the hospital. She again damaged her shoulder. There were no more attempts to surgically repair her shoulder. The case settled for $250,000 in the midst of trial after the orthopedic surgeon admitted liability (unpublished case).

TIP: Carefully review the medical record for evidence of documentation of allergies. The attorney will encounter the following abbreviations indicating that an inquiry was made and the patient denied allergies: NKA (No Known Allergies) or NKDA (No Known Drug Allergies). The nurse has fulfilled the standard of care by inquiring about allergies and should not be liable if the patient conceals a history of allergies.

D. Critically Ill Patient

The critically ill patient is particularly vulnerable to serious medication errors. This individual is already high-risk for dying or having a reduced quality of life. There are five categories of critically ill patients:

1. People who suffer life-threatening medical problems in the community. This includes a wide array of people and problems, including severe infections, heart attacks, stroke, drug and alcohol-related emergencies, liver, lung, kidney failure, and many other less common disorders. Some may be in the intensive care unit (ICU) due to a delay or failure of diagnosis and delay in treatment.

2. People with life-threatening, potentially surgical conditions, such as multiple traumas, head injury, ruptured and/or dissecting aorta, and acute abdominal emergencies. Some of these individuals may be in the ICU as a result of trauma related to a personal injury suit.

3. Elective surgical patients undergoing high-risk procedures that normally require an ICU bed (e.g., coronary artery bypass surgery, lung resection, or removal of a brain tumor), or have enough existing medical problems to warrant admission to an ICU post op setting (e.g., a patient with heart failure undergoing gall bladder surgery).

4. Patients who deteriorate while in the hospital and need to be admitted or readmitted to an ICU for medical or surgical problems. The list of conditions that cause these problems is long but is usually one of seven: chest pain, cardiac rhythm disturbance, low blood pressure, infection, bleeding, respiratory failure, cardiac arrest, or some combination thereof. Patients with unexpected problems at the time of low-risk elective surgery are also included. Medical malpractice cases may result from alleged deviations associated with deterioration, such as failure to diagnose or appropriately intervene before the patient's condition becomes life threatening.

5. The chronically, critically ill. This is a varied group of patients who continue to have critical care issues such as requiring a ventilator for prolonged periods of time, sometimes indefinitely. In this group are patients who return to ICUs on multiple occasions for reason such as recurring severe infections or bouts of respiratory failure. The hospital mortality rate of this group is extremely high.[86]

An overdose, an inadequate amount of medication, a medication infusion hung at the wrong rate, or any other type of serious medication error may be all that is necessary to cause physiological stress to an individual already in a compromised state.

Detection of a medication error may be difficult because critically ill patients may deteriorate independent of an er-

ror. Furthermore, the skills of an intensivist may be needed to separate the impact of the error from the factors resulting in the critically ill condition.

E. Patients Assigned to Student Nurses

Although each student providing patient care should be supervised by an instructor, every instance of medication administration may not necessarily be observed. Some errors originate from communication problems. For example, there may be confusion about who is to administer the medications, which medication doses have been given, and which have been held.[87] Since many clinical experiences end with a post conference that may not coincide with the end of the shift, drugs that need to be given after the student leaves the unit may be overlooked by the facility's staff.

TIP: The Joint Commission specifically addresses supervision of students in the Human Resources chapter of the Comprehensive Accreditation Manual for Hospitals. HR.01.02.07 states "Staff oversee the supervision of students when they provide patient care, treatment, and services as part of their training."[88]

28.11 Litigation of the Medication Error Claim

The hospital risk manager investigating the incident—as well as the attorney for the family or injured patient—first must determine an injury has occurred. Without an injury, and solid scientific evidence supporting causation of the injury by the drug (or absence of the drug), there should be no litigation. Causation can be determined by a toxicologist, pharmacologist, or physician trained in a particular specialty (such as a cardiologist or nephrologist evaluating cardiac and kidney toxicities).

A. Useful Discovery Items

In addition to medical records, internal pharmacy records not part of the medical record should be subpoenaed. Prior to computers, these records were only retained for relatively short periods of time. With computers, these records are usually available indefinitely. An additional benefit to the computer record is a "fingerprint" of any authorized person making entries or changes to the record. No records can be replaced. If controlled substances are involved, a separate record requirement of five years by the Drug Enforcement Administration usually exceeds local record retention requirements for departmental records outside the chart. If there are toxicology issues, the raw data of the toxicology analysis should be reviewed. Often called the "litigation package," commercial toxicology laboratories are frequently asked for chromatographs, standards, controls, and so on, beyond the basic toxicology report.

Policies and procedures of the nursing and pharmacy department for safe medication use outline the mission and objective of the various departments related to medication use. Additional policies and procedures related to PCA may be found in the anesthesia policies. Operating rooms and intensive care units may have specific policies and procedures.

B. Types of Experts Needed

Once causation is established as described above, many jurisdictions require a certificate of merit or affidavit of a healthcare professional to affirm a particular professional violated the standard of care, and the violation was a cause or contributing cause of the injury to the patient. The expert recruited must be from the same profession as the patient's caregiver (i.e., physician, nurse, or pharmacist).

C. When Early Settlement is Advised

Early settlement is advised when causation is determined and an error occurred. Even though the phrase "to err is human" is pertinent, patients do not expect to be harmed by error, and arguing an error was innocent and not a violation of the standard of care will probably be ineffective with the jury. One prominent attorney who represented an insurance company representing pharmacists was quoted: "If your pharmacist fills the prescription with the wrong drug or the wrong strength, admit liability. Focus on the causation only. Patients expect perfection when getting their prescriptions filled—don't you?"

28.12 Summary

The prevention of medication errors is a multifaceted and multidisciplinary problem. The serious repercussions from a medication error, both from a clinical sense and a legal perspective, drive healthcare professionals to adhere to the basics of medication ordering, transcription or transmission of orders, and dispensing and administering of medications. A medication error can result in a patient's death. Therefore, there cannot be any relaxing from adherence to the standard of care. Patients demand and deserve it!

Endnotes

1. Barker, K.N. et al., "Medication errors observed in 36 healthcare facilities," *Arch Intern Med* 2002: 162 (16): 1897-903.

2. Bates, DW et al., "Incidence of adverse drug events and potential adverse drug events: Implications for prevention," ADE Prevention Study Groups, *JAMA* 1995: 274 (1): 29-34.

3. Institute of Medicine. *To Err is Human: Building a Safer Health System.* Washington, D.C.: National Academy of Sciences, 1999.

4. Lazarou, J., B.H. Pomeranz, and P.N. Corey, "Incidence of adverse drug reactions in hospitalized patients: a meta-analysis of prospective studies," *JAMA* 279, no. 15 (April 15, 1998): 1200–1205.

5. Kaiser Family Foundation. "Five years after IOM Report on medical errors, nearly half of all consumers worry about the safety of their health care," 2004. Retrieved online at http://www.kff.org/kaiserpolls/pomr111704nr.cfm, last accessed 5/27/06.

6. Reason, J., "Safety," American College of Endocrinology/American Association of Clinical Endocrinologists, Patient Safety and Medical System Errors in *Diabetes and Endocrinology Consensus Conference*, Washington, D.C., 2005.

7. Lisby, M., L. P. Nielsen, and J. Mainz, "Errors in the medication process: frequency, type, and potential clinical consequences," *International Journal of Quality Health Care* 1 (February 17, 2005): 15–22.

8. Hicks, R., et al., *MEDMARX 5th Anniversary Data Report*. Rockville, Maryland: US Pharmacopeia, 2004.

9. Anonymous, "Medication Safety Issue Brief: A Fully Stocked Toolkit," *Hospitals and Health Networks* 77, no. 6 (June 2003). Series II, Part 1, 2.

10. Institute of Medicine, "Medication errors injure 1.5 million people and cost billions of dollars annually." 2006, http://www8.nationalacademies.org/onpinews/newsitem.aspx?RecordID=11623 last accessed 6/20/10

11. Brennan, T. A., L. L. Leape, and N. M. Laird, "Incidence of Adverse events and negligence in hospitalized patients: results from the Harvard Medical Practice Study," *New England Journal of Medicine* 324 (1991): 370–376. *Perspectives in Healthcare Risk Management*, 2-8, as quoted in Kohn, L., J. Corrigan, and M. Donaldson (eds.) *To Err is Human*, Washington, D.C.: National Academy Press, 2000.

12. See note 1.

13. "ISMP Survey on State Licensing Boards Response to Medical Error," http://www.ismp.org/s/survey200502R.asp, accessed 9/23/05.

14. Cohen, H. and A. Shastay. "Getting to the root of medication errors," *Nursing 2008,* December 2008, 39-47.

15. Flynn, E., et al., "Comparison of methods for detecting medication errors in 36 hospitals and skilled-nursing facilities," *American Journal of Health-System Pharmacy* 59, no. 5 (March 1, 2002): 436–446.

16. Wald, H. and K. G. Shojania, "Incident reporting," In *Making Health Care Safer: A Critical Analysis of Patient Safety Practices.* Rockville, Maryland: Agency for Healthcare Research and Quality, 2001.

17. Iyer, P., L. Cohen, and J. T. O'Donnell, "Medical Legal Aspects of Medication Error," In *Drug Injury: Liability, Analysis, and Prevention,* Second edition, ed. J. T. O'Donnell. Tucson, Arizona: Lawyers & Judges Publishing Co., 2005.

18. See note 14.

19. See note 8.

20. *Id.*

21. Iyer, P., and J. Barone. "Obtaining and Organizing Medical Records," In *Medical Legal Aspects of Medical Records, Second Edition,* eds. P. Iyer, B. Levin, Tucson, Arizona: Lawyers & Judges Publishing Co., 2010.

22. "Creating a culture of safety on an inpatient unit," *Focus on Patient Safety,* Vol. 9 Issue 2, 2006, 3-4.

23. Benjamin, D. M. and J. T. O'Donnell, "Medication Errors," In *Legal Medicine,* Seventh edition, ed. S. Sandbar. Schaumburg, Illinois: American College of Legal Medicine, 2006.

24. Stefancyk, A., "Postponing medication administration," *AJN,* April 2009, Vol 109, No. 4, 21-23.

25. See note 23.

26. Wilson D. G., R. G. McArtney, and R. G. Newcombe, "Medication Errors in Paediatric Practice: Insights from a Continuous Quality Improvement Approach," *European Journal of Pediatric Surgery* 157 (1998): 769–774.

27. Cohen, M. R., *Medication Errors,* 2–3, Washington, D.C.: American Public Health Association, 1999.

28. Burnum, J. G. "Preventability of Adverse Drug Reaction" *Annals of Internal Medicine* 85 (1976): 810.

29. Bates, D. W., L. L. Leape, and D. J. Cullen, et al., "Effect of Computerized Physician Order Entry and a Team Intervention on Prevention of Serious Medication Errors," *JAMA* 280, no. 15 (1998): 1311–1316.

30. Cohen, M. "Medication Errors," *Nursing 2009,* March 2009, 12.

31. Cohen, M. and H. Cohen, "Following a game plan for continued improvement, medication errors," *Nursing 95* (November 1995): 34–37.

32. See note 14.

33. Ketchum, K., Grass, C. and Padwojski, A., "Medication reconciliation," *AJN,* November 2005, Vol. 105, No. 11, 78-85.

34. See note 26.

35. *Id.*

36. See note 31.

37. Lesar, T., B. Lomaestro, and H. Pohl, "Medication prescribing errors in a teaching hospital," *Archives of Internal Medicine* 157 (1997): 1569–1574.

38. Lesar, T. S., L. Briceland, and D. S. Stein, "Factors Related to Errors in Medication Prescribing," *JAMA* 277, no. 4 (1997): 312–317.

39. See note 1.

40. O'Donnell, J. T., "From the Courtroom: Systems Failure-An Intrathecal Vincristine Tragedy," *Pharmacy Practice News* (January 2004).

41. See note 1.

42. "Bad 'marks' for order communication," *ISMP Medication Safety Alert,* http://www.ismp.org/msaarticles/badprint.htm, accessed 3/02/04.

43. "All is not as it seems," *ISMP Medication Safety Alert* 3, no. 9 (September 2005).

44. Garbutt, J. G., et al., "Safe medication prescribing: training and experience of medical students and house staff at a large teaching hospital," *Academic Medicine* 6 (June 2005): 594–599.

45. "Computerized ordering cuts medication errors," www.news.yahoo.com.

46. http://www.jointcommission.org/NR/rdonlyres/2329F8F5-6EC5-4E21-B932-54B2B7D53F00/0/06_dnu_list.pdf.

47. http://www.jointcommission.org/PatientSafety/NationalPatientSafetyGoals/abbr_tips.htm.

48. Iyer, P., "Legal Aspects of Charting," In *Medical Legal Aspects of Medical Records*, Second Edition, eds. P. Iyer, B. Levin, Tucson, Arizona: Lawyers & Judges Publishing Co., 2010.

49. O'Donnell, J. T. "Pharmacist Malpractice and the Infamous Courtney Case," In *Drug Injury: Liability, Analysis, and Prevention*, Second edition, ed. J. T. O'Donnell. Tucson, Arizona: Lawyers & Judges Publishing Co., 2005.

50. Kalman and Schlegel, "Standards of Practice for the Profession of Pharmacy," *American Pharmacy* 19, no. 3 (March 1979).

51. See note 14.

52. Fraleigh, J. "Injectable drug errors and syringe labeling," *RN*, March 2008, 21.

53. "Positive identification: not just for patients, but for drugs and solutions," *ISMP Medication Safety Alert* 3, no. 8 (August 1, 2005).

54. Cohen, M. "Tall man letters a big help." *Nursing 2009*, February 2009, 12.

55. Metules, T. and Bauer, J. JCAHO's Patient Safety Goals: Preventing Med Errors," *RN* January 2007, 39-43.

56. Green, M., "Nursing error and human nature," *Journal of Nursing Law* 9, no. 4 (2004): 7–44.

57. Lesar, T., "Errors in the use of medication dosage equations," *Archives of Pediatric and Adolescent Medicine* 152 (April 1998): 340–344.

58. Laska, L. (ed.),"Woman dies after endoscopic lithotripsy procedure for removal of kidney stone," *Medical Malpractice Verdicts, Settlements, and Experts* (April 2003): 58.

59. Laska, L. (ed.), "Failure to promptly administer antibiotics for kidney infection, resulting in death," *Medical Malpractice Verdicts, Settlements, and Experts* (June 2004): 17.

60. Laska, L. (ed.), "Patient dies after Fentanyl patches induce overdose," *Medical Malpractice Verdicts, Settlements, and Experts* (July 2003): 35.

61. Laska, L. (ed.), "Pitocin administered to pregnant woman who had undergone previous cesarean section," *Medical Malpractice Verdicts, Settlements, and Experts* (April 2003): 36.

62. http://www.jointcommission.org/SentinelEvents/SentinelEventAlert/sea_11.htm.

63. Davis, N. M., *Medical Abbreviations: 24,000 Conveniences at the Expense of Communications and Safety*. Eleventh edition. Huntington Valley, Pennsylvania: Neil M. Davis Associates, 2003.

64. O'Donnell, J. T., "Adverse Effects of Diabetic Drugs," In *Drug Injury: Liability, Analysis, and Prevention, Second edition*, ed. J. T. O'Donnell. Tucson, Arizona: Lawyers & Judges Publishing Co., 2005.

65. "Metabolic and nutritional diseases of the nervous system," In *Harrison's Principles of Internal Medicine*, Seventh edition, eds. Wintrobe, M. M., et al. New York: McGraw-Hill, 1974.

66. Laska, L. (ed.), "Diabetic overdosed with insulin soon after hospitalization," *Medical Malpractice Verdicts, Settlements, and Experts* (April 2005): 18.

67. O'Donnell, J. T., "Pain Medications and OxyContin," In *Drug Injury: Liability, Analysis, and Prevention*. Second edition, ed. J. T. O'Donnell, Chapter 30. Tucson, Arizona: Lawyers & Judges Publishing Co., 2005.

68. Laska, L. (ed.), "Overdose of Fentanyl following surgery for sigmoid diverticulitis," *Medical Malpractice Verdicts, Settlements, and Experts* (May 2005).

69. D'Arcy, Y. "Are opioids safe for your patient?," *Nursing 2009*, April 2009, 40-44.

70. www.ismp.org.

71. D'Arcy, Y. "Keeping your patient safe during PCA," Nursing 2008, *January 2008*, 50-55.

72. See note 69.

73. *Marie Lenoure, Special Administrator for the Estate of Victor LePore v. Oak Pak Hospital,* Cook County (IL) Circuit Court, Case No. 98 L 7257.

74. Laska, L. (ed.), "Doctors fail to order proper tests and nurses fail to inform doctor of change in status in woman following fall while on Coumadin," *Medical Malpractice Verdicts, Settlements, and Experts* (April 2005): 21.

75. Cohen, M. "Vindesine tragedy," *Nursing 2009*, March 2009, 12.

76. Laska, L. (ed.), "Failure to administer proper dose of 5-Fluoroouracil to tongue cancer patient," *Medical Malpractice Verdicts, Settlements, and Experts* (September 2005): 38.

77. Laska, L. (Ed), "Nursing home's nurse, woman's physician and pharmacy all faulted in failing to recognize that she was receiving rheumatoid arthritis medication daily, instead of once a week," *Medical Malpractice Verdicts, Settlements, and Experts*, April 2010, 16.

78. See note 14.

79. Engleman, S., "Pediatric Records," In *Medical Legal Aspects of Medical Records, Second Edition*, eds. P. Iyer, B. Levin, Tucson, Arizona: Lawyers & Judges Publishing Co., 2010.

80. Levine, S., et al., "Guidelines for preventing medication errors in pediatrics," *The Journal of Pediatric Pharmacology and Therapeutics* 6 (2001): 426–442.

81. Iyer, P., "Nursing home liability and its consequences," In *Nursing Home Litigation: Investigation and Case Preparation, Second Edition*, ed. P. Iyer. Tucson, Arizona: Lawyers & Judges Publishing Co., 2006.

82. Clark, T., "Medications and the Nursing Home Survey: Introduction," In *Medication Guide for the long-term care nurse*, ed. T. Clark. American Society of Consultant Pharmacists, 2003.

83. Vance, J., "Reducing medication errors in nursing homes," http://www.amda.com/caring/april2003/med-errors.htm.

84. Atlanta Legal Aid Society, Inc., "The silenced voice speaks out," http://www.law.emory.edu/alas/abuse.htm.

85. Gurwitz, et al., "Incidence and preventability of adverse drug events in nursing homes," *American Journal of Medicine* 109 (2000): 87.

86. Cohen, I., "Pain and Suffering in the Intensive Care Unit," In *Medical Legal Aspects of Pain and Suffering*, ed. P. Iyer. Tucson, Arizona: Lawyers & Judges Publishing Co., 2003.

87. Cohen, M. "Errors by nursing students: unique circumstances," *Nursing 2008*, March 2008, 12.

88. "Human Resources," *CAMH Refreshed Core*, The Joint Commission, January 2010, 6.

Additional Reading

Anderson, P. and Townsend, T. "Medication errors: Don't let them happen to you," *American Nurse Today*, March 2010, 23-27.

Burke, C. "Sidestepping unsafe abbreviations," *Nursing 2009*, January 2009, 21-2.

Cohen, H. "Reduce the risks of high-alert drugs," *Nursing 2007*, September 2007, 49-55.

Hutchinson, R. and Rodriguez, L. "Capnography and respiratory depression," *AJN*, February 2008, 35-39.

Rosenthal, K. "Avoiding common perils of drug administration," *Nursing 2007*, April 2007, 20-21.

Appendix 28.1
Omitted Medication

* All names have been changed.

Date

Steven Quigley Esq.
Rome and Rome
804 Walnut Tree Road
Ellison, MT

Estate of Gale Walker
Dear Mr. Quigley,

Thank you for forwarding the records of Mrs. Walker. I have reviewed the material listed below:

- Medical record for admission to Minor Medical Center 8/12/04-9/1/04
- Minor Medical Center Clinical Department Policy and Procedure-Medication System
- Rider for Question 2
- State of *** Department of Health and Senior Services report dated 1/4/05
- Deposition of Gale Russo
- Deposition of Cindy Maguire RN

Summary of medical events
On the day Mrs. Gale Walker was admitted to Minor Medical Center (8/14/04), she was an 83-year-old who had been experiencing severe anemia and increasing nausea for three weeks. The focus of the medical plan of care was to provide blood transfusions, determine why the patient was anemic, and to control her symptoms. In an effort to reduce the patient's nausea, Dr. Lipton provided a series of orders for Compazine beginning 8/23/04. After adjusting the Compazine orders in response to episodes of vomiting (on 8/24/04, 8/25/04, 8/26/04, 8/27/04 and 8/28/04), he ordered Compazine to be given by mouth every eight hours (6:00 A.M., 2:00 P.M., 10:00 P.M.) as needed (beginning on 8/27/04). The patient was to receive Metoclopramide (Regan) by IV push every eight hours (6:00 A.M., 2:00 P.M., 10:00 P.M.). On 8/28/04, in anticipation of a scheduled small bowel series, the patient was not to have anything to eat or drink except for medications as of midnight.

Nurse Cindy Maguire was assigned to care for the patient on the 7:00 A.M.-7:00 P.M. shift of 8/28/04 and 8/29/04. On 8/28/04, while under the care of Nurse Maguire, the patient vomited. The nursing notes for 8/29/04 state that the

patient was alert and resting in bed at 2:00 P.M. She was awaiting x-ray. At 2:15 P.M., she left the nursing unit for the small bowel series. The Reglan and Compazine were not administered before the patient left the nursing unit. The patient's medication administration record shows that the 2:00 P.M. doses were not administered because "the patient was in x-ray."

Keila Ringwald (the patient's daughter) testified that she called the patient's room about 2:15 P.M. and there was no answer. At 2:30 P.M. the patient's daughter called the nursing station and was told that the patient had just gone down (to Radiology.) At 3:00 P.M., the daughter was told that the patient was not back and that the test took about three hours.

The patient vomited in the Radiology Department, went into a respiratory arrest, and required intubation. She was transferred to the Intensive Care Unit, where she was placed on a ventilator. At 5:30 P.M., the daughter was informed by "Cindy" that the patient had been transferred to ICU after vomiting and inhaling the vomit.

After it was clear that the patient was not improving, a family conference was held about the patient's poor prognosis on 9/1/04. The patient was extubated and died about three hours later on 9/1/04.

Standard of Care
The policies of Minor Medical Center state that the hospital system provided a Schedule Meds Due List, which contained all of the medications scheduled for a specific hour. The list printed out 45 minutes before the medication was due to be given. The nurse was expected to review the medical care plan for odd hours and make a note of all irregular hours. The Scheduled Meds Due List was to be checked every hour during the shift. Medications could be given one hour before or after a scheduled dose.

The Department of Health and Senior Services investigated the incident and prepared a report on 1/4/05. The facility was cited for failure of the registered nurse to ensure that medications to control the patient's nausea and vomiting were administered prior to her transfer to the Radiology Department. The facility was cited for failure of the Radiology Department to have adequate policies and procedures addressing patient safety.

The deposition of Cindy Maguire was reviewed. She testified that she was told the patient was going for her small bowel series some time after lunch. Nurse Maguire testified that she did not administer the 2:00 P.M. medications because she did not realize that she had 2:00 P.M. medication orders until after the patient left the floor. She testified that she had administered these two 2:00 P.M. medications the previous day. Nurse Maguire testified that she was on the nursing unit when the patient left the unit for the Radiology Department, and that she would have looked at the medication list after 2:30 P.M. After recognizing that the Reglan and Compazine were to have been given at 2:00 P.M., the nurse testified that she highlighted the doses. If the patient had returned within a reasonable time (by 3:00 P.M.), the nurse would have given the medications and changed the schedule for the following doses. She heard the code called and estimated that it was very close to her dinner hour, which was 5:00 P.M.

The standard of care requires the reasonably prudent staff nurse to follow hospital policy regarding reviewing the lists of medications to be administered at specific times. Nurse Maguire deviated by not consulting the list of medications she was to administer at 2:00 P.M. The reasonably prudent nurse is expected to know that small bowel series involves taking a series of films, which will delay the return to the patient to the nursing unit. When a patient is going to be transported to the Radiology Department for a test that will not be brief, the reasonably prudent nurse is expected to consult the list of medications to see what medications are due and need to be administered before the patient leaves the nursing unit. I find from the review of all of the material supplied to me that Nurse Maguire deviated from the standard of care by failing to administer Compazine and Reglan, medications that were important to a patient who had a history of vomiting.

I hold these opinions with a reasonable degree of nursing probability.

Very truly,

Patricia Iyer MSN RN LNCC

Appendix 28.2

* All names have been changed

Date
Kelten Ranger, Jr. Esq.
Orange and Ranger
204 Prince Ave
Princeton, NH

Re: *Estate of Carol Lucite v. Minor Medical Center et al.*

Dear Mr. Ranger,

Thank you for forwarding the medical records of this patient. I have reviewed Mrs. Lucite's admission records to Minor Medical Center from 1/25/05-2/5/05 and her autopsy report.

Admission assessment

When Mrs. Lucite was admitted to the Behavioral Health Center of Minor Medical Center on 1/25/05, she was a 72-year-old, married woman. Her admitting diagnosis was alcohol abuse. Her husband accompanied her. Although she was alert and oriented, she had limited reliability as an informant, impaired concentration and was jittery. As the patient was intoxicated, the husband answered most of the questions. Her medical conditions included diabetes, heart disease, arthritis, and multiple myeloma. The section of the admission assessment form used to list the medications was left blank. The patient denied taking her medications that day and when asked why, the nurse documented "not responsible."

The multidisciplinary interventions documented on the treatment plan included (MD): "Safe detox, treatment of alcoholism, depression and medical problems." (Nursing): "Patient will be medicated appropriately throughout her detoxification. She will be aware of her medication and the purpose of taking them."

Methotrexate administration

On 1/25/05, Dr. Kelley phoned in orders for medications. "Methotrexate 2.5 mgs 6 tablets per day" was one of these orders. This order was taken by Lani Spitfire RN, and was signed by Dr. Kelley at some later point. According to a consultation dictated by Dr. Mark Erlinger, an internist, the patient had been taking Methotrexate 2.5 mg six per week (for arthritis). This consult was dictated on 1/26/05 and transcribed the following day, 1/27/05.

Methotrexate administration of 6 tablets once a day began on 1/26/05 and it was administered daily at 10:00 A.M.

on 1/27/05, 1/28/05, 1/29/05, 1/30/05, 1/31/05, 2/01/05 and 2/2/05. A telephone order was received from Dr. Losey on 2/2/05 at 5:50 P.M. to discontinue the drug.

Medical condition 1/25/05-2/3/05

As part of the treatment plan for her alcoholism, the patient was placed on a detoxification treatment plan, which included the use of Librium and Haldol as needed. On 1/26/05, shortly after the beginning of Methotrexate treatment, the patient was pleasant, cooperative, and somewhat shaky. She was described as cheerful and friendly on 1/27/05 and 1/28/05, Days Two and Three of Methotrexate administration. No specific medical complaints were noted on 1/29/05. As the week progressed, her medical condition deteriorated rapidly and significantly, as described below. The recognition that the patient was experiencing toxic effects of Methotrexate led to a transfer of the patient to a different nursing unit on 2/3/05. The section below describes her condition until that transfer took place.

Fever

Mrs. Lucite began running a fever on 1/30/05, her 5th day of Methotrexate treatment. Her temperature was elevated to 100.4° at 2:00 A.M., and remained at least 100° or higher (with one exception) until it hit a high of 101.7° on 2/1/05 at 4:00 A.M. Her temperature remained over 101° until it dropped to 97.4° on 2/2/05. It continued to fluctuate on 2/2/05 and 2/3/05. On 2/2/05 at 9:15 A.M., she complained of chills and requested a blanket for uncontrollable shaking. Her temperature was 100.7°. Her temperature was 101.8° at 1:30 P.M. on 2/2/05. On 2/3/05, the patient was trembling and sweating.

Incontinence

At 2:00 A.M. on 1/30/05, the patient became incontinent of urine with a foul odor present. An order was obtained to obtain a urine specimen by straight catheterization (not leaving the catheter in place.) On 1/31/05, A. Gagliardi, RN noted that the patient was incontinent. After the patient was incontinent on the bathroom floor and rug, a diaper was placed on her. She continued to get urine all over the floor that day. She was diapered again on 2/1/05 and continued to be incontinent.

Respiratory status

On 1/30/05, at 12:00 A.M., the patient was noted to have a moist non-reproductive cough with wheezing heard throughout her lungs. The wheezing was so loud that it could be heard without a stethoscope. Respiratory therapy was begun. At 4:00 A.M. and 5:00 A.M. that day, the patient's pulse oximeter reading was 92 percent (normal is 95 percent-100 percent). She continued to have difficulty breathing on 1/31/05. On 2/2/05 on the night shift, the patient's breathing pattern was described as irregular. She had labored breathing and wheezing at 8 A.M. on 2/2/05.

Pain

Mrs. Lucite complained of pain in her back on 2/2/05 and stated it was relieved by nebulizer treatments. She complained of a headache at 2:45 P.M. on 2/2/05. Pain from her sore mouth and throat is described in the "gastrointestinal" section below.

Mental and emotional status

The patient was described as confused and having difficulty following directions at 12:30 P.M. on 1/30/05, the first time these symptoms were noted. She was also described as depressed and tearful. On 1/31/05, A. Gagliardi, RN noted that the patient remained somewhat confused.

Gastrointestinal changes

The patient's blood sugar dropped to 25 at 1:00 P.M. on 1/30/05, the first time since admission that it had fallen to this critical low point (normal is 80-120). She was given oral glucose to raise it. The patient's appetite was poor at 6:30 P.M. that day. She was unable to finish her meals. On 1/31/05, A. Gagliardi, RN noted that the patient's diabetes was not controlled. Sores in her mouth were first documented on 1/31/05 by the psychiatrist. The nurses on 2/1/05 noted a sore throat and sores in her mouth. On 2/2/05, Dr. Erlinger documented that the patient had trouble eating due to her sore mouth. The patient was not eating well at that time. On 2/2/05, the patient's blood sugar varied between a low of 38 and a high of 72. The patient was continuing to eat "minimally" despite encouragement. Her blood sugar remained low at 68 at 1:00 A.M. on 2/3/05.

Lethargy

The patient was alert and taking part in activities in the psychiatric unit until 1/30/05. The patient was in bed all day on 1/30/05. The evening shift nurse encouraged her to get out of bed and walk. An unsteady gait was noted on 1/31/05. On the night that began at midnight on 1/31/05, the patient had difficulty falling asleep. The patient was in bed all day on 2/1/05 and 2/2/05. The patient was awake several times on the night shift that began on 2/3/05.

Status at the time of transfer to medical unit

On 2/2/05, the psychiatrist noted that the patient was worsening, was still incontinent and had poor breathing. Dr. Er-

linger was to evaluate her and possibly transfer her to the medical unit. At 2:55 P.M. on 2/2/05, the patient's complete blood count was analyzed. The patient had a 0.9 white blood cell count, which was described by the laboratory as a critically low value. The patient's white blood cell count had been 6.3 on admission on 1/25/05. (Normal levels are 5.0-10). On 2/3/05, Dr. Erlinger noted her decreased white blood cell count and stomatitis (sore mouth) and attributed it to the Methotrexate. Arrangements were made to transfer her to the medical unit.

After receiving what was to be her final dose of Methotrexate, at around 2:30 A.M. on 2/3/05, the patient was transferred to a medical floor. According to A. Gagliardi, RN, the patient was "having severe complications-elevated temperatures, low blood sugar levels, low white blood cell count." She was a possible transfer to a medical floor and appeared to be through detoxification.

Condition 2/3/05-2/5/05

Carol Lucite was admitted to a medical unit (1 West) at 12:30 P.M. on 2/3/05. She was alert and oriented with appropriate behavior. The problems noted on admission included:

- pale skin
- rash on her face, back and abdomen
- incontinence of urine
- reddened elbows
- diminished breath sounds in lower lobes of lungs
- constant sore throat and mouth affecting sleep, activity and appetite.

Medical problems 2/3/05-2/5/05

During the remaining days of Mrs. Lucite's life, she experienced the following problems, which are described below.

Fever

The patient's temperature was 101° at 2:30 P.M. on 2/3/05. Her temperature remained elevated at 8:30 P.M. and then dropped to 99° at 2:30 P.M. Her temperature remained below 100° on 2/4/05 and rose to 101° at 8:00 A.M. on 2/5/05. It dropped to 98.2° at 8:00 P.M. on 2/5/05 shortly before her death.

Incontinence

The first note documenting incontinence following the patient's transfer to 1 West was written at 12:00 midnight on the night that began as 2/5/05. The patient was incontinent of urine. Her genitalia were red and irritated.

Respiratory status

A nurse noted that Mrs. Lucite had a moist cough at 7:30 A.M. on 2/4/05. By 2:00 P.M., worsening coughing made it difficult for Mrs. Lucite to speak. He voice was very hoarse. The doctor was paged for orders. At 3:30 P.M. on 2/4/05, the patient was described as "gurgly" sounding with crackles and wheezes. By that time, it was very difficult to understand her. Her voice was hoarse and her mouth was reddened and swollen. Her respirations continued to sound gurgling as of 9:00 P.M. At 12:00 A.M. at the beginning of 2/5/05, the patient was described as "very gurgling." When she was suctioned, bloody drainage was removed from her mouth. Oral care was attempted two times.

Mental and emotional status

At 7:30 A.M. on 2/4/05, Mrs. Lucite was agitated and confused. At 3:30 P.M. on 2/4/05, the patient was again described as confused and agitated. She received three doses of Ativan that day. A note by Dr. Kelley on that day states that he was concerned lest sedation be given for restlessness and worsen her breathing compromise. Mrs. Lucite was very restless as of 9:00 P.M. on 2/4/05, and was continuously pulling off her blankets and tossing and turning. She was trying to get out of bed on that shift, and was described as very agitated. Restraints (type not specified) were used on the evening of 2/4/05 and the night shift of 2/4/05-2/5/05. On 2/5/05, Dr. Erlinger documented that the family and the patient did not want any aggressive intervention used such as ventilation or CPR. A "do not resuscitate" order was written.

Gastrointestinal

A nursing care plan documented on 2/3/05 states that Mrs. Lucite had abdominal pain. On 2/3/05, the patient's sore mouth reduced her ability to eat. That day, she took less than 50 percent of her meal due to her sore mouth. On 2/3/05, the patient took her own medications. Her blood sugar was only 59 at 5:00 P.M. but rose to 168 at 7:20 P.M. On 2/4/05, Dr. Erlinger noted that the patient's mouth was very sore. The patient's mouth was bleeding as of midnight on 2/5/05. At 8:50 A.M. on 2/5/05, she was given her first dose of Morphine 2 mgs for oral pain. This was repeated at 1:50 A.M., along with Ativan for restlessness. Morphine was again given to the patient at 1:30 P.M. She was unable to swallow pills that day.

Lethargy

Mrs. Lucite was described as having generalized weakness at 7:30 A.M. on 2/4/05. She was observed to be lethargic on the day shift of 2/5/05.

Rash

The patient's face and elbows were red at 7:30 A.M. on 2/4/05. A rash was covering her face, abdomen, and back as of 3:30 PM on 2/4/05 and was described as reddened and raised.

Tremors

Mrs. Lucite was observed to have tremors or shaking of her hands at 7:45 P.M. on 2/3/05. She continued to have tremors noted at 7:30 A.M. on 2/4/05.

Description of death

At 7:30 P.M. on 2/5/05, Mrs. Lucite was unresponsive. Her breathing was labored. It was impossible to measure the oxygen level in her blood. Her heart rate was rapid. A Foley catheter, which had been inserted on the day shift of 2/5/05, was draining clear yellow urine. The oxygen was turned up to 15 liters per minute (normal is 4-6.) An oxygen mask covered her face. Her family was at her bedside. At 8:00 P.M., the patient was given Morphine. Thirty minutes later, she died.

Autopsy and toxicity studies of the patient's blood led to the conclusion that the patient died from Methotrexate toxicity superimposed on diabetes, hypertension and chronic alcoholism.

Standards of care

The first step in the delivery of appropriate nursing care is to obtain assessment data. When a patient is admitted to the hospital, a standard part of the nursing admission assessment is to obtain information about the medications the patient was taking at home. When the patient is unreliable or unable to answer that question, the nurse is expected to determine if anyone else in the household can provide this information. Mrs. Lucite's husband, who accompanied his wife to the hospital, should have been asked to provide the nurses with a list of medications with their frequencies and dosages, or to bring in the actual pill containers for the nurse to use to document this information. This information should then be used to compare with medications ordered in the hospital. There is no indication that the nurse who admitted the patient to the hospital, Lani Spitfire, RN, made any attempt to learn the names, frequencies and doses of the medications the patient was taking. This was a deviation from the standard of care.

Nurses are expected to know the usual doses of medications they administer. The first opportunity to catch an inappropriate dose occurs when the nurse accepts or transcribes orders from a physician. Nurse Spitfire further deviated from the standard of care by accepting a telephone order for a medication that exceeded the recommended dosage. Methotrexate is used to treat a variety of conditions, including rheumatoid arthritis. The recommended starting dose is 7.5 mgs per week or divided dosage of 2.5 mgs orally at 12 hour intervals for three days given as a course once a week. The dosage is not to exceed 20 mgs/week. Mrs. Lucite was being given 15 mgs of Methotrexate a day. If Nurse Spitfire was unfamiliar with the indications for use of this drug and the expected dosage range, it was her obligation to consult standard pharmacology texts. This information is readily available on nursing units in the form of the Physicians Desk Reference or a nursing drug reference book. Some facilities have computerized information available. A clinical pharmacist should also be available for questions. The failure to question the Methotrexate order was a deviation from the standard of care.

Each nurse who administered Methotrexate deviated from the standard of care by failing to recognize that the dose ordered was outside of the therapeutic range and was too high. The standard of care requires the nurse to verify the dosage by consulting standard pharmacology tests, the pharmacist and the physician. On or around 1/27/05, the consultation completed by Dr. Mark Erlinger, which documented that the patient was receiving Methotrexate 2.5 mgs six per week, should have been readily available to the nursing staff. One of the purposes of the medical record is to communicate key information to other members of the healthcare staff. It is obvious that there was a complete lack of communication between all medical professionals, including nurses, pharmacists and doctors. The patient received eight days of Methotrexate without any evidence that any nurse questioned the dosage or referred to the consultation by Dr. Erlinger. The failure to question the Methotrexate order was a deviation from the standard of care.

I hold the opinion that the nurses deviated from the standard of care with a reasonable degree of nursing certainty.

Thank you for the opportunity to evaluate this case.

Very truly,

Patricia Iyer RN MSN LNCC

Chapter 29

Nurses Who Kill

Katherine Ramsland, PhD and Dana DeVito, RN

Synopsis
29.1 Introduction: The Serial Killer in Health Care
29.2 Differences Between Doctors and Nurses as HCSKs
    A. Their Respective Positions Fuel Different Motives
    B. Dr. Michael Swango and Dr. Harold Shipman
    C. Nurses More Prevalent
    D. Serial Murder versus Euthanasia
29.3 The Case of Charles Cullen
    A. Initial Suspicions
    B. Cullen's Revelations
    C. Response of Police
    D. A Murderer's History
    E. Response of Healthcare Institutions
    F. Special Problems for Investigators in Cases of HCSKs
    G. New Issues in Cullen Case
    H. Cullen's Advice
    I. Discovery of Red Flags and Reports Ignored
    J. Similarities to Other Cases
29.4 Summary of Other Cases
    A. Male HCSKs—Methods and Motives
    B. Female HCSKs—Methods and Motives
    C. Similarities
    D. Statistics—Prevalence and Increase
    E. Red Flags—Detecting Deviant Behavior
29.5 Forensic Nursing
    A. Definition
    B. History
    C. Contemporary Roles
29.6 Healthcare Institutions' Role in Screening Candidates
    A. Nurse Recruitment
    B. Human Resource Department
    C. Background Checks
    D. Risk Management Department
29.7 Healthcare Institutions' Role in Detecting and Monitoring
    A. Call for Nurse Database
    B. Response Since Cullen
29.8 Role of the Forensic Nurse in the Healthcare Setting
    A. Education and Training
    B. The Forensic Nurse and Risk Management
    C. Reporting Pathways
    D. Bridging the Gap Between Health Care and Law Enforcement
29.9 Policies in Response to Dr. Harold Shipman's Murder History
29.10 Update 2011
29.11 Conclusion
Endnotes
Additional Reading

29.1 Introduction: The Serial Killer in Health Care

Some nurses have assisted patients to die out of motives of mercy, but some kill for pleasure, thrill, or other self-centered reasons. This chapter is concerned primarily with the traits and behaviors of those nurses who kill patients in ways and for purposes that might encourage them to repeat their actions. They have become sufficiently numerous to be grouped as a subcategory of serial murder, which allows for a distinct definition, as well as a list of behavioral red flags to assist with risk assessment. A healthcare serial killer (HCSK) may be any type of employee in the healthcare system who uses his position to murder at least two patients in two separate incidents for self-centered purposes, with the psychological capacity for more killing. (The HCSK generally kills more than two people.) The killer may be a physician or nurse, male or female, or any of the support staff who work closely with key medical personnel. The authors focus specifically on nurses (male or female) who kill, because they outnumber predatory physicians. This chapter examines their motives, modus operandi, and other relevant factors, as well as the public's response. Since there are too many cases to detail in a single chapter, the authors selected Charles Cullen, among recent confessors in the United States, and list summaries of several other prominent cases. In addition, the chapter provides statistics from research about these killers and the ramifications for healthcare policies and procedures. Section 29.10 updates what has happened with the laws since this chapter was published in a previous edition.

TIP: Nurses who kill have learned how to exploit the atmosphere of trust in the healthcare community and to hasten deaths that may go unnoticed in an already vulnerable arena.

The first comprehensive study of HCSKs indicated that between 1975 and 2005, there were over 75 such cases in civilized societies (half in the U.S.), with more suspected and several that cannot be fully investigated.[1] A more recent study has shown that from 1970 to 2006, there were 90 criminal prosecutions of healthcare workers, 36 of them in the U.S.[2] No one knows how many people have been killed by nurses. A rare few enter the profession as predatory "angels of death," while many transform into killers on the job, sometimes via benign motives. Understandably, co-workers and potential patients want to know how to spot dangerous nurses before harm is done, but often these killers do not stand out. They may even be exemplary at what they do, and thus garner little suspicion. However, observant co-workers can spot the signs.

TIP: It is clear that patients must depend on hospitals and clinics to spot the red flags and do something about them. Too often these killers have been allowed to drift from one hospital to another, fired under a cloud of suspicion but rarely reported or brought to justice until incriminating evidence has reached shocking levels.

Institutions face challenges related to suspected killers. Hospital administrators claim that many laws have allowed that if they voice suspicions, especially to future employers of a suspect, they can be sued. But some hospitals are discovering they may be sued for *not* doing so, and their insurance carriers will not cover them.[3] The companies say intentional acts of murder are not considered part of professional practice. The hospitals, caught in a Catch-22, are on their own. When families sue those facilities that did not voice suspicions when asked or did not warn other potential employers of a suspected party, they receive a disturbing and expensive wake-up call. With new laws that now provide better protections for institutions, some employees are complaining about invasion of privacy. See Section 29.10.

The most susceptible patients are very young children, who are unable to report suspicious activity, and the elderly or very ill, who are expected to die anyway. Hospital staff members must understand the motives and modus operandi of their internal predators, and devise policies for dealing with them rather than hoping they just move on. Lawmakers are growing aware that they must support the importance of hospitals conducting thorough reviews and decline to give employment recommendations for people under strong suspicion.

29.2 Differences Between Doctors and Nurses as HCSKs
A. Their Respective Positions Fuel Different Motives
The available cases indicate that doctors often kill from the desire to feel a godlike sense of power over patients or from experimental curiosity. They view themselves as superior, and thus their decision to kill is often narcissistic and fueled by their fantasies of power and entitlement. Nurses, on the other hand, often feel put upon and undervalued. Their killing sprees, as evident from the examples described in this chapter, appear to have other motives, such as gaining attention, finding a small realm of power in an otherwise powerless world, assuaging depression, paying back an unfair system, and acting out to relieve frustration or workload pressures.

B. Dr. Michael Swango and Dr. Harold Shipman
Among the more notorious physicians who have murdered patients are Michael Swango, an international killer, and Harold Shipman, who contained his murders to England but has the largest victim toll to date for this subcategory of serial killer.

Swango traveled from one hospital to another in the U.S., poisoning patients with a syringe, and he was suspected of killing for two decades in seven different hospitals. He went to Zimbabwe, where he was finally stopped and brought back to the U.S. The investigation indicated he had been experimenting and had found satisfaction in ending the lives of patients. In 2001, he confessed to four murders and received life in prison.[4]

Harold Shipman started killing right out of medical school, and by the time he was done 25 years later, says the final British inquiry, he may have been responsible for as many as 250 deaths. He was sentenced to life and committed suicide in prison. Although patients adored him for making house calls, he categorized them with scornful epithets and felt superior to them. He displayed complete indifference to the suffering he had caused.[5]

C. Nurses More Prevalent
While there is no clear count of the number of physicians who have been identified and successfully prosecuted for killing patients (not including doctors who have killed family or strangers), it appears to be less than a dozen. Nurses, however, are a different matter. From the mid-1970s until mid-2003 in the United States (before Cullen, as discussed later in this chapter), there were 36 cases of serial murder among nurses and other healthcare workers. A survey shows

that the instances appear to be increasing, with at least 20 cases just in the past 15 years. In 2008, Australian nurse John Field examined 48 cases of nurses who killed, and identified 38 as serial killers.[6]

TIP: "Many experts speculate," says Kelly Pyrek, "that healthcare has contributed more serial killers than all other professions combined and that the field attracts a disproportionately high number of people with a pathological interest in life and death."[7]

D. Serial Murder versus Euthanasia

In a study that involved 852 nurses practicing in adult intensive care units, 19 percent admitted to having participated in some form of euthanasia. Only 30 percent believed the practice was unethical. A few had decided against carrying out a physician's orders so that a patient's death might be hastened. Generally, patients or their surrogates had made the request.[8] Most of these incidents involved genuine mercy-killing, wherein a patient was critically ill and it appeared that the most compassionate act, at their request, was to assist them to die. That is quite different from nurses who kill patients for personal reasons or decide on the patient's behalf that she should die.

29.3 The Case of Charles Cullen
A. Initial Suspicions

Charles Cullen is one of the most recent cases of a healthcare serial killer In the United States. Crossing several jurisdictions in seven counties in New Jersey and Pennsylvania, he was stopped after a 15-year spree at ten institutions that took the lives of numerous patients. As of January 2010, including Cullen's review of around 240 files, he had admitted to 29 murders and six attempted murders. Officials were still investigating other possible cases to link to him, but Cullen said he did not recall more than those with which he had been charged. His attorney said he has offered his last plea.[9]

The unveiling of Charles Cullen as a serial killer began when two people at Somerset Medical Center in Somerville, New Jersey, were given the wrong medication. The Reverend Florian Gall had come to the hospital in May 2003 for a routine procedure, and soon died. Jin Kyung Han, who was being treated for heart problems and cancer, was saved from an overdose of digoxin by an antidote but died later from unrelated causes. Other patients showed problematic test results as well and one died.

An internal investigation was launched and the Department of Health and Senior Services was notified. The involvement of Charles Cullen, 43, was found to be the common factor in the cases of four patients who had abnormal test results—high levels of insulin or digoxin. Yet Cullen continued to work. Then two more patients suffered from similar overdoses and Cullen was fired. On December 12, 2003, he was charged with the murder of Reverend Florian Gall and the attempted murder of Jin Kyung Han. He was suspected of using a lethal dose of digoxin, a heart medication, which he procured from hospital supplies via deceptive computer manipulation.

Cullen admitted he had indeed attempted to overdose these patients with drugs.[10]

B. Cullen's Revelations

Then Cullen dropped a bombshell. Over the past 16 years in ten different institutions, he said he had done the same thing to between 30 and 40 patients. He was clearly a healthcare serial killer of major proportions, and in the past year alone had dispatched 12 to 15 patients. To that date, only nurse's aide Donald Harvey had come close to that number.

In court at his arraignment, Cullen pleaded guilty to the charges and said he had no intention of fighting it. He did not want a lawyer, but in a quick turnabout accepted a public defender, who subsequently said Cullen might offer names in exchange for avoiding the death penalty.[11]

C. Response of Police

The New Jersey State police interrogated Cullen for seven hours on December 12, 2003. Cullen revealed his methods and motives in the cases they were investigating. He talked about how easy it was to go from one place to the next, moving on as soon as suspicions were voiced. He said some of his bosses knew of the errors he made, which had harmed patients, but they had overlooked them. He claimed he killed to end suffering, but clearly a number of patients were not suffering and were even on the mend when he decided to take their lives.

TIP: Cullen said he was aware in some places that people realized what he was doing, but he simply got fired or written up, or was pressured to leave. There were no other consequences; he did not get reported to the state boards.[12]

D. A Murderer's History

In the meantime, police and reporters compiled information. Cullen was the youngest of nine brothers and sisters. His father was a bus driver; his mother a homemaker. He grew up in a working-class neighborhood in a strongly religious Catholic family. His father died when he was an infant and his mother while he was in high school. Two of his siblings also died, and he cared for one of them.

In 1978, Cullen enlisted in the Navy, and attended a nursing school when he got out. By 1988, he was working at a hospital, one of many where he would stay only a short while. He got married and had two daughters, but soon was divorced. In 1998, he filed for bankruptcy and had debts and back payments in child support of over $65,000. The animal protection agency confiscated his dog.

In 1997, Cullen was taken to a hospital in New Jersey, suffering from depression. He refused to provide a blood sample. Just over two years later, he lit coals in a bathtub and sealed off his apartment to make a suicide attempt. A neighbor called the police.

As his debts mounted, Cullen moved from one position to another, and at St. Luke's in Bethlehem, Pennsylvania, he left to avoid an investigation into the deaths of 69 patients when an empty box of heart medication was found in a disposal bin. While a coroner determined there was no evidence of criminal conduct, there had been no toxicology reports on those patients, and only one autopsy had been performed. No bodies were exhumed. In short, it was a superficial investigation with no determination about the medications present in the bodies.[13]

E. Response of Healthcare Institutions

Administrators of Somerset Medical Center said they were unaware Cullen had been investigated elsewhere. When they checked his credentials, there were no red flags that would make them hesitate to hire him. All they received were his dates of employment.[14] It was at this facility where Cullen may have done his deadliest work, as he admitted to killing between 12 and 15 patients in only 13 months. Things would have been different had concerns been communicated by previous institutions. Hospital officials were upset that they faced a massive investigation and damage to their reputation in the community. At the time of this writing, several of the hospitals that employed Charles Cullen settled civil suits filed by the families of alleged victims.

F. Special Problems for Investigators in Cases of HCSKs

Healthcare providers in hospitals know how to use subtle means of murder, and they have access to drugs that can poison someone undetected. Unless some behavior inspires suspicion, they may effectively hide their crimes. A common thought is that older people are expected to die, so they are not as likely to have their deaths investigated. Children are not always able to communicate that someone has done something to them and thus they can become easy targets.

TIP: Even when patients complain that someone has injected them, it is often overlooked. Institutions protect their reputations, so "accidental" medication may be ignored or covered up.

Once a person has died, he is generally either embalmed or cremated, and in both cases, the evidence can be lost. Even an investigation into the cases of 69 patients at a hospital where Cullen actually did kill people failed to find anything clearly criminal. District attorneys need strong evidence for these cases and sometimes can only acquire circumstantial evidence or witness reports that they know will not add up sufficiently for juries. More than one HCSK who has been brought to trial has either been acquitted or convicted of only a small percentage of the suspicious deaths.

G. New Issues in Cullen Case

The Morning Call newspaper in Allentown, Pennsylvania, sued to make 400 pages of legal papers available that described a year full of problems in Cullen's sordid life.[15] Placing these events against the timeline of some of his confessed murders thus far, reporters determined that while Cullen claimed he had committed "mercy killings," the facts undermine that. More clearly, he was acting out during times of stress and failure. In 1993, his wife had filed for a restraining order against him, frightened that he might endanger her and their children. She said he had spiked people's drinks with lighter fluid, burned his daughters' books, forgotten his daughters at a babysitter's for a week, asked a funeral home about their rates, and was cruel to family pets.

On January 22, 1993, Cullen's wife served him with divorce papers, and a few weeks later he was arrested for stalking a girlfriend. He broke into the girl's home, then taunted her, and subsequently admitted himself into a psychiatric facility. On two occasions that same year, he was accused of domestic violence and tried to kill himself. As described below, he killed three elderly women in New Jersey during periods of stress.

Just days after fire inspectors went to Cullen's apartment in 1993 to check for hazards, he killed 90-year-old Lucy Mugavero.

In June that year, Cullen submitted to a polygraph (and passed) to show that he had not neglected his children or abused alcohol in their presence. In July, he killed 85-year-old Mary Natoli.

In August 1993, a caseworker reported that Cullen had not addressed his alcohol addiction or depression, so he recommended all visits with the children be supervised. Two weeks later, Cullen killed Helen Dean, 91.

The record for this one-year period clearly shows that when things went wrong, Cullen reacted with aggression toward those who could not protect themselves.

H. Cullen's Advice

Cullen offered to assist authorities in preventing others in his position from killing. In short, there should be protocols for accountability of staff and for drug-handling procedures. Among them would be installing surveillance cameras, the use of swipe cards and bar codes, and a daily count of lethal medications. He also said there should be a national database for updating employment history of healthcare workers.[16]

In his various responses, Cullen blames others. He holds hospital administrators responsible for not stopping him or reporting him. He blames the way hospitals operate, which is to say, he exploited the trust factor present in places where employees are believed to have patient well-being as a goal. One of his methods was to get medications by opening patients' medication drawers or closets, because no one tracked the drugs. When electronic drug tracking was put in place, he simply learned how to manipulate computer records. He left "tracks," but no one checked. There was no system in place for making people who got the drugs accountable for them. In another place, a storage room for drugs was never locked and it was easy for him to pilfer them. Yet these signals were often overlooked.

I. Discovery of Red Flags and Reports Ignored

In 1999, the Northampton County, Pennsylvania coroner voiced suspicions to several officials that there might be an "angel of death" at Easton Hospital. He believed a 78-year-old patient had been murdered. The coroner could not prove where the man had received a fatal dose of digoxin, since he had come to the hospital from a nursing home, nor who might have administered it. He requested an internal investigation at the hospital, based on reports from the patient's relative, but it was inconclusive. In 2002, he heard from a nurse at St. Luke's in nearby Bethlehem, Pennsylvania, about suspicious behavior by Nurse Charles Cullen, and contacted that county's district attorney. They made a comprehensive investigation but found no proof of criminal activity. Yet Cullen eventually admitted his part in the death of the Easton Hospital patient.[17]

Seven nurses at St. Luke's had reportedly done their own detective work and warned hospital administrators and the state police about Charles Cullen. In June 2002, they had found opened and unopened packages of drugs improperly discarded, and had seen Cullen leaving the rooms of patients who then expired. Cullen was pressured, so he resigned and moved on. But in March 2003, a pathologist concluded there was no apparent criminal activity. During that investigation, no one interviewed Cullen.[18]

In New Jersey, the son of Helen Dean had long suspected Cullen, because his mother had pointed out the nurse who had stuck her with a needle when no medication had been ordered. The son was certain his mother had been murdered, but an investigation turned up no evidence. Helen Dean was among the victims Cullen eventually listed.[19]

Steven Marcus, a toxicologist and executive director of New Jersey Poison Information and Education System, had warned Somerset Medical Center in July 2003 they had a poisoner on their staff. He spotted a cluster of at least four cases. Hospital officials dismissed his concerns and had even complained about Marcus to the state's health department, saying he had rushed to judgment and was pressuring them unduly.[20]

TIP: Cullen's problems were not reported to state boards; his poor performance was hidden from future employers; his theft of drugs went unnoted; and his mental instability was ignored. Thus, he moved undetected through the system, able to leap from one institution to another, kill patients without being detected or stopped, and gain a sense of invulnerability, which may have fueled his lethal escalation.

J. Similarities to Other Cases

In Atlanta, Georgia, convicted killer Richard Akin was fired from eight hospitals, but only one hospital told a prospective employer he had been fired and would not be rehired.[21] In like manner, other nurses have managed to leave a place where suspicions surrounded them and find a job elsewhere. There was no protocol in place to have their records available to prospective employers, in part because hospitals feared lawsuits from the employee when they had no proof of misbehavior, and in part because they hoped to avoid public exposure from a criminal investigation.

While Cullen's stated motive—mercy for seriously ill patients—may seem compassionate, other healthcare professionals convicted as killers have also made this claim, but a closer examination indicated otherwise. Nurse's aide Donald Harvey, who initially admitted to 80 "mercy-killings," seemed to enjoy the confessing as much as the killing.

TIP: Compartmentalizing, or using a persona of social functioning while also murdering people, is characteristic of many serial killers. They can act and think one way, yet also behave in ways that contradict it.

Serial killers, especially psychopathic ones, can be quite chameleonic, and killing becomes a way of life, not necessarily something they actively calculate for any given situation. In an environment where medical mistakes are made and people die as a result, it is not difficult to mimic that and get away with it. It satisfies some personal agenda; they will continue to do it.

29.4 Summary of Other Cases
A. Male HCSKs—Methods and Motives

Male nurses are disproportionately represented among caretakers who harm patients. While there are many more cases, quantitatively, of females who indulge in this behavior, Beatrice Yorker, Director of the School of Nursing at San Francisco State University, cites a striking statistic: the 146,000 male registered nurses represent 5 to 7 percent of nurses, yet this group comprises about one-third of those nurses in the U.S. since 1975 who have killed patients.[22]

Among them are:

- In 1987, Donald Harvey pled guilty in Indiana, Kentucky, and Ohio to 37 counts of murder and several counts of attempted murder, mostly by poisoning or smothering. A psychiatrist who examined him said he was a compulsive killer, murdering to relieve tension. To that point, Harvey has the most confirmed victims of any healthcare serial killer in America. He actually confessed to more than twice this number.[23]

- On Long Island in 1987, Richard Angelo, 26, said he would put himself into situations where he could be a hero, by injecting patients through their IV tubes to cause respiratory distress. Some survived, but some died. Two psychologists testified he suffered from dissociative identity disorder and had not recognized the risks to which he had put these patients. The jury convicted Angelo of two counts of second-degree murder, one count of second-degree manslaughter, one count of criminally negligent homicide, and six counts of assault.[24]

- Orville Lynn Majors, LPN, joined the nursing staff at Vermillion County Hospital in Clinton, Indiana, in 1993. Only around 26 people died there per year in the intensive care unit, but in 1994, the deaths rose to 101, with 63 during Majors' shifts. In only 22 months of his service there, 147 people died, most of them while he was working. An investigation revealed that Majors sometimes treated patients, something for which he had no authority. Investigators exhumed 15 bodies, finding that at least six deaths were consistent with the administration of epinephrine and potassium chloride. Although he was suspected in over one-hundred deaths, on October 17, 1999, Majors was only convicted of six counts of murder.[25]

Majors frequently killed patients in an isolation room behind a closed door in the ICU. Against regulations, he was left alone in the ICU, even though a registered nurse was supposed to be on duty. When he was assigned to a medical surgical unit instead of the ICU, he sometimes called the patient's physician to report that the patient looked ill and needed to be transferred to the ICU. After arranging for the transfer, he then killed the patient.[26]

- On January 14, 2004, Roger Andermatt was arrested in Switzerland for the murder of 22 patients and also charged with the attempted murder of three patients. He confessed to all the murders. The victims, aged 66 to 95, were in need of high levels of care. Nine patients were killed with medication, eight were smothered, and ten were killed with both. Andermatt claimed to have killed out of pity, although he added that he and his nursing team felt overworked by the volume of care they had to provide. He was convicted.[27]

B. Female HCSKs—Methods and Motives

While there are many overlapping methods and motives between male and female HCSKs, there are also some key differences. Among the most notorious of the female killers are the nurses described below:

- Genene Jones was convicted of using succinylcholine chloride, a drug that paralyzes the diaphragm, on a child who died. Jones was also convicted of attempting to kill another child, who was saved. She was suspected in many more murders of children at the San Antonio Medical Center in Texas in 1981 and 1982. On her shift, the pediatric ICU death rate rose 178 percent; a child under her care was ten times more likely to die and 23 times more likely to suffer a seizure. For one murder in which evidence of six others was introduced, she received 99 years. Nurse Jones was believed to enjoy the excitement attendant to the cardiac arrests of her victims.[28]

- Beverly Allitt attacked nine children and murdered four in a British hospital in Lincolnshire, England. On May 23, 1993, she was convicted and given 13 life sentences for murder, attempted murder, and causing grievous bodily harm. Seriously disturbed since adolescence, Allitt had reported many illnesses over the years and even mutilated herself on so many occasions that she had become a notorious patient for area doctors. Once Allitt was arrested, the only motive the police could determine was that she had been seeking attention. A pediatrician told the court she suffered from both Munchausen's syndrome, whereby people repeatedly and compulsively injure themselves to get attention, and Munchausen's syndrome by proxy, where they injure others for the same reason. To see both conditions in the same person, this expert said, was both rare and extreme, and he doubted she could be cured. The court did not consider it a mitigating circumstance.[29]

- Kristin Gilbert was convicted of killing four patients with epinephrine at a veterans hospital in Leeds, Massachusetts, apparently motivated by the thrill of the emergency.[30]
- Christine Malèvre was charged with the murder of seven patients in 1997 and 1998 at a lung hospital in Mantes-la-Jolie, France. She admitted to four and said her motive was compassion. Families of victims denied that those people had made any request for help. Malèvre was sentenced for six of the deaths to a prison term of ten years.[31]
- "Martha U" was convicted in 1996 of murder in the deaths of four elderly patients, and was suspected in nine other patient deaths. She had worked for 20 years in a geriatric nursing home and had used insulin to overdose the patients. In two cases, the patients apparently had angered her. Nevertheless, she insisted she had killed to end the patients' suffering.[32]

C. Similarities

The most common motives among healthcare serial killers are shown in Figure 29.1.

TIP: Healthcare serial killers generally administer an overdose or smothering, and they are quick to claim their motives were mercy or compassion. In most cases, those motives fall apart and other evidence is found that indicates they were predators. The best initial evidence against them is their repeated presence at or near a death just before the death occurred, and their attitudes about it.

- Misplaced compassion
- Desire to be a hero
- Gain attention
- Obtain a thrill
- Perform an experiment
- Need for a sense of power
- Relieve tension
- Disdain for patients
- Ease workload

Figure 29.1 Motives of Killers

D. Statistics—Prevalence and Increase

Since 1970, U.S. prosecutors have filed charges against 38 healthcare workers suspected of killing patients. Not all of the charges have stuck. Worldwide, according to Beatrice Yorker of the University of San Francisco School of Nursing, 72 healthcare workers have been charged in serial murder with a total of over 2,000 fatalities.[33]

Healthcare researcher and former surgical nurse Paula Lampe has collected information about HCSKs over the years. Since 1970, she has examined 83 cases of nurses from around the world (her figure is higher than Yorker's) who killed patients, 31 of whom were male (this percentage also diverges from other studies, offering a slightly higher percentage). Her findings indicate that what motivates many of these people is what she terms "feelings of transparency," by which she means lack of self-esteem. They kill to enhance their own sense of value and of power.[34]

A number of experts are attempting to devise ways to spot these killers earlier in their careers in order to make the administrators of hospitals and nursing homes take complaints about them more seriously.

E. Red Flags—Detecting Deviant Behavior

While arguments have arisen over the Cullen case in terms of ultimate responsibility, it is clear patients must depend on hospitals and clinics to spot the red flags and do something about them. Too often these killers have been allowed to drift from one hospital to another, fired under a cloud of suspicion but rarely brought to justice until incriminating evidence has reached shocking levels. While there is no distinct psychological type to look for, secretive behavior, missing medications, a preference for the night shift, spikes in unexpected deaths on a certain person's shift, and spotty past work records can be troublesome signals.

It takes a number of signals collectively to solidify suspicions. The signs of killers are found in Figure 29.2.

Killers are individuals who:

- like to predict when someone will die
- work on shifts during which a higher incidence of Code Blues or deaths occur
- like to arrive early or stay late on a shift
- have often been seen inside a patient's room shortly before that person's health unexpectedly deteriorated
- like to talk about death with colleagues or show odd behaviors related to the death (excitement, ownership, undue curiosity)
- prefer shifts where fewer colleagues are around
- are given macabre nicknames by patients or others on staff
- have been involved in other criminal activities
- appear to exhibit surreptitious behavior
- make colleagues anxious or suspicious
- crave attention
- try to prevent others from checking on patients
- hang around during the immediate death investigation

Figure 29.2 *Signs of Killers*

Other signals seem to have come up during a number of cases in which a person is investigated. Notably, several incidences are associated with this person at different institutions; some of the suspect substance was found in the person's home, and there are inconsistencies in their statements when asked about the incidences.

The following signals should be taken quite seriously:[35]

- Statistically, there is a higher death rate when the suspected person is on shift.
- The suspect deaths were unexpected.
- The death symptoms were also not expected, given the patient's illness or procedure.
- The suspect has moved around from one facility to another.
- Patients have complained about the person's treatment of them.
- The suspect is secretive or has a difficult time with personal relationships.
- The suspect has a history of mental instability or periodic depression.

While none of these items is itself sufficient to raise suspicion, a number of them in constellation should be alarm-ing to colleagues and facility administrators. Among those, the forensic nurse is generally the best prepared in knowing what to do.

29.5 Forensic Nursing
A. Definition
Forensic nursing is a dynamic and relatively new specialty in the practice of nursing. Nurses trained in forensic procedures combine nursing skill and knowledge of the legal system with clinical information about criminology. The specialty was formally recognized in 1991 by the American Academy of Forensic Sciences,[36] and its standards and scope of practice have been developed by the International Association of Forensic Nurses (IAFN), with the support of the American Nurses Association (ANA). In 1996, the ANA formally recognized the specialty. [37]

B. History
Prior to that auspicious moment, many brave pioneers were hard at work to achieve this status, and Linda Ledray, Ph.D. was among them.[38] In 1992 in Minneapolis, she organized a group of 72 sexual assault nurses. At that time, Ledray had performed sexual assault exams and written about the protocol for appropriate treatment. She believed the best way to improve her care and become a complete patient advocate was to meet with other nurses doing the same thing. Top on her list of questions were those involving how other nurses performed the rape examinations and what their success and failure rates were. After speaking with other practitioners, Ledray learned that nurses had discovered that the types of problems victims of sexual assault faced were best handled by nurses with specialized training and expertise in the criminal justice field. This meeting led to the founding of the IAFN. [39]

Today, thanks to a broad definition, forensic nursing includes more than just the subspecialty of sexual assault nurse examiners (SANE). The IAFN describes forensic nursing as the application of nursing science to public or legal proceedings; the application of the forensic aspects of health care combined with the bio-psychosocial education of the registered nurse in the scientific investigation; and treatment of trauma and death of victims and perpetrators of abuse, violence, criminal activity, and traumatic accidents.[40] Thus, the forensic nurse works in many fields, including death investigators, nurse coroners, forensic nurse consultants, nurse attorneys, correctional nurses, and legal nurse consultants—wherever medical-legal interests and forensic issues interact.[41]

C. Contemporary Roles
Forensic nurses are in a unique position as they are trained to see the legal side of medical practice. Forensics plays a

significant role in nursing, and indeed forensics is intrinsic to what nurses do in their daily practices. Yet since most nursing curriculums lack a forensic component, few nurses today are trained to be aware of this dimension of their work. Inservice courses provided by the healthcare institution or reimbursement for outside forensic nursing courses may be the only way to educate practicing nurses to think forensically. Refer to Lynch and Farrell[42] for additional information about the role of forensic nurses.

29.6 Healthcare Institutions' Role in Screening Candidates

A. Nurse Recruitment

Nurse recruitment in times of nursing shortages can become lax, allowing unqualified personnel to be hired. The shortage in qualified nurses will continue as the baby boomer generation ages. Refer to Chapter 2, *Where Have All the Nurses Gone?*, in Volume I, for additional information on the nursing shortage. We must thus examine the role that healthcare institutions play and the responsibilities they have to the public to insure those they hire to provide patient care are qualified.

This issue has surfaced repeatedly in the wake of the Charles Cullen case. Reducing the risk to patients, residents, and even visitors is of paramount importance for all healthcare institutions. But healthcare employers also face legal and risk management issues. They need to be protected when spotting dangerous workers and responding to reports from whistleblowers.

B. Human Resource Department

Human resource departments must safeguard against not only hiring but also retaining employees who pose a threat to safety. There have been multimillion dollar verdicts by juries against healthcare facilities for deaths and injuries caused to patients by employees who have been convicted of crimes previous to their employment.[43] Healthcare institutions may be held liable for failure to properly screen or follow reasonable policies and procedures for adequate candidate screening.

Both risk management and human resource departments must be aware of the protection they are provided under state and federal laws. Employment references are a tool used by most employers, but these can be ambiguous. Many employers would rather give no references than risk a defamation lawsuit.

TIP: The freedom to discuss freely, in good faith, prospective employees' strengths and weaknesses, as well as any suspicions a former employer may have, often cannot be exercised without fear of reprisal.

Alaska	Iowa	Oklahoma
Arizona	Kansas	Oregon
Arkansas	Louisiana	Rhode Island
California	Maine	South Carolina
Colorado	Maryland	South Dakota
Connecticut	Massachusetts	Tennessee
Delaware	Michigan	Texas
Florida	Montana	Utah
Georgia	Nevada	Virginia
Hawaii	New Mexico	West Virginia
Idaho	North Carolina	Wisconsin
Illinois	North Dakota	Wyoming
Indiana	Ohio	

Figure 29.3 *States that Have Protections for Employee Reference Checks*

In the wake of the Cullen case, previously nonexistent nationwide or statewide legal standards to protect healthcare facilities are beginning to develop. Thirty-eight states have already adopted laws protecting the employers.[44] Some of these states will protect an employer for good faith information, but only if it is truthful, as the protection is lost when an employer willfully or maliciously discloses false information in an attempt to prevent employment elsewhere. Some states protect the discussion of job performance and reasons for termination, unless a person who decides to sue can show evidence that is clear and convincing of reckless disclosure of false information or malicious intent on the part of the employer. States that have enacted these protections have standards for the burden of proof that must be overcome for an employee to even challenge an employer with success.[45]

States that currently have protections in place for employer reference checks are listed in Figure 29.3.[46] Employers in any state should protect their rights in writing. Human resource departments, as well as nurse recruiters, should consider a release document in the employment application that acknowledges the rights of all parties to discuss job performance and reasons for ending the employment. This document should be signed by the applicant. The employer should disclose that this document will be faxed, once signed, to previous employers and then kept in the personnel file for the future. This may allow a more candid discussion with the previous employer. Retaining this release allows the employer to provide a reference when the employee leaves.

The wording of such a release form should always be cleared with the facilities' risk management and legal departments. It should include an authorization for a thorough investigation of past employment and an agreement to release from all liability and responsibility any requests for information, as well as those institutions supplying the requested information. Most legal sources agree that the best protection an employer has is the truth. If the information shared is factual, the outcome of possible litigation is more likely to be positive for the employer. Even the consent forms will not protect an employer from a defamation lawsuit if the reference given was intentionally defamatory. Employers must be careful to document real performance problems and report these accurately. Each state law needs to be checked carefully to determine if the law protects a negative reference made in good faith.[47]

C. Background Checks

References are not the only tools available to employers. Investigative reports such as criminal background checks and credit reports may be used for screening candidates. Risk management departments can take a hard look at each position in the organization and determine whether or not these investigative reports should be required. The responsibility also falls upon the risk managers to be aware of the applicant's rights, which are provided under the Fair Credit Reporting Act. If the employer complies with the statute, federal protection is provided against invasion of privacy litigation. Again, an employer is required by this statute to obtain written permission to get access to criminal record and credit reports.[48]

At this time, there is no central database for criminal records for nurses. These searches therefore must be conducted on a state-by-state basis. The processes that states have in place to obtain these reports may vary as widely as the places in which these reports are kept. For example, records may be kept in the various states' attorney general or court administration offices.[49] Each state maintains a database of certified nursing assistants. Nursing home administrators are expected to query this database as part of a background check once a person is under consideration for hiring.

D. Risk Management Department

Risk managers should become familiar with the requirements of their state for obtaining background checks. They are also expected to know about adjoining jurisdictions, because employees may be drawn from bordering states.

When a healthcare facility has a policy for conditional hires or has employees working while waiting for the background checks to be completed, careful and direct supervision of these employees is crucial. There is a documented case of a person who was conditionally hired and then killed a nursing home resident during the 60 days it took to complete the background check.[50]

TIP: Employers should be aware that many of the perpetrators may not be deterred by the ongoing background check. If the healthcare facility has a policy of using temporary staffing agencies to fill vacancies in its workforce, it should require the agency to verify that its staff meets the same requirements.

Employment discrimination is an issue about which all employers need to remain vigilant. Employment policies need to protect constitutional rights of privacy. Some states have statutes that prohibit the use of certain criminal history information when hiring, and these same statutes and policies prohibit discrimination in employment based on criminal conviction records.[51] The guidelines published by the Equal Employment Opportunity Commission (EEOC) offer a format for job application and interview questions.

Human resource and risk management departments should be fully aware of the state laws, statutes, and policies addressing background and reference checks. Legal counsel can be sought to determine that the facility's policies meet all legal and regulatory requirements. If an outside agency is used to perform background checks, these agencies must be scrutinized to determine that they are reputable. In doing this the healthcare employer can also avoid the risk of being held legally responsible for failure to sufficiently screen candidates. All policies within the human resource and risk management departments should be put in writing and applied equally to each potential hire.

29.7 Healthcare Institutions' Role in Detecting and Monitoring
A. Call for Nurse Database

Healthcare employers run the risk of liability for negligent retention of an employee who causes harm to staff or patients during her employment. In New Jersey, where Cullen worked, legislators have suggested a national database for reporting disciplinary action against nurses, similar to the current national data bank for physicians, created in 1990 by Congress. The National Practitioner Data Bank is a federal program that collects information about doctors who have been sued successfully, whose hospital privileges have been revoked or curtailed, or who have been disciplined by the state medical boards.[52] Also operating is the Federation of State Medical Boards (FSMB), a centralized database used to compile reports from state medical boards. Most hospitals are now required to check this database before hiring any physician.

The Health Care Integrity and Protection Data Bank collects information on nurses who have been disciplined by state boards, but it is not open to the public at this time, making it impossible for employers to use this avenue to check potential hires.[53]

Nursys Data Bank, started several years ago by the National Council of State Boards of Nursing (NCSBN), is a way to share information among states.[54] Information regarding actions taken against a nurse's license is kept and made available here. Hospitals can check the nursing boards of each state, but they would fail to learn information other than the actions taken. This would not have helped in Cullen's case, as no action was ever taken against his license. He was investigated but never charged. State nursing boards and the NCSBN are active in raising awareness of just what should be reported.

B. Response Since Cullen

Since Cullen's revelations, there has been a nationwide call for discussion about databases that collect and distribute information about suspicious activities by nurses. Senator Frank Lautenberg and Senator Jon Corzine from New Jersey have spearheaded this effort in the hope of developing a federal database.[55]

Professional nursing agencies such as the New Jersey State Nurses Association (NJSNA) and the American Nurses Association (ANA) agree that the public's trust in the nursing profession is eroded greatly when a nurse intentionally harms a patient. Both agencies believe safeguards for the public require that a healthcare agency be self-reporting, similar to the procedures for the mandatory reporting of suspected child abuse cases. Suspicious activities, as well as data about frequent terminations, patient overdoses, high cardiac arrest or high rates of death associated with an individual nurse, could be reported and collected in a national data bank. This would provide a method for monitoring dangerous nursing professionals. Yet with the duty to report these activities, there must be legislation for immunity from lawsuits and the provision of whistleblower protection.

As of now, there are no standards or mandatory requirements for reporting suspicious activity of licensed nursing professionals. Senators Corzine and Lautenberg promoted legislation aimed at creating mandatory hospital reporting requirements. This legislation, unveiled in 2004 and named the Safe Healthcare Reporting Act, or SHARE Act, required any adverse employment action against a healthcare professional for reasons related to professional conduct or competence to be reported to professional licensing boards and the National Practitioner Databank.[56]

This bill was drafted to make reporting not only mandatory but enforceable. It proposes to effect this in several ways. First it would grant employers access to the Healthcare Integrity and Protection Databank, which has heretofore been accessible only to health insurers and the federal government. This databank collects information on healthcare fraud and abuse, including any actions taken by state licensing boards.[57] This bill also directs the Secretary of Health and Human Services to consolidate this databank with the National Practitioners Databank (NPDB).

Even though Congress expanded the National Practitioners Databank in 1987 to include reporting of disciplinary action taken against practitioners other than doctors, the Health Resources and Services Administration has failed to implement these provisions.[58] Under the SHARE Act, healthcare facilities would be required to not only report incidents but also to check the database to obtain information on prospective employees. Failure to do either could result in civil penalties of up to $50,000 per violation as well as being unable to participate in Medicare programs.[59] Whistleblowers Protection would also be provided under this legislation. Nurses and other employees who in good faith report violations would be protected from employment discrimination and retaliation.

The American Nurses Association (ANA) supports the efforts to fully include registered nurses in the NPDB. The ANA maintains that nurses should have the same responsibilities as physicians.[60] The ANA supports SHARE in its effort to provide nurses with the same due process rights for reviewing and contesting reports that physicians now use. Nurses would have adequate notice and be able to review the adverse report. The RN would have the ability to request a hearing before an arbitrator and have the right to be represented at this hearing by a lawyer or union representative. The right to review the final written report is also addressed.[61]

In a press release from the New Jersey Office of the Governor on May 3, 2005, acting Governor Richard J. Codey signed Senate Bill 1804, which strengthens the reporting requirements for healthcare facilities. This bill requires that all licensed healthcare professionals undergo criminal history background checks as a condition of renewal of their professional license.[62] Fingerprinting of nurses has been completed.

S1804 is known as the Health Care Professional Responsibility Reporting Act. Legislators claim this bill increases protections and allows facilities to report to other facilities disciplinary actions taken against employees. It also requires the disclosure to the State Division of Consumer Affairs of information regarding the behavior of professionals and facilities that would endanger patients. This may be a step in the right direction, although it must be noted there were never actions reported against Charles Cullen's license.

With the SHARE legislation pending, the healthcare facilities together with legal departments and risk management can develop internal pathways for reporting violations. Peer review systems and internal investigations are just methods of insuring safety to patients. Forensic nurses hired to work with risk management can help establish investigative procedures and internal reporting pathways. Hospitals can protect their establishments by implementing written policies and procedures.

29.8 Role of the Forensic Nurse in the Healthcare Setting
A. Education and Training
Nurses who add forensic training to their repertoire are exposed to such subjects as the handling of evidence, documentation at a crime scene, photo documentation, computer forensics, chain of custody issues, and ways to bridge the gap between law enforcement and health care. They may undertake an entire certification program, which may include as many as 36 credits, or they may take weekend seminars on the diverse topics. In either case, they will have information over and above their typical nursing duties that prepares them for forensic application.

B. The Forensic Nurse and Risk Management
Protection of patients requires co-workers to be observant of fellow staff. Before Cullen's history became well known, most nurses would not have been suspicious of another nurse. The role of the nurse as a patient advocate mandates the nurse take action to report behavior consistent with a deliberate attempt to harm or kill a patient. These concerns should be carried up the chain of command and ultimately to the risk manager (if the facility has one) or administrator.

With no data bank available at this time, and little or no forensic training offered in nursing curriculums today, the responsibility to develop a pathway for reporting suspicious activities by the professional staff falls on the risk management department. Nurses with forensic training are invaluable assets to these departments, because they are able to recognize a possible forensic situation. Their skills include understanding the protocol of a crime scene, recognizing what constitutes potential evidence, and knowing how to preserve evidence properly. Their attention to detail and ability to recognize the possible importance of every piece of evidence may lead to a suspect and/or solve a crime. They know that a body is a crime scene. They recognize the importance of documentation of findings and are aware of the significance of the absence of findings. In addition, they know when to call in law enforcement. Their skills come into play, as do their taking histories to get a full and accurate story or determine a discrepancy among several narratives. These specially trained nurses also know how to present the findings to doctors and law enforcement. Nurses with forensic training are able to give evidence in a court of law, be it civil or criminal.

C. Reporting Pathways
Risk management and nurse educators in healthcare facilities can collaborate to draft written policies and procedures to provide standard pathways for the reporting of suspicious activities of fellow nurses. These departments, in conjunction with a forensically trained nurse, can then interpret this information to spot trends, such as a high incidence of deaths on a specific person's shift, which may help insure the safety of all patients.

D. Bridging the Gap Between Health Care and Law Enforcement
Forensic nurses have knowledge of legal issues and investigative protocol, and thus are able to speak to detectives who arrive on the scene. They understand what may constitute evidence; they can assist in describing potential contamination of the scene. Additionally, they will inform police about who may have handled potential evidence. In the place of doctors, they can make court appearances, which frees up doctors to remain on the job. This is cost-effective for hospitals. In addition, forensic nurses can coach potential witnesses in courtroom protocol.

29.9 Policies in Response to Dr. Harold Shipman's Murder History
Other countries are responding to this crisis as well. After Shipman's conviction, the pharmacists who dispensed drugs to him came under investigation, but were cleared of misconduct.[63] Nevertheless, tighter procedures have been proposed for controlling drug dispensing, as an amendment to the Misuse of Drugs Regulation Act of 2001. The proposal includes making information available about all prescriptions from a single prescriber, and all healthcare providers being required to make an annual declaration about the drugs they have on their premises. Pharmacists, too, must gather more personal information before filling a prescription.[64]

In New Zealand, the Medical Council instituted proactive audits designed to catch doctors engaging in misconduct. Although it is expected to take a decade to audit them all, the process is already in place. Questionnaires are completed by 16 of each doctor's professional colleagues and paramedical colleagues, as well as ten randomly selected patients.[65]

29.10 Update 2011

There is currently no national requirement for licensure of healthcare professionals. State Boards of Nursing are the sole bodies responsible for regulating licensure. As private bodies, they cannot perform national criminal background checks. In the absence of any federal legislation regulating this process, changing the laws in each state is the only way for the boards to gain access to the FBI databases.[66]

The National Council of State Boards of Nursing (NCSBN) in Chicago, Illinois, has recommended FBI checks in its core licensure requirements since 1999, but lacks the authority to mandate them.[67] It does post information regarding state requirements for nurse licensure applicants. Those practitioners looking for more information are best served there. The NCSBN also offers resources for states that have not yet formulated their regulations.

Current laws and requirements vary from state to state. Thirty-four states now have federal criminal background check (CBC) requirements for all initial applicants as well as renewals and those who apply for reciprocity from out of state. States such as New Hampshire and North Dakota passed legislation for CBCs as recently as 2008. Three states are awaiting implementation of CBCs; two states have introduced legislation; and seven states have conditional CBC requirements.[68] These conditional requirements allow for CBCs only in a specified circumstance and these circumstances vary significantly. The state may simply require a CBC if the applicant self-reports a criminal conviction or answers a moral character question on the application in a suspicious manner. Although Cullen practiced in Pennsylvania, it is one of the states with conditional requirements. Pennsylvania requires CBCs only when an applicant reports a criminal history in response to a question on an application.

State Boards must also fund CBCs. At this time the average cost is $34.00 for each FBI check.[69] State boards understand that the public may want this done, but it requires resources these boards may not have. Texas, for example, has approximately 300,000 nurses, resulting in a cost of $10 million just for CBCs—not the cost of staff to process them.[70] If information is found, more work must be undertaken, and it must be done in a timely fashion.

An example of comprehensive legislation in response to the Cullen murders is a bill signed in New Jersey. Still stinging from the Cullen atrocities, in May 2005 Governor Richard J. Codey of New Jersey signed Senate Bill 1804, entitled the Health Care Professional Responsibility and Reporting Enhancement Act. It requires that a criminal history record background check be performed for all healthcare professionals licensed or certified by the New Jersey Division of Consumer Affairs.[71] All healthcare professionals must complete authorization forms and fingerprinting, which are then processed by the FBI. These requirements are for both initial licensure and condition of renewals. If licensees choose not to complete the process, their licenses will assume an inactive status, not to be reinstated until the background check is completed.

Healthcare professionals also have reporting obligations under this law. If they have information regarding the negligence, impairment or incompetence of a healthcare professional, they are obligated to notify the Division of Consumer Affairs. If the reporting professional works in the same institution, he must also notify the healthcare entity. This act requires not only New Jersey healthcare professionals but also healthcare entities to report, in writing, any and all information regarding incompetence or negligence of a healthcare worker employed by, or under contract to, provide services (including those from staffing registries). This law defined the healthcare entities, and included not only hospitals but also public health centers, diagnostic centers, nursing homes and even home health agencies. These notifications must be made within seven days of the action.[72]

Healthcare entities must also provide information to other entities that make inquiries. The entity must disclose whether it has provided any notice about the individual to the Division within a seven year period preceding the inquiry. This then dictates a recordkeeping requirement. The Act requires that all healthcare entities maintain records for seven years of all documented complaints and events related to patient care. Included are any disciplinary proceedings or actions against any healthcare professionals employed or contracted by the entity. For a period of four years, records of mortality, morbidity, readmission, complication and infection must be kept. If done without malice and with best practice procedures, neither professionals nor institutions are liable for civil damages arising out of the notification.[73]

However, not everyone is in agreement about the response to Cullen. Prior to the Bill, the New Jersey State Nurses Association (NJSNA) was involved in several meetings with legislators from their state. As stakeholders, they believed it was necessary to discuss the impact such a bill would have on the nurses and the profession. Andrea Aughenbaugh, RN, former CEO of NJSNA, was concerned that while it is imperative to protect patients, the action of one nurse should not negatively impact all nurses.[74] Many nurses feel that the broad scope of these laws causes the pendulum to swing too far in the other direction, impacting nurses too harshly.

There have been significant changes in New Jersey since the Cullen case. Nurses who in the past would have been counseled for making a medication error are now reported to the Board of Nursing. For example, if a nurse omits a medication and forgets to circle that it was not given, that is now considered tampering with the medical record and is reported to the Board. An investigation follows. The concept of a just culture that does not rely on punishment for minor errors cannot flourish in a post-Cullen environment.

An article in *Nursing Spectrum* sheds light on the problems of the New Jersey law.[75] Many nurses are finding that certain stipulations may be quite harmful, specifically in the way it spotlights RNs. Under the strict guidelines, nurses can be reported for behaviors that are due more to inexperience than malice or incompetence. Exacerbating the situation is the lack of inservice training and residency programs for new nurses.[76] Thus, for a young, inexperienced RN, the consequences of being reported to the state boards and Division of Consumer Affairs can be catastrophic. With a seven-day reporting requirement, the nurse has little time to organize a defense, and her record can be marred, even if no action is taken. The law also states that if a licensee resigns while under investigation, that too must be reported. Since this law was enacted, the reported cases have tripled in New Jersey, and many take months to adjudicate.[77] Thus, while there are good intentions for public safety underlying these laws, there might be a less damaging approach. These debates raise the issue to public consciousness, and at the date of this publication (2011), the discussions continue.

29.11 Conclusion

With HCSKs increasing in number, rare as they may still be, hiring institutions in the healthcare professions have a duty to screen employees for potential predators. A proactive approach needs to be developed instead of waiting for legislative mandates. Written policies and procedures for reporting suspicious activities, accurate documentation, and cogent coordination of all the data collected, along with protection for those who do report, should all be considered. With the cooperation and input of the legal, nursing, and risk management departments, red flags may appear sooner, and could be addressed, thus potentially avoiding patient injuries and deaths. Forensic training for nurses, or the employment of one of these specialized nurses, is invaluable to the healthcare institutions that hope to correct their vulnerabilities to the person who decides to start killing patients.

Endnotes

1. Lucy, D. and C. Aitken, "A review of the role of roster data and evidence of attendance in cases of suspected excess deaths in a medical context," *Law, Probability and Risk* 1 (2002): 141–160.

2. Sachs, Jessica Snyder, "Killers in the ICU," *Popular Science,* January 12, 2009. http://www.popsci.com/sci-tech/article/2009-01/killers-icu, accessed 6/22/10.

3. Wang, K. and M. Frassinelli, "Families and possible victims sue suspected killer nurse," *Newark Star Ledger* (March 7, 2004); Garlicki, D., "Families of patients not involved in criminal proceedings sue him, hospitals in civil court, alleging he caused loved ones' deaths," *Morning Call* (Mar 25, 2005). Cullen litigation. http://www.judiciary.state.nj.us/cullen/other_orders_prohac.htm accessed 6/22/10.

4. Stewart, J., *Blind Faith: How the Medical Establishment Let a Doctor Get away with Murder.* New York: Simon & Schuster, 1999.

5. Haxton, Nance, "Study Investigates serial killer nurses," ABC online, April 21, 2008. http://www.abc.net.au/pm/content/2008/s2223423.htm, accessed 6/22/10.

6. Waugh, R., "Telltale signs pointed to murder," *Yorkshire Post* (February 1, 2005).

7. Pyrek, K., "Healthcare serial killers: Recognizing the red flags," *Forensic Nurse* (September-October 2003): 1–5.

8. Asch, D. and M. DeKay, "Euthanasia among critical care nurses: Practices, attitudes, and social and professional correlates," *Medical Care* 35 (September 1997): 890–900.

9. Assad, M., "Cullen sentencing may begin soon," *Morning Call* (November 29, 2005); Matteson, S., "Serial killer admits another attempted murder while a nurse," *Asbury Park Press,* December 6, 2005.

10. Campbell, C., "AG uses one killer to catch others," *Newark Star Ledger* (November 21, 2004).

11. Hepp, Rick, "Nurse's lawyer seeks to bar death penalty," *Newark Star Ledger* (December 18, 2003).

12. "In his own words," *Newark Star Ledger* (September 12, 2004).

13. Kraus, S., "Seven nurses had warned about killer," *Morning Call* (July 10, 2005).

14. Hampson, R., "Angels of mercy: The dark side," *USA Today* (December 16, 2003).

15. Hepp, Rick, "Killer nurse blasts judge for unsealing violent past," *Newark Star Ledger* (June 10, 2004).

16. Assad, M., "Cullen gives tips for stopping killings: Serial killer nurse outlines flaws in hospital security and hiring practices," *Morning Call* (May 21, 2005).

17. Hepp, R., "Coroner had gut feeling about an 'angel of death'," *Newark Star Ledger* (October 3, 2004).

18. See note 10.

19. Alexander, M., "Killer on call," *Reader's Digest* (November 2004): 163–180.

20. "Did hospitals see no evil?" *CBSNews.com* (August 15, 2004).

21. See note 14.

22. See note 5 at 4.

23. Whalen, W. and B. Martin, *Defending Donald Harvey.* Cincinnati: Emmis Books, 2005.

24. *People v. Richard Angelo.* 88 NY2d 217, 666 NE2d 1333, 644 NYS2d 460 (1996).

25. "Former Nurse Guilty of Murder of Six Patients," *News Tribune* (October 18, 1999).

26. Turchland, F. and G. Carter, "Overview of investigation and prosecution of Orville Lynn Majors for the murder of 7 patients at the Vermillion County Hospital with an emphasis on the role of medical experts in the collection and presentation of evidence," presented April 2, 2004, American Association of Legal Nurse Consultants Conference.

27. "Swiss nurse is sentenced for 22 murders," *New York Times* (January 28, 2005).

28. Elkind, P., *The Death Shift: The True Story of Nurse Genene Jones and the Texas Baby Murders.* New York: Viking, 1983.

29. Manner, T., *Deadlier Than the Male: Stories of Female Serial Killers*, 254–291. London: Pan Books, 1995.

30. See note 1 at 147.

31. "Christina Malèvre appeals her sentence," October 2, 2003. www.worldrtd.net/news, accessed 6/22/10.

32. Lampe, P., *The Mother Teresa Syndrome*, Holland: Nelissen, 2002.

33. See note 7.

34. See note 30.

35. Ramsland, K., "Angels of death: the male nurses," www.crimelibrary.com. 2003, accessed 6/22/10.

36. Scope and Standards of Forensic Nursing Practice. International Association of Forensic Nurses, American Nurses Association. Washington, D.C.: American Nurses Publishing, 1999.

37. Stevens, S., *Forensic Nurse,* 1. New York: St. Martin's Press, 2004.

38. *Id.* at 2.

39. See note 35.

40. www.forensicnurse.org.

41. See note 35.

42. Lynch, V. and J. Farrell, "Forensic Records," In *Medical Legal Aspects of Medical Records,* eds. P. Iyer, B. Levin. Tucson, Arizona: Lawyers and Judges Publishing Co., 2010.

43. Quattrone, M., "Criminal background checks help ensure patient safety," *ASHRM* (Spring 2003).

44. Henry, Jr., W. R., "Employment references—Can you get (and give) an honest answer?" *Risk Vue*, Warren, McVeigh, & Griffin Inc. and Griffen Communications, Inc. April 2004.

45. *Id.*

46. *Id.*

47. *Id.*

48. See note 42.

49. *Id.*

50. *Id.*

51. *Id.*

52. Fong, T., "Necessary Knowledge," National Council of State Boards of Nursing. www.ncsbn.org, accessed 6/22/10.

53. *Id.*

54. Dunbar, Carol N., "Nurses who kill: Picking up the pieces after the Charles Cullen arrest," *Forensic Nurse* (March 2004).

55. See note 51.

56. "News From Frank Lautenberg," Lautenberg.senate. gov/Lautenberg/press/2003, accessed 6/22/10.

57. *Id.*

58. *Id.*

59. *Id.*

60. "Safe Healthcare Reporting (SHARE) Act," Nursing's Legislative and Regulatory Initiatives for the 109th Congress, 2005 American Nurses Association.

61. *Id.*

62. "Codey Signs Health Care Professional Responsibility And Reporting Enhancement Act," New Jersey Office of the Governor-Press Release. www.state.nj.us/cgi—bin/governor. May 3, 2005. Accessed 6/22/10.

63. Carter, H., "Disciplinary hearing for pharmacist," *Guardian Unlimited* (February 10, 2005).

64. "Prescription rules tightened," www.politics.co.uk. July 28, 2005. Accessed 6/22/10.

65. Meylan, G., "Patients to rate their GPs," www.stuff. co.nz. May 15, 2005. Accessed 6/22/10.

66. Shalo, Sibyl BSN, RN. AJN, *American Journal of Nursing*, March 2009.

67. *Id.*

68. NCSBN available at www.ncsbn.org, accessed 6/22/10.

69. Shalo, Sibyl BSN, RN. AJN, *American Journal of Nursing*, March 2009, pp. 25-26.

70. *Id.*

71. *Id.*

72. Fliszar, Gregory M. "'Nurse Cullen' Legislation requires New Jersey health care entities to report incompetence and negligence," Lexis-Nexis Matindale Hubbell, July 26, 2005.

73. *Id.*

74. New Jersey State Nurses Association. Available at www.njsna.org, accessed 6/22/10.

75. Frellick, Marcia. Nurse.com, *Nursing Spectrum*, Feb 23, 2009.

76. *Id.*

77. *Id.*

Additional Reading

ASHRM 2004 Advocacy Task Force. "A call for federal immunity to protect health care employers—and patients," *ASHRM Journal* 25, no. 1 (2005): 5–8.

Fliszar, Gregory M,. Pepper Hamilton, LLP, Philadelphia Office. *"Nurse Cullen' Legislation Requires NJ Health Care Entities to Report Incompetencies and Negligence"* LexisNexis Martindale Hubbell, July 26, 2005. Available at http://www.martindale.com/print.asxp

Frellick, Marcia, "This Could Be You: Cullen Law Under Scrutiny. Two New Jersey Attorneys Cite RNs as Unfair Targets and Are Working Hard to Change the Cullen Law," February 23, 2009. Nurse.com, *Nursing Spectrum*, Nurse Week. Available at http://news.nurse. com/article

Furbee, R., "Criminal poisoning: medical murderers," *Clinical Laboratory Medicine* 26 (2006): 255–273.

National Council of State Boards of Nursing (NCSBN). "State Information regarding Criminal Background Checks for Nurse Licensure Applicants." Dec. 2008. Available at http://www.ncsbn.org

New Jersey State Nursing Association "Acting Governor Codey signs Heath Care Professional Responsibility and Reporting Enhancement Act" May/ June 2005. ProQuest Information and Learning Company. BNet. Health Industry. Available at http://findarticles.com/p/ articles.

Ramsland, Katherine. *Inside the Minds of Healthcare Serial Killers*. Westport, CT: Praeger (2007).

Shalo, Sibyl BSN, RN. "Protecting the Public from Bad Nurses." AJN, *American Journal of Nursing*, March 2009 Volume109—Issue 3 AJN Reports. 2009 Lippincott Williams & Williams Inc. Available at http://journals.lww.com/ajnonline/fulltext/2009, pp. 25-26.

Socolof, Jon and Julie Jordon. "Best practices for health care background screen," *Journal of Health Care Compliance*, October 2006, pp. 5-9.

Appendix A

Medical Terminology, Abbreviations, Acronyms, and Symbols

Ann M. Peterson, EdD, MSN, RN, CS, LNCC

Medical Terminology

English words, and most medical terms, are drawn from other languages, most notably Latin and Greek. To determine the meaning of a word it is helpful to understand the basic components—the root, the prefix and the suffix. Generally, but not always, prefixes and suffixes combine with a root of a word derived from the same language, that is, Latin prefixes and suffixes combine Latin roots and Greek prefixes and suffixes with Greek roots.

The root, stem, or base of a word provides the primary meaning. The prefix added to the beginning of the root word changes the meaning. For example, one can add "un" before the root word "pleasant," or add "a" to "symptomatic." The suffix is added to the end of a word to modify its meaning and, often, its part of speech. For instance, adding "ly" to the end of the word "pleasant" changes the word from an adjective to an adverb. Breaking down the various components of a word or phrase will help the reader arrive at a definition. Define the suffix first followed by the prefix and then the root. (See Table A.1.)

Roots

The root provides the basic meaning of a word and can be descriptive (providing color, strength, size, shape, position and quantity) as is shown in the following examples

- Leukocyte describes the *body part* and *color*—white cell.
- Megaloblast suggests *strength* of an abnormally large immature blood cell that develops in large numbers in the bone marrow.
- Bariatrics describe the field of medicine dealing with *size,* i.e., obesity.
- Anklosis indicates the *shape,* i.e., bent or abnormally positioned joint.
- Dextrocardia denotes the *position* of the heart in the right side of the chest.

- Oliguria describes the *quantity* of urine.

Although a root can stand alone, it is usually combined with a suffix. For example gastro, meaning stomach, usually occurs with a suffix. The suffix "itis" means inflammation. Some words, such as gastroenteritis, have more than one root. (See Table A.2.) Prefixes and suffixes connect two consonantal roots with the letter "o," as in "neur + o + logy." However the "o" is dropped when joining to a vowel stem as in the word "neur + itis."

Prefixes

A prefix, generally an adverb or preposition, placed before a word will add to or alter the word's meaning. Consider the words order and **dis**order. (See Table A.3.)

Suffixes

The suffix, added at the end of a word, identifies the part of speech—noun, verb, and adjective. Some, such as phobia, can stand alone. Start with the suffix when attempting to define a word. (See Table A.4.)

Abbreviations and Acronyms
Legibility

An Institute of Medicine report, "To Err is Human: Building a Safer Health System," published in 2000, estimates that, in any given year, as many as 98,000 people die from medical errors that occur in hospitals. Many patient safety experts feel this number is too low. The original Harvard Practice Review studied New York State hospitals. Additional people die of negligence in other settings, such as offices, nursing homes, clinics, and so on. Illegible entries compromise patient safety and lead to disastrous legal ramifications.

In general, written medical documentation should be done in black ink; however, some institutions designate other colors for the evening and night nurses' notes or for telephone orders. Each entry should immediately follow the previous entry without leaving any blank space between the entries. If an error is made, a single line should be drawn through the erroneous words and the words written above followed by the initials of the writer making the correction. Erasures or liquid whiteout are unacceptable. If the note flows over onto a second page, each entry and page in the progress notes and the doctor's order sheet should be preceded by the date and time that documentation was made and should be followed by the writer's legal signature and license initials. For example: John Doe, RN.

Communication and Safety

The goal of medical records is to communicate information about a patient's health and care. Abbreviations, intended to save time and space, can be problematic if illegible or misinterpreted. Many abbreviations have more than one meaning, even within the same discipline, as the following points out.

"A 49-YO WF was admitted with CP and SOB. She was known to have MS and MI and had an MVR 2 years ago." The first question that arises is whether she is having chest pain or chest pressure. The poor woman also may have multiple sclerosis, but what if she has mitral stenosis? She could have a history of mitral stenosis and mitral incompetence, but maybe she has had a myocardial infarction. One hopes that the physician remembers that she had a mitral valve repair rather than a mitral valve replacement two years ago, so she doesn't receive anticoagulants unnecessarily, and so on. Like a physician's handwriting, the interpretation of medical abbreviations often is in the eye of the beholder.[1]

Knowing the field of medical practice will help, but not ensure, correct interpretation of abbreviations and acronyms. To prevent misunderstandings most healthcare facilities offer an official list of authorized abbreviations or use abbreviations recommended by The Joint Commission (formerly the Joint Commission on Accreditation of Healthcare Organizations or JCAHO). Medical personnel should only use standard approved abbreviations, acronyms and symbols.[2]

The concern over the lack of standard medical abbreviations, acronyms and symbols has long been recognized.[3] Given the magnitude of abbreviations, acronyms, and symbols in use (the 2005 *Stedman's Medical Speller* contained 120,000 entries based on more than 72,000 medical words, phrases, and acronyms), it is more practical to address what is NOT accepted. In an effort to reduce the risk to patient safety and professional liability, organizations such as The Joint Commission have published a list of abbreviations, acronyms, and symbols *not* to be used, and encouraged healthcare institutions to prepare a list of approved abbreviations to be used within the medical records. They should not be used on the face sheet, in the final diagnosis, or on the physician's order sheet.

The use of handwritten abbreviations and symbols can jeopardize patient safety due to illegibility and misinterpretation. As the list provided below demonstrates, there can be numerous interpretations, influenced by the practitioner's education, experience, background, writing style (upper case versus lower case, use of periods, and so on) and legibility, specialty area, and patient care setting. In an effort to reduce the risk to patients' safety, institutions and organizations such as The Joint Commission and the Institute for Safe Medication Practices (ISMP) have provided listings of often-misinterpreted abbreviations to be eliminated from all types of clinical documentation, including written laboratory reports.

TJC's *2004 National Patient Safety Goals* requires abbreviations, acronyms and symbols used to be standardized throughout the organization (Standard IM.3.10, EP #20). The Joint Commission's approved list of dangerous abbreviations, acronyms, and symbols *not to use* were required to appear on each accredited organization's "Do not use" list beginning January 1, 2004. In 2008, The Joint Commission reaffirmed and renumbered this safety goal as NPSG.02.02.01. The ISMP urges publishers and Information Systems vendors to adhere to a single universal standard and follow the recommended standards in their printed materials and has made available the *List of Error-Prone Abbreviations, Symbols, and Dose Designations* at http://www.ismp.org/tools/errorproneabbreviations.pdf.

Table A.1
Word Components

Word	Prefix	Root	Suffix
Autobiography A story of a person's life written by himself.	*Auto* is from the Greek word meaning "self."	*Bio* is from the Greek word meaning "life."	*Graph* is from the Greek word meaning graph which means "to write."
Angiotensin A chemical in the body that causes blood vessel constriction.	*Tensin* is from the Latin word "tendere" which means "to stretch."	*Angio* is from the Greek word "angeion" meaning "vessel."	
Appendicitis		*Appendix* comes from the Latin word "appendere" which means "to add something."	*Itis* is from the Greek language meaning "inflammation."
Vermiform	*Vermi* is from the Latin word "vermis" meaning "worm."	*Forma* is the Latin word meaning "form."	

Table A.2
Roots

Root	Meaning	Sample Word
acanth-	spine, prickle	**acanth**oma—tumor arising from the prickle-cell layer of the epidermis
aceto-	vinegar cup	**aceta**bulum—cup-shaped cavity that holds the femur head
acro-	extremity, tip, sharp	**acro**megaly—chronic metabolic condition characterized by marked enlargement of the bones of the face, jaw and extremities
adeno-	gland	**adeno**pathy—enlargement of a gland
agon-	contest, struggle	**agon**ist—contacting muscle opposing another muscle
angio-	vessel	**angio**genesis—ability to evoke blood vessel formation
ankyl-	bent, a joint locked in one position	**ankyl**osis—fusion of a joint
arthro-	joint	**arthro**scopy—examination of an interior joint via endoscopy
athero-	meal	**athero**sclerosis—formation of plaques on an arterial wall
azo-	nitrogen	**azo**temia—retention of an excessive amount of nitrogenous compounds in the blood
bac(t)-	rod	**bac**terium—rod shaped organism
balano-	acorn, glans	**balan**itis—inflammation of the glans penis
blast-	bud, sprout	**blast**in—any substance that provides nourishment for cell growth
bleph-	eyelid	**bleph**aritis—inflammation of the eyelids
bol-	throw	**bol**us—a dose of medicine injected all at once intravenously
brachi-	arm	**brachi**alis—muscle of the upper arm
brady-	slow	**brady**cardia—slow heart rate
calco-	heel, spur	**calc**aneal—relating to the heel bone
carpo-	wrist	**carp**al—pertaining to the wrist
caus-	burn	**caus**algia—burning pain
cephal-	head	**cepha**halgia—headache
cereb(r)-	brain	**cereb**ral hemorrhage—hemorrhage of a blood vessel in the brain
cervic-	neck	**cervic**odynia—neck pain
chlor(o)-	green	**chlor**oma—greenish malignant neoplasm
chol(e)-	bile	**chol**angitis—inflammation of the bile ducts
chondr-	cartilage	**chondr**omalacia—softening of the cartilage
chrom-	color	**chrom**otopssia—a form of color blindness
circum-	around	**circum**cision—cutting around
cirrh(o)-	red-yellow	**cirrh**osis—chronic degenerative disease of the liver
cornu-	horn	**corn**—a horny mass, resulting from chronic friction and pressure, over a bony prominence
cost(o)-	rib	**cost**ectomy—surgical removal of a rib
cox-	hip	**cox**a—head of the femur
Cranio-	skull	**cran**ium—skull
cubit-	elbow	**cubit**al—pertaining to the elbow
cutane	skin	**cutane**ous—pertaining to the skin

Root	Meaning	Sample Word
cyan-	dark blue	**cyan**osis—bluish discoloration of the skin or mucous membranes due to decreased tissue oxygenation
cysto-	urinary bladder	**cysto**scopy—direct visualization of the bladder
cyto-	cell	**cyto**toxic—poisonous to tissue cells
dacr-	tear (from the eye)	**dacr**yocystitis—infection of the tear duct
dacty-	finger	**dacty**litis—painful inflammation of the fingers or toes
dent	teeth	**dent**ist
derm(o)-, dermat(o)	skin	**derma**tologist
diplo-	double	**diplo**pia—double vision
dors(i)-, dors(o)-	back	**dors**um—back of
embol-	plug	**embol**us—a quantity of gas, tissue or foreign object that ciculates until it becomes lodged
enceph-	brain	**enceph**alopathy—any abnormality of the brain structure or function
entero-	intestine	**entero**itis—inflammation of the intestine
erythro-	red	**erythro**cyte—red blood cell
equi-	equal	**equi**librium—state of balance
fis-, fid-	split, cleave, divide	**fis**sure—cleft or groove in an organ
fora/foro	hole	**fora**men—opening in a bone
galact-	milk	**galact**orrhea—lactation not associated with childbirth or nursing. Symptom associated with pituitary gland tumor.
gangl-	knot	**gangl**ion—knotlike mass of nerve cells
gastr-	stomach, belly	**gastr**ic—pertaining to the stomach
genu	knee	**genu**flect—to bend the knee
gest-	bring forth, produce	**gest**ation—period of time from conception to birth
gingiv-	gums	**gingiv**itis—inflammation of the gums
glauc-	bluish grey	**glauc**oma—disease of the eye with increased pressure within the eyeball
gloss-	tongue	**gloss**odynia—pain in the tongue
gluco-	sweet	**gluco**se—simple sugar found in foods
glute-	buttocks	**glute**al—pertaining to the buttocks
glyco-	sugar	**glyco**genesis—the synthesis of glycogen from glucose
gnath(o)-	jaw	**gnath**ic—pertaining to the jaw
halluc	to wander in the mind	**halluc**ination—a sensory perception not triggered by an external sensation
helm-	worm	**helm**inthiasis—parasitic worm infestation
heme-	blood	**hema**turia—abnormal presence of blood in the urine
hemi-	half	**hemi**paresis—muscular weakness on one half of the body
hepat-	liver	**hepat**itis—inflammation of the liver
hidr-	sweat	**hidr**osos—sweat production
histo-	tissue, web, cloth	**histo**logy—science dealing with the microscopic identification of cells and tissues

Root	Meaning	Sample Word
hydro-	water	**hydro**ps—abnormal accumulation of clear watery fluid in the body
hystero-	uterus	**hyster**ectomy—surgical removal of the uterus
iatro-	physician	**iatro**genic—caused by treatment
ichth-	fish	**ichth**yosis—dry scaly skin condition
idio-	self, personal, private	**idio**pathic—unknown cause
ischi-	hip joint	**ischi**um—one of three parts of the hip bone
iso-	equal	**iso**metric—maintaining the same measurement
jejun-	hungry	**jejun**um—one of three portions of the small intestine
kera-	horny	**kera**tosis—overgrowth and thickening of the cornified epithelium
kerato-	cornea	**kera**tectomy—surgical removal of the cornea
kyph(o)-	hunch backed	**kyph**osis—abnormal convexity in the curvature of the thoracic spine
lab-	lips	**lab**ia—the lips
lachry-	tear (from the eye)	**lacri**mal—pertaining to tears
lacrim-	tear	**lacrim**al apparatus-structure hat secretes and drains tears from the eyeball
lact-,	milk	**lact**aion—synthesis and secretion of milk from the breasts
lapar-	loin, abdomen	**lapar**otomy—surgical incision into the peritoneal cavity
leiomyo-	smooth muscle	**leimyo**mata—smooth muscle tumor found in the esophagus, stomach, or small intestine
leuco- / leuko-	white	**leuko**cyte—white blood cell
liga(t)-	bind together, bandage	**liga**ments—bands of fibrous tissue that binds joints together and connect bones and cartilage
lingu-	tongue	**lingu**al artery—artery that supplies blood to the tongue
lip(o)	fat	**lip**osuction—technique for removing fatty tissue
lith-	stone	**lith**iasis—formation of calculi or stones in a body cavity or duct
mal(i)	abnormal, bad	**mal**ignant—virulent, destructive
mast(o)-	breast	**mast**ectomy—surgical removal of a breast
melano-	black	**melano**ma—malignant neoplasm-usually black or brown in color
medi- / mid-	middle	**mid**body—middle of the body
meso-	middle	**meso**derm—middle of three layers of developing embryo
multi-	many	**multi**form—more than one shape
my(o)-	muscle	**my**algia—muscle pain
myel(o)-	bone marrow	**myel**ocyte—immature white blood cell found in the bone marrow
myring(o)-	eardrum	**myring**ectomy—excision of the tympanic membrane (eardrum)
narco-	sleep	**narco**lepsy—sudden sleep attacks
necro-	dead	**necro**sis—localized tissue death
nephr-	kidney	**nephr**optosis—downward displacement of the kidney
neur-,	nerve	**neur**ology—science of the nervous system
ocul-	eye	**ocul**ar spot—abnormal opacity In the eye
odon-	tooth	**odon**tectomy—tooth extraction
olfact-	smell	**olfact**ory—pertaining to smell
oligo-	few, scarce	**olig**uria-scant urine

Root	Meaning	Sample Word
onco-	tumor, mass	**onco**logist—physician who specializes in the treatment of cancers
onycho-	nail (finger/toe)	**onycho**lysis—separation of the nail from the nail bed
oophor-	carrying egg	**oophor**ectomy—surgical removal of one or both ovaries
ophth-	eye	**ophth**almoscope—instrument used to examine the interior of the eye
orch-	testis	**orch**itis—inflammation of the testes
ortho-	straight	**ortho**pnea—condition in which a person must sit or stand to breathe comfortably
ossi-	bone	**ossi**cle—small bone within the ear
ot-	ear	**ot**ologist—physician trained in ear disorders
ov-	egg, ovum	**ov**iduct—fallopian tube which serves as a passage for the ovum to the uterus
palpebr-	eyelid	**palpebr**a superior—upper eyelid
peri-	surrounding	**peri**cardium—around the heart
phag-	eat	**phag**ocytosis—process where certain cells engulf and destroy microorganisms and cell debris
phlebo-	vein	**phlebo**tomy—incision of a vein for blood letting
phren-	mind, breath	**phren**ic nerve—one of the nerves that innervates the diaphragm
pleur-	ribs	**pleur**al cavity—the cavity that contains the lings
pneum-	luns	**pneum**onia—inflammation of the lungs
pod-	foot	**pod**iatrist—a physician who treats conditions of the foot
polio-	gray	**polio**encephalitis—inflammation of the gray matter of the brain
poly-	many	**poly**morphous—many shapes
procto-	rectum	**proct**itis—inflammation of the rectum and anus
pyelo-	vat, basin, pelvis	**pyelo**nephritis—inflammation of the pelvis and parenchyma of the kidney
pyo-	pus	**pyo**genic—pus producing
pyr(o)-	fever (cognate to "fire")	**pyr**exia—fever
ren(o)-	kidneys	**ren**al—pertaining to the kidneys
ret(ic)	net	**retic**ular—netlike pattern
rhabdo-	striated muscle	**rhabdo**myoma—tumor of striated muscle
rhino-	nose	**rhino**plasty—plastic surgery to change the nose structure
rub(r)-	red	**rub**ella—fine red viral rash
sacch(ar)-	sugar	**sacchar**ine—sugar substitute
sang(ui)	blood	**sangui**neous—pertaining to the blood
sarc(o)-	flesh	**sarco**ma—malignant soft tissue tumor
sclero-	hard	**sclero**derma—autoimmune condition in which the skin becomes firm and fixed to underlying tissues
scoli(o)-	twised	**scoli**osis—lateral curvature of the spine
sebo-	hard fat, skin oil	**sebo**rrhea—skin condition in which there is an overproduction of sebum resulting in oiliness or dry scales
semi	half	**semi**lunar—half-moon shaped

Root	Meaning	Sample Word
soma/somy	body	**soma**totype—body build
spondylo-	spine	**spondyl**itis—an inflammation of any of the spinal vertebrae
sphygmo-	heartbeat	**sphygmo**manometer—device for measuring blood pressure
sten(o)-	narrow	**sten**osis—abnormal narrowing of a bodily passageway
tachy-	fast, swift	**tachy**cardia—rapid heartbeat
ten(d)o-	stretch, tendon	**tend**on—band of tissue that attaches muscle to bone
terato-	monster	**terato**logy—study of causes and effects of congenital abnormalities
thel-	breast, covering layer	**thel**arche—the beginning of female pubertal breast development
thromb(o)-	blood clot	**thromb**olytic—pertaining to the dissolution of a blood clot
thyro-	oblong shield	**thyro**id—shield shaped gland
tono-	stretch	**ton**ic—pertaining to nerve fibers that respond to length changes of a muscle spindle
trache-	neck	**trache**a—air passage tube in the neck
tricho-	hair	**tricho**id—resembling a hair
umbilic-	navel	**umbilic**us—navel, depression in the center of the abdomen
ungui	nail, claw	**ungui**s—nail, claw
uro-	urine	**uro**gram—x-ray of the urinary tract
vacc-	cow	**vacc**inia—infectious disease of cattle
vaso-	blood vessel	**vaso**dilatation—distention of a blood vessel
vener-	sexual acts, lusty	**vener**eal—pertaining to sexual intercourse or genital contact
veno-	vein (as opposed to artery)	**veno**us—pertaining to the vein
vert-	turn	**vert**igo—dizziness
vesico-	bladder	**vesic**le—blister
xantho-	yellow	**xantho**ma—yellowish plaque that develops in the subcutaneous layer of skin
xeno-	stranger	**xeno**phobia—irrational fear of strangers
xero-	dry	**xero**derma—chronic dry rough skin
zoo-	animals	**zoo**toxin—poisonous substance from an animal
zygo-	yoke	**zygo**te—developing fertilized ovum

Table A.3
Prefixes

Prefix	Meaning	Sample Word
a	without	**a**symptomatic—without symptoms
a(n)-	without	**an**aerobe—without air
ab-	from	**ab**duct—move from
ab(s)-	away from	**abs**orb—to take up or receive
abdomin(o)-	abdomen, fat around the belly	**abdomen**
acous(o)-	hearing	**acous**tic
acr(o)-	topmost, extremity	**acr**odematitis—skin eruption of the hands and feet caused by a mite
ad-	towards	**ad**duction—move towards
aden(o), anden(i)-	fatty tissue	**adeno**lipoma—a fatty tumor
adip(o)-	fatty tissue	**adip**oscyte—a fat cell
adren(o)-	adrenal galnd	**adren**al crisis—life-threatening dysfunction of the adrenal gland
aesthesio-	sensation	**an**esthesi**a**—absence of normal sensation
alb-	white	**alb**inism—lack of melanim pigment
alg((i)-	pain	an**alg**esic— pain medication
allo-	other, another	**allo**genic—genetically different tissues from same species
ambi-	both	**ambi**dextrous—able to use both hands equally well
amino-	fetal sac	**amnio**tic fliud—fluid that surrounds the fetus
amphi-	on both sides, around	**amphi**theater—room with seats arranged in tiers around a central area
ana-	up to, back, again, movement from	**ana**stomosis—surgical bypass of a vessel or duct to allow flow from one part to the other
andr(o)-	man	**andr**osterone—male sex hormone
angio-	blood vessel	**angio**catheter—a tube inserted into th blood vessel
aniso-	different, unequal	**aniso**cytosis—variable and abnormal size of red blood cells
ante-	before, forwards	**ante**version—abnormal forward tilt of an organ
anti-	against, opposite	**anti**bacterial—substance that destroys or inhibits bacterial growth or replication
ap-, apo-	from, away	**apo**physis—outgrowth, usually from bone
arteri(o)-	the artery	**arteri**ogram—x-ray of an artery using radiopaque medium
arthr(o)-	joint or limb	**arthr**itis—inflammation of a joint
aur(i)-	the ear	**aur**al—pertaining to the ear or hearing
Bene	good	**ben**ign—non-cancerous
bi(s)-	twice, double	**bi**lateral—having two sides
bio-	life	**bio**logic—pertaining to living organisms
blast(o)-	germ	**blast**ogenic—originating in the germ plasm
brachio-	arm	**brachi**al artery—artery in upper arm
brachy-	short	**brachy**dactyly—abnormally short fingers and toes
bronchi-	windpipe	**bronchi**al tree—anatomic branches of the traches

Prefix	Meaning	Sample Word
bucc(o)-	cheek	**bucc**al—inside of cheek
burs(o)-	wine skin	**burs**a—fluid filled saclike cavity between movable body parts
capill-	hair	**capill**ary fracture—hairlike fracture
capit-	head	**capit**at—head shaped
carcin(o)-	cancer	**carcin**ogen-cancer producing substance
cardi(o)-	heart	**cardi**ac—pertaining to the heart
carp(o)-	wrist	**carp**al—pertaining to the wrist
cata-	down	**cata**bolism—breakdown of complex substances to simpler substances
cephal(o)-	head	**cephal**ometry—measurement of the head
cerebell(o)-	little brain	**cerebell**um-posterior part of the brain that controls balance and muscular coordination
cerebro-	brain	**cerebr**um—the largest part of the brain associated with thought, emotions and memory
cervic-	neck	**cervi**x—lower narrow outer part of the uterus that extends into the vagina
chemo-	chemistry	**chemo**therapy—treament of disease with chemicals
chir(o)-	hand	**chir**opractic—manipulation of the spinal column
chlor(o)-	green	**chlor**ophyll—green pigments found in plants
chol(e)-	bile	**chol**angiogram—x-ray of bile ducts
chrom(ato)-	color,	**chrom**atosis—abnormal skin pigmentation
cili-	eyelash	**cili**a—eyelashes
circum-	around	**circum**corneal—area surrounding the cornea
co-,com-, con-	together	**con**fluent—running together
colo-, colono-	pipe	**colo**n—portion of the large intestine
colp(o)-	vaginal canal	**colp**oscopy—examination of the vagina and cervix with a magnifying instrument
contra-	against	**contra**ceptive—serving to prevent pregnancy or conception
cor-	heart	**cor**onary—pertaining to the heart
Cry(o)	cold	**cry**otherapy—treating with cold
cyte-	cell	**cyto**logy—study of cells
de-	from, away from, down from	**de**cease—to depart from life
deca-	ten	**deca**gram—a unit of 10 grams
dextr(o)-	right	**dextr**ocaria—location of the heart
di(s)-	two	**dis**sect—cut apart
dia-	through, complete	**dia**gnose—determine the nature of a problem
di(a)s-	separation	**dia**stasis—forceful separation of two parts normally joined together
diplo-	double	**diplo**pia—double vision
dolicho-	long	**dolicho**cephalicx—long-headed
dur-	hard, firm	**dur**able—lasting, resistant to wear
dys-	bad, abnormal	**dys**phagia—difficulty swallowing

Prefix	Meaning	Sample Word
e-, ec-	out, from out of	**ec**crine—sweat gland secreting outwardly
ecto-	outside, external	**ecto**pic—away from its normal location
em-	in	**em**bed—fix into place
en-	into	**en**case—enclose
endo-	into	**endo**scopy—visualization of the inner cavities of the body
ent-	within	**ent**eric—pertaining to the intestines
epi-	on, up, against, high	**epi**thelium—tissue that covers a surface
eso-	I will carry	**eso**teric—meant for a select few
eu-	well, abundant, prosperous	**eu**phoric—state of well-being
eury-	broad, wide	**eury**thmic—wide variations in rhythm
ex-, exo-	out, from out of	**exo**phytic—tendency to grow outward
extra-	outside, beyond, in addition	**extra**cellular—occurring outside the cell
haplo-	single	**haplo**id—pertaining to a single set of chromosones
hypo-	below, deficient	**hypo**glycemia—low blood sugar
im-, in-	not	**in**ert—not moving
in-	into, to	**in**spiration—drawing air into the lungs
infra-	below, underneath	**infra**clavicular—below the clavicle
inter-	among, between	**inter**mittent—occurring at intervals
intra-	within, inside, during	**intra**muscular—into the muscle
intro-	inward, during	**intro**vert—withdrawn, self-absorbed
iso-	equal,same	**iso**metric—having equal measure
juxta-	adjacent to	**juxta**position—placement side-to-side or end-to-end
kerat(o)	horny	**kerat**osis—hard bump on the skin
macro-	large	**macro**glossia—excessively large tongue
medi-	middle	**medi**an—middle value
mega-	large	**mega**dose—excessively large dose
megalo-	very large	**megalo**cephaly—pathological overgrowth of the brain
meso-	middle	**meso**derm—middle of three layers of an embryo
meta-	beyond, between	**meta**stasis—spread of tumor cells
micro-	small	**micro**cytic—smaller than normal red blood cells
neo-	new	**neo**nate—newborn child
non-	not	**non**compliance—not adhering to therapeutic plan
ob-	before, against	**ob**tund—render insensitive to painful stimuli
oligo-	few	**oligo**uria—diminished amount of produced and passed urine
pachy-	thick	**pachy**cephaly—abnormal thickening of the skull
pan-	all	**pan**acea—cure-all
para-	beside, to the side of, wrong	**para**plegia—paralysis of the lower limbs

Prefix	Meaning	Sample Word
per-	by, through, throughout	**per**cutaneous—through the skin
peri-	around, round-about	**peri**odontal—area around a tooth
pleo-	more than usual	**pleo**morphism—existing in two or more distinct forms during a life cycle
poly-	many	**poly**cystic—presence of many cysts
post-	behind, after	**post**mortem—after death
pre-	before, in front, very	**pre**tibial—area in front of the tibia
pseudo-	false, fake	**pseudo**tumor—false tumor
quar(r)-	four	**quar**tan—occurring on the fourth day
re, red-	back, again	**re**duce—restore to original size
retro-	backwards, behind	**retro**flex—bent backward
semi-	half	**semi**lunar—half moon-shaped objects
sub-	under, beneath	**sub**cutaneous—beneath the skin
super-	above, in addition, over	**super**ficial—pertaining to the surface
supra-	above, on the upper side	**supra**pubic—above the symphysis pubis
syn-	together, with	**syn**ergy—two or muscles, nerves etc. working together
sys-	together, with	**sys**temic—pertaining to the whole
tetra-	four	**tetra**logy of Fallot—congenital heart anomaly consisting of four defects
trans-	across, beyond	**trans**cend—to rise above and beyond
tri-	three	**tri**mester—one of three 3-month periods
uni-	one	**uni**lateral—pertaining to one side
ultra-	beyond, besides, over	**ultra**centrifuge—high-speed centrifuge

Table A.4
Suffixes

Suffix	Meaning	Sample Word
-ac	pertaining to	cardi**ac**—pertaining to the heart
-al	pertaining to	abdomin**al**—pertaining to the abdomen
algia	pain	my**algia**—muscle aches or pains
-ase	fermenter	lact**ase**—enzyme that breaks down milk
-asthenia	weakness	my**asthenia**—abnormal muscle weakness
-centesis	puncture	amnio**centesis**—removal of amniotic fluid
-cide	killer	bacteri**cide**—destruction of bacteria
-c(o)ele	cavity, hollow	cyst**ocele**—protrusion of the bladder into the vaginal wall
-crine	secretion ("separation")	endo**crine** system—network of glands that secrete hormones
-cyte	cell	leuko**cyte**—white cell
-desis	binding	arthro**desis**-surgical fixation of a joint
-ectasis	expansion	bronchi**ectasis**—dilatation of the bronchial tubes
-ectomy	excision	thromb**ectomy**—removal of a blood clot
-emesis	vomiting	hemat**emesis**—vomiting blood
-em(ia)	blood	an**emia**—blood disorder characterized by low hemoglobin levels
-enchyme	filling, infusion	par**enchyma**—essential and distinctive tissue of an organ
-form	shaped like	bacilli**form**—rod shaped like a bacterium
-genesis	origin	sporo**genesis**—formation of spores
-gram	record	electrocardio**gram**—graphic record of the electrocardiograph tracings
-graph	to write	electrocardio**graph**—printout of the electrical activity of the heart
-iasis	full of	ancylostomo**iasis**—hookworm infection
-icle	small	part**icle**—a small piece
-ism	theory, characteristic of	relativ**ism**—"theory that knowledge is relative to the limited nature of the mind and the conditions of knowing"[1]
-itis	inflammation	appendic**itis**—inflammation of the appendix
-ity	makes a noun, of quality	reliabil**ity**—quality of being reliable
-ium, um	thing (makes a noun)	bacter**ium**—unicellular microorganism
-ize	do	social**ize**—act in a social manner
-lepsis	seizure	epi**lepsy**—seizure disorder
-logy	study of, reasoning about	histo**logy**—study of tissue
-lysis / -lytic	breaking down	hemo**lytic**—break down of red blood cells
-malacia	soft	chondro**malacia**—softening of cartilage
-megaly	large	hepato**megaly**—enlarged liver
-meter	measurement	spiro**meter**—instrument for measuring air flow in and out of the lungs
-oid	resembling, image of	aden**oid**—having a glandular appearance
-ol(e)	alcohol	ethan**ol**—intoxicating flammable element in liquor
-oma	tumor/lump	hemat**oma**—blood clot

Suffix	Meaning	Sample Word
-osis	full of	anatom**osis**—joining of two ducts or vessels
-paresis	weakness	hemi**paresis**—weakness on one side of the body
-pathy	disease of, suffering	neuro**pathy**—abnormal condition of the peripheral nerves
-penia	lack	thrombocyto**penia**—reduced number of platelets
-phage	eater	macro**phage**s—cells that ingest pathogens
-philia	attraction for	hemo**philia**—bleeding disorder
-phobia	fear	homo**phobia**—irrational fear or aversion to homosexuals
-plasia	formation	hyper**plasia**—abnormal increase in cells
-plasty	re-shaping	mammo**plasty**—plastic reshaping of the breasts
-plexy	stroke	apo**plexy**—hemorrhage within an organ
-plegia	stroke, paralysis	para**plegia**—motor or sensory loss in the lower limbs
-philia / -philo	affection for	cryo**philia**—preference for cold environments
-poiesis	production	erythro**poiesis**—formation of red blood cells
-ptosis	fall	colo**ptosis**—prolapse of the colon
-ptysis	spitting	hemo**ptysis**—spitting blood
-rhage	burst out	hemor**rhage**—bleeding
-rhea	discharge, flowing out	rhinor**rhea**—runny nose
-sis	idea (makes a noun, typically abstract)	synthe**sis**—combination of elements
-static	standing	bacterio**static**—restraining the reproduction of bacteria
-staxis	dripping	epi**staxis**—nosebleed
-stomy	"mouth-cut"	colo**stomy**—surgically created artificial anus
-tresia	Not whole	a**tresia**—absence of a normal body opening
-tripsy	crushing, pounding	litho**tripsy**—procedure for crushing stones in the urinary bladder or the urethra
-tomy	cut	thoraco**tomy**—surgical opening in the chest cavity
-ule	little version	ven**ule**—small vein

1. The Free Dictionary http://www.thefreedictionary.com (accessed 5/12/09)

Abbreviations and Acronyms: Know thy Source

An abbreviation is a shortened form of a word or phrase, used for convenience, which should be readily understood by the reader. Abbreviations may appear as upper or lower case letters and with or without periods. An acronym is an abbreviation of a name or formed from the initial letters of other words. Organization, corporations, famous people and countries often use acronyms—AMA, IBM, JFK, USA, with or without periods, which are readily recognizable by most readers. Some acronyms form pronounceable words and are readily recognized, such as WHO (World Health Organization) and OPEC (Organization of the Petroleum Exporting Countries).

Medical records are apt to contain multiple abbreviations and acronyms, the definition of some being more obvious than others. ER, referring to emergency room, is a popular abbreviation unlikely to cause confusion. AROM in a note written by a physical therapist means "active range of motion." An obstetrician will use the same acronym to mean artificial rupture of membranes. "BC" in a medical chart can have numerous meanings and the interpretation depends upon the context of the note. Is the writer referring to back care, blood count, birth control, and so on?

As indicated, there are multiple and divergent definitions ascribed to any one abbreviation or acronym. When initially written in a record, the writer should provide a definition to help alleviate confusion and misinterpretation by the reader. To assign the most appropriate meaning of abbreviations in medical records, the reader should first define medical diagnoses and the author's practice specialty.

The following list provides a sampling of abbreviations and acronyms found in medical records. In an effort to assist the reader, when appropriate, the applicable specialty area or type of medical record where the abbreviation or acronym is likely to be used and/or the area the reader can begin researching further information is provided in parentheses. (The author has italicized some notes of explanation in parentheses to assist the reader.)

A

@	at
A	active, assistance
A	arteriole
a	ante/before
A1	aortic first heart sound
A2	aortic second heart sound
A&B	apnea and bradycardia
A&BC	air and bone conduction
A&D	alcohol and drug
A&O	alert and oriented
A&P	anterior and posterior
A&P	auscultation and palpation
A&P	auscultation and percussion
A&W	alive and well
A/	acid-base ratio
A/G	albumin globulin ratio
A/O	alert and oriented
A/T	activity therapy
A/V	arteriovenous
A>B	air greater than bone (*Refers to sound conduction in the ear*)
A1	aortic first sound
A2	aortic second sound
AA	Alcoholics Anonymous
Aa	of each
AAA	abdominal aortic aneurysm
AAAHC	Accreditation Association for Ambulatory Care
AAAASF	American Association for Accreditation of Ambulatory Surgery Facilities
AABB	American Association of Blood Banks
AACME	Accreditation Council for Continuing Medical Education
ACGME	Accreditation Council for Graduate Medical Education
AACPDM	American Academy for Cerebral Palsy and Developmental Medicine
AACR	American Association for Cancer Research
AAE	American Association of Endodontists
AAFP	American Academy of Family Physicians
AAHKS	American Association of Hip and Knee Surgeons
AAHP	American Association of Health Plans
AAHS	American Association for Hand Surgery
AAHSA	American Association of Homes and Services for the Aging
AAL	anterior axillary line
AAMA	American Academy of Medical Administrators
AAMC	Association of American Medical Colleges
AAN	American Academy of Neurology
AAN	Attending admission note
AANOS	The American Academy of Neurological and Orthopaedic Surgeons
AANS	American Association of Neurological Surgeons

AAO	American Academy of Ophthalmology	Ab, ab	antibody
AAOFAS	American Association of Orthopaedic Foot and Ankle Surgeons	AB, Ab	abortion
		AB, Ab	antibiotic
AAOHN	American Association of Occupational Health Nurses	AB, abn	abnormal
		ABA	American Board of Anesthesiologists
AAOM	American Academy of Oral Medicine	Abb	abbreviation, abbreviated
AAOO	American Academy of Ophthalmology and Otolaryngology	ABC	airway, breathing, and circulation
		Abd	abdomen
AAOP	American Academy of Orthotists and Prosthetists	Abd	abduction
		ABE	acute bacterial endocarditis
AAOS	American Academy of Orthopaedic Surgery	ABE	American Board of Endodontics
		ABG	arterial blood gas (Laboratory)
AAOx3	awake, alert, and oriented × 3; i.e., to person, place, and time	ABI	ankle to brachial index (peripheral vascular)
AAP	American Academy of Pediatrics	ABJS	Association of Bone and Joint Surgeons
AAP	American Academy of Pedodontics		
AAP	American Academy of Periodontology	ABL	anticonvulsive blood level
AAP	American Association of Pathologists	ABMS	American Board of Medical Specialties
AAPA	American Academy of Physician Assistants		
		ABO	blood grouping system
AAPA	American Association of Pathologist Assistants	ABOS	American Board of Orthopaedic Surgery
AAPB	American Association of Pathologists and Bacteriologists	ABP	American Board of Pathology
		ABR	auditory brainstem response audiometry
AAPC	antibiotic-associated pseudomembranous colitis		
		ABS	arterial blood pressure
AAPCC	adjusted average per capita cost	Abs feb	while the fever is absent
AAPMC	antibiotic-associated pseudo-membranous colitis	ABTA	American Brain Tumor Association
		AC	acromioclavicular joint
AAPMR	American Academy of Physical Medicine and Rehabilitation	AC	air conduction
		ac	before meals
AAPPO	American Association of Preferred Providers Organization	AC	anterior chamber (may be graded, i.e., 4/4; 3/4; 2/4; 1/4; 0/4) (Ophthalmology)
AAPS	American Association of Plastic Surgeons		
		AC/A	accommodation convergence/accommodation ratio (Ophthalmology)
AAPS	Association of American Physicians and Surgeons		
		ACA	American Chiropractic Association
AAPSM	American Academy of Podiatric Sports Medicine	ACC	American College of Cardiology
		Acc	accommodation (Ophthalmology)
AARC	American Association for Respiratory Care	ACCP	American College of Chest Physicians
		ACD	anterior cervical discectomy (Orthopedics, Neurosurgery)
AAROM	active assistive range of motion		
AAT	alanine aminotransferase (Laboratory)	ACDF	anterior cervical discectomy and fusion (Orthopedics, Neurosurgery)
AATS	American Association for Thoracic Surgery		
		ACE	angiotensin converting enzyme (Pharmacology)
AAU	acute anterior uveitis		
AAWM	American Academy of Wound Management	ACF	anterior cervical fusion (Orthopedics, Neurosurgery)
AB	American Board of Pediatrics	ACFAS	American College of Foot and Ankle Surgeons
AB	blood group AB		

ACF	antecubital fossa (Intravenous site location)	ACPOC	Association of Children's Prosthetic-Orthotic Clinics
ACG	angle closure glaucoma (Ophthalmology)	ACPP	prostate-specific acid phosphatase (Laboratory)
ACHP	Alliance of Community Health Plans	ACR	adenomatosis of colon and rectum (Gastroenterology; Endocrinology)
ACI	acute coronary insufficiency		
acid phos	acid phosphatase (Laboratory)	ACR	adjusted community rating (Insurance)
ACJ	acromioclavicular joint (Orthopedic)	ACR	ambulance call report
ACL	anterior clavicular line (Physical assessment term referring to location)	ACR	American College of Radiology
		ACR	American College of Rheumatology
ACL	anterior cruciate ligament (Orthopedics, Physical Therapy)	ACRM	American Congress on Rehabilitation Medicine
ACLA	American Clinical Laboratory Association	ACRPI	Association of Clinical Research for the Pharmaceutical Industry
ACLR	anterior capsulolabral reconstruction (Orthopedics)	ACS	acute cervical strain; acute cervical sprain
ACLS	Advanced Cardiac Life Support	ACS	acute chest syndrome
ACM	acetaminophen (Pharmacology)	ACS	acute confusional state
ACM	anticonvulsant (Pharmacology)	ACS	American Cancer Society
ACMA	American Occupational Medical Association	ACS	American College of Surgeons
		ACSM	American College of Sports Medicine
ACMV	assist-controlled mechanical ventilation (Respiratory Therapy)	ACSV	aortocoronary saphenous vein
		ACSVBG	aortocoronary saphenous vein bypass graft
ACNM	American College of Nurse-Midwives		
ACNP	acute care nurse practitioner	ACSW	Academy of Certified Social Workers
ACNP	American College of Nuclear Physicians	ACT	activated clotting time (Laboratory)
		ACT	active motion
ACO	acute coronary occlusion	Act	activity, active
ACO	alert, cooperative, oriented	ACT	anticoagulant therapy (Pharmacology)
ACOA	adult children of alcoholics	ACT	anxiety control training
ACOEM	American College of Occupational and Environmental Medicine	ACT	asthma care training
		ACT	atropine coma therapy (Pharmacology)
ACOEP	American College of Osteopathic Emergency Physicians	ACTA	American Cardiology Technologists Association
ACOG	American College of Obstetricians and Gynecologist	ACTA	automatic computerized transverse axial (scanning) (Radiology)
ACOM	American College of Occupational Medicine	ACTH	adrenocorticotrophic hormone (Endocrinology)
ACOM	anterior communicating (Artery)	ACTS	acute cervical trauma syndrome
ACOMS	American College of Oral and Maxillofacial Surgeons	ACTZ	acetazolamide (Pharmacology)
		ACVB	aortocoronary venous bypass
ACOOG	American College of Osteopathic Obstetricians and Gynecologists	ACVD	acute cardiovascular disease
		ACVD	arteriosclerotic cardiovascular disease
ACOS	American College of Osteopathic Surgeons	ad lib	at pleasure, at discretion, freely as desired
ACP	American College of Pathologists	AD	adjuvant chemotherapy
ACP	American College of Pharmacists	AD	admission and discharge
ACP	American College of Prosthodontists	AD	admitting diagnosis
ACPM	American College of Preventive Medicine	AD	alternating days
		AD	Alzheimer's disease

AD	attending doctor	ADS	alternative delivery system (Insurance)
AD	atopic dermatitis (Dermatology)	ADV	advised
AD	auris dextra (right ear)	adv	against (Found on prescriptions)
ADA	American Dental Association	AE	above the elbow
ADA	Americans with Disabilities Act	AE	active and equal
ADA	anterior descending artery (Cardiology)	AE	adverse event
		AEB	as evidenced by
ADASP	Association of Directors of Anatomic and Surgical Pathology	AED	antiepileptic drug (Pharmacology)
		AED	automated external defibrillator (Cardiology, Emergency Medical Services)
ADC	AIDS dementia complex (Psychiatry)		
ADD	addiction	Aeg	the patient (Found on prescriptions)
Add	adduct; adduction	AEG	air encephalogram (Neurology)
Add	addition (Ophthalmology)	AER	auditory evoked response (Neurology)
ADD	attention deficit disorder (Psychology)	AER	average evoked response (Neurology)
ADD	average daily dose (Pharmacology)	AF	adult female
ADEA	American Dental Education Association	AF	African-American
		AF	amniotic fluid (Obstetrics)
adeno-Ca	adenocarcinoma (Oncology)	AF	aortic flow (Cardiology)
ADH	antidiuretic hormone (Pharmacology)	AF	atrial fibrillation; atrial flutter (Cardiology)
ADH	atypical ductal hyperplasia (Gynecology; Oncology)		
		AFB	acid-fast bacilli (Laboratory)
ADHD	attention deficit hyperactivity disorder (Psychology)	AFC	amniotic fluid cortisol (Obstetrics)
		AFDC	Aid to Families with Dependent Children
ADJ	adjacent		
ADJ	adjoining	A-Fib; Afib	atrial fibrillation (Cardiology)
ADJ	adjust, adjustment or manipulation (Chiropractic)	AFL	artificial limb
		A-Flutter	atrial flutter (Cardiology, Emergency Medical Services)
ADL	activities of daily living (i.e., bathing, dressing, toileting, feeding, and grooming)	AFO	ankle-foot orthoses (Physical Therapy)
		AFP	acute flaccid paralysis (Neurology)
Ad lib	as desired	AFP	alpha-fetoprotein (Obstetrics, Laboratory)
ADM scale	Acceptance of Disability Scale Modified	AGA	appropriate-for-gestational age (Obstetrics)
ADM	admission/admitted		
ADM	adrenal medulla (Endocrinology)	AGF	angle of greatest flexion (Physical Therapy)
ADM	advancement of the mandible (Dental)		
ADM	alcohol, drug, and mental disorders	AGG	aggravation
ADM	anterior deep masseter (Orthopedics, Physical Therapy)	AGN	acute glomerulonephritis (Renal)
		AGTT	abnormal glucose tolerance test (Laboratory)
ADM	atypical diabetes mellitus; adult onset diabetes mellitus (Endocrinology)		
		AH	abdominal hysterectomy (Gynecology)
ADM	auditory dominance model (Speech)	AH	arterial hypertension (Cardiology)
admin	administration	AH	auditory hallucinations (Psychiatry)
ADN	attending (doctor) discharge note	AHA	American Hospital Association
ADON	assistant director of nursing	AHC	acute hemorrhagic conjunctivitis (Refers to the eye)
ADP	abductor pollicis (Orthopedics, Physical Therapy)		
		AHC	acute hemorrhagic cystitis (Refers to the bladder) (Urology)
ADP	adenosine diphosphate (Pharmacology)	AHC	alternative health care (Insurance)
ADR	adverse drug reaction	AHCA	Agency for Health Care Administration

AHCA	American Health Care Association		AIDSLINE	online information on acquired immu-nodeficiency syndrome
AHCPR	Agency for Health Care Policy and Re-search		AIDS-OI	AIDS with opportunistic infections
AHD	acute heart disease		AIIS	anterior inferior iliac spine
AHD	antihypertensive drug		AIMS	Abnormal Involuntary Movement Scale (Neurology)
AHD	atherosclerotic heart disease		AION	anterior ischemic optic neuropathy (Ophthalmology)
AHD	autoimmune hemolytic disease (He-matology)		AIOSM	American Institute of Orthopaedic and Sports Medicine
AHEC	Area Health Education Center		AIS	adenocarcinoma in situ (Oncology)
AHF	acute heart failure		AIT	after image transfer (Ophthalmology)
AHIMA	American Health Information Manage-ment Association		AltSOT	alternate esotrophis (Ophthalmology)
AHIS	automated hospital information system		AltXOT	alternative exotropia (Ophthalmology)
AHJ	artificial hip joint		AJ	ankle jerk
AHM	ambulatory Holter monitor (Cardiol-ogy, Diagnostic)		AJKS	American Journal of Knee Surgery
AHMA	American Holistic Medicine Associa-tion		AJNR	American Journal of NeuroRadiology
			AJO	American Journal of Orthopaedics
AHR	atrial heart rate (Cardiology)		AK	above knee
AHRF	acute hypoxemic respiratory failure (Pulmonary)		AKA	above knee amputation
			AKA	also known as
AHRQ	Agency for Healthcare Research and Quality (formerly AHCPR)		AL	left ear (Not recommended)
			alb	albumin (Laboratory)
AHS	Academy of Health Sciences		alk phos	alkaline phosphatase (Laboratory)
AHS	American Hearing Society		ALL	acute lymphocytic leukemia (Oncol-ogy)
AHS	American Hospital Society		ALL	allergic; allergy
AHT	arterial hypertension		ALMI	anterior lateral myocardial infarction (Cardiology)
AI	active ingredient		
AI	aortic incompetence; aortic insuffi-ciency (Cardiology)		ALOS	average length of stay
			ALP	alkaline phosphatase (Laboratory)
AI	apical impulse (Cardiology)		ALPC	argon laser photocoagulation (Labora-tory)
AI	articulation index (Speech Pathology)		
AI	artificial insemination (Infertility)		ALRI	anterolateral rotatory instability (Physi-cal Therapy)
AI	atrial insufficiency (Cardiology)		
AI	autoimmune, autoimmunity (Endocri-nology)		ALS	acute lumbar strain
			ALS	amyotrophic lateral sclerosis (Neurol-ogy)
AICA	anterior inferior cerebellar artery (Anat-omy)		
			ALT	alanine aminotransferase (Formerly SGPT) (Laboratory)
AICA	anterior inferior communicating artery (Anatomy)		
			alt	alternate; alternating
AICD	automated internal cardioverter (Cardi-ology, Emergency Medical Services)		alt die	alternate days (Found on prescriptions)
			ALTHA	Acute Long Term Hospital Association
AID	autoimmune deficiency; autoimmune disease (Infectious Disease)		alt hore	alternate hours (Found on prescrip-tions)
AIDS	acquired immune deficiency syn-drome		alt noc	alternate nights (Found on prescrip-tions)
AIDSDRUGS	clinical trials of acquired immunodefi-ciency drugs		alv	alveolar
			AM A.M.	before noon
AIDS-KS	acquired immune deficiency syndrome with Kaposi's sarcoma		AM	adult male

AM	anteromedial	A-P & Lat	anterioposterior and lateral (*Physical assessment term referring to location*)
AM	before noon		
ama	against medical advice	AP	acute pancreatitis (Gastroenterology, Digestive Diseases)
AMA	American Medical Association		
AMB	ambulate; ambulatory	AP	acute pneumonia (Pulmonary)
AMCRA	American Managed Care and Review Association	AP	after parturition (Obstetrics)
		AP	alkaline phosphatase (Laboratory)
AMD	age-related macular degeneration (*also ARMD*) (Ophthalmology)	AP	angina pectoris (Cardiology)
		A-P	anterioposterior (*Physical assessment term referring to location*)
AMI	acute myocardial infarction (Cardiology)		
AMIA	American Medical Informatics Association	AP	anterior pituitary (Anatomy, Endocrinology)
AML	acute myelogenous leukemia (Oncology)	AP	anterioposterior (*Physical assessment term referring to location*)
AMP	adenosine monophosphate (biochemistry)	AP	aortic pressure (Cardiology)
		AP	apical pulse
amp	ampere (*Unit of electric current*)	AP	appendectomy; appendicitis; appendix
AMP	amphetamine (Pharmacology)		
AMP	amputation	AP	arterial pressure
AMSSM	American Medical Society for Sports Medicine	AP	aspiration pneumonia
		AP	atrial pacing (Cardiology)
Amt; amt	amount	AP	atrioventricular pathway (Anatomy)
ANA	American Nurses Association	APA	American Psychiatric Association
ANA	antinuclear antibody test (Laboratory)	APA	acetaminophen (Pharmacology)
ANAL	analgesic (Pharmacology)	APB	atrial premature beat (Cardiology)
ANES	anesthesia	APC	atrial premature contractions (Cardiology)
ANP	advanced nurse practitioner		
ANRI	acute nerve root irritation	APC	anterior polar cataract (Ophthalmology)
ANS	autonomic nervous system (Anatomy)		
ANT, ant.	anterior	APC	aspirin, phenacetin, caffeine (Pharmacology)
ante	before		
ANX	anxiety	APC	Ambulatory Payment Classification
AO	angle of	APD	afferent pupillary defect (Ophthalmology)
AO	aorta		
AOA	American Osteopathic Association	APH	anterior pituitary hormone (Endocrinology)
AOB	alcohol on breath		
AOD	arteriosclerotic occlusive disease	APH	aphasia (Neurology)
AODM	adult onset diabetes mellitus	APHA	American Public Health Association
AOFAS	American Orthopaedic Foot and Ankle Society	APL	abductor pollicis longus (Orthopedics, Physical Therapy)
AOI	Academia Ophthalmologica Internationalis	APMA	American Podiatric Medical Association
AOM	acute otitis media	APP	Alzheimer amyloid precursor protein (Neurology, Laboratory)
AOPA	American Orthotic and Prosthetic Association		
		APP	appendix
AORN	Association of Perioperative Registered Nurses	Appt	appointment
		APTA	American Physical Therapy Association
AOS	Academic Orthopaedic Society		
AOSSM	American Orthopaedic Society for Sports Medicine	APTT	automated partial thromboplastin time (Laboratory)

aq	water	ASHD	atherosclerotic heart disease
AR	active resistance (Physical Therapy)	ASHNR	American Society of Head and Neck Radiology
AR	admitting room		
AR	aortic regurgitation (Cardiology)	ASIA	American Spinal Injury Association
ARC	AIDS related complex	ASIS	anterior superior iliac spine (Anatomy)
ARC	anomalous retinal correspondence (Ophthalmology)	ASLME	American Society of Law, Medicine & Ethics
ARD	acute respiratory disease	ASMI	American Sports Medicine Institute
ARDS	adult respiratory distress syndrome	ASMI	atrial septal myocardial infarction (Cardiology)
ARE	active-resistance exercise (Physical Therapy)	ASNR	American Society of NeuroRadiology
ARF	acute renal failure (Renal)	ASO	administrative services only
ARF	acute respiratory failure (Pulmonary)	ASO	arteriosclerosis obliterans (Vascular)
ARF	acute rheumatic fever (Immunology)	ASOPA	American Society of Orthopaedic Physician's Assistants
ARM	anxiety reaction, mild (Psychiatry)		
ARNP	advanced registered nurse practitioner	ASPNR	American Society of Pediatric Neuro-Radiology
AROM	active range of motion (Physical Therapy)	ASPRS	American Society of Plastic and Reconstructive Surgeons
AROM	artificial rupture of membranes (Obstetrics)	ASR	age/sex rate (Insurance)
ARP	American Registry of Pathology	ASRT	American Society of Radiologic Technologists
ARRT	American Registry of Radiologic Technologists	ASS	anterior superior spine (*Physical assessment term referring to location*)
ART	artery		
ART	articulation	ASSH	American Society for Surgery of the Hand
ART	artificial	ASSR	American Society of Spine Radiology
as to	as tolerated	Asst	assistant
AS	anal sphincter	AST	alanine aminotransferase (Laboratory)
AS	ankylosing spondylitis (Immunology)	AST	aspartate aminotransferase (*Formerly SGOT*) (*Laboratory*)
AS	aortic stenosis (Cardiology)		
AS; ASC	arteriosclerosis	AST	Association of Surgical Technologists
AS	left ear	AST; Astigm.	Astigmatism (Ophthalmology)
ASA	acetylsalicylic acid (aspirin)	As tol	as tolerated
ASA	American Society of Anesthesiologists	ASTRO	American Society for Therapeutic Radiology and Oncology
ASAP	as soon as possible		
ASC	ascending (*Physical assessment term referring to location*)	ASU	ambulatory surgery unit
		ASVD	Arteriosclerotic Vascular Disease
ASCAD	arteriosclerotic coronary artery disease	AT	achilles tendon (Anatomy)
ASCO	American Society of Clinical Oncology	AT	activity therapist
		AT	anterior tibial (Anatomy)
ASCVD	arteriosclerotic cardiovascular disease	AT	athletic trainer
ASD	atrial septal defect (Cardiology)	ATA	American Telemedicine Association
ASDP	American Society of DermatoPathology	ATP	adenosine triphosphate (Biochemistry)
		ATP	attending physician
ASES	American Shoulder and Elbow Surgeons	Atr fib	atrial fibrillation (Cardiology)
		ATR	Achilles tendon reflex (Anatomy)
ASF	anterior spinal fusion (Neurology)	ATR	alpha-thalassemia-mental retardation (*syndrome*) (Hematology, Genetics)
ASH	American Society of Hematology		
ASH	asymmetrical septal hypertrophy (Cardiology)	Atr	atrophy

ATS	American Thoracic Society	AVH	acute viral hepatitis (Infectious Disease, Gastroenterology)
ATS	arteriosclerosis		
Atyp	atypical	AVL	automated volt left (Electrocardiography)
ATZ	atypical transformation zone (Pathology)	aVL	unipolar limb lead on the left arm in electrocardiography
AU	both ears, each ear	AVM	atrio-ventricular malformations (Cardiology)
Au	gold (Pharmacology, Biochemistry)		
AUA	American Urological Association	AVM	arteriovenous malformations (Cardiology)
AUB	normal uterine bleeding (Gynecology)		
Aud	auditory	AVN	atrioventricular node (Cardiology)
AUDIT	alcohol use disorders identification test	AVO	aortic valve opening (Cardiology)
		AVO	aortic valve orifice (Cardiology)
AUG	acute ulcerative gingivitis (Dental)	AVO	atrioventricular opening (Cardiology)
AUR	ambulatory utilization review	AVR	automated volt right (Electrocardiography)
AUS	acute urethral syndrome (Genitourinary)		
		AVR	unipolar limb lead on the right arm in electrocardiography
Aus	alcohol users		
aus, ausc	auscultation (Physical Assessment)	AVRI	acute viral respiratory infection
AUV	anterior urethral valve (Genitourinary)	AVS	aortic valve stenosis (Cardiology)
AV	anteversion (Physical assessment term referring to position)	AVS	arteriovenous shunt (Cardiology)
		AVSD	atrioventricular septal defect (Cardiology)
AV	aortic valve (Cardiology)		
AV	artificial ventilation, assisted ventilation (Respiratory Therapy)	AVT	Allen vision test (Ophthalmology)
		AVZ	avascular zone
AV/AF	anteverted, anteflexed (Physical assessment term referring to position)	AW	above waist
		Aw	airway
AV; av	avulsion	AW	alive and well
AV; A-V	arteriovenous; atrioventricular (Cardiovascular)	AW	alveolar wall (Pulmonary)
		AW	anterior wall (Physical assessment term referring to location)
AV; Av	avoirdupois (Pharmacology)		
AV; Av; av	average	AWOL	absent without leave
AVA	antiviral antibody (Laboratory)	AX	axial: axillary (Physical assessment term referring to location)
AVA	aortic valve area		
AVA	aortic valve atresia (Cardiology)	AZT	azidothymidine (Zidovudine) (Pharmacology)
AVA	arteriovenous anastomosis (Cardiology)		
AVB	atrioventricular block (Cardiology)	**B**	
AV block	atrioventricular block (Cardiology)	B; bal	bath
AVC	aberrant ventricular conduction (Cardiology)	B	bilateral (May be encircled) (Physical assessment term referring to location)
AVC	aortic valve closure (Cardiology)	B	Black
AVD	aortic valvular disease (Cardiology)	b	bone
AVD	atrioventricular dissociation (Cardiology)	B	born
		B	buccal
Avdp	avoirdupois (Pharmacology)	B&B	bowel and bladder
AVF	antiviral factor (Laboratory)	B&C	biopsy and curettage (Surgery, Pathology)
AVF	arteriovenous fistula (Cardiology)		
AVF	unipolar limb lead on the left leg in electrocardiography	b/c	because
		B/M	black male
AVG, avg	average	B-Mod	behavior modification

BA	blood alcohol	BD	behavioral disorder
BA	bone age	BD	Bechct disease (Immunology, Gastroenterology)
BA	brachial artery	BD	belladonna (Pharmacology)
BA	bronchial asthma	BD	bile duct (Anatomy)
Ba, BA	barium (Pharmacology)	BD	birth date
BAB	Babinski's sign (Neurological examination)	BD	blood donor
BAC	blood alcohol concentration (Laboratory)	BD	brain dead, brain death
Bact	bacteriologist; bacteriology, bacterium (Laboratory)	BD	bronchodilation, bronchodilator (Pulmonary, Pharmacology)
BaE	barium enema (Diagnostic)	BDI-PC	Beck Depression Inventory for Primary Care
BAER	brain stem auditory evoked response (Neurology)	BDR	background retinal correspondence (Ophthalmology)
BAL	blood alcohol level (Laboratory)	BE	barium enema
BAPS	biomechanical ankle platform (Physical Therapy)	BE	below the elbow
Barb, BARB	barbiturate, barbituric (Pharmacology)	BE	benzoylecgonine (cocaine) (Pharmacology)
BaS	barium swallow (Diagnostic)	BE	binocular visual efficiency (Ophthalmology)
Baso; basos	basophils (leukocytes) (Laboratory)	BE	blood vessel endothelium (Vascular)
BAT	blunt abdominal trauma	BE	blood volume expander (Hematology, Pharmacology)
BB	bad breath		
BB	bed bath	BE	both eyes (Ophthalmology)
BB	bed board	BE	brisk and equal (neurological examination)
BB	breakthrough bleeding (Gynecology)		
BB	breast biopsy (Oncology, Pathology)	BEAP	brainstem evoked auditory potential (Neurology)
BB	bundle branch (Cardiology)		
BBB	blood-brain barrier (Anatomy)	Beh Sp	behavior specialist
BBB	bundle branch block (Cardiology)	Beh Tech	behavior technician
BBBB	bilateral bundle-branch block (Cardiology)	BF	blood flow
		BF	bone fragment
BBD	benign breast disease	bf	boyfriend
BBS	benign breast syndrome	BG	blood glucose
BBS	bilateral breath sounds (Pulmonary examination)	BG	bone graft
		BHP	benign hypertrophic prostate (Urology)
BC	back care	BHS	beta hemolytic streptococcus (Laboratory)
BC	birth control		
BC	blood count	BHT	blunt head trauma
BC	blood culture	BI	bodily injury
BC	bone conduction (ear examination)	BI	bone injury
BC	brachiocephalic (Anatomy)	BI	brain injury
BC	breast cancer	BI	burn index (Surgery, Plastic Surgery)
BC/BS	Blue Cross/Blue Shield	Bic	Biceps
BCA	balloon catheter angioplasty (Diagnostic)	Bicarb	sodium bicarbonate
		BID	brought in dead
BCC	basal cell carcinoma (Oncology)	BID, b.i.d.	twice a day. (Not recommended)
BCC	benign cellular changes (pap smear) (Pathology)	BI; Bilat	bilateral
BCP	birth control pills	BILI	bilirubin (Anatomy, Hematology, Gastroenterology)
BCS	breast conservation surgery		

BIN	twice a night	BOW	bag of waters (Obstetrics)
BIO	binocular indirect ophthalmoscopy (Ophthalmology)	BP	bipolar
		BP; B/P	blood pressure
Biol	biological	BPD	biparietal diameter (Anatomy)
BIP	bronchiolitis obliterans with interstitial pneumonia (Pulmonary)	BPD	borderline personality disorder (Psychiatry)
BIPE	brief psychiatric examination	BPD	bronchopulmonary dysplasia
BiVAS	biventricular assist system (Cardiology)	BPH	benign prostatic hypertrophy (Urology)
BIW	twice a week (Not recommended)	BPI	Brief Pain Inventory
BJ	Bence Jones (proteinuria) (Laboratory)	BPM	beats per minute
BJ	biceps jerk (neurological examination)	BPRS	Brief Psychiatric Rating Scale
BJ	bone and joint	BR	bathroom
BJE	bones, joints, extremities	BR	bed rest
BJM	bones, joints, muscles	BRAP	branch retinal artery occlusion (Ophthalmology)
BK	back	BRB	bright red blood
BK	below the knee	BRBPR	bright red blood per rectum
BKA	below knee amputation; below-the-knee amputee	BRP	bathroom privileges
Bkwds	backwards	BRVO	branch retinal vein occlusion (Ophthalmology)
bl cult	blood culture		
BL	bilateral lower lung fields (Physical assessment term referring to location)	BS	blood sugar
		BS	bowel sounds
BL	blood loss	BS	breath sounds
Blad.	bladder	BS	bronchial secretion (Pulmonary)
bld	blood	BSA	body surface area
BLE	both lower extremities	BSA	bowel signs active
BLEED	(Mnemonic for gastro-intestinal hemorrhage)	BSAEP	brain stem auditory evoked potentials (Neurology)
BLS	basic life support	BSC	bedside commode
BM	body mass index (Nutrition)	BSE	breast self examination
BM	blood monitoring	BSI	blood stream infections
BM	body mass	BSL	baseline
BM	bone marrow	BSO	bilateral salpingo-oophorectomy (Surgery, Gynecology)
BM	bowel movement		
BM	basal metabolism	BSR	bowel sounds regular
BM/E	bowel movement with enema	BSU	Bartholin, Skene, urethral (glands) (Anatomy)
BMD	bone mineral density (Diagnostic)		
BMG	benign monoclonal gammopathy (Hematology, Immunology)	BT	bedtime
		BT	bladder tumor
BMJ	British Medical Journal	BT	bleeding time
BMR	basal metabolic rate (Nutrition)	BT	body temperature
BNO	bladder neck obstruction (Urology)	BT	brain tumor
BOE	bilateral otitis externa (External canal ear infection)	BT	breast tumor
		BTB	breakthrough bleeding (Gynecology)
		BTC	basal temperature chart
BOM	bilateral otitis media (Middle ear infection)	BTC	biliary tract complication (Gastroenterology)
		BTC	body temperature chart
BOO	bladder outlet obstruction (Urology)	BTD	biliary tract disease
BOP	blood, ova, parasites (Laboratory)	BTE	behind the ear (Hearing aid)
BOS	base of support		

BTL	bilateral tubal ligation (Obstetrics/Gynecology)	C/W	continue with
BTR	biceps tendon reflex (Anatomy)	C1–C7	cervical vertebrae (Anatomy)
BTW	back to work	Ca	calcium (Chemistry, Laboratory)
BTW	by the way	CA, Ca	cancer, carcinoma
BTZ	benzothiazepine (Pharmacology)	CA	cardiac arrest
BUE	both upper extremities	CA	caucasian adult
BUN	blood urea nitrogen (Laboratory)	CA	chronological age
BUN/CR	blood urea nitrogen/creatine ratio (Laboratory)	CAB	coronary artery bypass
		CABG	coronary artery bypass graft
BUO	bleeding of undetermined origin, bruising of undetermined origin	CAC	certified alcoholism counselor
		CAD	coronary artery disease
BUQ	both upper quadrants	CAE	carotid artery endarterectomy (Cardiovascular)
BUR	bilateral ureteral occlusion (Urology)		
BUS	Bartholin, urethral, and Skene glands (Anatomy)	CAF	caucasian adult female
		cal	calorie
BV	bacterial vaginosis (Gynecology)	CAM	caucasian adult male
BV	blood vessel	Cap	capitation (Insurance, Administration)
BV	blood volume	caps	capsules
BV	bronchovesicular (Pulmonary)	Car	carbapenem (Pharmacology)
BVD	back vertex distance (Ophthalmology)	CARF	Commission on Accreditation of Rehabilitation Facilities
BVP	back vertex power (Ophthalmology)		
BW	bed wetting	Cat	cataract (Ophthalmology)
BW	below waist	CAT	computed axial tomography (Diagnostic)
BW	biological warfare		
BW	biological weapon	cath	catheter
BW	birth weight	CBC	complete blood count
BW	black woman	CBD	common bile duct (Anatomy)
BW	body weight	CBG	capillary blood gas (Laboratory)
BWS	battered woman syndrome	CBI	continuous bladder irrigation (Urology)
BWX	bite wing x-ray (Dental)		
BX, Bx, biop	biopsy	CBP	comprehensive behavior plan
BZ. BZD	benzodiazepine (Pharmacology)	CBR	complete bed rest
		CBS	chronic brain syndrome
		CBT	carotid body tumor (Oncology)
		CBT	computed body tomography (Diagnostic)

C

c	with	CBV	cerebral blood volume
C	celsius, centigrade, complement	CBV	circulating blood volume
C	chlorine (Chemistry, Laboratory)	CBZ	carbamazepine *(Tegretol)* (Pharmacology)
C	clinical		
C&C	cold and clammy	CC	chief complaint
c&d	clean and dry (Assessment)	Cc	clean catch
C/D	cup/disc ratio (Ophthalmology)	CC	colony count
C&S	conjunctiva and sclera (Anatomy)	CC	Complicating condition
C&S	culture and sensitivity (Laboratory)	Cc	concave
C/M	counts per minute	CC	contrast cystogram (Diagnostic, Urology)
C/O, c/o	care of; complains of		
C/O	complaint of	CC	corpus callosum (Birth Defects)
C/S	C sect, Cesarean section (Obstetrics)	Cc	corrected
C/S	cycles per second	CC	creatinine clearance (Laboratory)
c/w	compatible with		

CC	critical care	CD	cystic duct (Anatomy)
CC	critical condition	CDC	Centers for Disease Control
CC	Crohn colitis (Digestive Diseases)	CDI (c, d, i)	clean, dry, intact (Assessment)
CC; cc	cc, cubic centimeter (Not recommended)	Cdiff	clostridium difficile (Laboratory)
		CDR	clinical dementia rating
CCA	circumflex coronary artery (Anatomy)	CDT	chronic disorganized type (Schizophrenia)
CCA	common carotid artery (Anatomy)		
CCB	calcium channel blocker (Pharmacology)	CDT	clock drawing test (Psychiatry)
		CE	angle (radiograph), center-edge angle
CCC	Council on Clinical Classification	CEA	carcinoembryonic antigen (Laboratory)
CCCR	closed chest cardiac resuscitation	ceph	cephalic vein (Intravenous site location)
CCCS	condom catheter collecting system		
CCE	cyanosis, clubbing, edema	Cervical dil	cervical dilation (Obstetrics)
CCF	compound comminuted fracture (Orthopedics)	CF	clofibrate (Pharmacology)
		cf	compare, refer to
CCF	congestive cardiac failure (Cardiology)	CF	complement fixation (Laboratory)
CCG	cholecystogram, cholecystography (Diagnostic)	CF	cystic fibrosis
		CFDI	color-flow duplex imaging (Diagnostic)
CCHIT	Certification Commission for Health Information Technology	CFM	continuous electronic fetal monitoring (Obstetrics)
CCI	chronic coronary insufficiency		
CCLI	composite clinical and Laboratory index	CFNS	chills, fever, night sweats
		CFR	Code of Federal Regulations
C-collar	cervical collar (Emergency Medical Services)	CG	contact guard
		CGA	contact guard assist (Physical Therapy)
CCM	critical care medicine	CGN	chronic glomerulonephritis (Renal)
CCMS	clean (urine) catch midstream	CGy	centi gray (Unit of radiation)
CCMSU	clean catch midstream urine	CH	chest
CCN	coronary care nursing	CH	chief
CCN	critical care nursing	CH	chronic
CCT	chronic catatonic type (Schizophrenia)	CH	crown-heel (Obstetrics, Diagnostic)
CCU	coronary/cardiac care unit	CHAMPUS	Civilian Health and Medical Program for Uniformed Services (Insurance)
CCW	counterclockwise		
CD	carbon dioxide	CHB	complete heart block
CD	cardiac disease	CHD	congenital dislocation of the hip
CD	cardiac dysrhythmia	CHD	congenital heart disease
CD	cardiovascular disease	CHD	coronary heart disease
CD	caudad, caudal (Physical assessment term referring to location)	Chemo	chemotherapy
		CHF	congestive heart failure
CD	cause of death	CHG	change
CD	celiac disease (Digestive Diseases)	CHI	closed head injury
CD	centration distance (Ophthalmology)	CHO	carbohydrate
CD	color Doppler (Diagnostic)	CHOL	serum cholesterol (Laboratory)
CD	common (bile) duct (Anatomy)	CHR	chronic
CD	communicable disease	CHR	chronological
CD	conduction disorder (Cardiology, Neurology)	CI	cardiac index
		CI	cardiac insufficiency
CD	contact dermatitis (Dermatitis)	CI	cerebral infarction
CD	Crohn disease (Digestive Diseases)	CI	confidence interval (Research)
CD	cut down (Intravenous Therapy)	CIC	crisis intervention clinic

CICU	cardiac intensive care unit	CLINPROT	clinical cancer protocols
CID	carpal instability, dissociative (Orthopedics)	CLL	cholesterol-lowering lipid (Laboratory, Pharmacology)
CID	cervical immobilization device (Emergency Medical Services)	CLMA	Clinical Laboratory Management Association
cig	cigarette	CLP	cleft lip with cleft palate
CIN	cervical intraepithelial neoplasia (grades I, II, III) (Pathology)	ClP	clinical pathology
		CLS	clinical laboratory scientist
CIND	carpal instability non-dissociative (Orthopedics)	CLT	certified laboratory technician; clinical laboratory technician
CIP	clinical investigation plan (Research)	CLT	clotting time (Laboratory)
circ	circulation	CM	cardiac murmur
circ	circumference	CM	cardiac muscle
CIS	carcinoma in situ (Oncology)	CM	cardiomyopathy
CJD	Creutzfeldt-Jakob disease (Neurology)	CM	carpometacarpal (Anatomy)
ck	check	CM	caucasian male
CK	creatine kinase (Laboratory)	cm	centimeter
CKD	chronic kidney disease	CM	cervical mucosa or mucus (Gynecology)
CL	chest and left arm (Lead in electrocardiography)	CM	circumferential measurement
Cl	chloride (Laboratory)	CM	clinical medicine
CL	cholelithiasis (Gastroenterology)	CM	congenital malformation
CL	clavicle (Anatomy)	CM	contrast medium (Diagnostic, Pharmacology)
CL	clear liquid		
CL	clearance	CM	costal margin (Physical assessment term referring to location)
Cl	cleft		
CL	cleft lip	CM	continuous murmur (Cardiology)
Cl	clinic, clinical	CM	tomorrow morning (Rehabilitation)
CL	clinical laboratory	CMA	certified medical assistant
Cl	clonus	CME	continuing medical education
Cl	closed, closure	CME	cystoid macula edema (Ophthalmology)
Cl, Clostr	clostridium (Laboratory)		
Cl	clotting	CMHC	community mental health center
Cl	cloudy	CMO	comfort measures only
CL	contact lens	CMP	cardiomyopathy
CL	corpus luteum (Anatomy, Gynecology)	CMP	competitive medical plan (Insurance)
CL	critical list	CMS	Centers for Medicare and Medicaid Services (Formerly HCFA)
CL; cl	clean		
CLA	cerebellar ataxia (Neurology)	CMS	circulation, motion, sensation
CLA	certified laboratory assistant	CMS 1500	a standard claim form for submission of charges (Formerly HCFA 1500)
Clav	clavicle (Anatomy)		
CLBBB	complete left bundle branch block (Cardiology)	CMT	chiropractic manipulative therapy (Chiropractic)
CLBP	chronic low back pain	CMV	cytomegalovirus (Infectious Diseases)
CLD	complete lower denture	CN	cranial nerve (Often followed by a Roman numeral from I to XII, e.g. CNII) (Anatomy)
CLD	chronic lung disease		
Cldy	cloudy		
CLH	corpus luteum hormone (Gynecology, Endocrinology)	CNA	certified nursing assistant
		CNS	central nervous system
CLIA	Clinical Laboratory Improvement Act	CNV	cranial nerve number 5

CNX	cranial nerve number 10	CPS	Children's Protective Services
CO	cardiac output	CPT	chronic paranoid type (*Schizophrenia*)
CO	check out	CPT	Current Procedural Terminology (Billing)
CO	childhood-onset		
Co	cobalt (Nuclear Medicine)	CQI	Continuous Quality Improvement (Risk Management)
CO2	carbon monoxide (Laboratory)		
COA	certificate of authority	CR	carrier replacement (Insurance)
COAG	coagulation (Laboratory, Hematology)	CR	clinical records
COB	coordination of benefits (Insurance)	CR	closed reduction (Orthopedics)
COBRA	Consolidated Omnibus Budget Reconciliation Act	CR	complete remission; complete response
COC	certificate of coverage	CR	conditional release
COC	continuity of care	CR	conditioned reflex
COG	center of gravity	Cr	creatinine (Laboratory)
Cog	cognitive	CRAO	central retinal artery occlusion (Ophthalmology)
col ct	colony count (Laboratory)		
COLD	chronic obstructive lung disease (Pulmonary)	Cr Cl	creatinine clearance (Laboratory)
		CR&C	closed reduction and cast (Orthopedics)
comp	complete		
Comp	compound	CRA	clinical research associate
CON	Certificate of Need	CRBBB	complete right bundle branch block (Cardiology)
conc	concentrate		
cont	continue	CRC	colorectal carcinoma
co-ord	coordination	CRC	community rating by class (Insurance)
COPD	chronic obstructive pulmonary disease	CRF	chronic renal failure
COPE	chronic obstructive pulmonary emphysema	CRI	chronic renal insufficiency
		CRNA	certified registered nurse anesthetist
COTA	certified occupational therapy assistant	CROM	cervical range of motion
CP	cerebral palsy	CRP	C-reactive protein (Laboratory)
CP	chest pain	CRRN	certified rehabilitation registered nurse
CP	cold pack	CRT	capillary refill time (Laboratory)
CP&PD	chest percussion and postural drainage (Respiratory Therapy)	CRT	certified
		CRT	chronic residual type (*Schizophrenia*)
CPAP	continuous positive airway pressure (Respiratory Therapy)	CRT	computerized renal tomography (Diagnostic)
CPB	cardiopulmonary bypass	CRTT	certified respiratory therapy technician
CPD	cephalopelvic disproportion (Obstetrics)	CRVO	central vein occlusion (Ophthalmology)
CPHA	Commission on Professional and Hospital Activities	CS	Cesarean section (Obstetrics)
		CS	cardiogenic shock (Cardiology)
CPK	creatine phosphokinase (Laboratory)	CS	carotid sinus (Cardiology)
CPM	clinical project manager	CS	central supply
CPM	continuous passive motion (Physical Therapy)	CS	cerebrospinal
		CS	cigarette smoker
CPM	counts per minute	CS	conscious sedation (Anesthesia)
CPM	cyclophosphamide (*Anti cancer drug*) (Pharmacology)	CS	conscious, consciousness
		Cs	consciousness
CPR	cardiopulmonary resuscitation	CS	convalescence, convalescent
CPR	checks with previous results	CS	coronary sclerosis (Cardiovascular)
CPR	C-reactive protein (Laboratory)	CS	coronary sinus (Cardiology)

CS	C-section, Cesarean section (Obstetrics)	CV	cervical vertebra (Anatomy)
		CV	color vision
CS	current smoker	CVA	cerebrovascular accident (Stroke)
CS	Cushing syndrome (Endocrinology)	CVA	costovertebral angle (Physical assessment term referring to location)
C-section	Cesarean section		
CSF	cerebrospinal fluid (Anatomy, Neurology)	CVAT	costovertebral angle tenderness
		CVC	central venous catheters (Intravenous Therapy)
CSF	coronary sinus flow (Diagnostic)		
CSF-WR	cerebrospinal fluid-Wassermann reaction (Laboratory)	CVD	cardiovascular disease
		CVF	confrontation visual field (Ophthalmology)
CSG	cholecystography, cholecystogram (Diagnostic)		
		CVI	Cerebrovascular Insufficiency
CSH	carotid sinus hypersensitivity (Cardiology)	CVP	central venous pressure
		CVS	cardiovascular system
CSH	chronic subdural hematoma (Neurology)	CVS	chorionic villous sampling (Obstetrics, Diagnostic)
CSP	cervical spine	CVAT	costovertebral angle tenderness
CSP	cyclosporine (Pharmacology)	CW	caseworker
C-spine	cervical spine	CW	chest wall
CT	carpal tunnel (Anatomy)	CW	clockwise
CT	cerebral thrombosis (Neurology, Hematology)	CW	close work (Ophthalmology)
		CW	crutch walking
CT	cervical traction (Orthopedics)	CWI	crutch walking instructions
CT	cervical-thoracic (Physical assessment term referring to location)	CWP	childbirth without pain
		CX	cervix (Anatomy)
CT	chemotherapy	CX	consciousness
CT	clinical trial	Cx	culture (Laboratory)
CT	Computerized Tomography (Diagnostic)	Cx	cervical spine (Chiropractic)
		CXR	chest x-ray
ct	count	cyl	cylinder (refraction) (Ophthalmology)
CT	cover test (Ophthalmology)	Cysto	cystoscopic exam (Urology, Diagnostic)
CTA	clear to auscultation (Refers to lung examination)		
CTAB	clear to auscultation bilaterally	CZP	clonazepam (Klonopin) (Pharmacology)
CTB	confined to bed		
CTNB	guided needle biopsy (Diagnostic, Pathology)	**D**	
		D	day
CTR	carpal tunnel release (Orthopedics)	D	diopter (lens strength) (Ophthalmology)
CTRS	certified therapeutic recreational specialist		
		D&C	dilatation and curettage (Gynecology)
CTS	carpal tunnel syndrome (Orthopedics, Neurology)	D&E	dilatation and evacuation (Gynecology)
Ctx	cervical traction (Orthopedics)	D&I	dry and intact (Wound dressings)
CU	cause unknown	D&V	diarrhea and vomiting
CU	clinical unit	d, /d	day, per day
Cu	cubic	D/A	date of accident
CUD	complete upper denture	D/A	date of admission
CULD	complete upper and lower dentures	d/c	diarrhea/constipation
CUT	chronic undifferentiated type	D/C	discharge
CV	cardiovascular	D/C	discontinue (Not recommended)

D/DW	dextrose in distilled water (Pharmacology, Intravenous Therapy)	DCI	duplicate coverage inquiry (Insurance)
D/H	drug history	DCIS	ductal carcinoma in situ (Type of breast cancer) (Oncology)
D/NS	dextrose in normal saline (Pharmacology, Intravenous Therapy)	DCR	dacrocystorhinostomy (Ophthalmology)
D/O	disorder	DD	developmental disabilities
D/W	dextrose in water (Pharmacology, Intravenous Therapy)	DD	discharge diagnosis
D/W	discuss with	DD	dry dressing
D1–D12	dorsal vertebrae (Thoracic vertebrae 1 through 12) (Anatomy)	DDD	degenerative disk disease (Orthopedics)
D1OW, 10%	aqueous dextrose solution (Pharmacology, Intravenous Therapy)	DDS	Doctor of Dental Surgery
		DDx	differential diagnosis
D5%DW	dextrose 5% in distilled water (Pharmacology, Intravenous Therapy)	DEA	diethylamine (Pharmacology)
		DEA	Drug Enforcement Agency
D5%NS	dextrose 5% in normal saline (Pharmacology, Intravenous Therapy)	DEC; dec	deceased
		Dec	decrease
D5LR	dextrose 5% with lactated ringers (Pharmacology, Intravenous Therapy)	decel	deceleration
		Deg	degeneration
D5W	dextrose 5% in water (Pharmacology, Intravenous Therapy)	Den	dental
		Derm	dermatology
DA	degenerative arthritis (Orthopedics, Immunology)	des	describe
		DES	diethylstilbestrol (Pharmacology)
DAB	dorsal abductors (Orthopedics)	Dev	deviation
DAFO	dynamic ankle/foot orthosis (Physical Therapy)	DF	dorsiflexion (Physical assessment term referring to position)
DAP	Draw a Person Test (Psychiatry)	DFA	direct fluorescent antibody test (Laboratory)
DAPRE	daily adjustable progressive resistive exercise (Physical Therapy)	DFCS	Department of Family and Children Services
DAPT	direct agglutination pregnancy test	DFM	deep friction massage
DAT	dementia of the Alzheimer's type	DI	date of injury
DAT	diet as tolerated	DI	diabetes insipitus
DAT	direct antibody testing (Laboratory)	Diag	diagnosis, diagnostic
DAW	dispense as written (Pharmacology)	DIC	disseminated intravascular coagulation (Hematology)
db	decibel		
DB	disability	DICOM	Digital Imaging and Communications in Medicine
DB; DOB	date of birth		
DBP	diastolic blood pressure	Dict	dictation
DBW	desirable body weight	DIFF; diff	differential (Blood count) (Laboratory)
DBW	diabetic black women	Dig	digoxin (Pharmacology)
DC	dioptres cylinder (Ophthalmology)	DIL, dil	dilated, dilatation
DC	direct current	DIL	dilute
DC	Doctor of Chiropractic	DIM	diminished
DC&B	dilation, curettage, and biopsy	DIP	distal interphalangeal (Physical assessment term referring to location)
DC; D/C	discharged, discontinue (Not recommended)	DIPJ	distal interphalangeal joint (Anatomy)
DCA	deferred compensation administrator (Insurance)	DIS	disabled
		DIS	disease
DCABG	double coronary artery bypass graft (Cardiac Surgery)	Disl	dislocate; dislocation
		disp	disposition, dispense

DIST	distal, distribution
DIST	distended
DIW	dextrose in water (Pharmacology, Intravenous Therapy)
DJD	degenerative joint disease (Orthopedics)
DKA	diabetic ketoacidosis (Gastroenterology)
DKB	deep knee bends
dl, deciliter	0.01 liters (100 ml)
DLA	dorsolateral area (Physical assessment term referring to location)
DLE	discoid lupus erythematosus (Dermatology, Immunology)
DLS	date last seen
DM	diabetes mellitus
DM	diastolic murmur (Cardiology)
DMD	daily maintenance dose
DMD	delayed mental development
DMD	depression and manic depression (Psychiatry)
DMD	disease modifying drug
DMD	Doctor of Dental Medicine
DMD	Duchenne muscular dystrophy (Neurology)
DME	durable medical equipment
DMSO	dimethyl sulfamethoxazole (Pharmacology)
DMT	dynamic muscle test (Physical Therapy)
DMV	dorsal metatarsal veins (Anatomy)
DNA	deoxyribonucleic acid (Biochemistry)
DNA	did not attend (clinic)
DNC	dominant-negative complementation (Genetics)
DND	died a natural death
DNI	do not intubate
DNI/DNR	do not intubate, do not resuscitate
DNKA	did not keep appointment
DNR	do not resuscitate
DNR	dorsal nerve root (Anatomy)
DNS	did not show for appointment
DNS	director of nursing service
DNS	doctor of nursing science
DO	doctor of osteopathy
DO	dorsal outflow (Cardiology)
DOA	day of admission
DOA	dead on arrival
DOB	date of birth
DOD	date of death
DOE	date of examination

DOE	dyspnea on exertion
DOH	department of health
DOI	date of injury
DOMS	delayed onset muscle soreness
DON	director of nursing
DOS	date of surgery
DOT	date of transfer
DP	deep pulse
DP	diastolic pressure
DP	distal pulses (Physical assessment tern referring to location)
DP; DPed	dorsalis pedis (Anatomy)
DPL	diagnostic peritoneal lavage
DPM	doctor of podiatric medicine
DPR	drug price review (Insurance)
DPT	days per thousand (Insurance)
DPT	diphtheria, pertussis, tetanus immunization
DR	delivery room
DR	diabetic retinopathy (Ophthalmology)
Dr	dram
DR	dressing
DRA	Deficit Reduction Act of 2005
DRE	digital rectal examination
DRG	diagnosis-related groups (Billing)
DRG	dorsal root ganglion (Anatomy, Neurology)
Drng	drainage
Drsg	dressing
DS	dioptres spherical (Ophthalmology)
DSD	dry sterile dressing
Dsg	dressing
DSG	dry sterile gauze
DSM	Diagnostic and Statistical Manual
DSM-IV	Diagnostic and Statistical Manual Fourth Edition
DT	date and time
DT	date of treatment
DT	due to
DT	delirium tremens (Neurology, Psychiatry)
DTP	diphtheria and tetanus toxoids with pertussis
DTP	distal tingling on percussion (Physical assessment term referring to sensation)
DTR	deep tendon reflex/es (Anatomy)
DTZ	diltiazem (Pharmacology)
DU	duodenal ulcer (Gastroenterology)
DUB	dysfunctional uterine bleeding (Gynecology)

DUE	drug use evaluation		ECCE	extracapsular cataract extraction (Ophthalmology)
DUR	drug utilization review (Risk Management)		ECF	extended care facility
DUS	divergent unilateral strabismus (Ophthalmology)		ECG	electrocardiogram
			ECHO	ultrasound cardiogram
DUS	Doppler ultrasound (Diagnostic)		ECRB	extensor carpi radialus brevis (Orthopedics; Physical Therapy)
DUS	Dusseldorf (Catheter)			
DUs	drug users		ECRL	extensor carpi radialus longus (Orthopedics; Physical Therapy)
Dus	duodenal ulcers			
Dv	double vibrations		ECT	electroconvulsive therapy (Psychiatry)
DV; DVA	distance vision; distance visual acuity (Ophthalmology)		ED	emergency department
			EDC	estimated date of confinement (Obstetrics)
DVD	dissociated vertical deviation (Ophthalmology)			
			EDI	electronic data interchange
DVERT	domestic violence emergency response team		EDTA	ethylendiminetetracetic acid (used in measuring kidney function) (Pharmacology)
DVI	deep venous insufficiency			
DVI	Doppler velocity index (Diagnostic)		EEG	electroencephalogram
DVP	domestic violence programs		EENT	eyes, ears, nose, and throat
DVP	Doppler velocity profile (Diagnostic)		EF	eccentric fixation (Ophthalmology)
DVR	double valve replacement (Cardiology)		EF	ejection fraction (Cardiology)
DVT	deep venous thrombosis		e.g.	for example
DW	daily weight		EGD	esophagogastroduodenoscopy (Diagnostic)
DW	dextrose in water (Pharmacology, Intravenous Therapy)			
			EHL	extensor hallicus longus (Anatomy)
DW	distilled water		EIA	essay immunosobent assay (Laboratory)
DW	doing well			
DWI	driving while impaired; driving while intoxicated		EIA	exercise induced asthma
			EIL	extension in lying (Physical Therapy)
DWR	delayed word recall		EJ	external jugular (Anatomy)
DWR	desirable weight range		EKG	electrocardiogram
DWSCL	daily wear contact lenses (Ophthalmology)		ELISA	enzyme-linked immunosorbent assay (Laboratory)
DX	dextran (Pharmacology)		Elix	elixir
DX	dicloxacillin (Pharmacology)		EM	emergency medical technician
DX	discharged		E/M	evaluation and management
DX	disease		EMD	electrical mechanical dissociation
Dx, dx	diagnosis		EMG	electromyelogram
DYFS	Division of Youth and Family Services		EMUO	early morning urine osmolarity (Laboratory test)
Dysp	dyspnea			
DZ	diazepam (Pharmacology)		EMS	electrical muscle stimulation (Chiropractic)
DZ	dizziness			
Dz	dozen		EMS	emergency medical service
			EMV	eyes, motor, verbal response (Glasgow coma scale) (Neurology)

E

EAC	external auditory canal		ENDO	endocrine
E	esotropia (Ophthalmology)		Endo	endodontics
EAP	employee assistance program		ENT	ears, nose, and throat
EBL	estimated blood loss		eo	eosinophil (Laboratory)
EBV	Epstein-Barr Virus (Infectious Diseases)		EOB	explanation of benefits (Insurance)

EOB	edge of bed
EOE	extraoral exam
EOG	electrooculogram (Ophthalmology)
EOI	evidence of insurability
EOM	end of month (Insurance)
EOM	extraocular movement (*Eye muscle*)
EOMB	explanation of medicare benefits (Insurance)
EOMI	extraocular movement intact
EOR	end of report (Emergency Medical Services)
Eos	eosinophil (Laboratory, Hematology)
EOY	end of year
EP	electrophysiology
Epi	epinephrine (Pharmacology)
EPO	Epogen (Pharmacology)
EPO	Exclusive Provider Organization (Insurance)
EPS	extrapyramidal symptoms (Neurology)
ER	emergency room
ER	external rotation (Physical Therapy)
ERCP	endoscopic retrograde cholangiopan-crea-tography (Diagnostic)
ERG	electroretinogram (Ophthalmology)
ERISA	Employee Retirement Income Security Act of 1974
ERM	epi-retinal membrane (Ophthalmology)
ERP	end range pain (Physical Therapy)
ES; E-stim	electrical stimulation (Physical Therapy)
Esp	especially
ESR	erythrocyte sedimentation rate (Laboratory)
ESRD	end-stage renal disease
EST	exercise stress test
ETOH	alcohol
et	and
ET	endotracheal
ETA	estimated time of arrival
ETCO2	end tidal carbon dioxide (Respiratory, Emergency Medical Services)
ETOH	ethanol
ETS	endotracheal suctioning
ETT	endotracheal tube
EUA	examination under anesthesia
EV	eversion
eval	evaluation
Ex	exercise
expt	expectorant
Ext	extraction; external

F

F	Fahrenheit
F	female; father
fa	forearm (Intravenous site location)
FADER	flexion, abduction, external rotation
FADIR	flexion, adduction, internal rotation
FASA	Federated Ambulatory Surgery Association
f/b	followed by
F/U	follow up
FB	foreign body
FBR	full body restraint
FBS	fasting blood sugar
FBS&2hPP	fasting blood sugar and 2-hour post prandial (Laboratory)
FEV	forced expectorant volume (*Lung test*)
FDL	flexor digitorum longus (Orthopedics, Physical Therapy)
FD	fixation disparity (Ophthalmology)
FDA	Food and Drug Administration
Fe	iron
FeSO4	ferrous sulfate (Pharmacology)
FFB	flexible fibroscopic bronchoscope (Diagnostic)
FFP	fresh frozen plasma (Hematology)
FFS	fee for service
FFW	front wheel walker Physical Therapy)
FH; F/H	family history
FHL	flexor hallicus longus (Anatomy)
fib	fibula (Anatomy)
FIL	flexion in lying (Physical Therapy)
FIM	functional independence measure (Physical Therapy)
fl	femtoliter (Pharmacology)
Fl	fluid
Flex	flexion
fl tr	fluoride treatment
fluoro	fluoroscopy (Diagnostic)
FM	full mouth
FMX	full mouth x-ray
FNP	family nurse practitioner
FOH	family ocular vision (Ophthalmology)
FOI	flight of ideas (Psychiatry)
FM	family meeting
FOB	foot of bed
FPD	fixed partial denture (Dental bridge)
Fr	French
FRC	functional residual capacity (Rehabilitation)
FRCP	Federal Rules of Civil Procedure

FROM	full range of motion (Physical Therapy)	glu	glucose
FS	fever scan *(Forehead thermometer)*	gm	gram
FS	finger stick	GM	grandmother
FSBG	fasting sugar blood glucose (Laboratory)	GN	graduate nurse
FSH	follicle stimulating hormone (Laboratory)	GP	general practitioner
		gr	grain
FSIQ	Full Scale Intelligence Quotient	GR	gravida (Obstetrics)
Ft	foot	Grad	gradually (Rehabilitation)
FTN	full term nursery	GSI	genuine stress incontinence (Urology)
FTT	failure to thrive	GSW	gunshot wound
funct	function	GTC	generalized tonic-clonic *(Seizures)*
FUO	fever of unknown origin	GTE	great toe extension
FVC	forced vital capacity	Gtt; gtt, gutt	drop
FWB	full weight bearing	GTT	glucose tolerance test (Laboratory)
Fx	fracture	Gtube	gastrointestinal tube
Fxn	function	GU	genitourinary
FY	Fiscal year	GVHR	graft vs. host reaction (Immunology)
		GXT	graded exercise tolerance *(Stress test)*
		Gy	grays *(Units of radiation)*
		GYN	Gynecology

G

g	gram		
G6PD	glucose-6 phosphate dehydrogenase (Genetics)	**H**	
		H	Hispanic
g/h	grooming and hygiene	h	hour
GA	general anesthesia	H&P	history and physical
GAD	generalized anxiety disorder (Psychiatry)	H/A; HA	headache
		HAC	Hospital acquired condition
GAF	Global Assessment of Functioning (Psychiatry)	h/o	history of
		H2O2	hydrogen peroxide
gastroc	gastrocnemius (Anatomy)	H2O	water
GB	gallbladder	HAA	Hospice Association of America
GBP	gabapentin *(Neurontin)* (Pharmacology)	HARC	harmonious abnormal retinal correspondence (Ophthalmology)
GC	gonorrhea, gonococcus, gonococcal (Infectious Diseases)	HbcAb	type B hepatitis core antibody (Laboratory)
GCS	Glascow Coma Scale (Neurology)	HBP	high blood pressure
GE	gastroesophageal (Anatomy)	HbsAb	type B hepatitis surface antibody (Laboratory)
GERD	gastroesophageal reflux disease (Gastroenterology)	HbsAG	type B hepatitis surface antigen (Laboratory
GF	glomerular filtration (Renal)	HC	hydrocortisone (Pharmacology)
gf	girlfriend	HC	head circumference
GF	grandfather	HCCA	Health Care Compliance Association
GFR	glomerular filtration rate (Renal)	HCFA	Health Care Finance Administration
GGT	gamma glutamyl transpeptidase (Genetics)	HCFA 1500	HCFA developed billing form
		HCG	Human Chorionic Gonadatropin (Laboratory)
GH	general health		
GH	glenorhumeral (Anatomy)	HCL	hairy cell leukemia (Oncology)
GH	growth hormone	HCO3	bicarbonate (Laboratory)
GHAA	Group Health Association of America	HCP	healthcare plan (Insurance)
GI	gastrointestinal		

HCPCS	Healthcare Common Procedure Coding System (Insurance)
HCPP	Health Care Prepayment Plan (Insurance)
Hct	hematocrit (Laboratory)
HCTZ	hydrochlorothiazide (Pharmacology)
HCVD	Hypertensive Cardiovascular Disease
HD	Hodgkin's disease (Oncology)
HDC	high dose chemotherapy (Oncology)
HDL	high-density lipoprotein (Laboratory)
HEDIS	Health Plan Employer Data and Information Set (Insurance)
HEENT	head, eyes, ears, nose, and throat
Heme	hematology
HEP	home exercise program (Physical Therapy)
Hgb	hemoglobin (Laboratory)
HH	hiatal hernia
HHA	home health agency; home health aide
HHC	home health care
HHNK	Hyperosmolor, hyperglycemic nonketotic syndrome
HHS	Health and Human Services
HI	head injury
HI	homicidal ideation
HIAA	Health Insurance Association of America
HICP	Health Insurance Purchasing Cooperative
Histo	histoplasmosis (Infectious Diseases)
HITECH	Health Information Technology for Economic and Clinical Health Act
HIV	human immunodeficiency virus (Infectious Diseases)
HKAFO	hip, knee, ankle, foot orthosis (Physical Therapy)
HJR	hepatojugular reflux (Anatomy)
HKB	hinged knee brace
hl	heparin lock (Intravenous)
HL-A	human leukocyte associated antigens (Laboratory)
HM	hand motion vision (Ophthalmology)
HMO	Health Maintenance Organization
HNP	herniated nucleus pulposus (Neurology)
HO	hold order
HO	house officer
HOB	head of bed
HOP	hospital outpatient

HOP-HAC	hospital outpatient-hospital acquired condition
Hosp	hospital
HP	hot pack (Physical Therapy)
Hpf	high-powered field (Laboratory)
HPI	history of present illness
HPLC	high-pressure liquid chromatography (Laboratory)
HPV	human papilloma virus (Laboratory, Infectious Disease)
HR	heart rate
HR	high risk
HRT	hormone replacement therapy (Pharmacology)
hs	at bedtime
HSA	health service agreement (Insurance)
HSM	hepatosplenomegaly (Anatomy)
HSP	health service plan (Insurance)
HST	health service technician
HSV	herpes simplex virus (Laboratory, Infectious Disease)
Ht	height
HTN	hypertension
HTLV	human T-cell leukemia lymphoma virus (Oncology)
HVD	Hypertensive Vascular Disease
HVGS	high voltage galvanic stimulation (Physical Therapy)
hw	heparin well (Intravenous)
Hx	history
Hyg	hygiene
Hz	hertz, cycles per second

I

I	incisal
I	independent
I	iris (Ophthalmology)
I&D	incision and drainage
I/J	insight/judgment (Psychiatry)
I&O	intake and output
I-131	radioactive iodine
IABP	intraaortic balloon pump (Cardiology)
IAC	internal auditory canal
IADL	instrumental acts of daily living
IAPB	International Agency for the Prevention of Blindness
IBNR	incurred but not reported
IBW	ideal body weight
ICCE	intracapsular cataract extraction (Ophthalmology)

ICD	implantable cardiac defibrillator	INNS	International Neuroblastoma Staging System
ICD	International Classification of Diseases	inoc	inoculation
ICD-9-CM	International Classification of Diseases, 9th Edition-Clinical Modification	In Pt	in-patient
ICD-10-CM	International Classification of Diseases, 10th Revision for Clinical Modification	Inpt	inpatient
		int	internal
ICDO	International Classification of Diseases for Oncology	int	intermittent device
		INV	inversion
ICF	intercellular fluid	Invol	involuntary
ICF	intermediate care facility	IOE	intraoral exam
ICF/MR	intermediate care facility/mental retardation	IOL	intra-ocular lens implant (Ophthalmology)
		IOM	Institute of Medicine
ICN	intensive care nursery	IOP	intraocular pressure (Ophthalmology)
ICO	International Congress of Ophthalmology	IOR	ideas of reference (Psychiatry)
ICS	intercostal space (Physical assessment term referring to location)	ip	intraperitoneal
		IP	interphalangeal
ict	icterus (Gastroenterology)	IPA	Individual Practice Association (Insurance)
ICU	Intensive Care Unit		
ICU	intermediate care unit	IPE	initial psychiatric examination
ID	identification	IPF	idiopathic pulmonary fibrosis
ID	intradermal	IPPB	intermittent positive pressure breathing (Respiratory Therapy)
id	same day (Rehabilitation)		
IDDM	Insulin Dependent Diabetes Mellitus	IPPS	Inpatient Prospective Payment System
IDT	interdisciplinary team	IQ	intelligence quotient
ie	that is	IR	internal rotation
IF	inferential	IRBBB	incomplete right bundle branch block (Cardiology)
IF	intrinsic factor		
IFN	Interferon (Pharmacology)	IRM	intermediate restorative material (Dental)
IFOS	International Federation of Ophthalmologic Societies		
		IRMA	intraretinal microvascular abnormality (Ophthalmology)
IgG	immunoglobulin G (Laboratory)		
IK	interstitial keratitis (Ophthalmology)	IRU	inpatient rehabilitation unit
IJ	internal jugular (Anatomy)	IS/IS	intensity of service/severity of illness— (Describes how sick a patient is and the level of healthcare services the patient requires.) (Administration)
IL2	interleukin2 (Pharmacology)		
IM; im	intramuscular		
IME	Independent Medical Evaluation		
IMI	inferior myocardial infarction (Cardiology)	ISP	individual service plan (Insurance)
		IST	intersegmental traction (Chiropractic)
IMM	immunologic	ITB	iliotibial band (Anatomy)
IMO	Integrated Multiple Option (Insurance)	ITP	idiopathic thrombocytopenia purpura (Hematology)
Imp	impression		
IMV	intermittent mandatory ventilation (Respiratory Therapy)	IU	international units (Not Recommended) (Pharmacology)
inc	increase	IUD	intrauterine device (Gynecology)
inf	infiltration	IUP	intrauterine pregnancy (Obstetrics)
INF	intravenous nutritional fluid	IV	intravenous
Inf	infusion	IVC	inferior vena cava (Anatomy)
inj	injection	IVDA	IV drug abuse
inj	injury	IVF	intravenous fluids
INH	isoniazid (Pharmacology)		

IVP	intravenous pyelogram (Diagnostic, Renal)
IWR	ideal weight range

J

JC	Joint Commission (now TJC)
JCAHO	The Joint Commission on Accreditation of Healthcare Organizations (now The Joint Commission, or TJC)
JCO	Journal of Clinical Oncology
jt	joint
JODM	juvenile onset diabetes mellitus
JRA	juvenile rheumatoid arthritis
JVD	jugular-venous distension
JVP	jugular-venous pulsation (Anatomy)

K

K	keratometry, keratometer reading (Ophthalmology)
K	potassium (Laboratory)
KAFO	knee ankle foot orthosis (Physical Therapy)
KB	ketone bodies (Laboratory)
KCL	Potassium Chloride (Intravenous Therapy Solution)
KCS	keratoconjunctivitis sicca (Ophthalmology)
Kg	kilogram
kj	knee jerk
Klebs	klebsiella (Laboratory)
KOH	potassium hydroxide (Laboratory)
KOR	keep open rate
KP	keratic precipitate (Ophthalmology)
KUB	kidney, ureter, bladder x-ray
KVO	keep vein open

L

L	left (May be encircled)
l	liter
L&D	Labor and Delivery (Obstetrics)
L/R	left hyperphoria (Ophthalmology)
L/RFD	L/R fixation disparity (Ophthalmology)
L1	1st lumbar vertebra, etc. (Total of 5) (Anatomy)
LA	long acting
lab	Laboratory
lac	laceration (Obstetrics)
LAD	left axis deviation (Cardiology)
LAE	left atrial enlargement (Cardiology)

LAH	left atrial hypertrophy (Cardiology)
lat	lateral
lAQ	long arc quad set (Physical Therapy)
Lax	laxative
Lb	pound
LB	low back, lumbar spine
LBBB	left bundle branch block (Cardiology)
LBP	lower back pain
LCL	lateral collateral ligament (Orthopedics, Physical Therapy)
LCM	left costal margin (Physical assessment term referring to location)
LCP	licensed clinical psychologist
LCSW	licensed clinical social worker
LDH	lactate dehydrogenase (Laboratory)
L-DOPA	levadopamine (Pharmacology)
LE prep	lupus erythematosus cell preparation (Laboratory)
LE	left eye (Ophthalmology)
LE	lower extremity
LFT	liver function tests (Laboratory)
Lg	large
LGA	large for gestational age (Obstetrics)
LH	lutenizing hormone (Obstetrics)
LHyperT	left hypertropia (Ophthalmology)
LHypoT	left hypotropia (Ophthalmology)
LiCo3	lithium carbonate (Pharmacology)
Lido	lidocaine (Pharmacology)
LIH	left inguinal hernia
LIMA	left internal mammary artery (Anatomy)
Liq	liquid
LJX	lateral jaw x-ray
LLb	long leg brace
LLC	long leg cast
LLE	left lower extremity
LLL	left lower lobe (Lung) (Physical assessment term referring to location)
LLQ	left lower quadrant (Abdomen) (Physical assessment term referring to location)
LLSB	left lower sternal border (Physical assessment term referring to location)
LM	landmark
LMP	last menstrual period
LMSW	licensed master social worker
LN	lymph node
LO	lens opacities (Ophthalmology)
LOA	left occipito-anterior (Physical assessment term referring to location)

LOA	loosening of associations (Psychiatry)	M	murmur (cardiac)
LOB	loss of balance	M/H	medical history
LOC	loss of consciousness; level of consciousness	M&N	Mydriacyl and neosynephrine solution (Ophthalmology, Pharmacology)
LOM	loss of memory	m/o	month old
LOS	length of stay	mab	median antebrachial vein (Intravenous site location)
LOS	line of sight		
LP	lumbar puncture	MAC	maximum allowable cost list (Prescription drug) (Insurance)
LPC	licensed professional counselor		
LPI	laser peripheral iredectomy (Ophthalmology)	MAFO	molded ankle foot orthosis (Physical Therapy)
LPN	licensed practical nurse	MAL	mid axillary line (Physical assessment term referring to location)
LR	light reflex		
LR	Lactated Ringer's solution (Pharmacology, Intravenous Therapy)	malign	malignant
		MAP	mean arterial pressure
L-S	lumbosacral (Anatomy)	MAO	monoamine oxidase (Pharmacology)
LSB	left sternal border (Physical assessment term referring to location)	MAOI	monoamine oxidase inhibitor (Pharmacology)
LSOT	left esotropia (Ophthalmology)	Mand	mandibular (Anatomy)
L-spine	lumbar spine (Anatomy)	MAST	medical anti-shock trousers
LTACH	long-term acute care hospital	max	maximum
LTG	long-term goal	MBC	minimum bacterial concentration (Laboratory)
LTG	low tension glaucoma (Ophthalmology)		
		MC	metacarpal (Anatomy)
LTM	long-term memory	MCC	major complicating condition
LTR	lower truck rotation (Physical Therapy)	Mcg	micrograms
L-trax	lumbar traction (Physical therapy)	MCH	mean corpuscular hemoglobin (Laboratory)
LUE	left upper extremity		
LUL	left upper lobe (Lung)	MCHC	mean corpuscular hemoglobin concentration (Laboratory)
LUQ	left upper quadrant (Abdomen)		
LV	left ventricle (Cardiology)	MCL	medial collateral ligament (Anatomy)
LVA	low vision aid (Ophthalmology)	MCL	mid-clavicular line (Physical assessment term referring to location)
LVE	left ventricle enlargement (Cardiology)		
LVH	left ventricle hypertrophy (Cardiology)	MCO	Managed Care Organization (Insurance)
LVN	licensed vocational nurse		
LVEF	left ventricular ejection fraction (Cardiology)	MCP; MP	metacarpophalangeal (joint)
		MCR	modified community rating (Insurance)
LVSF	left ventricular shortening fraction (Cardiology)	MCV	mean corpuscular volume (Laboratory)
		MD	medical doctor
LWBS	left without being seen	MDE	major depressive episode (Psychiatry)
Lx	lumpectomy (Surgery)	MDI	metered dose inhaler (Pharmacology)
Lymphs	lymphocytes (Laboratory, Hematology)	MDR	multi drug resistant
lytes	electrolytes (Laboratory)	MDS	Minimum Data Set (Tool to assess nursing home residents' needs and determine Medicare reimbursement)

M

m	meter	MDU	Mallett distance unit (Ophthalmology)
M/A	mood/affect	med	medial (Physical assessment term referring to location)
M; m	male		
M	mother	Med	medicine
M	manifest refraction (Ophthalmology)	Medigap	Medicare Supplement Insurance

Meds	medications	MR	Maddock rod (Ophthalmology)
Medsupp	Medicare Supplement Insurance	MR	mental retardation
MEq	milliequivalent	MR	myofascial release (Chiropractic)
mEq/l	milliequivalents per liter	MRE	most recent episode
met	metacarpal vein (Intravenous site location)	MRI	Magnetic Resonance Imaging
		MRN	medical record number
MET	muscle energy technique (Physical Therapy)	mRNA	messenger ribonucleic acid (Laboratory)
		MRSA	methicillin resistant staphylococcus aureus (Infectious Disease, Laboratory)
mets	metastases (Oncology)		
MFR	myofascial release (Physical Therapy)	MS	multiple sclerosis
Mg	magnesium (Laboratory)	MS	musculoskeleton
mg	milligram (0.0001 gram)	MSE	mental status exam
mg%	milligrams per hundred milliliter of serum or blood	Msg	massage (Physical Therapy)
		MSIII	medical student, 3rd year
MGF	maternal grandfather	MSIV	medical student, 4th year
MGM	maternal grandmother	MSL	midsternal line (Physical assessment term referring to location)
MH	mental health		
MH	moist heat (Physical Therapy)	MSN	master of science in nursing
MHC	mental health center; mental health counselor	MSO	Management Service Organization (Insurance)
MH/CD	mental health/chemical dependency	MSS	medical social services
MH/SA	mental health/substance abuse	MSSU	midstream specimen urine
MI	myocardial infarction (Cardiology)	MSW	master of social work
MIC	minimum inhibitory concentration (Laboratory)	MT	music therapy
		MTP	master treatment plan
min	minimum	MTP joint	metatarsophalangeal joint (Anatomy)
Misc	miscellaneous	MTP	minor treatment protocol
MJ	marijuana	MTP	master treatment plan
ml	milliliter or milliliters	MTX	methotrexate (Cancer drug)
MLE	midline episiotomy (Obstetrics)	MVA	motor vehicle accident
mm	millimeter	MVI	multivitamin injection
mM	millimole	MVM	mobilization with movement (Physical Therapy)
MM	muscle		
MMG	mammogram (Diagnostic)	MVP	mitral valve prolapse (Cardiology)
MMPI	Minnesota Multiphasic Personality Inventory (Psychology)	MVV	maximum voluntary ventilation (Respiratory Therapy)
MMR	measles/mumps/rubella	Mwing	Maddock wing (Ophthalmology)
MMSE	mini-mental status exam	MX	maxillary (Anatomy)
MMT	manual muscle test (Physical Therapy)	Mx	mastectomy (Surgery)
Mn	midnight		
MNU	Mallett near unit (Ophthalmology)	**N**	
mo	month	N	normal
mob	mobilization	N/A	not applicable
mod	moderate	n/v	nausea and vomiting
MOM	milk of magnesia (Pharmacology)	N/V/D	nausea, vomiting and diarrhea
Mono	infectious mononucleosis	N20/02	nitrous oxide and oxygen (Anesthesia)
mono	monocyte (Laboratory)	NA	nurse assistant
mos	months	Na	sodium (Laboratory)
MP	mouth prop (Dental)	NAATP	National Association of Addiction Treatment Providers
MP	metacarpophalangeal joint (Anatomy)		

NACC	National Association of Childbearing Centers	NH	nursing home
NaCl	sodium chloride (Laboratory, Intravenous Therapy)	NHL	non Hodgkin's lymphoma (Oncology)
NAD	no acute distress	NIC	Nursing Interventions Classification
NAG	narrow angle glaucoma (Ophthalmology)	NIDDM	non-insulin dependent diabetes mellitus
NAGS	neuro apophyseal glides (Physical Therapy)	Nitro	nitroglycerin (Pharmacology)
NAHC	National Association of Health Consultants	NK	not known
		NKA	no known allergies
NAHDO	National Association of Health Data Organizations	NKDA	no known drug allergies
		nl	normal
NAIC	National Association of Insurance Commissioners	NLP	no light perception (Ophthalmology)
		NMR	neuromuscular re-education (Chiropractic)
NAD	no acute distress	NMRI	nuclear Magnetic Resonance Imaging
NAD	no abnormality detected; no active disease	no.	number
		noc	night
NANDA	North American Nursing Diagnosis Association	NOC	Nursing Outcomes Classification
		non-par	non-participating provider (Insurance)
NAS	no added salt	NOS	not otherwise specified (Insurance)
NB	newborn	NP	nurse practitioner
NBM	nothing by mouth	NPA	National Prescription Audit
NBW	normal birth weight	NPA	non-participating provider approved (Insurance)
NC	nasal canula		
NCA	nurse controlled analgesia	NPC	no previous correction; near point of convergence (Ophthalmology)
NCAT	normocephalic atraumatic		
NCPDP	Nation Council of Prescription Drug Programs	NPH	neutral protamine hagedorn (insulin) (Pharmacology)
NCQA	The National Committee for Quality Assurance	NPL	no perception of light (Ophthalmology)
NCT	near cover test (Ophthalmology)	NPN	nonprotein nitrogen (Nutrition)
NCT	non-contact tonometry	NPO	nothing by mouth
NCV	nerve conduction velocity (Neurology)	NPN	non-participating provider not approved (Insurance)
ND	neural density filter (Ophthalmology)	NRC	normal retinal correspondence (Ophthalmology)
NDC	National Drug Code	NREM	non rapid eye movement (Neurology)
NDT	neurodevelopmental treatment (Neurology)	NS	normal saline
		NS	nuclear sclerosis (Ophthalmology)
NEC	necrotizing enterocolitis (Gastroenterology)	NSAID	nonsteroidal anti-inflammatory drug
		NSCLC	non-small cell lung cancer (Oncology)
NEC	not classified elsewhere	NSFTD	normal spontaneous full term delivery (Obstetrics)
NED	no evidence recurrent disease (Insurance)		
		NSG	nursing
Neg	negative	NSR	normal sinus rhythm
Neuro	neurology	NSS	Normal Saline Solution (Intravenous Therapy)
NeuroSurg	neurosurgery		
NFTD	normal full term delivery (Obstetrics)	NSU	neurosurgey unit
ng	nanogram (0.000000001 gram)	NSVD	normal spontaneous vaginal delivery (Obstetrics)
NG; NGT	nasogastric		
NGRI	not guilty by reason of insanity	NT	nasotracheal

NT	not tested
NTE	not to exceed
NTG	nitroglycerin (Pharmacology)
NTG	normotensive glaucoma (Ophthalmology)
NVI	neovascularization of iris (Ophthalmology)
NWB	non-weight bearing (Physical Therapy)
NWT	normal wearing time (Ophthalmology)

O

O	occlusal *(Surface of tooth)* (Dental)
O X 3	oriented times three
O/T; OT	occupational therapy
O2 cap	oxygen capacity
O2	oxygen
O2Sat	oxygen saturation (Laboratory, Pulmonary)
OA	open access (Insurance)
OA	osteoarthritis
OB	obstetrics
obl	oblique
OBRA	Omnibus Budget Reconciliation Act of 1987 *(Defines nursing home standards)*
obs	observation
OBS	Organic Brain Syndrome
OC	optical center (Ophthalmology)
OCBZ	oxycarbazepine *(Trileptal)* (Pharmacology)
Occ	occupation
OCD	obsessive-compulsive disorder (Psychiatry)
od	once a day (Ophthalmology)
OD	right eye *(Not recommended)*
OD	overall diameter (Ophthalmology)
ODD	oppositional defiant disorder (Psychiatry)
OE	otitis externa *(Outer ear)*
OH	oral hygiene
OHT	ocular hypertension (Ophthalmology)
OKC	open kinetic chain (Physical Therapy)
OM	otitis media *(Middle ear)*
OMB	ocular motor balance (Ophthalmology)
ONH	optic nerve head (Ophthalmology)
OOA	out of area (Insurance)
OOB	out of bed
OOPS	out-of-pocket-expenses (Insurance)
Op	operation

OP	overpressure (Physical Therapy)
OPC	order of protective custody
OPC	outpatient clinic
Ophth	ophthalmology
OPPS	Outpatient Prospective Payment System
OPV	oral polio vaccine
OR	operating room
ORIF	open reduction internal fixation (Orthopedic)
Orth; ortho	orthopedic
OS	left eye *(Not recommended)*
OSHA	Occupational Safety and Health Administration
OT	occupational therapist
OTC	over the counter
OTR	occupational therapist, registered
OU	both eyes *(Not recommended)*
Out Pt	outpatient
OTC	over the counter
Oz	ounce

P

p	after *(Written with a line drawn over letter)*
P	pulse
P/T	physical therapy
P2	pulmonic second sound (Anatomy, Cardiology)
PA	physician's assistant
P-A	posteroanterior *(Physical assessment term referring to location)*
PAAO	Pan American Association of Ophthalmology
PA-C	physician's assistant—certified
PAC	pre-admission certificate (Insurance)
PAC	premature atrial contraction (Cardiology)
PAGE	polyacrylamide gel electrophoresis (Diagnostic)
PAL	posterior axillary line *(Physical assessment term referring to location)*
Palp	palpitation
PAO2	alveolar oxygen (Laboratory; Pulmonary)
PaO2	peripheral arterial oxygen content (Laboratory)
PANSS	Positive and Negative Syndrome Scale (Psychiatry)
PAP; Pap	Papanicolaou's smear (Gynecology)

Par	participating provider (Insurance)	PEG	percutaneous gastrostomy (Gastroenterology)
PARA 1	having borne one child (*Number indicated number of children born*) (Obstetrics)	PEG	punctuate epithelial granularity (Ophthalmology)
PAT	paroxysmal atrial tachycardia (Cardiology)	PEK	punctuate epithelial keratitis (Ophthalmology)
Path; pathol	pathology	PEJ	percutaneous jejunostomy (Gastroenterology)
PAX	periapical x-ray		
PB	phenobarbital (Pharmacology)	Per	through or by
PBI	protein bound iodine (Laboratory)	Perio	periodontal (Dental)
PBS	phosphate-buffered saline (Pharmacology)	PERL	pupils equal and reactive to light
		PERRLA	pupils equal, round, reactive to light and
pc	after meals, post prandial		
PC	posterior chamber; posterior capsule (Ophthalmology)		accommodation
		PET	positron emission computed tomography (Diagnostic)
PCA	patient controlled analgesia		
PCH	personal care home	PFM	porcelain fused to metal (*Crown*) (Dental)
PCL	posterior cruciate ligament (Anatomy)		
PCN	penicillin (Pharmacology)	PFS	patellofemoral syndrome (Orthopedics)
PCN	Primary Care Network (Insurance)		
PCP	primary care physician	PFSH	past family social history
PCP	phencyclidine (Pharmacology)	PFT	pulmonary function tests
PCPM	per contract per month (Insurance)	Pg	pictogram (0.000000000001 gram)
PCR	Physician Contingency Reserve (Insurance)	PGF	paternal grandfather
		PGM	paternal grandmother
PCR	polymerase chain reaction (Laboratory)	pH	hydrogen ion concentration (Chemistry)
PCV	packed cell volume (Hematology)	PH	past history
PCWP	pulmonary capillary wedge pressure (Diagnostic)	PH	pinhole (Ophthalmology)
		Phos	phosphorus (Laboratory)
PD	papillary distance (Ophthalmology)	PHR	periodic health review
PDA	patient ductus arteriosis (Cardiovascular)	PI	pulmonary insufficiency
		PID	pelvic inflammatory disease
PDD	pervasive development disorder (Psychiatry)	PIP	proximal interphalangeal (*joint*)
		PIP	Personal Injury Protection (*Medical expense coverage by the client's own auto insurance carrier*) (Insurance)
PDL	periodontal ligament (Dental)		
PDR	Physicians Desk Reference		
PDR	proliferative diabetic retinopathy (Ophthalmology)	PIVM	passive intervertebral motion (Physical Therapy)
		PJC	porcelain jacket crown (Dental)
PDQ	Physicians Data Query	PKU	phenylketonuria (Laboratory)
PE, PHACO	phacoemulsification (Ophthalmology)	PL	light perception (Ophthalmology)
PE	physical examination	pl ct	platelet count (Laboratory)
PE	pulmonary edema	plt	platelet
PE	pulmonary embolism	PM; pm	afternoon
PEC	pre-existing condition (Insurance)	PMG	Primary Medical Group (Insurance)
Pedi	pediatric	PMH	past medical history
PEE	punctuate epithelial erosions (Ophthalmology)	PMI	point of maximal impulse (Cardiology)
		PMP	previous menstrual period
PEEP	positive end expiratory pressure (Respiratory Therapy)	PMS	premenstrual syndrome

PND	paroxysmal nocturnal dyspnea (Cardiology)	
PNF	proprioceptive neuromuscular facilitation (Neurology)	
PNS	peripheral nervous system	
PO; po	by mouth	
POA	Present on admission	
POAG	primary open angle glaucoma (Ophthalmology)	
POD	postoperative day (Followed by a number)	
POH	previous ocular history (Ophthalmology)	
polys	polymorphonuclear leucocytes (Also called neutrophils) (Laboratory)	
POS	point of service (Insurance)	
post	after; posterior	
Post-op	postoperative	
PPD	purified protein derivative (Pharmacology)	
PPDR	preproliferatuve diabetic retinopathy (Ophthalmology)	
PPO	preferred provider organization (Insurance)	
PPRC	Physician Payment Review Commission (Insurance)	
PPS	Prospective Payment System (Insurance)	
PPTL	postpartum tubal ligation (Obstetrics; Gynecology)	
PPVT-R	Peabody Picture Vocabulary Test-Revised (Psychology)	
PR	per rectum	
PRBC	packed red blood cells (Hematology, Intravenous Therapy)	
PRE	progressive resistive exercise (Physical Therapy)	
pre-op	preoperative	
prep	prepare for, preparation for	
PRICE	protect, rest, ice, compression, elevation (Physical Therapy)	
PRN; prn	as necessary, as needed	
PRO	Peer Review Organization, Physician Review Organization (Risk Management)	
Pro	pronation	
Prog	prognosis	
PRK	photorefractive keratectomy (Ophthalmology)	

PROM	passive range of motion (Physical Therapy)
Prophy	dental prophylaxis
PRP	pan-retinal photocoagulation (Ophthalmology)
PQRE	progressive quad resistance exercises (Physical Therapy)
PS	pulmonary stenosis
PSA	prostate specific antigen (Laboratory)
PSC	posterior subcapsular cataract (Ophthalmology)
PSI	Patient Safety Institute
PSIS	posterior superior iliac spine (Anatomy)
Psy; Psych	psychiatric
PsychD	Doctor of Psychology
Pt; pt	patient
PT	physical therapy
PT	prothrombin time (Laboratory)
PTA	prior to admission
PTA	physical therapy assistant
PTCA	percutaneous transluminal coronary angioplasty (Diagnostic)
PTE	pre-trial evaluation
Pt Ed	patient education
PTN	phenytoin (Dilantin) (Pharmacology)
PTSD	posttraumatic stress disorder (Psychiatry)
PTT	partial thromboplastin time (Laboratory)
Ptx	pelvic traction
PUD	peptic ulcer disease
PVC	premature ventricular contraction (Cardiology)
PVD	peripheral vascular disease (Vascular)
PVD	posterior vitreous detachment (Ophthalmology)
PWB	partial weight bearing (Physical Therapy)
Px	patient

Q

q	every; each
Q(x)H	every (x) hours
QA	quality assurance (Risk Management)
qAM	every morning
qd	every day (Not recommended)
qh	every hour (Not recommended)
qhs	every hour of sleep (Not recommended)

QI	quality improvement
qid	four times per day *(Not recommended)*
QM	quality management
QMB	qualified Medicare beneficiary (Insurance)
qod	every other day *(Not recommended)*
qPM	every afternoon
QS	quad sets (Physical Therapy)
QS	quantity sufficient (Urology)
qSHIFT	every shift

R

R	registration
R	respiration
R	right *(May be encircled)*
R&C	reasonable and customary (Insurance)
R/O	rule out
R/T	related to
RA	rheumatoid arthritis
rad	radius
RAD	right axis deviation (Cardiology)
RAE	right atrial enlargement (Cardiology)
RAH	right atrial hypertrophy (Cardiology)
RAI	Resident Assessment Instrument *(Includes the MDS, RAPS, and the care plan)* (Nursing Home Record)
RAIU	radioactive iodine uptake (Diagnostic)
RAN	resident admission note
RAP	Resident Assessment Protocol *(System that used the MDS to identify and define residents' problems)* (Nursing Home Record)
RAP	retinal artery pressure (Urology)
RAP	right atrial pressure (Cardiology)
RAPD	relative afferent papillary defect (Ophthalmology)
RBBB	right bundle branch block (Cardiology)
RBC	red blood cell (Laboratory, Hematology)
RPB	retinol-binding protein (Laboratory)
RC	rotator cuff (Anatomy)
RCT	rotator cuff tear (Orthopedics)
RCM	right costal margin *(Physical assessment term referring to location)*
RCT	randomized controlled trial (Research)
RCT	root canal therapy (Dental)
RD	registered dietitian
RD	retinal detachment (Ophthalmology)
RDH	registered dental hygienist
Re	regarding

RE	right eye (Ophthalmology)
readm	readmission
recd	received
REIL	repeated extension in lying (Physical Therapy)
REIS	repeated extension in standing (Physical Therapy)
Ret	retinoscopy (Ophthalmology)
retics	reticulocyte (Laboratory)
RFIL	repeated flexion in lying (Physical Therapy)
RFIS	repeated flexion in standing (Physical Therapy)
rehab	rehabilitation
reps	repetitions (Physical Therapy)
resp	respiration
ret	retraction (Physical Therapy)
retic(s)	reticulocyte(s) (Laboratory)
RF	rheumatoid factor (Laboratory)
RFP	request for proposal (Insurance)
Rh	rhesus blood factor (Laboratory)
RHD	rheumatic heart disease
RHyperT	right hypertropia (Ophthalmology)
RHypoT	right hypotropia (Ophthalmology)
RIA	radioimmunoassay (Diagnostic)
RICE	rest, ice, compression, and elevation
RIG	right inguinal hernia
RK	radial keratotomy (Ophthalmology)
RLE	right lower extremity
RLL	right lower lobe *(Lung)*
RLQ	right lower quadrant *(Abdomen)*
RMC	rating method code (Insurance)
RML	right middle lobe *(Lung)*
RN	registered nurse
RNFL	retinal nerve fiber layer (Ophthalmology)
ROM	range of movement
ROP	retinopathy of prematurity (Ophthalmology)
ROS	review of systems
rot	rotation
RP	retinal pigmentosa (Ophthalmology)
RPE	retinal pigmentosa epithelium (Ophthalmology)
RPD	removable partial denture
RPG	retrograde pyelogram (Radiology)
RPh	registered pharmacist
RROM	resistive range of motion (Physical Therapy)
RPR	rapid plasma reagent (Laboratory)

RR	recovery room
RR	respiratory rate
RRR	regular rate and rhythm (Heart examination)
RRT	Rapid Response Team
RS	rhythmic stabilization (Physical Therapy)
RSOT	right esotropia (Ophthalmology)
RT	recreational therapist
RTC	return to clinic
RUE	right upper extremity
RUG	Resource Utilization Group (Method that used MDS data to calculate reimbursements) (Insurance)
RUG	retrograde urethrogram (Diagnostic)
RUL	right upper lobe (Lung)
RUQ	right upper quadrant (Abdomen)
RV	residual volume (Respiratory Therapy)
RV	right ventricle (Cardiology)
RVE	right ventricular enlargement (Cardiology)
RVH	right ventricular hypertrophy (Cardiology)
RVS	Relative Value System (Method of assigning the cost of a procedure or service) (Insurance)
RVT	rate, volume, tone
Rx	prescription, treatment

S

S	sign
S	sister
S	supervision (May be encircled)
s	second
s	without (Written with a line drawn over letter)
S/P	status-post
S/P	suicide precautions
S/Sx; s/s	signs/symptoms
S1 & S2	first and second heart sounds (Heart examination)
S3 & S4	third and fourth heart sounds (Heart examination)
SA	sinoatrial (Cardiology)
SA	substance abuse
SAC	short arm cast
SAH	subarachnoid hemorrhage (Neurology)
SAID	specific adaptation to imposed demands
SART	sexual response team

SANE	sexual assault nurse examiner
SAQ	short arc quad set (Physical Therapy)
SB	side bending (Physical Therapy)
SBA	stand by assist (Physical Therapy)
SBAR	Situation Background Assessment Response
SBE	subacute bacterial endocarditis (Cardiology)
SBIS	side bending in standing (Physical Therapy)
SBO	small bowel obstruction
SBP	systolic blood pressure
SBS	short bowel syndrome (Gastroenterology)
SC	sternoclavicular (Physical assessment term referring to location)
SC; SQ	subcutaneous
sc	without refractive correction (Ophthalmology)
SC anemia	sickle cell anemia (Hematology)
SCC	squamous cell carcinoma (Oncology)
SCI	spinal cord injury
SC joint	sternoclavicular joint (Anatomy)
SCLC	small cell lung cancer (Oncology)
SCM	sternocleidomastoid muscle (Anatomy)
SC Trait	sickle cell trait (Genetics)
SCR	standard class rate (Insurance)
SDA	same day admission
SDAT	Senile Dementia Alzheimer's type
SDH	Subdural Hematoma
SE	side effects
SEAL	superior epithelial arcuate lesion (Ophthalmology)
sed	sedation
sed rate	sedimentation rate (Laboratory)
SF	stepfather (May be encircled)
SGA	small for gestational age (Obstetrics)
segs	segmented neutrophils (Laboratory, Hematology)
SEM	systolic ejection murmur (Cardiology)
SG	specific gravity (Laboratory)
SG	Swan-Ganz (Catheter)
SGA	small for gestational age (Obstetrics)
SGIS	side glide in standing (Physical Therapy)
SGOT	serum glutamic oxaloacetic transaminase (Laboratory)
SGPT	serum glutamic pyruvic transaminase (Laboratory)

SH	social history	SP	suicide precaution(s)
SHAPA	social history and psychosocial assess-ment	SPC	single point cane (Physical Therapy)
		SPF	sun protection factor
SHO	senior house officer	sp gr	specific gravity (Laboratory)
SI	sacroiliac (Anatomy, Chiropractic)	SPIN	standard prescriber identification num-ber (Insurance)
SI	steroid injection		
SI	suicidal ideation (Psychiatry)	SPK	superficial punctuate keratitis (Oph-thalmology)
SI/HI	suicidal/homicidal ideation		
SIADH	Syndrome of Inappropriate Antidiuretic Hormone	SQ; SC	subcutaneous (Dermatology)
		SR	superior rectus (Ophthalmology)
SIB	self-injurious behavior	SRN	subretinal neovascularization mem-brane (Ophthalmology)
sib(s)	sibling(s)		
SIC	standard industry code (Insurance)	STAT	immediately
SICU	surgical intensive care unit	STG	short-term goals
sig:	directions for use, label	STM	short-term memory
sl	saline lock (Intravenous Therapy)	STS	serological tests for syphilis (Labora-tory)
sl	slight; slightly		
SL	sublingual (Under the tongue)	SQ	subcutaneous
SLB	short leg brace	ss enema	soapsuds enema
SLC	short leg cast	SS	Social Security
SLE; SLX	slit lamp exam (Ophthalmology)	SSC	stainless steel crown (Dental)
SLE	systemic lupus erythematous (Immu-nology)	SSD	Sulfa Silvadene (an antibiotic in cream form)
SLH	supportive living home	SSD	social security disability
SLK	superior limbic keratoconjunctivitis (Ophthalmology)	SSI	supplemental security income
		SSN	social security number
SLM	slit-lamp microscope (Ophthalmology)	ST	speech therapy
SLP	speech/language pathologist	Staph	staphylococcus (Biology, Laboratory)
SLR	straight leg raise (Neurology, Physical Therapy)	STAT	immediately; at once
		STD	sexually transmitted disease
S-M	sensorimotor (Neurology)	STJ	subtabular joint (Physical Therapy)
Sm	small	Strep	streptococcus (Biology, Laboratory)
SM	stepmother (May be encircled)	STSG	split thickness skin graft (Surgery)
SMA; SMAC	sequential multiple analyzer (comput-er)	STW	soft tissue wound
		Subg	subgingival (Dental)
SMI	supplementary medical insurance	sup	supination (Physical Therapy)
SMO	slips made out	Supp	suppository
SMT	static muscle test (Physical Therapy)	Surg	surgery; surgical
SNF	skilled nursing facility	Susp	suspension (Pharmacology)
SO2	oxygen saturation (Laboratory)	SVC	service
SOAP	subjective, objective, assessment, plan (Progress note format)	SVD	spontaneous vaginal delivery (Obstet-rics)
SOB	shortness of breath	SVT	supra-ventricular tachycardia (Cardiol-ogy)
SOC	social		
SOD	statement of deficiency	SW	social worker
sol'n	solution	Sx	symptoms
SOM	serous otitis media (Fluid behind the middle ear)	Sz	seizure
		Sz D/O	seizure disorder
SPA	summary plan description (Insurance)	SZAF	schizoaffective (Psychiatry)

T

T; temp	temperature
T&A	tonsillectomy and adenoidectomy (Surgery)
T/A	toothache
T&C	type and cross (Hematology, Laboratory)
T&H	type and hold (Hematology, Laboratory)
T&S	type and screen (Laboratory)
T1	1st thoracic vertebra, etc. *(12 total)*
TA	applanation tonometry (Ophthalmology)
Tab, tabs	tablet, tablets
TAC	triamcinolone cream (Pharmacology)
TAH	total abdominal hysterectomy (Gynecology, Surgery)
TAH & BSO	total abdominal hysterectomy and bilateral salpingo oophorectomy (Gynecology)
TANF	Temporary Aid to Needy Families
TAS	therapeutic activity specialist
TAT	Thematic Apperception Test (Psychology)
TAT	turnaround time
TB; Tbc	tuberculosis
TBG	total binding globulin (Laboratory)
TBI	total body irradiation (Radiology)
TBI	traumatic brain injury
TBSA	total body surface area
tbsp	tablespoon
TC	thought content
TCA	tricyclic antidepressant (Pharmacology)
TCDB	turn, cough, deep breathe
TCH	marijuana
TCP	thrombocytopenia (Hematology)
TD	tardive dyskinesia (Psychiatry)
Td	tetanus/diphtheria toxoid
Temp Flg	temporary filling (Dental)
Ted hose	antiembolitic stockings
TENS	transcutaneous electrical neurostimulation (Anesthesia, Pain Control)
TFM	transverse friction massage (Physical Therapy)
TFT	thyroid function test (Laboratory)
TGB	tiagabine *(Gabatril)* (Pharmacology)
THA	total hip arthroplasty (Orthopedics)
Ther ex	therapeutic exercise
THR	total hip replacement
TIA	transient ischemic attack (Vascular)
TIBC	total iron binding capacity (Laboratory)
TID	three times daily *(Not recommended)*
TIW	three times per week *(Not recommended)*
TKA	total knee arthroplasty (Orthopedics)
TKR	total knee replacement (Orthopedics)
TL	temporary leave
T-L	thoracolumbar *(Physical assessment term referring to location)*
TLC	tender loving care
TLC	total lung capacity
tlc	triple lumen catheter (Intravenous Therapy)
TLSO	thoracic lumbar sacral orthosis (Physical Therapy)
TM	tympanic membrane *(ear drum)*
TMJ	temporomandibular joint (Anatomy)
TNF	tumor necrosis factor (Laboratory)
TNM	staging system-primary tumor (Oncology)
TNTC	too numerous to count (Laboratory)
TO	telephone order
TOF	tetralogy of fallot (Cardiology)
Tol	tolerate
TOPV	trivalent oral polio vaccine
TOS	thoracic outlet syndrome (Neurovascular)
Toxo	toxoplasmosis (Infectious Diseases)
TP	thought process
TPA	third party administrator (Insurance)
TPM	topiramate *(Topamax)* (Pharmacology)
TPN	total parenteral nutrition
TPR	temperature, pulse, respiration
TR	therapeutic recreation
Trach	tracheostomy
trans	transfer (Physical Therapy)
trax	traction (Physical Therapy)
Trich	trichomonas (Laboratory)
TSH	thyroid stimulating hormone (Laboratory)
tsp	teaspoon
TT	tetanus toxoid *(Vaccine)*
TT	thrombin time (Laboratory)
TTP	thrombotic thrombocytopenic purpura (Hematology)
TTWM	toe touch weight bearing (Physical Therapy)
TU	tuberculin units

TUR	transurethral resection (Urology)	URTI	upper respiratory tract infection
TURBT	transurethral bladder tumors (Urology)	US	ultra-sound (Diagnostic)
TURP	transurethral resection of prostate (Urology)	USP	United States Pharmacopoeia
		UT	upper trapezius muscle (Anatomy)
TV	tidal volume (Respiratory Therapy)	UTI	urinary tract infection
TV	trial visit	UV	ultraviolet
TVH	total vaginal hysterectomy (Gynecology, Surgery)	UVR	ultraviolet radiation

TW — thought withdrawal (Psychiatry)
Tx — treatment
tx plan — treatment plan

U

U	uncle *(May be encircled)*		
U&C	usual and customary (Insurance)		
UA; U/A	urinalysis (Laboratory)		
UAC	uric acid (Laboratory)		
UB-92	Uniform Billing Code 1992		
UBE	upper body ergometer (Physical Therapy)		
UBR	upper body restraints		
UCG	urine chorionic gonadotropin *(Pregnancy test)* (Laboratory)		
UCR	usual, customary, and reasonable (Insurance)		
ud	as directed		
UDS	urine drug screen		
UE	upper extremity		
ug	microgram (0.000001 gram)		
UGI w/SBFT	upper gastrointestinal series with small bowel follow through (Diagnostic)		
UGI	upper gastrointestinal		
ULTT	upper limb tension test (Physical Therapy)		
UM	utilization management		
UNK	unknown		
UP	ureteropelvic (Anatomy)		
UPIN	universal physician identification number		
UR	Utilization Review (Risk Management)		
URC	usual, customary, and reasonable (Insurance)		
UR/QA	utilization review/quality assurance (Risk Management)		
URI	upper respiratory infection		
Urol	urology		
URR	urea reduction ratio *(Laboratory test done to determine effectiveness of dialysis treatment in removing blood urea nitrogen)*		

V

-ve	negative
+ve	positive
V	vision (Ophthalmology)
V/A	visual acuity
V/Q	ventilation/perfusion (Respiratory Therapy)
VA	Veterans Administration
Va	visual acuity (Ophthalmology)
VAMC	Veterans Administration Medical Center
VCU	voiding cystourethrogram (Diagnostic)
VD	venereal disease
VDRL	Venereal Disease Research Laboratory
VE	voluntary effort
VEF	ventricular ejection fraction (Cardiology, Diagnostic)
VEP	visual evoked potential (Neurology)
VF	visual field (Ophthalmology)
VH	visual hallucinations (Psychiatry)
Vit	vitamin
Vit	vitreous (Ophthalmology)
VMA	vanillylmandelic acid (Laboratory)
VO; vo	verbal order
vol	volume
V-P	ventriculo-peritoneal *(shunt)* (Neurology)
VPA	valproic acid (Pharmacology)
VPC	ventricular premature complexes (Cardiology)
VR	vocational rehabilitation
VRE	vancomycin resistant enterococcus (Laboratory)
VS; V/S	vital signs
vs	versus
VSD	ventricular septal defect (Cardiology)
vss	vital signs stable
V Tach	ventricular tachycardia (Cardiology)
VTX	vitrectomy (Ophthalmology)

W

W	white

w/	with (Not recommended)
w/c	wheelchair
W/F	white female
W/M	white male
w/o	without
w/u	workup
WAIS	Wechsler Adult Intelligence Scale (Psychology)
WAIS-R	Wechsler Adult Intelligence Scale-Revised (Psychology)
WB	weight bearing (Physical Therapy)
WBAT	weight bearing as tolerated
WBC	white blood count
WBT	weight bearing transfers (Physical Therapy)
WD	well developed
WD	working distance (Ophthalmology)
WD/WN	well-developed and well-nourished
WFL	within functional limits (Physical Therapy)
whpl	whirlpool (Physical Therapy)
WISC	Wechsler Intelligence Scale for Children (Psychology)
WISC-R	Wechsler Intelligence Scale for Children-Revised (Psychology)
WISC-III	Wechsler Intelligence Scale for Children-Revised (3rd edition) (Psychology)
wk	week
WN	well nourished
WNL, wnl	within normal limits
WP	whirlpool (Physical Therapy)
WPPSI-R	Wechsler Preschool and Primary Scale of Intelligence-Revised (Psychology)
WPW Syndrome	Wolff-Parkinson-White Syndrome (Cardiology)
WRAT-R	Wide Range Achievement Test-Revised (Psychology)
Wt	weight
WTR	within therapeutic range

X

X	times
X	exoptrophia (Ophthalmology)
X-match	cross match (Laboratory)
XRT	x-ray therapy

Y

YAG	neodymium-yttrium aluminum garnet laser (Ophthalmology)
YO; y/o	year old
yr(s)	year(s)
ytd	year-to-date

Z

ZnO	zinc oxide
ZOE	zinc oxide and eugenol (Pharmacology)
ZSM	zonisamide (Zonegran)(Pharmacology)

Symbols

Symbols use characters or letters and characters to abbreviate. The following symbols may be found on a medical record, but like letter abbreviations are open to interpretation and should be used with caution.

&	and
@	t
$\bar{p}$	after (Written with a line drawn over the "p")
$\bar{s}$	without
x	except for; with the exception of (Written with a line drawn above the "x")
o	degree
0	absent, null
Ø	nothing, none
↑	increase
↓	decrease
+, ive+	positive
(-), -, ive-	negative
(+)	significant
(-)	insignificant
++, 2+	plus two (Often used to describe reflex response time)
+++, 3+	plus three
++++, 4+	plus four
<	less than
≤	less than or equal to
>	greater than (Not recommended)
		standing
—	lying
I¬	sitting
/	per
X	times
1X	one time, once
i	one
ii	two
iii	three
=	equal to; equals
≠	not equal

±	more or less, indefinite, plus or minus, minimal pain
_+	time interval
≙	no change
%	percent
1°	primary
2°	secondary
~	approximate
?	questionable
♀	normal female, living female
♂	normal male, living male
n	affected female, deceased female
qs	quantity sufficient
ψ	psychiatric

Endnotes

1. French, P.A., E. Ohman, and Magnus. "The Abbreviated Life of Acronyms." *American Heart Journal*. Vol 137 (4), April 1999.

2. The Use of Standardized Abbreviations, Acronyms, and Symbols is Addressed by JCAHO Standard IM.3 http://www.jcaho.org/accredited+organizations/ health+care+network/standards/field+reviews/net_ids_ mco_im_ xwalk.pdf. Retrieved December 1, 2003.

3. http://www.pubmedcentral.nih.gov/picrender.fcgi?artid =227556&action=stream&blobtype=pdf.   Retrieved December 3, 2003.

About the Editors

Patricia W. Iyer, MSN, RN, LNCC is one of the editors of this text and wrote or coauthored 12 chapters: *Roots of Patient Injury, Where Have all the Nurses Gone? Medical Errors: Roots of Litigation, Foundations of Nursing Practice, Pain and Suffering, Nursing Documentation, Patient Safety Initiatives, Subacute and Long-term Care Nursing Malpractice, Demonstrative Evidence, Working with Legal Nurse Consultants, Working with Nursing Expert Witnesses,* and *Medication Errors.* Ms. Iyer's experience as an author and editor began in 1980. She has written, coauthored, or edited over 125 articles, chapters, textbooks, case studies, and online courses. Prior to this text, her most recent editorial involvement was serving as the coeditor, with Barbara Levin, of *Medical Legal Aspects of Medical Records.* She is the chief editor of *Principles and Practices of Legal Nurse Consulting, Second Edition* (2003) the core curriculum of legal nurse consulting and *Business Principles for Legal Nurse Consultants* (2005). Most recently, she completed an online course for Sigma Theta Tau directed to legal issues for the new nurse.

Ms. Iyer is a frequent lecturer to attorneys, paralegals, nurses, and legal nurse consultants. She has appeared several times on Law Journal TV and on American Airlines inflight entertainment radio programming as part of a program on the nursing shortage. After entering the field of legal nurse consulting as a medical surgical expert witness in 1987, in 1989, she established Med League Support Services, Inc., an independent legal nurse consulting firm. Ms. Iyer has served on the national board of the American Association of Legal Nurse Consultants in the role of secretary, director at large, president elect, president, and past president. She served two years as the chair of the AALNC Education Committee, during which time she was the chief editor of the AALNC online legal nurse consulting course. AALNC awarded Ms. Iyer with the Lifetime Achievement Award in 2005 and the Volunteer of the Year Award in 2006. Certified by the American Association of Legal Nurse Consulting as a Legal Nurse Consultant Certified (LNCC), Ms. Iyer began her nursing career by earning a diploma in nursing from Muhlenberg Hospital School of Nursing in Plainfield, New Jersey. She earned her bachelor of science degree in nursing and a master of science degree in nursing from the University of Pennsylvania in Philadelphia. She can be reached at Med League Support Services, Inc., Flemington, New Jersey, or through patmedleague@gmail.com or www.medleague.com or www.patiyer.com.

Barbara J. Levin, BSN, RN, ONC, LNCC co-authored and updated the *Orthopaedic Malpractice* chapter and co-authored a new chapter: *Falls and Their Consequences.* Ms. Levin was a co-editor of *Medical Legal Aspects of Medical Records, Second Edition* (2010) and co-authored the chapter *Orthopaedic Records.* In addition, she was an associate editor of *Principles and Practices of Legal Nurse Consulting, Second Edition.* Ms. Levin is a certified orthopaedic nurse and has received recognition as a Clinical Scholar at Massachusetts General Hospital where she works in the orthopedic trauma unit. Her dedication to orthopaedics has inspired her to co-author the chapter *Orthopaedic Complications* for the National Association of Orthopaedic Nurses Core Curriculum.

Ms. Levin is an accomplished NAON instructor who teaches review classes to nurses in preparation for the ONC (orthopaedic nurses' certification) exam. She earned the distinction of Legal Nurse Consultant Certified and served as president of the American Association of Legal Nurse Consultants (2004-2005). She participated with the American Nurses Association to define and publish *Legal Nurse Consulting: Scope and Standards of Practice.* During Ms. Levin's term on the AALNC Board of Directors, she assisted in the development of the position statement *The Specialty Practice of Legal Nurse Consulting.* She also received the prestigious 2006 Partners in Excellence award for exemplary performance in "Outstanding Community Contributions." In 2007, Ms. Levin received the AALNC Member of the Year award. Ms. Levin draws on a wealth of nursing experience in a myriad of clinical settings. She has published and lectured to nurses nationwide about patient safety, orthopaedics, and documentation practices. Assisting facilities in redesigning key policies and procedures, Ms. Levin has improved patient safety and reporting of such incidents. Ms. Levin serves as a valued member of the Massachusetts Tribunal, working together with a judge and an attorney to determine the direction of medical malpractice claims. In her role as a legal nurse consultant, she educates at court mediations and has been an appreciated asset during these appearances. Ms. Levin and Ms. Iyer have collaborated on many projects which include teaching two programs to the International Council of Nurses, 2007 conference, in Yokohama, Japan. Additionally they have given presentations to nurses, physicians, medical students, nursing students, and attorneys nationally. Ms. Levin earned her bachelor of science degree in nursing from Boston University. She can be reached at bjllnc@aol.com.

Kathleen C. Ashton, PhD, APRN, BC is a Professor of Nursing in the Jefferson School of Nursing at Thomas Jefferson University in Philadelphia, Pennsylvania, and a Professor Emerita at Rutgers University in Camden, New Jersey, where she taught for 16 years. She has conducted numerous funded research studies on women and heart disease and has published her work in leading medical and nursing journals. She coauthored the *Critical Care Nursing Liability Issues* chapter.

She obtained her basic nursing education at Mercer Medical Center in Trenton, New Jersey, her BSN from Coe College in Iowa, her MS in nursing from the University of Maryland, and her Ph.D. from Temple University in Philadelphia. As a legal nurse consultant for over 15 years, she reviews cases for plaintiff and defense firms and serves as an expert witness at depositions and trials. She also serves on various boards for community and professional organizations and volunteers for medical missions to Lima, Peru where she practices as an Advanced Practice Nurse. She has received numerous awards for research, service and teaching, including the New Jersey Governor's Merit Award for

Advanced Practice Nursing. Dr. Ashton may be reached at ashton834@comcast.net.

Victoria Powell, RN, CCM, LNCC, CNLCP, CLCP, MSCC, CEAS is an editor of this text and co-author of the *Life Care Planning* chapter. Ms. Powell is the author of *Business Plan* and *Marketing* chapters for the core curriculum of nurse life care planning. She sits on the editorial board for the American Association of Nurse Life Care Planners and has written several articles on amputation for the publication. Ms. Powell is also an avid blogger. She is the owner and current president of VP Medical Consulting, a professional nurse consulting firm in central Arkansas. She provides case management services to the catastrophically injured and life care plans for both clinical use and litigation with a special interest in amputation. She holds certifications in case management, nurse life care planning, Medicare Set Aside, legal nurse consulting and ergonomic assessment. She has a worldwide client base.

Ms. Powell is a nationally recognized speaker, having made numerous presentations on a variety of business and health-related topics to healthcare providers, attorneys, public and civic groups. She currently serves as the state's chapter president for the AALNC and is the marketing chair for the AANLCP as well as a conference committee member. She is a current member of the American Association of Legal Nurse Consultants, American Association of Nurse Life Care Planners, National Association of Medicare Set-Aside Professionals, National Nurses in Business, Case Management Society of America, Academy of Certified Case Managers, and the Amputee Coalition of America. Ms. Powell is also one of the adjunct faculty for University of Florida's Forensic Science for Nurses. Ms. Powell began her nursing career in 1994 after having graduated from Baptist School of Nursing in Little Rock, Arkansas. She can be reached at VP Medical Consulting in Benton, Arkansas or by e-mailing victoria@vp-medical.com. For more information on Ms. Powell, visit www.vp-medical.com.

About the Contributors

Carol Ann Armenti, MA, JD is in private practice. Prior to establishing her current practice, she was a legal services staff attorney, whose practice consisted of representing low income individuals on healthcare matters. While there, she was President of the local bargaining unit of the Legal Service Workers, an affiliate of the United Auto Workers. She received both her bachelor of arts and master's degrees from Montclair State University in the fields of Language Arts and Educational Psychology, where she attained teaching licenses in English and Special Education. Specializing in adapting cognitive processing models to learning in non-traditional environments, Ms. Armenti acquired expertise in telecommunications and computer interfaces, leading to her successful implementation of the first free public access commercial online service. She successfully lobbied nationally for the Patients Rights Act, granting patients the right to access medical records, and the Breast and Cervical Screening program, providing free and low cost breast and cervical examinations for the early detection of cancer. Her efforts culminated in a commendation from the United States Senate for her service to others. She received her Juris Doctor from Seton Hall University with a concentration in Health Law Policy, and is admitted to practice in New Jersey and New York. She has received federal appointments from the Food and Drug Administration, National Institutes of Health, and the National Cancer Institute, as well as appointments from the State of New Jersey, where she resides with her family. Ms. Armenti lectures and publishes frequently on healthcare policy issues.

Gretchen Aumann, PhD, RN, at the time of publication, was employed as a nurse consultant at Medical Research Consultants in Houston. Ms. Aumann worked as an OB/GYN staff nurse and was an assistant professor of Obstetrics and Gynecology at the University of Pittsburgh School of Medicine. She has extensive clinical, perinatal teaching, and research experience. She was a member of the Nurses Association of the American College of Obstetrics and Gynecology, Sigma Theta Tau (International Honor Society for Nursing), the American Nurses Association, and the Society for Health and Human Values.

Jenny Beerman, MN, RN, LNCC practices nursing as clinical professor of nursing at the University of Kansas Hospital and recently as a medical/surgical and critical care nurse in a metropolitan Kansas City hospital. After graduating as a nurse in 1971, she obtained clinical nursing experience in a variety of medical/surgical and critical care areas, including trauma, telemetry, and medical and surgical intensive care units. She has worked as a cardiac clinical nurse specialist, was co-developer of a cardiac rehabilitation program, and has taught nursing in a wide variety of medical and surgical settings. Ms. Beerman served as the editor of the *Journal of Legal Nursing Consulting* from 1996 to 1998 and served on the board of the *Journal of Nursing Law* from 1999 to 2006. She has been a member of AALNC since 1989 and has testified at depositions and trials as an expert witness and expert fact witness. She is a member of the American Association of Critical Care Nurses as well as an author of several textbooks and journals on legal nursing topics. Ms. Beerman is a national speaker and holds a degree in psychology and a master's degree in nursing. She was named most outstanding nursing faculty member in 2004, 2006, and 2010 at the University of Kansas.

David M. Benjamin, PhD, FCP, FCLM is a doctorally prepared clinical pharmacologist and toxicologist, a trained arbitrator and mediator, as well as a nationally-recognized scholar in legal medicine, reducing medication errors, the drug development process and forensic toxicology. Dr. Benjamin completed his PhD in Pharmacology at the University of Vermont College of Medicine in 1972 and did his specialty training in Clinical Pharmacology & Toxicology at the University of Kansas Medical Center in 1972-73. He then spent 12 years in the pharmaceutical industry conducting clinical research, writing package inserts, and filing INDs and NDAs.

Barbara Mladenetz Weber Berry, MSN, RN served as VP of Patient Services at the Visiting Nurse Association of Mercer County, Trenton, New Jersey. Community health nursing was her passion as a student nurse and it became her professional career path for over 30 years. Ms. Berry holds a bachelor's in nursing from the College of New Jersey and a master's in nursing from the University of Pennsylvania with a major in community health nursing and a minor in education. She attained certifications in Nursing Administration, School Nursing from various institutions. Working in many capacities from field nurse to administrator, in both preventive health and morbidity home care programs, has given Ms. Berry a unique perspective about this nursing specialty. In conjunction with this, Ms. Berry is committed to education and exposing students to the field of community health nursing. She was a clinical faculty member in the College of New Jersey's baccalaureate nursing program for over ten years and taught leadership in nursing practice. She has also mentored graduate students pursuing degrees in nursing administration. Ms. Berry currently writes reviews for *Advance*, the bimonthly nursing journal, on topics related to home health care and nursing management.

Georgette M. Bieber, RNC, LNCC is a licensed registered nurse in New Jersey where she is the director of clinical services in Dellridge Health and Rehabilitation, a subacute and long-term care facility. She coauthored *Subacute and Long Term Care Nursing Malpractice*. As a legal nurse consultant she consults for attorneys providing medical record reviews regarding nursing malpractice and more recently has become actively involved in the corporate compliance process for long-term care facilities. She is certified as a legal nurse consultant by the American Association of Legal Nurse Consultants and has been in private practice for ten years. Ms. Bieber has served on a regional bioethics committee, has been a Director of Nursing and a member of NADONA since 1986. She has directed the establishment of nursing services for several new facilities, has been responsible for the safe transition of residents as facilities have closed and has assisted facilities to re-establish substantial compliance after surveys. Ms. Bieber continues to author policies and procedures regarding the provision of clinical services as well as corporate compliance for long-term care facilities. She received her training as a registered nurse at Bellevue Hospital affiliated with New York University and after working in critical care and neurology/neurosurgery she transitioned to long-term care.

Gloria Blackmon, AAS, RN, BSN, RN-BC, LNHA received an associate's degree in Nursing from Maryville College of St. Louis and a bachelor of science degree in nursing from the University of Missouri-St. Louis. Her clinical career has included acute medicine, physical rehabilitation, home health and gerontological nursing, in which she holds ANCC certification. Administratively, she has functioned as a coordinator in education and Alzheimer's unit development, a director of nursing in freestanding and hospital-based skilled nursing facilities, and is a licensed nursing home administrator. Ms. Blackmon established an independent medical-legal practice in 1996 while she continued a clinical practice. She has worked with Legal Aid, defense and plaintiff counsels. Experienced as an appointed independent monitor by a State Attorney General's office and expert witness, she also provides services to the insurance industry as a loss control analyst and onsite investigator. Ms. Blackmon has given numerous presentations at nursing facilities and to national audiences regarding long-term care issues. Frequently published, she has contributed articles to *Claims Magazine*, *LNC Resource*, *The Medical-Legal Institute Journals* and *E-Zine* and textbook chapters in *A Facility Based Risk Management Program—A Practical Guide For LTC Providers*, *Defensive Documentation For Long Term Care: Strategies for Creating a More Lawsuit-Proof Resident Record*, and *Problem Behaviors in Long Term Care*.

Rose Clifford, RN received her diploma of nursing from Jackson Memorial Hospital School of Nursing in Miami, Florida. She is the director of Medical Analysis Resources, Inc. in Cynthiana, Kentucky, and has worked in the legal nurse consulting field for 20 years. Her firm specializes in onsite financial analysis of medical records for due diligence, billing accuracy and corporate compliance with state, federal, and payer regulations. Services are provided to accounting firms, law firms, and insurance companies. She uses her knowledge of healthcare fraud to help explore the issues in medical malpractice and personal injury cases. Ms. Clifford lectures to nurses, attorneys, and paralegals on related topics. She was the co-founder and president of the Miami Chapter of the American Association of Legal Nurse Consultants and the past president of the Lexington Chapter of the American Association of Legal Nurse Consultants. She is a current member of the American Nurses Association, Kentucky Nurses Association, American Association of Legal Nurse Consultants, and the National Association of Nurses in Business.

Beth Cohen, MSN, RNC, ARNP is currently a medical surgical clinical nurse specialist at North Broward Medical Center in Deerfield Beach, Florida. Recently she was awarded the Clinical Practice Recognition Award from the Academy of Medical Surgical Nurses (AMSN), an international nursing professional organization. She has spoken nationally on a variety of medical surgical topics, including alcohol withdrawal and HIV/AIDS. Ms. Cohen is a coauthor of *AIDS Care at Home* that was written for the lay public. Ms. Cohen holds a bachelor's degree and a master's degree as an adult nurse practitioner from Columbia University School of Nursing in New York. She currently serves as the president of the local AMSN Sunshine Region Chapter.

Mindy Cohen, RN, MSN, LNCC is a legal nurse consultant and owner of the Villanova firm of Mindy Cohen & Associates, Inc. Nursing and Medical-Legal Consultants, in operation since 1995. Her firm offers medical litigation support services including medical record review, working with experts, discovery and trial support, pain and suffering reports, life care plans and cost projections, attending medical exams, etc. Areas of practice include medical malpractice, personal injury, product liability, toxic tort, workers' compensation, and criminal cases. Services are offered to law firms, insurance companies, government agencies, and risk management departments. Ms. Cohen has more than 25 years of diverse nursing experience in the hospital, home care, and rehabilitation settings. She has been a staff nurse and administrator in all three arenas, having held leadership and decision-making positions on such committees as Safety, Risk Management, and Quality Improvement. Ms. Cohen has taught nursing students at two Philadelphia area universities. She is a past president of the American Association of Legal Nurse Consultants and holds her LNCC, the only legal nurse consulting certification approved by the American Board of Nursing Specialties. She is an author, conference presenter and active member of professional nursing associations. She received her BSN and MSN degrees, with honors, from the University of Pennsylvania.

Trish Councell, BSN, RN graduated from Community College of Denver, Aurora in 1983 with an associate's degree in nursing and a bachelor of science degree from Metropolitan State College of Denver in 1989. She is currently president of Storm LNC in Aurora, Colorado. She has had eight years experience in the legal nurse consulting field including utilization review, workers' compensation and case management. She started out in medicine as an Emergency Medical Technician (EMT) spending two years on an ambulance crew. While going through nursing school she worked first as a nurse's aide then as a Licensed Practical Nurse (LPN). This broad background has given her a unique perspective of the medical field. She has over seven years emergency department experience including St. Anthony's Hospital in Denver, Colorado, a Level I trauma center and the University of Colorado Health Sciences Center in Aurora, Colorado. She has two years experience in telephone triage with Kaiser Permanente in Denver. She was instrumental in developing a computer program to enable smooth communication between the clinics and the Call Center. She chaired committees tasked with developing guidelines and protocols. Other experience includes inpatient, ICU, homecare and outpatient nursing. This broad background has given her a unique perspective of the medical field. She is a member of the American Association of Legal Nurse Consultants.

Luke Curtis, MD, MS, CIH is a medical writer/researcher and industrial hygienist living in Chicago, Illinois. He has an MD degree from St. Christopher's Medical College (Lutom, Great Britain) and an MS in public health *Summa Cum Laude* from the University of Illinois at Chicago. Dr. Curtis has extensive experience in infection control, nutrition, indoor air quality and environmental/occupational health science. He has completed ten infection control projects as an industrial hygienist. He has published 60 papers/articles in peer-reviewed medical journals. He has 14 publications in hospital infection control — including a review of 48 methods to prevent hospital acquired infections published in the July 2008 *Journal of Hospital Infection*. He has also published over 150 medical articles for the popular press. Dr. Curtis also published a 347-page book on Elder Nutrition (Xlibris Press, 2010).

Dana DeVito, RN has been a registered nurse for 27 years and a certified forensic nurse for two years. She attended both County College of Morris and Seton Hall University. She specialized in emergency nursing and has been twice certified in the specialty. While working in this field, she recognized the need for forensic training in the emergency department. Ms. DeVito obtained her certification in forensic nursing at Kaplan University. She is a member of the American College of Forensic Examiners and currently offers lectures and programs in forensic nursing.

Elaine K. Diegmann, CNM, ND, FACNM is the Director of the Nurse Midwifery Educational Program at the University of Medicine and Dentistry of New Jersey. She holds a BSN from the University of Pennsylvania, a master of science degree in education from Teachers College, Columbia University, and a Doctor of Nursing from Case Western Reserve University. She is a graduate of the UMDNJ Nurse Midwifery Program. Dr. Diegmann has presented on numerous clinical issues throughout the United States.

Her areas of expertise include soft tissue repair of the vagina and surrounding structures, labor dystocias, shoulder dystocia, and malpresentations. She continues in full scope clinical practice and delivered both of her grandsons on October 28, 2003 and August 30, 2005. Dr. Diegmann is a Fellow in the American College of Nurse Midwives and was elected a Master Educator in 2001.

Sean J. Doolan, Esq. graduated from Law School in 1994. He started his legal career as an Assistant District Attorney in Bronx County prosecuting white-collar crimes, and as the DWI prosecutor in Greene County, New York. He currently resides in Greene County, New York with his wife and son. Mr. Doolan has recently been honored to coauthor (along with Monica Kenny, Esq.) a chapter on litigation strategies in two books, both published by Lawyers & Judges Publishing Company: *Nursing Home Litigation: Investigation and Case Preparation, Second Edition*, and *Nursing Malpractice, Fourth Edition*. Mr. Doolan is also a guest lecturer at numerous nursing home/assisted living litigation and negligence seminars. Some of the organizations that he lectures for include: American Association of Legal Nurse Consultants (AALNC), Lorman Education Services, Professional Education Systems Institute, LLC (PESI), Greene County Department of Aging, New York Bar Association, Rockland County Bar Association, and the Albany County Bar Association. Mr. Doolan is a member of the Greene County, Albany County, Rockland County, and New York State Bar Associations, the New York State Trial Lawyers Association, and the American Association for Justice. He is also a member of the Nursing Home Group of the American Association for Justice.

Kelly L. Dyar, RN, CNN is currently a registered nurse with over 21 years of experience in the care of dialysis and nephrology patients. She has experience in the care of chronic hemodialysis, peritoneal dialysis and acute hemodialysis patients, as well as some experience in pheresis therapies. Mrs. Dyar has worked as a staff nurse with direct patient care responsibilities, as a home dialysis nurse training patients in peritoneal dialysis, and also for eight years as a facility administrator in which she had full responsibility for a large outpatient dialysis clinic. Mrs. Dyar is active as a member of the American Nephrology Nurses' Association since 1990 and has served as a local chapter officer and education committee member. Mrs. Dyar has been a certified nephrology nurse since 1994. Further professional activities include presenting on dialysis related topics in local, regional and national conferences. Mrs. Dyar provides legal consultation services and has served as an expert witness in litigation pertaining to dialysis nursing care. Mrs. Dyar received her diploma in nursing from Georgia Baptist School of Nursing and is currently a BSN candidate at the University of Phoenix.

Susan G. Engleman, MSN, RN, APRN-BC, PNP, CLCP is an advanced practice nurse who works both as a clinical nurse specialist for Pediatric Services and as a nurse practitioner for the Pediatric Pain Service at Memorial Hermann Children's Hospital, a level one trauma center, in Houston, Texas. In addition, Ms. Engleman is also a certified life care planner specializing in life care plans for children with catastrophic injuries or illnesses and has participated in the field of legal nurse consulting since 1989. Ms. Engleman is adjunct faculty at the University of Texas Health Science Center School of Nursing in Houston, Texas. She earned her bachelor of science degree in nursing from the University of Evansville in Evansville, Indiana, in 1984. She received her MSN in Critical Care Nursing with a focus in Pediatrics 1989 and a post-master's Pediatric Nurse Practitioner certificate in 1994 from the University of Texas in Houston. Ms. Engleman has many years of pediatric nursing experience in numerous roles practicing in a variety of settings including pediatric intensive care, intermediate care, acute care and home care. Prior to her employment with Memorial Hermann Children's Hospital, she served as Chief Operating Officer with Pediatric Special Care, a home care agency specializing in the care of children with special healthcare needs. Ms. Engleman is a member of several professional organizations and was the founding chapter president for the Houston Gulf Coast Chapter of the Society of Pediatric Nurses in 1993.

Linda Esposito, PhD, MPH, MSN, APRN-BC is an Advanced Practice Nurse with dual National Certifications as a Child/Adolescent Psychiatric and Mental Health Clinical Nurse Specialist and an Adult Psychiatric and Mental Health Nurse Practitioner. She received her bachelor of science degree in nursing with a minor in psychology from Jersey City State College; both a master of public health degree and a master of science degree and nursing from the University of Medicine and Dentistry of New Jersey; and a doctorate in Philosophy and Health Studies from Temple University. She has published widely in professional journals and currently has a private practice.

Austin A. Evans, Esq. is an associate in the medical/medical device, pharmaceutical and professional liability practice groups in the Philadelphia office of Lavin, O'Neil, Ricci, Cedrone & DiSipio. He defends many cases, on both the state and federal levels, involving diverse claims against international corporations. Mr. Evans has gained substantial experience defending a wide variety of claims against healthcare-related entities and has handled all aspects of defense, ranging from pre-suit investigations through trial. Mr. Evans graduated with a bachelor of science degree from the University of Georgia in 2002, where he was a research assistant in the cognitive psychology lab. He earned his juris doctor, with an advanced certificate in Health Law, from the University Of Pittsburgh School of Law in 2005, where he was elected to the Order of the Barristers. He also was a recipient of the Jonas Salk Health Fellowship from 2003–2004 and was a member of the National Health Law Moot Court team in 2004. Mr. Evans is admitted to practice in Pennsylvania and New Jersey state courts, the United States District Courts for the Eastern District of Pennsylvania and the District of New Jersey, as well as the United States Court of Appeals for the Third Circuit. He is currently a member of Defense Research Institute (DRI) and the Philadelphia Bar Association.

Mary E. Fakes, RN, MSN is currently the Coordinator of Emergency Nursing Programs at St. Louis Community College and EMS Educational Coordinator, Eureka Fire Protection District, Support Team. She has worked as a clinician, coordinator, educator and nursing consultant for more than 20 years in a wide variety of clinical and educational settings. She has worked as a nurse expert and testifying expert in a variety of healthcare cases. Her consulting expertise is in the the areas of adult and pediatric emergency nursing, resuscitation issues, prehospital care and care plan management in long-term care. She also holds a license as a funeral director and has served as a consultant in this field. Ms. Fakes began her nursing career as a diploma registered nurse from Deaconess School of Nursing in St. Louis, Missouri. She received her BSN from Deaconess College of Nursing in St. Louis, Missouri, and her MSN in Nursing Administration from the University of Phoenix, graduating with honors. She is active in the American Heart Association, serving as a Regional Faculty Member in the disciplines of ACLS, BLS, and PALS. In addition, she has served several terms as ACLS National Faculty in Missouri for the American Heart Association. Ms. Fakes is active in numerous health-related organizations in a variety of volunteer roles and frequently lectures on cardiac resuscitation and education issues.

Hilary J. Flanders, MPH, RN-BC, RRT is currently a staff nurse in the Respiratory Acute Care Unit (RACU), and a coach for the Electronic Medication Administration Process for Patient Safety (EMAPPS) at Massachusetts General Hospital. She holds a bachelor's degree in Respiratory Therapy from Northeastern University, a bachelor's degree in Nursing from the University of Massachusetts Boston, and a master's degree in Public Health from the University of Massachusetts, Amherst. Prior to working at Massachusetts General Hospital, she held several staff and travel nurse positions in intensive and intermediate care units. She is board certified in Medical-Surgical Nursing and Gerontological Nursing.

Patricia Goode, RN, ANP/FNP is an actively practicing nurse practitioner and legal nurse consultant with 30 years of experience. As the senior partner of Legal Nurse Consulting of Brevard, she provides a professionally focused review and evaluation of medical legal cases for attorneys, insurance companies, hospitals and other health care institutions and businesses. Ms. Goode is a member of the American Nurses Association, the Florida Nurses Association, Space Coast Clinicians, the American Academy of Nurse Practitioners, and the National Association of Certified Legal Nurse Consultants.

M. Elizabeth Greenberg, RN-BC, C-TNP, PhD has extensive experience in telehealth nursing practice, management, and research and is a nationally recognized leader in the field of telehealth nursing. For 16 years, Dr. Greenberg has practiced, studied, published, and presented in the field of telehealth and ambulatory care nursing. She has practiced telephone triage nursing in multispecialty pediatric and OB/GYN ambulatory care clinics. For two years she was manager of a regional after-hours telephone triage service where she was responsible for daily operations, staff education and development, quality assurance, marketing, and fiscal accountability. Over 90 providers from individual office, group practices, and organizations subscribed to this service, which addressed the health needs of 250,000 patients of all ages. Dr. Greenberg is currently an Assistant Clinical Professor at Northern Arizona University in Tucson, Arizona. She began her career over 26 years ago with an associate's degree in Nursing Science. She then received her BSN, MS, and PhD at the University of Arizona, College of Nursing. Dr. Greenberg holds national certifications in Telephone Nursing Practice and Ambulatory Care Nursing. She has been an active member of AAACN since 1999, a member of the *Viewpoint* Editorial Board since 2007 and is also a member of ANA and Sigma Theta Tau.

Agnes Grogan, BS, RN is a partner in V/G Associates, Inc. of Westminster, California. She is a founding member of the American Association of Legal Nurse Consultants at both national and chapter levels. Ms. Grogan's background in medical bill review is extensive and includes hospital bill audits, medical claim reviews for insurance adjusters, as well as plaintiff and defense attorneys. She has a nationwide client base and serves as a testifying expert in many instances. She has lectured nationally on medical fraud investigation and has presented extensively to attorneys, insurance adjusters, and legal nurse consultants on various aspects of bill review and medical fraud. Additionally, she has published several articles on the topic of medical billing and authored *Health Care Claims Analysis in Legal Nurse Consulting: Principles and Practices and Billing and Coding* in a Lawyers & Judges text entitled *Medical Legal Aspects of Medical Records*. She currently serves as the Chairman of the Legislation Committee for the American Association of Medical Audit Specialists.

Lorraine M. Harkavy, RN, MS has extensive experience in the specialty of infection control and prevention. Ms. Harkavy earned her bachelor of science degree at the University of Connecticut, and her master of science degree at Boston University. She is a past president of the international organization, the Association for Professionals in Infection Control and Epidemiology (APIC). As an infection control professional, Ms. Harkavy has worked with and consulted for acute-care and long-term acute-care hospitals, long-term care facilities, ambulatory care and surgery centers, and home care agencies. She has served as a consultant to various governmental agencies including the Centers for Disease Control and Prevention, the General Accounting Office and state agencies, and for the private sector including manufacturers of medical equipment and over-the-counter products. She was a vice president of a nationwide post-acute care firm and took responsibility for initiating a company-wide infection control and prevention program. Ms. Harkavy's work crosses many sectors of the healthcare industry, including the operating room, intensive care, postanesthesia care, private duty nursing, and education, having taught in hospital and collegiate schools of nursing.

Martie Hawkins, RN-BC, BSN, CWOCN, CCM is a certified Wound, Ostomy Continence Nurse Consultant with Horizon Home Care and Hospice. Her extensive nursing career includes over 27 years of nursing, 18 years of WOCN (ET) specialty nursing, and 14 years in legal nurse consulting. She is the owner of Hawkins Medical/Legal Consulting Company. She is a graduate of Florida Community College and University of North Florida in Jacksonville, Florida, Enterostomal Therapy Certification course from Emory University in Atlanta, Georgia, Certified Case Manager, Certified Geriatric Nurse, and holds an associate's degree in Arts—Paralegal/Legal Nurse Consulting from Kaplan College. She reviews medical records as an expert on wound, ostomies, and skin breakdowns for both plaintiff and defense attorneys throughout the United States. She has presented at several conferences around the country on topics such as prevention and treatment of pressure ulcers and the legal issues associated with pressure ulcers. Active in the Idaho Coalition for Prevention of Pressure Ulcers she provides education throughout the State of Idaho to acute care, long-term care, home care and assisted living employees.

Elizabeth E. Hill, PhD, RN, PLNC is currently a member of the clinical faculty at Johns Hopkins University School of Nursing, and owner of Hill Nurse Consulting, LLC. Dr. Hill holds a bachelor's degree in Nursing from Indiana University of Pennsylvania, master's degree in nursing from Pennsylvania State University, and a Doctor of Philosophy in Nursing from the University of Maryland, Baltimore. Since 2002, she has been known for her funded and published research in the area of falls and fall-related injury. She authored a "Safety" chapter for a new foundations of nursing textbook and serves on the editorial boards of *Nursing Research* and *Research in Gerontological Nursing*.

Donna Hunter-Adkins, BSN, RN, CEN, CCM, CRRN, CLCP, LNCC is President/CEO of Medical Claims Analysis & Management Services and is a registered nurse with over 30 years of nursing experience. She has practiced in the areas of emergency care and pre-hospital emergency care, having served for many years as the EMS Coordinator for a large metropolitan area. Her hospital experience includes working in the ED at the bedside and as an administrator and supervisor. Ms. Hunter-Adkins continues to consult with healthcare facilities and ambulance providers on standards of care and risk management issues. She has been an Affiliate Faculty with the American Heart Association in the areas of Basic and Advanced Cardiac Life Support for many years and has been certified as an instructor in the use of the AED. Ms. Hunter-Adkins serves as a mentor to nursing students and new nurses and lectures on the issues of the nursing process, standard of care issues and nursing documentation in addition to issues involving emergency care and risk management. She has taught at the university level and continues to lecture nationally on issues involving nursing issues, case management, life care planning, emergency care, expert witness preparation and standard of care issues. In 1993, she opened her business which focuses on liaison and consultation with insurance companies, healthcare providers, including ambulance services, individuals, attorneys, case management for the ill and injured, medical record reviews, detection of fraud and abuse, lifetime needs assessment and other issues, including civil and criminal cases. She has extensive experience in Life Care Planning and attended the first life care planning training program offered through the University of Florida, Department of Rehabilitation. She has been credentialed as a Certified Life Care Planner since 1995. She serves as a mentor to both novice and experienced life care planners. Ms. Hunter-Adkins has worked with plaintiff and defense attorneys who utilize life care plans in their cases. She has significant experience in testimony, in trial and at deposition. She has recently focused on litigation involving mass tort action.

Monica Kenny, Esq. is a sole practitioner with an office in Catskill, New York. She is a graduate of Albany Law School, where she was named the Arthur F. Mathew's Scholar, receiving a full scholarship. Ms. Kenny began her legal career earning a paralegal certificate from Marist College in 1999, and continued with her education at the State University at Albany, graduating *summa cum laude* with a bachelor's degree in Criminal Justice in 2002. Upon graduation from the State University at Albany, she was the recipient of the Donald J. Newman Award for Academic Achievement. Ms. Kenny previously worked for her coauthor, Sean J. Doolan, Esq., for over eight years. Mr. Doolan's practice includes personal injury litigation with a concentration on Nursing Home/Assisted Living Facility Abuse and Neglect. Ms. Kenny has been in private practice as a sole practitioner for approximately two years and practices primarily in the areas of family law, criminal defense, and civil practice.

Peter A. Kolbert, Esq. is a partner with the law firm of Wilson, Elser, Moskowitz, Edelman and Dicker, LLP. Mr. Kolbert's practice concentrates on health law. He has represented hospitals, physicians, nurses, and long-term care facilities in cases involving professional negligence. He has lectured extensively on medical-legal issues and has written on issues surrounding long-term care facilities litigation. Mr. Kolbert is admitted to practice law before the Courts of the State of New York, as well as the United States District Court for the Southern and Eastern Districts of New York. He is a former Assistant Corporation Counsel for the City of New York and obtained a bachelor of arts degree from the University of Massachusetts at Amherst and a Juris Doctor from Brooklyn Law School.

Ginny Lee, BBM, MBA/HCM, MSN, RN, an alumni of LeTourneau University and the University of Phoenix, lives in Benton, Arkansas. She has been a nurse for over 16 years and has worked in compliance and infection control for over eight years as both a director and compliance officer. She has performed adjunct activities including working with local quality improvement organizations and the Clark County Health Department and the State of Washington Pandemic and Emergency Preparedness Committees. She anticipates starting her doctorate of nurse practitioner in forensics in the fall of 2012.

Mary K. Leverock, RN, BSN, QAUR, is CEO of the consulting firm Healthcare Attorney-Client Consulting, Inc. in Miami, Florida. She also serves as senior consultant for Medical Analysis Recourses, Inc. in Cynthiana, Kentucky. Previously she had been a clinical research associate with the law firm of McDermott, Will & Emery. She earned her BSN from the University of Miami. Certified in Quality Assurance and Utilization Review, she has conducted compliance-related audits affecting state and federal level fraud and abuse issues. Additionally, she has worked with health law attorneys, as well as litigators on reimbursement and coverage issues for many types of providers from national corporations to individual providers. She has broad nursing experience in various clinical and management positions as well as expertise in medical record, coding, and reimbursement issues.

Susan Masoorli, RN has been active in the fields of intravenous therapy and vascular access for over 30 years. She has served on the Board of Directors for the Association of Vascular Access and was President of an Infusion Nurse Society local chapter. She has published over 200 articles in many peer-reviewed nursing journals. She is recognized nationally and internationally as a speaker on various intravenous therapy topics. She has developed training videos and workbooks on peripheral intravenous venipuncture techniques and central venous catheter care and maintenance. She has been offering intravenous therapy educational programs throughout the country for the past 20 years through the company she founded, Perivascular Nurse Consultants, Inc. She has been an expert witness on infusion therapy nursing malpractice cases since 1990.

Dianna McCorkle, BSN, RN, CNOR, active in perioperative nursing for over 25 years, has extensive experience in various perioperative roles as a staff nurse, educator, charge nurse, and department head. She is a veteran of the United States Navy Nurse Corps having honorably served both at home and abroad. She has held certification in perioperative nursing since 1992 and is an independent legal nurse consultant and expert witness for both plaintiff and defense cases since 2003. She is an active member of the Association of Operating Room Nurses and the American Association of Legal Nurse Consultants. She received her BS in Nursing from College Misericordia, Pennsylvania in 1975.

Joanne McDermott, MA, RN has worked in the maternal-newborn area of nursing for over 25 years. She received her bachelor of science degree in nursing in 1975 from the State University of New York and her master's degree in nursing education from New York University in 1985. She has worked as a staff nurse, assistant head nurse, clinical coordinator and assistant director of nursing. Currently, Ms. McDermott is an Assistant Professor of Nursing in Kansas City, Missouri. Ms. McDermott has experience in medical risk management as a claims analyst, and has reviewed medical-legal cases as an obstetrical nurse expert witness. She is a member of the Association of Women's Health, Obstetrical and Neonatal Nursing (AWHONN).

Wanda K. Mohr, PhD, RN, FAAN received her doctorate in nursing from the University of Texas at Austin in 1995. Presently she is a retired Associate Professor of Psychiatric Mental Health Nursing from University of Medicine and Dentistry School of Nursing. She is a certified advanced practice nurse in Child and Adolescent Psychiatric Mental Health Nursing. Dr. Mohr dedicated her career to studying the effects of exposure to violence on children's development. She is recognized for her work on institutional violence on troubled children, and has testified before the United States Congress representing national agencies that advocate for children's mental health. She is a recognized leader in the movement to reform conditions in mental health settings, with special emphasis on seclusion and restraint. She has over 30 years of clinical experience with troubled children and their families ranging across a variety of healthcare settings. Since completing her doctorate, she has authored over 70 professional journal articles, chapters, and books on the subject of mental health and has been consulted by a variety of state and federal agencies on the issue of children's responses to violence. Dr. Mohr is a fellow in the American Academy of Nursing and has been recognized by her peers with numerous national and international awards. She has conducted seven funded research studies from 1983 employing qualitative and quantitative research methods.

Nancy E. Mooney, MA, RNC, ONC is the Director of Nursing Administration at Lutheran Medical Center in Brooklyn, New York. Ms. Mooney started her nursing career as a diploma nurse from Kings County Hospital Center School of Nursing, Brooklyn, New York and earned her BSN at the University of North Carolina at Chapel Hill, and her master's degree in nursing education at New York University. With over 35 years of experience, Ms. Mooney has worked as a staff nurse, instructor, nurse manager, supervisor, and director. Her career spans working in the Indian Health Service to the Internet. Her clinical specialty has been orthopaedics and she has spoken at workshops across the country. She served as the President of the National Association of Orthopaedic Nurses (1996-1997) and remains active in that organization as the editor of NAON News, the official newsletter for NAON. She holds memberships in the Upsilon Chapter of Sigma Theta Tau, Nurses House, Inc., as well as other nursing organizations. Certified as both an orthopaedic nurse specialist and as a pain management nurse specialist, Ms. Mooney has published widely on these topics, as well as the topic of humor.

Scott A. Mullins AAS, EMT-P is a Battalion Chief and EMS Officer for the Eureka Fire Protection District in St. Louis County, Missouri. He has a BS in Fire and Safety Engineering Technology from the University of Cincinnati and is enrolled in the Executive Fire Officer Program at the National Fire Academy in Emmitsburg, Maryland. He is a Regional Faculty for the American Heart Association for the disciplines of Basic Life Support, Advanced Cardiac Life Support, and Pediatric Advanced Life Support. Battalion Chief Mullins has published articles in *Emergency Medical Services Magazine* and has been a reviewer for various paramedic textbooks. He recently served as President of the Greater St. Louis Region Fire EMS Officer's Association and was named the Administrator of the Year in 2002 for the Missouri Emergency Medical Services Association. He also is vice president of SAR Training and Consulting Inc. an EMS and medical training and consulting company that offers a variety of programs for corporate and medical provider clients in the St. Louis area.

Tammy J. Murphy, ASN, RN, CAP III is currently attending Graceland University and earning a BA-HCM (Health Care Management). She is also a graduate of Catherine Laboure' College in Boston. Ms. Murphy attended Kaplan College School of Paralegal-Legal Nurse Consulting in Boca Raton, Florida, and is a member of the Delta Epsilon Tau International Honor Society. Ms. Murphy has worked in the emergency department as charge nurse at the Jordan Hospital in Plymouth, Masachusetts, for 22 years. In 2001, she was the recipient of "Plymouth Area Emergency Medical Systems Nurse of the Year." She has been the chairperson of the Emergency Department Service Excellence team since 2005, consistently working on ways to improve the quality of care for their patients and families while in the emergency department. She has her own independent legal nurse consulting practice, Medical Legal Consulting Services where most of her work surrounds expert witnessing for the plaintiff and defense. She has served on the Board of Directors of the Southern New England Chapter of the American Association of Legal Nurse Consultants and is a past president. She has a background in oral surgery, home health care as well as pre-hospital emergency medical care.

Marian Nowak, RN, MSN, M.Ed., MPH served as a school nurse for 27 years in a suburban School Health Services Program. During her tenure she developed many quality improvement projects for both the school and community she served. Currently she is a doctoral student at Case Western Reserve University. Her academic accomplishments include achieving an MPH from Johns Hopkins University, M.Ed. from Temple University and a MSN from Thomas Jefferson University.

James O'Donnell, PharmD, FCP, ABCP is a Professor of Pharmacology and frequent consultant in litigation. He has worked on high profile cases in the national news. He is responsible for medical college instruction on adverse drug reactions and drug interactions and is the editor of several "Drug Injury" books and more than 200 publications addressing drug injury. Dr. O'Donnell earned his bachelor's and doctorate degrees in Pharmacy from the Universities of Illinois and Michigan, respectively, and earned a master's degree in clinical nutrition from Rush University. He is currently an Associate Professor and Course Director for Medical Pharmacology at the Rush University Medical Center. Dr. O'Donnell is also a Lecturer in the Department of Medicine at the University of Illinois College of Medicine. He is a Diplomate of the American Board of Clinical Pharmacology, a Fellow of the American College of Clinical Pharmacology, a Diplomate of the Board of Nutritional Specialties, Fellow in the American College of Nutrition, and member of several professional societies. He is a co-editor of Pharmacy Law, the editor of *Drug Injury: Liability, Analysis, and Prevention*, first and second editions, and co-editor of *The Process of New Drug Discovery and Development*. His publications include several chapters on medication errors in nursing malpractice books, and more than 200 articles on drug injury and prevention. In addition to his academic and editorial endeavors, he regularly consults in drug and pharmaceutical matters to industry, government, and law.

Valerie V. Parisi, RN, CRRN, CLCP of Doylestown, Pennsylvania, has a private consulting practice in medical case management and medical-legal consulting. Ms. Parisi has been an active registered nurse for 20 years and is certified by the Association of Rehabilitation Nurses as a certified rehabilitation nurse (CRRN). Ms. Parisi is also a life care planner and has pursued a post graduate certificate in this field through the University of Florida Intellicus program. Ms. Parisi has worked in the field of home health care for 14 years and has served as both a field nurse and case manager. She has experience working with general medical/surgical patients as well as patients requiring specialty care. This includes many years working with the high risk infant program. Ms. Parisi currently provides case management for those injured in work-related or motor vehicle accidents and has stayed abreast of the changes in home care as she recommends the appropriate health delivery systems for her clients. Ms. Parisi received a Diploma in Nursing from Thomas Jefferson University in Philadelphia, Pennsylvania.

Ann M. Peterson, EdD, MSN, RN, CS, LNCC has practiced as an independent legal nurse consultant since 1995. Located in Massachusetts, Dr. Peterson, a certified family nurse practitioner, consults with both defense and plaintiff firms nationwide drawing on her vast experiences as a clinician, educator, and healthcare administrator to review and opine on medical malpractice, nursing negligence, and criminal cases. The majority of her work over the past five years has been in the arena of nursing home litigation. In addition to being a contributor to this text and to *Medical Legal Aspects of Medical Records* (edited by Iyer, Levin and Shea), Dr. Peterson has authored numerous professional articles, has participated in Massachusetts' Medical Malpractice Tribunals, and been an active member of numerous public and professional organizations. She was a coeditor of the Principles and Practices of Legal Nurse Consulting, Third Edition.

JoAnn Pietro, JD, RN is a partner in the firm of Wahrenberger & Pietro LLP, Springfield, New Jersey, which specializes in medical malpractice and health care law. Ms. Pietro's concentration of practice is in representing health care professionals who are sued for malpractice, in professional licensure actions before professional boards, in employment, health care regulatory, and general practice matters and does guardianship law. She holds a diploma in Nursing from Holy Name School of Nursing, Teaneck, New Jersey, a bachelor of arts degree in labor studies from Rutgers University, Newark, New Jersey, and a Juris Doctor degree from the City University of New York Law School at Queens College. She served as the chapter editor of "Legal and Ethical Aspects of Psychiatric-Mental Health Nursing" in the *Psychiatric-Mental Health Nursing, Seventh Edition*, Lippincott Williams & Wilkins, 2007 and MD Advisor. Ms. Pietro has coauthored an article with Kathleen Gialanella, Esq. and David Gialanella entitled: *The New Jersey Health Care Professional Responsibility and Reporting Enhancement Act: Helpful or Harmful?* published in the New Jersey State Bar Association, Health & Hospital Law Section Newsletter, Volume 17, Number 1, March 2010. Currently Ms. Pietro is an adjunct professor at Felician College, New Jersey and teaches legal

issues in the nurse educator masters program. She has served as an Adjunct Professor at Teachers College, Columbia University, New York, School of Education, Department of Organization and Leadership where she taught healthcare policy and healthcare ethics to doctoral nurse executive candidates. She has lectured and written extensively on litigation and healthcare related topics. Ms. Pietro is a member of the American Association of Nurse Attorneys, and is Vice President of the New Jersey Chapter. She is a member of the New Jersey State Nurses Association. She has served as President of the Young Lawyers Division of the Essex County Bar Association and is a member of the New Jersey Bar Association and active in the Health Law Section, and she is the past Chair of the Essex County Bar Association Medical/Legal Committee. In 2007, she served as a Commissioner on the New Jersey Governor Corzine's Commission on Rationalizing Health Care Resources.

Katherine Ramsland, PhD holds graduate degrees in forensic psychology, clinical psychology, and philosophy. Currently, she teaches forensic psychology and criminal justice at DeSales University in Pennsylvania. She has published over 900 articles and 38 books, including *The Forensic Psychology of Criminal Minds*, *Beating the Devil's Game: A History of Forensic Science and Criminal Investigation*, *The Human Predator: A Historical Chronicle of Serial Murder and Forensic Investigation*, and *Inside the Minds of Healthcare Serial Killers*. She has been published in ten languages. Her background in forensic studies positioned her to assist former FBI profiler John Douglas on his book, *The Cases that Haunt Us*, to co-write a book with former FBI profiler, Gregg McCrary, *The Unknown Darkness*, and to collaborate on a forensic textbook with renowned criminalist Henry C. Lee, *The Real World of a Forensic Scientist*. For seven years, she contributed regularly to Court TV's Crime Library, and now writes a column on historic forensics for *The Forensic Examiner*, offers case analysis for the media, and speaks internationally about forensic psychology, forensic science, and serial murder. She has appeared in numerous cable network documentaries, as well as on such programs as The Today Show, 20/20, Montel Williams, NPR, Larry King Live and E! True Hollywood.

F. David Rodden, CRNA, MSN, MS graduated from the University of Delaware with a BSN, received an MSN from the University of Pennsylvania, and earned an MS in nurse anesthesia from the Medical College of Pennsylvania. He has experience in all areas of nurse anesthesia practice and was director of a nurse anesthesia program for 14 years, where he taught a course on the legal aspects of anesthesia practice. He has served as expert witness for plaintiffs and defendants and continues to have an interest in the professional aspects of anesthesia care. He is presently the chief nurse anesthetist at an active surgery center, providing anesthesia for children and adults having a variety of outpatient procedures.

Marlene Roman, MSN, RN, ARNP, CMSRN is currently the director of education at Kindred Hospital in Hollywood, Florida. Medical surgical nursing is her passion. She previously served as president of the Academy of Medical Surgical Nurses (AMSN), the only professional nursing organization that represents medical surgical nurses. She has served as editor of *MedSurg Matters*, the official publication of AMSN and as an editorial board member of *MedSurg Nursing Journal*. She also served as a board member and president of the Medical Surgical Nurses Certification Board (MSNCB). She recently accepted the position as chair of the Ambassador Program for both AMSN and MSNCB. Ms. Roman holds a bachelor's in nursing from Northeastern University in Boston, a master's in adult health education from Salem State College in Salem, Massachusetts, and a post-master's geriatric clinical nurse specialist/nurse practitioner from Florida Atlantic University in Boca Raton, Florida. She holds the credential CMSRN, certified medical surgical registered nurse. Recognized as a leader in medical surgical nursing, Ms. Roman was awarded the Anthony J. Jannetti award for outstanding contributions to medical surgical nursing. Ms. Roman is also committed to education and has worked as clinical faculty and most recently as an online instructor for nurses returning to the workforce at Broward College.

Carol Rutenberg, RN-BC, C-TNP, MNSc is a nationally recognized expert, speaker and author in the field of telephone triage. She has conducted research and has been recognized as the foremost authority on telephone triage and scope of practice. Ms. Rutenberg has hands-on experience, having been a telephone triage nurse in both the office and call center settings. President of Telephone Triage Consulting, Inc., Ms. Rutenberg speaks and consults nationally and internationally, specializing in professional education, program design and implementation, and risk management in telephone nursing practice. She also provides legal consultative services and has served as an expert witness in litigation pertaining to telephone triage and ambulatory care nursing. Ms. Rutenberg received her BSN from Baylor University and a master's degree in nursing administration (MNSc) from the University of Arkansas for Medical Sciences College of Nursing in Little Rock. She has been published in several peer-reviewed nursing journals and is a member of the Emergency Nurses Association, Sigma Theta Tau, and the Arkansas and American Nurses Associations. Ms. Rutenberg is an active member of the American Academy of Ambulatory Care Nursing (AAACN), having served in numerous capacities including revision of the Telehealth Nursing Practice Administration and Practice Standards and development of Position Statements on the Nurse Licensure Compact and the Role of the RN in Ambulatory Care. Ms. Rutenberg is honored to have received the AAACN President's "Above and Beyond" Award in 2008.

Kelly Shanley, MSN, RN is currently the Director of Quality and Patient Safety at the Caritas Carney Hospital in Dorchester, Massachusetts. She holds a master's degree in nursing from Walden University. Prior to the Director position at Carney Hospital, Ms. Shanley was a Quality Improvement Specialist at the New England Baptist Hospital in Boston. She has focused on Joint Commission readiness and quality issues in health care for the last four years, and has over 28 years of nursing experiences in varied specialties.

Nanette Sulik, MSN, RN, CSN is a Clinical Instructor of Nursing at the Rutgers University Camden College of Arts and Sciences in New Jersey where she teaches community health nursing, home and hospice care, and school nursing. She holds a MSN in Community Health Nursing and a BSN from LaSalle University. She maintains current clinical nursing experience in the areas of medical/surgical and home care nursing, and has taught nursing in a wide variety of community health and medical and surgical settings over the past 18 years. As part of the service mission of the university, she coordinates eight to ten community health service learning projects yearly with senior nursing students in the Camden community.

Jacqueline Vance, RNC, CDONA/LTC, a certified Gerontological Registered Nurse and a certified Director of Nursing in long-term care, is Director of Clinical Affairs for the American Medical Directors Association. In addition to overseeing, managing, and coordinating all projects in the Clinical Affairs Department, she manages the Clinical Practice Guideline Project. Ms. Vance has been a Director of Nursing in long-term care and has worked as a long-term care nursing consultant for a nationwide company. She is currently on the Board of Trustees-National Association Directors of Nursing Administration in Long Term Care (NADONA/LTC) and is Executive Director for Maryland. Ms. Vance is a recipient of several NADONA awards, including the National Nurse Administrator of the Year Award/Long-Term Care 2002. She is actively involved in her mission to improve the quality of care that seniors receive throughout the nation. Ms. Vance is a national presenter on educational topics focused on improving care for the elderly, and has authored multiple articles and manuals on that theme, including "Infections in Nursing Homes" in *Nursing Home Litigation: Investigation and Case Preparation*, edited by Patricia Iyer. She is on the editorial advisory boards of the *Internet Journal of Geriatrics* and *Gerontology, Assisted Living Consult*, and *McKnight's Long Term Care Medicine*. She is a contributing writer for *Caring for the Ages* magazine and a legal nurse consultant.

M. Terese Verklan, PhD, CCNS, RNC is an associate professor and clinical nurse specialist at the University of Texas Health Science Center at Houston. Her research investigates mechanisms of fetal heart rate variability and neonatal physiologic variability that may provide information regarding how the fetus/neonate is tolerating stresses of labor/delivery and transition to extrauterine life. Her clinical skills are maintained by working in a large tertiary neonatal intensive care unit providing a spectrum of care to high-risk neonates, including ECMO, total-body cooling, high-frequency ventilation and use of nitric oxide. In addition to writing research and clinical articles, she is a co-editor of Core Curriculum for Neonatal Intensive Care Nursing, as well as contributing to several chapters including Transition to Extrauterine Life, Neurologic Disorders and Legal Issues. She is a member of several editorial boards, as well as reviewer for nursing and medical journals. Dr. Verklan is frequently requested to speak on topics related to care of the high-risk neonate and advance practice nursing. She has played a key role in the development of the American Association of Critical Care Nurses Certification Corporation Clinical Nurse Specialist Examination (CCNS) for certification. She has also developed the

Neonatal Orientation and Education Program at the request of the Association of Women's Health, Obstetric and Neonatal Nurses, to be used for orienting new nurses to the special care and intensive care nurses across the United States. She has worked as a nurse expert and testifying expert in matters related to neonatal care and advanced practice nursing, and has a nationwide client base. Dr. Verklan also works as a consultant and resource for professional associations, manufacturers of neonatal products, and publishers of perinatal literature.

John C. Webber, Esq. is a senior associate with the law firm of Wilson, Elser, Moskowitz, Edelman and Dicker, LLP, in White Plains, New York. Mr. Webber focuses on legal issues related to health care, representing nurses, physicians, nursing homes, hospitals, and dentists. Before beginning his practice, Mr. Webber was a political consultant in Washington, D.C. He is a graduate of the University of Connecticut and Fordham University School of Law.

Index

A

abandonment, 136-137, 142, 144-145, 156, 189, 308, 405, 417, 419-420
abbreviations, 215, 234, 411, 451, 612, 832, 836, 840, 843, 848, 877-878, 890-891, 925
   do not use, 215
abductions, 7, 29-30, 73-75, 257, 646, 892, 909
abuse
   elder, 306-307, 311, 329, 409, 503, 516, 700-701
   emotional, 183, 306, 338
   financial, 183, 306, 800
   physical, 183, 294, 306-307, 316, 337
   sexual, 183, 307, 311, 337-338
   verbal, 183, 294, 307, 316, 337-338
Academy of Medical-Surgical Nurses, 201-202, 483, 485
accidental death, 430
accreditation of healthcare organization(s), see also Joint Commission, 408, 545, 692, 707, 878, 913
acute care, 110, 120, 160, 237, 244, 268, 281, 315, 318, 373, 403, 413, 487, 490, 525, 544, 673, 675-677, 685, 692, 696, 728, 737-738, 742, 756, 771-772, 774, 793, 801, 822, 893, 914
admissibility, 669
advance directives, 119, 319, 410, 423, 516-517, 524, 688, 698
Advanced Life Support (ALS), 105, 115, 431, 433, 455, 460, 478-479, 484-487, 572, 623, 798, 808, 895
Advanced Nurse Practitioners (ANP), see also nurse practitioners, 181, 476, 561, 812, 896
Advanced Practice Nurse (APN), 53-54, 57-58, 61, 63-64, 66, 69-72, 76, 79-80, 106, 181, 189, 199, 234, 281, 300, 356, 386, 476, 486, 561-565, 567-568, 608, 621, 636, 640, 812-813
Advanced Trauma Life Support (ATLS), 115, 479, 486-487
adverse drug reaction (ADR), 319, 701, 894
adverse outcomes, 13, 26, 117, 410, 571, 582-583, 595, 611, 627-628, 669, 701, 783, 792
affidavit of merit, 172
Against Medical Advice (AMA), 163, 204, 207, 383, 490, 514, 521, 524, 528, 532-535, 666, 792-793, 797, 817, 891, 895-896
Agency for Health Care Policy and Research (AHCPR), see also AHRQ, 728, 752, 759-760, 767, 894-895
Agency for Health Care Research and Quality (AHRQ), 201, 408, 488, 510, 728, 735, 737-738, 760-761, 767, 769, 829, 895
airway maintenance, 115, 579, 613
Albuterol, 239, 450, 601
alcohol withdrawal, 207, 808
Alfentanil, 577, 600
Allegra, 567, 808

allergic reactions, 145, 209, 239, 349, 381, 398, 444, 572, 739, 823, 848
allergies, 137, 158, 161, 165, 231, 241, 244, 286, 398, 451, 493, 497, 530, 567, 571, 609, 701, 728, 824, 830, 832, 836, 838-839, 843, 848, 895, 916
Alzheimer's, 204, 283, 286-289, 306, 309, 317-318, 326, 331, 337, 339, 341, 343, 802-803, 833-834, 893, 896, 906, 921
ambulatory care center, 483
American Academy of Orthopedic Surgeons, 254, 480, 776, 785, 892
American Academy of Pediatrics (AAP), 5, 28, 53, 55, 67, 71-72, 78, 353, 479-480, 892
American Academy of Science (AAS), 429, 571, 622-623
American Association of Colleges of Nursing, 562
American Association of Critical Care Nurses (AACN), 52-54, 79, 109-110, 115-116, 118, 124, 126
   outcome standards, 115
   standard(s), 110, 115
American Association of Nurse Anesthetists (AANA), 570-571, 575, 577-578, 583, 591, 594-595, 606-607, 612, 621-624, 626
   Guidelines, 606, 612
   Practice Manual, 575
American Association of Occupational Health Nursing (AAOHN), 892
American Board of Anesthesiology, 892
American College of Emergency Physicians, 476, 479-480
American College of Nurse Midwives (ACNM), 639-640, 642-643, 647, 649, 655, 893
American College of Obstetricians and Gynecologists (ACOG), 4-6, 17, 23, 25-26, 31, 33-35, 37, 39, 41, 53, 55, 63, 643-644, 893
American College of Surgeons (ACS), 434, 479-480, 498, 893
American Geriatrics Society, 767
American Health Care Association (AHCA), 293, 894-895
American Heart Association, 28, 55, 78, 96, 105, 434, 479-480
American Hospital Association, 6, 118, 123, 480, 692, 894
   Patient's Bill of Rights, 123
American Medical Association (AMA), 61, 163, 180, 204, 430, 479, 490, 514, 524, 528, 532, 534-535, 652, 663, 667, 792-793, 797, 817, 891, 895-896
American Nurses Association (ANA), 6, 52, 112, 115, 133, 164, 180-182, 186, 199-201, 251, 293, 297, 350, 358-359, 386, 407, 476, 480-483, 508, 515, 544-545, 562, 564, 639, 761, 770, 868, 871, 896
   Code for Nurses, 186, 515
   Standards of Care, 186
   Standards of Professional Performance, 481

American Nurses Credentialing Center, 545, 561-562
American Pharmaceutical Association, 839
American Psychiatric Nurses, 182, 485
American Society of Anesthesiologists (ASA), 162, 479-480, 570-
        571, 580, 582-585, 587, 589-592, 594-595, 599, 605-609,
        611, 619, 623-624, 626, 836, 897
American Society of Post Anesthesia Nurses (ASPAN), 133, 161-
        162, 172, 174-176, 594
American Society of Testing Materials (ASTM), 480
Americans with Disabilities Act (ADA), 348-349, 351, 365, 525,
        894
amniocentesis, 7, 13, 15, 17-19, 650, 889
        use and complications, 17-18
                cystic fibrosis, 17, 232, 649-650, 902
                Down's syndrome, 18, 524
                Duchenne's muscular dystrophy, 17-18
                galactosemia, 17
                hemophilia, 18, 271, 500, 890
                maple sugar urine disease, 17
                sickle cell disease, 7, 17-18, 585
                Tay-Sachs, 17
                thalassemia, 10, 13, 17-18
amnioinfusion, 7, 13-14, 44, 654
AMPLE algorithm, 497
anaphylaxis, 349, 398, 572
Anderson system, 260
anesthesia care, 132, 145, 151, 153-156, 158, 165, 172-174, 198,
        208, 220-221, 571, 573-574, 576-577, 580, 583, 586, 588,
        590, 592, 594, 597-598, 603-604, 606, 608, 617-619, 622-
        624, 626-628
        anesthesia care teams, 594, 623
        policies, 607
        products used in, 595
                anesthesia machine, 588, 595-596, 614
                medications, 598
                monitors, 596
        unique aspects of, 627
anesthesia, complications of, 609
anesthesia delivery, places of
        ambulatory surgery center (ASC), 606
        labor and delivery suite, 605
        office-based anesthesia, 606
        operating room, 604
anesthesia equipment, 576
anesthesia outcome, 623
Anesthesia Patient Safety Foundation (APSF), 570, 595, 628
anesthesia, practice of, 569-571, 607, 621
anesthesia record, 9, 148, 581-582, 587, 592, 599, 602, 605, 608,
        612-615, 617, 627
        automated, 617
anesthesia safety, improving, 599
        Patient Safety Foundation, 61, 570, 595
        Patient Safety Foundation Newsletter, 570
anesthesia, types of
        general anesthesia, 161, 572
        regional anesthesia, 573
        epidural anesthesia, 574-575
        spinal anesthesia, 574
        brachial plexus block, 575
        monitored anesthesia care, 576

anesthetist, 25, 106, 131, 134, 137, 139, 143, 156, 234, 562, 570-
        571, 575, 577-579, 583-584, 596, 599, 602-603, 606, 608,
        615, 619-623, 625-626, 716, 812-813, 904
angiogram, 111, 199, 526
angiography, 503, 532, 741
angioplasty, 231, 512, 526, 741, 899, 919
anorexia, 240, 372, 746
antepartum fetal surveillance, 16
anticoagulation therapy, 411
antidepressants, 294-295, 772, 923
antidotes, 584, 717, 822-823, 863
antiemetic, 593, 600-601
antisialogogues, 600
Apgar score, 7, 9, 14, 26-28, 32, 34, 36, 41, 58, 66, 68, 73, 86-88,
        641, 644-645, 651, 653
asphyxiation, 4, 14, 26, 28, 32, 42-45, 55, 66-67, 219, 303-304,
        643, 645
aspiration, 17, 44, 76, 100-101, 115, 206, 219, 231, 235-236, 238,
        242, 313, 504, 570, 572-573, 578, 587-588, 601, 605, 641,
        678-680, 734, 742, 762, 777, 782, 896
        prevention of, 219
aspirin, 275, 285, 587, 781-782, 836, 848, 896-897
assault, 189, 303, 306-311, 329, 337-338, 500, 502, 517, 667, 714,
        866, 868, 921
assisted-living facilities, 205, 281, 293, 306, 325-344, 405, 794,
        797, 811
Association of Perioperative Registered Nurses (AORN), 132-134,
        153, 896
Association of Women's Health, Obstetrical, Gynecological and
        Neonatal Nurses (AWHONN), 4-5, 15, 33, 52, 79, 605
atracurium, 600

B
Balanced Budget Act, 301
Basic Life Support (BLS), 105, 203, 413, 431, 433, 460, 464, 478-
        479, 484, 486-487, 652, 798, 900
Benzodiazepine, 185-186, 576, 600, 901
benzquinamide, 601
billing, 299, 426, 432-433, 438, 440, 617, 663-664, 669, 771, 785,
        791-796, 798-817, 827, 904, 907, 910, 924
bioengineering, 69, 507
biophysical profile (BPP), 6-7, 13, 15-16, 644, 652-653
Board of Nurse Examiners, 105
board(s) of nursing, 52, 54, 62, 72, 133, 329, 348, 387, 472-473,
        475-476, 481, 542, 544-545, 549, 562-563, 607, 714, 871,
        873-874
borrowed servant doctrine, 136-140, 625
Braden scale, 738
breathing problems, 98, 100-101, 232-233, 579, 857-858
bronchoscopy, 100, 117, 119, 241-243, 679
bronchospasms, 117, 244, 580, 603
Bupivicaine, 575, 600
butorphanol, 600

C
capnography, 579, 845
cardiac arrest, 17, 29, 76, 104-105, 117, 122, 145, 155, 158, 160,
        208, 219, 221, 237, 319, 378, 388, 394, 398, 433, 492, 494,
        511-513, 517, 526, 531, 574-575, 578-582, 584, 589-590,
        598, 603, 617, 624-625, 627, 714, 739, 841, 849, 871, 901

cardiovascular medications, 601

care planning process, 302, 316

care, refusal of, 204, 319, 354, 450-451, 456, 459, 462, 517, 520, 551, 553, 737, 753

catheter injury, 509, 708

catheterization, 199, 213, 231, 246, 474, 525, 606, 678-679, 688, 718, 840, 856

Center for Medicare and Medicaid Services (CMS), see also Health Care Financing Administration, 20, 69, 193, 290, 293-294, 296-297, 300-302, 307, 315, 386-388, 391, 405, 407-410, 563, 606, 626, 639, 652-653, 661, 663-667, 670, 677, 688, 691-692, 695-696, 771, 776, 783, 785, 791, 794, 803, 819, 903

Centers for Disease Control (CDC), 63, 118, 217, 349, 353, 387, 390-391, 397, 411, 471, 474, 480, 623, 663, 667, 670, 674, 676-680, 682, 684, 686, 688, 690, 693-694, 699, 708, 711, 713, 721-722, 769, 771, 902

cephalo-pelvic disproportion (CPD), 21, 35, 904

cerebral palsy, 4, 6, 14, 26, 34, 36, 41-42, 56, 66, 68-69, 95, 301, 351, 641, 643-644, 649-650, 891, 904

certification
    Certified Critical Registered Nurse (CCRN), 53, 569
    Certified in Emergency Nursing (CEN), 433-434, 469, 484-486
    Certified in Nursing Administration (CNA), 61, 283, 290-291, 307-308, 311, 476, 566, 578, 903
    Certified Life Care Planner (CLCP), 93, 401, 469

Certified Rehabilitation Registered Nurse (CRRN), 401, 469, 904

certification requirements, 200, 281

Certified Case Manager (CCM), 469, 725, 902

Certified Critical Care Nurse Specialists (CCNS), 51, 54

Certified Nurse Midwife (CNM), 14, 562, 637-640, 643-644, 655

Certified Nursing Assistant, 290, 292, 302, 326, 330, 338, 476, 696, 742, 759, 811, 870, 903

Certified Rehabilitation Registered Nurse (CRRN), 401, 469, 904

cesarean section, 6-9, 14-16, 18-19, 22, 24-26, 28-30, 32, 34-39, 41, 44, 86, 88, 135, 142, 144, 235, 493, 495, 575, 587, 591, 605, 620, 641, 644-646, 648-649, 651-654, 842, 901, 904-905

chain of command, 7, 19, 30, 36-38, 93-94, 98-99, 154, 272, 341, 420-421, 516-517, 522, 524-525, 528, 532, 535, 594, 754, 837, 872

charge nurse, 28, 74, 99, 125, 158, 173, 272, 282, 302, 308, 317, 374, 387, 491, 516-517, 784

charitable immunity, 136, 138-139, 141

charting, 38-39, 60, 79-80, 89, 116, 126, 163-164, 214, 297, 312, 319, 396, 412, 420, 533, 547, 565, 592, 656, 761
    flow sheets, 9, 60, 79, 122, 126, 186, 299-300, 412, 435, 480, 502, 531, 713

charting systems
    Charting By Exception (CBE), 80, 420, 533, 547
    narrative charting, 79, 126
    problem-oriented charting (SOAP), 79, 185, 385, 605, 680, 684, 922

chemical burns, 153, 218, 741

chemotherapy, 245, 280, 301, 403, 405, 407, 711-715, 717, 719, 748, 752, 809, 842-843, 846, 886-888, 893, 902, 905, 911

Chief Executive Officer, 306, 796, 801, 873

Chief Nursing Officer (CNO), 208, 210

child abuse, 79, 192, 354, 423, 516, 524, 871

childbirth, see delivery

chlorpromazine, 832, 835, 840

chronologies, see also timelines, 101, 530

cimetidine, 601

cipro, 712

circulation, inadequate, 95, 580-581, 726, 743

Cisplatin, 835, 846

clinical diagnosis, 111

clinical experience, 53, 79, 95, 113, 404, 562

clinical knowledge, 78-79, 485

Clinical Nurse Specialist (CNS), 53-54, 106, 113-115, 181, 199, 476, 562

clinical nursing, 122, 387, 482-483, 501
    anesthesia practice, 571, 596, 600, 606, 617, 621-622, 627-628
    evidence-based practice, 4, 54, 62, 79, 118, 201, 478, 481, 488, 654-655

clinical practice guideline, 4-5, 67, 243, 318, 387, 641, 654, 687, 695-696, 761, 767

closed claim study, 605

coagulopathy, 209, 573

code(s) of ethics, 180, 182, 186, 359, 515, 640

Code of Federal Regulations, 184, 307, 312, 352, 433-434, 902

Code Pink, 74

code sheet, 87, 122

code team, 122, 236

communication skills, 78, 420

community health, 350, 402, 808, 893

comparative negligence, 204, 444, 534, 772

compazine, 854-855

complication, 35, 38, 61, 96, 117-118, 166, 198, 208, 216-218, 255, 273-274, 377, 382-383, 393, 397-398, 534, 556, 587, 594, 611-612, 681, 708-710, 712-713, 722, 751, 827, 873, 900

Comprehensive Accreditation Manual, see also Joint Commission, 849

Computerized Physician Order Entry (CPOE), 215, 470, 533, 829-830

Consolidated Omnibus Budget Reconciliation Act (COBRA), 432, 490, 904

Consumer Protection Act, 340

Continuous Quality Improvement (CQI), 54, 492, 694, 904

Continuum of Care, 67, 279, 411, 414, 760, 829

contractions, 7, 9, 13, 16-17, 20-21, 25, 29, 31, 34-36, 38, 242, 258, 394, 495, 527, 601, 644-645, 649-652, 654, 730, 896, 917, 919

contractures, 734, 751, 757, 760, 762, 777

contributory negligence, 127, 504
    potentially contributing patient acts (PCPA), 204

controlled substances, 356, 459, 461, 463, 564, 627, 801, 816, 849

core curriculum, 80, 115, 481

crisis management, 583, 618-619, 627-628

critical care cases, screening, 126
    documentation, 126

critical care malpractice issues
    advance directives and organ procurement, 119
    airway maintenance, 115
    consent, 118
    do not resuscitate orders orders (DNR), 119, 299, 410, 423, 442, 450, 456, 459-460, 858, 907
    falls and restraints, 120, 771
    ICU psychosis, 120

nursing research, 123
pressure ulcers, 120
response to alarms and changes in condition, 121
critical care medicine
    admission criteria, 111-112, 114, 124-125, 505, 678, 849
    discharge criteria, 118, 125
    standing orders, 110
    trends, 123
    unit-based protocols, 110
critical care nursing
    areas of competence, 113
    certification, 53-54, 109-110, 113-115, 407, 434, 902
    continuing education, 110, 114
    nursing process in critical care, 111, 115
    personnel, 110, 113, 124
    prerequisites, 114
    standards of care, 52, 115, 123, 125, 594
critical care unit(s), 7, 29, 109-127, 155, 158, 203, 211, 216, 229, 243, 475, 484, 500, 505, 520, 526, 594, 599, 604, 619, 678-680, 717, 771, 827, 849, 854, 866, 902, 912
critical thinking, 57, 89, 202, 221, 474, 488, 546-548, 550-554, 556, 714, 837
crossclamp, 615
CT-scan, 99, 104, 202, 231-232, 241, 244-246, 273, 447, 475, 495-496, 501, 503-504, 526, 531-532, 568, 689, 720, 845
central venous pressure (CVP), 59, 592, 596, 614, 711, 714, 905
    monitoring, 59, 596
cystic fibrosis, 17, 232, 649-650, 902

D

Dantrolene, 601
debridement, 97, 260-262, 268, 271, 315-316, 681, 698, 717, 730-731, 741-742, 752, 754-755, 779
decubitus ulcer, see also pressure ulcers, 698, 754, 757-758, 780, 782
defendant nurse, see nurse defendants
defendants, identifying potential, 425, 619
defense experts, 149, 156, 207, 719
defenses
    charitable immunity, 136, 138-139, 141
    contributory negligence, 127, 504
    comparative negligence, 204, 444, 534, 772
    statute(s) of limitation, 365
defibrillation, 114, 122, 149, 231, 431, 433, 487, 507-509, 614, 894, 911-912
    early defibrillation, 487
delirium tremens (DTs), 207, 907
delivery
    breech presentation(s), 15, 22-23
    cesarean section (C/S), 6-9, 14-16, 18-19, 22, 24-26, 28-30, 32, 34-39, 41, 44, 86, 88, 135, 142, 144, 235, 493, 495, 575, 587, 591, 605, 620, 641, 644-646, 648-649, 651-654, 842, 901, 904-905
    shoulder dystocia, 9, 22-24, 44, 645-647, 652
    sponge and instrument counts, 19, 30, 37
    use of forceps, 23
    vacuum extraction assisted births, 23
    vaginal birth after a cesarean section (VBAC), 25-26, 38, 649
delivery suite, 473

delivery systems, 396, 471, 562, 618, 823, 847
delivery units, 19, 33-35, 63
dementia, 205, 285, 287, 306-307, 309-310, 312-314, 317-318, 326, 334-339, 343, 552, 687-688, 780, 816, 838, 894, 902, 906, 921
Department of Health and Human Services (DHHS), 356-357, 440, 510, 563, 620, 769, 792-793, 797, 800
departmental manuals, 607-608
deposition(s), see also nursing malpractice cases and expert witnesses
dermatology, 566, 691, 881-884, 894, 906-907, 922
Desflurane, 572-573, 590, 595, 600
diaphoresis, 233, 494, 510
diabetes, 7-10, 17, 28, 39, 64-66, 157, 161, 185, 212-215, 217, 283, 285-286, 349, 402, 494, 512-513, 524, 587, 645, 650, 668, 674, 677, 680-681, 688, 698, 728, 741, 746, 749-751, 754, 757, 830, 837, 856-858, 894, 896, 906-907, 912-913, 916
Diazepam, 600, 908
digoxin, 76, 417, 823, 830, 838, 843, 863, 865, 906
    toxicity, 417
diplopia, 881-884, 886-888
Diprivan, 835
directed verdict, 78
director of
    anesthesia, 594
    nursing, 282, 291, 319, 696, 894, 907
    patient care, 418
    perioperative nursing, 594
discharge instructions, 166, 277, 414, 482, 500, 514-515, 528, 531-532, 534
discharge planning, 112, 126, 134, 162, 176, 276, 299, 776
discovery, 7, 10, 35-36, 39, 56, 94, 118, 123, 144, 150, 199, 232, 273, 337, 341-342, 415, 420, 422, 484, 487, 512, 591, 594, 607-608, 618, 627, 638, 652, 685, 813-814, 823, 825-826, 830, 833, 849, 865
dispensing medications, 336-337, 341
diuretic, 587
dobutamine, 407, 601, 840
documentation, importance of, 403, 872
Droperidol, 593, 601
drug(s), see medications and medication errors
drug administration, see also medication administration, 35, 60, 62, 116, 123, 158, 327, 410, 483, 506, 563, 588, 590, 593, 607, 613, 618, 701, 713, 777, 807-809, 823, 831, 840-841, 847-849, 909
Drug Enforcement Administration, 563, 849, 906
drug information, 847
drug products, approved, 123, 807-808
drug reactions, adverse, 319, 701, 894
drug utilization review, 908
Duchenne's muscular dystrophy, 17-18, 422, 907
duplicate dose, 842
dysplasia, 900
dyspnea, 155, 232, 240, 243, 245-246, 450, 481, 497, 584, 907-908, 918-919
dysrhythmia, 111, 117, 123, 157-158, 497, 528, 902
dystocia, 9, 20-24, 44, 645-647, 652

E

echocardiograms, 64, 231-232, 246, 609

eclampsia, 10, 647
economic damages, 127, 340
economists, see forensic economist(s)
EDC, 10, 908
edrophonium, 600
elder abuse, 307, 329, 409, 503, 516, 700-701
electrocardiogram (EKG or ECG), 114, 133, 159, 198-199, 231-232, 403, 431, 437, 462, 487, 489, 494, 506, 512-513, 526-527, 583, 592, 596-597, 609, 613, 617-618, 625, 627, 889, 908
electrocautery, 151-152, 165, 234, 617, 739
electroencephalogram (EEG), 125, 231, 591, 908
electroconvulsive therapy, 607, 908
electronic fetal monitoring, 31-34, 37, 643, 902
electrosurgery, 152
elopement, see also wandering, 204, 207, 302, 316-318, 331, 334, 340
emergency department nursing assessment, 497
    AMPLE, 497
    Glasgow Coma Scale, 126, 454, 498-499, 908
    Trauma Score, 498-499
    treatment area assessment, 482, 498-499
emergency management
    first responder care, 486
    flight transport team, 487
    liability questions regarding prehospital care, 487
    monitor printouts, 487
    prehospital records, 452, 487
Emergency Medical Services (EMS)
    Advanced Life Support (ALS), 105, 115, 431, 433, 455, 460, 478-479, 484-487, 572, 623, 798, 808, 895
    Advanced Trauma Life Support (ATLS), 115, 479, 486-487
    Basic Life Support (BLS), 105, 203, 413, 431, 433, 460, 464, 478-479, 484, 486-487, 652, 798, 900
    Pediatric Advanced Life Support (PALS), 105, 115, 433-434, 479, 484
    trauma criteria, 485
Emergency Medical Treatment and Active Labor Act (EMTALA), 432, 470, 474, 480-481, 486-487, 490, 500, 518-523, 526-530
    dumping, 516, 518, 520, 522, 524, 526-527, 799
    required transport documents, 523
    transfer requirements, 522
Emergency Nurses Association (ENA), 472, 476-477, 480-486, 488, 490, 492-493, 497, 501-502, 506, 512, 518-519, 540, 545
emergency nursing
    evaluation, 511
    patient advocacy, 515
    patient education, 513-514
    standards of care, 470, 475, 478, 480, 483, 485, 529
    transfer and discharge of patients, 482, 500, 503, 512, 514-515, 518, 521, 523-525, 532, 534
emergency nursing and nursing diagnosis, 470, 497, 500, 504
emergency nursing, defenses, 533
    contributory or comparative negligence
        withholding information, 533
        leaving against medical advice, 204, 534
emergency nursing, negligence, 470, 529, 531, 533-534
    documentation red flags, 531
    documents to obtain in evaluating liability, 533

emergency department chart, 530
    screening the case, 529
    what to look for in the medical record, 124, 531, 697
emergency nursing, qualifications and skills
    care of the admitted patient, 505
    cervical and spinal immobilization, 505-506
    conscious sedation, 506
    emergency equipment, 506-507
    qualifications of the triage nurse, 485, 488
emergency nursing, consent issues, 118-119, 504, 517, 547, 608, 619
    advance directives in the ED, 517
    assault and battery by ED staff, 517
    refusal of tests, treatment, admission, medications by patients, 517
emergent care, 496, 675
Employee Retirement Income Security Act of 1974 (ERISA), 363-369, 909
endarterectomy, 157, 604, 901
endoscopy, 131, 199, 217, 567, 577, 579, 590, 675, 828, 840-841, 880-884, 887-888, 909
encephalopathy, 26, 36, 41, 43, 56, 65, 67-69, 117, 372-373, 422, 643-645, 689, 720, 881-884
Enflurane, 600
environmental control, 682
environmental safety, 608
Ephedrine, 601, 835
epidural anesthesia, 573-575, 581, 586-587, 605, 620
epinephrine, 60, 87, 96, 150, 349, 356, 358, 398, 576, 578, 598, 600-601, 626, 823, 835, 866-867, 909
errors
    categorization, 824
    detection, 511, 822-823
    sentinel events, 36, 67, 74, 120-121, 146, 148-149, 153, 254, 296, 305-306, 410, 608, 628, 813
erythema, 680, 731-732, 735-736, 739, 751-752
ethical issues, 359, 410, 797
Etomidate, 589, 600
euthanasia, 863
expert witness(es), see also nurse (nursing) expert witnesses

F
False Claims Act (FCA), 796, 799-800, 807, 809, 812-815
Federal Rules of Civil Procedure, 909
Federal Tort Claims Act (FTCA), 41, 442
fee schedule agreement, 793, 806, 812
Fentanyl, 339, 574, 576, 584-585, 600, 803, 825, 835, 842-844
fetal heart rate (FHR), 6-7, 9-10, 16, 18-19, 24-25, 30-39, 43, 86, 495, 642-644, 649, 651, 653
    characteristics of, 33
    electronic monitoring, 30-33, 643
first responders, 228, 429-435, 479, 486-488
five rights, see also medication administration, 61-62, 396, 839-840
float nurse(s), 476
flowsheet(s), 9, 22, 60, 76-77, 79, 122, 126, 186, 217, 299-300, 316, 384-386, 412, 435, 480, 485, 502, 531, 708-709, 713, 759, 826
Flumazenil, 600
fluoroscopy, 603, 712, 720, 833, 909

follow-up phone calls, 163-164, 176
foot drop, 222, 269-270, 274, 733
forceps, 22-23, 234, 645, 650, 652-653
foreign object(s), retained, 135, 146-148, 663, 667-668
forensic economist(s), 101
forensic nursing, 868-869
fraud, see health care fraud and abuse
Freedom of Information Act, 508
Friedman labor curve, 20-21

G

galactosemia, 17
gastritis, 515, 525, 648
gastroenteritis, 515, 686, 689, 699, 877
gastroenterologist, 576, 611, 718
gastroenterology, 94, 577, 893, 896, 898-900, 903, 907, 910, 912, 916, 918, 921
general anesthesia, maintenance of, 588
Gentamicin, 823
geriatric nursing, 811, 867
Glasgow Coma Scale, 126, 436, 454, 497-499, 908, 910
glycogen, 64-65, 843, 881-884
glycopyrrolate, 600-601
graduate medical education, 891
guidelines, see practice guidelines
gynecology, see also OB-GYN, 4, 6, 15, 53, 55, 63, 214-215, 639, 643-644, 649, 651, 893-894, 898-901, 903, 905, 907, 910, 912, 917, 919, 923-924

H

Haldol, 310, 838, 856
Halothane, 572-573, 590, 595, 598, 600
hand-off, 135-136, 153, 158, 164, 413, 471, 475, 483-484, 496, 535, 829
Health Care Financing Administration (HCFA), 480, 520-521, 562, 626, 663, 793, 812, 903, 910
health care fraud and abuse, 306, 416, 439, 791-792, 794-796, 798-804, 806-817, 871
    civil monetary penalties (CMP), 315, 521, 798, 816, 903
    fraud versus abuse, 794
    in medical malpractice cases, 813
    kickbacks, 796-797
    qui tam action(s), 796, 800, 807, 813-815
    schemes, 798
    self-referral, 796-797
Health Insurance Portability Accountability Act of 1996 (HIPAA), 184, 331, 437, 545, 565, 737, 793
Health Maintenance Organization (HMO), 363-368, 405, 425, 483, 527, 542-543, 664-665, 807-808, 911
hearsay rule, 669
Heimlich maneuver, 479
hemiparesis, 881-884, 890
hemiplegia, 77, 301
hemodialysis, 242-243, 372-378, 381-383, 387, 389-390, 398, 709, 718
hemodynamics, 757
hemoglobinopathies, 8
Heparin, 90, 233, 275, 379, 385-386, 584, 601, 712, 781-782, 825, 828-829, 831, 835, 842, 845, 911
hepatitis, 61, 391, 582, 682, 721, 881-884, 898, 910

high-risk pregnancy, 7-8, 13
histamine, 601, 837
histamine blocking agents, 601
Home Health Agency (HHA), 202, 402, 404-406, 410, 413-415, 417, 419, 421, 425, 737, 794, 797-798, 803-804, 809-811, 813, 815, 873, 911
home health care
    home care medical record, 410
        admission, 330, 410
        assessment, 411
        case management, 412
        flowsheets, 412
        laboratory results, 412
        medication administration record, 412
        miscellaneous, 412
        nursing care plan, 411
        plan of treatment, 411
        progress notes, 411-412
        therapies, 412
    providers, 404
        case manager, 276, 319, 404-405, 409-410, 414-415, 420, 425
        clinical supervisor, 404, 412
        companion, 404
        generalist and specialist nurses, 404, 407
        Home Health Aide, 202, 336, 404-408, 412, 414-416, 419-420, 426, 805, 911
        payor or insurance provider, 405
        rehabilitation therapist, 404, 409
    services offered in the home setting, 404
    settings, 405
    standards, 402, 405, 407-410, 414, 423-426, 483, 711
    types of care, 405
home health care liability issues
    case screening, 422-423
        appropriateness of the care, 423
        liability of the agency, 423
        potential defendants, 424
    defenses, 420
        agency issues, 421
        documentation, 314, 420, 546, 745
        noncompliance, 421
        standard-of-care issues, 420, 714
    failure to recognize changes in the patient's condition, 417
    improper provision of specialized services, 415
    patient abandonment, 417
    patient safety, 416
hospice care, 125, 280, 402-403, 405, 422, 501, 795, 805-806, 809, 910
hospital charts, 411, 822
hospital emergency department, 470, 487, 495, 504, 512, 521-522, 528
human resources, 307, 328, 849
Hydralazine, 601
hydrocephalus, 103
hyperalimentation, 60
hypercarbia, 55, 103, 572-573, 648
hyperglycemia, 66, 843
hyperinsulinemia, 65
hyperkalemia, 590
hypertonia, 69

hypnotics, 296, 572, 589, 591, 593, 595, 600

hypocalcemia, 70, 644

hypoglycemia, 16, 54, 64-66, 70-71, 88-89, 91, 442, 492, 668, 830, 843, 887-888

hypoglycemic, 16, 54, 64-66, 70-71, 88-89, 91, 442, 492, 668, 830, 843, 887-888

hypokalemia, 527

hypopituitarism, 67

hypothyroidism, 43, 67, 285-286, 696, 837

hypotonia, 57, 65, 69, 75, 395, 647

hypovolemic shock, 93, 101-102, 208

hypoxemia, 16, 26, 43-44, 55, 90-91, 103-104, 115-117, 220-221, 233-234, 238, 244-245, 572, 577, 580, 895

hypoxia, 22, 32, 42-43, 54-55, 58, 65, 90, 93-94, 96, 101, 104, 155-156, 234-235, 237, 243, 433, 532, 570, 578-579, 594, 603, 644, 743-744

I

iatrogenic injury, 76-77, 663, 882-884

inadequate care, provision of, 218

incident report(s), 35, 114, 122, 147, 304, 352, 409, 423, 517, 534, 783-784, 822-823

Infancy Protection Act, 638

infection control, 118, 274, 295, 328, 387, 390-391, 409, 481, 608, 622, 674, 676-677, 679, 681, 685-686, 688, 690-697, 699-701, 758

information, withholding, 183, 533

informed consent, 37, 51, 79, 118-119, 123, 136-137, 144, 148, 151, 164, 166, 179-180, 183-184, 189, 191, 193, 332, 384, 388, 409, 421, 517-518, 522, 524, 547, 569, 576, 580, 586, 595-596, 604, 607-609, 611, 619-620, 622, 649, 652, 654, 711, 714, 738

infusion pumps, 19, 34, 59-60, 122-123, 218, 385, 405, 508

initial nursing assessment, 411, 419-420, 700

injury, prevention of, 22, 60, 75, 151, 154, 260, 300, 303, 319, 380, 406, 472, 571, 576, 580, 602, 712, 753

Institute for Safe Medical Practices (ISMP), 823, 844, 878

Institute of Medicine (IOM), 61, 254, 471, 474, 536, 661-662, 670, 797, 822, 877, 912

insurance, see professional liability insurance

intake sheet, 414, 825-826

intensive care unit (ICU), 5, 26, 29, 51, 86, 95, 98-100, 109-127, 153, 155, 158, 211, 216, 228-229, 243, 276, 475, 486, 500, 520, 522, 526, 577, 584, 594, 599, 604, 664, 674, 676, 678-680, 717, 771, 774, 841, 849-850, 854, 863, 866, 902-903, 912, 922

intern(s), 126, 137, 140, 185, 511, 815

internist, 213, 228, 231, 856

intracranial pressure, increased, in infants, 93, 97-99, 101, 103, 112, 116, 237, 352, 480, 495, 509, 512

intravenous anticoagulants (heparin), 379, 842, 845

intravenous fluids (IVF), 59, 66, 76, 165, 208, 217-218, 244, 431, 512, 574-575, 604, 707-708, 719, 912

intravenous potassium chloride, 913

intravenous regional anesthesia, 575-576

Ipratroprium, 601

Isoflurane, 572-573, 590, 595, 600

J

Joint Commission, The (TJC)
    accreditation manual, 205, 328, 481
    National Patient Safety Goals (NPSGs), 148-149, 153, 211, 218, 329, 410-411, 416, 839-840
    standards, 118, 132, 150, 328-329, 408, 414, 503, 529, 624, 692

juries and jurors

K

Ketamine, 600

L

Labetolol, 601

labor
    abnormal labor, 20
    augmentation of, 5, 35
    Friedman curve(s), 20-21
    induction of, 7, 14-15, 18, 23, 34, 36, 644, 649-650
    labor and delivery unit, 13, 19-20, 33-36, 63, 475, 521, 605
    labor/delivery/recovery/postpartum unit (LDRP), 19-20
    physiology of, 20

Labor Act, 432, 470, 490, 518, 799

language barriers, 160, 477, 484, 510

laparoscopy, 152, 171-172, 174

laryngectomy, 285-286

Lasix, 160, 285, 450, 592, 825, 838

late entries in medical records, 38, 556, 667

latex allergy protocol, 161, 609

Leapfrog, 62, 669

legal nurse consultant (LNC), 9, 41, 94, 255, 273, 312, 330, 336, 420, 571, 674, 676, 679, 697, 711, 715, 769, 784-785, 803, 811, 824, 826, 868

Legal Nurse Consultant Certified (LNCC), 109, 253, 279, 469, 769, 821, 855, 859, 877

level I hospitals, 5-6

level II hospitals, 5

liability
    associated, 254, 275-277, 310-311, 316, 451, 491, 497-498, 503, 508-510, 515-516, 699-700, 847
    claims, 30, 147, 341, 363, 367, 424, 561, 587, 641, 667, 718
    evaluation, 315, 470, 510

liability, theories of, 136, 145, 151, 214, 335, 339, 402, 422, 625
    respondeat superior, 54, 56, 72, 136-138, 140-141, 368, 625
    vicarious liability, 136-138, 140, 214, 625, 641

licensure, 200, 203, 291, 327-328, 330-332, 339, 387-388, 402, 409, 414, 423, 431, 433, 436, 451, 462, 486, 516, 548-550, 554-555, 568, 607, 622, 626, 640, 795, 811, 873

Lidocaine, 600-601, 626, 913

life care plan, 101

life care planner, 45

life support, 105, 110, 113, 115, 206, 214, 216, 387, 413, 431, 433-434, 460, 464, 478-479, 484, 486-487, 507, 526, 529, 572, 598, 619, 623, 652-653, 798, 843, 893, 900

literature review, 709, 759

Lithium, 285, 913

lithotomy, 602-603

lithotripter, 606

living will, 119, 534

locality rule, 51

long-term care
    Ombudsman program, 329, 337
long-term care nursing, 279, 291, 795, 801, 803
    long-term-care record, 297
        MDS and change of condition, 302
        Minimum Data Set (MDS), 291, 293-294, 298, 300-302,
        794, 914, 920-921
        quarterly and annual reassessments, 301-302
        resident assessment protocol (RAP), 298, 300, 920
        Resource Utilization Groups (RUG), 300-301, 416, 776,
        794, 802, 856, 921
    prospective payment system (PPS), 300-301, 662-664, 912,
    917, 919
long-term care malpractice issues
    assessment and care planning process, 302
    common liability issues, 302
    defenses, 319
        preexisting illness or disputing the proximate cause, 319
        right to refuse care, 319
        standards of care were followed, 319
        unforeseeable injury, 319
    sources of liability, 281
        falls, 303, 310, 334
        burns, 305
        abuse, neglect and assaults by residents, 306
        pressure ulcers, 311
        wandering and elopement, 316
    staffing, 41, 201, 290, 342, 416
Lorazepam, 600, 825
lost earnings, 127, 157, 340, 367
Lovett Scale, 258

M

Magnet Commission, 79
Malignant Hyperthermia Association of the United States
    (MHAUS), 573
malnutrition, 306, 308, 311, 674, 689, 696, 745-749, 796, 801
managed care liability issues
    ERISA, 363-369, 909
        preemption, 364-369
Marcaine, 150
maternal child nursing, 105
maternity care, 4
meconium, 14, 17-18, 39, 43-44, 54, 641, 643, 653-654
medical expert, 313, 336, 338, 340, 348, 422, 500-501
medical gases, 600
medical malpractice cases, 239, 340, 521, 627, 753, 849
medical practice study, 93, 822
medical standard of care, 534
medical surgical nurses, 113, 200-203, 205-208, 210, 213, 215,
    218-219, 223, 483, 485
medical surgical nursing malpractice issues
    contributing factors, 201
        staffing, 201
    deviations from the standard of care, 208
medical surgical units, composition of, 199
medication administration, 821
    five rights, 61-62, 396, 839-840
        right dose, 839-840
        right drug, 839

        right patient, 839
        right route, 840
        right time, 840
medication error(s)
    adverse events, report of, 254, 439, 669, 777, 784
    detection of, 822
    prevention of, 661, 824, 839-840, 850
    types of errors, 824, 829-830, 833, 840-841, 849
        duplicate dose, 842
        mistakes and slips, 831
        omitted dose, 841-842
        prescribing errors, 825, 832, 840, 844, 848
        unordered drug error, 842
    wrong dose, 358, 509, 840, 846, 848
    wrong drug, 509, 830-832, 838, 840, 844, 850
    wrong patient, 133, 141, 148, 155, 509, 511, 667, 838-840
    wrong route, 100, 509, 841
    wrong site, 134, 148-149
    wrong time, 100, 509, 841
medications
    refusal of, 158, 332, 336, 356, 419, 421, 450, 517, 534
meningomyelocele, 18
mental health care, 181, 188, 194
mental illness, 181, 184, 186, 190, 192-194, 309, 336-337, 503,
    800-801
Meperidine, 461, 825, 832
Mepivicaine, 600
Methergine, 29
Methicillin, 685, 915
microcephaly, 36, 43
microsurgery, 150
Midazolam, 577, 590, 600, 612
midwifery, 14, 637-642, 644, 651, 653-656
minimum data set (MDS), 291, 293-294, 298, 300-302, 794, 914,
    920-921
misdiagnosis, 6, 99, 514, 535, 741
mitral valve, 878, 915
Mivacurium, 600
mixups, 159, 831
Monroe-Kellie doctrine, 103
morphine, 95, 97, 156, 159, 171-172, 205, 272, 319, 339, 450, 459,
    461, 574, 576, 599-600, 721, 800, 825, 832, 835-836, 842-
    843, 858
Morphine Patient-Controlled Analgesia, 272
myelogram, 220
myocardial infarction, 188, 231, 275, 318, 434, 494, 499, 511, 513,
    525-526, 548, 566, 581, 619, 878, 895-897, 912, 915
myocardium, 105

N

Naloxone, 600, 823, 844-845
Narcan, 156, 648, 823
narcotic antagonist(s), 600
narcotics, 59-60, 97, 115, 155-157, 216, 218, 220, 256, 356, 422,
    450, 461, 572, 574-576, 584, 587-589, 593, 596, 598, 600,
    605, 648, 748, 802, 823-824, 842-844
National Association of Neonatal Nurses (NANN), 52-53, 72-73, 79
National Association of Nurse Anesthetists, 621
National Association of Orthopaedic Nurses, 254, 256, 260, 263,
    265-267, 270-271, 275

National Association of Pediatric Nurse Associates and Practitioners (NAPNAP), 52

National Association of School Nurses, 348, 350, 358-359

National Certification Corporation (NCC), 53-54

National Committee for Quality Assurance (NCQA), 545, 916

National Council of State Boards of Nursing (NCSBN), 475-476, 480, 542, 544, 549, 871, 873

National Council of State Boards of Nursing computerized testing registered nurse examination (NCLEX-RN), 181

National Flight Nurses Association, 434, 480

National Gerontological Nursing Association, 485

National Institute of Health (NIH), 209, 351, 649, 767, 769

National Nursing Organizations, 358

National Patient Safety Goals (NPSGs), see also Joint Commission on Accreditation of Health Care Organizations, 148-149, 153, 210-211, 215, 218, 329, 410-411, 414, 416, 477, 496, 507, 770, 829, 831, 836, 839-841, 878

National Practitioner Data Bank (NPDB), 566, 621, 870-871

National Research Council Conference, 478

NCLEX-RN, see National Council of State Boards of Nursing computerized testing registered nurse examination

neglect, 79, 182-183, 185, 292, 303, 306-308, 325, 329, 336, 338, 354, 409, 439, 499, 700, 726, 728, 753, 757, 816

negligence, elements of, 529, 550, 785

neonatal intensive care unit (NICU), 5, 26, 45, 51, 53, 57-59, 61-62, 64, 70-73, 77, 86, 99, 125, 522, 531, 645

neonatal nursing
    Advanced Practice Nurse (APN), 53, 63, 71
        Neonatal Nurse Practitioner (NNP), 53-54, 62-63
        Clinical Nurse Specialist (CNS), 53, 106, 114, 476
    common causes of liability, 54
        intravenous therapy, 60
        hyperbilirubinemia, 66-67, 70
        hypoglycemia, 54, 64-66, 71, 88
        iatrogenic injuries, 77
        medication errors, 62
        neonatal kidnapping, 73
        respiratory distress, 57-58, 65
        resuscitation situations, 24, 28, 43, 54-56, 72, 78, 86, 479, 605-606, 647, 652, 654
        sepsis, 62-65
        stabilization and transport of the high-risk neonate, 72
    documentation, 9, 51, 73, 78
    informed consent, 51, 79
    intensive care nursing, 26, 51, 53, 57-59, 61, 64, 71-73, 77, 86, 125, 531, 645
    scope of practice, 53-54
    standard of care, 51, 55-56

neonatal resuscitation, 24, 28, 55-56, 78, 86, 606, 647, 652, 654
    Neonatal Resuscitation Program (NRP), 28, 55-56, 78, 86

neonatologists, 9, 28, 53-54, 57, 62, 64, 71-72, 87, 228, 606

Neostigmine, 600

nerve damage, 145, 148, 155, 157, 222, 242, 382, 483, 599

neuroimaging, 43

neurologist, 9, 14, 156, 213, 334, 555, 584

neurology, 882-884, 891, 894-897, 899-900, 902-903, 905, 907-911, 916, 919, 921-922, 924

neuromuscular blockade, 116, 590, 592, 599-600, 613-615
    train-of-four (TOF) stimulation, 116, 923

neuropathy, 157, 582, 599, 743, 750-751, 890, 895

neurosurgeon, 98, 259, 525

neurosurgery, 892, 916

neurotransmitters, 116

Nifedipine, 601

Nipride, 158

nitroglycerin, 233, 450, 528, 598, 601, 916-917

nitroprusside, 601

nitrous oxide, 572, 581, 583, 587, 590, 595, 598, 600, 915

No Known Allergies (NKA), 848, 916

No Known Drug Allergies (NKDA), 848, 916

noncompliance, patient, 203-204, 419-421

noninvasive blood pressure monitor (NIBPM), 618

nonstress test (NST), 6-7, 16-17, 648

Norcuron, 116

Norepinephrine, 60, 217, 601

normoblasts, 43

nurse anesthesia malpractice issues
    analysis of malpractice claims, 583
        induction and maintenance of general anesthesia, 588
        preanesthetic evaluation, 585-586, 589, 608-609
        safe emergence, 592
    analysis of the medical record, 607-608
        anesthesia record, 612
        postanesthesia evaluation, 618
        preanesthetic evaluation, 585-586, 589, 608-609
    defenses, 618
    potential defendants, 619
    sources of liability, 578
        airway and breathing problems, 579
        inadequate circulation, 580-581
        production pressure, 582

nurse anesthetists, 106, 131, 134, 137, 139, 143, 156, 234, 562, 570-571, 575, 578-579, 584, 606, 608, 619-623, 625-626, 716, 812-813, 904

nurse assistants, 338, 915

nurse attorneys, 476, 769, 868

nurse defendants, 143

nurse (nursing) expert witnesses, 52, 94, 127, 156, 207, 312, 330, 420, 563, 711, 715, 826, 848

nurse managers, 74, 114, 199, 269, 387, 486, 528

Nurse Practice Act, 6, 31, 52-54, 72, 106, 111, 118, 125, 133-134, 180, 208, 404, 407, 480-481, 549, 561-565, 567

nurse staffing, adequacy of, 40, 201
    involuntary loss of nurses
        downsizing, 45, 113, 127
    shortage of nurses, 45, 125, 472, 869
        specialty nurses, 564, 797

nurse midwives, 6, 9-10, 13-14, 18, 22-23, 29, 31, 37, 363, 562, 637-641, 643-652, 654-655, 813, 893

nursing certification, see certification

nursing chain of command, 154
    charge nurse, 28, 74, 99, 125, 158, 173, 272, 282, 308, 317, 374, 387, 491, 516-517, 784
    director of patient care, 418
    licensed practical nurse, 132, 150, 160, 199, 208, 282, 330, 404, 407, 914
    nurse manager, 74, 114, 199, 269, 387, 528
    staff nurse, 58, 80, 101, 110, 144, 154, 158, 200-201, 855
    Unlicensed Assistive Personnel (UAP), 101, 113-114, 124, 127, 132, 199-202, 281, 471, 474-476, 488, 490, 535, 547

nursing charting systems, see charting

nursing competency, 79, 186

nursing diagnosis, 57, 63-64, 110-112, 175, 180-181, 201, 222, 228, 302, 318, 330, 350, 352, 402, 404, 411, 470, 476, 482, 486, 491, 497, 500-504, 516, 529, 544, 548, 551, 566-567, 728, 757, 806, 827, 873, 916
nursing education, 114, 181, 190, 297, 386, 486, 562
    associate degree programs, 181
    baccalaureate degree programs, 181
    diploma programs, 181
nursing, evidence-based practice, 4, 54, 62, 79, 118, 201, 478, 481, 488, 654-655
nursing errors, 145, 203, 508, 552, 848
nursing expert witnesses, 127, 156, 420
nursing home
    infections, 674-675, 686, 691, 695-696, 700
    quality initiative, 294
    Quality Protection Act, 291
    records, 297-298, 822, 920
    reform, 291
    settlements, 292, 319
nursing organizations, 181-182, 352, 358, 407, 480, 639
nursing practice acts, 6, 31, 52-54, 72, 106, 111, 118, 125, 133-134, 180, 208, 404, 407, 480-481, 549, 561-565, 567
nursing process
    assessment, 111, 173, 201, 330, 431, 481, 508, 544, 548
    diagnosis, 201, 330, 431, 481, 502, 508, 548
    evaluation, 201, 330, 481, 508, 545, 548
    implementation, 112, 201, 330, 481, 508, 515
    planning, 112, 126, 201, 330, 481, 508, 515
nursing progress notes, 420, 425, 709
nursing responsibilities, 17-18, 29, 35, 61, 63, 70, 133, 155, 157, 220, 260, 502, 514, 750, 843-845
nursing shortage, 45, 290, 471, 869
nutritionist, 402, 404, 412, 415

O

obstetrical anesthesia, 575, 590, 605
obstetrical malpractice issues
    charting and documentation, 38
    defenses
        lymphocytes and normoblasts, 43
        meconium-stained amniotic fluid (MSAF), 43-44
        shoulder dystocia, 9, 22-24, 44, 645-647, 652
    staffing, 40
obstetrical services, categories of, 5
obstetrical standards of care, 4-7, 9, 19, 32
    deviations from, 6-7
obstetrics-gynecology (ob-gyn), 4, 34, 41, 901, 919
occupational safety, 480, 917
oligohydramnios, 15-17, 650, 652
Ombudsman, 297, 307, 329, 332, 337
omitted dose, 841-842
Omnibus Budget Reconciliation Act (OBRA), 291, 293-294, 296, 300, 303-304, 307, 432, 490, 688, 695, 797, 839, 904, 917
Oncology, 105, 214, 404, 712-713, 719, 809, 833-834, 894-897, 899, 901, 903, 906, 910-913, 915-916, 921, 923
Oncovin, 719
Operating Room Nurses Association, 164
ophthalmology, 61, 64, 71, 163, 352, 802, 891-925
ophthalmoscopy, 103, 883-884, 900
ophthalmologist, 71, 163, 802

opisthotonic, 69
opiate, 461, 587, 600, 843-844
order entry process, 834
organ procurement, 119-120, 439, 611
orthopedist, 221, 515, 717
orthotics, 750, 793
ostensible agency, 368
osteoarthritis, 917
osteoporosis, 240, 253, 258, 696, 778-781, 807
ototoxicity, 285
outcome standards, 115
outpatient surgery, 159, 198, 556, 666, 709
overdosage, 100
oversedation, 238, 844-845
over-the-counter drugs, 609, 848
oxacillin, 685
oximeters, 117-118, 172, 220, 242-243, 405, 580, 582, 591, 596, 602, 605, 613, 856-857
oxycontin, 353
oxygen, lack of, 55, 104, 117, 155, 228, 493, 509, 581, 585, 625, 744
oxygen supply, 578
oxygenation, 16-17, 25, 53, 55, 57, 89-90, 96, 102, 104, 209, 220, 242-243, 315, 450, 455, 508, 570-571, 576-577, 579, 586, 597, 606, 613, 742, 744, 749, 751, 755, 881-884
oxytocin, 19, 22, 29-30, 34-36, 38, 601, 644-645, 650
oxytoxics, 601

P

pain management, see also suffering, 154, 160, 280, 295, 316, 403, 481, 508, 593, 607, 621, 626, 742, 802, 844
pain medications, analgesic
    patient-controlled analgesia (PCA), 159, 199, 208, 218, 268, 272, 842-845, 850, 918
    routes of administration, 34, 90, 412, 846-847
painkiller(s), 217, 845
Pancuronium, 600, 831
papilledema, 103
paralegal, 711, 803, 811, 826
paralyzing agents, 590, 593
paramedics, 228-229, 234, 318, 394, 429, 431, 433-434, 436, 444, 450-451, 455, 460, 462, 464, 476, 479, 486-487, 494, 505, 507-508, 525-526, 528, 799, 872
paranoia, 207, 287, 302, 904
paraplegia, 100, 214, 422, 442, 887-888, 890
Parkinson's disease, 286, 688, 746, 803
pathogens, 102, 244, 348, 350, 357, 390, 513, 674-675, 680, 682-685, 690, 890
pathology, 7, 26, 42, 64, 68-69, 205, 264-265, 372, 571-572, 583, 642, 665, 727, 780, 782, 892, 894-895, 897-899, 903, 905, 918
pathologist, 43, 274, 406, 455, 865, 892, 922
pathophysiology, 53, 57, 72, 104, 113, 434, 570
patient
    advocacy, 154, 218, 480, 515-517, 524, 553, 564
    assessment, 19, 67, 95, 111, 113, 374, 417, 435, 451, 544, 547, 551, 553, 735
    assignment, 374
    Bill of Rights, 123
    care services, 418, 483, 638

controlled analgesia, 159, 208, 218, 268, 842-844, 918
dumping, 516, 518, 520, 522, 524, 526-527, 799
education, 9, 53, 159, 181, 193, 206, 219, 228, 236, 262, 264,
    276-277, 405, 412, 423, 425, 431, 470, 513-515, 542, 553,
    565, 733, 744, 834, 844, 846, 919
identification, 61, 414, 435, 451, 477, 481, 738, 839
monitoring, 159-161, 166, 220, 506, 578, 591
patient-to-nurse ratio, 35, 684, 801
transfer, 158, 298, 482, 837
transport, 435-436, 676, 798-799
Pavulon, 116, 831
pediatric advanced life support, 105, 115, 433, 479, 484
pediatric illnesses as sources of litigation, 101
    hypovolemic shock, 93, 101-102, 208
    increased intracranial pressure, 93, 97-99, 101, 103, 112, 116,
        237, 352, 480, 495, 509, 512
    respiratory failure, 93, 434
    sepsis, or septic shock, 93
pediatric malpractice issues
    assessment and monitoring, 95
    chain of command, 93-94, 98
    delegation, 93-94, 100
    errors, 99, 281, 475
    reporting and documentation, 97
pediatric nursing, 93-94, 96, 101, 104-106, 350, 483, 485
    scope of practice, 105
    standards of care, 105
pediatricians, 9, 28, 53-54, 63-64, 68, 72, 228, 235, 434, 494-495,
    530, 556, 599, 605-606, 620, 867
pediatrics, 5, 53, 55, 67, 71-72, 78, 99, 105, 107, 113, 206, 353,
    403, 479-480, 646-647, 812, 847, 892
    psychosocial aspects, 106
peer review, 521, 640, 653, 872, 919
penicillin, 62, 137, 676, 685, 712, 848, 918
performance evaluations, 423, 481
perianesthesia, 133, 161-162, 164, 173-175, 618, 621
pericardiocentesis, 450, 518
perinatal care, 5, 40, 53, 55, 72
perinatology, 605
perioperative nursing, 37, 131-133, 146, 159, 161, 164-165, 254,
    594, 602, 604
    complications, 166
    documentation, 164-165
    responsibilities, 133
    risk management, 164
    standard of care, 132
perioperative nursing malpractice issues
    legal theories
        abandonment, 144
        borrowed servant doctrine, 138
        captain of the ship doctrine, 137, 625
        informed consent, 144
        res ipsa loquitur, 141
        vicarious liability, 138, 140
    errors, 145
        injury from equipment, 150
        medication errors, 149
        retained foreign objects, 146
        sentinel events, 148, 254, 410, 608
    screening the case, 164
peripheral nerve stimulation (PNS) test, 116, 592, 919

personal injury, 228, 253, 341, 424, 521, 667, 669, 849, 918
personal items, unauthorized, 205
pharmaceuticals, 61-62, 207, 315, 473, 798, 807-809, 839-840,
    893
pharmacies, 402, 545, 566, 686, 840
pharmacist, 61-62, 100, 150, 218, 298, 318-319, 355, 404, 461,
    713, 776, 822-823, 825, 828-830, 833-834, 837-839, 846,
    850, 859, 872, 893, 920
pharmacology, 53, 471, 565, 840, 859, 892-894, 896, 898-899,
    901-919, 922-925
Phenergan, 217, 526, 712, 800
Phentolamine, 60, 96
Phenylephrine, 581-582, 593, 600-601
phenylketonuria (PKU), 918
phlebotomist, 199, 715
phlebotomy, 199, 474, 715, 883-884
physical status, 583, 608-609, 611, 727, 784
physical status classification, 608-609, 611
physicians, supervision by, 534, 620, 624, 626, 642
Physicians Desk Reference (PDR), 34, 859, 918
physiotherapy, 115, 680
Pitocin, 7, 21-22, 26, 28, 32, 34-36, 40, 642-643, 649, 651-654,
    842
policies, institutional, 52, 126, 203, 607, 621, 624, 713-714
polycythemia, 65, 67
polyhydramnios, 8, 15-16
polypharmacy, 205, 776, 847
postanesthesia care nursing, 158
    fast-tracking, 594
    liability issues, 578
    postanesthesia surveillance, 595
    standards, 156, 174
Post Anesthesia Care Unit (PACU), 109, 113, 125, 131-133, 136,
    145, 151, 153-159, 161-165, 171-174, 176-177, 198, 208-
    209, 220-221, 593-595, 604, 608, 612, 618
    guidelines, 172-173, 594, 608
    records, 618
posttraumatic stress disorder, 584, 587, 919
potassium chloride, 60, 100, 217, 379, 712, 717, 825, 832, 842,
    866, 913
potassium phosphate, 842
potentially contributing patient acts (PCPA), 204
Preferred Provider Organization (PPO), 363-364, 919
Prospective Payment System (PPS), 300-301, 662-664, 912, 917,
    919
practical nurses, 132, 150, 160, 199, 201, 208, 281-282, 290, 314,
    318, 326, 330, 402, 404, 407, 476, 696, 811, 914
practice guidelines
    clinical pathways, 110, 185, 404, 407, 411, 423, 526
    clinical practice guidelines, 4-5, 67, 243, 318, 387, 641, 654,
        687, 695-696, 761, 767
    practice parameters, 23, 140, 761
practice standards, 52, 115, 182, 186, 471, 478, 480-481, 485, 490,
    508, 545-546, 564, 622, 693
preanesthetic evaluation, 585-586, 589, 608-609
preexisting condition, 550, 580
preexisting illness, 319
prehospital trauma life support, 433-434, 479
pregnancy
    high-risk, 7-8, 13
        assessment, 13

biophysical profile (BPP), 6-7, 13, 15-16, 644, 652-653
contraction stress test (CST), 7, 16-17, 174
nonstress test (NST), 6-7, 16
oligohydramnios, 15-17, 650, 652
polyhydramnios, 8, 15-16
pregnancy, managing, 9
pregnancy induced hypertension (PIH), 7-10, 28, 39
prenatal testing unit, 17
prenatal visits, subsequent, 13
preoperative assessment, 160, 165, 254, 573
preoperative instructions, 159
prescriptive authority, 181, 387, 565
pressure ulcers, see also decubitus ulcers
    assessment, 120, 312, 316, 520, 733, 735, 737-738, 762
    prevention, 120, 282, 306, 312, 315-316, 408, 733, 737-738,
        749, 755-757, 760-761, 767
    stages, 274, 301-302, 312-313, 316, 335-336, 664, 668, 698,
        732-733, 736, 745, 747, 756, 758-759, 762, 767
    treatment of, 291, 299, 314-316, 408, 690, 733, 735, 737, 755-
        756, 760-761, 767
problem oriented charting, 79
procardia, 285
product liability, 151, 477, 595
professional liability insurance, 30, 570
    types of insurance, 792
progress notes, 9, 41, 99, 204, 298-300, 302, 313, 386, 411-412,
    420, 425, 617, 640, 708-709, 714-715, 717, 720, 756-757,
    824, 878
Promethazine, 601
prophylaxis, 63, 601, 919
Propofol, 574, 576-577, 589, 591, 595, 600
Prosequendum, 157
prostatectomy, 216, 574
prostatitis, 494, 687
prosthetics, 151, 205, 516, 680, 793, 802, 893, 896
proximate cause, 42-43, 60, 126, 136, 145, 147, 158, 187-188, 319,
    471, 530, 585, 655
pseudocholinesterase, 583, 609
psychiatric nursing, 105, 179, 190, 800-801
    standards of care, 180
psychiatric nursing malpractice issues
    insurance issues, 801, 912
    screening the case, 520
    failure to warn, 179, 188, 192, 213, 753, 837
psychiatrists, 181, 801, 809, 857, 866
psychosis, 120, 157, 287
psychotherapy, 181, 802-803
pulmonary artery pressure, monitoring, 596
punitive damages, 210, 292-293, 307-308, 311, 314, 328, 340, 367,
    701, 813
pyridostigmine, 600

Q

quality assurance, 126, 293, 340, 386, 391, 409, 426, 438, 479-480,
    492, 545, 547, 549-550, 564, 608, 617, 771, 776, 792, 806,
    813, 828, 833, 916, 919, 924
quality improvement, 54, 110, 175, 291, 294, 410, 470, 474, 477,
    492, 615, 642, 664, 677, 693-694, 904, 919-920

R

radiography, 57, 59, 73, 148, 233, 245, 264, 266-267, 712, 718,
    902
radiology, 114, 131, 166, 199, 220, 382-383, 503, 606, 615, 679,
    707-708, 711-713, 717, 780, 795, 833, 840, 854-855, 893,
    897, 920, 923
radiologists, 16, 37, 111, 131, 148, 216, 245, 480, 500, 525, 576,
    598, 623, 711, 713
Ranitidine, 601
regional anesthesia, 175, 570, 573-577, 581, 586-587, 605, 607,
    614, 623-624
Registered Nurse, Certified (RN-C), 51, 53-54, 197, 253, 279, 526,
    673
Reglan, 854-855
res ipsa loquitur, 136-137, 141-144, 146-147, 164, 229, 305, 597,
    599, 669
    examples of, 142-143
resident
    assessment, 298, 300, 920
    education, 317, 328, 737
    rights, 293, 310, 319-320, 327-328, 331-332, 338, 341
    services, 282-283, 289, 299, 301, 326, 328, 332, 336, 340,
        802
Resident Assessment Protocol (RAP), 298, 300, 920
    guidelines, 300
Resource Utilization Group (RUG), 300-301, 416, 776, 794, 802,
    856, 921
respiratory depressants, 216
respiratory distress, report of, 158, 718
respiratory distress syndrome (RDS), 64, 690, 897
Respiratory Nursing Society, 229, 251
respiratory status, monitoring, 220, 450
respondeat superior, 54, 56, 72, 136-138, 140-141, 368, 625
restraints, 117, 120-121, 155, 157, 183, 190-191, 193, 289, 293,
    299, 303-304, 310, 338, 447, 504-505, 509, 754, 776-777,
    858, 924
    alternatives, 121, 193
    psychiatric hospitals, use in, 191, 193
resuscitation
    do not resuscitate orders, 119, 410, 423, 442, 450, 456, 459-
        460, 858, 907
    neonatal, 23-24, 28, 54-56, 75-76, 78, 86, 479, 606, 647, 652-
        654
    termination of, 71, 283, 907, 918-920
reversal agents, 593, 614
Rh isoimmunization, 17
risk manager, 204, 319, 528, 826, 849, 872
risk of suicide, assessment of, 534
ritodrine, 7
Rocuronium, 589, 599-600
root cause analysis, 67, 74, 149, 254, 697
rules of civil procedure, 909
rules of evidence, 479
rule of nines, 767

S

Safe Medical Devices Act, 123, 304, 508
safe medication practices, 62, 830, 844, 878
same day surgery, 131-132, 136, 145, 152, 154-155, 159-160, 162-
    165, 171-172, 174-177, 198, 556, 606, 675

follow-up telephone calls, 163-164, 176, 555, 565
    preoperative instructions, 159
Schloendorff Rule, 141
sentinel events, 36, 67, 74, 120-121, 146, 148-149, 153, 254, 296,
    305-306, 410, 608, 628, 813
sepsis (septic shock), 62-65, 67, 93, 101-102, 113, 120, 148, 158,
    209-210, 308, 494-495, 513, 581, 678, 683, 689-690, 697-
    698, 711, 721, 740, 744-745, 747, 755, 841, 846
Sermchief, 111
severity of injury, 485, 745
Sevoflurane, 572-573, 590, 595, 600
sexual misconduct, 192
shift changes, 135, 164, 462, 649, 825, 828-829
shoulder dystocia, 9, 22-24, 44, 645-647, 652
    avulsion of the brachial plexus nerves, 23
    fractures, 23-24, 646
siderails, 120, 134, 157, 303-305, 335, 505, 532, 777
Silvadene, 316, 740, 922
skin assessment, 175, 230, 269, 314, 316, 384, 391, 682, 727-728,
    733, 737, 749-751, 759, 762
SOAP, 185, 385, 605, 680, 684, 922
Social Security Act, 664, 814
social services, 119, 162, 293, 299, 330, 412, 416, 503, 535, 805,
    915
Society of Critical Care Medicine (SCCM), 113
Society of Pediatric Nurses, 105, 483
socioeconomic factors, 8
sodium citrate, 601
Solu cortef, 398, 601, 848
spina bifida, 18, 351
spinal anesthesia, 570, 573-575
spirometers, 243, 680, 889
spirometry, 243-244, 782
sponge counts, 37, 140, 146-147, 165
staffing
    adequacy of, 19, 40, 114, 192, 200-201, 291, 307, 343, 358,
    475, 485, 506, 518, 546, 554, 684, 749, 753, 772
    downsizing, 45, 113, 127
    out-staffing, 502
    short staffing, 114, 307-308, 475, 518
    understaffing, 41, 66, 114, 124, 291, 475, 696, 795, 801
standards of care
    breaches by nurses, 56, 94, 98, 101-102, 106, 142, 209-210,
    330, 340, 342, 529-530, 813
    ethics and standards, 125, 180
standards of care, sources of
    nursing literature, 53, 115, 133, 188
    regulatory agencies, 52, 297, 328, 330, 387, 410, 424, 561,
    694-695, 785
standing orders, 36, 53, 69, 110-111, 116, 164, 215, 315, 350, 352,
    447, 450-451, 455, 462, 528, 546, 548, 688, 696, 728
state board(s) of nursing, 54, 133, 472, 475-476, 481, 542, 545,
    549, 562-563, 607, 714, 871, 873
state department(s) of health, 115, 133, 199, 297, 307, 640
state nurse practice act(s), 6, 31, 134, 208, 407, 481, 561-565
statute(s) of limitation, 365
steroids, 161, 239-240, 244, 259, 276, 286, 587, 601, 681, 752,
    781, 843, 848, 922
stridor, 104, 232, 497
subacute care, 197, 279-282, 726, 737
    defined, 281

liability issues, 302
    standards of care, 293
    subacute care in the hospital, 280-281, 726
    subacute care in the long-term-care hospital, 280-281, 726
    subacute care in the long-term-care facility, 279-282, 320,
    726, 803
succinylcholine, 116, 573, 583-584, 588-590, 598-600, 605, 866
sudden infant death syndrome, 422
Sufenta, 156
Sufentanil, 600, 835
suffocation, 236
suicide, 179, 184, 187-188, 190, 192, 336, 373, 471, 477, 481, 498-
    499, 534, 816, 862, 864, 921-922
summary judgment, 60, 158, 210, 335, 339, 341, 535, 617
supplemental answers, 172, 174
surgical fires, 148-149, 153
Surgical Site Infection (SSI), 663, 668, 674, 677, 680-683, 922
surgicenters, 606
Swan-Ganz lines, 7, 921
symptomatology, 57, 64
systolic blood pressure, 498-499, 921

T

tachycardia, 13, 29, 66, 70, 95, 101-103, 171-173, 239, 433-434,
    464, 527, 533, 573, 578, 581-582, 592, 643-644, 689, 884,
    918, 922, 924
tampering, 75, 205, 297, 618, 800, 826, 874
Tarasoff, 188, 192
tardive dyskinesia, 923
Tay-Sachs, 17
teaching hospitals, 127, 479, 623, 829, 832
telephone advice, 164, 492-494, 543, 545, 553
temporomandibular joint (TMJ), 923
terbutaline, 7
thalassemia, 10, 13, 17-18
therapeutic drug monitoring, 823
thermal burns, see also burns, 151, 603-604
Thiopental, 600
thoracentesis, 72, 233
thrombophlebitis, 709
thrombosis, 270, 274-275, 381-382, 597, 663, 709, 749, 780, 782,
    845, 905, 908
thyroidectomy, 594, 837
timelines, 9, 44, 296, 372, 411, 487, 565, 605, 608, 612, 656, 864
Tobia, 504
tomography, 66, 512, 901, 904-905, 918
tonsillectomy, 151, 923
total parenteral nutrition, 60, 280, 402, 711, 715, 718, 923
tourniquets, 58, 143, 165, 271, 576, 615
toxemia, 7, 28
toxicity, 67, 234, 239, 245, 417, 575-577, 601, 823, 834, 838-839,
    843, 846, 848-849, 858
toxicology, 172, 434, 511, 534, 574, 823, 849-850, 864-865
toxins, 41, 689
tracheostomy, 117, 119, 234-237, 243, 280, 301, 413, 417, 500,
    579, 586, 589, 593, 596, 679, 701, 923
tracings, storage of, 7
tralette, 164
tranquilizers, 461, 587
transcription errors, 829, 837

transfusions, 7, 13, 29, 59, 68-71, 77, 141, 199, 203, 208-209, 217, 254, 299, 301, 397, 481, 511, 518, 535, 571-572, 582, 590, 599, 625, 710, 713, 854
trauma center accreditation, 480, 485
trauma nurse course, 485
trauma nursing, 484-485
trauma patient, 126, 264, 276, 432, 434, 444, 452, 455-456, 478-480, 485, 487, 498, 500, 505, 518, 522, 603, 710, 779
trauma records, 456, 487
trauma severity index, 126
treatment, withholding, 517
tremors, 65, 239, 858
triage, 5, 206, 231, 455, 473, 475, 477-478, 481-482, 484-486, 488-496, 500, 511, 513, 517, 520, 523-524, 526, 529-535, 541-556, 738-739
    importance of, 488
    triage classifications, 488, 491, 494
    components of the triage system, 490
    telephone advice, 164, 492-494, 543, 545, 553
    performance standards for the triage nurse, 493
triage system, components of, 490, 496, 543
trials, 25, 118, 683, 808, 847, 895
trocars, 171, 582
tuberculosis, 99, 161, 231, 242, 245, 349, 391, 402, 686, 695, 923
tube feeding, 228, 282, 295, 301, 689, 746-747

U

ulceration, see also pressure ulcers, 312, 701, 743-744, 750, 755, 898
ultrasound (US), 9-10, 13-18, 22, 31, 44, 57, 64, 66, 77, 232, 532, 597, 645-646, 648, 652-653, 711-712, 715, 908
umbilical cord blood gas analysis, 26
Uniform Anatomical Gift Act, 119
Unique Provider Identification Number (UPIN), 813, 924
Unlicensed Assistive Personnel (UAP), 101, 113-114, 124, 127, 132, 199-202, 281, 471, 474-476, 488, 490, 535, 547
urinalysis, 13, 924
urological, 148, 898
urologist, 603

V

vaccine(s), 61, 353, 391, 688, 696, 917, 923
Valium, 95, 459, 461, 576
vasoconstriction, 44, 102, 752

vasodilation, 736
vasopressor, 59-60, 96, 574-575, 581-582, 593
Vecuronium, 572, 589, 600
venipuncture, 217, 715
vertebrae, 59, 258-259, 351, 436, 444, 505, 574, 780-781, 884, 901, 905-906, 913, 923
vertigo, 884
vesicants, 217, 712-713, 715, 717
vicarious liability, 136-138, 140, 214, 625, 641
videography, 95, 150
videos, 124, 219, 379, 504, 589, 615
Vinblastine, 835, 846
Vincristine, 833-835, 846
violent patient, potentially, 444
Visiting Nurse Agency (VNA), 401-402, 829
visiting nurse, 401-403, 422, 829
vital signs, monitoring, 35, 70, 72-73, 95, 155, 177, 208-209, 220, 450, 590

W

wandering, 287, 301, 303, 310, 316-318, 334, 341, 848
Warfarin, 587, 825, 834, 838, 842
wellness director, 331
wellness program, 327
whistleblowers, 190, 796, 809-811, 814-816, 869, 871
World Health Organization (WHO), 793, 891
wounds
    care, 281, 294, 312, 314-315, 335, 403-407, 421, 425, 514-515, 534, 594, 690, 698, 741, 750, 754, 756-757, 761-763, 767
    healing, 294, 316, 403, 419, 726-727, 729-730, 734, 742, 745, 748, 751-752, 754-756
    management, 407, 750, 754-755, 762, 767, 892
    ostomy, 314, 732, 754, 767
    photography, 314, 737-738
wrongful death, 111, 119, 340, 369, 383, 442, 507, 698, 700-701
    Wrongful Death Act, 119, 369, 701

X–Z

Xanax, 835-837
Zantac, 525, 835, 837
Zoloft, 843
Zyrtec, 835